D1422604

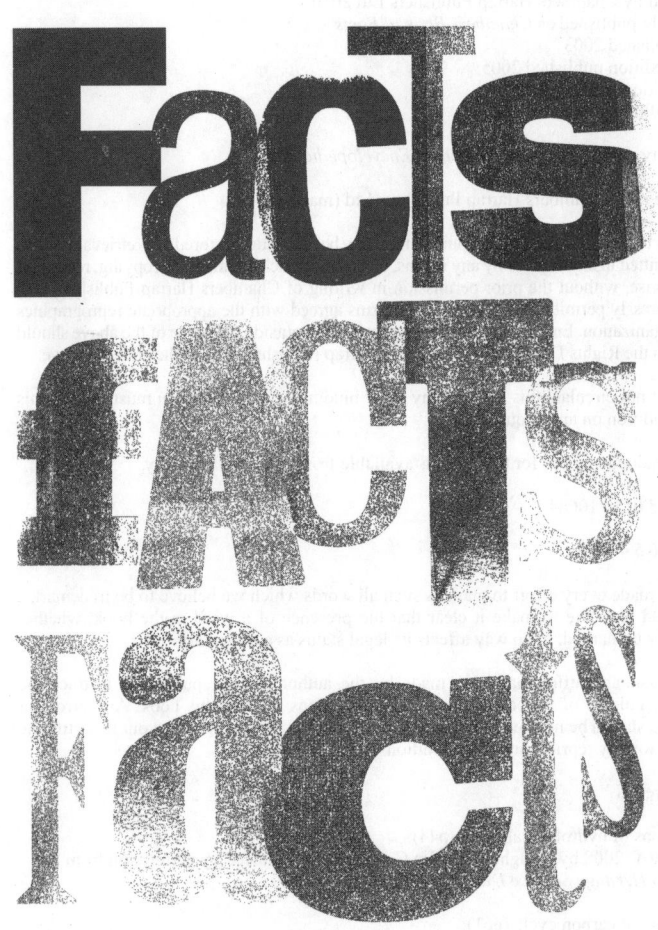

Chambers

CHAMBERS
An imprint of Chambers Harrap Publishers Ltd
7 Hopetoun Crescent, Edinburgh, EH7 4AY

Chambers Harrap is an Hachette UK company

© Chambers Harrap Publishers Ltd 2010

Chambers® is a registered trademark of Chambers Harrap Publishers Ltd

Published by Chambers Harrap Publishers Ltd 2010
Previously published as *Chambers Book of Facts*
First published 2003
Second edition published 2005
Third edition published 2007
Fourth edition published 2009

Previously published as *The Chambers Encyclopedia* 2001

Database right Chambers Harrap Publishers Ltd (makers)

All rights reserved. No part of this publication may be reproduced, stored in a retrieval system, or transmitted in any form or by any means, electronic, mechanical, photocopying, recording or otherwise, without the prior permission in writing of Chambers Harrap Publishers Ltd, or as expressly permitted by law, or under terms agreed with the appropriate reprographics rights organization. Enquiries concerning reproduction outside the scope of the above should be sent to the Rights Department, Chambers Harrap Publishers Ltd, at the address above.

You must not circulate this book in any other binding or cover and you must impose this same condition on any acquirer.

A CIP catalogue record for this book is available from the British Library.

ISBN 978 0550 10684 1

10 9 8 7 6 5 4 3 2 1

We have made every effort to mark as such all words which we believe to be trademarks. We should also like to make it clear that the presence of a word in the book, whether marked or unmarked, in no way affects its legal status as a trademark.

Every reasonable effort has been made by the author and the publishers to trace the copyright holders of material quoted and illustrations used in this book. Any errors or omissions should be notified in writing to the publishers, who will endeavour to rectify the situation for any reprints and future editions.

Image Credits

Illustrations of hydrological cycle (p44):
Copyright © 2008 by Houghton Mifflin Company. Reproduced by permission from *The American Heritage Science Dictionary*.

Illustration of carbon cycle (p61):
Copyright © 2002 by Houghton Mifflin Company. Reproduced by permission from *The American Heritage Student Science Dictionary*.

Illustrations of cloud images (p44–5):
Copyright © 2002 by Houghton Mifflin Company. Adapted and reproduced by permission from *The American Heritage Student Science Dictionary*.

www.chambers.co.uk

Designed by Chambers Harrap Publishers Ltd, Edinburgh
Typeset in Cheltenham and Optima by Chambers Harrap Publishers Ltd, Edinburgh
Printed and bound in India by Replika Press Pvt. Ltd.

Introduction

Chambers *Facts, Facts, Facts* is an authoritative and indispensable reference work. It provides an impressive array of up-to-date facts, figures and useful information from a diverse range of fields.

All material relating to specific fields is grouped under individual sections and subsections, enabling the user to find information on any particular topic with ease. There are 14 major subject areas: Space, Earth, Climate and Environment, Natural History, Human Body, Health and Nutrition, Science and Technology, History, Arts and Culture, Thought and Belief, Sports and Games, Time, Communication, Social Structure, and Nations of the World. Within these broad areas are clearly labelled subsections to guide the reader quickly to the relevant material. Tables, lists and diagrams, illustrations and maps complement the text.

This thematic arrangement means that it is easy to satisfy a specific query, or to broaden one's knowledge of a particular field by browsing around the section or subsection. Where material could be categorized under more than one heading, every effort has been made to locate the information in the place the reader would be most likely to look first. However, the detailed contents pages at the front and the extensive index at the back of the book can also be used to go straight to the information you want.

Whether you are seeking an answer to an urgent enquiry or dipping in at leisure, we hope you find this book useful and stimulating.

The Editors

Contributors

Editor
Liam Rodger

Contributors
Stuart Fortey
Hilary Marsden

Editorial Assistance
Deborah Smith

Data Management
Ruth O'Donovan

Prepress
Becky Pickard

Publishing Manager
Hazel Norris

Abbreviations

AD	Anno Domini		K	Kelvin
admin	administration		kcal	kilocalorie(s)
b.	born		kg	kilogram(s)
BC	Before Christ		kJ	kilojoules
b.c.	born circa		l	litre(s)
c	century		L	Lake
c.	circa		Lat	Latin
C	Celsius (Centigrade),		lb	pound(s)
	Central		l y	light year(s)
cc	cubic centimetre(s)		m	metre(s)
Chin	Chinese		Ma	millennia
CIS	Commonwealth of Independent		mi	mile(s)
	States		min	minute(s)
cm	centimetre(s)		mm	millimetre(s)
Co	County		Mt	Mount(ain)
cont.	continued		Mts	Mount(ain)s
cu	cubic		mya	million years ago
cwt	hundredweight		N	North(ern)
d.	died		n/a	not applicable
d.c.	died circa		no.	number
e	estimate		oz	ounce(s)
E	East(ern)		p(p)	page(s)
eg	for example		pop	population
Eng	English		Port	Portuguese
F	Fahrenheit		pt	pint(s)
fl oz	fluid ounce(s)		r.	reigned
fl	flourished (floruit)		R	River
Fr	French		Russ	Russian
ft	foot (feet)		S	South(ern)
g	gram(s)		sec	second(s)
gal	gallon(s)		Span	Spanish
Ger	German		sq	square
Gr	Greek		St	Saint
h	hour(s)		Sta	Santa
ha	hectare(s)		Ste	Sainte
Hung	Hungarian		Swed	Swedish
I(s)	Island(s)		TV	television
ie	that is		UT	Unified Team
in	inch(es)		v.	versus
Ir	Irish		vols.	volumes
Ital	Italian		W	West(ern)
Jap	Japanese		yd	yard(s)

See also

Common abbreviations pp598–604

Abbreviations and acronyms used in e-mail p609

Abbreviations and acronyms used in text messages p609

Chemistry abbreviations pp199–202

Computer languages p608

Currency abbreviations pp673–8

National holiday abbreviations p577

United Nations specialized agencies p646

Other conventions

Months are abbreviated to the first three letters (3 Jan 1817)

Contents

Space

The Sun	1	The 20 nearest stars	8
Solar system	2	Comets	8
Planets in the solar system	2	Annual meteor showers	9
Major satellites of the planets	2	Largest ground-based telescopes	9
Dwarf planets	3	Space launchers	11
The lunar 'seas'	3	Significant space missions	11
Phases of the Moon	4	NASA launches (crew-related)	13
Solar eclipses 2005–25	4	Shuttle flights 1998–2008	14
Lunar eclipses 2005–25	5	Major USSR/Russian launches (crew-related)	15
The constellations	6	Space records	17
The 20 brightest stars	7	Astronomers Royal	18

Earth

Atmosphere	19	Largest islands	28
Temperature and pressure of atmosphere	20	Major island groups	29
Structure of the Earth	20	Oceans	32
Plate tectonics	21	Largest seas	32
Continental drift	22	Largest lakes	32
Geological time scale	22	Longest rivers	33
Ice ages	24	Highest waterfalls	33
Fossils	24	Largest deserts	33
Classification of sedimentary rocks	25	Deepest caves	34
Principal metamorphic rocks	25	Highest mountains	34
Principal igneous rocks	26	Major volcanoes	35
Properties of common minerals	27	Major earthquakes	36
Properties of gemstones	27	Earthquake severity measurement	37
Mohs' hardness scale	28	Major tsunamis	38
Continents	28		

Climate and Environment

Climatic zones	39	Acid rain	45
Meteorological extremes	39	Tropical rainforest distribution	46
World temperatures	40	Forest area and rate of change	46
World temperature change	41	Environmental disasters on land	46
Wind force and sea disturbance	41	Major oil spills at sea	48
Windstorms	42	Major national parks and nature reserves	49
Hydrological cycle	44	World Heritage sites	51
Clouds	44	Shipping forecast areas	59

Natural History

Nitrogen cycle	60	Fungi	77
Carbon cycle	61	Animal kingdom	79
Classification of organisms	61	Mammals	79
Plant kingdom	62	Mammals: record holders	89
Cereals	62	Length of pregnancy in some mammals	89
Edible fruits (temperate and Mediterranean)	63	Birds	89
Edible fruits (tropical)	64	Birds: record holders	100
Herbs	64	Amphibians	100
Spices	66	Reptiles	102
Vegetables	67	Fish	105
Flowers (bulbs, corms, rhizomes and tubers)	69	Fish: record holders	109
Flowers (herbaceous)	70	Invertebrates	110
Flowers (shrubs)	72	Collective names for mammals, birds and fish	118
Trees (temperate and Mediterranean)	74	Species under threat	119
Trees (tropical)	76		

Human Body, Health and Nutrition

DNA	121	Supplementary medical treatments	139
The chromosomes	121	Complementary medicine	139
The skeleton	122	Commonly prescribed drugs	141
The muscles	122	Common illegal drugs	143
The skin	123	Immunization schedule for children up to	
The nervous system	123	age 18	144
The brain	124	Immunization for foreign travel	144
The glands	124	An A to Z of phobias	145
The digestive system	125	Measuring your Body Mass Index	147
The lymphatic system	125	Optimum weight according to height	147
ABO blood group system	126	Average daily energy requirements	147
The heart	126	Energy expenditure	148
The circulatory system	127	Dietary recommendations	149
The lungs	127	Composition of selected foods	150
CPR – cardio-pulmonary resuscitation	128	E numbers	152
The ear	128	Culinary terms of foreign origin	153
The eye	128	Chefs, restaurateurs and cookery writers	156
The reproductive organs	129	Varieties of wines and grapes	159
Main types of vitamin	130	Terms relating to wine-making and	
Main trace minerals	130	wine-tasting	160
Infectious diseases and infections	131	Wine bottle sizes	163
Major causes of death	135	Types of European cheese	163
Important discoveries in medicine	135		

Science and Technology

Scientific terms	164	SI units (international system of units)	208
Fields of scientific study	174	SI conversion factors	209
Scientists	177	SI prefixes	211
Nobel Prizes	186	Temperature conversion	211
Inventions	188	Common measures	212
Industrialists and entrepreneurs	192	Other measures	213
Physical constants	196	Conversion factors	214
Radiation	197	Conversion tables: length	215
Decibel scale	197	Conversion tables: area	216
Periodic table	198	Conversion tables: volume	217
Table of elements	199	Conversion tables: capacity	218
Properties of metals	202	Conversion tables: tyre pressure	220
Properties of polymers	203	Conversion tables: weight	220
Mathematical signs and symbols	204	International clothing sizes	222
Squares and roots	204	International pattern sizes	222
Areas and volumes of common shapes	205	International paper sizes	223
Conic sections	206	Engineering: bridges	224
Pythagoras's theorem	206	Engineering: tunnels	226
Numerical equivalents	207	Engineering: dams	227
Multiplication table	208	Engineering: tallest inhabited buildings	228

History

Chronology	229	Mughal emperors	283
Journeys of exploration	274	European monarchs	283
Major battles and wars	275	Emperors of the Holy Roman Empire	286
Seven Wonders of the World	280	Popes	287
Ancient Egyptian dynasties	280	Political leaders 1900–2008	289
Chinese dynasties	281	British Prime Ministers	339
Japanese emperors	281	Presidents of the USA	340
Roman kings and emperors	282		

Arts and Culture

Novelists	341	Motion picture Academy Awards	397
Literary prizes 1988–2008	355	Composers	399
Poets	356	Librettists and songwriters	403
Poets laureate	359	Operas and operettas	405
Playwrights	360	Opera singers	406
Plays of Shakespeare	362	Orchestras	407
Film and TV actors	363	Layout of an orchestra	408
Film directors	392	Jazz and blues musicians and singers	409

Pop and rock musicians and singers 417
Grammy awards 429
Musical symbols, terms and abbreviations 430
Tempo and expression marks 431
Other terms and abbreviations 431
Ballet and modern dance choreographers 432
Ballets 433
Ballet and modern dancers 435
Ballet and modern dance companies 436
Major painting styles 437
Artists 439

Turner Prize 1988–2008 444
Sculptors 444
Photographers 445
Fashion designers 450
Major architectural styles 453
Architects 454
Nobel Prizes 457
Museums and art galleries – Europe 459
Museums and art galleries – UK 461
Museums and art galleries – USA 462

Thought and Belief

Philosophers 464
Gods of Greek mythology 469
Gods of Roman mythology 469
Gods of Egyptian mythology 470
Gods of Norse mythology 470
Figures of myth and legend 471
Population distribution of major beliefs 489
Baha'i 492
Buddhism 492
Christianity 492
Major Christian denominations 493
The Ten Commandments 493
Major immovable Christian feasts 493
Movable Christian feasts 2005–2030 493
Saints' days 494
Patron saints of occupations 497
Confucianism 498
Major Chinese festivals 498

Hinduism 498
Major Hindu festivals 498
Islam 499
Major Islamic festivals 499
Jainism 499
Judaism 500
Major Jewish festivals 500
Shintoism 500
Major Japanese festivals 500
Sikhism 501
Taoism 501
Sacred texts of world religions 501
Other religions, sects and religious movements 502
Religious leaders and theologians 503
Templeton Prize 509
Religious symbols 510
Signs of the zodiac 511

Sports and Games

Olympic Games 512
Paralympic Games 513
Commonwealth Games 514
Sports 514

Champions 1992–2008 521
100 Champions in sport 559
Card, board and other indoor games 564
Hobbies and pastimes 566

Time

Perpetual calendar 1801–2040 569
Year equivalents 574
The seasons 575
Chinese animal years and times 1960–2019 575

Wedding anniversaries 575
Months' associations with gems and flowers 575
International time differences 576
National holidays 577

Communication

Languages: number of speakers 584
Speakers of English 585
Foreign words and phrases 585
Differences between British and US English 591
Proverbs 593
Some common similes 594
-isms 595
First name meanings in the UK and USA 596
Common abbreviations 598
Alphabets 605
British sign language: fingerspelling 607
US sign language: fingerspelling 607
Computer languages 608
Emoticons 608
Abbreviations and acronyms used in e-mail 609
Abbreviations and acronyms used in text
  messages 609
Typefaces 610

News agencies 610
National newspapers – UK 612
National newspapers – Europe 612
Major newspapers – USA 613
Symbols in general use 614
Clothes care symbols 614
Car index marks – UK 615
Car index marks – international 617
Road signs 619
UK road distances 624
European road distances 624
International E-road network ('Euroroutes') 625
UK airports 626
International airports 627
Airline designators 632
Air distances 634
Flying times 634
Deepwater ports of the world 635

Social Structure

World population estimates 638
Population of the six most populous nations 638
Major cities of the world 638
Largest cities by population 644
Largest metropolitan areas by population 645
United Nations 645
The Commonwealth 647
Commonwealth of Independent States 647
European Union 648
Europe – administrative divisions 649
County and unitary councils of England 659
Council areas of Wales 661
Council areas of Scotland 661

Districts of Northern Ireland 662
British islands 662
Political definitions 663
Legislative systems of government 664
Passage of a public bill to law in the UK 665
Passage of a public bill to law in the USA 666
Military ranks 667
Royal and aristocratic ranks 668
Honours: UK 668
Honours: Europe 668
Honours: USA 669
Forms of address 669

Nations of the World

A–Z of nations 673
Afghanistan 679
Albania 680
Algeria 681
Andorra 682
Angola 682
Antigua and Barbuda 683
Argentina 684
Armenia 686
Australia 687
Austria 689
Azerbaijan 690
The Bahamas 691
Bahrain 691
Bangladesh 692
Barbados 693
Belarus 694
Belgium 695
Belize 696
Benin 697
Bhutan 698
Bolivia 698
Bosnia and Herzegovina 699
Botswana 700
Brazil 701
Brunei 702
Bulgaria 703
Burkina Faso 704
Burundi 704
Cambodia 705
Cameroon 706
Canada 707
Cape Verde 709
Central African Republic 710
Chad 711
Chile 712
China 713
Colombia 715
Comoros 716
Congo 717
Congo, Democratic Republic of the 718
Costa Rica 719
Côte d'Ivoire 720
Croatia 721
Cuba 722
Cyprus 723
Czech Republic 724
Denmark 724
Djibouti 726
Dominica 726
Dominican Republic 727
East Timor 728
Ecuador 729
Egypt 730
El Salvador 731

Equatorial Guinea 732
Eritrea 732
Estonia 733
Ethiopia 734
Fiji 735
Finland 736
France 737
Gabon 739
The Gambia 740
Georgia 741
Germany 742
Ghana 744
Greece 745
Grenada 746
Guatemala 747
Guinea 748
Guinea-Bissau 748
Guyana 749
Haiti 750
Honduras 751
Hungary 752
Iceland 753
India 754
Indonesia 756
Iran 757
Iraq 758
Ireland 759
Israel 760
Italy 762
Jamaica 764
Japan 764
Jordan 766
Kazakhstan 767
Kenya 768
Kiribati 769
North Korea 769
South Korea 770
Kuwait 771
Kyrgyzstan 772
Laos 773
Latvia 773
Lebanon 774
Lesotho 775
Liberia 776
Libya 777
Liechtenstein 778
Lithuania 778
Luxembourg 779
Macedonia 780
Madagascar 781
Malawi 782
Malaysia 783
Maldives 784
Mali 785
Malta 786

Marshall Islands	786	Serbia	826
Mauritania	787	Seychelles	827
Mauritius	788	Sierra Leone	828
Mexico	789	Singapore	829
Federated States of Micronesia	790	Slovakia	829
Moldova	791	Slovenia	830
Monaco	792	Solomon Islands	831
Mongolia	792	Somalia	832
Montenegro	793	South Africa	833
Morocco	794	Spain	834
Mozambique	795	Sri Lanka	836
Myanmar (Burma)	796	Sudan	837
Namibia	797	Suriname	838
Nauru	798	Swaziland	839
Nepal	799	Sweden	840
The Netherlands	800	Switzerland	841
New Zealand	801	Syria	842
Nicaragua	802	Taiwan	843
Niger	803	Tajikistan	844
Nigeria	804	Tanzania	845
Norway	805	Thailand	846
Oman	806	Togo	847
Pakistan	807	Tonga	847
Palau	808	Trinidad and Tobago	848
Panama	809	Tunisia	849
Papua New Guinea	810	Turkey	850
Paraguay	811	Turkmenistan	851
Peru	811	Tuvalu	851
Philippines	812	Uganda	852
Poland	813	Ukraine	853
Portugal	815	United Arab Emirates	854
Qatar	816	United Kingdom	855
Romania	816	United States of America	863
Russia	817	Uruguay	870
Rwanda	819	Uzbekistan	871
St Christopher and Nevis	820	Vanuatu	872
St Lucia	821	Vatican City State	872
St Vincent and the Grenadines	821	Venezuela	873
Samoa	822	Vietnam	874
San Marino	823	Yemen	875
São Tomé and Príncipe	823	Zambia	876
Saudi Arabia	824	Zimbabwe	877
Senegal	825		

Index   879

SPACE

The Sun

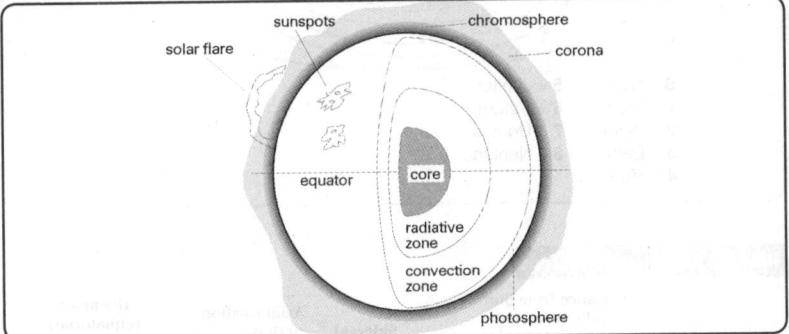

Physical characteristics of the Sun
Diameter 1 392 530km/864 950mi
Volume 1.414×10^{18}km³/3.388×10^{17}cu mi
Mass 1.9891×10^{30}kg/4.385×10^{30}lb

Density (water = 1)

Mean density of entire Sun	1.410g cm⁻³
Interior (centre of Sun)	150g cm⁻³
Surface (photosphere)	10^{-3}g cm⁻³
Chromosphere	10^{-6}g cm⁻³
Low corona	1.7×10^{-16}g cm⁻³

Temperature

Interior (centre)	15 000 000K
Surface (photosphere)	6050K
Sunspot umbra (typical)	4240K
Penumbra (typical)	5680K
Chromosphere	4300 to 50 000K
Corona	800 000 to 5 000 000K

Rotation (as seen from Earth)

Of solar equator	26.8 days
At solar latitude 30°	28.2 days
At solar latitude 60°	30.8 days
At solar latitude 75°	31.8 days

Chemical composition of photosphere

Element	% weight
Hydrogen	73.46
Helium	24.85
Oxygen	0.77
Carbon	0.29
Iron	0.16
Neon	0.12
Nitrogen	0.09
Silicon	0.07
Magnesium	0.05
Sulphur	0.04
Other	0.10

Solar system

Space

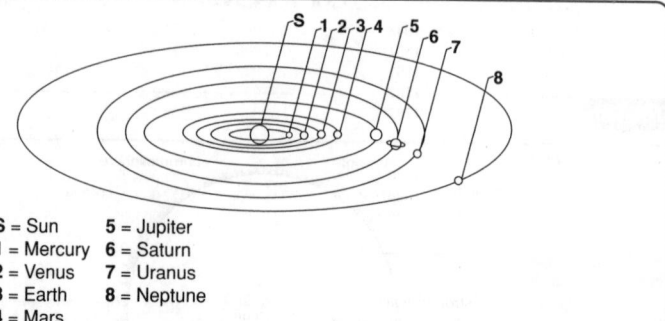

S = Sun   **5** = Jupiter
1 = Mercury **6** = Saturn
2 = Venus   **7** = Uranus
3 = Earth   **8** = Neptune
4 = Mars

Planets in the solar system

Planet	Distance from Sun (million km/mi)				Sidereal period	Axial rotation period (equatorial)	Diameter (equatorial)	
	Maximum		Minimum				km	mi
Mercury	69.4	43.0	46.8	29.0	88d	58d 16h	4878	3031
Venus	109.0	67.6	107.6	66.7	224.7d	243d	12104	7521
Earth	152.6	94.6	147.4	91.4	365.256d	23h 56m	12756	7927
Mars	249.2	154.5	207.3	128.5	687d	24h 37m 23s	6794	4222
Jupiter	817.4	506.8	741.6	459.8	11.86y	9h 50m 30s	142800	88700
Saturn	1512	937.6	1346	834.6	29.46y	10h 14m	120536	74900
Uranus	3011	1867	2740	1699	84.01y	16–28h[1]	51118	31765
Neptune	4543	2817	4466	2769	164.79y	18–20h[1]	49492	30754

y: years d: days h: hours m: minutes s: seconds km: kilometres mi: miles
[1] Different latitudes rotate at different speeds.

Major satellites of the planets

The number in parenthesis after the name of the planet is the total number of known satellites; data is for the major satellites.

	Year discovered	Distance from planet		Diameter	
		km	mi	km	mi
Earth (1)					
Moon	—	384000	239000	3476	2160
Mars (2)					
Phobos	1877	9380	5830	27	17
Deimos	1877	23460	14580	15	9
Jupiter (c.60)					
Io	1610	422000	262000	3630	2260
Europa	1610	671000	417000	3138	1950
Ganymede	1610	1070000	665000	5260	3270
Callisto	1610	1883000	1170000	4800	3000
Saturn (c.30)					
Mimas	1789	186000	116000	390	240
Enceladus	1789	238000	148000	500	310
Tethys	1684	295000	183000	1050	650
Dione	1684	377000	234000	1120	700
Rhea	1672	527000	327000	1530	950
Titan	1655	1222000	759000	5150	3200
Hyperion	1848	1481000	920000	300	190
Iapetus	1671	3560000	2212000	1460	900

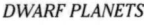

	Year discovered	Distance from planet km	Distance from planet mi	Diameter km	Diameter mi
Uranus (c.20)					
Miranda	1948	130000	81000	470	290
Ariel	1851	191000	119000	1160	720
Umbriel	1851	266000	165000	1170	725
Titania	1787	436000	271000	1580	980
Oberon	1787	583000	362000	1520	945
Neptune (11)					
Triton	1846	355000	221000	2700	1675
Nereid	1949	5515000	3427000	340	210
Proteus	1989	117600	73000	400	249

Dwarf planets

In 2006, the International Astronomical Union (IAU) created a new category of 'dwarf planets' and reclassified Pluto as such, along with two other celestial bodies. Dwarf planets are objects that orbit the sun and are massive enough to be nearly spherical in shape, but differ from planets as they do not have a clear neighbourhood around their orbit.

Dwarf planet	Region	Diameter	Classification date
Ceres	Asteroid belt	975 × 909km	Aug 2006
Eris	Scattered disc	2400 ± 100km	Aug 2006
Pluto	Kuiper belt	2306 ± 20km	Aug 2006

The lunar 'seas'

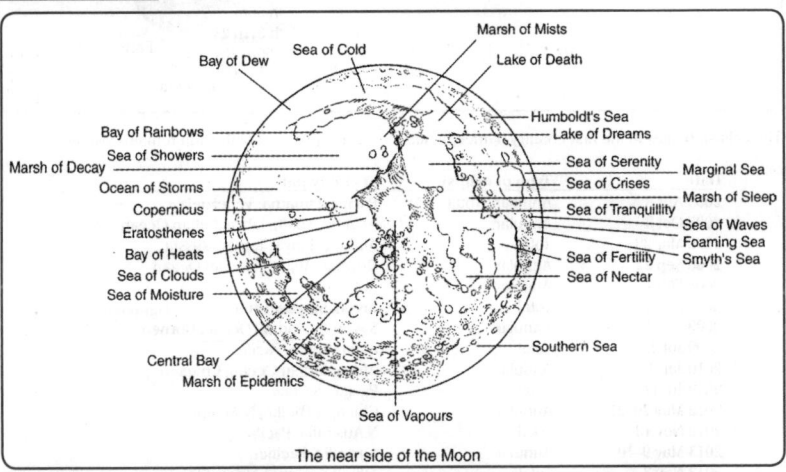

The near side of the Moon

Latin name	English name	Latin name	English name
Lacus Mortis	Lake of Death	Mare Serenitatis	Sea of Serenity
Lacus Somniorum	Lake of Dreams	Mare Smythii	Smyth's Sea
Mare Australe	Southern Sea	Mare Spumans	Foaming Sea
Mare Crisium	Sea of Crises	Mare Tranquillitatis	Sea of Tranquillity
Mare Fecunditatis	Sea of Fertility	Mare Undarum	Sea of Waves
Mare Frigoris	Sea of Cold	Mare Vaporum	Sea of Vapours
Mare Humboldtianum	Humboldt's Sea	Oceanus Procellarum	Ocean of Storms
Mare Humorum	Sea of Moisture	Palus Epidemiarum	Marsh of Epidemics
Mare Imbrium	Sea of Showers	Palus Nebularum	Marsh of Mists
Mare Ingenii[1]	Sea of Geniuses	Palus Putredinis	Marsh of Decay
Mare Marginis	Marginal Sea	Palus Somnii	Marsh of Sleep
Mare Moscoviense[1]	Moscow Sea	Sinus Aestuum	Bay of Heats
Mare Nectaris	Sea of Nectar	Sinus Iridum	Bay of Rainbows
Mare Nubium	Sea of Clouds	Sinus Medii	Central Bay
Mare Orientale[1]	Eastern Sea	Sinus Roris	Bay of Dew

[1] On the far side of the Moon.

Space

Phases of the Moon

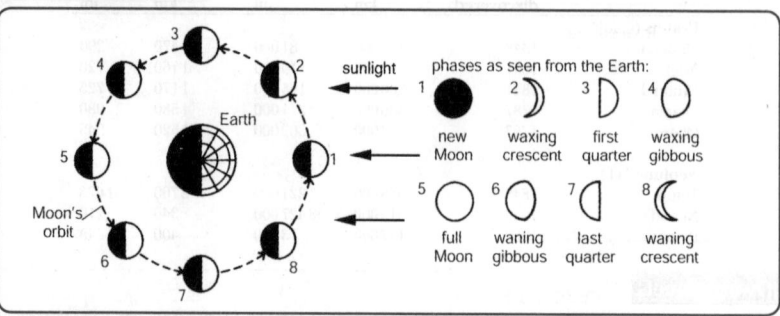

Solar eclipses 2005–25

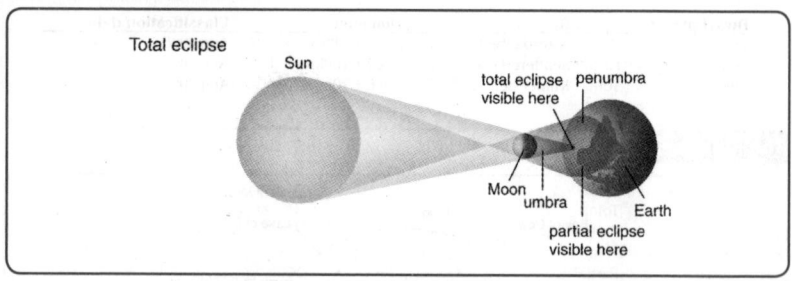

The eclipse begins in the first country named. In an annular eclipse, part of the Sun remains visible.

Date	Type of eclipse	Visibility path
2005 Apr 8	Annular / Total	Pacific, Panama, Venezuela
2005 Oct 3	Annular	Atlantic, Spain, Libya, Indian Ocean
2006 Mar 29	Total	Atlantic, Libya, Turkey, Russia
2006 Sep 22	Annular	Guyana, Atlantic, Indian Ocean
2008 Feb 7	Annular	Antarctic
2008 Aug 1	Total	Arctic, Siberia, China
2009 Jan 26	Annular	S Atlantic, Indian Ocean, Borneo
2009 Jul 22	Total	India, China, Pacific
2010 Jan 15	Annular	Africa, Indian Ocean, China
2010 Jul 11	Total	Pacific, S Chile
2012 May 20–21	Annular	China, N Pacific, N America
2012 Nov 13	Total	N Australia, Pacific
2013 May 9–10	Annular	Australia, Pacific
2013 Nov 3	Total	Atlantic, central Africa, Ethiopia
2015 Mar 20	Total	N Atlantic, Arctic
2016 Mar 9	Total	Indonesia, Pacific
2016 Sep 1	Annular	Atlantic, Africa, Madagascar, Indian Ocean
2017 Feb 26	Annular	Pacific, S America, Atlantic, Africa
2017 Aug 21	Total	Pacific, N America, Atlantic
2019 Jul 2	Total	Pacific, S America
2019 Dec 26	Annular	Middle East, Sri Lanka, Indonesia, Pacific
2020 Jun 21	Annular	Africa, Middle East, China, Pacific
2020 Dec 14	Total	S Pacific, S America, S Atlantic
2021 Jun 10	Annular	Canada, Greenland, Russia
2021 Dec 4	Total	Antarctic
2023 Apr 20	Total	Indonesia, Australia, Papua New Guinea
2023 Oct 14	Annular	N America, Central America, Colombia, Brazil
2024 Apr 8	Total	Mexico, N America
2024 Oct 2	Annular	Chile, Argentina

4

Lunar eclipses 2005-25

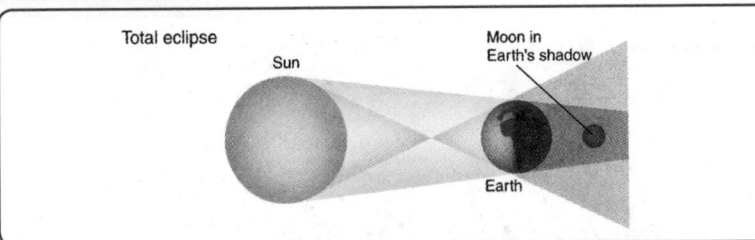

Total eclipse

Sun

Moon in Earth's shadow

Earth

Space

Date	Type of eclipse	Time of greatest eclipse UT[1]	Where visible
2005 Oct 17	Partial	12.03	E Asia, Pacific, N America
2006 Sep 7	Partial	18.51	Australia, Asia, E Africa
2007 Mar 3	Total	23.21	Americas, Europe, Asia, Africa
2007 Aug 28	Total	10.37	Australia, Pacific, part of N America
2008 Feb 21	Total	03.26	Americas, Europe, Africa
2008 Aug 16	Partial	21.10	Europe, Africa, W Asia
2009 Dec 31	Partial	19.22	Asia, Africa, Europe
2010 Jun 26	Partial	11.38	Pacific Rim
2010 Dec 21	Total	08.17	N and S America
2011 Jun 15	Total	20.13	Asia, Africa, Europe
2011 Dec 10	Total	14.32	Pacific, Australia, E Asia
2012 Jun 4	Partial	11.03	Pacific, Australasia
2013 Apr 25	Partial	20.08	Asia, Africa, Europe
2014 Apr 15	Total	07.46	N and S America
2014 Oct 8	Total	10.55	Pacific, Australia, W Americas
2015 Apr 4	Partial	12.00	Pacific, Australasia
2015 Sep 28	Total	02.47	Africa, Europe, Americas
2017 Aug 7	Partial	18.20	Asia, Africa, Australia
2018 Jan 31	Total	13.30	Pacific, Australia, Asia
2018 Jul 27	Total	20.22	Asia, Africa, part of Europe
2019 Jan 21	Total	05.12	Americas, part of Europe
2019 Jul 16	Partial	21.31	Asia, Africa, Europe
2021 May 26	Total	11.19	Asia, Australia, Pacific, America
2021 Nov 19	Partial	09.03	Americas, N Europe, E Asia, Pacific
2022 May 16	Total	04.11	Americas. Europe, Africa
2022 Nov 8	Total	10.59	Asia, Australia, Pacific, Americas
2023 Oct 28	Partial	20.14	Americas, Europe, Africa, Asia, Australia
2024 Sep 18	Partial	02.44	Americas, Europe, Africa
2025 Mar 14	Total	07.00	Pacific, Americas, Europe, Africa
2025 Sep 7	Total	18.12	Europe, Africa, Asia, Australia

[1] Universal Time, equivalent to Greenwich Mean Time (GMT).

Space

The constellations

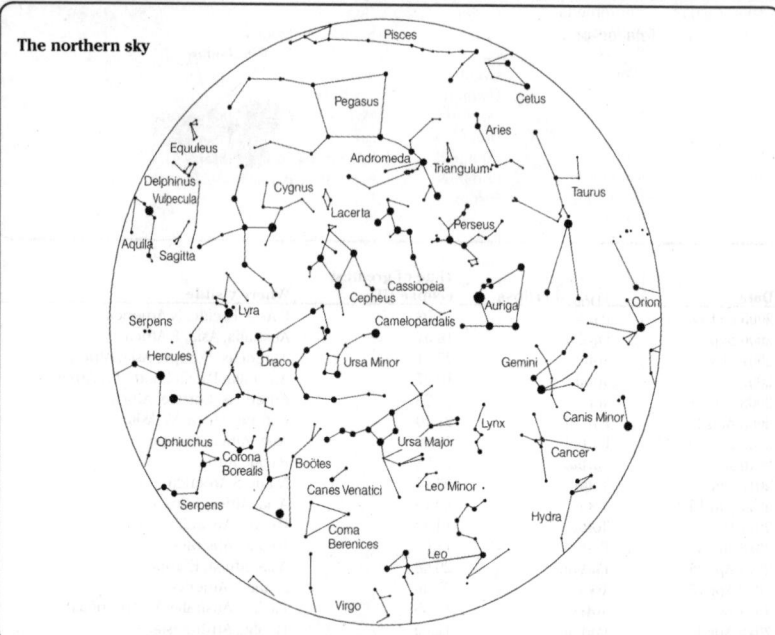

The northern sky

Pisces · Pegasus · Cetus · Aries · Equuleus · Andromeda · Triangulum · Taurus · Delphinus · Cygnus · Vulpecula · Lacerta · Perseus · Aquila · Sagitta · Cassiopeia · Cepheus · Auriga · Orion · Serpens · Lyra · Camelopardalis · Hercules · Draco · Ursa Minor · Gemini · Lynx · Canis Minor · Ophiuchus · Corona Borealis · Boötes · Ursa Major · Cancer · Serpens · Canes Venatici · Leo Minor · Hydra · Coma Berenices · Leo · Virgo

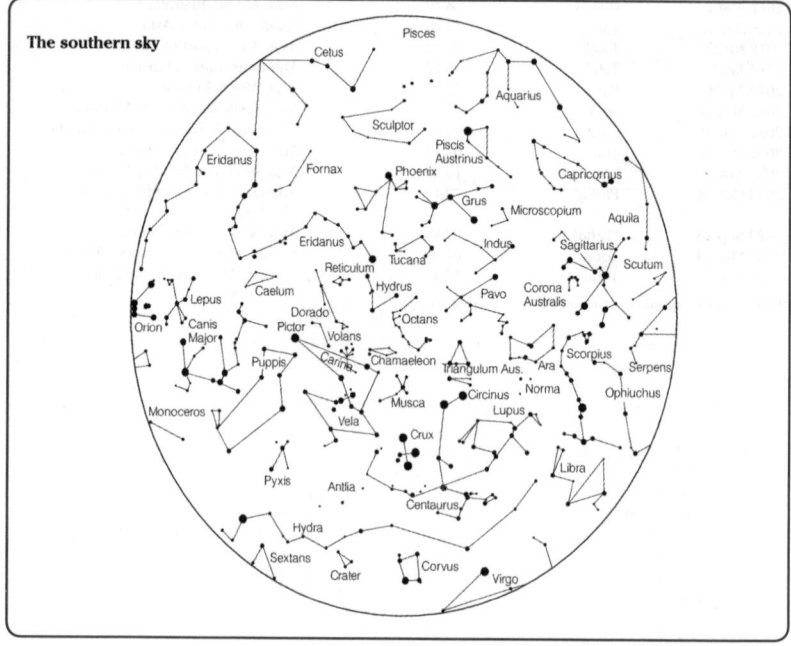

The southern sky

Pisces · Cetus · Aquarius · Sculptor · Piscis Austrinus · Eridanus · Fornax · Phoenix · Capricornus · Grus · Microscopium · Aquila · Eridanus · Tucana · Indus · Sagittarius · Scutum · Reticulum · Hydrus · Pavo · Corona Australis · Lepus · Caelum · Dorado · Octans · Orion · Canis Major · Pictor · Volans · Scorpius · Puppis · Carina · Chamaeleon · Triangulum Aus. · Ara · Serpens · Musca · Circinus · Norma · Ophiuchus · Monoceros · Vela · Lupus · Crux · Pyxis · Antlia · Libra · Centaurus · Hydra · Sextans · Crater · Corvus · Virgo

THE 20 BRIGHTEST STARS

Latin name	English name	Latin name	English name	Latin name	English name
Andromeda	Andromeda	Crater	Cup	Orion	Orion
Antlia	Air Pump	Crux	Southern Cross	Pavo	Peacock
Apus	Bird of Paradise	Cygnus	Swan	Pegasus	Winged Horse
Aquarius	Water Bearer	Delphinus	Dolphin	Perseus	Perseus
Aquila	Eagle	Dorado	Swordfish	Phoenix	Phoenix
Ara	Altar	Draco	Dragon	Pictor	Easel
Aries	Ram	Equuleus	Little Horse	Pisces	Fishes
Auriga	Charioteer	Eridanus	River Eridanus	Piscis Austrinus	Southern Fish
Boötes	Herdsman	Fornax	Furnace	Puppis	Ship's Stern
Caelum	Chisel	Gemini	Twins	Pyxis	Mariner's Compass
Camelopardalis	Giraffe	Grus	Crane	Reticulum	Net
Cancer	Crab	Hercules	Hercules	Sagitta	Arrow
Canes Venatici	Hunting Dogs	Horologium	Clock	Sagittarius	Archer
Canis Major	Great Dog	Hydra	Sea Serpent	Scorpius	Scorpion
Canis Minor	Little Dog	Hydrus	Water Snake	Sculptor	Sculptor
Capricornus	Sea Goat	Indus	Indian	Scutum	Shield
Carina	Keel	Lacerta	Lizard	Serpens	Serpent
Cassiopeia	Cassiopeia	Leo	Lion	Sextans	Sextant
Centaurus	Centaur	Leo Minor	Little Lion	Taurus	Bull
Cepheus	Cepheus	Lepus	Hare	Telescopium	Telescope
Cetus	Whale	Libra	Scales	Triangulum	Triangle
Chamaeleon	Chameleon	Lupus	Wolf	Triangulum Australe	Southern Triangle
Circinus	Compasses	Lynx	Lynx	Tucana	Toucan
Columba	Dove	Lyra	Harp	Ursa Major	Great Bear
Coma Berenices	Berenice's Hair	Mensa	Table	Ursa Minor	Little Bear
Corona Australis	Southern Crown	Microscopium	Microscope	Vela	Sails
Corona Borealis	Northern Crown	Monoceros	Unicorn	Virgo	Virgin
Corvus	Crow	Musca	Fly	Volans	Flying Fish
		Norma	Level	Vulpecula	Fox
		Octans	Octant		
		Ophiuchus	Serpent Bearer		

The 20 brightest stars

The apparent brightness of a star is represented by a number called its magnitude. The larger the number, the fainter the star. The faintest stars visible to the naked eye are slightly fainter than magnitude 6. Only about 6000 of the billions of stars in the sky are visible to the naked eye.

Star name	Distance (light years)	Apparent magnitude	Absolute magnitude
Sirius A	8.7	−1.46	+1.4
Canopus	98	−0.72	−3.1
Arcturus	36	−0.06	−0.3
Rigil Kentaurus	4.2	−0.01	+4.4
Vega	26.5	+0.04	+0.5
Capella	45	+0.05	−0.6
Rigel	900	+0.14	−7.1
Procyon	11.4	+0.37	+2.6
Betelgeuse	520	+0.41	−5.6
Achernar	118	+0.51	−2.3
Hadar	490	+0.63	−5.2
Altair	16.5	+0.76	+2.2
Aldebaran	68	+0.86	−0.7
Spica	220	+0.91	−3.3
Antares	520	+0.92	−5.1
Fomalhaut	22.6	+1.15	+2.0
Pollux	35	+1.16	+1.0
Deneb	1600	+1.26	−7.1
Beta Crucis	490	+1.28	−4.6
Regulus	84	+1.36	−0.7

Space

The 20 nearest stars

Star name	Distance (light years)	Apparent magnitude	Absolute magnitude
Proxima Centauri	4.3	+11.05	+15.5
Alpha Centauri A	4.3	−0.01	+4.4
Alpha Centauri B	4.3	+1.33	+5.7
Barnard's Star	5.9	+9.54	+13.3
Wolf 359	7.6	+13.53	+16.7
Lalande 21 185	8.1	+7.50	+10.5
Sirius A	8.6	−1.46	+1.4
Sirius B	8.6	+8.68	+11.6
Luyten 726-8A	8.9	+12.45	+15.3
UV 726-8B	8.9	+12.95	+15.3
Ross 154	9.4	+10.60	+13.3
Ross 248	10.3	+12.29	+14.8
Epsilon Eridani	10.8	+3.73	+6.1
Ross 128	10.8	+11.10	+13.5
Luyten 789-6	10.8	+12.18	+14.6
61 Cygni A	11.1	+5.22	+7.6
61 Cygni B	11.1	+6.03	+8.4
Epsilon Indi	11.2	+4.68	+7.0
Procyon A	11.2	+0.37	+2.7
Procyon B	11.2	+10.70	+13.0

Comets

The solid nucleus of a comet is usually several kilometres in diameter; it consists of ice, dust and solid particles like a large, dirty snowball. When the comet passes close to the Sun, a cloud of gas and dust is ejected from the nucleus, forming a huge head or coma, many thousands of kilometres in diameter. The radiations from the Sun elongate the gas and dust to form one or more tails, often extending millions of kilometres in space. These tails point away from the Sun, but as the comet recedes, the tail will decrease in length until the comet returns to its latent dirty snowball state.

Information for selected comets is given below.

Comet	First seen	Period of orbit (years)
Arend-Roland	1957	*not known*
Bennett	1970	1 680
Cruls	1882	758.4
Daylight Comet	1910	*not known*
De Chéseaux	1744	*not known*
Donati	1858	1 950
Encke	1786	3.3
Flauergues	1811	3 094
Great Comet	1843	512.6
Hale-Bopp	1995	2 400
Halley	240 BC	76.1
Humason	1961	3 000
Hyakutake	1996	18 000
Ikeya-Seki	1965	880
IRAS-Araki-Alcock	1983	*not known*
Kirch[1]	1680	8814
Kohoutek	1973	75 000
Lexell	1770	5.6
Morehouse	1908	*not known*
Mrkos	1957	*not known*
Pons-Winnecke	1819	6.34
Schwassmann-Wachmann 1	1925	15
Seki-Lines	1962	*not known*
Shoemaker-Levy 9	1993	collided with Jupiter, 1994
Swift-Tuttle	1862	125
Tago-Sato-Kosaka	1969	420 000
Tebbutt	1861	409.1
Tycho	1577	*not known*
West	1975	500 000
Wolf	1884	8.4

[1] Kirch also known as Newton.

Annual meteor showers

Meteors appear to radiate from named star region.

Shower	Dates	Maximum activity	Notes
Quadrantids	Jan 1–6	Jan 3–4	swift
Lyrids	Apr 19–25	Apr 22	
Alpha-Scorpiids	Apr 20–May 19	Apr 28–May 10	S Hemisphere
Eta Aquariids	May 1–8	May 5	
Delta Aquariids	Jul 15–Aug 10	Jul 28–Aug 5	S Hemisphere
Perseids	Jul 27–Aug 17	Aug 11–14	very reliable
Orionids	Oct 15–25	Oct 21	
Taurids	Oct 25–Nov 25	Nov 4–14	
Leonids	Nov 14–20	Nov 17–18	
Geminids	Dec 8–14	Dec 13–14	very reliable
Ursids	Dec 19–24	Dec 22–23	

Largest ground-based telescopes

Telescope name	Type	Observatory	Site (altitude m / ft)	Mirror / dish size	Founded
Anglo-Australian Telescope (AAT)	optical	Anglo-Australian Observatory	Siding Spring Mountain, NSW, Australia (1165m/3820ft)	3.9m	1974
Arecibo Telescope	radio	National Astronomy and Ionosphere Centre	Puerto Rico (496m / 1625ft)	304.8m	1963
Australia Telescope	radio	Commonwealth Scientific and Industrial Research Organization	Throughout NSW, Australia	7 × 22m, 1 × 64m	1990
Bol'shoi Teleskop Azimutal'nyi	optical	Special Astrophysical Observatory	Mt Pastukhov, Zelenchukskaya, Russia (2100m/6900ft)	6m	1976
—	optical	Byurakan Astrophysical Observatory	Mt Aragatz, Armenia (1500m/5000ft)	2.6m	1976
C Donald Shane Telescope	optical	Lick Observatory	Mt Hamilton, California, USA (1277m/4190ft)	3.05m	1959
California Submillimetre Observatory	submilli-metre	California Institute of Technology	Mauna Kea, Hawaii, USA (4160m/13650ft)	10.4m	1986
Canada–France–Hawaii Telescope (CFHT)	optical	Canada–France–Hawaii Telescope Corporation	Mauna Kea, Hawaii, USA (4180m/13720ft)	3.6m	1979
Effelsberg Radio Telescope	radio	Max Planck Institut für Radioastronomie	Effelsberg, nr Bonn, Germany	100m	1971
ESO New Technology Telescope,	optical	European Southern Observatory	Cerro Tololo, Chile (2160m/7100ft)	3.6m	1990
ESO 3.6m	optical	European Southern Observatory	Cerro La Silla, Chile (2400m/7850ft)	3.6m	1976
—	radio	Five College Radio Astronomy	New Salem, Massachusetts, USA	14m	1969
Gemini North Telescope, Gemini South Telescope	optical/ infrared	various	Mauna Kea, Hawaii, USA (4160m/13650ft), Cerro Pachón, Chile (2715m/8907ft)	2 × 8.1m	1999
George Ellery Hale Telescope	optical	Palomar Observatory	Palomar Mountain, California, USA (1700m/5600ft)	5.08m	1948
Gran Telescopio Canarias (GTC)	optical	Observatory Roque de los Muchachos	La Palma, Canary Is	10.4m	2006
—	optical	German–Spanish Astronomical Centre	Calar Alto, Spain (2160m/7100ft)	3.5m	1985
Harlan J Smith Telescope	optical	McDonald Observatory	Mt Locke, Texas, USA (2070m/6791ft)	2.7m	1968

Space

Space

Telescope name	Type	Observatory	Site (altitude m / ft)	Mirror / dish size	Founded
Hobby–Eberly Telescope	optical	McDonald Observatory	Mt Fowlkes, Texas, USA (2100m/6900ft)	11m	1997
Irénée du Pont Telescope	optical	Mt Wilson and Las Campanas Observatories	Cerro Las Campanas,Chile (2510m/8235ft)	2.57m	1977
IRAM Array	millimetre	Institut de Radio Astronomie Millimétrique	Plateau de Bure, France (2552m/8373ft)	4 × 15m	1979
Isaac Newton Telescope	optical	Observatory Roque de los Muchachos	La Palma, Canary Is (2336m/7660ft)	2.54m	1984
James Clerk Maxwell Telescope (JCMT)	submillimetre	Royal Observatory, Edinburgh	Mauna Kea, Hawaii, USA (4160m/13650ft)	15m	1987
Keck Telescope	optical/ infrared	California Association for Research and Astronomy (CARA)	Mauna Kea, Hawaii, USA (4160m/13650ft)	2 × 10m	1990
Large Binocular Telescope (LBT)	optical	Mount Graham International Observatory	Arizona, USA	2 × 8.4m	2007
Lovell Telescope	radio	Nuffield Radio Astronomy Laboratory (Jodrell Bank), University of Manchester	Jodrell Bank, Cheshire, UK	76m	1957
MERLIN (Multi-Element Radio-Linked Interfero-meter Network)	radio	Nuffield Radio Astronomy Laboratory (Jodrell Bank), University of Manchester	UK (Midlands and Wales)	5 × 25m, 1 × 32m, 1 × 76m	1980
Multiple Mirror Telescope	optical	Whipple Observatory	Mt Hopkins, Arizona, USA (2606m/8550ft)	6.5m	1979
NASA Infrared Telescope Facility (IRTF)	infrared	NASA	Mauna Kea, Hawaii, USA (4160m/13650ft)	3m	1979
—	millimetre	National Radio Astronomy Observatory (NRAO)	Kitt Peak, Arizona, USA (1920m/6300ft)	12m	1982
Nicholas U Mayall Telescope	optical	Kitt Peak National Observatory	Kitt Peak, Arizona, USA (2100m/6900ft)	4m	1973
Nobeyama Millimetre Array	millimetre	Nobeyama Radio Observatory	Nobeyama, Japan (1300m/4265ft)	5 × 10m	1986
Nobeyama Radio Telescope	radio	Nobeyama Radio Observatory	Nobeyama, Japan (1300m/4265ft)	45m	1970
Parkes Radio Telescope	radio	Australian National Radio Observatory	Nr Parkes, NSW, Australia (392m/1285ft)	64m	1961
Shajin Telescope	optical	Crimean Astrophysical Observatory	Simeis, Ukraine (680m/2230ft)	2.6m	1961
South African Large Telescope (SALT)	optical	South African Astro-nomical Observatory	South Africa	10.4m	2005
Subaru Telescope	optical/ infrared	National Astronomical Observatory of Japan	Mauna Kea, Hawaii, USA (4160m/13650ft)	8.2m	1999
Swedish/European Submillimetre Telescope	submillimetre	European Southern Observatory	Cerro Tololo, Chile (2160m/7100ft)	10m	1987
United Kingdom Infrared Telescope (UKIRT)	infrared	Royal Observatory, Edinburgh	Mauna Kea, Hawaii, USA (4180m/13720ft)	3.8m	1979
Very Large Array (VLA)	radio	National Radio Astro-nomy Observatories	Socorro, New Mexico, USA	27 × 25m	1980–1
Victor Blanco Telescope	optical	Cerro Tololo Inter-American Observatory	Cerro Tololo, Chile (2160m/7100ft)	4m	1976
William Herschel Telescope	optical	Observatory Roque de los Muchachos	La Palma, Canary Is (2332m/7650ft)	4.2m	1987

Space launchers

1. Vostok, USSR 1961
2. Mercury-Atlas, USA 1962
3. Apollo-Saturn V, USA 1968
4. US shuttle, 1981
5. Ariane, Europe 1981

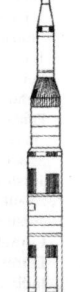
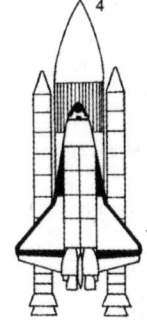
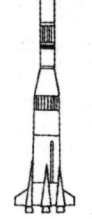

Space

Significant space missions

Launch date	Mission	Nation/ Agency	Event description
1957 Oct 4	Sputnik 1	USSR	First satellite to orbit Earth
1957 Nov 3	Sputnik 2	USSR	First living creature in space; dog (Laika) dies
1958 Feb 1	Explorer 1	USA	Discovered radiation belt (Van Allen)
1959 Jan 2	Luna 1	USSR	Escaped Earth's gravity
1959 Feb 17	Vanguard 2	USA	Took photo of Earth
1959 Sep 12	Luna 2	USSR	Made a lunar impact
1959 Oct 4	Luna 3	USSR	Took photo of far side of Moon
1960 Apr 1	TIROS 1	USA	First weather satellite
1960 Apr 13	Transit 1B	USA	First navigation satellite
1960 Aug 12	ECHO 1	USA	First communications satellite
1960 Aug 19	Sputnik 5	USSR	Two dogs recovered alive
1961 Apr 12	Vostok 1	USSR	First man in space; orbits Earth
1962 Aug 26	Mariner 2	USA	Venus flyby
1963 Jun 16	Vostok 6	USSR	First woman in space; orbits Earth
1964 Jul 28	Ranger VII	USA	Close-up television pictures of the Moon
1964 Nov 28	Mariner 4	USA	Mars flyby pictures
1965 Mar 18	Voshkod 2	USSR	First space walk
1965 Apr 6	Early Bird	USA	Commercial geostationary communications satellite
1965 Nov 16	Venera 3	USSR	Venus impact
1965 Nov 26	A-1 Asterix	France	First French satellite
1965 Dec 15	Gemini 7–A	USA	First manned rendezvous (with Gemini 7)
1966 Jan 31	Luna 9	USSR	Lunar soft landing
1966 Mar 16	Gemini 8	USA	First manned docking
1966 Mar 31	Luna 10	USSR	First lunar orbiter
1966 May 30	Surveyor 1	USA	Soft landing on Moon
1966 Aug 10	Lunar Orbiter 1	USA	US lunar orbiter
1967 Oct 22–28	Cosmos 186/188	USSR	Automatic docking
1967 Nov 29	WRESAT	Australia	First Australian satellite
1968 Sep 14	Zond 5	USSR	Animals orbit the Moon
1968 Dec 21	Apollo VIII	USA	First manned orbit of Moon
1969 Jan 14–15	Soyuz 4/5	USSR	Transfer of crews (Jan 16)
1969 Jul 16	Apollo XI	USA	First men on Moon
1970 Feb 11	Oshumi	Japan	First Japanese satellite
1970 Apr 24	Long March	China	First Chinese satellite
1970 Aug 17	Venera 7	USSR	Venus soft landing
1970 Sep 12	Luna 16	USSR	Unmanned sample return
1970 Nov 10	Luna 17	USSR	Unmanned Moon rover
1971 Apr 19	Salyut 1	USSR	First space station launched
1971 May 19	Mars 2	USSR	Mars orbit; first crash landing

Space

Launch date	Mission	Nation/ Agency	Event description
1971 May 28	Mars 3	USSR	Mars soft landing
1971 May 30	Mariner 9	USA	Mars orbit
1971 Oct 28	Prospero	UK	First UK satellite
1972 Mar 3	Pioneer 10	USA	Jupiter flyby; crossed Pluto orbit; escaped solar system
1973 Apr 6	Pioneer 11	USA	Jupiter flyby; Saturn flyby
1973 Nov 3	Mariner 10	USA	Venus flyby; three Mercury flybys
1975 Jun 8	Venera 9	USSR	Venus orbit
1975 Jul 15	Apollo/Soyuz	USA/ USSR	First manned international mission; craft dock in space
1975 Aug 20	Viking 1	USA	Spacecraft operations on Mars surface
1977 Aug 20	Voyager 2	USA	Jupiter flyby; Saturn flyby; Uranus flyby; Neptune flyby
1977 Sep 5	Voyager 1	USA	Jupiter flyby; Saturn flyby
1978 Aug 12	ISEE-C	USA	Comet intercept
1979 Dec 24	Ariane/CAT	ESA	European launcher
1980 Jul 18	Rohini	India	Indian-launched satellite
1981 Apr 12	STS 1	USA	First space shuttle flight
1981 Nov 12	STS 2	USA	Launch vehicle re-use
1983 Jun 27	Soyuz T9	USSR	Construction in space
1984 Dec 15	Vega 1	USSR	Comet Halley flyby
1985 Jul 2	Giotto	ESA	Close-up of comet Halley
1986	Mir	USSR	Main module of space station launched
1988 Nov 15	Buran	USSR	Unmanned space shuttle
1989 Oct 18	Galileo	USA	Close-up photographs of an asteroid
1990 Jan 24	Muses-A	Japan	Moon orbiter
1990 Apr 5	Pegsat	USA	First airborne launch
1990 Apr 24	Hubble Space Telescope	USA/ESA	Space telescope
1990 Dec 2	Soyuz TM11	USSR	Paying passenger flight
1991 Apr 5	CGRO	USA	Gamma-ray astronomy
1991 May 18	Soyuz TM12	USSR	First Briton (Helen Sharman) in space
1994 Jan 25	Clementine	USA	Lunar/asteroid exploration
1994 May 19	P. 91 (STEP 2)	USA	Explosion scattered space debris
1995 Nov 17	Infrared Space Observatory	ESA	Space observatory
1996 Feb 17	NEAR	USA	Asteroid rendezvous
1996 Nov 7	Mars Global Survey	USA	Mars survey
1996 Dec 4	Mars Pathfinder	USA	Mars surface exploration
1997 Feb 12	Haruka	Japan	Radio astronomy
1997 May 5	Iridium	USA	Communication constellation
1997 Oct 15	Cassini–Huygens	USA	Saturn/Titan study in 2004
1998 Jan 6	Lunar Prospector	USA	Lunar surface investigation
1998 Oct 24	Deep Space 1	USA	Ion propulsion spacecraft
1998 Oct 29	STS 95	USA	John Glenn's return to space
1998 Nov 20	Zarya	ISS (USA/ Russia/ESA/ Canada/ Japan)	First launch in International Space Station assembly
1998 Dec 11	MCO	USA	Mars climate survey
1999 Jan 3	MPL	USA	Mars surface investigation
1999 Feb 7	Stardust	USA	Capture and analysis of comet particles
1999 Nov 22	Shenzhou	China	First Chinese unmanned spacecraft
2000 Jul 12	Zvezda	ISS	International Space Station command module
2000 Jul 16	Cluster II	ESA	Earth's magnetosphere survey
2000 Aug 9	Cluster II	ESA	Earth's magnetosphere survey
2000 Oct 11	STS 92	USA	100th space shuttle flight
2000 Oct 31	Expedition 1	ISS	First residents of International Space Station
2001 Jan 24	Progress M1	Russia	Brought Mir back to earth
2001 Apr 28	Soyuz TM32	Russia	First space tourist goes to International Space Station
2003 Jun 2	Mars Express	ESA	Mars surface imaging; survey of Mars atmosphere and sub-surface
2003 Jun 10	Mars Rover Spirit	USA	Mars surface investigation
2003 Jul 7	Mars Rover Opportunity	USA	Mars surface investigation

Launch date	Mission	Nation/ Agency	Event description
2003 Oct 15	Shenzhou 5	China	First Chinese manned spacecraft
2004 Mar 2	Rosetta	ESA	Comet orbiter and lander
2004 Jun 21	SpaceShipOne	private	First private spacecraft
2004 Aug 3	Messenger	USA	Mercury orbiter
2005 Jan 12	Deep Impact	USA	First comet impact
2005 Aug 12	Mars Reconnaissance Orbiter	USA	Mars surface imaging
2005 Nov 9	Venus Express	ESA	Venus exploration
2006 Jan 19	New Horizons	USA	Pluto flyby; Jupiter flyby
2006 Sep 18	Expedition 14	USA	International Space Station crew delivery
2006 Oct 25	Solar Terrestrial Relations Observatories (STEREO)	USA	Solar imaging
2007 Aug 4	Phoenix	USA	Mars water investigation
2007 Sep 27	Dawn	USA	Asteroid orbiter
2007 Oct 24	Chang'e 1	China	First Chinese lunar orbiter
2008 Sep 19	Chandrayaan-1	India	First Indian lunar orbiter

NASA launches (crew-related)

Launch	Mission	Duration[1]	Crew	Comment
1961 May 5	Mercury MR3 (Freedom 7)	0:15	Shepard	First US manned suborbital flight
1961 Jul 21	Mercury MR4 (Liberty Bell 7)	0:16	Grissom	Suborbital flight
1961 Nov 29	Mercury MA5	3:16	Enos	Chimpanzee
1962 Feb 20	Mercury MA6 (Friendship 7)	4:55	Glenn	First US manned orbital flight
1962 May 24	Mercury MA7 (Aurora 7)	4:56	Carpenter	Orbital flight; manual re-entry
1962 Oct 3	Mercury MA8 (Sigma 7)	9:13	Schirra	6 orbits
1962 May 15	Mercury MA9 (Faith 7)	34:20	Cooper	22 orbits; last Mercury flight
1964 Apr 8	Gemini I			Test of launch vehicle compatability
1965 Jan 19	Gemini II			Unmanned suborbital test flight
1965 Mar 23	Gemini III	4:53	Grissom/Young	First manned Gemini flight
1965 Jun 3	Gemini IV	97:56	McDivitt/White	First spacewalk (by White, 36min)
1965 Aug 21	Gemini V	190:56	Cooper/Conrad	Simulated rendezvous manoeuvres
1965 Oct 25	Gemini VI			Orbit not achieved
1965 Dec 4	Gemini VII	330:35	Borman/Lovell	Part of mission without spacesuits
1965 Dec 15	Gemini VII-A	25:51	Schirra/Stafford	First space rendezvous (with Gemini VII)
1966 Mar 16	Gemini VIII	10:42	Armstrong/Scott	Rendezvous/docking with Agena target vehicle
1966 Jun 3	Gemini IX-A	72:21	Stafford/Cernan	Docking not achieved
1966 Jul 18	Gemini X	70:47	Young/Collins	First docked vehicle manoeuvres and spacewalks
1966 Sep 12	Gemini XI	71:17	Conrad/Gordon	Rendezvous/docking and spacewalks
1966 Nov 11	Gemini XII	94:35	Lovell/Aldrin	Rendezvous/docking and spacewalks
1967 Jan 27	Apollo I		Grissom/White/ Chaffee	Astronauts killed in command module in fire at launch site
1967 Nov 9	Apollo IV			First launch by Saturn V rocket; successful launch of unmanned module
1968 Jan 22–24	Apollo V			Flight test of lunar module in Earth orbit
1968 Oct 11	Apollo VII	260:09	Schirra/Eisele/ Cunningham	First manned Apollo flight in Earth orbit

Space

Launch	Mission	Duration[1]	Crew	Comment
1968 Dec 21	Apollo VIII	147:01	Borman/Lovell/ Anders	First manned orbit of Moon (10 orbits)
1969 Mar 3	Apollo IX	241:01	McDivitt/Scott/ Schweickart	First manned lunar module flight in Earth orbit
1969 May 18	Apollo X	192:03	Stafford/Young/ Cernan	First lunar module orbit of Moon
1969 Jul 16	Apollo XI	195:18	Armstrong[2]/Aldrin[2]/ Collins	First men on Moon, 20 Jul, Sea of Tranquillity
1969 Nov 14	Apollo XII	244:36	Conrad[2]/Bean[2]/ Gordon	Moon landing, 19 Nov, Ocean of Storms
1970 Apr 11	Apollo XIII	142:54	Lovell/Swigert/ Haise	Mission aborted, ruptured oxygen tank
1971 Jan 31	Apollo XIV	216:02	Shepard[2]/Mitchell[2]/ Roosa	Moon landing, 5 Feb, Fra Mauro area
1971 Jul 26	Apollo XV	295:12	Scott[2]/Irwin[2]/ Worden	Moon landing, 30 Jul, Hadley Rille; Lunar Roving Vehicle used
1972 Apr 16	Apollo XVI	265:51	Young[2]/Duke[2]/ Mattingly	Moon landing, 20 Apr, Descartes
1972 Dec 7	Apollo XVII	301:52	Cernan[2]/Schmitt[2]/ Evans	Longest Apollo mission, 11 Dec, Taurus-Littrow
1973 May 14	Skylab 1		Unmanned space station	Launched unmanned; uncontrolled re-entry 1979
1973 May 25	Skylab 2	672:50	Conrad/Kerwin/ Weitz	Repairs in orbit; duration record (28 days)
1973 Jul 28	Skylab 3	1427:09	Bean/Garriott/ Lousma	New duration record (59 days)
1973 Nov 16	Skylab 4	2017:15	Carr/Gibson/ Pogue	Final visit (84 days)
1975 Jul 15	Apollo–Soyuz Test Project	217:28	Stafford/Brand/ Slayton	Rendezvous/docking with Soyuz 19 (▶p15)

[1] (h:min).
[2] Astronauts who landed on the Moon; the remaining astronaut was the pilot of the command module.

Shuttle flights 1998–2008

Launch and landing dates	Flight/ Name	Commander/Pilot/ Number of other crew	Payload
1998 Jan 22–31	STS 89 (E)	Wilcutt/Edwards/5	MIR docking
1998 Apr 17–May 3	STS 90 (C)	Searfoss/Altman/5	Neurolab, GAS
1998 Jun 2–12	STS 91 (D)	Precourt/Pudwill/Gorie/4	MIR docking, Spacehab
1998 Oct 29–Nov 7	STS 95 (D)	Brown/Lindsey/5	Spacehab, Spartan 201
1998 Dec 4–15	STS 88 (E)	Cabana/Sturckow/4	International Space Station assembly
1999 May 27–Jun 6	STS 96 (D)	Rominger/Husband/5	International Space Station assembly
1999 Jul 23–27	STS 93 (C)	Collins/Ashby/3	AXAF, MSX
1999 Dec 19–27	STS 103 (D)	Brown/Kelly/5	Hubble servicing
2000 Feb 11–22	STS 99 (E)	Kregell/Pudwill/Gorie/4	SRTM, EarthKAM
2000 May 19–29	STS 101 (A)	Halsell/Horowitz/5	International Space Station assembly
2000 Sep 8–19	STS 106 (A)	Wilcutt/Altman/5	International Space Station assembly
2000 Oct 11–24	STS 92 (D)	Duffy/Melroy/5	International Space Station assembly
2000 Nov 30–Dec 11	STS 97 (E)	Jett/Bloomfield/3	International Space Station assembly
2001 Feb 7–20	STS 98 (A)	Cockrell/Polansky/3	International Space Station assembly
2001 Mar 8–21	STS 102 (D)	Wetherbee/Kelly/5	International Space Station crew exchange
2001 Apr 19–May 1	STS 100 (E)	Rominger/Ashby/5	International Space Station assembly
2001 Jul 12–24	STS 104 (A)	Lindsey/Hobaugh/3	International Space Station assembly
2001 Aug 10–22	STS 105 (D)	Horowitz/Sturckow/2	International Space Station crew exchange
2001 Dec 5–17	STS 108 (E)	Gorie/Kelly/5	International Space Station crew exchange
2002 Mar 1–12	STS 109 (C)	Altman/Carey/5	Hubble servicing
2002 Apr 8–19	STS 110 (A)	Bloomfield/Frick/5	International Space Station assembly
2002 Jun 5–19	STS 111 (E)	Cockrell/Lockhart/2	International Space Station crew exchange
2002 Oct 7–16	STS 112 (A)	Ashby/Melroy/4	International Space Station assembly
2002 Nov 23–Dec 7	STS 113 (E)	Wetherbee/Lockhart/5	International Space Station crew exchange

Launch and landing dates	Flight/Name	Commander/Pilot/Number of other crew	Payload
2003 Jan 16–Feb 1	STS 107 (C)[1]	Husband/McCool/5	SpaceHab-DM Research Mission, Freestar
2005 Jul 26–Aug 9	STS 114 (D)	Collins/Kelly/5	International Space Station assembly
2006 Jul 4–17	STS 121 (D)	Lindsey/Kelly/5	International Space Station crew exchange
2006 Sep 9–21	STS 115 (A)	Jett/Ferguson/4	International Space Station assembly
2006 Dec 9–22	STS 116 (D)	Polansky/Oefelein/6	International Space Station assembly
2007 Jun 8–22	STS 117 (A)	Sturckow/Archambault/5	International Space Station crew exchange
2007 Aug 8–21	STS 118 (E)	Kelly/Hobaugh/5	International Space Station assembly
2007 Oct 23–Nov 7	STS 120 (D)	Melroy/Zamka/5	International Space Station crew exchange
2008 Feb 7–20	STS 122 (A)	Frick/Poindexter/5	International Space Station crew exchange
2008 Mar 11–26	STS 123 (E)	Gorie/Johnson/5	International Space Station assembly
2008 May 31–Jun 14	STS 124 (D)	Kelly/Ham/6	International Space Station crew exchange
2008 Oct 8–19	STS 125 (A)	Altman/Johnson/5	Hubble servicing
2008 Nov 14–30	STS 126 (E)	Ferguson/Boe/6	International Space Station assembly

A: Atlantis C: Columbia D: Discovery E: Endeavour
[1] Columbia disintegrated on re-entry; all crew members perished.
Following the Columbia disaster, shuttle flights were suspended until Discovery's 'Return to Flight' mission in 2005.

Major USSR/Russian launches (crew-related)

Launch	Mission	Duration[1]	Crew	Comment
1961 Apr 12	Vostok 1	01:48	Gagarin	First space flight (1 orbit)
1961 Aug 6	Vostok 2	25:18	Titov	Day-long mission
1962 Aug 11	Vostok 3	94:22	Nikolayev	First dual mission
1962 Aug 12	Vostok 4	71:00	Popovich	First dual mission
1963 Jun 16	Vostok 6	70:50	Tereshkova	First woman in space
1964 Oct 12	Voshkod 1	24:17	Komarov/Feoktistov/Yegorov	Three man flight
1965 Mar 18	Voshkod 2	26:02	Belyayev/Leonov	First spacewalk (EVA)
1967 Apr 23	Soyuz 1	27:00	Komarov	Cosmonaut killed on re-entry
1969 Jan 14	Soyuz 4	71:14	Shatalov	Khrunov and Yeliseyev transferred from Soyuz 5
1969 Jan 15	Soyuz 5	72:46	Volynov/Khrunov/Yeliseyev	Docked with Soyuz 4
1971 Apr 22	Soyuz 10	48:00	Shatalov/Yeliseyev/Rukavishnikov	Docked with Salyut 1 space station but did not enter for undisclosed reason
1971 Jun 6	Soyuz 11	23 days	Dobrovolsky/Volkov/Patsayev	Docked with Salyut 1; crew killed on re-entry
1974 Jun 25	Salyut 3	214 days	Soyuz 14	Operational military space station
1974 Jul 4	Soyuz 14	16 days	Popovich/Artyukhin	Docked with Salyut 3
1974 Dec 26	Salyut 4	769 days	Soyuz 17/Soyuz 18/Soyuz 20	Space station; re-entered 2 Feb 77
1975 Jan 9	Soyuz 17	30 days	Gubarev/Grechko	Docked with Salyut 4
1975 Jul 15 (Apollo–Soyuz Test Project)	Soyuz 19	6 days	Kubasov/Leonov	First international space mission with USA; crew transfer
1976 Jun 22	Salyut 5	412 days	Soyuz 21/Soyuz 24	Space station; re-entered 8 Aug 77
1976 Jul 6	Soyuz 21	49 days	Volynov/Zholobov	Docked with Salyut 5
1976 Oct 14	Soyuz 23	2 days	Zudov/Rozhdestivensky	Attempted docking with Salyut 5
1977 Feb 7	Soyuz 24	18 days	Gorbatko/Glazkov	Docked with Salyut 5
1977 Sep 29	Salyut 6	1764 days	Soyuz 25 to Soyuz 40	Space station; re-entered 29 Jul 82
1977 Dec 10	Soyuz 26	96 days	Romanenko/Grechko	First prime crew Salyut 6; broke endurance record
1978 Jan 10	Soyuz 27	65 days	Dzhanibekov/Makarov	First visiting crew to Salyut 6
1978 Mar 2	Soyuz 28	8 days	Gubarev/Remek	Second visiting crew to Salyut 6
1978 Jun 15	Soyuz 29	140 days	Kovalenok/Ivanchenko	Second prime crew of Salyut 6
1979 Feb 25	Soyuz 32	108 days	Lyakhov/Ryumin	Third prime crew of Salyut 6; broke endurance record
1979 Dec 16	Soyuz T1	100 days		Redesigned Soyuz craft
1981 Mar 12	Soyuz T4	75 days	Kovalenok/Savinykh	Last prime crew of Salyut 6
1981 Mar 22	Soyuz 39	8 days	Dzhanibekov/Gurragcha	Mongolian cosmonaut

Space

Launch	Mission	Duration[1]	Crew	Comment
1981 May 14	Soyuz 40	8 days	Popov/Prunariu	Last visiting crew to Salyut 6
1982 Apr 19	Salyut 7	9 years	Soyuz T5 to Soyuz T15	Space station; re-entered 7 Feb 91
1982 May 14	Soyuz T5	106 days	Berezovoy/Ledebev	Crew broke endurance record
1982 Aug 19	Soyuz T7	113 days	Popov/Serebrov/ Savitskaya	Savitskaya, second woman in space
1983 Jun 27	Soyuz T9	149 days	Lyakhov/Alexandrov	Docked with Salyut 7
1983 Sep 27	Soyuz T10-1		Titov/Strekalov	Exploded on launch pad; crew safe
1984 Feb 8	Soyuz T10	263 days	Kizim/Solovyov/Atkov	Crew broke endurance record
1984 Jul 17	Soyuz T12	12 days	Dzhanibekov/Savitskaya/ Volk	Docked with Salyut 7; first female EVA
1985 Sep 17	Soyuz T14	65 days	Vasyutin/Volkov/Grechko	Docked with Salyut 7; mission terminated when Vasyutin fell ill
1986 Feb 19	MIR 1	Projected 13 years	Soyuz T15 onwards	Space station; designed for orbit; modular construction
1986 Mar 13	Soyuz T15	125 days	Kizim/Solovyov	Docked with both MIR and Salyut 7
1986 May 21	Soyuz TM1	9 days		Redesigned Soyuz T craft
1987 Mar 31	Kvant 1	in orbit		Astrophysical module attached to MIR
1987 Jul 22	Soyuz TM3	160 days	Viktorenko/Alexandrov/ Faris	Docked with MIR
1987 Dec 21	Soyuz TM4	179 days	Titov/Manarov/ Levchenko	Docked with MIR; Titov and Manarov completed 365-day flight
1989 Nov 26	Kvant 2	in orbit		Module attached to MIR on 6 Dec 89
1990 May 31	Kristall	in orbit		Material processing module added to MIR
1990 Dec 2	Soyuz TM11	175 days	Afanasyev/Manarov/ Akiyama	Docked with MIR; Japanese journalist on board
1991 May 18	Soyuz TM12	311 days	Artsebarsky/Krikalev/ Sharman (UK)	Docked with MIR; first British cosmonaut
1991 Oct 2	Soyuz TM13	175 days	Volkov/Aubakirov/ Vietiboeck (Austria)	Docked with MIR; partial crew rotation (Artsebarsky down)
1992 Mar 17	Soyuz TM14	146 days	Viktorenko/Kaleri/ Flade (Germany)	Docked with MIR; crew rotation (Volkov, Krikalev down)
1992 Jul 27	Soyuz TM15	189 days	A Solovyov/Avdeyev	2
1993 Jan 24	Soyuz TM16	179 days	Manakov/Poleshchuk	2
1993 Jul 1	Soyuz TM17	197 days	Tsibliev/Serebrov	2
1994 Jan 8	Soyuz TM18	182 days	Afanasyev/Usachyov/ Polyakov	2
1994 Jul 1	Soyuz TM19	126 days	Malenchenko/Musabayev	2
1994 Oct 3	Soyuz TM20	170 days	Viktorenko/Kondakova/ Merbold	2
1995 Mar 14	Soyuz TM21	181 days	Dezhurov/Strekalov/ Thagard	2
1995 May 20	Spektr Module	in orbit		Module attached to MIR
1995 Sep 3	Soyuz TM22	179 days	Gidzenko/Avdeyev/ Reiter	2
1996 Feb 21	Soyuz TM23	194 days	Onufrienko/Usachyov	2
1996 Apr 23	Priroda Module	in orbit		Module attached to MIR
1996 Aug 17	Soyuz TM24	197 days	Korzun/Kaleri	2
1997 Feb 10	Soyuz TM25	185 days	Tsibliev/Lazutkin/ Ewald	2
1997 Aug 5	Soyuz TM26	197 days	A Solovyov/Vinogradov	2
1998 Jan 29	Soyuz TM27	207 days	Musabayev/Budarin/ Eyharts	2
1998 Aug 13	Soyuz TM28	198 days	Padalka/Avdeyev/ Baturin	2

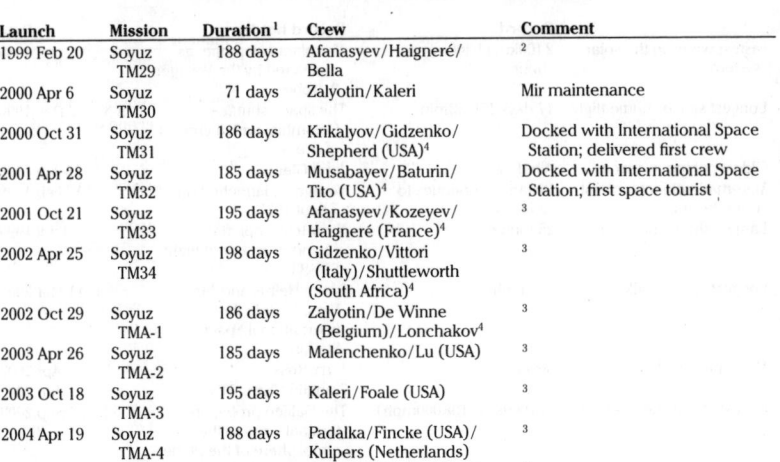

Launch	Mission	Duration[1]	Crew	Comment
1999 Feb 20	Soyuz TM29	188 days	Afanasyev/Haigneré/ Bella	[2]
2000 Apr 6	Soyuz TM30	71 days	Zalyotin/Kaleri	Mir maintenance
2000 Oct 31	Soyuz TM31	186 days	Krikalyov/Gidzenko/ Shepherd (USA)[4]	Docked with International Space Station; delivered first crew
2001 Apr 28	Soyuz TM32	185 days	Musabayev/Baturin/ Tito (USA)[4]	Docked with International Space Station; first space tourist
2001 Oct 21	Soyuz TM33	195 days	Afanasyev/Kozeyev/ Haigneré (France)[4]	[3]
2002 Apr 25	Soyuz TM34	198 days	Gidzenko/Vittori (Italy)/Shuttleworth (South Africa)[4]	[3]
2002 Oct 29	Soyuz TMA-1	186 days	Zalyotin/De Winne (Belgium)/Lonchakov[4]	[3]
2003 Apr 26	Soyuz TMA-2	185 days	Malenchenko/Lu (USA)	[3]
2003 Oct 18	Soyuz TMA-3	195 days	Kaleri/Foale (USA)	[3]
2004 Apr 19	Soyuz TMA-4	188 days	Padalka/Fincke (USA)/ Kuipers (Netherlands)	[3]
2004 Oct 14	Soyuz TMA-5	192 days	Chiao (USA)/Sharipov/ Shargin	[3]
2005 Apr 15	Soyuz TMA-6	179 days	Krikalev/Vittori (Italy)/ Phillips (USA)	[3]
2005 Oct 1	Soyuz TMA-7	182 days	McArthur (USA)/Tokarev	[3]
2006 Mar 30	Soyuz TMA-8	178 days	Vinogradov/Williams (USA)	[3]
2006 Sep 18	Soyuz TMA-9	216 days	Lopez-Alegria (USA)/ Tyurin/Williams (USA)	[3]
2007 Apr 7	Soyuz TMA-10	197 days	Yurchikhin/Kotov/Simonyi	[3]
2007 Oct 10	Soyuz TMA-11	192 days	Whitson (USA)/ Malenchenko/ Shukor (Mayaysia)	[3]
2008 Apr 8	Soyuz TMA-12	199 days	Volkov/Kononenko/Yi (S Korea)	[3]
2008 Oct 12	Soyuz TMA-13	ongoing	Finke (USA)/Louchakov/ Garriott (USA)	[3]

[1] (h:min).
[2] The purpose was basically the same for all the Soyuz spacecraft: they were all 'ferry' craft which were used to take crews to and from MIR, acting as 'lifeboats' in case of emergencies.
[3] The Soyuz spacecraft have served the International Space Station since late 2000 as 'lifeboats' in case of emergencies. A new craft is delivered approximately every six months and left at the Station while the crew return to Earth in the previous craft.
[4] Crews given are for the outward journey; each craft remains at the Station for six months and returns with a different crew.
[5] Soyuz TMA-9 scheduled to return to earth in March 2007.

Space records

	Record	Record holder	Date
First manned space flight		Yuri Gagarin aboard Vostok 1	12 Apr 1961
Largest rocket	110.6m (363ft) high, weighing 2903 tonnes (2857 tons)	Saturn V	9 Nov 1967
Most isolated space traveller	3596.4km (2234.75mi)	Alfred M Worden, during the Apollo15 lunar mission	30 Jul–1 Aug 1971
Lunar speed and distance record	18kph (11.2mph), over 33.8km (22.4mi)	John Young, driving the Apollo 16 rover	1 Apr 1972
Longest time spent on the surface of the moon	74h 59min	Apollo 17 lunar mission	7–19 Dec 1972
Longest time spent in orbit around the moon	147h 41min	Ronald E Evans, during the Apollo 17 lunar mission	7–19 Dec 1972
Closest approach to the sun by a spacecraft	Within 43.5 million km (27 million mi)	Helios 2, a probe launched on 15 Jan 1976	16 Apr 1976

Space

	Record	Record holder	Date
Fastest winds in the solar system	2100km (1300mi) per hour	The planet Neptune, as measured by the Voyager 2 probe	1989
Longest space shuttle flight	17 days 15h 53min	The space shuttle Columbia, with a crew of five	19 Nov–7 Dec 1996
Oldest person in space	Aged 77	John Glenn	15 Jan 1998
Man-made object furthest from the sun	Distance continues to increase	Voyager 1, launched on 5 Sept 1977	17 Feb 1998
Largest shuttle payload	25 tonnes	X-ray telescope the Chandra, on board flight STS-93	1 Jul 1999
Longest space walk	8h 56min	Susan Helms and Jim Voss, outside the International Space Station	11 Mar 2001
Most space flights	Seven	Jerry Ross	Apr 2002
		Franklin Chang-Diaz	Jun 2002
Fastest atmospheric entry	174000km (108000mph)	The Galileo probe, on terminal entry to the atmosphere of the planet Jupiter	21 Sep 2003
Fastest air-breathing aircraft	Top speed of Mach 9.68	NASA's Hyper-X (X-43A) research vehicle	16 Nov 2004
First privately funded manned spaceflight		Mike Melvill, SpaceShipOne	21 Jun 2004
Largest communications satellite	6.5 tonnes	Thaicom 4	11 Aug 2005
Fastest departure from earth	57600kph (35800mph)	New Horizons spacecraft, on way to explore Pluto	19 Jan 2006
Most time spent in space	803 days 9h 39min	Sergei Krikalev, aboard the International Space Station	10 Oct 2006
Most expensive individual space trip	$30 million (£20 million) (reputedly)	Richard Garriott, a US computer games designer, to go aboard the International Space Station	12–24 Oct 2008
Highest mountain in the solar system	27km (17mi) from base to peak	Olympus Mons, on the planet Mars	

Astronomers Royal

Astronomer Royal is an honorary title awarded to a distinguished British astronomer. Until 1972, the director of the Royal Greenwich Observatory automatically became the Astronomer Royal, but the two posts have since been separate.

Dates	Name
1675–1719	John Flamsteed
1720–42	Edmond Halley
1742–62	James Bradley
1762–4	Nathaniel Bliss
1765–1811	Nevil Maskelyne
1811–35	John Pond
1835–81	Sir George Airy
1881–1910	Sir William Christie
1910–33	Sir Frank Dyson
1933–55	Sir Harold Spencer Jones
1956–71	Sir Richard Woolley
1972–82	Sir Martin Ryle
1982–90	Sir Francis Graham-Smith
1991–5	Sir Arnold Wolfendale
1995–	Sir Martin Rees

EARTH

There are no universally agreed estimates of the natural phenomena given in this section. Surveys make use of different criteria for identifying natural boundaries, and use different techniques of measurement. The sizes of continents, oceans, seas, deserts, and rivers are particularly subject to variation.

Age 4 600 000 000 years (accurate to within a very small percentage of possible error)
Area 509 600 000 sq km / 197 000 000 sq mi
Mass 5 976 × 10^{24}kg
Land surface 148 000 000 sq km / 57 000 000 sq mi (c.29% of total area)

Water surface 361 600 000 sq km / 140 000 000 sq mi (c.71% of total area)
Circumference at equator 40 076km / 24 902mi
Circumference of meridian 40 000km / 24 860mi

Atmosphere

The Earth's atmosphere is composed of air, generally containing 78% nitrogen, 21% oxygen and 1% argon, together with carbon dioxide, hydrogen, ozone and methane, and traces of the other rare gases. The amount of water vapour present depends on the temperature and humidity. The atmosphere is divided into several layers.

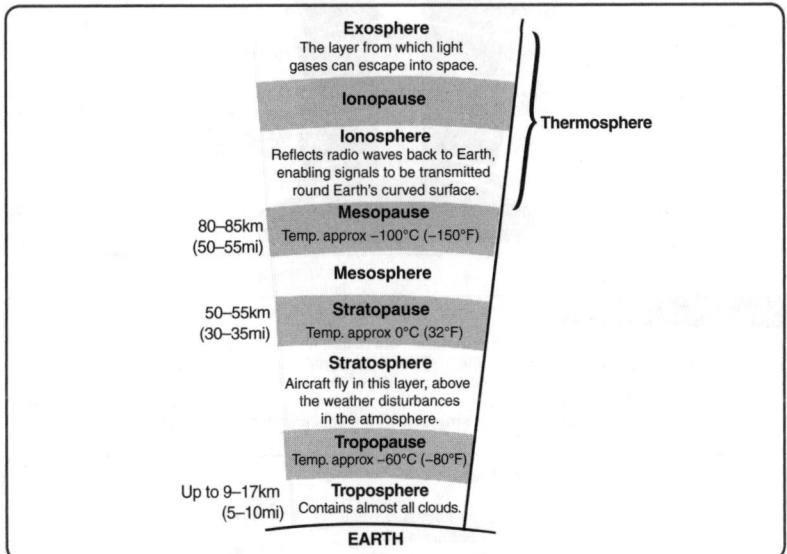

Earth

Temperature and pressure of atmosphere

The temperature of the atmosphere is the balance between convection and radiation. The amount of heat contained at any level depends on the pressure or density as well as the temperature. In the thermosphere the temperature may be as high as 2000°C/3600°F, but the pressure is only a millionth of a billionth of that at sea-level. The temperature falls steadily as the influence of solar radiation lessens, reaching a minimum about 80km/50mi above the ground; then it increases again. Temperatures decrease down through the stratosphere, where typical pressures are still only a hundredth of those on the surface, but down through the troposphere temperatures increase again.

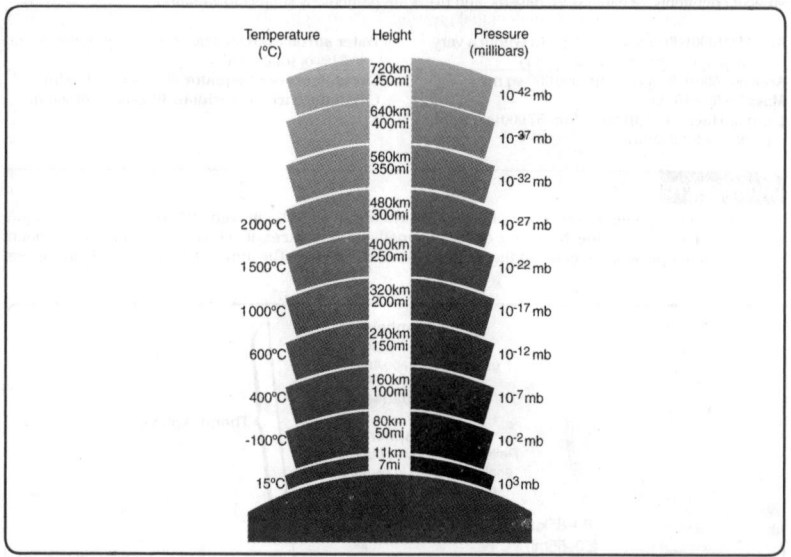

Structure of the Earth

At the centre of the Earth there is a molten metallic core of iron and nickel, possibly with a solid core at the very centre at a temperature of around 4000°C/7200°F. A silicate mantle overlies the core. The outermost crust is about 10km/6mi thick under the oceans and 30km/19mi thick where there are continents. A dozen or so crustal plates – the *lithosphere* – slide over the less rigid *asthenosphere*. Collisions between the plates produce folded mountains, and zones of seismic activity are concentrated along the plate boundaries.

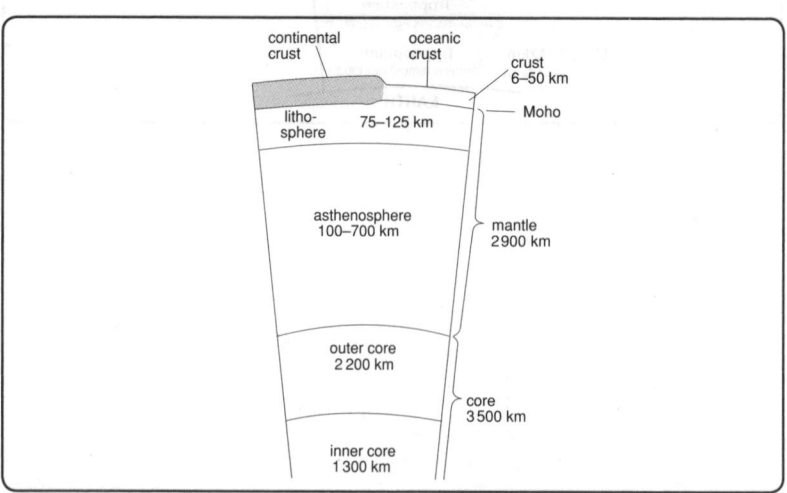

Plate tectonics

Plate tectonics is a widely accepted geological theory, developed in the late 1960s, according to which the Earth's crust is composed of a small number of large plates of solid rock, whose movements in relation to one another are responsible for continental drift. According to the theory, the plates of the Earth's crust are floating on the moving molten rock of the mantle which lies beneath the crust. It is believed that the plates move as a result of convection currents which occur deep within the mantle. New crust is formed at the edges of the plates where rising convection currents bring up new material from the mantle. Some plates may be 'sliding' in relation to one another along margins where there are huge fault systems, eg the San Andreas fault system off the coast of California. It is thought that mountain ranges are formed when one crustal plate pushes into another, forcing the land upward under great pressure. Plate movements can cause earthquakes as well as changes to the Earth's surface.

Earth

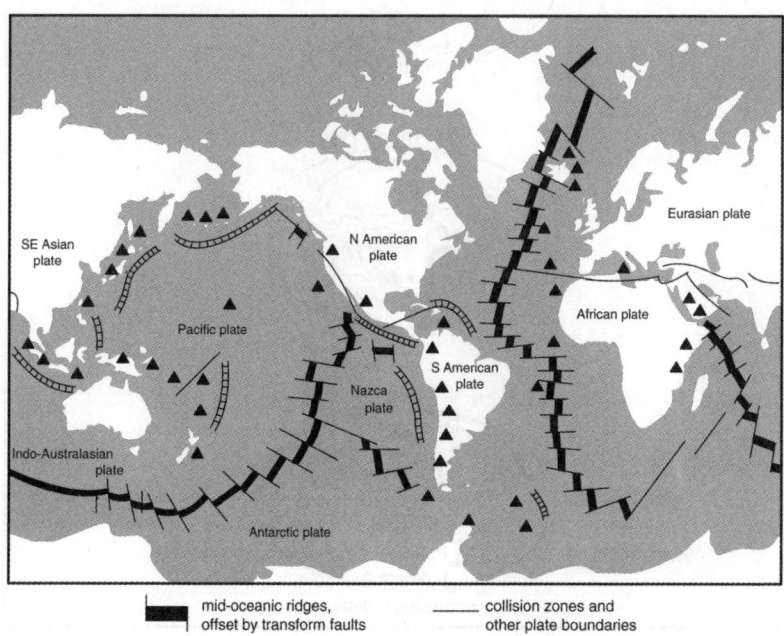

SE Asian plate

N American plate

Eurasian plate

Pacific plate

African plate

Nazca plate

S American plate

Indo-Australasian plate

Antarctic plate

▬▬ mid-oceanic ridges, offset by transform faults

⫿⫿⫿ oceanic trenches

▬▬ collision zones and other plate boundaries

▲ volcanoes

Earth

Continental drift

Continental drift is the theory that the continents were formed as a result of the breaking up of a single land mass into several smaller land masses, which slowly drifted apart across the Earth's surface.

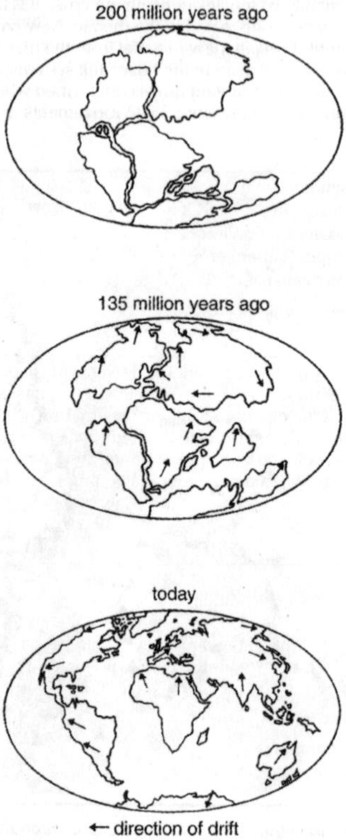

200 million years ago

135 million years ago

today

← direction of drift

Geological time scale

The various stages of the history of life on Earth are divided into aeons, based on fossil evidence and changes in climate. The aeons are further divided into eras, periods, series and sometimes stages. Three eras make up the most recent aeon, known as the Phanerozoic aeon. The most recent of these is the Cenozoic; further back in time are the eras known as Mesozoic and Palaeozoic. The period of time before the Phanerozoic aeon is called the Precambrian aeon, so named because it occurred before the earliest (Cambrian) period of the Palaeozoic era.

Precambrian aeon

The rocks that were formed during the Precambrian consisted of two divisions: the Archaean and the Proterozoic. Primitive plant life existed well back into the Archaean, and bacteria may have existed as early as 3,800 million years ago. In the most recent Proterozoic rocks there are impressions of soft-bodied animals and trace fossils (burrows and tracks) indicating a long period of earlier evolution.

Division	Era	Age (mya)[1]
Archaean		4600–2500
Proterozoic	Aphebian	2500–1650
	Riphean	1650–610
	Vendian	610–570

[1] mya = million years ago

Palaeozoic era

The Palaeozoic ('ancient life') is the oldest of the Phanerozoic eras. Until this time, only primitive life forms such as bacteria, algae and sponges existed. However, there was a sudden great expansion of animal life (the Cambrian explosion) at the start of the Palaeozoic. Creatures included molluscs and small marine organisms called trilobites; early plant life was also present. The Ordovician was a time of diverse sea life, including the first coral reefs, and amphibians evolved by the end of the Devonian. During the Carboniferous there was rich plant life in parts of the world, but a glacial climate existed in other regions known as the Gondwana continents. The trilobites died out in the Permian, a period of desert conditions in Britain.

Period	Age (mya)[1]
Cambrian	570–510
Ordovician	510–439
Silurian	439–408
Devonian	408–362
Lower Carboniferous	362–333
Upper Carboniferous	333–290
Permian	290–245

[1] mya = million years ago

Mesozoic era

Animals present during the Mesozoic ('middle life') era included spiral-shaped molluscs called ammonites, as well as reptiles and corals. The earliest period, the Triassic, had an impoverished range of animals and plants that followed the extinctions at the end of the Palaeozoic era. However, during the middle period, the Jurassic, there was diverse plant life in the warm climate, and reptiles, notably dinosaurs, were dominant on land. The first flowering plants developed and spread during the Cretaceous period. A mass extinction occurred at the end of the Cretaceous, when most birds, a large proportion of marine life and all remaining dinosaurs became extinct.

Period	Series	Age (mya)[1]
Triassic	Lower	245–241
	Middle	241–210
	Upper	210–208
Jurassic	Lower (Lias)	208–178
	Middle (Dogger)	178–161
	Upper (Malm)	161–146
Cretaceous	Lower	146–97
	Upper	97–65

[1] mya = million years ago

Cenozoic era

The Cenozoic ('recent life') era is divided into two sub-eras, Tertiary and Quaternary. In the early part of the Tertiary sub-era, the plants and animals of the Cretaceous (see Mesozoic era) gave way to more modern forms, with mammals replacing reptiles as the dominant animals. Later, in the Miocene, large-scale earth movements built many of the mountain ranges of the world, and provoked wide-scale volcanic activity. Modern landscape and geography were laid down in the Quaternary. The many stages of this sub-era were much influenced by the ice ages. Large mammals such as mastodons and woolly mammoths were present at the start of the Quaternary but became extinct during the late Pleistocene and early Holocene, when humans appeared and developed.

Sub-era[1]	Period[2]	Series	Age[3]
Tertiary	Palaeogene	Palaeocene	65–56.5 mya
		Eocene	56.5–35.4 mya
		Oligocene	35.4–23.3 mya
	Neogene	Miocene	23.3–5.2 mya
		Pliocene	5.2–1.64 mya
Quaternary		Pleistocene	1.64 mya to 10000 years ago
		Holocene	10000 years ago to present

[1] Also known as Period
[2] Also known as Epoch
[3] mya = million years ago

Ice ages

The most recent ice age occurred during the Pleistocene epoch in the Cenozoic era, and is generally known as 'the Ice Age'.

Era	Part of era
Precambrian	Early Proterozoic
Precambrian	Upper Proterozoic
Palaeozoic	Upper Carboniferous
Cenozoic	Pleistocene (and Holocene?)

Cycles of glaciation have occurred during the ice ages, with glacial periods being interspersed with slightly warmer interglacial periods. Some of the most recent glacial periods of the Ice Age are:

European name	American name	Time period
Günz	Nebraskan	520 000–490 000 years ago
Mindel	Kansan	430 000–370 000 years ago
Riss	Illinoian	130 000–100 000 years ago
Würm	Wisconsinian	40 000–18 000 years ago

Fossils

Fossils are produced when animals and plants decompose and become preserved within sedimentary rock.

Period	Fossil type
Cambrian	Trilobites and brachiopods
Ordovician	Graptolites, trilobites (small crustacea)
Silurian	Graptolites (thin, branching, free-swimming, coral-like)
Devonian	Goniatites, fish and plants
Lower Carboniferous	Corals and brachiopods
Carboniferous	Foraminifera, goniatites, fresh-water bivalves and plants
Permian	Foraminifera, ammonites and goniatites (ammonite ancestors)
Triassic	Ammonites
Jurassic	Ammonites plus ostracods (tiny crustacea) and bivalves
Lower Cretaceous	Ammonites
Upper Cretaceous	Foraminifera, echinoderms, bivalves and belemnites
Cenozoic	Foraminifera (plankton)

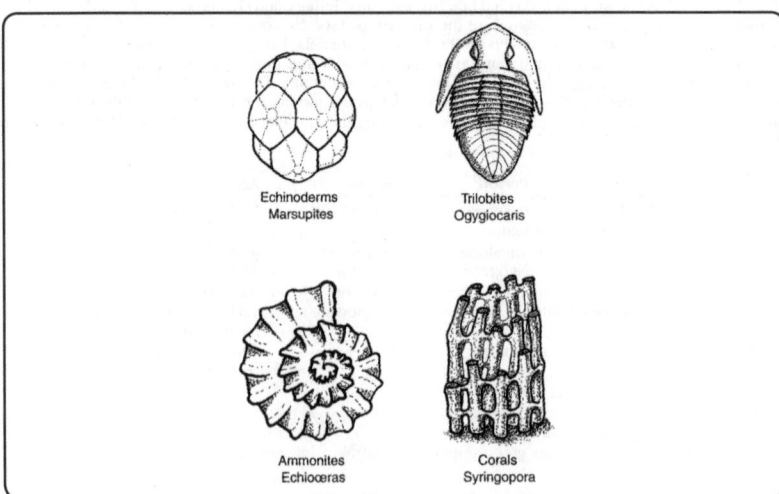

Echinoderms
Marsupites

Trilobites
Ogygiocaris

Ammonites
Echioceras

Corals
Syringopora

Classification of sedimentary rocks

Sedimentary rocks result from the deposition of materials transported by water, wind or ice. Clastic rocks are the eroded remnants of earlier rocks; chemical sediments are formed from precipitation out of solution; organic sediments are formed from living material.

Clastic

Conglomerate	Large, rounded, cemented
Breccia	Coarse, angular, cemented
Gritstone	Coarse
Sandstone	Medium
Greensand	With glauconite
Greywacke	Deep ocean sediments
Siltstone	Fine, with more quartz than shale
Loess	Fine, angular particles
Marl	Fine silt or clay with limestone cement
Shale	Very fine laminated clay and detritus
Mudstone	Clay and very fine grains cemented with iron or calcite
Clay	Very fine; absorbs water

Chemical

Limestone	Calcium carbonate
Chalk	Soft white limestone, mostly microfossils
Tufa	Calcium carbonate; precipitated from fresh water
Dolomite	Calcium and magnesium carbonate
Ironstone	Limestone or chert enriched in iron, often Precambrian
Chert and flint	Hard silicatious nodules or sheets in chalk or limestone

Organic

Peat	Plant material
Lignite	Soft, carbonaceous
Coal	Hard, brittle, carbonaceous
Jet	Hard, black, coal-like

Principal metamorphic rocks

Metamorphic rocks are produced when pressure and heat cause changes in existing rocks.

Name	Texture	Origin
Slate	Aligned minerals produce perfect cleavage; not necessarily aligned with bedding	Sedimentary shale and clay
Phyllite	As slate, but coarser, with small-scale folding	Medium grain sediments
Schist	Flaky minerals such as mica give glittery, foliated texture	Sediments buried deep in mountain belts, eg siltstones
Gneiss	Medium/coarse grain; quartz, feldspar and mica with darker layers or lines	High pressure and temperature, from sediment or granite; abundant deep under continents
Migmatite	Mixture of dark schist and light granitic rock; highly folded	Extensive deep metamorphism of sediments
Eclogite	Coarse grain; mostly green pyroxene and red garnet	Very high temperature and pressure close to mantle
Amphibolite	Coarse grain; often foliated; mostly hornblende	Highly metamorphosed igneous dolorite
Marble	Crystalline, soft and sugary; made of calcium carbonate	Limestone heated by igneous intrusion
Hornfels	Fine grain; dark coloured with quartz, mica and pyroxene	Sediments closest to hot igneous intrusion
Quartzite	Medium grain; of even texture with fused quartz crystals; very hard	Sandy sediment heated by intrusion or regional metamorphism
Serpentinite	Coarse grain; green serpentine minerals	Intense metamorphism of olivine-rich rock

Earth

Principal igneous rocks

Igneous rocks result from volcanic activity in the Earth's crust and upper mantle.

Earth

Rock	Texture	Type	Composition	Origin	Features	Varieties
Granite	Coarse	Acid	<20% quartz, K-feldspars, mica	Intrusive batholiths	Occasional phenocrysts	Pink, white and microgranite
Pegmatite	Coarse	Acid	<20% quartz, mica and feldspar	Deep batholiths and dykes	Very large crystals	Occasional rare minerals
Diorite	Coarse	Intermediate	Plagioclase feldspar and hornblende	Dykes associated with granite	Biotite and pyroxene	Granodiorite with quartz
Syenite	Coarse	Intermediate	Little or no quartz, otherwise like granite	Dykes and sills near granite	Often pink	Nepheline syenite, quartz syenite
Gabbro	Coarse	Basic	Plagioclase, pyroxene and olivine	Large layered intrusions	Layers of magnetite	Olivine gabbro
Larvikite	Coarse	Intermediate	Feldspar crystals with pyroxene, mica and amphibolite banks	Small sills	Popular for cladding banks	None
Anorthosite	Coarse	Basic	<90% plagioclase feldspar	Layered intrusions, on Moon	Aligned mineral grains	Can include olivine and pyroxene
Dolerite	Medium	Basic	>10% quartz with plagioclase and pyroxene	Dykes and sills near basalt	Dark colour	None
Dunite	Medium	Ultra-basic	Almost entirely olivine	Deep sourced intrusions	Can contain chromite	None
Kimberlite	Coarse	Ultra-basic	Dense ferro-magnesian minerals	Pipes of deep ancient volcanoes	Sometimes contains diamonds	None
Peridotite	Coarse	Ultra-basic	No quartz or feldspar, mostly olivine and garnet	Caught up in intrusions	Possibly derived from mantle	With pyroxene and hornblende
Rhyolite	Fine	Acid	As granite	Explosive volcanic eruptions	Phenocrysts and gas bubbles	Banded form
Obsidian	Glassy	Acid	Silica-rich glass	Rapid cooling of acid lava	Black, glassy	Snowflake obsidian
Lamprophyre	Medium	Acid to basic	Amphibole pyroxene and biotite	Dykes and sills around granite	Phenocrysts of biotite and hornblende	None
Andesite	Fine	Intermediate	Mainly plagioclase	Volcanoes above subduction zones	Dark with white phenocrysts	With vesicles of zeolite
Trachyte	Fine	Intermediate	>10% quartz, rich in alkali feldspar	Lava flows, dykes and sills	Not many	Sometimes porphyritic
Basalt	Fine	Basic	Plagioclase and pyroxene	Volcanic eruptions	Dark — the commonest lava	Bubbles and vesicles
Tuff	Fine	Acid to basic	Consolidated volcanic fragments	Thrown out by volcanic vents	Variable	Tuff-breccia, lapilli-tuff
Pumice	Fine	Acid to basic	Glass and minute silicate crystals	Rapidly quenched frothy lava	Can sometimes float	Bubbles and vesicles

Properties of common minerals

Earth

Name	Type	Mohs of hardness	Specific gravity	Crystal	Optical	Fracture
Talc	Silicate	1	2.6–2.8	Monoclinic	Pale green or grey, pearly lustre	Uneven
Graphite	Element	1–2	2.1–2.3	Trigonal/hexagonal	Grey metallic lustre	Perfect basal cleavage
Gypsum	Sulphate	2	2.32	Monoclinic	White to transparent	Splintery
Calcite	Carbonate	3	2.71	Trigonal/hexagonal	Double refraction	Perfect rhombic cleavage
Barytes	Sulphate	3–3.5	4.5	Orthorhombic	Pale, translucent	Perfect cleavage
Aragonite	Carbonate	3.5–4	2.95	Orthorhombic	Translucent white streak	Subconchoidal
Dolomite	Carbonate	3.5–4	2.85	Trigonal/hexagonal	Pale, translucent	Rhombohedral cleavage
Fluorite	Halide	4	3.18	Cubic	Many colours, fluorescent	Perfect octahedral cleavage
Apatite	Phosphate	5	3.1–3.2	Trigonal/hexagonal	Usually green	Uneven
Sodalite	Silicate	5.5–6	2.2–2.4	Cubic	Blue	Uneven
Pyrite	Sulphide	6–6.5	5.0	Cubic	'Fool's gold'	Uneven
Quartz	Oxide	7	2.65	Trigonal/hexagonal	Translucent, also microcrystalline	Uneven
Garnet	Silicate	7	3.5–4.3	Cubic	Various forms, often plum red	Uneven
Tourmaline	Silicate	7–7.5	3.0–3.2	Trigonal/hexagonal	Often pink or green	Uneven
Zircon	Silicate	7.5	4.3	Tetragonal	Often brown	Uneven
Beryl	Silicate	7–8	2.6–2.9	Trigonal/hexagonal	Many colours, emerald green	Uneven
Spinel	Oxide	7.5–8	3.5–4.1	Cubic	Many colours, vitreous lustre	Uneven
Corundum	Oxide	9	4.0–4.1	Trigonal/hexagonal	Various forms including ruby and sapphire	Uneven
Diamond	Element	10	3.52	Cubic	Transparent, sparkles if cut	Octahedral cleavage

Properties of gemstones

Nearly all gemstones are minerals. The four non-mineral gems are amber, coral, jet and pearl. The hardness of solid substances is expressed on the Mohs scale.

Gemstone	Colour	Mohs of hardness
Agate	brown, red, blue, green, yellow	7.0
Alexandrite	green, red	8.5
Amber	yellow, brown and other colours	2–2.5
Amethyst	violet	7.0
Aquamarine	sky blue, greenish blue	7.5
Beryl	green, blue, pink	7.5
Bloodstone	green with red spots	7.0
Chalcedony	all colours	7.0
Chrysoprase	apple green	7.0
Citrine	yellow	7.0
Coral	white, pink, red, orange, blue, violet and other colours	3.5–4
Diamond	colourless, tints of various colours	10.0
Emerald	green	7.5
Garnet	red and other colours	6.5–7.25
Jade	green, whitish, mauve, brown	7.0
Jasper	dark red, multi-coloured	7.0
Jet	black	2.5–4
Lapis lazuli	deep blue	5.5
Malachite	dark green banded	3.5
Moonstone	whitish with blue shimmer	6.0
Onyx	various colours with straight coloured bands	7.0
Opal	black, white, orange-red, rainbow coloured	6.0

Earth

Gemstone	Colour	Mohs of hardness
Pearl	cream, white, pink and other colours	2.5–4.5
Peridot	green	6.5
Ruby	red	9.0
Sapphire	blue and other colours	9.0
Serpentine	red and green	3.0
Soapstone	white, may be stained with impurities	2.0
Sunstone	whitish red-brown flecked with golden particles	6.0
Topaz	blue, green, pink, yellow, colourless	8.0
Tourmaline	brown-black, blue, pink, red, violet-red, yellow, green	7.5
Turquoise	greenish grey, sky blue	6.0
Zircon	all colours	7.5

Mohs' hardness scale

The relative hardness of solids can be expressed using a scale of numbers from 1 to 10, each relating to a mineral (1 representing talc, 10 representing diamond). The method was devised by Friedrich Mohs (1773–1839), a German mineralogist. Sets of hardness pencils are used to test specimens to see what will scratch them; other useful instruments include: fingernail (2.5), copper coin (3.5), steel knife (5.5), glass (6.0).

Talc	1	Calcite	3	Apatite	5	Quartz	7	Corundum	9
Gypsum	2	Fluorite	4	Orthoclase	6	Topaz	8	Diamond	10

Continents

	Area			Lowest point below sea level			Highest elevation		
	sq km	sq mi	%tlm[1]		m	ft		m	ft
Africa	30293000	11696000	(20.2%)	Lake Assal, Djibouti	156	512	Mt Kilimanjaro, Tanzania	5895	19340
Antarctica	13975000	5396000	(9.3%)	Bently sub-glacial trench	2538	8327	Vinson Massif	5140	16864
Asia	44493000	17179000	(29.6%)	Dead Sea, Israel/Jordan	400	1312	Mt Everest, China/Nepal	8848	29028
Europe[2]	10245000	3956000	(6.8%)	Caspian Sea, SW Asia	29	94	Mt El'brus, Russia	5642	18510
North America	24454000	9442000	(16.3%)	Death Valley, California	86	282	Mt McKinley, Alaska	6194	20320
Oceania	8945000	3454000	(6%)	Lake Eyre, S Australia	15	49	Puncak Jaya (New Guinea)	5030	16500
South America	17838000	6887000	(11.9%)	Península Valdés, Argentina	40	131	Aconcagua, Argentina	6960	22831

[1] Including the former western USSR.
[2] Percentage of total land mass.

Largest islands

	Area[1]			Area[1]	
	sq km	sq mi		sq km	sq mi
Australia[2]	7692300	2970000	Java	129000	49800
Greenland	2175600	840000	North Island, New Zealand	114000	44000
New Guinea	790000	305000	Cuba	110900	42800
Borneo	737000	285000	Newfoundland	109000	42100
Madagascar	587000	226600	Luzon	105000	40500
Baffin Island	507000	195800	Iceland	103000	39800
Sumatra	425000	164100	Mindanao	94600	36500
Honshu (Hondo)	228000	88000	Novaya Zemlya (two islands)	90600	35000
Great Britain	219000	84600	Ireland	84100	32500
Victoria Island, Canada	217300	83900	Hokkaido	78500	30300
Ellesmere Island, Canada	196000	75700	Hispaniola	77200	29800
Celebes	174000	67200	Sakhalin	75100	29000
South Island, New Zealand	151000	58300	Tierra del Fuego	71200	27500

[1] Areas are rounded to the nearest 100 sq km/sq mi. [2] Sometimes discounted, as a continent.

Major island groups

Name	Country	Sea/Ocean	Constituent islands
Aeolian	Italy	Mediterranean	Alicudi, Basiluzzo, Filicudi, Lipari, Salina, Stromboli, Vulcano
Åland	Finland	Gulf of Bothnia	over 300 islands including Ahvenanmaa, Eckero, Fasta Åland, Lemland, Lumparland, Vardo
Aleutian	USA	Pacific	five island groups: Andreanof, Four Mountains, Fox, Near, Rat
Alexander	Canada	Pacific	Admiralty, Baranof, Chichagof, Dall, Kupreanof, Prince of Wales, Revillagigedo, Wrangell
Andaman	India	Bay of Bengal	over 300 islands including Baratang, Little Andaman, Middle Andaman, N Andaman, Rutland, S Andaman
Antilles, Greater	—	Caribbean	Cuba, Hispaniola, Jamaica, Puerto Rico
Antilles, Lesser	—	Caribbean	three island groups: Leeward, Netherlands Antilles, Windward
Azores	Portugal	Atlantic	nine main islands: Corvo, Faial, Flores, Graciosa, Pico, Santa Maria, São Jorge, São Miguel, Terceira
Bahamas, The	The Bahamas	Atlantic	700 islands including Acklins, Andros, Berry, Cat, Cay, Crooked, Exuma, Grand Bahama, Great Abaco, Inagua, Long, Mayaguana, New Providence, Ragged
Balearic	Spain	Mediterranean	Cabrera, Formentera, Ibiza, Majorca, Menorca
Bay	Honduras	Caribbean	Guanja, Roatan, Utila
Bismarck Archipelago	Papua New Guinea	Pacific	c.200 islands including Admiralty, Duke of York, Lavonga, Mussau, New Britain, New Hanover, New Ireland, Vitu
Bissagos	Guinea-Bissau	Atlantic	15 islands including Caravela, Formosa, Orango, Roxa
Canadian Arctic Archipelago	Canada	Arctic	main islands: Baffin, Banks, Ellesmere, Victoria
Canary	Spain	Atlantic	main islands: Fuerteventura, Gomera, Graciosa, Gran Canaria, Hierro, Lanzarote, La Palma, Tenerife
Cape Verde	Cape Verde	Atlantic	10 islands divided into Barlaventos (windward) group: Boa Vista, Sal, Santa Luzia, Santo Antão, São Nicolau, São Vicente; and Sotaventos (leeward) group: Brava, Fogo, Maio, São Tiago
Caroline	—	Pacific	c.680 islands including Kusac, Palau, Ponape, Truk, Yap
Chagos Archipelago	UK	Indian	55 islands including Blenheim Reef, Diego Garcia, Egmont, Great Chagos Bank, Peros Banhos, Salomon, Speakers Bank
Channel	UK	English	Alderney, Jersey, Guernsey, Herm, Sark
Chonos Archipelago	Chile	Pacific	main islands: Benjamin, Chaffers, James, Luz, Melchior, Victoria
Commander	Russia	Bering Sea	Arii Kamen, Bering, Medny, Toporkov
Comoro	Comoros and France (Mayotte)	Mozambique Channel	Anjouan, Grand Comore, Mayotte, Mohéli, Pamanzi
Cook	New Zealand	Pacific	three island groups: High Cook (includes Mangaia, Rarotonga), Low, Northern Cook (includes Palmerston)
Cyclades	Greece	Aegean	c.220 islands including Amorges, Anafi, Andros, Antiparos, Delos, Ios, Kea, Mikonos, Milos, Naxos, Paros, Kithnos, Serifos, Tinos, Siros
Denmark	Denmark	Baltic	main islands: Zealand, Falster, Fyn, Lolland, North Jutland, Bornholm
Dodecanese	Greece	Aegean	12 islands including Astipalaia, Kalimnos, Karpathos, Kasos, Khalki, Kos, Leros, Patmos, Rhodes, Samos, Simi, Tilos,
Ellice	Tuvalu	Pacific	main islands: Funafuti, Nukefetau, Nukulailai, Nanumea
Falkland	UK	Atlantic	main islands: E Falkland, W Falkland
Faroe	Denmark	Atlantic	18 islands including Stromo, Ostero

Earth

Earth

Name	Country	Sea/Ocean	Constituent islands
Fiji	Fiji	Pacific	main islands: Vanua Levu, Viti Levu
Franz Josef Land ▶	Zemlya Frantsa-Iosifa		
Frisian, East	Germany and Denmark	North Sea	main islands: Baltrum, Borkum, Juist, Langeoog, Norderney, Spiekeroog, Wangerooge
Frisian, North	Germany and Denmark	North Sea	main islands: (German) Amrum, Föhr, Nordstrand, Pellworm, Sylt; (Danish) Fanø, Mandø, Rømø
Frisian, West	Netherlands	North Sea	main islands: Ameland, Griend, Schiermonnikoog, Texel, Terschelling, Vlieland
Galapagos	Ecuador	Pacific	main islands: Fernandina, Floreana, Isabela, San Cristobal, Santa Cruz, Santiago
Gilbert	Kiribati	Pacific	main islands: Abaiang, Abemama, Beru, Butaritari, Nonouti, Tabiteuea, Tarawa
Gotland	Sweden	Baltic	main islands: Gotland, Fårö, Karlsö
Greenland	Denmark	N Atlantic/Arctic	main islands: Greenland, Disko
Hawaiian	USA	Pacific	eight main islands: Hawaii, Kahoolawe, Kauai, Lanai, Maui, Molokai, Niihau, Oahu
Hebrides, Inner	UK	Atlantic	main islands: Coll, Eigg, Iona, Islay, Jura, Mull, Skye, Staffa, Tiree
Hebrides, Outer	UK	Atlantic	Barra, Benbecula, Harris, Lewis, N Uist, S Uist
Indonesia	Indonesia	Pacific	17508 islands and islets including Celebes, Java, Kalimantan, Lesser Sundas, Moluccas, New Guinea (Papua), Sumatra
Ionian	Greece	Aegean	main islands: Corfu, Cephalonia, Ithaca, Kythira, Lefkas, Paxos, Zakynthos
Japan	Japan	Pacific	main islands: Hokkaido, Honshu, Kyushu, Ryuku, Shikoku
Juan Fernández	Chile	Pacific	Más Afuera, Más a Tierra, Santa Clara
Kerguelen	France	Indian	Grande Terre (Kerguelen) and 300 islets
Kuril	Russia	Pacific	56 islands including Iturup, Kunashir, Onekotan, Paramushir, Shiaskhotan, Shikotanto, Shimushir, Shumsu, Urup
Laccadive	India	Arabian Sea	27 islands including Amindivi, Androth, Kavaratti, Laccadive, Minicoy
Line	Kiribati	Pacific	main islands: Christmas, Fanning, Washington
Lofoten	Norway	Norwegian Sea	main islands: Hinnøya, Austvågøy, Moskenesøya, Vestvågøy
Madeira	Portugal	Atlantic	Madeira, Desertas, Porto Santo, Selvagens
Malay Archipelago	Indonesia, Malaysia, Philippines	Pacific/Indian	main islands: Borneo, Celebes, Java, Luzon, Mindanao, New Guinea, Sumatra
Maldives	Maldives	Indian	19 clusters, main island: Male
Maltese	Malta	Mediterranean	main islands: Malta, Comino, Gozo
Mariana	USA	Pacific	14 islands including Agrihan, Anatahan, Alamagan, Guguan, Pagan, Rota, Saipan, Tinian
Marquesas	France	Pacific	Northern group: Eiao, Hatutu, Motu Iti, Moto Oa, Motu One, Nuku Hiva, Ua Huka, Ua Pu; Southern group: Fatu Hiva, Fatu Huku, Hiva Oa, Moho Tani, Motu Nao, Tahuata, Terihi
Marshall	Marshall Islands	Pacific	main islands: Bikini, Enewetak, Jaluit, Kwajalein, Majuro, Rongelap, Wotho
Mascarene	—	Indian	main islands: Mauritius, Réunion, Rodrigues
Melanesia	—	Pacific	main groups of islands: Bismarck Archipelago, Fiji, Maluku, New Caledonia, Palau, Papua New Guinea, Solomon Islands, Torres Strait, Vanuatu
Micronesia	—	Pacific	main groups of islands: Caroline, Gilbert, Guam, Mariana, Marshall, Nauru
Newfoundland	Canada	Atlantic	Prince Edward, Anticosti
New Hebrides	Vanuatu	Pacific	main islands: Espíritu Santo, Ambrym, Aurora, Éfaté, Épi, Erromanga, Malakula, Pentecôte, Tanna
New Siberian	Russia	Arctic	main islands: Faddeyevsky, Kotelny, Great Lyakhovsky, Little Lyakhovsky

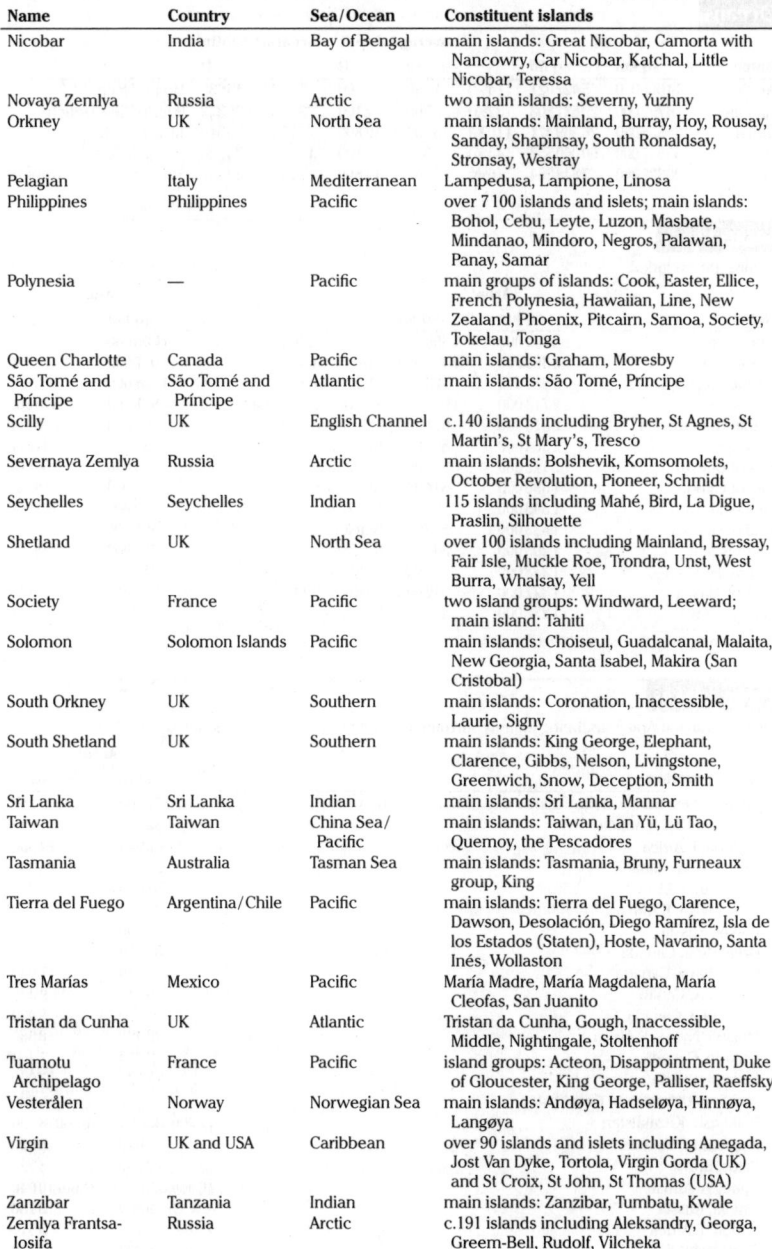

Name	Country	Sea/Ocean	Constituent islands
Nicobar	India	Bay of Bengal	main islands: Great Nicobar, Camorta with Nancowry, Car Nicobar, Katchal, Little Nicobar, Teressa
Novaya Zemlya	Russia	Arctic	two main islands: Severny, Yuzhny
Orkney	UK	North Sea	main islands: Mainland, Burray, Hoy, Rousay, Sanday, Shapinsay, South Ronaldsay, Stronsay, Westray
Pelagian	Italy	Mediterranean	Lampedusa, Lampione, Linosa
Philippines	Philippines	Pacific	over 7100 islands and islets; main islands: Bohol, Cebu, Leyte, Luzon, Masbate, Mindanao, Mindoro, Negros, Palawan, Panay, Samar
Polynesia	—	Pacific	main groups of islands: Cook, Easter, Ellice, French Polynesia, Hawaiian, Line, New Zealand, Phoenix, Pitcairn, Samoa, Society, Tokelau, Tonga
Queen Charlotte	Canada	Pacific	main islands: Graham, Moresby
São Tomé and Príncipe	São Tomé and Príncipe	Atlantic	main islands: São Tomé, Príncipe
Scilly	UK	English Channel	c.140 islands including Bryher, St Agnes, St Martin's, St Mary's, Tresco
Severnaya Zemlya	Russia	Arctic	main islands: Bolshevik, Komsomolets, October Revolution, Pioneer, Schmidt
Seychelles	Seychelles	Indian	115 islands including Mahé, Bird, La Digue, Praslin, Silhouette
Shetland	UK	North Sea	over 100 islands including Mainland, Bressay, Fair Isle, Muckle Roe, Trondra, Unst, West Burra, Whalsay, Yell
Society	France	Pacific	two island groups: Windward, Leeward; main island: Tahiti
Solomon	Solomon Islands	Pacific	main islands: Choiseul, Guadalcanal, Malaita, New Georgia, Santa Isabel, Makira (San Cristobal)
South Orkney	UK	Southern	main islands: Coronation, Inaccessible, Laurie, Signy
South Shetland	UK	Southern	main islands: King George, Elephant, Clarence, Gibbs, Nelson, Livingstone, Greenwich, Snow, Deception, Smith
Sri Lanka	Sri Lanka	Indian	main islands: Sri Lanka, Mannar
Taiwan	Taiwan	China Sea/Pacific	main islands: Taiwan, Lan Yü, Lü Tao, Quemoy, the Pescadores
Tasmania	Australia	Tasman Sea	main islands: Tasmania, Bruny, Furneaux group, King
Tierra del Fuego	Argentina/Chile	Pacific	main islands: Tierra del Fuego, Clarence, Dawson, Desolación, Diego Ramírez, Isla de los Estados (Staten), Hoste, Navarino, Santa Inés, Wollaston
Tres Marías	Mexico	Pacific	María Madre, María Magdalena, María Cleofas, San Juanito
Tristan da Cunha	UK	Atlantic	Tristan da Cunha, Gough, Inaccessible, Middle, Nightingale, Stoltenhoff
Tuamotu Archipelago	France	Pacific	island groups: Acteon, Disappointment, Duke of Gloucester, King George, Palliser, Raeffsky
Vesterålen	Norway	Norwegian Sea	main islands: Andøya, Hadseløya, Hinnøya, Langøya
Virgin	UK and USA	Caribbean	over 90 islands and islets including Anegada, Jost Van Dyke, Tortola, Virgin Gorda (UK) and St Croix, St John, St Thomas (USA)
Zanzibar	Tanzania	Indian	main islands: Zanzibar, Tumbatu, Kwale
Zemlya Frantsa-Iosifa	Russia	Arctic	c.191 islands including Aleksandry, Georga, Greem-Bell, Rudolf, Vilcheka

Earth

Oceans

Name	Area sq km	Area sq mi		Average depth m	Average depth ft	Greatest depth m	Greatest depth ft	
Arctic	14056000	5427021	(4%)	1330	4400	5680	18635	Molloy Deep
Atlantic	76762000	29637808	(22%)	3700	12100	8648	28372	Puerto Rico Trench
Indian	68556000	26469471	(19%)	3900	12800	7725	25344	Java Trench
Pacific	155557000	60060557	(43%)	4300	14100	11040	36220	Mariana Trench
Southern	20327000	7848254	(6%)	4500	14800	7235	23737	South Sandwich Trench

Largest seas

Oceans are excluded.

Name	Area[1] sq km	Area[1] sq mi	Name	Area[1] sq km	Area[1] sq mi
Coral Sea	4791000	1850000	Greenland Sea	1205000	465000
Arabian Sea	3863000	1492000	Arafura Sea	1037000	400000
S China (Nan) Sea	3685000	1423000	Philippine Sea	1036000	400000
Caribbean Sea	2718000	1050000	Sea of Japan (East Sea)	978000	378000
Mediterranean Sea	2516000	971000	E Siberian Sea	901000	348000
Bering Sea	2304000	890000	Kara Sea	883000	341000
Bay of Bengal	2172000	839000	E China Sea	664000	256000
Sea of Okhotsk	1590000	614000	Andaman Sea	565000	218000
Gulf of Mexico	1543000	596000	North Sea	520000	201000
Gulf of Guinea	1533000	592000	Black Sea	508000	196000
Barents Sea	1405000	542000	Red Sea	453000	175000
Norwegian Sea	1383000	534000	Baltic Sea	414000	160000
Gulf of Alaska	1327000	512000	Arabian Gulf	239000	92000
Hudson Bay	1232000	476000	St Lawrence Gulf	238000	92000

[1] Areas are rounded to the nearest 1000 sq km/sq mi.

Largest lakes

The Caspian and Aral Seas, being entirely surrounded by land, are classified as lakes.

Name/Location	Area[1] sq km	Area[1] sq mi
Caspian Sea, Iran/Russia/Turkmenistan/Kazakhstan/Azerbaijan	371000	143240[2]
Superior, USA/Canada	82260	31760[3]
Victoria, E Africa	62940	24300
Huron, USA/Canada	59580	23000[3]
Michigan, USA	58020	22400
Tanganyika, E Africa	32000	12360
Baikal, Russia	31500	12160
Great Bear, Canada	31330	12100
Great Slave, Canada	28570	11030
Erie, USA/Canada	25710	9930[3]
Winnipeg, Canada	24390	9420
Malawi/Nyasa, E Africa	22490	8680
Ontario, Canada	19270	7440[3]
Ladoga, Russia	18130	7000
Aral Sea, Uzbekistan/Kazakhstan	17160	6626[2]
Balkhash, Kazakhstan	17000–22000	6560–8490[2]
Maracaibo, Venezuela	13010	5020[4]
Patos, Brazil	10140	3920[4]
Chad, W Africa	10000–26000	3860–10040
Onega, Russia	9800	3780
Rudolf, E Africa	9100	3510
Eyre, Australia	8800	3400[4]
Titicaca, Peru/Bolivia	8300	3200

[1] Areas are rounded to the nearest 10 sq km/sq mi.
[2] Salt lakes.
[3] Average of areas given by Canada and USA.
[4] Salt lagoons.

Longest rivers

Name	Outflow	Length[1] km	mi
Nile-Kagera-Ruvuvu-Ruvusu-Luvironza	Mediterranean Sea (Egypt)	6690	4160
Amazon-Ucayali-Tambo-Ene-Apurimac	Atlantic Ocean (Brazil)	6570	4080
Mississippi-Missouri-Jefferson-Beaverhead-Red Rock	Gulf of Mexico (USA)	6020	3740
Chang Jiang (Yangtze)	E China Sea (China)	5980	3720
Yenisey-Angara-Selenga-Ider	Kara Sea (Russia)	5870	3650
Amur-Argun-Kerulen	Tartar Strait (Russia)	5780	3590
Ob-Irtysh	Gulf of Ob, Kara Sea (Russia)	5410	3360
Plata-Parana-Grande	Atlantic Ocean (Argentina/Uruguay)	4880	3030
Huang He (Yellow)	Yellow Sea (China)	4840	3010
Congo-Lualaba	S Atlantic Ocean (Angola/Democratic Republic of the Congo)	4630	2880
Lena	Laptev Sea (Russia)	4400	2730
Mackenzie-Slave-Peace-Finlay	Beaufort Sea (Canada)	4240	2630
Mekong	S China Sea (Vietnam)	4180	2600
Niger	Gulf of Guinea (Nigeria)	4100	2550

[1] Lengths are given to the nearest 10km/mi, and include the river plus tributaries comprising the longest watercourse.

Highest waterfalls

Name	Total height m	ft	Greatest single drop m	ft
Angel Falls, Venezuela	979	3212	807	2648
Tugela Falls, South Africa	948	3110	411	1350
Tres Hermanas (Three Sisters), Peru	914	3000	—	—
Olo'upena Falls, Hawaii, USA	900	2953	—	—
Vinnufossen, Norway	860	2822	420	1378
Baläifossen, Norway	850	2788	452	1482
Pu'uka'oku Falls, Hawaii, USA	840	2756	—	—
Browne Falls, New Zealand	836	2744	244	800
Strupenfossen, Norway	820	2690	—	—
Ramnefjellsfossen (Utigardsfossen), Norway	818	2685	600	1968

Largest deserts

Name/Location	Area[1] sq km	sq mi
Sahara, N Africa	8600000	3320000
Arabian, SW Asia	2330000	900000
Gobi, Mongolia and NE China	1166000	450000
Patagonian, Argentina	673000	260000
Great Victoria, SW Australia	647000	250000
Great Basin, SW USA	492000	190000
Chihuahuan, Mexico	450000	174000
Great Sandy, NW Australia	400000	154000
Sonoran, SW USA	310000	120000
Kyzyl Kum, Kazakhstan	300000	116000
Takla Makan, N China	270000	104000
Kalahari, SW Africa	260000	100000
Kara Kum, Turkmenistan	260000	100000
Kavir, Iran	260000	100000
Syrian, Saudi Arabia/Jordan/Syria/Iraq	260000	100000
Nubian, Sudan	260000	100000
Thar, India/Pakistan	200000	77000
Ust'-Urt, Kazakhstan	160000	62000
Bet-Pak-Dala, S Kazakhstan	155000	60000
Simpson, C Australia	145000	56000
Dzungaria, China	142000	55000
Atacama, Chile	140000	54000
Namib, SE Africa	134000	52000
Sturt, SE Australia	130000	50000
Bolson de Mapimi, Mexico	130000	50000
Ordos, China	130000	50000
Alashan, China	116000	45000

[1] Desert areas are very approximate, because clear physical boundaries may not occur.

Deepest caves

Name/Location	Depth	
	m	ft
Krubera-Voronja, Georgia	2191	7188
Illyuzia-Mezhonnogo-Snezhnaya, Georgia	1753	5751
Gouffre Mirolda, France	1733	5686
Lamprechtsofen Vogelschacht, Austria	1632	5354
Jean Bernard, France	1602	5256
Torca del Cerro del Cuevon, Spain	1589	5213
Sarma, Georgia	1543	5062
Shakta Vjacheslav Pantjukhina, Georgia	1508	4948
Sima de la Cornisa, Spain	1507	4944
Cehi 2, Slovenia	1502	4928
Sistema Cheve, Mexico	1484	4869
Sistema Huautla, Mexico	1475	4839
Sistema del Trave, Spain	1441	4728
Evren Gunay Dudeni, Turkey	1429	4688
Boj-Bulok, Uzbekistan	1415	4642

Highest mountains

Name	Height[1]		Location
	m	ft	
Everest	8850	29030	China/Nepal
K2	8610	28250	Kashmir/Jammu
Kangchenjunga	8590	28170	India/Nepal
Lhotse	8500	27890	China/Nepal
Kangchenjunga S Peak	8470	27800	India/Nepal
Makalu I	8470	27800	China/Nepal
Kangchenjunga W Peak	8420	27620	India/Nepal
Lhotse E Peak	8380	27500	China/Nepal
Dhaulagiri	8170	26810	Nepal
Cho Oyu	8150	26750	China/Nepal
Manaslu	8130	26660	Nepal
Nanga Parbat	8130	26660	Kashmir/Jammu
Annapurna I	8080	26500	Nepal
Gasherbrum I	8070	26470	Kashmir/Jammu
Broad Peak I	8050	26400	Kashmir/Jammu
Gasherbrum II	8030	26360	Kashmir/Jammu
Gosainthan	8010	26290	China
Broad Peak Central	8000	26250	Kashmir/Jammu
Gasherbrum III	7950	26090	Kashmir/Jammu
Annapurna II	7940	26040	Nepal
Nanda Devi	7820	25660	India
Rakaposhi	7790	25560	Kashmir
Kamet	7760	25450	India
Ulugh Muztagh	7720	25340	China (Tibet)
Tirich Mir	7690	25230	Pakistan
Muz Tag Ata	7550	24760	China
Imeni Ismail Samani Peak (Communism Peak)	7490	24590	Tajikistan
Pobedy Peak	7440	24410	China/Kyrgyzstan
Aconcagua	6960	22830	Argentina
Ojos del Salado	6910	22660	Argentina/Chile

[1] Heights are given to the nearest 10m/ft.

Earth

Major volcanoes

Name	Height m	ft	Major eruptions (years)	Last eruption (year)
Aconcagua (Argentina)	6959	22831	extinct	—
Kilimanjaro (Tanzania)	5928	19450	extinct	Pleistocene
Cotopaxi (Ecuador)	5897	19347	1877	1940
Popocatépetl (Mexico)	5483	17990	1519, 1663, 1896–2003, 2005–present	ongoing
Ararat (Turkey)	5137	16853	extinct	—
Klyuchevskoy (Russia)	4850	15910	1700–1966, 1986–90, 1994	2007
Rainier, Mt (USA)	4394	14416	300 BC, 1825	1894
Mauna Loa (Hawaii)	4171	13685	1852, 1859, 1868, 1880, 1887, 1919, 1950	1984
Erebus (Antarctica)	3794	12447	1947, 1972–present	ongoing
Fuji (Japan)	3776	12388	800, 1707	1707
Etna (Italy)	3239	10625	122, 1169, 1329, 1536, 1669, 1928, 1964, 1971, 1981, 1986, 1992, 1994, 2000, 2001	2008
Paricutín (Mexico)	3188	10460	1943–52	1952
Lassen Peak (USA)	3186	10453	1914–17	1917
Nyamuragira (Democratic Republic of the Congo)	3056	10026	1807, 1921–40, 1971, 1980, 1984, 1989, 1996, 2000, 2002	2006
Tambora (Sumbawa, Indonesia)	2868	9410	1815, 1880	1967
Bezymianny (Russia)	2800	9186	1955–6, 1981, 1997, 2001, 2004	2007
Ruapehu (New Zealand)	2797	9175	1945, 1953, 1969, 1975, 1986, 1995	2007
Mt St Helens (USA)	2549	8364	1480, 1482, 1800, 1831, 1835, 1842–3, 1980, 1990, 2004–present	ongoing
Mayon (Philippines)	2464	8084	1616, 1766, 1814, 1897, 1947, 1968, 1978, 1984, 1993, 1999, 2001	2006
Galunggung (Java)	2181	7155	1822, 1918, 1982	1984
Katmai (Alaska)	2047	6715	1912	1912
Lamington (Papua New Guinea)	1680	5512	1951	1956
Pinatubo, Mt (Philippines)	1486	4875	c.1450, 1991	1993
Hudson (Chile)	1905	6250	1971	1991
Grímsvötn (Iceland)	1725	5658	935, 1783–4, 1873, 1902–4, 1934, 1996, 1998	2004
Hekla (Iceland)	1491	4892	1693, 1845, 1947–8, 1970, 1981, 1991	2000
Taal (Philippines)	1311	1020	1716, 1749, 1754, 1911, 1965, 1969	1977
Pelée, Mont (Martinique)	1397	4584	1902, 1929–32	1932
Unzen (Japan)	1500	4921	1792, 1990–5	1996
El Chichón (Mexico)	1150	3773	1982	1982
Jorullo (Mexico)	1330	4255	1759–74	1774
Awu (Sangihe Is, Indonesia)	1320	4331	1711, 1812, 1856, 1892, 1966	2004
Vesuvius (Italy)	1289	4230	79, 472, 536, 685, 968, 1631, 1779, 1906	1944
Kilauea (Hawaii)	1222	4009	1823–1924, 1952, 1955, 1960, 1967–8, 1968–74, 1983–present	ongoing
Soufrière (St Vincent)	1220	4003	1718, 1812, 1902, 1971–2	1979
Tarawera (New Zealand)	1149	3770	1886	1886
Stromboli (Italy)	924	3031	1857–89, 1890–1907, 1910–31, 1934–present	ongoing
Soufrière Hills (Montserrat)	914	3000	1995–2003	2008
Krakatoa (Sumatra)	813	2667	1680, 1883, 1927, 1952–3, 1969, 1980, 1994–present	ongoing
Santoriní/Thíra (Greece)	367	1204	1470 BC, 197 BC, AD 46, 1570–3, 1650, 1707–11, 1866–70	1950
Vulcano (Italy)	503	1650	antiquity, 1444, 1730–40, 1786, 1873, 1888–90	1890
Eldfell (Iceland)	279	915	1973	1973
Surtsey (Iceland)	174	570	1963–7	1967

Earth

35

Major earthquakes

Earth

All magnitudes on the Richter scale. The energy released by earthquakes is measured on the logarithmic Richter scale. Thus:

2 Barely perceptible; 5 Rather strong; 7+ Very strong

Year	Location	Magni-tude	Deaths
2008	Sichuan (China)	8.0	69000+
2007	New Zealand	7.4	0
2007	Sumatra (Indonesia)	8.4	20+
2008	Peru	8.0	500+
2007	Solomon Islands	8.1	50+
2006	Kuril Is (Russia)	8.3	0
2006	Java (Indonesia)[1]	7.7	650+
2006	Java (Indonesia)[1]	6.3	5500+
2005	Dem. Rep. of Congo	6.8	2
2005	Kithira I (Greece)	6.9	0
2005	Kashmir	7.6	74500+
2005	Fukoka (Japan)	7.0	1
2005	Sumatra (Indonesia)	8.7	1300
2004	Indian Ocean	9.3	2
2004	Niigata state (N Japan)	6.8	25+
2004	Al Hoceima (NE Morocco)	6.3	560+
2003	Bam (Iran)	6.5	26000+
2003	N Algeria	6.7	2200+
2003	Xinjiang Region (China)	6.3	250+
2003	Colima (Mexico)	7.6	21+
2002	Papua New Guinea	7.6	5+
2002	Qazvin (Iran)	6.0	500+
2002	Hindu Kush (Afghanistan)	6.1	1800+
2001	Gujarat (India)	6.9	20000+
2001	El Salvador	7.7	675+
2000	Bengkulu (Sumatra)	7.9	115+
1999	Nantou Province (Taiwan)	7.6	2400+
1999	Izmit (NW Turkey)	7.4	17000+
1999	Armenia (Colombia)	6.0	1100+
1998	Badakhshan Province (Afghanistan)	7.1	5000+
1998	Rustaq (Afghanistan)	6.1	4000+
1997	Qayen (E Iran)	7.1	2400
1997	Ardabil (NW Iran)	5.5	965+
1996	Xinjiang Region (China)	6.9	26
1996	Biak I (Indonesia)	7.9	108
1996	Flores Sea (near Indonesia)	7.9	—
1996	Samar (Philippines)	7.9	—
1996	Lijiang, Yunan Province (China)	7.0	304
1995	Manzanillo (Mexico)	7.6	66
1995	S Mexico	7.3	—
1995	Sakhalin I (E Russia)	7.5	2000
1995	Kobe (Japan)	7.2	6300
1994	Hokkaido I (Japan) and Kuril Is (Russia) (undersea)	8.2	16+
1994	Bolivia (617km underground)	8.2	5
1994	Paez River Valley (SW Colombia)	6.8	269
1994	Java (Indonesia)	7.7	200
1994	Sumatra I (Indonesia)	7.2	215
1994	Halmahera I (Indonesia)	6.8	7+

Year	Location	Magni-tude	Deaths
1994	Los Angeles, California (USA)	6.8	61
1993	Maharashtra State (India)	6.5	22000
1993	Guam (Mariana Is)	8.1	—
1993	Okushiri and Hokkaido Is (N Japan)	7.8	185
1993	Papua New Guinea	6.8	60
1992	Maumere, Flores I (Indonesia)	7.5	1232
1992	Joshua Tree and Yucca Valley, California (USA)	7.4	2
1992	Erzincan (Turkey)	6.8	500
1992	Nusa Tenggara Is (Indonesia)	6.8	2500
1991	Uttar Pradesh (India)	6.1	1000
1991	Costa Rica/Panama	7.5	80
1991	Georgia	7.2	100
1991	Afghanistan	6.8	1000
1991	Pakistan	6.8	300
1990	Cabanatuan City (Philippines)	7.7	
1990	NW Iran	7.5	40000
1990	N Peru	5.8	200
1990	Romania	6.6	70
1990	Philippines	7.7	1600
1989	San Francisco (USA)	6.9	100
1988	Armenia	7.0	25000
1988	SW China	7.6	1000
1988	Nepal/India	6.9	900
1985	Mexico City (Mexico)	8.1	7200
1982	N Yemen	6.0	2800
1980	S Italy	7.2	4500
1980	El Asnam (Algeria)	7.3	5000
1978	NE Iran	7.7	25000
1976	Tangshan (China)	8.2	242000
1976	Guatemala City (Guatemala)	7.5	22778
1974	Kashmir (India)	6.3	5200
1972	Managua (Nicaragua)	6.2	5000
1972	S Iran	6.9	5000
1970	Chimbote (Peru)	7.7	66000
1968	NE Iran	7.4	11600
1964	Anchorage (USA)	8.5	131
1962	NW Iran	7.1	12000
1960	Agadir (Morocco)	5.8	12000
1939	Erzincan (Turkey)	7.9	23000
1939	Chillan (Chile)	7.8	30000
1935	Quetta (India)	7.5	60000
1932	Gansu (China)	7.6	70000
1927	Nan-shan (China)	8.3	200000
1923	Kwanto (Japan)	8.3	143000
1920	Gansu (China)	8.6	180000
1915	Avezzano (Italy)	7.5	30000
1908	Messina (Italy)	7.5	120000
1906	Valparaiso (Chile)	8.6	20000
1906	San Francisco (USA)	8.3	500
1868	Ecuador/Colombia	*	70000
1783	Calabria (Italy)	*	50000

Earth

Year	Location	Magnitude	Deaths	Year	Location	Magnitude	Deaths
1755	Lisbon (Portugal)	*	70 000	1556	Shensi (China)	*	830 000
1737	Calcutta (India)	*	300 000	1290	Chihli (China)	*	100 000
1730	Hokkaido (Japan)	*	137 000	1268	Silicia (Asia Minor)	*	60 000
1693	Catania (Italy)	*	60 000	856	Corinth (Greece)	*	45 000
1667	Caucasia (Caucasus)	*	80 000	526	Antioch (Turkey)	*	250 000

*Magnitude not available
[1] Earthquakes occurred in May and July 2006; the later one is shown first.
[2] Caused the tsunami which killed 225 000+ people in SE Asia.

Earthquake severity measurement

Modified Mercalli intensity scale (1956 Revision)

Intensity value	Description
I	Not felt; marginal and long-period effects of large earthquakes.
II	Felt by persons at rest, on upper floors or favourably placed.
III	Felt indoors; hanging objects swing; vibration like passing of light trucks; duration estimated; may not be recognized as an earthquake.
IV	Hanging objects swing; vibration like passing of heavy trucks, or sensation of a jolt like a heavy ball striking the walls; standing cars rock; windows, dishes, doors rattle; glasses clink; crockery clashes; in the upper range of IV, wooden walls and frames creak.
V	Felt outdoors; direction estimated; sleepers awoken; liquids disturbed, some spilled; small unstable objects displaced or upset; doors swing, close, open; shutters, pictures move; pendulum clocks stop, start, change rate.
VI	Felt by all; many frightened and run outdoors; persons walk unsteadily; windows, dishes, glassware break; knick-knacks, books, etc fall off shelves; pictures off walls; furniture moves or overturns; weak plaster and masonry D crack; small bells ring (church, school); trees, bushes shake visibly, or heard to rustle.
VII	Difficult to stand; noticed by drivers; hanging objects quiver; furniture breaks; damage to masonry D, including cracks; weak chimneys broken at roof line; fall of plaster, loose bricks, stones, tiles, cornices, also unbraced parapets and architectural ornaments; some cracks in masonry C; waves on ponds, water turbid with mud; small slides and caving in along sand or gravel banks; large bells ring; concrete irrigation ditches damaged.
VIII	Steering of cars affected; damage to masonry C and partial collapse; some damage to masonry B; none to masonry A; fall of stucco and some masonry walls; twisting, fall of chimneys, factory stacks, monuments, towers, elevated tanks; frame houses move on foundations if not bolted down; loose panel walls thrown out; decayed piling broken off; branches broken from trees; changes in flow or temperature of springs and wells; cracks in wet ground and on steep slopes.
IX	General panic; masonry D destroyed; masonry C heavily damaged, sometimes with complete collapse; masonry B seriously damaged; general damage to foundations; frame structures, if not bolted, shift off foundations; frames racked; serious damage to reservoirs; underground pipes break; conspicuous cracks in ground; in alluviated areas sand and mud ejected, earthquake fountains, sand craters.
X	Most masonry and frame structures destroyed with their foundations; some well-built wooden structures and bridges destroyed; serious damage to dams, dykes, embankments; large landslides; water thrown on banks of canals, rivers, lakes, etc; sand and mud shifted horizontally on beaches and flat land; rails bent slightly.
XI	Rails bent greatly; underground pipelines completely out of service.
XII	Damage nearly total; large rock masses displaced; lines of sight and level distorted; objects thrown into the air.

Notes:

Masonry A Good workmanship, mortar and design; reinforced, especially laterally, and bound together by using steel, concrete, etc; designed to resist lateral forces.

Masonry B Good workmanship and mortar; reinforced, but not designed in detail to resist lateral forces.

Masonry C Ordinary workmanship and mortar; no extreme weakness like failing to tie in at corners, but neither reinforced nor designed against horizontal forces.

Masonry D Weak materials, such as adobe; poor mortar; low standards of workmanship; weak horizontally.

Major tsunamis

Earth

Tsunamis are long-period ocean waves associated with earthquakes, volcanic explosions, or landslides. They are also referred to as *seismic sea waves* and popularly, but incorrectly, as *tidal waves*.

Year	Location of source	Height m	ft	Location of damage/deaths	Deaths
2007	Chile	6	20	Chile	3
2006	W Java, Indonesia	10	33	W Java	600+
2004	Sumatra, Indonesia	51	167	Indonesia, Sri Lanka, SE India, Thailand, Malaysia, Myanmar, Maldives, Bangladesh, Somalia, Kenya, Tanzania	225000+
1998	Papua New Guinea	10	33	Papua New Guinea	2200+
1996	Peru	4.9	16	Peru	12
1996	Irian Jaya, Indonesia	7	23	Indonesia	161
1996	Makassar Straits, Indonesia	4.9	16	Indonesia	9
1994	Mindoro I	15	49	Philippines	41
1994	Skagway, Alaska[1]	11	36	Skagway, Alaska	1
1994	Kuril Is	9	31	Kuril Is, Japan	12
1994	Java trench (Indian Ocean)	11	36	Java	223
1993	Sea of Japan	30.5	100	Japan, Russia	202
1992	Flores I (Indonesia)	26	85	Indonesia	400
1992	Nicaragua	9	30	Nicaragua	167
1983	Sea of Japan	15	49	Japan, Korea	103
1979	Indonesia	9.8	32	Indonesia	187
1976	Celebes Sea	30	98	Philippines	5000
1964	Alaska	32	105	Alaska, Aleutian Is, California	122
1960	Chile	25	82	Chile, Hawaii, Japan	1260
1957	Aleutian Is	15.9	52	Hawaii, Japan	0
1952	Kamchatka	18.3	60	Kamchatka, Kuril Is, Hawaii	many
1946	Aleutian Is	32	105	Aleutian Is, Hawaii, California	165
1946	Nankaido (Japan)	6.1	20	Japan	1997
1944	Kii (Japan)	7.6	25	Japan	998
1933	Sanriku (Japan)	28.3	93	Japan, Hawaii	3000
1923	E Kamchatka	20.1	66	Kamchatka, Hawaii	3
1918	S Kuril Is	11.9	39	Kuril Is, Russia, Japan, Hawaii	23
1896	Sanriku (Japan)	29.9	98	Japan	27122
1883	Sunda Strait	35.1	115	Java, Sumatra	36000
1877	Chile	22.9	75	Chile, Hawaii	many
1868	Chile	21	69	Chile, Hawaii	25000
1868	Hawaii	20.1	66	Hawaii	81
1854	Japan	6.1	20	Japan	3000
1800	Flores Sea	24.1	79	Indonesia	400–500
1792	Ariake Sea	9.1	30	Japan	9745
1783	Italy	?	?	Italy	30000
1771	Ryukyu Is	11.9	39	Ryukyu Is	11941
1775	Portugal	15.8	52	W Europe, Morocco, W Indies	60000
1746	Peru	24.1	79	Peru	5000
1741	Japan	9	30	Japan	1000+
1737	SE Kamchatka	29.9	98	Kamchatka, Kuril Is	?
1724	Peru	24.1	79	Peru	?
1707	Japan	11.6	38	Japan	30000
1692	W Indies	?	?	Jamaica	2000
1629	Banda Is	14.9	49	Indonesia	?
1611	Sanriku (Japan)	25	82	Japan	5000
1605	Japan	?	?	Japan	4000
1498	Kii (Japan)	?	?	Japan	5000

[1] Tsunami caused by the dock collapsing into the sea.

CLIMATE AND ENVIRONMENT

Climatic zones

The earth may be divided into zones, approximating to zones of latitude, such that each zone possesses a distinct type of climate.

The principal zones are:

■ **Tropical** One zone of wet climate near the equator (either constantly wet or monsoonal with wet and dry seasons, tropical savannah with dry winters); the average temperature is not below 18°C;
  Amazon forest
  Malaysia
  S Vietnam
  India
  Africa
  Congo Basin
  Indonesia
  SE Asia
  Australia
■ **Subtropical** Two zones of steppe and desert climate (transition through semi-arid to arid);
  Sahara
  Central Asia
  Mexico
  Australia
  Kalahari
■ **Mediterranean** Zones of rainy climate with mild winters; coolest month above 0°C but below 18°C;
  California
  South Africa
  S Europe
  parts of Chile
  SW Australia
■ **Temperate** Rainy climate (includes areas of temperate woodland, mountain forests, and plains

with no dry season; influenced by seas – rainfall all year, small temperate changes); average temperature between 3°C and 18°C;
  Most of Europe
  Asia
  NW / NE USA
  New Zealand
  Chile
■ **Boreal** Climate with a great range of temperature in the northern hemisphere (in some areas the most humid month is in summer and there is ten times more precipitation than the driest part of winter. In other areas the most humid month is in winter and there is ten times more precipitation than in the driest part of summer); in the coldest period temperatures do not exceed 3°C and in the hottest do not go below 10°C;
  Prairies of USA
  parts of South Africa
  parts of Russia
  parts of Australia
■ **Polar caps** Snowy climate (tundra and ice-cap) with little or no precipitation. There is permafrost in the tundra and vegetation includes lichen and moss all year, and grass in the summer; the highest annual temperature in the polar region is below 0°C and in the tundra the average temperature is 10°C;
  Arctic regions of Russia and N America
  Antarctica

Meteorological extremes

■ The hottest place is Dallol, Ethiopia, at 34.4°C/93.9°F (annual mean temperature).
■ The highest recorded temperature in the shade is 58°C/136.4°F at al'Aziziyah, Libya, on 13 September 1922.
■ The coldest place is Plateau Station, Antarctica, at -56.6°C/-69.8°F (annual mean temperature).
■ The lowest recorded temperature is -89.2°C/-128.6°F at Vostok, Antarctica, on 21 July 1983.
■ The driest place is the Atacama desert near Calama, Chile, where no rainfall was recorded in over 400 years to 1972.
■ The most rain to fall in 24 hours was 1870mm/74in which fell on Cilaos, Réunion, in the Indian Ocean, on 15–16 March 1952.
■ The wettest place is Mawsynram, Meghalaya State, India, where the annual average rainfall is 11870mm/467in.
■ The greatest amount of snow to fall in 12 months was 31102mm/1225in, at Paradise, Mt Rainier, in Washington, USA, in 1971–2.
■ The most rainy days in a year are the c.350 experienced on Mt Waialeale, Kauai, Hawaii, USA.
■ The least sunshine occurs at the North and South Poles, where the Sun does not rise for 182 days of winter.
■ The greatest amount of sunshine occurs in Yuma, Arizona, USA: with a mean average of 4055 hours of sun a year (91% of possible hours of sunlight).
■ The highest recorded surface wind speed is 371.75kph/231mph, at Mt Washington, New Hampshire, USA, on 12 April 1934.

World temperatures

The maps below show the average world temperatures for January and July.

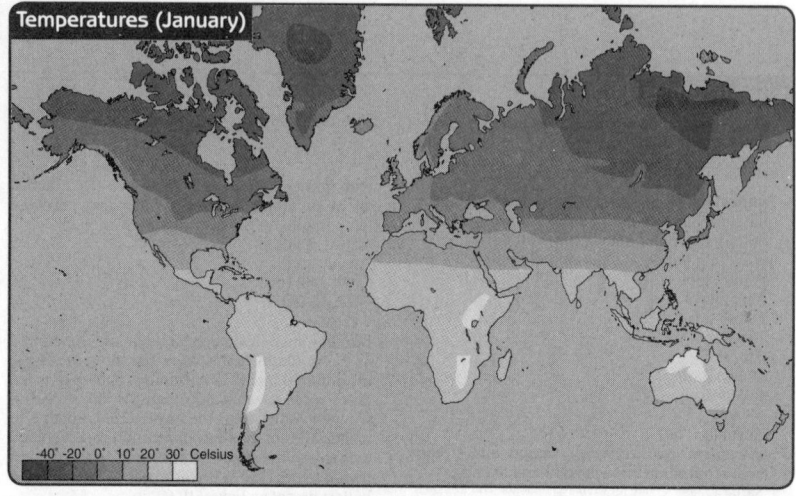

Temperatures (January)

-40° -20° 0° 10° 20° 30° Celsius

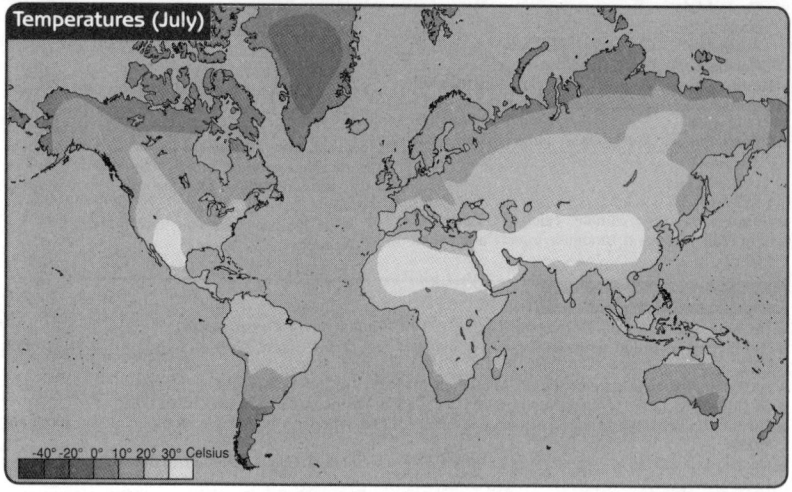

Temperatures (July)

-40° -20° 0° 10° 20° 30° Celsius

Climate and Environment

World temperature change

Global Average Near-Surface Temperature 1850–2008, relative to the average for 1961–90.

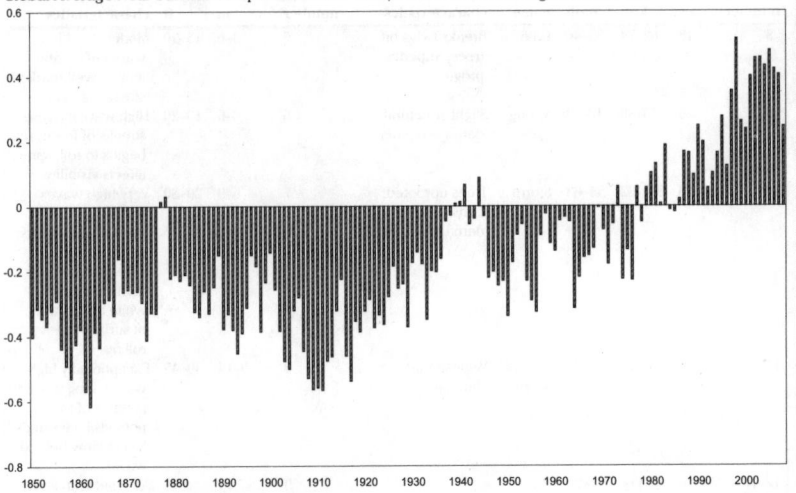

Data source: Hadley Centre for Climate Prediction and Research, Met Office

Climate and Environment

Wind force and sea disturbance

Beau-fort number	m/ sec	Windspeed kph	Windspeed mph	Wind name	Observable wind characteristics	Sea disturbance number	Average wave ht. m	Average wave ht. ft	Observable sea characteristics
0	1	<1	<1	Calm	Smoke rises vertically	0	0	0	Sea like a mirror
1	1	1–5	1–3	Light air	Wind direction shown by smoke drift, but not by wind vanes	0	0	0	Ripples like scales, without foam crests
2	2	6–11	4–7	Light breeze	Wind felt on face; leaves rustle; vanes moved by wind	1	0.3	0–1	More definite wavelets, but crests do not break
3	4	12–19	8–12	Gentle breeze	Leaves and small twigs in constant motion; wind extends light flag	2	0.3–0.6	1–2	Large wavelets; crests begin to break; scattered white horses
4	7	20–28	13–18	Moder-ate breeze	Raises dust, loose paper; small branches moved	3	0.6–1.2	2–4	Small waves become longer; fairly frequent white horses
5	10	29–38	19–24	Fresh breeze	Small trees in leaf begin to sway; crested wavelets on inland waters	4	1.2–2.4	4–8	Moderate waves with a more definite long form; many white horses; some spray possible
6	12	39–49	25–31	Strong breeze	Large branches in motion; difficult to use umbrellas; whistling heard in telegraph wires	5	2.4–4	8–13	Large waves form; more extensive white foam crests; some spray probable
7	15	50–61	32–38	Near gale	Whole trees in motion; inconvenience walking against wind	6	4–6	13–20	Sea heaps up; streaks of white foam blown along

Climate and Environment

Beau-fort number	m/sec	Windspeed kph	Windspeed mph	Wind name	Observable wind characteristics	Sea disturbance number	Average wave ht. m	Average wave ht. ft	Observable sea characteristics
8	18	62–74	39–46	Gale	Breaks twigs off trees; impedes progress	6	4–6	13–20	Moderately high waves of greater length; well-marked streaks of foam
9	20	75–88	47–54	Strong gale	Slight structural damage occurs	6	4–6	13–20	High waves; dense streaks of foam; sea begins to roll; spray affects visibility
10	26	89–102	55–63	Storm	Trees uprooted; considerable damage occurs	7	6–9	20–30	Very high waves with long overhanging crests; dense streaks of foam blown along; generally white appearance of surface; heavy rolling
11	30	103–17	64–72	Violent storm	Widespread damage	8	9–14	30–45	Exceptionally high waves; long white patches of foam; poor visibility; ships lost to view behind waves
12–17	⩾30	⩾118	⩾73	Hurricane		9	14	>45	Air filled with foam and spray; sea completely white; very poor visibility

Windstorms

A **cyclone** (abbreviated to C. in the table) is a circulation of winds in the atmosphere which rotates round a depression; rotation is anticlockwise in the northern hemisphere and clockwise in the southern.

A **hurricane** (abbreviated to H.) is a windstorm originating over tropical oceans in the northern hemisphere, with winds in excess of 74mph. Hurricanes are named by the National Hurricane Center, USA, in alphabetical sequence as they occur each year. Since 1978 names given have been alternately male/female. In the N Pacific they are known as **typhoons** (abbreviated to T.).

A **tornado** is a column of air rotating rapidly around a very low pressure centre.

Information on selected windstorms to 2008 is given.

Year	Name	Location	Deaths
2008	T. Fengshen	Philippines, China	1356
2008	C. Nargis	Sri Lanka, Myanmar	84000+
2007	H. Dean	Caribbean, Mexico, C America	32
2007	T. Sepat	Philippines, Taiwan, China	43
2006	T. Durian	Philippines, Vietnam	190
2006	T. Cimaron	Philippines	19
2006	H. Ernesto	N Caribbean, Florida, N Carolina	7
2005	H. Wilma	Atlantic Basin	23
2005	H. Rita	Gulf of Mexico	7
2005	H. Katrina	Gulf Coast, USA	1833
2005	T. Haitang	Taiwan, China	13
2005	H. Dennis	Florida, Cuba	42
2004	H. Jeanne	Puerto Rico, Haiti, Dominican Republic, Florida	1500+
2004	H. Ivan	Caribbean, Cuba, SW USA	100+
2003	H. Isabel	N Carolina	51+
2002	H. Isidore	Cuba, Yucatan Peninsula	7
2001	H. Michelle	Cuba, Honduras, Nicaragua	17+
2000	C. Eline	Madagascar, Mozambique	*
1999	Cyclone	Orissa	10000+
1999	H. Floyd	Florida, N Carolina, The Bahamas	57
1998	H. Mitch	C America (Honduras, Nicaragua), Florida	10000+
1998	H. Georges	NE Caribbean, Mississippi	602
1997	T. Linda	Vietnam, Thailand	453
1996	H. Fran	N Carolina	34

Year	Name	Location	Deaths
1995	H. Opal	NW Florida	19
1992	H. Andrew	S Florida, The Bahamas	88
1991	H. Bob	NE USA	17
1991	Cyclone	Bangladesh	200 000
1989	H. Hugo	S Carolina	49
1988	H. Gilbert	Caribbean, Mexico	318
1988	H. Joan	Caribbean	216
1987	Winter storm	S England, NW France	17
1985	H. Kate	Florida (Keys), NW Florida	16
1985	Cyclone	Bangladesh	11 000
1984	Ts. Ike and June	Philippines (Mindanao)	1 000
1980	H. Allen	S Texas	235
1979	H. David	Florida, E USA	2 400
1975	H. Eloise	NW Florida	100
1974	Tornadoes	C USA	322
1974	H. Fifi	C America (Honduras)	10 000
1974	C. Tracy	Australia (Darwin)	65
1972	H. Agnes	E Coast, USA	122
1970	Cyclone	Bangladesh	300 000
1969	H. Camille	Mississippi, Louisiana	256
1965	H. Betsy	SE Florida, SE Louisiana, Mississippi	75
1964	T. Louise	Philippines (Mindanao)	58
1964	H. Hilda	Central Louisiana	38
1964	H. Cleo	SE Florida	154
1963	H. Flora	Haiti, Cuba, Dominican Republic	7 000
1961	H. Carla	Texas	46
1960	H. Donna	Florida, E USA	50
1959	T. Vera	Ise Bay, Japan	5 098
1957	H. Audrey	Louisiana, N Texas	390
1955	H. Diane	NE USA	184
1954	H. Hazel	S Carolina, N Carolina	95
1954	H. Carol	NE USA	60
1954	Typhoon	Japan (Toyama, N Honshu)	3 000
1947	Hurricane	SE Florida, Louisiana, Mississippi	51
1945	Typhoon	Japan (Makurazaki)	3 756
1944	Hurricane	NE USA	390
1942	Cyclone	Bangladesh	61 000
1940	Hurricane	Georgia, S Carolina, N Carolina	50
1938	Hurricane	New England	600
1935	Hurricane	Florida (Keys)	408
1933	Hurricane	S Texas	40
1932	Hurricane	Texas (Freeport)	40
1932	Hurricane	Cuba	2 500
1931	Hurricane	Belize	2 000
1930	Hurricane	San Zenon, Santo Domingo, Dominican Republic	2 000
1928	Hurricane	Florida (Lake Okeechobee)	1 836
1926	Hurricane	Florida (Miami)	243
1922	Typhoon	China (Shantou)	28 000
1919	Hurricane	Florida (Keys), S Texas	600–900
1917	Typhoon	Japan (Honshu)	4 000
1915	Hurricane	N Texas (Galveston), Louisiana	550
1913	Tornado	Ohio, Indiana	700
1912	Typhoon	China (Wenchang)	50 000
1909	Hurricane	Louisiana (Grand Isle)	350
1906	Typhoon	Hong Kong	10 000
1906	Hurricane	SE Florida	164
1906	Hurricane	Mississippi, Alabama, Florida (Pensacola)	134
1900	Hurricane	N Texas (Galveston)	6 000
1906	Hurricane	SE Florida	164
1906	Hurricane	Mississippi, Alabama, Florida (Pensacola)	134
1900	Hurricane	N Texas (Galveston)	6 000
1899	Hurricane	San Ciriaco	3 369
1897	Typhoon	Philippines (Leyte)	10 000
1893	Hurricane	S Carolina, Georgia	1 000
1884	Typhoon	W Coast, Japan	2 000
1882	Cyclone	India (Bombay)	100 000

Climate and Environment

Year	Name	Location	Deaths
1881	Typhoon	China	300 000
1876	Cyclone	Bangladesh (Bakarganj)	215 000
1864	Cyclone	India (Calcutta)	50 000
1822	Cyclone	Bangladesh (Bakarganj)	50 000
1791	Hurricane	Cuba	3 000
1780	Hurricane	West Indies, Barbados, Martinique, St Vincent, Guadeloupe	24 000
1737	Cyclone	India (Calcutta)	300 000
1588	Winter storm	UK (sinking of the Spanish Armada)	20 000

* Indeterminate, due to severe flooding prior to cyclone.

Hydrological cycle

The hydrological cycle is the circulation of water between the Earth's surface and the atmosphere. Water moves from mountain streams to the sea, travelling along rivers. Evaporation from seas and lakes moves water into th e atmosphere, where it condenses to form clouds. Plants also lose water to the atmosphere; this is known as transpiration.

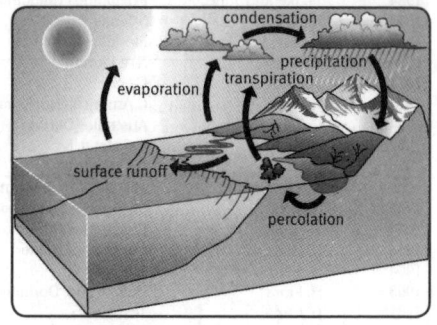

Clouds

Clouds are formed by the condensation or freezing of water vapour on minute particles in the atmosphere. They play an important role in regulating climate by absorbing and reflecting certain parts of the Sun's radiation. Cloud formation occurs when air masses move upward as a result of convection currents, unstable conditions, etc, and in so doing cool rapidly.

Clouds are usually classified according to their height and shape. Meteorologists measure cloud height in feet; to convert to metres, multiply by 0.3048.

Low clouds

The base of low clouds is usually surface–7 000ft.

- **Stratus (St)**
Cloud base: usually surface–1 500ft.
Colour: usually grey.

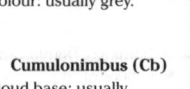

- **Cumulus (Cu)**
Cloud base: usually 1 200–6 000ft.
Colour: white in sunlight but dark underside.

- **Cumulonimbus (Cb)**
Cloud base: usually 1 000–5 000ft.
Colour: white above with dark underside.

- **Stratocumulus (Sc)**
Cloud base: usually 1200–7000ft.
Colour: grey or white, with shading.

Medium clouds

The base of medium clouds is usually 7 000–17 000ft, although Nimbostratus may be much lower.

- **Nimbostratus (Ns)**
Cloud base: usually 1500–10 000ft.
Colour: dark grey.

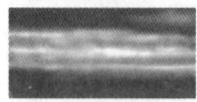

- **Altostratus (As)**
Cloud base: usually 8000–17 000ft.
Colour: greyish or bluish.

- **Altocumulus (Ac)**
Cloud base: usually 7000–17 000ft.
Colour: grey or white, with shading.

High clouds

The base of high clouds is usually 17 000–35 000ft. High clouds are composed of ice crystals.

■ **Cirrus (Ci)**
Cloud base: usually
17 000–35 000ft.
Colour: white.

■ **Cirrostratus (Cs)**
Cloud base: usually
17 000–35 000ft.
Colour: white.

■
Cirrocumulus (Cc)
Cloud base: usually
17 000–35 000ft.
Colour: white.

Acid rain

A term generally used for polluted rainfall associated with the burning of fossil fuels. It is implicated in damage to forests and the stonework of buildings, and increases the acid content of soils and lakes, harming crops and fish.

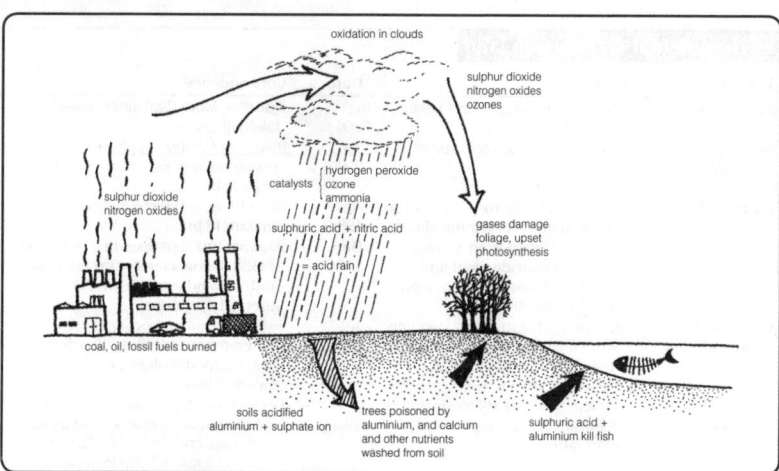

Tropical rainforest distribution

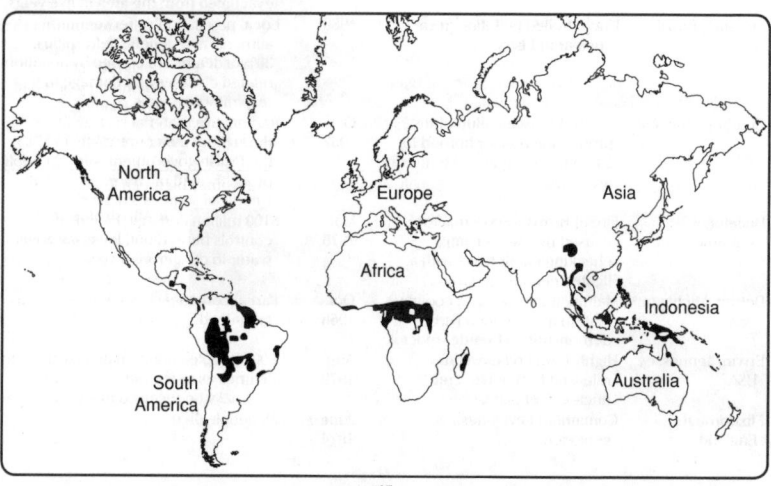

Climate and Environment

Forest area and rate of change

Deforestation has taken place largely as a result of economic pressures for more agricultural land. Deforestation has serious implications for the environment (as carbon dioxide is released into the atmosphere) and can also cause the degradation of topsoil, increasing the risk of rivers silting up and flooding. Rainforests, which are home to half the world's plant and animal species are in particular danger. The following data are taken from *State of the World's Forests 2005*, published by the Food and Agricultural Organization (FAO) of the United Nations.

Country/Area	Forest area 2000		Forest cover change 1990–2000	
	Total forest (1 000 ha)[1]	% of land area	Annual change (1 000 ha)	Annual rate of change (%)
Africa	649 866	21.8	-5 262	-0.8
Asia	547 796	17.8	-364	-0.1
Europe	1 039 251	46	881	0.1
North & Central America	549 304	25.7	-570	-0.1
Oceania	197 623	23.3	-365	-0.2
South America	885 618	50.5	-3 711	-0.4
World	3 869 455	29.6	-9 391	-0.2

[1] One hectare (ha) = 10 000 sq m. To convert ha to sq km, divide by 100; to convert ha to sq mi, multiply by 0.003861.

Environmental disasters on land

Location	Event	Date	Consequence
Abidjan, Ivory Coast	Toxic waste dumped in 11 sites round city	Sep 2006	7 deaths. More than 40 000 people taken ill.
Baia Mare, Romania	Cyanide leak from gold mine.	Jan 2000	Rivers and water supplies contaminated, fish stocks severely depleted.
Basle, Switzerland	Fire in Sandoz factory warehouse resulted in major chemical spill.	Nov 1980	River Rhine rendered lifeless for 200km/124mi.
Bhopal, India	Toxic gas leaked from a Union Carbide pesticide plant and enveloped a nearby slum area housing 200 000 people.	Dec 1984	Possibly 10 000 people died (officially 2 352). Survivors suffer ravaged lungs and/or blindness. 100km²/39mi² affected by the gas.
Camelford, Cornwall	20 tonnes of aluminium sulphate were flushed down local rivers after an accident at a water treatment works.	Jul 1988	60 000 fish killed. Local people suffered from vomiting, diarrhoea, blisters, mouth ulcers, rashes and memory loss.
Chernobyl, Ukraine	Nuclear reactor exploded, releasing a radioactive cloud over Europe.	Apr 1986	Fewer than 50 people were killed, but the radioactive cloud spread as far as Britain, contaminating farmland. 100 000 Ukrainian and Russian citizens may die of radiation-induced cancer, a further 30 000 fatalities are possible worldwide. 250 000 people evacuated from the area in five years.
Cubatão, Brazil	Uncontrolled pollution from nuclear industry.	1980s	Local population suffer serious ailments and genetic deformities. 30% of deaths are caused by pollution-related diseases and damage to respiratory systems.
Cumbria, England	Fire in Windscale plutonium production reactor burned for 24 hours and ignited 3 tonnes of uranium.	Oct 1957	Radioactive material spread throughout the countryside. In 1983 the British government said 39 people probably died of cancer as a result. Unofficial sources say 1 000.
Decatur, Alabama, USA	Fire at Browns Ferry reactor caused by a technician checking for air leaks with a lighted candle.	Mar 1975	$100 million damage. Electrical controls burned out, lowering cooling water to dangerous levels.
Detroit, Michigan, USA	Malfunction in sodium cooling system at the Enrico Fermi demonstration breeder reactor.	Oct 1966	Partial core meltdown. Radiation was contained.
Erwin, Tennessee, USA	Highly enriched uranium released from top-secret nuclear fuel plant.	Aug 1979	1 000 people contaminated (with up to 5 times as much radiation as would normally be received in a year).
Flixborough, England	Container of cyclohexane exploded.	June 1974	28 people died.

Climate and Environment

46

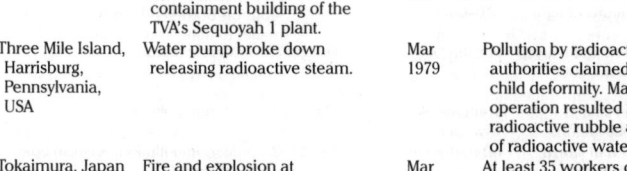

Location	Event	Date	Consequence
Goiânia, Brazil	Major radioactive contamination incident involving an abandoned radiotherapy unit containing radioactive caesium chloride salts.	Sep–Oct 1987	People evacuated; homes demolished; 249 people affected by sickness or death.
Gore, Oklahoma, USA	Cylinder of nuclear material burst after being improperly heated at Kerr-McGee plant.	Jan 1986	1 worker died, 100 hospitalized.
Idaho Falls, Idaho, USA	Accident at experiment reactor.	Jan 1961	3 workers killed. Damage contained, despite high radiation levels at the plant.
Jilin, China	Chemical plant explosion.	Nov 2005	Five people killed. Explosion caused a toxic slick covering 80km of the Songhua River.
Jiyyeh, Lebanon	Power station hit by Israeli bombing.	July 2006	Caused an oil spill affecting the Lebanese and Syrian coastlines.
Kasli, Russia	Chemical explosion in tanks containing nuclear waste.	Sep 1957	Radioactive material spread. Major evacuation of area.
Kuwait	Iraqi forces set alight 600 oil wells.	Feb 1991	Air pollution consisted of clouds of soot and oil particles which obscured the sun and fell as 'black rain'. Threat that it would turn into sulphur dioxide and fall as acid rain. Incidence of fatal bronchitis expected to increase. Possible serious contamination of agricultural land and water supplies particularly in Iraq's Tigris and Euphrates valleys.
Love Canal, near Niagara Falls, New York, USA	Dumping of drums containing hazardous waste at Love Canal, which by the 1970s were leaking toxic chemicals.	1940s to 1952	More than 240 families evacuated, countryside contaminated.
Lucens Vad, Switzerland	Coolant malfunction in an experimental underground reactor.	Jan 1969	Large amount of radiation released into cavern, which was then sealed.
Minimata Bay, Japan	Dumping of chemicals, including methyl mercury.	1953	Minimata disease, characterized by cerebral palsy, had killed more than 300 people by 1983. Thousands more suffered genetic abnormalities, brain disease and nervous disorders.
Monongahela River, Pennsylvania, USA	Storage tank ruptured and spilled 3 800 000 gallons of diesel oil into the Mononghela River.	Jan 1988	Water supply to 23 000 residents of Pittsburgh cut off. Oil slick spread into W Virginia, growing to 77km/48mi, and reached Steubenville, Ohio.
Monticello, Minnesota, USA	Water-storage space at Northern States Power Company's reactor overflowed.	Nov 1971	50 000 gallons of radioactive waste water dumped in Mississippi River. St Paul water system contaminated.
Rochester, New York, USA	Steam-generator pipe broke at the Rochester Gas & Electric Company's plant.	Jan 1982	Small amounts of radioactive steam escaped.
Seveso, N Italy	Leak of toxic TCDD gas containing the poison dioxin.	Jul 1976	Local population still suffering; in worst contaminated area, topsoil had to be removed and buried in a giant plastic-coated pit.
Sihanoukville, Cambodia	Around 3 000 tons of Taiwanese toxic waste dumped in a field.	Nov 1998	Reports of illness and death amongst scavengers who handled the waste.
Tennessee, USA	100 000 gallons of radioactive coolant leaked into the containment building of the TVA's Sequoyah 1 plant.	Feb 1981	8 workers contaminated.
Three Mile Island, Harrisburg, Pennsylvania, USA	Water pump broke down releasing radioactive steam.	Mar 1979	Pollution by radioactive gases. Some authorities claimed regional cancer, child deformity. Massive clean-up operation resulted in 150 tonnes of radioactive rubble and 250 000 gallons of radioactive water.
Tokaimura, Japan	Fire and explosion at power reactor and nuclear reprocessing plant.	Mar 1997	At least 35 workers contaminated.

Climate and Environment

Climate and Environment

Location	Event	Date	Consequence
Toulouse, France	AZF chemical factory exploded due to improper handling of ammonium nitrate.	Sep 2001	29 people killed, 2500 seriously injured; 40000 made temporarily homeless and several schools and hospitals evacuated.
Tsuruga, Japan	Accident during repairs of a nuclear plant.	Apr 1981	100 workers exposed to radioactive material.

Major oil spills at sea

Name	Location	Date	Consequence
Aegean Sea grounded and spilled 16000000 gallons and caught fire	La Coruña, Spain	Dec 1992	Marine pollution; 80km/50mi of Spanish coast polluted.
Amoco Cadiz, Cyprus-registered tanker, grounded and spilled 65562000 gallons	near Portshall, France	Mar 1978	Marine pollution; 160km/99mi of French coast polluted.
Aragon spilled 7350000 gallons	off Madeira Is	Dec 1989– Jan 1990	Marine pollution
Atlantic Empress and *Aegean Captain*; collision between tankers caused spillage of 88200000 gallons	off Trinidad and Tobago	Jul 1979	Marine pollution
Braer tanker, broke up and spilled 26000000 gallons	Shetland, Scotland	Jan 1993	Marine pollution
Burmah Agate collided and spilled 10700000 gallons	Galveston Bay, Texas	Nov 1979	Marine pollution
Castillo de Bellver tanker; fire caused spillage of 73500000 gallons	off Cape Town, South Africa	Aug 1983	Marine pollution
Diamond Grace, Panamanian-registered tanker, grounded and spilled 4000000 gallons	off Yokohama, Japan	Jul 1997	Marine pollution
Ekofisk oil field; blow-out caused spillage of 8200000 gallons	North Sea	Apr 1977	Marine pollution
Exxon Valdez, US tanker, grounded on Bligh Reef and spilled 10080000 gallons	Prince William Sound, Alaska	Mar 1989	1770km/1162mi of Alaskan coastline polluted. More than 3600 sq km/1390 sq mi of water fouled. Thousands of animals killed.
Gulf; Iraq pumped oil at a rate of 4200000 gallons a day into the sea	16km/10mi off coast near Kuwait City	Jan–Feb 1991	Threat to desalination plants and therefore to water supply; marine pollution
Hawaiian Patriot; fire caused spillage of 29106000 gallons	N Pacific	Feb 1977	Marine pollution
Hebei Spirit; collision with barge caused spillage of more than 10000 tons of crude oil	Yellow Sea, about 150km/95 miles south-west of Seoul	Dec 2007	Pollution of 300km/185mi of shoreline
Ixtoc oil well; blow-out caused spillage of 176400000 gallons	Gulf of Mexico	Jun 1979	Marine pollution
Keo; hull failure caused spillage of 88200000 gallons	off Massachusetts, USA	Nov 1969	Marine pollution
Khark 5, Iranian supertanker, spilled 19000000 gallons of heavy crude oil after an explosion in its hull	700km/435mi north of the Canary Is, Atlantic Ocean	Dec 1989	370km/230mi oil slick almost reached Morocco. About 40% evaporated and much sank to ocean floor, endangering fish and oysters.
Kirki, Greek tanker, broke up and spilled 5880000 gallons of light crude oil	off Cervantes, W Australia	Jul 1991	Pollution of conservation zones and lobster fishery.
Nowruz oil field; blow-out caused spillage of about 80000000 gallons	Persian Gulf	Feb 1983	Marine pollution
Othello collided and spilled 17640000–29405000 gallons	Tralhavet Bay, Sweden	Mar 1970	Marine pollution
Prestige; hull cracked in storm, sank, began to leak cargo of 20500000 gallons at rate of 33000 gallons a day	off north-western Spain	Dec 2002	Marine pollution; Spanish coast polluted

Name	Location	Date	Consequence
Sea Empress, Liberian-registered tanker, grounded and spilled 21 500 000 gallons	Milford Haven, Wales	Feb 1996	Marine pollution
Sea Star collided and spilled 33 810 000 gallons	Gulf of Oman	Dec 1972	Marine pollution
Selendang Ayu ran aground and spilled 300 000 gallons of thick fuel oil	Unalaska I, Alaska	Dec 2004	6 crew members killed when a rescue helicopter crashed. Over 700 birds coated in oil.
Solar I sank, spilling 130 000 gallons	Guimaras Strait, The Philippines	Aug 2006	Marine pollution, particularly in the Visayas Sea.
Storage tank rupture caused spillage of 8 400 000 gallons	Sewaren, New Jersey, USA	Nov 1969	Marine pollution
Tasman Spirit ran aground and spilled 28 000 tons of crude oil	Karachi, Arabian Sea	Aug 2003	Marine pollution
Torrey Canyon grounded and spilled 34 986 000 gallons	off Land's End, England	Mar 1967	Marine pollution
Urquiola grounded and spilled 29 400 000 gallons	La Coruña, Spain	May 1976	Marine pollution
World Glory; hull failure caused spillage of 13 524 000 gallons	off South Africa	Jun 1968	Marine pollution

Major national parks and nature reserves

The first national park was Yellowstone, Wyoming, which was obtained by the US government during the 1870s for the use and enjoyment of the people. By the late 1980s there were more than 3 000 national parks and wildlife reserves around the world. All together, they covered approximately 4 million km²/1.5 million mi². Below is a selection of the best known.

Name	Country	Area (km²) [1]	Special features
Altos de Campana	Panama	48	Great variety of plant zones
Amazonia	Brazil	9 940	Rainforest
Arctic National Wildlife Refuge	USA (Alaska)	79 318	Centre of oil exploration controversy
Badlands	USA	985	Prehistoric fossils; dramatically eroded hills
Banff	Canada	6 640	Spectacular glaciated scenery; hot springs
Beinn Eighe	UK	48	Original Scottish pine forest
Białowieza	Poland	105	Largest remnant of primeval forest; European bison
Burren	Ireland	15	Limestone pavement with remarkable plants
Camargue	France	131	Wetland; many rare birds, especially flamingoes
Canaima	Venezuela	30 000	World's highest waterfall, Angel Falls
Canyonlands	USA	1 365	Deep gorges, colourful rock, spectacular landforms
Carlsbad Caverns	USA	189	Huge limestone caverns with millions of bats
Carnarvon	Australia	2 980	Bush-tailed rock wallabies; aboriginal cave paintings
Chitwan	Nepal	932	Bengal tigers, gavials (type of Indian crocodile), Gangetic dolphins
Corbett	India	520	Indian tigers; gavials, muggers (both types of Indian crocodile)
Dartmoor	UK	954	Wild ponies
Death Valley	USA	13 628	Lowest point in W hemisphere; unique flora, fauna
Doñana	Spain	507	Wetland; rare birds and mammals; Spanish lynx
Everglades	USA	5 929	Swamp, mangrove; subtropical wildlife refuge
Etosha	Namibia	22 270	Swampland and bush; rare and abundant wildlife
Fiordland	New Zealand	12 570	Kiwis, keas, wekas, takahe, kakapo (all flightless birds, except for the kea)
Fuji-Hakone-Izu	Japan	1 218	Mt Fuji; varied animal and plant life
Galapagos Islands	Ecuador	7 665	Giant iguanas, giant tortoises
Gir	India	259	Asiatic lions
Glacier	USA (Montana)	4 102	Virgin coniferous forest; glaciers
Gran Paradiso	Italy	702	Alpine scenery; chamois, ibex

Climate and Environment

Name	Country	Area (km²) [1]	Special features
Grand Canyon	USA	4931	Mile-deep canyon, colourful walls; many life zones
Great Smoky Mountains	USA	2094	Varied wildlife including wild turkey, black bear
Hardangervidda	Norway	3422	Plateau of ancient rock; large wild reindeer herd
Hawaii Volcanoes	USA	920	Active volcanoes, rare plants and animals
Heron Island	Australia	0.17	Part of Great Barrier Reef; corals, invertebrates, fish
Hoge Veluwe	Netherlands	54	Largely stabilized dunes; wet and dry heath
Iguazú/Iguaçu	Argentina/Brazil	2250	Iguazú/Iguaçu Falls
Iztaccihuatl-Popocatépetl	Mexico	257	Snow-capped volcanoes
Kafue	Zambia	22400	Numerous animals and birds; black rhinoceros refuge
Kakadu	Australia	20277	Aboriginal rock art; crocodiles, water birds
Kaziranga	India	430	Indian one-horned rhinoceros, swamp deer
Kgalagadi	Botswana/ South Africa	38000	Desert, grassland; lions and large herds of game
Khao Yai	Thailand	2169	Large caves and waterfalls; many bird species
Kilimanjaro	Tanzania	754	Africa's highest peak, Mt Kilimanjaro; colobus monkeys
Kinabalu	Malaysia	754	Orchids; SE Asia's highest peak, Mt Kinabalu
Kosciusko	Australia	6469	Australia's highest peak, Mt Kosciusko; mountain pygmy possum
Kruger	South Africa	19485	Wide range of animals and birds; rare white rhinoceros
Lainzer Tiergarten	Austria	25	Ancient forest and meadow; wild boar, deer, moufflon (wild sheep)
Lake District	UK	2292	Lake and mountain scenery
Los Glaciares	Argentina/Chile	1618	Glacial landforms
Manu	Peru	15328	Small mammals, birds; Amazon/Andean ecosystems
Mercantour	France	685	Alpine scenery and flora
Mt Apo	Philippines	728	Volcanoes; monkey-eating eagles
Mt Cook	New Zealand	699	New Zealand's highest peak, Mt Cook
Mt Olympus	Greece	40	Maquis and forest; wild mountain goats
Muddus	Sweden	493	Glaciated area with forest and tundra; Lapp pasture
Namib-Naukluft	Namibia	49768	Only true desert in southern Africa
Ngorongoro	Tanzania	8300	Huge volcanic crater
North East Greenland	Greenland (Denmark)	972000	Largest national park in the world
Olympic	USA	3712	Rugged peaks, glaciers, dense forest; Roosevelt elk
Petrified Forest	USA (Arizona)	379	Tree-trunks millions of years old; colourful sands
Pfälzerwald	Germany	1793	Forest; European bison, moufflon (wild sheep), mountain goats
Phu Rua	Thailand	120	Mountain forest zones from tropical to pine
Redwood	USA	446	Virgin redwood; Roosevelt elk
Royal	Australia	150	World's second-oldest national park (1879)
Rwenzori	Uganda	996	Hippopotamuses, chimpanzees, baboons, colobus monkeys
Sagarmatha	Nepal	1148	Mt Everest; impeyan pheasant, Himalayan tahr (wild goat)
Sarek	Sweden	1970	Lapland; herds of reindeer
Sequoia and Kings Canyon	USA	3495	The largest tree on earth, the General Sherman Tree
Serengeti	Tanzania	14763	Huge animal migrations at start of dry season
Snowdonia	UK	2142	Glaciated mountain scenery; varied flora and fauna
Swiss	Switzerland	172	Alpine forests and flora; reintroduced ibex
Tatra	Poland/Slovakia	950	Bears, lynxes, marmots; mountain scenery
Tikal	Guatemala	574	Mayan ruins; rainforest animals
Toubkal	Morocco	360	Barbary apes, porcupines, hyenas, bald ibis
Tsavo	Kenya	20812	Vast range of wildlife
Ujung-Kulon	Indonesia	1229	Low-relief forest; Javan tiger, Javan rhinoceros
Uluru	Australia	1326	Desert; Uluru (Ayers Rock) and the Olgas
Victoria Falls	Zimbabwe/ Zambia	190	Spectacular waterfall

Name	Country	Area (km²) [1]	Special features
Virunga	Congo, Democratic Republic of	7800	Mountain gorillas; active volcanoes
Waterton Lakes	Canada	526	Varied flora and fauna
Waza	Cameroon	1700	Giraffes, elephants, ostriches, waterbuck
Wolong	China	2000	Giant pandas; also golden langurs, snow leopards
Wood Buffalo	Canada	44800	Refuge for American buffalo (bison), whooping crane
Yellowstone	USA	8991	World's greatest geyser area; bears, deer, elk, bison
Yosemite	USA	3080	High waterfalls; varied flora and fauna; giant sequoias

[1] To convert km² to mi², multiply by 0.386.

World Heritage sites

This list is up-to-date to December 2008. It comprises 878 properties selected by UNESCO as being of such outstanding natural, environmental or cultural importance that they merit exceptional international efforts to make them more widely known and to save them from damage and destruction.

- **Afghanistan**
  Minaret and archaeological remains of Jam
  Bamiyan Valley (archaeological site)
- **Albania**
  Butrint
  Berat and Gjirokastra (historic centres)
- **Algeria**
  Algiers (Kasbah)
  Al Qal'a of Beni Hammad
  Djémila (Roman ruins)
  M'Zab Valley
  Tassili N'Ajjer
  Timgad (Roman ruins)
  Tipasa (archaeological site)
- **Andorra**
  Madriu-Perafita-Claror Valley
- **Argentina**
  Córdoba (Jesuit block and estancias)
  Iguazú National Park
  Ischigualasto/Talampaya Natural Parks
  Jesuit Missions of the Guaranis (shared with Brazil)
  Quebrada de Humahuaca
  Los Glaciares National Park
  Península Valdés
  Río Pinturas (Cueva de las Manos)
- **Armenia**
  Echmiatsin (cathedral, churches) and Zvartnots (archaeological site)
  Geghard monastery and the Upper Azat Valley
  Haghpat and Sanahin monasteries
- **Australia**
  Central Eastern Australian Rainforest Reserves
  Fraser Island
  Great Barrier Reef
  Greater Blue Mountains Area
  Heard and McDonald Islands
  Kakadu National Park
  Lord Howe Island Group
  Macquarie Island
  Purnululu National Park
  Queensland (wet tropics)
  Riversleigh/Naracoorte (mammal fossil sites)
  Royal Exhibition Building and Carlton Gardens
  Shark Bay
  Sydney Opera House
  Tasmanian Wilderness
  Uluru-Kata Tjuta National Park
  Willandra Lakes region

- **Austria**
  Fertö/Neusiedlersee cultural landscape (shared with Hungary)
  Graz (historic centre)
  Hallstatt-Dachstein Salzkammergut cultural landscape
  Salzburg (historic centre)
  Schönbrunn palace and gardens
  Semmering Railway
  Vienna (historic centre)
  Wachau cultural landscape
- **Azerbaijan**
  Baku (walled city, with Shirvanshah's Palace and Maiden Tower)
  Gobustan Rock Art Cultural Landscape
- **Bahrain**
  Qal'at al-Bahrain (ancient harbour and capital of Dilmun)
- **Bangladesh**
  Bagerhat (historic mosque city)
  Paharpur (ruins of the Buddhist Vihara)
  Sundarbans (mangrove forest)
- **Belarus**
  Architectural, residential and cultural complex of the Radziwill family at Nesvizh
  Belovezhskaya Pushcha/Białowieża Forest (shared with Poland)
  Mir Castle complex
  Struve Geodetic Arc*
- **Belgium**
  Belfries of Belgium and France (shared with France)
  Bruges (historic centre)
  Brussels (Grand-Place)
  Flemish Béguinages
  Four lifts on the Canal du Centre, La Louvière and Le Roeulx
  Major town houses of Victor Horta (Brussels)
  Plantin-Moretus house-museum complex (2005)
  Spiennes (Neolithic flint mines)
  Tournai (Notre-Dame Cathedral)
- **Belize**
  Barrier Reef Reserve System
- **Benin**
  Abomey (royal palaces)
- **Bolivia**
  Fuerte de Samaipata
  Jesuit Missions of the Chiquitos
  Noel Kempff Mercado National Park

51

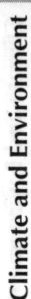

Climate and Environment

Potosi (mining town)
Sucre (historic city)
Tiwanaku
Bosnia and Herzegovina
Mostar (Old Bridge area)
Mehmed Paša Sokolović Bridge, Višegrad
Botswana
Tsodilo
Brazil
Bom Jesus do Congonhas (sanctuary)
Brasilia
Central Amazon conservation complex
Chapada dos Veadeiros and Emas National Parks
Diamantina (historic centre)
Discovery Coast Atlantic Forest Reserves
Fernando de Noronha and Atol das Rocas Reserves
Goiás (historic centre)
Iguaçu National Park
Jesuit Missions of the Guaranis (shared with
    Argentina)
Olinda (historic centre)
Ouro Preto (historic town)
Pantanal conservation area
Salvador da Bahia (historic centre)
São Luis (historic centre)
Serra da Capivara National Park
Atlantic Forest South-East Reserves
Bulgaria
Boyana Church
Ivanovo rock-hewn churches
Kazanlak (Thracian tomb)
Madara Rider
Nessebar (ancient city)
Pirin National Park
Rila Monastery
Srebarna Nature Reserve
Sveshtari (Thracian tomb)
Cambodia
Angkor
Temple of Preah Vihear
Cameroon
Dja Wildlife Reserve
Canada
Canadian Rocky Mountain Parks
Dinosaur Provincial Park
Gros Morne National Park
Head-Smashed-In Buffalo Jump complex
Joggins Fossil Cliffs
L'Anse aux Meadows Historic Park
Lunenburg (old town)
Miguasha National Park
Nahanni National Park
Quebec (historic area, old town)
Rideau Canal
SGang Gwaay
Tatshenshini-Alsek, Kluane National Park,
    Wrangell St Elias National Park and Reserve,
    and Glacier Bay National Park (shared with
    USA)
Waterton Glacier International Peace Park
    (shared with USA)
Wood Buffalo National Park
Central African Republic
Manovo-Gounda St Floris National Park
Chile
Chiloé Churches
Humberstone and Santa Laura saltpetre works
Rapa Nui National Park (Easter Island)
Sewell mining town
Valparaíso (historic quarter)
China
Beijing and Shenyang: imperial palaces of the
    Ming and Qing dynasties

Beijing: Summer Palace (imperial garden)
Beijing: Temple of Heaven (sacrificial altar)
Chengde (mountain resort and outlying temples)
Dazu (rock carvings)
Fujian Tulou
Great Wall
Huanglong area
Jiuzhaigou Valley area
Kaiping Diaolou and villages
Koguryo Kingdom (ancient capital cities and
    tombs)
Lhasa (Potala Palace complex)
Lijiang (old town)
Longmen Grottoes
Lushan National Park
Macao (historic centre)
Mausoleum of the first Qin emperor
Ming and Qing dynasties imperial tombs
Mogao caves
Mt Emei scenic area including Leshan Giant
    Buddha scenic area
Mt Huangshan
Mt Qingcheng and Dujiangyan irrigation system
Mt Sanqingshan National Park
Mt Taishan
Mt Wuyi
Ping Yao (ancient city)
Qufu (temple and cemetery of Confucius and the
    K'ung family mansion)
Sichuan giant panda sanctuaries
South China Karst
Suzhou (classical gardens)
Three Parallel Rivers of Yunnan protected areas
Wudang mountains (ancient building complex)
Wulingyuan area
Xidi and Hongcun (ancient villages)
Yin Xu
Yungang Grottoes
Zhoukoudian (Peking Man site)
Colombia
Cartagena (port, fortress and monuments)
Los Katios National Park
Malpelo Fauna and Flora Sanctuary
San Agustín Archaeological Park
Santa Cruz de Mompox (historic centre)
Tierradentro National Archaeological Park
Congo, Democratic Republic of the
Garamba National Park
Kahuzi-Biega National Park
Okapi Wildlife Reserve
Salonga National Park
Virunga National Park
Costa Rica
Cocos Island National Park
Guanacaste conservation area
La Amistad National Park (shared with Panama)
Côte d'Ivoire
Comoé National Park
Mt Nimba Nature Reserve (shared with Guinea)
Taï National Park
Croatia
Cathedral of St James, Šibenik
Dubrovnik (old city)
Plitvice Lakes National Park
Poreč (episcopal complex of the Euphrasian
    basilica in the historic centre)
Split (historic centre with Diocletian's Palace)
Stari Grad Plain
Trogir (historic city)
Cuba
Alejandro de Humboldt National Park
Camagüey (historic centre)
Cienfuegos (historic centre)

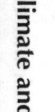

Desembarco del Granma National Park
First coffee plantations in SE Cuba
  (archaeological landscape)
Old Havana and its fortifications
San Pedro de la Roca Castle, Santiago de Cuba
Trinidad and the Valley de los Ingenios
Viñales Valley
- **Cyprus**
Choirokoitia
Paphos (archaeological site)
Troödos (painted churches)
- **Czech Republic**
Český Krumlov (historic centre)
Holašovice (historical village reservation)
Kroměříž (gardens and castle)
Kutná Hora (historic centre) with Church of
  St Barbara and the Cathedral of Our Lady at
  Sedlec
Lednice-Valtice cultural landscape
Litomyšl Castle
Olomouc (Holy Trinity Column)
Pilgrimage church of St John of Nepomuk, Zelena
  Hora
Prague (historic centre)
Telč (historic centre)
Trebíc (Jewish quarter and St Procopius Basilica)
Tugendhat Villa, Brno
- **Denmark**
Ilulissat Icefjord
Jelling (mounds, runic stones and church)
Kronberg Castle
Roskilde Cathedral
- **Dominica**
Morne Trois Pitons National Park
- **Dominican Republic**
Santo Domingo
- **Ecuador**
Galápagos Islands National Park
Quito (old city)
Sangay National Park
Santa Ana de los Rios de Cuenca (historic centre)
- **Egypt**
Abu Mena (Christian ruins)
Abu Simbel to Philae (Nubian monuments)
Cairo (Islamic district)
Memphis and its necropolis, with the Pyramid
  fields from Giza to Dahshur
St Catherine area
Thebes and its necropolis
Wadi Al-Hitan (Whale Valley)
- **El Salvador**
Joya de Cerén (archaeological site)
- **Estonia**
Struve Geodetic Arc*
Tallinn (historic centre, old town)
- **Ethiopia**
Aksum (archaeological site)
Awash Lower Valley
Fasil Ghebbi and Gondar monuments
Harar Jugol (fortified historic town)
Lalibela rock-hewn churches
Omo Lower Valley
Simien National Park
Tiya (carved steles)
- **Finland**
Kvarken Archipelago/High Coast (shared with
  Sweden)
Old Rauma
Petäjävesi Old Church
Sammallahdenmäki (Bronze Age burial site)
Struve Geodetic Arc*
Suomenlinna (fortress)
Verla groundwood and board mill

- **France**
Amiens Cathedral
Arc-et-Senans (royal saltworks)
Arles (Roman and Romanesque monuments)
Avignon (historic centre, papal palace and bridge)
Belfries of Belgium and France (shared with
  Belgium)
Bordeaux, Port of the Moon
Bourges Cathedral
Canal du Midi
Carcassonne (historic fortified city)
Chartres Cathedral
Corsica (Gulf of Girolata, Cape Porto, Scandola
  Natural Reserve and Calanche of Piana)
Fontainebleau (palace and park)
Fontenay (Cistercian abbey)
Le Havre
Loire Valley between Sully-sur-Loire and Chalonnes
Lyons (historic site)
Mont St Michel and its bay
Nancy (Place Stanislas, Place de la Carrière and
  Place d'Alliance)
New Caledonia (lagoons and reefs)
Orange (Roman theatre and triumphal arch)
Paris (banks of the Seine)
Pont du Gard (Roman aqueduct)
Provins
Pyrenees, Mt Perdu landscape (shared with Spain)
Rheims (Cathedral of Notre-Dame, St Remy
  Abbey and Palace of Tau)
Routes of Santiago de Compostela in France
St Emilion (jurisdiction)
St Savin sur Gartempe (abbey church)
Strasbourg (Grande Île)
Vauban (fortifications)
Versailles (palace and park)
Vezelay (basilica and hill)
Vézère (prehistoric sites and decorated caves)
- **Gabon**
Lopé-Okanda (ecosystem and relict cultural
  landscape)
- **The Gambia**
James Island and related sites
Senegambia stone circles (shared with Senegal)
- **Georgia**
Bagrati Cathedral and Gelati Monastery
Mtskheta (historic monuments)
Upper Svaneti region
- **Germany**
Aachen Cathedral
Bamberg
Bauhaus and its sites in Weimar and Dessau
Bremen (town hall and Roland on the
  Marketplace)
Brühl (Augustusburg and Falkenlust castles)
Cologne Cathedral
Dessau-Wörlitz (Garden Kingdom)
Dresden Elbe Valley
Frontiers of the Roman Empire (shared with UK)
Hildesheim (St Mary's Cathedral and St Michael's
  Church)
Lorsch (abbey and Altenmünster)
Lübeck (Hanseatic city)
Luther memorials in Eisleben and Wittenberg
Maulbronn monastery complex
Messel Pit (fossil site)
Modernism Housing Estates, Berlin
Museum Island, Berlin
Muskauer Park/Park Muzakowski (shared with
  Poland)
Potsdam and Berlin palaces and parks
Quedlinburg (collegiate church, castle and old
  town)

Climate and Environment

Rammelsberg mines and historic town of Goslar
Regensburg with Stadtamhof (old town)
Reichenau (monastic island)
Speyer Cathedral
Stralsund and Wismar (historic centres)
Trier (Roman monuments, cathedral and
  Liebfrauen church)
Upper Middle Rhine Valley
Völklingen ironworks
Wartburg Castle
Weimar (classical quarter)
Wies (pilgrimage church)
Würzburg Residence
Zollverein Coal Mine (industrial complex), Essen
■ **Ghana**
Ashante traditional buildings
Forts and castles, Volta, Greater Accra, Central
  and Western regions
■ **Greece**
Athens (Acropolis)
Bassae (temple of Apollo Epicurius)
Chorá (historic centre), with the monastery of
  St John 'the Theologian' and the cave of the
  Apocalypse on Pátmos
Corfu, Old Town
Daphni, Hossios Luckas and Nea Moni of Chios
  monasteries
Delos
Delphi (archaeological site)
Epidaurus (archaeological site)
Meteora
Mt Athos
Mycenae and Tiryns (archaeological site)
Mystras
Olympia (archaeological site)
Rhodes (medieval city)
Samos (Pythagoreion and Heraion)
Thessalonika (Paleochristian and Byzantine
  monuments)
Vergina (archaeological site)
■ **Guatemala**
Antigua Guatemala
Quirigua (archaeological site and ruins)
Tikal National Park
■ **Guinea**
Mt Nimba Nature Reserve (shared with Côte
  d'Ivoire)
■ **Haiti**
National Historic Park (citadel, Sans-Souci,
  Ramiers)
■ **Honduras**
Maya ruins of Copan
Río Plátano Biosphere Reserve
■ **Hungary**
Aggtelek Karst and Slovak Karst caves (shared
  with Slovakia)
Budapest (banks of the Danube, the Buda Castle
  quarter and Andrássy Avenue)
Fertő/Neusiedlersee cultural landscape (shared
  with Austria)
Hollókö (traditional village)
Hortobágy National Park
Pannonhalma, Millenary Benedictine Abbey and
  its natural environment
Pécs (early Christian necropolis, Sophianae)
Tokaj wine region
■ **Iceland**
Surtsey
Thingvellir National Park
■ **India**
Agra Fort
Ajanta caves
Bhimbetka rock shelters

Champaner-Pavagadh Archaelogical Park
Chhatrapati Shivaji Terminus (formerly Victoria
  Terminus)
Elephanta caves
Ellora caves
Fatehpur Sikri (Moghul city)
Goa (churches and convents)
Great Living Chola Temples
Hampi (monuments)
Humayun's Tomb, Delhi
Kaziranga National Park
Keoladeo National Park
Khajuraho (monuments)
Konarak (Sun Temple)
Mahabalipuram (monuments)
Mahabodhi temple complex, Bodh Gaya
Manas Wildlife Sanctuary
Mountain railways
Nanda Devi and Valley of Flowers National Parks
Pattadakal (monuments)
Qutb Minar and monuments, Delhi
Red Fort complex
Sanchi Buddhist monuments
Sundarbans National Park
Taj Mahal
■ **Indonesia**
Borobudur temple compounds
Komodo National Park
Lorentz National Park
Prambanan temple compounds
Sangiran (early man site)
Sumatra tropical rainforest heritage
Ujung Kulon National Park
■ **Iran**
Armenian Monastic Ensembles
Bam and its cultural landscape
Bisotun
Esfahan (Meidan Emam)
Pasargadae
Persepolis
Soltaniyeh
Takht-e Soleyman
Tchogha Zanbil Ziggurat and complex
■ **Iraq**
Ashur (Qal'at Sherqat)
Hatra
Samarra Archaeological City
■ **Ireland**
Skellig Michael
Valley of the Boyne (archaeological site)
■ **Israel**
Acre (old city)
Bahá'i Holy Places, Haifa and Western Galilee
Biblical Tels – Megiddo, Hazor, Beer Sheba
Incense Route – desert cities in the Negev
Jerusalem (old city and its walls)
Masada
Tel-Aviv (White City – the Modern Movement)
■ **Italy**
Aeolian Islands
Agrigento (archaeological area)
Alberobello (the trulli)
Amalfi (the coast)
Aquileia (archaelogical area and the patriarchal
  basilica)
Assisi (Basilica of San Francesco and other
  Franciscan sites)
Barumini, Sardinia ('nuraghi' defensive towers)
Casale (Villa Romana)
Caserta (18c palace, park, aqueduct of Vanvitelli
  and the San Leucio complex)
Castel del Monte
Cerveteri and Tarquinia (Etruscan necropolises)

Cilento and Vallo di Diano National Park with archaeological sites of Paestum and Velia, and the Certosa di Padula
Crespi d'Adda
Ferrara (Renaissance city) and the Po delta
Florence (historic centre)
Genoa (Strade Nuove and Palazzi dei Rolli system)
I Sassi di Matera
Mantua and Sabbioneta
Modena (cathedral, Torre Civica and Piazza Grande)
Naples (historic centre)
Padua (botanical garden)
Pienza (historic centre)
Pisa (Piazza del Duomo)
Pompeii, with Herculaneum and Torre Annunziata archaeological areas
Portovenere, Cinque Terre and the islands of Palmaria, Tino and Tinetto
Ravenna, early Christian monuments and mosaics
Rhaetian Railway in the Albula/Bernina landscapes (shared with Switzerland)
Rome (historic centre)
Sacri Monti of Piedmont and Lombardy
San Gimignano (historic centre)
Santa Maria delle Grazie with *The Last Supper* by Leonardo da Vinci, Milan
Siena (historic centre)
Syracuse and Pantalica (necropolis)
Turin residences of royal house of Savoy
Urbino (historic centre)
Valcamonica (rock drawings)
Val di Noto (late Baroque towns)
Val d'Orcia
Venice and its lagoon
Verona (city)
Vicenza (city) and Palladian villas of the Veneto
Villa Adriana, Tivoli
Villa d'Este, Tivoli
■ **Japan**
Ancient Kyoto (Kyoto, Uji and Otsu cities)
Ancient Nara (historic monuments)
Himeji-jo
Hiroshima Peace Memorial (Genbaku Dome)
Horyu-ji (Buddhist monuments)
Itsukushima Shinto shrine
Iwami Ginzan silver mine
Kii mountain range (sacred sites and pilgrimage routes)
Nikko (shrines and temples)
Ryuku Kingdom (Gusuku sites and related properties)
Shirakami-Sanchi
Shirakawa-go and Gokayama (historic villages)
Shiretoko
Yakushima
■ **Jordan**
Petra
Quseir Amra
Um er-Rasas (Kastrom Mefa'a)
■ **Kazakhstan**
Mausoleum of Khoja Ahmed Yasawi
Saryarka (steppe and lakes)
Tamgaly (petroglyphs within the archaeological landscape)
■ **Kenya**
Mt Kenya National Park and natural forest
Lake Turkana National Parks
Lamu (old town)
Mijikenda Kaya sacred forests
■ **Korea, North**
Koguryo Tombs complex

■ **Korea, South**
Ch'angdokkung Palace complex
Chongmyo Shrine
Gochang, Hwasun and Ganghwa Dolmen sites
Gyeongju historic areas
Haeinsa Temple, including the Tripitaka Koreana woodblocks
Hwasong Fortress
Jeju volcanic island and lava tubes
Seokguram Grotto and Bulguksa Temple
■ **Laos**
Luang Prabang
Vat Phou and associated ancient settlements
■ **Latvia**
Riga (historic centre)
Struve Geodetic Arc*
■ **Lebanon**
Anjar (archaeological site)
Baalbek
Byblos
Ouadi Qadisha and the Forest of the Cedars of God
Tyre (archaeological site)
■ **Libya**
Cyrene (archaeological site)
Ghadamès (old town)
Leptis Magna (archaeological site)
Sabratha (archaeological site)
Tadrart Acacus (rock-art sites)
■ **Lithuania**
Curonian Spit (shared with Russia)
Kernave (archaeological site)
Struve Geodetic Arc*
Vilnius (historic centre)
■ **Luxembourg**
City of Luxembourg, old quarters and fortifications
■ **Macedonia**
Ohrid region (natural and cultural heritage)
■ **Madagascar**
Atsinanana rainforests
Royal Hill of Ambohimanga
Tsingy de Bemaraha Nature Reserve
■ **Malawi**
Chongoni (rock art area)
Lake Malawi National Park
■ **Malaysia**
Gunung Mulu National Park
Kinabalu Park
Melaka and George Town (historic cities)
■ **Mali**
Cliffs of Bandiagara (land of the Dogons)
Djenné (old towns)
Timbuktu
Tomb of Askia
■ **Malta**
Hal Saflieni Hypogeum
Megalithic temples
Valetta (old city)
■ **Mauritania**
Ancient ksour of Ouadane, Chinguetti, Tichitt and Oualata
Banc d'Arguin National Park
■ **Mauritius**
Aapravasi Ghat
Le Morne cultural landscape
■ **Mexico**
Calakmul (ancient Maya city)
Campeche (historic fortified town)
Chichen Itza (pre-Hispanic city)
El Tajin (pre-Hispanic city)
El Vizcaino Whale Sanctuary
Franciscan missions in Sierra Gorda of Querétaro
Guadalajara (Hospicio Cabañas)

Climate and Environment

Guanajuato (historic town) and adjacent mines
Gulf of California (islands and protected areas)
Luis Barragán House and Studio, Mexico City
Mexico City (historic centre and Xochimilco)
Mexico City (central university campus)
Monarch butterfly biosphere reserve
Morelia (historic centre)
Oaxaca (historic centre) and Monte Albán
    (archaeological site)
Palenque (pre-Hispanic city and national park)
Paquimé, Casas Grandes (archaeological zone)
Popocatepetl (16c monasteries on the slopes)
Puebla (historic centre)
Querétaro (historic monuments zone)
San Miguel de Allende (fortified town) and
    sanctuary of Jesús Nazareno de Atotonilco)
Sian Ka'an (biosphere reserve)
Sierra de San Francisco (rock paintings)
Teotihuacán (pre-Hispanic city)
Tequila (agave landscape and industrial facilities)
Tlacotalpan (historic monuments zone)
Uxmal (pre-Hispanic town)
Xochicalco (archaeological monuments zone)
Zacatecas (historic centre)
■ **Moldova**
Struve Geodetic Arc*
■ **Mongolia**
Orkhon Valley (cultural landscape)
Uvs Nuur basin (shared with Russia)
■ **Montenegro**
Durmitor National Park
Kotor (natural and culturo-historical region)
■ **Morocco**
Aït-Ben-Haddou (fortified village)
Essaouira (Medina)
Fez (Medina)
Marrakesh (Medina)
Meknes (historic city)
Portuguese City of Mazagan (El Jadida)
Tétouan (Medina)
Volubilis (archaeological site)
■ **Mozambique**
Island of Mozambique
■ **Namibia**
Twyfelfontein or /Ui-//aes (petroglyphs)
■ **Nepal**
Kathmandu Valley
Lumbini (birthplace of Lord Buddha)
Royal Chitwan National Park
Sagarmatha National Park
■ **The Netherlands**
Amsterdam defence line
Beemster Polder
D F Wouda Steam Pumping Station
Kinderdijk-Elshout (mill network)
Rietveld Schröder House
Schokland and its surroundings
Willemstad (historic area, inner city and
    harbour), Netherlands Antilles
■ **New Zealand**
Sub-Antarctic Islands
Te Wahipounamu (SW New Zealand)
Tongariro National Park
■ **Nicaragua**
Ruins of León Viejo
■ **Niger**
Air and Ténéré Nature Reserves
'W' National Park
■ **Nigeria**
Osun-Osogbo sacred grove
Sukur (cultural landscape)
■ **Norway**
Alta (rock drawings)

Bergen (Bryggen area)
Røros (mining town)
Struve Geodetic Arc*
Urnes Stave Church
Vega Archipelago
West Norwegian Fjords (Geirangerfjord and
    Nærøyfjord)
■ **Oman**
Aflaj irrigation systems
Bahla Fort
Bat, Al-Khutm and Al-Ayn (archaeological sites)
Land of Frankincense
■ **Pakistan**
Lahore (fort and Shalamar gardens)
Mohenjo Daro (archaeological site)
Rohtas Fort
Takht-i-Bahi (Buddhist ruins) and Sahr-i-Bahlol
    (city remains)
Taxila (archaeological remains)
Thatta (historical monuments)
■ **Panama**
Coiba National Park and marine protection zone
Darien National Park
La Amistad National Park (shared with Costa
    Rica)
Panama (archaeological site and historic
    district)
Portobelo and San Lorenzo fortifications
■ **Papua New Guinea**
Kuk early agricultural site
■ **Paraguay**
Jesuit Missions of La Santísima Trinidad de
    Paraná and Jesús de Tavarangue
■ **Peru**
Arequipa (historic centre)
Chan Chan (archaeological site)
Chavin (archaeological site)
Cuzco (old city)
Huascarán National Park
Lima (historic centre)
Machu Picchu (historic sanctuary)
Manú National Park
Nasca and Pampas de Jumana (lines and
    geoglyphs)
Río Abiseo National Park
■ **Philippines**
Baroque churches of the Philippines
Puerto-Princesa Subterranean River National Park
Rice terraces of the Philippine Cordilleras
Tubbataha Reef Marine Park
Vigan (historic town)
■ **Poland**
Auschwitz concentration camp
Belovezhskaya Pushcha/Białowieża Forest
    (shared with Belarus)
Cracow (historic centre)
Jawor and Swidnica Churches of Peace
Kalwaria Zebrzydowska (Mannerist architectural
    and park landscape complex, and pilgrimage
    park)
Malbork (castle of the Teutonic Order)
Muskauer Park/Park Muzakowski (shared with
    Germany)
Torún (medieval town)
Warsaw (historic centre)
Wieliczka saltmines
Wooden churches of southern Little Poland
Wroclaw Centennial Hall
Zamość (old city)
■ **Portugal**
Alcobaça monastery
Alto Douro wine region
Angra do Heroismo (town centre), Azores

Batalha monastery
Belém Tower and Monastery of the Hieronymites, Lisbon
Côa Valley (rock-art sites)
Évora (historic centre)
Guimarães (historic centre)
Laurisilva, Madeira (laurel forest)
Oporto (historic centre)
Pico Island vineyard culture
Sintra (cultural landscape)
Tomar (Convent of Christ)
■ **Romania**
Biertan and its fortified church
Dacian fortresses, Orastie Mountains
Danube Delta
Horezu Monastery
Painted churches of northern Moldavia
Sighişoara (historic centre)
Wooden churches of Maramureş
■ **Russia**
Central Sikhote-Alin
Curonian Spit (shared with Lithuania)
Derbent (citadel, ancient city and fortress)
Ferrapontov Monastery
Golden Mountains of Altai
Kamchatka volcanoes
Kazan Kremlin
Kizhi Pogost
Kolomenskoye (Church of the Ascension)
Lake Baikal
Moscow (Kremlin and Red Square)
Novodevichy Convent
Novgorod (historic monuments)
St Petersburg (historic centre and monuments)
Sergiev Posad (Trinity Sergius Lavra complex)
Solovetsky Islands
Struve Geodetic Arc*
Uvs Nuur basin (shared with Mongolia)
Virgin Komi forests
Vladimir and Suzdal monuments
Western Caucasus
Wrangel Island Reserve
Yaroslavl (historic centre)
■ **St Christopher and Nevis**
Brimstone Hill Fortress National Park
■ **St Lucia**
Pitons Management Area
■ **San Marino**
San Marino historic centre and Mt Titano
■ **Saudi Arabia**
Al-Hijr archaeological site
■ **Senegal**
Djoudj Bird Sanctuary
Gorée Island
Niokolo-Koba National Park
Saint-Louis Island
Senegambia stone circles (shared with the Gambia)
■ **Serbia**
Gamzigrad-Romuliana, Palace of Galerius
Kosovo medieval monuments
Stari Ras and Sopoćani
Studenica Monastery
■ **Seychelles**
Aldabra Atoll
Vallée de Mai Nature Reserve
■ **Slovakia**
Aggtelek Karst and Slovak Karst caves (shared with Hungary)
Banská Štiavnica and technical monuments
Bardejov Town Conservation Reserve
Carpathian primeval beech forests (shared with Ukraine)
Spišský Hrad and cultural monuments

Vlkolínec
Wooden churches, Slovak part of Carpathian mountain area
■ **Slovenia**
Škocjan caves
■ **Solomon Islands**
East Rennell
■ **South Africa**
Cape Floral Region protected areas
Greater St Lucia Wetland Park
Mapungubwe (cultural landscape)
Richtersveld cultural and botanical landscape
Robben Island
Sterkfontein, Swartkrans, Kromdraai and environs (fossil hominid sites)
uKhahlamba/Drakensberg Park
Vredefort Dome
■ **Spain**
Alcalá de Henares (university and historic precinct)
Altamira Cave
Aragon (Mudejar architecture)
Aranjuez (cultural landscape)
Atapuerca (archaeological site)
Ávila (old town) with its Extra-Muros churches
Barcelona: Palau de la Música Catalana and Hospital de Sant Pau
Barcelona: works of Antoni Gaudí
Burgos Cathedral
Cáceres (old town)
Córdoba (historic centre)
Cuenca (historic walled town)
Doñana National Park
El Escurial (monastery and site)
Garajonay National Park (Canary Is)
Granada (Alhambra, Generalife and Albayzín)
Ibiza (biodiversity and culture)
Kingdom of Asturias (its churches) and monuments of Oviedo
Las Médulas
Lugo (Roman walls)
Mérida
Palmeral of Elche
Poblet Monastery
Pyrenees, Mt Perdu landscape (shared with France)
Rock art of the Mediterranean Basin on the Iberian Peninsula
Routes of Santiago de Compostela
Salamanca (old city)
San Cristóbal de La Laguna
San Millán Yuso and Suso monasteries
Santa Maria de Guadalupe (royal monastery)
Santiago de Compostela (old town)
Segovia (old town and aqueduct)
Seville (cathedral, Alcázar and Archivo de Indias)
Tárraco (archaeological ensemble)
Teide National Park
Toledo (historic city)
Úbeda and Baeza (Renaissance monumental ensembles)
Valencia, 'La Lonja de la Seda'
Vall de Boi (Catalan Romanesque churches)
Vizcaya Bridge
■ **Sri Lanka**
Anuradhapura (sacred city)
Dambulla (Golden Rock Temple)
Galle (old town and its fortifications)
Kandy (sacred city)
Polonnaruwa (ancient city)
Sigiriya (ancient city)
Sinharaja Forest Reserve
■ **Sudan**
Gebe Barkal and the sites of the Napatan region

Climate and Environment

■ **Suriname**
Central Suriname Nature Reserve
Paramaribo (historic inner city)
■ **Sweden**
Birka and Hovgården
Drottningholm Palace and domain
Engelsberg ironworks
Falun (mining area of the Great Copper Mountain)
Gammelstad (church village), Luleå
Karlskrona (naval port)
Kvarken Archipelago/High Coast (shared with Finland)
Laponian area
Skogskyrkogården
Southern Öland (agricultural landscape)
Struve Geodetic Arc*
Tanum (rock carvings)
Varberg Radio Station
Visby (Hanseatic town)
■ **Switzerland**
Bellinzone (three castles, defensive walls and town ramparts)
Berne (old city)
Jungfrau-Aletsch-Bietschhorn
Lavaux vineyard terraces
Monte San Giorgio
Müstair: Benedictine convent of St John
Rhaetian Railway in the Albula/Bernina landscapes (shared with Italy)
Swiss tectonic arena Sardona
St Gall convent
■ **Syria**
Aleppo (ancient city)
Bosra (ancient city)
Crac des Chevaliers and Qal'at Salah El-Din
Damascus (ancient city)
Palmyra (archaeological site)
■ **Tanzania**
Kilimanjaro National Park
Kilwa Kisiwani and Songa Mnara ruins
Kondoa (rock art sites)
Ngorongoro conservation area
Selous Game Reserve
Serengeti National Park
Zanzibar (stone town)
■ **Thailand**
Ayutthaya (historic city)
Ban Chiang (archaeological site)
Dong Phayayen-Khao Yai forest complex
Sukhothai (historic city) and associated towns
Thungyai-Huai Kha Khaeng wildlife sanctuaries
■ **Togo**
Koutammakou (land of the Batammariba)
■ **Tunisia**
Carthage (archaeological site)
Dougga/Thugga
El Djem (amphitheatre)
Ichkeul National Park
Kairouan
Kerkuane (Punic town and necropolis)
Sousse (Medina)
Tunis (Medina)
■ **Turkey**
Divriği (Great Mosque and hospital)
Göreme National Park and rock sites of Cappadocia
Hattusha (Hittite city)
Hierapolis-Pamukkale
Istanbul (historic areas)
Nemrut Dağ (archaeological site)
Safranbolu (old city)
Troy (archaeological site)
Xanthos-Letoon

■ **Turkmenistan**
Ancient Merv (state historical and cultural park)
Kunya-Urgench
Nisa (Parthian fortresses)
■ **Uganda**
Bwindi Impenetrable National Park
Kasubi (tombs of Buganda Kings)
Rwenzori Mountains National Park
■ **Ukraine**
Carpathian primeval beech forests (shared with Slovakia)
L'viv (historic centre)
St Sophia Cathedral and Kiev-Pechersk Lavra, Kiev
Struve Geodetic Arc *
■ **UK**
Bath (city)
Blaenavon (industrial landscape)
Blenheim Palace
Canterbury Cathedral, St Augustine's Abbey and St Martin's Church
Cornwall and West Devon mining landscape
Derwent Valley Mills
Dorset and East Devon coast
Durham castle and cathedral
Edinburgh Old and New Towns
Frontiers of the Roman Empire, including Hadrian's Wall (shared with Germany)
Giant's Causeway and its coast
Gough and Inaccessible Islands (South Atlantic Ocean)
Greenwich (maritime buildings and park)
Gwynedd castles and towns of King Edward I
Henderson Island (Pacific Ocean)
Ironbridge Gorge
Liverpool (maritime mercantile city)
New Lanark
Orkney (Neolithic areas)
Royal Botanic Gardens, Kew
Saltaire
St George, Bermuda (historic town and fortifications)
St Kilda (island)
Stonehenge, Avebury and related megalithic sites
Studley Royal Park and the ruins of Fountains Abbey
Tower of London
Westminster (palace and abbey) and St Margaret's Church
■ **USA**
Cahokia Mounds historic site
Carlsbad Caverns National Park
Chaco Culture National Historical Park
Everglades National Park
Grand Canyon National Park
Great Smoky Mountains National Park
Hawaii Volcanoes National Park
Independence Hall, Philadelphia
La Fortaleza and San Juan historic site, Puerto Rico
Mammoth Cave National Park
Mesa Verde National Park
Monticello and the University of Virginia in Charlottesville
Olympic National Park
Pueblo de Taos
Redwood National Park
Statue of Liberty
Tatshenshini-Alsek, Kluane National Park, Wrangell St Elias National Park and Reserve, and Glacier Bay National Park (shared with Canada)
Waterton Glacier International Peace Park (shared with Canada)
Yellowstone National Park

Yosemite National Park
■ **Uruguay**
Colonia del Sacramento (historic quarter)
■ **Uzbekistan**
Bukhara (historic centre)
Itchan Kala (historic city)
Samarkand
Shakhrisyabz (historic centre)
■ **Vanuatu**
Chief Roy Mata's domain
■ **Vatican City**
Rome properties of the Holy See outside the
Vatican City, and San Paolo Fuori le Mura
Vatican City
■ **Venezuela**
Canaima National Park
Coro and its port
Cuidad Universitaria de Caracas
■ **Vietnam**
Ha Long Bay

Hoi An (ancient town)
Hué monuments complex
My Son Sanctuary
Phong Nha-Ke Bang National Park
■ **Yemen**
San'a (old city)
Shibam (old walled city)
Socotra archipelago
Zabid (historic town)
■ **Zambia**
Mosi-oa-Tunya/Victoria Falls (shared with
Zimbabwe)
■ **Zimbabwe**
Khami Ruins National Monument
Great Zimbabwe National Monument
Mana Pools National Park and Sapi and Chewore
safari areas
Matobo Hills
Mosi-oa-Tunya/Victoria Falls (shared with
Zambia)

*Struve Geodetic Arc is shared by Belarus, Estonia, Finland, Latvia, Lithuania, Moldova, Norway, Russia, Sweden and Ukraine.

Climate and Environment

Shipping forecast areas

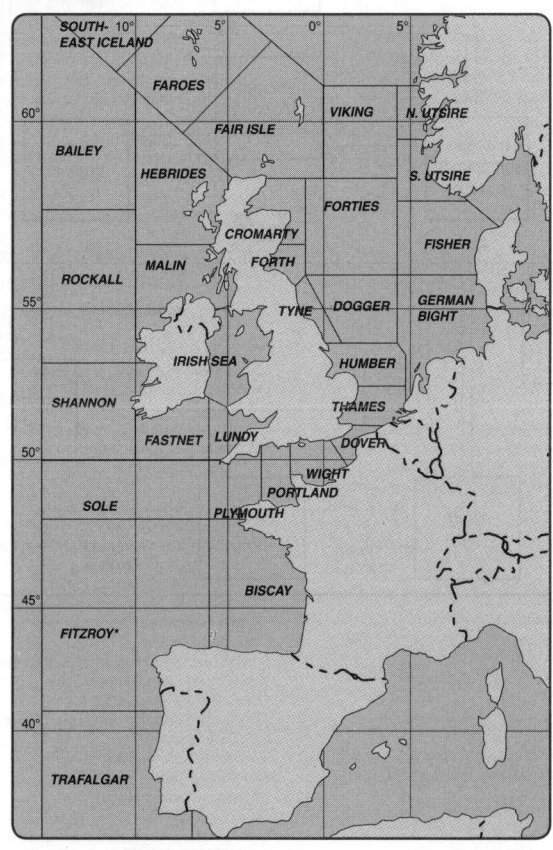

* Formerly Finisterre (renamed 2002)
Reproduced with data supplied by the Met Office.

NATURAL HISTORY

Natural History

Nitrogen cycle

The nitrogen cycle is the continuous circulation of nitrogen and its compounds between the atmosphere and the biosphere as a result of the activity of living organisms.

Nitrogen taken up by plants is incorporated into proteins, and when such plants are subsequently eaten by animals, it is incorporated into animal protein. The excreta of animals, together with the decomposing remains of dead plants and animals, are broken down by nitrifying bacteria to form ammonia. Ammonia is oxidized first to nitrites and then to nitrates in a process known as *nitrification*. The ammonia and nitrates may be used as plant nutrients. Nitrates are also converted to molecular nitrogen (which is released back to the atmosphere) by bacteria that live in waterlogged soils, in a process known as *denitrification*.

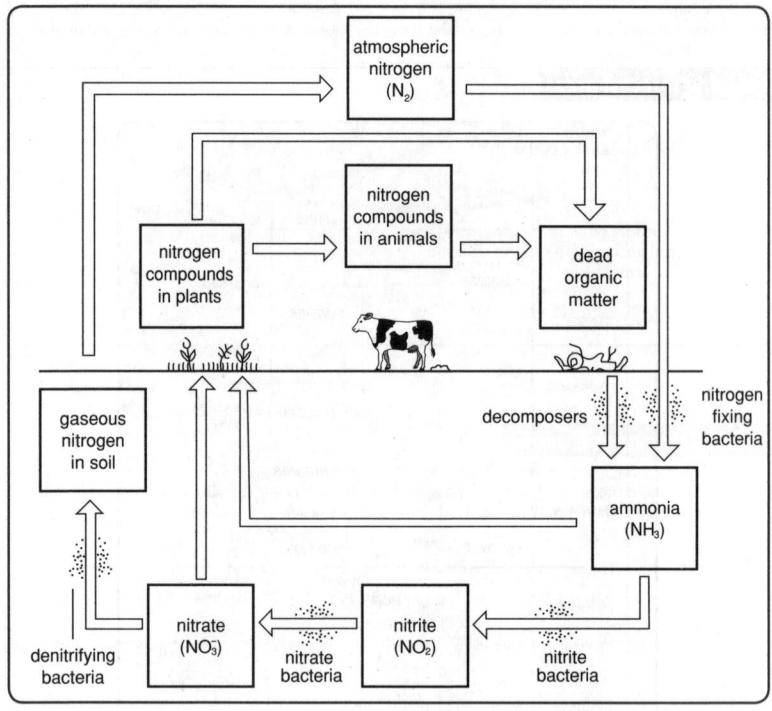

Carbon cycle

The carbon cycle is the biological circulation of carbon from the atmosphere into living organisms and, after their death, back again. Plants acquire carbon from the atmosphere by photosynthesis, while plants and animals release carbon back to the atmosphere by respiration. The consumption of plants by animals and the decomposition of dead organisms are also part of the cycle.

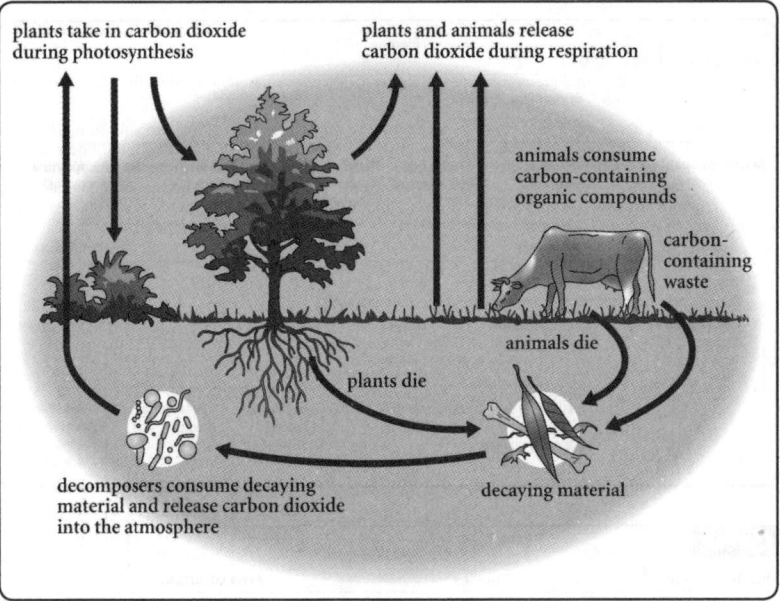

plants take in carbon dioxide during photosynthesis

plants and animals release carbon dioxide during respiration

animals consume carbon-containing organic compounds

carbon-containing waste

animals die

plants die

decomposers consume decaying material and release carbon dioxide into the atmosphere

decaying material

Natural History (sidebar)

Classification of organisms

Organisms with similar characteristics are often categorized into groups. The most commonly used classification system (taxonomy) has seven major levels; as well as these major levels, higher (super-) and lower (sub-) versions of the levels can be used.

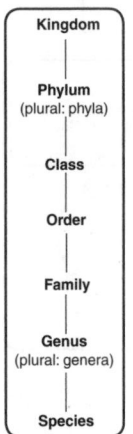

Kingdom

Phylum
(plural: phyla)

Class

Order

Family

Genus
(plural: genera)

Species

The generally recognized kingdoms are:

Eubacteria	bacteria
Archaea	archaeans (similar to bacteria)
Protista or protoctista	protists, eg amoebae, slime moulds, protozoa, some algae
Fungi	includes mushrooms, toadstools, yeasts, truffles
Plantae	plants
Animalia	animals

Natural History

Plant kingdom

Plants are multicellular organisms that can make their own carbohydrates (starch) from carbon dioxide and light energy by photosynthesis. Their cells have a wall that is made out of cellulose; this wall can sometimes become hardened with lignin to form wood. Plants are non-motile; they therefore react more slowly to external factors, such as light and food, than do organisms such as animals and bacteria.

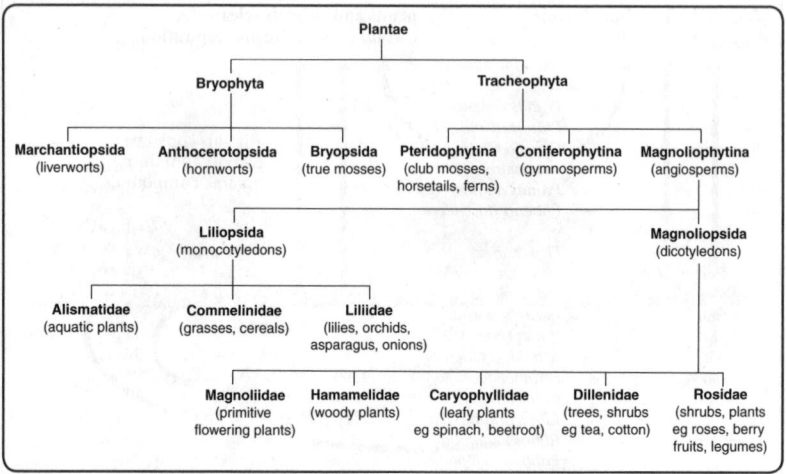

Cereals

English name	Species	Area of origin
barley	*Hordeum vulgare*	Middle East
maize (or corn, sweetcorn, Indian corn)	*Zea mays*	C America
millet, bulrush	*Pennisetum americanum*	tropics, warm temperate regions
millet, common	*Panicum miliaceum*	tropics, warm temperate regions
millet, foxtail (or Italian millet)	*Setaria italica*	tropics, warm temperate regions
oats	*Avena sativa*	Mediterranean basin
rice	*Oryza sativa*	Asia
rye	*Secale cereale*	Mediterranean, SW Asia
sorghum (or Kaffir corn)	*Sorghum bicolor*	Africa, Asia
wheat	Genus *Triticum*, 20 species	Mediterranean, W Asia

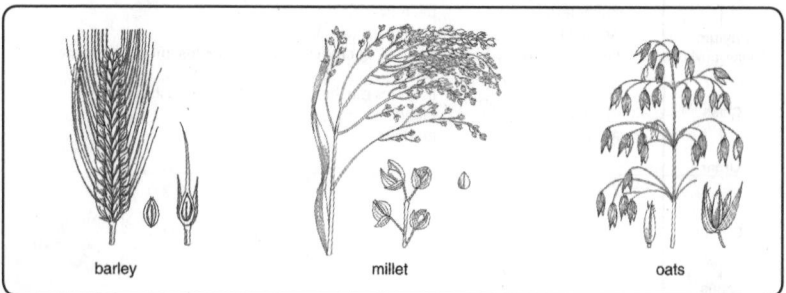

barley   millet   oats

Edible fruits (temperate and Mediterranean)

English name	Species	Colour	Area of origin
apple	*Malus pumila*	green, yellow, red	temperate regions
apricot	*Prunus armeniaca*	yellow, orange	Asia
bilberry	*Vaccinium myrtillus*	blue, black	Europe, N Asia
blackberry (or bramble)	*Rubus fruticosus*	purple, black	N hemisphere
blackcurrant	*Ribes nigrum*	black	Europe, Asia, Africa
blueberry	*Vaccinium corymbosum*	blue, purple, black	America, Europe
Cape gooseberry ► physalis			
cherry (sour)	*Prunus cerasus*	red	temperate regions
cherry (sweet)	*Prunus avium*	purple, red	temperate regions
clementine	*Citrus reticulata*	orange	W Mediterranean
cranberry	*Vaccinium oxycoccus*	red	N America
damson	*Prunus damascena*	purple	temperate regions
date	*Phoenix dactylifera*	yellow, red, brown	Persian Gulf
date-plum ► persimmon			
fig	*Ficus carica*	white, black, purple, green	W Asia
gooseberry	*Ribes grossularia*	green, red	Europe
grape	*Vitis vinifera*	green, purple, black	Asia
grapefruit	*Citrus × paradisi*	yellow	W Indies
greengage	*Prunus italica*	green	temperate regions
kiwi fruit	*Actinidia chinensis*	brown skin, green flesh	China
kumquat	*Fortunella margarita*	orange	China
lemon	*Citrus limon*	yellow	India, S Asia
lime	*Citrus aurantifolia*	green	SE Asia
loganberry	*Rubus loganobaccus*	red	America
loquat	*Eriobotrya japonica*	yellow	China, Japan
lychee	*Litchi chinensis*	reddish-brown skin, white flesh	China
mandarin (or tangerine)	*Citrus reticulata*	orange	China
medlar	*Mespilus germanica*	russet brown	SE Europe, Asia
melon	*Cucumis melo*	green, yellow	Egypt
minneola ► tangelo			
mulberry	*Morus nigra*	purple, red	W Asia
nectarine	*Prunus persica nectarina*	orange, red	China
orange	*Citrus sinensis*	orange	China
peach	*Prunus persica* var. *nectarina*	yellow, red	China
pear	*Pyrus communis*	yellow	Middle East, E Europe
persimmon (or date-plum)	*Diospyros kaki*	yellow, orange	E Asia
physalis (or Cape gooseberry)	*Physalis alkekengi*	yellow	S America
plum	*Prunus domestica*	red, yellow, purple, orange	temperate regions
pomegranate	*Punica granatum*	red, yellow	Persia
pomelo	*Citrus maxima*	yellow	Malaysia
quince	*Cydonia oblonga*	golden	Iran
raspberry	*Rubus idaeus*	red, crimson	N hemisphere
redcurrant	*Ribes rubrum*	red	Europe, Asia, Africa
rhubarb	*Rheum rhaponticum*	red, green, pink	Asia

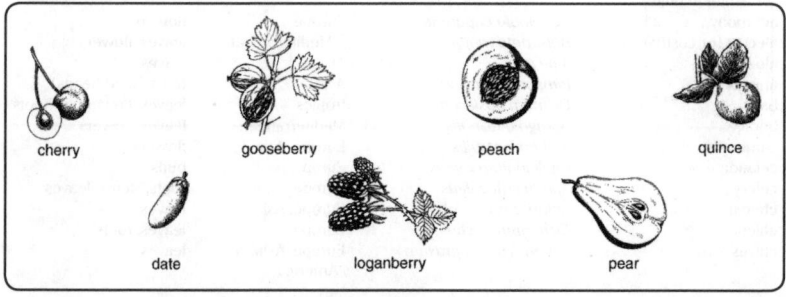

cherry gooseberry peach quince

date loganberry pear

Natural History

English name	Species	Colour	Area of origin
satsuma	*Citrus reticulata*	orange	Japan
strawberry	*Fragaria ananassa*	red	Europe, Asia
tangelo (or minneola, or ugli)	*Citrus × tangelo*	orange, yellow	N America
tangerine ▶ mandarin			
ugli ▶ tangelo			
watermelon	*Citrullus vulgaris*	green, yellow	Africa
white currant	*Ribes rubrum* cv.	white	W Europe

Edible fruits (tropical)

English name	Species	Colour	Area of origin
acerola	*Malpighia glabra*	yellow, red	S America
avocado	*Persea americana*	green, purple	C America, Mexico
banana	*Musa acuminita*	yellow	India, S Asia
breadfruit	*Artocarpus altilis*	greenish brown, yellow	Malaysia
carambola	*Averrhoa carambola*	yellow, green	S China
cherimoya	*Annona cherimola*	green skin, white flesh	Peru
guava	*Psidium guajava*	green, yellow	S America
mango	*Mangifera indica*	green, yellow, orange, red, purple	S Asia
papaya (or pawpaw)	*Carica papaya*	green, yellow, orange	tropics
passion fruit	*Passiflora edulis*	purple, yellow, brown	S America
pineapple	*Ananas comosus*	green, yellow	S America
sapodilla plum	*Manilkara zapota*	brown	C America
soursop	*Anona muricata*	green	C and S America
tamarind	*Tamarindus indica*	brown	Africa, S Asia

papaya   pineapple   soursop

Herbs

Herbs may be used for medicinal, cosmetic or culinary purposes. Any part of those marked * may be poisonous when ingested.

English name	Species	Origin	Part of plant used
aconite* (or monkshood or winter aconite)	*Aconitum napellus*	Europe, NW Asia	tuber
agrimony	*Agrimonia eupatoria*	Europe	flowers
alecost (or costmary)	*Balsimata major*	E Mediterranean	leaves, flowers
aloe	*Aloe vera*	Africa	leaves
aniseed	*Pimpinella anisum*	Asia	fruits (seed heads)
basil	*Ocimum basilicum*	tropics	leaves, flowering shoots
borage	*Borago officinalis*	Mediterranean	leaves, flowers
camomile	*Anthemis nobilis*	Europe, Asia	flowers
celandine	*Chelidonium majus*	Europe	buds
celery	*Apium graveolens*	Europe	roots, stems, leaves
chervil	*Anthriscus cerefolium*	Europe, Asia	leaves
chicory	*Cichorium intybus*	Europe	leaves, roots
chives	*Allium schoenoprasum*	Europe, Asia, N America	leaves

English name	Species	Origin	Part of plant used
coriander	Coriandrum sativum	N Africa, W Asia	leaves, fruits
dandelion	Taraxacum officinalis	Europe	leaves, roots
deadly nightshade*	Atropa belladonna	Europe, Asia	root
dill	Anethum graveolens	S Europe	leaves, fruits (seeds)
elderberry	Sambucus nigra	Europe	flowers, fruits
epazote	Chenopodium ambrosioides	C and S America	leaves
fennel, Florentine	Foeniculum vulgare var. azoricum	Mediterranean	leaves, stems, fruits (seeds)
feverfew	Tanacetum parthenium	SE Europe, W Asia	leaves, flowers
foxglove*	Digitalis purpurea	Europe	leaves
garlic	Allium sativum	Asia	bulbs
gentian	Gentiana lutea	Europe	rhizomes, roots
ginseng	Panax pseudo-ginseng	China	roots
guaiacum	Guaiacum officinale	Caribbean	leaves
heart's-ease (or wild pansy)	Viola tricolor	Europe	flowers
hemlock*	Conium maculatum	Europe	all parts
hemp (or ganja or cannabis or marijuana)	Cannabis sativa	Asia	leaves, flowers
henbane*	Hyoscyamus niger	Europe, W Asia, N Africa	leaves, fruits (seeds)
henna	Lawsonia inermis	Asia, Africa	leaves
horseradish	Armoracia rusticana	SE Europe, W Asia	roots, flowering shoots, leaves
hyssop	Hyssopus officinalis	S Europe	leaves, flowers
juniper	Juniperus communis	Mediterranean	fruits (berries), wood
lavender	Lavandula vera	Mediterranean	flowers, stems
leek	Allium porrum	Europe	stem, leaves
lemon	Citrus limon	Asia	fruits
lemon balm	Melissa officinalis	S Europe	leaves
lily of the valley	Convallaria majalis	Europe, N America	leaves, flowers
lime	Tilia cordata	Europe	flowers
liquorice	Glycyrrhiza glabra	Europe	roots
lovage	Levisticum officinale	W Asia	leaves, shoots, stems, roots
mandrake*	Mandragora officinarum	Himalayas, SE Europe, W Asia	roots
marjoram	Oreganum majorana	Africa, Mediterranean, Asia	leaves, shoots, stems
marsh mallow	Althaea officinalis	Europe, Asia	leaves, roots
maté	Ilex paraguariensis	S America	leaves
milfoil ▶ yarrow			
monkshood ▶ aconite			
mugwort	Artemesia vulgaris	Europe, Asia	leaves
myrrh	Commiphora myrrha	Arabia, Africa	resin
myrtle	Myrtus communis	Asia, Mediterranean	leaves, flower heads, fruits (berries)
nasturtium	Tropaeolom majus	Peru	leaves, flowers, fruits
onion	Allium cepa	Asia	bulbs
oregano	Origanum vulgare	Mediterranean	leaves, shoots, stems
parsley	Petroselinum crispum	Mediterranean	leaves, stems
peony	Paeonia officinalis	Europe, Asia, N America	roots, seeds
peppermint	Mentha × piperita	Europe	leaves
poppy, opium*	Papaver somniferum	Asia	fruits, seeds
purslane	Portulaca oleracea	Europe	leaves
rosemary	Rosmarinus officinalis	Mediterranean	leaves
rue	Ruta graveolens	Mediterranean	leaves, stems, flowers
saffron	Crocus sativus	Asia Minor	flowers
sage	Salvia officinalis	N Mediterranean	leaves
sorrel	Rumex acetosa	Europe	leaves
spearmint	Mentha spicata	Europe	leaves
tansy	Tanacetum vulgare	Asia	leaves, flowers
tarragon, French	Artemesia dracunculus	Asia, E Europe	leaves, stems
thyme	Thymus vulgaris	Mediterranean	leaves, stems, flowers
valerian	Valeriana officinalis	Europe, Asia	rhizomes, roots

English name	Species	Origin	Part of plant used
vervain	*Verbena officinalis*	Europe, Asia, N Africa	leaves, flowers
watercress	*Nasturtium officinale*	Europe, Asia	leaves, shoots, stems
witch-hazel	*Hamamelis virginiana*	N America, E Asia	leaves, shoots, bark
wormwood	*Artemesia absinthium*	Europe	leaves, flowering shoots
yarrow (or milfoil)	*Achillea millefolium*	Europe, W Asia	flower heads, leaves

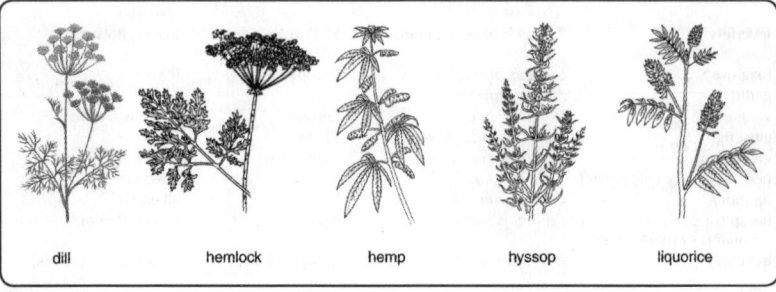

dill   hemlock   hemp   hyssop   liquorice

Spices

English name	Species	Origin	Part of plant used
allspice	*Pimenta dioica*	America, W Indies	fruits
annatto	*Bixa orellana*	S America, W Indies	seeds
asafoetida	*Ferula assa-foetida*	W Asia	sap
bay	*Laurus nobilis*	Mediterranean, Asia Minor	leaves
caper	*Capparis spinosa*	Europe	flower buds
caraway	*Carum carvi*	Europe, Asia	seeds
cardamom	*Elettaria cardamomum*	SE Asia	seeds
cayenne	*Capsicum annuum*	America, Africa	fruit pods
chilli pepper	*Capsicum frutescens*	America	fruit pods
cinnamon	*Cinnamomum zeylanicum*	India	bark
cloves	*Eugenia caryophyllus*	Moluccas	buds
cocoa	*Theobroma cacoa*	S America	seeds (beans)
coconut	*Cocus nucifera*	Polynesia	fruits
coriander	*Coriandrum sativum*	S Europe	fruits
cumin	*Cuminum cyminum*	Mediterranean	fruits (seed heads)
curry leaf	*Murraya koenigi*	India	leaves
fennel	*Foeniculum vulgare*	S Europe	fruits
fenugreek	*Trigonella foenum-graecum*	India, S Europe	seeds
ginger	*Zingiber officinale*	SE Asia	rhizomes
horseradish	*Armoracia rusticana*	E Europe	roots
mace	*Myristica fragrans*	Moluccas	seeds
mustard, black	*Brassica nigra*	Europe, Africa, Asia, America	seeds
mustard, white	*Sinapis alba*	Europe, Asia	seeds
nutmeg	*Myristica fragrans*	Indonesia	seeds
paprika	*Capsicum annuum*	S America	fruit pods
pepper	*Piper nigrum*	India	seeds
sandalwood	*Santalum album*	India, Indonesia, Australia	heartwood, roots

cumin   vanilla

English name	Species	Origin	Part of plant used
sassafras	*Sassafras albidum*	N America	root bark
sesame	*Sesamum indicum*	tropics	seeds
soya	*Glycine max*	China	fruit (beans)
tamarind	*Tamarindus indica*	Africa	fruits
turmeric	*Curcuma longa*	SE Asia	rhizomes
vanilla	*Vanilla planifolia*	C America	fruit pods

Natural History

Vegetables

English name	Species	Colour	Area of origin	Part eaten
artichoke, Chinese	*Stachys affinis*	white	China	tuber
artichoke, globe	*Cynara scolymus*	green, purple	Mediterranean	buds
artichoke, Jerusalem	*Helianthus tuberosus*	white	N America	tuber
asparagus	*Asparagus officinalis*	green, white	Europe, Asia	young shoots
aubergine (or eggplant)	*Solanum melongena*	purple, white	Asia, Africa	fruit
avocado	*Persea americana*	green, purple	C America	fruit
bean sprout	*Vigna radiata*	white, pale brown	China	shoots
bean, blackeyed	*Vigna unguiculata*	white/black	India, Iran	seeds
bean, borlotti (or Boston bean or pinto bean)	*Phaseolus vulgaris*	pink/brown	America	seeds
bean, broad	*Vicia faba*	white	Africa, Europe	seeds and pods
bean, flageolet	*Phaseolus vulgaris*	white, pale green	America	seeds
bean, French	*Phaseolus vulgaris*	green	America	pods
bean, haricot	*Phaseolus vulgaris*	white	America	seeds
bean, kidney	*Phaseolus vulgaris*	red	America	seeds
bean, runner	*Phaseolus coccineus*	green	America	pods
bean, soya	*Glycine max*	green	E Asia	seeds
beetroot	*Beta vulgaris*	white, dark red	Mediterranean	root
broccoli	*Brassica oleracea*	green, purple	Europe	buds and leaves
Brussels sprout	*Brassica oleracea* (gemmifera)	green	N Europe	buds
cabbage	*Brassica oleracea*	green, red, white	Europe, W Asia	leaves
cardoon	*Cynara cardunculus*	white, green	Mediterranean	inner stalks and flower heads
carrot	*Daucus carota*	orange	Asia	root
cauliflower	*Brassica oleracea* (botrytis)	white, green	Middle East	flower buds
celeriac	*Apium graveolens* var. *rapaceum*	white	Mediterranean	root
celery	*Apium graveolens* var. *dulce*	white, green	Europe, N Africa, America	stalks
chayote (or chocho)	*Sechium edule*	white, green	America	fruit
chickpea	*Cicer arietinum*	beige, golden, dark brown	W Asia	seeds
chicory	*Cichorium intybus*	red, green	Europe, W Asia	leaves
chinese leaf	*Brassica pekinensis*	white, green	E Asia, China	leaf stalks
chives	*Allium schoenoprasum*	green, white	Europe, N America	leaves
courgette (or zucchini)	*Cucurbita pepo*	green	S America, Africa	fruit
cucumber	*Cucumis sativus*	green	S Asia	fruit
eggplant ▶ aubergine				
endive	*Cichorium endivia*	yellow, green	S Europe, E Indies, Africa	leaves
fennel, Florentine	*Foeniculum vulgare* var. *dulce*	white, green	Europe	leaf stalks
kale (or borecole)	*Brassica oleracea* (acephala)	green	Europe	leaves
kohlrabi	*Brassica oleracea* (gongylodes)	white	Europe	stems
laver	*Porphyra leucosticta, P. umbilicalis*	purple-pink	Europe	leaves and stems

Natural History

English name	Species	Colour	Area of origin	Part eaten
leek	*Allium porrum*	green, white	Europe, N Africa	leaves and stems
lentil	*Lens culinaris*	white, green, pink, red	S Asia	seeds
lettuce	*Lactuca sativa*	green, white	Middle East	leaves
marrow	*Cucurbita pepo*	green	America	fruit
mooli	*Raphanus sativus*	white	E Africa	root
mushroom	*Agaricus campestris*	brown, white	worldwide	fruiting body
okra	*Abelmoschus esculentus*	green, white	Africa	pods and seeds
onion	*Allium cepa*	white, pink	C Asia	bulb
parsnip	*Pastinaca sativa*	white, yellow	Europe	root
pea	*Pisum sativum*	green	Asia, Europe	pods and seeds
pepper	*Capsicum annuum*	red, green, yellow	S America	fruit
potato	*Solanum tuberosum*	white	S America	tuber
pumpkin	*Cucurbita pepo*	yellow, orange	S America	fruit
radish	*Raphanus sativus*	red, white	China, Japan	root
salsify	*Tragopogon porrifolius*	white	S Europe	root
sorrel	*Rumex acetosa*	green	Europe	leaves
spinach	*Spinacea oleracea*	green	Asia	leaves
squash, winter	*Cucurbita maxima*	green, yellow, orange	America	fruit
squash, summer	*Cucurbita pepo*	yellow, orange, green	America	fruit
swede	*Brassica napus* (napobrassica)	yellow, white	Europe	root
sweet potato	*Ipomoea batatas*	white, yellow, red to purple	C America	tuber
swiss chard	*Beta vulgaris* subsp. *cicla*	green, white	Europe	leaves and stems
tomato	*Lycopersicon esculentum*	red	S America	fruit
turnip	*Brassica rapa*	white	Middle East	root
watercress	*Nasturtium officinale*	green	Europe, Asia	leaves and stems
yam	Genus *Dioscorea*, 60 species	white, orange	tropics	tuber

zucchini ► courgette

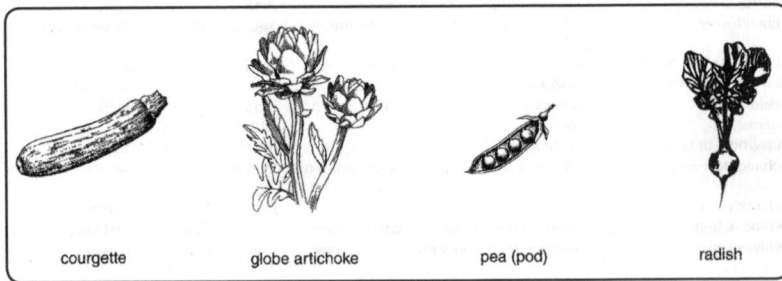

courgette   globe artichoke   pea (pod)   radish

Flowers (bulbs, corms, rhizomes and tubers)

English name	Genus/Family	Colour	Country/Continent of origin
acidanthera	*Acidanthera*	white	NE Africa
African lily (or lily-of-the-Nile)	*Agapanthus*	white, purple	S Africa
agapanthus	*Agapanthus*	blue, white	S Africa
allium	*Allium*	blue, lilac, white, rose	Asia, Europe
amaryllis (or belladonna lily)	*Amaryllis*	rose-pink	S Africa, tropical America
anemone	*Anemone*	white, lilac, blue	Mediterranean, Asia, Europe
belladonna lily ▶ amaryllis			
bluebell	*Hyacinthoides*	blue	Europe
carnassia	*Camassia*	white, cream, blue, purple	N America
chionodoxa (or glory of the snow)	*Chionodoxa*	blue, white, pink	Greece, Turkey
crinum	*Crinum*	rose-pink, white	S Africa
crocosmia	*Crocosmia*	orange	S Africa
crocus	*Crocus*	purple, rose, yellow, pink, orange	Mediterranean, Asia, Africa
crown imperial	*Fritillaria*	orange	N India
curtonus	*Curtonus*	orange	S Africa
cyclamen	*Cyclamen*	white, pink, red	Asia, Mediterranean
daffodil (or narcissus)	*Narcissus*	white, yellow, orange	Mediterranean, Europe
dogtooth violet ▶ erythronium			
erythronium (or dog-tooth violet)	*Erythronium*	purple, pink, white, yellow	Europe, Asia
fritillaria	*Fritillaria*	red, yellow	Europe, Asia, N America
galtonia	*Galtonia*	white	S Africa
gladiolus	*Gladiolus*	purple, yellow	Europe, Asia
glory of the snow ▶ chionodoxa			
harebell	*Campanula*	blue	N temperate regions
hippeastrum	*Hippeastrum*	pink, white, red	tropical America
hyacinth	*Hyacinthus*	blue, white, red	S Europe, Asia
hyacinth, grape	*Muscari*	blue	Europe, Mediterranean
hyacinth, wild	*Scilla*	blue, purple, pink, white	Asia, S Europe
iris	*Iris*	purple, white, yellow	N temperate regions
lthuriel's spear	*Brodiaea*	white, pink, blue	N America
lapeirousia	*Lapeirousia*	red	S Africa
lily	*Lilium*	white, pink, crimson, yellow, orange, red	China, Europe, America
lily-of-the-Nile ▶ African lily			
lily-of-the-valley	*Convallaria*	white	Europe, Asia, America
naked ladies	*Colchicum*	white, pink, purple	Asia, Europe
nerine	*Nerine*	pink, salmon	S Africa
ornithogalum	*Ornithogalum*	white, yellow	S Africa
peacock (or tiger flower)	*Tigridia*	white, orange, red, yellow	Asia
rouge, giant	*Tigridia*	white, yellow, red, lilac	Mexico
snake's-head	*Fritillaria*	purple, white	Europe
snowdrop	*Galanthus*	white	Europe
snowflake	*Leucojum*	white, green	S Europe

cyclamen

gladiolus

lily

Natural History

English name	Genus/Family	Colour	Country/Continent of origin
solfaterre	*Crocosmia × crocosmiflora*	orange, red	S Africa
Solomon's seal	*Polygonatum*	white	Europe, Asia
squill	*Scilla*	blue, purple	Europe, Asia, S Africa
sternbergia	*Sternbergia*	yellow	Europe
striped squill	*Puschkinia*	bluish-white	Asia
tiger flower ▶ peacock			
tiger lily	*Lilium*	orange	Asia
tulip	*Tulipa*	orange, red, pink, white, crimson, lilac	Europe, Asia
wand flower	*Dierama*	white, pink, mauve, purple	S Africa
winter aconite	*Eranthis*	yellow	Greece, Turkey

Flowers (herbaceous)

English name	Genus/Family	Colour	Country/Continent of origin
acanthus	*Acanthus*	white, rose, purple	Europe
African violet	*Saintpaulia*	violet, white, pink	Africa
alum root	*Heuchera*	rose, pink, red	N America
alyssum	*Alyssum*	white, yellow, pink	S Europe
anchusa	*Anchusa*	blue	Asia, S Europe
anemone	*Hepatica*	white, red-pink, blue	Europe, Caucasus
asphodel	*Asphodelus*	white, yellow	S Europe
aster	*Aster*	white, blue, purple, pink	Europe, Asia, N America
astilbe	*Astilbe*	white, pink, red	Asia
aubrietia	*Aubrieta*	purple	SE Europe
begonia	*Begonia*	pink	S America, the Pacific
bellflower	*Campanula*	blue, white	N temperate regions
bergamot	*Monarda*	white, pink, red, purple	N America
bistort	*Polygonum*	rose-pink	Japan, Himalayas
bleeding heart	*Dicentra*	pink, white, red	China, Japan, N America
bugbane	*Cimicifuga*	white	N America, Japan
busy lizzie	*Impatiens*	crimson, pink, white	tropics
buttercup	*Ranunculus*	yellow	temperate regions
carnation	*Dianthus*	white, pink, red	temperate regions
catmint	*Nepeta*	blue, mauve	Europe, Asia
celandine, giant	*Ranunculus*	white, copper-orange	Europe
Christmas rose	*Helleborus*	white, pink	Europe
chrysanthemum	*Chrysanthemum*	yellow, white	China
cinquefoil	*Potentilla*	orange, red, yellow	Europe, Asia
columbine (or granny's bonnet)	*Aquilegia*	purple, dark blue, pink, yellow	Europe
cupid's dart	*Catananche*	blue, white	Europe
dahlia	*Dahlia*	red, yellow, white	Mexico
daisy	*Bellis*	white, yellow, pink	Europe
delphinium	*Delphinium*	white, mauve, pink, blue	Europe, N America
echinacea	*Echinacea*	rose-red, purple	N America
edelweiss	*Leontopodium*	yellow, white	Europe, Asia
evening primrose	*Oenothera*	yellow	N America
everlasting flower (or immortelle)	*Helichrysum bracteatum*	yellow	Australia
everlasting flower, pearly	*Anaphalis*	white	N America, Himalayas
fleabane	*Erigeron*	white, pink, blue, violet	Australia
forget-me-not	*Myosotis*	blue	Europe
foxglove	*Digitalis*	white, yellow, pink, red	Europe, Asia
fraxinella	*Dictamnus*	white, mauve	Europe, Asia
gentian	*Gentiana*	blue, yellow, white, red	temperate regions
geranium	*Pelargonium*	scarlet, pink, white	temperate regions, subtropics
geum	*Geum*	orange, red, yellow	S Europe, N America
goat's-beard	*Aruncus*	white	N Europe
golden rod	*Solidago*	yellow	Europe
granny's bonnet ▶ columbine			
gypsophila	*Gypsophila*	white, pink	Europe, Asia

English name	Genus/Family	Colour	Country/Continent of origin
Hattie's pincushion (or the melancholy gentleman)	Astrantia	white, pink	Europe
heliopsis	Heliopsis	orange-yellow	N America
hellebore	Helleborus	plum-purple, white	Asia, Greece
herb Christopher	Actaea	white	N America
hollyhock	Alcaea	white, yellow, pink, red, maroon	Europe, China
hosta	Hosta	violet, white	China, Japan
immortelle ▶ everlasting flower			
kaffir lily	Schizostylis	red, pink	S Africa
kirengeshoma	Kirengeshoma	yellow	Japan
liatris	Liatris	heather-purple	N America
lobelia	Lobelia	white, red, blue, purple	Africa, N America, Australia
loosestrife	Lysimachia	rose-pink, purple	Europe
lotus	Lotus	yellow, pink, white	Asia, America
lupin	Lupinus	blue, yellow, pink, red	N America
marigold, African (or French marigold)	Tagetes	yellow, orange	Mexico
marigold, pot	Calendula	orange, apricot, cream	unknown
meadow rue	Thalictrum	yellow-white	Europe, Asia
mullein	Verbascum	yellow, white, pink, purple	Europe, Asia
nasturtium	Tropaeolum	yellow, red, orange	S America, Mexico
orchid	Orchidaea	red, purple, white, violet, green, brown, yellow, pink	tropics
ox-eye	Buphthalmum	yellow	Europe
pansy	Viola	white, yellow	temperate regions
peony	Paeonia	white, yellow, pink, red	Asia, Europe
Peruvian lily	Alstroemeria	cream, pink, yellow, orange, red	S America
petunia	Petunia	blue, violet, purple, white, pink	S America
phlox	Phlox	blue, white, purple, red	America
poppy	Papaver	red, orange, white, yellow, lilac	N temperate regions
primrose	Primula	yellow	N temperate regions
primula	Primula	white, pink, yellow, blue, purple	N temperate regions
red-hot poker	Kniphofia	white, yellow, orange, red	S Africa
salvia	Salvia	red, yellow, blue	S America, Europe, Asia
sea holly	Eryngium	blue, green-grey, white	Europe, S America
sidalcea	Sidalcea	lilac, pink, rose	N America
snapdragon	Antirrhinum	white, yellow, pink, red, maroon	Europe, Asia, S America
speedwell	Veronica	blue, white	Europe, Asia
spiderwort	Tradescantia	white, blue, pink, red, purple	N America
stokesia	Stokesia	white, blue, purple	N America
sunflower	Helianthus	yellow	N America
sweet pea	Lathyrus	purple, pink, white, red	Mediterranean
sweet william	Dianthus	white, pink, red, purple	S Europe
thistle, globe	Echinops	blue, white-grey	Europe, Asia
thistle, Scotch (or cotton thistle)	Onopordum	purple	Europe

| edelweiss | lotus | lupin | orchid |

Natural History

English name	Genus/Family	Colour	Country/Continent of origin
violet	*Viola*	mauve, blue	N temperate regions
water chestnut	*Trapa*	white, lilac	Asia
water lily	*Nymphaea*	white, blue, red, yellow	worldwide
wolfsbane	*Aconitum*	blue, white, rose, yellow	Europe, Asia
yarrow	*Achillea*	white, cream	Europe, W Asia

Flowers (shrubs)

English name	Genus / Family	Colour	Country/Continent of origin
abelia	*Abelia*	white, rose-purple	Asia, China, Mexico
abutilon	*Abutilon*	lavender-blue	S America
acacia (or mimosa or wattle)	*Acacia*	yellow	Australia, tropical Africa, tropical America
almond, dwarf	*Prunus*	white, crimson, rose-pink	Asia, Europe
ampelopsis	*Ampelopsis*	green (blue-black fruit)	Far East
anthyllis	*Anthyllis*	yellow	Europe
azalea	*Rhododendron*	pink, purple, white, yellow, crimson	N hemisphere
berberis	*Berberis*	yellow, orange	Asia, America, Europe
bottlebrush	*Callistemon*	red	Australia
bougainvillea	*Bougainvillea*	lilac, pink, purple, red, orange, white	S America
broom	*Cytisus*	yellow	Europe
buckthorn	*Rhamnus*	red, black	N hemisphere
buddleia	*Buddleja*	purple, yellow, white	China, S America
cactus	*Cactaceae*	red, purple, orange, yellow, white	America
calico bush (or mountain laurel)	*Kalmia*	white, pink	China
camellia	*Camellia*	white, pink, red	Asia
caryopteris	*Caryopteris*	blue, violet	Asia
ceanothus	*Ceanothus*	pink, blue, purple	N America
ceratostigma	*Ceratostigma*	purple-blue	China
Chinese lantern	*Physalis*	orange, red	Japan
cistus	*Cistus*	white, pink	Europe
clematis	*Clematis*	white, purple, violet, blue, pink, yellow	N temperate regions
clerodendron	*Clerodendron*	white, purple-red	China
colquhounia	*Colquhounia*	scarlet, yellow	Himalayas
cornelian cherry	*Cornus*	yellow	Europe
coronilla	*Coronilla*	yellow	S Europe
corylopsis	*Corylopsis*	yellow	China, Japan
cotoneaster	*Cotoneaster*	white (red fruit)	Asia
currant, flowering	*Ribes*	red, white, pink	N America
desfontainia	*Desfontainia*	scarlet-gold	S America
deutzia	*Deutzia*	white, pink	Asia
diplera	*Diplera*	pale pink	China
dogwood	*Cornus*	white	Europe, SW Asia
embothrium	*Embothrium*	scarlet	S America
escallonia	*Escallonia*	white, pink	S America
euchryphia	*Euchryphia*	white	Chile, Australasia
euryops	*Euryops*	yellow	S Africa
fabiana	*Fabiana*	white, mauve	S America
firethorn	*Pyracantha*	white (red, orange, yellow fruits)	China
forsythia	*Forsythia*	yellow	China
frangipani	*Plumeria*	white, pink, yellow	tropical America
fuchsia	*Fuchsia*	red, pink, white	C and S America, New Zealand
gardenia	*Gardenia*	white	tropics
garland flower	*Daphne*	pink, crimson, white, purple	Europe, Asia
garrya	*Garrya*	green	California and Oregon
gorse (or furze or whin)	*Ulex*	yellow	Europe, Britain
hawthorn	*Crataegus*	white (orange-red berries)	N America, Europe, N Africa

Natural History

English name	Genus / Family	Colour	Country/Continent of origin
heath, winter-flowering	Erica	white, pink, red	Africa, Europe
heather	Calluna	pink, purple, white	Europe, W Asia
hebe	Hebe	blue-white	New Zealand
helichrysum	Helichrysum	yellow	Australia, S Africa
hibiscus	Hibiscus	pink, mauve, purple, white, red	China, India
honeysuckle	Lonicera	white, yellow, pink, red	temperate regions
hydrangea	Hydrangea	white, pink, blue	Asia, America
hyssop	Hyssopus	bluish-purple	S Europe, W Asia
indigofera	Indigofera	rose-purple	Himalayas
ipomoea (or morning glory)	Ipomoea	white, red, blue	tropical America
japonica	Chaenomeles	white, pink, orange, red, yellow	N Asia
jasmine	Jasminum	white, yellow, red	Asia
Jerusalem sage	Phlomis	yellow	Europe
kerria	Kerria	yellow	China
kolkwitzia	Kolkwitzia	pink	China
laburnum	Laburnum	yellow	Europe, Asia
lavender	Lavandula	purple	Europe
leptospermum	Leptospermum	red, white	Australasia
lespedeza	Lespedeza	rose-purple	China, Japan
leycesteria	Leycesteria	claret	Himalayas
lilac (or syringa)	Syringa	purple, pink, white	Balkans
lion's tail	Leonotis	red	S Africa
magnolia	Magnolia	yellow, white, rose, purple	China, Japan
mahonia	Mahonia	yellow	Japan
malus	Malus	white, pink, red	N America, Asia
menziesa	Menziesa	wine-red	Japan
mimosa ▶ acacia			
mimulus	Mimulus	cream, orange, red	N America
mock orange	Philadelphus	white	Europe, Asia, N America
moltkia	Moltkia	violet-blue	Greece
morning glory ▶ ipomoea			
mother-of-pearl	Symphoricarpus	pink, white, red fruit	N America
mountain ash ▶ rowan			
myrtle	Myrtus	pink, white	Europe
oleander	Nerium	white, pink, purple, red	Mediterranean
olearia	Olearia	white, yellow	New Zealand
oleaster	Elaeagnus	yellow	Europe, Asia, N America
osmanthus	Osmanthus	white	China
pearl bush	Exochorda	white	China
peony	Paeonia	pink, red, white, yellow	Europe, Asia, N America
pieris	Pieris	white	China
poinsettia	Euphorbia	scarlet	Mexico
potentilla	Potentilla	yellow, red, orange	Asia
rhododendron	Rhododendron	red, purple, pink, white	S Asia
rhus	Rhus	foliage grey, purple, red	Europe, N America
ribbon woods	Hoheria	white	New Zealand
robinia	Robinia	rose-pink	N America
rock rose (or sun rose)	Helianthemum	white, yellow, pink, orange, red	Europe
rose	Rosa	pink, red, white, cream, yellow	N temperate regions
rosemary	Rosmarinus	violet	Europe, Asia
rowan (or mountain ash)	Sorbus	white (red, yellow berries)	Europe, Asia
sage, common	Salvia	green, white, yellow, reddish purple	S Europe
St John's wort	Hypericum	yellow	Europe, Asia
sea buckthorn	Hippophae	silver, orange	SW Europe
senecio	Senecio	yellow	New Zealand
skimmia	Skimmia	white	Japan, China
snowberry	Symphoricarpos	pink, white	N America
spiraea	Spiraea	white, pink, crimson	China, Japan

English name	Genus / Family	Colour	Country/Continent of origin
stachyurus	*Stachyurus*	pale yellow	China
staphylea	*Staphylea*	rose-pink	Europe, Asia
sun rose ▶ rock rose			
syringa ▶ lilac			
tamarisk	*Tamarix*	pink, white	Europe
thyme	*Thymus*	purple, white, pink	Europe
veronica	*Veronica*	white, pink, lilac, purple	New Zealand
viburnum	*Viburnum*	white, pink	Europe, Asia, Africa
Virginia creeper	*Parthenocissus*	foliage orange, red (blue-black fruits)	N America
wattle ▶ acacia			
weigela	*Weigela*	pink, red	N China
winter sweet	*Chimonanthus*	yellow	China
wisteria	*Wisteria*	mauve, white, pink	China, Japan
witch-hazel	*Hamamelis*	red, yellow	China, Japan

acacia

cactus

Trees (temperate and Mediterranean)

English name	Species	Deciduous/Evergreen	Continent of origin
alder, common	*Alnus glutinosa*	deciduous	Europe
almond	*Prunus dulcis*	deciduous	W Asia, N Africa
apple	*Malus pumila*	deciduous	Europe, W Africa
ash, common	*Fraxinus excelsior*	deciduous	Europe
aspen	*Populus tremula*	deciduous	Europe
bean tree, Red Indian	*Catalpa bignonioides*	deciduous	America, E Asia
beech, common	*Fagus sylvatica*	deciduous	Europe
beech, copper	*Fagus purpurea* ('Atropunicea')	deciduous	Europe
beech, noble	*Nothofagus obliqua*	deciduous	S America
birch, silver	*Betula pendula*	deciduous	Europe, America, Asia
box	*Buxus sempervirens*	evergreen	Europe, N Africa
Brazil nut	*Bertholletia excelsa*	evergreen	S America
camellia, deciduous	*Stewartia pseudo-camellia*	deciduous	Asia
castor-oil tree, prickly	*Eleutherococcus pictus*	deciduous	tropics
cedar of Lebanon	*Cedrus libani*	evergreen	Asia
cedar, smooth Tasmanian	*Athrotaxis cupressoides*	evergreen	Australia
cedar, white	*Thuja occidentalis*	evergreen	America
cherry, morello (or sour cherry)	*Prunus cerasus*	deciduous	Europe, Asia
cherry, wild (or gean)	*Prunus avium*	deciduous	Europe
chestnut, horse	*Aesculus hippocastanum*	deciduous	Asia, SW Europe
chestnut, sweet (or Spanish chestnut)	*Castanea sativa*	deciduous	Europe, Africa, Asia
crab apple	*Malus sylvestris*	deciduous	Europe, Asia
cypress, Lawson	*Chamaecyparis lawsoniana*	evergreen	America
deodar	*Cedrus deodara*	evergreen	Asia
dogwood, common	*Cornus sanguinea*	deciduous	Europe
elm, Dutch	*Ulmus × hollandica*	deciduous	Europe
elm, English	*Ulmus procera*	deciduous	Europe
elm, wych	*Ulmus glabra*	deciduous	Europe
fig	*Ficus carica*	evergreen	Asia

English name	Species	Deciduous/ Evergreen	Continent of origin
fir, Douglas	*Pseudotsuga menziesii*	evergreen	America
fir, red	*Abies magnifica*	evergreen	America
ginkgo	*Ginkgo biloba*	deciduous	Asia
grapefruit	*Citrus × paradisi*	evergreen	Asia
gum, blue	*Eucalyptus globulus*	evergreen	Australia
gum, cider	*Eucalyptus gunnii*	evergreen	Australia
gum, snow	*Eucalyptus panciflora*	evergreen	Australia
gutta-percha tree	*Eucommia ulmoides*	deciduous	China
hawthorn	*Crataegus monogyna*	deciduous	Europe
hazel, common	*Corylus avellana*	deciduous	Europe, W Asia, N Africa
hemlock, Western	*Tsuga heterophylla*	evergreen	America
holly	*Ilex aquifolium*	evergreen	Europe, N Africa, W Asia
hornbeam	*Carpinus betulus*	deciduous	Europe, Asia
Joshua-tree	*Yucca brevifolia*	evergreen	America
Judas-tree	*Cercis siliquastrum*	deciduous	S Europe, Asia
juniper, common	*Juniperus communis*	evergreen	Europe, Asia
laburnum, common	*Laburnum anagyroides*	deciduous	Europe
larch, European	*Larix decidua*	deciduous	Europe
larch, golden	*Pseudolarix kaempferi*	deciduous	E Asia
leatherwood	*Eucryphia lucida*	evergreen	Australia
lemon	*Citrus limon*	evergreen	Asia
lime	*Citrus aurantifolia*	evergreen	Asia
lime, small-leafed	*Tilia cordata*	deciduous	Europe
locust tree	*Robinia pseudoacacia*	deciduous	America
magnolia (or white laurel)	*Magnolia virginiana*	evergreen	America
maple, field (or common maple)	*Acer campestre*	deciduous	Europe
maple, sugar	*Acer saccharum*	deciduous	America
medlar	*Mespilus germanica*	deciduous	Europe
mimosa	*Acacia dealbata*	deciduous	Australia, Europe
mockernut	*Carya tomentosa*	deciduous	America
monkey puzzle	*Araucaria araucana*	evergreen	S America
mountain ash ▶ rowan			
mulberry, common	*Morus nigra*	deciduous	Asia
mulberry, white	*Morus alba*	deciduous	Asia
myrtle, orange bark	*Myrtus apiculata*	evergreen	S America
nutmeg, California	*Torreya californica*	evergreen	America
oak, California live	*Quercus agrifolia*	deciduous	America
oak, cork	*Quercus suber*	evergreen	S Europe, N Africa
oak, English (or common oak)	*Quercus robur*	deciduous	Europe, Asia, Africa
oak, red	*Quercus rubra*	deciduous	America
olive	*Olea europaea*	evergreen	S Europe
orange, sweet	*Citrus sinensis*	evergreen	Asia
pagoda-tree	*Sophora japonica*	deciduous	China, Japan
pear	*Pyrus communis*	deciduous	Europe, W Asia
pine, Austrian	*Pinus nigra* subsp. *nigra*	evergreen	Europe, Asia
pine, Corsican	*Pinus nigra* subsp. *laricio*	evergreen	Europe
pine, Monterey	*Pinus radiata*	evergreen	America
pine, Scots	*Pinus sylvestris*	evergreen	Europe
plane, London	*Platanus × hispanica*	deciduous	Europe
plane, Oriental	*Platanus orientalis*	deciduous	SE Europe, Asia
plum	*Prunus domestica*	deciduous	Europe, Asia
poplar, balsam	*Populus balsamifera*	deciduous	America, Asia
poplar, black	*Populus nigra*	deciduous	Europe, Asia
poplar, Lombardy	*Populus nigra* 'Italica'	deciduous	Europe
poplar, white	*Populus alba*	deciduous	Europe
quince	*Cydonia oblonga*	deciduous	Asia
raoul	*Nothofagus procera*	deciduous	S America
rowan (or mountain ash)	*Sorbus aucuparia*	deciduous	Europe
sassafras, American	*Sassafras albidum*	deciduous	America
service tree, true	*Sorbus domestica*	deciduous	Europe
silver fir, common	*Abies alba*	evergreen	Europe
spruce, Norway	*Picea abies*	evergreen	Europe
spruce, sitka	*Picea sitchensis*	evergreen	America, Europe

Natural History

Natural History

English name	Species	Deciduous/Evergreen	Continent of origin
strawberry tree	*Arbutus unedo*	evergreen	Europe
sycamore ('plane')	*Acer pseudoplatanus*	deciduous	Europe, W Asia
tamarack	*Larix laricina*	deciduous	N America
tree of heaven	*Ailanthus altissima*	deciduous	China
tulip tree	*Liriodendron tulipfera*	deciduous	America
walnut, black	*Juglans nigra*	deciduous	America
walnut, common	*Juglans regia*	deciduous	Europe, Asia
whitebeam	*Sorbus aria*	deciduous	Europe
willow, pussy (or goat willow or sallow willow)	*Salix caprea*	deciduous	Europe, Asia
willow, weeping	*Salix babylonica*	deciduous	Asia
willow, white	*Salix alba*	deciduous	Europe
yew, common	*Taxus baccata*	evergreen	N temperate regions

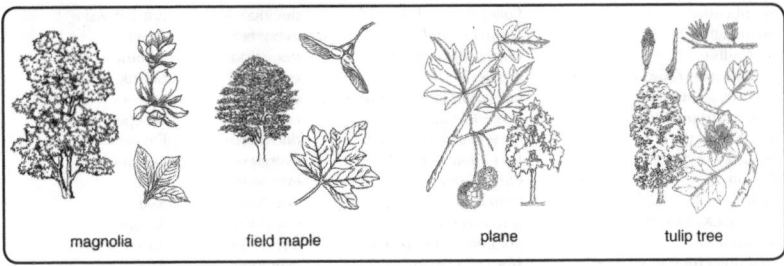

magnolia · field maple · plane · tulip tree

Trees (tropical)

Name	Species	Deciduous/Evergreen	Continent of origin
African tulip tree	*Spathodea campanulata*	evergreen	Africa
almond, tropical	*Terminalia catappa*	deciduous	Asia
angel's trumpet	*Brugmansia × candida*	deciduous	S America
autograph tree	*Clusia rosea*	evergreen	Asia
avocado	*Persea americana*	evergreen	C America, Mexico
bamboo	*Schizostachyum glauchifolium*	deciduous	America
banana	*Musa × paradisiaca*	plant dies after fruiting	Asia
banyan	*Ficus benghalensis*	evergreen	Asia
baobab (or dead rat's tree)	*Adansonia digitata*	deciduous	Africa
beach heliotrope	*Argusia argentea*	evergreen	S America
bo tree	*Ficus religiosa*	deciduous	Asia
bombax	*Bombax ceiba*	deciduous	Asia
bottlebrush	*Callistemon citrinus*	evergreen	Australia
breadfruit	*Artocarpus altilis*	evergreen	Asia
brownea	*Brownea macrophylla*	evergreen	C America
calabash	*Crescentia cujete*	evergreen	America
candlenut	*Aleurites moluccana*	evergreen	Asia
cannonball	*Courouptia guianensis*	evergreen	S America
chinaberry (or bead tree)	*Melia azedarach*	deciduous	Asia
Christmas-berry	*Schinus terebinthifolius*	evergreen	America
coconut palm	*Cocus nucifera*	evergreen	Asia
coffee tree	*Coffea liberica*	evergreen	Africa
Cook pine	*Araucaria columnaris*	evergreen	America
coral tree	*Erythrina coralloides*	deciduous	C America
coral shower	*Cassia grandis*	deciduous	Asia
cotton, wild	*Cochlospermum vitifolium*	deciduous	C and S America
crape myrtle	*Lagerstroemia indica*	deciduous	Asia
date palm	*Phoenix dactylifera*	evergreen	Asia and Africa
dragon tree	*Dracaena draco*	evergreen	Africa (Canary Is)
durian	*Durio zibethinus*	evergreen	Asia
ebony	*Diospyros ebenum*	evergreen	Asia
elephant's-ear	*Enderolobium cyclocarpum*	deciduous	S America

Name	Species	Deciduous/ Evergreen	Continent of origin
flame tree	*Delonix regia*	deciduous	Africa (Madagascar)
gold tree	*Cybistax donnell-smithii*	deciduous	Asia
golden rain	*Koelreuteria paniculata*	deciduous	Asia
golden shower	*Cassia fistula*	deciduous	Asia
guava	*Psidium guajeva*	evergreen	S America
ironwood (or casuarina)	*Casuarina equisetifolia*	deciduous	Australia and Asia
jacaranda	*Jacaranda mimosifolia*	deciduous	S America
jackfruit (or jack)	*Artocarpus heterophyllus*	evergreen	Asia
kapok tree	*Ceiba pentandra*	deciduous	Old and New World tropics
koa	*Acacia koa*	evergreen	Oceania (Hawaii)
lipstick tree	*Bixa orellanna*	evergreen	America
lychee	*Litchi chinensis*	evergreen	China
macadamia nut	*Macadamia integrifolia*	evergreen	Australia
mahogany	*Swietenia mahogoni*	evergreen	S America
mango	*Mangifera indica*	evergreen	Asia
mesquite	*Prosopis pallida*	evergreen	America
monkeypod (or rain tree)	*Albizia saman*	evergreen	S America
Norfolk Island pine	*Araucaria heterophylla*	evergreen	Oceania (Norfolk I)
octopus tree	*Schefflera actinophylla*	evergreen	Australia
ohi' a lehua	*Metrosideros collina*	evergreen	Oceania (Hawaii)
pandanus (or screw pine)	*Pandanus tectorius*	evergreen	Oceania
paperbark tree	*Melaleuca quinquenervia*	evergreen	Australia
powderpuff	*Calliandra haematocephala*	evergreen	S America
royal palm	*Roystonea regia*	evergreen	America (Cuba)
sandalwood	*Santalum album*	deciduous	Asia
sand-box tree	*Hura crepitans*	deciduous	Americas
sausage tree	*Kigelia pinnata*	evergreen	Africa
scrambled egg tree	*Cassia glauca*	evergreen	Americas
Surinam cherry	*Eugenia uniflora*	evergreen	S America
teak tree	*Tectona grandis*	evergreen	Asia
tiger's claw	*Erythrina variegata*	deciduous	Asia
yellow oleander	*Thevetia peruviana*	evergreen	Americas (W Indies)

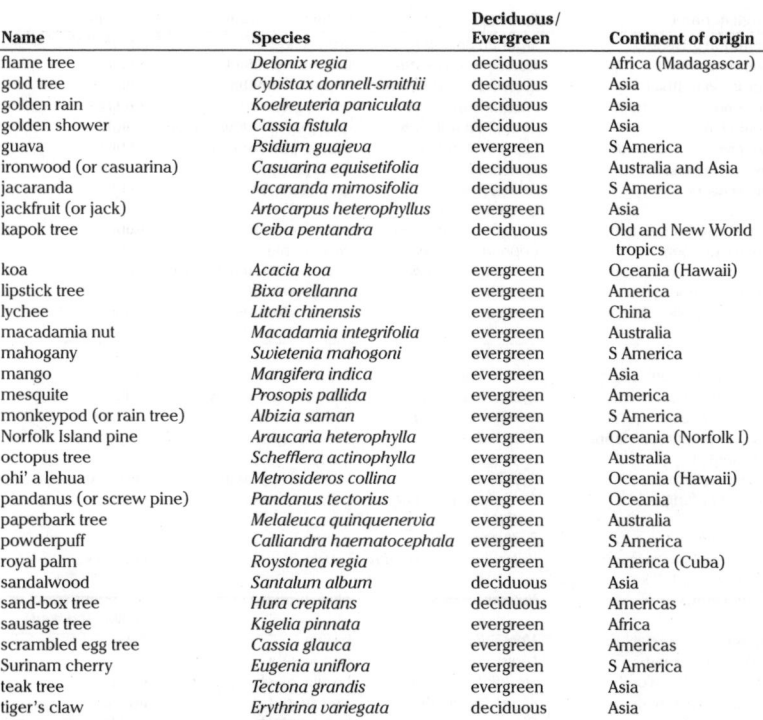

coconut palm   kapok tree   monkey puzzle

Fungi

English name	Species	Colour	Edibility
base toadstool (or ugly toadstool)	*Lactarius necator*	green, brown	poisonous
beautiful clavaria	*Ramaria formosa*	yellow, ochre, red, purple	poisonous
beefsteak fungus	*Fistulina hepatica*	red	edible
blusher	*Amanita fubescens*	red, brown	poisonous (raw) or edible (cooked)
brain mushroom	*Gyromitra esculenta*	chestnut, dark brown	poisonous
buckler agaric	*Entoloma clypeatum*	grey, brown	edible
Caesar's mushroom	*Amanita caesarea*	red, yellow	edible
chanterelle	*Cantharellus cibarius*	yellow, ochre	excellent
clean mycena	*Mycena pura*	purple	poisonous
clouded agaric	*Lepista nebularis*	grey, brown	poisonous
common earthball	*Scleroderma aurantium*	ochre, yellow, brown	poisonous

Natural History

English name	Species	Colour	Edibility
common grisette	*Amanita vaginita*	grey, yellow	edible
common morel	*Morchella esculenta*	light brown, black	edible
common puffball	*Lycoperdon perlatum*	white, cream, brown	edible
common stinkhorn	*Phallus impudicus*	white, green	inedible
death cap	*Amanita phalloides*	grey, green, yellow, brown	deadly
deceiver, common laccaria	*Laccaria laccata*	purple, pink, orange	edible
destroying angel	*Amanita virosa*	white, brown	deadly
dingy agaric	*Tricholoma portentosum*	grey, black, yellow, lilac	edible
dryad's saddle	*Polyporus squamosus*	yellow, brown	edible
fairies' bonnets	*Coprinus disseminatus*	grey, purple	worthless
fairy-ring champignon	*Marasmius oreades*	beige, ochre, red, brown	edible
field mushroom	*Agaricus campestris*	white, brown	excellent
firwood agaric	*Tricholoma auratum*	green, yellow, brown	edible
fly agaric	*Amanita muscaria*	red, orange, white	poisonous
garlic marosmius	*Marosmius scorodonius*	red, brown	edible
gypsy mushroom	*Rozites caperata*	yellow, ochre	edible
hedgehog mushroom	*Hydnum repandum*	white, beige, yellow	edible
honey fungus	*Armillaria mellea*	honey, brown, red	inedible
horn of plenty (or trumpet of the dead)	*Craterellus cornucopiodes*	brown, black	very good
horse mushroom	*Agaricus arvensis*	white, yellow, ochre	very good
Jew's ear fungus	*Auricularia auricula judae*	yellow, brown	edible
larch boletus	*Suillus grevillei*	yellow	edible
liberty cap (or 'magic mushroom')	*Psilocybe semilanceata*	brown	poisonous
lurid boletus	*Boletus luridus*	olive, brown, yellow	poisonous (raw) or edible (cooked)
morel	*Morchella*	brown	good
naked mushroom	*Lepista nuda*	purple, brown	edible
old man of the woods	*Strobilomyces floccopus*	brown, black	edible
orange-peel fungus	*Aleuria aurantia*	orange, red	edible
oyster mushroom	*Pleurotus ostreatus*	brown, black, grey, blue, purple	edible
panther cap (or false blusher)	*Amanita pantherina*	brown, ochre, grey, white	poisonous
parasol mushroom	*Macrolepiota procera*	beige, ochre, brown	excellent
penny-bun fungus	*Boletus edulis*	chestnut brown	excellent
Périgord truffle	*Tuber melanosporum*	black, red-brown	excellent
Piedmont truffle	*Tuber magnatum*	white	edible
purple blewits	*Tricholomopsis rutilans*	yellow, red	edible
saffron milk cap	*Lactorius delicioses*	orange, red	poisonous (raw) or edible (cooked)
St George's mushroom	*Calocybe gambosa*	white, cream	edible
Satan's boletus	*Boletus satanus*	grey	poisonous (raw) or edible (cooked)
scarlet-stemmed boletus	*Boletus calopus*	grey, brown	poisonous
shaggy ink cap (or lawyer's wig)	*Coprinus comatus*	white, ochre	edible
sickener (or emetic russula)	*Russula emetica*	pink, red	poisonous
stinking russula	*Russula foetens*	ochre, brown	poisonous
stout agaric	*Amanita spissa*	grey, brown	edible
strong scented garlic	*Tricholoma saponaceum*	grey, green, brown	poisonous

chanterelle

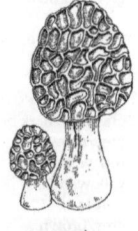

morel

common puffball

common stinkhorn

English name	Species	Colour	Edibility
sulphur tuft (or clustered woodlover)	*Hypholoma fasciculare*	yellow, red, brown	poisonous
summer truffle	*Tuber aestivum*	dark brown	very good
white truffle	*Tuber magnatum*	cream, pale brown	excellent
winter fungus (or velvet shank)	*Flammulina velutipes*	yellow, brown, ochre	edible
wood agaric	*Collybia dryophila*	yellow, brown, rust	edible
wood mushroom	*Agaricus sylvaticus*	grey, red, brown	edible
woolly milk-cap (or griping toadstool)	*Lactarius torminosus*	pink, brown	poisonous
yellow stainer	*Agaricus xanthodermus*	white, yellow, grey	poisonous
yellow-brown boletus (or slippery jack)	*Suillus luteus*	yellow, brown	edible

Natural History

Animal Kingdom

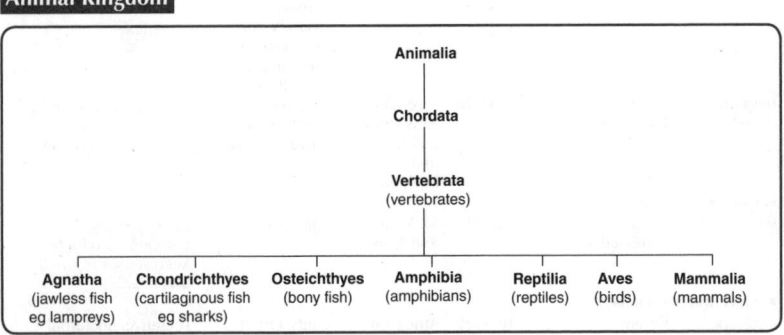

Animalia

Chordata

Vertebrata
(vertebrates)

Agnatha	Chondrichthyes	Osteichthyes	Amphibia	Reptilia	Aves	Mammalia
(jawless fish eg lampreys)	(cartilaginous fish eg sharks)	(bony fish)	(amphibians)	(reptiles)	(birds)	(mammals)

Mammals

Mammals are the group of animals to which humans belong. They are characterized by the presence of mammary glands in the female which produce milk on which the young can be nourished. They are divided into monotremes or egg-laying mammals; marsupials in which the young are born at an early stage of development and then grow outside the mother's womb, often in a pouch; and placental mammals in which the young are nourished in the womb by the mother's blood and are born at a late stage of development. A crucial aspect of mammals is the fact that their hair and skin glands allow them to regulate their temperatures from within, ie they are endothermic (warm-blooded). This confers on them a greater adaptability to more varied environments than that of reptiles. There are over 4000 species of mammals, most of which are terrestrial, the exceptions being species of bat which have developed the ability to fly, and cetaceans (including dolphins, porpoises and whales) which lead aquatic existences.

Generally, the size given in the table denotes length from head to tip of tail. To convert from cm to inches, multiply by 0.3937.

Name	Family/ Species	Size (cm)	Distribution	Food	Special features
■ **Monotremes**					
echidna, long-beaked	Species *Zaglossus bruijni*	45–90	New Guinea	earthworms	prominent beak; short spines scattered among fur
echidna, short-beaked	Species *Tachyglossidae aculeatus*	30–45	Australia, Tasmania and New Guinea	ants, termites	fur covered in protective spines; known to live up to 50 years in captivity
platypus	Family *Ornithorhynchidae*	45–60	E Australia and Tasmania	invertebrates, larvae	noted for its duck-like snout
■ **Marsupials**					
bandicoot	Family Peramelidae	15–56	Australia and New Guinea	insectivorous and omnivorous	highest reproductive rate of all marsupials
kangaroo	Family Macropodidae	to 165	Australia and New Guinea	grasses, plants	most popularly known of Australian mammals, noted for its bounding motion and prominent female pouch; includes all species of wallaby

Natural History

Name	Family/ Species	Size (cm)	Distribution	Food	Special features
kangaroo, rat	Family Macropodidae	28.4–30	Australia and New Guinea	grasses, plants	rabbit-sized version of its larger namesake
koala	Family Phascolarctidae	78	E Australia	eucalyptus leaves	marsupial with popular reputation; at one time seemed threatened with extinction but intensive management has significantly revived population numbers
mole, marsupial	Family Notoryctidae	13–15	Australia	insects, larvae	only Australian mammal that has specialized in burrowing
opossum	Family Didelphidae	7–55	C and S America	earthworms, fruit, insects, small vertebrates, crustaceans, fish, frogs, reptiles	generally known for its dreadful smell
possum, brushtail	Family Phalangeridae	34–70	Australia, New Guinea, Solomon Is and New Zealand	leaves, fruit, bark, eggs, invertebrates	the most commonly encountered of all Australian mammals
wallaby ▶ kangaroo					
wombat	Family Vombatidae	80–115	SE Australia and Tasmania	grasses	poor eyesight compensated for by keen senses of smell and hearing

■ **Placental mammals**

Name	Family/ Species	Size (cm)	Distribution	Food	Special features
aardvark	Family Orycteropodidae	105–130	Africa S of the Sahara	ants, termites	secretive, nocturnal creature; characterized by its long, tubular snout
anteater	Family Myrmecophagidae	16–22	C and S America	ants and sometimes termites	noted, particularly the giant anteater, for its elongated snout
antelope, dwarf	Tribe Neotragini	45–55	Africa	leaves, grass, fruit, buds	unusual among hoofed mammals in that the female is larger than the male
armadillo	Family Dasypodidae	12.5–100	southern N America, C and S America	vertebrates, insects, fungi, tubers, fruit, carrion	noted, particularly the giant armadillo, for its protective suit of armour
ass	Subgenus *Asinus*	200–210	Africa and Asia	grass, leaves	renowned as a beast of burden
baboon and mandrill	Genus *Papio*	56–80	Africa	fruit, plants, insects, small mammals	able to walk over long distances
badger	Family Mustelidae	50–100	Africa, Europe, Asia and N America	vertebrates, invertebrates, fruit, roots, earthworms	mainly nocturnal; European species characterized by its distinctive black and white markings
bat	Order Chiroptera	15–200 (wing-span)	worldwide except for the Arctic and Antarctic	insects, vertebrates, fish, fruit	the only vertebrate, except for birds, capable of sustained flight; noted for its powers of echolocation and tendency to cluster in large numbers
bear, black	Species *Ursus americanus*	130–180	N America	omnivorous	smaller and more secretive than the brown or grizzly bear, its greater ability to adapt has helped it to survive in greater numbers

Name	Family/ Species	Size (cm)	Distribution	Food	Special features
bear, grizzly (or brown bear)	Species *Ursus arctos*	200–280	NW America and former USSR	omnivorous	noted for its size (up to half a ton); much reduced population due to hunting, loss of natural habitat
beaver	Genus *Castor*	80–120	N America, Asia and Europe	plants, wood	renowned for its industry and ability to construct dams and lodges in streams and ponds
beaver, mountain	Family Aplondontidae	30–41	Pacific Coast of Canada and USA	leaves, plant materials	land-dwelling and burrowing animal; causes great damage to forest areas
bison, American	Species *Bison bison*	to 380	N America	grazing fodder	once numbered in millions on the prairies of N America, now survives only in parks and refuges
bison, European	Species *Bison bonasus*	to 290	former USSR	grazing fodder	became extinct in the wild in 1919, but has now been re-established in parts of the former USSR
boar	Family Suidae	58–210	Europe, Africa and Asia	plants, larvae, frogs, mice, earthworms	wild pig; characteristically ugly appearance; intelligent and highly adaptable; includes species of warthog
buffalo, wild water	Species *Bubalus arnee*	240–280	SE Asia	grazing fodder	adept at moving through the muddy areas which they inhabit
bushbaby	Subfamily Galaginae	12–32	Africa and S Asia	insects, fruit, gum	highly agile, arboreal creature
bushbuck	Species *Tragelaphus scriptus*	110–145	Africa S of the Sahara	grazing fodder	occupies habitats with dense cover; dark brown or chestnut coat with white markings
camel	Species *Camelus bactrianus*	190–230 (height of hump)	Mongolia	plants, vegetation	two humps
capybara	Family Hydrochoeridae	106–134	S America	grass	largest living rodent; lives in groups by the edge of water; traditionally hunted for its meat and skin
cat	Family Felidae	20–400	worldwide	carnivorous	acute sense of vision and smell
cattle	Family Bovidae	180–200	worldwide	grass	agricultural animal existing in both long-horned and polled or hornless breeds
chamois	Species *Rupicapra rupicapra*	125–135	Europe and Asia	grass, leaves, lichen	has adapted to alpine and subalpine conditions and to life on snowy mountains; part of its defence mechanism in fighting is its evasive running and dodging movement
cheetah	Family Felidae	112–135	Africa	hoofed animals up to 40kg, such as gazelles, impala, wilde-beest calves	the fastest of all land animals, reaching speeds of 100kph/62mph
chimpanzee	Genus *Pan*	70–85	W and C Africa	fruit, leaves, seeds, insects, small mammals	most intelligent of the great apes; recent studies suggest that adults teach their offspring how to use tools

Natural History

Name	Family/ Species	Size (cm)	Distribution	Food	Special features
chinchilla	Family Chinchillidae	25	S America	grazing fodder	widely hunted as food and for its valuable fur
civet	Family Viverridae	33–84	Africa and Asia	fruit, small mammals, birds, rodents, insects, small reptiles	cat-like carnivore; nocturnal hunter; economic source of civet oil
colugo	Genus *Cynocephalus*	33–42	SE Asia	leaves, shoots, buds, flowers	also known as flying lemur, a reference to the membrane which stretches from its neck to the tips of its fingers, toes and tail, allowing it to glide from tree to tree
coyote	Species *Canis latrans*	70–97	N America	squirrels, rabbits, mice, antelope, deer, mountain sheep	makes unique howling sound; regarded as agricultural pest for its attacks on farm animals, but also kills agricultural vermin
coypu	Species *Myocastor coypu*	50	S America	freshwater plants	highly aquatic rodent; burrows into banks; beaver-like qualities
deer	Family Cervidae	41–152	N and S America, Europe and Asia	grass, shoots, twigs, leaves, flowers, fruit	distinguished in the male by the presence of antlers, most characteristically used to attack other males during the rutting period; species include red deer, reindeer, waipiti, and the moose or elk
dingo	Species *Canis dingo*	150	Australasia	rabbits, lizards, grasshoppers, wild pigs, kangaroos	history of the dingo in Australia dates back 8000 years; descendant of the wolf; lives in packs
dog	Species *Canis familiaris*	20–75	worldwide	carnivorous	first animal to be domesticated; c.400 domestic breeds
dolphin	Family Delphinidae	120–400	worldwide	fish, squid	renowned for grace, agility, intelligence; highly developed social organization and communication systems
dolphin, river	Family Platanistidae	210–260	SE Asia and S America	fish, shrimp, squid, octopus	virtually blind, but with highly sensitive system of echolocation
dormouse	Family Gliridae	6–19	Europe, Africa, Turkey, Asia and Japan	omnivorous	halfway between mouse and squirrel both in form and behaviour
dromedary	Species *Camelus dromedarius*	190–230 (height of hump)	SW Asia, N Africa and Australia	plants, vegetation	domesticated camel with one hump; important as a beast of burden, and source of wool and milk
duiker	Subfamily Cephalophinae	55–72	Africa S of the Sahara	leaves, fruit, shoots, buds, seeds, bark, small birds, rodents	named after its habit of diving into cover when disturbed
eland	Genus *Taurotragus*	250–350	Africa	grazing fodder	elegant and highly mobile spiral-horned antelope; experiments in the agricultural domestication of the common eland have taken place in Africa

Name	Family/ Species	Size (cm)	Distribution	Food	Special features
elephant, African	Species *Loxodonta africana*	600–750	Africa S of the Sahara	grass, plants, leaves, twigs, flowers, fruit	largest living land mammal, with distinctive trunk and large tusks and ears; drastically reduced population
fox	Family Canidae	24–100	N and S America, Europe, Asia and Africa	rodents, birds, invertebrates, fruit, fish, rabbits, hares, earthworms	justified reputation for cunning, intelligence and resourcefulness
gazelle	Genus *Gazella*	122–166	Africa	leaves, grass, fruit	birth peaks adapted to coincide with abundance of feeding vegetation during the spring and early rains
gerbil	Subfamily Gerbillinae	6–7.5	Africa and Asia	seeds, fruits, leaves, stems, roots, bulbs, insects, snails	defence mechanisms include colour of skin closely allied to the environment for hiding purposes, wide field of vision, and the ability to hear low frequency sounds such as the beating of owls' wings; domesticated form is the Mongolian gerbil often kept as a pet
gerenuk	Genus *Litocranius*	140–160	Africa	leaves, shoots, flowers, fruit	graceful, delicate creature; rises on hind legs in order to extend its reach when feeding on the leaves of tall shrubs and bushes
gibbon	Family Hylobatidae	45–65	SE Asia	fruit, leaves, invertebrates	renowned for spectacular ability to move among trees using swinging movements of arms; loud and sophisticated voice
giraffe	Species *Giraffa camelopardalis*	380–470	Africa S of the Sahara	leaves, shoots, herbs, flowers, fruit, seed	distinguished by its mottled coat and the length of its neck which allows it to feed on foliage which is out of the reach of smaller mammals
gnu	Genus *Connochaetes*	194–209	Africa	grazing fodder	characterized by massive head and mane, bearded throat, and tail which reaches almost to the ground
goat, mountain	Species *Oreamnos americanus*	to 175	N America	grazing fodder	large, ponderous rock climber, adapted to living in snowy mountains of N America
goat, wild	Species *Capra aegagrus*	130–140	S Europe, Middle East and Asia	grazing fodder	subspecies includes domestic goat
gopher	Family Geomyidae	12–22.5	N America	plant materials	highly adapted to its burrowing and subterranean existence
gorilla	Genus *Gorilla*	150–170	C Africa	leaves and stems	largest living primate; the most intelligent of land animals (after humans); unjustified reputation for ferocity, perhaps based on its size, and habit of beating its chest in a show of aggression

Name	Family/ Species	Size (cm)	Distribution	Food	Special features
guinea pig	Genus *Cavia*	28	S America	herbs, grasses	tailless rodent; domesticated form is the *Cavia porcellus*
hamster	Subfamily Cricetinae	5.3–10.2	Europe, Middle East, former USSR and China	mainly seeds, shoots, root vegetables	familiar Western pet, but aggressive towards own species in the wild
hare	Genus *Lepus*	40–76	N and S America, Africa, Europe, Asia and Arctic	grass, herbs, plants, bark twigs	well-developed ability to run from predators; species include jack-rabbits and the arctic hare
hare, Patagonian	Genus *Dolichotis*	45	S America	grasses, herbs	unusual characteristic in a mammal of being strictly monogamous
hartebeest	Genus *Alcelaphus*	195–200	Africa	grass, vegetation	distinctive long face, sloping back
hedgehog	Subfamily Erinaceinae	10–15	Europe, Asia and Africa	earthworms, beetles, slugs, earwigs, caterpillars	ability to curl up and use prickly, spined back as protection
hippo-potamus	Family Hippopotamidae	150–345	Africa	terrestrial vegetation	large, heavy and barrel-shaped with short stumpy legs; wallows in water
horse	Subgenus *Equus*	200–210	worldwide in domesticated form; Asia, N and S America and Australia in the wild	grass, leaves	historically useful as a beast of burden and means of transport, and for agricultural, military and recreational purposes
hyena	Family Hyaeninae	85–140	Africa and Asia	carrion, mammals, insects, small vertebrates, eggs, fruit, vegetables	scavenger and hunter, with highly developed systems of communication; family includes the aardwolf
ibex	Species *Capra ibex*	85–143	C Europe, Asia and Africa	grazing fodder	large-horned creature saved from extinction in C Europe
impala	Genus *Aepyceros*	128–142	Africa	grass, leaves, flowers, fruit, seeds	attractive, graceful creature with fawn and mahogany coat; females and young gather in large herds; male has lyre-shaped horns
jackal	Genus *Canis*	65–106	Africa, SE Europe and Asia	fruit, invertebrates, reptiles, birds, small mammals, carrion	unfair reputation as cowardly scavenger
jaguar	Species *Panthera onca*	112–185	C and S America	deer, monkeys, sloths, birds, turtles, frogs, fish, small rodents	largest cat to be found in the Americas
jerboa	Family Dipodidae	4–26	N Africa, Turkey, Middle East and C Asia	seeds, vegetation, insects	long hind legs allow movement by hopping and jumping
lemming	Tribe Lemmini	10–11	N America and Eurasia	plants, bulbs, roots, mosses	Norway lemming is noted for its mass migration which sometimes results in drowning
lemur	Family Lemuridae	12–70	Madagascar, Africa	flowers, leaves, bamboo shoots	mainly nocturnal and arboreal

lemur, flying ► colugo

Name	Family/ Species	Size (cm)	Distribution	Food	Special features
leopard	Species *Panthera pardus*	100–190	Africa and Asia	mainly small mammals, birds	opportunistic, nocturnal hunter; adept at climbing trees
lion	Species *Panthera leo*	240–300	Africa and Asia	meat of animals which weigh 50–500kg	known as the 'King of Beasts'; the most socially organized of the cat family
llama	Species *Lama glama*	230–400	S America	plants and vegetation	S American beast of burden
lynx	Species *Felis lynx*	67–110	Europe and N America	rodents, small hoofed mammals	lives in cold northern latitudes; well adapted to travelling through deep snow
macaque	Genus *Macaca*	38–70	Asia and N Africa	mainly fruit, insects, leaves, crops, small animals	heavily built and partly terrestrial genus of monkey; includes the Rhesus monkey adapted to life in the Himalayas, and the Barbary apes imported into Gibraltar in the 18c
marmoset	Family Callitrichidae	17.5–40	S America	fruit, flowers, nectar, gum, frogs, snails, lizards, spiders, insects	small, colourful, squirrel-like monkeys; includes species of tamarins
marten	Genus *Martes*	30–75	N America, Europe and Asia	mice, squirrels, rabbits, grouse, fruit, nuts	one species, the fisher, unique for its ability to penetrate the quilled defences of the porcupine
mole	Family Talpidae	2.4–7.5	Europe, Asia and N America	earthworms, insect larvae, slugs	almost exclusively subterranean existence
mongoose	Family Viverridae	24–58	Africa, S Asia and SW Europe	vertebrates, insects, fruit, snakes	some species live in social groups; often seen in the tripod position, ie standing up on hind legs and tail
monkey, capuchin	Family Cebidae	25–63	S America	insects, fruit, leaves, seeds, other small mammals	mainly lives in social groupings for the purposes of defence, foraging for food, and rearing young
mouse ▶ rat					
narwhal	Species *Monodon monoceros*	400–500	former USSR, N America and Greenland	shrimp, cod, flounder	distinctive single tusk in the male can reach lengths of up to 3m
okapi	Species *Okapia johnstoni*	190–200	C Africa	mainly leaves and shoots	secretive and elusive creature; strange-looking mixture of giraffe and zebra
orang-utan	Species *Pongo pygmaeus*	150	forests of N Sumatra and Borneo	fruit, leaves, insects	sparse covering of long red-brown hair; adults have large naked fatty folds around face; life-span of 35 years in the wild; much diminished population
otter	Subfamily Lutrinae	40–123	N and S America, Europe, Asia and Africa	frogs, crabs, fish, aquatic birds	only truly amphibious members of the general weasel family; greatly reduced population due to persecution and loss of natural habitat
panda, giant	Species *Ailuropoda melanoleuca*	130–150	China	bamboo	rare; poor breeder; the success rate of breeding in captivity has been extremely low

Name	Family/ Species	Size (cm)	Distribution	Food	Special features
polar bear	Species *Ursus maritimus*	250–300	N polar regions	mainly seals, carcasses of large marine animals	unique for its large size, white coat and adaptation to aquatic living
porcupine (New World)	Family Erethizontidae	30–86	N and S America	bark, roots, shoots, leaves, berries, seeds, nuts, flowers	arboreal version of Old World porcupine; excellent climber
porcupine (Old World)	Family Hystricidae	37–47	Africa and Asia	roots, bulbs, fruit, berries	heavily quilled and spiny body
porpoise	Family Phocoenidae	120–150	N temperate zone, W Indo-Pacific, temperate and sub-antarctic waters of S America and Auckland Is	fish, squid, crustaceans	large range of sounds for the purpose of echolocation
puma	Species *Felis concolor*	105–196	N and S America	deer, rodents	wide-ranging hunter; includes subspecies cougar
rabbit, European	Genus *Oryctolagus*	38–58	Europe, Africa, Australia, New Zealand and S America	grass, herbs, roots, plants, bark	burrowing creature; opportunistic animal in widespread environment; noted for its breeding capacity; domesticated rabbits descended from this genus
raccoon	Genus *Procyon*	55	N, S and C America	frogs, fish, birds, eggs, fruit, nuts, small rodents, insects, corn	black masked face; distinctive ringed tail; reputation for mischief
rat (New World)	Subfamily Hesperomyinae	5–8	N and S America	seeds, grain, plants, nuts, fruit, fungi, insects, crustaceans, fish	numerous species adapted to living in all possible forms of habitat
rat (Old World)	Subfamily Murinae	4.5–8.2	Europe, Asia, Africa and Australia	omnivorous	large number of species; one of the most successful mammals at adapting to any form of environment
reedbuck	Genus *Redunca*	110–176	Africa	grass, leaves, crops	graceful, elegant animal; distinctive whistling sounds, leaping movements
rhinoceros	Family Rhinocerotidae	250–400	Africa and tropical Asia	plant foliage	name derives from horn growing from snout; use of the horn for commercial purposes has brought the animal to the verge of extinction
seal	Family Phocidae	117–490	mainly polar, subpolar and temperate seas	fish, squid, crustaceans	graceful swimmer and diver; some species have been the object of controversial culling procedures
sheep, American bighorn	Species *Ovis canadensis*	168–186	N America	grazing fodder	large horns and body similar to an ibex; clings to the vicinity of cliffs
sheep, barbary	Genus *Ammotragus*	155–165	N Africa	grazing fodder	large head and horns up to 84cm in length
sheep, blue	Genus *Pseudois*	91 (shoulder height)	Asia	grazing fodder	blue coat; curved horns

Name	Family/ Species	Size (cm)	Distribution	Food	Special features
shrew	Family Soricidae	3.5–4.8	Europe, Asia, Africa, N America and northern S America	insects, earthworms	generally poor eyesight compensated for by acute sense of smell and hearing
shrew, elephant	Order Macroscelidea	10.4–29.4	Africa	invertebrates, plants, fruit, seeds	distinctive creature with beady eyes, long pointed snout and short legs
skunk	Subfamily Mephitinae	40–68	N and S America	insects, small mammals, eggs, fruit	evil-smelling defence mechanism; major carrier of rabies
sloth, three-toed	Family Bradypodidae	56–60	S America	leaves	smaller version of the two-toed sloth; slightly more active both by day and night
sloth, two-toed	Family Megalonychidae	58–70	S America	leaves	arboreal, nocturnal creature noted for the slowness of its movement
springbok	Genus *Antidorcas*	96–115	S Africa	mainly grass	gregarious creature which migrates in herds of tens of thousands
springhare	Family Pedetidae	36–43	S Africa	grass and soil	burrowing creature like a miniature kangaroo; moves usually by hopping; hunted by humans as a source of food and for its skin
squirrel	Family Sciuridae	6.6–10	N and S America, Europe, Africa and Asia	nuts, seeds, plants, insects	large number of species living in a variety of environments and including arboreal, burrowing and flying creatures; species include the marmot and chipmunk; grey squirrel noted for its ability to strip bark and damage young trees
tapir	Genus *Tapirus*	180–250	C and S America and SE Asia	grass, leaves, vegetation, buds, fruit, shoots	strange-looking, nocturnal mammal with distinctive snout; all species exist in vastly reduced numbers
tarsier	Genus *Tarsius*	11–14	islands of SE Asia	insects, lizards, bats, birds, snakes	proportionally large eyes; extraordinary ability to rotate neck
tiger	Species *Panthera tigris*	220–360	India, Manchuria, China and Indonesia	hoofed animals, eg deer and wild pigs	solitary hunters; stalk for prey
vole	Tribe Microtini	10–11	N America, Europe, Asia and the Arctic	grasses, seeds, aquatic plants, insects	population fluctuates in regular patterns or cycles
walrus	Species *Odobenus rosmarus*	250–320	Arctic seas	marine molluscs and invertebrates	characterized by its thick folds of skin and twin tusks
waterbuck	Species *Kobus ellipsiprymnus*	177–235	Africa	grasses, reeds, rushes, aquatic vegetation	shaggy coat and heavy gait; gives off an oily, detectable secretion on its coat
weasel	Subfamily Mustelinae	15–55	Arctic, N and S America, Europe, Asia and Africa	rodents, rabbits, birds, insects, lizards, frogs	certain species have been exploited for their fur, eg mink, ermine; includes species of ferret and polecat
whale, beaked	Family Ziphiidae	400–1 280	worldwide	mainly squid	named after its distinctive, protuberant, dolphin-like beak

Natural History

Name	Family/Species	Size (cm)	Distribution	Food	Special features
whale, blue	Species *Balaenoptera musculus*	to 3000	Arctic and subtropics	krill	largest living animal
whale, grey	Species *Eschrichtius robustus*	1190–1520	N Pacific	fish, crustaceans, molluscs	long migration to breed, from the Arctic to the ocean floor subtropics; one of the most heavily barnacled of the whale species
whale, humpback	Species *Megaptera novaeangliae*	1600	worldwide	mainly fish, krill	highly acrobatic, with wide range of sounds; migrates between Arctic and mid-Pacific
whale, killer	Species *Orcinus orca*	900–1000	worldwide in cool coastal waters	fish, squid, birds, and other marine mammals	toothed whale; dorsal fin narrow and vertical; co-operative and highly co-ordinated hunter, with triangular fins and distinctive white and black colouring; not generally a threat to humans
whale, long-finned pilot	Species *Globicephala melaena*	600	temperate waters of the N Atlantic	cuttlefish, squid	best known for mysterious mass strandings on beaches
whale, sperm	Species *Physeter catodon*	to 2070	widespread in temperate and tropical waters	mainly squid	largest of the toothed whales; prodigious deep sea diver
whale, white (or beluga)	Species *Delphinapterus leucas*	300–500	N Russia, N America and Greenland	crustaceans, worms, molluscs	distinctive white skin; wide range of bodily, facial and vocal expressions
wild cat	Species *Felis silvestris*	50–80	Europe, India and Africa	small mammals, birds	domestic cat may be descended from the African wild cat
wolf, grey	Species *Canis lupus*	100–150	N America, Europe, Asia and Middle East	moose, deer, caribou	noted for hunting in packs
wolverine	Species *Gulo gulo*	to 83	Arctic and subarctic regions	small mammals, deer, caribou, birds, plants, carrion	heavily built; long, dark coat of fur; adapted for hunting in soft, deep snow
zebra	Subgenus *Hippotigris*	215–230	Africa	grass, leaves	famous for black and white stripes

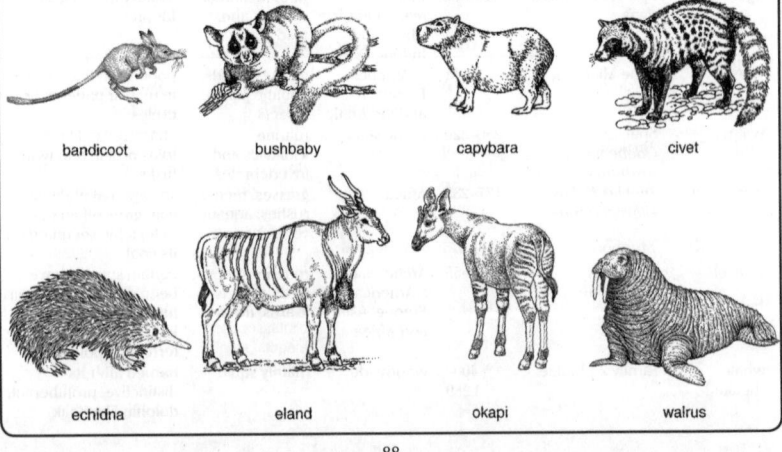

bandicoot   bushbaby   capybara   civet

echidna   eland   okapi   walrus

Mammals – record holders

Largest	The blue whale, up to 33m/110ft long and weighing up to 190 tonnes, is the largest known mammal. The largest existing land mammal is the male African elephant, standing up to 3.7m/12ft at the shoulder and weighing up to 7 tonnes.
Tallest	The giraffe stands up to 5.5m/18ft high.
Smallest	Savi's pygmy shrew has a body length of 3.6–5.3cm/1.4–2.1in and weighs 1.2–2.7g/0.4–0.9oz.
Fastest on land	The cheetah can reach 103kph/64mph, but only in short bursts. The pronghorn can maintain speeds of 50kph/31mph for several kilometres.
Most prolific breeder	A North American meadow vole produced 17 litters in a single year (4–9 babies per litter).
Most widespread	Humans are the most widely distributed mammals, closely followed by the house mouse and brown rat, which have accompanied humans to all parts of the world.

Natural History

Length of pregnancy in some mammals

Animal	Gestation period*	Animal	Gestation period*
camel	406	kangaroo	40
cat	62	lion	108
chimpanzee	237	mink	50
cow	280	monkey, rhesus	164
dog	62	mouse	21
dolphin	276	opossum	13
elephant, African	640	orang-utan	246–275
ferret	42	pig	113
fox	52	rabbit	32
giraffe	395–425	rat	21
goat	151	reindeer	215–245
guinea pig	68	seal, northern fur	350
hamster	16	sheep	148
hedgehog	35–40	skunk	62
horse	337	squirrel, grey	44
human	266	tiger	105–109
hyena	110	whale	365

* average number of days

Birds

Birds are warm-blooded, egg-laying, and, in the case of adults, feathered vertebrates of the class Aves; there are approximately 8600 species classified into 29 Orders and 181 Families. Birds are constructed for flight. The body is streamlined to reduce air resistance, the fore-limbs are modified as feathered wings, and the skeletal structure, heart and wing muscles, centre of gravity, and lung capacity are all designed for the act of flying. Two exceptions to this are the ratites or flightless birds which have become too large to be capable of sustained flight, eg the ostrich, kiwi and emu, and the penguin which has evolved into a highly aquatic creature. Birds are thought to have evolved from reptiles, their closest living relative being the crocodile.

Generally, the size given in the table denotes height. To convert cm to inches, multiply by 0.3937.

Name	Family	Size (cm)	Distribution	Food	Special features
■ Flightless birds					
cassowary	Casauriidae	150	Australia and New Guinea	fruit, plants, insects	claws capable of inflicting fatal wounds on humans
emu	Dromaiidae	160–190	Australia	plants, fruit, flowers, insects	highly mobile, nomadic population
kiwi	Apterygidae	35–55	New Zealand	earthworms, insects, seeds, berries	smallest of the Ratitae order; nocturnal
ostrich	Struthonidae	275	dry areas of Africa	mainly leaves, flowers, seeds of plants	fastest animal on two legs
rhea	Rheidae	100–150	grasslands of S America	leaves, roots, seeds, insects, small vertebrates	lives in flocks

Natural History

cassowary   emu   kiwi

Name	Family	Size (cm)	Distribution	Food	Special features
tinamou	Tinamidae	15–49	C and S America	seeds, fruit, insects, small animals	sustains flight over short distances
■ Birds of prey					
buzzard	Accipitridae	80	worldwide except Australasia and Malaysia	small mammals	spends much time perching; kills prey on ground
condor	Cathartidae	60–100	the Americas	carrion	Andean condor has largest wingspan of any living bird (up to 3m)
eagle, bald	Accipitridae	80–100	N America	fish, birds, mammals	name refers to white plumage on head and neck; national symbol of USA
eagle, golden	Accipitridae	80–100	N hemisphere	rabbits, hares, carrion	kills with talons; most numerous large eagle
eagle, harpy	Accipitridae	90	C America to Argentina	some birds, tree-dwelling mammals	the world's largest eagle; black, white and grey; large feet
eagle, sea	Accipitridae	70–120	coastline worldwide	fish	breeds on sea cliffs
falcon	Falconidae	15–60	worldwide	birds, carrion, large insects, small mammals	remarkable powers of flight and sight
harrier	Accipitridae	50	worldwide	small mammals, birds	hunts by flying low in regular search pattern
kite	Accipitridae	52–58	worldwide	insects, snails, small vertebrates, carrion	most varied and diverse group of hawks
osprey	Pandionidae	55–58	worldwide	fish	feet specially adapted for catching fish
owl	Strigidae	12–73	worldwide	mainly small mammals	acute sight and hearing; swallows prey whole; nocturnal
owl, barn	Tytonidae	30–45	worldwide	small vertebrates	feathered legs; nests high above ground

barn owl   condor   peregrine falcon   secretary bird

Name	Family	Size (cm)	Distribution	Food	Special features
secretary bird	Sagittaridae	100	Africa	rodents, reptiles, large beetles, grasshoppers	walks up to 30km/20mi per day
sparrowhawk	Accipitridae	to 27 (male), to 38 (female)	Eurasia, NW Africa, C and S America	small birds	long tail, small round wings
vulture (New World)	Cathartidae	60–100	the Americas	carrion, carcasses	lives in colonies; locates food mainly by sight; head often lacking long feathers
vulture (Old World)	Accipitridae	150–270 (wing-span)	worldwide except the Americas	carrion	no sense of smell
■ **Songbirds**					
accentor	Prunellidae	14–18	Palaearctic	insects, seeds	complex social organization and mating systems
bird of paradise	Paradisaeidae	12.5–100	New Guinea, Moluccas and Eastern Australia	frogs, nestling birds, insects, fruit, plants	brilliantly ornate plumage; elaborate courtship displays
bowerbird	Ptilinorhynchidae	25–37	Australia and New Guinea	mainly fruit, vegetable matter	male builds bowers to attract female for mating
bulbul	Pycnonotidae	13–23	Africa, Madagascar, S Asia and the Philippines	fruits, berries, insects	several species renowned for powerful, beautiful singing voice
bunting	Emberizidae	15–20	worldwide	seeds, crustaceans, insects	large family including species of sparrow, finch, and cardinals
butcherbird	Cracticidae	26–58	Australia, New Guinea and New Zealand	large insects, crustaceans, reptiles, small mammals, young birds	highly aggressive; sings loudly at dawn, thus has alternative name of 'bushman's clock'
cowbird	Icteridae	17–54	N and S America	fruit, seeds, crustaceans, insects	forages for food using distinctive gaping movements of the bill
crow	Corvidae	20–66	worldwide, except New Zealand	omnivorous	adaptable, intelligent; with complex social systems
dipper	Cinclidae	17–20	Europe, S Asia and W regions of N and S America	water insects, molluscs, crustaceans, worms, tadpoles, small fish	strong legs and toes allow mobility to walk under water
drongo	Dicruridae	18–38	S Asia and Africa	insects, lizards, small birds	pugnacious
finch	Fringillidae	11–19	Europe, N and S America, Africa and Asia	seeds	strong bill; melodious singing voice
flowerpecker	Dicaeidae	8–20	SE Asia and Australasia	berries, nectar, insects	short tongue specially adapted for feeding on nectar
flycatcher (Old World)	Muscicapidae	9–27	worldwide except N and S America	insects	tropical species brightly coloured; feeds on the wing
flycatcher, silky	Ptilogonidae	to 14	N and S America	insects	feeds on the wing
honeycreeper, Hawaiian	Drepanididae	10–20	Hawaiian Is	nectar, fruit, seeds, insects	widely varying bills between species adapted to different environments

BIRDS

bird of paradise chaffinch treecreeper waxwing

Name	Family	Size (cm)	Distribution	Food	Special features
honeyeater	Meliphagidae	10–32	Australasia, Pacific Is, Hawaii and S Africa	nectar, insects, fruits, berries	brush tongue adapted for nectar feeding
lark	Alaudidae	11–19	worldwide	seeds, flowers, leaves, insects	ground-dwelling; elaborate singing displays
leafbird	Irenidae	12–24	S Asia	insects, fruit	forest dwellers; ability to mimic sounds of other birds
magpie lark	Grallinidae	19–50	Australasia and New Guinea	insects, tadpoles, seeds, fruit	adaptation to urban surroundings makes it amongst the best-known birds in Australia
mockingbird	Mimidae	20–33	N and S America	invertebrates, fruit	great ability to mimic sounds
nuthatch	Sittidae	14–20	worldwide except S America and New Zealand	insects, invertebrates, seeds, nuts	name reflects ability of the European species to break open nuts
oriole (Old World)	Oriolidae	18–30	Europe, Africa, Asia, Philippines, New Guinea and Australia	insects, fruit	melodious singing voice
palmchat	Dulidae	18	Hispaniola and W Indies	berries, flowers and plants	communal nesting with individual compartments for each nesting pair
robin	Turdinae	13	worldwide except New Zealand	worms, snails, fruit, insects	territorial, uses song to deter intruders
shrike	Laniidae	15–35	Africa, N America, Asia and New Guinea	mainly insects	noted for its sharply hooked bill
shrike, cuckoo	Campephagidae	14–40	Africa, S Asia	mainly insects, caterpillars	peculiar courtship display; family includes colourful minivets
shrike, vanga	Vangidae	12–30	Madagascar	insects, frogs, small reptiles	dwindling population; some endangered species
sparrow	Ploceidae	10–20	African tropics in origin, now worldwide	seeds, insects, bread, household scraps	some species renowned for having adapted to an urban environment
starling	Sturnidae	16–45	Europe, Asia and Africa	fruit, insects, pollen, nectar, seeds	gregarious; nests in colonies, roosts communally
sunbird	Nectariniidae	8–16	Africa, SE Asia and Australasia	insects, nectar	named for its bright plumage

Natural History

92

Name	Family	Size (cm)	Distribution	Food	Special features
swallow	Hirundinidae	12–23	worldwide	insects	noted for strong and agile flight
thrush	Turdinae	12–26	worldwide, except New Zealand	worms, snails, fruit	loud and varied singing voice
tit	Paridae	11–14	N America, Europe, Asia and Africa	insects, seeds, vegetable matter, nuts	nests in holes, wide range of singing voice
treecreeper	Certhildae	12–15	N hemisphere and S Africa	insects, seeds	forages on trees for food
treecreeper, Australian	Climacteridae	15	Australia and New Guinea	mainly ants	forages for food on the trunks and limbs of trees
vireo	Vireonidae	10–17	N and S America	insects, fruit	distinctive thick and slightly hooked bill
wagtail	Motacillidae	14–17	worldwide, although rare in Australia	insects, seeds	spectacular song in flight
warbler, American	Parulidae	10–16	N and S America	insects, berries, vegetable matter	well developed and often complex songs
wattle-bird	Callaeidae	25–53	New Zealand	insects, fruit, invertebrates	distinctive fleshy fold of skin at base of bill
waxbill	Estrildidae	9–13.5	Africa, SE Asia and Australasia	mainly seeds, grain	several species drink by sucking, in the manner of pigeons and doves
waxwing	Bombycillidae	18	W hemisphere	fruit, berries, insects	wax-like, red tips on secondary flight feathers
white-eye	Zosteropidae	12	Africa, SE Asia and Australasia	insects, spiders, nectar, fruit	distinctive ring of tiny white feathers formed round the eyes
wood swallow	Artamidae	15–20	tropical Asia and Australasia	insects	tends to huddle together in small groups on branches of trees; elegant flyer and glider; highly aggressive towards other birds
wren	Troglodytidae	8–15	N and S America, Europe and Asia	invertebrates	nests play ceremonial role in courtship

■ **Waterfowl**

diver ► loon

Name	Family	Size (cm)	Distribution	Food	Special features
duck	Anatidae	wide range	worldwide	vegetation	gregarious; migratory
flamingo	Phoenicopterides	90–180	tropics, N America, S Europe	minute organisms	red/pink colour of plumage caused by diet
goose	Anatidae	wide range	N hemisphere	grass, underwater plants	migratory

great northern diver ► loon

Name	Family	Size (cm)	Distribution	Food	Special features
grebe	Podicipedidae	22–60	worldwide	insects, crustaceans, fish	highly aquatic, adapted for swimming and diving under water
hamerkop	Scopidae	56	Africa S of the Sahara, Madagascar, and S Arabia	mainly frogs and tadpoles, also small fish, shrimps, insects	builds a remarkably elaborate nest with entrance tunnel and internal chamber
heron	Ardeidae	30–140	worldwide	carnivorous; aquatic prey	mainly a wading bird
ibis	Threskiornithidae	50–100	warmer regions of all continents	crustaceans, insects, larvae, small fish, frogs, small reptiles	family also includes species of spoonbill named for shape of bill

Natural History

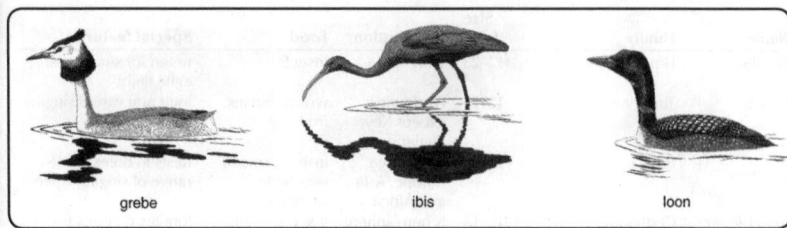

grebe   ibis   loon

Name	Family	Size (cm)	Distribution	Food	Special features
loon (or diver)	Gaviidae	66–95	high latitudes of the N hemisphere, migrating to temperate zones	mainly fish	highly territorial and aggressive; loud warning calls; also known as diver; includes great northern diver which can dive deeper than any other flying bird
screamer	Anhimidae	69–90	warmer parts of S America	herbivorous	highly vocal, trumpet-like alarm calls give it its name
shoebill	Balaenicipitidae	120	E Africa	fish, aquatic prey	also known as the whale-headed stork because it has a large head on a short neck
stork	Ciconiidae	60–120	S America, Asia, Africa and Australia	fish, insects, frogs, snakes, mice, lizards	known for its long bill and long neck
swan	Anatidae	100–160	worldwide, fresh water, sheltered shores and estuaries	underwater plants	very long neck

■ Shorebirds

Name	Family	Size (cm)	Distribution	Food	Special features
auk	Alcidae	16–76	cold waters of the N hemisphere	fish, plankton	same family as the extinct and flightless great auk; species include varieties of puffin and guillemot
avocet	Recurvirostridae	29–48	worldwide, except high latitudes	insects, larvae	particularly graceful walk; long slender legs give rise to alternative name of 'stilt'
courser	Glareolidae	15–25	Africa, S Europe, Asia and Australia	insects	inhabits dry, flat savanna, grassland and the shores of large rivers
curlew, stone	Burhinidae	36–52	Africa, Europe, Asia, Australia and parts of S America	eggs, insects, worms, molluscs, crustaceans, small vertebrates, amphibians	leg joints give alternative name of 'thick knee'
gull	Laridae	31–76	worldwide, scarce in the tropics	fish, marine invertebrates	highly gregarious with elaborate systems of communication
jacana	Jacanidae	17–53	tropics	insects, frogs, fish, invertebrates	ability to walk on floating vegetation gives alternative name of 'lily trotter'
oystercatcher	Haematopididae	40–45	tropical and temperate coastlines, except tropical Africa and S Asia	shellfish, worms, insects	powerful bill for breaking shells; despite the name, they do not eat oysters

gull   oystercatcher   snipe

Natural History

Name	Family	Size (cm)	Distribution	Food	Special features
phalarope	Phalaropidae	19–25	high latitudes of the N hemisphere	insects, crabs, shrimps	wading bird which also regularly swims
plover	Charadriidae	15–40	worldwide	shellfish, insects	swift runner; strong flyer
plover, crab	Dromadidae	38	coasts of E Africa, India, Persian Gulf, Sri Lanka and Madagascar	crabs	single species with mainly white and black plumage
sandpiper	Scolopacidae	12–60	worldwide	invertebrates, insects, berries	spectacular flight patterns
seedsnipe	Thinocoridae	17–28	W coast of S America	seeds, leaves	named after its diet
sheathbill	Chionididae	35–43	subantarctic and E coast of S America	plankton, algae, carcasses, offal	scavenger of a communal and quarrelsome nature
skimmer	Rhynchopidae	37–51	tropics and subtropics of N and S America, Africa, and S Asia	fish, shrimps	uniquely shaped bill aids capture of prey in shallow waters
skua	Stercorariidae	43–61	mainly high latitudes of the N hemisphere	fish, small seabirds, insects, eggs	known for chasing other seabirds until they disgorge their food
snipe, painted	Rostratulidae	19–24	S America, Africa, S Asia and Australia	molluscs, earthworms, seeds	spectacular female plumage; distinctive running action with lowered head

■ **Seabirds**

Name	Family	Size (cm)	Distribution	Food	Special features
albatross	Diomedidae	70–140	S hemisphere	fish	noted for its size and power of flight
cormorant (or shag)	Phalacrocoracidae	50–100	worldwide	fish, crustaceans	marine equivalent of falcons, used in fishing
darter	Anhingidae	80–100	tropical, subtropical, temperate regions	fish, insects	distinctive swimming action occasions name of 'snake-bird'
frigatebird	Fregatidae	70–110	tropical oceans	fish, young birds	enormous wings; adept at flying; forces other birds to disgorge their food
fulmar	Procellariidae	to 60	N and S oceans	fish	comes to land only to breed; can eject foul-smelling vomit to deter predators
gannet	Sulidae	up to 90	worldwide	fish, squid	complex behaviour during mating
guillemot	Alcidae	38–42	N hemisphere	fish, crustaceans, worms	eggs shaped so they do not roll off cliff ledge
pelican	Pelecanidae	140–180	tropics and subtropics	fish, crustaceans	known for its long bill

Natural History

| darter | gannet | puffin | shearwater |

Name	Family	Size (cm)	Distribution	Food	Special features
penguin	Spheniscidae	40–115	S hemisphere	fish, crustaceans, squid	flightless: wings modified as flippers; feathers waterproof; highly social
petrel, diving	Pelecanoididae	16–25	S hemisphere	fish	great resemblance to the auk
petrel, storm	Hydrobatidae	12–25	high latitudes of N and S hemispheres	fish, other marine organisms	considerable powers of migration
puffin	Alcidae	28–32	N hemisphere	fish, crustaceans	nests in burrows in very large colonies
shag ► cormorant					
shearwater	Procellariidae	28–91	subantarctic and subtropical zones	fish, plankton	many species known for long migrations
tropicbird	Phaethontidae	25–45	tropical seas	small fish and squid	elongated central tail feathers produce distinctive flight pattern

■ **Arboreal birds**

Name	Family	Size (cm)	Distribution	Food	Special features
barbet	Capitonidae	9–32	tropics, except Australasia	mainly fruits, berries, buds, insects	nests in holes made in rotten timber or sand banks
bee-eater	Meropidae	15–38	Africa, Asia and Australia	insects	colourful plumage
cuckoo	Cuculidae	15–90	worldwide	insects, especially caterpillars	some species lay eggs in the nests of other birds and rely on foster parents to feed the young
cuckoo-roller	Leptosomatidae	38–43	Madagascar and Comoros Is	large insects, chameleons	diminishing population due to destruction of natural habitat
honeyguide	Indicatoridae	10–20	Africa and S Asia	insects, beeswax	named for peculiar habit of eating the wax of honeycombs
hoopoe	Upupidae	31	Africa, SE Asia and S Europe	mainly small insects	named after its distinctive 'hoo hoo' call
hornbill	Bucerotidae	38–126	tropics of Africa and Australasia	fruit, insects, small animals	noted for its long, heavy bill
jacamar	Galbulidae	13–30	tropical America	insects	long, slender bill; attractive, green, metallic plumage
kingfisher	Alcedinidae	10–46	worldwide	fish, insects, shrimps, frogs, lizards, crabs, snails, worms	colourful plumage, strong bill; characteristic diving movements to catch prey
motmot	Momotidae	20–50	tropical America	insects, frogs, small reptiles, fruit	typically attractive, with distinctive long tail feathers

BIRDS

barbet · cuckoo · hornbill · woodpecker

Natural History

Name	Family	Size (cm)	Distribution	Food	Special features
mousebird	Coliidae	30–35	Africa S of the Sahara	leaves, fruit, seeds, nectar	distinguished by its crest and long tail
parrot	Psittacidae	10–100	mainly tropics of S hemisphere	seeds, nuts, berries, fruit, insects	mainly sedentary; unmelodic voice, not known to mimic sounds outside captivity
pigeon	Columbidae	17–90	worldwide, except high latitudes	seeds, flowers, fruit, berries, leaves, small snails	large family including species of dove, known for its distinctive cooing sound
puffbird	Bucconidae	14–32	tropical America	insects, lizards	named after its stout, puffy appearance
roller	Coraciidae	27–38	Africa, Europe, Asia, Australia	insects, frogs, fruit	named after its courtship display of diving from great heights in a rolling motion
sandgrouse	Pteroclididae	25–48	Africa, S Europe and S Asia	seeds, berries, insects	mainly terrestrial birds
tody	Todidae	10–12	Greater Antilles	mainly insects, seeds	captures its insect prey from the underside of leaves and twigs
toucan	Ramphastidae	34–66	S America	seeds, berries, fruits, insects, small animals	known for its bright plumage and immense bill
trogon	Trogonidae	25–35	tropics, except Australasia	mainly insects, fruit	colourful, attractive plumage
turaco	Musophagidae	35–76	Africa S of the Sahara	mainly fruit	noted for its loud and resounding call
woodhoopoe	Phoeniculidae	21–43	Africa S of the Sahara	insects, fruit	long graduated tail; strongly hooked bill; some species also called scimitar bill
woodpecker	Picidae	10–58	worldwide, except Australasia and Antarctica	insects, fruit, nuts	named after its manner of excavating wood and tree bark for food
■ Aerial feeders					
frogmouth	Podargidae	23–53	SE Asia and Australasia	beetles, scorpions, centipedes, frogs, snails, mice, small birds, fruit	distinctively shaped bill with extremely wide gape
hummingbird	Trochilidae	6–22	N and S America	nectar, insects	the humming sound is made by the wings when hovering
nightjar	Caprimulgidae	19–29	worldwide	mainly insects	nocturnal

97

Natural History

Name	Family	Size (cm)	Distribution	Food	Special features
nightjar, owlet-	Aegothelidae	23–44	Australasia	insects, small vertebrates	perches in upright owl-like way
oilbird	Steatornithidae	53	tropical S America	fruit	the only nocturnal fruit-eating bird
potoo	Nyctibiidae	23–51	tropical C and S America	insects	nocturnal bird, also known as 'tree-nighthawk'
swift	Apodidae	10–25	worldwide	insects	lands only on near-vertical surfaces; spends most of life flying
swift, crested	Hemiprocnidae	17–33	SE Asia and New Guinea	insects	named after the prominent crest on its head
■ Passerines[1]					
antbird	Formicariidae	8–36	parts of S America and W Indies	small insects, spiders, lizards, frogs	named after the habit some species have of following armies of ants to prey
bellbird	Cotingidae	9–45	C and S America	fruit	long, metallic sounding display call
broadbill	Eurylaimidae	13–28	tropical Africa and Asia, and the Philippines	mainly insects	noted for its colourful broad bill
false sunbird	Philepittidae	15	Madagascar	fruit	noted for the bright blue and emerald wattle which develops around the eyes of the male during breeding season
flycatcher (New World)	Tyrannidae	9–27	N and S America	insects	feeds on wing
flycatcher, tyrant	Tyrannidae	5–14	N and S America, W Indies and Galapagos Is	insects, fish, fruit	many species known for spectacular aerial courtship display
gnateater	Conopophagidae	14	parts of S America	insects	long thin legs; short tail
lyrebird	Menuridae	80–90	SE Australia	invertebrates	named after its extravagant tail which resembles a Greek lyre
manakin	Pipridae	9–15	C and S America	fruit, insects	highly elaborate courtship display
ovenbird	Furnariidae	to 25	S America	mainly insects	one species, the true ovenbird, builds substantial nests like mud-ovens
pitta	Pittidae	15–28	Africa, Asia and Australasia	mainly insects, spiders, worms, snails	long legs; short tail; colourful plumage
plantcutter	Phytotomidae	18–19	western S America	buds, shoots, leaves, fruit	bill is ideally adapted for feeding on fruit and plants; regarded as a horticultural and agricultural pest

hummingbird

swift

Natural History

Name	Family	Size (cm)	Distribution	Food	Special features
scrub-bird	Atrichornithidae	16–21	E and SW Australia	insects, small lizards, frogs	small terrestrial bird; long graduated tail
tapaculo	Rhinocryptidae	8–25	S and C America	insects, larvae, spiders	distinctive movable flap covers the nostril
woodcreeper	Dendrocolaptidae	20–37	S America and W Indies	insects, frogs, lizards	stiff tail feathers used as support in climbing trees to forage for food
wren, New Zealand	Xenicidae	8–10	New Zealand	insects	bird family thought to have colonized the islands in the Tertiary Period[2]

■ **Gamebirds and cranes**

Name	Family	Size (cm)	Distribution	Food	Special features
bustard	Otitidae	37–132	Africa, S Europe, Asia and Australia	plants, leaves, seeds, berries, insects, small reptiles and mammals, birds' eggs, nestlings	characterized by its frequent pauses during walking to observe its surroundings
coot	Rallidae	14–51	worldwide	small animals, vegetable food	conspicuous for its loud harsh vocal strains at night
crane	Gruidae	80–150	worldwide, except S America and Antarctica	omnivorous	characterized by its long legs
curassow	Cracidae	75–112	Southern N America and S America	leaves, insects, frogs	noted for agility in running along branches before taking flight
finfoot	Heliornithidae	30–62	tropics of America, and SE Asia	mainly insects	long, slender neck; agile on land and in water
grouse	Tetraonidae	30–90	N hemisphere	leaves, buds, berries, fruit, insects	many species threatened by hunting and use of pesticides
guinea fowl	Numididae	45–60	Africa	mainly insects, bulbs	virtually unfeathered head and neck; often domesticated
hoatzin	Opisthocomidae	60	tropical S America	leaves, fruit and flowers of the white mangrove, fish, crabs	musky odour; top-heavy, retarded flight; unique digestive system
kagu	Rhynochetidae	56	New Caledonia	earthworms	sole species; forest dwelling
limpkin	Aramidae	60–70	C and S America	large snails	sole species; noted for its wailing voice
mesite	Mesoenatidae	25–27	Madagascar	fruit, insects	highly terrestrial; sedentary; endemic to Madagascar
pheasant	Phasianidae	40–235	worldwide	seeds, shoots, berries, insects	elaborate courtship display
plains wanderer	Pedionomidae	16	SE Australia	insects, seeds, vegetable substances	male incubates the eggs and raises the young

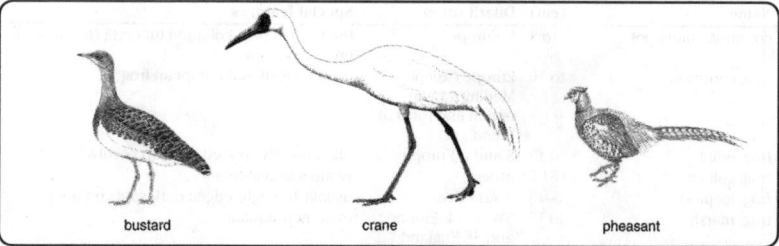

bustard   crane   pheasant

Name	Family	Size (cm)	Distribution	Food	Special features
quail, button	Turnicidae	11–19	Africa, S Asia and Australia	insects, seeds, plants	secretive; terrestrial; only three toes, hind toe absent
seriema	Cariamidae	75–90	S America	omnivorous, especially small snakes	heavily feathered head and crest
sun bittern	Eurypygidae	46	forest swamps of C and S America	insects, crustacea, minnows	complex markings
trumpeter	Psophiidae	43–53	tropical S America	berries, fruit, insects	named after its trumpeting call of warning or alarm
turkey	Meleagrididae	90–110	N America	fruit, seeds, vegetation, invertebrates	characterized by male's distinctive strutting displays during breeding

[1] Any bird of the worldwide order Passeriformes ('perching birds'), which comprises more than half the living species of birds; landbirds.
[2] See Geological time scale p.35.

Birds – record holders

Highest flyer   Ruppell's griffon vulture has been measured at 11 277m (about 7mi) above sea level.

Furthest migrator   The arctic tern travels at least 36 000km/18 641mi each year, flying from the Arctic to the Antarctic and back again.

Fastest flyer   The peregrine falcon can dive through the air at speeds exceeding 322kph/200mph. Species such as red-breasted merganser, eider, canvasback and spur-winged goose can probably reach 90–100kph/56–62mph on rare occasions.

Fastest animal on two legs   The ostrich can maintain a speed of 50kph/31mph for 15 minutes or more, and it is capable of bursts of up to 72kph/45mph, eg when escaping from predators.

Smallest   The bee hummingbird of Cuba is under 6cm/2.4in long and weighs 1.6–1.9g/0.06–0.07oz.

Greatest wingspan   The wandering albatross can reach 3.4m/11ft 1in..

Heaviest flying bird   The kori bustard weighs up to 22kg/49lb; swans weigh about 16kg/35lb.

Deepest diver   The emperor penguin can reach a depth of 483m/1 585ft. The great northern diver or loon can dive to about 80m/262ft — deeper than any other flying bird.

Most abundant   Africa's red-billed quelea is the most numerous wild bird, with a population guessed to be in the hundreds of millions; the largest gatherings can comprise about 30 million or more birds. The domestic chicken is the most abundant of all birds, numbering thousands of millions.

Most feathers   The greatest number of feathers counted on a bird was 25 216, on a swan.

Amphibians

Amphibians are a class of cold-blooded vertebrates including frogs, toads, newts and salamanders. There are approximately 4000 species. They have a moist, thin skin without scales, and the adults live partly or entirely on land, but can usually only survive in damp habitats. They return to water to lay their eggs, which hatch to form fish-like larvae or tadpoles that breathe by means of gills, but gradually develop lungs as they approach adulthood.

Generally, the size given in the table denotes length. To convert from cm to inches, multiply by 0.3937.

Name	Size (cm)	Distribution	Special features
common spadefoot	to 8	C Europe	toad with a pale-coloured tubercle (the spade) on its hind foot
frog, common	to 10	Europe except Mediterranean region and most of Iberia	most widespread European frog
frog, edible	to 12	S and C Europe	often heavily spotted; whitish vocal sacs
frog, goliath	to 81.5	Africa	world's largest frog
frog, leopard	5–13	N America	usually has light-edged dark spots on body
frog, marsh	to 15	SW and E Europe and SE England	extremely aquatic

Name	Size (cm)	Distribution	Special features
frog, painted	to 7	Iberia and SW France	usually smooth and yellow-brown, grey or reddish with dark spots
frog, parsley	to 5	W Europe	slender bodied, with a whitish underside
frog, poison-arrow	0.85–1.24	C and S America	smallest known amphibian; skin highly poisonous
hellbender	to 63	America	salamander with wrinkled folds of flesh on body
mudpuppy	18–43	N America	salamander with bright red external gills
natterjack	to 10	SW and C Europe	toad with bright yellow stripe along its back
newt, alpine	to 12	C Europe	dark mottled back and a uniformly orange belly and bluish spotted sides
newt, Bosca's	7–10	Iberian peninsula	similiar to smooth newt without a dorsal crest
newt, marbled	to 15	Iberia and W France	bright yellow or orange stripe on velvety green and black mottled back
newt, palmate	to 9	W Europe	palmate (webbed feet); short filament at end of breeding male's tail
newt, smooth	to 11	Europe	breeding male develops a wavy crest
newt, warty (great crested newt)	to 17	Europe except Iberia and Ireland	bright red, orange or yellow spotted belly and warty skin
salamander, alpine	to 15	C Europe	large glands on back of head
salamander, Chinese giant	114 (average)	China	world's largest amphibian
salamander, fire	to 25	C and S Europe	large glands on sides of head contain venomous secretion
salamander, goldstriped	15–16	Iberian peninsula	thin with shiny skin
salamander, spectacled	to 11	W Italy	only European salamander with four toes on hind feet
toad, common	to 15	Europe except N Scandinavia, Ireland and some Mediterranean islands	largest European toad; usually brownish or greyish with warty skin
toad, green	to 10	E Europe	distinctive colouring: grey or greenish with darker marbled markings
toad, marine	to 23.8	S America	world's largest toad
toad, midwife	to 5	W Europe	male carries strings of eggs wrapped around hind legs
toad, Surinam	to 20	S America	female incubates eggs on her back
toad, yellow-bellied	to 5	C and S Europe	usually bright yellow or orange, black-blotched belly
treefrog, common	to 5	C and S Europe	usually bright green; often found in trees high above ground

poison-arrow frog   fire salamander   midwife toad

Natural History

Reptiles

Reptiles are egg-laying vertebrates of the class Reptilia, having evolved from primitive amphibians; there are 6547 species divided into Squamata (lizards and snakes), Chelonia (tortoises and turtles), Crocodylia (crocodiles and alligators) and Rhynchocephalia (the tuatara).

Most reptiles live on the land, breathe with lungs, and have horny or plated skins. Reptiles require the rays of the sun to maintain their body temperature, ie they are cold-blooded or ectothermic. This confines them to warm, tropical and subtropical regions, but does allow some species to exist in particularly hot desert environments in which mammals and birds would find it impossible to survive. Extinct species of reptile include the dinosaur and pterodactyl.

Generally, the size given in the table denotes to length. To convert cm to inches, multiply by 0.3937.

Name	Family	Size (cm)	Distribution	Food	Special features
alligator	Alligatoridae	200–550	S USA, C and S America and E China	fish, birds, mammals, amphibians, reptiles	able to inflict fatalities on humans but attacks rare; only the American alligator is currently free from being an endangered species, noted for its longevity in protected environments
anguid	Anguidae	6–30	N and S America, Europe, Asia and NW Africa	small lizards, mice, birds' eggs, tadpoles, earthworms, spiders, scorpions, grasshoppers, moths, wasps, larvae	distinctive bony-plated scales which reach round the underside giving the creature a rigid appearance
boa	Boidae	200–400	Western N America, S America, Africa, Madagascar, Asia, Fiji, Solomon Is and New Guinea	birds, mammals	famous constricting snake; includes within its family species of anaconda
chameleon	Chamaeleontidae	2–28	Africa outside the Sahara, Madagascar, Middle East, S Spain, S Arabian peninsula, Sri Lanka, Crete, India and Pakistan	insects, spiders, scorpions, small birds, mammals	noted for its ability to change colour and blend into its environment
crocodile	Crocodylidae	150–750	pantropical and some temperate regions of Africa	vertebrates	distinguished from the alligator by the visible fourth tooth in the lower jaw; famous for its huge jaws, fierce appearance, and violent hunting and ambush techniques when capturing prey; populations have been decimated by the demand for luxury leather and several species are endangered
gecko	Gekkonidae	1.5–24	N and S America, Africa, S Europe, Asia and Australia	mainly insects	noted for its vocalization and ability to climb; able to shed its tail as a defence mechanism against predators
iguana	Iguanidae	to 200	C and S America, Madagascar, Fiji and Tonga	mainly insects	terrestrial and tree-dwelling lizard; active by day, able to survive in exceptionally high temperatures
lizard, beaded	Helodermatidae	33–45	SW USA, W Mexico to Guatemala	small mammals, birds, lizards, frogs, birds' eggs, insects, earth-worms, carrion	possesses a mildly venomous bite
lizard, blind	Dibamidae	12–16.5	SE Asia	insects	so named because the eyes are concealed within the skin

Natural History

Name	Family	Size (cm)	Distribution	Food	Special features
lizard, Bornean earless	Lanthanotidae	to 20	Borneo	fish, earthworms, birds' eggs	lacks an external ear opening; partly aquatic and a good swimmer; capable of short, rapid movements on land
lizard, chisel-tooth	Agamidae	4–35	Africa, Asia and Australia	insects, fruit, plants, eggs	named after its distinctive teeth; family includes the flying dragon which is able to glide from perch to perch
lizard, girdle-tailed	Cordylidae	5–27.5	Africa S of the Sahara, Madagascar	mainly insectivorous and carnivorous	terrestrial; active by day; adapted to arid environments
lizard, monitor	Varanidae	12–150	Africa, S Asia, Indo-Australian archipelago, Philippines, New Guinea and Australia	carrion, large snails, grasshoppers, beetles, scorpions, crocodiles' and birds' eggs, fish, lizards, snakes, birds, shrews, squirrels	consumes its prey whole in the manner of snakes; includes the Komodo dragon, the largest living lizard, which has a prodigious appetite and is capable of killing pigs and small deer
lizard, night	Xantisiidae	3.5–12	C America	mainly insects	most species active by night, secretive by day
lizard, snake	Pygopodidae	6.5–31	New Guinea and Australia	mainly insects	snake-like appearance; broad but highly extensible tongue
lizard, wall and sand	Lacertidae	4–22	Europe, Africa, Asia and Indo-Australian archipelago	mainly insects, snails, worms	highly conspicuous lizard living in open and sandy environments; terrestrial, active by day
lizard, worm	Amphisbaenidae	15–35	subtropical regions of N and S America, Africa, Middle East, Asia and Europe	mainly insects, snails, worms	worm-like, burrowing reptile; some of the species have the rare ability to move backwards and forwards
pipesnake	Aniliidae	<100	S America, SE Asia	snakes, eels	tail has brilliantly coloured red underside; burrows in swampy regions and feeds on other snakes
python	Pythonidae	100–1000	tropical and subtropical Africa, SE Asia, Australia, Mexico and C America	birds, mammals	capable of killing humans, especially children, by constriction
skink	Scincidae	2.8–35	tropical and temperate regions	crabs, insects, seeds	family of terrestrial, tree-dwelling or burrowing species, including highly adept swimmers and those able to swim through sand
snake, dawn blind	Anomalepidae	11–30	C and S America	ants, termites	short tail, indistinct head, one or two teeth in the lower jaw
snake, front-fanged	Elapidae	38–560	worldwide in warm regions	frogs, snakes, eels, rodents, lizards, and other vertebrates	highly venomous family with short fangs; responsible for numerous human fatalities; includes the mamba, the adder and the cobra with its broad, hooded head
snake, harmless	Colubridae	13–350	worldwide	wide variety of vertebrates	large family which includes terrestrial, burrowing, arboreal and aquatic species; called harmless because of the inability of most species to inject or produce venomous saliva
snake, shieldtail	Uropeltidae	20–50	S India and Sri Lanka	earthworms and insects	small burrowing snake, with tiny eyes, so called because the tail ends abruptly and forms a rough cylindrical shield

Natural History

Name	Family	Size (cm)	Distribution	Food	Special features
snake, thread	Leptotyphlopidae	15–90	C and S America, Africa and Asia	ants and termites	small and exceptionally slender burrowing snake
snake, typical blind	Typhlopidae	15–90	C and S America, Africa S of the Sahara, SE Europe, S Asia, Taiwan and Australia	ants, termites, larvae	burrowing snake with tiny, concealed eyes and no teeth on lower jaw
tortoise	Testudinidae	10–140	S Europe, Africa, Asia, C and S America	mainly herbivorous	includes smallest species of turtle, the speckled Cape tortoise (10cm), and one of the longest-lived turtles, the spur-thighed tortoise with a possible lifespan of over a century
tuatara	Sphenodontidae	45–61	islands off New Zealand	ground insects, geckos, skinks, birds' eggs	lizard-like reptile with a 'third eye' in the top of its head
turtle, Afro-American side-necked	Pelomedusidae	12–90	S America, Africa, Madagascar, Seychelles and Mauritius	herbivorous and omnivorous species	seabed-dweller that rarely requires to come to the surface
turtle, American mud and musk	Kinosternidae	11–27	N and S America	molluscs, insects, crustaceans, fish, plants	lives permanently or semi-permanently in fresh water; glands produce distinctive and evil-smelling secretion
turtle, Austro-American side-necked	Chelidae	14–48	S America, Australia and New Guinea	omnivorous and carnivorous species	family includes the peculiar looking matamata, the most adept of the ambush-feeders at the gape and suck technique of capturing prey
turtle, big-headed	Platysternidae	20	SE Asia	small invertebrates	distinctive large head which cannot be retracted; active at night; exceptionally good climber
turtle, Central American river	Dermatemydidae	to 65	Vera Cruz, Mexico, Honduras	fish, insects, fruit, leaves, plants	freshwater creature with well-developed shell
turtle, Mexican musk	Staurotypidae	to 38	Mexico to Honduras	worms, fish, newts	freshwater creature dwelling in marshes and swamps
turtle, pig-nosed softshell	Carettochelyidae	55 or over	New Guinea and N Australia	crustaceans, insects, molluscs, fish, aquatic plants, fruit	specialized swimmer named for its plateless skin and fleshy, pig-like snout
turtle, pond and river	Emydidae	11.4–80	N and C America, S Europe, N Africa, Asia and Argentina	insects, molluscs, vertebrates, plants	family ranges from tiny bog turtle (11.4cm) to the largest of the river turtles, the Malaysian giant turtle; includes box turtle with possible life span of over a century, also species of terrapin
turtle, sea	Cheloniidae	75–213	pantropical, and some subtropical and temperate regions	sponges, jellyfish, mussels, crabs, sea urchins, fish	rapid movement through water contrasts with characteristically slow movements of turtles on land
turtle, snapping	Chelydridae	47–66	N and C America	carrion, insects, fish, turtles, molluscs, plant food	large-headed, aggressive seabed dweller; includes other turtles in its diet; ambush feeder with rapid snapping movements; alligator snapping turtle has unique worm-like projection on the tongue which fills with blood, turns red, and acts as a lure to catch fish

Name	Family	Size (cm)	Distribution	Food	Special features
turtle, softshell	Trionychidae	30–115	N America, Africa, Asia and Indo-Australian archipelago	insects, crustaceans, fish	named after its leathered, plateless skin; noted for its prominent, pointed snout
viper	Viperidae	25–365	N and S America, Africa, Europe and Asia	vertebrates	famous, venomous family of snakes, including the rattlesnake, which vibrates its tail when disturbed, and the sidewinder with its distinctive sideways movements
whiptail and racerunner	Teiidae	37–45	N and S Asia	small mammals, birds, fish, frogs, tadpoles, lizards, insects, snails, plants	captured and eaten by S American Indians; the fat and flesh also used in traditional medicines
xenosaur	Xenosauridae	10–15	Mexico, Guatemala and S China	insects, tadpoles, fish	terrestrial, sedentary and secretive

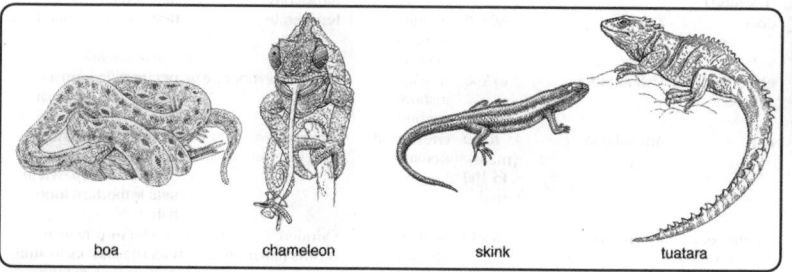

boa   chameleon   skink   tuatara

Fish

Generally, the size given in the table denotes length. To convert cm to inches, multiply by 0.3937.

Name	Family	Size (cm)	Habitat	Distribution	Special features
albacore	Scombridae	to 130	open waters	tropical, warm temperate	tuna fish with large pectoral fins; prized food and sport fish
anchovy	Engraulidae	9–12	surface ocean	temperate	important food fish in S Europe, Black Sea, Peru
anglerfish	Chaunacidae	5–8	deep ocean	tropical, temperate	large jaws; fishing lure at tip of modified dorsal ray
barracuda	Sphyraenidae	30–240	surface ocean	tropical, warm temperate	carnivorous; voracious; large teeth
blenny	Blennidae	20–49	seabed	temperate, tropical	devoid of scales; often found in rock pools
bonito	Scombridae	to 90	open sea, surface water	temperate, warm	commercially important; member of tuna family; food fish; sport fish
bream	Cyprinidae	41–80	freshwater lakes, rivers	temperate (N Europe)	deep-bodied; food fish
brill	Scophthalmidae	to 70	seabed	temperate	flatfish; eyes on left side; food fish
butterfly fish	Chaetodontidae	to 15	reefs	tropical	deep, compressed body; brightly coloured
carp	Cyprinidae	51–61	beds of freshwater lakes, rivers	temperate	important food fish; used in aquaculture
catfish	Ictaluridae	90–135	seabed	temperate (N America)	females lay eggs in nest scooped out in mud; important food fish

Natural History

Natural History

Name	Family	Size (cm)	Habitat	Distribution	Special features
chub	Cyprinidae	30–60	lakes, rivers	temperate (Europe)	popular sport fish
cod	Gadidae	to 120	ocean shelf	temperate, N hemisphere	common cod very important food fish
conger eel	Congridae	274	seabed, deep inshore pools	temperate	rounded cylindrical body; upper jaw longer than lower
dab	Pleuronectidae	20–40	shallow seabed	temperate (Europe)	flatfish; eyes on right side; food fish
dace	Cyprinidae	15–30	freshwater lakes, rivers	temperate (Europe, former USSR)	sport fish
damselfish	Pomacentridae	5–15	reefs, rocky shores	tropical, temperate	brightly coloured
dogfish	Scyliorhinidae	60–100	seabed	temperate (Europe)	skin very rough; food fish (sold as rock salmon)
dolphinfish (dorado)	Corypaenidae	to 200	surface	tropical, warm temperate	predatory; prized sport fish; food fish
dory	Zeidae	30–60	mainly shallow ocean	temperate	deep-bodied; food fish
eagle ray	Myliobatidae	to 200	mainly inshore seabed	tropical, temperate	pectoral fins form 'wings'; young born live
eel	Anguillidae	to 50 (male), to 100 (female)	rivers, mid-ocean	temperate	elongate cylindrical body form; adults live in rivers but spawn in sea; important food fish
electric eel	Electrophoridae	to 240	shallow streams	Orinoco, Amazon basins (S America)	produces powerful electric shocks to stun prey and as defence
electric ray (or torpedo ray)	Torpenidae	to 180	seabed	tropical, temperate	produces strong electric shocks to stun prey
file fish	Monacanthidae	5–13	reefs, shallow water	tropical, warm temperate	rough skin; food fish
flounder	Pleuronectidae	to 51	shallow seabed, saline estuaries, lakes	temperate (Europe)	flatfish (eyes may be on right or left side); locally important food fish
flying fish	Exocoetidae	25–50	surface ocean	tropical, warm temperate	enlarged pelvic and pectoral fins give ability to jump and glide above water surface
goatfish ▶ red mullet					
goby	Gobiidae	1–27	shallow seabed, rocky pools	tropical, temperate	pelvic fins joined to form single sucker-like fin
goldfish	Cyprinidae	to 30	freshwater ponds, rivers	temperate	popular ornamental fish
grenadier ▶ rat-tail					
grey mullet	Mugilidae	to 75	coastal seabed; occasionally tropical fresh waters	tropical, temperate	food fish
grouper	Serranidae	5–370	deep sea	tropical, warm temperate	common around reefs, prized sport and food fish
gurnard (or sea robin)	Triglidae	to 75	seabed	tropical, warm temperate	bony plates on head; many produce audible sounds
hake	Merlucciidae	to 180	continental shelf waters	temperate	large head and jaws; food fish

Name	Family	Size (cm)	Habitat	Distribution	Special features
halibut	Pleuronectidae	to 250	seabed	temperate (Atlantic)	flatfish; eyes on right side; prized food fish
herring	Clupeidae	to 40	surface ocean	temperate (N Atlantic, Arctic)	important food fish
lamprey	Petromyzonidae	to 91	streams, rivers; parasitic in open sea	temperate (N Atlantic)	primitive jawless fish; mouth sucker-like; food fish
lanternfish	Myctophidae	2–15	deep sea, but many migrate to surface at night	tropical, temperate	body has numerous light organs
lemon sole	Pleuronectidae	to 66	seabed	temperate	flatfish; specialized feeder on polychaete worms; food fish
loach	Cobitidae	to 15	freshwater lakes, rivers	temperate (Europe, Asia)	popular aquarium fish
mackerel	Scombridae	to 66	surface ocean	temperate (N Atlantic)	seasonal migrations; important food fish
manta ray (or devil ray)	Mobulidae	120–900 (width)	surface ocean	tropical	fleshy 'horns' at side of head; young born, not hatched
minnow	Cyprinidae	to 12	fast-flowing freshwater lakes, rivers	temperate (N Europe, Asia)	locally abundant
monkfish	Squatinidae	to 180	seabed	temperate (N Atlantic, Mediterranean)	pectoral fins very broad, tail slender, intermediate in shape between shark and ray; food fish
moorish idol	Zanclidae	to 22	reefs	tropical (Indo-Pacific)	body deep, tall dorsal and anal fins; bold black/white stripes with some yellow
moray eel	Muraenidae	to 130	rocky shores	temperate, tropical	pointed snout; long, sharp teeth; aggressive
parrotfish	Scaridae	25–190	reefs	tropical	jaw teeth fused to form parrot-like beak for scraping algal growth from reefs, and for breaking coral
perch	Percidae	30–50	freshwater lakes, rivers, Baltic Sea	temperate	food fish; sport fish
pike	Escocidae	to 130	freshwater lakes, rivers	temperate	snout pointed; jaws large; predatory; prized by anglers
pilchard (or sardine)	Clupeidae	to 25	surface	temperate (N Atlantic, Mediterranean)	important food fish, often canned
pipefish	Syngnathidae	15–160	shallow seas	tropical, warm temperate	slender segmented body; males of some species carry eggs in brood pouch
plaice	Pleuronectidae	50–90	shallow seabed	temperate (Europe)	flatfish; eyes on right side; important food fish
puffer	Tetraodontidae	3–25	inshore shallow seas, reefs	tropical, warm temperate	body often spiny; some organs and tissues very poisonous, but a food delicacy in Japan
rat-tail (or grenadier)	Macrouridae	40–110	close to deep-seabed	temperate, tropical	large head, tapering body; some species make sounds by resonating swim bladder

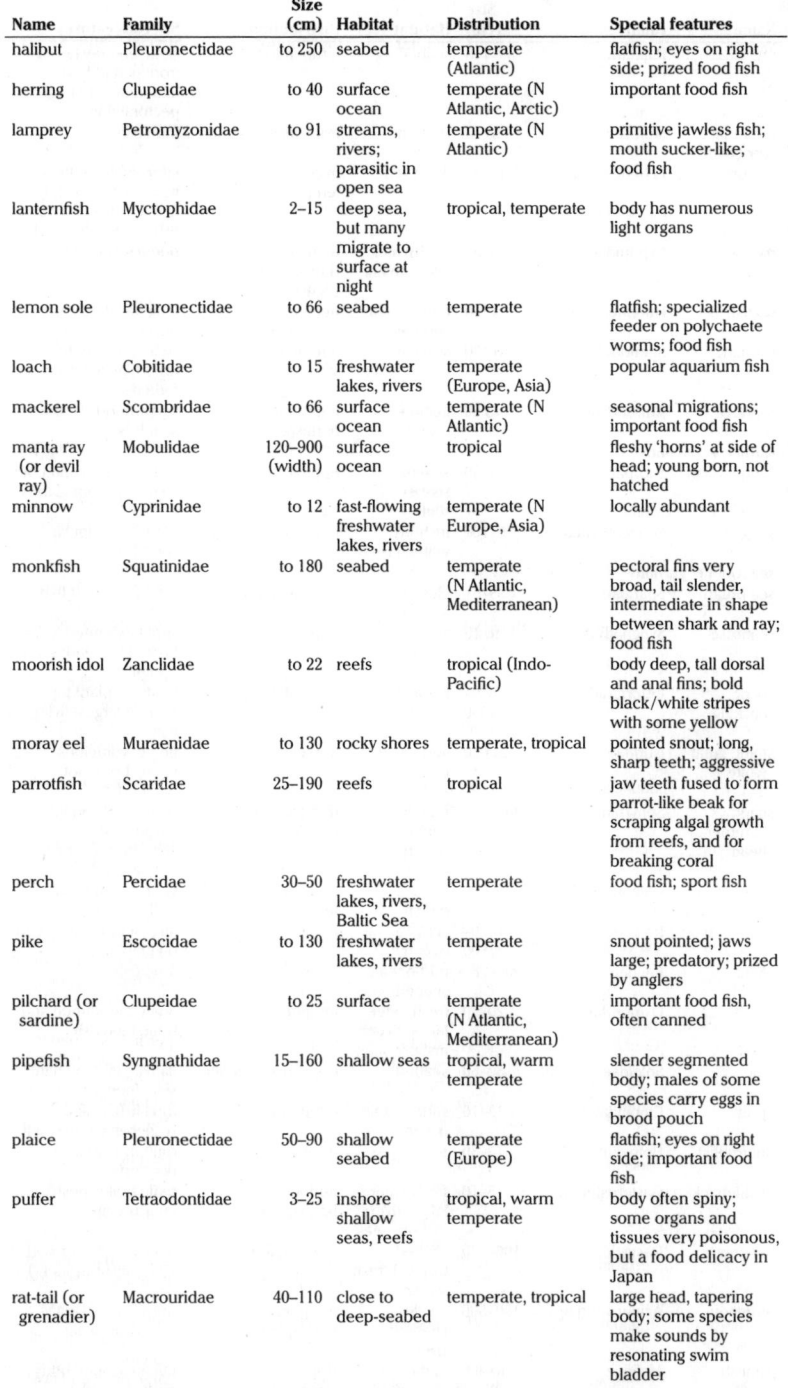

Natural History

Name	Family	Size (cm)	Habitat	Distribution	Special features
ray	Rajidae	39–113	seabed	temperate	skate and ray family; front part of body flattened with large pectoral fins
red mullet (or goatfish)	Mullidae	to 40	seabed	tropical, temperate	food fish
remora	Echeneidae	12–46	open sea	tropical, warm temperate	large sucking disc on head, with which it attaches itself to other fish, especially sharks
roach	Cyprinidae	35–53	freshwater lakes, rivers	temperate (Europe, former USSR)	popular sport fish
sailfish	Istiophoridae	to 360	open ocean surface	tropical, warm temperate	long, tall dorsal fin; prized sport fish
salmon	Salmonidae	to 150	surface ocean; rivers	temperate	swims upriver to breed; prized sport and food fish
sandeel	Ammodytidae	to 20	inshore seabed	temperate (N hemisphere)	very important food for seabirds
sardine ▶ pilchard					
scorpionfish	Scorpaenidae	to 50	shallow seabed, reefs	tropical, temperate	distinctive fin and body spines; venom glands
sea bass	Percichthyidae	60–100	inshore waters; reefs	tropical, temperate	food fish; popular sport fish
sea robin ▶ gurnard					
sea-bream	Sparidae	35–51	close to seabed	tropical, temperate	food fish; sport fish
seahorse	Syngnathidae	to 15	surface ocean	tropical, warm temperate	snout extended to form horse-like head; swims upright
shark, basking	Cetorhinidae	870–1350	surface ocean	tropical, temperate	feeds on plankton; second largest living fish
shark, great white	Isuridae	to 630	surface ocean	tropical	fierce; voracious; young born, not hatched
shark, hammer-head	Sphyrnidae	360–600	mainly surface ocean	tropical, warm temperate	head flattened into hammer shape; voracious; young born, not hatched
shark, tiger	Galeorhinidae	360–600	surface ocean	tropical, warm temperate	vertical stripes on body; fierce
shark, whale	Rhincodontidae	1020–1800	surface ocean	tropical	largest living fish; feeds on plankton
skate	Rajidae	200–285	mid-ocean, seabed	temperate	food fish
smelt	Osmeridae	20–30	freshwater lakes, rivers; inshore seas	temperate	related to salmon and trout; food fish
sole	Soleidae	30–60	seabed	tropical, temperate	flatfish; eyes on right side; food fish
sprat	Clupeidae	13–16	surface–mid-ocean	temperate	food fish; called whitebait when small
squirrelfish	Holocentridae	12–30	reefs	tropical	brightly coloured; nocturnal
stickleback	Gasterosteidae	5–10	freshwater lakes, rivers; inshore seas	temperate (N hemisphere)	male builds nest, guards eggs
stingray	Dasyatidae	106–140	seabed; tropical fresh waters	tropical, temperate	tail whip-like, armed with poison spine(s)
sturgeon	Acipenseridae	100–500	shallow seabed; rivers	temperate (N hemisphere)	primitive fish; eggs prized as caviar
sunfish	Molidae	to 400	surface–mid-open ocean	tropical, warm temperate	tail fin absent; body almost circular

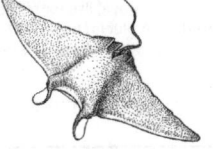

| hammerhead shark | lamprey | manta ray | turbot |

Natural History

Name	Family	Size (cm)	Habitat	Distribution	Special features
surgeonfish (or tang)	Acanthuridae	20–45	reefs	tropical, subtropical	brightly coloured; sharp spine on sides of tail can be erected for defence
swordfish	Xiphiidae	200–500	surface–mid-open ocean	tropical, temperate	upper jaw extended to form flat 'sword'; food and sport fish
tang ► surgeonfish					
triggerfish	Balistidae	10–60	seabed outside reefs	tropical	colourful; dorsal spine can be erected to wedge fish in crevice as defence; food fish, but can be poisonous
trout	Salmonidae	23–140	surface ocean; freshwater lakes, rivers	temperate	brown trout confined to fresh water; sea trout migratory; prized food fish
tuna, skipjack	Scombridae	to 100	mid-ocean	tropical, temperate	fast swimmer; important food fish
tuna, yellow-fin	Scombridae	to 200	surface ocean	tropical, warm temperate	elongated body, long dorsal and anal fins; important food fish
turbot	Scophthalamidae	50–100	shallow seabed	temperate (N Atlantic)	flatfish; eyes on left side of body; prized food fish
wrasse	Labridae	7–210	reefs, rocky coasts	tropical, warm temperate	brightly coloured

Fish – record holders

Fastest	Over short distances, the sailfish can reach a speed of 109kph/68mph; however marlins are the fastest over longer distances, and can reach a burst speed of 64–80kph/40–50mph.
Largest	The whale shark (*Rhincodon typus*) is said to reach over 18m/59ft, with the largest on record being 12.65m/41ft 5in, weighing an estimated 21.5 tonnes.
Smallest	The stout infantfish (*Schindleria brevipinguis*), found in Great Barrier Reef coral lagoons in Australia, measures 6.5–8.4mm/0.2–0.3in.
Smallest in British waters	Guillet's goby (*Lebetus guilleti*) reaches a maximum length of 24mm.
Most widespread	The distribution of the bristlemouths of genus *Cyclothone* is worldwide; *Cyclothone microdon* may even be found in the Arctic Ocean.
Most restricted	The devil's hole pupfish (*Cyprinodon diabolis*) inhabits only a small area of water above a rock shelf in a spring-fed pool in Ash Meadows, Nevada, USA.
Deepest dweller	In 1970 a brotulid, *Bassogigas profundissimus*, was recovered from a depth of 8300m/27231ft, making it the deepest living vertebrate.
Largest fish ever caught on a rod	In 1959 a great white shark measuring 5.13m/16ft 10in and weighing 1208kg/2664lb was caught off S Australia.
Largest freshwater fish found in Britain and Ireland	Reportedly, in 1815 a pike (*Esox lucius*) was taken from the River Shannon in Ireland weighing 41.7kg/92lb; however there is evidence of a pike weighing 32.7kg/72lb having been caught on Loch Ken, Scotland, in 1774.
Largest saltwater fish caught by anglers in the UK	In 1933 a tunny weighing 386kg/851lb was caught near Whitby, Yorkshire.
Longest-lived species	Some specimens of the lake sturgeon of N America are thought to be over 80 years old.

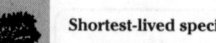

Shortest-lived species	Some species of the killifish (*Aplocheilidae* family), which are found in Africa, live for only 8 months in the wild.
Greatest distance covered by a migrating fish	A bluefin tuna was tagged in 1958 off Baja California and caught in 1963 south of Japan; it had covered a distance of 9335km/5800mi.

Invertebrates

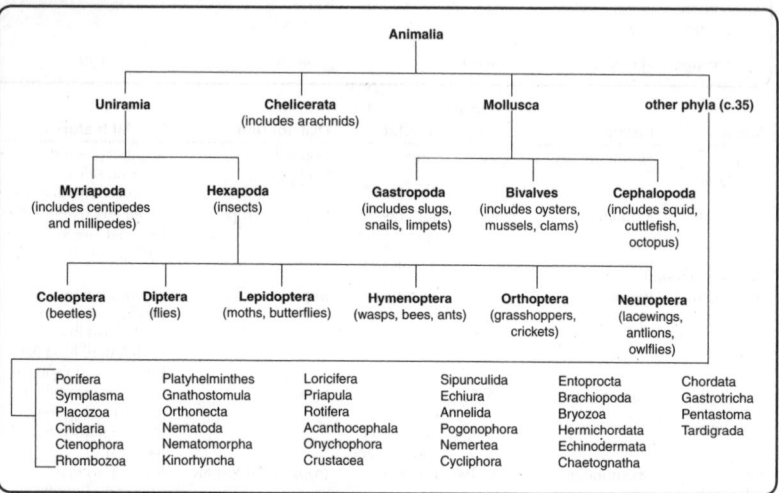

Animalia

Uniramia — Chelicerata (includes arachnids) — Mollusca — other phyla (c.35)

Myriapoda (includes centipedes and millipedes) — Hexapoda (insects) — Gastropoda (includes slugs, snails, limpets) — Bivalves (includes oysters, mussels, clams) — Cephalopoda (includes squid, cuttlefish, octopus)

Coleoptera (beetles) — Diptera (flies) — Lepidoptera (moths, butterflies) — Hymenoptera (wasps, bees, ants) — Orthoptera (grasshoppers, crickets) — Neuroptera (lacewings, antlions, owlflies)

Porifera	Platyhelminthes	Loricifera	Sipunculida	Entoprocta	Chordata
Symplasma	Gnathostomula	Priapula	Echiura	Brachiopoda	Gastrotricha
Placozoa	Orthonecta	Rotifera	Annelida	Bryozoa	Pentastoma
Cnidaria	Nematoda	Acanthocephala	Pogonophora	Hermichordata	Tardigrada
Ctenophora	Nematomorpha	Onychophora	Nemertea	Echinodermata	
Rhombozoa	Kinorhyncha	Crustacea	Cycliphora	Chaetognatha	

For molluscs, lengths given are normally maximum shell lengths, but (b) indicates body length; for spiders, lengths are body lengths, although legs may be much longer; for insects, sizes given are normally body lengths, but (w) indicates wingspan.

Name	Species	Length	Range and habitat	Notable features
MOLLUSCS: Phylum Mollusca				
■ **Slugs and snails/Gastropoda (c.50000 species)**				
abalone	*Haliotis* (several species)	<30cm	warm seas worldwide	feeds on seaweeds; mainly in coastal waters; collected for food and for the pearly shells
conch	*Strombus* (several species)	<33cm	tropical seas	feeds on seaweeds; shells with a broad 'wing', often used as trumpets
cone shell	*Conus* (c.600 species)	<23cm	warm seas worldwide	feeds on fish and molluscs paralysed with poison darts; some species dangerous to humans; beautiful shells much sought by collectors
cowrie	(c.150 species in several genera)	<10cm	warm seas worldwide	feeds on sea anemones and other small creatures; shiny, china-like shells were once used as money
limpet, common	*Patella vulgata*	<5.5cm	worldwide	feeds on seaweeds in intertidal zone; conical shell pulled tightly down on rocks when tide is out
limpet, slipper	*Crepidula fornicata*	<6cm	originally N America, now common on coasts of Europe	strains food particles from the water; slipper-like shells cling together in chains; a serious pest in oyster and mussel farms, settling on the shells and cutting off their food supplies
periwinkle, common	*Littorina littorea*	<2.5cm	N Atlantic and adjacent seas; rocky shores	feeds on seaweeds; thick, dull brown shell; the fishmonger's winkle
sea butterfly	(c.100 species in several genera)	<5cm	oceans worldwide; most common in warm waters	carnivorous, eating a variety of small marine creatures; with or without shells, they swim by flapping wing-like extensions of the foot

Name	Species	Length	Range and habitat	Notable features
slug, great grey	*Limax maximus*	<20cm (b)	Europe	mainly feeds on fungi and rotting matter; mottled grey and brown; common in gardens; mates in mid-air, hanging from a rope of slime
snail, giant African	*Achatina fulica*	<15cm	originally Africa, now tropical Asia and Pacific	vegetarian; a serious agricultural pest; lays hard-shelled eggs as big as those of a thrush
snail, great ramshorn	*Planorbarius corneus*	<3cm	Europe; still and slow-moving fresh water	vegetarian, often browsing on algae; shell forms a flat spiral; body has bright red blood
snail, roman	*Helix pomatia*	<5cm	C and S Europe; lime soils	vegetarian; often a pest, but cultivated for food in some areas
whelk	*Buccinum undatum*	<12cm	N Atlantic and neighbouring seas	carnivorous, feeding on living and dead animals; large numbers are collected for human consumption

■ **Bivalves/Lamellibranchia (c.8000 species)**

Name	Species	Length	Range and habitat	Notable features
cockle, common	*Cardium edule*	<5cm	European coasts	burrows in sand and mud near low-tide level; important food for fish and wading birds
mussel, common	*Mytilus edulis*	<11cm	coasts of Europe and eastern North America	bluish shell clings to rocks with tough threads; farmed on a large scale for human consumption, especially in S Europe
oyster	*Ostrea edulis*	<15cm	coasts of Europe and Africa	cements trough-shaped lower valve to stones, with flat upper valve sitting on it like a lid; large numbers farmed for human consumption
piddock	*Pholas dactylus*	<12cm	coasts of Europe and eastern North America	uses rasp-like shell to bore into soft rocks and wood, making an inescapable tomb; sucks in water and food through long siphons
razor-shell, pod	*Ensis siliqua*	<20cm	European coasts	long, straight shell, shaped like a cut-throat razor, is open at both ends; burrows in sand
scallop, great	*Pecten maximus*	<15cm	European coasts; usually below tide level	strongly ribbed, eared shells with one valve flatter than the other; lives freely on seabed and swims by opening and closing its valves

■ **Squids and octopuses/Cephalopoda (c.750 species)**

Name	Species	Length	Range and habitat	Notable features
cuttlefish, common	*Sepia officinalis*	<30cm	coastal waters of Atlantic and neighbouring seas	eats shrimps and other crustaceans, caught with tentacles; lives on seabed; flat, oval body can change colour; cuttle-bone is the internal shell
octopus, blue-ringed	*Hapalochlaena maculosa*	10cm (span)	Australian coasts	the most dangerous species, despite its size; the only octopus whose venom is known to have killed people
octopus, common	*Octopus vulgaris*	<3m (span)	Atlantic and Mediterranean coastal waters	eats small fish and crustaceans, killed by a poisonous bite; not dangerous to people
squid, common	*Loligo vulgaris*	<50cm	Atlantic and Mediterranean coastal waters	eats fish, crustaceans and smaller squid; cylindrical body with a triangular fin at the rear; deep pink in life, fading to grey after death

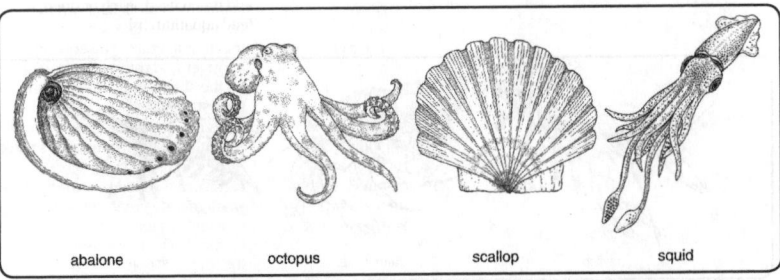

abalone   octopus   scallop   squid

Natural History

Name	Species	Length	Range and habitat	Notable features
squid, giant	*Architeuthis princeps*	<15m	oceans worldwide	largest invertebrate, although tentacles account for over half its length; eats fish, seals and small whales; main food of the sperm whale

CRUSTACEANS: Phylum Arthropoda
■ **Crustacea (c.30 000 species)**

Name	Species	Length	Range and habitat	Notable features
barnacle, acorn	*Semibalanus balanoides*	<1.5cm (diam.)	worldwide	cemented to intertidal rocks; the shell opens when the tide is in and the animal combs food particles from the water with its legs
crab, edible	*Cancer pagurus*	<20cm	eastern N Atlantic and neighbouring seas	scavenger; inhabits rocky coasts to depths of about 50m; widely caught for human consumption
crab, fiddler	*Uca* (many species)	<3cm	tropical seashores and mangrove swamps	scavengers; male has one big, colourful claw, often much bigger than the rest of his body
crab, hermit	(several species and genera)	<15cm	worldwide; mainly in coastal waters	scavengers; elongated, soft-bodied crabs use empty seashells as portable homes
crab, robber	*Birgus latro*	<45cm	islands and coasts of Indian and Pacific oceans	related to hermit crab, but does not live in discarded shells; terrestrial scavenger, feeds mainly on carrion; often climbs trees
crayfish, noble	*Astacus astacus*	<15cm	Europe	inhabits shallow, well aerated streams, feeding on other animals, living or dead; reared in large numbers for human consumption, especially in France
krill	*Euphausia superba*	<5cm	mainly the southern oceans	planktonic shrimp-like animal; the main food of the baleen whales and many other animals in the southern oceans
lobster, common	*Homarus gammarus*	<70cm	European coasts	scavenger; lives on rocky coasts down to depths of about 30m; bluish black in life; now rare in many places through overfishing
lobster, Norway	*Nephrops norvegicus*	<25cm	European seas	a spiny scavenger; lives on sandy and muddy seabeds at depths of 30–200m; marketed as scampi
lobster, spiny	*Palinurus vulgaris*	<45cm	Mediterranean and Atlantic; rocky coasts	very spiny, with stout antennae much longer than the body; no pincers; feeds on molluscs; a popular food in S Europe; also known as crayfish
prawn, common	*Palaemon serratus*	<10cm	European coasts; usually stony or rocky shores	scavenger; almost transparent in life; differs from shrimps in its serrated rostrum
shrimp, common	*Crangon crangon*	<7cm	coasts of Europe and eastern North America	eats other small animals, living or dead; common on sand and mud, and much used for human consumption; front legs stout and clawed
water flea	*Daphnia* (many species)	<0.5cm	worldwide; fresh water	reddish brown or greenish, abundant in muddy ponds and other fresh water; swims by waving long antennae; a major food of small fish and much used, living or dried, to feed aquarium fish

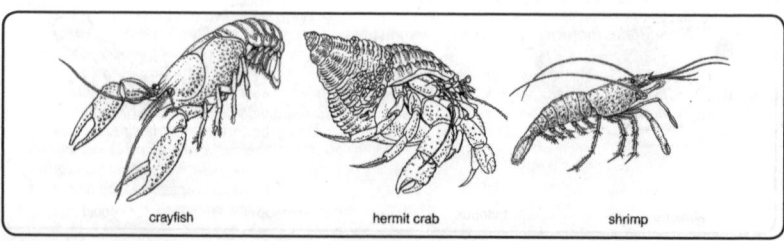

crayfish   hermit crab   shrimp

Name	Species	Length	Range and habitat	Notable features
woodlouse	(many genera and species)	<2.5cm	worldwide	scavengers; feed mainly on decaying plant material; the only major group of terrestrial crustaceans, but still confined to damp places; also called 'sowbugs' and 'slaters'

■ **SPIDERS: Phylum Arthropoda**
■ **Arachnida (c.40 000 species)**

Name	Species	Length	Range and habitat	Notable features
bird-eating spider	(c.800 species in several genera)	<10cm	warmer parts of the Americas and southern Africa	stout-bodied, hairy hunting spiders, often in trees, where they sometimes capture nestling birds; venom not dangerous to people, although the hairs may cause a painful rash; often called tarantulas
black widow	*Latrodectus mactans*	<1.6cm	most warm parts of the world, including S Europe	black with red markings beneath; a dangerous spider that has caused many human deaths, but bites are now quickly cured with antivenin; female sometimes eats the smaller male after mating
bolas spider	(several species and genera)	<1.5cm	N and S America, Africa and Australasia	catches moths by whirling a single thread of silk with a blob of sticky gum on the end
crab spider	(c.3 000 species in numerous genera)	<2cm	worldwide	mostly squat, crab-like spiders that lie in wait for prey – often in flowers – and grab it with their long front legs
funnel-web spider	*Atrax* (3 species)	<5cm	Australia	among the deadliest spiders, although antivenins are now available for treating bites; inhabit tubular webs in the ground or among rocks
garden spider	*Araneus diadematus*	<1.2cm	N hemisphere	black to ginger, with a white cross on the back; makes orb-webs up to 50cm across on fences and vegetation; not only in gardens
gladiator spider	*Dinopis* (several species)	<2.5cm	warm regions and some cooler parts of North America and Australia	slender spiders with enormous eyes; make sticky webs which they throw at passing prey, usually at night
house spider	*Tegenaria* (c.90 species)	<2cm	mostly N hemisphere	long-legged, fast-moving spiders, often seen running over floors at night; make scruffy triangular webs in neglected corners; harmless
jumping spider	(c.4 000 species in many genera)	<1.5cm	worldwide	large-eyed, day-active spiders that leap onto their prey; often brilliantly coloured
money spider	(many species and genera)	<0.6cm	worldwide, but most common in cooler areas of N hemisphere	believed to bring wealth or good fortune, perhaps because of the silvery appearance of their little hammock-like webs which cover grassland and glisten with dew on autumn mornings
orb-web spider	(c.2 500 species in many genera)	<3cm	worldwide	the makers of the familiar wheel-shaped webs, up to a metre or more in diameter; mostly brown, but some are very colourful; not dangerous
raft spider	*Dolomedes* (c.100 species)	<2.5cm	worldwide	hunting spiders that lurk at the edge of pools or on floating objects, picking up vibrations of prey (insects and small fish) and streaking after them
spitting spider	*Scytodes thoracica*	<0.6cm	worldwide; normally only in buildings	catches small insects by spitting strands of sticky, venom-coated gum at them
tarantula	*Lycosa narbonensis*	<3cm	S Europe	a wolf spider whose bite was believed to be curable only by performing a frantic dance – the tarantella; although painful, the bite is not really dangerous; the name is now often applied to the hairy bird-eating spiders

Natural History

black widow	house spider	orb-web spider	zebra spider

Name	Species	Length	Range and habitat	Notable features
trapdoor spider	(c.700 species in several genera)	<3cm	most warm parts of the world, including S Europe	live in burrows closed by hinged lids of silk and debris; spiders lie in wait under the lid and grab passing prey
water spider	*Argyroneta aquatica*	<1.5cm	Eurasia; in ponds and slow-moving streams	the world's only truly aquatic spider, living in an air-filled, thimble-shaped web fixed to water plants; darts out to catch passing prey
wolf spider	(c.2500 species in many genera)	<3cm	worldwide, but most common in cooler parts of N hemisphere	large-eyed hunting spiders, mostly ground-living; some chase their prey at speed; generally harmless but some of the larger species have dangerous bites
zebra spider	*Salticus scenicus*	<0.6cm	N hemisphere; often in and around houses	black and white jumping spider, commonly hunting on rocks and walls, especially those covered with lichen

- **INSECTS: Phylum Arthropoda**
- **Silverfish/Thysanura (c.370 species)**

silverfish	*Lepisma saccharina*	10mm	worldwide	wingless scavenger of starchy foods in houses

- **Mayflies/Ephemeroptera (c.2500 species)**

mayfly	*Hexagenia bilineata*	16mm	worldwide	flimsy insects with 2 or 3 long 'tails'; they grow up in water and have a very short adult life, often only a few hours

- **Damselflies and dragonflies/Odonata (c.5500 species)**

dragonfly	(many species)	<20–130mm	worldwide	long-bodied insects, with gauzy wings spanning up to 150mm; most fly rapidly and catch insects in mid-air; they grow up in water

- **Crickets and grasshoppers/Orthoptera (c.17000 species)**

cricket, bush	(thousands of species)	<150mm	worldwide, apart from coldest areas	omnivorous or insect-eating; like grasshoppers but with very long antennae; several N American species are called katydids
cricket, house	*Acheta domesticus*	<20mm	worldwide	scavenger in houses and rubbish dumps
locust, desert	*Schistocerca gregaria*	85mm	Africa and S Asia	herbivorous; swarms periodically destroy crops in Africa
locust, migratory	*Locusta migratoria*	<50mm	Africa and S Europe	herbivorous; swarm in Africa, but solitary in Europe

- **Stick insects and leaf insects/Phasmida (c.2500 species, mostly tropical)**

insect, leaf	(c.50 species)	<90mm	SE Asia	very flat, leaf-like, green or brown herbivores
insect, stick	(over 2400 species)	<350mm	warm areas, including S Europe	herbivorous; stick-like green or brown bodies with or without wings; often kept as pets

- **Earwigs/Dermaptera (c.1300 species)**

earwig	(many species)	<30mm	originally Africa, now worldwide	slender, brownish insects, with or without wings and always with prominent pincers at the rear; most are omnivorous scavengers

- **Cockroaches and mantids/Dictyoptera (c.5500 species)**

American cockroach	*Periplaneta americana*	40mm	worldwide	scavenger, living outside (if warm) or in buildings; chestnut brown
praying mantis	(c.2000 species)	<75mm	all warm areas	catches other insects with spiky front legs

Name	Species	Length	Range and habitat	Notable features
■ Termites/Isoptera (over 2000 species)				
termite	(many species)	<22mm	mostly tropical	small and ant-like, with or without wings; colonies in mounds of earth, in dead wood or underground; many are timber pests
■ Bugs/Hemiptera (c.70000 species)				
aphid	(numerous species)	<5mm	worldwide	sap-sucking insects, with or without wings; many, including blackfly and greenfly, are serious pests
bedbug	*Cimex lectularius*	5mm	worldwide	bloodsucking; hides by day and feeds at night, often attacking people in their beds
cicada	(numerous species)	<40mm (w)	worldwide, mainly in warm climates	sap-sucking; males make loud, shrill sounds; young stages live underground on roots; one American species takes 17 years to mature
froghopper	*Philaenus spumarius*	6mm	N hemisphere	sap-sucker; young stages live in froth, often called cuckoo-spit
pondskater	*Gerris lacustris*	10mm	N hemisphere	skims across the surface of still water and catches other insects
■ Thrips/Thysanoptera (over 3000 species)				
thrips	(many species)	2.5mm	worldwide	tiny winged or wingless herbivorous insects, many of which grow up in crops and cause much damage; they fly in huge numbers in sultry weather in summer and are often called thunder-bugs
■ Lacewings/Neuroptera (over 6000 species)				
antlion	*Myrmeleon formicarius*	90mm (w)	Eurasia	larvae make small pits in sandy soil and feed on ants and other insects that fall into them
green lacewing	(several genera and many species)	<50mm	worldwide	predators of aphids and other small insects in a wide range of habitats; delicate green wings
■ Scorpion flies/Mecoptera (c.400 species)				
scorpionfly	*Panorpa*	20mm	worldwide	scavenging insects in which the male abdomen is usually turned up like a scorpion's tail, although they are quite harmless
■ Butterflies and moths/Lepidoptera (c.150000 species)				
■ Butterflies (c.18000 species)				
birdwing butterfly	(several genera and species)	<300mm (w)	SE Asia and N Australia, tropical forests	they include the world's largest butterflies; many are becoming rare through collecting and loss of habitat
cabbage white butterfly	*Pieris brassicae*	<70mm (w)	Eurasia, N Africa, flowery places	caterpillar is a serious pest of cabbages and other brassicas
fritillary butterfly	(many genera and species)	<80mm (w)	mostly N hemisphere	mostly orange with black spots above and silvery spots below; live in woods and open spaces including arctic tundra
monarch butterfly	*Danaus plexippus*	<100mm (w)	mostly Pacific area and N America	orange with black markings; a great migrant; it hibernates in huge swarms in Mexico and southern USA; a rare visitor to Europe

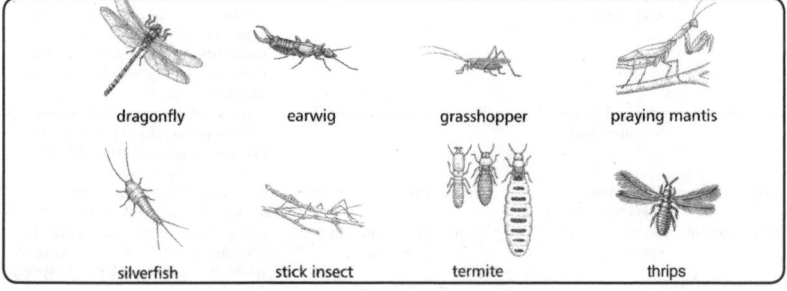

dragonfly   earwig   grasshopper   praying mantis

silverfish   stick insect   termite   thrips

Natural History

Name	Species	Length	Range and habitat	Notable features
skipper butterfly	(many genera and species)	<80mm (w)	worldwide	mostly small brown or orange grassland insects with darting flight
swallowtail butterfly	(many genera and species)	<120mm (w)	worldwide, but mostly tropical	large, usually colourful and with prominent 'tails' on hindwings; many becoming rare through collecting and loss of habitat

■ **Moths (c. 132 000 species)**

Name	Species	Length	Range and habitat	Notable features
burnet moth	*Zygaena* (many species)	<40mm (w)	Eurasia and N Africa	slow, night- and day-flying moths, protected by foul-tasting body fluids and gaudy black and red colours
clothes moth	(several species)	<15mm (w)	worldwide	small, often rather shiny moths whose caterpillars damage woollen fabrics; live mainly in buildings
death's-head hawk moth	*Acherontia atropos*	<135mm (w)	Africa and Eurasia	sturdy moth with a skull-like pattern on its thorax; larvae feed on potato and related plants
hummingbird hawk moth	*Macroglossum stellatarum*	<60mm (w)	Eurasia	day-flying, producing loud hum as it hovers in front of flowers to feed; larvae on bedstraws
pine pro-cessionary moth	*Thaumetopoea pityocampa*	<40mm (w)	S and C Europe	greyish moth whose larvae live in silken tents on pine trees and go out to feed in long processions at night; a serious forest pest
silk moth	*Bombyx mori*	<60mm (w)	native of China; now unknown in the wild	cream-coloured moth bred for the fine silk obtained from its cocoon (over 1km from one cocoon); larvae eat mulberry leaves; all cultured moths flightless
tiger moth	(many genera and species)	<100mm (w)	worldwide	mostly brightly coloured and hairy, with evil-tasting body fluids

■ **True flies/Diptera (c.90 000 species, a few without wings)**

Name	Species	Length	Range and habitat	Notable features
cranefly (or leather-jacket)	(many genera and species)	<35mm (w)	worldwide	slender, long-legged flies, often resting with wings outstretched; larvae of many are leatherjackets that damage crop roots
housefly	*Musca domestica*	7mm	worldwide	abundant on farms and rubbish dumps; becoming less common in houses; breeds in dung and other decaying matter and carries germs
hoverfly	(many genera and species)	<40mm	worldwide	many have amazing hovering ability; adults feed on pollen and nectar; many are black and yellow mimics of bees and wasps
mosquito	(many genera and species)	<15mm	worldwide	females are bloodsuckers; spread malaria and other diseases
tsetse fly	*Glossina* (c.20 species)	10mm	tropical Africa	bloodsuckers; spread human sleeping sickness, cattle diseases

■ **Fleas/Siphonaptera (c.1 800 species)**

Name	Species	Length	Range and habitat	Notable features
European flea	(many species)	3mm	worldwide	wingless, bloodsucking parasites feeding on birds and mammals; long hind legs enable them to jump many times their own lengths; the maggot-like larvae are not parasitic

■ **Bees, wasps and ants/Hymenoptera (over 120 000 species)**

Name	Species	Length	Range and habitat	Notable features
ant, army	(several genera and species)	<40mm	tropics	live in mobile colonies, some of over a million ants; kill any animal unable to get out of their way; workers much smaller than the 40mm-long queen; African species often called driver ants
ant, honeypot	(several genera and species)	20mm	deserts across the world	some workers gorge themselves with sugar-rich food and become living honeypots from which other ants can feed
ant, weaver	*Oecophylla* (several species)	10mm	Old World tropics	nest made from leaves, joined by sticky silk produced by the grubs
bee, bumble	*Bombus* (many species)	<35mm	worldwide, except Australia	plump, hairy bees living in annual colonies; only mated queen survives winter to start new colonies in spring

Natural History

Name	Species	Length	Range and habitat	Notable features
bee, honey	*Apis mellifera*	<20mm	worldwide (probably native of SE Asia)	less hairy than bumble bee; lives in permanent colonies, sometimes in hollow trees but mostly in artificial hives; stores honey for winter
hornet, European	*Vespa crabro*	<35mm	Eurasia and now America	large brown and yellow wasp; nests in hollow trees and feeds young on other insects
ichneumon	(thousands of genera and species)	<50mm	worldwide	parasites, mostly laying their eggs in young stages of other insects; the young grow inside their hosts and gradually kill them
sawfly	(numerous families)	<50mm	worldwide	named after the saw-like ovipositor of most females, used to cut slits in plants before egg-laying; larvae all vegetarians

■ **Beetles/Coleoptera (over 350 000 species; front wings usually form casing over body)**

Name	Species	Length	Range and habitat	Notable features
sexton beetle	*Nicrophorus* (several species)	<25mm	worldwide	often orange and black; beetles work in pairs to bury small dead animals, near which they then lay their eggs
click beetle (or wireworm)	(many genera and species)	<40mm	worldwide	bullet-shaped beetles which flick into the air to turn over, making a loud click; larvae, called wireworms, damage crop roots
Colorado beetle	*Leptinotarsa decemlineata*	10mm	N America and now Europe	black and yellow adults and pink grubs both seriously damage potato crops
deathwatch beetle	*Xestobium rufovillosum*	7mm	N hemisphere	tunnelling larvae do immense damage to old building timbers; adults tap wood as mating call; also found in dead trees
devil's coach-horse	*Staphylinus olens*	25mm	Eurasia	slender black beetle with short front wings; lives in gardens and often enters houses; also called cocktail because it raises its rear end
furniture beetle (or woodworm)	*Anobium punctatum*	5mm	worldwide	larvae, known as woodworm, tunnel in dead wood and cause much damage to furniture and building timbers
glow-worm	*Lampyris noctiluca*	15mm	Europe	wingless female glows with greenish light to attract males flying overhead; feeds on snails
goliath beetle	*Goliathus* (several species)	<150mm	Africa	world's heaviest beetles, up to 100g; fly well and feed on fruit
grain weevil	*Sitophilus granarius*	3mm	worldwide	a serious pest, breeding in and destroying all kinds of stored grain
ladybird	(c.3500 species in many genera)	10mm	worldwide	aphid-eating habits make them friends of gardeners; most are red or yellow, with various spot patterns
scarab beetle	*Scarabaeus* (many species)	30mm	most warm parts of the world	some form dung into balls and roll it around before burying it; known as tumblebugs in N America; introduced into Australia to deal with sheep and cattle dung
stag beetle	*Lucanus cervus*	50mm	Eurasia	males have huge antler-like jaws, with which they wrestle rivals

woodworm ► furniture beetle

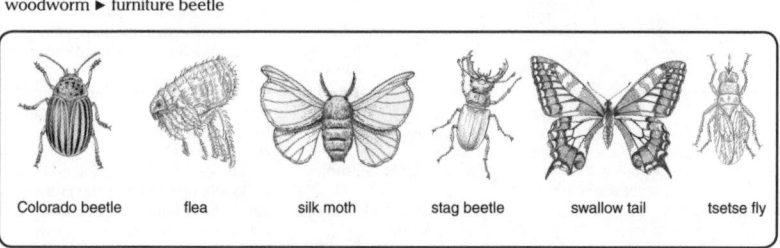

Colorado beetle   flea   silk moth   stag beetle   swallow tail   tsetse fly

Collective names for mammals, birds and fish

Natural History

Animal	Collective name	Animal	Collective name
ants	colony, nest, swarm	kittens	kindle, litter
apes	shrewdness	larks	bevy, exaltation
asses	pace	leopards	leap
baboons	troop	lions	pride
badgers	cete	locusts	plague, swarm
bears	sleuth, sloth	magpies	tiding, tittering
bees	colony, erst, grist, hive, nest, swarm	moles	labour
		monkeys	troop
birds	flight, flock, volery	mules	span
buffalo	gang, herd, obstinacy	nightingales	watch
caterpillars	army	otters	romp
cats	clowder, pounce	owls	parliament, stare
cattle	drove, herd	oxen	drove, herd, yoke
chickens	brood, clutch	oysters	bed
clams	bed	parrots	company, pandemonium
cockroaches	intrusion	partridges	covey
cranes	sedge, siege	peacocks	muster, ostentation
crocodiles	bask	penguins	colony, muster, parcel
crows	murder	pheasants	bevy, bouquet, nest, nid, nide, nye
deer	herd		
dogs	kennel, pack	pigs	litter
dolphins	school	plovers	congregation, wing
doves	dole	ponies	string
ducks	brace, flock, paddling, safe, team	porcupines	prickle
		porpoises	school, turmoil
eagles	convocation	quail	bevy, covey
elephants	herd, parade	rabbits	bury
elk	gang	rats	colony
ferrets	busyness	ravens	unkindness
fish	draught, school, shoal	rhinoceros	crash
flamingos	stand	rooks	building, parliament, rookery
flies	busyness, swarm	seals	herd, pod, rookery
foxes	leash, skulk	sharks	shiver
frogs	army	sheep	drove, flock, trip
geese	flock, gaggle, skein	sparrows	host
giraffes	tower	squirrels	dray, scurry
gnats	cloud, horde	starlings	murmuration
goats	herd, tribe, trip	storks	mustering
goldfinches	charm, chirm	swans	bevy, wedge
gorillas	band	swine	drift, sounder
grouse	pack	teal	spring
hares	down, husk, mute	tigers	ambush, streak
hawks	cast	toads	knot
hens	brood	trout	hover
herons	siege	turkeys	rafter
hippopotami	bloat	turtles	bale, dole, turn
hogs	drift	vipers	nest
horses	drove, herd, stable, team	whales	gam, herd, pod, school
hounds	cry, mute, pack	wolves	pack, rout, route
hyenas	cackle	woodcocks	fall
jellyfish	smack	woodpeckers	descent
kangaroos	herd, mob, troop	zebras	zeal

Species under threat

The world's animal and plant species are increasingly under threat of extinction. Although the threats are varied, human activities are now the main cause of extinctions, putting 99% of threatened species at risk. The acronym HIPPO is sometimes used to summarize the threats to species and ecosystems:

H   habitat destruction and degradation; this also includes human-induced climate change, which is an increasing problem; these factors affect 86% of threatened birds and mammals and 88% of threatened amphibians.

I   invasive species; this refers to non-native species (eg cats, rats, zebra mussels) which might be introduced to a place either deliberately or unintentionally and then start to destroy native species.

P   pollution.

P   population growth.

O   over-harvesting/hunting; this refers to unsustainable levels of harvesting, hunting or fishing bringing species to the brink of extinction.

The IUCN: The World Conservation Union produces the most comprehensive inventory of the conservation status of animal and plant species, the Red List of Threatened Species (www.iucnredlist.org), which is updated every year. Experts assess species for the Red List against five criteria: rate of decline, population size, area of geographic distribution, degree of population and distribution fragmentation. They then classify species into one of nine categories:

Extinct (EX)	when there is no doubt that the last individual in a taxon (any taxonomic group, eg subspecies, species, genus) has died; it is presumed extinct when exhaustive surveys in known or expected habitat throughout its range have failed to record an individual.
Extinct in the Wild (EW)	when a taxon is known to survive only in cultivation, in captivity or as a naturalized population outside the historic range.
Critically Endangered (CR)	when a taxon is facing an extremely high risk of extinction in the wild.
Endangered (EN)	when a taxon is facing a very high risk of extinction in the wild.
Vulnerable (VU)	when a taxon is facing a high risk of extinction in the wild.
Near Threatened (NT)	when a taxon is close to qualifying for, or is likely to qualify for, a threatened category in the near future unless conservation measures are taken.
Least Concern (LC)	when a taxon does not qualify for the previous categories; includes widespread and abundant taxa.
Data Deficient (DD)	when there is inadequate information to make an assessment of a taxon's risk of extinction based on its distribution and/or population status.
Not Evaluated (NE)	when a taxon has not yet been evaluated against the criteria.

The 2008 Red List assessed 44 838 species against the criteria. As at October 2008:

Number of species officially declared extinct	804
Number of species found only in cultivation or captivity	65
Number of species threatened with extinction in one of the three threatened categories*	16 928
Number of species improved in status since last assessment	40
Number of species declined in status since last assessment	183

* Critically Endangered, Endangered or Vulnerable; this includes 30% of amphibians, 12% of birds and 21% of mammals.

The Red List Indices, which measure trends in extinction risk by comparing the status of specific groups over time, show that the status of birds and amphibians in particular has been declining steadily since before the 1990s.

Group	Critically Endangered		Endangered		Vulnerable	
	1996–8	2008	1996–8	2008	1996–8	2008
Mammals	169	188	315	448	612	505
Birds	168	190	235	361	704	671
Reptiles	41	86	59	134	153	203
Amphibians	18	475	31	755	75	675
Fish	157	289	134	269	443	717
Insects	44	70	116	132	377	424
Molluscs	257	268	212	224	451	486
Plants	909	1575	1197	2280	3222	4602

Natural History

Natural History

Species under threat include:

■ **Habit destruction/degradation** pygmy hippopotamus (W Africa); golden-rumped sengi (elephant shrew) (Kenya); Aran rock lizard (Spain); Mariana crow (Northern Marianas Islands); spider tortoise (Madagascar)

■ **Climate change/pollution** polar bear (Arctic); Naufraga balearica (plant endemic to Majorca); Squalius keadicus (fish endemic to Greece)

■ **Invasive species** Pritchardia palm (Hawaii); tiger chameleon (Seychelles); giant bronze gecko (Seychelles); Campbell Islands teal (New Zealand)

■ **Over-harvesting/hunting** Cuban crocodile; gulper shark (Atlantic); common hippopotamus (C Africa); pygmy three-toed sloth (Panama)

Threatened species often require a combination of conservation measures to ensure their survival, such as research, species-specific actions, site- and habitat-based actions, policy responses, and communication and education. Current conservation programmes include those to conserve the African elephant, Bengal tiger (India), European bison, southern white rhinoceros (Africa), Asian vultures, grouse, pink pigeon (Mauritius), Siberian crane (Russia), marine and freshwater turtles, western grey whale, and ecosystems such as coral reefs and mangrove forests (SE Asia).

The Convention on Migratory Species and the Convention on International Trade in Endangered Species of Wild Fauna and Flora (CITES) was set up to ensure that trade in wild species does not threaten their survival. It protects about 5000 species of animals and 28 000 species of plants (www.cites.org/eng/resources/species. html) against overexploitation. It lists species in three Appendices, grouped according to how threatened they are by international trade.

Appendix I	species that are threatened with extinction (eg Asian elephant, gorilla, humpback whale, Brazilian rosewood, some orchid species); trade in these species is prohibited for commercial purposes; some non-commercial trade (eg for educational facilities) is allowed.
Appendix II	species that may become threatened unless trade is regulated (eg American black bear, Galapagos marine iguana, southern fur seal, American mahogany); trade is allowed if it is not detrimental to the survival of the species, but it is strictly regulated.
Appendix III	species that any signatory of the Convention has identified as being exploited in its country and in need of the help of other signatory countries to regulate international trade in it (eg Hoffmann's two-toed sloth from Costa Rica; African civet from Botswana).

CITES currently has programmes monitoring: the illegal killing of African and Asian elephants and illicit trade in ivory and other elephant products; sustainable trade in falcons for falconry; illicit trade in orang-utans (Asia); the status of trade in Hawksbill turtles; sustainable trade in bigleaf mahogany; and illegal trade in sturgeons and unsustainable harvesting of caviar.

HUMAN BODY, HEALTH AND NUTRITION

DNA

DNA, or deoxyribonucleic acid, is the genetic material of humans and other organisms. It contains the sugar deoxyribose and interlocking pairs of molecules known as bases. Genes are sequences of DNA that contain coded instructions for the transmission of genetic information from one generation to the next, and for the manufacture of all the proteins that are required for growth and development of a whole new organism.

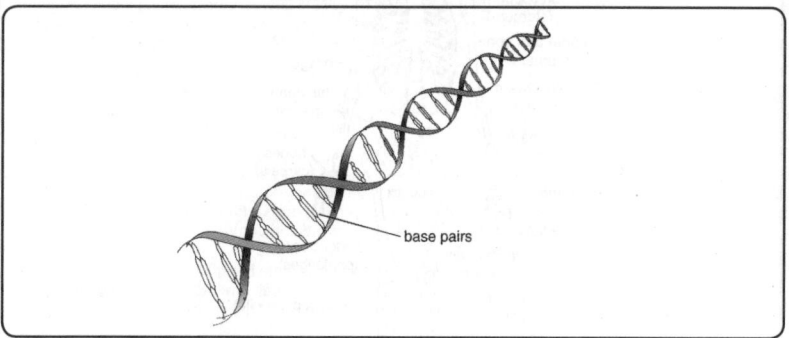

base pairs

The chromosomes

A chromosome is a rod-like portion of the DNA of a cell. Chromosomes perform an important part in cell division, and in the transmission of hereditary characteristics. Normally constant in number for any species, there are 22 pairs of chromosomes and two sex chromosomes in a typical human cell.

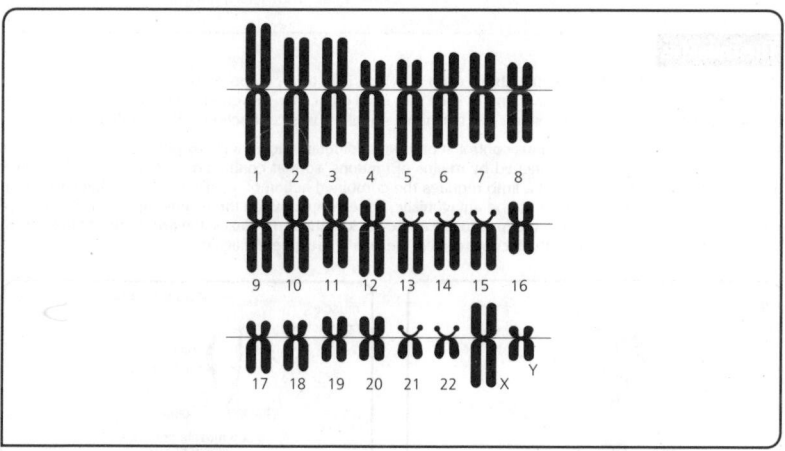

The skeleton

Human beings have an internal skeleton, or endoskeleton, made of bone and cartilage. It supports the tissues and organs of the body, and protects soft internal organs such as the lungs. The muscles are attached to the bones of the skeleton by means of tendons, which allow the muscles to pull against the bones when they contract, causing them to move. Bones are connected to each other by means of ligaments; the point of articulation or contact between two or more bones is known as a joint. Different types of joint allow varying degrees of movement. In total, the adult human skeleton has 206 bones.

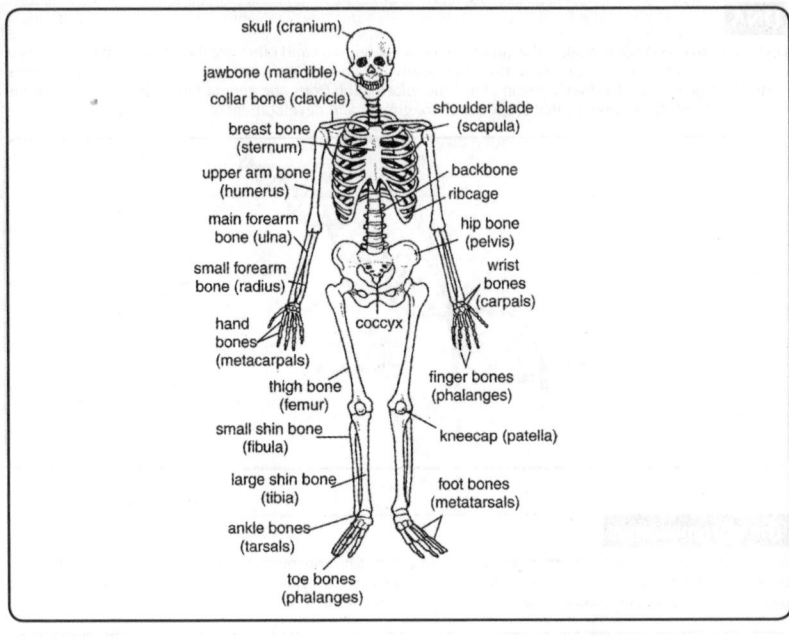

skull (cranium)
jawbone (mandible)
collar bone (clavicle)
breast bone (sternum)
shoulder blade (scapula)
upper arm bone (humerus)
backbone
ribcage
main forearm bone (ulna)
hip bone (pelvis)
small forearm bone (radius)
wrist bones (carpals)
hand bones (metacarpals)
coccyx
thigh bone (femur)
finger bones (phalanges)
small shin bone (fibula)
kneecap (patella)
large shin bone (tibia)
foot bones (metatarsals)
ankle bones (tarsals)
toe bones (phalanges)

The muscles

Muscles consist of bundles of small fibres, each of which is in turn composed of many protein myofibrils. These lengthen or shorten as their filaments slide past each other. This movement, which occurs in response to a stimulus from the nervous system, or a hormonal signal, causes contraction of the whole muscle.

Voluntary muscle is under conscious control. It produces voluntary movements by pulling against the bones of the skeleton, to which it is attached by means of tendons, so that contractions of such muscles cause the bones to move. Movement of a limb requires the combined action of a pair of muscles that can pull in opposite directions; these are said to be antagonistic. For example, when the biceps muscle at the front of the upper arm contracts, and the triceps muscle at the back of the arm relaxes, the arm bends at the elbow. When the triceps contracts and the biceps relaxes, the arm is straightened again.

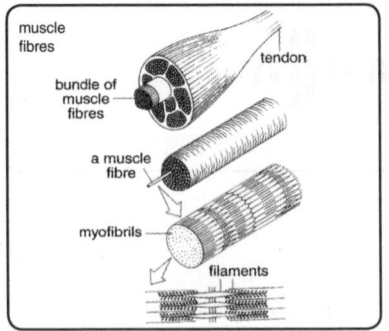

muscle fibres
tendon
bundle of muscle fibres
a muscle fibre
myofibrils
filaments

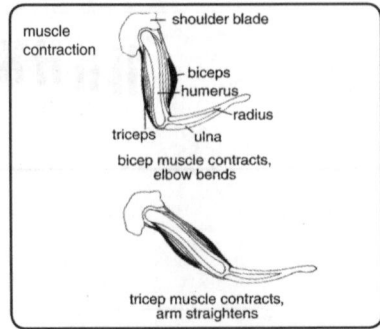

muscle contraction
shoulder blade
biceps
humerus
radius
triceps
ulna
bicep muscle contracts, elbow bends

tricep muscle contracts, arm straightens

Involuntary muscle (also called smooth muscle) maintains the movements of the internal body systems, and forms part of many internal organs such as the intestines, bladder and uterus. Cardiac muscle, found only in the heart, does not become fatigued, and continues to contract rhythmically even when it is disconnected from the nervous system.

The skin

The skin consists of a thin outer layer (the epidermis), which is continually being renewed as dead cells are shed from its surface, and a thicker underlying layer (the dermis). The latter is composed of a network of collagen and elastic fibres containing blood and lymph vessels, sensory nerve endings, hair follicles, sweat and sebaceous glands, and smooth muscle.

The skin is an important sense organ, sensitive to touch, pressure, changes in temperature, and painful stimuli. It prevents fluid loss and dehydration, and protects the body from invasion by micro-organisms and parasites. In humans and other warm-blooded animals it has an important role in temperature regulation, heat loss being achieved by sweating and by dilation of the skin capillaries. In order to conserve heat, the skin capillaries contract and the hairs on the surface are raised, trapping a layer of warm air next to the skin.

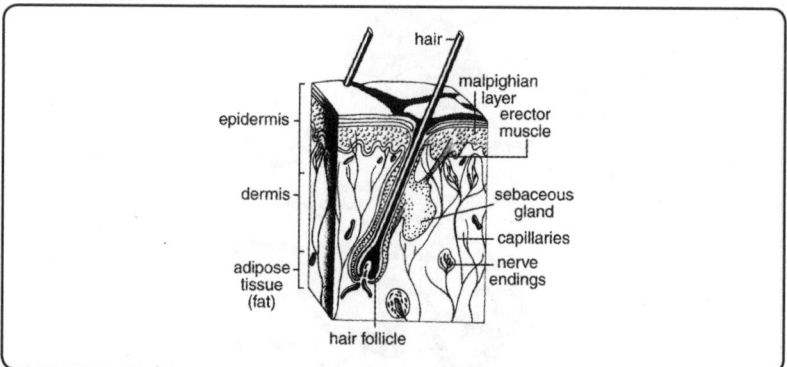

The nervous system

The central nervous system (CNS) consists of the brain and spinal cord, while the remainder of the nervous system is known as the peripheral nervous system (PNS). Sensory receptor cells and sense organs of the PNS collect sensory information in the form of nerve impulses (electrical or chemical signals). These are carried along sensory neurones (nerve cells) to the CNS for processing. The CNS relays a suitable response, again in the form of a nerve impulse, along motor neurones of the PNS to muscles or glands (often referred to as effectors).

The part of the PNS that controls the sensory and motor functions described above is called the somatic nervous system. Another part of the PNS, the autonomic nervous system, controls vital body functions that are not under conscious control, such as breathing and heartbeat.

Some peripheral nerves operate by means of reflexes, eg to produce rapid withdrawal of the hand from a hot object. These involve the transmission of sensory information only as far as the spinal cord, which then sends a response directly to the muscles without the need for processing of information in the brain.

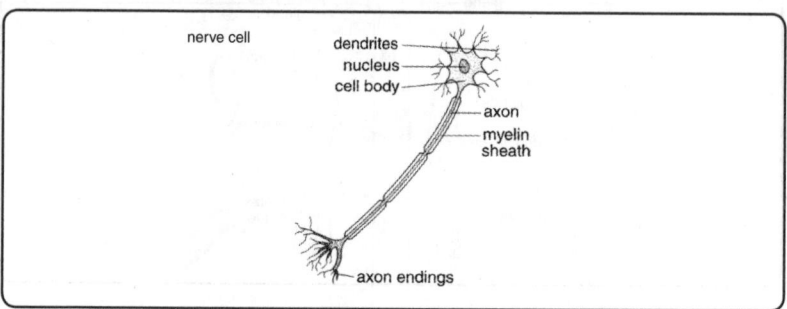

Human Body, Health and Nutrition

The brain

The human brain is part of the central nervous system. It contains more than ten billion nerve cells, and on average weighs about 1400g. It receives sensory information via spinal nerves from the spinal cord and cranial nerves from sense organs such as the eye and the ear. When this information has been processed within the brain, appropriate instructions are sent out along motor neurones to effector organs such as muscles.

The brain is enclosed within three membranes, the meninges, and is protected by the rigid bones of the skull. The forebrain consists of the cerebral hemispheres, the thalamus and the hypothalamus. The outermost layer of the cerebral hemispheres, which are deeply folded and cover most of the surface of the human brain, is known as the cerebral cortex. It is involved in the integration of all sensory input to the brain, including memory and learning, enabling behaviour to be based on past experience. The midbrain connects the forebrain to the hindbrain, which comprises the cerebellum, the medulla oblongata and the pons. The cerebellum co-ordinates complex muscular processes such as maintaining posture, and the medulla oblongata contains centres that regulate breathing, heartbeat and blood pressure.

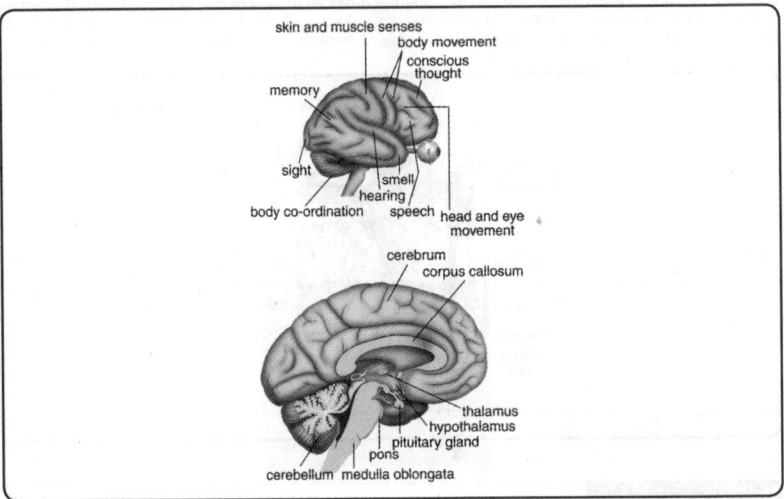

The glands

The hormonal, or endocrine, system works in tandem with the nervous system to control body activities. The hormonal communications system that exerts this control consists of a network of endocrine glands. These glands release many different hormones, or chemical messengers, each of which affects particular glands or tissues in other parts of the body. Hormones are carried to their target tissues by the bloodstream. By attaching themselves to receptors on cells in the target tissues, the hormones pass on their instructions.

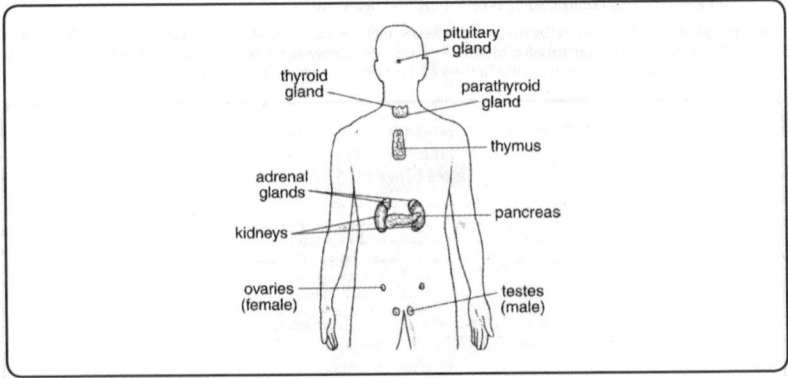

The digestive system

The body uses the food we eat to provide energy for growth and repair; however, the body cannot use the food until it has been processed by the digestive system. The processing is carried out along the alimentary canal, a tubular organ that extends from the mouth, where the food is ingested, to the anus, where waste material is eliminated. The alimentary canal consists of the mouth cavity, pharynx, oesophagus, stomach, duodenum, small intestine, large intestine and rectum. The movement of food along it is achieved by a wave of involuntary muscle contractions (peristalsis). Specialized regions such as the small intestine secrete different enzymes and absorb the products of digestion.

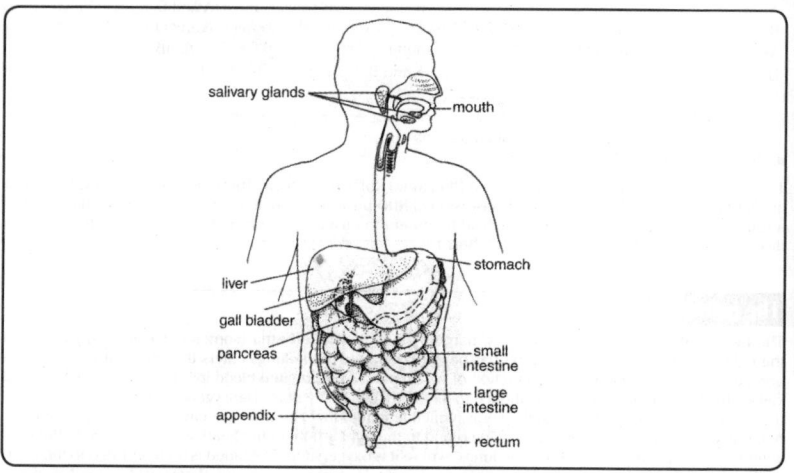

The lymphatic system

Lymph is a blood-derived colourless fluid that bathes all the tissues, cleansing them of cellular debris and bacteria. It contains lymphocytes and antibodies that prevent the spread of infection. A network of vessels, the lymphatic system, drains lymph from throughout the body to the lymph nodes, spleen and other lymphoid tissue where immune responses are initiated.

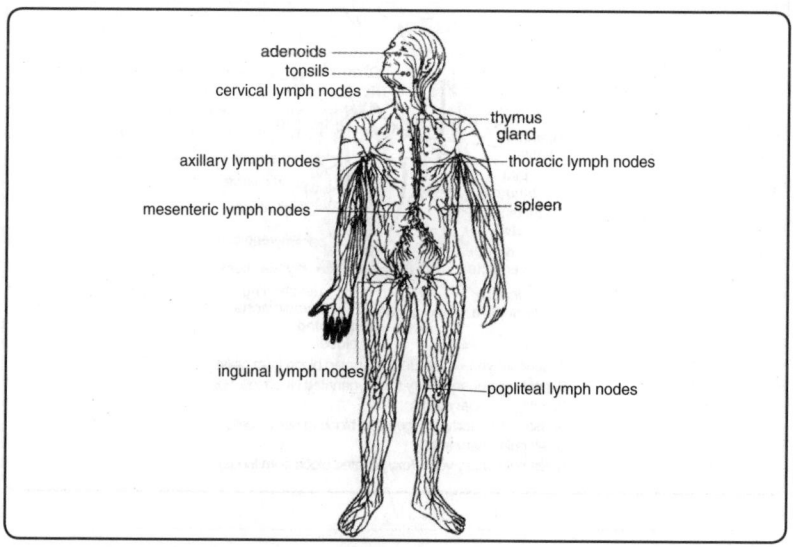

Human Body, Health and Nutrition

ABO blood group system

An individual's blood group is determined by genes inherited from their parents. The red blood cells of the A, B, AB and O groups carry, respectively, the A antigen, B antigen, both antigens and neither. The blood contains natural antibodies against any blood group antigens that are absent from the red cells. Before a transfusion, the blood of the recipient and donor is cross-matched to ensure that red cells from the donor are not given to a person possessing antibodies against them, as this could have fatal consequences.

Blood group	Antigens on red cells	Antibodies in plasma	Can receive blood type
A	A	B	A and O
B	B	A	B and O
AB[1]	A and B	none	A, B, AB, O
O[2]	none	A and B	O

[1] Universal recipient
[2] Universal donor

- **Rhesus factor**

The 'Rhesus factor' is a blood antigen called Rhesus D (RhD). As with the ABO blood groups, individuals who are RhD-negative must not be given a transfusion of RhD-positive blood. If a RhD-negative woman conceives a RhD-positive child, she may need medical treatment to ensure she does not react to the foetus ('Rhesus disease', or haemolytic disease of the newborn).

The heart

The heart is divided into four chambers, namely the right and left atria (sometimes called auricles), and the right and left ventricles. Blood that has been oxygenated in the lungs enters the left atrium of the heart and passes to the left ventricle, contraction of which passes oxygenated blood into the aorta, a major blood vessel that leads to the arteries and thence to all the tissues of the body. Deoxygenated blood from the body tissues is returned to the heart via the veins, which lead into the superior vena cava and inferior vena cava, two major blood vessels. These convey the blood to the right atrium of the heart, and from there to the right ventricle, which pumps blood on to the lungs, where it is oxygenated. The blood is then returned to the heart so that the cycle can begin again. The presence of several valves within the heart ensures that the blood can only flow in one direction.

The muscular contractions of the heart are self-sustaining, because it consists of a special type of muscle, known as cardiac muscle. This type of muscle does not become fatigued, and continues to contract rhythmically even when it is disconnected from the nervous system. The average rate of contraction, measured as the pulse rate, is about 72 beats per minute in men and about 80 beats per minute in women.

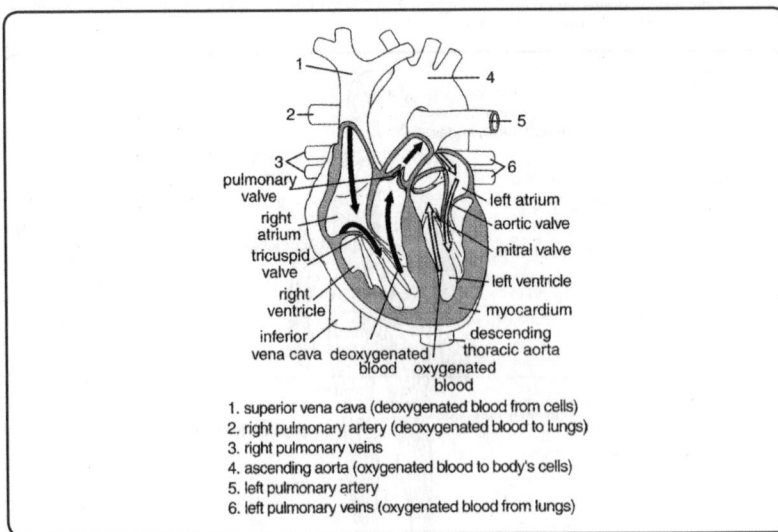

1. superior vena cava (deoxygenated blood from cells)
2. right pulmonary artery (deoxygenated blood to lungs)
3. right pulmonary veins
4. ascending aorta (oxygenated blood to body's cells)
5. left pulmonary artery
6. left pulmonary veins (oxygenated blood from lungs)

The circulatory system

The process by which blood is continuously moved throughout the body is shown in diagrammatic form below.

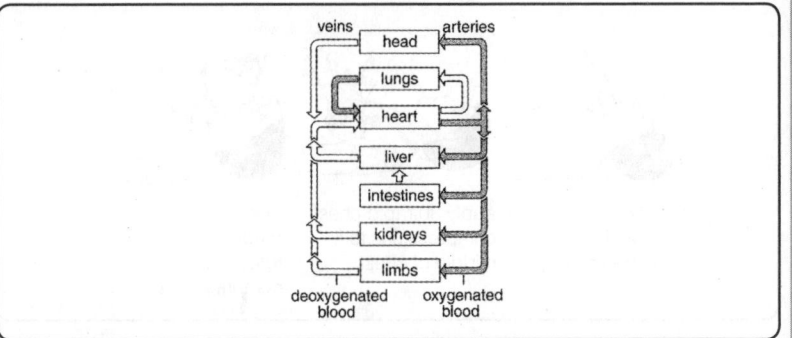

The lungs

The lungs are large spongy respiratory organs that remove carbon dioxide from the blood and replace it with oxygen. The surface area of the lungs is greatly increased by the presence of millions of tiny air sacs, known as alveoli. In humans, the total surface area of the alveoli is about 70m². Air containing oxygen is drawn into the lungs through the trachea (windpipe), which divides at its lower end to form two bronchi, which in turn divide into many fine tubes known as bronchioles. Each bronchiole terminates in a cluster of alveoli, which are lined with a thin moist membrane richly supplied with capillaries (very small blood vessels). Oxygen from the air on one side of the membrane passes through the thin walls of the alveoli into the capillaries, while carbon dioxide passes out of the capillaries into the lungs in the same way. Air is forced in and out of the lungs as a result of movements of the diaphragm (a sheet of muscle that separates the thorax from the abdomen). During inhalation the diaphragm is lowered, and the lungs expand to fill with air. During exhalation, the diaphragm is raised, and air is forcibly expelled from the lungs.

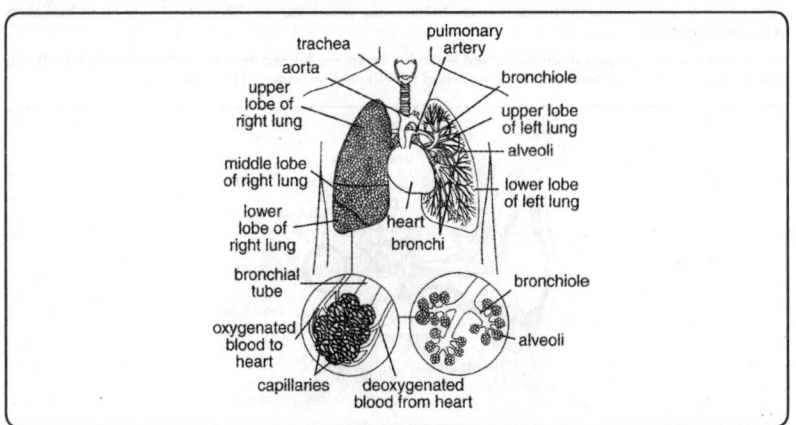

Human Body, Health and Nutrition

CPR – cardio-pulmonary resuscitation

CPR, or cardio-pulmonary resuscitation, is a method of stimulating the heart and lungs of a person who has stopped breathing, or is not breathing normally, to try to make him or her start breathing naturally again.

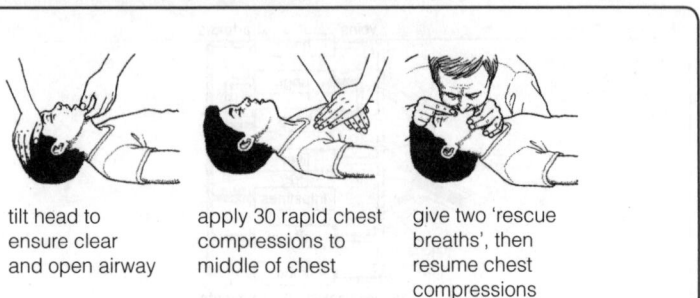

tilt head to
ensure clear
and open airway

apply 30 rapid chest
compressions to
middle of chest

give two 'rescue
breaths', then
resume chest
compressions

The ear

The ear consists of three parts. The outer ear transmits sound waves from outside the ear to the tympanic membrane (eardrum), and consists of a pinna (commonly referred to as the 'ear') that projects from the head and is made of a thin layer of cartilage covered with skin. It funnels sound into a channel that leads to the tympanic membrane. (In some mammals, eg dogs, the pinna can be moved independently in order to detect the direction of sounds.)

The middle ear is an air-filled cavity containing three small bones or ossicles, known as the malleus (hammer), incus (anvil) and stapes (stirrup). The Eustachian tube links the middle ear to the pharynx at the back of the throat, ensuring that the air pressure remains the same on both sides of the tympanic membrane. The ossicles transmit vibrations from the tympanic membrane to the fenestra ovalis (oval window), the upper of two membrane-covered openings that separate the middle ear from the fluid-filled inner ear. Vibrations from the fenestra ovalis are finally transmitted to the spiral-shaped cochlea in the inner ear. The cochlea is filled with fluid and lined with sensory cells (hair cells) that detect vibrations as movements of fluid and relay them as nerve impulses via the auditory nerve to the brain, where they are interpreted as the tone and pitch of the original sound.

The inner ear also contains three fluid-filled semicircular tubes, known as semicircular canals, which can detect movements of the head and are concerned with the maintenance of balance.

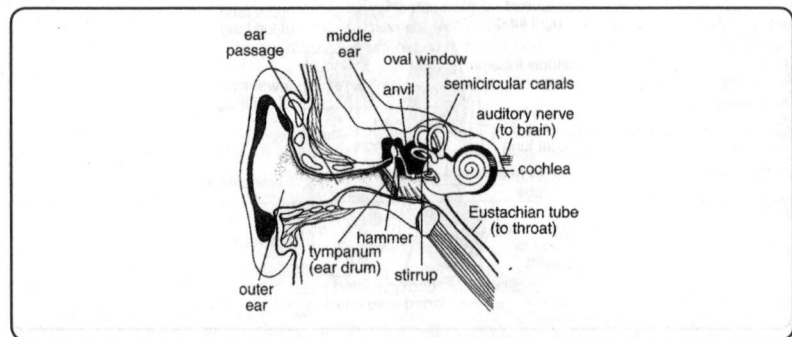

The eye

The eye is surrounded by a white fibrous outer layer (the sclera), which is modified at the front of the eye to form the transparent cornea. The sclera is lined by a vascular layer or choroid, which is in turn lined at the back of the eye by the retina. The retina contains millions of light-sensitive cells of two types: the rods (which function at low light levels, and are responsible for black and white vision), and the cones (which are responsible for colour vision).

Light enters the eye through the cornea, and passes through a watery medium (the aqueous humour) and then through the pupil, a small circular aperture in the iris. The iris is an adjustable ring of muscle that forms the coloured part of the eye, and controls the size of the pupil and thus the amount of light entering the eye.

Behind the iris lies the transparent lens, whose curvature is regulated by means of ciliary muscles. These contract to make the lens thin, for viewing distant objects, or relax to make it thicker, for viewing nearby objects. The shape of the lens is adjusted in this way so that light is directed through the jelly-like vitreous humour lying between the lens and the retina, and is focused onto the retina. The light-sensitive rods and cones of the latter then transmit nerve impulses via the optic nerve to the brain, where they are interpreted as vision.

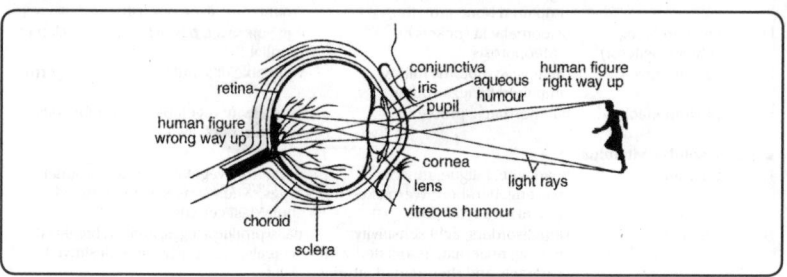

■ **Astigmatism**

In the normal eye, light travels through the lens to a single focal point, producing clear, undistorted vision. In the astigmatic eye, a defect in the lens produces distortion because not all light rays from it are brought to the same focus on the retina. It can be corrected by surgery or by wearing spectacles or contact lenses that produce exactly the opposite degree of distortion.

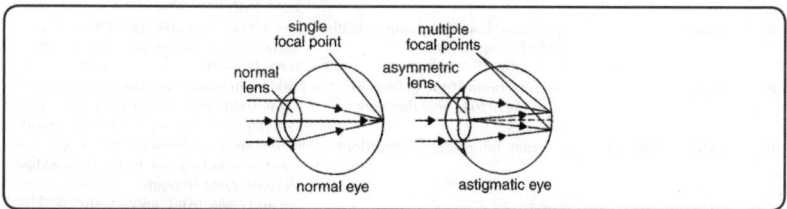

The reproductive organs

The male reproductive system is closely associated with the urinary system. The bladder stores urine, releasing it to the outside along the urethra, a tube inside the penis that also carries sperm during ejaculation. Sperm are made inside the testis and stored in coiled tubes called the epididymis until, during ejaculation, they are carried to the penis along the sperm duct or vas deferens. The prostate gland, which is located where the sperm ducts and urethra join, releases semen, the milky medium in which sperm are ejaculated from the penis.

Within the female reproductive system, a single sex cell, or ovum (egg), is released each month from one of the ovaries. It travels along the Fallopian tube to the uterus. The neck of the uterus, or cervix, forms a narrow opening between the uterus and the vagina.

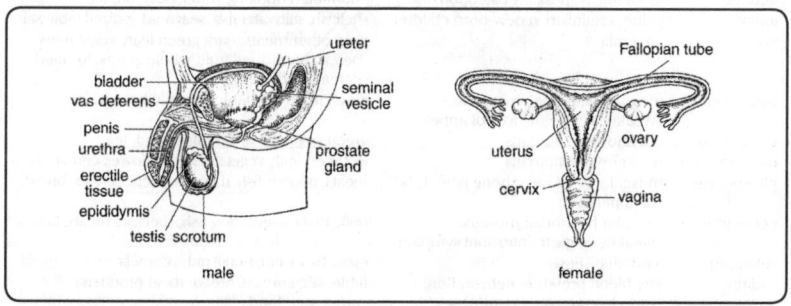

Human Body, Health and Nutrition

Main types of vitamin

■ Fat-soluble vitamins

Vit-amin	Chemical name	Deficiency symptoms	Source
A	retinol (carotene)	night blindness; rough skin; impaired bone growth	dairy products, egg yolk, fortified margarine, liver, oily fish
D	calciferols (eg cholecalciferol)	osteomalacia (rickets); osteoporosis	egg yolk, liver, oily fish; made on skin in sunlight
E	tocopherols	multiple symptoms follow impaired fat absorption	vegetable oils, nuts, seeds, wheatgerm
K	phytomenadione	haemorrhagic problems	green leafy vegetables, vegetable oils, cereals, beef, liver

■ Water-soluble vitamins

Vit-amin	Chemical name	Deficiency symptoms	Source
B_1	thiamin	headache, fatigue, muscle wasting; beri-beri; Wernicke–Korsakov's syndrome	pork, fruit, vegetables, dairy products, eggs, whole grains, some fortified breakfast cereals
B_2	riboflavin	skin disorders; light sensitivity; itching; anaemia; associated with cataracts and rheumatoid arthritis	dairy products, eggs, fortified breakfast cereals, rice, mushrooms; destroyed by light
B_3	niacin	pellagra (gastrointestinal problems, skin and, neurological symptoms)	milk, eggs, poultry, meats, wheat flour, maize flour
B_5	pantothenic acid	fatigue; gastrointestinal problems; sleep disturbances; neurological disorders	found in virtually all meat and vegetable foods; destroyed in heavily processed food
B_6	pyridoxine	anxiety and depression; weight gain or loss	liver, meats, milk, eggs, fruits, cereals, brown rice, soya beans, whole grains, nuts, leafy vegetables
B_7	biotin	dermatitis; hair loss; conjunctivitis; loss of co-ordination	liver, kidney, egg yolk, dried fruit, yeast extract; made by micro-organisms in large intestine
B_9	folic acid	anaemia; neural tube defects in offspring of folic acid-deficient mothers	liver, green leafy vegetables, some fruits, brown rice, yeast extract; cooking and processing can cause serious losses in food
B_{12}	cyanocobalamin	anaemia; neurological disorders	liver, kidney, other meats, fish, eggs, dairy products, some fortified breakfast cereals; none in plants
C	ascorbic acid	scurvy	soft and citrus fruits, green leafy vegetables, potatoes, liver, kidney; losses occur during storage and cooking

Main trace minerals

Mineral	Deficiency symptoms	Source
calcium	osteomalacia (rickets) in children; osteoporosis in adults	milk, cheese, most green leafy vegetables, soya beans, nuts, fortified cereals and flours
chromium	impaired regulation of blood sugar; weight loss; neuropathy	processed meats, whole grains, pulses, spices
copper	anaemia; bone abnormalities	nuts, shellfish, offal
fluoride	tooth decay; possibly osteoporosis	fluoridated drinking water, seafood, tea
iodine	goitre; cretinism in new-born children	shellfish, saltwater fish, seaweed, iodized table salt
iron	anaemia	liver, other meats, dark green leafy vegetables, beans, nuts, dried fruit, whole grains, fortified cereals and flours
magnesium	irregular heartbeat; muscular weakness; fatigue; loss of appetite	green leafy vegetables, nuts, whole grains
manganese	not known in humans	green vegetables, cereals, bread, tea
molybdenum	not known in humans	legumes, leafy vegetables, cauliflower, cereals, nuts
phosphorus	muscular weakness; bone pain; loss of appetite	meats, poultry, fish, dairy products, cereals, bread
potassium	irregular heartbeat; muscular weakness; gastrointestinal symptoms	milk, fruits, vegetables, fish, shellfish, meats, liver
selenium	Keshan disease	eggs, fish, offal, brazil nuts, cereals
sodium	low blood pressure, dehydration, muscle cramps (very rare)	table salt, cereals, bread, meat products, processed foods
zinc	impaired growth and development; nerve damage; impaired wound healing; loss of appetite; susceptibility to infection	meat, shellfish, dairy products, whole grains

Infectious diseases and infections

Name	Cause	Transmission	Incubation	Symptoms
AIDS (Acquired Immune Deficiency Syndrome)	human immunodeficiency virus (HIV; retrovirus family)	sexual intercourse, sharing of syringes, blood transfusion	several years	fever, lethargy, weight loss, diarrhoea, lymph node enlargement, viral and fungal infections
amoebiasis	*Entamoeba histolytica* amoeba	organism in contaminated food	up to several years	fever, diarrhoea, exhaustion, rectal bleeding
anthrax	*Bacillus anthracis* bacterium	animal hair	1–3 days	small red pimple on hand or face enlarges and discharges pus
appendicitis	usually *E. coli* bacterium	not transmitted	sudden onset	abdominal pain which moves from left to right after a few hours, nausea
bilharziasis (schisto-somiasis)	*Schistosoma haematobium* (also called Bilharzia), *S. mansoni* or *S. japonicum* parasites	certain snails living in calm water	varies with lifespan of parasite	fever, muscle aches, abdominal pain, headaches
bronchiolitis (babies only)	respiratory syncytical virus (RSV; paramyxovirus family)	droplet infection	1–3 days	blocked or runny nose, irritability
brucellosis	*Brucella abortus* or *B. meliteusis* bacteria	cattle or goats	3–6 days	fever, drenching sweats, weight loss, muscle and joint pains, confusion and poor memory
bubonic plague	*Yersinia pestis* bacterium	fleas	3–6 days	fever, muscle aches, headaches, exhaustion, enlarged lymph glands ('buboes')
chickenpox (varicella)	varicella-zoster virus (herpesvirus family)	droplet infection	14–21 days	blister-like eruptions, lethargy, headaches, sore throat
cholera	*Vibrio cholerae* bacterium	contaminated water	a few hours to 5 days	severe diarrhoea, vomiting
common cold (coryza)	rhinoviruses, adenoviruses	droplet infection	1–3 days	blocked or runny nose, sneezing, sore throat, runny eyes
conjunctivitis	viruses; bacteria eg *Staphylococcus* species; allergy	variable	variable	if viral, watery discharge from eyes; if bacterial, sticky yellow discharge from eyes
dengue fever (break-bone fever)	dengue fever virus (flavivirus family)	mosquito	5–6 days	fever, severe muscle cramps, enlarged lymph nodes
diphtheria	*Corynebacterium diphtheriae* bacterium	droplet infection	4–6 days	grey exudate across throat; swelling of throat tissues may lead to asphyxiation; toxin secreted by bacteria may seriously damage heart
dysentery	*Shigella* genus of bacteria	contaminated food or water	variable; can cause death within 48 hours	diarrhoea, with or without bleeding
gastroenteritis	bacteria, viruses and food poisoning	droplet infection of food	variable	varies from nausea to severe fever, vomiting and diarrhoea
German measles (rubella)	rubella virus (togavirus family)	droplet infection	18 days	1–2 days catarrh and sore throat, then red rash, enlargement of lymph nodes
glandular fever (infectious mono-nucleosis)	Epstein–Barr virus (herpesvirus family)	saliva of infected person	1–6 weeks	sore throat, fever, enlargement of tonsils and lymph nodes, lethargy, depression

Human Body, Health and Nutrition

Human Body, Health and Nutrition

Name	Cause	Transmission	Incubation	Symptoms
gonorrhoea	*Neisseria gonorrhoeae* bacterium	usually sexually transmitted	2–10 days	in men, burning sensation on urination and discharge from urethra; in women (if any), vaginal discharge
hepatitis	hepatitis A, B or C virus (picornavirus, hepadnavirus and flavivirus families)	contaminated food or water (type A); sexual relations, infected blood (types B and C)	3–6 weeks (type A); up to a few weeks (type B); over 10 years (type C)	often no symptoms, otherwise similar to flu; loss of appetite, tenderness below right ribs, jaundice
influenza (flu)	influenza A, B or C virus (orthomyxovirus family)	droplet infection	1–3 days	fever, sweating, muscle aches
kala-azar (leishmaniasis)	parasites of the genus *Leishmania*	sandfly	usually 1–2 months; can be up to 10 years	lymph gland, spleen and liver enlargement
laryngitis	same viruses that cause colds, ie adeno- and rhinoviruses	droplet infection	1–3 days	sore throat, coughing, hoarseness
lassa fever	lassa virus (arenavirus family)	urine	3 weeks	fever, sore throat, muscle aches and pains, haemorrhage into the skin
legionnaire's disease	*Legionella pneumophila* bacterium	water droplets in infected humidifiers, cooling towers; stagnant water in cisterns and shower heads	1–3 days	flu and pneumonia-like symptoms, fever, diarrhoea, mental confusion
leprosy	*Mycobacterium leprae* bacterium	droplet infection; minimally contagious	variable	insensitive white patches on skin, nodules, thickening of and damage to nerves
malaria	*Plasmodium falciparum, P. vivax, P. ovale* and *P. malariae* parasites	*Anopheles* mosquito	7–30 days (shortest for *P. falciparum*, longest for *P. malariae*)	severe swinging fever, cold sweats, shivers
Marburg (or green monkey) disease	Marburg virus (filovirus family)	transmission by unknown animal(s), body fluids	5–9 days	fever, diarrhoea; affects brain, kidneys and lungs
measles	measles virus (paramyxovirus family)	droplet infection	14 days	fever, severe cold symptoms, bloody red rash
meningitis	*Streptococcus pneumoniae* or *Neisseria meningitidis* bacteria; viruses eg enteroviruses; fungi eg *Cryptococcus* species	droplet infection	variable	severe headache, stiffness in neck muscles, dislike of the light, nausea, vomiting, confusion
MRSA	methicillin-resistant strains of *Staphylococcus aureus* bacteria	skin-to-skin contact	variable	various, including skin or wound infections or septicaemia
mumps	mumps virus (paramyxovirus family)	droplet infection	18 days	lethargy, fever, pain at the angle of the jaw, swelling of parotid gland(s)
orchitis	bacteria or viruses; if bacterial, urinary infection due to eg gonorrhoea; if viral, due to eg mumps	see cause	variable	painful red and swollen testes, fever, nausea

Name	Cause	Transmission	Incubation	Symptoms
osteomyelitis	bacteria eg *Staphylococcus* species	infection spreads from eg boil or impetigo	1–10 days	abrupt onset of fever, and pain at site of infected bone (usually tibia)
parotitis	bacteria eg *Staphylococcus aureus*; viruses eg mumps	common in mumps (viral), may follow severe febrile illness or abdominal operation	1–10 days	inflammation of one or both parotid glands
pericarditis	bacteria eg *Staphylococcus* species; viruses eg Coxsackie B	infection follows a chest disease or heart attack	variable	inflamed pericardium (fibrous bag which encloses the heart); tight chest pain
peritonitis	bacteria eg *E. coli* or *Staphylococcus aureus*; chemical irritation	usually appendicitis; perforation of the gut allows escape of barrel contents into peritoneal cavity	1–10 days	severe abdominal pain, vomiting, rigidity, shock
pharyngitis	viruses eg adenoviruses; bacteria eg *Streptococcus* species	droplet infection	3–5 days	sore throat, fever, pain on swallowing, enlarged neck glands
pneumonia	viruses eg influenza virus; bacteria eg *Streptococcus pneumoniae*	droplet infection	1–3 weeks	cough, fever, chest pain
poliomyelitis	three strains of polio virus (picornavirus family)	droplet infection and hand to mouth infection from faeces	7–14 days	affects spinal cord and brain; headache, fever, neck and muscle stiffness; may result in meningitis or paralysis
proctitis	sexually transmitted bacterial infections eg gonorrhoea	contact	variable	inflammation of the rectum and anus resulting from thrush, piles or fissures; pain on defecation
psittacosis	*Chlamydis psittaci* bacterium	infected birds (eg parrots)	1–2 weeks	headache, chest pain, fever, nausea
puerperal fever	*Streptococcus* infection within uterine cavity or vagina	follows childbirth	1–10 days	fever; often fatal in past, now rare
pyelitis (or pyelonephritis)	bacteria eg *E. coli*	kidney infection resulting from urinary tract infection	1–10 days	fever, rigor, loin pain, burning on passing urine
rabies	rabies virus (rhabdovirus family)	animal bite	2–6 weeks	headache, sickness, excitability, fear of drinking water, convulsions, coma and death
river blindness (or onchocerciasis)	*Onchocerca volvulus* worm	bites of infected flies of genus *Simulium*	worms mature in 2–4 months, may live 12 years	worms inhabit skin, causing nodules and sometimes blindness
salpingitis	Bacteria eg *Neisseria gonorrhoeae* or *Chlamydia trachomatis*	infection of the Fallopian tubes	variable	abdominal pain, fever, irregular periods, vaginal discharge
SARS (Severe Acute Respiratory Syndrome)	SARS virus (coronavirus family)	droplet infection; possibly also direct contact	2–10 days	fever, cough, breathing difficulty
scarlet fever	*Streptococcus pyogenes* bacterium	droplet infection or streptococci-infected milk or ice cream	2–4 days	sudden onset; headache, sore throat, fever, vomiting, red skin rash

Human Body, Health and Nutrition

Human Body, Health and Nutrition

Name	Cause	Transmission	Incubation	Symptoms
shingles	herpes-zoster virus (also causes chickenpox)	dormant virus in body becomes active following a minor infection	variable	pain, numbness, blisters
sinusitis	bacteria eg *Streptococcus pneumoniae*; indirect consequence of allergy or viral infection	droplet infection	1–3 days	fever, sinus pain, nasal discharge
sleeping sickness (or African try- panosomiasis)	1. *Trypanosoma brucei gambiense* or 2. *Tb. rhodesiense*	bites by infected tsetse fly	1. weeks– months; 2. 7–14 days	fever, lymph node enlargement, headache, behavioural change, drowsiness, coma, sometimes death
smallpox	variola major or minor virus	now eradicated worldwide, but was transmitted by direct contact	12 days	fever, rash followed by pustules on face and extremities
syphilis	*Treponema pallidum* bacterium	sexually transmitted: bacteria enter bloodstream through a mucous membrane, usually genital skin	ulcer after 2–6 weeks, skin rash after weeks or months	late syphilis damages brain, heart and main blood vessels, and unborn babies
tetanus	*Clostridium tetani* bacterium	bacteria from soil infect wounds	2 days–4 weeks	muscular spasms cause lockjaw and affect breathing; potentially fatal
thrush (or candidiasis)	*Candida albicans* yeast	the yeast is present on skin of most people and multiplies when resistance to infection is low, when hormonal balance is altered, or when taking antibiotics	variable	white spots on tongue and cheeks (oral thrush); irritant vaginal discharge (vaginal thrush); rash in genital area or between folds of skin (one form of 'nappy rash')
tonsillitis	usually same viruses responsible for colds; sometimes bacterial, eg *Streptococcus* species	droplet infection	1–3 days	red inflamed tonsils, sore throat
trachoma	*Chlamydia trachomatis* bacterium	poor hygiene: bacteria infect eye	5 days	conjunctivitis, swelling and scarring in cornea, often leading to blindness
tuberculosis	*Mycobacterium tuberculosis* bacterium	inhalation of bacteria from person with active tuberculosis pneumonia; drinking infected milk	up to several years	cough with bloodstained sputum, weight loss, chest pain
typhoid	*Salmonella typhi* bacterium	contaminated water or food	10–14 days	slow onset of fever, abdominal discomfort, cough, rash, constipation then diarrhoea, delirium, coma; potentially fatal
typhus	species of *Rickettsia* bacteria	bite by infected flea, tick, mite or louse, which carry the bacteria as parasites	7–14 days	fever, rigor, headache, muscular pain, rash

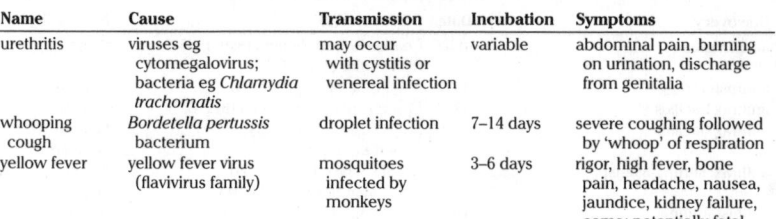

Name	Cause	Transmission	Incubation	Symptoms
urethritis	viruses eg cytomegalovirus; bacteria eg *Chlamydia trachomatis*	may occur with cystitis or venereal infection	variable	abdominal pain, burning on urination, discharge from genitalia
whooping cough	*Bordetella pertussis* bacterium	droplet infection	7–14 days	severe coughing followed by 'whoop' of respiration
yellow fever	yellow fever virus (flavivirus family)	mosquitoes infected by monkeys	3–6 days	rigor, high fever, bone pain, headache, nausea, jaundice, kidney failure, coma; potentially fatal

Major causes of death

Death from respiratory ailments, infectious diseases and injuries tends to be lower in the developed world due to preventative medicine, safer living conditions and powerful modern drugs; however, people in the developed world are more likely to die from cancer or heart disease.

The table below shows the estimated number of deaths in a year from selected causes in WHO (World Health Organization)-designated regions. The figures given represent thousands.

Cause of death	Africa	The Americas	SE Asia	Europe	Eastern Mediterranean	Western Pacific
Infectious and parasitic diseases	5625	397	2922	195	953	804
Respiratory infections	1118	226	1474	288	354	498
Maternal conditions	231	17	171	3	68	21
Perinatal conditions	554	175	1012	65	303	349
Nutritional deficiencies	143	61	189	12	53	27
Malignant neoplasms	410	1116	1160	1833	272	2318
Other neoplasms	9	29	19	39	24	29
Diabetes mellitus	80	253	263	142	55	192
Nutritional/endocrine disorders	26	62	39	34	29	52
Neuropsychiatric disorders	90	240	267	256	89	167
Sense organ disorders	0	0	1	0	1	0
Cardiovascular diseases	1036	1928	3911	4927	1079	3825
Respiratory diseases	257	398	874	404	155	1609
Digestive diseases	157	284	502	389	152	480
Diseases of the genito-urinary system	106	136	206	112	83	203
Skin diseases	19	13	15	12	5	4
Musculoskeletal diseases	7	29	17	26	3	26
Congenital abnormalities	56	58	149	38	83	108
Oral diseases	0	0	0	0	0	0
Unintentional injuries	488	321	1080	534	294	827
Intentional injuries	253	220	386	256	98	402

Source: *World Health Report 2004* (WHO, 2004)

Important discoveries in medicine

Discovery	Date	Discoverer(s)	Nationality
adrenal gland, function of	1856	Vulpian (1826–87)[1]	French
adrenaline	1901	Jokichi Takamine (1854–1922) based on work by Edward Sharpey-Schafer (1850–1935) and George Oliver (1841–1915)	Japanese UK
AIDS (Aquired Immune Deficiency Syndrome)	1981	scientists in Los Angeles	—
allergenic nature of hay fever	1906	Clemens Peter von Pirquet (1874–1929)	Austrian
allergy recognized in skin's reaction to tuberculin	1906	Clemens Peter von Pirquet (1874–1929)	Austrian
anaesthetic, epidural	1885	James Leonard Corning (1855–1923)	US
anaesthetic, general	c.1840	priority claimed by Crawford Long (1815–78) Gardner Cotton (1814–98) Horace Wells (1815–48) Charles Jackson (1805–80)	all US
anaesthetic, local (mandrake leaves and polenta)	described in *Natural History*	Pliny the Elder (23–79 AD)	Roman

Human Body, Health and Nutrition

Human Body, Health and Nutrition

Discovery	Date	Discoverer(s)	Nationality
anaphylaxis	1902	Charles Robert Richet (1850–1935)	French
		Paul Portier (1866–1962)	French
androsterone	1931	Adolf Butenandt (1903–95)	German
anthrax bacillus	1850	Casimir Joseph Davaine (1812–82)	French
anthrax bacillus	1876	Louis Pasteur (1822–95)	French
		Robert Koch (1843–1910)	German
anthrax, serum against	1895	Achille Sclavo (1861–1930)	Italian
		Émile Marchoux (1862–1943)	French
antihistamine	1937	Hans Staub (1890–1967)	Swiss
		Daniel Bovet (1907–92)	Swiss
antipyretic agent (lowers temperature)	4–5c BC	Hippocrates (c.460–c.377 or 359 BC)	Greek
antisepsis	1865	Joseph Lister (1827–1912)	UK
asepsis by boiling and by dry heat autoclave	1883	Octave Terrillon (1844–95)	French
		Louis-Félix Terrier (1837–1908)	French
asprin	1897	Felix Hoffmann (1868–1946)	German
atropine (isolated)	1819	Rudolph Brandes (1795–1842)	German
bacillus ▶ diphtheria, gangrene, tuberculosis, typhus bacillus	1673	Anton van Leeuwenhoek (1632–1723)	Dutch
benzodiazepines (tranquillizers)	1960	Leo Sternbach (1908–2005)	US
blood circulation	1628	William Harvey (1578–1677)	UK
blood groups A, O, B, AB	1901	Karl Landsteiner (1868–1943)	Austrian–US
blood groups M, N and P	1927	Karl Landsteiner (1868–1943)	Austrian–US
		Philip Levine (1900–87)	US
blood pressure greater than atmospheric pressure	1733	Stephen Hales (1677–1761)	UK
brain, electric activity in the (▶ EEG)	1875	Richard Caton (1842–1926)	UK
cellular division	1855	Rudolph Virchow (1821–1902)	German
chloroform, anaesthetic properties of	1847	James Young Simpson (1811–70)	UK
cholera vibrion	1883	Robert Koch (1843–1910)	German
chromosome X, heredity linked to sex	1909	Thomas Hunt Morgan (1866–1945)	US
chromosomes	1888	Thomas Hunt Morgan (1866–1945)	US
chromosomes (46) in man	1955	Joe Hin Tjio (1919–2001)	US
		Albert Levan (1905–1998)	Swedish
circadian rhythm of 25 hours	1972	Michel Siffre (1939–)	French
coagulation, role of fibrin in	1771	William Hewson (1739–74)	UK
coagulation (formation of fibrin following dissolution of fibrinogen under influence of thrombin)	1876	Olaf Hammarsten (1841–1932)	Swedish
cochlea or inner ear, stimulation mechanism of	1961	Georg von Békésy (1899–1972)	Hungarian–US
cortisone (adrenal cortex hormone) (isolated)	1934	Edward Calvin Kendall (1886–1972)	US
cyclosporin-A, immuno-suppressive properties of	1972	Jean-Francois Borel (1933–)	Swiss
digestive system	—	Claude Bernard (1813–78)	French
diphtheria bacillus	1882	Edwin Klebs (1834–1913)	Swiss–US
		Friedrich Löffler (1852–1915)	German
diphtheria, serum against	1892	Emil Adolf von Behring (1854–1917)	German
		Shibasaburo Kitasato (1852–1931)	Japanese
		Pierre Émile Roux (1853–1933)	French
disinfection of wounds, chemical	1825	Antoine Labarraque (1777–1850)	French
DNA, structure of	1953	Francis Crick (1916–2004)	UK
		James D Watson (1928–)	US
		Maurice Wilkins (1916–2004)	UK
		Rosalind Franklin (1920–58)	UK
Down's Syndrome, cause of ('the extra chromosome')	1958	Raymond Turpin (1895–1988)	French
		Marthe Gautier (1898–1995)	French
		Jérôme Lejeune (1926–1994)	French
electro-encephalogram (EEG) (spontaneous activity of the brain)	1929	Hans Berger (1873–1941)	German
endorphins	1975	John Hughes (1942–)	UK
		Roger Guillemin (1924–)	French–US

Discovery	Date	Discoverer(s)	Nationality
enzymes	1833	Anselme Payen (1795–1871)	French
		Jean-François Persoz (1805–68)	French
enzymes, restriction	1970	Hamilton Smith (1931–)	US
ether first used as anaesthetic	1846	William Thomas Morton (1819–68)	US
fertilization	1875	Oskar Hertwig (1849–1922)	German
gangrene, gas bacillus of	1878	Louis Pasteur (1822–95)	French
genes, chemical regulation by	1952	Jacques Monod (1910–76)	French
		Edwin Joseph Cohn (1892–1953)	US
gonococcus	1879	Albert Ludwig Siegmund Neisser (1855–1916)	German
heparin (anticoagulant secreted by liver cells)	1916	Jay McLean (1890–1957)	US
hepatitis-C virus	1989	Dr Qui-Lim-Choo's research team of the Chiron Corporation	US
heredity	1865	Gregor Mendel (1822–84)	Austrian
HIV virus (isolated)	1983	Luc Montagnier (1932–) and others	French
HLA (human leucocyte antigen) system (responsible for transplant rejection)	1950–77	Jean Dausset (1916–2009)	French
hormone ▶ adrenaline, cortisone, inhibin, insulin, progesterone, testosterone			
inhibin	1985	Roger Guillemin (1924–)	French–US
insulin (isolated)	1921	Frederick Grant Banting (1891–1941)	Canadian
		Charles Herbert Best (1899–1978)	Canadian
		John James McLeod (1876–1935)	Canadian
insulin	1921	Nicolae Paulescu (1869–1931)	Romanian
interferon	1957	Alick Isaacs (1921–67)	UK
		J Lindernann	Swiss
interleukin 2	1985	Steven Rosenberg (1940–)	US
interleukin 3	1986	Steven Clark	US
		Yu Chang Yang	US
leprosy bacillus	1869	Gerhard Hansen (1841–1912)	Norwegian
malaria, plasmodium protozoan as agent of	1880	Charles-Louis-Alphonse Laveran (1845–1922)	French
microbes	1762	M A Plenciz (1705–86)	Austrian
morphine	1805	Friedrich Serturner (1783–1841)	German
mosquitoes in infectious diseases, role of	1895	Ronald Ross (1857–1932)	UK
mosquitoes, transmission of filariae by	1883	Patrick Manson (1844–1922)	UK
nervous reaction, chemical transmission of	1936	Otto Loewi (1873–1961)	German–US
		Henry Hallet Dale (1875–1968)	UK
nitrous oxide (laughing gas)	1776	Joseph Priestley (1733–1804)	UK
nitrous oxide, analgesic and laughter-provoking effect of	1799	Humphry Davy (1778–1829)	UK
nucleic acid	1869	Johann Friedrich Miescher (1844–95)	Swiss
oestrogen produced by ovarian follicle	1924	Robert Courrier (1895–1986)	French
oestrone	1929	Edward Doisy (1893–1986)	US
		Adolf Butenandt (1903–95)	German
oncogenes	1981	Robert Weinberg (1942–)	US
		Geoffrey Cooper	US
		Michael Wigler (1947–)	US
ovulation, substances acting against	1921	Ludwig Haberlandt (1885–1932)	German
penicillin	1928	Alexander Fleming (1881–1955)	UK
phagocytes (cells which devour infective organisms)	1882–6	Ilya Ilich Mechnikov (1845–1916)	Russian
phenol, disinfectant properties of	1865	Joseph Lister (1827–1912)	UK
Phenytoin (for treatment of epilepsy)	1939	—	—
pituitary, secretion of growth hormone	1921	Herbert McLean Evans (1882–1971)	US
prion (proteinaceous infectious particles)	1982	Stanley Prusiner (1942–)	US
progesterone	1929	George Washington Corner (1889–1981)	US
		Edgar Allen (1892–1943)	US
protozoa (unicellular organisms)	1675	Anton van Leeuwenhoek (1632–1723)	Dutch

Human Body, Health and Nutrition

Human Body, Health and Nutrition

Discovery	Date	Discoverer(s)	Nationality
quinoline (later discovered to be antimicrobial agent)	1834	Friedlieb Ferdinand Runge (1795–1867)	German
rabies vaccination	1885	Louis Pasteur (1822–95)	French
red blood cells	1675 or 1684	Anton van Leeuwenhoek (1632–1723)	Dutch
relapsing fever, spirochaete of	1873	Otto Obermeier (1843–73)	German
respiration, use of oxygen in	1770–80	Antoine Lavoisier (1743–94)	French
rhesus factor	1939–40	Karl Landsteiner (1868–1943)	Austrian–US
		Philip Levine (1900–87)	US
RNA interference, discovery of causative agent for	1998	Andrew Fire (1959–)	US
		Craig Mello (1960–)	US
scurvy, lemon juice treatment of	c.1740	James Lind (1716–94)	UK
skin culture	1950	Howard Green	US
sleeping sickness, transmission by tsetse flies	1895	David Bruce (1855–1931)	UK
smallpox vaccination	1796	Edward Jenner (1749–1823)	UK
smallpox inoculation, introduction of	1718	Lady Mary Wortley Montagu (1689–1762)	UK
spermatozoa	1677	Anton van Leeuwenhoek (1632–1723)	Dutch
Staphylococcus and Streptococcus	1880	Louis Pasteur (1822–95)	French
streptomycin (antibiotic against tuberculosis)	1943	Selman Waksman (1888–1973)	US
sulphonamides (first antibiotics)	1935	Gerhard Domagk (1895–1964)	German
T-lymphocytes	1966	J David	US
		V Blum	US
testosterone (isolated)	1929	—	—
testosterone (synthesized)	1935	Leopold Stephen Ružička (1887–1976)	Swiss
tetanus, serum against	1890	Emil von Behring (1854–1917)	German
		Shibasaburo Kitasato (1852–1931)	Japanese
		Pierre-Paul-Émile Roux (1853–1933)	French
thyroxine (thyroid hormone) (isolated)	1914	Edward Calvin Kendall (1886–1972)	US
tomography	1915	André Bocage (1892–1953)	French
tuberculosis bacillus	1882	Robert Koch (1843–1910)	German
tubocurarine (muscle relaxant)	1935	Harold King (1887–1956)	UK
Tumor Necrosis Factor (TNF)	1975	E A Carswell	US
typhus bacillus	1880	Karl Joseph Eberth (1835–1926)	German
vaccination	c.10c	—	Turkey and China
vaccination ► rabies, smallpox			
viruses, cultivation of (on chicken embryos)	1931	Ernest William Goodpasture (1886–1960)	US
vitamin A	1913	Elmer Verner McCollum (1879–1967)	US
		Marguerite Davis (1887–1967)	US
		Thomas Burr Osborne (1859–1929)	US
		Lafayette Mendel (1872–1935)	US
vitamin B (niacin) (isolated)	1913	Casimir Funk (1884–1967)	Polish–US
vitamin B₁ (thiamin)	1897	Christiaan Eijkman (1858–1930)	Dutch
vitamin B₂ (riboflavin)	1933	Richard Kuhn (1900–67)	German
		Paul György (1893–1976)	German
		Theodor Wagner-Jauregg (1903–92)	German
vitamin B₃	1937	R J Madden	UK
		Frank Strong	UK
		Dilworth Wayne Woolley (1914–66)	Canadian
		Conrad Elvehjem (1901–62)	US
vitamin B₅	1933	Roger Williams (1893–1988)	US
vitamin B₆	1936	Thomas Birch	US
		Paul György (1893–1976)	German
vitamin B₉	1931	Lucy Wills (1888–1964)	UK
vitamin B₁₂	1927	George Minot (1885–1950)	US
		William Murphy (1892–1987)	US
vitamin B₁₂ (isolated)	1948	E L Smith	UK
		L F J Parke	UK
	same date in US	Edward Rickes	US
		Norman Brink	US
		Frank Koniuszy	US

Discovery	Date	Discoverer(s)	Nationality
		Thomas Wood	US
		Karl Folkers	US
vitamin C (isolated but not recognized as a vitamin)	1928	Albert von Nagyrapolt Szent Györgyi (1893–1986)	Hungarian–US
vitamin C (isolated)	1932	Charles Glen King (1896–1988)	US
vitamin D (role in prevention of rickets)[2]	1918	Edward Mellanby (1884–1955)	UK
vitamin D (isolated)	1924	Harry Steenbock (1886–1967)	US
		Alfred Hess (1875–1933)	German
		Mildred Weinstock	German
vitamin E	1923	Herbert McLean Evans (1882–1971)	US
		Katharine Scott Bishop (1889–1976)	US
vitamin K₁	1934	Henrik Dam (1895–1976)	Danish
		Fritz Schønheyder (1905–79)	Danish
vitamins, necessity of	1906	Sir Frederick Hopkins (1861–1947)	UK
X-rays	1892	Heinrich Hertz (1857–94)	German
X-rays, properties of	1895	Wilhelm von Röntgen (1845–1923)	German
yellow fever, transmission by stegmyia mosquito	1881	Ronald Ross (1857–1932)	UK
		Carlos Juan Finlay (1833–1915)	Cuban

[1]Vulpian = Edmé Félix Alfred Vulpian.
[2]Not known as Vitamin D at this time.

Supplementary medical treatments

The following treatments are carried out by regulated healthcare professionals, and may be recommended by a doctor.

art therapy Use of drawing and painting to encourage patients to explore and resolve deep-seated fears and emotions that they find difficult to express in words. Used to treat addiction, alcoholism, anorexia and other conditions.

chiropody ► podiatry

chiropractic Manipulation of the spine and other joints. Used to relieve musculoskeletal complaints, especially back and neck pain.

dietetics The treatment of food-related problems, disease and ill health through dietary advice.

dramatherapy Use of drama to help patients express the whole range of their emotions and to increase their insight and knowledge of themselves and others. Used in a wide variety of conditions.

music therapy Use of music to encourage positive changes in behaviour and emotional wellbeing, and the development of an increased sense of self-awareness. Patients are encouraged to use their voices as well as instruments to express themselves. Used to assist patients with learning and communication disabilities, mental health problems, addictions, challenging behaviour, emotional and behavioural difficulties, eating disorders and other conditions.

occupational therapy Used to help patients with physical, mental or social problems to live as fulfilling a life as possible. Occupational therapists give practical advice and assistance with adapting buildings and equipment, and work out ways in which activities can be modified to suit the individual.

osteopathy Diagnosis and treatment of disorders of the bones, joints, muscles, tendons and nerves. Commonly used to treat back and neck problems, tension headaches and sports injuries. Based on the concept that the musculoskeletal system plays a key role in the body's health. Osteopaths assess the damage, then manipulate the affected area.

physiotherapy Use of physical approaches to improve body function and movement. Used in the treatment of muscoloskeletal disorders, mental illness, stroke recovery and many other conditions. Also used in intensive care, occupational health, and care of the elderly.

podiatry Treatment of disorders primarily of the feet but also of the ankle, knee, leg and hip. Often known as chiropody, especially when referring to the treatment of minor ailments of the feet. Other specialisms include biomechanics and the treatment of athletes and dancers.

speech and language therapy The treatment of disorders involving communication, eating, drinking and swallowing, caused by physical disabilities, learning difficulties, hearing impairment or speech//voice disorders.

Complementary medicine

Complementary medicine is the treatment of diseases and disorders using procedures other than those traditionally practised in orthodox medicine. The term 'alternative medicine' is also used. The main types are explained below.

acupressure Ancient Chinese and Japanese healing massage using fingertip pressure on pain-relieving points around the body. These pressure points (acupoints) lie along the meridians (invisible body channels) used in **acupuncture**. Acupressure balances the flow of Qi (or Chi), the energy flowing through the meridians.

acupuncture Traditional Chinese method of healing in which symptoms are relieved by the insertion of special needles into one or more of 2000 specific points (acupoints) that lie along invisible channels called meridians. This ancient therapy

Human Body, Health and Nutrition

is believed to control the flow of Qi (or Chi), the energy flowing along the meridians. Used in the treatment of arthritis, allergy, back pain and many other disorders.

Alexander technique System of body awareness which involves retraining the body's movements, positions and posture during all activities, including sitting or reading. The method, which must be learned from qualified teachers, is believed to encourage good mental and physical health, and resistance to stress, by promoting harmony between mind and body. Named after Australian-born physiotherapist F M Alexander (d.1955).

aromatherapy Use of concentrated plant oils (such as bergamot, eucalyptus or rosemary) to treat conditions including stress, headache and arthritis. Extracts, or essential oils, are generally massaged into the skin by aromatherapists, but can also be inhaled or added to baths.

aura therapy An aura is said to be a magnetic field surrounding the body, visible to aura practitioners as lines of light. Aura therapy involves analysis of the aura, which is said to be indicative of a person's health, and balancing or recharging it to treat health problems.

autogenics Relaxation therapy used to reduce and control stress and fatigue by facilitating voluntary control of bodily tension. It is based on six taught mental exercises, which are repeated, sitting or lying down, twice or three times a day.

autosuggestion Form of self-**hypnotherapy** which empties the mind by the repetition of positive phrases or ideas to oneself in order to enhance wellbeing, relieve pain, and change attitudes or habits such as addictions and phobias.

Bach remedies or **Bach flower healing** Use of wild flower preparations, chosen according to an individual's particular personality and emotional state, to treat physical and psychological disorders. Named after British physician Edward Bach (1880–1936).

biochemic tissue salts Use of 12 mineral salts to cure disorders by restoring the natural salt balance within the body.

colour therapy Therapy based on the idea that the seven colours of the spectrum correspond to seven energy areas of the body known as chakras. The application of colour using coloured light, coloured water or other techniques is thought to rebalance the chakras.

cranial osteopathy Gentle manipulation of the bones of the skull and face to correct pressure changes to the brain and nerves in order to treat conditions such as migraine and neuralgia.

craniosacral therapy (CST) Gentle manipulation of the skull and face in order to release tensions and imbalances which are said to arise in the bones and membranes of the skull. Used to treat a wide range of physical and psychological symptoms.

crystal healing Selection and use of crystals that are said to promote healing and wellbeing in humans.

dance movement therapy Use of body movement to express deep feelings too difficult to explain in words. Used to treat depression and anxiety as well as more serious mental illnesses.

Feldenkrais method Technique of teaching people how to improve the way they move by learning how they are moving. The aim is to move with maximum efficiency and minimum movement. Believed to reduce risk of injury in eg dancers or athletes.

flotation therapy Therapy in which the patient floats for about an hour in a sealed saltwater-filled capsule (a flotation tank or float tank), with music

sometimes piped in. Used to relieve stress, pain and arthritis.

herbal medicine or **herbalism** Use of herbs to treat ailments, a practice that dates back thousands of years.

homeopathy Treatment of an illness using dilute doses of substances that produce symptoms similar to those of the illness itself (treating like with like). The aim is to restore the body's natural balance by boosting its healing powers.

hydrotherapy Use of water to stimulate the body's ability to heal itself, based on the fact that water is essential for life. Treatment includes hot and cold baths, and the steam baths found at spas and health farms. Used also to treat disability by developing movement in water.

hypnotherapy Use of suggestion under hypnosis to treat conditions including stress, phobias, and addiction to tobacco and alcohol.

iridology Diagnosis of disorders achieved by studying the patterns on the irises of the eyes. Iridologists believe that each section of the iris indicates the condition of a specific part of the body.

kinesiology Monitoring of muscle strength and tone, using gentle finger pressure, to indicate how the whole body is working. Based on the belief that muscle groups are linked to particular body organs. If imbalances are found, gentle massage is applied to pressure points to restore normal energy flow to muscles and their organs.

macrobiotics Dietary regime based on Chinese philosophy of yin (flexible and cool) and yang (strong and hot), balancing the two elements to complement an individual's nature and lifestyle. Believed to improve health and resistance to disease. In common usage, the term macrobiotics often refers to the devising and following of diets using whole grains and organically-grown fruit and vegetables, which are thought to prolong life.

massage Ancient therapy whereby one person uses hands and fingers to stroke, press and knead the body of another person who is lying horizontally. It is used to relax mind and body, and reduce tension, as well as treating disorders such as back pain.

meditation Achieving a tranquil mental state, without the use of drugs, to reduce tension, decrease blood pressure and regain confidence when stressed. This technique enables individuals to calm their bodies by controlling their thoughts. The meditative state is reached by focusing on a neutral thought or silently repeating a mantra while breathing in a controlled way.

moxibustion A form of **acupuncture**. A piece of burning moxa (a pithy material, eg sunflower pith or cotton wool) is placed on the head of an inserted acupuncture needle to heat it. Alternatively, the burning moxa is held above the acupuncture point to warm the skin. Both methods are used to relieve pain after operations, and for arthritis.

naturopathy Using natural cures to seek the underlying cause of illnesses rather than merely alleviating the symptoms. Naturopaths treat patients as whole individuals, taking into account their emotions and lifestyles. Evidently effective against stress and anxiety, as well as degenerative diseases such as emphysema and arthritis.

negative ion therapy Treatment whereby the body is exposed to harmless ions; claimed to effect various cures.

Pilates System of physical and mental training to improve strength, flexibility and posture through the co-ordination of movement and breathing. Used to treat back pain and other musculoskeletal conditions. Named after German deviser Joseph Pilates (1880–1967).

reflexology Treatment of disorders by massaging the feet. Reflexologists relate different zones of the feet to different organs or parts of the body by way of meridians or energy channels. By massaging a particular foot region, they treat a particular organ or part of the body by releasing blocks in the meridians.

reiki Form of Japanese natural therapy involving the laying on of hands or gentle massage. Aims to reduce stress and promote relaxation and healing, and is believed to work by restoring a universal life force that can pass from one person to another.

Rolfing Massaging of muscles and connective tissues in order to improve body posture and thereby improve the health and physical wellbeing of the whole body. Named after US physiotherapist Dr Ida Rolf (1897–1979).

shiatsu or shiatzu Ancient Japanese massage using the fingers or palms of the hand which, like

acupressure, involves the application of pressure to points lying along the body's meridians in order to control the energy flow (Qi). Used in the treatment of many conditions including migraine, back pain, stress and digestive problems.

t'ai chi ch'uan Technique whereby people focus on their body and emotions by performing slow, circular, dance-like movements. T'ai chi is believed to remedy imbalances in the movement of the body's natural energy, Qi, so improving a person's wellbeing. It is also used as a system of exercise and self-defence.

thalassotherapy Treatment to detoxify and relax the body, involving the application of mud and seaweed compresses, seawater baths and massage.

yoga System of physical, mental and spiritual training designed to make the body more relaxed and more flexible. It involves adopting a series of postures while maintaining an inner calm of concentrated awareness. Yoga is used to help pain, especially back pain, stress and many other conditions.

Commonly prescribed drugs

This list includes drugs that are commonly prescribed in the UK, the USA and other countries of the developed world. They are grouped according to their usage, and listed by their generic names, not by brand names.

ACE inhibitors Block the action of angiotensin-converting enzyme (ACE), allowing blood vessels to dilate. Used to treat angina, high blood pressure and heart failure.
Δ Captopril; Enalapril; Ramipril.

Anabolic steroids Used to help muscle repair following injury or, occasionally, to speed up recovery after a serious illness or major surgery. Abused by body-builders and athletes to improve their physique.
Δ Nandrolone.

Analgesic drugs Used to relieve pain. Non-opioid analgesics are used for mild pain; opioid analgesics for severe pain. Local anaesthetics are also used to relieve pain.
Δ **Non-opioid analgesics** Nefopam; NSAIDs; Paracetamol.
Δ **Opioid analgesics** Buprenorphine; Codeine; Dextropropoxyphene; Diamorphine, Dihydrocodeine; Morphine; Pentazocine; Pethidine; Tramadol.
Δ **Local anaesthetics** Lidocaine; Tetracaine.

Antacid drugs Neutralize stomach acids, relieving heartburn, peptic ulcers and other gastric complaints.
Δ Aluminium hydroxide; Magnesium carbonate; Magnesium trisilicate.

Anthelminthic drugs Kill parasitic worms such as tapeworms, threadworms and roundworms.
Δ Albendazole; Ivermectin; Levamisole; Mebendazole; Niclosamide; Piperazine; Praziquantel; Pyrantel; Tiabendazole.

Antianxiety drugs Used to reduce feelings of tension, nervousness and anxiety if they interfere with a person's ability to cope with everyday life.
Δ ▶ **Benzodiazepines**
Δ ▶ **Beta-blocker drugs**
Δ **Others** Buspirone.

Antibacterial drugs (antibiotics) Used to treat bacterial infections.
Δ Amoxicillin; Ampicillin; Benzylpenicillin; Chloramphenicol; Cefaclor; Cefalexin; Cefradine; Doxycycline; Erythromycin; Flucloxacillin; Gentamicin; Minocycline; Oxytetracycline; Phenoxymethyl penicillin; Streptomycin; Tetracycline; Trimethoprim.

Anticancer drugs Used to treat certain cancers. Some are cytotoxic, which means they kill cancer cells; others (marked *) are similar to sex hormones or hormone antagonists, and, although not curative, may provide palliation of symptoms. Therapeutic antibodies (marked +) target cancer cells for destruction by the immune system.
Δ Alemtuzumab+; Chlorambucil; Cyclophosphamide; Diethylstilbestrol*; Doxorubicin; Ethinylestradiol*; Etoposide; Fluorouracil; Lomustine; Medroxyprogesterone*; Megestrol*; Mercaptopurine; Methotrexate; Procarbazine; Rituximab+; Tamoxifen*; Trastuzumab+; Vincristine.

Anticoagulant drugs Used both to prevent and to treat strokes or heart attacks by stopping the abnormal formation of blood clots.
Δ Acenocoumarol; Heparin; Warfarin; Phenindione.

Antidepressant drugs Used to treat moderate or serious depression by stimulating the nervous system to elevate mood.
Δ ▶ **MAOIs**
Δ ▶ **SSRIs**
Δ ▶ **Tricyclic drugs**
Δ **Others** Mianserin; Trazodone; Venlafaxine.

Antidiarrhoeal drugs Used to make faeces more bulky, or to slow down gut mobility.
Δ Codeine; Co-phenotrope; Hyoscine; Kaolin; Loperamide.

Antiemetic drugs Used to treat vomiting and nausea resulting from travel sickness, anxiety, or side effects of other drugs (especially anticancer drugs).
Δ Chlorpromazine; Cinnarizine; Hyoscine; Metoclopramide; Ondansetron; Prochlorperazine; Promethazine.

Antifungal drugs Used to treat fungal infections including thrush, ringworm and athlete's foot.
Δ Amphotericin B; Clotrimazole; Econazole; Flucytosine; Griseofulvin; Ketoconazole; Miconazole; Nystatin; Terbinafine; Tolnaftate.

Antihistamine drugs Used to treat allergic reactions such as hay fever and urticaria. Some (marked *) tend to induce drowsiness, which can be useful when discomfort from itching disturbs sleep;

Human Body, Health and Nutrition

however, they should not be used when driving or operating machinery.

Δ Acrivastine; Alimemazine*; Cetirizine; Chlorphenamine*; Fexofenadine; Loratadine; Promethazine*; Triprolidine*.

Antihypertensive drugs Used to treat high blood pressure to reduce the risk of heart failure or stroke.

Δ ► **ACE inhibitors**
Δ ► **Beta-blocker drugs**
Δ ► **Calcium channel blocker drugs**
Δ ► **Diuretic drugs**
Δ **Others** Clonidine; Hydralazine; Methyldopa; Minoxidil; Prazosin.

Antimanic drugs Used to alleviate the extreme mood swings that occur in bipolar disorder (manic depression).

Δ Carbamazepine; Lithium.

Antimuscarinic drugs Block the transmission of impulses along parts of the nervous system. Used to treat asthma, irritable bowel syndrome, Parkinson's disease, urinary incontinence and other conditions.

Δ Atropine sulphate; Dicycloverine hydrochloride; Hyoscine butylbromide; Ipratropium; Orphenadrine; Trihexyphenidyl.

Antipsychotic drugs Used to treat symptoms such as delusions or hallucinations in psychotic disorders including schizophrenia. Also used as sedatives in cases of extreme aggression or agitation.

Δ Chlorpromazine; Clozapine; Flupentixol; Haloperidol; Olanzapine; Risperidone; Sulpiride.

Antirheumatic drugs Used to treat rheumatoid arthritis.

Δ ► **Corticosteroid drugs**
Δ ► **Immunosuppressant drugs**
Δ ► **NSAIDs**
Δ **Others** Chloroquine; Gold compounds; Penicillamine.

Antispasmodic drugs Used to control spasms in the wall of the bladder (causing irritable bladder) or intestine (causing irritable bowel syndrome).

Δ ► **Antimuscarinic drugs**
Δ **Others** Alverine citrate; Mebeverine hydrochloride; Peppermint oil.

Antiviral drugs Used to treat infections caused by viruses, including cold sores, shingles, herpes and influenza.

Δ Aciclovir; Idoxuridine; Inosine pranobex; Interferon; Oseltamivir; Zanamivir; Zidovudine.

Benzodiazepines Used to treat anxiety, panic attacks and insomnia. Some are also used as muscle relaxants and to treat epilepsy.

Δ Chlordiazepoxide hydrochloride; Diazepam; Lorazepam

Beta-blocker drugs Used to reduce heart rate in treating anxiety, high blood pressure and angina.

Δ Acebutolol; Atenolol; Metoprolol; Nadolol; Oxprenolol; Pindolol; Propranolol.

Bronchodilator drugs Widen the airways to the lungs. Used to treat asthma and bronchitis.

Δ Aminophylline; Fenoterol; Salbutamol; Terbutaline; Theophylline.

Calcium channel blocker drugs Reduce the workload of the heart by causing blood vessels to dilate. Used to treat irregular heartbeat, high blood pressure and angina.

Δ Amlodipine; Diltiazem; Nifedipine; Verapamil.

Cholesterol-lowering drugs Used to lower levels of cholesterol in the blood in patients with heart disease; most common are those in the statin group.

Δ Atorvastatin; Fluvastatin; Pravastatin; Simvastatin.

Corticosteroid drugs Wide-ranging uses include the treatment of rheumatoid arthritis, eczema and asthma, and Crohn's disease.

Δ Beclometasone; Betamethasone; Dexamethasone; Fludrocortisone; Hydrocortisone; Prednisolone.

Diuretic drugs Used to treat high blood pressure and oedema (fluid retention) by increasing the amount of water lost from the body in urine.

Δ Amiloride; Bendroflumethiazide; Bumetanide; Chlortalidone; Cyclopenthiazide; Furosemide; Hydrochlorothiazide; Spironolactone; Triamterene.

Hypoglycaemic drugs (oral) Used to lower levels of glucose in the blood to normal levels in patients with one form of diabetes (type 2).

Δ Chlorpropamide; Glibenclamide; Gliclazide; Glipizide; Tolbutamide.

Immunosuppressant drugs Used to suppress activity of the immune system so that it does not cause the rejection of a recently transplanted organ. Also used to treat autoimmune disorders such as rheumatoid arthritis.

Δ **Antiproliferation drugs** Azathioprine; Mycophenolate mofetil.
Δ ► **Corticosteroids**
Δ **Monoclonal antibodies** Basiliximab; Daclizumab.
Δ **Others** Cyclosporin; Tacrolimus.

MAOIs (monoamine oxidase inhibitors) Used to treat moderate or severe depression by increasing the levels of the neurotransmitters serotonin and noradrenaline in the brain. Foods rich in tyramine, eg cheese, red wine and yeast extracts, must be avoided when taking MAOIs.

Δ Isocarboxazid; Moclobemide; Phenelzine; Tranylcypromine.

NSAIDs (non-steroidal anti-inflammatory drugs) Used to relieve pain, stiffness and inflammation in patients suffering from conditions affecting the joints, muscles and bones. Also used to reduce fever and to relieve headaches, menstrual pain and back pain.

Δ Aspirin; Celecoxib; Diclofenac; Fenbufen; Fenoprofen; Flurbiprofen; Ibuprofen; Indometacin; Ketoprofen; Mefenamic acid; Naproxen; Piroxicam.

Oral contraceptive drugs Hormone-based preparations used by women to prevent conception by stopping the release of eggs from the ovaries or thickening the mucus to block entry of sperm into the uterus. Some oral contraceptives contain only a progestogen hormone, while 'combined' oral contraceptives contain both a progestogen and an oestrogen.

Δ **Progestogens** Gestodene; Norethisterone; Levonorgestrel.
Δ **Oestrogens** Ethinylestradiol; Mestranol.

SSRIs (selective serotonin re-uptake inhibitors) Used to treat moderate or severe depression by increasing the levels of the neurotransmitter serotonin in the brain. Some are also used to treat the eating disorder bulimia nervosa.

Δ Citalopram; Fluoxetine; Paroxetine; Sertraline.

Thrombolytic drugs Used to dissolve blood clots in cases of heart attack, stroke or thrombosis.

Δ Reteplase; Streptokinase; Tenecteplase.

Tricyclic drugs Used to treat moderate or severe depression by increasing the levels of the neurotransmitters serotonin and noradrenaline in the brain.

Δ Amitriptyline; Clomipramine; Imipramine; Lofepramine.

Common illegal drugs

Type	Name	How taken	Major effects	Hazards associated with abuse
Depressants	Barbiturates ('downers'): amobarbital, nembutal, seconal	Taken orally or injected	Euphoria, tiredness, reduction in anxiety, slurred speech, slowed breathing and heart rate, confusion.	Dependence, tolerance; combination with alcohol may cause death.
	Benzodiazepines ('benzos')	Taken orally or injected	Sedation, tiredness, reduction in anxiety.	Dependence, tolerance; combination with alcohol may cause death. Injection of liquid extracted from capsules can block blood vessels, leading to loss of the limb.
Narcotic analgesics	Heroin ('brown', 'H', 'horse', 'gear', 'smack')	Sniffed, smoked or injected	Euphoria, reduction in pain, slurred speech, tiredness, loss of self-control, mood swings.	Dependence, tolerance; risk of overdose, or poisoning if heroin is impure; injecting can cause gangrene; risk of HIV or hepatitis from needle sharing.
Psychedelics/ hallucinogens	Cannabis (marijuana, 'dope', 'hash', 'spliff', 'weed')	Smoked or taken in food or tea	Euphoria, altered perception of time and sensory phenomena, hunger.	Long-term use may cause paranoia and anxiety in vulnerable users.
	Ketamine ('green', 'K', 'special K')	Taken orally, injected or sniffed	Perceptual changes, reduced bodily sensation, 'out of body experiences', temporary paralysis.	Dependence, suppressed breathing and heart function, high blood pressure, panic attacks, depression, exacerbation of existing mental health problems. Anaesthetic effect can lead to self-injury.
	Lysergic acid diethylamide (LSD, 'acid', 'Lucy', 'rainbow', 'trips')	Taken orally	Distortion of auditory and visual imagery, hallucinations, increased/distorted feelings of sensory awareness, unpredictable behaviour.	Paranoia, flashbacks (recurrence of hallucinatory events without taking drug); exacerbation of existing mental health problems.
Solvents	Various adhesives, cleaning fluid	Sniffed	Confusion, feeling of wellbeing, giddiness.	Brain, liver and kidney damage; may cause heart failure and sometimes death.
Stimulants	Alkyl nitrites ('poppers', 'liquid gold'): amyl nitrite, butyl nitrite	Sniffed	Temporary feeling of euphoria, reported enhancement of sexual experiences.	Nausea, weakness, headache, impotence; can cause a rash around the mouth.
	Amphetamines ('uppers', 'speed', 'whizz'): benzedrine, dexedrine, methedrine	Taken orally, sniffed or injected	Feeling of self-confidence, hyperactivity, excitement, restlessness, racing pulse; often followed by depression.	Dependence, tolerance, paranoia, violent behaviour, weight loss, hallucinations; death from overdose.
	Cocaine ('C', 'coke', 'charlie', 'white')	Sniffed, smoked or injected	Temporary feeling of euphoria and self-confidence, appetite loss, increased heart rate; often followed by anxiety, agitation, depression.	Long-term use may cause mental impairment, hallucinations, damage to nasal passages; risk of seizures or death from overdose. Highly addictive.

Human Body, Health and Nutrition

Human Body, Health and Nutrition

Type	Name	How taken	Major effects	Hazards associated with abuse
	Crack cocaine	Smoked	Intense feelings of power and euphoria last for five minutes, followed by a 'crash' and a deep craving for another crack 'hit'.	Paranoia, violent behaviour, suicidal feelings, loss of sex drive, possible death from heart attack. Extremely addictive.
	MDMA ('E', 'Ecstasy', 'X')	Taken orally	Mood elevation, increased energy, euphoria.	Severe dehydration, slight possibility of sudden death.
	Methyl-amphetamine (meth-amphetamine, 'crystal meth', 'ice')	Taken orally, sniffed, injected or smoked	Feeling of exhilaration, increased arousal and activity levels, reduced tiredness, appetite loss, increased heart rate.	Dependence, tolerance, increased blood pressure, psychosis. Overdose can lead to organ failure, coma and death.

Immunization schedule for children up to age 18

Age	Vaccine	How given
2 months	Diphtheria, tetanus, pertussis (whooping cough), polio, *Haemophilus influenzae* type b	Combined injection (DTaP/IPV/Hib)
	Pneumococcal infection	Injection (Pneumococcal conjugate vaccine, PCV)
3 months	Diphtheria, tetanus, pertussis, polio, *Haemophilus influenzae* type b	Combined injection (DTaP/IPV/Hib)
	Meningitis C	Injection (MenC)
4 months	Diphtheria, tetanus, pertussis, polio, *Haemophilis influenzae* type b	Combined injection (DTaP/IPV/Hib)
	Meningitis C	Injection (MenC)
	Pneumococcal infection	Injection (PCV)
Around 12 months	*Haemophilus influenzae* type b, Meningitis C	Combined injection (Hib/MenC)
Around 13 months	Measles, mumps, rubella (German measles)	Combined injection (MMR)
	Pneumococcal infection	Injection (PCV)
3 years 4 months–5 years	Diphtheria, tetanus, pertussis, polio	Combined injection (dTaP/IPV or DTaP/IPV)
	Measles, mumps, rubella	Combined injection (MMR)
13–18 years	Diphtheria, tetanus, polio	Combined injection (Td/IPV)

Immunization for foreign travel

Immunization is recommended for travellers of all ages who are visiting countries where there is a chance of contracting serious or potentially fatal diseases. The information below is included for guidance only; travellers should check which immunizations are required for their particular destination, and whether they require immunization certificates. Malaria prophylaxis may also be recommended for some areas.

Disease	Area where immunization needed	Effective for
Cholera	Certificates of vaccination no longer officially required by any country. Rarely, unofficial requests are made for evidence of vaccination following an outbreak. Confirmation of non-requirement of vaccination can be obtained if such a request is anticipated.	N/A
Diphtheria	For longer stays in E Europe, S America, Africa, the Middle East, the Indian subcontinent, SE Asia, the Far East.	10 years
Hepatitis A	Recommended for travel outside western Europe, North America and Australasia.	5–10 years, if booster given after 6–12 months
Hepatitis B	For longer stays in C and S America, the Caribbean, Africa, the Middle East, the Indian subcontinent, SE Asia, the Far East.	Unknown
Japanese encephalitis	Recommended for travel during the transmission season in eastern parts of the Russian Federation, certain parts of Australia and the Pacific Islands, and for longer, rural travel in the Indian subcontinent, SE Asia, the Far East.	1–3 years

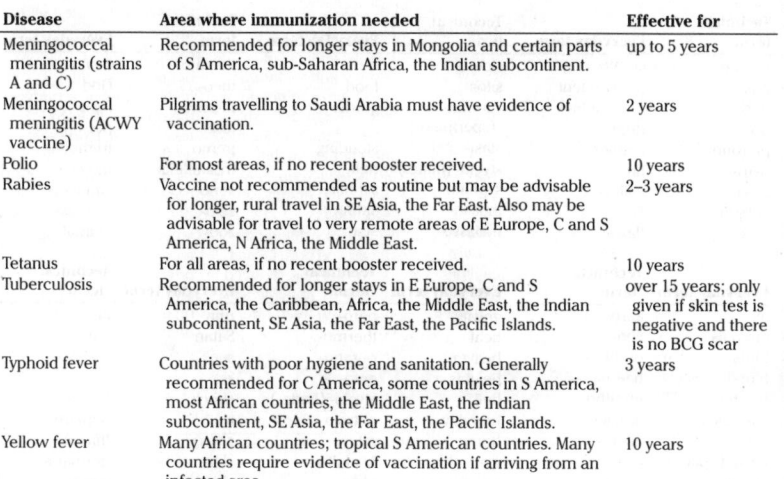

Disease	Area where immunization needed	Effective for
Meningococcal meningitis (strains A and C)	Recommended for longer stays in Mongolia and certain parts of S America, sub-Saharan Africa, the Indian subcontinent.	up to 5 years
Meningococcal meningitis (ACWY vaccine)	Pilgrims travelling to Saudi Arabia must have evidence of vaccination.	2 years
Polio	For most areas, if no recent booster received.	10 years
Rabies	Vaccine not recommended as routine but may be advisable for longer, rural travel in SE Asia, the Far East. Also may be advisable for travel to very remote areas of E Europe, C and S America, N Africa, the Middle East.	2–3 years
Tetanus	For all areas, if no recent booster received.	10 years
Tuberculosis	Recommended for longer stays in E Europe, C and S America, the Caribbean, Africa, the Middle East, the Indian subcontinent, SE Asia, the Far East, the Pacific Islands.	over 15 years; only given if skin test is negative and there is no BCG scar
Typhoid fever	Countries with poor hygiene and sanitation. Generally recommended for C America, some countries in S America, most African countries, the Middle East, the Indian subcontinent, SE Asia, the Far East, the Pacific Islands.	3 years
Yellow fever	Many African countries; tropical S American countries. Many countries require evidence of vaccination if arriving from an infected area.	10 years

Human Body, Health and Nutrition

An A to Z of phobias

Technical term	Everyday term	Technical term	Everyday term	Technical term	Everyday term
acero-	sourness	claustro-	closed spaces	kineso-	motion
achluo-	darkness	cnido-	stings	klepto-	stealing
acro-	heights	cometo-	comets	kopo-	fatigue
aero-	air	cyno-	dogs	kristallo-	ice
agora-	open spaces	demo-	crowds	lalio-	stuttering
aichuro-	points	demono-	demons	linono-	string
ailuro-	cats	dermato-	skin	logo-	words
akoustico-	sound	dike-	injustice	lysso- (mania-)	insanity
algo-	pain	dora-	fur	mastigo-	flogging
amaka-	carriages	eisoptro-	mirrors	mechano-	machinery
amatho-	dust	electro-	electricity	metallo-	metals
andro-	men	entomo-	insects	meteoro-	meteors
anemo-	wind	eoso-	dawn	miso-	contamination
angino-	narrowness	eremo-	solitude	mono-	one thing
anthropo-	man	erete-	pins	musico-	music
antlo-	flood	ereuthro-	blushing	muso-	mice
apeiro-	infinity	ergasio-	work	necro-	corpses
arachno-	spiders	geno-	sex	nelo-	glass
astheno-	weakness	geuma-	taste	neo-	newness
astra-	lightning	grapho-	writing	nepho-	clouds
ate-	ruin	gymno-	nudity	noso- (patho-)	disease
aulo-	flute	gyno-	women	ochlo-	crowds
aurora-	Northern Lights	haemato-	blood	ocho-	vehicles
bacilli-	microbes	hamartio-	sin	odonto-	teeth
baro-	gravity	haphe-	touch	oiko-	home
baso-	walking	harpaxo-	robbers	olfacto-	smell
batracho-	reptiles	hedono-	pleasure	ommato-	eyes
belone-	needles	helmintho-	worms	oneiro-	dreams
bronto- (tonitro-, kerauno-)	thunder	hodo-	travel	ophidio-	snakes
		homichlo-	fog	ornitho-	birds
		horme-	shock	ourano-	heaven
cheima-	cold	hydro-	water	pan- (panto-)	everything
chiono-	snow	hypegia-	responsibility	partheno-	girls
chrometo-	money	hypno-	sleep	patroio-	heredity
chromo-	colour	ideo-	ideas	penia-	poverty
chrono-	duration	kakorraphia-	failure	phasmo-	ghosts
chrystallo-	crystals	katagelo-	ridicule	phobo-	fears
		keno-	void	photo-	light

Human Body, Health and Nutrition

Technical term	Everyday term	Technical term	Everyday term	Technical term	Everyday term
pnigero-	smothering	sidero-	stars	thanato-	death
poine-	punishment	sito-	food	theo-	God
poly-	many things	sperma- (spermato-)	germs	thermo-	heat
poto-	drink			toxi-	poison
pterono-	feathers	stasi-	standing	tremo-	trembling
pyro-	fire	stygio- (hade-)	hell	triskaideka-	thirteen
rypo-	soiling	syphilo-	syphilis	xeno-	strangers
Satano-	Satan	thaaso-	sitting	zelo-	jealousy
sela-	flashes	thalasso-	sea	zoo-	animals

Everyday term	Technical term	Everyday term	Technical term	Everyday term	Technical term
air	aero-	gravity	baro-	ruin	ate-
animals	zoo-	heat	thermo-	Satan	Satano-
birds	ornitho-	heaven	ourano-	sea	thalasso-
blood	haemato-	heights	acro-	sex	geno-
blushing	ereutho-	hell	stygio- (hade-)	shock	horme-
carriages	amaka-	heredity	patroio-	sin	hamartio-
cats	ailuro-	home	oiko-	sitting	thaaso-
closed spaces	claustro-	ice	kristallo-	skin	dermato-
clouds	nepho-	ideas	ideo-	sleep	hypno-
cold	cheima-	infinity	apeiro-	smell	olfacto-
colour	chromo-	injustice	dike-	smothering	pnigero-
comets	cometo-	insanity	lysso- (mania-)	snakes	ophidio-
contamination	miso-	insects	entomo-	snow	chiono-
corpses	necro-	jealousy	zelo-	soiling	rypo-
crowds	ochlo-	light	photo-	solitude	eremo-
crystals	chrystallo-	lightning	astra-	sound	akoustico-
darkness	achluo-	machinery	mechano-	sourness	acero-
dawn	eoso-	man	anthropo-	spiders	arachno-
death	thanato-	many things	poly-	standing	stasi-
demons	demono-	men	andro-	stars	sidero-
disease	noso- (patho-)	metals	metallo-	stealing	klepto-
dogs	cyno-	meteors	meteoro-	stings	cnido-
dreams	oneiro-	mice	muso-	strangers	xeno-
drink	poto-	microbes	bacilli-	string	linono-
duration	chrono-	mirrors	eisoptro-	stuttering	lalio-
dust	amatho-	money	chrometo-	syphilis	syphilo-
electricity	electro-	motion	kineso-	taste	geuma-
everything	pan- (panto-)	music	musico-	teeth	odonto-
eyes	ommato-	narrowness	angino-	thirteen	triskaideka-
failure	kakorraphia-	needles	belone-	thunder	bronto- (tonitro-, kerauno-)
fatigue	kopo-	newness	neo-		
fears	phobo-	Northern Lights	aurora-		
feathers	pterono-	nudity	gymno-	touch	haphe-
fire	pyro-	one thing	mono-	travel	hodo-
flashes	sela-	open spaces	agora-	trembling	tremo-
flogging	mastigo-	pain	algo-	vehicles	ocho-
flood	antlo-	pins	erete-	void	keno-
flute	aulo-	pleasure	hedono-	walking	baso-
fog	homichlo-	points	aichuro-	water	hydro-
food	sito-	poison	toxi-	weakness	astheno-
fur	dora-	poverty	penia-	wind	anemo-
germs	sperma- (spermato-)	punishment	poine-	women	gyno-
		reptiles	batracho-	words	logo-
ghosts	phasmo-	responsibility	hypegia-	work	ergasio-
girls	partheno-	ridicule	katagelo-	worms	helmintho-
glass	nelo-	robbers	harpaxo-	writing	grapho-
God	theo-				

Measuring your Body Mass Index

Body Mass Index (BMI) can give an indication of obesity. In order to determine your BMI, find out your height in metres and weight in kilograms. To convert height in inches to metres, multiply the number of inches by 0.0254; to convert weight in pounds to kilos, multiply the number of pounds by 0.4536.

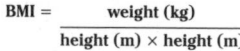

$$BMI = \frac{weight\ (kg)}{height\ (m) \times height\ (m)}$$

BMI values:
Less than 18 – underweight
18 to 25 – in the ideal weight range
25 to 30 – overweight
Over 30 – obese; endangering health

Optimum weight according to height

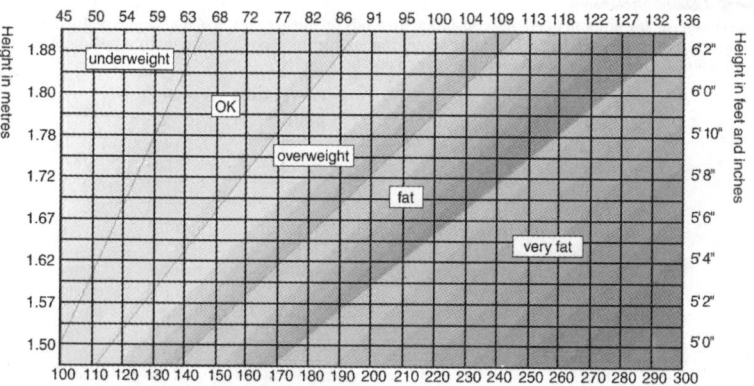

Weight in kilograms

Weight in pounds

Average daily energy requirements

CHILDREN	Energy used per day	
Age	kcals[1]	kJ[1]
0–3 months	550	2 300
3–6 months	760	3 200
6–9 months	905	3 800
9–12 months	1 000	4 200
8 years	2 095	8 800
15 years (female)	2 285	9 600
15 years (male)	3 000	12 600

ADULT FEMALES	Energy used per day	
Age	kcals[1]	kJ[1]
18–55 years		
Inactive	1 900	7 980
Active	2 150	9 030
Very active	2 500	10 500
Pregnant	2 380	10 000
Breastfeeding	2 690	11 300
Over 56 years		
Inactive	1 700	7 140
Active	2 000	8 400

Human Body, Health and Nutrition

Human Body, Health and Nutrition

ADULT MALES	Energy used per day	
Age	kcals[1]	kJ[1]
18–35 years		
Inactive	2500	10500
Active	3000	12600
Very active	3500	14700
36–55 years		
Inactive	2400	10080
Active	2800	11760
Very active	3400	14280
Over 56 years		
Inactive	2200	9240
Active	2500	10500

[1]kcals = kilocalories; kJ = kilojoules.

Energy expenditure

During exercise, the amount of energy consumed depends on the age, sex, size and fitness of the individual, and how vigorous the exercise is. This table shows the approximate energy used up by a person of average size and fitness carrying out certain activities over a one-hour period.

	Energy used per hour	
Activity	kcals[1]	kJ[1]
Badminton	340	1428
Climbing stairs	620	2604
Cycling	660	2772
Football	540	2268
Gardening, heavy	420	1764
Gardening, light	270	1134
Golf	270	1134
Gymnastics	420	1764
Hockey	540	2268
Housework	270	1134
Jogging	630	2646
Rugby	540	2268
Squash	600	2520
Standing	120	504
Staying in bed	60	252
Swimming	720	3024
Tennis	480	2016
Walking, brisk	300	1260
Walking, easy	180	756

[1]kcals = kilocalories; kJ =kilojoules.

Dietary recommendations

■ **Dietary recommendations to protect the heart**
Eat less fat, especially saturated fats, and avoid sugary and processed foods.
Avoid obesity.
Eat plenty of fibre-rich foods, including foods containing soluble fibre (eg oats).
Cut down on salt — too much salt can increase your blood pressure.
Eat at least 5 portions (400g) of a variety of fruit and vegetables each day.

■ **Dietary recommendations to reduce cancer risks**
Eat foods rich in fibre daily: these help to prevent bowel and colon cancers.
Eat at least five portions (400g) of a variety of fruit and vegetables each day: these are rich in fibre and
vitamins.
Eat less fat. There seems to be a close correlation between fat consumption and breast cancer.
Consume alcohol only in moderation. Excessive alcohol intake has been linked to cancers of the bowel,
liver, mouth, oesophagus, stomach and throat, especially in smokers.
Eat fewer smoked and salted foods. High consumption of salt-cured meat and fish and nitrate-cured meat
has been linked to throat and stomach cancers. There is also a link between eating pickled foods and
stomach cancer.
Keep body weight at recommended level.

■ **Dietary recommendations to lose weight**
To be healthy, a diet designed to reduce body weight needs to be in tune with the body's physiology. An
effective diet should promote the loss of fatty, or adipose, tissue from the body so that its overall fat content
is reduced. To do this successfully, the dieter should eat a well-balanced, high-carbohydrate, high-fibre,
low-fat diet with an energy content of between 1200 and 1500 calories per day, combining this with regular
exercise. Foods that can be consumed in this kind of low-calorie diet are shown (*below*) as Type A and Type
B foods; Type C foods should be avoided, and fat-containing Type B foods, such as meat, should be eaten in
moderation.

■ **Dieting tips**
Reduce alcohol intake to a minimum.
Avoid convenience foods because many contain 'hidden' fats and sugar.
Exercise at least three times a week.
Remove fat from meat, and fatty skin from poultry.
Avoid frying food — bake, grill, microwave or steam instead.
Avoid mayonnaise and rich sauces.
If you overeat, work out why you do it (eg through boredom or depression) and find other ways of relieving
these feelings.
Plan meals for the next day the night before, or early in the morning, to avoid impulse eating of high-calorie
foods.
Use a smaller plate to make smaller helpings look larger than they really are.
Eat regularly. Do not miss meals but try to eat 3–5 small meals each day.
Avoid second helpings.
Avoid between-meal snacks, except for raw fruit and vegetables if very hungry.
Eat at a table rather than eg in front of the television, which may encourage you to eat more and faster.
Take more time when eating — chew well.

Type A foods	Type B foods	Type C foods
Vegetarian foods	**Vegetarian foods**	**Meat, fish and dairy foods**
Cereals (unsweetened)	Dried fruit	Bacon
Fruits — all except avocados	Margarine, mono- or polyunsaturated	Beef, fatty cuts
Vegetables — all, including potatoes	Nuts	Butter
Vegetable protein, eg tofu	Pasta, especially wholewheat	Cheeses, apart from low-fat
Wholemeal bread	Pulses, such as beans and lentils	Duck
	Rice, especially wholegrain	Fish, fried
Meat, fish and dairy foods	Vegetable oils	Ice cream
Chicken and other poultry (not		Lamb, fatty cuts
duck) with skin removed		Mayonnaise
Cod, haddock and other non-oily fish	**Meat, fish and dairy foods**	Milk, full cream
Mussels and other shellfish	Beef, lean cuts	Pâté
Salmon (if tinned, in brine or water)	Eggs	Pork, fatty cuts
Tuna (if tinned, in brine or water)	Lamb, lean cuts	Salami
Yoghurt (plain, low fat)	Oily fish such as herring or mackerel	Sausages
	Pork, lean cuts	
	Sardines (if tinned, in brine)	
		Convenience foods
		Biscuits
		Burgers
		Cakes
		Chips
		Chocolate
		Crisps

Human Body, Health and Nutrition

Composition of selected foods

Approximate values given are for 100g of the food named.

Food	Kilo-calories[1]	Protein (g)	Carbo-hydrates (g)	Fat (g)	Fibre (g)
almonds	564	19	20	54	15
apples	38	trace	15	trace	2
apricots, dried	182	5	67	1	24
apricots, raw	25	1	13	trace	2
asparagus, cooked	18	2	4	trace	1
aubergine (or eggplant), cooked	14	1	4	trace	2
avocados	221	2	6	16	2
bacon, back, grilled	271	15	2	24	0
bacon, streaky, grilled	308	16	2	27	0
bananas	85	1	22	trace	2
beans, broad, cooked	46	4	66	1	4
beans, dried white, cooked	118	8	21	7	25
beans, green, cooked	25	2	5	trace	4
beef, rump steak, grilled	218	30	0	12	0
beetroot, cooked	43	1	7	trace	2
biscuits, chocolate digestive	506	6	64	25	4
biscuits, digestive	486	7	62	23	5
blackberries, raw	29	1	13	1	7
blackcurrants	29	2	14	trace	9
brazil nuts, raw	618	14	11	67	9
bread, white	232	10	58	2	3
bread, wholemeal	216	10	55	3	9
broccoli, cooked	26	3	5	trace	4
brussel sprouts, cooked	18	4	6	trace	3
butter, salted	740	1	trace	82	0
cabbage, cooked	11	2	trace	trace	2
cabbage, raw	25	2	5	trace	3
carrots, cooked	20	1	5	trace	3
carrots, raw	25	1	6	trace	3
cauliflower, cooked	22	2	4	trace	2
celery, raw	36	1	2	trace	2
cheese, Brie	314	19	2	23	0
cheese, Cheddar	414	25	2	32	0
cheese, cottage	96	17	2	4	0
cheese, Edam	314	30	trace	23	0
cherries, raw	70	1	17	trace	1
chickpeas, dry	320	20	50	6	15
chicken, meat only, roast	142	19	0	4	0
chocolate bar, plain	510	4	63	29	0
cod, cooked	94	19	0	1	0
corn (on the cob)	91	3	21	1	5
courgettes, cooked	14	1	3	trace	1
crab, cooked	129	18	1	5	0
cream, double	446	2	3	48	0
crisps	517	6	40	37	11
cucumber, raw	15	1	3	trace	trace
dates	214	2	73	1	7
egg, boiled	163	13	1	12	0
eggplant, ▶ aubergine					
figs, dried	214	4	69	1	19
flour, white	350	9	80	1	4
flour, wholemeal	318	13	56	2	10
grapefruit	41	1	11	trace	trace
grapes, raw	69	1	16	1	1
haddock, cooked	96	19	0	1	0
ham, lean	168	22	0	5	0
honey	289	trace	82	0	0
jam	261	1	79	trace	1
lamb chop, boned, grilled	353	24	0	29	0
leeks, cooked	25	1	7	0	4
lentils, cooked	106	8	19	trace	4
lettuce, raw	12	1	3	trace	1
liver, cooked	254	20	6	13	0

COMPOSITION OF SELECTED FOODS

Food	Kilo-calories[1]	Protein (g)	Carbo-hydrates (g)	Fat (g)	Fibre (g)
lobster, cooked	119	20	trace	3	0
mackerel, cooked	188	25	0	11	0
margarine	730	trace	1	80	0
melon, honeydew	21	1	5	trace	1
melon, water	21	trace	5	trace	1
milk, cow's, skimmed	36	4	5	trace	0
milk, cow's, whole	65	4	5	4	0
mushrooms, raw	14	3	4	trace	2
mussels, cooked	86	17	0	1	0
nectarines	64	1	17	trace	2
oatmeal, cooked	399	2	10	1	7
oats, porridge	377	10	70	7	7
oil, vegetable	900	0	0	100	0
onions, raw	38	2	9	trace	1
orange juice	45	1	10	trace	0
oranges, peeled, raw	49	1	12	trace	2
parsnip, cooked	50	1	17	trace	4
pasta, dry	353	12	71	2	4
peaches, raw	38	1	8	trace	1
peanuts, fresh	571	26	19	48	8
pears, raw	61	1	15	trace	2
peas, fresh, cooked	54	5	4	trace	5
pepper, green, raw	14	1	5	trace	1
pepper, red, raw	20	1	7	trace	1
pineapple, raw	46	trace	14	trace	1
pork chop, boned, grilled	328	28	0	24	0
potatoes, baked in skin	86	3	21	trace	2
potatoes, boiled in skin	75	2	17	trace	2
prawns, cooked	107	18	0	1	0
prunes	136	1	77	trace	14
raisins	246	3	77	trace	7
raspberries, raw	25	1	14	1	7
rice, brown, cooked	129	3	26	1	1
rice, white, cooked	121	3	33	trace	1
salmon, cooked	196	20	0	13	0
spinach, cooked	23	3	4	trace	6
strawberries, raw	37	1	8	1	2
sugar	394	0	100	0	0
swede, cooked	18	1	4	trace	3
tomatoes, raw	14	1	5	trace	1
tuna, canned in brine	118	28	0	1	0
turkey, meat only, roast	140	36	0	3	0
turnip, cooked	14	1	5	trace	2
walnuts	525	15	16	64	5
yogurt, skimmed milk	50	3	5	2	0
yogurt, whole milk	62	3	5	3	0

[1] To convert kilocalories into kilojoules, multiply by 4.184.

Human Body, Health and Nutrition

E numbers

Human Body, Health and Nutrition

Glossary	Description
acidifiers	impart a sharp flavour; control acidity, eg for setting jams; include some numbers within range E300–399
anti-caking agents	prevent particles sticking together to enable the product to flow freely, eg in salt and icing sugar; include some numbers within range E550–599
anti-foaming agents	prevent excessive froth and scum formation during boiling; include some numbers within range E430–439, E900, E905
antioxidants	prevent or inhibit the harmful effects of oxidation in fat and oils, thus preventing fatty foods from turning rancid; also used to prevent discoloration due to oxidation eg in cut fruits; include some numbers within range E300–321
azo dyes	have a particular chemical structure and may be responsible for allergic reactions eg attacks of asthma and eczema, nettle rash, watering eyes and nose, blurred vision and hyperactivity in children; include E102, E107, E110, E122, E123, E124, E128, E151, E154, E155, E181
bases	added to reduce acidity or increase alkalinity; also react with acids to make carbon dioxide for aeration; mainly found within range E500–599
bleaching agents	artificially bleach and whiten flour; include some numbers within range E925–930
buffers	maintain the acid–alkali balance at a constant level; include E262, E263, E326, E327, some numbers within range E331–340, some numbers within range E350–365, E380, E450, E503, E578
bulking agents	add to the bulk of foods without increasing their energy value, eg in slimming products; include some numbers within range E400–499
chelating agents	▶ **sequestrants**
coal tar dyes	dyes formerly made from coal, now made industrially; may have same configuration as **azo dyes**; include those additives listed under azo dyes above plus E104, E127, E131, E132, E133
colours	make food, particularly processed food, look more attractive and 'realistic'; include numbers within range E100–199
emulsifiers	plant gums, chemicals or plant derivatives which allow the mixing of fats and oils with water and enhance smooth creamy textures; also slow down process of baked foods going stale (▶ **stabilizers**); mainly found within range E400–499
emulsifying salts	mixture of citrates, phosphates and tartrates added during processing of cheese to prevent it turning stringy; include some numbers within range E330–340, E380, E450, some numbers within range E540–549
firming agents	calcium and magnesium salts that ensure fruits and vegetables retain their crispness and firmness and do not go soft during processing; include E170, E226, E227, E263, E327, E333, E341, E352, some numbers within range E500–529, E578
flavour modifiers or enhancers	reduce or enhance taste or smell of a food without imparting their own smell or flavour; mainly found within range E620–639
glazing agents	provide a protective coating or shiny appearance; include numbers within range E900–909
humectants	prevent food from drying out by absorbing water from the atmosphere; include E325, E406, E420–422
improving agents	used to whiten flour and alter the consistency of bread; also called flour treatment agents; include numbers within range E920–930
plasticizers	make a substance more flexible; include E422 and E478
preservatives, antibacterial, antimicrobial etc	inhibit growth of bacteria, fungi and viruses which cause food poisoning or food decay, thus increasing storage time; mainly found within range E200–299
release agents	used to coat machinery or food to prevent sticking during manufacture, and also to enable food to slip easily out of packaging; include E552, E553, E572, E901, E907
sequestrants	attach themselves to trace metals eg iron or copper to prevent them speeding up oxidation and thus causing the deterioration of food; also render toxic trace metals harmless; include E262, E263, some numbers within range E330–341, E353, E370, E450, E509, E516, some numbers within range E570–579
stabilizers	like **emulsifiers**, they prevent mixtures from separating out and enhance smooth creamy textures; they also delay the process of baked foods going stale; mainly found within range E400–499
sweeteners	used as a substitute for sugar to sweeten food; include E420, E421, numbers within range E950–969
thickeners	increase the viscosity of a food; usually of plant origin (except E551, silicon dioxide); mainly found within range E400–499

Culinary terms of foreign origin

aïoli a garlic-flavoured mayonnaise. [French; from Provençal *ai*, garlic]

à la carte said of a meal in a restaurant, with each dish priced and ordered separately. [French, = from the menu]

à la mode said of beef, larded and stewed with vegetables; said of desserts, served with ice cream (North American). [French, = in fashion]

al dente said of pasta and vegetables, cooked so as to remain firm when bitten. [Italian, = to the tooth]

antipasto (*plural* **antipasti**, **antipastos**) food served at the beginning of a meal to sharpen the appetite. [Italian]

aperitif an alcoholic drink taken before a meal to stimulate the appetite. [from French *apéritif*; from Latin *aperire*, to open]

aqua vitae a strong alcoholic drink, especially brandy. [Latin, = water of life]

au gratin covered with breadcrumbs and / or grated cheese, cooked in the oven and / or browned under the grill, so that a crisp, golden topping is formed. [French, = literally 'with the burnt scrapings'; from *gratter*, to scrape]

au naturel cooked plainly, or uncooked; served without dressing. [French, = in the natural state]

bain-marie a vessel of hot or boiling water in which a container of food can be cooked gently or kept warm. [French, = bath of Mary; from Latin *balneum Mariae*; origin uncertain, perhaps from Mary, or Miriam, sister of Moses, who reputedly wrote a book on alchemy]

baklava or **baclava** a rich cake of Middle Eastern origin made of layers of flaky pastry with a filling of honey, nuts and spices. [Turkish]

balti 1 a style of Indian cooking originating in Britain, in which food is both cooked and served in a pan resembling a wok. **2** the pan in which this is cooked. [Hindi, = bucket]

béarnaise (sauce) a rich sauce made from egg yolks, butter, shallots, tarragon, chervil and wine vinegar. [French; after *Béarn*, a region in SW France]

béchamel (sauce) a white sauce flavoured with onion and herbs and sometimes enriched with cream. [French; named after the Marquis de Béchamel (d.1703), a French courtier who attended Louis XIV]

bhaji an Indian appetizer of vegetables, chickpea flour, and spices, formed into a ball and deep-fried. [Hindi]

biriani or **biryani** (*plural* **birianis** or **biryanis**) a type of spicy Indian dish consisting mainly of rice, with meat or fish and vegetables, etc. [Urdu]

bisque a thick rich soup, usually made from shellfish, cream, and wine. [French]

blanch 1 to prepare (vegetables or meat) for cooking or freezing by boiling in water for a short time. **2** to remove the skins (from almonds etc) by soaking them in boiling water. [from Old French *blanchir*]

blancmange a cold sweet jelly-like pudding made with milk. [from Old French *blanc*, white + *manger*, food]

blanquette a dish made with white meat such as chicken or veal, cooked in a white sauce. [from French *blanquette* (related to English *blanket*); from Old French *blankete*; from *blanc*, white]

Bolognese said especially of pasta, served with a tomato and meat sauce, usually also containing mushrooms, garlic, etc. [named after Bologna in N Italy]

bombe a dessert, usually ice cream, frozen in a round or melon-shaped mould. [French, = bomb]

bonne femme said of a dish, eg sole bonne femme, cooked simply and garnished with fresh vegetables and herbs. [from French *à la bonne femme*, in the manner of a good wife]

bouillabaisse a thick spicy fish soup from Provence. [French]

bouillon a thin clear soup made by boiling meat and vegetables in water, often used as a basis for thicker soups. [French; from *bouillir*, to boil]

bouquet garni a bunch or small packet of mixed herbs used to add flavour to food, usually removed before serving. [from French *bouquet* + *garnir*, to garnish]

bourguignon said of meat dishes, stewed with onion, mushrooms and Burgundy wine. [French, = Burgundian]

braise to cook (meat etc) slowly with a small amount of liquid in a closed dish. [from French *braiser*, from *braise*, live coals]

brochette a small metal or wooden skewer for holding food together or steady while it is being cooked. [French; a diminutive of *broche*, brooch or needle]

brioche a type of bread-like cake made with a yeast dough, eggs, and butter. [French]

brûlé usually said of a dessert, having brown sugar on top and cooked so that the sugar melts. [French, = burnt]

cacciatore or **cacciatora** said of meat, especially chicken or veal, cooked with tomatoes, mushrooms, onions and herbs. [Italian, = hunter]

calamari *plural noun* squid. [Italian, plural of *calamaro*, squid]

calzone a folded round of pizza dough stuffed with a savoury filling. [Italian, = trouser leg]

canapé a type of food served at parties, etc consisting of a small piece of bread or toast spread or topped with something savoury. [French, = sofa]

cannelloni a kind of pasta in the form of large tubes, served with a filling of meat, cheese, etc. [Italian; from *cannello*, tube]

cappuccino (*plural* **cappuccinos**) coffee with frothy hot milk and usually chocolate powder on top. [Italian]

ceviche (Mexican cookery) raw fish marinated in lime juice and served as an hors d'oeuvre. [American Spanish]

chapati or **chapatti** in Indian cooking, a thin flat portion of unleavened bread. [from Hindi *capati*]

chasseur said of a sauce or food cooked in a sauce containing mushrooms, shallots, white wine and herbs. [French, = hunter]

Chateaubriand or **chateaubriand** a thick steak cut from grilled fillet of beef, usually served with fried potatoes and mushrooms. [named after François René, Vicomte de Chateaubriand (1768–1848), French author and statesman]

chiffon a light frothy mixture, made with beaten whites of eggs. [French, = rag]

choux pastry a very light pastry made with eggs. [from French *pâte choux*, cabbage pastry]

ciabatta Italian bread with a sponge-like texture, made with olive oil. [Italian, = slipper]

consommé thin clear soup made from meat stock. [French; from *consommer*, to eat, consume]

cordon bleu *noun* (*plural* **cordons bleus**) a cook of the highest standard; *adjective* said of a cook or cookery, being of the highest standard. [French, = blue ribbon]

coupe a dessert made with fruit and ice cream. [French, = glass, cup]

couscous a N African dish of crushed wheat steamed and served eg with meat. [French; from Arabic *kuskus*]

crème 1 cream, or a creamy food. **2** a liqueur. [French, = cream]

crème fraîche cream thickened with a culture of bacteria, used in cooking. [French, = fresh cream]

crêpe or **crepe** a thin pancake. [French; from Latin *crispus*, crisp]

croissant a crescent-shaped bread roll, made with a high proportion of fat, and flaky in consistency. [French, = crescent]

croquante a crisp pie or tart; a crisp cake containing almonds. [French]

croquette a ball or roll of eg minced meat, fish, or potato, coated in breadcrumbs and fried. [French; from *croquer*, to crunch]

croûte a thick slice of fried bread for serving entrées (▶ **en croûte**). [French, = crust]

croûton a small cube of fried or toasted bread, served in soup, salads, etc. [French; a diminutive of *croûte*, crust]

dal or **dahl** or **dhal 1** any of various edible dried split pea-like seeds. **2** a cooked dish made of any of these seeds. [from Hindi *dal*, to split]

doner kebab thin slices cut from a block of minced and seasoned lamb grilled on a spit, eaten on unleavened bread. [from Turkish *döner*, rotating]

enchilada (*plural* **enchiladas**) a Mexican dish consisting of a flour tortilla with a meat filling, served with a chilli-flavoured sauce. [from Spanish *enchilar*, to season with chilli]

en croûte wrapped in pastry and baked. [from French *croûte*, crust]

entrecôte a boneless steak cut from between two ribs. [French; from *entre*, between + *côte*, rib]

entrée 1 a small dish served after the fish course and before the main course at a formal dinner. **2** (chiefly USA) a main course. [French, = entrance]

escalope a thin slice of boneless meat, especially veal. [French]

espresso (*plural* **espressos**) **1** coffee made by forcing steam or boiling water through ground coffee beans. **2** the machine for making it. [Italian, = pressed out]

farce stuffing or force-meat. [French]

farci stuffed. [from French *farce*, stuffing; from Latin *farcire*, to stuff]

fettuccine pasta in the form of flat wide ribbons. [Italian, a diminutive (plural) of *fettuccia*, tape]

fines herbes *plural noun* a mixture of herbs for use in cooking. [French, = fine herbs]

flambé *adjective* said of food, soaked in brandy and set alight before serving; *verb* (**flambéed**, **flambéing**) to serve (food) in this way. [from French *flamber*, to expose to flame]

florentine *adjective* containing or served with spinach, eg eggs florentine; *noun* a biscuit on a chocolate base covered on one side with preserved fruit and nuts. [from Latin *Florentinus*, from *Florentia* (Florence)]

focaccia a flat round of Italian bread topped with olive oil and herbs or spices. [Italian, = cake]

fondue 1 a Swiss dish of hot cheese sauce into which bits of bread are dipped. **2** a steak dish (also called **fondue bourguignonne**), the pieces of meat being cooked at the table by dipping them

briefly into hot oil or stock. [French; from *fondre*, to melt]

frankfurter a type of spicy smoked sausage. [from German *Frankfurter Wurst*, Frankfurt sausage]

fricassee a cooked dish usually of pieces of meat or chicken served in a sauce. [from Old French *fricasser*, to cook chopped food in its own juice]

fromage frais a creamy low-fat cheese with the consistency of whipped cream. [French, = fresh cheese]

fusilli pasta shaped into short thick spirals. [Italian]

galantine a dish of boneless cooked white meat or fish served cold in jelly. [Old French]

garam masala a mixture of ground spices used to make curry. [Hindi, = hot mixture]

garni trimmed, garnished. [French; from *garnir*, to garnish]

gateau or **gâteau** (*plural* **gateaux**, **gateaus**, **gâteaux**) a large rich cake, especially filled with cream and decorated with fruit, nuts, etc. [French]

ghee butter made from cow's or buffalo's milk, purified by heating, used in Indian cooking. [from Hindi *ghi*]

glacé *adjective* **1** coated with a sugary glaze; candied: eg glacé cherries. **2** said of icing on cakes etc, made with icing sugar and liquid. **3** said of drinks etc, frozen or served with ice, eg mousse glacée; *verb* (**glacéed**, **glacéing**) **1** to crystallize fruit etc. **2** to ice cakes etc with glacé icing. [French]

gnocchi an Italian dish of small dumplings made with flour, cooked potato, or semolina, poached and served with various sauces. [Italian, = lumps]

gougère a kind of choux pastry that has grated cheese added to it before baking. [French]

goujons small strips of fish or chicken coated in seasoned flour, egg and breadcrumbs, and deep-fried. [from French *goujon*, gudgeon (the fish)]

gratin the golden brown crust covering a gratinated food or dish; ▶ **au gratin**.

gratinate to cook with a topping of buttered breadcrumbs and/or cheese browned until crisp; to cook au gratin; ▶ **au gratin**. [from French *gratiner*, to cook au gratin]

gratiné cooked or served au gratin; ▶ **au gratin**. [from French *gratiner*, to cook au gratin]

gremolata a colourful, flavoursome garnish, made of chopped parsley, lemon or orange peel, garlic, etc. [Italian]

haute cuisine cookery (especially French) of a very high standard. [French, = high cooking]

hors d'oeuvre a savoury appetiser served at the beginning of a meal. [French, = out of the work]

hummus or **hommos** or **houmus** a Middle Eastern hors d'oeuvre or dip consisting of pureed cooked chickpeas and tahini paste, flavoured with lemon juice and garlic. [from Turkish *humus*]

jardinière an accompaniment of mixed vegetables for a meat dish. [from French *jardinière*, feminine of *jardinier*, gardener]

jus juice; gravy. [French]

kofta (*plural* **koftas**) (Indian cookery) minced and seasoned meat or vegetables, shaped into balls and fried. [Hindi, = pounded meat]

lasagne pasta in the form of thin flat sheets, often cooked in layers with a mixture of meat and tomatoes, and a cheese sauce. [Italian]

lyonnaise made with sautéed sliced potatoes and onions or potatoes in an onion sauce. [named after Lyon, France]

macaroni (*plural* **macaronis,macaronies**) pasta in the form of short tubes. [from Italian *maccaroni*]

mascarpone a soft Italian cream cheese. [Italian]

mayonnaise a cold creamy sauce made of egg yolk, oil, vinegar or lemon juice, and seasoning. [French]

meringue a crisp cooked mixture of sugar and egg whites, or a cake made from this. [French]

mesclun a mixed green salad of young leaves and shoots of rocket, chicory, fennel, etc. [French; from Niçois *mesclumo*, mixture]

minestrone thick soup containing vegetables and pasta. [Italian; from *minestrare*, to serve]

moussaka a dish made with minced meat, aubergines, onions, tomatoes, etc, covered with a cheese sauce and baked, traditionally eaten in Greece, Turkey and the Balkans. [Greek]

mousse 1 a dessert made from a whipped mixture of cream, eggs and flavouring, eaten cold. 2 a similar meat or fish dish. [French, = froth]

mozzarella a soft white Italian cheese, especially used as a topping for pizza. [Italian]

muesli a mixture of crushed grain, nuts and dried fruit, eaten with milk, especially for breakfast. [Swiss German]

mulligatawny a thick curry-flavoured meat soup, originally made in E India. [from Tamil *milagu-tannir*, pepper-water]

nan a slightly leavened Indian bread, similar to pitta bread. [Hindi]

navarin a stew of lamb or mutton with root vegetables such as turnip. [French]

nougat a chewy sweet containing nuts etc. [French; from Latin *nux*, nut]

nouvelle cuisine a simple style of cookery characterized by much use of fresh produce and elegant presentation. [French, = new cookery]

omelette (*especially USA* **omelet**) a dish of beaten eggs fried in a pan, often folded round a savoury or sweet filling such as cheese or jam. [from Old French *alemette*; from *lemelle*, knife-blade]

paella a Spanish dish of rice, fish, or chicken, vegetables and saffron. [Catalan; from Latin *patella*, pan]

pakora an Indian dish of chopped spiced vegetables formed into balls, coated in batter, and deep-fried. [Hindi]

papillote 1 frilled paper used to decorate the bones of chops, etc. 2 oiled or greased paper in which meat is cooked and served. [French, apparently from *papillon*, butterfly]

Parmesan a hard dry Italian cheese, especially served grated with pasta dishes. [from Italian *Parmegiano*, from Parma]

passata an Italian sauce of puréed and sieved tomatoes. [Italian, = passed (ie through a sieve)]

pasta 1 a dough made with flour, water, and eggs shaped in a variety of forms such as spaghetti, macaroni, lasagne, etc. 2 a cooked dish of this, usually with a sauce. [Italian; from Latin *pasta*, paste, dough; from Greek *pasta*, barley porridge]

pâté a spread made from ground or chopped meat, fish or vegetables blended with herbs, spices, etc. [French; formerly meaning pie or pasty]

patisserie a shop selling fancy cakes, sweet pastries, etc. [from French *pâtisserie*; from Latin *pasta*, dough]

pesto an Italian sauce originating in Liguria and made from fresh basil leaves, pine kernels, olive oil, garlic and Parmesan cheese. [Italian; from *pestare*, to crush, pound]

petit four (*plural* **petits fours**) a small sweet biscuit, usually decorated with icing. [French, = little oven]

pilaf or **pilaff** or **pilau** an oriental dish of spiced rice with chicken, fish, etc. [from Turkish *pilaw*]

pizza a circle of dough spread with cheese, tomatoes, etc and baked, made originally in Italy. [Italian]

polenta an Italian dish of cooked ground maize. [Italian; from Latin *polenta*, hulled and crushed grain]

poppadum or **poppadom** a paper-thin pancake grilled till crisp for serving with Indian dishes. [Tamil]

praline a sweet consisting of nuts in caramelized sugar. [named after Marshal Duplessis-Praslin (1598–1675), a French soldier whose cook invented it]

pretzel a salted and glazed biscuit in the shape of a knot. [German]

profiterole a small sweet or savoury confection of choux pastry. [French; said to be a diminutive from *profiter*, to profit]

prosciutto finely cured uncooked ham, often smoked. [Italian = pre-dried]

provençale a style of cookery that traditionally uses olive oil, tomatoes, onion, garlic and white wine, eg eggs à la provençale, and, in meat dishes, requires slow-cooking. [named after the area of Provence, SE France]

pumpernickel a dark heavy coarse rye bread, eaten especially in Germany. [German, = lout, perhaps literally 'stink-devil' or 'fart-devil']

purée *noun* a quantity of fruit or vegetables reduced to a pulp by liquidizing or rubbing through a sieve; *verb* (**purées, puréed**) to reduce to a purée. [from French *purer*, to strain]

puri a small cake of unleavened Indian bread, deep-fried and served hot. [Hindi]

quenelle a dumpling of fish, chicken, veal, etc. [French]

quesadilla (Mexican cookery) a tortilla filled with cheese, chillis, etc, folded and fried or grilled. [Mexican Spanish; diminutive of *queseda*; from *quese*, cheese]

quiche a tart with a savoury filling usually made with eggs. [French; from German *Kuchen*, cake]

ragout a highly seasoned stew of meat and vegetables. [from French *ragoût*]

ramekin 1 a small baking dish for a single serving of food. 2 an individual serving of food, especially of a savoury dish containing cheese and eggs, served in a ramekin. [from French *ramequin*]

ratafia 1 a flavouring essence made with the essential oil of almonds. 2 a cordial or liqueur flavoured with fruit kernels and almonds. 3 an almond-flavoured biscuit or small cake. [French; probably from Creole or *tafia*, a type of rum]

ratatouille a southern French stew made with tomatoes, peppers, courgettes, aubergines, onions, and garlic. [French]

ravioli *plural noun* small, square pasta cases with a savoury filling of meat, cheese, etc. [Italian]

rijsttafel an Indonesian rice dish served with a variety of foods. [Dutch, = rice table]

risotto (*plural* **risottos**) an Italian dish of rice cooked in a meat or seafood stock with onions, tomatoes, cheese, etc. [from Italian *riso*, rice]

roti (*plural* **rotis**) 1 a cake of unleavened bread, traditionally made in parts of India and the Caribbean. 2 a kind of sandwich made of this wrapped around curried vegetables, seafood, or chicken. [Hindi, = bread]

roulade meat, cake or soufflé mixture served rolled up, usually with a filling. [French]

roux (*plural* **roux**) a cooked mixture of flour and fat, used to thicken sauces. [from French *beurre roux*, brown butter]

rugelach or **ruggelach** *plural noun* (Jewish cookery) small crescent-shaped pastries filled with fruit, nuts, cheese, etc. [from Yiddish *rugelekh*, plural of *rugele*]

salami (*plural* **salamis**) a highly seasoned type of sausage, usually served sliced. [Italian]

salsa (Mexican cookery) a spicy sauce made with tomatoes, onions, chillies and oil. [Spanish and Italian *salsa*, sauce]

salsa verde Italian green sauce, made with anchovies, garlic, capers, oil and herbs. [Spanish and Italian *salsa*, sauce]

samosa a small deep-fried triangular spicy meat or vegetable pasty of Indian origin. [Hindi]

sauerkraut shredded cabbage pickled in salt water, a popular German dish. [from German *sauerkraut*, sour cabbage]

sauté *verb* (**sautés**, **sautéd** or **sautéed**, **sautéing** or **sautéeing**) to fry gently for a short time; *adjective* fried in this way: eg sauté potatoes. [French, = tossed; from *sauter*, to jump]

schnapps in N Europe, any strong dry alcoholic spirit, especially Dutch gin distilled from potatoes. [German, = dram of liquor]

schnitzel a veal cutlet. [German]

sorbet a dish of sweetened fruit juice, frozen and served as a kind of ice cream; a water ice. [French; from Arabic *sharbah*, drink]

soufflé a light sweet or savoury baked dish, a frothy mass of whipped egg whites with other ingredients mixed in. [French; from *souffler*, to puff up]

spaghetti pasta in the form of long thin string-like strands. [Italian; from *spago*, cord]

stroganoff a dish, also called **beef stroganoff**, that is traditionally made with strips of sautéed fillet steak, onions and mushrooms, cooked in a lightly spiced, creamy white wine sauce and served with pilaf rice; there are many variations on this, including one that uses only vegetables. [named after Count Paul Stroganov, a 19c Russian diplomat]

strudel a baked roll of thin pastry with a filling of fruit, especially apple. [German, = whirlpool, ie from the rolling]

table d'hôte (*plural* **tables d'hôte**) a meal with a set number of choices and a set number of courses

offered for a fixed price, especially to residents in a hotel. [French, = host's table]

tagliatelle pasta made in the form of long narrow ribbons. [Italian]

tandoori food cooked on a spit over charcoal in a clay oven. [from Hindi *tandoor*, clay oven]

tapas light savoury snacks or appetizers, especially those based on Spanish foods and cooking techniques and served with drinks. [from Spanish *tapa*, cover or lid]

thermidor *postpositive adjective* (eg lobster thermidor) denoting a method of preparation, the flesh being mixed with a cream sauce seasoned with mustard, and served in the shell. [from Greek *therme*, heat, and *doron* gift; Thermidor was the eleventh month of the French Revolutionary calendar, 19 July–17 August]

tikka in Indian cookery, meat that is marinated in yoghurt and spices and cooked in a clay oven. [Hindi]

timbale a dish of meat or fish, etc cooked in a cup-shaped mould or shell. [from French *timbale*; from Spanish *atabal*; from Arabic *at-tabl*, the drum]

tortilla (*plural* **tortillas**) a thin round Mexican maize cake cooked on a griddle and usually eaten hot, with a filling or topping of meat or cheese. [Spanish; a diminutive of *torta*, cake]

tournedos (*plural* **tournedos**) a small round thick fillet of beef. [French]

vacherin a dessert made with meringue and whipped cream, usually with ice cream, fruit, nuts, etc. [French]

velouté a smooth white sauce made with stock [French, = velvety]

vermicelli 1 pasta in very thin strands, thinner than spaghetti. 2 tiny splinters of chocolate used for desserts and cake decoration. [Italian, = little worms]

vinaigrette a salad dressing made by mixing oil, vinegar and seasonings, especially mustard. [French; from *vinaigre*, vinegar]

vol-au-vent a small round puff-pastry case with a savoury filling. [French, = flight in the wind]

wurst any of various types of large German sausage. [German, = something rolled; related to Latin *vertere*, to turn]

yakitori a Japanese dish of boneless pieces of chicken grilled on skewers and basted with a thick sweet sauce of sake, mirin and soy sauce. [Japanese; from *yaki*, grill + *tori*, bird]

zabaglione a dessert made from egg yolks, sugar and wine whipped together.

Chefs, restaurateurs and cookery writers

Beard, James (1903–85) US chef and cookery writer. An influential teacher, he wrote many books including *The James Beard Cookbook* (1959) and *James Beard's American Cookery* (1972).

Beeton, Mrs Isabella Mary, née **Mayson** (1836–65) English cookery writer. Her *Book of Household Management* first appeared in a magazine owned by her husband, Samuel Beeton, in 1859–60. It made her a household name.

Blanc, Raymond René (1949–) French chef and restaurateur. He began to cook in 1975 in England and opened Les Quat' Saisons in Oxford in 1977, and Le Manoir aux Quat' Saisons (two Michelin stars) in 1984. Books include *Blanc Vite* (1999) and *Foolproof French Cookery* (2002). His reality TV programme *The Restaurant* began in 2007.

Blumenthal, Heston (1966–) English chef and broadcaster. He is the chef and owner of the

Fat Duck restaurant (three Michelin stars). His scientific approach to the principles of cooking was made more widely known by his television series *In Search of Perfection* (2006) and accompanying publications.

Bocuse, Paul (1926–) French restaurateur and cookery writer. He took over the family business, Restaurant Bocuse or L'Auberge du Pont de Collonges, and runs the French Pavilion at Disneyworld, Orlando. Books include *La Bonne chère* (1995).

Carluccio, Antonio Mario Gaetano (1937–) Italian restaurateur, cookery writer and broadcaster. He became restaurateur at Neal Street Restaurant in 1981 (proprietor since 1989) and has since opened a number of restaurants and food shops in south-east England. His books include *An Invitation to Italian Cooking* (1986), *A Passion for Pasta* (1993),

Antonio Carluccio's Italian Feast (1996, also television series) and Passion for Pasta (2003).

Child, Julia, née **McWilliams** (1912–2004) US cookery writer and broadcaster. She co-founded a cooking school in Paris in 1951, co-wrote Mastering the Art of French Cooking in 1961, among other books, and hosted several television series including The French Chef (1963–76).

Claiborne, Craig (1920–2000) US food critic and cookery writer. He was food editor of the New York Times (1957–88). Books included the New York Times Cook Book (1961) and Craig Claiborne's Memorable Meals (1985).

David, Elizabeth (1913–92) English cookery writer. She drew on her time spent abroad to write such influential books as French Provincial Cooking (1960).

Delmonico, Lorenzo (1813–81) Swiss-born US restaurateur. After arriving in New York with his uncles in 1832, he opened Delmonico's c.1834. He started a new restaurant culture by introducing European standards and foods (eg fresh salads, vegetables) and longer opening hours.

Diat, Louis Felix (1885–1957) French-born US restaurateur. Known as 'Monsieur Louis', he was chef at the New York Ritz-Carlton hotel's famous restaurant (1910–51) and championed French cooking there and through his books, eg Cooking à la Ritz (1941). He created vichyssoise.

Dickson Wright, Clarissa (1946–) English cook, cookery writer and broadcaster. A professional cook, she came to fame with the television series Two Fat Ladies (1996–9) and related publications. Since the death of **Jennifer Paterson**, she has published a number of cookery books and co-presented television programmes on field sports and traditional country pursuits

Dimbleby, Josceline Rose (1943–) English cookery writer. She wrote for Sainsbury's from 1978 and was cookery editor for the Sunday Telegraph from 1982. Books include Salads for all Seasons (1981) and Josceline Dimbleby's Complete Cookbook (1997).

Eriksen, Gunn (1956–) Norwegian-born Scottish chef and restaurateur. From 1980, she and her husband, Fred Brown, ran a Michelin-starred restaurant at their Altnaharrie Inn across Loch Broom from Ullapool, until her severe back problems forced them to close in 2001.

Escoffier, Auguste (c.1847–1935) French chef. He used his culinary skills in the Franco–Prussian War and at the Grand Hotel in Monte Carlo before going to the London Savoy and then to the Carlton. He invented the bombe Nero and pêche melba.

Farmer, Fannie Merritt (1857–1915) US cookery expert. She was a director of the Boston Cooking School and edited its bestselling cook book (now called 'Fannie Farmer's') in 1896 before founding Miss Farmer's School of Cookery, the first to cater for housewives and nurses rather than servants and teachers.

Fearnley-Whittingstall, Hugh (1965–) English cookery writer and broadcaster. Formerly a sous-chef at the River Café, his television programmes Cook on the Wild Side, TV Dinners and the River Cottage series gained him a reputation as a back-to-basics and sometimes unorthodox cook. In 2008 he broadcast Hugh's Chicken Run to campaign for free-range chickens. Books include The River Cottage Cookbook (2003) and Hugh Fearlessly Eats It All (2006).

Fisher, F(rances) K(ennedy), née **Kennedy** (1908–92) US cookery writer. Her books, which are like collections of culinary essays celebrating US regional food, include How to Cook a Wolf (1942) and The Art of Eating (1976).

Floyd, Keith (1943–) English cookery writer and broadcaster. He is known for the flamboyant style of his television programmes and for his many Floyd on ... books, eg Floyd on France, Floyd on Fish.

Franey, Pierre (1921–96) French-born US chef and restaurateur. He was chef at Le Pavillon in New York, collaborated on books and articles with **Craig Claiborne**, and published his own articles written for the New York Times.

Gray, Rose (1939–) British chef and restaurateur. In 1987 she and **Ruth Rogers** opened the successful Italian-cooking based River Café in Hammersmith, London. The River Café Cook Book and other titles, plus a cookery school, followed.

Grigson, (Heather) Jane, née **McIntyre** (1928–90) English cookery writer. She was correspondent for the Observer and wrote the cookery classics English Food (1974), Jane Grigson's Vegetable Book (1978) and Jane Grigson's Fruit Book (1982), all influenced by her country lifestyle.

Grigson, Sophie (Hester Sophia Frances) (1959–) English cookery writer and broadcaster, and cookery correspondent for several newspapers. Television series and books include Travels à la Carte (1994), Taste of the Times (1997), Complete Sophie Grigson Cookbook (2001) and The First-time Cook (2004).

Grossman, Loyd Daniel Gilman (1950–) US chef, broadcaster and cookery writer. He presented the television series Masterchef (1990–9). Books include The World on a Plate (1997).

Guérard, Michel Etienne (1933–) French chef, restaurateur and cookery writer. His restaurant Les Prés d'Eugénie in Eugénie les Bains has three Michelin stars. Books include Minceur Exquise (1989).

Harvey, Frederick Henry (1835–1901) British-born US restaurateur. Starting in 1876 at the railroad depot in Kansas, he created a chain of restaurants along the Atchison, Topeka and Santa Fe railroad; these became known for their good food, fresh linens, and their trained waitresses or 'Harvey Girls'.

Heathcote, Paul (1960–) English chef and restaurateur. His first restaurant was Paul Heathcote's Longridge Restaurant; others include Heathcote's Brasserie in Preston and Simply Heathcote's in Manchester.

Hom, Ken(neth) (1949–) US chef, cookery writer and broadcaster. He has earned renown as a food consultant and for popularizing Chinese cooking. His books and television series include Hot Wok (1996) and Foolproof Asian Cookery (2003).

Jaffrey, Madhur (1933–) Indian-born US cookery writer, broadcaster and actress. She began publishing the recipes sent to her by her mother in India. Books include Flavours of India (1995) and Madhur Jaffrey's Ultimate Curry Bible (2003).

Johnstone, (Christian) Isobel, pseudonym **Margaret Dods** (1781–1857) Scottish cookery writer and novelist. She had a huge success in 1826 with 'Meg Dods' Cookery', properly The Cook and Housewife's Manual by Mistress Margaret Dods.

Kerr, Graham Victor (1934–) New Zealand cookery writer and broadcaster. He became known for his widely-screened television show The Galloping Gourmet, and for such books as Galloping Gourmets (1969) and Graham Kerr's Kitchen (1995).

Ladenis, Nico (Nicholas Peter) (1934–) Kenyan

chef and restaurateur. He and his wife opened the Chez Nico restaurant, specializing in French cuisine, in 1971; other ventures include Incognico and Deca, now managed by his daughters. Books include *My Gastronomy* (1987) and *Nico* (1996).

Lawson, Nigella (1960–) English cookery writer and broadcaster. Her television series and related books include *How to Eat* (1998), *How to Be a Domestic Goddess* (2000), *Feast* (2004) and *Nigella Express* (2007).

Leith, Prue (Prudence Margaret) (1940–) English chef, restaurateur and cookery writer. She started Leith's restaurant in 1969 (one Michelin star) and Leith's School of Food and Wine in 1975. Books include *Leith's Cookery Bible* (1991).

Little, (Robert) Alastair (1950–) English chef and restaurateur. He opened two eponymous London restaurants in 1985 and 1995, but now runs a delicatessen, Tavola, in West London. Books include *Keep it Simple* (1993) and *Alastair Little's Italian Kitchen* (1996).

Mosimann, Anton (1947–) Swiss chef, restaurateur, cookery writer and broadcaster. He was chef at the Dorchester Hotel, London, and opened the restaurant Mosimann's in 1988. Books include *Anton Mosimann – Naturally!* (1991).

Nairn, Nick (1959–) Scottish chef and broadcaster. A Michelin-star winner, he now concentrates on his catering business and cookery school in Aberfoyle, Perthshire. Books include *Nick Nairn's New Scottish Cookery Book* (2004) and his television series and related books include *Nick Nairn's Wild Harvest* (1996).

Novelli, Jean-Christophe (1961–) French chef and restaurateur. He worked in the UK with Keith Floyd and later opened his own restaurant, Maison Novelli, in 1996. He has received a Michelin star at four of his various ventures. He now divides his time between his cookery school and his gastropub in Hertfordshire.

Oliver, Jamie (1975–) English chef, cookery writer, broadcaster and restaurateur. His successful television series and related books include *The Naked Chef* (1999), *The Return of the Naked Chef* (2000) and *Jamie's Dinners* (2004). *Jamie's School Dinners* (2005) tackled the poor quality of school food and led to a national campaign while *Jamie's Ministry of Food* (2008) tried the same approach with an entire town – Rotherham in Yorkshire.

Paterson, Jennifer (1928–99) English cook, cookery writer and broadcaster. A professional cook who also wrote for *The Spectator* and *The Oldie*, she came to fame with **Clarissa Dickson-Wright** in the television series *Two Fat Ladies* (1996–9) and related publications.

Patten, Marguerite (1915–) English cook, cookery writer and broadcaster. A food adviser to the government during World War II, she presented her first cookery series on the BBC in 1947. Her many books include *Cooking in a Hurry* (1973) and *We'll Eat Again* (2004) and she was an adviser to the television series *The 1940s House* (2001).

Prudhomme, Paul (1940–) US chef, restaurateur, cookery writer and broadcaster. In 1979 he opened K-Paul's Louisiana Kitchen in New Orleans which is known for its cajun and creole cooking. He often appears on television and his books include *Chef Paul Prudhomme's Louisiana Tastes* (2000).

Ramsay, Gordon (1967–) Scottish chef, restaurateur and broadcaster. He trained under Marco Pierre White, the Roux brothers, Guy Savoy and Joël Robuchon, and the restaurants he runs include Restaurant Gordon Ramsay (three

Michelin stars), Pétrus (two Michelin stars), Gordon Ramsay at Claridges (one Michelin star), Maze (one Michelin star) and Boxwood Café in the Berkeley Hotel, Knightsbridge, in London and he has opened restaurants in Tokyo, New York, Dubai, Prague and Versailles. Television series include *Ramsay's Kitchen Nightmares*, (2004–), *Hell's Kitchen* (2004–), *The F-Word* (2005–) and *Cookalong Live* (2008–).

Rhodes, Gary (1960–) English chef, restaurateur and broadcaster. He worked at the Castle Hotel, Taunton, and the Greenhouse in Mayfair, London, before launching his own restaurants. Books include *New British Classics* (2001).

Robuchon, Joël (1945–) French chef and restaurateur. He runs L'Atelier de Joël Robuchon in Paris (one Michelin star), Las Vegas, New York, Hong Kong (three Michelin stars) and Tokyo. Books include *Simply French* (1991).

Roden, Claudia (1941?–) Egyptian-born cookery writer and broadcaster. An authority on Middle Eastern and Mediterranean cuisine, she has a particular interest in the social and historical context of food. Her books include *A Book of Middle Eastern Food* (1968), *The Book of Jewish Food* (1999) and *Simple Mediterranean Cookery* (2006).

Rogers, Ruth (19?–) US-born chef and restaurateur. After a career in publishing, in 1987 she and **Rose Gray** opened the successful Italian-cooking based River Café in Hammersmith, London. *The River Café Cook Book* and other titles, plus a cookery school, followed.

Rombauer, Irma, née **Louisa von Starkloff** (1877–1962) US cookery writer. She wrote the perpetual bestseller, *The Joy of Cooking* (illustrated and revised in later editions by her daughter Marion Rombauer Becker, 1903–76). An encyclopedic collection of classic American and European recipes, culinary techniques and food preparation instructions, it has sold around 8 million copies, and has had an immeasurable influence on American cuisine.

Roux, Albert Henri (1935–) **and Michel André** (1941–) French chefs and restaurateurs. They opened Le Gavroche in London in 1967, which is now run by Albert's son, Michel Jr; Michel's son Alain now runs the Waterside Inn (three Michelin stars) in Bray, Berkshire. Their television appearances include *At Home with the Roux Brothers* (1988), and books include *Desserts: A Lifelong Passion* (1994).

Sardi, (Melchior Pio Vi) Vincent (1885–1969) Italian-born US restaurateur. From c.1907 he lived in New York City, where Sardi's, his restaurant in the theatre district, became a favourite haunt of many theatre-goers.

Savoy, Guy (1953–) French chef and restaurateur. His restaurants in Paris include the Restaurant Guy Savoy which has three Michelin stars. Books include *Simple French Recipes for the Home Cook* (2004).

Smith, Delia (1941–) English cookery writer and broadcaster. She followed her first of many books, *How to Cheat at Cooking* (1971, updated edition 2008), with several television series and bestsellers, eg *Delia's How to Cook* (1998) and *The Delia Collection: Italian* (2004).

Soyer, Alexis (1809–58) French chef. The most famous of his time, he was chef in the Reform Club in London (1837–50). He wrote *Culinary Campaign in the Crimea* (1857) after trying to reform the food supply system in the Crimea by introducing the 'Soyer stove'.

Spry, Constance (1886–1960) English flower

arranger and cookery writer. She ran flower shops and cookery schools, held advisory positions and wrote *The Constance Spry Cookbook* (1956).
Stein, Rick (1947–) English chef and restaurateur. Specializing in seafood, he runs the Seafood Restaurant and the Padstow Seafood School in Cornwall. He became known through the television series *Taste of the Sea* (1995) and *Fruits of the Sea* (1997) and has written many other cookery books including *Rick Stein's Food Heroes* (2002).
Two Fat Ladies ► **Clarissa Dickson Wright, Jennifer Paterson**
White, Marco Pierre (1961–) English chef and restaurateur. He learned from Albert Roux, Nico Ladenis and Raymond Blanc, and opened his

first (of several) restaurants, Harveys, in 1987. Publications include *Canteen Cuisine* (1995) and *The Mirabelle Cookbook* (1999).
Wishart, Martin (1969–) Scottish chef and restaurateur. He trained with many well-known chefs, including Albert Roux and Marco Pierre White, and opened his Restaurant Martin Wishart in Leith in 1999. He gained a Michelin star in 2001.
Worrall Thompson, Antony (1952–) English chef, restaurateur and cookery writer. His London restaurants have included Ménage à Trois, 190 Queensgate, Dell'ugo and he still runs Notting Grill and Kew Grill. He appears regularly on television in *Ready Steady Cook* and *Saturday Kitchen*.

Varieties of wines and grapes

Wines are often named after the grape from which they are made, or the region or château in which they are produced.

Alsace mainly dry, white wine produced in the Alsace region of NE France; the wines are named after the grapes, eg Riesling, Gewürztraminer, Sylvaner, Pinot Blanc and Pinot Gris.
Anjou Blanc a dry white wine produced in the western Loire region of France and made from blends of such grape varieties as Chenin Blanc, Chardonnay and Sauvignon.
Asti Spumante a sweet, aromatic sparkling wine made from the Muscat grape and named after the town of Asti in Piedmont, Italy.
Auslese an expensive full-flavoured, sweet wine made in Germany from exceptionally high-quality mature grapes, particularly the Riesling grape.
Beaujolais a large area in southern Burgundy, France, famous for light, fruity red wines made from the Gamay grape.
Beaujolais Nouveau a young red wine from the Beaujolais area, available in late November.
Beaune French town in the centre of Burgundy with its own vineyard sites which are known for their soft, fragrant red wines.
Bordeaux French city and seaport in the centre of the famous wine-producing region of Bordeaux in SW France where red wines (known as claret) and white wines are produced. The finest wines come from the areas Médoc, Graves, St-Émilion and Pomerol.
Burgundy 1 famous wine-producing region in France, divided into five districts: Chablis, Côte d'Or, Chalonnais, Mâconnais and Beaujolais. 2 a French wine made in the Burgundy region; most are red, some are white, all are dry. Burgundy's vineyards are divided into the Grands crus, Premier crus, and the remainder which are named after communes. 3 any similar red wine.
Cabernet Sauvignon 1 a red-wine grape which is the basis of most Bordeaux wine; an adaptable variety originally from Bordeaux, it is now grown throughout the world. 2 the wine produced from this grape.
Carignan a red-wine grape used to make table wine and dessert wine; grown in the Midi, N and C America, N Africa and Australia.
Chablis a dry white wine made from the Chardonnay grape in the Burgundy region of central France, named after the small French town near to where it is made.
Chardonnay 1 a white grape variety used in

Burgundy and Champagne; originally from Burgundy, it is now also grown in California, Australia, New Zealand, etc. 2 a dry white wine made from this grape.
Chateauneuf-du-Pape a district of the Rhône region of France known especially for its expensive red wine; the wine is blended, using mainly Grenache, Syrah and Cinsault grapes.
Chenin Blanc a white-wine grape widely grown in the Loire Valley in France, and in South Africa (called Steen) and California; it is used to make Vouvray and Saumur wines.
Chianti a dry, usually red, blended Italian wine made in Tuscany.
Cinsault a red-wine grape grown especially in the Rhône valley and, being low in tannin, is used in blended wines eg Chateauneuf-du-Pape.
Colombard a white-wine grape, used especially in South Africa.
Corbières a district of the Languedoc-Roussillon area where red, white and rosé wines are made.
Côtes du Rhône the appellation for the lesser red, white and rosé wines produced in the Rhône valley.
Dão a mountain district in northern Portugal where mainly red wine is produced.
Fitou a red wine produced from the Carignan grape in the Languedoc-Roussillon area of France.
Frascati a full-bodied, fragrant white wine made in the town of Frascati, S Italy.
Gamay a red-wine grape used widely in France and elsewhere; used in Beaujolais, and in Anjou as a base for rosé wines.
Gewürztraminer a spicy variety of white grape grown especially in the Alsace region which is used to make a medium-dry aromatic wine.
Grenache a fruity grape used for making strong, sweet wines; grown in Europe (especially Spain), N Africa, Australia, C and N America; used in rosé wines and in blended wines eg Chateauneuf-du-Pape.
Graves a large area within the Bordeaux region in France which produces red and white wines.
Lambrusco a red- or white-wine grape; used to make a light, sweet sparkling red wine of the same name in northern Italy.
Liebfraumilch a white blended wine from the Rhine region of Germany; by law it is made with Riesling, Sylvaner and Müller-Thurgau grapes from the regions of Rheinhessen, Nahe, Rheinpfalz or Rheingau.

Human Body, Health and Nutrition

Mâcon a town in southern Burgundy where white and red wine is produced.

Madeira a fortified wine made on the N Atlantic island of Madeira.

Malaga a dark dessert wine from Andalucia, Spain, made from grapes that are partially sun-dried before use.

Marsala a brown, fortified wine made in the town of Marsala, Sicily.

Médoc the premier area of Bordeaux in France known for its fine red wines; many famous châteaux are situated here, eg Château Mouton-Rothschild.

Merlot 1 an important variety of black grape often used in blends with Cabernet Sauvignon and in many soft fruity wines for drinking young. 2 a red wine that is produced in France, Italy and the USA from, or mainly from, this variety of grape.

Minervois a well-rated district in the Languedoc-Roussillon area which produces well-balanced, robust red wines made from Carignan, Cinsault and Grenache grapes.

Moselle or **Mosel** the region around the Moselle river which runs through NE France, Luxembourg and Germany; it is known for its light, crisp, perfumed dry white wine made mainly from the Riesling grape.

Müller-Thurgau a white-wine grape widely used in Germany, as well as in California, England and New Zealand; similar to the Muscat grape in flavour.

Muscadet 1 a white-wine grape successfully grown in the Loire valley in France. 2 a dry white wine, the best-known of those made in the Loire eg Muscadet de Sèvre-et-Maine.

Muscat or **Muscadelle** or **Moscatello** names of a large family of white and red grapes; they have a musky smell, and are dried for raisins as well as used to make scented, grapey wines; most wines made from the Muscat grape are sweet, except those made in Alsace.

Niersteiner a well-known German wine made from the Riesling grape in the Nierstein district of the Rheinhessen region in Germany.

Pinot an important variety of black and white grape grown throughout the world. Pinot Noir is the traditional grape of Burgundy and is used in making champagne; as it is difficult to grow elsewhere, it is an irresistible challenge to wine-makers.

Pinotage a red-wine grape used especially in South Africa.

Pomerol a district of Bordeaux which produces red and white vines, including the high-quality red wine Château Petrus.

Riesling a white-wine grape grown most successfully in Germany, but also in Alsace, Austria and elsewhere; it is used to make wine ranging from dry to very sweet.

Rioja a small wine-making area in NE Spain, which produces mainly dry red wine.

St-Émilion a fine, fruity red wine made particularly from the Merlot grape in the St-Émilion area of Bordeaux.

Sancerre a district in the Loire Valley known especially for its pale, dry white wines, and for its rosés, which are made from the Pinot Noir grape.

Saumur a district of Anjou in NW France where both still and sparkling wines are made.

Sauternes an appellation used by five communes (Sauternes, Barsac, Bommes, Fargues and Preignac) in the Graves district of Bordeaux which produce sweet white wine, mainly from the Sémillon grape.

Sauvignon Blanc a white-wine grape used in Bordeaux and Sancerre; makes excellent wine in New Zealand and California.

Sémillon a white grape used in Bordeaux whites, especially the Sauternes district where is it harvested half rotten and therefore with a high concentration of sugar; it is also successful in Australia's Hunter Valley region.

Soave a light, dry, flowery white wine made near the village of Soave, NE Italy.

Spätlese a German term for wine made from grapes that have been harvested late, resulting in a wine with more body and sweetness than other German white wines.

Sylvaner a German white-wine grape used to make fruity wines and grown in Europe, N and S America and Australia.

Syrah a red-wine grape, the foremost grape of the hot Rhône valley; particularly at home in Australia, where it is known as Shiraz.

Tarragona a wine region in Spain, where much red and white table wine, and the sweet, red fortified wine Tarragona are produced.

Valpolicella a light, fragrant red wine made near the village of Valpolicella in the Veneto region of NE Italy.

Vouvray a usually sweet, but always fresh and fruity, white wine produced from the Chenin Blanc grape in Touraine, in the Loire Valley.

Zinfandel a red-wine grape used widely in California for making dry red wine.

Terms relating to wine-making and wine-tasting

acetic tasting or smelling of vinegar, due to the presence of acetic acid; caused by oxidization or by faulty fermentation or bottling.

acidity the taste caused by the natural organic acids in wine, which in the correct proportions make a wine well-balanced.

aftertaste the taste that remains in the mouth or comes into it after tasting wine.

appellation contrôlée and **appellation d'origine contrôlée** (French; abbreviation AC or AOC) 1 the system which within France designates and controls the names especially of wine, but also of cognac, armagnac, calvados and some foods, guaranteeing the authenticity of the producing region and the methods of production, and which outside France protects the generic names from misappropriation. 2 the highest designation of French wine awarded under this system.

argol the harmless crystalline potassium deposit that is left on the sides of wine vats during fermentation. Also called tartrate.

balance a noun describing a wine's combination of alcoholic strength, acidity, residual sugar and tannins.

big amply flavoured, often with a high alcohol content.

body the 'weight' of a wine on the palate, or the sensation of fullness it imparts due to its density or viscosity. Wines range from being light-bodied to full-bodied.

bouquet the delicate smell of wine. [French; a diminutive of *bois*, a wood]

breathe to develop flavour when exposed to the air.

brut said especially of champagne: very dry.

Buck's fizz or **buck's fizz** a drink consisting of champagne, or sparkling white wine, and orange juice. [named after Buck's Club, London]

chambré said of wine: at room temperature.

character having positive, distinctive characteristics.

château used in names of wines, especially from the Bordeaux area: a vineyard estate around a castle or house.

claret a French red wine, especially from the Bordeaux area.

clarity the quality of being clear and pure; the clarity of a wine is an indication of both its condition (faulty wine often appears cloudy), and of how much clarification (the removal of suspended material, the lees) has been carried out.

clean pure-tasting and pure-smelling; a term usually applied to white wine.

coarse rough or crude; lacking refinement.

common plain and of no distinctive character, though not necessarily low quality.

corked said of wine: spoiled as a result of having a faulty cork, which has affected the taste of the wine.

crisp with a dry, refreshing taste; usually said of white wines with a pleasantly high level of acidity.

cru specialist term for a high-quality vineyard; often translated in English as 'growth'; eg grand cru, premier cru.

decant to pour (wine etc) from one bottle or container to another, leaving any sediment behind.

decanter an ornamental bottle with a stopper, used for decanted wine, sherry, whisky, etc.

demijohn a large bottle with a short narrow neck and one or two small handles, used for storing eg wine.

DOC *abbreviation* said of wine: *Denominazione di Origine Controllata* (Italian), the Italian equivalent of **appellation contrôlée**. Compare **DOCG**.

DOCG *abbreviation* said of wine: *Denominazione di Origine Controllata Garantita* (Italian), a designation of wines, guaranteeing quality, strength, etc. Compare **DOC**.

dry said of wine etc: not sweet.

earthy with a flavour and bouquet enhanced by characteristics of the soil in which the vine was grown (usually applicable only to grapes grown in a hot climate).

en primeur said of tasting, buying or investing in wine: when the wine is new.

fat full-bodied and viscous, but unbalanced due to insufficient acidity.

fine an ill-defined term, usually referring to the superior wines of the classic regions of Europe, eg Bordeaux and Burgundy.

finesse refinement; having the best possible characteristics a wine can have.

finish aftertaste.

flabby lacking in acidity; like a fat wine, well flavoured but with little 'bite'.

flinty usually said of highly rated white wines: having a dry, clean, hard taste reminiscent of gun flint; eg Pouilly Blanc Fumé.

flowery containing the scent of flowers in the bouquet.

fortify to add extra alcohol to (wine) in the course of production, in order to produce sherry, port, etc.

fresh refreshing.

frizzante an Italian term for semi-sparkling.

fruity smelling strongly of fruit, eg blackberries, blackcurrants, gooseberries or raspberries as well as grapes.

full or **full-bodied** having a rich flavour or quality.

generous rich, invigorating.

glühwein or **Glühwein** mulled wine, especially as prepared in Germany, Austria, etc.

grand cru produced by a famous vineyard or group of vineyards.

grapey having a strong flavour of grapes, eg wine made from the Muscat grape.

grappa a brandy (originally from Italy) distilled from what is left after the grapes have been pressed for wine-making.

green too acid, usually due to having been made from unripe grapes.

hanepoot a kind of grape for eating and wine-making.

hard with an unpleasant excess of tannin and lack of fruit; hard wines usually improve with time.

hearty usually said of red wines, eg from the Rhône valley: with a generous, warm flavour.

heavy too alcoholic; or full-bodied but lacking in finesse.

hock a white wine, originally only the one made in Hochheim, on the River Main, in Germany, but now applied to all white wines from the Rhine valley.

honest ordinary and undistinguished; unremarkable, eg an honest wine.

hot too alcoholic.

lay down to store (wine) in a cellar.

lees the sediment that settles at the bottom of liquids and alcoholic drinks, especially wine.

legs ► **tears**

length persistence of flavour on the palate; length is an indicator of quality.

light pleasantly slender in body and low in alcohol.

lively said of white wine: young and fresh, often with a slight natural sparkle.

long with an impressively enduring aftertaste, usually indicating high quality.

maceration in the making of red wine, the process in which the tannins etc are dissolved from the skins, seeds and stem fragments of the grapes to be added to the juice or new wine.

madeirized said of white wines: tinged with brown because of old age.

magnum a champagne or wine bottle that holds approximately 1.5 litres, ie twice the normal amount.

malic acid (formula $H_6C_4O_5$) an acid found in unripe fruits, and occurring in wines.

malmsey a strong sweet wine originally from Greece but now usually from Spain, Madeira, etc.

marc 1 the leftover skins and stems of grapes used in winemaking. 2 a kind of brandy made from these.

mature having a fully developed flavour.

medium neither dry nor sweet.

mellow fully flavoured with age; well matured.

mirin a sweet rice wine used in Japanese cookery.

mull to spice, sweeten and warm, eg mulled wine.

muscatel a rich sweet white wine made from Muscat grapes.

must the juice of grapes or other fruit before it is completely fermented to become wine.

noble rot on white grapes: a rot caused by the fungus *Botrytis cinerea*, which aids the production of sweet white wine.

nose a scent or aroma, especially a wine's bouquet.

nutty usually said of sherries or red wines: having a flavour reminiscent of nuts, eg walnuts or hazelnuts, which usually indicates good quality.

oenology the study or knowledge of wine (*adjective* **oenological**, *noun* **oenologist**).

oenophile a lover or connoisseur of wine; an oenologist.

Human Body, Health and Nutrition

oxidation a fault caused by exposure to oxygen, making any wine smell bad and making white wine darker.

palate an ability to discriminate between wines, different qualities of wine, etc.

pétillant lightly sparkling; a French term for a wine sparkling more than when *perlant* but not as much as when *mousseux*.

pipe 1 a cask or butt of varying capacity, but usually about 105 gallons in Britain (equal to 126 US gallons or 477 litres), used for wine or oil. 2 a measure of this amount.

piquant usually said of white wine: with an agreeably sharp flavour caused by high levels of acidity, eg wine from some areas of the Rhine, Loire and Mosel.

plonk *colloq* cheap, undistinguished wine.

port a sweet dark-red or tawny fortified wine. [from Oporto, the city in Portugal from where it was originally exported]

prädikat 1 in Germany: a distinction awarded to a wine, based on the ripeness of the grapes used to produce it. 2 a wine that qualifies for this award.

race said of wine: the special flavour by which its origin may be recognized.

rack to draw off (wine or beer) from its sediment.

racy said of wine: with a distinctive flavour imparted by the soil.

rape the refuse of grapes left after wine-making and used in making vinegar.

red biddy *colloq* a cheap alcoholic drink made from red wine and methylated spirits.

remuage in wine-making, the process of turning the bottles so that the sediment collects at the cork end for removal.

retsina a Greek white or rosé wine flavoured with pine resin.

Rhenish Rhine wine.

Rhine wine an imprecise term for any wine made from grapes grown in the valley of the River Rhine.

ripe said of the flavour or taste of wine: rich or strong.

robust said of wine: with a full, rich quality.

rosé a light-pink wine properly made by removing the skins of red grapes after fermentation has begun; it is sometimes also made by mixing red and white wines.

rouge *in full* vin rouge, French red wine.

sack a dry white wine from Spain, Portugal and the Canary Islands.

sangria a Spanish drink of red wine, fruit juice, sugar and spices.

sec 1 said of wine: dry. 2 said of champagne: medium sweet.

Sekt a German term for sparkling wines.

severe very sharp, almost astringent; this sourness is usually due to the wine being too acid and/or immature.

sharp sour-tasting, but not as sour as a severe wine; sharpness may be intentional, or a fault caused by immaturity or by the use of unripe grapes.

sherry 1 a fortified wine ranging in colour from pale gold to dark brown. 2 *loosely* a similar type of wine produced elsewhere. [from Jerez de la Frontera, the S Spanish town where it is produced].

short opposite of long; with little or no aftertaste.

smooth pleasantly textured with a mellow flavour.

soft a term describing the impact of the wine on the palate.

spicy with a flavour of spices and herbs, eg wines made from the Gewürztraminer grape.

spritzer a drink of white wine and soda water.

spritzig 1 a slightly sparkling, usually German, wine. 2 in wine-tasting: the slight prickle on the tongue that is effected by this kind of wine.

spumante an Italian term for fully sparkling, usually sweet wine, eg Asti Spumante.

stalky with an unpleasant taste of damp twigs; a fault caused by leaving the grape stalks in contact with the grapes for too long.

stum *noun* partly fermented grape juice that is added to a wine which has lost its strength, flavour, sharpness, etc in order to perk it up; *verb* to add stum to (a wine) and so restart the fermentation process.

sulphurous acid or (*USA*) **sulfurous acid** (formula H_2SO_3) a colourless weakly acidic solution of sulphur dioxide in water that acts as a preservative in wine-making. A sulphury wine contains too much sulphur, but usually improves an hour or two after opening.

supple usually said of red wine: a term evoking pliability in describing the impact on the palate.

sweet said of wine: having some taste of sugar or fruit; not dry.

tannin any of several substances in the pips, skins and stalks of the grapes which give a distinctive flavour to red wine. The tannin should mellow as the wine matures; if not, the wine tastes hard and disagreeable and is described as tannic.

tart very sharp.

tartar a deposit that forms a hard brownish-red crust on the insides of wine casks during fermentation.

tears (rhymes with 'ears') a noun used to describe the droplets that cling to the glass just above the surface of a glass of wine; a wine high in alcohol.

temperature an ideal tasting temperature for both red and white wines is 15°–20°C/59°–68°F.

thin insipid and watery.

tierce a former measure of wine, equal to one-third of a pipe, ie approx. 35 British or 42 US gallons (159 litres).

tun *noun* a large cask or liquid measure equivalent to 252 British or 303 US gallons (1146 litres) of wine; *verb* to put or store (liquid, eg ale, beer or wine) in a tun.

ullage 1 the amount of wine etc by which a container falls short of being full. 2 the quantity of liquid lost from a container through leakage, evaporation, etc. 3 *slang* the dregs remaining in a glass.

vault a wine cellar.

VDQS *abbreviation*: *vins délimités de qualité supérieure* (French); wines of superior quality from approved vineyards, the interim wine quality designation between vin de pays and appellation contrôlée.

velvety said of the feel of the wine, not the flavour: very soft and smooth.

vermouth an alcoholic drink consisting of wine flavoured with aromatic herbs, originally wormwood.

vin de pays country or local wine.

vin ordinaire inexpensive table wine for everyday use.

vine any of various woody climbing plants that produce grapes.

vineyard a plantation of grape-bearing vines, especially for wine-making.

vinho verde a light, sharp young Portuguese wine.

viniculture the cultivation of grapes for wine-making.

vino *slang* wine, especially of poor quality.

vinosity a wine-like character; the characteristic qualities of a particular wine; an acceptable standard, with good, balanced characteristics.

vinous 1 belonging or relating to, or resembling, wine. 2 caused by or indicative of an excess of wine, eg a vinous complexion.

vintage said of wine: good quality and from a specified year.

vintner *formal* a wine-merchant.

viticulture the cultivation of grapes for making wine; viniculture.

weighty usually said of full-bodied red wine: with great depth and character.

well-balanced having good balance.

white said of wine: made from white grapes or from skinned black grapes.

wine cellar 1 a cellar in which to store wines. 2 the stock of wine stored there.

wine cooler a receptacle for cooling wine in bottles, ready for serving.

wine glass 1 a drinking-glass typically consisting of a small bowl on a stem, with a wide base flaring out from the stem. 2 the capacity of this; a wineglassful.

wine list a list of the wines available, eg in a restaurant.

wine tasting 1 the sampling of a variety of wines. 2 a gathering specifically for this.

wine vault 1 a vaulted wine cellar. 2 a place where wine is tasted or drunk.

winepress in the manufacture of wine: a machine in which grapes are pressed to extract the juice.

winery *chiefly USA* a place where wine is prepared and stored.

wineskin *historical* the skin of a goat or sheep sewn up and used for holding wine.

wino *slang* someone, especially a down-and-out, addicted to cheap wine; an alcoholic.

winy or **winey** having a wine-like flavour.

woody with a flavour of wood; if overpowering, this may be a fault caused by the wine being left too long in the cask, or a problem with the cask.

yeasty with a smell of yeast, suggesting a second fermentation has happened or is about to happen.

Wine bottle sizes

Name	Capacity	
wine bottle	75 cl	(26⅜ fl oz) (standard size)
magnum	1.5 l	(2 standard bottles)
flagon	1.13 l or 2 pints	
jeroboam	3 l	(4 standard bottles)

Name	Capacity	
rehoboam	4.5 l	(6 standard bottles)
methuselah	6 l	(8 standard bottles)
salmanazar	9 l	(12 standard bottles)
balthazar	12 l	(16 standard bottles)
nebuchadnezzar	15 l	(20 standard bottles)

Types of European cheese

Cheese	Type and characteristics
■ **England**	
Cheddar	hard; cow's milk; white to yellow
Cheshire	hard; cow's milk; white to palest yellow
Lancashire	hard; cow's milk; white; crumbly
Leicester	hard; cow's milk; orange; crumbly
Stilton	semihard; cow's milk; mould-ripened; blue-veined
■ **France**	
Brie	soft; cow's milk; downy rind
Camembert	soft; cow's milk; downy rind
Pont l'Évêque	soft; cow's milk; washed rind
Port Salut	semisoft; cow's milk; yellow
Reblochon	soft; cow's milk; pressed
Roquefort	semihard; ewe's milk; blue-veined
Saint Paulin	semisoft; cow's milk; yellow
Vacherin	soft; cow's milk; soft interior with hard rind
■ **Germany**	
Münster	semisoft; cow's milk; bacteria-ripened
Tilsit	semihard; cow's milk; bacteria-ripened

Cheese	Type and characteristics
■ **Greece**	
Feta	soft; ewe's or goat's milk; salty
■ **Italy**	
Dolcelatte	semisoft; cow's milk; mould-ripened; blue/green-veined
Gorgonzola	semihard; cow's milk; mould-ripened; blue/green-veined
Parmesan	very hard; cow's milk; bacteria-ripened; long cure
Romano	very hard; cow's, ewe's or goat's milk; bacteria-ripened
■ **Netherlands**	
Edam	semihard; skimmed cow's milk; mild; red wax rind
Gouda	semihard; cow's milk; mild; yellow wax rind
■ **Spain**	
Manchego	semisoft–hard; ewe's milk; mild or sharp depending on length of cure
■ **Switzerland**	
Emmenthal	hard; cow's milk; creamy; large holes
Gruyère	hard; cow's milk; small holes
Sapsago	very hard; soured cow's milk; light green (clover mixed with the curd)

Human Body, Health and Nutrition

SCIENCE AND TECHNOLOGY

Scientific terms

Bold type indicates that a definition of a word or phrase in an entry is given elsewhere in the glossary.

In this glossary 10^{12} is used to mean 1 followed by 12 zeros and 10^{-27} is used to mean 1 occurring 27 places after a decimal point.

aberration In an image-forming system, such as a curved mirror or lens, the failure to produce a true image when different colours of light or light incident on different parts of the mirror or lens are focused to different positions.

absolute alcohol Water-free **ethanol**.

absolute zero The lowest possible temperature for all substances, when the **molecules** of any substance possess no heat energy. A figure of $-273.15°C$ is generally accepted as the value of absolute zero.

absorption In chemistry, the process by which one substance is incorporated into the structure of another substance, as when water is soaked up by a sponge. Compare **adsorption**.

ac ▶ **alternating current**

acid Normally, a substance which (a) dissolves in water to form a solution that contains hydrogen **ions** and that has a pH of below 7, (b) dissolves metals with the liberation of hydrogen gas, or (c) more generally, a substance which tends to lose a **proton** or to accept an **electron** pair.

acid rain Rain that is unnaturally **acid** as a result of pollution of the atmosphere with oxides of nitrogen and sulphur from the burning of coal and oil.

acoustic imaging Determination of distance and direction of objects, such as submarines, by the reception of the reflection of a sound pulse. Also known as sonar.

acquired character In zoology, a modification of an organ during the lifetime of an individual due to use or disuse, and not inherited from a previous generation. ▶ **natural selection**.

adaptation In zoology, a physical or behavioural change in an organism that makes it better suited to its natural environment and increases its chances of survival. ▶ **natural selection**.

adiabatic process In physics, a process which occurs without interchange of heat with the surroundings.

adsorption In chemistry, the process by which one substance collects on the surface of another but is not incorporated into the structure of it. Compare **absorption**.

aerosol (1) A system in the form of a **colloid**, such as a mist or a fog, in which the dispersion medium is a gas. (2) Pressurized container with built-in spray mechanism used for packaging insecticides, deodorants, paints, etc.

aerospace The Earth's atmosphere together with the space beyond; the branch of technology or of industry concerned with the flight of spacecraft through this.

algae A group of simple organisms that contain **chlorophylls**, have no roots, stems or leaves, and live in water or in damp conditions.

alkali A substance which, when dissolved in water, forms a solution that contains hydroxyl **ions** (negatively charged ions containing oxygen and hydrogen) and that has a **pH value** higher than 7.

allotropy The existence of two or more forms (allotropes) of an **element** in one phase of matter (ie solid, liquid or gas). For example, graphite and diamond are allotropes of carbon.

alloy A mixture of metals, or of a metal with a non-metal in which the metal is the major component.

alpha particle A positively charged particle, equivalent to the **nucleus** of a helium **atom**, that is emitted from a radioactive **isotope**. Often written α particle. ▶ **radioactivity**.

alternating current Generally abbreviated to ac. An electric **current** in which the direction of flow changes at regular intervals. Compare **dc**.

AM (amplitude modulation) ▶ **modulation**

amino acid An **organic molecule** containing an amino group (NH_2) and a carboxyl group (COOH). Amino acids play an important part in biological processes, often combining in different forms to produce **proteins**.

amorphous Existing in a non-crystalline or disordered form. Glass is an amorphous solid.

amu ▶ **atomic mass unit**

anaerobic Taking place or surviving in the absence of oxygen. Anaerobic respiration is the liberation of energy which does not require the presence of oxygen.

anion A negatively charged **ion**, ie an **atom** or **molecule** that has gained one or more **electrons**.

anisotropic Having physical properties, eg strength or the ability to conduct electrical **current**, that are different in different directions.

annihilation In nuclear physics, the process in which a **subatomic particle** and its **antiparticle** are destroyed as they collide, releasing a burst of **radiation**.

annual A plant that flowers and dies within a period of one year from germination.

annulus A ring-shaped structure or object, such as a washer.

anode A positively charged **conductor** used in conjunction with a **cathode** to lead an electric current into or out of a solid, liquid or gas.

antibody A defensive protein produced in an organism in response to the action of a foreign body, such as a bacterial toxin.

anticyclone A distribution of atmospheric pressure in which the pressure increases towards the centre. Winds in such a system circulate in a clockwise direction in the northern hemisphere and in a counterclockwise direction in the southern hemisphere.

antigen A substance that stimulates the production of an **antibody**.

antiparticle The antiparticle of a given **subatomic particle** has the same mass but opposite values for all its other properties, such as charge. A particle and its antiparticle, eg an **electron** and a **positron**, destroy each other on contact in the process of **annihilation**.

aperture (1) The opening, usually circular, through which light enters an optical system such as a camera lens; its area may be varied by an iris diaphragm to control the amount of light passing. ► **f-number**. (2) The rectangular opening at which motion-picture film is exposed in a camera or projector.

Archimedes' principle The principle that when a body is wholly or partly immersed in a fluid it experiences an upwards force equal to the weight of fluid it displaces.

aromatic compounds Organic compounds containing **benzene** or with similar chemical properties.

asteroid One of thousands of rocky objects found in the **solar system**, normally between the orbits of Mars and Jupiter, ranging in size from 1 to 1&thsp;000 km.

astigmatism (1) In medicine, unequal curvature of the focusing surfaces of the eye, which prevents incident light rays from reaching a common focus point on the retina, resulting in blurred eyesight. (2) In physics, a defect in an optical system on account of which, instead of a point image being formed of a point object, two short line images (focal lines) are produced at slightly different positions and at right angles to each other.

astronomical unit The mean distance of the Earth from the Sun, about 149 600 000 km or 93 000 000 mi.

atom The smallest particle of an element that can take part in a chemical reaction. Atoms consist of a central nucleus containing **protons** and **neutrons**, surrounded by shells of **electrons**.

atomic mass unit A unit of mass equal to exactly one twelfth of the mass of a neutral **atom** of the most abundant **isotope** of carbon (1.660×10^{-27} kg).

atomic number The number of protons in the nucleus of an atom of an element, equal also to the number of electrons orbiting the nucleus.

aurora Luminous curtains or streamers of light seen in the night sky at high latitudes, caused when electrically charged particles from the Sun are guided by the Earth's magnetic field to the polar regions, there colliding with atoms in the upper atmosphere. Known as aurora borealis in the northern hemisphere and aurora australis in the southern hemisphere.

background radiation Radiation that causes **ionization** and that comes from natural sources such as the Earth's rocks, soil and atmosphere.

bacteria A large group of single-cell microorganisms that are found in all living things and natural environments. Some bacteria live as parasites and produce toxins that cause disease.

bacteriophage A **virus** that infects bacteria.

base (1) In chemistry, any of a class of compounds that react with acids and some metals to form salts. A base that dissolves in water is an **alkali**. (2) In genetics, the molecules that determine the sequences in **DNA** and **RNA**. Adenine, guanine and cytosine are found in DNA and RNA, thymine in DNA only and uracil in RNA only.

benthos Collectively, the immobile animal and plant life living on the sea bottom.

benzene A colourless, liquid aromatic compound derived from petroleum, used to make various chemical products. Its **molecules** consist of a ring or closed chain of six carbon **atoms** each with a single hydrogen atom attached.

beta particle An **electron** or **positron** that is emitted from a radioactive **isotope**. Often written β particle. ► **radioactivity**.

biennial A plant that flowers and dies between its first and second years from germination and that does not flower in its first year.

Big Bang The hypothetical violent explosion that created the universe, between 12 billion and 14 billion years ago. The Big Bang Theory states that all the matter and energy of the universe was once an unimaginably dense mass and that the universe has been expanding from the explosion of this mass ever since.

bioassay An experiment designed to determine how much of a substance is present by measuring its biological effect, eg on the growth of an organism.

biogenesis The formation of living organisms from their ancestors and of minute **cell** structures from their predecessors.

bioluminescence The production of light by living organisms, such as glow-worms, some deep-sea fish, some bacteria and some fungi.

biosphere The parts of the Earth and the atmosphere surrounding it that are able to support life, generally accepted as extending upwards at least to a height of 10 000 m (33 000 ft) and downwards to the depths of the ocean, and a few hundred metres below the land surface. The term may also be applied theoretically to other planets.

bit In computer science, a digit in binary notation, ie 0 or 1. It is the smallest unit of storage (from *Binary dig IT*).

black hole A region in space from which matter and energy cannot escape. A black hole could be a **star** or the central part of a **galaxy** that has collapsed in on itself to the point where the speed required for matter to escape exceeds the speed of light.

buckminsterfullerene A **molecule** consisting of 60 carbon **atoms** arranged symmetrically to form a nearly-spherical structure. Commonly referred to as buckyballs.

byte In computer science, a fixed number of **bits**, often eight, that correspond to a single character and are operated on as a unit.

calculus The branch of mathematics dealing with continuously varying quantities or functions. It can be used to calculate, for example, the area bounded by a curve.

carat or **karat** (1) A standard weight for precious stones, equal to 200 milligrams. (2) The standard of fineness for gold, such that 24 carats represents pure gold, and 23 carat gold has $\frac{1}{24}$ part impurity.

carbohydrate Any of a group of compounds of carbon, hydrogen and oxygen, the last two being in the same proportion as in water. They form the main source of energy in food as sugars and starches.

carbon dating or **radiocarbon dating** A technique for estimating the age of an **organic** material from the amount of a radioactive **isotope** of carbon in it. The quantity of the radioactive carbon naturally decreases with time once an organism has died. ► **radioactivity**

carcinogen A substance that can cause cancer.

carnivore A flesh-eating animal.

catalysis The acceleration or retardation of a chemical reaction by a substance, a catalyst, that itself undergoes no permanent chemical change and that can be recovered when the chemical reaction is completed.

cathode A negatively charged **conductor** used in

conjunction with an **anode** to lead an electric current into or out of a solid, liquid or gas.

cation A positively charged ion, ie an **atom** or **molecule** that has lost one or more **electrons**.

caustic Said of an **alkali** that is destructive or corrosive to living tissue; an alkaline agent that burns or destroys living tissue.

cell In biology, the unit from which plants and animals are composed.

cellulose A **carbohydrate** forming the chief component of **cell** walls in plants and in wood. A carbohydrate that is insoluble in water and is the main component of cell walls in plants. Its fibrous nature makes it an important ingredient in the manufacture of paper, textiles and other products.

Celsius scale The **SI** name for the temperature scale in which the freezing point of water is 0°C and the boiling point is 100°C under normal atmospheric pressure. Also called the centigrade scale.

centigrade scale ▶ **Celsius scale**

centrifuge A machine that uses the force produced by rotation to separate molecules from solution, particles and solids from liquids, and liquids that do not mix from each other.

CFCs Chlorofluorocarbons, synthetic compounds that react with ozone when released into the atmosphere, resulting in damage to the ozone layer.

CGS unit Abbreviation for Centimetre-Gram-Second unit, based on the centimetre, the gram and the second as the fundamental units of length, mass and time. For most purposes superseded by **SI**. ▶ **SI units** (p208.)

chaos theory The theory which describes how the behaviour of a system which obeys well-known physical laws can become unpredictable if a very large number of accurately known quantities or a very extensive description of its initial state is required to predict its development. This leads to unpredictability in eg weather forecasting.

chip The popular name for an **integrated circuit**.

chlorophylls Green pigments involved in the process of **photosynthesis**. *Chlorophyll a* is the primary photosynthetic pigment in all organisms that release oxygen, ie all plants and **algae**.

cholesterol A white fatty molecule found in nerve tissues, gall stones, and in other tissues of the body. It is a main component of cell membranes and, in vertebrates, of blood, where increased levels are thought to cause diseases of the arteries.

chromosome One of the rod-like structures found in the **nucleus** of a **cell**, which carry the genes and perform an important role in cell division and transmission of hereditary features.

clone An organism, **cell** or group of cells that is produced asexually from a single ancestor and that has an almost identical **genotype**. Clones can occur naturally, as when a plant produces a new and identical plant from a runner, or as the product of genetic engineering.

colloid A solid dispersed through a liquid such that, though apparently dissolved, it cannot pass through a membrane.

comet A small member of the solar system, made of ice, dust and gas, becoming visible as it approaches the Sun. A bright nucleus is often seen, and sometimes one or more tails that point away from the Sun.

commensalism A relationship between two different species in which one species, the commensal, benefits from the relationship and the other derives no benefit but is not harmed. Compare **symbiosis**.

conductor A material through which heat or electrical energy can pass.

congenital Said of diseases or deformities that are present at birth but are not passed on from a previous generation.

continental drift A hypothesis to explain the distribution of the continents and oceans and the structural, geological and physical similarities which exist between them. The continents are believed to have been formed from one large land mass and to have drifted apart. ▶ **plate tectonics**.

convection The transfer of heat in a **fluid** by means of a current that circulates as a result of temperature differences. The regions of higher temperature, being less dense, rise, while the regions of lower temperature move down to take their place.

Coriolis effect The effect whereby an object falling freely towards the Earth is slightly deviated from a straight line and will fall to a point east of the point directly below its initial position, due to the rotation of the Earth underneath as it falls.

cosmic rays Highly penetrating rays from interstellar space, consisting of particles such as **protons**, **electrons** and **positrons**.

cracking The breaking down of heavier crude-oil **molecules** to form lighter molecules by heat, pressure and the use of **catalysis**.

current The flow of electric charge in a substance (solid, liquid or gas).

cyclone (1) A region of low pressure, or depression. (2) A tropical revolving storm in the Arabian Sea, Bay of Bengal and South Indian Ocean.

Darwinian theory ▶ **natural selection**

desertification Formation of deserts from zones previously supporting plant life by the action of drought and/or increased populations of humans and grass-eating animals.

diffraction The spreading of light or other waves passing through a narrow opening or by the edge of an opaque body.

diffusion The movement of **molecules** or **ions** from an area of high concentration towards an area of low concentration, continuing until concentration is uniform.

dimorphism (1) In chemistry, the existence of two distinct forms of an **element** or compound, eg diamond and graphite as forms of carbon. (2) In biology, the existence of two types of individual within a species. Examples are animals that show marked differences between male and female (sexual dimorphism), animals that have two different kinds of offspring, and colonial species in which the members of the colony are of two different kinds.

direct current Generally abbreviated to dc. An electric current which flows in one direction only. Compare **alternating current**.

dispersion The separation of visible light into its various colours when it passes between media of different density, such as air and glass. It occurs because light passing between the media is deviated from a straight path by an amount that depends on the wavelength, ie the colour, and is observable, for example, when white light passes through a prism.

diurnal (1) Occurring during, or once during, a period of twenty-four hours. The term is used, for example, in astronomy and meteorology to indicate the variations of an astronomical quantity or weather phenomenon during an average day. (2) Of animals, active during the day. (3) Of flowers, opening during the day and closing at night.

DNA or **deoxyribonucleic acid**   In its double-stranded form, the genetic material of organisms. Usually, two strands of DNA form a double-helix, with the strands running in opposite directions. DNA is a major component of chromosomes.

dominant A term used to describe a version (allele) of a **gene** that shows its effect in those individuals who received that allele from only one parent. The dominant allele overrides the effects of other alleles. The term is also used to describe an inherited feature that is encoded by a dominant allele.

Doppler effect The apparent change of frequency of light or sound because of the relative motion of the source of radiation and the observer, eg the change in frequency of sound heard when an ambulance siren is moving towards or away from an observer.

dry ice   Solid (frozen) carbon dioxide, used in refrigeration (storage) and engineering.

dwarf planet An object that is in orbit round the Sun, is large enough to maintain an approximately round shape under gravity, is not a moon of another planet, but has not cleared its orbit of smaller objects. Pluto is now classified as a dwarf planet.

dwarf star The name given to a small low-luminosity star. ▶ **white dwarf**.

ecosystem A community consisting of animals, plants and their environment, often studied in terms of the interactions between living and non-living parts, and the flow of materials and energy between these parts.

electric field A region in which there is an electrical charge. Any charged particle entering the region therefore experiences a force.

electrode A **conductor** whereby an electric current is led into or out of a solid, liquid or gas. ▶ **anode**, **cathode**.

electrolysis   A chemical change, generally decomposition of a compound, based on **ionization**. Such a change is brought about by passing a current through a solution of the chemical, or the chemical in its molten state.

electromagnetic wave   A wave of energy comprising an **electric field** and a **magnetic field**, each of which is a transverse wave. These two individual waves are interdependent and mutually perpendicular. The spectrum of electromagnetic waves comprises **gamma radiation**, **X-rays**, **ultraviolet radiation**, visible light, **infrared radiation**, **microwaves** and **radio waves**. The speed in free space for all such waves is around 300000 km (186000 mi) per sec.

electron A subatomic particle with negative electric charge, which with the **proton** and **neutron**, is a basic constituent of the **atom**.

element A simple substance, composed of **atoms**, that cannot be resolved into simpler substances by normal chemical means.

El Niño A periodic large-scale warming of the surface of the eastern Pacific Ocean, especially off the coast of Peru and Ecuador. It affects the patterns of trade winds and is associated with weather anomalies and extreme weather conditions in the Pacific region; for example, flooding in normally dry regions and drought in regions that normally have high rainfall. Compare **La Niña**.

emulsion   (1) In chemistry, a suspension in the form of a **colloid** of one liquid in another. (2) In photography, a suspension of finely divided crystals in a medium such as gelatine, which

provides the light-sensitive coating on film, glass plates and paper.

endothermic   Said of a chemical reaction that is accompanied by the absorption of heat. Compare **exothermic**.

entropy   In thermal processes, a quantity that measures the extent to which the energy of a system is available for conversion to work.

enzyme   Any protein that provides **catalysis** for a metabolic process. Each enzyme can only catalyse a limited set of reactions.

epicentre The point on the surface of the Earth that lies immediately above the point of origin of an earthquake or nuclear explosion.

equinox Either of the two instants of time at which the Sun crosses the projected plane of the Earth's equator and the hours of daylight and darkness are almost equal, around 21 March and 23 September.

ethanol or **ethyl alcohol** An alcohol with chemical formula C_2H_5OH, the active substance in alcoholic drinks.

evolution   In biology, very gradual changes in the form of organisms owing both to genetic variations and to natural selection. Such changes are responsible for the development of modern complex organisms from earlier simpler ones.

exothermic   Said of a chemical reaction that is accompanied by the evolution of heat. Compare **endothermic**.

f-number   A measure of the **aperture** of a lens, representing its light transmission; it expresses the diameter of the lens diaphragm as a fraction of its focal length, eg f / 8, also written f:8 or f8.

Fahrenheit scale   The temperature scale in which the freezing point of water is 32°F and the boiling point is 212°F.

fault   A fracture in rocks along which some displacement has taken place. The displacement may vary from a few millimetres to thousands of metres. Movement along faults is the most common cause of earthquakes.

feedback A process in which part of the information that a system outputs is fed back into the input. Positive feedback enhances the output, as happens in an electrical circuit when a random amplified noise from a microphone is picked up by an amplifier and further amplified. Negative feedback regulates systems, as when a rising level of carbon dioxide in the human body causes the lungs to expel more carbon dioxide.

fermentation   The process in which **organic** substances slowly decompose as a result of the action of microorganisms or enzymes. An important fermentation process is the alcoholic fermentation of sugar.

fibre optics ▶ **optical fibre**

field theory ▶ **unified field theory**

fission   (1) In biology, the reproduction of some single-cell organisms from a single parent in which the **cell** divides into two more or less equal parts. (2) ▶ **nuclear fission**.

fluid A liquid or a gas.

fossil The relic or trace of some plant or animal which has been preserved by natural processes in rocks of the past.

fractal A geometrical entity characterized by a basic pattern that is repeated at ever decreasing sizes.

fraternal twins ▶ **twins**

fusion (1) ▶ **nuclear fusion**. (2) The conversion of a solid into a liquid state. ▶ **atom**.

galaxy (1) The name given to the belt of faint stars which encircles the heavens and which is known as the Milky Way. (2) The term is also used for the entire system of dust, gases and stars within which the Sun moves. (3) More generally, the term is used to mean any extra-galactic nebula, each being a vast collection of stars, dust and gas.

galvanized iron Iron which has been subjected to galvanizing, eg zinc coating, to prevent corrosion due to moisture.

gamma radiation High-energy **electromagnetic waves** emitted after **nuclear reactions**, or by radioactive atoms during the process of radioactive decay. ▶ **radioactivity**.

gene One of the units of **DNA** that are arranged in linear fashion on the **chromosome** and are responsible for passing on specific features from parents to offspring.

genetic code The system by which **genes** pass on instructions that ensure transmission of features inherited from previous generations.

genetic engineering The techniques involved in artificially changing the **genes** of an organism, with the aim of producing or eliminating a trait in an organism, or of enabling an organism to produce a biological substance (eg insulin) that it cannot normally produce. The techniques have numerous medical and commercial applications.

genome The full set of **chromosomes** of an individual; the total number of **genes** in such a set.

genotype The genetic constitution of an individual; a group of individuals all of which possess the same genetic constitution.

genus In biology, a taxonomic rank of closely related forms, which is lower than family and is further subdivided into species.

geomorphology The structure and development of land forms, including those under the sea; the study of this.

geostationary Said of an orbit lying above the equator, in which an artificial satellite moves at the same speed as the Earth rotates, thus maintaining position above a fixed point on the Earth's surface. Such a satellite would have an altitude of 35 800 km (22 200 mi) above the Earth's surface.

geothermal power Power generated by using the heat energy of rocks in the Earth's crust.

gestation In mammals, the act of retaining and nourishing the young in the uterus; pregnancy.

giant star A large and luminous star with low average density.

gravitational waves Waves that move through a gravitational field. Accelerating masses are expected to radiate gravitational waves, but so far this has not been observed directly.

greenhouse effect The phenomenon by which thermal energy from the Sun, reflected by the Earth's surface, is trapped within the Earth's atmosphere by the presence of certain gases (known as greenhouse gases). The main greenhouse gases are carbon dioxide, methane, water vapour and nitrous oxide.

gyroscope or **gyro** An apparatus in which a wheel spinning about an axis, moving freely within a ring-shaped frame, returns to its original level whenever the frame is displaced. Gyroscopes are essential components in modern navigation and stabilization equipment on ships.

herbaceous Said of a soft and green plant organ, or a plant without persistent woody tissues above ground.

herbivore A grass-eating animal.

hermaphrodite An organism that has both male and female reproductive organs in a single individual. Earthworms and some flowering plants are hermaphrodites; hermaphroditism can also occur anomalously in humans.

histamine A substance that is present in all tissues of the body and is released into the blood under certain circumstances, eg when the skin is cut or burnt or during allergic reactions (eg hay fever). Large releases cause the contraction of nearly all smooth muscle, a fall of arterial blood pressure and shock.

hologram A photograph made without use of a lens by means of interference between two parts of a split **laser** beam. Such a photograph, when suitably illuminated, displays a three-dimensional image.

hormone Any of various substances that regulate biological processes including growth and metabolism. Hormones are released by glands into the bloodstream.

hybrid In biology, the offspring of a cross between two different strains, varieties, races or species.

identical twins ▶ **twins**

igneous rocks Rocks that are formed by the solidification of lava or **magma**. Granite and basalt are igneous rocks.

immunity The state of having a high resistance to a disease due to the formation of **antibody** in response to the presence of **antigen**.

imprinting (1) In behavioural biology, an aspect of learning in some species, through which attachment to the important parental figure develops and their social preferences become restricted to their own species. (2) In genetics, a phenomenon whereby an individual's two copies of a **gene** (one inherited from each parent) are expressed differently, the differences being determined by which parent each is from.

in vitro fertilization (IVF) The process of fertilizing an egg outside the living body, in laboratory apparatus.

indigenous Native to a particular region; not imported.

inertia The tendency of a body, proportional to its mass, to oppose a change in motion when an external force is applied.

infinity A number that is larger than any quantified concept. For many purposes it may be considered as one divided by zero.

infrared radiation **Electromagnetic waves** in the approximate wavelength range from 0.000075 to 0.1 cm, lying between visible light and **microwaves** in the spectrum.

infrasound The range of sound frequencies below the usual audible limit, ie of less than around 20 cycles per sec or hertz.

inorganic Said of chemical compounds that do not contain carbon bonded to hydrogen. Such compounds generally occur outside living organisms. Compare **organic**.

integer Any whole number, including zero and negative numbers.

integrated circuit A very small circuit consisting of interconnected **semiconductor** devices in a single structure, which cannot be subdivided without destroying its intended function.

ion Strictly, any **atom** or **molecule** which has resultant electric charge due to loss or gain of **electrons**. Free electrons are sometimes loosely classified as negative ions.

ionization The formation of **ions** by breaking down **molecules**, or adding or removing **electrons** to/from **atoms** by various methods.

irrational number A number that is neither an

integer nor a ratio of two integers. The square roots of many integers are irrational numbers. Compare **rational number**.

isobar A line drawn on a map through places that have the same atmospheric pressure at a given time.

isomer A chemical compound that has the same composition and mass as another, but different chemical or physical properties because its atoms are arranged in a different structure.

isotope One of a set of chemically identical species of **atom** that have the same number of **protons**, but different numbers of **neutrons**.

jet stream A fairly well-defined core of strong wind that occurs more than 7000 m (20 000 ft) above the Earth. It is around 320–480 km (200–300 mi) wide and has wind speeds up to around 320 kph (200 mph).

Kelvin scale Temperature scale in which **absolute zero** is assigned the value zero and the temperature interval is the same as that of the Celsius scale. The unit is abbreviated as K; the freezing point of water (0°C) on this scale is 273.15 K.

La Niña A periodic cooling of the surface of the eastern Pacific Ocean, which causes abnormal weather conditions more or less opposite to those caused by **El Niño**.

laser *L*ight *A*mplification by *S*timulated *E*mission of *R*adiation. A source of intense light of a very narrow wavelength that can travel long distances without diffusing. Laser light is emitted when the atoms of a substance are excited by sending a light wave of a particular frequency through the substance.

LED ▶ **light-emitting diode**

light-emitting diode A **semiconductor** device that emits light when an electric current is passed through it, as used eg for displays in digital clocks and electronic calculators. Abbreviated as LED.

light-year A measure of astronomical distance, equal to the distance travelled by light in space during a year, which is approximately 9.46×10^{12} km or 5.88×10^{12} mi.

lipids or **lipoids** General terms for oils, fats, waxes and related products found in living tissues.

litmus A powder, obtained from certain lichens, that is used as an indicator of **pH value**, because its colour changes to red in the presence of **acid** and to blue in the presence of **alkali**.

luminescence The emission of light that occurs other than as a result of heating, and therefore occurs at a relatively cool temperature.

Mach number The ratio of the speed of a body, or of the flow of a fluid, to the speed of sound in the same medium. At Mach 1, the speed of the body is that of sound; below Mach 1, it is **subsonic**; above Mach 1, it is **supersonic**.

magma Molten rock formed beneath the Earth's surface, which incorporates dissolved water and other gases. It rises either to the surface, as lava, or to whatever level it can reach, before crystallizing again.

magnetic field A field of force that exists around certain metal objects, allowing them to attract other metals. Such fields are also associated with electric **current** and the motions of **electrons** in **atoms**.

magnitude (1) In mathematics and physics, the size of a property. (2) In astronomy, a measure of the apparent or absolute brightness of an astronomical object. The brightest stars visible to the naked eye are of around the first magnitude and the dimmest of around the sixth

matrix (1) In mathematics, a system of numbers arranged in a rectangular formation, representing information about a mathematical system and useful in solving some types of equation. (2) In cell biology, the material between **cells** within a **tissue**.

metamorphic rocks Rocks formed by alteration of existing rocks by heat, pressure or other processes in the Earth's crust. Marble and slate are metamorphic rocks.

meteor A 'shooting star'. A small body that enters the Earth's atmosphere from the space between the planets and burns up owing to friction, flashing across the sky and generally ceasing to be visible before it falls to Earth.

microwave background A weak signal of **radio waves**, which is detectable in every direction in the sky with almost identical intensity. It is believed to be the relic of the early hot phase of the universe following the **Big Bang**.

microwaves Those electromagnetic waves with wavelengths between 1 mm and 30 cm, lying between **radio waves** and **infrared radiation** in the spectrum.

Milky Way ▶ **galaxy**

minor planet A term used generally in professional astronomy for **asteroid**. Also known as planetoid.

MKSA Metre-Kilogram(me)-Sec-Ampere system of units, adopted by the International Electrotechnical Commission, in place of all other systems of units. ▶ **SI**.

modulation The process of impressing information (code, speech, video, data, etc) onto a higher frequency carrier wave. In frequency modulation (FM) the information is recorded as a variation in frequency, with constant amplitude, and in amplitude modulation (AM) as a variation in amplitude at constant frequency. Used in radio and television broadcasting.

mole The **SI** unit of the amount of a substance, defined as the amount that contains as many entities (**atoms**, **molecules**, **ions**, etc) as there are atoms in twelve grams of carbon-12, an **isotope** of carbon.

molecule A group of two or more **atoms** bonded together by shared electrons. Molecules are capable of independent existence and have properties characteristic of the chemical compound of which they are the basic unit. Molecular substances are those which have discrete molecules, such as water; diamond and sodium chloride are examples of non-molecular substances.

mutation In biology, a genetic change that can be transmitted to offspring as an inheritable divergence from previous generations.

nadir In astronomy, the point on the celestial sphere that is vertically below the observer. Compare **zenith**.

natural selection A theory of evolution stating that those organisms that are best adapted to their environment, as a result of random **mutations** in their genes, have the best chances of surviving and passing on their genetic information to their offspring. It is often referred to as the Darwinian theory.

neap tides A tide in which the difference between water levels at high and low tide is relatively small. Neap tides occur when the Sun's tidal influence is working against that of the Moon. Compare **spring tides**.

nebula (1) In strict usage, true clouds of interstellar dust and gas. (2) Loosely, any astronomical object that appears as a hazy smudge of light in

Science and Technology

an optical telescope; this usage predates modern astronomy.

neuron or **neurone** A nerve cell and its processes.

neutrino A fundamental **subatomic particle** with zero charge and zero mass which only interacts weakly with matter and is therefore difficult to detect. Neutrinos are thought to be responsible for carrying away the energy that is observed to be 'missing' in some forms of radioactivity.

neutron An uncharged subatomic particle, with mass approximately equal to that of the **proton**, which is found in the **nucleus** of the **atom**.

neutron star A very small dense star that results from the collapse of a massive **star**. Electrons and **protons** of atoms in the stellar material combine to form **neutrons**.

noble gases The elements helium, neon, argon, krypton, xenon and radon, which, owing to their stable structures, do not take part in all the usual chemical reactions. Also known as inert gases, rare gases.

node (1) In physics, a point of minimum disturbance in a wave. (2) In botany, the point on a plant stem from which one or more leaves develop.

nova A star that suddenly brightens by a factor of 10 000 or more, believed to occur when gas from a nearby star explodes on its surface.

nuclear energy In principle, the energy stored in an atomic **nucleus**, which binds together the constituent particles. More usually, the energy released during nuclear reactions involving regrouping of such particles (eg **fission** or **fusion** processes).

nuclear fission The spontaneous or induced disintegration of a heavy atomic **nucleus** into two or more lighter fragments. The energy released in the process is referred to as **nuclear energy**.

nuclear fusion The process of forming a new atomic **nucleus** by combining lighter ones. The energy released in the process is referred to as **nuclear energy** or fusion energy.

nuclear reaction A process in which an atomic **nucleus** interacts with another nucleus or particle, producing changes in energy and nuclear structure.

nucleon A general name for a **neutron** or proton.

nucleus (1) In biology, a compartment within a **cell**, bounded by a double membrane and containing the genomic **DNA**. (2) In physics, a structure within an **atom**, which is composed of **protons** and **neutrons** and which constitutes almost all the mass of the atom.

omnivore An animal that eats both plants and animals.

oncogene A **gene** that can become overactive and cause the development of cancer.

optical fibre A fibre of ultra-pure glass or plastic, through which data can be transmitted as pulses of light, rather than as electric currents. The use of such fibres is commonly referred to as fibre optics and is steadily replacing the use of traditional cables in communications systems.

order of magnitude The approximate size or number of something, usually measured in a scale from one value to ten times that value.

organic Said of compounds that contain carbon bonded to hydrogen. Owing to the ability of carbon atoms to combine together in long chains, these compounds are far more numerous than those of other elements and are the basis of living matter.

orogenesis The tectonic process whereby mountain chains are formed through movement of the Earth's crust.

orthogenesis The evolution of organisms systematically in definite directions and not accidentally in many directions; determinate variation.

osmosis The movement of water or a solvent from an area of lower concentration to an area of higher concentration, through a semi-permeable membrane, which continues until the level of concentration is equal on both sides of the membrane.

oxidation The addition of oxygen to a compound. More generally, any reaction involving the loss of **electrons** from an **atom**. It is always accompanied by **reduction**.

ozone layer The region of the Earth's atmosphere, between about 20 and 40 km (12.5 and 25 mi) above the surface, where ozone makes up a greater proportion of the air than at any other height. This layer exerts a vital influence by absorbing much of the **ultraviolet radiation** in sunlight and preventing it from reaching the Earth's surface where it has considerable biological effect.

parasite An organism that lives in or on another organism (the host) and derives nourishment from it without rendering it any service in return.

parsec The unit of length used for distances beyond the solar system, approximately equal to 3.26 **light-years**.

parthenogenesis The development of a new individual from a single, unfertilized reproductive cell, often an egg; occurs in bees and certain other insects.

pasteurization Reduction of the number of microorganisms in a liquid, eg milk, by heating it to a temperature of between 62.8° and 65.5°C (145 and 150°F) for 30 minutes.

pathogen An organism, eg a **parasite**, bacterium or **virus**, that causes disease.

perennial A plant that lives for more than two years.

periodic table A table in which all the chemical **elements** are arranged by **atomic number**. The rows (periods) correspond to the filling of successive shells of electrons in the atom, while the columns (groups) correspond to the number of outer electrons present. Elements in the same column have similar properties.

pH value A number used to express degrees of acidity or alkalinity in solutions. The scale ranges from 0 to 14; a pH above 7 indicates alkalinity and one below 7 indicates acidity. A pH of 7 indicates that the substance is neutral. See **acid** and **alkali**.

phage ▶ **bacteriophage**

phosphorescence A type of **luminescence** that continues after the source of radiation that causes it is removed.

photochemical reaction A chemical reaction that is brought about by light or **ultraviolet radiation**.

photoelectric effect The emission of **electrons** from a substance that is struck by **photons**, usually photons from visible light or ultraviolet radiation.

photon The smallest unit of energy in light or other **electromagnetic waves**. Photons have no electrical charge or mass, and travel at the speed of light.

photosensitive Sensitive to the action of visible or invisible radiation.

photosynthesis The process in which green plants, algae and some bacteria, by means of chlorophyll, use energy from light to produce carbohydrates from carbon dioxide and water.

planet An object that is in orbit round the Sun or another star, is large enough to maintain an approximately round shape under gravity and has cleared its orbit of smaller objects. There are officially eight planets in our solar system, Pluto now being classified as a **dwarf planet**.

plankton   Minute animals and plants that drift in seas and rivers and constitute a major source of food for many larger animals. Plankton consists of, among other organisms, bacteria, certain algae and tiny crustaceans

plasma   (1) In physics, a gaseous discharge that occurs naturally in the atmosphere of stars and in interstellar space. It contains a balanced number of positively and negatively charged **ions**, and is a good conductor of electricity. (2) In biology, the watery fluid containing salts, protein and other organic compounds, in which the cells of the blood are suspended.

plasma membrane   The bounding membrane of **cell**s, which controls the entry of molecules and the interaction of cells with their environment.

plate tectonics   The theory that the Earth's crust and upper mantle is divided into plate-like sections that move as distinct masses. This movement is regarded as being responsible for the formation of the Earth's major physical features and processes such as mid-ocean ridges, mountain building, earthquake zones and volcanic belts.

polarization   (1) In chemistry, the separation of the positive and negative charges of the molecules of a substance, typically done by placing the substance in an electric field. (2) In physics, the process of controlling the direction of the electric and magnetic fields of an **electromagnetic wave** eg light.

Polaroid®   The trademark for a range of photographic and optical products, including a transparent light-polarizing plastic sheet and methods of instant photography in black-and-white and colour. ▶ **polarization**.

polymer   Any of various chemical compounds consisting of molecules built up of many identical units called monomers. Cellulose is an example of a naturally occurring polymer, while nylon is a synthetic polymer.

polymorphism   (1) The presence in a population of two or more forms of a particular gene. (2) The occurrence of different physical forms of the same organism, as in the case of bees, which exist as queens, workers and drones.

positron   A **subatomic particle** that has the same mass as an electron but the opposite (ie a positive) charge. Positrons are antiparticles to electrons.

precession of the equinoxes   The variation in the direction of the Earth's axis of rotation caused mainly by the attraction of the Sun and Moon on the equatorial bulge of the Earth, the change describing a full cone with a period of around 25800 years.

primary colours   In physics, either of two sets of coloured light that can be combined in different proportions to produce all the colours of the spectrum. Red, green and blue are known as the additive primaries. When they are mixed in equal proportions, they produce white light. The additive primaries are combined to form the subtractive primaries cyan, magenta and yellow. When these are combined in equal proportions, they produce black.

protein   Any member of a group of complex, nitrogen-containing **organic** compounds that play an important part in biological processes. They are made up of **amino acids**.

proton A positively charged subatomic particle, with

mass approximately equal to that of the **neutron**, that is found in the **nucleus** of the **atom**. The nucleus of a hydrogen atom is a single proton.

quantum theory   The theory that matter and energy are made up of tiny units called quanta that behave both as particles and as waves.

quark   A fundamental **subatomic particle**, currently seen as any of six types: bottom, top, up, down, charmed and strange. Although not yet observed directly, these are suggested to be the units out of which all other subatomic particles are formed.

quasar   Any of a number of distant, compact objects far beyond our **galaxy**, which look star-like on a photograph but appear to be much more distant than any star that we would be able to observe. The word is a contraction of quasi-stellar object. Quasars emit very bright light, possibly due to the acceleration of matter towards **black hole**s.

radar   A system that uses the reflection of pulsed **radio waves** to detect distant objects and measure their speed and direction of movement (from RAdio Detection And Ranging).

radiation   (1) Any energy in the form of **electromagnetic waves** or photons. Heat and light are forms of radiation. (2) (also called ionizing radiation) Emissions of **subatomic particle**s that arise when the nuclei of certain heavy elements, eg radium and uranium, disintegrate spontaneously. These emissions can cause considerable harm to organisms exposed to them.

radio galaxy   A **galaxy** that emits a large quantity of **radio waves**.

radio waves   Those **electromagnetic waves** of a frequency suitable for radio transmission, with a wavelength greater than around 10&thsp;cm, ie with a longer wavelength than **microwaves**.

radioactivity   Spontaneous disintegration of a **nucleus** of certain natural heavy **elements** (eg radium or uranium), which results in the emission of particles or gamma radiation. Also called radioactive decay.

rational number   A number that is either an **integer** or can be expressed a ratio of two integers eg $\frac{3}{4}$ Compare **irrational number**.

recessive   A term used to describe a version (allele) of a **gene** that only shows its effect in those individuals who received that allele from both parents. A recessive allele is overridden by the effects of other alleles. The term is also used to describe an inherited feature that is encoded by a recessive allele.

recombination   The rearrangement of genes that takes place naturally when cells divide during reproduction. It can also be induced by genetic engineering to alter the genetic make-up of a cell.

red giant   A large, cool, luminous star thought to be in a late stage of its evolution, when most of its hydrogen has been exhausted by **nuclear reaction** to helium.

redshift   An increase in the wavelength of light, accompanied by a decrease in its frequency, as the source of light moves away from the observer. The phenomenon is observable in distant galaxies and is regarded as an indication that the universe is expanding.

reduction   Any process in which an electron is added to an **atom** or an **ion**. Always occurs accompanied by **oxidation**.

refraction   The process in which waves (light, sound, etc) bend when passing from one medium to another of different density. Refraction explains why a straight object standing in a half-filled glass of water appears to bend at the surface of the water.

relative atomic mass The mass of atoms of an element given on the scale where 1 unit is equal to 1.660×10^{-27} kg. The scale assigns the value 12 to the carbon-12 **isotope** of carbon.

relativity The interdependence of matter, time and space, as discussed in two theories developed by Albert Einstein. The Special Theory of Relativity (1905) postulates that all motion is relative and that the velocity of light is the same for all observers, and predicts the effects of these assumptions, including variations in the size and mass of objects and in the rate of passage of time, depending on the speed of the observer. The General Theory of Relativity (1916) predicts the variations involved due to acceleration and gravitation.

remote sensing A method in which remote detectors are used to collect data for transmission to a central computer; observation and collection of scientific data without direct contact, especially observation of the Earth's surface from the air or from space using **electromagnetic waves**.

resonance In a vibrating or oscillating system, a rapid increase in the amplitude of the wave that occurs when a constant force is applied at regular intervals matching the frequency of the wave.

respiration (1) Breathing, the process by which an organism exchanges gases, especially taking in oxygen and giving out carbon dioxide. (2) The process by which glucose and other food substances are broken down to release energy, accompanied by the production of carbon dioxide and water as waste products.

Richter scale A scale of measurement from 1 to 10, used to indicate the magnitude of an earthquake.

RNA or **ribonucleic acid** A type of nucleic acid that is present in cells, where it is the primary agent for transferring information from the **genome** to the **protein** synthetic machinery. It also holds genetic information in certain **viruses**.

saprobe An organism that gets nourishment from decaying organic matter, including fungi and some bacteria. Also called saprotrophs; used to be known as saprophytes.

saturated compounds An organic compound in which all the carbon atoms are joined by single bonds, making it incapable of combining with any additional atoms. Compare **unsaturated compounds**.

scalar A quantity that has magnitude but no direction, eg mass or temperature. Compare **vector**.

sedimentary rocks Rocks that form from sediments deposited by ice, water and wind. These sediments include fragments of fossils and shells, and pieces of other rocks. Limestone and shale are sedimentary rocks.

semiconductor A material that has a higher resistance to the flow of electricity than a **conductor**, but a lower resistance than an insulator. Semiconductors are used in a wide range of electronic devices.

sex determination The process by which the sex of an organism is determined. In vertebrates and many other organisms, sex is determined by the possession of a particular combination of **chromosomes**. In mammals, the female's chromosomes are designated XX and the male's XY.

SI The system of coherent metric units (Système International d'Unités) proposed for international acceptance in 1960. It is based on seven units: the metre, kilogram, second, ampere, kelvin, mole

and candela. It has replaced the **CGS** system for most purposes.

sidereal time Time measured by considering the movement of the Earth relative to the distant stars (rather than to the Sun, which is the basis of civil time). A sidereal day is 3 minutes 56 seconds shorter than a solar day.

silicon chip ▶ **chip**

sine wave A mathematical function that describes a waveform of a single frequency, indefinitely repeated in time. Its displacement can be expressed as the sine (or cosine) of a linear function of time or distance, or both.

solar system The Sun and the bodies moving about it under gravity; bodies that comprise not only the major planets but also their moons, several **dwarf planets** and a vast number of **asteroids**, **comets** and **meteors**.

solstice One of the two instants in the year when the Sun reaches its furthest point north or south of the equator. The summer solstice is the longest day of the year, and occurs in the northern hemisphere around 21 June, when the Sun reaches the tropic of Cancer; the winter solstice is the shortest day of the year and occurs in the northern hemisphere around 21 December, when the Sun reaches the tropic of Capricorn. (In the southern hemisphere the dates are reversed.)

sonar *SO*und *N*avigation *A*nd *R*anging; ▶ **acoustic imaging**

sonic boom A noise phenomenon consisting of two loud explosive noises, caused by the shock waves projected from an aircraft travelling at **supersonic** speed. The waves create pressures that may be of sufficient intensity to cause damage to buildings etc.

species A group of individuals that actually or potentially interbreed with each other to produce fertile offspring, but cannot do so with other such groups. They show continuous **variation** within the group but they have distinct differences from other such groups.

spore A single-cell asexual reproductive body produced by some simple plants, and by fungi and bacteria; sometimes extended to other reproductive bodies.

spring tides A tide in which the difference between water levels at high and low tide is relatively great. Spring tides occur when the Sun's and Moon's tidal influences are working together. Compare **neap tides**.

stalactite A deposit of calcium carbonate which hangs icicle-like from the roofs of limestone caverns.

stalagmite An upward-growing conical formation of calcium carbonate, precipitated from dripping solutions on the floors and walls of limestone caverns.

star A sphere of gas and dust held together entirely by its own gravitational field and generating energy by means of **nuclear fusion** reactions in its deep interior.

stellar evolution The sequence of events and changes covering the entire life-cycle of a star.

subatomic particle A basic unit of matter, such as an electron, from which atoms are made.

subsonic Said of an object or flow which moves with a speed less than that of sound. ▶ **Mach number**, **supersonic**

superconductivity The property of some pure metals and metallic alloys at very low temperature of having negligible resistance to the flow of an electric current. Each material has its own critical

temperature above which it is a normal conductor. When a current is established, it persists almost indefinitely.

supergiant star A star of very high luminosity, enormous size and low density.

supernova A very bright **nova** resulting from an explosion that blows a star's material into space, leaving an expanding cloud of gas and sometimes a central compact object.

supersonic Faster than the speed of sound in that medium. Erroneously used for ultrasonic. ▶ **Mach number, subsonic, ultrasonic**

symbiosis A mutually beneficial partnership between organisms of different kinds, especially such an association where one lives within the other. Compare **commensalism**.

Système International d'Unités ▶ **SI**

thermonuclear energy Energy released by a nuclear **fusion** reaction that occurs because of the high thermal energy of the interacting particles.

tissue A collection of similar cells that together form a particular type of fabric, eg muscle.

tornado An intensely destructive, advancing whirlwind formed from strongly ascending air current; also, in West Africa, the squall following thunderstorms between the wet and dry seasons.

transition metal Any of a group of metallic elements, eg copper and iron, that have an incomplete inner electron shell. Such elements form alloys easily and are excellent electrical conductors. Also known as transition elements. ▶ **atom**.

transuranic element Any element with an atomic number greater than that of uranium, ie with 93 or more protons in each atomic nucleus. These do not occur naturally but more than twelve have been artificially produced, including neptunium, plutonium, curium and lawrencium.

tsunami A series of waves produced in the ocean by violent movement of the sea floor, most commonly submarine faulting accompanied by an earthquake. Its amplitude in mid-ocean is very small; as it approaches land, the amplitude builds up and all the energy of the original disturbance is concentrated with devastating results. Erroneously called a tidal wave.

turbulence The irregular motion of particles within a fluid, which at any point varies rapidly in magnitude and direction.

twins (1) Identical twins arise from the same fertilized egg which has subsequently divided into two, each half developing into a separate individual. (2) In mammals, non-identical twins are produced from separate eggs fertilized at the same time.

typhoon A tropical revolving storm in the China Sea and western North Pacific.

ultrasonic A term used to describe sound frequencies above the upper limit of the normal range of hearing, at or about 20 000 cycles per sec, or 20 kilohertz. Ultrasonics is the general term for the study and application of ultrasonic sound and vibrations.

ultrasound **Ultrasonic** sound used by some animals (eg bats, dolphins) for localization and communication, and in a variety of industrial applications.

ultraviolet radiation **Electromagnetic wave** in a wavelength range from 0.00004 to 0.000001 cm approximately, ie between the visible and X-ray regions of the spectrum.

uncertainty principle The principle that there is a fundamental limit to the precision with which a position co-ordinate of a particle and its momentum in that direction can be simultaneously known. Also, there is a fundamental limit to the knowledge of the energy of a particle when it is measured for a finite time.

unified field theory As yet an unverified attempt to link the properties of all force fields in physics into a unified system.

unsaturated compound An organic compound in which two or more of the carbon atoms are joined by double or triple bonds, making it capable of combining with additional atoms. Compare **saturated compound**.

valency A measure of the ability of an **atom**, **molecule** or **ion** to combine with other such entities, expressed as the number of electrons it donates, accepts or shares when it forms a bond.

Van Allen radiation belts Two belts encircling the Earth within which electrically charged particles from the Sun are trapped.

variation In biology, the differences between the offspring of a single mating; the differences between the individuals of a race, subspecies, or species; the differences between analogous groups of higher rank.

vector (1) In mathematics, a quantity that has both magnitude and direction, eg force or velocity. Compare **scalar**. (2) In biology, an organism that can transmit disease-causing microorganisms from one host to another without being harmed itself, eg mosquitoes or ticks. (3) In genetics, a piece of DNA that is used to transfer genes between cells or organisms.

very high frequencies Those between 30 000 000 and 300 000 000 cycles per sec or between 30 and 300 megahertz. Abbreviated as VHF.

virtual reality Computer simulation which takes into account the motion of an observer to produce the illusion of reality in a computer-created situation, using complex graphics and sound reproduction.

virus A **pathogen**, usually protein-coated particles of **DNA** or **RNA**, capable of increasing rapidly inside a living cell.

vitamins **Organic** substances required in relatively small amounts in the diet for the proper functioning of the organism, comprising vitamins A, C, D, E, K and the vitamins of the B complex.

white dwarf A small dim star in the final stages of its evolution. The masses of known white dwarfs do not exceed 1.4 times that of the Sun, with a typical diameter about the same as that of the Earth.

X-chromosome ▶ **sex determination**

X-rays **Electromagnetic waves** in the wavelength range from 0.0000000001 to 0.000001 cm approximately, ie between the ultraviolet and gamma-ray regions of the spectrum.

Y-chromosome ▶ **sex determination**

zenith In astronomy, the point on the celestial sphere that is vertically above the observer's head. Compare **nadir**.

zodiac A name, of Greek origin, given to the belt of stars, about 18° wide, through which the Sun appears to pass through the year. The zodiac lies approximately in the plane of the motions of the Sun, Moon and planets.

Fields of scientific study

Science and Technology

acoustics The science of mechanical waves including production and propagation properties.

actinobiology The study of the effects of radiation upon living organisms.

aerodynamics The branch of fluid mechanics that deals with the dynamics of gases, particularly the study of forces acting upon bodies in motion in air.

aerology The study of the free atmosphere.

aeronautics All activities concerned with aerial locomotion.

aerothermodynamics The branch of thermodynamics relating to the heating effects associated with the dynamics of a gas; in particular the physical effects produced in the air flowing over an aircraft or spacecraft during launch and re-entry.

aetiology or **etiology** The medical study of the causes of disease.

algology The study of algae.

angiology The study of the structure of blood and lymph vascular systems.

astronautics The science of space flight.

astronomy The study of all classes of celestial object and the universe as a whole.

astrophysics The branch of astronomy that applies the laws of physics to the study of stars, galaxies and interstellar space.

autecology The study of the ecology of any individual species. Compare **synecology**.

autonomics The study of self-regulating systems for process control and performance optimization.

bacteriology The scientific study of bacteria.

ballistics The branch of physics that deals with the motion of projectiles, eg bullets and missiles.

balneology The scientific study of baths and bathing, and of their application to disease.

bioclimatology The study of the effects of climate on living organisms.

biology The study of living organisms and systems; the life sciences collectively, including botany, anatomy, physiology, zoology, etc.

biometeorology The study of the effects of atmospheric conditions on living things.

biophysics The study of biological phenomena using the laws of physics.

biosystematics The study of the relationships between different types of organism with reference to the laws of classification of organisms; taxonomy.

biotechnology The use of organisms or their components in industrial or commercial processes, eg the use of genetic manipulation to develop new plant varieties for agriculture.

botany The scientific study of plants.

cardiology The branch of medical science that deals with the function and diseases of the heart.

chemistry The study of the composition of substances and the changes that they undergo.

chromatics The science of colours as affected by phenomena determined by their differing wavelengths.

cladistics A method of classifying organisms into groups (taxa) based on 'recency of common descent' as judged by the possession of shared derived (ie not primitive) characteristics.

climatology The study of climate and its causes.

cosmology The study of the universe on the largest scales of length and time, particularly the propounding of theories concerning its origin, nature, structure and evolution. A cosmology is any model said to represent the observed universe. Western cosmology is entirely scientific in its approach, and has produced two famous models, the Big Bang and steady-state cosmology.

cryogenics The study of materials at very low temperatures.

crystallography The study of the chemical structure of crystals and their classification into types.

cybernetics The study of control and communications processes in complex electronic and mechanical systems and in biological systems, especially humans. Cybernetic research often involves attempts to replicate human systems by artificial means.

cytogenetics The study of the structure and function of the chromosomes within cells, and of chromosomal abnormalities and their inheritance.

cytology The study of the structure and functions of cells.

dendrochronology The science of reconstructing past climate conditions by analysing the growth rings in tree trunks.

dermatology The branch of medical science that deals with the skin and its diseases.

dynamics The branch of applied mathematics and physics that studies the way in which force produces motion. Also called kinetics. Compare **kinematics**.

ecology The scientific study of the relationships between living organisms and their environment, including the distribution and abundance of living organisms (ie exactly where they occur and precisely how many there are).

econometrics The application of statistical methods to economic phenomena.

ecophysiology The branch of physiology concerned with how organisms are adapted to their natural environment.

electrocardiography The study of electric currents produced in cardiac muscular activity.

electrodynamics The branch of physics that deals with the phenomenon of electric charges that are flowing in a current. Also electrokinetics. Compare **electrostatics**.

electromagnetics or **electromagnetism** The science of the properties of, and relationships between, magnetism and electric currents.

electromyography The study of electric currents set up in muscle fibres by bodily movement.

electronics The study and application of the flow of electrons (as electric current) through different materials or devices.

electrophysiology The study of electrical phenomena associated with living organisms, particularly nervous conduction.

electrostatics The branch of physics that deals with the phenomenon of electric charges substantially at rest. Compare **electrodynamics**.

embryology The study of the formation and development of embryos.

endocrinology The branch of biology or medicine that deals with the endocrine glands, which produce and secrete hormones.

energetics The abstract study of the energy relations of physical and chemical changes. ▶ **thermodynamics**.

entomology The branch of zoology that deals with the study of insects.

epidemiology The branch of medicine that deals with the causes and spread of diseases in the population, examining the role of external influences such as infection, diet or toxic substances, and devising appropriate preventive or curative measures.

epistemics The scientific study of the perceptual, intellectual and linguistic processes by which knowledge and understanding are acquired and communicated.

ergonomics The study of the relationships between people and the objects with which they interact, including furniture, machinery and working tools, usually with the aim of improving work performance and minimizing physical discomfort. It incorporates aspects of anatomy, physiology and psychology.

ethology An approach to the study of animal behaviour in which attempts to explain behaviour combine questions about its immediate causation, development, function and evolution.

etiology ▶ **aetiology**

eugenics The study of the means whereby the characteristics of human populations might be improved by the application of genetics.

exobiology The study of (possible) living systems that may exist elsewhere in the universe.

fluidics The science of liquid flow in tubes etc, which bears a marked resemblance to electron flow in conductors. The interaction of streams of fluid can be used for the control of instruments or industrial processes without the use of moving parts.

fractography The microscopic study of fractures in metal surfaces.

genecology The branch of ecology which seeks genetic explanations of the patterns of distribution of plants and animals in time and space.

genetic engineering The techniques involved in artificially changing the genes of an organism to produce or eliminate a trait, or to enable production of a biological substance that the organism cannot normally produce.

genetics The study of the process by which differences between individuals are passed on from one generation to the next; and of how the information in the genes is used in the development and functioning of the adult organism.

geochronology The branch of geology in which the study of rocks and fossils is applied to dating the Earth.

geology The study of the structure, history and physical properties of the Earth, including such disciplines as **geophysics**, **palaeontology** and **stratigraphy**.

geophysics The study of the physical properties of the Earth, which makes use of the data available from **seismology**, **meteorology**, **oceanography** and other disciplines.

gerontology The scientific study of the processes of ageing.

gynaecology or **gynecology** The branch of medical science that deals with the functions and diseases of women's reproductive organs.

histology The study of the minute structure of tissues in organisms.

horology The science of time measurement, or of the construction of timepieces.

hydraulics ▶ **hydrodynamics**

hydrodynamics The branch of dynamics that studies the motion produced in fluids by applied forces. The practical application of this is known as hydraulics.

hydrogeology The branch of geology that deals with the distribution and movement of groundwater in the Earth's soil and rocks.

hydrography The investigation of seas and other bodies of water, including surveying, charting and the study of tides and currents.

hydrology The study of water, including rain and snow as well as water on the Earth's surface, covering its properties, distribution and use.

hydroponics The technique of growing plants without soil. The roots can be in a nutrient solution or in an inert medium percolated by such a solution.

hydrostatics The branch of statics that studies the forces arising from the presence of fluids.

immunology The study of the biological responses of a living organism to its invasion by living bacteria, viruses or parasites, and its defence against these; also the study of the body's reaction to foreign substances.

kinematics The branch of applied mathematics that deals with the way in which velocities and accelerations of various parts of a moving system are related, without reference to the forces that cause the motion. Compare **dynamics**.

kinetics (1) In chemistry and biology, the study of the rates at which chemical reactions and biological processes proceed. (2) ▶ **dynamics**.

laryngology The branch of medical science that treats diseases of the larynx and adjacent parts of the upper respiratory tract.

limnology The study of lakes.

lithology The systematic description of rocks, more especially sedimentary rocks. ▶ **petrology**.

magnetism The branch of physics that covers **magnetic fields** and their effects on materials.

magnetohydrodynamics The study of the interactions between an electrically conducting fluid and a magnetic field, which act on one another to cause motion that can be used to generate electricity.

magnetostatics The study of steady-state magnetic fields.

malacology The study of molluscs.

mathematics The study of the logical consequences of sets of axioms. Pure mathematics, roughly speaking, comprises those branches studied for their own sake or their relation to other branches. The most important of these are algebra, analysis and topology. The term applied mathematics is usually restricted to applications in physics. Applications in other fields, eg economics, mainly statistical, are sometimes referred to as applicable mathematics.

mechanics The study of the forces acting on bodies and of the motions they produce. It is subdivided into **dynamics**, **kinematics**, **statics**.

metallography The study of the structure of metals and their alloys.

meteorology The study of the Earth's atmosphere in its relation to weather and climate.

metrology The science of measuring.

micropalaeontology The study of microfossils, tiny fossils that can only be seen with a microscope.

mineralogy The study of the chemical composition, physical properties and occurrence of minerals.

morphology The study of the structure and forms of organisms, as opposed to the study of their functions.

mycology The study of fungi.

myology The study of muscles.

neuroendocrinology The study of interactions between the nervous system and endocrine organs, particularly pituitary gland and hypothalamic region of the brain.

neurology The study of the nervous system.

Science and Technology

neuropathology   The study of diseases of the nervous system.

nosology   The branch of medical science that deals with the classification of diseases.

nucleonics   The science and technology of nuclear studies.

obstetrics   The branch of medical science that deals with the problems and management of pregnancy and labour.

oceanography   The study of the oceans, including geological, chemical, physical and biological processes.

odontology   The study of structure and diseases of the teeth.

oncology   The branch of medical science that deals with cancer.

oölogy   The study of ova (eggs).

ophthalmology   The study of the eye and its diseases.

optics   The study of light. Physical optics deals with the nature of light and its wave properties, while geometrical optics looks at problems of reflection and refraction.

organography   A descriptive study of the organs of plants or animals.

ornithology   The study of birds.

orthopaedics or **orthopedics**   The branch of surgery that deals with deformities arising from injury or disease of bones or of joints.

osteology   The study of bones.

otology   The part of medical science that deals with the ear and its diseases.

otorhinolaryngology   The part of surgical science that deals with diseases of the ear, nose and throat.

palaeoclimatology   The study of climatic conditions in the earliest periods of history, using evidence from fossils, sediments and their structures, geophysics and geochemistry.

palaeoecology   The study of organisms preserved as fossils in terms of their mode of life, their interrelationships and their environment.

palaeogeography   The study of the relative positions of land and water at particular periods in the geological past.

palaeontology   The study of fossil animals and plants.

palaeopathology   The study of disease of previous eras from examination of bodily remains or evidence from ancient writings.

palaeozoology   The study of fossil animals. ▶ **palaeontology**.

palynology   The study of fossil spores and pollen. They are very resistant to destruction and in many sedimentary rocks are the only fossils that can be used to determine the relationships of strata.

parapsychology   The study of certain alleged phenomena, the paranormal, that are beyond the scope of ordinary psychology, eg ESP, psychokinesis, etc.

parasitology   The study of parasites and their habits (usually confined to animal parasites).

pathology   The branch of medical science that deals with the causes and nature of disease, and with the bodily changes brought about by disease.

pedology   The study of soil.

petrology   The study of the origin, structure and chemical and mineral composition of rocks.

pharmacodynamics   The branch of pharmacology that deals with the action of drugs on the body, including therapeutic effects and side effects. Compare **pharmacokinetics**.

pharmacokinetics   The branch of pharmacology that deals with the effects the body has on drugs, eg the route and speed of elimination. Compare **pharmacodynamics**.

pharmacology   The scientific study of the interaction between drugs and the body.

phenology   The study of plant development in relation to the seasons.

phenomenology   In psychiatry, the description and classification of an individual's mental activity, including subjective experience and perceptions, mental performance (eg memory) and the somatic accompaniments of mental events (eg heart rate).

phonetics   The study of speech and vocal acoustics.

photobiology   The study of light as it affects living organisms.

phycology   The study of algae.

physics   The study of the forces that exist between objects and the interrelationship between matter and energy. It encompasses electrical, mechanical, magnetic, radioactive and thermal phenomena.

physiography   The science of the surface of the Earth and the interrelations of air, water and land.

phytology   ▶ **botany**

phytopathology   Plant pathology; the study of plant diseases, especially of plants in relation to their parasites.

phytosociology   The study of the distribution of plant species and the relationships between broad groupings of plants known as syntaxa.

planetology   The study of the composition, origin and distribution of matter in the planets of the solar system.

prosthetics   That branch of surgical science involved in supplying artificial parts to the body.

proxemics   The study of the human use of physical space in social interaction and communication.

psychodynamics   A theory of the workings of the mind.

psychometrics   The application of mathematical and statistical concepts to psychological data, particularly in the areas of mental testing and experimental data.

psychopathology   The study of psychological disorders.

psychopharmacology   The study and use of drugs that influence behaviour, emotions, perception and thought by acting on the central nervous system.

psychophysics   The branch of psychology that studies the relationship between characteristics of physical stimuli and the psychological experiences they produce.

quantum mechanics   The branch of mechanics, based on quantum theory, that is used to predict the behaviour of elementary subatomic particles.

radiobiology   The branch of biology that deals with the effect of radiation on living organisms.

radiology or **röntgenology**   The science and application of X-rays, gamma-rays and other penetrating radiation.

rheology   The study of the deformation and flow of materials, including properties such as elasticity, viscosity and plasticity.

robotics   The study of the design and use of robots, particularly for their use in manufacturing and related processes.

röntgenology   ▶ **radiology**

seismology   The study of earthquakes, particularly their shock waves. Studies of the speed and refraction of seismic waves enable the deeper structure of the Earth to be investigated.

semiology The branch of medical science that deals with the symptoms of disease.

semiotics The study of communication.

serology The scientific study of blood serum, especially the analysis of the antibodies found in it.

sonics The study of mechanical vibrations in matter.

spelaeology or **speleology** The study of the fauna and flora of caves.

statics The branch of applied mathematics that deals with the way in which forces combine with each other usually so as to produce equilibrium.

statistics The branch of mathematics that deals with the collection and analysis of numerical data.

stratigraphy The branch of geology that deals with the formation, structure and fossil content of sedimentary rocks.

superaerodynamics Aerodynamics as applied at very low air densities occurring above 30 480 m/100 000 ft, ie for spacecraft on ascending and re-entry trajectories.

symptomatology The study of disease symptoms.

synecology The study of relationships between communities and their environment. Compare **autecology**.

systematics The branch of biology which deals with classification and nomenclature.

tectonics The study of the major structural features of the Earth's crust.

teratology The study of biological malformations or abnormal growths, as an aid to the understanding of normal developmental processes.

thermionics The study of the processes involved in the emission of electrons from hot bodies.

thermodynamics The branch of physics that deals with heat and heat-related phenomena.

topology The study of those properties of shapes and space that are independent of distance.

toxicology The branch of medical science that deals with the nature and effects of poisons.

urodynamics The study of urine flow.

urology The branch of medical science that deals with diseases and abnormalities of the urinary tract and their treatment.

virology The study of viruses.

zoogeography The study of animal distribution.

zoology The scientific study of all aspects of animals.

zootaxy The science of the classification of animals.

Scientists

Airy, Sir George Biddell (1802–92) English astronomer and geophysicist, born Alnwick. Astronomer Royal (1835–81) who reorganized the Greenwich Observatory. Initiated measurement of Greenwich Mean Time, determined the mass of the Earth from gravity experiments in mines, and carried out extensive work in optics.

Alzheimer, Alois (1864–1915) German psychiatrist and neuropathologist, born Markbreit. Gave full clinical and pathological description of presenile dementia (Alzheimer's disease) (1907).

Ampère, André Marie (1775–1836) French mathematician and physicist, born Lyons. Laid the foundations of the science of electrodynamics. His name is given to the basic SI unit of electric current (ampere, amp).

Appleton, Sir Edward Victor (1892–1965) English physicist, born Bradford. Researched propagation of wireless waves, and discovered the existence of a layer of electrically charged particles in the upper atmosphere (the Appleton layer) which plays an essential role in radio communication. Received the Nobel Prize for physics (1947) for studies of Earth's atmosphere.

Archimedes (c.287–212 BC) Greek mathematician, born Syracuse. Discovered formulae for the areas and volumes of plane and solid geometrical figures using methods which anticipated theories of integration to be developed 1800 years later. Also founded the science of hydrostatics; in popular tradition remembered for the cry of 'Eureka' when he discovered the principle of upthrust on a floating body.

Aristotle (384–322 BC) Greek philosopher and scientist, born Stagira. One of the most influential figures in the history of Western thought and scientific tradition. Wrote enormous amounts on biology, zoology, physics and psychology.

Avogadro, Amedeo (1776–1856) Italian physicist, born Turin. Formulated the hypothesis (Avogadro's law) that equal volumes of gas contain equal numbers of molecules, when at the same temperature and pressure.

Axelrod, Julius (1912–2004) US pharmacologist, born New York City. Discovered an enzyme that inhibits neural impulses, laying the basis for significant advances in the treatment of disorders such as schizophrenia. Joint winner of the 1970 Nobel Prize for physiology or medicine.

Babbage, Charles (1791–1871) English mathematician, born Teignmouth. Attempted to build two calculating machines – the 'difference engine', to calculate logarithms and similar functions by repeated addition performed by trains of gear wheels, and the 'analytical engine', to perform much more varied calculations. Babbage is regarded as the pioneer of modern computers.

Bacon, Francis, Viscount St Albans (1561–1626) English statesman and natural philosopher, born London. Creator of scientific induction; stressed the importance of experiment in interpreting nature, giving significant impetus to future scientific investigation.

Baird, John Logie (1888–1946) Scottish engineer, born Helensburgh. Gave first public demonstration of a television image in 1926. Researched radar and infrared television, and succeeded in producing 3-D and colour images (1944), as well as projection onto a screen and stereophonic sound.

Barnard, Christiaan Neethling (1922–2001) South African surgeon, born Beaufort West. Performed first successful heart transplant in December 1967 at Groote Schuur Hospital. Although the recipient died 18 days later from pneumonia, a second patient operated on in January 1968 survived for 594 days.

Beaufort, Sir Francis (1774–1857) Irish naval officer and hydrographer, born Navan, County Meath. Devised the Beaufort scale of wind force and a tabulated system of weather registration.

Becquerel, Antoine Henri (1852–1908) French physicist, born Paris. While researching fluorescence (the ability of substances to give off visible light), discovered radioactivity in the form of rays emitted by uranium salts, leading to the beginnings of modern nuclear physics. For this he

Science and Technology

Science and Technology

shared the 1903 Nobel Prize for physics with Marie and Pierre Curie.

Bell, Alexander Graham (1847–1922) Scottish–US inventor, born Edinburgh. After researching and teaching methods in speech therapy and experimenting with various acoustical devices, produced the first intelligible telephonic transmission on 5 June 1875, and patented the telephone in 1876. Founded the Bell Telephone Company in 1877.

Bishop, (John) Michael (1936–) US molecular biologist and virologist, born York, Pennsylvania. Awarded 1989 Nobel Prize for physiology or medicine (jointly with Harold Varmus, 1939–), for their discovery of oncogenes. This discovery is crucial to the understanding of cancer mechanisms.

Blumberg, Baruch Samuel (1925–) US biochemist, born New York. Awarded 1976 Nobel Prize for physiology or medicine (jointly with Daniel Gadjusek), for his development of a vaccine against Hepatitis B.

Bohr, Niels Henrik David (1885–1962) Danish physicist, born Copenhagen. Greatly extended the theory of atomic structure by explaining the spectrum of hydrogen by means of an atomic model and quantum theory (1913). Awarded the Nobel Prize for physics in 1922. Assisted in atom bomb research in America during World War II.

Boltzmann, Ludwig Eduard (1844–1906) Austrian physicist, born Vienna. Carried out important work on the kinetic theory of gases and established Boltzmann's law, or the principle of equipartition of energy.

Boyle, The Hon Robert (1627–91) Irish physicist and chemist, born Munster. One of the first members of the Royal Society. Carried out experiments on air, vacuum, combustion and respiration, and in 1662 arrived at Boyle's law, which states that the pressure and volume of a gas are inversely proportional at constant temperature.

Brahe, Tycho or **Tyge** (1546–1601) Danish astronomer, born Knudstrup, Sweden (then under Danish crown). After seeing the partial solar eclipse of 1569, became obsessed with astronomy. Accurately measured and compiled catalogues of the positions of stars, providing vital information for later astronomers, and recorded unique observations of a new star in Cassiopeia in 1572 (a nova now known as Tycho's star).

Brenner, Sydney (1927–) British molecular biologist, born Germiston, South Africa. With Francis Crick, carried out experiments to determine the nature of the genetic code. Established the nematode (roundworm) *Caenorhabditis elegans* as an important model organism for studying genetics, cell biology and development; for this he shared the 2002 Nobel Prize for physiology or medicine with Robert Horvitz (1947–) and John Sulston (1942–).

Brunel, Isambard Kingdom (1806–59) English engineer and inventor, born Portsmouth. Helped to plan the Thames Tunnel and later planned the Clifton Suspension Bridge. Designed the first steamship to cross the Atlantic and the first ocean screw-steamer. In 1833 appointed engineer to the Great Western Railway and constructed all tunnels, bridges and viaducts on that line; also constructed and improved many docks.

Celsius, Anders (1701–44) Swedish astronomer, born Uppsala. Devised the centigrade, or 'Celsius', scale of temperature. Also advocated the introduction of the Gregorian calendar, and made observations of the aurora borealis, or northern lights.

Chadwick, Sir James (1891–1974) English physicist, born near Macclesfield. Studied radioactivity and, as a result of the Curies' work, was able to confirm the existence of the neutron, which Rutherford had postulated in 1920. Built Britain's first cyclotron in 1935 and assisted in atomic bomb research in America during World War II.

Chandrasekhar, Subrahmanyan (1910–95) Indian US astrophysicist, born Lahore (now in Pakistan). Showed that at the end of their lives, stars of less than a certain critical mass will collapse to form white dwarfs. Shared the 1983 Nobel Prize for physics with William Fowler (1911–95).

Charles, Jacques-Alexandre-César (1746–1823) French experimental physicist, born Beaugency. Formulated Charles's law, which relates the volume of a gas at constant pressure to its absolute temperature.

Copernicus, Nicolaus (1473–1543) Polish astronomer, born Toruń. Studied mathematics, optics, perspective and canon law before pursuing a varied career involving law, medicine and astronomy. Published a theory in 1543 that the Sun is at the centre of the Universe; this was not initially accepted owing to opposition from the Church, which held that the Universe was Earth-centred.

Coulomb, Charles Augustin de (1736–1806) French physicist, born Angoulême. Experimented on friction, and invented the torsion balance for measuring the force of magnetic and electrical attraction. The unit of electric charge (coulomb) is named after him.

Crick, Francis Harry Compton (1916–2004) English biologist, born Northampton. Constructed a molecular model of the complex genetic material deoxyribonucleic acid (DNA). Later research on nucleic acids led to far-reaching discoveries concerning the genetic code. Joint winner of the Nobel Prize for physiology or medicine in 1962 with James Watson (1928–).

Curie, Marie (originally **Manya**) née **Sklodowska** (1867–1934) Polish–French physicist, born Warsaw. Worked on magnetism and radioactivity, isolating radium and polonium. Shared the Nobel Prize for physics in 1903 with her husband, Pierre Curie (1859–1906), and Antoine Henri Becquerel (1852–1908). Became professor of physics at the Sorbonne in 1906; awarded the Nobel Prize for chemistry in 1911. Element 96 is named curium after the Curies.

Curie, Pierre (1859–1906) French chemist and physicist, born Paris. Carried out research on magnetism and radioactivity with his wife, Marie Curie (1867–1934), for which they were jointly awarded the Nobel Prize for physics in 1903, with Antoine Henri Becquerel (1852–1908).

Cuvier, Georges (Léopold Chrétien Frédéric Dagobert) (1769–1832) French anatomist, born Montbéliard. Linked comparative anatomy and palaeontology through studies of animal and fish fossils, and is known as the father of comparative anatomy and palaeontology. Also originated the natural system of animal classification. He opposed the theory of evolution, instead favouring catastrophism (a series of mass extinctions).

Dalton, John (1766–1844) English chemist, born Eaglesfield, near Cockermouth. Researched mixed gases, the force of steam, the elasticity of vapours and deduced the law of partial pressures, or Dalton's law. Also made important contributions in atomic theory.

Darwin, Charles Robert (1809–82) English naturalist, born Shrewsbury. Recommended as naturalist for a scientific survey of South American waters (1831–6) on HMS *Beagle*, during which he made many geological and zoological discoveries that led him to speculate on the origin of species. In 1859 published his theory of evolution in *The Origin of Species by Means of Natural Selection*.

Davy, Sir Humphry (1778–1829) English chemist, born Penzance. Experimented with newly discovered gases, and discovered the anaesthetic effect of nitrous oxide (laughing gas). Discovered the new metals potassium, sodium, barium, strontium, magnesium and calcium. Also investigated volcanic action, devised safety lamps for use in mining and was important in promoting science within industry.

Dawkins, Richard (1941–) British zoologist, born Nairobi, Kenya. Developed views on evolution in books such as *The Selfish Gene* (1976), *The Blind Watchmaker* (1986), *Climbing Mount Improbable* (1996) and *The Ancestor's Tale* (2004). Introduced the concept of the 'meme', a unit of cultural transmission.

Delbrück, Max (1906–81) German–US biophysicist, born Berlin. Made significant contributions to the creation of bacterial and bacteriophage genetics, and in 1946 showed that viruses can recombine genetic material. Joint winner of the 1969 Nobel Prize for physiology or medicine with Alfred Hershey (1908–1997) and Salvador Luria (1912–1991) for his work in viral genetics.

Descartes, René (1596–1650) French philosopher and mathematician, born near Tours. Creator of analytical or co-ordinate geometry, also named after him as Cartesian geometry. Also theorized extensively in physics and physiology, and is regarded as the father of modern philosophy.

Dirac, Paul Adrien Maurice (1902–84) English mathematical physicist, born Bristol. Published a complete mathematical formulation of the relativity theory of Albert Einstein after work on quantum mechanics. Joint winner of the 1933 Nobel Prize for physics with Erwin Schrödinger (1887–1961).

Doherty, Peter Charles (1940–) Australian immunologist, born Brisbane. Joint winner of 1996 Nobel Prize for physiology or medicine (with Swiss immunologist Rolf M Zinkernagel, 1944–) for his research into the human immune system. Also received the Paul Ehrlich Prize in 1983 and became FRS in 1987.

Doppler, Christian Johann (1803–53) Austrian physicist, born Salzburg. Published a paper in 1842 describing the Doppler effect, an increase and decrease of wave frequency observed when a wave source and the observer respectively approach or recede from one another.

Duchenne, Guillaume Benjamin Amand (1806–75) French physician, born Boulogne. Pioneer in electrophysiology and founder of electrotherapeutics. First to describe locomotor ataxia, in 1858. Also described pseudohypertrophic muscular atrophy, now known as Duchenne Muscular Dystrophy.

Dulbecco, Renato (1914–) Italian–US biologist, born Catanzaro. Showed how certain viruses can transform some cells into a cancerous state, giving a valuable simple model system for which he shared the 1975 Nobel Prize for physiology or medicine with David Baltimore (1938–) and Howard Temin (1934–94).

Edison, Thomas Alva (1847–1931) US inventor and physicist, born Milan, Ohio. Took out more than 1000 patents, including the gramophone (1877), the incandescent light bulb (1879) and an improved microphone for Bell's telephone. Also discovered thermionic emission, formerly called the Edison effect.

Ehrlich, Paul (1854–1915) German bacteriologist, born Strehlen (now Strzelin), Silesia. Pioneer in haematology and chemotherapy, he synthesized salvarsan as a treatment for syphilis. Also propounded the side-chain theory in immunology, for which he was joint winner of the 1908 Nobel Prize for physiology or medicine with Ilya Metchnikov (1845–1916).

Einstein, Albert (1879–1955) German–Swiss–US mathematical physicist, born Ulm, Bavaria. Achieved world fame through his special and general theories of relativity (1905 and 1916); also studied gases and discovered the photoelectric effect, for which he was awarded the Nobel Prize for physics in 1921. Element 99 was named einsteinium after him.

Ernst, Richard Robert (1933–) Swiss physical chemist, born Winterthur. Awarded the 1991 Nobel Prize for chemistry for innovations in nuclear magnetic resonance (NMR) spectroscopy. Also received the 1986 Benoist Prize and the 1990 Ampère Prize.

Euclid (fl.300 BC) Greek mathematician who taught in Alexandria, where he appears to have founded a mathematical school. His *Elements of Geometry* is the earliest substantial Greek mathematical treatise to have survived, and is probably the most widely known mathematical work.

Euler, Leonhard (1707–83) Swiss mathematician, born Basel. Published over 800 different books and papers on mathematics, physics and astronomy, introducing many new functions and carrying out important work in calculus. Introduced many important mathematical notations, including e (the base of the natural logarithm) and i (the square root of -1). Also studied motion and celestial mechanics.

Eysenck, Hans Jurgen (1916–97) German–British psychologist, born Berlin. Researched the variations in human personality and intelligence, and frequently championed the view that genetic factors are to a large extent responsible for psychological differences between people.

Fahrenheit, Gabriel Daniel (1686–1736) German physicist, born Danzig. Devised the alcohol thermometer (1709) and later invented the mercury thermometer (1714). Also devised the temperature scale named after him, and was the first to show that the boiling point of liquids varies at different atmospheric pressures.

Faraday, Michael (1791–1867) English chemist and physicist, born Grenoble. Discovered electromagnetic induction (1831), the laws of electrolysis (1833) and the rotation of polarized light by magnetism (1845). First to isolate benzene and to synthesize chlorocarbons. The unit of electrical capacitance, the farad, is named after him.

Fermat, Pierre de (1601–65) French mathematician, born Beaumont. Made many discoveries about the properties of numbers, probability, geometry and optics. A proof of his so-called 'last theorem' was announced in 1993 by Andrew Wiles (1953–).

Fermi, Enrico (1901–54) Italian–US nuclear physicist, born Rome. Published a statistical method of calculating atomic properties. In 1943 succeeded in splitting the nuclei of uranium atoms to produce artificial radioactive substances; awarded the 1938 Nobel Prize for physics for this work. Constructed the first US nuclear reactor at Chicago (1942). Element 100 was named fermium after him, and a class of subatomic particle is now known as the fermion.

Feynman, Richard Phillips (1918–88) US physicist, born New York City. Made considerable theoretical advances in quantum electrodynamics, for which he was joint winner of the 1965 Nobel Prize for physics with Julian Schwinger (1918–94) and Sinitiro Tomonaga (1906–79). Involved in building the first atomic bomb during World War II.

Fleming, Sir Alexander (1881–1955) Scottish bacteriologist, born Loudoun, Ayrshire. Was the first to use anti-typhoid vaccines on humans, and pioneered the use of salvarsan to treat syphilis. In 1928 discovered penicillin by chance. For this he was joint winner of the 1945 Nobel Prize for physiology or medicine with Ernst Chain (1906–79) and Sir Howard Florey (1898–1968), who developed large-scale production of the drug.

Foucault, Jean Bernard Léon (1819–68) French physicist, born Paris. Determined the velocity of light using a revolving mirror, and proved that light travels more slowly in water than in air (1850). In 1851, by means of a freely suspended pendulum, he proved that the Earth rotates. In 1852 he constructed the gyroscope and in 1857 the Foucault prism.

Franklin, Rosalind Elsie (1920–58) English X-ray crystallographer, born London. Together with Maurice Wilkins (1916–2004), used X-ray crystallography techniques to obtain data on the structure of DNA. This work was instrumental in allowing James Watson (1928–) and Francis Crick (1916–2004) to deduce the helical structure of DNA. Franklin died before she could be considered for the Nobel Prize later awarded to Watson, Crick and Wilkins.

Freud, Sigmund (1856–1939) Austrian neurologist and founder of psychoanalysis, born Freiburg. Developed the technique of conversational 'free association' in place of hypnosis, and refined psychoanalysis as a method of treatment. Argued that dreams are disguised manifestations of repressed sexual desires, and propounded theories of infantile sexuality and the division of the unconscious mind into the 'Id', the 'Ego' and the 'Super-Ego'.

Frisch, Karl von (1886–1982) Austrian ethologist and zoologist, born Vienna. Developed ethology using field observation of animals combined with ingenious experiments. Showed that forager bees communicate information (on the location of food sources) in part by use of coded dances (waggle dances). Joint winner of the Nobel Prize for physiology or medicine in 1973 with Konrad Lorenz (1903–89) and Nikolaas Tinbergen (1907–88).

Gadolin, Johan (1760–1852) Finnish chemist, born Turku. He is remembered for his investigations of the rare earth elements, analysing a new black mineral from Ytterby, Sweden, and isolating from it a rare earth mineral, yttria, in 1794. This was an important step towards identifying the remaining undiscovered elements. Element 64 was named gadolinium after him.

Gajdusek, (Daniel) Carleton (1923–2008) US virologist, born Yonkers, New York. Studied the origin and dissemination of the infectious disease kuru amongst the Fore people of Papua New Guinea, work that eventually led to the theory that kuru, BSE and CJD are caused by novel infectious proteins known as prions. Joint winner of the 1976 Nobel Prize for physiology or medicine with Baruch Blumberg (1925–).

Galen (c.130–c.201 AD) Greek physician, born Pergamum. Wrote on medical and philosophical subjects, collated all the medical knowledge of his time, and was an active experimentalist. Venerated for many centuries as the standard authority on medical matters.

Galilei, Galileo, known as **Galileo** (1564–1642) Italian astronomer, mathematician and natural philosopher, born Pisa. Inferred the value of a pendulum for exact measurement of time, proved that all falling bodies, great or small, descend due to gravity at the same rate. Perfected the refracting telescope and pursued astronomical observations that revealed mountains and valleys on the Moon, four satellites of Jupiter, and sunspots. These observations convinced him of the correctness of the Copernican theory that the Earth moves around the Sun. His advocation of the Copernican theory led to his imprisonment by the Inquisition; he remained under house arrest until his death.

Galvani, Luigi (1737–98) Italian physiologist, born Bologna. Proposed the theory of 'animal electricity' or 'galvanism', later shown to be attributable to other sources. Gave his name to the galvanometer, used from 1820 to detect electric current.

Gauss, Carl Friedrich (1777–1855) German mathematician, astronomer and physicist, born Brunswick. Made significant new advances in number theory, studied errors of observation and devised the method of least squares for fitting a curve to a data set. Also carried out much work on pure mathematics, studied the Earth's magnetism and was involved in the development of the magnetometer, as well as giving a mathematical theory of optical systems of lenses.

Gay-Lussac, Joseph Louis (1778–1850) French chemist and physicist, born Saint-Léonard. Established the law governing the expansion of gases in relation to their temperature, independently of Jacques Charles. Also formulated the law of combining volumes of gases (Gay-Lussac's law).

Geiger, Hans Wilhelm (1882–1945) German physicist, born Neustadt-an-der-Haart. Investigated beta-ray radioactivity and, with Walther Müller (1905–79), devised a counter to measure it.

Gell-Mann, Murray (1929–) US theoretical physicist, born New York City. Developed the theory of 'strangeness' to explain the behaviour of subatomic particles. With George Zweig introduced the concept of quarks as the basic building blocks of certain subatomic particles such as protons and neutrons. Awarded the 1969 Nobel Prize for physics.

Gould, Stephen Jay (1941–2002) US palaeontologist, born New York City. His ideas on evolution, history and culture appeared in popular collections of essays such as *Bully for Brontosaurus* (1991). He became best known for his theory of 'punctuated equilibrium', or rapid evolutionary change followed by stasis.

Halley, Edmond (1656–1742) English astronomer and mathematician, born London. Studied the solar system and correctly predicted the return (in 1758, 1835 and 1910) of a comet that had been observed in 1583, and is now named after him.

Harvey, William (1578–1657) English physician, born Folkestone. Discovered the circulation of the blood, and proposed that the heart is a muscle that pumps the blood around the body.

Hawking, Stephen William (1942–) English theoretical physicist, born Oxford. Research on relativity led him to study gravitational singularities such as the 'Big Bang', out of which the Universe is thought to have originated, and 'black holes', which result from the death of stars. His book *A Brief History of Time* is a popular account of modern cosmology. Since the 1960s he has suffered from a highly disabling progressive neuromotor disease.

Heisenberg, Werner Karl (1901–76) German theoretical physicist, born Würzburg. Developed quantum mechanics and formulated the principle of indeterminacy (uncertainty principle), for which he was awarded the 1932 Nobel Prize for physics.

Helmholtz, Hermann (Ludwig Ferdinand von) (1821–94) German physiologist and physicist, born Potsdam. Researched physiology of vision, the ear and the nervous system as well as making important contributions in fluid dynamics, studies of vibrations and the spectrum, and studies of the development of electric current within a galvanic battery.

Henle, Friedrich Gustav Jakob (1809–85) German anatomist, born Fürth. Discovered the portion of the kidney nephron, known as the loop of Henle, that allows water and salt to be reabsorbed from the urine. Wrote treatises on systematic anatomy.

Herschel, Sir John Frederick William (1792–1871) English astronomer, born Slough. Son of Sir William Herschel; continued his father's research and discovered 525 nebulae and clusters. Pioneered celestial photography and researched photoactive chemicals and the wave theory of light.

Herschel, Sir (Frederick) William (1738–1822) German–British astronomer, born Hanover. Made a reflecting telescope (1773–4) with which he discovered the planet Uranus in 1781. Also discovered satellites of Uranus and Saturn, the rotation of Saturn's rings and Saturn's rotation period. Researched binary stars, nebulae and the Milky Way.

Hertz, Heinrich Rudolph (1857–94) German physicist, born Hamburg. Confirmed James Clerk Maxwell's predictions in 1887 by his discovery of invisible electromagnetic waves, of the same fundamental form as light waves. The SI unit of frequency is named hertz after him.

Hippocrates (d.377 or 359 BC) Greek physician, born Cos. Known as the 'father of medicine', and revered as the most celebrated physician of antiquity. His followers developed his (erroneous) theories that four fluids or 'humours' of the body are the primary seats of disease. His name is remembered in the 'Hippocratic oath'.

Hooke, Robert (1635–1703) English chemist, physicist and architect, born Freshwater, Isle of Wight. Anticipated the invention of the steam engine, formulated Hooke's Law of the extension and compression of elastic bodies, and anticipated Isaac Newton's inverse square law of gravitation. Constructed the first reflecting telescope and inferred the rotation of Jupiter. Also materially improved or invented the compound microscope, the quadrant and a marine barometer.

Hubble, Edwin Powell (1889–1953) US astronomer, born Marshfield, Missouri. Demonstrated that some nebulae are independent galaxies. In 1929 discovered galaxy 'redshift', the phenomenon whereby distant galaxies are receding from us and the apparent speed of recession of a galaxy is proportional to its distance from us.

Hunt, Sir (Richard) Tim(othy) (1943–) English biologist, born Neston, Cheshire. Made important discoveries regarding the regulation of the cell cycle, allowing more accurate cancer diagnostics. Appointed Principal Scientist at the Cancer Research UK's London Institute in 1991. Joint winner of the 2001 Nobel Prize for physiology or medicine with Leland Hartwell (1939–) and Sir Paul Nurse (1949–).

Hutton, James (1726–97) Scottish geologist, born Edinburgh. Pioneered modern geology by proposing the theory of uniformitarianism, emphasizing that the formation of rocks is a continuous process and that the same processes have taken place throughout time.

Huxley, Thomas Henry (1825–95) English biologist, born Ealing. Assistant surgeon on a surveying expedition to the South Seas (1846–50), during which he collected marine invertebrate specimens and carried out comparative anatomical research. Became the foremost scientific supporter of Charles Darwin's theory of evolution. Also studied fossils and later turned to philosophy and theology.

Huygens, Christiaan (1629–93) Dutch physicist, born The Hague. Made the first pendulum clock (1657), based on a suggestion by Galileo (1564–1642), and developed Galileo's doctrine of accelerated motion under gravity. Discovered the rings and fourth satellite of Saturn and the laws of collision of elastic bodies, and first proposed the wave theory of light.

Jansky, Karl Guthe (1905–50) US radio engineer, born Norman, Oklahoma. Discovered astronomical radio sources by chance while investigating interference on short-wave radio telephone transmissions, initiating the science of radio astronomy. The SI unit of radio emission strength, the jansky, is named after him.

Jeans, Sir James Hopwood (1877–1946) English physicist and astronomer, born Ormskirk, near Southport. Made important contributions to the dynamical theory of gases, radiation, quantum theory and stellar evolution; best known for his role in popularizing physics and astronomy.

Jeffreys, Sir Alec John (1950–) English molecular biologist, born Oxford. Developed the technique of 'DNA fingerprinting', in which DNA from an individual can be broken down and separated into a unique pattern of fragments.

Jenner, Edward (1749–1823) English physician, born Berkeley. In 1796 made the revolutionary discovery of vaccination by inoculating a child first with cowpox and then with smallpox, and finding that the child failed to develop the disease. Within five years vaccination was being practised in many parts of the world.

Joule, James Prescott (1818–89) English physicist, born Salford. Showed experimentally that heat is a form of energy and established the mechanical equivalent of heat; this became the basis for the theory of conservation of energy. With Lord Kelvin he studied temperatures of gases and formulated the absolute scale of temperature. The joule, a unit of work or energy, is named after him.

Jung, Carl (Gustav) (1875–1961) Swiss psychiatrist, born Kesswil. After collaborating with Sigmund Freud, went on to develop his own theories of 'analytical psychology'. Described psychological types ('extraversion/introversion'), and propounded the concepts of the 'collective unconscious' and the psyche as a 'self-regulating system', expressing itself in the process of 'individuation'.

Science and Technology

Kant, Immanuel (1724–1804) German philosopher, born Königsberg, Prussia (now Kaliningrad, Russia). Researched astronomy and geophysics, and predicted the existence of the planet Uranus before its discovery. His philosophical works had enormous influence.

Katz, Sir Bernard (1911–2003) German–British biophysicist, born Leipzig. Discovered how the neural transmitter acetylcholine is released by neural impulses. Joint winner of the 1970 Nobel Prize for physiology or medicine with Ulf von Euler (1905–83) and Julius Axelrod (1912–2004).

Kelvin, William Thomson, 1st Baron (1824–1907) Irish–Scottish physicist and mathematician, born Belfast. Solved important problems in electrostatics, proposed the absolute, or Kelvin, temperature scale and established the second law of thermodynamics simultaneously with Rudolf Clausius. Also investigated geomagnetism and hydrodynamics, and invented instruments.

Kepler, Johannes (1571–1630) German astronomer, born Württemberg. Formulated laws of planetary motion describing elliptical orbits and forming the starting point of modern astronomy. Also made discoveries in optics, physics and geometry.

Kirchhoff, Gustav Robert (1824–87) German physicist, born Königsberg, Prussia (now Kaliningrad, Russia). Carried out important research in electricity, heat, optics and spectrum analysis. His work led to the discovery of caesium and rubidium (1859).

Krebs, Sir Edwin Gerhard (1918–) US biochemist, born Lansing, Iowa. Elected FRS in 1947. Together with Edmond Fischer (1920–), showed that glycogen enzymes are regulated by the addition and removal of phosphate groups, for which work they were awarded the 1992 Nobel Prize for physiology or medicine. Krebs later studied the structure and properties of the enzymes that carry out these additions and removals.

Krebs, Sir Hans Adolf (1900–81) German–British biochemist, born Hildesheim. Discovered the series of chemical reactions known as the urea cycle (1932). Joint winner of the 1953 Nobel Prize for physiology or medicine for research into metabolic processes, particularly the 'Krebs cycle'.

Kroto, Sir Harold Walter (1939–) English chemist, born Wisbech, Cambridgeshire. Distinguished for his work in detecting unstable molecules, especially those found in space, and the discovery of the C₆₀ form of carbon (buckminsterfullerene). Joint winner of the 1996 Nobel Prize for chemistry (with Robert Curl, 1933– , and Richard Smalley, 1943–2005) for the C₆₀ work.

Lamarck, Jean (Baptiste Pierre Antoine de Monet) Chevalier de (1744–1829) French naturalist, born Bazentin. Made the basic distinction between vertebrates and invertebrates. Postulated that species could change over time (transmutation), preparing the way for the Darwinian theory of evolution, although his proposal that acquired characteristics can be inherited by later generations has largely been superseded by natural selection as a mechanism for evolution.

Langmuir, Irving (1881–1959) US physical chemist, born New York City. Worked at the General Electric Company for 41 years, and his many inventions include the gas-filled tungsten lamp and an improved vacuum pump. Awarded the 1932 Nobel Prize for chemistry for his work on solid and liquid surfaces.

Laplace, Pierre Simon, Marquis de (1749–1827) French mathematician and astronomer, born Beaumont-en-Auge. Researched the stability of planetary orbits and developed the nebular hypothesis of planetary origin. Also formulated the fundamental differential equation in physics that bears his name, and the modern form of probability theory.

Lavoisier, Antoine Laurent (1743–1794) French chemist, born Paris. Showed that air is a mixture of gases, identifying both oxygen and nitrogen. Devised the modern method of naming chemical compounds, and helped to introduce the metric system. Guillotined in revolutionary Paris for his role as a government tax-collector.

Lawrence, Ernest Orlando (1901–58) US physicist, born Canton, South Dakota. Constructed the first cyclotron for the production of artificial radioactivity (1929), allowing the development of the atomic bomb. Became the first director of the radiation laboratory at Berkeley, California, in 1936 and received the Nobel Prize for physics in 1939. Element 103 was named lawrencium after him.

Leibniz, Gottfried Wilhelm (1646–1716) German mathematician and philosopher, born Leipzig. Discovered calculus around the same time as Isaac Newton; also made original contributions in the fields of optics, mechanics, statistics, logic and probability, and laid the foundations of 18c philosophy.

Leishman, Sir William Boog (1865–1926) Scottish bacteriologist, born Glasgow. Discovered an effective vaccine for inoculation against typhoid and was first to discover the parasite (leishmania) of the disease kala-azar (also known as leishmaniasis).

Linnaeus, Carolus (Carl von Linné) (1707–78) Swedish naturalist and physician, born Raceshult. Introduced the modern binomial system of scientific nomenclature for plants and animals.

Lister, Joseph, Lord (1827–1912) English surgeon, born Upton. Professor in Glasgow, Edinburgh and London whose greatest work was the introduction of the antiseptic system (1867), which revolutionized modern surgery. He was the first medical man to be elevated to the peerage.

Lorentz, Hendrik Antoon (1853–1928) Dutch physicist, born Arnhem. Carried out important work in electromagnetism; joint winner of the Nobel Prize for physics in 1902 (with Pieter Zeeman, 1865–1943) for explaining the effect whereby atomic spectral lines are split in the presence of magnetic fields.

Lorenz, Konrad Zacharias (1903–89) Austrian zoologist and ethologist, born Vienna. Regarded as the father of ethology, favouring the study of the instinctive behaviour of animals in the wild. In 1935 published observations on imprinting in young birds by which hatchlings 'learn' to recognize substitute parents, and argued that while aggressive behaviour in humans is inborn, it may be channelled into other forms of activity, whereas in other animals it is purely survival-motivated.

Lyell, Sir Charles (1797–1875) Scottish geologist, born Kinnordy, Fife. Popularized the principle of uniformitarianism in geology, which proposes that geological changes have been gradual and produced by forces still at work rather than by catastrophic changes. His work significantly influenced Charles Darwin, although Lyell never accepted the theory of evolution by natural selection.

Mach, Ernst (1838–1916) Austrian physicist and

philosopher, born Turas, Moravia. Carried out experimental work on projectiles and the flow of gases. His name has been given to the ratio of the speed of an object through a gas to the speed of sound in the same gas (Mach number) and to the angle of a shock wave to the direction of motion (Mach angle).

Malpighi, Marcello (1628–94) Italian anatomist, born near Bologna. Discovered capillary blood vessels and made many pioneering discoveries in microscopic anatomy.

Marconi, (Marquis) Guglielmo (1874–1937) Italian physicist and inventor, born Bologna. Experimented with converting electromagnetic waves into electricity and achieved wireless telegraphy in 1895. In 1898 transmitted signals across the English Channel and in 1901 succeeded in sending Morse code signals across the Atlantic. Joint winner of the 1909 Nobel Prize for physics with Karl Braun (1850–1918). Later developed short-wave radio equipment and established a worldwide radio telegraph network for the British government.

Marshall, Barry J(ames) (1951–) Australian microbiologist, born Kalgoorlie, Western Australia. Collaborated with J Robin Warren to show that most stomach ulcers are caused by the *Helicobacter pylori* bacterium and can be treated with antibiotics. Marshall famously demonstrated this by infecting himself with the bacterium, becoming sick, and curing himself. With Warren, shared the 2005 Nobel Prize in physiology or medicine.

Maxwell, James Clerk (1831–79) Scottish physicist, born Edinburgh. Produced a mathematical theory of electromagnetism and identified light as electromagnetic radiation. Also suggested that invisible electromagnetic waves could be generated in a laboratory, as later carried out by Hertz. Other research included the kinetic theory of gases, the nature of Saturn's rings, colour perception and colour photography.

Medawar, Sir Peter Brian (1915–87) British zoologist and immunologist, born Rio de Janeiro. Pioneered experiments in skin grafting and the prevention of rejection in transplant operations. Joint winner of the Nobel Prize for physiology or medicine in 1960 with Sir Frank Macfarlane Burnet (1899–1985).

Mendel, Gregor Johann (1822–84) Austrian biologist and botanist, born near Udrau, Silesia. Became an abbot in 1868. Researched inheritance characteristics in plants, leading to the formulation of Mendel's law of segregation and the law of independent assortment. These principles became the basis of modern genetics.

Mendeleyev, Dmitri Ivanovich (1834–1907) Russian chemist, born Tobolsk. Formulated the periodic law and hence devised the periodic table, from which he predicted the existence of several elements that were subsequently discovered. Element 101 was named mendelevium after him.

Michaelis, Leonor (1875–1949) German–US biochemist, born Berlin. Made early deductions on enzyme action and is best known for the Michaelis–Menten equation describing the kinetics of enzyme-catalysed reactions. Also discovered that thioglycolic acid can dissolve keratin, thus enabling the development of the permanent wave ('perm') for hair.

Michelson, Albert Abraham (1852–1931) German–US physicist, born Strelno (now Strzelno, Poland). Carried out the famous Michelson–Morley experiment confirming the non-existence of

'ether', a result that set Einstein on the road to the theory of relativity. Became the first American scientist to win a Nobel Prize (physics) in 1907.

Millikan, Robert Andrews (1868–1953) US physicist, born Illinois. Awarded the Nobel Prize for physics in 1923 for determining the charge on the electron; also carried out important work on cosmic rays.

Milstein, César (1927–2002) British molecular biologist and immunologist, born Bahía Blanca, Argentina. Together with Georges Köhler (1946–95), devised the hybridoma technique for the production of monoclonal antibodies. Milstein and Köhler shared the 1984 Nobel Prize for physiology or medicine with Niels Jerne (1911–94).

Mullis, Kary Banks (1944–) US biochemist, born Lenoir, North Carolina. Developed the 'polymerase chain reaction' (PCR) technique, which allows tiny amounts of DNA to be copied millions of times. This has many analytical uses, including forensics and diagnosis of viral infections. Joint winner of the 1993 Nobel Prize for chemistry with Michael Smith (1932–2000). His more recent work has focused on the chemical manipulation of the immune system.

Napier, John (1550–1619) Scottish mathematician, born Edinburgh. Famous for the invention of logarithms to simplify computation, and for devising a calculating machine using a set of rods, known as 'Napier's Bones'.

Newton, Sir Isaac (1642–1727) English scientist and mathematician, born Woolsthorpe, Lincolnshire. Formulated his complete theory of gravitation by 1684. Also carried out important work in optics, concluding that the different colours of light making up white light are refracted differently, developed the reflecting telescope, and invented calculus around the same time as Leibniz.

Nurse, Sir Paul M(axime) (1949–) English biologist, born Norwich. Made important discoveries regarding the regulation of the cell cycle, allowing more accurate cancer diagnostics. Appointed Principal Scientist at the London Institute of the Imperial Cancer Research Fund (now part of Cancer Research UK) in 1991. Joint winner of the 2001 Nobel Prize for physiology or medicine with Leland Hartwell (1939–) and Sir Tim Hunt (1943–).

Ohm, Georg Simon (1787–1854) German physicist, born Erlangen. In 1827 published 'Ohm's law', relating voltage, current and resistance in an electrical circuit. The SI unit of electrical resistance is named after him.

Oppenheimer, (Julius) Robert (1904–67) US nuclear physicist, born New York City. Led the atomic bomb development project at Los Alamos during World War II and continued to play an important role in US atomic energy policy after the war. Opposed the development of the hydrogen bomb, and was suspended from secret nuclear research in 1953.

Parkinson, James (1755–1824) English physician, born London. Gave the first description of paralysis agitans, or Parkinson's disease. Described appendicitis and perforation of the appendix, and was first to recognize perforation as a cause of death.

Pascal, Blaise (1623–62) French mathematician and physicist, born Clermont-Ferrand. Carried out important work in geometry, invented a calculating machine, and demonstrated that air pressure decreases with altitude as previously predicted and developed probability theory. The SI unit of pressure (pascal) and the modern

Science and Technology

computer programming language, Pascal, are named after him.

Pasteur, Louis (1822–95) French chemist, born Dôle. Father of modern bacteriology. Discovered the possibility of attenuating the virulence of injurious micro-organisms by exposure to air, by variety of culture, or by transmission through various animals, and demonstrated that the attenuated organisms could be used for immunization. From this he developed vaccinations against anthrax and rabies. Introduced pasteurization (moderate heating) to kill disease-producing organisms in wine, milk and other foods. Also discovered that certain molecules can exist in two distinct chiral ('handed') forms.

Pauli, Wolfgang (1900–58) Austrian–US theoretical physicist, born Vienna. Formulated the exclusion principle (1924), which states that no two electrons can be in the same energy state. This led to important advances in the application of quantum theory to the periodic table of elements. He was awarded the Nobel Prize for physics in 1945.

Pauling, Linus (1901–94) US chemist, born Portland, Oregon. He made important discoveries concerning chemical bonding and complex molecular structures; this led him into work on the chemistry of biological molecules and the chemical basis of hereditary disease. He was awarded the 1954 Nobel Prize for chemistry, and also the 1962 Nobel Peace Prize for his campaigning against nuclear weapons.

Pavlov, Ivan Petrovich (1849–1936) Russian physiologist, born near Ryazan. Studied the physiology of circulation, digestion and 'conditioned' or acquired reflexes, believing the brain's only function to be to couple neurones to produce reflexes. Awarded the Nobel Prize for physiology or medicine in 1904.

Perutz, Max Ferdinand (1914–2002) Austrian–British biochemist, born Vienna. Studied the structure of haemoglobin, for which work he was the joint winner of the 1962 Nobel Prize for chemistry with John Kendrew (1917–97).

Planck, Max Karl Ernst (1858–1947) German theoretical physicist, born Kiel. Researched thermodynamics and black-body radiation. This led him to formulate quantum theory (1900), which assumes that energy changes take place in small discrete instalments or quanta. Awarded the Nobel Prize for physics in 1918.

Ptolemy or **Claudius Ptolemaeus** (c.90–168 AD) Egyptian astronomer and geographer, believed born Ptolemaeus Hermion. Corrected and improved the astronomical work of his predecessors to form the Ptolemaic System, described by Plato and Aristotle, with the Earth at the centre of the Universe and heavenly bodies revolving round it; beyond this lay the sphere of the fixed stars. Also compiled geographical catalogues and maps.

Purkinje, Jan Evangelista (1787–1869) Czech physiologist, born Libochowitz. Carried out research on the eye, brain, heart, muscles, embryology, digestion and sweat glands. Studied 'Purkinje's figure', an effect by which one can see in one's own eye the shadows of the retinal blood vessels, and 'Purkinje's cells', cells in the middle layer of the cerebellar cortex. Also discovered the 'Purkinje fibres' that conduct electrical impulses within the heart, causing it to contract in a co-ordinated manner.

Pythagoras (6c BC) Greek mathematician and philosopher, born Samos. Associated with mathematical discoveries involving the chief

musical intervals, the relations of numbers and the relations between the lengths of sides of right-angled triangles (Pythagoras's theorem). Profoundly influenced Plato and later astronomers and mathematicians.

Ramón y Cajal, Santiago (1852–1934) Spanish physician and histologist, born Petilla de Aragon. Carried out important work on the brain and nerves, isolated the neuron and discovered how nerve impulses are transmitted to brain cells. Joint winner of the 1906 Nobel Prize for physiology or medicine with Camillo Golgi (1843–1926).

Rathke, Martin Heinrich (1793–1860) German biologist, born Danzig (now Gdańsk, Poland). Discovered gill-slits and gill-arches in embryo birds and mammals. 'Rathke's pocket' is the name given to the small pit on the dorsal side of the oral cavity of developing vertebrates.

Rayleigh, John William Strutt, 3rd Baron (1842–1919) English physicist, born near Maldon, Essex. Carried out valuable research on vibratory motion, the theory of sound and the wave theory of light. With Sir William Ramsay (1852–1916) discovered argon (1894). Awarded the Nobel Prize for physics in 1904.

Réaumur, René Antoine Ferchault de (1683–1757) French natural philosopher, born La Rochelle. Developed methods for producing iron, steel and porcelain, and became a leading naturalist. His alcohol and water thermometer (1731) introduced the Réaumur temperature scale.

Richter, Charles Francis (1900–85) US seismologist, born near Hamilton, Ohio. Devised the scale of earthquake strength that bears his name (1927–35).

Röntgen, Wilhelm Konrad von (1845–1923) German physicist, born Lennep, Prussia. Discovered the electromagnetic rays that he called X-rays (also known as Röntgen rays) in 1895. For his work on X-rays he was joint winner of the Rumford medal in 1896 and winner of the 1901 Nobel Prize for physics. Also carried out important work on the heat conductivity of crystals, the specific heat of gases, and the electromagnetic rotation of polarized light.

Rutherford, Ernest, 1st Baron Rutherford of Nelson (1871–1937) New Zealand–British physicist, born Spring Grove, near Nelson. Made the first successful wireless transmissions over two miles. Discovered the three types of uranium radiations, formulated a theory of atomic disintegration and determined the nature of alpha particles; this led to a new atomic model in which the mass is concentrated in the nucleus. Also discovered that alpha-ray bombardment could produce atomic transformation, and predicted the existence of the neutron. Awarded the Nobel Prize for chemistry in 1908.

Schrödinger, Erwin (1887–1961) Austrian physicist, born Vienna. Originated the study of wave mechanics as part of the quantum theory with the celebrated Schrödinger wave equation, for which he was joint winner of the 1933 Nobel Prize for physics with P A M Dirac (1902–1984). Also made contributions to field theory.

Schwann, Theodor (1810–82) German physiologist, born Neuss. Discovered the digestive enzyme pepsin, investigated muscle contraction, demonstrated the role of micro-organisms in putrefaction and extended the cell theory, previously applied to plants, to animal tissues. Also discovered Schwann cells, which form a sheath around nerve fibres to aid the transmission of impulses.

Sharp, Phillip Allen (1944–) US molecular biologist, born Kentucky. Invented the mapping technique used in the analysis of RNA molecules. This led to the discovery that genes are split into several sections or exons, separated by stretches of DNA (introns) that appear to carry no genetic information. Shared the 1993 Nobel Prize for physiology or medicine with Richard Roberts (1943–).

Sörensen, Sören Peter Lauritz (1868–1939) Danish biochemist, born Havrabjerg, Slagelsi. Carried out pioneering research on hydrogen ion concentration, and invented the pH scale for measuring acidity in 1909.

Szent-Györgyi, Albert von Nagyrapolt (1893–1986) Hungarian–US biochemist, born Budapest. Discovered actin, which interacts with myosin and the energy source ATP during muscle contraction. Isolated vitamin C and studied cellular respiration; for this work he was awarded the Nobel Prize for physiology or medicine in 1937.

Tesla, Nikola (1856–1943) Yugoslav–US physicist and electrical engineer, born Smiljan (now in Croatia). His many inventions included improved dynamos, transformers, electric bulbs, and the high-frequency coil that now bears his name. He also did much to promote the use of alternating current for electricity suppy.

Thomson, Sir Joseph John (1856–1940) English physicist, born Cheetham Hill, near Manchester. Studied gaseous conductors of electricity and the nature of cathode rays; this led to his discovery of the electron. Also pioneered mass spectrometry and discovered the existence of different isotopes of elements. Awarded the Nobel Prize for physics in 1906.

Thomson, Sir William ▶ Kelvin, 1st Baron

Tinbergen, Nikolaas (1907–88) Dutch ethologist, born The Hague. Co-founder with Konrad Lorenz of the science of ethology (the study of animal behaviour in natural surroundings). Analysed social behaviour of certain animals and insects as an evolutionary process with considerable relevance to human behaviour, especially courtship and aggression. Joint winner of the 1973 Nobel Prize for physiology or medicine with Karl von Frisch (1886–1982) and Konrad Lorenz (1903–89).

Van de Graaff, Robert Jemison (1901–67) US physicist, born Tuscaloosa, Alabama. Conceived of an improved type of electrostatic generator, in which electric charge could be built up on a hollow metal sphere. Constructed the first model, later to be known as the Van de Graaff generator, which could generate potentials of over a million volts. Developed the generator for use as a particle accelerator for atomic and nuclear physicists. The generator was also adapted to produce high-energy X-rays for cancer treatment and for examination of the interior structure of heavy artillery.

Varmus, Harold (1939–) US molecular biologist, born New York. Awarded the 1989 Nobel Prize for physiology or medicine (jointly with Michael Bishop, 1936–) for the discovery of oncogenes, genes that can become overactive and cause cancer.

Volta, Alessandro Giuseppe Anastasio, Count (1745–1827) Italian physicist, born Como. Developed an electric battery able to produce a continuous flow of electrical current. Invented the electrophorus (a precursor to the induction motor) and the electroscope (a device for detecting electricity).

Also made investigations into heat and gases, and discovered methane. His name is given to the SI unit of electric potential difference, the volt.

Von Neumann, John (1903–57) Hungarian–US mathematician, born Budapest. Worked on the atomic bomb project at Los Alamos during World War II and later designed some of the earliest computers. Went on to invent the idea of self-replicating machines.

Waals, Johannes Diderik van der (1837–1923) Dutch physicist, born Leiden. Formulated the van der Waals equation, which defines the physical state of a gas or liquid, and investigated the weak attractive forces (van der Waals forces) between molecules. Awarded the Nobel Prize for physics in 1910.

Warburg, Otto Heinrich (1883–1970) German biochemist, born Freiburg, Baden. Carried out important research into cellular metabolism and especially that of cancer cells. Awarded the 1931 Nobel Prize for physiology or medicine; was offered a second Nobel Prize in 1944 but, as a Jew, was prevented by Hitler from accepting it.

Watson, James Dewey (1928–) US biologist, born Chicago. Deduced with Francis Crick (1916–2004) the two-stranded helical structure of DNA, for which they shared the 1962 Nobel Prize for physiology or medicine. Later became professor at Harvard and Director of the Cold Spring Harbor Laboratory in New York.

Watt, James (1736–1819) Scottish engineer and inventor, born Greenock. Developed and improved early models of the steam engine, and manufactured it from 1774. The watt, a unit of power, is named after him, and the term horsepower was first used by him.

Weinberg, Steven (1933–) US physicist, born New York City. In 1967 published the 'electroweak' theory of atomic interaction; for this he shared the 1979 Nobel Prize for physics with Abdus Salam (1926–96) and Sheldon Glashow (1932–). Published *The First Three Minutes* (about the early history of the universe) in 1977.

Wien, Wilhelm (1864–1928) German physicist, born Gaffken, East Prussia. Received the Nobel Prize for physics in 1911 for work on the radiation of energy from black bodies. Research also included investigation of X-rays and hydrodynamics.

Wiles, Sir Andrew John (1953–) English mathematician, born Cambridge. In 1995 published a proof of 'Fermat's last theorem', the conjecture made by the French mathematician Pierre de Fermat (1601–65) that the equation $x^n + y^n = z^n$ has no solutions for $n>2$. Awarded a special plaque by the International Mathematical Union in 1998, as he was too old to be awarded the Fields Medal. He was knighted in 2000.

Wilkins, Maurice Hugh Frederick (1916–2004) British physicist, born New Zealand. Together with Rosalind Franklin, used X-ray crystallography techniques to obtain data on the structure of DNA. This work was instrumental in allowing James Watson and Francis Crick to deduce the helical structure of DNA. Shared the 1962 Nobel Prize for physiology or medicine with Watson and Crick.

Young, Thomas (1773–1829) English physicist and physician, born Milverton, Somerset. Carried out experiments involving the generation of interference patterns by splitting beams of light, in support of the wave theory of light. Also made valuable contributions in haemodynamics, insurance and deciphering the inscriptions on the Rosetta Stone.

Science and Technology

Nobel Prizes

Nobel Prizes for chemistry, physics and physiology or medicine were first awarded in 1901.

Year	Chemistry	Physics	Physiology/Medicine
1937	Sir Norman Haworth, Paul Karrer	Clinton Davisson, Sir George Thomson	Albert von Szent-Györgyi
1938	Richard Kuhn	Enrico Fermi	Corneille Heymans
1939	Adolf Butenandt, Leopold Ružička	Ernest Orlando Lawrence	Gerhard Domagk
1940–2	No award		
1943	George de Hevesy	Otto Stern	Henrik Dam, Edward Doisy
1944	Otto Hahn	Isidor Isaac Rabi	Joseph Erlanger, Herbert Gasser
1945	Artturi Ilmari Virtanen	Wolfgang Pauli	Sir Ernst Chain, Sir Alexander Fleming, Baron (Howard) Florey
1946	James Batcheller Sumner, John Howard Northrop, Wendell Meredith Stanley	Percy Williams Bridgman	Hermann Joseph Muller
1947	Sir Robert Robinson	Sir Edward Victor Appleton	Carl Cori, Gerty Cori, Bernardo Houssay
1948	Arne Wilhelm Kaurin Tiselius	Baron (Patrick) Blackett	Paul Hermann Müller
1949	William Francis Giauque	Hideki Yukawa	Walter Hess, Antonio Egas Moniz
1950	Otto Paul Hermann Diels, Kurt Alder	Cecil Frank Powell	Philip Hench, Edward Kendall, Tadeus Reichstein
1951	Edwin Mattison McMillan, Glenn Theodore Seaborg	Sir John Douglas Cockcroft, Ernest Thomas Sinton Walton	Max Theiler
1952	A J P Martin, Richard Synge	Felix Bloch, Edward Mills Purcell	Selman Abraham Waksman
1953	Hermann Staudinger	Frederik Zernike	Sir Hans Krebs, Fritz Lipmann
1954	Linus Carl Pauling	Max Born, Walther Bothe	John Enders, Frederick Robbins, Thomas Weller
1955	Vincent du Vigneaud	Willis Lamb, Polykarp Kusch	Axel Hugo Theodor Theorell
1956	Sir Cyril Hinshelwood, Nikolay Semenov	William Shockley, John Bardeen, Walter Brattain	André Cournand, Werner Forssmann, Dickinson W Richards
1957	Lord Alexander R Todd	Chen Ning-Yang, Tsung-Dao Lee	Daniel Bovet
1958	Frederick Sanger	Pavel Cherenkov, Il'ja Frank, Igor Tamm	George Beadle, Edward Tatum, Joshua Lederberg
1959	Jaroslav Heyrovsky	Emilio Segrè, Owen Chamberlain	Arthur Kornberg, Severo Ochoa
1960	Willard Frank Libby	Donald A Glaser	Sir Macfarlane Burnet, Sir Peter Medawar
1961	Melvin Calvin	Robert Hofstadter, Rudolf Ludwig Mössbauer	Georg von Békésy
1962	Max Ferdinand Perutz, Sir John Cowdery Kendrew	Lev Davidovich Landau	Francis Crick, James Watson, Maurice Wilkins
1963	Karl Ziegler, Guilio Natta	Eugene Winger, Maria Goeppert-Mayer, Hans Jensen	Sir John Eccles, Sir Alan Hodgkin, Sir Andrew Huxley
1964	Dorothy Hodgkin	Charles H Townes, Nicolay Basov, Aleksandr Prokhorov	Konrad Bloch, Feodor Lynen
1965	Robert Burns Woodward	Sin-itiro Tomonaga, Julian Schwinger, Richard Feynman	François Jacob, André Lwoff, Jacques Monod
1966	Robert S Mulliken	Alfred Kastler	Peyton Rous, Charles Huggins
1967	Manfred Eigen, Ronald Norrish, Baron (George) Porter of Luddenham	Hans Albrecht Bethe	Ragnar Granit, Haldan Keffer Hartline, George Wald
1968	Lars Onsager	Luis W Alvarez	Robert Holley, Har Gobind Khorana, Marshall Nirenberg
1969	Sir Derek H R Barton, Odd Hassel	Murray Gell-Mann	Max Delbrück, Alfred D Hershey, Salvador E Luria
1970	Luis Federico Leloir	Louis Eugène Néel, Hannes Olof Alfvén	Sir Bernard Katz, Ulf von Euler, Julius Axelrod
1971	Gerhard Herzberg	Dennis Gabor	Earl W Sutherland, Jr
1972	Stanford Moore, William H Stein, Christian B Anfinsen	John Bardeen, Leon N Cooper, J Robert Schrieffer	Gerald M Edelman, Rodney R Porter

Science and Technology

Year	Chemistry	Physics	Physiology/Medicine
1973	Ernst Otto Fischer, Sir Geoffrey Wilkinson	Leo Esaki, Ivar Giaever, Brian D Josephson	Karl von Frisch, Konrad Lorenz, Nikolaas Tinbergen
1974	Paul J Flory	Sir Martin Ryle, Antony Hewish	Albert Claude, Christian de Duve, George E Palade
1975	Sir John Warcup Cornforth, Vladimir Prelog	Aage N Bohr, Ben R Mottelson, L James Rainwater	David Baltimore, Renato Dulbecco, Howard Temin
1976	William N Lipscomb	Burton Richter, Samuel Chao Chung Ting	Baruch S Blumberg, D Carleton Gajdusek
1977	Ilya Prigogine	Philip W Anderson, Sir Neville F Mott, John H van Vleck	Roger Guillemin, Andrew V Schally, Rosalyn Yalow
1978	Peter D Mitchell	Pyotr L Kapitsa, Arno A Penzias, Robert W Wilson	Werner Arber, Daniel Nathans, Hamilton O Smith
1979	Herbert C Brown, Georg Wittig	Steven Weinberg, Sheldon L Glashow, Abdus Salam	Allan M Cormack, Sir Godfrey N Hounsfield
1980	Paul Berg, Walter Gilbert, Frederick Sanger	James W Cronin, Val L Fitch	Baruj Benacerraf, George D Snell, Jean Dausset
1981	Kenichi Fukui, Roald Hoffman	Nicolaas Bloembergen, Arthur L Schawlow, Kai M Siegbahn	Roger W Sperry, David H Hubel, Torsten N Wiesel
1982	Sir Aaron Klug	Kenneth G Wilson	Sune K Bergström, Bengt I Samuelsson, Sir John Vane
1983	Henry Taube	Subramanyan Chandrasekhar, William A Fowler	Barbara McClintock
1984	Robert B Merrifield	Carlo Rubbia, Simon van der Meer	Niels K Jerne, Georges J F Köhler, César Milstein
1985	Herbert A Hauptman, Jerome Karle	Klaus von Klitzing	Joseph L Goldstein, Michael S Brown
1986	Dudley R Herschbach, Yuan Tseh Lee, John C Polanyi	Gerd Binnig, Heinrich Rohrer, Ernst Ruska	Stanley Cohen, Rita Levi-Montalcini
1987	Charles J Pedersen, Donald J Cram, Jean-Marie Lehn	J Georg Bednorz, K Alexander Müller	Susumu Tonegawa
1988	Johann Deisenhofer, Robert Huber, Hartmut Michel	Leon M Lederman, Melvin Schwartz, Jack Steinberger	Sir James W Black, Gertrude B Elion, George H Hitchings
1989	Sidney Altman, Thomas R Cech	Hans G Dehmelt, Wolfgang Paul, Norman F Ramsey	J Michael Bishop, Harold E Varmus
1990	Elias James Corey	Jerome I Friedman, Henry W Kendall, Richard E Taylor	Joseph E Murray, E Donnall Thomas
1991	Richard R Ernst	Pierre-Gilles de Gennes	Erwin Neher, Bert Sakmann
1992	Rudolph A Marcus	Georges Charpak	Edmond H Fischer, Edwin G Krebs
1993	Kary Banks Mullis, Michael Smith	Russell A Hulse, Joseph H Taylor Jr	Richard J Roberts, Phillip A Sharp
1994	George Olah	Clifford G Shull, Bertram N Brockhouse	Alfred G Gilman, Martin Rodbell
1995	F Sherwood Roland, Mario J Molina, Paul J Crutzen	Martin L Perl, Frederick Reines	Edward B Lewis, Christiane Nüsslein-Volhard, Eric F Wieschaus
1996	Sir Harold W Kroto, Robert F Curl, Jr, Richard E Smalley	David M Lee, Douglas D Osheroff, Robert C Richardson	Peter C Doherty, Rolf M Zinkernagel
1997	Jens C Skou, John E Walker, Paul D Boyer	Steven Chu, William D Phillips, Claude Cohen-Tannoudji	Stanley B Prusiner
1998	Walter Kohn, John A Pople	Robert B Laughlin, Horst L Störmer, Daniel C Tsui	Robert F Furchgott, Louis J Ignarro, Ferid Murad
1999	Ahmed H Zewail	Gerardus 't Hooft, Martinus J G Veltman	Günter Blobel
2000	Alan J Heeger, Alan G MacDiarmid, Hideki Shirakawa	Zhores I Alferov, Herbert Kroemer, Jack S Kilby	Arvid Carlsson, Paul Greengard, Eric Kandel
2001	William S Knowles, Ryoji Noyori, K Barry Sharpless	Eric A Cornell, Wolfgang Ketterle, Carl E Wieman	Leland H Hartwell, R Timothy Hunt, Sir Paul Nurse
2002	John B Fenn, Koichi Tanaka, Kurt Wüthrich	Raymond Davis Jr, Masatoshi Koshiba, Riccardo Giacconi	Sydney Brenner, H Robert Horvitz, John E Sulston
2003	Peter Agre, Roderick MacKinnon	Alexei A Abrikosov, Vitaly L Ginzburg, Anthony J Leggett	Paul C Lauterbur, Sir Peter Mansfield
2004	Aaron Ciechanover, Avram Hershko, Irwin Rose	David J Gross, H David Politzer, Frank Wilczek	Richard Axel, Linda B Buck
2005	Yves Chauvin, Robert H Grubbs, Richard R Schrock	Roy J Glauber, John L Hall, Theodor W Hänsch	Barry J Marshall, J Robin Warren
2006	Roger D Kornberg	John C Mather, George F Smoot	Andrew Z Fire, Craig C Mello

Science and Technology

Science and Technology

Year	Chemistry	Physics	Physiology/Medicine
2007	Gerhard Ertl	Albert Fert, Peter Grünberg	Mario R Capecchi, Sir Martin J Evans, Oliver Smithies
2008	Osamu Shimomura, Martin Chalfie, Roger Y Tsien	Yoichiro Nambu, Makoto Kobayashi, Toshihide Maskawa	Harald zur Hausen, Françoise Barré-Sinoussi, Luc Montagnier

Inventions

Name	Date	Inventor (nationality)*
adding machine (mechanical)	1623	Wilhelm Schickard (Ger)
adhesive (rubber-based glue)	1850	anon
adhesive (epoxy resin)	1958	Certas Co
aeroplane (steam powered)	1886	Clement Ader (Fr)
aeroplane	1903	Orville and Wilbur Wright (US)
aeroplane (swing-wing)	1954	Barnes Wallis (UK)
aerosol	1926	Erik Rotheim (Nor)
airship (non-rigid)	1851	Henri Giffard (Fr)
airship (rigid)	1900	Graf Ferdinand von Zeppelin (Ger)
ambulance	1792	Jean Dominique Larrey (Fr)
aspirin (introduction into medicine)	1899	Felix Hoffmann (Ger)
atomic bomb	1939–45	Otto Frisch (Aus), Niels Bohr (D), Rudolf Peierls (Ger), Robert Oppenheimer (US) and others
balloon (first manned flight)	1783	Jacques and Joseph Montgolfier (Fr)
barbed wire (first patent)	1867	Lucien B Smith (US)
barbed wire (manufacture)	1874	Joseph Glidden (US)
barbiturates (preparation of barbituric acid)	1863	Adolf von Baeyer (Pruss)
barometer	1643	Evangelista Torricelli (Ital)
battery (electric)	1800	Alessandro Volta (Ital)
bicycle	1839–40	Kirkpatrick MacMillan (UK)
bifocal lens	1780	Benjamin Franklin (US)
blood (artificial oxygen-carrying substitute)	1966	Clark and Gollan (US)
bronze (copper with tin)	c.3700 BC	Pre-dynastic Egypt
bunsen burner	1855	Robert Wilhelm Bunsen (Pruss)
burglar alarm	1858	Edwin T Holmes (US)
cable-car	1866	W Ritter (Ger) or anon (US)
calendar (modern)	525	Dionysius Exiguus (Scythian)
camera (polaroid)	1947	Edwin Land (US)
canning	1810	Nicolas Appert (Fr)
cannon	2c BC	Archimedes (Gr)
car (three-wheeled steam tractor)	1769	Nicolas Cugnot (Fr)
car (internal combustion)	1884	Gottlieb Daimler (Ger)
car (petrol)	1886	Karl Benz (Ger)
car (air-conditioning)	1902	J Wilkinson (US)
car (disc brakes)	1902	Frederick W Lanchester (UK)
car (speedometer)	1902	Thorpe and Salter (UK)
carbon fibres	1964	Courtaulds Ltd (UK)
carburettor	1876	Gottlieb Daimler (Ger)
carpet sweeper	1876	Melville Bissell (US)
cash register	1892	William Burroughs (US)
celluloid	1870	John W Hyatt (US)
cement (Portland)	1824	Joseph Aspdin (UK)
chocolate (solid)	1819	François-Louis Cailler (Swiss)
chocolate (solid, milk)	1875	Daniel Peter (Swiss)
chronometer	1735	John Harrison (UK)
cinema	1895	Auguste and Louis Lumière (Fr)
cinema (wide screen)	1900	Raoul Grimoin-Sanson (Fr)
clock (mechanical)	725	I-Hsing (Chinese)
clock (pendulum)	1657	Christiaan Huygens (NL)
clock (quartz)	1929	Warren Alvin Marrison (US)
coffee (instant)	1937	Nestlé (Swiss)
compact disc	1979	Philips (NL) and Sony (Japanese)
compass (discovery of magnetite)	1c	China
compass (first record of mariner's compass)	1187	Alexander Neckam (UK)

Name	Date	Inventor (nationality)*
computer (mechanical, fully programmable)	1835	Charles Babbage (UK)
computer (electronic, digital, stored program)	1949	J Presper Eckert, John W Mauchly, John von Neumann (US)
concrete	1c	anon, Rome
concrete (reinforced)	1892	François Hennebique (Fr)
contact lenses	1887	Adolph E Fick (Ger)
contraceptive pill	1950	Gregory Pincus (US)
corrugated iron	1853	Pierre Carpentier (Fr)
credit card	1950	Ralph Scheider (US)
crossword	1913	Arthur Wynne (US) in *New York World*
crystal (glass)	c.1450	anon, Venice
decompression chamber	1929	Robert H Davis (UK)
dental plate	1817	Anthony A Plantson (US)
dental plate (rubber)	1854	Charles Goodyear (US)
detergents	1916	anon, Germany
diesel engine	1892	Rudolf Diesel (Ger)
dishwasher (automatic)	1889	Mrs W A Cockran (US)
drill (pneumatic)	1861	Germain Sommelier (Fr)
drill (electric, hand)	1895	Wilhelm Fein (Ger)
electric chair	1888	Harold P Brown and E A Kenneally (US)
electric flat iron	1882	Henry W Seeley (US)
electric generator	1831	Michael Faraday (UK)
electric guitar	1931	Adolph Rickenbacker, Barth and Beauchamp (US)
electric heater	1887	W Leigh Burton (US)
electric light bulb	1879	Thomas Alva Edison (US)
electric motor (AC)	1888	Nikola Tesla (US)
electric motor (DC)	1870	Zenobe Gramme (Belg)
electric oven	1889	Bernina Hotel, Switzerland
electrocardiography	1903	Willem Einthoven (NL)
electromagnet	1824	William Sturgeon (UK)
encyclopedia	c.47 BC	Marcus Terentius Varro (Roman)
endoscope	1827	Pierre Segalas (Fr)
escalator	1892	Jesse W Reno (US)
explosives (nitroglycerine)	1847	Ascanio Sobrero (Ital)
explosives (dynamite)	1866	Alfred Nobel (Swed)
extinguisher	1866	François Carlier (Fr)
facsimile machine (fax)	1907	Arthur Korn (Ger)
ferrofluids	1968	Ronald Rosensweig (US)
film (moving outlines)	1874	Jules Janssen (Fr)
	1888	Louis Le Prince (Fr)
	1891	Thomas Alva Edison (US)
film (with soundtrack)	1896	Lee De Forest (US)
forceps (obstetric)	c.1630	Peter Chamberlen (UK)
freeze-drying	1906	Arsene D'Arsonval and Georges Bordas (Fr)
galvanometer	1834	André Marie Ampère (Fr)
gas lighting	1792	William Murdock (UK)
gearbox (automatic)	1910	Hermann Fottinger (Ger)
glass (heat-resistant)	1884	Carl Zeiss (Ger)
glass (stained)	pre-850	Europe
glass (toughened)	1893	Leon Appert (Fr)
glass fibre	1713	René de Réaumur (Fr)
glass fibre (industrial)	1931	Owens Illinois Glass Co (US)
glassware	c.2600 BC	Egypt
glider	1853	George Cayley (UK)
gramophone	1877	Thomas Alva Edison (US)
gun	245 BC	Ctesibius (Gr)
gyro-compass	1911	Elmer A Sperry (US)
heart (artificial)	1937	Vladimir P Demikhov (USSR)
	1982	Robert Jarvik (US)
heat pump	1851	William Thomson, Lord Kelvin (UK)
helicopter	1907	Louis and Jacques Breguet (Fr)
holography	1948	Dennis Gabor (Hung/UK)
hovercraft	1955	Christopher Cockerell (UK)
integrated circuit (concept)	1952	Geoffrey Dummer (UK)
interferometry	1802	Thomas Young (UK)
interferometer	1856	J-C Jamin (Fr)

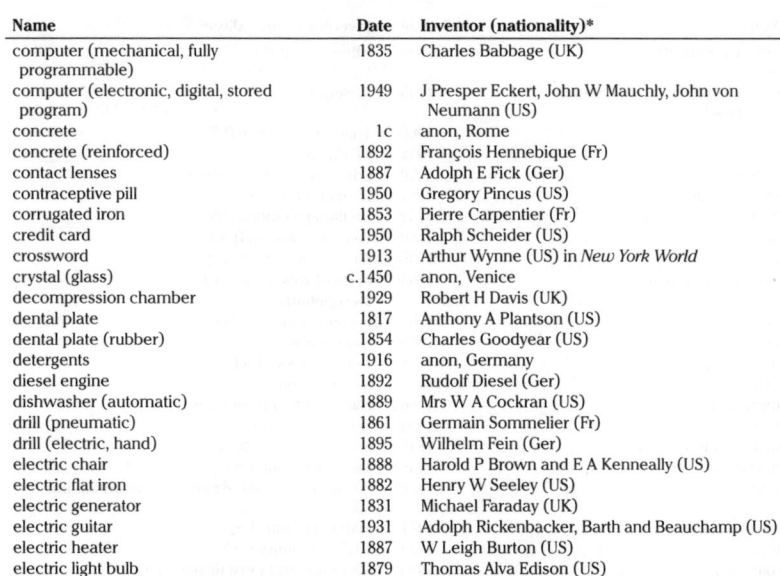

Science and Technology

Name	Date	Inventor (nationality)*
iron (working of)	c.1323 BC	Hittites, Anatolia
jeans	1872	Levi-Strauss (US)
kidney, artificial (haemodialysis machine)	1945	Willem Kolff (NL)
laser	1960	Theodore Maiman (US)
launderette	1934	J F Cantrell (US)
lawnmower	1830	Edwin Beard Budding (UK)
lift (mechanical)	1851	Elisha G Otis (US)
lightning conductor	1752	Benjamin Franklin (US)
linoleum	1860	Frederick Walton (UK)
lithography	1796	Aloys Senefelder (Bav)
locomotive (railed)	1804	Richard Trevithick (UK)
lock	c.4000 BC	Mesopotamia
loom (power)	1785	Edmund Cartwright (UK)
loudspeaker	1900	Horace Short (UK)
machine gun	1718	James Puckle (UK)
maps	c.2250 BC	Mesopotamia
margarine	1868	Hippolyte Mergé-Mouriès (Fr)
match	1680	Robert Boyle (UK)
match (safety)	1845	Anton von Schrotter (Ger)
microchip	1958	Jack Saint Clair Kilby (US)
microphone	1876	Alexander Graham Bell and Thomas Alva Edison (US)
microprocessor	1971	Marcian E Hoff (US)
microscope	1590	Zacharias Janssen (NL)
microscope (electron)	1933	Max Knoll and Ernst Ruska (Ger)
microscope (scanning tunnelling)	1982	Gerd Binnig and Heinrich Rohrer (Swiss)
microscope (atomic force)	1985	Gerd Binnig and Heinrich Rohrer (Swiss)
microwave oven	1945	Percy Le Baron Spencer (US)
missile (air-to-air)	1943	Herbert Wagner (Ger)
motorcycle	1885	Gottlieb Daimler (Ger)
neon lamp	1910	Georges Claude (Fr)
newspaper	59 BC	Julius Caesar (Roman)
non-stick pan	1954	Marc Grégoir (Fr)
novel (serialized)	1836	Charles Dickens, Chapman and Hall Publishers (UK)
nylon	1937	Wallace H Carothers (US)
optical fibres	c.1955	Navinder S Kapany (Ind)
optical sound recording	1920	Lee De Forest (US)
pacemaker (implantable)	1956	Wilson Greatbach (US)
paint (fluorescent)	1933	Joe and Bob Switzer (US)
paint (acrylic)	1964	Reeves Ltd (UK)
paper	AD 105	Ts'ai Lun (Chinese)
paper clip	1900	Johann Vaaler (Nor)
parachute	c.2c BC	China
parachute (jump)	1797	André-Jacques Garnerin (Fr)
parachute (patent)	1802	André-Jacques Garnerin (Fr)
parchment	2c BC	Eumenes II of Pergamum (reigned 197–159 BC)
parking meter	1932	Carlton C Magee (US)
pasteurization	1863	Louis Pasteur (Fr)
pen (fountain)	1884	Lewis Waterman (US)
pen (ball-point)	1938	Laszlo Biro (Hung)
pencil	1795	Nicholas Jacques Conté (Fr)
pentium processor	1995	Intel (US)
phonograph	1877	Thomas Alva Edison (US)
photoelectric cell	1896	Julius Elster and Hans F Geitel (Ger)
phototypesetting	1894	Eugene Porzott (Hung)
photographic lens (for camera obscura)	1812	William H Wollaston (UK)
photographic film	1889	George Eastman (US)
photography (on metal)	1816	Joseph Nicéphore Niepce (Fr)
photography (on paper)	1838	William Henry Fox Talbot (UK)
photography (colour)	1861	James Clerk Maxwell (UK)
pianoforte	1720	Bartolomeo Cristofori (Ital)
plastics	1868	John W Hyatt (US)
pocket calculator	1972	Jack Saint Clair Kilby, James Van Tassell and Jerry D Merryman (US)
porcelain	c.960	China

Name	Date	Inventor (nationality)*
pressure cooker	1679	Denis Papin (Fr)
printing press (wooden)	c.1450	Johannes Gutenberg (Ger)
printing press (rotary)	1845	Richard Hoe (US)
propeller (boat, hand-operated)	1775	David Bushnell (US)
propeller (ship)	1844	Isambard Kingdom Brunel (UK)
radar (theory)	1900	Nikola Tesla (Croat)
	1922	Guglielmo Marconi (Ital)
radar (application)	c.1930	A Hoyt Taylor and Leo C Young (US)
radio telegraphy (discovery and production of sound waves)	1888	Heinrich Hertz (Ger)
radio (transatlantic)	1901	Guglielmo Marconi (Ital)
rails (iron)	1738	Abraham Darby (UK)
railway (underground)	1843	Charles Pearson (UK)
railway (electric)	1878	Ernst Werner von Siemens (Ger)
rayon	1883	Joseph Swan (UK)
razor (safety)	1895	King Camp Gillette (US)
razor (electric)	1928	Jacob Schick (US)
record (flat disc)	1888	Emil Berliner (Ger)
record (long-playing microgroove)	1948	Peter Goldmark (US)
refrigerator (compressed ether)	1855	James Harrison (UK)
refrigerator (absorption)	1857	Ferdinand Carré (Fr)
revolver	1835	Samuel Colt (US)
Richter seismographic scale	1935	Charles Francis Richter (US)
rocket (missile)	1232	Mongols, China
rubber (latex foam)	1929	E A Murphy, W H Chapman and John Dunlop (US)
rubber (butyl)	1937	Robert Thomas and William Sparks, Exxon (US)
rubber (vulcanized)	1939	Charles Goodyear (US)
Rubik cube	1975	Erno Rubik (Hung)
safety-pin	1849	Walter Hunt (US)
satellite (artificial)	1957	USSR
saw	c.4000 BC	Egypt
scanner	1973	Godfrey N Hounsfield (UK)
scotch tape	1930	Richard Drew (US)
screw	3c BC	Archimedes (Gr)
serotherapy	1890	Emil von Behring (Ger)
sewing machine	1830	Barthelemy Thimonnier (Fr)
ship (steam)	1775	Jacques C Perier (Fr)
ship (turbine)	1894	Charles Parsons (UK)
ship (metal hull and propeller)	1844	Isambard Kingdom Brunel (UK)
silicon chip	1961	Texas Instruments (US)
silk (reeling)	c.2640 BC	Hsi Ling Shi (Chinese)
skin (artificial)	c.1980	John Tanner (US), Bell (US), Neveu (Fr), Ioannis Yannas (Gr), Howard Green (US) and Jacques Thivolet (Fr)
skyscraper	1882	William Le Baron Jenney (US)
slide rule	1621	William Oughtred (UK)
soap	c.2500 BC	Sumer, Babylonia
soda (extraction of)	c.16c BC	Egypt
space shuttle	1981	NASA (US)
spectacles	c.1280	Alessandro della Spina and Salvino degli Armati (Ital)
spinning frame	1768	Richard Arkwright (UK)
spinning jenny	c.1764	James Hargreaves (UK)
spinning-mule	1779	Samuel Crompton (UK)
stapler	1868	Charles Henry Gould (UK)
starter motor	1912	Charles F Kettering (US)
steam engine	1698	Thomas Savery (UK)
steam engine (condenser)	1769	James Watt (UK)
steam engine (piston)	1705	Thomas Newcomen (UK)
steel (production)	1854	Henry Bessemer (UK) and William Kelly (US)
steel (stainless)	1913	Henry Brearley (UK)
stethoscope	1816	René Théophile Hyacinthe Laennec (Fr)
stereotype	1725	William Ged (UK)
submarine	c.1620	Cornelis Brebbel or Van Drebbel (NL)
sun-tan cream	1936	Eugène Schueller (Fr)
suspension bridge	25 BC	China
syringe (scientific)	1646	Blaise Pascal (Fr)

Science and Technology

Name	Date	Inventor (nationality)*
syringe (hypodermic)	c.1835	Charles Gabriel Pravaz (Fr)
table tennis	1890	James Gibb (UK)
tampon	1930	Earl Hass (US)
tank	1916	Ernest Swinton (UK)
telegraph (electric)	1774	Georges Louis Lesage (Swiss)
telegraph (transatlantic cable)	1866	William Thomson, Lord Kelvin (UK)
telegraph code	1837	Samuel F B Morse (US)
telephone (first practical)	1876	Alexander Graham Bell (US)
telephone (automatic exchange)	1889	Alman B Strowger (US)
telephone, mobile cellular (first commercially available)	1983	Motorola (US)
telescope (refractor)	1608	Hans Lippershey (NL)
telescope (space)	1990	Edwin Hubble (US)
television (mechanical)	1926	John Logie Baird (UK)
television (colour)	1940	Peter Goldmark (US)
tennis	1873	Walter G Wingfield (UK)
thermometer	3c BC	Ctesibius (Gr)
thermometer (mercury)	1714	Gabriel Fahrenheit (Ger)
timeclock	1894	Daniel M Cooper (US)
toaster	1927	Charles Strite (US)
traffic lights	1868	J P Knight (UK)
traffic lights (automatic)	1914	Alfred Benesch (US)
transformer	1831	Michael Faraday (UK)
tranquillizers	1952	Henri Laborit (Fr)
transistor	1948	John Bardeen, Walter Brattain and William Shockley (US)
travel agency	1841	Thomas Cook (UK)
traveller's cheques	1891	American Express Travel Agency (US)
turbojet	1928	Frank Whittle (UK)
typewriter	1829	William Burt (US)
typewriter (electric)	1872	Thomas Alva Edison (US)
tyre (pneumatic, coach)	1845	Robert William Thomson (UK)
tyre (pneumatic, bicycle)	1888	John Boyd Dunlop (UK)
ultrasonography (obstetric)	1958	Ian Donald (UK)
universal joint	c.140 BC	Fang Feng (Chinese)
vacuum cleaner (steam powered)	1871	Ives W McGaffrey (US)
vacuum cleaner (electric)	1901	Hubert Cecil Booth (UK)
vending machine	1883	Percival Everitt (UK)
ventilator	1858	Théophile Guibal (Fr)
videophone	1927	American Telegraph and Telephone Co
video recorder	1956	Ampex Co (US)
washing machine (electric)	1907	Hurley Machine Co (US)
watch	1462	Bartholomew Manfredi (Ital)
watch (waterproof)	1927	Rolex (Swiss)
wheel	c.3500 BC	Mesopotamia
windmill	c.600	Syria
word processor	1965	IBM (US)
writing (pictography)	c.3000 BC	Egypt
xerography	1938	Chester Carlson (US)
zip-fastener	1893	Whitcomb L Judson (US)

*Aus: Austrian Bav: Bavarian Belg: Belgian Croat: Croatian D: Danish Fr: French Ger: German Gr: Greek Hung: Hungarian Ind: Indian Ital: Italian NL: Dutch Nor: Norwegian Pruss: Prussian Swed: Swedish

Industrialists and entrepreneurs

Agnelli, Giovanni (1866–1945) Italian, born Villa Perosa, Piedmont. Founder of Fiat (Fabbrica Italiana Automobili Torino) in 1899. Appointed as a senator in 1923 and mobilized Italian industry in World War II.

Astor, John Jacob, 1st Baron Astor of Hever (1886–1971) Anglo-American, born New York City. Elected MP for Dover (1922) and chairman of the Times Publishing Company.

Astor, William Waldorf, 1st Viscount (1848–1919) Anglo-American, born New York City. After period as US minister to Italy, emigrated to Britain to

become newspaper proprietor, acquiring the *Pall Mall Gazette*, *Pall Mall Magazine* and, in 1911, *The Observer*.

Austin, Herbert, 1st Baron Austin of Longbridge (1866–1941) English, born Buckinghamshire. After working in engineering shops in Australia, returned to England and produced his first three-wheel car with the Wolseley Co in 1895, forming his own company in 1905. Conservative MP from 1918 to 1924.

Barclay, Robert (1843–1913) English. Founder of Barclay and Co Ltd with the merger of 20 banks in

1896. In 1917 the name was changed to Barclay's Bank Limited.

Beaverbrook, Max (William Maxwell Aitken), 1st Baron (1879–1964) Anglo-Canadian, born Maple, Ontario. Originally stockbroker, before entering British parliament (1911–16); became Minister of Information (1918). Later acquired a number of major British newspapers, including the *Daily Express*.

Benz, Karl Friedrich (1844–1929) German, born Karlsruhe. Engineer and car manufacturer who developed the two-stroke engine. Founded Benz & Co and produced one of the earliest petrol-driven vehicles; the company later merged to become Daimler-Benz.

Birdseye, Clarence (1886–1956) American, born Brooklyn, New York City. Co-founder of the General Seafoods Co in 1924, after developing a process for freezing foods in small packages. Later president of Birdseye Frosted Foods (1930–4) and Birdseye Electric Company (1935–8). He is credited with around 300 patents.

Boeing, William Edward (1881–1956) American, born Detroit, Michigan. Formed Pacific Aero Products Co in 1916 to build seaplanes. Renamed as the Boeing Airplane Co in 1917, it became the largest aircraft manufacturer in the world. Also formed Boeing Air Transport Co airline in 1927.

Branson, Sir Richard Charles Nicholas (1950–) English entrepreneur and businessman, born London. Started the Virgin mail-order business in 1969. Opened the first branch of his record chain in 1971 and founded his record label in 1973. Founded Virgin Atlantic Airlines in 1984, and sold Virgin Music in 1992 for £560m to expand the airline. Launched Virgin Radio in 1993 (sold to Chris Evans's Ginger Productions in 1997) and bought MGM UK high-street cinemas in 1995. Introduced personal banking services and Virgin Trains into the Virgin Group in the 1990s. By 1998 the Virgin Group consisted of 200 companies, with an annual turnover of £1.8 billion. In 2004, signed a £14m agreement to have five spacecraft built, and expects his Virgin Galactic company to offer space flights to paying passengers.

Brierley, Sir Ron(ald Alfred) (1937–) New Zealand entrepreneur, born Wellington. Founded Brierley Investments in 1961. Sold his Industrial Equities conglomerate just before 1987 crash and became chairman of Guinness Peat Group in 1990.

Burrell, Sir William (1861–1958) Scottish, born Glasgow. Ship-owner and art collector. Accumulated 8,000 works of art, which he donated to the city of Glasgow in 1944.

Butlin, Sir William Edmund (1899–1980) English, born South Africa. Holiday camp promoter; opened his first camp at Skegness in 1936 and expanded the business in the UK and abroad after World War II.

Cadbury, George (1839–1922) English, born Birmingham. Quaker businessman, son of John Cadbury. Took over his father's business in 1861 and established for the workers the model village of Bournville, near Birmingham. Became the proprietor of the *Daily News* in 1902.

Cadbury, John (1801–89) English, born Birmingham. Quaker businessman, founder of Cadbury's cocoa and chocolate business.

Carnegie, Andrew (1835–1918) Scottish, born Dunfermline. Invested in oil lands and a business which grew into the largest iron and steel works in the USA. Retired in 1901, a multimillionaire.

Chandos, Oliver Lyttelton, 1st Viscount (1893–1972) English, born London. Managing director of the British Metal Corporation from 1928. In 1940 entered the House of Commons and was made President of the Board of Trade. Resigned from politics to return to business in 1954.

Christie, James (1730–1803) English, born London. Founder of Christie's auctioneers in 1766.

Citroën, André Gustave (1878–1935) French, born Paris. Responsible for mass production of armaments during World War I. Later became a manufacturer of small low-priced cars but lost control of the Citroën company in 1934.

Conran, Sir Terence Orby (1931–) English, born Esher, Surrey. Businessman and designer who founded and ran the Habitat Company (1971). Has since been involved in management of Richard Shops, Conran Stores, Mothercare and several restaurants.

Cunard, Sir Samuel (1787–1865) Canadian, born Halifax. Merchant and ship-owner who emigrated to Britain in 1838 to found the British and North American Royal Mail Steam Packet Company, later known as the Cunard Line, for the new steam mail service between Britain and the USA.

du Pont Nemours, Eleuthère Irénée (1771–1834) French–American, born Paris. Worked in father's printing plant until 1797. Emigrated to the USA and in 1802 established a gunpowder factory that developed into one of the world's largest chemical concerns.

du Pont, Pierre Samuel (1870–1954) American, born Wilmington, Delaware. Joined the family gunpowder company. As its president (1915–20), introduced and developed many new industrial management techniques. Became president of General Motors in 1920.

Dunlop, John Boyd (1840–1921) Scottish, born Dreghorn, Ayrshire. Credited with inventing the pneumatic tyre. In 1889 formed the business that became the Dunlop Rubber Company Ltd; produced pneumatic tyres for bicycles, and later for cars.

Firestone, Harvey Samuel (1868–1938) American, born Columbiana, Ohio. Sold solid rubber carriage tyres in Chicago and in 1900 founded Firestone Tire and Rubber Company, which grew to be one of the biggest industrial corporations in the USA. Pioneered pneumatic tyres for Ford Model T, and non-skid treads. Started rubber plantations in Liberia in 1924.

Ford, Henry (1863–1947) American, born Greenfield, Michigan. Apprentice to a machinist at the age of 15; produced his first petrol-driven car in 1893. In 1903 founded Ford Motor Company and pioneered mass-production techniques.

Ford, Henry II (1917–87) American, born Dearborn, Michigan. Seized control of the Ford Motor Company from his grandfather Henry Ford in 1945. Stepped down as chief executive officer in 1979 and as chairman in 1980, but remained as member of the board of directors.

Frick, Henry Clay (1849–1919) American, born West Overton, Pennsylvania. Millionaire at 30 after forming company to supply the Pittsburgh steelworks with coke. Became chairman of the Carnegie steel company in 1889. A ruthless employer, he was shot and stabbed after forcefully breaking a strike in 1892, but subsequently recovered. Became a director of United States Steel in 1901.

Gates, Bill (William Henry) (1955–) American, born Seattle. Founded Microsoft Corporation in 1975 and licensed computer operating system

(MS-DOS) to IBM in 1980. This system and their applications software have been phenomenally successful. By the turn of the century, Microsoft earned revenues in excess of $19 billion, with over 32000 employees in 60 countries. In recent years the company has faced anti-trust litigation over its perceived monopoly in the market. He and his wife founded the Bill and Melinda Gates Foundation (2000) to promote global health and education.

Getty, Jean Paul (1892–1976) American, born Minneapolis, Minnesota. Entered the oil business in his early twenties and went on to acquire and control more than 100 companies. Also acquired an enormous and valuable art collection.

Guinness, Sir Benjamin Lee (1798–1868) Irish, born Dublin. Inherited Guinness's Brewery (founded 1759) and made it the largest business of its kind in the world. First Lord Mayor of Dublin (1851) and MP (1865–8).

Gulbenkian, Calouste Sarkis (1869–1955) British–Ottoman Turkish, born Scutari. Entered father's oil business in Baku in 1888. Later organized international oil company mergers and negotiated oil concessions between the USA and Saudi Arabia.

Hammer, Armand (1899–1990) American, born New York City. Exported grain to the USSR in exchange for furs, dealing with Lenin and subsequent Soviet leaders. Founded the A Hammer Pencil Company in 1925 and maintained strong connections with the USSR, occasionally acting as intermediary between Soviet and American governments. Bought and expanded the small Occidental Petroleum Corporation in 1957, and founded Hammer Galleries Inc in New York in 1930.

Heinz, Henry John (1844–1919) American, born Pittsburgh, Pennsylvania. Co-founder of food manufacturing and packing company F & J Heinz, and president of the reorganized business H J Heinz Co from 1905 to 1919. Promoted the pure food movement in the USA, and pioneered staff welfare work.

Hilton, Conrad Nicholson (1887–1979) American, born San Antonio, New Mexico. Took over the family inn in 1918, then built up a chain of hotels in major cities in the USA. Formed the Hilton Hotels Corporation in 1946 and Hilton International in 1948, and continued to expand until 1966 when his son became president.

Honda, Soichiro (1906–91) Japanese, born Iwata Gun. Became a garage apprentice in 1922 and opened his own garage in 1928. By 1934 had opened a piston-ring production factory and later produced motorcycles. President of Honda Corporation (1948–73), remaining as a director, and appointed 'supreme advisor' in 1983.

Hoover, William Henry (1849–1932) American, born Ohio. After running a tannery business, bought the patent of an electric cleaning machine from a janitor and formed Electric Suction Sweeper Co in 1908 (later renamed Hoover) to manufacture and market it throughout the world.

Hughes, Howard Robard (1905–76) American, born Houston, Texas. Inherited his father's oil-drilling equipment company and used the profits to make Hollywood films. After working as a pilot, became involved in designing, building and flying aircraft, then abruptly returned to filmmaking. From 1966 lived in complete seclusion but continued to control his vast business interests.

Iacocca, Lee (Lido Anthony) (1924–) American, born Allentown, Pennsylvania. Worked for Ford Motor Co, rising to become president in 1970. In 1978 joined Chrysler Corporation as president and chief executive officer, restoring profitability during serious financial difficulties. Retired from Chrysler in 1992 and, in 2000, founded a brand of food products based on olive oil.

Jobs, Steven (1955–) American, born San Fransisco. With Stephen Wozniak (1950–) he set up Apple Computer Co in 1976, which became the fastest-growing company in the USA. Jobs left Apple in 1985 and founded NeXT Inc, and the following year co-founded Pixar, the computer animation studio responsible for the *Toy Story* films (1995, 1999), *Finding Nemo* (2003) and *The Incredibles* (2004). Rejoined Apple in 1997 as CEO, and oversaw the development of the iMac, iBook and iPod brands.

King, John Leonard, Baron King of Wartnaby (1917–2005) English industrialist. Became chairman of Dennis Motor Holdings in 1970 and Babcock and Wilcox Ltd in 1972. Was appointed chairman of British Airways in 1981 and then life president in 1993.

Krupp, Alfred (1812–87) German, born Essen. Inherited his father's iron forge and began manufacturing arms in 1837. Established a steel plant and became an international arms supplier. Also acquired large mines, collieries and docks.

Lyons, Sir Joseph (1848–1917) English, born London. Starting with a teashop in Piccadilly, made J Lyons and Co Ltd one of the largest catering businesses in Britain.

Marks, Simon, 1st Baron Marks of Broughton (1888–1964) English, born Leeds. Son of a Jewish immigrant from Poland from whom he inherited 60 Marks and Spencer 'penny bazaars'. With Israel (later Lord) Seif, established Marks and Spencer as a major high-quality retail chain.

Maxwell (Ian) Robert (1923–91) English, born Czechoslovakia. Founder of Pergamon Press and Labour MP (1964–70). As well as controlling Mirror Group Newspapers and the Maxwell Communication Corporation, he had extensive private business interests. After his death massive debts were revealed.

Morita, Akio (1921–99) Japanese, born Nagoya. Founded Sony electronics firm together with Masaru Ibuka (1908–97) in 1958. Among Sony's most important products have been early tape recorders (c.1950) and the 'Walkman' (1980).

Murdoch, (Keith) Rupert (1931–) Australian–American, born Melbourne. After becoming Australia's second largest publisher, expanded abroad acquiring newspapers in London and New York, including *The Sun*, *The Times* and the *New York Post*. Expanded his communications empire in 1989 with the purchase of Collins the publishers and the inauguration of Sky Television. Later bought 20th Century Fox film studios and New World Communications, and created the Fox Network, becoming the owner of television stations that reached up to 40 per cent of viewers.

Nobel, Alfred (1833–96) Swedish, born Stockholm. Explosives expert who invented dynamite and gelignite. Created an industrial empire to manufacture his many inventions and left his fortune to endow annual Nobel Prizes. Element 102 was named nobelium after him.

Nuffield, William Richard Morris, 1st Viscount (1877–1963) English, born Worcester. Started in a bicycle repair business and by 1910 was manufacturing prototypes of Morris Oxford cars at Cowley in Oxford. He was the first British manufacturer to develop mass production of cheap cars.

Olivetti, Adriano (1901–60) Italian, born Ivrea. Vastly increased and developed his father's typewriter firm. Widely noted for his social concerns.

Onassis, Aristotle Socrates (1906–75) Greek, born Smyrna, Turkey. Made his fortune in the tobacco trade and built up one of the world's largest independent fleets of ships. Also a pioneer in the construction of supertankers. Married Jacqueline Kennedy, widow of American president John F Kennedy.

Packer, Kerry Francis Bullmore (1937–2005) Australian, born Sydney. Inherited from his father the media company Australian Consolidated Press. Was involved in disputes and legal battles with national cricket bodies due to his creation and broadcasting of 'World Series Cricket'.

Pilkington, Sir Lionel Alexander Bethune (Sir Alastair) (1920–95) English, born Calcutta (now Kolkata). Member of a family firm of glass-makers, who researched and developed methods of producing defect-free plate glass.

Pulitzer, Joseph (1847–1911) Hungarian–American, born Makó, Hungary. Emigrated to the USA in 1864 and joined the army. Later in St Louis he became a reporter, then began to acquire and revitalize old newspapers, including the New York World (1883). Established in his will the annual Pulitzer prizes for literature, drama, music and journalism.

Rockefeller, John Davison (1839–1937) American, born Richford, New York. Founded the Standard Oil Co in 1870 and through it secured control of the oil trade of America. Gave over $500 million in aid of medical research, universities and Baptist churches; in 1913 established Rockefeller Foundation 'to promote the well-being of mankind'.

Roddick, Anita Lucia (1942–2007) English, born Brighton. Founded the Body Shop International plc to sell natural cosmetics. The company has around 2,100 stores in 55 countries, and was bought by L'Oréal in 2006.

Rolls, Charles Stewart (1877–1910) English, born London. Motor car manufacturer who founded C S Rolls & Co in 1902 and, later, Rolls-Royce Ltd with Sir Henry Royce. In 1910 made the first non-stop double crossing of the English Channel by aeroplane.

Rothermere, Harold Sydney Harmsworth, 1st Viscount (1868–1940) Irish, born London. Newspaper magnate, founder of the Glasgow Daily Record and the Sunday Pictorial. Also controlled the Daily Mail, Sunday Dispatch and the Daily Mirror, for which he developed a circulation of three million in 1922.

Rowntree, Joseph (1836–1925) English, born York. With his brother became a partner in a cocoa factory in York in 1869, and built up welfare organizations for employees.

Royce, Sir (Frederick) Henry (1863–1933) English, born near Peterborough. Founder of electrical and mechanical engineering firm Royce Ltd (1884) and co-founder of Rolls-Royce Ltd, manufacturer of car and aeroplane engines. Designed engines used in Spitfires and Hurricanes in World War II.

Sainsbury, Alan John, Baron Sainsbury of Drury Lane (1902–98) English, born Hornsey, Middlesex. Joined the family grocery business in 1921 and from 1967 was joint president of the major supermarket chain J Sainsbury plc.

Selfridge, Harry Gordon (1858–1947) Anglo-American, born Ripon, Wisconsin. Chicago trader who in 1906 on a visit to London initiated the Selfridge business; the Oxford Street store opened in 1909.

Sieff, Israel Moses, Baron Sieff of Brimpton (1889–1972) English, born Manchester. With Simon Marks, developed Marks and Spencer. Joint managing director from 1926 to 1967 and succeeded Lord Marks as chairman (1964–7).

Sinclair, Sir Clive (Marles) (1940–) English, born Surrey. Launched an electronics company that has developed and successfully marketed pocket calculators, miniature televisions and personal computers. Also manufactured the Sinclair C5 'personal transport' vehicle powered by a small electric motor and rechargeable batteries.

Sugar, Alan Michael (1947–) English, born London. Founded the computer and electronics company Amstrad (the name is a contraction of Alan M Sugar Trading) in 1968. The company expanded rapidly during the personal computer boom of the 1980s, but ran into problems with the slump at the end of that decade, losing, at one stage, £1 million per week. As a result, Sugar bought the company back into private ownership, and it now produces telecommunications and audiovisual equipment. Sugar was chairman of Tottenham Hotspur football club from 1991 to 2001, and hosted the UK version of the reality television show The Apprentice (2005 onwards).

Tate, Sir Henry (1819–99) English, born Chorley, Lancashire. Patented a method for cutting sugar cubes (1872) and formed a major sugar refinery. Gave to the nation the Tate Gallery (1897) containing his own valuable private collection.

Tiffany, Charles Lewis (1812–1902) American, born Killingby, Connecticut. Goldsmith and jeweller who began dealing in 1837, and by 1883 was one of the largest silverware manufacturers in the USA. Held appointments to 23 royal patrons, including the Tsar of Russia and Queen Victoria.

Trump, Donald J (1946–) American, born New York City. Assisted his father in business ventures when young. Went on to become a billionaire real estate developer with interests in Manhattan, Miami, Chicago and Atlantic City; his landmark properties include Trump Tower and the Plaza Hotel. Hosted the US reality television show The Apprentice (2004 onwards).

Turner, Ted (Robert Edward) (1938–) American, born Cincinnati. Created the first 'superstation', WTBS, in the mid-1970s and created Cable News Network (CNN) in 1980. In 1985 he bought MGM and established a movie channel on television in 1988. Time Warner Inc merged with Turner Broadcasting System in 1996, creating the world's largest media company, with Turner as its vice-chairman, and in 2001 Time Warner merged with America Online (AOL), the internet provider. Turner stood down in 2003.

Wang, An (1920–89) American–Chinese, born Shanghai. Graduated in science from Shanghai, then studied applied physics at Harvard. Invented the magnetic core memory, an early form of computer memory, and founded Wang Laboratories in Boston in 1951 to produce calculators and desktop computers.

Woolworth, Frank Winfield (1852–1919) American, born Rodman, Jefferson County, New York. From inexpensive fixed-price goods stores, built up a chain of over a thousand stores controlled from a New York headquarters. Most development outside the USA was after the death of the founder.

Science and Technology

Physical constants

2002 recommended values of the main fundamental physical constants of physics and chemistry.

Science and Technology

Quantity	Symbol	Value	Units
Universal constants			
speed of light in vacuum	c	299 792 458	m s^{-1}
permeability of vacuum	μ_0	$4\pi \times 10^{-7}$	N A^{-2}
		= 12.566370614...	10^{-7} N A^{-2}
permittivity of vacuum, $1/\mu_0\gamma^2$	ε_0	8.854187817...	10^{-12} F m^{-1}
Newtonian constant of gravitation	G	6.6742	10^{-11} m^3 kg^{-1} s^{-2}
Planck constant	h	6.6260693	10^{-34} J s

Quantity	Symbol	Value	Units
$h/2\pi$	$\hbar$	1.05457168	10^{-34} J s
Electromagnetic constants			
elementary charge	e	1.60217653	10^{-19} C
	e/h	2.417978940	10^{14} A J^{-1}
magnetic flux quantum, $h/2e$	Φ_0	2.06783372	10^{-15} Wb
Josephson frequency-voltage quotient	$2e/h$	4.83597879	10^{14} Hz V^{-1}
Bohr magneton, $e\hbar/2m_e$	μ_B	9.27400949	10^{-24} J T^{-1}
nuclear magneton, $e\hbar/2m_p$	μ_N	5.05078343	10^{-27} J T^{-1}
Atomic constants			
fine-structure constant, $\mu_0ce^2/2h$	α	7.297352568	10^{-3}
	α^{-1}	137.0359991	
Rydberg constant, $m_ec\alpha^2/2h$	R_∞	10973731.568	m^{-1}
Bohr radius, $\alpha/4\pi R_\infty$	a_0	0.5291772108	10^{-10} m
quantum of circulation	$h/2m_e$	3.636947550	10^{-4} m^2 s^{-1}
	h/m_e	7.2738951	10^{-4} m^2 s^{-1}
Electron			
electron mass	m_e	9.1093826	10^{-31} kg
		5.4857990945	10^{-4} u
electron-muon mass ratio	m_e/m_μ	4.83633167	10^{-3}
electron-proton mass ratio	m_e/m_p	5.4461702173	10^{-4}
electron specific charge	$-e/m_e$	-1.75881962	10^{11} C kg^{-1}
Compton wavelength, h/m_ec	λ_C	2.426310238	10^{-12} m
$\lambda_C/2\pi = \alpha a_0 = \alpha^2/4\pi R_\infty$	$\lambdabar_C$	3.861592678	10^{-13} m
classical electron radius, α^2a_0	r_e	2.817940325	10^{-15} m
electron magnetic moment	μ_e	-928.476412	10^{-26} J T^{-1}
electron g factor, $2(1+a_e)$	g_e	-2.0023193043718	
electron-proton magnetic moment ratio	μ_e/μ_p	-658.2106862	
Muon			
muon mass	m_μ	1.88353140	10^{-28} kg
		0.1134289264	u
muon magnetic moment	μ_μ	-4.49044799	10^{-26} J T^{-1}
muon g factor, $2(1 + a_\mu)$	g_μ	-2.0023318396	
muon-proton magnetic moment ratio	μ_μ/μ_p	-3.183345118	
Proton			
proton mass	m_p	1.67262171	10^{-27} kg
		1.00727646688	u
proton Compton wavelength, h/m_pc	$\lambda_{C,p}$	1.3214098555	10^{-15} m
$\lambdabar_{C,p}/2\pi$	$\lambdabar_{C,p}$	2.103089104	10^{-16} m
proton magnetic moment	μ_p	1.41060671	10^{-26} J T^{-1}
in Bohr magnetons	μ_p/μ_B	1.521032206	10^{-3}
in nuclear magnetons	μ_p/μ_N	2.792847351	
proton gyromagnetic ratio	γ_p	26752.2128	10^4 s^{-1} T^{-1}
	$\gamma_p/2\pi$	42.577469	MHz T^{-1}
uncorrected (H_2O, sph., 25°C)	γ'_p	2.67522205	10^8 s^{-1} T^{-1}
	$\gamma'_p/2\pi$	42.5774813	MHz T^{-1}

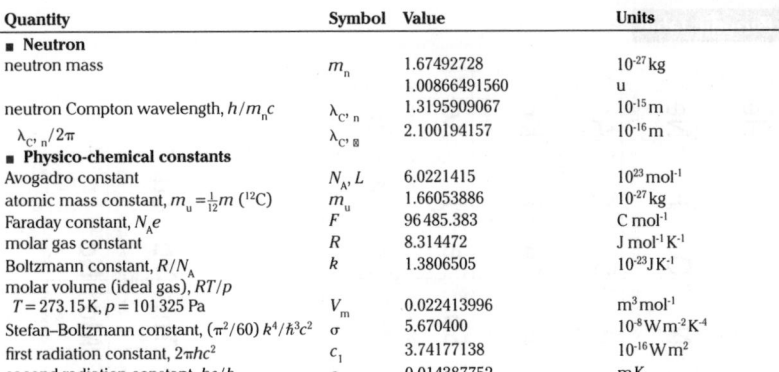

Quantity	Symbol	Value	Units
■ **Neutron**			
neutron mass	m_n	1.67492728	10^{-27} kg
		1.00866491560	u
neutron Compton wavelength, $h/m_n c$	$\lambda_{C,n}$	1.3195909067	10^{-15} m
$\lambda_{C,n}/2\pi$	$\lambda_{C,n}$	2.100194157	10^{-16} m
■ **Physico-chemical constants**			
Avogadro constant	N_A, L	6.0221415	10^{23} mol^{-1}
atomic mass constant, $m_u = \frac{1}{12} m$ (^{12}C)	m_u	1.66053886	10^{-27} kg
Faraday constant, $N_A e$	F	96 485.383	C mol^{-1}
molar gas constant	R	8.314472	J mol^{-1} K^{-1}
Boltzmann constant, R/N_A	k	1.3806505	10^{-23} J K^{-1}
molar volume (ideal gas), RT/p			
$T = 273.15$ K, $p = 101\,325$ Pa	V_m	0.022413996	m^3 mol^{-1}
Stefan–Boltzmann constant, $(\pi^2/60)\,k^4/\hbar^3 c^2$	σ	5.670400	10^{-8} W m^{-2} K^{-4}
first radiation constant, $2\pi hc^2$	c_1	3.74177138	10^{-16} W m^2
second radiation constant, hc/k	c_2	0.014387752	m K

Radiation

Radiation	Approximate wavelengths	Discovered by	Date	Uses
Radio waves	>10 cm	Heinrich Hertz (German)	1888	communications; radio and TV broadcasting
Microwaves	1 mm–10 cm	Heinrich Hertz (German)	1886	communications; radar; microwave ovens
Infrared	10^{-3}–7.8×10^{-7} m	William Herschel (German–British)	1800	night and smoke vision systems; intruder alarms; weather forecasting; missile guidance systems
Visible	7.8×10^{-7}–3×10^{-7} m	—	—	human eyesight
Ultraviolet	3×10^{-7}–10^{-8} m	Johann Ritter (German)	1801	forensic science; medical treatment
X-rays	10^{-8}–3×10^{-11} m	Wilhelm Röntgen (German)	1895	medical X-ray photographs; material structure analysis
Gamma rays	$<3 \times 10^{-11}$ m	Ernest Rutherford (British)	1902	medical diagnosis

Decibel scale

Source	Decibel level (dB)	Source	Decibel level (dB)
Breathing	10	Traffic	60–90
Whisper	20	Pneumatic drill	110
Conversation	50–60	Jet aircraft	120
Vacuum cleaner	80	Space vehicle launch	140–170

Science and Technology

Periodic table

element symbol — atomic number
element name

1 H hydrogen																	2 He helium
3 Li lithium	4 Be beryllium											5 B boron	6 C carbon	7 N nitrogen	8 O oxygen	9 F fluorine	10 Ne neon
11 Na sodium	12 Mg magnesium											13 Al aluminium	14 Si silicon	15 P phosphorus	16 S sulphur	17 Cl chlorine	18 Ar argon
19 K potassium	20 Ca calcium	21 Sc scandium	22 Ti titanium	23 V vanadium	24 Cr chromium	25 Mn manganese	26 Fe iron	27 Co cobalt	28 Ni nickel	29 Cu copper	30 Zn zinc	31 Ga gallium	32 Ge germanium	33 As arsenic	34 Se selenium	35 Br bromine	36 Kr krypton
37 Rb rubidium	38 Sr strontium	39 Y yttrium	40 Zr zirconium	41 Nb niobium	42 Mo molybdenum	43 Tc technetium	44 Ru ruthenium	45 Rh rhodium	46 Pd palladium	47 Ag silver	48 Cd cadmium	49 In indium	50 Sn tin	51 Sb antimony	52 Te tellurium	53 I iodine	54 Xe xenon
55 Cs caesium	56 Ba barium	57–71 *	72 Hf hafnium	73 Ta tantalum	74 W tungsten	75 Re rhenium	76 Os osmium	77 Ir iridium	78 Pt platinum	79 Au gold	80 Hg mercury	81 Tl thallium	82 Pb lead	83 Bi bismuth	84 Po polonium	85 At astatine	86 Rn radon
87 Fr francium	88 Ra radium	89–103 **	104 Rf rutherfordium	105 Db dubnium	106 Sg seaborgium	107 Bh bohrium	108 Hs hassium	109 Mt meitnerium	110 Uun ununnilium	111 Uuu unununium	112 Uub ununbium						

*Lanthanide series

57 La lanthanum	58 Ce cerium	59 Pr praseodymium	60 Nd neodymium	61 Pm promethium	62 Sm samarium	63 Eu europium	64 Gd gadolinium	65 Tb terbium	66 Dy dysprosium	67 Ho holmium	68 Er erbium	69 Tm thulium	70 Yb ytterbium	71 Lu lutetium

**Actinide series

89 Ac actinium	90 Th thorium	91 Pa protactinium	92 U uranium	93 Np neptunium	94 Pu plutonium	95 Am americium	96 Cm curium	97 Bk berkelium	98 Cf californium	99 Es einsteinium	100 Fm fermium	101 Md mendelevium	102 No nobelium	103 Lr lawrencium

Table of elements

Atomic weights are taken from the 1983 list of the International Union of Pure and Applied Chemistry. For radioactive elements, the mass number of the most stable isotope is given in square brackets.

Symbol	Element	Derived from	Atomic No.	Weight	Discovered by	Date
Ac	actinium	Greek, *aktis* = ray	89	[227]	André-Louis Debierne (1874–1949)	1899
Ag	silver	Anglo-Saxon, *seolfor*	47	107.8682	Prehistoric	—
Al	aluminium	Latin, *alumen* = alum	13	26.98154	Friedrich Wöhler (1800–82)	1828
Am	americium	America	95	[243]	Glenn Theodore Seaborg (1912–99), Ralph James and others	1944
Ar	argon	Greek, *argos* = inactive	18	39.948	John Rayleigh (1842–1919) and William Ramsay (1852–1916)	1894
As	arsenic	Latin, *arsenicum*	33	74.9216	Prehistoric	—
At	astatine	Greek, *astatos* = unstable	85	[210]	Emilio Segrè (1905–89), Dale Corson and Mackenzie	1940
Au	gold	Anglo-Saxon, *gold*	79	196.9665	Prehistoric	—
B	boron	*Bor*ax + carb*on*	5	10.811	Humphry Davy (1778–1829)	1808
Ba	barium	Greek, *barys* = heavy	56	137.33	Humphry Davy (1778–1829)	1808
Be	beryllium	Greek, *beryllion* = beryl	4	9.01218	Friedrich Wöhler (1800–82)	1828
Bh	bohrium	Niels Bohr	107	[262]	Joint Insititute for Nuclear Research Dubna, USSR	1976
Bi	bismuth	German (origin unknown)	83	208.9804	Basil Valentine	1450
Bk	berkelium	Berkeley, California	97	[247]	Glenn Theodore Seaborg (1912–99) and others	1950
Br	bromine	Greek, *bromos* = stench	35	79.904	Antoine Balard (1802–76)	1826
C	carbon	Latin, *carbo* = charcoal	6	12.011	Prehistoric	—
Ca	calcium	Latin, *calx* = lime	20	40.078	Humphry Davy (1778–1829)	1808
Cd	cadmium	Greek, *kadmeia* = calamine	48	112.41	Friedrich Stromeyer (1776–1848)	1817
Ce	cerium	Planet Ceres	58	140.12	Jöns Jacob Berzelius (1779–1848)	1803
Cf	californium	California	98	[251]	Glenn Theodore Seaborg (1912–99) and others	1950
Cl	chlorine	Greek, *chloros* = green	17	35.453	Carl Wilhelm Scheele (1742–86)	1774
Cm	curium	Pierre and Marie Curie	96	[249]	Glenn Theodore Seaborg (1912–99), Ralph James and others	1944
Co	cobalt	German, *Kobold* = goblin	27	58.9332	Georg Brandt (1694–1768)	1739
Cr	chromium	Greek, *chroma* = colour	24	51.9961	Nicolas-Louis Vauquelin (1763–1829)	1797
Cs	cesium/ caesium	Latin, *caesium* = bluish-grey	55	132.9054	Robert Bunsen (1811–99)	1860
Cu	copper	Cyprus	29	63.546	Prehistoric	—
Db	dubnium	Dubna, a Russian town	105	[261]	Joint Institute for Nuclear Research, Dubna, USSR	1967
Dy	dysprosium	Greek, *dysprositos*	66	162.50	Paul Émile Lecoq de Boisbaudran (1838–1912)	1886
Er	erbium	Ytterby, a Swedish town	68	167.26	Carl Gustaf Mosander (1797–1858)	1843
Es	einsteinium	Albert Einstein	99	[252]	Albert Ghiorso and others	1952
Eu	europium	Europe	63	151.96	Eugène Demarcay (1852–1903)	1896
F	fluorine	Latin, *fluo* = flow	9	18.998403	Carl Wilhelm Scheele (1742–86)	1771

Symbol	Element	Derived from	Atomic No.	Weight	Discovered by	Date
Fe	iron	Anglo-Saxon, *iren*	26	55.847	Prehistoric	—
Fm	fermium	Enrico Fermi	100	[257]	Albert Ghiorso and others	1952
Fr	francium	France	87	[223]	Marguerite Perey (1909–75)	1939
Ga	gallium	Latin, *Gallia* = France	31	69.723	Paul Émile Lecoq de Boisbaudran (1838–1912)	1875
Gd	gadolinium	Johan Gadolin	64	157.25	Jean Charles Galissard de Marignac (1817–94)	1880
Ge	germanium	Latin, *Germania*	32	72.59	Clemens Winkler (1838–1904)	1886
H	hydrogen	Greek, *hydor* = water + *gen*	1	1.00794	Henry Cavendish (1731–1810)	1766
He	helium	Greek, *helios* = sun	2	4.002602	William Ramsay (1852–1916)	1895
Hf	hafnium	*Hafnia* = Copenhagen	72	178.49	Dirk Coster (1889–1950) and Georg Hevesey (1885–1966)	1923
Hg	mercury	Mercury (myth)	80	200.59	Prehistoric	—
Ho	holmium	*Holmia* = Stockholm	67	164.9304	Per Teodor Cleve (1840–1905)	1879
Hs	hassium	Latin, *Hassius* = Hess, state in Germany	108	[265]	GSI, Darmstadt, Germany	1984
I	iodine	Greek, *iodes* = violet	53	126.9045	Bernard Courtois (1777–1838)	1811
In	indium	Its indigo spectrum	49	114.82	Ferdinand Reich (1799–1882) and Hieronymous Richter (1824–98)	1863
Ir	iridium	Latin, *iris* = rainbow	77	192.22	Smithson Tennant (1761–1815)	1803
K	potassium	English, *potash*	19	39.0983	Humphry Davy (1778–1829)	1807
Kr	krypton	Greek, *kryptos* = hidden	36	83.80	William Ramsay (1852–1916) and Morris William Travers (1872–1961)	1898
La	lanthanum	Greek, *lanthanō* = conceal	57	138.9055	Carl Gustaf Mosander (1797–1858)	1839
Li	lithium	Greek, *lithos* = stone	3	6.941	Johan August Arfvedson	1817
Lr	lawrencium	Ernest Lawrence	103	[260]	Albert Ghiorso and others	1961
Lu	lutetium	*Lutetia*, ancient name of Paris	71	174.967	Georges Urbain (1872–1938) and Karl Auer, Baron von Welsbach (1858–1929)	1907
Md	mendelevium	Dmitri Mendeleyev	101	[258]	Glenn Theodore Seaborg (1912–99) and others	1955
Mg	magnesium	Magnesia, district in Thessaly	12	24.305	Antoine Bussy (1794–1882)	1829
Mn	manganese	Latin, *magnes* = magnet	25	54.9380	Johan Gottlieb Gahn (1745–1818)	1774
Mo	molybdenum	Greek, *molybdos* = lead	42	95.94	Peter Jacob Hjelm (1746–1813)	1782
Mt	meitnerium	Lise Meitner	109	[266]	GSI, Darmstadt, Germany	1982
N	nitrogen	Greek, *nitron* = salpetre	7	14.0067	Daniel Rutherford (1749–1819)	1772
Na	sodium	English, *soda*	11	22.98977	Humphry Davy (1778–1829)	1807
Nb	niobium	Niobe (Greek myth)	41	92.9064	Charles Hatchett (1765–1847)	1801
Nd	neodymium	Greek, *neos* = new and *didymos* = twin	60	144.24	Karl Auer, Baron von Welsbach (1858–1929)	1885
Ne	neon	Greek, *neos* = new	10	20.179	William Ramsay (1852–1916) and Morris William Travers (1872–1961)	1898
Ni	nickel	Swedish, abbreviation of *kopparnickel*	28	58.69	Baron Axel Fredrik Cronstedt (1722–65)	1751
No	nobelium	Alfred Nobel	102	[259]	Albert Ghiorso, Glenn Theodore Seaborg (1912–99) and others	1957

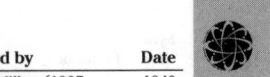

Science and Technology

Symbol	Element	Derived from	Atomic No.	Weight	Discovered by	Date
Np	neptunium	Planet Neptune	93	[237]	Edwin McMillan (1907–91) and Philip Hauge Abelson (1913–2004)	1940
O	oxygen	Greek, *oxys* = acid + *gen*	8	15.9994	Joseph Priestley (1733–1804)	1774
Os	osmium	Greek, *osme* = odour	76	190.2	Smithson Tennant (1761–1815)	1803
P	phosphorus	Latin, from Greek 'light-bearing'	15	30.97376	Hennig Brand	1669
Pa	protactinium	Greek, *protos* = first + *actinium*	91	[231]	Otto Hahn (1879–1968) and Lise Meitner (1878–1968)	1917
Pb	lead	Anglo-Saxon, *lead*	82	207.2	Prehistoric	—
Pd	palladium	Planet Pallas	46	106.42	William Hyde Wollaston (1766–1828)	1804
Pm	promethium	Prometheus, stealer of fire from heaven (Greek myth)	61	[145]	Clinton Laboratories, Oak Ridge, Tennessee	1940
Po	polonium	Poland	84	[209]	Marie Curie (1867–1934)	1898
Pr	praseodymium	Greek, *prasios* = green and *didymos* = twin	59	140.9077	Karl Auer, Baron von Welsbach (1858–1929)	1885
Pt	platinum	Spanish, *platina* = silver	78	195.08	Antonio de Ulloa	1735
Pu	plutonium	Planet Pluto	94	[244]	Glenn Theodore Seaborg (1912–99), Edwin McMillan (1907–91), Wahl and Kennedy	1940
Ra	radium	Latin, *radius* = ray	88	[226]	Marie (1867–1934) and Pierre (1859–1906) Curie	1898
Rb	rubidium	Latin, *rubidus* = red	37	85.4678	Robert Bunsen (1811–99)	1860
Re	rhenium	German, *Rhein*	75	186.207	Walter (1893–1960) and Ida Tacke (1896–1978) Noddack	1925
Rf	rutherfordium	Ernest Rutherford	104	[262]	Joint Institute for Nuclear Research, Dubna, USSR	1964
Rh	rhodium	Greek, *rhodon* = rose	45	102.9055	William Hyde Wollaston (1766–1828)	1804
Rn	radon	Radium emanation	86	[222]	Friedrich Dorn (1848–1916)	1901
Ru	ruthenium	Latin, *Ruthenia* = Russia	44	101.07	Carl Ernst Claus (1796–1864)	1845
S	sulphur/sulfur	Latin, *sulfur*	16	32.066	Prehistoric	—
Sb	antimony	Latin, *antimonium*	51	121.75	Prehistoric	—
Sc	scandium	Scandinavia	21	44.95591	Lars Fredrik Nilson (1840–99)	1879
Se	selenium	Greek, *selene* = moon	34	78.96	Jacob Berzelius (1779–1848)	1817
Sg	seaborgium	Glenn Seaborg	106	[263]	Joint Institute for Nuclear Research, Dubna, USSR	1974
Si	silicon	Latin, *silex* = flint	14	28.0855	Jacob Berzelius (1779–1848)	1823
Sm	samarium	Samarski, a Russian savant	62	150.36	Paul Émile Lecoq de Boisbaudran (1838–1912)	1879
Sn	tin	Anglo-Saxon, *tin*	50	118.710	Prehistoric	—
Sr	strontium	Strontian, a Scottish village	38	87.62	Humphry Davy (1778–1829)	1808
Ta	tantalum	Tantalus (Greek myth)	73	180.9479	Anders Gustaf Ekeberg (1767–1813)	1802
Tb	terbium	Ytterby, a Swedish town	65	158.9254	Carl Gustaf Mosander (1797–1858)	1843
Tc	technetium	Greek, *technetos* = artificial	43	[99]	Emilio Segrè (1905–89) and Carlo Perrier	1937
Te	tellurium	Latin, *tellus* = earth	52	127.60	Franz Joseph Müller, Baron von Reichenstein (1740–1825)	1782
Th	thorium	God Thor	90	232.0381	Jacob Berzelius (1779–1848)	1828

Symbol	Element	Derived from	Atomic No.	Weight	Discovered by	Date
Ti	titanium	Latin, *Titanes* = sons of the earth	22	47.88	William Gregor (1761–1817)	1789
Tl	thallium	Greek, *thallos* = budding twig	81	204.383	William Crookes (1832–1919)	1862
Tm	thulium	Greek and Roman *Thule* = Northland	69	168.9342	Per Teodor Cleve (1840–1905)	1879
U	uranium	Planet Uranus	92	238.0289	Martin Heinrich Klaproth (1743–1817)	1789
V	vanadium	Goddess Vanadis (Freya)	23	50.9415	Nils Gabriel Sefström (1765–1829)	1830
W	tungsten	Swedish, heavy stone	74	183.85	Don Fausto d'Elhujar (1755–1833)	1781
Xe	xenon	Greek, *xenos* = stranger	54	131.29	William Ramsay (1852–1916) and Morris William Travers (1872–1961)	1898
Y	yttrium	Ytterby, a Swedish town	39	88.9059	Johan Gadolin (1760–1852)	1794
Yb	ytterbium	Ytterby, a Swedish town	70	173.04	Jean Charles Galissard de Marignac (1817–94)	1878
Zn	zinc	German, *zink*	30	65.39	—	c.1500
Zr	zirconium	Persian, *zargun* = gold-coloured	40	91.224	Jacob Berzelius (1779–1848)	1824

Properties of metals

Name	Symbol	Valence no.	Atomic no.	Melting point (°C)
Aluminium	Al	3	13	660.37
Antimony (stibium)	Sb	3 or 5	51	630.74
Barium	Ba	2	56	725
Beryllium	Be	2	4	1278 ± 5
Bismuth	Bi	3 or 5	83	271.3
Cadmium	Cd	1 or 2	48	320.9
Caesium	Cs	1	55	28.40 ± 0.01
Calcium	Ca	2	20	839 ± 2
Cerium	Ce	3 or 4	58	798
Chromium	Cr	2, 3 or 6	24	1857 ± 20
Cobalt	Co	2 or 3	27	1495
Copper (cuprum)	Cu	1 or 2	29	1083.4 ± 0.2
Gallium	Ga	3	31	29.78
Gold (aurum)	Au	1 or 3	79	1064.43
Iridium	Ir	2 or 4	77	2410
Iron (ferrum)	Fe	2 or 3	26	1535
Lanthanum	La	3	57	918
Lead (plumbum)	Pb	2 or 4	82	327.5
Lithium	Li	1	3	180.5
Magnesium	Mg	2	12	648.8 ± 0.5
Manganese	Mn	2, 3, 4, 6 or 7	25	1244 ± 3
Mercury (hydrargyrum)	Hg	1 or 2	80	−38.87
Molybdenum	Mo	2 or 6	42	2617
Nickel	Ni	2 or 3	28	1453
Osmium	Os	2 or 8	76	3045 ± 30
Palladium	Pd	2 or 4	46	1554
Platinum	Pt	3 or 4	78	1772
Plutonium	Pu	—	94	641
Potassium (kalium)	K	1	19	63.25
Rubidium	Rb	1	37	38.89
Silver (argentum)	Ag	1	47	961.93
Sodium (natrium)	Na	1	11	97.81 ± 0.03
Tin (stannum)	Sn	2 or 4	50	231.97
Titanium	Ti	3 or 4	22	1660 ± 10
Tungsten (wolfram)	W	4 or 6	74	3410 ± 20
Uranium	U	2 or 6	92	1132 ± 0.8
Vanadium	V	5	23	1890 ± 10
Zinc	Zn	2	30	419.58

Properties of polymers

Polymer	Density (kg m^{-3})	Tensile strength (MN m^{-2})	Heat capacity (J g^{-1}K^{-1})	Resistivity (Ω cm)
Acetals	1 420	65	1.46	10^{15}
Cellulose	1 480–1 530	80–240	1.3–1.5	10^7–10^{14}
Cellulose acetate				
Moulded	1 220–1 340	12–58	1.26–1.8	10^{10}–10^{14}
Sheet	1 280–1 320	30–52	1.26–2.1	10^{11}–10^{15}
Cellulose nitrate (celluloid)	1 350–1 400	50	1.3–1.7	10^{10}
Epoxy cast resins	1 110–1 400	26–85	1.0	10^{12}–10^{17}
Nylon–6 (Poly-E-caprolactam)	1 120–1 170	45–90	1.6	10^{12}–10^{15}
Nylon–66 (Polyhexamethylene adipamide)	1 130–1 150	60–80	1.7	10^{14}–10^{15}
Polyacrylonitrile	1 160–1 180	200	—	10^{14}
Polycarbonates	1 200	52–62	1.17–1.25	10^{16}
Polyethylene (polythene)				
Low density	910–925	4–15	—	10^{15}–10^{18}
Medium density	926–940	8–22	—	10^{15}–10^{18}
High density	940–965	20–36	—	10^{15}–10^{18}
Polyisoprene				
Natural rubber	906–913	—	1.88	10^6
Hard rubber	1 130–1 180	39	1.38	10^{16}
Polypropylene	902–906	28–36	1.92	>10^{16}
Polystyrene	1 040–1 090	30–100	1.3–1.5	>10^6
Polyurethane				
Cast liquid	1 100–1 500	1–65	1.8	10^{11}–10^{15}
Elastomer	1 110–1 250	29–55	1.8	10^{11}–10^{13}
Polyvinylchloride (PVC)	1 300–1 400	50	0.84–1.17	10^{16}
Silicone cast resin	1 300	—	—	10^{14}–10^{15}

Science and Technology

Mathematical signs and symbols

+	plus; positive; underestimate	∞	infinity
−	minus; negative; overestimate	→	approaches the limit
±	plus or minus; positive or negative; degree of accuracy	√	square root
		$\sqrt[3]{}$, $\sqrt[4]{}$	cube root, fourth root, etc.
∓	minus or plus; negative or positive	!	factorial ($4! = 4 \times 3 \times 2 \times 1$)
×	multiplies (colloq. 'times') (6×4)	%	per cent
·	multiplies (colloq. 'times') (6.4); scalar product of two vectors ($A \cdot B$)	′	prime; minute(s) of arc; foot/feet
÷	divided by ($6 \div 4$)	″	double prime; second(s) of arc; inch(es)
/	divided by; ratio of (6/4)	⌒	arc of circle
—	divided by; ratio of ($\frac{6}{4}$)	°	degree of arc
=	equals	∠, ∠s	angle(s)
≠, ≠	not equal to	⋎	equiangular
≡	identical with	⊥	perpendicular
≢, ≢	not identical with	∥	parallel
:	ratio of (6 : 4); scalar product of two tensors (X : Y)	○, Ⓢ	circle(s)
::	proportionately equals (1 : 2 :: 2 : 4)	△, ▲	triangle(s)
≈	approximately equal to; equivalent to; similar to	□	square(s)
		▭	rectangle
>	greater than	▱	parallelogram
≫	much greater than	≅	congruent to
≯	not greater than	∴	therefore
<	less than	∵	because
≪	much less than	m̲	measured by
≮	not less than	△	increment
⩾, ≥, ≧	equal to or greater than	Σ	summation
⩽, ≤, ≦	equal to or less than	Π	product
∝	directly proportional to	∫	integral sign
( )	parentheses	▽	del: differential operator
[ ]	brackets	∩	union
{ }	braces	∪	interaction
—	vinculum: division ($\overline{a-b}$); chord of circle or length of line ($\overline{AB}$); arithmetic mean ($\overline{X}$)		

Squares and roots

No.	Square	Cube	Square root	Cube root	No.	Square	Cube	Square root	Cube root
1	1	1	1.000	1.000	13	169	2197	3.606	2.351
2	4	8	1.414	1.260	14	196	2744	3.742	2.410
3	9	27	1.732	1.442	15	225	3375	3.873	2.466
4	16	64	2.000	1.587	16	256	4096	4.000	2.520
5	25	125	2.236	1.710	17	289	4913	4.123	2.571
6	36	216	2.449	1.817	18	324	5832	4.243	2.621
7	49	343	2.646	1.913	19	361	6859	4.359	2.668
8	64	512	2.828	2.000	20	400	8000	4.472	2.714
9	81	729	3.000	2.080	25	625	15625	5.000	2.924
10	100	1000	3.162	2.154	30	900	27000	5.477	3.107
11	121	1331	3.317	2.224	40	1600	64000	6.325	3.420
12	144	1728	3.464	2.289	50	2500	125000	7.071	3.684

Science and Technology

Areas and volumes of common shapes

The Greek letter π is used in some of the formulae below, and represents the ratio of the circumference of a circle to its diameter. Its value is approximately equal to 3.14159.

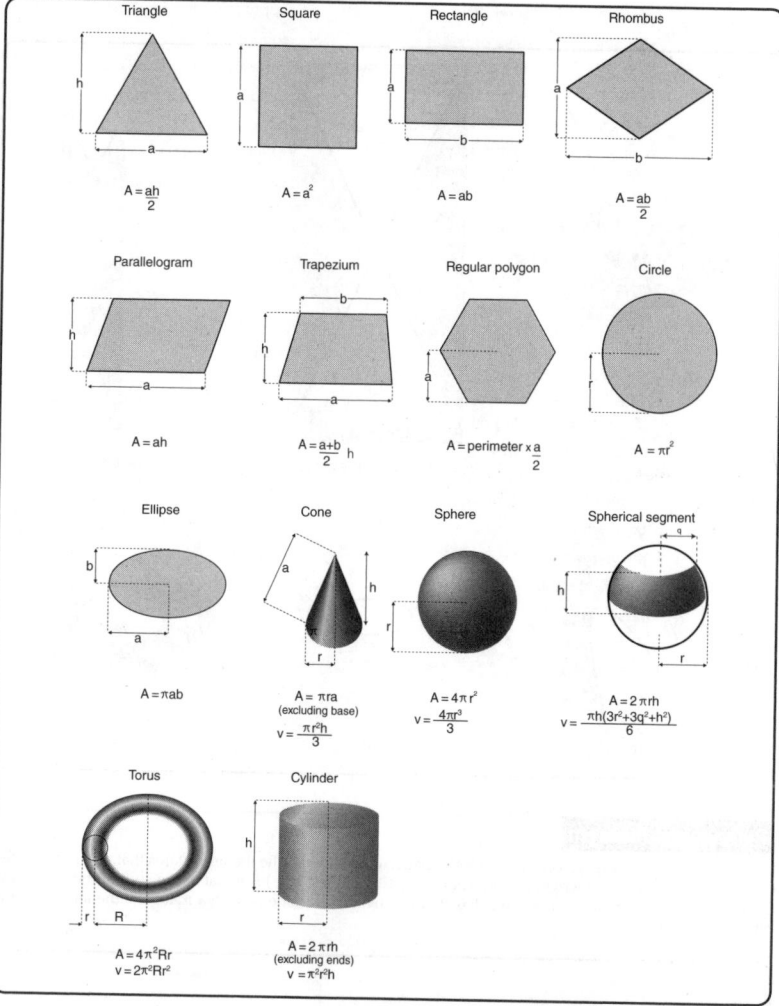

Triangle

$A = \dfrac{ah}{2}$

Square

$A = a^2$

Rectangle

$A = ab$

Rhombus

$A = \dfrac{ab}{2}$

Parallelogram

$A = ah$

Trapezium

$A = \dfrac{a+b}{2}\, h$

Regular polygon

$A = \text{perimeter} \times \dfrac{a}{2}$

Circle

$A = \pi r^2$

Ellipse

$A = \pi ab$

Cone

$A = \pi ra$ (excluding base)

$V = \dfrac{\pi r^2 h}{3}$

Sphere

$A = 4\pi r^2$

$V = \dfrac{4\pi r^3}{3}$

Spherical segment

$A = 2\pi rh$

$V = \dfrac{\pi h(3r^2 + 3q^2 + h^2)}{6}$

Torus

$A = 4\pi^2 Rr$

$V = 2\pi^2 Rr^2$

Cylinder

$A = 2\pi rh$ (excluding ends)

$V = \pi^2 r^2 h$

Science and Technology

Science and Technology

Conic sections

A conic section is the curved figure producedwhen a plane (flat surface) intersects a cone. Depending on the angle at which it cuts through the cone, it may be a circle, ellipse, hyperbola or parabola. V is the vertex of the right cone.

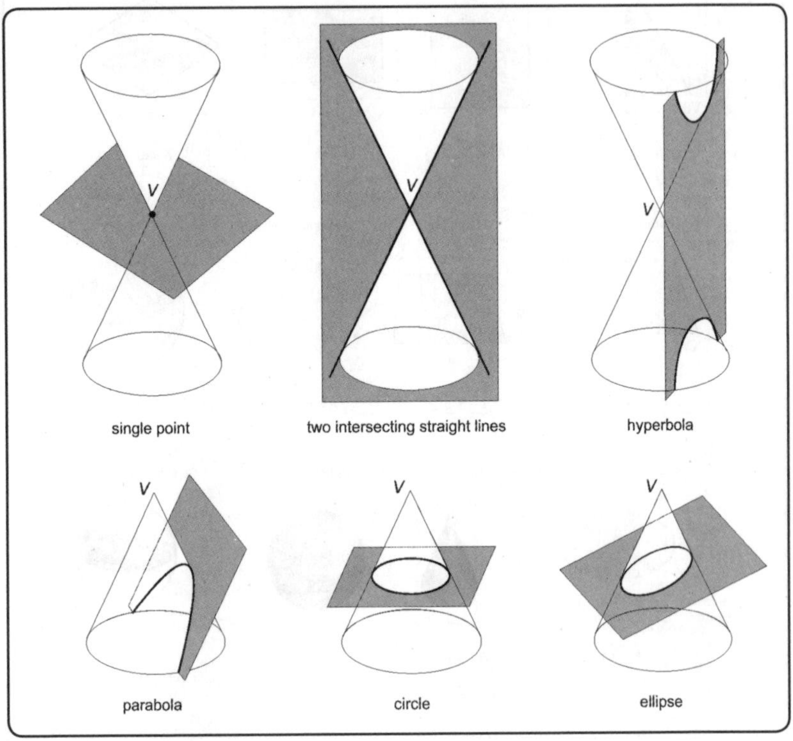

single point   two intersecting straight lines   hyperbola

parabola   circle   ellipse

Pythagoras' theorem

Named after the Greek philosopher and mathematician Pythagoras, the theorem states that, in a right-angled triangle, the square of the length of the hypotenuse (the longest side) is equal to the sum of the squares of the two other sides. It can be used to calculate the length of any side of such a triangle if the lengths of the other sides are known.

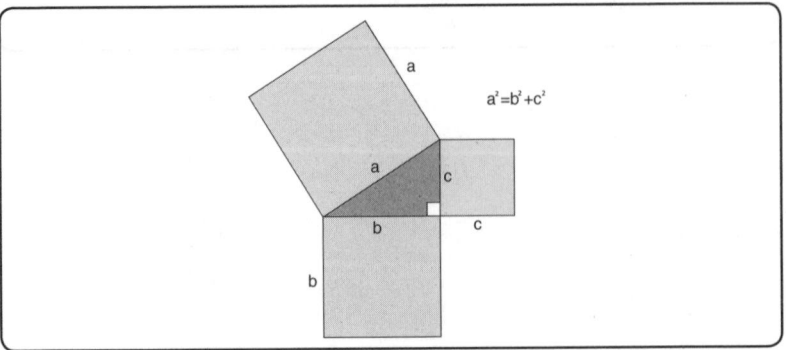

$$a^2 = b^2 + c^2$$

Numerical equivalents

Arabic	Roman	Greek	Binary no.	Arabic	Roman	Greek	Binary no.
1	I	α'	1	19	XIX	$\iota\theta'$	10011
2	II	β'	10	20	XX	κ'	10100
3	III	γ'	11	30	XXX	λ'	11110
4	IV	δ'	100	40	XL	μ'	101000
5	V	ε'	101	50	L	ν'	110010
6	VI	σ'	110	60	LX	ξ'	111100
7	VII	ζ'	111	70	LXX	o'	1000110
8	VIII	η'	1000	80	LXXX	π'	1010000
9	IX	θ'	1001	90	XC	$,o'$	1011010
10	X	ι'	1010	100	C	ρ'	1100100
11	XI	$\iota\alpha'$	1011	200	CC	σ'	11001000
12	XII	$\iota\beta'$	1100	300	CCC	τ'	100101100
13	XIII	$\iota\gamma'$	1101	400	CD	υ'	110010000
14	XIV	$\iota\delta'$	1110	500	D	φ'	111110100
15	XV	$\iota\varepsilon'$	1111	1000	M	$,\alpha$	1111101000
16	XVI	$\iota\sigma'$	10000	5000	$\overline{V}$	$,\varepsilon$	1001110001000
17	XVII	$\iota\zeta'$	10001	10000	$\overline{X}$	$,\iota$	10011100010000
18	XVIII	$\iota\eta'$	10010	100000	$\overline{C}$	$,\rho$	11000011010100000

%	D[1]	F[2]	%	D	F	%	D	F	%	D	F	%	D	F
1	0.01	$\frac{1}{100}$	$12\frac{1}{2}$	0.125	$\frac{1}{8}$	24	0.24	$\frac{6}{25}$	36	0.36	$\frac{9}{25}$	49	0.49	$\frac{49}{100}$
2	0.02	$\frac{1}{50}$	13	0.13	$\frac{13}{100}$	25	0.25	$\frac{1}{4}$	37	0.37	$\frac{37}{100}$	50	0.50	$\frac{1}{2}$
3	0.03	$\frac{3}{100}$	14	0.14	$\frac{7}{50}$	26	0.26	$\frac{13}{50}$	38	0.38	$\frac{19}{50}$	55	0.55	$\frac{11}{20}$
4	0.04	$\frac{1}{25}$	15	0.15	$\frac{3}{20}$	27	0.27	$\frac{27}{100}$	39	0.39	$\frac{39}{100}$	60	0.60	$\frac{3}{5}$
5	0.05	$\frac{1}{20}$	16	0.16	$\frac{4}{25}$	28	0.28	$\frac{7}{25}$	40	0.40	$\frac{2}{5}$	65	0.65	$\frac{13}{20}$
6	0.06	$\frac{3}{50}$	$16\frac{2}{3}$	0.167	$\frac{1}{6}$	29	0.29	$\frac{29}{100}$	41	0.41	$\frac{41}{100}$	70	0.70	$\frac{7}{10}$
7	0.07	$\frac{7}{100}$	17	0.17	$\frac{17}{100}$	30	0.30	$\frac{3}{10}$	42	0.42	$\frac{21}{50}$	75	0.75	$\frac{3}{4}$
8	0.08	$\frac{2}{25}$	18	0.18	$\frac{9}{50}$	31	0.31	$\frac{31}{100}$	43	0.43	$\frac{43}{100}$	80	0.80	$\frac{4}{5}$
$8\frac{1}{3}$	0.083	$\frac{1}{12}$	19	0.19	$\frac{19}{100}$	32	0.32	$\frac{8}{25}$	44	0.44	$\frac{11}{25}$	85	0.85	$\frac{17}{20}$
9	0.09	$\frac{9}{100}$	20	0.20	$\frac{1}{5}$	33	0.33	$\frac{33}{100}$	45	0.45	$\frac{9}{20}$	90	0.90	$\frac{9}{10}$
10	0.10	$\frac{1}{10}$	21	0.21	$\frac{21}{100}$	$33\frac{1}{3}$	0.333	$\frac{1}{3}$	46	0.46	$\frac{23}{50}$	95	0.95	$\frac{19}{20}$
11	0.11	$\frac{11}{100}$	22	0.22	$\frac{11}{50}$	34	0.34	$\frac{17}{50}$	47	0.47	$\frac{47}{100}$	100	1.00	1
12	0.12	$\frac{3}{25}$	23	0.23	$\frac{23}{100}$	35	0.35	$\frac{7}{20}$	48	0.48	$\frac{12}{25}$			

[1] Decimal [2] Fraction

Fraction	Decimal	Fraction	Decimal	Fraction	Decimal	Fraction	Decimal
$\frac{1}{2}$	0.5000	$\frac{7}{8}$	0.8750	$\frac{10}{11}$	0.9090	$\frac{19}{20}$	0.9500
$\frac{1}{3}$	0.3333	$\frac{1}{9}$	0.1111	$\frac{1}{12}$	0.0833	$\frac{1}{32}$	0.0312
$\frac{2}{3}$	0.6667	$\frac{2}{9}$	0.2222	$\frac{5}{12}$	0.4167	$\frac{3}{32}$	0.0937
$\frac{1}{4}$	0.2500	$\frac{4}{9}$	0.4444	$\frac{7}{12}$	0.5833	$\frac{5}{32}$	0.1562
$\frac{3}{4}$	0.7500	$\frac{5}{9}$	0.5556	$\frac{11}{12}$	0.9167	$\frac{7}{32}$	0.2187
$\frac{1}{5}$	0.2000	$\frac{7}{9}$	0.7778	$\frac{1}{16}$	0.0625	$\frac{9}{32}$	0.2812
$\frac{2}{5}$	0.4000	$\frac{8}{9}$	0.8889	$\frac{3}{16}$	0.1875	$\frac{11}{32}$	0.3437
$\frac{3}{5}$	0.6000	$\frac{1}{10}$	0.1000	$\frac{5}{16}$	0.3125	$\frac{13}{32}$	0.4062
$\frac{4}{5}$	0.8000	$\frac{3}{10}$	0.3000	$\frac{7}{16}$	0.4375	$\frac{15}{32}$	0.4687
$\frac{1}{6}$	0.1667	$\frac{7}{10}$	0.7000	$\frac{9}{16}$	0.5625	$\frac{17}{32}$	0.5312
$\frac{5}{6}$	0.8333	$\frac{9}{10}$	0.9000	$\frac{11}{16}$	0.6875	$\frac{19}{32}$	0.5937
$\frac{1}{7}$	0.1429	$\frac{1}{11}$	0.0909	$\frac{13}{16}$	0.8125	$\frac{21}{32}$	0.6562
$\frac{2}{7}$	0.2857	$\frac{2}{11}$	0.1818	$\frac{15}{16}$	0.9375	$\frac{23}{32}$	0.7187
$\frac{3}{7}$	0.4286	$\frac{3}{11}$	0.2727	$\frac{1}{20}$	0.0500	$\frac{25}{32}$	0.7812
$\frac{4}{7}$	0.5714	$\frac{4}{11}$	0.3636	$\frac{3}{20}$	0.1500	$\frac{27}{32}$	0.8437
$\frac{5}{7}$	0.7143	$\frac{5}{11}$	0.4545	$\frac{7}{20}$	0.3500	$\frac{29}{32}$	0.9062
$\frac{6}{7}$	0.8571	$\frac{6}{11}$	0.5454	$\frac{9}{20}$	0.4500	$\frac{31}{32}$	0.9687
$\frac{1}{8}$	0.1250	$\frac{7}{11}$	0.6363	$\frac{11}{20}$	0.5500		
$\frac{3}{8}$	0.3750	$\frac{8}{11}$	0.7272	$\frac{13}{20}$	0.6500		
$\frac{5}{8}$	0.6250	$\frac{9}{11}$	0.8181	$\frac{17}{20}$	0.8500		

Science and Technology

Multiplication table

	2	3	4	5	6	7	8	9	10	11	12	13	14	15	16	17	18	19	20	21	22	23	24	25
2	4	6	8	10	12	14	16	18	20	22	24	26	28	30	32	34	36	38	40	42	44	46	48	50
3	6	9	12	15	18	21	24	27	30	33	36	39	42	45	48	51	54	57	60	63	66	69	72	75
4	8	12	16	20	24	28	32	36	40	44	48	52	56	60	64	68	72	76	80	84	88	92	96	100
5	10	15	20	25	30	35	40	45	50	55	60	65	70	75	80	85	90	95	100	105	110	115	120	125
6	12	18	24	30	36	42	48	54	60	66	72	78	84	90	96	102	108	114	120	126	132	138	144	150
7	14	21	28	35	42	49	56	63	70	77	84	91	98	105	112	119	126	133	140	147	154	161	168	175
8	16	24	32	40	48	56	64	72	80	88	96	104	112	120	128	136	144	152	160	168	176	184	192	200
9	18	27	36	45	54	63	72	81	90	99	108	117	126	135	144	153	162	171	180	189	198	207	216	225
10	20	30	40	50	60	70	80	90	100	110	120	130	140	150	160	170	180	190	200	210	220	230	240	250
11	22	33	44	55	66	77	88	99	110	121	132	143	154	165	176	187	198	209	220	231	242	253	264	275
12	24	36	48	60	72	84	96	108	120	132	144	156	168	180	192	204	216	228	240	252	264	276	288	300
13	26	39	52	65	78	91	104	117	130	143	156	169	182	195	208	221	234	247	260	273	286	299	312	325
14	28	42	56	70	84	98	112	126	140	154	168	182	196	210	224	238	252	266	280	294	308	322	336	350
15	30	45	60	75	90	105	120	135	150	165	180	195	210	225	240	255	270	285	300	315	330	345	360	375
16	32	48	64	80	96	112	128	144	160	176	192	208	224	240	256	272	288	304	320	336	352	368	384	400
17	34	51	68	85	102	119	136	153	170	187	204	221	238	255	272	289	306	323	340	357	374	391	408	425
18	36	54	72	90	108	126	144	162	180	198	216	234	252	270	288	306	324	342	360	378	396	414	432	450
19	38	57	76	95	114	133	152	171	190	209	228	247	266	285	304	323	342	361	380	399	418	437	456	475
20	40	60	80	100	120	140	160	180	200	220	240	260	280	300	320	340	360	380	400	420	440	460	480	500
21	42	63	84	105	126	147	168	189	210	231	252	273	294	315	336	357	378	399	420	441	462	483	504	525
22	44	66	88	110	132	154	176	198	220	242	264	286	308	330	352	374	396	418	440	462	484	506	528	550
23	46	69	92	115	138	161	184	207	230	253	276	299	322	345	368	391	414	437	460	483	506	529	552	575
24	48	72	96	120	144	168	192	216	240	264	288	312	336	360	384	408	432	456	480	501	528	552	576	600
25	50	75	100	125	150	175	200	225	250	275	300	325	350	375	400	425	450	475	500	525	550	575	600	625

SI units (International system of units)

Concept	Symbol	Name of unit	Abbreviation of unit name
Length	l	metre*	m
Mass	m	kilogramme*	kg
Time	t	second*	s
Electric current	I	ampere*	A
Thermodynamic temperature	T	kelvin*	K
Luminous intensity	I	candela*	cd
Amount of substance		mole*	mol
Plane angle	α, β, θ, etc	radian	rad
Solid angle	Ω, ω	steradian	sr
Area	A, a	square metre	m^2
Volume	V, v	cubic metre	m^3
Velocity	v, u	metre/second	$m\,s^{-1}$
Acceleration	a	metre/second^2	$m\,s^{-2}$
Density	ρ	kilogramme/metre^3	$kg\,m^{-3}$
Mass rate of flow	m, M	kilogramme/second	$kg\,s^{-1}$
Volume rate of flow	V	cubic metre/second	$m^3 s^{-1}$
Moment of inertia	I	kilogramme metre^2	$kg\,m^2$
Momentum	p	kilogramme metre/sec	$kg\,m\,s^{-1}$
Angular momentum	$I\omega$	kilogramme metre^2/sec	$kg\,m^2 s^{-1}$
Force	F	newton	N
Torque (moment of force)	$T (M)$	newton metre	N m
Work (energy, heat)	$W (E)$	joule	J
Potential energy	V	joule	J
Kinetic energy	$T (W)$	joule	J
Heat (enthalpy)	$Q (H)$	joule	J
Power	P	watt	W
Pressure (stress)	$p\ (\sigma, f)$	newton/metre^2	$N\,m^{-2}$
Surface tension	$\gamma\ (\sigma)$	newton/metre	$N\,m^{-1}$
Viscosity, dynamic	η, μ		$N\,s\,m^{-1}$

Science and Technology

Concept	Symbol	Name of unit	Abbreviation of unit name
Viscosity, kinematic	υ		$m^2\,s^{-1}$
Temperature	θ, T	degree Celsius, kelvin	°C, K
Velocity of light	c	metre/second	$m\,s^{-1}$
Permeability of vacuum	μ_0	henry/metre	$H\,m^{-1}$
Permittivity of vacuum	ε_0	farad/metre	$F\,m^{-1}$
Electric charge	Q	coulomb	C
Electric potential (potential difference)	V	volt	V
Electric field strength (electric force)	E	volt/metre	$V\,m^{-1}$
Electric resistance	R	ohm	Ω
Conductance	G	siemens	S
Electric flux	Ψ	coulomb	$\Psi = Q$
Electric flux density (displacement)	D	coulomb/metre²	$C\,m^{-2}$
Frequency	f	hertz	Hz
Permittivity	ε	farad/metre	$F\,m^{-1}$
Relative permittivity	ε_r		
Magnetic field strength	H	amp. turn/metre	$A\,t\,m^{-1}$
Magnetic flux	Φ	weber	Wb
Magnetic flux density	B	tesla	T
Permeability	μ	henry/metre	$H\,m^{-1}$
Relative permeability	μ_r		
Mutual inductance	M	henry	H
Self inductance	L	henry	H
Capacitance	C	farad	F
Reactance	X	ohm	Ω
Impedance	Z	ohm	Ω
Susceptance	B	siemens	S
Admittance	Y	siemens	S
Total voltamperes	S	volt amp	VA
Reactive voltamperes	Q	volt amp reactive	VAr
Power factor	p.f.	—	—
Luminous flux	Φ	lumen	lm
Illumination	E	lux	lx

*SI base units; all other units listed are SI derived units.

SI conversion factors

This table gives the conversion factors for many British and other units which are still in common use, showing their equivalents in terms of the international system of units (SI). The column labelled 'SI equivalent' gives the SI value of one unit of the type named in the first column, eg 1 calorie is 4.186 J.

Unit name	Symbol	Quantity	SI equivalent	Unit
acre		area	0.405	hm²
ångström*	Å	length	0.1	nm
astronomical unit	AU	length	0.150	Tm
atomic mass unit	amu	mass	1.661×10^{-27}	kg
bar*	bar	pressure	0.1	MPa
barn*	b	area	100	fm²
barrel (US) = 42 US gal	bbl	volume	0.159	m³
British thermal unit	Btu	energy	1.055	kJ
calorie	cal	energy	4.186	J
cubic foot	ft³	volume	0.028	m³
cubic inch	in³	volume	16.387	cm³
cubic yard	yd³	volume	0.765	m³
curie*	Ci	activity of radionuclide	37	GBq
degree = 1/90 rt angle	°	plane angle	$\pi/180$	rad
degree Celsius	°C	temperature	1	K
degree Centigrade	°C	temperature	1	K
degree Fahrenheit	°F	temperature	5/9	K
degree Rankine	°R	temperature	5/9	K
dyne	dyn	force	10	μN
electronvolt	eV	energy	0.160	aJ
erg	erg	energy	0.1	μJ

Unit name	Symbol	Quantity	SI equivalent	Unit
fathom (6 ft)		length	1.829	m
fermi		length	1	fm
foot	ft	length	30.48	cm
foot per second	ft s^{-1}	velocity	$\begin{cases} 0.305 \\ 1.097 \end{cases}$	m s^{-1} km h^{-1}
gallon (UK)*	gal	volume	4.546	dm^3
gallon (US)* = 231 in^3	gal	volume	3.785	dm^3
gallon (UK) per mile		consumption	2.825	dm^3 km^{-1}
gauss	Gs, G	magnetic flux density	100	μT
grade = 0.01 rt angle		plane angle	π/200	rad
grain	gr	mass	0.065	g
hectare*	ha	area	1	hm^2
horsepower	hp	energy	0.746	kW
inch	in	length	2.54	cm
kilogram-force	kgf	force	9.807	N
knot*		velocity	1.852	km h^{-1}
light year	l.y.	length	9.461×10^{15}	m
litre	l	volume	1	dm^3
maxwell	Mx	magnetic flux	10	nWb
metric carat		mass	0.2	g
micron	μ	length	1	μm
mile (nautical)*		length	1.852	km
mile (statute)		length	1.609	km
mile per hour (mph)	mile h^{-1}	velocity	1.609	km h^{-1}
minute = (1/60)°	′	plane angle	π/10 800	rad
oersted	Oe	magnetic field strength	1/(4π)	kA m^{-1}
ounce (avoirdupois)	oz	mass	28.349	g
ounce (troy) = 480 gr		mass	31.103	g
parsec	pc	length	30 857	Tm
phot	ph	illuminance	10	klx
pint (UK)	pt	volume	0.568	dm^3
poise	p	viscosity	0.1	Pa s
pound	lb	mass	0.454	kg
pound-force	lbf	force	4.448	N
pound-force/in^{-2}		pressure	6.895×10^3	kPa
poundal	pdl	force	0.138	N
pounds per square inch	psi	pressure	6.895×10^3	kPa
rad*	rad	absorbed dose	0.01	Gy
rem*	rem	dose equivalent	0.01	Sv
right angle = π/2 rad		plane angle	1.571	rad
röntgen*	R	exposure	0.258	mC kg^{-1}
second = (1/60)′	″	plane angle	π/648	mrad
slug		mass	14.594	kg
solar mass	M	mass	1.989×10^{30}	kg
square foot	ft^2	area	9.290	dm^2
square inch	in^2	area	6.452	cm^2
square mile (statute)		area	2.590	km^2
square yard	yd^2	area	0.836	m^2
standard atmosphere	atm	pressure	0.101	MPa
stere	st	volume	1	m^3
stilb	sb	luminance	10	kcd m^{-2}
stokes	St	viscosity	1	cm^2 s^{-1}
therm = 10^5 Btu		energy	0.105	GJ
ton = 2 240 lb		mass	1.016	Mg
ton-force	tonf	force	9.964	kN
ton-force/in^{-2}		pressure	15.444	MPa
tonne	t	mass	1	Mg
torr mmHg }	torr	pressure	0.133	kPa
X unit		length	0.100	pm
yard	yd	length	0.915	m

*In temporary use with SI.

SI prefixes

Factor	Prefix	Symbol	Factor	Prefix	Symbol	Factor	Prefix	Symbol
10^{24}	yotta	Y	10^3	kilo	k	10^{-9}	nano	n
10^{21}	zetta	Z	10^2	hecto	h	10^{-12}	pico	p
10^{18}	exa	E	10^1	deca	da	10^{-15}	femto	f
10^{15}	peta	P	10^{-1}	deci	d	10^{-18}	atto	a
10^{12}	tera	T	10^{-2}	centi	c	10^{-21}	zepto	z
10^9	giga	G	10^{-3}	milli	m	10^{-24}	yocto	y
10^6	mega	M	10^{-6}	micro	µ			

Science and Technology

Temperature conversion

To convert	To	Equation
°Fahrenheit	°Celsius	$-32, \times 5, \div 9$
°Fahrenheit	°Rankine	$+459.67$
°Fahrenheit	°Réaumur	$-32, \times 4, \div 9$
°Celsius	°Fahrenheit	$\times 9, \div 5, +32$
°Celsius	Kelvin	$+273.15$
°Celsius	°Réaumur	$\times 4, \div 5$
Kelvin	°Celsius	-273.15
°Rankine	°Fahrenheit	-459.67
°Réaumur	°Fahrenheit	$\times 9, \div 4, +32$
°Réaumur	°Celsius	$\times 5, \div 4$

Carry out operations in sequence.

Degrees Fahrenheit (F) → Degrees Celsius (Centigrade) (C)

(F) →	(C)	(F) →	(C)	(F) →	(C)	(F) →	(C)	(F) →	(C)
1	−17.2	42	5.5	83	28.3	124	51.1	165	73.9
2	−16.7	43	6.1	84	28.9	125	51.7	166	74.4
3	−16.1	44	6.7	85	29.4	126	52.2	167	75.0
4	−15.5	45	7.2	86	30.0	127	52.8	168	75.5
5	−15.0	46	7.8	87	30.5	128	53.3	169	76.1
6	−14.4	47	8.3	88	31.1	129	53.9	170	76.7
7	−13.9	48	8.9	89	31.7	130	54.4	171	77.2
8	−13.3	49	9.4	90	32.2	131	55.0	172	77.8
9	−12.8	50	10.0	91	32.8	132	55.5	173	78.3
10	−12.2	51	10.5	92	33.3	133	56.1	174	78.9
11	−11.6	52	11.1	93	33.9	134	56.7	175	79.4
12	−11.1	53	11.7	94	34.4	135	57.2	176	80.0
13	−10.5	54	12.2	95	35.0	136	57.8	177	80.5
14	−10.0	55	12.8	96	35.5	137	58.3	178	81.1
15	−9.4	56	13.3	97	36.1	138	58.9	179	81.7
16	−8.9	57	13.9	98	36.7	139	59.4	180	82.2
17	−8.3	58	14.4	99	37.2	140	60.0	181	82.8
18	−7.8	59	15.0	100	37.8	141	60.5	182	83.3
19	−7.2	60	15.5	101	38.3	142	61.1	183	83.9
20	−6.7	61	16.1	102	38.9	143	61.7	184	84.4
21	−6.1	62	16.7	103	39.4	144	62.2	185	85.0
22	−5.5	63	17.2	104	40.0	145	62.8	186	85.5
23	−5.0	64	17.8	105	40.5	146	63.3	187	86.1
24	−4.4	65	18.3	106	41.1	147	63.9	188	86.7
25	−3.9	66	18.9	107	41.7	148	64.4	189	87.2
26	−3.3	67	19.4	108	42.2	149	65.0	190	87.8
27	−2.8	68	20.0	109	42.8	150	65.5	191	88.3
28	−2.2	69	20.5	110	43.3	151	66.1	192	88.8
29	−1.7	70	21.1	111	43.9	152	66.7	193	89.4
30	−1.1	71	21.7	112	44.4	153	67.2	194	90.0
31	−0.5	72	22.2	113	45.0	154	67.8	195	90.5
32	0	73	22.8	114	45.5	155	68.3	196	91.1
33	0.5	74	23.3	115	46.1	156	68.9	197	91.7
34	1.1	75	23.9	116	46.7	157	69.4	198	92.2
35	1.7	76	24.4	117	47.2	158	70.0	199	92.8
36	2.2	77	25.0	118	47.8	159	70.5	200	93.3
37	2.8	78	25.5	119	48.3	160	71.1	201	93.9
38	3.3	79	26.1	120	48.9	161	71.7		
39	3.9	80	26.7	121	49.4	162	72.2		
40	4.4	81	27.2	122	50.0	163	72.8		
41	5.0	82	27.8	123	50.5	164	73.3		

Science and Technology

Degrees Celsius (Centigrade) (C) →Degrees Fahrenheit (F)

(C) →	(F)	(C) →	(F)	(C) →	(F)	(C) →	(F)	(C) →	(F)
1	33.8	22	71.6	43	109.4	64	147.2	85	185.0
2	35.6	23	73.4	44	111.2	65	149.0	86	186.8
3	37.4	24	75.2	45	113.0	66	150.8	87	188.6
4	39.2	25	77.0	46	114.8	67	152.6	88	190.4
5	41.0	26	78.8	47	116.6	68	154.4	89	192.2
6	42.8	27	80.6	48	118.4	69	156.2	90	194.0
7	44.6	28	82.4	49	120.2	70	158.0	91	195.8
8	46.4	29	84.2	50	122.0	71	159.8	92	197.6
9	48.2	30	86.0	51	123.8	72	161.6	93	199.4
10	50.0	31	87.8	52	125.6	73	163.4	94	201.2
11	51.8	32	89.6	53	127.4	74	165.2	95	203.0
12	53.6	33	91.4	54	129.2	75	167.0	96	204.8
13	55.4	34	93.2	55	131.0	76	168.8	97	206.6
14	57.2	35	95.0	56	132.8	77	170.6	98	208.4
15	59.0	36	96.8	57	134.6	78	172.4	99	210.2
16	60.8	37	98.6	58	136.4	79	174.2	100	212.0
17	62.6	38	100.4	59	138.2	80	176.0		
18	64.4	39	102.2	60	140.0	81	177.8		
19	66.2	40	104.0	61	141.8	82	179.6		
20	68.0	41	105.8	62	143.6	83	181.4		
21	69.8	42	107.6	63	145.4	84	183.2		

Common measures

■ Metric units		Imperial equivalent
Length		
	1 millimetre	0.03937 in
10 mm	1 centimetre	0.39 in
10 cm	1 decimetre	3.94 in
100 cm	1 metre	39.37 in
1000 m	1 kilometre	0.62 mile
Area		
	1 square millimetre	0.0016 sq in
	1 square centimetre	0.155 sq in
100 sq cm	1 square decimetre	15.5 sq in
10 000 sq cm	1 square metre	10.76 sq ft
10 000 sq m	1 hectare	2.47 acres
Volume		
	1 cubic centimetre	0.061 cu in
1000 cu cm	1 cubic decimetre	61.024 cu in
1000 cu dm	1 cubic metre	35.31 cu ft
		1.308 cu yds
Liquid volume		
	1 litre	1.76 pints
100 litres	1 hectolitre	22 gallons
Weight		
	1 gram	0.035 oz
1 000 g	1 kilogram	2.2046 lb
1 000 kg	1 tonne	0.9842 ton

■ Imperial units		Metric equivalent
Length		
	1 inch	2.54 cm
12 in	1 foot	30.48 cm
3 ft	1 yard	0.9144 m
1 760 yd	1 mile	1.6093 km
Area		
	1 square inch	6.45 sq cm
144 sq in	1 square foot	0.0929 m^2
9 sq ft	1 square yard	0.836 m^2
4840 sq yd	1 acre	0.405 ha

Imperial units		Metric equivalent
640 acres	1 square mile	259 ha

Volume

	1 cubic inch	16.3871 cm³
1728 cu in	1 cubic foot	0.028 m³
27 cu ft	1 cubic yard	0.765 m³

Liquid volume

	1 pint	0.57 litres
2 pints	1 quart	1.14 litres
4 quarts	1 gallon	4.55 litres

Weight

	1 ounce	28.3495 g
16 oz	1 pound	0.4536 kg
14 lb	1 stone	6.35 kg
8 stones	1 hundredweight	50.8 kg
20 cwt	1 ton	1.016 tonnes

Other measures

Nautical
1 span = 9 inches = 23 centimetres
8 spans = 1 fathom = 6 feet
1 cable's length = 1/10 nautical mile
1 nautical mile (old) = 6080 feet
1 nautical mile (international) = 6076.1 feet = 1.151 statute miles (= 1852 metres)
60 nautical miles = 1 degree
3 nautical miles = 1 league (nautical)
1 knot = 1 nautical mile per hour
1 ton (shipping) = 42 cubic feet
1 ton (displacement) = 35 cubic feet
1 ton (register) = 100 cubic feet
Crude oil (petroleum)
1 barrel = 35 imperial gallons = 42 US gallons
Paper (writing)
25 sheets = 1 quire
20 quires = 1 ream = 500 sheets
Printing
1 point = 0.3515 millimetres
1 pica = 4.2175 millimetres = 12 points
Timber
1000 millisteres = 1 stere = 1 cubic metre
1 board foot = 144 cubic inches (12 × 12 × 1 inch)
1 cord foot = 16 cubic feet
1 cord = 8 cord feet
1 hoppus foot = 4/π cubic feet (round timber)
1 Petrograd standard = 165 cubic feet
Cloth
1 ell = 45 inches
1 bolt = 120 feet = 32 ells
Brewing
4.5 gallons = 1 pin
2 pins = 9 gallons = 1 firkin
4 firkins = 1 barrel = 36 gallons
6 firkins = 1 hogshead = 54 gallons
4 hogsheads = 1 tun
Horses (height)
1 hand = 4 inches = 10 centimetres

Conversion factors

Science and Technology

■ Imperial to metric			Multiply by
Length			
inches	→	millimetres	25.4
inches	→	centimetres	2.54
feet	→	metres	0.3048
yards	→	metres	0.9144
statute miles	→	kilometres	1.6093
nautical miles	→	kilometres	1.852
Area			
square inches	→	square centimetres	6.4516
square feet	→	square metres	0.0929
square yards	→	square metres	0.8361
acres	→	hectares	0.4047
square miles	→	square kilometres	2.5899
Volume			
cubic inches	→	cubic centimetres	16.3871
cubic feet	→	cubic metres	0.0283
cubic yards	→	cubic metres	0.7646
Capacity			
UK fluid ounces	→	litres	0.0284
US fluid ounces	→	litres	0.0296
UK pints	→	litres	0.5682
US pints	→	litres	0.4732
UK gallons	→	litres	4.546
US gallons	→	litres	3.7854
Weight			
ounces (avoirdupois)	→	grams	28.3495
ounces (troy)	→	grams	31.1035
pounds	→	kilograms	0.4536
tons (long)	→	tonnes	1.016

■ Metric to imperial			Multiply by
Length			
millimetres	→	inches	0.0394
centimetres	→	inches	0.3937
metres	→	feet	3.2808
metres	→	yards	1.0936
kilometres	→	statute miles	0.6214
kilometres	→	nautical miles	0.54
Area			
square centimetres	→	square inches	0.155
square metres	→	square feet	10.764
square metres	→	square yards	1.196
hectares	→	acres	2.471
square kilometres	→	square miles	0.386
Volume			
cubic centimetres	→	cubic inches	0.061
cubic metres	→	cubic feet	35.315
cubic metres	→	cubic yards	1.308
Capacity			
litres	→	UK fluid ounces	35.1961
litres	→	US fluid ounces	33.8150
litres	→	UK pints	1.7598
litres	→	US pints	2.1134
litres	→	UK gallons	0.2199
litres	→	US gallons	0.2642

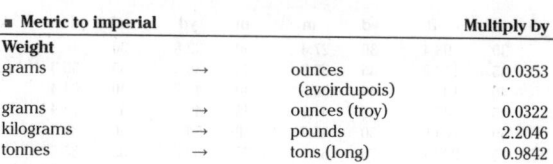

■ Metric to imperial			Multiply by
Weight			
grams	→	ounces (avoirdupois)	0.0353
grams	→	ounces (troy)	0.0322
kilograms	→	pounds	2.2046
tonnes	→	tons (long)	0.9842

Conversion tables: length

in	cm	in	cm	cm	in
⅛	0.3	16	40.6	1	0.39
¼	0.6	17	43.2	2	0.79
⅜	1	18	45.7	3	1.18
½	1.3	19	48.3	4	1.57
⅝	1.6	20	50.8	5	1.97
¾	1.9	21	53.3	6	2.36
⅞	2.2	22	55.9	7	2.76
1	2.5	23	58.4	8	3.15
2	5.1	24	61	9	3.54
3	7.6	25	63.5	10	3.94
4	10.2	26	66	11	4.33
5	12.7	27	68.6	12	4.72
6	15.2	28	71.1	13	5.12
7	17.8	29	73.7	14	5.51
8	20.3	30	76.2	15	5.91
9	22.9	40	101.6	16	6.30
10	25.4	50	127	17	6.69

cm	in	in	mm	mm	in
24	9.45	$\frac{1}{8}$	3.2	1	0.04
25	9.84	$\frac{1}{4}$	6.4	2	0.08
26	10.24	$\frac{3}{8}$	9.5	3	0.12
27	10.63	$\frac{1}{2}$	12.7	4	0.16
28	11.02	$\frac{5}{8}$	15.9	5	0.20
29	11.42	$\frac{3}{4}$	19	6	0.24
30	11.81	$\frac{7}{8}$	22.2	7	0.28
31	12.20	1	25.4	8	0.31
32	12.60	2	50.8	9	0.35
33	12.99	3	76.2	10	0.39
34	13.39	4	101.6	11	0.43
35	13.78	5	127	12	0.47
36	14.17	6	152.4	13	0.51
37	14.57	7	177.8	14	0.55
38	14.96	8	203.2	15	0.59
39	15.35	9	228.6	16	0.63
40	15.75	10	254	17	0.67

Exact conversions   1 in = 2.54 cm   1 cm = 0.3937 in   1 in = 25.40 mm   1 mm = 0.0394 in

ft	m	m	ft	yd	m	m	yd	mi	km	km	mi*
1	0.3	1	3.3	1	0.9	1	1.1	1	1.6	1	0.6
2	0.6	2	6.6	2	1.8	2	2.2	2	3.2	2	1.2
3	0.9	3	9.8	3	2.7	3	3.3	3	4.8	3	1.9
4	1.2	4	13.1	4	3.7	4	4.4	4	6.4	4	2.5
5	1.5	5	16.4	5	4.6	5	5.5	5	8.0	5	3.1
6	1.8	6	19.7	6	5.5	6	6.6	6	9.7	6	3.7
7	2.1	7	23.0	7	6.4	7	7.7	7	11.3	7	4.3
8	2.4	8	26.2	8	7.3	8	8.7	8	12.9	8	5.0
9	2.7	9	29.5	9	8.2	9	9.8	9	14.5	9	5.6
10	3.0	10	32.8	10	9.1	10	10.9	10	16.1	10	6.2
15	4.6	15	49.2	15	13.7	15	16.4	15	24.1	15	9.3
20	6.1	20	65.5	20	18.3	20	21.9	20	32.2	20	12.4
25	7.6	25	82.0	25	22.9	25	27.3	25	40.2	25	15.5

Science and Technology

ft	m	m	ft	yd	m	m	yd	mi	km	km	mi*
30	9.1	30	98.4	30	27.4	30	32.8	30	48.3	30	18.6
35	10.7	35	114.8	35	32.0	35	38.3	35	56.3	35	21.7
40	12.2	40	131.2	40	36.6	40	43.7	40	64.4	40	24.9
45	13.7	45	147.6	45	41.1	45	49.2	45	72.4	45	28.0
50	15.2	50	164.0	50	45.7	50	54.7	50	80.5	50	31.1
75	22.9	75	246.1	75	68.6	75	82.0	55	88.5	55	34.2
100	30.5	100	328.1	100	91.4	100	109.4	60	96.6	60	37.3
200	61.0	200	656.2	200	182.9	200	218.7	65	104.6	65	40.4
300	91.4	300	984.3	220	201.2	220	240.6	70	112.7	70	43.5
400	121.9	400	1312.3	300	274.3	300	328.1	75	120.7	75	46.6
500	152.4	500	1640.4	400	365.8	400	437.4	80	128.7	80	49.7
600	182.9	600	1968.5	440	402.3	440	481.2	85	136.8	85	52.8
700	213.4	700	2296.6	500	457.2	500	546.8	90	144.8	90	55.9
800	243.8	800	2624.7	600	548.6	600	656.2	95	152.9	95	59.0
900	274.3	900	2952.8	700	640.1	700	765.5	100	160.9	100	62.1
1000	304.8	1000	3280.8	800	731.5	800	874.9	200	321.9	200	124.3
1500	457.2	1500	4921.3	880	804.7	880	962.4	300	482.8	300	186.4
2000	609.6	2000	6561.7	900	823.0	900	984.2	400	643.7	400	248.5
2500	762.0	2500	8202.1	1000	914.4	1000	1093.6	500	804.7	500	310.7
3000	914.4	3000	9842.5	1500	1371.6	1500	1640.4	750	1207.0	750	466.0
3500	1066.8	3500	11482.9	2000	1828.8	2000	2187.2	1000	1609.3	1000	621.4
4000	1219.2	4000	13123.4	2500	2286.0	2500	2734.0	2500	4023.4	2500	1553.4
5000	1524.0	5000	16404.2	5000	4572.0	5000	5468.1	5000	8046.7	5000	3106.9

* Statute miles

Exact conversions   1 ft = 0.3048 m   1 m = 3.2808 ft   1 yd = 0.9144 m
                    1 m = 1.0936 yd   1 mi = 1.6093 km   1 km = 0.6214 mi

Conversion tables: area

sq in	sq cm	sq cm	sq in	sq ft	sq m	sq m	sq ft	acres	hect-ares	hect-ares	acres
1	6.45	1	0.16	1	0.09	1	10.8	1	0.40	1	2.5
2	12.90	2	0.31	2	0.19	2	21.5	2	0.81	2	4.9
3	19.35	3	0.47	3	0.28	3	32.3	3	1.21	3	7.4
4	25.81	4	0.62	4	0.37	4	43.1	4	1.62	4	9.9
5	32.26	5	0.78	5	0.46	5	53.8	5	2.02	5	12.4
6	38.71	6	0.93	6	0.56	6	64.6	6	2.43	6	14.8
7	45.16	7	1.09	7	0.65	7	75.3	7	2.83	7	17.3
8	51.61	8	1.24	8	0.74	8	86.1	8	3.24	8	19.8
9	58.06	9	1.40	9	0.84	9	96.9	9	3.64	9	22.2
10	64.52	10	1.55	10	0.93	10	107.6	10	4.05	10	24.7
11	70.97	11	1.71	11	1.02	11	118.4	11	4.45	11	27.2
12	77.42	12	1.86	12	1.11	12	129.2	12	4.86	12	29.7
13	83.87	13	2.02	13	1.21	13	139.9	13	5.26	13	32.1
14	90.32	14	2.17	14	1.30	14	150.7	14	5.67	14	34.6
15	96.77	15	2.33	15	1.39	15	161.5	15	6.07	15	37.1
16	103.23	16	2.48	16	1.49	16	172.2	16	6.47	16	39.5
17	109.68	17	2.64	17	1.58	17	183	17	6.88	17	42
18	116.13	18	2.79	18	1.67	18	193.8	18	7.28	18	44.5
19	122.58	19	2.95	19	1.77	19	204.5	19	7.69	19	46.9
20	129.03	20	3.10	20	1.86	20	215.3	20	8.09	20	49.4
25	161.29	25	3.88	25	2.32	25	269.1	25	10.12	25	61.8
50	322.58	50	7.75	50	4.65	50	538.2	50	20.23	50	123.6
75	483.87	75	11.63	75	6.97	75	807.3	75	30.35	75	185.3
100	645.16	100	15.50	100	9.29	100	1076.4	100	40.47	100	247.1
125	806.45	125	19.38	250	23.23	250	2691	250	101.17	250	617.8
150	967.74	150	23.25	500	46.45	500	5382	500	202.34	500	1235.5
				750	69.68	750	8072.9	750	303.51	750	1853.3
				1000	92.90	1000	10763.9	1000	404.69	1000	2471.1
								1500	607.03	1500	3706.6

Exact conversions   1 in² = 6.4516 cm²   1 cm² = 0.155 in²   1 ft² = 0.0929 m²
                     1 m² = 10.7639 ft²   1 acre = 0.4047 hectares   1 hectare = 2.471 acres

sq mi*	→	sq km		sq km	→	sq mi*
1		2.6		1		0.39
2		5.2		2		0.77
3		7.8		3		1.16
4		10.4		4		1.54
5		12.9		5		1.93
6		15.5		6		2.32
7		18.1		7		2.70
8		20.7		8		3.09
9		23.3		9		3.47
10		25.9		10		3.86
20		51.8		20		7.72
21		54.4		21		8.11
22		57.0		22		8.49
23		59.6		23		8.88
24		62.2		24		9.27
25		64.7		25		9.65
30		77.7		30		11.58
40		103.6		40		15.44
50		129.5		50		19.31
100		259.0		100		38.61
200		518.0		200		77.22
300		777.0		300		115.83
400		1036.0		400		154.44
500		1295.0		500		193.05
600		1554.0		600		231.66
700		1813.0		700		270.27
800		2072.0		800		308.88
900		2331.0		900		347.49
1000		2590.0		1000		386.1
1500		3885.0		1500		579.2
2000		5180.0		2000		772.2

* Statute miles
Exact conversions 1 sq mi = 2.589999 sq km
1 sq km = 0.3861 sq mi

Science and Technology

Conversion tables: volume

cu in	cu cm	cu cm	cu in	cu ft	cu m	cu m	cu ft	cu yd	cu m	cu m	cu yd
1	16.39	1	0.06	1	0.03	1	35.3	1	0.76	1	1.31
2	32.77	2	0.12	2	0.06	2	70.6	2	1.53	2	2.62
3	49.16	3	0.18	3	0.08	3	105.9	3	2.29	3	3.92
4	65.55	4	0.24	4	0.11	4	141.3	4	3.06	4	5.23
5	81.93	5	0.30	5	0.14	5	176.6	5	3.82	5	6.54
6	93.32	6	0.37	6	0.17	6	211.9	6	4.59	6	7.85
7	114.71	7	0.43	7	0.20	7	247.2	7	5.35	7	9.16
8	131.10	8	0.49	8	0.23	8	282.5	8	6.12	8	10.46
9	147.48	9	0.55	9	0.25	9	317.8	9	6.88	9	11.77
10	163.87	10	0.61	10	0.28	10	353.1	10	7.65	10	13.08
15	245.81	15	0.92	15	0.42	15	529.7	15	11.47	15	19.62
20	327.74	20	1.22	20	0.57	20	706.3	20	15.29	20	26.16
50	819.35	50	3.05	50	1.41	50	1765.7	50	38.23	50	65.40
100	1638.71	100	6.10	100	2.83	100	3531.5	100	76.46	100	130.80

Exact conversions $1\,in^3 = 16.3871\,cm^3$ $1\,ft^3 = 0.0283\,m^3$ $1\,yd^3 = 0.7646\,m^3$
$1\,cm^3 = 0.0610\,in^3$ $1\,m^3 = 35.3147\,ft^3$ $1\,m^3 = 1.3080\,yd^3$

Conversion tables: capacity

■ Liquid measure

Science and Technology

UK fluid ounces	litres	US fluid ounces	litres	litres	UK fluid ounces	US fluid ounces
1	0.0284	1	0.0296	1	35.2	33.8
2	0.0568	2	0.0592	2	70.4	67.6
3	0.0852	3	0.0888	3	105.6	101.4
4	0.114	4	0.118	4	140.8	135.3
5	0.142	5	0.148	5	176.0	169.1
6	0.170	6	0.178	6	211.2	202.9
7	0.199	7	0.207	7	246.4	236.7
8	0.227	8	0.237	8	281.6	270.5
9	0.256	9	0.266	9	316.8	304.3
10	0.284	10	0.296	10	352.0	338.1
11	0.312	11	0.326	11	387.2	372.0
12	0.341	12	0.355	12	422.4	405.8
13	0.369	13	0.385	13	457.5	439.6
14	0.397	14	0.414	14	492.7	473.4
15	0.426	15	0.444	15	527.9	507.2
20	0.568	20	0.592	20	703.9	676.3
50	1.42	50	1.48	50	1 759.8	1 690.7
100	2.84	100	2.96	100	3519.6	3381.5

Exact conversions   1 UK fl oz = 0.0284 l   1 l = 35.1961 UK fl oz
   1 US fl oz = 0.0296 l   1 l = 33.8140 US fl oz

UK pints	litres	US pints	litres	litres	UK pints	US pints
1	0.57	1	0.47	1	1.76	2.11
2	1.14	2	0.95	2	3.52	4.23
3	1.70	3	1.42	3	5.28	6.34
4	2.27	4	1.89	4	7.04	8.45
5	2.84	5	2.37	5	8.80	10.57
6	3.41	6	2.84	6	10.56	12.68
7	3.98	7	3.31	7	12.32	14.79
8	4.55	8	3.78	8	14.08	16.91
9	5.11	9	4.26	9	15.84	19.02
10	5.68	10	4.73	10	17.60	21.13
11	6.25	11	5.20	11	19.36	23.25
12	6.82	12	5.68	12	21.12	25.36
13	7.38	13	6.15	13	22.88	27.47
14	7.95	14	6.62	14	24.64	29.59
15	8.52	15	7.10	15	26.40	31.70
20	11.36	20	9.46	20	35.20	42.27
50	28.41	50	23.66	50	87.99	105.67
100	56.82	100	47.32	100	175.98	211.34

Exact conversions   1 UK pt = 0.5682 l   1 US pt = 0.4732 l   1 l = 1.7598 UK pt, 2.1134 US pt
   1 UK pt = 1.20 US pt   1 US pt = 0.83 UK pt   1 US cup = 8 fl oz

UK gallons	litres	US gallons	litres	litres	UK gallons	US gallons
1	4.55	1	3.78	1	0.22	0.26
2	9.09	2	7.57	2	0.44	0.53
3	13.64	3	11.36	3	0.66	0.79
4	18.18	4	15.14	4	0.88	1.06
5	22.73	5	18.93	5	1.10	1.32
6	27.28	6	22.71	6	1.32	1.58
7	31.82	7	26.50	7	1.54	1.85
8	36.37	8	30.28	8	1.76	2.11
9	40.91	9	34.07	9	1.98	2.38
10	45.46	10	37.85	10	2.20	2.64
11	50.01	11	41.64	11	2.42	2.91
12	54.55	12	45.42	12	2.64	3.17
13	59.10	13	49.21	13	2.86	3.43
14	63.64	14	52.99	14	3.08	3.70
15	68.19	15	56.78	15	3.30	3.96
16	72.74	16	60.57	16	3.52	4.23

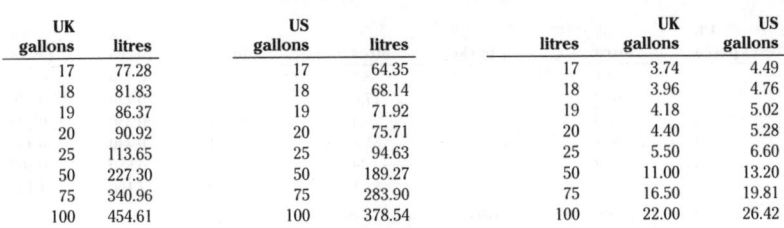

UK gallons	litres	US gallons	litres	litres	UK gallons	US gallons
17	77.28	17	64.35	17	3.74	4.49
18	81.83	18	68.14	18	3.96	4.76
19	86.37	19	71.92	19	4.18	5.02
20	90.92	20	75.71	20	4.40	5.28
25	113.65	25	94.63	25	5.50	6.60
50	227.30	50	189.27	50	11.00	13.20
75	340.96	75	283.90	75	16.50	19.81
100	454.61	100	378.54	100	22.00	26.42

Exact conversions 1 UK gal = 4.546 l   1 US gal = 3.7854 l   1 l = 0.220 UK gal, 0.2642 US gal

■ Conversion tables: capacity

UK gal	US gal	US gal	UK gal
1	1.2	1	0.8
2	2.4	2	1.7
3	3.6	3	2.5
4	4.8	4	3.3
5	6	5	4.2
6	7.2	6	5
7	8.4	7	5.8
·8	9.6	8	6.7
9	10.8	9	7.5
10	12	10	8.3
11	13.2	11	9.2
12	14.4	12	10
13	15.6	13	10.8
14	16.8	14	11.7
15	18	15	12.5
20	24	20	16.6
25	30	25	20.8
50	60	50	41.6

Exact conversions   1 UK gal = 1.200929 US gal   1 US gal = 0.832688 UK gal

■ Dry capacity measures

UK bushels	cu m	litres	US bushels	cu m	litres
1	0.037	36.4	1	0.035	35.2
2	0.074	72.7	2	0.071	70.5
3	0.111	109.1	3	0.106	105.7
4	0.148	145.5	4	0.141	140.9
5	0.184	181.8	5	0.175	176.2
10	0.369	363.7	10	0.353	352.4

Exact conversions   1 UK bushel = 0.0369 m^3 1 US bushel = 0.9353 m^3
1 UK bushel = 36.3677 l   1 US bushel = 35.2381 l

cu m	UK bushels	US bushels	litres	UK bushels	US bushels
1	27.5	28.4	1	0.027	0.028
2	55.0	56.7	2	0.055	0.057
3	82.5	85.1	3	0.082	0.085
4	110	113	4	0.110	0.114
5	137	142	5	0.137	0.142
10	275	284	10	0.275	0.284

Exact conversions   1 m^3 = 27.4962 UK bu   1 l = 0.0275 UK bu
1 m^3 = 28.3776 US bu   1 l = 0.0284 US bu

Science and Technology

UK pecks	litres	US pecks	litres	litres	UK pecks	US pecks
1	9.1	1	8.8	1	0.110	0.113
2	18.2	2	17.6	2	0.220	0.226
3	27.3	3	26.4	3	0.330	0.339
4	36.4	4	35.2	4	0.440	0.454
5	45.5	5	44	5	0.550	0.567
10	90.9	10	88.1	10	1.100	1.135

Exact conversions   1 UK pk = 9.0919 l   1 l = 0.1100 UK pk = 0.1135 US pk
1 US pk = 8.8095 l

US quarts	cu cm	litres	US pints	cu cm	litres
1	1 101	1.1	1	551	0.55
2	2 202	2.2	2	1 101	1.10
3	3 304	3.3	3	1 652	1.65
4	4 405	4.4	4	2 202	2.20
5	5 506	5.5	5	2 753	2.75
10	11 012	11	10	5 506	5.51

Exact conversions   1 US qt = 1 101.2209 cm^3 1 US pt = 550.6105 cm^3
1 US qt = 1.1012 l   1 US pt = 0.5506 l

Conversion tables: tyre pressures

lb per sq in	kg per sq in	lb per sq in	kg per sq in
10	0.7	26	1.8
15	1.1	28	2
20	1.4	30	2.1
24	1.7	40	2.8

Conversion tables: weight

oun-ces*	grams	grams	oun-ces*	pounds	kilo-grams	pounds	kilo-grams	kilo-grams	pounds	kilo-grams	pounds
1	28.3	1	0.04	1	0.45	19	8.62	1	2.2	19	41.9
2	56.7	2	0.07	2	0.91	20	9.07	2	4.4	20	44.1
3	85	3	0.11	3	1.36	25	11.34	3	6.6	25	55.1
4	113.4	4	0.14	4	1.81	30	13.61	4	8.8	30	66.1
5	141.7	5	0.18	5	2.27	35	15.88	5	11	35	77.2
6	170.1	6	0.21	6	2.72	40	18.14	6	13.2	40	88.2
7	198.4	7	0.25	7	3.18	45	20.41	7	15.4	45	99.2
8	226.8	8	0.28	8	3.63	50	22.68	8	17.6	50	110.2
9	255.1	9	0.32	9	4.08	60	27.24	9	19.8	60	132.3
10	283.5	10	0.35	10	4.54	70	31.78	10	22	70	154.4
11	311.7	20	0.71	11	4.99	80	36.32	11	24.3	80	176.4
12	340.2	30	1.06	12	5.44	90	40.86	12	26.5	90	198.5
13	368.5	40	1.41	13	5.90	100	45.36	13	28.7	100	220.5
14	396.9	50	1.76	14	6.35	200	90.72	14	30.9	200	440.9
15	425.2	60	2.12	15	6.80	250	113.40	15	33.1	250	551.2
16	453.6	70	2.47	16	7.26	500	226.80	16	35.3	500	1 102.3
		80	2.82	17	7.71	750	340.19	17	37.5	750	1 653.5
		90	3.18	18	8.16	1 000	453.59	18	39.7	1 000	2 204.6
		100	3.53								

* avoirdupois
Exact conversions   1 oz (avdp) = 28.3495 g   1 g = 0.0353 oz (avdp)   1 lb = 0.454 kg   1 kg = 2.205 lb
Tons: long, UK 2 240 lb; short, US 2 000 lb

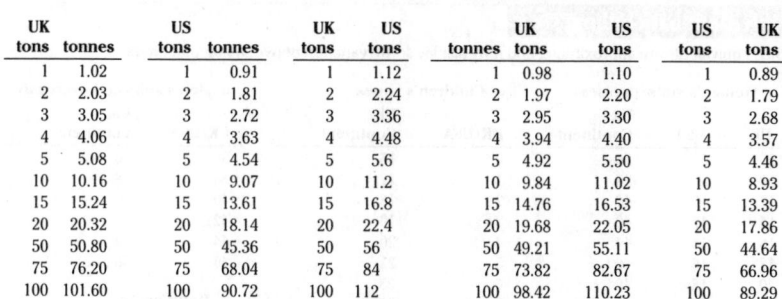

Science and Technology

UK tons	tonnes	US tons	tonnes	UK tons	US tons	tonnes	UK tons	US tons	US tons	UK tons
1	1.02	1	0.91	1	1.12	1	0.98	1.10	1	0.89
2	2.03	2	1.81	2	2.24	2	1.97	2.20	2	1.79
3	3.05	3	2.72	3	3.36	3	2.95	3.30	3	2.68
4	4.06	4	3.63	4	4.48	4	3.94	4.40	4	3.57
5	5.08	5	4.54	5	5.6	5	4.92	5.50	5	4.46
10	10.16	10	9.07	10	11.2	10	9.84	11.02	10	8.93
15	15.24	15	13.61	15	16.8	15	14.76	16.53	15	13.39
20	20.32	20	18.14	20	22.4	20	19.68	22.05	20	17.86
50	50.80	50	45.36	50	56	50	49.21	55.11	50	44.64
75	76.20	75	68.04	75	84	75	73.82	82.67	75	66.96
100	101.60	100	90.72	100	112	100	98.42	110.23	100	89.29

Exact conversions 1 UK ton = 1.0160 tonnes 1 US ton = 0.9072 tonne 1 UK ton = 1.1199 US tons
1 tonne = 0.9842 UK ton = 1.1023 US tons 1 US ton = 0.8929 UK ton
Hundredweights: long, UK 112 lb; short, US 100 lb

UK cwt	kilograms	US cwt	kilograms	UK cwt	US cwt	kilograms	UK cwt	US cwt	US cwt	UK cwt
1	50.8	1	45.4	1	1.12	1	0.0197	0.022	1	0.89
2	102	2	90.7	2	2.24	2	0.039	0.044	2	1.79
3	152	3	136	3	3.36	3	0.059	0.066	3	2.68
4	203	4	181	4	4.48	4	0.079	0.088	4	3.57
5	254	5	227	5	5.6	5	0.098	0.11	5	4.46
10	508	10	454	10	11.2	10	0.197	0.22	10	8.93
15	762	15	680	15	16.8	15	0.295	0.33	15	13.39
20	1016	20	907	20	22.4	20	0.394	0.44	20	17.86
50	2540	50	2268	50	56	50	0.985	1.10	50	44.64
75	3810	75	3402	75	84	75	1.477	1.65	75	66.96
100	5080	100	4536	100	112	100	1.970	2.20	100	89.29

Exact conversions 1 UK cwt = 50.8023 kg   1 US cwt = 45.3592 kg   1 UK cwt = 1.1199 US cwt
1 kg = 0.0197 UK cwt = 0.0220 US cwt   1 US cwt = 0.8929 UK cwt

stones	pounds	stones	pounds	stones	kilograms
1	14	11	154	1	6.35
2	28	12	168	2	12.70
3	42	13	182	3	19.05
4	56	14	196	4	25.40
5	70	15	210	5	31.75
6	84	16	224	6	38.10
7	98	17	238	7	44.45
8	112	18	252	8	50.80
9	126	19	266	9	57.15
10	140	20	280	10	63.50

1 st = 14 lb   1 lb = 0.07 st   1 st = 6.350 kg   1 kg = 0.1575 st

International clothing sizes

Size equivalents are approximate, and may display some variation between manufacturers.

Science and Technology

■ Women's suits/dresses

UK	USA	UK/Continent
8	6	36
10	8	38
12	10	40
14	12	42
16	14	44
18	16	46
20	18	48
22	20	50
24	22	52

■ Adults' shoes

UK	USA	UK/Continent
4	$5\frac{1}{2}$	37
$4\frac{1}{2}$	6	38
5	$6\frac{1}{2}$	38
$5\frac{1}{2}$	7	39
6	$7\frac{1}{2}$	39
$6\frac{1}{2}$	8	40
7	$8\frac{1}{2}$	41
$7\frac{1}{2}$	$8\frac{1}{2}$	42
8	$9\frac{1}{2}$	42
$8\frac{1}{2}$	$9\frac{1}{2}$	43
9	$10\frac{1}{2}$	43
$9\frac{1}{2}$	$10\frac{1}{2}$	44
10	$11\frac{1}{2}$	44
$10\frac{1}{2}$	$11\frac{1}{2}$	45
11	12	46

■ Children's shoes

UK/USA	UK/Continent
0	15
1	17
2	18
3	19
4	20
5	22
6	23
7	24
8	25
$8\frac{1}{2}$	26
9	27
10	28
11	29
12	30
13	32

■ Women's hosiery

UK/USA	UK/Continent
8	0
$8\frac{1}{2}$	1
9	2
$9\frac{1}{2}$	3
10	4
$10\frac{1}{2}$	5

■ Men's suits and overcoats

UK/USA	UK/Continent
36	46
38	48
40	50
42	52
44	54
46	56

■ Men's socks

UK/USA	UK/Continent
$9\frac{1}{2}$	38–39
10	39–40
$10\frac{1}{2}$	40–41
11	41–42
$11\frac{1}{2}$	42–43

■ Men's shirts

UK/USA	UK/Continent
12	30–31
$12\frac{1}{2}$	32
13	33
$13\frac{1}{2}$	34–35
14	36
$14\frac{1}{2}$	37
15	38
$15\frac{1}{2}$	39–40
16	41
$16\frac{1}{2}$	42
17	43
$17\frac{1}{2}$	44–45

International pattern sizes

Size	Bust cm	Bust in	Waist cm	Waist in	Hip cm	Hip in	Back waist length cm	Back waist length in
■ Young junior/teenage								
5/6	71	28	56	22	79	31	34.5	$13\frac{1}{2}$
7/8	74	29	58	23	81	32	35.5	14
9/10	78	$30\frac{1}{2}$	61	24	85	$33\frac{1}{2}$	37	$14\frac{1}{2}$
11/12	81	32	64	25	89	35	38	15
13/14	85	$33\frac{1}{2}$	66	26	93	$36\frac{1}{2}$	39	$15\frac{3}{8}$
15/16	89	35	69	27	97	38	40	$15\frac{3}{4}$
■ Misses								
6	78	$30\frac{1}{2}$	58	23	83	$32\frac{1}{2}$	39.5	$15\frac{1}{2}$
8	80	$31\frac{1}{2}$	61	24	85	$33\frac{1}{2}$	40	$15\frac{3}{4}$
10	83	$32\frac{1}{2}$	64	25	88	$34\frac{1}{2}$	40.5	16
12	87	34	67	$26\frac{1}{2}$	92	36	41.5	$16\frac{1}{4}$
14	92	36	71	28	97	38	42	$16\frac{1}{2}$
16	97	38	76	30	102	40	42.5	$16\frac{3}{4}$
18	102	40	81	32	107	42	43	17
20	107	42	87	34	112	44	44	$17\frac{1}{4}$

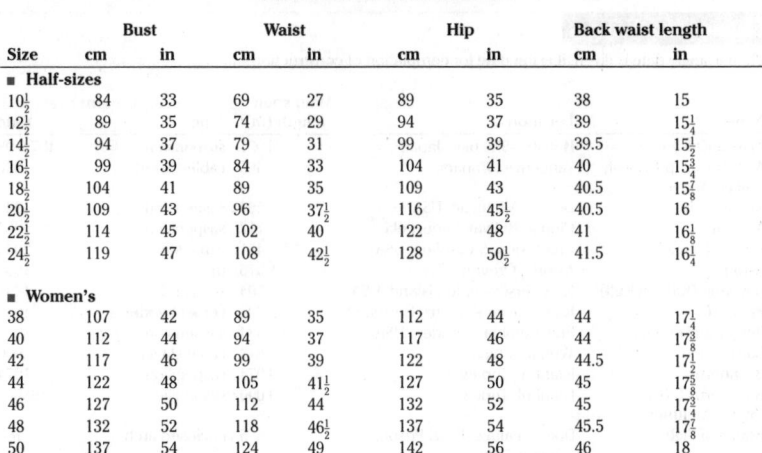

Size	Bust cm	Bust in	Waist cm	Waist in	Hip cm	Hip in	Back waist length cm	Back waist length in
Half-sizes								
$10\frac{1}{2}$	84	33	69	27	89	35	38	15
$12\frac{1}{2}$	89	35	74	29	94	37	39	$15\frac{1}{4}$
$14\frac{1}{2}$	94	37	79	31	99	39	39.5	$15\frac{1}{2}$
$16\frac{1}{2}$	99	39	84	33	104	41	40	$15\frac{3}{4}$
$18\frac{1}{2}$	104	41	89	35	109	43	40.5	$15\frac{7}{8}$
$20\frac{1}{2}$	109	43	96	$37\frac{1}{2}$	116	$45\frac{1}{2}$	40.5	16
$22\frac{1}{2}$	114	45	102	40	122	48	41	$16\frac{1}{8}$
$24\frac{1}{2}$	119	47	108	$42\frac{1}{2}$	128	$50\frac{1}{2}$	41.5	$16\frac{1}{4}$
Women's								
38	107	42	89	35	112	44	44	$17\frac{1}{4}$
40	112	44	94	37	117	46	44	$17\frac{3}{8}$
42	117	46	99	39	122	48	44.5	$17\frac{1}{2}$
44	122	48	105	$41\frac{1}{2}$	127	50	45	$17\frac{5}{8}$
46	127	50	112	44	132	52	45	$17\frac{3}{4}$
48	132	52	118	$46\frac{1}{2}$	137	54	45.5	$17\frac{7}{8}$
50	137	54	124	49	142	56	46	18

International paper sizes

A series

	mm	in
A0	841×1189	33.11×46.81
A1	594×841	23.39×33.1
A2	420×594	16.54×23.39
A3	297×420	11.69×16.54
A4	210×297	8.27×11.69
A5	148×210	5.83×8.27
A6	105×148	4.13×5.83
A7	74×105	2.91×4.13
A8	52×74	2.05×2.91
A9	37×52	1.46×2.05
A10	26×37	1.02×1.46

B series

	mm	in
B0	$1\,000 \times 1414$	39.37×55.67
B1	707×1000	27.83×39.37
B2	500×707	19.68×27.83
B3	353×500	13.90×19.68
B4	250×353	9.84×13.90
B5	176×250	6.93×9.84
B6	125×176	4.92×6.93
B7	88×125	3.46×4.92
B8	62×88	2.44×3.46
B9	44×62	1.73×2.44
B10	31×44	1.22×1.73

C series

	mm	in
C0	917×1297	36.00×51.20
C1	648×917	25.60×36.00
C2	458×648	18.00×25.60
C3	324×458	12.80×18.00
C4	229×324	9.00×12.80
C5	162×229	6.40×9.00
C6	114×162	4.50×6.40
C7	81×114	3.20×4.50
DL	110×220	4.33×8.66
C7/6	81×162	3.19×6.38

All sizes in these series have sides in the proportion of $1 : \sqrt{2}$, except sizes DL and C7/6.
A series is used for writing paper, books and magazines; B series for posters; C series for envelopes.

Science and Technology

Engineering: bridges

When a single date is given, it is the date for completion of construction.

Name	Location	Main span length (m)[1]	Type	Date
Akashi-Kaikyo	Honshu–Shikoku, Japan	1991	suspension	1978–98
Alex Fraser (previously called Annacis)	Vancouver, Canada	465	cable-stayed	1986
Ambassador	Detroit, Michigan, USA	564	suspension	1929
Angostura	Ciudad Bolivar, Venezuela	712	suspension	1967
Arthur Ravenel Jr	Charleston, S Carolina, USA	471	cable-stayed	2005
Astoria	Astoria, Oregon, USA	376	truss	1966
Bayonne (Kill van Kull)	New Jersey–Staten Island, USA	504	steel arch	1931
Bendorf	Rhine River, Koblenz, Germany	208	cement girder	1965
Benjamin Franklin	Philadelphia–Camden, USA	534	suspension	1926
Baishazhou	Wuhan, China	618	cable-stayed	2000
Bosphorus	Istanbul, Turkey	1074	suspension	1974
Bosphorus II (Fatih Sultan Mehmet)	Istanbul, Turkey	1090	suspension	1986–8
Bridge of Sighs	Doge's Palace–Pozzi Prison, Venice, Italy	c.5	enclosed arch	16c
Britannia tubular rail	Menai Strait, Wales	420	plate girder	1845–50
Brooklyn	Brooklyn–Manhattan Island, New York City, USA	487	suspension	1869–83
Clifton	Bristol, England	214	suspension	1836–64
Commodore Barry	Chester, Pennsylvania, USA	501	cantilever	1974
Evergreen Point	Seattle, Washington, USA	2293	floating pontoon	1963
Forth (rail)	Firth of Forth, South Queensferry, Scotland	521	cantilever	1882–90
Forth Road Bridge (road)	Firth of Forth, South Queensferry, Scotland	1006	suspension	1958–64
George Washington	Hudson River, New York City, USA	1067	suspension	1927–31
Gladesville	Sydney, Australia	305	concrete arch	1964
Golden Gate	San Francisco, California, USA	1280	suspension	1937
Great Belt (Storebælt) East	Halsskov–Kudshoved, Denmark	1624	suspension	1998
Greater New Orleans	Mississippi River, Louisiana, USA	486	cantilever	1988
High Coast	Veda, Västernorrland, Sweden	1210	suspension	1997
Howrah (railroad)	Hooghly River, Kolkata, India	457	cantilever	1936–43
Humber Estuary	Hull–Grimsby, England	1410	suspension	1973–81
Humen	Humen, China	888	suspension	1997
Ironbridge	Coalbrookdale, Shropshire, England	31	(first) cast-iron arch	1779
Jiangyin Yangtze	Jiangsu Province, China	1385	suspension	1999
Kap Shui Mun	Lantau I–Ma Wan I, Hong Kong	430	cable-stayed (double-deck road/rail)	1997
Kincardine	Forth River, Scotland	111	movable	1936
Kurushima-Kaikyo II	Oshima–Mashima, Japan	1020	suspension	1999
Lake Pontchartrain Causeway	Maudeville–Jefferson, Louisiana, USA	38.4 km (total length)	twin concrete trestle	1969
Lion's Gate	Vancouver, Canada	473	suspension	1938
London	Southwark–City of London	46	concrete arch	1973
Lupu	Shanghai, China	550	(longest) steel arch	2003
McCall's Ferry	Susquehanna River, Lancaster, Pennsylvania, USA	108	wooden covered	1815
Mackinac Straits	Michigan, USA	1158	suspension	1957
Mega Bridge (Dipangkorn Rasmijoti)	Bangkok, Thailand	398	cable-stayed	2006
Meiko Chuo	Tokyo Bay, Japan	590	cable-stayed	1998
Menai Strait	Menai Strait, N Wales	177	suspension	1820–6 (reconstructed 1940)
Millau	River Tarn, France	342	suspension	2004
Minami Bisan-Seto	Honshu–Shikoku, Japan	1100	suspension	1988

Name	Location	Main span length (m)[1]	Type	Date
Nanjing II	Nanjing, China	628	cable-stayed	2001
Nanjing III	Nanjing, China	648	cable-stayed	2005
New River Gorge	Fayetteville, West Virginia, USA	518	steel arch	1978
Niagara Falls (rail)	Niagara Falls, New York, USA	250	suspension	1855 (survived until 1897)
Nordsund	Norway	222	cantilever	1987
Normandie	Le Havre, France	856	cable-stayed	1995
Øresund	Flinterenden, Denmark–Malmö, Sweden	490	cable-stayed	2000
Pont d'Avignon	Rhône River, France	c.60	arch	1177–87
Ponte Infante Dom Henrique	Oporto, Portugal	280	concrete arch	2002
Pontypridd	S Wales	43	single-span arch	1756
Quebec (railroad)	St Lawrence, Canada	549	(largest-span) cantilever	1918
Qingzhou Min River	Fuzhou, China	605	cable-stayed	2001
Rainbow	Canada–USA, Niagara Falls	286	steel arch	1941
Rama IX	Bangkok, Thailand	450	cable-stayed	1987
Ravenswood (William S Ritchie)	West Virginia, USA	274	cantilever	1981
Rialto	Grand Canal, Venice, Italy	29	single-span arch	1588–91
Rio-Niteroi	Guanabara Bay, Brazil	300	box and plate girder	1974
Runyang	Zhenjiang, China	1 490	suspension	2005
Salazar (25 de Abril)	Tagus River, Lisbon, Portugal	1 013	suspension	1966
Severn	Beachley, England	988	suspension	1961–6
Severn II	Severn Estuary, England	456	cable-stayed	1996
Shibanpo	Chongqing, China	330	concrete girder	2006
Skarnsundet	Norway	530	cable-stayed	1991
Sky Train Bridge (rail)	Vancouver, Canada	350	cable-stayed	1990
Sutong	Suzhou, Jiangsu, China	1 088	cable-stayed	2008
Sydney Harbour	Sydney, Australia	503	steel arch	1923–32
Syratalviadukt	Plauen, Germany	90	masonry arch	1905
Tacoma Narrows (New)	Puget Sound, Washington, USA	853	suspension	2007
Tagus II	Lisbon, Portugal	420	cable-stayed	1997
Tatara, Great	Japan	890	cable-stayed	1999
Tay (road)	Dundee, Scotland	76	box girder	1966
Thatcher Ferry (Bridge of the Americas)	Panama Canal, C America	344	arch	1962
Tower	Thames River, London	79	bascule	1886–94
Transbay (San Francisco-Oakland Bay)	San Francisco, California, USA	705	suspension	1936
Trans-Tokyo Bay Highway	Kawasaki–Kisarazu, Japan	590	box girder	1997
Trois-Rivières (Laviolette)	St Lawrence River, Quebec, Canada	336	cantilever	1967
Tsing Ma	Tsing Yi I–Ma Wan I, Hong Kong	1 377	suspension (double deck)	1997
Vasco da Gama	Tagus Estuary, Lisbon, Portugal	450	cable-stayed	1998
Verrazano Narrows	Brooklyn–Staten Island, New York Harbour, USA	1298	suspension	1959–64
Veterans Memorial	Gramercy, Louisiana, USA	445	cantilever	1995
Victoria Jubilee	St Lawrence River, Montreal, Canada	100	open steel	1854–9
Wanxian	Wanzhou, China	420	concrete arch	1997
Wheeling	Wheeling, Virginia, USA	308	suspension	1849
Wushan	Chongqing, China	460	steel arch	2005
Xihoumen	Zhoushan, China	1 650	suspension	2008
Xiling Yangtze	Yichang, Hubei, China	900	suspension	1996
Yokohama Bay (road)	Japan	460	cable-stayed	1989
Zoo	Cologne, Germany	259	cantilever	1966

[1] To convert m to ft, multiply by 3.2808.

Science and Technology

Engineering: tunnels

When a single date is given, it is the date for completion of construction.

Science and Technology

Name	Use	Location	Length[1]	Date
Aki	rail	Japan	13 km	1975
Box	rail	Wiltshire, England	3 km	1841
Cascade	rail	Washington, USA	13 km	1929
Channel	rail	Cheriton, England–Sargette, France	50 km	1987–94
Chesapeake Bay Bridge-Tunnel	road	USA	28 km	1964
Chesbrough	water supply	Chicago, USA	3 km	1867
Cumberland Mountain	underground parking	Cumberland Gap, USA	1402 m	1996
Dai-shimizu	rail	Honshu, Japan	22 km	1979
Delaware Aqueduct	water supply	Catskill Mts, New York, USA	169 km	1937–44
Detroit River	rail	Detroit, Michigan, USA–Windsor, Ontario, Canada	2 km	1910
Eupalinus	water supply	Samos, Greece	1037 m	c.525 BC
FATIMA (Magerøy)	road	Norway	6820 m (longest undersea road)	1998
Fenguoshan	rail	China–Tibet	1338 m (highest rail tunnel)	2006
Flathead	rail	Washington, USA	13 km	1970
Fredhällstunneln	road	Stockholm, Sweden	210 m	1996
Fréjus	rail	Modane, France–Bardonecchia, Italy	13 km	1857–71
Fucino	drainage	Lake Fucino, Italy	6 km	41
Great Apennine	rail	Vernio, Italy	19 km	1934
Hokuriku	rail	Japan	15 km	1962
Holland	road	Hudson River, New York City–Jersey City, New Jersey, USA	3 km	1927
Hoosac	rail	Massachusetts, USA	8 km	1876
Hsuehshan	road	Taiwan	13 km	2006
Hyperion	sewer	Los Angeles, California, USA	8 km	1959
Kanmon	rail	Kanmon Strait, Japan	19 km	1975
Keijo	rail	Japan	11 km	1970
Kilsby Ridge	rail	London–Birmingham line, England	2 km	1838
Laerdal	road	Bergen–Oslo, Norway	24.5 km (longest road tunnel)	2000
Languedoc (Canal du Midi)	canal	Malpas, France	157 m	1666–92
Lierasen	rail	Norway	11 km	1973
London and Southwark Subway	rail	London, England	11 km	1890
Lötschberg	rail	Switzerland	15 km	1913
Mersey	road	Mersey River, Birkenhead–Liverpool, England	4 km	1934
Moffat	rail	Colorado, USA	10 km	1928
Mont Blanc	road	France–Italy	12 km	1965
Mt MacDonald	rail	Canada	15 km	1989
NEAT (St Gotthard)	rail	Switzerland	57 km	under construction
NEAT (Lötschberg Base)	rail	Switzerland	35 km (longest land tunnel)	2007
North Cape	road	Norway	7 km	1999
Orange-Fish River	irrigation	South Africa	82 km (longest irrigation tunnel)	1975
Øresund	road-rail	Copenhagen, Denmark–Malmö, Sweden	3750 m (longest immersed tube)	2000
Owingsburg Landing	canal	Pennsylvania, USA	137 m	1828
Päijänne	water supply	Finland	120 km	1982
Posilipo	road	Naples–Pozzuoli, Italy	6 km	c.36 BC

Name	Use	Location	Length[1]	Date
Rennsteig	road	Germany	8 km	2003
Rogers Pass	rail	Calgary–Vancouver, Canada	15 km	1982–8
Rogers Pass	road	British Columbia, Canada	35 km	1989
Rokko	rail	Osaka–Kōbe, Japan	16 km	1972
Seikan	rail	Tsugaru Strait, Honshu–Hokkaido, Japan	54 km (longest undersea rail)	1964–88
Shin-shimizu	rail	Japan	13 km	1961
Simplon I and II	rail	Brigue, Switzerland–Iselle, Italy	20 km	1906 and 1922
St Gotthard	rail	Switzerland	15 km	1882
St Gotthard	road	Göschenen, Switzerland–Airolo, Italy	16 km	1980
(First) Thames	pedestrian; rail after 1865	Wapping–Rotherhithe, London, England	366 m	1825–43
Tower Subway	rail	London, England	411 m	1869–70
Tronquoy	canal	France	1 099 m	1810
Vaglia	rail	Florence–Bologna line, Italy	18 km	under construction

[1] To convert m to ft, multiply by 3.2808; to convert km to mi, multiply by 0.6214.

Engineering: dams

When a single date is given, it is the date for completion of construction.

Name	River, country	Height (m)[1]	Date
Afsluitdijk Sea	Zuider Zee, Netherlands	20 (largest sea dam, length 31 km)	1927–32
Alberto Lleras	Orinoco, Colombia	243	1989
Aswan High	Nile, Egypt	111	1970
Atatürk	Euphrates, Turkey	184	1990
Bakun	Rajang, Malaysia	204	2002
Chicoasén	Grijalva, Mexico	263	1980
Chivor	Cundinamarca, Colombia	237	1975
Cipasang	Cimanuk, Indonesia	200	under construction
Daniel Johnson	Manicouagan, Canada	214	1968
Ertan	Yalong, China	240	1998
Esmerelda	Batá, Colombia	237	1975
Grand Coulee	Columbia (Franklin D Roosevelt Lake), USA	168	1933–42
Grand Dixence	Dixence, Switzerland	285	1961
Guavio	Guaviare, Colombia	245	1989
Hoover	Colorado (Lake Mead), USA	221	1931–6
Inguri	Inguri, Georgia	272	1980
Itaipú	Paraná, Paraguay/Brazil border	189; length 8 km (world's largest hydroelectric complex)	opened 1982, completed 1991
Kambaratinsk	Naryn, Kyrgyzstan	255	under construction
Katse	Malibamatso, Lesotho	182	1996
Kiev	Dneiper, Ukraine	256	1964
Kishau	Tons, India	253	1995
Longtan	Hongshui, China	285	under construction
Manuel M Torres	Grijalva, Mexico	261	1981
Mauvoisin	Drance de Bagnes, Switzerland	237	1957
Mica	Columbia, Canada	244	1973
New China (Three Gorges)	Chang Jiang (Yangtze), China	175	under construction
Nurek	Vakhsh, Tajikistan	310 (tallest)	1980
Oroville	Feather, California, USA	235	1968
Pati	Paraná, Argentina	109 (most massive: vol 238 180 000 m³)	under construction
Rogun	Vakhsh, Tajikistan	335 (tallest projected)	under construction
San Roque	Agno, Philippines	210	2004

Science and Technology

Name	River, country	Height (m)[1]	Date
Sardar Sarovar	Narmada, India	163	2006
Sayansk	Yenisey, Russia	236	1980
Tehri	Bhagirathi, India	261	1997
Thames Barrier	Thames, England	spans 520 (largest tidal barrier)	1984
Vaiont	Vaiont, Italy	265	1961 (damaged by landslide 1963)
Xiaolangdi	Huang He, China	154	2001
Xiaowan	Lancang, China	292	under construction

[1] To convert m to ft, multiply by 3.2808.

Engineering: tallest inhabited buildings

Name	Location	Height (m)[1] of construction	Completion Date
Burj Dubai	Dubai, United Arab Emirates	818	2009
Taipei 101	Taipei, Taiwan	509	2004
World Financial Centre	Shanghai, China	492	2008
Petronas Twin Towers	Kuala Lumpur, Malaysia	452	1998
Nanjing Greenland Financial Center	Nanjing, China	450	2009
Willis Tower (formerly Sears Tower)	Chicago, USA	442	1974
Guangzhou West Tower	Guangzhou, China	440	2009
Jin Mao Building	Shanghai, China	421	1999
Two International Finance Centre	Hong Kong, China	415	2003
Trump International Hotel	Chicago, USA	415	2009
CITIC Plaza	Guangzhou, China	391	1997
Shun Hing Square	Shenzen, China	384	1996
Empire State Building	New York City, USA	381	1931
Central Plaza	Hong Kong	374	1992
Bank of China Tower	Hong Kong	367	1990
Bank of America Tower	New York City, USA	366	2008
Almas Tower	Dubai, United Arab Emirates	360	2008
Emirates Office Tower	Dubai, United Arab Emirates	355	2000
Tuntex Sky Tower	Kaohsiung, Taiwan	348	1997
Aon Center	Chicago, USA	346	1973

[1] To convert m to ft, multiply by 3.2808.

Prehistory to 5000 BC

- Primitive hominids (*Australopithecus*) appear in Africa c.4 000 000 BC.

- c.2 000 000 BC, *Homo habilis* is found in Africa, hunting small game and using stones as tools, such as hand axes, to cut meat and pound bones for their marrow.

- *Homo erectus* emerges in eastern and south-eastern Asia c.1 500 000 BC, living beside rivers and lakes, and spreads to Europe by c.700 000 BC. Fire is used for the first time to cook meat.

- The earliest true human being, *Homo sapiens*, appears in Europe c.400 000 BC.

- Neanderthal man is living in caves in Europe c.120 000 BC, using crude flint tools, looking after the sick and aged, and burying the dead.

- From c.100 000 BC Cro-Magnon man (*Homo sapiens sapiens*) begins to spread from Africa into Asia and China, and by 50 000 BC Australia is reached. A wider range of stone tools is used as well as other materials such as wood and bone. Furs and leather are worn. Materials are traded over considerable distances. The woolly mammoth is hunted.

- North America begins to be peopled c.30 000 BC as human beings cross from Siberia to Alaska by a land bridge that is later cut by the Bering Strait. Giant bison and mammoths are hunted in the grasslands.

- Southern African decorated stone tablets dating from c.27 000 BC are the first examples of painting. Cave painting develops c.17 000 BC with such fine examples as Lascaux in France and Altamira in Spain.

- Female figurines with exaggerated sexual characteristics are carved in many parts of Europe.

- By 20 000 BC the last Ice Age is at its height. In Australia paintings are made on rocks.

- Tools with stone blades are made c.15 000 BC. Beads and pendants are worn.

- The range of human weaponry expands, with knives, spears and bows in use c.12 000 BC.

- Farming begins c.10 000 BC in various parts of the world, notably the Fertile Crescent in the Middle East.

- Previously nomadic societies begin to make permanent settlements c.9000 BC. Wild cereals are harvested, and dogs, goats and pigs are domesticated. Human occupation in the Americas extends to the southern extremes of South America.

- c.8000 BC villages built using mud bricks appear in Syria and Palestine. Jericho, the earliest walled town, is inhabited before 7500 BC. Forest spreads in northern Europe as the ice sheet gradually retreats. Wild cattle and elk are hunted. Cattle are herded in the Sahara region. Pulses and cereals are cultivated.

- Sheep and cattle are domesticated in the Near East c.7000 BC. Linen is used to make textiles and pure copper is beaten for ornaments. In South America root crops are cultivated, while rice begins to be grown in China.

- The first known pottery and woollen textiles are made in central Turkey c.6000 BC. Lead is smelted. Farming spreads to south-eastern Europe, while oak forests extend into northern Europe. Cattle are used to pull ploughs in the Near East. Cereals begin to be cultivated in North Africa, while millet is grown in China, and wheat and barley in Pakistan.

History

History and politics	Religion and philosophy

5000 BC–AD 1

- Successive civilizations arise in Mesopotamia, including the Sumerians and the empire of Akkad. The Sumerians invent the wheel and write in cuneiform script.
- Farming spreads to Europe; olives and grapes are cultivated in the Mediterranean region, as is maize in Mexico and rice in India and China.
- Egypt is united under one pharaoh and the first pyramids are built. Hieroglyphics are devised, the 365-day calendar is established, papyrus is first used, and the cat is domesticated.
- In Greece, a civilization evolves from the Cycladic culture through the Minoan and Mycenean periods, trading with Egypt and building extensive palaces.

5000 BC

c.5000 BC Foundation of the city of Eridu in Mesopotamia. It is traditionally regarded as the first city.

5000 BC Civilizations develop in Fayoum and Nubia.

4000 BC Colonization of the Pacific islands.

3372 BC First date in the Mayan calendar.

c.3100 BC Building of Stonehenge, England, is begun.

3000 BC

3000 BC Towns are built on the Peruvian coast.

3000 BC Lake Chad begins to dry up.

c.2334 BC Sargon of Akkad establishes the Akkadian Empire in southern Mesopotamia. He is one of the first great empire builders.

c.2300–1750 BC Flourishing of Indus Valley civilization around the River Indus in Pakistan.

c.2150 BC Collapse of Akkadian Empire in Mesopotamia.

2040 BC End of First Intermediate Period in Egypt. Beginning of Middle Kingdom.

c.2400 BC In Egyptian religion, Osiris is made both the god of fertility and the god of the dead. His son is Anubis.

2000 BC

2000 BC First settlers arrive in New Guinea.

2000 BC Migration of Bantu south from Central Africa.

1950 BC End of empire of Ur, Sumeria.

1595 BC Hittites conquer Babylon.

1300 BC First settlers arrive in Fiji, Tonga and Samoa.

c.1270 BC Israelites leave Egypt.

c.1200 BC Legendary Trojan Wars between the Greeks and the Trojans.

1200–600 BC Olmec civilization flourishes in Mexico.

1122 BC End of Shang Dynasty in China, replaced by the Zhou Dynasty.

c.1100–612 BC Assyrian Empire.

c.2000 BC Birth of Abraham.

Abraham is traditionally regarded as the father of the three great monotheistic religions: Judaism, Christianity and Islam.

c.1500 BC Start of the Vedic period of Hindu literature. The writings produced are known collectively as the *Veda*.

1500 BC Stone temples are built in Mexico.

c.1290 BC Moses leads the Hebrews out of Egypt, and after a long period in the wilderness receives the Ten Commandments at Mount Sinai.

Science and technology	Arts and culture

5000 BC–AD 1

- The Indus valley civilization arises in India, based on the city of Mohenjo-Daro. The Olmecs dominate Mexico, creating huge ceremonial earthworks and massive sculpures.
- The Greek city-state develops, with Athens and Sparta as the major powers. Colonies are set up throughout the Mediterranean. The first coins are struck. Alexander the Great conquers the Persian Empire.
- The city of Rome rises to power and extends its rule, its government evolving from republic to empire.
- China becomes united under a single emperor; the Great Wall is built.
- The Mayan culture arises in Guatemala and Mexico.

Science and technology	Arts and culture	
5000 BC Maize grown in Mexico.	**c.3500** BC In Ancient Egypt the later Gerzean or Naqada II culture begins, characterized by buff-coloured pottery decorated with scenes in purplish paint.	**5000** BC
c.4500 BC Beginning of Neolithic period (new Stone Age) in Europe.		
c.3700 BC Bronze (an alloy of copper and tin) is invented in Egypt.	**3200** BC Sumerians invent cuneiform writing.	
3500 BC Potatoes grown in South America.		
c.3500 BC The wheel is invented in Mesopotamia.		
3500 BC Copper in use in Thailand.		
3000 BC Agriculture develops in Mexico.	**c.3000** BC The earliest known form of pictograph writing is in use in Egypt.	**3000** BC
3000 BC Wheeled vehicles in use in the Middle and Near East.	**c.3000** BC The Sumerian predecessors of the Babylonians write poetry, of which fragments remain.	
c.2700 BC Acupuncture is first developed in China.		
c.2600 BC Glassware is invented in Egypt.	**c.3000** BC On Egyptian tomb walls, stylized pictures of the deceased and his or her servants are painted.	
c.2500 BC Soap is invented in Sumer, Babylonia.	**c.2600** BC Work begins on the Great Pyramid of Khufu at Giza.	
c.2300 BC The earliest surviving maps are land surveys for the purposes of taxation in use by the Babylonians.		
c.2300 BC Beginning of Bronze Age in central Europe.		
c.1900 BC Work begins on the Minoan palace complex at Knossos, Crete.	**c.2000** BC Part of the *Epic of Gilgamesh* is written down on clay tablets in Babylonia, the earliest known great poetic work.	**2000** BC
Knossos was noted for the sophistication of its art and architecture. It flourished c.1900–1400 BC, and was dominated by the Minoan palace. It is associated in legend with Minos, the labyrinth of Theseus, and the Minotaur.	**c.2000** BC Tales are recorded in Egypt.	
	c.1750 BC Death of Amorite king of Babylon Hammurabi.	
	Hammurabi ruled from c.1792–c.1750 BC, and is best known for his Code of Laws (a tablet inscribed with it is in the Louvre, Paris).	
c.1340 BC Egyptian pharaoh Tutankhamun is buried in a magnificent tomb at Thebes.		
c.1323 BC Hittites in Anatolia begin working iron.	**c.1550** BC Fine pottery is made at Knossos, Crete, and the palace is decorated with frescoes.	
1300 BC The first canal across the isthmus of Suez is dug, linking the Nile delta with the Red Sea.		

History

History and politics	Religion and philosophy
1000 BC	
c.962 BC Solomon succeeds his father David as King of Israel. His reign is characterized by an elaborate building programme and expansion in trade and political contacts.	**c.630 BC** Birth of Persian religious leader and prophet Zoroaster (d.c.553 BC).
c.900 BC Etruscans settle in Italy.	**c.600 BC** The *Upanishads*, the last section of the Hindu scriptures (the *Veda*) are composed in Sanskrit.
850 BC Chavín culture appears in Peru.	**600 BC** Foundation of Taoism in China by philosopher and sage Lao-tzu.
800 BC Development of India's caste system.	
814 BC Carthage founded by the Phoenicians.	**551 BC** Birth of Chinese philosopher Confucius (d.479 BC).
753 BC Foundation of Rome.	
750 BC Kush conquer Egypt.	Confucius emerged as a great moral teacher who tried to replace the old religious observances with moral values as the basis of social and political order.
721 BC Assyrians conquer Israel.	
666 BC Assyrians defeat Kush and conquer Egypt.	
550 BC Foundation of Persian Achaemenid Empire by Cyrus II, the Great (c.600–529 BC).	
539 BC Carthaginians defeated by the Greeks.	**c.540 BC** Birth in India of Vardhamana Mahavira, founder of Jainism.
525 BC Persia conquers Egypt.	
510 BC Last king of Rome deposed; foundation of the Roman Republic.	
500 BC	
c.500 BC Gallianazo and Salinar cultures flourish in Peru.	**c.500 BC** Buddhism is founded in India by Prince Siddhartha Gautama (c.560–480 BC), who became Buddha ('the enlightened') through meditation.
c.499 BC Persian Empire at its height.	
490 BC Athenians defeat the Persians with an overwhelming victory at the Battle of Marathon.	
431–404 BC Peloponnesian War between the Greek city-states of Athens and Sparta.	**469 BC** Birth of Greek philosopher Socrates (d.399 BC).
400 BC Nok culture in West Africa.	
332 BC King of Macedonia, Alexander the Great (356–323 BC), conquers Egypt.	One of the three great figures in ancient philosophy, Socrates' pivotal influence was such that all earlier Greek philosophy is classified as 'pre-Socratic'.
330 BC Alexander the Great defeats Darius III (c.381–330 BC), King of Persia, ending the Achaemenid Dynasty.	
323 BC On the death of Alexander the Great, Ptolemy I (c.367–283 BC) obtains Egypt, founding the Ptolemaic Dynasty.	**384 BC** Birth of Greek philosopher and scientist Aristotle (d.322 BC).
321 BC The extensive Mauryan Empire is founded in India by Chandra Gupta.	**c.372 BC** Chinese philosopher and sage Mencius born (d.c.289 BC).
312 BC Macedonian general Seleucus I Nicator (c.358–281 BC) founds the Seleucid Dynasty.	Mencius helped to develop and popularize the Confucian ideas and founded a school to promote their study.
c.300 BC Rome rises to power.	
264–146 BC Punic Wars; a series of wars between Rome and Carthage.	**c.348 BC** Death of Greek philosopher Plato (b.c.428 BC).
221 BC Shi Huangdi (c.259–210 BC), Chinese emperor and founder of the Qin Dynasty, creates the first unified Chinese empire.	**300 BC** Greek philosopher and founder of Stoicism, Zeno of Citium (c.334–c.265 BC), founds a school in the *Stoa poikile* ('painted porch'), from where the Stoics get their name.
218 BC Carthaginian soldier Hannibal (247–182 BC) crosses the Alps into Italy with an army including elephants.	
206 BC In China Liu Bang (256–195 BC) founds the Han Dynasty after a rebellion overthrows the Qin Dynasty.	**c.273–232 BC** Mauryan emperor Aśoka organizes Buddhism as the state religion of India, whilst giving freedom to other religious sects.

History

Science and technology

c.1000 BC Start of the Iron Age in south and central Europe.

781 BC Chinese astronomers observe a solar eclipse.

c.700 BC Lydians develop a system of coined money in south-west Asia Minor.

600 BC The massive Temple of Zeus in Sicily is built.

585 BC Greek natural philosopher and astronomer Thales (c.620–c.555 BC), traditionally regarded as the founder of Greek philosophy, accurately predicts a solar eclipse.

c.580 BC Greek philosopher, mystic and mathematician Pythagoras born (d.c.500 BC).

Pythagoras is associated with mathematical discoveries involving the chief musical intervals, the relations of numbers, the theorem of right-angled triangles which bears his name, and with more fundamental beliefs about the understanding and representation of the world of nature through numbers.

c.575 BC The Ishtar Gate, a huge and elaborate gateway into the city of Babylon, is built.

c.500 BC The Chinese begin to use single-gate locks on their canals.

c.460 BC Birth of Greek physician and 'father of medicine' Hippocrates (d. 377/359 BC).

Skilled in diagnosis and prognosis, Hippocrates gathered together all the work of his predecessors which he believed to be sound, and laid the early foundations of scientific medicine. The Hippocratic oath has been seen as the foundation of Western medical ethics.

447 BC The Parthenon is built in Athens.

c.335 BC Birth of Greek anatomist Herophilus (d.c.280 BC). He founded the Alexandrian school of anatomy and was the first to dissect the human body to compare it with that of other animals.

c.300 BC Greek mathematician Euclid writes his *Elements*, a treatise on geometry in 13 books. It is the earliest substantial mathematical treatise to have survived, and is probably better known than any other mathematical book.

c.287 BC Birth of Greek mathematician Archimedes (d.212 BC).

Archimedes is remembered as the inventor of the Archimedean screw (which is still used for raising water) and for the 'Archimedes' principle'. He also demonstrated the powers of levers in moving large weights. In mathematics Archimedes discovered the formulae for the areas and volumes of cylinders, spheres, parabolas, and other plane and solid figures.

c.250 BC Greek mathematician, astronomer and geographer Erastosthenes (c.276–194 BC) calculates the circumference of the Earth with considerable accuracy.

221 BC Construction of the Great Wall of China begins.

Arts and culture

c.900 BC Greek epic poet Homer writing.　　1000 BC

A major figure of Ancient Greek literature, Homer was regarded in Greek and Roman antiquity as the author of the *Iliad* (dealing with episodes in The Trojan War) and the *Odyssey* (dealing with Odysseus's adventures on his return from Troy).

776 BC The traditional date of the first Olympic Games, held at Olympia in western Greece.

c.700 BC Greek writer Hesiod writes his epic poems *Opera et dies* ('Works and Days') and *Theogonia* ('Theogony').

c.610 BC Greek lyric poet Sappho of Lesbos born (d.c.580 BC). It is from her that the four-line sapphic stanza takes its name and the term 'lesbian' has acquired its meaning.

c.534 BC Greek poet and reputed founder of Greek drama Thespis, wins the first prize for tragedy at a festival in Athens.

c.496 BC Birth of Athenian tragedian Sophocles　500 BC
(d.405 BC). One of the great figures of Greek drama, *Oedipus Tyrranus* is generally regarded as his masterpiece.

431 BC Greek tragic dramatist Euripides (484/480–406 BC) writes *Medea*.

c.430 BC Greek sculptor Phidias completes his *Statue of Zeus* at Olympia, one of the Seven Wonders of the World.

c.385 BC Greek comic dramatist Aristophanes dies (b.c.448 BC). Of the 50 plays he wrote, 11 are extant.

c.350 BC Greek sculptor Praxiteles completes his most celebrated work *Aphrodite of Cnidos*.

c.300 BC Greek historian and high priest of Heliopolis, Manetho, writes his history (in Greek) of the 30 dynasties of Egypt.

c.280 BC The *Colossus of Rhodes*, a giant statue of the sun-god Helios and one of the Seven Wonders of the World, is completed by Greek sculptor Chares of Lyndos.

224 BC Roman comic dramatist Plautus (c.250–184 BC) begins to write.

History

History and politics	Religion and philosophy
200 BC	
185 BC End of Mauryan Empire in India.	**c.200 BC** The Old Testament is translated into Greek.
149–146 BC The Third Punic War (between the Roman Republic and the Carthaginian Empire) results in the destruction of Carthage.	**136 BC** Confucianism becomes the official state ideology in China, due largely to the influence of scholar and philosopher Dong Zhongshu (c.179–104 BC).
63 BC Conquest of Jerusalem by Roman Pompey (106–48 BC). Palestine becomes a province of Rome.	
45 BC Roman general and statesman Julius Caesar (100/102–44 BC) defeats Pompey's legates in Spain and is appointed dictator.	**c.4 BC** Birth of Jesus Christ in Bethlehem.
30 BC Egypt becomes a Roman province following the seizure of Alexandria. Suicides of Cleopatra (b.69 BC) and Mark Antony (b.c.83 BC).	
27 BC Foundation of Roman Empire with Augustus (63 BC–AD 14) as first emperor.	

AD 1–299

■ The Roman Empire is at its height, including Britain as far north as the Antonine Wall (built c.143) in southern Scotland. The presence of its merchants is recorded at the Imperial Court in China (166). The prized status of Roman citizen is granted to all free inhabitants of the Empire (212).

■ Chinese civilization continues to advance with such innovations as a simple practical compass (271). Contact with other cultures increases: a Chinese ambassador visits Persia (97), and Chinese silks are brought by camel to Dimashq (Damascus) (220).

AD 1	
1 Bantu people begin to migrate to East Africa.	**c.30** Jesus Christ is crucified.
9 Plans to extend the Roman frontier from the Rhine to the Elbe are abandoned when three Roman legions are ambushed and annihilated by Germanic tribes in the Teutoburg Forest.	**c.40** Hellenistic Jewish philosopher Philo Judaeus (c.20 BC–c.40 AD)leads a deputation to the Emperor Caligula to plead on behalf of Jews who refuse to worship him.
25 Chinese capital moves east from Changan to Luoyang. Start of Eastern Han Dynasty.	**64** Fire destroys two-thirds of Rome. Christians are blamed and many are put to death.
43 Romans invade Britain, led by Emperor Claudius I (10 BC–AD 54).	
60 In England, Boudicca, Queen of the Iceni, leads an unsuccessful rebellion against Roman rule.	**68** The *Dead Sea Scrolls* are hidden in a cave near Qumran on the Dead Sea during the Roman invasion of the area.
70 Jerusalem is destroyed by the Romans.	
78 Height of Kushan Empire in northern India and Central Asia under King Kaniska.	**c.75** Buddhism is introduced to China.
79 Mount Vesuvius in southern Italy erupts, burying Pompeii under ashes.	
100	
100 Foundation of the city of Teotihuacán in Mexico.	**c.120** Development of Gnosticism.
117 Death of Roman emperor Trajan (b.c.53). His reign saw the Roman Empire at its greatest extent.	**c.125** Syrian Gnostic philosopher Basilides founds a sect in Alexandria. His disciples (Basilidians) are active into the 4c.
122–8 Hadrian's Wall is built as the northern frontier of Roman Britain.	

Science and technology

129 BC Greek astronomer and mathematician Hipparchos (c.180–125 BC) completes his catalogue of 850 stars, giving their positions in celestial latitude and longitude. This work remained of prime importance until the 17c.

c.40 BC Death of Greek physician Asclepiades (b.124 BC). He advanced the doctrine that disease results from discord in the corpuscles of the body, and recommended good diet and exercise as a cure.

Arts and culture

c.200 BC Sculptors carve the reliefs on the stupa at Bharhut, India.

200 BC

166 BC Roman comic dramatist Terence (c.195–159 BC) writes his first play, *Andria* ('The Girl from Andros').

150 BC The *Venus de Milo*, a statue of Aphrodite, is carved in Greece.

90 BC Hydraulic organs are first played by Romans.

27 BC Roman scholar and writer Marcus Terentius Varro dies (b.116 BC). His works include the *Disciplinarum Libri IX*, an encyclopedia of the liberal arts.

19 BC Death of Roman poet Virgil (b.70 BC). One of the greatest poets of antiquity, the *Aeneid* is unfinished at his death.

AD 1–299

■ An anonymous text called *A Voyage around the Red Sea* (1c) describes nautical trading routes from the Red Sea to East Africa and as far east as the Ganges Delta.

■ In Africa, the Aksum civilization begins to dominate Ethiopia (50), and Bantu-speaking peoples migrate into the southern part of the continent (265).

■ The Mayan civilization develops in Central America around centres such as Tikal and Palenque (c.284).

c.30 Roman writer and physician Aulus Cornelius Celsus writes his *De Medicina*, giving accounts of symptoms and treatments of diseases, surgical methods and medical history.

c.62 Greek mathematician Hero of Alexandria invents the *aeolipile*, the earliest known steam engine.

78 Chinese scholar and inventor Chang Heng born (d.139). Among several other inventions, he is credited with the construction of the world's first seismograph.

82 The Colosseum in Rome is completed.

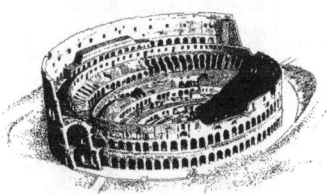

c.90 Death of Greek physician Pedanius Dioscorides (b.c.40). His *De materis medica* was the standard work on substances used in medicine for many centuries.

8 Roman poet Ovid (43 BC–AD 17) completes his *Metamorphoses*, a collection of mythological tales in 15 books.

AD 1

Later acclaimed as a master of the elegiac couplet, Ovid had his first literary success with a collection of love poems, the *Amores* ('Loves'), followed by *Heroides* ('Heroines'). The *Ars Amandi* or *Ars Amatoria* ('The Art of Love'), a handbook of seduction, appeared about 1 BC, followed by the *Remedia Amoris* ('Cures for Love').

c.46 Greek historian, biographer and philosopher Plutarch born (d.c.120). His best-known work is *Parallel Lives*.

c.50 Translator of Aesop's fables into Latin verse Phaedrus dies (b.c.15 BC). In addition to reproducing the fables of Aesop, he invented his own and also borrowed from other sources.

65 Roman philosopher, statesman and tragedian Seneca commits suicide after his implication in the conspiracy of Piso (b.c.4 BC).

82 Chinese historian Ban Gu (32–92) completes his history of the Western Han Dynasty, initiating an unparalleled tradition of dynastic histories.

c.100 Greek physician Aretaeus writes his great work, discussing the causes, symptons and cures of diseases.

105 Paper is invented in China by Zai Lun (c.50–118); it is made from tree bark and rags.

118 The Pantheon in Rome is rebuilt by the emperor Hadrian (76–138).

c.114 Chinese historian and moralist Ban Zhao dies (b.45). She helped complete Ban Gu's history of the Western Han Dynasty, and her book of moral admonitions for women had a lasting influence on attitudes towards women in China.

100

120 Roman historian Tacitus dies (b.c.55). His major work is the 12-volume *Historiae* ('Histories').

History

	History and politics	Religion and philosophy
130	**138** Antoninus Pius (86–161) succeeds Hadrian (76–138) as Roman emperor. His reign is peaceful and happy. **161** Marcus Aurelius (121–80) becomes Roman emperor on the death of Antoninus Pius. **184** Start of Yellow Turban Rebellion in China, which weakens Han rule. **192–7** Period of civil war in the Roman Empire following the death of the emperor Commodus. **197–9** Roman emperor Lucius Septimius Severus (146–211) defeats the Parthians.	**132** Jewish leader Simon Bar Kokhba (d.135) leads an unsuccessful rebellion against the Romans in Judea, precipitating the diaspora. **c.178** Roman philosopher Celsus publishes his *True Discourse*, one of the first anti-Jewish and anti-Christian polemics.
200	**c.200** Burial mounds are built by Native Americans in Ohio. **220** Collapse of Han Dynasty in China, followed by the Three Kingdoms Period. **c.224** In Persia, Ardashir I (d.241) overthrows Ardavan, last of the Parthian kings, and founds the Sassanid Dynasty. **c.240** Kushan Empire in northern India declines. **250** Yamato dominates Japan. **260** Roman emperor Valerian (c.193–260) is defeated by the Persians at Edessa. He dies in captivity. **280** Jin Dynasty completes the reunification of China, ending the Three Kingdoms Period. **293** Roman emperor Diocletian (245–313) establishes the tetrarchy, with the Roman Empire ruled by two emperors, each assisted by a Caesar.	**c.205** Greek philosopher Plotinus born (d.270). His 54 works established the foundations of Neoplatonism as a philosophical system. **c.224** Sassanid king Ardashir I makes Zoroastrianism the state religion of Persia. **c.250** Death of Indian Buddhist monk-philosopher Nāgājuna (b.c.150). He was the founder of the Madhyamika or Middle Path school of Buddhism. **285** Confucianism reaches Japan.

300–599

- The Roman Empire declines in the face of barbarian incursions. Byzantium, rebuilt and renamed Constantinople, becomes the imperial capital (330), then the empire is split (395) between West (ruled from Milan) and East (ruled from Constantinople).
- Christianity spreads throughout the Roman Empire, especially after the conversion of the Emperor Constantine (312).
- Westward movement of Huns triggers migrations of other peoples such as the Ostrogoths and Vandals into Roman territory.

300	**c.300** Rise of the Maya civilization in southern Mexico. **c.300** The first settlers arrive in Tahiti. **c.320** Founding of Gupta Dynasty in India by Chandra Gupta I. **330** Constantinople becomes the capital of the Roman Empire. **350** Kingdom of Axum (Ethiopia) conquers the kingdom of Kush in Nubia. **370** Europe is invaded by Huns from Asia. **378** At the Battle of Adrianople, the Romans are defeated by the Visigoths. **c.380** Expansion of the Gupta Empire in India under Chandra Gupta II. **395** The Roman Empire is formally split into two, the Eastern Empire (Byzantine Empire) and the Western Empire, on the death of Emperor Theodosius I (b.c.343).	**324** Christianity becomes the official religion of the Roman Empire. **329** Palestinian hermit St Hilarion (c.291–371) founds the first monastery in Palestine. **350** Christianity reaches Ethiopia. **386** St Jerome (c.342–420) begins the first Latin translation of the Bible from the Hebrew (the Vulgate Bible). **397** Numidian Christian St Augustine of Hippo (354–430) writes his *Confessions*.

Science and technology

c.130 Egyptian astronomer and geographer Ptolemy (c.90–168) completes his *Almagest*, a 'great compendium of astronomy'. His Earth-centred view of the universe dominated cosmological thought until the work of Copernicus in the 16c.

c.150 Soranus of Ephesus, a Greek gynaecologist, produces *On Midwifery and the Diseases of Women*.

c.201 Greek physician Galen dies (b.c.130).

Long venerated as the standard authority on medical matters, Galen studied the function of the bodily organs through experimentation and the dissection of animals. Galen was also the first to use the pulse as a diagnostic aid.

206 Work begins on the Baths of Caracella in Rome.

c.250 Greek mathematician Diophantus writes his *Arithmetica*, dealing with the solution of algebraic equations. In contrast to earlier Greek works it uses a rudimentary algebraic notation, instead of a purely geometric one.

Arts and culture

c.140 Roman lawyer and satirist Juvenal dies (b.c.55). Both Dryden and Dr Johnson would later be influenced by Juvenal's satires of Roman life and society.

180 Greek historian Arrian dies (b.c.95). His chief work is the *Anabasis Alexandrou*, a history of the campaigns of Alexander the Great.

c.250 The earliest known Sanskrit dramatist Bhasa active. The author of plays on religious and legendary themes, his greatest work is *Svapnavasavadatta* ('The Dream of Vasavadatta').

c.264 Palestinian theologian and scholar Eusebius of Caesarea born (d.340). His most important work, *Ecclesiastical History*, is a record of the chief events in the Christian Church down to 324.

c.290 One of the earliest Greek novelists Heliodorus writes *Aethiopica*, which describes the love of Theagenes and Chariclea.

130

200

300–599

- The Romans leave Britain (410), which is invaded and settled by Angles, Saxons and Jutes.
- The civilization of Teotihuacán dominates Mexico. Mayan civilization is at its height c.600.
- The middle of the 4c sees the height of Buddhist sculpture, painting, and temple construction. Buddhism reaches Japan from Korea c.550.
- Chinese mathematicians are capable of solving linear equations and reducing fractions. In India, the decimal system is invented.
- Silkworms are brought from China to the Byzantine Empire c.540.

c.326 Work begins on Old Saint Peter's Basilica, Rome, at the order of Emperor Constantine I (c.274–337).

c.340 Greek mathematician Pappus of Alexandria writes his mathematical *Collection*, covering a wide range of geometrical problems.

343 Chinese alchemist Ge Hong dies (b.c.280).

Ge Hong's most famous book, *Bao-pu zi* ('He who holds to Simplicity'), contains accounts of methods of producing solutions of minerals in order to make immortality elixirs. He also describes the apparent production of gold from other metals.

c.375 The first metal stirrups are used on horses in China. Unlike earlier leather stirrups that were aids to mounting, metal stirrups were to help warriors fight from horseback.

c.330 Roman historian Ammianus Marcellinus born (d.390). He wrote a history of the Roman Empire from AD 98.

340 Roman poet Claudian born (d.410). The last of the great Latin poets, his works include the epic poem *The Rape of Proserpine*.

365 Chinese poet Tao Qian born (d.427). One of the great poets of China, Tao Qian employed a less artificial style than his contemporaries. He also wrote short stories.

c.380 Chandra Gupta II becomes head of the Gupta Empire. His reign sees peace and religious tolerance alongside the flourishing of Indian art, architecture and sculpture.

300

History

	History and politics	Religion and philosophy
400	**c.400** Moche culture now well established in Peru.	**c.400** The Palestinian Talmud is completed.
	c.400 Polynesians reach Easter Island.	**402** Chinese Buddhist monk Fa Xian makes a pilgrimage to India to find holy texts. He left a valuable account of Indian Buddhism.
	400 Hepthalites ('White Huns') invade Sassanian Empire (Persia).	
	410 Rome is sacked by the Visigoths led by Alaric I (c.390–461).	**451** Italian pope Leo I (c.390–461) summons the Council of Chalcedon.
	429 Vandals found North African kingdom.	
	434 Attila (c.406–53) becomes King of the Huns.	**c.475** Roman philosopher and politician Anicius Manlius Severinus Boethius born (d.524). His most famous work is *De Consolatione Philosophiae* ('The Consolation of Philosophy').
	c.450 Flourishing of Nazca people in Peru.	
	451 Attila the Hun is defeated when he invades Gaul.	
	455 Vandals sack Rome.	
	476 Emperor Romulus Augustulus is overthrown by Germanic warrior Odoacer (433–93), ending the Western Roman Empire.	
	486 Clovis (465–511) overthrows the last Roman governor in Gaul.	
	493 Theodoric the Great (c.455–526) assassinates Odoacer and becomes Ostrogoth king of Italy.	
500	**534** North African Vandal kingdom destroyed by the Byzantines under General Belisarius (505–65).	**515** Italian monk St Benedict of Nursia (c.480–c.547) composes his *Regula Monachorum*, which became the common rule of all Western monasticism.
	534 Franks conquer Burgundian kingdom.	
	535 North Africa becomes part of the Byzantine Empire.	**563** St Columba founds the monastery at Iona.
	535 Byzantine emperor Justinian I (c.482–565) declares war on the Ostrogoths, reclaiming Italy for the Empire.	**570** Prophet Muhammad born (d.c.632) in Mecca.
	540 End of Gupta Dynasty in northern and parts of central and western India after attacks by the Hepthalites ('White Huns').	**594** Buddhism becomes the official religion of Japan.
	552 Juan-juan Empire destroyed by Nomadic Turks led by Bumin, who founds the Turk Empire with control over central Asia.	**597** Italian prelate Augustine (d.604) is made Bishop of the English and establishes his church at Canterbury.
	558 Clotaire becomes King of all Franks.	
	568 Lombards invade northern Italy and found a kingdom around the River Po.	
	581 Yang Jian overthrows the Northern Zhou Dynasty, founding the Sui Dynasty and unifying China (by 589) after three centuries of division.	

600–899

■ China, united under the Tang Dynasty, sees a flowering of literature, especially the poetry of Li Bo and Du Fu.

■ The Islamic era begins with the Hegira of Muhammad, and Arab expansion carries the faith throughout North Africa, the Near East and into Spain.

■ The Muslim world sees the introduction of paper from China c. 751, and there are great advances in mathematics, medicine and astronomy.

	History and politics	Religion and philosophy
600	**613–19** Sassanid king of Persia Chosroes II (d.628) conquers Syria, Palestine, Egypt and parts of Asia Minor, almost defeating the Byzantine Empire.	**622** Muhammad's migration to Medina, the Hegira, marks the beginning of the Islamic calendar.
	618 Tang Dynasty replaces Sui Dynasty in China, founded by frontier general Li Yuan (566–635).	**c.625** Irish monk St Adomnan born (d.704). An abbot at Iona, his *Vita Sancti Columbae* reveals a great deal about the religious community there.
	628–33 Byzantine emperor Heraclius (c.575–641) defeats the Persians and restores lost territories in the East.	
	632 Muhammad dies and the caliphate is instituted.	
	634–42 Second caliph Omar (c.581–644) builds up an empire comprising Persia, Syria and all North Africa, conquering lands recently won by the Byzantines and ending the Sassanian Empire.	

Science and technology	Arts and culture	
415 Greek philosopher Hypatia is murdered by a Christian mob (b.c.370).	**c.410** Latin Christian poet Marcus Aurelius Clemens Prudentius dies (b.348). He is the best known of the early Christian verse-makers.	**400**
Hypatia was the first notable female astronomer and mathematician, and head of the Neoplatonist school in Alexandria.	**438** The Theodosian Code, a law code by Byzantine emperor Theodosius II (401–50), is published.	
432 The Santa Maria Maggiore basilica is built in Rome.	**c.450** India's greatest dramatist Kálidása writes his drama *Sákuntala*.	
c.460 Work begins on the Buddhist cave temples at Yun-kang, China.	**c.480** North African scholar and writer Martianus Minneus Felix Capella writes his *Satiricon*, a kind of encyclopedia in verse and prose.	
499 Indian astronomer and mathematician Aryabatha (476–c.550) completes his *Aryabhatiya*, a work summarizing mathematical knowledge in his time.	**c.480** Greek epic poet Musaeus writes *Hero and Leander*.	
c.500 In North America the Inuit begin hunting whales and seals.	**c.500** Greek anthologist Johannes Stobaeus compiles an anthology from 500 Greek poets and prose-writers, which preserves fragments from many lost works.	**500**
510 Chinese develop block-book printing, in which a wooden block is carved with the characters of text, inked, and then used to produce multiple copies.	**538** Frankish prelate and historian Gregory of Tours born (d.594). His *Historia Francorum* ('History of the Franks') is the chief authority for the history of Gaul in the 6c.	
525 Scythian scholar Dionysius Exiguus (d.556) fixes the dating of the Christian era in his *Cyclus Paschalis*.	**565** Byzantine historian Procopius dies (b.c.499). His works include *Historiae* (on the Persian, Vandal and Gothic wars) and *Anecdota* or *Historia Arcana* ('Secret History').	
532–7 The church of Hagia Sophia is built in Constantinople under the direction of Justinian I, emperor of the Byzantine Empire.	**570** Romano-British historian and monk St Gildas dies (b.c.493). His famous treatise *De Excidio et Conquestu Britanniae* is the only extant history of the Celts.	
550 The astrolabe, a scientific instrument for showing the positions of the Sun and bright stars at any given time, is developed. It is used for astronomy and in navigation.		

600–899

■ In the 790s the Vikings begin their raids in western Europe.

■ Under Charlemagne, crowned Emperor of the West in 800, western Europe experiences a revival of scholarship.

■ The Cyrillic alphabet is created (863) and spreads through eastern Europe.

■ The infirmaries of abbeys and monasteries in western Europe become centres for the care of the ill.

607–10 A great canal system is built in China, connecting the Yellow and Yangtze rivers.	**c.600** Chinese artist Yen Liben born (d.673). One of the most important painters of the early Tang Dynasty, his extant works include 'Portraits of the Emperors'.	**600**
628 Indian astronomer and mathematician Brahmagupta (598–c.665) completes his *Brahma-sphuta-siddhanta* ('The Opening of the Universe').	**636** Spanish prelate St Isidore of Seville dies (b.c.560). He is best known for his *Etymologiae*, a weighty encyclopedia of knowledge, and a standard reference work throughout the Middle Ages.	

History

History and politics	Religion and philosophy
640	

640

650 All Polynesian islands are now colonized except New Zealand.

661 Mu'Awiyah (c.602–80) becomes first Umayyad caliph. He extends the caliphate in North Africa and Afghanistan.

668 The three rival kingdoms of Korea are united by the Silla Dynasty.

689 Frankish king Pepin II (d.714) defeats the Frisians, adding western Frisia to the Frankish kingdom.

690 Wu Zetian (d.705) becomes Emperor of China, the only woman ever to do so.

698 Carthage is destroyed by Arabs.

Religion and philosophy

c.640 In China, Ch'an Buddhism develops.

c.645 Buddhism is recognized in Tibet.

c.650 The revelations of Muhammad are collected and written down as the *Koran*.

661 Beginning of the major Sunni–Shiite division within Islam.

664 Synod of Whitby chooses Roman Christianity over Celtic Christianity in England.

700

c.700 The Kingdom of Ghana expands due to trade across the Sahara.

711 Spain invaded by Muslims from North Africa, who defeat the Visigoths.

736 Frankish ruler Charles Martel (c.688–741) defeats Muslim invaders from Spain at Poitiers.

c.750 The Pala Dynasty, the ruling dynasty in Bihar and Bengal, India, is founded by Gopala.

c.750 In Mexico the city of Teotihuacán is sacked by the invading Toltec.

750 In India the Rashtrakuta Dynasty is founded, soon dominating the entire area of northern Maharashtra.

750 'Abbasid Dynasty founded, replacing Umayyad Dynasty.

751 Pepin III, the Short (c.715–68) becomes King of the Franks.

755 In Tang China the Rebellion of An Lushan, although crushed, leaves the dynasty weakened.

756 Islamic Empire starts to break up into separate countries.

771 Charlemagne (747–814) becomes sole King of the Franks.

773 Charlemagne defeats the Lombards in Italy.

793 Beginning of Viking raids on England.

794 Japanese capital moved from Nara to Heian (present-day Kyoto). Start of the Heian Era.

Religion and philosophy

c.700 Lindisfarne Gospels, an illuminated manuscript of the Gospels, is created at Lindisfarne.

718 Anglo-Saxon missionary Boniface (c.680–c.754) sets out to preach the gospel to all the tribes of Germany.

726 Iconoclasm movement starts when Byzantine emperor Leo III (c.680–741) prohibits the use of icons in public worship.

750 Death of Hindu philosopher and theologian Śankara (b.c.700).

Śankara was the most famous exponent of *Advaita* (the *Vedanta* school of Indian philosophy), and is the source of the main currents of modern Hindu thought.

c.754 Death of Greek theologian and hymn-writer of the Eastern Church, St John of Damascus. Among his works is an encyclopedia of Christian theology, the *Fount of Wisdom*.

800

c.800 Rajput Dynasties begin to dominate northern India.

800 Establishment of the Holy Roman Empire with the coronation of Charlemagne as emperor.

802 King Jayavarman II asserts Khmer independence and the Angkorean Dynasty is founded.

Religion and philosophy

c.800 Large and sophisticated Hindu temples are built in eastern India.

Science and technology

644 Earliest known reference to a windmill, in Persia.

673 In the Battle of Cyzicus, the Byzantines use 'Greek fire' (a highly inflammable liquid, which is set alight and shot towards the enemy), invented by the architect Callinicus.

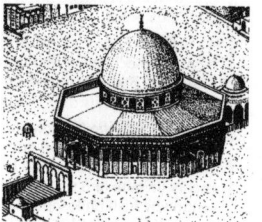

685–91 In Jerusalem the Dome of the Rock is built by Umayyad caliph 'Abd al-Malik (646/647–705).

700 Water wheels are used throughout Europe to drive mills.

705–15 Caliph al-Walid I (c.668–715) builds the Great Mosque of Damascus.

c.721 Arab alchemist Jabir ibn Hayyan born (d.c.815). He wrote a number of works on alchemy and metaphysics which were widely circulated in the Middle Ages.

725 Chinese inventor I-Hsing (682–727) produces a mechanical clock, the first Chinese clock to strike the hours and half-hours.

751 Knowledge of papermaking reaches Samarkand, Central Asia.

784–96 Offa, King of Mercia (d.796), builds the great earthwork known as Offa's Dyke to protect his frontiers against the Welsh.

787 Birth of Arab astronomer and astrologer Albumazar (d.885). In Baghdad he was the leading astrologer of his day, and he produced valuable work on the nature of tides.

793 A paper factory is established at Baghdad.

c.800 First use of bow and arrow in Mississippi valley.

c.800 Arab mathematician al-Khwarizmi born (d.c.850). His writings in Latin translation were influential in transmitting Indian and Arab mathematics to medieval Europe.

804 Arab scholar Hunayn ibn Ishaq born (d.873). His translations of Greek writers such as Galen and Aristotle made Greek thought available to Arab philosophers and scientists.

Arts and culture

658 Caedmon, an uneducated herdsman and the earliest English poet known by name, composes his 'Hymn of Creation'. **640**

c.673 Anglo-Saxon monk and scholar Bede born (d.735). His greatest work, *Historia Ecclesiastica Gentis Anglorum* ('Ecclesiastical History of the English People'), was completed in 731. It is the single most valuable source for early English history.

699 Chinese painter and poet Wang Wei born (d.759). He linked painting with poetry in nature and mood, and may have pioneered monochrome ink painting.

c.700 Anglo-Saxon poet and scholar Cynewulf born (d.c.800). The four poems attributed to him are contained in the *Exeter Book* and the *Vercelli Book*. **700**

712 Chinese poet Du Fu born (d.770). He was one of the foremost lyricists in the Chinese language.

c.725 The Old English epic poem *Beowulf* is written.

Beowulf was the earliest European epic poem to be written in a vernacular language. Surviving in the single late-10c 'Cotton manuscript' it describes the heroic life of Beowulf the dragon-slayer.

c.737 Alcuin born (d.804). A Northumbrian scholar and adviser to the Emperor Charlemagne, his works include poems, works on grammar, treatises, lives of saints, and over 200 letters.

754 Chinese emperor Xuan Zong (681–761) founds the Hanlin Academy.

c.760 Arab poet Abu Nuwas born (d.814). Considered one of the greatest poets of the 'Abbasid period, he was a favourite at the court in Baghdad and figures in the *Arabian Nights*.

762 Chinese poet Li Bo dies (b.701). He was regarded as the greatest poet in China, and wrote colourful verse on wine, women and nature.

c.800 Monks at Kells, Ireland, complete the *Book of Kells*, an illuminated manuscript of the Gospels. **800**

807 Arab poet Abu Tammam born (d.c.850). He compiled a celebrated anthology of early Arab poetry, the *Hamasu*.

History

History and politics	Religion and philosophy
820	

825 In England Egbert (d.839) ends Mercian dominance at the Battle of Ellendun.

827 Muslim Aghlabids conquer Sicily.

843 The Carolingian Empire is divided into three by the Treaty of Verdun.

843 Kenneth MacAlpin (d.858) becomes King of Picts and Scots.

c.850 West African trading kingdom of Kanem established near Lake Chad.

866 Danes invade south-east England.

867 Byzantine emperor Basil I (c.812–86) founds the Macedonian Dynasty.

868 In a break from the 'Abbasid caliphate, the Tulunid Dynasty is founded in Egypt by Turk Ahmad ibn Tulun.

882 Oleg (d.912) unites Novgorod and Kiev, founding the first Russian state.

886 Anglo-Saxon king of Wessex Alfred the Great (849–99) formalizes the partition of England, with the Danelaw under Viking rule.

c.896 Magyar chieftain Árpád (d.c.907) occupies modern Hungary.

896 Danish Vikings settle at the mouth of the Seine in France.

824 Chinese moralist Han Yu dies (b.768). He attacked Buddhism and promoted a revival of Confucian thought.

843 Period of iconoclasm in the Byzantine Church comes fully to an end with icons placed firmly within Orthodox belief.

845 In China Emperor Wu-tsung begins persecution of Buddhists, destroying Buddhist temples and shrines.

c.865 *De Divisione Naturae*, an attempt to fuse Christian and Neoplatonic doctrines, and to reconcile faith and reason, is written by Irish philosopher John Scotus Erigena (c.810–c.877).

867 Patriarch of Constantinople Photius (c.820–91) separates the Eastern Church from Rome.

c.870 Arab philosopher al-Kindi dies (b.c.800). He was one of the first to spread Greek thought into the Arab world, and was known as 'the philosopher of the Arabs'.

900–999

■ The Toltec state rises to power in Mexico, based on the city of Tula.

■ The Vikings continue to explore, colonize and establish settlements, reaching Kiev and Constantinople in the east, and Greenland and North America in the west, and holding Normandy as a duchy under the French king.

■ The Byzantine Empire undergoes a period of expansion through military successes, especially under Emperor Basil II.

900	

c.900 Decline of Maya civilization in South America.

907 End of Tang Dynasty in China, followed by the Five Dynasties and Ten Kingdoms Period, a time of social and political turmoil.

910 Arab Fatimid Dynasty established in North Africa.

911 Rollo (c.860–c.932), Viking founder of the duchy of Normandy, arrives in France.

913 Koryo Dynasty founded by Wang Kon in Korea.

937 Anglo-Saxon king Athelstan (c.895–939) defeats the Scots, Welsh and Vikings at the Battle of Brunanburh.

945 Shiite Buyids take control of Baghdad, but allow the Sunni 'Abbasid caliph to retain his position.

c.909 Anglo-Saxon prelate St Dunstan born (d.988). He transformed Glastonbury into a centre of religious learning and re-established monasticism in England.

923 Arab historian at-Tabari dies (b.839). He wrote a major commentary on the *Koran* and a history of the world from creation.

935 Jewish philosopher Ben Joseph Sa'adia (882–942) writes *The Book of Beliefs and Opinions*.

950	

955 Otto I (912–73), Holy Roman Emperor, defeats the Hungarian Magyars at the Battle of Lechfield.

960 General Zhao Guangyin founds the Song Dynasty and begins to reunite China.

969 Fatimids conquer Egypt and build a new capital at Cairo.

c.950 Islamic philosopher Abu Nasr al-Farabi dies (b.878). Influenced by Plato's *Republic*, he published a utopian political philosophy, known under the title *The Perfect City*.

Science and technology

827 Ptolemy's *Almagest*, an encyclopedia of anatomy and mathematics, is translated into Arabic.

c.850 A medical school emerges at Salerno in southern Italy.

c.865 Persian physician and alchemist ar-Razi (Rhazes) born (d.923/932).

Ar-Razi wrote many medical works, some of which were translated into Latin and had considerable influence in the Middle Ages. He successfully distinguished smallpox from measles, and was considered the greatest physician of the Arab world.

868 The *Diamond Sutra* is the earliest datable printed document, produced in China using carved wooden blocks.

Arts and culture

c.820 Frankish historian Einhard (c.770–840)   **820**
writes his *Life of Charlemagne*, the greatest biographical work of the Middle Ages.

846 Chinese lyric poet Bo Juyi dies (b.772). His work was so admired that his poems were collected by imperial order and engraved on stone tablets.

859 The Islamic university of Qarawiyin is founded in Fès, Morocco.

871–99 In England, under the reign of King Alfred, the *Anglo-Saxon Chronicle* is first assembled, an account of Anglo-Saxon and Norman England.

c.880 Japanese poet Ono No Komachi dies (b.c.810). She is known in Japan as one of the 'Six Poetic Geniuses'.

c.897 Japanese artist Kose Kanaoka dies (b.c.802). He was one of the first important secular artists in Japan.

900–999

- Buddhism spreads into Korea.
- In the Muslim world, the text of the Koran is finalized (935), and Cairo is founded as the capital of the Fatimid Dynasty. A caliphate is established at Córdoba in Spain.
- The Fujiwara family establishes its domination as regents of the Japanese emperors.
- The 990s see the rise of Dublin as the chief city of Ireland, and the first Irish coins are struck there.
- Venetian merchants are granted trading privileges in Constantinople.

918 First hospitals for the mentally ill are established in Baghdad and Cairo.

929 Arab mathematician and astronomer al-Battani dies (b.c.858). He was the author of a collection of astronomical tables, 'On Stellar Motion', and improved upon Ptolemy's astronomical calculations.

c.940 Pope Sylvester II (Gerbert of Aurillac) born (d.1003). Skilled in chemistry, mathematics and philosophy, he wrote about the abacus and the astrolabe, and worked on celestial globes.

c.950 The first 'motte and bailey' castles are built between the Loire and Rhine rivers.

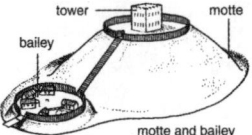

motte and bailey

905 *Kokinshu*, an anthology of Japanese   **900**
poetry, is completed.

915 Arab poet al-Mutanabbi born (d.965). One of the greatest Arab poets, his work was influential for centuries to come.

c.935 German playwright Hrostwitha born (d.1000). A Benedictine nun, she wrote six comedies in Latin, the first known plays written by a woman.

c.935 Persian poet Firdausi born (d.c.1020). His masterpiece *Shah Náma* ('Book of Kings') is based on actual events from the annals of Persia.

c.970 Japanese writer Murasaki Shikibu   **950**
born (d.c.1015). Her *Genji Monogatari* ('The Tale of the Genji') is the first great work in Japanese and is regarded by many as the first novel.

970 University of al-Azhar founded in Cairo by the Fatimids.

History

History

History and politics

Religion and philosophy

975

977 Turkish Ghaznevid Dynasty founded in Afghanistan, western Iran and northern India.

985 Norwegian sailor Erik the Red founds Norse colonies on Greenland.

987 Hugh Capet (c.938–96) becomes King of France. The Capetian Dynasty he founded ruled France until 1328.

988 Vladimir I (c.956–1015), Grand Prince of Kiev, converts to Christianity, and adopts the Greek Orthodox rite from Byzantium as the official religion of Russia.

1000–1099

■ The Viking expansion loses its impetus, and their power in Ireland is broken by Brian Boru at the Battle of Clontarf (1014). Their Norman descendants, however, aggressively acquire territory with the conquest of England and areas of the Mediterranean, especially in Italy.

■ The work of the Persian philosopher Avicenna epitomizes Eastern influence on European scholasticism and medicine.

■ The *Domesday Book* surveys and values all the lands in England.

1000

1000 New Zealand is settled by Polynesians.

1003 Icelandic explorer Leif Eriksson becomes one of the first Europeans to reach America.

1014 Rajendra I becomes ruler of the Cholas of southern India. He extended the kingdom to include Sri Lanka.

1014 Vikings defeated at the Battle of Clontarf, Ireland.

1028 Canute (c.995–1035), King of Denmark and England, conquers Norway.

1040 Duncan I, King of Scots, overthrown and killed by Macbeth (b.c.1010).

1040 Ghaznevids defeated by Seljuk Turks.

1017 Influential Tamil Brahmin philosopher Ramanuja born (d.1137). He prepared the way for the *bhakti* or devotional strain of Hinduism.

1033 Birth of Italian theologian and philosopher St Anselm (d.1109). He is especially remembered for his ontological proof for the existence of God.

1040 French Jewish scholar Rashi (Rabbi Shlomo Yitzhaqi) born (d.1105). His commentaries on the Bible were influential throughout the Middle Ages, and beyond.

1050

1058 Muslim Almoravids invade Morocco, founding a new capital at Marrakesh (c.1070).

1060–71 Normans, under Roger I (1031–1101), take Calabria and Sicily from the Saracens.

1066 Harold II (b.c.1022) is defeated at the Battle of Hastings and the Norman Conquest of England is successful.

1071 Byzantine forces defeated by Seljuk Turks at Manzikart.

1075 Seljuks take Syria and Palestine.

1076 Almoravids sack the capital of western Sudanese Kingdom of Ghana, breaking its power.

1086 *Domesday Book*, a survey of all lands in England, ordered by William the Conqueror (1027–87).

1086 Almoravids invade Spain from North Africa.

1094 El Cid (c.1043–99) defeats the Moors and takes Valencia.

1099 First Crusade (1095–9) captures Jerusalem.

1054 East–West Schism divides the Orthodox Church of Byzantium and the Catholic Church of Rome.

1058 Islamic philosopher, theologian and jurist al-Ghazali born (d.1111). A prolific author, one of his major works was *The Revival of the Religious Sciences*.

1075 Investiture Controversy, a conflict between reforming popes and lay rulers over the leadership of Christian society (until 1122).

Science and technology	Arts and culture	
c.975 Arab numerals are first used in Europe.	**975** The *Exeter Book*, one of the most important collections of Old English poetry, is copied and later given to Exeter Cathedral.	**975**
968 Persian astronomer al-Sufi dies (b.903). He made some corrections to the work of Ptolemy and wrote the *Book of Fixed Stars*.		
998 Muslim astronomer and mathematician Abu al-Wafa' dies (b.940). As well as his contributions to astronomy, he had an important influence on the development of trigonometry.	**990** Norwegian court poet Eyvindur, also known as Skáldaspillir ('the Plagiarist') dies.	

1000–1099

- Coffee drinking becomes established in Persia and Arabia, and rice becomes the staple diet of China after being introduced from what is now Vietnam.
- The rise to dominance in Asia Minor of the Seljuk Turks, taking Baghdad and defeating the Byzantines at Manzikert, is seen by the Western Church as threatening pilgrimage routes to the Holy Land, leading Pope Urban II to preach the First Crusade.
- The feudal system becomes established throughout most of Europe.

c.1000 Gunpowder used in Chinese warfare.	**c.1000** Easter Island inhabitants start to carve huge stone statues.	**1000**
1024 The first paper money is introduced in China.	**c.1020** Anglo-Saxon churchman and writer Ælfric ('the Grammarian') dies (b.c.955). He was the greatest vernacular prose writer of his time.	
1037 Persian philosopher and physician Avicenna (Ibn Sina) dies (b.980). His medical system was to be the standard in many medical schools up until the 17c.		
c.1040 Arab mathematician Alhazen (Ibn al-Haytham) dies (b.c.965). His work on optics gave the first account of atmospheric refraction and reflection from curved surfaces, and the structure of the eye.	**1036** Chinese painter, calligrapher, poet, philosopher and politician Su Dongpo born (d.1101).	
	c.1048 Persian poet, mathematician and astronomer Omar Khayyám born (d.c.1122). Initially famous for scientific achievements, he is now remembered for the poetry of *The Rubáiyát of Omar Khayyám*.	
1048 Persian scientist al-Biruni dies (b.973). An outstanding scholar, he wrote on astronomy, mathematics, medicine, physics and history.		
c.1050 Chinese alchemist Pi Sheng invents the first movable type for use in printing. He created reusable type from a hardened mixture of clay and glue.	**1077** The Bayeux Tapestry is completed.	**1050**
c.1072 Arab physician Avenzoar (Ibn Zohr) born (d.1162). He published influential medical works describing such conditions as kidney stones and pericarditis.	The Bayeux Tapestry is an embroidered wall-hanging in coloured wool on linen, and narrates events leading up to the invasion of England by William of Normandy, and the Battle of Hastings in 1066.	
1095 Chinese administrator, engineer and scientist Shen Gua dies (b.1031).	**c.1078** Byzantine politician and teacher of philosophy Michael Psellus dies (b.c.1018). His *Chronographia* recounts the reigns of Byzantine emperors from 976 onwards.	
Shen Gua's compilation of about 600 observations, *Brush Talks from Dream Brook*, is now one of the most important sources of information on early Chinese science and technology.	**1088** First official university in Europe is founded at Bologna, Italy.	

History

History and politics	Religion and philosophy

1100–1199

- In the Holy Land, the Knights Templar order is founded (c.1119). Saladin conquers the Crusader strongholds of Jerusalem and Acre (1187), provoking the Third Crusade, which recaptures Acre (1191).
- The formal knightly tournament develops in France and spreads to England.
- Playing cards appear in China (c.1120), while the game of draughts arises in Europe. Chess is introduced into England c.1150.
- Gothic architecture flourishes in Europe, notably in the construction of Chartres Cathedral.

History and politics	Religion and philosophy
1100 **1106** Henry I (1068–1135), King of England, conquers Normandy from his brother, Robert Curthose (c.1054–1134), at the Battle of Tinchebrai.	**c.1100** Spanish-Jewish philosopher Abraham ibn Daud born (d.c.1180). He was the first to draw systematically on Aristotle.
1108 Louis VI, the Fat (1081–1137) crowned King of France.	**c.1119** Foundation of the religious and military order the Knights Templar to protect pilgrims to the Holy Land.
1113 Suryavarman II (d.c.1150) establishes sole rule over the Khmer Empire.	
1122 Jurchen nomads found Jin Dynasty in northern China.	**1122** Concordat of Worms, an agreement which brings a temporary end to the Investiture Controversy.
1135 Stephen (c.1097–1154) takes the English throne, leading to civil war with Matilda, the Empress Maud (1102–67).	
1139 Alfonso I (1110–85) defeats the Moors at Ourique, and proclaims himself first king of Portugal, so securing Portuguese independence from León.	**1130** Philosopher Zhu Xi born (d. 1200). His commentaries on Confucian classics became accepted orthodoxy from the 14c.
1147 Almoravid Dynasty overthrown by Almohad Dynasty in north-west Africa.	**1142** French philosopher and scholar Peter Abelard dies (b.1079).
1147–9 Second Crusade ends after disastrous campaigns in Syria and Anatolia, and an unsuccessful siege at Damascus.	
1150 **1154** Henry II (1113–89) crowned King of England, founding the Plantagenet Dynasty.	**1154** Pope Adrian IV (c.1100–59), originally Nicholas Breakspear, becomes the only Englishman to hold the office of pope.
1167 Establishment of the Lombard League in northern Italy against Emperor Frederick I, Barbarossa (c.1123–90).	**c.1156** Carmelite order founded at Mount Carmel, Palestine.
1168 In central Mexico the last Toltec king is driven from the capital Tula.	**1159** Divisions within the Roman Catholic Church lead to the election of a pope (Alexander III) and an antipope (Victor IV).
1170 Thomas à Becket murdered in Canterbury Cathedral.	
1171 Muslim sultan Saladin (1138–93) abolishes the Fatimid Dynasty in Egypt and founds the Ayyubid Dynasty.	**1169–95** Islamic philosopher Ibn Rushd (known in Europe as Averroës) writes influential commentaries on the works of Aristotle.
1180–5 Gempei War in Japan between rival Minamoto and Taira clans.	
1187 Saladin overwhelms Christian forces at Hattin and captures Jerusalem.	**1173** Thomas à Becket canonized.
1189 Richard I, the Lionheart (1157–99) becomes King of England.	**1177** Treaty of Venice restores single papacy.
1189–92 Third Crusade ends without recapture of Jerusalem but with successful close to the siege at Acre and the capture of Cyprus.	**1190** Jewish philosopher Moses Maimonides (1135–1204) completes his greatest work, *Guide to the Perplexed*.
1192 In Japan Minamoto Yoritomo (1147–99) takes the title shogun and institutes the shogunate.	**1191** Growth of Zen Buddhism in Japan due to introduction of Rinzai sect by the Buddhist monk Eisai (1141–1215).
1192 Muslim victory at the Second Battle of Tarain gives Muhammad Ghuri (d.1206) control of all north India as far as Delhi.	

Science and technology	Arts and culture

1100–1199

- In the Americas, the Toltec Empire of Mexico collapses after invasions by Chichimecs, who take its capital, Tula (1168), and Aztecs. The Inca Empire is dominant in the Andes region.
- Many of the great European universities are founded, including Oxford and Paris.
- The Cambodian Khmers are at the height of their power and greatly expand their capital at Angkor.
- In west Africa, Yoruba city-states begin to arise (c. 1150).
- The system of trial by jury is introduced in England in 1166.

1101 Chinese astronomer and inventor Su Song dies (b.1020). He designed an elaborate water clock, housed in a tower some 10m in height, and probably accurate to within 100 seconds a day.

c.1113 Work starts on the temple of Angkor Wat in Cambodia, instigated by Suryavarman II.

c.1125 Adelard of Bath translates an Arabic version of Euclid's treatise on geometry, *Elements*, into Latin.

c.1130 First windmills in use in Europe (invented in 7c Persia).

c.1132 Work begins on the first church in the Gothic style, St Denis Abbey, Paris.

> After the fall of the Roman Empire, the dominant architectural style to emerge was the Romanesque, characterized by the use of round arches, clear plans and elevations and, typically, a two-tower façade. The Gothic style that followed resulted from the development of the ribbed vault to support the roof, and flying buttresses that allowed the walls to be thinner. It was typified by high-pointed arches.

c.1100 The Old French epic poem *La Chanson de Roland* ('The Song of Roland') is written. It is a masterpiece of *chansons de gestes* ('songs of deeds'), epic poems which centre on Charlemagne and the Crusades. **1100**

c.1136 *Historia Regum Britanniae* ('History of the Kings of Britain') written by Geoffrey of Monmouth.

> Welsh chronicler and ecclesiastic Geoffrey of Monmouth studied at Oxford, was Archdeacon of Llandaff (c.1140), and was appointed Bishop of St Asaph (1152). His *Historia Regum Britanniae* traced the descent of British kings back to the Trojans, and he claimed to have based it on old Welsh chronicles which he alone had seen. It brought enduring romance by introducing the legends of King Arthur to European literature.

1148 Byzantine princess Anna Comnena dies (b.1083). She is known for her *Alexiad*, a life of her father (Alexius I Comnenus) which contains an account of the First Crusade.

c.1150 Italian scholar Gerard of Cremona translates important medical works by Galen, Rhazes and Avicenna, increasing European medical knowledge.

1151 First European paper made at Xativa in Spain.

1163 Foundation stone of the Gothic cathedral Notre Dame de Paris is laid.

1174 Work begins on the bell tower at Pisa, Italy, later to become known as the Leaning Tower of Pisa.

c.1187 First record of a magnetic compass used as a navigational aid in Alexander Neckam's *De utensilibus*.

c.1150 Establishment of a university in Paris, France. **1150**

1155 Robert Wace (c.1115–83) completes his *Roman de Brut*, based on Geoffrey of Monmouth's *Historiae Regum Britanniae*.

c.1155–70 Anglo-Norman poet Thomas writes the earliest extant text of the legend of Tristan and Iseult.

c.1160 French poet and fable writer Marie de France writes the *Lais*, 14 romantic narratives based on Celtic material.

c.1167 Rapid development of the University of Oxford after Henry II bans English attendance at the University of Paris.

1176 First Eisteddfod held in Wales.

c.1183 Chrétien de Troyes, French poet and troubadour dies. His works include *Yvain et Lancelot*, *Érec et Énide* and *Cligès*.

> Troubadours, poets composing lyrics on courtly love, first appeared in Provence, and flourished from the 11c to the 13c. Most commonly the love is unfulfilled, and the hero of such romances loves the lady of his desire absolutely and ever increasingly, existing only to serve her. Such a relationship was based on the subject's dependence on his lord. The ideas of courtly love spread quickly through Europe and had a major effect on subsequent lyric poetry in that area.

History

History and politics	Religion and philosophy

1200–1299

- Continuing Christian zeal to redeem the Holy Land is perverted into the Fourth Crusade's sack of Constantinople (1204), yet inspires the tragic Children's Crusade (1212); the French king Louis IX dies while crusading against Tunis (1270).
- The Franciscan order of monks gains papal approval in 1209–10, as does the Dominican order in 1216.
- England achieves a measure of internal peace with the signing of the Magna Carta (1215), but conflict with its neighbours includes the conquest of Wales (1277–82) and defeat in Scotland at Stirling Bridge by William Wallace (1297).

1200

1200 The Muslim Delhi Sultanate is founded in N India.

1202–4 Fourth Crusade takes Zara then Constantinople.

1206 Temujin (c.1162–1227) establishes Mongol Empire, taking the title Genghis Khan ('Universal Ruler').

1211 Mongol armies enter China.

1215 Magna Carta ('Great Charter'), which began England's constitutional development, sealed at Runnymede by King John (1167–1216).

1216 King John dies and is succeeded by Henry III (1207–72).

1217–21 Fifth Crusade captures Damietta but fails in the Nile Delta.

1228–9 Sixth Crusade takes Jerusalem.

1229 The Berber Hafsid Dynasty replaces Almohads in Tunisia and eastern Algeria.

c.1235 Sundiata (d.1255) founds the Mali Empire in western Sudan.

1237–8 Mongols capture Moscow and Vladimir.

1240 Russian hero and saint Alexander Nevski (c.1220–63) defeats Swedish invaders in a battle on the River Neva.

1244 Jerusalem is lost to a joint Egyptian and Khwarazmian army.

c.1200 Indian philosopher Gangeśa founds the *Navya-nyaya* school of Hindu philosophy in Mithila, Bihar.

1209 Franciscan Order founded by St Francis of Assisi (1181–1226).

1209–28 A crusade in the south of France destroys the heretical Albigenses.

1225 Italian scholastic philosopher and theologian St Thomas Aquinas born (d.1274).

> Thomas Aquinas's influence on the theological thought of succeeding ages was immense. His best-known writings are the *Summa contra Gentiles*, which deals chiefly with the principles of natural religion, and the *Summa Theologiae*, which includes the famous 'five ways' or proofs of the existence of God.

1250

1250 Saladin's Ayyubid Sultanate in Egypt is overthrown by the Mamluks.

1258 Hulagu (c.1217–65), grandson of Genghis Khan, captures Baghdad, and the Ilkhanid Dynasty rules in Iran and the central Islamic lands.

1260 Mongols defeated by Mamluks in the Battle of Ayn Julut. This effectively stops the Mongols westward advance.

1269 The Berber Marinid Dynasty replaces Almohad rule in Morocco.

1273 Rudolf I (1218–91) becomes King of Germany, founding the Habsburg Dynasty.

c.1274 William Wallace born (d.1305), Scottish knight and champion of the independence of Scotland.

1279 In China the Southern Song Dynasty is destroyed by the Mongols. Kublai Khan (1214–94), grandson of Genghis Khan, becomes Emperor of China.

c.1280 Creation of the Hanseatic League, an association formed to protect trading interests in northern Europe.

1281 Mongols are defeated when they attempt to invade Japan. When a typhoon struck the Mongol invaders, the Japanese saw it as a kamikaze ('divine wind').

1282 Sicilian Vespers; a massacre of the French in Sicily which began the Sicilian revolt against French rule.

1291 Creation of Swiss Confederation.

c.1297 Hindu Gujarat is conquered by the Delhi Sultanate.

1298 Edward I (1239–1307) defeats Wallace at Falkirk.

1250 Spanish Kabbalist Moses de León born (d.1305). He is the presumed author of *The Book of Splendour*, an influential work on Jewish mysticism.

1253 Death of Dogen (b.1200), founder of the Soto school of Japanese Zen Buddhism.

1263 Death of Japanese Buddhist Shinran (b.1173). Shinran founded the Pure Land school known as Jodo Shinshu ('True Pure Land').

c.1265 Scottish Franciscan philosopher and theologian John Duns Scotus born (d.1308). He rivalled Aquinas as the greatest theologian of the Middle Ages.

1273 Persian lyric poet and mystic Jalal ad-Din ar-Rumi dies (b.1207). In 1226 he founded a sect, and his disciples were later referred to in the West as the Whirling Dervishes.

1282 Death of Japanese Buddhist monk Nichiren (b.1222).

1290 Jews are expelled from England.

Science and technology	Arts and culture

History

1200–1299

- In Asia the Mongols are united under Genghis Khan (1206), who extends his empire from China to the Black Sea. Under his descendants, the Mongols sack Baghdad (1258), ravage eastern Europe, and complete the conquest of China, with Kublai Khan becoming the first Yuan Emperor (1279–94).

- By 1226 glass is being used in England to make bottles and windows.

- Marco Polo leaves Europe (1271) and journeys to China, travelling across central Asia and through the Gobi Desert. His account of his travels sparks great western interest in the east.

- The Mali Empire is established in West Africa and controls trade across the Sahara.

c.1200 Emperor Lalibela has great churches hewn out of solid rock in Ethiopia.	c.1200 German poet Gottfried von Strassburg writes his version of the legend of *Tristan and Isolde*.	1200
c.1214 English philosopher and scientist Roger Bacon born (d.1292).	c.1200 Chinese artist Xia Gui (fl.1180–1230) produces work for the Song Dynasty court. He was one of China's masters of landscape painting.	
Bacon's views on the primacy of mathematical proof and on experimentalism have often seemed strikingly modern, and he published many works on mathematics, philosophy and logic, the importance of which was only recognized in later centuries.	1209 Rioting in Oxford leads some scholars to move to Cambridge and development of the University of Cambridge begins.	
c.1236 French Jewish astronomer Jacob ben Machir ibn Tibbon born (d.c.1312). In addition to important works of translation he also devised a quadrant which was used by mariners.	1220 German poet Wolfram von Eschenbach dies (b.c.1170). It was from his epic *Parzifal* that Wagner derived the libretto of his opera *Parsifal*.	
	c.1235 French poet Guillaume de Lorris writes the first part (c.4000 lines) of the dream-vision poem *Roman de la Rose*.	
1238 Work begins on the Alhambra, the palace and fortress of the Moorish kings in Granada, Spain.	1241 Icelandic poet and historian Snorri Sturluson dies (b.1179). His main works were the *Prose Edda* and the *Heimskringla*, a series of sagas about Norwegian kings.	
c.1250 Italian mathematician Leonardo Fibonacci dies (b.c.1170).	1259 English chronicler Matthew Paris dies. His *Chronica Majora* established him as the finest chronicler of the 13c.	1250
Leonardo Fibonacci popularized the modern Arabic system of numerals, which originated in India. His major works were *Liber abaci* ('The Book of Calculation'), and *Liber quadratorum* ('The Book of Square Numbers'). He discovered the 'Fibonacci Sequence' of integers, and was the first outstanding mathematician of the Middle Ages.	c.1260 Birth of Italian painter and founder of the Sienese school Duccio di Buoninsegna (d.c.1320).	
	1260 Italian sculptor Nicola Pisano (c.1225–c.1284) sculpts the panels of the pulpit in the Baptistry in Pisa.	
c.1252 Completion of *Alfonsine Tables* in Spain. These astronomical tables were used to calculate eclipses and planetary positions for over two centuries.	1264 French encyclopedist Vincent de Beauvais dies (b.c. 1190). He gathered together the knowledge of the Middle Ages in his *Speculum Majus* ('Great Mirror').	
c.1269 French scientist and soldier Petrus Peregrinus is the first to describe the properties of magnets in his *Epistola de magnete*. He also invented a compass with a graduated scale.	c.1267 Italian painter and architect Giotto (di Bondone) born (d.1337). He was the most innovative artist of his time, and is generally regarded as the founder of the Florentine school.	
c.1270 Mondino dei Liucca born (d.1326). He published the first manual of anatomy at Bologna after carrying out his own dissections.	c.1277 French poet and satirist Jean de Meung adds 18 000 lines to the *Roman de la Rose* — a work which was influential in the coming centuries.	
c.1280 Invention of spectacles by Alessandro della Spina and Salvino degli Armati in Italy.	c.1284 Catalan author Ramon Lull (c.1232–c.1316) writes his allegorical novel *Blanquerna*.	
	c.1292 Persian poet Sádi (Sheikh Muslih Addin) dies (b.c.1184). His most celebrated writing is the *Gulistan* ('Rose Garden'), a moral work in prose and verse.	

History

History and politics	Religion and philosophy

1300–1399

- c.1300 the kingdom of Benin in West Africa is founded.
- c.1300 the Ottoman Turks begin their drive west to threaten the Byzantine Empire; by the century's end they control the Balkans.
- c.1325 the Aztecs found their capital Tenochtitlán. The Chimú state extends its rule in the central Andes of Peru.
- Gunpowder is introduced into Europe and the cannon makes its appearance on the battlefield.

1300

c.1300 Sultan Osman I (c.1259–c.1326) founds the Ottoman Empire in Turkey.

1305 William Wallace hanged by the English.

1307 Mansa Musa becomes ruler of the empire of Mali. He is best known for the splendour of his pilgrimage to Mecca.

1314 Under Robert Bruce (1274–1329) the Scots gain a decisive victory over Edward II's English forces at the Battle of Bannockburn.

c.1325 Aztecs found city of Tenochtitlán on Lake Texcoco in Mexico.

1331 The Byzantine town of Nicaea in Asia Minor falls to the Ottomans.

1336 The last great medieval Hindu state of Vijayanagar is founded in southern India.

1337 Edward III (1312–77) declares war on France. This begins a series of wars which became known as the Hundred Years' War.

1338 In Japan the Ashikaga Shogunate is founded.

1347–51 Black Death ravages Europe.

The Black Death originated in Asia and was spread from a Mongol invading army in the Crimea, then along trade routes to Europe by infected fleas living on rats. In Europe the Black Death caused the demise of around one third of the population (25 million people).

1309 Pope Clement V (c.1260–1314) moves the seat of the papacy from Rome to Avignon.

1327 German theologian and mystic Johannes Eckhart dies (b.c.1260). He taught mystic pantheism, which influenced later religious mysticism and speculative philosophy.

1332 Arab philosopher Ibn Khaldun born (d.1406). He wrote a monumental history of the Arabs, best known by its *Muqaddima*, or introduction.

c.1349 Influential English philosopher William of Ockham dies (b.c.1285). His best-known philosophical contributions are his successful defence of nominalism against realism, and the philosophical principle of 'Ockham's razor'.

1350

1355 Death of Stephen Dushan, King and Emperor of Serbia (b.c.1308). During his reign he extended Serbian rule into Macedonia, Bulgaria and Albania.

1361–3 Second outbreak of the Black Death in Europe.

1368 Ming Hongwu (1328–98) drives out the Mongols and founds the Ming Dynasty in China.

1369 Tatar Timur (1336–1405) ascends the throne of Samarkand.

c.1370 In Peru Nançen Pinco becomes ruler of the Chimú, and the Chimú state expands.

1381 Wat Tyler (d.1381) leads the Peasants' Revolt in south-east England, caused by the three oppressive poll taxes of 1377–81. It was quickly suppressed.

1385 Portugal gain independence from Spain after the Portuguese victory at the Battle of Aljubarrota.

1386–95 Timur subdues nearly all Persia, Mesopotamia, Georgia and the territory of the Golden Horde.

1389 Serbia falls to the Turks.

1392 Yi Song-gye (1335–92) founds the Yi Dynasty in Korea.

1397 The Kalmar Union sees Erik of Pomerania (c.1381–1459) crowned king of Denmark, Sweden and Norway.

1398 Timur invades India.

1378 The return of the papacy to Rome causes the Great Schism (until 1417), a period of deep crisis for the papal monarchy when there were two, and later three, rival popes.

1380 Death of Italian mystic St Catherine of Siena (b.1347). She wrote many devotional pieces, letters and poems; her *Dialogue* is the best known of her works.

1384 English religious reformer John Wycliffe dies (b.c.1329).

Wycliffe asserted the right of every man to examine the Bible for himself and promoted the first English translation of the Bible.

Science and technology	Arts and culture

1300–1399

- Italy experiences a cultural reflowering, with such works as Dante's *Divine Comedy* (c.1307–21), Boccaccio's *Decameron* (1348–58), Petrarch's *Canzoniere* (c.1351–3) and the paintings of Giotto.
- The Black Death appears in China c.1333, and spreads west, reaching Britain by 1348 and killing millions in Europe alone.
- In 1337 England embarks on war with France that is to last for more than a century.
- In China the Ming Dynasty (from 1368) sees a period of great craftsmanship in porcelain and bronze.

c.1300 French scholastic philosopher Jean Buridan born (d.1358). He published works on mechanics, optics and logic.	**1301** Chinese landscape painter, calligrapher and poet Ni Zan born (d.1374).	**1300**
c.1300 First use of the treadle in Europe.	**1304** Italian scholar and poet Petrarch born (d.1374). He was one of the earliest and greatest of modern lyric poets.	
c.1310 A Spanish alchemist and author, writing under the name Geber, begins to produce books on chemical and alchemical theory and practice.	**c.1307** Italian poet Dante Alighieri (1265–1321) begins his most celebrated work *Divina Commedia* ('Divine Comedy'), a poem which narrates a journey through Hell and Purgatory, and finally to Paradise. As well as providing a view of the highest culture and knowledge of the age, this work also established Italian as a literary language.	

It was through Geber's works that the discoveries of the early Arab chemists, along with many basic laboratory techniques, were relayed to Europe. His works continued to be influential until the 16c.

1311 Earliest dated portolan chart (a type of navigational chart used in Europe in the Middle Ages) produced by Petrus Vesconte in Genoa.

c.1320 First European use of cannon in warfare.

1348 Italian horologist Giovanni de' Dondi (1318–89) begins work on a complicated astronomical clock. In addition to the usual planetary motions it showed the feasts of the Church calculated in accordance with a perpetual calendar and was far ahead of its time.

c.1337 Leading Chinese dramatist Wang Shifu dies (b.c.1250).

c.1345 English poet Geoffrey Chaucer born (d.1400).

The most influential English poet of the Middle Ages, Geoffrey Chaucer's first work as a poet was the *Book of the Duchess*, written in 1369. His greatest work, probably begun in the late 1380s and not completed, was *The Canterbury Tales*, recounting, with a prologue, the tales told by a group of pilgrims on their journey to Canterbury.

1368 French surgeon Guy de Chauliac dies (b.c.1300).	**1358** Italian writer Giovanni Boccaccio (1313–75) completes his greatest work, the *Decameron*, begun some 10 years before, with medieval subject matter and classical form.	**1350**

Born in Chauliac, Auvergne, Guy de Chauliac became the most famous surgeon of the Middle Ages. His *Chirurgia Magna* (1363) was translated into French over a century later and used as a manual by generations of doctors.

c.1370 Bohemian Hussite leader John Ziska born (d.1424).

During the Hussite wars, Ziska made the first important use of mobile field artillery, mounting his guns on wagons drawn by bullocks or horses so they could be used against enemy cavalry and infantry, as well as against fortifications.

1386 Work begins on Milan Cathedral, the third largest church in Europe.

c.1363 Japanese actor and playwright Zeami Motokiyo born (d.1443). Along with his father, he had great influence in shaping Noh theatre as it still exists today.

1366 Italian artist Taddeo Gaddi dies (b.c.1300). His finest work is seen in the frescoes of Santa Croce, Florence.

c.1375 One of the greatest English poems of the period, *Sir Gawayne and the Green Knight*, is composed by an unknown author.

1378 Russian-Byzantine painter Theophanes the Greek (c.1335–c.1405) paints frescoes in the Church of Our Saviour of the Transfiguration in Novgorod.

1384 Flemish sculptor Claus Sluter (c.1305–1405) begins work on the tomb of Philip the Bold in Dijon.

1385 English poet William Langland (c.1332–c.1400) writes *The Vision of Piers Plowman*, a medieval alliterative poem on spiritual pilgrimage.

History

History and politics	Religion and philosophy
1400–1499	

- The Chinese admiral and diplomat Zheng He leads a series of voyages west, reaching as far as east Africa (1405–33).
- The Portuguese capture of Ceuta in 1415 is the first step in their acquisition of an empire.
- c.1425 the first oil paintings are produced, in Italy.
- Partly through the inspiration of Joan of Arc, the French drive the English from all France, except Calais, by 1453, aided by the English internal conflict of the Wars of the Roses.
- The fall of Constantinople to the Ottoman Turks in 1453 marks the end of the Byzantine Empire.

	History and politics	Religion and philosophy
1400	**1401** The Welsh, led by Owen Glendower (c.1350–c.1416), rebel against Henry IV (c.1366–1413).	**1415** Bohemian religious reformer Jan Hus burnt at the stake for heresy (b.c.1369). The anger of his followers lead to the Hussite Wars; Hus's ideas were influential on the Protestant reformers of the 16c.
	1402 Ottoman Turks are defeated by Timur at the Battle of Ankara.	
	1413 Thai armies sack Angkor Thom, the ancient capital of the Khmer Empire. The city is abandoned and not rediscovered until 1861.	
		1417 Great Schism in the Catholic Church comes to an end with the election of Martin V (1368–1431) as pope at the Council of Constance.
	1415 The French are defeated by Henry V (1387–1422) of England at the Battle of Agincourt.	
	1420 Ming Dynasty capital moves from Nanjing to Beijing.	**1440** Indian mystic and poet Kabir born (d.1518).
	1431 French patriot and martyr St Joan of Arc (b.c.1412) is burnt at the stake, having halted the English ascendancy in France during the Hundred Years' War.	Kabir tried to unite Hindu and Muslim thought, and his preaching was a forerunner of Sikhism, which was established by his disciple Nanak.
	1434 Cosimo de' Medici (1389–1464) establishes the Medici principate in Florence.	
	c.1437 Montezuma I (c.1390–1464) becomes Aztec emperor of Mexico.	**1448** Russian Orthodox Church becomes autonomous.
	1448 First European fort built by Portuguese at Arguin in Mauritania.	
1450	**1453** End of the Hundred Years' War. Only Calais (lost in 1558) and the Channel Islands remain English territories.	**1469** Guru Nanak born (d.1539), Indian religious leader and founder of Sikhism.
	1453 Byzantine Empire extinguished with the taking of Constantinople by the Ottoman Turks.	**1471** German religious writer Thomas à Kempis dies (b.1379). Among his many writings was the influential devotional work *Imitatio Christi* ('The Imitation of Christ').
	1454 Peace of Lodi ends conflicts between the warring states of Italy.	
	1455 Wars of the Roses begin. A series of civil wars in England named from the emblems of the two rival branches of the House of Plantagenet, York (white rose) and Lancaster (red rose).	**1472** Chinese Neo-Confucian philosopher Wang Yangming born (d.1529).
	c.1460 Songhai Empire rises to power in the former Mali Empire in West Africa.	**1478** The Spanish Inquisition, a tribunal for prosecuting heresy, is founded by papal bull.
	1467 Onin War in Japan (until 1477); a struggle between rival daimyo (feudal lords) in a dispute over shogunal succession.	**1483** Martin Luther born (d.1546), German religious reformer and founder of the Reformation.
	c.1470 In Peru the Inca conquer the Chimú.	
	1479 The crowns of Aragon and Castile are united, forming the basis of modern Spain.	**1492** Spaniard Rodrigo Borgia (1431–1503) becomes Pope Alexander VI.
	1480 Ivan III of Moscow (1440–1505) defeats the Mongol Golden Horde.	**c.1494** Birth of English translator of the Bible William Tyndale (d.1536).
	1485 The end of the Wars of the Roses, when Henry VII (1457–1509), founder of the Tudor Dynasty, defeats Richard III (1452–85) at the Battle of Bosworth Field.	
	1488 Swabian League formed, a German alliance of towns, knights and princes to protect the Holy Roman Empire.	
	1492 Christians conquer Granada and end the last Muslim dynasty in Spain, the Nasrid.	
	1494 Start of the Italian Wars, a long series of conflicts which lasted until 1559.	

Science and technology	Arts and culture

History

1400–1499

- c.1470 the Incas overthrow the Chimú state and dominate Peru; their crops include potatoes and cotton.
- A sea route to Asia from the Atlantic is opened when the Portuguese explorer Bartolomeu Dias rounds the Cape of Good Hope in 1488, and his compatriot Vasco da Gama follows this to make the first European sea voyage to India and back (1497–9).
- Christopher Columbus lands in the Caribbean Islands in 1492, and four years later establishes the first European settlement in the New World on Hispaniola. In 1497 John Cabot lands in Newfoundland.

Science and technology	Arts and culture	
c.1403 In the field of printing, Koreans are the first to cast movable type in bronze.	**1411** St Andrews University, the first university in Scotland, is founded.	**1400**
1420 Tatar prince and astronomer Ulugh-Beg (1394–1449) founds an observatory at Samarkand. He went on to prepare new planetary tables and a new star catalogue.	**1420** Japanese painter and priest Toyu Sesshu born (d.1506).	
1423 Austrian astronomer and mathematician Georg von Purbach born (d.1461). In astronomy his observational work resulted in the publication of a table of lunar eclipses, and in mathematics he is thought to have been the first to introduce sines into trigonometry.	**1424** French writer and courtier Alain Chartier (c.1390–c.1440) writes his much imitated poem, *La Belle dame sans merci*, ('The Beautiful Woman with No Mercy').	
	1432 Flemish painter Jan van Eyck (c.1389–1441) paints the famous altarpiece *The Adoration of the Holy Lamb*, at the church of Saint Bavon, Ghent.	
1436 Italian architect Leon Battista Alberti (1404–72) writes his *Della Pittura*, containing the first description of perspective construction.	**1440** English mystic Margery Kempe dies (b.c.1373). Between 1432 and 1436 she dictated *The Book of Margery Kempe*, a remarkable early autobiography.	
	1446 Italian architect Filippo Brunelleschi dies (b.1377). He is best known for the dome of Florence Cathedral.	
c.1450 German goldsmith Johannes Gutenberg (1400–68) invents a mould for casting movable type and the first printing press. In 1455 he produces his first printed work, the Gutenberg Bible. This is credited as being the first European book printed with movable type.	**c.1450** Dutch painter Hieronymus Bosch born (d.1516). He is best known for his depictions of a bizarre, nightmarish world. His masterpiece is *The Garden of Earthly Delights*.	**1450**
	1452 Italian painter, sculptor, architect and engineer Leonardo da Vinci born (d.1519).	
1472 German mathematician and astronomer Regiomontanus dies (b.1436). He worked on *Ephemerides*, which was used extensively by Christopher Columbus (1451–1506), and established the study of algebra and trigonometry in Germany.	**1466** Florentine sculptor Donatello dies (b.c.1386). His celebrated bronze statue of David is a key work of the Renaissance.	
	1471 English writer Sir Thomas Malory dies. His masterpiece *Le Morte d'Arthur* is a prose romance of Arthurian legends.	
1475 English printer and translator William Caxton (c.1422–1491), produces the first printed book in English, *The Recuyell of the Historyes of Troye*, at Bruges.	**1472** Italian architect Michelozzo di Bartolommeo dies (b.1396). He was court architect to Cosimo de' Medici.	
1476 Caxton sets up a printing press at Westminster.	**1475** Italian sculptor, painter and poet Michelangelo born (d.1564). He is by far the most brilliant representative of the Italian Renaissance.	
1483 Leonardo da Vinci designs flying machines and a parachute.	**c.1482–4** Florentine painter Sandro Botticelli (1445–1510) paints *The Birth of Venus*.	
1490–2 German geographer and navigator Martin Behaim (1440–1507) constructs the oldest extant terrestrial globe.	**1498** Leonardo da Vinci completes his fresco *The Last Supper*.	
1494 German mineralogist and metallurgist Georgius Agricola born (d.1555). His *De Re Metallica* is a valuable record of mining, ore-smelting and metalworking in his lifetime.		

History

History and politics	Religion and philosophy

1500–1599

- The Portuguese send the first African slaves to the New World, to Brazil (1503). In 1511 they add Malacca to their growing empire.
- In 1518 smallpox breaks out in the Caribbean, one of many diseases introduced by Europeans.
- In 1519 the Portuguese navigator Ferdinand Magellan discovers a passage from the Atlantic to another ocean, which he names the Pacific, and crosses to the Philippines.
- Among the produce introduced to Europe from the New World are potatoes, tobacco, chocolate and quinine. In return, horses and cattle are introduced to the Americas.
- Protestantism comes into being in the Reformation.

1500

1501 Isma'il I (1487–1524) founds the Safavid Dynasty in Persia.

1502 Montezuma II (1466–1520) becomes the last Aztec emperor of Mexico.

1510 Portuguese conquer Goa.

1516–17 In Egypt the Mamluks are defeated by the Ottomans.

1520 Suleyman I, the Magnificent (1494–1566) becomes Ottoman Sultan.

1521 Hernán Cortés (1485–1547), Spanish conqueror of Mexico, takes the Aztec capital Tenochtitlán.

1523 Gustav I Vasa (1496–1560) breaks the Kalmar Union, establishing the state of Sweden and the Vasa Dynasty.

1526 Delhi Sultanate is destroyed by Babur (1483–1530) who becomes the first Mogul emperor of India.

1529 The first Ottoman siege of Vienna is unsuccessful.

1533 Francisco Pizarro (c.1478–1541), Spanish conqueror of Peru, takes the Inca capital of Cuzco.

1533 Ivan IV, the Terrible (1530–84) becomes Grand Prince of Moscow. He was the first prince to assume the title 'tsar'.

1540 Afghan chieftain Sher Shan (c.1486–1545) takes control of the Mogul Empire in India.

1517 Martin Luther draws up his list of 95 theses questioning the authority of the Church, and nails them to the door at Wittenberg Church. The Protestant Reformation begins.

1518 Swiss religious reformer Huldreich Zwingli (1484–1531) begins preaching in Zurich.

1534 The Act of Supremacy ends the pope's formal authority in England, and Henry VIII (1491–1547) is made head of the English Church.

1534 St Ignatius of Loyola founds the religious order of the Society of Jesus (Jesuits).

1545–63 The Council of Trent takes place, a series of councils of the Catholic Church to reform some doctrines and reaffirm others. It formed part of the Counter-Reformation.

1550

1556 Akbar the Great (1542–1605) becomes Mogul emperor of India, defeating the Afghan threat and extending the empire's territories.

1557 China allows Portuguese settlement in Macao.

1558 Elizabeth I (1533–1603) becomes Queen of England.

1568 Start of the Eighty Years' War; uprisings and wars against Spanish Habsburg rule by 17 provinces in the Low Countries.

1568 Japanese warrior Oda Nobunaga (1534–82) begins to unify of Japan after two centuries of feudal warfare.

1571 Christian forces defeat the Ottomans in the Battle of Lepanto, a naval battle fought off the coast of Greece.

1578 Moroccans overcome Portuguese in north-west Africa.

1587 Elizabeth I has Mary Queen of Scots (1542–87) executed.

1583 Newfoundland claimed for England.

1588 The Spanish Armada, a fleet of 130 ships sent by Philip II of Spain (1527–98) to invade England, is defeated.

1590 Japanese soldier Hideyoshi Toyotomi (1536–98) unifies all Japan.

1591 Songhai Empire falls to invading Moroccan army.

1598 French Wars of Religion come to an end (began 1562) with the Edict of Nantes.

1555 Catholicism and Lutheranism are allowed to coexist in Germany following the Peace of Augsburg treaty.

1559 *Index Librorum Prohibitorum* ('Index of Forbidden Books') drawn up by the Roman Catholic Church.

1564 French theologian and reformer John Calvin dies (b.1509). One of the most important reformers of the 16c, he systematized Protestant doctrine and organized its ecclesiastical discipline.

1574 Indian Hindi devotional poet Tulsīdās (1532–1623) begins his *Rāmacaritamānas* ('The Holy Lake of Rāma's Deeds'), a popular Eastern Hindi version of the Rāmāyana epic.

1577 Sikh Guru Ram Das (1534–81) founds Amritsar, later to become the centre of the Sikh religion.

Science and technology	Arts and culture

1500–1599

- Ottoman power is strengthened under Sultan Suleyman I, the Magnificent but his siege of Vienna fails (1529).
- The Inca Empire is conquered by Spain by 1535.
- The first mention in print of cricket being played in England is made in 1550.
- Sir Francis Drake is the first Englishman to circumnavigate the globe (1577–80); Sir Walter Raleigh attempts to found colonies in Virginia.
- Anglo-Spanish rivalry comes to a head with the launch, and defeat, of the Spanish Armada (1588).
- An early form of ballet emerges in France in the 1590s.

c.1505 German locksmith Peter Henlein develops a mainspring as an alternative to weight-driven clocks, and pocket watches are made in Europe.

c.1510 French surgeon Ambroise Paré born (d.1590). Regarded by many as 'the father of modern surgery', he improved the treatment of gunshot wounds, and substituted ligature of the arteries for cauterization after amputation.

1512 Flemish geographer and cartographer Gerardus Mercator born (d.1594). To aid navigators, in 1569 he introduced a map projection (Mercator's map projection), which has been used for nautical charts ever since.

1518 English humanist and physician Thomas Linacre (c.1460–1524) founds the Royal College of Physicians.

1543 Theory of the Sun-centred universe is published by Polish astronomer Nicolaus Copernicus (1473–1543).

1543 Belgian anatomist Andreas Vesalius (1514–64) completes his greatest work, *De Humani Corporis Fabrica*. Based on the actual dissection of human cadavers, the book set a new level of clarity and accuracy in anatomy.

1562 Italian anatomist Gabriele Falloppio dies (b.1523). He particularly studied bones and the reproductive organs, and the Fallopian tube is named after him.

1570 Flemish geographer Abraham Ortelius (1527–98) produces *Theatrum Orbis Terrarum*, the first great atlas.

1576 Danish astronomer Tycho Brahe (1546–1601) establishes the Uraniborg Observatory. He is considered the greatest pre-telescope observer.

1587 Italian architect and engineer Antonio da Ponte (1512–c.1595) designs the Rialto Bridge in Venice.

1590 Italian astronomer, mathematician and natural philosopher Galileo Galilei (1564–1642) discovers that all bodies fall at the same rate.

1590 Dutch spectacle-maker Zacharias Janssen invents the compound microscope.

1593 Death of Chinese physician, naturalist and biologist Li Shizhen (b.1518). His great work was the *Ben Cao Gang Mu* ('Great Pharmacopoeia') which he spent 30 years compiling.

c.1500 German painter Lucas Cranach, the Elder (1472–1553) paints the *Crucifixion* at the Stadtkirche, Weimar.

1501–4 Michelangelo fashions his *David* out of a single colossal block of marble.

1504 Leonardo da Vinci begins the *Mona Lisa*.

1508–12 Michelangelo paints the frescoes on the ceiling of the Sistine Chapel.

1509 Dutch humanist and scholar Desiderius Erasmus (c.1466–1536) writes the famous *Encomium Moriae* ('In Praise of Folly').

1513 Italian statesman, writer and political philosopher Niccolò Machiavelli writes his masterpiece, *The Prince*.

1516 English politician and scholar Sir Thomas More writes *Utopia*.

1532 French satirist François Rabelais (1483/1494–1553) begins the series of books for which he is best known with *Pantagruel*.

1538 Venetian painter Titian (c.1488–1576), one of the greatest artists of the Renaissance, paints the *Venus of Urbino*.

1559 Japanese painter Kano Motonobu dies (b.1476). He achieved a synthesis of Kanga (ink painting in the Chinese style) with the lively colours of the Japanese style.

1564 William Shakespeare born (d.1616), English playwright, poet, actor and dramatist.

From 1594 Shakespeare acted with the Lord Chamberlain's players, later 'the King's Men', for whom he wrote many of his 37 plays. His works brought him success in the fields of comedy, history and tragedy. His success at the Globe was accompanied by acclaim at the court. His plays are still performed worldwide.

1578–80 English dramatist and novelist John Lyly (c.1554–1606) writes his hugely popular romance *Euphues*.

1590 The first three books of English poet Edmund Spenser's (c.1552–99) *The Faerie Queene* are published.

1593 English dramatist Christopher Marlowe is fatally stabbed in a tavern brawl (b.1564). His works include *Tamburlaine the Great*, *Dr Faustus*, and *The Jew of Malta*.

1596–8 Italian artist Caravaggio (1573–1610) paints *The Supper at Emmaus*.

1599 The Globe Theatre in London opens with Shakespeare's *Henry V*.

1500

1550

History

History and politics	Religion and philosophy

1600–1699

- In 1603 James VI of Scotland becomes James I of England, beginning the troubled Stuart era which sees civil war, execution of one king (Charles I) and deposition of another (James II).
- England's empire expands with its first permanent settlements in the Americas and India. Emigration to Massachusetts follows the landing of the Mayflower Pilgrims in 1620.
- The Dutch East India Company makes its base at Batavia (Jakarta) in 1619 and founds a colony at the Cape of Good Hope (1652). It is a Dutch ship from Macao that introduces tea to Europe c.1630, and it is in Amsterdam that the first weekly newspaper appears (1620).

1600

1600 In West Africa the Oyo Empire begins to flourish.

1600 In Japan, after the Battle of Sekigahara, Tokugawa Ieyasu (1543–1616) takes power, claiming the title shogun and establishing the Tokugawa Shogunate in 1603.

1605 The Gunpowder Plot, a conspiracy by Catholic gentry to blow up the English parliament, fails.

1607 Virginia becomes the first English colony in North America.

1608 French navigator and Governor of New France, Samuel de Champlain (c.1570–1635), founds Quebec.

1613 In Russia Mikhail Romanov (1596–1645) is elected tsar, founding the Romanov Dynasty.

1618 The start of the Thirty Years' War, a long and intermittent power struggle between the kings of France and the Habsburg rulers of the Holy Roman Empire and Spain.

1619 Dutch empire established in the East Indies.

1620 Pilgrim Fathers establish Plymouth colony in America.

1624 New Amsterdam (New York City) is founded by the Dutch.

1633 Japan bans foreign contact.

1642–8 English Civil Wars, between supporters of parliament and supporters of Charles I (1600–49), caused by parliamentary opposition to what it considered growing royal power.

1644 Manchus conquer China, overthrowing the Ming Dynasty and establishing the Qing Dynasty.

1648 The Peace of Westphalia ends the Thirty Years' War, and recognizes Dutch independence.

1649 Charles I of England is executed. The monarchy is abolished and Oliver Cromwell (1599–1658) establishes the Commonwealth.

1650

1652 Cape Town is founded by the Dutch East India Company.

1652–74 Anglo-Dutch Wars, three naval wars between England and the Dutch Republic, caused mainly by commercial and colonial rivalry.

1656 Mehmet Köprülü (d.1661) becomes Ottoman grand vizier. His work, and that of his successors, helped stabilize the Ottoman Empire.

1658 Aurangzeb (1618–1707) is the last and most magnificent of the Mogul emperors of India.

1659 The Treaty of the Pyrenees ends hostilities between France and Spain.

---

c.1602 Whilst imprisoned for heresy, Italian philosopher Tommaso Campanella (1568–1639) writes his Utopian work, *City of the Sun*.

1604 Neo-Confucian Donglin Academy established near Shanghai.

1604 The principal Sikh scripture, the *Adi Granth*, is compiled by the fifth Sikh guru, Guru Arjan (1536–1606), and installed in the newly completed Golden Temple in Amritsar.

1611 The Authorized Version, or King James Bible, is completed.

1624 English religious leader George Fox born (d.1691), founder of the Society of Friends, or 'Quakers'.

A Puritan by upbringing, at the age of 19 George Fox rebelled against the formalism of the established Church, and the State's control of it. He travelled around the country attracting many followers. In 1646 he had a divine revelation that inspired him to teach a gospel of brotherly love, and called his society the 'Friends of Truth'.

1648 Turkish Jewish mystic Sabbatai Zebi (1626–76) declares himself the Messiah and gains a large following.

1650 French philosopher and mathematician René Descartes dies (b.1596).

Descartes is usually regarded as the father of modern philosophy. His works include the *Discours de la méthode* (1637), *Meditationes de prima Philosophiae* (1641), and *Principia Philosophiae* (1644). These set out the fundamental Cartesian doctrines, including the proposition, *je pense, donc je suis* or *cogito ergo sum* ('I think, therefore I am').

1652 Russian religious leader and reformer Nikon (1606–81) becomes Patriarch of the Russian Church.

Science and technology	Arts and culture

History

1600–1699

- From 1642 the Dutch navigator Abel Janszoon Tasman discovers Tasmania, New Zealand, and explores the coast of Australia.
- While much of Europe is ravaged in the Thirty Years' War, Mogul power in India is at its height and Shah Jahan completes the Taj Mahal (1643).
- London suffers plague and fire but extensive rebuilding begins under the architect Christopher Wren.
- The French explorer Robert Cavelier de la Salle explores the Mississippi to its mouth (1682) and claims Louisiana for France.

1600 English physician William Gilbert (1544–1603) publishes his *De Magnete*, in which he establishes the magnetic nature of the Earth.

1608 Dutch optician Hans Lippershey (c.1570–c.1619) invents the telescope.

1610 Galileo perfects the refraction telescope and uses it in the course of many astronomical revelations, including the mountains of the Moon and the existence of four of Jupiter's satellites.

1614 Scottish mathematician John Napier (1550–1617) describes his invention of logarithms in *Mirifici Logarithmorum Canonis Descriptio*.

1620 Dutch-British inventor Cornelis Jacobszoon Drebbel (c.1572–1633) successfully tests his invention of a rudimentary submarine in the River Thames.

1621 English mathematician William Oughtred (1575–c.1660) invents the earliest type of slide rule.

1628 English physician William Harvey (1578–1657) publishes his *Exercitatio Anatomica de Motu Cordis et Sanguinis*, in which the circulation of the blood is first described.

1632 Galileo defends the Copernican system of a Sun-centred universe in his *Dialogue on the Two Principal Systems of the World*.

c.1632 Work begins on the Taj Mahal mausoleum outside Agra in India.

1644 Italian physicist and mathematician Evangelista Torricelli (1608–47) gives the first description of a mercury barometer or 'Torricellian tube'.

1647 French mathematician Blaise Pascal (1623–62) patents an adding machine.

1650 German engineer and physicist Otto von Guericke (1602–86) develops a primitive vacuum pump.

1654 The correspondence of French mathematicians Pierre de Fermat (1601–65) and Blaise Pascal (1623–62) lays the foundations of probability theory.

1656 English mathematician John Wallis (1616–1703) publishes *Arithmetica Infinitorum*. Wallis also introduced the symbol ∞ for infinity.

1657 Dutch physicist Christiaan Huygens (1629–93) invents the pendulum clock.

1605 Spanish writer Miguel de Cervantes (1547–1616) publishes the first part of *Don Quixote*.

1606 English dramatist Ben Jonson (1572–1637) writes *Volpone*.

1607 Italian composer Claudio Monteverdi (1567–1643) writes his first opera, *Orfeo*.

1612 American poet Anne Bradstreet is born (d.1672). Her most famous work is the volume of poems *The Tenth Muse lately sprung up in America*.

1614 Flemish painter Peter Paul Rubens (1577–1640) completes his triptych *Descent from the Cross*.

1623 Seven years after Shakespeare's death, two of his former fellow-actors, John Heminges and Henry Condell, collect and publish the 36 plays of the First Folio.

1623 English dramatist John Webster (c.1580–c.1625) writes *The Duchess of Malfi*.

1627 German composer Heinrich Schütz's *Dafne*, the first German opera, is produced in Torgau.

1631 English poet John Donne dies (b.c.1572).

1641 Sir Anthony Van Dyck dies (b.1599), Flemish painter and one of the great masters of portraiture of the 17c.

1642 Dutch painter Rembrandt (1606–69) produces his most famous work, *The Company of Captain Frans Banning Cocq and Lieutenant Willem van Ruytenburch* ('The Night Watch').

c.1644 Italian violin maker Antonio Stradivari born (d. 1737).

1650 Italian composer Giacomo Carissimi (1605–74) writes the oratorio *Jephthe*.

1650 Welsh religious poet Henry Vaughan (1622–95) prints his *Silex Scintillans* ('Sparkling Flint'), a volume of mystical and religious poems.

1652 French painter Georges de La Tour dies (b.1593).

1654 Dutch poet and dramatist Joost van den Vondel (1587–1679) writes *Lucifer*, a masterpiece of great religious drama.

1656 Spanish artist Diego de Silva y Velásquez (1599–1660) paints one of his masterpieces, *Las Meniñas* ('Maids of Honour').

1600

1650

History

History and politics	Religion and philosophy
1660	
1660 In England the monarchy is restored, with Charles II (1630–85) of the House of Stuart taking the throne.	**1677** Death of Dutch theologian and philosopher Benedict de Spinoza (b.1632). His *Ethics* is published posthumously.
1664 The English take control of the Dutch colony of New Amsterdam, renaming it New York.	**1679** Death of English political philosopher Thomas Hobbes (b.1588). His major work was *Leviathan*.
1666 Great Fire of London.	
1670–71 In Russia Stenka Razin (c.1630–71) leads an unsuccessful Cossack and peasant revolt.	**1685** In France the Edict of Nantes, which guaranteed at least limited religious toleration, is revoked.
1688 In England the Glorious Revolution sees James VII and II (1633–1701) flee, and William III (1650–1702) and Mary II (1662–94) established by parliament as joint monarchs.	**1690** *Essay concerning Human Understanding* published by English empiricist philosopher John Locke (1632–1704).
1689 In Africa the Ashanti confederacy is founded by Osei Tutu (d.1712).	**1697** French philosopher and critic Pierre Bayle (1647–1706) completes his *Dictionnaire historique et critique* ('Historical and Critical Dictionary').
1689 The Treaty of Nerchinsk settles border disputes between tsarist Russia and the Qing Dynasty.	
1689–97 King William's War; the first of the great wars between France and England for the control of North America.	**1699** Gobind Singh (1666–1708), last of the ten Sikh Gurus, institutes the Khalsa, a Sikh brotherhood marked by a new code of discipline, the 'Five Ks' and adoption of the name Singh for males and Kaur for females.
1690 William III's forces defeat those of James VII and II at the Battle of the Boyne, Ireland.	
1692 Salem Witch Trials in colonial Massachusetts.	
1692 In Scotland the Jacobite Macdonalds are killed at the Massacre of Glencoe.	
1696 Peter I, the Great (1672–1725) becomes sole Tsar of Russia on the death of his half-brother Ivan.	

1700–1799

- England and Scotland are united in 1707, but Scottish resentment of this helps fuel the Jacobite rebellions of 1715 and 1745.
- The Danish navigator Vitas Bering is sent by Russia to explore Alaska (1728) and finds the strait that is now named after him.
- Britain wins the struggle with France for control of North America but is forced to grant independence to the colonies that become the United States.
- English navigator James Cook charts the coasts of Canada, Australia and New Zealand, explores the Pacific and discovers Hawaii.
- French explorer Louis de Bougainville carries out the first French voyage of circumnavigation, 1766–9, and charts many South Pacific islands.

1700	
1700–21 Great Northern War between Sweden and the alliance of Russia, Denmark and Poland; Russia dominates the Baltic.	**1704** German philosopher and mathematician Gottfried Leibniz (1646–1716) completes his response to John Locke, the *New Essays on Human Understanding*.
1701 Elector Frederick III of Brandenburg (1657–1713) is crowned King Frederick I of Prussia.	
1701–13 War of the Spanish Succession; England, Holland and Austria declare war on France and Spain.	**1709** Irish Anglican Bishop and philosopher George Berkeley (1685–1753) publishes his *Essay towards a New Theory of Vision*.
1703 St Petersburg founded by Peter the Great.	
1704 Gibraltar taken from Spain by English forces.	**1713** Jansenism is condemned by papal bull.
1707 Act of Union unites England and Scotland.	
1710 War of Mascates; Brazilian natives revolt against the Portuguese.	
1713 The Treaty of Utrecht ends the War of the Spanish Succession.	
1715 Jacobite rebellion in Britain.	
1718 France founds New Orleans.	

Science and technology

1662 Irish physicist and chemist Robert Boyle (1627–91) arrives at 'Boyle's law', which states that the pressure and volume of gas are inversely proportional.

1669 German chemist Hennig Brand discovers phosphorus.

1676 The Royal Greenwich Observatory is completed.

1679 French scientist Denis Papin (1647–c.1712) invents the 'steam digester' (a prototype pressure cooker).

1680 English astronomer Edmond Halley (1656–1742) correctly predicts the return of a comet (in 1758, 1835 and 1910) that had been observed in 1583 (Halley's comet).

1684 English scientist and mathematician Sir Isaac Newton (1642–1727) expounds his gravitation theory in *De Motu Corporum*.

1687 Isaac Newton publishes his greatest work, *Philosophiae Naturalis Principia Mathematica*, which includes his three laws of motion.

1689 English physician Thomas Sydenham dies (b.1624). His works, with their astute descriptions of diseases, were reprinted and translated throughout the 18c.

1694 Italian anatomist and microscopist Marcello Malpighi dies (b.1628). An early pioneer of histology, he conducted a remarkable series of microscopic studies.

1698 The first practical high-pressure steam engine for pumping water out of mines is invented in England by Thomas Savery (c.1650–1715).

Arts and culture

1660 English Admiralty official Samuel Pepys (1633–73) begins his celebrated diary. **1660**

1665 English poet John Milton (1608–74) completes his most famous work, *Paradise Lost*.

1666 French playwright Molière (1622–73) produces his comic masterpiece *Le Misanthrope*.

1668 John Dryden (1631–1700) is appointed Poet Laureate.

1675 Dutch painter Jan Vermeer dies (b.1632).

1677 French dramatist and poet Jean Racine (1639–99) writes *Phèdre*.

1678 English writer John Bunyan (1628–88) completes the first part of *The Pilgrim's Progress*.

1678 English metaphysical poet Andrew Marvell dies (b.1621).

1688 Aphra Behn (1604–89), perhaps the first professional woman writer in England, publishes her novel *Oroonoko*.

1689 English composer Henry Purcell (1659–95) completes *Dido and Aeneas*, now regarded as the first great English opera.

1694 Japanese poet Matsuo Basho dies (b.1644). He is responsible for turning the 17-syllable haiku into a serious art form.

1700–1799

■ The British found Australia's first permanent European settlement, the penal colony of New South Wales (1788).

■ Revolution in France (1789) leads to war in Europe, and Napoleon Bonaparte comes to power as First Consul. The first income tax is introduced in Britain to help fund the war with France.

■ A metric system and a new calendar, as well as the guillotine, are among the innovations in Revolutionary France.

■ Europe sees a flowering in classical music, with composers such as Mozart and Beethoven producing their great works.

1701 English agriculturalist Jethro Tull (1674–1740) invents a seed-drill which plants seeds in rows.

1704 *Opticks* published by English scientist Sir Isaac Newton (1642–1727).

1709 English iron-master Abraham Darby (c.1678–1717) is the first to use coke successfully in the smelting of iron.

1712 English inventors Thomas Savery and Thomas Newcomen (1663–1729) construct a practical working engine widely used in collieries.

1714 German instrument maker Daniel Fahrenheit (1686–1736) invents an accurate mercury thermometer and devises the Fahrenheit temperature scale.

1700 American colonial merchant Samuel Sewall (1685–1759) writes his anti-slavery essay *The Selling of Joseph*. **1700**

c.1709 Italian harpsichord-maker Bartolommeo Cristofori (1655–1731) invents the pianoforte.

1712 English poet Alexander Pope (1688–1744) publishes his mock epic *The Rape of the Lock*.

1715 Italian composer Alessandro Scarlatti (1659–1725) writes his opera *Il Tigrane*.

1717 German-born English composer George Handel (1685–1759) composes his *Water Music*.

1719 *Robinson Crusoe* published by English writer Daniel Defoe (1660–1731).

History

History and politics

1720

1720 The Bering Strait between Russia and Alaska is discovered by Vitus Bering (1681–1741), Danish navigator.

1720 The South Sea Bubble financial crisis ruins many investors in Britain.

1722 Safavid Dynasty overthrown by the Afghans.

1728 The Treaty of Liakhta is signed by China and Russia in an attempt to solve border disputes and increase trade.

1736 Nadir Shah (1688–1747) becomes King of Persia.

1736–96 Chinese empire under Qianlong (1711–99) expands to include Tibet, Mongolia, Turkestan, Annam, Burma and Nepal.

1737 The town of Richmond, Virginia is founded by William Byrd (1674–1744).

1740–8 War of the Austrian Succession.

1741 Prussia conquers Silesia in the first Silesian War.

1745 Jacobite rebellion in Britain.

1746 Defeat at Culloden ends the Forty-Five Jacobite rebellion.

1746 Chin-ch'uan rebellion in China.

1755 The Portuguese city of Lisbon is devastated by an earthquake.

1756–63 Seven Years' War; Austria, France, Russia, Sweden and Saxony oppose Prussia, Britain and Portugal.

1757 British forces under Robert Clive (1725–74) defeat Siraj ud-Daula (c.1732–57), Nawab of Bengal.

1759 British and Hanoverian forces defeat the French at Minden.

1759 British general James Wolfe (1727–59) defeats the French on the Plains of Abraham near Quebec, winning Canada for Britain but dying in the battle.

1761 Hyder Ali (1722–82) becomes ruler of Mysore, India.

1761 The Afghans defeat the Marathas at Panipat, India.

1768 Ali Bey (1728–73) becomes Sultan of Egypt and establishes independence from the Ottoman Empire.

1770 English navigator Captain James Cook (1728–79) lands at Botany Bay, Australia.

1772 Poland is partitioned between Russia, Austria and Prussia.

1775–83 American Revolution.

1776 The American Continental Congress adopts the Declaration of Independence, proclaiming separation from Britain.

1776–86 Fulani Emirates founded.

1780 Joseph II (1741–90) becomes sole ruler of Austria on the death of his mother, Maria Theresa (b.1717), and introduces reforms.

1783 American independence is established by the Peace of Paris.

Religion and philosophy

1726 The *Fifteen Sermons* of English moral philosopher Joseph Butler (1692–1752) are published.

1730s Wahhabite reformist religious movement within Islam begins to develop.

1738 The Methodist Church is founded by John Wesley (1703–91) and his brother Charles (1707–88), as an evangelical movement within the Church of England.

1739–40 *A Treatise of Human Nature* is published anonymously in London by Scottish philosopher David Hume (1711–76).

c.1740 High point of the First Great Awakening, a Christian revival movement in the American colonies, led by Jonathan Edwards (1703–58) and George Whitefield (1714–70).

1746 *Pensées philosophiques* published by French writer and philosopher Denis Diderot (1713–84).

c.1750 Polish Jewish teacher and healer Baal-Shem-Tov (1699–1760) founds modern Hasidism.

1758 Swedish mystic and scientist Emanuel Swedenborg (1688–1772) publishes *The New Jerusalem*.

1762 French philosopher Jean Jacques Rousseau (1712–78) publishes *Du contrat social*, which greatly influences French revolutionary thought.

1764 The Jesuits are expelled from France (and from Spain in 1767).

1773 The Jesuits are suppressed by Pope Clement XIV (1705–74).

1776 A community of Christian revivalist Shakers is set up by Ann Lee (1736–84) near Albany, New York.

1781 German philosopher Immanuel Kant (1724–1804) produces his *Kritik der reinen Vernunft* ('Critique of Pure Reason').

1783 Moses Mendelssohn (1729–86), an important figure in the Jewish Enlightenment, writes *Jerusalem*, which advocates Judaism as the religion of reason.

Science and technology	Arts and culture	
1724 Dutch physician and botanist Hermann Boerhaave (1668–1738) writes his classic *Elementa Chemiae* ('Elements of Chemistry').	**1721** Johann Sebastian Bach, German composer (1685–1750), finishes his *Brandenburg Concertos*.	**1720**
1725 Italian historical philosopher Giambattista Vico (1668–1774) publishes his major work *Scienza Nuova* ('The New Science').	**1721** French philosopher Charles Montesquieu (1689–1755) completes his *Lettres persanes* ('Persian Letters').	
1730s Swedish naturalist Carolus Linnaeus (1707–78) publishes his system of classification for plants and animals.	**1725** *The Four Seasons* completed by Venetian composer Antonio Vivaldi (1678–1741).	
1731 Invention of the quadrant, an instrument used in measuring angles in navigation, by English astonomer John Hadley (1682–1744).	**1726** Jonathan Swift (1667–1745), Anglo-Irish clergyman and satirist, publishes *Gulliver's Travels*.	
1733 Mechanization of the textile industry is advanced by the invention of the flying-shuttle loom by English inventor John Kay (1704–64).	**1731** *Manon Lescaut* published by French novelist Abbé Prévost (1697–1763).	
c.1740 English inventor Benjamin Huntsman (1704–76) develops a crucible process, improving steel production.	**1733** French composer and musical theorist Jean Philippe Rameau (1638–1764) completes his opera *Hippolyte et Aricie*.	
1742 Invention of the centigrade (Celsius) temperature scale by Swedish astronomer Anders Celsius (1701–44).	**1738** Kirov Ballet founded in St Petersburg.	
1749–67 French naturalist Georges Buffon (1707–88) produces his monumental *Histoire Naturelle*.	**1740** *Pamela*, an epistolary novel, is published by English novelist Samuel Richardson (1689–1761).	
	1742 Handel completes his *Messiah*.	
	1743–5 English painter and engraver William Hogarth (1697–1764) completes his moral narrative *Marriage à la mode* series.	
	1749 English novelist Henry Fielding (1707–54) publishes *Tom Jones*.	
1752 The Gregorian calendar is adopted in Britain.	**1751** The first volume of the *Encyclopédie*, a major reference work of the Enlightenment, is published in France.	**1750**
1757 British naval officer John Campbell invents the sextant, allowing mariners to use the angle of a celestial object above the horizon to determine latitude and longitude at sea.	**1755** English writer Samuel Johnson (1709–84) publishes his *Dictionary of the English Language*.	
1764 British inventor James Hargreaves (1720–78) invents the spinning jenny, which allows one person to spin several yarns at once.	**1759** French writer Voltaire (1694–1778) publishes his satirical novel *Candide*.	
1765 Scottish engineer James Watt (1736–1819) improves the steam engine by adding a separate condenser.	**1760** English painter Joshua Reynolds (1723–92) completes his portrait of Georgiana, Countess Spencer.	
1766 English chemist Henry Cavendish (1731–1810) discovers hydrogen.	**1761** Publication of *Fingal*, a supposed translation from an ancient work by the legendary Gaelic poet Ossian, but in fact largely the work of the Scottish poet James Macpherson (1736–96).	
1774 English clergyman and scientist Joseph Priestley (1733–1804) discovers oxygen.		
c.1775 Start of the Industrial Revolution.	**1762** German composer Christoph Gluck (1714–87) completes his opera *Orfeo ed Euridice*.	
The Industrial Revolution began in Britain with the mechanization of the cotton and woollen industries of Lancashire, central Scotland, and the West Riding of Yorkshire. The mechanization of heavier industries (iron and steel) was slower, but sustained the Industrial Revolution in its second phase from c.1830.	**1768** Italian painter Canaletto dies (b.1697).	
	1770 English painter Thomas Gainsborough (1727–88) completes his *Blue Boy*.	
	1776 Bolshoi Ballet founded in Moscow.	
	1778 The opera house La Scala opens in Milan.	
1781 German-born British astronomer William Herschel (1738–1822) discovers Uranus.	**1778** *Evelina* is published anonymously. It is English novelist Fanny Burney's (1752–1840) first and best novel.	
1783 French aeronautical inventors Joseph (1740–1810) and his brother Jacques (1745–99) Montgolfier conduct the world's first manned balloon flight.	*Evelina* describes the entry of a country girl into the gaieties of London life, and shows a natural style. As a portrayer of the domestic scene, Burney was a forerunner of Jane Austen, whom she influenced.	

History

History and politics

1789 George Washington (1732–99) becomes the first President of the United States.

1789 The French Revolution begins; fall of the Bastille.

1793 Louis XVI (1754–93), King of France, is executed by revolutionary authorities.

1794 The Qajar Dynasty of Persian rulers is founded, retaining power until 1925.

1798 Rising in Ireland by the United Irishmen fails.

1799 Tipu Sultan (c. 1753–99), ruler of Mysore, is defeated and killed by British forces.

1799 Napoleon Bonaparte (1769–1821) seizes power in France as First Consul.

Religion and philosophy

1789 English philosopher Jeremy Bentham (1748–1832) publishes his *Introduction to the Principles of Morals and Legislation*.

1790s The Second Great Awakening takes place in the American colonies.

1792 English political writer Thomas Paine (1737–1809) publishes *The Rights of Man*.

1795 The Methodist Church breaks away from the Church of England.

1800–1899

- White settlement in North America pushes steadily west, especially after the Lewis and Clark expedition (1804–6) opens up a route to the Pacific.
- Industrialization advances rapidly, first in Britain then in Europe, as does urbanization. Britain's first census is carried out in 1801. Among the century's innovations are the steamship, the railway, the telephone, the motor car, cinema and the bra.
- It is an age of political reforms, some achieved by peaceful political activity, others by revolutionary unrest, especially in the widespread European agitation in 1848. In this period, Britain alone sees four main Reform Acts.

1803 With the Louisiana Purchase from France, the USA acquires full control of the Mississippi Valley.

1804 Islamic religious leader Usman dan Fodio (1754–1817) launches the war that establishes the Fulani Empire in central Africa.

1805 Battle of Trafalgar; Horatio Nelson (1758–1805) defeats the combined fleets of France and Spain but is mortally wounded.

1806 The Holy Roman Empire comes to an end when Emperor Francis II (1768–1835) is forced to abdicate by Napoleon.

1811 In Britain workers known as Luddites destroy newly introduced textile machinery.

1812 Napoleon invades Russia; his army suffers disastrous losses in a forced retreat.

1813 Napoleon is defeated at Leipzig by the forces of Austria, Prussia, Russia and Sweden.

1814 Napoleon is forced to abdicate and retire to Elba.

1815 Napoleon, having regained power, is finally defeated at Waterloo by Wellington (1769–1852) and Blücher (1742–1819), and exiled to St Helena.

1818 Shaka (1787–1828) founds the Zulu Kingdom in southern Africa.

1819 Singapore is acquired for the British East India Company by Sir Stamford Raffles (1781–1826).

1807 German philosopher Georg Hegel (1770–1831) publishes his first great work *Phänomenologie des Geistes* ('The Phenomenology of Mind').

Hegel was the last and perhaps the most important of the great German idealist philosophers. Although his philosophy can be difficult and obscure, it has been a great influence on later philosophies, including Marxism, Positivism and Existentialism.

1814 Pope Pius VII (1742–1823) formally re-establishes the Jesuits.

1819 German philosopher Arthur Schopenhauer (1788–1860) publishes *The World as Will and Idea*, emphasizing the primacy of the human will.

Science and technology	Arts and culture
1785 The power loom for spinning cotton is invented by English clergyman and inventor Edmund Cartwright (1743–1823).	**1786** Austrian composer Wolfgang Amadeus Mozart (1756–91) completes his opera *The Marriage of Figaro*. **1785**
1793 US inventor Eli Whitney (1765–1825) invents the cotton gin, a machine that separates seeds from fibre.	**1786** Scottish poet Robert Burns (1759–96) publishes his *Poems, Chiefly in the Scottish Dialect*.
1796 English physician Edward Jenner (1749–1823) makes the revolutionary discovery of vaccination, and successfully inoculates a child against smallpox.	**1789** English poet William Blake (1757–1827) publishes his *Songs of Innocence. Songs of Experience* follows in 1794.
1798 In France US engineer Robert Fulton (1765–1815) constructs the first practical submarine.	**1798** *Lyrical Ballads*, the work of English poets William Wordsworth (1770–1850) and Samuel Taylor Coleridge (1772–1834), is published.
	1799 Discovery at Rosetta (Raschid) in Egypt of the Rosetta Stone, a slab of basalt engraved with a trilingual inscription in Greek and Egyptian hieroglyphic and demotic, later to prove the key to the language of ancient Egypt.

1800–1899

- In South America former colonies of Spain and Portugal win their independence; in the North, the United States is torn by civil war.

- The British East India Company extends its power in India, but after the suppression of the Indian Mutiny rule passes to the British crown (1858). Queen Victoria becomes Empress of India.

- Turning its back on feudalism, Japan begins to modernize.

- Organized sport grows in popularity, especially in Britain, where the Football Association is founded in 1863.

- In 1887 Australia beat England in the first cricket Test match, in Melbourne.

1800 Italian physicist Alessandro Volta (1745–1827) invents the electrochemical battery, the first source of continuous electricity.	**1800** Spanish painter Francisco Goya (1746–1828) paints his *Family of Charles IV*. **1800**
1801 Italian astronomer Giuseppe Piazzi (1746–1826) discovers the first minor planet (or asteroid), which he names Ceres.	**1802** German composer Ludwig van Beethoven (1770–1827) completes his 'Moonlight' sonata.
1806 The Beaufort Scale of wind speed is devised by British admiral Sir Francis Beaufort (1774–1857).	**1810** Scottish novelist and poet Sir Walter Scott (1771–1832) publishes *The Lady of the Lake*.
1807 The first commercial steamboat service is introduced in New York by engineer Robert Fulton (1765–1815).	**1810–14** Spanish artist Francisco Goya (1746–1828) creates the series of etchings *The Disasters of War*.
1807 Swedish chemist Jöns Jacob Berzelius (1779–1848) begins the work that leads him to draw up a table of atomic weights using oxygen as a base, devising the modern system of chemical symbols.	**1811** *Sense and Sensibility* is published by English novelist Jane Austen (1775–1817).
1809 Gas-powered street lighting is introduced in London.	**1812** Publication of the first volume of *Grimm's Fairy Tales* by German brothers Jacob (1785–1863) and Wilhelm (1786–1859) Grimm.
1812 French chef Nicolas Appert (1749–1841) opens the world's first commercial canning factory.	**1812** The first volume of *Childe Harold's Pilgrimage* by British poet George Gordon, Lord Byron (1788–1824), is published to instant acclaim.
1816 French physician René Lännec (1781–1826) invents the stethoscope.	**1816** Italian composer Gioacchino Rossini (1792–1868) produces his masterpiece, the comic opera *The Barber of Seville*.
	1818 English writer Mary Shelley (1797–1851) publishes her first and most impressive novel *Frankenstein, or the Modern Prometheus*.

History and politics

1820

1821 The Greeks begin a war of independence against Turkey, realising their goal in 1832.

1822 Liberia is founded as a homeland for freed US slaves.

1823 Monroe Doctrine declares US hostility to further European colonization or political interference in the western hemisphere.

1825–8 Argentine–Brazilian War; fought to decide possession of the Banda Oriental territory.

1826 Ottoman Sultan Mahmud II (1785–1839) ends the power of the professional military corps of Janissaries by massacring them.

1827 The British and French fleets destroy a Turkish and Egyptian fleet at Navarino.

1833 Slavery is abolished in the British Empire.

1836 Beginning of the Great Trek of the Boers from Cape Colony to escape British rule.

1836–42 First Anglo-Afghan War.

1839–42 First of the Opium Wars, fought between Britain and China over the opium trade.

1840 Britain annexes New Zealand.

1845–51 Irish famine, caused by the failure of the potato crop, leads to massive population loss through starvation and emigration.

1846–48 Mexican War between Mexico and the USA.

1848 A wave of revolutions sweeps central and western Europe. The Second Republic is established in France.

1850

1850–64 The Taiping Rebellion against the Qing Dynasty in China costs millions of lives before it is crushed.

1852 President Louis-Napoleon of France (1808–73) dissolves the constitution of the Second Republic and assumes the title of Emperor Napoleon III.

1854 Britain and France join in the Crimean War on the side of Turkey against Russia.

1856–7 Persia at war with Britain after taking Herat (Afghanistan).

1856–60 Second Opium War.

1857–8 The Indian Mutiny, an uprising against British rule in India, begins with a mutiny of Indian troops in British service. It leads to the transfer of government from the East India Company to the British Crown.

1861–5 US Civil War.

1861 Emancipation of the Russian serfs.

1863 US President Lincoln (1809–65) abolishes slavery in the USA.

1864 Geneva Convention founds the International Red Cross.

Religion and philosophy

1828 Indian religious reformer Rammohun Roy (1774–1833) founds the Brahmo Samaj, a theistic movement which argues that reason should form the basis of Hinduism.

1829 Catholic Emancipation legislation in Britain allows Catholics to become MPs.

1830 The Church of Jesus Christ of the Latter-Day Saints (Mormons) is founded in the USA by Joseph Smith (1805–44).

1833 Beginning of the Oxford Movement in the Church of England, aimed at reviving high doctrine and ceremony.

1843 Publication of *Either/Or* by Danish philosopher Søren Kierkegaard (1813–55), one of the founders of Existentialism.

1844 The Muslim Babist sect is founded when Persian mystic Mirza Ali Muhammad (1819–50) declares himself the 'Bab' (gate) between man and God. Babism was the forerunner of the Baha'i faith.

1848 The Christadelphians, a Christian sect, is founded in the USA by John Thomas (1805–71).

1859 English utilitarian philosopher John Stuart Mill (1806–73) publishes *On Liberty*.

1862 English philosopher Herbert Spencer (1820–1903) publishes the first volume of his *System of Synthetic Philosophy*. An evolutionist, he supported Darwin and coined the phrase 'survival of the fittest'.

1863 Formation of the Seventh Day Adventist Church in the USA, led by Ellen Gould White (1827–1915).

1863 Foundation of the Baha'i faith in Persia by Mirza Husayn Ali (1817–92).

History

Science and technology	Arts and culture	
1821 English scientist Michael Faraday (1791–1867) invents the electric motor and generator.	**1820** Publication of *Lamia and Other Poems* by English poet John Keats (1795–1821), which contains his best-known work, including the great 'Odes'.	1820
1825 The first passenger steam railway comes into service, between Stockton and Darlington in north-east England.	**1821** English landscape painter John Constable (1776–1837) completes *The Haywain*.	
1826 French scientist and pioneer of photography Nicéphore Niepce (1765–1833) produces the first photographic image, using a bitumen-coated pewter plate.	**1823** Beethoven completes his Symphony No 9.	
1827 Scottish botanist Robert Brown (1773–1858) first observes the movement of fine particles in a liquid, subsequently named 'Brownian movement'.	**1825** Russian poet and writer Alexander Pushkin (1799–1837) publishes *Boris Godunov*.	
	1828 US lexicographer Noah Webster (1758–1843) publishes *An American Dictionary of the English Language*.	
1831 English naturalist Charles Darwin (1809–82) begins the voyage of the *Beagle*, making many of the discoveries which later allow him to develop his idea of the origin of species.	**1830** French composer Hector Berlioz (1803–69) completes his *Symphonie fantastique*.	
	1832 Japanese Ukiyo-e painter and wood engraver Ando Hiroshige (1797–1858) completes his *Fifty-three Stages of the Tokaido*.	
1833 English mathematician Charles Babbage (1792–1871) initiates a major step in the development of the computer with his design for an 'analytical engine', intended to be programmable to carry out mathematical functions.	**1836** Serial publication begins of *The Pickwick Papers*, the first novel by Charles Dickens (1812–70).	
1837 English physicist Sir Charles Wheatstone (1802–75) patents an electric telegraph.	Dickens is the most widely-known English writer after Shakespeare. His novels are a vivid portrayal of social life in Victorian England and they continue to find a receptive audience, not only in book form, but also as film and stage adaptations.	
1839 US inventor Charles Goodyear (1800–60) discovers the process of vulcanizing rubber.		
1846 German astronomer Johann Galle (1812–1910) is the first person to observe the planet Neptune.	**1848** Foundation of the Pre-Raphaelite Brotherhood, a group of English artists aiming to revolutionize Victorian art.	
1848 The absolute (Kelvin) scale of temperature is devised by British physicist William (later Lord) Kelvin (1824–1907).		
1850 Invention of the bunsen burner, named after the German scientist Robert Bunsen (1811–99).	**1851** The Great Exhibition in London celebrates British industry.	1850
1850 German physiologist and physicist Hermann von Helmholtz (1821–94) invents an ophthalmoscope.	**1851** US author Herman Melville (1819–91) publishes *Moby Dick*, considered one of the greatest US novels.	
1851 French physicist Jean Bernard Léon Foucault (1819–68) uses a freely-suspended pendulum to convincingly demonstrate the rotation of the Earth.	**1852** US novelist Harriet Beecher Stowe (1811–96) publishes *Uncle Tom's Cabin*, an anti-slavery novel.	
1855 English metallurgist Henry Bessemer (1813–98) patents his process for converting pig-iron into steel.	**1853** Italian composer Giuseppe Verdi (1813–1901) completes his operas *Il Trovatore* and *La Traviata*.	
1859 Darwin publishes *The Origin of Species*.	**1857** French novelist Gustave Flaubert (1821–80) publishes *Madame Bovary*, for which he is unsuccessfully prosecuted for immorality.	
1860 Florence Nightingale (1820–1910) establishes the first institution for the training of nurses.	**1858** German-born French composer Jacques Offenbach (1819–80) completes his *opéra bouffe, Orpheus in the Underworld*.	
1863 French chemist Louis Pasteur (1822–95) develops the technique of 'pasteurization'.	**1863** *Le Déjeuner sur l'herbe*, by French painter Edouard Manet (1832–83), causes a scandal with its provocative portrayal of a naked woman.	
1863 The first underground railway is opened in London.		

History

History and politics	Religion and philosophy
1865	
1867 The USA buys Alaska from Russia.	**1865** English religious leader William Booth (1829–1912) begins the Christian Mission in London's East End. It becomes the Salvation Army in 1878.
1868 The Meiji Restoration in Japan sees the overthrow of the last Shogun and the restoration of imperial rule.	
1868 The British Trades Union Congress is founded.	
1870–1 Franco-Prussian War; a crushing defeat for France leads to the fall of Napoleon III.	**1869–70** First Vatican Council called by Pope Pius IX (1792–1878); the doctrine of papal infallibility is declared.
1871 The King of Prussia becomes Emperor Wilhelm I (1797–1888) of the united Germany.	
1875 Britain buys the Suez Canal.	**1872** In the USA, the international Bible Students' Association (Jehovah's Witnesses) is founded by Charles Taze Russell (1852–1916).
1876 Queen Victoria of Great Britain and Ireland (1819–1901) is declared Empress of India.	
1879 Zulu Kingdom defeated by the British.	
1880–1 The First Boer War; it ends with the defeat of Britain at Majuba Hill.	**1882** In the Sudan Muhammad Ahmed (1843–85) claims to be the Islamic saviour the Mahdi.
1881 Tsar Alexander II of Russia (b.1818) is assassinated by revolutionary terrorists.	
1885 Foundation of the Indian National Congress, a political organization aimed at independence from Britain.	**1884** Death of Indian Hindu reformer Keshub Chunder Sen (b.1838).
	1890 Death of English theologian, cardinal and leader of the Oxford Movement, John Henry Newman (b. 1801).
1892 Scottish labour leader Keir Hardie (1856–1915) becomes the first Labour MP.	
1893 New Zealand is the first country to give women the right to vote.	
1894 French army captain Alfred Dreyfus (1859–1935) is wrongly convicted of passing military secrets to Germany; his case becomes a national *cause célèbre*.	
1898 The USA gains Puerto Rico and the Philippines in the Spanish–American War.	
1899–1902 The Second Boer War.	

1900–2000

- Early technological advances include the domestic refrigerator and powered flight.
- The ever more powerful and efficient weapons produced by modern industry help kill millions in World War I. The newly developed aeroplane becomes militarily important. In Britain long-lasting effects of the wartime drive for efficiency are British Summer Time and the licensing laws.
- Revolution in Russia leads to the first communist state (1917).
- Inspired by the Suffragettes, British women win the right to vote in 1918, followed two years later by women in the USA. Many women go out to work for the first time during the two world wars.
- Unemployment and poverty characterize the worldwide depression of the 1930s.

History and politics	Religion and philosophy
1900	
1900 The Boxer Rising in China is put down by a combined force of foreign powers.	**1901** Pentecostalism, a Christian renewal movement, is established in Topeka, Kansas.
1901 Death of Queen Victoria of Great Britain after a reign of 64 years.	
1901 The Commonwealth of Australia is established, with Canberra as its capital.	**1902** US philosopher William James (1842–1910) publishes *The Varieties of Religious Experience*.
1904–5 Russo-Japanese War; Russia suffers naval and military disasters before eventual defeat.	**1904** German sociologist Max Weber (1864–1920) publishes *The Protestant Ethic and the Spirit of Capitalism*.
1905 An unsuccessful revolution in Russia results in the country's first constitution and parliament.	
1908 In Turkey the reformist Young Turks stage a revolution and depose the Sultan.	

Science and technology

1866 A transatlantic telegraph cable is laid.

1866 Swedish chemist and industrialist Alfred Nobel (1833–96) invents dynamite.

1869 A transcontinental railway is established in the USA with the meeting of the Union and Pacific railroads.

1876 Scots-born US inventor Alexander Graham Bell (1847–1922) patents his telephone.

1878 Electric street lighting is introduced in London.

1882 The world's first hydroelectric plant comes into operation in Wisconsin, USA.

1883 The first fully automatic machine gun, the Maxim gun, is invented by US-born British inventor Sir Hiram Maxim (1840–1916).

1884 German engineer Gottlieb Daimler (1834–1900) produces a petrol-burning internal-combustion engine.

1888 Scottish veterinarian and inventor John Dunlop (1840–1921) invents the pneumatic tyre.

1889 The Eiffel Tower, designed by French engineer Gustave Eiffel (1832–1923), is completed in Paris.

1895 German physicist Wilhelm Röntgen (1845–1923) discovers X-rays.

1897 German engineer Rudolf Diesel (1858–1913) demonstrates his compression-ignition engine.

1898 French physicists Marie (1867–1934) and Pierre (1859–1906) Curie isolate polonium and radium.

Arts and culture

1865 Russian writer Leo Tolstoy (1828–1910) publishes the first part of his masterpiece, the novel *War and Peace*.　　**1865**

1869 First performance of the opera *Das Rheingold* by German composer Richard Wagner (1813–83).

1874 *Impression, soleil levant*, a painting by French artist Claude Monet (1840–1926), gives the name to the Impressionist school of painters.

1875 French composer Georges Bizet (1838–75) completes *Carmen* shortly before his death.

1876 US writer Mark Twain (1835–1910) publishes *Tom Sawyer*.

1879 Norwegian dramatist Henrik Ibsen (1828–1906) writes *A Doll's House*.

1884 The first part of the *Oxford English Dictionary* is published.

1886 The *Statue of Liberty*, designed by French sculptor Auguste Bartholdi (1834–1904), is unveiled.

1891 English author Thomas Hardy (1840–1928) publishes *Tess of the D'Urbervilles*.

1895 First performance of *The Importance of Being Earnest* by Irish writer Oscar Wilde (1854–1900).

1899 English composer Edward Elgar (1857–1934) completes his *Enigma Variations*.

1900–2000

- World War II sees the development of total war, with the mass bombing of enemy cities, and ends with the use of the most destructive weapon yet known, the atomic bomb.
- Humankind ventures into outer space.
- Popular culture comes into its own with the spread of radio and television broadcasting and the rise of pop music as a genre.
- With the introduction of the PC, computers increasingly dominate the workplace and daily life. Millions of people worldwide use the Internet for communication, entertainment and business.

1901 Italian Guglielmo Marconi (1847–1937) sends the first transatlantic wireless message.

1901 Austrian-born US pathologist Karl Landsteiner (1868–1943) discovers the four major blood groups (A, O, B, AB).

1902 The Aswan Dam on the Nile is completed.

1903 The first powered flight of a heavier-than-air craft is carried out by Orville Wright (1871–1948) and his brother Wilbur (1867–1912) at Kitty Hawk, North Carolina.

1905 German-born US physicist Albert Einstein (1879–1955) publishes a paper on his special theory of relativity.

1908 US automobile engineer Henry Ford (1863–1947) begins production of the Model T.

1909 French aviator Louis Blériot (1872–1936) makes the first flight across the English Channel.

1900 First performance of the opera *Tosca* by Italian composer Giacomo Puccini (1858–1924).　　**1900**

1901 Russian composer Sergei Rachmaninov (1873–1943) composes his piano concerto *No.2 in C Minor*.

1904 French sculptor Auguste Rodin (1840–1917) completes *Le Penseur* ('The Thinker').

1904 Russian writer Anton Chekhov (1860–1904) completes his play *The Cherry Orchard*.

1907 Spanish artist Pablo Picasso (1881–1973) completes *Les Demoiselles d'Avignon*, regarded as the first Cubist painting.

1908 English novelist E M Forster (1879–1970) publishes *A Room with a View*.

History

History

History and politics	Religion and philosophy
1910	
1910 The Union of South Africa is established as a dominion of the British Empire.	**1911** Birth of Indian cult leader Maharishi Mahesh Yogi.
1910–17 Revolution in Mexico.	Maharishi Mahesh Yogi founded the science of creative intelligence and, as an exponent of the relaxation technique called transcendental meditation, he became one of the first Eastern gurus to attract a Western following.
1911 Revolution in China leads to the overthrow of the Qing Dynasty and the establishment of a republic.	
1912–13 Balkan Wars; Turkey loses almost all of its territory in Europe.	
1914 World War I begins.	
1916 In Dublin Irish nationalists stage the Easter Rising.	**1912** Austrian social philosopher Rudolf Steiner (1861–1925) founds anthroposophy, a modern spiritual movement, in Switzerland.
1917 The USA enters World War I.	
1917 The Russian Revolution overthrows the imperial regime and brings the first communist government to power.	
1917 The Balfour Declaration by British Foreign Secretary Arthur Balfour (1848–1930) promises Zionists a national home in Palestine.	**1918** Formal foundation of the Native American Church, combining native religion with certain elements of Christianity.
1918 World War I ends.	**1919** Swiss theologian Karl Barth (1886–1968) publishes his commentary of St Paul's Epistle to the Romans.
1918 In Britain women over the age of 30 receive the right to vote.	
1919 The League of Nations is established to preserve international peace.	**1922** Austrian-born British philosopher Ludwig Wittgenstein (1889–1951) publishes his *Tractatus Logico-philosophicus*.
1922 Fascist leader Benito Mussolini (1883–1945) comes to power in Italy.	
1925 German politician Adolf Hitler (1889–1945) writes his political testament *Mein Kampf* while in prison.	**1927** German philosopher Martin Heidegger (1889–1976) publishes *Being and Time*.
1929 The New York Stock Exchange collapses, triggering the Depression.	
1930	
1931 Japan invades Manchuria.	**1931** Tibetan Buddhist teacher and monk Geshe Kelsang Gyatso born. He is the founder of the New Kadampa Tradition of Buddhism.
1932 The Kingdom of Saudi Arabia is established.	
1933 Adolf Hitler (1889–1945) becomes Chancellor of Germany.	**1931** The Nation of Islam is founded in the USA by Wallace Ford Muhammad (b.c.1877), also known as Wali Farad.
1933 US President Franklin D Roosevelt (1882–1945) begins to implement his New Deal programme for national recovery.	
1934 Chinese communists under Mao Zedong (1893–1976) begin their `Long March', withdrawing from south-eastern to north-western China.	**1933** Death of Buddhist Anagarika Dharmapala (b.1864). He wrote and spoke as the champion of Buddhist reformism, and in his later years campaigned for the return of Buddhist sacred sites in North India into Buddhist hands.
1936–9 Spanish Civil War; it ends with the overthrow of the Republican government.	
1939 World War II breaks out.	
1940 The victory of the RAF over the Luftwaffe in the Battle of Britain causes Hitler to postpone plans to invade the UK.	**1940** Foundation of the Taizé religious community by Swiss monk Roger Schutz-Marsauche (1915–).
1941 Germany invades Russia.	**1943** French writer and philosopher Jean-Paul Sartre (1905–80) publishes *Being and Nothingness*, one of the seminal texts of Existentialism.
1941 A Japanese air attack on the US base at Pearl Harbor, Hawaii brings the USA into World War II.	
1942 The British victory over the German Afrika Corps at El Alamein in Egypt is a turning point in the North African campaign.	
1944 Landings in Normandy on D-Day (June 6) begin the Allied liberation of Europe.	

History

Science and technology

1910–13 *Principia Mathematica* is produced by English philosophers and mathematicians Bertrand Russell (1872–1970) and Alfred Whitehead (1861–1947).

1914 The US Corps of Engineers completes the building of the Panama Canal.

1916 The British Army makes the first use of the military tank, in the Battle of the Somme.

1919 The first non-stop transatlantic flight is made by English aviators John Alcock (1892–1919) and Arthur Whitten Brown (1886–1948).

1920 US soldier John Brown (1860–1940) invents the 'Thompson' gun.

1924 A vaccine (BCG) against tuberculosis is introduced in France after being discovered by the bacteriologists Albert Calmette (1863–1933) and Camille Guérin (1872–1961).

1926 Scottish electrical engineer John Logie Baird (1888–1946) gives the first demonstration of a television image.

1927 *The Jazz Singer*, the first cinema film with a soundtrack ('talking picture'), is released by the US Warner Brothers company.

1927 US aviator Charles Lindbergh (1902–74) makes the first non-stop solo transatlantic flight.

1928 Penicillin is discovered by Scottish bacteriologist Alexander Fleming (1881–1955).

1929 US astronomer Edwin Hubble (1889–1953) announces his discovery that the universe is expanding.

1930 US astronomer Clyde Tombaugh (1906–97) discovers the planet Pluto.

1932 English physicist James Chadwick (1891–1974) discovers and names the neutron.

1935 US seismologist Charles Richter (1900–85) completes the Richter scale of earthquake measurement.

1935 The first practical radar system is developed by Scottish physicist Robert Watson-Watt (1892–1973).

1936 English mathematician Alan Turing (1912–54) makes an outstanding contribution to the development of computer science, outlining a theoretical 'universal' machine.

1937 British aeronautical engineer Frank Whittle (1907–96) invents the jet engine.

1937 Nylon is invented in the USA by industrial chemist Wallace Hume Carothers (1896–1937).

1938 US inventor Chester Carlson (1906–68) discovers the basic principles of 'xerography' (patented in 1940).

1942 Italian-born US physicist Enrico Fermi (1901–54) builds the world's first nuclear reactor.

1943 French naval officer and underwater explorer Jacques Cousteau (1910–97) invents the aqualung diving apparatus.

1944 The first jet fighter aircraft (the German Messerschmitt Me262) makes its appearance in combat.

Arts and culture

c.1910 Russian-born French artist Wassily Kandinsky (1866–1944) begins to produce the first abstract paintings.   **1910**

1912 French novelist Marcel Proust (1871–1922) publishes the first volume of *À la recherche du temps perdu*.

1913 German writer Thomas Mann (1871–1950) publishes the novella *Death in Venice*.

1914–16 English composer Gustav Holst (1874–1934) composes *The Planets*.

1915 Release of *The Birth of a Nation*, by US filmmaker D W Griffith (1875–1948).

1916 The Dada movement is founded in Zurich.

1920 Posthumous publication of *Poems* by Wilfred Owen (1893–1918), reflecting the horror of trench warfare in World War I.

1920 New Zealand author Katherine Mansfield (1888–1923) publishes *Bliss, and other stories*.

1922 *Ulysses* by Irish writer James Joyce (1882–1941) is published in Paris. It helps revolutionize the 20c novel, but because it is considered obscene, it is not published in Britain and the USA until 1936.

1924 US composer George Gershwin (1898–1937) completes his *Rhapsody in Blue*.

1925 Austrian writer Franz Kafka's (1883–1924) *The Trial* is published posthumously.

1925 US novelist F Scott Fitzgerald captures the spirit of the 1920s in *The Great Gatsby*.

1927 The British Broadcasting Corporation begins its radio service.

1931 Surrealist Spanish artist Salvador Dalí (1904–89) paints *The Persistence of Memory*.   **1930**

1932 *Brave New World*, a novel by English author Aldous Huxley (1894–1963), depicts a dystopian future in which people are scientifically bred.

1933 Spanish poet and playwright Federico García Lorca (1898–1936) writes *Blood Wedding*.

1934 *Tropic of Cancer*, a novel by US author Henry Miller (1891–1980), is published in Paris but banned in Britain and the USA because of sexual explicitness.

1936 Russian composer Sergei Prokofiev (1891–1953) completes *Peter and the Wolf*.

1937 Picasso paints *Guernica*, a depiction of the destruction of that town by bombing in the Spanish Civil War.

1938 British sculptor Henry Moore (1898–1986) completes *Recumbent Figure*.

1940 *For Whom the Bell Tolls* is published by US writer Ernest Hemingway (1899–1961).

1941 Release of *Citizen Kane*, a US film directed by Orson Welles (1915–85), often acclaimed as the greatest film ever made.

1943 The musical *Oklahoma!* is written by US composers Oscar Hammerstein II (1895–1960) and Richard Rodgers (1902–79).

History

History and politics	Religion and philosophy
1945 **1945** World War II ends; Germany surrenders (May); Japan also capitulates (August) after the USA drops atomic bombs on Hiroshima and Nagasaki.	**1945** Austrian-born British philosopher Karl Popper (1902–94) publishes *The Open Society and its Enemies*.
1947 The Truman Doctrine, announced by US President Truman (1884–1972), promises US aid to countries threatened by communist interference.	**1948** Foundation of the World Council of Churches.
1948 Israel proclaims its independence.	**1954** The Church of Scientology is founded, based on L Ron Hubbard's (1911–86) *Dianetics: The Modern Science of Mental Health*.
1948 Assassination of Indian leader Mahatma Gandhi (b.1869).	
1949 NATO formed.	**1954** South Korean religious leader Sun Myung Moon (1920–) founds the Unification Church.
1949 The Communists take power in China.	
1950–3 Korean War; United Nations forces defend South Korea against invasion by communist North Korea and China.	**1956** British philosopher A J Ayer (1910–89) publishes *The Problem of Knowledge*.
1953 Death of Soviet revolutionary and leader Joseph Stalin (b.1879).	
1954 French withdraw from Indochina.	
1956 Suez Crisis; Egypt nationalizes the Suez Canal, prompting occupation of the canal zone by Britain and France, who are forced to withdraw by US and Russian pressure.	
1957 Treaty of Rome establishes a European Economic Community comprising France, West Germany, Italy, Belgium, Netherlands and Luxembourg.	
1959 The Communists come to power in Cuba under Fidel Castro (1927–).	
1960 **1961** The East German government builds a wall in Berlin to prevent its citizens moving from East to West.	**1962–5** The Second Vatican Council, called by Pope John XXIII (1881–1963), initiates far-reaching reforms in Catholicism.
1963 US President John F Kennedy is assassinated (b.1917).	**1965** US black nationalist leader Malcolm X is killed by Black Muslim assassins (b.1925).
1964–75 Vietnam War between communist North Vietnam and non-communist South Vietnam; USA involved until 1973.	
1966–76 The Cultural Revolution in China. Mao Zedong (1893–1976) encourages youth to persecute intellectuals.	**1966** The Catholic Church decides to publish no further editions of its index of prohibited books.
1967 In the Six-Day War, Israel quickly defeats an alliance of Egypt, Syria and Jordan.	**1966** The Hindu cult The International Society for Krishna Consciousness (Hare Krishna) is founded in the USA by A C Bhaktivedanta Swami Prabhupada (1896–1977).
1968 US civil rights leader Martin Luther King, Jr (b.1929) is assassinated.	
1968 Warsaw Pact troops invade Czechoslovakia to crush the liberalizing Dubček regime.	
1969 Northern Ireland enters a period of unrest and violence.	**1967** French philosopher Jacques Derrida (1930–2004), founder of the deconstruction school of criticism, publishes *L'écriture et la différence*.
1971 Civil war in Pakistan sees Bangladesh declare independence.	
1973 US troops are withdrawn from Vietnam.	**1970** The complete New English Bible, in modern English, is published.
1973 Yom Kippur War follows a surprise attack by Egypt and Syria on Israel.	**1971** Peruvian theologian Gustavo Gutiérrez (1928–) completes his seminal work *A Theology of Liberation*.
1973 Chilean Socialist President Salvador Allende (b.1908) is killed when his government is overthrown by the armed forces.	
1974 US President Richard Nixon (1913–94) resigns under threat of impeachment over the Watergate affair.	**1978** Polish cardinal Karol Wojtyła (1920–2005) becomes Pope John Paul II, the first non-Italian pope since the 16c.
1979 The Shah of Iran is deposed and an Islamic republic is set up under Ayatollah Khomeini (1900–89).	

Science and technology

1947 US test pilot Charles 'Chuck' Yeager (1923–) makes the first supersonic flight, in the Bell X-1 rocket aircraft.

1948 The transistor is invented in the USA, contributing greatly to the development of computers.

1952 The hydrogen bomb is tested by the USA.

1953 The helical structure of DNA is discovered by English molecular biologist Francis Crick (1916–2004) and US biologist James Watson (1928–).

1954 Invention of the contraceptive pill.

1956 The first practical videotape recorder is demonstrated by US engineers Raymond Dolby (1933–) and Charles Ginsburg (1920–92).

1957 The Soviet Union launches the world's first artificial satellite, Sputnik 1.

1959 The Soviet space probe Luna 3 takes a photograph of the far side of the Moon.

1960 US physicist Theodore Maiman (1927–2007) produces the first laser.

1961 Soviet airman Yuri Gagarin (1934–68) becomes the first human to travel in space.

1962 The USA launches Telstar I, a communications satellite which relays the first transatlantic television signals.

1965 US physicists Arno Penzias (1933–) and Robert Wilson (1936–) discover microwave background radiation, a remnant of the Big Bang.

1966 The genetic code is elucidated by US biochemist Marshall Nirenberg (1927–) and others.

1967 The first successful heart transplant operation is carried out by South African surgeon Christiaan Barnard (1922–2001).

1969 US astronaut Neil Armstrong (1930–) becomes the first man to set foot on the Moon during the Apollo 11 mission.

1971 The introduction of the microprocessor is a great step forward in the development of computers.

1972 The pocket calculator is invented in the USA.

1975 First personal computer (Altair 8800) commercially available.

1976 The Anglo-French aircraft Concorde, the world's first supersonic airliner, enters regular service.

1978 The first 'test-tube baby' (ie conceived using *in-vitro* fertilization) is born, in the UK.

Arts and culture

1945 English author George Orwell (1903–50) publishes *Animal Farm*, a satire on totalitarianism.   **1945**

1951 Publication of *Catcher in the Rye*, a novel by US writer J D Salinger (1919–).

1952 US composer John Cage (1912–92) produces *4'33"* (silent throughout).

1953 Irish playwright Samuel Beckett (1906–89) writes his *Waiting for Godot*.

1954–5 J R R Tolkien (1892–1973) publishes *The Lord of the Rings*.

1955 'Rock Around the Clock' by Bill Haley (1925–81) and the Comets is one of the first hit singles of the rock and roll era.

1956 Death of US artist Jackson Pollock (b.1912). He was the first exponent of tachism or action painting in the USA.

1956 First performance of *Look Back in Anger*, a play by English dramatist John Osborne (1929–94), which introduces the prototype of the 'angry young man' as hero.

1957 Publication of *On the Road*, a novel by US author Jack Kerouac (1922–69), which captures the discontent and restlessness of the 'Beat Generation'.

1959 Russian-born US novelist Vladimir Nabokov (1899–1977) publishes *Lolita*.

1960 Publication of *Rabbit, Run* by US novelist John Updike (1932–2009).   **1960**

1961 US novelist Joseph Heller (1923–99) publishes *Catch-22*, creating both a bestseller and a new English expression.

1962 British pop group The Beatles (1960–70) have their first hit single 'Love Me Do'. They go on to inspire 'Beatlemania' and change the face of popular music.

1962 US artist Andy Warhol (c.1926–87) produces his multiple portrait of Marilyn Monroe, *Marilyn Diptych*.

1967 The Beatles release their album *Sergeant Pepper's Lonely Hearts Club Band*.

1973 US novelist Thomas Pynchon (1937–) publishes *Gravity's Rainbow*.

1973 Sydney Opera House opens.

1976 US composer Philip Glass (1937–) writes *Einstein on the Beach*.

1977 Millions mourn the death of 'The King', Elvis Presley (b. 1935).

1977 Release of *Star Wars*, a science-fiction blockbuster film by US director George Lucas (1944–).

1979 Czech-born French novelist Milan Kundera (1929–) publishes *The Book of Laughter and Forgetting*.

History

	History and politics	Religion and philosophy
1980	**1980** Black majority rule comes into force in Zimbabwe.	**1989** The 14th Dalai Lama (Tenzin Gyatso, b.1935) receives the Nobel Prize for Peace in recognition of his commitment to the non-violent liberation of Tibet.
	1980–8 Millions of lives are lost in the Iran–Iraq War.	
	1982 Falklands War; Britain retakes the Falkland Islands after invasion by Argentina.	
	1984 Indian Prime Minister Indira Gandhi (b.1917) is assassinated by Sikh extremists.	**1994** The Church of England ordains women priests.
	1986 Chernobyl nuclear reactor disaster, Ukraine, USSR.	**1995** Pope John Paul II participates in historic meetings aimed at discussing relations between the Orthodox and Roman Catholic churches.
	1988 Mikhail Gorbachev (1931–) becomes Soviet head of state and begins a programme of reform and restructuring.	
	1989 The Chinese Army crushes mass anti-government protests in Beijing's Tiananmen Square.	
	1990 East and West Germany are reunited.	
	1991 In the Gulf War a US-led United Nations coalition expels Iraqi forces from Kuwait.	
	1991 USSR breaks up; civil war in Yugoslavia.	
	1992 Yugoslavia breaks up; Czechoslovakia splits in two.	
	1994 Nelson Mandela (1918–) is elected South Africa's first black President.	
	1994 World Trade Organization founded.	
	1997 Britain returns Hong Kong to China.	
	1998 A tentative peace agreement is reached in Northern Ireland (Good Friday Agreement).	
	1999 Launch of the Euro, the single currency of the European Union.	
	1999 Inauguration of new Scottish Parliament and Welsh Assembly.	
	1999 NATO attacks Serbia over treatment of Albanians in Kosovo.	
2000	**2000** The leaders of North and South Korea have their first summit meeting in 50 years.	**2003** Rowan Williams is enthroned as Archbishop of Canterbury.
	2000 Israel and Palestine pursue peace, but the administration of Jerusalem remains a stumbling block and violence ensues.	**2003** Gene Robinson is consecrated as Episcopal Bishop of New Hampshire. He is the first openly homosexual bishop to be appointed.
	2001 World Trade Center, New York, destroyed in terrorist attack, killing thousands. The USA and its allies overthrow the Taliban regime in Afghanistan who were believed to be sheltering those responsible.	**2005** German cardinal Josef Ratzinger (1927–) becomes Pope Benedict XVI.
	2002 The Euro becomes the official currency of 12 states in the European Union.	**2005** John Sentamu is enthroned as Archbishop of York. He is the first black archbishop in the Church of England.
	2002 East Timor gains its independence from Indonesia.	
	2002 India and Pakistan come to the brink of war over Kashmir.	**2008** Pope Benedict XVI, on his first visit to the USA, expresses his shame at the recent scandals involving paedophile priests.
	2003 The USA and its allies overthrow Saddam Hussein's regime in Iraq.	
	2004 A massive earthquake off the coast of Indonesia causes a tsunami, affecting areas around the Indian Ocean. Over 225 000 people are killed.	
	2005 Suicide bombings on three Tube trains and a bus in London kill 52 people.	
	2006 Hamas wins Palestinian legislative elections. Many donor nations withhold aid from Palestinian authority.	
	2007 Power-sharing agreement in Northern Ireland.	
	2007 North Korea agrees to dismantle its nuclear facilities in return for fuel and aid.	
	2008 Fidel Castro steps down as Cuban leader after 49 years in power.	
	2008 Worldwide banking crisis. Governments resort to unprecedented emergency financial measures.	

History

Science and technology	Arts and culture	
1981 First use of the US space shuttle, a reusable crewed launch vehicle.	**1980** Italian novelist Umberto Eco (1932–) publishes *The Name of the Rose*.	**1980**
1983 Compact discs first come on the market.	**1982** Chilean novelist Isabel Allende (1942–) publishes *House of the Spirits*, a bestselling novel in the 'magical realist' style.	
1984 The Apple Macintosh personal computer is introduced.		
1984 The technique of 'DNA fingerprinting' is developed by English molecular biologist Alec Jeffreys (1950–).	**1982** US writer Alice Walker (1944–) publishes *The Color Purple*.	
	1984 English poet Ted Hughes (1930–98) is appointed Poet Laureate.	
1986 The Soviet space station Mir is launched as the first permanently manned space station.	**1987** US novelist Toni Morrison (1931–) publishes *Beloved*.	
1987 Work begins on the Channel Tunnel between England and France (completed 1994).	**1988** British novelist Salman Rushdie (1947–) publishes *The Satanic Verses*.	
1988 *A Brief History of Time*, an account of cosmology by English theoretical physicist Stephen Hawking (1942–), becomes a popular bestseller.	**1990** English composer Harrison Birtwistle (1934–) completes the opera *Gawain*.	
	1993 English sculptor Rachel Whiteread (1963–) completes *House*.	
1989 Creation of the World Wide Web.	**1993** British artist Damien Hirst (1965–) causes a sensation with his *Mother and Child, Divided*.	
1990 Start of the Human Genome Project.		
1990 The space shuttle *Discovery* launches the Hubble Space telescope; a problem with its primary mirror is soon apparent.	**1996** The new Globe Theatre opens in London.	
1993 British mathematician Andrew Wiles (1953–) announces his proof of Fermat's last theorem.	**1997** British author J K Rowling (1965–) publishes the first Harry Potter book, *Harry Potter and the Philospher's Stone*.	
1997 The first successful cloning of an animal results in 'Dolly' the sheep, at the Roslin Institute, Scotland.	**1998** Poet Laureate Ted Hughes (1930–98) publishes *Birthday Letters*.	
	1999 English poet Andrew Motion (1952–) is appointed Poet Laureate.	
2000 Researchers in the USA and Britain publish the first draft of the human genome map.	**2000** In London, Bankside Power Station reopens as the Tate Modern gallery.	**2000**
2000 The International Space Station is manned with its first long-term crew.	**2000** Northern Irish poet Seamus Heaney (1939–) publishes *Beowulf*.	
2002 The first synthetic virus is created, following the genome sequence for polio.	**2002** German professor Gunther von Hagens causes controversy with his *Body Worlds* exhibition in London of cadavers.	
2003 Scientists sequencing the human genome announce its completion.	**2004** British composer Sir Peter Maxwell Davies is appointed as Master of the Queen's Music.	
2004 NASA's *Spirit* lander sends back detailed pictures of the surface of Mars.		
2004 The international Cassini–Huygens spacecraft reaches Saturn.	**2004** *Reflecting Absence*, a design by architect Michael Arad and landscape architect Peter Walker, is chosen for the World Trade Center site memorial.	
2005 French surgeons carry out world's first face transplant.	**2006** Cartoons of Muhammad in a Danish newspaper lead to angry protests across the Muslim world.	
2006 Trials begin of a device that detects limb movement-related brain activity in paralysed people and converts it into signals that can be recognized by a computer.	**2008** End of three-month strike by Writers' Guild of America which threatened to halt US film and TV productions.	
2006 A vaccine that protects against certain strains of human papilloma virus, a major cause of cervical cancer, is licensed for use.		
2007 The first evidence of water vapour is detected in the atmosphere of a planet beyond the solar system.		
2007 Scientists in the USA and Japan announce they have made embryonic stem cells from ordinary skin cells.		
2008 The Large Hadron Collider particle accelerator at CERN in Switzerland goes into operation.		

Journeys of exploration

History

More is known about exploration that originated in Europe than anywhere else; lack of documentation means there is little detailed knowledge of non-European explorers, such as the Polynesians in the Pacific. This table comprises mainly European explorers; 'discovers' is used to indicate the first recorded visit by a European.

Date	Name	Exploration
490 BC	Hanno	Makes voyage round part of the coast of Africa
325 BC	Alexander the Great	Leads fleet along the N Indian coast and up the Persian Gulf
84 AD	Agricola	His fleet circumnavigates Britain
c.985	Erik the Red	Explores Greenland's coast and founds settlements there
1003	Leif Ericsson	Voyages to N America and discovers 'Vinland' (possibly Nova Scotia)
1405–33	Admiral Zheng He	Fleets of Chinese junks explore the Indian Ocean, reaching the African coast
1418	João Gonçalves Zarco	Discovers Madeira (dispatched by Henry the Navigator)
1434	Gil Eanes	Sails round Cape Bojadar (dispatched by Henry the Navigator)
1446	Dinís Dias	Discovers Cape Verde and the Senegal River (dispatched by Henry the Navigator)
1488	Bartolomeu Dias	Sails round the Cape of Storms (Cape of Good Hope)
1492	Christopher Columbus	Discovers the New World
1493	Christopher Columbus	Discovers Puerto Rico, Antigua and Jamaica
1497	John Cabot	Explores the coast of Newfoundland
1497	Vasco da Gama	Voyages round the Cape of Good Hope
1498	Vasco da Gama	Explores coast of Mozambique and discovers sea route to India
1498	Christopher Columbus	Discovers Trinidad and Venezuela
1499	Amerigo Vespucci	Discovers mouth of the River Amazon
1500	Pedro Alvares Cabral	Discovers Brazil
1500	Diogo Dias	Discovers Madagascar
1500	Gaspar Corte Real	Explores east coast of Greenland and Labrador
1501	Amerigo Vespucci	Explores S American coast
1502	Christopher Columbus	Explores Honduras and Panama
1513	Vasco Núñez de Balboa	Crosses the Panama Isthmus to discover the Pacific Ocean
1520	Ferdinand Magellan	Discovers the Straits of Magellan
1521	Ferdinand Magellan	Discovers the Philippines
1524	Giovanni da Verrazano	Discovers New York Bay and the Hudson River
1526	Sebastian Cabot	Explores the Rio de la Plata
1534	Jacques Cartier	Explores the Gulf of St Lawrence
1535	Jacques Cartier	Navigates the St Lawrence River
1536	Pedro de Mendoza	Founds Buenos Aires and explores Parana and Paraguay rivers
1539	Hernando de Soto	Explores Florida
1540	García López de Cárdenas	Discovers the Grand Canyon
1580	Francis Drake	Completes circumnavigation of the globe
1585	John Davis	Discovers Davis Strait on expedition to Greenland
1595	Walter Raleigh	Explores the Orinoco River
1610	Henry Hudson	Discovers Hudson's Bay
1616	William Baffin	Discovers Baffin Bay during search for the NW Passage
1617	Walter Raleigh	Begins expedition to Guiana
1642	Abel Janszoon Tasman	Discovers Van Diemen's Land (Tasmania) and New Zealand
1678	Robert Cavelier de la Salle	Explores the Great Lakes of Canada
1682	Robert Cavelier de la Salle	Follows the course of the Mississippi River to the Gulf of Mexico
1692	Ijsbrand Iders	Explores the Gobi Desert
1736	Anders Celsius	Undertakes expedition to Lapland
1761	Carsten Niebuhr	Undertakes expedition to Arabia
1766	Louis de Bougainville	Voyage of discovery in Pacific, names Navigator Is
1769	James Cook	Names Society Is; charts coasts of New Zealand and E Australia
1770	James Cook	Lands at Botany Bay, Australia
1772	James Bruce	Explores Abyssinia and the confluence of the Blue Nile and White Nile
1774	James Cook	Discoveries and rediscoveries in the Pacific; discovers and names S Georgia and the S Sandwich Is
1778	James Cook	Discovers Hawaiian group; surveys N American coast as far as the Bering Strait
1787	Horace Saussure	Makes first ascent of Mont Blanc
1790	George Vancouver	Explores the coast of NW America
1795	Mungo Park	Explores the course of the Niger

Date	Name	Exploration
1804–6	Meriwether Lewis and William Clark	Follow the Missouri and Columbia rivers to the Pacific
1818	John Ross	Attempts to discover NW Passage
1819	John Barrow	Enters Barrow Straits in the N Arctic
1823	Walter Oudney	Discovers Lake Chad in C Africa
1841	David Livingstone	Discovers Lake Ngami
1845	John Franklin	Attempts to discover NW Passage
1854	Richard Burton and John Speke	Explore interior of Somaliland
1855	David Livingstone	Discovers the Victoria Falls on the Zambesi River
1858	Richard Burton and John Speke	Discover Lake Tanganyika
1860	Robert Burke and William Wills	First expedition to cross the interior of Australia, south to north
1872–6	British Challenger expedition	Explores ocean floor, mapping depths, taking core samples and discovering 4417 new species
1875	Henry Morton Stanley	Traces the Congo to the Atlantic
1888	Fridtjof Nansen	Crosses Greenland
1893	Fridtjof Nansen	Attempts to reach N Pole
1905	Roald Amundsen	Sails through NW Passage
1909	Robert Peary	Reaches N Pole
1911	Roald Amundsen	Reaches S Pole
1912	Robert Scott	Reaches S Pole
1914	Ernest Shackleton	Leads expedition to the Antarctic
1953	Edmund Hillary and Tenzing Norgay	Make first ascent of Mt Everest
1961	Yuri Gagarin	Becomes first man in space
1969	Neil Armstrong and Buzz Aldrin	Make first landing on the moon
1997	Mars Pathfinder expedition	Unmanned rover explores surface of Mars
2005	Cassini–Huygens mission to Saturn	Huygens probe lands of Titan, largest moon of Saturn

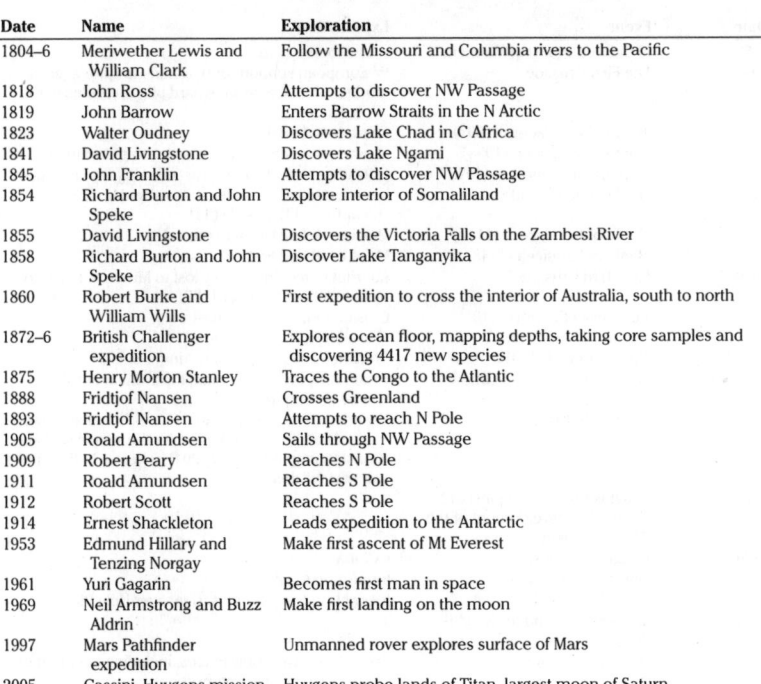

History

Major battles and wars

Date	Event	Explanation
c.1200 BC	Trojan Wars	Greeks v Trojans
490–479 BC	Persian Wars	Persia v Greek city states
490 BC	Battle of Marathon	Athens defeat of Persia
460–445 BC	First Peloponnesian War	Sparta v Athens
431–404 BC	Second Peloponnesian War	Sparta, Corinth, Persia v Athens
334–323 BC	Conquests of Alexander Great Battle of Granicus (334 BC) Battle of Issus (333 BC) Battle of Gaugamela (331 BC)	v Persia, Indian states
306 BC	Battle of Ipsus	'Battle of the Kings', warring 'successors' of Alexander the Great
264–241 BC	First Punic War	Rome v Carthage
218–202 BC	Second Punic War	Rome v Carthage
149–146 BC	Third Punic War	Destruction of Carthage
112–106 BC	Numidian War	Rome v Juguertia, King of Numidia
73–71 BC	Revolt of Spartacus	Slaves v Rome
58–51 BC	Gallic Wars of Caesar	Rome v Celtic tribes of Gaul (ancient France)
55 BC	Caesar's expedition to Britain	Rome v British tribes
48 BC	Battle of Pharsalus	Julius Caesar's defeat of Pompey
31 BC	Battle of Actium	Octavian's defeat of Anthony and Cleopatra
AD 70	Siege of Jerusalem	Rome v Israel (destruction of the Temple)
AD 84	Battle of Mons Graupius	Rome (Agricola) v Scottish tribes
AD 375–454	Hun raids on the Roman Empire	Attila v tribes of Gaul and Italy
665	Battle of Basra	Arabs conquered by Muslims
771–814	Conquests of Charles the Great (Charlemagne)	v Saxons, Lombards, Arabs (in Spain)
800–1016	Viking raids	v Britain, Normandy, Russia, Spain, Morocco, Italy
1066	Battle of Hastings and Norman Conquest of England	William (the Conqueror) v Harold II (King of Anglo Saxons)

History

Date	Event	Explanation
1089–94	El Cid's conquest of Valencia	v the Moors
1095–9	The First Crusade	W European support for Byzantine Empire against Turks; ostensibly to safeguard pilgrim routes to the Holy Places
	Battle of Dorylaeum (1097)	Crusaders defeat Turks
	Capture of Antioch (1098)	Crusaders defeat Turks; crusader state founded
	Capture of Jerusalem (1099)	Crusaders defeat Turks; crusader kingdom founded
1147–9	The Second Crusade	Intended to aid crusader states after Muslim recapture of Edessa (1144)
	Battle of Dorylaeum (1147)	Muslims defeat German crusaders
	Battle of Laodicea (1148)	Muslims defeat French crusaders
1089–92	The Third Crusade	Attempt to regain territory lost to Muslims; failed to retake Jerusalem (lost 1187)
	conquest of Cyprus (1191)	Crusader kingdom established
	capture of Acre (1191)	Crusader defeat of Muslims
	Battle of Arsuf (1191)	Crusader defeat of Muslims under Saladin
1190–1227	Conquests of Genghis Khan	v Naimans, Uigurs, N China, Kara-Chitai empire, Kharezm empire
1202–4	The Fourth Crusade	Intended to recover the Holy Places but diverted to part of Dalmatia (conquered for the Venetians) and Constantinople (sacked 1204), where a Latin empire was established
1211–1227	Genghis Khan's conquest of N China and development of the Mongol empire	
1206–1405	Mongol conquests	v China
1208–29	Albigensian Crusade	Inquisition v Cathars
1217–21	The Fifth Crusade	Inconclusive expeditions to recover Holy Places
1220	Fall of Samarkand to Genghis Khan	
1228–9	The Sixth Crusade	Crusaders regain Holy Places, including kingdom of Jerusalem, by negotiation
1248–54	The Seventh Crusade	Unsuccessful attempt to recapture Jerusalem (lost 1244)
1270–2	The Eighth Crusade	Attempt to recapture territory lost to Mameluks (1265, 1268); 11-year truce negotiated but all crusaders driven from Palestine by 1291
1282–1302	War of the Sicilian Vespers	Sicilian rebels v French rulers
1297–1305	Revolt of William Wallace	Scots v English
1314	Battle of Bannockburn	Scots (under Robert Bruce) v English
1337–1453	Hundred Years' War	England v France
	Battle of Sluys (1340)	English defeat of French
	Battle of Crécy (1346)	English defeat of French
	Battle of Poitiers (1356)	English defeat of French
	Battle of Agincourt (1415)	English defeat of French
1360–1405	Conquests of Tamerlane (Timur)	v Mongols, Persia, Russia, India
1388	Battle of Otterburn (Chevy Chase)	Scots' defeat of English (under Sir Henry Percy, 'Hotspur')
1403	Battle of Shrewsbury	Glendower and Percys defeated by Henry V
1411	Battle of Harlaw	Highland v Lowland Scots
1429	Siege of Orleans	Joan of Arc's defeat of English
1453	Fall of Constantinople	Turkish conquest of Byzantine Empire
1455–85	Wars of the Roses	Series of civil wars in England (House of York v House of Lancaster)
	Battle of St Albans (1455)	First battle of war: Yorkist victory
	Battle of Bosworth Field (1485)	Lancastrian victory: death of Richard III, accession of Henry VII
1491–2	Siege of Granada	Spanish defeat of Moors
1494–1559	Habsburg–Valois wars	
1513	Battle of Flodden	English defeat of Scots
1542	Battle of Solway Moss	English defeat of Scots
1546–7	War of the Schmalkaldic League	France v German Protestant Estates
1562	Massacre at Vassy	Huguenots killed by de Guise
1562–98	French Wars of Religion	Catholics v Huguenots
1568–1648	Dutch Wars of Independence	Successful revolt of Netherlands v Philip II of Spain
1571	Battle of Lepanto	Spanish and Italian defeat of Turkish navy
1572	St Bartholomew's Day Massacre	Slaughter of French Huguenots by Charles IX
1585–9	War of the Three Henries	Henry IV secures succession to French throne

History

Date	Event	Explanation
1587	Sack of Cadiz by Drake	Defeat of Philip II's Spanish ships
1588	Defeat of the Spanish Armada	English defeat of Spanish navy
1592–9	Japanese invasion of Korea	
1596–1603	Tyrone's Rebellion in Ireland	Irish v English
1605	Gunpowder Plot	Catholic conspiracy against James I and the English Parliament
1609–14	War of the Julich Succession	Protestant v Catholic powers of Europe
1618–48	Thirty Years' War	French king v Habsburg rulers
1620	Battle of the White Mountain (Prague)	Defeat of Bohemian Protestants
1628–31	War of the Mantuan Succession	France v Spain
1639	First Bishops' War	Scotland v England
1640	Second Bishops' War	Scots' defeat of English
1641–9	Great Irish Rebellion	Ireland v England
1642–6	English Civil War	Royalist forces of Charles I v Parliamentarians under Cromwell
	Battle of Marston Moor (1644)	Parliamentary defeat of Royalists
1688	The Glorious Revolution	William III and Mary II ascend English throne after flight of James II
1688–97	War of the League of Augsburg	European alliance's defeat of Louis XIV
1689	Battle of Killiecrankie	Highland Scots' defeat of government
1690	Battle of the Boyne	Defeat of James II's Catholic forces by Protestant William III
1692	Glencoe Massacre	Slaughter of McDonalds by Campbells (anti-Jacobite forces)
1701–14	War of the Spanish Succession	Grand Alliance v Louis XIV of France
1702–13	Queen Anne's War	Britain v France
1704	Battle of Blenheim	Allied troops' defeat of Louis XIV
1715–16	Jacobite Rebellion	Led by Earl of Mar v Hanoverians
	Battle of Sherrifmuir (1715)	Hanoverians v Jacobites, indecisive battle
1739–43	War of Jenkins' Ear	Britain v Spain
1740–8	War of the Austrian Succession	Prussia v Austria
1745–6	Jacobite Rebellion	Led by Charles Edward Stuart (Bonnie Prince Charlie)
	Battle of Prestonpans (1745)	Jacobite defeat of Hanoverians
	Battle of Culloden (1746)	Jacobite Highlanders crushed by Hanoverian forces
1756–63	Seven Years' War	Austria, France, Russia, Sweden and Saxony v Prussia, Britain and Portugal
	Battle of Quebec (1759)	British defeat of French
1763–6	Pontiac's War	Unsuccessful uprising of Native Americans v British colonists
1775–83	US War of Independence	American settlers v British government forces
	Battle of Bunker Hill (1775)	First battle of war; heavy British losses
	Battle of Stillwater or Saratoga (1777)	American defeat of British
	Battle of Yorktown (1781)	American defeat of British; decisive campaign of war
1789–92	French Revolution	Popular movement overthrowing *ancien régime* to establish new constitution
1792–1802	French Revolutionary Wars	French campaigns v various neighbouring states
	Battle of Valmy (1792)	French defeat of Prussians
	Battle of Aboukir Bay or the Nile (1798)	Napoleon's French fleet destroyed by Nelson
1800–15	Napoleonic Wars	Fought to preserve new French constitution and influence under Napoleon Bonaparte
	Battle of Austerlitz (1805)	French defeat of Austro-Russian army
	Battle of Trafalgar (1805)	British defeat of Napoleonic fleet
1808–14	Peninsular War	France v Britain
	Battle of Corunna (1809)	British commander Sir John Moore killed by French
1812	Napoleon's retreat from Moscow	
1814–16	Gurkha War	Gurkhas v British in India
1815	Battle of Waterloo	Napoleon defeated by Allied forces under Duke of Wellington
1821–32	Greek War of Independence	Greek rebellion v Turkish rule
1836	Texan War of Independence, Battle of the Alamo	Americans v Mexican rule
1838–9	Boer–Zulu War	
1839–42	First Opium War in China	British defeat of China
1843–51	Siege of Montevideo	Combined Argentine–Uruguayan army v Montevideo with French and British support

History

Date	Event	Explanation
1844–7	First Maori War	Maoris v British settlers in New Zealand
1846–7	Mexican War	USA v Mexico
1853–6	Crimean War	Britain v Russia
	Battle of Balaclava (1856)	Unsuccessful Russian attack on British base; heavy British losses
1856–60	Second Opium War in China	British defeat of China
1857–8	Mormon Utah War	Mormons v Federal Government of USA
1859	John Brown's raid on Harpers Ferry	Abolitionist attack on Federal arsenal
1859–61	Italian War of Unification	Austria v Italy and France
	Battle of Solferino (1859)	French defeat of Austria
1860–72	Second Maori War	Maoris v British settlers in New Zealand
1861–5	American Civil War	North (Union states) v South (Confederate)
	Battle of Shiloh (1862)	Heavy losses to both sides
	Battle of Gettysburg (1863)	Unionist defeat of Confederates
	Battles of Petersburg (1864)	Successful Unionist campaign v Confederates
1866	Seven Weeks' War	Prussia and Italy's defeat of Austria and allies
1876	Battle of Little Bighorn (Custer's Last Stand)	Defeat of US cavalry under General Custer by Sioux and Cheyenne
1879	Zulu War	British defeat of Zulus
1879–84	War of the Pacific	Chile v Peru and Bolivia
1880–1	First Boer War	Boers' defeat of British
1885	Fall of Khartoum	Mahdi defeat of Egyptians; death of British General Gordon
1890	Massacre of Wounded Knee	US defeat of Sioux
1899–1901	Boxer Uprising	Unsuccessful anti-foreign uprising in China
1899–1902	Great (Second) Boer War	Boers v British
	Battle of Ladysmith (1900)	Sieges of the British by the Boers
	Battle of Mafeking (1900)	
1911–12	Chinese Revolution	Overthrow of Manchu dynasty
1914–18	World War I	Triple Entente (Britain, France and Russia) v Triple Alliance (Germany, Austria–Hungary and Italy)
	Battles of Liège, Marne, Ypres and Tannenberg (1914)	Allied v German forces
	Dardanelles and Gallipoli campaigns (1915)	Unsuccessful Allied operations in Turkey
	Battles of Loos and Ypres (1915)	Britain v Germany
	Battle of Jutland (1916)	British fleet v German fleet
	Battle of Verdun (1916)	France v Germany
	Battle of Passchendaele (1917)	Third battle of Ypres, Britain v Germany
	Battles of Amiens, Antwerp and the Second Battle of the Somme (1918)	Allied v German forces
1916	Easter Rising in Dublin	Unsuccessful revolt by Irish nationalists v British rule
1917	Russian Revolution	Overthrow of monarchy and beginning of Communism
1918	Hungarian Revolution	Communist revolt
1932–7	Communist rebellion in China	
1935–6	Italian invasion of Abyssinia (Ethiopia)	Mussolini's troops v Abyssinia under Haile Selassie
1936–9	Spanish Civil War	Republicans v Nationalists
	Battle of Ebro River (1938)	Nationalist defeat of Republicans
1939–45	World War II	Allied forces (Britain, France, USA, USSR) v Germany, Italy, Japan
	Battle of Flanders, Evacuation of Dunkirk, Fall of France; Battle of Britain (1940)	Allied forces v Germany
	Babi Yar Massacre (1941)	German slaughter of Jews
	Bombing of Pearl Harbor (1941)	Japanese attack on US naval base
	Battle of Stalingrad and Moscow (1941–2)	Soviet defeat of Germany
	Battle of Tobruk (1941–2)	Allied v German forces in N Africa
	Battle of Midway Island (1942)	US defeat of Japanese air force
	Battle of El Alamein (1942)	British defeat of Rommel's Afrika Corps
	Battle of Singapore (1942)	Japanese siege and occupation
	Battle of Salerno, invasion of Sicily (1943)	Allied defeat of German and Italian forces in Italy
	Burma campaigns (1943–5)	British–Indian forces v Japan

History

Date	Event	Explanation
	D-Day invasion of Normandy (1944)	Allied defeat of German forces in France
	Battle of Anzio, Battle of Monte Cassino (1944)	Allied forces v Germany in Italy
	Battle of Arnhem (1944), Battle of the Bulge (1944–5)	Eventual Allied defeat of German forces in Low Countries
	Battle of Iwo Jima (1945)	Allied capture of Japanese airbase
	Battle of the Rhine (1945)	Allied defeat of Germany
1945–9	Chinese Civil War	Communist v non-communist forces
1946–54	French War of Indochina	Nationalist revolt v France
1947–8	Indian civil war	Pakistan v India
1950–3	Korean War	Communist v non-communist forces
1952–6	Mau-Mau uprisings in Kenya	Kikuyu revolt v white settlers
1956	Suez Invasion	Israel, Britain and France v Egypt
1956–1975	Vietnam War	North Vietnam (communist) v South Vietnam (non-communist) and US forces
1960–5	Civil war in the Congo (DR)	Mobutu seizes power in 1965, beginning 30-year dictatorship
1961	Bay of Pigs invasion	Cuban defeat of exiles supported by USA
1962–74	Mozambique War of Independence	Nationalist revolt against Portuguese rule
1967	Six-Day War	Israel v Arab states
1967–70	Nigerian–Biafran War	Nigerian defeat of Biafran separatists
1968	Soviet invasion of Czechoslovakia	Defeat of attempt at liberalization of communism
1968	Tet offensive in Vietnam	Viet Cong v South Vietnam and USA
1970–1	Jordanian civil war	Jordan v Palestinian guerillas
1970–5	Cambodian War	Cambodia, South Vietnam and USA v North Vietnam, Viet Cong and Khmer Rouge
1971	Civil war in Pakistan	East v West Pakistan
1974	Turkish invasion of Cyprus	Turkey v Greek Cypriots
1975–89	Lebanese civil war	Shia Muslims, Palestinians v Sunni Muslims, Maronite Christians, with interventions by Syria and Israel
1975–2002	Angolan civil war	Internal fighting after independence
1978–9	Ugandan civil war	Ugandan exiles and Tanzanian defeat of Idi Amin Dada's regime
1978	Israeli invasion of S Lebanon	Israel v Palestinian Liberation Organization (PLO)
1979–1992	Soviet invasion of Afghanistan	Afghan resistance to Soviet invasion and to the Soviet-backed government remaining after their withdrawal in 1988
1979	Iranian Revolution	Islamic republic established under Ayatollah Khomeini
1980–8	Iran–Iraq War	
1982	Falklands War	British defeat of Argentina
1982–90	Nicaraguan civil war	Contras (supported by USA) v Sandinistas (socialist junta)
1983	Invasion of Grenada	US troops on peace-restoring mission
1983–	Civil war in Sri Lanka	Tamil separatists v Sinhalese government
1986	Civil war in Haiti	Military coup and new constitution
1990–6	Civil war in Rwanda	Tutsi v Hutu groups
1991	Gulf War	Iraqi invasion of Kuwait in 1990 resulted in the defeat of Iraq by US-led allies (29 countries, including UK)
1991–5	Civil war in Yugoslavia	Declaration of independence from Yugoslavia by Slovenia, Macedonia, Croatia (1991) and Bosnia-Herzegovina (1992) developed into civil war between Croats, Bosnians (mainly Slavic Muslims) and Serbs, lasting longest in Bosnia-Herzegovina
1992–2001	Civil war in Afghanistan	Disputes between Islamic factions, and opposition to the Taliban regime
1996–2002	Civil war in the Democratic Republic of Congo (formerly Zaire)	Tutsi rebels invade and stage a coup; civil war continued with military intervention from neighbouring foreign armies
1997–9	Civil war in Sierra Leone	Military coup and subsequent violence by Revolutionary United Front
1999	Nato air-strikes on Serbia	Nato attacked Serbian military resources following the ethnic cleansing of Kosovo Albanians from their homes
2001	US and allied strikes on Afghanistan	US-led coalition overthrew the Taliban regime thought to be sheltering Al Qaeda terrorists

History

Date	Event	Explanation
2003	Iraq War	US-led coalition invaded Iraq, overthrowing the dictatorship of Saddam Hussein
2003–	Darfur conflict	Sudanese military and Janjaweed militia v rebel groups in western Sudan, with mass killings of civilians
2006	Israeli attacks on S Lebanon	Israel v Hizbollah guerrillas
2008–9	Israeli attack on Gaza	Israel v Hamas militia

Seven Wonders of the World

Originally compiled by Antipater of Sidon, a Greek poet, c.100 BC.

Pyramids of Egypt	Oldest and only surviving 'wonder'. Built c. 2000 BC as royal tombs, about 80 are still standing. The largest, the Great Pyramid of Cheops, at el-Gizeh, was 147m (481ft) high.
Hanging Gardens of Babylon	Terraced gardens adjoining Nebuchadnezzar's palace said to rise from 23–91m (75–300ft). Supposedly built by the king about 600 BC to please his wife, a princess from the mountains, but they are also associated with the Assyrian Queen Semiramis.
Statue of Zeus at Olympia	Carved by Phidias, the 12m (40ft) statue marked the site of the original Olympic Games c. 400 BC. It was constructed of ivory and gold, and showed Zeus (Jupiter) on his throne.
Temple of Artemis (Diana) at Ephesus	Constructed of Parian marble and more than 122m (400ft) long with over 100 columns 18m (60ft) high, it was begun about 350 BC and took some 120 years to build. Destroyed by the Goths in AD 262.
Mausoleum at Halicarnassus	Erected by Queen Artemisia in memory of her husband King Mausolus of Caria (in Asia Minor), who died 353 BC. It stood 43m (140ft) high. All that remains are a few pieces in the British Museum and the word 'mausoleum' in the English language.
Colossus of Rhodes	Gigantic bronze statue of sun-god Helios (or Apollo); stood about 36m (117ft) high, dominating the harbour entrance at Rhodes. The sculptor Chares supposedly laboured for 12 years before he completed it in 280 BC. It was destroyed by an earthquake in 224 BC.
Pharos of Alexandria	Marble lighthouse and watchtower built about 270 BC on the island of Pharos in Alexandria's harbour. Possibly standing 122m (400ft) high, it was destroyed by an earthquake in 1375.

Ancient Egyptian dynasties

Date BC	Dy-nasty	Period	Date BC	Dy-nasty	Period
c.3100–2890	I	**Early Dynastic Period**	1567–1320	XVIII	**New Kingdom**
c.2890–2686	II	(First use of stone in building.)	1320–1200	XIX	(Began with colonial
			1200–1085	XX	expansion, ended in
c.2686–2613	III	**Old Kingdom**			divided rule.)
c.2613–2494	IV	(The age of the great	1085–945	XXI	**Third Intermediate Period**
c.2494–2345	V	pyramid builders.	945–745	XXII	(Revival of prosperity and
c.2345–2181	VI	Longest reign in history:	745–718	XXIII	restoration of cults.)
		Pepi II, 90 years.)	718–715	XXIV	
c.2181–2173	VII	**First Intermediate Period**	715–668	XXV	
c.2173–2160	VIII	(Social order upset; few	664–525	XXVI	**Late Period**
c.2160–2130	IX	monuments built.)	525–404	XXVII	(Completion of Nile–Red
c.2130–2040	X		404–399	XXVIII	Sea canal. Alexander the
c.2133–1991	XI		399–380	XXIX	Great reached Alexandria
			380–343	XXX	in 332 BC.)
1991–1786	XII	**Middle Kingdom**	343–332	XXXI	
1786–1633	XIII	(Golden age of art and craftsmanship.)			
1786–c.1603	XIV	**Second Intermediate Period**			
1674–1567	XV	(Country divided into			
c.1684–1567	XVI	principalities.)			
c.1660–1567	XVII				

Chinese dynasties

Regnal dates	Name	Regnal dates	Name
c.22c–18c BC	Xia Dynasty	AD 317–420	Eastern Jin (Chin) Dynasty
c.18c–12c BC	Shang or Yin Dynasty	AD 420–589	Southern Dynasties
c.1122/1066–771 BC	Western Chou Dynasty	581–618	Sui Dynasty
771–256 BC	Eastern Chou Dynasty	618–907	Tang Dynasty
403–222 BC	Warring States Period	907–60	Five Dynasties and Ten
222–206 BC	Qin (Ch'in) Dynasty		Kingdoms Period
206 BC–AD 9	Western ('Former') Han	960–1279	Song (Sung) Dynasty
	Dynasty	1122–1234	Jin (Jurchen) Dynasty
AD 8–23	Interregnum (Wang Mang)	1279–1368	Yuan (Mongol) Dynasty
AD 25–220	Eastern Han Dynasty	1368–1644	Ming Dynasty
AD 220–80	Three Kingdoms Period	1644–1911	Qing (Manchu) Dynasty
AD 266–317	Western Jin (Chin) Dynasty		

Japanese emperors

The first 14 emperors (to Chuai) are regarded as legendary, and the regnal dates for the 15th to the 28th emperor (Senka), taken from the early Japanese chronicle, 'Nihon shoki', are not considered to be authentic.

The reign of an emperor is known by a name that is not necessarily the emperor's personal name.

Regnal dates	Name	Regnal dates	Name	Regnal dates	Name
660–585 BC	Jimmu	707–15	Gemmei	1210–21	Juntoku
581–549 BC	Suizei		(Empress)	1221	Chukyo
549–511 BC	Annei	715–24	Gensho (Empress)	1221–32	Go-Horikawa
510–477 BC	Itoku	724–49	Shomu	1232–42	Shijo
475–393 BC	Kosho	749–58	Koken (Empress)[2]	1242–6	Go-Saga
392–291 BC	Koan	758–64	Junnin	1246–59	Go-Fukakusa
290–215 BC	Korei	764–70	Shotoku	1259–74	Kameyama
214–158 BC	Kogen		(Empress)[2]	1274–87	Go-Uda
158–98 BC	Kaika	770–81	Konin	1287–98	Fushimi
97–30 BC	Sujin	781–806	Kammu	1298–1301	Go-Fushimi
29 BC–AD 70	Suinin	806–9	Heizei	1301–8	Go-Nijo
AD 71–130	Keiko	809–23	Saga	1308–18	Hanazono
AD 131–90	Seimu	823–33	Junna	1318–39	Go-Daigo
AD 192–200	Chuai	833–50	Nimmyo	1339–68	Go-Murakami
AD 270–310	Ojin	850–8	Montoku	1368–83	Chokei
AD 313–99	Nintoku	858–76	Seiwa	1383–92	Go-Kameyama
AD 400–5	Richu	876–84	Yozei		
AD 406–10	Hanzei	884–7	Koko	■ *Northern Court*	
AD 412–53	Ingyo	887–97	Uda		
AD 453–6	Anko	897–930	Daigo	1331–3	Kogon
AD 456–79	Yuryaku	930–46	Suzaku	1336–48	Komyo
AD 480–4	Seinei	946–67	Murakami	1348–51	Suko
AD 485–7	Kenzo	967–9	Reizei	1352–71	Go-Kogon
AD 488–98	Ninken	969–84	En-yu	1371–82	Go-Enyu
AD 498–506	Buretsu	984–6	Kazan	1382–1412	Go-Komatsu
507–31	Keitai	986–1011	Ichijo	1412–28	Shoko
531–5	Ankan	1011–16	Sanjo	1428–64	Go-Hanazono
535–9	Senka	1016–36	Go-Ichijo	1464–1500	Go-Tsuchimikado
539–71	Kimmei	1036–45	Go-Suzaku	1500–26	Go-Kashiwabara
572–85	Bidatsu	1045–68	Go-Reizei	1526–57	Go-Nara
585–7	Yomei	1068–72	Go-Sanjo	1557–86	Ogimachi
587–92	Sushun	1072–86	Shirakawa	1586–1611	Go-Yozei
592–628	Suiko (Empress)	1086–1107	Horikawa	1611–29	Go-Mizuno-o
629–41	Jomei	1107–23	Toba	1629–43	Meisho (Empress)
642–5	Kogyoku	1123–41	Sutoku	1643–54	Go-Komyo
	(Empress)[1]	1141–55	Konoe	1654–63	Go-Sai
645–54	Kotoku	1155–8	Go-Shirakawa	1663–87	Reigen
655–61	Saimei (Empress)[1]	1158–65	Nijo	1687–1709	Higashiyama
662–71	Tenji	1165–8	Rokujo	1709–35	Nakamikado
671–2	Kobun	1168–80	Takakura	1735–47	Sakuramachi
673–86	Temmu	1180–3	Antoku	1747–62	Momozono
686–97	Jito (Empress)	1183–98	Go-Toba	1762–70	Go-Sakuramachi
697–707	Mommu	1198–1210	Tsuchimikado		(Empress)

History

Regnal dates	Name	Regnal dates	Name	Regnal dates	Name
1770–9	Go-Momozono	1846–66	Komei	1926–89	Shōwa
1779–1817	Kokaku	1867–1912	Meiji	1989–	Heisei
1817–46	Ninko	1912–26	Taisho		

[1] Same empress although reigns have different names.
[2] Same empress although reigns have different names.

Roman kings and emperors

The founding of Rome by Romulus is a Roman literary tradition. Rome was ruled by kings until the last of them was expelled in 510 BC and a republic was established. In the power struggle that followed the assassination in 44 BC of the dictator Julius Caesar, Octavian emerged victorious, becoming the first Roman emperor in 27 BC under the title Augustus.

Dates of emperors overlap where there are periods of joint rule (eg Marcus Aurelius and Lucius Verus) and where the government of the empire divides between east and west.

Regnal dates	Name	Regnal dates	Name
■ *Kings*		AD 253–60	Valerian
753–715 BC	Romulus	AD 253–68	Gallienus
715–673 BC	Numa Pompilius	AD 268–9	Claudius II (the Goth)
673–642 BC	Tullus Hostilius	AD 269–70	Quintillus
642–616 BC	Ancus Marcius	AD 270–5	Aurelian
616–578 BC	Tarquinius Priscus	AD 275–6	Tacitus
578–534 BC	Servius Tullius	AD 276	Florian
534–509 BC	Tarquinius Superbus	AD 276–82	Probus
		AD 282–3	Carus
■ *Emperors*		AD 283–5	Carinus
27 BC–AD 14	Augustus (Caesar Augustus)	AD 283–4	Numerian
AD 14–37	Tiberius	AD 284–305	Diocletian (East)
AD 37–41	Caligula (Gaius Caesar)	AD 286–305	Maximian (West)
AD 41–54	Claudius	AD 305–11	Galerius (East)
AD 54–68	Nero	AD 305–6	Constantius I
AD 68–9	Galba	AD 306–7	Severus (West)
AD 69	Otho	AD 306–12	Maxentius (West)
AD 69	Vitellius	AD 306–37	Constantine I
AD 69–79	Vespasian	AD 308–24	Licinius (East)
AD 79–81	Titus	AD 337–40	Constantine II
AD 81–96	Domitian	AD 337–50	Constans I
AD 96–8	Nerva	AD 337–50	Constantius II
AD 98–117	Trajan	AD 350–1	Magnentius
AD 117–138	Hadrian	AD 360–3	Julian
AD 138–161	Antoninus Pius	AD 364–75	Valentinian I (West)
AD 161–180	Marcus Aurelius	AD 364–78	Valens (East)
AD 161–9	Lucius Verus	AD 365–6	Procopius (East)
AD 176–192	Commodus	AD 375–83	Gratian (West)
AD 193	Pertinax	AD 375–92	Valentinian II (West)
AD 193	Didius Julianus	AD 379–95	Theodosius I
AD 193–211	Septemius Severus	AD 395–408	Arcadius (East)
AD 198–217	Caracalla	AD 395–423	Honorius (West)
AD 209–12	Geta	AD 408–50	Theodosius II (East)
AD 217–18	Macrinus	AD 421–3	Constantius III (West)
AD 218–22	Elagabalus	AD 423–55	Valentinian III (West)
AD 222–35	Alexander Severus	AD 450–7	Marcian (East)
AD 235–38	Maximin	AD 455	Petronius Maximus (West)
AD 238	Gordian I	AD 455–6	Avitus (West)
AD 238	Gordian II	AD 457–74	Leo I (East)
AD 238	Maximus	AD 457–61	Majorian (West)
AD 238	Balbinus	AD 461–7	Libius Severus (West)
AD 238–44	Gordian III	AD 467–72	Anthemius (West)
AD 244–9	Philip	AD 472–3	Olybrius (West)
AD 249–51	Decius	AD 474–80	Julius Nepos (West)
AD 251	Hostilian	AD 474	Leo II (East)
AD 251–3	Gallus	AD 474–91	Zeno (East)
AD 253	Aemilian	AD 475–6	Romulus Augustus (West)

Mughal emperors

The second Mughal emperor, Humayun, lost his throne in 1540, became a fugitive, and did not regain his title until 1555.

Regnal dates	Name	Regnal dates	Name
1526–30	Babur	1719	Rafi-ud-Daulat
1530–56	Humayun	1719	Neku-siyar
1556–1605	Akbar I (the Great)	1719	Ibrahim
1605–27	Jahangir	1719–48	Muhammad Shah
1627–58	Shah Jahan	1748–54	Ahmad Shah
1658–1707	Aurangzeb (Alamgir)	1754–9	Alamgir II
1707–12	Bahadur Shah I (Shah Alam I)	1759–1806	Shah Alam II
1712–13	Jahandar Shah	1806–37	Akbar II
1713–19	Farruk-siyar	1837–57	Bahadur Shah II
1719	Rafid-ud-Darajat		

European monarchs

Austria

The head of the German branch of the Habsburg Dynasty held the (elective) title of Holy Roman Emperor with few interruptions from medieval times until 1804, when the title 'Emperor of Austria' was adopted.

Regnal dates	Name
■ *Habsburg Dynasty*	
1440–93	Frederick III
1493–1519	Maximilian I
1519–58	Charles V
1558–64	Ferdinand I
1564–76	Maximilian II
1576–1612	Rudolf II
1612–19	Matthias
1619–37	Ferdinand II
1637–57	Ferdinand III
1658–1705	Leopold I
1705–11	Joseph I
1711–40	Charles VI
1740–2	*Interregnum*
1742–5	Charles VII
1745–65	Francis I
1765–90	Joseph II
1790–2	Leopold II
1792–1835	Francis II
1835–48	Ferdinand I
1848–1916	Francis Joseph
1916–18	Charles I

Belgium

Belgium became an independent kingdom in 1831. A national congress elected Prince Leopold of Saxe-Coburg as king.

Regnal dates	Name
1831–65	Leopold I
1865–1909	Leopold II
1909–34	Albert I
1934–51	Leopold III
1951–93	Baudouin
1993–	Albert II

Denmark

Regnal dates	Name
1448–81	Christian I
1481–1513	John
1513–23	Christian II
1523–34	Frederick I
1534–59	Christian III
1559–88	Frederick II
1588–1648	Christian IV
1648–70	Frederick III
1670–99	Christian V
1699–1730	Frederick IV
1730–46	Christian VI
1746–66	Frederick V
1766–1808	Christian VII
1808–39	Frederick VI
1839–48	Christian VIII
1848–63	Frederick VII
1863–1906	Christian IX
1906–12	Frederick VIII
1912–47	Christian X
1947–72	Frederick IX
1972–	Margrethe II

England

Regnal dates	Name
■ *West Saxon Kings*	
802–39	Egbert
839–58	Æthelwulf
858–60	Æthelbald
860–5	Æthelbert
866–71	Æthelred
871–99	Alfred
899–924	Edward (the Elder)
924–39	Athelstan
939–46	Edmund
946–55	Edred
955–9	Edwy
959–75	Edgar
975–8	Edward (the Martyr)
978–1016	Æthelred (the Unready)
1016	Edmund (Ironside)

Regnal dates	Name
■ *Danish Kings*	
1016–35	Knut (Canute)
1035–7	Harold *Regent*
1037–40	Harold I (Harefoot)
1040–2	Hardaknut
1042–66	Edward (the Confessor)
1066	Harold II
■ *House of Normandy*	
1066–87	William I (the Conqueror)
1087–1100	William II (Rufus)
1100–35	Henry I
■ *House of Blois*	
1135–54	Stephen
■ *House of Plantagenet*	
1154–89	Henry II
1189–99	Richard I (Cœur de Lion)
1199–1216	John
1216–72	Henry III
1272–1307	Edward I
1307–27	Edward II
1327–77	Edward III
1377–99	Richard II
■ *House of Lancaster*	
1399–1413	Henry IV
1413–22	Henry V
1422–61	Henry VI
■ *House of York*	
1461–70	Edward IV
■ *House of Lancaster*	
1470–1	Henry VI
■ *House of York*	
1471–83	Edward IV
1483	Edward V
1483–5	Richard III
■ *House of Tudor*	
1485–1509	Henry VII
1509–47	Henry VIII
1547–53	Edward VI

History

Regnal dates	Name
1553–8	Mary I
1558–1603	Elizabeth I

Finland

Finland was under Swedish control from the 13c until it was ceded to Russia in 1809 by the Treaty of Friedrichsham. Russian rulers then assumed the title of Grand Duke of Finland. In 1917 it became an independent monarchy. However in November 1918, after initially accepting the throne the previous month, Landgrave Frederick Charles of Hesse, the brother-in-law of the German Emperor William II, withdrew his acceptance because of the Armistice and the ensuing abdication of William II. The previous regent remained in power until a republic was declared in July 1919.

Regnal dates	Name
1918	Dr Pehr Evind Svinhufvud *Regent*
1918	Landgrave Frederick Charles of Hesse (withdrew acceptance)
1918–19	Dr Pehr Evind Svinhufvud

France

France became a republic in 1793, and an empire in 1804 under Napoleon Bonaparte. The monarchy was restored in 1814 and then once more dissolved in 1848.

Regnal dates	Name
■ *House of Capet*	
987–996	Hugh Capet
996–1031	Robert II
1031–60	Henry I
1060–1108	Philip I
1108–37	Louis VI
1137–80	Louis VII
1180–1223	Philip II Augustus
1223–6	Louis VIII
1226–70	Louis IX
1270–85	Philip III
1285–1314	Philip IV
1314–16	Louis X
1316	John I
1316–22	Philip V
1322–8	Charles IV
■ *House of Valois*	
1328–50	Philip VI
1350–64	John II
1364–80	Charles V
1380–1422	Charles VI

Regnal dates	Name
1422–61	Charles VII
1461–83	Louis XI
1483–98	Charles VIII
1498–1515	Louis XII
1515–47	Francis I
1547–59	Henry II
1559–60	Francis II
1560–74	Charles IX
1574–89	Henry III
■ *House of Bourbon*	
1589–1610	Henry IV (of Navarre)
1610–43	Louis XIII
1643–1715	Louis XIV
1715–74	Louis XV
1774–93	Louis XVI
1793–1814	*Republican and Bonapartist regimes*
1814–24	Louis XVIII
1824–30	Charles X
1830–48	Louis-Philippe

Germany

Modern Germany was united under Prussia in 1871; it became a republic (1919) after World War I and the abdication of William II in 1918.

Regnal dates	Name
1871–88	William I
1888	Frederick
1888–1918	William II

Greece

In 1832 the Greek National Assembly elected Otto of Bavaria as King of modern Greece. In 1917 Constantine I abdicated the throne in favour of his son Alexander. In 1920 a plebiscite voted for his return. In 1922 he again abdicated. In 1923 the monarchy was deposed and a republic was proclaimed in 1924. In 1935 a plebiscite restored the monarchy until in 1967 a military junta staged a coup. The monarchy was formally abolished in 1973; Greece became a republic again in 1975.

Regnal dates	Name
1832–62	Otto of Bavaria
1863–1913	George I (of Denmark)
1913–17	Constantine I
1917–20	Alexander
1920–2	Constantine I
1922–3	George II
1924–35	*Republic*
1935–47	George II
1947–64	Paul
1964–7	Constantine II

Italy

Modern Italy became a united kingdom in 1861; it became a republic in 1946.

Regnal dates	Name
1861–78	Victor Emmanuel II
1878–1900	Humbert I
1900–46	Victor Emmanuel III
1946	Humbert II

Luxembourg

The Duchy of Luxembourg formally separated from the Netherlands in 1890.

Regnal dates	Name
1890–1905	Adolf of Nassau
1905–12	William
1912–19	Marie Adélaïde
1919–64	Charlotte
1964–2000	John
2000–	Henry

The Netherlands

The House of Orange were hereditary Stadholders and Captains-General of the Netherlands until the French Revolutionary Wars, taking the title 'King of the United Provinces of the Netherlands' after the post-Napoleonic settlement reunited the southern and northern provinces.

Regnal dates	Name
1572–84	William the Silent
1584–1625	Maurice
1625–47	Frederick Henry
1647–50	William II
1672–1702	William III
1747–51	William IV
1751–95	William V
1794–1813	*French Revolutionary and Bonapartist regimes*
1813–40	William I
1840–9	William II
1849–90	William III
1890–1948	Wilhelmina
1948–80	Juliana
1980–	Beatrix

Portugal

The Count of Portugal assumed the title 'King of Portugal' in 1139. From 1383 to 1385 the Portuguese throne was the subject of a dispute between John of Castile and John of Aviz. In 1826 Peter IV (I of Brazil) renounced his right to the Portuguese throne in order to remain in Brazil. His abdication was contingent upon his successor and daughter, Maria II, marrying her uncle, Miguel. In 1828 Miguel usurped the throne on his own behalf. In 1834 Miguel was deposed and Maria II was restored to the throne. In 1910 Manuel II was deposed and Portugal became a republic.

Regnal dates	Name
1112–85	Alfonso I
1185–1211	Sancho I
1211–23	Alfonso II
1223–45	Sancho II
1245–79	Alfonso III
1279–1325	Diniz
1325–57	Alfonso IV
1357–67	Peter I
1367–83	Ferdinand

■ *House of Avis*
1385–1433	John I
1433–8	Edward
1438–81	Alfonso V
1481–95	John II
1495–1521	Manuel I
1521–57	John III
1557–78	Sebastian

■ *House of Habsburg*
1580–98	Philip I (II of Spain)
1598–1621	Philip II (III of Spain)
1621–40	Philip III (IV of Spain)

■ *House of Braganza*
1640–56	John IV
1656–83	Alfonso VI
1683–1706	Peter II
1706–50	John V
1750–77	Joseph
1777–1816	Maria I
1777–86	Peter III (King Consort)
1816–26	John VI
1826	Peter IV (Emperor of Brazil, as Peter I, 1822–31)
1826–8	Maria II
1828–34	Miguel
1834–53	Maria II
1853–61	Peter V (Emperor of Brazil, as Peter II, 1831–89)
1861–89	Luis
1889–1908	Charles
1908–10	Manuel II

Russia

In 1610 Vasili Shuisky was deposed as Tsar and the throne remained vacant until the election of Michael Romanov in 1613. In 1682 a condition of the succession was that the two step-brothers, Ivan V and Peter I (the Great) should jointly be proclaimed as Tsars. In 1917 the empire was overthrown and Tsar Nicholas II was forced to abdicate.

Regnal dates	Name
1283–1303	Daniel
1303–25	Yuri
1325–41	Ivan I
1341–53	Simeon
1353–9	Ivan II
1359–89	Dimitri Donskoi
1389–1425	Vasili I
1425–62	Vasili II
1462–1505	Ivan III (the Great)
1505–33	Vasili III
1533–84	Ivan IV (the Terrible)
1584–98	Feodor I
1598–1605	Boris Godunov
1605	Feodor II
1605–6	Dimitri II
1606–10	Vasili IV Shuisky

■ *House of Romanov*
1613–45	Michael
1645–76	Alexei
1676–82	Feodor III
1682–96	Ivan V
1682–1725	Peter I (the Great)
1725–7	Catherine I
1727–30	Peter II
1730–40	Anne
1740–1	Ivan VI
1741–62	Elizabeth
1762	Peter III
1762–96	Catherine II (the Great)
1796–1801	Paul
1801–25	Alexander I
1825–55	Nicholas I
1855–81	Alexander II
1881–94	Alexander III
1894–1917	Nicholas II

Scotland

When the Athol line died out in 1290, the crown was awarded to John Balliol by adjudication of Edward I of England; Edward declared John Balliol to have forfeited the throne for contumacy in 1296 and took the government of Scotland into his own hands. In 1332 Edward Balliol, son of John Balliol, was crowned King of Scots; he was expelled a few months later but was restored and reigned 1333–6.

Regnal dates	Name
1005–34	Malcolm II

■ *House of Athol*
1034–40	Duncan I
1040–57	Macbeth
1057–8	Lulach
1058–93	Malcolm III
1093–4	Donald III (Donald Bane)

Regnal dates	Name
1094	Duncan II
1094–7	Donald III (Donald Bane)
1097–1107	Edgar
1107–24	Alexander I
1124–53	David I
1153–65	Malcolm IV
1165–1214	William I
1214–49	Alexander II
1249–86	Alexander III
1286–90	Margaret
1290–2	*Interregnum*

■ *House of Balliol*
1292–96	John Balliol
1296–1306	*Interregnum*

■ *House of Bruce*
1306–29	Robert I (the Bruce)
1329–71	David II

■ *House of Stewart*
1371–90	Robert II
1390–1406	Robert III
1406–37	James I
1437–60	James II
1460–88	James III
1488–1513	James IV
1513–42	James V
1542–67	Mary, Queen of Scots
1567–1625	James VI[1]

[1] In 1603, James VI succeeded Elizabeth I on the English throne (Union of the Crowns) and united the thrones of Scotland and England.

Spain

Philip V abdicated in favour of Luis in 1724, but returned to the throne in the same year following Luis' death. After the French invasion of Spain in 1808, Napoleon set up Joseph Bonaparte as king. In 1814 Ferdinand was restored to the crown. In 1868 a revolution deposed Isabella II. In 1870 Amadeus of Savoy was elected as king. In 1873 he resigned the throne and a temporary republic was formed. In 1874 Alfonso XII restored the Bourbon dynasty to the throne. In 1931 Alfonso XIII was deposed and a republican constitution was proclaimed. From 1939 Franco ruled Spain under a dictatorship until his death in 1975 and the restoration of King Juan Carlos.

Regnal dates	Name

■ *House of Habsburg*
1516–56	Charles I (Emperor Charles V)
1556–98	Philip II
1598–1621	Philip III
1621–65	Philip IV
1665–1700	Charles II

History

Regnal dates	Name
House of Bourbon	
1700–24	Philip V
1724	Luis
1724–46	Philip V
1746–59	Ferdinand VI
1759–88	Charles III
1788–1808	Charles IV
1808	Ferdinand VII
1808–14	*Bonapartist regime*
1814–33	Ferdinand VII
1833–68	Isabella II
1870–3	Amadeus of Savoy
1873–4	*First Republic*
1874–85	Alfonso XII
1886–1931	Alfonso XIII
1931–75	*Second Republic and Franco dictatorship*
1975–	Juan Carlos

Sweden

Sigismund, a Catholic, was driven from the throne by the Protestant nobility, led by his uncle, who became regent before accepting the crown in 1604. On Christina's abdication in 1654, she nominated her cousin as heir. In 1720, Ulrika Eleonora abdicated in favour of her husband, Frederick of Hesse, who died without heirs, when the throne passed to Adolf Frederick, whose succession was imposed by Russia as a term of an armistice. The childless Charles XIII was succeeded by the French marshal Jean Baptiste Jules Bernadotte, selected as heir by the Diet in 1810.

Regnal dates	Name
House of Vasa	
1523–60	Gustav I
1560–8	Erik XIV
1568–92	John III
1592–9	Sigismund
1599–1604	*Regency*
1604–11	Charles IX
1611–32	Gustav II Adolf
1632–54	Christina
House of Zweibrucken	
1654–60	Charles X Gustav
1660–97	Charles XI
1697–1718	Charles XII
1718–20	Ulrika Eleonora
House of Hesse	
1720–51	Fredrik
House of Oldenburg-Holstein-Gottorp	
1751–71	Adolf Fredrick
1771–92	Gustav III
1792–1809	Gustav IV Adolf
1809–18	Charles XIII
House of Bernadotte	
1818–44	Charles XIV John
1844–59	Oscar I
1859–72	Charles XV
1872–1907	Oscar II
1907–50	Gustav V
1950–73	Gustav VI Adolf
1973–	Carl XVI Gustav

United Kingdom

Regnal dates	Name
House of Stuart	
1603–25	James I (VI of Scotland)
1625–49	Charles I
Commonwealth and Protectorate	
1649–53	Council of State
1653–8	Oliver Cromwell Lord Protector
1658–9	Richard Cromwell Lord Protector
House of Stuart (restored)	
1660–85	Charles II
1685–8	James II (VII of Scotland)
1689–94	William III (*jointly with* Mary II)
1694–1702	William III (*alone*)
1702–14	Anne
House of Hanover	
1714–27	George I
1727–60	George II
1760–1820	George III
1820–30	George IV
1830–7	William IV
1837–1901	Victoria
House of Saxe-Coburg-Gotha	
1901–10	Edward VII
House of Windsor	
1910–36	George V
1936	Edward VIII
1936–52	George VI
1952–	Elizabeth II

Emperors of the Holy Roman Empire

Regnal dates	Name
800–14	Charles I (Charlemagne)
814–40	Louis I (the Pious)
840–3	*Civil war*
843–55	Lothair I
855–75	Louis II
875–7	Charles II (the Bald)
877–81	*Interregnum*
881–7	Charles III (the Fat)
887–91	*Interregnum*
891–4	Guido of Spoleto
892–8	Lambert of Spoleto[1]
896–9	Arnulf[2]
901–5	Louis III
905–24	Berengar
911–18	Conrad I[2 4]
919–36	Henry I (the Fowler)[4]
936–73	Otto I (the Great)
973–83	Otto II
983–1002	Otto III
1002–24	Henry II (the Saint)
1024–39	Conrad II
1039–56	Henry III (the Black)

Regnal dates	Name
1056–1106	Henry IV
1077–80	Rudolf[2 4]
1081–93	Hermann[2 4]
1093–1101	Conrad[2 4]
1106–25	Henry V
1125–37	Lothair II
1138–52	Conrad III[4]
1152–90	Frederick I (Barbarossa)
1190–7	Henry VI
1198–1214	Otto IV
1198–1208	Philip[2 4]
1215–50	Frederick II
1246–7	Henry Raspe[2 4]
1247–56	William of Holland[2 4]
1250–4	Conrad IV[4]
1254–73	*Great Interregnum*
1257–72	Richard[2 4]
1257–75	Alfonso (Alfonso X of Castile)[2 4]
1273–91	Rudolf I[4]
1292–8	Adolf[4]
1298–1308	Albert I[4]
1308–13	Henry VII

Regnal dates	Name		Regnal dates	Name
1314–26	Frederick (III)[3][4]		1612–19	Matthias[4]
1314–46	Louis IV		1619–37	Ferdinand II[4]
1346–78	Charles IV		1637–57	Ferdinand III[4]
1378–1400	Wenceslas[4]		1658–1705	Leopold I[4]
1400–10	Rupert[4]		1705–11	Joseph I[4]
1410–37	Sigismund		1711–40	Charles VI[4]
1438–9	Albert II[4]		1740–2	*Interregnum*
1440–93	Frederick III		1742–5	Charles VII[4]
1493–1519	Maximilian I[4]		1745–65	Francis I[4]
1519–56	Charles V[4]		1765–90	Joseph II[4]
1556–64	Ferdinand I[4]		1790–2	Leopold II[4]
1564–76	Maximilian II[4]		1792–1806	Francis II[4]
1576–1612	Rudolf II[4]			

[1] Co-emperor
[2] Rival
[3] Co-regent
[4] Ruler not crowned at Rome; therefore, strictly speaking, only King of Germany

Popes

Antipopes (those who claimed to be pope in opposition to those canonically chosen) are given in square brackets. All dates are AD.

until c.64	Peter	402–17	Innocent I	678–81	Agatho
c.64–c.76	Linus	417–18	Zosimus	682–3	Leo II
c.76–c.90	Anacletus	418–22	Boniface I	684–5	Benedict II
c.90–c.99	Clement I	[418–19	Eulalius]	685–6	John V
c.99–c.105	Evaristus	422–32	Celestine I	686–7	Conon
c.105–c.117	Alexander I	432–40	Sixtus III	[687	Theodore]
c.117–c.127	Sixtus I	440–61	Leo I	[687–92	Paschal]
c.127–c.137	Telesphorus	461–8	Hilarius	687–701	Sergius I
c.137–c.140	Hyginus	468–83	Simplicius	701–5	John VI
c.140–c.154	Pius I	483–92	Felix III (II)	705–7	John VII
c.154–c.166	Anicetus	492–6	Gelasius I	708	Sisinnius
c.166–c.175	Soter	496–8	Anastasius II	708–15	Constantine
175–89	Eleutherius	498–514	Symmachus	715–31	Gregory II
189–98	Victor I	[498, 501–5	Laurentius]	731–41	Gregory III
198–217	Zephyrinus	514–23	Hormisdas	741–52	Zacharias
217–22	Callistus I	523–6	John I	752	Stephen II (*not*
[217–c.235	Hippolytus]	526–30	Felix IV (III)		*consecrated*)
222–30	Urban I	530–2	Boniface II	752–7	Stephen II (III)
230–5	Pontian	[530	Dioscorus]	757–67	Paul I
235–6	Anterus	533–5	John II	[767–9	Constantine (II)]
236–50	Fabian	535–6	Agapetus I	[768	Philip]
251–3	Cornelius	536–7	Silverius	768–72	Stephen III (IV)
[251–c.258	Novatian]	537–55	Vigilius	772–95	Adrian I
253–4	Lucius I	556–61	Pelagius I	795–816	Leo III
254–7	Stephen I	561–74	John III	816–17	Stephen IV (V)
257–8	Sixtus II	575–9	Benedict I	817–24	Paschal I
259–68	Dionysius	579–90	Pelagius II	824–7	Eugenius II
269–74	Felix I	590–604	Gregory I	827	Valentine
275–83	Eutychianus	604–6	Sabinianus	827–44	Gregory IV
283–96	Caius	607	Boniface III	[844	John]
296–304	Marcellinus	608–15	Boniface IV	844–7	Sergius II
308–9	Marcellus I	615–18	Deusdedit *or*	847–55	Leo IV
310	Eusebius		Adeodatus I	855–8	Benedict III
311–14	Miltiades	619–25	Boniface V	[855	Anastasius (III)]
314–35	Sylvester I	625–38	Honorius I	858–67	Nicholas I
336	Mark	640	Severinus	867–72	Adrian II
337–52	Julius I	640–2	John IV	872–82	John VIII
352–66	Liberius	642–9	Theodore I	882–4	Marinus I
[355–65	Felix (II)]	649–55	Martin I	884–5	Adrian III
366–84	Damasus I	654–7	Eugenius I[1]	885–91	Stephen V (VI)
[366–7	Ursinus]	657–72	Vitalian	891–6	Formosus
384–99	Siricius	672–6	Adeodatus II	896	Boniface VI
399–401	Anastasius I	676–8	Donus	896–7	Stephen VI (VII)

History

History

897	Romanus	1118–19	Gelasius II	[1425–30	Benedict (XIV)]
897	Theodore II	[1118–21	Gregory (VIII)]	1431–47	Eugenius IV
898–900	John IX	1119–24	Callistus II	[1439–49	Felix (V)]
900–3	Benedict IV	1124–30	Honorius II	1447–55	Nicholas V
903	Leo V	[1124	Celestine (II)]	1455–8	Callistus III
[903–4	Christopher]	1130–43	Innocent II	1458–64	Pius II
904–11	Sergius III	[1130–8	Anacletus (II)]	1464–71	Paul II
911–13	Anastasius III	[1138	Victor (IV)][2]	1471–84	Sixtus IV
913–14	Lando	1143–4	Celestine II	1484–92	Innocent VIII
914–28	John X	1144–5	Lucius II	1492–1503	Alexander VI
928	Leo VI	1145–53	Eugenius III	1503	Pius III
928–31	Stephen VII (VIII)	1153–4	Anastasius IV	1503–13	Julius II
931–5	John XI	1154–9	Adrian IV	1513–21	Leo X
936–9	Leo VII	1159–81	Alexander III	1522–3	Adrian VI
939–42	Stephen VIII (IX)	[1159–64	Victor (IV)][2]	1523–34	Clement VII
942–6	Marinus II	[1164–8	Paschal (III)]	1534–49	Paul III
946–55	Agapetus II	[1168–78	Callistus (III)]	1550–5	Julius III
955–64	John XII	[1179–80	Innocent (III)]	1555	Marcellus II
[963–5	Leo (VIII)]	1181–5	Lucius III	1555–9	Paul IV
964–6	Benedict V	1185–7	Urban III	1559–65	Pius IV
965–72	John XIII	1187	Gregory VIII	1566–72	Pius V
973–4	Benedict VI	1187–91	Clement III	1572–85	Gregory XIII
[974, 984–5	Boniface (VII)]	1191–8	Celestine III	1585–90	Sixtus V
974–83	Benedict VII	1198–1216	Innocent III	1590	Urban VII
983–4	John XIV	1216–27	Honorius III	1590–1	Gregory XIV
985–96	John XV	1227–41	Gregory IX	1591	Innocent IX
996–9	Gregory V	1241	Celestine IV	1592–1605	Clement VIII
[997–8	John (XVI)]	1243–54	Innocent IV	1605	Leo XI
999–1003	Sylvester II	1254–61	Alexander IV	1605–21	Paul V
1003	John XVII	1261–4	Urban IV	1621–3	Gregory XV
1004–9	John XVIII	1265–8	Clement IV	1623–44	Urban VIII
1009–12	Sergius IV	1271–6	Gregory X	1644–55	Innocent X
1012–24	Benedict VIII	1276	Innocent V	1655–67	Alexander VII
[1012	Gregory (VI)]	1276	Adrian V	1667–9	Clement IX
1024–32	John XIX	1276–7	John XXI[3]	1670–6	Clement X
1032–44	Benedict IX	1277–80	Nicholas III	1676–89	Innocent XI
1045	Sylvester III	1281–5	Martin IV	1689–91	Alexander VIII
1045	Benedict IX	1285–7	Honorius IV	1691–1700	Innocent XII
	(second	1288–92	Nicholas IV	1700–21	Clement XI
	pontificate)	1294	Celestine V	1721–4	Innocent XIII
1045–6	Gregory VI	1294–1303	Boniface VIII	1724–30	Benedict XIII
1046–7	Clement II	1303–4	Benedict XI	1730–40	Clement XII
1047–8	Benedict IX (third	1305–14	Clement V	1740–58	Benedict XIV
	pontificate)	1316–34	John XXII	1758–69	Clement XIII
1048	Damasus II	[1328–30	Nicholas (V)]	1769–74	Clement XIV
1048–54	Leo IX	1334–42	Benedict XII	1775–99	Pius VI
1055–7	Victor II	1342–52	Clement VI	1800–23	Pius VII
1057–8	Stephen IX (X)	1352–62	Innocent VI	1823–9	Leo XII
[1058–9	Benedict (X)]	1362–70	Urban V	1829–30	Pius VIII
1059–61	Nicholas II	1370–8	Gregory XI	1831–46	Gregory XVI
1061–73	Alexander II	1378–89	Urban VI	1846–78	Pius IX
[1061–72	Honorius (II)]	[1378–94	Clement (VII)]	1878–1903	Leo XIII
1073–85	Gregory VII	1389–1404	Boniface IX	1903–14	Pius X
[1080,	Clement (III)]	[1394–1423	Benedict (XIII)]	1914–22	Benedict XV
1084–1100		1404–6	Innocent VII	1922–39	Pius XI
1086–7	Victor III	1406–15	Gregory XII	1939–58	Pius XII
1088–99	Urban II	[1409–10	Alexander (V)]	1958–63	John XXIII
1099–1118	Paschal II	[1410–15	John (XXIII)]	1963–78	Paul VI
[1100–2	Theodoric]	1417–31	Martin V	1978	John Paul I
[1102	Albert]	[1423–9	Clement (VIII)]	1978–2005	John Paul II
[1105–11	Sylvester (IV)]			2005–	Benedict XVI

[1] Elected during the banishment of Martin I.
[2] Different individuals.
[3] There was no John XX.

Political leaders 1900–2008

Countries and organizations are listed alphabetically, with former or alternative names given in parentheses. Rulers are named chronologically since 1900 or (for new nations) since independence. For some major English-speaking nations, relevant details are also given of pre-20c rulers, along with a note of any political affiliation. The list does not distinguish successive terms of office by a single ruler. Listings complete to December 2008.

There is no universally agreed way of transliterating proper names in non-Roman alphabets; variations from the spellings given are therefore to be expected, especially in the case of Arabic rulers. Minor variations in the titles adopted by heads of state, or in the name of an administration, are not given; these occur most notably in countries under military rule.

Afghanistan

■ Afghan Empire
Monarch

1881–1901	Abdur Rahman Khan
1901–19	Habibullah Khan
1919–29	Amanullah Khan
1929	Habibullah Ghazi
1929–33	Nadir Shah
1933–73	Zahir Shah

President
■ Republic of Afghanistan
1973–8	Mohammad Daoud Khan

■ Democratic Republic of Afghanistan
Revolutionary Council
1978–9	Nour Mohammad Taraki
1979	Hafizullah Amin

Soviet invasion
1979–86	Babrak Karmal
1986–7	Haji Mohammad Chamkani *Acting*
1987–92	Mohammad Najibullah
1992	Sebghatullah Mojaddedi *Acting*

General Secretary
1978–86	*As President*
1986–92	Mohammad Najibullah

President
■ Islamic State of Afghanistan
1992–2001	Burhanuddin Rabbani[1]

Chairman Interim Government
2001–4	Hamid Karzai

President
■ Islamic Republic of Afghanistan[2]
2004–	Hamid Karzai

[1] Ousted by the Taliban in 1996, but remained titular head of state; Taliban de facto rulers 1996–2001.
[2] Islamic Transitional State of Afghanistan until 2004.

Prime Minister
1929–46	Sardar Mohammad Hashim Khan
1946–53	Shah Mahmoud Khan Ghazi
1953–63	Mohammad Daoud
1963–5	Mohammad Yousef
1965–7	Mohammad Hashim Maiwandwal
1967–71	Nour Ahmad Etemadi
1972–3	Mohammad Mousa Shafiq
1973–9	*As President*
1979–81	Babrak Karmal
1981–8	Sultan Ali Keshtmand
1988–9	Mohammad Hasan Sharq
1989–90	Sultan Ali Keshtmand
1990–2	Fazal Haq Khaliqyar
1992–3	Abdul Sabour Fareed

1993–6	Gulbuddin Hekmatyar

Albania

Monarch
1928–39	Zog I (Ahmed Zogu)
1939–44	*Italian rule*

President
■ People's Socialist Republic (from 1946)
1944–85	Enver Hoxha
1985–92	Ramiz Alia

■ Republic of Albania (from 1991)
1992–7	Sali Berisha
1997–2002	Rexhep Mejdani
2002–7	Alfred Moisiu
2007–	Bamir Topi

Prime Minister
1914	Turhan Pashë Përmëti
1914	Esad Toptani
1914–18	Abdullah Rushdi
1918–20	Turhan Pashë Përmëti
1920	Sulejman Deluina
1920–1	Iljaz Bej Vrioni
1921	Pandeli Evangeli
1921	Xhafer Ypi
1921–2	Omer Vrioni
1922–4	Ahmed Zogu
1924	Iljaz Bej Vrioni
1924–5	Fan Noli
1925–8	Ahmed Zogu
1928–30	Koço Kota
1930–5	Pandeli Evangeli
1935–6	Mehdi Frashëri
1936–9	Koço Kota
1939–41	Shefqet Verlaci
1941–3	Mustafa Merlika-Kruja
1943	Eqrem Libohova
1943	Maliq Bushati
1943	Eqrem Libohova
1943	*Provisional Executive Committee* (Ibrahim Biçakçlu)
1943	*Council of Regents* (Mehdi Frashëri)
1943–4	Rexhep Mitrovica
1944	Fiori Dine
1944–54	Enver Hoxha
1954–81	Mehmed Shehu
1981–91	Adil Carcani
1991	Ylli Buffi
1991	Fatos Nano
1991–2	Vilson Ahmeti
1992–7	Aleksander Meksi
1997	Bashkim Fino
1997–8	Fatos Nano
1998–9	Pandeli Majko

History

1999–2002	Ilir Meta
2002	Pandeli Majko
2002–5	Fatos Nano
2005–	Sali Berisha

Algeria

President

1962–5	Ahmed Ben Bella
1965–78	Houari Boumédienne
1979–92	Chandli Benjedid
1992	High Commission of State: Chair Mohamed Boudiaf
1992–4	Ali Kafi
1994–9	Liamine Zeroual
1999–	Abdelaziz Bouteflika

Prime Minister

1962–3	Ahmed Ben Bella
1963–79	No Prime Minister
1979–84	Mohamed Ben Ahmed Abdelghani
1984–8	Abdelhamid Brahimi
1988–9	Kasdi Merbah
1989–91	Mouloud Hamrouche
1991–2	Sid Ahmed Ghozali
1992–3	Belaid Abdessalam
1993–4	Redha Malek
1994–5	Mokdad Sifi
1995–8	Ahmed Ouyahia
1998–9	Ismail Hamdani
1999–2000	Ahmed Benbitour
2000–3	Ali Benflis
2003–6	Ahmed Ouyahia
2006–8	Abdelaziz Belkhadem
2008–	Ahmed Ouyahia

Andorra

There are two heads of state, called Co-Princes: the President of France (see p 304) and the Bishop of Urgell, Spain (Joan Enric Vives i Sicilia since 2003).

President of the Executive Council

1982–4	Óscar Ribas Reig
1984–90	Josep Pintat Solens
1990–4	Óscar Ribas Reig
1994–2005	Marc Forné Molné
2005–	Albert Pintat Santolària

Angola

President

| 1975–9 | Antonio Agostinho Neto |
| 1979– | José Eduardo dos Santos |

Prime Minister

1975–8	Lopo do Nasciemento
1978–91	No Prime Minister
1991–2	Fernando van Dúnem
1992–6	Marcolino Moco
1996–97	Fernando van Dúnem
1999–2002	No Prime Minister
2002–8	Fernando dos Santos
2008–	Antonio Paulo Kassoma

Antigua and Barbuda

Head of State: British monarch, represented by Governor-General

Prime Minister

1981–94	Vere Cornwall Bird
1994–2004	Lester Bird
2004–	Baldwin Spencer

Argentina

President

1898–1904	Julio Argentino Roca
1904–6	Manuel Quintana
1906–10	José Figueroa Alcorta
1910–14	Roque Sáenz Peña
1914–16	Victorino de la Plaza
1916–22	Hipólito Yrigoyen
1922–8	Marcelo T de Alvear
1928–30	Hipólito Yrigoyen
1930–2	José Félix Uriburu
1932–8	Augustin Pedro Justo
1938–40	Roberto M Ortiz
1940–3	Ramón S Castillo
1943–4	Pedro P Ramírez
1944–6	Edelmiro J Farrell
1946–55	Juan Perón
1955–8	Eduardo Lonardi
1958–62	Arturo Frondizi
1962–3	José María Guido
1963–6	Arturo Illia
1966–70	Juan Carlos Onganía
1970–1	Roberto Marcelo Levingston
1971–3	Alejandro Agustin Lanusse
1973	Héctor J Cámpora
1973–4	Juan Perón
1974–6	Martínez de Perón
1976–81	Military Junta (Jorge Rafaél Videla)
1981	Military Junta (Roberto Eduardo Viola)
1981–2	Military Junta (Leopoldo Galtieri)
1982–3	Reynaldo Bignone
1983–8	Raúl Alfonsín
1988–99	Carlos Saúl Menem
1999–2001	Fernando de la Rúa
2001	Three Interim Presidents
2002–3	Eduardo Duhalde
2003–7	Nestor Kirchner
2007–	Cristina Fernandez de Kirchner

Armenia

President

1991–8	Levon Ter-Petrossian
1998–2008	Robert Kocharyan
2008–	Serge Sarkisian

Prime Minister

1991–2	Gagik Haroutunian
1992–3	Khosrov Haroutunian
1993–6	Hrand Bagratian
1996–7	Armen Sarkissian
1997–8	Robert Kocharyan
1998–9	Armen Darbinian
1999	Vazgen Sarkissian
1999–2000	Aram Sarkissian
2000–7	Andranik Markarian
2007–8	Serge Sarkisian
2008–	Tigran Sarkisian

Australia

Head of State: British monarch, represented by Governor General

Prime Minister

1901–3	Edmund Barton *Prot*
1903–4	Alfred Deakin *Prot*
1904	John Christian Watson *Lab*
1904–5	George Houston Reid *Free*
1905–8	Alfred Deakin *Prot*
1908–9	Andrew Fisher *Lab*
1909–10	Alfred Deakin *Fusion*
1910–13	Andrew Fisher *Lab*
1913–14	Joseph Cook *Lib*
1914–15	Andrew Fisher *Lab*
1915–17	William Morris Hughes *Nat Lab*
1917–23	William Morris Hughes *Nat*
1923–9	Stanley Melbourne Bruce *Nat*
1929–32	James Henry Scullin *Lab*
1932–9	Joseph Aloysius Lyons *Un*
1939	Earle Christmas Page *Co*
1939–41	Robert Gordon Menzies *Un*
1941	Arthur William Fadden *Co*
1941–5	John Joseph Curtin *Lab*
1945	Francis Michael Forde *Lab*
1945–9	Joseph Benedict Chifley *Lab*
1949–66	Robert Gordon Menzies *Lib*
1966–7	Harold Edward Holt *Lib*
1967–8	John McEwen *Co*
1968–71	John Grey Gorton *Lib*
1971–2	William McMahon *Lib*
1972–5	Edward Gough Whitlam *Lab*
1975–83	John Malcolm Fraser *Lib*
1983–91	Robert James Lee Hawke *Lab*
1991–6	Paul Keating *Lab*
1996–2007	John Howard *Lib*
2007–	Kevin Rudd *Lab*

Co = Country	*Nat Lab* = National Labor
Free = Free Trade	*Prot* = Protectionist
Lab = Labor	*Un* = United
Lib = Liberal	
Nat = Nationalist	

Austria

President

1918–20	Karl Sätz
1920–8	Michael Hainisch
1928–38	Wilhelm Miklas
1938–45	*German rule*
1945–50	Karl Renner
1950–7	Theodor Körner
1957–65	Adolf Schärf
1965–74	Franz Jonas
1974–86	Rudolf Kirchsläger
1986–92	Kurt Waldheim
1992–2004	Thomas Klestil
2004–	Heinz Fischer

Chancellor

1918–20	Karl Renner
1920–1	Michael Mayr
1921–2	Johann Schober
1922	Walter Breisky
1922	Johann Schober
1922–4	Ignaz Seipel
1924–6	Rudolph Ramek
1926–9	Ignaz Seipel

1929–30	Ernst Streeruwitz
1930	Johann Schober
1930	Carl Vaugoin
1930–1	Otto Ender
1931–2	Karl Buresch
1932–4	Engelbert Dollfus
1934–8	Kurt von Schuschnigg
1938–45	*German rule*
1945	Karl Renner
1945–53	Leopold Figl
1953–61	Julius Raab
1961–4	Alfons Gorbach
1964–70	Josef Klaus
1970–83	Bruno Kreisky
1983–6	Fred Sinowatz
1986–97	Franz Vranitzky
1997–2000	Viktor Klima
2000–7	Wolfgang Schüssel
2007–8	Alfred Gusenbauer
2008–	Werner Faymann

Azerbaijan

President

1991–2	Ayaz Mutalibov
1992	Yakub Mamedov *Acting*
1992–3	Abul Faz Elchibey
1993–2003	Heidar Aliyev
2003–7	Ilham Aliyev
2007–	Hubert Ingraham

Prime Minister

1991–2	Hassan Hasanov
1992	Feirus Mustafayev *Acting*
1992–3	Rakhim Guseinov
1993	Ali Masimov *Acting*
1993	Panakh Guseinov
1993–4	Surat Guseinov
1994–6	Fuad Kuliyev
1996–2003	Artur Rasizade
2003	Ilham Aliyev
2003–	Artur Rasizade

The Bahamas

Head of State: British monarch, represented by Governor General

Prime Minister

1973–92	Lynden O Pindling
1992–2002	Hubert Ingraham
2002–7	Perry Christie
2007–	Hubert Ingraham

Bahrain

Emir

1971–99	Isa bin Salman al-Khalifa
1999–2002	Hamad bin Isa al-Khalifa

King

2002–	Hamad bin Isa al-Khalifa

Prime Minister

1971–	Khalifa bin Salman al-Khalifa

Bangladesh

President

1971–2	Sayed Nazrul Islam *Acting*
1972	Mujibur Rahman

History

291

1972–3	Abu Saeed Chowdhury
1973–5	Mohammad Mohammadullah
1975	Mujibur Rahman
1975	Khondaker Mushtaq Ahmad
1975–7	Abu Saadat Mohammad Sayem
1977–81	Zia Ur-Rahman
1981–2	Abdus Sattar
1982–3	Abdul Fazal Mohammad Ahsanuddin Chowdhury
1983–90	Hossain Mohammad Ershad
1990–1	Shehabuddin Ahmed *Acting*
1991–6	Abdur Rahman Biswas
1996–2001	Shehabuddin Ahmed
2001–2	A Q M Badruddoza Chowdhury
2002–	Iajuddin Ahmed

Prime Minister

1971–2	Tajuddin Ahmed
1972–5	Mujibur Rahman
1975	Mohammad Monsur Ali
1975–9	*Martial Law*
1979–82	Mohammad Azizur Rahman
1982–4	*Martial Law*
1984–5	Ataur Rahman Khan
1986–8	Mizanur Rahman Chowdhury
1988–90	Kazi Zafar Ahmed
1991–6	Khaleda Zia
1996	Mohammad Habibur Rahman
1996–2001	Sheikh Hasina Wajed
2001–6	Khaleda Zia
2006–	*Caretaker government pending election*

Barbados

Head of State: British monarch, represented by Governor General

Prime Minister

1966–76	Errol Walton Barrow
1976–85	J M G (Tom) Adams
1985–6	H Bernard St John
1986–7	Errol Walton Barrow
1987–94	L Erskine Sandiford
1994–2008	Owen Arthur
2008–	David Thompson

Belarus

Chair of Supreme Soviet

| 1991–4 | Stanislav Shushkevich |
| 1994–6 | Mecheslav Grib |

President

| 1994– | Alexander Lukashenko |

Prime Minister

1990–4	Vyacheslav Kebich
1994–6	Mikhail Chigir
1996–2000	Sergei Ling
2000–1	Uladzimir Yarmoshyn
2001–3	Gennady Vasilyevich Novitsky
2003–	Sergei Sidorski

Belgium

Monarch

1865–1909	Léopold II
1909–34	Albert I
1934–44	Léopold III

1944–50	Prince Charles *Regent*
1950–93	Baudouin I *Regent 1950–1*
1993–	Albert II

Prime Minister

1899–1907	Paul de Smet de Nayer
1907–8	Jules de Trooz
1908–11	Frans Schollaert
1911–18	Charles de Broqueville
1918	Gerhard Cooreman
1918–20	Léon Delacroix
1920–1	Henri Carton de Wiart
1921–5	Georges Theunis
1925	Alois van de Vyvere
1925–6	Prosper Poullet
1926–31	Henri Jaspar
1931–2	Jules Renkin
1932–4	Charles de Broqueville
1934–5	Georges Theunis
1935–7	Paul van Zeeland
1937–8	Paul Émile Janson
1938–9	Paul Spaak
1939–45	Hubert Pierlot
1945–6	Achille van Acker
1946	Paul Spaak
1946	Achille van Acker
1946–7	Camille Huysmans
1947–9	Paul Spaak
1949–50	Gaston Eyskens
1950	Jean Pierre Duvieusart
1950–2	Joseph Pholien
1952–4	Jean van Houtte
1954–8	Achille van Acker
1958–61	Gaston Eyskens
1961–5	Théodore Lefèvre
1965–6	Pierre Harmel
1966–8	Paul Vanden Boeynants
1968–72	Gaston Eyskens
1973–4	Edmond Leburton
1974–8	Léo Tindemans
1978	Paul Vanden Boeynants
1979–81	Wilfried Martens
1981	Marc Eyskens
1981–91	Wilfried Martens
1992–9	Jean-Luc Dehaene
1999–2008	Guy Verhofstadt
2008–	Yves Leterme

Belize

Head of State: British monarch, represented by Governor General

Prime Minister

1981–4	George Cadle Price
1985–9	Manuel Esquivel
1989–93	George Cadle Price
1993–8	Manuel Esquivel
1998–2008	Said Musa
2008–	Dean Barrow

Benin

President

■ **Dahomey**

1960–3	Hubert Coutoucou Maga
1963–4	Christophe Soglo
1964–5	Sourou Migan Apithy
1965	Justin Tométin Ahomadegbé

1965	Tairou Congacou
1965–7	Christophe Soglo
1967–8	Alphonse Amadou Alley
1968–9	Émile Derlin Zinsou
1969–70	*Presidential Committee* (Maurice Kouandété)
1970–2	*Presidential Committee* (Hubert Coutoucou Maga)
1972–5	Mathieu Kérékou

■ **People's Republic of Benin**

| 1975–90 | Mathieu (*from 1980* Ahmed) Kérékou |

■ **Republic of Benin**

1990–1	Ahmed Kérékou
1991–6	Nicéphore Soglo
1996–2006	Ahmed Kérékou
2006–	Yayi Boni

Prime Minister

1958–9	Sourou Migan Apithy
1959–60	Hubert Coutoucou Maga
1960–4	*As President*
1964–5	Justin Tométin Ahomadegbé
1965–7	*As President*
1967–8	Maurice Kouandété
1968–90	*As President*
1990–1	Nicéphore Soglo
1991–6	*As President*
1996–8	Adrien Houngbedji
1998	*Post abolished*

Bhutan

Monarch (Druk Gyalpo)

1907–26	Uggyen Wangchuk
1926–52	Jigme Wangchuk
1952–72	Jigme Dorji Wangchuk
1972–2006	Jigme Singye Wangchuk
2006–	Jigme Khesar Namgyel Wangchuk

Prime Minister

1952–64	Jigme Palden Dorji
1964	Lhendup Dorji *Acting*
1964–98	*No Prime Minister*

Chair of Council of Ministers (annually rotating post)

1998–99	Jigme Thinley
1999–2000	Sangay Ngedup
2000–1	Yeshey Zimba
2001–2	Khandu Wangchuk
2002–3	Kinzang Dorji
2003–4	Jigme Thinley
2004–5	Yeshey Zimba
2005–6	Sangay Ngedup
2006–7	Khandu Wangchuk

Prime Minister

| 2008– | Jigme Thinley |

Bolivia

President

1899–1904	José Manuel Pando
1904–9	Ismael Montes
1909–13	Heliodoro Villazón
1913–17	Ismael Montes
1917–20	José N Gutiérrez Guerra
1920–5	Bautista Saavedra

1925–6	José Cabina Villanueva
1926–30	Hernando Siles
1930	Roberto Hinojusa *President of Revolutionaries*
1930–1	Carlos Blanco Galindo
1931–4	Daniel Salamanca
1934–6	José Luis Tejado Sorzano
1936–7	David Toro
1937–9	Germán Busch
1939	Carlos Quintanilla
1940–3	Enrique Peñaranda y del Castillo
1943–6	Gualberto Villaroel
1946	Nestor Guillen
1946–7	Tomas Monje Gutiérrez
1947–9	Enrique Hertzog
1949	Mamerto Urriolagoitía
1951–2	Hugo Ballivián
1952	Hernán Siles Suazo
1952–6	Víctor Paz Estenssoro
1956–60	Hernán Siles Suazo
1960–4	Víctor Paz Estenssoro
1964–5	René Barrientos Ortuño
1965–6	René Barrientos Ortuño *and* Alfredo Ovando Candía
1966	Alfredo Ovando Candía
1966–9	René Barrientos Ortuño
1969	Luis Adolfo Siles Salinas
1969–70	Alfredo Ovando Candía
1970	Rogelio Mirando
1970–1	Juan José Torres Gonzales
1971–8	Hugo Banzer Suárez
1978	Juan Pereda Asbún
1978–9	*Military Junta* (David Padilla Arericiba)
1979	Walter Guevara Arze
1979–80	Lydia Gueiler Tejada
1980–1	*Military Junta* (Luis García Meza)
1981–2	*Military Junta* (Celso Torrelio Villa)
1982	Guido Vildoso Calderón
1982–5	Hernán Siles Suazo
1985–9	Víctor Paz Estenssoro
1989–93	Jaime Paz Zamora
1993–97	Gonzalo Sánchez de Lozada
1997–2001	Hugo Bánzer Suárez
2001–2	Jorge Quiroga Ramírez
2002–3	Gonzalo Sánchez de Lozada
2003–5	Carlos Mesa
2005–6	Eduardo Rodriguez *Acting*
2006–	Evo Morales

Bosnia and Herzegovina

*President**

■ **Republic**

1990–8	Alija Izetbegović
1998–9	Žvko Radišić
1999–2000	Ante Jelavić
2000	Alija Izetbegović
2000–1	Živko Radišić
2001–2	Jozo Križanović
2002	Beriz Belkić
2002–3	Mirko Šarović, Borislav Paravac, Dragan Čović
2004–6	Sulejman Tihić, Borislav Paravac, Ivo Miro Jovic
2006–	Nebojsa Radmanovic, Zeljko Komsic, Haris Silajdžic

* Tripartite presidency rotating every eight months since 2002

History

- **Federation**

1994–7	Krešimir Zubak
1997	Vladimir Šoljić
1997–8	Ejup Ganić
1999–2000	Ivo Andrić-Lužanski
2000–1	Ejup Ganić
2001–2	Karlo Filipović
2002–3	Safet Halilović
2003–7	Niko Lozančić
2007–	Borjana Kristo

- **Republika Srpska**

1992–6	Radovan Karadzic
1996–8	Biljana Plavšić
1998–9	Nikola Poplašen
2000–2	Mirko Šarović
2002–6	Dragan Čavić
2006–7	Milan Jelic
2007	Rajko Kuzmanovic

Prime Minister
- **Republic**

1990–2	Jure Pelivan
1992–3	Mile Akmadzic
1993–6	Haris Silajdžic
1996–7	Hasan Muratovic
1997–9	Boro Bosic *co-PM*
1997–2000	Haris Silajdžic *co-PM*
1999–2000	Svetozar Mihajlovic *co-PM*
2000	Spasoje Tusevljak
2000–1	Martin Raguz
2001	Bozidar Matic
2001–2	Zlatko Lagurndzija
2002	Dragan Mikerevic
2002–7	Adnan Terzic
2007–	Nikola Spiric

- **Federation**

1994–6	Haris Silajdžic
1996	Izudin Kapetanovic
1996–2001	Edhem Bicakcić
2001	Dragan Čović *Acting*
2001–3	Alija Behmen
2003–7	Ahmet Hadzipasic
2007–	Nedzad Brankovic

- **Republika Srpska**

1992–3	Branko Djeric
1993–4	Vladimir Lukic
1994–5	Dusan Kozic
1995–6	Rajko Kasagic
1996–8	Gojko Klickovic
1998–2001	Milorad Dodik
2001–3	Mladen Ivanic
2003–5	Dragan Mikerevic
2005–6	Pero Bukejlovic
2006–	Milorad Dodik

Botswana

President

1966–80	Seretse Khama
1980–98	Ketumile Masire
1998–2008	Festus Mogae
2008–	Ian Khama

Brazil

President

1898–1902	Manuel Ferraz de Campos Sales
1902–6	Francisco de Paula Rodrigues Alves
1906–9	Alfonso Pena
1909–10	Nilo Peçanha
1910–14	Hermes Rodrigues da Fonseca
1914–18	Venceslau Brás Pereira Gomes
1918–19	Francisco de Paula Rodrigues Alves
1919–22	Epitácio Pessoa
1922–6	Artur da Silva Bernardes
1926–30	Washington Luís Pereira de Sousa
1930–45	Getúlio Dorneles Vargas
1945–51	Eurico Gaspar Dutra
1951–54	Getúlio Dorneles Vargas
1954–5	João Café Filho
1955	Carlos Coimbra da Luz
1955–6	Nereu de Oliveira Ramos
1956–61	Juscelino Kubitschek de Oliveira
1961	Jânio da Silva Quadros
1961–3	João Belchior Marques Goulart
1963	Pascoal Ranieri Mazilli
1963–4	João Belchior Marques Goulart
1964	Pascoal Ranieri Mazilli
1964–7	Humberto Castelo Branco
1967–9	Artur da Costa e Silva
1969–74	Emílio Garrastazu Médici
1974–9	Ernesto Geisel
1979–85	João Baptista de Oliveira Figueiredo
1985–90	José Sarney
1990–2	Fernando Collor de Mello
1992–4	Itamar Franco
1994–2002	Fernando Henrique Cardoso
2002–	Luiz Inacio 'Lula' da Silva

Brunei

Monarch (Sultan)

| 1967– | Muda Hassanal Bolkiah Mu'izzadin Waddaulah |

Bulgaria

- **Tsardom of Bulgaria**
Monarch

1887–1908	Ferdinand *Prince*
1908–18	Ferdinand I
1918–43	Boris III
1943–6	Simeon II

President
- **People's Republic of Bulgaria**

1946–7	Vasil Kolarov
1947–50	Mincho Naichev
1950–8	Georgi Damianov
1958–64	Dimitro Ganev
1964–71	Georgi Traikov
1971–89	Todor Zhivkov
1989–90	Petar Mladenov

- **Republic of Bulgaria**

1990–7	Zhelyu Zhelev
1997–2002	Petar Stoyanov
2002–	Georgi Parvanov

Premier

| 1946–9 | Georgi Dimitrov |

1949–50	Vasil Kolarov
1950–6	Vulko Chervenkov
1956–62	Anton Yugov
1962–71	Todor Zhivkov
1971–81	Stanko Todorov
1981–6	Grisha Filipov
1986–90	Georgy Atanasov
1990	Andrei Lukanov
1990–1	Dimitur Popov

First Secretary

1946–53	Vulko Chervenkov
1953–89	Todor Zhivkov
1989–90	Petar Mladenov
1990	Alexander Lilov

Prime Minister

1991–2	Filip Dimitrov
1992–4	Lyuben Berov
1994–5	Renate Indzhova *Acting*
1995–7	Zhan Videnov
1997	Stefan Sofiyanski *Acting*
1997–2001	Ivan Kostov
2001–5	Simeon Saxe-Coburg-Gotha (Simeon II)
2005–	Sergey Stanishev

Burkina Faso

President

■ Upper Volta

1960–6	Maurice Yaméogo
1966–80	Sangoulé Lamizana
1980	Saye Zerbo

People's Salvation Council

1982–3	Jean-Baptiste Ouedraugo *Chairman*

National Revolutionary Council

1983–4	Thomas Sankara *Chairman*

■ Burkina Faso

1984–7	Thomas Sankara *Chairman*
1987–	Blaise Compaoré

Prime Minister

1992–4	Youssouf Ouedraogo
1994–6	Roch Christian Kaboré
1996–2000	Kadré Désiré Ouedraogo
2000–7	Paramanga Ernest Yonli
2007–	Tertius Zongo

Burma ► Myanmar, Union of

Burundi

■ Ruanda-Urundi

Monarch

1962–6	Mwambutsa IV
1966	Ntare V

■ Republic of Burundi

President

1966–77	Michel Micombero
1977–87	Jean-Baptiste Bagaza
1987–93	*Military Junta* (Pierre Buyoya)
1993	Melchior Ndadaye
1994	Cyprien Ntaryamira
1994–6	Sylvestre Ntibantunganya

1996–2003	Pierre Buyoya
2003–5	Domitien Ndayizeye
2005–	Pierre Nkurunziza

Prime Minister

1961	Joseph Cimpaye
1961	Louis Rwagasore
1962–3	André Muhirwa
1963–4	Pierre Ngendandumwe
1964–5	Albin Nyamoya
1965	Pierre Ngendandumwe
1965	Pie Masumbuko *Acting*
1965	Joseph Bamina
1965–6	Léopold Biha
1966–76	Michel Micombero
1976–8	Edouard Nzambimana
1978–87	*No Prime Minister*
1987–8	Pierre Buyoya
1988–93	Adrien Sibomana
1993–4	Sylvie Kinigi
1994–5	Anatole Kanyenkiko
1995–6	Antoine Nduwayo
1996–8	Pascal-Firmin Ndimira
1998–	*No Prime Minister*

Cambodia

Monarch

1941–55	Norodom Sihanouk II
1955–60	Norodom Suramarit

Head of State

1960–70	Prince Norodom Sihanouk

■ Khmer Republic (from 1970)

1970–2	Cheng Heng *Acting Head of State*
1972–5	Lon Nol
1975–6	Prince Norodom Sihanouk
1976–81	Khieu Samphan
1981–91	Heng Samrin

■ Government in exile (until 1991)

President

1970–5	Prince Norodom Sihanouk
1982–93	Prince Norodom Sihanouk

■ Kingdom of Cambodia

Monarch (King)

1993–2004	Norodom Sihanouk
2004–	Norodom Sihamoni

Prime Minister

1945–6	Son Ngoc Thanh
1946–8	Prince Monireth
1948–9	Son Ngoc Thanh
1949–51	Prince Monipong
1951	Son Ngoc Thanh
1951–2	Huy Kanthoul
1952–3	Norodom Sihanouk II
1953	Samdech Penn Nouth
1953–4	Chan Nak
1954–5	Leng Ngeth
1955–6	Prince Norodom Sihanouk
1956	Oum Chheang Sun
1956	Prince Norodom Sihanouk
1956	Khim Tit
1956	Prince Norodom Sihanouk
1956	Sam Yun
1956–7	Prince Norodom Sihanouk
1957–8	Sim Var

History

History

1958	Ek Yi Oun
1958	Samdech Penn Nouth *Acting*
1958	Sim Var
1958–60	Prince Norodom Sihanouk
1960–1	Pho Proung
1961	Samdech Penn Nouth
1961–3	Prince Norodom Sihanouk
1963–6	Prince Norodom Kantol
1966–7	Lon Nol
1967–8	Prince Norodom Sihanouk
1968–9	Samdech Penn Nouth
1969–72	Lon Nol

■ **Khmer Republic (from 1970)**

1972	Sisovath Sivik Matak
1972	Son Ngoc Thanh
1972–3	Hang Thun Hak
1973	In Tam
1973–5	Long Boret
1975–6	Samdech Penn Nouth
1976–9	Pol Pot
1979–81	Khieu Samphan
1981–5	Chan Si
1985–93	Hun Sen

Government in exile (until 1991)

| 1970–3 | Samdech Penn Nouth |
| 1982–91 | Son Sann |

■ **Kingdom of Cambodia**

1993–7	Norodom Ranariddh *First Prime Minister*
	Hun Sen *Second Prime Minister*
1997	Ung Huot *First Prime Minister*
	Hun Sen *Second Prime Minister*
1998–	Hun Sen

Cameroon

President

| 1960–82 | Ahmadun Ahidjo |
| 1982– | Paul Biya |

Prime Minister

1960	Ahmadou Ahidjo
1960–1	Charles Assalé
1961–75	*No Prime Minister*
1975–82	Paul Biya
1982–3	Bello Bouba Maigari
1983–4	Luc Ayang
1991–2	Sadou Hayatou
1992–6	Simon Achidi Achu
1996–2004	Peter Mafany Musonge
2004–	Ephraïm Inoni

Canada

Head of State: British monarch, represented by Governor General

Prime Minister

1896–1911	Wilfrid Laurier *Lib*
1911–20	Robert Borden *Con/Un*
1920–1	Arthur Meighen *Un/Con*
1921–6	William Lyon Mackenzie King *Lib*
1926	Arthur Meighen *Con*
1926–30	William Lyon Mackenzie King *Lib*
1930–5	Richard Bedford Bennett *Con*
1935–48	William Lyon Mackenzie King *Lib*
1948–57	Louis St Laurent *Lib*

1957–63	John George Diefenbaker *Con*
1963–8	Lester Bowles Pearson *Lib*
1968–79	Pierre Elliott Trudeau *Lib*
1979–80	Joseph Clark *Con*
1980–4	Pierre Elliott Trudeau *Lib*
1984	John Turner *Lib*
1984–93	Brian Mulroney *Con*
1993	Kim Campbell *Con*
1993–2004	Jean Chrétien *Lib*
2004–6	Paul Martin *Lib*
2006–	Stephen Harper *Con*

Con = Conservative; *Lib* = Liberal; *Un* = Unionist

Cape Verde

President

1975–91	Arístides Pereira
1991–2001	Antonio Mascarenhas Monteiro
2001–	Pedro Pires

Prime Minister

1975–91	Pedro Pires
1991–2000	Carlos Wahnon Veiga
2000–1	António Gualberto do Rosário
2001–	José Maria Neves

Central African Republic

President

1960–6	David Dacko
1966–79	Jean-Bédel Bokassa (*from 1977, Emperor Bokassa I*)
1979–81	David Dacko
1981–93	André Kolingba
1993–2003	Ange-Félix Patassé
2003–	François Bozizé

Prime Minister

1991–2	Edouard Frank
1992–3	Thimothée Malendoma
1993	Enoch Derant Lakoué
1993–5	Jean-Luc Mandaba
1995–6	Gabriel Koyambounou
1996–7	Jean-Paul Ngoupandé
1997–9	Michel Gbezera-Bria
1999–2001	Anicet Georges Dologuélé
2001–3	Martin Ziguélé
2003	Abel Goumba
2003–5	Célestin Gaombalet
2005–8	Élie Doté
2008–	Faustin Archange Touadera

Chad

President

1960–75	François Tombalbaye
1975–9	*Supreme Military Council* (Félix Malloum)
1979	Goukouni Oueddi
1979	Mohammed Shawwa
1979–82	Goukouni Oueddi
1982–90	Hissène Habré
1990–	Idriss Déby

Prime Minister

1991–2	Jean Alingue Bawoyeu
1992–3	Joseph Yodemane
1993	Fidèle Moungar
1993–5	Delwa Kassire Koumakoye

1995-7	Koibla Djimasta
1997-9	Nassour Ouaidou Guelendouksia
1999-2002	Negoum Yamassoum
2002-3	Haroun Kabadi
2003-5	Moussa Faki Mahamat
2005-7	Pascal Yoadimnadji
2007-8	Nourradine Delwa Kassire Coumakoye
2008-	Youssouf Saleh Abbas

Chile

President

1900-1	Federico Errázuriz Echaurren
1901	Aníbal Zañartu *Vice President*
1901-3	Germán Riesco
1903	Ramón Barros Luco *Vice President*
1903-6	Germán Riesco
1906-10	Pedro Montt
1910	Ismael Tocornal *Vice President*
1910	Elías Fernández Albano *Vice President*
1910	Emiliano Figueroa Larraín *Vice President*
1910-15	Ramón Barros Luco
1915-20	Juan Luis Sanfuentes
1920-4	Arturo Alessandri
1924-5	*Military Juntas*
1925	Arturo Alessandri
1925	Luis Barros Borgoño *Vice President*
1925-7	Emiliano Figueroa
1927-31	Carlos Ibáñez
1931	Pedro Opaso Letelier *Vice President*
1931	Juan Esteban Montero *Vice President*
1931	Manuel Trucco Franzani *Vice President*
1931-2	Juan Estaban Montero
1932	*Military Juntas*
1932	Carlos G Dávila *Provisional President*
1932	Bartolomé Blanche *Provisional President*
1932	Abraham Oyanedel *Vice President*
1932-8	Arturo Alessandri Palma
1938-41	Pedro Aguirre Cerda
1941-2	Jerónimo Méndez Arancibia *Vice President*
1942-6	Juan Antonio Ríos Morales
1946-52	Gabriel González Videla
1952-8	Carlos Ibáñez del Campo
1958-64	Jorge Alessandri Rodríguez
1964-70	Eduardo Frei Montalva
1970-3	Salvador Allende Gossens
1973-90	Augusto Pinochet Ugarte
1990-3	Patricio Aylwin Azócar
1993-9	Eduardo Frei Ruíz-Tagle
2000-6	Ricardo Lagos Escobar
2006-	Michelle Bachelet

China

■ Qing (Ch'ing) dynasty
Emperor

1875-1908	Guangxu (Kuang-hsü)
1908-12	Xuantong (Hsüan-t'ung)

Prime Minister

1901-3	Ronglu (Jung-lu)
1903-11	Prince Qing (Ch'ing)
1912	Lu Zhengxiang (Lu Cheng-hsiang)
1912	Yuan Shikai (Yüan Shih-k'ai)

■ Republic of China
President

1912	Sun Yat-sen (Sun Yixian) *Provisional*
1912-16	Yuan Shikai (Yüan Shih-k'ai)
1916-17	Li Yuanhong (Li Yüan-hung)
1917-18	Feng Guozhang (Feng Kuo-chang)
1918-22	Xu Shichang (Hsü Shih-ch'ang)
1921-5	Sun Yat-sen *Canton Administration*
1922-3	Li Yuanhong
1923-4	Cao Kun (Ts'ao K'un)
1924-6	Duan Qirui (Tuan Ch'i-jui)
1926-7	*Civil Disorder*
1927-8	Zhang Zuolin (Chang Tso-lin)
1928-31	Chiang K'ai-shek (Jiang Jieshi)
1931-2	Cheng Minxu (Ch'eng Ming-hsü) *Acting*
1932-43	Lin Sen (Lin Sen)
1940-4	Wang Jingwei (Wang Ching-wei) *In Japanese-occupied territory*
1943-9	Chiang K'ai-shek
1945-9	*Civil War*
1949	Li Zongren (Li Tsung-jen)

Premier

1912	Tang Shaoyi (T'ang Shao-i)
1912-13	Zhao Bingjun (Chao Ping-chün)
1912-13	Xiong Xiling (Hsiung Hsi-ling)
1914	Sun Baoyi (Sun Pao-chi)
1915-16	*no Premier*
1916-17	Duan Qirui (Tuan Ch'i-jui)
1917-18	Wang Shizhen (Wang Shih-chen)
1918	Duan Qirui
1918-19	Qian Nengxun (Ch'ien Neng-hsün)
1919	Gong Xinzhan (Kung Hsin-chan)
1919-20	Jin Yunpeng (Chin Yün-p'eng)
1920	Sa Zhenbing (Sa Chen-ping)
1920-1	Jun Yunpeng
1921-2	Liang Shiyi (Liang Shih-i)
1922	Zhou Ziqi (Chow Tzu-ch'i) *Acting*
1922	Yan Huiqing (Yen Hui-ch'ing)
1922	Wang Chonghui (Wang Ch'ung-hui)
1922-3	Wang Daxie (Wang Ta-hsieh)
1923	Zhang Shaozeng (Chang Shao-ts'eng)
1923-4	Gao Lingwei (Kao Ling-wei)
1924	Sun Baoyi (Sun Pao-ch'i)
1924	Gu Weijun (Ku Wei-chün) *Acting*
1924	Yan Huiqing
1924-5	Huang Fu (Huang Fu) *Acting*
1925	Duan Qirui
1925-6	Xu Shiying (Hsü Shih-ying)
1926	Jia Deyao (Chia Te-yao)
1926	Hu Weide (Hu Wei-te)
1926	Yan Huiqing
1926	Du Xigui (Tu Hsi-kuei)
1926-7	Gu Weijun
1927	*Civil Disorder*

President of the Executive Council

1928-30	Tan Yankai (T'an Yen-k'ai)
1930	T V Soong (Sung Tzu-wen) *Acting*
1930	Wang Jingwei (Wang Ching-wei)
1930-1	Chiang K'ai-shek
1931-2	Sun Fo (Sun Fo)
1932-5	Wang Jingwei
1935-7	Chiang K'ai-shek
1937-8	Wang Chonghui (Wang Ch'ung-hui) *Acting*
1938-9	Kong Xiangxi (K'ung Hsiang-hsi)

History

1939–44	Chiang K'ai-shek
1944–7	T V Soong
1945–9	*Civil War*
1948	Wang Wenhao (Wong Wen-hao)
1948–9	Sun Fo
1949	He Yingqin (Ho Ying-ch'in)
1949	Yan Xishan (Yen Hsi-shan)

■ **People's Republic of China**
President

1949–59	Mao Zedong (Mao Tse-tung)
1959–68	Liu Shaoqi (Liu Shao-ch'i)
1968–75	Dong Biwu (Tung Pi-wu)
1975–6	Zhu De (Chu Te)
1976–8	Sung Qingling (Sung Ch'ing-ling)
1978–83	Ye Jianying (Yeh Chien-ying)
1983–8	Li Xiannian (Li Hsien-nien)
1988–93	Yang Shangkun (Yang Shang-k'un)
1993–2003	Jiang Zemin (Chiang Tse-min)
2003–	Hu Jintao

Prime Minister

1949–76	Zhou Enlai (Chou En-lai)
1976–80	Hua Guofeng (Huo Kuo-feng)
1980–7	Zhao Ziyang (Chao Tzu-yang)
1987–98	Li Peng (Li P'eng)
1998–2003	Zhu Rongji
2003–	Wen Jiabao

Communist Party
Chairman

1935–76	Mao Zedong
1976–81	Hua Guofeng
1981–2	Hu Yaobang (Hu Yao-pang)

General Secretary

1982–7	Hu Yaobang
1987–9	Zhao Ziyang
1989–2002	Jiang Zemin
2002–	Hu Jintao

Colombia

President

1900–4	José Manuel Marroquín *Vice President*
1904–9	Rafael Reyes
1909–10	Ramón González Valencia
1910–14	Carlos E Restrepo
1914–18	José Vicente Concha
1918–21	Marco Fidel Suárez
1921–2	Jorge Holguín *President Designate*
1922–6	Pedro Nel Ospina
1926–30	Miguel Abadía Méndez
1930–4	Enrique Olaya Herrera
1934–8	Alfonso López
1938–42	Eduardo Santos
1942–5	Alfonso López
1945–6	Alberto Lleras Camargo *President Designate*
1946–50	Mariano Ospina Pérez
1950–3	Laureano Gómez
1953–7	Gustavo Rojas Pinilla
1957	*Military Junta*
1958–62	Alberto Lleras Camargo
1962–6	Guillermo León Valencia
1966–70	Carlos Lleras Restrepo
1970–4	Misael Pastrana Borrero
1974–8	Alfonso López Michelsen

1978–82	Julio César Turbay Ayala
1982–6	Belisario Betancur
1986–90	Virgilio Barco Vargas
1990–4	César Gaviria Trujillo
1994–8	Ernesto Samper Pizano
1998–2002	Andrés Pastrana Arango
2002–	Álvaro Uribe Vélez

Comoros, Union of the

President

1976–78	Ali Soilih
1978–89	Ahmed Abdallah Abderemane
1989–96	Said Mohammed Djohar
1996–8	Mohammed Taki Abdoulkarim
1998–9	Tadjiddine Ben Said Massounde *Interim President*
1999–2002	Azali Assoumani
2002	Hamada Madi Boléro *Interim President*
2002–6	Azali Assoumani
2006–	Ahmed Abdallah Sambi

Prime Minister

1976–8	Abdallah Mohammed
1978–82	Salim Ben Ali
1982–4	Ali Mroudjae
1984–92	*No Prime Minister*
1992	Mohammed Taki Abdoulkarim
1993	Ibrahim Abdermane Halidi
1993	Said Ali Mohammed
1993–4	Ahmed Ben Cheikh Attoumane
1994	Mohammed Abdou Madi
1994–5	Halifa Houmadi
1995–6	Caambi el-Yachourtu
1996	Tadjiddine Ben Said Massounde
1996–7	Ahmed Abdou
1997–8	Nourdine Bourhane
1998–9	Abbas Djoussouf
1999–2000	Bianrifi Tarmidi
2000–2	Hamada Madi Boléro

Congo

President

1960–3	Abbé Fulbert Youlou
1963–8	Alphonse Massemba-Debat
1968	Marien Ngouabi
1968	Alphonse Massemba-Debat
1968–9	Alfred Raoul
1969–77	Marien Ngouabi
1977–9	Joachim Yhomby Opango
1979–92	Denis Sassou-Nguesso
1992–7	Pascal Lissouba
1997–	Denis Sassou-Nguesso

Prime Minister

1958	Jacques Opangault
1958–60	Fulbert Youlou
1960–3	*No Prime Minister*
1963–6	Pascal Lissouba
1966–8	Ambroise Noumazalaye
1968–9	Alfred Raoul
1969–73	*No Prime Minister*
1973–5	Henri Lopès
1975–84	Louis Sylvain Goma
1984–9	Ange-Édouard Poungui
1989–90	Alphonse Poaty-Souchlaty
1990–1	Pierre Moussa *Acting*

1991	Louis Sylvain Goma
1991–2	André Milongo
1992	Stéphane Maurice Bongho-Nouarra
1992–3	Claude Antoine Dacosta
1993–6	Joachim Yhombi-Opango
1996–7	Charles David Ganao
1997	Bernard Kolelas
1997–2005	*No Prime Minister*
2005–	Isidore Mvouba

Congo, Democratic Republic of the

President

1960–5	Joseph Kasavubu
1965–97	Mobutu Sese Seko (*formerly* Joseph Mobutu)

■ **Democratic Republic of the Congo**

1997–2001	Laurent Kabila
2001–	Joseph Kabila

Prime Minister

1960	Patrice Lumumba
1960	Joseph Ileo
1960–1	*College of Commissioners*
1961	Joseph Ileo
1961–4	Cyrille Adoula
1964–5	Moïse Tshombe
1965	Evariste Kimba
1965–6	Mulamba Nyungu wa Kadima
1966–77	*As President*
1977–80	Mpinga Kasenga
1980	Bo-Boliko Lokonga Monse Mihambu
1980–1	Nguza Karl I Bond
1981–3	Nsinga Udjuu
1983–6	Léon Kengo Wa Dondo
1986–8	*No Prime Minister*
1988	Sambura Pida Nbagui
1988–90	Léon Kengo Wa Dondo
1990–1	Lunda Bululu
1991	Mulumba Lukeji
1991	Etienne Tshisekedi
1991	Bernardin Mungul Diaka
1991–2	Karl I Bond
1992–3	Etienne Tshisekedi
1993–4	Faustin Birindwa
1994–7	Léon Kengo Wa Dondo
1997	Etienne Tshisekedi
1997	Likulia Bolongo
2006–8	Antoine Gizenga
2008–	Adolphe Muzito

Costa Rica

President

1894–1902	Rafael Yglesias y Castro
1902–6	Ascención Esquivel Ibarra
1906–10	Cleto González Víquez
1910–12	Ricardo Jiménez Oreamuno
1912–14	Cleto González Víquez
1914–17	Alfredo González Flores
1917–19	Federico Tinoco Granados
1919	Julio Acosta García
1919–20	Juan Bautista Quiros
1920–4	Julio Acosta García
1924–8	Ricardo Jiménez Oreamuno
1928–32	Cleto González Víquez
1932–6	Ricardo Jiménez Oreamuno

1936–40	León Cortés Castro
1940–4	Rafael Ángel Calderón Guardia
1944–8	Teodoro Picado Michalski
1948	Santos Léon Herrera
1948–9	*Civil Junta* (José Figueres Ferrer)
1949–52	Otilio Ulate Blanco
1952–3	Alberto Oreamuno Flores
1953–8	José Figueres Ferrer
1958–62	Mario Echandi Jiménez
1962–6	Francisco José Orlich Bolmarcich
1966–70	José Joaquín Trejos Fernández
1970–4	José Figueres Ferrer
1974–8	Daniel Oduber Quirós
1978–82	Rodrigo Carazo Odio
1982–6	Luis Alberto Monge Álvarez
1986–90	Oscar Arias Sánchez
1990–4	Rafael Angel Calderón Fournier
1994–8	José Maria Figueres Olsen
1998–2002	Miguel Angel Rodríguez Echevarría
2002–6	Abel Pacheca de la Espriella
2006–	Oscar Arias Sanchez

Côte d'Ivoire

President

1960–93	Félix Houphouët-Boigny
1993–9	Henri Konan-Bédié
1999–2000	Robert Guëi
2000–	Laurent Gbagbo

Prime Minister

1958–9	Auguste Denise
1959–60	Félix Houphouët-Boigny
1960–90	*No Prime Minister*
1990–3	Alassane Dramane Ouattara
1993–9	Daniel Kablan Duncan
1999	Robert Guëi
2000	Seydou Diarra
2000–3	Pascal Affi N'Guessan
2003–5	Seydou Diarra
2005–6	Charles Konan Banny
2007–	Guillaume Soro

Croatia

President

1992–9	Franjo Tudjman
1999–2000	Vlatko Pavletić *Acting*
2000	Zlatko Tomčić *Acting*
2000–	Stjepan Mesić

Prime Minister

1990	Stjepan Mesić
1990–1	Josip Manolić
1991–2	Franjo Gregurić
1992–3	Hrvoje Šarinić
1993–5	Nikica Valentić
1995–2000	Zlatko Mateša
2000–3	Ivica Racan
2003–	Ivo Sanader

Cuba

President

1902–6	Tomas Estrada Palma
1906–9	*US rule*
1909–13	José Miguel Gómez
1913–21	Mario García Menocal
1921–5	Alfredo Zayas y Alfonso

History

1925–33	Gerardo Machado y Morales
1933	Carlos Manuel de Céspedes
1933–4	Ramón Grau San Martín
1934–5	Carlos Mendieta
1935–6	José A Barnet y Vinagres
1936	Miguel Mariano Gómez y Arias
1936–40	Federico Laredo Bru
1940–4	Fulgencio Batista
1944–8	Ramón Grau San Martín
1948–52	Carlos Prío Socarrás
1952–9	Fulgencio Batista
1959	Manuel Urrutia
1959–76	Osvaldo Dorticós Torrado
1959–76	Fidel Castro Ruz *Prime Minister and First Secretary*
1976–2008	Fidel Castro Ruz *President*
2008–	Raul Castro Ruz *Acting President 2006–8*

Cyprus

President
1960–77	Archbishop Makarios III
1977–88	Spyros Kyprianou
1988–93	Georgios Vassiliou
1993–2003	Glafcos Clerides
2003–8	Tassos Papadopoulos
2008–	Demetris Christofias

Czechoslovakia

No longer in existence, but included for reference.

President
1918–35	Tomáš Garrigue Masaryk
1935–8	Edvard Beneš
1938–9	Emil Hácha

German Occupation
1938–45	Edvard Beneš *President in Exile*
1939–45	Emil Hácha *State President*
1939–45	Jozef Tiso *Slovak Republic President*

Post-war
1945–8	Edvard Beneš
1948–53	Klement Gottwald
1953–7	Antonín Zápotocký
1957–68	Antonín Novotný
1968–75	Ludvík Svoboda
1975–89	Gustáv Husák
1989–93	Václav Havel

Prime Minister
1918–19	Karel Kramář
1919–20	Vlastimil Tusar
1920–1	Jan Černý
1921–2	Edvard Beneš
1922–6	Antonín Švehla
1926	Jan Černý
1926–9	Antonín Švehla
1929–32	František Udržal
1932–5	Jan Malypetr
1935–8	Milan Hodža
1938	Jan Syrový
1938–9	Rudolf Beran
1940–5	Jan Šrámek *in exile*
1945–6	Zdeněk Fierlinger
1946–8	Klement Gottwald
1948–53	Antonín Zápotocký

1953–63	Viliám Široký
1963–8	Josef Lenárt
1968–70	Oldřich Černik
1970–88	Lubomír Štrougal
1988–9	Ladislav Adamec
1989–92	Marian Calfa
1992	Jan Strasky

First Secretary
1948–52	Rudolf Slánsky
1953–68	Antonín Novotný
1968–9	Alexander Dubček
1969–87	Gustáv Husák
1987–9	Miloš Jakeš
1989	Karel Urbánek
1989–93	Ladislav Adamec

▶ separate entries for the **Czech Republic** and **Slovakia** from 1993.

Czech Republic

President
1993–2003	Václav Havel
2003–	Václav Klaus

Prime Minister
1993–7	Václav Klaus
1997–8	Josef Tosovsky
1998–2002	Miloš Zeman
2002–4	Vladimír Špidla
2004–5	Stanislav Gross
2005–6	Jiri Paroubek
2006–	Mirek Topolanek

Denmark

Monarch
1863–1906	Kristian IX
1906–12	Frederik VIII
1912–47	Kristian X
1947–72	Frederik IX
1972–	Margrethe II

Prime Minister
1900–1	Hannibal Sehested
1901–5	J H Deuntzer
1905–8	J C Christensen
1908–9	Niels Neergaard
1909	Ludvig Holstein-Ledreborg
1909–10	C Th Zahle
1910–13	Klaus Berntsen
1913–20	C Th Zahle
1920	Otto Liebe
1920	M P Frlls
1920–4	Niels Neergaard
1924–6	Thorvald Stauning
1926–9	Thomas Madsen-Mygdal
1929–42	Thorvald Stauning
1942	Wilhelm Buhl
1942–3	Erik Scavenius
1943–5	*No government*
1945	Wilhelm Buhl
1945–7	Knud Kristensen
1947–50	Hans Hedtoft
1950–3	Erik Eriksen
1953–5	Hans Hedtoft
1955–60	Hans Christian Hansen
1960–2	Viggo Kampmann
1962–8	Jens Otto Krag

1968–71	Hilmar Baunsgaard
1971–2	Jens Otto Krag
1972–3	Anker Jørgensen
1973–5	Poul Hartling
1975–82	Anker Jørgensen
1982–93	Poul Schlüter
1993–2001	Poul Nyrup Rasmussen
2001–	Anders Fogh Rasmussen

Djibouti

President
| 1977–99 | Hassan Gouled Aptidon |
| 1999– | Ismaïl Omar Guelleh |

Prime Minister
1977–8	Abdallah Mohammed Kamil
1978–2001	Barkat Gourad Hamadou
2001–	Dileïta Mohamed Dileïta

Dominica

President
1977	Louis Cools-Lartigue *Interim President*
1978–9	Frederick E Degazon
1979–80	Jenner Armour *Acting*
1980–4	Aurelius Marie
1984–93	Clarence Augustus Seignoret
1993–8	Crispin Anselm Sorhaindo
1998–2003	Vernon Shaw
2003–	Nicholas Liverpool

Prime Minister
1978–9	Patrick Roland John
1979–80	Oliver Seraphine
1980–95	Mary Eugenia Charles
1995–2000	Edison James
2000	Rosie Douglas
2000–4	Pierre Charles
2004–	Roosevelt Skerrit

Dominican Republic

President
1899–1902	Juan Isidro Jiménez
1902–3	Horacio Vásquez
1903	Alejandro Wos y Gil
1903–4	Juan Isidro Jiménez
1904–6	Carlos Morales
1906–11	Ramon Cáceres
1911–12	Eladio Victoria
1912–13	Adolfo Nouel y Bobadilla
1913–14	José Bordas y Valdés
1914	Ramon Báez
1914–16	Juan Isidro Jiménez
1916–22	*US occupation* (Francisco Henríquez y Carrajal)
1922–4	*US occupation* (Juan Batista Vicini Burgos)
1924–30	Horacio Vásquez
1930	Rafael Estrella Urena
1930–8	Rafael Leónidas Trujillo y Molina
1938–40	Jacinto Bienvenudo Peynado
1940–2	Manuel de Jesus Troncoso de la Concha
1942–52	Rafael Leónidas Trujillo y Molina
1952–60	Hector Bienvenido Trujillo
1960–2	Joaquín Videla Balaguer

1962	Rafael Bonnelly
1962	*Military Junta* (Huberto Bogaert)
1962–3	Rafael Bonnelly
1963	Juan Bosch Gavino
1963	*Military Junta* (Emilio de los Santos)
1963–5	Donald Reid Cabral
1965	*Civil War*
1965	Elias Wessin y Wessin
1965	Antonio Imbert Barreras
1965	Francisco Caamaño Deñó
1965–6	Héctor Garcia Godoy Cáceres
1966–78	Joaquín Videla Balaguer
1978–82	Antonio Guzmán Fernández
1982–6	Salvador Jorge Blanco
1986–96	Joaquín Videla Balaguer
1996–2000	Leonel Fernández Reyna
2000–4	Hipólito Mejía
2004–	Leonel Fernández Reyna

East Timor

President
| 2002–7 | Xanana Gusmão |
| 2007– | Jose Ramós-Horta |

Prime Minister
2002–6	Mari Alkatiri
2006–7	José Ramos-Horta
2007–	Xanana Gusmão

Ecuador

President
1895–1901	Eloy Alfaro
1901–5	Leónides Plaza Gutiérrez
1905–6	Lizardo García
1906–11	Eloy Alfaro
1911	Emilio Estrada
1911–12	Carlos Freile Zaldumbide
1912–16	Leónides Plaza Gutiérrez
1916–20	Alfredo Baquerizo Moreno
1920–4	José Luis Tamayo
1924–5	Gonzálo S Córdova
1925–6	*Military Juntas*
1926–31	Isidro Ayora
1931–2	*Four Acting Presidents*
1932–3	Juan de Dios Martínez Mera
1933–4	Abelardo Montalvo
1934–5	José María Velasco Ibarra
1935	Antonio Pons
1935–7	Federico Páez
1937–8	Alberto Enriquez Gallo
1938	Manuel María Borrero
1938–9	Aurelio Mosquera Narváez
1939–40	Julio Enrique Moreno
1940–4	Carlos Alberto Arroya del Río
1944–7	José María Velasco Ibarra
1947	Carlos Mancheno
1947–8	Carlos Julio Arosemena Tola
1948–52	Galo Plaza Lasso
1952–6	José María Velasco Ibarra
1956–60	Camilo Ponce Enríquez
1960–1	José María Velasco Ibarra
1961–3	Carlos Julio Arosemena Monroy
1963–6	*Military Junta*
1966	Clemente Yerovi Indaburu
1966–8	Otto Arosemena Gómez

History

1968–72	José María Velasco Ibarra
1972–6	Guillermo Rodríguez Lara
1976–9	*Military Junta*
1979–81	Jaime Roldós Aguilera
1981–4	Oswaldo Hurtado Larrea
1984–8	León Febres Cordero
1988–92	Rodrigo Borja Cevallos
1992–6	Sixto Durán Ballén
1996–7	Abdalá Bucaram Ortiz
1997	Rosalia Arteaga *Acting*
1997–8	Fabián Alarcón Rivero
1998–2000	Jamil Mahuad Witt
2000–3	Gustavo Noboa Bejerano
2003–5	Lucio Gutiérrez *voted out of office*
2005–7	Alfredo Palacio *Vice President*
2007–	Rafael Correa

Egypt

Khedive

1895–1914	Abbas Helmi II

Sultan

1914–17	Hussein Kamel
1917–22	Ahmed Fouad

▪ Kingdom of Egypt
Monarch

1922–36	Fouad I
1936–7	Farouk *Trusteeship*
1937–52	Farouk I

▪ Republic of Egypt
President

1953–4	Mohammed Najib
1954–70	Gamal Abdel Nasser
1970–81	Mohammed Anwar El-Sadat
1981–	Mohammed Hosni Mubarak

Prime Minister

1895–1908	Mustafa Fahmy
1908–10	Butros Ghali
1910–14	Mohammed Said
1914–19	Hussein Rushdi
1919	Mohammed Said
1919–20	Yousuf Wahba
1920–1	Mohammed Tewfiq Nazim
1921	Adli Yegen
1922	Abdel Khaliq Tharwat
1922–3	Mohammed Tewfiq Nazim
1923–4	Yehia Ibrahim
1924	Saad Zaghloul
1924–6	Ahmed Zaywan
1926–7	Adli Yegen
1927–8	Abdel Khaliq Tharwat
1928	Mustafa An-Nahass
1928–9	Mohammed Mahmoud
1929–30	Adli Yegen
1930	Mustafa An-Nahass
1930–3	Ismail Sidqi
1933–4	Abdel Fattah Yahya
1934–6	Mohammed Tewfiq Nazim
1936	Ali Maher
1936–7	Mustafa An-Nahass
1937–9	Mohammed Mahmoud
1939–40	Ali Maher
1940	Hassan Sabri
1940–2	Hussein Sirry
1942–4	Mustafa An-Nahass

1944–5	Ahmed Maher
1945–6	Mahmoud Fahmy El-Nuqrashi
1946	Ismail Sidqi
1946–8	Mahmoud Fahmy El-Nuqrashi
1948–9	Ibrahim Abdel Hadi
1949–50	Hussein Sirry
1950–2	Mustafa An-Nahass
1952	Ali Maher
1952	Najib El-Hilali
1952	Hussein Sirry
1952	Najib El-Hilali
1952	Ali Maher
1952–4	Mohammed Najib
1954	Gamal Abdel Nasser
1954	Mohammed Najib
1954–62	Gamal Abdel Nasser
1958–61	*United Arab Republic*
1962–5	Ali Sabri
1965–6	Zakariya Mohyi Ed-Din
1966–7	Mohammed Sidqi Soliman
1967–70	Gamal Abdel Nasser
1970–2	Mahmoud Fawzi
1972–3	Aziz Sidki
1973–4	Mohammed Anwar El-Sadat
1974–5	Abdel Aziz Hijazy
1975–8	Mamdouh Salem
1978–80	Mustafa Khalil
1980–1	Mohammed Anwar El-Sadat
1981–2	Mohammed Hosni Mubarak
1982–4	Fouad Monyi Ed-Din
1984	Kamal Hassan Ali
1985–6	Ali Lotfi
1986–96	Atif Sidqi
1996–9	Ahmed Kamal Al-Ganzouri
1999–2004	Atif Muhammed Obeid
2004–	Ahmed Nazif

El Salvador

President

1899–1903	Tomás Regalado
1903–7	Pedro José Escalon
1907–11	Fernando Figueroa
1911–13	Manuel Enrique Araujo
1913–14	Carlos Meléndez *President Designate*
1914–15	Alfonso Quiñónez Molina *President Designate*
1915–18	Carlos Meléndez
1918–19	Alfonso Quiñónez Molina *Vice President*
1919–23	Jorge Meléndez
1923–7	Alfonso Quiñónez Molina
1927–31	Pio Romero Bosque
1931	Arturo Araujo
1931	*Military Administration*
1931–4	Maximiliano H Martinez *Vice President*
1934–5	Andrés I Menéndez *Provisional President*
1935–44	Maximiliano H Martinez
1944	Andrés I Menéndez *Vice President*
1944–5	Osmin Aguirre y Salinas *Provisional President*
1945–8	Salvador Castaneda Castro
1948–50	*Revolutionary Council*
1950–6	Oscar Osorio
1956–60	José María Lemus

1960–1	*Military Junta*
1961–2	*Civil-Military Administration*
1962	Rodolfo Eusebio Cordón *Provisional President*
1962–7	Julio Adalberto Rivera
1967–72	Fidel Sánchez Hernández
1972–7	Arturo Armando Molina
1977–9	Carlos Humberto Romero
1979–82	*Military Juntas*
1982–4	*Government of National Unanimity* (Alvaro Magaña)
1984–9	José Napoleón Duarte
1989–94	Alfredo Cristiani
1994–9	Armando Calderón Sol
1999–2004	Francisco Flores Perez
2004–	Elias Antonio (Tony) Saca

Equatorial Guinea

President

| 1968–79 | Francisco Macias Nguema |
| 1979– | Teodoro Obiang Nguema Mbasogo |

Prime Minister

1963–8	Bonifacio Ondó Edu
1968–82	*No Prime Minister*
1982–92	Cristino Seriche Bioko
1992–6	Silestre Siale Bileka
1996–2001	Ángel Serafín Seriche Dougan
2001–4	Cándido Muatetema Rivas
2004–6	Miguel Abia Bitea Borico
2006–8	Ricardo Mangue Obama Nfubea
2008–	Ignacio Milam Tang

Eritrea

President

| 1993– | Isaias Afewerki |

Estonia

President

1990–2	Arnold Rüütel
1992–2001	Lennart Meri
2001–6	Arnold Rüütel
2006–	Toomas Hendrik Ilves

Prime Minister

1990–2	Edgar Savisaar
1992	Tiit Vähi
1992–4	Mart Laar
1994–5	Andres Tarand
1995–7	Tiit Vähi
1997–9	Mart Siimann
1999–2002	Mart Laar
2002–3	Siim Kallas
2003–5	Juhan Parts
2005–	Andrus Ansip

Ethiopia

Monarch

1889–1911	Menelik II
1911–16	Lij Iyasu (Joshua)
1916–28	Zawditu
1928–74	Haile Selassie *Emperor from 1930*

■ **Provisional Military Administrative Council**

Chairman

| 1974–7 | Teferi Benti |
| 1977–87 | Mengistu Haile Mariam |

■ **People's Democratic Republic**

President

1987–91	Mengistu Haile Mariam
1991	Tesfaye Gebre Kidan *Acting*
1991–5	Meles Zenawi

Prime Minister

1987–9	Fikre Selassie Wogderess
1989–91	Haile Yimenu *Acting*
1991	Tesfaye Dinka *Acting*
1991–5	Tamirat Layne *Acting*

■ **Federal Democratic Republic**

President

| 1995–2001 | Negasso Gidada |
| 2001– | Girma Wolde-Giorgis |

Prime Minister

| 1995– | Meles Zenawi |

Fiji

Head of State 1970–87: British monarch, represented by Governor General

Prime Minister

| 1970–87 | Kamisese Mara |
| 1987 | Timoci Bavadra |

■ **Interim Administration**

Governor General

| 1987 | Penaia Ganilau |
| 1987 | *Military Administration* (Sitiveni Rabuka) |

■ **Republic**

President

1987	Sitiveni Rabuka *Chairman*
1987–94	Sir Penaia Ganilau
1994–2000	Sir Kamisese Mara
2000	*Interim Military Government* (Frank Bainimarama)
2001–	Josefa Iloilo (*Acting President until 2000–1*)
2006–7	Frank Bainimarama *Interim President*

Prime Minister

1987–92	Kamisese Mara
1992–9	Sitiveni Rabuka
1999–2000	Mahendra Chaudhry
2000	Tevita Momoedonu *Acting*
2000	Epeli Nailatika *Interim Prime Minister*
2000–1	Laisenia Qarase
2001	Tevita Momoedonu
2001–6	Laisenia Qarase
2006–7	Jona Senilagakali *Interim Prime Minister*
2007–	Frank Bainimarama *Interim Prime Minister*

Finland

President

| 1919–25 | Kaarlo Juho Ståhlberg |

History

1925–31	Lauri Kristian Relander
1931–7	Pehr Evind Svinhufvud
1937–40	Kyösti Kallio
1940–4	Risto Ryti
1944–6	Carl Gustaf Mannerheim
1946–56	Juho Kusti Paasikivi
1956–81	Urho Kekkonen
1982–94	Mauno Koivisto
1994–2000	Martti Ahtisaari
2000–	Tarja Halonen

Prime Minister

1917–18	Pehr Evind Svinhufvud
1918	Juho Kusti Paasikivi
1918–19	Lauri Johannes Ingman
1919	Kaarlo Castrén
1919–20	Juho Vennola
1920–1	Rafael Erich
1921–2	Juho Vennola
1922	Aino Kaarlo Cajander
1922–4	Kyösti Kallio
1924	Aino Kaarlo Cajander
1924–5	Lauri Johannes Ingman
1925	Antti Agaton Tulenheimo
1925–6	Kyösti Kallio
1926–7	Väinö Tanner
1927–8	Juho Emil Sunila
1928–9	Oskari Mantere
1929–30	Kyösti Kallio
1930–1	Pehr Evind Svinhufvud
1931–2	Juhu Emil Sunila
1932–6	Toivo Kivimäki
1936–7	Kyösti Kallio
1937–9	Aino Kaarlo Cajander
1939–41	Risto Ryti
1941–3	Johann Rangell
1943–4	Edwin Linkomies
1944	Andreas Hackzell
1944	Urho Jonas Castrén
1944–5	Juho Kusti Paasikivi
1946–8	Mauno Pekkala
1948–50	Karl August Fagerholm
1950–3	Urho Kekkonen
1953–4	Sakari Tuomioja
1954	Ralf Törngren
1954–6	Urho Kekkonen
1956–7	Karl August Fagerholm
1957	Väinö Johannes Sukselainen
1957–8	Rainer von Fieandt
1958	Reino Ilsakki Kuuskoski
1958–9	Karl August Fagerholm
1959–61	Väinö Johannes Sukselainen
1961–2	Martti Miettunen
1962–3	Ahti Karjalainen
1963–4	Reino Ragnar Lehto
1964–6	Johannes Virolainen
1966–8	Rafael Paasio
1968–70	Mauno Koivisto
1970	Teuvo Ensio Aura
1970–1	Ahti Karjalainen
1971–2	Teuvo Ensio Aura
1972	Rafael Paasio
1972–5	Kalevi Sorsa
1975	Keijo Antero Liinamaa
1975–7	Martti Miettunen
1977–9	Kalevi Sorsa
1979–82	Mauno Koivisto
1982–7	Kalevi Sorsa

1987–91	Harri Holkeri
1991–5	Esko Aho
1995–2003	Paavo Lipponen
2003	Anneli Jääteenmaki
2003–	Matti Vanhanen

France

President

■ **Third Republic**

1899–1906	Emile Loubet
1906–13	Armand Fallières
1913–20	Raymond Poincaré
1920	Paul Deschanel
1920–4	Alexandre Millerand
1924–31	Gaston Doumergue
1931–2	Paul Doumer
1932–40	Albert Lebrun

■ **Fourth Republic**

| 1947–54 | Vincent Auriol |
| 1954–8 | René Coty |

■ **Fifth Republic**

1958–69	Charles de Gaulle
1969–74	Georges Pompidou
1974–81	Valéry Giscard d'Estaing
1981–95	François Mitterrand
1995–2007	Jacques Chirac
2007–	Nicolas Sarkozy

Prime Minister

■ **Third Republic**

1899–1902	Pierre Waldeck-Rousseau
1902–5	Emile Combes
1905–6	Maurice Rouvier
1906	Jean Sarrien
1906–9	Georges Clemenceau
1909–11	Aristide Briand
1911	Ernest Monis
1911–12	Joseph Caillaux
1912–13	Raymond Poincaré
1913	Aristide Briand
1913	Jean Louis Barthou
1913–14	Gaston Doumergue
1914	Alexandre Ribot
1914–15	René Viviani
1915–17	Aristide Briand
1917	Alexandre Ribot
1917	Paul Painlevé
1917–20	Georges Clemenceau
1920	Alexandre Millerand
1920–1	Georges Leygues
1921–2	Aristide Briand
1922–4	Raymond Poincaré
1924	Frédéric François-Marsal
1924–5	Édouard Herriot
1925	Paul Painlevé
1925–6	Aristide Briand
1926	Édouard Herriot
1926–9	Raymond Poincaré
1929	Aristide Briand
1929–30	André Tardieu
1930	Camille Chautemps
1930	André Tardieu
1930–1	Théodore Steeg
1931–2	Pierre Laval
1932	André Tardieu

1932	Édouard Herriot
1932–3	Joseph Paul-Boncour
1933	Édouard Daladier
1933	Albert Sarrault
1933–4	Camille Chautemps
1934	Édouard Daladier
1934	Gaston Doumergue
1934–5	Pierre-Étienne Flandin
1935	Fernand Bouisson
1935–6	Pierre Laval
1936	Albert Sarrault
1936–7	Léon Blum
1937–8	Camille Chautemps
1938	Léon Blum
1938–40	Édouard Daladier
1940	Paul Reynaud
1940	Philippe Pétain

■ **Vichy Government**

1940–4	Philippe Pétain

■ **Provisional Government of the French Republic**

1944–6	Charles de Gaulle
1946	Félix Gouin
1946	Georges Bidault

■ **Fourth Republic**

1946–7	Léon Blum
1947	Paul Ramadier
1947–8	Robert Schuman
1948	André Marie
1948	Robert Schuman
1948–9	Henri Queuille
1949–50	Georges Bidault
1950	Henri Queuille
1950–1	René Pleven
1951	Henri Queuille
1951–2	René Pleven
1952	Edgar Faure
1952–3	Antoine Pinay
1953	René Mayer
1953–4	Joseph Laniel
1954–5	Pierre Mendès-France
1955–6	Edgar Faure
1956–7	Guy Mollet
1957	Maurice Bourgès-Maunoury
1957–8	Félix Gaillard
1958	Pierre Pfimlin
1958–9	Charles de Gaulle

■ **Fifth Republic**

1959–62	Michel Debré
1962–8	Georges Pompidou
1968–9	Maurice Couve de Murville
1969–72	Jacques Chaban Delmas
1972–4	Pierre Mesmer
1974–6	Jacques Chirac
1976–81	Raymond Barre
1981–4	Pierre Mauroy
1984–6	Laurent Fabius
1986–8	Jacques Chirac
1988–91	Michel Rocard
1991–2	Édith Cresson
1992–3	Pierre Bérégovoy
1993–5	Édouard Balladur
1995–7	Alain Juppé
1997–2002	Lionel Jospin
2002–5	Jean-Pierre Raffarin
2005–7	Dominique de Villepin
2007–	François Fillon

Gabon

President

1960–7	Léon M'ba
1967–	Omar (Bernard-Albert, *to 1973*) Bongo

Prime Minister

1960–75	*As President*
1975–90	Léon Mébiame (Mébiane)
1991–3	Casimir Oyé M'ba
1993–8	Paulin Obame-Nguema
1999–2006	Jean-François Ntoutoume-Emane
2006–	Jean Eyeghe Ndong

The Gambia

President

1965–94	Dawda Kairaba Jawara
1994–	Yahya Jammeh *Head of military junta 1994–6*

Georgia

President

1991–2	Zviad Gamsakhurdia
1992	*Military Council*
1992–2003	Eduard Shevardnaze
2003–4	Nino Burdschanadse *Acting*
2004–	Mikhail Saakashvili

Prime Minister

1990–1	Tengiz Sigua
1991	Murman Omanidze *Acting*
1991–2	Bessarion Gugushvili
1992–3	Tengiz Sigua
1993	Eduard Shevardnadze *Acting*
1993–5	Otar Patsatsia
1995–8	Niko Lekishvili
1998–2000	Vazha Lordkipanidze
2000–1	Giorgi Arsenishvili
2001–3	Avtandil Djorbenadze
2003–5	Zurab Zhvania
2005–7	Zurab Noghaideli
2007–8	Lado Gurgenidze
2008–	Grigol Mgaloblishvili

Germany

■ **German Empire**
Emperor

1888–1918	Wilhelm II *abdicated* 1918

Chancellor

1909–17	Theobald von Bethmann Hollweg
1917	Georg Michaelis
1917–18	Georg Graf von Hertling
1918	Prince Max von Baden
1918	Friedrich Ebert

■ **German Republic**
President

1919–25	Friedrich Ebert
1925–34	Paul von Hindenburg

Reich Chancellor

1919	Philipp Scheidemann

History

1919–20	Gustav Bauer
1920	Hermann Müller
1920–1	Konstantin Fehrenbach
1921–2	Karl Joseph Wirth
1922–3	Wilhelm Cuno
1923	Gustav Stresemann
1923–4	Wilhelm Marx
1925–6	Hans Luther
1926–8	Wilhelm Marx
1928–30	Hermann Müller
1930–2	Heinrich Brüning
1932	Franz von Papen
1932–3	Kurt von Schleicher
1933	Adolf Hitler

Chancellor and Führer

1933–45	Adolf Hitler (*Führer from 1934*)
1945	Karl Dönitz

■ **German Democratic Republic (East Germany)**
President

1949–60	Wilhelm Pieck

Chairman of the Council of State

1960–73	Walter Ernst Karl Ulbricht
1973–6	Willi Stoph
1976–89	Erich Honecker
1989	Egon Krenz
1989–90	Gregor Gysi *General Secretary as Chairman*

Premier

1949–64	Otto Grotewohl
1964–73	Willi Stoph
1973–6	Horst Sindermann
1976–89	Willi Stoph
1989–90	Hans Modrow
1990	Lothar de Maizière

■ **German Federal Republic (West Germany)**
President

1949–59	Theodor Heuss
1959–69	Heinrich Lübke
1969–74	Gustav Heinemann
1974–9	Walter Scheel
1979–84	Karl Carstens
1984–90	Richard von Weizsäcker

Chancellor

1949–63	Konrad Adenauer
1963–6	Ludwig Erhard
1966–9	Kurt Georg Kiesinger
1969–74	Willy Brandt
1974–82	Helmut Schmidt
1982–90	Helmut Kohl

■ **Germany**
President

1990–4	Richard von Weizsäcker
1994–9	Roman Herzog
1999–2004	Johannes Rau
2004–	Horst Köhler

Chancellor

1990–8	Helmut Kohl
1998–2005	Gerhard Schröder
2005–	Angela Merkel

Ghana

President

1960–6	Kwame Nkrumah

National Liberation Council
Chairman

1966–9	Joseph Arthur Ankrah
1969	Akwasi Amankwa Afrifa
1969–70	*Presidential Committee*

President

1970–2	Edward Akufo-Addo

Chairman

1972–8	*National Redemption Council* (Ignatius Kuti Acheampong)
1978–9	*Supreme Military Council* (Fred W Akuffo)
1979	*Armed Forces Revolutionary Council* (Jerry John Rawlings)

President

1979–81	Hilla Limann

Provisional National Defence Council
Chairman

1981–2001	Jerry John Rawlings (*President from 1992*)

President

2001–	John Agyekum Kufuor

Prime Minister

1960–9	*As President*
1969–72	Kufi Abrefa Busia
1972–8	*As President*
1978–	*No Prime Minister*

Greece

■ **Kingdom of Greece**
Monarch

1863–1913	George I
1913–17	Constantine I
1917–20	Alexander
1920–2	Constantine I
1922–3	George II
1923–4	Paul Koundouriotis *Regent*

■ **Republic**
President

1924–6	Paul Koundouriotis
1926	Theodore Pangalos
1926–9	Paul Koundouriotis
1929–35	Alexander T Zaïmis

■ **Kingdom of Greece**
Monarch

1935	George Kondylis *Regent*
1935–47	George II
1947–64	Paul
1964–7	Constantine II
1967–73	*Military Junta*
1973	George Papadopoulos *Regent*

■ **New Republic**
President

1973	George Papadopoulos
1973–4	Phaedon Gizikis
1974–5	Michael Stasinopoulos

1975–80	Constantine Tsatsos
1980–5	Constantine Karamanlis
1985–90	Christos Sartzetakis
1990–5	Constantine Karamanlis
1995–2005	Constantine Stephanopoulos
2005–	Karolos Papoulias

Prime Minister

1899–1901	George Theotokis
1901–2	Alexander T Zaïmis
1902–3	Theodore Deligiannis
1903	George Theotokis
1903	Demetrius G Rallis
1903–4	George Theotokis
1904–5	Theodore Deligiannis
1905	Demetrius G Rallis
1905–9	George Theotokis
1909	Demetrius G Rallis
1909–10	Kyriakoulis P Mavromichalis
1910	Stephen N Dragoumis
1910–15	Eleftherios K Venizelos
1915	Demetrius P Gounaris
1915	Eleftherios K Venizelos
1915	Alexander T Zaïmis
1915–16	Stephen Skouloudis
1916	Alexander T Zaïmis
1916	Nicholas P Kalogeropoulos
1916–17	Spyridon Lambros
1917	Alexander T Zaïmis
1917–20	Eleftherios K Venizelos
1920–1	Demetrius G Rallis
1921	Nicholas P Kalogeropoulos
1921–2	Demetrius P Gounaris
1922	Nicholas Stratos
1922	Peter E Protopapadakis
1922	Nicholas Triandaphyllakos
1922	Sortirios Krokidas
1922	Alexander T Zaïmis
1922–3	Stylianos Gonatas
1924	Eleftherios K Venizelos
1924	George Kaphandaris
1924	Alexander Papanastasiou
1924	Themistocles Sophoulis
1924–5	Andreas Michalakopoulos
1925–6	Alexander N Chatzikyriakos
1926	Theodore Pangalos
1926	Athanasius Eftaxias
1926	George Kondylis
1926–8	Alexander T Zaïmis
1928–32	Eleftherios K Venizelos
1932	Alexander Papanastasiou
1932	Eleftherios K Venizelos
1932–3	Panagiotis Tsaldaris
1933	Eleftherios K Venizelos
1933	Nicholas Plastiras
1933	Alexander Othonaos
1933–5	Panagiotis Tsaldaris
1935	George Kondylis
1935–6	Constantine Demertzis
1936–41	John Metaxas
1941	Alexander Koryzis
1941	*Chairman of Ministers* George II
1941	*German Occupation* (Emmanuel Tsouderos)
1941–2	George Tsolakoglou
1942–3	Constantine Logothetopoulos
1943–4	John Rallis

Government in exile

1941–4	Emmanuel Tsouderos
1944	Sophocles Venizelos
1944–5	George Papandreou

Post-war

1945	Nicholas Plastiras
1945	Peter Voulgaris
1945	Damaskinos, Archbishop of Athens
1945	Panagiotis Kanellopoulos
1945–6	Themistocles Sophoulis
1946	Panagiotis Politzas
1946–7	Constantine Tsaldaris
1947	Demetrius Maximos
1947	Constantine Tsaldaris
1947–9	Themistocles Sophoulis
1949–50	Alexander Diomedes
1950	John Theotokis
1950	Sophocles Venizelos
1950	Nicholas Plastiras
1950–1	Sophocles Venizelos
1951	Nicholas Plastiras
1952	Demetrius Kiusopoulos
1952–5	Alexander Papagos
1955	Stephen C Stefanopoulos
1955–8	Constantine Karamanlis
1958	Constantine Georgakopoulos
1958–61	Constantine Karamanlis
1961	Constantine Dovas
1961–3	Constantine Karamanlis
1963	Panagiotis Pipinellis
1963	Stylianos Mavromichalis
1963	George Papandreou
1963–4	John Parskevopoulos
1964–5	George Papandreou
1965	George Athanasiadis-Novas
1965	Elias Tsirimokos
1965–6	Stephen C Stefanopoulos
1966–7	John Paraskevopoulos
1967	Panagiotis Kanellopoulos
1967–74	*Military Junta*
1967	Constantine Kollias
1967–73	George Papadopoulos
1973	Spyridon Markezinis
1973–4	Adamantios Androutsopoulos
1974–80	Constantine Karamanlis
1980–1	George Rallis
1981–9	Andreas Papandreou
1989	Tzannis Tzannetakis
1989–90	Xenofon Zolotas
1990–3	Constantine Mitsotakis
1993–6	Andreas Papandreou
1996–2004	Costas Simitis
2004–	Costas Karamanlis

Grenada

Head of State: British monarch, represented by Governor General

Prime Minister

1974–9	Eric M Gairy
1979–83	Maurice Bishop
1983–4	Nicholas Brathwaite *Chairman of Interim Council*
1984–9	Herbert A Blaize
1989–90	Ben Jones
1990–5	Nicholas Brathwaite
1995–2008	Keith Mitchell

History

History

2008–	Tillman Thomas

Guatemala

President
1898–1920	Manuel Estrada Cabrera
1920–2	Carlos Herrera y Luna
1922–6	José María Orellana
1926–30	Lázaro Chacón
1930	Baudillo Palma
1930–1	Manuel María Orellana
1931	José María Reyna Andrade
1931–44	Jorge Ubico Castañeda
1944	Federico Ponce Vaidez
1944–5	Jacobo Arbenz Guzmán
1945–51	Juan José Arévalo
1951–4	Jacobo Arbenz Guzmán
1954	*Military Junta* (Carlos Díaz)
1954	Elfego J Monzón
1954–7	Carlos Castillo Armas
1957	*Military Junta* (Oscar Mendoza Azurdia)
1957	Luis Arturo González López
1957–8	*Military Junta* (Guillermo Flores Avendaño)
1958–63	Miguel Ydígoras Fuentes
1963–6	*Military Junta* (Enrique Peralta Azurdia)
1966–70	Julio César Méndez Montenegro
1970–4	Carlos Araña Osorio
1974–8	Kjell Eugenio Laugerud García
1978–82	Romeo Lucas García
1982	Angel Aníbal Guevara
1982–3	Efraín Rios Montt
1983–6	Oscar Humberto Mejía Victores
1986–91	Marco Vinicio Cerezo Arévalo
1991–3	Jorge Serrano Elias
1993–6	Ramiro de León Carpio
1996–2000	Álvaro Arzú Irigoyen
2000–4	Alfonso Portillo Cabrera
2004–8	Oscar Berger
2008–	Alvaro Colom Caballeros

Guinea

President
1961–84	Ahmed Sékou Touré
1984–	Lansana Conté

Prime Minister
1958–72	Ahmed Sékou Touré
1972–84	Louis Lansana Beavogui
1984–5	Diarra Traore
1985–96	*No Prime Minister*
1996–9	Sidia Toure
1999–2004	Lamine Sidime
2004	François Lonseny Fall
2004–6	Cellou Dalein Diallo
2006–7	*No Prime Minister*
2007–8	Lansana Kouyaté
2008–	Ahmed Tidiane Souaré

Guinea-Bissau

President
1974–80	Luis de Almeida Cabral
1980–4	*Revolutionary Council* (João Bernardo Vieira)
1984–99	João Vieira
1999–2000	Malai Bacai Sanhá *Interim President*
2000–3	Kumba Yalla
2003	Veríssimo Correia *Interim President*
2003–5	Henrique Rosa *Interim President*
2005–	João Vieira

Prime Minister
1992–4	Carlos Correia
1994–7	Manuel Saturnino da Costa
1997–8	Carlos Correia
1998–2000	Francisco Fadul
2000–1	Caetano N'Tchama
2001	Faustino Imbali
2001–2	Alamara Nhassé
2002–3	Mário Pires
2003–4	Artur Sanhá
2004–5	Carlos Gomes Júnior
2005–7	Aristides Gomes
2007–8	Martinho N'Dafa Cabi
2008–	Carlos Correia

Guyana

President
1970	Edward A Luckhoo
1970–80	Arthur Chung
1980–5	Linden Forbes Sampson Burnham
1985–92	Hugh Desmond Hoyte
1992–7	Cheddi Bharrat Jagan
1997	Samuel Hinds
1997–9	Janet Jagan
1999–	Bharrat Jagdeo *Interim President* 1999–2001

Prime Minister
1966–85	Linden Forbes Sampson Burnham
1985–92	Hamilton Green
1992–7	Samuel Hinds
1997	Janet Jagan
1997–	Samuel Hinds

Haiti

President
1896–1902	P A Tirésias Simon Lam
1902	Boisrond Canal
1902–8	Alexis Nord
1908–11	Antoine Simon
1911–12	Michel Cincinnatus Leconte
1912–13	Tancrède Auguste
1913–14	Michael Oreste
1914	Oreste Zamor
1914–15	Joseph Davilmare Théodore
1915	Jean Velbrun-Guillaume
1915–22	Philippe Sudre Dartiguenave
1922–30	Joseph Louis Bornó
1930	Étienne Roy
1930–41	Sténio Joseph Vincent
1941–6	Élie Lescot
1946	*Military Junta* (Frank Lavaud)
1946–50	Dumarsais Estimé
1950	*Military Junta* (Frank Lavaud)
1950–6	Paul E Magloire
1956–7	François Sylvain
1957	*Military Junta*
1957	Léon Cantave
1957	Daniel Fignolé
1957	Antoine Kebreau
1957–71	François Duvalier ('Papa Doc')

1971–86	Jean-Claude Duvalier ('Baby Doc')
1986–8	Henri Namphy
1988	Leslie Manigat
1988	Henri Namphy
1988–90	Prosper Avril
1990–1	Ertha Pascal-Trouillot
1991	Jean-Bertrand Aristide
1991	Raoul Cédras
1991–2	Joseph Nérette
1992–3	Marc-Louis Bazin
1993–4	Jean-Bertrand Aristide
1994	Émile Jonassaint
1994–6	Jean-Bertrand Aristide
1996–2000	René Préval
2000–4	Jean-Bertrand Aristide
2004–6	Boniface Alexandre *Interim President*
2006–	René Préval

Prime Minister

1988	Martial Célestin
1988–91	*No Prime Minister*
1991	René Préval
1991–2	Jean-Jacques Honorat *Interim Prime Minister*
1992–3	Marc Bazin
1993–4	Robert Malval
1994–5	Smarck Michel
1995–6	Claudette Werleigh
1996–7	Rosny Smarth
1998–2001	Jacques-Édouard Alexis
2001–2	Jean-Marie Cherestal
2002–4	Yvon Neptune
2004–6	Gérard Latortue *Interim Prime Minister*
2006–8	Jacques-Édouard Alexis
2008–	Michèle Pierre-Louis

Honduras

President

1900–3	Terencio Sierra
1903	Juan Angel Arias
1903–7	Manuel Bonilla Chirinos
1907–11	Miguel R Dávila
1912–15	Manuel Bonilla Chirinos
1915–20	Francisco Bertrand
1920–4	Rafael López Gutiérrez
1924–5	Vicente Tosta Carrasco
1925–8	Miguel Paz Barahona
1929–32	Vicente Mejía Clindres
1932–49	Tiburcio Carías Andino
1949–54	Juan Manuel Gálvez

Head of State

1954–6	Julio Lozano Diaz
1956–7	*Military Junta*

President

1958–63	José Ramón Villeda Morales

Head of State

1963–5	Oswaldo López Arellano

President

1965–71	Oswaldo López Arellano
1971–2	Ramón Ernesto Cruz

Head of State

1972–5	Oswaldo López Arellano

1975–8	Juan Alberto Melgar Castro
1978–82	Policarpo Paz García

President

1982–6	Roberto Suazo Córdova
1986–9	José Azcona Hoyo
1989–93	Rafael Leonardo Callejas
1993–7	Carlos Roberto Reina
1997–2002	Carlos Roberto Flores Facussé
2002–6	Ricardo Maduro
2006–	Manuel Zelaya Rosales

Hungary

Monarch

1900–16	Franz Josef I
1916–18	Charles IV

President

1919	Mihály Károlyi
1919	*Revolutionary Governing Council* (Sándor Garbai)
1920–44	Miklós Horthy *Regent*
1944–5	*Provisional National Assembly*
1946–8	Zoltán Tildy
1948–50	Árpád Szakasits
1950–2	Sándor Rónai
1952–67	István Dobi
1967–87	Pál Losonczi
1987–8	Károly Németh
1988–9	Brunó Ferenc Straub
1989–90	Mátyás Szürös
1990–2000	Árpád Göncz
2000–5	Ferenc Madl
2005–	Laszlo Solyom

Premier

1899–1903	Kálmán Széll
1903	Károly Khuen-Héderváry
1903–5	István Tisza
1905–6	Géza Fejérváry
1906–10	Sándor Wekerle
1910–12	Károly Khuen-Héderváry
1912–13	Lázló Lukács
1913–17	István Tisza
1917	Móric Esterházy
1917–18	Sándor Wekerle
1918–19	Mihály Károlyi
1919	Dénes Berinkey
1919	*Revolutionary Governing Council*
1919	Gyula Peidl
1919	István Friedrich
1919–20	Károly Huszár
1920	Sándor Simonyi-Semadam
1920–1	Pál Teleki
1921–31	István Bethlen
1931–2	Gyula Károlyi
1932–6	Gyula Gömbös
1936–8	Kálman Darányi
1938–9	Béla Imrédy
1939–41	Pál Teleki
1941–2	Lázló Bárdossy
1942–4	Miklós Kállay
1944	Döme Sztójay
1944	Géza Lakatos
1944	Ferenc Szálasi
1944–5	*Provisional National Assembly* (Béla Dálnoki Miklós)
1945–6	Zoltán Tildy

1946–7	Ferenc Nagy
1947–8	Lajos Dinnyés
1948–52	István Dobi
1952–3	Mátyás Rákosi
1953–5	Imre Nagy
1955–6	András Hegedüs
1956	Imre Nagy
1956–8	János Kádár
1958–61	Ferenc Münnich
1961–5	János Kádár
1965–7	Gyula Kállai
1967–75	Jenö Fock
1975–87	György Lázár
1987–8	Károly Grosz
1988–90	Miklás Németh
1990–3	József Antall
1993–4	Péter Boross
1994–8	Gyula Horn
1998–2002	Viktor Orban
2002–4	Peter Medgyessy
2004–	Ferenc Gyurcsany

First Secretary

1949–56	Mátyás Rákosi
1956	Ernö Gerö
1956–88	János Kádár
1988–90	Károly Grosz

Iceland

President

1944–52	Sveinn Björnsson
1952–68	Ásgeir Ásgeirsson
1968–80	Kristján Eldjárn
1980–96	Vigdís Finnbogadóttir
1996–	Ólafur Ragnar Grimsson

Prime Minister

1900–1	C Goos
1901–4	P A Alberti
1904–9	Hannes Hafstein
1909–11	Björn Jónsson
1911–12	Kristján Jónsson
1912–14	Hannes Hafstein
1914–15	Sigurður Eggerz
1915–17	Einar Arnórsson
1917–22	Jón Magnússon
1922–4	Sigurður Eggerz
1924–6	Jón Magnússon
1926–7	John þorláksson
1927–32	Tryggvi þórhallsson
1932–4	Ásgeir Ásgeirsson
1934–42	Hermann Jónasson
1942	Ólafur Thors
1942–4	Björn þórðarsson
1944–7	Ólafur Thors
1947–9	Stefán Jóhann Stefánsson
1949–50	Ólafur Thors
1950–3	Steingrímur Steinþórsson
1953–6	Ólafur Thors
1956–8	Hermann Jónasson
1958–9	Emil Jónsson
1959–61	Ólafur Thors
1961	Bjarni Benediktsson
1961–3	Ólafur Thors
1963–70	Bjarni Benediktsson
1970–1	Jóhann Hafstein
1971–4	Ólafur Jóhannesson

1974–8	Geir Hallgrímsson
1978–9	Ólafur Jóhannesson
1979	Benedikt Gröndal
1980–3	Gunnar Thoroddsen
1983–7	Steingrímur Hermannsson
1987–8	Thorsteinn Pálsson
1988–91	Steingrímur Hermannsson
1991–2004	Davíd Oddsson
2004–6	Halldór Ásgrímsson
2006–	Geir Hilmar Haarde

India

President

1950–62	Rajendra Prasad
1962–7	Sarvepalli Radhakrishnan
1967–9	Zakir Husain
1969	Varahagiri Venkatagiri *Acting*
1969	Mohammed Hidayatullah *Acting*
1969–74	Varahagiri Venkatagiri
1974–7	Fakhruddin Ali Ahmed
1977	B D Jatti *Acting*
1977–82	Neelam Sanjiva Reddy
1982–7	Giani Zail Singh
1987–92	Ramaswami Venkataraman
1992–7	Shankar Dayal Sharma
1997–2002	Kocheril Raman Narayanan
2002–7	A P J Abdul Kalam
2007–	Pratibha Patil

Prime Minister

1947–64	Jawaharlal Nehru
1964	Gulzari Lal Nanda *Acting*
1964–6	Lal Bahadur Shastri
1966	Gulzari Lal Nanda *Acting*
1966–77	Indira Gandhi
1977–9	Morarji Desai
1979–80	Charan Singh
1980–4	Indira Gandhi
1984–9	Rajiv Gandhi
1989–90	Vishwanath Pratap Singh
1990–1	Chandra Shekhar
1991–6	P V Narasimha Rao
1996	Atal Behari Vajpayee
1996–7	H D Deve Gowda
1997	Inder Kumar Gujral
1998–2004	Atal Behari Vajpayee
2004–	Manmohan Singh

Indonesia

President

1945–9	Ahmed Sukarno

■ **Republic**

1949–66	Ahmed Sukarno
1966–98	T N J Suharto
1998–9	B J Habibie
1999–2001	Abdurrahman Wahid
2001–4	Megawati Sukarnoputri
2004–	Susilo Bambang Yudhoyono

Prime Minister

1945	R A A Wiranatakusumah
1945–7	Sutan Sjahrir
1947–8	Amir Sjarifuddin
1948	Mohammed Hatta
1948–9	Sjarifuddin Prawiraranegara
1949	Susanto Tirtoprodjo

History

1949	Mohammed Hatta
1950	Dr Halim
1950–1	Mohammed Natsir
1951–2	Sukiman Wirjosandjojo
1952–3	Dr Wilopo
1953–5	Ali Sastroamidjojo
1955–6	Burhanuddin Harahap
1956–7	Ali Sastroamidjojo
1957–9	Raden Haji Djuanda Kurtawidjaja
1959–63	Ahmed Sukarno
1963–6	S E Subandrio
1966–	*No Prime Minister*

Iran

Shah

1896–1907	Muzaffar Ad-Din
1907–9	Mohammed Ali
1909–25	Ahmad Mirza
1925–41	Mohammed Reza Khan
1941–79	Mohammed Reza Pahlavi

■ **Islamic Republic**
Leader of the Islamic Revolution

| 1979–89 | Ayatollah Ruhollah Khomeini |
| 1989– | Ayatollah Sayed Ali Khamenei |

President

1980–1	Abolhassan Bani-Sadr
1981	Mohammed Ali Rajai
1981–9	Sayed Ali Khamenei
1989–97	Ali Akbar Hashemi Rafsanjani
1997–2005	Mohammad Khatami
2005–	Mahmoud Ahmadinejad

Prime Minister

1979	Shahpur Bakhtiar
1979–80	Mehdi Bazargan
1980–1	Mohammed Ali Rajai
1981	Mohammed Javad Bahonar
1981	Mohammed Reza Mahdavi-Kani
1981–9	Mir Hossein Moussavi

Iraq

Monarch

1921–33	Faisal I
1933–9	Ghazi I
1939–58	Faisal II (*Regent* 1939–53, Abdul Illah)

■ **Republic**
Commander of the National Forces

| 1958–63 | Abdul Karim Qassem |

Head of Council of State

| 1958–63 | Mohammed Najib Ar-Rubai |

President

1963–6	Abd as-Salam Arif
1966–8	Abd ar-Rahman Arif
1968–79	Ahmad Hassan al-Bakr
1979–2003	Saddam Hussein
2003–4	*US-controlled Transitional Administration*
2004–5	Ghazi Yawer *Interim President*
2005–	Jalal Talabani *Interim President 2005–6*

Prime Minister

| 1958–63 | Abdul Karim Qassem |
| 1963 | Ahmad Hassan al-Bakr |

1963–5	Tahir Yahya
1965	Arif Abd ar-Razzaq
1965–6	Abd ar-Rahman al-Bazzaz
1966–7	Naji Talib
1967	Abd ar-Rahman Arif
1967–8	Tahir Yahya
1968	Abd ar-Razzaq an-Naif
1968–79	Ahmad Hassan al-Bakr
1979–91	Saddam Hussein
1991	Sadun Hammadi
1991–3	Mohammed Hamzah az-Zubaydi
1993–4	Ahmad Hussein Khudayir as-Samarrai
1994–2003	Saddam Hussein
2003–4	*US-controlled Transitional Administration*
2004–5	Iyad Allawi *Interim Prime Minister*
2005–6	Ibrahim al-Jaafari *Interim Prime Minister*
2006–	Nouri Jawad al-Maliki

Ireland

Head of State until 1937: British monarch, represented by a Governor General

President

1937–8	*Presidential Commission*
1938–45	Douglas Hyde
1945–59	Sean Thomas O'Kelly
1959–73	Éamon de Valera
1973–4	Erskine H Childers
1974–6	Carroll Daly
1976–90	Patrick J Hillery
1990–7	Mary Robinson
1997–	Mary McAleese

Prime Minister

1919–21	Éamon de Valera
1922	Arthur Griffiths
1922–32	William Cosgrave
1932–48	Éamon de Valera
1948–51	John Aloysius Costello
1951–4	Éamon de Valera
1954–7	John Aloysius Costello
1957–9	Éamon de Valera
1959–66	Sean Lemass
1966–73	John Lynch
1973–7	Liam Cosgrave
1977–9	John Lynch
1979–82	Charles Haughey
1982–7	Garrett Fitzgerald
1987–92	Charles Haughey
1992–4	Albert Reynolds
1994–7	John Bruton
1997–2008	Bertie Ahern
2008–	Brian Cowen

Israel

President

1948–52	Chaim Weizmann
1952–63	Itzhak Ben-Zvi
1963–73	Zalman Shazar
1973–8	Ephraim Katzair
1978–83	Yitzhak Navon
1983–93	Chaim Herzog
1993–2000	Ezer Weizman
2000–7	Moshe Katsav
2007–	Shimon Peres

History

Prime Minister

1948–53	David Ben-Gurion
1954–5	Moshe Sharett
1955–63	David Ben-Gurion
1963–9	Levi Eshkol
1969–74	Golda Meir
1974–7	Yitzhak Rabin
1977–83	Menachem Begin
1983–4	Yitzhak Shamir
1984–8	Shimon Peres
1988–92	Yitzhak Shamir
1992–5	Yitzhak Rabin
1995–6	Shimon Peres *Acting*
1996–9	Binyamin Netanyahu
1999–2001	Ehud Barak
2001–6	Ariel Sharon
2005–	Ehud Olmert *Interim Prime Minister 2005–6*

Italy

■ Kingdom of Italy
Monarch

1900–46	Victor Emmanuel III
1946	Humbert II

■ Italian Republic
President

1946–8	Enrico de Nicola
1948–55	Luigi Einaudi
1955–62	Giovanni Gronchi
1962–4	Antonio Segni
1964–71	Giuseppe Saragat
1971–8	Giovanni Leone
1978–85	Alessandro Pertini
1985–92	Francesco Cossiga
1992–9	Oscar Luigi Scalfaro
1999–2006	Carlo Azeglio Ciampi
2006–	Giorgio Napolitano

Prime Minister

1900–1	Giuseppe Saracco
1901–3	Giuseppe Zanardelli
1903–5	Giovanni Giolitti
1905–6	Alessandro Fortis
1906	Sydney Sonnino
1906–9	Giovanni Giolitti
1909–10	Sydney Sonnino
1910–11	Luigi Luzzatti
1911–14	Giovanni Giolitti
1914–16	Antonio Salandra
1916–17	Paolo Boselli
1917–19	Vittorio Emmanuele Orlando
1919–20	Francesco Saverio Nitti
1920–1	Giovanni Giolitti
1921–2	Ivanoe Bonomi
1922	Luigi Facta
1922–43	Benito Mussolini
1943–4	Pietro Badoglio
1944–5	Ivanoe Bonomi
1945	Ferrucio Parri
1945–53	Alcide de Gasperi
1953–4	Giuseppe Pella
1954	Amintore Fanfani
1954–5	Mario Scelba
1955–7	Antonio Segni
1957–8	Adone Zoli
1958–9	Amintore Fanfani
1959–60	Antonio Segni
1960	Fernando Tambroni
1960–3	Amintore Fanfani
1963	Giovanni Leone
1963–8	Aldo Moro
1968	Giovanni Leone
1968–70	Mariano Rumor
1970–2	Emilio Colombo
1972–4	Giulio Andreotti
1974–6	Aldo Moro
1976–8	Giulio Andreotti
1979–80	Francisco Cossiga
1980–1	Arnaldo Forlani
1981–2	Giovanni Spadolini
1982–3	Amintore Fanfani
1983–7	Bettino Craxi
1987	Amintore Fanfani
1987–8	Giovanni Goria
1988–9	Ciriaco de Mita
1989–92	Giulio Andreotti
1992–3	Giuliano Amato
1993–4	Carlo Azeglio Ciampi
1994	Silvio Berlusconi
1995–6	Lamberto Dini
1996–8	Romano Prodi
1998–2000	Massimo D'Alema
2000–1	Giuliano Amato
2001–6	Silvio Berlusconi
2006–8	Romano Prodi
2008–	Silvio Berlusconi

Jamaica

Head of State: British monarch, represented by Governor General

Prime Minister

1962–7	Alexander Bustamante
1967	Donald Sangster
1967–72	Hugh Shearer
1972–80	Michael Manley
1980–9	Edward Seaga
1989–92	Michael Manley
1992–2006	Percival Patterson
2006–7	Portia Simpson Miller
2008–	Bruce Golding

Japan

Monarch (Emperor)

1867–1912	Mutsuhito (Meiji Era)
1912–26	Yoshihito (Taisho Era)
1926–89	Hirohito (Showa Era)
1989–	Akihito (Heisei Era)

Prime Minister

1900–1	Hirobumi Ito
1901–6	Taro Katsura
1906–8	Kimmochi Saionji
1908–11	Taro Katsura
1911–12	Kimmochi Saionji
1912–13	Taro Katsura
1913–14	Gonnohyoe Yamamoto
1914–16	Shigenobu Okuma
1916–18	Masatake Terauchi
1918–21	Takashi Hara
1921–2	Korekiyo Takahashi
1922–3	Tomosaburo Kato
1923–4	Gonnohyoe Yamamoto

1924	Keigo Kiyoura
1924–6	Takaaki Kato
1926–7	Reijiro Wakatsuki
1927–9	Giichi Tanaka
1929–31	Osachi Hamaguchi
1931	Reijiro Wakatsuki
1931–2	Tsuyoshi Inukai
1932–4	Makoto Saito
1934–6	Keisuke Okada
1936–7	Koki Hirota
1937	Senjuro Hayashi
1937–9	Fumimaro Konoe
1939	Kiichiro Hiranuma
1939–40	Nobuyuki Abe
1940	Mitsumasa Yonai
1940–1	Fumimaro Konoe
1941–4	Hideki Tojo
1944–5	Kuniaki Koiso
1945	Kantaro Suzuki
1945	Naruhiko Higashikuni
1945–6	Kijuro Shidehara
1946–7	Shigeru Yoshida
1947–8	Tetsu Katayama
1948	Hitoshi Ashida
1948–54	Shigeru Yoshida
1954–6	Ichiro Hatoyama
1956–7	Tanzan Ishibashi
1957–60	Nobusuke Kishi
1960–4	Hayato Ikeda
1964–72	Eisaku Sato
1972–4	Kakuei Tanaka
1974–6	Takeo Miki
1976–8	Takeo Fukuda
1978–80	Masayoshi Ohira
1980–2	Zenko Suzuki
1982–7	Yasuhiro Nakasone
1987–9	Noboru Takeshita
1989	Sasuke Uno
1989–91	Toshiki Kaifu
1991–93	Kiichi Miyazawa
1993	Morihiro Hosokawa
1994	Tsutomu Hata
1994–6	Tomiichi Murayama
1996–8	Ryutaro Hashimoto
1998–2000	Keizo Obuchi
2000	Mikio Aoki *Acting*
2000–1	Yoshiro Mori
2001–6	Junichiro Koizumi
2006–7	Shinzo Abe
2007–8	Yasuo Fukuda
2008–	Taro Aso

Jordan

Monarch

1921–51	Abdullah I ibn Hussein
1951–2	Talal I
1952–99	Hussein ibn Talal
1999–	Abdullah II ibn Hussein

Prime Minister

1921	Rashid Tali
1921	Muzhir Ar-Raslan
1921–3	Rida Ar-Riqabi
1923	Muzhir Ar-Raslan
1923–4	Hassan Khalid
1924–33	Rida Ar-Riqabi
1933–8	Ibrahim Hashim

1939–45	Taufiq Abul-Huda
1945–8	Ibrahim Hashim
1948–50	Taufiq Abul-Huda
1950	Said Al-Mufti
1950–1	Samir Ar-Rifai
1951–3	Taufiq Abul-Huda
1953–4	Fauzi Al-Mulqi
1954–5	Taufiq Abul-Huda
1955	Said Al-Mufti
1955	Hazza Al-Majali
1955–6	Ibrahim Hashim
1956	Samir Ar-Rifai
1956	Said Al-Mufti
1956	Ibrahim Hashim
1956–7	Suleiman Nabulsi
1957	Hussein Fakhri Al-Khalidi
1957–8	Ibrahim Hashim
1958	Nuri Pasha Al-Said
1958–9	Samir Ar-Rifai
1959–60	Hazza Al-Majali
1960–2	Bahjat Talhuni
1962–3	Wasfi At-Tall
1963	Samir Ar-Rifai
1963–4	Sharif Hussein bin Nasir
1964	Bahjat Talhuni
1965–7	Wasfi At-Tall
1967	Sharif Hussein bin Nasir
1967	Saad Jumaa
1967–9	Bahjat Talhuni
1969	Abdul Munem Rifai
1969–70	Bahjat Talhuni
1970	Abdul Munem Rifai
1970	*Military Junta* (Mohammed Daud)
1970	Mohamed Ahmed Tugan
1970–1	Wasfi At-Tall
1971–3	Ahmad Lozi
1973–6	Zeid Rifai
1976–9	Mudar Badran
1979–80	Sharif Abdul Hamid Sharaf
1980	Kassem Rimawi
1980–4	Mudar Badran
1984–5	Ahmad Ubayat
1985–9	Zeid Ar-Rifai
1989	Sharif Zaid ibn Shaker
1989–91	Mudar Badran
1991	Taher Al-Masri
1991–3	Sharif Zaid ibn Shaker
1993–5	Abdel Salam Al-Majali
1995–7	Abdul Karim Kabariti
1997–8	Abdel Salam Al-Majali
1998–9	Fayez Tarawneh
1999–2000	Abdul Raouf Rawabdeh
2000–3	Ali Abu Ragheb
2003–5	Faisal al-Fayez
2005	Adnan Badran
2005–7	Marouf al-Bakhet
2007–	Nader Dahabi

Kazakhstan

President

1991–	Nursultan Nazarbayev

Prime Minister

1991–4	Sergei Tereshchenko
1994–7	Akezhan Kazhageldin
1997–9	Nurlan Balgimbayev
1999–2002	Kasymzhomart Tokaev

2002–3	Imangali Tasmagambetov
2003–7	Daniyal Akhmetov
2007–	Karim Masimov

Kenya

President

1963–78	Mzee Jomo Kenyatta
1978–2002	Daniel arap Moi
2002–	Mwai Kibaki

Prime Minister

| 2008– | Raila Odinga |

Kiribati

President

1979–82	Ieremia T Tabai
1982–3	Council of State (Rota Onorio)
1983–91	Ieremia T Tabai
1991–4	Teatao Teannaki
1994	Council of State (Tekire Tameura/Ata Teaotai)
1994–2003	Teburoro Tito
2003	Council of State (Tion Otang)
2003–	Anote Tong

Korea, Democratic People's Republic of (North Korea)

President

1948–57	Kim Doo-bong
1957–72	Choi Yong-kun
1972–94	Kim Il Sung
1994–7	position vacant
1998–	Kim Il Sung (deceased) Eternal President

Chairman of National Defence Commission

| 1993– | Kim Jong Il |

Prime Minister

1948–76	Kim Il Sung
1976–7	Park Sung-chul
1977–84	Li Jong-ok
1984–6	Kang Song-san
1986–8	Yi Kun-mo
1988–92	Yon Hyong-muk
1992–7	Kang Song-san
1997–2003	Hong Song-nam
2003–7	Pak Pong-ju
2007–	Kim Yong Il

Korea, Republic of (South Korea)

President

1948–60	Syngman Rhee
1960	Ho Chong Acting
1960	Kwak Sang-hun Acting
1960	Ho Chong Acting
1960–3	Yun Po-sun
1963–79	Park Chung-hee
1979–80	Choi Kyu-hah
1980	Park Choong-hoon Acting
1980–8	Chun Doo-hwan
1988–92	Roh Tae-woo
1993–7	Kim Young-sam
1997–2003	Kim Dae-jung

2003–8	Roh Moo Hyun suspended Mar–May 2004
2004	Ko Kun Acting President, Mar–May
2008–	Lee Myung-bak

Prime Minister

1948–50	Lee Pom-sok
1950	Shin Song-mo Acting
1950–1	John M Chang
1951–2	Ho Chong Acting
1952	Lee Yun-yong Acting
1952	Chang Taek-sang
1952–4	Paik Too-chin
1954–6	Pyon Yong-tae
1956–60	Syngman Rhee
1960	Ho Chong
1960–1	John M Chang
1961	Chang To-yong
1961–2	Song Yo-chan
1962–3	Kim Hyun-chul
1963–4	Choe Tu-son
1964–70	Chung Il-kwon
1970–1	Paik Too-chin
1971–5	Kim Jong-pil
1975–9	Choi Kyu-hah
1979–80	Shin Hyun-hwak
1980	Park Choong-hoon Acting
1980–2	Nam Duck-woo
1982	Yoo Chang-soon
1982–3	Kim Sang-hyup
1983–5	Chin Lee-chong
1985–8	Lho Shin-yong
1988	Lee Hyun-jae
1988–90	Kang Young-hoon
1990–1	Ro Jai-bong
1991–2	Chung Won-shik
1992–3	Hyun Soong-jong
1993	Hwang In-sung
1993–4	Lee Hoi-chang
1994	Lee Yung-duck
1994–5	Yi Hong-ku
1995–7	Lee Soo-sung
1997–8	Koh Kun
1998–2000	Kim Jong-pil
2000	Park Tae-joon
2000	Lee Hun-jai Acting
2000–2	Lee Han-dong
2002–3	Kim Suk-soo
2003–4	Ko Kun
2004–6	Lee Hae-chan
2006–7	Han Myung-sook
2008–	Han Seung-soo

Kosovo

President

| 2006– | Fatmir Sejdiu |

Prime Minister

| 2007– | Hashim Thaci |

Kuwait

Emir

Family name: Al-Sabah

1896–1915	Mubarak
1915–17	Jaber II
1917–21	Salem Al-Mubarak

1921–50	Ahmed Al-Jaber
1950–65	Abdallah Al-Salem
1965–77	Sabah Al-Salem
1978–2006	Jaber Al-Ahmed Al-Jaber
2006	Saad Al-Abdallah Al-Salem (*abdicated*)
2006–	Sabah Al-Ahmed Al-Jaber

Prime Minister

1962–3	Jaber Al-Ahmed Al-Jaber
1963–5	Sabah Al-Salem
1965–78	Jaber Al-Ahmed Al-Jaber
1978–2003	Saad Al-Abdallah Al-Salem
2003–6	Sabah Al-Ahmed Al-Jaber
2006–	Nasser Al-Muhammad Al-Ahmad

Kyrgyzstan

President

| 1991–2005 | Askar Akayev |
| 2005– | Kurmanbek Bakiyev |

Prime Minister

1991	Nasirdin Isanov
1991–2	Andrey Yordan *Acting*
1992–3	Tursunbek Chyngyshev
1993–8	Apas Jumagulov
1998	Kubanychbek Djumaliyev
1998	Boris Silayev *Acting*
1998–9	Jumabek Ibraimov
1999	Boris Silayev *Acting*
1999–2000	Amangeldy Muraliyev
2000–2	Kurmanbek Bakiyev
2002–5	Nikolai Tanayev
2005	Kurmanbek Bakiyev
2005	Medetbek Kerimkulov *Acting*
2005–7	Felix Kulov
2007	Almazbek Atambeyev
2007–	Igor Chudinov

Laos

Monarch

| 1904–59 | Sisavang Vong |
| 1959–75 | Savang Vatthana |

■ **Lao People's Democratic Republic**

President

1975–87	Souphanouvong
1987–91	Phoumi Vongvichit
1991–2	Kaysone Phomvihane
1992–8	Nouhak Phoumsavan
1998–2006	Khamtai Siphandon
2006–	Choummaly Sayasone

Prime Minister

1951–4	Souvanna Phouma
1954–5	Katay Don Sasorith
1956–8	Souvanna Phouma
1958–9	Phoui Sahanikone
1959–60	Sunthone Patthamavong
1960	Kou Abhay
1960	Somsanith
1960	Souvana Phouma
1960	Sunthone Patthamavong
1960	Quinim Pholsena
1960–2	Boun Oum Na Champassac
1962–75	Souvanna Phouma
1975–91	Kaysone Phomvihane

1991–8	Khamtai Siphandon
1998–2001	Sisavath Keobounphan
2001–6	Bounnhang Vorachit
2006–	Bouasone Bouphavanh

Latvia

President

1990–3	Anatolijs Gorbunovs
1993–9	Guntis Ulmanis
1999–2007	Vaira Vike-Freiberga
2007–	Valdis Zatlers

Prime Minister

1990–3	Ivars Godmanis
1993–4	Valdis Birkavs
1994–5	Maris Gailis
1995–7	Andris Skele
1997–8	Guntars Krasts
1998–9	Vilis Kristopans
1999–2000	Andris Skele
2000–2	Andris Berzins
2002–4	Einars Repse
2004	Indulis Emsis
2004–7	Aigars Kalvitis
2007–	Ivars Godmanis

Lebanon

President

1943–52	Bishara Al-Khoury
1952–8	Camille Shamoun
1958–64	Fouad Shehab
1964–70	Charle Hilo
1970–6	Suleiman Frenjieh
1976–82	Elias Sarkis
1982	Bashir Gemayel
1982–8	Amin Gemayel
1988–9	*No President*
1989	Rene Muawad
1989–98	Elias Hrawi
1998–2007	Émile Lahoud
2008–	Michel Suleiman

Prime Minister

1943	Riad Solh
1943–4	Henry Pharaon
1944–5	Riad Solh
1945	Abdul Hamid Karame
1945–6	Sami Solh
1946	Saadi Munla
1946–51	Riad Solh
1951	Hussein Oweini
1951–2	Abdullah Yafi
1952	Sami Solh
1952	Nazem Accari
1952	Saeb Salam
1952	Fouad Chehab
1952–3	Khaled Chehab
1953	Saeb Salam
1953–5	Abdullah Yafi
1955	Sami Solh
1955–6	Rashid Karami
1956	Abdullah Yafi
1956–8	Sami Solh
1958–60	Rashid Karami
1960	Ahmad Daouq
1960–1	Saeb Salam
1961–4	Rashid Karami

1964–5	Hussein Oweini
1965–6	Rashid Karami
1966	Abdullah Yafi
1966–8	Rashid Karami
1968–9	Abdullah Yafi
1969–70	Rashid Karami
1970–3	Saeb Salam
1973	Amin al-Hafez
1973–4	Takieddine Solh
1974–5	Rashid Solh
1975	Noureddin Rifai
1975–6	Rashid Karami
1976–80	Selim al-Hoss
1980	Takieddine Solh
1980–4	Chafiq al-Wazan
1984–8	Rashid Karami
1988–90	Michel Aoun/Selim al-Hoss
1990–2	Umar Karami
1992–8	Rafiq al-Hariri
1998–2000	Selim al-Hoss
2000–4	Rafiq al-Hariri
2004–5	Omar Karami
2005	Najib Mikati *Interim Prime Minister*
2005–	Fouad Siniora

Lesotho

Monarch

1966–70	Moshoeshoe II
1970	Leabua Jonathan *Head of State*
1970	'MaMohato Lerotholi *Queen Regent*
1970–90	Moshoeshoe II
1990	'MaMohato Lerotholi *Queen Regent*
1990–5	Letsie III
1995–6	Moshoeshoe II
1996	'MaMohato Lerotholi *Queen Regent*
1996–	Letsie III

Prime Minister

| 1966–86 | Leabua Jonathan |

Chairman of Military Council

| 1986–91 | Justin Metsing Lekhanya |
| 1991–3 | Elias Tutsoane Ramaema |

Prime Minister

1993–4	Ntsu Mokhehle
1994	Hae Phoofolo *Interim Prime Minster*
1994–8	Ntsu Mokhehle
1998–	Bethuel Pakalitha Mosisili

Liberia

President

1900–4	Garretson Wilmot Gibson
1904–12	Arthur Barclay
1912–20	Daniel Edward Howard
1920–30	Charles Dunbar Burgess King
1930–43	Edwin J Barclay
1943–71	William V S Tubman
1971–80	William Richard Tolbert

People's Redemption Council
Chairman

| 1980–6 | Samuel K Doe |

President

| 1986–90 | Samuel K Doe |
| 1991–4 | Amos Sawyer *Interim President* |

Council of State
Chairman

1994–5	David Kpormakor
1995–6	Wilton Sankawulo
1996–7	Ruth Perry

President

1997–2003	Charles Taylor
2003	Moses Zeh Blah *Interim President*
2003–6	Gyude Bryant *Transitional President*
2006–	Ellen Johnson-Sirleaf

Libya

Monarch

| 1951–69 | Mohammed Idris Al-Mahdi Al-Senussi |

Revolutionary Command Council
Chairman

| 1969–77 | Muammar Al-Gaddafi (Qaddafi) |

General Secretariat
Secretary General

1977–9	Muammar Al-Gaddafi
1979–84	Abdul Ati Al-Ubaidi
1984–6	Mohammed Az-Zaruq Rajab
1986–90	Omar Al-Muntasir
1990–4	Abu Zayd 'Umar Durda
1994–	Zanati Mohammed Al-Zanati

Leader of the Revolution

| 1969– | Muammar Al-Gaddafi |

Liechtenstein

Prince

1858–1929	Johann II
1929–38	Franz von Paula
1938–89	Franz Josef II
1989–	Hans Adam II

Prime Minister

1928–45	Franz Josef Hoop
1945–62	Alexander Friek
1962–70	Gérard Batliner
1970–4	Alfred J Hilbe
1974–8	Walter Kieber
1978–93	Hans Brunhart
1993	Markus Büchel
1994–2001	Mario Frick
2001–	Otmar Hasler

Lithuania

President

1990–3	Vytautas Landsbergis
1993–8	Algirdas Brazauskas
1998–2003	Valdas Adamkus
2003–4	Rolandas Paksas
2004	Arturas Paulauskas *Acting*
2004–	Valdas Adamkus

Prime Minister

1990–1	Kazimiera Prunskienė
1991	Albertas Simenas
1991–2	Gediminas Vagnorius

1992	Aleksandras Abisala
1992–3	Bronislovas Lubys
1993–6	Adolfas Slezevicius
1996	Laurynas Stankevicius
1996–9	Gediminas Vagnorius
1999	Irena Degutienë *Acting*
1999	Rolandas Paksas
1999	Irena Degutienë *Acting*
1999–2000	Andrius Kubilius
2000–1	Rolandas Paksas
2001	Eugenijus Gentvilas *Acting*
2001–6	Algirdas Brazauskas
2006–8	Gediminas Kirkilas
2008–	Andrius Kubilius

Luxembourg

Grand Duke / Duchess

1890–1905	Adolf
1905–12	William IV
1912–19	Marie Adelaide
1919–64	Charlotte (*in exile 1940–4*)
1964–2000	Jean
2000–	Henri

Prime Minister

1889–1915	Paul Eyschen
1915	Mathias Mongenast
1915–16	Hubert Loutsch
1916–17	Victor Thorn
1917–18	Léon Kaufmann
1918–25	Emil Reuter
1925–6	Pierre Prum
1926–37	Joseph Bech
1937–53	Pierre Dupong (*in exile 1940–4*)
1953–8	Joseph Bech
1958	Pierre Frieden
1959–69	Pierre Werner
1969–79	Gaston Thorn
1979–84	Pierre Werner
1984–95	Jacques Santer
1995–	Jean-Claude Juncker

Macedonia, Former Yugoslav Republic of

President

1991–5	Kiro Gligorov
1995–8	Stojan Andov *Acting*
1998–9	Kiro Gligorov
1999–2004	Boris Trajkovski
2004	Ljupco Jordanovski *Interim President*
2004–	Branko Crvenkovski

Prime Minister

1991–2	Branko Crvenkovski
1992–6	Petar Gosev
1996–8	Branko Crvenkovski
1998–2002	Ljubco Georgievski
2002–4	Branko Crvenkovski
2004	Hari Kostov
2004–6	Vlado Buckovski
2006–	Nikola Gruevski

Madagascar

President

1960–72	Philibert Tsiranana
1972–5	Gabriel Ramanantsoa
1975	Richard Ratsimandrava

1975	Gilles Andriamahazo
1975–93	Didier Ratsiraka
1993–7	Albert Zafy
1997–2002	Didier Ratsiraka
2002–	Marc Ravalomanana

Prime Minister

1960–75	*As President*
1975–6	Joël Rakotomala
1976–7	Justin Rakotoriaina
1977–88	Désiré Rakotoarijaona
1988–91	Victor Ramahatra
1991–3	Guy Willy Razanamasy
1993–5	Francisque Ravony
1995–6	Emmanuel Rakotovahiny
1996–7	Norbert Ratsirahonana
1997–8	Paskal Rakotmavo
1998–2002	Tantely Andrianarivo
2002–6	Jacques Sylla
2006–	Charles Rabemananjara

Malawi

President

1966–94	Hastings Kamuzu Banda
1994–2004	Bakili Muluzi
2004–	Bingu wa Mutharika

Malaysia

Head of State (Yang di-Pertuan Agong)

1957–63	Abdul Rahman
1963–5	Syed Putra Jamalullah
1965–70	Ismail Nasiruddin Shah
1970–5	Abdul Halim Muadzam Shah
1975–9	Yahya Petra Ibrahim
1979–84	Haji Ahmad Shah Al-Mustain Billah
1984–9	Mahmood Iskandar Shah
1989–94	Azlan Muhibuddin Shah
1994–9	Jaafar Ibni Abdul Rahman
1999–2001	Salehuddin Abdul Aziz Shah
2001	Mizal Zainal Abidin *Acting*
2001–6	Syed Sirajuddin Putra Jamalullail
2006–	Mizan Zainal Abidin ibn Almarhum

Prime Minister

■ **Malaya**

1957–63	Abdul Rahman Putra Al-Haj

■ **Malaysia**

1963–70	Abdul Rahman Putra Al-Haj
1970–6	Abdul Razak bin Hussein
1976–9	Haji Hussein bin Onn
1979–97	Mahathir bin Mohamad
1997	Anwar Ibrahim *Acting*
1997–2003	Mahathir bin Mohamad
2003–	Abdullah Ahmad Badawi

Maldives

Monarch (Sultan)

1954–68	Mohammed Farid Didi

■ **Republic**

President

1968–78	Ibrahim Nasir
1978–2008	Maumoon Abdul Gayoom
2008–	Mohamed Nasheed

History

Mali

President

1960–8	Modibo Keita
1969–91	Moussa Traoré
1991–2	Amadou Toumani Touré
1992–2002	Alpha Oumar Konaré
2002–	Amadou Toumani Touré

Prime Minister

1986–88	Mamadou Dembelé
1988–91	*No Prime Minister*
1991–2	Soumana Sacko
1992–3	Younoussi Touré
1993–4	Abdoulaye Sekou Sow
1994–2000	Ibrahim Boubacar Keita
2000–2	Mande Sidibe
2002–4	Ahmed Mohamed ag Hamani
2004–7	Ousmane Issoufi Maiga
2007–	Modibo Sidbe

Malta

President

1974–6	Anthony Mamo
1976–81	Anton Buttigieg
1981–2	Albert Hyzler *Acting*
1982–7	Agatha Barbara
1987–9	Paul Xuereb *Acting*
1989–94	Vincent Tabone
1994–9	Ugo Mifsud Bonnici
1999–2004	Guido de Marco
2004–	Edward Fenech Adami

Prime Minister

1962–71	G Borg Olivier
1971–84	Dom Mintoff
1984–7	Carmelo Mifsud Bonnici
1987–96	Edward Fenech Adami
1996–8	Alfred Sant
1998–2004	Edward Fenech Adami
2004–	Lawrence Gonzi

Marshall Islands

President

1979–96	Amata Kabua
1996–7	Kunio Lemari *Acting*
1997–2000	Imata Kabua
2000–8	Kessai Note
2008–	Litokwa Tomeing

Mauritania

President

1961–78	Mokhtar Ould Daddah
1979	Mustapha Ould Mohammed Salek
1979–80	Mohammed Mahmoud Ould Ahmed Louly
1980–4	Mohammed Khouna Ould Haydallah
1984–2004	Maaouya Ould Sidi Ahmed Taya

Chairman, Military Council for Justice and Democracy

2005–7	Ely Ould Mohammed Vall
2007–8	Sidi Ould Cheikh Abdallahi
2008–	Mohamed Ould Abdelaziz

Prime Minister

1992–6	Sidi Mohammed Ould Boubaker
1996–7	Cheikh el Avia Ould Mohammed Khouna
1997–8	Mohammed Lemine Ould Guig
1998–2003	Cheikh el Avia Ould Mohammed Khouna
2003–5	Seghair Ould M'bareck
2005–7	Sidi Mohammed Ould Boubaker
2007–8	Zeine Ould Zeidane
2008	Yahya Ould Ahmed al Wagh
2008–	Moulaye Ould Mohamed Laghdaf

Mauritius

Head of State 1968–92: British monarch, represented by Governor General

■ Republic

President

1992	Veerasamy Ringadoo
1992–2002	Cassam Uteem
2002	Angidi Chettiar
2002	Arianga Pillay *Interim President*
2002–3	Karl Offmann
2003–	Sir Anerood Jugnauth

Prime Minister

1968–82	Seewoosagur Ramgoolam
1982–95	Anerood Jugnauth
1995–2000	Navin Ramgoolam
2000–3	Anerood Jugnauth
2003–5	Paul Berengér
2005–	Navinchandra Ramgoolam

Mexico

President

1876–1911	Porfirio Diaz
1911	Francisco León de la Barra
1911–13	Francisco I Madero
1913–14	Victoriano Huerta
1914	Francisco Carvajal
1914	Venustiano Carranza
1914–15	Eulalio Gutiérrez *Provisional President*
1915	Roque González Garza *Provisional President*
1915	Francisco Lagos Chazaro *Provisional President*
1917–20	Venustiano Carranza
1920	Adolfo de la Huerta
1920–4	Alvaro Obregón
1924–8	Plutarco Elías Calles
1928–30	Emilio Portes Gil
1930–2	Pascual Ortíz Rubio
1932–4	Abelardo L Rodríguez
1934–40	Lazaro Cardenas
1940–6	Manuel Avila Camacho
1946–52	Miguel Alemán
1952–8	Adolfo Ruiz Cortines
1958–64	Adolfo López Mateos
1964–70	Gustavo Díaz Ordaz
1970–6	Luis Echeverría
1976–82	José López Portillo
1982–8	Miguel de la Madrid Hurtado
1988–94	Carlos Salinas de Gortari
1994–2000	Ernesto Zedillo Ponce de León
2000–6	Vicente Fox Quesada

2006–   Felipe Calderon

Micronesia, Federated States of

President
1991–7   Bailey Olter (Pohnpei)
1997–9   Jacob Nena (Kosrae)
1999–2003   Leo Falcam (Pohnpei)
2003–7   Joseph Urusemal
2007–   Emmanuel ('Manny') Mori

Moldova

President
1991–6   Mircea Snegur
1996–2001   Petru Lucinschi
2001–   Vladimir Voronin

Prime Minister
1991–2   Valery Muravsky
1992–7   Andrei Sangheli
1997–9   Ion Ciubuc
1999   Ion Sturza
1999–2001   Dumitru Barghis
2001–8   Vasile Tarlev
2008–   Zinaida Greceanii

Monaco

Head of State (Prince)
1889–1922   Albert I
1922–49   Louis II
1949–2005   Rainier III
2005–   Albert II

Mongolia

Prime Minister
1924–8   Tserendorji
1928–32   Amor
1932–6   Gendun
1936–8   Amor
1939–52   Korloghiin Choibalsan
1952–74   Yumsjhagiin Tsedenbal

Chairman of the Praesidium
1948–53   Gonchighlin Bumatsende
1954–72   Jamsarangiin Sambu
1972–4   Sonomyn Luvsan
1974–84   Yumsjhagiin Tsedenbal
1984–90   Jambyn Batmunkh

President
1990–7   Punsalmaagiyn Ochirbat
1997–2005   Natsagiyn Bagabandi
2005–   Nambariyn Enkhbayar

Premier
1974–84   Jambyn Batmunkh
1984–90   Dumaagiyn Sodnom
1990–2   Dashiyn Byambasuren
1992–6   Puntsagiyn Jasray
1996–8   Mendsaihany Enkhsahan
1998   Tsahiagiyin Elbegdorj
1998–9   Janlaviyn Narantsatsralt
1999–2000   Rinchinnyamiyn Amarjagal
2000–4   Nambaryn Enkhbayar
2004   Chultern Ulaan *Acting*
2004–6   Tsakhiagiin Elbegdorj

2006–8   Miyeegombo Enkhbold
2008–   Sanjaa Bayar

Montenegro

For 1993–2006 ► **Serbia and Montenegro**.

President
2006–   Filip Vujanovic
Prime Minister
2002–6   Milo Djukanovic
2006–8   Zeljko Sturanovic
2008–   Milo Djukanovic

Morocco

Monarch
1927–61   Mohammed V
1961–99   Hassan II
1999–   Mohammed VI

Prime Minister
1955–8   Si Mohammed Bekkai
1958   Ahmad Balfrej
1958–60   Abdullah Ibrahim
1960–3   *As Monarch*
1963–5   Ahmad Bahnini
1965–7   *As Monarch*
1967–9   Moulay Ahmed Laraki
1969–71   Mohammed Ben Hima
1971–2   Mohammed Karim Lamrani
1972–9   Ahmed Othman
1979–83   Maati Bouabid
1983–6   Mohammed Karim Lamrani
1986–92   Izz Id-Dien Laraki
1992–4   Mohammed Karim Lamrani
1994–8   Abdellatif Filali
1998–2002   Abderrahmane el-Yousifi
2002–7   Driss Jettou
2007–   Abbas el-Fassi

Mozambique

President
1975–86   Samora Machel
1986–2005   Joaquim Chissano
2005–   Armando Guebuza

Prime Minister
1986–94   Mario de Graça Machungo
1994–2004   Pascoal Mocumbi
2004–   Luisa Diogo

Myanmar, Union of (Burma)

The Socialist Republic of the Union of Burma offically became the Union of Myanmar in 1989, following the military coup of 1988, but it is still often referred to as Burma.

President
1948–52   Sao Shwe Thaik
1952–7   Agga Maha Thiri Thudhamma Ba U
1957–62   U Wing Maung
1962   Sama Duwa Sinwa Nawng

Revolutionary Council
1962–74   Ne Win

State Council
1974–81   Ne Win

History

1981–8	U San Yu
1988	U Sein Lwin
1988	Maung Maung
1988–92	Saw Maung
1992–	Than Shwe

Prime Minister

1947–56	U Nu
1956–7	U Ba Swe
1957–8	U Nu
1958–60	Ne Win
1960–2	U Nu
1962–74	Ne Win
1974–7	U Sein Win
1977–8	U Maung Maung Ka
1988	U Tun Tin
1988–92	Saw Maung
1992–2003	Than Shwe
2003–4	Khin Nyunt
2004–7	Soe Win
2007–	Thein Sein

Namibia

President

| 1990–2005 | Sam Daniel Nujoma |
| 2005– | Hifikepunye Pohamba |

Prime Minister

1990–2002	Hage Geingob
2002–5	Theo-Ben Gurirab
2005–	Nahas Angula

Nauru

President

1968–76	Hammer DeRoburt
1976–8	Bernard Dowiyogo
1978	Lagumot Harris
1978–86	Hammer DeRoburt
1986	Kennan Adeang
1986–9	Hammer DeRoburt
1989	Kenas Aroi
1989–95	Bernard Dowiyogo
1995–6	Lagumot Harris
1996	Bernard Dowiyogo
1996	Kennan Adeang
1996–7	Reuben Kun
1997–8	Kinza Clodumar
1998–9	Bernard Dowiyogo
1999–2000	Rene Harris
2000–1	Bernard Dowiyogo
2001–3	Rene Harris
2003	Bernard Dowiyogo
2003	Derog Gioura *Acting*
2003	Ludwig Scotty
2003–4	Rene Harris
2004–7	Ludwig Scotty
2007–	Marcus Stephen

Nepal

Monarch

1881–1911	Prithvi Bir Bikram Shah
1911–50	Tribhuvan Bir Bikram Shah
1950–2	Bir Bikram
1952–5	Tribhuvan Bir Bikram Shah
1956–72	Mahendra Bir Bikram Shah
1972–2001	Birendra Bir Bikram Shah Dev

| 2001 | Dipendra Bir Bikram Shah Dev |
| 2001–8 | Gyanendra Bir Bikram Shah Dev |

President

| 2008– | Ram Baran Yadav |

Prime Minister

1901–29	Chandra Sham Sher Jang Bahadur Rana
1929–31	Bhim Cham Sham Sher Jang Bahadur Rana
1931–45	Juddha Sham Sher Rana
1945–8	Padma Sham Sher Jang Bahadur Rana
1948–51	Mohan Sham Sher Jang Bahadur Rana
1951–2	Matrika Prasad Koirala
1952–3	*King also Prime Minister*
1953–5	Matrika Prasad Koirala
1955–6	Mahendra Bir Bikram Shah
1956–7	Tanka Prasad Acharya
1957–9	*King also Prime Minister*
1959–60	Sri Bishawa Prasad Koirala
1960–3	*No Prime Minister*
1963–5	Tulsi Giri
1965–9	Surya Bahadur Thapa
1969–70	Kirti Nidhi Bista
1970–1	*King also Prime Minister*
1971–3	Kirti Nidhi Bista
1973–5	Nagendra Prasad Rijal
1975–7	Tulsi Giri
1977–9	Kirti Nidhi Bista
1979–83	Surya Bahadur Thapa
1983–6	Lokendra Bahadur Chand
1986–91	Marich Man Singh Shrestha
1991–4	Girija Prasad Koirala
1994–5	Man Mohan Adhikari
1995–7	Sher Bahadur Deuba
1997	Lokendra Bahadur Chand
1997	Surya Bahadur Thapa
1998–9	Girija Prasad Koirala
1999–2000	Krishna Prasad Bhattari
2000–1	Girija Prasad Koirala
2001–2	Sher Bahadur Deuba
2002–3	Lokendra Bahadur Chand
2003–4	Surya Bahadur Thapa
2004–5	Sher Bahadur Deuba
2005–6	*King also Prime Minister*
2006–8	Girija Prasad Koirala *Interim Prime Minister*
2008–	Pushpa Kamal Dahal (Prachanda)

The Netherlands

Monarch

1890–1948	Wilhelmina
1948–80	Juliana
1980–	Beatrix

Prime Minister

1897–1901	Nicholas G Pierson
1901–5	Abraham Kuyper
1905–8	Theodoor H de Meester
1908–13	Theodorus Heemskerk
1913–18	Pieter W A Cort van der Linden
1918–25	Charles J M Ruys de Beerenbrouck
1925–6	Hendrikus Colijn
1926	Dirk J de Geer
1926–33	Charles J M Ruys de Beerenbrouck
1933–9	Hendrikus Colijn

1939–40	Dirk J de Geer
1940–5	Pieter S Gerbrandy (in exile)
1945–6	Willem Schermerhorn/Willem Drees
1946–8	Louis J M Beel
1948–51	Willem Drees/Josephus R H van Schaik
1951–8	Willem Drees
1958–9	Louis J M Beel
1959–63	Jan E de Quay
1963–5	Victor G M Marijnen
1965–6	Joseph M L T Cals
1966–7	Jelle Zijlstra
1967–71	Petrus J S de Jong
1971–3	Barend W Biesheuvel
1973–7	Joop M Den Uyl
1977–82	Andreas A M van Agt
1982–94	Ruud F M Lubbers
1994–2002	Wim Kok
2002–	Jan Peter Balkenende

New Zealand

Head of State: British monarch, represented by Governor General

Prime Minister

1893–1906	Richard John Seddon *Lib*
1906	William Hall-Jones *Lib*
1906–12	Joseph George Ward *Lib/Nat*
1912	Thomas Mackenzie *Nat*
1912–25	William Ferguson Massey *Ref*
1925	Francis Henry Dillon Bell *Ref*
1925–8	Joseph Gordon Coates *Ref*
1928–30	Joseph George Ward *Lib/Nat*
1930–5	George William Forbes *Un*
1935–40	Michael Joseph Savage *Lab*
1940–9	Peter Fraser *Lab*
1949–57	Sidney George Holland *Nat*
1957	Keith Jacka Holyoake *Nat*
1957–60	Walter Nash *Lab*
1960–72	Keith Jacka Holyoake *Nat*
1972	John Ross Marshall *Nat*
1972–4	Norman Eric Kirk *Lab*
1974–5	Wallace Edward Rowling *Lab*
1975–84	Robert David Muldoon *Nat*
1984–89	David Russell Lange *Lab*
1989–90	Geoffrey Palmer *Lab*
1990	Mike Moore *Lab*
1990–7	James Bolger *Nat*
1997–9	Jenny Shipley *Nat*
1999–2008	Helen Clark *Lab*
2008–	John Key *Nat*

Lab = Labour; *Lib* = Liberal; *Nat* = National; *Ref* = Reform; *Un* = United

Nicaragua

President

1893–1909	José Santos Zelaya
1909–10	José Madriz
1910–11	José Dolores Estrada
1911	Juan José Estrada
1911–17	Adolfo Díaz
1912	Luis Mena *rival President*
1917–21	Emiliano Chamorro Vargas
1921–3	Riego Manuel Chamorro
1923–4	Martínez Bartolo
1925–6	Carlos Solórzano
1926	Emiliano Chamorro Vargas
1926–8	Adolfo Díaz

1926	Juan Bautista Sacasa *rival President*
1928–32	José Marcia Moncada
1933–6	Juan Bautista Sacasa
1936	Carlos Brenes Jarquin
1937–47	Anastasio Somoza García
1947	Leonardo Argüello
1947	Benjamin Lascayo Sacasa
1947–50	Victor Manuel Román y Reyes
1950–6	Anastasio Somoza García
1956–63	Luis Somoza Debayle
1963–6	René Schick Gutiérrez
1966–7	Lorenzo Guerrero Gutiérrez
1967–72	Anastasio Somoza Debayle
1972–4	*Triumvirate*
1974–9	Anastasio Somoza Debayle
1979–84	*Government Junta of National Reconstruction*
1984–90	Daniel Ortega Saavedra
1990–7	Violeta Barrios de Chamorro
1997–2002	Arnoldo Alemán Lacayo
2002–7	Enrique Bolaños Geyer
2007–	Daniel Ortega Saavedra

Niger

President

1960–74	Hamani Diori
1974–87	Seyni Kountché
1987–91	Ali Saibou
1993–6	Mahamane Ousmane
1996–9	Ibrahim Baré Maïnassara
1999	Daouda Malam Wanke
1999–	Mamadou Tandja

Prime Minister

1958–60	Hamani Diori
1960–83	*No Prime Minister*
1983	Mamane Oumarou
1983–8	Ahmid Algabid
1988–9	Mamane Oumarou
1990–1	Aliou Mahamidou
1991–3	Amadou Cheiffou
1993–4	Mahamadou Issoufou
1994–5	Abdoulaye Souley
1995	Amadou Boubacar Cissé
1995–6	Hama Amadou
1996	Boukary Adji
1996–7	Amadou Boubacar Cissé
1997–2000	Ibrahim Assane Mayaki
2000–7	Hama Amadou
2007–	Seini Oumarou

Nigeria

President

1960–6	Nnamdi Azikiwe

Prime Minister

1960–6	Abubakar Tafawa Balewa

Military Government

1966	J T U Aguiyi-Ironsi
1966–75	Yakubu Gowon
1975–6	Murtala R Mohamed
1976–9	Olusegun Obasanjo

President

1979–83	Alhaji Shehu Shagari

History

321

History

Military Government

1983–4	Mohammadu Buhari
1985–93	Ibrahim B Babangida
1993	Ernest Shonekan *Interim President*
1993–8	Sani Abacha
1998–9	Abdulsalami Abubakar

President

1999–2007	Olusegun Obasanjo
2007–	Umau Musa Yar'Adua

North Korea ▶ Korea, Democratic People's Republic of

Norway

Union with Sweden dissolved on independence in 1905

Monarch

1905–57	Haakon VII
1957–91	Olav V
1991–	Harald V

Prime Minister

1898–1902	Johannes Steen
1902–3	Otto Albert Blehr
1903–5	George Francis Hagerup
1905–7	Christian Michelsen
1907–8	Jørgen Løvland
1908–10	Gunnar Knudsen
1910–12	Wollert Konow
1912–13	Jens Bratlie
1913–20	Gunnar Knudsen
1920–1	Otto Bahr Halvorsen
1921–3	Otto Albert Blehr
1923	Otto Bahr Halvorsen
1923–4	Abraham Berge
1924–6	Johan Ludwig Mowinckel
1926–8	Ivar Lykke
1928	Christopher Hornsrud
1928–31	Johan Ludwig Mowinckel
1931–2	Peder L Kolstad
1932–3	Jens Hundseid
1933–5	Johan Ludwig Mowinckel
1935–45	Johan Nygaardsvold
1945–51	Einar Gerhardsen
1951–5	Oscar Torp
1955–63	Einar Gerhardsen
1963	John Lyng
1963–5	Einar Gerhardsen
1965–71	Per Borten
1971–2	Trygve Bratteli
1972–3	Lars Korvald
1973–6	Trygve Bratteli
1976–81	Odvar Nordli
1981	Gro Harlem Brundtland
1981–6	Kåre Willoch
1986–9	Gro Harlem Brundtland
1989–90	Jan P Syse
1990–6	Gro Harlem Brundtland
1996–7	Thorbjørn Jagland
1997–2000	Kjell Magne Bondevik
2000–1	Jens Stoltenberg
2001–5	Kjell Magne Bondevik
2005–	Jens Stoltenberg

Oman

Sultan

1888–1913	Faisal bin Turki
1913–32	Taimur bin Faisal
1932–70	Said bin Taimur
1970–	Qaboos bin Said

Prime Minister

1970–2	Tariq bin Taimur
1972–	*As Sultan*

Pakistan

President

1956–8	Iskander Mirza
1958–69	Mohammad Ayoub Khan
1969–71	Agha Mohammad Yahya Khan
1971–3	Zulfikar Ali Bhutto
1973–8	Fazal Elahi Chawdry
1978–88	Mohammad Zia Ul-Haq
1988–93	Ghulam Ishaq Khan
1993	Wasim Sajjad *Acting*
1993–7	Farooq Ahmad Khan Leghari
1997	Wasim Sajjad *Acting*
1998–2001	Muhammed Rafiq Tarar
2001–8	Pervez Musharraf
2008–	Asif Ali Zardari

Prime Minister

1947–51	Liaqat Ali Khan
1951–3	Khawaja Nazimuddin
1953–5	Mohammad Ali
1955–6	Chawdry Mohammad Ali
1956–7	Hussein Shahid Suhrawardi
1957	Ismail Chundrigar
1957–8	Malik Feroz Khan Noon
1958	Mohammad Ayoub Khan
1958–73	*No Prime Minister*
1973–7	Zulfikar Ali Bhutto
1977–85	*No Prime Minister*
1985–8	Mohammad Khan Junejo
1988	Mohammad Aslam Khan Khattak
1988–90	Benazir Bhutto
1990	Ghulam Mustafa Jatoi
1990–3	Mian Mohammad Nawaz Sharif
1993–6	Benazir Bhutto
1996–7	Meraj Khalid *Acting*
1997–9	Mian Mohammad Nawaz Sharif
1999–2002	*No Prime Minister*
2002–4	Mir Zafarullah Khan Jamali
2004	Chaudhry Shujaat Hussain
2004–8	Shaukat Aziz
2008–	Yusuf Raza Gilani

Palau

President

1981–5	Haruo Remeliik
1985	Thomas Remengesau *Acting*
1985	Alfonso Oiterong
1985–8	Lazarus Salii
1988–9	Thomas Remengesau
1989–93	Ngiratkel Etpison
1993–2000	Kuniwo Nakamura
2001–	Tommy Remengesau

History

Palestinian Autonomous Areas

Leader of Palestinian National Authority

1994–2004	Yasser Arafat
2004	Ahmed Qureia *Acting for Arafat*
2004	Rauhi Fattouh *Acting*
2005–	Mahmoud Abbas (Abu Mazen)

Prime Minister

2003	Mahmoud Abbas (Abu Mazen)
2003–6	Ahmed Qureia (Abu Ala)
2006–7	Ismail Haniyeh
2007–	Salam Khaled Fayyad

Panama

President

1904–8	Manuel Amador Guerrero
1908–10	José Domingo de Obaldia
1910	Federico Boyd
1910	Carlos Antonio Mendoza
1910–12	Pablo Arosemena
1912	Rodolfo Chiari
1912–16	Belisario Porras
1916–18	Ramón Maximiliano Valdés
1918	Pedro Antonio Diaz
1918	Cirilo Luis Urriola
1918–20	Belisario Porras
1920	Ernesto T Lefevre
1920–4	Belisario Porras
1924–8	Rodolfo Chiari
1928	Tomás Gabriel Duque
1928–31	Florencio Harmodio Arosemena
1931	Harmodio Arias
1931–2	Ricardo Joaquín Alfaro
1932–6	Harmodio Arias
1936–9	Juan Demóstenes Arosemena
1939	Ezequiel Fernández Jaén
1939–40	Augusto Samuel Boyd
1940–1	Arnulfo Arias Madrid
1941	Ernesto Jaén Guardia
1941	José Pezet
1941–5	Ricardo Adolfo de la Guardia
1945–8	Enrique Adolfo Jiménez Brin
1948–9	Domingo Diaz Arosemena
1949	Daniel Chanis
1949	Roberto Francisco Chiari
1949–51	Arnulfo Arias Madrid
1951–2	Alcibiades Arosemena
1952–5	José Antonio Remón
1955	José Ramón Guizado
1955–6	Ricardo Manuel Arias Espinosa
1956–60	Ernesto de la Guardia
1960–4	Roberto Francisco Chiari
1964–8	Marco A Robles
1968	Arnulfo Arias Madrid
1968	*Military Junta*
1968–9	Omar Torrijos Herrera
1969–78	Demetrio Basilio Lakas
1978–82	Aristides Royo
1982–4	Ricardo de la Esoriella
1984	Jorge Enrique Illueca Sibauste
1984–5	Nicolás Ardito Barletta
1985–8	Eric Arturo Delvalle
1988–9	Manuel Solís Palma
1989–94	Guillermo Endara Galimany
1994–9	Ernesto Pérez Balladares
1999–2004	Mireya Moscoso Rodriguez
2004–	Martín Torrijos

Papua New Guinea

Head of State: British monarch, represented by Governor General

Prime Minister

1975–80	Michael T Somare
1980–2	Julius Chan
1982–5	Michael T Somare
1985–8	Paias Wingti
1988–92	Rabbie Namaliu
1992–4	Paias Wingti
1994–7	Julius Chan
1997	John Giheno *Acting*
1997	Julius Chan
1997–9	Bill Skate
1999–2002	Sir Mekere Morauta
2002–	Sir Michael Somare

Paraguay

President

1898–1902	Emilio Aceval
1902	Héctor Carvallo
1902–4	Juan Antonio Escurra
1904–5	Juan Gaona
1905–6	Cecilio Baez
1906–8	Benigno Ferreira
1908–10	Emiliano González Navero
1910–11	Manuel Gondra
1911	Albino Jara
1911	Liberato Marcial Rojas
1912	Pedro Peña
1912	Emiliano González Navero
1912–16	Eduardo Schaerer
1916–19	Manuel Franco
1919–20	José P Montero
1920–1	Manuel Gondra
1921	Félix Paiva
1921–3	Eusebio Ayala
1923–4	Eligio Ayala
1924	Luis Alberto Riart
1924–8	Eligio Ayala
1928–31	José Particio Guggiari
1931–2	Emiliano González Navero
1932	José Particio Guggiari
1932–6	Eusebio Ayala
1936–7	Rafael Franco
1937–9	Félix Paiva
1939–40	José Félix Estigarribia
1940–8	Higino Moríñigo
1948	Juan Manuel Frutos
1948–9	Juan Natalicio González
1949	Raimundo Rolón
1949	Felipe Molas López
1949–54	Federico Chaves
1954	Tomás Romero Pareira
1954–89	Alfredo Stroessner
1989–93	Andrés Rodríguez
1993–8	Juan Carlos Wasmosy
1998–9	Raúl Cubas Grau
1999–2003	Luis González Mácchi
2003–8	Nicanor Duarte Frutos
2008–	Fernando Lugo

Peru

President

1899–1903	Eduardo López de Romaña

History

1903–4	Manuel Candamo
1904	Serapio Calderón
1904–8	José Pardo y Barreda
1908–12	Augusto B Leguía
1912–14	Guillermo Billinghurst
1914–15	Oscar R Benavides
1915–19	José Pardo y Barreda
1919–30	Augusto B Leguía
1930	Manuel Ponce
1930–1	Luis M Sánchez Cerro
1931	Leoncio Elías
1931	Gustavo A Jiménez
1931	David Samanez Ocampo
1931–3	Luis M Sánchez Cerro
1933–9	Oscar R Benavides
1939–45	Manuel Prado
1945–8	José Luis Bustamante y Rivero
1948–56	Manuel A Odría
1956–62	Manuel Prado
1962–3	*Military Junta*
1963–8	Fernando Belaúnde Terry
1968–75	*Military Junta* (Juan Velasco Alvarado)
1975–80	*Military Junta* (Francisco Morales Bermúdez)
1980–5	Fernando Belaúnde Terry
1985–90	Alan García Pérez
1990–2000	Alberto Keinya Fujimori
2000–1	Valentín Paniagua *Interim President*
2001–6	Alejandro Toledo Manrique
2006–	Alan García Pérez

Prime Minister

1900	Enrique Coronel Zegarra y Cortés
1900–1	Domingo M Almenara Butler
1901–2	Cesáreo Chacaltana Reyes
1902	Cesáreo Octavio Deustua Escarza
1902–3	Eugenio Larrabure y Unanue
1903–4	José Pardo y Barreda
1904	Alberto Elmore Fernández de Córdoba
1904–7	Augusto B Leguía y Salcedo
1907	Agustín Tovar
1907–8	Carlos A Washburn Salas
1908–9	Eulogio Romero Salcedo
1909–10	Rafael Fernández de Villanueva Cortez
1910	Javier Prado y Ugarteche
1910	Germán Schreiber Waddington
1910	José Salvador Cavero
1910–11	Enrique C Basadre Stevenson
1911–12	Agustín G Ganoza Cavero
1912	Elías Malpartida
1912–13	Enrique Varela
1913	Federico Luna y Peralta
1913	Aurelio Sousa Matute
1913–14	Enrique Varela
1914	Pedro E Muñiz
1914	Manuel Melitón Carvajal
1914	Aurelio Sousa Matute
1914–15	Germán Schreiber Waddington
1915	Carlos Isaac Abrill
1915–17	Enrique de la Riva-Agüero y Looz Corswaren
1917–18	Francisco Tudela y Varela
1918–19	Germán Arenas y Loayza
1919	Juan Manuel Zuloaga
1919–22	Germán Leguía y Martínez Jakeway
1922–4	Julio Enrique Ego Aguirre
1924–6	Alejandrino Maguiña
1926–9	Pedro José Rada y Gamio

1929–30	Benjamín Huamán de los Heros
1930–1	Fernando Sarmiento
1931–2	Germán Arenas y Loayza
1932	Francisco R Lanatta
1932	Luis A Flores
1932	Ricardo Rivadeneira
1932–3	José Matías Manzanilla Barrientos
1933	Jorge Prado y Ugarteche
1933–4	José de la Riva-Agüero y Osma
1934–5	Carlos Arenas y Loayza
1935–6	Manuel Esteban Rodríguez
1936–9	Ernesto Montagne Markholz
1939	Alberto Rey de Castro y Romaña
1939–44	Alfredo Solf y Muro
1944–5	Manuel Cisneros Sánchez
1945–6	Rafael Belaúnde y Diez Canseco
1946–7	Julio Ernesto Portugal Escobedo
1947	José Alcamora
1948	Roque Augusto Saldías Maninat
1948	Armando Revoredo Iglesias
1948–54	*No Prime Minister*
1954–6	Roque Augusto Saldías Maninat
1956–7	Manuel Cisneros Sánchez
1958–9	Luis Gallo Porras
1959–61	Pedro Gerardo Beltrán Espantos
1961–2	Carlos Moreyra y Paz Soldán
1962–3	Nicolás Lindley López
1963	Julio Óscar Trelles Montes
1963–5	Fernando Schwalb López Aldana
1965–7	Daniel Becerra de la Flor
1967	Edgardo Seoane Corrales
1967–8	Raúl Ferrero Rebagliati
1968	Oswaldo Hercelles García
1968	Miguel Mujica Gallo
1968–73	Ernesto Montagne Sánchez
1973–5	Edgardo Mercado Jarrín
1975	Francisco Morales Bermúdez
1975–6	Óscar Vargas Prieto
1976	Jorge Fernández Maldonado Solari
1976–8	Guillermo Arbulú Galliani
1978–9	Óscar Molina Pallochia
1979–80	Pedro Richter Prada
1980–3	Manuel Ulloa Elías
1983–4	Fernando Schwalb López Aldana
1984	Sandro Mariátegui Chiappe
1984–5	Luis Pércovich Roca
1985–7	Luis Alva Castro
1987–8	Guillermo Larco Cox
1988–9	Armando Villanueva del Campo
1989	Luis Alberto Sánchez
1989–90	Guillermo Larco Cox
1990–1	Juan Carlos Hurtado Miller
1991	Carlos Torres y Torres Lara
1991–2	Alfonso de los Heros
1992–3	Óscar de la Puente Raygada
1993–4	Alfonso Bustamante y Bustamante
1994–5	Efraín Goldenberg Schreiber
1995–6	Dante Córdova Blanco
1996–8	Alberto Pandolfi
1998	Javier Valle Riestra
1998–9	Alberto Pandolfi
1999	Víctor Joy Way
1999–2000	Alberto Bustamante Belaúnde
2000	Federico Salas Guevara
2001	Javier Perez de Cuellar
2001–2	Roberto Daniño Zapata
2002–3	Luis Solari de la Fuente
2003	Beatriz Merino

2003–5	Carlos Ferrero
2005–6	Pedro Kuczynski
2006–8	Jorge del Castillo
2008–	Yehude Simon Munaro

Philippines

President

■ Commonwealth

1935–44	Manuel L Quezon (*in exile from 1942*)

Japanese Occupation

1943–4	José P Laurel

■ Commonwealth

1944–6	Sergio Osmeña

■ First Republic

1946–8	Manuel A Roxas
1948–53	Elpidio Quirino
1953–7	Ramon Magsaysay
1957–61	Carlos P Garcia
1961–5	Diosdado Macapagal
1965–72	Ferdinand E Marcos

Martial law

1972–81	Ferdinand E Marcos

■ New Republic

1981–6	Ferdinand E Marcos
1986–92	Corazon C Aquino
1992–8	Fidel V Ramos
1998–2001	Joseph Estrada
2001–	Gloria Macapagal-Arroyo

Poland

■ Republic of Poland
President

1945–7	Bolesław Bierut *Acting*
1947–52	Bolesław Bierut
1952–64	Aleksander Zawadzki
1964–8	Edward Ochab
1968–70	Marian Spychalski
1970–2	Józef Cyrankiewicz
1972–85	Henryk Jabłonski
1985–90	Wojciech Jaruzelski
1990–5	Lech Wałesa
1995–2005	Aleksander Kwaśniewski
2005–	Lech Kaczynski

Prime Minister

1947–52	Józef Cyrankiewicz
1952–4	Bolesław Bierut
1954–70	Józef Cyrankiewicz
1970–80	Piotr Jecoszewicz
1980	Edward Babiuch
1980–1	Józef Pinkowski
1981–5	Wojciech Jaruzelski
1985–8	Zbigniew Messner
1988–9	Mieczyslaw Rakowski
1989	Czeslaw Kiszczak
1989–90	Tadeusz Mazowiecki
1991	Jan Bielecki
1991–2	Jan Olszewski
1992	Waldemar Pawlak
1992–3	Hanna Suchocka
1993–5	Waldemar Pawlak
1995–6	Józef Oleksy

1996–7	Wlodzimierz Cimoszewicz
1997–2001	Jerzy Buzek
2001–4	Leszek Miller
2004–5	Marek Belka
2005–6	Kazimierz Marcinkiewicz
2006–7	Jaroslaw Kaczynski
2007–	Donald Tusk

First Secretary

1945–8	Władysław Gomułka
1948–56	Bolesław Bierut
1956	Edward Ochab
1956–70	Władysław Gomułka
1970–80	Edward Gierek
1980–1	Stanisław Kania
1981–9	Wojciech Jaruzelski
1989	Mieczyslaw Rakowski

Portugal

President

■ First Republic

1910–11	Teófilo Braga
1911–15	Manuel José de Arriaga
1915	Teófilo Braga
1915–17	Bernardino Machado
1917–18	Sidónio Pais
1918–19	João do Canto e Castro
1919–23	António José de Almeida
1923–5	Manuel Teixeira Gomes
1925–6	Bernardino Machado

■ New State

1926	*Military Junta* (José Mendes Cabeçadas)
1926	*Military Junta* (Manuel de Oliveira Gomes da Costa)
1926–51	António Oscar Fragoso Carmona
1951–8	Francisco Craveiro Lopes
1958–74	Américo de Deus Tomás

■ Second Republic

1974	*Military Junta* (António Spínola)
1974–6	*Military Junta* (Francisco da Costa Gomes)

■ Third Republic

1976–86	António dos Santos Ramalho Eanes
1986–96	Mário Soares
1996–2006	Jorge Sampaio
2006–	Anibal Cavaço Silva

Prime Minister

1932–68	António de Oliveira Salazar
1968–74	Marcelo Caetano
1974	Adelino da Palma Carlos
1974–5	Vasco Gonçalves
1975–6	José Pinheiro de Azevedo
1976–8	Mário Soares
1978	Alfredo Nobre da Costa
1978–9	Carlos Alberto de Mota Pinto
1979	Maria de Lurdes Pintasilgo
1980–1	Francisco de Sá Carneiro
1981–3	Francisco Pinto Balsemão
1983–5	Mário Soares
1985–95	Aníbal Cavaço Silva
1995–2001	António Guterres
2002–4	José Manuel Durão Barroso

History

| 2004–5 | Pedro Santana Lopes |
| 2005– | José Sócrates |

Qatar

Emir
Family name: al-Thani
1971–2	Ahmad bin Ali
1972–95	Khalifah bin Hamad
1995–	Hamad bin Khalifa

Prime Minister
1971–96	*As Emir*
1996–2007	Abdullah bin Khalifa
2007–	Hamad bin Jassem al-Thani

Romania

Monarch
1881–1914	Carol I
1914–27	Ferdinand I
1927–30	Michael *Prince*
1930–40	Carol II
1940–7	Michael I

■ Republic
President
1947–8	Mihai Sadoveanu *Interim*
1948–52	Constantin I Parhon
1952–8	Petru Groza
1958–61	Ion Georghe Maurer
1961–5	Georghe Gheorghiu-Dej
1965–7	Chivu Stoica
1967–89	Nicolae Ceauşescu
1989–96	Ion Iliescu
1996–2000	Emil Constantinescu
2000–4	Ion Iliescu
2004–	Traian Basescu

Prime Minister
1900–1	Petre P Carp
1901–6	Dimitrie A Sturdza
1906–7	Gheorge Grigore Cantacuzino
1907–9	Dimitrie A Sturdza
1909	Ionel Brătianu
1909–10	Mihai Pherekyde
1910–11	Ionel Brătianu
1911–12	Petre P Carp
1912–14	Titu Maiorescu
1914–18	Ionel Brătianu
1918	Alexandru Averescu
1918	Alexandru Marghiloman
1918	Constantin Coandă
1918	Ionel Brătianu
1919	Artur Văitoianu
1919–20	Alexandru Vaida-Voevod
1920–1	Alexandru Averescu
1921–2	Take Ionescu
1922–6	Ionel Brătianu
1926–7	Alexandru Averescu
1927	Ionel Brătianu
1927–8	Vintila I C Brătianu
1928–30	Juliu Maniu
1930	Gheorghe C Mironescu
1930	Juliu Maniu
1930–1	Gheorghe C Mironescu
1931–2	Nicolae Iorga
1932	Alexandru Vaida-Voevod
1932–3	Juliu Maniu

1933	Alexandru Vaida-Voevod
1933	Ion G Duca
1933–4	Constantin Angelescu
1934–7	Gheorghe Tătărescu
1937	Octavian Goga
1937–9	Miron Cristea
1939	Armand Călinescu
1939	Gheorghe Argeşanu
1939	Constantine Argetoianu
1939–40	Gheorghe Tătărescu
1940	Ion Gigurtu
1940–4	Ion Antonescu
1944	Constantin Savbnătescu
1944–5	Nicolae Rădescu
1945–52	Petru Groza
1952–5	Gheorghe Gheorghiu-Dej
1955–61	Chivu Stoica
1961–74	Ion Gheorghe Maurer
1974–80	Manea Mănescu
1980–3	Ilie Verdet
1983–9	Constantin Dăscălescu
1989–91	Petre Roman
1991–2	Theodor Stolojan
1992–6	Nicolae Vacaroiu
1996–8	Victor Ciorbea
1998	Gavril Dejeu *Interim Prime Minister*
1998–9	Radu Vasile
1999	Alexandru Athanesiu *Interim Prime Minister*
1999–2000	Mugur Isarescu
2000–4	Adrian Nastase
2004	Eugen Bejinariu *Interim Prime Minister*
2004–8	Calin Popescu-Tariceanu
2008–	Emil Boc

General Secretary
| 1955–65 | Georghe Gheorghiu-Dej |
| 1965–89 | Nicolae Ceauşescu |

Russia

Monarch (Tsar)
| 1894–1917 | Nicholas II |

For 1917–91 ▶ **USSR**.
President
1991–9	Boris Yeltsin
2000–8	Vladimir Putin
2008–	Dmitry Medvedev

Prime Minister
1991–2	Boris Yeltsin
1992	Yegor Gaidar *Acting*
1992–8	Viktor Chernomyrdin
1998	Sergei Kiriyenko
1998	Viktor Chernomyrdin *Acting*
1998–9	Yevgeny Primakov
1999	Sergei Stepashin
1999–2000	Vladimir Putin
2000–4	Mikhail Kasyanov
2004	Viktor Khristenko
2004–7	Mikhael Fradkov
2007–8	Viktor Zubkov
2008–	Vladimir Putin

Rwanda

President
| 1962–73 | Grégoire Kayibanda |
| 1973–94 | Juvénal Habyarimana |

1994	Theodore Sindikubgabo *Interim President*
1994–2000	Pasteur Bizimungu
2000–	Paul Kagame (*under transitional regime, 2000–3*)

Prime Minister

1991–2	Sylvestre Nsanzimana
1992–4	Dismas Nsengiyaremye
1994	Jean Kambanda *Acting*
1994–5	Faustin Twagiramungu
1995–2000	Pierre-Célestin Rwigyema
2000–	Bernard Makuza

St Christopher and Nevis

Head of State: British monarch, represented by Governor General

Prime Minister

1983–95	Kennedy A Simmonds
1995–	Denzil Douglas

St Lucia

Head of State: British monarch, represented by Governor General

Prime Minister

1979	John Compton
1979–81	Allan Louisy
1981–3	Winston Francis Cenac
1983–96	John Compton
1996–7	Vaughan Lewis
1997–2006	Kenny Anthony
2006–7	Sir John Compton
2007–	Stephenson King

St Vincent and the Grenadines

Head of State: British monarch, represented by Governor General

Prime Minister

1979–84	Milton Cato
1984–2000	James Fitz-Allen Mitchell
2000–1	Arnhim Eustace
2001–	Ralph Gonsalves

Samoa

Head of State (elected monarch)

1962–3	Tupua Tamesehe Mea'ole *and* Malietoa Tanumalfi II *jointly*
1963–2007	Malietoa Tanumafili II
2007–	Tuiatua Tupua Tamasese Efi

Prime Minister

1962–1970	Fiame Mata'afa Faumuina Mulinu'u II
1970–6	Tupua Tamasese Leolofi IV
1976–82	Tupuola Taisi Efi
1982	Va'ai Kolone
1982	Tupuola Taisi Efi
1982–6	Tofilau Eti Alesana
1986–8	Va'ai Kolone
1988–98	Tofilau Eti Alesana
1998–	Tuilaepa Sailele Malielegaoi

San Marino

Heads of State (Captains-Regent)
Two captains-regent, elected every six months

São Tomé and Príncipe

President

1975–91	Manuel Pinto da Costa
1991–2001	Miguel Trovoada
2001–	Fradique de Menezes

Prime Minister

1974–5	Leonel Maria d'Alva
1975–8	Miguel Trovoada
1978–88	*No Prime Minister*
1988–91	Celestino Rocha da Costa
1991–2	Daniel Lima dos Santos Daio
1992–4	Norberto José d'Alva Costa Alegre
1994	Evaristo Carvalho
1994–5	Carlos da Graça
1995–6	Armindo Vaz d'Almeida
1996–9	Raul Bragança
1999–2002	Guilherme Posser da Costa
2002	Gabriel Costa
2002–4	Maria das Neves
2004–5	Damião Vaz d'Almeida
2005–6	Maria do Carmo Silveira
2006–8	Tomé Vera Cruz
2008	Patrice Trovoada
2008–	Joaquim Rafael Branco

Saudi Arabia

Monarch
Family name: al-Saud

1932–53	Abdulaziz bin Abdur-Rahman
1953–64	Saud bin Abdul Aziz
1964–75	Faisal bin Abdul Aziz
1975–82	Khalid bin Abdul Aziz
1982–96	Fahd bin Abdul Aziz
1996	Abdullah bin Abdul Aziz *Acting*
1996–2005	Fahd bin Abdul Aziz
2005–	Abdullah bin Abdul Aziz

Senegal

President

1960–80	Léopold Sédar Senghor
1981–2000	Abdou Diouf
2000–	Abdoulaye Wade

Prime Minister

1958–62	Mamadou Dia
1962–70	*No Prime Minister*
1970–80	Abdou Diouf
1981–3	Habib Thiam
1983	Moustapha Niasse *Interim Prime Minister*
1983–91	*No Prime Minister*
1991–8	Habib Thiam
1998–2000	Mamadou Lamine Loum
2000–1	Moustapha Niasse
2001–2	Madior Boye
2002–4	Idrissa Seck
2004–7	Macky Sall
2007–	Cheikh Hadjibou Somare

History

Serbia

For 1993–2006 ▶ **Serbia and Montenegro**.

President
2006–   Boris Tadić

Prime Minister
2006–8   Vojislav Kostunica
2008–   Mirko Cvetkovic

Serbia and Montenegro

■ **Federal Republic of Yugoslavia**
President
1992–3   Dobrica Cosic
1993   Milos Radulovic *Acting*
1993–7   Zoran Lilic
1997   Srdja Bozovic *Acting*
1997–2000   Slobodan Milosevic
2000–3   Vojislav Kostunica

Prime Minister
1992–3   Milan Panic
1993–8   Radoje Kontic
1998–2000   Momir Bulatovic
2000–1   Zoran Zizic
2001–3   Dragisa Pesic

■ **Serbia and Montenegro**
President
2003–6   Svetozar Marović

■ **Serbia**
President
1992–7   Slobodan Milosevic
1997   Vojislav Šešelj
1997–2002   Milan Milutinovic
2002–4   Nataša Mićić *Acting President*
2004   Dragin Marsicanin *Acting*
2004   Vojislav Mihailovic *Acting*
2004   Predrag Markovic *Acting*
2004–6   Boris Tadić

■ **Montenegro**
President
1993–7   Momir Bulatovic
1997–2002   Milo Djukanović
2002–3   Filip Vujanović *Acting*
2003   Rifat Rastoder/Dragan Kujovic
             Acting
2003–6   Filip Vujanović

Seychelles

President
1976–7   James R Mancham
1977–2004   France-Albert René
2004–   James Michel

Sierra Leone

Head of State 1961–71: British monarch, represented by Governor General.

■ **Republic**
President
1971   Christopher Okero Cole
1971–85   Siaka Stevens
1985–92   Joseph Saidu Momoh

1992–6   Valentine Strasser
1996–7   Ahmad Tejan Kabbah
1997   *Military coup* (Johnny Koroma)
1998–2007   Ahmad Tejan Kabbah
2007–   Ernest Bai Koroma

Prime Minister
1961–4   Milton Margai
1964–7   Albert Michael Margai
1967   Siaka Stevens
1967   David Lansana
1967   Ambrose Genda
1967–8   *National Reformation Council*
             (Andrew Saxon-Smith)
1968   John Bangura
1968–71   Siaka Stevens
1971–5   Sorie Ibrahim Koroma
1975–8   Christian Alusine Kamara Taylor
1978–   *No Prime Minister*

Singapore

President (Yang di-Pertuan Negara)
1959–70   Yusof bin Ishak
1970–81   Benjamin Henry Sheares
1981–5   Chengara Veetil Devan Nair
1985–93   Wee Kim Wee
1993–9   Ong Teng Cheong
1999–   Sellapan Rama Nathan

Prime Minister
1959–90   Lee Kuan Yew
1990–2004   Goh Chok Tong
2004–   Lee Hsien Loong

Slovakia

For 1918–93 ▶ **Czechoslovakia**.

President
1993–8   Michal Kovác
1998–9   *No President*
1999–2004   Rudolf Schuster
2004–   Ivan Gašparović

Prime Minister
1993–4   Vladimír Mečiar
1994   Jozef Moravčik
1994–8   Vladimír Mečiar
1998–2006   Mikuláš Dzurinda
2006–   Robert Fico

Slovenia

President
1991–2002   Milan Kučan
2002–7   Janez Drnovsek
2007–   Danilo Türk

Prime Minister
1990–2   Lojze Peterle
1992–2000   Janez Drnovšek
2000   Andrej Bajuk
2000–2   Janez Drnovsek
2002–4   Anton Rop
2004–8   Janez Jansa
2008–   Borut Pahor

Solomon Islands

Head of State: British monarch, represented by Governor General

Prime Minister

1978–82	Peter Kenilorea
1982–4	Solomon Mamaloni
1984–6	Peter Kenilorea
1986–9	Ezekiel Alebua
1989–93	Solomon Mamaloni
1993–4	Francis Billy Hilly
1994–7	Solomon Mamaloni
1997–2000	Bartholomew Ulufa'alu
2000–1	Manasseh Sogavare
2001–6	Sir Allan Kemakeza
2006	Snyder Rini
2006–7	Manasseh Sogavare
2007–	Derek Sikua

Somalia

President

1961–7	Aden Abdallah Osman
1967–9	Abdirashid Ali Shermarke

Supreme Revolutionary Council

1969–80	Mohammed Siad Barre

■ **Republic**

1980–91	Mohammed Siad Barre
1991–2000	*Civil War*
2000	Abdullahi Derow Isaq *Acting*
2000–4	Abd-al-Qassim Salat Hasan
2004–	Abdullahi Yusuf Ahmed

Prime Minister

1960	Mohammed Haji Ibrahim Egal
1960–4	Abdirashid Ali Shermarke
1964–7	Abdirizak Haji Hussein
1967–9	Mohammed Haji Ibrahim Egal
1969–70	Mohammed Siad Barre
1970–87	*No Prime Minister*
1987–90	Mohammed Ali Samater
1990–1	Mohammed Hawadie Madar
1991	Umar Arteh Ghalib
1991–2000	*Civil War*
2000–1	Ali Khalif Galaid
2001–3	Hassan Abshir Farah
2003–4	Abdi Yusuf Mohammed
2004–7	Ali Mohamed Gedi
2007	Salim Aliyow Ibrow *Acting*
2007–	Nur Hassan Hussein

South Africa

Head of State 1910–61: British monarch, represented by Governor General

■ **Republic**

President

1961–7	Charles Robberts Swart
1967	Theophilus Ebenhaezer Dönges
1967–8	Jozua François Nandé
1968–75	Jacobus Johannes Fouché
1975–8	Nicolaas Diederichs
1978–9	Balthazar Johannes Vorster
1979–84	Marais Viljoen
1984–9	Pieter Willem Botha
1989–94	Frederick Willem de Klerk

1994–9	Nelson Mandela
1999–2008	Thabo Mbeki
2008–	Kgalema Motlanthe *Interim*

Prime Minister

1910–19	Louis Botha *SAf*
1919–24	Jan Christiaan Smuts *SAf*
1924–39	James Barry Munnick Hertzog *Nat*
1939–48	Jan Christiaan Smuts *Un*
1948–54	Daniel François Malan *Nat*
1954–8	Johannes Gerardus Strijdom *Nat*
1958–66	Hendrik Frensch Verwoerd *Nat*
1966–78	Balthazar Johannes Vorster *Nat*
1978–84	Pieter Willem Botha *Nat*
1984–	*No Prime Minister*

Nat = National; *SAf* = South African Party; *Un* = United

South Korea ► Korea, Republic of

Spain

Monarch

1886–1931	Alfonso XIII

■ **Second Republic**

President

1931	Niceto Alcalá Zamora y Torres
1931	Manuel Azaña Díaz
1931–6	Niceto Alcalá Zamora y Torres
1936	Diego Martínez Barrio *Acting*

Civil War

1936–9	Manuel Azaña Díaz

Prime Minister

1900–1	Marcelo de Azcárraga y Palmero
1901–2	Práxedes Mateo Sagasta
1902–3	Francisco Silvela y Le-Vielleuze
1903	Raimundo Fernández Villaverde
1903–4	Antonio Maura y Montaner
1904–5	Marcelo de Azcárraga y Palmero
1905	Raimundo Fernández Villaverde
1905	Eugenio Montero Ríos
1905–6	Segismundo Moret y Prendergast
1906	José López Domínguez
1906	Segismundo Moret y Prendergast
1906–7	Antonio Aguilar y Correa
1907–9	Antonio Maura y Montaner
1909–10	Segismundo Moret y Prendergast
1910–12	José Canalejas y Méndez
1912	Álvaro Figueroa y Torres
1912–13	Manuel García Prieto
1913–15	Eduardo Dato y Iradier
1915–17	Álvaro Figueroa y Torres
1917	Manuel García Prieto
1917	Eduardo Dato y Iradier
1917–18	Manuel García Prieto
1918	Antonio Maura y Montaner
1918	Manuel García Prieto
1918–19	Álvaro Figueroa y Torres
1919	Antonio Maura y Montaner
1919	Joaquín Sánchez de Toca
1919–20	Manuel Allendesalazar
1920–1	Eduardo Dato y Iradier
1921	Gabino Bugallal Araujo *Acting*
1921	Manuel Allendesalazar
1921–2	Antonio Maura y Montaner

History

1922	José Sánchez Guerra y Martínez
1922–3	Manuel García Prieto
1923–30	Miguel Primo de Rivera y Oraneja
1930–1	Dámaso Berenguer y Fusté
1931	Juan Bautista Aznar-Cabañas
1931	Niceto Alcalá Zamora y Torres
1931–3	Manuel Azaña Díaz
1933	Alejandro Lerroux y García
1933	Diego Martínez Barrio
1933–4	Alejandro Lerroux y García
1934	Ricardo Samper Ibáñez
1934–5	Alejandro Lerroux y García
1935	Joaquín Chapaprieta y Terragosa
1935–6	Manuel Portela Valladares
1936	Manuel Azaña Díaz
1936	Santiago Casares Quiroga
1936	Diego Martínez Barrio
1936	José Giral y Pereyra
1936–7	Francisco Largo Caballero
1937–9	Juan Negrín López

■ **Nationalist Government**
Head of State

| 1936–75 | Francisco Franco Bahamonde |

Chairman of the Council of Ministers

| 1939–73 | Francisco Franco Bahamonde |

■ **Kingdom of Spain (from 1975)**
Monarch

| 1975– | Juan Carlos I |

Prime Minister

1973	Torcuato Fernández Miranda y Hevía *Acting*
1973–6	Carlos Arias Navarro
1976–81	Adolfo Suárez
1981–2	Calvo Sotelo
1982–96	Felipe González
1996–2004	José María Aznar
2004–	José Zapatero

Sri Lanka

■ **Ceylon**
Head of State 1948–72: British monarch, represented by Governor General.

Prime Minister

1947–52	Don Stephen Senanayake
1952–3	Dudley Shelton Senanayake
1953–6	John Lionel Kotelawala
1956–9	Solomon West Ridgeway Dias Bandaranaike
1959–60	Vijayananda Dahanayake
1960	Dudley Shelton Senanayake
1960–5	Sirimavo Bandaranaike
1965–70	Dudley Shelton Senanayake

■ **Sri Lanka**
President

1972–8	William Gopallawa
1978–89	Junius Jayawardene
1989–93	Ranasinghe Premadasa
1994–2005	Chandrika Bandaranaike Kumaratunga
2005–	Mahinda Rajapakse

Prime Minister

1970–7	Sirimavo Bandaranaike
1977–89	Ranasinghe Premadasa
1989–93	Dingiri Banda Wijetunge
1993–4	Ranil Wickremasingh
1994	Chandrika Bandaranaike Kumaratunga
1994–2000	Sirimavo Bandaranaike
2000–1	Ratnasiri Wickremanayake
2001–4	Ranil Wickremasinghe
2004–5	Mahinda Rajapakse
2005–	Ratnasiri Wickremanayake

Sudan

Head of State

1956–8	*Council of State*
1958–64	Ibrahim Abboud
1964–5	*Council of Sovereignty*
1965–9	Ismail Al-Azhari
1969–85	Jaafar Mohammed Nimeiri *President from 1971*

■ **Transitional Military Council**

| 1985–6 | Abd Al-Rahman Siwar Al-Dahab *Chairman* |

■ **Supreme Council**

| 1986–9 | Ahmad Al-Mirghani *Chairman* |

■ **Revolutionary Command Council**

| 1989– | Omar Hassan Ahmed Al-Bashir *Chairman*; *President from 1993* |

Prime Minister

1955–6	Ismail Al-Azhari
1956–8	Abdullah Khalil
1958–64	*As President*
1964–5	Serr Al-Khatim Al-Khalifa
1965–6	Mohammed Ahmed Mahjoub
1966–7	Sadiq Al-Mahdi
1967–9	Mohammed Ahmed Mahjoub
1969	Babiker Awadalla
1969–76	*As President*
1976–7	Rashid Al-Tahir Bakr
1977–85	*As President*
1985–6	*Transitional Military Council* (Al-Jazuli Dafallah)
1986–9	*Supreme Council* (Sadiq Al-Mahdi)
1989–	*No Prime Minister*

Suriname

President

1975–80	J H E Ferrier
1980–2	Henk Chin-a-Sen
1982–8	L F Ramdat-Musier *Acting*
1988–90	Ramsewak Shankar
1990–1	Johan Kraag
1991–6	Ronald Venetiaan
1996–2000	Jules Wijdenbosch
2000–	Ronald Venetiaan

National Military Council
Chairman

| 1980–7 | Desi Bouterse |
| 1987 | Iwan Granoogst *Acting Premier* |

Prime Minister

| 1975–80 | Henk Arron |
| 1980 | Henk Chin-a-Sen |

1980–2	No Prime Minister
1982–3	Henry Weyhorst
1983–4	Errol Alibux
1984–6	Wim Udenhout
1986–7	Pretaapnarain Radhakishun
1987–8	Jules Wijdenbosch
1988–90	Henk Arron
1990–1	Jules Wijdenbosch
1991–6	Jules Ajodhia

Vice President / Chairman of Council of Ministers

1996–2000	Pretaapnarain Radhakishun
2000–5	Jules Ajodhia
2005–	Ram Sardjoe

Swaziland

Monarch

1967–82	Sobhuza II *Chief since 1921*
1982–3	Dzeliwe *Queen Regent*
1983	Sozisa Dlamini *Regent*
1983–6	Ntombi *Queen Regent*
1986–	Mswati III

Prime Minister

1967–78	Prince Makhosini
1978–9	Prince Maphevu Dlamini
1979–83	Prince Mbandla Dlamini
1983–6	Prince Bhekimpi Dlamini
1986–9	Sotsha Dlamini
1989–93	Obed Dlamini *Acting*
1993–6	Jameson Mbilini Dlamini
1996–2003	Barnabas Sibusiso Dlamini
2003	Paul Shabangu
2003–8	Absalom Themba Dlamini
2008–	Barnabas Sibusiso Dlamini

Sweden

Monarch

1872–1907	Oskar II
1907–50	Gustav V
1950–73	Gustav VI Adolf
1973–	Carl XVI Gustaf

Prime Minister

1900–2	Fredrik von Otter
1902–5	Erik Gustaf Boström
1905	Johan Ramstedt
1905	Christian Lundeberg
1905–6	Karl Staaf
1906–11	Arvid Lindman
1911–14	Karl Staaf
1914–17	Hjalmar Hammarskjöld
1917	Carl Swartz
1917–20	Nils Edén
1920	Hjalmar Branting
1920–1	Louis de Geer
1921	Oscar von Sydow
1921–3	Hjalmar Branting
1923–4	Ernst Trygger
1924–5	Hjalmar Branting
1925–6	Rickard Sandler
1926–8	Carl Gustaf Ekman
1928–30	Arvid Lindman
1930–2	Carl Gustaf Ekman
1932	Felix Hamrin
1932–6	Per Albin Hansson
1936	Axel Pehrsson-Branstorp
1936–46	Per Albin Hansson

1946–69	Tage Erlander
1969–76	Olof Palme
1976–8	Thorbjörn Fälldin
1978–9	Ola Ullsten
1979–82	Thorbjörn Fälldin
1982–6	Olof Palme
1986–91	Ingvar Carlsson
1991–4	Carl Bildt
1994–6	Ingvar Carlsson
1996–2006	Göran Persson
2006–	Fredrik Reinfeldt

Switzerland

President (annually rotating post)

1900	Walter Hauser
1901	Ernst Brenner
1902	Joseph Zemp
1903	Adolf Deucher
1904	Robert Comtesse
1905	Marc-Emile Ruchet
1906	Ludwig Forrer
1907	Eduard Müller
1908	Ernst Brenner
1909	Adolf Deucher
1910	Robert Comtesse
1911	Marc-Emile Ruchet
1912	Ludwig Forrer
1913	Eduard Müller
1914	Arthur Hoffmann
1915	Giuseppe Motta
1916	Camille Decoppet
1917	Edmund Schulthess
1918	Felix Calonder
1919	Gustave Ador
1920	Giuseppe Motta
1921	Edmund Schulthess
1922	Robert Haab
1923	Karl Scheurer
1924	Ernest Chuard
1925	Jean-Marie Musy
1926	Heinrich Häberlin
1927	Giuseppe Motta
1928	Edmund Schulthess
1929	Robert Haab
1930	Jean-Marie Musy
1931	Heinrich Häberlin
1932	Giuseppe Motta
1933	Edmund Schulthess
1934	Marcel Pilet-Golaz
1935	Rudolf Minger
1936	Albert Meyer
1937	Giuseppe Motta
1938	Johannes Baumann
1939	Philipp Etter
1940	Marcel Pilet-Golaz
1941	Ernst Wetter
1942	Philipp Etter
1943	Enrico Celio
1944	Walter Stampfli
1945	Eduard von Steiger
1946	Karl Kobelt
1947	Philipp Etter
1948	Enrico Celio
1949	Ernst Nobs
1950	Max Petitpierre
1951	Eduard von Steiger
1952	Karl Kobelt

History

History

1953	Philipp Etter
1954	Rodolphe Rubattel
1955	Max Petitpierre
1956	Markus Feldmann
1957	Hans Streuli
1958	Thomas Holenstein
1959	Paul Chaudet
1960	Max Petitpierre
1961	Friedrich Wahlen
1962	Paul Chaudet
1963	Willy Spühler
1964	Ludwig von Moos
1965	Hans Peter Tschudi
1966	Hans Schaffner
1967	Roger Bonvin
1968	Willy Spühler
1969	Ludwig von Moos
1970	Hans Peter Tschudi
1971	Rudolf Gnägi
1972	Nello Celio
1973	Roger Bonvin
1974	Ernst Brugger
1975	Pierre Graber
1976	Rudolf Gnägi
1977	Kurt Furgler
1978	Willi Ritschard
1979	Hans Hürlimann
1980	Georges-André Chevallaz
1981	Kurt Furgler
1982	Fritz Honegger
1983	Pierre Aubert
1984	Leon Schlumpf
1985	Kurt Furgler
1986	Alphons Egli
1987	Pierre Aubert
1988	Otto Stich
1989	Jean-Pascal Delamuraz
1990	Arnold Koller
1991	Flavio Cotti
1992	René Felber
1993	Adolf Ogi
1994	Otto Stich
1995	Kaspar Villiger
1996	Jean-Pascal Delamuraz
1997	Arnold Koller
1998	Flavio Cotti
1999	Ruth Dreifuss
2000	Adolf Ogi
2001	Moritz Leuenberger
2002	Kaspar Villinger
2003	Pascal Couchepin
2004	Joseph Deiss
2005	Samuel Schmid
2006	Moritz Leuenberger
2007	Micheline Calmy-Rey
2008	Pascal Couchepin
2009	Hans-Rudolf Merz

Syria

President

1943–9	Shukri Al-Quwwatli
1949	Husni Az-Zaim
1949–51	Hashim Al-Atassi
1951–4	Adib Shishaqli
1954–5	Hashim Al-Atassi
1955–8	Shukri Al-Quwwatli
1958–61	*Part of United Arab Republic*

1961–3	Nazim Al-Qudsi
1963	Luai Al-Atassi
1963–6	Amin Al-Hafiz
1966–70	Nureddin Al-Atassi
1970–1	Ahmad Al-Khatib
1971–2000	Hafez Al-Assad
2000–	Bashar Al-Assad

Prime Minister

1946–8	Jamil Mardam Bey
1948–9	Khalid Al-Azm
1949	Husni Az-Zaim
1949	Muhsi Al-Barazi
1949	Hashim Al-Atassi
1949	Nazim Al-Qudsi
1949–50	Khalid Al-Azm
1950–1	Nazim Al-Qudsi
1951	Khalid Al-Azm
1951	Hassan Al-Hakim
1951	Maruf Ad-Dawalibi
1951–3	Fauzi As-Salu
1953–4	Adib Shishaqli
1954	Shewqet Shuqair
1954	Sabri Al-Asali
1954	Said Al-Ghazzi
1954–5	Faris Al-Khuri
1955	Sabri Al-Asali
1955–6	Said Al-Ghazzi
1956–8	Sabri Al-Asali
1958–61	*Part of United Arab Republic*
1961	Abd Al-Hamid As-Sarraj
1961	Mamun Kuzbari
1961	Izzat An-Nuss
1961–2	Maruf Ad-Dawalibi
1962	Bashir Azmah
1962–3	Khalid Al-Azm
1963	Salah Ad-Din Al-Bitaar
1963	Sami Al-Jundi
1963	Salah Ad-Din Al-Bitaar
1963–4	Amin Al-Hafez
1964	Salah Ad-Din Al-Bitaar
1964–5	Amin Al-Hafez
1965	Yousif Zeayen
1966	Salah Ad-Din Al-Bitaar
1966–8	Yousif Zeayen
1968–70	Nureddin Al-Atassi *Acting*
1970–1	Hafez Al-Assad
1971–2	Abdel Rahman Khleifawi
1972–6	Mahmoud bin Saleh Al-Ayoubi
1976–8	Abdul Rahman Khleifawi
1978–80	Mohammed Ali Al-Halabi
1980–7	Abdel Rauof Al-Kasm
1987–2000	Mahmoud Al-Zubi
2000–3	Muhammad Mustafa Mero
2003–	Muhammad Naji Al-Otari

Taiwan (Republic of China)

President

1950–75	Chiang Kai-shek
1975–8	Yen Chia-kan
1978–87	Chiang Ching-kuo
1987–2000	Lee Teng-hui
2000–8	Chen Shui-bian
2008–	Ma Ying-jeou

President of Executive Council

1950–4	Ch'eng Ch'eng

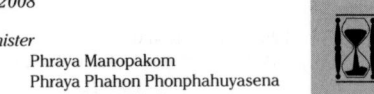

1954–8	O K Yui
1958–63	Ch'eng Ch'eng
1963–72	Yen Chia-ken
1972–8	Chiang Ching-kuo
1978–84	Sun Yun-suan
1984–9	Yu Kuo-hwa
1989–90	Lee Huan
1990–3	Hau Pei-tsun
1993–6	Lien Chan

Prime Minister

1996–7	Lien Chan
1997–2000	Vincent Siew
2000	Tang Fei
2000–2	Chang Chun-hsiung
2002–5	Yu Shyi-kun
2005–6	Frank Hsieh
2006–8	Su Tseng-chang
2008	Liu Chao-shiuan

Tajikistan

President

1991–2	Rakhman Nabiev
1992	Akbarsho Iskandrov *Acting*
1992–	Imomali Rakhmonov

Prime Minister

1991–2	Akbar Mirzoyev
1992–3	Abdumalik Abdullojanov
1993–4	Abduljalil Samadov *Acting*
1994–6	Jamshed Karimov
1996–9	Yahya Azimov
1999–	Akil Akilov

Tanzania

President

1964–85	Julius Kambarage Nyerere
1985–95	Ali Hassan Mwinyi
1995–2005	Benjamin William Mkapa
2005–	Jakaya Mrisho Kikwete

Prime Minister

1964–72	Rashid M Kawawa *Vice*
1972–7	Rashid M Kawawa
1977–80	Edward M Sokoine
1980–3	Cleopa D Msuya
1983–4	Edward M Sokoine
1984–5	Salim A Salim
1985–90	Joseph S Warioba
1990–4	John Malecela
1994–5	Cleopa Msuya
1995–2005	Frederick Sumaye
2005–8	Edward Lowassa
2008–	Mizengo Kayanza Peter Pinda

Thailand

Monarch

1868–1910	Chulalongkorn, Rama V
1910–25	Vajiravudh, Rama VI
1925–35	Prajadhipok, Rama VII
1935–46	Ananda Mahidol, Rama VIII
	(*regency 1935–45*)
1938–45	Nai Pridi Phanomyong *Regent*
1946–	Bhumibol Adulyadej, Rama IX
	(*regency 1946–50*)

Prime Minister

1932–3	Phraya Manopakom
1933–8	Phraya Phahon Phonphahuyasena
1938–44	Luang Plaek Pibulsonggram
	(Pibun)
1944–5	Nai Khuang Aphaiwong
1945	Thawi Bunyaket
1945–6	Mom Rachawongse Seni Pramoj
1946	Nai Khuang Aphaiwong
1946	Nai Pridi Phanomyong
1946–7	Luang Thamrong Nawasawat
1947–8	Nai Khuang Aphaiwong
1948–57	Luang Plaek Pibulsonggram
	(Pibun)
1957	Sarit Thanarat
1957	Nai Pote Sarasin
1957–8	Thanom Kittikatchorn
1958–63	Sarit Thanarat
1963–73	Thanom Kittikatchorn
1973–5	Sanya Dharmasaki
1975–6	Mom Rachawongse Kukrit Pramoj
1976	Seni Pramoj
1976–7	Thanin Kraivichien
1977–80	Kriangsak Chammanard
1980–7	Prem Tinsulanonda
1987–91	Chatichai Choonhaven
1991–2	Anand Panyarachun
1992	Suchinda Kraprayoon
1992	Anand Panyarachun
1992–5	Chuan Leekpai
1995–6	Banharn Silpa-Archa
1996–7	Chavalit Yongchaiyudh
1997–2001	Chuan Leekpai
2001–6	Thaksin Shinawatra
2006–8	Surayud Chulanont *Interim Prime Minister*
2008	Samak Sundaravej
2008–	Somchai Wongsawat

Togo

President

1960–3	Sylvanus Olympio
1963–7	Nicolas Grunitzky
1967–2005	Gnassingbé Eyadéma
2005–	Faure Gnassingbé

Prime Minister

1991–4	Joseph Koukou Koffigoh
1994–6	Edem Kodjo
1996–9	Kwassi Klutse
1999–2000	Eugene Koffi Adoboli
2000–2	Messan Agbeyome Kodjo
2002–5	Koffi Sama
2005–6	Edem Kodjo
2006–7	Yawovi Madji Agboyibo
2007–8	Komlan Mally
2008–	Gilbert Houngbo

Tonga

Monarch

1893–1918	George Tupou II
1918–65	Salote Tupou III
1965–2006	Taufa'ahau Tupou IV
2006–	Siaosi (George) Tupou V

Prime Minister

1970–91	Fatafehi Tu'ipelehake

History

1991–2000	Baron Vaea
2000–6	Prince 'Ulukalala Lavaka Ata
2006–	Feleti Sevele

Trinidad and Tobago

Head of State 1962–76: British monarch, represented by Governor General
■ *Republic*
President

1976–87	Ellis Emmanuel Clarke
1987–97	Noor Mohammed Hassanali
1997–2003	Arthur Robinson
2003–	George Maxwell Richards

Prime Minister

1962–81	Eric Williams
1981–6	George Chambers
1986–91	Raymond Robinson
1991–5	Patrick Manning
1995–2001	Basdeo Panday
2001–	Patrick Manning

Tunisia

Bey

| 1943–57 | Muhammad VIII |

President

| 1957–87 | Habib Bourguiba |
| 1987– | Zine El-Abidine Ben Ali |

Prime Minister

1956–7	Habib Bourguiba
1957–69	*No Prime Minister*
1969–70	Bahi Ladgham
1970–80	Hadi Nouira
1980–6	Mohammed Mezali
1986–7	Rashid Sfar
1987	Zine El-Abidine Ben Ali
1987–9	Hadi Baccouche
1989–99	Hamed Karoui
1999–	Mohammed Ghannouchi

Turkey

Sultan of the Ottoman Empire

1876–1909	Abdülhamit
1909–18	Mehmet Reşat
1918–22	Mehmet Vahideddin

■ **Turkish Republic**
President

1923–38	Mustafa Kemal Atatürk
1938–50	İsmet İnönü
1950–60	Celal Bayar
1961–6	Cemal Gürsel
1966–73	Cevdet Sunay
1973–80	Fahri S Korutürk
1980	Ihsan Çaglayangil *Acting*
1982–9	Kenan Evren
1989–93	Turgut Özal
1993–2000	Süleyman Demirel
2000–7	Ahmet Necdet Sezer
2007–	Abdullah Gül

Prime Minister

1923–4	İsmet İnönü
1924–5	Ali Fethi Okyar
1925–37	İsmet İnönü

1937–9	Celal Bayar
1939–42	Dr Refik Saydam
1942–6	Şükrü Saracoğlu
1946–7	Recep Peker
1947–9	Hasan Saka
1949–50	Şemşettin Günaltay
1950–60	Adnan Menderes
1960–1	Cemal Gürsel
1961–5	İsmet İnönü
1965	S Hayri Ürgüplü
1965–71	Süleyman Demirel
1971–2	Nihat Erim
1972–3	Ferit Melen
1973–4	Naim Talu
1974	Bülent Ecevit
1974–5	Sadi Irmak
1975–7	Süleyman Demirel
1977	Bülent Ecevit
1977–8	Süleyman Demirel
1978–9	Bülent Ecevit
1979–80	Süleyman Demirel
1980–3	Bülent Ülüsü
1983–9	Turgut Özal
1989–91	Yildirim Akbulut
1991	Mesut Yilmaz
1991–3	Süleyman Demirel
1993–6	Tansu Çiller
1996	Mesut Yilmaz
1996–7	Necmettin Erbakan
1997–8	Mesut Yilmaz
1999–2002	Bülent Ecevit
2002–3	Abdullah Gül
2003–	Recep Tayyip Erdoğan

Turkmenistan

President

| 1991–2006 | Saparmurad Niyazov |
| 2006– | Gurbanguly Berdymukhamedov *Acting 2006–7* |

Prime Minister

| 1991–2 | Khan Akhmedov |
| 1992– | *As President* |

Tuvalu

Head of State: British monarch, represented by Governor General

Prime Minister

1978–81	Toalipi Lauti
1981–9	Tomasi Puapua
1989–93	Bikenibeu Paeniu
1993–6	Kamuta Lataasi
1996–9	Bikenibeu Paeniu
1999–2000	Ionatana Ionatana
2000–1	Lagitupu Tuilimu *Acting*
2001	Faimalaga Luka
2001–2	Koloa Talake
2002–4	Saufatu Sopoanga
2004–6	Maatia Toafa
2006–	Apisai Ielemia

Uganda

President

1963–6	Edward Muteesa II
1967–71	Milton Obote
1971–9	Idi Amin

1979 Yusuf Lule
1979–80 Godfrey Binaisa
1981–5 Milton Obote
1985–6 *Military Council* (Tito Okello)
1986– Yoweri Museveni

Prime Minister
1962–71 Milton Obote
1971–81 *No Prime Minister*
1981–5 Eric Oterna Alimadi
1985 Paulo Muwanga
1985–6 Abraham N Waliggo
1986–91 Samson B Kisekka
1991–4 George Cosmas Adyebo
1994–9 Kintu Musoke
1999– Apolo Nsibambi

Ukraine

President
1991–4 Leonid Kravchuk
1994–2005 Leonid Kuchma
2005– Viktor Yushchenko

Prime Minister
1990–2 Vitold Fokin
1992 Valentin Symonenko
1992–3 Leonid Kuchma
1993–4 Yukhim Zvyahilski *Acting*
1994–5 Vitalii Masol
1995–6 Yevhenii Marchuk
1996–7 Pavlo Lazarenko
1997 Vasyl Durdynets *Acting*
1997–9 Valery Pustovoytenko
1999–2001 Viktor Yushchenko
2001–2 Anatoli Kinakh
2002–5 Viktor Yanukovych
2005 Mykola Azarov *Acting*
2005 Yuliya Tymoshenko
2005–6 Yuri Yekhanurov
2006–7 Viktor Yanukovych
2007– Yuliya Tymoshenko

United Arab Emirates

President
1971–2004 Zayed bin Sultan al-Nahyan
2004– Khalifa bin Zayed al-Nahyan

Prime Minister
1971–9 Maktoum bin Rashid al-Maktoum
1979–91 Rashid bin Said al-Maktoum
1991–2006 Maktoum bin Rashid al-Maktoum
2006– Mohammed bin Rashid al-Maktoum

■ Abu Dhabi
Tribe: al Bu Falah *or* al Nahyan (Bani Yas)
Family name: al-Nahyan
Shaikh
1855–1909 Zayed
1909–12 Tahnoun
1912–22 Hamdan
1922–6 Sultan
1926–8 Saqr
1928–66 Shakhbout
1966–2004 Zayed
2004– Khalifa

■ Ajman
Tribe: al Bu Kharayban (Naim)
Family name: al-Nuaimi
Shaikh
1900–10 Abdel-Aziz
1910–28 Humaid
1928–81 Rashid
1981– Humaid

■ Dubai
Tribe: al Bu Flasah (Bani Yas)
Family name: al-Maktoum
Shaikh
1894–1906 Maktoum
1906–12 Butti
1912–58 Said
1958–90 Rashid
1990–2006 Maktoum
2006– Mohammed

■ Fujairah
Tribe: Sharqiyyin
Family name: al-Sharqi
Shaikh
1952–75 Mohammed
1975– Hamad

■ Ras al-Khaimah
Tribe: Huwalah
Family name: al-Qasimi
Shaikh
1921–48 Sultan
1948– Saqr

■ Sharjah
Tribe: Huwalah
Family name: al-Qasimi
Shaikh
1883–1914 Saqr
1914–24 Khaled
1924–51 Sultan
1951–65 Saqr
1965–72 Khaled
1972–87 Sultan
1987 Abdel-Aziz
1987– Sultan

■ Umm al-Qaiwain
Tribe: al-Ali
Family name: al-Mualla
Shaikh
1873–1904 Ahmad
1904–22 Rashid
1922–3 Abdullah
1923–9 Hamad
1929–81 Ahmad
1981– Rashid

United Kingdom

For list of monarchs, see pp 283–4, 285, 286.
For list of prime ministers from 1721, see p 339.

United States of America

For list of presidents and vice presidents from 1789, see p 340.

History

History

Uruguay

President

1899–1903	Juan Lindolfo Cuestas
1903–7	José Batlle y Ordóñez
1907–11	Claudio Williman
1911–15	José Batlle y Ordóñez
1915–19	Feliciano Viera
1919–23	Baltasar Brum
1923–7	José Serrato
1927–31	Juan Capisteguy
1931–8	Gabriel Terra
1938–43	Alfredo Baldomir
1943–7	Juan José de Amézaga
1947	Tomás Berreta
1947–51	Luis Batlle Berres
1951–2	Andrés Martínez Trueba

Chairman of the National Government Council

1952–5	Andrés Martínez Trueba
1955–6	Luis Batlle Berres
1956–7	Alberto F Zubiría
1957–8	Alberto Lezama
1958–9	Carlos L Fischer
1959–60	Martín R Etchegoyen
1960–1	Benito Nardone
1961–2	Eduardo Victor Haedo
1962–3	Faustino Harrison
1963–4	Daniel Fernández Crespo
1964–5	Luis Giannattasio
1965–6	Washington Beltrán
1966–7	Alberto Heber Usher

President

1967	Oscar Daniel Gestido
1967–72	Jorge Pacheco Areco
1972–6	Juan María Bordaberry Arocena
1976–81	Aparicio Méndez
1981–4	Gregorio Conrado Álvarez Armelino
1984–90	Julio María Sanguinetti Cairolo
1990–4	Luis Alberto Lacalle Herrera
1994–9	Julio María Sanguinetti
1999–2005	Jorge Batlle Ibáñez
2005–	Tabaré Vázquez

USSR (Union of Soviet Socialist Republics)

No longer in existence, but included for reference.

President

1917	Leo Kamenev
1917–19	Yakov Sverlov
1919–46	Mikhail Kalinin
1946–53	Nikolai Shvernik
1953–60	Klimentiy Voroshilov
1960–4	Leonid Brezhnev
1964–5	Anastas Mikoyan
1965–77	Nikolai Podgorny
1977–82	Leonid Brezhnev
1982–3	Vasily Kuznetsov *Acting*
1983–4	Yuri Andropov
1984	Vasily Kuznetsov *Acting*
1984–5	Konstantin Chernenko
1985	Vasily Kuznetsov *Acting*
1985–8	Andrei Gromyko
1988–90	Mikhail Gorbachev

Executive President

1990–91	Mikhail Gorbachev
1991	Gennady Yanayev *Acting*
1991	Mikhail Gorbachev

Chairman (Prime Minister)
Council of Ministers

1917	Georgy Lvov
1917	Aleksandr Kerensky

Council of People's Commissars

1917–24	Vladimir Ilyich Lenin
1924–30	Aleksei Rykov
1930–41	Vyacheslav Molotov
1941–53	Josef Stalin

Council of Ministers

1953–5	Georgiy Malenkov
1955–8	Nikolai Bulganin
1958–64	Nikita Khrushchev
1964–80	Alexei Kosygin
1980–5	Nikolai Tikhonov
1985–90	Nikolai Ryzhkov
1990–1	Yuri Maslyukov *Acting*
1991	Valentin Pavlov
1991	Ivan Silayev *Acting*

General Secretary

1922–53	Josef Stalin
1953	Georgiy Malenkov
1953–64	Nikita Khrushchev
1964–82	Leonid Brezhnev
1982–4	Yuri Andropov
1984–5	Konstantin Chernenko
1985–91	Mikhail Gorbachev

For period from 1990/1 ► separate entries for former constitutent states of USSR.

Uzbekistan

President

1991–	Islam Karimov

Prime Minister

1991–5	Abdulhashim Mutalov
1995–2003	Otkir Sultonov
2003–	Shavkat Mirziyayev

Vanuatu

President

1980–9	George Sokomanu (*formerly* Kalkoa)
1989–94	Fred Timakata
1994–9	Jean-Marie Leye
1999–2004	John Bani
2004	Roger Abiut *Interim President*
2004	Alfred Maseng
2004	Roger Abiut *Interim President*
2004	Josias Moli *Interim President*
2004–	Kalkot Mataskelekele

Prime Minister

1980–91	Walter Lini
1991	Donald Kalpokas
1991–5	Maxime Carlot Korman
1995–6	Serge Vohor
1996	Maxime Carlot Korman
1996–8	Serge Vohor

1998–9	Donald Kalpokas
1999–2001	Barak Sopé
2001–4	Edward Natapei
2004	Serge Vohor
2004–8	Ham Lini
2008–	Edward Natapei

Venezuela

President

1899–1908	Cipriano Castro
1908–36	Juan Vicente Gomez
1936–41	Eleazar Lopez Contreras
1941–5	Isaias Medina Angarita
1945–7	*Military Junta* (Rómulo Betancourt)
1947–8	Romulo Gallegos
1948–50	*Military Junta* (Carlos Delgado Chalbaud)
1950–9	*Military Junta* (Marcos Pérez Jiménez)
1959–64	Rómulo Betancourt
1964–9	Raul Leoni
1969–74	Rafael Caldera Rodriguez
1974–9	Carlos Andres Pérez
1979–84	Luis Herrera Campins
1984–9	Jaime Lusinchi
1989–93	Carlos Andres Pérez
1994–9	Rafael Caldera Rodríguez
1999–	Hugo Chávez Frías

Vietnam

President
■ **Democratic Republic of Vietnam (North Vietnam)**

1945–69	Ho Chi Minh
1969–76	Ton Duc Thang

■ **State of Vietnam (South Vietnam)**

1949–55	Bao Dai

■ **Republic of Vietnam (South Vietnam)**

1955–63	Ngo Dinh Diem
1963–4	Duong Van Minh
1964	Nguyen Khanh
1964–5	Phan Khac Suu
1965–75	Nguyen Van Thieu
1975	Tran Van Huong
1975	Duong Van Minh
1975–6	*Provisional Revolutionary Government* (Huynh Tan Phat)

■ **Socialist Republic of Vietnam**

1976–80	Ton Duc Thang
1980–1	Nguyen Hun Tho *Acting*
1981–7	Truongh Chinh
1987–92	Vo Chi Cong
1992–7	Le Duc Anh
1997–2006	Tran Duc Luong
2006–	Nguyen Minh Triet

Prime Minister
■ **Democratic Republic of Vietnam (North Vietnam)**

1955–76	Pham Van Dong

■ **State of Vietnam (South Vietnam)**

1949–50	Nguyen Van Xuan
1950	Nguyen Phan Long

1950–2	Tran Van Huu
1952	Tran Van Huong
1952–3	Nguyen Van Tam
1953–4	Buu Loc
1954–5	Ngo Dinh Diem

■ **Republic of Vietnam (South Vietnam)**

1955–63	Ngo Dinh Diem
1963–4	Nguyen Ngoc Tho
1964	Nguyen Khan
1964–5	Tran Van Huong
1965	Phan Huy Quat
1965–7	Nguyen Cao Ky
1967–8	Nguyen Van Loc
1968–9	Tran Van Huong
1969–75	Tran Thien Khiem
1975	Nguyen Ba Can
1975–6	Vu Van Mau

■ **Socialist Republic of Vietnam**
Premier

1976–87	Pham Van Dong
1987–8	Pham Hung
1988	Vo Van Kiet *Acting*
1988–91	Do Muoi
1991–7	Vo Van Kiet
1997–2006	Phan Van Khai
2006–	Nguyen Tan Dung

Secretary General

1960–80	Le Duan
1986	Truong Chinh
1986–91	Nguyen Van Linh
1991–7	Do Muoi
1997–2001	Le Kha Phieu
2001–	Nong Duc Manh

Western Samoa ►Samoa

Yemen

■ **North Yemen**
Monarch (Imam)

1918–48	Yahya Mohammed bin Mohammed
1948–62	Ahmed bin Yahya
1962–70	Mohammed bin Ahmed
1962	*Civil war*

President
Yemen Arab Republic

1962–7	Abdullah Al-Sallal
1967–74	Abdur Rahman Al-Iriani
1974–7	*Military Command Council* (Ibrahim Al- Hamadi)
1977–8	Ahmed bin Hussein Al-Ghashmi
1978–90	Ali Abdullah Saleh

Prime Minister

1964	Hamud Al-Jaifi
1965	Hassan Al-Amri
1965	Ahmed Mohammed Numan
1965	*As President*
1965–6	Hassan Al-Amri
1966–7	*As President*
1967	Muhsin Al-Aini
1967–9	Hassan Al-Amri
1969–70	Abd Allah Kurshumi

History

History

1970–1	Muhsin Al-Aini
1971	Abdel Salam Sabra *Acting*
1971	Ahmed Mohammed Numan
1971	Hassan Al-Amri
1971–2	Muhsin Al-Aini
1972–4	Qadi Abdullah Al-Hijri
1974	Hassan Makki
1974–5	Muhsin Al-Aini
1975	Abdel Latif Deifallah *Acting*
1975–90	Abdel-Aziz Abdel-Ghani

■ **South Yemen**
President
People's Democratic Republic of Yemen

1967–9	Qahtan Mohammed Al-Shaabi
1969–78	Salim Ali Rubai
1978	Ali Nasir Mohammed
	Husani
1978–80	Abdel Fattah Ismail
1980–6	Ali Nasir Mohammed Husani
1986–90	Haidar Abu Bakr Al-Attas

Prime Minister

1969	Faisal Abd Al-Latif Al-Shaabi
1969–71	Mohammed Ali Haithem
1971–85	Ali Nasir Mohammed Husani
1985–6	Haidar Abu Bakr Al-Attas
1986–90	Yasin Said Numan

■ **Republic of Yemen**
President

| 1990– | Ali Abdullah Saleh |

Prime Minister

1990–3	Haidar Abu Bakr Al-Attas
1993–7	Abdel-Aziz Abdel-Ghani
1997	Farag Said Ben Ghanem
1998–2001	Abdul Ali Al-Karim Al-Iryani
2001–7	Abd al-Qadir Abd al-Rahman Bajammal
2007–	Ali Mohammed Mujawar

Yugoslavia

No longer in existence, but included for reference.

Monarch

| 1921–34 | Aleksandar II |
| 1934–45 | Petar II (*in exile from 1941*) |

Chairman, National Assembly

| 1945–53 | Ivan Ribar |

President

| 1953–80 | Josip Broz Tito |

Collective Presidency

1980	Lazar Koliševski
1980–1	Cvijetin Mijatović
1981–2	Serghei Kraigher
1982–3	Petar Stambolić
1983–4	Mika Spiljak
1984–5	Veselin Duranović
1985–6	Radovan Vlajković
1986–7	Sinan Hasani
1987–8	Lazar Mojsov
1988–9	Raif Dizdarević
1989–90	Janez Drnovšek
1990–1	Borisav Jovic

| 1991 | Stipe Mesic |
| 1991–2 | Branko Kostic *Acting* |

Prime Minister

1929–32	Pear Živkovic
1932	Vojislav Marinković
1932–4	Milan Srškić
1934	Nikola Uzunović
1934–5	Bogoljub Jevtić
1935–9	Milan Stojadinović
1939–41	Dragiša Cvetković
1941	Dušan Simović

Government in exile

1942	Slobodan Jovanović
1943	Miloš Trifunović
1943–4	Božidar Purić
1944–5	Ivan Šubašić
1945	Drago Marušić

Home government

1941–4	Milan Nedić
1943–63	Josip Broz Tito
1963–7	Petar Stambolić
1967–9	Mika Špiljak
1969–71	Mitja Ribičič
1971–7	Džemal Bijedić
1977–82	Veselin Duranović
1982–6	Milka Planinc
1986–9	Branko Mikulić
1989–91	Ante Marković
1992	Aleksandar Mitrovic *Acting*

Communist Party
First Secretary

| 1937–52 | Josip Broz Tito |

League of Communists

| 1952–80 | Josip Broz Tito |

League of Communists Central Committee
President

1979–80	Stevan Doronjski *Acting*
1980–1	Lazar Mojsov
1981–2	Dušan Dragosavac
1982–3	Mitja Ribičič
1983–4	Dragoslav Marković
1984–5	Ali Sukrija
1985–6	Vidoje Žarkovic
1986–7	Milanko Renovica
1987–8	Boško Krunić
1988–9	Stipe Suvar
1989–90	Milan Pancevski
1990	Miomir Grbović

For period from 1991/2 ► **Bosnia and Herzegovina, Croatia, Macedonia, Montenegro, Serbia** and **Slovenia**.

Zaire ► Congo, Democratic Republic of

Zambia

President

1964–91	Kenneth Kaunda
1991–2002	Frederick Chiluba
2002–8	Levy Mwanawasa
2008–	Rupiah Banda

Prime Minister

1964–73	Kenneth Kaunda
1973–5	Mainza Chona
1975–7	Elijah Mudenda
1977–8	Mainza Chona
1978–81	Daniel Lisulu
1981–5	Nalumino Mundia
1985–9	Kebby Musokotwane
1989–91	Malimba Masheke

Zimbabwe

President

1980–7	Canaan Sodindo Banana
1987–	Robert Gabriel Mugabe

Prime Minister

1980–7	Robert Gabriel Mugabe
2008–	Morgan Tsvangirai *Designate*

British Prime Ministers

1721–42	Robert Walpole *Whig*
1742–3	Earl of Wilmington (Spencer Compton) *Whig*
1743–54	Henry Pelham *Whig*
1754–6	Duke of Newcastle (Thomas Pelham-Holles) *Whig*
1756–7	Duke of Devonshire (William Cavendish) *Whig*
1757–62	Duke of Newcastle *Whig*
1762–3	Earl of Bute (John Stuart) *Tory*
1763–5	George Grenville *Whig*
1765–6	Marquess of Rockingham (Charles Watson Wentworth) *Whig*
1766–70	Duke of Grafton (Augustus Henry Fitzroy) *Whig*
1770–82	Lord North (Frederick North) *Tory*
1782	Marquess of Rockingham *Whig*
1782–3	Earl of Shelburne (William Petty-Fitzmaurice) *Whig*
1783	Duke of Portland (William Henry Cavendish) *Coal*
1783–1801	William Pitt *Tory*
1801–4	Henry Addington *Tory*
1804–6	William Pitt *Tory*
1806–7	Lord Grenville (William Wyndham) *Whig*
1807–9	Duke of Portland *Tory*
1809–12	Spencer Perceval *Tory*
1812–27	Earl of Liverpool (Robert Banks Jenkinson) *Tory*
1827	George Canning *Tory*
1827–8	Viscount Goderich (Frederick John Robinson) *Tory*
1828–30	Duke of Wellington (Arthur Wellesley) *Tory*
1830–4	Earl Grey (Charles Grey) *Whig*
1834	Viscount Melbourne (William Lamb) *Whig*
1834–5	Robert Peel *Con*
1835–41	Viscount Melbourne *Whig*
1841–6	Robert Peel *Con*
1846–52	Lord John Russell *Lib*
1852	Earl of Derby (Edward George Smith Stanley) *Con*
1852–5	Lord Aberdeen (George Hamilton-Gordon) *Peelite*

1855–8	Viscount Palmerston (Henry John Temple) *Lib*
1858–9	Earl of Derby *Con*
1859–65	Viscount Palmerston *Lib*
1865–6	Lord John Russell *Lib*
1866–8	Earl of Derby *Con*
1868	Benjamin Disraeli *Con*
1868–74	William Ewart Gladstone *Lib*
1874–80	Benjamin Disraeli *Con*
1880–5	William Ewart Gladstone *Lib*
1885–6	Marquess of Salisbury (Robert Gascoyne-Cecil) *Con*
1886	William Ewart Gladstone *Lib*
1886–92	Marquess of Salisbury *Con*
1892–4	William Ewart Gladstone *Lib*
1894–5	Earl of Rosebery (Archibald Philip Primrose) *Lib*
1895–1902	Marquess of Salisbury *Con*
1902–5	Arthur James Balfour *Con*
1905–8	Henry Campbell-Bannerman *Lib*
1908–15	Herbert Henry Asquith *Lib*
1915–16	Herbert Henry Asquith *Coal*
1916–22	David Lloyd George *Coal*
1922–3	Andrew Bonar Law *Con*
1923–4	Stanley Baldwin *Con*
1924	James Ramsay MacDonald *Lab*
1924–9	Stanley Baldwin *Con*
1929–31	James Ramsay MacDonald *Lab*
1931–5	James Ramsay MacDonald *Nat*
1935–7	Stanley Baldwin *Nat*
1937–40	Neville Chamberlain *Nat*
1940–5	Winston Churchill *Coal*
1945–51	Clement Attlee *Lab*
1951–5	Winston Churchill *Con*
1955–7	Anthony Eden *Con*
1957–63	Harold Macmillan *Con*
1963–4	Alec Douglas-Home *Con*
1964–70	Harold Wilson *Lab*
1970–4	Edward Heath *Con*
1974–6	Harold Wilson *Lab*
1976–9	James Callaghan *Lab*
1979–90	Margaret Thatcher *Con*
1990–7	John Major *Con*
1997–2007	Anthony Blair *Lab*
2007–	Gordon Brown *Lab*

Coal = Coalition; *Con* = Conservative; *Lab* = Labour; *Lib* = Liberal; *Nat* = National Government

History

Presidents of the USA

President (Vice President in parentheses)

1789–97	George Washington (1st) (John Adams)
1797–1801	John Adams (2nd) *Fed* (Thomas Jefferson)
1801–9	Thomas Jefferson (3rd) *Dem-Rep* (Aaron Burr, 1801–5) (George Clinton, 1805–9)
1809–17	James Madison (4th) *Dem-Rep* (George Clinton, 1809–12) *no Vice President 1812–13* (Elbridge Gerry, 1813–14) *no Vice President 1814–17*
1817–25	James Monroe (5th) *Dem-Rep* (Daniel D Tompkins)
1825–9	John Quincy Adams (6th) *Dem-Rep* (John C Calhoun)
1829–37	Andrew Jackson (7th) *Dem* (John C Calhoun, 1829–32) *no Vice President 1832–3* (Martin van Buren, 1833–7)
1837–41	Martin van Buren (8th) *Dem* (Richard M Johnson)
1841	William Henry Harrison (9th) *Whig* (John Tyler)
1841–5	John Tyler (10th) *Whig no Vice President*
1845–9	James Knox Polk (11th) *Dem* (George M Dallas)
1849–50	Zachary Taylor (12th) *Whig* (Millard Fillmore)
1850–3	Millard Fillmore (13th) *Whig no Vice President*
1853–7	Franklin Pierce (14th) *Dem* (William R King, 1853) *no Vice President 1853–7*
1857–61	James Buchanan (15th) *Dem* (John C Breckinridge)
1861–5	Abraham Lincoln (16th) *Rep* (Hannibal Hamlin, 1861–5) (Andrew Johnson, 1865)
1865–9	Andrew Johnson (17th) *Dem-Nat no Vice President*
1869–77	Ulysses Simpson Grant (18th) *Rep* (Schuyler Colfax, 1869–73) (Henry Wilson, 1873–5) *no Vice President 1875–7*
1877–81	Rutherford Birchard Hayes (19th) *Rep* (William A Wheeler)
1881	James Abram Garfield (20th) *Rep* (Chester A Arthur)
1881–5	Chester Alan Arthur (21st) *Rep no Vice President*
1885–9	Grover Cleveland (22nd) *Dem* (Thomas A Hendricks, 1885) *no Vice President 1885–9*
1889–93	Benjamin Harrison (23rd) *Rep* (Levi P Morton)
1893–7	Grover Cleveland (24th) *Dem* (Adlai E Stevenson)
1897–1901	William McKinley (25th) *Rep* (Garrat A Hobart, 1897–9) *no Vice President 1899–1901* (Theodore Roosevelt, 1901)
1901–9	Theodore Roosevelt (26th) *Rep no Vice President 1901–5* (Charles W Fairbanks, 1905–9)
1909–13	William Howard Taft (27th) *Rep* (James S Sherman, 1909–12) *no Vice President 1912–13*
1913–21	Woodrow Wilson (28th) *Dem* (Thomas R Marshall)
1921–3	Warren Gamaliel Harding (29th) *Rep* (Calvin Coolidge)
1923–9	Calvin Coolidge (30th) *Rep no Vice President 1923–5* (Charles G Dawes, 1925–9)
1929–33	Herbert Clark Hoover (31st) *Rep* (Charles Curtis)
1933–45	Franklin Delano Roosevelt (32nd) *Dem* (John N Garner, 1933–41) (Henry A Wallace, 1941–5) (Harry S Truman, 1945)
1945–53	Harry S Truman (33rd) *Dem no Vice President 1945–9* (Alben W Barkley, 1949–53)
1953–61	Dwight David Eisenhower (34th) *Rep* (Richard M Nixon)
1961–3	John Fitzgerald Kennedy (35th) *Dem* (Lyndon B Johnson)
1963–9	Lyndon Baines Johnson (36th) *Dem no Vice President 1963–5* (Hubert H Humphrey, 1965–9)
1969–74	Richard Milhous Nixon (37th) *Rep* (Spiro T Agnew, 1969–73) *no Vice President 1973, Oct–Dec* (Gerald R Ford, 1973–4)
1974–7	Gerald Rudolph Ford (38th) *Rep no Vice President 1974, Aug–Dec* (Nelson A Rockefeller, 1974–7)
1977–81	Jimmy Carter (39th) *Dem* (Walter F Mondale)
1981–9	Ronald Wilson Reagan (40th) *Rep* (George H W Bush)
1989–93	George Herbert Walker Bush (41st) *Rep* (J Danforth Quayle)
1993–2001	William Jefferson Blythe IV Clinton (42nd) *Dem* (Albert Gore)
2001–9	George Walker Bush (43rd) *Rep* (Richard B Cheney)
2009–	Barack Hussein Obama II (44th) *Dem* (Joseph R Biden)

Dem = Democrat; *Fed* = Federalist; *Nat* = National Union; *Rep* = Republican

ARTS AND CULTURE

Novelists

Selected works are listed.

Abrahams, Peter (Henry) (1919–) South African novelist, born Vrededorp, near Johannesburg; *The View from Coyaba* (1985).

Achebe, Chinua (originally **Albert Chinualumogu**) (1930–) Nigerian novelist, born Ogidi; *Things Fall Apart* (1958), *Anthills of the Savannah* (1987).

Ackroyd, Peter (1949–) English novelist, poet, critic, born London; *Notes for a New Culture* (1976), *The Last Testament of Oscar Wilde* (1983), *Hawksmoor* (1985), *Chatterton* (1987), *First Light* (1989), *English Music* (1992), *Milton in America* (1996), *London: The Biography* (2002), *Shakespeare* (2005).

Adams, Douglas (Noël) (1952–2001) English novelist, short-story writer, born Cambridge; *The Hitch Hiker's Guide to the Galaxy* (1979), *Life, the Universe and Everything* (1982), *Mostly Harmless* (1992).

Adams, Richard (George) (1920–) English novelist, short-story writer, born Newbury, Berkshire; *Watership Down* (1972), *Shardik* (1974), *The Girl in a Swing* (1980), *The Day Gone By* (autobiography) (1990).

Alcott, Louisa May (1832–88) US children's writer, born Germantown, Philadelphia; *Little Women* (1868–9), *Little Men* (1871), *Jo's Boys* (1886).

Aldiss, Brian (Wilson) (1925–) English novelist, poet, short-story writer, playwright, critic, born Dereham, Norfolk; *Helliconia Spring* (1982), *Helliconia Summer* (1983), *Helliconia Winter* (1985), *Forgotten Life* (1988), *Dracula Unbound* (1991), *Remembrance Day* (1993), *Jocasta* (2004).

Aldridge, (Harold Edward) James (1918–) Australian novelist, short-story writer, playwright, born White Hills, Victoria; *The Diplomat* (1949), *The Hunter* (1950), *The Last Exile* (1961), *The True Story of Spit MacPhee* (1986), *The True Story of Lola MacKellar* (1993), *The Girl from the Sea* (2002).

Alvarez, Al(fred) (1929–) English novelist, poet, critic, born London; *The Savage God: A Study of Suicide* (non-fiction) (1971), *Hers* (1974), *Day of Atonement* (1991), *Night* (1995), *Where Did It All Go Right?* (autobiography) (1999), *The Writer's Voice* (2005).

Ambler, Eric (1909–98) English novelist, playwright screenwriter, born London; *The Mask of Dimitrios* (1939), *The Intercom Conspiracy* (1970), *The Care of Time* (1981), *The Story So Far* (1993).

Amis, Sir Kingsley (William) (1922–95) English novelist, poet, born London; *Lucky Jim* (1954), *That Uncertain Feeling* (1955), *Jake's Thing* (1978), *The Old Devils* (1986, Booker Prize).

Amis, Martin (Louis) (1949–) English novelist, short-story writer, born Oxford; *The Rachel Papers* (1973), *Money* (1984), *London Fields* (1989), *Time's Arrow* (1991), *The Information* (1995), *Experience* (2000), *Yellow Dog* (2003), *House of Meetings* (2006).

Anand, Mulk Raj (1905–2004) Indian novelist, short-story writer, born Peshawar; *Untouchable* (1935), *The Big Heart* (1945).

Angelou, Maya (Marguerite Annie) (née **Johnson**) (1928–) US novelist, poet, playwright, born St Louis, Missouri; *I Know Why the Caged Bird Sings* (1970), *All God's Children Need Travelling Shoes* (1986), *Wouldn't Take Nothing for My Journey Now* (1993), *Even the Stars Look Lonesome* (1998), *A Song Flung up to Heaven* (2002).

Apuleius, Lucius (c.123–after 170 AD) Roman writer, born Madaurus, Numidia, Africa; *Golden Ass* (the only Roman novel to survive complete), *Apologia*.

Archer, Jeffrey (Howard) Archer, Baron (1940–) English novelist, short-story writer, born London; *Not a Penny More, Not a Penny Less* (1975), *Kane and Abel* (1979), *First Among Equals* (1984), *Honour Among Thieves* (1993), *The Fourth Estate* (1996), *False Impressions* (2006).

Asimov, Isaac (1920–92) US novelist, short-story writer, born Petrovichi, Russia; *I Robot* (1950), *Foundation* (1951), *The Disappearing Man and Other Stories* (1985), *Nightfall* (1990).

Atwood, Margaret (Eleanor) (1939–) Canadian novelist, poet, short-story writer, born Ottawa; *The Handmaid's Tale* (1985), *Cat's Eye* (1988), *The Robber Bride* (1993), *The Blind Assassin* (2000, Booker Prize), *Oryx and Crake* (2003), *The Penelopiad* (2005).

Auchincloss, Louis (Stanton) (1917–) US novelist, short-story writer, born Lawrence, New York; *The Great World and Timothy Colt* (1956), *A World of Profit* (1968), *Diary of a Yuppie* (1986), *Fellow Passengers* (1989), *Lady of Situations* (1990), *Tales of Yesteryear* (1994), *The Young Apollo* (2006).

Austen, Jane (1775–1817) English novelist, born Steventon, Hampshire; *Sense and Sensibility* (1811), *Pride and Prejudice* (1813), *Mansfield Park* (1814), *Emma* (1816), *Persuasion* (1818).

Bainbridge, Dame Beryl (Margaret) (1934–) English novelist, born Liverpool; *The Dressmaker* (1973), *Injury Time* (1977), *An Awfully Big Adventure* (1989), *Every Man for Himself* (1996), *Master Georgie* (1998), *According to Queeney* (2001).

Baldwin, James Arthur (1924–87) US novelist, playwright, born Harlem, New York City; *Go Tell it on the Mountain* (1954), *Tell Me How Long the Train's Been Gone* (1968), *Just Above My Head* (1979).

Ballantyne, R(obert) M(ichael) (1825–94) Scottish novelist, born Edinburgh; *The Coral Island* (1857), *The Gorilla Hunters* (1862).

Ballard, J(ames) G(raham) (1930–2009) English novelist, born Shanghai, China; *The Drowned World* (1962), *The Terminal Beach* (1964), *Empire of the Sun* (1984), *The Kindness of Women* (1991), *Super-Cannes* (2000), *Kingdom Come* (2006).

Balzac, Honoré de (1799–1850) French novelist, born Tours; *Comédie humaine* (1827–47), *Illusions perdues* (1837–43).

Banks, Iain (Menzies) (1954–) Scottish novelist, born Dunfermline; *The Wasp Factory* (1984), *The Bridge* (1986), *The Crow Road* (1992), *Whit* (1995), *Excession* (1996), *A Song of Stone* (1997), *Dead Air*

(2002), *The Steep Approach to Garbadale* (2007).

Banks, Lynne Reid (1929–) English novelist, playwright, and children's writer, born London; *The L-Shaped Room* (1960), *The Adventures of King Midas* (1976), *The Indian in the Cupboard* (1980), *The Warning Bell* (1984), *The Magic Hare* (1992), *Tiger, Tiger* (2004).

Banville, John (1945–) Irish novelist, born Wexford; *Birchwood* (1973), *Dr Copernicus* (1976), *Kepler* (1981), *Book of Evidence* (1989), *The Untouchables* (1997), *The Sea* (2005, Man Booker Prize).

Barker, Pat (Patricia Margaret) (1943–) English novelist, short-story writer, born Thornaby-on-Tees; *Union Street* (1982), *Blow Your House Down* (1984), *The Century's Daughter* (1986), *The Man Who Wasn't There* (1989), *Regeneration* (1991), *The Eye in the Door* (1993), *The Ghost Road* (1995, Booker Prize, Best of Booker 2008), *Border Crossing* (2001), *Double Vision* (2003), *Life Class* (2007).

Barnes, Julian (Patrick) (1946–) English novelist, born Leicester; *Metroland* (1980), *Flaubert's Parrot* (1984), *Staring at the Sun* (1986), *A History of the World in 10½ Chapters* (1989), *Love, Etc* (1992), *Something to Declare* (2002), *Arthur and George* (2005).

Barstow, Stan(ley) (1928–) English novelist, short-story writer, playwright, born Horbury, Yorkshire; *A Kind of Loving* (1960), *A Raging Calm* (1968), *Just You Wait and See* (1986), *Next of Kin* (1991), *In My Own Good Time* (2001).

Barth, John (Simmons) (1930–) US novelist, short-story writer, born Cambridge, Maryland; *The Floating Opera* (1956), *Chimera* (1974), *The Tidewater Tales* (1987), *The Last Voyage of Somebody the Sailor* (1991), *Where Three Roads Meet* (2005).

Bates, H(erbert) E(rnest) (1905–74) English novelist, short-story writer, born Rushden, Northamptonshire; *Fair Stood the Wind for France* (1944), *The Jacaranda Tree* (1949), *Love for Lydia* (1952), *The Darling Buds of May* (1958).

Bawden, Nina (Mary) (née Mabey) (1925–) English writer, born London; *The Birds on the Trees* (1970), *Carrie's War* (1973), *The Peppermint Pig* (1975), *Walking Naked* (1981), *The Ice House* (1983), *Circles of Deceit* (1987), *Family Money* (1991), *A Nice Change* (1997).

Bedford, Sybille (née von Schoenebeck) (1911–2006) British novelist, born Charlottenburg, Germany; *A Legacy* (1956), *Jigsaw: An Unsentimental Education* (1989), *As It Was* (essays) (1990).

Beerbohm, Sir (Henry) Max(imilian) (1872–1956) English novelist, born London; *Zuleika Dobson* (1912).

Behn, Aphra (1640–89) English novelist, playwright, born Wye, Kent; *The Rover* (play) (1678), *Oroonoko* (1688).

Bellow, Saul (1915–2005) American novelist, born Quebec, Canada; *Henderson the Rain King* (1959), *Herzog* (1964), *Humboldt's Gift* (1975, Pulitzer Prize 1976) *The Dean's December* (1982), *The Actual* (1997), *Ravelstein* (2000); Nobel Prize for literature 1976.

Bely, Andrei (pseudonym of **Boris Nikolayvich Bugayev**) (1880–1934) Russian novelist, poet, born Moscow; *The Silver Dove* (1910), *Petersburg* (1913).

Benedictus, David (Henry) (1938–) English novelist, playwright, born London; *The Fourth of June* (1962), *A World of Windows* (1971), *Local Hero* (novelization of screenplay) (1983), *The Stamp Collector* (1994).

Bennett, (Enoch) Arnold (1867–1931) English novelist, born Hanley, Staffordshire; *Anna of the Five Towns* (1902), *The Old Wives' Tale* (1908), *Clayhanger* series (1910–18).

Berger, John (Peter) (1926–) English novelist, playwright, born London; *A Painter of Our Time* (1958), *A Fortunate Man* (non-fiction) (1967), *G* (1972, Booker Prize), *To the Wedding* (1995), *Photocopies* (1996), *Here is Where We Meet* (2005), *From A to X* (2008).

Berger, Thomas (Louis) (1924–) US novelist, born Cincinnati, Ohio; *Little Big Man* (1964), *Arthur Rex* (1978), *The Houseguest* (1988), *Suspects* (1996).

Binchy, Maeve (1940–) Irish novelist, short-story writer, born Dublin; *Light a Penny Candle* (1982), *Echoes* (1985), *Firefly Summer* (1987), *Circle of Friends* (1990), *Copper Beech* (1992), *The Glass Lake* (1994), *Tara Road* (1998), *Whitethorn Woods* (2006).

Blackmore, R(ichard) D(oddridge) (1825–1900) English novelist, born Longworth, Berkshire; *Lorna Doone* (1869).

Bleasdale, Alan (1946–) English novelist, playwright, born Liverpool; *Scully* (1975), *The Boys from the Blackstuff* (TV series) (1982), *Are You Lonesome Tonight?* (musical) (1985), *GBH* (TV series) (1991), *Jake's Progress* (TV series) (1995).

Blyton, Enid (Mary) (1897–1968) English children's writer, born London; best-known characters include Noddy, the Famous Five and the Secret Seven. Published over 600 books.

Böll, Heinrich (1917–85) German novelist, born Cologne; *And Never Said a Solitary Word* (1953), *The Unguarded House* (1954), *The Bread of Our Early Years* (1955); Nobel Prize for literature 1972.

Borges, Jorge Luis (1899–1986) Argentinian poet, short-story writer, born Buenos Aires; *Ficciones* (1944), *El Aleph* (1949), *Labyrinths* (1962).

Bowen, Elizabeth (Dorothea Cole) (1899–1973) Anglo-Irish novelist, short-story writer, born Dublin; *The Death of the Heart* (1938), *The Heat of the Day* (1949).

Bowles, Paul (Frederick) (1910–99) US novelist, short-story writer, born New York City; *The Sheltering Sky* (1949), *Pages from Cold Point and Other Stories* (1968), *Midnight Mass* (stories) (1981).

Boyd, William (Andrew Murray) (1952–) Scottish novelist, short-story writer, born Accra, Ghana; *A Good Man in Africa* (1981), *An Ice-Cream War* (1982), *Brazzaville Beach* (1990), *Nat Tate: An American Artist* (1998), *Armadillo* (1998), *Restless* (2006).

Bradbury, Sir Malcolm (Stanley) (1932–2000) English novelist, born Sheffield; *Eating People is Wrong* (1959), *The History Man* (1975), *Dr Criminale* (1992).

Bradbury, Ray(mond) (Douglas) (1920–) US novelist, short-story writer, born Waukegan, Illinois; *The Martian Chronicles* (short stories) (1950), *Fahrenheit 451* (1953), *Something Wicked this Way Comes* (1962), *A Graveyard for Lunatics* (1990), *Farewell Summer* (2006).

Bradford, Barbara Taylor (1933–) English novelist, born Leeds; *A Woman of Substance* (1979), *Hold the Dream* (1985), *Love in Another Town* (1995), *Just Rewards* (2005).

Bragg, Melvyn Bragg, Baron (1939–) English novelist, playwright, short-story writer, born Wigton; *The Hired Man* (1969), *A Time to Dance* (1991), *The Soldier's Return* (1999), *Crossing the Lines* (2003), *Remember Me* (2008).

Braine, John (Gerard) (1922–86) English novelist, born Bradford; *Room at the Top* (1957).

Brink, André (Philippus) (1935–) South African novelist, short-story writer, playwright, born Vrede, Orange Free State; *Looking on Darkness* (1973), *Rumours of Rain* (1978), *A Dry White Season* (1979), *States of Emergency* (1988), *On the Contrary* (1993), *Imaginings of Sand* (1996), *Praying Mantis* (2005), *Other Lives* (2008).

Brittain, Vera (Mary) (1893–1970) English novelist, poet, born Newcastle-under-Lyme, Staffordshire; *Testament of Youth* (1933), *Testament of Friendship* (1940), *Testament of Experience* (1957) (all autobiographies).

Bromfield, Louis (1896–1956) US novelist, short-story writer, born Mansfield, Ohio; *Early Autumn* (1926), *Until the Day Break* (1942).

Brontë, Anne (1820–49) English novelist, poet, born Thornton, Yorkshire; *Agnes Grey* (1847), *The Tenant of Wildfell Hall* (1848).

Brontë, Charlotte (1816–55) English novelist, poet, born Thornton, Yorkshire; *Jane Eyre* (1847), *Shirley* (1849), *Villette* (1853).

Brontë, Emily (1818–48) English novelist, poet, born Thornton, Yorkshire; *Wuthering Heights* (1847).

Brooke-Rose, Christine (1926–) English novelist, born Geneva, Switzerland; *The Languages of Love* (1957), *Thru* (1975), *Amalgamemnon* (1984), *Textermination* (1991), *Remake* (1996), *Life, End of* (2006).

Brookner, Anita (1928–) English novelist, born London; *Hotel du Lac* (1984, Booker Prize), *Family and Friends* (1985), *Brief Lives* (1990), *Altered States* (1996), *Visitors* (1997), *Leaving Home* (2005).

Brophy, Brigid (Antonia) (1929–95) English novelist, short-story writer, playwright, born London; *The Crown Princess and Other Stories* (1953), *The King of a Rainy Country* (1956), *In Transit* (1969).

Brown, George Douglas (1869–1902) Scottish novelist, born Ochiltree, Ayrshire; *The House with the Green Shutters* (1901).

Brown, George Mackay (1921–96) Scottish novelist, poet, short-story writer, playwright, born Orkney; *Greenvoe* (1972), *Beside the Ocean of Time* (1994).

Buchan, John (1875–1940) Scottish novelist, poet, born Perth; *The Thirty-Nine Steps* (1915), *Greenmantle* (1916), *Sir Walter Scott* (biography) (1932).

Buck, Pearl (née **Sydenstricker**) (1892–1973) US novelist, born Hillsboro, West Virginia; *The Good Earth* (1913), *Pavilion of Women* (1946); Nobel Prize for literature 1938.

Bulgakov, Mikhail (Afanasievich) (1891–1940) Russian novelist, short-story writer, born Kiev; *Diavoliada* (1925), *The Master and Margarita* (1967).

Bunyan, John (1628–88) English novelist, born Elstow, near Bedford; *Pilgrim's Progress* (1678).

Burgess, Anthony (pseudonym of **John Anthony Burgess Wilson**) (1917–93) English novelist, born Manchester; *A Clockwork Orange* (1962), *The Malayan Trilogy* (1972), *Earthly Powers* (1980), *Kingdom of the Wicked* (1985), *Any Old Iron* (1989).

Burnett, Frances Hodgson (1849–1924) Anglo-US children's writer, playwright, born Manchester; *Little Lord Fauntleroy* (1886), *The Little Princess* (1905), *The Secret Garden* (1909).

Burney, Fanny (Frances, later **Mme d'Arblay)** (1752–1840) English novelist, born King's Lynn; *Evelina* (1778), *Cecilia* (1782).

Burroughs, Edgar Rice (1875–1950) US novelist, born Chicago; *Tarzan of the Apes* (1914), *The Land that Time Forgot* (1924).

Burroughs, William S(eward) (1914–97) US novelist, born St Louis, Missouri; *The Naked Lunch* (1959), *The Soft Machine* (1961), *The Wild Boys* (1971), *Exterminator!* (1974), *My Education: A Book of Dreams* (1995).

Byatt, Dame A(ntonia) S(usan) (1936–) English novelist, born Sheffield; *The Shadow of a Sun* (1964), *The Virgin in the Garden* (1978), *Possession* (1990, Booker Prize), *Babel Tower* (1996), *The Biographer's Tale* (2000), *A Whistling Woman* (2002).

Calvino, Italo (1923–87) Italian novelist, short-story writer, born Santiago de Las Vegas, Cuba; *Invisible Cities* (1972), *The Castle of Crossed Destinies* (1969), *If on a Winter's Night a Traveller* (1979).

Camus, Albert (1913–60) French novelist, playwright, born Mondovi, Algeria; *The Outsider* (1942), *The Plague* (1948), *The Fall* (1957); Nobel Prize for literature 1957.

Canetti, Elias (1905–94) Bulgarian novelist, born Ruse, Bulgaria; *Auto da Fé* (1935, trans 1946), *Crowds and Power* (1960, trans 1962); Nobel Prize for literature 1981.

Capote, Truman (1924–84) US playwright, novelist, short-story writer, born New Orleans; *Other Voices, Other Rooms* (1948), *Breakfast at Tiffany's* (1958).

Carey, Peter (Philip) (1943–) Australian novelist, short-story writer, born Bacchus Marsh, Victoria; *Illywhacker* (1985), *Oscar and Lucinda* (1988, Booker Prize), *True History of the Kelly Gang* (2001, Booker Prize), *His Illegal Self* (2008).

Carr, Philippa ▶ Holt, Victoria

Carroll, Lewis (pseudonym of **Charles Lutwidge Dodgson**) (1832–98) English children's writer, nonsense poet and mathematician, born Daresbury, near Warrington; *Alice's Adventures in Wonderland* (1865), *Through the Looking-Glass and What Alice Found There* (1871).

Carter, Angela (1940–92) English novelist, poet, playwright, born London; *The Magic Toyshop* (1967), *The Infernal Desire Machines of Dr Hoffman* (1972), *Nights at the Circus* (1984), *Wise Children* (1991).

Cartland, (Mary) Barbara (Hamilton) (1901–2000) English novelist, born Birmingham; *Wings on My Heart* (1954), *The Husband Hunters* (1976), *The Castle Made for Love* (1985), *Love Solves the Problem* (1995).

Carver, Raymond (1939–88) US short-story writer, poet, born Clatskanie, Oregon; story collections: *Will You Please Be Quiet, Please?* (1976), *What We Talk About When We Talk About Love* (1981), *Cathedral* (1983); poetry collections: *Where Water Comes Together with Other Water* (1985), *Ultramarine* (1985).

Cather, Willa (Silbert) (1876–1947) US novelist, poet, born near Winchester, Virginia; *O Pioneers!* (1913), *My Antonia* (1918), *One of Ours* (1922), *The Professor's House* (1925), *My Mortal Enemy* (1926), *Death Comes for the Archbishop* (1927), *Sapphira and the Slave Girl* (1940).

Cela, Camilo José (1916–2002) Spanish novelist, born Iria Flavia; *La familia de Pascual Duarte* (1942), *La Colmena* (1951), *Mazurca para dos muertos* (1984); Nobel Prize for literature 1989.

Cervantes (Saavedra), Miguel de (1547–1616) Spanish novelist and poet, born Alcala de Henares; *La Galatea* (1585), *Don Quixote* (1605–15).

Chandler, Raymond (1888–1959) US novelist, born Chicago; *The Big Sleep* (1939), *Farewell, My Lovely* (1940), *The High Window* (1942), *The Lady in the Lake* (1943), *The Long Goodbye* (1953).

Chatwin, Bruce (1940–89) English novelist, born

Sheffield; *In Patagonia* (1977), *The Viceroy of Ouidah* (1980), *On The Black Hill* (1982), *The Songlines* (1987), *Utz* (1988).

Chesterton, G(ilbert) K(eith) (1874–1936) English novelist, poet, born London; *The Napoleon of Notting Hill* (1904), *The Innocence of Father Brown* (1911).

Christie, Dame Agatha (Mary Clarissa) (née **Miller**) (1890–1976) English novelist, born Torquay, Devon; *Murder on the Orient Express* (1934), *Death on the Nile* (1937), *A Murder is Announced* (1950), *Curtain* (1975).

Clarke, Sir Arthur C(harles) (1917–2008) English novelist, short-story writer, born Minehead, Somerset; *Childhood's End* (1953), *2001: A Space Odyssey* (1968), *The Fountains of Paradise* (1979), *The Garden of Rama* (1991), *The Hammer of God* (1993).

Clavell, James (du Maresq) (1922–94) US novelist, playwright, born England; *King Rat* (1962), *Tai-Pan* (1966), *Shogun* (1975).

Cleary, Jon (Stephen) (1917–) Australian novelist, born Sydney; *You Can't See Around Corners* (1947), *The Sundowners* (1951), *The High Commissioner* (1966), *Pride's Harvest* (1991), *Dark Summer* (1992), *Endpeace* (1996), *Morning's Gone* (2006).

Coetzee, J(ohn) M(ichael) (1940–) South African novelist, born Cape Town; *Life and Times of Michael K* (1983, Booker Prize), *Disgrace* (1999, Booker Prize), *Slow Man* (2006); Nobel Prize for literature 2003.

Colette, Sidonie Gabrielle (1873–1954) French novelist, born Saint-Sauveur-en-Puisaye, Burgundy; *Claudine à l'école* (1900), *Chéri* (1920), *La Fin de Chéri* (1926), *Gigi* (1943).

Collins, (William) Wilkie (1824–89) English novelist, born London; *The Woman in White* (1860), *No Name* (1862), *Armadale* (1866), *The Moonstone* (1868).

Compton-Burnett, Dame Ivy (1884–1969) English novelist, born Pinner, Middlesex; *A House and its Head* (1935), *A Family and a Fortune* (1939), *Manservant and Maidservant* (1947).

Condon, Richard (Thomas) (1915–96) US novelist, born New York City; *The Manchurian Candidate* (1959), *Winter Kills* (1974), *Prizzi's Honor* (1982).

Connell, Evan S(helby) (1924–) US novelist, born Kansas City, Missouri; *Mrs Bridge* (1959), *The Diary of a Rapist* (1966), *Mr Bridge* (1969), *The Alchymist's Journal* (1991).

Conrad, Joseph (originally **Jozef Teodor Konrad Nalecz Korzeniowski**) (1857–1924) Anglo-Polish novelist, short-story writer, born Berdichev, Poland (now Ukraine); *Lord Jim* (1900), *Heart of Darkness* (1902), *Nostromo* (1904), *The Secret Agent* (1907), *Chance* (1914).

Cookson, Dame Catherine (Ann) (1906–98) English novelist, born Tyne Dock, County Durham; *Tilly Trotter* (1956), *The Glass Virgin* (1969), *The Black Candle* (1989).

Cooper, Jilly (1937–) English novelist, born Hornchurch, Essex; *Men and Supermen* (1972), *Class* (1979), *Riders* (1985), *Rivals* (1988), *Polo* (1990), *Appassionata* (1996), *Score* (1999), *Wicked!* (2006).

Cooper, William (pseudonym of **Harry Summerfield Hoff**) (1910–2002) English novelist, born Crewe, Cheshire; *Scenes from Provincial Life* (1950), *Disquiet and Peace* (1956), *Immortality At Any Price* (1991).

Crane, Stephen (1871–1900) US novelist, born New Jersey; *The Red Badge of Courage* (1895).

Dahl, Roald (1916–90) Welsh children's writer, short-story writer, playwright, born Llandaff, Glamorgan; *Over to You* (1946), *Someone Like You* (1954), *Kiss, Kiss* (1960) (all short stories), *James and the Giant Peach* (1961), *Charlie and the Chocolate Factory* (1964), *Matilda* (1988).

Davidson, Lionel (1922–) English novelist, born Hull, Yorkshire; *The Rose of Tibet* (1962), *Smith's Gazelle* (1971), *The Chelsea Murders* (1978).

Davies, (William) Robertson (1913–95) Canadian novelist, playwright, born Thamesville, Ontario; *The Rebel Angels* (1981), *The Deptford Trilogy* (1970–5), *What's Bred in the Bone* (1985).

de Beauvoir, Simone (1908–86) French novelist, born Paris; *The Second Sex* (1949, trans 1953), *Les Mandarins* (1954), *Memoirs of a Dutiful Daughter* (1959).

Defoe, Daniel (1660–1731) English novelist, born Stoke Newington, London; *Robinson Crusoe* (1719), *Moll Flanders* (1722), *A Journal of the Plague Year* (1722).

Deighton, Len (Leonard Cyril) (1929–) English novelist, born London; *The Ipcress File* (1962), *Funeral in Berlin* (1964), *Spy Hook* (1988), *Spy Line* (1989), *Spy Sinker* (1990), *Faith* (1994), *Hope* (1995), *Charity* (1996).

Delafield, E M (pseudonym of **Edmée Elizabeth Monica Dashwood**) (née **de la Pasture**) (1890–1943) English novelist, born Llandogo, Monmouth, Wales; *The Diary of a Provincial Lady* (1931).

DeLillo, Don (1936–) US novelist, born New York City; *End Zone* (1972), *Ratner's Star* (1976), *The Names* (1982), *White Noise* (1985), *Mao II* (1991), *Underworld* (1997), *Falling Man* (2007).

de Quincey, Thomas (1785–1859) English novelist, born Manchester; *Confessions of an English Opium Eater* (1822).

Desai, Anita (née **Mazumbar**) (1937–) Indian novelist, short-story writer, born Mussoorie; *Cry, The Peacock* (1963), *Clear Light of Day* (1980), *In Custody* (1984), *Baumgartner's Bombay* (1987), *Journey to Ithaca* (1995), *Fasting, Feasting* (1999).

De Vries, Peter (1910–93) US novelist, born Chicago; *The Tunnel of Love* (1954), *The Meckerel Plaza* (1958), *Slouching Towards Kalamazoo* (1983).

Dickens, Charles (1812–70) English novelist, born Landport, Portsmouth; *Oliver Twist* (1837–9), *David Copperfield* (1849–50), *Bleak House* (1852–3), *Great Expectations* (1860–1).

Dickens, Monica (1915–92) English novelist, born London; *One Pair of Hands* (1939), *Spring Comes to World's End* (1973).

Didion, Joan (1934–) US novelist, essayist, born Sacramento, California; *Run River* (1963), *Slouching Towards Bethlehem* (1968), *A Book of Common Prayer* (1977), *Democracy* (1984), *The Last Thing He Wanted* (1996), *The Year of Magical Thinking* (2005).

Dinesen, Isak (pseudonym of **Baroness Karen Blixen**) (1885–1962) Danish novelist, born Rungsted; *Seven Gothic Tales* (1934), *Out of Africa* (1937).

Disraeli, Benjamin (1804–81) English novelist, politician, born London; *Coningsby* (1844), *Sybil* (1846), *Tancred* (1847).

Donleavy, J(ames) P(atrick) (1926–) Irish–US novelist, playwright, born Brooklyn, New York City; *The Ginger Man* (1955), *Schultz* (1980), *Are You Listening, Rabbi Low?* (1987), *The Lady Who Liked Clean Rest Rooms* (1995).

Dos Passos, John Roderigo (1896–1970) US novelist, born Chicago; *Manhattan Transfer* (1925), *USA* (1930–6).

Dostoevsky, Fyodor Mikhailovich (1821–81)

Russian novelist, born Moscow; *Notes from the Underground* (1864), *Crime and Punishment* (1866), *The Brothers Karamazov* (1880).

Doyle, Sir Arthur Conan (1859–1930) Scottish novelist, short-story writer, born Edinburgh; *The Memoirs of Sherlock Holmes* (1894), *The Hound of the Baskervilles* (1902), *The Lost World* (1912).

Doyle, Roddy (1958–) Irish novelist, born Dublin; *The Commitments* (1987), *Paddy Clarke, Ha Ha Ha* (1993, Booker Prize), *The Woman Who Walked into Doors* (1996), *A Star Called Henry* (1999), *Paula Spencer* (2006).

Drabble, Margaret (1939–) English novelist, short-story writer, born Sheffield; *The Millstone* (1965), *The Ice Age* (1977), *The Gates of Ivory* (1991), *The Witch of Exmoor* (1996), *The Sea Lady* (2006).

Duffy, Maureen (Patricia) (1933–) English novelist, playwright, born Worthing, Sussex; *That's How It Was* (1962), *The Microcosm* (1966), *The Paradox Players* (1967), *Occam's Razor* (1993), *Alchemy* (2004).

Dumas, Alexandre (in full **Alexandre Dumas Davy de la Pailleterie**), known as **Dumas père** (1802–70) French novelist, playwright, born Villers-Cotterêts, Aisne; *The Three Musketeers* (1844–5).

Dumas, Alexandre, known as **Dumas fils** (1824–95) French novelist, playwright, born Paris; *La Dame aux camélias* (1848).

du Maurier, Dame Daphne (1907–89) English novelist, born London; *Jamaica Inn* (1936), *Rebecca* (1938), *Frenchman's Creek* (1942), *My Cousin Rachel* (1951).

Dunmore, Helen (1952–) English novelist, poet and children's writer, born Yorkshire; *The Apple Fall* (poems 1983), *Zennor in Darkness* (1993), *A Spell of Winter* (1995), *The Siege* (2001), *Counting the Stars* (2008).

Dunn, Nell (Mary) (1936–) English novelist, playwright, born London; *Up the Junction* (1963), *Poor Cow* (1967), *The Only Child* (1978), *Cancer Tales* (2002).

Durrell, Gerald Malcolm (1925–95) English writer, born Jamshedpur, India; *The Overloaded Ark* (1953), *My Family and Other Animals* (1956).

Durrell, Lawrence George (1912–90) English novelist, poet, born Julundur, India; *The Alexandria Quartet* (1957–60).

Eco, Umberto (1932–) Italian novelist, born Alessandria, Piedmont; *The Name of the Rose* (1980), *Foucault's Pendulum* (1989), *The Island of the Day Before* (1995), *Baudolino* (2002), *The Mysterious Flame of Queen Loana* (2005).

Edgeworth, Maria (1767–1849) Irish novelist, born Blackbourton, Oxfordshire; *Castle Rackrent* (1800), *The Absentee* (1809).

Eliot, George (originally **Mary Ann**, later **Marian Evans**) (1819–80) English novelist, born Arbury, Warwickshire; *Adam Bede* (1858), *The Mill on the Floss* (1860), *Middlemarch* (1871–2), *Daniel Deronda* (1874–6).

Elkin, Stanley (Lawrence) (1930–95) US novelist, short-story writer, born Brooklyn, New York City; *Criers and Kibitzers, Kibitzers and Criers* (1966), *The Living End* (1979), *George Mills* (1982), *The Magic Kingdom* (1985).

Ellis, Alice Thomas (pseudonym of **Anna Margaret Haycraft**) (née **Lindholm**) (1932–2005) English novelist, born Liverpool; *The Sin Eater* (1977), *The 27th Kingdom* (1982), *The Inn at the Edge of the World* (1990), *Fairy Tale* (1996).

Elton, Ben (Benjamin Charles) (1959–) English novelist, born Catford, South London; *Stark* (1989), *Gridlock* (1991), *Popcorn* (1996), *Inconceivable*

(1999), *High Society* (2002), *The First Casualty* (2005).

Fairbairns, Zoë (Ann) (1948–) English novelist, born Tunbridge Wells, Kent; *Stand We At Last* (1983), *Daddy's Girls* (1991), *Other Names* (1998).

Farmer, Philip José (1918–) US novelist, short-story writer, born Terre Haute, Indiana; *To Your Scattered Bodies Go* (1977), *The Magic Labyrinth* (1980), *Nothing Burns in Hell* (1998).

Fast, Howard (Melvin) (1914–2003) US novelist, playwright, born New York City; *The Last Frontier* (1941), *Spartacus* (1951), *The Immigrants* (1977).

Faulkner, William Harrison (1897–1962) US novelist, born near Oxford, Mississippi; *Sartoris* (1929), *The Sound and the Fury* (1929), *Absalom, Absalom!* (1936); Nobel Prize for literature 1949.

Feinstein, Elaine (1930–) English novelist, poet, born Bootle, Lancashire; *The Circle* (1970), *The Border* (1984), *All You Need* (1989), *Dark Inheritance* (2001).

Fielding, Henry (1707–54) English novelist, born Sharpham Park, near Glastonbury, Somerset; *Joseph Andrews* (1742), *Tom Jones* (1749).

Figes, Eva (née **Unger**) (1932–) British novelist, born Berlin, Germany; *Winter Journey* (1967), *Light* (1983), *The Tree of Knowledge* (1990), *The Tenancy* (1993), *Tales of Innocence and Experience* (2003).

Fitzgerald, F(rancis) Scott (Key) (1896–1940) US novelist, short-story writer, born St Paul, Minnesota; *The Beautiful and the Damned* (1922), *The Great Gatsby* (1925), *Tender is the Night* (1934).

Fitzgerald, Penelope (Mary) (née **Knox**) (1916–2000) English novelist, born Lincoln; *The Bookshop* (1978), *Offshore* (1979, Booker Prize), *The Gate of Angels* (1990), *The Blue Flower* (1995).

Flaubert, Gustave (1821–80) French novelist, born Rouen; *Madame Bovary* (1857), *Salammbô* (1862).

Fleming, Ian (Lancaster) (1908–64) English novelist, born London; author of the 'James Bond' novels, eg *Casino Royale* (1953), *From Russia with Love* (1957), *Dr No* (1958), *Goldfinger* (1959), *The Man with the Golden Gun* (1965).

Ford, Ford Madox (originally **Ford Hermann Hueffer**) (1873–1939) English novelist, poet, born Merton, Surrey; *The Fifth Queen* (1906), *The Good Soldier* (1915), *Parade's End* (1924–8).

Ford, Richard (1944–) US novelist, born Jackson, Mississippi; *A Piece of My Heart* (1976), *The Sportswriter* (1986), *Independence Day* (1995, Pulitzer Prize 1996), *Lay of the Land* (2006).

Forester, C(ecil) S(cott) (1899–1966) British novelist, born Cairo, Egypt; *Payment Deferred* (1926), *The African Queen* (1935), *The Happy Return* (1937).

Forster, E(dward) M(organ) (1879–1970) English novelist, short-story writer, born London; *A Room with a View* (1908), *Howards End* (1910), *A Passage to India* (1922–4).

Forsyth, Frederick (1938–) English novelist, short-story writer, born Ashford, Kent; *The Day of the Jackal* (1971), *The Odessa File* (1972), *The Fourth Protocol* (1984), *The Fist of God* (1993), *The Afghan* (2006).

Fowles, John (Robert) (1926–2005) English novelist, born Leigh-on-Sea, Essex; *The Collector* (1963), *The Magus* (1965, revised 1977), *The French Lieutenant's Woman* (1969), *The Ebony Tower* (1974), *The Tree* (1979).

Frame, Janet Paterson (1924–2004) New Zealand novelist, short-story writer, born Dunedin; *The Lagoon: Stories* (1951), *Scented Gardens for the Blind* (1963), *Living in the Maniototo* (1979), *The Carpathians* (1988); autobiographies: *To the Is-*

Iand (1982), *An Angel at My Table* (1984), *The Envoy from Mirror City* (1985).

Francis, Dick (Richard Stanley) (1920–) English novelist, born Tenby, Pembrokeshire; *Dead Cert* (1962), *Slay-Ride* (1973), *The Edge* (1988), *Comeback* (1991), *To The Hilt* (1996), *10lb Penalty* (1997), *Under Orders* (2006).

Fraser, Lady Antonia (née **Pakenham**) (1932–) English novelist, biographer, born London; *Mary, Queen of Scots* (1969), *Quiet as a Nun* (1977), *A Splash of Red* (1981), *Have a Nice Death* (1983), *Political Death* (1994), *Love and Louis XIV* (2001).

Frayn, Michael (1933–) English novelist, playwright, born Mill Hill, London; *The Tin Men* (1965), *A Very Private Life* (1968), *Sweet Dreams* (1973), *A Landing on the Sun* (1990), *Headlong* (1999), *Spies* (2002).

Freeling, Nicholas (1927–2003) English novelist, born London; *Love in Amsterdam* (1962), *Tsing-Boum* (1969), *Sand Castles* (1990), *A Dwarf Kingdom* (1996).

French, Marilyn (1929–) US novelist, born New York City; *The Women's Room* (1977), *The Bleeding Heart* (1980), *Her Mother's Daughter* (1987), *The War Against Women* (1992), *In the Name of Friendship* (2006).

Fuller, Roy (Broadbent) (1912–91) English novelist, poet, born Failsworth, Lancashire; *The Second Curtain* (1953), *The Ruined Boys* (1959), *My Child, My Sister* (1965).

Gaddis, William (1922–98) US novelist, born New York City; *The Recognitions* (1955), *JR* (1976), *Carpenter's Gothic* (1985), *A Frolic of His Own* (1994).

Galsworthy, John (1867–1933) English novelist, playwright, born Coombe, Surrey; *The Man of Property* (1906), *The Forsyte Saga* (1906–31); Nobel Prize for literature 1932.

García Márquez, Gabriel (1928–) Colombian novelist, born Aracataca; *One Hundred Years of Solitude* (1970), *Chronicle of a Death Foretold* (1982), *Love in the Time of Cholera* (1985), *The General in His Labyrinth* (1991), *Of Love and Other Demons* (1995); Nobel Prize for literature 1982.

Garner, Helen (1942–) Australian novelist, born Geelong; *Monkey Grip* (1977), *Cosmo Cosmolino* (1992), *The Last Days of Chez Nous* (screenplay) (1993), *The Spare Room* (2008).

Gaskell, Mrs Elizabeth (Cleghorn) (née **Stevenson**) (1810–65) English novelist, born Chelsea, London; *Mary Barton* (1848), *Cranford* (1853), *North and South* (1855), *Sylvia's Lovers* (1863).

Gerhardie, William Alexander (1895–1977) English novelist, born St Petersburg, Russia; *The Polyglots* (1925), *Resurrection* (1934).

Gibbon, Lewis Grassic (pseudonym of **James Leslie Mitchell**) (1901–35) Scottish novelist, born near Auchterless, Aberdeenshire; trilogy *Sunset Song* (1932), *Cloud Howe* (1933), *Grey Granite* (1934).

Gibbons, Stella (Dorothea) (1902–89) English novelist, born London; *Cold Comfort Farm* (1933).

Gide, André (Paul Guillaume) (1860–1951) French novelist, born Paris; *The Immoralist* (1902), *The Vatican Cellars* (1914); Nobel Prize for literature 1947.

Gilliat, Penelope (Ann Douglas, née **Conner)** (1932–93) English novelist, short-story writer, born London; *One by One* (1965), *The Cutting Edge* (1978), *Mortal Matters* (1983).

Gissing, George Robert (1857–1903) English novelist, short-story writer, born Wakefield, Yorkshire; *New Grub Street* (1891), *The Odd Women* (1893), *The Private Papers of Henry Ryecroft* (1902).

Glasgow, Ellen (1873–1945) US novelist, born Richmond, Virginia; *Barren Ground* (1925), *The Sheltered Life* (1932), *In This Our Life* (1941).

Godden, (Margaret) Rumer (1907–98) English novelist, poet, children's author, born Eastbourne, Sussex; *Black Narcissus* (1939), *Breakfast with the Nikolides* (1942), *The Greengage Summer* (1958), *Coromandel Sea Change* (1991), *Pippa Passes* (1994).

Godwin, William (1756–1836) English novelist, born Wisbech, Cambridgeshire; *Caleb Williams* (1794), *Mandeville* (1817).

Goethe, Johann Wolfgang von (1749–1832) German novelist, poet, born Frankfurt am Main; *The Sorrows of Young Werther* (1774).

Gogol, Nikolai Vasilievich (1809–52) Russian novelist, short-story writer, playwright, born Sorochinstsi, Poltava; *The Overcoat* (1835), *Diary of a Madman* (1835), *Dead Souls* (1842).

Gold, Herbert (1924–) US novelist, born Cleveland, Ohio; *Birth of a Hero* (1951), *The Man Who Was Not With It* (1956), *My Last Two Thousand Years* (autobiography) (1972), *She Took My Arm as if She Loved Me* (1997).

Golding, (Sir) William (Gerald) (1911–93) English novelist, born St Columb Minor, Cornwall; *Lord of the Flies* (1954), *The Inheritors* (1955), *Pincher Martin* (1956), *The Spire* (1964), *Darkness Visible* (1979), *Rites of Passage* (1980, Booker Prize), *The Paper Men* (1984), *Close Quarter* (1987), *Fire Down Below* (1989); Nobel Prize for literature 1983.

Goldman, William (1931–) US novelist, playwright, born Chicago; *Boys and Girls Together* (1964), *The Princess Bride* (1973), *The Silent Gondoliers* (1983), *Misery* (screenplay) (1990), *Absolute Power* (1997).

Goldsmith, Oliver (1728–74) Anglo-Irish playwright, novelist, poet, born Pallasmore, County Longford; *The Vicar of Wakefield* (1766).

Gordimer, Nadine (1923–) South African novelist, short-story writer, born Springs, Transvaal; *Occasion for Loving* (1963), *A Guest of Honour* (1971), *The Conservationist* (1974, Booker Prize), *A Sport of Nature* (1987), *None to Accompany Me* (1994), *Get a Life* (2005); Nobel Prize for literature 1991.

Gorky, Maxim (pseudonym of **Aleksei Maksimovich Peshkov**) (1868–1936) Russian novelist, short-story writer, born Nizhni Novgorod (New Gorky); *The Mother* (1906–7), *Childhood* (1913), *The Life of Klim Samgin* (1925–36).

Gosse, Sir Edmund William (1849–1928) English novelist, poet, born London; *Father and Son* (1907).

Graham, Winston (Mawdsley) (1911–2003) English novelist, born Victoria Park, Manchester; *Ross Poldark* (1945), *The Little Walls* (1955), *Marnie* (1961), *Poldark's Cornwall* (1983), *The Ugly Sister* (1998).

Grahame, Kenneth (1859–1932) Scottish children's writer, born Edinburgh; *Dream Days* (1898), *The Wind in the Willows* (1908).

Grass, Günter (Wilhelm) (1927–) German novelist, born Danzig; *The Tin Drum* (1962), *A Broad Field* (1995), *My Century* (1999), *Crabwalk* (2003); Nobel Prize for literature 1999.

Graves, Robert (Ranke) (1895–1985) English novelist, poet, born London; *I Claudius* (1934), *Claudius the God* (1934).

Gray, Alasdair (James) (1934–) Scottish novelist, short-story writer, poet, born Glasgow; *Lanark* (1981), *Unlikely Stories, Mostly* (stories) (1983), *Janine* (1984), *Poor Things* (1992, Whitbread

Novel Award), *A History Maker* (1994), *Old Men in Love* (2007).

Greene, (Henry) Graham (1904–91) English novelist, playwright, born Berkhamsted, Hertfordshire; *Brighton Rock* (1938), *The Power and the Glory* (1940), *The Third Man* (1950), *The Honorary Consul* (1973).

Grenville, Kate (1950–) Australian novelist, born Sydney; *Lilian's Story* (1986), *Dreamhouse* (1987), *The Idea of Perfection* (1999), *The Secret River* (2005).

Grossmith, George (1847–1912) and **Weedon** (1852–1919) English writers, entertainers, both born London; *The Diary of a Nobody* (1892).

Guterson, David (1956–) US novelist, short-story writer, born Seattle, Washington; *The Country Ahead of Us, The Country Behind* (stories) (1989), *Snow Falling on Cedars* (1995), *East of the Mountains* (1999), *The Other* (2008).

Haddon, Mark (1962–) English novelist and children's writer, born Northampton; *The Curious Incident of the Dog in the Night-Time* (2003), *A Spot of Bother* (2006).

Haggard, Sir (Henry) Rider (1856–1925) English novelist, born Bradenham Hall, Norfolk; *King Solomon's Mines* (1885), *She* (1887), *Allan Quatermain* (1887).

Hailey, Arthur (1920–2004) Canadian novelist, playwright, born Luton, Bedfordshire; *Flight into Danger* (1958), *Airport* (1968), *The Evening News* (1990), *Detective* (1997).

Hammett, (Samuel) Dashiell (1894–1961) US novelist, born St Mary's County, Maryland; *Red Harvest* (1929), *The Maltese Falcon* (1930), *The Glass Key* (1931), *The Thin Man* (1934).

Hammond Innes, (Ralph) (1913–98) English novelist, playwright, born Horsham, Sussex; *The Trojan Horse* (1940), *Atlantic Fury* (1962), *Isvik* (1991), *Delta Connection* (1996).

Hardy, Thomas (1840–1928) English novelist, poet, born Higher Bockhampton, Dorset; *Far from the Madding Crowd* (1874), *The Mayor of Casterbridge* (1886), *Tess of the D'Urbervilles* (1891), *Jude the Obscure* (1895).

Hartley, L(eslie) P(oles) (1895–1972) English novelist, short-story writer, born near Peterborough; *The Shrimp and the Anemone* (1944), *The Go-Between* (1953), *The Hireling* (1957).

Hawthorne, Nathaniel (1804–64) US novelist, short-story writer, born Salem, Massachusetts; *The Scarlet Letter* (1850), *The House of the Seven Gables* (1851).

Hazzard, Shirley (1931–) US novelist, short-story writer, born Sydney, Australia; *People in Glass Houses* (1967), *The Transit of Venus* (1980), *Countenance of Truth* (1990), *Greene on Capri: A Memoir* (2000).

Heinlein, Robert A(nson) (1907–88) US novelist, born Missouri; *Stranger in a Strange Land* (1962), *The Moon is a Harsh Mistress* (1967).

Heller, Joseph (1923–99) US novelist, born Brooklyn, New York City; *Catch-22* (1961), *Something Happened* (1974), *Closing Time* (1994).

Hemingway, Ernest (Millar) (1899–1961) US novelist, short-story writer, born Oak Park (Chicago), Illinois; *A Farewell to Arms* (1929), *For Whom the Bell Tolls* (1940), *The Old Man and the Sea* (1952); Nobel Prize for literature 1954.

Hesse, Hermann (1877–1962) German novelist, born Calw, Württemberg; *Rosshalde* (1914), *Steppenwolf* (1927), *The Glass Bead Game* (1943); Nobel Prize for literature 1946.

Heyer, Georgette (1902–74) English novelist, born London; *The Black Moth* (1929), *Footsteps in the Dark* (1932), *Regency Buck* (1935), *The Corinthian* (1940), *The Grand Sophy* (1950), *Bath Tangle* (1955), *The Nonesuch* (1962), *Frederica* (1965).

Highsmith, (Mary) Patricia (1921–95) US novelist, short-story writer, born Fort Worth, Texas; *Strangers on a Train* (1950), *The Talented Mr Ripley* (1956), *Ripley's Game* (1974).

Hill, Susan (Elizabeth) (1942–) English novelist, short-story writer, born Scarborough, Yorkshire; *I'm the King of the Castle* (1970), *Strange Meeting* (1972), *The Woman in Black* (1983), *Mrs de Winter* (1993), *The Risk of Darkness* (2006).

Hilton, James (1900–54) English novelist, born Leigh, Lancashire; *Lost Horizon* (1933), *Goodbye Mr Chips* (1934).

Hines, (Melvin) Barry (1939–) English novelist, playwright, born Barnsley, Yorkshire; *A Kestrel for a Knave* (1968), *The Gamekeeper* (1975), *The Heart of It* (1994), *Elvis over England* (1998).

Hoban, Russell (Conwell) (1925–) US novelist, playwright, children's writer, born Lansdale, Pennsylvania; *Turtle Diary* (1975), *Riddley Walker* (1980), *Pilgermann* (1983), *Come Dance with Me* (2005).

Hogg, James, 'the Ettrick Shepherd' (1770–1835) Scottish novelist, poet, born Ettrick, Selkirkshire; *Confessions of a Justified Sinner* (1824).

Holt, Victoria (pseudonym of **Eleanor Alice Burford Hibbert**) (1906–93) English novelist, born London, also wrote as Philippa Carr, Jean Plaidy; *Catherine de' Medici* (1969, as JP), *Will You Love Me in September* (1981, as PC), *The Captive* (1989, as VH).

Holtby, Winifred (1898–1935) English novelist, born Rudston, Yorkshire; *The Crowded Street* (1924), *The Land of Green Ginger* (1927), *South Riding* (1936).

Horgan, Paul (1903–95) US novelist, poet, short-story writer, born Buffalo, New York; *The Fault of Angels* (1933), *Rome Eternal* (1957), *Mexico Bay* (1982).

Howard, Elizabeth Jane (1923–) English novelist, born London; *The Sea Change* (1959), *After Julius* (1965), *The Light Years* (1990), *Marking Time* (1991), *Casting Off* (1995), *Slipstream* (autobiography) (2002).

Hughes, Thomas (1822–96) English novelist, born Uffington, Berkshire; *Tom Brown's Schooldays* (1857).

Hugo, Victor (Marie) (1802–85) French novelist, dramatist, poet, born Besançon; *Notre Dame de Paris* (1831), *Les Misérables* (1862).

Hulme, Keri (Ann Ruhi) (1947–) New Zealand novelist, born Christchurch; *The Bone People* (1983, Booker Prize 1985), *Stonefish* (2004).

Hunter, Evan (originally **Salvatore A Lambino**) (1926–2005) US novelist, playwright, short-story writer, born New York City; *The Blackboard Jungle* (1954), *Strangers When We Meet* (1958), *The Paper Dragon* (1966), *Last Summer* (1968), *Privileged Conversation* (1996); also writes as Ed McBain.

Hurston, Zora Neale (1903–60) US novelist, born Eatonville, Florida; *Their Eyes Were Watching God* (1937), *Moses, Man of the Mountain* (1939).

Huxley, Aldous (Leonard) (1894–1963) English novelist, born Godalming, Surrey; *Brave New World* (1932), *Eyeless in Gaza* (1936), *Island* (1962).

Innes, Michael ► Stewart, J I M

Irving, John (Winslow) (1942–) US novelist, short-story writer, born Exeter, New Hampshire; *The World According to Garp* (1978), *The Hotel*

New Hampshire (1981), A Prayer for Owen Meany (1988), A Son of the Circus (1994), Until I Find You (2005).

Isherwood, Christopher (William Bradshaw) (1904–86) Anglo-US novelist, born Disley, Cheshire; Mr Norris Changes Trains (1935), Goodbye to Berlin (1939), Down There on a Visit (1962).

Ishiguro, Kazuo (1954–) British novelist, short-story writer, born Nagasaki, Japan; The Remains of the Day (1989, Booker Prize), The Unconsoled (1995), When We Were Orphans (2000), Never Let Me Go (2005).

James, Henry (1843–1916) US novelist, born New York City; Portrait of a Lady (1881), The Bostonians (1886), The Turn of the Screw (1889), The Awkward Age (1899), The Ambassadors (1903).

James, P(hylis) D(orothy) (1920–) English novelist, born Oxford; Cover Her Face (1962), Taste for Death (1986), Devices and Desires (1989), Original Sin (1994), The Lighthouse (2005), The Private Patient (2008).

Jelinek, Elfriede (1946–) Austrian novelist, poet, playwright, born Mürzzuschlag, Styria; Wonderful Times, Wonderful Times (1990), The Piano Teacher (1988), Lust (1992), Greed (2006); Nobel Prize for literature 2004.

Jhabvala, Ruth Prawer (1927–) British novelist, born Cologne, Germany; Heat and Dust (1975, Booker Prize), In Search of Love and Beauty (1983), Poet and Dancer (1993), The Householder (2001), My Nine Lives (2004).

Jong, Erica (née Mann) (1942–) US novelist, poet, born New York City; Fear of Flying (1973), Fear of Fifty (1994), Sappho's Leap (2003).

Joyce, James (Augustine Aloysius) (1882–1941) Irish novelist, poet, born Dublin; Dubliners (1914), A Portrait of the Artist as a Young Man (1914–15), Ulysses (1922), Finnegans Wake (1939).

Kafka, Franz (1883–1924) Austrian novelist, short-story writer, born Prague; Metamorphosis (1916), The Trial (1925), The Castle (1926), America (1927).

Kaplan, Johanna (1942–) US novelist, short-story writer, born New York City; Other People's Lives (1975), O My America! (1980).

Kazantazakis, Nikos (1883–1957) Greek novelist, poet, playwright, born Heraklion, Crete; Zorba the Greek (1946).

Keane, Molly (1904–96) Anglo-Irish novelist, born County Kildare, Ireland; Devoted Ladies (1934), Good Behaviour (1981), Time After Time (1983).

Kelman, James (Alexander) (1946–) Scottish novelist, short-story writer, playwright, born Glasgow; The Busconductor Hines (1984), A Chancer (1985), Greyhound for Breakfast (stories) (1987), A Disaffection (1989), How late it was, how late (1994, Booker Prize), Translated Accounts (2001).

Keneally, Thomas (Michael) (1935–) Australian novelist, short-story writer, playwright, born Sydney; Bring Larks and Heroes (1967), Three Cheers for the Paraclete (1968), The Survivor (1969), Schindler's Ark (1982, Booker Prize), Woman of the Inner Sea (1992), The Widow and Her Hero (2007).

Kennedy, Margaret (Moore) (1896–1967) English novelist, playwright, born London; The Ladies of Lyndon (1923), The Constant Nymph (1924), The Fool of the Family (1930).

Kerouac, Jack (Jean-Louis) (1922–69) US novelist, born Lowell, Massachusetts; On the Road (1957), The Dharma Bums (1958).

Kesey, Ken (Elton) (1935–2001) US novelist, short-story writer, born La Junta, Colorado; One Flew

Over the Cuckoo's Nest (1962), Demon Box (stories) (1987), Sailor Song (1992), Last Go Round (1994).

King, Francis (Henry) (1923–) English novelist, short-story writer, born Adelboden, Switzerland; To the Dark Tower (1946), The Dividing Stream (1951), The Widow (1957), The Custom House (1961), Visiting Cards (1990), Ash on an Old Man's Sleeve (1996), With My Little Eye (2007).

King, Stephen (Edwin) (1947–) US novelist, short-story writer, born Portland, Maine; Carrie (1974), The Shining (1977), Christine (1983), Pet Sematary (1983), Misery (1988), Four Past Midnight (1990), The Plant (Internet novel) (2000), Lisey's Story (2006).

Kingsley, Charles (1819–75) English novelist, born Holne vicarage, Dartmoor; Westward Ho! (1855), The Water-Babies (1863), Hereward the Wake (1866).

Kipling, Rudyard (1865–1936) English novelist, poet, short-story writer, born Bombay (now Mumbai), India; Barrack-room Ballads (1892), The Jungle Book (1894), Kim (1901), Just So Stories (1902); Nobel Prize for literature 1907.

Kundera, Milan (1929–) French novelist, born Brno, Czechoslovakia (now Czech Republic); Life is Elsewhere (1973), The Farewell Party (1976), The Unbearable Lightness of Being (1984), Immortality (1991), Testaments Betrayed (1995), Ignorance (2002).

Laclos, Pierre (Ambroise François) Choderlos de (1741–1803) French novelist, born Amiens; Les Liaisons Dangereuses (Dangerous Liaisons) (1782).

La Fayette, Marie Madeleine Pioche de Lavergne, Comtesse de (1634–93) French novelist, born Paris; Zaide (1670), La Princesse de Clèves (1678).

Lamming, George (Eric) (1927–) Barbadian novelist, born Carrington Village; In the Castle of My Skin (1953), Season of Adventure (1960), Natives of My Person (1972).

Lampedusa, Giuseppe Tomasi di (1896–1957) Italian novelist, born Palermo, Sicily; Il Gattopardo (The Leopard) (1958).

Lawrence, D(avid) H(erbert) (1885–1930) English novelist, poet, short-story writer, born Eastwood, Nottinghamshire; Sons and Lovers (1913), The Rainbow (1915), Women in Love (1920), Lady Chatterley's Lover (1928).

Le Carré, John (pseudonym of David John Moore Cornwell) (1931–) English novelist, born Poole, Dorset; Tinker, Tailor, Soldier, Spy (1974), The Honourable Schoolboy (1977), Smiley's People (1980), The Little Drummer Girl (1983), A Perfect Spy (1986), The Russia House (1989), The Secret Pilgrim (1991), Our Game (1995), The Tailor of Panama (1996), A Most Wanted Man (2008).

Lee, (Nelle) Harper (1926–) US novelist, born Monroeville, Alabama; To Kill a Mockingbird (1960, Pulitzer Prize 1961).

Lee, Laurie (1914–97) English novelist, poet, born Slad, Gloucestershire; Cider with Rosie (1959), As I Walked Out One Midsummer Morning (1969).

Le Fanu, (Joseph) Sheridan (1814–73) Irish novelist, short-story writer, born Dublin; Uncle Silas (1864), In a Glass Darkly (1872).

Le Guin, Ursula K(roeber) (1929–) US novelist, poet, short-story writer, born Berkeley, California; Rocannon's World (1966), The Left Hand of Darkness (1969), Searoad (1991), Fish Soup (1992), Unlocking the Air and Other Stories (1996), The Telling (2000), Lavinia (2008).

Lehmann, Rosamond (Nina) (1903–90) English novelist, born London; Dusty Answer (1927),

Invitation to the Waltz (1932), *The Ballad and the Source* (1944).

Lessing, Doris (May) (née **Tayler**) (1919–) Rhodesian novelist, short-story writer, born Kermanshah, Iran; *The Grass is Singing* (1950), *The Golden Notebook* (1962), *Canopus in Argos Archives* (1979–83), *The Good Terrorist* (1985), *The Grandmothers* (2003); Nobel Prize for literature 2007.

Levi, Primo (1919–87) Italian novelist, born Turin; *If this is a Man* (1947), *The Periodic Table* (1984).

Lewis, C(live) S(taples) (1898–1963) Irish novelist, literary scholar and religious writer, born Belfast; trilogy *Out of the Silent Planet* (1938), *Perelandra* (1939), *That Hideous Strength* (1945); *The Screwtape Letters* (1940), *The Chronicles of Narnia* (1950–6), *Mere Christianity* (collected broadcast talks) (1952).

Lewis, (Harry) Sinclair (1885–1951) US novelist, born Sauk Center, Minnesota; *Main Street* (1920), *Babbitt* (1922), *Martin Arrowsmith* (1925), *Elmer Gantry* (1927); Nobel Prize for literature 1930.

Lively, Penelope (Margaret) (née **Low**) (1933–) English novelist, born Cairo, Egypt; *The Road to Lichfield* (1977), *Moon Tiger* (1987, Booker Prize), *City of the Mind* (1991), *Heat Wave* (1996), *Consequences* (2007).

Lodge, David (John) (1935–) English novelist, born London; *The British Museum is Falling Down* (1965), *Changing Places* (1975), *Small World* (1984), *Nice Work* (1988), *Paradise News* (1991), *Therapy* (1995), *Thinks…* (2001), *Author, Author* (2004), *Deaf Sentence* (2008).

London, Jack (John) Griffith (1876–1916) US novelist, born San Francisco; *Call of the Wild* (1903), *White Fang* (1907), *Martin Eden* (1909).

Lowry, (Clarence) Malcolm (1909–57) English novelist, born New Brighton, Merseyside; *Under The Volcano* (1947).

Lurie, Alison (1926–) US novelist, born Chicago; *Love and Friendship* (1962), *The War Between the Tates* (1974), *Foreign Affairs* (1984, Pulitzer Prize 1985), *Women and Ghosts* (short stories) (1994), *The Last Resort* (1998), *Truth and Consequences* (2005).

Macaulay, Dame (Emilie) Rose (1881–1958) English novelist, born Rugby, Warwickshire; *Dangerous Ages* (1921), *The World, My Wilderness* (1950), *The Towers of Trebizond* (1956).

MacDonald, George (1824–1905) Scottish novelist, born Huntly, Aberdeenshire; *Robert Falconer* (1868), *The Princess and the Goblin* (1872), *Lilith* (1895).

McEwan, Ian (Russell) (1948–) English novelist, short-story writer, playwright, born Aldershot, Hampshire; *The Cement Garden* (1978), *The Child in Time* (1987), *The Innocent* (1990), *Amsterdam* (1998, Booker Prize), *Atonement* (2001), *Saturday* (2005), *On Chesil Beach* (2007).

McIlvanney, William (Angus) (1936–) Scottish novelist, poet, born Kilmarnock, Ayrshire; *Remedy is None* (1966), *Docherty* (1975), *Laidlaw* (1977), *The Big Man* (1985), *The Weekend* (2006).

MacInnes, Colin (1914–76) English novelist, born London; *City of Spades* (1959), *Absolute Beginners* (1959).

MacKenzie, Sir (Edward Montague) Compton (1883–1972) English novelist, born West Hartlepool, Cleveland; *Sinister Street* (1914), *Whisky Galore* (1947).

MacKenzie, Henry (1745–1831) Scottish novelist, born Edinburgh; *The Man of Feeling* (1771).

MacLean, Alistair (1922–87) Scottish novelist, born

Glasgow; *The Guns of Navarone* (1957), *Ice Station Zebra* (1963), *Where Eagles Dare* (1967), *Force Ten from Navarone* (1968).

Mahfouz, Naguib (1911–2006) Egyptian novelist, born Cairo; *The Cairo Trilogy* (1956–7), *The Thief and the Dogs* (1961), *Adrift on the Nile* (1966), *God's World* (1973), *Arabian Nights and Days* (1995); Nobel Prize for literature 1988.

Mailer, Norman (Kingsley) (1923–2007) US novelist, born Long Branch, New Jersey; *The Naked and the Dead* (1948), *Barbary Shore* (1951), *An American Dream* (1965), *Armies of the Night* (1968, Pulitzer Prize 1969), *The Executioner's Song* (1979, Pulitzer Prize 1980), *Oswald's Tale* (1995).

Malamud, Bernard (1914–86) US novelist, born Brooklyn, New York City; *The Fixer* (1966), *The Tenants* (1971).

Malouf, David (1934–) Australian novelist, poet, born Brisbane; *An Imaginary Life* (1978), *Harland's Half Acre* (1984), *Remembering Babylon* (1993), *Every Move You Make* (2006).

Mankowitz, (Cyril) Wolf (1924–98) English novelist, short-story writer, playwright, born London; *Make Me an Offer* (1952), *The Bespoke Overcoat* (play) (1954), *A Kid for Two Farthings* (1953), *Exquisite Cadaver* (1990).

Mann, Thomas (1875–1955) German novelist, born Lübeck; *Buddenbrooks* (1901), *Death in Venice* (1912), *The Magic Mountain* (1924); Nobel Prize for literature 1929.

Manning, Olivia (1908–80) English novelist, short-story writer, born Portsmouth; *The Balkan Trilogy* (1960–5), *The Levant Trilogy* (1977–80).

Mansfield, Katherine (pseudonym of **Katherine Mansfield Beauchamp**) (1888–1923) New Zealand short-story writer, born Wellington; *Prelude* (1918), *Bliss and Other Stories* (1920), *The Garden Party and Other Stories* (1922).

Markandaya, Kamala (pseudonym of **Kamala Purnaiya Taylor**) (1924–2004) Indian novelist, born Madras (now Chennai); *Nectar in a Sieve* (1954), *A Silence of Desire* (1960), *The Coffer Dams* (1969).

Mars-Jones, Adam (1954–) English short-story writer, critic, born London; *Lantern Lecture and Other Stories* (1981), *The Darker Proof; Stories From a Crisis* (with Edmund White) (1987), *The Waters of Thirst* (1993), *Blind Bitter Happiness* (1997), *Pilcrow* (2008).

Marsh, Ngaio (1899–1982) New Zealand novelist, born Christchurch; *Death in a White Tie* (1958), *A Grave Mistake* (1978).

Martel, Yann (1963–) Canadian novelist, born Salamanca, Spain; *Self* (1996), *Life of Pi* (2002, Man Booker Prize), *We Ate the Children Last* (2004).

Massie, Allan (Johnstone) (1938–) Scottish novelist, journalist, born Singapore; *The Last Peacock* (1980), *A Question of Loyalties* (1989), *The Sins of the Fathers* (1991), *King David* (1995), *Caligula* (2004), *Charlemagne and Roland* (2007).

Maugham, (William) Somerset (1874–1965) English novelist, born Paris; *Of Human Bondage* (1915), *The Moon and Sixpence* (1919), *The Razor's Edge* (1945).

Maupassant, Guy de (1850–93) French short-story writer, novelist, born Miromesnil; *Claire de Lune* (1884), *Bel Ami* (1885).

Mauriac, François (1885–1970) French novelist, born Bordeaux; *Le Baiser au Lépreux* (1922); Nobel Prize for literature 1952.

Melville, Herman (1819–1909) US novelist, poet, born New York City; *Moby Dick* (1851).

Meredith, George (1828–1909) English novelist,

poet, born Portsmouth; *The Egoist* (1879), *Diana of the Crossways* (1885).

Michener, James A(lbert) (1907–97) US novelist, short-story writer, born New York City; *Tales of the South Pacific* (1947, Pultizer Prize 1948), *Hawaii* (1959), *Chesapeake* (1978), *Miracle in Seville* (1995).

Miller, Henry Valentine (1891–1980) US novelist, born New York City; *Tropic of Cancer* (1934), *Tropic of Capricorn* (1938), *The Rosy Crucifixion Trilogy* (1949–60).

Milne, A(lan) A(lexander) (1882–1956) English children's writer, born London; *Winnie-the-Pooh* (1926), *Now We are Six* (1927), *The House at Pooh Corner* (1928).

Mishima, Yukio (pseudonym of **Hiraoka Kimitake**) (1925–70) Japanese novelist, born Tokyo; *Confessions of a Mask* (1960), *The Temple of the Golden Pavilion* (1959), *The Sea of Fertility* (1969–71).

Mitchell, (Charles) Julian (Humphrey) (1935–) English novelist, playwright, born Epping, Essex; *The White Father* (1964), *The Undiscovered Country* (1968), *Another Country* (play) (1981), *Falling Over England* (play) (1994).

Mitchell, Margaret (1900–49) US novelist, born Atlanta, Georgia; *Gone with the Wind* (1936).

Mitchison, Naomi (Margaret) (née **Haldane**) (1897–1999) Scottish novelist, poet, playwright, born Edinburgh; *The Corn King and The Spring Queen* (1931); *The Big House* (1950); memoirs: *Small Talk* (1973), *All Change Here* (1975), *You May Well Ask* (1979).

Mitford, Nancy (1904–73) English novelist, born London; *Love in a Cold Climate* (1949), *Don't Tell Alfred* (1960).

Mo, Timothy (Peter) (1950–) British novelist, born Hong Kong; *The Monkey King* (1978), *Sour Sweet* (1982), *An Insular Possession* (1986), *The Redundancy of Courage* (1991), *Brownout on Breadfruit Boulevard* (1995), *Renegade or Halo2* (1999).

Monsarrat, Nicholas (John Turney) (1910–79) English novelist, born Liverpool; *The Cruel Sea* (1951), *The Story of Esther Costello* (1953).

Moorcock, Michael (1939–) English novelist, short-story writer, born London; *Gloriana* (1978), *Byzantium Endures* (1983), *The City in the Autumn Stars* (1986), *Stormbringer* (1993), *Silverheart* (2000).

Moore, Brian (1921–99) Irish–Canadian novelist, born Belfast, Northern Ireland; *The Luck of Ginger Coffey* (1960), *The Temptation of Eileen Hughes* (1981), *The Colour of Blood* (1987), *Lies of Silence* (1990), *The Statement* (1995).

Morpurgo, Michael (1943–) English children's writer, born St Albans; *War Horse* (1982), *The Wreck of the Zanzibar* (1995), *The Butterfly Lion* (1996), *Kensuke's Kingdom* (1999), *Private Peaceful* (2003).

Morrison, Toni (Chloe Anthony) (née **Wofford**) (1931–) US novelist, born Lorain, Ohio; *The Bluest Eye* (1970), *Sula* (1973), *Song of Solomon* (1977), *Tar Baby* (1981), *Beloved* (1987, Pulitzer Prize 1988), *Jazz* (1992), *Paradise* (1998), *Love* (2003); Nobel Prize for literature 1993.

Mortimer, Sir John (Clifford) (1923–2009) English novelist, short-story writer, playwright, born London; *A Cat Among the Pigeons* (1964), *Rumpole of the Bailey* (1978), *Paradise Postponed* (1985), *Under the Hammer* (1994), *Scales of Justice* (2005).

Mortimer, Penelope (Ruth) (née **Fletcher**) (1918–

99) Welsh novelist, playwright, born Rhyl; *A Villa in Summer* (1954), *The Pumpkin Eater* (1962), *My Friend Says It's Bullet-Proof* (1967), *The Home* (1971), *About Time* (autobiography) (1993).

Mosley, Nicholas (3rd Baron Ravensdale) (1923–) English novelist, born London; *Spaces of the Dark* (1951), *Accident* (1965), *Hopeful Monsters* (1991), *Children of Darkness and Light* (1996), *The Hesperides Tree* (2001), *Inventing God* (2003).

Murdoch, Dame (Jean) Iris (1919–99) Irish novelist, philosopher, born Dublin; *The Bell* (1958), *The Sea, The Sea* (1978, Booker Prize), *The Philosopher's Pupil* (1983), *The Green Knight* (1993).

Nabokov, Vladimir Vladimirovich (1899–1977) Russian–US novelist, poet, born St Petersburg; *Lolita* (1955), *Look at the Harlequins!* (1974).

Naipaul, Sir V(idiadhar) S(urajprasad) (1932–) Trinidadian novelist, born Chaguanas; *A House for Mr Biswas* (1961), *In a Free State* (1971, Booker Prize), *A Bend in the River* (1979), *A Way in the World* (1994), *Magic Seeds* (2004); Nobel Prize for literature 2001.

Nesbit, Edith (1858–1924) English children's writer, born London; *The Story of the Treasure Seekers* (1899), *The Would-Be-Goods* (1901), *Five Children and It* (1902), *The Railway Children* (1906), *The Enchanted Castle* (1907).

Newby, P(ercy) H(oward) (1918–97) English novelist, born Crowborough, Sussex; *The Picnic at Sakkara* (1955), *Revolution and Roses* (1957), *The Barbary Light* (1962), *Something About Women* (1995).

Ngugi wa Thiong'o (formerly wrote as **James T Ngugi**) (1938–) Kenyan novelist, short-story writer, playwright, born Kamiriithu; *The River Between* (1963), *Weep Not, Child* (1964), *Petals of Blood* (1977), *Moving the Centre* (1994), *Wizard of the Crow* (2004).

Nye, Robert (1939–) English novelist, poet, short-story writer, playwright, born London; *Falstaff* (1976), *Merlin* (1978), *The Life and Death of My Lord Gilles de Rais* (1990), *Mrs Shakespeare: The Complete Works* (1993), *The Late Mr Shakespeare* (1998).

Oates, Joyce Carol (1938–) US novelist, short-story writer, born Lockport, New York; *A Garden of Earthly Delights* (1967), *Them* (1969), *Wonderland* (1971), *What I Lived For* (1994), *I'll Take You There* (2003), *Black Girl, White Girl* (2006).

O'Brien, Edna (1932–) Irish novelist, short-story writer, born Tuamgraney, County Clare; *The Country Girls* (1960), *August is a Wicked Month* (1964), *A Pagan Place* (1971), *Lantern Slides* (stories) (1990), *Time and Tide* (1992), *Wild Decembers* (1999), *The Light of Evening* (2006).

O'Brien, Flann (pseudonym of **Brian O'Nolan**, also wrote as **Myles na gCopaleen**) (1911–66) Irish novelist, born Strabane; *At Swim-Two-Birds* (1939), *The Dalkey Archive* (1964), *The Third Policeman* (1967).

Oë, Kenzaburo (1935–) Japanese novelist, born Uchiko, Shikoku; *A Personal Matter* (1968), *The Silent Cry* (1974), *Hiroshima Notes* (1981), *Somersault* (2003); Nobel Prize for literature 1994.

O'Flaherty, Liam (1897–1984) Irish novelist, short-story writer, born Inishmore, Aran Islands; *The Informer* (1926), *Two Lovely Beasts* (1948).

O'Hara, John (Henry) (1905–70) US novelist, short-story writer, born Pottsville, Pennsylvania; *Spring Sowing* (1924), *Appointment in Samarra* (1934), *The Doctor's Son* (1935), *Butterfield 8* (1935), *Pal Joey* (1940).

Okri, Ben (1959–) Nigerian novelist, born Minna; *The Famished Road* (1991, Booker Prize), *Dangerous Love* (1996), *Starbook* (2007).

Oliphant, Margaret (1828–97) Scottish novelist, born Wallyford, Midlothian; *The Athelings* (1857), *Salem Chapel* (1863).

Ondaatje, (Philip) Michael (1943–) Canadian novelist, poet, born Ceylon (now Sri Lanka); *Coming Through Slaughter* (1976), *The English Patient* (1991, Booker Prize 1992), *Anil's Ghost* (2000), *Divisadero* (2007).

Orwell, George (pseudonym of **Eric Arthur Blair**) (1903–50) English novelist, born Bengal, India; *Down and Out in Paris and London* (1933), *The Road to Wigan Pier* (1937), *Animal Farm* (1945), *Nineteen Eighty-Four* (1949).

Ouida (pseudonym of **Marie-Louise de la Ramée**) (1839–1908) English novelist, born Bury St Edmunds; *Held in Bondage* (1865), *Under Two Flags* (1867), *Folle-Farine* (1871).

Ozick, Cynthia (1928–) US novelist, short-story writer, born New York City; *Trust* (1966), *The Pagan Rabbit and Other Stories* (1971), *The Cannibal Galaxy* (1983), *The Messiah of Stockholm* (1987), *The Puttermesser Papers* (1997), *The Bear Boy* (2005).

Pamuk, Orhan (1952–) Turkish novelist, born Istanbul; *The White Castle* (1985), *The Black Book* (1990), *My Name is Red* (2000), *Snow* (2002); Nobel Prize for literature 2006.

Pasternak, Boris (Leonidovich) (1890–1960) Russian novelist, born Moscow; *Doctor Zhivago* (1957); Nobel Prize for literature 1958.

Paton, Allan (Stewart) (1903–88) South African novelist, short-story writer, born Pietermaritzburg, Natal; *Cry, the Beloved Country* (1948).

Peacock, Thomas Love (1785–1866) English novelist, poet, born Weymouth; *Melincourt* (1817), *Nightmare Abbey* (1818).

Peake, Mervyn (Laurence) (1911–68) English novelist, poet, born Kuling, China; *Titus Groan* (1946), *Gormenghast* (1950), *Titus Alone* (1959).

Plaidy, Jean ▶ **Holt, Victoria**

Poe, Edgar Allan (1809–49) US short-story writer, poet, born Boston, Massachusetts; *Tales of the Grotesque and Arabesque* (eg 'The Fall of the House of Usher') (1840), *The Pit and the Pendulum* (1843).

Porter, Harold (Hal) (1911–84) Australian novelist, playwright, poet, short-story writer, born Melbourne; *A Handful of Pennies* (1958), *The Right Thing* (1971).

Porter, Katherine Anne (Maria Veronica Callista Russell) (1890–1980) US novelist, short-story writer, born Indian Creek, Texas; *Pale Horse, Pale Rider* (1939), *Ship of Fools* (1962).

Powell, Anthony (Dymoke) (1905–2000) English novelist, born London; *A Dance to the Music of Time* (1951–75), *The Fisher King* (1986).

Powys, John Cowper (1872–1963) English novelist, born Shirley, Derbyshire; *Wolf Solent* (1929), *Owen Glendower* (1940).

Pratchett, Terry (1948–) English novelist, born Beaconsfield, Buckinghamshire; *The Colour of Magic* (1983), *Only You Can Save Mankind* (1992), *Carpe Jugulum* (1998), *Watersmith* (2006).

Priestley, J(ohn) B(oynton) (1894–1984) English novelist, playwright, born Bradford, Yorkshire; *The Good Companions* (1929), *Angel Pavement* (1930).

Pritchett, Sir V(ictor) S(awdon) (1900–97) English novelist, short-story writer, playwright, born Ipswich, Suffolk; *Nothing like Leather* (1935), *Dead*

Man Leading (1937), *Mr Beluncle* (1951), *The Key to My Heart* (1963), *Man of Letters* (essays) (1985).

Proulx, E Annie (1935–) US novelist, short-story writer, born Norwich, Connecticut; *Postcards* (1993), *The Shipping News* (1993, Pulitzer Prize 1994), *That Old Ace in the Hole* (2002), *Fine Just the Way It Is* (2008).

Proust, Marcel (1871–1922) French novelist, born Paris; *Remembrance of Things Past* (1913–27).

Pullman, Philip (1946–) English novelist and children's writer, born Norwich; *Sally Lockhart* quartet (1985–94), New Cut Gang series (1994–5), His Dark Materials trilogy: *Northern Lights* (1995), *The Subtle Knife* (1997), *The Amber Spyglass* (2000); *The Firework-Maker's Daughter* (1995), *The Scarecrow and His Servant* (2004).

Puzo, Mario (1920–99) US novelist, born New York City; *The Godfather* (1969), *The Last Don* (1996), *Omerta* (2000).

Pynchon, Thomas (1937–) US novelist, born Long Island, New York; *V* (1963), *Gravity's Rainbow* (1973), *Vineland* (1990), *Mason & Dixon* (1997), *Against the Day* (2006).

Queen, Ellery (pseudonym of **Patrick Dannay** (1905–82) and his cousin **Manfred B Lee** (1905–71)) US novelists and short-story writers, both born Brooklyn, New York City; *The French Powder Mystery* (1930), *The Tragedy of X* (1940), *The Glass Village* (1954).

Radcliffe, Ann (1764–1823) English novelist, born London; *The Mysteries of Udolpho* (1794), *The Italian* (1797).

Rankin, Ian James (1960–) Scottish novelist, born Fife; *The Flood* (1985), *Knots and Crosses* (1987), *Black and Blue* (1997), *Resurrection Men* (2002), *Exit Music* (2007).

Ransome, Arthur (Mitchell) (1884–1967) English children's writer, born Leeds; *Swallows and Amazons* (1930), *Peter Duck* (1932).

Rao, Raja (1909–2006) Indian novelist, short-story writer, born Hassan, Mysore; *Kanthapura* (1938), *The Serpent and the Rope* (1960), *The Cat and Shakespeare* (1965).

Raphael, Frederic (Michael) (1931–) US novelist, short-story writer, playwright, born Chicago; *The Limits of Love* (1960), *Lindmann* (1963), *The Glittering Prizes* (1970), *Heaven and Earth* (1985), *Fame and Fortune* (2007).

Read, Piers Paul (1941–) English novelist, born Beaconsfield, Buckinghamshire; *The Junkers* (1968), *Monk Dawson* (1969), *The Villa Golitsyn* (1981), *A Season in the West* (1988), *A Patriot in Berlin* (1995), *Alice in Exile* (2001).

Remarque, Erich Maria (1898–1970) German novelist, born Osnabrück; *All Quiet on the Western Front* (1929), *The Road Back* (1931), *The Black Obelisk* (1957).

Renault, Mary (pseudonym of **Eileen Mary Challans**) (1905–83) English novelist, born London; *The King Must Die* (1958), *Fire from Heaven* (1969), *The Persian Boy* (1972).

Rendell, Ruth (Barbara), Baroness (1930–) English novelist, born London, also writes as Barbara Vine; *A Judgement in Stone* (1977), *The Killing Doll* (1980), *Heartstones* (1987), *The Water's Lovely* (2006); as Barbara Vine: *The House of Stairs* (1989), *Blood Doctor* (2002), *The Birthday Present* (2008).

Rhys, Jean (pseudonym of **Ella Gwendolyn Rees Williams**) (1894–1979) British novelist, short-story writer, born Dominica, West Indies; *After Leaving Mackenzie* (1930), *Wide Sargasso Sea* (1966), *Tigers are Better Looking* (1968).

Arts and Culture

Richardson, Dorothy M(iller) (1873–1957) English novelist, born Abingdon, Berkshire; *Pilgrimage* (twelve vols, 1915–38).

Richardson, Harry Handel (pseudonym of **Ethel Florence Lindesay Richardson**) (1870–1946) Australian novelist, born Melbourne; *The Getting of Wisdom* (1910), *Ultima Thule* (1929).

Richardson, Samuel (1689–1761) English novelist, born near Derby; *Pamela* (1740), *Clarissa* (1747–8), *Sir Charles Grandison* (1753–4).

Richler, Mordecai (1931–2001) Canadian novelist, born Montreal, Quebec; *The Apprenticeship of Duddy Kravitz* (1959), *St Urbain's Horseman* (1971), *Solomon Gursky Was Here* (1990), *This Year in Jerusalem* (1994).

Robbins, Harold (pseudonym of **Francis Kane**) (1916–97) US novelist, born Hell's Kitchen, New York City; *Never Love a Stranger* (1948), *A Stone for Danny Fisher* (1951), *The Carpetbaggers* (1961), *The Betsy* (1971), *Tycoon* (1996).

Rolfe, Frederick William (styled **Baron Corvo**) (1860–1913) English novelist, born London; *Hadrian the Seventh* (1904), *The Desire and Pursuit of the Whole* (1934).

Roth, Henry (1906–95) US novelist, short-story writer, born Tysmenica, Austro-Hungary (now Ukraine); *Call It Sleep* (1934).

Roth, Philip Milton (1933–) US novelist, short-story writer, born Newark, New Jersey; *Goodbye Columbus* (1959), *Portnoy's Complaint* (1969), *The Great American Novel* (1973), *My Life as a Man* (1974), *Patrimony* (1991), *American Pastoral* (1997, Pulitzer Prize 1998), *The Plot Against America* (2004), *Exit Ghost* (2007).

Rowling, J(oanne) K(athleen) (1965–) English children's writer, born Chipping Sodbury, Bristol; *Harry Potter and the Philosopher's Stone* (1997), *Harry Potter and the Goblet of Fire* (2000), *Harry Potter and the Deathly Hallows* (2007).

Rushdie, (Ahmed) Salman (1947–) British novelist, short-story writer, born Bombay (now Mumbai), India; *Midnight's Children* (1981, Booker Prize), *Shame* (1983), *The Satanic Verses* (1988), *The Moor's Last Sigh* (1995), *Shalimar the Clown* (2005), *The Enchantress of Florence* (2008).

Sackville-West, Vita (Victoria May) (1892–1962) English poet, novelist, short-story writer, born Knole, Kent; *The Edwardians* (1930), *All Passion Spent* (1931).

Sade, Donatien Alphonse François, Comte de, (known as **Marquis**) (1740–1814) French novelist, born Paris; *Les 120 Journées de Sodome* (1784), *Justine* (1791), *La Philosophie dans le boudoir* (1793), *Juliette* (1798), *Les Crimes de l'amour* (1800).

Saint-Exupéry, Antoine de (1900–44) French novelist, born Lyons; *Flight to Arras* (1942), *The Little Prince* (1943).

Saki (pseudonym of **Hector Hugh Munro**) (1870–1916) British novelist, short-story writer, born Akyab, Burma (now Myanmar); *The Chronicles of Clovis* (1912), *The Unbearable Bassington* (1912).

Salinger, J(erome) D(avid) (1919–) US novelist, born New York; *The Catcher in the Rye* (1951), *Franny and Zooey* (1961), *Hapworth 16, 1924* (1965).

Sand, George (pseudonym of **Amandine Aurore Lucille Dupin, Baronne Dudevant**) (1804–76) French novelist, born Paris; *Lélia* (1833), *La Petite Fadette* (1849).

Saroyan, William (1908–81) US novelist, playwright, short-story writer, born Fresno, California; *The Daring Young Man on the Flying Trapeze* (1934), *My Name is Aram* (1940), *The Human Comedy* (1942).

Sartre, Jean-Paul (1905–80) French novelist, playwright, born Paris; *Nausea* (1949), *The Roads to Freedom* (1945–7); Nobel Prize for literature 1964.

Sayers, Dorothy L(eigh) (1893–1957) English novelist, short-story writer, born Oxford; *Lord Peter Views the Body* (1928), *Gaudy Night* (1935).

Schreiner, Olive (1855–1920) South African novelist, born Wittebergen Mission Station, Cape of Good Hope; *The Story of an African Farm* (1883), *Trooper Peter Halkett of Mashonaland* (1897).

Scott, Sir Walter (1771–1832) Scottish novelist, poet, born Edinburgh; *Waverley* (1814), *Rob Roy* (1817), *The Heart of Midlothian* (1818), *The Bride of Lammermoor* (1819), *Ivanhoe* (1820).

Selby, Hubert, Jr (1928–2004) US novelist, short-story writer, born Brooklyn, New York City; *Last Exit to Brooklyn* (1964), *The Room* (1971), *Requiem for a Dream* (1978), *Song of the Silent Snow* (1986), *The Willow Tree* (1998).

Seth, Vikram (1952–) Indian novelist, poet, born Calcutta (now Kolkata); *The Golden Gate* (1986), *A Suitable Boy* (1993), *An Equal Music* (1999).

Sharpe, Tom (Thomas Ridley) (1928–) English novelist, born London; *Riotous Assembly* (1971), *Porterhouse Blue* (1973), *Blott on the Landscape* (1975), *Wilt* (1976), *Grantchester Grind* (1995), *The Midden* (1996), *Wilt in Nowhere* (2004).

Shelley, Mary (Wollstonecraft) (née **Godwin**) (1797–1851) English novelist, born London; *Frankenstein* (1818), *The Last Man* (1826), *Perkin Warbeck* (1830).

Shields, Carol (Ann) (née **Warner**) (1935–2003) Canadian novelist, born Illinois, USA; *Small Ceremonies* (1976), *Happenstance* (1980), *Swann: A Mystery* (1987), *The Republic of Love* (1992), *The Stone Diaries* (1993, Pulitzer Prize 1995), *Larry's Party* (1997, Orange Prize 1998), *Dressing Up for the Carnival* (2000).

Sholokhov, Mikhail Alexandrovich (1905–84) Russian novelist, born near Veshenskayal; *And Quiet Flows the Don* (1928–40), *The Upturned Soil* (1940); Nobel Prize for literature 1965.

Shute, Nevil (pseudonym of **Nevil Shute Norway**) (1899–1960) Anglo-Australian novelist, born Ealing, London; *The Pied Piper* (1942), *A Town Like Alice* (1950), *On the Beach* (1957).

Sillitoe, Alan (1928–) English novelist, poet, short-story writer, born Nottingham; *Saturday Night and Sunday Morning* (1958), *The Loneliness of the Long Distance Runner* (1959), *The Broken Chariot* (1998), *A Man of His Time* (2004).

Simenon, Georges (1903–89) French writer, born Liège, Belgium; almost 100 novels featuring Jules Maigret, and 400 other novels: *The Death of Monsieur Gallet* (1932), *The Crime of Inspector Maigret* (1933).

Simon, Claude (Henri Eugène) (1913–2005) French novelist, born Tananarive, Madagascar; *The Wind* (1959), *The Flanders Road* (1962), *Triptych* (1977); Nobel Prize for literature 1985.

Singer, Isaac Bashevis (1904–91) US novelist, playwright, born Radzymin, Poland; *The Family Moskat* (1950), *The Satan in Goray* (1955); Nobel Prize for literature 1978.

Smith, Alexander McCall (1948–) Scottish novelist and children's writer, born Zimbabwe; *No. 1 Ladies' Detective Agency* (1998), *Tears of the Giraffe* (2000), *The Sunday Philosophy Club* (2004), *Blue Shoes and Happiness* (2006).

Smith, Iain Crichton (Gaelic **Iain Mac A'Ghobhainn**) (1928–98) Scottish novelist, poet, short-story writer, playwright, born Glasgow; *Consider the*

Lilies (1968), *Murdo and Other Stories* (1981), *The Dream* (1990).

Smith, Zadie (1975–) English novelist, born London; *White Teeth* (2000), *The Autograph Man* (2002), *On Beauty* (2005).

Smollett, Tobias George (1721–71) Scottish novelist, born Dalquharn, Dunbartonshire; *Roderick Random* (1748), *The Adventures of Peregrine Pickle* (1751), *The Expedition of Humphrey Clinker* (1771).

Snow, C(harles) P(ercy) (1905–80) English novelist, born Leicester; *Strangers and Brothers* (1940–70).

Solzhenitsyn, Aleksandr Isayevich (1918–2008) Russian novelist, born Kislovodsk, Caucasus; *One Day in the Life of Ivan Denisovich* (1963), *Cancer Ward* (1968), *The First Circle* (1969), *The Gulag Archipelago 1918–56* (3 vols 1974–8); Nobel Prize for literature 1970.

Spark, Dame Muriel (Sarah) (née **Camberg**) (1918–2006) Scottish novelist, short-story writer, poet, born Edinburgh; *The Ballad of Peckham Rye* (1960), *The Prime of Miss Jean Brodie* (1961), *The Girls of Slender Means* (1963), *The Mandelbaum Gate* (1965), *A Far Cry from Kensington* (1988), *Reality and Dreams* (1996), *Aiding and Abetting* (2000).

Spring, Howard (1889–1965) Welsh novelist, born Cardiff; *Oh Absalom* (1938).

Stead, C(hristian) K(arlson) (1932–) New Zealand novelist, poet, born Auckland; *Smith's Dream* (1971), *All Visitors Ashore* (1984), *Sister Hollywood* (1990), *The Singing Whakapapa* (1994), *Mansfield* (2004).

Stein, Gertrude (1874–1946) US novelist, short-story writer, born Allegheny, Pennsylvania; *Three Lives* (1909), *Tender Buttons* (1914).

Steinbeck, John Ernest (1902–68) US novelist, born Salinas, California; *Of Mice and Men* (1937), *The Grapes of Wrath* (1939), *Cannery Row* (1945), *East of Eden* (1952); Nobel Prize for literature 1962.

Stendhal (pseudonym of **Henri Marie Beyle**) (1788–1842) French novelist, born Grenoble; *Le Rouge et le noir* (1830), *La Chartreuse de Parme* (1839).

Sterne, Lawrence (1713–68) Irish novelist, born Clonmel, Tipperary; *Tristram Shandy* (1759–67), *A Sentimental Journey* (1768).

Stevenson, Robert Louis (Balfour) (1850–94) Scottish novelist, short-story writer, poet, born Edinburgh; *Travels with a Donkey* (1879), *Treasure Island* (1883), *Kidnapped* (1886), *The Strange Case of Dr Jekyll and Mr Hyde* (1886), *Weir of Hermiston* (1896).

Stewart, J(ohn) I(nnes) M(ackintosh) (1906–94) Scottish novelist, born Edinburgh; *A Use of Riches* (1957), *The Last Tresilians* (1963); as Michael Innes: *Hamlet, Revenge!* (1937), *Appleby and the Ospreys* (1986).

Stewart, Mary (Florence Elinor) (1916–) English novelist, born Sunderland; *This Rough Magic* (1964), *The Last Enchantment* (1979), *The Prince and the Pilgrim* (1995).

Stoker, Bram (Abraham) (1847–1912) Irish novelist, short-story writer, born Dublin; *Dracula* (1897).

Stone, Robert (Anthony) (1937–) US novelist, born Brooklyn, New York City; *Dog Soldiers* (1974), *A Flag for Sunrise* (1982), *Outerbridge Reach* (1992), *Bay of Souls* (2003).

Storey, David (Malcolm) (1933–) English novelist, playwright, born Wakefield, Yorkshire; *This Sporting Life* (1960), *Radcliffe* (1963), *Saville* (1976, Booker Prize), *A Prodigal Child* (1982), *Thin-Ice Skater* (2004).

Stowe, Harriet (Elizabeth) Beecher (1811–96) US novelist, born Litchfield, Connecticut; *Uncle Tom's Cabin* (1852).

Styron, William (Clark) (1925–2006) US novelist, born Newport News, Virginia; *The Confessions of Nat Turner* (1967, Pulitzer Prize 1968), *Sophie's Choice* (1979), *A Tidewater Morning* (1993).

Swift, Graham (Colin) (1949–) English novelist, born London; *The Sweet Shop Owner* (1980), *Waterland* (1983), *Out of This World* (1988), *Ever After* (1992), *Last Orders* (1996, Booker Prize), *The Light of Day* (2003), *Tomorrow* (2007).

Swift, Jonathan (1667–1745) Irish novelist, poet, born Dublin; *A Tale of a Tub* (1704), *Gulliver's Travels* (1726).

Symons, Julian (Gustave) (1912–94) English novelist, poet, short-story writer, playwright, born London; *The Thirty-First of February* (1950), *The Colour of Murder* (1957), *Sweet Adelaide* (1980).

Tennant, Emma (Christina) (1937–) English novelist, born London; *Hotel de Dream* (1978), *Alice Fell* (1980), *Pemberley* (1993), *Elinor and Marianne* (1996), *The Amazing Marriage* (2006).

Thackeray, William Makepeace (1811–63) English novelist, born Calcutta (now Kolkata), India; *Vanity Fair* (1847–8), *Pendennis* (1848–50).

Theroux, Paul (Edward) (1941–) US novelist, short-story writer, travel writer, born Medford, Massachusetts; *The Mosquito Coast* (1981), *The Kingdom by the Sea* (travel) (1983), *Riding the Iron Rooster* (travel) (1988), *My Secret History* (1989), *My Other Life* (1996), *Blinding Light* (2006).

Thomas, D(onald) M(ichael) (1935–) English novelist, poet, born Redruth, Cornwall; *The White Hotel* (1981); *Ararat* (1983), *Swallow* (1984), *Sphinx* (1986), *Summit* (1987), *Lying Together* (1990), *Eating Pavlova* (1994), *Charlotte* (2000).

Tolkien, J(ohn) R(onald) R(euel) (1892–1973) English novelist, born Bloemfontein, South Africa; *The Hobbit* (1937), *The Lord of the Rings* (1954–5).

Tolstoy, Count Leo Nikolayevich (1828–1910) Russian novelist, born Yasnaya Polyana, Central Russia; *War and Peace* (1863–9), *Anna Karenina* (1873–7), *Resurrection* (1899).

Tranter, Nigel Godwin (1909–99) Scottish novelist, born Glasgow; over 100 novels including *The Steps to the Empty Throne* (1969), *The Path of the Hero King* (1970), *The Price of the King's Peace* (1971), *Honours Even* (1995).

Tremain, Rose (née **Thomson**) (1943–) English novelist, short-story writer, playwright, born London; *The Cupboard* (1981), *The Colonel's Daughter and Other Stories* (1984), *Restoration* (1989), *Sacred Country* (1992), *The Way I Found Her* (1997), *Music and Silence* (1999), *The Colour* (2003), *The Road Home* (2008).

Trevor, William (properly **William Trevor Cox**) (1928–) Irish novelist, short-story writer, born Mitchelstown, County Cork; *Fools of Fortune* (1983), *The Silence in the Garden* (1988), *Two Lives* (1991), *Felicia's Journey* (1994), *The Story of Lucy Gault* (2002), *Cheating at Canasta* (2007).

Trollope, Anthony (1815–82) English novelist, born London; *Barchester Towers* (1857), *Can You Forgive Her?* (1864), *The Way We Live Now* (1875).

Trollope, Joanna (1943–) English novelist, born Gloucestershire; *Eliza Stanhope* (1978), *The Choir* (1988), *A Village Affair* (1989), *The Rector's Wife* (1991), *Second Honeymoon* (2006).

Tuohy, Frank (John Francis) (1925–99) English novelist, short-story writer, born Uckfield, Sussex; *The Animal Game* (1957), *The Warm Nights of*

Arts and Culture

Arts and Culture

January (1960), *The Ice Saints* (1964), *Fingers in the Door* (stories) (1970), *Collected Stories* (1984).

Turgenev, Ivan Sergeevich (1818–83) Russian novelist, born province of Oryel; *Sportsman's Sketches* (1852), *Fathers and Children* (1862).

Tutuola, Amos (1920–97) Nigerian novelist, short-story writer, born Abeokuta; *The Palm-Wine Drinkard and His Dead Palm-Wine Tapster in the Deads' Town* (1952), *The Wild Hunter in the Bush of the Ghosts* (1982), *Pauper, Brawler and Slanderer* (1987), *The Village Witchdoctor and Other Stories* (1990).

Twain, Mark (pseudonym of **Samuel Langhorne Clemens**) (1835–1910) US novelist, born Florida, Missouri; *The Celebrated Jumping Frog of Calaveras County* (1865), *The Adventures of Tom Sawyer* (1876), *The Prince and the Pauper* (1882), *The Adventures of Huckleberry Finn* (1884), *A Connecticut Yankee in King Arthur's Court* (1889).

Tyler, Anne (1941–) US novelist, short-story writer, born Minneapolis, Minnesota; *If Morning Ever Comes* (1964), *Morgan's Passing* (1980), *The Accidental Tourist* (1985), *Breathing Lessons* (1988, Pulitzer Prize 1989), *Ladder of Years* (1995), *A Patchwork Planet* (1998), *The Amateur Marriage* (2003), *Digging to America* (2007).

Updike, John (Hoyer) (1932–2009) US novelist, short-story writer, born Shillington, Pennsylvania; *Rabbit, Run* (1960), *Pigeon Feathers and Other Stories* (1962), *Rabbit is Rich* (1981, Pulitzer Prize 1982), *The Witches of Eastwick* (1984), *Rabbit at Rest* (1990, Pulitzer Prize 1991), *Terrorist* (2006).

Upward, Edward (Falaise) (1903–) English novelist, born Romford, Essex; *Journey to the Border* (1938), *In the Thirties* (1962), *The Rotten Elements* (1969), *A Renegade in Springtime* (2003).

Uris, Leon (Marcus) (1924–2003) US novelist, born Baltimore, Maryland; *Battle Cry* (1953), *Exodus* (1958), *The Haj* (1984), *Redemption* (1995).

Van der Post, Sir Laurens (Jan) (1906–96) South African novelist, playwright, born Philippolis; *Flamingo Feather* (1955), *Journey into Russia* (1964), *A Far-Off Place* (1974).

Vansittart, Peter (1920–2008) English novelist, born Bedford; *Quintet* (1976), *The Death of Robin Hood* (1981), *Parsifal* (1988), *In the Fifties* (1995), *Secret Protocols* (2006).

Vargas Llosa, Mario (1936–) Peruvian novelist, born Arequipa; *The Time of the Hero* (1962), *The Green House* (1966), *Aunt Julia and the Scriptwriter* (1977), *The War at the End of the World* (1981), *The Feast of the Goat* (2000), *The Bad Girl* (2006).

Verne, Jules (1828–1905) French novelist, born Nantes; *Voyage to the Centre of the Earth* (1864), *Twenty Thousand Leagues under the Sea* (1870).

Vidal, Gore (Eugene Luther, Jr) (1925–) US novelist, short-story writer, playwright, born West Point, New York; *Williwaw* (1946), *The City and the Pillar* (1948), *The Judgement of Paris* (1952), *Myra Breckenridge* (1968), *Creation* (1981), *Lincoln* (1984), *Empire* (1987), *Hollywood* (1989), *The Golden Age* (2000).

Vine, Barbara ▶ **Rendell, Ruth**

Voltaire, François-Marie Arouet de (1694–1778) French novelist, poet, born Paris; *Zadig* (1747), *Candide* (1759).

Vonnegut, Kurt, Jr (1922–2007) US novelist, short-story writer, born Indianapolis, Indiana; *Cat's Cradle* (1963), *Slaughterhouse-Five* (1969), *Hocus Pocus* (1990), *Timequake* (1997).

Wain, John (Barrington) (1925–94) English novelist, poet, short-story writer, playwright, born Stoke-on-Trent, Staffordshire; *Hurry on Down* (1953), *The Young Visitors* (1965), *Where the Rivers Meet* (1988).

Walker, Alice (Malsenior) (1944–) US novelist, short-story writer, born Eatonville, Georgia; *The Third Life of Grange Copeland* (1970), *Meridian* (1976), *The Color Purple* (1982, Pulitzer Prize 1983), *Now is the Time to Open Your Heart* (2004).

Walpole, Horace (1717–97) English novelist, poet, born London; *Letter from Xotto to his Friend Lien Chi at Pekin* (1757), *Anecdotes of Painting in England* (1761–71), *The Castle of Otranto* (1764), *The Mysterious Mother* (1768), *Historic Doubts on the Life and Reign of King Richard the Third* (1768).

Warner, Marina (Sarah) (1946–) English novelist, born London; *In a Dark Wood* (1977), *The Skating Party* (1982), *The Lost Father* (1988), *The Mermaids in the Basement* (1993), *The Leto Bundle* (2001).

Warren, Robert Penn (1905–89) US novelist, poet, born Guthrie, Kentucky; *Night Rider* (1939), *All the King's Men* (1943).

Waterhouse, Keith (Spencer) (1929–) English novelist, playwright, born Leeds, Yorkshire; *Billy Liar* (1959), *Office Life* (1978), *Bimbo* (1990), *Unsweet Charity* (1992), *Palace Pier* (2005).

Waugh, Evelyn (Arthur St John) (1903–66) English novelist, born Hampstead, London; *Decline and Fall* (1928), *A Handful of Dust* (1934), *Brideshead Revisited* (1945).

Weldon, Fay (originally **Franklin Birkinshaw**) (1931–) English novelist, born Alvechurch, Worcestershire; *Down Among the Women* (1971), *Female Friends* (1975), *Life and Loves of a She-Devil* (1983), *Worst Fears* (1996), *Mantrapped* (2004), *The Spa Decameron* (2007).

Wells, H(erbert) G(eorge) (1866–1946) English novelist, born Bromley, Kent; *The Time Machine* (1895), *The War of the Worlds* (1898), *The History of Mr Polly* (1910).

Welsh, Irvine (1958–) Scottish novelist, born Edinburgh; *Trainspotting* (1993), *Filth* (1998), *Porno* (2002), *The Bedroom Secrets of the Master Chefs* (2006), *Crime* (2008).

Welty, Eudora (1909–2001) US novelist, short-story writer, born Jackson, Mississippi; *A Curtain of Green* (1941), *The Robber Bridegroom* (1944), *The Golden Apples* (1949), *The Ponder Heart* (1954), *The Optimist's Daughter* (1972, Pulitzer Prize 1973), *A Writer's Eye: Collected Book Reviews* (1994).

Wesley, Mary (pseudonym of **Mary Aline Siepmann**) (née **Farmar**) (1912–2002) English novelist, born Englefield Green, Berkshire; *The Camomile Lawn* (1984), *A Sensible Life* (1990), *Part of the Furniture* (1997).

West, Morris (Langlo) (1916–99) Australian novelist, playwright, born Melbourne, Victoria; *Children of the Sun* (non-fiction) (1957), *The Devil's Advocate* (1959), *Summer of the Red Wolf* (1971), *The Clowns of God* (1981), *The World is Made of Glass* (1983), *The Ringmaster* (1991), *Vanishing Point* (1996).

West, Dame Rebecca (pseudonym of **Cecily Isabel Andrews**) (née **Fairfield**) (1892–1983) Irish novelist, born County Kerry; *The Harsh Voice* (1935), *The Mountain Overflows* (1957).

Wharton, Edith (Newbold) (1862–1937) US novelist, short-story writer, born New York; *The House of Mirth* (1905), *Ethan Frome* (1911), *The Age of Innocence* (1920).

White, Antonia (pseudonym of **Eirene Adeline Botting**) (1899–1980) English novelist, born

London; *Beyond the Glass* (1954), *Frost in May* (1983).

White, Patrick Victor Martindale (1912–90) Australian novelist, playwright, short-story writer, born London; *Voss* (1957), *The Vivisector* (1970), *A Fringe of Leaves* (1976); Nobel Prize for literature 1973.

White, T(erence) H(anbury) (1906–64) English novelist, poet, born Bombay (now Mumbai), India; *Darkness at Pemberley* (1932), *The Once and Future King* (1958).

Wilde, Oscar (Fingal O'Flahertie Wills) (1854–1900) Irish novelist, short-story writer, playwright, poet, born Dublin; *The Happy Prince and Other Tales* (1888), *The Picture of Dorian Gray* (1890).

Wilder, Thornton Niven (1897–1976) US novelist, playwright, born Madison, Wisconsin; *The Bridge of San Luis Rey* (1927), *The Woman of Andros* (1930), *Heaven's My Destination* (1935).

Wilding, Michael (1942–) Australian novelist, short-story writer, born Worcester, England; *Living Together* (1974), *The West Midland Underground* (1975), *Pacific Highway* (1982), *Under Saturn* (1988), *Somewhere New* (1996).

Wilson, A(ndrew) N(orman) (1950–) English novelist, born London; *Kindly Light* (1979), *Wise Virgin* (1982), *Daughters of Albion* (1991), *A Watch in the Night* (1996), *Winnie and Wolf* (2007).

Wilson, Jacqueline (1945–) English children's writer, born Bath; *The Story of Tracy Beaker* (1991), *The Bed and Breakfast Star* (1994), *Double Act* (1995), *The Illustrated Mum* (1999), *Best Friends* (2004).

Winterson, Jeanette (1959–) English novelist, born Manchester; *Oranges Are Not the Only Fruit* (1985), *The Passion* (1987), *Sexing the Cherry* (1989), *Gut Symmetries* (1997), *Lighthousekeeping* (2004), *The Stone Gods* (2007).

Wodehouse, Sir P(elham) G(renville) (1881–1975) English novelist, short-story writer, born Guildford, Surrey; *The Inimitable Jeeves* (1923), *Carry on, Jeeves* (1925).

Wolfe, Thomas Clayton (1900–38) US novelist, born Asheville, North Carolina; *Look Homeward, Angel* (1929), *Of Time and the River* (1935), *From Death to Morning* (1935).

Wolfe, Tom (Thomas Kennerly) (1931–) US novelist, journalist, born Richmond, Virginia; *The Kandy-Kolored Tangerine-Flake Streamline Baby* (1965), *The Electric Kool-Aid Acid Test* (1968), *The Right Stuff* (1979), *The Bonfire of the Vanities* (1st novel) (1988), *A Man in Full* (1998), *I Am Charlotte Simmons* (2004).

Wolff, Tobias (1945–) US novelist, short-story writer, born Birmingham, Alabama; *In the Garden of the North American Martyrs* (stories) (1981), *The Barracks Thief* (1984), *Back in the World* (stories) (1985), *The Night in Question* (stories) (1996), *Old School* (2003).

Woolf, (Adeline) Virginia (1882–1941) English novelist, born London; *Mrs Dalloway* (1925), *To The Lighthouse* (1927), *Orlando* (1928), *A Room of One's Own* (1929), *The Waves* (1931).

Wouk, Herman (1915–) US novelist, playwright, born New York City; *The Caine Mutiny* (1951, Pulitzer Prize 1952), *The Winds of War* (1971), *War and Remembrance* (1978), *Inside, Outside* (1985), *The Hope* (1993), *The Glory* (1994), *A Hole in Texas* (2004).

Wright, Richard Nathaniel (1908–60) US novelist, short-story writer, born Mississippi; *Native Son* (1940), *Eight Men* (1961).

Wyndham, John (pseudonym of **John Wyndham Parkes Lucas Beynon Harris**) (1903–69) English novelist, born Knowle, Warwickshire; *The Day of the Triffids* (1951), *The Kraken Wakes* (1953), *The Chrysalids* (1955), *The Midwich Cuckoos* (1957), *The Trouble with Lichen* (1960), *Consider Her Ways* (1961) (short stories), *Chocky* (1968).

Yerby, Frank (Garvin) (1916–91) US novelist, born Augusta, Georgia; *The Golden Hawk* (1948), *The Dahomean* (1971), *A Darkness at Ingraham's Crest* (1979).

Yourcenar, Marguerite (pseudonym of **Marguerite de Crayencour**) (1903–87) French novelist, poet, born Brussels; *Memoirs of Hadrian* (1941).

Zamyatin, Evgeny Ivanovich (1884–1937) Russian novelist, short-story writer, born Lebedyan; *We* (1921), *The Dragon: Fifteen Stories* (1966).

Zola, Émile (1840–1902) French novelist, born Paris; *Thérèse Raquin* (1867), *Les Rougon-Macquart* (1871–93), *Germinal* (1885).

Arts and Culture

Literary prizes 1988–2008

■ **Man Booker Prize (UK)**

1988	Peter Carey, *Oscar and Lucinda*
1989	Kazuo Ishiguro, *The Remains of the Day*
1990	A S Byatt, *Possession*
1991	Ben Okri, *The Famished Road*
1992	Michael Ondaatje, *The English Patient*; Barry Unsworth, *Sacred Hunger*
1993	Roddy Doyle, *Paddy Clarke, Ha Ha Ha*
1994	James Kelman, *How late it was, how late*
1995	Pat Barker, *The Ghost Road*
1996	Graham Swift, *Last Orders*
1997	Arundhati Roy, *The God of Small Things*
1998	Ian McEwan, *Amsterdam*
1999	J M Coetzee, *Disgrace*
2000	Margaret Atwood, *The Blind Assassin*
2001	Peter Carey, *True History of the Kelly Gang*
2002	Yann Martel, *Life of Pi*
2003	D B C Pierre, *Vernon God Little*
2004	Alan Hollinghurst, *The Line of Beauty*
2005	John Banville, *The Sea*
2006	Kiran Desai, *The Inheritance of Loss*
2007	Anne Enright, *The Gathering*
2008	Aravind Adiga, *The White Tiger*

■ **Orange Prize for Fiction (women writers)**

1998	Carol Shields, *Larry's Party*
1999	Suzanne Berne, *A Crime in the Neighborhood*
2000	Linda Grant, *When I Lived in Modern Times*
2001	Kate Grenville, *The Idea of Perfection*
2002	Ann Patchett, *Bel Canto*
2003	Valerie Martin, *Property*
2004	Andrea Levy, *Small Island*
2005	Lionel Shriver, *We Need to Talk About Kevin*
2006	Zadie Smith, *On Beauty*
2007	Chimamanda Ngozi Adichie, *Half of a Yellow Sun*
2008	Rose Tremain, *The Road Home*

Arts and Culture

■ **Prix Goncourt (France)**

1988 Erik Orsenna, *L'Exposition coloniale*
1989 Jean Vautrin, *Un Grand Pas vers le Bon Dieu*
1990 Jean Rouaud, *Les Champs d'Honneur*
1991 Pierre Combescot, *Les Filles du Calvaire*
1992 Patrick Chamoiseau, *Texaco*
1993 Amin Maalouf, *Le Rocher de Tanios*
1994 Didier van Cauwelaert, *Un Aller simple*
1995 Andréï Makine, *Le Testament français*
1996 Pascale Roze, *Le Chasseur Zéro*
1997 Patrick Rambaud, *La Bataille*
1998 Paule Constant, *Confidence pour confidence*
1999 Jean Echenoz, *Je m'en vais*
2000 Jean-Jacques Schuhl, *Ingrid Caven*
2001 Jean-Christophe Rufin, *Rouge Brésil*
2002 Pascal Quignard, *Les ombres errantes*
2003 Jacques-Pierre Amette, *La maîtresse de Brecht*
2004 Laurent Gaudé, *Le soleil des Scorta*
2005 François Weyergans, *Trois jours chez ma mère*
2006 Jonathan Littel, *Les Bienveillantes*
2007 Gilles Leroy, *Alabama Song*
2008 Atiq Rahimi, *Syngué Sabour: Pierre de Patience*

■ **Pulitzer Prize in Letters: Fiction (USA)**

1988 Toni Morrison, *Beloved*
1989 Anne Tyler, *Breathing Lessons*
1990 Oscar Hijuelos, *The Mambo Kings Play Songs of Love*
1991 John Updike, *Rabbit at Rest*
1992 Jane Smiley, *A Thousand Acres*
1993 Robert Olen Butler, *A Good Scent From A Strange Mountain*
1994 E Annie Proulx, *The Shipping News*
1995 Carol Shields, *The Stone Diaries*
1996 Richard Ford, *Independence Day*
1997 Steven Millhauser, *Martin Dressler: The Tale of an American Dreamer*
1998 Philip Roth, *American Pastoral*
1999 Michael Cunningham, *The Hours*
2000 Jhumpa Lahiri, *Interpreter of Maladies*
2001 Michael Chabon, *The Amazing Adventures of Kavalier & Clay*
2002 Richard Russo, *Empire Falls*
2003 Jeffrey Eugenides, *Middlesex*
2004 Edward P Jones, *The Known World*
2005 Marilynne Robinson, *Gilead*
2006 Geraldine Brooks, *March*
2007 Cormac McCarthy, *The Road*
2008 Junot Diaz, *The Brief Wondrous Life of Oscar Wao*

Poets

Selected volumes of poetry are listed.

Abse, Dannie (Daniel) (1923–) Welsh, born Cardiff; *After Every Green Thing* (1948), *Tenants of the House* (1957), *There Was a Young Man from Cardiff* (1991), *Arcadia, One Mile* (1998) *Running Late* (2006).

Adcock, (Kareen) Fleur (1934–) New Zealander, born Auckland; *The Eye of the Hurricane* (1964), *In Focus* (1977), *The Incident Book* (1986), *Poems 1960–2000* (2000).

Aiken, Conrad (Potter) (1889–1973) American, born Georgia; *Earth Triumphant* (1914), *Preludes for Memnon* (1931).

Akhmatova, Anna (pseudonym of **Anna Andreevna Gorenko**) (1889–1966) Russian, born Odessa; *Evening* (1912), *Poem without a Hero* (1940–62), *Requiem* (1963).

Angelou, Maya (Marguerite Annie) (née **Johnson**) (1928–) American, born St Louis, Missouri; *And Still I Rise* (1978), *I Shall Not Be Moved* (1990), *The Complete Collected Poems of Maya Angelou* (1995).

Apollinaire, Guillaume (pseudonym of **Wilhelm Apollinaris de Kostrowitzky**) (1880–1918) French, born Rome; *Alcools* (1913), *Calligrammes* (1918).

Ariosto, Ludovico (1474–1535) Italian, born Reggio; *Orlando Furioso* (1532).

Auden, W(ystan) H(ugh) (1907–73) British, naturalized US citizen, born York; *Another Time* (1940), *The Sea and the Mirror* (1944), *The Age of Anxiety* (1947).

Baudelaire, Charles (Pierre) (1821–67) French, born Paris; *Les Fleurs du mal* (1857).

Beer, Patricia (1919–99) English, born Exmouth, Devon; *The Loss of the Magyar* (1959), *The Lie of the Land* (1983), *Friend of Heraclitus* (1993).

Belloc, (Joseph) Hillaire (Pierre) (1870–1953) British, born St Cloud, France; *Cautionary Tales* (1907), *Sonnets and Verse* (1923).

Berryman, John (1914–72) American, born McAlester, Oklahoma; *Homage to Mistress Bradsheet* (1966), *Dream Songs* (1969).

Betjeman, Sir John (1906–84) English, born Highgate, London; *Mount Zion* (1931), *New Bats in Old Belfries* (1945), *A Nip in the Air* (1972).

Bishop, Elizabeth (1911–79) American, born Worcester, Massachusetts; *North and South* (1946), *Geography III* (1978).

Blake, William (1757–1827) English, born London; *The Marriage of Heaven and Hell* (1793), *The Visions of the Daughters of Albion* (1793), *Songs of Innocence and Experience* (1794), *Vala*, or *The Four Zoas* (1800), *Milton* (1810).

Blunden, Edmund (Charles) (1896–1974) English, born Yalding, Kent; *The Waggoner and Other Poems* (1920).

Brodsky, Joseph (originally **Iosif Aleksandrovich Brodsky**) (1940–96) Russian–American, born Leningrad (now St Petersburg); *Longer and Shorter Poems* (1965), *To Urania: Selected Poems 1965–1985* (1988); Nobel Prize for literature 1987.

Brooke, Rupert (Chawner) (1887–1915) English, born Rugby; *Poems* (1911); *1914 and Other Poems* (1915), *New Numbers* (1915).

Brooks, Gwendolyn (Elizabeth) (1917–2000) American, born Topeka, Kansas; *A Street in Bronzeville* (1945), *Annie Allen* (1949, Pulitzer Prize 1950), *In The Mecca* (1968), *Blacks* (1987).

Browning, Elizabeth Barrett (née **Barrett**) (1806–61) English, born Coxhoe Hall, near Durham; *Sonnets from the Portuguese* (1850), *Aurora Leigh* (1855).

Browning, Robert (1812–89) English, born Camberwell, London; *Bells and Pomegranates* (1841–6), *Men and Women* (1855), *The Ring and the Book* (1868–9).

Burns, Robert (1759–96) Scottish, born Alloway, Ayr; *Poems, Chiefly in the Scottish Dialect* (1786), *Tam o'Shanter* (1790).

Byron, George Gordon, 6th Baron (1788–1824)

Arts and Culture

English, born London; *Hours of Idleness* (1807), *Childe Harolde's Pilgrimage* (1817), *Don Juan* (1819–24).

Catullus, Gaius Valerius (c.84–c.54 BC) Roman, born Verona; lyric poet, over 100 poems survive.

Causley, Charles (1917–2003) English, born Launceston, Cornwall; *Union St* (1957), *Johnny Alleluia* (1961), *Underneath the Water* (1968), *All Day Saturday* (1994), *Collected Poems for Children* (1996).

Chaucer, Geoffrey (c.1343–1400) English, born London; *Book of the Duchess* (1370), *Troilus and Cressida* (c.1385), *The Canterbury Tales* (1387–1400).

Clampitt, Amy (1920–94) American, born Iowa; *The Kingfisher* (1983), *Archaic Figure* (1987), *Westward* (1990).

Clare, John (1773–1864) English, born Helpstone, Northamptonshire; *Poems Descriptive of Rural Life* (1820), *The Shepherd's Calendar* (1827).

Coleridge, Samuel Taylor (1772–1834) English, born Ottery St Mary, Devon; *Poems on Various Subjects* (1796), 'Kubla Khan' (1797), 'The Rime of the Ancient Mariner' (1798), *Christabel and Other Poems* (1816), *Sibylline Leaves* (1817).

Cowper, William (1731–1800) English, born Great Berkhampstead, Hertfordshire; *The Task* (1785).

Crabbe, George (1754–1823) English, born Aldeburgh, Suffolk; *The Village* (1783).

cummings, e(dward) e(stlin) (1894–1962) American, born Cambridge, Massachusetts; *Tulips and Chimneys* (1923), *XLI Poems* (1925), *is 5* (1926).

Dante Alighieri (1265–1321) Italian, born Florence; *Vita Nuova* (1294), *Divine Comedy* (1321).

Day-Lewis, Cecil (1904–72) Irish, born Ballintubbert, Laois; *Overtures to Death* (1938), *The Aeneid of Virgil* (1952).

de la Mare, Walter (1873–1956) English, born Charleston, Kent; *The Listeners* (1912), *The Burning Glass and Other Poems* (1945).

Dickinson, Emily (Elizabeth) (1830–86) American, born Amherst, Massachusetts; only seven poems published in her lifetime; posthumous publications, eg *Poems* (1890).

Donne, John (c.1572–1631) English, born London; *Satires & Elegies* (1590s), *Holy Sonnets* (1610–11), *Songs and Sonnets*; most verse published posthumously.

Doolittle, Hilda (known as **H D**) (1886–1961) American, born Bethlehem, Pennsylvania; *Sea Garden* (1916), *The Walls Do Not Fall* (1944), *Helen in Egypt* (1961).

Dryden, John (1631–1700) English, born Adwinckle All Saints, Northamptonshire; *Astrea Redux* (1660), *Absalom and Achitophel* (1681), 'Mac Flecknoe' (1684).

Duffy, Carol Ann (1955–) Scottish, born Glasgow; *Standing Female Nude* (1985), *Mean Time* (1993), *The World's Wife* (1999), *Rapture* (2005), *The Hat* (2007).

Dunbar, William (c.1460–c.1520) Scottish, birthplace probably E Lothian; 'The Thrissill and the Rois' (1503), 'Lament for the Makaris' (c.1507).

Dunn, Douglas (Eaglesham) (1942–) Scottish, born Inchinnan, Renfrewshire; *Love or Nothing* (1974), *Elegies* (1985), *Dante's Drum-kit* (1993), *The Year's Afternoon* (2000).

Dutton, Geoffrey (Piers Henry) (1922–98) Australian, born Kapunda; *Antipodes in Shoes* (1958), *Poems, Soft and Loud* (1968), *A Body of Words* (1977), *New and Selected Poems* (1993).

Eliot, T(homas) S(tearns) (1888–1965) American (British citizen 1927), born St Louis, Missouri; *Prufrock and Other Observations* (1917), *The*

Waste Land (1922), *Ash Wednesday* (1930), *Four Quartets* (1944); Nobel Prize for Literature 1948.

Éluard, Paul (pseudonym of **Eugène Grindel**) (1895–1952) French, born Saint-Denis; *La Vie immédiate* (1934), *Poésie et vérité* (1942).

Emerson, Ralph Waldo (1803–84) American, born Boston, Massachusetts; poems published posthumously in *Complete Works* (1903–4).

Empson, Sir William (1906–84) English, born Yokefleet, E Yorkshire; *Poems* (1935), *The Gathering Storm* (1940).

Fanthorpe, U(rsula) A(skham) (1929–) English poet, born Kent; *Side Effects* (1978), *Safe as Houses* (1995), *Consequences* (2000), *Queuing for the Sun* (2003).

Fitzgerald, Edward (1809–83) English, born near Woodbridge, Suffolk; translator of *The Rubaiyat of Omar Khayyam* (1859).

Frost, Robert (Lee) (1874–1963) American, born San Francisco; *North of Boston* (1914), *Mountain Interval* (1916), *New Hampshire* (1923), *In the Clearing* (1962).

Ginsberg, Allen (1926–97) American, born Newark, New Jersey; *Howl and Other Poems* (1956), *Empty Mirror* (1961), *The Fall of America* (1973).

Graves, Robert (Ranke) (1895–1985) English, born London; *Fairies and Fusiliers* (1917).

Gray, Thomas (1716–71) English, born London; 'Elegy Written in a Country Churchyard' (1751), *Pindaric Odes* (1757).

Gunn, Thom(son William) (1929–2004) English, born Gravesend, Kent; *The Sense of Movement* (1957), *Touch* (1967), *Jack Straw's Castle* (1976), *The Passages of Joy* (1982), *The Man with Night Sweats* (1992), *Boss Cupid* (2000).

Heaney, Seamus (Justin) (1939–) Northern Irish, born Castledawson, County Derry; *Death of a Naturalist* (1966), *Door into the Dark* (1969), *Field Work* (1979), *Seeing Things* (1991), *Spirit Level* (1995), *Beowulf: A New Translation* (2000), *District and Circle* (2006); Nobel Prize for literature 1995.

Henri, Adrian (Maurice) (1932–2000) English, born Birkenhead; *The Mersey Sound: Penguin Modern Poets 10* (with Roger McGough and Brian Patten) (1967), *Tonight at Noon* (1968), *From the Loveless Motel* (1980), *Wish You Were Here* (1990), *Not Fade Away* (1994), *Robocat* (1998).

Henryson, Robert (c.1430–1506) Scottish, birthplace unknown; *Testament of Cresseid, Morall Fables of Esope the Phrygian*.

Herbert, George (1593–1633) English, born Montgomery, Wales; *The Temple* (1633).

Herrick, Robert (1591–1674) English, born London; *Hesperides* (1648).

Hill, Geoffrey (William) (1932–) English, born Bromsgrove, Worcestershire; *King Log* (1968), *Mercian Hymns* (1971), *Tenebrae* (1978), *Canaan* (1996), *Without Title* (2006).

Hodgson, Ralph (Edwin) (1871–1962) English, born Yorkshire; *Poems* (1917), *The Skylark and Other Poems* (1958).

Homer (10c–8c BC) Greek, birthplace and existence disputed; he is credited with the writing or writing down of *The Iliad* and *The Odyssey*.

Hopkins, Gerard Manley (1844–89) English, born Stratford, London; 'The Wreck of the Deutschland' (1876), posthumously published *Poems* (1918).

Horace, Quintus Horatius Flaccus (65–8 BC) Roman, born Venusia, Apulia; *Epodes* (30 BC), *Odes* (23–13 BC).

Housman, A(lfred) E(dward) (1859–1936) English, born Flockbury, Worcestershire; *A Shropshire Lad* (1896), *Last Poems* (1922).

Arts and Culture

Hughes, Ted (1930–98) English, born Mytholmroyd, Yorkshire; *The Hawk in the Rain* (1957), *Lupercal* (1960), *Wodwo* (1967), *Crow* (1970), *Cave Birds* (1975), *Season Songs* (1976), *Gaudete* (1977), *Moortown* (1979), *Wolfwatching* (1989), *Birthday Letters* (1998).

Jennings, Elizabeth (Joan) (1926–2001) English, born Boston, Lincolnshire; *Poems* (1953), *The Mind Has Mountains* (1966), *The Animals' Arrival* (1969), *Relationships* (1972), *Praises* (1998).

Johnson, Samuel (1709–84) English, born Lichfield, Staffordshire; *The Vanity of Human Wishes* (1749).

Kavanagh, Patrick (1905–67) Irish, born Inniskeen; *Ploughman and Other Poems* (1936), *The Great Hunger* (1942).

Keats, John (1795–1821) English, born London; *Endymion* (1818), *Lamia and Other Poems* (1820).

Keyes, Sidney (Arthur Kilworth) (1922–43) English, born Dartford, Kent; *The Iron Laurel* (1942), *The Cruel Solstice* (1943).

La Fontaine, Jean de (1621–95) French, born Château-Thierry, Champagne; *Contes et nouvelles en vers* (1665), *Fables choisies mises en vers* (1668).

Langland or **Langley, William** (c.1332–c.1400) English, birthplace uncertain, possibly Ledbury, Herefordshire; *Piers Plowman* (1362–99).

Larkin, Philip (Arthur) (1922–85) English, born Coventry; *The North Ship* (1945), *The Whitsun Weddings* (1964), *High Windows* (1974).

Lear, Edward (1812–88) English, born London; *Book of Nonsense* (1846).

Longfellow, Henry (Wadsworth) (1807–82) American, born Portland, Maine; *Voices of the Night* (1839), *Ballads and Other Poems* (1842), *Hiawatha* (1855).

Lowell, Amy (Laurence) (1874–1925) American, born Brookline, Massachusetts; *A Dome of Many-Colored Glass* (1912), *Legends* (1921).

Lowell, Robert (Traill Spence, Jr) (1917–77) American, born Boston, Massachusetts; *Lord Weary's Castle* (1946), *Life Studies* (1959), *Prometheus Bound* (1967).

Macaulay, Thomas (Babington) (1800–59) English, born Rothey Temple, Leicestershire; *The Lays of Ancient Rome* (1842).

MacCaig, Norman (Alexander) (1910–96) Scottish, born Edinburgh; *Far Cry* (1943), *Riding Lights* (1955), *A Round of Applause* (1962), *A Man in My Position* (1969), *Voice-Over* (1988).

MacDiarmid, Hugh (pseudonym of **Christopher Murray Grieve**) (1892–1978) Scottish, born Langholm, Dumfriesshire; *A Drunk Man Looks at the Thistle* (1926).

McGough, Roger (1937–) English, born Liverpool; *The Mersey Sound: Penguin Modern Poets 10* (with Adrian Henri and Brian Patten) (1967), *Gig* (1973), *Waving at Trains* (1982), *An Imaginary Menagerie* (1988), *The Spotted Unicorn* (1998), *The Way Things Are* (1999), *Everyday Eclipses* (2002).

MacLean, Sorley (Gaelic **Somhairle Macgill-Eain**) (1911–96) Scottish, born Isle of Raasay, off Skye; *Reothairt is Contraigh* (Spring Tide and Neap Tide) (1977).

MacNeice, (Frederick) Louis (1907–63) Irish, born Belfast; *Blind Fireworks* (1929), *Solstices* (1961).

Mallarmé, Stéphane (1842–98) French, born Paris; *L'Après-midi d'un faune* (1876), *Poésies* (1899).

Marvell, Andrew (1621–78) English, born Winestead, near Hull; *Miscellaneous Poems by Andrew Marvell, Esq.* (1681).

Masefield, John (Edward) (1878–1967) English, born Ledbury, Herefordshire; *Salt-Water Ballads* (1902).

Millay, Edna St Vincent (1892–1950) American, born Rockland, Maine; *A Few Figs from Thistles* (1920), *The Ballad of Harp-Weaver* (1922).

Milton, John (1608–74) English, born London; *Lycidas* (1637), *Paradise Lost* (1667), *Samson Agonistes* (1671).

Moore, Marianne (Craig) (1887–1972) American, born Kirkwood, Missouri; *The Pangolin and Other Verse* (1936).

Motion, Andrew (1952–) English, born London; *The Pleasure Steamers* (1978), *Love in a Life* (1991), *Salt Water* (1997), *Public Property* (2002).

Muir, Edwin (1887–1959) Scottish, born Deerness, Orkney; *First Poems* (1925), *Chorus of the Newly Dead* (1926), *Variations on a Time Theme* (1934), *The Labyrinth* (1949), *New Poems* (1949–51).

Nash, (Frederick) Ogden (1902–71) American, born Rye, New York; *Free Wheeling* (1931).

Ovid (in full **Publius Ovidius Naso**) (43 BC– c.17 AD) Roman, born Sulmo; *Amores* (c.16 BC), *Metamorphoses*, *Ars Amatoria*.

Owen, Wilfred (Edward Salter) (1893–1918) English, born Oswestry, Shropshire; most poems published posthumously, 1920, by Siegfried Sassoon; *'Dulce et decorum est'*.

Patten, Brian (1946–) English, born Liverpool; *The Mersey Sound: Penguin Modern Poets 10* (1967), *Notes to the Hurrying Man* (1969), *Grinning Jack* (1990), *Armada* (1996), *The Blue and Green Ark* (1999), *Selected Poems* (2007).

Paz, Octavio (1914–98) Mexican, born Mexico City; *Sun Stone* (1963), *The Bow and the Lyre* (1973), *Collected Poems 1957–87* (1987), *Glimpses of India* (1995); Nobel Prize for literature 1990.

Petrarch (in full **Francesco Petrarca**) (1304–74) Italian, born Arezzo; *Canzoniere*, *Trionfi*.

Plath, Sylvia (1932–63) American, born Boston, Massachusetts; *The Colossus and Other Poems* (1960), *Ariel* (1965), *Crossing the Water* (1971).

Pope, Alexander (1688–1744) English, born London; *An Essay on Criticism* (1711), *The Rape of the Lock* (1712), *The Dunciad* (1728–42), *Essay on Man* (1733–4).

Porter, Peter (Neville Frederick) (1929–) Australian, born Brisbane; *Poems, Ancient and Modern* (1964), *English Subtitles* (1981), *The Automatic Oracle* (1987), *Millennial Fables* (1994), *Max is Missing* (2001), *Afterburner* (2004).

Pound, Ezra (Weston Loomis) (1885–1972) American, born Haile, Idaho; *The Cantos* (1917, 1948, 1959).

Pushkin, Aleksandr (Sergeyevich) (1799–1837) Russian, born Moscow; *Eugene Onegin* (1828), *Ruslam and Lyudmilla* (1820).

Raine, Kathleen (Jessie) (1908–2003) English, born London; *Stone and Flower* (1943), *The Hollow Hill* (1965), *Living with Mystery* (1992).

Rich, Adrienne (Cecile) (1929–) American, born Baltimore, Maryland; *The Diamond Cutters* (1955), *Snapshots of a Daughter-in-Law* (1963), *The Will to Change* (1971), *Dark Fields of the Republic* (1995), *The School Among the Ruins* (2004).

Riding, Laura (née **Reichenfeld**) (1901–91) American, born New York; *The Close Chaplet* (1926).

Rilke, Rainer Maria (1875–1926) Austrian, born Prague; *Die Sonette an Orpheus* (1923), *Duino Elegies* (1939).

Rimbaud, (Jean Nicholas) Arthur (1854–91) French, born Charleville, Ardennes; *Le Bateau ivre* (1871), *Les Illuminations* (1886).

Arts and Culture

Rochester, John Wilmot, Earl of (1647–80) English, born Ditchley, Oxfordshire; *A Satyre Against Mankind* (1675).

Roethke, Theodore Huebner (1908–63) American, born Saginaw, Michigan; *Open House* (1941), *The Lost Son and Other Poems* (1948).

Rosenberg, Isaac (1890–1918) English, born Bristol; *Night and Day* (1912), *Youth* (1915), *Poems* (1922).

Saint-John Perse (pseudonym of **Marie René Auguste Alexis Saint-Léger Léger**) (1887–1975) French, born St Léger des Feuilles; *Anabase* (1924), *Exil* (1942), *Chroniques* (1960); Nobel Prize for literature 1960.

Sassoon, Siegfried (Lorraine) (1886–1967) English, born Brenchley, Kent; *Counter-Attack and Other Poems* (1917), *The Road to Ruin* (1933).

Schwarz, Delmore (1913–66) American, born New York City; *In Dreams Begin Responsibilities* (1938), *Vaudeville for a Princess and Other Poems* (1950).

Seifert, Jaroslav (1901–86) Czech, born Prague; *City of Tears* (1921), *All Love* (1923), *A Helmet of Earth* (1945); Nobel Prize for literature 1984.

Shelley, Percy Bysshe (1792–1822) English, born Field Place, Horsham, Sussex; *Alastor* (1816), *The Revolt of Islam* (1818), *Julian and Maddalo* (1818), *The Triumph of Life* (1822).

Sidney, Sir Philip (1554–86) English, born Penshurst, Kent; *Arcadia* (1580), *Astrophel and Stella* (1591).

Sitwell, Dame Edith (Louisa) (1887–1964) English, born Scarborough; *Façade* (1922), *Colonel Fantock* (1926).

Smart, Christopher (1722–71) English, born Shipbourne, Kent; *Jubilate Agno* (first published 1939).

Smith, Stevie (pseudonym of **Florence Margaret Smith**) (1902–71) English, born Hull; *Not Waving but Drowning: Poems* (1957).

Spender, Sir Stephen (Harold) (1909–95) English, born London; *Poems* (1933).

Spenser, Edmund (1552–99) English, born London; *The Shepheardes Calender* (1579), *The Faerie Queene* (1590, 1596).

Stevens, Wallace (1879–1955) American, born Reading, Pennsylvania; *Harmonium* (1923), *Transport to Summer* (1947).

Swinburne, Algernon Charles (1837–1909) English, born London; *Poems and Ballads* (1866), *Songs before Sunrise* (1871), *Tristram of Lyonesse* (1882).

Szymborska, Wislawa (1923–) Polish, born Kórnik; *A Large Number* (1976), *People on the Bridge* (1986), *View with a Grain of Sand* (1996), *Poems New and Collected 1957–1997* (1998), *Miracle Fair* (2001), *Monologue of a Dog* (2005); Nobel Prize for literature 1996.

Tennyson, Alfred, Lord (1809–92) English, born Somersby, Lincolnshire; *Poems* (1832) (eg 'The Lotus-Eaters' and 'The Lady of Shalott'), *The Princess* (1847), *In Memoriam* (1850), *Idylls of the King* (1859), *Maud* (1885).

Thomas, Dylan (Marlais) (1914–53) Welsh, born Swansea; *Twenty-five Poems* (1936), *Deaths and Entrances* (1946), *In Country Sleep and Other Poems* (1952).

Thomas, (Philip) Edward (1878–1917) English, born London; *Six Poems* (1916), *Last Poems* (1918).

Thomas, R(onald) S(tuart) (1913–2000) Welsh, born Cardiff; *Stones of the Field* (1947), *Song at the Year's Turning* (1955), *The Bread of Truth* (1963), *Between Here and Now* (1981), *Counterpoint* (1990), *No Truce with the Furies* (1995).

Thomson, James (1700–48) Scottish, born Ednam, Roxburghshire; *The Seasons* (1730), *The Castle of Indolence* (1748).

Verlaine, Paul (1844–96) French, born Metz; *Fêtes galantes* (1869), *Sagesse* (1881).

Virgil (in full **Publius Vergilius Maro**) (70–19 BC) Roman, born near Mantua; *Eclogues* (37 BC), *Georgics* (29 BC), *The Aeneid* (19 BC).

Walcott, Derek Alton (1930–) West Indian, born St Lucia; *Castaway* (1965), *Fortunate Traveller* (1982), *The Bounty* (1997), *Tiepolo's Hound* (2000), *The Prodigal* (2005); Nobel Prize for literature 1992.

Webb, Francis Charles (1925–73) Australian, born Adelaide; *A Drum for Ben Boyd* (1948), *The Ghost of the Cock* (1964).

Whitman, Walt (1819–92) American, born West Hills, Long Island, New York; *Leaves of Grass* (1855–89).

Wordsworth, William (1770–1850) English, born Cockermouth; *Lyrical Ballads* (with S T Coleridge, 1798), *The Prelude* (1799, 1805, 1850), *The Excursion* (1814).

Wright, Judith (Arundell) (1915–2000) Australian, born Armidale, New South Wales; *The Moving Image* (1946), *Birds* (1962), *Alive* (1973), *The Cry for the Dead* (1981), *Collected Poems 1942–1985* (1994).

Wyatt, Sir Thomas (1503–42) English, born Allington Castle, Kent; poems first published in *Tottel's Miscellany* (1557).

Yeats, W(illiam) B(utler) (1865–1939) Irish, born Sandymount, County Dublin; *The Wanderings of Oisin and Other Poems* (1889), *The Wind Among the Reeds* (1894), *The Wild Swans at Coole* (1917), *Michael Robartes and the Dancer* (1921), *The Winding Stair and Other Poems* (1933); Nobel Prize for literature 1923.

Zephaniah, Benjamin Obadiah Iqbal (1958–) English poet and writer, born Birmingham; *Pen Rhythm* (1980), *The Dread Affair* (1985), *Too Black, Too Strong* (2001), *We are Britain* (2002), *Teacher's Dead* (2007).

Poets laureate

1617	Ben Jonson[1]	1813	Robert Southey
1638	Sir William Davenant[1]	1843	William Wordsworth
1668	John Dryden	1850	Alfred, Lord Tennyson
1689	Thomas Shadwell	1896	Alfred Austin
1692	Nahum Tate	1913	Robert Bridges
1715	Nicholas Rowe	1930	John Masefield
1718	Laurence Eusden	1968	Cecil Day-Lewis
1730	Colley Cibber	1972	Sir John Betjeman
1757	William Whitehead	1984	Ted Hughes
1785	Thomas Warton	1999	Andrew Motion
1790	Henry Pye		

[1] The post was not officially established until 1668.

Playwrights

Selected plays are listed.

Aeschylus (c.525–c.456 BC) Athenian; *The Oresteia trilogy (Agamemnon, Choephoroe, Eumenides)* (458 BC), *Prometheus Bound, Seven Against Thebes*.

Albee, Edward Franklin, III (1928–) American, born Washington, DC; *The American Dream* (1960), *Who's Afraid of Virginia Woolf?* (1962), *A Delicate Balance* (1966, Pulitzer Prize 1967), *Seascape* (1974, Pulitzer Prize 1975), *Three Tall Women* (1991, Pulitzer Prize 1994), *The Goat, or Who is Sylvia?* (2002).

Anouilh, Jean (1910–87) French, born Bordeaux; *Antigone* (1944), *Médée* (1946), *L'Alouette* (1953), *Beckett, or the Honour of God* (1960).

Aristophanes (c.448–c.385 BC) Athenian; *The Acharnians* (425 BC), *The Knights* (424 BC), *The Clouds* (423 BC), *The Wasps* (422 BC), *The Birds* (414 BC), *Lysistrata* (411 BC), *The Frogs* (405 BC).

Ayckbourn, Sir Alan (1939–) English, born London; *Absurd Person Singular* (1973), *Absent Friends* (1975), *Joking Apart* (1979), *Way Upstream* (1982), *Woman in Mind* (1985), *Henceforward* (1987), *Wildest Dreams* (1991), *Communicating Doors* (1994), *The Champion of Paribanou* (1998), *The Boy Who Fell Into a Book* (2000), *If I Were You* (2006), *Life and Beth* (2008).

Beaumont, Sir Francis (1584–1616) English, born Grace-Dieu, Leicestershire, and **John Fletcher** *Philaster* (1609), *The Maid's Tragedy* (1610).

Beckett, Samuel (Barclay) (1906–89) Irish, born Foxrock, near Dublin; *Waiting for Godot* (1955), *Endgame* (1958), *Krapp's Last Tape* (1958), *Happy Days* (1961), *Not I* (1973); Nobel Prize for literature 1969.

Behan, Brendan (Francis) (1923–64) Irish, born Dublin; *The Quare Fellow* (1956), *The Hostage* (1958).

Bennett, Alan (1934–) English, born Leeds; *Beyond the Fringe* (1960), *Forty Years On* (1968), *The Old Country* (1977), *An Englishman Abroad* (1983, television), *Talking Heads* (1988, television monologues), *The Madness of George III* (1991), *The History Boys* (2004).

Bond, (Thomas) Edward (1934–) English, born North London; *Early Morning* (1967), *Lear* (1971), *Summer* (1982), *The War Plays* (1985), *Olly's Prison* (1992), *Coffee* (1995), *Eleven Vests* (1997), *The Crime of the 21st Century* (2001).

Brecht, (Eugen) Bertolt (Friedrich) (1898–1956) German, born Augsburg; *Threepenny Opera* (libretto 1928), *Galileo* (1938–9), *Mutter Courage und ihre Kinder* (Mother Courage and Her Children) (1941), *Der Gute Mensch von Setzuan* (The Good Woman of Setzuan) (1943), *Der Kaukasische Kreidekreis* (The Caucasian Chalk Circle) (1949).

Brieux, Eugène (1858–1932) French, born Paris; *Les Trois Filles de M Dupont* (1897), *The Red Robe* (1900).

Chapman, George (c.1559–1634) English, born near Hitchin, Hertfordshire; *Bussy D'Ambois* (1607).

Chekhov, Anton Pavlovich (1860–1904) Russian, born Taganrog; *The Seagull* (1895), *Uncle Vanya* (1900), *Three Sisters* (1901), *The Cherry Orchard* (1904).

Congreve, William (1670–1729) English, born Bardsey, near Leeds; *Love for Love* (1695), *The Way of the World* (1700).

Corneille, Pierre (1606–84) French, born Rouen; *Le Cid* (1636), *Horace* (1639), *Polyeucte* (1640).

Coward, Sir Noël Peirce (1899–1973) English, born

Teddington, Middlesex; *Hay Fever* (1925), *Private Lives* (1933), *Blithe Spirit* (1941).

Dekker, Thomas (c.1570–1632) English, born London; *The Whore of Babylon* (1606).

Dryden, John (1631–1700) English, born Aldwinkle; *The Indian Queen* (1664), *Marriage à la Mode* (1672), *All for Love* (1678), *Amphitryon* (1690).

Eliot, T(homas) S(tearns) (1888–1965) American, naturalized British, born St Louis, Missouri; *Murder in the Cathedral* (1935), *The Family Reunion* (1939), *The Cocktail Party* (1950).

Esson, (Thomas) Louis (Buvelot) (1879–1943) Australian, born Edinburgh; *The Drovers* (1920), *Andeganora* (1937).

Euripides (c.480–406 BC) Athenian; *Medea* (431 BC), *Electra* (413 BC), *The Bacchae* (407 BC).

Fletcher, John (1579–1625) English, born Rye, Sussex; *The Faithful Shepherdess* (1610), *A Wife for a Month* (1624).

Fo, Dario (1926–) Italian, born Lombardy; *Mistero Buffo* (1969), *Accidental Death of an Anarchist* (1970), *Can't Pay! Won't Pay!* (1974), *The Pope and the Witch* (1989), *The Devil in Drag* (1997); Nobel Prize for literature 1997.

Ford, John (1586–c.1640) English, born Devon; *'Tis Pity She's a Whore* (1633), *Perkin Warbeck* (1634).

Galsworthy, John (1867–1933) English, born Coombe, Surrey; *Strife* (1909), *Justice* (1910); Nobel Prize for literature 1932.

Genet, Jean (1910–86) French, born Paris; *The Maids* (1948), *The Balcony* (1956), *The Screens* (1961).

Giraudoux, (Hippolyte) Jean (1882–1944) French, born Bellac; *Judith* (1931), *Ondine* (1939).

Goethe, Johann Wolfgang von (1749–1832) German, born Frankfurt am Main; *Faust* (1808, 1832).

Gogol, Nikolai (Vasilievich) (1809–52) Russian, born Ukraine; *The Inspector General* (1836).

Goldsmith, Oliver (1728–74) Irish, born Pallas, County Longford; *She Stoops to Conquer* (1773).

Greene, Robert (1558–92) English, born Norwich; *Orlando Furioso* (1594), *James the Fourth* (1598).

Hare, Sir David (1947–) English, born London; *Slag* (1970), *Plenty* (1978), *Pravda* (1985, with Howard Brenton), *The Secret Rapture* (1988), *Amy's View* (1997), *Stuff Happens* (2005), *Gethsemane* (2008).

Hauptmann, Gerhart Johann Robert (1862–1946) German, born Obersalzbrunn, Silesia; *Before Sunrise* (1889), *The Weavers* (1892); Nobel Prize for literature 1912.

Hebbel, (Christian) Friedrich (1813–63) German, born Wesselburen, Dithmarschen; *Judith* (1841), *Maria Magdalena* (1844).

Hewett, Dorothy (Coade) (1923–2002) Australian, born Wickepin, West Australia; *The Chapel Perilous* (1972), *This Old Man Comes Rolling Home* (1976), *Golden Valley* (1984), *Nowhere* (2001).

Heywood, Thomas (c.1574–1641) English, born Lincolnshire; *A Woman Killed with Kindness* (1603), *The Fair Maid of the West* (1631), *The English Traveller* (1633).

Hibberd, Jack (1940–) Australian, born Warracknabeal, Victoria; *Dimboola* (1969), *White with Wire Wheels* (1967), *A Stretch of the Imagination* (1971), *Squibs* (1984), *The Prodigal Son* (1997).

Howard, Sidney (Coe) (1891–1939) American, born Oakland, California; *They Knew What They Wanted* (1924), *The Silver Cord* (1926).

Ibsen, Henrik (1828–1906) Norwegian, born Skien;

Peer Gynt (1867), *A Doll's House* (1879), *The Pillars of Society* (1880), *The Wild Duck* (1884), *Hedda Gabler* (1890), *The Master Builder* (1892).

Inge, William Motter (1913–73) American, born Kansas; *Picnic* (1953), *Where's Daddy?* (1966).

Ionesco, Eugène (1912–94) French, born Romania; *The Bald Prima Donna* (1948), *The Picture* (1958), *Le Rhinocéros* (1960).

Jonson, Ben(jamin) (c.1572–1637) English, born Westminster, London; *Every Man in His Humour* (1598), *Sejanus* (1603), *Volpone* (1606), *The Alchemist* (1610), *Bartholomew Fair* (1614).

Kaiser, Georg (1878–1945) German, born Magdeburg; *The Burghers of Calais* (1914), *Gas* (1920).

Kane, Sarah (1971–99) English, born Essex; *Blasted* (1995), *Phaedra's Love* (1996), *Cleansed* (1998), *Crave* (1998), *4.48 Psychosis* (1999)

Kushner, Tony (1956–) American, born New York City; *Yes, Yes, No, No* (1985), *Angels in America* (1992, Pulitzer Prize 1993), *Slavs!* (1995), *Henry Box Brown* (1997), *Homebody/Kabul* (2001).

Kyd, Thomas (1558–94) English, born London; *The Spanish Tragedy* (1587).

Lawler, Ray(mond Evenor) (1922–) Australian, born Melbourne; *Summer of the Seventeenth Doll* (1955), *The Man Who Shot the Albatross* (1970), *Kid Stakes* (1975), *Other Times* (1976), *Godsend* (1982).

Lochhead, Liz (1947–) Scottish, born Motherwell; *Blood and Ice* (1982), *Mary Queen of Scots Got Her Head Chopped Off* (1987), *Misery Guts* (2002), *Good Things* (2006).

Lorca, Federico García (1899–1936) Spanish, born Fuente Vaqueros; *Blood Wedding* (1933), *The House of Bernarda Alba* (1945).

Maeterlinck, Maurice, Count (1862–1949) Belgian, born Ghent; *La Princesse Maleine* (1889), *Pélleas et Mélisande* (1892), *The Blue Bird* (1909).

Mamet, David Alan (1947–) American, born Chicago; *Sexual Perversity in Chicago* (1974), *Duck Variations* (1974), *American Buffalo* (1975), *Edmond* (1982), *Glengarry Glen Ross* (1984, Pulitzer Prize), *Oleanna* (1992), *Death Defying Acts* (1996), *Wag the Dog* (screenplay) (1997), *Romance* (2005), *November* (2007).

Marlowe, Christopher (1564–93) English, born Canterbury; *Tamburlaine the Great* (in two parts, 1587), *Dr Faustus* (1588), *The Jew of Malta* (c.1589), *Edward II* (1592).

Marston, John (1576–1634) English, born Wardington, Oxfordshire; *Antonio's Revenge* (1602), *The Malcontent* (1604).

Miller, Arthur (1915–2005) American, born New York City; *All My Sons* (1947), *Death of a Salesman* (1949), *The Crucible* (1952), *A View from the Bridge* (1955), *The Misfits* (1961), *After the Fall* (1964), *The Creation of the World and Other Business* (1972), *Playing for Time* (1981), *Danger: Memory!* (1987), *The Ride Down Mount Morgan* (1991), *The Last Yankee* (1992), *Broken Glass* (1994), *Homely Girl* (1995), *Mr Peter's Connections* (1998).

Molière (pseudonym of **Jean-Baptiste Poquelin**) (1622–73) French, born Paris; *Le Bourgeois Gentilhomme* (The Bourgeois Gentleman) (1660), *Tartuffe* (1664), *Le Misanthrope* (The Misanthropist) (1666), *Le Malade Imaginaire* (The Hypochondriac) (1673).

O'Casey, Sean (originally **John Casey**) (1880–1964) Irish, born Dublin; *Juno and the Paycock* (1924), *The Plough and the Stars* (1926).

O'Neill, Eugene Gladstone (1888–1953) American, born New York City; *Beyond the Horizon* (1920),

Desire under the Elms (1924), *Mourning Becomes Electra* (1931), *Long Day's Journey into Night* (1941), *The Iceman Cometh* (1946); Nobel Prize for literature 1936.

Orton, Joe (John Kingsley) (1933–67) English, born Leicester; *Entertaining Mr Sloane* (1964), *Loot* (1965), *What the Butler Saw* (1969).

Osborne, John (James) (1929–94) Welsh, born Fulham, London; *Look Back in Anger* (1956), *The Entertainer* (1957), *Inadmissible Evidence* (1965), *The Hotel in Amsterdam* (1968), *West of Suez* (1971), *Almost a Vision* (1976), *Déjà Vu* (1989).

Otway, Thomas (1652–85) English, born Milland, Sussex; *Don Carlos* (1676), *The Orphan* (1680), *Venice Preserv'd* (1682).

Patrick, John (1905–95) American, born Louisville, Kentucky; *The Teahouse of the August Moon* (1953).

Pinter, Harold (1930–2008) English, born East London; *The Birthday Party* (1957), *The Caretaker* (1959), *The Homecoming* (1964), *Landscape* (1967), *Old Times* (1970), *No Man's Land* (1974), *Betrayal* (1978), *A Kind of Alaska* (1982), *Party Time* (1991), *Ashes to Ashes* (1996), *Celebration* (1999), *Remembrance of Things Past* (2000); Nobel Prize for literature 2005.

Pirandello, Luigi (1867–1936) Italian, born near Agrigento, Sicily; *Six Characters in Search of an Author* (1921), *Henry IV* (1922); Nobel Prize for literature 1934.

Plautus, Titus Maccius (c.250–184 BC) Roman; *Menachmi, Miles Gloriosus*.

Potter, Dennis (Christopher George) (1935–94) English, born Forest of Dean; for television: *Vote, Vote, Vote for Nigel Barton* (1965), *Pennies from Heaven* (1978), *The Singing Detective* (1986), *Lipstick on Your Collar* (1993), *Karaoke* (1994).

Racine, Jean (1639–99) French, born near Soissons; *Andromaque* (1667), *Phèdre* (1677), *Bajazet* (1672), *Esther* (1689).

Rattigan, Sir Terence (1911–77) English, born London; *French without Tears* (1936), *The Winslow Boy* (1946), *The Browning Version* (1948), *Separate Tables* (1954).

Romeril, John (1945–) Australian, born Melbourne; *Chicago, Chicago* (1970), *I Don't Know Who to Feel Sorry For* (1969), *The Kelly Dance* (1984), *Love Suicides* (1997), *Miss Tanaka* (2002).

Russell, Willy (William) (1947–) English, born Whiston, Merseyside; *Educating Rita* (1979), *Blood Brothers* (1983), *Shirley Valentine* (1986).

Sackville, Thomas (1553–1608) English, born Buckhurst, Sussex; *Gorboduc* (1592).

Sartre, Jean-Paul (1905–80) French, born Paris; *The Flies* (1943), *Huis Clos* (1945), *The Condemned of Altona* (1961).

Schiller, Johann Christoph Friedrich von (1759–1805) German, born Marbach; *The Robbers* (1781), *Wallenstein* (1799), *Maria Stuart* (1800).

Seneca, Lucius Annaeus (c.4 BC–AD 65) Roman, born Cordoba; *Hercules, Medea, Thyestes*.

Seymour, Alan (1927–) Australian, born Perth; *Swamp Creatures* (1957),*The One Day of the Year* (1960), *Donny Johnson* (1965).

Shaffer, Sir Peter (Levin) (1926–) English, born Liverpool; *The Royal Hunt of the Sun* (1964), *Equus* (1973), *Amadeus* (1979), *Yonadab* (1985), *The Gift of the Gorgon* (1992).

Shakespeare, William ▶ Plays of Shakespeare over

Shaw, George Bernard (1856–1950) Irish, born Dublin; *Arms and the Man* (1894), *Man and Superman* (1903), *Pygmalion* (1913), *Saint Joan*

Arts and Culture

(1924); Nobel Prize for literature 1925.

Shepard, Sam (originally **Samuel Shepard Rogers**) (1943–) American, born Fort Sheridan, Illinois; *La Turista* (1967), *The Tooth of Crime* (1972), *Buried Child* (1978, Pulitzer Prize), *True West* (1979), *Fool for Love* (1983), *A Lie of the Mind* (1985), *Simpatico* (1993), *Eyes for Consuela* (1998), *God of Hell* (2004), *Kicking a Dead Horse* (2007).

Sheridan, Richard Brinsley (1751–1816) Irish, born Dublin; *The Rivals* (1775), *The School for Scandal* (1777), *The Critic* (1779).

Sherwood, Robert (Emmet) (1896–1955) American, born New Rochelle, New York; *Idiot's Delight* (1936), *Abe Lincoln in Illinois* (1938), *There Shall Be No Night* (1940).

Sophocles (496–406 BC) Athenian, born Colonus; *Antigone*, *Oedipus Rex*, *Oedipus at Colonus*.

Soyinka, Wole (in full **Akinwande Oluwole Soyinka**) (1934–) Nigerian, born Abeokuta, West Nigeria; *The Swamp Dwellers* (1958), *The Strong Breed* (1962), *The Road* (1964), *The Bacchae of Euripides* (1973), *Opera Wonyosi* (1978), *From Zia, with Love* (1991), *The Beatification of Area Boy* (1995), *King Baabu* (2001); Nobel Prize for literature 1986.

Stoppard, Sir Tom (Thomas Straussler) (1937–) English, born Czechoslovakia (now Czech Republic); *Rosencrantz and Guildenstern are Dead* (1966), *The Real Inspector Hound* (1968), *Travesties* (1974), *Every Good Boy Deserves Favour* (1978), *Rough Crossing* (1984), *Arcadia* (1993), *Indian Ink* (1995), *Shakespeare in Love* (screenplay) (1998), *Coast of Utopia* (trilogy) (2002), *Rock'n'Roll* (2006).

Strindberg, (Johan) August (1849–1912) Swedish, born Stockholm; *Master Olof* (1877), *Miss Julie* (1888), *The Dance of Death* (1901).

Synge, (Edmund) J(ohn) M(illington) (1871–1909) Irish, born near Dublin; *The Well of Saints* (1905), *The Playboy of the Western World* (1907).

Webster, John (c.1578–c.1632) English, born London; *The White Devil* (1612), *The Duchess of Malfi* (1614).

Wesker, Arnold (1932–) English, born London; *Chicken Soup with Barley* / *Roots* / *I'm Talking about Jerusalem* (trilogy) (1958–60), *The Kitchen* (1959), *Chips with Everything* (1962), *The Friends* (1970), *Denial* (1997), *Longitude* (2002).

Wilde, Oscar (Fingal O'Flahertie Wills) (1854–1900) Irish, born Dublin; *Lady Windermere's Fan* (1892), *The Importance of Being Earnest* (1895).

Wilder, Thornton (Niven) (1897–1975) American, born Wisconsin; *Our Town* (1938), *The Merchant of Yonkers* (1938), *The Skin of Our Teeth* (1942), *The Matchmaker* (1954, later a musical *Hello, Dolly!*, 1964).

Williams, Tennessee (originally **Thomas Lanier Williams**) (1911–83) American, born Mississippi; *The Glass Menagerie* (1944), *A Streetcar Named Desire* (1947), *Cat on a Hot Tin Roof* (1955), *Sweet Bird of Youth* (1959).

Williamson, David Keith (1942–) Australian, born Melbourne; *The Removalists* (1971), *The Club* (1977), *Sons of Cain* (1985), *Money & Friends* (1991), *Up For Grabs* (2000), *Influence* (2005).

Wycherly, William (1641–1715) English, born Clive, near Shrewsbury; *The Gentleman Dancing-Master* (1672), *The Country Wife* (1675).

Plays of Shakespeare

William Shakespeare (1564–1616), English playwright and poet, born Stratford-upon-Avon.

Title	Date	Category
The Two Gentlemen of Verona	1590–1	comedy
Henry VI Part One	1592	history
Henry VI Part Two	1592	history
Henry VI Part Three	1592	history
Titus Andronicus	1592	tragedy
Richard III	1592–3	history
The Taming of the Shrew	1593	comedy
The Comedy of Errors	1594	comedy
Love's Labour's Lost	1594–5	comedy
Richard II	1595	history
Romeo and Juliet	1595	tragedy
A Midsummer Night's Dream	1595	comedy
King John	1596	history
The Merchant of Venice	1596–7	comedy
Henry IV Part One	1596–7	history
The Merry Wives of Windsor	1597–8	comedy
Henry IV Part Two	1597–8	history
Much Ado About Nothing	1598	comedy
Henry V	1598–9	history
Julius Caesar	1599	tragedy
Hamlet, Prince of Denmark	1600–1	tragedy
As You Like It	1599–1600	comedy
Twelfth Night, or What You Will	1601	comedy
Troilus and Cressida	1602	tragedy
Measure for Measure	1603	dark comedy
Othello	1603–4	tragedy
All's Well That Ends Well	1604–5	dark comedy
Timon of Athens	1605	tragedy
The Tragedy of King Lear	1605–6	tragedy
Macbeth	1606	tragedy
Antony and Cleopatra	1606	tragedy
Pericles	1607	romance
Coriolanus	1608	tragedy
The Winter's Tale	1609	romance
Cymbeline	1610	romance
The Tempest	1611	romance
Henry VIII	1613	history

Film and TV actors

Selected films and television productions are listed. Original and full names of actors are given in parentheses.

Arts and Culture

Adjani, Isabelle (1955–   ) French, born Paris; *The Story of Adele H* (1975), *Possession* (1981), *Quartet* (1981), *One Deadly Summer* (1983), *Subway* (1985), *Ishtar* (1987), *Camille Claudel* (1988), *La Reine Margot* (1994), *Adolphe* (2002).

Agutter, Jenny (1952–   ) British, born Taunton; *The Railway Children* (1970), *Walkabout* (1971), *Logan's Run* (1976), *The Eagle Has Landed* (1976), *Equus* (1977), *The Man in the Iron Mask* (TV 1977), *An American Werewolf in London* (1981), *Silas Marner* (TV 1985), *Blue Juice* (1995) *Spooks* (TV 2002–3), *The Invisibles* (TV 2008).

Aiello, Danny (1933–   ) American, born New York City; *Fort Apache, The Bronx* (1981), *Once Upon a Time in America* (1984), *The Purple Rose of Cairo* (1985), *Moonstruck* (1987), *Do the Right Thing* (1989), *Harlem Nights* (1989), *Léon* (1994), *Dinner Rush* (2000), *Brooklyn Lobster* (2005).

Aimée, Anouk (Françoise Sorya) (1932–   ) French, born Paris; *Les Amants de Vérone* (1949), *La Dolce Vita* (1960), *Lola* (1961), *Un Homme et une Femme* (1966), *Justine* (1969), *Flagrant Desire* (1985), *Prêt-À-Porter* (1994), *Une pour toutes* (1999).

Albert, Eddie (Eddie Albert Heimberger) (1906–2005) American, born Rock Island, Illinois; *Brother Rat* (1938), *Four Wives* (1939), *Smash-Up* (1947), *Carrie* (1952), *Roman Holiday* (1953), *Oklahoma!* (1955), *Attack!* (1956), *The Roots of Heaven* (1958), *Green Acres* (TV 1965–70), *The Longest Yard* (1974), *Switch* (TV 1975–6), *Dreamscape* (1984), *The Big Picture* (1989).

Alda, Alan (1936–   ) American, born New York City; *Paper Lion* (1968), *M*A*S*H* (TV 1972–83), *California Suite* (1978), *Same Time Next Year* (1978), *Sweet Liberty* (1986), *A New Life* (1988), *Crimes and Misdemeanors* (1989), *Betsy's Wedding* (1990), *Manhattan Murder Mystery* (1993), *Mad City* (1997), *The Aviator* (2004), *The West Wing* (TV 2004–6).

Allen, Woody (Allen Stewart Konigsberg) (1935–   ) American, born Brooklyn, New York City; *What's New, Pussycat?* (1965), *Casino Royale* (1967), *Bananas* (1971), *Play It Again, Sam* (1972), *Sleeper* (1973), *Annie Hall* (1977), *Manhattan* (1979), *Hannah and Her Sisters* (1986), *New York Stories* (1989), *Crimes and Misdemeanors* (1989), *Shadows and Fog* (1992), *Husbands and Wives* (1992), *Manhattan Murder Mystery* (1993), *Mighty Aphrodite* (1995), *Everyone Says I Love You* (1996), *Deconstructing Harry* (1997), *The Curse of the Jade Scorpion* (2001).

Alley, Kirstie (1955–   ) American, born Wichita, Kansas; *Star Trek II: The Wrath of Khan* (1982), *Blind Date* (1983), *Champions* (1983), *Runaway* (1984), *North and South* (TV 1986), *Summer School* (1987), *Cheers* (TV 1987–93), *Shoot to Kill* (1988), *Look Who's Talking* (1989), *Madhouse* (1990), *Sibling Rivalry* (1990), *Look Who's Talking Too* (1991), *Look Who's Talking Now* (1993), *It Takes Two* (1995), *Drop Dead Gorgeous* (1999), *Veronica's Closet* (TV 1997–2000).

Allyson, June (Ella Geisman) (1917–2006) American, born Westchester, New York City; *Two Girls and a Sailor* (1944), *Music for Millions* (1944), *Little Women* (1949), *The Glenn Miller Story* (1954), *The Shrike* (1955), *The June Allyson Show* (TV 1959–61).

Ameche, Don (Dominic Felix Amici) (1908–93) American, born Kenosha, Wisconsin; *Ramona* (1936), *In Old Chicago* (1938), *The Three Musketeers* (1939), *Midnight* (1939), *The Story of Alexander Graham Bell* (1939), *Swanee River* (1939), *Four Sons* (1940), *Down Argentine Way* (1940), *That Night in Rio* (1941), *Heaven Can Wait* (1943), *Trading Places* (1983), *Cocoon* (1985), *Coming to America* (1988), *Things Change* (1988), *Oscar* (1991), *Corrina, Corrina* (1994).

Anderson, Dame Judith (Frances Margaret Anderson) (1897–1992) Australian, born Adelaide; *Rebecca* (1940), *The Ten Commandments* (1956), *Cat on a Hot Tin Roof* (1958), *A Man Called Horse* (1970), *Star Trek III: The Search for Spock* (1984).

Andress, Ursula (1936–   ) Swiss, born Berne; *Dr No* (1962), *She* (1965), *What's New, Pussycat?* (1965), *Casino Royale* (1967), *The Clash of the Titans* (1981).

Andrews, Anthony (1948–   ) British, born London; *Danger UXB* (TV 1978), *Brideshead Revisited* (TV 1981), *The Scarlet Pimpernel* (TV 1982), *Under the Volcano* (1984), *The Lighthorsemen* (1987), *Lost in Siberia* (1991), *Haunted* (1995).

Andrews, Dame Julie (Julia Elizabeth Wells) (1935–   ) British, born Walton-on-Thames, Surrey; *Mary Poppins* (1964), *The Sound of Music* (1965), *Torn Curtain* (1966), *Thoroughly Modern Millie* (1967), *Star!* (1968), *SOB* (1981), *Victor/Victoria* (1982), *The Man Who Loved Women* (1983), *Tchin Tchin* (1990), *Relative Values* (2000), *The Princess Diaries* (2001), *The Princess Diaries 2* (2004).

Ann-Margret (Ann-Margret Olsson) (1941–   ) Swedish-American, born Valsjöbyn, Jämtland, Sweden; *State Fair* (1962), *Bye Bye Birdie* (1963), *The Cincinnati Kid* (1965), *Carnal Knowledge* (1971), *Tommy* (1975), *52 Pick-Up* (1986), *A New Life* (1988), *Newsies* (1991), *Grumpy Old Men* (1994), *Any Given Sunday* (1999), *The Break-Up* (2006), *Memory* (2006).

Archer, Anne (1947–   ) American, born Los Angeles; *Bob and Carol and Ted and Alice* (TV 1973), *Paradise Alley* (1978), *Green Ice* (1980), *Fatal Attraction* (1987), *Love at Large* (1990), *Body of Evidence* (1992), *Patriot Games* (1992), *Short Cuts* (1993), *Clear and Present Danger* (1994), *The Rules of Engagement* (2000), *Cut Off* (2006).

Arquette, Rosanna (1959–   ) American, born New York City; *Shirley* (TV 1979), *SOB* (1981), *The Executioner's Song* (TV 1982), *Desperately Seeking Susan* (1983), *After Hours* (1985), *The Big Blue* (1988), *New York Stories* (1989), *The Black Rainbow* (1990), *The Player* (1992), *Nowhere to Run* (1993), *Pulp Fiction* (1994), *Crash* (1996), *The Whole Nine Yards* (2000), *Dead Cool* (2004), *I-See-You.Com* (2006), *What About Brian* (TV 2006–7).

Ashcroft, Dame Peggy (1907–91) British, born Croydon, Greater London; *The Thirty-Nine Steps* (1935), *Quiet Wedding* (1940), *Edward and Mrs Simpson* (TV 1978), *A Passage to India* (1984), *The Jewel in the Crown* (TV 1984), *Madame Sousatzka* (1988), *She's Been Away* (TV 1990).

Asher, Jane (1946–   ) British, born London; *The Masque of the Red Death* (1964), *Deep End* (1971), *Dreamchild* (1985), *Paris by Night* (1988), *Tirante el Blanco* (2006).

Astaire, Fred (Frederick Austerlitz) (1899–1987) American, born Omaha, Nebraska; *Flying Down to Rio* (1933), *Top Hat* (1935), *Easter Parade* (1948); *Funny Face* (1957), *It Takes a Thief* (TV 1965–9),

Finian's Rainbow (1968).

Astor, Mary (Lucille Langhanke) (1906–87) American, born Quincy, Illinois; *Beau Brummell* (1924), *Don Juan* (1926), *Dodsworth* (1936), *The Prisoner of Zenda* (1937), *The Great Lie* (1941), *The Maltese Falcon* (1941), *The Palm Beach Story* (1942), *Meet Me in St Louis* (1944), *Act of Violence* (1948), *Little Women* (1949), *Return to Peyton Place* (1961).

Atkinson, Rowan (1955–) British, born Consett, Co. Durham; *The Black Adder* (TV 1984), *Blackadder II* (TV 1985), *Blackadder III* (TV 1986), *Blackadder Goes Forth* (TV 1989), *The Tall Guy* (1989), *The Witches* (1990), *Mr Bean* (TV 1990–4), *Bean: The Ultimate Disaster Movie* (1997), *Johnny English* (2003), *Keeping Mum* (2005), *Mr Bean's Holiday* (2007).

Attenborough, Richard Samuel Attenborough, Baron (1923–) British, born Cambridge; *In Which We Serve* (1942), *The Man Within* (1942), *Brighton Rock* (1947), *The Guinea Pig* (1949), *The Great Escape* (1963), *Brannigan* (1975), *Jurassic Park* (1993), *Miracle on 34th Street* (1994), $E = MC^2$ (1995), *The Lost World: Jurassic Park* (1997), *Elizabeth* (1998), *Puckoon* (2002).

Avalon, Frankie (Francis Thomas Avallone) (1939–) American, born Philadelphia, Pennsylvania; *The Alamo* (1960), *Voyage to the Bottom of the Sea* (1962), *Beach Blanket Bingo* (1965), *Fireball 500* (1966), *Grease* (1978), *Blood Song* (1982).

Aykroyd, Dan (1952–) Canadian, born Ottawa, Ontario; *1941* (1979), *The Blues Brothers* (1980), *Neighbors* (1981), *Twilight Zone* (1983), *Ghostbusters* (1984), *Spies Like Us* (1986), *Dragnet* (1987), *Ghostbusters II* (1989), *My Stepmother is an Alien* (1989), *Driving Miss Daisy* (1989), *Loose Cannons* (1990), *My Girl* (1991), *Chaplin* (1992), *Coneheads* (1993), *Casper* (1995), *Sgt Bilko* (1996), *Blues Brothers 2000* (1998), *Crossroads* (2002), *Bright Young Things* (2003), *50 First Dates* (2004).

Bacall, Lauren (Betty Joan Perske) (1924–) American, born New York City; *To Have and Have Not* (1944), *The Big Sleep* (1946), *How to Marry a Millionaire* (1953), *The Fan* (1981), *Mr North* (1988), *Misery* (1990), *Prêt-À-Porter* (1994), *The Mirror Has Two Faces* (1996), *Dogville* (2003).

Bacon, Kevin (1958–) American, born Philadelphia, Pennsylvania; *Animal House* (1978), *Friday the 13th* (1980), *Footloose* (1984), *She's Having a Baby* (1988), *Tremors* (1989), *Flatliners* (1990), *The Big Picture* (1990), *JFK* (1991), *A Few Good Men* (1992), *The River Wild* (1994), *Apollo 13* (1995), *Sleepers* (1996), *Stir of Echoes* (1999), *Mystic River* (2003), *The Woodsman* (2004), *Where the Truth Lies* (2005), *Death Sentence* (2007).

Baker, Tom (1934–) British, born Liverpool; *Nicholas and Alexandra* (1971), *Doctor Who* (TV 1975–81), *The Life and Loves of a She-Devil* (TV 1987), *The Chronicles of Narnia* (TV 1990), *Little Britain* (TV 2003–5).

Baldwin, Alec (1958–) American, born Massapequa, New York; *Sweet Revenge* (TV 1984), *She's Having a Baby* (1988), *Beetlejuice* (1988), *Working Girl* (1988), *Married to the Mob* (1988), *The Hunt for Red October* (1990), *Miami Blues* (1990), *Alice* (1991), *Glengarry Glen Ross* (1992), *Malice* (1993), *The Shadow* (1994), *Bookworm* (1997), *Notting Hill* (1999), *Pearl Harbor* (2001), *The Aviator* (2004), *Running with Scissors* (2006).

Ball, Lucille (1911–89) American, born Jamestown, New York; *Top Hat* (1935), *Stage Door* (1937), *The Affairs of Annabel* (1938), *Five Came Back* (1939),

The Big Street (1942), *Du Barry was a Lady* (1943), *Without Love* (1945), *Ziegfeld Follies* (1946), *Her Husband's Affairs* (1947), *Fancy Pants* (1950), *I Love Lucy* (TV 1951–5), *The Long Long Trailer* (1954), *The Facts of Life* (1956), *The Lucy Show* (TV 1962–8), *Yours Mine and Ours* (1968), *Here's Lucy* (TV 1968–73), *Life with Lucy* (TV 1976).

Bancroft, Anne (Anna Maria Italiano) (1931–2005) American, born The Bronx, New York City; *The Miracle Worker* (1962), *The Graduate* (1968), *Silent Movie* (1976), *The Elephant Man* (1980), *84 Charing Cross Road* (1987), *Torch Song Trilogy* (1988), *The Assassin* (1992), *Malice* (1993), *How To Make an American Quilt* (1995), *Dracula: Dead and Loving It* (1995), *Great Expectations* (1998).

Bankhead, Tallulah (1902–68) American, born Huntsville, Alabama; *Tarnished Lady* (1931), *Lifeboat* (1944), *A Royal Scandal* (1945).

Bardot, Brigitte (Camille Javal) (1934–) French, born Paris; *And God Created Woman* (1956), *En Cas de Malheur* (1958), *Viva Maria!* (1965).

Barkin, Ellen (1954–) American, born The Bronx, New York City; *Diner* (1982), *The Adventures of Buckeroo Banzai* (1984), *The Big Easy* (1987), *Siesta* (1987), *Sea of Love* (1990), *Johnny Handsome* (1990), *Switch* (1991), *Mac* (1993), *Trigger Happy* (1996), *Drop Dead Gorgeous* (1999), *She Hate Me* (2004), *Ocean's Thirteen* (2007).

Barrymore, Drew (1975–) American, born Los Angeles; *ET* (1982), *Firestarter* (1984), *Irreconcilable Differences* (1984), *Cat's Eye* (1984), *Poison Ivy* (1992), *Batman Forever* (1995), *Never Been Kissed* (1999), *Charlie's Angels* (2000), *Riding in Cars with Boys* (2001), *Confessions of a Dangerous Mind* (2002), *50 First Dates* (2004), *Fever Pitch* (2005), *Music and Lyrics* (2007).

Barrymore, Ethel (Edith Blythe) (1879–1959) American, born Philadelphia, Pennsylvania; *Rasputin and the Empress* (1932), *None but the Lonely Heart* (1944), *The Farmer's Daughter* (1947), *Young at Heart* (1954).

Barrymore, John (John Blythe) (1882–1942) American, born Philadelphia, Pennsylvania; *Dr Jekyll and Mr Hyde* (1920), *Show of Shows* (1929), *Rasputin and the Empress* (1932), *Dinner at 8* (1933), *Midnight* (1939), *The Great Profile* (1940).

Barrymore, Lionel (Lionel Blythe) (1878–1954) American, born Philadelphia, Pennsylvania; *Peter Ibbetson* (1917), *The Copperhead* (1918), *The Bells* (1926), *Sadie Thompson* (1928), *A Free Soul* (1931), *Rasputin and the Empress* (1932), *Grand Hotel* (1932), *Dinner at 8* (1933), *David Copperfield* (1934), *Captains Courageous* (1937), *A Family Affair* (1937), *Young Dr Kildare* (1938), *Calling Dr Gillespie* (1942), *On Borrowed Time* (1939), *Three Wise Fools* (1946), *It's a Wonderful Life* (1946), *Duel in the Sun* (1946), *Key Largo* (1948).

Basinger, Kim (1953–) American, born Athens, Georgia; *From Here to Eternity* (TV 1980), *Hard Country* (1981), *Never Say Never Again* (1983), *The Natural* (1984), *9½ Weeks* (1985), *Blind Date* (1987), *Batman* (1989), *My Stepmother is an Alien* (1989), *The Marrying Man* (1990), *Wayne's World 2* (1993), *Prêt-À-Porter* (1994), *Kansas City* (1996), *LA Confidential* (1997), *8 Mile* (2002), *Even Money* (2006).

Bates, Alan (1934–2003) British, born Allestree, Derbyshire; *A Kind of Loving* (1962), *Whistle Down the Wind* (1962), *Zorba the Greek* (1965), *Far from the Madding Crowd* (1967), *Women in Love* (1969), *The Rose* (1979), *A Prayer for the Dying* (1987), *We Think the World of You* (1988),

Hamlet (1990), Grotesque (1995), Gosford Park (2001).

Bates, Kathy (Kathleen Doyle Bates) (1948–) American, born Memphis, Tennessee; Misery (1990), Titanic (1997), Primary Colors (1998), About Schmidt (2002), Six Feet Under (TV 2003–5), P.S. I Love You (2007).

Béart, Emmanuelle (1965–) French, born Gassin; Manon des Sources (1986), Mission: Impossible (1996), 8 Women (2002), The Story of Marie and Julien (2003), L'Enfer (2005), The Witnesses (2007).

Beatty, Ned (1937–) American, born Louisville, Kentucky; Deliverance (1972), Nashville (1975), Network (1976), All the President's Men (1976), Superman (1978), Friendly Fire (TV 1979), Incredible Shrinking Woman (1981), Superman II (1981), The Toy (1983), Hopscotch (1983), The Big Easy (1987), The Fourth Protocol (1987), Switching Channels (1988), Just Cause (1995), Cookie's Fortune (1999), Sweet Land (2005).

Beatty, Warren (Henry Warren Beaty) (1937–) American, born Richmond, Virginia; Splendor in the Grass (1961), The Roman Spring of Mrs Stone (1961), All Fall Down (1962), Bonnie and Clyde (1967), The Parallax View (1974), Shampoo (1975), Heaven Can Wait (1978), Reds (1981), Ishtar (1987), Dick Tracy (1990), Bugsy (1991), Love Affair (1994), Bulworth (1998), Town and Country (2001).

Bedelia, Bonnie (1948–) American, born New York City; They Shoot Horses, Don't They? (1969), Love and Other Strangers (1970), Heart Like a Wheel (1983), The Prince of Pennsylvania (1988), Die Hard (1988), Die Hard II: Die Harder (1990), Presumed Innocent (1990), Anywhere But Here (1999), The Division (TV 2001–4).

Belmondo, Jean-Paul (1933–) French, born Neuilly-sur-Seine, Paris; À Bout de Souffle (1959), Moderato Cantabile (1960), Un Singe en Hiver (1962), That Man from Rio (1964), Les Misérables (1995).

Belushi, James (1954–) American, born Chicago; Trading Places (1983), Salvador (1986), About Last Night (1987), Red Heat (1988), Only the Lonely (1991), Curly Sue (1991), Last Action Hero (1993), Separate Lives (1995), Jingle All The Way (1996), Return to Me (2000), According to Jim (TV 2001–8).

Belushi, John (1949–82) American, born Chicago; Animal House (1978), 1941 (1979), The Blues Brothers (1981), Neighbors (1981).

Berenger, Tom (1949–) American, born Chicago; The Big Chill (1983), Platoon (1987), Shoot to Kill (1988), Betrayed (1988), Last Rites (1988), Born On The Fourth Of July (1990), Sliver (1993), The Substitute (1996), Training Day (2001), Stiletto (2008).

Bergen, Candice (1946–) American, born Beverly Hills, California; The Group (1966), The Magus (1969), Carnal Knowledge (1971), Rich and Famous (1981), Gandhi (1982), Miss Congeniality (2000), Sweet Home Alabama (2002), Boston Legal (TV 2004–8).

Bergman, Ingrid (1915–82) Swedish, born Stockholm; Intermezzo (1939), Dr Jekyll and Mr Hyde (1941), Casablanca (1943), For Whom the Bell Tolls (1943), Gaslight (1943), Spellbound (1945), Anastasia (1946), Notorious (1946), Indiscreet (1958), Cactus Flower (1969), Murder on the Orient Express (1974), Autumn Sonata (1978).

Berkoff, Stephen (1937–) British, born London; Octopussy (1983), Beverly Hills Cop (1984), Rambo

(1985), War and Remembrance (TV 1989), Charlie (2004).

Bernhardt, Sarah (Henriette Rosine Bernhardt) (1884–1923) French, born Paris; Queen Elizabeth (1912).

Berry, Halle (Maria) (1966–) American, born Cleveland, Ohio; Boomerang (1992), The Flintstones (1994), Introducing Dorothy Dandridge (TV 1999), X-Men trilogy (2000–6), Monster's Ball (2001), Die Another Day (2002), Catwoman (2004), Their Eyes Were Watching God (TV 2005), Perfect Stranger (2007).

Bisset, Jacqueline (1944–) British, born Weybridge, Surrey; Cul-de-Sac (1966), Casino Royale (1967), Bullitt (1968), The Grasshopper (1970), Murder on the Orient Express (1974), The Deep (1977), Rich and Famous (1981), Class (1983), Under the Volcano (1984), High Season (1987), Wild Orchid (1990), Joan of Arc: The Virgin Warrior (2000), Swing (2003).

Blanchett, Cate (Catherine Elise Blanchett) (1969–) Australian, born Melbourne; Oscar and Lucinda (1997), Elizabeth (1998), The Talented Mr Ripley (1999), Charlotte Gray (2001), The Shipping News (2001), Lord of the Rings trilogy (2001–3), The Aviator (2004), Little Fish (2005), Babel (2006), Notes on a Scandal (2006), I'm Not There (2007), The Curious Case of Benjamin Button (2008).

Blessed, Brian (1937–) British, born Mexborough, South Yorkshire; Z Cars (TV 1962–5), I, Claudius (TV 1976), Flash Gordon (1980), Henry V (1989), Robin Hood: Prince of Thieves (1991), Much Ado About Nothing (1993), Macbeth (1997), As You Like It (2006).

Bloom, Claire (Patricia Claire Blume) (1931–) British, born London; Look Back in Anger (1959), The Haunting (1963), The Spy who Came in from the Cold (1966), Clash of the Titans (1981), Crimes and Misdemeanors (1989), Daylight (1996).

Bogarde, Sir Dirk (Derek Niven Van Den Bogaerde) (1921–99) Anglo-Dutch, born Hampstead, London; A Tale of Two Cities (1958), Victim (1961), The Servant (1963), Darling (1965), Death in Venice (1971), Providence (1977), These Foolish Things (1990).

Bogart, Humphrey (DeForest) (1899–1957) American, born New York City; Broadway's Like That (1930), The Petrified Forest (1936), High Sierra (1941), The Maltese Falcon (1941), Casablanca (1942), To Have and Have Not (1944), The Big Sleep (1946), The Treasure of the Sierra Madre (1947), The African Queen (1952), The Barefoot Contessa (1954), The Caine Mutiny (1954).

Bonham-Carter, Helena (1966–) British, born London; Lady Jane (1985), A Room with a View (1985), Hamlet (1990), Where Angels Fear to Tread (1991), Howards End (1992), Frankenstein (1994), Twelfth Night (1996), The Wings of the Dove (1997), Fight Club (1999), Planet of the Apes (2001), Harry Potter and the Order of the Phoenix (2007), Sweeney Todd (2007).

Borgnine, Ernest (Ermes Borgnino) (1917–) American, born Hamden, Connecticut; From Here to Eternity (1953), Bad Day at Black Rock (1954), Marty (1955), The Best Things in Life are Free (1956), The Vikings (1958), Pay or Die (1960), McHale's Navy (TV 1962–5), The Dirty Dozen (1967), Ice Station Zebra (1968), The Wild Bunch (1969), The Poseidon Adventure (1972), Convoy (1978), The Black Hole (1979), Escape from New York (1981), Airwolf (TV 1984–6), Blueberry (2004).

Bow, Clara (1905–65) American, born Brooklyn,

Arts and Culture

New York City; *Mantrap* (1926), *It* (1927), *Wings* (1927).

Bowie, David (David Robert Jones) (1947–) British, born Brixton, South London; *The Man Who Fell to Earth* (1976), *The Hunger* (1983), *Merry Christmas Mr Lawrence* (1983), *Labyrinth* (1986), *The Last Temptation of Christ* (1988), *Twin Peaks: Fire Walk With Me* (1992), *Basquiat* (1996), *The Prestige* (2006).

Branagh, Kenneth (1960–) British, born Belfast; *A Month in the Country* (1988), *Henry V* (1989), *Dead Again* (1991), *Peter's Friends* (1992), *Much Ado About Nothing* (1993), *Frankenstein* (1994), *Othello* (1995), *Hamlet* (1996), *Love's Labour's Lost* (2000), *Rabbit-Proof Fence* (2002), *Harry Potter and the Chamber of Secrets* (2002), *Conspiracy* (TV 2002), *Warm Springs* (TV 2005).

Brandauer, Klaus Maria (1944–) Austrian, born Bad Aussee; *Mephisto* (1980), *Never Say Never Again* (1983), *Colonel Redl* (1984), *Out of Africa* (1985), *Streets of Gold* (1986), *The Russia House* (1990), *White Fang* (1991), *Rembrandt* (1999).

Brando, Marlon (1924–2004) American, born Omaha, Nebraska; *A Streetcar Named Desire* (1951), *Viva Zapata* (1952), *Julius Caesar* (1953), *The Wild One* (1953), *On the Waterfront* (1954), *Guys and Dolls* (1955), *The Teahouse of the August Moon* (1956), *One-Eyed Jacks* (1961), *Mutiny on the Bounty* (1962), *The Godfather* (1972), *Last Tango in Paris* (1972), *Superman* (1978), *Apocalypse Now* (1979), *A Dry White Season* (1988), *Don Juan de Marco* (1995).

Bridges, Jeff (1949–) American, born Los Angeles; *The Last Picture Show* (1971), *Thunderbolt and Lightfoot* (1974), *Stay Hungry* (1976), *King Kong* (1976), *Against All Odds* (1983), *Starman* (1984), *Jagged Edge* (1985), *The Morning After* (1986), *The Fabulous Baker Boys* (1989), *Texasville* (1990), *The Fisher King* (1991), *The Vanishing* (1992), *Fearless* (1993), *The Mirror Has Two Faces* (1996), *Arlington Road* (1999), *K-PAX* (2001), *The Contender* (2000), *Seabiscuit* (2003), *Iron Man* (2008).

Bridges, Lloyd (1913–98) American, born San Leandro, California; *Home of the Brave* (1949), *Try and Get Me* (1951), *The Rainmaker* (1956), *Sea Hunt* (TV 1957–60), *The Goddess* (1958), *The Love War* (TV 1970), *Roots* (TV 1977), *Airplane* (1980), *Hot Shots!* (1991), *Honey, I Blew Up the Kid* (1992), *Hot Shots! Part Deux* (1993).

Broderick, Matthew (1962–) American, born New York City; *War Games* (1983), *Ladyhawke* (1984), *Ferris Bueller's Day Off* (1986), *Biloxi Blues* (1988), *Torch Song Trilogy* (1988), *Family Business* (1989), *Glory* (1989), *The Freshman* (1990), *The Cable Guy* (1996), *Inspector Gadget* (1999), *The Producers* (2005), *Then She Found Me* (2007).

Bronson, Charles (Charles Buchinski) (1921– 2003) American, born Ehrenfield, Pennsylvania; *Drumbeat* (1954), *Vera Cruz* (1954), *The Magnificent Seven* (1960), *The Dirty Dozen* (1967), *The Mechanic* (1972), *The Valachi Papers* (1972), *Death Wish* (1974), *Hard Times* (1975), *Telefon* (1977), *Death Wish II* (1982), *Death Wish III* (1985), *Death Wish IV* (1987), *Murphy's Law* (1987), *The Indian Runner* (1991), *Death Wish V* (1993).

Brooks, Louise (Leslie Gettman) (1906–85) American, born Cherryvale, Kansas; *Pandora's Box* (1929), *Diary of a Lost Girl* (1930).

Brooks, Mel (Melvin Kaminski) (1926–) American, born New York City; *Blazing Saddles* (1974), *Silent Movie* (1976), *High Anxiety* (1978), *History of the World: Part One* (1981), *Spaceballs* (1987), *Robin Hood: Men in Tights* (1993), *Dracula: Dead and Loving It* (1995), *Svitati* (1999).

Brown, Bryan (1947–) Australian, born Panania; *A Town Like Alice* (TV 1981), *The Thorn Birds* (TV 1983), *Eureka Stockade* (TV 1985), *F/X: Murder by Illusion* (1985), *Rebel* (1985), *Taipan* (1985), *The Shiralee* (TV 1987), *Cocktail* (1988), *Gorillas in the Mist* (1988), *Dead Heart* (1996), *Risk* (2000).

Brynner, Yul (1915–85) Swiss–Russian, naturalized American, born Sakhalin, Siberia; *The King and I* (1956), *The Brothers Karamazov* (1958), *The Magnificent Seven* (1960), *Return of the Seven* (1966).

Bullock, Sandra (Annette) (1964–) American, born Arlington, Virginia; *Demolition Man* (1993), *Speed* (1994), *While You Were Sleeping* (1995), *Forces of Nature* (1999), *Miss Congeniality* (2000), *Murder by Numbers* (2002), *Crash* (2004), *The Lake House* (2006).

Burton, Richard (Richard Walter Jenkins) (1925– 84) British, born Pontrhydyfen, S Wales: *My Cousin Rachel* (1952), *Alexander the Great* (1956), *Look Back in Anger* (1959), *Cleopatra* (1962), *The Night of the Iguana* (1964), *The Spy Who Came in from the Cold* (1965), *Who's Afraid of Virginia Woolf?* (1966), *The Taming of the Shrew* (1967), *Where Eagles Dare* (1969), *Equus* (1977), *Exorcist II: The Heretic* (1977), *Absolution* (1979), *1984* (1984).

Caan, James (1939–) American, born The Bronx, New York City; *Brian's Song* (TV 1971), *The Godfather* (1972), *The Godfather, Part II* (1974), *Rollerball* (1975), *A Bridge Too Far* (1977), *Alien Nation* (1989), *Misery* (1990), *Eraser* (1996), *Mickey Blue Eyes* (1999), *Las Vegas* (TV 2003–7).

Cage, Nicolas (Nicholas Coppola) (1964–) American, born Long Beach, California; *Rumblefish* (1983), *The Cotton Club* (1984), *Birdy* (1985), *Peggy Sue Got Married* (1986), *Raising Arizona* (1987), *Moonstruck* (1987), *Vampire's Kiss* (1988), *Wild at Heart* (1990), *Leaving Las Vegas* (1995), *The Rock* (1996), *Con Air* (1997), *Face Off* (1997), *Snake Eyes* (1998), *Gone in Sixty Seconds* (2000), *Captain Corelli's Mandolin* (2001), *Adaptation* (2002), *World Trade Center* (2006), *Bangkok Dangerous* (2008).

Cagney, James (Francis Jr) (1899–1986) American, born New York City; *Public Enemy* (1931), *Lady Killer* (1933), *A Midsummer Night's Dream* (1935), *The Roaring Twenties* (1939), *Yankee Doodle Dandy* (1942), *White Heat* (1949), *Love Me or Leave Me* (1955), *Mister Roberts* (1955), *One, Two, Three* (1961), *Ragtime* (1981).

Caine, Sir Michael (Maurice Micklewhite) (1933–) British, born London; *Zulu* (1963), *The Ipcress File* (1965), *Alfie* (1966), *The Italian Job* (1969), *Sleuth* (1972), *The Man Who Would Be King* (1975), *The Eagle Has Landed* (1976), *California Suite* (1978), *Dressed to Kill* (1980), *Death Trap* (1983), *Educating Rita* (1983), *Hannah and Her Sisters* (1986), *Bullseye* (1990), *Noises Off* (1992), *Blue Ice* (1992), *Blood and Wine* (1996), *Little Voice* (1998), *The Cider House Rules* (1999), *The Quiet American* (2002), *The Prestige* (2006), *Sleuth* (2007).

Callow, Simon (1949–) British, born London; *Amadeus* (1984), *A Room With a View* (1985), *Maurice* (1987), *Four Weddings and a Funeral* (1994), *Shakespeare in Love* (1998), *The Phantom of the Opera* (2004).

Cardinale, Claudia (1939–) Italian, born Tunis, Tunisia; *The Pink Panther* (1963), *Once Upon a Time in the West* (1969), *Escape to Athena* (1979), *Fitzcarraldo* (1982), *A Man in Love* (1987), *Torrents of Spring* (1988), *Son of the Pink Panther* (1993).

Carlyle, Robert (1961–) British, born Glasgow; *Riff Raff* (1990), *Priest* (1994), *Hamish Macbeth* (TV 1994–7), *Carla's Song* (1996), *Trainspotting* (1996), *The Full Monty* (1997), *Face* (1997), *Angela's Ashes* (1999), *The Beach* (2000), *Human Trafficking* (TV 2005), *Eragon* (2006), *28 Weeks Later* (2007).

Caron, Leslie (Claire Margaret) (1931–) French, born Boulogne-Billancourt, near Paris; *An American in Paris* (1951), *Lili* (1953), *The Glass Slipper* (1954), *Daddy Long Legs* (1955), *Gigi* (1958), *Fanny* (1961), *The L-Shaped Room* (1962), *Father Goose* (1964), *QB VII* (TV 1974), *Chocolat* (2000), *Le Divorce* (2003).

Carradine, John (Richmond Reed Carradine) (1906–88) American, born New York City; *Five Came Back* (1939), *Stagecoach* (1939), *The Grapes of Wrath* (1940), *Bluebeard* (1944), *House of Frankenstein* (1945), *The Man Who Shot Liberty Valance* (1962), *Peggy Sue Got Married* (1986).

Carrey, Jim (James Eugene Carrey) (1962–) Canadian, born Newmarket, Ontario; *Earth Girls Are Easy* (1989), *The Mask* (1994), *Ace Ventura: Pet Detective* (1994), *Dumb and Dumber* (1994), *Batman Forever* (1995), *Liar Liar* (1997), *The Truman Show* (1998), *Man on the Moon* (1999), *Me, Myself and Irene* (2000), *How the Grinch Stole Christmas* (2000), *Eternal Sunshine of the Spotless Mind* (2004), *Fun with Dick and Jane* (2005).

Cassavetes, John (1929–89) American, born New York City; *Johnny Staccato* (TV 1959), *The Dirty Dozen* (1967), *Rosemary's Baby* (1969), *The Fury* (1978), *Minnie and Moskovitz* (1979), *Whose Life is it Anyway?* (1981), *Tempest* (1982).

Chamberlain, Richard (1935–) American, born Beverly Hills, California; *Dr Kildare* (TV 1961–6), *The Music Lovers* (1970), *Lady Caroline Lamb* (1972), *The Three Musketeers* (1973), *The Slipper and the Rose* (1976), *The Man in the Iron Mask* (1977), *The Last Wave* (1978), *Shogun* (TV 1980), *The Thorn Birds* (TV 1983), *Strength and Honour* (2007).

Chaplin, Charlie (Sir Charles Spencer) (1889–1977) British, born London; *The Tramp* (1915), *Easy Street* (1917), *A Dog's Life* (1918), *The Kid* (1921), *The Gold Rush* (1924), *City Lights* (1931), *Modern Times* (1936), *The Great Dictator* (1940), *Monsieur Verdoux* (1947), *Limelight* (1952).

Chaplin, Geraldine (1944–) American, born Santa Monica, California; *Doctor Zhivago* (1965), *The Three Musketeers* (1973), *Nashville* (1975), *White Mischief* (1987), *The Moderns* (1988), *Chaplin* (1992), *The Age of Innocence* (1993), *Jane Eyre* (1996), *Heidi* (2005).

Charisse, Cyd (Tula Ellice Finklea) (1921–2008) American, born Amarillo, Texas; *Ziegfeld Follies* (1946), *Singin' in the Rain* (1952), *The Band Wagon* (1953), *Brigadoon* (1954), *It's Always Fair Weather* (1955), *Invitation to the Dance* (1957), *Two Weeks in Another Town* (1962).

Chase, Chevy (Cornelius Crane Chase) (1943–) American, born New York City; *Foul Play* (1978), *Caddyshack* (1980), *Seems Like Old Times* (1980), *Vacation* (1983), *European Vacation* (1984), *Fletch* (1985), *Spies Like Us* (1985), *The Three Amigos* (1986), *The Couch Trip* (1988), *Caddyshack II* (1988), *Funny Farm* (1988), *Fletch Lives* (1988), *Christmas Vacation* (1989), *Last Action Hero* (1993), *Vegas Vacation* (1997), *Funny Money* (2006).

Cher (Cherilyn Sarkisian La Piere) (1946–) American, born El Centro, California; *Silkwood* (1983), *Mask* (1985), *Moonstruck* (1987), *Suspect* (1987), *The Witches of Eastwick* (1987),

Mermaids (1990), *Faithful* (1995), *Tea with Mussolini* (1999).

Chevalier, Maurice (1888–1972) French, born Paris; *The Innocents of Paris* (1929), *One Hour with You* (1932), *Love Me Tonight* (1932), *The Love Parade* (1932), *Gigi* (1958).

Christie, Julie (1941–) British, born Chukua, Assam, India; *The Fast Lady* (1963), *Billy Liar* (1963), *Doctor Zhivago* (1965), *Darling* (1965), *Fahrenheit 451* (1966), *Far from the Madding Crowd* (1967), *The Go-Between* (1971), *Don't Look Now* (1974), *Shampoo* (1975), *Heaven Can Wait* (1978), *Heat and Dust* (1982), *Power* (1985), *The Gold Diggers* (1988), *Dragon Heart* (1996), *Hamlet* (1996), *Afterglow* (1997), *Finding Neverland* (2004), *Away From Her* (2007).

Clark, Petula (1932–) British, born Epsom, Surrey; *Finian's Rainbow* (1968), *Goodbye Mr Chips* (1969).

Cleese, John (Marwood) (1939–) British, born Weston-super-Mare; *The Frost Report* (TV 1966), *At Last the 1948 Show* (TV 1967), *Monty Python's Flying Circus* (TV 1969–74), *Monty Python and the Holy Grail* (1974), *Fawlty Towers* (TV 1975, 1979), *Life of Brian* (1979), *The Meaning of Life* (1983), *Clockwise* (1985), *A Fish Called Wanda* (1988), *Fierce Creatures* (1996), *The World is Not Enough* (1999), *Harry Potter and the Philosopher's Stone* (2001), *Harry Potter and the Chamber of Secrets* (2002), *Die Another Day* (2002), *Man About Town* (2006).

Clift, (Edward) Montgomery (1920–66) American, born Omaha, Nebraska; *Red River* (1946), *The Search* (1948), *A Place in the Sun* (1951), *From Here to Eternity* (1953), *Suddenly Last Summer* (1959), *Freud* (1962).

Clooney, George (Timothy) (1961–) American, born Lexington, Kentucky; *ER* (TV 1994–2000), *From Dusk to Dawn* (1996), *O Brother, Where Art Thou* (2000), *The Perfect Storm* (2000), *Ocean's Eleven* (2001), *Confessions of a Dangerous Mind* (2002), *Ocean's Twelve* (2004), *Syriana* (2005), *Good Night and Good Luck* (2005), *Ocean's Thirteen* (2007), *Burn After Reading* (2008).

Close, Glenn (1947–) American, born Greenwich, Connecticut; *The World According to Garp* (1982), *The Big Chill* (1983), *The Natural* (1984), *Jagged Edge* (1985), *Maxie* (1985), *Fatal Attraction* (1987), *Dangerous Liaisons* (1988), *Reversal of Fortune* (1990), *Hamlet* (1990), *Meeting Venus* (1991), *Hook* (1991), *The Paper* (1994), *Mary Reilly* (1996), *101 Dalmatians* (1996), *Mars Attacks!* (1996), *Cookie's Fortune* (1999), *The Stepford Wives* (2004).

Cobb, Lee J (Lee Jacoby) (1911–76) American, born New York City; *Golden Boy* (1939), *The Moon is Down* (1943), *Anna and the King of Siam* (1946), *The Dark Past* (1948), *On the Waterfront* (1954), *The Man in the Gray Flannel Suit* (1956), *Twelve Angry Men* (1957), *The Brothers Karamazov* (1958), *The Virginian* (TV 1962–6), *Come Blow Your Horn* (1963), *Death of a Salesman* (TV 1966), *Coogan's Bluff* (1968), *The Young Lawyers* (TV 1970–1), *The Exorcist* (1973).

Coburn, James (1928–2002) American, born Laurel, Nebraska; *The Magnificent Seven* (1960), *The Great Escape* (1963), *Charade* (1963), *Our Man Flint* (1966), *In Like Flint* (1966), *A Fistful of Dynamite* (1971), *California Suite* (1978), *Young Guns II* (1990), *Sister Act 2: Back in the Habit* (1993), *Maverick* (1995), *Eraser* (1996).

Collins, Joan (Henrietta) (1933–) British, born London; *Lady Godiva Rides Again* (1951), *The Virgin Queen* (1955), *The Bitch* (1979), *Dynasty*

Arts and Culture

(TV 1981–9), *Decadence* (1993), *In the Bleak Midwinter* (1995).

Coltrane, Robbie (Anthony Robert McMillan) (1950–) British, born Rutherglen, Glasgow; *Mona Lisa* (1986), *The Fruit Machine* (1987), *Tutti Frutti* (TV 1987), *Henry V* (1989), *Nuns on the Run* (1990), *The Pope Must Die* (1991), *Cracker* (TV 1993–6), *Golden Eye* (1995), *The World is Not Enough* (1999), *Harry Potter* series (2001–), *Ocean's Twelve* (2004),

Connery, Sir (Thomas) Sean (1930–) British, born Edinburgh; *Dr No* (1963), *Marnie* (1964), *From Russia With Love* (1964), *Goldfinger* (1965), *Thunderball* (1965), *You Only Live Twice* (1967), *The Molly Maguires* (1969), *The Anderson Tapes* (1970), *Diamonds are Forever* (1971), *Zardoz* (1973), *Murder on the Orient Express* (1974), *The Man Who Would Be King* (1975), *Robin and Marian* (1976), *Meteor* (1979), *Time Bandits* (1981), *Never Say Never Again* (1983), *Highlander* (1985), *The Name of the Rose* (1986), *The Untouchables* (1987), *The Presidio* (1988), *Indiana Jones and the Last Crusade* (1989), *The Hunt for Red October* (1990), *The Russia House* (1990), *Medicine Man* (1991), *Rising Sun* (1992), *Dreadnought* (1992), *Broken Dreams* (1992), *First Knight* (1995), *The Rock* (1996), *Entrapment* (1999), *The League of Extraordinary Gentlemen* (2003).

Conti, Tom (1941–) British, born Paisley; *Glittering Prizes* (TV 1976), *Merry Christmas Mr Lawrence* (1983), *Reuben Reuben* (1983), *Saving Grace* (1984), *Miracles* (1985), *Heavenly Pursuits* (1985), *Shirley Valentine* (1989), *Out of Control* (1998), *Rabbit Fever* (2006).

Cooper, Gary (Frank J Cooper) (1901–61) American, born Helena, Montana; *The Winning of Barbara Worth* (1926), *The Virginian* (1929), *A Farewell to Arms* (1932), *City Streets* (1932), *The Lives of a Bengal Lancer* (1935), *Sergeant York* (1941), *For Whom the Bell Tolls* (1943), *The Fountainhead* (1949), *High Noon* (1952), *Friendly Persuasion* (1956).

Costner, Kevin (1955–) American, born Los Angeles; *Silverado* (1985), *The Untouchables* (1987), *No Way Out* (1987), *Bull Durham* (1988), *Field of Dreams* (1989), *Revenge* (1990), *Dances with Wolves* (1990), *Robin Hood: Prince of Thieves* (1991), *JFK* (1991), *The Bodyguard* (1992), *A Perfect World* (1993), *The War* (1994), *Waterworld* (1995), *Tin Cup* (1996), *Message in a Bottle* (1999), *The Upside of Anger* (2005).

Cotten, Joseph (1905–94) American, born Petersburg, Virginia; *Citizen Kane* (1941), *The Magnificent Ambersons* (1942), *Journey into Fear* (1942), *Shadow of a Doubt* (1943), *Portrait of Jennie* (1948), *The Third Man* (1949), *Niagara* (1952), *Tora! Tora! Tora!* (1971).

Courtenay, Tom (1937–) British, born Hull; *The Loneliness of the Long Distance Runner* (1962), *Billy Liar* (1963), *Doctor Zhivago* (1965), *The Dresser* (1983), *Let Him Have It* (1991), *Last Orders* (2001), *Nicholas Nickleby* (2002), *The Golden Compass* (2007).

Crawford, Joan (Lucille Le Sueur) (1906–77) American, born San Antonio, Texas; *Our Dancing Daughters* (1928), *Our Blushing Brides* (1933), *Dancing Lady* (1933), *The Women* (1939), *Mildred Pierce* (1945), *Possessed* (1947), *What Ever Happened to Baby Jane?* (1962), *Trog* (1970).

Crosby, Bing (Harry Lillis Crosby) (1903–77) American, born Tacoma, Washington; *King of Jazz* (1930), *Mississippi* (1935), *Road to Singapore* (1940), *Road to Zanzibar* (1941), *Holiday Inn*

(1942), *Road to Morocco* (1942), *Going My Way* (1944), *The Bells of St Mary's* (1945), *Blue Skies* (1946), *A Connecticut Yankee in King Arthur's Court* (1949), *White Christmas* (1954), *The Country Girl* (1954), *High Society* (1956), *Road to Hong Kong* (1962).

Crowe, Russell (Ira) (1964–) New Zealander, born Wellington; *Romper Stomper* (1992), *LA Confidential* (1997), *The Insider* (1999), *Gladiator* (2000), *A Beautiful Mind* (2001), *Master and Commander* (2003), *Cinderella Man* (2005), *American Gangster* (2007).

Cruise, Tom (Tom Cruise Mapother IV) (1962–) American, born Syracuse, New York; *Top Gun* (1985), *The Color of Money* (1986), *Cocktail* (1988), *Rain Man* (1988), *Born on the Fourth of July* (1989), *Days of Thunder* (1990), *Far and Away* (1992), *A Few Good Men* (1992), *The Firm* (1993), *Interview with the Vampire* (1994), *Mission: Impossible* (1996), *Jerry Maguire* (1996), *Eyes Wide Shut* (1999), *Mission: Impossible 2* (2000), *Vanilla Sky* (2001), *Minority Report* (2002), *Collateral* (2004), *Mission: Impossible 3* (2006), *Valkyrie* (2008).

Cruz, Penélope (Penélope Cruz Sánchez) (1974–) Spanish, born Madrid; *Belle Epoque* (1992), *All About My Mother* (1999), *All the Pretty Horses* (2000), *Vanilla Sky* (2001), *Captain Corelli's Mandolin* (2001), *Blow* (2001), *Non ti muovere* (2004), *Sahara* (2005), *Volver* (2006), *Elegy* (2008).

Crystal, Billy (1947–) American, born Long Beach, New York; *This Is Spinal Tap* (1984), *Throw Momma from the Train* (1987), *The Princess Bride* (1987), *When Harry Met Sally ...* (1989), *City Slickers* (1991), *Mr Saturday Night* (1992), *Hamlet* (1996), *Analyze This* (1999), *Analyze That* (2002).

Culp, Robert (1930–) American, born Oakland, California; *I Spy* (TV 1965–7), *Bob and Carol and Ted and Alice* (1969), *The Greatest American Hero* (TV 1981–2), *The Gladiator* (TV 1986), *The Pelican Brief* (1993), *Everybody Loves Raymond* (TV 1996–2004).

Curtis, Jamie Lee (1958–) American, born Los Angeles; *Operation Petticoat* (TV 1978), *Halloween* (1979), *The Fog* (1980), *Halloween II* (1981), *Love Letters* (1983), *Trading Places* (1983), *Perfect* (1985), *A Fish Called Wanda* (1988), *Dominick and Eugene* (1988), *Blue Steel* (1990), *My Girl* (1991), *Fierce Creatures* (1996), *Virus* (1999), *The Tailor of Panama* (2001), *Freaky Friday* (2003).

Curtis, Tony (Bernard Schwartz) (1925–) American, born New York City; *Houdini* (1953), *Trapeze* (1956), *The Vikings* (1958), *Some Like it Hot* (1959), *Spartacus* (1960), *The Boston Strangler* (1968), *The Persuaders* (TV 1971–2), *Insignificance* (1985).

Cusack, Cyril (James) (1910–93) Irish, born Durban, South Africa; *Odd Man Out* (1947), *The Blue Lagoon* (1949), *The Spy Who Came in From the Cold* (1965), *Fahrenheit 451* (1966), *Day of the Jackal* (1973), *1984* (1984), *Little Dorrit* (1987), *My Left Foot* (1989), *The Fool* (1990).

Cushing, Peter (1913–94) British, born Kenley, Surrey; *The Man in the Iron Mask* (1939), *Hamlet* (1948), *1984* (TV 1955), *The Curse of Frankenstein* (1957), *Dracula* (1958), *The Mummy* (1959), *The Hound of the Baskervilles* (1959), *Dr Who and the Daleks* (1965), *Sherlock Holmes* (TV 1968), *Tales from the Crypt* (1972), *Horror Express* (1972), *Star Wars* (1977), *Biggles* (1986).

Dafoe, Willem (1955–) American, born Appleton, Wisconsin; *Platoon* (1986), *The Last Temptation of Christ* (1988), *Mississippi Burning* (1988), *Wild At Heart* (1990), *Body of Evidence* (1992), *Tom and*

Viv (1994), Clear and Present Danger (1994), The English Patient (1996), eXistenZ (1999), Spider-Man (2002), Inside Man (2006).

Dalton, Timothy (1944–) British, born Colwyn Bay, Wales; The Lion in Winter (1968), Mary Queen of Scots (1971), Agatha (1979), Flash Gordon (1980), Centennial (TV 1981–2), The Living Daylights (1987), License to Kill (1989), The Rocketeer (1991), Hot Fuzz (2007).

Damon, Matt (Matthew Paige Damon) (1970–) American, born Cambridge, Massachusetts; Good Will Hunting (1997), Saving Private Ryan (1998), The Talented Mr Ripley (1999), All the Pretty Horses (2000), Ocean's Eleven (2001), Confessions of a Dangerous Mind (2002), The Bourne Supremacy (2004), Ocean's Twelve (2004), The Departed (2006), The Bourne Ultimatum (2007).

Dance, Charles (1946–) British, born Rednal, Worcestershire; For Your Eyes Only (1981), The Jewel in the Crown (TV 1984), The Golden Child (1985), Plenty (1985), Good Morning Babylon (1987), White Mischief (1987), Pascali's Island (1988), Phantom of the Opera (TV 1990), Last Action Hero (1993), Hilary and Jackie (1998), Gosford Park (2001), Bleak House (TV 2005).

Daniels, Jeff (1955–) American, born Athens, Georgia; Terms of Endearment (1983), The Purple Rose of Cairo (1985), Arachnophobia (1990), Speed (1994), Dumb and Dumber (1994), The Hours (2002), The Squid and the Whale (2005), Good Night and Good Luck (2005).

Danson, Ted (1947–) American, born San Diego, California; The Onion Field (1979), Body Heat (1981), Cheers (TV 1982–93), Creepshow (1982), Three Men and a Baby (1988), Cousins (1989), Dad (1990), Three Men and a Little Lady (1990), Made In America (1993), Loch Ness (1995), Saving Private Ryan (1998), Mad Money (2008).

Davenport, Nigel (1928–) British, born Shelford, Cambridge; A Man for All Seasons (1966), The Virgin Soldiers (1969), Living Free (1972), The Island of Dr Moreau (1977), Longitude (2000).

Davis, Bette (1908–89) American, born Lowell, Massachusetts; Dangerous (1935), Jezebel (1938), The Great Lie (1941), All About Eve (1950), What Ever Happened to Baby Jane? (1962), Strangers (TV 1979), The Whales of August (1987).

Davis, Geena (1956–) American, born Wareham, Massachusetts; Tootsie (1982), Fletch (1985), The Fly (1986), Beetlejuice (1988), The Accidental Tourist (1989), Earth Girls Are Easy (1989), Thelma and Louise (1991), A League of Their Own (1993), The Long Kiss Goodnight (1996), The Commander in Chief (TV 2005–6).

Davis, Judy (1955–) Australian, born Perth; My Brilliant Career (1979), Who Dares Wins (1982), A Passage to India (1987), High Tide (1987), Naked Lunch (1991), Barton Fink (1991), Husbands and Wives (1992), Deconstructing Harry (1997), The Man Who Sued God (2001), Swimming Upstream (2003), Marie Antoinette (2006).

Day, Doris (Doris von Kappelhoff) (1924–) American, born Cincinnati, Ohio; Romance on the High Seas (1948), Calamity Jane (1953), Young at Heart (1954), Love Me or Leave Me (1955), The Pajama Game (1957), Pillow Talk (1959), That Touch of Mink (1962), With Six You Get Egg Roll (1968), The Doris Day Show (TV 1968–73).

Day-Lewis, Daniel (1958–) Irish, born London; Gandhi (1982), My Beautiful Laundrette (1985), Room with a View (1985), The Unbearable Lightness of Being (1988), My Left Foot (1989), The Last of the Mohicans (1992), The Age of Innocence

(1993), In the Name of the Father (1993), The Crucible (1996), The Boxer (1998), Gangs of New York (2002), There Will Be Blood (2007).

Dean, James (Byron) (1931–55) American, born Fairmount, Indiana; East of Eden (1955), Rebel without a Cause (1955), Giant (1956).

De Havilland, Olivia (1916–) British, born Tokyo, Japan; Midsummer Night's Dream (1935), The Adventures of Robin Hood (1938), Gone with the Wind (1939), The Dark Mirror (1946), The Heiress (1949), My Cousin Rachel (1952).

De Mornay, Rebecca (1962–) American, born Los Angeles; Risky Business (1984), Runaway Train (1985), And God Created Woman (1988), Feds (1988), Backdraft (1991), The Hand that Rocks the Cradle (1992), Wedding Crashers (2005).

Dench, Dame Judi (Judith Olivia Dench) (1934–) British, born York; A Fine Romance (TV 1981–4), A Room With a View (1985), 84 Charing Cross Road (1987), Henry V (1989), Jack and Sarah (1995), Hamlet (1996), Mrs Brown (1997), Shakespeare in Love (1998), Tea with Mussolini (1999), Chocolat (2000), Iris (2001), The Shipping News (2001), Mrs Henderson Presents (2005), Casino Royale (2006), Notes on a Scandal (2006), Cranford (TV 2007).

Deneuve, Catherine (Catherine Dorleac) (1943–) French, born Paris; Les Parapluies de Cherbourg (1964), Repulsion (1965), Belle de Jour (1967), Tristana (1970), The Hunger (1983), Indochine (1991), Les Voleurs (1996), Dancer in the Dark (2000), 8 Women (2002), Palais Royale (2005).

De Niro, Robert (1943–) American, born New York City; Mean Streets (1973), The Godfather, Part II (1974), 1900 (1976), Taxi Driver (1976), The Deer Hunter (1978), Raging Bull (1980), King of Comedy (1982), Brazil (1985), Angel Heart (1987), The Untouchables (1987), Midnight Run (1988), Stanley & Iris (1989), We're No Angels (1990), Goodfellas (1990), Awakenings (1990), Backdraft (1991), Cape Fear (1991), Mad Dog and Glory (1992), This Boy's Life (1992), Frankenstein (1994), Casino (1995), Heat (1995), Sleepers (1996), Jackie Brown (1998), Ronin (1998), Analyze This (1999), Meet the Parents (2000), Analyze That (2002), Meet The Fockers (2004), The Good Shepherd (2006).

Depardieu, Gérard (1948–) French, born Châteauroux; Get Out Your Handkerchiefs (1977), The Last Metro (1980), The Return of Martin Guerre (1981), Danton (1982), Police (1985), Jean de Florette (1986), The Woman Next Door (1987), Cyrano de Bergerac (1990), Green Card (1990), Mon Père, Ce Héros (1991), Tous les Matins du Monde (1991), Christopher Columbus (1992), Germinal (1992), Le Colonel Chabert (1994), Les Anges Gardiens (1995), Unhook the Stars (1996), Hamlet (1996), The Man in the Iron Mask (1998), The Closet (2001), La Vie en Rose (2007).

Depp, Johnny (1963–) American, born Owensboro, Kentucky; Nightmare on Elm Street (1984), Platoon (1986), Edward Scissorhands (1990), What's Eating Gilbert Grape? (1993), Ed Wood (1994), Fear and Loathing in Las Vegas (1998), Sleepy Hollow (1999), Blow (2001), Pirates of the Caribbean (2003), Finding Neverland (2004), The Libertine (2004), Charlie and the Chocolate Factory (2005), Sweeney Todd (2007).

Dern, Bruce (MacLeish) (1936–) American, born Chicago; Marnie (1964), They Shoot Horses Don't They? (1969), Silent Running (1972), The Great Gatsby (1974), Coming Home (1978), The Driver (1978), That Championship Season (1982), 1969 (1988), The 'Burbs (1989), After Dark My Sweet

Arts and Culture

(1990), *Last Man Standing* (1996), *The Haunting* (1999), *Believe in Me* (2006).

Dern, Laura (Elizabeth) (1966–) American, born California; *Mask* (1985), *Blue Velvet* (1986), *Wild at Heart* (1990), *Rambling Rose* (1991), *Jurassic Park* (1993), *Citizen Ruth* (1996), *Dr T and the Women* (2000), *We Don't Live Here Anymore* (2004), *Inland Empire* (2006).

DeVito, Danny (1944–) American, born Neptune, New Jersey; *One Flew Over the Cuckoo's Nest* (1975), *Taxi* (TV 1978–82), *Romancing the Stone* (1983), *Terms of Endearment* (1984), *The Jewel of the Nile* (1985), *Ruthless People* (1986), *Throw Momma from the Train* (1987), *Twins* (1988), *War of the Roses* (1989), *Batman Returns* (1992), *Renaissance Man* (1994), *Junior* (1994), *Get Shorty* (1995), *Matilda* (1996), *LA Confidential* (1997), *Man on the Moon* (1999), *Big Fish* (2003).

Diaz, Cameron (Michelle) (1972–) American, born San Diego, California; *The Mask* (1994), *My Best Friend's Wedding* (1997), *There's Something About Mary* (1998), *Any Given Sunday* (1999), *Being John Malkovich* (1999), *Charlie's Angels* (2000), *Shrek* (2001), *Vanilla Sky* (2001), *Gangs of New York* (2002), *The Holiday* (2006).

DiCaprio, Leonardo (Wilhelm) (1974–) American, born Hollywood; *This Boy's Life* (1993), *What's Eating Gilbert Grape* (1993), *Total Eclipse* (1995), *Romeo and Juliet* (1996), *Titanic* (1997), *The Beach* (2000), *Gangs of New York* (2002), *Catch Me If You Can* (2002), *The Aviator* (2004), *The Departed* (2006), *Blood Diamond* (2006), *Revolutionary Road* (2008).

Dietrich, Marlene (Maria Magdalena von Losch) (1901–92) German–American, born Berlin; *The Blue Angel* (1930), *Morocco* (1930), *Blond Venus* (1932), *Shanghai Express* (1932), *The Scarlet Empress* (1934), *The Devil is a Woman* (1935), *Desire* (1936), *Destry Rides Again* (1939), *A Foreign Affair* (1948), *Rancho Notorious* (1952), *Judgement at Nuremberg* (1961).

Dillon, Matt (1964–) American, born Larchmont, New York; *The Outsiders* (1983), *Rumble Fish* (1983), *The Flamingo Kid* (1984), *Target* (1985), *Big Town* (1987), *Drugstore Cowboy* (1989), *A Kiss Before Dying* (1991), *Singles* (1992), *Mr Wonderful* (1994), *Albino Alligator* (1996), *Wild Things* (1998), *One Night At McCool's* (2001), *Crash* (2004), *You, Me and Dupree* (2006).

Donat, Robert (1905–58) British, born Manchester; *The Count of Monte Cristo* (1934), *The Thirty-Nine Steps* (1935), *The Citadel* (1938), *Goodbye Mr Chips* (1939), *The Winslow Boy* (1948), *The Inn of the Sixth Happiness* (1958).

Donohoe, Amanda (1962–) British, born London; *Castaway* (1987), *The Lair of the White Worm* (1988), *The Rainbow* (1989), *LA Law* (TV 1990–2), *Paper Mask* (1990), *The Madness of King George* (1994), *Liar Liar* (1997), *Wild About Harry* (2000).

Dors, Diana (Diana Fluck) (1931–84) British, born Swindon, Wiltshire; *Oliver Twist* (1948), *Yield to the Night* (1956), *Deep End* (1970), *There's a Girl in My Soup* (1970), *The Amazing Mr Blunden* (1972), *Theatre of Blood* (1973), *Steaming* (1984).

Douglas, Kirk (Issur Danielovitch Demsky) (1916–) American, born Amsterdam, New York; *The Strange Love of Martha Ivers* (1946), *Lust for Life* (1956), *Gunfight at the OK Corral* (1957), *Paths of Glory* (1957), *The Vikings* (1958), *Spartacus* (1960), *The Man from Snowy River* (1982), *Oscar* (1991), *Greedy* (1994), *Diamonds* (1999).

Douglas, Michael (1944–) American, born New Brunswick, New Jersey; *The Streets of San Francisco* (TV 1972–5), *The China Syndrome* (1980), *The Star Chamber* (1983), *Romancing the Stone* (1984), *The Jewel of the Nile* (1985), *Fatal Attraction* (1987), *Wall Street* (1987), *Black Rain* (1989), *War of the Roses* (1989), *Shining Through* (1991), *Basic Instinct* (1992), *Falling Down* (1993), *Disclosure* (1994), *The Ghost and the Darkness* (1996), *The Game* (1997), *A Perfect Murder* (1998), *Traffic* (2000), *Wonder Boys* (2000), *The Sentinel* (2006).

Dreyfuss, Richard (1947–) American, born Brooklyn, New York City; *American Graffiti* (1973), *Jaws* (1975), *Close Encounters of the Third Kind* (1977), *The Goodbye Girl* (1977), *Whose Life is it Anyway?* (1981), *Down and Out in Beverly Hills* (1986), *Stakeout* (1987), *Tin Men* (1987), *Always* (1989), *What About Bob?* (1991), *Rosencrantz and Guildernstern are Dead* (1991), *Lost in Yonkers* (1993), *Another Stakeout* (1993), *The American President* (1995), *Trigger Happy* (1996), *Poseidon* (2006).

Dunaway, (Dorothy) Faye (1941–) American, born Bascom, Florida; *Bonnie and Clyde* (1967), *Little Big Man* (1970), *Chinatown* (1974), *The Towering Inferno* (1974), *Network* (1976), *The Eyes of Laura Mars* (1978), *The Champ* (1979), *Mommie Dearest* (1981), *Barfly* (1987), *Burning Secret* (1988), *The Handmaid's Tale* (1990), *Scorchers* (1991), *Silhouette* (TV 1991), *Don Juan de Marco* (1995), *Albino Alligator* (1996), *The Thomas Crown Affair* (1999).

Durbin, Deanna (Edna Mae Durbin) (1921–) Canadian, born Winnipeg, Manitoba; *Three Smart Girls* (1936), *One Hundred Men and a Girl* (1937), *Mad About Music* (1938), *Three Smart Girls Grow Up* (1939), *It Started With Eve* (1941), *Christmas Holiday* (1944), *Lady on a Train* (1945).

Duvall, Robert (1930–) American, born San Diego, California; *To Kill a Mockingbird* (1962), *The Godfather* (1972), *The Godfather, Part II* (1974), *Apocalypse Now* (1979), *The Great Santini* (1980), *Tender Mercies* (1983), *The Natural* (1984), *Colors* (1988), *The Handmaid's Tale* (1990), *Days of Thunder* (1990), *Newsies* (1992), *Geronimo* (1993), *The Paper* (1994), *The Scarlet Letter* (1995), *Phenomenon* (1996), *The Apostle* (1997), *A Civil Action* (1998), *John Q* (2002), *We Own the Night* (2007).

Duvall, Shelley (1949–) American, born Houston, Texas; *Thieves Like Us* (1974), *Annie Hall* (1977), *The Shining* (1980), *Popeye* (1980), *Roxanne* (1987), *Suburban Commando* (1991), *The Portrait of a Lady* (1996), *Home Fries* (1998).

Eastwood, Clint (1930–) American, born San Francisco, California; *Rawhide* (TV 1958–65), *A Fistful of Dollars* (1964), *For a Few Dollars More* (1965), *The Good, The Bad, and the Ugly* (1966), *Coogan's Bluff* (1968), *Paint Your Wagon* (1969), *Where Eagles Dare* (1969), *Play Misty for Me* (1971), *Dirty Harry* (1972), *High Plains Drifter* (1973), *Magnum Force* (1973), *The Enforcer* (1976), *Every Which Way But Loose* (1978), *Escape from Alcatraz* (1979), *Sudden Impact* (1983), *Heartbreak Ridge* (1986), *The Dead Pool* (1989), *The Rookie* (1990), *Unforgiven* (1992), *In the Line of Fire* (1993), *A Perfect World* (1993), *The Bridges of Madison County* (1995), *Absolute Power* (1997), *True Crime* (1999), *Mystic River* (2003), *Million Dollar Baby* (2004).

Eden, Barbara (Barbara Huffman) (1934–) American, born Tucson, Arizona; *Voyage to the Bottom of the Sea* (1961), *I Dream of Jeannie* (TV 1965–70), *Harper Valley PTA* (1978), *Harper Valley PTA* (TV 1981).

Ekberg, Anita (1931–) Swedish, born Malmö; *La Dolce Vita* (1959), *The Summer is Short* (1962), *Bambola* (1996).

Ekland, Britt (Britt-Marie Ekland) (1942–) Swedish, born Stockholm; *The Man with the Golden Gun* (1974), *Casanova* (1977), *Scandal* (1989), *Beverly Hills Vamp* (1988).

Elliott, Denholm (1922–92) British, born London; *Here We Go Round the Mulberry Bush* (1967), *A Bridge too Far* (1977), *Raiders of the Lost Ark* (1981), *Brimstone and Treacle* (1982), *Trading Places* (1983), *The Razor's Edge* (1984), *A Private Function* (1984), *A Room with a View* (1985), *Maurice* (1987), *Indiana Jones and the Last Crusade* (1989), *Toy Soldiers* (1991).

Estevez, Emilio (1962–) American, born New York City; *The Outsiders* (1983), *Repo Man* (1984), *Breakfast Club* (1984), *St Elmo's Fire* (1985), *Stakeout* (1987), *Young Guns* (1988), *Freejack* (1991), *The Mighty Ducks* (1992), *Judgement Night* (1993), *Bobby* (2006).

Evans, Dame Edith (1888–1976) British, born London; *The Queen of Spades* (1948), *The Importance of Being Earnest* (1951).

Everett, Rupert (1959–) British, born Norfolk; *Another Country* (1984), *Dance with a Stranger* (1985), *The Comfort of Strangers* (1990), *Prêt-À-Porter* (1994), *The Madness of King George* (1994), *My Best Friend's Wedding* (1997), *An Ideal Husband* (1999), *A Midsummer Night's Dream* (1999), *The Importance of Being Earnest* (2002), *Separate Lies* (2005), *St Trinian's* (2007).

Fairbanks, Douglas, Jr (1909–2000) American, born New York City; *Catherine the Great* (1934), *The Prisoner of Zenda* (1937), *Sinbad the Sailor* (1947).

Fairbanks, Douglas, Sr (Douglas Elton Ullman) (1883–1939) American, born Denver, Colorado; *The Mark of Zorro* (1920), *The Three Musketeers* (1921), *Robin Hood* (1922), *The Thief of Baghdad* (1924), *The Black Pirate* (1926).

Falk, Peter (1927–) American, born New York City; *It's a Mad, Mad, Mad, Mad World* (1963), *The Great Race* (1965), *Columbo* (TV 1971–8, 1989–2000), *The Princess Bride* (1987), *Vibes* (1988), *Aunt Julia and the Scriptwriter* (1991), *The Player* (1992), *Undisputed* (2002).

Farrow, Mia (Maria Farrow) (1945–) American, born Los Angeles; *Peyton Place* (TV 1964–7), *Rosemary's Baby* (1968), *The Great Gatsby* (1973), *Death on the Nile* (1978), *A Wedding* (1978), *A Midsummer Night's Sex Comedy* (1982), *The Purple Rose of Cairo* (1985), *Hannah and Her Sisters* (1986), *Another Woman* (1988), *New York Stories* (1989), *Alice* (1991), *Shadows and Fog* (1992), *Husbands and Wives* (1992), *Reckless* (1995), *Coming Soon* (1999), *Be Kind Rewind* (2008).

Fell, Norman (1924–98) American, born Philadelphia, Pennsylvania; *The Graduate* (1967), *Bullitt* (1968), *The Man from UNCLE* (TV 1968), *Three's Company* (TV 1977–8), *The Ropers* (TV 1979–80).

Field, Sally (1946–) American, born Pasadena, California; *Gidget* (TV 1965), *The Flying Nun* (TV 1967–9), *Sybil* (TV 1976), *Stay Hungry* (1976), *Heroes* (1977), *Smokey and the Bandit* (1977), *Hooper* (1978), *Norma Rae* (1979), *Beyond the Poseidon Adventure* (1979), *Smokey and the Bandit II* (1980), *Absence of Malice* (1981), *Places in the Heart* (1984), *Punchline* (1988), *Steel Magnolias* (1990), *Not Without my Daughter* (1991), *Soapdish* (1991), *Mrs Doubtfire* (1993), *Forrest Gump* (1994), *Legally Blonde 2* (2003).

Fields, W C (William Claude Dukenfield) (1879– 1946) American, born Philadelphia, Pennsylvania; *Pool Sharks* (1915), *International House* (1933), *It's a Gift* (1934), *David Copperfield* (1935), *My Little Chickadee* (1940), *The Bank Dick* (1940), *Never Give a Sucker an Even Break* (1941).

Fiennes, Ralph (Ralph Nathaniel Fiennes) (1962–) British, born Ipswich, Suffolk; *Wuthering Heights* (1992), *Schindler's List* (1993), *Quiz Show* (1994), *The English Patient* (1996), *Oscar and Lucinda* (1998), *The End of the Affair* (1999), *Red Dragon* (2002), *The Constant Gardener* (2005), *In Bruges* (2008).

Finch, Peter (Frederick George Peter Ingle Finch) (1916–77) British, born London; *The Shiralee* (1957), *The Nun's Story* (1959), *Far from the Madding Crowd* (1967), *Sunday, Bloody Sunday* (1971), *Network* (1976).

Finney, Albert (1936–) British, born Salford, Lancashire; *The Entertainer* (1960), *Saturday Night and Sunday Morning* (1960), *Tom Jones* (1963), *Charlie Bubbles* (1968), *Murder on the Orient Express* (1974), *Annie* (1982), *The Dresser* (1983), *Under the Volcano* (1984), *The Green Man* (TV 1990), *Miller's Crossing* (1990), *Karaoke* (TV 1996), *Washington Square* (1997), *Erin Brockovich* (2000), *Traffic* (2000), *Big Fish* (2003), *The Bourne Ultimatum* (2007).

Firth, Colin (**Andrew**) (1960–) British, born Grayshott, Hampshire; *Another Country* (1984), *A Month in the Country* (1987), *Valmont* (1989), *Pride and Prejudice* (TV 1995), *Fever Pitch* (1997), *Bridget Jones's Diary* (2001), *The Importance of Being Earnest* (2002), *Girl with a Pearl Earring* (2003), *Bridget Jones: The Edge of Reason* (2004), *And When Did You Last See Your Father?* (2007), *Then She Found Me* (2007), *Mamma Mia!* (2008).

Firth, Peter (1953–) British, born Bradford, Yorkshire; *Equus* (1977), *Tess* (1980), *Life Force* (1985), *Letter to Brezhnev* (1985), *A State of Emergency* (1986), *Amistad* (1997), *Mighty Joe Young* (1998), *The Gathering Storm* (TV 2002), *Spooks* (TV 2002–).

Fisher, Carrie (1956–) American, born Beverly Hills, California; *Shampoo* (1975), *Star Wars* (1977), *The Blues Brothers* (1980), *The Empire Strikes Back* (1980), *Under the Rainbow* (1981), *Return of the Jedi* (1983), *Hannah and Her Sisters* (1986), *The 'Burbs* (1989), *When Harry Met Sally … * (1989), *Loverboy* (1990), *Sibling Rivalry* (1990), *Soapdish* (1991), *This is My Life* (1991), *So I Married an Axe Murderer* (1992), *Scream 3* (2000), *Wonderland* (2003).

Fletcher, Louise (1934–) American, born Birmingham, Alabama; *One Flew Over the Cuckoo's Nest* (1975), *Exorcist II: The Heretic* (1977), *The Cheap Detective* (1978), *Brainstorm* (1983), *Firestarter* (1984), *The Boy Who Could Fly* (1985), *Cruel Intentions* (1999).

Flynn, Errol (1909–59) Australian–American, born Hobart, Tasmania; *Captain Blood* (1935), *The Charge of the Light Brigade* (1936), *The Adventures of Robin Hood* (1938), *The Sea Hawk* (1940), *The Sun Also Rises* (1957).

Fonda, Henry (**James**) (1905–82) American, born Grand Island, Nebraska; *The Moon's Our Home* (1936), *A Farmer Takes A Wife* (1938), *Young Mr Lincoln* (1939), *The Grapes of Wrath* (1940), *The Lady Eve* (1941), *The Oxbow Incident* (1943), *My Darling Clementine* (1946), *Twelve Angry Men* (1957), *Stage Struck* (1957), *Fail Safe* (1964), *The Boston Strangler* (1968), *On Golden Pond* (1981).

Fonda, Jane (**Seymour**) (1937–) American, born New York City; *Walk on the Wild Side* (1961),

Barbarella (1968), *They Shoot Horses, Don't They?* (1969), *Klute* (1971), *Julia* (1977), *Coming Home* (1978), *The Electric Horseman* (1979), *The China Syndrome* (1980), *Nine to Five* (1981), *On Golden Pond* (1981), *The Morning After* (1986), *Old Gringo* (1989), *Stanley and Iris* (1989), *Monster in Law* (2005), *Georgia Rule* (2007).

Fonda, Peter (1939–) American, born New York City; *Easy Rider* (1969), *Futureworld* (1976), *Cannonball Run* (1981), *Mercenary Fighters* (1988), *Escape From LA* (1996), *The Laramie Project* (2002), *Ghost Rider* (2007).

Fontaine, Joan (Joan de Havilland) (1917–) British, born Tokyo, Japan; *Rebecca* (1940), *Suspicion* (1941), *Jane Eyre* (1943), *Frenchman's Creek* (1944), *From This Day Forward* (1946), *Letter from an Unknown Woman* (1948), *Born to Be Bad* (1950).

Ford, Harrison (1942–) American, born Chicago; *American Graffiti* (1973), *Star Wars* (1977), *Force 10 from Navarone* (1978), *The Frisco Kid* (1979), *Hanover Street* (1979), *Apocalypse Now* (1979), *The Empire Strikes Back* (1980), *Raiders of the Lost Ark* (1981), *Blade Runner* (1982), *Return of the Jedi* (1983), *Indiana Jones and the Temple of Doom* (1984), *Witness* (1985), *Mosquito Coast* (1986), *Frantic* (1988), *Working Girl* (1988), *Indiana Jones and the Last Crusade* (1989), *Presumed Innocent* (1990), *Regarding Henry* (1991), *Patriot Games* (1992), *The Fugitive* (1993), *Clear and Present Danger* (1994), *The Devil's Own* (1996), *Random Hearts* (1999), *What Lies Beneath* (2000), *K-19: The Widowmaker* (2002), *Indiana Jones and the Kingdom of the Crystal Skull* (2008).

Foster, Jodie (Alicia Christian Foster) (1962–) American, born Los Angeles, California; *Alice Doesn't Live Here Anymore* (1974), *Bugsy Malone* (1976), *Taxi Driver* (1976), *Candleshoe* (1977), *Freaky Friday* (1977), *The Accused* (1988), *Stealing Home* (1988), *Catchfire* (1990), *Silence of the Lambs* (1991), *Little Man Tate* (1991), *Shadows and Fog* (1992), *Sommersby* (1993), *Maverick* (1994), *Nell* (1994), *Contact* (1997), *Anna and the King* (1999), *Panic Room* (2002), *Flightplan* (2005), *The Brave One* (2007).

Fox, James (1939–) British, born London; *The Magnet* (1950), *The Loneliness of the Long Distance Runner* (1963), *Those Magnificent Men in Their Flying Machines* (1965), *Thoroughly Modern Millie* (1967), *Performance* (1970), *A Passage to India* (1984), *Greystoke* (1984), *The Whistle Blower* (1987), *High Season* (1987), *Hostage* (1992), *Never Ever* (1996), *Mickey Blue Eyes* (1999), *Charlie and the Chocolate Factory* (2005).

Fox, Michael J (1961–) Canadian, born Edmonton, Alberta; *Letters from Frank* (TV 1979), *Family Ties* (TV 1982–9), *Back to the Future* (1985), *Teenwolf* (1985), *The Secret of My Success* (1987), *Bright Lights Big City* (1988), *Casualties of War* (1989), *Back to the Future II* (1989), *Back to the Future III* (1990), *The Hard Way* (1991), *Doc Hollywood* (1991), *For Love or Money* (1993), *Life with Mikey* (1993), *Don't Drink the Water* (TV 1994), *The American President* (1995), *Blue in the Face* (1995), *Mars Attacks!* (1996), *Spin City* (TV 1996–2001), *Boston Legal* (TV 2006).

Freeman, Morgan (1937–) American, born Memphis, Tennessee; *The Electric Company* (TV 1971–6), *Driving Miss Daisy* (1989), *Glory* (1989), *The Bonfire of the Vanities* (1990), *Robin Hood: Prince of Thieves* (1991), *Unforgiven* (1992), *The Shawshank Redemption* (1994), *Se7en* (1995), *Deep Impact* (1998), *The Sum of All Fears* (2002),

Million Dollar Baby (2004), *The Dark Knight* (2008).

Fry, Stephen (John) (1957–) English, born London; *A Handful of Dust* (1988), *A Fish Called Wanda* (1988), *A Bit of Fry and Laurie* (TV 1989– 95), *Jeeves and Wooster* (TV 1990–3), *Peter's Friends* (1992), *Wilde* (1997), *Gosford Park* (2001), *A Cock and Bull Story* (2005).

Gabin, Jean (Jean-Alexis Moncorgé) (1904–76) French, born Paris; *Pepé le Moko* (1936), *La Grande Illusion* (1937), *Quai des Brumes* (1938), *Le Jour se lève* (1939), *Touchez Pas Au Grisbi* (1953), *Archimède Le Clochard* (1958), *Un Singe en Hiver* (1962), *Le Chat* (1971), *L'Année Sainte* (1976).

Gable, (William) Clark (1901–60) American, born Cadiz, Ohio; *Red Dust* (1932), *It Happened One Night* (1934), *Mutiny on the Bounty* (1935), *San Francisco* (1936), *Gone with the Wind* (1939), *The Hucksters* (1947), *Mogambo* (1953), *Teacher's Pet* (1958), *The Misfits* (1961).

Gabor, Zsa Zsa (Sari Gabor) (1918–) Hungarian, born Budapest; *Lovely to Look at* (1952), *Moulin Rouge* (1952), *Lili* (1953), *Public Enemy Number One* (1954), *Queen of Outer Space* (1959), *Up the Front* (1972).

Gambon, Sir Michael (1940–) Irish, born Dublin; *Turtle Diary* (1985), *The Singing Detective* (TV 1986), *Paris by Night* (1989), *The Cook, The Thief, His Wife and Her Lover* (1989), *Sleepy Hollow* (1999), *Gosford Park* (2001), *Harry Potter* series (2004–), *Amazing Grace* (2006).

Garbo, Greta (Greta Lovisa Gustafsson) (1905–90) Swedish–American, born Stockholm; *Flesh and the Devil* (1927), *Anna Christie* (1930), *Grand Hotel* (1932), *Queen Christina* (1933), *Anna Karenina* (1935), *Camille* (1936), *Ninotchka* (1939).

Gardner, Ava (Lucy Johnson) (1922–90) American, born Smithfield, North Carolina; *The Killers* (1946), *The Hucksters* (1947), *Show Boat* (1951), *Pandora and the Flying Dutchman* (1951), *The Snows of Kilimanjaro* (1952), *Mogambo* (1953), *The Barefoot Contessa* (1954), *The Sun Also Rises* (1957), *The Night of the Iguana* (1964).

Garland, Judy (Frances Gumm) (1922–69) American, born Grand Rapids, Minnesota; *The Wizard of Oz* (1939), *Babes in Arms* (1939), *For Me and My Gal* (1942), *Meet Me in St Louis* (1944), *Ziegfeld Follies* (1946), *The Clock* (1945), *Easter Parade* (1948), *Summer Stock* (1950), *A Star is Born* (1954).

Garner, James (James Scott Baumgarner) (1928–) American, born Norman, Oklahoma; *Maverick* (TV 1957–62), *The Great Escape* (1963), *The Americanization of Emily* (1964), *The Skin Game* (1971), *Rockford Files* (TV 1974–80), *The Fan* (1980), *Victor/Victoria* (1982), *Maverick* (1994), *My Fellow Americans* (1996), *Space Cowboys* (2000), *The Notebook* (2004), *The Ultimate Gift* (2006).

Garr, Teri (1949–) American, born Lakewood, Ohio; *Young Frankenstein* (1974), *Oh God* (1977), *Close Encounters of the Third Kind* (1977), *The Black Stallion* (1978), *One from the Heart* (1982), *Tootsie* (1982), *The Sting II* (1982), *Mr Mom* (1983), *First Born* (1984), *After Hours* (1985), *Full Moon in Blue Water* (1988), *Prêt-À-Porter* (1994), *Dumb and Dumber* (1994), *Michael* (1996), *Dick* (1999), *Life Without Dick* (2002).

Gassman, Vittorio (1922–2000) Italian, born Genoa; *Il Cavaliere Misterioso* (1948), *Riso Amaro* (1948), *La Vie est un Roman* (1983), *Sleepers* (1996).

Gere, Richard (1949–) American, born Philadelphia, Pennsylvania; *American Gigolo* (1980), *An Officer and a Gentleman* (1982),

Breathless (1983), *The Cotton Club* (1984), *Internal Affairs* (1990), *Pretty Woman* (1990), *Sommersby* (1993), *First Knight* (1995), *Primal Fear* (1996), *The Jackal* (1997), *Runaway Bride* (1999), *Dr T and the Women* (2000), *The Mothman Prophecies* (2002), *Chicago* (2002), *I'm Not There* (2007).

Gibson, Mel (1956–) American–Australian, born Peekskill, New York; *Tim* (1979), *Mad Max* (1979), *Gallipoli* (1981), *Mad Max 2: The Road Warrior* (1982), *The Year of Living Dangerously* (1982), *Mad Max Beyond Thunderdome* (1985), *Lethal Weapon* (1987), *Tequila Sunrise* (1988), *Lethal Weapon 2* (1989), *Bird on a Wire* (1990), *Air America* (1990), *Hamlet* (1990), *Lethal Weapon 3* (1992), *Forever Young* (1992), *The Man Without A Face* (1993), *Braveheart* (1995), *Ransom* (1996), *Conspiracy Theory* (1997), *The Patriot* (2000), *What Women Want* (2000), *Signs* (2002).

Gielgud, Sir John (Arthur) (1904–2000) British, born London; *Julius Caesar* (1953), *The Charge of the Light Brigade* (1968), *Oh What a Lovely War* (1969), *Murder on the Orient Express* (1974), *Providence* (1977), *Brideshead Revisited* (TV 1981), *Arthur* (1981), *Gandhi* (1982), *Prospero's Books* (1991), *Haunted* (1995), *Hamlet* (1996), *Elizabeth* (1998).

Gish, Lillian (Diana) (Lillian de Guiche) (1893–1993) American, born Springfield, Ohio; *An Unseen Enemy* (1912), *Birth of a Nation* (1915), *Intolerance* (1916), *Broken Blossoms* (1919), *Way Down East* (1920), *Duel in the Sun* (1946), *Night of the Hunter* (1955), *The Whales of August* (1987).

Glover, Danny (1947–) American, born San Francisco, California; *Silverado* (1985), *Witness* (1985), *Lethal Weapon* (1987), *Lethal Weapon 2* (1989), *Predator 2* (1990), *Lethal Weapon 3* (1992), *The Saint of Fort Washington* (1993), *Bopha!* (1993), *Lethal Weapon 4* (1998), *The Patriot* (2000), *The Royal Tenenbaums* (2001), *Saw* (2004).

Goldberg, Whoopi (Caryn Johnson) (1949–) American, born Manhattan, New York City; *The Color Purple* (1985), *Burglar* (1985), *Jumping Jack Flash* (1986), *Ghost* (1990), *Soapdish* (1991), *Sister Act* (1992), *The Player* (1992), *Made in America* (1993), *Sister Act 2: Back in the Habit* (1993), *Corrina Corrina* (1994), *Star Trek: Generations* (1994), *Girl Interrupted* (1999).

Goldblum, Jeff (1952–) American, born Pittsburgh, Pennsylvania; *Death Wish* (1974), *Nashville* (1975), *Invasion of the Body Snatchers* (1978), *The Big Chill* (1983), *Silverado* (1985), *The Fly* (1985), *Vibes* (1988), *The Tall Guy* (1989), *Earth Girls Are Easy* (1989), *Mister Frost* (1990), *The Player* (1992), *Fathers and Sons* (1992), *Jurassic Park* (1993), *Nine Months* (1995), *Independence Day* (1996), *The Lost World: Jurassic Park* (1997), *Cats and Dogs* (2001), *Man of the Year* (2006).

Goodman, John (1952–) American, born St Louis, Missouri; *True Stories* (1986), *The Big Easy* (1987), *Roseanne* (TV 1988–97), *Sea of Love* (1990), *Always* (1990), *Stella* (1990), *Arachnophobia* (1990), *King Ralph* (1991), *The Flintstones* (1994), *Pie in the Sky* (1996), *The Borrowers* (1997), *Blues Brothers 2000* (1998), *The Big Lebowski* (1998), *O Brother, Where Art Thou?* (2000), *One Night At McCool's* (2001), *Speed Racer* (2008).

Granger, Stewart (James Lablanche Stewart) (1913–93) British, born London; *The Man in Grey* (1943), *Waterloo Road* (1944), *Caesar and Cleopatra* (1945), *Captain Boycott* (1947), *King Solomon's Mines* (1950), *Scaramouche* (1952), *The Prisoner*

of Zenda (1952), *Beau Brummell* (1954), *The Wild Geese* (1977).

Grant, Cary (Archibald Alexander Leach) (1904–86) Anglo-American, born Bristol, England; *This is the Night* (1932), *The Awful Truth* (1937), *Bringing Up Baby* (1938), *His Girl Friday* (1940), *Arsenic and Old Lace* (1944), *Notorious* (1946), *To Catch a Thief* (1953), *North by Northwest* (1959).

Grant, Hugh (1960–) British, born London; *Maurice* (1987), *Bitter Moon* (1992), *Four Weddings and a Funeral* (1994), *Nine Months* (1995), *An Awfully Big Adventure* (1995), *Sense and Sensibility* (1995), *Extreme Measures* (1996), *Notting Hill* (1999), *Mickey Blue Eyes* (1999), *Bridget Jones's Diary* (2001), *About A Boy* (2002), *Two Weeks Notice* (2002), *Love Actually* (2003), *Bridget Jones: The Edge of Reason* (2004), *Music and Lyrics* (2007).

Grant, Lee (Lyova Rosenthal) (1927–) American, born New York City; *Detective Story* (1951), *The Landlord* (1970), *Shampoo* (1975), *The Voyage of the Damned* (1976), *Damien: Omen II* (1978), *Big Town* (1987), *It's My Party* (1996), *Dr T and the Women* (2000), *Mulholland Dr.* (2001).

Greenwood, Joan (1921–87) British, born Chelsea, London; *Whisky Galore* (1949), *Kind Hearts and Coronets* (1949), *The Man in the White Suit* (1951), *The Importance of Being Earnest* (1952), *Tom Jones* (1963), *Little Dorrit* (1987).

Griffith, Melanie (1957–) American, born New York City; *Something Wild* (1987), *Working Girl* (1988), *Stormy Monday* (1988), *Pacific Heights* (1990), *Bonfire of the Vanities* (1990), *Paradise* (1991), *Shining Through* (1992), *Born Yesterday* (1993), *Nobody's Fool* (1994), *Lolita* (1996), *Forever Lulu* (2000), *Tempo* (2003).

Griffiths, Richard (1947–) English, born Thornaby-on-Tees; *It Shouldn't Happen to a Vet* (1975), *Pie in the Sky* (TV 1994–7), *Harry Potter* series (2001–), *The History Boys* (2006).

Guinness, Sir Alec (1914–2000) British, born London; *Oliver Twist* (1948), *Kind Hearts and Coronets* (1949), *The Lavender Hill Mob* (1951), *The Man in the White Suit* (1951), *Father Brown* (1954), *The Ladykillers* (1955), *The Bridge on the River Kwai* (1957), *The Horse's Mouth* (1958), *Our Man in Havana* (1960), *Tunes of Glory* (1962), *Lawrence of Arabia* (1962), *Doctor Zhivago* (1966), *Star Wars* (1977), *Tinker, Tailor, Soldier, Spy* (TV 1979), *Smiley's People* (TV 1981), *Return of the Jedi* (1983), *A Passage to India* (1984), *Little Dorrit* (1987).

Guttenberg, Steve (1958–) American, born Massapequa, New York; *Diner* (1981), *Police Academy* (1984), *Police Academy II* (1985), *Cocoon* (1985), *Short Circuit* (1986), *The Bedroom Window* (1986), *Three Men and a Baby* (1988), *High Spirits* (1988), *Three Men and a Little Lady* (1990), *Airborne* (1998), *Veronica Mars* (TV 2005–6).

Gwynne, Fred (1926–93) American, born New York City; *Car 54 Where are You?* (TV 1961–2), *The Munsters* (TV 1964–5), *Munster Go Home* (1966), *The Cotton Club* (1984), *Fatal Attraction* (1987), *Kane and Abel* (TV 1988), *Pet Sematary* (1989), *Shadows and Fog* (1992), *My Cousin Vinny* (1992).

Hackman, Gene (1931–) American, born San Bernardino, California; *Bonnie and Clyde* (1967), *French Connection* (1971), *The Poseidon Adventure* (1972), *Young Frankenstein* (1974), *French Connection II* (1975), *A Bridge Too Far* (1977), *Superman* (1978), *Superman II* (1981), *Target* (1985), *Superman IV* (1987), *Bat 21* (1988), *Full Moon in Blue Water* (1988), *Mississippi Burning* (1989), *The Package* (1989), *Loose Cannons*

(1990), *Postcards from the Edge* (1990), *Class Action* (1990), *Unforgiven* (1992), *The Firm* (1993), *Geronimo* (1993), *Get Shorty* (1995), *The Birdcage* (1996), *The Chamber* (1996), *Extreme Measures* (1996), *Absolute Power* (1997), *Enemy of the State* (1999), *The Royal Tenenbaums* (2001), *Runaway Jury* (2003).

Hagman, Larry (Larry Hageman) (1931–) American, born Fort Worth, Texas; *Ensign Pulver* (1964), *I Dream of Jeannie* (TV 1965–70), *The Eagle Has Landed* (1976), *Superman* (1978), *Dallas* (TV 1978–90), *Nixon* (1995), *Primary Colors* (1998).

Hamill, Mark (1951–) American, born Oakland, California; *Star Wars* (1977), *The Big Red One* (1979), *The Empire Strikes Back* (1980), *Return of the Jedi* (1983), *Slipstream* (1988), *Flash II* (1991), *Village of the Damned* (1995).

Hamlin, Harry (1951–) American, born Pasadena, California; *Clash of the Titans* (1981), *Dragonslayer* (1981), *Space* (TV 1985), *LA Law* (TV 1986–92), *Veronica Mars* (TV 2004–6).

Hanks, Tom (1956–) American, born Oakland, California; *Bachelor Party* (1983), *Splash!* (1984), *Dragnet* (1987), *Big* (1988), *Punchline* (1988), *The 'Burbs* (1989), *Turner and Hooch* (1990), *Bonfire of the Vanities* (1991), *A League of Their Own* (1992), *Sleepless in Seattle* (1993), *Philadelphia* (1993), *Forrest Gump* (1994), *Apollo 13* (1995), *That Thing You Do* (1996), *Saving Private Ryan* (1998), *You've Got Mail* (1998), *The Green Mile* (1999), *Cast Away* (2000), *Road to Perdition* (2002), *The Da Vinci Code* (2006), *Charlie Wilson's War* (2007).

Hannah, Daryl (1960–) American, born Chicago; *Blade Runner* (1982), *Splash!* (1984), *Clan of the Cave Bear* (1986), *Legal Eagles* (1986), *Roxanne* (1987), *Wall Street* (1987), *High Spirits* (1988), *Steel Magnolias* (1989), *Crazy People* (1990), *Memoirs of an Invisible Man* (1992), *The Last Days of Frankie the Fly* (1997), *Run for the Money* (2002), *Kill Bill: Vol 1* (2004), *Kill Bill: Vol 2* (2005).

Hardy, Oliver (Norvell Hardy Junior) (1892–1957) American, born near Atlanta, Georgia; *Putting Pants on Philip* (1927), *The Battle of the Century* (1927), *Two Tars* (1928), *The Perfect Day* (1929), *The Music Box* (1932), *Babes in Toyland* (1934), *Bonnie Scotland* (1935), *Way Out West* (1937), *The Flying Deuces* (1939), *Atoll K* (1950).

Harlow, Jean (Harlean Carpentier) (1911–37) American, born Kansas City, Missouri; *Red Dust* (1932), *Hell's Angels* (1930), *Platinum Blonde* (1931), *Red-Headed Woman* (1932), *Bombshell* (1933), *Dinner at 8* (1933), *Libelled Lady* (1936).

Harrelson, Woody (1961–) American, born Midland, Texas; *Cheers* (TV 1985–93), *Wildcats* (1986), *Ted and Venus* (1991), *White Men Can't Jump* (1992), *Indecent Proposal* (1993), *Natural Born Killers* (1994), *Kingpin* (1996), *The People vs Larry Flynt* (1996), *The Thin Red Line* (1998), *EdTV* (1999), *No Country for Old Men* (2007).

Harris, Julie (Julia Harris) (1925–) American, born Grosse Point, Michigan; *The Member of the Wedding* (1953), *East of Eden* (1955), *The Haunting* (1963).

Harris, Richard (1930–2002) Irish, born County Limerick; *The Guns of Navarone* (1961), *Mutiny on the Bounty* (1962), *This Sporting Life* (1963), *Camelot* (1967), *A Man Called Horse* (1969), *Cromwell* (1970), *The Cassandra Crossing* (1977), *Orca – Killer Whale* (1977), *The Wild Geese* (1978), *The Field* (1990), *Gladiator* (2000), *Harry Potter and the Philosopher's Stone* (2001), *Harry Potter and the Chamber of Secrets* (2002).

Harrison, Sir Rex (Reginald Carey Harrison) (1908–90) British, born Huyton, Lancashire; *Major Barbara* (1940), *Blithe Spirit* (1945), *Anna and the King of Siam* (1946), *The Ghost and Mrs Muir* (1947), *The Reluctant Debutante* (1958), *The Constant Husband* (1955), *Cleopatra* (1962), *My Fair Lady* (1964), *Dr Dolittle* (1967).

Hauer, Rutger (1944–) Dutch, born Amsterdam; *Nighthawks* (1981), *Blade Runner* (1982), *Eureka* (1983), *The Osterman Weekend* (1983), *The Hitcher* (1985), *Flesh & Blood* (1985), *Wanted Dead or Alive* (1986), *The Legend of the Holy Drinker* (1989), *Blind Fury* (1990), *On a Moonlit Night* (1991), *Split Second* (1992), *Buffy the Vampire Slayer* (1992), *Past Midnight* (1992), *Nostradamus* (1994), *Crossworlds* (1996), *Confessions of a Dangerous Mind* (2002), *Minotaur* (2006).

Hawn, Goldie (Jeanne) (1945–) American, born Washington DC; *Laugh In* (TV 1968–73), *Cactus Flower* (1969), *There's a Girl in My Soup* (1970), *Butterflies are Free* (1971), *Sugarland Express* (1974), *Shampoo* (1975), *Foul Play* (1978), *Seems Like Old Times* (1980), *Private Benjamin* (1980), *Best Friends* (1982), *Swing Shift* (1984), *Bird on a Wire* (1990), *Deceived* (1991), *Housesitter* (1992), *Death Becomes Her* (1992), *The First Wives Club* (1996), *The Banger Sisters* (2002).

Hawthorne, Sir Nigel (Barnard) (1929–2001) British, born Coventry; *Yes Minister* (TV 1980–92), *Yes, Prime Minister* (TV 1986–8), *The Madness of King George* (1994), *Richard III* (1995), *Twelfth Night* (1996), *A Reasonable Man* (1999).

Hay, Will (1889–1949) British, born Stockton-on-Tees; *Good Morning Boys* (1937), *Old Bones of the River* (1938), *Oh Mr Porter* (1938), *Ask a Policeman* (1939), *The Ghost of St Michaels* (1941), *My Learned Friend* (1944).

Hayward, Susan (Edythe Marrener) (1917–75) American, born Brooklyn, New York City; *Smash-Up: The Story of a Woman* (1947), *With a Song In My Heart* (1952), *I'll Cry Tomorrow* (1955), *I Want to Live!* (1958), *Where Love Has Gone* (1964), *Valley of the Dolls* (1967), *The Revengers* (1972).

Hayworth, Rita (Margarita Carmen Cansino) (1918–87) American, born New York City; *Only Angels Have Wings* (1939), *The Lady in Question* (1940), *The Strawberry Blonde* (1940), *Blood and Sand* (1941), *You'll Never Get Rich* (1941), *Cover Girl* (1944), *Gilda* (1946), *The Lady from Shanghai* (1948), *Separate Tables* (1958).

Hepburn, Audrey (Audrey Kathleen Ruston) (1929–93) Anglo-Dutch, born Brussels, Belgium; *Roman Holiday* (1953), *War and Peace* (1956), *Funny Face* (1957), *The Nun's Story* (1959), *Breakfast at Tiffany's* (1961), *My Fair Lady* (1964), *How to Steal a Million* (1966), *Wait Until Dark* (1967), *Robin and Marian* (1976), *Always* (1989).

Hepburn, Katharine (1907–2003) American, born Hartford, Connecticut; *A Bill of Divorcement* (1932), *Morning Glory* (1933), *Stage Door* (1937), *Bringing Up Baby* (1938), *Holiday* (1938), *The Philadelphia Story* (1940), *Woman of the Year* (1942), *Adam's Rib* (1949), *The African Queen* (1951), *Long Day's Journey into Night* (1962), *Guess Who's Coming to Dinner* (1967), *Suddenly Last Summer* (1968), *The Lion in Winter* (1968), *Rooster Cogburn* (1975), *On Golden Pond* (1981), *Love Affair* (1994).

Hershey, Barbara (formerly Barbara Seagull, originally Herzstein) (1948–) American, born Hollywood, California; *Last Summer* (1968), *The Flood* (TV 1976), *The Stunt Man* (1978), *Angel on My Shoulder* (TV 1980), *The Entity* (1983), *The Right Stuff* (1983), *The Natural* (1984), *Hannah* *and Her Sisters* (1986), *Tin Men* (1987), *A World Apart* (1988), *The Last Temptation of Christ* (1988), *Beaches* (1988), *Barton Fink* (1990), *Naked Lunch* (1991), *The Public Eye* (1991), *A Dangerous Woman* (1993), *Splitting Heirs* (1993), *The Portrait of a Lady* (1996), *Passion* (1999), *Lantana* (2002), *Riding the Bullet* (2004).

Heston, Charlton (John Charlton Carter) (1923–2008) American, born Evanston, Illinois; *Arrowhead* (1953), *The Ten Commandments* (1956), *Touch of Evil* (1958), *Ben-Hur* (1959), *El Cid* (1961), *The Greatest Story Ever Told* (1965), *The War Lord* (1965), *Khartoum* (1966), *Planet of the Apes* (1968), *Will Penny* (1968), *Earthquake* (1973), *Airport* (1975), *The Four Musketeers* (1975), *Almost an Angel* (1990), *Wayne's World 2* (1993), *Tombstone* (1993), *Hamlet* (1996), *Any Given Sunday* (1999).

Hiller, Dame Wendy (1912–2003) British, born Bramhall, Cheshire; *Major Barbara* (1940), *I Know Where I'm Going* (1945), *Separate Tables* (1958), *Sons and Lovers* (1960), *A Man for All Seasons* (1966), *Murder on the Orient Express* (1974), *Voyage of the Damned* (1976), *The Elephant Man* (1980), *The Lonely Passion of Judith Hearne* (1987).

Hoffman, Dustin (1937–) American, born Los Angeles; *The Graduate* (1967), *Midnight Cowboy* (1969), *Little Big Man* (1970), *Papillon* (1973), *Lenny* (1974), *Marathon Man* (1976), *All the President's Men* (1976), *Kramer vs Kramer* (1979), *Tootsie* (1982), *Death of a Salesman* (TV 1984), *Rain Man* (1988), *Dick Tracy* (1990), *Hook* (1991), *Hero* (1992), *Outbreak* (1995), *Sleepers* (1996), *Wag The Dog* (1997), *Sphere* (1998), *Finding Neverland* (2004), *Perfume* (2006).

Hogan, Paul (1939–) Australian, born Lightning Ridge, New South Wales; *Crocodile Dundee* (1986), *Crocodile Dundee II* (1988), *Almost an Angel* (1990), *Lightning Jack* (1994), *Flipper* (1996), *Crocodile Dundee in Los Angeles* (2001), *Strange Bedfellows* (2004).

Holbrook, Hal (Harold Holbrook) (1925–) American, born Cleveland, Ohio; *The Group* (1966), *The Bold Ones* (1970–1), *That Certain Summer* (TV 1972), *Magnum Force* (1973), *All the President's Men* (1976), *Capricorn One* (1976), *Julia* (1977), *The Fog* (1980), *Creepshow* (1982), *The Star Chamber* (1982), *Into the Wild* (2007).

Holden, William (William Franklin Beedle, Jr) (1918–82) American, born O'Fallon, Illinois; *Golden Boy* (1939), *Rachel and the Stranger* (1948), *Sunset Boulevard* (1950), *Born Yesterday* (1950), *Stalag 17* (1953), *Love is a Many-Splendored Thing* (1955), *Picnic* (1955), *The Bridge on the River Kwai* (1957), *Casino Royale* (1967), *The Wild Bunch* (1969), *The Towering Inferno* (1974), *Network* (1976), *Damien: Omen II* (1978), *The Earthling* (1980), *SOB* (1981), *When Time Ran Out* (1981).

Holm, Sir Ian (Ian Holm Cuthbert) (1931–) English, born Goodmayes, Essex; *The Bofors Gun* (1968), *The Lost Boys* (TV 1978), *Chariots of Fire* (1981), *Henry V* (1989), *The Madness of King George* (1994), *The Sweet Hereafter* (1997), *King Lear* (TV 1998), *The Lord of the Rings: The Fellowship of the Ring* (2001), *The Aviator* (2004).

Hope, Bob (Leslie Townes Hope) (1903–2003) Anglo-American, born Eltham, London; *Thanks for the Memory* (1938), *The Cat and the Canary* (1939), *Road to Singapore* (1940), *The Ghost Breakers* (1940), *Road to Zanzibar* (1941), *My Favorite Blonde* (1942), *Road to Morocco* (1942), *The Paleface* (1948), *Fancy Pants* (1950), *The Facts*

of Life (1960), *Road to Hong Kong* (1961), *How to Commit Marriage* (1969).

Hopkins, Sir Anthony (1937–) Welsh–American, born Port Talbot, Wales; *The Lion in Winter* (1968), *When Eight Bells Toll* (1971), *War and Peace* (TV 1972), *Magic* (1978), *The Elephant Man* (1980), *The Bounty* (1983), *84 Charing Cross Road* (1986), *Desperate Hours* (1991), *Silence of the Lambs* (1991), *Spotswood* (1991), *Howards End* (1992), *Charlie* (1992), *The Innocent* (1992), *Dracula* (1992), *The Remains of the Day* (1993), *Shadowlands* (1993), *The Road to Wellville* (1994), *Legends of the Fall* (1994), *Nixon* (1995), *Surviving Picasso* (1996), *Amistad* (1997), *Meet Joe Black* (1998), *Hannibal* (2001), *Red Dragon* (2002), *Bobby* (2006), *Beowulf* (2007).

Hopper, Dennis (1936–) American, born Dodge City, Kansas; *Rebel Without a Cause* (1955), *Giant* (1956), *Cool Hand Luke* (1967), *Easy Rider* (1969), *Apocalypse Now* (1979), *Blue Velvet* (1986), *River's Edge* (1986), *Blood Red* (1990), *Catchfire* (1990), *Paris Trout* (1991), *The Indian Runner* (1991), *Money Men* (1992), *True Romance* (1993), *Speed* (1994), *Basquiat* (1996), *10th and Wolf* (2006).

Hordern, Sir Michael (1911–95) British, born Berkhamsted, Hertfordshire; *The Constant Husband* (1955), *The Spanish Gardener* (1956), *Dr Syn – Alias the Scarecrow* (1963), *A Funny Thing Happened on the Way to the Forum* (1966), *The Bed-Sitting Room* (1969), *The Slipper and the Rose* (1976), *The Missionary* (1982), *Paradise Postponed* (TV 1986), *The Fool* (1990).

Hoskins, Bob (Robert William) (1942–) British, born Bury St Edmunds, Suffolk; *Pennies from Heaven* (TV 1978), *The Long Good Friday* (1980), *The Honorary Consul* (1983), *The Cotton Club* (1984), *Brazil* (1985), *Mona Lisa* (1986), *A Prayer for the Dying* (1987), *Who Framed Roger Rabbit* (1988), *Mermaids* (1990), *Shattered* (1991), *Hook* (1991), *The Inner Circle* (1992), *Rainbow* (1995), *Nixon* (1995), *The Secret Agent* (1996), *Parting Shots* (1998), *Last Orders* (2001), *Mrs Henderson Presents* (2005), *Hollywoodland* (2006).

Howard, Leslie (Leslie Howard Stainer) (1890–1943) British, born London; *Of Human Bondage* (1934), *The Scarlet Pimpernel* (1935), *Pygmalion* (1938), *Gone with the Wind* (1939).

Howard, Trevor (Wallace) (1916–88) British, born Cliftonville, Kent; *The Way Ahead* (1944), *Brief Encounter* (1946), *Green for Danger* (1946), *The Third Man* (1949), *The Heart of the Matter* (1953), *The Key* (1958), *Sons and Lovers* (1960), *Mutiny on the Bounty* (1962), *The Charge of the Light Brigade* (1968), *Ryan's Daughter* (1970), *The Night Visitor* (1971), *Catholics* (TV 1973), *Conduct Unbecoming* (1975), *Meteor* (1979), *Gandhi* (1982), *White Mischief* (1987), *The Unholy* (1988).

Hudson, Rock (Roy Scherer, Jr) (1925–85) American, born Winnetka, Illinois; *Magnificent Obsession* (1954), *Giant* (1956), *Written on the Wind* (1956), *The Tarnished Angel* (1957), *Pillow Talk* (1959), *Send Me No Flowers* (1964), *Seconds* (1966), *Darling Lili* (1969), *McMillan and Wife* (TV 1971–5), *McMillan* (TV 1976), *Embryo* (1976), *The Martian Chronicles* (TV 1980), *Dynasty* (TV 1985).

Hulce, Tom (1953–) American, born Whitewater, Wisconsin; *September 30, 1955* (1977), *Animal House* (1978), *Amadeus* (1984), *Dominick and Eugene* (1988), *Parenthood* (1989), *Shadow Man* (1990), *The Inner Circle* (1991), *Fearless* (1993), *Wings of Courage* (1995).

Hunter, Holly (1958–) American, born Conyers, Georgia; *Raising Arizona* (1987), *Once Around*

Arts and Culture

Arts and Culture

(1990), *The Piano* (1993), *The Firm* (1993), *The Positively True Adventures of the Alleged Texas Cheerleader-Murdering Mom* (TV 1993), *Copycat* (1995), *Crash* (1996), *A Life Less Ordinary* (1997), *O Brother, Where Art Thou?* (2000), *Moonlight Mile* (2002), *Thirteen* (2003), *Saving Grace* (TV 2007–).

Hunter, Kim (Janet Cole) (1922–2002) American, born Detroit, Michigan; *A Matter of Life and Death* (1945), *A Streetcar Named Desire* (1951), *Deadline USA* (1952), *The Swimmer* (1968), *Planet of the Apes* (1968), *Beneath the Planet of the Apes* (1970), *Escape from the Planet of the Apes* (1971).

Huppert, Isabelle (1955–) French, born Paris; *César et Rosalie* (1972), *La Dentellière* (1977), *Heaven's Gate* (1980), *The Possessed* (1987), *Une Affaire des Femmes* (1988), *Madame Bovary* (1991), *Pas de scandale* (1999), *La Pianiste* (2001, *8 Women* (2002), *Gabrielle* (2006).

Hurt, John (1940–) British, born Chesterfield, Derbyshire; *A Man for All Seasons* (1966), *10 Rillington Place* (1971), *The Naked Civil Servant* (TV 1975), *Midnight Express* (1978), *Alien* (1979), *The Elephant Man* (1980), *History of the World Part One* (1981), *Champions* (1983), *1984* (1984), *Spaceballs* (1987), *White Mischief* (1987), *Scandal* (1989), *Frankenstein Unbound* (1990), *King Ralph* (1991), *Rob Roy* (1995), *Darkening* (1996), *Captain Corelli's Mandolin* (2001), *The Proposition* (2005).

Hurt, William (1950–) American, born Washington, DC; *Altered States* (1981), *The Janitor* (1981), *Body Heat* (1981), *Gorky Park* (1983), *Kiss of the Spider Woman* (1985), *Children of a Lesser God* (1986), *Broadcast News* (1987), *The Accidental Tourist* (1989), *Alice* (1990), *The Doctor* (1991), *The Plague* (1992), *Second Best* (1994), *Smoke* (1995), *Jane Eyre* (1995), *Michael* (1996), *Lost in Space* (1998), *Artificial Intelligence: AI* (2001), *A History of Violence* (2005), *Into the Wild* (2007).

Hussey, Olivia (1951–) British, born Buenos Aires, Argentina; *Romeo and Juliet* (1968), *Lost Horizon* (1973), *Jesus of Nazareth* (TV 1977), *Death on the Nile* (1978), *The Man with Bogart's Face* (1980), *Ivanhoe* (TV 1982), *El Grito* (2000).

Huston, Anjelica (1951–) American, born Los Angeles; *The Last Tycoon* (1976), *Frances* (1982), *This is Spinal Tap* (1984), *Prizzi's Honor* (1985), *The Dead* (1987), *Gardens of Stone* (1987), *A Handful of Dust* (1988), *Mr North* (1988), *The Witches* (1990), *The Grifters* (1990), *The Addams Family* (1991), *Bitter Moon* (1992), *Addams Family Values* (1993), *Manhattan Murder Mystery* (1994), *The Crossing Guard* (1995), *Agnes Browne* (1999), *The Royal Tenenbaums* (2001), *Iron Jawed Angels* (TV 2004), *The Darjeeling Limited* (2007).

Hyde-White, Wilfrid (1903–91) British, born Gloucester; *The Third Man* (1949), *My Fair Lady* (1964), *The Associates* (TV 1979), *Buck Rogers* (TV 1980–2), *Oh God Book Two* (1980).

Irons, Jeremy (1948–) British, born Cowes; *The French Lieutenant's Woman* (1981), *Brideshead Revisited* (TV 1981), *Swann in Love* (1984), *The Mission* (1985), *Dead Ringers* (1988), *Reversal of Fortune* (1990), *Kafka* (1991), *Waterland* (1992), *Damage* (1992), *M Butterfly* (1992), *Die Hard with a Vengeance* (1995), *Stealing Beauty* (1996), *Lolita* (1996), *The Fourth Angel* (2001), *Elizabeth I* (TV 2005), *Appaloosa* (2008).

Jackson, Glenda (1936–) British, born Liverpool; *Women in Love* (1969), *Sunday, Bloody Sunday* (1971), *Mary Queen of Scots* (1971), *Elizabeth R* (TV 1971), *A Touch of Class* (1972), *Hedda* (1975), *Stevie* (1978), *Turtle Diary* (1985), *Business as*

Usual (1987), *Salome's Last Dance* (1988), *The Rainbow* (1989), *Doombeach* (1990).

Jackson, Gordon (1923–90) British, born Glasgow; *Whisky Galore* (1948), *Tunes of Glory* (1960), *The Great Escape* (1963), *The Ipcress File* (1965), *The Prime of Miss Jean Brodie* (1969), *Upstairs Downstairs* (TV 1970–5), *The Medusa Touch* (1977), *The Professionals* (TV 1977–81), *A Town Like Alice* (TV 1980), *The Shooting Party* (1984), *The Whistle Blower* (1987), *Beyond Therapy* (1987).

Jacobi, Sir Derek (1938–) British, born Leytonstone, London; *The Odessa File* (1964), *I Claudius* (TV 1976), *Burgess and MacLean* (TV 1977), *Mr Pye* (TV 1986), *Little Dorrit* (1987), *The Fool* (1990), *Hamlet* (1996), *Gladiator* (2000), *Gosford Park* (2001), *The Golden Compass* (2007).

Johansson, Scarlett (1984–) American, born New York City; *The Horse Whisperer* (1998), *An American Rhapsody* (2000), *Ghost World* (2001), *Girl with a Pearl Earring* (2003), *Lost in Translation* (2003), *A Love Song for Bobby Long* (2004), *Match Point* (2005), *Scoop* (2006), *The Prestige* (2006), *The Other Boleyn Girl* (2008).

Johnson, Don (1949–) American, born Flatt Creek, Missouri; *From Here to Eternity* (1979), *Miami Vice* (TV 1984–90), *The Long Hot Summer* (TV 1985), *Dead Bang* (1988), *The Hot Spot* (1990), *Harley Davidson and the Marlboro Man* (1991), *Paradise* (1991), *Born Yesterday* (1993), *Guilty as Sin* (1993), *Tin Cup* (1996), *Nash Bridges* (TV 1996–2001).

Jolie, Angelina (Angelina Jolie Voight) (1975–) American, born Los Angeles, California; *George Wallace* (TV 1997), *The Bone Collector* (1999), *Girl, Interrupted* (1999), *Gone in Sixty Seconds* (2000), *Lara Croft, Tomb Raider* (2001), *Mr and Mrs Smith* (2005), *Changeling* (2008).

Jones, James Earl (1931–) American, born Arkabutla, Mississippi; *The Great White Hope* (1970), *Jesus of Nazareth* (TV 1977), *Exorcist II: The Heretic* (1977), *Roots II* (TV 1979), *Conan the Barbarian* (1982), *Beastmaster* (1982), *Coming to America* (1988), *Field of Dreams* (1989), *Three Fugitives* (1988), *Best of the Best* (1989), *The Hunt for Red October* (1990), *Clear and Present Danger* (1994).

Jones, Jennifer (Phyllis Isley) (1919–) American, born Tulsa, Oklahoma; *The Song of Bernadette* (1943), *Duel in the Sun* (1946), *Portrait of Jennie* (1948), *Carrie* (1951), *Love is a Many-Splendored Thing* (1955), *A Farewell to Arms* (1958), *Tender is the Night* (1961), *The Towering Inferno* (1974).

Julia, Raul (1940–94) Puerto Rican, born San Juan; *The Eyes of Laura Mars* (1978), *One From the Heart* (1982), *Tempest* (1982), *Kiss of the Spider Woman* (1985), *The Morning After* (1986), *Moon over Parador* (1988), *Tequila Sunrise* (1989), *Romero* (1990), *Presumed Innocent* (1990), *The Rookie* (1990), *Frankenstein Unbound* (1990).

Karloff, Boris (William Henry Pratt) (1887–1969) Anglo-American, born London; *Frankenstein* (1931), *The Mask of Fu Manchu* (1931), *The Lost Patrol* (1934), *The Raven* (1935), *The Bride of Frankenstein* (1935), *The Body Snatcher* (1945).

Kaye, Danny (David Daniel Kaminski) (1913–87) American, born New York City; *Up in Arms* (1944), *The Secret Life of Walter Mitty* (1947), *Hans Christian Andersen* (1952), *White Christmas* (1954), *The Court Jester* (1956), *The Five Pennies* (1959).

Keaton, Buster (Joseph Francis Keaton) (1895–1966) American, born Piqua, Kansas; *Our Hospitality* (1923), *The Navigator* (1924), *The General* (1927), *San Diego I Love You* (1944), *Sunset Boulevard*

(1950), *Limelight* (1952), *It's a Mad, Mad, Mad, Mad World* (1963).

Keaton, Diane (Diane Hall) (1946–) American, born Los Angeles, California; *The Godfather* (1972), *The Godfather, Part II* (1974), *Sleeper* (1973), *Annie Hall* (1977), *Manhattan* (1979), *Reds* (1981), *Shoot the Moon* (1982), *Baby Boom* (1987), *The Good Mother* (1988), *The Godfather, Part III* (1990), *Success* (1991), *Father of the Bride* (1991), *Manhattan Murder Mystery* (1993), *Father of the Bride II* (1995), *The First Wives Club* (1996), *Marvin's Room* (1996), *The Other Sister* (1999), *Something's Gotta Give* (2003), *The Family Stone* (2005).

Keaton, Michael (Michael Douglas) (1951–) American, born Carapolis, Pennsylvania; *Night Shift* (1982), *Mr Mom* (1983), *Beetlejuice* (1988), *Batman* (1989), *The Dream Team* (1989), *Clean and Sober* (1989), *Pacific Heights* (1990), *Batman Returns* (1992), *Much Ado About Nothing* (1993), *My Life* (1993), *The Paper* (1994), *Desperate Measures* (1997), *Jack Frost* (1998), *White Noise* (2005).

Keitel, Harvey (1939–) American, born Brooklyn, New York City; *Mean Streets* (1973), *Taxi Driver* (1976), *Bad Timing* (1980), *The Last Temptation of Christ* (1988), *The January Man* (1989), *Bugsy* (1991), *Thelma and Louise* (1991), *Reservoir Dogs* (1992), *The Bad Lieutenant* (1992), *Sister Act* (1992), *The Piano* (1993), *Pulp Fiction* (1994), *Smoke* (1995), *Clockers* (1995), *Blue in the Face* (1995), *Get Shorty* (1995), *Head Above Water* (1996), *Copland* (1997), *Holy Smoke* (1999), *Red Dragon* (2002), *The Shadow Dancer* (2005).

Kelly, Gene (Eugene Curran Kelly) (1912–96) American, born Pittsburgh, Pennsylvania; *For Me and My Gal* (1942), *Cover Girl* (1944), *Anchors Aweigh* (1945), *Ziegfeld Follies* (1946), *The Pirate* (1948), *The Three Musketeers* (1948), *On the Town* (1949), *Summer Stock* (1950), *An American in Paris* (1951), *Singin' in the Rain* (1952), *Brigadoon* (1954), *Invitation to the Dance* (1956), *Les Girls* (1957), *Marjorie Morningstar* (1958), *Inherit the Wind* (1960), *Sins* (TV 1987).

Kelly, Grace (Patricia) (1928–82) American, born Philadelphia, Pennsylvania; *High Noon* (1952), *Mogambo* (1953), *Dial M for Murder* (1954), *Rear Window* (1954), *The Country Girl* (1954), *To Catch a Thief* (1955), *High Society* (1956).

Kennedy, George (1925–) American, born New York City; *Charade* (1963), *The Flight of the Phoenix* (1967), *The Dirty Dozen* (1967), *Cool Hand Luke* (1967), *Sarge* (TV 1971), *Thunderbolt and Lightfoot* (1974), *Earthquake* (1974), *The Blue Knight* (TV 1975–6), *The Eiger Sanction* (1977), *Death on the Nile* (1979), *Bolero* (1984), *Delta Force* (1985), *Creepshow 2* (1987), *Dallas* (TV 1988–91), *Naked Gun* (1989), *Naked Gun 2½: The Smell of Fear* (1991), *Naked Gun 33⅓: The Final Insult* (1994).

Kerr, Deborah (Deborah Jane Kerr-Trimmer) (1921–2007) British, born Helensburgh, Scotland; *Major Barbara* (1940), *Love on the Dole* (1941), *The Life and Death of Colonel Blimp* (1943), *Perfect Strangers* (1945), *I See a Dark Stranger* (1945), *Black Narcissus* (1947), *From Here to Eternity* (1953), *The King and I* (1956), *Tea and Sympathy* (1956), *An Affair to Remember* (1957), *Separate Tables* (1958), *The Sundowners* (1960), *The Innocents* (1961), *The Night of the Iguana* (1964), *Casino Royale* (1967), *Prudence and the Pill* (1968), *The Assam Garden* (1985).

Kidman, Nicole (1967–) Australian–American, born Honolulu, Hawaii; *Days of Thunder* (1990),

To Die For (1995), *The Portrait of a Lady* (1996), *Practical Magic* (1998), *Eyes Wide Shut* (1999), *Moulin Rouge!* (2001), *The Others* (2001), *The Hours* (2002), *Dogville* (2003), *Cold Mountain* (2003), *Birth* (2004), *Fur* (2006), *Margot at the Wedding* (2007), *Australia* (2008).

Kingsley, Sir Ben (Krishna Banji) (1943–) Anglo-Indian, born Snaiton, Yorkshire; *Gandhi* (1982), *Betrayal* (1982), *Turtle Diary* (1985), *Testimony* (1987), *Pascali's Island* (1988), *Without a Clue* (1988), *Slipstream* (1989), *Bugsy* (1991), *Sneakers* (1992), *Schindler's List* (1993), *Death and the Maiden* (1993), *Species* (1996), *Parting Shots* (1998), *Sexy Beast* (2000), *House of Sand and Fog* (2003), *Elegy* (2008).

Kinski, Klaus (Claus Gunther Nakszynski) (1926–91) Polish, born Sopot (Zoppot), Danzig; *For a Few Dollars More* (1965), *Dr Zhivago* (1965), *Aguirre: Wrath of God* (1972), *Nosferatu* (1978), *Fitzcarraldo* (1982), *Codename: Wildgeese* (1984).

Kinski, Nastassja (Nastassja Nakszynski) (1959–) German, born Berlin; *Tess* (1979), *Cat People* (1982), *One from the Heart* (1982), *Paris, Texas* (1984), *Maria's Lovers* (1985), *Revolution* (1985), *Torrents of Spring* (1989), *On a Moonlit Night* (1991), *The Secret* (1991), *Night Sun* (1992), *Terminal Velocity* (1994), *One Night Stand* (1997), *Town and Country* (2001), *Paradise Found* (2003).

Kline, Kevin (1947–) American, born St Louis, Missouri; *Sophie's Choice* (1983), *The Big Chill* (1983), *Silverado* (1985), *Cry Freedom* (1987), *A Fish Called Wanda* (1988), *January Man* (1989), *Love You to Death* (1990), *Soap Dish* (1991), *Dave* (1993), *Paris Match* (1995), *Fierce Creatures* (1996), *The Ice Storm* (1998), *Wild Wild West* (1999), *De-lovely* (2004), *Trade* (2007).

Knightley, Keira (Christina) (1985–) British, born Teddington, Middlesex; *Bend It Like Beckham* (2002), *Doctor Zhivago* (TV 2002), *Pirates of the Caribbean: The Curse of the Black Pearl* (2003), *Love Actually* (2003), *Pride & Prejudice* (2005), *Pirates of the Caribbean: Dead Man's Chest* (2006), *Pirates of the Caribbean: At World's End* (2007), *Atonement* (2007), *The Edge of Love* (2008), *The Duchess* (2008).

Ladd, Alan (1913–64) American, born Hot Springs, Arkansas; *This Gun for Hire* (1942), *The Glass Key* (1942), *The Blue Dahlia* (1946), *The Great Gatsby* (1949), *Shane* (1953), *The Carpetbaggers* (1964).

Lamarr, Hedy (Hedwig Eva Maria Kiesler) (1913–2000) Austrian, born Vienna; *Algiers* (1938), *White Cargo* (1942), *Samson and Delilah* (1949).

Lambert, Christopher (1957–) French, born Long Island, USA; *Greystoke* (1984), *Subway* (1985), *Highlander* (1985), *The Sicilian* (1987), *Highlander II: The Quickening* (1991), *Knight Moves* (1993), *Gunmen* (1994), *The Hunted* (1994), *Mortal Kombat* (1995), *Highlander III: The Sorcerer* (1995), *Highlander: Endgame* (2000), *Day of Wrath* (2006).

Lamour, Dorothy (Mary Leaton Dorothy Slaton) (1914–96) American, born New Orleans, Louisiana; *The Jungle Princess* (1936), *The Hurricane* (1937), *Road to Singapore* (1940), *Road to Zanzibar* (1941), *Manhandled* (1948), *Creepshow 2* (1987).

Lancaster, Burt (Stephen Burton) (1913–94) American, born New York City; *Brute Force* (1947), *The Flame and the Arrow* (1950), *Come Back Little Sheba* (1953), *From Here to Eternity* (1953), *Vera Cruz* (1954), *Gunfight at the OK Corral* (1957), *Elmer Gantry* (1960), *Birdman of Alcatraz* (1962), *The Professionals* (1966), *The Swimmer* (1967), *1900* (1976), *Atlantic City* (1980), *Local Hero* (1983),

Rocket Gibraltar (1988), *Field of Dreams* (1988).

Lange, Hope (Elsie Ross) (1931–2003) American, born Redding Ridge, Connecticut; *Bus Stop* (1956), *Peyton Place* (1957), *Death Wish* (1974), *Nightmare on Elm Street II* (1985), *Blue Velvet* (1986), *Tune in Tomorrow* (1990), *Clear and Present Danger* (1994), *Just Cause* (1995).

Lange, Jessica (1949–) American, born Cloquet, Minnesota; *King Kong* (1976), *All That Jazz* (1979), *The Postman Always Rings Twice* (1981), *Tootsie* (1982), *Frances* (1982), *Country* (1984), *Sweet Dreams* (1985), *Crimes of the Heart* (1986), *Far North* (1988), *Music Box* (1989), *Men Don't Leave* (1990), *Blue Sky* (1991), *Cape Fear* (1991), *Night and The City* (1992), *Losing Isaiah* (1995), *Rob Roy* (1995), *Titus* (1999), *Prozac Nation* (2001), *Big Fish* (2003), *Normal* (2003), *Bonneville* (2006).

Lansbury, Angela (Brigid) (1925–) American, born London; *National Velvet* (1944), *Gaslight* (1944), *The Picture of Dorian Gray* (1945), *The Private Affairs of Bel Ami* (1947), *The Three Musketeers* (1948), *The Reluctant Debutante* (1958), *The Long Hot Summer* (1958), *The Dark at the Top of the Stairs* (1960), *The Manchurian Candidate* (1962), *The Greatest Story Ever Told* (1965), *Bedknobs and Broomsticks* (1971), *Death on the Nile* (1978), *The Lady Vanishes* (1979), *Lace* (TV 1984), *Company of Wolves* (1984), *Murder She Wrote* (TV 1984–96).

Laughton, Charles (1899–1962) British, born Scarborough; *The Sign of the Cross* (1932), *The Private Life of Henry VIII* (1932), *The Barretts of Wimpole Street* (1934), *Ruggles of Red Gap* (1935), *Mutiny on the Bounty* (1935), *Les Misérables* (1935), *Rembrandt* (1936), *The Hunchback of Notre Dame* (1939), *Hobson's Choice* (1954), *Witness for the Prosecution* (1957), *Advise and Consent* (1962).

Laurel, Stan (Arthur Stanley Jefferson) (1890–1965) Anglo-American, born Ulverston, Lancashire; *Nuts in May* (1917), *Monsieur Don't Care* (1925); for films with Hardy ▶ **Hardy, Oliver**.

Laurie, Piper (Rosetta Jacobs) (1932–) American, born Detroit, Michigan; *The Hustler* (1961), *Carrie* (1976), *Tim* (1979), *The Thorn Birds* (TV 1983), *Return to Oz* (1985), *Children of a Lesser God* (1986), *Twin Peaks* (TV 1991), *Other People's Money* (1991), *Storyville* (1992), *Wrestling Ernest Hemingway* (1993), *The Crossing Guard* (1995), *The Faculty* (1998), *Hounddog* (2007).

Law, Jude (1972–) British, born London; *Wilde* (1997), *The Wisdom of Crocodiles* (1998), *Onegin* (1999), *The Talented Mr Ripley* (1999), *Artificial Intelligence: AI* (2001), *Road to Perdition* (2002), *Cold Mountain* (2003), *Closer* (2004), *The Aviator* (2004), *Sleuth* (2007).

Lee, Bruce (Lee Jun Fan) (1940–73) American–Chinese, born San Francisco, California; *The Big Boss* (1971), *Fist of Fury* (1972), *Way of the Dragon* (1972), *Enter the Dragon* (1973), *Game of Death* (1978).

Lee, Christopher (1922–) British, born London; *The Curse of Frankenstein* (1956), *Dracula* (1958), *The Mummy* (1959), *The Face of Fu Manchu* (1965), *Rasputin the Mad Monk* (1965), *Horror Express* (1972), *The Three Musketeers* (1973), *The Man With the Golden Gun* (1974), *Return from Witch Mountain* (1976), *Howling II* (1985), *The Land of Faraway* (1988), *Gremlins 2: The New Batch* (1990), *Police Academy 7: Mission to Moscow* (1994), *The Knot* (1996), *Ivanhoe* (TV 1997), *Sleepy Hollow* (1999), *The Lord of the Rings: The Fellowship of the Ring* (2001), *Star Wars: Attack of the Clones* (2002), *The Lord of the Rings: The*

Two Towers (2002), *Star Wars: Revenge of the Sith* (2005), *Charlie and the Chocolate Factory* (2005), *The Golden Compass* (2007).

Lee, Spike (Shelton Jackson Lee) (1957–) American, born Atlanta, Georgia; *She's Gotta Have It* (1986), *School Daze* (1988), *Do the Right Thing* (1989), *Mo' Better Blues* (1990), *Jungle Fever* (1991), *Malcolm X* (1992), *Summer of Sam* (1999), *The 25th Hour* (2002).

Leigh, Janet (Jeanette Helen Morrison) (1927–2004) American, born Merced, California; *Little Women* (1949), *That Forsyte Woman* (1949), *Houdini* (1953), *My Sister Eileen* (1955), *The Vikings* (1958), *Psycho* (1960), *The Manchurian Candidate* (1962), *The Fog* (1980).

Leigh, Vivien (Vivian Hartley) (1913–67) British, born Darjeeling, India; *Dark Journey* (1937), *A Yank at Oxford* (1938), *Gone with the Wind* (1939), *Lady Hamilton* (1941), *Caesar and Cleopatra* (1945), *Anna Karenina* (1948), *A Streetcar Named Desire* (1951), *The Roman Spring of Mrs Stone* (1961), *Ship of Fools* (1965).

Lemmon, Jack (John Uhler Lemmon III) (1925–2001) American, born Boston, Massachusetts; *It Should Happen to You* (1953), *Mister Roberts* (1955), *Some Like It Hot* (1959), *The Apartment* (1960), *Irma La Douce* (1963), *The Great Race* (1965), *The Odd Couple* (1968), *The Prisoner of Second Avenue* (1975), *The China Syndrome* (1979), *Missing* (1982), *Dad* (1990), *JFK* (1991), *The Player* (1992), *Glengarry Glen Ross* (1992), *Short Cuts* (1993), *The Grass Harp* (1995), *Hamlet* (1996), *The Odd Couple II* (1998).

Lewis, Jerry (Joseph Levitch) (1926–) American, born Newark, New Jersey; *My Friend Irma* (1949), *The Bellboy* (1960), *Cinderfella* (1960), *The Nutty Professor* (1963), *It's a Mad, Mad, Mad, Mad World* (1963), *The Family Jewels* (1965), *King of Comedy* (1983), *Smorgasbord* (1983), *Cookie* (1988), *Funny Bones* (1995).

Lithgow, John (1945–) American, born Rochester, New York; *Blow Out* (1973), *High Anxiety* (1978), *The World According to Garp* (1982), *Twilight Zone* (1983), *Terms of Endearment* (1983), *The Day After* (TV 1983), *2010* (1984), *Footloose* (1984), *Distant Thunder* (1988), *Memphis Belle* (1990), *Ricochet* (1991), *Raising Cain* (1992), *The Pelican Brief* (1993), *Shrek* (2001), *Dreamgirls* (2006).

Lloyd, Christopher (1938–) American, born Stanford, Connecticut; *Star Trek III: The Search for Spock* (1984), *Back to the Future* (1985), *Who Framed Roger Rabbit* (1988), *Track 29* (1988), *Eight Men Out* (1988), *Back to the Future II* (1989), *Back to the Future III* (1990), *Why Me?* (1990), *The Addams Family* (1991), *Addams Family Values* (1993), *My Favourite Martian* (1999).

Lloyd, Harold (Clayton) (1893–1971) American, born Burchard, Nebraska; *High and Dizzy* (1920), *Grandma's Boy* (1922), *Safety Last* (1923), *Why Worry?* (1923), *The Freshman* (1925), *The Kid Brother* (1927), *Feet First* (1930), *Movie Crazy* (1932).

Lockwood, Margaret (Margaret Day) (1916–90) British, born Karachi, India; *Lorna Doone* (1934), *The Beloved Vagabond* (1936), *The Lady Vanishes* (1938), *Night Train to Munich* (1940), *The Man in Grey* (1943), *The Wicked Lady* (1945), *Cast a Dark Shadow* (1947), *The Slipper and the Rose* (1976).

Lollobrigida, Gina (1927–) Italian, born Subiaco; *Belles de Nuit* (1952), *Bread, Love and Dreams* (1953), *Beautiful but Dangerous* (1955), *Trapeze* (1956), *Woman of Straw* (1964).

Lom, Herbert (Herbert Charles Angelo Kuchacevich

ze Schluderpacheru) (1917–) Czech, born Prague; *The Seventh Veil* (1946), *Dual Alibi* (1947), *State Secret* (1950), *The Ladykillers* (1950), *Phantom of the Opera* (1962), *A Shot in the Dark* (1964), *Murders in the Rue Morgue* (1972), *The Return of the Pink Panther* (1974), *The Pink Panther Strikes Again* (1977), *Revenge of the Pink Panther* (1978), *The Lady Vanishes* (1979), *Whoops Apocalypse* (1986), *Ten Little Indians* (1989), *The Pope Must Die* (1991), *Son of the Pink Panther* (1993).

Loren, Sophia (Sofia Scicolone) (1934–) Italian, born Rome; *Woman of the River* (1955), *Boy on a Dolphin* (1957), *The Key* (1958), *El Cid* (1961), *Two Women* (1961), *The Millionairess* (1961), *Marriage Italian Style* (1964), *Cinderella Italian Style* (1967), *A Special Day* (1977), *Prêt-À-Porter* (1994), *Grumpier Old Men* (1995), *Between Strangers* (2002).

Lorre, Peter (Laszlo Lowenstein) (1904–64) Hungarian, born Rosenberg; *M* (1931), *Mad Love* (1935), *Crime and Punishment* (1935), *The Maltese Falcon* (1941), *Casablanca* (1942), *The Mask of Dimitrios* (1944), *Arsenic and Old Lace* (1944), *The Beast With Five Fingers* (1946), *20 000 Leagues Under the Sea* (1954), *The Raven* (1963).

Lowe, Rob (1964–) American, born Charlottesville, Virginia; *Class* (1983), *Oxford Blues* (1984), *St Elmo's Fire* (1985), *Youngblood* (1985), *About Last Night* (1987), *Illegally Yours* (1987), *Masquerade* (1988), *Wayne's World* (1991), *Tommy Boy* (1995), *Austin Powers: The Spy Who Shagged Me* (1999), *The West Wing* (TV 1999–2003, 2006), *Austin Powers in Goldmember* (2002), *Brothers and Sisters* (TV 2006–).

Lugosi, Bela (Bela Ferenc Denzso Blasko) (1882–1956) Hungarian–American, born Lugos (now Romania); *Dracula* (1930), *The Murders in the Rue Morgue* (1931), *White Zombie* (1932), *International House* (1933), *The Black Cat* (1934), *Son of Frankenstein* (1939), *Abbott and Costello Meet Frankenstein* (1948), *Plan 9 from Outer Space* (1956).

Lumley, Joanna (1946–) British, born Srinagar, India; *On Her Majesty's Secret Service* (1969), *General Hospital* (TV 1974–5), *The New Avengers* (TV 1976–7), *Sapphire and Steel* (TV 1979), *Trail of the Pink Panther* (1982), *Curse of the Pink Panther* (1983), *Shirley Valentine* (1989), *Absolutely Fabulous* (TV 1992–2005), *Maybe Baby* (2000), *Jam & Jerusalem* (TV 2006–).

McCallum, David (1933–) British, born Glasgow; *The Great Escape* (1963), *The Man from UNCLE* (TV 1964–7), *The Greatest Story Ever Told* (1965), *Colditz* (TV 1972), *The Invisible Man* (TV 1975), *Sapphire and Steel* (TV 1979), *The Watcher in the Woods* (1980), *Return of the Man from UNCLE* (TV 1983), *Mother Love* (1989), *Cherry* (1999).

McCarthy, Andrew (1962–) American, born New York City; *Class* (1983), *Pretty in Pink* (1986), *Mannequin* (1987), *Less Than Zero* (1987), *Fresh Horses* (1988), *Kansas* (1988), *Weekend at Bernie's* (1989), *Only You* (1992), *Dead Funny* (1994), *New World Disorder* (1999), *Kingdom Hospital* (2004).

McCowen, Alec (Alexander Duncan McCowen) (1925–) British, born Tunbridge Wells; *The Cruel Sea* (1953), *The One That Got Away* (1957), *The Loneliness of the Long Distance Runner* (1962), *The Witches* (1966), *Frenzy* (1972), *Never Say Never Again* (1983), *Forever Young* (1984), *The Assam Garden* (1985), *Cry Freedom* (1987), *Henry V* (1989), *The Age of Innocence* (1993), *Gangs of New York* (2002).

MacDowell, Andie (Rosalie Anderson MacDowell)

(1958–) American, born Gaffney, South Carolina; *St Elmo's Fire* (1985), *Sex, Lies and Videotape* (1990), *Green Card* (1990), *The Player* (1992), *Groundhog Day* (1993), *Short Cuts* (1993), *Four Weddings and a Funeral* (1993), *Michael* (1996), *Town and Country* (2001), *Beauty Shop* (2005).

McGoohan, Patrick (1928–2009) Irish–American, born Long Island, New York; *The Dam Busters* (1954), *Hell Drivers* (1957), *Danger Man* (TV 1960– 7), *The Prisoner* (TV 1968–9), *Ice Station Zebra* (1968), *Escape from Alcatraz* (1979), *A Time to Kill* (1996).

McGregor, Ewan (1971–) British, born Crieff; *Lipstick on Your Collar* (TV 1993), *Shallow Grave* (1994), *Blue Juice* (1995), *The Pillow Book* (1995), *Emma* (1995), *Trainspotting* (1996), *Brassed Off* (1996), *A Life Less Ordinary* (1997), *Little Voice* (1998), *Star Wars: The Phantom Menace* (1999), *Moulin Rouge!* (2001), *Star Wars: Attack of the Clones* (2002), *Down with Love* (2003), *Big Fish* (2003), *Young Adam* (2003), *Miss Potter* (2006), *Cassandra's Dream* (2007).

McKellen, Sir Ian (1939–) English, born Burnley; *Walter* (TV 1982), *Richard III* (1995), *Rasputin* (TV 1996), *Gods and Monsters* (1998), *X Men* trilogy (2000–6), *Lord of the Rings* trilogy (2001–3), *The Da Vinci Code* (2006).

McKern, Leo (Reginald McKern) (1920–2002) Australian, born Sydney; *Time without Pity* (1957), *The Mouse That Roared* (1959), *A Jolly Bad Fellow* (1964), *A Man for All Seasons* (1966), *Ryan's Daughter* (1970), *The Omen* (1976), *Candleshoe* (1977), *Rumpole of the Bailey* (TV 1978–92), *The Blue Lagoon* (1980), *The French Lieutenant's Woman* (1981), *Ladyhawke* (1984), *Monsignor Quixote* (TV 1986), *Travelling North* (1986), *Good King Wenceslas* (TV 1994).

MacLaine, Shirley (Shirley Beaty) (1934–) American, born Richmond, Virginia; *The Trouble with Harry* (1955), *Ask any Girl* (1959), *The Apartment* (1959), *Irma La Douce* (1963), *Sweet Charity* (1968), *Terms of Endearment* (1983), *Madame Sousatzka* (1988), *Postcards from the Edge* (1990), *Used People* (1992), *Guarding Tess* (1994), *The Evening Star* (1996), *Bruno* (2000), *In Her Shoes* (2005), *Closing the Ring* (2007).

Macnee, (Daniel) Patrick (1922–) British, born London; *The Life and Death of Colonel Blimp* (1943), *Hamlet* (1948), *Scrooge* (1951), *Les Girls* (1957), *The Avengers* (TV 1960–8), *The New Avengers* (TV 1977–8), *The Sea Wolves* (1980), *This is Spinal Tap* (1984), *A View to a Kill* (1985), *Chill Factor* (1990).

McQueen, Steve (Terence Steven McQueen) (1930– 80) American, born Slater, Missouri; *Wanted Dead or Alive* (TV 1958), *The Blob* (1958), *The Magnificent Seven* (1960), *The Great Escape* (1963), *Love with the Proper Stranger* (1963), *The Cincinnatti Kid* (1965), *Bullitt* (1968), *Le Mans* (1971), *Getaway* (1972), *Papillon* (1973), *The Towering Inferno* (1974), *An Enemy of the People* (1977).

Madonna (Madonna Louise Veronica Ciccone) (1958–) American, born Bay City, Michigan; *Desperately Seeking Susan* (1985), *Shanghai Surprise* (1986), *Who's That Girl?* (1987), *Dick Tracy* (1990), *A League of Their Own* (1992), *Body of Evidence* (1993), *Blue in the Face* (1995), *Four Rooms* (1995), *Girl 6* (1996), *Evita* (1996), *The Next Best Thing* (2000), *Swept Away* (2002).

Malkovich, John (1953–) American, born Christopher, Illinois; *The Killing Fields* (1984), *Places in the Heart* (1984), *Empire of the Sun* (1987), *Dangerous Liaisons* (1988), *Crazy People*

(1990), *The Sheltering Sky* (1990), *Of Mice and Men* (1992), *In the Line of Fire* (1993), *Mary Reilly* (1996), *Being John Malkovich* (1999), *Je rentre à la maison* (2001), *Ripley's Game* (2002), *Klimt* (2006), *Burn After Reading* (2008).

Mansfield, Jayne (Vera Jayne Palmer) (1933–67) American, born Bryn Mawr, Pennsylvania; *The Girl Can't Help It* (1957), *The Sheriff of Fractured Jaw* (1959), *Too Hot to Handle* (1960), *The Challenge* (1960), *Promises! Promises!* (1965).

Martin, Steve (1945–   ) American, born Waco, Texas; *Sgt Pepper's Lonely Hearts Club Band* (1978), *The Jerk* (1978), *Muppet Movie* (1979), *Pennies from Heaven* (1981), *Dead Men Don't Wear Plaid* (1982), *The Man With Two Brains* (1983), *The Lonely Guy* (1984), *All of Me* (1984), *The Three Amigos* (1986), *The Little Shop of Horrors* (1986), *Planes, Trains and Automobiles* (1987), *Roxanne* (1987), *Dirty Rotten Scoundrels* (1989), *Parenthood* (1989), *My Blue Heaven* (1990), *LA Story* (1991), *Father of the Bride* (1991), *Housesitter* (1992), *A Simple Twist of Faith* (1994), *Sgt Bilko* (1995), *Bowfinger* (1999), *Shopgirl* (2005), *The Pink Panther* (2006).

Marvin, Lee (1924–87) American, born New York City; *The Wild One* (1954), *Attack* (1957), *The Killers* (1964), *Cat Ballou* (1965), *The Dirty Dozen* (1967), *Paint Your Wagon* (1969), *Gorky Park* (1983), *Dirty Dozen 2: The Next Mission* (TV 1985).

Marx Brothers, The: Chico (Leonard Marx) (1887–1961); **Harpo** (Adolph Marx) (1888–1964); **Groucho** (Julius Henry Marx) (1890–1977); **Zeppo** (Herbert Marx) (1901–79) all American, born New York City; (joint) *The Cocoanuts* (1929), *Monkey Business* (1931), *Horse Feathers* (1932), *Duck Soup* (1933), *A Night at the Opera* (1935), *A Day at the Races* (1937), *A Night in Casablanca* (1946).

Mason, James (1909–84) British, born Huddersfield; *I Met a Murderer* (1939), *The Night Has Eyes* (1942), *The Man in Grey* (1943), *Fanny by Gaslight* (1944), *The Seventh Veil* (1945), *The Wicked Lady* (1946), *Odd Man Out* (1946), *Pandora and the Flying Dutchman* (1951), *The Desert Fox* (1951), *Five Fingers* (1952), *The Prisoner of Zenda* (1952), *Julius Caesar* (1953), *20 000 Leagues Under the Sea* (1954), *A Star is Born* (1954), *Journey to the Center of the Earth* (1959), *Lolita* (1962), *The Pumpkin Eater* (1964), *Georgy Girl* (1966), *The Blue Max* (1966), *The Deadly Affair* (1967), *Voyage of the Damned* (1976), *Heaven Can Wait* (1978), *The Boys from Brazil* (1978), *Murder by Decree* (1979), *Evil Under the Sun* (1982), *The Verdict* (1982), *Yellowbeard* (1983), *The Shooting Party* (1984).

Massey, Raymond (1896–1983) American, born Toronto, Canada; *The Old Dark House* (1932), *The Scarlet Pimpernel* (1935), *Things to Come* (1936), *The Prisoner of Zenda* (1937), *Abe Lincoln in Illinois* (1940), *Arsenic and Old Lace* (1944), *The Fountainhead* (1949), *East of Eden* (1955), *I Spy* (TV 1955), *Dr Kildare* (TV 1961–6).

Mastroianni, Marcello (1924–96) Italian, born Fontana Liri, near Frosinone; *I Miserabili* (1947), *White Nights* (1957), *La Dolce Vita* (1959), *Divorce Italian Style* (1962), *Yesterday, Today and Tomorrow* (1963), *8½* (1963), *Casanova* (1970), *Diamonds for Breakfast* (1968), *Ginger and Fred* (1985), *The Two Lives of Mattia Pascal* (1988), *Traffic Jam* (1988), *Used People* (1992), *Prêt-À-Porter* (1993), *Beyond the Clouds* (1996).

Matthau, Walter (Walter John Matthow) (1920–2000) American, born New York City; *A Face in the Crowd* (1957), *King Creole* (1958), *Charade* (1963), *Mirage* (1965), *The Fortune Cookie* (1966), *A Guide for the Married Man* (1967), *The Odd Couple*

(1968), *Hello Dolly* (1969), *Cactus Flower* (1969), *Kotch* (1971), *Earthquake* (1974), *The Taking of Pelham One Two Three* (1974), *Hopscotch* (1980), *Pirates* (1986), *The Couch Trip* (1988), *JFK* (1991), *Grumpy Old Men* (1993), *Out to Sea* (1997).

Mature, Victor (1913–99) American, born Louisville, Kentucky; *One Million BC* (1940), *My Darling Clementine* (1946), *Kiss of Death* (1947), *Samson and Delilah* (1949), *The Robe* (1953), *The Egyptian* (1954), *Safari* (1956), *The Long Haul* (1957), *After the Fox* (1966).

Maura, Carmen (1945–   ) Spanish, born Madrid; *Dark Habits* (1983), *What Have I Done to Deserve This?* (1984), *Law of Desire* (1987), *Women on the Verge of a Nervous Breakdown* (1988), *Baton Rouge* (1988), *How to Be a Woman and Not Die Trying* (1991), *Lisboa* (1999), *La Comunidad* (2000), *Volver* (2006).

Mercouri, Melina (1920–94) Greek, born Athens; *Stella* (1954), *Never on Sunday* (1960), *Topkapi* (1964).

Midler, Bette (1945–   ) American, born Honolulu, Hawaii; *The Rose* (1979), *Down and Out in Beverly Hills* (1986), *Ruthless People* (1986), *Outrageous Fortune* (1987), *Beaches* (1988), *Big Business* (1988), *Stella* (1989), *For the Boys* (1991), *Hocus Pocus* (1993), *Gypsy* (1993), *Get Shorty* (1995), *The First Wives Club* (1996), *Bette* (TV 2000), *The Stepford Wives* (2004), *Then She Found Me* (2007).

Mills, Hayley (1946–   ) British, born London; *Tiger Bay* (1959), *Pollyanna* (1960), *The Parent Trap* (1961), *Whistle Down the Wind* (1961), *The Moonspinners* (1965), *Forbush and the Penguins* (1971), *Deadly Strangers* (1974), *After Midnight* (1989).

Mills, Sir John (Lewis Ernest Watts Mills) (1908–2005) British, born Felixstowe, Suffolk; *Those Were the Days* (1934), *Cottage to Let* (1941), *In Which We Serve* (1942), *Waterloo Road* (1944), *The Way to the Stars* (1945), *Great Expectations* (1946), *The October Man* (1947), *Scott of the Antarctic* (1948), *The History of Mr Polly* (1949), *The Rocking Horse Winner* (1950), *The Colditz Story* (1954), *Hobson's Choice* (1954), *Town on Trial* (1957), *Tiger Bay* (1959), *Swiss Family Robinson* (1959), *Tunes of Glory* (1960), *Ryan's Daughter* (1970), *Lady Caroline Lamb* (1972), *The Big Sleep* (1978), *The 39 Steps* (1978), *Quatermass* (TV 1979), *Young at Heart* (TV 1980–1), *Gandhi* (1982), *Sahara* (1983), *Who's That Girl?* (1987), *Hamlet* (1996).

Minnelli, Liza (1946–   ) American, born Los Angeles; *Cabaret* (1972), *New York New York* (1977), *Arthur* (1981), *Stepping Out* (1991).

Mirren, Dame Helen (Ilyena Lydia Mironov) (1945–   ) British, born London; *Miss Julie* (1973), *Excalibur* (1981), *Cal* (1984), *2010* (1985), *Heavenly Pursuits* (1985), *White Nights* (1986), *Mosquito Coast* (1986), *Pascali's Island* (1988), *The Cook, The Thief, His Wife and Her Lover* (1989), *The Comfort of Strangers* (1990), *Where Angels Fear to Tread* (1991), *Prime Suspect* (TV 1991–2006), *The Hawk* (1993), *The Madness of King George* (1994), *Gosford Park* (2001), *Calendar Girls* (2003), *Elizabeth I* (TV 2005), *The Queen* (2006).

Mitchum, Robert (1917–97) American, born Bridgeport, Connecticut; *The Story of GI Joe* (1945), *Pursued* (1947), *Crossfire* (1947), *Out of the Past* (1947), *The Big Steal* (1949), *Night of the Hunter* (1955), *Home from the Hill* (1960), *The Sundowners* (1960), *Cape Fear* (1962), *The List of Adrian Messenger* (1963), *Ryan's Daughter* (1970), *Farewell My Lovely* (1975), *The Big Sleep*

(1978), *The Winds of War* (TV 1983), *War and Remembrance* (TV 1987), *Mr North* (1988), *Scrooged* (1988), *Cape Fear* (1991), *Tombstone* (1993), *Backfire* (1994).

Modine, Matthew (1959–) American, born Utah; *Private School* (1983), *Streamers* (1983), *Birdy* (1984), *Vision Quest* (1985), *Full Metal Jacket* (1988), *Married to the Mob* (1989), *Memphis Belle* (1990), *Pacific Heights* (1990), *Short Cuts* (1993), *Any Given Sunday* (1999), *Kettle of Fish* (2006).

Monroe, Marilyn (Norma Jean Mortenson or Baker) (1926–62) American, born Los Angeles; *How to Marry a Millionaire* (1953), *Gentlemen Prefer Blondes* (1953), *The Seven Year Itch* (1955), *Bus Stop* (1956), *Some Like It Hot* (1959), *The Misfits* (1960).

Montand, Yves (Ivo Levi) (1921–91) French, born Monsumagno, Italy; *The Wages of Fear* (1953), *Let's Make Love* (1962), *Jean de Florette* (1986), *Manon des Sources* (1986).

Moore, Demi (Demi Guines) (1962–) American, born Roswell, New Mexico; *St Elmo's Fire* (1986), *About Last Night* (1987), *We're No Angels* (1990), *Ghost* (1990), *The Butcher's Wife* (1991), *A Few Good Men* (1992), *Indecent Proposal* (1993), *Disclosure* (1994), *The Scarlet Letter* (1995), *Striptease* (1996), *GI Jane* (1997), *Deconstructing Harry* (1997), *Passion of Mind* (2000), *Bobby* (2006), *Mr Brooks* (2007).

Moore, Dudley (1935–2002) British, born Dagenham, Essex; *Bedazzled* (1967), *Foul Play* (1978), *'10'* (1979), *Arthur* (1981), *Lovesick* (1983), *Unfaithfully Yours* (1983), *Micki and Maude* (1984), *Best Defense* (1985), *Santa Claus* (1985), *Arthur 2: On the Rocks* (1988), *Like Father, Like Son* (1989), *Crazy People* (1990), *Blame it on the Bellboy* (1992).

Moore, Roger (George) (1927–) British, born London; *Ivanhoe* (TV 1957), *The Saint* (TV 1963–8), *The Persuaders* (TV 1971–2), *Live and Let Die* (1973), *The Man with the Golden Gun* (1974), *Shout at the Devil* (1976), *The Spy Who Loved Me* (1977), *The Wild Geese* (1978), *Escape to Athena* (1979), *Moonraker* (1979), *For Your Eyes Only* (1981), *The Cannonball Run* (1981), *Octopussy* (1983), *A View to a Kill* (1985), *The Quest* (1996), *Boat Trip* (2002).

Moorehead, Agnes (1906–74) American, born Clinton, Massachusetts; *Citizen Kane* (1941), *The Magnificent Ambersons* (1942), *Jane Eyre* (1943), *The Lost Moment* (1947), *The Woman in White* (1948), *Johnny Belinda* (1948), *Summer Holiday* (1948), *The Bat* (1959), *How the West was Won* (1963), *Bewitched* (TV 1964–71).

Moranis, Rick (1953–) Canadian, born Toronto, Ontario; *Strange Brew* (1982), *Ghostbusters* (1984), *Brewster's Millions* (1985), *Little Shop of Horrors* (1986), *Spaceballs* (1987), *Ghostbusters II* (1989), *Parenthood* (1989), *Honey, I Shrunk the Kids* (1990), *My Blue Heaven* (1990), *LA Story* (1991), *Honey, I Blew Up the Kid* (1992), *The Flintstones* (1994), *Brother Bear* (2001).

Moreau, Jeanne (1928–) French, born Paris; *Les Amants* (1958), *Ascenseur Pour L'Échafaud* (1957), *Jules et Jim* (1961), *Eva* (1962), *The Trial* (1963), *Journal d'une Femme de Chambre* (1964), *Viva Maria* (1965), *Nikita* (1990), *La Vieille Qui Marchait Dans La Mer* (1991), *Ever After* (1998).

Morgan, Frank (Francis Phillip Wupperman) (1890–1949) American, born New York City; *Hallelujah I'm a Bum* (1933), *Bombshell* (1933), *The Great Ziegfeld* (1936), *Trouble for Two* (1936), *Piccadilly Jim* (1936), *Dimples* (1936), *The Last of Mrs Cheyney* (1937), *The Wizard of Oz* (1939), *Boom*

Town (1940), *Tortilla Flat* (1942), *The Human Comedy* (1943), *The Three Musketeers* (1948).

Morgan, Harry (Harry Bratsburg) (1915–) American, born Detroit, Michigan; *High Noon* (1952), *December Bride* (TV 1954–8), *The Teahouse of the August Moon* (1956), *Dragnet* (TV 1969), *M*A*S*H* (TV 1976–83), *Aftermash* (TV 1983), *Dragnet* (TV 1987).

Murphy, Eddie (1961–) American, born Brooklyn, New York City; *48 Hours* (1982), *Trading Places* (1983), *Beverly Hills Cop* (1985), *The Golden Child* (1986), *Beverly Hills Cop II* (1987), *Coming to America* (1988), *Harlem Nights* (1989), *Another 48 Hours* (1990), *Boomerang* (1992), *Distinguished Gentleman* (1992), *Beverly Hills Cop III* (1994), *The Nutty Professor* (1995), *Doctor Dolittle* (1998), *Nutty Professor II: The Klumps* (2000), *Shrek* (2001), *Dreamgirls* (2006).

Murray, Bill (1950–) American, born Evanston, Illinois; *Meatballs* (1977), *Caddyshack* (1980), *Stripes* (1981), *Tootsie* (1982), *Ghostbusters* (1984), *Razor's Edge* (1984), *Little Shop of Horrors* (1986), *Scrooged* (1988), *Ghostbusters II* (1989), *What About Bob?* (1991), *Mad Dog and Glory* (1992), *Groundhog Day* (1993), *Ed Wood* (1994), *Kingpin* (1996), *Cradle Will Rock* (1999), *The Royal Tenenbaums* (2001), *Lost in Translation* (2003), *The Life Aquatic with Steve Zissou* (2004), *Broken Flowers* (2005), *The Darjeeling Limited* (2007).

Neal, Patricia (1926–) American, born Packard, Kentucky; *The Fountainhead* (1949), *The Hasty Heart* (1950), *Diplomatic Courier* (1952), *Breakfast at Tiffany's* (1961), *Hud* (1963), *A Face in the Crowd* (1957), *All Quiet on the Western Front* (TV 1980), *Cookie's Fortune* (1999).

Neeson, Liam (1952–) British, born Ballymena, Northern Ireland; *Excalibur* (1981), *Suspect* (1987), *Satisfaction* (1988), *High Spirits* (1988), *The Good Mother* (1988), *The Dead Pool* (1988), *The Big Man* (1990), *Dark Man* (1990), *Husbands and Wives* (1992), *Schindler's List* (1993), *Nell* (1994), *Rob Roy* (1995), *Michael Collins* (1996), *Star Wars: The Phantom Menace* (1999), *Star Wars: Attack of the Clones* (2002), *K-19: The Widowmaker* (2002), *Kinsey* (2004), *Seraphim Falls* (2006).

Neill, Sam (1947–) New Zealander, born Omagh, Northern Ireland; *The Final Conflict* (1982), *Reilly: Ace of Spies* (TV 1983), *Robbery Under Arms* (TV 1985), *Plenty* (1985), *Kane and Abel* (TV 1988), *A Cry in the Dark* (1988), *Evil Angels* (1988), *The Hunt for Red October* (1990), *Jurassic Park* (1993), *The Horse Whisperer* (1998), *The Dish* (2000), *Little Fish* (2005), *The Tudors* (TV 2007).

Newman, Paul (1925–2008) American, born Cleveland, Ohio; *Somebody Up There Likes Me* (1956), *The Long Hot Summer* (1958), *The Hustler* (1961), *Hud* (1963), *The Prize* (1963), *Cool Hand Luke* (1967), *Butch Cassidy and the Sundance Kid* (1969), *Judge Roy Bean* (1972), *The Sting* (1973), *Absence of Malice* (1981), *The Verdict* (1982), *The Color of Money* (1986), *Blaze* (1990), *Mr and Mrs Bridge* (1990), *The Hudsucker Proxy* (1994), *Nobody's Fool* (1994), *Twilight* (1998), *Road to Perdition* (2002).

Nicholson, Jack (1937–) American, born Neptune, New Jersey; *The Little Shop of Horrors* (1960), *Easy Rider* (1969), *Five Easy Pieces* (1970), *Carnal Knowledge* (1971), *The Last Detail* (1974), *Chinatown* (1974), *One Flew Over the Cuckoo's Nest* (1975), *Tommy* (1975), *The Shining* (1980), *The Postman Always Rings Twice* (1981), *Reds* (1981), *Terms of Endearment* (1983), *Prizzi's Honor* (1985), *The Witches of Eastwick* (1987),

Batman (1989), *The Death of Napoleon* (1991), *Man Trouble* (1992), *A Few Good Men* (1992), *Hoffa* (1992), *Wolf* (1994), *The Crossing Guard* (1995), *Blood and Wine* (1996), *Mars Attacks!* (1996), *As Good as it Gets* (1997), *About Schmidt* (2002), *The Departed* (2006), *The Bucket List* (2007).

Nielsen, Leslie (1926–) Canadian, born Regina, Saskatchewan; *Forbidden Planet* (1956), *The Poseidon Adventure* (1972), *Airplane* (1980), *Prom Night* (1980), *Police Squad* (TV 1982), *Soul Man* (TV 1986), *The Patriot* (TV 1987), *Fatal Confession* (TV 1987), *Naked Gun* (1988), *Repossessed* (1990), *Naked Gun 2½: The Smell of Fear* (1991), *Naked Gun 33⅓: The Final Insult* (1994), *Dracula: Dead and Loving It* (1995), *Spy Hard* (1996), *2001: A Space Travesty* (2000), *Superhero Movie* (2008).

Nimoy, Leonard (1931–) American, born Boston, Massachusetts; *Star Trek* (TV 1966–8), *Mission Impossible* (TV 1970–2), *Invasion of the Body Snatchers* (1978), *Star Trek: The Motion Picture* (1979), *Star Trek II: The Wrath of Khan* (1982), *Star Trek III: The Search for Spock* (1984), *Star Trek IV: The Voyage Home* (1986), *Star Trek V: The Final Frontier* (1989), *Star Trek VI: The Undiscovered Country* (1991).

Niven, David (James David Graham Niven) (1910–83) British, born London; *The Prisoner of Zenda* (1937), *Wuthering Heights* (1939), *Bachelor Mother* (1939), *Raffles* (1940), *The Way Ahead* (1944), *A Matter of Life and Death* (1946), *Carrington VC* (1955), *Around the World in Eighty Days* (1956), *Separate Tables* (1958), *The Guns of Navarone* (1961), *The Pink Panther* (1964), *Casino Royale* (1967), *Candleshoe* (1977), *Death on the Nile* (1978), *Escape to Athena* (1979), *Trail of the Pink Panther* (1982), *Curse of the Pink Panther* (1982).

Nolte, Nick (1941–) American, born Omaha, Nebraska; *Rich Man Poor Man* (TV 1976), *Cannery Row* (1982), *48 Hours* (1982), *Down and Out in Beverly Hills* (1986), *Weeds* (1987), *New York Stories* (1989), *Three Fugitives* (1989), *Another 48 Hours* (1990), *Cape Fear* (1991), *Prince of Tides* (1991), *The Player* (1992), *Lorenzo's Oil* (1992), *Blue Chips* (1993), *I Love Trouble* (1994), *Jefferson in Paris* (1995), *Nightwatch* (1996), *The Thin Red Line* (1998), *The Beautiful Country* (2004), *Hotel Rwanda* (2004), *Tropic Thunder* (2008).

Oberon, Merle (Estelle Merle O'Brien Thompson) (1911–79) Anglo-Indian, born Bombay (now Mumbai), India; *The Scarlet Pimpernel* (1935), *The Divorce of Lady X* (1938), *Wuthering Heights* (1939), *That Uncertain Feeling* (1941), *A Song to Remember* (1943).

Oldman, Gary (1959–) British, born New Cross, South London; *Sid and Nancy* (1986), *Prick Up Your Ears* (1987), *Rosencrantz and Guildernstern are Dead* (1990), *JFK* (1991), *Bram Stoker's Dracula* (1992), *True Romance* (1993), *Leon* (1994), *The Scarlet Letter* (1995), *The Fifth Element* (1996), *Lost in Space* (1998), *Hannibal* (2001), *Harry Potter* series (2004–), *The Dark Knight* (2008).

Olivier, Sir Laurence (1907–89) British, born Dorking; *The Divorce of Lady X* (1938), *Wuthering Heights* (1939), *Rebecca* (1940), *Pride and Prejudice* (1940), *Henry V* (1944), *Hamlet* (1948), *Richard III* (1956), *The Prince and the Showgirl* (1958), *The Devil's Disciple* (1959), *The Entertainer* (1960), *Sleuth* (1972), *Marathon Man* (1976), *A Bridge Too Far* (1977), *Brideshead Revisited* (TV 1981), *A Voyage Round My Father* (TV 1982), *The Jigsaw Man* (1984), *The Bounty* (1984), *A Talent for Murder* (TV 1986), *War Requiem* (1988).

O'Neal, Ryan (Patrick Ryan O'Neal) (1941–) American, born Los Angeles; *Peyton Place* (TV 1964–8), *Love Story* (1970), *What's Up, Doc?* (1972), *Paper Moon* (1973), *Nickelodeon* (1976), *A Bridge Too Far* (1977), *Green Ice* (1980), *Fever Pitch* (1985), *Tough Guys Don't Dance* (1987), *Chances Are* (1989), *Zero Effect* (1998).

O'Neal, Tatum (1963–) American, born Los Angeles; *Paper Moon* (1973), *Nickelodeon* (1976), *International Velvet* (1978), *Little Darlings* (1980), *Little Noises* (1991), *Basquiat* (1996), *The Scoundrel's Wife* (2002).

O'Sullivan, Maureen (1911–98) Irish, born Boyle; *Tarzan the Ape Man* (1932), *Tarzan and His Mate* (1934), *The Barretts of Wimpole Street* (1934), *Pride and Prejudice* (1940), *Never Too Late* (1965), *Hannah and Her Sisters* (1986), *Peggy Sue Got Married* (1986), *Stranded* (1987).

O'Toole, Peter (Seamus) (1932–) Irish, born Connemara; *Lawrence of Arabia* (1962), *How to Steal a Million* (1966), *The Lion in Winter* (1968), *Goodbye Mr Chips* (1969), *The Ruling Class* (1972), *The Stunt Man* (1980), *My Favourite Year* (1982), *The Last Emperor* (1987), *High Spirits* (1988), *Wings of Fame* (1989), *Isabelle Eberhardt* (1990), *King Ralph* (1991), *Worlds Apart* (1992), *Phantoms* (1998), *Venus* (2006), *The Tudors* (TV 2008).

Pacino, Al (Alfredo Pacino) (1940–) American, born New York City; *The Godfather* (1972), *The Godfather, Part II* (1974), *Dog Day Afternoon* (1975), *Scarface* (1983), *Revolution* (1984), *Sea of Love* (1990), *Dick Tracy* (1990), *The Godfather, Part III* (1990), *Frankie and Johnny* (1991), *Glengarry Glen Ross* (1992), *Scent of a Woman* (1992), *Carlito's Way* (1993), *Heat* (1995), *Donnie Brasco* (1997), *The Insider* (1999), *Insomnia* (2002), *Angels in America* (TV 2003), *Ocean's Thirteen* (2007).

Page, Geraldine (1924–87) American, born Kirksville, Missouri; *Summer and Smoke* (1961), *Sweet Bird of Youth* (1962), *Dear Heart* (1965), *The Happiest Millionaire* (1966), *Interiors* (1978), *Harry's War* (1980), *Honky Tonk Freeway* (1981), *The Pope of Greenwich Village* (1984), *The Trip to Bountiful* (1985).

Palance, Jack (Walter Palanuik) (1919–2006) American, born Lattimer, Pennsylvania; *Panic in the Streets* (1950), *Shane* (1953), *The Big Knife* (1953), *Arrowhead* (1953), *They Came to Rob Las Vegas* (1968), *Oklahoma Crude* (1973), *Ripley's Believe It or Not* (TV 1982–6), *Gor* (1988), *Batman* (1988), *Young Guns* (1988), *Tango and Cash* (1989), *City Slickers* (1991), *Tombstone* (1993), *The Incredible Adventures of Marco Polo* (1998).

Palin, Michael (1943–) British, born Sheffield; *Monty Python's Flying Circus* (TV 1969–74), *And Now for Something Completely Different* (1970), *Monty Python and the Holy Grail* (1974), *Three Men in a Boat* (TV 1975), *Jabberwocky* (1976), *Ripping Yarns* (TV 1976–80), *The Life of Brian* (1978), *The Meaning of Life* (1982), *The Missionary* (1982), *Brazil* (1985), *A Fish Called Wanda* (1988), *American Friends* (1990), *GBH* (TV 1991), *Fierce Creatures* (1996).

Paltrow, Gwyneth (1972–) American, born Los Angeles, California; *Jefferson in Paris* (1995), *Emma* (1996), *Sliding Doors* (1998), *Shakespeare in Love* (1998), *The Talented Mr Ripley* (1999), *The Royal Tenenbaums* (2001), *Possession* (2002), *Proof* (2005), *Iron Man* (2008).

Peck, (Eldred) Gregory (1916–2003) American, born La Jolla, California; *The Keys to the Kingdom* (1944), *Spellbound* (1945), *Duel in the Sun* (1946), *Gentleman's Agreement* (1947), *The Macomber Affair* (1947), *The Paradine Case* (1947), *Twelve*

O'Clock High (1949), The Gunfighter (1950), Captain Horatio Hornblower (1951), The Million Pound Note (1954), The Purple Plain (1955), The Man in the Gray Flannel Suit (1956), The Big Country (1958), The Guns of Navarone (1961), Cape Fear (1962), To Kill a Mockingbird (1962), The Omen (1976), Old Gringo (1989), Other People's Money (1991), Cape Fear (1991).

Penn, Sean (1960–) American, born Burbank, California; Fast Times at Ridgemont High (1982), The Falcon and the Snowman (1985), At Close Range (1986), Shanghai Surprise (1986), Colors (1988), Casualties of War (1989), We're No Angels (1989), State of Grace (1990), Carlito's Way (1993), Dead Man Walking (1995), The Thin Red Line (1998), I Am Sam (2001), Mystic River (2003), 21 Grams (2003), All the King's Men (2006), Milk (2008).

Perkins, Anthony (1932–92) American, born New York City; Desire Under the Elms (1957), Psycho (1960), Five Miles to Midnight (1962), Murder on the Orient Express (1974), For the Term of His Natural Life (TV 1982), Psycho II (1983), Crimes of Passion (1984), Psycho III (1986), Naked Target (1991).

Pesci, Joe (1943–) American, born Newark, New Jersey; Raging Bull (1980), Lethal Weapon 2 (1989), Goodfellas (1990), Home Alone (1990), JFK (1991), My Cousin Vinny (1992), Lethal Weapon 3 (1992), Home Alone 2 (1992), A Bronx Tale (1993), Jimmy Hollywood (1994), Casino (1995), Lethal Weapon 4 (1998).

Pfeiffer, Michelle (1957–) American, born Santa Ana, California; Grease 2 (1982), Scarface (1983), Sweet Liberty (1982), Into the Night (1985), The Witches of Eastwick (1987), Dangerous Liaisons (1988), Tequila Sunrise (1988), Married to the Mob (1989), The Fabulous Baker Boys (1989), The Russia House (1990), Frankie and Johnny (1991), Batman Returns (1992), The Age of Innocence (1993), Wolf (1994), Up Close and Personal (1995), A Midsummer Night's Dream (1999), What Lies Beneath (2000), I Am Sam (2001), White Oleander (2002), Hairspray (2007).

Philipe, Gérard (1922–59) French, born Cannes; The Idiot (1946), Le Diable au Corps (1947), Une Si Jolie Petite Plage (1949), Fanfan la Tulipe (1952), Les Belles de Nuit (1952), Knave of Hearts (1954), Montparnasse 19 (1958), Les Liaisons Dangereuses (1959).

Phoenix, River (1970–93) American, born Madras, Oregon; Mosquito Coast (1986), Running on Empty (1988), Little Nikita (1988), Indiana Jones and the Last Crusade (1989), I Love You to Death (1990), Dogfight (1991), My Own Private Idaho (1991), Sneakers (1992), The Thing Called Love (1993).

Pickford, Mary (Gladys Mary Smith) (1893–1979) Canadian, born Toronto, Ontario; The Violin Maker of Cremona (1909), Rebecca of Sunnybrook Farm (1917), Poor Little Rich Girl (1917), Pollyanna (1919), Little Lord Fauntleroy (1921), Tess of the Storm Country (1922), The Taming of the Shrew (1929), Coquette (1929), Secrets (1933).

Pitt, Brad (William Bradley Pitt) (1963–) American, born Shawnee, Oklahoma; Thelma and Louise (1991), A River Runs Through It (1992), Kalifornia (1993), True Romance (1993), Interview with the Vampire (1994), Legends of the Fall (1994), Se7en (1995), Twelve Monkeys (1995), Sleepers (1996), Seven Years in Tibet (1997), Fight Club (1999), The Mexican (2001), Ocean's Eleven (2001), Troy (2004), Mr and Mrs Smith (2005), Babel (2006), The Assassination

of Jesse James (2007), The Curious Case of Benjamin Button (2008).

Pleasence, Donald (1919–95) British, born Worksop; Robin Hood (TV 1955–7), Dr Crippen (1962), The Great Escape (1963), The Caretaker (1964), Cul-de-Sac (1966), Fantastic Voyage (1966), You Only Live Twice (1967), Escape to Witch Mountain (1975), The Eagle Has Landed (1977), Oh God (1977), Telefon (1977), Halloween (1978), Escape from New York (1981), The Barchester Chronicles (TV 1982), Hanna's War (1988), Ground Zero (1988), Ten Little Indians (1989), Shadows and Fog (1992).

Plowright, Joan (1929–) British, born Brigg, Lincolnshire; The Entertainer (1960), Drowning by Numbers (1988), Love You to Death (1990), Tea with Mussolini (1999), Callas Forever (2002), Mrs Palfrey at the Claremont (2005).

Plummer, Christopher (1929–) Canadian, born Toronto, Ontario; The Fall of the Roman Empire (1964), The Sound of Music (1965), Waterloo (1970), The Man Who Would Be King (1975), The Return of the Pink Panther (1975), International Velvet (1978), Hanover Street (1979), Somewhere in Time (1980), The Janitor (1981), Dreamscape (1984), Where the Heart Is (1990), Liar's Edge (1992), Impolite (1992), Malcolm X (1992), Twelve Monkeys (1995), Crackerjack (1996), The Insider (1999), A Beautiful Mind (2001), Syriana (2005).

Poitier, Sidney (1927–) American, born Miami, Florida; No Way Out (1950), Cry, the Beloved Country (1952), The Blackboard Jungle (1955), The Defiant Ones (1958), Porgy and Bess (1959), Lilies of the Field (1963), To Sir with Love (1967), In the Heat of the Night (1967), Guess Who's Coming to Dinner (1967), Little Nikita (1988), Shoot to Kill (1988), Sneakers (1992), To Sir with Love II (1996), The Jackal (1997).

Powell, Robert (1944–) British, born Salford, Lancashire; The Italian Job (1969), Jesus of Nazareth (TV 1977), The 39 Steps (1978), Frankenstein (TV 1984), Hannay (TV 1988).

Powers, Stefanie (Stefania Federkiewicz) (1942–) American, born Hollywood, California; Experiment in Terror (1962), Fanatic (1964), Stagecoach (1966), The Girl from UNCLE (TV 1966), Herbie Rides Again (1973), Escape to Athena (1979), Hart to Hart (TV 1979–83), Family Secrets (TV 1984), Someone is Watching (2000), Rabbit Fever (2006).

Presley, Elvis (Aaron) (1935–77) American, born Tupelo, Mississippi; Love Me Tender (1956), Jailhouse Rock (1957), King Creole (1958), GI Blues (1960), Girl Happy (1965), That's the Way It Is (1971).

Price, Vincent (1911–93) American, born St Louis, Missouri; Tower of London (1940), Dragonwyck (1946), His Kind of Woman (1941), House of Wax (1953), The Story of Mankind (1957), The Fly (1958), The Fall of the House of Usher (1961), The Raven (1963), The Tomb of Ligeia (1964), City Under the Sea (1965), House of a Thousand Dolls (1967), The House of Long Shadows (1983), Dead Heat (1988), Edward Scissorhands (1991).

Pryor, Richard (1940–2005) American, born Peoria, Illinois; Busy Body (1967), Lady Sings the Blues (1972), Silver Streak (1976), Blue Collar (1978), Stir Crazy (1980), Superman III (1982), Brewster's Millions (1985), Jo Jo Dancer Your Life is Calling (1986), Harlem Nights (1989), Lost Highway (1997).

Quaid, Dennis (1954–) American, born Houston, Texas; Breaking Away (1978), Caveman (1980), The Night the Lights Went Out in Georgia (1980), Bill (TV 1981), All Night Long (1981), The Right

Arts and Culture

Arts and Culture

Stuff (1983), Jaws 3D (1983), Dreamscape (1984), The Big Easy (1986), Innerspace (1987), Suspect (1987), DOA (1988), Great Balls of Fire (1989), Come See the Paradise (1990), Postcards from the Edge (1990), Wilder Napalm (1992), Undercover Blues (1993), Wyatt Earp (1995), Dragon Heart (1996), Any Given Sunday (1999), Traffic (2000), Far From Heaven (2002), The Day After Tomorrow (2004), Vantage Point (2008).

Quaid, Randy (1950–) American, born Houston, Texas; The Last Picture Show (1971), What's Up, Doc? (1972), Paper Moon (1973), Midnight Express (1978), Vacation (1983), Parents (1988), Caddyshack II (1988), Christmas Vacation (1989), Days of Thunder (1990), Texasville (1990), Kingpin (1996), Hard Rain (1998), Brokeback Mountain (2005), Goya's Ghosts (2006).

Quayle, Sir Anthony (1913–89) British, born Ainsdale, Lancashire; Ice Cold in Alex (1958), The Guns of Navarone (1961), Lawrence of Arabia (1962).

Quinn, Anthony (Rudolph Oaxaca) (1915–2001) Irish–American, born Chihuahua, Mexico; Viva Zapata (1952), La Strada (1954), Lust for Life (1956), The Guns of Navarone (1961), Zorba the Greek (1964), The Shoes of the Fisherman (1968), Revenge (1989), Ghosts Can't Do It (1990), Jungle Fever (1991), Mobsters (1991), Last Action Hero (1993).

Rampling, Charlotte (1946–) British, born Sturmer; Georgy Girl (1966), The Damned (1969), Zardoz (1973), Orca (1977), Stardust Memories (1980), The Verdict (1982), Max mon Amour (1986), Angel Heart (1987), Paris by Night (1988), DOA (1988), Head Games (1996), Wings of the Dove (1997), Sous le Sable (2000), Swimming Pool (2003), Lemming (2005), The Duchess (2008).

Rathbone, (Philip St John) Basil (1892–1967) British, born Johannesburg, South Africa; David Copperfield (1935), Anna Karenina (1935), Captain Blood (1935), Romeo and Juliet (1936), The Adventures of Robin Hood (1938), The Hound of the Baskervilles (1939), The Adventures of Sherlock Holmes (1939), Spider Woman (1944), Heartbeat (1946), The Court Jester (1956).

Reagan, Ronald (Wilson) (1911–2004) American, born Tampico, Illinois; Kings Row (1942), Desperate Journey (1942), The Hasty Heart (1949), Bedtime for Bonzo (1951), The Killer (1964).

Redford, (Charles) Robert (1937–) American, born Santa Monica, California; Barefoot in the Park (1967), Butch Cassidy and the Sundance Kid (1969), The Candidate (1972), The Great Gatsby (1973), The Sting (1973), The Way We Were (1973), All the President's Men (1976), The Natural (1984), Out of Africa (1985), Legal Eagles (1986), Havana (1990), Sneakers (1992), Indecent Proposal (1993), Up Close and Personal (1995), The Horse Whisperer (1998), The Clearing (2004), Lions for Lambs (2007).

Redgrave, Sir Michael (Scudamore) (1908–85) British, born Bristol; The Lady Vanishes (1938), The Way to the Stars (1945), The Browning Version (1951), The Importance of Being Earnest (1952), The Dam Busters (1955), The Quiet American (1958), The Innocents (1961), Nicholas and Alexandra (1971).

Redgrave, Vanessa (1937–) British, born London; Morgan! (1965), Blow-Up (1966), Camelot (1967), Mary, Queen of Scots (1971), Julia (1977), Playing for Time (TV 1980), The Bostonians (1984), Wetherby (1985), Three Sovereigns for Sarah (TV 1985), Prick Up Your Ears (1987), Consuming

Passions (1988), What Ever Happened to Baby Jane? (1991), Howards End (1992), Little Odessa (1994), Mission: Impossible (1996), Deep Impact (1998), Girl, Interrupted (1999), The Gathering Storm (TV 2003), Venus (2006), Atonement (2007).

Reed, Oliver (Robert Oliver Reed) (1938–99) British, born Wimbledon, London; The Damned (1962), The Jokers (1966), Women in Love (1969), The Brood (1980), Condorman (1981), Castaway (1987), Gor (1988), Return of the Musketeers (1989), The Pit and the Pendulum (1991), Severed Ties (1992), Funny Bones (1995), Gladiator (2000).

Reeve, Christopher (1952–2004) American, born New York City; Superman (1978), Superman II (1980), Somewhere in Time (1980), Monsignor (1982), Death Trap (1982), Superman III (1983), The Bostonians (1984), Superman IV (1987), Switching Channels (1988), Noises Off (1992), The Remains of the Day (1993), Morning Glory (1993), Speechless (1994), Village of the Damned (1995), Rear Window (1998).

Reeves, Keanu (1964–) American, born Beirut, Lebanon; River's Edge (1986), The Night Before (1988), Dangerous Liaisons (1988), Bill and Ted's Excellent Adventure (1989), Parenthood (1989), Love You to Death (1990), Bill and Ted's Bogus Journey (1991), My Own Private Idaho (1991), Dracula (1992), Much Ado About Nothing (1993), Little Buddha (1993), Speed (1994), Even Cowgirls Get the Blues (1994), A Walk in the Clouds (1995), Feeling Minnesota (1995), The Matrix (1999), Hard Ball (2001), The Matrix Reloaded (2003), The Lake House (2006), Street Kings (2008).

Reynolds, Burt (1936–) American, born Waycross, Georgia; Gunsmoke (TV 1965–7), Deliverance (1972), Nickelodeon (1976), Smokey and the Bandit (1977), Hooper (1978), Smokey and the Bandit II (1980), The Cannonball Run (1981), Sharky's Machine (1981), The Best Little Whorehouse in Texas (1982), Stroker Ace (1983), The Man Who Loved Women (1983), City Heat (1984), Switching Channels (1988), Breaking In (1989), Evening Shade (TV 1990–4), Cop-and-a-Half (1992), The Player (1992), The Maddening (1995), Striptease (1996), Trigger Happy (1996), Boogie Nights (1997), Driven (2001), The Longest Yard (2005).

Richardson, Miranda (1958–) British, born Southport; Dance with a Stranger (1984), The Innocent (1985), Blackadder II (TV 1986), Empire of the Sun (1987), A Month in the Country (1988), Die Kinder (TV 1990), The Fool (1990), Enchanted April (1991), Damage (1992), The Crying Game (1992), Tom and Viv (1994), Paradise Pages (1995), Kansas City (1996), Sleepy Hollow (1999), The Hours (2002), The Phantom of the Opera (2004), Harry Potter and the Goblet of Fire (2005).

Richardson, Sir Ralph (1902–83) British, born Cheltenham; Bulldog Jack (1935), Q Planes (1939), The Four Feathers (1939), Anna Karenina (1948), The Fallen Idol (1948), The Heiress (1949), Richard III (1956), Oscar Wilde (1960), Long Day's Journey into Night (1962), Dr Zhivago (1966), The Wrong Box (1967), A Doll's House (1973), The Man in the Iron Mask (1977), Time Bandits (1980), Dragonslayer (1981), Greystoke (1984).

Rickman, Alan (1947–) British, born London; The Barchester Chronicles (TV 1982), Die Hard (1988), Robin Hood: Prince of Thieves (1991), Truly, Madly, Deeply (1991), Close My Eyes (1991), Sense and Sensibility (1995), Michael Collins (1996), Rasputin (TV 1996), Galaxy Quest (1999), Harry Potter series (2001–), Perfume (2006), Sweeney Todd (2007).

Rigg, Dame Diana (1938–) British, born Doncaster, Yorkshire; *The Avengers* (TV 1965–7), *On Her Majesty's Secret Service* (1969), *Theatre of Blood* (1973), *Diana* (TV 1973–4), *Evil Under the Sun* (1981), *Mother Love* (TV 1989), *Snow White* (1989), *The Mrs Bradley Mysteries* (TV 1998–9), *The Painted Veil* (2006).

Robards, Jason (Jr) (1922–2000) American, born Chicago; *Tender is the Night* (1961), *Long Day's Journey into Night* (1962), *The Hour of the Gun* (1967), *Once Upon a Time in the West* (1969), *Tora! Tora! Tora!* (1970), *All the President's Men* (1976), *Julia* (1977), *Melvin and Howard* (1980), *The Legend of the Lone Ranger* (1981), *The Day After* (1983), *Sakharov* (TV 1984), *The Long Hot Summer* (TV 1985), *Bright Lights, Big City* (1988), *The Good Mother* (1988), *Parenthood* (1989), *Reunion* (1989), *Storyville* (1992), *Philadelphia* (1993), *The Trial* (1993), *The Paper* (1994), *Beloved* (1998).

Robbins, Tim (Timothy Francis Robbins) (1958–) American, born New York City; *Bull Durham* (1988), *Cadillac Man* (1990), *Jacob's Ladder* (1990), *The Player* (1992), *Bob Roberts* (1992), *Short Cuts* (1993), *The Hudsucker Proxy* (1994), *The Shawshank Redemption* (1994), *Nothing to Lose* (1996), *Arlington Road* (1999), *High Fidelity* (2000), *Mystic River* (2003), *War of the Worlds* (2005).

Roberts, Julia (1967–) American, born Smyrna, Georgia; *Mystic Pizza* (1988), *Steel Magnolias* (1989), *Flatliners* (1990), *Pretty Woman* (1990), *Sleeping with the Enemy* (1991), *Hook* (1991), *The Player* (1992), *The Pelican Brief* (1993), *Prêt-À-Porter* (1994), *Michael Collins* (1996), *My Best Friend's Wedding* (1997), *Notting Hill* (1999), *Runaway Bride* (1999), *Erin Brockovich* (2000), *The Mexican* (2001), *Ocean's Eleven* (2001), *Confessions of a Dangerous Mind* (2002), *Closer* (2004), *Ocean's Twelve* (2004), *Charlie Wilson's War* (2007).

Robinson, Edward G (Emanuel Goldenberg) (1893–1973) American, born Bucharest, Romania; *Little Caesar* (1930), *Five Star Final* (1931), *The Whole Town's Talking* (1935), *The Last Gangster* (1937), *A Slight Case of Murder* (1938), *The Amazing Dr Clitterhouse* (1938), *Dr Ehrlich's Magic Bullet* (1940), *Brother Orchid* (1940), *The Sea Wolf* (1941), *Double Indemnity* (1944), *The Woman in the Window* (1944), *Scarlet Street* (1945), *All My Sons* (1948), *Key Largo* (1948), *House of Strangers* (1949), *Two Weeks in Another Town* (1962), *The Cincinnati Kid* (1965), *Soylent Green* (1973).

Rogers, Ginger (Virginia Katherine McMath) (1911–95) American, born Independence, Missouri; *Young Man of Manhattan* (1930), *42nd Street* (1933), *Flying Down to Rio* (1933), *The Gay Divorcee* (1934), *Top Hat* (1935), *Follow the Fleet* (1936), *Stage Door* (1937), *Bachelor Mother* (1939), *Kitty Foyle* (1940), *Roxie Hart* (1942), *Lady in the Dark* (1944).

Rogers, Will (William Penn Adair Rogers) (1879–1935) American, born Oolagah, Indian Territory (now Oklahoma); *Jubilo* (1919), *State Fair* (1933), *Judge Priest* (1934), *David Harum* (1934), *Handy Andy* (1934), *Life Begins at Forty* (1935), *Steamboat Round the Bend* (1935).

Rooney, Mickey (Joe Yule, Jr) (1920–) American, born Brooklyn, New York City; *A Midsummer Night's Dream* (1935), *A Family Affair* (1937), *Judge Hardy's Children* (1938), *Boys' Town* (1938), *Babes in Arms* (1939), *The Human Comedy* (1943), *National Velvet* (1944), *Summer Holiday* (1948), *The Bold and the Brave* (1956), *Breakfast at*

Tiffany's (1961), *It's a Mad, Mad, Mad, Mad World* (1963), *Leave 'Em Laughing* (TV 1980), *Bill* (TV 1981), *Erik the Viking* (1989), *Home for Christmas* (TV 1990), *The Toy Maker* (1991), *The Legend of Wolf Mountain* (1992), *That's Entertainment! III* (1994), *Heidi* (1996), *The First of May* (1999), *Night at the Museum* (2006).

Rossellini, Isabella (1952–) Italian, born Rome; *White Nights* (1985), *Blue Velvet* (1986), *Siesta* (1987), *Zelly and Me* (1988), *Cousins* (1989), *Wild at Heart* (1990), *Death Becomes Her* (1992), *Fearless* (1993), *Wyatt Earp* (1994), *The Funeral* (1996), *Left Luggage* (1998), *The Architect* (2006).

Roth, Tim (1961–) British, born London; *A World Apart* (1988), *The Cook, The Thief, His Wife and Her Lover* (1989), *Vincent and Theo* (1990), *Rosencrantz and Guildenstern are Dead* (1990), *Reservoir Dogs* (1992), *Bodies, Rest and Motion* (1993), *Pulp Fiction* (1994), *Rob Roy* (1995), *Deceiver* (1997), *Planet of the Apes* (2001), *The Incredible Hulk* (2008).

Rourke, Mickey (1956–) American, born Schenectady, New York; *Body Heat* (1981), *Rumble Fish* (1983), *9½ Weeks* (1985), *The Year of the Dragon* (1985), *Angel Heart* (1987), *A Prayer for the Dying* (1987), *Johnny Handsome* (1990), *Wild Orchid* (1990), *Harley Davidson and the Marlboro Man* (1991), *Desperate Hours* (1991), *White Sands* (1992), *Bullet* (1995), *Exit in Red* (1996), *The Rainmaker* (1997), *Sin City* (2005), *The Wrestler* (2008).

Russell, Jane (1921–) American, born Bemidji, Minnesota; *The Outlaw* (1943), *The Paleface* (1948), *Gentlemen Prefer Blondes* (1953).

Russell, Kurt (1951–) American, born Springfield, Massachusetts; *The Quest* (TV 1976), *Elvis* (TV 1979), *Escape from New York* (1981), *The Thing* (1982), *Silkwood* (1983), *Swing Shift* (1984), *Big Trouble in Little China* (1986), *Tequila Sunrise* (1988), *Tango and Cash* (1990), *Backdraft* (1991), *Unlawful Entry* (1992), *Tombstone* (1993), *Escape from LA* (1996), *Breakdown* (1997), *Vanilla Sky* (2001), *Poseidon* (2006), *Death Proof* (2007).

Rutherford, Dame Margaret (1892–1972) British, born London; *Blithe Spirit* (1945), *The Happiest Days of Your Life* (1950), *The Importance of Being Earnest* (1952), *The Smallest Show on Earth* (1957), *Murder She Said* (1961), *The VIPs* (1963), *Murder Most Foul* (1964), *Murder Ahoy* (1964).

Ryan, Meg (1962–) American, born Fairfield, Connecticut; *Rich and Famous* (1981), *Top Gun* (1985), *Innerspace* (1987), *DOA* (1988), *Promised Land* (1988), *The Presidio* (1988), *When Harry Met Sally ...* (1989), *Joe Versus the Volcano* (1990), *The Doors* (1991), *Prelude to a Kiss* (1992), *Sleepless in Seattle* (1993), *Flesh and Bone* (1993), *French Kiss* (1995), *Courage Under Fire* (1996), *Easy Women* (1996), *You've Got Mail* (1998), *Hanging Up* (2000), *In the Cut* (2003), *The Women* (2008).

Ryan, Robert (1909–73) American, born Chicago; *Gangway for Tomorrow* (1943), *Crossfire* (1947), *The Set-Up* (1949), *Clash by Night* (1952), *God's Little Acre* (1958), *Odds Against Tomorrow* (1959), *Billy Budd* (1962), *The Dirty Dozen* (1967), *The Wild Bunch* (1969).

Ryder, Winona (Winona Laura Horowitz) (1971–) American, born Winona, Michigan; *Beetlejuice* (1988), *Heathers* (1989), *Great Balls of Fire* (1989), *Mermaids* (1990), *Night on Earth* (1992), *Dracula* (1992), *The Age of Innocence* (1993), *Reality Bites* (1994), *Little Women* (1994), *How to Make an American Quilt* (1995), *The Crucible* (1996), *Alien:*

Resurrection (1997), *Girl, Interrupted* (1999), *Mr Deeds* (2002), *A Scanner Darkly* (2006).

Sabu (Sabu Dastagir) (1924–63) Indian, born Karapur, Mysore; *Elephant Boy* (1937), *The Thief of Baghdad* (1940), *The Jungle Book* (1942), *The End of the River* (1947), *Black Narcissus* (1947).

Sanders, George (1906–72) British, born St Petersburg, Russia; *Lancer Spy* (1937), *Rebecca* (1940), *The Saint's Double Trouble* (1940), *The Moon and Sixpence* (1942), *The Picture of Dorian Gray* (1944), *Scandal in Paris* (1946), *The Ghost and Mrs Muir* (1947), *Forever Amber* (1947), *The Private Affairs of Bel Ami* (1947), *Lady Windermere's Fan* (1949), *All About Eve* (1950), *Village of the Damned* (1960), *A Shot in the Dark* (1964).

Sands, Julian (1958–) British, born Otley, Yorkshire; *Oxford Blues* (1982), *The Killing Fields* (1984), *A Room with a View* (1985), *Gothic* (1987), *Siesta* (1987), *Vibes* (1988), *Warlock* (1989), *Arachnophobia* (1990), *Impromptu* (1990), *Grand Isle* (1991), *Naked Lunch* (1991), *Husbands and Lovers* (1992), *Boxing Helena* (1993), *Warlock, Part II* (1993), *Leaving Las Vegas* (1995), *One Night Stand* (1997), *The Scoundrel's Wife* (2002), *The Trail* (2006).

Sarandon, Susan (Susan Abigail Tomalin) (1946–) American, born New York City; *Dragonfly* (1977), *Atlantic City* (1981), *The Hunger* (1983), *The Witches of Eastwick* (1987), *Bull Durham* (1988), *A Dry White Season* (1989), *White Palace* (1991), *Thelma and Louise* (1991), *Light Sleeper* (1991), *Lorenzo's Oil* (1992), *The Client* (1994), *Little Women* (1994), *Dead Man Walking* (1995), *Stepmom* (1998), *Irresistible* (2006).

Savalas, Telly (Aristotle Savalas) (1924–94) Greek–American, born Garden City, New York; *Birdman of Alcatraz* (1962), *The Battle of the Bulge* (1965), *The Dirty Dozen* (1967), *On Her Majesty's Secret Service* (1969), *Horror Express* (1972), *Visions of Death* (1972), *Kojak* (TV 1973–7), *Escape to Athena* (1979), *Kojak* (TV 1989–90), *Backfire* (1994).

Scheider, Roy (1932–2008) American, born Orange, New Jersey; *French Connection* (1971), *Jaws* (1975), *Jaws 2* (1978), *All That Jazz* (1979), *Blue Thunder* (1982), *Still of the Night* (1982), *2010* (1984), *52 Pick-Up* (1986), *Night Game* (1989), *The Russia House* (1990), *Naked Lunch* (1991), *Romeo Is Bleeding* (1994), *The Rainmaker* (1997).

Schwarzenegger, Arnold (1947–) American, born Thal, near Graz, Austria; *Conan the Barbarian* (1982), *Conan the Destroyer* (1984), *The Terminator* (1984), *Red Sonja* (1985), *Predator* (1987), *The Running Man* (1987), *Twins* (1988), *Red Heat* (1989), *Total Recall* (1990), *Kindergarten Cop* (1990), *Terminator 2: Judgement Day* (1991), *The Last Action Hero* (1993), *True Lies* (1994), *Junior* (1994), *Eraser* (1996), *Batman and Robin* (1997), *Collateral Damage* (2002), *Terminator 3: Rise of the Machines* (2003).

Scofield, (David) Paul (1922–2008) British, born Hurstpierpoint, Sussex; *That Lady* (1955), *A Man for All Seasons* (1966), *Henry V* (1989), *Hamlet* (1990), *Quiz Show* (1994), *The Crucible* (1996).

Scott, George C (1927–99) American, born Wise, Virginia; *Anatomy of a Murder* (1959), *The Hustler* (1962), *The List of Adrian Messenger* (1963), *Dr Strangelove* (1963), *Patton* (1970), *The Hospital* (1972), *Fear on Trial* (TV 1976), *The Changeling* (1980), *Taps* (1981), *Oliver Twist* (1982), *Firestarter* (1984), *A Christmas Carol* (TV 1984), *The Last Days of Patton* (TV 1986), *The Exorcist III* (1990), *Malice* (1993), *Family Rescue* (TV 1996).

Selleck, Tom (1945–) American, born Detroit,

Michigan; *Coma* (1977), *Magnum* (TV 1981–9), *High Road to China* (1983), *Lassiter* (1984), *Runaway* (1984), *Three Men and a Baby* (1988), *Three Men and a Little Lady* (1990), *Christopher Columbus: The Discovery* (1992), *Mr Baseball* (1992), *The Love Letter* (1999), *Las Vegas* (TV 2007–8).

Sellers, Peter (1925–80) British, born Southsea; *The Smallest Show on Earth* (1957), *The Ladykillers* (1959), *I'm All Right Jack* (1959), *Only Two Can Play* (1962), *Lolita* (1962), *Dr Strangelove* (1963), *The Pink Panther* (1963), *A Shot in the Dark* (1964), *Return of the Pink Panther* (1975), *The Pink Panther Strikes Again* (1976), *Revenge of the Pink Panther* (1978), *Being There* (1979).

Seymour, Jane (Joyce Frankenberg) (1951–) British, born Hillingdon, Middlesex; *Live and Let Die* (1972), *Battle Star Galactica* (TV 1978), *East of Eden* (TV 1981), *Somewhere in Time* (1980), *The Scarlet Pimpernel* (TV 1982), *War and Remembrance* (TV 1988), *Matters of the Heart* (1991), *Angel of Death* (1991), *Dr Quinn, Medicine Woman* (TV 1992–8), *Wedding Crashers* (2005).

Sharif, Omar (Michael Shalhoub) (1932–) Egyptian, born Alexandria; *Lawrence of Arabia* (1962), *Genghis Khan* (1965), *Doctor Zhivago* (1965), *Che!* (1969), *Green Ice* (1980), *The 13th Warrior* (1999), *Monsieur Ibrahim et les Fleurs du Coran* (2003), *Hidalgo* (2004).

Shatner, William (1931–) Canadian, born Montreal, Quebec; *Star Trek* (TV 1966–8), *Horror at 37000 Feet* (TV 1974), *Big Bad Mama* (1974), *Star Trek: The Motion Picture* (1979), *The Kidnapping of the President* (1980), *Star Trek II: The Wrath of Khan* (1982), *T J Hooker* (TV 1982–6), *Star Trek III: The Search for Spock* (1984), *Star Trek IV: The Voyage Home* (1987), *Star Trek V: The Final Frontier* (1989), *Star Trek VI: The Undiscovered Country* (1991), *Star Trek: Generations* (1994), *Miss Congeniality* (2000), *Boston Legal* (TV 2004–6).

Sheen, Charlie (Carlos Irwin Estevez) (1965–) American, born Santa Monica, California; *Ferris Bueller's Day Off* (1986), *Wall Street* (1987), *Platoon* (1987), *Eight Men Out* (1988), *Major League* (1989), *The Rookie* (1990), *Navy Seals* (1990), *Back Track* (1991), *Hot Shots!* (1991), *Hot Shots! Part Deux* (1993), *The Three Musketeers* (1993), *Terminal Velocity* (1994), *Being John Malkovich* (1999), *Two and a Half Men* (TV 2003–).

Sheen, Martin (Ramon Estevez) (1940–) American, born Dayton, Ohio; *Catch-22* (1970), *Badlands* (1973), *The Execution of Private Slovik* (TV 1974), *The Little Girl Who Lives Down the Lane* (1976), *Apocalypse Now* (1979), *Gandhi* (1982), *The Dead Zone* (1983), *Firestarter* (1984), *Wall Street* (1987), *Siesta* (1987), *Da* (1988), *Judgement in Berlin* (1988), *Stockade* (1990), *JFK* (1991), *Gettysburg* (1993), *Finnegan's Wake* (1993), *Hot Shots! Part Deux* (1993), *A Hundred and One Nights* (1994), *The American President* (1995), *The West Wing* (TV 1999–2006), *Bobby* (2006), *The Departed* (2006).

Shepard, Sam (Samuel Shepard Rogers) (1943–) American, born Fort Sheridan, Illinois; *The Right Stuff* (1983), *Country* (1984), *Crimes of the Heart* (1986), *Baby Boom* (1987), *Steel Magnolias* (1989), *Bright Angel* (1990), *Voyager* (1990), *Thunderheart* (1992), *The Pelican Brief* (1993), *Swordfish* (2001), *Black Hawk Down* (2001), *The Notebook* (2004).

Shepherd, Cybill (1950–) American, born Memphis, Tennessee; *The Last Picture Show* (1971), *Taxi Driver* (1976), *The Lady Vanishes* (1979), *The Long Hot Summer* (TV 1985),

Moonlighting (TV 1985–9), *Texasville* (1990), *Alice* (1991), *Married to It* (1991), *Once Upon a Crime* (1992), *Cybill* (TV 1995–8), *Open Window* (2006).

Sher, Sir Anthony (1949–) South African, born Cape Town, South Africa; *Richard III* (play, 1985, Olivier Award), *Stanley* (play, 1997, Olivier Award), *Mrs Brown* (1997), *Shakespeare in Love* (1998), *Primo* (2005), *God on Trial* (TV 2008).

Sim, Alastair (1900–76) British, born Edinburgh; *Inspector Hornleigh* (1939), *Green for Danger* (1946), *The Happiest Days of Your Life* (1950), *Scrooge* (1951), *Laughter in Paradise* (1951), *The Belles of St Trinians* (1954).

Simmons, Jean (1929–) British, born London; *Great Expectations* (1946), *Black Narcissus* (1946), *Hamlet* (1948), *The Blue Lagoon* (1948), *The Big Country* (1958), *Elmer Gantry* (1960), *Spartacus* (1960), *The Grass is Greener* (1961), *The Thorn Birds* (TV 1983), *Going Undercover* (1988), *Great Expectations* (TV 1991), *Sense and Sensibility* (TV 1990), *How to Make an American Quilt* (1995).

Sinatra, Frank (Francis Albert Sinatra) (1915–98) American, born Hoboken, New Jersey; *Anchors Aweigh* (1945), *On the Town* (1949), *From Here to Eternity* (1953), *The Man With the Golden Arm* (1955), *Pal Joey* (1957), *The Manchurian Candidate* (1962), *The Detective* (1963).

Sinden, Sir Donald (1923–) British, born Plymouth; *Doctor in the House* (1954), *The National Health* (1973), *The Day of the Jackal* (1973), *The Island at the Top of the World* (1973), *Two's Company* (TV 1977–80), *Never the Twain* (TV 1981–91), *The Canterville Ghost* (TV 1996), *Judge John Deed* (TV 2001–).

Singer, Marc (1948–) Canadian, born Vancouver, British Columbia; *BeastMaster* (1982), *If You Could See What I Hear* (1982), *V* (TV 1983), *V – The Final Battle* (TV 1984–5), *Dallas* (TV 1986), *Born to Race* (1988), *Angel Blade* (2002).

Slater, Christian (1969–) American, born New York City; *The Name of the Rose* (1986), *Tucker: The Man and His Dream* (1988), *Heathers* (1989), *Young Guns II* (1990), *Pump Up the Volume* (1990), *Robin Hood: Prince of Thieves* (1991), *Kuffs* (1992), *Where the Day Takes You* (1992), *True Romance* (1993), *Jimmy Hollywood* (1994), *Interview with the Vampire* (1994), *Broken Arrow* (1996), *Very Bad Things* (1998), *The Contender* (2000), *Bobby* (2006).

Smith, Sir C Aubrey (Charles Aubrey Smith) (1863–1948) British, born London; *Love Me Tonight* (1932), *Morning Glory* (1933), *Lives of a Bengal Lancer* (1935), *The Prisoner of Zenda* (1937), *The Four Feathers* (1939), *Rebecca* (1940), *And Then There Were None* (1945), *An Ideal Husband* (1947), *Little Women* (1949).

Smith, Dame Maggie (1934–) British, born Ilford, Essex; *The VIPs* (1963), *The Pumpkin Eater* (1964), *The Prime of Miss Jean Brodie* (1969), *Travels with My Aunt* (1972), *California Suite* (1978), *A Private Function* (1984), *A Room With a View* (1985), *The Lonely Passion of Judith Hearne* (1987), *Hook* (1991), *Sister Act* (1992), *The Secret Garden* (1993), *Sister Act 2: Back in the Habit* (1993), *Richard III* (1995), *The First Wives Club* (1996), *Washington Square* (1997), *Tea with Mussolini* (1999), *Gosford Park* (2001), *Harry Potter* series (2001–), *Ladies in Lavender* (2004), *Becoming Jane* (2007).

Smith, Will (Willard Christopher Smith Jr) (1968–) American, born Philadelphia, Pennsylvania; *The Fresh Prince of Bel-Air* (TV 1990–96), *Six Degrees of Separation* (1993), *Bad Boys* (1995), *Independence Day* (1996), *Men in Black* (1997), *Enemy of the State*

(1998), *Ali* (2001), *Men in Black II* (2002), *Hitch* (2005), *I Am Legend* (2007), *Hancock* (2008).

Spacek, Sissy (Mary Elizabeth Spacek) (1949–) American, born Quitman, Texas; *Badlands* (1973), *Carrie* (1976), *The Coal Miner's Daughter* (1981), *Missing* (1982), *The River* (1984), *Crimes of the Heart* (1986), *In the Bedroom* (2001), *Nine Lives* (2005), *An American Haunting* (2005).

Spacey, Kevin (1959–) American, born South Orange, New Jersey; *Glengarry Glen Ross* (1992), *The Usual Suspects* (1995), *Se7en* (1995), *LA Confidential* (1997), *American Beauty* (1999), *K-PAX* (2001), *The Shipping News* (2001), *The Life of David Gale* (2003), *Superman Returns* (2005), *21* (2008).

Spader, James (1960–) American, born Boston, Massachusetts; *Pretty in Pink* (1986), *Jack's Back* (1988), *Sex, Lies and Videotape* (1989), *The Rachel Papers* (1989), *Bad Influence* (1990), *White Palace* (1991), *True Colors* (1991), *Storyville* (1992), *Bob Roberts* (1992), *Wolf* (1994), *Stargate* (1994), *Crash* (1996), *Curtain Call* (1999), *Boston Legal* (TV 2004–8).

Stallone, Sylvester (1946–) American, born New York City; *Rocky* (1976), *Paradise Alley* (1978), *Rocky II* (1979), *Nighthawks* (1981), *First Blood* (1981), *Rocky III* (1981), *Rambo: First Blood Part II* (1985), *Rocky IV* (1985), *Rambo II* (1986), *Over the Top* (1987), *Rambo III* (1988), *Lock Up* (1989), *Tango and Cash* (1990), *Rocky V* (1990), *Oscar* (1991), *Stop, Or My Mom Will Shoot* (1992), *Cliffhanger* (1992), *Demolition Man* (1993), *The Specialist* (1994), *Judge Dredd* (1995), *Daylight* (1996), *Copland* (1997), *Get Carter* (2000), *Rocky Balboa* (2006), *Rambo* (2008).

Stamp, Terence (1939–) British, born Stepney, London; *The Collector* (1965), *Far from the Madding Crowd* (1967), *Superman* (1978), *Superman II* (1981), *Company of Wolves* (1985), *Legal Eagles* (1986), *Wall Street* (1987), *The Sicilian* (1988), *Alien Nation* (1988), *Young Guns* (1988), *Genuine Risk* (1990), *Stranger in the House* (1991), *Priscilla Queen of the Desert* (1994), *Star Wars: The Phantom Menace* (1999), *These Foolish Things* (2006), *Wanted* (2008).

Stanton, Harry Dean (1926–) American, born Kentucky; *How the West Was Won* (1962), *Cool Hand Luke* (1967), *The Godfather, Part II* (1974), *Alien* (1979), *The Rose* (1979), *Private Benjamin* (1980), *Christine* (1983), *Repo Man* (1984), *Paris, Texas* (1984), *Pretty in Pink* (1986), *Mr North* (1988), *Stars and Bars* (1988), *The Last Temptation of Christ* (1988), *Twister* (1989), *Wild at Heart* (1990), *Twin Peaks: Fire Walk With Me* (1992), *Fear and Loathing in Las Vegas* (1998), *Inland Empire* (2006), *Big Love* (TV 2006–8).

Stanwyck, Barbara (Ruby Stevens) (1907–90) American, born Brooklyn, New York City; *Broadway Nights* (1927), *Miracle Woman* (1931), *Night Nurse* (1931), *The Bitter Tea of General Yen* (1933), *Baby Face* (1933), *Annie Oakley* (1935), *Stella Dallas* (1937), *Union Pacific* (1939), *The Lady Eve* (1941), *Meet John Doe* (1941), *Ball of Fire* (1941), *Double Indemnity* (1944), *The Strange Love of Martha Ivers* (1946), *Sorry Wrong Number* (1948), *The Furies* (1950), *Executive Suite* (1954), *Walk on the Wild Side* (1962), *The Big Valley* (TV 1965–9), *The Thorn Birds* (TV 1983).

Staunton, Imelda (Mary Philomena Bernadette) (1956–) English, born London; *Much Ado About Nothing* (1993), *Shakespeare in Love* (1998), *Rat* (2000), *Vera Drake* (2004), *Freedom Writers* (2007).

Arts and Culture

Steiger, Rod (Rodney Stephen Steiger) (1925–2002) American, born Westhampton, New York; *On the Waterfront* (1954), *Oklahoma!* (1955), *The Court Martial of Billy Mitchell* (1955), *The Harder They Fall* (1956), *Al Capone* (1958), *The Pawnbroker* (1964), *Doctor Zhivago* (1965), *In the Heat of the Night* (1967), *The Amityville Horror* (1979), *American Gothic* (1988), *The January Man* (1988), *Men of Respect* (1990), *Guilty as Charged* (1991), *Taking Liberties* (1993), *The Specialist* (1994), *Mars Attacks!* (1996), *End of Days* (1999).

Stevenson, Juliet (Anne Virginia) (1956–) British, born Essex; *Drowning by Numbers* (1988), *Truly, Madly, Deeply* (1991), *The Trial* (1993), *Emma* (1996), *Cider with Rosie* (TV 1998), *Play* (2000), *Nicholas Nickleby* (2002), *And When Did You Last See Your Father?* (2007), *A Previous Engagement* (2008).

Stewart, James (Maitland) (1908–97) American, born Indiana, Pennsylvania; *Seventh Heaven* (1937), *You Can't Take It With You* (1938), *Mr Smith Goes to Washington* (1939), *Destry Rides Again* (1939), *The Shop around the Corner* (1940), *The Philadelphia Story* (1940), *It's a Wonderful Life* (1946), *Harvey* (1950), *Broken Arrow* (1950), *The Glenn Miller Story* (1954), *Rear Window* (1954), *The Man from Laramie* (1955), *Vertigo* (1958), *Anatomy of a Murder* (1959), *Mr Hobbs Takes a Vacation* (1962), *Shenandoah* (1965), *The Big Sleep* (1978), *North and South II* (TV 1986).

Stockwell, Dean (1936–) American, born Hollywood, California; *The Green Years* (1946), *The Boy with Green Hair* (1948), *Kim* (1950), *Compulsion* (1959), *Sons and Lovers* (1959), *McCloud: Twas the Fight Before Christmas* (TV 1977), *Paris, Texas* (1984), *Dune* (1984), *The Legend of Billie Jean* (1985), *Blue Velvet* (1986), *Gardens of Stone* (1987), *Tucker: The Man and His Dream* (1988), *The Blue Iguana* (1988), *Married to the Mob* (1988), *Quantum Leap* (TV 1989–93), *Smokescreen* (1990), *Back Track* (1991), *The Player* (1992), *Chasers* (1994), *Midnight Blue* (1996).

Stoltz, Eric (1961–) American, born Whittier, California; *Fast Times at Ridgemont High* (1982), *Mask* (1985), *Some Kind of Wonderful* (1987), *Sister Sister* (1988), *Haunted Summer* (1988), *Fly II* (1989), *Memphis Belle* (1990), *The Waterdance* (1992), *Bodies, Rest and Motion* (1993), *Killing Zoë* (1993), *Pulp Fiction* (1994), *Little Women* (1994), *Rob Roy* (1995), *The Rules of Attraction* (2002).

Stone, Sharon (1958–) American, born Meadville, Pennsylvania; *Deadly Blessing* (1981), *Action Jackson* (1987), *Total Recall* (1990), *He Said She Said* (1991), *Basic Instinct* (1992), *Diary of a Hitman* (1992), *Sliver* (1993), *Last Action Hero* (1993), *Intersection* (1994), *Casino* (1995), *Diabolique* (1996), *The Mighty* (1998), *Gloria* (1999), *Basic Instinct 2* (2006), *When a Man Falls* (2007).

Streep, Meryl (Mary Louise Streep) (1949–) American, born Summit, New Jersey; *Julia* (1977), *The Deer Hunter* (1978), *Kramer vs Kramer* (1979), *Manhattan* (1979), *The French Lieutenant's Woman* (1981), *Sophie's Choice* (1982), *Silkwood* (1983), *Plenty* (1985), *Out of Africa* (1985), *Ironweed* (1987), *A Cry in the Dark* (1988), *She-Devil* (1989), *Postcards from the Edge* (1990), *Death Becomes Her* (1992), *The River Wild* (1994), *The Bridges of Madison County* (1995), *Music of the Heart* (1999), *Adaptation* (2002), *The Hours* (2002), *The Manchurian Candidate* (2004), *The Devil Wears Prada* (2006), *A Prairie Home Companion* (2006), *Mamma Mia!* (2008).

Streisand, Barbra (Joan) (1942–) American, born Brooklyn, New York City; *Funny Girl* (1968), *Hello Dolly* (1969), *On a Clear Day You Can See Forever* (1970), *What's Up, Doc?* (1972), *The Way We Were* (1973), *A Star is Born* (1976), *Yentl* (1983), *Nuts* (1987), *Prince of Tides* (1991), *The Mirror Has Two Faces* (1996), *Meet the Fockers* (2004).

Sutherland, Donald (1935–) Canadian, born St John, New Brunswick; *The Dirty Dozen* (1967), *M*A*S*H* (1970), *Klute* (1971), *Casanova* (1976), *1900* (1976), *The Eagle Has Landed* (1977), *Animal House* (1978), *Invasion of the Body Snatchers* (1978), *Ordinary People* (1980), *A Dry White Season* (1989), *Backdraft* (1991), *Buffy the Vampire Slayer* (1992), *The Poet* (1996), *Instinct* (1999), *Space Cowboys* (2000), *Pride and Prejudice* (2005), *Fool's Gold* (2008).

Sutherland, Kiefer (1967–) American, born London, UK; *Bright Lights, Big City* (1985), *Stand By Me* (1987), *The Lost Boys* (1987), *The Killing Time* (1987), *1969* (1988), *Promised Land* (1988), *Young Guns* (1988), *Renegades* (1989), *Chicago Joe and the Showgirl* (1989), *Flatliners* (1990), *Young Guns II* (1990), *Article 99* (1991), *A Few Good Men* (1992), *Twin Peaks: Fire Walk With Me* (1992), *The Vanishing* (1992), *The Three Musketeers* (1993), *Double Cross* (1995), *Truth or Consequences* (1996), *Ground Control* (1998), *24* (TV 2001–7).

Swank, Hilary (Ann) (1974–) American, born Lincoln, Nebraska; *Buffy the Vampire Slayer* (1992), *Boys Don't Cry* (1999), *Insomnia* (2002), *Million Dollar Baby* (2004), *Iron Jawed Angels* (TV 2004), *The Black Dahlia* (2006), *Freedom Writers* (2007).

Swanson, Gloria (Gloria May Josephine Svensson) (1897–1983) American, born Chicago; *Male and Female* (1919), *The Affairs of Anatol* (1921), *Manhandled* (1924), *Sadie Thompson* (1928), *Queen Kelly* (1928), *Sunset Boulevard* (1950).

Swayze, Patrick (1952–) American, born Houston, Texas; *The Outsiders* (1983), *Red Dawn* (1984), *Young Blood* (1985), *North and South* (TV 1986), *North and South II* (TV 1986), *Dirty Dancing* (1987), *Road House* (1989), *Next of Kin* (1989), *Ghost* (1990), *Point Break* (1991), *City of Joy* (1992), *Father Hood* (1993), *Tall Tale* (1995), *Three Wishes* (1995), *Donnie Darko* (2001), *Keeping Mum* (2007).

Tandy, Jessica (1909–94) British, born London; *Dragonwyck* (1946), *The Birds* (1963), *Honky Tonk Freeway* (1981), *The World According to Garp* (1982), *Still of the Night* (1982), *The Bostonians* (1984), *Cocoon* (1985), *The House on Carroll Street* (1988), *Cocoon: The Return* (1988), *Driving Miss Daisy* (1989), *Fried Green Tomatoes* (1991).

Taylor, Dame Elizabeth (Rosemond) (1932–) British, born London; *National Velvet* (1944), *Little Women* (1949), *The Father of the Bride* (1950), *A Place in the Sun* (1951), *Giant* (1956), *Raintree Country* (1957), *Cat on a Hot Tin Roof* (1958), *Butterfield 8* (1960), *Cleopatra* (1962), *Who's Afraid of Virginia Woolf?* (1966), *Reflections in a Golden Eye* (1967), *The Taming of the Shrew* (1967), *Suddenly Last Summer* (1968), *A Little Night Music* (1977), *The Mirror Crack'd* (1981), *Malice in Wonderland* (TV 1985), *Poker Alice* (TV 1986), *Young Toscanini* (1988), *Sweet Bird of Youth* (TV 1989), *Faithful* (1992), *The Flintstones* (1994).

Taylor, Robert (Spangler Arlington Brugh) (1911–69) American, born Filley, Nebraska; *Magnificent Obsession* (1935), *Camille* (1936), *Three Comrades* (1938), *A Yank at Oxford* (1938), *Waterloo Bridge* (1940), *Bataan* (1943), *Song of Russia* (1943), *Quo Vadis* (1951), *Ivanhoe* (1952), *Knights of the Round*

Table (1953), Party Girl (1958), The Detectives (TV 1959–61), The Miracle of the White Stallions (1962).

Taylor, Rod(ney Sturt) (1929–) Australian, born Sydney; The Time Machine (1960), The Birds (1963), The VIPs (1963), Thirty-Six Hours (1964), The Glass Bottom Boat (1966), A Rage in Harlem (1991), Open Season (1995).

Tearle, Sir Godfrey (1884–1953) British, born New York City; Romeo and Juliet (1908), The Thirty-Nine Steps (1935), One of Our Aircraft is Missing (1942), The Titfield Thunderbolt (1953).

Temple, Shirley (1928–) American, born Santa Monica, California; Little Miss Marker (1934), Curly Top (1935), Dimples (1936), Heidi (1937), The Little Princess (1939).

Terry-Thomas (Thomas Terry Hoar-Stevens) (1911–90) British, born Finchley, London; Private's Progress (1956), Carleton Browne of the FO (1958), The Naked Truth (1958), I'm All Right, Jack (1959), It's a Mad, Mad, Mad, Mad World (1963), How to Murder Your Wife (1965), Those Magnificent Men in Their Flying Machines (1965).

Theron, Charlize (1975–) South African, born Benoni, Gauteng; The Devil's Advocate (1997), Mighty Joe Young (1998), The Cider House Rules (1999), Monster (2003), The Life and Death of Peter Sellers (2004), North Country (2005), Hancock (2008).

Thompson, Emma (1959–) British, born London; Tutti Frutti (TV 1987), Fortunes of War (TV 1987), Henry V (1989), Dead Again (1989), Howards End (1992), Much Ado About Nothing (1993), The Remains of the Day (1993), In the Name of the Father (1993), Junior (1994), Carrington (1995), Sense and Sensibility (1995), Primary Colors (1998), Love Actually (2003), Angels in America (TV 2003), Nanny McPhee (2005), Stranger than Fiction (2006), Brideshead Revisited (2008).

Thurman, Uma (Karuna) (1970–) American, born Boston, Massachusetts; Dangerous Liaisons (1988), Pulp Fiction (1994), A Month by the Lake (1995), Hysterical Blindness (TV 2002), Kill Bill: Vol 1 (2003), Kill Bill: Vol 2 (2004), The Producers (2005), Be Cool (2005), My Super Ex-Girlfriend (2006).

Tierney, Gene (Eliza) (1920–91) American, born Brooklyn, New York City; The Return of Frank James (1940), Tobacco Road (1941), Belle Starr (1941), Heaven Can Wait (1943), Laura (1944), Leave Her to Heaven (1945), The Ghost and Mrs Muir (1947), Whirlpool (1949), Toys in the Attic (1963), The Pleasure Seekers (1964).

Tilly, Meg (1960–) Canadian, born Texada; Fame (1980), The Big Chill (1983), Psycho II (1983), Agnes of God (1985), Masquerade (1988), Valmont (1989), The Two Jakes (1991), Leaving Normal (1992), Body Snatchers (1994), Double Cross (1994), Journey (TV 1995).

Tomlin, Lily (1939–) American, born Detroit, Michigan; Nine to Five (1980), The Incredible Shrinking Woman (1981), All of Me (1984), Big Business (1988), Shadows and Fog (1992), The Beverly Hillbillies (1993), Short Cuts (1993), Even Cowgirls Get the Blues (1993), Blue in the Face (1995), Flirting with Disaster (1996), Tea with Mussolini (1999), The West Wing (TV 2002–6), A Prairie Home Companion (2006).

Tracy, Spencer (1900–67) American, born Milwaukee, Wisconsin; Twenty Thousand Years in Sing Sing (1932), The Power and the Glory (1933), A Man's Castle (1933), Fury (1936), San Francisco (1936), Libeled Lady (1936), Captains Courageous (1937), Boys' Town (1938), Stanley and Livingstone (1939), Northwest Passage (1939), Edison the Man

(1940), Dr Jekyll and Mr Hyde (1941), Woman of the Year (1942), The Seventh Cross (1944), State of the Union (1948), Adam's Rib (1949), Father of the Bride (1950), Bad Day at Black Rock (1955), The Last Hurrah (1958), Inherit the Wind (1960), Judgement at Nuremberg (1961), It's a Mad, Mad, Mad, Mad World (1963), Guess Who's Coming to Dinner (1967).

Travolta, John (1954–) American, born Englewood, New Jersey; Welcome Back Kotter (TV 1975–8), Carrie (1976), Saturday Night Fever (1977), Grease (1978), Blow Out (1981), Staying Alive (1983), Two of a Kind (1984), Perfect (1985), Look Who's Talking (1989), Look Who's Talking Too (1991), Chains of Gold (1991), Pulp Fiction (1994), White Man's Burden (1995), Get Shorty (1995), Broken Arrow (1996), Phenomenon (1996), Michael (1996), The Thin Red Line (1998), Swordfish (2001), Hairspray (2007).

Turner, Kathleen (1954–) American, born Springfield, Missouri; The Doctors (TV 1977–8), Body Heat (1981), The Man With Two Brains (1983), Romancing the Stone (1984), Crimes of Passion (1984), The Jewel of the Nile (1985), Prizzi's Honor (1985), Peggy Sue Got Married (1986), Switching Channels (1988), Julia and Julia (1988), The Accidental Tourist (1989), War of the Roses (1989), V I Warshawski (1991), House of Cards (1992), Serial Mom (1994), Moonlight and Valentino (1995), The Virgin Suicides (1999).

Turner, Lana (Julia Jean Mildred Frances Turner) (1920–95) American, born Wallace, Indiana; Dr Jekyll and Mr Hyde (1940), Somewhere I'll Find You (1942), The Three Musketeers (1948), Peyton Place (1957).

Turturro, John (1957–) American, born Brooklyn, New York City; Raging Bull (1980), Hannah and Her Sisters (1986), Do the Right Thing (1989), Miller's Crossing (1990), Barton Fink (1991), Mac (1992), Fearless (1993), O Brother, Where Art Thou? (2000), Secret Window (2004), You Don't Mess with the Zohan (2008).

Tushingham, Rita (1940–) British, born Liverpool; A Taste of Honey (1961), Girl with Green Eyes (1964), The Knack (1965), Dr Zhivago (1965), Judgement in Stone (1986), Resurrected (1988), Paper Marriage (1992), An Awfully Big Adventure (1995), Swing (1999), Being Julia (2004).

Ullmann, Liv (1938–) Norwegian, born Tokyo, Japan; Persona (1966), The Emigrants (1972), Face to Face (1975), Autumn Sonata (1978), Dangerous Moves (1983), Gaby – The True Story (1987), La Amiga (1988), The Rose Garden (1989), Mindwalk (1990), The Ox (1991), The Long Shadow (1992).

Ustinov, Sir Peter (Alexander) (1921–2004) British, born London; Private Angelo (1949), Hotel Sahara (1951), Quo Vadis (1951), Beau Brummell (1954), The Sundowners (1960), Spartacus (1960), Romanoff and Juliet (1961), Topkapi (1964), Logan's Run (1976), Death on the Nile (1978), Evil Under the Sun (1982), Appointment with Death (1988), Lorenzo's Oil (1992), Stiff Upper Lips (1997), The Bachelor (1999).

Valentino, Rudolph (Rodolpho Alphonso Guglielmi di Valentina d'Antonguolla) (1895–1926) Italian-American, born Castellaneta, Italy; The Four Horsemen of the Apocalypse (1921), The Sheikh (1921), Blood and Sand (1922), The Young Rajah (1922), Monsieur Beaucaire (1924), The Eagle (1925), The Son of the Sheikh (1926).

Van Cleef, Lee (1925–89) American, born Somerville, New Jersey; High Noon (1952), For a Few Dollars More (1967), The Good, the Bad and the Ugly

Arts and Culture

(1967), *Return of Sabata* (1971), *The Magnificent Seven Ride* (1972), *Escape from New York* (1981), *Codename: Wildgeese II* (1986), *The Heist* (1988).

Van Damme, Jean-Claude (1961–) Belgian, born Brussels; *No Retreat No Surrender* (1985), *Kickboxer* (1989), *Universal Soldier* (1992), *Nowhere to Run* (1993), *Timecop* (1994), *Streetfighter* (1994), *The Quest* (1996), *Legionnaire* (1998), *Derailed* (2002), *Until Death* (2007).

Van Dyke, Dick (1925–) American, born West Plains, Missouri; *The Dick Van Dyke Show* (TV 1961–6), *Mary Poppins* (1964), *Chitty Chitty Bang Bang* (1968), *The Comic* (1969), *Dropout Father* (TV 1982), *Dick Tracy* (1990), *Diagnosis Murder* (TV 1993–2001).

Vaughn, Robert (Francis) (1932–) American, born New York City; *The Magnificent Seven* (1960), *The Man from UNCLE* (TV 1964–7), *The Towering Inferno* (1974), *Superman III* (1983), *Delta Force* (1985), *Black Moon Rising* (1986), *The Sender* (1997), *Happy Hour* (2003), *Hustle* (TV 2004–).

Vincent, Jan-Michael (1944–) American, born Denver, Colorado; *The Mechanic* (1972), *The World's Greatest Athlete* (1973), *Bite the Bullet* (1974), *Hooper* (1978), *Hard Country* (1981), *Airwolf* (TV 1982–6), *The Winds of War* (TV 1983), *Alienator* (1989), *Beyond the Call of Duty* (1992), *Extreme* (1993), *Redline* (1995), *Russian Roulette* (1996), *White Boy* (2002).

von Stroheim, Erich (Erich Oswald Stroheim) (1885–1957) Austrian, born Vienna; *Foolish Wives* (1921), *La Grande Illusion* (1937), *Five Graves to Cairo* (1943), *Sunset Boulevard* (1950).

von Sydow, Max (Carl Adolf) (1929–) Swedish, born Lund; *The Seventh Seal* (1956), *The Face* (1959), *The Greatest Story Ever Told* (1965), *Hawaii* (1966), *Through a Glass Darkly* (1966), *Hour of the Wolf* (1967), *The Emigrants* (1972), *The Exorcist* (1973), *Exorcist II: The Heretic* (1977), *Flash Gordon* (1980), *Never Say Never Again* (1983), *Hannah and Her Sisters* (1986), *Pelle, the Conqueror* (1988), *Awakenings* (1990), *Dr Grassler* (1990), *The Father* (1990), *The Ox* (1991), *The Touch* (1992), *Needful Things* (1993), *Judge Dredd* (1995), *Snow Falling on Cedars* (1999), *Minority Report* (2002), *Heidi* (2005).

Wagner, Robert (John) (1930–) American, born Detroit, Michigan; *The Silver Whip* (1953), *Prince Valiant* (1954), *A Kiss Before Dying* (1956), *The True Story of Jesse James* (1957), *All the Fine Young Cannibals* (1959), *The Condemned of Altona* (1963), *The Pink Panther* (1963), *It Takes a Thief* (TV 1965–7), *Colditz* (TV 1972–3), *The Towering Inferno* (1974), *Switch* (TV 1975–7), *Hart to Hart* (TV 1979–84), *Trail of the Pink Panther* (1982), *Curse of the Pink Panther* (1983), *Delirious* (1993), *The Bruce Lee Story* (1993), *Austin Powers: International Man of Mystery* (1997), *Austin Powers: The Spy Who Shagged Me* (1999), *Austin Powers in Goldmember* (2002).

Walken, Christopher (1943–) American, born Astoria, New York; *Annie Hall* (1977), *The Deer Hunter* (1978), *The Dogs of War* (1981), *Pennies from Heaven* (1981), *The Dead Zone* (1983), *Brainstorm* (1983), *A View to a Kill* (1984), *At Close Range* (1986), *The Milagro Beanfield War* (1987), *Biloxi Blues* (1988), *Puss in Boots* (1988), *The Comfort of Strangers* (1990), *Batman Returns* (1992), *True Romance* (1993), *Wayne's World 2* (1993), *Pulp Fiction* (1994), *Things to Do in Denver When You're Dead* (1995), *Sleepy Hollow* (1999), *Catch Me If You Can* (2002), *Hairspray* (2007).

Walters, Julie (1950–) British, born Birmingham;

Educating Rita (1983), *She'll Be Wearing Pink Pyjamas* (1984), *Car Trouble* (1986), *Prick Up Your Ears* (1987), *Personal Services* (1987), *Buster* (1987), *Killing Dad* (1989), *Stepping Out* (1991), *Sister My Sister* (1995), *Intimate Relations* (1996), *Billy Elliott* (2000), *Harry Potter* series (2001–) *Calendar Girls* (2003), *Driving Lessons* (2006), *Mamma Mia!* (2008).

Wanamaker, Sam (1919–93) American, born Chicago; *Those Magnificent Men in Their Flying Machines* (1965), *The Spy Who Came in from the Cold* (1965), *Voyage of the Damned* (1976), *Death on the Nile* (1978), *Private Benjamin* (1980), *Raw Deal* (1986), *Superman IV* (1986), *Baby Boom* (1987), *Judgement in Berlin* (1988), *Guilty by Suspicion* (1991).

Warner, David (1941–) British, born Manchester; *Morgan* (1966), *The Bofors Gun* (1968), *The Engagement* (1970), *The Omen* (1976), *Holocaust* (TV 1978), *The 39 Steps* (1978), *Time Bandits* (1981), *The French Lieutenant's Woman* (1981), *Tron* (1982), *The Man with Two Brains* (1983), *Company of Wolves* (1984), *Mr North* (1988), *Hanna's War* (1988), *Star Trek V: The Final Frontier* (1989), *The Secret Life of Ian Fleming* (1990), *Star Trek VI: The Undiscovered Country* (1991), *The Unnameable Returns* (1992), *Tryst* (1994), *Darkening* (1996), *Titanic* (1997), *Avatar* (2004).

Washington, Denzel (1954–) American, born Mt Vernon, New York; *St Elsewhere* (TV 1982–9), *Cry Freedom* (1987), *Queen and Country* (1988), *Glory* (1989), *Mo' Better Blues* (1990), *Mississippi Masala* (1991), *Ricochet* (1991), *Malcolm X* (1992), *Philadelphia* (1993), *The Pelican Brief* (1993), *Much Ado About Nothing* (1993), *Devil in a Blue Dress* (1995), *Crimson Tide* (1995), *Courage Under Fire* (1996), *The Preacher's Wife* (1996), *Training Day* (2001), *John Q* (2002), *Antwone Fisher* (2002), *Inside Man* (2006), *American Gangster* (2007).

Wayne, John (Marion Robert Morrison) (1907–79) American, born Winterset, Iowa; *The Big Trail* (1930), *Stagecoach* (1939), *The Long Voyage Home* (1940), *Red River* (1948), *She Wore a Yellow Ribbon* (1949), *Sands of Iwo Jima* (1949), *The Quiet Man* (1952), *The High and the Mighty* (1954), *The Searchers* (1956), *Rio Bravo* (1959), *The Alamo* (1960), *True Grit* (1969), *The Shootist* (1976).

Weaver, Sigourney (Susan Weaver) (1949–) American, born New York City; *Alien* (1979), *The Janitor* (1981), *The Year of Living Dangerously* (1982), *Ghostbusters* (1984), *Aliens* (1986), *Gorillas in the Mist* (1988), *Working Girl* (1988), *Ghostbusters II* (1989), *Alien 3* (1992), *1492* (1992), *Dave* (1993), *Death and The Maiden* (1994), *Copycat* (1995), *Ice Storm* (1996), *Alien: Resurrection* (1997), *Galaxy Quest* (1999), *Holes* (2003), *Imaginary Heroes* (2004), *The Girl in the Park* (2007).

Welch, Raquel (Raquel Tejada) (1940–) American, born Chicago; *Fantastic Voyage* (1966), *One Million Years BC* (1967), *Myra Breckenridge* (1970), *The Three Musketeers* (1974), *The Four Musketeers* (1975).

Welles, Orson (1915–85) American, born Kenosha, Wisconsin; *Citizen Kane* (1941), *Journey into Fear* (1942), *The Stranger* (1945), *The Lady from Shanghai* (1947), *The Third Man* (1949), *The Trial* (1962), *Touch of Evil* (1965), *A Man For All Seasons* (1966), *Casino Royale* (1967), *Voyage of the Damned* (1976), *History of the World Part One* (1981).

West, Mae (1892–1980) American, born Brooklyn, New York City; *She Done Him Wrong* (1933), *I'm No Angel* (1933), *My Little Chickadee* (1939), *Myra Breckenridge* (1970).

Widmark, Richard (1914–2008) American, born Sunrise, Minnesota; *Kiss of Death* (1947), *Night and the City* (1950), *How the West Was Won* (1963), *The Bedford Incident* (1965), *Madigan* (1968), *Madigan* (TV 1972), *Murder on the Orient Express* (1974), *Who Dares Wins* (1982), *Hanky Panky* (1982), *Against all Odds* (1983), *True Colors* (1991).

Wilder, Gene (Jerome Silberman) (1935–) American, born Milwaukee, Wisconsin; *Bonnie and Clyde* (1967), *The Producers* (1967), *Willy Wonka and the Chocolate Factory* (1971), *Blazing Saddles* (1974), *Young Frankenstein* (1974), *The Frisco Kid* (1979), *Stir Crazy* (1982), *Hanky Panky* (1982), *The Woman in Red* (1984), *Haunted Honeymoon* (1986), *See No Evil Hear No Evil* (1989), *Funny About Love* (1991).

Williams, Kenneth (1926–88) British, born London; *Carry on Sergeant* (1958), *Follow that Camel* (1968), *Carry on Dick* (1974).

Williams, Robin (1952–) American, born Chicago; *Mork and Mindy* (TV 1978–82), *Popeye* (1980), *The World According to Garp* (1982), *Good Morning Vietnam* (1987), *Dead Poets Society* (1989), *Cadillac Man* (1990), *Awakenings* (1990), *Dead Again* (1991), *The Fisher King* (1991), *Hook* (1991), *Toys* (1992), *Ferngully* (1992), *Being Human* (1992), *Mrs Doubtfire* (1993), *Jumanji* (1995), *Hamlet* (1996), *Father's Day* (1997), *Good Will Hunting* (1997), *Bicentennial Man* (1999), *One Hour Photo* (2002), *Insomnia* (2002), *Man of the Year* (2006).

Williams, Treat (Richard Williams) (1951–) American, born Rowayton, Connecticut; *The Eagle Has Landed* (1977), *Hair* (1977), *1941* (1979), *Once Upon a Time in America* (1984), *Dempsey* (TV 1985), *Smooth Talk* (1985), *A Streetcar Named Desire* (1986), *The Men's Club* (1986), *Dead Heat* (1988), *Heart of Dixie* (1990), *The Phantom* (1995), *Deep Rising* (1998), *What Happens in Vegas* (2008).

Williamson, Nicol (1938–) British, born Hamilton, near Glasgow; *Inadmissible Evidence* (1967), *The Bofors Gun* (1968), *The Reckoning* (1969), *Excalibur* (1981), *Sakharov* (TV 1985), *Return to Oz* (1985), *Black Widow* (1986), *The Exorcist III* (1990).

Willis, Bruce (1955–) American, born Idar-Oberstein, West Germany; *Moonlighting* (TV 1985–9), *Blind Date* (1987), *Die Hard* (1988), *Die Hard 2: Die Harder* (1990), *Bonfire of the Vanities* (1991), *Hudson Hawk* (1991), *Billy Bathgate* (1991), *The Last Boy Scout* (1991), *Death Becomes Her* (1992), *Striking Distance* (1993), *Pulp Fiction* (1994), *Nobody's Fool* (1994), *Die Hard with a Vengeance* (1995), *Twelve Monkeys* (1995), *The Fifth Element* (1996), *The Jackal* (1997), *The Sixth Sense* (1999), *Hart's War* (2002), *Sin City* (2005), *Lucky Number Slevin* (2006), *Live Free or Die Hard* (2007).

Winslet, Kate (Elizabeth) (1975–) English, born Reading; *Heavenly Creatures* (1994), *Sense and Sensibility* (1995), *Hamlet* (1996), *Titanic* (1997), *Quills* (2000), *Iris* (2002), *Eternal Sunshine of the Spotless Mind* (2004), *Finding Neverland* (2004), *Little Children* (2006), *The Reader* (2008), *Revolutionary Road* (2008).

Winger, Debra (1955–) American, born Columbus, Ohio; *Urban Cowboy* (1980), *Cannery Row* (1981), *An Officer and a Gentleman* (1982), *Terms of Endearment* (1983), *Legal Eagles* (1986), *Black Widow* (1987), *Made in Heaven* (1987), *Betrayed* (1988), *The Sheltering Sky* (1990), *Wilder Napalm* (1992), *A Dangerous Woman* (1993), *Shadowlands*

(1993), *Forget Paris* (1995), *Eulogy* (2004).

Winters, Shelley (Shirley Schrift) (1922–2006) American, born St Louis, Missouri; *A Double Life* (1948), *The Big Knife* (1955), *The Night of the Hunter* (1955), *The Diary of Anne Frank* (1959), *Lolita* (1962), *A Patch of Blue* (1965), *Alfie* (1966), *The Poseidon Adventure* (1972), *SOB* (1981), *Purple People Eater* (1988), *Stepping Out* (1991), *Backfire* (1994), *The Portrait of a Lady* (1996).

Wisdom, Sir Norman (1915–) British, born London; *Trouble in Store* (1955), *Man of the Moment* (1955), *Just My Luck* (1958), *There was a Crooked Man* (1960), *On the Beat* (1962), *A Stitch in Time* (1963), *Sandwich Man* (1966), *The Night They Raided Minsky's* (1968), *What's Good for the Goose* (1969), *Five Children and It* (2004).

Witherspoon, (Laura Jeanne) Reese (1976–) American, born New Orleans, Louisiana; *Freeway* (1996), *Pleasantville* (1998), *Cruel Intentions* (1999), *Election* (1999), *Legally Blonde* (2001), *Sweet Home Alabama* (2002), *Walk the Line* (2005), *Rendition* (2007).

Wood, Natalie (Natalia Nikolaevna Zakharenko) (1938–81) American, born San Francisco, California; *Miracle on 34th Street* (1947), *The Ghost and Mrs Muir* (1947), *Rebel Without a Cause* (1955), *The Searchers* (1956), *Marjorie Morningstar* (1958), *All The Fine Young Cannibals* (1959), *Splendor in the Grass* (1961), *West Side Story* (1961), *Love with the Proper Stranger* (1964), *The Great Race* (1965), *This Property is Condemned* (1966), *Bob and Carol and Ted and Alice* (1969), *From Here to Eternity* (TV 1979), *Meteor* (1979), *Brainstorm* (1983).

Woods, James (1947–) American, born Vernal, Utah; *The Choirboys* (1977), *Videodrome* (1983), *Salvador* (1986), *Best Seller* (1987), *Cop* (1988), *The Boost* (1988), *The Getaway* (1994), *Nixon* (1995), *Contact* (1997), *John Q* (2002).

Woodward, Joanne (1930–) American, born Thomasville, Georgia; *Three Faces of Eve* (1957), *No Down Payment* (1957), *The Long Hot Summer* (1958), *The Stripper* (1963), *A Big Hand for the Little Lady* (1966), *Rachel, Rachel* (1968), *Summer Wishes, Winter Dreams* (1973), *The Glass Menagerie* (1987), *Mr and Mrs Bridge* (1990), *Philadelphia* (1993), *Breathing Lessons* (TV 1994).

York, Michael (1942–) British, born Fulmer; *Accident* (1967), *Romeo and Juliet* (1968), *Cabaret* (1972), *Lost Horizon* (1973), *The Three Musketeers* (1973), *The Four Musketeers* (1974), *Jesus of Nazareth* (TV 1977), *The Island of Dr Moreau* (1977), *The White Lions* (1980), *Space* (TV 1985), *The Far Country* (TV 1986), *Sword of Gideon* (TV 1986), *Return of the Musketeers* (1989), *The Four Minute Mile* (1992), *The Ring* (1996), *Austin Powers: International Man of Mystery* (1997), *Austin Powers: The Spy Who Shagged Me* (1999), *Austin Powers in Goldmember* (2002).

Zellweger, Renée (1969–) American, born Katy, Texas; *Jerry Maguire* (1996), *Nurse Betty* (2000), *Bridget Jones's Diary* (2001), *Chicago* (2002), *Cold Mountain* (2003), *Bridget Jones: The Edge of Reason* (2004), *Miss Potter* (2006), *Leatherheads* (2008).

Zeta-Jones, Catherine (1969–) British, born Swansea; *The Darling Buds of May* (TV 1991), *The Mask of Zorro* (1998), *Entrapment* (1999), *Traffic* (2000), *High Fidelity* (2000), *Chicago* (2002), *Intolerable Cruelty* (2003), *Ocean's Twelve* (2004), *No Reservations* (2007).

Arts and Culture

Arts and Culture

Film directors

Selected films are listed.

Aldrich, Robert (1918–83) American, born Cranston, Rhode Island; *Apache* (1954), *Vera Cruz* (1954), *Kiss Me Deadly* (1955), *Attack!* (1957), *What Ever Happened to Baby Jane?* (1962), *The Dirty Dozen* (1967).

Allen, Woody (Allen Stewart Konigsberg) (1935–) American, born Brooklyn, New York City; *What's Up, Tiger Lily?* (1966), *Bananas* (1971), *Everything You Wanted to Know About Sex, But Were Afraid to Ask* (1972), *Play it Again, Sam* (1972), *Sleeper* (1973), *Love and Death* (1975), *Annie Hall* (1977), *Interiors* (1978), *Manhattan* (1979), *A Midsummer Night's Sex Comedy* (1982), *Hannah and Her Sisters* (1986), *Radio Days* (1987), *Crimes and Misdemeanors* (1990), *Alice* (1991), *Shadows and Fog* (1992), *Husbands and Wives* (1992), *Manhattan Murder Mystery* (1993), *Bullets Over Broadway* (1994), *Mighty Aphrodite* (1996), *Deconstructing Harry* (1997), *Celebrity* (1998), *Sweet and Lowdown* (1999), *The Curse of the Jade Scorpion* (2001), *Melinda and Melinda* (2004), *Match Point* (2005), *Scoop* (2006), *Vicky Cristina Barcelona* (2008).

Almodóvar, Pedro (1949–) Spanish, born Calzada de Calatrava; *Women on the Verge of a Nervous Breakdown* (1988), *Tie Me Up! Tie Me Down!* (1990), *High Heels* (1991), *Kika* (1993), *Live Flesh* (1997), *All About My Mother* (1999), *Talk to Her* (2002), *Volver* (2006).

Altman, Robert (1925–2006) American, born Kansas City, Missouri; *The James Dean Story* (1957), *M*A*S*H* (1970), *McCabe and Mrs Miller* (1971), *The Long Goodbye* (1973), *Nashville* (1975), *Popeye* (1980), *Come Back to the 5 & Dime Jimmy Dean Jimmy Dean* (1982), *Fool for Love* (1985), *Aria* (1987), *Vincent and Theo* (1990), *The Player* (1992), *Short Cuts* (1993), *Prêt-À-Porter* (1994), *Kansas City* (1996), *The Gingerbread Man* (1998), *Cookie's Fortune* (1999), *Gosford Park* (2001), *A Prairie House Companion* (2006).

Antonioni, Michelangelo (1912–2007) Italian, born Ferrara; *L'Avventura* (1959), *La Notte* (1960), *L'Eclisse* (1962), *Blow-Up* (1966), *The Passenger* (1975), *Beyond the Clouds* (1995), *Eros* (2004).

Asquith, Anthony (1902–68) British, born London; *Underground* (1930), *Pygmalion* (1937), *French without Tears* (1939), *Quiet Wedding* (1940), *The Demi-Paradise* (1943), *Fanny by Gaslight* (1944), *The Way to the Stars* (1945), *The Browning Version* (1950), *The Importance of Being Earnest* (1952), *Orders to Kill* (1958), *The VIPs* (1963).

Attenborough, Richard (Samuel) Attenborough, Baron (1923–) British, born Cambridge; *Oh! What a Lovely War* (1968), *A Bridge Too Far* (1977), *Gandhi* (1982), *A Chorus Line* (1985), *Cry Freedom* (1987), *Chaplin* (1992), *Shadowlands* (1993), *In Love and War* (1996), *Grey Owl* (1998), *Closing the Ring* (2007).

Badham, John (1939–) American, born Luton, England; *The Law* (TV 1974), *Saturday Night Fever* (1977), *Whose Life is it Anyway?* (1981), *Blue Thunder* (1982), *War Games* (1983), *American Flyers* (1984), *Short Circuit* (1986), *Stakeout* (1987), *Bird on a Wire* (1989), *The Assassin* (1992), *Another Stakeout* (1993), *Floating Away* (1998).

Beatty, Warren (Henry Warren Beaty) (1937–) American, born Richmond, Virginia; *Heaven Can Wait* (1978), *Reds* (1981), *Dick Tracy* (1990), *Bulworth* (1998).

Bergman, (Ernst) Ingmar (1918–2007) Swedish, born Uppsala; *Crisis* (1945), *Prison* (1948), *Sawdust and Tinsel* (1953), *The Face* (1955), *Smiles of a Summer Night* (1955), *The Seventh Seal* (1957), *Wild Strawberries* (1957), *The Virgin Spring* (1959), *Through a Glass Darkly* (1961), *The Silence* (1963), *Shame* (1968), *Cries and Whispers* (1972), *The Magic Flute* (1974), *Autumn Sonata* (1978), *Fanny and Alexander* (1983).

Bertolucci, Bernardo (1940–) Italian, born Parma; *Love and Anger* (1969), *The Conformist* (1970), *Last Tango in Paris* (1972), *1900* (1976), *The Last Emperor* (1987), *The Sheltering Sky* (1990), *Little Buddha* (1993), *Stealing Beauty* (1996), *Besieged* (1998), *The Dreamers* (2003).

Besson, Luc (1959–) French, born Paris; *The Last Battle* (1983), *Subway* (1985), *The Big Blue* (1988), *Nikita* (1990), *Leon* (1994), *The Fifth Element* (1997), *The Messenger: The Story of Joan of Arc* (1999), *Arthur and the Invisibles* (2007).

Bogdanovich, Peter (1939–) American, born Kingston, New York; *Targets* (1967), *The Last Picture Show* (1971), *Paper Moon* (1973), *What's Up, Doc?* (1972), *Nickelodeon* (1976), *Mask* (1985), *Illegally Yours* (1987), *Texasville* (1990), *Noises Off* (1992), *The Thing Called Love* (1993), *The Cat's Meow* (2001).

Boorman, John (1933–) English, born Epsom, Surrey; *Point Blank* (1967), *Hell in the Pacific* (1969), *Deliverance* (1972), *Zardoz* (1974), *Excalibur* (1981), *The Emerald Forest* (1984), *Hope and Glory* (1987), *Where the Heart Is* (1990), *Beyond Rangoon* (1995), *The Tailor of Panama* (2001), *The Tiger's Tail* (2006).

Bresson, Robert (1901–99) French, born Bromont-Lamothe; *Les Dames du Bois de Boulogne* (1946), *Journal d'un Curé de Campagne* (1950), *Pickpocket* (1959), *Au hasard, Balthazar* (1966), *Une Femme douce* (1969), *L'Argent* (1983).

Brook, Peter (Stephen Paul) (1925–) British, born London; *Lord of the Flies* (1963), *King Lear* (1971), *Carmen* (1983), *The Mahabharata* (TV 1989).

Brooks, Mel (Melvin Kaminski) (1926–) American, born Brooklyn, New York City; *The Producers* (1966), *Blazing Saddles* (1974), *Young Frankenstein* (1974), *High Anxiety* (1977), *History of the World Part One* (1981), *Spaceballs* (1987), *Life Stinks* (1991), *Robin Hood: Men in Tights* (1993), *Dracula: Dead and Loving It* (1995).

Buñuel, Luis (1900–83) Spanish, born Calanda; *Un Chien Andalou* (with Salvador Dalí) (1928), *L'Âge d'Or* (1930), *Los Olvidados* (1950), *Robinson Crusoe* (1952), *El* (1953), *Nazarin* (1958), *Viridiana* (1961), *The Exterminating Angel* (1962), *Belle de Jour* (1967), *The Discreet Charm of the Bourgeoisie* (1972), *The Phantom of Liberty* (1974), *That Obscure Object of Desire* (1977).

Burton, Tim (1958–) American, born Burbank, California; *Beetlejuice* (1988), *Batman* (1989), *Edward Scissorhands* (1990), *Batman Returns* (1992), *Ed Wood* (1994), *Mars Attacks!* (1996), *Sleepy Hollow* (1999), *Planet of the Apes* (2001), *Big Fish* (2003), *Corpse Bride* (2005), *Sweeney Todd* (2007).

Capra, Frank (1897–1991) Italian-American, born Bisacquino, Sicily; *Platinum Blonde* (1932), *American Madness* (1932), *Lady for a Day* (1933), *It Happened One Night* (1934), *Mr Deeds Goes to Town* (1936), *Lost Horizon* (1937), *You Can't Take It With You* (1938), *Mr Smith Goes to Washington* (1939), *Meet John Doe* (1941), *Arsenic and Old Lace* (1944), *It's a Wonderful Life* (1946).

Carné, Marcel (1909–96) French, born Batignolles,

Paris; *Quai des Brumes* (1938), *Le Jour se lève* (1939), *Les Enfants du Paradis* (1944).

Carpenter, John (1948–) American, born Carthage, New York; *Dark Star* (1974), *Assault on Precinct 13* (1976), *Halloween* (1978), *The Fog* (1979), *Escape from New York* (1981), *The Thing* (1982), *Christine* (1983), *Starman* (1984), *Big Trouble in Little China* (1986), *Prince of Darkness* (1987), *Memoirs of an Invisible Man* (1992), *Escape From LA* (1996), *Vampires* (1998), *Ghosts of Mars* (2001).

Chabrol, Claude (1930–) French, born Paris; *Beau Serge* (1958), *Les Cousins* (1959), *Les Biches* (1968), *La Femme Infidèle* (1969), *Le Boucher* (1969), *Les Noces rouges* (1973), *Masques* (1987), *Une Affaire des Femmes* (1989), *Rein ne va plus* (1997), *Merci pour le Chocolat* (2000), *La Fleur du Mal* (2003), *L'ivresse du Pouvoir* (2006), *La Fille coupée en deux* (2007).

Clair, René (René Lucien Chomette) (1891–1981) French, born Paris; *An Italian Straw Hat* (1927), *Sous Les Toits de Paris* (1929), *Le Million* (1931), *À Nous la liberté* (1931), *I Married a Witch* (1942), *It Happened Tomorrow* (1944), *And Then There Were None* (1945), *Les Belles de Nuit* (1952), *Porte des Lilas* (1956), *Tout l'or du Monde* (1961).

Cocteau, Jean (1889–1963) French, born Maisons-Lafitte; *Le Sang d'un poète* (1930), *La Belle et La Bête* (1946), *Orphée* (1950), *Le Testament d'Orphée* (1959).

Coen, Ethan (1957–) and **Joel** (1954–) American, both born St Louis Park, Minnesota; *Blood Simple* (1984), *Raising Arizona* (1987), *Miller's Crossing* (1990), *Barton Fink* (1991), *The Hudsucker Proxy* (1994), *Fargo* (1995), *The Big Lebowski* (1998), *O Brother, Where Art Thou?* (2000), *The Man Who Wasn't There* (2001), *Intolerable Cruelty* (2003), *The Ladykillers* (2004), *No Country for Old Men* (2007), *Burn After Reading* (2008).

Coppola, Francis Ford (1939–) American, born Detroit, Michigan; *The Godfather* (1972), *The Godfather, Part II* (1974), *Apocalypse Now* (1979), *One from the Heart* (1982), *The Outsiders* (1983), *Rumble Fish* (1983), *The Cotton Club* (1984), *Peggy Sue Got Married* (1987), *Gardens of Stone* (1987), *Tucker: The Man and His Dream* (1988), *The Godfather, Part III* (1991), *Dracula* (1992), *The Rainmaker* (1997), *Youth Without Youth* (2007).

Corman, Roger (1926–) American, born Detroit, Michigan; *Not of This Earth* (1957), *Bucket of Blood* (1959), *Fall of the House of Usher* (1960), *The Little Shop of Horrors* (1960), *The Pit and the Pendulum* (1961), *The Intruder* (1962), *The Raven* (1963), *The Man with the X-ray Eyes* (1963), *The Masque of the Red Death* (1964), *The Tomb of Ligeia* (1964), *Frankenstein Unbound* (1990).

Cronenberg, David (1943–) Canadian, born Toronto, Ontario; *Shivers* (1976), *Rabid* (1977), *The Brood* (1978), *Scanners* (1980), *Videodrome* (1983), *The Dead Zone* (1983), *The Fly* (1985), *Dead Ringers* (1988), *Naked Lunch* (1991), *M Butterfly* (1992), *Crash* (1996), *eXistenZ* (1999), *Spider* (2002), *A History of Violence* (2005), *Eastern Promises* (2007).

Curtiz, Michael (Mihály Kertész) (1888–1962) American–Hungarian, born Budapest, Hungary; *Noah's Ark* (1929), *Mammy* (1930), *Doctor X* (1932), *The Mystery of the Wax Museum* (1933), *Black Fury* (1935), *Captain Blood* (1935), *Charge of the Light Brigade* (1936), *The Adventures of Robin Hood* (1938), *Angels with Dirty Faces* (1938), *The Sea Hawk* (1940), *The Sea Wolf* (1941), *Yankee Doodle Dandy* (1942), *Casablanca* (1943), *Mildred*

Pierce (1945), *White Christmas* (1954), *We're No Angels* (1955), *King Creole* (1958).

Dante, Joe (1946–) American, born Morristown, New Jersey; *Piranha* (1978), *The Howling* (1980), *Gremlins* (1984), *Explorers* (1985), *Innerspace* (1987), *The 'Burbs* (1989), *Amazon Women on the Moon* (1987), *Gremlins 2: The New Batch* (1990), *Small Soldiers* (1998), *Looney Tunes: Back in Action* (2003).

de Mille, Cecil B(lount) (1881–1959) American, born Ashfield, Massachusetts; *Male and Female* (1919), *King of Kings* (1927), *The Ten Commandments* (1923–1956), *The Greatest Show on Earth* (1952).

Demme, Jonathan (1944–) American, born Long Island, New York; *Citizens Band* (1977), *Swing Shift* (1984), *Swimming to Cambodia* (1987), *The Silence of the Lambs* (1991), *Philadelphia* (1993), *Beloved* (1998), *The Manchurian Candidate* (2004), *Rachel Getting Married* (2008).

de Palma, Brian (1940–) American, born Newark, New Jersey; *Greetings* (1968), *Carrie* (1976), *The Fury* (1978), *Dressed to Kill* (1980), *Blow Out* (1981), *Scarface* (1983), *Body Double* (1984), *The Untouchables* (1987), *Casualties of War* (1989), *Bonfire of the Vanities* (1990), *Carlito's Way* (1993), *Mission: Impossible* (1996), *Mission to Mars* (2000), *The Black Dahlia* (2006), *Redacted* (2007).

Donner, Richard (1930–) American, born New York City; *The Omen* (1976), *Superman* (1978), *Inside Moves* (1980), *The Final Conflict* (1981), *Ladyhawke* (1984), *The Goonies* (1985), *Lethal Weapon* (1987), *Scrooged* (1988), *Lethal Weapon 2* (1989), *Lethal Weapon 3* (1992), *Maverick* (1994), *Conspiracy Theory* (1997), *Lethal Weapon 4* (1998), *16 Blocks* (2006).

Eastwood, Clint (1930–) American, born San Francisco, California; *Play Misty for Me* (1971), *The Outlaw Josey Wales* (1976), *Pale Rider* (1985), *Birdy* (1988), *Unforgiven* (1992), *The Bridges of Madison County* (1995), *Absolute Power* (1997), *True Crime* (1999), *Space Cowboys* (2000), *Mystic River* (2003), *Million Dollar Baby* (2004), *Flags of Our Fathers* (2006), *Letters from Iwo Jima* (2006), *Changeling* (2008).

Eisenstein, Sergei Mikhailovich (1898–1948) Russian, born Riga; *Stride* (1924), *Battleship Potemkin* (1925), *Alexander Nevsky* (1938), *Ten Days that Shook the World* (1928), *The Magic Seed* (1941), *Ivan the Terrible* (1942–6).

Fassbinder, Rainer Werner (1946–82) German, born Bad Wörishofen; *Fear Eats the Soul* (1974), *The Marriage of Maria Braun* (1979).

Fellini, Federico (1920–93) Italian, born Rimini; *I Vitelloni* (1953), *La Strada* (1954), *La Dolce Vita* (1960), *8½* (1963), *Satyricon* (1969), *Fellini's Rome* (1972), *Casanova* (1976), *Orchestra Rehearsal* (1979), *City of Women* (1981), *The Ship Sails On* (1983), *Ginger and Fred* (1986).

Fleming, Victor (1883–1949) American, born Pasadena, California; *Mantrap* (1926), *The Virginian* (1929), *The Wet Parade* (1932), *Red Dust* (1932), *Treasure Island* (1934), *Test Pilot* (1938), *Gone with the Wind* (1939), *The Wizard of Oz* (1939), *Dr Jekyll and Mr Hyde* (1941), *A Guy Named Joe* (1943).

Forbes, Bryan (John Theobold Clarke) (1926–) British, born London; *The L-shaped Room* (1962), *The Slipper and the Rose* (1976), *International Velvet* (1978), *The Naked Face* (1984).

Ford, John (1895–73) American, born Cape Elizabeth, Maine; *The Tornado* (1917), *The Iron Horse* (1924), *Arrowsmith* (1931), *The Informer* (1935), *Stagecoach* (1939), *Young Mr Lincoln*

(1939), *The Grapes of Wrath* (1940), *My Darling Clementine* (1946), *The Quiet Man* (1952), *The Searchers* (1956), *The Man Who Shot Liberty Valance* (1962).

Forman, Miloš (1932–) Czech, born Kaslov; *Taking Off* (1971), *One Flew Over the Cuckoo's Nest* (1975), *Amadeus* (1984), *The People vs Larry Flynt* (1996), *Man on the Moon* (1999), *Goya's Ghosts* (2006).

Frears, Stephen (1941–) British, born Leicester; *The Hit* (1984), *My Beautiful Laundrette* (1985), *Prick Up Your Ears* (1987), *Sammy and Rosie Get Laid* (1987), *Dangerous Liaisons* (1988), *The Grifters* (1990), *The Snapper* (1993), *Mary Reilly* (1995), *High Fidelity* (2000), *Dirty Pretty Things* (2002), *Mrs Henderson Presents* (2005), *The Queen* (2006).

Friedkin, William (1935–) American, born Chicago; *The French Connection* (1971), *The Exorcist* (1973), *The Guardian* (1990), *Rules of Engagement* (2000), *Bug* (2006).

Gilliam, Terry (1940–) American, born Minneapolis, Minnesota; *Jabberwocky* (1977), *Time Bandits* (1980), *Brazil* (1985), *The Adventures of Baron Munchausen* (1988), *The Fisher King* (1991), *Twelve Monkeys* (1995), *Fear and Loathing in Las Vegas* (1998), *The Brothers Grimm* (2005), *Tideland* (2005).

Godard, Jean-Luc (1930–) French, born Paris; *À Bout de Souffle* (1960), *Alphaville* (1965), *Le Plus Vieux Métier du Monde* (1967), *Sauve Qui Peut La Vie* (1980), *Hail Mary* (1985), *Nouvelle Vague* (1990), *The Old Place* (1998), *Notre Musique* (2004).

Greenaway, Peter (1942–) British, born Newport, Gwent; *The Draughtman's Contract* (1982), *The Belly of an Architect* (1987), *Drowning by Numbers* (1988), *The Cook, The Thief, His Wife and Her Lover* (1989), *Prospero's Books* (1991), *The Baby of Macon* (1993), *The Pillow Book* (1995), *8½ Women* (1999), *Nightwatching* (2007).

Griffith, D(avid) W(ark) (1875–1948) American, born La Grange, Kentucky; *Judith of Bethulia* (1913), *The Birth of a Nation* (1915), *Intolerance* (1916), *Hearts of the World* (1918), *Broken Blossoms* (1919), *Orphans of the Storm* (1922).

Hall, Sir Peter (Reginald Frederick) (1930–) British, born Bury St Edmunds, Suffolk; *Work is a Four Letter Word* (1968), *Perfect Friday* (1971), *Akenfield* (1974), *Never Talk to Strangers* (1995).

Hawks, Howard (Winchester) (1896–1977) American, born Goshen, Indiana; *The Dawn Patrol* (1930), *Scarface* (1932), *Twentieth Century* (1934), *Barbary Coast* (1935), *Bringing Up Baby* (1938), *His Girl Friday* (1940), *To Have and Have Not* (1944), *The Big Sleep* (1946), *Red River* (1948), *Gentlemen Prefer Blondes* (1953), *Rio Bravo* (1959).

Hill, George Roy (1921–2002) American, born Minneapolis, Minnesota; *The World of Henry Orient* (1964), *Thoroughly Modern Millie* (1967), *Butch Cassidy and the Sundance Kid* (1969), *Slaughterhouse 5* (1972), *The Sting* (1973), *The World According to Garp* (1982), *Funny Farm* (1988).

Hitchcock, Sir Alfred (Joseph) (1899–1980) British, born Leytonstone, London; *The Lodger* (1926), *Blackmail* (1929), *Murder* (1930), *The Thirty-Nine Steps* (1935), *The Lady Vanishes* (1938), *Rebecca* (1940), *Spellbound* (1945), *Notorious* (1946), *The Paradine Case* (1947), *Strangers on a Train* (1951), *Rear Window* (1954), *Dial M for Murder* (1955), *Vertigo* (1958), *North by Northwest* (1959), *Psycho* (1960), *The Birds* (1963), *Marnie* (1964), *Frenzy* (1972), *Alfred Hitchcock Presents* (TV 1955–61).

Huston, John (Marcellus) (1906–87) Irish–American, born Nevada, Missouri; *The Maltese Falcon* (1941), *Key Largo* (1948), *The Treasure of the Sierra Madre* (1948), *The Asphalt Jungle* (1950), *The African Queen* (1951), *Moulin Rouge* (1952), *The Misfits* (1960), *Freud* (1962), *Night of the Iguana* (1964), *Casino Royale* (1967), *Fat City* (1972), *The Man Who Would Be King* (1975), *Annie* (1982), *Prizzi's Honor* (1985), *The Dead* (1987).

Ivory, James Francis (1928–) American, born Berkeley, California; *Shakespeare Wallah* (1965), *Heat and Dust* (1982), *The Bostonians* (1984), *A Room with a View* (1985), *Maurice* (1987), *Mr and Mrs Bridge* (1990), *Howards End* (1992), *The Remains of the Day* (1993), *Jefferson in Paris* (1995), *Surviving Picasso* (1996), *The Golden Bowl* (2000), *The White Countess* (2005), *The City of Your Final Destination* (2007).

Jarman, (Michael) Derek (1942–94) British, born Northwood, Middlesex; *Sebastiane* (1976), *Jubilee* (1977), *The Tempest* (1979), *Caravaggio* (1985), *The Last of England* (1987), *The Garden* (1990), *Edward II* (1991), *Wittgenstein* (1993).

Jackson, Peter (1961–) New Zealander, born Pukerua Bay, North Island; *Heavenly Creatures* (1994), *The Lord of the Rings* trilogy (2001–3), *King Kong* (2005).

Jordan, Neil (1950–) Irish, born Sligo; *Angel* (1982), *The Company of Wolves* (1984), *Mona Lisa* (1986), *High Spirits* (1988), *The Crying Game* (1992), *Interview with the Vampire* (1994), *Michael Collins* (1996), *The Butcher Boy* (1997), *The End of the Affair* (1999), *The Good Thief* (2002), *Breakfast on Pluto* (2005), *The Brave One* (2007).

Kasdan, Lawrence (1949–) American, born Miami Beach, Florida; *Body Heat* (1981), *The Big Chill* (1983), *Silverado* (1985), *The Accidental Tourist* (1989), *Love You to Death* (1990), *Wyatt Earp* (1994), *French Kiss* (1995), *Mumford* (1999), *Dreamcatcher* (2003).

Kaufman, Philip (1936–) American, born Chicago; *Invasion of the Body Snatchers* (1978), *The Wanderers* (1979), *The Right Stuff* (1983), *The Unbearable Lightness of Being* (1988), *Henry and June* (1990), *Quills* (2000), *Twisted* (2004).

Kazan, Elia (Elia Kazanjoglou) (1909–2003) American, born Istanbul, Turkey; *Boomerang* (1947), *Gentleman's Agreement* (1947), *Pink* (1949), *A Streetcar Named Desire* (1951), *Viva Zapata* (1952), *On the Waterfront* (1954), *East of Eden* (1955), *Baby Doll* (1956), *A Face in the Crowd* (1957), *Splendor in the Grass* (1962), *America, America* (1963), *The Arrangement* (1969), *The Visitors* (1972), *The Last Tycoon* (1976).

Kieslowski, Krzysztof (1941–96) Polish, born Warsaw; *Camera Buff* (1979), *A Short Film About Killing* (1988), *The Double Life of Veronique* (1991), *Three Colours: Blue* (1993), *White* (1993), *Red* (1994).

Kubrick, Stanley (1928–99) American, born The Bronx, New York City; *The Killing* (1956), *Paths of Glory* (1957), *Spartacus* (1960), *Lolita* (1962), *Dr Strangelove* (1964), *2001: A Space Odyssey* (1968), *A Clockwork Orange* (1971), *Barry Lyndon* (1975), *The Shining* (1980), *Full Metal Jacket* (1987), *Eyes Wide Shut* (1999).

Kurosawa, Akira (1910–98) Japanese, born Tokyo; *Rashomon* (1950), *The Idiot* (1951), *Living* (1952), *The Seven Samurai* (1954), *Throne of Blood* (1957), *The Lower Depths* (1957), *The Hidden Fortress* (1958), *Dersu Uzala* (1975), *The Shadow Warrior* (1981), *Ran* (1985), *Dreams* (1990), *Rhapsody in August* (1991).

Landis, John (1950–) American, born Chicago;

Arts and Culture

Schlock (1971), *Kentucky Fried Movie* (1977), *Animal House* (1978), *The Blues Brothers* (1980), *An American Werewolf in London* (1981), *Twilight Zone* (1983), *Trading Places* (1983), *Into the Night* (1985), *Spies Like Us* (1985), *The Three Amigos* (1986), *Coming to America* (1988), *Oscar* (1991), *Innocent Blood* (1992), *Beverly Hills Cop III* (1994), *Blues Brothers 2000* (1998).

Lang, Fritz (1890–1976) German, born Vienna, Austria; *Destiny* (1921), *Dr Mabuse the Gambler* (1922), *Siegfried* (1923), *Metropolis* (1926), *Spies* (1927), *M* (1931), *The Testament of Dr Mabuse* (1932), *You Only Live Once* (1937), *The Return of Frank James* (1940), *The Woman in the Window* (1944), *The Big Heat* (1953), *Beyond a Reasonable Doubt* (1956), *While the City Sleeps* (1955).

Lean, Sir David (1908–91) British, born Croydon; *Pygmalion* (1938), *In Which We Serve* (1942), *Blithe Spirit* (1945), *Brief Encounter* (1946), *Great Expectations* (1946), *The Sound Barrier* (1952), *Hobson's Choice* (1954), *Summer Madness* (1955), *Bridge on the River Kwai* (1957), *Lawrence of Arabia* (1962), *Doctor Zhivago* (1965), *Ryan's Daughter* (1970), *A Passage to India* (1984).

Lee, Ang (1954–) Chinese, born Pingtung, Taiwan; *Sense and Sensibility* (1995), *The Ice Storm* (1997), *Crouching Tiger, Hidden Dragon* (2000), *Hulk* (2003), *Brokeback Mountain* (2005), *Lust, Caution* (2007).

Lee, Spike (Shelton Jackson Lee) (1957–) American, born Atlanta, Georgia; *She's Gotta Have It* (1986), *School Daze* (1988), *Do the Right Thing* (1989), *Mo' Better Blues* (1990), *Jungle Fever* (1991), *Malcolm X* (1992), *Crooklyn* (1994), *Girl 6* (1996), *He Got Game* (1998), *Summer of Sam* (1999), *25th Hour* (2002), *Inside Man* (2006), *When the Levees Broke* (2006), *Miracle at St Anna* (2008).

Leigh, Mike (1943–) British, born Salford; *Bleak Moments* (1971), *Nuts in May* (1976), *Abigail's Party* (1977), *High Hopes* (1988), *Life is Sweet* (1990), *Naked* (1993), *Secrets and Lies* (1996), *Career Girls* (1997), *Topsy-Turvy* (1999), *All or Nothing* (2002), *Vera Drake* (2004), *Happy-Go-Lucky* (2008).

Leone, Sergio (1922–89) Italian, born Rome; *A Fistful of Dollars* (1964), *For a Few Dollars More* (1965), *The Good the Bad and the Ugly* (1967), *Once upon a Time in the West* (1969), *A Fistful of Dynamite* (1972), *Once upon a Time in America* (1984).

Levinson, Barry (1942–) American, born Baltimore, Maryland; *Diner* (1982), *The Natural* (1984), *The Young Sherlock Holmes* (1985), *Tin Men* (1987), *Good Morning Vietnam* (1987), *Rain Man* (1988), *Avalon* (1990), *Bugsy* (1991), *Toys* (1992), *Disclosure* (1994), *Sleepers* (1996), *Wag the Dog* (1997), *Sphere* (1998), *Bandits* (2001), *Man of the Year* (2006), *What Just Happened?* (2008).

Lucas, George (1944–) American, born Modesto, California; *THX–1138: 4EB/Electronic Labyrinth* (1965), *American Graffiti* (1973), *Star Wars* (1977), *Star Wars: The Phantom Menace* (1999), *Attack of the Clones* (2002), *Revenge of the Sith* (2005).

Lumet, Sidney (1924–) American, born Philadelphia, Pennsylvania; *The Pawnbroker* (1965), *Serpico* (1974), *Dog Day Afternoon* (1975), *Network* (1976), *The Verdict* (1982), *Night Falls on Manhattan* (1994), *Gloria* (1999), *Find Me Guilty* (2005), *Before the Devil Knows You're Dead* (2007).

Lynch, David (Keith) (1946–) American, born Missoula, Montana; *Eraserhead* (1976), *The Elephant Man* (1980), *Dune* (1984), *Blue Velvet* (1986), *Wild at Heart* (1990), *Twin Peaks* (TV 1990–1), *Twin Peaks: Fire Walk With Me* (1992), *Lost Highway* (1997), *Mulholland Drive* (2001), *Inland Empire* (2006).

McBride, Jim (1941–) American, born New York City; *Breathless* (1983), *The Big Easy* (1986), *Great Balls of Fire* (1989), *The Wrong Man* (1992), *The Informant* (1997).

Mankiewicz, Joseph Leo (1909–93) American, born Wilkes-Barre, Pennsylvania; *All About Eve* (1950), *The Barefoot Contessa* (1954), *Guys and Dolls* (1954), *Suddenly Last Summer* (1959), *Sleuth* (1972).

Miller, George (1945–) Australian, born Brisbane; *Mad Max* (1979), *Mad Max 2: The Road Warrior* (1982), *Mad Max Beyond Thunderdome* (1985), *The Witches of Eastwick* (1987), *Lorenzo's Oil* (1992), *Babe: Pig in the City* (1998), *Happy Feet* (2006).

Miller, Jonathan (Wolfe) (1934–) British, born London; *The Magic Flute* (1986), *The Tempest* (1988).

Minnelli, Vincente (1913–86) American, born Chicago; *Ziegfeld Follies* (1946), *An American in Paris* (1951), *Lust for Life* (1956), *Gigi* (1958).

Nichols, Mike (Michael Igor Peschkowsky) (1931–) American–German, born Berlin, Germany; *Who's Afraid of Virginia Woolf?* (1966), *The Graduate* (1967), *Catch-22* (1970), *Working Girl* (1988), *Postcards from the Edge* (1990), *Wolf* (1994), *The Birdcage* (1996), *Primary Colors* (1998), *Closer* (2004), *Charlie Wilson's War* (2007).

Olivier, Laurence (Kerr) Olivier, Baron (1907–89) British, born Dorking, Surrey; *Henry V* (1944), *Hamlet* (1948), *Richard III* (1956), *The Prince and the Showgirl* (1958), *The Entertainer* (1960).

Parker, Alan (1944–) British, born London; *Bugsy Malone* (1976), *Midnight Express* (1978), *Fame* (1980), *Shoot the Moon* (1981), *Pink Floyd: The Wall* (1982), *Angel Heart* (1987), *Mississippi Burning* (1988), *Come See the Paradise* (1990), *The Commitments* (1991), *Evita* (1996), *Angela's Ashes* (1999), *The Life of David Gale* (2003).

Pasolini, Pier Paolo (1922–75) Italian, born Bologna; *Accatone!* (1961), *The Gospel According to St Matthew* (1964), *Oedipus Rex* (1967), *Medea* (1970).

Peckinpah, Sam (1925–84) American, born Fresno, California; *The Deadly Companions* (1961), *Major Dundee* (1965), *The Wild Bunch* (1969), *Straw Dogs* (1971), *Bring Me the Head of Alfredo Garcia* (1974), *Cross of Iron* (1977).

Polanski, Roman (1933–) Polish, born Paris; *Knife in the Water* (1962), *Repulsion* (1965), *Cul-de-Sac* (1966), *Rosemary's Baby* (1968), *Macbeth* (1971), *Chinatown* (1974), *Tess* (1979), *Pirates* (1985), *Frantic* (1988), *Bitter Moon* (1992), *Death and the Maiden* (1994), *The Ninth Gate* (1999), *The Pianist* (2002), *Oliver Twist* (2005).

Pollack, Sydney (1934–2008) American, born South Bend, Indiana; *They Shoot Horses, Don't They?* (1969), *The Electric Horseman* (1979), *Absence of Malice* (1981), *Tootsie* (1982), *Out of Africa* (1985), *Havana* (1990), *The Firm* (1993), *Random Hearts* (1999), *The Interpeter* (2005).

Powell, Michael (Latham) (1905–90) British, born Bekesbourne, near Canterbury; with **Emeric Pressburger** (1902–88) Hungarian–British, born Miskolc, Hungary; *The Spy in Black* (1939), *The Thief of Baghdad* (1940), *The Life and Death of Colonel Blimp* (1943), *Black Narcissus* (1946), *A Matter of Life and Death* (1946), *The Red Shoes* (1948).

Ray, Satyajit (1921–92) Indian, born Calcutta (now Kolkata); *Pather Panchali* (1954), *The Music Room* (1958), *The World of Apu* (1959), *The Kingdom of Diamonds* (1980), *Pickoo* (1982), *The Home and The World* (1984).

Redford, (Charles) Robert (1936–) American, born Santa Monica, California; *Ordinary People* (1980), *The Milagro Beanfield War* (1987), *A River*

Runs Through It (1992), Quiz Show (1994), The Horse Whisperer (1998), The Legend of Bagger Vance (2000), Lions for Lambs (2007).

Reed, Sir Carol (1906–76) British, born London; The Young Mr Pitt (1942), The Way Ahead (1944), The Fallen Idol (1948), The Third Man (1949), An Outcast of the Islands (1952), The Man Between (1953), Our Man in Havana (1959), Oliver! (1968).

Reiner, Carl (1922–) American, born The Bronx, New York City; Oh God (1977), The Jerk (1979), Dead Men Don't Wear Plaid (1982), The Man with Two Brains (1983), Summer School (1987), That Old Feeling (1997).

Reiner, Rob (1947–) American, born The Bronx, New York City; This is Spinal Tap (1984), Stand by Me (1987), The Princess Bride (1988), When Harry Met Sally ... (1989), Misery (1990), A Few Good Men (1992), North (1994), The American President (1995), The Story of Us (1999), Rumour Has It (2005), The Bucket List (2007).

Renoir, Jean (1894–1979) French, born Paris; Une Partie de Campagne (1936), La Règle du Jeu (1939), The Southerner (1945).

Robbins, Tim (Timothy Francis Robbins) (1958–) American, born West Covina, California; No Small Affair (1984), Bob Roberts (1992), Dead Man Walking (1995), Cradle Will Rock (1999).

Roeg, Nicolas (Jack) (1928–) British, born London; Performance (1970), Walkabout (1971), Don't Look Now (1973), The Man Who Fell to Earth (1976), Bad Timing (1979), Eureka (1983), Insignificance (1985), Castaway (1986), Black Widow (1988), Track 29 (1988), The Witches (1990), Heart of Darkness (1994), Two Deaths (1995), Puffball (2007).

Rossellini, Roberto (1906–77) Italian, born Rome; The White Ship (1940), Rome, Open City (1945), Paisan (1946), Germany, Year Zero (1947), Stromboli (1950), Voyage to Italy (1953), General Della Rovera (1959).

Russell, Ken (Henry Kenneth Alfred Russell) (1927–) British, born Southampton; Women in Love (1969), The Devils (1971), Crimes of Passion (1984), Gothic (1987), Lair of the White Worm (1989), The Rainbow (1989), Whore (1991), Tales of Erotica (1996), Trapped Ashes (2006).

Schlesinger, John (Richard) (1926–2003) British, born London; A Kind of Loving (1962), Billy Liar! (1963), Midnight Cowboy (1969), Sunday, Bloody Sunday (1971), Marathon Man (1976), Honky Tonk Freeway (1981), An Englishman Abroad (TV 1982), Madame Sousatzka (1988), Pacific Heights (1990), The Innocent (1993), The Next Best Thing (2000).

Scorsese, Martin (1942–) American, born Queens, New York; Mean Streets (1973), Alice Doesn't Live Here Any More (1974), Taxi Driver (1976), Raging Bull (1980), King of Comedy (1982), After Hours (1985), The Color of Money (1986), The Last Temptation of Christ (1988), GoodFellas (1990), Cape Fear (1991), The Age of Innocence (1992), Casino (1995), Kundun (1997), Gangs of New York (2002), The Aviator (2004), The Departed (2006), Shine a Light (2008).

Scott, Sir Ridley (1937–) British, born South Shields; Alien (1979), Blade Runner (1982), Black Rain (1989), Thelma and Louise (1991), 1492 (1992), G I Jane (1997), Gladiator (2000), Hannibal (2001), Black Hawk Down (2001), Matchstick Men (2003), A Good Year (2006), American Gangster (2007).

Siegel, Don (1912–91) American, born Chicago; Riot in Cell Block 11 (1954), Invasion of the Body Snatchers (1956), Baby Face Nelson (1957), Coogan's Bluff (1968), Two Mules for Sister Sara (1969), Dirty Harry (1971), Charley Varrick (1973), The Shootist (1976), Telefon (1977), Escape from Alcatraz (1979).

Soderbergh, Steven (1963–) American, born Atlanta, Georgia; sex, lies and videotape (1989), King of the Hill (1993), Erin Brockovich (2000), Traffic (2000), Ocean's Eleven (2001), Solaris (2002), Ocean's Twelve (2004), The Good German (2006), Ocean's Thirteen (2007), Che (2008).

Spielberg, Steven (1946–) American, born Cincinnati, Ohio; Duel (TV 1972), Sugarland Express (1973), Jaws (1975), Close Encounters of the Third Kind (1977), Raiders of the Lost Ark (1981), ET (1982), Twilight Zone (1983), The Color Purple (1985), Indiana Jones and the Temple of Doom (1984), Empire of the Sun (1987), Indiana Jones and the Last Crusade (1989), Hook (1992), Jurassic Park (1993), Schindler's List (1993), The Lost World: Jurassic Park (1997), Amistad (1997), Saving Private Ryan (1998), Minority Report (2002), Munich (2005), Indiana Jones and the Kingdom of the Crystal Skull (2008).

Stone, Oliver (1946–) American, born New York City; Platoon (1987), Wall Street (1987), Born on the Fourth of July (1989), The Doors (1991), JFK (1991), Heaven and Earth (1993), Natural Born Killers (1994), Nixon (1995), Any Given Sunday (1999), World Trade Center (2006), W. (2008).

Tarantino, Quentin (1963–) American, born Knoxville, Tennessee; Reservoir Dogs (1993), Pulp Fiction (1994), Jackie Brown (1997), Kill Bill: Vol 1 (2003), Kill Bill: Vol 2 (2004), Death Proof (2007).

Tati, Jacques (Jacques Tatischeff) (1908–82) French, born Le Pecq; Jour de fête (1947), Monsieur Hulot's Holiday (1952), Mon Oncle (1958), Playtime (1968), Traffic (1981).

Tavernier, Bertrand (1941–) French, born Lyons; L'Horloger de Saint-Paul (1973), La Mort en direct (1979), Dimanche à la Campagne (1984), La Vie et rien d'autre (1989), Daddy Nostalgie (1990), L 627 (1992), Capitaine Conan (1996), It All Starts Today (1999), Safe Conduct (2002), Holy Lola (2004).

Truffaut, François (1932–84) French, born Paris; Jules et Jim (1961), The Bride Wore Black (1967), Baisers volés (1968), L'Enfant Sauvage (1969), Day for Night (1973), The Last Metro (1980).

Visconti, Luchino (Count Don Luchino Visconti Di Morone) (1906–76) Italian, born Milan; Ossessione (1942), The Leopard (1963), The Damned (1969), Death in Venice (1971).

Weir, Peter (1944–) Australian, born Sydney; The Cars That Ate Paris (1974), Picnic at Hanging Rock (1975), Gallipoli (1981), The Year of Living Dangerously (1982), Witness (1985), Mosquito Coast (1986), Dead Poets Society (1989), Green Card (1990), Fearless (1993), The Truman Show (1998), Master and Commander (2004).

Welles, (George) Orson (1915–85) American, born Kenosha, Wisconsin; Citizen Kane (1941), The Magnificent Ambersons (1942), Jane Eyre (1943), Macbeth (1948), Othello (1951), Touch of Evil (1958), The Trial (1962), Chimes at Midnight (1966).

Wenders, Wim (1945–) German, born Düsseldorf; Summer in the City (1970), Alice in the Cities (1974), Kings of the Road (1976), Paris, Texas (1984), Wings of Desire (1987), Until the End of the World (1991), Faraway, So Close (1993), Beyond the Clouds (co-director 1995), The End of Violence (1997), Buena Vista Social Club (1999), The Million Dollar Hotel (2000), Don't Come Knocking (2005).

Wilder, Billy (1906–2002) Austrian–American, born Sucha, Austria; Double Indemnity (1944), The Lost Weekend (1945), Sunset Boulevard (1950), The Seven Year Itch (1955), Some Like It Hot (1959), The Apartment (1960), Avanti! (1972).

Wise, Robert (1914–2005) American, born Winchester, Indiana; The Body Snatcher (1945),

The Day the Earth Stood Still (1951), *West Side Story* (1961), *The Sound of Music* (1965), *Star Trek: The Motion Picture* (1979).

Wyler, William (1902–1981) German–American, born Mulhouse, Alsace; *The Little Foxes* (1941), *Mrs Miniver* (1942), *The Best Years of Our Lives* (1946), *Friendly Persuasion* (1956), *Ben-Hur* (1959), *Funny Girl* (1968).

Zeffirelli, Franco (Gianfranco Corsi) (1923–) Italian, born Florence; *The Taming of the Shrew* (1966), *Romeo and Juliet* (1968), *Brother Sun, Sister Moon* (1973), *Jesus of Nazareth* (TV 1977), *The Champ* (1979), *Endless Love* (1981), *La Traviata* (1982), *Otello* (1986), *Hamlet* (1990),

Jane Eyre (TV 1995), *Tea with Mussolini* (1999), *Callas Forever* (2002).

Zemeckis, Robert (1952–) American, born Chicago; *I Wanna Hold Your Hand* (1978), *Romancing The Stone* (1984), *Back to the Future* (1985), *Who Framed Roger Rabbit?* (1988), *Back to the Future II* (1989), *Back to the Future III* (1990), *Death Becomes Her* (1992), *Forrest Gump* (1994), *Contact* (1997), *What Lies Beneath* (2000), *Cast Away* (2000), *The Polar Express* (2004), *Beowulf* (2007).

Zinnemann, Fred (1907–97) Austrian–American, born Vienna, Austria; *High Noon* (1952), *From Here to Eternity* (1953), *A Man for All Seasons* (1966), *Five Days One Summer* (1982).

Motion picture Academy Awards

Awarded by the Academy of Motion Picture Arts and Sciences; popularly known as Oscars.

Year	Best film (director)	Best actor	Best actress
1927/8	*Wings* (William A Wellman)	Emil Jannings *The Last Command*, *The Way of All Flesh*	Janet Gaynor *7th Heaven*, *Street Angel*, *Sunrise*
1928/9	*The Broadway Melody* (Harry Beaumont)	Warner Baxter *In Old Arizona*	Mary Pickford *Coquette*
1929/30	*All Quiet on the Western Front* (Lewis Milestone)	George Arliss *Disraeli*	Norma Shearer *The Divorcee*
1930/1	*Cimarron* (Wesley Ruggles)	Lionel Barrymore *A Free Soul*	Marie Dressler *Min and Bill*
1931/2	*Grand Hotel* (Edmund Goulding)	Wallace Beery *The Champ*; Fredric March *Dr Jekyll and Mr Hyde*	Helen Hayes *The Sin of Madelon Claudet*
1932/3	*Cavalcade* (Frank Lloyd)	Charles Laughton *The Private Life of Henry VIII*	Katharine Hepburn *Morning Glory*
1934	*It Happened One Night* (Frank Capra)	Clark Gable *It Happened One Night*	Claudette Colbert *It Happened One Night*
1935	*Mutiny on the Bounty* (Frank Lloyd)	Victor McLaglen *The Informer*	Bette Davis *Dangerous*
1936	*The Great Ziegfeld* (Robert Z Leonard)	Paul Muni *The Story of Louis Pasteur*	Luise Rainer *The Great Ziegfeld*
1937	*The Life of Émile Zola* (William Dieterle)	Spencer Tracy *Captains Courageous*	Luise Rainer *The Good Earth*
1938	*You Can't Take It with You* (Frank Capra)	Spencer Tracy *Boys' Town*	Bette Davis *Jezebel*
1939	*Gone with the Wind* (Victor Fleming)	Robert Donat *Goodbye Mr Chips*	Vivien Leigh *Gone with the Wind*
1940	*Rebecca* (Alfred Hitchcock)	James Stewart *The Philadelphia Story*	Ginger Rogers *Kitty Foyle*
1941	*How Green Was My Valley* (John Ford)	Gary Cooper *Sergeant York*	Joan Fontaine *Suspicion*
1942	*Mrs Miniver* (William Wyler)	James Cagney *Yankee Doodle Dandy*	Greer Garson *Mrs Miniver*
1943	*Casablanca* (Michael Curtiz)	Paul Lukas *Watch on the Rhine*	Jennifer Jones *The Song of Bernadette*
1944	*Going My Way* (Leo McCarey)	Bing Crosby *Going My Way*	Ingrid Bergman *Gaslight*
1945	*The Lost Weekend* (Billy Wilder)	Ray Milland *The Lost Weekend*	Joan Crawford *Mildred Pierce*
1946	*The Best Years of Our Lives* (William Wyler)	Fredric March *The Best Years of Our Lives*	Olivia de Havilland *To Each His Own*
1947	*Gentleman's Agreement* (Elia Kazan)	Ronald Colman *A Double Life*	Loretta Young *The Farmer's Daughter*
1948	*Hamlet* (Laurence Olivier)	Laurence Olivier *Hamlet*	Jane Wyman *Johnny Belinda*
1949	*All the King's Men* (Robert Rossen)	Broderick Crawford *All the King's Men*	Olivia de Havilland *The Heiress*
1950	*All About Eve* (Joseph L Mankiewicz)	Jose Ferrer *Cyrano de Bergerac*	Judy Holliday *Born Yesterday*
1951	*An American in Paris* (Vincente Minnelli)	Humphrey Bogart *The African Queen*	Vivien Leigh *A Streetcar Named Desire*
1952	*The Greatest Show on Earth* (Cecil B DeMille)	Gary Cooper *High Noon*	Shirley Booth *Come Back, Little Sheba*

Arts and Culture

Year	Best film (director)	Best actor	Best actress
1953	*From Here to Eternity* (Fred Zinnemann)	William Holden *Stalag 17*	Audrey Hepburn *Roman Holiday*
1954	*On the Waterfront* (Elia Kazan)	Marlon Brando *On the Waterfront*	Grace Kelly *The Country Girl*
1955	*Marty* (Delbert Mann)	Ernest Borgnine *Marty*	Anna Magnani *The Rose Tattoo*
1956	*Around the World in 80 Days* (Michael Anderson)	Yul Brynner *The King and I*	Ingrid Bergman *Anastasia*
1957	*The Bridge on the River Kwai* (David Lean)	Alec Guinness *The Bridge on the River Kwai*	Joanne Woodward *The Three Faces of Eve*
1958	*Gigi* (Vincente Minnelli)	David Niven *Separate Tables*	Susan Hayward *I Want to Live!*
1959	*Ben-Hur* (William Wyler)	Charlton Heston *Ben-Hur*	Simone Signoret *Room at the Top*
1960	*The Apartment* (Billy Wilder)	Burt Lancaster *Elmer Gantry*	Elizabeth Taylor *Butterfield 8*
1961	*West Side Story* (Jerome Robbins, Robert Wise)	Maximilian Schell *Judgement at Nuremberg*	Sophia Loren *Two Women*
1962	*Lawrence of Arabia* (David Lean)	Gregory Peck *To Kill a Mockingbird*	Anne Bancroft *The Miracle Worker*
1963	*Tom Jones* (Tony Richardson)	Sidney Poitier *Lilies of the Field*	Patricia Neal *Hud*
1964	*My Fair Lady* (George Cukor)	Rex Harrison *My Fair Lady*	Julie Andrews *Mary Poppins*
1965	*The Sound of Music* (Robert Wise)	Lee Marvin *Cat Ballou*	Julie Christie *Darling*
1966	*A Man for All Seasons* (Fred Zinnemann)	Paul Scofield *A Man for All Seasons*	Elizabeth Taylor *Who's Afraid of Virginia Woolf?*
1967	*In the Heat of the Night* (Norman Jewison)	Rod Steiger *In the Heat of the Night*	Katharine Hepburn *Guess Who's Coming to Dinner*
1968	*Oliver!* (Carol Reed)	Cliff Robertson *Charly*	Katharine Hepburn *The Lion in Winter*; Barbra Streisand *Funny Girl*
1969	*Midnight Cowboy* (John Schlesinger)	John Wayne *True Grit*	Maggie Smith *The Prime of Miss Jean Brodie*
1970	*Patton* (Franklin J Schaffner)	George C Scott *Patton*	Glenda Jackson *Women in Love*
1971	*The French Connection* (William Friedkin)	Gene Hackman *The French Connection*	Jane Fonda *Klute*
1972	*The Godfather* (Francis Ford Coppola)	Marlon Brando *The Godfather*	Liza Minnelli *Cabaret*
1973	*The Sting* (George Roy Hill)	Jack Lemmon *Save the Tiger*	Glenda Jackson *A Touch of Class*
1974	*The Godfather, Part II* (Francis Ford Coppola)	Art Carney *Harry and Tonto*	Ellen Burstyn *Alice Doesn't Live Here Anymore*
1975	*One Flew Over the Cuckoo's Nest* (Miloš Forman)	Jack Nicholson *One Flew Over the Cuckoo's Nest*	Louise Fletcher *One Flew Over the Cuckoo's Nest*
1976	*Rocky* (John G Avildsen)	Peter Finch *Network*	Faye Dunaway *Network*
1977	*Annie Hall* (Woody Allen)	Richard Dreyfuss *The Goodbye Girl*	Diane Keaton *Annie Hall*
1978	*The Deer Hunter* (Michael Cimino)	Jon Voight *Coming Home*	Jane Fonda *Coming Home*
1979	*Kramer vs Kramer* (Robert Beaton)	Dustin Hoffman *Kramer vs Kramer*	Sally Field *Norma Rae*
1980	*Ordinary People* (Robert Redford)	Robert de Niro *Raging Bull*	Sissy Spacek *Coal Miner's Daughter*
1981	*Chariots of Fire* (Hugh Hudson)	Henry Fonda *On Golden Pond*	Katharine Hepburn *On Golden Pond*
1982	*Gandhi* (Richard Attenborough)	Ben Kingsley *Gandhi*	Meryl Streep *Sophie's Choice*
1983	*Terms of Endearment* (James L Brooks)	Robert Duvall *Tender Mercies*	Shirley MacLaine *Terms of Endearment*
1984	*Amadeus* (Miloš Forman)	F Murray Abraham *Amadeus*	Sally Field *Places in the Heart*
1985	*Out of Africa* (Sydney Pollack)	William Hurt *Kiss of the Spider Woman*	Geraldine Page *The Trip to Bountiful*
1986	*Platoon* (Oliver Stone)	Paul Newman *The Color of Money*	Marlee Matlin *Children of a Lesser God*
1987	*The Last Emperor* (Bernardo Bertolucci)	Michael Douglas *Wall Street*	Cher *Moonstruck*
1988	*Rain Man* (Barry Levinson)	Dustin Hoffman *Rain Man*	Jodie Foster *The Accused*
1989	*Driving Miss Daisy* (Bruce Beresford)	Daniel Day-Lewis *My Left Foot*	Jessica Tandy *Driving Miss Daisy*
1990	*Dances with Wolves* (Kevin Costner)	Jeremy Irons *Reversal of Fortune*	Kathy Bates *Misery*

Year	Best film (director)	Best actor	Best actress
1991	*The Silence of the Lambs* (Jonathan Demme)	Anthony Hopkins *The Silence of the Lambs*	Jodie Foster *The Silence of the Lambs*
1992	*Unforgiven* (Clint Eastwood)	Al Pacino *Scent of a Woman*	Emma Thompson *Howards End*
1993	*Schindler's List* (Steven Spielberg)	Tom Hanks *Philadelphia*	Holly Hunter *The Piano*
1994	*Forrest Gump* (Robert Zemeckis)	Tom Hanks *Forrest Gump*	Jessica Lange *Blue Sky*
1995	*Braveheart* (Mel Gibson)	Nicolas Cage *Leaving Las Vegas*	Susan Sarandon *Dead Man Walking*
1996	*The English Patient* (Anthony Minghella)	Geoffrey Rush *Shine*	Frances McDormand *Fargo*
1997	*Titanic* (James Cameron)	Jack Nicholson *As Good as it Gets*	Helen Hunt *As Good as it Gets*
1998	*Shakespeare in Love* (John Madden)	Roberto Benigni *Life is Beautiful*	Gwyneth Paltrow *Shakespeare in Love*
1999	*American Beauty* (Sam Mendes)	Kevin Spacey *American Beauty*	Hilary Swank *Boys Don't Cry*
2000	*Gladiator* (Ridley Scott)	Russell Crowe *Gladiator*	Julia Roberts *Erin Brockovich*
2001	*A Beautiful Mind* (Ron Howard)	Denzel Washington *Training Day*	Halle Berry *Monster's Ball*
2002	*Chicago* (Rob Marshall)	Adrien Brody *The Pianist*	Nicole Kidman *The Hours*
2003	*The Lord of the Rings: The Return of the King* (Peter Jackson)	Sean Penn *Mystic River*	Charlize Theron *Monster*
2004	*Million Dollar Baby* (Clint Eastwood)	Jamie Foxx *Ray*	Hilary Swank *Million Dollar Baby*
2005	*Crash* (Paul Haggis)	Philip Seymour Hoffman *Capote*	Reese Witherspoon *Walk the Line*
2006	*The Departed* (Martin Scorsese)	Forest Whitaker *The Last King of Scotland*	Helen Mirren *The Queen*
2007	*No Country for Old Men* (Joel and Ethan Coen)	Daniel Day-Lewis *There Will Be Blood*	Marion Cotillard *La Vie en Rose*
2008	*Slumdog Millionaire* (Danny Boyle)	Sean Penn *Milk*	Kate Winslet *The Reader*

Composers

Selected works are listed.

Adams, John (Coolidge) (1947–) American, born Worcester, Massachusetts; works include opera (eg *Nixon in China*), compositions for chorus and orchestra (eg *Harmonium*) and orchestral pieces (eg *Short Ride in a Fast Machine*).

Albéniz, Isaac (1860–1909) Spanish, born Camprodón, Catalonia; works include operas and works for piano based on Spanish folk music (eg *Iberia*).

Arnold, Sir Malcolm (Henry) (1921–2006) English, born Northampton; works include symphonies, concertos, ballets, operas, vocal, choral, chamber and orchestral music (eg *Tam O'Shanter*) and film scores (eg *Bridge over the River Kwai*).

Bach, Johann Sebastian (1685–1750) German, born Eisenach; prolific composer, works include over 190 cantatas and oratorios, concertos, chamber music, keyboard music, and orchestral works (eg *Toccata and Fugue in D minor*, *The Well-tempered Clavier*, *Six Brandenburg Concertos*, *St Matthew Passion*, *Mass in B minor*, *Goldberg Variations*, *The Musical Offering*, *The Art of Fugue*).

Bartók, Béla (1881–1945) Hungarian, born Nagyszentmiklós; works include six string quartets, *Sonata for 2 pianos and percussion*, concertos (for piano, violin, viola and *Concerto for Orchestra*), opera (*Duke Bluebeard's Castle*), two ballets (*The Wooden Prince*, *The Miraculous Mandarin*), songs, choruses, folksong arrangements.

Beethoven, Ludwig van (1770–1827) German, born Bonn; works include 33 piano sonatas (eg the 'Pathétique', 'Moonlight', *Waldstein*, *Appassionata*), nine symphonies (eg *Eroica*, 'Pastoral', *Choral Symphony No.9*), string quartets, concertos, songs and the opera *Fidelio*.

Berg, Alban (1885–1935) Austrian, born Vienna; works include songs (*Four Songs*), operas (*Wozzeck*, the unfinished *Lulu*), a violin concerto and a string quartet (*Lyric Suite*).

Berio, Luciano (1925–2003) Italian, born Oneglia; works include compositions using tapes and electronic music (eg *Mutazioni*, *Omaggio a James Joyce*), works for solo instruments (*Sequenzas*), stage works (eg *Laborintus II*, *Opera*), symphonies (*Synfonia*) and vocal works.

Berlioz, (Louis) Hector (1803–69) French, born Côte St André, near Grenoble; works include the overture *Le Carnival romain*, the cantata *La Damnation de Faust*, symphonies (eg *Symphonie fantastique*, *Roméo et Juliette*) and operas (eg *Béatrice et Bénédict*, *Les Troyens*).

Bernstein, Leonard (1918–90) American, born Laurence, Massachusetts; works include ballets (*Jeremiah*, *The Age of Anxiety*, *Kaddish*), symphonies (eg *Fancy Free*, *The Dybbuk*), and musicals (eg *Candide*, *West Side Story*, *On The Town*, *Songfest*, *Halil*).

Birtwistle, Sir Harrison (1934–) English, born Accrington, Lancashire; works include operas (eg *The Mask of Orpheus*, *The Minotaur*), 'dramatic pastorals' (eg *Down by the Greenwood Side*) and orchestral pieces (eg *The Triumph of Time*).

Bizet, Georges (1838–75) French, born Paris; works include operas (eg *Carmen*, *Les Pêcheurs de Perles*, *La Jolie Fille de Perth*), incidental music to Daudet's play *L'Arlésienne* and a symphony.

Boulez, Pierre (1925–) French, born Montbrison; works include three piano sonatas, and works for piano and flute (eg *Sonatine*).

Brahms, Johannes (1833–97) German, born Hamburg; works include songs, four symphonies, two piano concertos, choral work (eg *A German Requiem*), orchestral work (eg *Variations on a Theme of Haydn*), programme work (eg *Tragic Overture*), also the *Academic Festival Overture* and *Hungarian Dances*.

Britten, (Edward) Benjamin, Baron Britten of Aldeburgh (1913–76) English, born Lowestoft; composer of orchestral works (eg *The Young Person's Guide to the Orchestra*), choral symphonic works, operas (eg *Peter Grimes*, *The Turn of the Screw*), song cycles (eg *Our Hunting Fathers*, *On This Island* (text by W H Auden)).

Bruckner, Anton (1824–96) Austrian, born Ansfelden; works include nine symphonies, a string quartet, choral-orchestral Masses and other church music (eg *Te Deum*).

Cage, John (1912–92) American, born Los Angeles; works include unorthodox modern compositions (eg *Sonatas and Interludes for the Perpared Piano*).

Carter, Elliott (Cook), Jr (1908–) American, born New York City; works include quartets, symphonies, concertos, songs and chamber music.

Chabrier, Emmanuel (1841–94) French, born Ambert; works include operas (*Gwendoline*, *Le Roi malgré lui*, *Briséis*) and an orchestral rhapsody (*España*).

Chausson, Ernest (1855–99) French, born Paris; works include songs and orchestral works (eg *Poème*).

Chopin, Frédéric (François) (1810–49) Polish, born Zelazowa Wola, near Warsaw; wrote almost exclusively for piano – nocturnes, polonaises, mazurkas, preludes, concertos, and a funeral march.

Copland, Aaron (1900–90) American, born Brooklyn, New York City; ballets (eg *Billy The Kid*, *Appalachian Spring*), film scores (eg *Our Town*), symphonies, concertos (eg *Clarinet Concerto*), orchestral music (eg *El Salón Mexico*) and songs.

Corelli, Arcangelo (1653–1713) Italian, born Fusignano, near Bologna; works include twelve concertos (eg *Concerto for Christmas Night*) and solo and trio sonatas for violin.

Couperin, François (1668–1733) French, born Paris; works include chamber music, four books containing 240 harpsichord pieces, motets and other church music.

Debussy, (Achille) Claude (1862–1918) French, born St Germaine-en-Laye, near Paris; songs (eg the cantata *L'Enfant prodigue*), opera (*Pelléas et Mélisande*), orchestral works (eg *Prélude à l'après-midi d'un faune*, *La Mer*), chamber and piano music (eg *La Cathédrale engloutie*).

Delius, Frederick (1862–1934) English (of German Scandinavian descent), born Bradford; works include songs (eg *A Song of Summer*), concertos, operas (eg *Koanga*, *A Village Romeo and Juliet*), chamber music and orchestral variations (eg *Appalachia*, *Sea Drift*, *A Mass of Life*).

Dukas, Paul (1865–1935) French, born Paris; works include a symphonic poem (*L'Apprenti sorcier*) and opera (*Ariane et Barbe-Bleue*).

Dutilleux, Henri (1916–) French, born Angers; works include a piano sonata, two symphonies, a violin concerto, a string quartet (*Ainsi la nuit*) and compositions for two pianos.

Dvořák, Antonin (Leopold) (1841–1904) Czech, born near Prague; works include songs, concertos, choral music (eg *Hymnus*), chamber music, symphonies (notably *From the New World*) and operas (eg *Rusalka* and the *Slavonic Dances*).

Elgar, Sir Edward (William) (1857–1934) English, born Broadheath, near Worcester; works include chamber music, two symphonies, oratorios (eg *The Dream of Gerontius*, *The Apostles*, *The Kingdom*), songs and the orchestral work *Enigma Variations*.

Falla, Manuel de (1876–1946) Spanish, born Cádiz; works include opera (eg *La Vida Breve*), ballet (eg *The Three-Cornered Hat*, *Love the Magician*) and orchestral suites (eg *Nights in the Gardens of Spain*).

Fauré, Gabriel (Urbain) (1845–1924) French, born Pamiers; works include songs (eg *Après un rêve*), chamber music, choral music (eg the *Requiem*), operas and orchestral music (eg *Masques et bergamasques*).

Franck, César (Auguste) (1822–90) naturalized French, born Liège, Belgium; works include tone-poems, oratorios (eg *Les Béatitudes*), sonatas for violin and piano, *Symphony in D minor* and *Variations symphoniques* for piano and orchestra.

Gershwin, George (1898–1937) American, born Brooklyn, New York City; Broadway musicals (eg *Lady Be Good*, *Of Thee I Sing*), songs (notably 'I Got Rhythm', 'The Man I Love'), operas (eg *Porgy and Bess*), and concert works (eg *Rhapsody in Blue*, *Concerto in F*, *An American in Paris*).

Glass, Philip (1937–) American, born Baltimore, Maryland; works include stage pieces (eg *Einstein on the Beach*), film scores (eg *Hamburger Hill*) and the opera *Orphee*.

Gluck, Christoph (Willibald) (1714–87) Austro-German, born Erasbach, Bavaria; operas include *Orfeo ed Euridice*, *Iphigénie en Aulide*, *Alceste*, *Paride ed Elena*, *Iphigénie en Tauride*.

Goodall, Howard (1958–) English, born Bromley; works include many television themes (eg *Blackadder*, *QI*), musicals (eg *The Hired Man*, *A Winter's Tale*), choral works (eg *In Memoriam Anne Frank*, *Psalm 23*) and organ works.

Gounod, Charles (François) (1818–93) French, born Paris; works include operas (eg *Le Médecin malgré lui*, *Faust*, *Philémon et Baucis*, *Roméo et Juliette*), masses, hymns, anthems and songs.

Grainger, Percy (Aldridge) (1882–1961) Australian, born Melbourne; works include songs, piano and chamber music (eg *Molly on the Shore*, *Mock Morris*, *Shepherd's Hey*).

Grieg, Edvard (Hagerup) (1843–1907) Norwegian, born Bergen; works include songs, a piano concerto, orchestral suites, violin sonatas, choral music, and incidental music for *Peer Gynt*.

Handel, George Frideric (1685–1759) naturalized English, born Halle, Saxony; prolific output including over 27 operas (eg *Almira*, *Rinaldo*), 20 oratorios (eg *The Messiah*, *Saul*, *Israel in Egypt*, *Samson*, *Jephthah*), orchestral suites (eg the *Water Music* and *Music for the Royal Fireworks*), organ concertos and chamber music.

Haydn, (Franz) Joseph (1732–1809) Austrian, born

Rohrau, Lower Austria; prolific output including 104 symphonies (eg the 'Surprise' or 'London' Symphonies), string quartets and oratorios (notably *The Creation*, *The Seasons*) and concertos.

Holst, Gustav (Theodore) (originally **von Holst**) (1874–1934) English of Swedish origin, born Cheltenham; works include ballet music, operas (eg *The Perfect Fool*, *At the Boar's Head*), orchestral suites (eg *The Planets*, *St Paul's Suite*) and choral music (eg *The Hymn of Jesus*, *Ode to Death*).

Honegger, Arthur (1892–1955) French, born Le Havre; works include five symphonies and dramatic oratorios (*King David*, *Joan of Arc at the Stake*).

Ireland, John (Nicholson) (1879–1962) English, born Bowden, Cheshire; works include sonatas, piano music, songs (eg 'Sea Fever'), the rhapsody *Mai-dun* and orchestral works (eg *The Forgotten Rite*, *These Things Shall Be*).

Ives, Charles (1874–1954) American, born Danbury, Connecticut; works include five symphonies, chamber music (eg *Concord Sonata*) and songs.

Janáček, Leoš (1854–1928) Czech, born Hukvaldy, Moravia; works include chamber, orchestral and choral music (eg the song cycle *The Diary of One Who Has Vanished*), operas (eg *Janufa*, *The Cunning Little Vixen*, *From the House of the Dead*), two string quartets and a mass.

Lalo, (Victor Antoine) Édouard (1823–92) French, born Lille. Works include compositions for violin (eg *Symphonie espagnole*), opera (eg *Le Roi d'Ys*) and ballet (*Namouna*).

Ligeti, György (Sándor) (1923–2006) Hungarian, born Dicsőszentmárton; works include orchestral compositions (eg *Apparitions*, *Lontano*), choral works (eg *Requiem*) and music for harpsichord, organ, and wind and string ensembles.

Liszt, Franz (1811–86) Hungarian, born Raiding; 400 original compositions including symphonic poems, piano music (eg *Hungarian Rhapsodies*) and oratorios (eg *Christus*).

Lloyd Webber, Andrew, Baron Lloyd-Webber (1948–) English, born London; works include *Joseph and the Amazing Technicolor Dreamcoat*, *Jesus Christ Superstar*, *Evita* (lyrics Tim Rice), *Cats* (libretto T S Eliot), *Phantom of the Opera*, *Aspects of Love* and *The Woman in White*.

MacMillan, James (Loy) (1959–) Scottish, born Kilwinning, Ayrshire; works include concertos (eg *Veni, Veni, Emmanuel*, percussion concerto), works for orchestra (eg *The Confession of Isobel Gowdie*), choral works (eg *Seven Last Words from the Cross*) and opera (eg *Inés de Castro*).

Mahler, Gustav (1860–1911) Austrian, born Kalist, Bohemia; works include ten symphonies, songs, the cantata *Das klagende Lied* and the song-symphony *Das Lied von der Erde* (The Song of the Earth).

Maxwell Davies, Sir Peter (1934–) English, born Manchester; works include operas (eg *Taverner*), songs (eg *Eight Songs for a Mad King*), symphonies, concertos and chamber ensembles. Appointed Master of the Queen's Music in 2004.

Mendelssohn, (Jacob Ludwig) Felix (1809–47) German, born Hamburg; prolific output, including concert overtures (eg *Fingal's Cave*, *A Midsummer Night's Dream*), symphonies (*Symphony in C minor*, *Scottish*, *Italian*), violin and piano concertos, quartets, operas and oratorios (eg *Elijah*).

Messiaen, Olivier (Eugène Prosper Charles) (1908–92) French, born Avignon; works include compositions for piano (*Vingt regards sur l'enfant Jésus*, *Catalogue d'oiseaux*), the symphony

Turangalila, an oratorio (*La Transfiguration de Notre Seigneur Jésus-Christ*) and an opera (*St François d'Assisi*).

Milhaud, Darius (1892–1974) French, born Aix-en-Provence; works include several operas, incidental music for plays, ballets (eg the jazz ballet *La Création du monde*), symphonies and orchestral, choral and chamber works.

Monteverdi, Claudio (Giovanni Antonio) (1567–1643) Italian, born Cremona; works include sacred works (eg *Vespers of 1610*), cantatas and operas (eg *Orfeo*, *Il Ritorno d'Ulisse*, *L'Incoronazione di Poppea*).

Mozart, (Johann Chrysostom) Wolfgang Amadeus (1756–91) Austrian, born Salzburg; 600 compositions including symphonies (eg 'Jupiter', *Linz*, *Prague*), concertos, string quartets, sonatas, operas (eg *Marriage of Figaro*, *Don Giovanni*, *Così fan tutte*, *Die Entführung aus dem Serail*, *Die Zauberflöte*), and church music (eg *Requiem Mass*).

Mussorgsky, Modest (1839–81) Russian, born Karevo; works include operas (eg *Boris Godunov*), song cycles and instrumental works (eg *Pictures at an Exhibition*, *Night on the Bare Mountain*).

Nielsen, Carl (August) (1865–1931) Danish, born Furen; works include operas (eg *Saul and David*, *Masquerade*), symphonies (eg 'The Inextinguishable'), string quartets, choral music, piano music and orchestral works (eg *Helios Overture*).

Offenbach, Jacques (1819–80) German, born Cologne; works include operettas (eg *Orphée aux enfers*, *La Belle Hélène*, *Barbe-bleue*, *La Vie Parisienne*) and the grand opera *Les Contes d'Hoffmann*.

Orff, Carl (1895–1982) German, born Munich; works include the scenic cantata *Carmina Burana* and the operatic pieces *Antigone*, *Oedipus* and *Prometheus*.

Palestrina, Giovanni Pierluigi da (c.1525–1594) Italian, born Palestrina, near Rome; works include chamber music, masses, choral music (eg *Song of Songs*) and madrigals.

Parry, Sir (Charles) Hubert (Hastings) (1848–1918) English, born Bournemouth, Hampshire; works include three oratorios, an opera, five symphonies, and many other pieces. Best-known work is the unison chorus *Jerusalem*.

Penderecki, Krzysztof (1933–) Polish, born Debica; works include compositions for strings (eg *Trenofiarom Hiroszimy*), operas (eg *Die schwarze Maske*) and concertos (eg *Flute Concerto*).

Poulenc, Francis (1899–1963) French, born Paris; works include much chamber music and the ballet *Les Biches*. Best known for his considerable output of songs, such as *Fêtes Galantes*.

Prokofiev, Sergei (1891–1953) Russian, born Sontsovka, Ukraine; works include eleven operas (eg *The Gambler*, *The Love for Three Oranges*, *War and Peace*), ballets (eg *Romeo and Juliet*), seven symphonies (eg the 'Classical'), concertos, sonatas, cantatas (eg *We are Seven*), film scores (eg *Alexander Nevsky*), and the 'children's piece' *Peter and the Wolf*.

Puccini, Giacomo (Antonio Domenico Michele Secondo Maria) (1858–1924) Italian, born Lucca; 12 operas (eg *Manon Lescaut*, *La Bohème*, *Tosca*, *Madama Butterfly*, *Turandot*).

Purcell, Henry (1659–95) English, born London; works include songs (eg 'Nymphs and Shepherds', 'Arise, ye Subterranean Winds'), sonatas, string fantasies, church music and opera (eg *Dido and Aeneas*).

Rachmaninov, Sergei Vasilyevich (1873–1943) Russian, born Nizhny Novgorod; works include operas, three symphonies, four piano concertos, the tone-poem *Isle of the Dead*, and *Rhapsody on a Theme of Paganini* for piano and orchestra.

Rameau, Jean Philippe (1683–1764) French, born Dijon; works include over 30 ballets and operas (eg *Hippolyte et Aricie, Castor et Pollux*) and harpsichord pieces.

Ravel, Maurice (1875–1937) French, born Ciboure; works include piano compositions (eg *Ma Mère L'Oye, Gaspard de la nuit*), string quartets, operas (eg *L'Heure espagnole, L'Enfant et les sortilèges*), ballets (eg *Daphnis and Chloé*), the 'choreographic poem' *La Valse* and the miniature ballet *Boléro*.

Rimsky-Korsakov, Nikolai Andreyevich (1844–1908) Russian, born Tikhvin, Novgorod; works include orchestral music (eg the symphonic suite *Sheherazade, Capriccio Espagnol, Russian Easter Festival Overture*) and 15 operas (eg *Sadko, The Snow Maiden, The Golden Cockerel*).

Rossini, Gioacchino Antonio (1792–1868) Italian, born Pesaro; works include many operas (eg *Il Barbiere di Siviglia, Otello, Guillaume Tell*) and a number of vocal and piano pieces.

Saint-Saëns, (Charles) Camille (1835–1921) French, born Paris; works include four symphonic poems (eg *Danse macabre*), piano, violin and cello concertos, symphonies, the opera *Samson et Dalila*, church music (eg *Messe solennelle*), and *Le Carnaval des animaux* for two pianos and orchestra.

Satie, Erik (Alfred Leslie) (1866–1925) French, born Honfleur; works include ballets (eg *Parade*), lyric dramas and whimsical piano pieces (eg *Gymnopédies*).

Scarlatti, (Giuseppe) Domenico (1685–1757) Italian, born Naples; works include over 600 harpsichord sonatas.

Schönberg, Arnold (1874–1951) naturalized American, born Vienna, Austria; works include chamber music, concertos and symphonic poems (eg *Pelleas and Melisande*), the choral-orchestral *Gurrelieder*, string music (eg *Verklärte Nacht*) and opera (*Moses and Aaron*).

Schubert, Franz (Peter) (1797–1828) Austrian, born Vienna; prolific output, works include symphonies, piano sonatas, string quartets and songs (eg *Gretchen am Spinnrade, Erlkönig, Die schöne Müllerin, Winterreise, Schwanengesang*).

Schumann, Robert (Alexander) (1810–56) German, born Zwickau, Saxony; works include piano music (eg *Fantasiestücke*), songs (eg the cycles *Dichterliebe* and *Frauenliebe und Leben*), chamber music, and four symphonies (eg *Rhenish*).

Scriabin, Alexander (1872–1915) Russian, born Moscow; works include a piano concerto, three symphonies, two tone-poems (eg *Poem of Ecstasy*), ten sonatas, studies and preludes.

Shostakovich, Dmitri (1906–75) Russian, born St Petersburg; works include 15 symphonies, operas (eg *The Nose, A Lady Macbeth of Mtsensk*), concertos, string quartets and film music.

Sibelius, Jean (1865–1957) Finnish, born Tavastehus; works include symphonic poems (eg *The Swan of Tuonela, Finlandia, The En Saga*), songs, a violin concerto and seven symphonies.

Stanford, Sir Charles Villiers (1852–1924) Irish, born Dublin; works include oratorios (eg *The Three Holy Children*), choral pieces (eg *Magnificat, Songs of the Sea*), organ preludes, operas, chamber music and orchestral music.

Stockhausen, Karlheinz (1928–2007) German, born Mödrath, near Cologne; works include orchestral music (eg *Gruppen*), choral and instrumental compositions.

Strauss, Johann, (the Younger) (1825–99) Austrian, born Vienna; works include over 400 waltzes (eg *The Blue Danube, Wine, Women, and Song, Tales from the Vienna Woods, Voices of Spring, The Emperor*), and operettas (eg *Die Fledermaus*).

Strauss, Richard (1864–1949) German, born Munich; works include symphonic poems (eg *Don Juan, Till Eulenspiegels lustige Streiche, Also Sprach Zarathustra, Tod und Verklärung, Don Quixote, Ein Heldenleben*) and operas (eg *Der Rosenkavalier, Ariadne auf Naxos, Capriccio*).

Stravinsky, Igor (1882–1971) Russian, born Oranienbaum, near St Petersburg (naturalized French, then American); works include operas (eg *The Rake's Progress*), oratorios (eg *Oedipus Rex*), concertos, ballets (eg *The Firebird, The Rite of Spring, Petrushka, Pulcinella, Orpheus, Agon*), and the musical play *Elegy for JFK* for voice and clarinets.

Tavener, Sir John (Kenneth) (1944–) English, born London; works include the cantata *The Whale*, the choral-orchestral work *Ultimos ritos*, the sacred opera *Thérèse*, as well as pieces such as *The Protecting Veil* for cello and strings.

Tchaikovsky, Piotr Ilyich (1840–93) Russian, born Kamsko-Votkinsk; works include ten operas (eg *Eugene Onegin, The Queen of Spades*), a violin concerto, six symphonies, three ballets (*The Nutcracker, Swan Lake, The Sleeping Beauty*) and tone-poems (eg *Romeo and Juliet, Capriccio Italien*).

Telemann, George Philipp (1681–1767) German, born Magdeburg; prolific composer, works include 600 overtures, 40 operas, 200 concertos, sonatas, suites, and oratorios (eg *Der Tag des Gerichts*).

Tippett, Sir Michael (Kemp) (1905–98) English, born London; works include operas (eg *The Midsummer Marriage, King Priam, The Knot Garden, The Ice Break*), concertos, symphonies, cantatas and oratorios (eg *A Child of Our Time*).

Varèse, Edgard (1883–1965) American, born Paris; works are almost entirely orchestral (eg *Metal, Ionization, Hyperprism*).

Vaughan Williams, Ralph (1872–1958) English, born Down Ampney, Gloucestershire; works include songs, symphonies (eg *London Symphony, Pastoral Symphony*), orchestral works (eg *Fantasia on a Theme by Thomas Tallis*), choral-orchestral works (eg *Sea Symphony*), operas (eg *Hugh the Drover*), the ballet *Job*, and film music (eg *Scott of the Antarctic*).

Verdi, Giuseppe (1813–1901) Italian, born le Roncole, near Busseto; works include church music (eg *Requiem*) and operas (eg *Nabucco, Rigoletto, Il Trovatore, La Traviata, La Forza del Destino, Aïda, Otello, Falstaff*).

Vivaldi, Antonio (1678–1741) Italian, born Venice; prolific output, works include over 400 concertos (eg *L'Estro Armonico, The Four Seasons*), 40 operas and an oratorio, *Juditha Triumphans*.

Wagner, (Wilhelm) Richard (1813–83) German, born Leipzig; operas include *Lohengrin*, the *Ring* cycle (*Das Rheingold, Die Walküre, Siegfried, Götterdämmerung*), *Die Meistersinger, Tristan und Isolde, Parsifal*.

Walton, Sir William (Turner) (1902–83) English, born Oldham; works include concertos, operas (eg *Troilus and Cressida*), cantatas (eg *Belshazzar's*

Feast), ballet music for *The Wise Virgins* and film music (eg *Henry V*).

Weber, Carl Maria (Friedrich) von (1786–1826) German, born Eutin, near Lübeck; works include operas (eg *Der Freischütz, Oberon, Euryanthe*), concertos, symphonies, sonatas, cantatas (eg *Kampf und Sieg*) and songs.

Webern, Anton (Friedrich Wilhelm) von (1883–1945) Austrian, born Vienna; works include a symphony, three cantatas, *Four Pieces for Violin and Pianoforte, Five Pieces for Orchestra*, a concerto for nine instruments, and songs.

Weill, Kurt (1900–50) German composer, born Dessau; works include songspiel (eg *Mahagonny*), operas (eg *Threepenny Opera, Rise and Fall of the*

City of Mahagonny), ballet (eg *The Seven Deadly Sins*), musical comedy and light opera (eg *Lady in the Dark, Street Scene, Lost in the Stars*).

Whitehead, Gillian (1941–) New Zealand, born Whangerei; works include compositions for choir and chamber orchestra (eg *Inner Harbour*), for soprano and instrumental ensemble (eg *Hotspur*), for opera (eg *Eleanor of Aquitaine*) and for strings (eg *Pakuru*).

Xenakis, Iannis (1922–2001) French, born Romania; works include compositions for piano and orchestra (eg *Erikhthon*), *Shaar* for strings, *Tetras* for string quartet, solo pieces (eg *Nomos Alpha* for cello, *Herma* for piano) and *Pithoprakta* for 50 instruments.

Librettists and songwriters

A selection of songs is listed. Original and full names of songwriters are given in parentheses.

Arlen, Harold (Hyman Arluck) (1905–86) US composer, lyricist, born Buffalo, New York; over 500 songs, including 'Between the Devil and the Deep Blue Sea', 'Stormy Weather', 'Get Happy' (lyrics by Ted Koehler), *A Star is Born* (1953) ('The Man that Got Away') (lyrics Ira Gershwin); *The Wizard of Oz* (1939) ('Over the Rainbow') (lyrics E Y Harburg, 1896–1981).

Bacharach, Burt (1928–) US composer and lyricist, born Kansas City, Missouri; 'Twenty Four Hours from Tulsa', 'Anyone Who Had a Heart', 'Walk On By', 'The Look of Love', 'Alfie', 'What's New, Pussycat', 'I Say a Little Prayer', 'Raindrops Keep Fallin' on My Head', 'That's What Friends Are For'.

Berlin, Irving (Israel Baline) (1888–1989) US, lyricist, born Temus, Siberia; composer; *Annie Get Your Gun* (1946), *Call Me Madam* (1950); over 900 songs, including 'Alexander's Ragtime Band', 'There's No Business Like Show Business', 'White Christmas', 'God Bless America', 'Oh, How I Hate to Get Up in the Morning'.

Bernstein, Leonard (1918–90) US composer, lyricist, born Laurence, Massachusetts; composer of opera, symphonies, songs; *West Side Story* (1958) ('America', 'Tonight') (lyrics Stephen Sondheim); songs include 'You Got Me', 'New York, New York'.

Boito, Arrigo (Enrico) (1842–1918) Italian composer and librettist, born Padua; work includes librettos for Verdi's *Otello* (1886) and *Falstaff* (1893).

Brown, Nacio Herb (1896–1964) US composer, lyricist, born Deming, New Mexico; *Broadway Melody* (1929) (lyrics Arthur Freed, 1894–1973); *Singin' in the Rain* (1952) (lyrics Freed); songs include 'You Were Meant to Me'.

Cahn, Sammy (Samuel Cohen) (1913–93) US lyricist, born New York; 'I've Heard That Song Before', 'I'll Walk Alone', 'It's Magic' (with Jule Styne); 'All the Way', 'High Hopes' (with Jimmy van Heusen).

Carmichael, Hoagy (Hoagland Howard Carmichael) (1899–1981) US songwriter and pianist, born Bloomington, Indiana; wrote many popular and enduring songs, eg 'Riverboat Shuffle', 'Stardust', 'Georgia on My Mind', 'Lazy River', 'I Get Along Without You Very Well', 'Lamplighter's Serenade' (Frank Sinatra's first solo recording).

Cohan, George M(ichael) (1878–1942) US composer, lyricist, born Providence, Rhode Island; *Little Johnny Jones* (1904) ('Give My Regards to Broadway'); 'The Talk of the Town' (1907).

Coward, Sir Noël Peirce (1899–1973) English composer, lyricist, playwright, born Teddington; *Words and Music* (revue) (1932) ('Mad Dogs and Englishmen', 'Someday I'll Find You').

Da Ponte, Lorenzo (Emanuele Conegliano) (1749–1838) Italian poet and librettist, born Ceneda, near Venice; work includes librettos for Mozart's *The Marriage of Figaro* (1786), *Don Giovanni* (1787) and *Così fan tutte* (1790).

Dylan, Bob (Robert Allen Zimmerman) (1941–) US songwriter, musician, born Duluth, Minnesota; 'Blowin' in the Wind', 'The Times They are A-Changin'', 'It's Alright Ma, I'm Only Bleeding', 'Mr Tambourine Man', 'Subterranean Homesick Blues', 'Like a Rolling Stone', 'Knockin' on Heaven's Door', 'Tangled up in Blue', 'Lay, Lady, Lay'.

Ellington, (Edward Kennedy) 'Duke' (1899–1974) US pianist, composer, bandleader, born Washington, DC; 2,000 works, including songs, instrumentals, film music; 'It Don't Mean a Thing if it Ain't Got That Swing' (lyrics Irving Mills), 'Best Wishes' (lyrics Ted Koehler), 'Creole Love Call' (vocal, no lyrics).

Fields, Dorothy (1905–74) US lyricist, born Allenhurst, New Jersey; 'I Can't Give You Anything But Love' (with Jimmy McHugh, from *Blackbirds of 1928*, 1928); 'On the Sunny Side of the Street', 'Exactly Like You' (with Jimmy McHugh); 'Lovely to Look At', 'The Way You Look Tonight' (with Jerome Kern); *Stars in Your Eyes* (1939) (with Arthur Schwartz); *Sweet Charity* (1966) ('Big Spender') (with Cy Coleman).

Gershwin, George (Jacob Gershvin) (1898–1937) US composer, born Brooklyn, New York City; and **Ira Gershwin** (Israel Gershvin) (1896–1983) US lyricist, born New York City; *Lady, Be Good!* (1924) ('The Man I Love', 'How Long Has This Been Going On?'), *Girl Crazy* (1930), *Porgy and Bess* (1935) ('Summertime') (lyrics Ira Gershwin and DuBose Heyward); songs include 'You Can't Take That Away from Me', 'Nice Work if You Can Get It', 'Love Walked In', 'They All Laughed'.

Gilbert, Sir William Schwenck (1836–1911) English librettist, born London; and **Sir Arthur Seymour Sullivan** (1842–1900) English composer, born London; operettas and songs include *HMS Pinafore* (1878) ('When I was a Lad'), *The Mikado* (1885) ('A Wand'ring Minstrel I'), *The Gondoliers* (1889) ('Take a Pair of Sparkling Eyes').

Herman, Jerry (1932–) US composer, lyricist, born New York City; *Hello Dolly!* (1964), *Mame* (1966), *La Cage aux Folles* (1983).

Kern, Jerome (David) (1885–1945) US composer, born New York City; 'The Way You Look Tonight' (lyrics Dorothy Fields); 'Ol' Man River', 'They Didn't Believe Me' (lyrics Herbert Reynolds); *Show Boat* (1927) (lyrics Oscar Hammerstein II).

Lennon, John (Winston) (1940–80) English songwriter, musician, born Liverpool; and **(James) Paul McCartney** (1942–) English songwriter, musician, born Liverpool; 'Please Please Me', 'Yesterday', 'All You Need Is Love', 'Strawberry Fields Forever', 'I Want to Hold Your Hand', 'Michelle', 'Eleanor Rigby', 'Ticket to Ride', 'Help'.

Lerner, Alan Jay (1918–86) US librettist, lyricist, playwright, born New York City; and **Frederick Loewe** (1904–88) German–American composer, born Berlin; *Brigadoon* (1947), *Paint Your Wagon* (1951), *My Fair Lady* (1956), *Gigi* (1958) (film).

Livingston, Jay (1915–2001) US composer, lyricist, born McDonald, Pennsylvania; and **Ray Evans** (1915–2007) US lyricist, born Salamanca, New York; 'The Cat and the Canary', 'Mona Lisa', 'Whatever Will Be, Will Be (Que Sera Sera)', 'Dear Heart'.

Loesser, Frank (Henry) (1910–69) US composer, lyricist, born New York City; *Guys and Dolls* (1950) ('I've Never Been in Love Before', 'Luck Be a Lady'); lyrics for 'The Boys in the Back Room' (music Frederick Hollander); lyrics for 'The Lady's in Love with You' and 'Some Like it Hot'.

MacColl, Ewan (James Miller) (1915–89) Scottish folk-singer, composer, collector, born Salford, Lancashire; 'The Shoals of Herring', 'Dirty Old Town', 'Freeborn Man', 'The First Time Ever I Saw Your Face'.

McHugh, Jimmy (James Frances McHugh) (1894–1969) US composer, born Boston, Massachusetts; with Dorothy Fields, as above; 'I'm Shooting High' (with Ted Koehler).

Mancini, Henry (1924–94) US composer of songs and film music, born Cleveland, Ohio; over 80 films, eg *Breakfast at Tiffany's* (1961); songs include 'Moon River' (lyrics Johnny Mercer), 'Days of Wine and Roses', 'Charade'.

Mercer, Johnny (Herndon) (1909–76) US lyricist, born Savannah, Georgia; 1,500 songs for over 70 films and seven Broadway musicals; songs with Henry Mancini, as above; 'Blues in the Night', 'That Old Black Magic' (music Harold Arlen); 'Jeepers Creepers' (music Harry Warren); lyrics for *Seven Brides for Seven Brothers* (1954).

Novello, Ivor (David Ivor Davies) (1893–1951) Welsh composer, songwriter, born Cardiff; 'Keep the Home Fires Burning', musical plays including *Glamorous Night* (1935), *The Dancing Years* (1939), *King's Rhapsody* (1949).

Porter, Cole (1891–1964) US composer, lyricist, born Peru, Indiana; *Gay Divorcee* (1932), *Anything Goes* (1934), *Du Barry Was a Lady* (1939) ('Well, Did You Evah!'), *Kiss Me Kate* (1948) ('So in Love'); songs include 'I'm in Love Again', 'Let's Do It, Let's Fall in Love', 'Just One of Those Things'.

Rice, Sir Timothy (Miles Bindon) (1944–) English lyricist, born Amersham, Buckinghamshire;

Joseph and the Amazing Technicolor Dreamcoat (1968) ('Any Dream Will Do'); *Jesus Christ Superstar* (1970) ('Jesus Christ Superstar', 'I Don't Know How to Love Him'), *Evita* (1978) ('Don't Cry for Me, Argentina') (with Andrew Lloyd Webber); *Chess* (1984) (with Benny Andersson and Björn Ulvaeus); *Aladdin* (1992) (with Alan Menken), *The Lion King* (1994) (with Elton John).

Rodgers, Richard (1902–79) US composer, born Long Island, New York; with **Lorenz Hart** (1895–1943) US lyricist, born New York City: *The Girl Friend* (1926), *Babes in Arms* (1937), 'Manhattan'; with **Oscar Hammerstein II** (1895–1960) US librettist, born New York City: *Oklahoma!* (1943) ('Oh, What a Beautiful Morning'), *South Pacific* (1949), *The King and I* (1959) ('Shall We Dance?'), *The Sound of Music* (1959) ('Do-Re-Mi', 'Edelweiss').

Romberg, Sigmund (1887–1951) US composer, born Nagykanizsa, Hungary; *The Desert Song* (1926), *The New Moon* (1928), ('Lover Come Back to Me'), *The Student Prince* (1924), *Girl of the Golden West* (1938).

Simon, Paul (1941–) US songwriter, musician, born Newark, New Jersey; 'I am a Rock', 'Bridge over Troubled Water', 'Mrs Robinson', 'Cecilia', 'Keep the Customer Satisfied', 'Homeward Bound', 'The Boxer', 'The Sound of Silence', 'You Can Call Me Al'.

Sondheim, Stephen (Joshua) (1930–) US composer, lyricist, born New York City; *West Side Story* (1958) (music Leonard Bernstein), *A Funny Thing Happened on the Way to the Forum* (1962), *A Little Night Music* (1973) ('Send in the Clowns'), *Sunday in the Park with George* (1984), *Assassins* (1990).

Styne, Jule (Julius Kerwin Stein) (1905–94) US composer, born London, England; 'There Goes That Song Again', 'I'll Walk Alone', 'It's Magic' (with Sammy Cahn); *Gentlemen Prefer Blondes* (1949) ('Diamonds are a Girl's Best Friend') (with Leo Robin).

Taupin, Bernie (1950–) English lyricist, born Anwick, Lincolnshire; with Elton John: 'Candle in the Wind', 'Crocodile Rock', 'Don't Go Breaking My Heart', 'Goodbye Yellow Brick Road', 'Rocket Man'; for film *Brokeback Mountain*, 'A Love That Will Never Grow Cold' (2005).

Warren, Harry (Salvatore Antonio Guaragna) (1893–1981) US composer of songs, film scores, born Brooklyn, New York City; 'You're My Everything', 'We're in the Money', 'Chattanooga Choo-Choo', 'Jeepers Creepers' (with Johnny Mercer); with **Al Dubin** (1891–1945) US lyricist, born Zurich, Switzerland: *42nd Street* (1932), 'The Boulevard of Broken Dreams', 'I Only Have Eyes for You'.

Weill, Kurt (1900–50) German composer, born Dessau; *Threepenny Opera* (1928) ('Mack the Knife') (lyrics Bertolt Brecht), *Lady in the Dark* (1941) (lyrics Ira Gershwin), *Street Scene* (1947) (lyrics Langston Hughes), *Lost in the Stars* (1949) (lyrics Maxwell Anderson).

Operas and operettas

Arts and Culture

Name	Composer	Date
Aïda	Verdi	1871
Akhnaten	Philip Glass	1984
Albert Herring	Britten	1947
Alceste	Gluck	1767
Andrea Chénier	Umberto Giordano	1896
Ariadne auf Naxos	Richard Strauss	1916
Armide et Renaud	Lully	1686
Un Ballo in Maschera	Verdi	1859
The Barber of Seville	Rossini	1816
The Bartered Bride	Smetana	1866
Béatrice et Bénédict	Berlioz	1862
The Beggar's Opera	Pepusch	1728
Billy Budd	Britten	1951
La Bohème	Puccini	1896
Boris Godunov	Mussorgsky	1874
Capriccio	Richard Strauss	1942
Carmen	Bizet	1875
Cavalleria Rusticana	Mascagni	1890
La Cenerentola (Cinderella)	Rossini	1817
La Clemenza di Tito	Mozart	1791
The Consul	Gian-Carlo Menotti	1950
Così Fan Tutte	Mozart	1790
The Cunning Little Vixen	Janáček	1924
The Damnation of Faust	Berlioz	1846
Death in Venice	Britten	1973
Dido and Aeneas	Purcell	1689
Don Carlos	Verdi	1867
Don Giovanni	Mozart	1787
Don Pasquale	Donizetti	1843
Duke Bluebeard's Castle	Bartók	1918
The Egyptian Helen	Richard Strauss	1928
Einstein on the Beach	Philip Glass	1976
Elegy for Young Lovers	Hans Werner Henze	1961
Elektra	Richard Strauss	1909
Eugene Onegin	Tchaikovsky	1879
The Fair Maid of Perth	Bizet	1867
Falstaff	Verdi	1893
Faust	Gounod	1859
La Fille du Régiment	Donizetti	1840
Fidelio	Beethoven	1814
Die Fledermaus	Johann Strauss	1874
The Flying Dutchman	Wagner	1843
La Gioconda	Amilcare Ponchielli	1876
The Golden Cockerel	Rimsky-Korsakov	1909
The Gondoliers	Gilbert and Sullivan	1889
Le Grand Macabre	Ligeti	1978
Hansel and Gretel	Humperdinck	1893
HMS Pinafore	Gilbert and Sullivan	1878
Hugh the Drover	Vaughan Williams	1924
The Ice Break	Tippett	1977
Idomeneo	Mozart	1781
L'Incoronazione di Poppea	Monteverdi	1642
Iphigénie en Tauride	Gluck	1779

Name	Composer	Date
Jenufa	Janáček	1904
Katya Kabanova	Janáček	1921
King Priam	Tippett	1962
Lady Macbeth of Mtsensk	Shostakovich	1934
Lohengrin	Wagner	1850
The Love for Three Oranges	Prokofiev	1920
Lucia di Lammermoor	Donizetti	1835
Lucrezia Borgia	Donizetti	1833
Lulu	Berg	1937
Macbeth	Verdi	1847
Madama Butterfly	Puccini	1904
The Magic Flute	Mozart	1791
Les Mamelles de Tirésias	Poulenc	1947
Manon	Massenet	1884
Manon Lescaut	Puccini	1893
The Marriage of Figaro	Mozart	1786
Maskarade	Nielsen	1906
The Mask of Orpheus	Harrison Birtwistle	1986
Die Meistersinger von Nürnberg	Wagner	1868
The Merry Widow	Lehár	1905
The Merry Wives of Windsor	Otto Nicolai	1849
The Midsummer Marriage	Tippett	1955
The Mikado	Gilbert and Sullivan	1885
Moses und Aron	Schönberg	1954
Nabucco	Verdi	1842
Nixon in China	John Adams	1987
Norma	Bellini	1831
Noye's Fludde	Britten	1958
Oedipus Rex	Stravinsky	1927
Orfeo ed Euridice	Gluck	1762
Orpheus in the Underworld	Offenbach	1858
Otello	Verdi	1887
Pagliacci	Leoncavallo	1892
Parsifal	Wagner	1882
The Pearl Fishers	Bizet	1863
Pelléas et Mélisande	Debussy	1902
Peter Grimes	Britten	1945
Porgy and Bess	Gershwin	1935
Punch and Judy	Harrison Birtwistle	1968
I Puritani	Bellini	1835
The Rake's Progress	Stravinsky	1951
The Rape of Lucretia	Britten	1946
Rigoletto	Verdi	1851
The Ring	Wagner	1876
Der Rosenkavalier	Richard Strauss	1911
Le Rossignol	Stravinsky	1914
Salome	Richard Strauss	1911
Samson et Dalila	Saint-Saëns	1877
Semele	Handel	1744
Simon Boccanegra	Verdi	1857
La Sonnambula	Bellini	1831
The Tales of Hoffmann	Offenbach	1881
Tannhäuser	Wagner	1845
The Threepenny Opera	Weill	1928

Name	Composer	Date
Tosca	Puccini	1900
La Traviata	Verdi	1853
Tristan und Isolde	Wagner	1865
The Trojans	Berlioz	1863
Il Trovatore	Verdi	1853
Turandot	Puccini	1926
The Turn of the Screw	Britten	1954

Name	Composer	Date
I Vespri Siciliani	Verdi	1855
Werther	Massenet	1892
Where the Wild Things Are	Oliver Knussen	1980
William Tell	Rossini	1829
Wozzeck	Berg	1925

Opera singers

Allen, Sir Thomas (Boaz) (1944–) English baritone, born Seaham.

Anderson, Marian (1902–93) US contralto, born South Philadelphia.

Austral, Florence (Florence Wilson) (1892–1968) Australian soprano, born Richmond, West Melbourne.

Bailey, Norman (Stanley) (1933–) English baritone, born Birmingham.

Baker, Dame Janet (Abbott) (1933–) English mezzo-soprano, born Hatfield, Yorkshire.

Barstow, Dame Josephine (Clare) (1940–) English soprano, born Sheffield.

Bartoli, Cecilia (1966–) Italian mezzo-soprano, born Rome.

Battistini, Mattia (1856–1928) Italian baritone, born Rome.

Battle, Kathleen (1948–) US soprano, born Portsmouth, Ohio.

Berganza, Teresa (1935–) Spanish mezzo-soprano, born Madrid.

Bergonzi, Carlo (1924–) Italian tenor, born Polisene.

Björling, Jussi (1911–60) Swedish tenor, born Stora Tuna.

Bonci, Alessandro (1870–1940) Italian tenor, born Cesena.

Borgatti, Giuseppe (1871–1950) Italian tenor, born Cento.

Borgioli, Dino (1891–1960) Italian tenor, born Florence.

Bowman, James (1941–) English countertenor, born Oxford.

Brannigan, Owen (1908–73) English, bass baritone, born Annitsford, Northumberland.

Butt, Dame Clara (1872–1936) English contralto, born Southwick, Sussex.

Caballé, Montserrat (1933–) Spanish soprano, born Barcelona.

Callas, Maria (Maria Anna Sofia Cecilia Kalogeropoulos) (1923–77) US soprano of Greek parents, born New York City.

Carden, Joan Maralyn (1937–) Australian soprano, born Melbourne.

Carreras, José (1946–) Spanish tenor, born Barcelona.

Caruso, Enrico (1873–1921) Italian tenor, born Naples.

Collier, Marie (1926–71) Australian soprano, born Ballarat.

Craig, Charles (1919–97) English tenor, born London.

Davies, Ryland (1943–) Welsh tenor, born Cwym, Ebbw Vale.

de Luca, Giuseppe (1876–1950) Italian baritone, born Rome.

De Lucia, Fernando (1860–1925) Italian tenor, born Naples.

de Reszke, Jean (Jan Mieczislaw) (1850–1925) Polish tenor, born Warsaw.

Del Monaco, Mario (1915–82) Italian tenor, born Florence.

Deller, Alfred (George) (1912–79) English countertenor, born Margate.

Di Stefano, Giuseppe (1921–2008) Italian tenor, born near Catania, Sicily.

Domingo, Placido (1941–) Spanish tenor, born Madrid.

Evans, Sir Geraint (Llewellyn) (1922–92) Welsh baritone, born Pontypridd, South Wales.

Ewing, Maria (Louise) (1950–) US mezzo-soprano, born Detroit.

Farrar, Geraldine (1882–1967) US soprano, born Melrose, Massachusetts.

Farrell, Eileen (1920–2002) US soprano, born Willimantic, Connecticut.

Ferrier, Kathleen (1912–53) English contralto, born Higher Walton, Lancashire.

Fischer-Dieskau, Dietrich (1925–) German baritone, born Zehlendorf, Berlin.

Flagstad, Kirsten (1895–1962) Norwegian soprano, born Hamar.

Fleming, Renée (1959–) US soprano, born Indiana, Pennsylvania.

Forrester, Maureen (1930–) Canadian contralto, born Montreal.

Fremstad, Olive (1871–1951) US soprano, born Stockholm.

Freni, Mirella (1935–) Italian soprano, born Modena.

Galli-Curci, Amelita (1882–1963) Italian soprano, born Milan.

Galli-Marie, Celestine (1840–1905) French mezzo-soprano, born Paris.

Garrett, Lesley (1955–) English soprano, born Thorne, Doncaster.

Gedda, Nicolai (1925–) Swedish tenor, born Stockholm.

Gigli, Beniamino (1890–1957) Italian tenor, born Recanati.

Gobbi, Tito (1913–84) Italian baritone, born Bassano del Grappa.

Harper, Dame Heather (1930–) Northern Irish soprano, born Belfast.

Hendricks, Barbara (1948–) US soprano, born Stephens, Arizona.

Horne, Marilyn (1934–) US mezzo-soprano, born Bradford, Pennsylvania.

Hotter, Hans (1909–2003) Austrian bass-baritone, born Offenbach-am-Main, Germany.

Jurinac, Sena (1921–) Yugoslav (now Bosnian) soprano, born Travnik.

Kollo, René (1937–) German tenor, born Berlin.

Kraus, Alfredo (1927–99) Spanish tenor, born Las Palmas, Canary Islands.

Lanza, Mario (Alfredo Arnold Coccozza) (1921–59) US tenor, born Philadelphia, Pennsylvania.

Lehmann, Lilli (1848–1929) German soprano, born Würzburg.

Lehmann, Lotte (1888–1976) German soprano, born Perleberg.

Lind, Jenny ('the Swedish Nightingale') (1820–87) Swedish soprano, born Stockholm.

Los Angeles, Victoria de (Victoria Gómez Cima) (1923–2005) Spanish soprano, born Barcelona.

Ludwig, Christa (1928–) German mezzo-soprano, born Berlin.

Luxon, Benjamin (1937–) English baritone, born Redruth, Cornwall.

McCormack, John (1884–1945) Irish tenor, born Athlone.

Major, Dame Malvina (Lorraine) (1943–) New Zealand soprano, born Hamilton.

Martinelli, Giovanni (1885–1969) Italian tenor, born Montagnana.

Melba, Dame Nellie (Helen Mitchell) (1861–1931) Australian soprano, born Burnle, near Richmond, Melbourne.

Melchior, Lauritz (1890–1973) Danish tenor, born Copenhagen.

Migenes-Johnson, Julia (1945–) US soprano, born New York City.

Milanov, Zinka (1906–89) Croatian soprano, born Zagreb.

Nash, Heddle (1896–1961) English tenor, born London.

Nilsson, Birgit (1918–2005) Swedish soprano, born near Karup.

Norman, Jessye (1945–) US soprano, born Augusta, Georgia.

Patti, Adelina (Adela Juana Maria Patti) (1843–1919) Italian soprano, born Madrid.

Pavarotti, Luciano (1935–2007) Italian tenor, born Modena.

Pears, Sir Peter (1910–86) English tenor, born Farnham, Surrey.

Pinza, Ezio (1892–1957) Italian bass, born Rome.

Ponselle, Rosa (Melba) (1897–1981) US soprano, born Meriden, Connecticut.

Popp, Lucia (1939–93) Czech soprano, born Llhorsaká.

Prey, Hermann (1929–98) German baritone, born Berlin.

Price, (Mary Violet) Leontyne (1927–) US soprano, born Laurel, Mississippi.

Scholl, Andreas (1967–) German countertenor, born Eltville am Rhein.

Schumann, Elisabeth (1889–1952) US soprano, born Merseburg, Germany.

Schwarzkopf, Dame Elisabeth (1915–2006) Austrian–British soprano, born Jarotschin, near Poznan, Poland.

Scotto, Renata (1934–) Italian soprano, born Savona.

Shirley-Quirk, John (1931–) English bass-baritone, born Liverpool.

Siepi, Cesare (1923–) Italian bass, born Milan.

Söderström, Elisabeth (1927–) Swedish soprano, born Stockholm.

Stratas, Teresa (1938–) Canadian soprano, born Toronto.

Studer, Cheryl (1955–) US soprano, born Midland, Michigan.

Sutherland, Dame Joan (1926–) Australian soprano, born Sydney.

Tauber, Richard (1891–1948) Austrian–British tenor, born Linz.

Tear, Robert (1939–) Welsh tenor, born Barry, South Wales.

Tebaldi, Renata (1922–2004) Italian soprano, born Pesaro.

Te Kanawa, Dame Kiri (1944–) New Zealand soprano, born Gisborne.

Terfel, Bryn (1965–) Welsh bass-baritone, born Pwllheli, Gwynedd.

Tetrazzini, Luisa (1871–1940) Italian soprano, born Florence.

Teyte, Dame Maggie (1888–1976) English soprano, born Wolverhampton.

Tibbett, Lawrence Mervil (1896–1960) US baritone, born Bakersfield, California.

Turner, Dame Eva (1892–1990) English soprano, born Oldham.

Van Dam, José (1940–) Belgian bass-baritone, born Brussels.

Vickers, Jon(athan) Stewart (1926–) Canadian tenor, born Prince Albert.

Von Otter, Anne Sofie (1955–) Swedish mezzo-soprano, born Stockholm.

Wiener, Otto (1911–2000) Austrian baritone, born Vienna.

Orchestras

Name	Date founded	Location
Academy of Ancient Music	1973	UK (London)
Academy of St Martin-in-the-Fields	1959	UK (London)
Australian Chamber	1975	Sydney
BBC Concert Orchestra	1952	UK (London)
BBC Philharmonic	1934	UK (Manchester)
BBC Scottish Symphony	1935	UK (Glasgow)
BBC Symphony	1930	UK (London)
BBC National Orchestra of Wales	1935	UK (Cardiff)
Berliner Philharmoniker	1882	Germany
Boston Symphony	1881	USA
Bournemouth Symphony	1893	UK
Chicago Symphony	1891	USA
City of Birmingham Symphony	1920	UK
Cleveland Symphony	1918	USA
Concertgebouw	1888	Netherlands (Amsterdam)
Detroit Symphony	1914	USA
English Chamber	1948	UK (London)
Hallé	1858	UK (Manchester)
Israel Philharmonic	1936	Israel (Tel Aviv)
London Philharmonic	1904	UK
London Symphony	1904	UK
Los Angeles Philharmonic	1904	USA

Name	Date founded	Location
Melbourne Symphony	1906	Australia
Milan La Scala	1778	Italy
Minnesota	1903	USA (Minneapolis)
National Symphony	1931	USA (Washington DC)
NBC Symphony	1937–54	USA (New York)
New Orleans Philharmonic Symphony	1936	USA
New York Philharmonic	1842	USA
New York Symphony	1878	USA
Northern Sinfonia	1958	UK (Newcastle-upon-Tyne)
Orchestre Symphonique de Montréal	1842	Canada
Oslo Philharmonic	1919	Norway
Philadelphia	1900	USA
The Philharmonia	1945	UK (London)
Pittsburgh Symphony	1926	USA
Royal Liverpool Philharmonic	1840	UK
Royal Philharmonic	1946	UK (London)
Royal Scottish National	1891	UK (Glasgow)
St Petersburg Philharmonic	1921	Russia
San Francisco	1911	USA
Santa Cecilia Academy	1895	Italy (Rome)
Scottish Chamber	1974	UK (Edinburgh)
Seattle Symphony	1903	USA
Staatskapelle	1923	Germany (Dresden)
Sydney Symphony	1934	Australia
Toronto Symphony	1922	Canada
Ulster	1966	UK (Belfast)
Vienna Philharmonic	1842	Austria
Vienna Symphony	1900	Austria
West-Eastern Divan	1999	Spain (Seville)

Layout of an orchestra

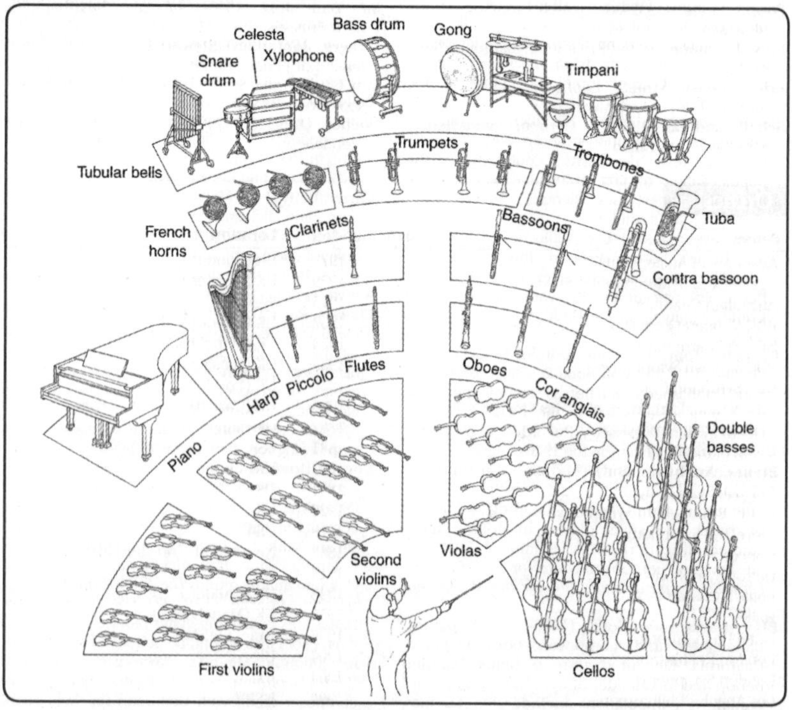

Layout of an orchestra showing: Celesta, Snare drum, Xylophone, Bass drum, Gong, Timpani, Tubular bells, Trumpets, Trombones, Tuba, French horns, Clarinets, Bassoons, Contra bassoon, Harp, Piccolo, Flutes, Oboes, Cor anglais, Piano, Double basses, Second violins, Violas, First violins, Cellos

Jazz and blues musicians and singers

Selected songs, compositions and albums are listed.

Adderley, 'Cannonball' (Julian Edwin) (1928–75) US alto saxophonist, bandleader and composer, born Tampa, Florida. Played blues and funk, one of the first to electrify the saxophone; made hits out of Afro-American themes; 'Sermonette', 'This Here', 'Work Song'.

Armstrong, Louis (Daniel) ('Satchmo') (1900–71) US trumpeter and singer, born New Orleans. First major jazz virtuoso and exponent of 'scat' singing (vocal imitation of an instrument); appeared in more than 50 films, also very successful commercially; 'Mack the Knife', 'Blueberry Hill', 'Hello Dolly!'.

Ayler, Albert (1936–70) US tenor saxophonist, born Cleveland, Ohio. Influenced from youth by gospel and religious bands; début at 16 with Little Walter as sax player; developed Free Jazz style; 'Bells', 'Ghosts'.

Baker, Chet (Chesney Henry Baker) (1929–88) US trumpeter and singer, born Yale, Oklahoma. One of the most lyrical trumpeters in jazz history, at centre of West Coast 'cool jazz' scene; had success with Gerry Mulligan's pianoless quartet with 'My Funny Valentine'.

Barbieri, Gato (Leandro J Barbieri) (1934–) Argentinian clarinettist, tenor saxophonist and composer, born Rosario, Argentina. Made début playing the requinto (clarinet) in the 'milonga' bands, then developed own styles, from Free Jazz to Latin; tenor sax player of tropical alcoves and clubs; won Grammy for film soundtrack *Last Tango in Paris* (1972); *Caliente!, Che Corazon*.

Basie, 'Count' (William Allen) (1904–84) US pianist and bandleader, born Red Bank, New Jersey. Major big band (16-piece) leader of the swing era; Kansas City style music; compositions include 'One O'Clock Jump' and 'Jumpin' at the Woodside'.

Bechet, Sidney (Joseph) (1897–1959) US clarinettist and soprano saxophonist, born New Orleans. Began in New Orleans style; contributed to the popularization of jazz, mingling tradition with accessible tunes; 'Les Oignons', 'Petite Fleur', 'Dans les Rues d'Antibes'.

Beiderbecke, (Leon) Bix (1903–31) US cornettist and pianist, born Davenport, Iowa. First great white jazz musician, characterized by his richly harmonic tone and soft, warm sonority; 'I'm Comin' Virginia', 'In the Dark', 'In a Mist' (piano solos).

Bennett, Tony (Anthony Dominick Benedetto) (1926–) US jazz and popular singer, born New York. Established reputation as singer in the 1950s, graduating towards jazz in the 1960s; 'I Left My Heart in San Francisco'. Recorded two albums with pianist Bill Evans in the 1970s.

Blakey, Art(hur) ('Bu') (Abdullah ibn Buhaina) (1919–90) US drummer and bandleader, born Pittsburgh, Pennsylvania. Leading exponent of 'hard bop' style; played in double time; studied African rhythms; leader of The Jazz Messengers; composed score for 1985 film *Des Femmes Disparaissent; Oh, By the Way, New York Scene*.

Bley, Carla (née Borg) (1938–) US pianist, bandleader and composer, born Oakland, California. Elegant rhythm 'n' blues, blended bebop and folk; leader of own band and record company; compositions include 'Ida Lupino',

'Sing Me Softly of the Blues' and Gary Burton's masterpiece 'A Genuine Tong Funeral'.

Broonzy, Big Bill (William Lee Conley Broonzy) (1893–1958) US singer, musician and composer, born Scott, Mississippi. Guitar accompanist and composer to the great blues players of his generation; played in ragtime style, also encompassing folksong, rural and urban blues; 'See See Rider', 'Trouble in Mind', his own 'Texas Tornado' and 'Bossie Woman' and recordings of John Hampton's 1938–9 *Spirituals to Sing* concerts.

Brown, Sandy (Alexander Brown) (1929–75) Anglo-Indian clarinettist, bandleader and composer, born Izatnagar, India. Outstanding blues player. Originally influenced by Louis Armstrong's Hot Five and the New Orleans style, then by West Indian calypso and African folk.

Brubeck, Dave (David Warren Brubeck) (1920–) US pianist, bandleader and composer, born Concord, California. Pupil of Schoenberg and Milhaud; uses odd rhythms, the rondo form, fugue-like passages; made popular by Paul Desmond's 'Take Five'; compositions include 'The Duke', 'In Your own Sweet Way', 'Unsquare Dance'.

Burton, Gary (1943–) US vibraphonist and bandleader, born Anderson, Indiana. Has habit of 'discovering' new talent, eg Tommy Smith. Also involved in music education and publishing. Many successful album recordings, including Carla Bley's *A Genuine Tong Funeral* and *Alone at Last*.

Byrd, Charlie (1925–99) US guitarist, born Chuckatuck, Virginia. Specialist on nylon-string guitar; very versatile; played jazz, classical and South American in the same concerts; prolific recordings include *Jazz / Samba* with Stan Getz.

Calloway, Cab(ell) (1907–94) US bandleader and singer, born Rochester, New York. His band succeeded Duke Ellington's at Harlem's Cotton Club in 1931. Known for his signature tune *Minnie the Moocher* and his scat-style catchphrases.

Carter, Betty (Lillie Mae Jones) (1930–98) US singer, born Flint, Michigan. Sang with bebop musicians, including Charlie Parker and Dizzie Gillespie. A brilliant vocal improviser, who was popular in the 1950s. Rediscovered in the 1970s after setting up own record label, Bet-Car.

Charles, Ray ('The Genius') (Ray Charles Robinson) (1930–2004) US singer, pianist and composer, born Albany, Georgia. Successful soul artist (despite blindness) with sensitive, vibrant voice and sincere, expressive preacher's tone; often accompanied by big bands; 'Swanee River Rock', 'What'd I Say', 'Georgia on My Mind', 'Hit the Road Jack', 'I Can't Stop Loving You', film theme 'Ruby'.

Cherry, Don(ald Eugene) (1936–95) US trumpeter, cornetist, bandleader and composer, born Oklahoma City. Exponent of improvised music; considered himself not playing the trumpet but singing with it; came to prominence in Ornette Coleman's Free Jazz quartet and on the John Coltrane quartet album *The Avant-Garde*.

Christian, Charlie (1916–42) US guitarist, born Dallas, Texas. Electric guitar pioneer, establishing it as a solo instrument; helped lay basis of bebop revolution in Minton's Playhouse; played with Benny Goodman. Early death due to TB. Shared composer credit with Goodman for 'Solo Flight'

Arts and Culture

Arts and Culture

and 'Seven Come Eleven'; also 'Blues in C', 'Waitin' for Benny'.

Clarke, Kenny ('Klook') (Kenneth Spearman Clarke) (1914–85) US drummer, bandleader and composer, born Pittsburgh, Pennsylvania. Inventor of bebop drums; father of modern percussionists; co-led Clarke–Boland big band. Compositions include 'Epistrophy' with Thelonious Monk, 'Salt Peanuts' with Dizzy Gillespie.

Cole, Nat 'King' (Nathaniel Adams Coles) (1919–65) US singer, pianist and composer, born Montgomery, Alabama. Inventor of modern concept of trio, using piano, guitar and double bass. Won popularity as a singer; 'Straighten up and Fly Right', 'Too Young', 'Unforgettable', 'Answer Me, My Love', 'Ballerina', 'Stardust'.

Coleman, Ornette (1930–) US alto and tenor saxophonist, trumpeter and composer, born Fort Worth, Texas. Experimented in free-form jazz and atonality to mixed acclaim; now regarded as major innovator; invented word 'harmelodic' (improvised coloration). Albums include *Something Else!* and *The Shape of Jazz to Come*.

Collins, Albert (1932–93) US blues guitarist and singer, born Leona, Texas. A cousin of Lightnin' Hopkins, he inherited the Texas blues guitar tradition of Hopkins and T-Bone Walker. He had a regional hit in 1958 with 'The Freeze', and became known for an 'icy', spare guitar sound. He recorded in a crossover blues-funk style in the late 1960s, but did little more of real note until he signed with Alligator Records in 1977. He joined Robert Cray and Johnny Copeland on the best-selling *Showdown* (1985).

Coltrane, John (William) (1926–67) US tenor and soprano saxophonist, bandleader and composer, born Hamlet, North Carolina. One of the most influential performers of the post-bebop era. Developed and experimented with improvisation, influenced by Indian ragas, African pentatonic scales and the polyphonic music of the Pygmies; *Giant Steps, A Love Supreme*.

Corea, Chick (Armando Anthony Corea) (1941–) Italian–US pianist and composer, born Chelsea, Massachusetts. His taste for diversity makes him hard to classify; plays from acoustics to electronics and from Latin rhythms to bebop, Free Jazz to classical; replaced Herbie Hancock in Miles Davis's group for *In a Silent Way* and *Bitches Brew*; 'Return to Forever', 'Crystal Silence', 'Armando's Rhumba', *Now He Sings, Now He Sobs* (1968), *The Ultimate Adventure* (2006).

Cray, Robert (1953–) US singer, blues guitarist, born Columbus, Georgia. One of the most successful blues artists of the last 20 years, Cray's clean guitar style is coupled with a soul-infused singing voice. Frontman with the Robert Cray Band since 1974, recordings include *Don't Be Afraid of the Dark* (1988) and *Shoulda Been Home* (2001).

Cullum, Jamie (1979–) English pianist, singer and composer, born Romford. Rooted in jazz, he nevertheless draws on a wide range of musical styles, including pop and hip-hop; often uses a 'stompbox' (a small wooden box which is tapped with the foot to provide a rhythmic self-accompaniment); plays solo and in trios and small ensembles; came to prominience with the album *Heard It All Before* (1999); *Catching Tales* (2005).

Dankworth, Sir John (Philip William) (1927–) English alto saxophonist, bandleader and composer, born London. A student of the Royal Academy of Music, he later converted stables at his

home to be a workshop for young musicians. Hits include novelty 'Experiments with Mice', 'African Waltz'; ballet *Lysistrata*; film score *Saturday Night and Sunday Morning*; piece for orchestra *What the Dickens*.

Davis, Miles ('Prince of Darkness') (Miles Dewey Davis III) (1926–91) US trumpeter and bandleader, born Alton, Illinois. One of the most popular and adaptable jazz musicians of all time. Recording début with 'Now's the Time', 'Billie Bounce', 'Koko'. Working with Gil Evans, he led a nonet that inspired the 'cool jazz' school. Albums include *The Birth of the Cool* (a turning point in jazz history), *Kind of Blue*; recorded music for Louis Malle's film *Ascenseur pour l'Échafaud* (1957).

Dolphy, Eric (Allan) (1928–64) US alto saxophonist, clarinettist, flautist and composer, born Los Angeles. Music rooted in Afro-American tradition but with birdsong-like improvisation comprising screeches, airiness and wild escapades, eg in 'Gazelloni' on *Out to Lunch* and 'Jim Crow' on *Other Aspects*.

Domino, Fats (Antoine Domino) (1928–) US singer, pianist, born New Orleans, Louisiana; 'Every Night About This Time', 'It's Midnight', 'Ain't That a Shame', 'Blue Monday', 'Blueberry Hill'.

Dorsey, Tommy ('the Sentimental Gentleman of Swing') (Thomas Francis Dorsey) (1905–56) US trombonist and big-band leader, born Shenandoah, Pennsylvania. Characteristic sweet-toned instrumental style with seamless legato; formed Dorsey Brothers Orchestra in 1928 with brother Jimmy; became the Tommy Dorsey Orchestra in 1934, which had nearly 200 hits 1935–53 including 'I'm Getting Sentimental Over You', 'Marie', 'Indian Summer', 'In the Blue of Evening' (with Frank Sinatra), 'Boogie Woogie'.

Eldridge, Roy (David) ('Little Jazz') (1911–89) US trumpeter, pianist, drummer, bass player and bandleader, born Pittsburgh, Pennsylvania. Virtuoso who influenced Louis Armstrong and Dizzy Gillespie. Famous trumpet soloist, often playing in the high register; played with top bands, eg McKinney's Cotton Pickers and the Fletcher Henderson Orchestra; vocal duet hit with Anita O'Day 'Let Me Off Uptown', also countless recordings, including *Dale's Wail* with Oscar Peterson, *The Trumpet Battle* with Charlie Shavers and Lester Young.

Elis, Don(ald Johnson) (1934–78) US trumpeter, bandleader and composer, born Los Angeles. Worked in both jazz and contemporary music, experimenting with oriental instruments and compositions, and incorporating string quartets; music full of virtuosity collages and improvisation, but poorly represented on disc.

Ellington, 'Duke' (Edward Kennedy) (1899–1974) US pianist, bandleader and composer, born Washington, DC. One of the most important jazz composers and players. Produced about 2000 works including 'Mood Indigo', 'Sophisticated Lady', 'Take the A Train', film music for *Anatomy of a Murder* (1959) and *Paris Blues* (1961).

Evans, Bill (William John Evans) (1929–80) US pianist and composer, born Plainfield, New Jersey. Most influential pianist of his generation. Won several Grammies, eg for *Conversations with Myself*; 'Waltz for Debby', 'N Y C's No Lark' (for Sonny Clark).

Evans, Gil (Ian Ernest Gilmore Green) (1912–88) Canadian composer, pianist and bandleader, born Toronto. Collaboration with Miles Davis led to emergence of 'cool jazz' style; one of the first modern jazz arrangers to combine electronics and rock influences with bebop and swing. Compositions include 'Boplicity' and 'Moon Dreams' for Davis's *Birth of the Cool*, 'Concierto de Aranjuez' for *Sketches of Spain*, electric album *Svengali*.

Fitzgerald, Ella (1917–96) US singer, born Newport News, Virginia. Talented jazz singer; famous for scat singing (vocal imitation of an instrument) and improvisation; starred in drummer Chick Webb's orchestra; sang with Duke Ellington's and Count Basie's bands; performed *Porgy and Bess* with Louis Armstrong; 'Stone Cold Dead in the Market', 'Mack the Knife', 'Party Blues'.

Franklin, Aretha ('Lady Soul', 'Queen of Soul') (1942–) US singer, born Memphis, Tennessee. Daughter of Detroit preacher and gospel singer; many million-selling singles; recorded 'Respect' with Ray Charles and 'Lady Soul' with Otis Redding; masterpiece album *Amazing Grace*; *Love All the Hurt Away*, *One Lord, One Faith, One Baptism*, *So Damn Happy*.

Garbarek, Jan (1947–) Norwegian saxophonist, born Mysen, Norway. Despite being inspired by Coltrane, his influence is very much European, drawing on the moods and haunting melodies from his Scandinavian roots; has played and recorded with George Russell's sextet and orchestra in Sweden, and with the medieval folk group the Hilliard Ensemble (*Officium*, 1996); style described as 'distilled thought'.

Garner, Erroll (1921–77) US pianist, born Pittsburgh, Pennsylvania. Self-taught artist with a gift for melody; combined old and new styles; his own lingering style became known as the 'Garner amble'; known for 'Play Piano Play', 'Laura', 'Misty'; awarded gold disc for *Concert by the Sea* (1958).

Getz, Stan(ley) ('The Sound') (1927–91) US tenor saxophonist and bandleader, born Philadelphia. Most important white jazz saxophonist for 40 years of his life. Characteristic smooth, light tone and articulate phrasing. Popularized bossa nova jazz style in the 1960s; 'Focus', 'Desafinado', 'The Girl from Ipanema'.

Gillespie, 'Dizzy' (John Birks) (1917–93) US trumpeter, bandleader and composer, born Cheraw, South Carolina. Great pioneering virtuoso and innovator; created bebop style (with Charlie Parker); introduced African rhythms into jazz; compositions include classics 'Night in Tunisia', 'Groovin' High', 'Dizzy Atmosphere', 'Anthropology'.

Goodman, Benny ('the King of Swing') (Benjamin David Goodman) (1909–86) US clarinettist, bandleader and composer, born Chicago. The first white performer to integrate black musicians into his own band; in 1962 played in first American jazz band to perform in the Soviet Union; clean, joyful style; sextet recordings include 'Six Appeal', 'Seven Come Eleven', 'Wholly Cats', 'Breakfast Feud', 'Jersey Bounce', 'Why Don't You Do Right' (sung by Peggy Lee).

Gordon, Dexter (Keith) (1923–90) US tenor saxophonist, born Los Angeles. One of the first to play bop tenor; developed modern ballad style and keen harmonic tone (which Coltrane and Rollins studied); 'The Chase', 'The Duel', 'Daddy Plays the Horn', *Gotham City*; also acted in play *The Connection* and film *Round Midnight* (1986).

Grappelli, Stephane (1908–97) French violinist, born Paris. Founder member (with Django Reinhardt) of Quintette du Hot Club de France, which had a European influence on jazz in the 1930s. Adapted violin to jazz; master of swing-based style; recorded swing versions of the 'Marseillaise' called 'Echoes of France', and of J S Bach's *Concerto in D Minor*. Duets with Yehudi Menuhin include *Tea for Two* and *Strictly for the Birds*.

Guy, Buddy (1936–) US singer and guitarist, born Lettsworth, Louisiana. Began at 13 with home-made guitar and progressed to centre of Chicago blues scene in the 1950s and 1960s; 'Stone Crazy', début album *A Man And His Blues*, compilation with other Chicago bands *In The Beginning*.

Hampton, Lionel ('Hamp') (1909–2002) US vibraphonist, born Louisville, Kentucky. Made vibraphone a solo instrument, first recording with Louis Armstrong; played in Benny Goodman's band before forming own big band in 1940; 'Flyin' Home' (famous solo by Illinois Jacquet).

Hancock, Herbie (Herbert Jeffrey Hancock) (1940–) US pianist and composer, born Chicago. Child classical musician, but dedicated to jazz; played in Miles Davis's quintet for five years, seeing developments towards jazz rock; with own band turned to electric and electronic means. Music blends rhythm 'n' blues and soul blues, or blues and swing; 'Watermelon Man', 'Rock It'; soundtrack of Bertrand Tavernier's film *Round Midnight* (1986) won an Oscar; *River: The Joni Letters* (2007) is a tribute to Joni Mitchell.

Handy, W(illiam) C(hristopher) (1873–1958) US musician and composer, born Florence, Alabama. In 1903 he formed his own band in Memphis, Tennessee, and drew on various genres of African-American music, including spirituals, folk ballads, work songs and early jazz, to develop the form of music known as the blues. His earliest known composition, 'The Memphis Blues', was followed by 'St Louis Blues', 'Beale Street Blues', 'Yellow Dog Blues', 'Careless Love' and many others. Long known as the 'father of the blues', he used that epithet as the title of his autobiography, published in 1958.

Hawkins, Coleman (Randolph) ('Bean', 'Hawk') (1904–69) US tenor saxophonist, born St Joseph, Missouri. Elevated tenor sax to status of solo instrument, hence title 'father of the saxophone'. Abandoned staccato style to develop melodic fluid tone. Compositions include 'Queer Notions'. Hits include masterpiece 'Body and Soul', 'The Man I Love', 'Picasso'.

Henderson, (James) Fletcher ('Smack') (1897–1952) US bandleader, pianist and arranger, born Cuthbert, Georgia. Pioneer of the big-band formation. Perfected technique of writing for separate sections and set standard for the swing era. Joined Benny Goodman's band as pianist and arranger and contributed to its success with 'King Porter Stomp' and 'Blue Skies'.

Henderson, Joe (1937–2001) US saxophonist, bandleader and composer, born Lima, Ohio. Established reputation as a sideman, most notably to Herbie Hancock. Recorded under own name for Blue Note from 1963 onwards. In the 1990s recorded a series of award-winning records for the Verve label.

Herman, Woody (Woodrow Charles Herman) (1913–87) US clarinettist, saxophonist, singer, bandleader and composer, born Milwaukee, Wisconsin. He was a forerunner of 'cool jazz'. His first band, The Band That Plays The Blues, had 1939 hit 'Woodchopper's Ball'. His First Herd band was famous: Igor Stravinsky composed *Ebony Concerto* for him; the second had 'Four Brothers' reed section and recorded 'Early Autumn', which includes Stan Getz's influential solo.

Hines, Earl (Kenneth) ('Fatha') (1903–83) US pianist and bandleader, born Duquesne, Pennsylvania. Often associated with trumpeter Louis Armstrong (they had an influential duet recording 'Weather Bird'), Hines's trumpet-style of piano playing was a significant development among jazz pianists. One of the first jazz pianists to play and record solo; 'Boogie Woogie on St Louis Blues', 'Jelly Jelly', 'Second Balcony Jump', 'The Earl', 'Rosetta'.

Hodges, Johnny ('Jeep', 'Rabbit') (Jonn Cornelius Hodges) (1906–70) US alto and soprano saxophonist, born Cambridge, Massachusetts. Dominant in alto scene before Charlie Parker; constant member of Duke Ellington's band (except 1951–5); technically orthodox but aesthetically inimitable, known for 'I Got It Bad', 'On the Sunny Side of the Street', 'Warm Valley' and 'In a Sentimental Mood' (later recorded by Coltrane in his honour).

Holiday, Billie ('Lady Day') (Eleanora Fagan) (1915–59) US singer, born Baltimore, Maryland. Talented singer with a tragic destiny; noticed as a cabaret singer, she became famous alongside Benny Goodman and Lester Young, toured with Artie Shaw and made a film, *New Orleans*, with Louis Armstrong before drug addiction killed her; 'Strange Fruit', 'Lover Man', 'God Bless the Child'.

Hooker, John Lee (1917–2001) US singer and guitarist, born Clarksdale, Mississippi. Popular blues musician with relaxed vocal style; often sang alone and accompanied himself on guitar; began in gospel choirs and became one of the most influential of trad bluesmen; 'Boogie Chillen', 'Boogie With the Hook', 'It Serves Me Right to Suffer'; made *Hooker and Heat* with band Canned Heat; own albums include *Do the Boogie* and *Sittin' Here Thinkin'*.

Hopkins, Lightnin' (Sam Hopkins) (1912–82) US blues singer and guitarist, born Centerville, Texas. He cut his first record in 1946, and is thought to be the most recorded of all blues artists, although his use of pseudonyms to avoid contractual problems has made an accurate count difficult. He was 'rediscovered' singing in clubs in 1959, and his acoustic country blues style won favour with the folk revival audiences of the early 1960s. He was an inimitable raconteur as well as an idiosyncratic singer and guitarist, and he is one of the most important artists to have worked in the country blues tradition.

Howlin' Wolf (Chester Arthur Burnett) (1910–76) US blues singer, guitarist and harmonica player, born West Point, Mississippi. He began playing blues as a child, and was able to amalgamate several strains of country and urban blues into a distinctive, individual style. He was already a mature artist before recording his first record in Memphis in 1951, and settled in Chicago in 1953, where he was a giant of the emerging electric blues scene. He was one of the most intensely exciting of all blues performers, and recorded a number of classics of the genre, many of which were later covered by rock bands like The Rolling Stones and The Doors in the 1960s. .

Ibrahim, Abdullah (Dollar Brand, originally Adoph Johannes Brand) (1934–) South African pianist, born Cape Town. Formed the Jazz Epistles group, recording the country's first black jazz album. Worked with Duke Ellington in America in the 1960s. Also plays cello, soprano saxophone and flute. Known for jazz interpretations of melodies and rhythms of his African childhood.

Jackson, Milt(on) ('Bags') (1923–99) US vibraphonist, born Detroit, Michigan. Most important vibraphonist of the bebop era. Co-founder with John Lewis of Modern Jazz Quartet, with which his career is linked; 'La Ronde' and 'Vendome' are the MJQ's mascots.

James, Elmore (Elmore Brooks) (1918–63) US blues guitarist and singer, born Richmond, Mississippi. He taught himself to play on a homemade guitar, and was profoundly influenced by meeting Robert Johnson in 1937. He began performing with Sonny Boy Williamson (originally Rice Miller, 1910–65), and went on to establish the most important slide guitar style in modern blues. He made his first recording in 1952, and had an immediate hit with his adaptation of a Robert Johnson song, 'Dust My Broom', which became his best-known record. He moved to Chicago, but always remained in touch with his roots in the Mississippi Delta.

Jarrett, Keith (1945–) US pianist and composer, born Allentown, Pennsylvania. With his idiosyncratic style of playing, going wild on the keys and embellishing his solos with big 'free' lyrical passages, he became very popular; played with Miles Davis, among others; *Facing You, Sun Bear Concerts*.

Jefferson, Blind Lemon (1897–1929) US blues guitarist and singer, born Couchman, Texas. He was born blind. His recorded legacy of almost 100 songs was made between 1926 and his death (including some gospel and spiritual material using the pseudonym Deacon L J Bates). He was the first blues singer to establish a repertoire of his own songs, rather than buying from commercial songwriters, and his performing style, notably his intricate, improvisational guitar playing, was enormously influential in the development of the music.

Johnson, J J (James Louis Johnson) (1924–2001) US trombonist, pianist, baritone saxophonist and composer, born Indianapolis, Indiana. Father of the modern jazz trombone who invented bebop trombone playing, being the first slide trombonist to match the requirements of speed and articulation, as shown when he played with Charlie Parker; compositions include 'Rodeo for Quartet and Orchestra'; *All-Star Jam, The Eminent J J Johnson, The Bosses*.

Johnson, James P(rice) (1894–1955) US pianist and composer, born New Brunswick, New Jersey. Pioneer of stride with 'Carolina Shout'; often accompanied the great female blues singers; swinging style influential on eg Duke Ellington and Thelonious Monk; composer of symphonic works and hits 'Old Fashioned Love', 'Charleston' (with Cecil Mack).

Johnston, Lonnie (Alonzo Johnson) (1889–1970) US guitarist, born New Orleans. Major blues figure in New Orleans, introduced guitar in its modern form as a solo instrument; invented style of playing note by note; 'Stardust', 'Confused', 'Swinging with Lonnie'.

Johnson, Robert (1911–38) US blues singer and guitarist, born Hazelhurst, Mississippi. He is perhaps the most famous name in blues. He was a virtuoso self-taught guitarist, and although he recorded only 29 songs, their impact on the development of blues has been incalculable. Little is known of his life, but the legend that he acquired his skills by selling his soul to the Devil has taken root in blues mythology. His real impact is due not only to his musical skills, but also to the passionate, haunted intensity of his singing and playing. Most of his surviving songs, recorded in only two sessions in 1936 and 1937, have acquired classic status.

Jones, Elvin (Ray) (1927–2004) US drummer, born Pontiac, Michigan. Versatile, inventive, self-taught drummer who eschewed the restrictions of continuous tempo and created complicated polyrhythms, producing the river, a new tornado of sound in jazz. Played in Coltrane's quartet for six years; *Live at the Village Vanguard, Heart to Heart* (with Davis); appeared in film dedicated to him, *Different Drummer*.

Jones, Quincy (Delight) (1933–) US trumpeter, bandleader, composer and arranger, born Illinois. Famous as arranger and producer, but also successful solo musician. Michael Jackson's mentor and producer of the *Thriller* album; 'Killer Joe '70', 'Just Once', 'Summer in the City' (Grammy winner).

Joplin, Scott (1866–1917) US ragtime pianist and composer, born NE Texas. Originator and experimenter of 'ragtime' music. *Maple Leaf Rag* sold more than a million copies, but he died unfulfilled; Gunther Schiller made *Treemonisha* into a Broadway hit in the 1970s; 'The Entertainer' was used in the soundtrack of the film *The Sting* (1973).

Kenton, Stan(ley Newcomb) (1912–79) US pianist, composer and bandleader, born Wichita, Kansas. Exponent of 1950s big band 'progressive' jazz style; later bands had unusual five-trombone sections. Music considered loud and pretentious by some, but innovative by others; won Grammy 1961 for *West Side Story*.

Kidd, Carol (1944–) Scottish singer, born Glasgow. Formed permanent trio at the age of 17. Became known in London clubs in late 1970s and later appeared in radio and television. Won various awards in the 1990s.

King, B B (Riley B King) (1925–) US blues singer and guitarist, born Itta Bena, Mississippi. Famous as singer and influential for economical guitar style. Prolific recording success includes 'Three O'Clock Blues', 'Sweet Black Angel' and 1981 Grammy-winner *There Must be a Better World Somewhere*.

Kirk, (Rhasaan) Roland (1936–77) US multi-instrumentalist, born Columbus, Ohio. Music rooted in gospel and blues; polyinstrumentalist despite blindness; could play three saxophones at once, sang into his flute and played whistle, siren, bagpipes, etc.

Krupa, Gene (1909–73) US drummer and bandleader, born New York City. Exuberant soloist who made the drummer a solo instrumentalist; played with Benny Goodman; formed own band; had hit 'Sing Sing Sing' with Goodman small group, and 'Rockin' Chair' with trumpeter Roy Eldridge; also 'Chickery Chick', 'Bonaparte's Retreat' and compilation *World's Greatest Drummer*; appeared in several films, eg *Some Like It Hot* (1939) and *The Benny Goodman Story* (1956).

Lacy, Steve (Steven Norman Lackritz) (1934–2004) US soprano saxophonist and composer, born New York City. Concentrated on soprano sax and developed own rough-edged tone; in the 1950s was sideman to the best soloists of the Dixieland revival, then was partner to Cecil Taylor (*In Transition*), then to Thelonious Monk; first record in his own name, *Soprano Today*, included some of Monk's music, as did much of his work.

Leadbelly or **Lead Belly** (Huddie William Ledbetter) (1888–1949) US folk and blues singer and guitarist, born Mooringsport, Louisiana. Little is known of his early life, but at 15 he could play several instruments. He was twice sentenced to long prison terms, for murder in 1917 and intent to murder in 1930, but received an early pardon on each occasion. While serving the second sentence, he was heard by folk researcher Alan Lomax, who helped secure his release. He moved to New York, where he became a seminal figure in the burgeoning folk scene, alongside Woody Guthrie and Pete Seeger. His rough-hewn vocals and blues-soaked twelve-string guitar style was hugely influential into the rock era, while songs like 'Good Night Irene' and 'The Midnight Special' became folk-blues standards.

Lewis, John (Aaron) (1920–2001) US pianist and composer, born LaGrange, Illinois. Succeeded Monk as pianist in Dizzy Gillespie's big band; influential in the first bebop era; recorded with Charlie Parker and Miles Davis; formed the Modern Jazz Quartet in 1951; uncluttered, confident yet bluesy style; celebrated Monk with version of 'Round Midnight'; also composed 'Toccata for Trumpet' which shows Bach's influence, 'Move' and 'Rouge' in Davis's *Birth of the Cool*.

Lunceford, Jimmie (James Melvin Lunceford) (1902–47) US alto saxophonist and bandleader, born Fulton, Missouri. His band, the Chickasaw Syncopaters, was a great addition to the history of big bands, playing music by Sy Oliver and having outstanding success with 'Tain't What You Do (It's The Way That You Do It)', 'Rhythm is our Business' and 'Blues in the Night'; 'Honeydripper', 'Got a Right to Cry', 'Rag Mop', 'Pink Champagne'.

Lyttelton, Humphrey ('Humph') (1921–2008) English trumpeter and bandleader, born Eton, Berkshire. Mainstream jazz musician; celebrated 40 continuous years as bandleader in 1988; pioneer in the British revivalist movement; introduced three-saxophone section and original tunes from English and West Indian folk roots; albums include *Bad Penny Blues*, *Trouble in Mind* (with Elkie Brooks).

McLaughlin, John (1942–) English electric guitarist and bandleader, born Doncaster. Impressive speed and rhythm technique; music developed into synthesis of African-American and Indian music. Took part in birth of jazz-rock with Miles Davis; formed Mahavishnu Orchestra; first album *Extrapolation*; plays one track in 1986 film soundtrack *Round Midnight*; *Floating Point* (2008).

Marsalis, Wynton (1961–) US trumpeter and bandleader, born New Orleans. Classical soloist and jazz performer; played Haydn's *Concerto for Trumpet* at age 14; joined Art Blakey's Jazz Messengers at 18; first recording was with the 'giants' Herbie Hancock, Ron Carter and Tony Williams; style combines extension of bebop with sense of swing; won Grammy 1984 as both best classical and jazz soloist. Albums include 1987's *Standard Time*.

Metheny, Pat (1954–) US guitarist and composer, born Lee's Summit, Missouri. Musically open-minded, appeals to bebop, rock and Free Jazz fans; blends acoustics and electronics; composed music for John Schlesinger's *The Falcon and the Snowman* (sung by David Bowie); *Song X* (with Ornette Coleman), *Bright Side of Life*, *American Garage*, *Offramp*, *The Way Up*.

Mezzrow, Mezz (Milton Mesirow) (1899–1972) US reeds player (especially clarinet), born Chicago. Began playing sax in jail; played as a professional musician with eg Eddie Condon, Sidney Bechet; *Paris* and two volumes of *The King Jazz Story* with Bechet.

Miller, (Alton) Glenn (1904–44) US bandleader and trombonist, born Clarinda, Iowa. Very popular as dance band leader, especially during war years. Characteristic style was produced by doubling the lead tenor with a clarinet; 'In the Mood', 'Moonlight Serenade'.

Mingus, Charles (Jr) (1922–79) US double bassist, pianist, composer and bandleader, born Nogales, Arizona. One of the most important composers in 20th-century black music; 'Pussy Cat Dues', 'Boogie Stop Shuffle', 'Jelly Roll', 'Goodbye Pork Pie Hat', *Tijuana Moods*.

Monk, Thelonious (Sphere) (1917–82) US pianist and composer, born Rocky Mount, North Carolina. Famous 'Prophet' or 'High Priest' of bebop, with which he experimented at Minton's Playhouse in Harlem. Leading composer in jazz history; 'Round Midnight' and 'Straight No Chaser' are classics.

Montgomery, Wes (John Leslie Montgomery) (1923–68) US guitarist, born Indianapolis, Indiana. Influential, innovative and versatile self-taught guitarist; worked with Lionel Hampton; mellow sound due to plucking strings with thumb instead of plectrum; *The Incredible Jazz Guitar of Wes Montgomery*.

Morton, Jelly Roll (Ferdinand-Joseph LaMenthe) (1890–1941) US bandleader, composer and pianist, born New Orleans. First great composer in jazz, and a link between ragtime and jazz; formed successful band the Red Hot Peppers, who may have been the first to combine arranged ensemble pieces with improvisation; 'Georgia Stomp', 'Grandpa's Spells', 'Wolverine Blues', 'King Porter Stomp'.

Mulligan, Gerry ('Jeru') (Gerald Joseph Mulligan) (1927–96) US baritone saxophonist, born New York City. Talented arranger and popular musician who made the baritone saxophone a solo instrument; wrote 'Jeru', 'Boplicity', 'Venus de Milo' and 'Godchild' for Davis's *Birth of the Cool*.

Oliver, King (Joseph Nathan Oliver) (1885–1938) US cornettist and bandleader, born New Orleans. By the collective improvisation of Oliver's 'Dippermouth Blues', jazz was freed from the polyphonic concept of the New Orleans style; the Chicago style developed which retained swing but had many elements (marches, melodies, polkas, etc). Oliver is thus one of the 'fathers' of jazz; innovative cornet player, using newly invented mute; 'landmark' hits include 'West End Blues', 'Canal Street Blues' and 'Doctor Jazz'.

Ory, Kid (Edward Ory) (1886–1973) US trombonist, singer, bandleader and composer, born La Prince, Louisiana. A master of New Orleans 'tailgate' trumpet style, playing rhythmic bass as well as solo; led and played in various successful bands, eg Kid Ory's Sunshine Orchestra, the first black jazz band to record, and Louis Armstrong's Hot Five. From 1942 he was active in the New Orleans Revival, though he'd been there from the start. Compositions include 'Muskrat Ramble'; appeared as bandleader in *The Benny Goodman Story* (1956); albums include *Kid Ory's Creole Jazz Band* 1944–5.

Parker, Charlie ('Bird', 'Yardbird') (Charles Christopher Parker) (1920–55) US alto saxophonist, bandleader and composer, born Kansas City, Missouri. Influential modern jazz performer in post-1940s, whose ideas formed the basis of the bebop style; innovative association with trumpeter

Dizzy Gillespie in bebop quintets; compositions include 'Now's the Time' and 'Ornithology'.

Pass, Joe (Giuseppe Passalaqua) (1929–94) US guitarist, born New Brunswick, New Jersey. Most influential swing guitarist since Wes Montgomery, comparable to pianist Oscar Peterson in speed and vigour; world-famous as sideman with eg Peterson, Count Basie, Ella Fitzgerald, Duke Ellington; own albums include *Virtuoso* and *University of Akron Concert*.

Pedersen, Niels-Henning Ørsted (1946–2005) Danish pianist and bassist, born Osted. Established reputation as one of the top jazz bassists in the world. Flexible in style, he could play mainsteam to avant-garde. Much in demand with touring soloists. Has played extensively with pianist Oscar Peterson.

Peterson, Oscar (Emmanuel) (1925–2007) Canadian pianist and composer, born Montreal. Reliable accompanist and flamboyant soloist; permanent member of Jazz at the Philharmonic; also performed with double-bass player Niels-Henning Ørsted Pedersen and guitarist Joe Pass; solo albums include *My Favourite Instrument*, *At Salle Pleyel*, *Affinity* and *Jazz Portrait of Frank Sinatra*.

Pine, Courtney (1964–) English tenor and soprano saxophonist and bass clarinettist, bandleader and composer, born London. Originally Coltrane-inspired, this talented saxophonist of Jamaican origin has formed two bands, The Jazz Warriors and The World's First Saxophone Posse; 1986 album *Journey to the Urge Within* includes tune 'Miss Interpret'; also contributed to soundtrack of film *Angel Heart* (1987); *Underground, Resistance*.

Portal, Michel (1935–) French soprano, alto and tenor saxophonist and clarinettist, born Bayonne. Jazz and classical, uses different instruments for each style; a pioneer of Free Jazz in France; founded 'Unit', an open, informed group where American and European guests were welcomed; film music includes *La Cecilia* and *L'Ombre Rouge*.

Powell, Bud (Earl Powell) (1924–66) US pianist and composer, born New York City. A great virtuoso, very important in bebop movement, and in jazz history generally; encouraged by Thelonious Monk in the 1940s, he made many recordings with other virtuosos and solo, including 'Cheryl', 'Dana Lee', 'Chasin' the Bird', 'Un Poco Loco', 'Passion Thoroughfare', 'Bouncing With Bud'; the character Gordon in 1986 film *Round Midnight* is based on Powell.

Rainey, Gertrude Pridgett ('Ma Rainey') (1886–1939) US blues singer, born Columbus, Georgia. She began her career as a singer with the Rabbit Foot Minstrels, and claimed that she first introduced blues into her act in 1902, after hearing a girl in Missouri sing a song about the man who had deserted her. She won a large following among African-American Southerners and toured with Bessie Smith, who was her protégée. From 1923 to 1928 she made a series of recordings on the Paramount label, which won her an audience in the North. Often called the 'Mother of the Blues', she is considered to be the first of the great black blues singers, with a style of singing that preserves the continuity from early African-American music to jazz. Her best-known songs include 'See See Rider' and 'Slow Driving Moan'.

Reinhardt, Django (Jean-Baptiste Reinhardt) (1910–53) Belgian guitarist, born Liverchies, Belgium. Self-taught musician of gypsy background and the first European to have an influence on swing-style

American guitarists, despite losing two fingers in a caravan fire; joined with Stephane Grapelli (1908–97) to form the Quintette du Hot Club de France, which inaugurated a French-style jazz; toured with the Duke Ellington orchestra, changing from acoustic to electric guitar; compositions include 'Love's Melody' and 'Improvisation', also (with Grapelli) 'HQC Strut', 'Daphne', 'Djangology'.

Roach, Max(well) (1924–2007) US drummer, bandleader and composer, born New York City. Key member of bebop movement and a 'giant' of modern jazz; being the first to 'swing' on the drums and use them for 'melody', he created the very influential legato rhythmic feeling; *The Freedom Suite* (waltzes), *We Insist – Freedom Now Suite*, *Money Jungle* (with Duke Ellington), *Drums Unlimited*.

Rollins, Sonny ('Newk') (Theodore Walter Rollins) (1930–) US tenor saxophonist and composer, born New York City. Powerful improviser and important voice in the 'hard bop' movement, joining Clifford Brown and Max Roach; used Caribbean calypso eg in 'Saint Thomas' and 'Don't Stop the Carnival'; 'Tenor Madness', 'Olea', 'Airegin', *Saxophone Colossus*, *Sonny Please*.

Shaw, Artie (Arthur Jacob Arshawsky) (1910–2004) US clarinettist, bandleader and composer, born Norwalk, Connecticut. Like Benny Goodman in tone and innovation, he was also one of the first to present a mixed black and white band, which had a 'cooler' atmosphere due to its reliance on strings; 'Begin the Beguine', 'Summit Ridge Drive', 'Frenesi', 'Dancing in the Dark'.

Shepp, Archie (1937–) US saxophonist, pianist, singer and bandleader, born Fort Lauderdale, Florida. Created formula of three horns, bass and drums which became the Free Jazz standard; developed frantic solo style in orchestral context; jazz for him was 'Great Black Music'; faithful to blues and gospel traditions and embraced West African trends eg in *Mama Too Tight* and *Magic of Ju-Ju*; also *Four for Trane* and *Ascension* with Coltrane.

Shorter, Wayne (1933–) US tenor and soprano saxophonist, bandleader and composer, born Newark, New Jersey. Played in Art Blakey's Jazz Messengers and Miles Davis's quintet (whose development towards jazz rock he helped); formed own group Weather Report, then continued in electric jazz style; the ethereal 'Mysterious Traveller' and dance-like 'Heavy Weather' contributed to *Round Midnight* (1986) film soundtrack; *Alegria* (Grammy 2004).

Silver, Horace (Ward Martin Tavares) (1928–) US bandleader and composer, born Norwalk, Connecticut. Leading figure, with Art Blakey, of the hard bop style, and main exponent of funky jazz; first pianist and musical director of The Jazz Messengers; compositions have flavour of blues and gospel; 'Doodlin', 'The Preacher', 'Señor Blues' and 'Opus de Funk'.

Simone, Nina (Eunice Wayman) (1933–2003) US singer, pianist and composer, born North Carolina. Performance varied from gospel through blues and soul to modern jazz, excelling in all registers; repertoire included Gershwin; best known compositions 'To Be Young, Gifted and Black', 'I Loves You Porgy', 'Mississippi Goddam', 'Central Park Blues', 'My Baby Just Cares For Me'.

Smith, Bessie (1894–1937) US singer, born Chattanooga, Tennessee. Advertised as 'The Empress of the Blues'; hers was a blues-based repertoire including recordings accompanied by leading musicians (eg Louis Armstrong). Realistic songs depict poverty and love pains often flavoured by angry feminism, eg 'Downhearted Blues'; made short film *St Louis Blues* (1929).

Smith, Tommy (1967–) Scottish saxophonist and composer, born Edinburgh. Cosmopolitan musician with broad ideas and lavish tonality; disciple of John Coltrane, with a 'European' feeling for textures and moods in his playing; in his first album *Step By Step* he plays his own compositions, with John Scofield and Jack De Johnette; also *Peeping Tom*, *Alone at Last*.

Solal, Martial (1927–) Algerian pianist, composer and bandleader, born Algiers. Improviser with boundless imagination who defies classification, and who can render standard pieces unrecognizable by his artistry; compositions include *Suite in D Flat* for jazz quartet, and for the film *À Bout De Souffle*; *Longitude* (2008).

Sun Ra (Herman Blount or Sonny Lee) (1914–93) US pianist, composer and bandleader, born Birmingham, Alabama. Pioneer of electronic music, little is known of him before the 1950s; his influential Arkestra functioned as a cooperative, and combined the traditions of the swing era with the freedom of bop; dedicated his music 'to the Creator of the Universe'.

Surman, John (1944–) English multi-instrumentalist, composer and bandleader, born Tavistock, Devon. Emerging from a classical background with folk, ethnic and church music roots, he was sideman of French-born bluesman Alexis Korner before becoming world-famous as soloist; *The Trio*, *The Amazing Adventures of Simon Simon*, *In Darkness Let Me Dwell* (John Dowland songs).

Taylor, Cecil (Percival) (1929–) US pianist, bandleader and composer, born New York City. An exponent of the avant-garde due to his powerful free style of improvisation; very energetic and fast player who treats his piano like a percussion instrument; worked with saxophonist Jimmy Lyons for many years; *Conquistador*, *Unit Structures*, *For Olim*.

Teagarden, Jack ('Mr T') (1905–64) US trombonist and bandleader, born Texas. Great classical jazz figure with warm, natural tone; inventor of jazz trombone; also sang with Louis Armstrong; 'That's an Awful Serious Thing', 'I'm Gonna Stomp Mr Henry Lee' (with Eddie Condon), 'You Rascal You', 'Chances Are', 'Someone Stole Gabriel's Horn', 'A Hundred Years From Today'.

Tatum, Art(hur, Jr) (1909–56) US pianist, born Toledo, Ohio. The most influential of the swing-style pianists, and considered unequalled; despite near-blindness from birth his technique was astonishing and he became famous as the greatest in the history of jazz; 'Body and Soul', 'Tea For Two', 'Tiger Rag'.

Thielemans, 'Toots' (Jean-Baptiste) (1922–) Belgian guitarist and harmonica player, born Brussels. Converted from the accordian to the guitar and harmonica by Django Reinhardt, he also played with Benny Goodman, Lester Young, Count Basie and Stan Getz in America and Europe; Quincy Jones's favourite soloist; played film soundtrack *Midnight Cowboy* (1969); successes include album *Affinity*, and 'Bluesette', a composition which followed an evening improvising with Stephane Grapelli.

Tormé, Mel(vin Howard) (1925–99) US jazz and popular singer, born Chicago. He studied piano and drums as a youngster, then led his own pop

Arts and Culture

group, The Mel-Tones. He worked as an arranger after leaving the army in 1946, and began to build his reputation as a sophisticated singer of both jazz and pop music. His soft, slightly husky voice earned him the unwelcome nickname of 'The Velvet Fog', but his impeccable control of phrasing, pitch and expression were much admired by musicians. He recorded classic albums with arranger Marty Paitch throughout his career, and worked regularly with pianist George Shearing from the early 1980s. He wrote hundreds of songs, as well as novels and books on music, including an autobiography, and a biography of drummer Buddy Rich.

Tracey, Stan (1926–) English pianist, bandleader and composer, born London. Important contributor to European jazz scene; being self-taught meant an unconventional and individual technique; percussive piano style; compositions include jazz suites *Under Milk Wood*, *The Bracknell Connection*, *Genesis*, also for album *We Love You Madly*; *Solo: Trio* (1998).

Tristano, Lennie (Leonard Joseph Tristano) (1919–78) US pianist and composer, born Chicago. Blind by age 11; 'Pianist of the Year' 1948; great jazz teacher and 'father confessor to all the avant-garde musicians in the city (Chicago)'; anticipated the 1960s Free Jazz movement in eg 'Intuition', 'Digression', 'Yesteryear'.

Tyner, McCoy (Alfred) (1938–) US pianist and composer, born Philadelphia, Pennsylvania. Part of epochal Coltrane quartet, where the calmness of his playing was a background to the furious solos; later joined Ike and Tina Turner for *Sahara*; 1973 best record prize for *Enlightenment*; *Double Trios* includes revived standard and classic bebop numbers, eg 'Lover Man'; *Infinity* (1995, with Michael Brecker).

Vaughan, Sarah (Lois) ('Sassy', 'the Divine One') (1924–90) US singer, born Newark, New Jersey. Encouraged by Ella Fitzgerald, she began her career in Earl Hines's and Billy Eckstein's bands; wide vocal range, keen sense of improvisation; attracted by new bebop, she recorded with its inventors, eg Dizzy Gillespie and Charlie Parker; 'Things Must Change', 'Make Yourself Comfortable', 'Whatever Lola Wants', 'Broken-Hearted Melody'.

Walker, T-Bone (Aaron Thibeaux Walker) (1910–75) US guitarist, singer and songwriter, born Linden, Texas. One who achieved perfect cohesion between voice and electric sound; teenage friends with Charlie Christian (both were influential in guitar-playing field); made name as blues player with 'T-Bone Blues' in 1939; 'Call It Stormy Monday'; won Grammy in 1968 for *Good Feelin'*.

Waller, Fats (Thomas Wright Waller) (1904–43) US pianist, singer, bandleader and composer, born New York City. Professional musician at 15 and master of the New York 'Stride' piano style; talented musician but popular for singing and humour; prolific composer; 'Honeysuckle Rose', 'Ain't Misbehavin'', 'Black and Blue', 'I'm Crazy Bout My Baby', 'Two Sleepy People'; appeared in films, eg *Stormy Weather* (1943).

Washington, Dinah (Ruth Lee Jones) (1924–63) US singer, born Tuscaloosa, Alabama. Originally 'discovered' by Lionel Hampton, she became the 'Queen of the Blues' whose vibrato voice expressed the aspirations and disappointments of the Black community; 'Baby, Get Lost', 'This Bitter Earth', 'What a Difference a Day Makes', 'Baby (You've Got What It Takes)', 'It Could Happen To You'.

Waters, Ethel (1900–77) US singer, born Chester, Pennsylvania. Began in blues style and became a highly regarded 1930s pop singer; also worked in cabaret and film; 'Stormy Weather', 'A Hundred Years From Today' (with Benny Goodman and Jack Teagarden), 'Come Up and See Me Sometime' (from Mae West film).

Waters, Muddy (McKinley Morganfield) (1913–83) US singer, guitarist, bandleader and composer, born Rolling Fork, Mississippi. Popular blues player from 1943; sang with passionate gravelly voice; achieved fame worldwide and his pupils are many of the 'greats' in jazz; 'Rolling Stone', 'I've Got My Mojo Working', 'Hoochie Coochie Man', 'She's 19 Years Old'.

Weber, Eberhard (1940–) German bass player, bandleader and composer, born Stuttgart. Exponent of European (rather than American) music. Plays with five-string 'electro-bass', having made it a front-line instrument for rhythm to melody and improvisation; eschews American blues roots and, like Jan Garbarek, blends romanticism with evocative or moody sounds; successful first album *The Colours of Chloe*; *Endless Days* (2001).

Webster, Ben(jamin Francis) (1909–1973) US saxophonist, born Kansas City, Missouri. Leading instrumentalist of the swing era. Worked with many of leading musicians of the period including Duke Ellington. Went on to become much sought after soloist.

Williams, Tony (1945–97) US drummer and composer, born Chicago. Contributed to evolution of jazz-rock; percussionist in Miles Davis's quartet; made fame as 1970s symbol of modern drumming; drummer for Eric Dolphy's *Out to Lunch* and Davis's *Filles de Kilimanjaro*; latterly played modern jazz and jazz fusion; *Spring, Lifetime, Emergency, Turn It Over, The Joy of Flying*.

Winding, Kai (1922–83) Danish–US trombonist, born Aarhus, Denmark. Played with many of the jazz 'greats', eg co-leading quintet with J J Johnson, restoring trombone to important position; toured with Gillespie, Monk and Hampton; played on Davis's *Birth of the Cool*; had hit with 'More' (*Mondo Cane* (1963) film theme), also *More Brass, Betwixt And Between Jazz Showcase*.

Young, Lester (Willis) ('Prez') (1909–59) US tenor saxophonist, born Woodville, Mississippi. A forerunner of 'cool jazz', which was the opposite of the 1930s saxophone style (eg Coleman Hawkins); pioneer of linear improvisation (J J Johnson); eschewed accepted concepts of melody, rhythm and swing; made reputation with Count Basie's Band; recordings with them include 'Tickle Toe', 'Every Tub', 'One O'Clock Jump'; also 'Lady Be Good', 'Taxi War Dance', 'Rock-A-Bye Basie'.

Pop and rock musicians and singers

Selected singles and albums are listed.

Abba Swedish group, 1970s to early 1980s; members include Bjorn Ulvaeus (1945–) singer, guitarist, born Gothenburg; Agnetha Faltskog (1950–) singer, born Jankoping; Anni-Frid Lyngstad (1945–) singer, born Narvik, Norway; Benny Andersson (1946–) singer, keyboardist, born Stockholm; *Waterloo* (1974), *Arrival* (1976), *Voulez-Vous* (1979), *Super Trouper* (1980), *The Visitors* (1981).

AC/DC Australian heavy metal group, mid-1970s to present; members include Bon Scott (originally Ronald Belford Scott) (1946–80) vocalist, born Kirriemuir, Scotland; Brian Johnson (1947–) vocalist, born North Shields, England; Angus Young (1958–) guitarist, born Glasgow, Scotland; Malcolm Young (1953–) guitarist, born Glasgow, Scotland; Phil Rudd (1954–) drummer, born Melbourne, Australia; *High Voltage* (1976), *If you want blood, you've got it* (1978), *Highway to Hell* (1979), *Dirty Deeds Done Dirt Cheap* (1981), *For Those About to Rock* (1981), *Blow Up Your Video* (1988), *Stiff Upper Lip* (2000), *Black Ice* (2008).

Adams, Bryan (1959–) Canadian singer, guitarist, songwriter, born Vancouver, British Columbia; 'Everything I Do', *Cuts Like a Knife* (1983), *You Want It, You Got It* (1984), *Reckless* (1985), *Into the Fire* (1987), *Waking Up The Neighbours* (1991), *So Far So Good* (1993), *18 'Til I Die* (1997), *Spirit: Stallion of the Cimarron* (2002), *Room Service* (2004), *11* (2008).

Aerosmith US group, 1970s to present; members include Steve Tyler (1948–) vocalist, born New York City; Joe Perry (1950–) guitarist, born Boston, Massachusetts; Tom Hamilton (1951–) bassist, born Colorado Springs; Joey Kramer (1950–) drummer, born New York City; 'Come Together', 'Dream On', 'Angel', 'Dude Looks Like a Lady', 'Love in an Elevator', 'Jamie's Got a Gun', *Aerosmith* (1973), *Toys in the Attic* (1975), *Permanent Vacation* (1987), *Pump* (1989), *Get a Grip* (1993), *Big Ones* (1994), *Just Push Play* (2001), *Honkin' on Bobo* (2004).

The Animals British group, 1960s; split up in 1960s, reformed 1983; members include Eric Burdon (1941–) vocalist, born Newcastle upon Tyne; Alan Price (1942–) keyboardist, born County Durham, John Steel (1941–) drummer, born Newcastle-upon-Tyne; 'House of the Rising Sun', 'We've Gotta Get Out of this Place', *Animals* (1964), *Ark* (1983).

Arctic Monkeys British group, formed Sheffield, 2003 to present; members include Alex Turner (1986–) guitarist, vocalist; Jamie Cook (1985–) guitarist; Nick O'Malley (1985–) guitarist; Matt Helders (1986–) drummer; Andy Nicholson, guitarist; 'I Bet You Look Good on the Dancefloor', 'When the Sun Goes Down', 'Leave Before the Lights Come On', 'Brianstorm', *Whatever People Say I Am, That's What I'm Not* (2006), *Favourite Worst Nightmare* (2007).

Armatrading, Joan (1950–) British singer, guitarist, born St Kitts Island, Caribbean; *Joan Armatrading* (1976), *To the Limit* (1978), *Walk Under Ladders* (1981), *The Key* (1983), *Sleight of Hand* (1986), *The Shouting Stage* (1988), *Hearts and Flowers* (1990), *Square the Circle* (1992), *What's Inside* (1995), *Lovers Speak* (2003), *Into the Blues* (2007).

Baez, Joan (1941–) US singer, guitarist, born Staten Island, New York; 'The Night They Drove Ol' Dixie Down' (1972), *Any Day Now* (1968), *Farewell, Anjelica* (1975), *Diamonds and Rust* (1975), *Gone from Danger* (1997), *Dark Chords on a Big Guitar* (2003), *Bowery Songs* (2005); *Day After Tomorrow* (2008).

Bassey, Dame Shirley (1937–) British singer, born Tiger Bay, Cardiff, Wales; 'Goldfinger', 'Big Spender', 'Diamonds are Forever', *The Birthday Concert* (1998), *Forever Gold* (2006).

The Beach Boys US group, 1960s to 1990s; members include Brian (1942–) bassist, vocalist; Dennis (1944–83) drummer, vocalist; and Carl (1946–98) Wilson guitarist, vocalist; all born Hawthorne, California; Mike Love (1941–) vocalist; 'Surfin' USA', 'Help Me Rhonda', 'Barbara Ann', 'Good Vibrations', 'Fun, Fun, Fun', 'I Get Around', 'California Girls', 'Little Deuce Coupe', 'God Only Knows', 'Wouldn't It Be Nice', *Pet Sounds* (1966).

The Beatles British group, 1960s; John (Winston) Lennon (1940–80) singer/songwriter, guitarist; (James) Paul McCartney (1942–) singer/ songwriter, guitarist; George Harrison (1943–2001) singer/songwriter, guitarist; Ringo Starr (originally Richard Starkey) (1940–) singer/songwriter, drummer; all born Liverpool; 'Love Me Do', 'She Loves You', 'From Me to You', 'I Want to Hold Your Hand', 'Yesterday', 'Day Tripper', 'Paperback Writer', 'I am the Walrus', 'Penny Lane', 'Strawberry Fields Forever', 'Hey Jude', *Please Please Me* (1963), *With the Beatles* (1963), *A Hard Day's Night* (1964), *Beatles for Sale* (1964), *Help!* (1965), *Rubber Soul* (1965), *Revolver* (1966), *Sergeant Pepper's Lonely Hearts Club Band* (1967), *Magical Mystery Tour* (1967), *Yellow Submarine* (1968), *The White Album* (1968), *Abbey Road* (1969), *Let it Be* (1970), *Love* (2006).

The Bee Gees Anglo-Australian group, 1960s to present; members include Barry (1946–), Robin (1949–), and Maurice (1949–2003) Gibb; all born Isle of Man; 'Massachusetts', 'Jive Talkin'', 'How Deep is Your Love?', 'Staying Alive', 'Night Fever', *Children of the World* (1976), *ESP* (1987), *Size Isn't Everything* (1993), *Still Waters* (1997), *This is Where I Came In* (2001), *Number Ones* (2004).

Berry, Chuck (Charles Edward Anderson Berry) (1926–) US singer/songwriter, guitarist; born St Louis, California; 'Maybellene', 'Sweet Little Sixteen', 'Too Much Monkey Business', 'Rock and Roll Music', 'School Days', 'No Particular Place to Go', 'Johnny B Goode', 'Nadine', 'My Ding-a-Ling'.

Björk (1965–) Icelandic singer/songwriter, born Reykjavik; 'Venus as a Boy', 'It's Oh so Quiet', 'Big Time Sensuality', *Debut* (1993), *Post* (1995), *Homogenic* (1997), *Vespertine* (2001), *Medúlla* (2004), *Drawing Restraint 9* (2005), *Volta* (2007).

Black Sabbath British heavy rock group, 1969 to present; members include Ozzy Osbourne (1948–) vocalist; Tony Iommi (1948–) guitarist; both born Birmingham; *Paranoid* (1971), *Sabbath Bloody Sabbath* (1973), *Dehumanizer* (1992), *Cross Purposes* (1994), *Forbidden* (1995), *Past Lives* (2002).

Blondie US group, 1970s to present; members include Deborah Harry (1945–) vocalist, born Miami, Florida (solo 'Feel the Spin', 'French Kissin' in the USA', 'Free to Fall', 'I Want That Man'); Chris Stein (1950–) guitarist, born Brooklyn, New York City; 'Denis', 'Heart of Glass', 'Union City Blue', 'Call Me', 'The Tide is High', *Blondie* (1976), *Plastic Letters* (1977), *Parallel Lines* (1978), *Auto American* (1980), *The Hunter* (1982), *No Exit* (1999), *Curse of Blondie* (2004).

Blur British group, formed Colchester, late 1980s to present; members include Damon Albarn (1968–) singer, born London; Graham Coxon (1969–) guitarist, born Bournemouth; Alex

Arts and Culture

James (1968–) bassist, born Hanover, Germany; vocalist; Dave Rowntree (1964–) drummer, born Colchester, Essex; 'Parklife', 'For Tomorrow', 'Beetlebum', *Leisure* (1991), *Modern Life is Rubbish* (1993), *Parklife* (1994), *The Great Escape* (1995), *Blur* (1997), *13* (1999), *Think Tank* (2003).

Bolan, Marc (and T Rex) (Mark Feld) (1947–77) British singer/songwriter, guitarist, born London; 'Get It On', 'Metal Guru', 'Children of the Revolution', 'Jeepster', *Unicorn* (1970).

Booker T and the MGs US group, 1960s; Booker T Jones (1944–) vocalist, organist, born Memphis, Tennessee; Donald 'Duck' Dunn (1941–) bassist, born Memphis; Steve Cropper (1941–) guitarist, born Willow Springs, Missouri; 'To be a Lover', *Green Onions* (1962).

Bowie, David (David Robert Jones) (1947–) British singer/songwriter, guitarist, born Brixton, London; 'The Laughing Gnome', 'Space Oddity', 'Life on Mars', 'Jean Genie', 'Andy Warhol', 'Rebel Rebel', 'Ashes to Ashes', 'Blue Jean', 'China Girl', 'Let's Dance', 'Modern Love', *The Man who Sold the World* (1970), *Hunky Dory* (1971), *The Rise and Fall of Ziggy Stardust and the Spiders from Mars* (1972), *Diamond Dogs* (1974), *Heroes* (1977), *Let's Dance* (1983), *Tonight* (1984), *Never Let Me Down* (1987), *Black Tie White Noise* (1993), *Earthling* (1997), *Heathen* (2002), *Reality* (2003).

Brown, James (1928–2006) US singer/songwriter, drummer, pianist, born Barnwell, South Carolina; 'Papa's Got a Brand New Bag', 'It's a Man's Man's Man's World', 'Ain't It Funky Now', 'Sex Machine', 'Get Up Offa That Thing'.

Bush, Kate (1958–) British singer/songwriter, keyboardist, born Plumstead; 'Wuthering Heights', 'The Man with the Child in His Eyes', 'Wow', 'Running Up That Hill', *Never Forever* (1980), *The Dreaming* (1982), *Hounds of Love* (1986), *The Sensual World* (1989), *The Red Shoes* (1993), *Aerial* (2005).

The Byrds US group, 1960s to 1970s; Roger McGuinn (1942–) guitarist, born Chicago; Chris Hillman (1944–) bassist, mandolin player, vocalist, born Los Angeles; David Crosby (1941–) vocalist, guitarist; Michael Clarke (1943–93) drummer, born New York City; 'Mr Tambourine Man', 'Eight Miles High', *Mr Tambourine Man* (1965), *Turn, Turn, Turn* (1966), *Fifth Dimension* (1966).

The Carpenters US group, 1970s to 1980s; members include Karen Carpenter (1950–83) vocalist, drummer; Richard Carpenter (1946–) vocalist, keyboardist; both born New Haven, Connecticut; *Close to You* (1970), *Yesterday Once More* (1974), *Voice of the Heart* (1983), *Only Yesterday* (1990), *Interpretations* (tribute album) (1994).

Cash, Johnny (1932–2003) US singer/songwriter, guitarist, born Kingsland, Arkansas; 'Don't Take Your Guns to Town', 'Ring of Fire', 'A Boy Named Sue', 'The Man in Black', 'A Thing Called Love', 'Hurt', *Johnny Cash at San Quentin* (1969), *The Man In Black – The Definitive Collection* (1994), *American Recordings IV: The Man Comes Around* (2002).

Charles, Ray (Ray Charles Robinson) (1930–2004) US singer/songwriter, pianist, born Albany, Georgia; 'I Got a Woman', 'Lonely Avenue', 'You Are My Sunshine', 'Crying Time', 'Hit the Road, Jack', *The Genius of Ray Charles* (1959), *Heart to Heart – 20 Hot Hits* (1980), *The Collection* (1990), *Genius Loves Company* (2004).

Cher (Cherilyn Sarkisian La Piere) (1946–) US singer/songwriter, born El Centro, California; (with Sonny Bono) 'I Got You Babe', 'Just You', 'All I Ever Need Is You'; 'Gypsys, Tramps and Thieves', 'Half Breed', 'The Shoop Shoop Song', 'Believe', *Love*

Hurts (1991), *It's a Man's World* (1995), *Believe* (1998), *Living Proof* (2002), *All I Really Want to Do* (2005).

Clapton, Eric (1945–) British singer/songwriter, guitarist, born Ripley, Surrey (was in 1960s groups The Yardbirds and Cream); 'Layla', 'Lay Down Sally', 'Wonderful Tonight', 'I Shot the Sheriff', 'Tulsa Time', 'Cocaine', 'I've Got a Rock 'n' Roll Heart', *Derek and the Dominos* (with Duane Allman) (1970); *461 Ocean Boulevard* (1974), *Slowhand* (1977), *Just One Night* (1980), *Money and Cigarettes* (1983), *August* (1986), *Journey Man* (1989), *24 Nights* (1991), *Unplugged* (1992), *From The Cradle* (1994), *Reptile* (2001), *Back Home* (2005).

The Clash British group, late 1970s to 1980s; members include Joe Strummer (originally John Mellors) (1952–2002) guitarist, vocalist, born Ankara, Turkey; Mick Jones (1955–) guitarist, vocalist, born London; Paul Simonon (1956–) bassist, born London; Topper' Headon (1956–) drummer, born Dover; 'I Fought the Law', 'Rock the Casbah', 'Should I Stay or Should I Go', *The Clash* (1977), *Cost of Living* (1979), *London Calling* (1979), *Combat Rock* (1982), *Cut the Crap* (1985).

Cochran, Eddie (1938–60) US singer, guitarist, born Oklahoma City; 'Three Steps to Heaven', 'Summertime Blues', 'C'mon Everybody', 'Something Else'.

Cocker, Joe (1944–) British singer/songwriter, born Sheffield; 'With a Little Help from My Friends', 'You Are So Beautiful', 'Up Where We Belong' (with Jennifer Warnes), *Mad Dogs and Englishmen* (1970), *I Can Stand a Little Rain* (1974), *Unchain My Heart* (1987), *Night Calls* (1992), *Have a Little Faith* (1997), *Heart and Soul* (2004), *Hymn for My Soul* (2007).

Cohen, Leonard (1934–) Canadian singer/songwriter, guitarist, born Montreal, Quebec; 'Suzanne', 'Famous Blue Raincoat', *Songs of Leonard Cohen* (1968), *Songs of Love and Hate* (1970), *Various Positions* (1984), *I'm Your Man* (1988), *The Future* (1992), *Ten New Songs* (2001), *Dear Heather* (2004).

Coldplay British group, late 1990s to present; Chris Martin (1977–) vocalist and keyboardist, born Devon; Will Champion (1977–) drummer, born Southampton; Guy Berryman (1978–) bass guitarist, born Fife, Scotland; Jonny Buckland (1977–) lead guitarist, born London; 'Trouble', 'Yellow', *Parachutes* (2000), *A Rush of Blood to the Head* (2002), *X and Y* (2005), *Viva la Vida* (2008).

Cooke, Sam (Sam Cook) (1935–64) US singer/songwriter, born Chicago, Illinois; 'You Send Me', 'A Change Is Gonna Come', 'Wonderful World', *Sam Cooke at the Copa* (1964).

Cooper, Alice (Vincent Furnier) (1948–) US singer/songwriter, born Detroit, Michigan; 'School's Out', 'Poison', 'Hey Stoopid', *Love it to Death* (1971), *School's Out* (1972), *Trash* (1989), *Hey Stoopid* (1991), *The Last Temptation* (1994), *Dragontown* (2001), *Dirty Diamonds* (2005), *Along Came a Spider* (2008).

Costello, Elvis (Declan Patrick McManus) (1955–) British singer/songwriter, guitarist, born Paddington, London; 'Watching the Detectives', '(I Don't Want To Go To) Chelsea', 'Accidents Will Happen', 'Alison', 'Shipbuilding', 'Don't Let Me Be Misunderstood', *My Aim is True* (1977), *This Year's Model* (with The Attractions) (1978), *Armed Forces* (1979), *Almost Blue* (1981), *Imperial Bedroom* (1982), *Goodbye Cruel World* (1984), *King of America* (1986), *Spike* (1989), *When I Was Cruel* (2002), *The Delivery Man* (2004), *The River in Reverse* (2006), *Momofuku* (2008).

Cream British group, late 1960s; members include Eric Clapton (1945–) singer, guitarist; Jack Bruce (1943–) singer, bassist; Ginger Baker (1939–) drummer; 'I Feel Free', 'Sunshine of Your Love', 'Strange Brew', 'Badge', 'Crossroads', *Fresh Cream* (1966), *Disraeli Gears* (1967), *Wheels of Fire* (1968), *Goodbye* (1969).

Creedence Clearwater Revival US group, late 1960s to early 1970s; members include John Cameron Fogerty (1945–) (solo 'Rockin' All Over the World', *Centerfield* (1985)), Tom Fogerty (1941–90), both guitarists and vocalists, born Berkeley, California; Doug Clifford (1945–) drummer, born Palo Alto; Stu Cook (1945–) bassist, born Oakland; 'Susie Q', 'Proud Mary', 'Bad Moon Risin'', 'Green River', 'Born on the Bayou', 'Down on the Corner', 'I Heard it through the Grapevine', 'Fortunate Son', 'Travellin' Band', 'Up, around the Bend', *Creedence Clearwater Revival* (1968), *Pendulum* (1970), *Mardi Gras* (1972).

Crosby, Stills, Nash and Young US group, late 1960s to present; David Crosby (originally David van Cortland) (1941–) guitarist, vocalist, born Los Angeles; Graham Nash (1942–) vocalist, born Blackpool, England; Stephen Stills (1945–) guitarist, vocalist, pianist, born Dallas; Neil Young (1945–) guitarist, vocalist, pianist, born Toronto; 'Ohio', *Déjà vu* (1970), *Four Way Street* (1971), *Allies* (1983), *Looking Forward* (1999).

Crow, Sheryl (1962–) US singer/songwriter, born Kennett, Missouri; 'Every Day is a Winding Road', 'All I Wanna Do', *Tuesday Night Music Club* (1993), *Sheryl Crow* (1996), *C'mon C'mon* (2002), *Wildflower* (2005), *Detours* (2008).

Culture Club British group, 1980s; split up 1987, reformed in 1998; members include Boy George (originally George O'Dowd) (1961–) vocalist, born Eltham; Jon Moss (1957–) drummer, born London; 'Karma Chameleon', *Colour By Numbers* (1983), *Don't Mind if I Do* (1999).

The Cure British group, mid-1970s to present; members include Robert Smith (1959–) guitarist, singer/songwriter, born Crawley, Sussex; Laurence Tolhurst (1959–) drummer, keyboardist; 'Killing an Arab', 'Boys Don't Cry', 'Love Cats', 'The Caterpillar', 'Close to Me', 'Standing on the Beach', 'In Between Days', *Boy's Don't Cry* (1980), *Faith* (1981), *Pornography* (1982), *The Head on the Door* (1985), *Disintegration* (1989), *Mixed Up* (1990), *Wish* (1992), *Bloodflowers* (2000), *The Cure* (2004), *4:13 Dream* (2008).

Davis, Sammy, Jr (1925–90) American singer, born New York City; 'Something's Gotta Give', 'That Old Black Magic', 'Candy Man', *Starring Sammy Davis Jr* (1955), *Just for Lovers* (1955), *The Wham of Sam* (1960).

The Dead Kennedys American group, late 1970s to 1980s; members include Jello Biafra (originally Eric Boucher) (1958–) vocalist; East Bay Ray (aka Ray Valium) guitarist; Klaus Flouride bassist; Ted drummer; 'California Über Alles', 'Kill the Poor', 'Too Drunk to Fuck', 'Holiday in Cambodia', *Fresh Fruit for Rotten Vegetables* (1980), *Plastic Surgery Disaster* (1982), *Frankenchrist* (1985), *Live at the Deaf Club* (2004).

Deep Purple British heavy rock group, late 1960s to present; members include Ian Gillan (1945–) vocalist, born Hounslow; David Coverdale (1951–) vocalist, born Saltburn; Ritchie Blackmore (1945–) guitarist, born Weston-super-Mare; Jon Lord (1941–) keyboardist, born Leicester; Roger Glover (1945–) bassist; Ian Paice (1948–) drummer; 'Black Night', 'Smoke on the Water', *Shades of Deep Purple* (1968), *Deep Purple* (1969), *Deep Purple In Rock* (1970), *Made in Japan* (1972), *Perfect Strangers* (1984), *The Battle Rages On* (1993), *Abandon* (1998), *Rapture of the Deep* (2005).

Denver, John (John Henry Deutschendorf) (1943–97) US singer/songwriter, born New Mexico; 'Take Me Home Country Roads', 'Annie's Song', 'I'm Sorry', *Back Home Again* (1974), *An Evening With John Denver* (1975), *Perhaps Love* (1981), *One World* (1986).

Depeche Mode British group, 1980s to present; Andy Fletcher (1961–); Martin Gore (1961–); Vince Clarke (1960–); Dave Gahan (1962–); Alan Wilder (1959–) keyboardist; *Speak and Spell* (1981), *Black Celebration* (1986), *Music for the Masses* (1987), *Violator* (1990), *Songs of Faith and Devotion* (1993), *Exciter* (2001), *Useless* (2006).

Destiny's Child US group 1990s to present: Beyoncé Knowles (1981–) singer (solo 'Crazy in Love', *Dangerously in Love* (2003)), born Houston, Texas; Kelly Rowland (1981–) singer (solo *Simply Deep* (2002)), born Atlanta, Georgia; Michelle Williams (1980–) singer (solo *Heart to Yours* (2002)), born Rockford, Illinois; 'Survivor', 'Say my Name', *The Writing's on the Wall* (1999), *Destiny Fulfilled* (2004).

Diamond, Neil (Leslie) (1941–) US singer/songwriter, guitarist, born Coney Island, New York; 'Song Sung Blue', 'You Don't Bring Me Flowers' (with Barbra Streisand), 'Love on the Rocks', *Beautiful Noise* (1976), *The Jazz Singer* (1980), *Heartlight* (1982), *Headed for the Future* (1986), *Lovescape* (1991), *Up On The Roof – Songs From The Brill Building* (1993), *Three Chord Opera* (2001), *12 Songs* (2005), *Home Before Dark* (2008).

Diddley, Bo (Ellas McDaniel) (1928–) US singer, guitarist, born McComb, Mississippi; 'Bo Diddley'/'I'm a Man', 'Road Runner', 'Do Wah Diddy Diddy', *Got My Own Bag of Tricks* (1971).

Dire Straits British group, late 1970s to 1990s; members include Mark Knopfler (1949–) singer/songwriter, guitarist, born Glasgow (solo soundtrack *Local Hero* (1983)); David Knopfler (1951–) guitarist, replaced by Hal Lindes (1953–); John Illsley (1949–) bassist, born London; Pick Withers (1948–) drummer; Alan Clark (1952–) keyboardist; 'Romeo and Juliet', 'Tunnel of Love', 'So Far Away', 'Money for Nothing', 'Walk of Life', *Dire Straits* (1978), *Communiqué* (1979), *Making Movies* (1981), *Brothers in Arms* (1985), *Money for Nothing* (1988), *On Every Street* (1991), *On The Night* (1993).

The Doors US group, late 1960s to early 1970s; members include Jim Morrison (1943–71), singer/songwriter, born Melbourne, Florida; Ray Manzarek (1939–) keyboardist, born Chicago; Robby Krieger (1946–) guitarist, born Los Angeles; John Densmore (1945–) drummer, born Los Angeles; 'Light My Fire', 'The End', 'When the Music's Over', 'LA Woman', 'Hello, I Love You', 'Touch Me', 'Riders on the Storm', *The Doors* (1967), *Strange Days* (1967), *Waiting for the Sun* (1968), *An American Prayer* (1978), *In Concert* (1991).

Duran Duran British group, 1980s to present; members include Simon Le Bon (1958–) vocalist, born Watford, Hertfordshire; Nick Rhodes (originally Nicholas Bates) (1962–) keyboardist, born Birmingham; John Taylor (1960–) bassist, born Birmingham; Roger Taylor (1960–) drummer; Andy Taylor (1961–) guitarist; 'Planet Earth', 'Hungry Like the Wolf', 'Save a Prayer', 'Rio', 'Wild Boys', *Duran Duran* (1981), *Rio* (1982), *Arena* (1984), *Notorious* (1986), *Decade* (1989), *Liberty* (1990), *Thankyou* (1995), *Pop Trash* (2000), *Astronaut* (2004), *Red Carpet Massacre* (2007).

Arts and Culture

Arts and Culture

Dylan, Bob (Robert Allen Zimmerman) (1941–) US singer/songwriter, guitarist, born Duluth, Minnesota; 'Blowin' in the Wind', 'Mr Tambourine Man', 'Desolation Row', 'Like a Rolling Stone', 'Maggie's Farm', 'All Along the Watchtower', 'Lay Lady Lay', *The Freewheelin' Bob Dylan* (1963), *The Times They Are A-Changin'* (1963), *Another Side of Bob Dylan* (1964), *Bringing It All Back Home* (1965), *Blonde on Blonde* (1966), *John Wesley Harding* (1968), *Nashville Skyline* (1969), *Blood on the Tracks* (1974), *The Basement Tapes* (1975), *Slow Train Coming* (1979), *Infidels* (1983), *World Gone Wrong* (1993), *Time Out of Mind* (1997), *Love and Theft* (2001), *Live 1964* (2004), *Modern Times* (2006).

Dynamite, Ms (Niomi MacLean-Daley (1981–) British singer/songwriter, born London; *A Little Deeper* (2002), *Judgement Days* (2005), *A Little Darker* (2006).

The Eagles US group, 1970s; members include Glenn Frey (1948–) singer, guitarist, born Detroit, Michigan; Don Henley (1947–) singer, drummer, born Texas (solo 'Dirty Laundry', 'Boys of Summer', *Building the Perfect Beast* (1984)); Bernie Leadon (1947–) guitarist replaced by Joe Walsh (1947–) guitarist, singer/songwriter, born Wichita, Kansas (solo 'Life's Been Good', *But Seriously Folks* (1976), *Got Any Gum?* (1987)); Randy Meisner (1946–) bassist, born Nebraska; 'Best of My Love', 'Lyin' Eyes', 'New Kid in Town', 'Heartache Tonight', *Eagles* (1972), *Desperado* (1973), *One of these Nights* (1975), *Hotel California* (1976), *Eagles Live* (1980), *Hell Freezes Over* (1994), *Long Road out of Eden* (2007).

Earth, Wind and Fire US group, 1970s to present; Maurice White (1941–) vocalist, drummer, born Memphis, Tennessee; Verdine White (1951–) bassist; Philip Bailey (1951–) vocalist, born Denver, Colorado; Larry Dunn (1953–) keyboardist, born Colorado; Johnny Graham (1951–) guitarist, born Kentucky; Al McKay (1948–) guitarist, born Louisiana; Andrew Woolfolk (1950–) reeds, born Texas; Ralph Johnson (1951–) drummer, born California; 'Shining Star', 'Got to Get you into My Life', 'Boogie Wonderland', *Open Our Eyes* (1974), *That's The Way of the World* (1975), *In the Name of Love* (1997), *Illumination* (2005).

Electric Light Orchestra British group, 1970s to 1980s; members include Jeff Lynne (1947–) guitarist, vocalist; Roy Wood (1946–) guitarist, vocalist; Bev Bevan (1944–) drummer; all born Birmingham; 'Roll Over Beethoven', 'Evil Woman', 'Hold On Tight', 'Mr Blue Sky', 'Last Train to London', *Out of the Blue* (19867), *Zoom* (2001).

Elliott, Missy (1971–) US singer/songwriter, born Portsmouth, Virginia; 'The Rain', 'Work It', *Supa Dupa Fly* (1997), *Da Real World* (1999), *Mrs E ... So Addictive* (2001), *This is Not a Test!* (2003), *The Cookbook* (2005).

Eminem (1972–) US singer/songwriter, born St Joseph, Missouri; 'Stan', 'My Name is', *The Slim Shady LP* (1999), *The Marshall Mathers LP* (2000), *Encore* (2004).

Eno, Brian (1948–) British singer/songwriter, keyboardist, born Woodbridge, Suffolk (was in early 1970s Roxy Music line-up); *My Life In the Bush Of Ghosts* (with David Byrne) (1981), *More Net* (1992), *Wah Wah* (1994), *Sonora Portraits* (1999), *Another Day on Earth* (2005).

Eurythmics British group, 1980s; members include David Allan Stewart (1952–) songwriter, keyboardist, guitarist, born Sunderland, England; Annie Lennox (1954–) singer/songwriter, born Aberdeen, Scotland; 'Love is a Stranger', 'Who's that Girl?', 'Here Comes the Rain Again', 'Sexcrime', 'Thorn in My Side', 'It's Alright (Baby's Coming Back)', 'Sisters are Doin' it for Themselves' (with Aretha Franklin), 'When Tomorrow Comes', *Sweet Dreams are Made of This* (1982), *Touch* (1983), *1984* (1984), *Be Yourself Tonight* (1985), *Revenge* (1986), *Savage* (1987), *We Too are One* (1989), *Peace* (1999).

The Everly Brothers US group, 1960s; Don (1937–), Phil (1939–), born Brownie, Kentucky; 'Bye Bye Love', 'Little Susie', 'Dream', *EB 84* (1984).

Ferry, Bryan (1945–) British singer, born Washington, County Durham (was founder-member of Roxy Music, 1970); 'Slave to Love', 'Don't Stop the Dance', *Boys and Girls* (1985), *Bête Noire* (1987), *Taxi* (1993), *Mamouna* (1994), *Frantic* (2002), *Dylanesque* (2007).

Flack, Roberta (1939–) US singer/songwriter, pianist; 'Killing Me Softly With His Song', 'Back Together Again', 'Tonight I Celebrate My Love', *And Donny Hathaway* (1972), *Killing Me Softly* (1973), *Born To Love* (1983), *Set the Night to Music* (1991).

Fleetwood Mac Anglo-US group, late 1960s to present; members include Peter Green (originally Peter Greenbaum) (1946–) singer/songwriter, guitarist, born London; Mick Fleetwood (1942–) drummer, born Redruth, Cornwall; John McVie (1945–) bassist; Christine McVie (1943–) singer/songwriter, keyboardist; Lindsey Buckingham (1949–) singer/sonwriter, guitarist, born Palo Alto, California; Stevie (Stephanie) Nicks (1948–) singer/songwriter, born Phoenix, Arizona (solo *Bella Donna* (1982), *The Wild Heart* (1983), *Rock A Little* (1985)); 'Albatross', 'Oh Well', 'Big Love', 'Little Lies', *Fleetwood Mac* (1975), *Rumours* (1977), *Mirage* (1982), *Tango in the Night* (1987), *Behind The Mask* (1990), *Time* (1995), *The Dance* (1997), *Say You Will* (2003).

Frankie Goes to Hollywood British group, early 1980s; Holly Johnson (1960–) and Paul Rutherford (1959–) vocalists; Mark O'Toole (1964–) bassist; Peter Gill (1960–) drummer; Brian Nash (1963–) guitarist; 'Relax!', 'Two Tribes', 'The Power of Love', 'Ferry Across the Mersey', *Welcome to the Pleasure Dome* (1984).

Franklin, Aretha (1942–) US singer, born Memphis, Tennessee; 'Think', 'Respect', *I Never Loved A Man The Way I Love You* (1967), *Lady Soul* (1968), *Amazing Grace* (1972), *Everything I Feel in Me* (1974), *Almighty Fire* (1978), *Aretha* (1980), *Love All The Hurt Away* (1981), *Get It Right* (1983), *Through The Storm* (1989), *Love Songs* (2001), *So Damn Happy* (2003).

Franz Ferdinand Scottish group, formed Glasgow, 2002 to present; members include Alex Kapranos (1972–) guitarist, vocalist, born Almondsbury, Gloucestershire; Bob Hardy (1980–) guitarist, born Bradford; Nick McCarthy (1974–) guitarist, born Blackpool; Paul Thomson (1976–) drummer, born Edinburgh; 'Take Me Out', 'The Dark of the Matinée', 'Do You Want To', *Franz Ferdinand* (2004), *You Could Have It So Much Better* (2005), *Tonight: Franz Ferdinand* (2009).

Gaye, Marvin (Pentz) (1939–84) US singer/songwriter, pianist, drummer, born Washington, DC; 'Hitch Hike', 'Can I Get a Witness', 'I Heard it through the Grapevine', 'What's Goin' On', 'Sexual Healing', *What's Goin' On* (1971), *Let's Get it On* (1973), *Here My Dear* (1979), *Midnight Love* (1982).

Genesis British group, late 1960s to present; members include (at various times) Peter Gabriel (1950–) singer/songwriter, born Cobham, Surrey (solo 'Games without Frontiers', 'Sledgehammer', *So* (1986), *Up* (2002)); Phil Collins (1951–)

singer/songwriter, drummer, born London (solo 'You Can't Hurry Love', 'One More Night', *Face Value* (1981), *No Jacket Required* (1985), *Testify* (2002)); Tony Banks (1950–) keyboardist; Michael Rutherford (1950–) guitarist, bassist, vocalist; *Nursery Cryme* (1971), *Selling England by the Pound* (1973), *The Lamb Lies Down on Broadway* (1974), *Duke* (1980), *Genesis* (1983), *Invisible Touch* (1986), *We Can't Dance* (1991), *Turn it On Again* (1999).

The Grateful Dead US group, late 1960s to present; members include Jerry Garcia (originally Jerome Garcia) (1942–95) guitarist, born San Francisco, California; 'Dark Star', *Live Dead* (1970), *Europe* (1972), *Blues for Allah* (1975), *In the Dark* (1987), *Dylan and the Dead* (with Bob Dylan) (1988).

Guns n' Roses US group, late 1980s to present; Axl Rose (1962–) singer; Slash (1965–) guitarist; Matt Sorum (1960–) drummer; 'Sweet Child O' Mine', 'Welcome to the Jungle', 'Night Train', 'Patience', 'You Could Be Mine', *Appetite for Destruction* (1987), *G N' R Lies* (1988), *The Spaghetti Incident?* (1993), *Chinese Democracy* (2008).

Haley, Bill (1925–81) US singer/songwriter, guitarist, born Highland Park, Michigan; (with The Comets) 'Crazy Man Crazy', 'Shake Rattle and Roll', 'Rock Around the Clock', 'See You Later, Alligator', 'Rudy's Rock'.

Harris, Emmylou (1947–) US singer/songwriter, born Birmingham, Alabama; 'Blue Kentucky Girl', *Pieces of the Sky* (1975), *Wrecking Ball* (1995), *Stumble into Grace* (2003), *All I Intended to Be* (2008).

Harrison, George (1943–2001) British singer/songwriter, guitarist, born Liverpool; 'My Sweet Lord', 'All Those Years Ago', 'Got My Mind Set On You', 'When We Was Fab', *All Things Must Pass* (1970), *Cloud Nine* (1987), *Brainwashed* (posthumously, 2002).

Hendrix, Jimi (James Marshall Hendrix) (1942–70) US singer/songwriter, guitarist, born Seattle, Washington; (with the Experience) 'Voodoo Chile', 'Hey Joe', 'Purple Haze', 'The Wind Cries Mary', 'Crosstown Traffic', 'All Along the Watchtower', *Are You Experienced?* (1967), *Axis: Bold As Love* (1968), *Electric Ladyland* (1968).

The Hollies British group, 1960s to present; members include Allan Clarke (1942–) vocalist, born Salford; Graham Nash (1942–) guitarist, vocalist, born Blackpool replaced by Terry Sylvester (1945–) born Liverpool; Tony Hicks (1945–) guitarist, born Nelson; Eric Haydock (1943–) bassist, born Stockport replaced by Bernie Calvert (1942–) born Burnley; Bobby Elliott (1943–) drummer, born Burnley; 'Searchin'', 'Just One Look', 'He Ain't Heavy, He's My Brother', 'The Air That I Breathe', *Staying Power* (2006).

Holly, Buddy (Charles Hardin Holley) (1936–59) US singer/songwriter, guitarist, violinist, born Lubbock, Texas; (with The Crickets) 'That'll Be the Day', 'Oh Boy!', 'Not Fade Away', 'Peggy Sue', 'Every Day', 'Rave On'.

Houston, Whitney (1963–) US singer, born Newark, New Jersey; 'Saving All My Love For You', 'How Will I Know', 'Greatest Love', 'I Wanna Dance With Somebody (Who Loves Me)', 'Where Do Broken Hearts Go', 'My Name is Not Susan', *Whitney Houston* (1985), *Whitney* (1987), *I'm Your Baby Tonight* (1990), *The Bodyguard* (1992) (soundtrack), *The Preacher's Wife* (1996) (soundtrack), *My Love is Your Love* (1998), *Just Whitney* (2002), *One Wish* (2003).

The Human League British group, late 1970s to present; members include Philip Oakey (1955–) singer; Susanne Sully (1963–) singer; Joanne Catherall (1962–) singer; Ian Burden (1957–)

bassist; Jo Callis (1955–) guitarist; 'Don't You Want Me' (1981), '(Keep Feeling) Fascination', 'Mirror Man', 'Louise', *Dare* (1981), *Crash* (1986), *Romantic?* (1990), *Octopus* (1995), *Secrets* (2001).

INXS Australian group, 1980s to 1990s; Michael Hutchence (1960–97) singer, born Sydney; Andrew Farriss (1959–) keyboardist; Jon Farriss (1961–) drummer; Tim Farriss (1957–) guitarist; Kirk Pengilly (1958–) guitarist, saxophonist; Garry Beers (1957–) drummer; 'Original Sin', 'This Time', 'Never Tear Us Apart', 'Need You Tonight', *Shabooh Shoobah* (1982), *The Swing* (1984), *Listen Like Thieves* (1985), *Kick* (1987), *X* (1990), *Full Moon, Dirty Hearts* (1993).

Iron Maiden British heavy metal group, mid-1970s to present; members include Steve Harris (1957–) bassist, born London; Dave Murray (1955–) guitarist, born London; Adrian Smith (1957–) guitarist, born London; Paul Di'Anno (1959–) singer, born Chingford, Essex replaced by Bruce Dickinson (1958–) born Worksop; Nicko McBain (1954–) drummer, born London; Janick Gers (1957–) guitarist; 'Running Free', 'Run to the Hills', *Iron Maiden* (1980), *The Number of the Beast* (1982), *Somewhere In Time* (1986), *Seventh Son of a Seventh Son* (1988), *Running Free/Sanctuary* (1990), *Fear of the Dark* (1992), *The X Factor* (1995), *Brave New World* (2000), *Dance of Death* (2003), *A Matter of Life and Death* (2006).

The Isley Brothers US group; Kelly (originally O'Kelly) (1937–86), Rudolph (1939–), Ronald (1941–) Isley; all born Cincinnati, Ohio; 'Shout', 'Twist and Shout', 'This Old Heart of Mine (Is Weak For You)', *Harvest for the World* (1976).

Jackson, Michael (Joe) (1958–2009) US singer/songwriter, born Gary, Indiana; (was in The Jacksons, American group, 1960s to 1970s); 'Billy Jean', 'Beat It', 'The Girl is Mine', 'Say Say Say' (with Paul McCartney); 'I Can't Stop Loving You' (with Siedah Garrett), *Ben* (1972), *Off the Wall* (1979), *Thriller* (1982), *Bad* (1987), *Dangerous* (1991), *HIStory – Past Present and Future Book 1* (1995), *Blood on the Dancefloor* (2000), *Invincible* (2001).

The Jam British group, mid-1970s to early 1980s; members include Paul Weller (1958–) singer/songwriter, guitarist, born Woking, Surrey (solo *Stanley Road* (1995), *Heliocentric* (2000), *Studio 150* (2004), *22 Dreams* (2008)); Bruce Foxton (1955–) bassist, born Woking; Rick Buckler (1955–) drummer; 'Going Underground', 'Eton Rifles', 'Town Called Malice', 'Beat Surrender', 'Dream of Children', *In the City* (1977).

Jarre, Jean-Michel (1948–) French keyboardist, composer, born Lyons; *Oxygène* (1977), *Equinoxe* (1978), *Magnetic Fields* (1981), *The Concerts In China* (1982), *Rendez Vous* (1986), *Revolutions* (1988), *Waiting For Cousteau* (1990), *Chronologie* (1993), *Metamorphoses* (2000), *Téo & Téa* (2007).

Joel, Billy (William Martin Joel) (1949–) US singer/songwriter, pianist, born Hicksville, Long Island, New York; 'Say Goodbye to Hollywood', 'Just The Way You Are', 'My Life', 'It's Still Rock 'n' Roll to Me', 'Tell Her About it', 'Uptown Girl', 'We Didn't Start the Fire', *The Stranger* (1977), *52nd Street* (1978), *The Nylon Curtain* (1982), *An Innocent Man* (1983), *The Bridge* (1986), *Storm Front* (1989), *River of Dreams* (1993), *12 Gardens Live* (2006).

John, Sir Elton (Reginald Kenneth Dwight) (1947–) British singer/songwriter, pianist, born Pinner, Middlesex; 'Your Song', 'Crocodile Rock', 'Don't Go Breakin' My Heart' (with Kiki Dee), 'Little Jeannie', 'Candle In The Wind', 'Wrap Her Up', 'Nikita', 'Sacrifice', 'Candle In The Wind' (rewritten version for the late Princess Diana's funeral), *Tumbleweed Connection* (1970), *Don't Shoot Me, I'm Only The Piano Player* (1973), *Good Bye Yellow Brick Road* (1973), *A Single Man* (1979), *Too Low for Zero, Ice on Fire* (1985), *Sleeping With The Past* (1989), *The One* (1992), *Duets* (1993), *Made In England* (1995), *One Night Only* (2000), *Peachtree Road* (2004), *The Captain and the Kid* (2006).

Jones, Norah (1979–) US singer/songwriter, born New York; 'Don't Know Why', 'Come Away With Me', *Come Away With Me* (2002), *Feels Like Home* (2004), *Not Too Late* (2007).

Jones, Tom (Thomas Jones Woodward) (1940–) British singer, drummer, born Pontypridd, S Wales; 'It's Not Unusual', 'What's New, Pussycat?', 'Green Green Grass of Home', 'I'll Never Fall In Love Again', *Delilah*, *After Dark* (1989), *Carrying a Torch* (1991), *The Lead and How To Swing It* (1994), *Reload* (1999), *Mr Jones* (2002), *Tom Jones and Jools Holland* (2004).

Joplin, Janis (1943–70) US singer/songwriter, born Port Arthur, Texas; 'Piece of My Heart', *Cheap Thrills* (1968), *I Got Dem Ol' Kozmic Blues Again, Mama!* (1969), *Pearl* (1971).

Kaiser Chiefs British group, formed Leeds, 2003 to present; members include Ricky Wilson (1978–) vocalist, born Keighley; Andrew White (1974–), guitarist; Simon Rix (1977–) guitarist; Nick Baines, keyboardist; Nick Hodgson (1977–) drummer; 'Oh My God', 'I Predict a Riot', 'Everyday I Love You Less and Less', *Employment* (2005), *Yours Truly, Angry Mob* (2007).

King, B B (Riley B King) (1925–) US guitarist, singer/songwriter, born Itta Bena, near Indianola, Mississippi; *Live at the Regal* (1965), *Confessin' the Blues* (1966), *Blues Is King* (1967), *Indianola Mississippi Seeds* (1970), *Live in Stock County Jail* (1971), *There Must Be A Better World Somewhere* (1981), *Six Silver Strings* (1985), *Reflections* (2003), *One Kind Favor* (2008).

King, Ben E (Benjamin Earl Nelson) (1938–) US singer, born Henderson, North Carolina; 'Stand By Me', 'Spanish Harlem'.

King, Carole (Carole Klein) (1942–) US singer/songwriter; 'It Might As Well Rain Until September', 'It's Too Late', 'You've Got A Friend', 'Will You Love Me Tomorrow', *Tapestry* (1971), *Wrap Around Joy* (1974), *Pearls* (1980), *Love Makes the World* (2001).

The Kinks British group, 1960s to 1980s; Ray Davies (1944–) singer/songwriter, guitarist (solo 'A Quiet Life'); Dave Davies (1947–) singer, guitarist; both born Muswell Hill, London; Mick Avory (1944–) drummer, born Hampton, Middlesex; Peter Quaife (1943–) bassist, born Tavistock, Devon; 'You Really Got Me', 'All Day and All of the Night', 'Dedicated Follower of Fashion', 'Sunny Afternoon', 'Waterloo Sunset', 'Autumn Almanac', 'Lola', 'Come Dancing', 'Don't Forget to Dance', *Village Green Preservation Society* (1968), *Lola vs Powerman & The Moneyground Pt 1* (1970), *State of Confusion* (1983), *To the Bone* (1994).

Kiss US group, 1970s to present; members include Paul Stanley (originally Paul Stanley Eisen) (1952–) guitarist, born New York City; Gene Simmons (originally Gene Klein) (1949–) bassist, born Haifa, Israel; Peter Criss (originally Peter Crisscoula) (1945–) drummer, born New York City; Ace (Paul) Frehley (1951–) guitarist, born New York City; 'Rock and Roll All Nite', 'Beth', 'I was Made for Lovin' You', 'Tears are Fallin'', *Dressed to Kill* (1975), *Double Platinum* (1978), *Lick It Up* (1983), *Crazy Nights* (1987), *Revenge* (1992), *Alive* (1993), *Psycho Circus* (1998).

Knight, Gladys (1944–) US singer, band leader (The Pips, American group, late 1960s), born Atlanta, Georgia; (with The Pips) 'I Heard It Through The Grapevine', 'Help Me Make It Through The Night', 'Midnight Train To Georgia', 'On And On', *Imagination* (1973), *Visions* (1983), *Life* (1985); *Before Me* (2006).

Kraftwerk German group, 1970s to present; Ralf Hütter (1946–) and Florian Schneider (1947–); 'Radio Activity', 'The Model', 'Trans Europe Express', 'Computer Love', 'Tour de France', *Autobahn* (1975), *Man Machine* (1978), *Computer World* (1981), *Trans Europe Express* (1982), *The Mix* (1991), *Tour de France Soundtracks* (2003).

lang, k d (Kathryn Dawn Lang) (1962–) Canadian singer, born Alberta; 'Constant Craving', *Shadowland* (1988), *Absolute Torch and Twang* (1989), *Ingénue* (1992), *All You Can Eat* (1995), *Drag* (1997), *Invincible Summer* (2000), *Hymns of the 49th Parallel* (2005), *Watershed* (2008).

Led Zeppelin British group, late 1960s to 1980s; members include Jimmy Page (1944–) guitarist, born Heston, London; Robert Plant (1948–) vocalist, born Bromwich, Staffordshire; John Paul Jones (originally John Baldwin) (1946–) bassist, born Sidcup; John Bonham (1948–80) drummer, born Redditch; *Led Zeppelin I* (1969), *Led Zeppelin II* (1970), *Led Zeppelin III* (1970), *Led Zeppelin IV* (1971), *Houses of the Holy* (1973), *Physical Graffiti* (1975), *In Through The Out Door* (1979), *Coda* (1982), *Remasters* (1990), *BBC Sessions* (1997).

Lee, Peggy (Norma Delores Egstrom) (1920–2002) US singer, born Jamestown, North Dakota; 'Manana', 'Fever'.

Lennon, John Winston (1940–80) British singer/songwriter, guitarist, keyboardist, born Liverpool; 'Give Peace A Chance', 'Working Class Hero', 'Jealous Guy', 'Merry Xmas (War Is Over)', 'Whatever Gets You Through The Night', *Imagine* (1971), *Rock 'n' Roll* (1975), *Double Fantasy* (1980).

Lewis, Jerry Lee (1935–) US pianist, singer, born Ferriday, Louisiana; 'Great Balls of Fire', 'Whole Lotta Shakin' Goin' On', 'High School Confidential', 'Breathless'.

Little Richard (Richard Wayne Penniman) (1935–) US singer/songwriter, pianist, born Macon, Georgia; 'Tutti Frutti', 'Long Tall Sally', 'Rip It Up', 'The Girl Can't Help It', 'Lucille', 'Jenny, Jenny', 'Good Golly, Miss Molly', 'Lawdy Miss Clawdy', *Life Time Friend* (1986).

Lynyrd Skynyrd US group, 1970s; reformed late 1990s; members include Ronnie Van Zandt (1949–77) vocalist, born McCombe, Minnesota; 'Sweet Home Alabama', 'Freebird', *Pronounced Leh-nerd Skin-nerd* (1973), *Second Helping* (1974), *Street Survivors* (1977), *Gold and Platinum* (1979), *Edge of Forever* (1999), *Vicious Cycle* (2003).

McCartney, Sir Paul (1942–) British singer/songwriter, guitarist, born Liverpool; 'Wonderful Christmastime', 'Coming Up', 'Ebony and Ivory' (with Stevie Wonder), 'No More Lonely Nights', *Tug of War* (1982), *Pipes of Peace* (1983), *Give My Regards To Broad Street* (1984), *Flowers In The Dirt* (1989), *Off The Ground* (1993), *Flaming Pie* (1997), *Driving Rain* (2001), *Ecce Cor Meum* (2006), *Memory Almost Full* (2007).

McLean, Don (1945–) US singer/songwriter, born New Rochelle, New York; 'And I Love You So', 'Vincent', 'Castles in the Air', *American Pie* (1971), *Chain Lightning* (1981), *Dominion* (1983).

Madness British group, late 1970s to 1990s; members include Graham 'Suggs' McPherson (1961–) vocalist, born Hastings, Sussex; Mike

Barson (1958–) keyboardist, Lee Thompson (1957–) saxophonist; Chris Foreman (1958–) guitarist; Mark Bedford (1961–) bassist; Daniel 'Woody' Woodgate (1960–) drummer; Chas Smash (originally Cathal Smith) (1959–) vocalist, trumpeter; 'House Of Fun', 'Our House', 'Baggy Trousers', 'Ghost Train', *One Step Beyond* (1979), *Utter Madness* (1986), *Wonderful* (1999).

Madonna (Madonna Louise Veronica Ciccone) (1958–) US singer/songwriter, born Rochester, Michigan; 'Holiday', 'Crazy For You', 'Like a Virgin', 'Into The Groove', 'Live To Tell', 'Vogue', *Madonna* (1983), *Like a Virgin* (1984), *True Blue* (1986), *Who's that Girl?* (1987), *Like a Prayer* (1989), *The Immaculate Collection* (1990), *Erotica* (1992), *Bedtime Stories* (1994), *Ray of Light* (1998), *Music* (2000), *American Life* (2003), *Confessions on a Dance Floor* (2005), *I'm Going to Tell You a Secret* (2006), *Hard Candy* (2008).

The Mamas and the Papas US group, late 1960s; members include John Philips (1935–2001) singer/songwriter, guitarist, born Parris Island, South Carolina; Dennis Doherty (1941–2007) born Halifax, Nova Scotia; Michelle Phillips (originally Holly Michelle Gilliam) (1944–) born Long Beach, California; 'Mama' Cass Elliot (originally Ellen Naomi Cohen) (1943–74) vocalist, born Baltimore, Maryland; 'California Dreamin', 'Monday, Monday', 'Dedicated to the One I Love', 'San Francisco'.

Manfred Mann British group, 1960s to 1980s; members include Manfred Mann (originally Michael Lubowitz) (1940–) keyboardist, born Johannesburg, South Africa; Paul Jones (originally Paul Pond) (1942–) vocalist, harmonica player, born Portsmouth; '5-4-3-2-1', 'Do Wah Diddy Diddy', 'If You Gotta Go, Go Now', 'Pretty Flamingo', 'Blinded By The Light', *The Roaring Silence* (1986).

Manic Street Preachers British group, 1990s to present; members include James Dean Bradfield (1969–), vocalist and guitarist, born Newport, Gwent; Nicky Wire (originally Jones) (1969–), bassist, born Blackwood, Gwent; Sean Moore (1970–) drummer, born Blackwood, Gwent; Richey Edwards (1966– , missing since 1995, 'presumed dead' 2008) lyricist/guitarist, born Blackwood, Gwent; 'Motorcycle Emptiness', 'A Design for Life', 'If you tolerate this your children will be next', *The Holy Bible* (1994), *Everything Must Go* (1996), *This Is My Truth Tell Me Yours* (1998), *Lifeblood* (2004), *Send Away the Tigers* (2007).

Manilow, Barry (Barry Alan Pincus) (1946–) US singer/songwriter, pianist, born Brooklyn, New York City; 'Mandy', 'I Write the Songs', 'Looks Like We Made It', 'Copacabana (At the Copa)', *Barry Manilow* (1974), *Barry Manilow II* (1975), *A Touch More Magic* (1983), *Showstoppers* (1991), *Summer of '78* (1996), *Ultimate Manilow* (2002).

Marley, Bob (Robert Nesta Marley) (1945–81) Jamaican singer/songwriter, guitarist, born Rhoden Hall, St Ann's Parish, Jamaica; (with The Wailers) 'No Woman, No Cry', 'I Shot the Sheriff', 'Exodus', 'Buffalo Soldier', *Catch a Fire* (1972), *Rastaman Vibration* (1976), *Uprising* (1980).

Mayall, John (1933–) British singer/songwriter, guitarist, harmonica player, born Macclesfield; *Bluesbreakers – John Mayall with Eric Clapton* (1965), *Crusader* (1967), *A Hard Road* (1967), *The Turning Point* (1970), *Wake Up Call* (1993), *Stories* (2002), *Road Dogs* (2005), *In the Palace of the King* (2007).

Michael, George (Yorgos Kyriatou Panayiotou) (1963–) British singer/songwriter (was in Wham!, British 1980s group), born Finchley, London; 'Careless Whisper', 'Fastlove', 'I Want Your

Sex', *Faith* (1987), *Listen Without Prejudice* (1990), *Older* (1996), *Songs from the Last Century* (1999), *Patience* (2004).

Miller, Steve (1943–) US singer/songwriter, guitarist, born Milwaukee, Wisconsin; 'Rock 'n' Me', *The Joker* (1973), *Fly Like An Eagle* (1976), *Abracadabra* (1982), *Living In The 20th Century* (1986), *Wide River* (1993).

Minogue, Kylie (1968–) Australian singer, born Melbourne; 'Spinning Around', 'Can't Get You Out of My Head', 'Slow', 'I Believe in You', *Kylie* (1987), *Enjoy Yourself* (1989), *Rhythm of Love* (1990), *Kylie Minogue* (1994), *Light Years* (2000), *Fever* (2001), *Body Language* (2003), *X* (2007).

Mitchell, Joni (Roberta Joan Anderson) (1943–) Canadian singer/songwriter, guitarist, born McLeod, Alberta; 'Big Yellow Taxi', 'Help Me', *Joni Mitchell* (1968), *Clouds* (1969), *Ladies of the Canyon* (1970), *Blue* (1971), *Dog Eat Dog* (1985), *Chalk Mark in a Rain Storm* (1988), *Night Ride Home* (1991), *Turbulent Indigo* (1994), *Travelogue* (2002), *Shine* (2007).

The Monkees US group, late 1960s; members include Mickey Dolenz (1945–) vocalist, drummer, born Los Angeles; Davy Jones (1946–) vocalist, born Manchester, England; Peter Tork (originally Peter Torkelson) (1944–) bassist, born Washington, DC; Mike Nesmith (1942–) guitarist; 'I'm a Believer', 'Daydream Believer', *The Monkees* (1966), *Pool It* (1987).

The Moody Blues British group, mid-1960s to 1990s; members include Justin Hayward (1946–) guitarist, John Lodge (1945–) bassist; Mike Pinder (1941–) keyboardist; Graeme Edge (1941–) drummer; Ray Thomas (1941–) flautist, saxophonist, vocalist; 'Nights in White Satin', *Days of Future Passed* (1967), *Keys To The Kingdom* (1991).

Morrison, Van (George Ivan Morrison) (1945–) Northern Irish singer/songwriter, guitarist, born Belfast; (with Them, 1960s Irish group) 'Baby Please Don't Go', 'Brown Eyed Girl', *Blowin' Your Mind* (1967), *Enlightenment* (1990), *Hymns To The Silence* (1991), *Too Long in Exile* (1993), *Days Like This* (1995), *Down the Road* (2002), *Pay the Devil* (2006), *Keep It Simple* (2008).

Motörhead British heavy metal group, late 1970s to present; members include Lemmy (originally Ian Kilminster) (1945–) vocalist, born Stoke-on-Trent; *Overkill* (1979), *Bomber* (1979), *Ace of Spades* (1980), *No Sleep 'Til Hammersmith* (1981), *Orgasmatron* (1986), *No Sleep At All* (1988), *1916* (1991), *Everything Louder than Everyone Else* (1999), *Motörizer* (2008).

Nelson, Ricky (Eric Hilliard Nelson) (1940–85) US singer, guitarist, born Teaneck, New Jersey; 'Travelin' Man', 'Hello Mary Lou'.

Newman, Randy (Randolph Newman) (1943–) US singer/songwriter, pianist, born Los Angeles; 'I Love LA', 'Gone Dead Train', *Sail Away* (1972), *Trouble In Paradise* (1983), *The Natural* (1984) (soundtrack), *Parenthood* (1990) (soundtrack), *Awakenings* (1991) (soundtrack), *Toy Story* (1996) (soundtrack), *Meet the Parents* (2000) (soundtrack), *Meet the Fockers* (2004) (soundtrack), *Harps and Angels* (2008).

Nirvana US group, late 1980s to mid-1990s; members include Kurt Cobain (1967–94) vocalist, guitarist, born Aberdeen, Washington; Krist Novoselic (1965–) bassist, born Croatia; Dave Grohl (1969–) drummer, born Warren, Ohio; 'Smells like Teen Spirit', *Nevermind* (1991), *Unplugged in New York* (1994).

Oasis British group, formed Manchester 1992 as Rain; members include Liam Gallagher (1972–)

vocalist; Noel Gallagher (1967–) guitarist; Paul 'Bonehead' Arthurs (1965–) guitarist, replaced by Gem Archer; Paul McGuigan (1971–) guitarist, replaced by Andy Bell; Tony McCarroll drummer, replaced by Alan White; *Definitely Maybe* (1994), *(What's The Story) Morning Glory* (1995), *Be Here Now* (1997), *Heathen Chemistry* (2002), *Don't Believe the Truth* (2005).

Oldfield, Mike (1953–) British multi-instrumentalist, composer, born Reading, Berkshire; 'Blue Peter', 'Moonlight Shadow', *Tubular Bells* (1973), *Hergest Ridge* (1974), *Ommadawn* (1975), *Killing Fields* (1984), *Islands* (1987), *The Songs of Distant Earth* (1994), *Voyager* (1996), *Tres Lunas* (2002), *Light & Shade* (2005).

Orbison, Roy (1936–88) US singer/songwriter, guitarist, born Vernon, Texas; 'Only the Lonely', 'Crying', 'Dream Baby', '(Oh) Pretty Woman', 'In Dreams', 'Blue Bayou'.

Osbourne, Ozzy (John Michael Osbourne) (1948–) British rock musician, born Birmingham; formerly of Black Sabbath, solo since 1979; *Blizzard of Oz* (1980), *Diary of a Madman* (1981), *No Rest for the Wicked* (1988), *Ozzmosis* (1995), *Down to Earth* (2001), *Black Rain* (2007).

Palmer, Robert (1949–2003) British singer, born W Yorkshire, England; 'Every Kinda People', 'Bad Case Of Loving You (Doctor Doctor)', 'Some Guys Have All The Luck', 'Addicted To Love', 'She Makes My Day', *Riptide* (1985), *Drive* (2003).

Parton, Dolly (1946–) US singer/songwriter, born Sevier County, Tennessee; 'Jolene', 'Here You Come Again', 'Nine to Five', 'I Will Always Love You', 'Islands in the Stream' (with Kenny Rogers), *Just Because I'm a Woman* (1968), *Coat of Many Colours* (1971), *Grass is Blue* (1999), *Little Sparrow* (2001), *Halos and Horns* (2002), *Those Were the Days* (2005), *Backwoods Barbie* (2008).

Peter, Paul and Mary US trio, 1960s to 1980s; Peter Yarrow (1938–) guitarist, vocalist, born New York City; Paul Stookey (1937–) guitarist, vocalist, born Baltimore, Maryland; Mary Travers (1937–) vocalist, born Louisville, Kentucky; 'If I Had A Hammer', 'Blowin' In The Wind', 'Puff The Magic Dragon', 'Leavin' On A Jet Plane', *Peter, Paul & Mary* (1962), *In The Wind* (1963), *Peter, Paul & Mommy* (1969), *No Easy Walk To Freedom* (1986).

Pickett, Wilson (1941–2006) US singer, born Prattville, Alabama; 'In The Midnight Hour', '634-5789', 'Hey Jude'.

Pink Floyd British group, late 1960s to present; members include 'Syd' (Roger Keith) Barrett (1946–2006) singer/songwriter, guitarist; Roger Waters (1944–) singer/songwriter; David Gilmour (1944–) singer/songwriter, guitarist; all born Cambridge; *The Piper at the Gates of Dawn* (1967), *A Saucerful of Secrets* (1968), *Ummagumma* (1969), *Meddle* (1971), *Dark Side of the Moon* (1973), *Wish You Were Here* (1975), *The Wall* (1979), *The Final Cut* (1983), *A Momentary Lapse of Reason* (1987), *A Delicate Sound of Thunder* (1988), *The Division Bell* (1994), *Pulse* (1995), *Echoes* (2001).

Pitney, Gene (1941–2006) US singer, born Hartford, Connecticut; 'The Man Who Shot Liberty Valance', '24 Hours From Tulsa'.

The Pogues Anglo-Irish group, 1980s to 1990s; members include Shane MacGowan (1957–) vocalist, born Tunbridge Wells; Philip Chevron (originally Philip Ryan) (1957–) guitarist, born Dublin; James Fearnley (1954–) accordionist, born Manchester; Andrew Ranken (1953–) drummer, born London; Jem Finer (originally Jeremy Max Finer) (1955–) banjo player, born

Dublin; Spider Stacy (originally Peter Richard Stacy) (1958–) tin whistle player, born Eastbourne; 'Dirty Old Town', 'Sally Maclennane', 'A Pair of Brown Eyes', 'Irish Rover' (with the Dubliners), *Red Roses For Me* (1984), *Rum, Sodomy & The Lash* (1985), *If I Should Fall From Grace With God* (1988), *Peace and Love* (1989), *Hell's Ditch* (1990), *Waiting For Herb* (1993).

The Police British group, late 1970s to 1980s; members include Sting (originally Gordon Sumner) (1951–), singer/songwriter, bassist, born Wallsend, Northumberland (solo 'Set Them Free', 'Russians', 'Fields of Gold', 'Desert Rose', *The Dream of the Blue Turtles* (1985), *Nothing Like The Sun* (1987), *Brand New Day* (1999), *Sacred Love* (2003)); Stewart Copeland (1952–) drummer, born Alexandria, Virginia; Andy Summers (1942–) guitarist, born Lancaster; 'Can't Stand Losing You', 'Roxanne', 'Message In A Bottle', 'Walking On The Moon', 'Don't Stand So Close To Me', 'Every Little Thing She Does Is Magic', 'Every Breath You Take', *Outlandos d'Amour* (1978), *Regatta de Blanc* (1979), *Zenyatta Mondatta* (1980), *Ghost in the Machine* (1981), *Synchronicity* (1983).

Pop, Iggy (James Newell Osterburg) (1947–) US singer/songwriter, drummer, born Ypsilanti, Michigan; 'I Wanna Be Your Dog', *The Stooges* (1969), *Raw Power* (1973) (with the Stooges); 'Nightclubbing', 'The Passenger', 'Real Wild Child', 'Well Did You Evah' (with Deborah Harry), *The Idiot* (1976), *Lust for Life* (1977), *Blah Blah Blah* (1986), *Instinct* (1988), *Brick By Brick* (1990), *American Caesar* (1993), *A Damned Stooge With A Pistol* (1997), *Penetration* (2005).

Presley, Elvis (Aaron) (1935–77) US singer, guitarist, born Tupelo, Mississippi; 'Heartbreak Hotel', 'Hound Dog', 'Love Me Tender', 'All Shook Up', 'Jailhouse Rock', 'One Night', 'A Fool Such as I', 'It's Now or Never', 'Are You Lonesome Tonight', *G I Blues* (1961), *Blue Hawaii* (1961), *Roustabout* (1964), *From Elvis in Memphis* (1969).

The Pretenders British group, late 1970s to present; members include Chrissie Hynde (1951–) singer/songwriter, guitarist, born Akron, Ohio; 'Back on the Chain Gang', 'Brass in Pocket', *Pretenders* (1979), *Single Records* (1988), *Packed!* (1990), *Last Independents* (1994), *The Isle Of View* (1995), *¡Viva El Amor!* (1999), *Loose Screw* (2002).

Prince (Prince Rogers Nelson) (1958–) US singer/songwriter, guitarist, keyboardist, drummer, born Minneapolis, Minnesota; 'Little Red Corvette', 'Delirious', 'When Doves Cry', 'Let's Go Crazy', 'Raspberry Beret', 'Kiss', *Prince* (1979), *Dirty Mind* (1980), *Controversy* (1981), *1999* (1982), *Purple Rain* (with The Revolution) (1984), *Around The World In A Day* (1985), *Parade* (1986), *Sign o' the Times* (1987), *Love Sexy* (1988), *Diamonds and Pearls* (1991), *Symbol* (1992), *Come* (1994), *The Gold Experience* (1995), *Musicology* (2004), *3121* (2006), *Planet Earth* (2007).

Public Enemy US group, 1980s to present; members include Chuck D (originally Carlton Ridenhour) (1960–) vocalist; Flavor Flav (originally William Drayton) (1959–) vocalist, instrumentalist; Terminator X (originally Norman Rogers) (1966–) DJ; Professor Griff (originally Richard Griffin) (1960–) vocalist; *Yo! Bum Rush the Show* (1987), *It Takes A Nation of Millions To Hold Us Back* (1988), *Fear of a Black Planet* (1990), *He Got Game* (1998) (soundtrack), *Revolverlution* (2002), *Rebirth of a Nation* (2006), *How You Sell Soul to a Soulless People Who Sold Their Soul?* (2007).

Pulp British group, formed Sheffield 1981 as Arabacus

Pulp; members include Jarvis Cocker (1962–) vocalist, guitarist, pianist; Simon Hinkler, keyboardist; Peter Broam, bassist; David Hinkler, keyboardist; Gary Wilson, trombonist; guest vocalists Saskia Cocker and Gill Taylor; guest keyboardist Tim Allcard; 'Common People', 'Underwear', 'Disco 2000', *IT* (1983), *Freaks* (1987), *Separations* (1991), *His 'n' Hers* (1994), *Different Class* (1995), *This is Hardcore* (1998), *We Love Life* (2001).

Queen British group, 1970s to present; members include Freddie Mercury (originally Farookh Bulsara) (1946–91) singer/songwriter, born Zanzibar; Brian May (1947–) guitarist, born Hampton, Middlesex; John Deacon (1951–) bassist, born Leicester; Roger Taylor (originally Roger Meddows-Taylor) (1949–) drummer, born Norfolk; 'Killer Queen', 'Bohemian Rhapsody', 'We are the Champions', 'Somebody to Love', 'Another one Bites the Dust', 'Crazy Little Thing Called Love', 'Under Pressure' (with David Bowie), 'Radio Ga-Ga', *Queen II* (1974), *Sheer Heart Attack* (1974), *A Night at the Opera* (1975), *A Day at the Races* (1976), *The Game* (1980), *Hot Space* (1982), *The Works* (1984), *A Kind of Magic* (1986), *The Miracle* (1989), *Innuendo* (1991), *Made In Heaven* (1995), *The Cosmos Rocks* (2008).

Radiohead British group, late 1980s to present; members include Thom Yorke (1968–), vocalist, guitarist; Ed O'Brien (1968–), guitarist, vocalist; Jon Greenwood (1971–), guitarist; Colin Greenwood (1969–), bassist; Phil Selway (1967–), drummer; *Pablo Honey* (1993) *The Bends* (1995), *OK Computer* (1997), *Kid A* (2000), *Amnesiac* (2001), *Hail to the Thief* (2003), *In Rainbows* (2007).

Ray, Johnnie (1927–90) US singer, born Rosebud, Oregon; 'Cry'/'The Little White Cloud That Cried', 'Walkin' My Baby Back Home', 'Just Walking In The Rain', 'You Don't Owe Me A Thing', 'I'll Never Fall In Love Again', *The Big Beat* (1957).

Redding, Otis (1941–67) US singer/songwriter, born Dawson, Georgia; 'I've Been Loving You Too Long', 'Try a Little Tenderness', 'Mr Pitiful', 'Satisfaction', '(Sittin' On The) Dock of the Bay', 'Respect', *The Otis Redding Story* (1968).

Reed, Lou (Louis Firbank) (1944–) US singer/songwriter, born Long Island, New York (was founder-member of The Velvet Underground in 1965); 'Walk On The Wild Side', 'I Love You Suzanne', *Lou Reed* (1972), *Transformer* (1972), *Rock 'n' Roll Animal* (1974), *Coney Island Baby* (1976), *Street Hassle* (1978), *New Sensations* (1984), *New York* (1989), *Magic and Loss* (1992), *The Best of Lou Reed and The Velvet Underground* (1995), *Ecstasy* (2000), *The Raven* (2003).

Martha and The Vandellas US group, 1960s; members include Martha Reeves (1941–) singer; Rosalyn Ashford (1943–) singer; Betty Kelly (1944–) singer until 1967; all born Detroit, Michigan; 'Nowhere To Run', 'I'm Ready For Love', 'Jimmy Mack', 'Dancing In The Street'.

REM US group, 1980s to present; members include Michael Stipe (1960–) vocalist; Peter Buck (1956–) guitarist; Michael Mills (1958–) bassist; Bill Berry (1958–) drummer until 1997; 'World Leader Pretend', 'The One I Love', 'Stand', 'Superman', 'Orange Crush', 'Losing my Religion', 'Everybody Hurts', *Murmur* (1983), *Reckoning* (1984), *Life's Rich Pageant* (1986), *Number 5: Document* (1987), *Green* (1989), *Out of Time* (1991), *Automatic For The People* (1992), *Monster* (1994), *Reveal* (2001), *Around the Sun* (2004), *Accelerate* (2008).

Richard, Sir Cliff (Harry Rodger Webb) (1940–)

British singer/songwriter, guitarist, born Lucknow, India; over 100 hits including 'Livin' Doll', 'The Young Ones', 'Summer Holiday', 'Congratulations', *21 Today* (1961), *Rock & Roll Juvenile* (1971), *Love Songs* (1981), *Wired For Sound* (1981), *Now You See Me, Now You Don't* (1982), *Dressed For The Occasion* (1983), *Always Guaranteed* (1987), *Private Collection* (1988), *The Album* (1993), *Songs From Heathcliff* (1995), *Wanted* (2001), *Two's Company* (2006).

Richie, Lionel (Lionel Brockman Richie, Jr) (1949–) US singer/songwriter, pianist, born Tuskegee, Alabama; 'All Night Long', 'Say You', *Can't Slow Down* (1983), *Dancing On The Ceiling* (1986), *Back To Front* (1992), *Coming Home* (2006).

The Righteous Brothers US duo, 1960s to 1970s; Bobby Hatfield (1940–2003) singer, born Beaver Dam, Wisconsin; Bill Medley (1940–) singer, born Los Angeles; 'You've Lost That Lovin' Feelin'', 'Just Once In My Life', 'Unchained Melody', 'Ebb Tide', 'Rock And Roll Heaven'.

Robinson, Smokey (William Robinson, Jr) (1940–) US singer/songwriter, born Detroit, Michigan; (with The Miracles, American group, 1960s) 'Shop Around', 'The Tracks Of My Tears', 'I Second That Emotion'; 'Being With You', *Where There's Smoke* (1979), *Smoke Signals* (1986).

The Rolling Stones British group, 1960s to present; members include 'Mick' (Michael Philip) Jagger (1943–) vocalist, harmonica-player, born Dartford, Kent (solo 'Just Another Night', 'Dancing In The Street' (with David Bowie), *She's The Boss* (1985)); Keith Richards (1943–) guitarist, born Dartford, Kent; Bill Wyman (originally William Perks) (1936–) bassist, born Penge, London, replaced by Darryl Jones; Charlie Watts (1941–) drummer, born Neasden, London; Brian Jones (originally Lewis Brian Hopkin-Jones) (1942–69) guitarist, born Cheltenham, replaced by Mick Taylor (1948–) born Hertfordshire, replaced by Ron Wood (1947–) born Hillingdon, Middlesex; Ian Stewart (1938–85) keyboardist; 'It's All Over Now', 'Little Red Rooster', 'The Last Time', '(I Can't Get No) Satisfaction', 'Get Off My Cloud', '19th Nervous Breakdown', 'Paint It Black', 'Let's Spend The Night Together', 'Jumpin' Jack Flash', 'Sympathy For The Devil', 'Honky Tonk Women', 'Brown Sugar', 'Miss You', *The Rolling Stones* (1964), *Aftermath* (1966), *Beggar's Banquet* (1968), *Let it Bleed* (1969), *Sticky Fingers* (1971), *Exile on Main Street* (1972), *Some Girls* (1978), *Emotional Rescue* (1980), *Tattoo You* (1981), *Undercover* (1983), *Dirty Work* (1986), *Steel Wheels* (1989), *Voodoo Lounge* (1994), *Bridges to Babylon* (1997), *Live Licks* (2002), *A Bigger Bang* (2005).

Ross, Diana (1944–) US singer, born Detroit, Michigan; with the Supremes, 1960s group; 'Ain't No Mountain High Enough', 'Baby Love', 'Stop! In the Name of Love', 'You Can't Hurry Love', 'You Keep Me Hangin' On', 'Where Did Our Love Go', 'I'm Gonna Make You Love Me'; with Lionel Richie: 'Endless Love'; 'Upside Down', 'I'm Coming Out', 'My Old Piano', 'Chain Reaction', *Diana* (1980), *Eaten Alive* (1985) *Red Hot Rhythm 'n' Blues* (1987), *The Force Behind The Power* (1991), *Take Me Higher* (1995), *Love and Life* (2001), *Blue* (2006).

Roxy Music British group, 1970s to early 1980s; members include Bryan Ferry (1945–) singer, born Washington, County Durham; Brian Eno (1948–) songwriter, keyboardist, born Woodbridge, Suffolk; Phil Manzanera (originally Philip Targett-Adams) (1941–) guitarist, born London; Andy Mackay (1946–) saxophonist; 'Virginia Plain', 'Do The Strand', 'Street Life', 'Love is the Drug', 'Dance Away', 'Angel Eyes', 'Jealous Guy', 'My Only Love',

Roxy Music (1972), *Stranded* (1973), *Siren* (1975), *Manifesto* (1980), *Avalon* (1982).

Santana, Carlos (1947–) Mexican guitarist, vocalist, born Autlan de Novarra, Jalisco, Mexico; (with band Santana, late 1960s to present) 'Black Magic Woman', *Santana* (1969), *Abraxas* (1970), *Amigos* (1976), *Moonflower* (1977), *Zebop!* (1981), *Freedom* (1987), *Supernatural* (1999), *Ceremony* (2003), *Ultimate Santana* (2007).

Sedaka, Neil (1939–) US singer/songwriter; 'Breaking Up Is Hard To Do', 'Laughter In The Rain', 'Bad Blood', *Laughter And Tears: Best of Neil Sedaka Today* (1976).

The Sex Pistols British punk group, 1970s; members include Johnny Rotten (originally John Lydon) (1956–) vocalist; Steve Jones (1955–) guitarist; Paul Cook (1956–) drummer; Sid Vicious (originally John Simon Ritchie) (1958–79) singer, bassist; 'Anarchy in the UK', 'God Save The Queen', 'Pretty Vacant', 'Holidays In The Sun', 'My Way', 'Something Else', 'C'mon Everybody', 'Silly Thing', *Never Mind the Bollocks – Here's The Sex Pistols* (1977), *Some Product* (1978), *Flogging a Dead Horse* (1979), *The Great Rock 'n' Roll Swindle* (1980), *Kiss This* (1992), *Filthy Lucre Live* (1996).

The Shadows British group, late 1950s to present; members include Hank Marvin (originally Brian Rankin) (1941–) guitarist, born Newcastle upon Tyne; Bruce Welch (1941–) guitarist, born Newcastle upon Tyne; Jet Harris (originally Terry Harris) (1939–) bassist, born London; Tony Meehan (1943–2005) drummer, born London; 'Apache', 'Kon Tiki', 'Wonderful Land', 'Dance On', 'Foot Tapper', 'Don't Cry For Me Argentina', *Moonlight Shadows* (1986), *Reflection* (1990), *Shadows In The Night* (1993).

The Shangri-las US group, mid-1960s; Betty Weiss singer; Mary Weiss; Marge and Mary Ann Ganser; 'Leader of the Pack', 'Past, Present and Future'.

Shannon, Del (1939–90) US singer, born Coopersville, Michigan; 'Runaway', *Little Town Flirt* (1963), *Drop Down And Get Me* (1983).

Shaw, Sandie (Sandra Goodrich) (1947–) British singer, born Dagenham, Essex; 'There's Always Something There To Remind Me', 'Long Live Love', 'Puppet on a String', 'Hand In Glove', 'Are You Ready To Be Heartbroken?', *Nothing Less Than Brilliant* (1994).

Simon, Carly (1945–) US singer/songwriter, born New York City; 'You're So Vain', 'Nobody Does It Better', 'Coming Round Again', 'Let The River Run', *No Secrets* (1972), *Moonlight Serenade* (2005), *This Kind of Love* (2008).

Simon, Paul (1941–) US singer/songwriter, guitarist, born Newark, New Jersey; with Art Garfunkel (1942–) singer, born Forest Hills, New York; 'The Sound of Silence', 'Mrs Robinson', 'Bridge over Troubled Water', 'The Boxer', 'Scarborough Fair', 'Homeward Bound', *Bridge over Troubled Water* (1970); 'You Can Call Me Al', *Paul Simon* (1972), *Graceland* (1986), *Rhythm of the Saints* (1990), *You're the One* (2000), *Surprise* (2006).

Simply Red British group, 1980 to present; members include Mick Hucknall (1960–) singer/songwriter; Tony Bowers (1952–) bassist; Chris Joyce (1957–) drummer; Fritz McIntyre (1956–) keyboardist; Sylvan Richardson guitarist; 'Money's Too Tight To Mention', 'Holding Back The Years', *Picture Book* (1985), *Men And Women* (1987), *A New Flame* (1989), *Stars* (1991), *Life* (1995), *Blue* (1998), *Home* (2003), *Simplified* (2005), *Stay* (2007).

Sinatra, Frank (Francis Albert Sinatra) (1915–98) US singer, born Hoboken, New Jersey; 'I've Got You

Under My Skin', 'Strangers In The Night', 'The Lady Is A Tramp', 'Theme From New York, New York', 'My Way', *Songs For Swingin' Lovers* (1956), *Come Fly with Me* (1962).

Sly and the Family Stone US funk and soul group, 1960s to 1970s; members include Sly Stone (originally Sylvester Stewart) (1944–) vocalist, guitarist, keyboardist; Freddie Stone (1946–) guitarist; Cynthia Robinson (1946–) trumpeter; Larry Graham (1946–) guitarist; Rosemary Stone (1945–) vocalist, pianist; 'Dance To The Music', 'Everyday People', *Greatest Hits* (1970), *There's A Riot Goin' On* (1971).

Smith, Patti (1946–) US singer/songwriter, born Chicago; 'Because the Night', *Horses* (1976), *Easter* (1978), *Dream Of Life* (1988), *Peace and Noise* (1997), *Gung Ho* (2000), *Trampin'* (2004), *Twelve* (2007).

The Smiths British group, 1980s; members include (Steven Patrick) Morrissey (1959–) singer/songwriter (solo 'Everyday Is Like Sunday', *Viva Hate* (1988), *You are the Quarry* (2004)); Johnny Marr (1963–) guitarist, songwriter; both born Manchester; 'Hand In Glove', 'Bigmouth Strikes Again', 'Boy With The Thorn In His Side', 'Panic', *The Smiths* (1984), *Meat Is Murder* (1985), *Hatful of Hollow* (1985), *The Queen Is Dead* (1986), *Strangeways, Here We Come* (1987), *Rank* (1988).

Spears, Britney (Jean) (1981–) US singer, born Kentwood, Louisiana; *Baby One More Time* (1999), *Oops!... I Did It Again* (2000), *Britney* (2001), *In the Zone* (2003), *B in the Mix* (2005), *Blackout* (2007).

The Spice Girls British group, 1990s to 2000; Posh Spice (Victoria Adams) (1975–); Sporty Spice (Melanie Chisholm) (1974–); Ginger Spice (Geri Halliwell) (1972–); Scary Spice (Melanie Brown) (1975–) and Baby Spice (Emma Bunton) (1976–); 'Say You'll Be There', '2 Become 1', 'Spice Up Your Life', *Spice* (1996), *Forever* (2000).

Springfield, Dusty (Mary O'Brien) (1939–99) British singer, born Hampstead, London; 'I Only Want To Be With You', 'You Don't Have To Say You Love Me', *Dusty In Memphis* (1969), *Reputation* (1990), *A Very Fine Love* (1995).

Springsteen, Bruce (Frederick Joseph) (1949–) US singer/songwriter, guitarist, born Freehold, New Jersey; 'Hungry Heart', 'Dancing In The Dark', 'Brilliant Disguise', *Greetings from Ashbury Park, NJ* (1973), *Born to Run* (1975), *Darkness on the Edge of Town* (1978), *The River* (1980), *Nebraska* (1982), *Born in the USA* (1985), *Tunnel of Love* (1987), *Human Touch* (1992), *Lucky Town* (1992), *The Ghost of Tom Joad* (1995), *The Rising* (2002), *Devils and Dust* (2005), *Magic* (2007), *Working on a Dream* (2009).

Status Quo British group, 1970s to present; members include Francis Rossi (1949–) guitarist, vocalist; Richard Parfitt (1948–) guitarist, vocalist; Alan Lancaster (1949–) bassist; John Coghlan (1946–) drummer; all born London; 'Down, Down', 'Caroline', 'You're in the Army Now', *Piledriver* (1973), *Hello* (1973), *On The Level* (1975), *Blue For You* (1976), *Rockin' All Over the World* (1978), *Back To Back* (1983), *In The Army Now* (1986), *Rocking All Over The Years* (1990), *Live Alive Quo* (1992), *Thirsty Work* (1994), *Famous in the Last Century* (2000), *In Search of the Fourth Chord* (2007).

Steely Dan US group, 1970s to present; Walter Becker (1950–) bassist, guitarist; Donald Fagen (1948–) keyboardist; 'Reelin' In The Years', *Aja* (1977), *Gaucho* (1980), *Gold* (1982), *Alive In America* (1995), *Two Against Nature* (2000), *Everything Must Go* (2003).

Stevens, Cat (Yusuf Islam, originally Steven Demitri Georgiou) (1947–) British singer/songwriter, born

London; 'Lady D'Arbanville', 'Wild World', 'Peace Train', 'Morning Has Broken', *Tea For The Tillerman* (1971), *Teaser & The Firecat* (1971), *Catch Bull At Four* (1972), *Foreigner* (1973), *Buddha And The Chocolate Box* (1974), *An Other Cup* (2006).

Stewart, Rod(erick David) (1945–) British singer/songwriter, guitarist, born London; *Long Player* (1971) (with the Faces); 'Maggie May', 'You Wear It Well', 'Sailing', 'Do Ya Think I'm Sexy?', 'I Don't Want To Talk About It', 'Passion', 'Baby Jane', 'Stay with Me', 'Young Turks', 'The Motown Song', *Every Picture Tells A Story* (1971), *Atlantic Crossing* (1975), *Blondes Have More Fun* (1978), *Tonight I'm Yours* (1981), *Body Wishes* (1983), *Every Beat Of My Heart* (1986), *Out Of Order* (1988), *Vagabond Heart* (1991), *Unplugged And Seated* (1993), *A Spanner In The Works* (1995), *Stardust...The Great American Songbook Vol III* (2004), *Still the Same* (2006).

The Stranglers British group, mid-1970s to present; members include Hugh Cornwell (1949–) vocalist, guitarist; Jean-Jacques Burnel (1952–) vocalist, bassist; 'Peaches', 'Walk On By', 'Golden Brown', 'Always The Sun', '96 Tears', *Rattus Norvegicus* (1977), *No More Heroes* (1977), *Feline* (1983), *Aural Structure* (1984), *Dreamtime* (1986), *Ten* (1990), *Stranglers In The Night* (1992), *About Time* (1992), *Coup de Grace* (1998), *Suite XVI* (2006).

The Streets (Mike Skinner) (1978–) British rapper, born Birmingham; 'Fit But You Know It', 'Dry Your Eyes', 'When You Wasn't Famous', *A Grand Don't Come for Free* (2004), *The Hardest Way to Make an Easy Living* (2006).

Streisand, Barbra (Joan) (1942–) US singer/songwriter, born Brooklyn, New York City; (with Neil Diamond) 'You Don't Bring Me Flowers'; 'Guilty', *Stoney End* (1971), *The Way We Were* (1974), *Streisand Superman* (1977), *Emotion* (1984), *One Voice* (1987), *A Love Like Ours* (1999), *The Movie Album* (2003), *Guilty Pleasures* (2005).

Summer, Donna (Donna Adrian Gaines) (1948–) US singer, born Boston, Massachusetts; 'Love To Love You Baby', 'I Feel Love', 'Last Dance', 'Hot Stuff', 'Highway Runner', 'He's A Rebel', 'Forgive Me', 'Dinner With Gershwin', *Live And More* (1978), *Bad Girls* (1979), *The Wanderer* (1980), *She Works Hard For The Money* (1983), *All Systems Go* (1987), *Another Place and Time* (1989), *Crayons* (2008).

Talking Heads US group, mid-1970s to 1991; members include David Byrne (1952–) singer/songwriter, guitarist, born Dumbarton, Scotland; Chris Frantz (1951–) drummer, born Fort Campbell, Kentucky; Martina 'Tina' Weymouth (1950–) bassist, born Coronado, California; Jerry Harrison (1949–) keyboardist, born Milwaukee, Wisconsin; 'Psycho Killer', 'Burning Down the House', 'Road to Nowhere', 'And She Was', *Talking Heads* (1977), *Fear of Music* (1979), *Remain in Light* (1980), *Speaking In Tongues* (1983), *Little Creatures* (1985), *True Stories* (1986), *Naked* (1988), *Once In a Lifetime/Sand In The Vaseline* (1992).

Taylor, James (1948–) US singer/songwriter, guitarist, born Boston, Massachusetts; 'You've Got A Friend', *Mud Slide Slim And The Blue Horizon* (1971), *One Man Dog* (1972), *Gorilla* (1975), *That's Why I'm Here* (1986), *Never Die Young* (1988), *October Road* (2002).

The Temptations US group, 1960s to present; members have included David Ruffin (1941–91) singer; Eddie Kendricks (1939–92) singer; Dennis Edwards (1943–) singer; Melvin Franklin (1942–95) singer; Otis Williams (1941–); Damon Harris (1950–); over 80 hit singles since 1962; 'Just My Imagination (Running Away With Me)', 'Treat Her Like a Lady', 'Papa Was

A Rolling Stone', *Diana Ross & The Supremes Join The Temptations* (1968), *All Directions* (1972), *Truly For You* (1984), *Phoenix Rising* (1998).

Thin Lizzy Irish heavy rock group, 1970s to mid-1980s; members include Phil Lynott (1951–86) vocalist, bassist (solo 'Yellow Pearl', 'Nineteen'); Brian Downey (1951–) drummer; Eric Bell (1947–) guitarist, born Belfast; Gary Moore (1952–) vocalist, guitarist, born Dublin; Brian Robertson (1956–) guitarist, born Glasgow; Scott Gorham (1951–) guitarist, born Santa Monica, California; 'Whiskey In The Jar', 'The Boys Are Back In Town', *Jailbreak* (1976), *Live And Dangerous* (1978), *Black Rose* (1979), *China Town* (1980), *Adventures of Thin Lizzy* (1981), *Thunder and Lightning* (1983).

Turner, Tina (Annie Mae Bullock) (1938–) US singer/songwriter, born Nutbush, Tennessee; with Ike Turner (1931–) singer, pianist, born Clarksdale, Mississippi; 'River Deep, Mountain High', 'Nutbush City Limits', *The Best of Ike and Tina Turner* (1976); 'Let's Stay Together', 'What's Love Got to Do with It', 'Better Be Good To Me', 'We Don't Need Another Hero', *Private Dancer* (1984), *Break Every Rule* (1986), *Live In Europe* (1988), *Foreign Affair* (1989), *Simply The Best* (1991), *What's Love Got To Do With It* (1993) (soundtrack), *Twenty Four Seven* (2000).

Twain, Shania (Eileen Regina Edwards) (1965–) Canadian singer/songwriter, born Windsor, Ontario; 'That Don't Impress Me Much', 'Man! I Feel Like a Woman', *The Woman in Me* (1995), *Come on Over* (1997), *Up!* (2002), *Greatest Hits* (2004).

UB40 British group, 1980s to present; members include Ali Campbell (1959–) singer, guitarist; Robin Campbell (1954–) guitarist; Jim Brown (1957–) drummer; Brian Travers (1959–) saxophonist; Earl Falconer (1959–) bassist; Norman Hassan (1958–) percussionist; Mickey Virtue (1957–) keyboardist; 'Red Red Wine', 'I Got You Babe', 'Don't Break My Heart', 'Sing Our Own Song', *Signing Off* (1982), *Labour Of Love* (1983), *Baggariddim* (1985), *Rat In The Kitchen* (1986), *Labour of Love II* (1989), *Promises and Lies* (1993), *Homegrown* (2003), *Who You Fighting For* (2005).

U2 Irish group, 1980s to present; members include Bono (originally Paul Hewson) (1960–) vocalist, born Dublin; The Edge (originally David Evans) (1961–) guitarist; Larry Mullen (1961–) drummer; Adam Clayton (1960–) bassist; 'New Year's Day', 'Pride (In The Name of Love)', 'Sunday, Bloody Sunday', 'With Or Without You', 'Desire', 'Beautiful Day', 'Vertigo', *War* (1983), *Live Under a Blood Red Sky* (1983), *The Unforgettable Fire* (1984), *The Joshua Tree* (1987), *Rattle and Hum* (1988), *Achtung Baby* (1991), *Zooropa* (1993), *Pop* (1997), *All That You Can't Leave Behind* (2000), *How to Dismantle an Atomic Bomb* (2004).

Valens, Ritchie (originally **Richard Valenzuela**) (1941–59) US singer/songwriter, guitarist, born Pacoima, California; 'Come On, Let's Go', 'Donna', 'La Bamba'.

Vandross, Luther (1951–2005) US soul singer; 'Never Too Much', 'Here And Now', *Give Me The Reason* (1986), *Any Love* (1988), *Dance with my Father* (2003).

Van Halen US group, late 1970s to present; members include David Lee Roth (1955–) vocalist, born Bloomingdale, Indiana (solo 'California Girls', 'Yankee Rose', *Eat 'Em and Smile* (1986), *Skyscraper* (1987)); Sammy Hagar (1951–) singer/songwriter, guitarist, born Monterey, California (solo 'I've Done Everything For You', 'Your Love is Driving Me Crazy', 'Two Sides of Love', 'I Can't Drive 55', *Three Lock Box* (1983), *Voice of America* (1984)); Eddie Van

Arts and Culture

Halen (1955–) guitarist; Alex Van Halen (1953–) drummer; both born the Netherlands; Michael Anthony (1955–) bassist; 'You Really Got Me', 'Jump', 'Panama', 'Hot For Teacher', 'Why Can't This Be Love', *Van Halen* (1978), *Women And Children First* (1980), *Fair Warning* (1981), *Diver Down* (1982), *1984* (1984), *5150* (1986), *OU812* (1988), *For Unlawful Carnal Knowledge* (1991), *Balance* (1995), *Best of Both Worlds* (2004).

Vega, Suzanne (1959–) US singer/songwriter, guitarist, born Santa Monica, California; 'Marlene On The Wall', 'Small Blue Thing', 'Left Of Center', 'Luka', 'Tom's Diner', *Suzanne Vega* (1985), *Solitude Standing* (1987), *Days of Open Hand* (1990), *99.9°F* (1992), *Retrospective* (2003), *Beauty & Crime* (2007).

The Velvet Underground US group, late 1960s; members include John Cale (1940–) guitarist, viola player, born Garnant, Wales; Nico (originally Christa Paffgen) (1938–88) vocalist, born Cologne, Germany; Lou Reed (originally Louis Firbank) (1944–) singer/songwriter, guitarist, born Long Island, New York; *The Velvet Underground & Nico* (1967), *White Light, White Heat* (1968), *The Velvet Underground* (1969), *Loaded* (1970), *Live at Max's Kansas City* (1972), *1969 Velvet Underground Live* (1974), *VU* (1985), *Live MCMXCIII* (1993).

The Verve British group, 1990s; members include Richard Ashcroft (1971–) vocalist; Nick McCabe, guitarist; Simon Jones, bassist; Peter Salisbury, drummer; *A Storm In Heaven* (1993), *A Northern Soul* (1995), *Urban Hymns* (1997).

Vincent, Gene (Vincent Eugene Craddock) (1935–71) US singer, born Norfolk, Virginia; (with the Blue Caps) 'Be-Bop-a-Lula', 'Pistol Packin' Mama', 'Bird Doggin'.

Waits, Tom (1949–) US singer/songwriter, pianist, born Pamona, California; *Small Change* (1976), *Swordfishtrombones* (1983), *The Asylum Years* (1984), *Rain Dogs* (1985), *Frank's Wild Years* (1987), *Big Time* (1988), *Bone Machine* (1992), *The Black Rider* (1993), *Mule Variations* (1999), *Alice* (2002), *Bloody Money* (2002), *Real Gone* (2004).

Warwick, Dionne (Marie Dionne Warwicke) (1940–) US singer/songwriter, pianist, born East Orange, New Jersey; 'There Came You' (with The Spinners); (Dionne & Friends) 'That's What Friends Are For'; *Dionne* (1979), *Heartbreaker* (1982), *So Amazing* (1983), *Without Your Love* (1985), *Love Songs* (1990), *My Friends and Me* (2006).

Westlife Irish group, 1990s to present; members include Shane Filan (1979–), Mark Feehily (1980–), Kian Egan (1980–) all born Sligo, Ireland; Nicky Byrne (1978–), Bryan McFadden (1978–) both born Dublin; 'Flying Without Wings', 'Swear it Again', 'Queen of my Heart', 'Mandy', *Westlife* (1999), *World of Our Own* (2001), *Turnaround* (2003), *Allow Us to Be Frank* (2004), *Back Home* (2007).

Wham! British group, 1980s; George Michael (originally Yorgos Kyriatou Panayiotou) (1963–) singer/songwriter, born Finchley, London; Andrew Ridgely (1963–) singer, guitarist, born Bushey, Hertsfordshire; 'Young Guns (Go For It)', 'Club Tropicana', 'Wake Me Up Before You Go-Go', 'Freedom', 'Last Christmas', 'I'm Your Man', 'Edge of Heaven', *Fantastic* (1983), *Make It Big* (1984), *The Final* (1986).

White, Barry (1944–2003) US singer/songwriter, born Galveston, Texas; 'Can't Get Enough Of Your Love, Babe', *Can't Get Enough* (1974), *Right Now Barry White* (1987), *The Right Night And Barry White* (1987), *The Icon Is Love* (1995), *Staying Power* (1999).

The White Stripes US group; members include Jack White (1975–) singer/songwriter, guitarist, born Detroit, Michigan; Meg White (1974–) drummer,

singer, born Detroit, Michigan; *White Blood Cells* (2001), *Elephant* (2003), *Get Behind Me Satan* (2005), *Icky Thump* (2007).

The Who British group, late 1960s to present; members include Pete Townshend (1945–) singer/songwriter, guitarist (solo *Who Came First* (1972)); Roger Daltry (1944–) vocalist, born London (solo *After The Fire* (1985)); John Entwhistle (1944–2002) bassist, French horn player; Keith Moon (1947–78) drummer; all born London; 'Substitute', 'Won't Get Fooled Again', 'You Better You Bet', *My Generation* (1966), *The Who Sell Out* (1967), *Tommy* (1969), *Who's Next* (1971), *Quadrophenia* (1973), *Face Dances* (1981), *It's Hard* (1982), *Who's Last* (1984), *Who's Better Who's Best* (1988), *Join Together* (1990), *30 Years of Maximum R&B* (1994), *Endless Wire* (2006).

Williams, Robbie (1974–) British singer/songwriter, born Stoke-on-Trent (with Take That, 1990s) 'It Only Takes a Minute', 'Back for Good'; 'Angels', 'She's the One', 'Millennium', *Life Thru a Lens* (1997), *Sing When You're Winning* (2000), *Escapology* (2002), *Intensive Care* (2005), *Rudebox* (2006).

Winehouse, Amy (Jade) (1983–) British singer/songwriter, born London; 'Stronger Than Me', 'Rehab'; 'Valerie', 'Love is a Losing Game', *Frank* (2003), *Back to Black* (2006).

Wonder, Stevie (Steveland Judkins or Stevland Morris) (1950–) US singer/songwriter, harmonica player, keyboardist, born Saginaw, Michigan; 'Fingertips', 'Superstition', 'You Are The Sunshine Of My Life', 'Isn't She Lovely', 'Master Blaster', 'Happy Birthday', 'I Just Called to Say I Love You', 'Part-Time Lover', 'Ebony and Ivory' (with Paul McCartney), *Stevie Wonder/The 12 Year Old Genius* (1961), *Music of My Mind* (1972), *Talking Book* (1972), *Innervisions* (1973), *Songs in the Key of Life* (1976), *Hotter than July* (1980), *In Square Circle* (1985), *Characters* (1987), *Jungle Fever* (1991) (soundtrack), *Conversation Peace* (1995), *A Time 2 Love* (2005).

Yardbirds British group, 1960s; members include Keith Relf (1943–76) singer, harmonica player, born Richmond, Surrey; Paul Samwell-Smith (1943–) bassist, born Twickenham, Middlesex; Chris Dreja (1946–) guitarist, born Surbiton, Surrey; Eric Clapton (1945–) guitarist; Jeff Beck (1944–) guitarist; Jimmy Page (1944–) bassist, guitarist; 'Good Morning Little Schoolgirl', 'For Your Love', 'I'm A Man', 'Happening Ten Years Time Ago'.

Yes British group, 1970s to present; members include Jon Anderson (1944–) vocalist, born Lancashire; Rick Wakeman (1949–) keyboardist, born London; Steve Howe (1947–) guitarist, born London; Chris Squire (1948–) bassist, born London; 'Owner of a Lonely Heart', *Fragile* (1972), *Close to the Edge* (1972), *90125* (1983), *Big Generator* (1987), *Union* (1991), *Talk* (1994), *Magnification* (2001).

Young, Neil (1945–) Canadian singer/songwriter, guitarist, born Toronto; 'Heart Of Gold', *After the Gold Rush* (1970), *Harvest* (1972), *Tonight's the Night* (1975), *Zuma* (1975), *Rust Never Sleeps* (1979), *Reactor* (1981), *Landing On Water* (1986), *Freedom* (1989), *Ragged Glory* (1990), *Harvest Moon* (1992), *Sleeps With Angels* (1994), *Mirror Ball* (1995), *Are You Passionate?* (2002), *Prairie Wind* (2005), *Living with War* (2006), *Chrome Dreams II* (2007).

Zappa, Frank (Francis Vincent Zappa, Jr) (1940–93) US singer/songwriter, guitarist, bandleader (The Mothers of Invention, American 1970s group), born Baltimore, Maryland; 'Valley Girl', *Apostrophe* (1974), *Joe's Garage* (1979), *Ship Arriving Too Late To Save A Drowning Witch* (1982), *The Perfect Stranger And Other Works* (1985), *Guitar* (1988).

ZZ Top US group, 1970s to present; Billy Gibbons

vocalist, guitarist; Dusty Hill vocalist, bassist; Frank Beard drummer; 'Gimme All Your Lovin'', 'Sharp Dressed Man', 'Legs', 'Sleeping Bag', *Tres Hombres* (1973), *Tejas* (1976), *Deguello* (1979), *Eliminator* (1983), *Afterburner* (1985), *Recycler* (1990), *Antenna* (1994), *XXX* (1999), *Mescalero* (2003).

Grammy awards

Grammy awards are awarded annually, in a number of categories, by the US National Academy of Recording Arts and Sciences. They were first awarded in 1958.

Year	Best record	Best album
1958	Domenico Modugno 'Nel Blu Dipinto Di Blu (Volare)'	Henry Mancini *Peter Gunn*
1959	Bobby Darin 'Mack the Knife'	Frank Sinatra *Come Dance with Me*
1960	Percy Faith 'Theme from *A Summer Place*'	Bob Newhart *Button Down Mind*
1961	Henry Mancini 'Moon River'	Judy Garland *Judy at Carnegie Hall*
1962	Tony Bennett 'I Left My Heart in San Francisco'	Vaughn Meader *The First Family*
1963	Henry Mancini 'The Days of Wine and Roses'	Barbra Streisand *The Barbra Streisand Album*
1964	Stan Getz, Astrud Gilberto 'The Girl from Ipanema'	Stan Getz, João Gilberto *Getz / Gilberto*
1965	Herb Alpert 'A Taste of Honey'	Frank Sinatra *September of My Years*
1966	Frank Sinatra 'Strangers in the Night'	Frank Sinatra *A Man and His Music*
1967	5th Dimension 'Up, Up and Away'	The Beatles *Sgt Pepper's Lonely Hearts Club Band*
1968	Simon and Garfunkel 'Mrs Robinson'	Glen Campbell *By the Time I Get to Phoenix*
1969	5th Dimension 'Aquarius/Let the Sunshine In'	Blood, Sweat and Tears *Blood, Sweat and Tears*
1970	Simon and Garfunkel 'Bridge Over Troubled Water'	Simon and Garfunkel *Bridge Over Troubled Water*
1971	Carole King 'It's Too Late'	Carole King *Tapestry*
1972	Roberta Flack 'The First Time Ever I Saw Your Face'	Various *The Concert for Bangla Desh*
1973	Roberta Flack 'Killing Me Sofly with His Song'	Stevie Wonder *Innervisions*
1974	Olivia Newton-John 'I Honestly Love You'	Stevie Wonder *Fulfillingness' First Finale*
1975	Captain and Tennille 'Love Will Keep Us Together'	Paul Simon *Still Crazy After All These Years*
1976	George Benson 'This Masquerade'	Stevie Wonder *Songs in the Key of Life*
1977	Eagles 'Hotel California'	Fleetwood Mac *Rumours*
1978	Billy Joel 'Just the Way You Are'	Bee Gees *Saturday Night Fever*
1979	The Doobie Brothers 'What a Fool Believes'	Billy Joel *52nd Street*
1980	Christopher Cross 'Sailing'	Christopher Cross *Christopher Cross*
1981	Kim Carnes 'Bette Davis Eyes'	John Lennon, Yoko Ono *Double Fantasy*
1982	Toto 'Rosanna'	Toto *Toto IV*
1983	Michael Jackson 'Beat It'	Michael Jackson *Thriller*
1984	Tina Turner 'What's Love Got to Do with It'	Lionel Richie *Can't Slow Down*
1985	USA for Africa 'We Are the World'	Phil Collins *No Jacket Required*
1986	Steve Winwood 'Higher Love'	Paul Simon *Graceland*
1987	Paul Simon 'Graceland'	U2 *The Joshua Tree*
1988	Bobby McFerrin 'Don't Worry, Be Happy'	George Michael *Faith*
1989	Bette Midler 'Wind Beneath My Wings'	Bonnie Raitt *Nick of Time*
1990	Phil Collins 'Another Day in Paradise'	Quincy Jones *Back on the Block*
1991	Natalie Cole with Nat 'King' Cole 'Unforgettable'	Natalie Cole with Nat 'King' Cole *Unforgettable*
1992	Eric Clapton 'Tears in Heaven'	Eric Clapton *Unplugged*
1993	Whitney Houston 'I Will Always Love You'	Whitney Houston *The Bodyguard*
1994	Sheryl Crow 'All I Wanna Do'	Tony Bennett *MTV Unplugged*
1995	Seal 'Kiss From a Rose'	Alanis Morissette *Jagged Little Pill*
1996	Eric Clapton 'Change the World'	Celine Dion *Falling into You*
1997	Shawn Colvin 'Sunny Came Home'	Bob Dylan *Time Out of Mind*
1998	Celine Dion 'My Heart Will Go On'	Lauryn Hill *The Miseducation of Lauryn Hill*
1999	Santana, featuring Rob Thomas 'Smooth'	Santana *Supernatural*
2000	U2 'Beautiful Day'	Steely Dan *Two Against Nature*
2001	U2 'Walk On'	Various *O Brother, Where Art Thou?*
2002	Norah Jones 'Don't Know Why'	Norah Jones *Come Away With Me*
2003	Coldplay 'Clocks'	OutKast *Speakerboxxx / The Love Below*
2004	Ray Charles, Norah Jones 'Here We Go Again'	Ray Charles and others *Genius Loves Company*
2005	Green Day 'Boulevard of Broken Dreams'	U2 *How to Dismantle an Atomic Bomb*
2006	Dixie Chicks 'Not Ready to Make Nice'	Dixie Chicks *Taking the Long Way*
2007	Amy Winehouse 'Rehab'	Herbie Hancock *River: The Joni Letters*
2008	Robert Plant, Alison Krauss 'Please Read the Letter'	Alison Krauss, Robert Plant *Raising Sand*

Arts and Culture

Musical symbols, terms and abbreviations

Arts and Culture

■ Symbols

The staff or stave

staff/stave; additional ('leger') lines are added above or below as required

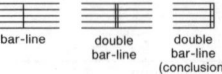

bar-line   double bar-line   double bar-line (conclusion)   brace, joining staves; read staves simultaneously

Clefs

These are in common use (the note Middle C is shown in each case):

treble (G) clef   bass (F) clef   alto or viola (C) clef   tenor (C) clef

In older music the C clef is found on any of the five lines of the staff.

Accidentals

♯	sharp, raising the pitch of a note by a semitone
𝄪	double sharp, raising the pitch of a note by two semitones
♭	flat, lowering the pitch of a note by a semitone
♭♭	double flat, lowering the pitch of a note by two semitones
♮	natural, cancelling the effect of a previous accidental

Note lengths

⊐ (or ⊏)	breve (double whole-note)
o	semibreve (whole-note)
d	minim (half-note)
	crotchet (quarter-note)
	quaver (eighth-note)
	semiquaver (1/16 note)
	demisemiquaver (1/32 note)
	hemidemisemiquaver (1/64 note)

chord: two or more notes sounded simultaneously

Ties (⌒, ⌣) are used to combine the lengths of two or more notes of the same pitch; dots are used to extend the length of a note by one-half, eg:

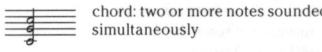

Beams are often used to group together quavers (eighth-notes) or shorter notes into larger units, eg:

Time signatures

The lower figure indicates the unit of measurement, the upper figure the number of these units in a bar, eg:

$\frac{2}{2}$ (or 𝄵)	two minims (half-notes) or their equivalent in a bar
$\frac{4}{4}$ (or 𝄴)	four crotchets (quarter-notes) or their equivalent in a bar
$\frac{3}{8}$	three quavers (eighth-notes) or their equivalent in a bar
$\frac{9}{16}$	nine semiquavers (1/16-notes) or their equivalent in a bar

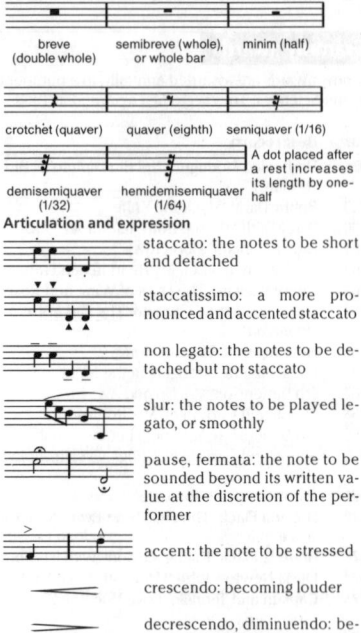

breve (double whole)   semibreve (whole), or whole bar   minim (half)

crotchet (quaver)   quaver (eighth)   semiquaver (1/16)

demisemiquaver (1/32)   hemidemisemiquaver (1/64)

A dot placed after a rest increases its length by one-half

Articulation and expression

staccato: the notes to be short and detached

staccatissimo: a more pronounced and accented staccato

non legato: the notes to be detached but not staccato

slur: the notes to be played legato, or smoothly

pause, fermata: the note to be sounded beyond its written value at the discretion of the performer

accent: the note to be stressed

crescendo: becoming louder

decrescendo, diminuendo: becoming quieter

♩ = 84   placed at the beginning of a piece or section, an indication of the tempo (eg 84 crotchet beats per minute); often preceded by 'MM' (Metronom Maelzel)

Ornaments

arpeggio: a chord whose notes are played one at a time in rapid (normally upward) succession rather than simultaneously

acciaccatura: a short grace note, that does not take any time from the note on which it leans

apoggiatura: an ornamental note, that is not essential to the melody but which leans on the following note, taking half its time from it

mordent ('lower' mordent): sounding approximately

pralltriller, inverted (or 'upper') mordent: sounding approximately

trill, shake: the rapid and continuous alternation of the written note and the note immediately above it

turn: sounding (depending on tempo and context) approximately

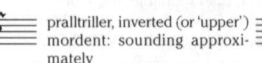

Key signatures
(Major keys: capital letters; minor keys: lower-case letters)

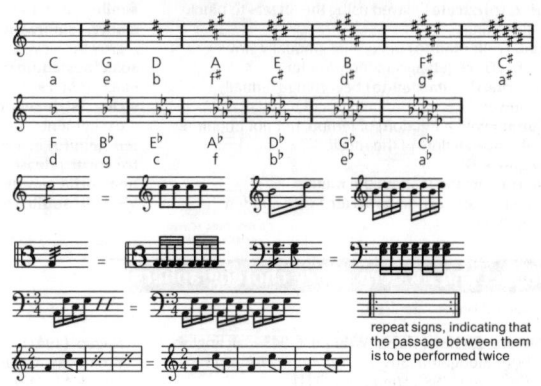

Repetition
In instrumental music repeated notes, figures and even whole sections are sometimes shown in abbreviated form, eg:

repeat signs, indicating that the passage between them is to be performed twice

Tempo and expression marks

Italian terms placed at the head of a piece or section to indicate its tempo and general expression have changed in meaning over the years and are rarely precise. The following list gives some indication of how the more common terms are generally understood today.

adagio slow
agitato agitated
allegro quick and lively
allegretto fairly quick and lively
andante 'going'; slow and steady
andantino a little quicker than andante
animato animated, lively
appasionato impassioned
assai 'very' (**allegro assai** very fast)
brio 'spirit', 'fire' (**allegro con brio** fast and energetic)
cantabile flowing and melodious
dolente sadly
energico energetic, vigorous
espressivo expressive
feroce fierce
fuoco 'fire' (**con fuoco** with fire)
furioso furious

giocoso lively or humorous
grave slow, solemn
grazioso graceful
larghetto fairly slow
largo slow and dignified
legato smooth and flowing
leggiero light
lento slow
maestoso majestic
marciale in the style of a march
marziale in a military style
meno 'less'(**meno mosso** slower)
moderato moderate, at a moderate pace
molto 'much', 'very' (**molto lento** very slow)
moto 'motion' (**con moto** quickly)
pesante heavy, ponderous
piacevole pleasant or playful
più 'more' (**più mosso** faster)

poco 'little' (**poco adagio** rather slowly)
prestissimo faster than **presto**
presto very fast
quasi 'as if', 'almost' (**andante, quasi allegretto**)
risoluto with emphasis, boldly
scherzando playful
semplice simple, in an unforced style
sotto voce very softly
strepitoso loud, noisy, boisterous
tanto, troppo 'so much', 'too much' (**allegro non tanto** fast but not very fast; **lento ma non troppo** slow, but not becoming too slow)
veloce with great rapidity
vivace lively
vivo vigorous, brisk

Other terms and abbreviations

This section lists symbols and terms that might be found in a musical score.

a tempo in time (ie revert to the previous or original tempo)
accel. (accelerando) with increasing speed
alla breve played quickly with two beats to the bar instead of four
allarg. (allargando) slowing
arco with the bow
cal. (calando) dying away
colla voce 'with the voice'; follow closely the singer's tempo
col legno 'with the wood'; play a string instrument with the stick of the bow
con sordino with the mute
cres. (crescendo) becoming louder
DC, da capo (al fine) go back to the beginning of the piece or movement (and play to the end marked **Fine**)
decresc. (decrescendo) becoming quieter
dim. (diminuendo) becoming quieter
dol (dolce) gently or sweetly

DS, dal segno go back to the sign
f (forte) loud; **ff (fortissimo)**, **fff** increasing degrees of loudness
Fine ▶DC
fz (forzato) with sudden emphasis
gliss. (glissando) slide quickly from one note to another
GP 'general pause'; a rest for the whole ensemble
MM metronom Maelzel
marc. (marcato) emphatic, accented
mf (mezzo forte) moderately loud
mp (mezzo piano) moderately quiet
ossia 'or', 'alternatively'
ottava, 8va, 8 play a passage an octave higher or lower; **coll ottava, col 8va, col 8** play the written notes together with their octaves
p (piano) quiet, soft; **pp (pianissimo)**, **ppp** increasing (but imprecise) degrees of softness
ped. depress the sustaining (loud) pedal on a piano, release indicated by *

Arts and Culture

pizz. (pizzicato) played using the fingers to pluck the strings

rall. (rallentando) becoming gradually slower

rinf., rfz, rf getting suddenly louder

rit., ritard. (ritardando) becoming gradually slower

rubato with a freedom of tempo, but not impairing the overall flow of the music

segno ▶ DS

senza sordino without the mute

sf., sfz., (sforzando, sforzato) with sudden emphasis

simile play in the same manner as before

smorz. (smorzando) gradually fading away, growing slower and softer

sost. (sostenuto) steady and sustained

stacc. (staccato) short and abrupt

string. (stringendo) with increasing speed and excitement

ten (tenuto) in a sustained manner

tre corde release the soft pedal on the piano

una corda play using the soft pedal on the piano

VS (volti subito) turn the page quickly

Ballet and modern dance choreographers

Selected ballets are listed.

Alston, Richard John William (1948–) English, born Stoughton, Sussex; *Rumours, Visions* (1969), *Red Run* (1998), *Shimmer* (2004).

Ashton, Sir Frederick William Mallandaine (1904–88) English, born Guayaquil, Ecuador; *Façade* (1931), *Les Rendezvous* (1933), *Cinderella* (1948), *Daphnis and Chloe* (1951), *Ondine* (1958), *The Two Pigeons* (1961), *The Dream* (1964), *Rhapsody* (1980).

Balanchine, George (Georgi Balanchivadze) (1904–83) Russian–American, born St Petersburg; *Apollo* (1928), *The Prodigal Son* (1929), *Bourrée Fantasque* (1949), *Jeu de cartes* (1937), *Agon* (1957), *The Seven Deadly Sins* (1958), *Davidsbündlertänze* (1980).

Béjart, Maurice (Maurice Jean Berger) (1927–2007) French, born Marseilles; *The Firebird* (1970), *Notre Faust* (1975), *Choreographic Offering* (1971), *Kabuki* (1986), *MutationX* (1998).

Bourne, Matthew (1960–) English, born London; *Overlap Lovers* (1987), *Swan Lake* (all male production, 1995), *Car Man* (2000), *Play Without Words* (2002), *Edward Scissorhands* (2006).

Bournonville, August (1805–79) Danish, born Copenhagen; *La Sylphide* (1836), *Napoli* (1842), *La Ventana* (1854).

Bruce, Christopher (1945–) English, born Leicester; *Ancient Voices of Children* (1975), *Ghost Dances* (1981), *Swansong* (1987), *Four Scenes* (1998).

Childs, Lucinda (1940–) American, born New York City; *Einstein on the Beach* (1976), *Relative Calm* (1981), *Available Light* (1983), *Premier Orange* (1984), *Rhythm Plus* (1991), *One and One* (1992), *Ten Part Suite* (2005).

Cranko, John (1927–73) South African, born Rustenburg; *Beauty and the Beast* (1949), *Pineapple Doll* (1951), *The Prince of the Pagodas* (1957), *Jeu de Cartes* (1965), *Onegin* (1965), *Taming of the Shrew* (1969), *Traces* (1973).

Cunningham, Merce (1919–2009) American, born Centralia, Washington; *Suite for Five* (1956), *Antic Meet* (1958), *Aeon* (1961), *Scramble* (1967), *Duets* (1980), *Loosestrife* (1991), *Occasion Piece* (1999), *Split Sides* (2003).

Darrell, Peter (1929–87) English, born Richmond, Surrey; *A Wedding Present* (1962), *Beauty and the Beast* (1969), *Tales of Hoffmann* (1972), *Swan Lake* (1977).

Davies, Siobhan (Susan Davies) (1950–) English, born London; *New Galileo* (1984), *Bridge the Distance* (1985), *Different Trains* (1990), *Winnsboro Cotton Mill Blues* (1992), *Plants and Ghosts* (2002), *Bird Song* (2004).

de Mille, Agnes George (1905–93) American, born New York City; *Three Virgins and a Devil* (1941), *Rodeo* (1942), *Fall River Legend* (1948), and for Broadway, *Oklahoma!* (1943), *Gentlemen Prefer Blondes* (1949).

de Valois, Dame Ninette (Edris Stannus) (1898–2001) Irish, born Baltiboys, County Wicklow; *Job* (1931), *La Création du monde* (1931), *The Rake's Progress* (1935), *Checkmate* (1937), *Don Quixote* (1950).

Diaghilev, Sergei Pavlovich (1872–1929) Russian, born Selistchev barracks, province of Novgorod; producer, impressario, and founder of Ballet Russes; not a choreographer himself, he fostered the talents of Balanchine, Fokine, Nijinsky.

Fokine, Michel (Mikhail Mikhaylovich Fokine) (1880–1942) Russian–American dancer and choreographer, born St Petersburg; *Les Sylphides* (1907), *Petroushka* (1911).

Graham, Martha (1894–1991) American, born Pittsburgh; *Lamentation* (1930), *Frontier* (1935), *Appalachian Spring* (1958).

Ivanov, Lev (Ivanovich) (1834–1901) Russian, born Moscow; *The Enchanted Forest* (1887), *The Nutcracker* (1892), *Swan Lake* (with Petipa, 1895).

Jooss, Kurt (1901–79) German, born Wasseralfingen; *Petrushka* (1930), *The Green Table* (1932), *Pulcinella* (1932), *The Mirror* (1935).

Limón, José (1908–72) American, born Culiacan, Mexico; *La Malinche* (1949), *The Moor's Pavane* (1949), *The Traitor* (1954), *Miss Brevis* (1958), *Carlotta* (1972).

Loring, Eugene (1914–82) American, born Milwaukee; *Yankee Clipper* (1937), *Billy the Kid* (1938).

Macmillan, Sir Kenneth (1929–92) Scottish, born Dunfermline, Fife; *The Rite of Spring* (1962), *Romeo and Juliet* (1965), *Anastasia* (1971), *The Four Seasons* (1975), *Mayerling* (1978), *Isadora* (1981).

Massine, Léonide (Fedorovich) (1895–1979) Russian–American, born Moscow; *Parade* (1917), *La Boutique Fantasque* (1919), *The Three-Cornered Hat* (1919), *Bachanale* (1939).

Morris, Mark (William) (1956–) American, born Seattle, Washington; *L'Allegro, il Penseroso ed il Moderato* (1988), *Dido and Aeneas* (1989), *The Hard Nut* (1991), *Resurrection* (2002), *Rock of Ages* (2004), *Up and Down* (2006).

Nijinska, Bronislova (Fominitshna) (1891–1972) Russian–Polish–American, born Minsk, Russia; *Le Renard* (1922), *Les Noces* (1923, 1966), *Les Biches* (1924, 1964), *La Valse* (1929), *The Snow Maiden* (1942).

Nikolais, Alwin (1910–93) American, born Southington, Connecticut; *Noumenon* (1953), *Kaleidoscope* (1956), *Imago* (1963), *Sanctum* (1964), *Gallery* (1978), *Schema* (1980), *Arc-en-Ciel* (1987).

Perrot, Jules (Joseph) (1810–92) French, born Lyons; *Ondine* (1843), *Les Éléments* (1847), *Faust* (1848), *Markobomba* (1854).

Petipa, Marius (1818–1910) French, born Marseilles; *Pharoah's Daughter* (1862), *La Bayadère* (1877), *The Sleeping Beauty* (1890), *Cinderella* (1893), *Swan Lake* (1895), *Raymonda* (1898).

Petit, Roland (1924–) French, born Paris; *Le Rossignol et la rose* (1944), *Les Forains* (1945), *Le Jeune homme et la mort* (1946), *Nana* (1976), *Marcel Proust Remembered* (1980), *Clavigo* (1999).

Robbins, Jerome (Jerome Rabinowitz) (1918–98) American, born New York; *Fancy Free* (1944), *Interplay* (1945), *The Pied Piper* (1951), *Afternoon of a Faun* (1953), *West Side Story* (1957, musical), and for Broadway, eg *The King and I* (1951).

St-Léon, Arthur (1821–70) French, born Paris; *Le Violon du diable* (1849), *La Fille mal gardée* (1866), *La Source* (1866), *Coppélia* (1870).

Tetley, Glen (1926–2007) American, born Cleveland, Ohio; *Pierrot lunaire* (1962), *Voluntaries* (1973), *The Tempest* (1979), *La Ronde* (1987), *Oracle* (1994).

Tharp, Twyla (1941–) American, born Portland, Indiana; *Eight Jelly Rolls* (1971), *Push Comes to Shove* (1976), *Hair* (1978, film), *The Catherine Wheel* (1983, film), *White Nights* (1985, film), *Jump Start* (1995), *Movin' Out* (2002, musical), *Even the King* (2003).

Tudor, Antony (William Cook) (1908–87) English, born London; *Undertow* (1945), *Lady of the Camellias* (1951), *Shadowplay* (1967), *The Tiller in the Field* (1978).

Ballets

Ballet	Composer	Choreographer	First performance
Anastasia	Tchaikovsky, Martinu	Macmillan	1971
Apollon Musagète	Stravinsky	Bolm	1928
Appalachian Spring	Copland	Graham	1944
L'Après-midi d'un faune	Debussy	Nijinsky	1912
La Bayadère	Minkus	Petipa	1877
Les Biches	Poulenc	Nijinska	1924
Billy the Kid	Copland	Loring	1938
Bolero	Ravel	Béjart	1961
La Boutique Fantasque	Rossini, arr. Respighi	Massine	1919
The Burrow	Martin	Macmillan	1958
Cain and Abel	Panufnik	Macmillan	1968
Carmen	Bizet	Petit	1949
Le Chant du rossignol	Stravinsky	Massine	1920
Checkmate	Bliss	de Valois	1937
Cinderella	Prokofiev	Ashton	1948
Concerto Barocco	Bach	Balanchine	1940
Coppélia	Delibes	St Léon	1870
Don Quixote	Minkus	Petipa	1869
Duo Concertant	Stravinsky	Balanchine	1972
Ebony Concerto	Stravinsky	Carter	1957
Elite Syncopations	Joplin	Macmillan	1974
Enigma Variations	Elgar	Ashton	1968
Façade	Walton	Ashton	1931
Fall River Legend	Gould	de Mille	1948
Fancy Free	Bernstein	Robbins	1944
La Fille mal gardée	Various (French popular songs and airs)	Dauberval	1789
The Firebird	Stravinsky	Fokine	1910
The Four Seasons	Verdi	Macmillan	1975
The Four Temperaments	Hindemith	Balanchine	1946
Giselle	Adam	Coralli and Perro (later revised by Petipa)	1841
The Gods Go A-Begging	Handel	Balanchine	1928
Hamlet	Tchaikovsky	Helpmann	1942
Harlequinade	Drigo	Balanchine	1965
Las Hermanas	Martin	Macmillan	1963
Illumination	Britten	Ashton	1950
The Invitation	Seiber	Macmillan	1960
Isadora	Rodney Bennett	Macmillan	1981
Ivan the Terrible	Prokofiev, arr. Chulaki	Grigorovich	1975
Jeu de cartes	Stravinsky	Balanchine	1937
Le Jeune homme et la mort	Bach	Petit	1946
The Judas Tree	Elias	Macmillan	1992
Jewels	Fauré, Stravinsky and Tchaikovsky	Balanchine	1967
Knight Errant	Richard Strauss	Tudor	1968

Arts and Culture

Ballet	Composer	Choreographer	First performance
The Lady and the Fool	Verdi, arr. Mackerras	Cranko	1954
Lady of Shallot	Sibelius	Ashton	1931
Lament of the Waves	Masson	Ashton	1970
Legend of Joseph	Richard Strauss	Fokine	1914
Legend of Judith	Mordecai	Graham	1962
La Luna	Bach	Béjart	1991
Le Malade imaginaire	Rota	Béjart	1976
Manon	Massenet	Macmillan	1974
The Masques	Poulenc	Ashton	1933
Mathilde	Wagner	Béjart	1965
Mayerling	Liszt	Macmillan	1978
A Midsummer Night's Dream	Mendelssohn	Balanchine	1962
A Month in the Country	Chopin, arr. Lanchbery	Ashton	1976
Monumentum pro Gesualdo	Stravinsky	Balanchine	1960
The Moor's Pavane	Purcell	Limón	1949
Night Journey	Schuman	Graham	1947
Night Shadow	Rieti	Balanchine	1946
Les Noces	Stravinsky	Nijinska	1923
Nocturne	Delius	Ashton	1936
The Nutcracker	Tchaikovsky	Ivanov	1892
Ondine	Henze	Ashton	1958
Onegin	Tchaikovsky, arr. Stolze	Cranko	1965
Orpheus	Stravinsky	Balanchine	1948
Les Papillons	Schumann, arr. Tcherepnin	Fokine	1913
Parade	Satie	Massine	1917
Les Patineurs	Mayerbeer, arr. Lambert	Ashton	1937
Petroushka	Stravinsky	Fokine	1911
Pineapple Poll	Sullivan, orch. Mackerras	Cranko	1951
Present Histories	Schubert	Tuckett	1991
Prince Igor	Borodin	Fokine	1909
The Prince of the Pagodas	Britten	Cranko	1957
The Prodigal Son	Prokofiev	Balanchine	1929
The Rake's Progress	Gordon	de Valois	1935
Raymonda	Glazunov	Petipa	1898
Le Renard	Stravinsky	Nijinska	1922
Les Rendezvous	Auber, arr. Lambert	Ashton	1933
Requiem	Fauré	Macmillan	1976
Rhapsody	Rachmaninov	Ashton	1980
Rituals	Bartók	Macmillan	1975
Rodeo	Copland	de Mille	1942
Romeo and Juliet	Prokofiev	Lavrovsky	1940
Rooms	Hopkins	Sokolow	1955
Russian Soldier	Prokofiev	Fokine	1942
Les Saisons	Glazunov	Petipa	1900
Le Sacre du printemps (The Rite of Spring)	Stravinsky, Roerich	Nijinsky	1913
Scènes de ballet	Stravinsky	Dolin	1944
Schéhérazade	Rimsky-Korsakov	Fokine	1910
Scotch Symphony	Mendelssohn	Balanchine	1952
Serenade	Tchaikovsky	Balanchine	1934
The Seven Deadly Sins	Weill	Balanchine	1933
The Sleeping Beauty	Tchaikovsky	Petipa	1890
Song of the Earth	Mahler	Macmillan	1965
Spartacus	Khachaturian	Grigorovich	1968
Le Spectre de la Rose	Weber	Fokine	1911
Stoics Quartet	Mendelssohn	Burrows	1991
Summerspace	Feldman	Cunningham	1958
Swan Lake	Tchaikovsky	Petipa and Ivanov	1895
La Sylphide	Løvenskjold	Bournonville	1836
Les Sylphides (Chopiniana)	Chopin, variously orchestrated	Fokine	1909
Symphonic Variations	Franck	Ashton	1946
Symphonie fantastique	Berlioz	Massine	1936
Symphony in C	Bizet	Balanchine	1947
Symphony in Three Movements	Stravinsky	Blanchine	1972
Tales of Hoffman	Offenbach, arr. Lanchbery	Darrell	1973
The Taming of the Shrew	Scarlatti-Stolze	Cranko	1969

Ballet	Composer	Choreographer	First performance
The Three-Cornered Hat	de Falla	Massine	1919
Les Vainqueurs	Wagner, and Indian and Tibetan music	Béjart	1969
La Valse	Ravel	Nijinska	1929
Variations	Stravinsky	Balanchine	1966
La Ventana	Lumbye and Holm	Bournonville	1854
Voluntaries	Poulenc	Tetley	1973
The Walk to the Paradise Garden	Delius	Ashton	1972
A Wedding Bouquet	Berners	Ashton	1937

Ballet and modern dancers

Ashley, Merrill (Linda Michelle Merrill) (1950–) American, born St Paul, Minnesota.

Baker, Josephine (Freda Josephine McDonald) (1906–75) American, born St Louis, Missouri.

Baryshnikov, Mikhail (Nikolaievich) (1948–) Russian, born Riga.

Bausch, Pina (1940–) German, born Solingen.

Bessmertnova, Natalia (1941–2008) Russian, born Moscow.

Bujones, Fernando (1955–2005) American, born Florida.

Bull, Deborah (Clare) (1963–) English, born Derby.

Bussell, Darcey (Andrea) (1969–) English, born London.

Camargo, Maria Anna de (1710–70) French, born Brussels.

Carlson, Carolyn (1943–) American, born California.

Chauviré, Yvette (1917–) French, born Paris.

Clark, Michael (1962–) Scottish, born Kintore, near Aberdeen.

Danilova, Alexandra (Dionysievna) (1903–97) Russian–American, born Peterhof.

De Keersmaeker, Anne Teresa (1960–) Belgian, born Mechelen.

Dolin, Sir Anton (Sydney Francis Patrick Chippendall Healey-Kay) (1904–83) English, born Slinfold, Sussex.

Dowell, Sir Anthony (1943–) English, born London.

Duncan, Isadora (1878–1927) American, born San Francisco.

Dunham, Katherine (1909–2006) American, born Chicago.

Dunn, Douglas (1942–) American, born Palo Alto, California.

Dupond, Patrick (1959–) French, born Paris.

Eglevsky, André (1917–77) Russian–American, born Moscow.

Elssler, Fanny (Franziska Elssler) (1810–84) Austrian, born Gumpendorf.

Farrell, Suzanne (1945–) American, born Cincinnati, Ohio.

Fonteyn, Dame Margot (Peggy Hookham) (1919–91) English, born Reigate, Surrey.

Fracci, Carla (1936–) Italian, born Milan.

Genée, Dame Adeline (Anina Jensen) (1878–1970) Danish, born Hinnerup.

Gilpin, John (1930–83) English, born Southsea.

Gore, Walter (1910–79) Scottish, born Waterside.

Gorsky, Alexander Alexeivich (1871–1924) Russian, born St Petersburg.

Gregory, Cynthia (1946–) American, born Los Angeles.

Grey, Dame Beryl (Beryl Svenson) (1927–) English, born London.

Grisi, Carlotta (1819–99) Italian, born Visinada.

Hamilton, Gordon (1918–59) Australian, born Sydney.

Haydée, Marcia (Marcia Haydee Salaverry Pereira de Silva) (1939–) Brazilian, born Niteroi.

Helpmann, Sir Robert (1909–86) Australian, born Mount Gambier.

Jasinski, (Czeslaw) Roman (1907–91) Polish–American, born Warsaw.

Kain, Karen (1951–) Canadian, born Hamilton, Ontario.

Karsavina, Tamara Platonovna (1885–1978) Russian–British, born St Petersburg.

Kaye, Nora (Nora Koreff) (1920–87) American, born New York.

Kent, Allegra (1937–) American, born Los Angeles.

Kirkland, Gelsey (1952–) American, born Bethlehem, Pennsylvania.

Lichine, David (David Lichenstein) (1910–72) Russian–American, born Rostov-na-Donu.

Makarova, Natalia (1940–) Russian, born St Petersburg.

Markova, Dame Alicia (Lilian Alicia Marks) (1910–2004) English, born London.

Martins, Peter (1946–) Danish, born Copenhagen.

Mauri, Rosita (1849–1923) Spanish, born Tarragona.

Neary, Patricia (1942–) American, born Miami, Florida.

Nemchinova, Vera (Nicolayevna) (1899–1984) Russian, born Moscow.

Nijinsky, Vaslav Fomich (1889–1950) Russian, born Kiev.

Nureyev, Rudolf Hametovich (1938–93) Russian–British, born on a train between Lake Baikal and Irkutsk, Siberia.

Page, Ruth (1899–1991) American, born Indianapolis.

Panov, Valery (Matvevich) (1938–) Russian, born Vitebsk.

Panova, Galina (1949–) Russian, born Archangel.

Petipa, Lucien (1815–98) French, born Marseilles.

Petipa, Marie (Mariusovna II) (1857–1930) Russian, born St Petersburg.

Petronio, Stephen (1956–) American, born Nutley, New Jersey.

Plisetskaya, Maya Mikailovna (1925–) Russian, born Moscow.

Rambert, Dame Marie (Cyvia Rambam, then Miriam Ramberg) (1888–1982) Polish–British, born Warsaw.

Riabouchinska, Tatiana (1917–2000) Russian–American, born Moscow.

Rubinstein, Ida Lvovna (1885–1960) Russian, born

St Petersburg.

Seymour, Lynn (Lynn Springbett) (1939–)
Canadian, born Wainwright.

Shearer, Moira (Moira King) (1926–2006) Scottish,
born Dunfermline.

Shearer, Sybil (1912–2005) American, born Toronto.

Sibley, Dame Antoinette (1939–) English, born
Bromley.

Sleep, Wayne (1948–) English, born Plymouth.

Somes, Michael (1917–94) British, born Horsley.

Spessivtseva, Olga Alexandrovna (1895–1991)
Russian–American, born Rostov.

Taglioni, Marie (1804–84) Swedish–Italian, born
Stockholm.

Tallchief, Maria (1925–) American, born Fairfax,
Oklahoma.

Trefilova, Vera Alexandrovna (1875–1943) Russian,
born St Petersburg.

Ulanova, Galina (Sergeyevna) (1910–98) Russian,
born St Petersburg.

Villella, Edward (1936–) American, born
Bayside, New York.

Ballet and modern dance companies

Name	Date founded	Location
Alvin Ailey American Dance Theater	1958	New York
American Ballet Theater	1940	New York
Australian Ballet	1962	Melbourne
Australian Dance Theatre	1965	Adelaide
Ballet Gulbenkian	1965	Lisbon
Ballet Jooss	1933	Cambridge
Ballet Rambert	1926	London
Ballet Russe de Monte Carlo	1938	Monte Carlo
Ballets des Champs Élysées	1944	Paris
Ballets de Paris	1948	France
Ballets Russes de Sergei Diaghilev (now Kirov Ballet)	1909–29	Paris and St Petersburg
Ballets Trockadero de Monte Carlos	1974	New York
Ballet-Théâtre Contemporain	1968	Amiens
Ballet West	1963	Salt Lake City, Utah
Béjart Ballet Lausanne (formerly Ballet du XXe siècle, 1960)	1987	Lausanne
Birmingham Royal Ballet (formerly Sadler's Wells Royal Ballet)	1946	Birmingham
Bolshoi Ballet	1776	Moscow
Borovansky Ballet	1942	Melbourne
Boston Ballet	1963	Boston, USA
Central Ballet of China	1959	Beijing
Cholmondeleys, The	1984	London
City Ballet of London	1996	London
Dance Theater of Harlem	1961	New York
Dutch National Ballet	1986	Amsterdam
DV8 Physical Theatre	1986	London
English National Ballet (formerly London Festival Ballet)	1950	London
Feld Ballet NY	1974	New York
Grands Ballets Canadiens de Montreal	1957	Montreal
Hong Kong Ballet	1979	Hong Kong
Houston Ballet	1968	Houston
Joffrey Ballet of Chicago (formerly Joffrey Ballet)	1956	Chicago
José Limón Dance Company	1946	New York
Kirov Ballet	1935	St Petersburg
Lar Lubovitch Dance Company	1968	New York
London Festival Ballet (originally Festival Ballet)	1949	London
Maly Ballet	1915	St Petersburg
Mark Morris Dance Group	1980	New York
Martha Graham Dance Company	1927	New York
Merce Cunningham Dance Company	1953	New York
Miami City Ballet	1986	Miami
Murray Louis and Nikolais Dance Company	1989	New York
National Ballet	1948	Maryland
National Ballet of Canada	1951	Toronto
National Ballet of Cuba (formerly Ballet Alicia Alonso, 1948)	1959	Havana
National Ballet of Mexico	1949	Mexico City
Netherland Dance Theatre	1959	The Hague
New York City Ballet	1948	New York
Northern Ballet Theatre (formerly Northern Dance Theatre, based in Manchester)	1969	Leeds
Paris Opéra Ballet	1669	Paris

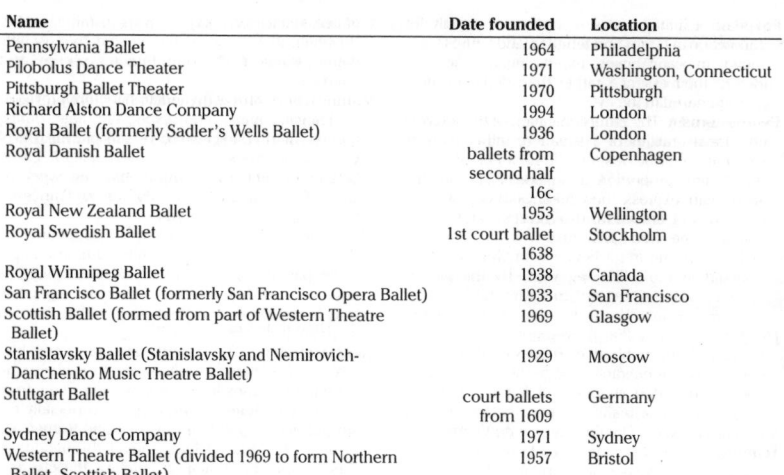

Name	Date founded	Location
Pennsylvania Ballet	1964	Philadelphia
Pilobolus Dance Theater	1971	Washington, Connecticut
Pittsburgh Ballet Theater	1970	Pittsburgh
Richard Alston Dance Company	1994	London
Royal Ballet (formerly Sadler's Wells Ballet)	1936	London
Royal Danish Ballet	ballets from second half 16c	Copenhagen
Royal New Zealand Ballet	1953	Wellington
Royal Swedish Ballet	1st court ballet 1638	Stockholm
Royal Winnipeg Ballet	1938	Canada
San Francisco Ballet (formerly San Francisco Opera Ballet)	1933	San Francisco
Scottish Ballet (formed from part of Western Theatre Ballet)	1969	Glasgow
Stanislavsky Ballet (Stanislavsky and Nemirovich-Danchenko Music Theatre Ballet)	1929	Moscow
Stuttgart Ballet	court ballets from 1609	Germany
Sydney Dance Company	1971	Sydney
Western Theatre Ballet (divided 1969 to form Northern Ballet, Scottish Ballet)	1957	Bristol

Arts and Culture

Major painting styles

Abstract Art A non-representational 20c style developed as a means of expressing inner reality in pictorial form. Some abstract pictures bear no resemblance to reality, whereas others feature a highly subjective treatment or 'abstraction' of recognizable subjects (as in Cubism). The earliest consciously abstract paintings were by Wassily Kandinsky (1910) and Frantisek Kupka (*Amorpha: Fugue in Two Colours*, 1912), both inspired by music, the universal abstract language. Abstract art led to other movements such as Neo-Plasticism, Constructivism and American Abstract Expressionism.

Abstract Expressionism A term relating to the vivid, non-representational work of a group of artists in 1940s New York, who were united by their emphasis on the expression inherent in the texture and colour of the paint itself, and the interaction of artist, paint and canvas; eg work by Mark Rothko, Arshile Gorky, Franz Kline, Jackson Pollock.

Action Painting A form of Abstract Expressionism; the technique of creating a picture that emphasizes the physical process of painting eg by throwing, splashing, dribbling or pouring on the paint. Its early exponents included Jackson Pollock, who also used knives on his canvases, dragged things across them and rode a bicycle on them, and Willem de Kooning.

Baroque An extravagant, confident and highly decorative style (c.1600–1720) which inherited movement from Mannerism and a sense of grandeur and solidity from High Renaissance. It was associated with the reinvigorated Catholic Church in Europe and often expressed intense religious emotion. In secular art, such as that commissioned by Louis XIV for Versailles, it served to express the glory of royalty; eg work by Rubens.

Buddhist Buddhism (founded 6c BC, India's national religion 3c BC), coupled with the patronage of such rulers as the Mauryan emperor Asoka and the Kushan ruler Kanishka, had a major influence on Indian art and architecture. From 1c AD Buddha, previously represented by the lotus flower, a wheel, or by his throne, could be shown in human form, which gave rise to many highly ornate statues.

Constructivism A term usually applied to a form of abstract art that began in Russia c.1917, using machine-age materials such as steel, glass and plastic. Leading practitioners included Vladimir Tatlin, and the brothers Antoine Pevsner and Naum Gabo. In Russia this impetus was channelled into industrial design (Soviet Constructivism). Pevsner and Gabo left Russia in the early 1920s, and their ideas subsequently influenced abstract artists in the West (International Constructivism).

Cubism A radical movement founded 1908 by Georges Braque and Pablo Picasso which revolutionized European painting and sculpture and continued in its purest form until the 1920s. Objects were no longer depicted from a single, fixed viewpoint, but were broken up into a multiplicity of facets, so that several different aspects of an object could be seen simultaneously; eg also work by Juan Gris, Fernand Léger, Stuart Davis.

Dada and **Surrealism** Two important, closely related movements in Europe and America. Both were pointedly anti-rationalist, laying emphasis on incongruous or shocking effects, but a key difference was that Dada (1916–22), arising from the mood of despair following World War I, was predominantly nihilistic, while Surrealism (1924–c.1940), which aimed to release and explore the creative powers of the subconscious mind using dreamlike effects, was much more positive in spirit; eg work by Ernst, Duchamp, Man Ray, Schwitters (Dada); Dalí, Magritte (Surrealism).

Dutch Art, 17c The golden age in Dutch art (c.1609–70) began when the Netherlands gained its freedom from Spain; its subjects tended to celebrate the country's hard-won peace and prosperity, eg seascapes, landscapes, portraits of successful merchants, domestic scenes and still lifes. There was little religious art because of the Protestant ethos; eg work by Frans Hals, Vermeer, Rembrandt.

Arts and Culture

Egyptian Painting and sculpture were mainly for decoration of tombs and temples, and figures were shown in static poses, expressing a schematic idea of their essence rather than depicting how they appeared to the eye.

Expressionism The communication of the internal emotional realities of a situation, rather than its external 'realistic' aspect. Traditional ideas of beauty and proportion are disregarded, so that artists can express their feelings more strongly by means of distortion, exaggeration and jarring colours. The term was first used in Germany in 1911, but the trend began with Van Gogh and Gauguin in the 1880s; eg work by the groups known as *Die Brücke* (incl Ernst Kirchner) and *Der Blaue Reiter* (incl Wassily Kandinsky) in Germany.

Fauvism An early 20c movement by a group of French painters dubbed *les Fauves* ('wild beasts'). Their work was characterized by the use of brilliant colours, distorted shapes and flat composition, without regard to realism or perspective; eg work by Matisse, André Derain, Maurice de Vlaminck.

Feminist Art Art not simply made by women, but exploring issues specifically relating to women's identity and experience. The movement began in the 1960s and involved reviving the reputations of neglected women artists of the past as well as promoting the work of contemporary women artists; eg Judy Chicago, Miriam Schapiro.

Gothic A style of Christian art (12–16c) characterized by stylized figures wearing flowing garments.

Greek Greek painters and sculptors were the first to master naturalistic depiction of the human body. Most of the surviving painting is on vases or wall fragments. Greek art is broken down into four periods: Geometric (9c–8c BC, named after a style of vase decoration); Archaic (700–480 BC); Classical (480–323 BC, when Greek art reached its greatest harmony and majesty); and Hellenistic (323–27 BC).

High Renaissance The period c.1490–1520 in Rome, Florence and Venice, during which the ideals of the Renaissance are thought to have been given most complete expression in art; eg work by Leonardo da Vinci, Michelangelo, Raphael, Titian, Andrea del Sarto.

Impressionism A style which aims to give a general impression of feelings and events rather than a formal or structural treatment of them. It was born in 1874 when a number of French artists who had difficulty in having their work accepted for the official Paris Salon organized their own group exhibition. Impressionist pictures are typically bright and cheerful, depicting contemporary life in a fresh and immediate way, and conveying the impression of a scene without minute detail; eg work by Monet, Manet, Pissarro, Renoir, Sisley, Degas, Cassatt.

International Gothic A style of art which flourished in W Europe (c.1375–c.1425), characterized by jewel-like colour, graceful shapes and realistic details. The style was seen especially in miniature paintings, drawings, and tapestries, often representing secular themes from courtly life.

Islamic Despite vast regional variations, there is an underlying unity in Islamic art, which reflects the main features of Islam (founded 7c AD): Mecca and the ornate niche in every mosque showing its direction; mosques; minarets, from which the faithful are called to prayer; and domes, symbolizing the heavens. Islamic theology forbids representation of the human figure in religious art, so decoration is abstract, eg complex geometrical patterns incorporating flowing Arabic script. However, in secular art illuminated manuscripts were produced showing hunting scenes and courtly life.

Mannerism A form of art and architecture prevalent in France, Spain, and especially Italy during the 16c. It is characterized by the playful use of Classical elements and *trompe l'oeil* effects in bizarre or dramatic compositions; eg work by Giulio Romano, Jacopa da Pontormo, Francesco Parmigianino, Giambologna.

Medieval The Middle Ages were dominated by Romanesque and Gothic architecture, and large-scale painting and sculpture existed mainly as adjuncts to these styles. Otherwise, painting mainly appeared as stained glass, which reached its zenith in 12c France.

Neoclassicism A movement (late 18c–early 19c) which arose partly as a reaction to Rococo and Baroque excesses in decoration, and partly from a renewed interest in the antique, especially the simplicity and grandeur of Greek and Roman art. Centred in Rome, it later spread throughout W Europe and N America. In painting, the classical themes and subjects were powerfully and dramatically represented in works by Jacques Louis David (eg *The Oath of the Horatii*, 1784).

Neo-Expressionism A term used to describe an international representational style which arose in the late 1970s. Works are sometimes abstract, sometimes figurative and sometimes bordering between the two, but are usually large in scale and tend to go to extremes of aggressive rawness in technique and feeling. They are characterized by a theatrical, melodramatic flavour conveyed by strong brushstrokes and colours, and distorted shapes; eg work by Julian Schnabel, Anselm Kiefer.

Neo-Plasticism A style of abstract painting in which geometrical patterns are formed of patches of pure flat colour enclosed by intersecting vertical and horizontal lines. It encompasses the 1920s style and theories of Dutch painter and theosophist Piet Mondrian, who tried to express an ideal of universal harmony in his austerely geometrical works.

Pop Art A modern art form based on the commonplace and ephemeral aspects of 20c urban life, such as soup cans, comics, movies and advertising. Pioneer British Pop Artists in the mid-1950s include Peter Blake, Eduardo Paolozzi, Richard Hamilton; leading American contributors in the 1960s included Jasper Johns, Andy Warhol, Roy Lichtenstein.

Post-Impressionism An umbrella term (coined 1910 by Roger Fry) for a number of trends in French painting that developed in the wake of Impressionism c.1880–1905. Its features included focus on structure and renewed importance of the subject; the decorative and symbolic, rather than naturalistic, use of colour and line; and emotional intensity conveyed by brilliant colour and swirling brushstrokes; eg work by Cézanne, Gauguin, Van Gogh.

Post-Modernism Most commonly an architectural or literary term, Post-Modernist refers to art works that blend disparate styles and make knowing use of cultural references, as in Pop Art.

Pre-Raphaelite A highly symbolic style characterizing the work of a group of mid-19c artists in London (the Pre-Raphaelite Brotherhood). Rejecting the formal academic art and neoclassicism prevalent at the time, they turned for inspiration to the brightly coloured work of Italian artists active before Raphael (1483–1520), and painted historical, literary and religious subjects with moral fervour, vivid colour, rich detail and elaborate symbolism; eg work by Holman Hunt, Dante Gabriel Rossetti, John Everett Millais.

Primitivism The result of the influence on modern artists of the art of the indigenous peoples of Africa, Oceania, and the Americas, which was seen to contain a sense of vitality and truth that had been polished out of western painting and sculpture; eg work by Ernst Kirchner, Modigliani, Picasso, Gauguin.

Realism A term which until the end of the 19c referred to naturalism, or the true-to-life depiction of subjects, eg late 16c work by Caravaggio. In France c.1840–80 it was a specific term relating to the depiction of unidealized subject-matter taken from everyday life, deliberately chosen to make a social or political point; eg work by Gustave Courbet and Honoré Daumier. In the late 20c, realism may refer simply to the move away from abstract art towards a more representational style, though it may also refer to the kind of abstract art that opposes superficial appearances and focuses on inner truth as 'reality'.

Renaissance A style prevalent in Europe (14–16c)

reflecting classical Greek and Roman styles. Little Roman painting had survived to be copied, but the ancient artists' fidelity to nature became a basic tenet of the Renaissance style; eg work by Masaccio (the first to master perspective), Albrecht Dürer, Pieter Brueghel.

Rococo A florid European style born in France (c.1700). Partly a development from Baroque art and partly a reaction against it, Rococo art is characterized by elaborate ornamental details and asymmetrical patterns, and was most successful as a style of interior decoration. Whereas Baroque art is sometimes sombre and often religious, it is much lighter (often intentionally playful) in spirit and usually secular. It flourished until the 1760s in France and the late 18c elsewhere; eg work by Watteau, Boucher and Fragonard.

Romanticism An intellectual trend (late 18c–mid-19c) that regarded the emotions and self-expression, rather than beauty of form or structure, as the basis of composition. Typical themes were wild or mysterious landscapes and dramatic scenes from literature; there was also interest in dreams and nightmares and in extremes of feelings and behaviour; eg work by Delacroix, Caspar David Friedrich, J M W Turner, Goya.

Artists

Selected paintings are listed.

Altdorfer, Albrecht (c.1480–1538) German, born Regensburg; *Danube Landscape* (1520), *Alexander's Victory* (1529).

Andrea del Sarto (Andrea d'Agnolo di Francesco) (1486–1530) Italian, born Florence; *Miracles of S Filippo Benizzi* (1509–10), *Madonna del Sacco* (1525).

Angelico, Fra (Guido di Pietro) (c.1400–55) Italian, born Vicchio, Tuscany; *Coronation of the Virgin* (1430–5), *San Marco altarpiece* (c.1440).

Auerbach, Frank (1931–) Anglo-German, born Berlin; *Mornington Crescent* (1967), *Jake* (1990), *Ruth* (2000).

Bacon, Francis (1909–92) British, born Dublin; *Three Figures at the Base of a Crucifixion* (1945), *Two Figures with a Monkey* (1973), *Triptych Inspired by the Oresteia of Aeschylus* (1981).

Banksy (date and place of birth uncertain) British; well-known graffiti artist; stencilled images and words on urban walls throughout the world.

Beardsley, Aubrey (Vincent) (1872–98) British, born Brighton; illustrations to Malory's *Morte d'Arthur* (1893), Wilde's *Salome* (1894).

Bell, Vanessa (1879–1961) British, born Kensington, London; *Still Life on Corner of a Mantlepiece* (1914).

Bellini, Gentile (c.1429–1507) Italian, born Venice; *Procession of the Relic of the True Cross* (1496), *Miracle at Ponte di Lorenzo* (1500).

Blackadder, Elizabeth (1931–) British, born Falkirk; *Interior with Self-Portrait* (1972), *White Anemones* (1983), *Texas Flame* (1986), *Still Life with Pagoda* (1998), *Irises* (2004).

Blake, Sir Peter (1932–) British, born Dartford, Kent; *On the Balcony* (1955–7), design for the Beatles' album *Sergeant Pepper's Lonely Hearts Club Band* (1967), *The Meeting* (1981); many screenprints.

Blake, William (1757–1827) British, born London; illustrations for his own *Songs of Innocence and Experience* (1794), *Newton* (1795), illustrations for the *Book of Job* (1826).

Böcklin, Arnold (1827–1901) Swiss, born Basel; *Pan in the Reeds* (1857), *The Island of the Dead* (1880).

Bomberg, David (1890–1957) British, born Birmingham; *In the Hold* (1913–14), *The Mud Bath* (1913–14).

Bonnard, Pierre (1867–1947) French, born Paris; *Young Woman in Lamplight* (1900), *Dining Room in the Country* (1913), *Seascape of the Mediterranean* (1941).

Bosch, Hieronymus (Jerome van Aken) (c.1450–1516) Dutch, born 's-Hertogenbosch, Brabant; *The Temptation of St Anthony*, *The Garden of Earthly Delights* (work undated).

Botticelli, Sandro (Alessandro di Mariano Filipepi) (1444–1510) Italian, born Florence; *Primavera* (c.1478), *The Birth of Venus* (c.1485), *Mystic Nativity* (1500).

Boucher, François (1703–70) French, born Paris; *Reclining Girl* (1751), *The Rising* and *The Setting of the Sun* (1753).

Braque, Georges (1882–1963) French, born Argenteuil-sur-Seine; *Still Life with Violin* (1910), *The Portuguese* (1911), *Blue Wash-Basin* (1942).

Brueghel, Pieter, (the Elder) (c.1525–69) Dutch, born Bruegel, near Breda; *Road to Calvary* (1564), *Massacre of the Innocents* (c.1566), *The Blind Leading the Blind* (1568), *The Peasant Wedding* (1568), *The Peasant Dance* (1568).

Burne-Jones, Sir Edward (Coley) (1833–98) British, born Birmingham; *The Beguiling of Merlin* (1874), *The Arming of Perseus* (1877), *King Cophetua and the Beggar Maid* (1883–4).

Burra, Edward (1905–76) British, born London; *Dancing Skeletons* (1934), *Soldiers* (1942), *Scene in Harlem (Simply Heavenly)* (1952).

Canaletto (Giovanni Antonio Canal) (1697–1768) Italian, born Venice; *Stone Mason's Yard* (c.1730).

Caravaggio (Michelangelo Merisi da Caravaggio) (1573–1610) Italian, born Caravaggio, near

Burgamo; *The Supper at Emmaus* (c.1598–1600), *Martyrdom of St Matthew* (1599–1600), *The Death of the Virgin* (1605–6).

Cassatt, Mary (1844–1926) American, born Pittsburgh, Pennsylvania; *The Blue Room* (1878), *Lady at the Tea Table* (1885), *Morning Toilette* (1886), *The Tramway* (1891), *The Bath* (1892).

Cézanne, Paul (1839–1906) French, born Aix-en-Provence; *The Black Marble Clock* (c.1869–70), *Maison du Pendu* (c.1873), *Bathing Women* (1900–5), *Le Jardinier* (1906).

Chagall, Marc (1887–1985) Russian–French, born Vitebsk; *The Musician* (1912–13), *Bouquet of Flying Lovers* (1947).

Chicago, Judy (Judy Gerowitz) (1939–) American, born Chicago; *The Dinner Party* (1974–9), *Holocaust Project* (1985–93).

Chirico, Giorgio de (1888–1978) Italian, born Volos, Greece; *Portrait of Guillaume Apollinaire* (1914), *The Jewish Angel* (1916), *The Return of Ulysses* (1968).

Christo (Christo Javacheff) (1935–) American, born Gabovra, Bulgaria, and **Jean-Claude** (Jean-Claude de Guillebon) (1935–) American, born Casablanca, Morocco; *Surrounded Islands* (1980–3), *Wrapped Reichstag* (1995), *The Gates* (2005).

Cimabue (Benciviene di Pepo) (c.1240–c.1302) Italian, born Florence; *Crucifix* (date unknown), *Saint John the Evangelist* (1302).

Claude Lorraine (in full **Claude Le Lorrain**) (Claude Gêllée) (1600–82) French, born near Nancy; *The Mill* (1631), *The Embarkation of St Ursula* (1641), *Ascanius Shooting the Stag of Silvia* (1682).

Constable, John (1776–1837) British, born East Bergholt, Suffolk; *A Country Lane* (c.1810), *The White Horse* (1819), *The Hay Wain* (1821), *Stonehenge* (1835).

Corot, Jean Baptiste Camille (1796–1875) French, born Paris; *Bridge at Narni* (1827), *Souvenir de Marcoussis* (1869), *Woman Reading in a Landscape* (1869).

Correggio (**Antonio Allegri da**) (c.1494–1534) Italian, born Correggio; *The Agony in the Garden* (c.1528).

Courbet, (Jean Désiré) Gustave (1819–77) French, born Ornans; *The After-Dinner at Ornans* (1848–9), *The Bathers* (1853), *The Painter's Studio* (1855), *The Stormy Sea* (1869).

Cranach, Lucas, (the Elder) (1472–1553) German, born Kronach, near Bamberg; *The Crucifixion* (1503), *The Fountain of Youth* (1550).

Dalí, Salvador (Felipe Jacinto) (1904–89) Spanish, born Figueras, Gerona; *The Persistence of Memory* (1931), *The Transformation of Narcissus* (1934), *Christ of St John of the Cross* (1951).

Daumier, Honoré (1808–78) French, born Marseilles; many caricatures and lithographs; *The Legislative Paunch* (1834), *The Third Class Carriage* (1840s), paintings on the theme of *Don Quixote*.

David, Jacques Louis (1748–1825) French, born Paris; *Death of Socrates* (1788), *The Death of Marat* (1793), *The Rape of the Sabines* (1799), *Madame Récamier* (1800).

Davis, Stuart (1894–1964) American, born Philadelphia; *The President* (1917), *House and Street* (1931), *Visa* (1951), *Premiere* (1957).

Degas, (Hilaire Germain) Edgar (1834–1917) French, born Paris; *Cotton-brokers Office* (1873), *L'Absinthe* (1875–6), *Little Fourteen-year-old Dancer* (sculpture) (1881), *Dancer at the Bar* (c.1900).

de Kooning, Willem (1904–97) American, born Rotterdam, the Netherlands; *Woman I–V* (1952–3),

Montauk Highway (1958), *Pastorale* (1963).

Delacroix, (Ferdinand Victor) Eugène (1798–1863) French, born St-Maurice-Charenton; *Dante and Virgil in Hell* (1822), *Liberty Guiding the People* (1831), *Jacob and the Angel* (1853–61).

Derain, André Louis (1880–1954) French, born Chatou; *Mountains at Collioure* (1905), *Westminster Bridge* (1907), *The Bagpiper* (1910–11).

Dix, Otto (1891–1969) German, born Gera-Unternhaus; *The Match Seller* (1920), *The War* (1924).

Doré, (Louis Auguste) Gustave (1832–83) French, born Strasbourg; illustrations to Dante's *Inferno* (1861), Milton's *Paradise Lost* (1866).

Duccio di Buoninsegna (c.1260–c.1320) Italian; *Maestà* (Siena Cathedral altarpiece) (1308–11).

Duchamp, (Henri Robert) Marcel (1887–1968) French–American, born Blainville, Normandy; *Nude Descending a Staircase* (1912), *The Bride Stripped Bare by Her Bachelors, Even* (1915–23).

Dufy, Raoul (1877–1953) French, born Le Havre; *Posters at Trouville* (1906), illustrations to Guillaume Apollinaire's *Bestiary* (1911), *Riders in the Wood* (1931).

Dürer, Albrecht (1471–1528) German, born Nuremberg; *Adam and Eve* (1507), *Adoration of the Magi* (1504), *Adoration of the Trinity* (1511).

Eardley, Joan (1921–63) British, born Warnham, Sussex; *Winter Sea IV* (1958), *Two Children* (1962).

Emin, Tracey (1964–) English, born London; *Everyone I Have Ever Slept With* (1995), *My Bed* (1998), *Top Spot* (film) (2004).

Ernst, Max(imillian) (1891–1976) German–American–French, born Brühl, near Cologne, Germany; *Europe After the Rain* (1940–2), *The Elephant Célébes* (1921), *Moonmad* (sculpture) (1944), *The King Playing with the Queen* (sculpture) (1959).

Escher, M(aurits) C(ornelis) (1898–1972) Dutch, born Leeuwarden; *Day and Night* (1938), *Convex and Concave* (1955).

Eyck, Jan van (c.1389–1441) Dutch, born Maaseyck, near Maastricht; *The Adoration of the Holy Lamb* (Ghent altarpiece) (1432), *Man in a Red Turban* (1433), *Arnolfini Marriage Portrait* (1434), *Madonna by the Fountain* (1439).

Fragonard, Jean Honoré (1732–1806) French, born Grasse; *Coresus Sacrificing Himself to Save Callirhoe* (1765), *The Swing* (c.1766), four canvases for Mme du Barry entitled *The Progress of Love* (1771–3).

Freud, Lucian (1922–) German–British, born Berlin; *Woman with a Daffodil* (1945), *Interior in Paddington* (1951), *Hotel Room* (1953–4), *Reflection* (1985).

Friedrich, Caspar David (1774–1840) German, born Pomerania; *The Cross in the Mountains* (1807–8).

Fuseli, Henri (Johann Heinrich Füssli) (1741–1825) Anglo-Swiss, born Zurich; *The Nightmare* (1781), *Appearance of the Ghost* (1796).

Gainsborough, Thomas (1727–88) British, born Sudbury, Suffolk; *Peasant Girl Gathering Sticks* (1782), *The Watering Place* (1777).

Gauguin, (Eugène Henri) Paul (1848–1903) French, born Paris; *The Vision After the Sermon* (1888), *The White Horse* (1898), *Women of Tahiti* (1891), *Tahitian Landscape* (1891), *Where Do We Come From? What Are We? Where Are We Going?* (1897–8), *Golden Bodies* (1901).

Géricault, Théodore (1791–1824) French, born Rouen; *Light Cavalry Officer* (c.1812), *Raft of the Medusa* (1819).

Ghirlandaio, Domenico (Domenico di Tommaso Bigordi) (1449–94) Italian, born Florence; *Virgin of Mercy* (1472), *St Jerome* (1480), *Nativity* (1485).

Giorgione (da Castelfranco) or Giorgio Barbarelli (c.1478–1511) Italian, born Castelfranco; *The Tempest* (c.1508), *Three Philosophers* (c.1508), *Portrait of a Man* (1510).

Giotto (di Bondone) (c.1266–1337) Italian, born near Florence; frescoes in Arena Chapel, Padua (1304–12), *Ognissanti Madonna* (1311–12).

Goes, Hugo van der (c.1440–82) Dutch, born probably Ghent; *Portinari Altarpiece* (1475).

Gorky, Arshile (Vosdanig Manoog Adoian) (1905–48) American, born Khorkom Vari, Turkish Armenia; *The Artist and His Mother* (c.1926–36), series *Image in Xhorkam* (from 1936), *The Liver is the Cock's Comb* (1944), *The Betrothal II* (1947).

Goya (y Lucientes), Francisco (José) de (1746–1828) Spanish, born Fuendetodos; *Family of Charles IV* (1799), *Los Desastres de la Guerra* (1810–14), *Black Paintings* (1820s).

Greco, El (Domenico Theotocopoulos) (1541–1614) Greek, born Candia, Crete; *Lady in Fur Wrap* (c.1577–8), *El Espolio* ('The Disrobing of Christ') (1577–9), *The Saviour of the World* (1600), *Portrait of Brother Hortensio Felix Paravicino* (1609), *Toledo Landscape* (c.1610).

Gris, Juan (José Victoriano González) (1887–1927) Spanish, born Madrid; *Sunblind* (1914), *Still Life with Dice* (1922), *Violin and Fruit Dish* (1924).

Grosz, George (1893–1959) German–American, born Berlin; *Fit for Active Service* (1918), *The Face of the Ruling Class* (1921), *Ecce Homo* (1927).

Grünewald, Matthias (Mathis Nithardt or Gothardt) (c.1480–1528) German, born probably Würzburg; *Isenheim Altarpiece* (1515).

Hals, Frans (c.1580–1666) Dutch, born Antwerp; *The Laughing Cavalier* (1624), *Banquet of the Company of St Adrian* (1627), *Gypsy Girl* (c.1628–30), *Man in a Slouch Hat* (c.1660–6).

Hamilton, Richard (1922–) British, born London; *Hommage à Chrysler Corp* (1952), *Just what is it that makes today's homes so different, so appealing?* (1956), *Study of Hugh Gaitskell as a Famous Monster of Film Land* (1964), *The Citizen* (1981–3).

Hilliard, Nicholas (c.1547–1619) British, born Exeter; miniature of *Queen Elizabeth I* (1572), *Henry Wriothesley* (1594).

Hirst, Damien (1965–) British, born Bristol; *The Physical Impossibility of Death in the Mind of Someone Living* (1991), *The Asthmatic Escaped* (1991), *Mother and Child, Divided* (1993), *For the Love of God* (2007).

Hockney, David (1937–) British, born Bradford, Yorkshire; *We Two Boys Together Clinging* (1961), *The Rake's Progress* (1963), *A Bigger Splash* (1967), *Invented Man Revealing a Still Life* (1975), *Dancer* (1980), *A Bigger Grand Canyon* (1998).

Hodgkin, Sir Howard (1932–) English, born London; *Dinner at Smith Square* (1975–9), *Goodbye to the Bay of Naples* (1980–2), *Rain* (1984–9), *Dirty Mirror* (2000).

Hogarth, William (1697–1764) British, born Smithfield, London; *Before and After* (1731), *A Rake's Progress* (1733–5).

Hokusai, Katsushika (1760–1849) Japanese, born Tokyo; *Tametomo and the Demon* (1811), *Mangwa* (1814–19), *Hundred Views of Mount Fuji* (1835).

Holbein, Hans, (the Younger) (1497–1543)

German, born Augsburg; *Bonifacius Amerbach* (1519), *Solothurn Madonna* (1522), *Sir Thomas Moore* (1527), *Anne of Cleves* (1539).

Hundertwasser, Friedensreich (Friedrich Stowasser) (1928–2000) Austrian, born Vienna; *Many Transparent Heads* (1949–50), *The End of Greece* (1963), *The Court of Sulaiman* (1967).

Hunt, (William) Holman (1827–1910) British, born London; *Our English Coasts* (1852), *Claudio and Isabella* (1853), *The Light of the World* (1854), *Isabella and the Pot of Basil* (1867).

Ingres, Jean August Dominique (1780–1867) French, born Montauban; *Gilbert* (1805), *La Source* (1807–59), *Bather* (1808), *Turkish Bath* (1863).

John, Augustus (Edwin) (1878–1961) British, born Tenby; *The Smiling Woman* (1908), *Portrait of a Lady in Black* (1917).

John, Gwen (1876–1939) British, born Haverfordwest, Pembrokeshire; *Girl with Bare Shoulders* (1909–10).

Johns, Jasper (1930–) American, born Allendale, South Carolina; *Flag* (1954–5), *Beer Cans* (sculpture) (1961), *Seasons* (1985).

Kandinsky, Wassily (1866–1944) Russian–French, born Moscow; *Kossacks* (1910–11), *Swinging* (1925), *Two Green Points* (1935), *Sky Blue* (1940).

Kiefer, Anselm (1945–) German, born Donaueschingen, Baden; *Occupations* (1969), *Parsifal III* (1973), *Innenraum* (1982), *Lilith* (1989), *Let a Thousand Flowers Bloom* (2000).

Kirchner, Ernst Ludwig (1880–1938) German, born Aschaffenburg; *Recumbent Blue Nude with Straw Hat* (1908–9), *The Drinker* (1915), *Die Amselfluh* (1923).

Kitaj, R(onald) B(rooks) (1932–2007) American, born Cleveland, Ohio; *The Ohio Gang* (1964), *If Not, Not* (1975–6), *The Oak Tree* (1991).

Klee, Paul (1879–1940) Swiss, born Münchenbuchsee, near Berne; *Der Vollmond* (1919), *Rose Garden* (1920), *Twittering Machine* (1922), *A Tiny Tale of a Tiny Dwarf* (1925), *Fire in the Evening* (1929).

Klimt, Gustav (1862–1918) Austrian, born Baumgarten, near Vienna; *Music* (1895), *The Kiss* (1907–8), *Judith II (Salome)* (1909).

Kline, Franz Joseph (1910–62) American, born Wilkes-Barre, Pennsylvania; *Orange and Black Wall* (1939), *Chief* (1950), *Mahoning* (1956).

Kokoschka, Oskar (1886–1980) Anglo-Austrian, born Pöchlarn; *The Dreaming Boys* (1908).

Kupka, Frantisek (1871–1957) Czech, born in Opocno, East Bohemia; *Girl with a Ball* (1908), *Amorpha: Fugue in Two Colours* (1912), *Working Steel* (1921–9).

Landseer, Sir Edwin (Henry) (1803–73) British, born London; *The Old Shepherd's Chief Mourner* (1837), *The Monarch of the Glen* (1850).

La Tour, Georges (Dumesnil) de (1593–1652) French, born Vic-sur-Seille, Lorraine; *St Jerome Reading* (1620s), *The Denial of St Peter* (1650).

Léger, Fernand (1881–1955) French, born Argentan; *Contrast of Forms* (1913), *Black Profile* (1928), *The Great Parade* (1954).

Lely, Sir Peter (Pietar van der Faes) (1618–80) Anglo-Dutch, born Soest, Westphalia; *The Windsor Beauties* (1668), *Admirals* series (1666–7).

Leonardo da Vinci (Leonardo di Ser Piero da Vinci) (1452–1519) Italian, born Vinci; *The Last Supper* (1495–7), *Madonna and Child with St Anne* (begun 1503), *Mona Lisa* (1500–6), *The Virgin of the Rocks* (c.1508).

Lichtenstein, Roy (1923–97) American, born New

York City; *Whaam!* (1963), *As I Opened Fire* (1964).

Lippi, Fra Filippo, called **Lippo** (c.1406–69) Italian, born Florence; *Tarquinia Madonna* (1437), *Barbadori Altarpiece* (begun 1437).

Lochner, Stefan (c.1400–51) German, born Meersburg am Bodensee; *The Adoration of the Magi* (c.1448), triptych in Cologne Cathedral.

Lowry, L(aurence) S(tephen) (1887–1976) English, born Manchester; *Salford Street Scene* (1928), *Coming from the Mill* (1930), *Industrial Landscape* (1955).

Macke, August (1887–1914) German, born Meschede; *Greeting* (1912), *The Zoo* (1912), *Girls Under Trees* (1914).

Magritte, René (François Ghislain) (1898–1967) Belgian, born Lessines, Hainault; *The Menaced Assassin* (1926), *Loving Perspective* (1935), *Presence of Mind* (1960).

Manet, Édouard (1832–83) French, born Paris; *Le Déjeuner sur l'herbe* (1863), *La Brioche* (1870), *A Bar at the Folies-Bergères* (1882).

Mantegna, Andrea (1431–1506) Italian, born Vicenza; *San Zeno Altarpiece* (1457–9), *Triumphs of Caesar* (c.1486–94), *Madonna of Victory* (1495).

Martini, Simone (c.1284–1344) Italian, born Siena; *S Caterina Polyptych* (1319), *Annunciation* (1333).

Masaccio (Tommaso di Giovanni di Simone Guidi) (1401–28) Italian, born Castel San Giovanni di Val d'Arno; polyptych for the Carmelite Church in Pisa (1426), frescoes in Sta Maria del Carmine, Florence (1424–7).

Masson, André (Aimé René) (1896–1987) French, born Balgny, Oise; *Massacres* (1933), *The Labyrinth* (1939).

Matisse, Henri (Emile Benoit) (1869–1954) French, born Le Cateau-Cambrésis; *La Desserte* (1908), *Notre Dame* (1914), *The Large Red Studio* (1948), *L'Escargot* (1953).

Memling, Hans (c.1440–94) Flemish, born Seligenstadt, Germany; *Madonna Enthroned* (1468), *Marriage of St Catherine* (c.1479), *Shrine of St Ursula* (1489).

Michelangelo (di Lodovico Buonarroti) (1475–1564) Italian, born Caprese, Tuscany; *The Pietà* (sculpture) (1497), *David* (sculpture) (1501–4), *Madonna* (c.1502), ceiling of the Sistine Chapel, Rome (1508–12), *The Last Judgement* (begun 1537).

Millais, Sir John Everett (1829–96) British, born Southampton; *Ophelia* (1851–2), *The Bridesmaid* (1851), *Tennyson* (1881), *Bubbles* (1886).

Millet, Jean-François (1814–75) French, born Grouchy; *Sower* (1850), *The Gleaners* (1857).

Miró, Joan (1893–1983) Spanish, born Montroig; *Catalan Landscape* (1923–4), *Maternity* (1924).

Modigliani, Amedeo (1884–1920) Italian, born Leghorn (Livorno), Tuscany; *The Jewess* (1908), *Moïse Kisling* (1915), *Reclining Nude* (c.1919), *Jeanne Hébuterne* (1919).

Mondrian, Piet (Pieter Cornelis Mondriaan) (1872–1944) Dutch, born Amersfoort; *Still Life with Gingerpot II* (1911), *Composition with Red, Black, Blue, Yellow, and Grey* (1920), *Broadway Boogie-Woogie* (1942–3).

Monet, Claude (1840–1926) French, born Paris; *Impression: Sunrise* (1872), *Haystacks* (1890–1), *Rouen Cathedral* (1892–5), *Waterlilies* (1899 onwards).

Moreau, Gustave (1826–98) French, born Paris; *Oedipus and the Sphinx* (1864), *Apparition* (1876), *Jupiter and Semele* (1889–95).

Morisot, Berthe (Marie Pauline) (1841–95) French,

born Bourges; *The Harbour at Cherbourg* (1874), *In the Dining Room* (1886).

Morris, William (1834–96) British, born Walthamstow, London; *Queen Guinevere* (1858).

Motherwell, Robert (Burns) (1915–91) American, born Aberdeen, Washington; *Gauloises* (1967), *Opens* (1968–72).

Munch, Edvard (1863–1944) Norwegian, born Löten; *The Scream* (1893), *Mother and Daughter* (c.1897), *Self-Portrait between the Clock and the Bed* (1940–2).

Nash, Paul (1899–1946) British, born London; *We Are Making a New World* (1918), *Menin Road* (1919).

Newman, Barnett (1905–70) American, born New York; *The Moment* (1946), *Onement I* (1948), *Vir Heroicus Sublimis* (1950–1).

Nicholson, Ben (1894–1982) British, born Denham, London; *White Relief* (1935), *November 11, 1947* (1947).

Nolde, Emil (Emil Hansen) (1867–1956) German, born Nolde; *The Missionary* (1912), *Candle Dancers* (1912).

Oliver, Isaac (c.1560–1617) Anglo-French, born Rouen; *Self-Portrait* (c.1590), *Henry, Prince of Wales* (c.1612).

Palmer, Samuel (1805–81) British, born London; *Repose of the Holy Family* (1824), *The Magic Apple Tree* (1830), *Opening the Fold* (1880).

Parmigianino (Girolamo Francesco Maria Mazzola) (1503–40) Italian, born Parma; frescoes in S Giovanni Evangelista, Parma (c.1522), *Self-Portrait in a Convex Mirror* (1524), *The Madonna of the Long Neck* (c.1535).

Pasmore, (Edwin John) Victor (1908–98) British, born Chelsham, Surrey; *The Evening Star* (1945–7), *Black Symphony – the Pistol Shot* (1977).

Perugino (Pietro di Cristoforo Vannucci) (c.1450–1523) Italian, born Città della Pieve, Umbria; *Christ Giving the Keys to Peter* (fresco in the Sistine Chapel) (c.1483).

Picabia, Francis (Marie) (1879–1953) French, born Paris; *I See Again in Memory My Dear Undine* (1913), *The Kiss* (1924).

Picasso, Pablo (Ruiz) (1881–1973) Spanish, born Malaga; *Mother and Child* (1921), *Three Dances* (1925), *Guernica* (1937), *The Charnel House* (1945), *The Artist and His Model* (1968).

Piero della Francesca (c.1420–92) Italian, born Borgo san Sepolcro; *Madonna of the Misericordia* (1445–8), *Resurrection* (c.1450).

Piper, John (1903–92) British, born Epsom; *Windsor Castle* watercolours (1941–2), *Council Chamber, House of Commons* (1941); also stage designs and illustrated publications.

Pissarro, Camille (Jacob) (1830–1903) French, born St Thomas, West Indies; *Landscape at Chaponval* (1880), *The Boieldieu Bridge at Rouen* (1896), *Boulevard Montmartre* (1897).

Pollock, (Paul) Jackson (1912–56) American, born Cody, Wyoming; *Guardians of the Secret* (1943), *No 14* (1948), *Blue Poles* (1952).

Pontormo, Jacopo da (1494–1552) Italian; frescoes eg of the *Passion* (1522–5), *Deposition* (c.1525).

Poussin, Nicolas (1594–1665) French, born Les Andelys, Normandy; *The Adoration of the Golden Calf* (1624), *Inspiration of the Poet* (c.1628), *Seven Sacraments* (1644–8), *Self-Portrait* (1650).

Raeburn, Sir Henry (1756–1823) British, born Edinburgh; *Rev Robert Walker Skating* (1784, although the attribution is now in doubt), *Isabella McLeod, Mrs James Gregory* (c.1798).

Ramsay, Allan (1713–84) British, born Edinburgh; *The Artist's Wife* (1754–5).

Raphael (Raffaello Santi or Sanzio) (1483–1520) Italian, born Urbino; *Assumption of the Virgin* (1504), *Madonna of the Meadow* (1505–6), *Transfiguration* (1518–20).

Redon, Odilon (1840–1916) French, born Bordeaux; *Woman with Outstretched Arms* (c.1910–14).

Rembrandt (Harmenszoon van Rijn) (1606–69) Dutch, born Leiden; *Anatomy Lesson of Dr Tulp* (1632), *Blinding of Samson* (1636), *The Night Watch* (1642), *The Conspiracy of Claudius* (1661–2).

Renoir, (Jean Pierre) Auguste (1841–1919) French, born Limoges; *Woman in Blue* (1874), *Woman Reading* (1876), *The Bathers* (1887).

Reynolds, Sir Joshua (1723–92) British, born Plympton Earls, near Plymouth; *Portrait of Miss Bowles with Her Dog* (1775), *Master Henry Hoare* (1788).

Riley, Bridget (Louise) (1931–) British, born London; *Pink Landscapes* (1959–60), *Zig-Zag* (1961), *Fall* (1963), *Apprehend* (1970), *Shadow Play* (1990).

Rivera, Diego (1886–1957) Mexican, born Guanajuato; *Man at the Crossroads* (1933), *Detroit Industry* (1932–3), *Man, Controller of the Universe* (1934).

Rosa, Salvator (1615–73) Italian, born Arenella, near Naples; *Self-Portrait with a Skull* (1656), *Humana Fragilitas* (c.1657).

Rossetti, Dante Gabriel (1828–82) British, born London; *Beata Beatrix* (1849–50), *Ecce Ancilla Domini!* (1850), *Astarte Syriaca* (1877).

Rothko, Mark (Marcus Rothkovitch) (1903–70) Latvian–American, born Dvinsk; *The Omen of the Eagle* (1942), *Red on Maroon* (1959), *Seagram Murals* (1958–9).

Rousseau, Henri (Julien Félix), known as **Le Douanier** (1844–1910) French, born Laval; *Monsieur et Madame Stevene* (1884), *Sleeping Gipsy* (1897), *Portrait of Joseph Brunner* (1909).

Rubens, Sir Peter Paul (1577–1640) Flemish, born Siegen, Westphalia; *Marchesa Brigida Spinola-Doria* (1606), *Hélène Fourment with Two of Her Children* (c.1637).

Sargent, John Singer (1856–1925) American, born Florence; *Madame X* (1884), *Lady Agnew* (1893), *Gassel* (1918).

Schiele, Egon (1890–1918) Austrian, born Tulln; *Autumn Tree* (1909), *Pregnant Woman and Death* (1911), *Edith Seated* (1917–18).

Schnabel, Julian (1951–) American, born New York City; *The Unexpected Death of Blinky Palermo in the Tropics* (1981), *Humanity Asleep* (1982), *Basquiat* (film) (1996).

Seurat, Georges (Pierre) (1859–91) French, born Paris; *Bathers at Asnières* (1884), *Sunday on the Island of La Grande Jatte* (1885–6), *Le Cirque* (1891).

Sickert, Walter (Richard) (1860–1942) British, born Munich; *La Hollandaise* (1905–6), *Ennui* (c.1914).

Sisley, Alfred (1839–99) French, born Paris; *Avenue of Chestnut Trees near La Celle Saint-Cloud* (1868), *Molesey Weir, Hampton Court* (1874).

Spencer, Sir Stanley (1891–1959) British, born Cookham-on-Thames, Berkshire; *The Resurrection* (1927), *The Leg of Mutton Nude* (1937).

Steen, Jan (Havicksz) (1627–79) Dutch, born Leiden; *A Woman at Her Toilet* (1663), *The World Upside Down* (1663).

Stubbs, George (1724–1806) British, born Liverpool; *Whistlejacket* (c.1762), *Anatomy of*

---

the Horse (1766), *Hambletonian, Rubbing Down* (1799).

Sutherland, Graham (Vivian) (1903–80) British, born London; *Entrance to a Lane* (1939), *Crucifixion* (1946), *A Bestiary and Some Correspondences* (1968).

Tanguy, Yves (1900–55) French–American, born Paris; *He Did What He Wanted* (1927), *The Invisibles* (1951).

Tatlin, Vladimir Yevgrafovich (1885–1953) Russian, born Moscow; painted reliefs, relief constructions, corner reliefs (all 1914 onwards); design for *Monument to the Third International* (1920).

Tintoretto (Jacopo Robusti) (1518–94) Italian, born probably Venice; *The Miracle of the Slave* (1548), *St George and the Dragon* (c.1558), *The Golden Calf* (c.1560).

Titian (Tiziano Veccellio) (c.1488–1576) Italian, born Pieve di Cadore; *The Assumption of the Virgin* (1516–18), *Bacchus and Ariadne* (1522–3), *Pesaro Madonna* (1519–26), *Crowning with Thorns* (c.1570).

Toulouse-Lautrec, Henri (Marie Raymond de) (1864–1901) French, born Albi; *The Jockey* (1899), *At the Moulin Rouge* (1895), *The Modiste* (1900).

Turner, Joseph Mallord William (1775–1851) British, born London; *Frosty Morning* (1813), *The Shipwreck* (1805), *Crossing the Brook* (1815), *The Fighting Téméraire* (1839), *Rain, Steam and Speed* (1844).

Uccello, Paolo (Paolo di Dono) (c.1396–1475) Italian, born Pratovecchio; *The Flood* (c.1445), *The Rout of San Romano* (1454–7).

Utamaro, Kitagawa (1753–1806) Japanese, born Edo (modern Tokyo); *Ohisa* (c.1788), *The Twelve Hours of the Green Houses* (c.1795).

Van der Weyden, Rogier (c.1400–64) Flemish, born Tournai; *Deposition* (c.1436), *Polyptych of the Last Judgement* (c.1445–9), *Portrait of a Woman* (c.1460).

Van Dyck, Sir Anthony (1599–1641) Flemish, born Antwerp; *Marchesa Elena Grimaldi* (c.1625), *The Deposition* (1634–5), *Le Roi à la chasse* (c.1638).

Van Gogh, Vincent (Willem) (1853–90) Dutch, born Groot-Zundert, near Breda; *The Potato Eaters* (1885), *Self-Portrait with Bandaged Ear* (1888), *The Harvest* (1888), *The Sunflowers* (1888), *Starry Night* (1889), *Cornfields with Flight of Birds* (1890).

Velázquez, Diego (Rodríguez de Silva y) (1599–1660) Spanish, born Seville; *The Immaculate Conception* (c.1618), *The Waterseller of Seville* (c.1620), *The Surrender of Breda* (1634–5), *Pope Innocent X* (1650), *Las Meninas* (c.1656).

Vermeer, Jan or **Johannes** (1632–75) Dutch, born Delft; *A Lady with a Gentleman at the Virginals* (c.1665), *The Astronomer* (1668), *Christ in the House of Mary and Martha* (date unknown), *The Lacemaker* (date unknown).

Veronese (Paolo Caliari) (1528–88) Italian, born Verona; *The Feast in the House of Levi* (1573), *Marriage at Cana* (1573), *Triumph of Venice* (c.1585).

Verrocchio, Andrea del (Andrea di Michele di Francesco Cioni) (c.1435–c.1488) Italian, born Florence; *Baptism of Christ* (c.1470), *David* (sculpture) (c.1475).

Vlaminck, Maurice de (1876–1958) French, born Paris; *The Red Trees* (1906), *Tugboat at Chatou* (1906).

Warhol, Andy (Andrew Warhola) (1928–87) American, born McKeesport, Pennsylvania; *Marilyn* (1962), *Electric Chair* (1963).

Arts and Culture

Watteau, (Jean) Antoine (1684–1721) French, born Valenciennes; *The Pilgrimage to the Island of Cythera* (1717), *L'Enseigne de Gersaint* (1721).

Whistler, James (Abbott) McNeill (1834–1903) American, born Lowell, Massachusetts; *The Artist's Mother* (1871), *Nocturne in Blue and Silver: Old Battersea Bridge* (1872–5), *Falling Rocket* (1875).

Wood, Grant (1891–1942) American, born Iowa; *American Gothic* (1930), *Spring Turning* (1936).

Wright (of Derby), Joseph (1734–97) British, born Derby; *Experiment with an Air Pump* (1766), *The Alchemist in Search of the Philosopher's Stone Discovers Phosphorus* (1795).

Wyeth, Andrew (Newell) (1917–2009) American, born Chadds Ford, Pennsylvania; *Christina's World* (1948).

Turner Prize 1988–2008

The Turner Prize was founded in 1984 by the Patrons of New Art. It is an award of £25 000 given to contemporary British artists under the age of 50 for an outstanding exhibition of work in the past 12 months.

Year	Winners
1988	Tony Cragg, sculptor
1989	Richard Long, land artist
1990	no prize awarded
1991	Anish Kapoor, sculptor
1992	Grenville Davey, sculptor
1993	Rachel Whiteread, sculptor
1994	Antony Gormley, sculptor
1995	Damien Hirst, painter and conceptual and installation artist
1996	Douglas Gordon, video artist
1997	Gillian Wearing, photographer and video artist
1998	Chris Ofili, painter
1999	Steve McQueen, video artist
2000	Wolfgang Tillmans, photographer

Year	Winners
2001	Martin Creed, conceptual and installation artist
2002	Keith Tyson, conceptual and installation artist
2003	Grayson Perry, ceramicist
2004	Jeremy Deller, performance artist and photographer
2005	Simon Starling, conceptual and installation artist
2006	Tomma Abts, painter
2007	Mark Wallinger, conceptual and installation artist
2008	Mark Leckey, video artist

Sculptors

Selected works are listed.

Andre, Carl (1935–) American, born Quincy, Massachusetts; *Equivalent VIII* (1966), *144 Magnesium Square* (1969), *Twelfth Copper Corner* (1975), *Bloody Angle* (1985), *Armadillo* (1998).

Armitage, Kenneth (1916–2002) British, born Leeds; *People in the Wind* (1950), *Sprawling Woman* (1958), *Figure and Clouds* (1972), *Richmond Oak* (1985–90).

Arp, Hans (Jean) (1887–1966) French, born Strasbourg; *Eggboard* (1922), *Kore* (1958).

Barlach, Ernst (1870–1938) German, born Wedel; *Moeller-Jarke Tomb* (1901), *Have Pity!* (1919).

Bernini, Gian Lorenzo (1598–1680) Italian, born Naples; *Neptune and Triton* (1620), *David* (1623), *Ecstasy of St Theresa* (1640s), *Fountain of the Four Rivers* (1648–51).

Beuys, Joseph (1921–86) German, born Kleve; *Fat Chair* (1964), *Snowfall* (1965).

Bologna, Giovanni da (also called **Giambologna**) (1529–1608) French, born Douai; *Mercury* (1564–5), *Rape of the Sabines* (1579–83).

Bourgeois, Louise (1911–) American, born Paris; *Labyrinthine Tower* (1963), *Destruction of the Father* (1974), *Spiders* (1995), *Maman* (1999).

Brancusi, Constantin (1876–1957) Romanian-French, born Hobitza, Gorj; *The Kiss* (1909), *Torso of a Young Man* (1922).

Calder, Alexander (1898–1976) American, born Philadelphia, Pennsylvania; *Stabiles and Mobiles* (1932), *A Universe* (1934).

Canova, Antonio (1757–1822) Italian, born Possagno; *Theseus* (1782), *Cupid and Psyche* (1787), *Pauline Borghese as Venus* (1805–7).

Caro, Sir Anthony (1924–) British, born London; *Sailing Tonight* (1971–4), *Veduggio Sound* (1973),

Ledge Piece (1978), *Night Movements* (1987–90), *The Barbarians* (1999–2002).

Cellini, Benvenuto (1500–71) Italian, born Florence; salt cellar of *Neptune and Ceres* (1543), *Cosimo de' Medici* (1545–7), *Perseus with the Head of Medusa* (1564).

Deacon, Richard (1949–) British, born Bangor, Wales; *Double Talk* (1987), *Never Mind* (1993), *Show and Tell* (1997), *Just Us* (2000).

Donatello (originally **Donnato di Niccolò di Betto Bardi**) (c.1386–1466) Italian, born Florence; *St Mark* (1411–12), *St George Killing the Dragon* (c.1417), *Feast of Herod* (1423–5), *Gattamelata* (1447–53), *Judith and Holofernes* (after 1459).

Epstein, Sir Jacob (1880–1959) Anglo-American, born New York City; *Rima* (1925), *Genesis* (1930), *Ecce Homo* (1934–5), *Adam* (1939), *Christ in Majesty* (Llandaff Cathedral), *St Michael and the Devil* (façade of Coventry Cathedral) (1958–9).

Frink, Dame Elisabeth (1930–93) British, born Thurlow, Suffolk; *Horse Lying Down* (1975), *Running Man* (1985), *Seated Man* (1986).

Gabo, Naum (originally **Naum Neemia Pevsner**) (1890–1977) American, born Bryansk, Russia; *Kinetic Construction* (1920), *No.1* (1943).

Gaudier-Brzeska, Henri (1891–1915) French, born St Jean de Braye, near Orléans; *Red stone dancer* (1913).

Ghiberti, Lorenzo (c.1378–1455) Italian, born in or near Florence; *St John the Baptist* (1412–15), *St Matthew* (1419–22), *The Gates of Paradise* (1425–52).

Giacometti, Alberto (1901–66) Swiss, born Bogonova, near Stampa; *Head* (c.1928), *Woman with Her Throat Cut* (1932).

Goldsworthy, Andy (1956–) British, born Cheshire; *Hazel Stick Throws* (1980), *Slate Cone* (1988), *The Wall* (1988–9), *Arch at Goodwood* (2002).

González, Julio (1876–1942) Spanish, born Barcelona; *Angel* (1933), *Woman Combing Her Hair* (1936), *Cactus People* (1930–40).

Gormley, Antony (1950–) English, born London; *Natural Selection* (1981), *Another Place* (1997), *Angel of the North* (1998), *Domain Field* (2003).

Hepworth, Dame (Jocelyn) Barbara (1903–75) British, born Wakefield, Yorkshire; *Figure of a Woman* (1929–30), *Large and Small Forms* (1945), *Single Form* (1963).

Leonardo da Vinci (1452–1519) Italian, born Vinci, between Pisa and Florence; *St John the Baptist*.

Kapoor, Anish (1954–) Indian, born Mumbai; *1000 Names* (1989–90), *Marsyas* (2002), *Cloud Gate* (2004).

Michelangelo (in full Michelangelo di Lodovico Buonarotti) (1475–1564) Italian, born Caprese, Tuscany; *Cupid* (1495), *Bacchus* (1496), *Pieta* (1497), *David* (c.1500).

Moore, Henry (Spencer) (1898–1986) British, born Castleford, Yorkshire; *Recumbent Figure* (1938), *Fallen Warrior* (1956–7).

Oldenburg, Claes (1929–) American, born Stockholm, Sweden; *Giant Clothespin* (1975), *The Course of the Knife* (1985), *Match Cover* (1992), *Cupid's Span* (2002).

Paolozzi, Sir Eduardo Luigi (1924–2005) British, born Leith, Edinburgh; *Krokodeel* (c.1956–7),

Japanese War God (1958), *Medea* (1964), *Piscator* (1981), *Daedalus* (1993), *London to Paris* (2000).

Pheidias (c.490–c.417 BC) Greek, born Athens; *Athena Promachos* (460–450 BC), marble sculptures of the Parthenon (447–432 BC).

Pisano, Andrea (c.1270–1349) Italian, born Pontedera; bronze doors of the *Baptistry* of Florence (1330–6).

Pisano, Giovanni (c.1248–c.1320) Italian, born Pisa; *Fontana Magiore*, Perugia (1278), *Duomo pulpit*, Pisa (1302–10).

Pisano, Nicola (c.1225–c.1284) Italian, birthplace unknown; *Baptistry* at Pisa (1260).

Praxiteles (5c BC) Greek, born probably Athens; *Hermes Carrying the Boy Dionysus* (date unknown).

Robbia, Luca della (in full Luca di Simone di Marco della Robbia) (c.1400–1482) Italian, born Florence; *Cantoria* (1432–7).

Rodin, (François) Auguste (René) (1840–1917) French, born Paris; *The Age of Bronze* (1875–6), *The Gates of Hell* (1880–1917), *The Burghers of Calais* (1884), *The Kiss* (1889), *The Thinker* (1904).

Schwitters, Kurt (1887–1948) German, born Hannover; *Merzbau* (1920–43).

Tinguely, Jean (1925–91) Swiss, born Fribourg; *Baluba No 3* (1959), *Métamécanique No 9* (1959), *Homage to New York* (1960), *EOSX* (1967).

Whiteread, Rachel (1963–) British, born London; *Torso* (1991), *House* (1993), *Orange Bath* (1996), *Embankment* (2005).

Photographers

Adams, Ansel (Easton) (1902–84) American, born San Francisco. Notable for broad landscapes of western America, especially the Yosemite in the 1930s. One of the founders of Group f/64 (1932). Publications include *Taos Pueblo* (1930) and *Born Free and Equal* (1944).

Adams, Marcus Algernon (1875–1959) English, born Southampton. Portrait photographer who established studio in 1919 specializing in formal children's portraits with soft-focus style. His portraits of three generations of the British royal family, taken from 1926 until his retirement in 1957, were published worldwide.

Adamson, Robert (1821–48) Scottish, born Berunside. Pioneer in photography. With David Octavius Hill applied the calotype process of making photographic prints on silver chloride paper for a commission to portray the founders of the Free Church of Scotland in 1843.

Akiyama, Shotaro (1920–2003) Japanese, born Tokyo. Worked for a Japanese motion picture company before becoming a freelance photographer for a number of publishers in 1951.

Anschütz, Ottomar (1846–1907) German, born Lissa (now in Poland). Pioneer of instantaneous photography and one of the first to make a series of pictures of moving animals and people, making a substantial contribution to the invention of the cinematograph.

Arbus, Diane (née Nemerov) (1923–71) American, born New York City. After work in conventional fashion photography, sought to portray people 'without their masks'. Achieved fame in the 1960s with ironic studies of social pests and the deprived classes, but became increasingly depressed, eventually committing suicide.

Arnold, Eve (1913–) American photojournalist,

born Philadelphia. First woman to photograph for Magnum Photos in 1951. Famous for pictures of women, the poor and the elderly, as well as celebrities such as Marilyn Monroe.

Atget, (Jean) Eugène (Auguste) (1856–1927) French, born Libourne, near Bordeaux. Studied at the Conservatoire d'Art Dramatique, Paris (1879–81), before working as a stage actor, comedian and painter. His photographic work (1898–1925) was discovered in 1926 in Paris by Berenice Abbott.

Avedon, Richard (1923–2004) American, born New York City. Studied photography at the New School for Social Research, New York and served in the photography section of the US merchant navy (1942–4). Established his own studio in New York and worked freelance for *Harper's Bazaar*, *Vogue* and *Life*. Worked for the *New Yorker* from 1992.

Bailey, David (Royston) (1938–) English, born London. Originally specialized in freelance fashion photography from 1959, later extending to portraits expressing the spirit of the 1960s and to studies of the nude. Also writes extensively on photography and has been director of television commercials and documentaries since the 1970s. CBE 2001.

Beaton, Sir Cecil (Walter Hardy) (1904–80) English, born London. Outstanding photographer of fashion and celebrities, including royalty. Also designed scenery and costumes for ballet, operatic, theatrical and film productions. Publications include *My Royal Past* (1939), *The Glass of Fashion* (1959), *The Magic Image* (1975), as well as several volumes of autobiography (1961–78).

Bischof, Werner (1916–54) Swiss, born Zurich. Freelance graphic artist and photographer in Zurich (1932–6) and later magazine photographer for *Life*, *Picture Post* and *Paris Match*.

Blumenfeld, Erwin (1897–1969) American, born Berlin, Germany. Self-taught photographer, associated with Dadaist artists in Amsterdam (1918–23). Worked as a fashion photographer for *Verve* and *Vogue* in Paris before opening a studio in New York in 1943.

Bourke-White, Margaret (White, Margaret) (1904–71) American, born New York City. Photo-journalist for *Life* magazine from 1936, for which she covered World War II. First woman photographer to be attached to US armed forces. Also produced reports of the siege of Moscow (1941) and opening of the concentration camps in 1944, later covering troubles around the world. Books include *Halfway to Freedom* (1946) and an autobiography, *Portrait of Myself* (1963).

Brady, Matthew B (1823–96) American, born near Lake George, New York. Operated portrait studio in New York using daguerrotype from 1844, and later recorded the American Civil War with the Union armies, an effort which ruined him financially so that he died in poverty in a New York almshouse.

Brandt, Bill (1904–83) English, born London. Studied with Man Ray in Paris in 1929. In 1930s produced striking social records and during World War II worked for ministry of information recording conditions in London in the Blitz. Subsequently turned to landscape and studies of the nude. Collections include *The English at Home* (1936), *A Night in London* (1938), *Perspective of Nudes* (1961), *Shadows of Light* (1966).

Brassaï (Halász, Gyula) (1899–1984) French, born Brasso, Transylvania, Hungary (now Romania). From 1930 recorded underworld and nightlife of Paris. Refused to photograph during the German occupation, but worked in Picasso's studios, returning to photography after World War II.

Bullock, Wynn (Percy Wingfield Bullock) (1902–75) American, born Chicago. Studied photography at the Art Center School, Los Angeles (1938–40). Worked in commercial postcard photography and later taught at the Institute of Design at the University of California.

Burgin, Victor (1941–) English, born Sheffield. Influenced by conceptual art of the 1960s. Concentrates on black-and-white images with text superimposed onto them, forcing the viewer to participate. Publications include *Some Cities* (1996) and *Relocating: Victor Burgin* (2002).

Cameron, Julia Margaret (née **Pattle**) (1815–79) British, born Calcutta (now Kolkata), India. Became outstanding amateur photographer in the 1860s, and received permanent acclaim for close-up portraits of Victorian celebrities.

Capa, Robert (Friedmann, André) (1913–54) American, born Budapest, Hungary. Recorded the Spanish Civil War (1935–7), China under Japanese attack (1938), World War II in Europe and subsequently the early days of the state of Israel. Killed by a land mine in the Indo-China fighting.

Cartier-Bresson, Henri (1908–2004) French, born Paris. Presented his first photographic exhibition in 1933; later visited Mexico and America and worked as assistant to film director Jean Renoir. After World War II developed his human interest style of black-and-white photography in worldwide travels. Was a co-founder of Magnum Photos. Publications include *Images à la sauvette* (The Decisive Moment, 1952), *The Europeans* (1955).

Chim, David Seymour (**David Szymin**) (1911–56) American, born Warsaw, Poland. Freelance photographer who worked for *Vu* and *Ce Soir* in Paris, and throughout Europe and N Africa.

Established his own studio in New York (1940–2) and was a co-founder of Magnum Photos, Paris and New York.

Clergue, Lucien (Georges) (1934–) French, born Arles. Self-taught freelance teacher at Arles from 1960. Founder of Recontres Internationales de la Photographie, Arles (1970).

Coburn, Alvin Langdon (1882–1966) British, born Boston, Massachusetts. Established a studio in New York (1901–2) and worked as an independent photographer in Boston, London, California and Wales. Associated with the Vorticist Group in London (1917–18).

Cosindas, Marie (1925–) American, born Boston, Massachusetts. Attended photography workshops under Ansel Adams in Boston in 1961 and has worked as a freelance photographer since 1960. Received Guggenheim Fellowship in 1967.

Crawford, Osbert Guy Stanhope (1886–1957) British, born Bombay (now Mumbai), India. Identified potential of aerial photography in archaeology, resulting in the collection *Wessex from the Air* (1928).

Cunningham, Imogen (1883–1976) American, born Portland, Oregon. Opened portrait studio in Seattle (1910) specializing in soft-focus sentimental-style portraits and still-life flower studies. Later converted to sharply defined images, and was still teaching at the Art Institute in San Francisco in her nineties.

Curtis, Edward Sheriff (1868–1952) American, born Madison, Wisconsin. From 1896 recorded the North American Indian tribes and their way of life, publishing first 20 volumes in 1907. Took around 40000 negatives, stressing the Indians' peaceful arts and culture.

Daguerre, Louis Jacques Mandé (1787–1851) French, born Cormeilles. Inventor of the 'daguerrotype', a process in which a photographic image is obtained on a copper plate coated with a layer of metallic silver sensitized to light by iodine vapour.

Davidson, Bruce (1933–) American, born Chicago. Studied photography at Rochester Institute of Technology and since 1958 has worked freelance for *Life*, *Queen*, *Vogue* and other magazines in New York, Paris and Los Angeles. Frank portraits of people in their social settings.

DeCarava, Roy (1919–) African–American, born New York City. His work includes pictures of life in Harlem, jazz musicians and civil rights protests. Received Guggenheim Fellowship in 1952.

Dodgson, Charles Lutwidge (Carroll, Lewis) (1832–98) English, born Daresbury, near Warrington. Pioneer photographer, mainly interested in portrait photography.

Doisneau, Robert (1912–94) French, born Gentilly, Seine. Studied lithography in Paris (1926–9) and worked as a photographer from 1930, including industrial photography and as a photojournalist. Awarded the Kodak Prize (1947) and the Niepce Prix (1956).

Donovan, Terence Daniel (1936–96) British, born London. Known for his fashion work in the 1960s, in which he photographed glamorous models against harsh urban backgrounds. Also made commercials and documentaries.

Draper, Henry (1837–82) American, born Prince Edward County, Virginia. Pioneer of astronomical photography who produced photographs of the Orion nebula and over 100 stellar spectra.

Duclos du Hauron, Louis (1837–1920) French, born Langon. Outlined principles of additive and subtractive colour separation in *Les Couleurs* *en Photographie* (1869). Described practical photographic methods which he patented in *Photographie en Couleur* (1878), and proposed the anaglyph method of viewing stereoscopic images.

Eakins, Thomas (1844–1916) American, born Philadelphia, Pennsylvania. Extended advances made by Muybridge in his studies of figures in motion. His composite plates inspired Duchamp's *Nude Descending a Staircase.*

Eastman, George (1854–1932) American, born Waterville, New York. Produced a successful roll-film (1884), the 'Kodak' box camera (1888) and pioneered experiments which made possible the moving-picture industry. Formed the Eastman Kodak Co in 1892 and produced the Brownie camera in 1900.

Edgerton, Harold Eugene (1903–90) American, born Fremont, Nebraska. Engineer who specialized in high-speed photography. Produced a krypton–xenon gas arc which was employed in photographing the capillaries in the white of the eye without harming the patient.

Eisenstaedt, Alfred (1898–1995) American, born Dirschau, West Prussia (now Tczew, Poland). One of the original photojournalists on *Life* magazine (1936–72). Voted Photographer of the Year in 1951. Publications include *Witness to Our Time* (1966), *The Eye of Eisenstaedt* (1969) and *Photojournalism* (1971).

Evans, Walker (1903–75) American, born St Louis, Missouri. Architectural and social photographer who recorded rural life in the Southern states and people in New York City subways. Publications include *American Photographs* (1938) and *Many Are Called* (1966).

Feininger, Andreas (Bernhard Lyonel) (1906–99) American, born Paris. Self-taught photographer, involved in industrial and architectural photography in Stockholm (1933–9). Worked as a freelance photographer in New York and as a war photographer for the US Office of War Information (1941–2).

Fenton, Roger (1819–69) English, born Lancashire. Photographed in Russia in 1852 and was a founder of the Photographic Society (later the Royal) in 1853. In 1855 went to the Crimea as the world's first accredited war photographer. Later travelled in Britain producing architectural and landscape studies.

Frank, Robert (1924–) Swiss, born Zurich. After working as a photographer in Zurich (1943–4) moved to America in 1947 and worked freelance for *Harper's Bazaar* and *Life* in New York. Later worked in film-making and received the Guggenheim Fellowship (1955). Known for the book *The Americans* (1959), containing bold images of US society, with a text by Jack Kerouac.

Frith, Francis (1822–98) English, born Chesterfield. Topographical photographer who produced the first photographic traveller's records to be seen in Britain during travel in Egypt and the Near East between 1856 and 1859. Established nationwide service of photographs of local scenes as prints in Britain, a business which survived commercially until 1971.

Genthe, Arnold (1869–1942) American, born Berlin. Commercial portrait photographer who emigrated to America in 1896 and established a studio in San Francisco (1897–1906). Concentrated on dance and theatrical portraits.

Gill, Sir David (1843–1914) Scottish, born Aberdeen. Astronomer who pioneered use of photography for charting the heavens.

Godwin, Fay Simmonds (1931–2005) English, born Berlin. Best known for landscape photography, including Welsh and Scottish scenes. Publications include *The Oldest Road* (1975, co-authored with J R C Anderson), *Glassworks and Secret Lives* (1999) and *Landmarks* (2001).

Haas, Ernst (1921–86) Austrian, born Vienna. Studied photography in Vienna and worked freelance for *Vogue* and *Life* in Paris (1948–50) before moving to America in 1950.

Halsman, Philippe (1906–79) American, born Riga, Latvia. Self-taught photographer who established a studio in Paris and worked for *Vogue* and *Voilà* (1931–40). Emigrated to America in 1940 and became President of the American Society of Magazine Photographers, New York (1944, 1954) and received a Life Achievement Award (1975).

Hardy, Bert (1913–95) English, born London. Photojournalist on staff of *Picture Post* until 1957, except for service as Army photographer from 1942 to 1946, during which he recorded concentration camps. Later assignments took him to the Korean and Vietnam wars. Became involved in advertising until his retirement in 1967.

Hill, David Octavius (1802–70) Scottish, born Perth. Pioneer in photography. With Robert Adamson applied the calotype process of making photographic prints on silver chloride paper for a commission to portray the founders of the Free Church of Scotland in 1843.

Hine, Lewis W(ickes) (1874–1940) American, born Oshkosh, Wisconsin. Expressed social concern through photographic studies of Ellis Island immigrants and child labour. During World War I documented the plight of refugees for the American Red Cross and recorded the construction of the Empire State Building in *Men at Work* (1932). Later registered the effects of the Depression for a US government project.

Hiro (Yasuhiro Wakabayashi) (1930–) Japanese, born Shanghai, China. Moved to New York in 1954 and established a studio there in 1958. Worked freelance for *Harper's Bazaar* from 1958, and received the Photographer of the Year award from the American Society of Magazine Photographers.

Karsh, Yousuf (1908–2002) Canadian, born Mardin, Turkey. Apprenticed to a Boston portraitist (1928–31) and in 1932 opened a studio in Ottawa. Appointed official portrait photographer to the Canadian government in 1935. Produced wartime studies of national leaders and continued to portray statesmen, artists and writers throughout the world.

Kertész, André (1894–1985) Hungarian–American, born Budapest. Photographer with Hungarian army during World War I and later an acclaimed reporter of the 'human condition' in Paris. Worked for Condé-Nast publications and other magazines in New York in the 1930s and 1940s. After a major retrospective exhibition at the New York Museum of Modern Art in 1964 received belated official recognition.

Lange, Dorothea (originally **Nutzhorn**) (1895–1965) American, born Hoboken, New Jersey. Established studio in San Francisco in 1919, and later recorded rural life in the south and west of America during the depression years from 1935. With her husband collaborated on the book *An American Exodus: A Record of Human Erosion* (1939). After World War II worked as a freelance reporter in Asia, South America and the Middle East.

Arts and Culture

Lartigue, Jacques-Henri (Charles Auguste) (1894–1986) French, born Courbvoie, Seine. Adopted informal approach to photography, elevating the snapshot into a creative art form. *Diary of a Century* is a collection recording the elegance of the inter-war years in France.

Leibovitz, Annie (1949–) American, born Connecticut. Known for photographs of celebrities. Worked for *Rolling Stone* in the 1970s and has been chief photographer for *Vanity Fair* since 1983. Won Innovation in Photography Award in 1987. Publications include *Photographs 1970–90* in 1992, and *Women* in 1999.

Levitt, Helen (1913–) American, born New York City. Known for documentation of urban life. Work published in *Time*, the *New York Post* and *Harper's Bazaar*. Also worked in film during the 1940s and 1950s.

Lichfield, Patrick, 5th Earl of (1939–2005) English. After working as an assistant, opened his own studio and from 1981 achieved success in travel and publicity photography and royal portraits.

Mapplethorpe, Robert (1946–89) American, born Long Island, New York. Developed his style in the 1970s. Renowned for his black-and-white photography, his work concentrated on nudes, flowers and formal portraits, and his homoerotic images created controversy. Publications include *Black Book* (1986) and *Flowers* (1993).

Marey, Étienne Jules (1830–1903) French, born Beaune. Physiologist who pioneered scientific cinematography in studies of animal movement (1887–1900). Improved camera design and reduced exposure time to around 1/25000 of a second to photograph insect flight.

Martin, Paul (1864–1942) Anglo-French, born Herbenville, France. Made use of a disguised camera to record working people in the streets of London and on holiday at the seaside (1888–98), recording the realities of late-Victorian everyday life in *London by Gaslight* (1896). Turned professional in 1899.

McBean, Angus (Rowland) (1904–90) Welsh, born Newbridge, Monmouth. Theatrical photographer from 1934, noted for an individualistic approach to portraiture, use of photographic montage, collage and double-exposure to achieve surrealistic effects. Withdrew from professional photography after 1969.

McCullin, Don(ald) (1935–) English, born London. Studied painting (1948–50) and later became a photographic assistant in aerial reconnaissance with the RAF (1953–5). Worked abroad as freelance photographer and as staff photographer for the *Sunday Times* (1964–84). Uncompromising photographer of war and conflict zones. Publications include *A Life's Work in Photography* (1995) and *Don McCullin* (2001).

Miller, Lee (1907–77) American, born Poughkeepsie, New York. Known for her documentary work and fashion photography. Photographer for *Vogue* before and after World War II. During war worked as official war correspondent for the US forces.

Moholy-Nagy, László (Nagy, László) (1895–1946) American, born Bucsborsod, near Mohol, south Hungary. Produced first 'photograms' (non-representational photographic images made directly without a camera) in 1923 and later became recognized as a leading avant-garde artist in Germany in the European New Photographers movement (1925–35), his work including film-making and typography integrated with photographic illustration. Moved to the USA in 1937.

Morath, Inge (1923–2002) Austrian, born Graz. Photographer and writer; wife of playwright Arthur Miller from 1962. She first joined Magnum Photos as an editor, then developed a talent for photography. Publications include *Venice Observed* (1956), *In Russia* (1969) and *Border Spaces* (2002).

Mountford, Charles Percy (1890–1976) Australian, born Hallett, South Australia. Ethnologist who wrote a series of books, illustrated with his own photographs, about Aboriginal Australians and their culture. Later directed feature films on Aboriginal life from 1950.

Muybridge, Eadweard (Muggeridge, Edward James) (1830–1904) Anglo-American, born Kingston-on-Thames. Became professional photographer in 1866 and later chief photographer to the American government. In 1880 devised the zoopraxiscope to show picture sequences, achieving a rudimentary kind of cinematography. *Animal Locomotion* (1887) gives the results of his extensive survey of animal and human movement.

Nadar (Tournachon, Gaspard-Felix) (1820–1910) French, born Paris. Photographer, artist and journalist who produced lively portraits of distinguished literary and artistic contemporaries and the first 'photo-interview' series of photographs captioned with the sitter's replies to his questions. Proposed the use of aerial photographs for map-making and in 1858 took the first photographs from a balloon, of Paris.

Newman, Arnold (Abner) (1918–2006) American, born New York City. Assistant portrait photographer (1938–9) and later Director of the Newman Portrait Studio, Miami Beach (1942–5). Worked freelance for publications including the *New Yorker*; books include *Arnold Newman* (2000).

Newton, Helmut (1920–2004) Australian, born Berlin, Germany. Apprentice to a theatre and fashion photographer in Berlin (1936–40) and freelance photographer for *Elle*, *Queen*, *Marie-Claire* and *Vogue* from 1958. Known particularly for his later work: dominant female nudes.

Niepce, Joseph Nicéphore (1765–1833) French, born Chalon-sur-Saône. Chemist who succeeded in producing a photograph on metal (1826), said to be the world's first. Later co-operated with others in further research.

Nilsson, Lennart (1922–) Swedish, born Rome. Freelance press photographer, acclaimed for several portraits such as *Sweden in Profiles* (1954), who later pioneered microfilm showing the anatomy of plants and animals. Perfected special lenses to film inside the human body, enabling him to produce pictures of the human foetus in the womb from conception to birth: *Ett barn blir till* (1965, The Everyday Miracle: A Child is Born).

Parer, Damien (1912–44) Australian, born Malvern, Victoria. Official cameraman with the 2nd Australian Imperial Forces. Filmed action at the siege of Tobruk in the Middle East, later working in Greece, Syria and New Guinea. His documentary film *Kokoda Front* was the first Australian film to win an Oscar. Killed while filming American troops landing at Peleliu, Caroline Islands.

Parkinson, Norman (originally **Parkinson Smith, Ronald William**) (1913–90) English, born London. Opened studio in 1934 and became a well-known portrait and fashion photographer, his work being used widely in quality magazines. Later advertising work in the 1950s involved worldwide travel. Settled in Tobago in 1963.

Parks, Gordon (Alexander Buchanan) (1912–2006) American, born Fort Scott, Kansas. Self-taught photographer; worked for the US Office of War Information (1943–5) and as a freelance fashion photographer in Minneapolis (1937–42). After working as a documentary filmmaker in America and Saudi Arabia, became an independent photographer, film writer and director for Warner Brothers, MGM and Paramount Pictures.

Penn, Irving (1917–) American, born Plainfield, New Jersey. Served as an ambulance driver and documentary photographer in the American Field Service in Italy and India (1944–5). Later worked for *Vogue* in New York (1943–4) and as a freelance advertising photographer from 1952.

Porter, Eliot (Furness) (1901–90) American, born Winnetka, Illinois. Self-taught photographer who concentrated on his photographic career from 1939, in particular in landscape and wildlife photography. Received the Conservation Award from the US Department of the Interior (1967).

Rankin (originally **Rankin Waddell**) (1966–) Scottish, born Glasgow. Co-founded *Dazed and Confused* style magazine (1991) and is known for celebrity and fashion work; books include *Nudes* (1999).

Ray, Man (Rabinovich, Emanuel) (1890–1976) American, born Philadelphia, Pennsylvania. After making a number of Surrealist films in Paris, published and exhibited many photographs and 'rayographs' (photographic images made without a camera) in the 1930s, returning to America in 1940.

Ritts, Herb (1952–2002) American, born Los Angeles. Celebrity photographer with shots in such leading magazines as *Vogue* and *Harper's Bazaar*. Also worked on music videos and commercials.

Robinson, Henry Peach (1830–1901) English, born Ludlow. Opened studio in Leamington Spa in 1857, but moved from formal portraiture to 'high art photography', often creating scenes using composites of several separate images of costumed models and painted settings in the mid-Victorian style. Wrote *Pictorial Effect in Photography* (1869).

Rodchenko, Alexander Mikhailovich (1891–1956) Russian, born St Petersburg. Photographer, painter and designer whose most original photographic works were documentary photographs of the new communist society.

Rosenblum, Walter (1919–) American, born New York City. After studying photography in New York, worked as a photographer for the US army in Europe (1943–5), becoming the most decorated photographer in the army. Awarded the Guggenheim Fellowship in 1979.

Rothstein, Arthur (1915–85) American, born New York City. Photo officer for the US army in India, Burma and China (1943–6) and picture editor for the Office of War Information, New York (1942–3). Founder of the American Society of Magazine Photographers (1941).

Saint Joseph, John Kenneth Sinclair (1912–94) English, born Worcestershire. Professor of aerial photographic studies at Cambridge (1948–80), developing large photographic archive with emphasis on systematic reconnaissance and low-level oblique photography of natural landscapes and archaeological monuments in their landscape setting. *Medieval England: An Aerial Survey* (1958, 1979), *Roman Britain from the Air* (1983) are collections of some of the results.

Salgado, Sebastião Ribeiro, Jr (1944–) Brazilian, born Aimorés, Minas Gerais. Photo-reporter who only uses black-and-white, a member of Magnum 1979–94. Works include *Workers* (1992), *Migrations* (2000) and *Africa* (2007).

Salomon, Erich (1886–1944) German, born Berlin. Prisoner-of-war in France (1915–18). Began freelance photographic career in 1927, working for *L'Illustration* of Paris and *Fortune* of New York. Died at Auschwitz with his wife and son.

Sander, August (1876–1964) German, born Herdorf am Sieg. Planned a massive photographic documentary study, *Men in the 20th Century*, but only the first part, *Faces of Our Times* (1929), was published as his social realism was discouraged by the Nazi Ministry of Culture after 1934. Surviving material has provided penetrating portraits of all levels of German life in the early part of the century.

Sheeler, Charles (1883–1965) American, born Philadelphia, Pennsylvania. Worked as industrial photographer from 1912, producing creative industrial records, especially of the skyscrapers of Manhattan in *Mannahatta* (1920). Commissioned to record the building of the Ford Motor installation at River Rouge, Michigan (1927).

Sielmann, Heinz (1917–2006) German, born Königsberg. Interested in animal photography, started making films in 1938, for which he won three German Oscars (1953–5). Developed techniques enabling photography in inaccessible animal lairs which revolutionized the study of animal behaviour.

Siskind, Aaron (1903–91) American, born New York City. Self-taught freelance photographer from 1932. Co-editor of the Chicago poetry and photographic magazine *Choice* (1961–70).

Smith, W(illiam) Eugene (1918–78) American, born Wichita, Kansas. Staff photographer for *Newsweek* in New York (1937–8) and later freelance for magazines including *Harper's Bazaar* and *Life*. Pacific war correspondent (1942–5) and photographer for Hitachi in New York and Japan (1959–77). .

Smythe, Francis Sydney (1900–49) English, born Maidstone. Mountaineer whose many books, including *Kamet Conquered* (1932), *Adventures of a Mountaineer* (1940) and *Over Welsh Hills* (1941) contain acclaimed mountain photography.

Snowdon, Antony Charles Robert Armstrong-Jones, 1st Earl of (1930–) English, born London. Freelance photographer from 1951 and artistic adviser for many publications. Famous for informal portraits of the famous, he has also photographed disabled people and has produced documentaries for television on similar themes.

Steichen, Edward Jean (1879–1973) American, born Luxembourg. Practised painting and photography in Europe until 1914. Noted for his studies of the nude. A founder of the American Photo-Secession Group, he later served in the photographic division of the US army during World War I, and in the 1920s achieved success in fashion photography. Head of US Naval Film Services during World War II and director of photography at the New York Museum of Modern Art (1945–62), organizing the world-famous exhibition *The Family of Man* (1945).

Stieglitz, Alfred (1864–1946) American, born Hoboken, New Jersey. Studied engineering and photography in Berlin and later was a founder of the Photo-Secession Group in 1902, devoted to artistic expression in photography. Exerted great influence through his magazine *Camera Work* (1903–17) and his gallery of modern art. Other work includes studies of New York architecture, clouds and portraits.

Strand, Paul (1890–1976) American, born New York City. Became commercial photographer in 1912, committed to 'straight' photography of precision and clarity. Produced documentary films during the 1920s and 1930s, but from the 1940s concentrated on still photography for records of his life in many different parts of the world.

Sutcliffe, Frank Meadow (1853–1941) English, born near Whitby, Yorkshire. Received numerous international awards for studies of the vanishing world of English farmhands and fisher-folk in the local country and seacoast between 1881 and 1905. From late 1890s made use of new lightweight cameras to obtain natural snapshots rather than formal poses.

Talbot, William Henry Fox (1800–77) English, born Melbury, Dorset. Announced his invention of photography, a system of making photographic prints on silver chloride paper, in 1839. In 1841 patented the calotype, the first process for photographic negatives from which prints could be made. Also discovered a method of instantaneous flash photography. His *Pencil of Nature* (1844) was the first photographically illustrated book to be published.

Testino, Mario (1954–) Peruvian, born Lima. Portrait and fashion photographer, who began his career when he moved to London in 1976. He has photographed many celebrities, including Diana, Princess of Wales. Publications include *Any Objections?* (1996), *Alive* (2001) and *Portraits* (2002).

Van der Elsken, Ed(uard) (1925–90) Dutch, born Amsterdam. Self-taught freelance photographer in Amsterdam (1947–50), Paris (1950–5) and Edam, the Netherlands after 1955. Also freelance film-maker.

Weber, Bruce (1946–) American, born Greensburg, Pennsylvania. Known for his work on fashion campaigns for Calvin Klein, Ralph Lauren and other top designers in which he concentrates on the male body. Also works in film.

Weegee (Fellig, Arthur) (1899–1968) American, born Lemburg, Austria (now Lviv, Ukraine). Emigrated to the USA with his parents in 1910. Freelance press photographer noted for his candid shots of New York's seedy night life, especially crime scenes and police arrests.

Weston, Edward (Henry) (1886–1958) American, born Highland Park, Illinois. Became recognized as modernist, emphasizing sharp images and precise definition in landscapes, portraits and still-life. First photographer to receive a Guggenheim Fellowship with which he travelled widely throughout the American West.

White, Minor (Martin) (1908–76) American, born Minneapolis, Minnesota. Developed the realism of the photographic sequence and the abstraction of the 'equivalent', the visual metaphor in which he continued Stieglitz's symbolism of natural formations. In 1946 moved to San Francisco and worked with Ansel Adams. Founded the periodicals *Aperture* (1952) and *Image* (1953–7).

Winogrand, Garry (1928–84) American, born New York. Striking images of US society from the 1960s onwards.

Fashion designers

Amies, Sir (Edwin) Hardy (1909–2003) English, born London. Couturier and dressmaker by appointment to Queen Elizabeth II. Renowned especially for tailored suits for women. Founded his own fashion house in 1946 and started designing for men also in 1959.

Armani, Giorgio (1935–) Italian, born Piacenza. Became designer for Nino Cerruti in 1961 and also freelanced before setting up the Giorgio Armani company in 1975. Designed first for men, then women, including loose-fitting jackets and blazers.

Ashley, Laura (née **Mountney**) (1925–85) Welsh, born Merthyr Tydfil. Started business with husband Bernard Ashley in 1953, manufacturing furnishing materials and wallpapers with patterns based mainly on 19th-century document sources. Later experimented with designing and making clothes, transforming the business from one shop to an international chain of boutiques.

Balenciaga, Cristóbal (1895–1972) Spanish, born Guetaria. Opened dressmaking and tailoring shops in Madrid and Barcelona in 1915. Moved to Paris in 1937 because of the Spanish Civil War. His clothes were noted for dramatic simplicity and elegant design.

Balmain, Pierre Alexandre (1914–82) French, born St Jean-de-Maurienne. Worked for Edward Molyneux and Lucien Lelong before opening his own house in 1945. Famous for elegant simplicity, his designs included evening dresses, tailored suits, sportswear and stoles. Also designed for the theatre and cinema.

Blahnik, Manolo (1942–) Spanish, born Santa Cruz de la Palma, Canary Islands. After studying in Geneva and in Paris, he moved to London in 1970. Self-taught as a shoe designer, he opened his first shop in 1973, quickly gaining renown. His work was exhibited at the Design Museum in 2003.

Boateng, Ozwald (c.1967–) English, born London. Began designing clothes as a teenager, and making bespoke suits in the early 1990s. Appointed creative director of Givenchy in 2003. Credited with reinvigorating Savile Row tailoring.

Cardin, Pierre (1922–) French, born Venice, Italy. Worked in fashion houses and on costume design in Paris after World War II and opened his own house in 1953. Since then has been prominent in fashion for both women and men.

Chanel, Gabrielle (known as **Coco**) (1883–1971) French, born Saumur. Orphaned at an early age, she worked with her sister as a milliner until 1912, when she opened a shop of her own. Later opened couture houses in Deauville and Paris, producing designs combining simple elegance and comfort. Also introduced the vogue for costume jewellery and the evening scarf. Retired in 1938, but made a successful comeback in 1954.

Choo, Jimmy (Datuk Jimmy Choo Yeang Keat) (1961–) Malaysian, born Penang. From a family of shoemakers, he trained at the London School of Fashion and established his business in London in 1986, designing elegant hand-made shoes, much favoured by celebrities. He has not been involved in the Jimmy Choo business since 2001, and now runs his own couture house in London.

Claiborne, Liz (1929–) Belgian–American, born Brussels. Designed for Youth Guild Inc, New York

City, before founding own company in 1976. Her designs are targeted at the working woman. She retired in 1989, though the company continues.

Conran, Jasper (1959–) English, born London. Son of Sir Terence Conran, he trained in art and design in New York before joining Fiorucci briefly as a designer in 1977. Produced his first collection of easy-to-wear, quality clothes in London in 1978.

Courrèges, André (1923–) French, born Pau. Trained by Balenciaga from 1952 to 1960, he opened his own house in 1961. Famous for stark, futuristic, 'Space Age' designs, he introduced the miniskirt (1964) and has featured white 'go-go' boots and trouser suits for women.

De la Renta, Oscar (1932–) American, born Santo Domingo, Dominican Republic. Worked at Balenciaga's couture house in Madrid, joined the house of Lanvin-Castillo in Paris (1961) then Elizabeth Arden in New York (1963), before starting his own company in 1965. Has reputation for opulent, ornately trimmed clothes, particularly evening dresses, but also designs daywear and accessories.

Dior, Christian (1905–57) French, born Granville, Normandy. Began designing clothes in 1935, and founded his own Paris house in 1947. Achieved worldwide fame with his long-skirted 'New Look' and subsequently the 'A-line' and 'the Sack'.

Farhi, Nicole (1946–) Anglo-French, born Nice, France. Started working in London on French Connection and the Stephen Marks label. Launched own company in 1983 and became well known for simple, comfortable, but elegant clothing.

Galliano, John (originally **Galliano, Juan Carlos**) (1960–) Gibraltan, born Gibraltar. Graduated from St Martin's School of Art and Design, London in 1984. Inspired by a range of cultural and historical references. Became designer-in-chief at Givenchy in 1995. Left in 1996 to become designer-in-chief at the House of Dior.

Gaultier, Jean-Paul (1952–) French, born Paris. Worked with Cardin for two years (1969–71), then at Patou. In 1976, began working as a freelance designer, drawing inspiration from the London street-scene, which he glamorized for the Paris market. He is now one of the most influential Paris designers.

Givenchy, Hubert James Marcel Taffin de (1927–) French, born Beauvais. After training and working with a number of well-known designers, opened his own house in 1952. His Bettina blouse in white cotton became internationally famous, and his clothes are noted for their elegance and quality. He retired in 1995.

Hamnett, Katharine (1947–) English, born Gravesend, Kent. After studying fashion at St Martin's School of Art and Design in London, worked as a freelance designer, setting up a short-lived company (1969–74) and then her own business in 1979. Draws inspiration for designs from workwear and from movements such as the peace movement.

Hartnell, Sir Norman (Bishop) (1901–78) English, born Honiton, Devon. Started his own couturier business in 1923, receiving the Royal Warrant in 1940. Produced costumes for leading actresses, wartime 'utility' dresses, the WRAC uniform and Princess Elizabeth's wedding and coronation gowns.

Hulanicki, Barbara (1936–) Born Palestine of Polish parents. Launched Biba's Postal Boutique in 1963. Opened three stores in London which became fashion mecca of the 1960s. Biba closed in 1976.

Jacobs, Marc (1963–) American, born New York City. Trained in New York, he designed his first collection under his name in 1987. He has continued to develop clothes and accessories under his own name since joining Perry Ellis (1989–97) and Louis Vuitton (since 1997).

Karan, Donna (originally **Donna Faske**) (1948–) American, born Forest Hills, New York. Became Director of Design at Anne Klein in 1974. Launched Donna Karan Company in 1984, which became Donna Karan International in 1996. She sold the company in 2001.

Kenzo Takada (1939–) Japanese, born Kyoto. After studying art, worked in Japan before producing freelance collections in Paris from 1964. Started a shop called Jungle Jap in 1970. Creates clothes with both oriental and western influences, and is a trendsetter in the field of knitwear.

Klein, Anne Hannah (née **Hannah Golofski**) (1921–74) American, born New York City. Started as sketcher on Seventh Avenue in 1938, and established Anne Klein & Co in 1968. Designed practical sportswear for women.

Klein, Calvin Richard (1942–) American, born New York City. Graduated from New York's Fashion Institute of Technology in 1962, and set up his own firm in 1968. Quickly achieved recognition and is known for understatement and the simple but sophisticated style of his clothes, including 'designer jeans'.

Lacroix, Christian (1951–) French couturier, born Arles, Provence. After studying fashion history, worked for a leather firm with Guy Paulin, a ready-to-wear designer. In 1981 joined Jean Patou; in 1987 opened the House of Lacroix in Paris. Made his name with ornate and frivolous clothes.

Lagerfeld, Karl (1938–) German, born Hamburg. Won an International Wool Secretariat competition in 1954 and worked with Balmain in Paris. After three years he left to begin freelance work with a number of design houses, including Chloë, Ballantyne, Fendi and Valentino. Since 1983 he has designed for Chanel. His talents lie particularly in meticulous cut, extravagant beading, furs and knitwear.

Lang, Helmut (1956–) Austrian, born Vienna. From 1979 has owned made-to-measure shop in Vienna. Launched his first ready-to-wear collection in 1984. .

Laroche, Guy (1923–89) French, born La Rochelle, near Bordeaux. Worked in millinery, first in Paris then on Seventh Avenue, New York, before returning to Paris where he worked for Dessès for eight years; started his own business in 1957, achieving a reputation for skilful cutting. From 1966 his designs included menswear.

Lauren, Ralph (originally **Ralph Lipschitz**) (1939–) American, born The Bronx, New York City. In 1967 joined Beau Brummel Neckwear and created the Polo range for men, later including womenswear. Famous for his American styles, such as the 'prairie look' and 'frontier fashions'.

McCartney, Stella (Nina) (1971–) English, born London. At age 15 she worked for Christian Lacroix, and then spent a number of years on Savile Row. Graduated from St Martin's School of Art and Design, London in 1995. Succeeded Karl Lagerfeld as chief designer for Chloë in

1997, leaving in 2001 to found her own house.

McQueen, Alexander (1969–) British, born London. Showed final collection at St Martin's School of Art and Design, London in 1992. From 1996 to 2001 he was Chief Designer at Givenchy and now runs his own house.

Mainbocher (originally **Main Rousseau Bocher**) (1891–1976) American, born Chicago. After service in World War I stayed on in Paris, eventually becoming a fashion artist with *Harper's Bazaar* and later editor of French *Voguet* until 1929. Started his couture house in Paris in 1930; created the Duchess of Windsor's wedding dress (1937).

Missoni, Tai Ottavio (1921–) Italian, born Dubrovnik, Yugoslavia (now Croatia). Founded the Missoni company in Milan with his wife, Rosita, in 1953. At first manufactured knitwear to be sold under other labels, but later created, under their own label, innovative knitwear notable for its sophistication and distinctive colours and patterns.

Miyake, Issey (1938–) Japanese, born Hiroshima. Spent six years in Paris and New York fashion houses before showing his first collection in Tokyo in 1963. Distinctive style combines eastern and western influences in garments which have an almost theatrical quality.

Molyneux, Edward Henry (1891–1974) English, born London. After studying art, worked for Lucile. Opened his own couture house in Paris in 1919 with branches in London, Monte Carlo, Cannes and Biarritz, and became famous for the elegant simplicity of tailored suits with pleated skirts, and evening wear.

Montana, Claude (1949–) French, born Paris. Began designing jewellery in London, and then moved to leather and knitwear companies. Designed his first ready-to-wear collection in 1976.

Mortensen, Erik (1926–98) Danish. From 1948, attached to the Balmain fashion house in Paris, taking over the management after the death of Pierre Balmain in 1982. Left Balmain in 1992 and worked for Jean-Louis Scherrer until 1994.

Muir, Jean Elizabeth (1928–95) English, born London. Started as sales assistant with Liberty's in London, then moved to Jaeger in 1956. In 1961 started on her own as Jane & Jane and in 1966 established her company Jean Muir. Her clothes are noted for their classic shapes, softness and fluidity.

Oldfield, Bruce (1950–) English, born London. As a freelance designer sold sketches to Yves Saint Laurent and designed for Bendel's store in New York. Showed his first collection in 1975 in London. His designs include evening dresses for royalty and screen stars and ready-to-wear clothes.

Ozbek, Rifat (1953–) Turkish, born Istanbul. Beginning with small collections, now has multi-million pound business. His designs cover many styles and display cross-cultural references.

Patou, Jean (1880–1936) French, born Normandy. In 1912 opened Maison Parry in Paris and in 1913 sold his collection outright to an American buyer. After war service he successfully opened again as a couturier in 1919. Noted for his designs for sports stars and actresses and for his perfume 'Joy'.

Poiret, Paul (1879–1944) French, born Paris. Worked for Jacques Doucet and Worth before opening his own fashion house in 1904. Influenced by the exotic oriental costumes of the Ballets Russes, his designs featured turbans and harem pants. After World War I did not re-establish his prominence and died in poverty.

Prada, Miucca (1949–) Italian, born Milan. Studied political science, then in 1978 with her husband, Patrizio Bertelli, she took over running the house founded by her grandfather in 1913. She developed a new style for accessories, and launched her first ready-to-wear collection in 1989 and the Miu Miu range in 1992. Her plain, stylish approach has proved very popular.

Pucci, Emilio, Marchese di Barsento (1914–92) Italian, born Naples. Member of Italy's Olympic ski team (1933–4) and later member of the Italian parliament (1963–72), he started designing ski clothes in 1947 and in 1950 opened his own couture house, creating print dresses for women. Became renowned for use of bold patterns and brilliant colour.

Quant, Mary (1934–) English, born London. Began fashion design when she opened a small boutique in Chelsea in 1955. Her clothes became extremely fashionable in the 1960s when the geometric simplicity of her designs and the originality of her colours became an essential feature of the 'swinging Britain' era.

Rhodes, Zandra (1940–) English, born Chatham, Kent. After studying art, designed and printed textiles and, with others, opened The Fulham Road Clothes Shop, afterwards setting up on her own. Showed her first dress collection in 1969. Noted for distinctive, exotic designs in chiffons and silks.

Ricci, Nina (1883–1970) Italian, born Turin. Became a dressmaker's apprentice at 13 and a head designer at 20. Opened her own couture house in Paris in 1932 with her jeweller husband Louis. Known for a high standard of workmanship that appealed to elegant, wealthy clients.

Saint Laurent, Yves (originally **Henri Donat Mathieu**) (1936–2008) French, born Oran, Algeria. Employed by Christian Dior in 1955 after winning an International Wool Secretariat design competition. Took over the house on Dior's death in 1957. In 1962 opened his own house and launched the first of his 160 Rive Gauche boutiques in 1966, selling ready-to-wear clothes, a trend which many other designers were to follow. He retired in 2002.

Schiaparelli, Elsa (1890–1973) Italian–French, born Rome. After living in America, moved to Paris and started business in 1929. Her designs were inventive and sensational, and she was noted for her use of bright colour and traditional fabrics, featuring zippers and buttons, and outrageous hats. Opened a salon in New York in 1949, and retired in 1954.

Ungaro, Emanuel Maffeolti (1933–) French, born Aix-en-Provence. Worked for small Paris tailoring firm and later with Balenciaga, before opening his own house in 1965, with Sonia Knapp designing his fabrics. Initially featured rigid lines, but later produced softer styles. Produced his first ready-to-wear lines in 1968.

Valentino (originally **Valentino Garavani**) (1933–) Italian, born Rome. Studied fashion in Milan and Paris, then worked for Jean Dessès and Guy Laroche in Paris. Opened his own house in Rome in 1959, and achieved worldwide recognition with his 1962 show in Florence. Opened numerous ready-to-wear boutiques. Sold the House of Valentino in 1998, but remains chief designer.

Versace, Gianni (1946–97) Italian, born Calabria. Launched first women's wear collection in 1978. Opened boutique and designed first menswear collection in 1979. Has designed for various ballet productions. Was shot dead outside his American home.

Westwood, Vivienne (1941–) English, born London. Began clothes design on meeting Malcolm McLaren, manager of The Sex Pistols. They established a shop in London and became known as the leading creators of punk clothing. Since her split from McLaren in 1983, has become accepted by the mainstream.

Worth, Charles Frederick (1825–95) Anglo-French, born Bourne, Lincolnshire. Achieved success as a fashion designer in Paris, gaining the patronage of the Empress Eugénie. His establishment in the Rue de la Paix became the centre of the fashion world.

Yamamoto, Yohji (1943–) Japanese, born Tokyo. Started his own company in 1972 producing his first collection in 1976 in Tokyo. After some time in Paris, opened a new headquarters in London in 1987. Designs loose, functional clothes for men and women, which conceal rather than emphasize the body.

Major architectural styles

Art Nouveau A deliberately new style, c.1890–1910, uninfluenced by past art, characterized mainly by undulating plant-like forms (particularly as surface decoration) and coloured materials; eg *Glasgow School of Art* by Charles Rennie Mackintosh.

Baroque The dominant European style of the 17c and early 18c, typically bold and exuberant, using Renaissance forms with a new freedom; eg gardens, fountains and palace at *Versailles*, France; Early Baroque: façade for *St Peter's* by Carlo Moderno; High Baroque: work by Gian Lorenzo Bernini and Francesco Borromini in Italy; Late Baroque: work by Balthasar Neumann and Johann Bernhard Fischer von Erlach.

Brutalism A reaction in the 1950s against the sleek sophistication of the International Modern style, characterized by chunky forms and exposed concrete; eg *Chandigarh*, the new capital of the Punjab, India, by Le Corbusier.

Byzantine The style of the Byzantine empire, which flourished 4–15c, its capital being Constantinople (originally Byzantium, now Istanbul). It blends Roman and eastern influences and its most typical form is the large domed church, lavishly decorated with mosaics; eg *Hagia Sophia*, Istanbul.

Gothic The style that succeeded Romanesque throughout Europe, characterized most obviously by the use of pointed arches and also by rib vaults, flying buttresses and elaborate window tracery. It began in France in the 1140s and flourished in many places into the 16c, windows generally becoming an increasingly prominent feature; eg *Cathedrals of Lincoln* and *Salisbury*, England; *Cathedral of Chartres*, France.

Gothic Revival A revival of the Gothic style of the Middle Ages, beginning in the 18c and flourishing in the 19c, particularly in Britain; it was used in buildings of all kinds – religious, civil, commercial and domestic; eg *Houses of Parliament*, London, by Sir Charles Barry and Augustus W N Pugin; *Grace Church*, New York City, by James Renwick.

Greek The style characteristic of ancient Greece and its Mediterranean colonies from the 7 BC, when stone building was revived, to the 1c BC, when Greece was absorbed into the Roman Empire. The most important Greek buildings were temples, and the beautifully proportioned columns that became typical of them were immensely influential on Roman and on much

subsequent European architecture; eg *Parthenon*, Athens.

High Tech An approach popular since the 1970s in which architects stress the technological aspects of a building, typically by giving dramatic visual expression to structural elements or services (pipes, air ducts and so on) that are usually hidden from view; eg *Pompidou Centre*, Paris, and the *Lloyds Building*, London, both by Richard Rogers.

International Modern or **International Style** A sleek, functional style that dominated progressive architecture in Europe and America in the 1930s and 1940s; eg *Bauhaus*, Dessau, Germany, by Walter Gropius; *Fallingwater*, Mill Run, Pennsylvania by Frank Lloyd Wright.

Neoclassicism A revival of the styles of ancient Greece and Rome in the late 18c and early 19c; eg *Charlotte Square*, Edinburgh, by Robert Adam; *Hôtel Dieu*, Lyons, by Jacques Soufflot.

Post-Modernism A trend, beginning in the 1970s, in which the cool rationalism of International Modern style was abandoned in favour of stylistic eclecticism; eg *Brant-Johnson House* in Vail, Colorado, by Robert Venturi; *Piazza d'Italia*, New Orleans, by Charles Willard Moore.

Renaissance A revival or 'rebirth' of the classical art of ancient Rome, beginning in Italy in the early 15c and spreading over Europe until the advent of Baroque; eg the circular *Tempietto of S Pietro*, Montoria, Rome, by Donato Bramante; *Banqueting House*, Whitehall, London, by Inigo Jones.

Rococo A style that emerged from Baroque in the early 18c; like Baroque, it tended to make vigorous use of curved forms, but it was lighter and more playful; eg *Residenztheater*, Munich, by François de Cuvilliés.

Roman The style of the ancient Romans, which spread over their empire, at its peak 1–4c AD; the Romans took much of the 'vocabulary' of classical architecture from the Greeks (particularly systematic use of columns), but added many features of their own, and excelled in the sheer size of their buildings and engineering projects; eg *Pantheon*, Rome; *Colosseum*, Rome.

Romanesque The style prevailing in most of Europe in the 11c and 12c, characterized by massive strength of construction, and the use of round-headed arches and windows (as opposed to the pointed arches of the Gothic style that succeeded it); eg *San Miniato al Monte*, Florence.

Architects

Selected works are listed.

Arts and Culture

Aalto, (Hugo) Alvar (Henrik) (1898–1976) Finnish, born Kuortane; *Convalescent Home*, Paimio, near Turku (1929–30), *Town Hall*, Saynatsab (1950–2), *Finlandia Concert Hall*, Helsinki (1971).

Adam, Robert (1728–92) Scottish, born Kirkcaldy; *General Register House* (begun 1774), *Charlotte Square* (1791), *University of Edinburgh, Old College* (1789–94), all Edinburgh; *Culzean Castle*, Ayrshire (1772–92).

Adam, William (1689–1748) Scottish, born Maryburgh; *Hopetoun House*, near Edinburgh (1721).

Alberti, Leon Battista (1404–72) Italian, born Genoa; façade of the *Palazzo Rucellai*, Florence (1460), *San Andrea*, Mantua (1470).

Ando, Tadao (1941) Japanese, born Osaka; *Rokko Housing Two*, Kobe (1993), *Pulitzer Foundation*, St Louis (2001).

Anthemias of Tralles (dates unknown) Greek, born Tralles, Lydia; *Hagia Sophia*, Constantinople (now Istanbul) (532–7).

Apollodorus of Damascus (dates unknown) Greek, born Syria; *Trajan's Forum*, Rome, *The Baths of Trajan*, Rome.

Asplund, Erik Gunnar (1885–1940) Swedish, born Stockholm; *Stockholm City Library* (1924–7), *Law Courts*, Gothenburg (1934–7).

Baker, Sir Herbert (1862–1946) English, born Kent; *Groote Schuur*, near Cape Town (1892–1902), *Union Government Buildings*, Pretoria (1907).

Barry, Sir Charles (1795–1860) English, born London; *Royal Institution of the Arts*, Manchester (1824), *Houses of Parliament*, London (opened 1852).

Behrens, Peter (1868–1940) German, born Hamburg; *Turbine Assembly Works*, Berlin (1909), *German Embassy*, St Petersburg (1912).

Berlage, Hendrick Petrus (1856–1934) Dutch, born Amsterdam; *Amsterdam Bourse* (1903), *Holland House*, London (1914), *Gemeente Museum*, The Hague (1934).

Bernini, Gian Lorenzo (1598–1680) Italian, born Naples; *St Peter's Baldacchino* (1625), *Cornaro Chapel* in the Church of Santa Maria della Vittoria (1645–52), both Rome.

Borromini, Francesco (1599–1667) Italian, born Bissone, on Lake Lugano; *S Carlo alle Quattro Fontane* (1637–41), *S Ivo della Sapienza* (1642–61), both Rome.

Boullée, Étienne-Louis (1728–99) French, born Paris; *Hôtel de Brunoy*, Paris (1772), *Monument to Isaac Newton* (never built) (1794).

Bramante, Donato (originally **Donato di Pascuccio d'Antonio**) (1444–1514) Italian, born near Urbino; *San Maria presso S Satiro*, Milan (begun 1482), *Tempietto of S Pietro*, Rome (1502).

Breuer, Marcel Lajos (1902–81) Hungarian–American, born Pécs, Hungary; *UNESCO Building*, Paris (1953–8).

Brosse, Salomon de (1565–1626) French, born Verneuil-sur-Oise; *Luxembourg Palace*, Paris (1615–20), *Louis XIII's Hunting Lodge*, Versailles (1624–6).

Brunelleschi, Filippo (1377–1446) Italian, born Florence; *San Lorenzo*, Florence (begun 1418), Dome of *Florence Cathedral* (begun 1420), *Ospedale degli Innocenti*, Florence (1419).

Bryce, David (1803–76) Scottish, born Edinburgh; *Fettes College* (1863–9), *former Royal Infirmary* (begun 1870), both Edinburgh.

Burnham, David Hudson (1846–1912) American, born Henderson, New York; *Reliance Building*, Chicago (1890–5), *Monadnock Building*, Chicago (1890–1), *Selfridge Building*, London (1908).

Burton, Decimus (1800–81) English, born London; *Regent's Park Colosseum* (1823), *Arch at Hyde Park Corner* (1825), both London.

Butterfield, William (1814–1900) English, born London; *Keble College*, Oxford (1866–86), *St Augustine's College*, Canterbury (1844–73), *All Saints'*, Margaret Street, London (1849–59).

Calatrava, Santiago (1951–) Spanish, born Valencia; *Puente del Alamillo*, Seville(1992), *Milwaukee Art Museum*, Milwaukee (2001), *Turning Torso*, Malmo (2005).

Campen, Jacob van (1595–1657) Dutch, born Haarlem; *Maurithuis*, The Hague (1633), *Amsterdam Theatre* (1637), *Amsterdam Town Hall* (1647–55).

Candela, Felix (1910–97) Spanish–Mexican, born Madrid; *Sports Palace* for Olympic Games, Mexico City (1968).

Chambers, Sir William (1726–96) Scottish, born Stockholm; *Somerset House* (1776), *pagoda in Kew Gardens* (1757), both London.

Chermayeff, Serge (1900–96) American, born the Caucasus Mountains, Russia; *De La Warr Pavilion*, Bexhill (1933–5).

Churriguera, Don José (1650–1725) Spanish, born Salamanca; *Salamanca Cathedral* (1692–4).

Coates, Wells (Wintemute) (1895–1958) English, born Tokyo; *Isokon Building*, London (1933–4), *Telek Cinema*, Festival of Britain Exhibition (1951).

Cockerell, Charles Robert (1788–1863) English, born London; *Fitzwilliam Museum*, Cambridge (1837–40), *Taylorian Institute*, Oxford (1841–5).

Cortona, Pietro Berrettini da (1596–1669) Italian, born Cortona; *Villa Sacchetti*, Castel Fusano (1626–7), *San Firenze*, Florence (1645).

Cuvilliés, François de (1695–1768) Bavarian, born Belgium; *Amelienburg Pavilion* at Schloss Nymphenburg, near Munich (1734–9), *Residenztheater*, Munich (1750–3).

Dance, George, (the Elder) (1700–68) English, born London; *Mansion House*, London (1739).

Dance, George, (the Younger) (1741–1825) English, born London; *rebuilt Newgate Prison* (1770–83).

Delorme, Philibert (c.1510–70) French, born Lyons; *Châteaux of Anet, Meudon, Saint Germain-en-Laye* (1547–55), *Tuileries* (1565–70).

Doesburg, Theo van (originally **Christian Emil Marie Kupper**) (1883–1931) Dutch, born Utrecht; *L'Art Nouveau Shop*, Paris (1896), *Keller und Reiner Art Gallery*, Berlin (1898).

Doshi, Balkrishna Vithaldas (1927–) Indian, born Poona; *City Hall*, Toronto (1958), *Indian Institute of Management*, Ahmedabad (1951–7).

Dudok, Willem Marinus (1884–1974) Dutch, born Amsterdam; *Hilversum Town Hall* (1928–30), *Bijenkorf Department Store*, Rotterdam (1929).

Engel, Johann Carl Ludwig (1778–1840) Finnish, born Berlin; layout of Helsinki (1818–26).

Erickson, Arthur Charles (1924–2009) Canadian, born Vancouver; *Simon Fraser University Buildings*, British Columbia (1963), *Lethbridge University*, Alberta (1971).

Fischer von Erlach, Johann Bernard (1656–1723) Austrian, born Graz; *Karlskirche*, Vienna (1716), *Hofbibliotek*, Vienna (1723), *Kollegienkirche*, Salzburg (1707).

Foster, Norman Foster, Baron (1935–) English, born Manchester; *Willis Faber Dumas Building*, Ipswich (1975), *Sainsbury Centre*, University of East Anglia (1978), *Hong Kong and Shanghai Bank*, Hong Kong (1979–85), *Beijing Airport*, China (2003–8).

Francesco di Giorgio (1439–1501/2) Italian, born Siena; *Church of San Bernardino all'Osservanza*, Siena (1474–84), *Palazzo Ducale*, Gubbio (1476–82).

Gabriel, Ange-Jacques (1698–1782) French, born Paris; *Pavillon de Pompadour*, Fontainebleau (begun 1749), Paris; layout of *Place de la Concorde*, Paris (1753), *Petit Trianon*, Versailles (1761–8).

Garnier, Tony (Antoine) (1869–1948) French, born Lyons; *Grange Blanche Hospital*, Lyons (1911–27), *Stadium*, Lyons (1913–18), *Hôtel de Ville*, Boulogne-Bilancourt (1931–3).

Gaudí (i Cornet), Antoni (1852–1926) Spanish, born Reus, Tarragona; *Casa Vicens* (1878–80), *Sagrada Familia* (1884 onwards), *Casa Batlló* (1904–17), *Casa Milá* (1905–9), all Barcelona.

Geddes, Sir Patrick (1854–1932) Scottish, born Perth; *Ramsay Garden*, Edinburgh (1892), *Edinburgh Zoo* (1913), *Scots College*, Montpellier, France (1924).

Gehry, Frank (1929–) US–Canadian, born Toronto; *Los Angeles Children's Museum* (1979), *Dancing House*, Prague (1996), *Guggenheim Museum*, Bilbao (1997), *Maggie's Centre*, Dundee (2003).

Gibbs, James (1682–1754) Scottish, born Aberdeen; *St-Martin-in-the-Fields*, London (1722–6), *King's College Fellows' Building*, Cambridge (1724–49).

Gilbert, Cass (1859–1934) American, born Zanesville, Ohio; *Woolworth Building*, New York City (1913).

Gilly, Friedrich (1772–1800) German, born Berlin; *Funerary Precinct and Temple* to Frederick II, the Great of Prussia (1796), *Prussian National Theatre*, Berlin (1798).

Giulio Romano (properly **Giulio Pippi de' Gianuzzi**) (c.1492–1546) Italian, born Rome; *Palazzo del Tè*, Mantua (1526), *Church of S Petronio* façade, Bologna (1546).

Greenway, Francis Howard (1777–1837) Anglo-Australian, born Bristol; *Macquarie Lighthouse*, Sydney Harbour (1818), *St James' Church*, Sydney (1824).

Gropius, Walter (1883–1969) German–American, born Berlin; *Fagus Shoe Factory*, Alfeld (1911), *Bauhaus*, Dessau (1925), both Germany; *Harvard University Graduate Centre* (1950), Massachusetts.

Guarini, Guarino (originally **Camillo**) (1624–83) Italian, born Modena; *San Lorenzo* church, Turin (1668–80), *Capella della SS Sindone* church, Turin (1668), *Palazzo Carignano*, Racconigi (1679).

Hadid, Zaha (1950–) Iraqi–British, born Baghdad; *Vitra Fire Station*, Weil am Rhein (1994), *BMW Central Building*, Leipzig (2005), *Maggie's Centre*, Kirkcaldy (2006).

Hamilton, Thomas (1784–1858) Scottish, born Glasgow; *Royal High School* (1825–9), *Royal College of Physicians Hall* (1844–5), *George IV Bridge* (1827–34), all Edinburgh.

Haussmann, Georges Eugène (1809–91) French, born Paris; layout of *Bois de Boulogne*, *Bois de Vincennes*, Paris (1853–70).

Hawksmoor, Nicholas (1661–1736) English, born Nottinghamshire; *St Mary Woolnoth Church* (1716–24), *St George's*, Bloomsbury (1716–30), both London.

Hildebrandt, Johann Lukas von (1668–1745) Austrian, born Genoa; *Lower and Upper Belvedere*, Vienna, (1714–15, 1720–3).

Hoffmann, Josef (1870–1956) Austrian, born Pirnitz; *Purkersdorf Sanatorium* (1903–5), *Stociet House*, Brussels (1905–11).

Holland, Henry (1746–1806) English, born London; *Carlton House*, London (1783–96), *Brighton Pavilion* (1787).

Howard, Sir Ebenezer (1850–1928) English, born London; *Letchworth Garden City* (1903).

Itkinos and Callicrates (dates and place of birth unknown) Greek; *The Parthenon*, Athens (447/6–438 BC).

Jacobsen, Arne (1902–71) Danish, born Copenhagen; *Town Hall of Aarhus* (with Erik Møller, 1938–42), *SAS Tower*, Copenhagen (1960), all Denmark; *St Catherine's College*, Oxford (1959).

Jefferson, Thomas (1743–1826) American, born Shadwell, Virginia; *Monticello*, Albemarle County (1769), *Virginia State Capitol* (1796).

Johnson, Philip Cortelyou (1906–2005) American, born Cleveland, Ohio; *Seagram Building*, New York City (1945), *Glass House*, New Canaan, Connecticut (1949–50), *New York State Theater*, Lincoln Center (1964).

Jones, Inigo (1573–1652) English, born London; *The Queen's House*, Greenwich (1616–18, 1629–35), *Banqueting House*, Whitehall, London (1619–22).

Kahn, Louis Isadore (1901–74) American architect, born Osel (now Saaremaa), Estonia; *Richards Medical Research Building*, Pennsylvania (1957–61), *Kimbell Art Musuem*, Fort Worth (1867–72).

Koolhaas, Rem (1944–) Dutch, born Rotterdam; *Kunsthal*, Rotterdam (1992), *Casa da Música*, Oporto (2001–5).

Labrouste, (Pierre François) Henri (1801–75) French, born Paris; *Bibliothèque Sainte Geneviève* (1838–50), *Bibliothèque Nationale* reading room (1860–7), both Paris.

Lasdun, Sir Denys Louis (1914–2001) English, born London; *Royal College of Musicians* (1958–64), *National Theatre* (1965–76), both London.

Le Corbusier (pseudonym of **Charles Édouard Jeanneret**) (1887–1965) French, born La Chaux-de-Fonds, Switzerland; *Salvation Army Hostel*, Paris (begun 1929), *Chapel of Ronchamp*, near Belfort (1950–4), *Chandigarh*, Punjab (1951–6), *Museum of Modern Art*, Tokyo (1957).

Ledoux, Claude Nicolas (1736–1806) French, born Dormans, Champagne; *Château*, Louveciennes (1771–3), *Theatre*, Besançon (1771–3).

Leonardo da Vinci (1452–1519) Italian, born Vinci; *Mariolo de Guiscardi House*, Milan (1497), *La Veruca Fortress*, near Pisa (1504), *Villa Melzi*, Vaprio, Milan (1513).

Lescot, Pierre (c.1510–78) French, born Paris; screen of *St Germain l'Auxerrois* (1541–4), rebuilt one wing of the *Louvre*, Paris (1546).

Lethaby, William Richard (1857–1931) English, born Barnstaple; *Avon Tyrell*, Hampshire (1891–2), *Eagle Insurance Buildings*, Birmingham (1899–1900).

Le Vau or **Levau, Louis** (1612–70) French, born Paris; *Hôtel Lambert*, Paris (1640–4), part of *Palace of Versailles* (from 1661), *Collège des Quatre Nations*, Paris (1661).

Libeskind, Daniel (1946–) Polish-American, born Łódź; *Jewish Museum*, Berlin (1999), *Imperial War Museum North*, Manchester (2002).

Loos, Adolf (1870–1933) Austrian, born Brno, Moravia; *Steiner House*, Vienna (1910).

Lorimer, Sir Robert Stodart (1864–1929) Scottish, born Edinburgh; *Thistle Chapel, St Giles*, Edinburgh (1909–11), *Scottish National War Memorial*, Edinburgh Castle (1923–8).

Lutyens, Sir Edwin Landseer (1869–1944) English,

Arts and Culture

Arts and Culture

born London; *Cenotaph*, Whitehall, London (1919–20), *Liverpool Roman Catholic Cathedral* (1929–c.1941, only crypt completed), *Viceroy's House*, New Delhi (1921–5).

Mackintosh, Charles Rennie (1868–1928) Scottish, born Glasgow; *Glasgow School of Art* (1897–9), *Hill House*, Helensburgh (1902–3).

Mackmurdo, Arthur Heygate (1851–1942) English, born London; *Gordon Institute for Boys*, St Helens (1890).

Maderna or **Maderno, Carlo** (1556–1629) Italian, born Capalago; *S Susanna* (1597–1603), façade of *St Peter's* (1606–12), *Palazzo Barberini* (1628–38), all Rome.

Mansard or **Mansart, François** (1598–1666) French, born Paris; *Sainte-Marie de la Visitation*, Paris (1632), north wing of *Château de Blois* (1635).

Mansard or **Mansart, Jules Hardouin** (1645–1708) French, born Paris; *Grand Trianon, Palace of Versailles* (1678–89).

Mendelsohn, Eric (1887–1953) German, born Allenstein; *De La Warr Pavilion*, Bexhill (1933–5), *Anglo-Palestine Bank*, Jerusalem (1938).

Michelozzo di Bartolommeo (1396–1472) Italian, born Florence; *Villa Medici*, Fiesole (1458–61), *San Marco*, Florence (begun 1437).

Mies van der Rohe, Ludwig (1886–1969) German–American, born Aachen; *Seagram Building*, New York City (1956–8), *Public Library*, Washington (1967).

Miralles, Enric (1955–2000) Spanish, born Catalonia; *Santa Caterina Market*, Barcelona (2001), *Scottish Parliament Building*, Edinburgh (2002).

Moneo, José Rafael (1937–) Spanish, born Tudela; *National Museum of Roman Art*, Mérida (1980–4), *Prado Extension*, Madrid (2000–5).

Moore, Charles Willard (1925–93) American, born Benton Harbor, Michigan; *Sea Ranch Condominium Estate*, Glendale, California (1965), *Piazza d'Italia*, New Orleans (1975–8).

Nash, John (1752–1835) English, born London; layout of *Regent's Park* and *Regent Street*, London (1811 onwards), *Brighton Pavilion* (1815).

Nervi, Pier Luigi (1891–1979) Italian, born Sondrio; *Berta Stadium*, Florence (1930–2), *Olympic Stadia*, Rome (1960), *San Francisco Cathedral* (1970).

Neumann, (Johann) Balthasar (1687–1753) German, born Eger; *Würzburg Palace* (1730–43), *Schloss Bruchsal* (1738–53).

Niemeyer, Oscar (1907–) Brazilian, born Rio de Janeiro; *Church of St Francis of Assisi*, Belo Horizonte, Brazil (1942–4), *Niemeyer House*, Rio de Janeiro (1953), *Museum of Contemporary Art*, Niteroi, Brazil (1996).

Nouvel, Jean (1945–) French, born Fumel; *Arab World Institute*, Paris (1981–7), *Torre Agbar*, Barcelona (2001–4).

Oud, Jacobus Johann Pieter (1890–1963) Dutch, born Purmerend; *Alida Hartog-Ond House*, Purmerend (1906), *Café de Unie*, Rotterdam (1924), *Convention Centre*, The Hague (1957–63).

Palladio, Andrea (1508–80) Italian, born Padua; *Godi-Porto* (villa at Lonedo) (1540), *La Malcontenta* (villa near Padua) (1560), *San Giorgio Maggiore*, Venice (begun 1566).

Paxton, Sir Joseph (1801–65) English, born Milton-Bryant, near Woburn; building for *Great Exhibition* of 1851, later re-erected as the *Crystal Palace*, Sydenham (1852–4).

Pei, I(eoh) M(ing) (1917–) Chinese–American, born Canton; *Mile High Center*, Denver (1954–9), *John Hancock Tower*, Boston (1973), *Glass*

Pyramids, the Louvre, Paris (1983–9).

Perret, Auguste (1874–1954) French, born Brussels; *Théâtre des Champs Élysées*, Paris (1911–13), *Musée des travaux publics*, Paris (1936).

Piano, Renzo (1937–) Italian, born Genoa; *Centre George Pompidou*, Paris (with Richard Rogers) (1971), *Kansai International Air Terminal*, Osaka (1994), *Padre Pio Pilgrimage Church*, San Giovanni Rotondo, Italy (2004).

Piranesi, Giambattista (1720–78) Italian, born Venice; *Santa Maria Arentina*, Rome (1764–6).

Pisano, Nicola (c.1225–c.1284) Italian, born Tuscany; *Pisa Baptistry* (1260), façade renovation of *Pisa Cathedral* (1260–70).

Playfair, William Henry (1789–1857) Scottish, born London; *National Gallery of Scotland* (1850–7), *Royal Scottish Academy* (1832–5), *Surgeon's Hall* (1829–32), all Edinburgh.

Poelzig, Hans (1869–1936) German, born Berlin; *Exhibition Hall*, Posen (1910–11), *Salzburg Festival Theatre* (1920–2).

Pugin, Augustus Welby Northmore (1812–52) English, born London; drawings, decorations and sculpture for the *Houses of Parliament*, London (1836–7), *Birmingham Cathedral* (1839–41).

Renwick, James (1818–95) American, born New York; *Smithsonian Institution*, Washington (1844–55), *Grace Church*, New York (1846), *St Patrick's Cathedral*, New York (1858–79).

Rietveld, Gerrit Thomas (1888–1964) Dutch, born Utrecht; *Schröder House*, Utrecht (1924), *Van Gogh Museum*, Amsterdam (1963–4).

Rogers, Richard George Rogers, Baron (1933–) English, born Florence; *Pompidou Centre*, Paris (1971–9), *Lloyd's*, London (1979–85), *National Assembly for Wales* (1998–2005), *Madrid Barajas Airport*, Madrid (1997–2005), *Heathrow Terminal 5*, London (2008).

Saarinen, Eero (1910–61) Finnish–American, born Kirkknonummi; *Jefferson Memorial Arch*, St Louis (1948–64), *American Embassy*, London (1955–60).

Saarinen, (Gottlieb) Eliel (1873–1950) Finnish–American, born Rantasalmi; *Cranbrook Academy of Art*, Michigan (1934–40).

Sanmichele, Michele (c.1484–1559) Italian, born Verona; *Capella Pelegrini*, Verona (1527–57), *Palazzo Grimani*, Venice (1551–9).

Sansovino, Jacopo (1486–1570) Italian, born Florence; *Library* and *Mint*, Venice.

Schinkel, Karl Friederich (1781–1841) German, born Neurippen, Brandenburg; *War Memorial on the Kreuzberg* (1818), *Old Museum*, Berlin (1823–30).

Scott, Sir George Gilbert (1811–78) English, born Gawcott, Buckinghamshire; *Albert Memorial*, London (1862–3), *St Pancras Station and Hotel*, London (1865), *Glasgow University* (1865).

Serlio, Sebastiano (1475–1554) Italian, born Bologna; *Grand Ferrare*, Fontainebleau (1541–8), *Château*, Ancy-le-Franc, Tonnerre (from 1546).

Shaw, (Richard) Norman (1831–1912) English, born Edinburgh; *Old Swan House*, Chelsea (1876), *New Scotland Yard*, London (1888).

Siza, Álvaro (1933–) Portuguese, born Matosinhos; *Faculty of Architecture*, Oporto (1987–93), *Public Library*, Viana do Castelo (2006–8).

Smirke, Sir Robert (1781–1867) English, born London; *Covent Garden Theatre*, London (1809), *British Museum*, London (1823–47).

Smythson, Robert (c.1535–1614) English, place of birth unknown; *Wollaton Hall*, Nottingham (1580–8), *Hardwick Hall*, Derbyshire (1591–7).

Soane, Sir John (1753–1837) English, born near Reading; altered interior of *Bank of England* (1788–1833), *Dulwich College Art Gallery* (1811–14).

Sottsass, Ettore, Jr (1917–2007) Italian, born Innsbruck; *Apartment Building*, Turin (1934), *Galleria del Cavalliro*, Venice (1956).

Soufflot, Jacques Germain (1713–80) French, born Irancy; *Hôtel Dieu*, Lyons (1741), *St Geneviève* (Panthéon), Paris (begun 1757).

Spence, Sir Basil Urwin (1907–76) Scottish, born India; Pavilions for *Festival of Britain* (1951), *Coventry Cathedral* (1951–62).

Stirling, Sir James (1926–92) Scottish, born Glasgow; *History Faculty*, Cambridge (1965–8), *Florey Building*, Queen's College, Oxford (1966), *Neue Staatsgalerie*, Stuttgart (1980–4).

Street, George Edmund (1824–81) English, born Woodford, Essex; *London Law Courts* (1870–81).

Stuart, James (1713–88) English, born London; rebuilt interior of *Chapel of Greenwich Hospital* (1779).

Sullivan, Louis Henry (1856–1924) American, born Boston, Massachusetts; *Wainwright Building*, St Louis (1890), *Carson, Pirie and Scott Store*, Chicago (1899–1904).

Tange, Kenzo (1913–2005) Japanese, born Tokyo; *Hiroshima Peace Centre* (1949–55), *Shizoka Press and Broadcasting Centre*, Tokyo (1966–7).

Utzon, Jørn (1918–2008) Danish, born Copenhagen; *Sydney Opera House* (1956–68), *Kuwait House of Parliament* (1972–8).

Vanbrugh, Sir John (1664–1726) English, born London; *Castle Howard* (1699–1726), *Blenheim Palace* (1705–20).

Velde, Henri Clemens van de (1863–1957) Belgian, born Antwerp; *Werkbund Theatre*, Cologne (1914), *Museum Kröller-Muller*, Otterloo (1937–54).

Venturi, Robert Charles (1925–) American, born Philadelphia, Pennsylvania; *Brant-Johnson House*, Vail, Colorado (1976), *Sainsbury Wing* of the National Gallery, London (1986–91).

Vignola, Giacomo Barozzi da (1507–73) Italian, born Vignola; *Villa di Papa Giulio* (1550–5), church of the *Gesu*, Rome (1586–73).

Viollet-le-Duc, Eugène Emmanuel (1814–79) French, born Paris; restored cathedral of *Notre Dame*, Paris (1845–64), *Château de Pierrefonds* (1858–70).

Vitruvius (in full **Marcus Vitruvius Pollio**) (1c BC) Roman; wrote the ten-volume *De Architectura* (35 BC), the only extant Roman treatise on architecture.

Voysey, Charles Francis Annesley (1857–1941) English, born London; *Grove Town Houses*, Kensington (1891–2), *Sanderson's Wallpaper Factory*, Chiswick (1902).

Wagner, Otto (1841–1918) Austrian, born Penzing, near Vienna; stations for *Vienna Stadtbahn* (1894–7), *Post Office Savings Bank*, Vienna (1904–6).

Waterhouse, Alfred (1830–1905) English, born Liverpool; *Manchester Town Hall* (1867–77), *Natural History Museum*, South Kensington, London (1873–81).

Webb, Sir Aston (1849–1930) English, born London; *Admiralty Arch* (1903–10), *Imperial College of Science* (1906), eastern façade of *Buckingham Palace* (1912), all London.

Webb, Philip (1831–1915) English, born Oxford; *Red House*, Bexley (1859), *Clouds*, Wiltshire (1881–6), *Standen*, East Grinstead (1891).

Wood, John, (the Elder) (1704–54) English. *Queen Square*, Bath (1729–36).

Wood, John, (the Younger) (1728–82) English. *Royal Crescent*, Bath (1767–75), *Assembly Rooms*, Bath (1769–71).

Wren, Sir Christopher (1632–1723) English, born East Knoyle, Wiltshire; *Pembroke College Chapel*, Cambridge (1663–5), *Sheldonian Theatre*, Oxford (1664), *Royal Greenwich Observatory* (1675–6), *St Paul's*, London (1675–1710), *Greenwich Hospital* (1696).

Wright, Frank Lloyd (1869–1959) American, born Richland Center, Wisconsin; *Johnson Wax Factory*, Racine, Wisconsin (1936–9), *Fallingwater*, Mill Run, Pennsylvania (1936), *Guggenheim Museum*, New York (begun 1942).

Wyatt, James (1746–1813) English, born Staffordshire; *London Pantheon* (1772), *Gothic Revival Country House*, Fonthill Abbey, Wiltshire (1796–1813).

Nobel Prizes

Nobel Prizes for Peace and Literature were first awarded in 1901.

Year	Peace	Literature	Economic Science
1906	Theodore Roosevelt	Giosuè Carducci	
1907	Ernesto Moneta, Louis Renault	Rudyard Kipling	
1908	Klas Arnoldson, Fredrik Bajer	Rudolf Eucken	
1909	August Beernaert, Paul Henri Benjamin Balluet (Baron de Constant de Rebecque)	Selma Lagerlöf	
1910	Bureau International Permanent de la Paix	Paul von Heyse	
1911	Tobias Asser, Alfred Fried	Maurice Maeterlinck	
1912	Elihu Root	Gerhart Hauptmann	
1913	Henri La Fontaine	Rabindranath Tagore	
1914	No award	No award	
1915	No award	Romain Rolland	
1916	No award	Verner von Heidenstam	
1917	Comité International de la Croix-Rouge	Karl Gjellerup, Henrik Pontoppidan	
1918	No award	No award	
1919	Thomas Woodrow Wilson	Carl Spitteler	
1920	Léon Bourgeois	Knut Hamsun	

Arts and Culture

Year	Peace	Literature	Economic Science
1921	Karl Branting, Christian Lange	Anatole France	
1922	Fridtjof Nansen	Jacinto Benavente y Martinez	
1923	No award	William Butler Yeats	
1924	No award	Wladslaw Reymont	
1925	Sir Austen Chamberlain, Charles Dawes	George Bernard Shaw	
1926	Aristide Briand, Gustav Stresemann	Grazia Deledda Madesani	
1927	Ferdinand Buisson, Ludwig Quidde	Henri Bergson	
1928	No award	Sigrid Undset	
1929	Frank B Kellogg	Thomas Mann	
1930	Nathan Söderblom	Sinclair Lewis	
1931	Jane Addams, Nicholas Butler	Erik Axel Karlfeldt	
1932	No award	John Galsworthy	
1933	Sir Norman Angell	Ivan Bunin	
1934	Arthur Henderson	Luigi Pirandello	
1935	Carl von Ossietzky	No award	
1936	Carlos Saavedra Lamas	Eugene O'Neill	
1937	Viscount Cecil of Chelwood	Roger Martin du Gard	
1938	Office International Nansen pour les Réfugiés	Pearl Buck	
1939	No award	Frans Emil Sillanpää	
1940–3	No award	No award	
1944	Comité International de la Croix-Rouge	Johannes Vilhelm Jensen	
1945	Cordell Hull	Gabriela Mistral	
1946	Emily Balch, John R Mott	Hermann Hesse	
1947	The Friends Service Council, The American Friends Service Committee (the Quakers)	André Gide	
1948	No award	T S Eliot	
1949	Baron Boyd Orr of Brechin	William Faulkner	
1950	Ralph Bunche	Bertrand Russell	
1951	Léon Jouhaux	Pär Lagerkvist	
1952	Albert Schweitzer	François Mauriac	
1953	George C Marshall	Sir Winston Churchill	
1954	Office of the UN High Commissioner for Refugees	Ernest Hemingway	
1955	No award	Halldór Laxness	
1956	No award	Juan Ramón Jiménez	
1957	Lester B Pearson	Albert Camus	
1958	Georges Pire	Boris Pasternak	
1959	Philip Noel-Baker	Salvatore Quasimodo	
1960	Albert Lutuli	Saint-John Perse	
1961	Dag Hammarskjöld	Ivo Andric	
1962	Linus Pauling	John Steinbeck	
1963	Comité International de la Croix-Rouge, Ligue des Sociétés de la Croix-Rouge	George Seferis	
1964	Martin Luther King, Jr	Jean-Paul Sartre (declined)	
1965	United Nations Children's Fund	Mikhail Sholokhov	
1966	No award	Shmuel Yosef Agnon, Nelly Sachs	
1967	No award	Miguel Angel Asturias	
1968	René Cassin	Kawabata Yasunari	
1969	International Labour Organization	Samuel Beckett	Ragnar Frisch, Jan Tinbergen
1970	Norman Borlaug	Aleksandr Solzhenitsyn	Paul Samuelson
1971	Willy Brandt	Pablo Neruda	Simon Kuznets
1972	No award	Heinrich Böll	Sir John Hicks, Kenneth Arrow
1973	Henry Kissinger, Le Duc Tho (declined)	Patrick White	Wassily Leontief
1974	Seán MacBride, Eisaku Sato	Eyvind Johnson, Harry Martinson	Gunnar Myrdal, Friedrich von Hayek
1975	Andrei Sakharov	Eugenio Montale	Leonid Kantorovich, Tjalling Koopmans

Year	Peace	Literature	Economic Science
1976	Mairead Corrigan, Betty Williams	Saul Bellow	Milton Friedman
1977	Amnesty International	Vicente Alexandre	James Meade, Bertil Ohlin
1978	Menachem Begin, Anwar Sadat	Isaac Bashevis Singer	Herbert Simon
1979	Mother Teresa	Odysseus Elytis	Sir Arthur Lewis, Theodore Schultz
1980	Adolfo Pérez Esquivel	Czesław Miłosz	Lawrence Klein
1981	Office of the UN High Commissioner for Refugees	Elias Canetti	James Tobin
1982	Alfonso García Robles, Alva Myrdal	Gabriel García Márquez	George Stigler
1983	Lech Wałesa	William Golding	Gerard Debreu
1984	Desmond Tutu	Jaroslav Seifert	Sir Richard Stone
1985	International Physicians for the Prevention of Nuclear War	Claude Simon	Franco Modigliani
1986	Elie Wiesel	Wole Soyinka	James Buchanan, Jr
1987	Oscar Arias Sánchez	Joseph Brodsky	Robert Solow
1988	UN Peacekeeping Forces	Naguib Mahfouz	Maurice Allais
1989	Tenzin Gyatso (Dalai Lama)	Camilo José Cela	Trygve Haavelmo
1990	Mikhail Gorbachev	Octavio Paz	Harry Markowitz, Merton Miller, William Sharpe
1991	Aung San Suu Kyi	Nadine Gordimer	Ronald Coase
1992	Rigoberta Menchú Tum	Derek Walcott	Gary Becker
1993	Nelson Mandela, F W de Klerk	Toni Morrison	Robert Fogel, Douglass North
1994	Yasser Arafat, Shimon Peres, Yitzhak Rabin	Kenzaburo Öe	John Harsanyi, John Nash, Reinhard Selten
1995	Joseph Rotblat and the Pugwash Conferences on Science and World Affairs	Seamus Heaney	Robert Lucas, Jr
1996	Carlos Filipe Ximenes Belo, José Ramos-Horta	Wislawa Szymborska	James Mirrlees, William Vickrey
1997	Jody Williams and the International Campaign to Ban Landmines	Dario Fo	Robert Merton, Myron Scholes
1998	John Hume, David Trimble	José Saramago	Amartya Sen
1999	Médecins Sans Frontières	Günter Grass	Robert Mundell
2000	Kim Dae Jung	Gao Xingjian	James Heckman, Daniel McFadden
2001	United Nations, Kofi Annan	V S Naipaul	George A Akerlof, A Michael Spence, Joseph E Stiglitz
2002	Jimmy Carter	Imre Kertész	Daniel Kahneman, Vernon L Smith
2003	Shirin Ebadi	J M Coetzee	Robert F Engle III, Clive W J Granger
2004	Wangari Maathai	Elfriede Jelinek	Finn E Kydland, Edward C Prescot
2005	Mohamed ElBaradei and the International Atomic Energy Authority	Harold Pinter	Robert J Aumann, Thomas C Schelling
2006	Muhammad Yunus	Orhan Pamuk	Edmund S Phelps
2007	Intergovernmental Panel on Climate Change, Al Gore	Doris Lessing	Leonid Hurwicz, Eric S Maskin, Roger B Myerson
2008	Martti Ahtisaari	Jean-Marie Gustave Le Clézio	Paul Krugman

Arts and Culture

Museums and art galleries – Europe

A selection of important museums and galleries is given.

Amsterdam, Netherlands
 Anne Frank's House
 Museum of Amsterdam
 Rijksmuseum
 Stedelijk Museum of Modern Art
 Van Gogh Museum
Ankara, Turkey
 Archaeological Museum
Antwerp, Belgium

 Folklore Museum
 Maritime Museum
 Royal Museum of Fine Art
 Rubens's House
Athens, Greece
 Acropolis Museum
 Byzantine Museum
 Goulandris Natural History Museum
 National Archaeological Museum

Arts and Culture

Museum of Decorative Arts
Museum of Modern Art
Barcelona, Spain
Catalan Museum of Art
Joan Miró Foundation
Picasso Museum
Basle, Switzerland
Basle Historical Museum
Basle Art and Contemporary Art Museum
Berlin, Germany
The Bauhaus Archives and Museum of Design
Berlin Museum
Jewish Museum
Memorial Museum of the German Resistance
Museum of Transport and Technology
New National Gallery
Old National Gallery
Pergamon Museum
Bilbao, Spain
Guggenheim Museum
Bruges, Belgium
Groeninge Museum
Memling Museum
Brunswick, Germany
Museum of Brunswick
Brussels, Belgium
Museum of Brussels
Museum of Modern Art
Railway Museum
Royal Museum of the Army
Budapest, Hungary
Hungarian National Museum
Cologne, Germany
Cologne Art Collective
Diocesan Museum
Museum of the City of Cologne
Schnütgen Museum
Copenhagen, Denmark
Copenhagen City Museum
National Museum
State Museum of Art
Theatre Museum
Delphi, Greece
Archaeological Museum
Dresden, Germany
Semper Gallery
State Gallery of Art
Grünes Gewölbe
Dublin, Ireland
Dublin Civic Museum
Guinness Museum
National Gallery of Ireland
National Museum of Ireland
National Transport Museum
Essen, Germany
Folkwang Museum
Figueres, Spain
Dalí Museum
Florence, Italy
Accademia Gallery
Bardini Museum
Bargello Museum
Museum of the History of Science
Pitti Palace
Uffizi Gallery
Frankfurt, Germany
Goethe Museum
Historical Museum
Modern Art Gallery
Freiburg im Breisgau, Germany
Augustiner Museum
Museum of Modern Art
Museum of Natural History

Geneva, Switzerland
International Museum of the Reformation
Museum of Art and History
Voltaire Museum
Genoa, Italy
Gallery of Modern Art
Palazzo Bianco
Palazzo Rosso
Hamburg, Germany
Altona Museum
Hamburg Art Gallery
Museum of Art and History
Helsinki, Finland
Helsinki City Museum
Museum of Applied Arts
Museum of Finnish Architecture
Sports Museum of Finland
Istanbul, Turkey
Archaeological Museum
Hagia Sophia Museum
Museum of the Ancient Orient
Topkapi Palace Museum
Leipzig, Germany
Museum of Art
Liège, Belgium
Museum of Firearms
Museum of Modern Art
Museum of Walloon Life
Lisbon, Portugal
Calouste Gulbenkian Museum
Museum of Archaeology and Ethnology
Museum of Art
Museum of Contemporary Art
Museum of Decorative Arts
Madrid, Spain
Museum of Madrid
National Archaeological Museum
National Museum of Ethnology
National Museum of Decorative Arts
Palace of El Pardo
The Prado Museum
Reina Sofia
Milan, Italy
Brera Picture Gallery
Castle of the Sforzas
Gallery of Modern Art
La Scala Museum of Theatre History
Leonardo da Vinci Museum of Science and
Technology
Moscow, Russia
Armory Museum
Central Lenin Museum
Pushkin Museum of Fine Arts
Tretyakov Art Gallery
Munich, Germany
Alte Pinakothek
Bavarian National Museum
City Museum
Deutsches Museum
Folklore Museum
Residence Museum
Naples, Italy
Archaeological Museum
Palazzo Capodimonte
Olympia, Greece
Museum of Ancient Olympia
Oslo, Norway
Edvard Munch Museum
National Gallery
Norwegian Folk Museum
Ski Museum
Paris, France
Auguste Rodin Museum

Carnavalet Museum
The Louvre
Musée d'Orsay
Museum of Modern Art at the Pompidou
 Centre
Museum of Technology
Prague, Czech Republic
 National Museum
 State Jewish Museum
Rome, Italy
 Borghese Gallery
 National Gallery of Ancient Art
 National Museum of Popular Art
 Vatican Museums
Rotterdam, The Netherlands
 Museum Boijmans Van Beuningen
 Rotterdam Museum: The Double Palmtree
 Rotterdam Museum: Schielandshuis
St Petersburg, Russia
 Museum of the History of Religion and Atheism
 Russian Museum
 State Hermitage Museum
Salzburg, Austria
 Mozart's Birthplace
 Residence Gallery
Siena, Italy
 Siena Art Gallery
 Siena Museum
Stockholm, Sweden
 National Museum of Antiquities
 Nordic Museum

Stockholm City Museum
The Hague, The Netherlands
 Netherlands Costume Museum
 Sikkens Museum of Signs
Thessaloniki, Greece
 Archaeological Museum
 Museum of Byzantine Culture
Toledo, Spain
 El Greco Museum
 Museum of the Alcazar of Toledo
Utrecht, The Netherlands
 Catharine Convent State Museum
 Netherlands Railway Museum
Venice, Italy
 Accademia Gallery
 Correr Museum
 Treasury of St Mark's
Versailles, France
 Château de Versailles
 Lambinet Museum
Vienna, Austria
 Belvedere Gallery
 Museum of the History of Art
 Museum of Lower Austria
 Treasury of the Holy Roman Empire
Warsaw, Poland
 National Museum
Zürich, Switzerland
 House for Art
 Swiss National Museum

Arts and Culture

Museums and art galleries – UK

Aberdeen, Scotland
 Aberdeen Art Gallery
Bangor, Wales
 Museum of Welsh Antiquities
 Bangor Art Gallery
Bath, England
 Museum of East Asian Art
 Victoria Art Gallery
Beaulieu, England
 National Motor Museum
Belfast, Northern Ireland
 Ulster Museum
Blaenafon, Wales
 National Mining Museum of Wales
Birmingham, England
 The Barber Institute of Fine Arts
 Birmingham Museum and Art Gallery
 National Motorcycle Museum
Bristol, England
 Arnolfini Gallery
 Blaise Castle House Museum
 Bristol Industrial Museum
 Bristol City Museums and Art Gallery
Cambridge, England
 The Fitzwilliam Museum
 Imperial War Museum (Duxford)
 Kettle's Yard
 Museum of Classical Archaeology
Cardiff, Wales
 National Museum and Gallery
 Museum of Welsh Life (at St Fagans)
Coventry, England
 Transport Museum
Edinburgh, Scotland
 City Art Centre
 Dean Gallery
 Museum of Childhood
 National Gallery of Scotland
 National Museum of Flight (East Fortune)

National Museum of Scotland
 Queen's Gallery, Palace of Holyroodhouse
 Scottish National Gallery of Modern Art
 Scottish National Portrait Gallery
Glasgow, Scotland
 Kelvingrove Art Gallery and Museum
 The Burrell Collection
 Gallery of Modern Art
 Hunterian Art Gallery and Museum
 Museum of Transport
 People's Palace Museum
Leeds, England
 City Art Gallery
 Leeds Industrial Museum
 Royal Armouries
Leicester, England
 Leicester Gas Museum
Liverpool, England
 Liverpool Museum
 Merseyside Maritime Museum
 Museum of Liverpool Life
 Tate, Liverpool
 Walker Art Gallery
London, England
 The British Museum
 Courtauld Gallery
 Design Museum
 Dulwich Picture Gallery
 Imperial War Museum
 Institute of Contemporary Arts
 London Transport Museum
 Museum of Instruments
 Museum of London
 Museum of the Moving Image
 The National Gallery
 National Maritime Museum
 The National Portrait Gallery
 Natural History Museum
 Pollock's Toy Museum

Arts and Culture

Science Museum
The Serpentine Gallery
Tate Britain
Tate Modern
Victoria and Albert Museum
The Wallace Collection
Wellcome Museum of the History of Medicine
Manchester, England
Imperial War Museum North
Museum of Science and Industry in Manchester
Manchester City Art Gallery
Manchester Jewish Museum
The Manchester Museum
Whitworth Art Gallery
Newcastle upon Tyne, England
Laing Art Gallery
Museum of Antiquities
Newcastle Discovery Museum
Oxford, England
Ashmolean Museum of Art and Archaeology
The Bate Collection of Historical Instruments
Christ Church Picture Gallery

Museum of Modern Art
Museum of the History of Science
Pitt Rivers Museum
Reading, England
Museum of English Rural Life
St Ives, England
Tate St Ives
Sheffield, England
Abbeydale Industrial Hamlet
Kelham Island Museum
Sheffield City Museum and Mappin Art Gallery
Southampton, England
Southampton City Art Gallery
Southampton Maritime Museum
Swansea, Wales
Glynn Vivian Art Gallery
National Waterfront Museum
York, England
National Railway Museum
York Castle Museum
York City Art Gallery
Yorkshire Museum

Museums and art galleries – USA

Atlanta, Georgia
High Museum of Art
Baltimore, Maryland
Baltimore Museum of Art
Walters Art Gallery
Boston, Massachusetts
Isabella Stewart Gardner Museum
Museum of Fine Arts
Museum of Science and Hayden Planetarium
Buffalo, New York
Albright-Knox Art Gallery
Cambridge, Massachusetts
Fogg Art Museum
MIT Museum
Arthur M Sackler Museum
Charleston, South Carolina
Charleston Museum
Chicago, Illinois
Art Institute of Chicago
Museum of Contemporary Art
Cincinnati, Ohio
Cincinnati Art Museum
Museum Center at Union Terminal
Cleveland, Ohio
Cleveland Museum of Art
Dallas, Texas
Dallas Museum of Art
Denver, Colorado
Denver Art Museum
Museum of Natural History
Des Moines, Iowa
Living History Farms (at Urbandale)
Detroit, Michigan
Detroit Institute of Arts
Henry Ford Museum
Dodge City, Kansas
Boot Hill Museum
Fort Lauderdale, Florida
Museum of Discovery and Science
Fort Myers, Florida
Edison Winter Home
Gainsville, Florida
Florida State Museum
Hartford, Connecticut
Wadsworth Museum
Honolulu, Hawaii
Honolulu Academy of Arts

Houston, Texas
Baker Planetarium, and the Museum of Medical Science
Burke Museum of Fine Arts
The Contemporary Arts Museum
Menil Collection
Indianapolis, Indiana
Children's Museum
Indianapolis Museum of Art
Jackson, Mississippi
Mississippi Museum of Art
Kansas City, Missouri
The Kemper Museum of Contemporary Art and Design
Nelson Atkins Museum of Art
Los Angeles, California
California Museum of Science and Industry
George C Page Museum of La Brea Discoveries
Getty Center
Getty Villa (at Malibu)
Los Angeles County Museum of Art
Museum of Contemporary Art
Natural History Museum
Memphis, Tennessee
Memphis Brooks Museum of Art
Minneapolis, Minnesota
Minneapolis Institute of Arts
Walker Art Center
New Haven, Connecticut
The Yale Art Gallery
New Orleans, Louisiana
Delgado Museum of Art
Louisiana State Museum
New York City, New York
American Museum of the Moving Image
American Museum of Natural History
Brooklyn Museum
Frick Collection
Gallery of Modern Art
Metropolitan Museum of Art and the Cloisters
Morgan Library
Museum of Holography
Museum of Modern Art
Museum of the American Indian
Museum of the City of New York
Solomon R Guggenheim Museum
Whitney Museum of American Art

Oklahoma City, Oklahoma
  National Cowboy Hall of Fame
Pasadena, California
  Norton Simon Museum
Philadelphia, Pennsylvania
  Academy of Natural Sciences
  Barnes Foundation Collection (in Merion, Pennsylvania)
  Franklin Institute Science Museum
  Museum of American Art
  Philadelphia Museum of Art
  Rodin Museum
  Rosenbach Museum
  University Museum of Archaeology and Anthropology
Pittsburgh, Pennsylvania
  Carnegie Museum of Art
  Carnegie Museum of Natural History
Plymouth, Massachusetts
  Plymouth Plantation
Portland, Oregon
  Oregon Art Institute
Reno, Nevada
  Harrah's Auto Collection
Rochester, New York
  Rochester Memorial Art Gallery
Salt Lake City, Utah
  The Museum of Church History and Art
San Francisco, California
  Asian Art Museum
  California Academy of Sciences
  California Palace of the Legion of Honor
  M H De Young Memorial Museum
  San Francisco Museum of Art

Santa Fe, New Mexico
  El Rancho de las Golondrinas (at Cienega)
  Museum of Indian Art and Culture
  Museum of International Folk Art
San Marino, California
  Huntington Library and Art Gallery
Sarasota, Florida
  Ringling Museum of Art
Seattle, Washington
  Seattle Art Museum
Toledo, Ohio
  Toledo Museum of Art
Tulsa, Oklahoma
  Philbrook Art Centre
Washington, District of Columbia
  American Indian Museum
  Corcoran Gallery of Art
  Dumbarton Oaks Collection
  Freer Gallery of Art
  Museum of Modern Art of Latin America
  National Air and Space Museum
  National Archives
  National Gallery of Art
  National Museum of American Art
  National Museum of American History
  Smithsonian Institute
  Washington Gallery of Modern Art
Williamsburg, Virginia
  Abby Aldrich
  Rockefeller Folk Art Collection
  Colonial Williamsburg
Williamstown, Massachusetts
  Sterling and Francine Clark Art Institute

Arts and Culture

THOUGHT AND BELIEF

Philosophers

Anaxagoras (500–428 BC) Greek, born Clazomenae. Believed that matter is infinitely divisible into particles containing a mixture of all qualities and that mind is a pervasive formative agency in the creation of material objects.

Anaximander (611–547 BC) Greek, born Miletus. Proposed that basic matter is the *apeiron*, the infinite or indefinite. Speculated that the Earth is unsupported at the centre of the Universe and that humans developed from another species.

Aristotle (384–322 BC) Greek, born Stagira, Macedonia. One of the most important philosophers and scientists in the history of Western thought, writing extensively on logic, metaphysics, ethics, politics, rhetoric, poetry, biology, zoology, physics and psychology. Best-known works include *Metaphysics, Nicomachean Ethics, Politics, Poetics,* the *De Anima,* the *Organon.*

Austin, John L(angshaw) (1911–60) English, born Lancaster. Professor at Oxford University and leading figure in 'Oxford Philosophy' movement. Examined ordinary linguistic usage to resolve philosophical perplexities. Best-known works: *Philosophical Papers* (1961), *Sense and Sensibilia* (1962), *How to Do Things with Words* (1962).

Averroës, Ibn Rushd (1126–98) Muslim, born Cordova, Spain. Famous medieval Islamic philosopher who also wrote on jurisprudence and medicine. Most important works were the *Commentaries on Aristotle* which offered a partial synthesis of Greek and Arabic philosophical traditions.

Ayer, Sir Alfred (Jules) (1910–89) English, born London. Professor at London and Oxford Universities. *Language, Truth and Logic* (1936) gives an account of the logical positivist, anti-metaphysical doctrines with which he became involved in the 1930s, and aroused great hostility when published. Later publications include *The Problem of Knowledge* (1956), *The Central Questions of Philosophy* (1972). Knighted in 1970.

Bacon, Francis, Viscount St Albans (1561–1626) English, born London. Important philosopher and statesman, knighted in 1603. Abandoned deductive logic of Aristotle and stressed the importance of experiment in interpretation of nature. Philosophical works include *The Advancement of Learning* (1605), *De Augmentis Scientiarum* (1623), *Novum Organum* (1620). He also wrote many religious and professional works.

Bacon, Roger (c.1214–92) English, born probably Ilchester, Somerset. Philosopher, scientist and Franciscan monk with reputation for unconventional learning in magic and alchemy, and imprisoned for heresy. Also published many works on mathematics, philosophy, and logic whose importance was recognized in later centuries.

Bentham, Jeremy (1748–1832) English, born London. Philosopher, jurist and social reformer: advocated utilitarianism in *A Fragment on Government* (1776) and *Introduction to the Principles of Morals and Legislation* (1789). Published many works on penal and social reform, economics and politics.

Berkeley, Bishop George (1685–1753) Irish, born near Kilkenny. Developed the belief that the contents of the material world are 'ideas' that only exist when perceived by a mind in *Essay towards a New Theory of Vision* (1709), *A Treatise concerning the Principles of Human Knowledge* (1710), *Three Dialogues between Hylas and Philonous* (1713). Expressed concern about social corruption and national decadence and wrote on social reform and religion.

Berlin, Sir Isaiah (1909–97) British, born Riga, Russia. Oxford professor whose philosophical works include *Karl Marx* (1939), *Historical Inevitability* (1954), *Two Concepts of Liberty* (1953), *Vico and Herder* (1976) and four volumes of essays.

Boethius, Anicius Manlius Severinus (c.475–524) Roman, born probably Rome. Produced translations of and commentaries on Aristotle. During a period of imprisonment for treason for which he was later executed, he wrote *De Consolatione Philosophiae,* which explains the mutability of all earthly fortune and demonstrates that happiness can only be attained by virtue.

Burke, Edmund (1729–97) Irish, born Dublin. Statesman and philosopher whose political thought has become the philosophy of modern Conservatism. Works include *Observations on the Present State of the Nation* (1769), *On the Causes of the Present Discontents* (1770).

Carnap, Rudolf (1891–1970) German–American, born Wuppertal. Leading member of the 'Vienna Circle' of logical positivists who dismissed most traditional metaphysics as a source of meaningless answers to pseudo-problems. Works include *Der logische Aufbau der Welt* (1928), *Logische Syntax der Sprache* (1934), *Meaning and Necessity* (1947), *The Logical Foundations of Probability* (1950).

Comte, Auguste (1798–1857) French, born Montpelier. Usually regarded as the founder of sociology. His 'positivism' sought to expound the laws of social evolution, to describe the organization of all branches of human knowledge, and to establish a science of society as a basis for social planning. Works include *Cours de Philosophie positive* (1830–42), *Système de Politique positive* (1851–4).

Cousin, Victor (1792–1867) French, born Paris. An eclectic in philosophy; published many historical studies and commentaries on other philosophers. Most original work is *Du Vrai, du Beau, et du Bien* (1854).

Croce, Benedetto (1866–1952) Italian, born Pescasserolli. Developed phenomenology of the mind in which four principal activities, art and philosophy (theoretical), political economy and ethics (practical), complement each other. His theory of aesthetics is described in *Lo Spirito* and his opposition to totalitarianism is expressed in *History as the Story of Liberty* (1941).

Cudworth, Ralph (1617–88) English, born Aller, Somerset. Leading member of the Cambridge Platonists. *The True Intellectual System of the*

Universe (1678) aimed to refute determinism and materialism and to establish the reality of a supreme divine intelligence; *Treatise concerning Eternal and Immutable Morality* is a posthumous publication discussing ethics.

Davidson, Donald Herbert (1917–2003) American, born Springfield, Massachusetts. One of the most influential recent analytical philosophers, who has made contributions to the philosophy of language, mind and action in *Essays on Action and Events* (1980) and *Structure and Content of Truth* (1990).

de Beauvoir, Simone (1908–80) French, born Paris. Sorbonne professor, novelist and feminist who contributed substantially to the existentialist movement. Works include *Le Deuxième Sexe* (1949), translated as *The Second Sex* (1953).

Democritus (c.460–370 BC) Greek, born Abdera, Thrace. Prolific ancient philosopher publishing works on ethics, physics, mathematics, cosmology and music, although only fragments of his writings remain. Best known for physical speculations, in particular the belief that the world consists of an infinite number of minute particles whose different combinations account for different properties.

Derrida, Jacques (1930–2004) French, born El Biar, Algeria. Work spans literary criticism, psychoanalysis, linguistics and philosophy. Founded the school of criticism known as 'deconstruction'.

Descartes, René (1596–1650) French, born La Haye, near Tours. Usually regarded as the founder of modern philosophy. *Discourse de la Méthode* (1637), *Meditationes de Prima Philosophia* (1641) and *Principia Philosophiae* (1644) set out his ideas on philosophical methods, propositions and religious beliefs. Famous for the dictum, 'I think, therefore I am' (cogito ergo sum) and for his dualism of mind and body, he also made important contributions in astronomy and mathematics.

Dewey, John (1859–1952) American, born Burlington, Vermont. Exponent of pragmatism whose philosophy stressed the instrumental function of ideas and judgements in problem solving. Also published widely on psychology and education. Works include *The School and Society* (1899), *Reconstruction in Philosophy* (1920), *Experience and Nature* (1925), *The Quest for Certainty* (1929), *Experience and Education* (1938).

Diogenes (412–323 BC) Greek, born Sinope, Pontus. Continued the pre-Socratic tradition of speculation about the primary constituent of the world, which he identified as air, operating as an active and intelligent life-force.

Duns Scotus, John (c.1266–1308) Scottish, born probably Duns, Berwickshire. Philosopher whose beliefs represented a strong reaction against Aristotle and Aquinas; he propounded the primacy of the individual and the freedom of the individual will. His writings were mainly commentaries on the Bible and other philosophers.

Empedocles (490–430 BC) Greek, born Acragas, Sicily. Philosopher, poet, doctor, statesman and soothsayer who described a cosmic cycle in which earth, air, fire and water periodically combine and separate under the forces of Love and Hate as well as beliefs on the transmigration and redemption of souls.

Epicurus (341–270 BC) Greek, born Samos. Advocated a philosophy designed to promote detachment, serenity and freedom from fear, and the belief that pleasure is the only good and the only goal of morality.

Feuerbach, Ludwig (Andreas) (1804–72) German,

born Landshut, Bavaria. Attacked conventional Christianity in *Das Wesen des Christentums* (1847), translated as *The Essence of Christianity*, arguing that God is the projection of human ideals and human nature.

Fichte, Johann Gottlieb (1762–1814) German, born Rammenau, Saxony. Posited the Ego as the basic reality, affirming itself in the act of consciousness and constructing the external world as its field of action. He elaborates this system in *Grundlage des Naturrechts* (1796) and *System der Sittenlehre* (1798).

Foucault, Michel (1926–84) French, born Poitiers. Believed that prevailing social attitudes are manipulated by those in power to define such categories as insanity, illness, sexuality and criminality and these are used to identify and oppress 'deviants'. Translations of his work include *The Order of Things* (1970), *Madness and Civilization* (1971), *The Archaeology of Knowledge* (1972), *The History of Sexuality* (1984).

Frege, (Friedrich Ludwig) Gottlob (1848–1925) German, born Wismar. Regarded as the founder of modern mathematical logic and the philosophy of language. Main works are *Begriffsschrift* (1879), *Die Grundlagen der Arithmetik* (1884) and *Die Grundgesetze der Arithmetik* (1893, 1903).

Gödel, Kurt (1906–78) American, born Brünn, Austria-Hungary (now Brno, Czechoslovakia). Logician and mathematician whose theorem, published in 1931, demonstrated the existence of formally undecidable elements in any formal system of arithmetic.

Gorgias (c.485–380 BC) Greek, born Leontini, Sicily. Advocated a philosophy which was an extreme form of scepticism or nihilism; that nothing exists, that if it did it would be unknowable, that if it were knowable it would be incommunicable to others. He is portrayed in Plato's dialogue, the *Gorgias*.

Habermas, Jürgen (1929–) German, born in Düsseldorf. Philosopher and socialist whose central theme is the possibility of a rational political commitment to socialism in societies in which science and technology are dominant.

Hamilton, Sir William (1788–1856) Scottish, born Glasgow. Philosopher whose main work *Lectures on Metaphysics and Logic*, published posthumously (1856–60), presented views on perception and knowledge. Important figure in the revival of philosophy in Britain at this time.

Hegel, Georg Wilhelm Friedrich (1770–1831) German, born Stuttgart. Idealist philosopher whose major works include *Phänomenologie des Geistes* (1807), *Wissenschaft der Logik* (1812, 1816), *Encyclopädie der philosophischen Wissenschaften in Grundrisse* (1817). Although his philosophy is difficult and obscure it has remained influential until the present.

Heidegger, Martin (1889–1976) German, born Messkirch, Baden. Philosopher whose writings examine the nature and predicament of human existence, classify modes of 'Being' and discuss the human mode of existence characterized by participation and involvement in the world of objects. His major work is *Sein und Zeit* (*Being and Time*, 1927).

Heraclitus (c.540–460 BC) Greek, born Ephesus. Believed that everything is in a state of flux and that fire is the ultimate constituent of the world. Only fragments remain of his book *On Nature*.

Herbert (of Cherbury), Edward, 1st Baron (1583–1648) English, born Eyton, Shropshire. Soldier, statesman and philosopher who argued in *De Religione Gentilum* (1645) that all religions recognize five main articles, from the acknowledgement of a supreme God to the concept that there are rewards and punishments in a future state.

Hobbes, Thomas (1588–1679) English, born Malmesbury. Political philosopher whose major work *Leviathan* (1651) presented and connected his thoughts on metaphysics, psychology and political philosophy. His materialistic philosophy described how the world is a mechanical system consisting of bodies in motion in which human beings are wholly selfish and enlightened self-interest explains the existence of the sovereign state and prevents 'a war of every man against every man'. He was banned from publishing in England in 1666 after being accused of being an atheist.

Hume, David (1711–76) Scottish, born Edinburgh. Philosopher and historian whose beliefs concerning perception, causation, personal identity, and ethics are still influential. Most important works include *A Treatise of Human Nature* (1739–40), *Essays Moral and Political* (1741, 1742), *Enquiry concerning Human Understanding* (1748), *Political Discourses* (1752), *Dialogues concerning Natural Religion* (published posthumously, 1779).

Husserl, Edmund (Gustav Albrecht) (1859–1938) German, born Prossnitz, Austrian Empire. Defender of philosophy as an a priori discipline and founder of Phenomenology: the systematic investigation of consciousness and its objects by suspending belief in the empirical world.

James, William (1842–1910) American, born New York City. Philosopher and psychologist who developed the pragmatist ideas of Charles Peirce; beliefs are true because they work, not vice versa. These ideas, and discussions of ethics and religion are given in *The Will to Believe* (1907), *Pragmatism* (1907), *The Varieties of Religious Experience* (1902), *The Meaning of Truth* (1909).

Jaspers, Karl (Theodor) (1883–1969) German, born Oldenburg. One of the founders of existentialism; his beliefs are developed in *Philosophie* (1932).

Kant, Immanuel (1724–1804) German, born Königsberg, Prussia. Influential scientist and philosopher, whose main interest was in the role of reason. He argued that the immediate objects of perception depend not only on our sensations but also on our perceptual equipment and that some properties we observe in objects are due to the nature of the observer. Ethics, aesthetics and politics are also discussed in *Critique of Pure Reason* (1781), *Critique of Practical Reason* (1788), *Critique of Judgement* (1790), *Perpetual Peace* (1795).

Kierkegaard, Søren Aabye (1813–55) Danish, born Copenhagen. A founder of existentialism who tried to reinstate the central importance of the individual and the significant choices each of us makes informing our future selves, and wrote in many works about the necessity for individual choice rather than prescribed dogma.

Langer, Suzanne K(nauth) (1895–1985) American, born New York City. Published important works in linguistic analysis and aesthetics; *Philosophy in a New Key* (1942), *Feeling and Form* (1953), *Problems of Art* (1957), *Mind: an Essay on Human Feeling* (1967–82).

Leibniz, Gottfried Wilhelm (1647–1716) German, born Leipzig. Mathematician and philosopher who believed that the world is composed of an infinity of simple immaterial 'monads' which form a hierarchy, the highest of which is God. Had greatest influence as a mathematician.

Locke, John (1632–1704) English, born Wrington, Somerset. Philosopher who defended natural rights, constitutional law and the liberty of the individual. *Essay concerning Human Understanding* (1690) explores the nature and scope of human reason and seeks to establish that 'all knowledge is founded on and ultimately derives from sense ... or sensation'.

Lukacs, George (1885–1971) Hungarian, born Budapest. Marxist philosopher who wrote prolifically on literature and aesthetics. His major work on Marxism was *History and Class Consciousness* (1923).

Mach, Ernst (1838–1916) Austrian, born Turas, Moravia. Physicist and philosopher whose writings laid the foundations of logical positivism.

MacIntyre, Alasdair Chalmers (1929–) Scottish, born Glasgow. Wide-ranging in his interests, his work has been particularly focused on ethics, drawing insight from Aristotle and Aquinas. Works include *After Virtue* (1981), *Three Rival Versions of Moral Enquiry* (1990).

Maimonides, Moses (Moses ben Maimon) (1135–1204) Jewish, born Córdoba, Spain. Physician and philosopher who tried to harmonize the thought of Aristotle and Judaism in *Guide to the Perplexed* (1190).

Marcuse, Herbert (1898–1979) American, born Berlin. Radical political theorist who analysed the repressions imposed by the unconscious mind in *Eros and Civilization* (1955) and condemned the 'repressive tolerance' of modern industrial society which both stimulated and satisfied superficial material desires of the masses at the cost of more fundamental needs and freedoms in *One Dimensional Man* (1964).

Marx, Karl (1818–83) German, born Trier. Social, political and economic philosopher in the German idealistic tradition. Founded the theory of historical materialism, and in his *Economic and Philosophical Manuscripts of 1844* (posthumously published, 1932) developed the notion of the alienation of man under capitalism. His most famous publication *Das Kapital* (Vol 1 1867, Vols 2 & 3 posthumously published 1884, 1894) was one of the most influential works of the 19th century.

Merleau-Ponty, Maurice (1908–61) French, born Rochefort-sur-mer. Philosopher who rejected extremes of both behaviouristic psychology and subjectivist accounts; the world is neither wholly 'given', nor wholly 'constructed' for the perceiving subject, but is essentially ambiguous and enigmatic. Major works are *La Structure du Comportement* (1942) and *Phénoménologie de la Perception* (1945).

Mill, J(ohn) S(tuart) (1806–73) English, born London. Philosopher and social reformer, leading exponent of the British empiricism and utilitarian traditions who also restored the importance of cultural values. Active in politics, he campaigned for women's suffrage and supported the Advanced Liberals. Major works include *A System of Logic* (1843), *On Liberty* (1859), *The Subjection of Women* (1869).

Montesquieu, Charles-Louis de Secondat, Baron de la Brède et de (1689–1755) French, born near Bordeaux. Became an advocate, but turned to scientific research and literary work. Best known for his comparative study of legal and political issues, *De l'ésprit des lois* (1748), which was a major influence on 18c Europe.

Moore, George (Edward) (1873–1958) English, born London. Cambridge professor of mental philosophy and logic who emphasized the intellectual virtues of clarity, precision and honesty, identifying as a principal task of philosophy the analysis of ordinary concepts and arguments. Works include *Principia Ethica* (1903), *Ethics* (1916).

More, Henry ('the Cambridge Platonist') (1614–87) English, born Grantham, Lincolnshire. Followed the philosophies of Plato, Plotinus and Descartes and attempted to demonstrate the compatibility of reason and faith. Later became interested in occultism and mysticism. Main works: *Philosophical Poems* (1647), *An Antidote against Atheism* (1653), *The Immortality of the Soul* (1659), *Enchiridion Ethicum* (1666), *Divine Dialogues* (1668).

Murdoch, Dame (Jean) Iris (1919–99) Irish novelist, playwright and philosopher. Published three important philosophical works in the Platonic tradition: *The Sovereignty of the Good* (1970), *The Fire and the Sun* (1977) and *Metaphysics as a Guide to Morals* (1992). These deal with the relationships between art and philosophy, and between love, freedom, knowledge and morality.

Nietzsche, Friedrich (Wilhelm) (1844–1900) German, born Röcken, Saxony. Philosopher who produced many unconventional works expressing repudiation of Christian and liberal ethics, detestation of democratic ideals, the celebration of the *Übermensch* (superman) who can create and impose his own law, and the death of God. Best-known writings include *Unzeitgemässe Betrachtungen* (*Untimely Meditations*, 1873–6), *Die Fröliche Wissenschaft* (*The Gay Science*, 1882), *Also Sprach Zarathustra* (*Thus Spake Zarathustra*, 1883–92), *Jenseits von Gut und Böse* (*Beyond Good and Evil*, 1886).

Ockham, William of (1285–1349) English, born Ockham, Surrey. Philosopher, theologian and political writer whose controversial religious views led to disputes with the Catholic church. Defended nominalism against realism and introduced 'Ockham's razor', the belief that a theory should not propose the existence of anything more than is needed for its explanation. Works include *Summa Logicae, Quodlibta Septem*.

Ortega y Gasset, José (1883–1955) Spanish, born Madrid. Argued that great philosophies demarcate the cultural horizons of their epochs. Works include *Meditaciones del Quijote* (1914), *Tema de nuestro tiempo* (1923), *La Rebelión de Las Masas* (1930).

Parmenides (c.515–c.445 BC) Greek, born Elea, S Italy. Argued in *On Nature* for the impossibility of motion, plurality and change, and set an agenda of problems for subsequent pre-Socratic philosophers.

Peirce, Charles (Sanders) (1839–1914) American, born Cambridge, Massachusetts. Philosopher, logician and mathematician, best known as the founder of pragmatism.

Philo Judeaus (c.20 BC–c.40 AD) Hellenistic Jew, born Alexandria. Prolific author who attempted to synthesize Greek philosophy and Jewish scripture.

Plato (c.428–c.348 BC) Greek, born probably Athens. One of the most important philosophers of all time. Pupil of Socrates and teacher of Aristotle, his writings consist of philosophical dialogues and letters discussing the definition of moral virtues, the theory of knowledge as recollection, the immortality of the soul, and contrasts of transient and timeless aspects of the world. The *Republic* presents Plato's political utopia.

Plotinus (c.205–70) Greek, born possibly Lycopolis, Egypt. Neoplatonist philosopher who advocated asceticism and the contemplative life, and greatly influenced early Christian theology.

Popper, Sir Karl (Raimund) (1902–94) Austrian, born Vienna. Rejected philosophical systems with totalitarian political implications from Plato to Marx and stressed the importance of 'falsifiability': true scientific theories must specify in advance the conditions under which they could be tested and refuted. Main works include *Die Logik der Forschung* (1934, trans. *The Logic of Scientific Discovery*, 1959), *The Open Society and its Enemies* (1945), *The Poverty of Historicism* (1957).

Protagoras (c.490–c.420 BC) Greek, born Abdera. Sophist philosopher, with a sceptical or relativistic view of human knowledge; his many works are lost and most information about him comes from Plato's dialogues.

Pythagoras (6c BC) Greek, born Samos. Philosopher and mathematician whose life is surrounded in myth and legend. Emphasized moral asceticism and purification; also associated with mathematical discoveries involving musical intervals and relations of numbers. He had a profound influence on later philosophers and scientists.

Quine, Willard van Orman (1908–2000) American, born Akron, Ohio. Influential professor of philosophy who challenged the standard sharp distinctions between analysis and synthetic truths and between science and metaphysics; also presented a systematic linguistic philosophy. Best-known works: *Two Dogmas of Empiricism* (1951), *From a Logical Point of View* (1953), *Word and Object* (1960), *The Roots of Reference* (1973).

Rawls, John (1921–2002) American, born Baltimore, Maryland. Social and political philosopher concerned mainly with the question of justice in publications including *A Theory of Justice* (1962), *Justice as Fairness* (1991), *Political Liberalism* (1993).

Reichenbach, Hans (1891–1953) German, born Hamburg. Made important contributions to technical probability theory and wrote widely on logic and the philosophical bases of science in *Philosophie der Raum-Zeit-Lehre* (1927–8), *Elements of Symbolic Logic* (1947), *The Rise of Scientific Philosophy* (1951).

Ricoeur, Paul (1913–2005) French, born Valence, Drôme. Influential figure in both French and Anglo-American philosophy, covering a wide range of problems on the nature of language, interpretation, human action and will, freedom and evil. Major works include *Philosophy of the Will* (1950–60), *The Living Metaphor* (1975).

Rorty, Richard (1931–2007) American, born New York City. Drew on philosophers such as Nietzsche and Heidegger, and literary sources, in a liberal and pragmatic critque of analytical philosophy. Works include *Contingency, Irony, and Solidarity* (1989).

Rousseau, Jean Jacques (1712–78) French–Swiss, born Geneva, Switzerland. Largely self-taught, he wrote *Discours sur l'origine de l'inégalité parmi les hommes* (1755), which emphasizes the essential goodness of humankind. His masterpiece was *Du contrat social* (1762), which introduced the slogan 'Liberty, Equality, Fraternity'. Fled to England in 1762, where he wrote most of his *Confessions* (published posthumously, 1782).

Russell, Bertrand (Arthur William), 3rd Earl (1872–1970) English, born Trelleck, Monmouthshire.

Philosopher, mathematician, prolific author and controversial figure, who was imprisoned in 1918 during World War I as an active pacifist and in 1961 for taking part in a sit-down demonstration in Whitehall, London. Wrote wide-ranging literature on mathematics, philosophy, politics, education and morals, such as *The Principles of Mathematics* (1903), *The Problems of Philosophy* (1912), *Theory and Practice of Bolshevism* (1919), *On Education* (1926), *Marriage and Morals* (1932).

Ryle, Gilbert (1900–76) English, born Brighton, Sussex. Influential exponent of linguistic philosophy. *The Concept of Mind* (1949) was directed against the traditional theory that mind and matter are distinct and problematically related. Other works: *Dilemmas* (1954), *Plato's Progress* (1966).

Santayana, George (Jorge Augustín Nicolás Ruiz de Santayana) (1863–1952) Spanish–American, born Madrid. Naturalistic and materialistic critic of the transcendental claims of religion and German idealism, who believed that our knowledge of the external world depends on an act of 'animal faith'. Main philosophical works: *The Sense of Beauty* (1896), *The Life of Reason* (1905–6), *Scepticism and Animal Faith* (1923), *Realms of Being* (1927–40), *Platonism and the Spiritual Life* (1927).

Sartre, Jean-Paul (1905–80) French, born Paris. Philosopher, dramatist and novelist who developed characteristic atheistic existentialist doctrines from an early anarchistic tendency; these are expressed in the autobiographical novel *La Nausée* (1938) and in *Le Mur* (1938). Awarded, but declined to accept, the Nobel Prize for literature in 1964.

Schelling, Friedrich (Wilhelm Joseph) von (1775–1854) German, born Leonburg. Idealist philosopher who examined the relation of the self to the objective world and argued that consciousness itself is the only immediate object of knowledge and that only in art can the mind become fully aware of itself. Works include *Ideen zur einer Philosophie der Natur* (1797), *System des transzendentalen Idealismus* (1800).

Schlick, Moritz (1882–1936) German, born Berlin. Leader of the 'Vienna Circle' of logical positivists who wrote on ethics, which he argued was a factual science of the causes of human actions. Main publications: *Allgemeine Erkenntnislehre* (*General Theory of Knowledge*, 1918), *Fragen der Ethik* (*Problems of Ethics*, 1930).

Schopenhauer, Arthur (1788–1860) German, born Danzig. Philosopher who emphasized the active role of Will as the creative but covert and irrational force in human nature and argued that art represented the sole kind of knowledge that was not subservient to the Will; his work is often characterized as a systematic philosophical pessimism. Major work: *Die Welt als Wille und Vorstellung* (*The World as Will and Idea*, 1819).

Scruton, Roger (1944–) English. Conservative political philosopher who champions the achievements of Western culture and institutions.

Shaftesbury, Anthony Ashley Cooper, 3rd Earl of (1671–1713) English, born London. Moral philosopher and politician who argued that we possess natural 'moral sense' and affections directed to the good of the species and in harmony with the larger cosmic order in *Characteristics of Men, Manners, Opinions, Times* (1711).

Socrates (469–399 BC) Greek, born Athens. One of the most important philosophers in history, responsible for a decisive shift of philosophical interest from speculation about the natural world and cosmology to ethics and conceptual analysis. His reputation

for eliciting contradictions in the philosophies of others may have contributed to demands for his conviction for 'impiety' and 'corrupting the youth'; he was sentenced to die by drinking hemlock.

Spencer, Herbert (1820–1903) British, born Derby. Philosopher with interest in evolutionary theory which he expounded in *Principles of Psychology* (1855). Also applied his evolutionary theories to ethics and sociology and became an advocate of 'Social Darwinism', the view that societies naturally evolve in competition for resources and that the 'survival of the fittest' is therefore morally justified. Works include *System of Synthetic Philosophy* (1862–93), *Social Statistics* (1851), *Education* (1861), *The Man Versus the State* (1884).

Spinoza, Baruch (Benedict de) (1632–77) Dutch, born Amsterdam. Rationalist philosopher who advocated a strictly historical approach to the interpretation of biblical sources and argued that complete freedom of philosophical and scientific speculation was appropriate. His major work, the *Ethics* (1677, posthumous), described a complete, deductive metaphysical system intended to be a proof derived with mathematical certainty of what is good for human beings.

Tarski, Alfred (1902–83) Polish, born Warsaw. Logician and mathematician who gave a definition of 'truth' in formal logical languages in *Der Wahrheitsbetriff in den Formalisierten Sprachen* (*The Concept of Truth in Formalized Languages*, 1933).

Thales (c.620–c.555 BC) Greek, born Miletus. Traditionally the founder of European philosophy. Proposed the first natural cosmology, identifying water as the original substance and the basis of the universe. Also had wide-ranging practical and scientific interests.

Weil, Simone (1909–43) French, born Paris. Combined sophisticated scholarly and philosophical interests with dedicated involvement and interest in the oppressed and exploited. Translated philosophical and spiritual works include *Gravity and Grace* (1952), *The Need for Roots* (1952), *Waiting for God* (1951), *Oppression and Liberty* (1958).

Whitehead, A(lfred) N(orth) (1861–1947) English, born Ramsgate. Mathematician and idealist philosopher. *Process and Reality* (1929) attempted a metaphysics comprising psychological as well as physical experience, with events as the ultimate component of reality. Other works include *Adventures of Ideas* (1933) and *Modes of Thought* (1938).

Williams, Sir Bernard Arthur Owen (1929–2003) English, born Essex. Philosopher whose work was wide-ranging. Particularly influential in his contributions to moral philosophy, including *Morality: an Introduction to Ethics* (1972), *Ethics and the Limits of Philosophy* (1985), *Shame and Necessity* (1993), and *Truth and Truthfulness* (2002).

Wittgenstein, Ludwig (Josef Johann) (1889–1951) Austrian, born Vienna. Philosopher who studied the nature and limits of language. *Logisch-philosophische Abhandlung* (1921) describes how meaningful language must consist in propositions that are 'pictures' of the facts of which the world is composed and therefore many claims of speculative philosophy must be rejected. *Philosophical Investigations* (1953, posthumous) comes to different conclusions, pointing to the variety and subtlety in language and exploring its functions.

Zeno of Elea (c.490–c.420 BC) Greek, born Elea, Italy. A disciple of Parmenides who devised famous paradoxes which purported to show the impossibility of motion and spatial division.

Gods of Greek mythology

Adonis	God of vegetation and rebirth
Aeolus	God of the winds
Alphito	Barley goddess of Argos
Aphrodite	Goddess of love and beauty
Apollo	God of prophecy, music, youth, archery and healing
Ares	God of war
Arethusa	Goddess of springs and fountains
Artemis	Goddess of fertility, chastity and hunting
Asclepius	God of healing
Athene	Goddess of prudence and wise council; protectress of Athens
Atlas	A Titan who bears up the earth
Attis	God of vegetation
Boreas	God of the north wind
Cronus	Father of Zeus
Cybele	Goddess of the earth
Demeter	Goddess of the harvest
Dionysus	God of wine, vegetation and ecstasy
Eos	Goddess of the dawn
Eros	God of love
Gaia	Goddess of the earth
Ganymede	God of rain
Hades/Pluto	God of the underworld
Hebe	Goddess of youth
Hecate	Goddess of the moon
Helios	God of the sun
Hephaestus	God of fire
Hera	Goddess of marriage and childbirth; queen of heaven
Hermes	Messenger of the gods
Hestia	Goddess of the hearth
Hypnos	God of sleep
Iris	Goddess of the rainbow
Morpheus	God of dreams
Nemesis	God of destiny
Nereus	God of the sea
Nike	Goddess of victory
Oceanus	God of the river Oceanus
Pan	God of male sexuality and of herds
Persephone	Goddess of the underworld and of corn
Poseidon	God of the sea
Rhea	The original mother goddess; wife of Cronus
Selene	Goddess of the moon
Thanatos	God of death
Zeus	Overlord of the Olympian gods and goddesses; god of the sky and all its properties

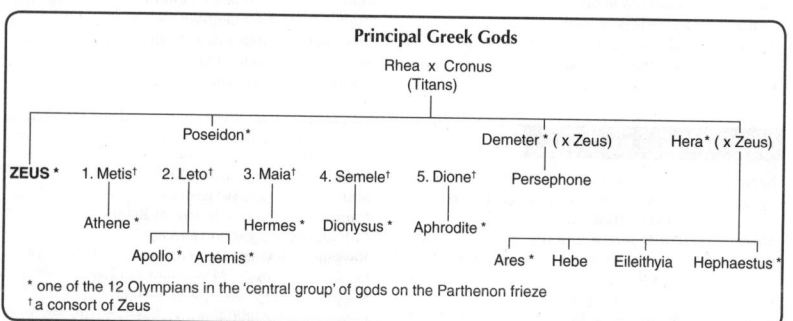

Principal Greek Gods

Rhea x Cronus
(Titans)

ZEUS * 1. Metis† 2. Leto† 3. Maia† 4. Semele† 5. Dione† Persephone
Poseidon* Demeter * (x Zeus) Hera* (x Zeus)

Athene * Hermes * Dionysus * Aphrodite *
Apollo * Artemis * Ares * Hebe Eileithyia Hephaestus *

* one of the 12 Olympians in the 'central group' of gods on the Parthenon frieze
† a consort of Zeus

Gods of Roman mythology

Apollo	God of the sun
Bacchus	God of wine and ecstasy
Bellona	Goddess of war
Ceres	Goddess of corn
Consus	God of seed sowing
Cupid	God of love
Diana	Goddess of fertility and hunting
Egreria	Goddess of fountains and childbirth
Epona	Goddess of horses
Fauna	Goddess of fertility
Faunus	God of crops and herbs
Feronia	Goddess of spring flowers
Fides	God of honesty
Flora	Goddess of fruitfulness and flowers
Fortuna	Goddess of chance and fate
Genius	Protective god of individuals, groups and the state
Janus	God of entrances, travel, the dawn
Juno	Goddess of marriage, childbirth, light
Jupiter	God of the sky and its attributes (sun, moon, thunder, rain, etc)
Lares	Gods of the house
Liber Pater	God of agricultural and human fertility
Libitina	Goddess of funeral rites
Luna	Goddess of the moon
Maia	Goddess of fertility
Mars	God of war
Mercury	Messenger of the gods; also god of merchants
Minerva	Goddess of war, craftsmen, education and the arts
Mithras	The sun god; god of regeneration
Neptune	God of the sea
Ops	Goddess of the harvest
Orcus	God of death
Pales	Goddess of flocks
Penates	Gods of food and drink
Picus	God of woods

Thought and Belief

Thought and Belief

Pluto/Dis	God of the underworld
Pomona	Goddess of fruit trees
Portunus	God of husbands
Proserpina	Goddess of the underworld
Rumina	Goddess of nursing mothers
Saturn	God of fertility and agriculture
Silvanus	God of trees and forests
Venus	Goddess of spring, gardens and love
Vertumnus	God of fertility
Vesta	Goddess of the hearth
Victoria	Goddess of victory
Vulcan	God of fire

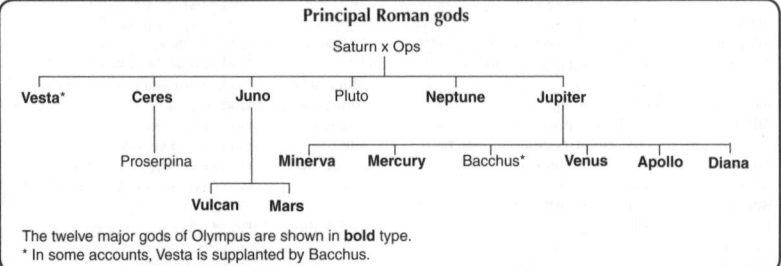

Principal Roman gods

Saturn x Ops

Vesta* Ceres Juno Pluto Neptune Jupiter

Proserpina Minerva Mercury Bacchus* Venus Apollo Diana

Vulcan Mars

The twelve major gods of Olympus are shown in **bold** type.
* In some accounts, Vesta is supplanted by Bacchus.

Gods of Egyptian mythology

Amun-Re	Universal god
Anubis	God of funerals
Apis	God of fertility
Aten	Unique god
Geb	God of the earth
Hathor	Goddess of love
Horus	God of light
Isis	Goddess of magic
Khnum	Goddess of creation
Khonsou	Son of Amun-Re
Maat	Goddess of order
Nephthys	Goddess of funerals
Nut	God of the sky
Osiris	God of vegetation
Ptah	God of creation
Sekhmet	Goddess of might
Seth	God of evil
Thoth	Supreme scribe

Gods of Norse mythology

Aegir	God of the sea
Aesir	Race of warlike gods, including Odin, Thor, Tyr
Alcis	Twin gods of the sky
Balder	Son of Odin and favourite of the gods
Bor	Father of Odin
Bragi	God of poetry
Fafnir	Dragon god
Fjorgynn	Mother of Thor
Frey	God of fertility
Freyja	Goddess of libido
Frigg	Goddess of fertility; wife of Odin
Geflon	Goddess who received virgins after death
Heimdall	Guardian of the bridge Bifrost
Hel	Goddess of death; Queen of Niflheim, the land of mists
Hermod	Son of Odin
Hoder	Blind god who killed Balder
Hoenir	Companion to Odin and Loki
Idunn	Guardian goddess of the golden apples of youth; wife of Bragi
Kvasir	God of wise utterances
Logi	Fire god
Loki	God of mischief
Mimir	God of wisdom
Nanna	Goddess wife of Balder
Nehallenia	Goddess of plenty
Nerthus	Goddess of earth
Njord	God of ships and the sea
Norns	Goddesses of destiny
Odin, (Woden, Wotan)	Chief of the Aesir family of gods, the 'father' god; the god of battle, death, inspiration
Otr	Otter god
Ran	Goddess of the sea
Sif	Goddess wife of Thor
Sigyn	Goddess wife of Loki
Thor (Donar)	God of thunder and sky; good crops
Tyr	God of battle
Ull	Stepson of Thor, an enchanter
Valkyries	Female helpers of the gods of war
Vanir	Race of benevolent gods, including Njord, Frey, Freyja
Vidar	Slayer of the wolf, Fenrir
Weland, (Volundr, Wayland, Weiland)	Craftsman god

Figures of myth and legend

Selected figures from religion, myth and legend are given. **Bold** type indicates that a figure is described elsewhere in the list.

Achilles Greek hero; son of **Peleus** and the goddess **Thetis**; his body invulnerable to injury, except his ankle, due to being held by the ankles when he was dipped in the R Styx (in another version **Cheiron** replaced his ankle bone with one taken from the fast-running giant Damysos); killed with an arrow in the heel by **Paris** or **Apollo**.

Actaeon Greek hero; a hunter who came upon **Artemis**, the goddess of chastity, while she was bathing and therefore naked; she threw water at him, changing him into a stag, so that he was pursued and then killed by his own hounds.

Adad Mesopotamian god of storms; known throughout the area of Babylonian influence; the Assyrians called him **Hadad**, and in the Bible he is Rimmon, the god of thunder; helped to cause the Great Flood in Gilgamesh; his symbol was the lightning held in his hand and his animal the bull.

Adapa Akkadian hero; one of the seven Apkallu, beings of great brilliance and genius, and envoy of the god **Ea**, the divine creator of Man, who lost the opportunity of immortality due to disagreements between Ea and **Anu**, the god of heaven.

Aditi Indian goddess; mother of the gods and all beings, and the guardian of childbirth; outside the divine world, she represented *everything* at the same time, being the total, the beginning, the end and the opposites; adopted by Buddhist tradition.

Adonis God of Phoenician origin; son of Myrrha, the daughter of the king of Syria who had been turned into a tree; spent one third of the year with **Persephone**, goddess of hell, and two thirds with **Aphrodite** after a decision by **Zeus**; mortally wounded by a wild boar in a battle.

Aegir Norse god of the sea; a giant, who collected dead sailors in his hall on the island of Hlesey; here also he sometimes gave banquets to the gods.

Aegisthus Greek hero; son of **Thyestes**; while **Agamemnon** was absent at Troy he became the lover of **Clytemnestra**; together they killed Agamemnon on his return to Argo; later killed by **Orestes**.

Aeneas Greek hero; son of **Aphrodite**, and bravest of the Trojans after **Hector** whose command he replaced in the fight against the Greeks; sailed to coast of Italy and is said to have given Rome its divine origin; subject of the *Aeneid* by Virgil.

Aeolus Greek god of the winds; in the *Odyssey*, Aeolus lived on an island, and gave **Odysseus** the winds tied in a bag so that his ship would not be blown off course; the ship had nearly reached Ithaca when Odysseus's men opened the bag, thinking it contained treasure; as a result, the ship was blown far away.

Aesculapius ▶ Asclepius

Agamemnon Greek king of Argos; commander of the Greek army in the Trojan War; Homer calls him 'king of men'; on his return he was murdered by his wife **Clytemnestra**.

Agni Indian god of fire; immortal god, regarded as the guide and protector of men; had two faces, one calm, one terrible, and gave both life and death.

Ahura Mazda Indo-Iranian god; had the form of the sun and nine wives; creator of other living beings and formed the world by his thought; his powers made plants grow and allowed fire to give its heat, water to quench thirst, animals to reproduce and armies to be victorious.

Ajax Two Greek heroes of the Trojan War; one was the son of Telamon, king of Salamis, therefore known as Telamonian Ajax and was proverbial for his size and strength; in all the worst situations he 'stood like a tower'; when the armour of the dead **Achilles** was not given to him, he went mad and killed himself. The second was the son of Oileus, king of Locris; returning from Troy, he provoked the anger of the gods, and was killed by **Poseidon** as he reached the shore of Greece.

Alcestis Greek heroine; she saved her husband, Admetus, who was doomed to die, by offering to die in his place; the action so impressed **Heracles** that he wrestled with the messenger of death and brought her back to life.

Alcmaeon Greek hero; to avenge the death of his father, Amphiaros, he killed his mother, and was pursued by the **Erinyes** until he came to a land which had not seen the sun at the time of his mother's death; he found this recently emerged land at the mouth of the River Achelous; **Apollo** commanded him to lead the expedition of the **Epigoni** against Thebes.

Alcyone ▶ Halcyone

Alexander ▶ Paris

Amaterasu Japanese goddess of the sun and light; considered to be the divine origin of the imperial dynasty; shut herself in a cave after a conflict with her brother Susa-no-o, plunging the world into darkness; returned light to the world when the gods managed to tempt her out.

Amazons Warrior-women of Greek myth; people of the Amazon state, where men were only tolerated for work of a servile nature; removed one breast so that they would not be restricted in the practice of archery and spear-throwing; said to be descendants of the god of war, **Ares**, and the **Nymph**, Harmony; crushed the Atlantians, occupied Gorgon and the greater part of Libya, fought with **Priam** during the Trojan war and invaded Attica; their leader, Hippolyta, married **Theseus**.

Amen ▶ Amun-Re

Amitabha The divine Buddha; one of five 'meditation Buddhas' sent by Adi Buddha, the original Buddha; wished to gather together all those who would pray to him with faith, to enjoy perfect happiness until they entered Nirvana.

Amma Dogon god; origin of all creation; with the earth gave birth to twins who were sacrificed to make the earth fertile, then brought back to life in the form of a human couple; created the sun and divided the world into two domains; his myth led to the practice of male circumcision.

Ammon, Amon ▶ Amun-Re

Amphitrite Greek goddess of the sea; married to **Poseidon**; the mother of **Triton** and other minor deities.

Amphitryon In Greek mythology, the husband of Alcmene; in his absence, **Zeus** took his shape and so became the father of **Heracles**.

Amun-Re (Amen, Ammon, Amon) Egyptian god; Amun was the local god of Thebes, considered as the god of air or fertility, who had the form of a man, but sometimes also the head of a ram; was likened to the sun-god Re, thus becoming Amun-Re; the pharaohs developed his cult.

Anahita Persian goddess of dawn and fertility; became a spirit of prosperity, collaborating in the

Thought and Belief

work of creation, fighting for justice and initiating men into religious rites.

Anchises In Roman mythology, the Trojan father of **Aeneas**; the *Aeneid* gives an account of Aeneas's piety in carrying Anchises on his shoulders out of the blazing city of Troy.

Androcles Roman slave; escaped from his master, met a lion, and extracted a thorn from its paw; when recaptured, he was made to confront a lion in the arena, and found it was the same animal, so that his life was spared.

Andromache In Greek mythology, the wife of **Hector**, the hero of Troy; after the fall of the city she became the slave of **Neoptolemus**.

Andromeda In Greek mythology, the daughter of Cepheus, king of the Ethiopians; to appease **Poseidon**, she was fastened to a rock by the seashore as an offering to a sea monster; rescued by **Perseus**, who used the **Gorgon**'s head to change the monster to stone; the persons named in the story were all turned into constellations.

Angels Messengers of God; nine choirs were divided into three ranks; the seraphim, cherubim and thrones; the dominions, powers and virtues; and the principalities, archangels and angels. The first class was to praise and worship God, and the last was to assist the course of the stars, nations and people; angels or lesser gods would pass on messages, give orders or bring help to men.

Angra Mainyu Persian **demon**; creator of darkness and of evil things; belonged to death, filth and rottenness, inspiring disgust.

Anna Perenna Roman goddess; represented as an old woman, and worshipped in a sacred wood situated north of Rome; named Perenna, meaning eternity, when she became a **Nymph**; approached by Mars (**Ares**) when she was old and asked to be an intermediary between himself and Minerva (**Athene**); realizing this was impossible, she substituted herself for the chaste goddess and made fun of Mars.

Angra Mainyu

Antigone Greek heroine; the guardian of the family; defied the dictator **Creon** to follow the wishes of the gods to fulfil the rite of burial for warriors considered as traitors, and for this was buried alive by Creon in the family tomb, where she hanged herself.

Anu Sumerian god of heaven; earthly royalty was descended from him, and as the god of Uruk, he gave back the city to Rim-Sin of the Larsa dynasty, who later conquered the neighbouring cities by Anu's strength.

Anubis Egyptian god; guide of souls to the world beyond; often represented with a human body and the head of a jackal or dog.

Aphrodite (Venus) Greek goddess of love who reigned over the hearts and senses of men; a proud and cruel goddess who punished all those who would not succumb to her; as a bribe, offered **Paris** the most beautiful mortal, **Helen**, causing the Trojan war; her worship was assimilated by the Romans with that of Venus, a goddess of ancient Italy.

Apis Egyptian god of strength and fecundity; represented as a bull for whom divine honours were reserved; Menes, the first Egyptian pharaoh, was said to have started the cult of Apis about 3000 BC.

Apollo Greek and Roman god; son of **Zeus**; young and handsome, seer, poet and musician, he was

said to be the most powerful of the gods; often identified with the sun, his nature also had a terrifying side and even his friends were afraid of him; said to have been responsible for the death of **Achilles**.

Arachne In Greek mythology, a weaver from Lydia; challenged **Athene** to a contest; when Arachne's work was seen to be superior, Athene destroyed the web and Arachne hanged herself; Athene saved her, but changed her into a spider.

Ares (Mars) Greek god of war; a supreme fighter who cared little for the interests he defended, and delighted in bloody massacres; fought with **Athene**, the sons of **Poseidon** and **Heracles**; identified with the Roman god Mars, said to be the father of **Romulus**, the founder of Rome.

Arethusa Greek **Nymph**; pursued by the river god Alpheus from Arcadia in Greece to Ortygia in Sicily; the myth attempts to account for the freshwater fountain which appears in the harbour of Syracuse and is believed to have flowed under the Ionian Sea.

Argonauts Greek heroes; sailed in the *Argo* to find the Golden Fleece; under **Jason**'s leadership they sailed through the Symplegades (presumably the Dardanelles) and along the Black Sea coast to Colchis; their return is variously described, and may have included a river-passage to the North Sea.

Argus Greek watchman with a hundred eyes, appointed by **Hera** to watch over **Io**; after Argus was killed by **Hermes**, the eyes were placed in the tail of the peacock; also the name of **Odysseus**'s dog.

Ariadne In Greek mythology, the daughter of King **Minos** of Crete; enabled **Theseus** to escape from the labyrinth by giving him a ball of thread; he fled with her, but deserted her on the island of Naxos; there she eventually became the wife of **Dionysus**.

Aristaeus Greek god of the countryside; a minor deity who introduced beekeeping, vines, and olives; pursued **Eurydice**, the wife of **Orpheus**, who trod on a snake and died; in revenge her sister **dryads** killed his bees; **Proteus** told him to sacrifice cattle to appease the dryads, and in nine days he found bees generated in the carcasses.

Arjuna Indian hero; in the *Bhagavadgita*, a poem in the *Mahabharata*, he hesitates before entering the battle, knowing the killing which will ensue; his charioteer, Krishna, urges him to fulfil the action which is his duty as a warrior, explaining that the whole universe needs the fulfilment of actions which advance God's will.

Artemis (Diana) Greek goddess; daughter of **Zeus** and sister of **Apollo**; defender of virginity and modesty, and warrior who turned against anyone who attempted to force her against her will; also the protectress of women in labour and newborn children; identified with the Roman goddess Diana, a huntress.

Arthur Celtic medieval hero; brought up by **Merlin** and crowned king of Britain, King Arthur; armed with his magical sword Excalibur, he rid his country of monsters and giants, drove out the invaders, conquered the continent to reach Rome and in some stories as far as Palestine, from where he brought back the Cross of Christ.

Asclepius (Aesculapius) Greek and Roman god of the earth; son of **Apollo**, he acquired the magic powers to cure and revitalize from **Cheiron** the **Centaur**; used his powers to serve mortals, curing the sick and bringing the dead back to life; became

Thought and Belief

a god when killed by **Zeus**, who was enraged that Asclepius had upset the natural order by restoring **Hippolytus** to life.

Astarte ► Ishtar

Atalanta Greek heroine; nurtured by a she-bear and grew up to be a strong huntress; refused to marry any man who would not take part in a foot-race with her; those who lost were killed; eventually Hippomenes (or Milanion) threw three golden apples of the **Hesperides** at her feet, so that her attention was diverted and she lost.

Aten Egyptian god; showed himself to mankind in the form of the solar disc, gave life, was the creator of all things, and all things depended on him; had no connection with the other, numerous gods.

Athene (Minerva) Greek goddess of restraint and forethought; daughter of **Zeus**, virgin and warrior, whose protégés were **Odysseus**, **Heracles** and **Achilles**; fought with the Achaeans in the Trojan war, and enemy of **Ares**; in competition with **Poseidon**, won the possession of Attica, beginning the era of civilization for the city of Athens; identified with the Roman god Minerva.

Atlas Greek **Titan**; made to hold up the heavens with his hands, as a punishment for taking part in the revolt against the Olympians; when books of maps came to be published, he was often portrayed as a frontispiece, hence the term 'atlas'.

Atreus Greek king of Argos; quarrelled with his brother **Thyestes**, and placed the flesh of Thyestes' children before him at a banquet; the father of **Agamemnon** and **Menelaus**.

Atropos ► Moerae

Attis (Atys) Greek god of vegetation; connected with the Asiatic cult of **Cybele**; died after castrating himself, and was resurrected; the story was later associated with the spring festival.

Aurora ► Eos

Autolycus In Greek mythology, the maternal grandfather of **Odysseus**, who surpassed all men in thieving; he was said to be a son of **Hermes**.

Baal Phoenician god of fertility and fecundity; known as king of the gods, and with his sister Anat was responsible for the universal prosperity of people and animals; his victory over the god of the sea gave sailors the courage to set their boats on water.

Bacchus ► Dionysus

Balder Norse god of sovereignty and power; son of **Odin** and **Frigg**; unlike the other power gods, he was kind and pleasant; a jealous god **Loki** conspired to kill him, and on death he went to the home of Hel, the terrible; the goddess of hell agreed to free him on condition that every creature would weep for him; all did, except an old woman (Loki in disguise), so that Balder would have to remain in hell until the battle (*Ragnarok*) which will bring about the end of the world.

Baal

Basilisk (Cockatrice) Greek monster; a small dragon-like creature combining features of the snake and the cockerel; its eye could freeze and kill, hence the expression: 'If looks could kill'; equivalent to the Cockatrice, which was hatched by a serpent from the egg of a cock.

Bellerophon Greek hero; sent to Lycia with a letter telling the king to put him to death; the king set him impossible adventures, notably the killing of the **Chimera**; in later accounts it is said that **Athene** helped him to tame **Pegasus**.

Berserker Norse warrior; fought in a 'bear-shirt'

in such a frenzy that he was impervious to wounds; the name is the origin of the phrase 'to go berserk'.

Bes Egyptian god; depicted as a bandy-legged dwarf who was horrific in appearance, but congenial in temperament; the protector in childbirth, and guardian of the family.

Bladud Legendary king of Britain; discovered the hot spring at Bath and founded the city; one story is that he was a leper who found that the mud cured him.

Brahma Indian god; the creator; divided himself into two to make a couple bringing **Sarasvati**, feminine energy, into existence; he then developed four heads so that he could always see Sarasvati as she constantly circled him; he was also given four arms to show his power; organized the world, and laid down the rules of *karma*, the standard of reward for one's actions.

Bran Celtic hero; known as Bendigeid Vran, the son of Llyr; invaded Ireland to help his sister, and died there; his seven followers cut off his head and buried it on the site of the Tower of London, from where it protects the whole island of Britain. In another legend, he was an Irish voyager who set out to find the Other World with 27 companions; on their return, as they approached the shore, people asked who they were, and said that the only Bran they knew was the hero of the ancient tale of *The Voyages of Bran*, so Bran wandered away forever.

Brigit (Brighid) Irish goddess of fire and the hearth; also of poetry and handicrafts; in the Christian era a number of her attributes were taken over by St Brigid.

Brunhild (Brunhilde, Brynhild) Norse **Valkyrie** who has assumed human form; **Odin** places her behind a wall of flame where she lies in an enchanted sleep; she is woken by **Sigurd**, who is able to leap the barrier on his horse Grani; tricked into marrying Gunnar, she finally kills herself on Sigurd's funeral pyre; in the similar Nibelungen legend, she is the wife of Gunther.

Bunyip In Australian aboriginal mythology, the source of evil; not to be thought of as a spirit or as a human; the **Rainbow Snake**, the mother of life, confined Bunyip to a waterhole; it haunts dark and gloomy places.

Cadmus Greek hero; son of Agenor, king of Tyre; set off in pursuit of his sister **Europa**, arrived in Greece, and founded the city of Thebes, teaching the natives to write; sowed dragon's teeth, from which armed men sprang up.

Calchas Greek seer; advised that **Iphigeneia** should be sacrificed at Aulis; at Troy he told **Agamemnon** to return Chryseis, the daughter of the priest of **Apollo**, to stop the plague; died in a combat of 'seeing'.

Calliope Greek **Muse** of epic poetry; sometimes said to be the mother of **Orpheus**.

Callisto Arcadian **Nymph**; attendant upon **Artemis**; loved by **Zeus**, she became pregnant, and was sent away from the virgin band; **Hera** changed her into a she-bear and after 15 years had passed, her son tried to spear her; taking pity on them, Zeus changed her into the constellation Ursa Major.

Cassandra Greek heroine; daughter of **Priam**, king of Troy; favoured by **Apollo**, who gave her the gift of prophecy; because she did not return his love, he decreed that while she would always tell the truth, she would never be believed; at the fall of Troy she was allotted to **Agamemnon**, and murdered on her arrival in Argos.

Thought and Belief

Castor and Pollux Greek heroes; twin sons of **Leda**; Pollux the son of **Zeus** and Castor the son of Tyndareus, king of Sparta, but both born at the same time; Castor was a good fighter and Pollux a skilled boxer, and the twins were inseparable; during their search for the Golden Fleece with the **Argonauts**, they saved the ship, the *Argos*, from a storm; when Castor was killed in a fight, Zeus agreed to Pollux's pleas for Castor to share his immortality so that he would not be separated from his brother.

Cecrops (Kekrops) Greek ancestor and first king of the Athenians; born from the earth, and formed with snakelike appendages instead of legs; during his reign, **Athene** and **Poseidon** fought for the possession of Athens; buried in the Erechtheum.

Centaurs Mythical Greek monsters; half man, half horse, aggressive and unintelligent with reputations for raping and kidnapping, with two exceptions: **Cheiron**, tutor of **Apollo**, **Jason** and **Achilles**, and Pholus, friend of **Heracles**, who were kindly Centaurs.

Cerberus Greek dog; guards the entrance to the underworld; originally fifty-headed, later with three heads; any living souls visiting hell gave 'a sop to Cerberus', ie a honey-cake, to quieten him; **Heracles** carried him off as one of his labours.

Ceres ▶ **Demeter**

Cernunnos Celtic god of plenty; represented with the ears and antlers of a stag, often accompanied by a serpent with the head of a ram; master of wild, earthly and aquatic animals.

Chac Mayan rain-god; characterized by two wide eyes, a long turned-up nose and two curved fangs; in the East he was red, in the North, white, in the West, black and in the South, yellow; made thunder and rain and was regarded as beneficent and friend of man.

Cernunnos

Charon Greek ferryman of the underworld; carried the shades or souls of the dead across the R Styx; sometimes other rivers are substituted in literature, such as Acheron and Lethe; the Greeks placed a small coin in the mouth of a corpse as Charon's fee.

Cheiron Greek **Centaur**; son of **Cronus** and Philyra the **Oceanid**, who kept a school for princes in Thessaly; educated **Asclepius** in the art of medicine and music, **Jason** the **Argonaut**, **Odysseus** and **Achilles**; wounded by one of **Heracles**'s poisoned arrows, he gladly gave up his immortality to be rid of pain.

Chimera (Chimaera) Greek monster; had the head of a lion, the body of a goat (the name means 'she-goat'), and the tail of a serpent, which breathed fire.

Circe Greek enchantress; in the *Odyssey*, detained **Odysseus** and his followers on the island of Aeaea; her house was full of wild beasts; transformed Odysseus's men into swine with a magic drink, but he was able to defeat her charms through the protection of the herb moly.

Clio Greek **Muse** of history and lyre-playing.

Clotho ▶ **Moerae**

Clytemnestra (Clytemestra) In Greek mythology, the twin sister of **Helen** and the wife of **Agamemnon**; murdered her husband on his return from Troy, assisted by her lover, **Aegisthus**; killed in revenge by her son, **Orestes**.

Cockatrice ▶ **Basilisk**

Consentes Dii (Di) Twelve Roman gods; their statues, grouped in male/female pairs, stood in the Forum; probably Jupiter/Juno, Neptune/Minerva, Mars/Venus, Apollo/Diana, Volcanus/Vesta and Mercury/Ceres (▶ **Zeus**/**Hera**, **Poseidon**/**Athene**, **Ares**/**Aphrodite**, **Apollo**/**Artemis**, **Hephaestus**/**Vesta** and **Hermes**/**Demeter**).

Creon (Kreon) Greek kings; the name (meaning 'ruler') is applied especially to the brother of **Jocasta**, regent of Thebes, who awarded the throne to **Oedipus**; later, after the siege of the city by the seven Champions, he commanded that **Polynices** should not be buried, and condemned **Antigone** for disobedience.

Cressida In medieval accounts of the Trojan War, the daughter of Calchas, a Trojan priest; beloved by **Troilus**, a Trojan prince, she deserted him for **Diomedes** when transferred to the Greek camp.

Cronus (Kronos) Greek ruler of the universe (the second ruler); a **Titan**, the youngest son of **Uranus**, who rebelled against his father; during his rule people lived in the Golden Age; probably a pre-Greek deity, he is incorrectly, but popularly, confused with Chronos 'Time', because he too devoured his children.

Cu Chulainn Irish hero and supreme warrior; halted the progress of enemies united against his country; finally killed by Lugaid, the son of one of his victims.

Cupid ▶ **Eros**

Cybele Phrygian goddess of the earth; made through the mutilation of a hermaphrodite monster by the gods, she lived in forests and mountains.

Cyclopes Greek mythological monsters; one-eyed giants who worked as smiths and were associated with volcanic activity; the Cyclops **Polyphemus** was outwitted and blinded by **Odysseus**.

Daedalus Athenian inventor; worked for King **Minos** in Crete and constructed the labyrinth; later he escaped to Sicily with wings he had made for himself and **Icarus**; there he made the golden honeycomb kept at Mt Eryx; any archaic work of skill was ascribed to him, and he was a patron deity of craftsmen in Ancient Greece.

Danaans (Danaoi) Collectively, the Greeks who joined together in the expedition to Troy.

Danae Greek heroine; daughter of King Acrisius of Argos; when an oracle prophesied that her son would kill his grandfather, Acrisius imprisoned her in a bronze tower, where **Zeus** visited her in the form of a golden shower; she gave birth to a son, **Perseus**, who accidentally killed Acrisius with a discus.

Danaoi ▶ **Danaans**

Danu Celtic mother-goddess; associated with hills and the earth.

Daphne Greek heroine; daughter of a river-god, Ladon (or, in another story, Peneios); pursued by the god **Apollo**, she was saved by being turned into a laurel, which became Apollo's sacred tree.

Daphnis Sicilian shepherd; half-brother of **Pan**, who was loved by a **Nymph**; he did not return her love, so she blinded him; became the inventor of pastoral poetry; in another story he would love nobody; when he died, all the beings of the island mourned him.

Deirdre In Irish legends, a girl destined to cause evil; grew up to be the most beautiful girl in Ireland; although intended for King Conchobhar, she was abducted by Naoise, a young king, and lived with him for seven years; when Naoise was killed by treachery, she was forced to marry Conchobhar, and killed herself.

Demeter (Ceres) Greek goddess of corn; presided over the interplay between life and death, and provided food; forced a compromise after **Hades** imprisoned her daughter **Persephone** in the underworld allowing her to return to the world above between spring and autumn; identified with the Roman goddess Ceres.

demons Evil celestial beings who force men to do evil and also do harm to men themselves, taking on the appearance of foreign gods, led by Satan; invisible and innumerable, they originally preferred to live in isolated and unclean places like deserts and ruins, and were greatly feared, especially at night; exorcisms are religious rites to remove demonic influences when a demon is thought to inhabit the body of a person, stripping him or her of self control and moral awareness.

Deucalion Greek hero; son of **Prometheus**; when **Zeus** flooded the world, Deucalion and his wife Pyrrha built an 'ark' which grounded on the top of Parnassus; as the only survivors, they asked how the human race was to be restored; an oracle told them 'to throw the bones of their mother over their shoulders'; they correctly interpreted this oracle, and threw stones (the bones of their mother Earth) which turned into human beings.

Diana ▶ **Artemis**

Dido Greek heroine; in the *Aeneid*, the daughter of the king of Tyre, who founded Carthage; **Aeneas** was diverted to Africa by storms, and told her his story; they fell in love, but when Aeneas deserted her she committed suicide by throwing herself upon a pyre.

Diomedes (Diomede) Greek hero; fought in the Trojan War, even taking on the gods in battle; also a wise counsellor, the partner of **Odysseus** in various schemes; in the medieval version of the story, he became the lover of **Cressida**.

Dionysus (Bacchus) Greek god of wine and the vine; lord of exuberance and drunkenness, he upset everything that got in his way, did not respect laws or customs and wandered about in caves; said to have made his followers coarse and vulgar, taught them to drink wine and caused madness.

Dragons Legendary animals present in Chinese, Greek and Indian mythology, and medieval Christian legends; had the claws of a lion, the wings of an eagle, a powerful serpent's tail and breathed fire; sometimes represented as the guardian of treasure, eg guarding the Golden Fleece, as an incarnation of Satan, as a primordial principle and as the symbol of the power of the emperor of China.

Dryads Greek mythological **Nymphs**; originally connected with oak trees, but more usually referring to a wood nymph, living in or among the trees; were usually friendly, but could frighten travellers.

Durga Indian goddess; wife of **Shiva** and his feminine part, and both the creator and destroyer of the world; a force for leading astray as well as for salvation, and a warrior who enjoyed battle and bloodshed.

Ea ▶ **Enki**

Echidna Greek monster; half woman and half snake, and the mother of various other monsters, eg **Hydra**.

Echo Greek **Nymph**; in one legend, beloved by **Pan**, and torn to pieces, only her voice surviving; in another story, punished by **Hera** so that she could only repeat the last words of another speaker; loved **Narcissus**, who rejected her, so that she wasted away to a voice.

Electra Heroine of Greek tragedies (but not in Homer); daughter of **Agamemnon** and **Clytemnestra**, who assisted her brother **Orestes** when he came to Argos to avenge his father, and who later married his friend Pylades; her personality is developed in different ways by the playwrights.

Endymion Greek shepherd of Mt Latmos; loved by the moon-goddess **Selene**; **Zeus** put him to sleep, while Selene looked after his flocks, and visited him every night; one of the mythological figures who was said to have founded the Olympic Games, as king of Elis.

Enki (Ea) Sumerian god who organized life on earth and developed the world; invented man and made a mould from him so that he could be reproduced, and created plants and livestock.

Enlil Sumerian god and keeper of sovereign power who maintained the order of the world; originally ruled over proletarian gods who became exhausted by their work and rebelled; it was agreed that man should be created to take over a part of the labours necessary for the maintenance of the world; later the prosperity and din of mankind, whose number was steadily increasing, irritated Enlil, who sent epidemics, suffering, death and worldwide flood.

Eos (Aurora) Greek goddess of the dawn; daughter of **Helios**, mother of **Memnon**; abducted various mortals; when she took the mortal Tithonus, **Zeus** granted her request that he should be made immortal, but she forgot to ask for perpetual youth, so he grew older and older, finally shrinking to no more than a voice or, possibly, the cicada insect.

Epigoni Greek heroes; collectively, the 'next generation'; after the failure of the **Seven against Thebes**, their sons made another expedition and succeeded; this was shortly before the Trojan War.

Epona Gallic goddess and guardian of horses; patron of civil and military horsemen, travellers and those on their way to the Great Beyond; sometimes seen as a goddess of fertility and also identified with **Rhiannon**.

Erato Greek **Muse** of lyric poetry and hymns.

Erechtheus Greek king of Athens; born from the earth and nurtured by **Athene**; sacrificed his daughter Chthonia to secure victory over the Eleusinians, but was killed by **Poseidon**; the Erechtheum, a temple on the Acropolis, is probably on the site of his palace.

Erinyes (Furies) Greek goddesses; inhabitants of hell who were responsible for punishing bloody crimes; named Alecto, Tisiphone and Megara, they were represented as winged spirits who had long hair entwined with snakes, and carried whips and torches; tortured their victims and drove them mad.

Eris Greek heroine; daughter of Night and the sister of **Ares**; a late story tells how she was present at the wedding of **Peleus** and **Thetis** and threw a golden apple 'for the fairest'; this brought **Hera**, **Athene**, and **Aphrodite** into contention, and was the first cause of the Trojan War; the name means 'strife' in Greek.

Eros (Cupid) Greek god, responsible for keeping the world together and for the continuation of the species; his power to inspire sexual desires could make people lose their reason and paralyse their will power; became Cupid for the Romans.

Eteocles Greek hero; elder of **Oedipus**'s two sons, whom he cursed; became king of Thebes after his father's death, and refused to share power with his brother **Polynices**; the **Seven against**

Thebes attacked the city, and Eteocles was killed by Polynices.

Eumenides A euphemistic name given to the **Erinyes** after being domesticated at Athens in Aeschylus's play of the same name; the name means 'the kindly ones'.

Europa (Europe) Greek heroine; daughter of Agenor, king of Tyre, who was abducted by **Zeus** in the shape of a bull, and swam with her on his back to Crete; her children were **Minos** and **Rhadamanthus**.

Eurydice Greek **Dryad**; wife of **Orpheus**; after her death, Orpheus went down to the underworld and persuaded **Hades** to let her go by the power of his music; the condition was that she should follow him, and that he should not look at her until they reached the light; not hearing her footsteps, he looked back, and she disappeared back into the underworld.

Euterpe Greek **Muse** of flute-playing.

Fates ▶ **Moerae**

Faunus Roman god of agriculture; responsible for the fertility of plants and the energy of living nature; reproduced himself in fauns, **satyrs** who were half man, half goat.

Finn mac Cumhal Irish hero; warrior and magician who avenged his father who was killed in battle and reorganized his elite troops, whose qualities were intelligence, cunning, faithfulness, a hatred of money and respect for women; possessed the gift of receiving visions when he bit his thumb.

Flora Roman goddess of flowers and flowering plants; appears with the spring; given a temple in 238 BC; her games were celebrated on 28 April.

Fortuna Roman goddess of fortune; introduced by King Servius Tullius (578–534 BC); in the Middle Ages was highly revered as a divine and moral figure, redressing human pride; her wheel is frequently referred to and depicted, as at St Etienne in Beauvais, where figures can be seen climbing and falling off.

Freyja Norse goddess of love, fertility, fecundity, victory and peace, and sister of **Freyr**; took on the form of a falcon to travel between one world and the other.

Freyr (Frey) Norse god of fertility and fecundity and brother of **Freyja**; presided over love, wealth and orgies, brought sun and rain to make crops grow; mainly worshipped by women.

Frigg (Frigga) Norse goddess of married love; wife of **Odin** (often confused with **Freyja**).

Furies ▶ **Erinyes**

Gaea (Gaia, Ge, Tellus) Greek goddess; 'the earth' personified, and later the goddess of the whole earth (not a particular piece of land); came into being after Chaos, and was the wife of **Uranus**, producing numerous children; the Romans identified her with Tellus.

Galahad, Sir One of King **Arthur**'s knights; son of **Lancelot** and Elaine; distinguished for his purity, he alone was able to succeed in the adventures of the Siege Perilous and the Holy Grail.

Galatea Greek **Nymph**; a sea nymph, wooed by **Polyphemus** the **Cyclops** with uncouth love-songs; in some versions Polyphemus destroys his rival Acis with a rock; in other versions he happily marries Galatea; probably a Sicilian story.

Ganesha Indian god; master of intelligence and the patron of artists and writers who was given by **Brahma** the task of copying the *Mahabharata*; represented with the head of an elephant; a popular god, he put obstacles in the way of those who neglected him, and spared others.

Ganesha

Ganymede In Greek mythology, the son of Tros, a Trojan prince; **Zeus** sent a storm-wind, or (later and more usually) an eagle, who carried Ganymede up to Olympus, where he became the cupbearer; in return his father was given a stud of exceptional horses.

Gawain (Gawayne) One of King **Arthur**'s knights; son of King Lot of Orkney, whose character varies in different accounts; in the medieval *Sir Gawayn and the Grene Knight*, he is a noble hero undergoing a test of faith; in other stories he is a jeering attacker of reputations, especially that of **Lancelot**.

Gawayne ▶ **Gawain**

Genii Spirits of mythology throughout the world; their forces were less beneficent than those of **angels**, but less wicked than those of **demons**; regarded as the doubles of objects, beings and events.

Giants Large, strong and often stupid beings from mythology throughout the world; in the Bible, the product of an unnatural union between fallen angels and the daughters of men; taught men the rudiments of the knowledge they had from being able to see from high up; for the Greeks, sons of the earth representing youth, strength and virility, who could only be killed by a god and a man together.

Gigantes Greek giants; sons of earth and Tartaros, with snakelike legs; made war on the Olympian gods, were defeated, and are buried under various volcanic islands; the Gigantomachy ('war of the giants') was the subject of large-scale sculpture, as at Pergamum; a subgroup, the Aloadi, piled Mt Pelion upon Mt Ossa.

Gilgamesh Sumerian hero; tyrannical king of Uruk and intrepid adventurer; began an adventure in search for immortality, but failed, and returned to Uruk to accept his fate and resume his former life.

Gorboduc Legendary king of Britain; first heard about in Geoffrey of Monmouth's *History*; when he grew senile, his two sons Ferret and Porrex quarrelled over the inheritance; he was the subject of an early Elizabethan tragedy in the Senecan style, written by Norton and Sackville (1561).

Gorgons Three mythical Greek monsters; represented with hair made of angry serpents, tusks like a boar's, hands of bronze and golden wings; anyone who looked at them was turned to stone; Euryale represented sexual excess, Stheno, social perversion, and **Medusa**, vanity; Medusa's head was cut off by **Perseus**, and the children of **Poseidon** emerged from the wound.

Graces In Greek mythology, three daughters of **Zeus** and **Hera**; embodied beauty and social accomplishments; sometimes called Aglaia, Euphrosyne and Thalia.

Graiae In Greek mythology, three sisters with the characteristics of extreme old age; had one eye and one tooth between them; **Perseus** took the eye and made them tell the route to the **Gorgons**, who were their sisters.

Griffin (Gryphon) Greek monster; originated in tales of the Arimaspians, who hunted the creature for its gold; had a lion's body, and an eagle's head, wings, and claws; collected fragments of gold to build its nest, and, instead of an egg, laid an agate.

Gryphon ▶ **Griffin**

Guan Di (Kuan Ti) Chinese god of war; based on a historical person who died in the 3c AD; made a god in 1594, and greatly revered.

Gudrun Norse heroine; wife of **Sigurd** the Volsung; after his death she married Atli (the legendary Attila) who put her brothers to death; in revenge she served up his sons in a dish, and then destroyed him by fire; in the similar German story she is known as Kriemhild.

Guinevere King **Arthur**'s queen; originally Guanhamara in Geoffrey of Monmouth's *History*, and there are other spellings; in later romances, much is made of her affair with Sir **Lancelot** (an example of courtly love); in Malory's epic poem she survives Arthur's death and enters a nunnery.

Hadad Assyrian god of storms, known as **Adad** by the Mesopotamians; invoked in curses when begged to send torrential rain to the lands of enemies, but also brought agricultural fertility.

Hades (Pluto) Greek god of hell; brother of **Zeus** and **Poseidon**; invisible god who ruled the dead, assisted by **demons**; forbade his subjects to leave his domain and became enraged when anyone tried to steal his prey; the most hated of the gods among mortals; identified by the Romans as Pluto.

Halcyone (Alcyone) In Greek mythology, daughter of **Aeolus**, who married Ceyx, son of the morning star; either for impiety, or because she mourned his death at sea, both were changed into seabirds (halcyons, or kingfishers, who are fabled to calm the sea); sometimes described instead as one of the **Pleiades**.

Hamadryads Greek **Nymphs**; tree nymphs who were offended or died when the trees containing them were harmed.

Hanuman Indian monkey god, son of the god of the winds, Vayu; as soon as he was born, he rushed towards the sun believing it to be a ripe fruit, crashing into all the planets on the way; as protector, he destroyed the death rays emitted by the planets and was known as the god of athletes and gymnasts.

Hanuman

Harpies Greek genii/spirits; represented as three women with wings or birds with the heads of women; seized children and souls and tortured their victims.

Harpocrates ► Horus

Hathor Egyptian goddess; portrayed as a woman bearing the sun between two cow's horns representing the intoxication of pleasure, love and fertility; identified by the Greeks with **Aphrodite**.

Hebe Greek goddess of youth and youthful beauty; daughter of **Zeus** and **Hera**; became cupbearer to the Olympians, and was married to **Heracles** after he was deified.

Hecabe ► Hecuba

Hecate Greek goddess of witchcraft, spooks, and magic; not in Homer, she appears in Hesiod, and seems to represent the powerful mother-goddess of Asia Minor; worshipped with offerings at places where three roads cross, and so given three bodies in sculpture.

Hector Hero of Greek mythology; the bravest Trojan, who led out their army to battle; the son of **Priam**, and married to **Andromache**; **Achilles** killed him

and dragged his body behind his chariot; Priam ransomed it at the end of the *Iliad*.

Hecuba (Hecabe) Greek heroine; wife of **Priam**, king of Troy, and mother of 18 children, including **Hector** and **Cassandra**; after the Greeks took Troy, she saw her sons and her husband killed, and was sent into slavery.

Heimdallr Norse god; born of nine mothers, he could see everything and never closed his eyes; the guardian of the gods' abode; at the moment of the end of the world, it was said that he would blow his trumpet to call all the gods to hold a council.

Hel (Hela) In Norse mythology, the youngest child of **Loki**; half her body was living human flesh, the other half decayed; assigned by **Odin** to rule Helheim (the underworld) and to receive the spirits of the dead who do not die in battle.

Helen Greek heroine; daughter of **Zeus** and **Leda**, sister to **Clytemnestra**, **Castor** and **Pollux**; the most beautiful of women who captivated all men, and as a result was the cause of the Trojan War when she was abducted by **Paris**; granted immortality by Zeus and **Apollo**.

Helios Greek god of the sun; represented as a charioteer with four horses; in early times Helios was not worshipped, except at Rhodes; in the late classical period, there was an Imperial cult of the sun, Sol Invictus.

Hellen In ancient Greek genealogies, the eldest son of **Deucalion**; father of Doros, Xuthos and Aiolos, who were the progenitors of the Dorian, Ionian, and Aeolic branches of the Greek race; the Greeks (or Hellenes) were named after him.

Hephaestus (Volcanus, Vulcan) Greek god of fire; son of **Zeus** and **Hera**; lame (either because his mother dropped him from Olympus when she realized how ugly he was, or because Zeus threw him down onto the island when he took his mother's side in a marital dispute); volcanoes were his workshops and the **Cyclopes** his assistants in his work as a blacksmith and jeweller; identified by the Romans as Vulcan.

Hera (Juno) Greek goddess; married her brother **Zeus**; conceived some of her sons without any male assistance by hitting the ground with her hand or eating a lettuce; pursued with a vengeance Zeus's mistresses and their children, putting enormous snakes into **Heracles**' cradle, forcing Zeus to hide his illegitimate children by transforming them into animals or enclosing them in the earth; identified by the Romans as Juno; her name means 'lady'.

Heracles (Hercules) Greek hero; demonstrated amazing strength from birth, choking the serpents sent to him by the jealous **Hera**; many achievements are attributed to him including the 12 labours of Eurystheus; he delivered Troy from a monster but came back to wreak havoc on the city because it did not pay his salary; succeeded in injuring **Hades** and **Hera** with his arrows and won immortality; identified by the Romans as Hercules.

Hercules ► Heracles

Hermaphroditus Greek god; a minor god with bisexual characteristics, the son of **Hermes** and **Aphrodite**; the **Nymph** Salmacis, unloved by him, prayed to be united with him; this was granted by combining them in one body.

Hermes (Mercury) Greek god of the spoken word and son of **Zeus**; intermediary who went from men to Olympus and Olympus to **Hades**; as the god of commerce, the only person to achieve immortality as a result of a contract; identified by the Romans as Mercury.

Hero and Leander Greek lovers; lived on opposite sides of the Hellespont; Hero was the priestess of **Aphrodite** at Sestos, and Leander, who lived at Abydos, swam across each night guided by her light; when this was extinguished in a storm, he was drowned, and Hero committed suicide by throwing herself into the sea.

Hesperides In Greek mythology, the daughters of the evening star (Hesper); guarded the Golden Apples together with the dragon, Ladon; sang as they circled the tree, which was given by **Gaia** to **Hera** as a wedding present; when **Heracles** had to fetch the apples, he either killed the dragon, or sent it to sleep, or, more usually, persuaded **Atlas** to get them for him while he took over Atlas's function of holding up the sky.

Hestia (Vesta) Greek goddess of hearth and home; sister of **Zeus** and **Hera**; never intervened in the stormy history of the gods and became the central point, the meeting place; identified by the Romans as Vesta.

Hiawatha Native American hero; appeared in *The Song of Hiawatha*, which retells Native American legends in the manner and metre of the Finnish *Kalevala*; Hiawatha is educated by his grandmother Nokomis, and marries Minnehaha.

Hippolytus Greek hero; son of **Theseus** and Hippolyta, leader of the **Amazons**; Theseus's new wife, **Phaedra**, made advances to Hippolytus, which were refused, so she falsely accused Hippolytus of rape; Theseus invoked a curse, **Poseidon** sent a frightening sea monster, and Hippolytus was thrown from his chariot and killed.

Horae In Greek mythology, 'the seasons'; implied the right or fitting time for something to happen; given various names either connected with fertility or peace.

Horatii and **Curiatii** Early Roman legend used to justify appeals; under Tullus Hostilius there was war between Rome and Alba; two groups of three brothers were selected from Rome (the Horatii) and Alba (the Curiatii) to fight, the winners to decide the battle; all were killed except one, Horatius; when his sister, who was betrothed to a Curiatius, abused her, he murdered her, but was acquitted after appealing to the Roman people.

Horus (Harpocrates) Egyptian god; husband of **Hathor**, brother of **Seth** and ancestor of the dynasties of the pharaohs; had a falcon's head and ruled the air, his eyes being the sun and the moon; became universal king of the earth after defeating Seth, who had seized power after murdering Horus's father.

Huang-ti Chinese cultural hero; legendary emperor, patron of alchemists, doctors and seers, and one of the fathers of Taoism; born miraculously after his mother was made pregnant by lightning from the Great Bear; invented chariots, ships and houses, and understood that every activity in the world had to be preceded by putting the individual body in order; discovered the way of the Tao in a dream and searched for ways of attaining immortality.

Huitzilopochtli Aztec god of war and protector of the city; symbolized in the midday sun and represented with hummingbird feathers on his head and left leg, a black face and brandishing a serpent of turquoise or fire; massacred all his brothers and sisters immediately after he was born, as they planned to kill his mother; as a soothsayer

Huitzilopochtli

he communed with the priests at night and as a cruel god, tore out the hearts of those who disobeyed him.

Hydra Greek monster; many-headed child of **Typhon** and **Echidna**, which lived in a swamp at Lerna; since the heads grew again when struck off, **Heracles** could kill it only with the assistance of Iolaos, who cauterized the places where the heads grew; the name means 'water snake'.

Hygeia Greek goddess; the daughter of **Asclepius**; a minor deity, her name was a personification of the word for 'health'.

Hymen Greek god of marriage; in Ancient Greece and Rome, the cry of 'O Hymen Hymenaie' at weddings (later a marriage song) led to the invention of a being called Hymen of Hymenaeus, who was assumed to have been happily married, and therefore suitable for invocation as a god of marriage; depicted as a youth with a torch.

Hyperboreans Greek unvisited people of fabled virtue and prosperity; lived in the land 'beyond the North Wind'; in Herodotus they worshipped **Apollo** and sent offerings to Delos; could refer to a lost Greek colony in what is now Romania, or even to the Swedes at the end of the trans-European amber route.

Hyperion Greek **Titan**; son of **Uranus** and **Gaia**, and father of **Eos** (the Dawn), **Helios** (the sun), and **Selene** (the moon); later, as in Shakespeare and Keats, identified with the sun.

Iapetus Greek **Titan**; father of **Prometheus** and **Atlas**; grandfather of **Deucalion**; the close resemblance to Japhet may indicate borrowing from near Eastern sources.

Icarus In Greek mythology, the son of **Daedalus**; his father made him wings to escape from Crete, but he flew too near the sun; the wax holding the wings melted and he fell into the Aegean at a point now known as the Icarian Sea.

Idomeneus Leader of the Cretans; a descendant of **Minos** who assisted the Greeks at Troy; caught in a storm at sea, he vowed to sacrifice the first thing he met on his safe return; this was his own son; after carrying out the sacrifice he was driven into exile.

Inanna Sumerian goddess of love and war; stole the *me* (meaning everything that makes up civilization) from **Enki** to give to her city, Uruk; attempted to seize power of the underworld from her sister but failed; in rage at her husband's lack of sympathy for her resulting predicament, she ordered the **demons** to torture him and imprison him in hell.

Indra Indian god; an athlete and exemplary warrior who gave life and light, created the ox and the horse, gave the cow milk and made all women fertile; crushed the evil **demon** Vrtra, allowing the dawn and the sunrise to be created.

Io Greek heroine; beloved by **Zeus**, who turned her into a heifer to save her from **Hera**'s jealousy; Hera kept her under the gaze of the **Argus**; but she escaped with **Hermes**' help; was then punished with a gadfly which drove her through the world until she arrived in Egypt; there Zeus changed her back into human shape, and she gave birth to Epaphos, ancestor of many peoples.

Iphigeneia Greek priestess; daughter of **Agamemnon** and **Clytemnestra**; was about to be

Thought and Belief

sacrificed at Aulis as the fleet could not sail to Troy, because the winds were against it, but at the last moment was saved by **Artemis**, who made her a priestess in the country of the Tauri (the Crimea); finally her brother **Orestes** saved her.

Irene In Greek mythology, a personification of 'peace'; one of the **Horae**.

Iris Greek goddess of the rainbow; became the messenger of the gods, especially of **Zeus** in Homer, and of **Hera** in later writers; depicted sitting under Hera's throne.

Ishtar (Astarte) Mesopotamian goddess; as the star of the morning, personified war, and as the star of the evening, personified love; came to the aid of the sexually impotent and was cruel and determined as a hostile warrior; established the fame of Assyria and was responsible for the cruelty of its kings.

Isis Egyptian goddess; mother of **Horus**; wore a solar disc and the horns of a cow, and was known as the protectress of love and mistress of destiny; obtained her powers by trickery and as a magician, cured her son who had been bitten by a snake.

Isolde ► Tristan and Isolde

Itzamma Mayan god of heaven; the creator and civilizer of mankind, with the appearance of an old toothless man with sunken cheeks and a prominent nose, he gave places their names and distributed land between the different tribes; sometimes depicted as an enormous serpent which represented the sky.

Iuppiter ► Zeus

Ixion Greek king of Thessaly; the first murderer; also the father of the **Centaurs**; for attempting to rape **Hera** he was bound to a wheel of fire, usually located in the underworld.

Izanagi no Mikoto and **Izanami no Mikoto** Japanese male and female gods; in the creation myth these were the first beings who created islands in the water and the other gods; Izanami died when she gave birth to fire; Izanagi followed her to the land of the dead (Yomi), but she turned against him and pursued him; finally he had to block the exit from Yomi with a large rock and Izanami then became the goddess of the underworld.

Janus Roman god of beginnings; a two-faced god who personified clear-sightedness; protected **Saturn** when he was being hunted by Jupiter (**Zeus**); invented money, the cultivation of soil and legislation.

Jason Greek hero; son of the king of Iolcus, who was deposed by his half-brother, Pelias; Jason claimed the power from Pelias, who challenged him to demonstrate his worthiness of the crown by bringing back the Golden Fleece, guarded by an ever-wakeful dragon, hoping that Jason would never return from such an impossible mission; a ship, the *Argo*, was built for the mission, and Jason overcame many obstacles to return with the Golden Fleece; the king did not keep his promise, and weary of war, Jason stole the fleece and left.

Jimmu Tenno First emperor of Japan in the Shinto religion; said to be descended from **Amaterasu**, and to have reigned between 660 and 585 BC, dying at the age of 127; probably a real person, subsequently deified.

Jocasta In Greek legend, the wife of King Laius of Thebes and mother of **Oedipus**; later unwittingly became the wife of her son; she is called Epikaste in Homer; bore Oedipus four children: **Eteocles, Polynices, Antigone** and Ismene; killed herself when she discovered her incest.

Julunggul ► Rainbow Snake

Juno ► Hera

Jupiter ► Zeus

Kama Indian god of love; represented with a bow and arrow; as soon as he was born, looked around him and asked who he was going to set on fire; always ready to initiate love in men or in the gods.

Kami Japanese spirits; manifestations of natural forces and superior to men; there were 80 million kami, to personify anything big or inexplicable at a time when animals, rivers, lakes and seas were objects of veneration; the drink saké was the offering preferred by the kami.

Kane ► Tane

Kekrops ► Cecrops

Kreon ► Creon

Krishna Indian god; a lovable child and merciless warrior; endowed with exceptional strength and intelligence, he killed the monster Baku who had taken the form of a crane, and fought with Kaliya, the king of serpents; his life with 16 000 wives and 180 000 children was interspersed with numerous battles against **demons**; has become the only god in many Hindu sects.

Krishna

Kronos ► Cronus

Kuan Ti ► Guan Di

Kumarbi Hurrian god; deposed from the divine throne by the storm-god, **Teshub**; became the father of an enormous stone man in the hope that this son could overthrow the storm-god, but this was prevented by the other gods.

Lachesis ► Moerae

Laius Greek king of Thebes; father of **Oedipus**; he married **Jocasta**, and was warned by an oracle that their son would destroy him; this happened when Oedipus, assumed to be dead, returned from Corinth and accidentally killed Laius during a quarrel on the road.

Lakshmi Indian goddess of happiness, beauty and prosperity; the wife of **Vishnu**, she was the incarnation of the great god's power.

Lakshmi

Lancelot, Sir (Launcelot du Lac) The most famous of King **Arthur**'s knights, though he is a relatively late addition to the legend; the son of King Ban of Benwick, the courtly lover of **Guinevere**, and the father of **Galahad** by Elaine; in spite of his near-perfection as a knight, he was unable to achieve the Grail adventure; he arrived too late to help Arthur in the last battle.

Laocoon Trojan prince; a priest of **Apollo**, who objected to the plan to bring the Wooden Horse into Troy; two serpents came out of the sea and killed him, together with his two sons.

Lapiths In Greek mythology, a people of Thessaly; Perithous, king of the Lapiths, invited the **Centaurs** to his wedding with Hippodameia; a terrible fight took place between the two groups, in which the Centaurs were defeated.

Lares Roman gods; protectors of inhabited places; depicted as two boys accompanied by a dog; divided into two groups; *lares compitales* were found in the country, at crossroads and in meeting places; *lares familiares* were guardians of the family home.

Latinus Roman ancestor and eponymous king of the Latins; descended from **Circe** (according to

Hesiod) or from **Faunus** (according to Virgil); in the *Aeneid*, Latinus gives his daughter Lavinia to **Aeneas**.

Latona ▶ **Leto**

Launcelot du Lac ▶ **Lancelot, Sir**

Leander ▶ **Hero and Leander**

Lear Legendary king of Britain; son of **Bladud**, who reigned for 60 years; in his old age two of his daughters, Goneril and Regan, conspired against him, but the third daughter, Cordelia, saved him and became queen after his death (the story is changed by Shakespeare, so that she died before his eyes); Leicester is named after him.

Leda In Greek mythology, the wife of Tyndareus, king of Sparta, and mother, either by him or **Zeus**, of **Castor** and **Pollux**, **Helen**, and **Clytemnestra**; a frequent subject in art is Zeus courting Leda in the form of a swan; Helen was believed to have been hatched from an egg, preserved at Sparta into historic times.

Lemminkäinen Finnish hero; in the *Kalevala*, has to undertake impossible tasks, such as shooting the swan of Tuonela; this causes his death, and his mother has to reanimate him; his ride through a land of horrors inspired Sibelius.

Lemures Roman ghosts; wandered about outside the house on 9, 11 and 13 May (the Lemuria).

Leto (Latona) Greek **Titan**; mother by **Zeus** of the twins **Apollo** and **Artemis**; they were born at Delos, because in her jealousy **Hera** would allow no land to harbour Leto; luckily, at that time Delos was a floating island.

Leviathan Phoenician monster; personification of evil, believed to have come out of the primal chaos; sparks of fire shot from his mouth and smoke poured from his nostrils; always present, hidden in each individual.

Lif and **Lifthrasir** In Norse mythology, the mother and father of the new race of human beings after Ragnarok (the last battle); the names presumably mean 'life' and 'strong life'.

Lilith In Jewish legend, the first wife of Adam; or, more generally, a **demon** woman.

Lohengrin In Germanic legend, the son of Parsifal (**Perceval, Sir**); left the temple of the Grail and was carried to Antwerp in a boat drawn by swans; there he saved Princess Elsa of Brabant, and intended to marry her; however, she asked forbidden questions about his origin, and he was forced to leave her, the swan-boat taking him back to the Grail temple.

Loki Norse god; represented deceit, disorder, malevolence and perversity; fathered horrible monsters and put obstacles in the way of happiness; as a magician, had the power to transform himself into different animals and insulted and offended the other gods.

Lotus-eaters (Lotophagi) People encountered by **Odysseus**; lived on 'a flowery food' which makes those who eat it forget their own country, and wish to live always in a dreamy state; Odysseus had to force his men to move on.

Lucretia (Lucrece) Roman wife of Collatinus; raped by Sextus, son of Tarquinius Superbus; after telling her story, she committed suicide; the incident led to the expulsion of the Tarquins from Rome.

Lud Legendary king of Britain; first walled the principal city, from that time called Kaerlud after him, and eventually London; buried near Ludgate, which preserves his name.

Lug Irish god; skilled in many arts and fulfilled the office of all gods; proclaimed by the king to be the wisest of the wise and given the task of organizing

the battle which conquered the Fomoiri, evil beings who occupied Ireland and oppressed its inhabitants.

Lycurgus Greek king of Thrace; opposed **Dionysus** and was blinded; his name is shared by the founder of the Spartan constitution, with its military caste-system (the date when this originated has been much disputed, and is now thought to be c.600 BC, much too late for the legendary Lycurgus to have participated).

Maat Egyptian goddess; represented the social and cosmic order and the guardian of ethics and rites; there at the beginning of the universe, she maintained order in heaven as on earth, and was responsible for the seasons, night and day, the movement of the stars and rainfall.

Maenads Greek 'mad women'; followed **Dionysus** on his journeys; dressed in animal-skins and so strong that they could uproot trees and kill wild animals, eating the flesh raw; also known as Bacchae or Bacchantes.

Manes In Roman religion, 'the dead'; the concept developed from the spirits of the dead in general, to the gods of the underworld, Di Manes, the ancestors of the family, and the spirits of individuals in grave-stone inscriptions.

Marduk Babylonian god; represented life, civilization and progress; created the winds and raised the tempest, distressing the first-born gods who declared war on him but were defeated; Marduk created heaven, earth and man; when the god of death succeeded by a ruse in making him rise from his seat, the sun stopped shining, the roads became infested with brigands, and man ate man until Marduk took his place again.

Marduck

Mars ▶ **Ares**

Marsyas Greek **satyr**; challenged **Apollo** to a flute-contest; defeated and flayed alive by the god, his blood or tears formed a river of the same name.

Medea Greek witch; daughter of Aeetes, the king of Colchis, who assisted **Jason** in obtaining the Golden Fleece; on their return to Iolcos, she renewed the youth of Aeson, and tricked the daughters of Pelias into performing a similar ritual, so that they destroyed their own father; when deserted by Jason at Corinth, she fled in her aerial chariot after killing her children.

Medusa Greek **Gorgon**; depicted with staring eyes and snakes for hair.

Meleager Greek hero; at his birth the **Moerae** appeared and prophesied that he would die when the brand then on the fire had burnt away; his mother, Althaea, removed it and kept it; when the quarrel over the Calydonian boar took place and her brothers were killed, she threw the brand onto the fire, so that he died.

Melias ▶ **Nymphs**

Melpomene Greek **Muse** of tragedy.

Memnon In Greek mythology, a prince from Ethiopia; son of **Eos**; killed at Troy by **Achilles**; the Greeks thought that one of the gigantic statues at Thebes represented him; it gave out a musical sound at sunrise.

Menelaus King of Sparta; younger brother of **Agamemnon**, who married **Helen**; took part in the Trojan War and was delayed in Egypt on his return;

finally settled down at Sparta with Helen again.

Mercury ► **Hermes**

Merlin Good wizard or sage whose magic was used to help King **Arthur**; son of an incubus and a mortal woman, and therefore indestructible, but was finally entrapped by Vivien, the Lady of the Lake, and bound under a rock for ever; famous for his prophecies.

Mermaid Legendary sea creature; had the body of a woman and the tail of a fish, a fiction possibly based on early encounters with seals or sea cows; in stories their singing attracts mortal men to love them; their male counterparts were mermen.

Midas King of Phrygia; as a reward for helping the **Satyr** Silenus, **Dionysus** gave Midas a wish, and he asked that anything he touched should turn to gold; however, this caused so many difficulties (eg in eating and drinking) that he asked to be released; he was told to bathe in the River Pactolus, which thereafter had golden sands.

Minerva ► **Athene**

Minos Greek hero; son of **Zeus**, who took the form of a bull in order to impregnate **Europa**; claimed power as king of Crete and took part in military expeditions to avenge the murder of his son and to force Athens to provide men and women to feed to the **Minotaur**; became a judge in hell after being drowned in his bath.

Minotaur Greek monster; son of **Pasiphae** and a bull from the sea, half bull and half human; the name means **Minos**'s bull; kept in a labyrinth made by **Daedalus**, and killed by **Theseus** with the help of **Ariadne**.

Mithra Indo-European god; represented friendship, benevolence, non-hostility and compromise; depicted as a 'killer of the bull', plunging a sword into a dying bull's body, from which all herbs and beneficial plants were born; closely associated with the sun.

Mnemosyne Greek **Titan**; daughter of earth and heaven, and mother of all the **Muses**; her name means 'Memory'.

Modimo African god; originally from Zimbabwe, and considered to be the creator; when appearing in the east, he distributed good things and belonged to the element water; appearing in the west, he was a destroyer, responsible for drought, cyclones and earthquakes, and represented the element fire; his name was taboo and spoken only by priests or seers, and he could only be reached by imperfect beings.

Moerae (Fates, Parcae) Three Greek goddesses; named Atropos, Clotho and Lachesis, daughters of **Zeus**; the first spun a thread which signified birth, the second unravelled the thread, symbolizing the unravelling of life, and the third cut the thread, signifying death; they were the personification of inflexible law, representing destiny and the limits which could not be overstepped; in Rome assimilated to the Parcae, who were originally birth **demons**.

Moloch Biblical god of the Canaanites and other peoples; in his cult children were sacrificed by fire; a rebel angel in Milton's *Paradise Lost*, his name is used for any excessive and cruel religion.

Monsters Wild, unmanageable forces which appear as enemies in all mythologies; in general, a mixture of living creatures (eg horse and man for **Centaurs** and fish and woman for **Sirens**); signified irrational forces, the death necessary for new life and the anarchical energy which preceded and produced creation and order.

Morgan le Fay Legendary enchantress; 'Morgan the Fairy', King **Arthur**'s sister, and generally hostile towards him; one of the three queens who received him at his death.

Morpheus Roman god of sleep; one of the sons of Somnus ('sleep') who sent or impersonated images of people in the dreamer's mind; later, as in Spenser, the god of sleep.

Muses Nine Greek goddesses; daughters of **Zeus**, each with the vocation to promote an area of the arts: epic poetry, mime, history, the flute, dance, lyric poetry, tragedy, comedy, astronomy; they favoured communication, delighted the gods and inspired poets; See **Calliope**, **Polyhymnia**, **Clio**, **Euterpe**, **Terpsichore**, **Erato**, **Melpomene**, **Thalia**, **Urania**.

Myrmidons Greek band of warriors from Thessaly; went to the Trojan War with **Achilles**.

Naiads Greek **Nymphs**; inhabited springs, rivers, and lakes.

Narcissus Greek hero; the symbol of self-love, he was told by a seer that he would live to a ripe old age as long as he never looked at himself; caring for no one but himself, he drove his friends and those who fell in love with him to despair; the goddess **Nemesis** decided to avenge his victims by leading him to a spring in which he saw his own reflection, which he immediately fell in love with, and moving towards it, he fell into the spring and drowned; from his body was born the flower which bears his name.

Nausicaa Greek heroine; in Homer's *Odyssey*, the daughter of King Alcinous; when **Odysseus** landed in Phaeacia, alone and naked, she was doing the laundry by the sea shore; she took him home to her father's palace.

Nemesis Greek goddess of moderation; ruled over the distribution of wealth, taking revenge on arrogance and punishing excess; said to have prevented the Persians from seizing the city of Athens.

Neoptolemus Greek warrior; son of **Achilles**, his original name being Pyrrhus; went with **Odysseus** to persuade **Philoctetes** to come to Troy; at the end of the war he killed **Priam** and enslaved **Andromache**; for this, **Apollo** prevented him from reaching his home, and he was killed in a dispute at Delphi.

Nephthys Egyptian goddess; wife of **Seth**; cared for and protected the dead; took sides with her husband's enemies and when he was vanquished, killed and torn to pieces, helped to find the fragments of his body and put them back together, bringing him to life; Nephthys and her sister were the guardians of the tomb.

Neptune ► **Poseidon**

Nereids Greek **Nymphs**; 50 or (in some accounts) 100 daughters of **Nereus**; lived with their father in the depths of the sea.

Nereus Greek god of the sea; the wise old man of the sea who always told the truth; Heracles had to wrestle with him to find the location of the Golden Apples.

Nergal Babylonian god of death; son of the god of heaven, he loved catastrophes, epidemics and war, and made death his personal territory; later acquired the power of the ruler of the underworld; tricked **Marduk** into rising up from his seat, resulting in chaos throughout the world, until Marduk regained his position.

Nessus Greek **Centaur**; attacked **Heracles**' wife, Deinira; Heracles shot him, and the dying Centaur told Deinira that his blood would be a cure for infidelity; later, through jealousy, she put the blood

Thought and Belief

on a shirt, or made Heracles wear Nessus's shirt; this coated him with poison, so that he died.

Nestor A Greek leader in the Trojan War; in the *Iliad*, Homer portrays him as a long-winded sage, whose advice is often not taken; in the *Odyssey*, he is still living at Pylos, where a Mycenaean palace was discovered in the 1930s.

Nibelungen Medieval German race of dwarfs; lived in Norway and possessed a famous treasure; the *Nibelungenlied* recounts how Siegfried obtained the treasure and his later misfortunes; Wagner conflated this with other legends for his opera cycle.

Nike (Victoria) Greek goddess of victory, either in war or in an an athletic contest; the frequent subject of sculpture, often shown as a winged figure; identified by the Romans as Victoria.

Ninurta Sumerian god of war; chosen by the gods to fight against Anzu, who had stolen the tablets of destiny; on victory, he became champion of the gods.

Niobe Greek heroine; proud of having seven sons and seven daughters, she insulted mothers who had few children; her insults to **Leto** earned the revenge of Leto's son and daughter, **Apollo** and **Artemis**, and their father, **Zeus**, who murdered Niobe's children, left them without burial for nine days and turned her to stone on Mt Sipylus.

Nix (Nixie) European water sprite; occasionally entrapped people in her pool; not to be confused with the deity **Nyx** in Greek mythology.

Njord Norse god; father of **Freyr** and **Freyja**; succeeded **Odin** as sovereign and maintained peace and prosperity.

Norns Three Norse goddesses; Urdr represented the past, Verdandi, the present, and Skuld, the future; decided the fates of men and gods without reason or interest, dealing out as much good as evil.

Nox, Nux ▶ **Nyx**

Nymphs Greek goddesses; symbolized the beauty and charm of nature; for the most part, Nymphs were daughters of **Zeus** with lives lasting several centuries; dark formidable powers, whose beauty could lead to madness, and provoked sudden terror at midday; grouped into **Melias**, **Naiads**, **Nereids**, **Oreads**, **Dryads** and **Oceanids**.

Nyx (Nox, Nux) Greek goddess; a very ancient deity ('Night'), born of Chaos, and mother of Aither and Day, the **Hesperides**, and the **Moerae**; in the Orphic religion, Night was the original first principle; she laid an egg from which sprang other gods.

Oberon European king of the fairies; appears in European literature such as Shakespeare's *A Midsummer Night's Dream* and Wieland's *Oberon*.

Oceanids Greek **Nymphs**; inhabited the ocean and other watery places; daughters of **Oceanus** and Tethys.

Oceanus Greek **Titan**; son of **Uranus** and **Gaia**; a benign god who personified the stream of Ocean which was assumed to surround the world, as known to the Greeks.

Odin (Woden, Wotan) Norse god; keeper of all knowledge, represented as an old one-eyed bearded man wearing a multicoloured robe and a wide-brimmed hat; his horse had eight legs and galloped through the air, on the ocean as well as on ground; a cruel sovereign, he inspired deceit and was fond of human sacrifices; preserved the head of the decapitated giant Mimir, who was famous for his knowledge, and consulted it whenever he had some mystery to unravel.

Odysseus (Ulysses) Greek hero; a leader of the Achaeans in the Trojan War; returning to Greece, he became separated by a windstorm from his companions and overcame **Cyclopes**, **Sirens**, gods and magicians to return; his adventures are described in Homer's *Odyssey*.

Oedipus Greek hero; afflicted from birth by the curse that he would kill his father, marry his mother and be at the root of an endless series of misfortunes which would lead to the ruin of his family; because of this, his father abandoned him, and he was adopted by King Polybus; when the child was older and learned of the curse, he became frightened for the king, whom he believed to be his father and went into voluntary exile; he later killed his father in a fight when they met coincidentally; after being crowned king, he unknowingly married his mother, widowed by the death of his father.

Ogmios Celtic god; an old wrinkled man who wore a lion's skin and carried a club, a bow and a quiver; could draw or tow men attached by their ears to a gold chain, the end of which passed through the god's pierced tongue; attracted his followers by magic.

Olympians Greek gods and goddesses; collectively, the major gods and goddesses who were thought to live on Mt Olympus, the highest mountain in Ancient Greece, situated in a range between Macedonia and Thessaly.

Ops Roman goddess of plenty, the consort of **Saturn**, identified with **Rhea**.

Oreads ▶ **Nymphs**

Orestes In Greek legend, the son of **Agamemnon** and **Clytemnestra**; after his father's murder he went into exile, but returned to kill **Aegisthus** and his mother, for which he was pursued by the **Erinyes**.

Orion Greek gigantic hunter; beloved by **Eos** and killed by **Artemis**; changed into a constellation, and this generated further astronomical stories, for example, that he pursues the **Pleiades**.

Orpheus Greek hero; a musician and poet, he had the power to enchant gods, men, animals and inanimate objects who followed him under his spell; married the **Nymph Eurydice** who was taken to hell after dying from the bite of a serpent; Orpheus charmed the rulers of hell who agreed to release Eurydice on the condition that Orpheus did not turn round to look at her as she followed him out of hell; his doubts that she was following made him eventually turn round, to see Eurydice disappear into the underworld forever.

Osiris Egyptian god of vegetation; provided laws and customs and gave the fruits of the earth; his jealous brother **Seth** conspired to kill him by trapping him in a wooden chest and sinking it in a river; his wife **Isis** recovered the body and managed to make Osiris father a son, to take vengeance on her enemies.

Ouranus ▶ **Uranus**

Pan Greek god of animal instinct; half man, half goat with a long wrinkled face and two horns on his head; son of **Hermes**, he lived in hills and woods; constantly pursued by **Nymphs** and those who became possessed by him took on his characteristics.

Pandarus Trojan prince; in Homer's *Iliad*, was killed by **Diomedes**; in later developments of the story of **Troilus** and **Cressida**, he became her uncle and their 'go-between' (hence 'pander').

Pandora Greek heroine; the first woman on earth,

who led men to their downfall by seduction and entrapment; a gift from **Zeus** to man, made in the form of the immortal goddesses, Pandora was divine in appearance but human in reality; with her she brought a box which she had been forbidden to open; overcome with curiosity, she opened the box and let out all the evils of the world, such as disease, death, lies and theft, which spread throughout nature.

Pan Gu Chinese first being of creation; broke open the primal egg from within, held up the sky, and prevented it from bearing down upon the earth; the world was then made from parts of him, so that his body became the mountains, his hair the stars, and his eyes the sun and moon.

Parasurama Indian hero; united the religious purity of a Brahman with the impurity of a warrior; cut off his mother's head as requested by his father, who believed her to have produced the racial impurity; in 21 battles, freed the world of the kshatriya warriors.

Parcae ▶ Moerae

Paris (Alexander) Greek hero; a prince of Troy, the son of **Priam**; because of a prophecy, he was exposed at birth on Mt Ida, where he was loved by Oenone, a **Nymph**; there he also chose **Aphrodite** as the fairest of three goddesses; she offered him the most beautiful woman in the world; he abducted **Helen**, causing the Trojan war; wounded by **Philoctetes**, and in his death-agony asked Oenone for help, which she refused.

Parsifal ▶ Perceval, Sir

Pasiphae In Greek mythology, the daughter of **Helios**; wife of **Minos**, king of Crete; loved a bull sent by **Poseidon**, and became the mother of the **Minotaur**.

Patroclus Greek warrior; faithful follower of **Achilles** at Troy; went into battle wearing Achilles's armour, but was cut down by **Hector**; his death made Achilles return to the battle.

Pegasus Greek winged horse; sprang from the body of the **Medusa** after her death; **Bellerophon** caught it with **Athene**'s assistance; various fountains sprang from the touch of its foot, such as Hippocrene on Mt Helicon; finally it was placed in the sky as a constellation.

Peleus Greek king of Phythia in Thessaly; had to capture Thetis, a **Nereid**, before he could marry her; the gods attended the wedding feast; the father of **Achilles**.

Pelops Greek hero; protégé of **Poseidon**; eaten unknowingly by **Demeter** at birth as a result of his father's attempt to test the keenness of the gods; the other gods resurrected him to restore their reputation; protected by Poseidon on Olympus until his father led him to steal the nectar and ambrosia of the gods to give to mortals, for which he was forced to return to earth; drove his chariot drawn by winged horses to win the chance to marry Hippodameia; one of the mythological figures said to have founded the Olympic Games, in memory of his victory.

Penates Roman guardians of the storeroom; 'Lares and Penates' were the household gods; the *penates publici* were the 'luck' of the Roman state, originally brought by **Aeneas** from Troy and kept at Lavinium.

Penelope In Greek legend, the wife of **Odysseus**; faithfully waited 20 years for his return from Troy; tricked her insistent suitors by weaving her web (a shroud for Odysseus's father, Laertes, which had to be finished before she could marry), and undoing her work every night.

Pentheus In Greek mythology, the king of Thebes; did not welcome **Dionysus**; disguising himself as a woman, he tried to spy on the orgiastic rites of the **Maenads**, who tore him to pieces, his mother leading them on.

Perceval, Sir (Parsifal) One of King **Arthur**'s knights; went in quest of the Holy Grail; in the German version (Parzival) his bashfulness prevented him from asking the right questions of the warden of the Grail castle, so that the Fisher King was not healed.

Peri Persian good fairy or genie; Peri-Banou, for example, was the name of a beautiful fairy in the *Arabian Nights*.

Persephone (Proserpina) Greek goddess of the underworld; daughter of **Demeter** and **Zeus**, originally called Kore ('maiden'); while gathering flowers at Enna in Sicily was abducted by **Hades** and made queen of the underworld; there she ate the seeds of the pomegranate, which meant (in fairy lore) that she was bound to stay; however, a compromise was arranged so that she could return for half of every year (an allegory of the return of spring).

Perseus Greek hero; shut in a chest and thrown into the sea by his grandfather; washed up on the island of Seriphos; after he grew up, the island's tyrant demanded that he bring him the gift of the head of a **Gorgon**; with the help of **Hermes** and the **Nymphs**, he slew **Medusa** and returned with her head; married **Andromeda** after freeing her from the sea monster to whom she was promised; unknowingly killed his grandfather, fulfilling an oracle which predicted this.

Perun Slavic god of rain and fertility; represented as a human being with a silver head and golden moustache; controlled the seasons and destroyed the countries of wicked men with hail.

Phaedra Greek heroine; daughter of **Minos** and the second wife of **Theseus**; while he was away she fell in love with her stepson **Hippolytus**; he rejected her, so she killed herself, but left a note accusing him of trying to rape her; Theseus called on **Poseidon** to grant a promised favour, and punish Hippolytus with death.

Phaethon Greek hero; son of **Helios**; challenged to prove his ancestry by his friends, he asked to drive his father's chariot for a day; as he was inexperienced in this, the horses bolted, the chariot veered off its route and everything in their path was set on fire; the earth complained to the king of Olympus, and **Zeus** struck down the charioteer.

Phenix ▶ Phoenix

Philemon and Baucis Greek old man and wife; the only ones to entertain the Greek gods **Zeus** and **Hermes** when they visited the earth to test people's hospitality; in return they were saved from a flood, made priest and priestess, and allowed to die at the same time, when they were changed into trees.

Philoctetes Greek hero; son of Poeas, who inherited the bow of **Heracles** and its poisoned arrows; on the way to Troy was bitten by a snake, and the wound stank, so that he was left behind on the island of Lemnos; it was prophesied that only with the arrows of Heracles could Troy be taken, so **Diomedes** and **Odysseus** came to find Philoctetes; his wound was healed and he entered the battle, killing **Paris**.

Philomela (Philomel) and Procne (Progne) In Greek mythology, daughters of Pandion, king of Athens; Procne married Tereus, king of Thrace,

Thought and Belief

who raped Philomela and removed her tongue; but she was able to tell Procne by a message in her embroidery; Procne served up her son Itys, or Itylos, in a meal to his father; while pursuing the sisters, the gods changed Tereus into the hoopoe, Philomela into the swallow, and Procne into the nightingale; in Latin legend, the birds of the sisters are reversed.

Phoebe Greek **Titan**, identified with the moon; later she was confused with **Artemis**.

Phoenix (Phenix) Legendary bird; lived for a long time; killed itself on a funeral pyre, but was then reborn from the ashes.

Pleiades In Greek mythology, the seven daughters of **Atlas** and **Pleione**; Maia, Taygete, Elektra, Alkyone, Asterope, Kelaino and Merope; after their deaths they were transformed into the star-cluster of the same name.

Pluto ▶ **Hades**

Pollux ▶ **Castor and Pollux**

Polyhymnia Greek **Muse** of dance, mime and acting.

Polynices (Polyneices) Greek hero; second son of **Oedipus**, who led the **Seven against Thebes**; **Creon**'s refusal to bury him led eventually to the death of **Antigone**.

Polyphemus Greek **Cyclops**; imprisoned **Odysseus** and some of his companions in his cave; Odysseus blinded Polyphemus's one eye, and told him that 'No one' had hurt him; as a result, when he called on the other Cyclopes for help, and they asked who had attacked him, they did not understand his answer; Odysseus's band escaped by hiding under the sheep when they were let out of the cave to graze.

Pomona Roman goddess of fruit trees and their fruit, especially apples and pears.

Poseidon (Neptune) Greek god of the sea; represented wielding a trident and being pulled by monsters in a chariot; could evoke storms and set fire to rocks; took part in the construction of the walls of Troy, then called up a monster to devastate the area when he did not receive payment; Neptune was a Roman water god who was later associated with Poseidon.

Prajapati Indian god; master of creatures and posterity, he was born aged a thousand years from a primordial egg; created the gods, the evil spirits, man, melodies and the sun, then wasted away, exhausted by his tasks.

Priam In Greek legend, the king of Troy; son of Laomedon, and husband of **Hecuba**; presented in the *Iliad* as an old man; when **Hector** was killed, went secretly to **Achilles** to beg his son's body for burial; at the sack of Troy, he was killed by **Neoptolemus**.

Priapus Greek god; represented as a small bearded man with an oversized penis; in some traditions, the son of **Zeus** and **Aphrodite**; Zeus's jealous wife **Hera** made sure that the child was born with the extraordinary deformity to which he owes his name; Aphrodite abandoned him in the mountains; the guard of the orchard, he scared off thieves and threatened females with sexual violence.

Procrustes Thief of Attica; in the legend of **Theseus**, made travellers lie on his bed, and either cut or lengthened them to fit it; his name means 'the stretcher'; Theseus gave him the same treatment, and killed him.

Prometheus Greek hero; symbolized the revolt of man against the gods and brought to humanity all the good things refused it by the gods; punished for this when **Zeus** sent mankind the gift of **Pandora**,

who spread evils throughout the world; became immortal after exchanging death for immortality with **Cheiron** the **Centaur**.

Proserpina ▶ **Persephone**

Proteus Greek god of the sea; associated with seals, and a shape-changer; he gave answers to questions after a wrestling match; was sometimes to be found on the island of Pharos, in Egypt, where **Menelaus** wrestled with him.

Psyche Greek personification of 'the soul'; usually represented by a butterfly; in the story told by Apuleius, was beloved by Cupid (**Eros**), who hid her in an enchanted palace, and visited her at night, forbidding her to look at him; her sisters persuaded her to light a lamp; she saw Cupid, but was separated from him, and given impossible tasks by Venus (**Aphrodite**), who impeded her search for him.

Ptah Egyptian god; principal god of the city of Memphis, known as the creator and master of craftsmen; subsequently regarded as a healing god in the form of a flat-headed dwarf and as a protective spirit.

Purusha Primordial being of India; thought to be a gigantic man who covered the earth and went beyond it; heaven made up three-quarters of his being, and the fourth quarter consisted of all mortal creatures.

Pwyll Celtic hero; wise prince of Dyfed who as a service to the king of Annwn killed the king's permanent enemy; courteous and powerful, he emerged victorious from a thousand trials.

Ptah

Pygmalion In Greek mythology, a king of Cyprus; made a statue of a beautiful woman; he prayed to **Aphrodite**, and the sculptured figure came to life.

Pyramus and Thisbe Two lovers; kept apart by their parents, they conversed through a crack in the wall between their houses, and agreed to meet at Ninus's tomb outside the city of Babylon; finding Thisbe's bloodstained cloak, Pyramus thought she had been killed by a lion, and committed suicide; when she found him, Thisbe killed herself on his sword; incorporated into Shakespeare's *A Midsummer Night's Dream*.

Python Greek monster; lived at Delphi and was killed by **Apollo** when he took over the shrine; the name Pythia continued in use, and the Pythian games were celebrated there.

Qat Hero of Oceania; born from a rock which had been hollowed out in the centre to allow his birth; organizer of life, he created man and then death to allow renewal; initiated day and night; canoed away to a far country, taking with him the hopes of mankind.

Querinus Roman god; initially a god of the city who watched over the material well being of the community; also likened to **Ares** by the Greeks, and to **Romulus**, founder of Rome.

Quetzalcoatl Aztec god of vegetation and wind; depicted as a bearded man wearing a mask, earrings and a conical hat; son of the sun-god and one of the five goddesses of the moon; created mankind from the bones of the ancient dead; taught measurement of time and how to discover the movement of the stars.

Quetzalcoatl

Ra ▶ Re

Rainbow Snake (Julunggul) Australian Aboriginal fertility spirit; both male and female, creator and destroyer, known as Julunggul; associated with streams and waterholes, from which it emerges in the creation story and leaves special markings on the ground.

Rama Indian hero; incarnation of the god **Vishnu** on earth; was taught magic spells to allow him to conquer the rakasa, the **demons**; saved his wife from abduction and was made king; after his wife had been swallowed up by the earth, gave up his royal status, and went to the river Sarayu to be carried off to heaven.

Re (Ra) Egyptian god; the ancient sun-god of Heliopolis; as the creator, he emerged from the primeval waters at the beginning of time; depicted as a falcon with the sun's disc on his head; at night he appears as a ram-headed god who sails through the underworld.

Rhadamanthus (Rhadamanthys) In Greek mythology, a Cretan, son of **Zeus** and **Europa**; did not die but was taken to Elisium, where he became the just judge of the dead.

Rhea (Rheia) Greek **Titan**; sister and wife of **Cronus**, and mother of **Zeus** and other Olympian gods; when Cronus consumed his children, Rhea gave him a stone instead of Zeus, who was saved and later rebelled against his father.

Rhiannon Celtic heroine; mistress of horses and horsemen; refused all her suitors out of love for **Pwyll**, who prepared to marry her; Pwyll, however, agreed to grant a supplicant, Gnawl, any wish, and he claimed Rhiannon; Pwyll later set her free from Gnawl through trickery and became her husband; accused of infanticide after her son mysteriously disappeared, but the child later reappeared.

Roc Arabian mythical creature; an enormous bird encountered by travellers in the Indian Ocean, capable of carrying off an elephant.

Rod Slavic god; initially the god of husbandmen but also a universal god, the god of heaven, the thunderbolt and rain; responsible for the nation's increase and closely linked with the worship of ancestors; later dethroned by **Perun**.

Romulus and Remus In Roman legend, the twin sons of Mars (**Ares**) and the Vestal Virgin Rhea Silvia; an example of an invented myth, to explain the name of the city; thrown into the Tiber, which carried them to the Palatine, where they were suckled by a she-wolf; in building the wall of Rome, Remus made fun of the work and was killed by Romulus or one of his followers; having founded Rome, Romulus was later carried off in a thunderstorm.

Rosmerta Gallo-Roman goddess; represented as a woman standing draped in a long robe, holding a cornucopia and a patera; invoked to obtain fertility, fruitfulness and everything essential for a better life.

Rudra Indian god; a being with a thousand eyes and a thousand feet, with plaited hair, a black belly, a red back and armed with a bow and arrows; the great destroyer, he cast evil spells over men and beasts, and spread terror and illness.

Sakhmet ▶ Sekhmet

Sarapis ▶ Serapis

Sarasvati Indian goddess; wife of **Brahma**; personification of the word of the god Veda; carried the book of Veda, a musical instrument and a rosary composed of the letters of the alphabet; mother of the scriptures, the sciences and the arts; also associated with water.

Sarpedon Warrior of Greek mythology; in the *Iliad*, a son of **Zeus**, who led the Lycian troops on the Trojan side, and made an important speech on the duties of a warrior; killed by **Patroclus**, and carried off by Sleep and Death to Lycia.

Saturn Roman god; master of agriculture who invented the dressing of the vine, taught man agricultural methods and provided the first laws; depicted as being armed with a scythe; associated with the Golden Age, synonymous with religious festivals and feasts.

Satyr Greek god; a minor deity associated with **Dionysus**; usually depicted with goat-like ears, tail, and legs; rural, wild and lustful, the satyrs were said to be the brothers of the **Nymphs**.

Scylla Greek sea monster; usually located in the Straits of Messina opposite to Charybdis; originally a woman, she was changed by **Circe** or **Amphitrite** into a snake with six heads; in the *Odyssey* she snatched six men from **Odysseus**'s ships.

Sekhmet (Sakmet, Sakhmet, Sekmet) Egyptian goddess; wife of the god **Ptah**; depicted with the head of a lioness and the body of a woman; a terrible bloodthirsty goddess, responsible for epidemics, death, carnage and war; also had the power of healing.

Selene Greek goddess of the moon; depicted as a charioteer (the head of one of her horses may be seen among the Elgin Marbles).

Semele In Greek mythology, the daughter of Cadmus, and mother by **Zeus** of **Dionysus**; asked Zeus to appear in his glory before her, and was consumed in fire, but it made her son immortal.

Semiramis In Greek mythology, a queen of Assyria; founded many cities, including Nineveh and Babylon.

Serapis (Sarapis) Egyptian god; a compound deity, combining the names and aspects of two Egyptian gods, **Osiris** and **Apis**, to which were further added features of major Greek gods, such as **Zeus** and **Dionysus**; introduced to Alexandria by Ptolemy I in an attempt to unite Greeks and Egyptians in common worship.

Sesostris Egyptian king; alleged to have conquered vast areas of Europe, Asia and N Africa; probably a compound of the three Egyptian pharaohs (20c–19c BC) and Rameses II (13c BC).

Seth Egyptian god; depicted as a strange being with a forked tail, a long gaunt body, huge ears and protruding eyes; represented all evils and caused all disasters; fought the **demon** Apopis every morning and every evening and as a result of this permanent conflict, the equilibrium of forces and universal harmony were born.

Seven against Thebes Seven Greek Champions; attacked Thebes to deprive **Eteocles** of his kingship; led by his brother **Polynices**; the names of the other six were Tydeus, Adrastus (or Eteoklos), Capaneus, Hippomedon, Parthenopaeus and Amphiarus; defeated by another seven champions at the seven gates of Thebes; all were killed in battle, except for Amphiarus, whom the earth swallowed alive, and Adrastus, who escaped; later the sons of the Seven, the **Epigoni**, led by Adrastus, succeeded in destroying the city.

Seven Sleepers of Ephesus In medieval legend, seven persecuted Christians who fled into a cave at the time of the Emperor Decius (AD250); slept for 200 years, emerging in 447 at the time of Theodosius II; the story was thought to confirm the resurrection of Christ.

Thought and Belief

Shamash Babylonian god; depicted bearing a head-dress with four rows of horns and a large beard, wearing a long robe and holding a staff and a hoop; symbolized by a solar disc rising between two mountains or by a spoked wheel; god of light and justice, he gave light to the world and distributed punishment and reward.

Shango African god of thunder; dispensed justice using the thunderbolt which was regarded as the god's punishment; the victim of his punishment was compelled to pay heavy fines and to appease him by means of sacrifices; originally a cruel king whose subjects drove him away; he hanged himself from a tree leaving a hole from which emerged an iron chain; finding the tree without the body, his supporters concluded that he had become a god.

Shiva Indian god; representing darkness, his three eyes were filled with snakes; had four arms and a girdle made of skulls; danced amid devils on cremation sites, representing the world's constructive and destructive periods; withdrew to the mountains after the suicide of his wife but later came back to produce a son to kill a **demon** which threatened the world; carried out many heroic deeds and was regarded as a beneficent force.

Sibyl (Sibylla) Roman prophetess; uttered mysterious wisdom; **Aeneas** met the Cumaean Sibyl, who was inspired by **Apollo** and whose prophecies were written on leaves; she had been given 1000 years of life, and eventually shrank to a tiny creature hung up in a bottle; later there were said to be ten Sibyls; the Sibylline Books were nine books of prophecy offered by the Sibyl to Tarquinus Priscus, who refused to pay her price; she destroyed three, and came again, with the same result; she destroyed three more, and then Tarquin bought the remainder for the price originally asked.

Sigurd In Norse mythology, the son of Sigmund the Volsung; killed Fafnir the dragon and won **Brunhild**; married **Gudrun**, having forgotten Brunhild, and was killed by Gudrun's brother Gutthorn; virtually the same story is told of Siegfried in German legends.

Sileni Greek followers of **Dionysus**; depicted with horse ears, tail and legs, or as old men in need of support (Pappo+ sileni); could give good advice to humans if captured; plural form of **Silenus**.

Silenus Greek demigod; fostered and educated **Dionysus**; represented as a festive old man, usually quite drunk.

Silvanus (Sylvanus) Roman god of uncultivated land, especially woodland; he was therefore strange, and dangerous, like **Pan**.

Sin Sumerian god; represented the moon; depicted seated on a throne, with a long beard, holding an axe, a sceptre and a staff; his predictions were binding on the gods and man, and an eclipse was his most formidable sign, announcing catastrophe.

Sirens Three Greek demonesses; became half woman, half bird when they asked the gods for wings, to look for **Persephone** who had been taken to the underworld by **Hades**; one held a lyre, the second sang and the third played the flute; devoured sailors lured to their island by their enchanting sounds.

Sisyphus In Greek mythology, a Corinthian king who was a famous trickster; in one story he caught and bound Thanatos (Death); in the underworld was condemned to roll a large stone up a hill from which it always rolled down again.

Sita Indian heroine; emerged from a furrow in a ploughed field; married **Rama** and was abducted by Ravana; on reunion with her husband, was tested by fire and exiled as he believed she had been unfaithful; requested the earth to open up and swallow her forever.

Skanda Indian hero; son of **Shiva** and chief of the divine armies; killed the **demon** Taraka who threatened the world.

Skyamsen ▶ **Thunderbird**

Soma Indian moon-god; marked the rhythm of the days and months and was the nectar of immortality, a divine drink essential to the gods.

Sucellus Gallic god; depicted with a tunic, cowl and boots, holding a club or sceptre and a vase, indicating that he was a sovereign and the dispenser of food; married to the river goddess.

Svarog Slavic god of fire; dispenser of all wealth, and judge and protector of monogamy; also a magician and soothsayer.

Sventovit Slavic god of war; depicted holding a trumpet and a bow; also the god of fertility, fruitfulness and destiny; his horse had the gift of divination, and its movement could reveal the meaning of oracles it wished to communicate.

Sylvanus ▶ **Silvanus**

Syrinx Greek **Nymph**; pursued by **Pan**, she called on the earth to help, and so sank down into it and became a reedbed; Pan cut some of the reeds, and made the pan-pipes.

Tammuz (Thammuz) Babylonian god of vegetation; beloved by **Ishtar** (in Assyria by Astarte); returned from the dead and died again each year.

Tane (Kane) Divinity from the Pacific Islands; kept heaven and earth apart, permitting the world to exist; misfortune and death were born from his destructive war with his enemy, the god Tangaroa.

Tantalus In Greek mythology, a king of Sisyphos in Lydia; committed terrible crimes; stole the food of the gods, so becoming immortal, and served them his son **Pelops** in a dish; for this he was punished in the underworld; he sits in a pool which recedes when he bends to drink, and the grapes over his head elude his grasp.

Taranis Gallic god; master of the universe, who inspired fear by sending thunder and lightning; at the same time, brought the gentle rain which fed the earth and made crops grow; demanded human sacrifices; his victims were shut in wooden cages which were set alight, and severed heads were offered to him.

Tarpeia Roman woman who betrayed the Capitol to the Sabines, in return for 'what they wore on their left arms' (meaning gold rings); in their disgust, they threw their shields on her and crushed her to death.

Telemachus Greek hero; in the *Odyssey*, the son of **Odysseus** and **Penelope**; set out to find his father, visiting **Nestor** and **Menelaus**; later helped Odysseus fight Penelope's suitors.

Tellus ▶ **Gaea**

Tengri Mongol god of heaven; imposed the order of the natural world, the organization and movements of the stars and the government of the Mongol empire; distributed good luck and wealth and showed his anger by sending thunderstorms.

Terminus Roman god of boundary marks; his statue or bust was sometimes placed there; his stone on the Capitol was within the temple of Jupiter Optimus Maximus (**Zeus**), but was not allowed to be covered in.

Terpsichore Greek **Muse** of dance and lyric poetry.

Thought and Belief

Teshub Hurrian god of the thunderstorm; depicted holding an axe and thunderclouds; dethroned the king of heaven to become the supreme god and battled victoriously against the deposed king who sought his revenge.

Teutates Gallic god; a warrior god, sometimes compared to Mars (**Ares**) and Mercury (**Hermes**); depicted beside a serpent with a ram's head; a cruel god who demanded human sacrifices; the victims were drowned in a vat of water.

Tezcatlipoca Aztec god; depicted in human form with a stripe of black paint across his face and a mirror replacing one of his feet; said to have been mutilated by the mythical crocodile on which the earth was supposed to rest; reigned over the four worlds destroyed prior to the creation of the present one; with his mirror could see everything and was aware of both human actions and thoughts; a malevolent wizard who brought the custom of human sacrifice to Mexico.

Thalia (Thaleia) Greek **Muse** of comedy and idyllic poetry.

Thammuz ▶ **Tammuz**

Themis Greek goddess of established law and justice; a consort of **Zeus**, she was the mother of the **Horae** and the **Moerae**.

Theseus Greek hero; set out for Athens to find his father, the king, and slew many monsters on the way; fought those who tried to depose his father and killed the **Minotaur**; assumed power and defended Attica against the **Amazons** who almost won but in the end were forced to sign a peace treaty (he married their leader, Hippolyta); later became powerless and was forced into exile before being killed when thrown into a ravine.

Thetis Greek goddess; mother of **Achilles**; saved **Zeus** from a conspiracy to remove his power; an oracle predicted that her son would be more powerful than his father, and fearing this, Zeus forced her to marry a mortal; an unhappy goddess, she failed in her determined attempts to make her children immortal.

Thor Nordic god; son of **Odin**; armed with a hammer which returned automatically to the hand of the one who hurled it, and doubled his strength by wearing a magic belt; fond of tricks and practical jokes; killed the serpent of Midgard, but was himself killed by its venom.

Thoth (Hermes) Egyptian god; skilled at calculation, secretary to the gods and master of effective speech; also a magician and capable of providing cures; identified by the Greeks as Hermes.

Thunderbird (Skyamsen) Totem figure of NW Native American religion; lightning flashed from its eye and it fed on killer whales; the chief of the Thunderbirds was Golden Eagle (Keneun).

Thyestes In Greek mythology, a son of **Pelops**; inherited the curse upon that house; his brother **Atreus** set before him a dish made of the flesh of Thyestes' children; later became the father of **Aegisthus**.

Thunderbird **Tiamat** Akkadian goddess; a primordial divinity who represented salt water; became angry after an old god was murdered by a younger one; decided to create monsters as gods, and in the resulting confrontation was killed by **Marduk**; from one half of her corpse, heaven was created, and from the other half, Marduk formed dry land.

Tiresias In Greek mythology, a blind Theban prophet; takes a prominent part in Sophocles' plays about **Oedipus** and **Antigone**; later legends account for his wisdom by saying that he had experienced the life of both sexes.

Titania Greek female **Titan**; identified with the moon; in Shakespeare's *A Midsummer Night's Dream* she is the queen of the fairies, who is tricked into falling in love with Bottom the Weaver.

Titans Greek gods; members of the older generation of gods, the children of **Uranus** and **Gaia**; after **Zeus** and the Olympians took power, the Titans made war on them; but they were defeated and imprisoned in Tartarus; one or two, notably **Prometheus**, helped Zeus; may represent memories of pre-Greek Mediterranean gods.

Tlaloc Aztec god of mountains, rain and springs; represented as a man painted black with huge round eyes with circles or serpents around them, and long fangs; ordered the distribution of rain and hurricanes; sometimes killed by means of a thunderbolt; his victims were buried with a piece of dry wood which would come back to life in Tlaloc's paradise.

Tlazolteotl Aztec goddess of lust; represented as a young girl wearing a rubber mask and a crescent-shaped ornament in her nose; responsible for conjugal infidelities and at the same time the granter of pardon; also the goddess of renewal.

Triglav Slavic god; had three heads and a golden veil which covered his eyes and mouth, signifying his desire to disregard human faults; a soothsayer, priest, warrior and nourisher.

Tristan and Isolde Celtic heroes; Tristan was a master harp-player and huntsman; Isolde was the daughter of the king of Ireland, who was to marry Mark the king of Cornwall, and become queen; through a misunderstanding, Tristan and Isolde drank from the same love potion and became bound by an indissoluble love; discovered to be meeting secretly, Tristan and the queen were condemned to be burned alive, and both fled; King Mark searched for them, and finding them asleep, became seized with pity, leaving his sword between them and replacing a ring on Isolde's finger; moved by his generosity, the lovers returned to the court, where Isolde was accepted, but Tristan was sent into exile.

Triton In Greek mythology, the son of **Poseidon** and **Amphitrite**; depicted in art as a fish from the waist down, and blowing a conch-shell; beings of similar form (mermen) who serve Poseidon are often referred to as Tritons.

Troilus In Greek legend, a prince of Troy; son of **Priam** and **Hecuba**, who was killed by **Achilles**; in medieval stories, the lover of **Cressida**.

Tuatha de Danann Irish race of wise beings; came to Ireland in c.1500 BC, and became the ancient gods of the Irish; the name means 'the people of the goddess Danu'; conquered by the Milesians, and retreated into tumuli near the R Boyne.

Tyche Greek goddess of chance or luck; prominent in the Hellenistic period; depicted as blind, or, with a wall, as the luck of a city.

Typhoeus ▶ **Typhon**

Typhon (Typhoeus) Greek monster; had 100 heads and was brought forth by **Gaea**; a serious challenge to **Zeus**, who hurled his thunderbolts and thrust him down into Tartarus; in another story, said to be buried under Etna.

Tyr Nordic god; courageous and bold, he guaranteed right and justice; lost one arm in the courageous act of restraining the horrible wolf Fenrir.

Thought and Belief

Ulysses ▶ Odysseus

Unicorn Creature of medieval legend; a horse with a single horn on its forehead; probably based on stories of the rhinoceros; could be captured only by a virgin putting its head in her lap.

Urania Greek **Muse** of astronomy.

Uranus (Ouranus) Greek god of the sky; father of the Titans; a very abstract figure, not the subject of worship or of art, he was displaced by **Cronus**; equivalent to Roman Caelus, 'the heavens'.

Uther Pendragon Legendary king of Britain; father of King **Arthur** by Ygerna, the wife of Duke Gorlois of Cornwall.

Vahagn Armenian deity; born of water and fire, and married to the goddess of the stars; god of victory and destroyer of obstacles; created the Milky Way when he stole some straw one night and fled in haste across the sky, leaving wisps of straw across his path.

Väinämöinen Finnish sage, shaman and bard; dominates the epic *Kalevala*; sought the sampo, the magic cauldron of plenty, and invented the kantele or harp.

Valkyries Nordic goddesses; goddesses of fertility and the angels of battle; 40 are recorded as magicians and combat goddesses who selected those who were doomed to die, apportioning death not as a punishment, but as a reward.

Varuna Indian god and guardian of world order; ordered nature and supervised sacrificial rites; his domain consisted of darkness and the waters, and the stars were his thousand eyes; also producing evil, he caused earthquakes and sent disease, but possessed and provided the remedies.

Venus ▶ Aphrodite

Vesta ▶ Hestia

Vesta Roman goddess of the hearth; particularly known for the cult dedicated to her; her temple in the Roman Forum was served by virgins who were walled up alive at the Colline Gate if they failed to remain chaste; a fire was kept lit in her honour all year round.

Viracocha Incan god; the creator and civilizer, he created the first men, but disappointed by them, he changed some into stone statues and destroyed the others by fire; recreated humanity, accompanied by the sun and moon, then provided mountains, rivers and farmland to permit them to live in a civilized way; after this mission, disappeared over the horizon, and his return is still awaited; protector of the emperor of the Incas.

Vishnu Indian god; originally a dwarf who wanted to secure dominion over the world, he became the god of space, who gave the world its stability; the origin of the fertility of both nature and man; appeared in the form of heroes and animals each time the world needed him.

Vishnu

Visvamitra Indian hero; tried to equal the Brahman Vasistha by leading a life of increasing rigid asceticism; finally achieved his aim by stopping eating and breathing for a number of years.

Volcanus ▶ Hephaestus

Vulcan ▶ Hephaestus

Wak Ethiopian god; kept heaven at a distance from the earth and covered it with stars; created man on the flat earth, then buried him for seven years while he made fire rain down to create the mountains; when after this, man sprang back to life, he said that he had slept only for a brief moment; this was said to be why man is awake for most of the day; later created woman.

Wayland Norse, German, and Old English legendary inventor; known as Wayland the Smith; lame, having been maimed by King Nidud; many heroes carry swords made by him; his 'Smithy', is a dolmen on the Berkshire Downs, UK.

Woden, Wotan ▶ Odin

Xipe Totec Aztec god of springtime, renewal and nocturnal rain; inspired Mexican ceremonies with human sacrifices and mock battles; during the ceremonies the priests flayed the sacrifices and wore their skins.

Xiuhtecuhtli Aztec god of the hearth, fire, the sun and volcanoes; also associated with peppers and the pine, the tree from which torches were made.

Yama The first Indian man; the first mortal who on death became king of the dead; came to look for those who had used up their lifetimes; produced excessive increases of the human population when one day he became distracted and did not make a single man die.

Yggdrasil In Norse mythology, a giant ash; the World-Tree, which supported the sky, held the different realms of gods and men in its branches, and had its roots in the underworld.

Yu the Great Chinese hero; a thin, ill man who hopped about on one foot; dug out the mountains and allowed waters to flow from a catastrophic flood, working for 13 years without returning home; became a god and travelled the world to plan it; first emperor of the Hsia Dynasty.

Zanhary Madagascan god; creator god and father of heaven; terrifying, and spoke in thunder and lightning; a double god, the Zanhary from below created man and Zanhary from above gave him life; the two gods disagreed over women and became enemies, separating the worlds above and below forever.

Zeus (Jupiter, Iuppiter) Greek god of all gods; god of light and weather, and arbiter among gods and among men; had many wives and affairs with mortal women to whom he appeared in various guises, eg as a shower of gold, a bull or a swan; hanged his jealous wife **Hera** from Olympus with anvils fastened to her ankles.

Population distribution of major beliefs

Figures are for nation states only, have been compiled from the most accurate recent available information and where possible are correct to the nearest 1%. Within Islam the relative proportion of Sunnis and Shiites is indicated where possible, or the majority sect is given. No reliable information was available for North Korea.

■ Baha'i

Kiribati	2%
Marshall Islands	1%
Tuvalu	1%

■ Buddhism

Australia	2%
Bhutan	75%
Brunei	13%
Cambodia	95%
Canada	1%
China	8%
France	1%
Indonesia	1%
Japan	70%[4]
Korea, South	23%
Laos	67%
Malaysia	19%
Mongolia	50%
Myanmar (Burma)	89%
Nepal	11%
Singapore	42%
Sri Lanka	68%
Taiwan	35%
Thailand	95%
Vietnam	12%

■ Christianity

◊ Protestantism (includes all non-Roman Catholic denominations and forms of Christianity)

Albania	20%
Angola	15%
Antigua and Barbuda	82%
Argentina	2%
Armenia	95%
Australia	41%
Austria	5%
Azerbaijan	5%
Bahamas	83%
Bahrain	9%[1]
Barbados	71%
Belarus	41%
Belgium	10%
Belize	27%
Benin	16%
Bermuda	52%
Bolivia	5%
Bosnia and Herzegovina	31%
Botswana	72%[1]
Brazil	15%
Brunei	10%[1]
Bulgaria	84%
Burundi	5%
Cambodia	2%
Cameroon	20%
Canada	28%
Central African Republic	25%

Chad	14%
Chile	15%
China	4%[1]
Colombia	12%
Congo	5%
Congo, Dem. Rep of	20%
Costa Rica	16%
Côte d'Ivoire	33%[1]
Croatia	5%
Cuba	5%
Cyprus	78%
Czech Republic	2%
Denmark	83%
Djibouti	2%
Dominica	28%
Dominican Republic	18%
East Timor	1%
Ecuador	8%
Egypt	10%
El Salvador	24%
Equatorial Guinea	6%
Eritrea	32%
Estonia	28%
Ethiopia	55%
Fiji	46%
Finland	85%
France	3%
Gambia	8%[1]
Georgia	83%
Germany	34%
Ghana	54%
Greece	98%
Grenada	47%
Guatemala	31%
Guinea	8%[1]
Guinea Bissau	10%[1]
Guyana	49%
Haiti	16%
Honduras	3%
Hungary	23%
Iceland	89%
India	2%[1]
Indonesia	6%
Iraq	2%[1]
Ireland	5%
Israel	2%
Jamaica	62%
Japan	1%[1]
Jordan	6%[1]
Kazakhstan	46%
Kenya	45%
Kiribati	40%
Korea, South	20%
Kyrgyzstan	20%
Laos	1%
Latvia	35%
Lebanon	34%[1]
Lesotho	45%

Liberia	40%[1]
Liechtenstein	9%
Lithuania	6%
Macedonia	65%
Madagascar	41%[1]
Malawi	70%[1]
Malaysia	9%[1]
Mali	2%
Marshall Islands	85%
Mauritius	9%
Mexico	6%
Micronesia, Federated States of	47%
Moldova	98%
Monaco	5%
Montenegro	74%
Mozambique	17%
Myanmar (Burma)	4%[1]
Namibia	85%[1]
Nauru	46%
Netherlands	20%
New Zealand	41%
Nicaragua	24%
Niger	5%[1]
Nigeria	40%[1]
Norway	89%
Pakistan	2%[1]
Palau	23%
Panama	15%
Papua New Guinea	69%
Paraguay	7%
Peru	2%
Philippines	12%
Poland	2%
Portugal	2%
Qatar	9%[1]
Romania	94%
Russia	22%
Rwanda	37%
St Kitts and Nevis	50%
St Lucia	24%
St Vincent and the Grenadines	75%
Samoa	78%
São Tomé and Príncipe	7%
Senegal	5%[1]
Serbia	86%
Seychelles	11%
Sierra Leone	10%[1]
Singapore	10%
Slovakia	15%
Slovenia	3%
Solomon Islands	78%
Somalia	2%[1]
South Africa	80%[1]

Sri Lanka	6%[1]
Sudan	5%[1]
Suriname	48%[1]
Swaziland	40%
Sweden	87%
Switzerland	32%
Syria	10%[1]
Taiwan	3%
Tajikistan	3%
Tanzania	35%[1]
Togo	29%[1]
Tonga	63%
Trinidad and Tobago	32%
Turkmenistan	9%
Tuvalu	96%
UAE	9%[1]
Uganda	42%
UK	72%[1]
Ukraine	94%
Uruguay	11%
USA	53%
Uzbekistan	9%
Vanuatu	70%
Venezuela	2%
Vietnam	1%
Zambia	87%[1]
Zimbabwe	75%[1]

◊ Roman Catholicism

Albania	10%
Andorra	95%
Angola	38%
Antigua and Barbuda	10%
Argentina	92%
Armenia	4%
Australia	26%
Austria	74%
Bahamas	14%
Barbados	4%
Belarus	7%
Belgium	75%
Belize	50%
Benin	27%
Bermuda	15%
Bolivia	95%
Bosnia and Herzegovina	15%
Brazil	74%
Burkina Faso	10%
Burundi	62%
Cambodia	2%
Cameroon	20%
Canada	43%
Cape Verde	98%
Central African Republic	25%
Chad	20%
Chile	70%
Colombia	87%
Comoros	2%

Thought and Belief

Congo	45%	Poland	90%	Algeria (Sunni)	99%	Kuwait (Sunni 60%)	85%

Congo 45%
Congo, Dem. Rep. of 50%
Costa Rica 76%
Croatia 88%
Cuba 60%
Czech Republic 27%
Denmark 1%
Djibouti 4%
Dominica 61%
Dominican Republic 69%
East Timor 98%
Ecuador 85%
El Salvador 57%
Equatorial Guinea 87%
Eritrea 5%
Fiji 7%
France 51%
Gabon 55%
Germany 34%
Ghana 15%
Grenada 53%
Guatemala 57%
Guyana 8%
Haiti 80%
Honduras 97%
Hungary 52%
Iceland 2%
Indonesia 3%
Ireland 87%
Italy 83%
Jamaica 3%
Kenya 33%
Kiribati 52%
Korea, South 6%
Laos 1%
Latvia 22%
Lesotho 45%
Libya 1%
Liechtenstein 78%
Lithuania 79%
Luxembourg 90%
Macedonia 1%
Mali 3%
Malta 98%
Marshall Islands 8%
Mauritius 24%
Mexico 76%
Micronesia, Federated States of 50%
Monaco 90%
Montenegro 4%
Mozambique 24%
Nauru 33%
Netherlands 30%
New Zealand 12%
Nicaragua 58%
Norway 1%
Palau 42%
Panama 85%
Papua New Guinea 27%
Paraguay 90%
Peru 81%
Philippines 81%

Poland 90%
Portugal 85%
Romania 5%
Rwanda 56%
St Kitts and Nevis 25%
St Lucia 67%
St Vincent and the Grenadines 13%
Samoa 20%
San Marino 95%
São Tomé and Príncipe 70%
Serbia 6%
Seychelles 82%
Singapore 5%
Slovakia 69%
Slovenia 58%
Solomon Islands 19%
Spain 94%
Swaziland 20%
Sweden 2%
Switzerland 42%
Taiwan 1%
Tonga 16%
Trinidad and Tobago 26%
Tuvalu 1%
Uganda 42%
Ukraine 2%
Uruguay 45%
USA 24%
Vanuatu 13%
Vatican 100%
Venezuela 96%
Vietnam 7%

■ Druze
Israel 2%
Lebanon 5%
Syria 3%

■ Hinduism
Australia 1%
Bangladesh 16%
Bhutan 25%
Canada 1%
Fiji 34%
Guyana 28%
India 81%
Indonesia 2%
Kenya 1%
Malaysia 6%
Mauritius 48%
Nepal 81%
Oman 13%
Pakistan 2%
Qatar 1%
Seychelles 2%
Singapore 5%
Sri Lanka 7%
Suriname 27%
Trinidad and Tobago 22%
UK 1%

■ Islam
Afghanistan (Sunni 80%) 99%
Albania (Sunni) 70%

Algeria (Sunni) 99%
Andorra 2%
Argentina 2%
Australia 2%
Austria 4%
Azerbaijan (Shia) 93%
Bahrain (Shia 70%) 81%
Bangladesh (Sunni) 83%
Barbados 1%
Belgium 2%
Benin 24%
Bosnia and Herzegovina (Sunni) 40%
Brunei 67%
Bulgaria 12%
Burkina Faso (mostly Sunni) 50%
Burundi 10%
Cambodia 4%
Cameroon 20%
Canada 2%
Central African Republic 15%
Chad 53%
China 2%
Comoros (Sunni) 98%
Congo 2%
Congo, Dem, Rep. of 10%
Côte d'Ivoire 39%
Croatia 1%
Cyprus 18%
Denmark 4%
Djibouti (Sunni) 94%
East Timor 1%
Egypt (Sunni) 90%
Equatorial Guinea 1%
Eritrea (Sunni) 60%
Ethiopia (Sunni) 40%
Fiji 7%
France 9%
Gabon 1%
Gambia (Sunni) 90%
Georgia 11%
Germany 4%
Ghana 16%
Greece 1%
Guinea (mostly Sunni) 85%
Guinea-Bissau 50%
Guyana 7%
India (mostly Sunni) 13%
Indonesia 86%
Iran (Shia 89%) 98%
Iraq (Shia 62%) 97%
Israel 16%
Italy 1%
Jordan (Sunni) 92%
Kazakhstan 47%
Kenya 10%

Kuwait (Sunni 60%) 85%
Kyrgyzstan (mostly Sunni) 75%
Lebanon (Sunni 28%) 56%
Liberia 20%
Libya (Sunni) 97%
Liechtenstein 5%
Luxembourg 2%
Macedonia 33%
Madagascar 7%
Malawi (mostly Sunni) 20%
Malaysia 60%
Maldives (Sunni) 100%
Mali (mostly Sunni) 90%
Malta 1%
Mauritania (Sunni) 100%
Mauritius (mostly Sunni) 17%
Mongolia 4%
Montenegro 17%
Morocco (mostly Sunni) 99%
Mozambique 18%
Myanmar (mostly Sunni) 4%
Nepal 4%
Netherlands 6%
New Zealand 1%
Niger (mostly Sunni) 80%
Nigeria (mostly Sunni) 50%
Norway 2%
Oman 86%
Pakistan (mostly Sunni) 95%
Philippines 5%
Qatar (mostly Sunni) 78%
Russia 15%
Rwanda 5%
Saudi Arabia (mostly Sunni) 100%
Senegal (Sunni) 94%
Serbia 3%
Seychelles 1%
Sierra Leone 60%
Singapore 15%
Slovenia 2%
Somalia (Sunni) 98%
South Africa 1%
Spain 2%
Sri Lanka 8%
Sudan 70%
Suriname 20%
Swaziland 10%
Switzerland 4%
Syria (Sunni 74%) 90%
Tajikistan (Sunni 85%) 90%
Tanzania 35%
Thailand 4%

Togo (Sunni)	20%
Trinidad and Tobago	6%
Tunisia (Sunni)	98%
Turkey (Sunni)	99%
Turkmenistan (mostly Sunni)	89%
UAE	76%
Uganda	12%
UK	3%
USA	1%
Uzbekistan	88%
Yemen (Sunni 70%)	100%
Zimbabwe	1%

■ Judaism

Argentina	1%
Canada	1%
Croatia	1%
France	1%
Hungary	1%
Israel	76%
Moldova	2%
UK	1%
Ukraine	1%
USA	2%

■ Non-religious belief/unaffiliated

Antigua and Barbuda	6%
Australia	15%
Austria	14%
Bahamas	3%
Barbados	21%
Belarus	50%
Belgium	15%
Belize	9%
Bermuda	20%
Botswana	21%
Brazil	8%
Brunei	5%
Canada	16%
Chile	8%
Costa Rica	3%
Côte d'Ivoire	16%
Croatia	5%
Czech Republic	59%
Denmark	7%
Dominica	6%
Dominican Republic	11%
El Salvador	17%
Estonia	66%
Finland	15%
France	4%
Gabon	5%
Germany	26%
Guyana	4%
Haiti	1%
Hungary	14%
Iceland	3%
Ireland	4%
Italy	14%
Jamaica	21%
Kiribati	4%

Korea, South	49%
Liechtenstein	7%
Lithuania	10%
Marshall Islands	2%
Mexico	3%
Mongolia	40%
Netherlands	42%
New Zealand	44%
Nicaragua	16%
Palau	16%
Paraguay	1%
Peru	1%
Portugal	13%
St Lucia	6%
São Tomé and Príncipe	20%
Singapore	15%
Slovakia	13%
Slovenia	14%
South Africa	17%
Suriname	19%
Switzerland	16%
Togo	51%
Trinidad and Tobago	3%
UK	16%
Uruguay	28%
USA	16%
Vietnam	76%

■ Rastafarianism

Antigua and Barbuda	2%
Dominica	1%
Grenada	5%
Jamaica	1%
St Lucia	2%

■ Shintoism

| Japan | 84%[4] |

■ Sikhism

Canada	1%
India	2%
UK	1%

■ Taoism

| Singapore | 9% |
| Taiwan | 33% |

■ Traditional beliefs

Angola	47%
Armenia	1%
Benin	17%
Botswana	6%
Burkina Faso	40%
Burundi	23%
Cameroon	40%[2]
Central African Republic	35%
Chad	7%
Congo	48%
Congo, Dem. Rep. of	15%
Côte d'Ivoire	12%
Cuba	54%
Equatorial Guinea	5%
Eritrea	2%
Ethiopia	4%

Gambia	2%
Ghana	15%[3]
Guatemala	5%
Guinea	7%
Guinea-Bissau	40%
Haiti	2%
Kenya	11%[3]
Liberia	40%
Madagascar	52%
Malaysia	3%
Mali	5%[2]
Mozambique	23%
Namibia	15%
Nigeria	10%
Palau	9%
Paraguay	1%
Senegal	1%
Sierra Leone	40%
Suriname	5%
Tanzania	35%
Togo	33%
Trinidad and Tobago	6%
Vanuatu	6%

■ Unspecified/others

Afghanistan	1%
Algeria	1%
Antigua and Barbuda	1%
Argentina	4%
Armenia	1%
Australia	14%
Austria	3%
Azerbaijan	2%
Bahamas	1%
Bahrain	10%
Bangladesh	1%
Barbados	4%
Belarus	2%
Belgium	3%
Belize	14%
Benin	16%
Bermuda	13%
Bosnia and Herzegovina	14%
Botswana	1%
Brazil	3%
Brunei	5%
Bulgaria	4%
Cambodia	5%
Canada	12%
Chile	5%
Colombia	1%
Congo, Dem. Rep. of	5%
Costa Rica	5%
Croatia	1%
Cyprus	4%
Czech Republic	9%
Denmark	6%
Dominica	5%
El Salvador	2%
Eritrea	3%
France	31%
Georgia	1%

Germany	2%
Greece	1%
Guyana	4%
Haiti	3%
Hungary	11%
Iceland	6%
India	1%
Ireland	4%
Italy	2%
Jamaica	12%
Japan	15%
Kazakhstan	7%
Kiribati	3%
Korea, South	1%
Kuwait	15%
Kyrgyzstan	5%
Laos	32%
Latvia	43%
Lesotho	10%
Lithuania	5%
Macedonia	2%
Malaysia	3%
Marshall Islands	4%
Mexico	14%
Micronesia, Federated States of	3%
Nauru	8%
Nepal	4%
Netherlands	2%
New Zealand	3%
Nicaragua	2%
Norway	8%
Oman	1%
Palau	10%
Peru	2%
Philippines	2%
Portugal	1%
Qatar	14%
Romania	1%
Slovenia	23%
Solomon Islands	3%
Swaziland	30%
Sweden	1%
Switzerland	1%
Taiwan	5%
Thailand	1%
Togo	1%
Tonga	21%
Trinidad and Tobago	11%
Turkmenistan	2%
UAE	15%
Uganda	3%
UK	7%
Ukraine	3%
Uruguay	15%
USA	3%
Uzbekistan	3%
Vanuatu	11%
Venezuela	1%
Vietnam	3%
Zambia	12%

[1] Includes Roman Catholics [2] Includes no religious belief
[3] Includes unspecified other faiths [4] Many Japanese practise both Buddhism and Shinto

Thought and Belief

Thought and Belief

Baha'i

Founded 1863 in Persia.

Founder Mirza Husayn Ali (1817–92), known as Baha'u'llah (Glory of God). He declared himself the prophet foretold by Mirza ali Mohammed (1819–50), a direct descendant of Muhammad, who proclaimed himself to be the Bab ('gate' or 'door').

Sacred texts Most Holy Book, The Seven Valleys, The Hidden Words and The Bayan.

Beliefs Baha'i teaches the oneness of God, the unity of all faiths, the inevitable unification of humankind, the harmony of all people, universal education, and obedience to government. It does not predict an end to this world or any intervention by God but believes there will be a change within man and society.

Organization There is a network of elected local and national level bodies, and an elected international governing body. Although there is little formal ritual (most assemblies are simply gatherings of the faithful), there are ceremonies for marriages and funerals, and there are shrines and temples.

Buddhism

Founded c.500 BC in India.

Founder Prince Siddhartha Gautama (c.560–c.480 BC) who became Buddha ('the enlightened') through meditation.

Sacred texts The Pali Canon or Tripitaka made up of the Vinaya Pitaka (monastic discipline), Sutta Pitaka (discourses of the Buddha) and the Abhidhamma Pitaka (analysis of doctrines). Other texts: the Mahayana Sutras, the Milindapanha (Questions of Milinda) and the Bardo Thodol (Tibetan Book of the Dead).

Beliefs Buddha's teaching is summarized in the Four Noble Truths; suffering is always present in life; desire is the cause of suffering; freedom from suffering can be achieved by Nirvana (perfect peace and bliss); the Eightfold Path leads to Nirvana. Karma, by which good and evil deeds result in appropriate reward or punishment, and the cycle of rebirth can be broken by taking the Eightfold Path. All Buddhas are revered but particularly Gautama.

Organization There is a monastic system which aims to create favourable conditions for spiritual development. This involves meditation, personal discipline and spiritual exercises in the hope of liberation from self. Buddhism has proved very flexible in adapting its organization, ceremony and pattern of belief to different cultural and social conditions. There are numerous festivals and ceremonies, and pilgrimage is of great spiritual value.

Divisions There are two main traditions in Buddhism. Theravada Buddhism adheres to the teachings of the earliest Buddhist writings; salvation can be attained only by the few who accept the severe discipline and effort necessary to achieve it. Mahayana Buddhism developed later and is more flexible and creative, embracing popular piety. It teaches that salvation is possible for everyone and introduced the doctrine of the bodhisattva (one who attains enlightenment but out of compassion forestalls passing into Nirvana to help others achieve enlightenment). As Buddhism spread, other schools sprang up including Zen, Lamaism, Tendai, Nichiren and Soka Gakkai.

Major festivals Weekly Uposatha Days, Buddha's Birth, Enlightenment, First Sermon and Death are observed in the different countries where Buddhism is practised but often on different dates. In some of these countries there are additional festivals in honour of Buddha.

Christianity

Founded 1C AD.

Founder Jesus Christ 'the Son of God' (c.4 BC–c.30 AD).

Sacred texts The Bible consisting of the Old and New Testaments. The New Testament written between AD 30 and AD 150 consists of the Gospels, the Acts of the Apostles, the Epistles and the Apocalypse.

Beliefs A monotheistic world religion, centred on the life and works of Jesus of Nazareth in Judaea, who proclaimed the most important rules of life to be love of God, followed by love of one's neighbour. Christians believe that Jesus was the Son of God who was put to death by crucifixion as a sacrifice in order to save humanity from the consequences of sin and death, and was raised from the dead; he makes forgiveness and reconciliation with God possible, and ensures eternal life for the repentant believer. The earliest followers of Jesus were Jews who believed him to be the Messiah or 'Saviour' promised by the prophets in the Old Testament. Christians believe he will come again to inaugurate the 'Kingdom of God'.

Organization Jesus Christ appointed 12 men to be his disciples:

1 Peter (brother of Andrew)
2 Andrew (brother of Peter)
3 James, son of Zebedee (brother of John)
4 John (brother of James)
5 Philip
6 Bartholomew
7 Thomas
8 Matthew
9 James of Alphaeus
10 Simon the Canaanite (in Matthew and Mark) or Simon 'the Zealot' (in Luke and the Acts)
11 Judas Iscariot

(Thaddeus in the book of Matthew and Mark is the twelfth disciple, while in Luke and the Acts the twelfth is Judas or James. Matthias succeeded to Judas's place.) Soon after the resurrection the disciples gathered for the festival of Pentecost and received special signs of the power of God, the Holy Spirit. The disciples became a defined new body, the Church. Through the witness of the Apostles and their successors, the Christian faith quickly spread and in AD 315 became the official religion of the Roman Empire. It survived the 'Dark Ages' to become the basis of civilization in the Middle Ages in Europe.

Divisions Major divisions — separated as a result of differences of doctrine and practice — are the Orthodox or Eastern Church, the Roman Catholic Church, acknowledging the Bishop of Rome as head, and the Protestant Churches stemming from the split with the Roman Church in the 16c. All Christians recognize the authority of the Bible, read at public worship, which takes place at least every Sunday, to celebrate the resurrection of Jesus Christ. Most Churches recognize at least two sacraments (Baptism and the Eucharist, Mass, or Lord's Supper) as essential.

Major Christian denominations

Baptists Originated in radical Reformation objections to infant baptism, demands for Church–State separation; John Smyth, English Separatist in 1609; Roger Williams, 1638, Providence, Rhode Island.

Church of England Henry VIII separated the English Catholic Church from Rome in 1534, for political reasons.

Lutherans Martin Luther (1483–1546) in Wittenberg, Germany, in 1517 objected to Catholic doctrine of salvation by merit and sale of indulgences; break complete by 1519.

Methodists John Wesley (1703–91) began movement in 1738, within Church of England.

Orthodox Original Christian proselytizing in 1c; broke with Rome in 1054, after centuries of doctrinal disputes and diverging traditions.

Pentecostal See **Pentecostalism** on p 503.

Presbyterians Originated in Calvinist Reformation in 1500s; differed with Lutherans over sacraments, and church government. John Knox (c.1513–1572) founded Scottish Presbyterian Church about 1560.

Roman Catholic Traditionally in the naming of St Peter as the first vicar by Jesus; historically, in early Christian proselytizing and the conversion of imperial Rome in the 4c.

United Church of Christ Union of the Congregational and Christian Churches with the Evangelical and Reformed Church. An ecumenical Protestant Church, it allows for variation in organization and interpretation of doctrine but reflects its Reformed theological background.

The Ten Commandments

I I am the Lord your God, who brought you out of the land of Egypt, out of the house of bondage. You shall have no other gods before me.

II You shall not make for yourself a graven image. You shall not bow down to them or serve them.

III You shall not take the name of the Lord your God in vain.

IV Remember the sabbath day, to keep it holy.

V Honour your father and your mother.

VI You shall not kill.

VII You shall not commit adultery.

VIII You shall not steal.

IX You shall not bear false witness against your neighbour.

X You shall not covet.

The Ten Commandments appear in two different places in the Bible – Exodus 20:17 and Deuteronomy 5:6–21. Most Protestant, Anglican and Orthodox Christians enumerate the Commandments differently from Roman Catholics and Lutherans.

Major immovable Christian feasts

For saints' days ▶**Saints' days** p 494

1 Jan	Solemnity of Mary, Mother of God
6 Jan	Epiphany
7 Jan	Christmas Day (*Eastern Orthodox*)[1]
11 Jan	Baptism of Jesus
25 Jan	Conversion of Apostle Paul
2 Feb	Presentation of Jesus (*Candlemas Day*)
22 Feb	The Chair of Peter, Apostle
25 Mar	Annunciation of the Virgin Mary
24 Jun	Birth of John the Baptist
6 Aug	Transfiguration
15 Aug	Assumption of the Virgin Mary
22 Aug	Queenship of Mary
8 Sep	Birthday of the Virgin Mary
14 Sep	Exaltation of the Holy Cross
2 Oct	Guardian Angels
1 Nov	All Saints
2 Nov	All Souls
9 Nov	Dedication of the Lateran Basilica
21 Nov	Presentation of the Virgin Mary
8 Dec	Immaculate Conception
25 Dec	Christmas Day
28 Dec	Holy Innocents

[1] Fixed feasts in the Julian Calendar used by Eastern Orthodox churches fall 13 days later than the Gregorian Calendar date.

Movable Christian feasts 2005–2030

Year	Ash Wednesday	Easter	Ascension	Whit Sunday (Pentecost)	Trinity Sunday	Sundays after Trinity	Corpus Christi	First Sunday in Advent
2005	9 Feb	27 Mar	5 May	15 May	22 May	26	26 Jun	27 Nov
2006	1 Mar	16 Apr	25 May	4 Jun	11 Jun	24	15 Jun	3 Dec
2007	21 Feb	8 Apr	17 May	27 May	3 Jun	25	7 Jun	2 Dec
2008	6 Feb	23 Mar	1 May	11 May	18 May	27	22 May	30 Nov
2009	25 Feb	12 Apr	21 May	31 May	7 Jun	24	11 Jun	29 Nov
2010	17 Feb	4 Apr	13 May	23 May	30 May	25	3 Jun	28 Nov

Year	Ash Wednesday	Easter	Ascension	Whit Sunday (Pentecost)	Trinity Sunday	Sundays after Trinity	Corpus Christi	First Sunday in Advent
2011	9 Mar	24 Apr	2 Jun	12 Jun	19 Jun	22	23 Jun	27 Nov
2012	22 Feb	8 Apr	17 May	27 May	3 Jun	25	7 Jun	2 Dec
2013	13 Feb	31 Mar	9 May	19 May	26 May	26	30 May	1 Dec
2014	5 Mar	20 Apr	29 May	8 Jun	15 Jun	23	19 Jun	30 Nov
2015	18 Feb	5 Apr	14 May	24 May	31 May	25	4 Jun	29 Nov
2016	10 Feb	27 Mar	5 May	15 May	22 May	26	26 May	27 Nov
2017	1Mar	16 Apr	25 May	4 Jun	11 Jun	24	15 Jun	3 Dec
2018	14 Feb	1 Apr	10 May	20 May	27 May	26	31 May	2 Dec
2019	6 Mar	21 Apr	30 May	9 Jun	16 Jun	23	20 Jun	1 Dec
2020	26 Feb	12 Apr	21 May	31 May	7 Jun	24	11 Jun	29 Nov
2021	17 Feb	4 Apr	13 May	23 May	30 May	25	3 Jun	28 Nov
2022	2 Mar	17 Apr	26 May	5 Jun	12 Jun	23	16 Jun	27 Nov
2023	22 Feb	9 Apr	18 May	28 May	4 Jun	25	8 Jun	3 Dec
2024	14 Feb	31 Mar	9 May	19 May	26 May	26	30 May	1 Dec
2025	5 Mar	20 Apr	29 May	8 Jun	15 Jun	23	19 Jun	30 Nov
2026	18 Feb	5 Apr	14 May	24 May	31 May	25	4 June	29 Nov
2027	10 Feb	28 Mar	6 May	16 May	23 May	26	27 May	28 Nov
2028	1 Mar	16 Apr	25 May	4 Jun	11 Jun	24	15 Jun	3 Dec
2029	14 Feb	1 Apr	10 May	20 May	27 May	26	31 May	2 Dec
2030	6 Mar	21 Apr	30 May	9 June	16 Jun	23	20 Jun	1 Dec

Ash Wednesday, the first day of Lent, can fall at the earliest on 4 February and at the latest on 10 March.

Palm (Passion) Sunday is the Sunday before Easter; Good Friday is the Friday before Easter; Holy Saturday (often referred to as Easter Saturday) is the Saturday before Easter; Easter Saturday, in traditional usage, is the Saturday following Easter.

Easter Day can fall at the earliest on 22 March and at the latest on 25 April. Ascension Day can fall at the earliest on 30 April and at the latest on 3 June. Whit Sunday can fall at the earliest on 10 May and at the latest on 13 June. There are not fewer than 22 and not more than 27 Sundays after Trinity. The first Sunday of Advent is the Sunday nearest to 30 November.

Saints' days

Selected Saints' days are given below. The official recognition of Saints, and the choice of a Saint's Day, varies greatly between different branches of Christianity, calendars and localities. Only major variations are included below, using the following abbreviations:

C Coptic E Eastern G Greek W Western

■ January

1 Basil (E), Fulgentius, Telemachus
2 Basil and Gregory of Nazianzus (W), Macarius of Alexandria, Seraphim of Sarov
3 Geneviève
4 Angela of Foligno
5 Simeon Stylites (W)
7 Cedda, Lucian of Antioch (W), Raymond of Penyafort
8 Atticus (E), Gudule, Severinus
9 Hadrian the African
10 Agatho, Marcian
12 Ailred, Benedict Biscop
13 Hilary of Poitiers
14 Kentigern
15 Macarius of Egypt, Maurus, Paul of Thebes
16 Honoratus
17 Antony of Egypt
19 Wulfstan
20 Euthymius, Fabian, Sebastian
21 Agnes, Fructuosus, Maximus (E), Meinrad
22 Timothy (G), Vincent
23 Ildefonsus
24 Babylas (W), Francis de Sales
25 Gregory of Nazianzus (E)
26 Paula, Timothy and Titus, Xenophon (E)
27 Angela Merici
28 Ephraem Syrus (E), Paulinus of Nola, Thomas Aquinas
29 Gildas
31 John Bosco, Marcella

■ February

1 Brigid, Pionius
3 Anskar, Blaise (W), Werburga, Simeon (E)
4 Gilbert of Sempringham, Isidore of Pelusium, Phileas
5 Agatha, Avitus
6 Dorothy, Paul Miki and companions, Vedast
8 Theodore (G), Jerome Emiliani
9 Teilo
10 Scholastica
11 Benedict of Aniane, Blaise (E), Caedmon, Gregory II
12 Meletius
13 Agabus (W), Catherine dei Ricci, Priscilla (E)
14 Cyril and Methodius (W), Valentine (W)
16 Flavian (E), Pamphilus (E), Valentine (G)
18 Bernadette (France), Colman, Flavian (W), Leo I (E)
20 Wulfric
21 Peter Damian
23 Polycarp
25 Ethelbert, Tarasius, Walburga
26 Alexander (W), Porphyrius

27 Leander
28 Oswald of York

■ **March**
1 David
2 Chad, Simplicius
3 Ailred
4 Casimir
6 Chrodegang
7 Perpetua and Felicity
8 Felix, John of God, Pontius
9 Frances of Rome, Gregory of Nyssa, Pacian
10 John Ogilvie, Macarius of Jerusalem, Simplicius
11 Constantine, Oengus, Sophronius
12 Gregory (the Great)
13 Nicephorus
14 Benedict (*E*)
15 Clement Hofbauer
17 Gertrude, Joseph of Arimathea (*W*), Patrick
18 Anselm of Lucca, Cyril of Jerusalem, Edward
19 Joseph
20 Cuthbert, John of Parma, Martin of Braga
21 Serapion of Thmuis
22 Catherine of Sweden, Nicholas of Fluë
23 Turibius de Mongrovejo
30 John Climacus

■ **April**
1 Hugh of Grenoble, Mary of Egypt (*E*), Melito
2 Francis of Paola, Mary of Egypt (*W*)
3 Richard of Chichester
4 Isidore of Seville
5 Juliana of Liège, Vincent Ferrer
7 Hegesippus, John Baptist de la Salle
8 Agabus (*E*)
10 Fulbert
11 Gemma Galgani, Guthlac, Stanislaus
12 Julius I, Zeno
13 Martin I
15 Aristarchus, Pudus (*E*), Trophimus of Ephesus
17 Agapetus (*E*), Stephen Harding
18 Mme Acarie
19 Alphege, Leo IX
21 Anastasius (*E*), Anselm, Beuno, Januarius (*E*)
22 Alexander (*C*)
23 George
24 Egbert, Fidelis of Sigmaringen, Mellitus
25 Mark, Phaebadius
27 Zita
28 Peter Chanel, Vitalis and Valeria
29 Catherine of Siena, Hugh of Cluny, Peter Martyr, Robert
30 James (the Great) (*E*), Pius V

■ **May**
1 Asaph, Joseph the Worker, Walburga
2 Athanasius
3 Philip and James (the Less) (*W*)
4 Gotthard
5 Hilary of Arles
7 John of Beverley
8 John (*E*), Peter of Tarantaise
10 Antoninus, Comgall, John of Avila, Simon (*E*)
11 Cyril and Methodius (*E*), Mamertus
12 Epiphanius, Nereus and Achilleus, Pancras

14 Matthias (*W*)
16 Brendan, John of Nepomuk, Simon Stock
17 Robert Bellarmine, Paschal Baylon
18 John I
19 Dunstan, Ivo, Pudens (*W*), Pudentiana (*W*)
20 Bernardino of Siena
21 Helena (*E*)
22 Rita of Cascia
23 Ivo of Chartres
24 Vincent of Lérins
25 Aldhelm, Bede, Gregory VII, Mary Magdalene de Pazzi
26 Philip Neri, Quadratus
27 Augustine of Canterbury
30 Joan of Arc

■ **June**
1 Justin Martyr, Pamphilus
2 Erasmus, Marcellinus and Peter, Nicephorus (*G*), Pothinus
3 Charles Lwanga and companions, Clotilde, Kevin
4 Optatus, Petrock
5 Boniface
6 Martha (*E*), Norbert
7 Paul of Constantinople (*W*), Willibald
8 William of York
9 Columba, Cyril of Alexandria (*E*), Ephraem (*W*)
11 Barnabas, Bartholomew (*E*)
12 Leo III
13 Anthony of Padua
15 Orsisius, Vitus
17 Alban, Botulph
19 Gervasius and Protasius, Jude (*E*), Romuald
20 Alban
21 Alban of Mainz, Aloysius Gonzaga
22 John Fisher and Thomas More, Niceta, Pantaenus (*C*), Paulinus of Nola
23 Etheldreda
24 Birth of John the Baptist
25 Prosper of Aquitaine
27 Cyril of Alexandria (*W*), Ladislaus
28 Irenaeus
29 Peter and Paul
30 First Martyrs of the Church of Rome

■ **July**
1 Cosmas and Damian (*E*), Oliver Plunkett
3 Anatolius, Thomas
4 Andrew of Crete (*E*), Elizabeth of Portugal, Ulrich
5 Anthony Zaccaria
6 Maria Goretti
7 Palladius, Pantaenus
8 Kilian, Aquila and Prisca (*W*)
11 Benedict (*W*), Pius I
12 John Gualbert, Veronica
13 Henry II, Mildred, Silas
14 Camillus of Lellis, Deusdedit, Nicholas of the Holy Mountain (*E*)
15 Bonaventure, Jacob of Nisibis, Swithin, Vladimir
16 Eustathius, Our Lady of Mt Carmel
17 Ennodius, Leo IV, Marcellina, Margaret (*E*), Scillitan Martyrs
18 Arnulf, Philastrius
19 Macrina, Symmachus
20 Aurelius, Margaret (*W*)

Thought and Belief

Thought and Belief

21 Lawrence of Brindisi, Praxedes
22 Mary Magdalene
23 Apollinaris, Bridget of Sweden
25 Anne and Joachim (*E*), Christopher, James (the Great) (*W*)
26 Anne and Joachim (*W*)
27 Pantaleon
28 Innocent I, Samson, Victor I
29 Lupus, Martha (*W*), Olave
30 Peter Chrysologus, Silas (*G*)
31 Giovanni Colombini, Germanus, Joseph of Arimathea (*E*), Ignatius of Loyola

■ **August**
1 Alphonsus Liguori, Ethelwold
2 Eusebius of Vercelli, Stephen I
4 Jean-Baptiste Vianney
6 Hormisdas
7 Cajetan, Sixtus II and companions
8 Dominic
9 Matthias (*G*)
10 Laurence, Oswald of Northumbria
11 Clare, Susanna
13 Maximus (*W*), Pontian and Hippolytus, Radegunde
14 Maximilian Kolbe
15 Arnulf, Tarsicius
16 Roch, Simplicianus, Stephen of Hungary
17 Hyacinth
19 John Eudes, Sebaldus
20 Bernard, Oswin, Philibert
21 Jane Frances de Chantal, Pius X
23 Rose of Lima, Sidonius Apollinaris
24 Bartholomew (*W*), Ouen
25 Joseph Calasanctius, Louis IX, Menas of Constantinople
26 Blessed Dominic of the Mother of God, Zephyrinus
27 Caesarius, Monica
28 Augustine of Hippo
29 Beheading of John the Baptist, Sabina
30 Pammachius
31 Aidan, Paulinus of Trier

■ **September**
1 Giles, Simeon Stylites (*E*)
2 John the Faster (*E*)
3 Gregory (the Great)
4 Babylas (*E*), Boniface I
5 Zacharias (*E*)
9 Peter Claver, Sergius of Antioch
10 Finnian, Nicholas of Tolentino, Pulcheria
11 Deiniol, Ethelburga, Paphnutius
13 John Chrysostom (*W*)
15 Catherine of Genoa, Our Lady of Sorrows
16 Cornelius, Cyprian of Carthage, Euphemia, Ninian
17 Robert Bellarmine, Hildegard, Lambert, Satyrus
19 Januarius (*W*), Theodore of Tarsus
20 Agapetus or Eustace (*W*)
21 Matthew (*W*)
23 Adamnan, Linus
25 Sergius of Rostov
26 Cosmas and Damian (*W*), Cyprian of Antioch, John (*E*)
27 Frumentius (*W*), Vincent de Paul
28 Exuperius, Wenceslaus

29 Michael (*Michaelmas Day*), Gabriel and Raphael
30 Jerome, Otto

■ **October**
1 Remigius, Romanos, Teresa of the Child Jesus
2 Leodegar (Leger)
3 Teresa of Lisieux, Thomas de Cantilupe
4 Ammon, Francis of Assisi, Petronius
6 Bruno, Thomas (*G*)
9 Demetrius (*W*), Denis and companions, Dionysius of Paris, James (the Less) (*E*), John Leonardi
10 Francis Borgia, Paulinus of York
11 Atticus (*E*), Bruno, Nectarius
12 Wilfrid
13 Edward the Confessor
14 Callistus I, Cosmas Melodus (*E*)
15 Lucian of Antioch (*E*), Teresa of Avila
16 Gall, Hedwig, Lullus, Margaret Mary Alacoque
17 Ignatius of Antioch, Victor
18 Luke
19 John de Bréboeuf and Isaac Jogues and companions, Paul of the Cross, Peter of Alcantara
21 Hilarion, Ursula
22 Abercius
23 John of Capistrano
24 Anthony Claret
25 Crispin and Crispinian, Forty Martyrs of England and Wales, Gaudentius
26 Demetrius (*E*)
28 Firmilian (*E*), Simon and Jude
30 Serapion of Antioch
31 Wolfgang

■ **November**
1 All Saints, Cosmas and Damian (*E*)
2 Eustace (*E*), Victorinus
3 Hubert, Malachy, Martin de Porres, Pirminius, Winifred
4 Charles Borromeo, Vitalis and Agricola
5 Elizabeth (*W*)
6 Illtyd, Leonard, Paul of Constantinople (*E*)
7 Willibrord
8 Elizabeth (*E*), Willehad
9 Simeon Metaphrastes (*E*)
10 Justus, Leo I (*W*)
11 Martin of Tours (*W*), Menas of Egypt, Theodore of Studios
12 Josaphat, Martin of Tours (*E*), Nilus the Ascetic
13 Abbo, John Chrysostom (*E*), Nicholas I
14 Dubricius, Gregory Palamas (*E*)
15 Albert the Great, Machutus
16 Edmund of Abingdon, Eucherius, Gertrude (the Great), Margaret of Scotland, Matthew (*E*)
17 Elizabeth of Hungary, Gregory Thaumaturgus, Gregory of Tours, Hugh of Lincoln
18 Odo, Romanus
19 Mechthild, Nerses
20 Edmund the Martyr
21 Gelasius
22 Cecilia

23	Amphilochius, Clement I (W), Columban, Felicity, Gregory of Agrigentum
25	Clement I (E), Mercurius, Mesrob
26	Siricius
27	Barlam and Josaphat
28	Simeon Metaphrastes
29	Cuthbert Mayne
30	Andrew, Frumentius (G)

■ **December**

1	Eligius
2	Chromatius
3	Francis Xavier
4	Barbara, John Damascene, Osmund
5	Clement of Alexandria, Sabas
6	Nicholas
7	Ambrose

10	Miltiades
11	Damasus, Daniel
12	Jane Frances de Chantal, Spyridon (E), Vicelin
13	Lucy, Odilia
14	John of the Cross, Spyridon (W)
16	Eusebius
18	Frumentius (C)
20	Ignatius of Antioch (G)
21	Peter Canisius, Thomas
22	Anastasia (E), Chrysogonus (E)
23	John of Kanty
26	Stephen (W)
27	John (W), Fabiola, Stephen (E)
29	Thomas à Becket, Trophimus of Arles
31	Sylvester

Patron saints of occupations

Accountants	Matthew	Messengers	Gabriel
Actors	Genesius, Vitus	Metalworkers	Eligius
Advertisers	Bernardino of Siena	Midwives	Raymond Nonnatus
Architects	Thomas (Apostle)	Miners	Anne, Barbara
Artists	Luke, Angelico	Motorists	Christopher
Astronauts	Joseph (Cupertino)	Musicians	Cecilia, Gregory the Great
Astronomers	Dominic	Nurses	Camillus de Lellis, John of God
Athletes	Sebastian	Philosophers	Thomas Aquinas, Catherine of Alexandria
Authors	Francis de Sales		
Aviators	Our Lady of Loreto	Poets	Cecilia, David
Bakers	Honoratus	Police	Michael
Bankers	Bernardino (Feltre)	Politicians	Thomas More
Barbers	Cosmas and Damian	Postal workers	Gabriel
Blacksmiths	Eligius	Priests	Jean-Baptiste Vianney
Bookkeepers	Matthew	Printers	John of God
Book trade	John of God	Prisoners	Leonard
Brewers	Amand, Wenceslaus	Radio workers	Gabriel
Builders	Barbara, Thomas (Apostle)	Sailors	Christopher, Erasmus, Francis of Paola
Butchers	Luke		
Carpenters	Joseph	Scholars	Thomas Aquinas
Chemists	Cosmas and Damian	Scientists	Albert the Great
Comedians	Vitus	Sculptors	Luke, Louis
Cooks	Lawrence, Martha	Secretaries	Genesius
Dancers	Vitus	Servants	Martha, Zita
Dentists	Apollonia	Shoemakers	Crispin, Crispinian
Doctors	Cosmas and Damian, Luke	Singers	Cecilia, Gregory
Editors	Francis de Sales	Soldiers	George, Joan of Arc, Martin of Tours, Sebastian
Farmers	Isidore		
Firemen	Florian	Students	Thomas Aquinas
Fishermen	Andrew, Peter	Surgeons	Luke, Cosmas and Damian
Florists	Dorothy, Teresa of Lisieux	Tailors	Homobonus
Gardeners	Adam, Fiacre	Tax collectors	Matthew
Glassworkers	Luke, Lucy	Taxi drivers	Fiacre
Gravediggers	Joseph of Arimathea	Teachers	Gregory the Great, John Baptiste de la Salle
Grocers	Michael		
Hotelkeepers	Amand, Julian the Hospitaler	Theologians	Augustine, Alphonsus Liguori, Thomas Aquinas
Housewives	Martha		
Jewellers	Eligius	Television workers	Gabriel
Journalists	Francis de Sales	Undertakers	Dismas, Joseph of Arimathea
Labourers	James, John Bosco	Waiters	Martha
Lawyers	Ivo, Thomas More	Writers	Lucy
Librarians	Jerome, Catherine of Alexandria		
Merchants	Francis of Assisi		

Thought and Belief

Confucianism

Founded 6c BC in China.

Founder K'ung Fu-tse (Confucius) (c.551–479 BC).

Sacred texts Shih Ching, Li Ching, Shu Ching, Chu'un Ch'iu, I Ching.

Beliefs The oldest school of Chinese thought, Confucianism did not begin as a religion. Confucius was concerned with the best way to behave and live in this world and was not concerned with the afterlife. He emerges as a great moral teacher who tried to replace the old religious observances with moral values as the basis of social and political order. He laid particular emphasis on the family as the basic unit in society and the foundation of the whole community. He believed that government was a matter of moral responsibility, not just manipulation of power.

Organization Confucianism is not an institution and has no church or clergy. However, ancestor-worship and veneration of the sky have their sources in Confucian texts. Weddings and funerals follow a tradition handed down by Confucian scholars. Social life is ritualized and colour and patterns of clothes have a sacred meaning.

Divisions There are two ethical strands in Confucianism. One, associated with Confucius and Hsun Tzu (c.298–238 BC), is conventionalistic: we ought to follow the traditional codes of behaviour for their own sake. The other, associated with Mencius (c.371–289 BC) and medieval neo-Confucians, is intuitionistic: we ought to do as our moral natures dictate.

Major Chinese festivals

January/February	Chinese New Year	August	All Souls' Festival
February/March	Lantern Festival	September	Mid-Autumn Festival
March/April	Festival of Pure Brightness	September/October	Double Ninth Festival
		November/December	Winter Solstice
May/June	Dragon Boat Festival		
July/August	Herd Boy and Weaving Maid Festival		

Hinduism

Founded c.1500 BC by Aryan invaders of India with their Vedic religion.

Sacred texts The Vedas ('knowledge'), including the Upanishads which contain much that is esoteric and mystical. Also included are the epic poems Ramayana and the Mahabharata. Best known of all is the Bhagavad Gita, part of the Mahabharata.

Beliefs Hinduism emphasizes the right way of living (dharma) and embraces many diverse religious beliefs and practices rather than a set of doctrines. It acknowledges many gods who are seen as manifestations of an underlying reality. Devout Hindus aim to become one with the 'absolute reality' or Brahman. Only after a completely pure life will the soul be released from the cycle of rebirth. Until then the soul will be repeatedly reborn. Samsara refers to the cycle of birth and rebirth. Karma is the law by which consequences of actions within one life are carried over into the next.

Organization There is very little formal structure. Hinduism is concerned with the realization of religious values in every part of life, yet there is a great emphasis on the performance of complex demanding rituals under the supervision of a Brahman priest and teacher. There are three categories of worship: temple, domestic and congregational. The most common ceremony is prayer (puja). Many pilgrimages take place and there is an annual cycle of festivals.

Divisions As there is no concept of orthodoxy in Hinduism, there are many different sects worshipping different gods. The three most important gods are Brahman, the primeval god, Vishnu, the preserver, and Shiva, both destroyer and creator of life. The three major living traditions are those devoted to Vishnu, Shiva and the goddess Shakti. Folk beliefs and practices exist together with sophisticated philosophical schools.

Major Hindu festivals

Chaitra S 9	Ramanavami (Birthday of Lord Rama)	Asvina S 15	Lakshmi-puja (Homage to Goddess Lakshmi)
Asadha S 2	Rathayatra (Pilgrimage of the Jagannatha Chariot at Puri)	Asvina K 15	Diwali, Dipavali (String of Lights)
Sravana S 11–15	Jhulanayatra (Swinging the Lord Krishna)	Kartikka S 15	Guru Nanak Jananti (Birthday of Guru Nanak)
Sravana S 15	Rakshabandhana (Tying on Lucky Threads)	Magha K 5	Sarasvati-puja (Homage to Goddess Sarasvati)
Bhadrapada K 8	Janamashtami (Birthday of Lord Krishna)	Magha K 13	Maha-sivaratri (Great Night of Lord Shiva)
Asvina S 7–10	Durga-puja (Homage to Goddess Durga) (*Bengal*)	Phalguna S 14	Holi (Festival of Fire)
Asvina S 1–10	Navaratri (Festival of Nine Nights)	Phalguna S 15	Dolayatra (Swing Festival) (*Bengal*)

S = Sukla ('waxing fortnight') K = Krishna ('waning fortnight')

Islam

Founded 7c AD.

Founder Muhammad (c.570–c.632).

Sacred texts The Koran, the word of God as revealed to Muhammad, and the Hadith, a collection of the prophet's sayings.

Beliefs A monotheistic religion, God is the creator of all things and holds absolute power over man. All persons should devote themselves to lives of grateful and praise-giving obedience to God as they will be judged on the Day of Resurrection. It is acknowledged that Satan often misleads humankind but those who have obeyed God or have repented of their sins will dwell in paradise. Those sinners who are unrepentant will go to hell. Muslims accept the Old Testament and acknowledge Jesus Christ as an important prophet, but they believe the perfect word of God was revealed to Muhammad. Islam imposes five pillars of faith on its followers: belief in one God and his prophet, Muhammad; salat, formal prayer preceded by ritual cleansing five times a day, facing Mecca; saum, fasting during the month of Ramadan; Hajj, pilgrimage to Mecca at least once; zakat, a religious tax on the rich to provide for the poor.

Organization There is no organized priesthood but great respect is accorded to descendants of Muhammad and holy men, scholars and teachers such as mullahs and ayatollahs. The Shari'a is the Islamic law and applies to all aspects of life, not just religious practices.

Divisions There are two main groups within Islam. The Sunni are the majority and the more orthodox. They recognize the succession from Muhammad to Abu Bakr, his father-in-law, and to the next three caliphs. The Shiites are followers of Ali, Muhammad's cousin and son-in-law. They believe in 12 imams, perfect teachers, who still guide the faithful from paradise. Shi'ah practice tends towards the ecstatic. There are many other subsects including the Sufis, the Ismailis and the Wahhabis.

Major Islamic festivals

1 Muharram	New Year's Day; starts on the day which celebrates Muhammad's departure from Mecca to Medina in AD 622.	1 Shawwal	'Feast of Breaking the Fast' (Id al-Fitr); marks the end of Ramadan.
12 Rabi I	Birthday of Muhammad (Mawlid al-Nabi) AD 572; celebrated throughout month of Rabi I.	8–13 Dhu-I-Hijja	Annual pilgrimage ceremonies at and around Mecca; month during which the great pilgrimage (Hajj) should be made.
27 Rajab	'Night of Ascent' (Laylat al-Miraj) of Muhammad to Heaven.	10 Dhu-I-Hijja	Feast of the Sacrifice (Id al-Adha).
1 Ramadan	Beginning of month of fasting during daylight hours.		
27 Ramadan	'Night of Power' (Laylat al-Qadr); sending down of the Koran to Muhammad.		

Jainism

Founded 6c BC in India.

Founder Vardhamana Mahavira (c.540–468 BC).

Sacred texts Svetambara canon of scripture and Digambara texts.

Beliefs Jainism is derived from the ancient jinas ('those who overcome'). They believe that salvation consists in conquering material existence through adhering to a strict ascetic discipline, thus freeing the 'soul' from the working of karma for eternal, all-knowing bliss. Liberation requires detachment from worldly existence, an essential part of which is Ahimsa, non-injury to living beings. Jains are also strict vegetarians.

Organization Like Buddhists, the Jains are dedicated to the quest for liberation and the life of the ascetic. However, rather than congregating in monastic centres, Jain monks and nuns have developed a strong relationship with lay people. There are temple rituals resembling Hindu puja. There is also a series of lesser vows and specific religious practices that give the lay person an identifiable religious career.

Divisions There are two categories of religious and philosophical literature. The Svetambara have a canon of scripture consisting of 45 texts, including a group of 11 texts in which the sermons and dialogues of Mahavira himself are collected. The Digambara hold that the original teachings of Mahavira have been lost but that their texts preserve accurately the substance of the original message. This disagreement over scriptures has not led to fundamental doctrinal differences.

Judaism

Founded c.2000 BC.

Founder Abraham (c.2000–1650 BC), with whom God made a covenant, and Moses (15c–13c BC), who gave the Israelites the law.

Sacred texts The Hebrew Bible, consisting of 24 books, the most important of which are the Torah or Pentateuch — the first five books. Also the Talmud made up of the Mishna, the oral law, and the Gemara, an extensive commentary.

Beliefs A monotheistic religion, the Jews believe God is the creator of the world, delivered the Israelites out of bondage in Egypt, revealed his law to them, and chose them to be a light to all humankind. However varied their communities, Jews see themselves as members of a community whose origins lie in the patriarchal period. Ritual is very important and the family is the basic unit of ritual.

Organization Originally a theocracy, the basic institution is now the synagogue, operated by the congregation and led by a rabbi of their choice. The chief rabbis in France and Britain have authority over those who accept it; in Israel the two chief rabbis have civil authority in family law. The synagogue is the centre for community worship and study. Its main feature is the 'ark' (a cupboard) containing the handwritten scrolls of the Pentateuch. Daily life is governed by a number of practices and observances: male children are circumcised, the Sabbath is observed, and food has to be correctly prepared. The most important festival is the Passover, which celebrates the liberation of the Israelites from Egypt.

Divisions Today most Jews are descendants of either the Ashkenazim or the Sephardim, each with marked cultural differences. There are also several religious branches of Judaism from ultra-liberal to ultra-conservative, reflecting different points of view regarding the binding character of the prohibitions and duties prescribed for Jews.

Major Jewish festivals

1–2 Tishri	Rosh Hashana (New Year)	10 Tevet	Asara be-Tevet (Fast of 10th Tevet)
3 Tishri	Tzom Gedaliahu (Fast of Gedaliah)	13 Adar	Taanit Esther (Fast of Esther)
10 Tishri	Yom Kippur (Day of Atonement)	14–15 Adar	Purim (Feast of Lots)
15–21 Tishri	Sukkot (Feast of Tabernacles)	15–22 Nisan	Pesach (Passover)
22 Tishri	Shemini Atzeret (8th Day of the Solemn Assembly)	5 Iyar	Israel Independence Day
		6–7 Sivan	Shavuot (Feast of Weeks)
23 Tishri	Simchat Torah (Rejoicing of the Law)	17 Tammuz	Shiva Asar be-Tammuz (Fast of 17th Tammuz)
25 Kislev to 2–3 Tevet	Hanukkah (Feast of Dedication)	9 Av	Tishah beAv (Fast of 9th Av)

Shintoism

Founded 8c AD in Japan.

Sacred texts Kojiki and Nihon Shoki.

Beliefs Shinto 'the teaching' or 'way of the gods', came into existence independently from Buddhism which was coming to the mainland of Japan at that time. It subsequently incorporated many features of Buddhism. Founded on the nature-worship of Japanese folk religions, it is made up of many elements; animism, veneration of nature and ancestor-worship. Its gods are known as kami and there are many ceremonies appealing to these kami for benevolent treatment and protection. Great stress is laid on the harmony between humans, their kami and nature. Moral and physical purity is a basic law. Death and other pollutions are to be avoided. Shinto is primarily concerned with life and this world and the good of the group. Followers must show devotion and sincerity but aberrations can be erased by purification procedures.

Organization As a set of prehistoric agricultural ceremonies, Shinto was never supported by a body of philosophical or moralistic literature. Shamans originally performed the ceremonies and tended the shrines, then gradually a particular tribe took over the ceremonies. In the 8c Shinto became political when the imperial family were ascribed divine origins and state Shintoism was established.

Divisions In the 19c Shinto was divided into Shrine (jinga) Shinto and Sectarian (kyoko) Shinto. Jinga became a state cult and it remained the national religion until 1945.

Major Japanese festivals

Public holidays in Japan are listed on p 580. In addition, the following festivals should be noted:

1–3 Jan	Oshogatsu (New Year)	7 Jul	Hoshi matsuri *or* Tanabata (Star Festival)
3 Mar	Ohinamatsuri (Doll's *or* Girls' Festival)	13–31 Jul	Obon (Buddhist All Souls)
5 May	Tango no Sekku (Boys' Festival)		

Sikhism

Founded 15c in India.

Founder Guru Nanak (1469–1539).

Sacred text Adi Granth.

Beliefs Nanak preached tolerance and devotion to one God before whom everyone is equal. Sikh is the Sanskrit word for disciple. Nanak's doctrine sought a fusion of Brahmanism and Islam on the grounds that both were monotheistic. God is the true Guru and his divine word has come to humanity through the ten historical gurus. The line ended in 1708, since when the Sikh community has been called guru.

Organization There is no priestly caste and all Sikhs are empowered to perform rituals connected with births, marriages, and deaths. Sikhs worship in their own temples but they evolved distinct features like the langar, 'kitchen', a communal meal where people of any religion or caste could eat. Rest houses for travellers were also provided. The tenth guru instituted an initiation ceremony, the Khalsa. Initiates wear the Five Ks (uncut hair, steel bangle, comb, shorts, ceremonial sword) and a turban. Members of the Khalsa add the name Singh (lion) to their name and have to lead pure lives and follow a code of discipline. Sikhs generally rise before dawn, bathe and recite the japji, a morning prayer. Hindu festivals from northern India are observed.

Divisions There are several religious orders of Sikhs based either on disputes over the succession of gurus or points of ritual and tradition. The most important current issue is the number of Khalsa Sikhs cutting off their hair and beards and relapsing into Hinduism.

Taoism

Founded 600 BC in China.

Founder Lao-tzu (6c BC).

Sacred texts Chuang-tzu, Lao-tzu (Tao-te-ching).

Beliefs Taoism is Chinese for 'the school of the tao' and the 'Taoist religion'. Tao ('the way') is central in both Confucianism and Taoism. The former stresses the tao of humanity, the latter the tao of nature, harmony with which ensures appropriate conduct. Taoist religion developed later and was probably influenced by Buddhist beliefs. The doctrine emphasizes that good and evil action decide the fate of the soul. The Taoists believe that the sky, the earth and water are deities; that Lao-tzu is supreme master; that the disciple masters his body and puts evil spirits to flight with charms; that body and spirit are purified through meditation and by taking the pill of immortality to gain eternal life; and that the way is handed down from master to disciple. Religious Taoism incorporated ideas and images from philosophical Taoist texts, especially the Tao-te-ching but also the theory of Yin-Yang, the quest for immortality, mental and physical discipline, interior hygiene, internal alchemy, healing and exorcism, a pantheon of gods and spirits, and ideals of theocratic states. The Immortals are meant to live in the mountains far from the tumult of the world.

Organization This is similar to Buddhism in the matter of clergy and temple. The jiao is a ceremony to purify the ground. Zhon-gyual is the only important religious festival, when the hungry dead appear to the living and Taoist priests free the souls of the dead from suffering.

Divisions Religious Taoism emerged from many sects. These sects proliferated between 618 and 1126 AD and were described collectively as Spirit Cloud Taoists. They form the majority of Taoist priests in Taiwan, where they are called 'Masters of Methods' or Red-headed Taoists. The more orthodox priests are called 'Tao Masters' or Black-headed Taoists.

Sacred texts of world religions

Baha'i Most Holy Book, The Seven Valleys, The Hidden Words, The Bayan

Buddhism Tripitaka, Mahayana Sutras, Milindapanha, Bardo Thodol

Christianity Old Testament: Genesis, Exodus, Leviticus, Numbers, Deuteronomy, Joshua, Judges, Ruth, 1 Samuel, 2 Samuel, 1 Kings, 2 Kings, 1 Chronicles, 2 Chronicles, Ezra, Nehemiah, Esther, Job, Psalms, Proverbs, Ecclesiastes, Song of Solomon, Isaiah, Jeremiah, Lamentations, Ezekiel, Daniel, Hosea, Joel, Amos, Obadiah, Jonah, Micah, Nahum, Habakkuk, Zephaniah, Haggai, Zechariah, Malachi. New Testament: Matthew, Mark, Luke, John, Acts of the Apostles, Romans, 1 Corinthians, 2 Corinthians, Galatians, Ephesians, Philippians, Colossians, 1 Thessalonians, 2 Thessalonians, 1 Timothy, 2 Timothy, Titus, Philemon, Hebrews, James, 1 Peter, 2 Peter, 1 John, 2 John, 3 John, Jude, Revelation. Apocrypha (Revised standard version 1957): 1 Esdras, 2 Esdras, Tobit, Judith, Additions to Esther, Wisdom of Solomon, Ecclesiasticus, Epistle of Jeremiah, Baruch, Prayer of Azariah and the Song of the Three Young Men, (History of) Susanna, Bel and the Dragon, Prayer of Manasseh, 1 Maccabees, 2 Maccabees. (The Authorized version incorporates Jeremiah into Baruch; the prayer of Azariah is simply called the Song of the Three Holy Children. The Roman Catholic Church includes Tobit, Judith, all of Esther, Maccabees 1 and 2, Wisdom of Solomon, Ecclesiasticus, and Baruch in its canon.)

Confucianism Shih ching, Li ching, Shu ching, Chu'un Ch'iu, I Ching

Hinduism The Vedas (including the Upanishads), Ramayana, Mahabharata and the Bhagavad Gita

Islam The Koran, the Hadith

Jainism Svetambara canon, Digambara texts

Judaism The Hebrew Bible: Torah (Pentateuch): Genesis, Exodus, Leviticus, Numbers, Deuteronomy. Also the books of the Prophets, Psalms, Chronicles and Proverbs. The Talmud including the Mishna and Gemara. The Zohar (Book of Splendour) is a famous Cabalistic book.

Shintoism Kojiki, Nihon Shoki

Sikhism Adi Granth

Taoism Chuang-tzu, Lao-tzu (Tao-te-ching)

Thought and Belief

Other religions, sects and religious movements

Thought and Belief

Adventist A member of one of the many Christian groups which believe the second coming of Christ will happen very soon. ▶ **Seventh Day Adventists**

anthroposophy A modern spiritual movement founded in Switzerland in 1912 by Rudolf Steiner (1861–1925). *Anthropos* (meaning 'man') suggests it is more human-centred than God-centred; fundamental to anthroposophy is the aim to develop the whole human being — socially, intellectually and spiritually — and to restore the innate human capacity for spiritual perception, which has been dulled by materialism. Anthroposophy has influenced many areas of activity, particularly the foundation of special schools around the world.

charismatic movement A modern international, transdenominational Christian movement of spiritual renewal, which has its roots in the Pentecostal Church. Taking a variety of forms in Roman Catholic, Protestant, and Eastern Orthodox churches, it emphasizes the present reality and work of the Holy Spirit in the life of the Church and the individual. It may be characterized by the practice of speaking in tongues (glossolalia), prophecy and healing.

Christadelphians A Christian sect, founded in 1848 in the USA by John Thomas (1805–71). They claim that Christ will soon come again to establish a theocracy lasting for a millennium and based in Jerusalem. They are congregational in organization and have no ordained ministers. They believe in the complete accuracy of the Bible, and claim that only true believers will go on to life after death and that adult followers must be baptized to attain full salvation.

ecumenism A movement seeking to unify the different churches and denominations within Christianity. Modern ecumenism stems from the Edinburgh Missionary Conference (1910) and led to the formation in 1948 of the World Council of Churches. It encourages dialogue between churches, unions where possible, joint acts of worship, and joint service in the community.

evangelicalism A term (from Greek 'to announce the good news') which since the Reformation has been applied to the Protestant Churches due to their principles of justification through faith alone, and the supreme authority accorded to Scripture (ie not to church tradition or institutional figures). Although the term goes beyond denominational divisions, and has featured throughout the history of the Christian Church, in later years it has been applied more narrowly to Protestant Churches which emphasize biblical authority, and personal experience of conversion, commitment and ongoing relationship with Jesus Christ. Evangelicals believe in and are inspired by the necessity of carrying the Christian faith to those not already within the community of the Christian Church.

Freemasonry An international, secretive adult male fraternity who meet in clubs called lodges for social enjoyment and mutual assistance, united by their belief in a supreme being and in the immortal soul. The organization comes under attack for the secrecy concerning its activities, both towards outsiders and between the different levels of freemasons. Modern Freemasonry in the UK began in the early 18c, and is known for its rituals and signs of recognition that date back to ancient non-Christian religions and to the practices of the medieval craft guild of the stonemasons (in England).

Fundamentalism A conservative theological movement seeking to preserve the essential doctrines of the Christian faith, eg the Virgin birth and the resurrection of Christ. Its roots lie in the 19c when traditional assumptions began to be challenged by the concept of evolution and the growth of biblical criticism. The term dates from a 1920s Protestant movement in the USA which was characterized by a literal interpretation of the Bible. It was revived in the late 20c to describe some Christian and Muslim movements.

Hare Krishna Popular name for a Hindu cult founded in the USA in 1965 by His Divine Grace A C Bhaktivedanta Swami Prabhupada as The International Society for Krishna Consciousness. It focuses on love for Krishna (an incarnation of the god Vishnu) and promotes wellbeing through consciousness of God based on the ancient Vedic texts of India, eg the *Bhagavad Gita*. Its saffron-robed devotees are sometimes seen gathered in town centres chanting the mantra 'Hare Krishna'; they are vegetarians, avoid intoxicants and gambling, and are celibate apart from procreation within marriage.

Jehovah's Witnesses A millenarian movement organized in the USA in 1884 by Charles Taze Russell (1852–1916), then by Joseph Franklin Rutherford (1869–1942). They have their own translation of the Bible, which they interpret literally, and view themselves as entirely distinct from orthodox Christianity. They believe in the imminent second coming of Christ, and that their place in heaven depends on their obedience to God. Expected to 'witness' through house-to-house visiting, they avoid worldly involvement, and refuse to obey laws which they view as a contradiction of the law of God (eg taking oaths and military service). Their newspaper is called *The Watchtower* and their churches 'Kingdom Halls'.

Mormons, properly **The Church of Jesus Christ of Latter-day Saints** A religious sect which since 1847 has been based in Salt Lake City, Utah. The sect was founded in 1830 by Joseph Smith (d.1844) and was polygamous until 1890. They base their beliefs on *The Book of Mormon* and on Smith's own revelations, *Doctrine and Covenants* and *The Pearl of Great Price*; these texts tell of the coming of a millennium when Christ will rule from a New Jerusalem established in America. Smith claimed to have received visions of the Angel Moroni and a new revelation of the prophet Mormon on golden tablets which he translated as *The Book of Mormon*. Mormons believe that God was a physical being like them, that humans progress from a spiritual state with God, to mortality and then on to an afterlife, that they too can become gods, and that the incarnation of Jesus was unique only because it was the first.

New Age A modern cultural trend encompassing a wide range of concepts concerned with the union of mind, body, and spirit. New Age expresses itself in an interest in a variety of beliefs and disciplines such as mysticism, meditation, astrology, and holistic medicine, including the pseudoscientific application of the 'healing powers' of crystals. Many adherents of New Age anticipate the dawning of an astrological or spiritual age in which humans will realize a 'higher' existence and experience true peace and harmony.

502

Pentecostalism A Christian renewal movement which began in the early 1900s in the USA — in Topeka, Kansas (1901) and Los Angeles (1906) — inspired by the coming of the Holy Spirit upon the disciples (Acts 2) and in reaction to the loss of evangelical fervour among Methodists and other denominations. Pentecostals believe in the blessing and empowering of Christians through the gifts of the Holy Spirit, eg speaking in tongues, prophecy and healing, and in the literal interpretation of the Bible. Their churches are characterized by missionary zeal, informal worship, enthusiastic singing, and the practice of spiritual gifts.

Plymouth Brethren A fundamentalist Christian sect founded in 1827 by a group of evangelicals in Dublin, Ireland, under John Nelson Darby (1800–82). It spread to England in 1832 and met in Plymouth. Millenarian in outlook, the sect is characterized by a simplicity of belief, practice and style of life based on the New Testament. There are no ordained priests and no maintained church buildings since meetings are held in members' homes.

Quakers, properly **The Society of Friends** A Christian sect rooted in radical Puritanism, founded in England by George Fox (1624–91). A colony for persecuted Quakers was founded in Pennsylvania in 1682 by William Penn (1644–1718). Belief in the 'inner light', a living contact with the divine Spirit, is the basis of its meetings for worship, where Friends gather in silence until moved by the Spirit to speak. Many meetings now have programmed orders of worship. Quakers are often actively involved in promoting tolerance, justice and peace.

Scientology A movement developed in the USA in the 1950s by L Ron Hubbard (1911–86). Based on his *Dianetics: The Modern Science of Mental Health*, which outlines a type of counselling for curing emotional illnesses and for enhancing life, it strives to open the minds of adherents to all great truths and to self-determination. The Church of Scientology (founded 1954) has made several controversial religious and scientific claims.

Seventh Day Adventists A section of the American Adventist movement of 1831 that stemmed from the preaching of William Miller (1782–1849). Many followers left the movement when Miller's prophecy that Christ would return to earth in 1843 or 1844 did not materialize. Some turned to the teaching of Ellen Gould White (1827–1915), particularly the importance of honouring the Sabbath (Friday evening to Saturday evening), and formed the Seventh Day Adventists (1863). They believe Christ's second coming is imminent, but delayed until the Adventist message is preached worldwide. They also observe Old Testament dietary laws, abstain from alcohol, and practise adult baptism by total immersion.

transcendental meditation or **TM** A meditation technique based in part on Hindu meditation, but with no doctrinal content and practised by both religious and non-religious people. Rediscovered by Guru Dev, it came to prominence after 1958 through Dev's disciple Maharishi Mahesh Yogi, who travelled widely teaching TM. Practitioners are taught to meditate for 20 minutes twice a day, sometimes repeating a silent mantra, as a means of reducing stress, achieving relaxation and gaining self understanding. The ultimate goal is 'god-realization'.

Zoroastrianism An ancient religion of Persian origin founded or reformed by Zoroaster, which teaches the existence of two equally opposed divine beings, one good and the other evil. It was forced out of Persia by the expansion of Islam. Zoroastrians believe that the spirit of evil, Ahriman, will finally be overcome by Ahura Mazda ('Wise Lord') or God, only if individuals play their part in saving the world. Their body of scripture is known as the *Avesta*, and rites of worship are performed by priests.

Religious leaders and theologians

Abelard, Peter (1079–1142) French, born near Nantes. Philosopher and theologian. Secretly married his pupil Héloïse, whose relatives exacted revenge by castrating him, after which he became a monk and she a nun. His adversaries, headed by Bernard of Clairvaux, accused him of heresies, and he died on his way to Rome to defend himself. Abelard and Héloïse compiled a famous collection of their correspondence.

Abraham (**Abram**) (c.2000–1650 BC) Biblical character regarded as the ancestor of Israel and of several other nations; also an important figure in Islam. God called him to travel from the Chaldaean town of Ur to Canaan, promising him a land and descendants which would become a great nation (Genesis 12, 15). At 100 years of age he and his previously barren wife Sarah had a son, Isaac, who he nearly had to sacrifice as a test of faith (Genesis 21, 22).

Ali (d.661) Cousin and son-in-law of Muhammad, and fourth caliph. Married the prophet's daughter Fatima, thus founding the Fatimid Dynasty. Shia Muslims believe him to be the only true successor to Muhammad.

Anselm, St (1033–1109) Italian, born near Aosta. Theologian and philosopher who became abbot of the Abbey of Bec (1078) and later Archbishop of Canterbury (1093). Frequently in conflict with his masters over Church rights, Anselm was a major figure in early scholastic philosophy, remembered especially for his ontological proof for the existence of God.

Aquinas, St Thomas (1225–74) Italian, born Roccasecca, near Aquino. Combined Christian doctrine with the teachings of Aristotle. Wrote on principles of natural religion in *Summa contra Gentiles* (1259–64) and on proving the existence of God in *Summa Theologiae* (1266–73). Had considerable influence on theological thought of following ages.

Arius (c.250–336 AD) Libyan theologian, founder of the heresy known as Arianism. In c.319 AD he claimed that, in the doctrine of the Trinity, the Son was not co-equal or co-eternal with the Father, but only the first and highest of all finite beings. Fierce controversy followed, resolved at the Council of Nicaea (325), which condemned Arianism and affirmed the equality and unity of the three persons of the Trinity.

Athanasius, St (c.296–373 AD) Greek theologian and prelate, born Alexandria. Distinguished himself at the Council of Nicaea (AD 325) and was chosen Patriarch of Alexandria and Primate of Egypt. As a result of his stand against the heretic Arius, he was dismissed from his See on several occasions by emperors sympathetic to the Arian cause.

Thought and Belief

Augustine of Hippo, St (AD 354–430) Italian, born North Africa. One of the most influential Christian theologians, he was influenced primarily by Manicheanism, then Neoplatonism, before converting to Christianity in 386. Famous works are the *Confessions* (AD 400), *The City of God* (AD 412–27).

Baha'u'llah (Mirza Husayn Ali) (1817–92) Persian religious leader and founder of the Islamic Baha'i sect. Initially a follower of the Persian Babi sect, he was imprisoned in 1852, then exiled. In 1863 he proclaimed himself to be the prophet foretold by Bab-ed-din, and became the leader of the new Baha'i faith.

Barth, Karl (1886–1968) Swiss, born Basle. Protestant theologian, the major exponent of Reformed theology. His commentary (1919) on St Paul's Epistle to the Romans established his theological reputation, and he became a professor at Göttingen (1921), Münster (1925) and Bonn (1930). After refusing to take an unconditional oath to Hitler he was dismissed, and so became professor at Basle (1935–62). Other works include *Church Dogmatics* (1932–67).

Becket, St Thomas (à) (1118–70) English, born London. Became Chancellor (1155) and Archbishop of Canterbury (1162) but clashed with Henry II over Henry's desire to reduce the power of the Church. Henry's wish to be rid of this 'turbulent priest' led to Becket's murder in Canterbury Cathedral (29 December 1170). Pilgrimages to his burial place in Trinity Chapel are the subject of Chaucer's *Canterbury Tales* (c.1387–1400).

Bede, St ('the Venerable Bede') (c.673–735) Anglo-Saxon historian and theologian, born near Monkwearmouth, Durham. His most valuable work is the *Ecclesiastical History of the English People*, virtually the only source of English history before 731.

Besant, Annie (1847–1933) English, born London. Social reformer who became Vice-President of the National Secular Society (1874), and turned to theosophy after meeting Madame Blavatsky (1889); also championed nationalism and education in India and was President of the Indian National Congress (1917–23).

Blavatsky, Helena Petrovna (1831–91) Russian. Helped to found the Theosophical Society in New York (1875), and later carried on her work in India. Her psychic powers were widely acclaimed but did not survive scientific investigation. Writings include *Isis Unveiled* (1877).

Bodhidharma (6c) Indian, born near Madras (now Chennai). Monk and founder of the Ch'an (or Zen) sect of Buddhism. In 520 he travelled to China, where he had a famous audience with the emperor. He argued that merit leading to salvation could not be accumulated through good deeds, and taught meditation as the way to return to Buddha's spiritual precepts.

Boff, Leonardo (1938–) Brazilian, born Concordia. Franciscan liberation theologian, ordained in 1964, and Professor of Ethics, Philosophy of Religion and Ecology at the State University of Rio de Janeiro. His best-known work, *Jesus Christ Liberator* (1972), offers hope and justice for the oppressed rather than religious support of the status quo in Church and Society.

Bonhoeffer, Dietrich (1906–45) German, born Breslau. Lutheran pastor and theologian who left Germany in 1933 in protest against Nazi anti-Jewish legislation, then returned (1935) to become head of a pastoral seminary until its closure by the Nazis in 1937. Deeply involved in the German resistance movement, he was arrested (1943), imprisoned and hanged. His most influential works are *Ethics* (1949) and the posthumously published *Letters and Papers from Prison* (1951).

Booth, William (1829–1912) English, born Nottingham. In 1865 he founded the Salvation Army (so named in 1878) to do mission work in London's East End, waging war against such evils as sweated labour and child prostitution. His wife Catherine (1829–90) was an active partner in the work, as were his children Bramwell (1856–1929), Kate (1859–1955) and Evangeline (1865–1950).

Brunner, (Heinrich) Emil (1889–1966) Swiss, born Winterthur. Pastor and theologian, the author of nearly 400 books and articles, notably *The Mediator* (1927) and *The Divine Imperative* (1937). *The Divine–Human Encounter* (1944) reveals his debt to Martin Buber's 'I–Thou' understanding of the relationship between God and Man.

Buber, Martin (1878–1965) Jewish, born Vienna. Published many works on social and ethical problems and is best known for the religious philosophy expounded in *Ich und Du* (1922), contrasting personal relationships of mutuality and reciprocity with utilitarian or objective relationships.

Buddha (Prince Siddhartha Gautama) (c.560–c.480 BC) Founder of Buddhism, born the son of the rajah of the Sakya tribe ruling in Kapilavastu, Nepal. Aged about 30 he left the luxuries of the court, his beautiful wife, and all earthly ambitions for the life of an ascetic; after several years of severe austerities he saw in the contemplative life the perfect way to self-enlightenment. Taught for around 40 years, and gained many disciples and followers.

Bultmann, Rudolf Karl (1884–1976) German, born Wiefelstede. Protestant theologian who maintained that it was almost impossible to know anything about the historical Jesus, and that the Gospels needed to be 'de-mythologized' of their supernatural content; faith in a transcendent Christ, however, was still possible. Works include *Jesus and the Word* (1934), *The Gospel of John* (1941), *Theology of the New Testament* (1952–5) and *Jesus Christ and Mythology* (1960).

Calvin, John (1509–64) French, born Noyon. Protestant reformer and theologian active as a preacher and propagandist in France and Switzerland, founding a theocracy in Geneva which controlled most of the city's affairs. He left a double legacy to Protestantism by systematizing its doctrine and organizing its ecclesiastical discipline. Works include the influential *Institutes of the Christian Religion* (1536) and commentaries on most of the Old and New Testaments (published 1617).

Clement of Alexandria, St (Titus Flavius Clemens) (c.150–c.215 AD) Church Father, probably born in Athens, who became head of the catechetical school at Alexandria (c.180–201 AD). His most famous pupil was Origen. His chief surviving works are *Who is the Rich Man that is Saved* and the trilogy of *The Missionary*, *The Tutor* and *The Miscellanies*.

Confucius (K'ung Fu-tse, 'the Master K'ung') (551–479 BC) Chinese, born state of Lu (modern Shantung). Moral teacher who tried to replace old religious observances with moral values as the basis of social and political order, emphasizing the importance of respect and benevolence.

Thought and Belief

'Confucianism' became, and remained until recently, the state religion of China. His teachings are recorded in the *Analects*, written by his pupils after his death.

Cupitt, Don (1934–) English, born Oldham. Theologian and priest best known for the radical views expressed in his book *Sea of Faith* (1984), which became a successful television series. Other works include *Taking Leave of God* (1980) and *Reforming Christianity* (2001).

Dalai Lama (Tenzin Gyatso) (1935–) Spiritual and temporal head of Tibet, born Takster. He was designated the 14th incarnation of the Dalai Lama in 1937, and ruled Tibet from 1940 until 1959, when he fled to exile in India following China's suppression of a Tibetan uprising. Each successive Dalai Lama is held to be a reincarnation of the previous one, and is regarded as a manifestation of the Bodhisattva Avalokiteshvara. He won the Nobel peace prize in 1989.

Eckhart, Johannes (known as **Meister Eckhart**) (c.1260–c.1327) German, born Hochheim. Priest and theologian whose mystic pantheism influenced later religious mysticism and speculative philosophy. In 1325 he was accused of heresy by the Archbishop of Cologne, and two years after his death his writings were condemned by Pope John XXII.

Erasmus, Desiderius (1466–1536) Dutch, born Rotterdam. Influential Renaissance humanist and scholar who published many popular works including *Adagia* (*Adages*, 1500, 1508), *Enchiridion Militis Christiani* (*Handbook of a Christian Soldier*, 1503) and *Encomium Moriae* (*In Praise of Folly*, 1509).

Eusebius of Caesarea (c.264–340 AD) Palestinian theologian and Bishop of Caesarea, known as the Father of Church History. His great work, the *Ecclesiastical History*, is a record of the Christian Church down to AD 324.

Fox, George (1624–91) English, born Fenny Drayton, Leicestershire. Founder of the Society of Friends or 'Quakers', he argued for God-given inward light and against sacerdotalism and all social conventions. His life was a record of persecutions, imprisonments and missionary travel to several parts of the world.

Francis of Assisi, St (originally **Giovanni Bernadone**) (c.1181–1226) Italian, born Assisi. Left a worldly life in 1205 to care for the poor and the sick, and live as a hermit. His followers formed the Franciscan order, which by 1219 had 5000 members. Preached widely in Europe and the Holy Land, and on returning to Italy (1224) is said to have received the stigmata.

Gandhi, Mohandas Karamchand (known as **Mahatma**, 'of great soul') (1869–1948) Indian, born Poorbandar. Studied law in London, but in 1893 went to South Africa, where he opposed discriminatory legislation against Indians. Returned to India in 1914, and as leader of the Indian National Congress advocated a policy of non-violent non-cooperation to achieve independence; jailed for conspiracy (1922–4). After independence (1947) his attempts to stop the Hindu–Muslim conflict in Bengal led to his assassination by a Hindu fanatic. Revered worldwide as a pacifist and moral teacher.

Garvey, Marcus (1887–1940) Jamaican, born St Ann's Bay. Founded the Universal Negro Improvement Association (1914) which promoted worldwide black unity and pride. Wrote and taught in New York from 1916; called for a return to Africa and established the Black Star Line, a steamship line owned and operated by blacks.

Ghazali, Abu Hamid Mohammed al- (1058–1111) Persian, born Tus (near the modern Meshed). Islamic philosopher, theologian and jurist. Following a spiritual crisis (1095) he abandoned his position of Professor of Philosophy at Baghdad for the ascetic life of a mendicant sufi, later founding a monastic community at Tus. Works include *The Intentions of the Philosophers* and *The Revival of the Religious Sciences*.

Gobind Singh (1666–1708) Indian, born Patna. Last of the ten Sikh Gurus, he completed the process by which the Sikhs developed from the quietist faith of Guru Nanak to a militant creed. Established a small Sikh state in the Punjab foothills by military means, and instituted the Khalsa (a Sikh brotherhood marked by a new code of discipline), the 'Five Ks' regulating personal appearance, and common adoption of the name Singh for males and Kaur for females.

Graham, William Franklin ('**Billy**') (1918–) American, born Charlotte, North Carolina. Ordained a minister of the Southern Baptist Church in 1940, he quickly gained a reputation as a preacher. Since the 1950s he has conducted a series of highly organized revivalist crusades in the USA, the UK, South America and Europe.

Guru Nanak (1469–1539) Indian, born near Lahore, present-day Pakistan. Religious leader and founder of Sikhism. Though originally a Hindu, his doctrine, set out later in the *Adi Granth*, sought a fusion of Brahmanism and Islam on the grounds that both were monotheistic, although Nanak's own ideas leaned rather towards pantheism.

Gutiérrez, Gustavo (1928–) Peruvian, born Lima. Liberation theologian and priest, whose seminal *A Theology of Liberation* (1971) is dedicated to the needs of the poor and oppressed. Other works include *The Power of the Poor in History* (1984) and *Las Casas: In Search of the Poor of Jesus Christ* (1994).

Hick, John Harwood (1922–) English. Theologian and philosopher of religion known for his concern with questions of evil, the soul, eternal life, and the status of Christianity among the world religions, raised in works such as *Faith and Knowledge* (1966), *God has Many Names* (1982) and *The Fifth Dimension* (2004).

Huddleston, Trevor (1913–98) English, born Bedford. Anglican missionary and human rights campaigner. He entered the Community of the Resurrection and in 1943 he went to Johannesburg, where he became provincial of the order (1949–55); from 1960 to 1983 his posts included Bishop of Masasi (in Tanzania) and Archbishop of the Indian Ocean. After retiring he returned to London to become Chairman of the Anti-Apartheid Movement (1981).

Hutter, Jakob (d.1536) Swiss, born Moos. Anabaptist minister who founded the Hutterian Brethren (or Hutterites) in Moravia (1528), but was condemned and burned as a heretic in South Tyrol. The Brethren were organized in communal farms and espoused pacifism, adult baptism and rejection of oaths, and later became widespread in the USA.

Ignatius Loyola, St (originally **Iñigo López de Recalde**) (1491–1556) Spanish, born Loyola Castle, Guipúzcoa. Soldier and founder of the Jesuits. While convalescing he experienced a religious awakening and renounced military life; in 1534 with Frances Xavier he founded the Society of Jesus, establishing schools and sending

Thought and Belief

out missionaries to Japan, India and Brazil. Works include the influential *Spiritual Exercises*.

Irenaeus, St (c.130–c.200 AD) Greek, born Asia Minor. Theologian, bishop and Father of the Greek Church, chiefly remembered for his opposition to Gnosticism (especially the Valentinians), on which he wrote his *Against Heresies*.

Jansen, Cornelius (Otto) (1585–1638) Dutch, born Acquoi. Roman Catholic theologian and Bishop of Ypres, founder of the reform movement known as Jansenism. His major work *Augustinus* (published 1640) sought to prove that St Augustine's teachings were opposed to those of the Jesuit schools, and was condemned by Pope Urban VIII in 1642; controversy raged in France until a large number of Jansenists emigrated to the Netherlands.

Jenkins, David Edward (1925–) English, born Bromley, Kent. Theologian and prelate who was appointed Bishop of Durham (1984–94) amidst controversy over his interpretation of the Virgin Birth and the Resurrection. Writings include *The Contradiction of Christianity* (1976) and *The Calling of a Cuckoo* (2002).

Jesus Christ (Jesus of Nazareth) (c.4 BC–c.30 AD) Jewish teacher, born Bethlehem, the central figure of Christianity, which holds that he is the Son of God who was crucified and resurrected to redeem humanity from sin. In Islam he is considered a prophet second only to Muhammad. Began his ministry (mainly recorded in the New Testament Gospels) with baptism by John in the River Jordan (Luke 3.1), after which he gathered a group of 12 disciples and began healing the sick and demon-possessed, performing miracles, and proclaiming the coming of the kingdom of God, but was executed by order of the Roman procurator Pontius Pilate.

John of the Cross, St (originally **Juan de Yepes y Álvarez**) (1542–91) Spanish, born Fontiveros. Founded the Discalced Carmelites with St Teresa (1568); imprisoned in Toledo (1577), where he wrote a number of poems highly regarded in Spanish mystical literature. After escaping, he became Vicar Provincial of Andalusia (1585–7).

Kempis, Thomas à (Thomas Hemerken) (1379–1471) German, born Kempen. In 1400 he entered the Augustinian convent of Agnietenberg near Zwolle, was ordained in 1413, chosen sub-prior in 1429, and died there as superior. His many writings include the influential devotional work *The Imitation of Christ* (c.1415–24).

King, Martin Luther (1929–68) American, born Atlanta, Georgia. Minister and civil rights leader who challenged the segregation laws of the Southern states, and after 1965 turned his attention to social conditions in the North. Received the Kennedy peace prize and the Nobel peace prize (both 1964); assassinated in Memphis, Tennessee.

Knox, John (c.1513–72) Scottish, born Haddington, Lothian. Protestant religious reformer and chaplain to Edward VI. On Mary I's accession (1553) he fled to Geneva, where he was much influenced by Calvin. Returned to Scotland permanently in 1559 where he founded the Church of Scotland (1560). Contributed to the Second Book of Common Prayer; other writings include *First Blast of the Trumpet against the Monstrous Regiment of Women* (1558).

Küng, Hans (1928–) Swiss, born Sursee. Roman Catholic theologian whose questioning of Catholic doctrine has found an audience especially among lay people. Works such as *Infallible? An Inquiry* (1971) provoked the Vatican authorities

to withdraw his licence to teach as a Catholic theologian in 1979; other writings include *Does God Exist?* (1980).

Lao-tzu (Lao Zi) (6c BC) Chinese philosopher and sage, the founder of Taoism. Probably a legendary figure, he is represented as the older contemporary of Confucius, against whom most of his teaching is directed. *The Tao Te Ching* ('Way of Power'), the most venerated of the three classical texts of Taoism, is attributed to him, though it dates from 300 years after his death.

Luther, Martin (1483–1546) German, born Eisleben. Priest and religious reformer whose notoriety began after a visit to Rome in 1510–11, where he was angered by the sale of indulgences. Drew up 95 theses attacking the papal system (1517), which he nailed on the church door at Wittenberg. Violent controversy followed; the drawing up of the Augsburg Confession, where he was represented by Melanchthon, marked the culmination of the German Reformation (1530). His translation of the Bible is a landmark of German literature.

Maharishi Mahesh Yogi (originally **Mahesh Prasad Varma**) (1917–2008) Indian, born Jabalpur. Founder of Transcendental Meditation, a relaxation technique which first became popular in the West in the 1950s and 1960s; went on to found the Spiritual Regeneration movement, aimed at solving world problems through meditation.

Mahavira, Vardhamana (c.540–468 BC) Indian, born near Vaisali. Founder of Jainism, he renounced the world aged about 30 to lead a severely ascetic life. His sermons and dialogues, stressing non-injury to all living things, are believed by some Jain adherents to be collected in the Svetambara canon of scripture.

Manes (Mani) (c.216–76 AD) Prophet active in Persia from AD 240, the founder of Manichaeism, which holds that the material world represents an invasion of the realm of light by the powers of darkness. The Zoroastrians condemned the sect and executed Manes, but it spread rapidly in the West, and survived until the 10c.

Mbiti, John Samuel (1931–) Kenyan pastor, theologian and Director of the World Council of Churches Ecumenical Institute (1972–80). His writings maintain that the Christian message can be seen as a fulfilment of traditional African beliefs, and include *African Religions and Philosophy* (1969) and *Bible and Theology in African Christianity* (1987).

Melanchthon, Philip (originally **Philip Schwarzerd**) (1497–1560) German, born Bretten. Protestant reformer who became Luther's fellow-worker and composed the Augsburg Confession (1530). After Luther's death he led the German Reformation movement, but his concessions to the Catholics led to painful controversies. Works include the influential *Loci Communes* (1521).

Mencius (Meng-tzu) (c.372–c.298 BC) Chinese, born Shantung. Philosopher who popularized and developed Confucian ideas and made many proposals for social and political reform; his beliefs are recorded in a book compiled after his death, *Book of Meng-tzu*.

Moltmann, Jürgen (1926–) German, born Hamburg. Reformed theologian whose espousal of a theology of hope marked a reaction against the individualistic existential approach of Rudolf Bultmann. Best known for trilogies such as *Theology of Hope* (1967), *The Crucified God* (1974) and *The Church in the Power of the Spirit* (1977).

Moses (c.15c–13c BC) Biblical character, a prophet

506

and lawgiver, who escaped the slaughter of all male Jewish babies and was brought up in the Egyptian court. Was called by God to lead the enslaved Hebrews out of Egypt, which involved the miraculous crossing of the Red Sea (Exodus 14) and the revelation of the Ten Commandments on Mount Sinai (Exodus 20). Traditionally considered the author of the Pentateuch.

Muhammad (Mohammed, Mahomet) (c.570–c.632) Arab prophet and founder of Islam, born Mecca. His teachings were based on revelations of the word of Allah (God), transcribed in the Koran, which holds that God's mercy is principally to be obtained by prayer, fasting and almsgiving. Established a strong following in Medina by 622, and in 629 seized control of Mecca by armed force, thus securing the new religion in Arabia. Died in the home of Ayeshah, the favourite of his nine wives. His tomb in the mosque at Medina is venerated throughout Islam.

Muhammad, Elijah (originally **Elijah Poole**) (1897–1975) American, born near Sandersville, Georgia. Leader of the Black Muslims from 1934, and advocate of racial separation; imprisoned during World War II for discouraging his followers from registering for the draft. His national representative from 1963 was Louis Farrakhan (1933–), who later succeeded him as leader of the Nation of Islam.

Nagarjuna (c.150–c.250 AD) Indian Buddhist monk-philosopher, the founder of the Madhyamika or Middle Path school of Buddhism. His teachings concentrate on the contradictions inherent in philosophy while stressing the liberating power of enlightenment.

Newman, John Henry, Cardinal (1801–90) English, born London. Prelate and theologian, a vigorous member of the Oxford Movement until its dissolution (1841) and later a convert to Catholicism (1845). Joined the Oratorians in Rome, then established his own community in Birmingham; made cardinal in 1879. Works include the spiritual autobiography *Apologia pro Vita Sua* (1864).

Niebuhr, Reinhold (1892–1971) American, born Wright City, Missouri. Theologian who became an evangelical pastor in working-class Detroit (1915–28) and Professor of Christian Ethics in the Union Theological Seminary, New York (1928–1960). An advocate of Christian Realism, his works include *Moral Man and Immoral Society* (1932), *Faith and History* (1949) and *Structure of Nations and Empires* (1959).

Origen (c.185–c.254 AD) Christian scholar, theologian, and an early Greek Father of the Church, born probably in Alexandria. Head of the catechical school in Alexandria (c.211–232 AD); imprisoned and tortured during the persecution under Decius in 250. His views on the unity of God and speculations about the salvation of the Devil were condemned by Church Councils in the 5c–6c.

Otto, Rudolf (1869–1937) German, born Peine. Theologian and philosopher who, following several journeys to the East, published *The Idea of the Holy* (1923), in which he defines religious experience as a non-rational but objective sense of the 'numinous', inspiring both awe and a promise of exaltation and bliss. Other works include *The Philosophy of Religion* (1931) and *Mysticism East and West* (1932).

Paley, William (1743–1805) English, born Peterborough. Theologian and priest who, in works such as *Evidences of Christianity* (1794) and *Natural Theology* (1802), aimed to derive a

proof of Christian belief from the order inherent in creation. Other works such as *Principles of Moral and Political Philosophy* (1785) expounded a form of utilitarianism.

Pannenberg, Wolfhart (1928–) German, born Stettin (now Poland). Lutheran theologian whose work, *Jesus – God and Man* (1964), opposes Bultmann's programme of demythologization with the claim that the resurrection of Jesus is central to the Christian faith. Other works include the three-volume *Systematic Theology* (1988–93).

Paul, St (also known as **Saul of Tarsus**) (d.c.64 AD) New Testament figure born of Jewish parents in Tarsus, Cilicia. Originally a fervent Pharisee and persecutor of Christians, he converted to Christianity after a vision of Christ during a journey to Damascus (c.34–5 AD), and became a passionate evangelist and missionary, especially to Gentiles, throughout the Roman world. After imprisonment in Jerusalem and Rome c.60–4 AD he was probably executed under Nero. Thirteen New Testament letters and some other works are traditionally attributed to him.

Rahner, Karl (1904–84) German, born Freiburg. Roman Catholic theologian and priest whose writings maintain a dialogue between traditional dogma and contemporary existential questions. Advised Vatican Council II. Best known for his *Theological Investigations* (1961–81); other works include *Prayers for a Lifetime* (1984) and the autobiographical interviews *I Remember* (1985).

Rajneesh, Bhagwan Shree (originally **Rajneesh Chandra Mohan**) (1931–90) Indian exponent of yogic spirituality who attracted many Westerners to his ashram in Poona in the 1970s, relocating to Oregon in 1981. His flamboyant lifestyle and advocacy of free sexual expression met with some scepticism, but a nucleus of devotees remained loyal up to his death in 1990.

Ramakrishna Paramahasa (originally **Gadadhar Chattopadhyaya**) (1836–86) Indian, born Hooghly. Hindu religious teacher who formed a religious order which bore his name and established its headquarters in Calcutta (now Kolkata). Among his chief tenets is that all religions are paths to the same goal; his most noteworthy disciple was Swami Vivekananda.

Ramsey, Ian Thomas (1915–72) English, born Kearsley, near Bolton. Theologian and Bishop of Durham (1966–72), respected for his intellectual contribution to the Church of England's stance on educational and social matters. His theological work includes *Models and Mystery* (1964) and *Models for Divine Activity* (1973).

Robinson, J(ohn) A(rthur) T(homas) (1919–83) English, born Canterbury. Theologian and Bishop of Woolwich (1959–69) best known for his bestselling book *Honest to God* (1963), which he described as an attempt to explain the Christian faith to modern man. Other works include *Jesus and His Coming* (1957) and *Redating the New Testament* (1976).

Roger, Brother (originally **Roger Louis Schütz**) (1915–2005) Swiss, born Provence. Founder of a quasi-monastic community at Taizé, France, where the weekly services of prayer and reflection have, since the late 1950s, been attended each year by thousands of people from around the world. Devoted himself to reconciliation of the different Christian churches and particularly addressed Christian youth. On the verge of retirement, he was stabbed to death at a service by a schizophrenic woman.

Thought and Belief

Thought and Belief

Ruether, Rosemary Radford (1936–) American, born Minneapolis, Minnesota. Theologian who has written extensively on women and the need to affirm the feminine dimension of religion. Works include *New Woman/New Earth* (1975), *Sexism and God-Talk* (1983) and *Women–Church* (1985).

Russell, Charles Taze (known as **Pastor Russell**) (1852–1916) American, born Pittsburgh, Pennsylvania. Founder of the Jehovah's Witnesses movement, a sect with a literalist interpretation of the Bible and an apocalyptic bent.

Sankara (Samkara, Sankaracharya) (c.700–50) Indian, born Kalati. Philosopher and theologian who is the most famous exponent of Advaita or non-dualistic Vedanta, and is the source of the main currents of modern Hindu thought. His teaching that Brahma alone has true existence, and the goal of the self is to become one with the Divine, influenced Ramakrishna. Founded monastic centres throughout India.

Schleiermacher, Friedrich (Ernst Daniel) (1768–1834) German, born Breslau. Theologian, philosopher and priest widely held to be the founder of modern Protestant theology; led the movement which brought about the union of the Lutheran and Reformed Churches in Prussia (1817). His most important work is *The Christian Faith* (1821–2).

Schweitzer, Albert (1875–1965) German, born Kaysersberg. Medical missionary, theologian, musician and philosopher. Despite his international reputation in music and theology, he turned to studying medicine (1905), and after qualifying (1913) departed with his wife to set up a hospital to fight leprosy and sleeping sickness in Lambaréné, French Equatorial Africa. Awarded the Nobel peace prize in 1952. Religious writings include *The Quest of the Historical Jesus* (1906).

Smith, Joseph (1805–44) American, born Sharon, Vermont. Founder of Mormonism, he was told in a vision of a hidden gospel written on golden plates, the *Book of Mormon*, which was unearthed in 1827. Despite ridicule and hostility, the new 'Church of Jesus Christ of Latter-day Saints' (founded 1830) rapidly gained converts, and continues to be influential in the USA and worldwide.

Steiner, Rudolf (1861–1925) Austrian, born Kraljevec. Social philosopher, the founder of anthroposophy, he established his first 'school of spiritual science' in Dornach, Switzerland (1912), integrating ideas of psychology, ecology and physical therapy. Many schools and research institutions arose from his ideas, notably the Rudolf Steiner Schools for children with special needs.

Strauss, David Friedrich (1808–74) German, born Ludwigsburg. Theologian who sought to prove in his controversial *Life of Jesus* (1835) that the gospel history is a collection of myths, each containing nevertheless a nucleus of historical truth. Other works include *The Old and New Faiths* (1872), several biographies, and lectures on Voltaire (1870).

Swami Vivekananda (originally **Narendranath Dutt**) (1863–1902) Indian, born Calcutta (now Kolkata). Hindu missionary and chief disciple of Ramakrishna Paramahasa, a persuasive exponent of Hinduism in the West; organized the now worldwide Ramakrishna Mission.

Swedenborg, Emanuel (originally **Swedberg**) (1688–1772) Swedish, born Stockholm. Mystic and scientist who wrote on algebra, navigation, astronomy and chemistry, but became increasingly convinced that he had direct access to the spiritual world, which he explored in such works as *Heavenly Arcana* (1749–56) and *The New Jerusalem* (1758). In 1787 his followers in London formed the Church of the New Jerusalem.

Teilhard de Chardin, Pierre (1881–1955) French, born Sarcenat. Geologist, palaeontologist, Jesuit priest and philosopher whose unorthodox ideas led to a ban on his teaching and publishing. His major work, *The Phenomenon of Man* (1955), argues that humanity is in a continuous process of evolution towards a perfect spiritual state.

Teresa of Ávila, St (1515–82) Spanish, born Ávila. Carmelite nun noted for her asceticism and ecstatic visions. To re-establish the ancient Carmelite rule, in 1562 she founded the first of her 16 religious houses, and in 1568 she helped St John of the Cross found the first community of reformed Carmelite friars. Among her writings are her autobiography *The Way of Perfection* and the mystical work *The Interior Castle*.

Teresa of Calcutta, Mother (originally **Agnes Gonxha Bojaxhiu**) (1910–97) Albanian, born Skopje (now Macedonia). Roman Catholic nun and missionary in India. Became principal of a convent school in Calcutta (now Kolkata), but in 1948 left to work alone in the slums, especially with destitute children. Opened her House for the Dying in 1952, and in 1957 began work with lepers and in many disaster areas of the world. Awarded the Nobel peace prize in 1979.

Tertullian (c.160–220AD) Theologian and Father of the Latin Church, born Carthage, whose opposition to worldliness in the Church culminated in his becoming a leader of the Montanist sect (c.207AD). The first to produce major Christian works in Latin, he had a profound influence on the development of ecclesiastical language, and also wrote against heathens, Jews and heretics.

Tillich, Paul (Johannes) (1886–1965) German, born Starzeddel, Prussia. Protestant theologian and philosopher, an early critic of the Nazis whose main work *Systematic Theology* (1951–63) combines elements of existentialism and the ontological tradition in Christian thought. He explained faith as a reality transcending finite existence rather than a belief in a personal God, leading to oversimplified accusations of atheism. Popular works include *The Courage to Be* (1952), *Dynamics of Faith* (1957).

Tutu, Desmond Mpilo (1931–) South African, born Klerksdorp. Became an Anglican parish priest (1960) and rapidly rose to become Bishop of Lesotho (1977), the first black Bishop of Johannesburg (1984) and Archbishop of Cape Town (1986). A fierce critic of the apartheid system, he has nevertheless condemned the use of violence. Awarded the Nobel peace prize in 1984; chaired the Truth and Reconciliation Commission from 1995.

Wesley, John (1703–91) English, born Epworth, Lincolnshire. Priest and founder of Methodism. His evangelistic zeal led to persecution and isolation from the Church, and he was driven to preach to huge crowds in the open air in Bristol, where he founded the first Methodist chapel (1739). An energetic traveller and prolific writer, he produced grammars, histories, biographies, collections of hymns, his own sermons and journals, and a magazine.

Wycliffe, John (c.1330–84) English, born near Richmond, North Yorkshire. Religious reformer and rector of Lutterworth who wrote many popular tracts in English (as opposed to Latin) attacking the Church hierarchy, and issued the first English translation of the Bible. His opinions were condemned by the Church and his followers known derisively as 'Lollards'.

Young, Brigham (1801–77) American, born Whitingham, Vermont. Mormon leader who became one of the 12 apostles of the Mormon Church in 1835, and succeeded Joseph Smith as President (1844); later founded Salt Lake City. Appointed Governor of Utah in 1850, but was replaced in 1857 when an army was sent to establish federal law and suppress polygamy in the territory.

Zoroaster (Zarathushtra, Zaradusht) (c.630–

c.553 BC) Iranian religious leader and prophet, the founder or reformer of the Parsee religion known as Zoroastrianism. His visions of Ahura Mazda led him to preach against polytheism, and as the centre of a group of chieftains, he carried on a struggle for the establishment of a holy agricultural state against Turanian and Vedic aggressors.

Zwingli, Huldreich or **Ulrich** (1484–1531) Swiss, born Wildhaus. Protestant reformer and priest who opposed the selling of indulgences and espoused the Reformed doctrines, but in 1524 disagreed with Martin Luther over the question of the Eucharist. War between the cantons followed, and he was killed in an attack on Zurich.

Templeton Prize

Awarded for progress toward research or discoveries about spiritual realities.

1973	Mother Teresa, India
1974	Brother Roger, France
1975	Sir Sarvepalli Radhakrishnan, India
1976	Cardinal Leon Joseph Suenens, Belgium
1977	Chiara Lubich, Italy
1978	Rev Prof Thomas F Torrance, UK
1979	Rev Nikkyo Niwano, Japan
1980	Prof Ralph Wendell Burhoe, USA
1981	Dame Cecily Saunders, UK
1982	Rev Dr Billy Graham, USA
1983	Aleksandr Solzhenitsyn, USSR
1984	Rev Michael Bourdeaux, UK
1985	Sir Alister Hardy, UK
1986	Rev Dr James I McCord, USA
1987	Rev Prof Stanley L Jaki, Hungary/USA
1988	Dr Inamullah Khan, Pakistan
1989	Very Rev Lord MacLeod of Fiunary, UK; Prof Carl Friedrich von Weizsäcker, Germany
1990	Baba Amte, India; Prof L Charles Birch, Australia
1991	Rt Hon Lord Jakobovits, UK
1992	Rev Dr Kyung-Chik Han, South Korea
1993	Charles W Colson, USA
1994	Michael Novak, USA
1995	Paul Charles William Davies, UK
1996	William Rohl Bright, USA
1997	Pandurang Shastri Athavale, India
1998	Sir Sigmund Sternberg, Hungary/UK
1999	Ian Graeme Barbour, USA
2000	Prof Freeman J Dyson, USA
2001	Rev Canon Dr Arthur Peacocke, UK
2002	Rev Dr John C Polkinghorne, UK
2003	Prof Holmes Rolston III
2004	George F R Ellis
2005	Prof Charles H Townes, USA
2006	Prof John D Barrow, UK
2007	Prof Charles Taylor, Canada
2008	Prof Michael Heller, Poland

Thought and Belief

Thought and Belief

Religious symbols

Christian

Father	God Son	Holy Spirit
All-seeing eye	Fish	Sevenfold flame

The Trinity

Equilateral Triangle	Triangle in circle	Circle within triangle

Jewish

Seven-branched candlestick The Menorah   Abraham

Pentateuch (The Law)   Doorposts and lintel (Passover)

Twelve tribes of Israel   Star of David

Crosses

Barbée   Trefly   Canterbury   Celtic   Cercelée   Cross crosslet

Crux ansata   Globical   Graded (Calvary)   Greek   Iona   Jerusalem

Latin   Maltese   Millvine   Papal   Patée   Patée formée   Patriarchal (or Lorraine)

Potent   Raguly or Ragulée   Russian Orthodox   St Andrew's (Saltire)   St Peter's   Tau (St Anthony's)

Ankh (Egyptian)	Yin-yang (Taoism; symbol of harmony)	Torii (Shinto)	Om (Hinduism, Buddhism, Jainism; sacred syllable)	Ik Oankar (Sikhism; symbol of God)	Swastika	Yantra: Sri Cakra (wheel of fortune)

Signs of the zodiac

In astronomy, the zodiac is an imaginary belt in the heavens which extends 8° on either side of the Sun's ecliptic. It is divided into twelve equal parts, each of which once contained one of the zodiacal constellations, although some no longer do.

In astrology, the zodiac is a chart or diagram representing this band of the sky and the signs of the zodiac contained within it, although the signs may no longer coincide with the constellations after which they are named. The dates of transit from one sign to another vary slightly from year to year; those given below are approximate.

Sign	Dates	Sign	Dates
Aries	21 March–19 April	Libra	23 September–23 October
Taurus	20 April–20 May	Scorpio	24 October–21 November
Gemini	21 May–21 June	Sagittarius	22 November–21 December
Cancer	22 June–22 July	Capricorn	22 December–19 January
Leo	23 July–22 August	Aquarius	20 January–18 February
Virgo	23 August–22 September	Pisces	19 February–20 March

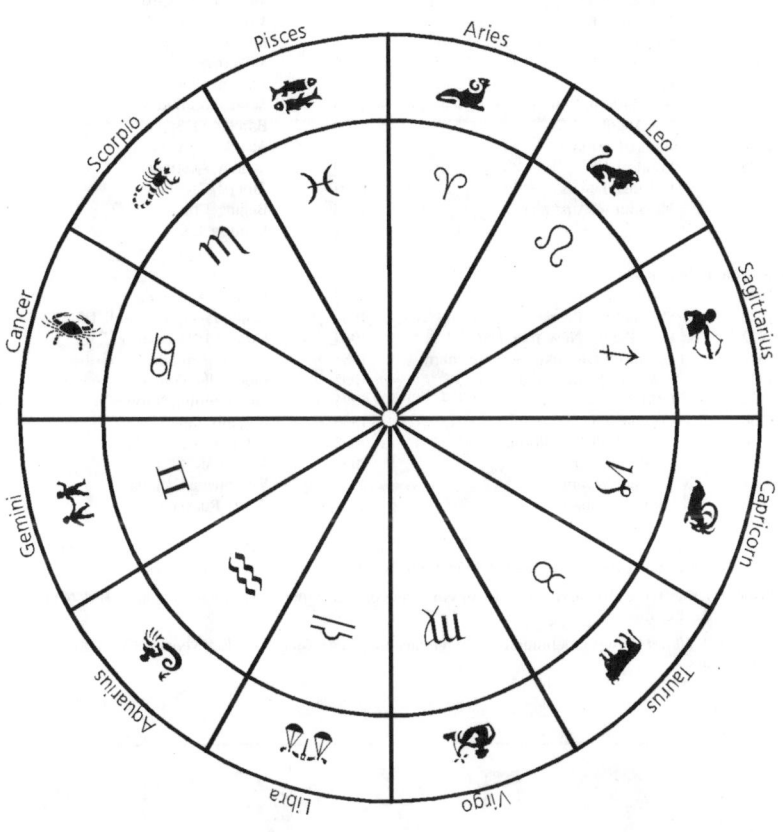

SPORTS AND GAMES

Olympic Games

First Modern Olympic Games took place in 1896, founded by Frenchman Baron de Coubertin (1863–1937); held every four years; women first competed in 1900; first separate Winter Games celebrations in 1924.

Venues

■ Summer Games

1896	Athens, Greece	1960	Rome, Italy
1900	Paris, France	1964	Tokyo, Japan
1904	St Louis, USA	1968	Mexico City, Mexico
1908	London, UK	1972	Munich, W Germany
1912	Stockholm, Sweden	1976	Montreal, Canada
1920	Antwerp, Belgium	1980	Moscow, USSR
1924	Paris, France	1984	Los Angeles, USA
1928	Amsterdam, Netherlands	1988	Seoul, South Korea
1932	Los Angeles, USA	1992	Barcelona, Spain
1936	Berlin, Germany	1996	Atlanta, USA
1948	London, UK	2000	Sydney, Australia
1952	Helsinki, Finland	2004	Athens, Greece
1956	Melbourne, Australia	2008	Beijing, China
		2012	London, UK

■ Winter Games

1924	Chamonix, France	1976	Innsbruck, Austria
1928	St Moritz, Switzerland	1980	Lake Placid, New York, USA
1932	Lake Placid, New York, USA	1984	Sarajevo, Yugoslavia
1936	Garmisch-Partenkirchen, Germany	1988	Calgary, Canada
1948	St Moritz, Switzerland	1992	Albertville, France
1952	Oslo, Norway	1994	Lillehammer, Norway
1956	Cortina, Italy	1998	Nagano, Japan
1960	Squaw Valley, California, USA	2002	Salt Lake City, USA
1964	Innsbruck, Austria	2006	Turin, Italy
1968	Grenoble, France	2010	Vancouver, Canada
1972	Sapporo, Japan	2014	Sochi, Russia

The 1956 equestrian events were held at Stockholm, Sweden, owing to quarantine laws in Australia.

Olympic Games were also held in 1906 in Athens, Greece, to commemorate the tenth anniversary of the birth of the modern Games.

In 1994, the Winter Games celebrations were readjusted to take place every four years between the Summer Games years.

Leading medal winners

Summer Games (including 2008)	Gold	Silver	Bronze	Total
1 USA	933	729	641	2303
2 Russia[1]	549	458	438	1445
3 Germany[2]	247	284	319	850
4 Great Britain	208	255	249	712
5 France	190	207	230	627
6 Italy	190	157	174	521
7 Sweden	141	159	174	474
8 Hungary	159	141	158	458
9 Australia	134	141	169	444
10 East Germany	153	129	127	409

Winter Games	Gold	Silver	Bronze	Total
1 Russia[1]	121	89	86	296
2 Norway	96	100	84	280
3 Germany[2]	79	80	58	217
4 USA	78	81	58	217
5 Austria	51	64	71	186
6 Finland	41	58	52	151
7 Canada	37	38	44	119
8 Sweden	43	32	43	118
9 Switzerland	38	37	43	118
10 East Germany	39	36	35	110

[1] Includes medals won by the former USSR team, and by the Unified Team (Armenia, Azerbaijan, Belarus, Georgia, Kazakhstan, Kyrgyzstan, Moldova, Russia, Tajikistan, Turkmenistan, Ukraine and Uzbekistan) in 1992.
[2] Includes medals won as West Germany 1968–88.

Paralympic Games

Summer Games first held in Stoke Mandeville, England, in 1952 (solely for competitors from the UK and the Netherlands), then once every four years from 1960; Winter Games first held in Örnsköldsvik, Sweden, in 1976, then once every four years until 1992, after which they were held once every four years from 1994, to coincide with the Winter Olympic Games.

Leading medal winners

Summer Games (1984–2008)	Gold	Silver	Bronze	Total
1 USA	444	409	431	1284
2 Great Britain	361	364	352	1077
3 Germany	307	340	319	966
4 Australia	248	258	247	753
5 France	247	256	236	739
6 Canada	274	220	243	737
7 China	232	187	135	554
8 Spain	186	161	186	533
9 Sweden	158	133	90	381
10 Poland	120	141	114	375

Winter Games (1984–2006)	Gold	Silver	Bronze	Total
1 Germany	97	85	83	265
2 Austria	95	80	83	258
3 USA	92	93	64	249
4 Norway	103	75	65	243
5 Russia[1]	52	52	34	138
6 Switzerland	35	54	48	137
7 France	43	41	43	127
8 Finland	54	31	39	124
9 Canada	24	33	38	95
10 Japan	14	24	25	63

[1] Includes medals won by the former USSR team, and by the Unified Team (Armenia, Azerbaijan, Belarus, Georgia, Kazakhstan, Kyrgyzstan, Moldova, Russia, Tajikistan, Turkmenistan, Ukraine and Uzbekistan) in 1992.

Source: International Paralympic Committee

Sports and Games

Sports and Games

Commonwealth Games

First held as the British Empire Games in 1930; became the British Empire and Commonwealth Games in 1954; current title adopted in 1970; take place every four years and between Olympic summer games.

Venues

1930	Hamilton, Canada
1934	London, England
1938	Sydney, Australia
1950	Auckland, New Zealand
1954	Vancouver, Canada
1958	Cardiff, Wales
1962	Perth, Australia
1966	Kingston, Jamaica
1970	Edinburgh, Scotland
1974	Christchurch, New Zealand
1978	Edmonton, Canada
1982	Brisbane, Australia
1986	Edinburgh, Scotland
1990	Auckland, New Zealand
1994	Victoria, Canada
1998	Kuala Lumpur, Malaysia
2002	Manchester, England
2006	Melbourne, Australia
2010	New Delhi, India
2014	Glasgow, Scotland

Leading medal winners

Nation	Gold	Silver	Bronze	Total
1 Australia	731	619	556	1906
2 England	578	554	569	1701
3 Canada	413	443	462	1318
4 New Zealand	124	168	238	530
5 Scotland	82	94	154	330
6 South Africa	92	92	96	280
7 India	102	97	72	271
8 Wales	49	69	97	215
9 Kenya	59	47	56	162
10 Nigeria	39	47	57	143

Sports

aikido Ancient Japanese art of self-defence; combination of karate and judo deriving from ancient jujitsu; two main systems; *Tomiki-ryo* and *ki-aikido*.

American football ▶ football

angling Fishing with rod, line and hook in the form of freshwater, fly, game and deep-sea fishing. Rules govern time of year when different types of fishing take place, and type and amount of bait used. Oldest fishing club is in Ellem, Scotland.

archery Shooting with a bow and arrow at a circular target divided into ten scoring zones, the smallest of which is coloured gold and worth ten points; popular as sport from 17c. In competition, arrows are fired from 30, 50, 70 and 90 metres (men), and 30, 50, 60 and 70 metres (women).

athletics Tests of running, jumping, throwing and walking skills. The running or **track** events range from the 100m (328ft) sprint to the 42.2km / 26.2mi marathon; jumping and throwing or **field** events consist of high jump, long jump, triple jump and pole vault, and the discus throw, shot put, javelin throw and hammer throw (men only). Multi-event competitions are the **decathlon** (10) for men and the **heptathlon** (7) for women. Athletics dates to c.3800 BC Egypt; International Amateur Athletic Federation founded 1912.

badminton Indoor game, two or four players, played on court 13.4m/44ft long and 5.2m/17ft wide (6.1m/20ft wide for doubles), using rackets, a shuttlecock (cork or plastic half sphere with 'feathers') and a raised central net; object is to volley the shuttlecock over the net so that the opponent is unable to return it; name derives from Badminton House, the seat of the Duke of Beaufort, where game played 19c, but it dates from China over 2200 years ago.

bagatelle Restricted form of billiards, played on a table with nine numbered cups instead of pockets; takes many different forms which vary according to local conditions.

baseball Team game played by two sides of 25 possible players on a diamond-shaped field which has bases at the corners, each 27.43m/90ft apart. Essential pieces of equipment are long cylindrical bats, the solid ball 'pitched' from the 'mound', and the glove worn by each fielder; team 'at bat' tries to score most runs by having its players circle the three bases and touch home plate before being put out by the team 'in the field'; players out if their hit is caught, if they are tagged with the ball when 'off-base', if the base is touched by the ball before they arrive at it, or if they 'strike out', ie fail to hit the ball after three pitches have been judged strikes by the umpire; 'home run' scored when player hits ball, circles all three bases and crosses home plate; game consists of nine innings; popularly believed to have been invented in 1839 by a West Point cadet, Abner Doubleday, at Cooperstown, New York.

basketball Five-a-side team ball game played on a hard surface court approx 28m/92ft by 15m/49ft, with a bottomless basket 3.05m/10ft above the ground at each end; object is to move the ball by a series of passing and bouncing moves and throw it through the opponent's basket; invented by James Naismith in 1891 at Springfield, Massachusetts, but similar game believed to have been played in 10c Mexico.

biathlon Combined test of cross-country skiing and rifle shooting. It is used as a form of military training, based on the old military patrol race. Men's individual competitions are over 10 and 20km (6.2 and 12.4mi), and women's over 5 and 10km (3.1 and 6.2mi). At designated points on the course, competitors have to fire either standing or prone at a fixed target.

billiards Indoor table game played in many different forms. The standard green baize-covered table measures 3.66m/12ft by 1.83m/6ft and has six pockets into which the players use a tapered pole or *cue* to 'pot' the one red or two white balls to score, the balls going in off another ball. Scoring also achieved by making 'cannons' (hitting the white ball so that it successively hits the two others). Originally an outdoor game, its origins are uncertain; an early reference is 1429 when Louis XI of France owned a billiard table.

bobsledding Propelling oneself along snow or ice on a sledge, popular as a sport since 19c; special luge run was created at Davos, Switzerland, in 1879. Most popular competitive forms; **luge tobogganing** on a small sledge and **bobsleighing** in a steel-bodied two- or four-person toboggan down special tracks at speeds of up to 130kph/80mph; earliest known sledge dates to c.6500 BC Finland.

bowling Delivering a rubber or plastic ball along a 18.3m/60ft wooden lane to knock down pins; in **tenpin bowling** these are often mechanically replaced; popularized by third- and fourth-century German churchgoers, who would roll a ball at a *kegel*, a club used for protection; a hit would absolve them from sin. The game of nine pins was taken to the USA by Dutch and German immigrants; when outlawed, 10th pin introduced as a way around the legislation.

bowls Indoor or outdoor game played as singles, pairs, triples or fours. **Lawn bowls** ('flat green') is played on a flat level rink; **crown green bowls** is played on an uneven green raised at the centre (usually singles and pairs only); object is to deliver your bowl nearest to the *jack*, a small target ball; similar game believed to have been played by the Egyptians in c.5200 BC. Glasgow solicitor William Mitchell drew up rules for modern bowls in 1848.

boxing Fist-fighting between two people, usually men, in a roped ring 4.3–6.1m/14–20ft square. Professional championship bouts constitute 12 three-minute rounds; amateur bouts three rounds, unless one fighter is knocked out or retires, the referee halts the fight, or a fighter is disqualified. The 17 weight divisions range from straw-weight for fighters under 48kg/105lb to heavyweight, normally over 88kg/195lb. Boxing dates from Greek and Roman times; first known match in Britain 1681 when Duke of Albemarle organized one between his butler and butcher in New Hall, Essex. First rules drawn up 1743, when each round lasted until one fighter was knocked down; gloves and three-minute rounds introduced 1867.

bull-fighting National sport in Spain, where it is called *corrida de toros* and the leading *matadors* are national heroes. *Picadors* are sent into the bull ring to weaken the bull before the matador enters the arena to make the final killing.

caber tossing Throwing a 3–4m/10–13ft tree trunk or *caber*, often practised in Highland Games gatherings in Scotland. The competitor has the caber placed vertically in his hands; he runs with it and tosses it so that it revolves longitudinally and lands with the base as near to the 12 o'clock position from him as possible.

canoeing Water sport practised by one to four people in canoes, developed 1865 by the British barrister John MacGregor. Competition usually consists of a river slalom course using poles suspended between the river banks to mark out the gates. Two types of competition canoe: the *kayak*, which has a keel (the canoeist sits in the boat), and the *Canadian canoe*, which has no keel (the canoeist kneels).

clay-pigeon shooting or **trap shooting** Pastime and sport in which shotguns are fired at clay targets (*clays*) in the air; these simulate birds in flight and are launched by an automatic or manually operated machine.

cricket Bat and ball eleven-a-side team game. A wicket consisting of three stumps (wooden sticks) surmounted by a pair of bails (smaller sticks) is placed at each end of a grassy pitch 20.1m/22yd in length. Each team takes it in turn to bat (with long flat-sided wooden bats) and bowl (with a solid ball), the object being to defend the two wickets while trying to score as many runs as possible. A bowler delivers an 'over' of six balls to a batsman standing in front of one of the wickets before a different bowler attacks the other wicket. If the batsman hits a ball (and in certain other circumstances), he may exchange places with the other batsman, thus scoring at least one run. A ball reaching the boundary of the field scores four runs automatically, and six if it has not bounced on the way. A batsman can be got out by being 'caught' (a fielder catches the ball before it reaches the ground), 'bowled' (the ball from the bowler knocks the bails off the stumps), 'stumped' (the wicketkeeper knocks the bails off the stumps with the ball while the defending batsman is standing outside his 'safe ground' or 'crease'), 'run out' (the bails on the wicket towards which one of the batsmen is running are knocked off before the safe ground is reached), 'leg before wicket' or 'lbw' (when the lower part of the batsman's leg prevents the ball from the bowler reaching the wicket) and 'hit wicket' (the batsman accidentally knocks the bails off the stumps. Once ten batsmen have been dismissed, the innings comes to a close, but a team can stop its innings or 'declare' if it thinks it has made enough runs. Each team has two innings, and the one with the greater number of runs at the end of the match wins. A similar game was played in the mid-16c; first known county match 1719; test matches usually last five days; county championship three or four, and limited-over competitions normally concluded in one day, lasting for a specific number of overs per side. Earliest known laws: 1744; Marylebone Cricket Club (MCC) founded 1787; first test match: Melbourne 1877.

croquet A ball-and-mallet game for two to four players, played on a lawn about 32m/105ft long and 25m/84ft wide, on which six hoops have been arranged, with a small stake in the centre of the lawn. The object is to strike your own ball (blue, red, yellow or black) through the hoops in a prescribed order, a process which can be delayed by an opponent's ball hitting your ball out of the way. The central peg marks the finish and the first to hit it with his/her ball is the winner.

curling Similar to bowls but played on ice using special smooth, heavy round stones fitted with handles. The object is to slide the stones, which curl in different directions depending on the twist as they are released, near to a circular target or *house* marked on the ice, the centre of which is called the *tee*. A match lasts for a certain number of *heads* or shots, or by time. Sweeping the ice in front of a stone can make it travel further.

cycling Bicycle riding as a sport can take several forms: *time trials* are raced against the clock; *cyclocross* is a mixture of cycling and cross-country running, carrying the bike; *track racing* takes place on purpose-built concrete or wooden velodromes; *criteriums* are races around town or city centres; *road races* are normally in excess of 150km/100mi in length, between two points or several circuits of a predetermined course; *stage races* involve many days' racing over more than 150km/100mi. First cycle race Paris 1868, won by James Moore of England.

cyclocross ▶ cycling

darts Indoor game of throwing three 13cm/5in darts from a distance of 2.4m/8ft at a circular board which has its 'bull' or centre 1.7m/5ft 8in from the floor. The standard board is divided into 20 segments numbered 1–20 (not in numerical order); each contains smaller segments which either double or treble that number's score if hit. The centre ring (the bull) is worth 50 points, and the area around it (the outer) is worth 25 points. Most popular game '501': players start at that figure and deduct all scores from it, aiming to reduce the starting score exactly to zero; final shot must consist of a double.

decathlon Ten-event track-and-field competition held over two days, usually for men: 100m, long jump, shot put, high jump, 400m, 110m hurdles, discus, pole vault, javelin, and 1500m. Points are awarded in each event.

discus throw Athletics field event using a circular disc of wood with metal plates, weighing 2kg/4.4lb for men and 1kg/2.2lb for women. It is thrown with one hand from within the confines of a circle 2.5m/8ft 2in in diameter.

diving Jumping from an elevated rigid or sprung board into a swimming pool, often performing a variety of twists and somersaults. Style gains marks, as does successfully completing the dive, based on the level of difficulty of each attempt (which is used as a multiplying factor). Springboard events take place from a board 3m/9ft 10in above the water; platform diving from a rigid board 10m/32ft 10in above the water.

falconry Sport in which birds of prey are trained to hunt animals and other birds, also known as **hawking**. Two kinds of falcon: *long-winged* birds (eg the peregrine), used in open country, which swoop on their prey from a great height, and *short-winged* birds, or accipiters, which perch on the falconer's gloved fist or tree branch until they see their prey, and then rely on speed. The birds are hooded until such time as they are ready to 'work'.

fencing Sword fighting, using a light *foil*, heavier *épée*, or *sabre* (curved handle, narrow blade). Different target areas exist for each weapon, and protective clothing registers hit electronically. It can be traced back to the Egyptians of c.1300 BC and was popular in the Middle Ages.

fishing ▶ angling

fives A handball game played on a three or four-walled court (which in Rugby fives is 5.49m/18ft wide, 8.54m/28ft long, with front wall 4.57m/15ft high, back wall 1.83m/6ft high and side walls sloping) by two or four players with a hard white ball, hit with gloved hands. It is derived from the French game *jeu de paume*. First recorded game 1825 at Eton College; another variation is Winchester fives.

football A field team game using an inflated ball, which has developed several different forms: **1 Association football or soccer** An eleven-a-side team game played on a grass or synthetic pitch measuring 90–120m/100–130yd in length, and 45–90m/50–100yd wide; goal nets measure 7.3m/8yd wide by 2.4m/8ft high; object is to move the ball around using the foot or head until it can be put into the net, thus scoring a goal. Only the goalkeeper within a specific area is allowed to touch the ball with the hand while it is in play. Ancient Greeks, Chinese, Egyptians and Romans all played a form of football; it became an organized game in 19c Britain, in schools and universities; standard rules drawn up 1848; Football Association formed 1863; first FA Cup final played 1872; first World Cup Uruguay 1930. **2 American football** Players wear heavy padding and helmets, and passing of the ball by hand, including forward passing, is permitted; played on a rectangular field 91m/100yd by 49m/53yd, divided gridiron-like into 4.6m/5yd segments; object is to score 'touchdowns' by moving the ball into the opposing team's 'end zone' (area behind the posts), but progress has to be made upfield by a series of 'plays': a team must make 9.1m/10yd of ground within four plays, otherwise they lose possession of the ball. Six points are awarded for a touchdown and one for an 'extra point', for kicking the ball between the posts and over the crossbar — the equivalent of a conversion in rugby. A goal kicked from anywhere on the field (a 'field goal') is worth three points. Teams consist of more than 40 members, but only 11 are allowed on the field at any one time; special units of players have different roles so they change eg when the team changes from attacking to defending. First intercollegiate game 1869. **3 Australian Rules football** A handling and kicking game with few rules, a cross between Association football and rugby, with 18 players on an oval pitch measuring c.165m/180yd long by c.137m/150yd wide. The object is to score by kicking the ball between the opponent's goal posts (six points). Smaller posts are positioned either side of the main goal: a ball kicked through that area scores one point; first recorded game played 1858. **4 Gaelic football** Mixture of rugby, soccer and Australian Rules football, played by teams of 15 on a rectangular pitch 82m/269ft wide and 137m/450ft long with goals resembling rugby posts with soccer-style nets attached; points scored by either putting the ball into the goal net (three), or over the crossbar and between the uprights (one); first game resembling Gaelic football took place 1712 at Slane, Ireland. **5 rugby football ▶ rugby**.

foxhunting Mounted blood sport involving chasing and killing a wild fox using foxhounds (similar to the beagle); hunt is controlled by a Master of Hounds, the hounds by the Huntsman; season lasts November to April. It developed in the UK in the late 17c. From 1949 there was a movement to get the sport banned in the UK; hunting with dogs was outlawed in Scotland in 2002 and in England and Wales in 2005.

golf Outdoor sport played on a course 4500–6500m/5000–7000yd long, usually with 18 but sometimes 9 holes; object is to hit a small rubber-cored ball using a long-handled metal- or (formerly) wooden-faced club from a flat starting point or *tee* along a *fairway* to a hole positioned on an area of smooth grass or *green*; additional hazards: trees, bushes, streams, sand-filled *bunkers* and the *rough*, or uncut grass beside the fairway; winner completes the course using the lowest number of strokes. The *par* is the expected number of strokes a good player needs to complete a hole; one stroke above par is called a *bogey*; one stroke below par is a *birdie*; two strokes below an *eagle*; three strokes below an *albatross*; a hole completed in one stroke is a *hole in one*. A similar game was played by the Dutch c.1300, known as *kolf* or *colf*. *Gouf* was definitely played in Scotland in the 15c; world's first club, the Gentlemen Golfers of Edinburgh, formed 1744.

greyhound racing Spectator sport which takes place on an enclosed circular or oval track where greyhound dogs (on whose success bets are usually placed) are lured to run by a mechanical hare; invented California 1919.

gymnastics Physical exercises. Men compete on the parallel bars, pommel horse, high bar, rings, horse vault and floor exercise, and women on the asymmetrical bars, beam, horse vault and floor exercise. Judges award marks out of ten, looking for control, suppleness, balance and ingenuity. The ancient Greeks and Romans performed such exercises for health purposes; modern techniques date from late 18c Germany.

hammer throw Athletics field event; hammer weighing 7.6kg/16lb is thrown using one hand from within the confines of a circle 2.13m/7ft in diameter (protected by a wire cage). Six throws are allowed, the object being to attain the greatest distance.

handball Indoor and outdoor game first played in Germany c.1890; resembles Association football, but played with the hands. Indoor game played seven-a-side on a court 40m/43.8yd long and 20m/21.9yd wide, with goals 2m/6ft 6in high and 3m/9ft 9in wide; outdoor game (**field handball**) played on a field with eleven on each side.

hang gliding Flying in a glider with a delta-shaped wing, usually having launched from a high place. The pilot is suspended by a harness from the light frame holding the wing, and controls the direction of the craft by body movement. Providing the angle of attack is maintained, lift is generated. A hang glider with a motor and wing span increased to 10m/33ft is called a *micro-light*, which typically has a speed of 90kph/55mph. Hang gliding was pioneered in the 1890s in Germany.

harness racing Horse race with rider seated in a small two-wheeled cart or *sulky*; horses trot or pace; races run on an oval dirt track measuring 800–1500m/0.5–1mi in circumference; first introduced 1554 Holland, popularized mid-19c USA.

hawking ▶ falconry

heptathlon Seven-event track-and-field competition held over two days, usually for women: 100m hurdles, shot put, high jump, 200m, long jump, javelin and 800m; replaced pentathlon in 1981.

high jump Athletics field event; competitors attempt to clear a bar without any aids; height increased gradually; three failed attempts means disqualification. The winner clears the greatest height, or has the fewest failures.

hockey or (USA) **field hockey** Stick-and-ball game played by two teams of eleven on a pitch 91m/100yd long and 54m/60yd wide, the object being to move the ball around with the sticks until a player can score from within the semicircle of radius 14.64m/16yd in front of the opposing side's goal; game is split into two halves of 35 minutes; ancient Greeks played a similar game c.2500BC; modern hockey dates from 1875.

horse-racing Racing of horses against one another, each ridden by a jockey. Two categories: **flat racing** for thoroughbred horses on a flat grass or dirt surface over a predetermined distance from 1 to 4km/5 furlongs to 2.5mi, and **national hunt racing** in which the horses negotiate either movable hurdles or fixed fences over a distance up to 6.5km/4.5mi. The ancient Egyptians took part in horse races in c.1200BC; popularized in 12c England. Most monarchs have supported the sport, hence its name 'the sport of kings'. ▶ **harness racing**, **hurdles** and **steeplechase**.

hurdles Horse race in which the horses jump hurdles of at least 106.7cm/3ft 6in in height; hurdles are easily knocked down so that horses can continue the race.

hurdling Athletics event in which the competitors race to clear ten obstacles (hurdles) placed on the track; race distances: 110m and 400m for men, 100m and 400m for women; hurdle height varies: 106.7cm/3ft 6in for the 110m; 91.4cm/3ft for the 400m and 84cm/2ft 9in for the 100m.

hurling or **hurley** Irish 15-a-side field game played with curved sticks and a ball; object to hit ball into opposing team's goal: under the crossbar scores three points; above the crossbar but between the posts scores one; played since 1800BC; standardized in 1884 following the formation of the Gaelic Athletic Association.

ice hockey Fast game played by two teams of six on an ice rink 56–61m/184–200ft long and 26–30m/85–98ft wide with sticks and a small rubber *puck*; aim is to score goals by using the stick to hit the puck into the opposing team's goal; players wear ice skates and protective clothing; possibly first played 1850s Canada.

ice skating 1 figure skating Artistic dancing on ice for individuals and pairs; first known skating club formed mid-18c London; first artificial rink opened 1876 Baker Street. **2 speed skating** Competitors race against one another on an oval ice track over distances between 500 and 10000m/550 and 11000yd.

javelin throw Athletics field event; throwing a spear-like javelin which consists of three parts: pointed metal head, shaft and grip; men's javelin is 2.6–2.7m/8ft 6in–8ft 10in in length and weighs 800g/1.8lb; women's is 2.2–2.3m/7ft 2in–7ft 6in and weighs at least 600g/1.3lb; the competitor runs to a specified mark with the javelin in one hand, and throws it; for throw to count, metal head must touch ground before any other part; first mark made by the head is the point used for measuring the distance achieved.

judo Unarmed combat sport of late 19c Japanese origin. Contestants wear a *judogi* or loose-fitting suit and compete on a mat which breaks their falls. When one cannot break a hold, surrender is signalled by slapping the mat; ability is graded from fifth to first Kyu, and then first to twelfth Dan — only Dr Jigoro Kano, who devised the sport, has been awarded twelfth Dan. Different coloured belts indicate grades; eg white for novice, brown (three degrees) and black (nine degrees).

jujitsu Japanese martial art of unarmed offence and self-defence used by the Samurai; forms basis of **judo**, **aikido** and **karate**; thought to have been introduced early 17c by Chinese monk, Chen Yuan-ping.

karate Martial art of unarmed combat, dating from 17c; developed Japan 20c; name adopted 1930s; aim is to be in total control of the body's muscular power, so it can be used with great force and accuracy at any instant. Experts may show their mental and physical training by eg breaking various thicknesses of wood, but in fighting an opponent, blows do not actually make contact; levels of prowess symbolized by coloured belts.

kendo Japanese martial art of sword fighting, now practised with *shinai*, or bamboo swords; object is to land two scoring blows on opponent's target area. *Kendokas* (participants) wear traditional dress of the Samurai period, including face masks and aprons; grades according to ability are from sixth to first Kyu, then from first to tenth Dan; earliest reference is 8c.

kung fu Chinese unarmed combat dating from the sixth century, when it was practised at the Shaolin Temple; best known form is *wing chun*.

lacrosse Stick-and-ball field game; teams of 10 (men's) or 12 (women's) play on a pitch measuring about 100–110m/110–120yd by 55–75m/60–82yd; stick measures at least 90cm/3ft and has thongs forming a triangular net at one end in which ball is caught and carried, and thrown into opponents' goal (just under 2m/6ft square); derived from Native American game of *baggataway*; stick supposedly resembled a bishop's crozier, so French settlers called it *la crosse*; played since 15c; spread to Europe early 19c, and to Britain 1867.

long jump Athletics field event; contestant runs up to the take-off mark and leaps into a sandpit; length of the jump measured from front of take-off line to nearest break in the sand made by any part of the competitor's body; also called **broad jump** in North America.

lugeing Travelling across ice on a toboggan sled, usually made of wood with metal runners; rider sits upright or lies back (but lies on the stomach in tobogganing). Competitors in single or two-seater luges race against time on a predetermined run of at least 1000m/1094yd; luge is approximately 1.5m/5ft in length, steered by the feet and a hand rope. ▶ **bobsledding**.

marathon Long-distance running race, normally on open roads, over 42km 195m/26mi 385yd (distance first used at 1908 London Olympics so competitors could finish exactly in front of the royal box); race introduced at the 1896 Olympic Games to commemorate the run of the Greek courier (according to legend, Pheidippides) who ran the c.24mi/39km from Marathon to Athens in 490 BC with the news of a Greek victory over the Persian army. In the 1980s the **half marathon** over 21km/13mi 194yd also became popular.

martial arts ▶ **aikido**, **judo**, **jujitsu**, **karate**, **kendo**, **kung fu** and **taekwondo**.

motocross or **scrambling** Motorcycle racing over a circuit of rough terrain, taking advantage of natural hazards eg streams and hills; uses sturdier motorcycles than those for road use; competitions usually categorized by engine size; first motocross race held 1924 at Camberley, Surrey.

motorcycle racing Speed competitions for motorcycles which for the annual season-long grand prix are categorized by the engine sizes 80cc, 125cc, 250cc, MotoGp, Superbike and Sidecar. Other forms include **speedway**, **motocross** and motorcycle trials riding.

motor racing Racing finely-tuned motor cars, either purpose-built or modified production vehicles; season-long (Mar–Nov) Formula One world championship involves usually 16 races at different venues worldwide; other popular forms include stock-car racing, hill-climbing, sports-car racing and **rallying**; first race 1894, between Paris and Rouen.

mountain biking Cycle racing over rugged, hilly terrain. Two main categories: **cross-country** over a closed circuit of at least 6km on narrow paths, forests and streams with races lasting about two hours; **downhill** time trial or mass start down a steep hill with banked sections and jumps.

mountaineering Climbing a mountain aided by ropes and other accessories, which for tall peaks can take weeks; most popular form in UK is rock climbing; in higher places elsewhere the form is snow and ice climbing.

netball Women's seven-a-side court game invented in the USA and developed from basketball; court is 30.5m/100ft long and 15.25m/50ft wide; object is to score goals by passing the inflated ball between players and throwing it through opponent's hoop suspended on a post 3.05m/10ft high. Players must not touch each other or run with the ball.

octopush A form of hockey played underwater, devised 1954 by English subaqua divers; teams of six; players use miniature hockey sticks and a *puck* or *squid*, which must hit the opposing team's end of the swimming pool to score a goal.

orienteering Cross-country running and routefinding aided by map and compass; competitors set off at intervals and have to find their way to official check-points; devised as a sport in Sweden in 1918, based on military training techniques; became an international sport 1960s.

paddle tennis Bat-and-ball game for two or four people, invented USA c.1920; rules similar to lawn tennis, but court is half the size; bat wooden and ball made of sponge.

parachuting Jumping out of an aircraft and landing with the aid of a parachute; competitions involve landing within a specific area; participant can choose to freefall for a few thousand feet before opening the chute, normally c.750m/2500ft.

pelota Generic name for various hand, glove, racket or bat-and-ball games, all developed from French *jeu de paume*; most popular form **Pelote Basque**: it uses a walled court (*trinquete*), players wear a shaped wicker basket attached to their forearm in which they catch and propel the ball. Pelota is one of the world's fastest games.

pentathlon 1 Five-event track-and-field competition, usually for women: 100m hurdles, shot put, high jump, long jump, and 800m; replaced by **heptathlon** in 1981. **2 modern pentathlon** Five-sport competition based on military training, comprising showjumping, épée fencing, pistol shooting, swimming and cross-country running.

point-to-point Horse races for amateur riders over a cross-country course, normally farmland; organized by hunts; horses used are regular hunting horses; original courses went from one point to another (hence name), but are now often over circular or oval courses with mixture of artificial and natural fences.

pole vault Athletics field event; jumping contest for height using fibreglass pole for leverage to clear a bar, which is raised progressively; three attempts may be made to clear the height before attempting a new one.

polo Stick-and-ball game; played by teams of four on horseback on a pitch measuring 274m/300yd by 146m/160yd; object is to hit the ball into the opposing team's 7.3m/8yd-wide and 3m/10ft-high goal using a long-handled mallet; match lasts about an hour, divided into seven-minute *chukkas*, the number of which varies according to competition; a pony is not expected to play more than two chukkas; game derives its name from Tibetan *pulu*; first played in central Asia c.500 BC.

pool US table game played in many forms, using 15 balls, a *cue* similar to that used in billiards and snooker, and a table half the size of a standard billiard table, with six round pockets; in UK most popular form is eight-ball pool, where the object is to pot all balls of your colour and finally the black (or No. 8) ball.

potholing or (USA) **spelunking** Exploration and study of caves and other underground features, originally to survey extent, physical history and structure, and natural history. When practised as a hobby people descend through access points (potholes) to follow courses of underground rivers and streams; scientific term: speleology.

powerboat racing Inshore and offshore racing of boats fitted with high-powered and finely-tuned engines; first race of note Calais to Dover 1903.

quoits Outdoor game demanding great accuracy; metal ring is thrown at a peg; became popular mid-14c England; horseshoe pitching developed from quoits.

rackets or (USA) **racquets** Racket-and-ball game; played by two or four players on walled court; probably forerunner to many racket-and-ball games; thought to have originated Middle Ages, and to have developed 18c at the Fleet debtors' prison, London.

rallying Motor racing on open roads and in forests, sometimes lasting several days; driver and navigator require skill and endurance; uses modified production cars.

real tennis Indoor racket-and-ball game similar to rackets; played on walled court with specifically designed hazards; derivation of the 11c *jeu de paume*; racket developed 16c and the game became very popular in the 17c; also known as 'royal' or 'court' tennis, and a minority sport today.

rodeo US sport; mainly competitive riding and a range of skills deriving from cowboy ranching practices; events include bronco riding with and without saddle (where the cowboy must stay on a wild bucking horse for a set time holding on with only one hand, points being awarded for style to the horse and rider), bull riding, steer wrestling, calf roping and team roping.

roller skating First seen 1760 in Belgium; developed as a sport late 19c, following invention of the modern four-wheeled skate in 1863. Competitions exist as for ice skating; individual, pairs, dancing and speed skating on a track.

rounders Outdoor bat-and-ball game; baseball may derive from it; teams of nine players; object, after hitting the ball, which is bowled from the centre of the pitch, is to score a rounder by running around the outside of the four posts without being put out (by the ball being caught, the batter being tagged between posts, or the post ahead of the batter being 'stopped' by a fielder touching it with the hand holding the ball); first reference to rounders 1774.

rowing Propulsion of a boat by oars; involves two or more rowers, each with an oar, and often with a coxswain; **sculling** involves rowers with two oars each; rowing as an organized sport dates from 1715 (first rowing of the Doggetts Coat and Badge race on the R Thames, London).

rugby Team ball game played with oval ball on a pitch 68m/74yd wide and 100m/110yd long; developed 1823 from football (when William Webb Ellis of Rugby school picked up the ball and ran with it); H-shaped goalposts at each end of field are 5.5m/18ft wide, with a crossbar 3m/10ft above the ground; object is to score a *try* by grounding ball in opposing team's scoring area behind goal line. The 15-a-side **Rugby Union** game and 13-a-side **Rugby League** are now both professional games, with some rule differences: eg the scoring (League in brackets): try 5 (4), conversion 2 (2), penalty 3 (2), dropped goal 3 (1). Rugby League was formed by the breakaway Northern Union after a dispute with the Rugby Football Union about pay in 1895.

sailing Travelling over water in a suitable craft, usually a small single or double-sided dinghy,

often with outboard motor or auxiliary engine for use in no wind; **yachting** involves racing small, light sailing vessels with crews of one, two or three; large ocean-going yachts may be 25m/80ft or more in length; several classes of racing yacht in Olympic and international competitions, eg the Admiral's Cup and America's Cup.

scrambling ▶ motocross

sculling ▶ rowing

sepek takrow Three-a-side court game played on badminton court with ball made from rattan palm; ball is propelled over centre net (lower than in badminton) by players using any part of the body other than arms or hands; popular in SE Asia, particularly Philippines, Malaysia (as 'kick') and Thailand (as 'rattan ball').

shinty Twelve-a-side stick-and-ball game originating in Ireland more than 1500 years ago, now popular in the Scottish Highlands; played on pitch up to 155m/170yd long and 73m/80yd wide; aim is to score goals by propelling the leather-covered cork and worsted ball, using curved sticks or *camans*, into the opposing team's goal or *hail*.

shooting Competitive shooting takes many forms and uses different types of weapon; most popular weapons: the standard pistol, small-bore rifle, full-bore rifle, air rifle and air pistol. All events involve shooting at still or moving targets (**▶ clay pigeon shooting**). Using firearms for sport developed in 15c. Hunting for game, eg grouse or pheasant shooting, has specifically defined seasons.

shot put Athletics field event; the shot is a brass or iron sphere weighing 7.26kg/16lb for men and 4kg/8lb 13oz for women. It is propelled, using only one hand, from a starting position under the chin. The thrower must not leave the 2.1m/7ft diameter throwing circle. In competition six throws are allowed.

skiing Propelling oneself along snow while standing on skis, aided by poles; named from Norwegian *ski*, 'snowshoe'; two forms of competition skiing: **Alpine skiing**, consisting of the downhill, slalom (zigzag courses through markers) and ski-jumping, and **Nordic skiing** or **langlaufing** (on narrower skis to which only the toe is attached), incorporating cross-country skiing and the **biathlon**. Other forms: **ski-flying** (ski-jumping from a high take-off point), **skijoring** (being towed behind a vehicle or horse), hang gliding on skis and parapenting on skis.

skydiving or **freefalling** Jumping from an aircraft and freefalling, often performing a wide range of stunts or forming patterns by holding hands with other skydivers, to a height of 600m/2000ft, when the parachute must be opened.

snooker Indoor game played on a standard billiard table by two (or occasionally four) players; aim is to 'pot' the 21 coloured balls (arranged on the table at the start) by hitting them with the white ball, itself hit using a tapered pole or *cue*. Fifteen of the balls are red; these must be potted alternately with the coloured ones. This sequence is called a *break* and continues until a mistake is made; reds remain in pockets but coloureds are returned to the table until no reds are left, when they are potted in ascending order; game ends when the black is finally potted. Points 1–7 relate to colours, in order: red, yellow, green, brown, blue, pink, black.

snowboarding Winter sport popular since 1970s, inspired by surfing; competitors stand on a board about 5ft long; **slalom, giant slalom** and **super-giant slalom** involve downhill racing against the clock through gates placed at different distances apart; **freestyle** involves performing judged tricks in a 'half-pipe', ie a snow-covered half-cylinder.

soccer ▶ football

softball   Smaller version of **baseball**, played on diamond-shaped pitch of sides measuring 18.3m/60ft; ball is larger as well as softer; teams of nine; game lasts for nine innings per team, each innings lasting until a team has three players out; object is to complete a circuit of the diamond without being put out, eg by being caught out, struck out, or tagged between bases by a player with the ball. Pitching is underarm in softball, overarm in baseball; two forms: *fast pitch* and *slow pitch*; in the latter the bowler must deliver ball in arc between 12ft/3.66m and 6ft/1.83m minimum.

speedway   Motorcycle racing on machines with no brakes and only one gear, usually on an oval track and involving four riders at once. Other forms include *long track* racing and *ice speedway*.

squash or **squash rackets**   Strenuous indoor racket-and-ball game played (in English singles) on an enclosed court measuring 9.75m/32ft long by 6.4m/21ft wide; small rubber ball is hit alternately by players against the front wall, so that it cannot be returned; developed 1817 from **rackets** at Harrow school.

steeplechase   **1** National hunt horse-racing; horses negotiate fixed fences normally 0.9–1.2m/3–4ft high; first one in Ireland in 1752; most famous is Grand National. ▶ **horse-racing**. **2** Track race run over 3000m and comprising 28 0.9m/3ft (for men) and 0.76m/2ft 6in (for women) hurdles and seven water jumps.

stock-car racing   Motor racing; in USA highly supercharged production cars race around a concreted track; in UK 'bangers' (old cars) race on a round or oval track; the aim is to be the last car still moving at the end of the race; some 'rough' tactics are allowed to try to eliminate other drivers.

street hockey   Hockey played on roller skates; popular in USA and Europe; five members to each team play on an enclosed rink.

sumo wrestling   A Japanese national sport; competition takes place in a 3.66m/12ft diameter circle; object is to force opponent out of ring or to ground; sumo wrestlers are very heavy and eat vast amounts of food to increase weight and body size.

surfing   Riding waves, either with the body alone, or with the aid of a board; object is to ride along the face of a wave before it breaks; board is usually about 1.8m/6ft long, but a longer one is used for competition; originated in Oceania, developed in Hawaii and has flourished in modern times there and in California and Australia.

swimming   Propelling oneself through water without mechanical aids. Four strokes: *breast stroke*, the slowest stroke, developed in the 16c; *front crawl* or *freestyle*, the fastest stroke; *backstroke*; and *butterfly*, developed in the USA in the 20c. In competitions there are also relays, involving four swimmers, and medley races, combining all four strokes. Olympic-size pool is 50m/55yd long, with eight lanes; race lengths from 50m/55yd to 1500m/1640yd (800m/875yd for women); earliest reference to swimming as a sport is 36 BC Japan.

table tennis or **ping pong**   Indoor bat-and-ball game played by two or four players; uses small wooden bats covered in rubber or sponge and a hollow plastic ball; table measures 2.75m/9ft by

1.52m/5ft and has a 15.25cm/6in-high net across it; ball must be hit over the net and into opposing half of table, to be returned without volleying; object is to play unreturnable shots; in doubles, players must hit ball alternately; winner is first to reach eleven points with at least a two-point lead; thought to have been first played 1880s.

taekwondo   Martial art developed in Korea by General Choi Hong Hi; officially part of Korean tradition and culture since 1955, now popular as a sport.

tennis, lawn   Racket-and-ball game for two or four players; court measures 23.77m/78ft long by 8.23m/27ft wide (singles), or 10.97m/36ft wide (doubles); net 0.9m/3ft high is stretched across centre; rackets have oval heads strung with nylon or gut; playing surface can be grass, clay, shale, concrete, wood, or other man-made materials; object is to play unreturnable strokes, thus scoring points; progression of scoring is 15, 30, 40, deuce if both reach 40, and game; set won by winning six games with a two-game lead (or one in a 'short' set); a very close set can be decided using a tie-break. In doubles, players may hit the ball in any order, but must serve in rotation. 'Field tennis' was played 18c but game similar to modern game was invented 1873 as *sphairistike* in Wales by Walter Wingfield.

tenpin bowling ▶ bowling

tobogganing ▶ bobsledding and lugeing

trampolining   Performing acrobatics on a sprung canvas sheet stretched across a frame, first used at turn of 20c as a circus attraction; developed as a sport following design of modern trampoline in 1936. In competition, marks gained for performing difficult manoeuvres; popular forms are synchronized trampolining and tumbling.

trap shooting ▶ clay pigeon shooting

triple jump   Athletics field event; takes place in same place as long jump, governed by same rules. After the run-up, competitors must take off and hop on the same foot; second phase is a step onto the other foot, followed by a jump; previously called the *hop, step and jump*.

triathlon   Swimming, running and cycling event. Olympic distance comprises 1500m swim, 40km cycle ride and 10km run. Also shorter distances, the most popular being sprint: 750m swim, 20km cycle and 5km run. Ironman comprises 2.4mi swim, 112mi cycle and 26.2mi (marathon) run. Thought to originate in France in 1920s, and popularized by Hawaiian Iron Man in 1970s.

tug-of-war   Athletics event of strength; two teams (normally eight men) pull against each other from opposite ends of a long thick rope; aim is to pull the opponents over a predetermined mark. Ancient Chinese and Egyptians participated in similar events; first rules drawn up 1879.

volleyball   Indoor court game; two teams of six play on a court measuring 18m/59ft by 9m/29ft which has a raised net stretched across the centre; aim is to score points by grounding the inflated ball on opponent's side after hitting it over net with the arms or hands; ball may not be hit more than three times on one team's side of the net.

walking   Either a leisurely pursuit (eg **fell walking**) or a competitive sport on roads or tracks which has strict rules; eg raised foot must touch ground before the other leaves it.

water polo   Sport played by two seven-a-side teams in a swimming pool; aim is to score by propelling inflated ball into opposing team's goal at end of the pool, without touching the bottom; developed in Britain in 1869; originally called 'football in water'.

water skiing Being towed by a motor boat on one or two skis, using a 20m/21.8yd-long rope. Competitions held for jumping, slalom and acrobatics.

weightlifting Test of strength by lifting weights attached to both ends of a metal pole or *barbell*. Competitors have to make two successful lifts: the *snatch*, taking the bar to an outstretched position above the head in one movement (held for two seconds), and the *clean and jerk* or *jerk* which is achieved in two movements, first onto the chest, then above the head with outstretched arms; aggregate weight of the two lifts gives a competitor's total, and the weights are gradually increased. Another form is *powerlifting*, which calls for sheer strength rather than technique, and

takes three forms: the *squat*, *dead lift* and *bench press*. Weightlifting was part of Ancient Olympic Games; introduced as sport c.1850.

wrestling Fighting person to person without striking; aim is to throw opponent to the ground; most popular forms are *freestyle*, where the legs can be used to hold and trip, and *Graeco-Roman* where holds below the waist are not allowed and legs cannot be used to hold and trip. Men compete in divisions from 55kg to 120kg; women from 48kg to 72kg. Other forms: *sumo*, the national sport in Japan; *Sambo* in Russia; *Kushti* in Iran; *Glima* in Iceland; *Schwingen* in Switzerland; and *Yagli*, the national sport in Turkey; also UK variations *Devon and Cornwall* and *Cumberland and Westmoreland*.

yachting ▶ **sailing**

Sports and Games

Champions 1992–2008

For 1992 Summer Olympic events the designation (UT) is given for members of the Unified Team (Armenia, Azerbaijan, Belarus, Georgia, Kazakhstan, Kyrgyzstan, Moldova, Russia, Tajikistan, Turkmenistan, Ukraine and Uzbekistan).

Angling

■ **World Freshwater Championship**
First held in 1954; takes place annually.

Individual

1992	David Wesson (Australia)
1993	Mario Barras (Portugal)
1994	Bob Nudd (England)
1995	Pierre Jean (France)
1996	Alan Scotthorne (England)
1997	Alan Scotthorne (England)
1998	Alan Scotthorne (England)
1999	Bob Nudd (England)
2000	Jacobo Falsini (Italy)
2001	Umberto Ballabeni (Italy)
2002	Juan Blasco (Spain)
2003	Alan Scotthorne (England)
2004	Tamás Walter (Hungary)
2005	Guido Nullens (Belgium)
2006	Tamás Walter (Hungary)
2007	Alan Scotthorne (England)
2008	Will Raison (England)

Team

1992	Italy
1993	Italy
1994	England
1995	France
1996	Italy
1997	Italy
1998	England
1999	Spain
2000	Italy
2001	England
2002	Spain
2003	Hungary
2004	France
2005	England
2006	England
2007	Italy
2008	England

■ **World Fly Fishing Championship**
First held in 1981; takes place annually.

Individual

1992	Pierluigi Cocito (Italy)
1993	Russell Owen (Wales)
1994	Pascal Cognard (France)
1995	Jeremy Herrmann (England)
1996	Pierluigi Cocito (Italy)
1997	Pascal Cognard (France)
1998	Tomas Starychfojtu (Czech Republic)
1999	Ross Stewart (Australia)
2000	Pascal Cognard (France)
2001	Vladimír Šedivý (Czech Republic)
2002	Jérôme Brossutti (France)
2003	Stefano Cotugno (Italy)
2004	Miroslav Antal (Slovakia)
2005	Bertrand Jacquemin (France)
2006	Antonín Pešek (Czech Republic)
2007	Marek Walczyk (Poland)
2008	Martin Droz (Czech Republic)

Team

1992	Italy
1993	England
1994	Czech Republic
1995	England
1996	Czech Republic
1997	France
1998	Czech Republic
1999	Australia
2000	France
2001	France
2002	France
2003	France
2004	Slovakia
2005	France
2006	Czech Republic
2007	France
2008	Czech Republic

Archery

■ World Championships
First held in 1931; took place annually until 1959; since then, every two years. Results are for recurve bows.

Individual (Men)
1993	Park Kyung-Mo (South Korea)
1995	Lee Kyung-Chul (South Korea)
1997	Kim Kyung-Ho (South Korea)
1999	Hong Sung-Chil (South Korea)
2001	Jung Ki Yeon (South Korea)
2003	Michele Frangilli (Italy)
2005	Chung Jae Hun (South Korea)
2007	Im Dong Hyun (South Korea)

Team (Men)
1993	France
1995	South Korea
1997	South Korea
1999	Italy
2001	South Korea
2003	South Korea
2005	South Korea
2007	South Korea

Individual (Women)
1993	Kim Hyo-Jung (South Korea)
1995	Natalia Valeyeva (Moldova)
1997	Kim Du-Ri (South Korea)
1999	Lee Eun-Kyung (South Korea)
2001	Sung Hyun Park (South Korea)
2003	Yun Mi-jin (South Korea)
2005	Lee Sung Jin (South Korea)
2007	Natalia Valeeva (Italy)

Team (Women)
1993	South Korea
1995	South Korea
1997	South Korea
1999	Italy
2001	China
2003	South Korea
2005	South Korea
2007	South Korea

Athletics

■ World Championships
First held in Helsinki, Finland in 1983, then in Rome, Italy in 1987; since 1995 every two years.

Event (Men)	Winners
1997	
100m	Maurice Greene (USA)
200m	Ato Boldon (Trinidad)
400m	Michael Johnson (USA)
800m	Wilson Kipketer (Denmark)
1500m	Hicham El Guerrouj (Morocco)
5000m	Daniel Komen (Kenya)
10000m	Haile Gebrselassie (Ethiopia)
Marathon	Abel Antón (Spain)
3000m steeplechase	Wilson Kipketer (Denmark)
110m hurdles	Allen Johnson (USA)
400m hurdles	Stephane Diagana (France)
20km walk	Daniel Garcia (Mexico)
50km walk	Robert Korzeniowski (Poland)
4 × 100m relay	Canada
4 × 400m relay	USA
High jump	Javier Sotomayor (Cuba)
Long jump	Iván Pedroso (Cuba)
Triple jump	Yoelvis Quesada (Cuba)
Pole vault	Sergei Bubka (Ukraine)
Shot	John Godina (USA)
Discus	Lars Riedel (Germany)
Hammer	Heinz Weis (Germany)
Javelin	Marius Corbett (South Africa)
Decathlon	Tómas Dvorák (Czech Republic)
1999	
100m	Maurice Greene (USA)
200m	Maurice Greene (USA)
400m	Michael Johnson (USA)
800m	Wilson Kipketer (Denmark)
1500m	Hicham El Guerrouj (Morocco)
5000m	Salah Hissou (Morocco)
10000m	Haile Gebrselassie (Ethiopia)
Marathon	Abel Antón (Spain)
3000m steeplechase	Christopher Koskei (Kenya)
110m hurdles	Colin Jackson (Great Britain)
400m hurdles	Fabrizio Mori (Italy)
20km walk	Ilya Markov (Russia)
50km walk	German Skurygin (Russia)
4 × 100m relay	USA
4 × 400m relay	USA
High jump	Vyacheslav Voronin (Russia)
Long jump	Ivan Pedroso (Cuba)
Triple jump	Charles Michael Friedek (Germany)
Pole vault	Maksim Tarasov (Russia)
Shot	C J Hunter (USA)
Discus	Anthony Washington (USA)
Hammer	Karsten Kobs (Germany)
Javelin	Aki Parviainen (Finland)
Decathlon	Tomás Dvorák (Czech Republic)
2001	
100m	Maurice Greene (USA)
200m	Konstantinos Kederis (Greece)
400m	Avard Moncur (Bahamas)
800m	André Bucher (Switzerland)
1500m	Hicham El Guerrouj (Morocco)
5000m	Richard Limo (Kenya)
10000m	Charles Kamathi (Kenya)
Marathon	Gezahegne Abera (Ethiopia)
3000m steeplechase	Reuben Kosgei (Kenya)
110m hurdles	Allen Johnson (USA)
400m hurdles	Felix Sanchez (Dominican Republic)
20km walk	Roman Rasskazov (Russia)
50km walk	Robert Korzeniowski (Poland)
4 × 100m relay	USA
4 × 400m relay	Jamaica
High jump	Buss Martin (Germany)
Long jump	Ivan Pedroso (Cuba)
Triple jump	Jonathan Edwards (Great Britain)
Pole vault	Dmitry Markov (Russia)
Shot	John Godina (USA)
Discus	Lars Riedel (Germany)
Hammer	Szymon Ziólkowski (Poland)
Javelin	Jan Zelezný (Czech Republic)
Decathlon	Tomás Dvorák (Czech Republic)

2003

100m	Kim Collins (Saint Kitts and Nevis)
200m	John Capel (USA)
400m	Jerome Young (USA)
800m	Djabir Saïd-Guerni (Algeria)
1500m	Hicham El Guerrouj (Morocco)
5000m	Eliud Kipchoge (Kenya)
10000m	Kenenisa Bekele (Ethiopia)
Marathon	Jaoud Gharib (Morocco)
3000m steeplechase	Saif Shaheen (Qatar)
110m hurdles	Allen Johnson (USA)
400m hurdles	Felix Sanchez (Dominican Republic)
20km walk	Jefferson Pérez (Ecuador)
50km walk	Robert Korzeniowski (Poland)
4 × 100m relay	USA
4 × 400m relay	USA
High jump	Jacques Freitag (South Africa)
Long jump	Dwight Phillips (USA)
Triple jump	Christian Olsson (Sweden)
Pole vault	Giuseppe Gibilisco (Italy)
Shot	Andrei Mikhnevich (Belarus)
Discus	Virgilijus Alekna (Lithuania)
Hammer	Ivan Tikhon (Belarus)
Javelin	Sergei Makarov (Russia)
Decathlon	Tom Pappas (USA)

2005

100m	Justin Gatlin (USA)
200m	Justin Gatlin (USA)
400m	Jeremy Wariner (USA)
800m	Rashid Ramzi (Bahrain)
1500m	Rashid Ramzi (Bahrain)
5000m	Benjamin Limo (Kenya)
10000m	Kenenisa Bekele (Ethiopia)
Marathon	Jaoud Gharib (Morocco)
3000m steeplechase	Saif Shaheen (Qatar)
110m hurdles	Ladji Doucoure (France)
400m hurdles	Bershawn Jackson (USA)
20km walk	Jefferson Pérez (Ecuador)
50km walk	Sergey Kirdyapkin (Russia)
4 × 100m relay	France
4 × 400m relay	USA
High jump	Yuriy Kyrmarenko (Ukraine)
Long jump	Dwight Phillips (USA)
Triple jump	Walter Davis (USA)
Pole vault	Rens Blom (Netherlands)
Shot	Adam Nelson (USA)
Discus	Virgilijus Alekna (Lithuania)
Hammer	Ivan Tikhon (Belarus)
Javelin	Andrus Varnik (Estonia)
Decathlon	Bryan Clay (USA)

2007

100m	Tyson Gay (USA)
200m	Tyson Gay (USA)
400m	Jeremy Wariner (USA)
800m	Alfred Yego (Kenya)
1500m	Bernard Lagat (USA)
5000m	Bernard Lagat (USA)
10000m	Kenenisa Bekele (Ethiopia)
Marathon	Luke Kibet (Kenya)
3000m steeplechase	Brimin Kipruto (Kenya)
110m hurdles	Liu Xiang (China)
400m hurdles	Kerron Clement (USA)
20km walk	Jefferson Pérez (Ecuador)
50km walk	Nathan Deakes (Australia)
4 × 100m relay	USA
4 × 400m relay	USA
High jump	Donald Thomas (Bahamas)
Long jump	Irving Saladino (Panama)
Triple jump	Nelson Évora (Portugal)
Pole vault	Brad Walker (USA)
Shot	Reese Hoffa (USA)
Discus	Gerd Kanter (Estonia)
Hammer	Ivan Tikhon (Belarus)
Javelin	Tero Pitkämäki (Finland)
Decathlon	Roman Šebrle (Czech Republic)

Event (Women)	Winners

1997

100m	Marion Jones (USA)
200m	Zhanna Pintussevich (Ukraine)
400m	Cathy Freeman (Australia)
800m	Ana Fidelia Quirot (Cuba)
1500m	Carla Sacramento (Portugal)
5000m	Gabriela Szabo (Romania)
10000m	Sally Barsosio (Kenya)
Marathon	Hiromi Suzuki (Japan)
100m hurdles	Ludmila Engquist (Sweden)
400m hurdles	Nezha Bidouane (Morocco)
10km walk	Annarita Sidoti (Italy)
4 × 100m relay	USA
4 × 400m relay	Germany
High jump	Hanne Haugland (Norway)
Long jump	Lyudmila Galkina (Russia)
Triple jump	Sarka Kasparkova (Czech Republic)
Shot	Astrid Kumbernuss (Germany)
Discus	Beatrice Faumuina (New Zealand)
Javelin	Trine Hattestad (Norway)
Heptathlon	Sabine Braun (Germany)

1999

100m	Marion Jones (USA)
200m	Inger Miller (USA)
400m	Cathy Freeman (Australia)
800m	Ludmilla Formanova (Czech Republic)
1500m	Svetlana Masterkova (Russia)
5000m	Gabriela Szabo (Romania)
10000m	Gete Warni (Ethiopia)
Marathon	Jong Song-Ok (North Korea)
100m hurdles	Gail Devers (USA)
400m hurdles	Daimi Pernia (Cuba)
20km walk	Liu Hongyu (China)
4 × 100m relay	Bahamas
4 × 400m relay	Russia
High jump	Inga Babakova (Ukraine)
Long jump	Niurka Montalvo (Spain)
Triple jump	Paraskevi Tsiamita (Greece)
Pole vault	Stacy Dragila (USA)
Shot	Astrid Kumbernuss (Germany)
Discus	Franka Dietzsch (Germany)
Hammer	Michaela Melinte (Romania)
Javelin	Mirela Manjani-Tzelili (Greece)
Heptathlon	Eunice Barber (France)

2001

100m	Zhanna Pintusevich-Block (Ukraine)
200m	Marion Jones (USA)
400m	Amy Mbacke Thiam (Senegal)
800m	Maria Mutola (Mozambique)

Sports and Games

1500m	Gabriela Szabo (Romania)
5000m	Olga Yegorova (Russia)
10000m	Derartu Tulu (Ethiopia)
Marathon	Lidia Simon (Romania)
100m hurdles	Anjanette Kirkland (USA)
400m hurdles	Nezha Bidouane (Morocco)
20km walk	Olimpiada Ivanova (Russia)
4 × 100m relay	USA
4 × 400m relay	USA
High jump	Hestrie Cloete (South Africa)
Long jump	Fiona May (Italy)
Triple jump	Tatyana Lebedeva (Russia)
Shot	Yanina Korolchik (Belarus)
Discus	Natalya Sadova (Russia)
Javelin	Osleidys Menéndez (Cuba)
Pole vault	Stacy Dragila (USA)
Hammer	Yipsi Moreno (Cuba)
Heptathlon	Yelena Prokhorova (Russia)

2003

100m	Torri Edwards (USA)
200m	Anastasiya Kapachinskaya (Russia)
400m	Ana Guevara (Mexico)
800m	Maria Mutola (Mozambique)
1500m	Tatyana Tomashova (Russia)
5000m	Tirunesh Dibaba (Ethiopia)
10000m	Berhane Adere (Ethiopia)
Marathon	Catherine Ndereba (Kenya)
100m hurdles	Perdita Felicien (Canada)
400m hurdles	Jana Pittman (Australia)
4 × 100m relay	France
4 × 400m relay	USA
20km walk	Yelena Nikolayeva (Russia)
High jump	Hestrie Cloete (South Africa)
Long jump	Eunice Barber (Italy)
Triple jump	Tatyana Lebedeva (Russia)
Pole vault	Svetlana Feofanova (Russia)
Shot	Svetlana Krivelyova (Russia)
Discus	Irina Yatchenko (Belarus)
Hammer	Yipsi Moreno (Cuba)
Javelin	Mirela Manjani-Tzelili (Greece)
Heptathlon	Carolina Kluft (Sweden)

2005

100m	Lauryn Williams (USA)
200m	Allyson Felix (USA)
400m	Tonique Williams Darling (Bahamas)
800m	Zulia Calatayud (Cuba)
1500m	Tatyana Tomashova (Russia)
5000m	Tirunesh Dibaba (Ethiopia)
10000m	Tirunesh Dibaba (Ethiopia)
Marathon	Paula Radcliffe (UK)
3000m steeplechase	Docus Inzikuru (Uganda)
100m hurdles	Michelle Perry (USA)
400m hurdles	Yuliya Pechonkina (Russia)
4 × 100m relay	USA
4 × 400m relay	Russia
20km walk	Olimpiada Ivanova (Russia)
High jump	Kajsa Bergqvist (Sweden)
Long jump	Tianna Madison (USA)
Triple jump	Trecia Smith (Jamaica)
Pole vault	Yelena Isinbayeva (Russia)
Shot	Nadezhda Ostapchuk (Belarus)
Discus	Franka Dietzsch (Germany)
Hammer	Olga Kuzenkova (Russia)
Javelin	Osleidys Menendez (Cuba)

Heptathlon	Carolina Kluft (Sweden)

2007

100m	Veronica Campbell (Jamaica)
200m	Allyson Felix (USA)
400m	Christine Ohuruogu (UK)
800m	Janeth Jepkosgei (Kenya)
1500m	Maryam Jamal (Bahrain)
5000m	Meseret Defar (Ethiopia)
10000m	Tirunesh Dibaba (Ethiopia)
Marathon	Catherine Ndereba (Kenya)
3000m steeplechase	Yekaterina Volkova (Russia)
100m hurdles	Michelle Perry (USA)
400m hurdles	Jana Rawlinson (Australia)
4 × 100m relay	USA
4 × 400m relay	USA
20km walk	Olga Kaniskina (Russia)
High jump	Blanka Vlašić (Croatia)
Long jump	Tatiana Lebedeva (Russia)
Triple jump	Yargelis Savigne (Cuba)
Pole vault	Yelena Isinbayeva (Russia)
Shot	Valerie Vili (New Zealand)
Discus	Franka Dietzsch (Germany)
Hammer	Betty Heidler (Germany)
Javelin	Barbora Špotáková (Czech Republic)
Heptathlon	Carolina Klüft (Sweden)

Badminton

■ World Championships

First held in 1977; initially took place every three years; from 1983 every two years; from 2005 annually (except Olympic years).

Men

1993	Joko Suprianto (Indonesia)
1995	Heryanto Arbi (Indonesia)
1997	Peter Rasmussen (Denmark)
1999	Sun Jun (China)
2001	Hendra Wan (Indonesia)
2003	Xia Xuanze (China)
2005	Taufik Hidayat (Indonesia)
2006	Lin Dan (China)
2007	Lin Dan (China)

Women

1993	Susi Susanti (Indonesia)
1995	Ye Zhaoying (China)
1997	Ye Zhaoying (China)
1999	Camilla Martin (Denmark)
2001	Gong Ruina (China)
2003	Zhang Ning (China)
2005	Xie Xingfang (China)
2006	Xie Xingfang (China)
2007	Zhu Lin (China)

■ Thomas Cup

An international team event for men's teams; inaugurated 1949, now held every two years.

1992	Malaysia
1994	Indonesia
1996	Indonesia
1998	Indonesia
2000	Indonesia
2002	Indonesia
2004	China
2006	China
2008	China

Baseball field

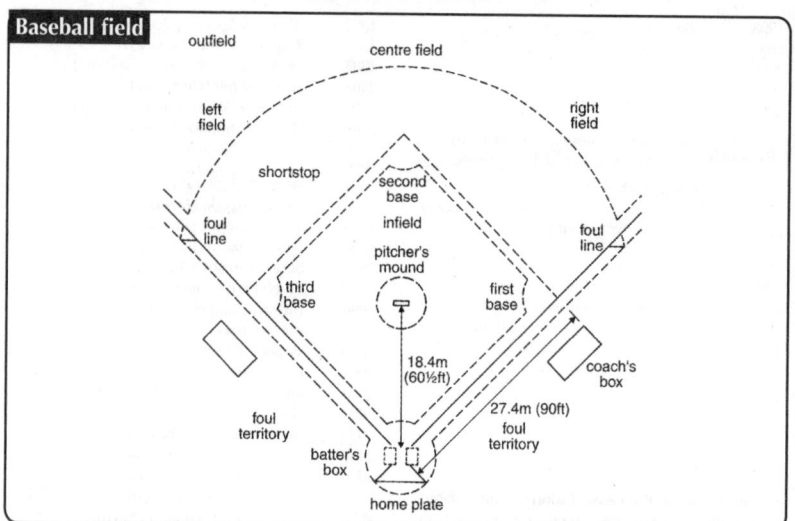

outfield

centre field

left field

right field

shortstop

second base

infield

foul line

foul line

pitcher's mound

third base

first base

18.4m (60½ft)

coach's box

foul territory

27.4m (90ft) foul territory

batter's box

home plate

■ Uber Cup

An international event for women's teams; first held in 1957; now held every two years.

1992	China
1994	Indonesia
1996	Indonesia
1998	China
2000	China
2002	China
2004	China
2006	China
2008	China

■ All-England Championship

Badminton's premier event prior to the inauguration of the World Championships; first held in 1899.

Men

1992	Liu Jun (China)
1993	Heryanto Arbi (Indonesia)
1994	Heryanto Arbi (Indonesia)
1995	Poul-Erik Hoyer-Larsen (Denmark)
1996	Poul-Erik Hoyer-Larsen (Denmark)
1997	Dong Jiong (China)
1998	Sun Jun (China)
1999	Peter Gade Christensen (Denmark)
2000	Xia Xuanze (China)
2001	Pulella Gopichand (India)
2002	Chen Hong (China)
2003	Muhammad Hafiz Hashim (Malaysia)
2004	Lin Dan (China)
2005	Hong Chen (China)
2006	Lin Dan (China)
2007	Lin Dan (China)
2008	Chen Yin (China)

Women

1992	Tang Jiuhong (China)
1993	Susi Susanti (Indonesia)
1994	Susi Susanti (Indonesia)
1995	Lim Xiao Qing (Sweden)
1996	Bang Soo Hyun (South Korea)
1997	Ye Zhaoying (China)
1998	Ye Zhaoying (China)
1999	Ye Zhaoying (China)
2000	Zichao Gong (China)
2001	Zichao Gong (China)
2002	Camilla Martin (Denmark)
2003	Mi Zhou (China)
2004	Gong Ruina (Denmark)
2005	Xie Xingfang (China)
2006	Xie Xingfang (China)
2007	Xie Xingfang (China)
2008	Tine Rasmussen (Denmark)

Baseball

■ World Series

First held in 1903; takes place each October, the best of seven matches; professional baseball's leading event, the end-of-season meeting between the winners of the two major baseball leagues in North America, the National League (NL) and American League (AL).

1992	Toronto Blue Jays (AL)
1993	Toronto Blue Jays (AL)
1994	*not held*
1995	Atlanta Braves (NL)
1996	New York Yankees (AL)
1997	Florida Marlins (NL)
1998	New York Yankees (AL)
1999	New York Yankees (AL)
2000	New York Yankees (AL)
2001	Arizona Diamondbacks (NL)
2002	Anaheim Angels (AL)
2003	Florida Marlins (NL)
2004	Boston Red Sox (AL)
2005	Chicago White Sox (AL)
2006	St Louis Cardinals (NL)
2007	Boston Red Sox (AL)
2008	Philadelphia Phillies (NL)

■ World Cup

Instituted in 1938; currently held every two years.

1994	Cuba

1998	Cuba
2001	Cuba
2003	Cuba
2005	Cuba
2007	USA

Basketball

■ **World Championship**
First held 1950 for men, 1953 for women; takes place approximately every four years.

Men

1994	USA
1998	Yugoslavia
2002	Yugoslavia
2006	Spain

Women

1994	Brazil
1998	USA
2002	USA
2006	Australia

■ **National Basketball Association Championship**
First held in 1947; the major competition in professional basketball in North America, end-of-season play-off involving the champion teams from the Eastern Conference (EC) and Western Conference (WC).

1992	Chicago Bulls (EC)
1993	Chicago Bulls (EC)
1994	Houston Rockets (WC)
1995	Houston Rockets (WC)
1996	Chicago Bulls (EC)
1997	Chicago Bulls (EC)
1998	Chicago Bulls (EC)
1999	San Antonio Spurs (WC)
2000	Los Angeles Lakers (WC)
2001	Los Angeles Lakers (WC)
2002	Los Angeles Lakers (WC)
2003	San Antonio Spurs (WC)
2004	Detroit Pistons (EC)
2005	San Antonio Spurs (WC)
2006	Miami Heat (EC)
2007	San Antonio Spurs (WC)
2008	Boston Celtics (EC)

Biathlon

■ **World Championships**
First held in 1958; take place annually; the Olympic champion is the automatic world champion in Olympic years; women's championship first held in 1984.

Men
10km

1992	Mark Kirchner (Germany)
1993	Mark Kirchner (Germany)
1994	Serguei Tchepikov (Russia)
1995	Patrice Bailly-Salins (France)
1996	Vladimir Dratchev (Russia)
1997	Wilfried Pallhuber (Italy)
1998	Ole Einar Bjoerndalen (Norway)
1999	Frank Luck (Germany)
2000	Frode Andresen (Norway)
2001	Paul Rostovtsev (Russia)
2002	Ole Einar Bjoerndalen (Norway)

2003	Ole Einar Bjoerndalen (Norway)
2004	Raphael Poiree (France)
2005	Ole Einar Bjoerndalen (Norway)
2006	Sven Fischer (Germany)
2007	Ole Einar Bjoerndalen (Norway)
2008	Maxim Tchondov (Russia)

20km

1992	Yevgeny Redkine (CIS)
1993	Franz Zingerle (Austria)
1994	Sergei Tarasov (Russia)
1995	Tomaz Sikora (Poland)
1996	Sergei Tarasov (Russia)
1997	Ricco Gross (Germany)
1998	Halvard Hanevold (Norway)
1999	Ricco Gross (Germany)
2000	Wolfgang Rottman (Austria)
2001	Paavo Puurunen (Finland)
2002	Ole Einar Bjoerndalen (Norway)
2003	Halvard Hanevold (Norway)
2004	Raphael Poiree (France)
2005	Roman Dostal (Czech Republic)
2006	Michael Greis (Germany)
2007	Raphael Poirée (France)
2008	Emil Hegle Svendsen (Norway)

Women
7.5km

1992	Anfissa Restzova (CIS)
1993	Myriam Bedard (Canada)
1994	Myriam Bedard (Canada)
1995	Anne Briand (France)
1996	Olga Romansko (Russia)
1997	Olga Romansko (Russia)
1998	Galina Koukleva (Russia)
1999	Martina Zellner (Germany)
2000	Liv Grete Skjelbreid (Norway)
2001	Kati Wilhelm (Germany)
2002	Kati Wilhelm (Germany)
2003	Sylvie Becaert (France)
2004	Liv Grete Poiree (Norway)
2005	Uschi Disl (Germany)
2006	Florence Baverel-Robert (France)
2007	Magdalena Neuner (Germany)
2008	Andrea Henkel (Germany)

15km

1992	Antje Misersky (Germany)
1993	Petra Schaaf (Germany)
1994	Myriam Bedard (Canada)
1995	Corinne Niogret (France)
1996	Emmanuelle Claret (France)
1997	Magdalena Forsberg (Sweden)
1998	Yekaterina Dafovska (Bulgaria)
1999	Olena Zubrilova (Ukraine)
2000	Corinne Niogret (France)
2001	Magdalena Forsberg (Sweden)
2002	Andrea Henkel (Germany)
2003	Katerina Holubcoua (Czech Republic)
2004	Olga Pyleva (Russia)
2005	Andrea Henkel (Germany)
2006	Svetlana Ishmouratova (Russia)
2007	Linda Grubben (Norway)
2008	Ekaterina Iourieva (Russia)

Billiards

■ **World Professional Championship**
First held in 1870, organized on a challenge basis; became a knockout event in 1909; discontinued in 1934; revived in 1951 as a challenge system; reverted to a knockout event in 1980.

1992	Geet Sethi (India)
1993	Geet Sethi (India)
1994	Peter Gilchrist (England)
1995	Geet Sethi (India)
1996	Mike Russell (England)
1997	*not held*
1998	Geet Sethi (India)
1999	Mike Russell (England)
2000	Mike Russell (England)
2001	Peter Gilchrist (England)
2002	Mike Russell (England)
2003	Mike Russell (England)
2004	Mike Russell (England)
2005	Chris Shutt (England)
2006	Geet Sethi (India)
2007	Mike Russell (England)
2008	Mike Russell (England)

Bobsleighing and tobogganing

■ **World Championships**
First held in 1930 (four-man) and in 1931 (two-man); Olympic champions automatically become world champions.

Two-man

1992	Gustav Weder/Donat Acklin (Switzerland)
1993	Christoph Langen/Peer Joechel (Germany)
1994	Gustav Weder/Donat Acklin (Switzerland)
1995	Christoph Langen/Olaf Hampel (Germany)
1996	Christoph Langen/Markus Zimmermann (Germany)
1997	Reto Goetschi/Guido Acklin (Switzerland)
1998	Guenther Huber/Antonio Tartaglia (Italy)
1999	Guenther Huber/Ubaldo Ranzi (Italy)
2000	Christoph Langen/Markus Zimmermann (Germany)
2001	Christoph Langen/Marco Jacobs (Germany)
2002	Christoph Langen/Markus Zimmermann (Germany)
2003	Kevin Kuske/Andre Lange (Germany)
2004	Pierre Lueders/Giulio Zardo (Canada)
2005	Pierre Lueders/Lascelles Brown (Canada)
2006	Andre Lange/Kevin Kuske (Germany)
2007	Andre Lange/Kevin Kuske (Germany)
2008	Andre Lange/Kevin Kuske (Germany)

Four-man

1991	Germany
1992	Austria
1993	Switzerland
1994	Germany
1995	Germany
1996	Germany
1997	Germany
1998	Germany
1999	France
2000	Germany
2001	Germany
2002	Germany
2003	Germany
2004	Germany
2005	Germany
2006	Germany
2007	Switzerland
2008	Germany

■ **Luge World Championships**
First held in 1955; annually until 1981, then every two years until 1989, then annually. Not held in Olympic years.

Men's single-seater

1993	Werdel Suckow (USA)
1995	Armin Zoeggeler (Italy)
1996	Jana Bode (Germany)
1997	Georg Hackl (Germany)
1999	Armin Zoeggeler (Italy)
2000	Jens Müller (Germany)
2001	Armin Zoeggeler (Italy)
2003	Armin Zoeggeler (Italy)
2004	David Möller (Germany)
2005	Armin Zoeggeler (Italy)
2007	David Möller (Germany)
2008	Felix Loch (Germany)

Women's single-seater

1993	Gerda Weissensteiner (Italy)
1995	Gabriele Kohlisch (Germany)
1996	Susi Erdmann (Germany)
1997	Susi Erdmann (Germany)
1999	Sonja Wiedemann (Germany)
2000	Sylke Otto (Germany)
2001	Sylke Otto (Germany)
2003	Sylke Otto (Germany)
2004	Silke Kraushaar (Germany)
2005	Sylke Otto (Germany)
2007	Tatjana Hüfner (Germany)
2008	Tatjana Hüfner (Germany)

Bowls

■ **World Outdoor Championships**
Instituted for men in 1966 and for women in 1969; held every four years.

Men's Singles

1992	Tony Allcock (England)
1996	Tony Allcock (England)
2000	Jeremy Henry (Ireland)
2004	Steve Glasson (Australia)
2008	Safnan Said (Malaysia)

Men's Pairs

1992	Scotland
1996	Ireland
2000	Scotland
2004	Canada
2008	New Zealand

Men's Triples

1992	Israel
1996	Scotland
2000	New Zealand
2004	Scotland
2008	Scotland

Men's Fours

1992	Scotland
1996	England
2000	Wales
2004	Scotland
2008	New Zealand

■ **Leonard Trophy**
Men's team award.

1992	Scotland
1996	Scotland
2000	Australia
2004	Scotland
2008	New Zealand

Women's Singles

1992	Margaret Johnston (Ireland)
1996	Carmen Anderson (Norfolk Is)
2000	Margaret Johnston (Ireland)
2004	Margaret Johnston (Ireland)
2008	Val Smith (New Zealand)

Women's Pairs

1992	Ireland
1996	Ireland
2000	Scotland
2004	New Zealand
2008	New Zealand

Women's Triples

1992	Scotland
1996	South Africa
2000	New Zealand
2004	South Africa
2008	South Africa

Women's Fours

1992	Scotland
1996	Australia
2000	New Zealand
2004	England
2008	Australia

■ *Taylor Trophy*
Women's team award.

1992	Scotland
1996	South Africa
2000	England
2004	England
2008	Australia

■ **World Indoor Championships**
First held in 1979; take place annually.

Men's singles

1992	Ian Schuback (Australia)
1993	Richard Corsie (Scotland)
1994	Andy Thomson (England)
1995	Andy Thomson (England)
1996	David Gourlay, Jr (Scotland)
1997	Hugh Duff (Scotland)
1998	Paul Foster (Scotland)
1999	Alex Marshall (Scotland)
2000	Robert Weale (Wales)
2001	Darren Burnett (Scotland)
2002	Tony Allcock (England)
2003	Alex Marshall (Scotland)
2004	Alex Marshall (Scotland)
2005	Paul Foster (Scotland)

2006	Mervyn King (England)
2007	Alex Marshall (Scotland)
2008	Alex Marshall (Scotland)

■ **Waterloo Handicap**
First held in 1907 and annually at Blackpool's Waterloo Hotel; the premier event of Crown Green Bowling.

1992	Brian Duncan
1993	Alan Broadhurst
1994	Bill Hilton
1995	Ken Strutt
1996	Lee Heaton
1997	Andrew Cairns
1998	Michael Jagger
1999	Ivan Smout
2000	Carl Armitage
2001	Glynn Cookson
2002	Stan Frith
2003	Glynn Cookson
2004	Noel Burrows
2005	John Bailey
2006	Andrew Moss
2007	Chris Mordue
2008	Gary Ellis

Boxing

■ **World Heavyweight Champions**
The first world heavyweight champion under Queensbury Rules with gloves was James J Corbett in 1892.

		Recognizing body
1992–3	Riddick Bowe (USA)[1]	WBA/WBC/IBF
1992–3	Michael Moorer (USA)	WBO
1993–4	Evander Holyfield (USA)	WBA/IBF
1992–4	Lennox Lewis (UK)	WBC
1993	Tommy Morrison (USA)	WBO
1993–4	Michael Bentt (USA)	WBO
1994–5	Herbie Hide (UK)	WBO
1994	Michael Moorer (USA)	WBA/IBF
1994–5	Oliver McCall (USA)	WBC
1994–5	George Foreman (USA)[2][3]	WBA/IBF
1995–6	Riddick Bowe (USA)	WBO
1995–6	Bruce Seldon (USA)	WBA
1995–6	Frank Bruno (UK)	WBC
1995–6	Frans Botha (South Africa)[4]	IBF
1996	Mike Tyson (USA)[5]	WBA/WBC
1996–7	Henry Akinwande (UK)	WBO
1996–7	Michael Moorer (USA)	IBF
1996–7	Evander Holyfield (USA)	WBA
1997–9	Evander Holyfield (USA)	WBA/IBF
1997–9	Lennox Lewis (UK)	WBC
1997–9	Herbie Hide (UK)	WBO
1999–2000	Vitali Klitschko (Ukraine)	WBO
1999–2000	Lennox Lewis (UK)[6]	UND (WBA/WBC/IBF)
2000	Chris Byrd (USA)	WBO
2000–1	Evander Holyfield (USA)	WBA
2000–1	Lennox Lewis (UK)	WBC/IBF
2001–3	John Ruiz (USA)	WBA
2000–3	Vladimir Klitschko (Ukraine)	WBO
2001	Hasim Rahman (USA)	WBC/IBF

2001–2	Lennox Lewis (UK)[7]	WBC/IBF
2002–4	Lennox Lewis (UK)	WBC
2002–6	Chris Byrd (USA)	IBF
2003	Corrie Sanders (South Africa)	WBO
2003–4	Roy Jones, Jr (USA)	WBA
2004–6	Lamon Brewster (USA)	WBO
2004–5	John Ruiz (USA)	WBA
2004–5	Vitali Klitschko (Ukraine)	WBC
2005	James Toney (USA)[8]	WBA
2005	John Ruiz (USA)	WBA
2005–6	Hasim Rahman (USA)	WBC
2005–7	Nikolay Valuev (Russia)	WBA
2006	Sergei Liakhovich (Belarus)	WBO
2006–	Vladimir Klitschko (Ukraine)	IBF
2006–8	Oleg Maskaev (Russia)	WBC
2006–7	Shannon Briggs (USA)	WBO
2007–8	Ruslan Chagaev (Uzbekistan)	WBA
2007–8	Sultan Ibragimov (Russia)	WBO
2008–	Samuel Peter (Nigeria)	WBC
2008–	Nikolay Valuev (Russia)	WBA
2008–	Vladimir Klitschko (Ukraine)	WBO

[1] Stripped of WBC title in 1992
[2] Gave up IBF title in 1995
[3] Stripped of WBA title in 1995
[4] Stripped of IBF title in 1996
[5] Gave up WBC title in 1996
[6] Stripped of WBA title in 2000
[7] Gave up IBF title in 2002
[8] Stripped of title in 2005

UND = Undisputed Champion; WBC = World Boxing Council; WBA = World Boxing Association; IBF = International Boxing Federation; WBO = World Boxing Organization

Canoeing

■ **Olympic Games**
The most prestigious competition in the canoeing calendar, included at every Olympic celebration since 1936; the Blue Riband event in the men's competition is the Kayak Singles over 1000 metres, and in the women's the Kayak Singles over 500 metres.

Single kayak (Men)

1992	Clint Robinson (Australia)
1996	Knut Holmann (Norway)
2000	Knut Holmann (Norway)
2004	Eirik Larsen (Norway)
2008	Knut Holmann (Norway)

Single kayak (Women)

1992	Birgit Schmidt (Germany)
1996	Rita Koban (Hungary)
2000	Josefa Guerrini (Italy)
2004	Natasa Janics (Hungary)
2008	Inna Osypenko-Radomska (Ukraine)

Chess

■ **World Champions**
World Champions have been recognized since 1886. The first international tournament was held in London in 1851, and won by Adolf Anderssen (Germany); first women's champion recognized in 1927.

Men

1985–93	Gary Kasparov (USSR)
1993–9	Anatoly Karpov (Russia)
1999–2000	Alexander Khalifman (Russia)
2000–2	Viswanathan Anand (India)
2002–4	Ruslan Ponomariov (Ukraine)
2004–5	Rustam Kasimdzhanov (Uzbekistan)
2005–6	Vesalin Topalov (Bulgaria)
2006–7	Vladimir Kramnik (Russia)
2007–	Viswanathan Anand (India)

Women

1978–91	Maya Chiburdanidze (USSR)
1991–6	Xie Jun (China)
1996–9	Zsuzsanna Polgar (Hungary)
1999–2001	Xie Jun (China)
2001–4	Zhu Chen (China)
2004–6	Antoaneta Stefanova (Bulgaria)
2006–8	Xu Yuhua (China)
2008	Alexandra Kosteniuk (Russia)

Contract bridge

■ **World Team Championship**
The game's biggest championship; men's contest (The Bermuda Bowl) first held in 1950, and now takes place every two years, with the exception of 1999; women's contest (The Venice Cup) first held in 1974, and since 1985 has been concurrent with the men's event.

Men

1993	Netherlands
1995	USA
1997	France
2000	USA
2001	USA II
2003	USA I
2005	Italy
2007	Norway

Women

1993	USA
1995	Germany
1997	USA
2000	Netherlands
2001	Germany
2003	USA I
2005	France
2007	USA 1

■ **World Bridge Games**
First held in 1960 as World Team Olympiad; since then, every four years.

Open

1992	France
1996	France
2000	Italy
2004	Italy
2008	Italy

Sports and Games

Sports and Games

Cricket field positions

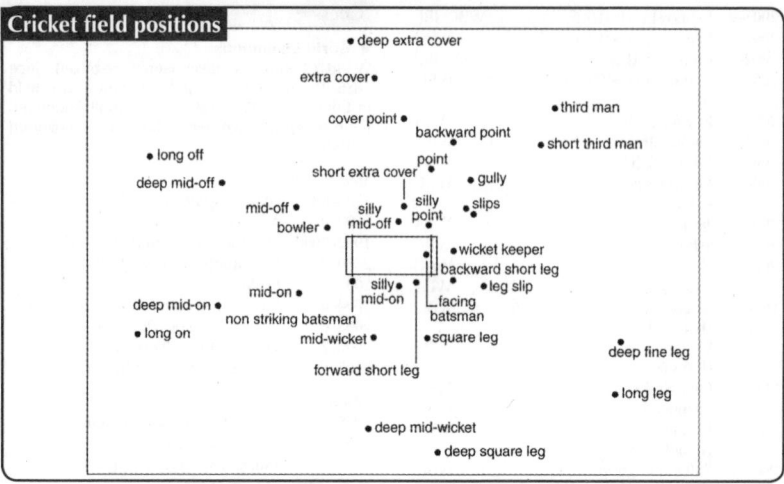

Women

1992	Austria
1996	USA
2000	USA
2004	Russia
2008	England

Cricket

■ World Cup
First played in England in 1975; usually held every four years; the 1987 competition, held in India and Pakistan, was the first to be played outside England.

1996	Sri Lanka
1999	Australia
2003	Australia
2007	Australia

■ County Championship
The oldest cricket competition in the world; first won by Sussex in 1827; not officially recognized until 1890, when a proper points system was introduced.

1992	Essex
1993	Middlesex
1994	Warwickshire
1995	Warwickshire
1996	Leicestershire
1997	Glamorgan
1998	Leicestershire
1999	Surrey
2000	Surrey
2001	Yorkshire
2002	Surrey
2003	Sussex
2004	Warwickshire
2005	Nottinghamshire
2006	Sussex
2007	Sussex
2008	Durham

■ Pro 40 League
First held in 1969; known as the John Player League until 1987, the Refuge Assurance League until 1991, the Axa Equity and Law League until 1999, the CGU League until 2000, the Norwich Union National Cricket League until 2003, and the Totesport National Cricket League until 2005.

1992	Middlesex
1993	Glamorgan
1994	Warwickshire
1995	Kent
1996	Surrey
1997	Warwickshire
1998	Lancashire
1999	Lancashire
2000	Gloucestershire
2001	Kent
2002	Glamorgan
2003	Surrey
2004	Glamorgan
2005	Essex
2006	Essex
2007	Worcestershire
2008	Sussex

■ Friends Provident Trophy
First held in 1963; known as the Gillette Cup until 1981, the NatWest Bank Trophy until 2000 and the Cheltenham & Gloucester Trophy until 2006.

1992	Northamptonshire
1993	Warwickshire
1994	Worcestershire
1995	Warwickshire
1996	Lancashire
1997	Essex
1998	Lancashire
1999	Gloucestershire
2000	Gloucestershire
2001	Somerset
2002	Yorkshire
2003	Gloucestershire
2004	Gloucestershire
2005	Hampshire
2006	Sussex

2007 Durham
2008 Essex

■ Benson and Hedges Cup
Competition ran from 1972 to 2002.

1992 Hampshire
1993 Derbyshire
1994 Warwickshire
1995 Lancashire
1996 Lancashire
1997 Surrey
1998 Essex
1999 Gloucestershire
2000 Gloucestershire
2001 Surrey
2002 Warwickshire

■ Twenty20 Cup
First held in 2003.

2003 Surrey
2004 Leicestershire
2005 Somerset
2006 Leicestershire
2007 Kent
2008 Middlesex

■ Pura Milk Cup
Australia's leading domestic competition; contested inter-state since 1891–2; known as the Sheffield Shield until 1999.

1992 Western Australia
1993 New South Wales
1994 New South Wales
1995 Queensland
1996 South Australia
1997 Queensland
1998 Western Australia
1999 Western Australia
2000 Queensland
2001 Queensland
2002 Queensland
2003 New South Wales
2004 Victoria
2005 New South Wales
2006 Queensland
2007 Tasmania
2008 New South Wales

Croquet

■ MacRobertson Shield
Croquet's leading tournament; held spasmodically since 1925; contested by teams from Great Britain, New Zealand, Australia and, since 1993, the USA.

1993 Great Britain & Ireland
1996 Great Britain
2000 Great Britain
2003 Great Britain
2006 Great Britain

Cross country running

■ World Championships
First international championship held in 1903, but only included runners from England, Ireland, Scotland and Wales; recognized as an official world championship from 1973; first women's race in 1967.

Individual (Men)
1992 John Ngugi (Kenya)
1993 William Sigei (Kenya)
1994 William Sigei (Kenya)
1995 Paul Tergat (Kenya)
1996 Paul Tergat (Kenya)
1997 Paul Tergat (Kenya)
1998 Paul Tergat (Kenya)
1999 Paul Tergat (Kenya)
2000 Mohammed Mourhit (Belgium)
2001 Mohammed Mourhit (Belgium)
2002 Kenenisa Bekele (Ethiopia)
2003 Kenenisa Bekele (Ethiopia)
2004 Kenenisa Bekele (Ethiopia)
2005 Kenenisa Bekele (Ethiopia)
2006 Kenenisa Bekele (Ethiopia)
2007 Zersenay Tadese (Eritrea)
2008 Kenenisa Bekele (Ethiopia)

Team (Men)
1992 Kenya
1993 Kenya
1994 Kenya
1995 Kenya
1996 Kenya
1997 Kenya
1998 Kenya
1999 Kenya
2000 Kenya
2001 Kenya
2002 Kenya
2003 Kenya
2004 Ethiopia
2005 Ethiopia
2006 Kenya
2007 Kenya
2008 Kenya

Individual (Women)
1992 Lynn Jennings (USA)
1993 Albertina Dias (Portugal)
1994 Helen Chepngeno (Kenya)
1995 Derartu Tulu (Ethiopia)
1996 Gete Wami (Ethiopia)
1997 Derartu Tulu (Ethiopia)
1998 Sonia O'Sullivan (Ireland)
1999 Gete Wami (Ethiopia)
2000 Derartu Tulu (Ethiopia)
2001 Paula Radcliffe (England)
2002 Paula Radcliffe (England)
2003 Werknesh Kidane (Ethiopia)
2004 Benita Johnson (Australia)
2005 Tirunesh Dibaba (Ethiopia)
2006 Tirunesh Dibaba (Ethiopia)
2007 Lornah Kiplagat (Netherlands)
2008 Tirunesh Dibaba (Ethiopia)

Team (Women)
1992 Kenya
1993 Kenya
1994 Portugal

1995	Kenya
1996	Kenya
1997	Ethiopia
1998	Kenya
1999	Ethiopia
2000	Ethiopia
2001	Kenya
2002	Ethiopia
2003	Ethiopia
2004	Ethiopia
2005	Ethiopia
2006	Ethiopia
2007	Ethiopia
2008	Ethiopia

Curling

■ World Championships
First men's championship held in 1959; first women's championship in 1979; takes place annually.

Men

1992	Switzerland
1993	Canada
1994	Canada
1995	Canada
1996	Canada
1997	Sweden
1998	Canada
1999	Scotland
2000	Canada
2001	Sweden
2002	Canada
2003	Canada
2004	Sweden
2005	Canada
2006	Scotland
2007	Canada
2008	Canada

Women

1992	Sweden
1993	Canada
1994	Canada
1995	Sweden
1996	Canada
1997	Canada
1998	Sweden
1999	Sweden
2000	Canada
2001	Canada
2002	Scotland
2003	USA
2004	Canada
2005	Sweden
2006	Sweden
2007	Canada
2008	Canada

Cycling

■ Tour de France
World's premier cycling event; first held in 1903.

1992	Miguel Indurain (Spain)
1993	Miguel Indurain (Spain)
1994	Miguel Indurain (Spain)
1995	Miguel Indurain (Spain)
1996	Bjarne Riis (Denmark)

1997	Jan Ullrich (Germany)
1998	Marco Pantani (Italy)
1999	Lance Armstrong (USA)
2000	Lance Armstrong (USA)
2001	Lance Armstrong (USA)
2002	Lance Armstrong (USA)
2003	Lance Armstrong (USA)
2004	Lance Armstrong (USA)
2005	Lance Armstrong (USA)
2006	Oscar Pereiro (Spain)
2007	Alberto Contador (Spain)
2008	Carlos Sastre (Spain)

■ World Road Race Championships
Men's race first held in 1927; first women's race in 1958; takes place annually.

Professional Men

1992	Gianni Bugno (Italy)
1993	Lance Armstrong (USA)
1994	Luc Leblanc (France)
1995	Abraham Olano (Spain)
1996	Johan Museeuw (Belgium)
1997	Laurent Brochard (France)
1998	Oskar Camenzind (Switzerland)
1999	Oscar Freire Gomez (Spain)
2000	Romans Vainsteins (Latvia)
2001	Oscar Freire Gomez (Spain)
2002	Mario Cipollini (Italy)
2003	Igor Astorloa (Spain)
2004	Oscar Freire Gomez (Spain)
2005	Tom Boonen (Belgium)
2006	Paolo Bettini (Italy)
2007	Paolo Bettini (Italy)
2008	Alessandro Ballan (Italy)

Women

1992	Kathryn Watt (Australia)
1993	Leontien van Moorsel (Holland)
1994	Monica Valvik (Norway)
1995	Jeannie Longo (France)
1996	Barbara Heeb (Switzerland)
1997	Alessandra Cappellotto (Italy)
1998	Diana Ziliute (Lithuania)
1999	Edita Pucinskaite (Lithuania)
2000	Zinaida Stahurskaia (Belarus)
2001	Rosa Polikeviciute (Lithuania)
2002	Susanne Ljungskog (Sweden)
2003	Susanne Ljungskog (Sweden)
2004	Judith Arndt (Germany)
2005	Regina Schleicher (Germany)
2006	Marianne Vos (Netherlands)
2007	Marta Bastianelli (Italy)
2008	Nicole Cooke (UK)

Cyclocross

■ World Championships
First held in 1950 as an open event; separate professional and amateur events from 1967 to 1993. Since 1994 held as an open event, known as the Elite.

Professional

1992	Mike Kluge (Germany)
1993	Dominique Arnould (France)

Amateur

1992	Daniele Pontoni (Italy)
1993	Henrik Djernis (Denmark)

Open

1994	Paul Herijgers (Belgium)
1995	Dieter Runkel (Switzerland)

Elite

1996	Adri van der Poel (Netherlands)
1997	Daniele Pontoni (Italy)
1998	Mario de Clerq (Belgium)
1999	Mario de Clerq (Belgium)
2000	Richard Groenendaal (Netherlands)
2001	Erwin Vervecken (Belgium)
2002	Mario de Clerq (Belgium)
2003	Bart Wellens (Belgium)
2004	Bart Wellens (Belgium)
2005	Sven Nijs (Belgium)
2006	Erwin Vervecken (Belgium)
2007	Erwin Vervecken (Belgium)
2008	Lars Boom (Netherlands)

Darts

■ Embassy World Professional Championship

Run by the British Darts Organisation and first held at Nottingham in 1978.

1992	Phil Taylor (England)
1993	John Lowe (England)
1994	John Part (Canada)
1995	Richie Burnett (Wales)
1996	Steve Beaton (England)
1997	Les Wallace (Scotland)
1998	Raymond van Barneveld (Netherlands)
1999	Raymond van Barneveld (Netherlands)
2000	Ted Hankey (England)
2001	John Walton (England)
2002	Tony David (Australia)
2003	Raymond van Barneveld (Netherlands)
2004	Andy Fordham (England)
2005	Raymond van Barneveld (Netherlands)
2006	Jelle Klaasen (Netherlands)
2007	Martin Adams (England)
2008	Mark Webster (Wales)

■ World Cup

A team competition first held at Wembley in 1977; takes place every two years.

Team (Men)

1993	England
1995	England
1997	Wales
1999	England
2001	England
2003	England
2005	Finland
2007	England

Individual (Men)

1993	Roland Schollen (Denmark)
1995	Martin Adams (England)
1997	Raymond van Barneveld (Netherlands)
1999	Raymond van Barneveld (Netherlands)
2001	Martin Adams (England)
2003	Raymond van Barneveld (Netherlands)
2005	Dick van Dijk (Netherlands)
2007	Mark Webster (Wales)

■ World Championship

Run by the World Darts Council (now Professional Darts Corporation) since 1994.

1994	Dennis Priestley (England)
1995	Phil Taylor (England)
1996	Phil Taylor (England)
1997	Phil Taylor (England)
1998	Phil Taylor (England)
1999	Phil Taylor (England)
2000	Phil Taylor (England)
2001	Phil Taylor (England)
2002	Phil Taylor (England)
2003	John Part (Canada)
2004	Phil Taylor (England)
2005	Phil Taylor (England)
2006	Phil Taylor (England)
2007	Raymond van Barneveld (Netherlands)
2008	John Part (Canada)

Draughts

■ British Open Championship

The leading championship in Britain; first held in 1926; now takes place every two years.

1992	Hugh Devlin (Ireland)
1994	Bill Edwards (Wales)
1996	Jack Francis (Barbados)
1998	Pat McCarthy (Republic of Ireland)
2000	William Docherty (Scotland)
2002	Ron King (Barbados)
2004	Colin Young (Scotland)
2006	Mustafa Durdyev (Turkmenistan)
2008	Rawle Allicock (England)

Equestrian events

■ World Championships

Show Jumping championships first held in 1953 (for men) and 1965 (for women); since 1978 they have competed together and on equal terms; team competition introduced in 1978; Three Day Event and Dressage championships introduced in 1966; all three now held every four years. Renamed the World Equestrian Games in 1990. Dressage split into two classes, Classic and Freestyle, in 2006.

Show Jumping (Individual)

1994	Franke Sloothaak (Germany)
1998	Rodrigo Pessoa (Brazil)
2002	Dermott Lennon (Ireland)
2006	Jos Lansink (Belgium)

Show Jumping (Team)

1994	Germany
1998	Germany
2002	France
2006	Netherlands

Three Day Event (Individual)

1994	Vaughn Jefferis (New Zealand)
1998	Blyth Tait (New Zealand)
2002	Jean Teulere (France)
2006	Zara Phillips (UK)

Three Day Event (Team)

1994	Great Britain
1998	New Zealand
2002	USA
2006	Germany

Dressage – Classic (Individual)

1994	Anky van Grunsven (Netherlands)
1998	Isabell Werth (Germany)

2002	Nadine Capellmann (Germany)
2006	Isabell Werth (Germany)

Dressage – Freestyle (Individual)

2006	Anky van Grunsven (Netherlands)

Dressage (Team)

1994	Germany
1998	Germany
2002	Germany
2006	Germany

Fencing

■ World Championships

Held annually since 1921 (between 1921–35, known as European Championships). Not held in Olympic years. Women's Sabre was introduced in 1999.

Foil Individual (Men)

1993	Alexander Koch (Germany)
1994	Rolando Tuckers (Cuba)
1995	Dimitriy Chevtchenko (Russia)
1997	Sergei Golubitsky (Ukraine)
1998	Sergei Golubitsky (Ukraine)
1999	Sergei Golubitsky (Ukraine)
2001	Salvatore Sanzo (Italy)
2002	Simone Vanni (Italy)
2003	Peter Joppich (Germany)
2005	Salvatore Sanzo (Italy)
2006	Peter Joppich (Germany)
2007	Peter Joppich (Germany)

Foil Team (Men)

1993	Germany
1994	Italy
1995	Cuba
1997	France
1998	Poland
1999	France
2001	France
2002	Germany
2003	Italy
2005	France
2006	France
2007	France

Foil Individual (Women)

1993	Francesca Bortolozzi (Italy)
1994	Reka Szabo-Lazar (Romania)
1995	Laura Badea (Romania)
1997	Giovanna Trillini (Italy)
1998	Sabine Bau (Germany)
1999	Valentina Vezzali (Italy)
2001	Valentina Vezzali (Italy)
2002	Svetlani Boiko (Russia)
2003	Valentina Vezzali (Italy)
2005	Valentina Vezzali (Italy)
2006	Margherita Granbassi (Italy)
2007	Valentina Vezzali (Italy)

Foil Team (Women)

1993	Germany
1994	Romania
1995	Italy
1997	Italy
1998	Italy
1999	Germany
2001	Italy
2002	Russia

2003	Poland
2005	South Korea
2006	Russia
2007	Poland

Épée Individual (Men)

1993	Pavel Kolobkov (Russia)
1994	Pavel Kolobkov (Russia)
1995	Eric Srecki (France)
1997	Eric Srecki (France)
1998	Hughes Obry (France)
1999	Arnd Schmitt (Germany)
2001	Paulo Milanoli (Italy)
2002	Pavel Kolobkov (Russia)
2003	Fabrice Jeannet (France)
2005	Pavel Kolobkov (Russia)
2006	Wang Lei (China)
2007	Krisztián Kulcsár (Hungary)

Épée Team (Men)

1993	Italy
1994	France
1995	Germany
1997	Cuba
1998	Hungary
1999	France
2001	Hungary
2002	France
2003	Russia
2005	France
2006	France
2007	France

Épée Individual (Women)

1993	Oksana Jermakova (Estonia)
1994	Laura Chiesa (Hungary)
1995	Joanna Jakimiuk (Poland)
1997	Miraide Garcia-Soto (Cuba)
1998	Laura Flessel (France)
1999	Laura Flessel-Colovic (France)
2001	Claudia Bokel (Germany)
2002	Hee Hyun (Korea)
2003	Natalia Conrad (Ukraine)
2005	Danuta Dmowska (Poland)
2006	Tímea Nagy (Hungary)
2007	Britta Heidemann (Germany)

Épée Team (Women)

1993	Hungary
1994	Spain
1995	Hungary
1997	Hungary
1998	France
1999	Hungary
2001	Russia
2002	Hungary
2003	Russia
2005	France
2006	China
2007	France

Sabre Individual (Men)

1993	Grigory Kirienko (Russia)
1994	Felix Becker (Germany)
1995	Grigory Kirienko (Russia)
1997	Stanislav Pozdniakov (Russia)
1998	Luigi Tarantino (Italy)
1999	Damien Touya (France)
2001	Stanislav Pozdniakov (Russia)

2002	Stanislav Pozdniakov (Russia)
2003	Vladimir Lukashenko (Ukraine)
2005	Mihai Covaliu (Romania)
2006	Stanislav Pozdniakov (Russia)
2007	Stanislav Pozdniakov (Russia)

Sabre Team (Men)

1993	Hungary
1994	Russia
1995	Italy
1997	France
1998	Hungary
1999	France
2001	Russia
2002	Russia
2003	Russia
2005	Russia
2006	France
2007	Hungary

Sabre Individual (Women)

1999	Elena Jemayeva (Azerbaijan)
2000	Elena Jemayeva (Azerbaijan)
2001	Anne Lise Touya (France)
2002	Xue Tan (China)
2003	Dorina Mihai (Romania)
2005	Anne Lise Touya (France)
2006	Rebecca Ward (USA)
2007	Elena Netchaeva (Russia)

Sabre Team (Women)

1999	Italy
2000	USA
2001	Russia
2002	Russia
2003	Italy
2005	USA
2006	France
2007	France

Football, American

▪ Super Bowl

First held in 1967; takes place each January; an end-of-season meeting between the champions of the two major US leagues, the National Football Conference (NFC) and the American Football Conference (AFC).

1992	Washington Redskins (NFC)
1993	Dallas Cowboys (NFC)
1994	Dallas Cowboys (NFC)
1995	San Francisco 49ers (NFC)
1996	Dallas Cowboys (NFC)
1997	Green Bay Packers (NFC)
1998	Denver Broncos (AFC)
1999	Denver Broncos (AFC)
2000	St Louis Rams (NFC)
2001	Baltimore Ravens (AFC)
2002	New England Patriots (AFC)
2003	Tampa Bay Buccaneers (NFC)
2004	New England Patriots (AFC)
2005	New England Patriots (AFC)
2006	Pittsburgh Steelers (AFC)
2007	Indianapolis Colts (AFC)
2008	New York Giants (NFC)

Football, Association

▪ FIFA World Cup

Association Football's premier event; first contested for the Jules Rimet Trophy in 1930; Brazil won it outright after winning for the third time in 1970; since then teams have competed for the FIFA (*Féderation Internationale de Football Association*) World Cup; held every four years.

Post-war winners

1950	Uruguay
1954	West Germany
1958	Brazil
1962	Brazil
1966	England
1970	Brazil
1974	West Germany
1978	Argentina
1982	Italy
1986	Argentina
1990	West Germany
1994	Brazil
1998	France
2002	Brazil
2006	Italy

▪ European Championship

Held every four years since 1960; qualifying group matches held over the two years preceding the final.

All winners

1960	USSR
1964	Spain
1968	Italy
1972	West Germany
1976	Czechoslovakia
1980	West Germany
1984	France
1988	Netherlands
1992	Denmark
1996	Germany
2000	France
2004	Greece
2008	Spain

▪ South American Championship

Known as Copa América; first held in 1916, for South American national sides; there were two tournaments in 1959, won by Argentina and Uruguay; discontinued in 1967, but revived eight years later.

1991	Argentina
1993	Argentina
1995	Uruguay
1997	Brazil
1999	Brazil
2001	Colombia
2004	Brazil
2007	Brazil

▪ European Champions Cup

The leading club competition in Europe; open to the League champions of countries affiliated to UEFA (Union of European Football Associations); commonly known as the 'European Cup'; inaugurated in the 1955–6 season; played annually.

1992	Barcelona (Spain)
1993	Olympique Marseille (France)
1994	AC Milan (Italy)
1995	Ajax Amsterdam (Holland)

Sports and Games

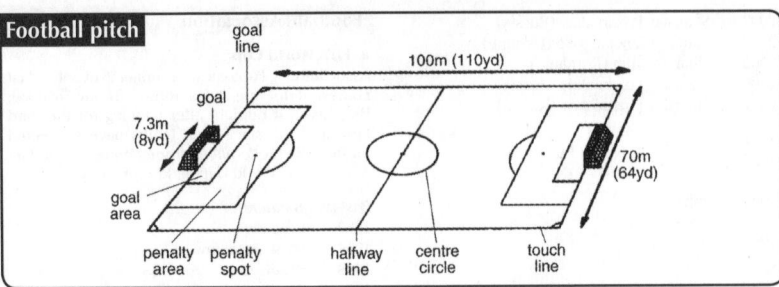

Football pitch

goal line

100m (110yd)

goal

7.3m (8yd)

70m (64yd)

goal area

penalty area | penalty spot | halfway line | centre circle | touch line

1996	Juventus (Italy)
1997	Borussia Dortmund (Germany)
1998	Real Madrid (Spain)
1999	Manchester United (England)
2000	Real Madrid (Spain)
2001	Bayern Munich (Germany)
2002	Real Madrid (Spain)
2003	AC Milan (Italy)
2004	Porto (Portugal)
2005	Liverpool (England)
2006	Barcelona (Spain)
2007	AC Milan (Italy)
2008	Manchester United (England)

■ **Football Association Challenge Cup (FA Cup)**
The world's oldest club knockout competition (the 'FA cup'), held annually; first contested in the 1871–2 season; first final at the Kennington Oval on 16 March 1872; first winners were The Wanderers.

1992	Liverpool
1993	Arsenal
1994	Manchester United
1995	Everton
1996	Manchester United
1997	Chelsea
1998	Arsenal
1999	Manchester United
2000	Chelsea
2001	Liverpool
2002	Arsenal
2003	Arsenal
2004	Manchester United
2005	Arsenal
2006	Liverpool
2007	Chelsea
2008	Portsmouth

■ **Football League (Premier League)**
The oldest league in the world, and regarded as the toughest; founded in 1888; consists of four divisions; the current complement of 92 teams achieved in 1950.

1992–3	Manchester United
1993–4	Manchester United
1994–5	Blackburn Rovers
1995–6	Manchester United
1996–7	Manchester United
1997–8	Arsenal
1998–9	Manchester United
1999–2000	Manchester United
2000–1	Manchester United
2001–2	Arsenal

2002–3	Manchester United
2003–4	Arsenal
2004–5	Chelsea
2005–6	Chelsea
2006–7	Manchester United
2007–8	Manchester United

Football, Australian Rules

■ **Australian Football League**
First held in 1897 as the Victoria Football League (1897–1989); inaugural winners were Essendon.

1992	West Coast
1993	Essendon
1994	West Coast
1995	Carlton
1996	North Melbourne
1997	Adelaide
1998	Adelaide
1999	North Melbourne
2000	Essendon
2001	Brisbane
2002	Brisbane
2003	Brisbane
2004	Adelaide
2005	Sydney
2006	West Coast
2007	Geelong
2008	Hawthorn

Football, Gaelic

■ **All-Ireland Championship**
First held in 1887; takes place in Dublin on the third Sunday in September each year.

1992	Donegal
1993	Derry
1994	Down
1995	Dublin
1996	Meath
1997	Kerry
1998	Galway
1999	Meath
2000	Kerry
2001	Galway
2002	Armagh
2003	Tyrone
2004	Kerry
2005	Tyrone
2006	Kerry
2007	Kerry
2008	Tyrone

Sports and Games

Gliding

■ **World Championships**
First held in 1937; current classes are Open, Standard and 15m; the Open class is the principal event, held every two years or so until 1978 and again since 1981.

1993	Andy Davis (Great Britain)
1995	Raymond Lynskey (New Zealand)
1997	Gerard Lherm (France)
1999	Holger Karow (Germany)
2001	Oscar Goudriaan (South Africa)
2003	Holger Karow (Germany)
2006	Michael Sommer (Germany)
2008	Michael Sommer (Germany)

Golf

■ **The Open**
First held at Prestwick in 1860, and won by Willie Park; takes place annually; regarded as the world's leading golf tournament.

1992	Nick Faldo (Great Britain)
1993	Greg Norman (Australia)
1994	Nick Price (Zimbabwe)
1995	John Daly (USA)
1996	Tom Lehman (USA)
1997	Justin Leonard (USA)
1998	Mark O'Meara (USA)
1999	Paul Lawrie (Great Britain)
2000	Tiger Woods (USA)
2001	David Duval (USA)
2002	Ernie Els (South Africa)
2003	Ben Curtis (USA)
2004	Todd Hamilton (USA)
2005	Tiger Woods (USA)
2006	Tiger Woods (USA)
2007	Padraig Harrington (Ireland)
2008	Padraig Harrington (Ireland)

■ **United States Open**
First held at Newport, Rhode Island, in 1895, and won by Horace Rawlins; takes place annually.

1992	Tom Kite (USA)
1993	Lee Janzen (USA)
1994	Ernie Els (South Africa)
1995	Corey Pavin (USA)
1996	Steve Jones (USA)
1997	Ernie Els (South Africa)
1998	Lee Janzen (USA)
1999	Payne Stewart (USA)
2000	Tiger Woods (USA)
2001	Retief Goosen (South Africa)
2002	Tiger Woods (USA)
2003	Jim Furyk (USA)
2004	Retief Goosen (South Africa)
2005	Michael Campbell (New Zealand)
2006	Geoff Ogilvy (Australia)
2007	Angel Cabrera (Argentina)
2008	Tiger Woods (USA)

■ **US Masters**
First held in 1934; takes place at the Augusta National course in Georgia every April.

1992	Fred Couples (USA)
1993	Bernhard Langer (Germany)
1994	José-María Olazábal (Spain)
1995	Ben Crenshaw (USA)

1996	Nick Faldo (Great Britain)
1997	Tiger Woods (USA)
1998	Mark O'Meara (USA)
1999	José-María Olazábal (Spain)
2000	Vijay Singh (Fiji)
2001	Tiger Woods (USA)
2002	Tiger Woods (USA)
2003	Mike Weir (Canada)
2004	Phil Mickelson (USA)
2005	Tiger Woods (USA)
2006	Phil Mickelson (USA)
2007	Zach Johnson (USA)
2008	Trevor Immelmann (South Africa)

■ **United States PGA Championship**
The last of the season's four 'Majors'; first held in 1916, and a match-play event until 1958; takes place annually.

1992	Nick Price (Zimbabwe)
1993	Paul Azinger (USA)
1994	Nick Price (Zimbabwe)
1995	Steve Elkington (Australia)
1996	Mark Brooks (USA)
1997	Davis Love III (USA)
1998	Vijay Singh (Fiji)
1999	Tiger Woods (USA)
2000	Tiger Woods (USA)
2001	David Toms (USA)
2002	Rich Beem (USA)
2003	Shaun Micheel (USA)
2004	Vijay Singh (Fiji)
2005	Phil Mickelson (USA)
2006	Tiger Woods (USA)
2007	Tiger Woods (USA)
2008	Padraig Harrington (Ireland)

■ **Ryder Cup**
The leading international team tournament; first held at Worcester, Massachusetts, in 1927; takes place every two years between teams from the USA and Europe (Great Britain 1927–71; Great Britain and Ireland 1973–7).

1993	USA	15–13
1995	Europe	14½–13½
1997	Europe	14½–13½
1999	USA	14½–13½
2002	Europe	15½–12½
2004	Europe	18½–9½
2006	Europe	18½–9½
2008	USA	16½–11½

Greyhound racing

■ **Greyhound Derby**
The top race of the British season, first held in 1927; run at the White City every year (except 1940) until its closure in 1985; since then all races run at Wimbledon.

1992	Farloe Melody
1993	Ringa Hustle
1994	Moral Standards
1995	Moaning Lad
1996	Shanless Slippy
1997	Some Picture
1998	Tom's the Best
1999	Chart King
2000	Rapid Ranger

2001	Rapid Ranger
2002	Allen Gift
2003	Droopys Hewitt
2004	Droopys Scholes
2005	Westmead Hawk
2006	Westmead Hawk
2007	Westmead Lord
2008	Loyal Honcho

Gymnastics

■ **World Championships**
First held in 1903.

Individual (Men)

1993	Vitaly Scherbo (Belarus)
1994	Ivan Ivankov (Belarus)
1995	Li Xiaoshuang (China)
1997	Ivan Ivankov (Belarus)
1999	Nikolay Krukov (Russia)
2001	Feng Jing (China)
2003	Paul Hamm (USA)
2005	Hiroyuki Tomita (Japan)
2006	Yang Wei (China)
2007	Yang Wei (China)

Team (Men)

1993	*no team prize*
1994	China
1995	China
1997	China
1999	China
2001	Belarus
2003	China
2006	China
2007	China

Individual (Women)

1993	Shannon Miller (USA)
1994	Shannon Miller (USA)
1995	Lilia Podkopayeva (Ukraine)
1997	Svetlana Khorkina (Russia)
1999	Maria Olaru (Romania)
2001	Svetlana Khorkina (Russia)
2003	Svetlana Khorkina (Russia)
2005	Chellsie Memmel (USA)
2006	Vanessa Ferrari (Italy)
2007	Shawn Johnson (USA)

Team (Women)

1993	*no team prize*
1994	Romania
1995	Romania
1997	Romania
1999	Romania
2001	Romania
2003	USA
2006	China
2007	USA

Handball

■ **World Championships**
First men's championships held in 1938, both indoors and outdoors (latter discontinued in 1966); first women's outdoor championships in 1949 (discontinued in 1960); first women's indoor championships in 1957; take place every two years.

Men

1993	Russia
1995	France
1997	Russia
1999	Sweden
2001	France
2003	Croatia
2005	Spain
2007	Germany

Women

1993	Germany
1995	South Korea
1997	Denmark
1999	Norway
2001	Russia
2003	France
2005	Russia
2007	Russia

Hang gliding

■ **World Championships**
First held officially in 1976; since 1979, take place every two years.

Individual: Class 1

1993	Tomás Suchanek (Czech Republic)
1995	Tomás Suchanek (Czech Republic)
1997	John Pendry (Great Britain)
1999	Manfred Ruhmer (Austria)
2001	Manfred Ruhmer (Austria)
2003	Manfred Ruhmer (Austria)
2005	Oleg Bondarchuk (Ukraine)
2007	Attila Bertok (Hungary)

Team

1993	USA
1995	Australia
1997	Switzerland
1999	Brazil
2001	Austria
2003	Austria
2005	Australia
2007	Great Britain

Hockey

■ **World Cup**
Men's tournament first held in 1971, and every four years since 1978; women's tournament first held in 1974, and now takes place every three or four years.

Men

1994	Pakistan
1998	Netherlands
2002	Germany
2006	Germany

Women

1994	Australia
1998	Australia
2002	Argentina
2006	Netherlands

■ **Olympic Games**
Regarded as hockey's leading competition; first held in 1908; included at every celebration since 1928; women's competition first held in 1980.

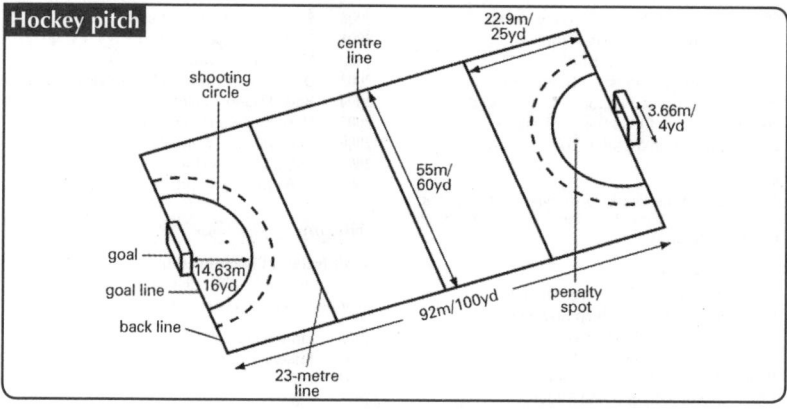

Hockey pitch

shooting circle

centre line

22.9m/25yd

3.66m/4yd

55m/60yd

goal

14.63m/16yd

goal line

back line

92m/100yd

penalty spot

23-metre line

Men

1992	Germany
1996	Netherlands
2000	Netherlands
2004	Australia
2008	Germany

Women

1992	Spain
1996	Australia
2000	Australia
2004	Germany
2008	Netherlands

Horse-racing

■ **The Derby**

The 'Blue Riband' of the Turf; run at Epsom over 1½ miles; first run in 1780.

Horse (Jockey)

1992	Dr Devious (John Reid)
1993	Commander in Chief (Michael Kinane)
1994	Erhaab (Willie Carson)
1995	Lammtarra (Walter Swinburn)
1996	Shaamit (Michael Hills)
1997	Benny the Dip (Willie Ryan)
1998	High Rise (Olivier Peslier)
1999	Oath (Kieren Fallon)
2000	Sinndar (Johnny Murtagh)
2001	Galileo (Michael Kinane)
2002	High Chaparral (John Murtagh)
2003	Kris Kin (Kieren Fallon)
2004	North Light (Kieren Fallon)
2005	Motivator (Johnny Murtagh)
2006	Sir Percy (Martin Dwyer)
2007	Authorized (Martin Dwyer)
2008	New Approach (Kevin Manning)

■ **The Oaks**

Raced at Epsom over 1½ miles; for fillies only; first run in 1779.

Horse (Jockey)

1992	User Friendly (George Duffield)
1993	Intrepidity (Michael Roberts)
1994	Balanchine (Frankie Dettori)
1995	Moonshell (Frankie Dettori)
1996	Lady Carla (Pat Eddery)
1997	Reams of Verse (Kieren Fallon)

1998	Shahtoush (Michael Kinane)
1999	Ramruma (Kieren Fallon)
2000	Love Divine (Richard Quinn)
2001	Imagine (Michael Kinane)
2002	Kazzia (Frankie Dettori)
2003	Casual Look (Martin Dwyer)
2004	Ouija Board (Kieren Fallon)
2005	Eswarah (Richard Hills)
2006	Alexandrova (Kieren Fallon)
2007	Light Shift (Ted Durcan)
2008	Look Here (Seb Sanders)

■ **One Thousand Guineas**

Run over 1 mile at Newmarket; for fillies only; first run in 1814.

Horse (Jockey)

1992	Hatoof (Walter Swinburn)
1993	Sayyedati (Walter Swinburn)
1994	Las Meninas (John Reid)
1995	Harayir (Richard Hills)
1996	Bosra Sham (Pat Eddery)
1997	Sleepytime (Kieren Fallon)
1998	Cape Verdi (Frankie Dettori)
1999	Wince (Kieren Fallon)
2000	Lahan (Richard Hills)
2001	Ameerat (Philip Robinson)
2002	Kazzia (Frankie Dettori)
2003	Russian Rhythm (Kieren Fallon)
2004	Attraction (Kevin Darley)
2005	Virginia Waters (Kieren Fallon)
2006	Speciosa (Michael Fenton)
2007	Finsceal Beo (Kevin Manning)
2008	Natagora (Christophe Lemaire)

■ **Two Thousand Guineas**

Run at Newmarket over 1 mile; first run in 1809.

Horse (Jockey)

1992	Rodrigo de Traiano (Lester Piggott)
1993	Zafonic (Pat Eddery)
1994	Mister Baileys (Jason Weaver)
1995	Pennekamp (Thierry Jarnet)
1996	Mark of Esteem (Frankie Dettori)
1997	Entrepreneur (Michael Kinane)
1998	King of Kings (Michael Kinane)
1999	Island Sands (Frankie Dettori)
2000	King's Best (Kieren Fallon)
2001	Golan (Kieren Fallon)

Sports and Games

2002	Rock of Gibraltar (Johnny Murtagh)
2003	Refuse to Bend (Pat Smullen)
2004	Haafhd (Richard Hills)
2005	Footstepsinthesand (Kieren Fallon)
2006	George Washington (Kieren Fallon)
2007	Cockney Rebel (Olivier Peslier)
2008	Henrythenavigator (Johnny Murtagh)

■ **St Leger**
The oldest of the five English classics; first run in 1776; raced at Doncaster annually over 1 mile 6 furlongs 127 yards.

Horse (Jockey)

1992	User Friendly (George Duffield)
1993	Bob's Return (Philip Robinson)
1994	Moonax (Pat Eddery)
1995	Classic Cliche (Frankie Dettori)
1996	Shantou (Frankie Dettori)
1997	Silver Patriarch (Pat Eddery)
1998	Nedawi (John Reid)
1999	Mutafaweq (Richard Hills)
2000	Millenary (Richard Quinn)
2001	Milan (Michael Kinane)
2002	Bollin Eric (Kevin Darley)
2003	Brian Boru (Jamie Spencer)
2004	Rule of Law (Kerrin McEvoy)
2005	Scorpion (Frankie Dettori)
2006	Sixties Icon (Frankie Dettori)
2007	Lucarno (Jimmie Fortune)
2008	Conduit (Frankie Dettori)

■ **Grand National**
Steeplechasing's most famous race; first run at Maghull in 1836; at Aintree since 1839; war-time races at Gatwick 1916–18.

Horse (Jockey)

1992	Party Politics (Carl Llewellyn)
1993	*race declared void* Esha Ness (John White) first past the post
1994	Minnehoma (Richard Dunwoody)
1995	Royal Athlete (Jason Titley)
1996	Rough Quest (Mick Fitzgerald)
1997	Lord Gyllene (Tony Dobbin)
1998	Earth Summit (Carl Llewellyn)
1999	Bobbyjo (Paul Carberry)
2000	Papillon (Ruby Walsh)
2001	Red Marauder (Richard Guest)
2002	Bindaree (Jim Culloty)
2003	Monty's Pass (Barry Geraghty)
2004	Amberleigh House (Graham Lee)
2005	Hedgehunter (Ruby Walsh)
2006	Numbersixvalverde (Niall Madden)
2007	Silver Birch (Robbie Power)
2008	Comply or Die (Timmy Murphy)

■ **Prix de l'Arc de Triomphe**
The leading end-of-season race in Europe; raced over 2400 metres at Longchamp; first run in 1920.

Horse (Jockey)

1992	Subotica (Thierry Jarnet)
1993	Urban Sea (Eric Saint-Martin)
1994	Carnegie (Thierry Jarnet)
1995	Lammtarra (Frankie Dettori)
1996	Helissio (Olivier Peslier)
1997	Peintre Celebre (Olivier Peslier)
1998	Sagamix (Olivier Peslier)
1999	Montjeu (Michael Kinane)

2000	Sinndar (Johnny Murtagh)
2001	Sakhee (Frankie Dettori)
2002	Marienbard (Frankie Dettori)
2003	Dalakhani (Christoph Soumillon)
2004	Bago (Thierry Gillet)
2005	Hurricane Run (Kieren Fallon)
2006	Rail Link (Stephane Pasquier)
2007	Dylan Thomas (Kieren Fallon)
2008	Zarkava (Christophe Soumillon)

Hurling

■ **All-Ireland Championship**
First contested in 1887; played on the first Sunday in September each year.

1992	Limerick
1993	Kilkenny
1994	Offaly
1995	Clare
1996	Wexford
1997	Clare
1998	Offaly
1999	Cork
2000	Kilkenny
2001	Tipperary
2002	Kilkenny
2003	Kilkenny
2004	Cork
2005	Cork
2006	Kilkenny
2007	Kilkenny
2008	Kilkenny

Ice hockey

■ **World Championship**
First held in 1930; takes place annually (except 1980); up to 1968 Olympic champions also regarded as world champions.

1992	Sweden
1993	Russia
1994	Canada
1995	Finland
1996	Czech Republic
1997	Canada
1998	Sweden
1999	Czech Republic
2000	Czech Republic
2001	Czech Republic
2002	Slovakia
2003	Canada
2004	Canada
2005	Czech Republic
2006	Sweden
2007	Canada
2008	Russia

■ **Stanley Cup**
The most sought-after trophy at club level; the end-of-season meeting between the winners of the two conferences in the National Hockey League in the USA and Canada.

1992	Pittsburgh Penguins
1993	Montreal Canadiens
1994	New York Rangers
1995	New Jersey Devils
1996	Colorado Avalanche

Ice hockey rink

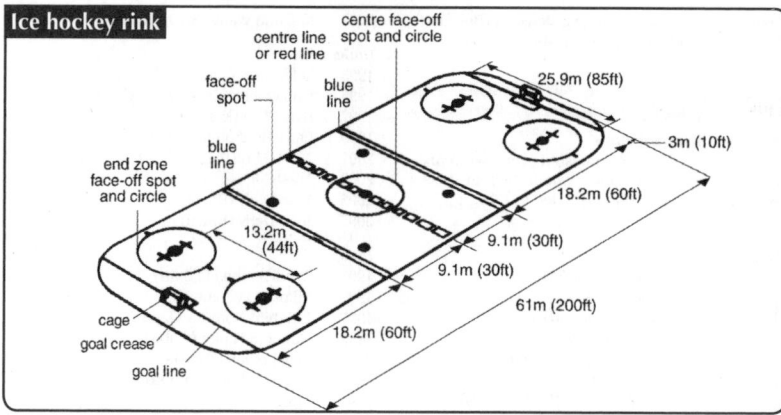

1997	Detroit Red Wings
1998	Detroit Red Wings
1999	Dallas Stars
2000	New Jersey Devils
2001	Colorado Avalanche
2002	Detroit Red Wings
2003	New Jersey Devils
2004	Tampa Bay Lightning
2005	*Cancelled over salary dispute*
2006	Carolina Hurricanes
2007	Anaheim Ducks
2008	Detroit Red Wings

Ice skating

▪ World Championships

First men's championships in 1896; first women's event in 1906; pairs first contested in 1908; Ice Dance officially recognized in 1952.

Men

1992	Viktor Petrenko (CIS)
1993	Kurt Browning (Canada)
1994	Elvis Stojko (Canada)
1995	Elvis Stojko (Canada)
1996	Todd Eldredge (USA)
1997	Elvis Stojko (Canada)
1998	Alexei Yagudin (Russia)
1999	Alexei Yagudin (Russia)
2000	Alexei Yagudin (Russia)
2001	Yevgeny Plushenko (Russia)
2002	Alexei Yagudin (Russia)
2003	Yevgeny Plushenko (Russia)
2004	Yevgeny Plushenko (Russia)
2005	Stéphane Lambiel (Switzerland)
2006	Stéphane Lambiel (Switzerland)
2007	Brian Joubert (France)
2008	Jeremy Buttle (Canada)

Women

1992	Kristi Yamaguchi (USA)
1993	Oksana Baiul (Ukraine)
1994	Yuka Sato (Japan)
1995	Lu Chen (China)
1996	Michelle Kwan (USA)
1997	Tara Lipinski (USA)
1998	Michelle Kwan (USA)
1999	Maria Butyrskaya (Russia)
2000	Michelle Kwan (USA)
2001	Michelle Kwan (USA)
2002	Irina Slutskaya (Russia)
2003	Michelle Kwan (USA)
2004	Shizuka Arakawa (Japan)
2005	Irina Slutskaya (Russia)
2006	Kimmie Meissner (USA)
2007	Miki Ando (Japan)
2008	Mao Asada (Japan)

Pairs

1992	Artur Dmtriev/Natalya Mishkutienok (USSR)
1993	Lloyd Eisler/Isabelle Brasseur (Canada)
1994	Vadim Naumov/Evgenia Shiskova (Russia)
1995	Rene Novotny/Radka Kovarikova (Czech Republic)
1996	Andrei Bushkov/Marina Eltsova (Russia)
1997	Ingo Steuer/Mandy Woetzel (Germany)
1998	Anton Sikharulidze/Elena Berezhnaya (Russia)
1999	Anton Sikharulidze/Elena Berezhnaya (Russia)
2000	Alexei Tikhonov/Maria Petrova (Russia)
2001	David Pelletier/Jamie Sale (Canada)
2002	Xue Shen/Zhao Hongbo (China)
2003	Xue Shen/Zhao Hongbo (China)
2004	Maxim Marinin/Tatiana Totmianina (Russia)
2005	Maxim Marinin/Tatiana Totmianina (Russia)
2006	Tong Jian/Pang Qing (China)
2007	Zhao Hongbo/ Xue Shen (China)
2008	Robin Szolkowy/ Aliona Savchenko (Germany)

Ice Dance

1992	Sergei Ponomarenko/Marina Klimova (CIS)
1993	Alesandr Zhulin/Maia Usova (Russia)
1994	Yevgeni Platov/Oksana Gritschuk (Russia)
1995	Yevgeni Platov/Oksana Gritschuk (Russia)
1996	Yevgeni Platov/Oksana Gritschuk (Russia)
1997	Yevgeni Platov/Oksana Gritschuk (Russia)
1998	Oleg Ovsyannikov/Anjelika Krylova (Russia)
1999	Oleg Ovsyannikov/Anjelika Krylova (Russia)
2000	Gwendal Peizerat/Marina Anissina (France)
2001	Maurizio Margaglio/Barbara Fusar-Poli (Italy)
2002	Ilia Averbukh/Irina Lobacheva (Russia)
2003	Victor Kraatz/Shae-Lynn Bourne (Canada)
2004	Roman Kostomarov/Tatiana Navka (Russia)
2005	Roman Kostomarov/Tatiana Navka (Russia)
2006	Maxim Staviski/Albena Denkova (Bulgaria)

2007 Maxim Staviski/Albena Denkova (Bulgaria)
2008 Olivier Schoenfelder/Isabelle Delobel
(France)

Judo

■ **World Championships**
First held in 1956, now contested every two years;
current weight categories established in 1999;
women's championship instituted in 1980.

Men
Open Class
1993 Rafael Kubacki (Poland)
1995 David Douillet (France)
1997 Rafael Kubacki (Poland)
1999 Shinichi Shinohara (Japan)
2001 Aleksandr Mikhaylin (Russia)
2003 Keiji Suzuki (Japan)
2005 Dennis van der Geest (Netherlands)
2007 Yasuyuki Muneta (Japan)

Over 100kg
1993 David Douillet (France)
1995 David Douillet (France)
1997 David Douillet (France)
1999 Shinichi Shinohara (Japan)
2001 Aleksandr Mikhaylin (Russia)
2003 Yauyuki Muneta (Japan)
2005 Alexander Mikhalin (Russia)
2007 Teddy Riner (France)

Under 100kg
1993 Antal Kovacs (Hungary)
1995 Pawel Nastula (Poland)
1997 Pawel Nastula (Poland)
1999 Kosei Inoue (Japan)
2001 Kosei Inoue (Japan)
2003 Kosei Inoue (Japan)
2005 Keiji Suzuki (Japan)
2007 Luciano Corrêa (Brazil)

Under 90kg
1993 Yoshoi Nakamura (Japan)
1995 Jeon Ki Young (South Korea)
1997 Jeon Ki Young (South Korea)
1999 Hidehiko Yoshida (Japan)
2001 Frédéric Demoutfaucon (France)
2003 Hwang Hee-tae (South Korea)
2005 Hiroshi Izumi (Japan)
2007 Irakli Tsirekidze (Georgia)

Under 81kg
1993 Jeon Ki Young (South Korea)
1995 Toshihiko Koga (Japan)
1997 Cho In-chul (South Korea)
1999 Graeme Randall (Great Britain)
2001 Cho In-chul (South Korea)
2003 Florian Wanner (Germany)
2005 Guillaume Elmont (Netherlands)
2007 Tiago Camilo (Brazil)

Under 73kg
1993 Yung Chung Hoon (South Korea)
1995 Daisuke Hideshima (Japan)
1997 Kenzo Nakamura (Japan)
1999 Jimmy Pedro (USA)
2001 Vital Makarov (Russia)
2003 Won Hee Lee (Russia)
2005 Akos Braun (Hungary)

2007 Ki-Chun Wang (South Korea)

Under 66kg
1993 Yukimasa Nakamura (Japan)
1995 Udo Quellmalz (Germany)
1997 Hyuk Kim (Korea)
1999 Larbi Benboudaoud (France)
2001 Arash Miresmaeili (Iran)
2003 Arash Miresmaeili (Iran)
2005 João Derly (Brazil)
2007 João Derly (Brazil)

Under 60kg
1993 Ryudi Sanoda (Japan)
1995 Nikolai Ojeguine (Russia)
1997 Tadahiro Nomura (Japan)
1999 Manuelo Poulot (Cuba)
2001 Anis Lounifi (Tunisia)
2003 Min Ho-Choi (South Korea)
2005 Craig Fallon (UK)
2007 Ruben Houkes (Netherlands)

Women
Open Class
1993 Beata Maksymow (Poland)
1995 Monique van der Lee (Netherlands)
1997 Daina Beltran (Cuba)
1999 Daina Beltran (Cuba)
2001 Céline Lebrun (France)
2003 Tong Wen (China)
2005 Midor Shintani (Japan)
2007 Maki Tsukada (Japan)

Over 78kg
1993 Johanna Hagen (Germany)
1995 Angelique Seriese (Netherlands)
1997 Christine Cicot (France)
1999 Beata Maksymow (Poland)
2001 Yuan Hua (China)
2003 Sun Fuming (China)
2005 Wen Tong (China)
2007 Wen Tong (China)

Under 78kg
1993 Chun Huileng (China)
1995 Castellano Luna (Cuba)
1997 Noriko Anno (Japan)
1999 Noriko Anno (Japan)
2001 Noriko Anno (Japan)
2003 Noriko Anno (Japan)
2005 Yurisel Laborde (Cuba)
2007 Yurisel Laborde (Cuba)

Under 70kg
1993 Cho Min Sun (South Korea)
1995 Cho Min Sun (South Korea)
1997 Kate Howey (Great Britain)
1999 Sibelis Veranes (Cuba)
2001 Masae Ueno (Japan)
2003 Masae Ueno (Japan)
2005 Edith Bosch (Netherlands)
2007 Gévrise Emane (France)

Under 63kg
1993 Gella van de Cayeve (Belgium)
1995 Jung Sung Sook (South Korea)
1997 Servenr Vandenhende (France)
1999 Keiko Maedo (Japan)
2001 Gella van de Caveye (Belgium)
2003 Daniela Krukower (Argentina)

| 2005 | Lucie Decosse (France) |
| 2007 | Driulis González (Cuba) |

Under 57kg

1993	Nicola Fairbrother (Great Britain)
1995	Driulis González (Cuba)
1997	Isabel Fernandez (Spain)
1999	Driulis González (Cuba)
2001	Yurisledes Lupety (Cuba)
2003	Sun Hui Kye (North Korea)
2005	Sun Hui Kye (North Korea)
2007	Sun Hui Kye (North Korea)

Under 52kg

1993	Rodriguez Verdecia (Cuba)
1995	Marie-Claire Restoux (France)
1997	Marie-Claire Restoux (France)
1999	Noriko Narasaki (Japan)
2001	Sun Hui Kye (North Korea)
2003	Amarilis Savon (Cuba)
2005	Li Ying (China)
2007	Junjie Shi (China)

Under 48kg

1993	Ryoko Tamura (Japan)
1995	Ryoko Tamura (Japan)
1997	Ryoko Tamura (Japan)
1999	Ryoko Tamura (Japan)
2001	Ryoko Tamura (Japan)
2003	Ryoko Tamura (Japan)
2005	Yanet Bermoy (Cuba)
2007	Ryoko Tani (Japan)

Karate

■ **World Championships**
First held in Tokyo in 1970; taken place every two years since 1980, when women first competed; there are team competitions plus individual competitions at Kumite and Kata. Since 1992 there have been separate men's and women's teams.

Kumite

Men		Women	
1992	Spain	1992	Great Britain
1994	France	1994	Spain
1996	France	1996	Great Britain
1998	France	1998	Turkey
2000	France	2000	France
2002	Spain	2002	Spain
2004	France	2004	Turkey
2006	Spain	2006	Japan
2008	Turkey	2008	Germany

Kata

Men		Women	
1992	Japan	1992	Japan
1994	Japan	1994	Japan
1996	Japan	1996	Japan
1998	Japan	1998	Japan
2000	Japan	2000	France
2002	Japan	2002	France
2004	Italy	2004	Japan
2006	Italy	2006	France
2008	France	2008	Japan

Lacrosse

■ **World Championships**
First held for men in 1967; for women in 1969; taken place every four years since 1974; since 1982 the women's event has been called the World Cup.

Men

1994	USA
1998	USA
2002	USA
2006	Canada

Women

1993	USA
1997	USA
2001	USA
2005	Australia

■ **Iroquois Cup**
The sport's best-known trophy; contested by English club sides annually since 1890.

1992	Cheadle
1993	Heaton Mersey
1994	Cheadle
1995	Cheadle
1996	Stockport
1997	Mellor
1998	*not held*
1999	*not held*
2000	Cheadle
2001	*not held*
2002	Heaton Mersey
2003	Cheadle
2004	Stockport
2005	*not held*
2006	*not held*
2007	Manchester Waconians
2008	Wilmslow

Modern pentathlon

■ **World Championships**
Held annually since 1949 with the exception of Olympic years, when the Olympic champions automatically become world champions.

Individual

1992	Arkadiusz Skrzypaszek (Poland)
1993	Richard Phelps (Great Britain)
1994	Dmitri Svatovski (Russia)
1995	Dmitri Svatovski (Russia)
1996	Alexander Parygin (Kazakhstan)
1997	Sebastien Deleigne (France)
1998	Sebastien Deleigne (France)
1999	Gabor Balogh (Hungary)
2000	Dmitri Svatovski (Russia)
2001	Gabor Balogh (Hungary)
2002	Michal Sedlecky (Czech Republic)
2003	Eric Walther (Germany)
2004	Andrey Moiseev (Russia)
2005	Zhenhua Qian (China)
2006	Edvinas Krungolkas (Lithuania)
2007	Viktor Horvath (Hungary)
2008	Andrey Moiseev (Russia)

Team

1992	Poland
1993	Hungary
1994	France

1995	Poland
1996	Poland
1997	Hungary
1998	Mexico
1999	Hungary
2000	*not held*
2001	Hungary
2002	Germany
2003	Hungary
2004	Russia
2005	Russia
2006	Lithuania
2007	Germany
2008	Belarus

Motor cycling

■ World Championships
First organized in 1949; current titles for MotoGP, 250cc, 125cc; Formula One and Endurance world championships also held annually; the most prestigious title is the MotoGP (formerly 500cc) category.

500cc
1992	Wayne Rainey (USA)
1993	Kevin Schwantz (USA)
1994	Michael Doohan (Australia)
1995	Michael Doohan (Australia)
1996	Michael Doohan (Australia)
1997	Michael Doohan (Australia)
1998	Michael Doohan (Australia)
1999	Alex Criville (Spain)
2000	Kenny Roberts (USA)
2001	Valentino Rossi (Italy)

MotoGP
2002	Valentino Rossi (Italy)
2003	Valentino Rossi (Italy)
2004	Valentino Rossi (Italy)
2005	Valentino Rossi (Italy)
2006	Nicky Hayden (USA)
2007	Casey Stoner (Australia)
2008	Valentino Rossi (Italy)

■ Isle of Man TT Races
The most famous of all motorcycle races; take place each June; first held 1907; principal race is the Senior TT.

Senior TT
1992	Steve Hislop (Great Britain)
1993	Phil McCallen (Ireland)
1994	Steve Hislop (Great Britain)
1995	Joey Dunlop (Ireland)
1996	Phil McCallen (Ireland)
1997	Phil McCallen (Ireland)
1998	Ian Simpson (Great Britain)
1999	David Jefferies (Great Britain)
2000	David Jefferies (Great Britain)
2001	*not held*
2002	David Jefferies (Great Britain)
2003	Adrian Archibald (Northern Ireland)
2004	Adrian Archibald (Northern Ireland)
2005	John McGuinness (England)
2006	John McGuinness (England)
2007	John McGuinness (England)
2008	John McGuinness (England)

Motor racing

■ World Championship
A Formula One drivers' world championship instituted in 1950; constructor's championship instituted in 1958.

	driver	*constructor*
1992	Nigel Mansell (Great Britain)	*Williams*
1993	Alain Prost (France)	*Williams*
1994	Michael Schumacher (Germany)	*Williams*
1995	Michael Schumacher (Germany)	*Benetton*
1996	Damon Hill (Great Britain)	*Williams*
1997	Jacques Villeneuve (Canada)	*Williams*
1998	Mika Hakkinen (Finland)	*McLaren*
1999	Mika Hakkinen (Finland)	*Ferrari*
2000	Michael Schumacher (Germany)	*Ferrari*
2001	Michael Schumacher (Germany)	*Ferrari*
2002	Michael Schumacher (Germany)	*Ferrari*
2003	Michael Schumacher (Germany)	*Ferrari*
2004	Michael Schumacher (Germany)	*Ferrari*
2005	Fernando Alonso (Spain)	*Renault*
2006	Fernando Alonso (Spain)	*Renault*
2007	Kimi Räikkönen (Finland)	*Ferrari*
2008	Lewis Hamilton (Great Britain)	*Ferrari*

■ Le Mans 24-Hour Race
The greatest of all endurance races; first held in 1923.

1992	Derek Warwick (UK)
	Mark Blundell (UK)
	Yannick Dalmas (France)
1993	Geoff Brabham (Australia)
	Christophe Bouchut (France)
	Eric Helary (France)
1994	Yannick Dalmas (France)
	Hurley Haywood (USA)
	Mauro Baldi (Italy)
1995	Yannick Dalmas (France)
	J J Lehto (Finland)
	Masanori Sekiya (Japan)
1996	Manuel Reuter (Germany)
	Davy Jones (USA)
	Alexander Wurz (Austria)
1997	Michele Alboreto (Italy)
	Stefan Johansson (Sweden)
	Tom Kristensen (Denmark)
1998	Allan McNish (UK)
	Laurent Aiello (France)
	Stephane Ortelli (France)
1999	Pierluigi Martini (Italy)
	Joachim Winkelhock (Germany)
	Yannick Dalmas (France)
2000	Frank Biela (Germany)
	Tom Kristensen (Denmark)
	Emanuele Pirro (Italy)
2001	Frank Biela (Germany)
	Tom Kristensen (Denmark)
	Emanuele Pirro (Italy)
2002	Frank Biela (Germany)
	Tom Kristensen (Denmark)
	Emanuele Pirro (Italy)

2003	Tom Kristensen (Denmark)
	Rinaldo Capello (Italy)
	Guy Smith (UK)
2004	Tom Kristensen (Denmark)
	Rinaldo Capello (Italy)
	Seiji Ara (Japan)
2005	J J Lehto (Finland)
	Tom Kristensen (Denmark)
	Marco Werner (Germany)
2006	Frank Biela (Germany)
	Emanuele Pirro (Italy)
	Marco Werner (Germany)
2007	Frank Biela (Germany)
	Emanuele Pirro (Italy)
	Marco Werner (Germany)
2008	Rinaldo Capello (Italy)
	Alan McNish (UK)
	Tom Kristensen (Denmark)

■ Indianapolis 500

First held in 1911; raced over the Indianapolis Raceway as part of the Memorial Day celebrations at the end of May each year.

1992	Al Unser (USA)
1993	Emerson Fittipaldi (Brazil)
1994	Al Unser (USA)
1995	Jacques Villeneuve (Canada)
1996	Buddy Lazier (USA)
1997	Arie Luyendyk (Netherlands)
1998	Eddie Cheever (USA)
1999	Kenny Brack (Sweden)
2000	Juan Montoya (Colombia)
2001	Helio Castroneves (Brazil)
2002	Helio Castroneves (Brazil)
2003	Gil de Ferran (Brazil)
2004	Buddy Rice (USA)
2005	Dan Wheldon (UK)
2006	Sam Hornish (USA)
2007	Dario Franchitti (UK)
2008	Scott Dixon (New Zealand)

■ Monte Carlo Rally

The world's leading rally; first held in 1911.

1992	Didier Auriol (France)
	Bernard Occelli (France)
1993	Didier Auriol (France)
	Bernard Occelli (France)
1994	François Delecour (France)
	Daniel Grataloup (France)
1995	Carlos Sainz (Spain)
	Luis Moya (Spain)
1996	Patrick Bernardini (France)
	Bernard Occelli (France)
1997	Piero Liatti (Italy)
	Fabrizia Pons (Italy)
1998	Carlos Sainz (Spain)
	Luis Moya (Spain)
1999	Tommi Mäkinen (Finland)
	Risto Mannisenmäki (Finland)
2000	Tommi Mäkinen (Finland)
	Risto Mannisenmäki (Finland)
2001	Tommi Mäkinen (Finland)
	Risto Mannisenmäki (Finland)
2002	Tommi Mäkinen (Finland)
	Kaj Lindstrom (Finland)
2003	Sébastien Loeb (France)
	Daniel Elena (Monaco)
2004	Sébastien Loeb (France)
	Daniel Elena (Monaco)
2005	Sébastien Loeb (France)
	Daniel Elena (Monaco)
2006	Marcus Grönholm (Finland)
	Timo Rautiainen (Finland)
2007	Sébastien Loeb (France)
	Daniel Elena (Poland)
2008	Sébastien Loeb (France)
	Daniel Elena (Poland)

Netball

■ World Championships

First held in 1963, then every four years.

1995	Australia
1999	Australia
2003	New Zealand
2007	Australia

Orienteering

■ World Championships

First held in 1966; held every two years to 1978 and 1979–2003; every year since 2003.

Individual (Men)

1993	Alan Mogensen (Denmark)
1995	Jörgen Mårtensson (Sweden)
1997	Peter Thoresen (Denmark)
1999	Bjornar Valstad (Norway)
2001	Jörgen Rostrup (Finland)
2003	Thomas Bührer (Switzerland)
2004	Bjornar Valstad (Norway)
2005	Andrey Khramov (Russia)
2006	Jani Lakenen (Finland)
2007	Matthias Merz (Switzerland)
2008	Daniel Hubmann (Switzerland)

Individual (Women)

1993	Marita Skogum (Sweden)
1995	Katalin Olah (Hungary)
1997	Hanne Staff (Norway)
1999	Kirsi Bostrom (Finland)
2001	Simone Luder (Switzerland)
2003	Simone Luder (Switzerland)
2004	Karolina Hojsgaard (Sweden)
2005	Simone Niggli-Luder (Switzerland)
2006	Simone Niggli-Luder (Switzerland)
2007	Heli Jukkola (Finland)
	Minna Kauppi (Finland)
2008	Dana Brožková (Czech Republic)

Relay (Men)

1993	Switzerland
1995	Switzerland
1997	Denmark
1999	Norway
2001	Finland
2003	Sweden
2004	Norway
2005	Norway
2006	Russia
2007	Russia
2008	Great Britain

Relay (Women)

1993	Sweden
1995	Finland
1997	Sweden
1999	Norway

Sports and Games

Polo field

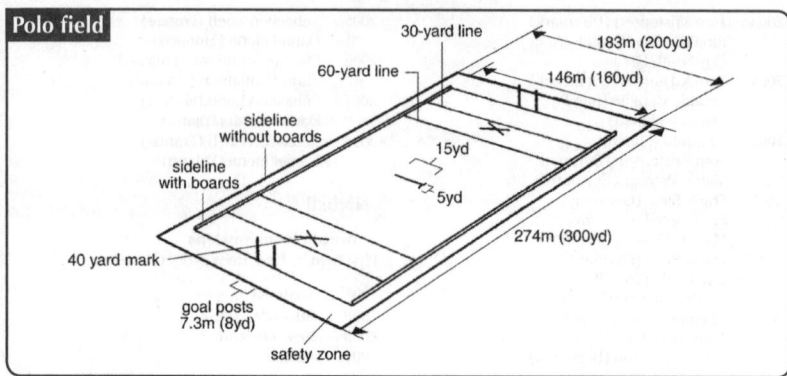

30-yard line
60-yard line
183m (200yd)
146m (160yd)
sideline without boards
15yd
sideline with boards
5yd
274m (300yd)
40 yard mark
goal posts 7.3m (8yd)
safety zone

2001	Finland
2003	Switzerland
2004	Sweden
2005	Switzerland
2006	Finland
2007	Finland
2008	Finland

Polo

■ **Veuve Clicquot Gold Cup**
First held in 1956, replacing the Champion Cup; the British Open Championship for club sides, played at Cowdray Park, Sussex; formerly called the Cowdray Park Gold Cup.

1992	Black Bears
1993	Alcatel
1994	Ellerston Blacks
1995	Ellerston Whites
1996	C S Brooks
1997	Labegorce
1998	Ellerston
1999	Pommery
2000	Geebung
2001	Dubai
2002	Black Bears
2003	Hildon Sport
2004	Azzurra
2005	Dubai
2006	Black Bears
2007	Lechuza Caracas
2008	Loro Piana

Powerboat racing

■ **World Championship**
Instituted in 1982; held in many categories, with Formula One and Formula Two being the principal competitions; Formula One was not held between 1987 and 1989; Formula Two was discontinued in 1989 and revived for one year in 1997.

Formula One

1992	Fabrizio Bocca (Italy)
1993	Guido Cappellini (Italy)
1994	Guido Cappellini (Italy)
1995	Guido Cappellini (Italy)
1996	Guido Cappellini (Italy)
1997	Scott Gilman (USA)
1998	Jonathan Jones (Great Britain)

1999	Guido Cappellini (Italy)
2000	Scott Gilman (USA)
2001	Guido Cappellini (Italy)
2002	Guido Cappellini (Italy)
2003	Guido Cappellini (Italy)
2004	Francesco Cantando (Italy)
2005	Guido Cappellini (Italy)
2006	Scott Gillman (USA)
2007	Sami Seliö (Finland)
2008	Jay Price (Qatar)

Formula Two

1997	Mark Rolls (Great Britain)

Real tennis

■ **World Championship**
Organized on a challenge basis; the first world champion was M Clerge (France) c.1740, regarded as the first world champion of any sport.

1981–7	Chris Ronaldson (Great Britain)
1987–94	Wayne Davies (Australia)
1994–	Robert Fahey (Australia)

Roller skating

■ **World Championships**
Figure skating world championships were first organized in 1947.

Men Combined

1992	Sandro Guerra (Italy)
1993	Samo Kokorovec (Italy)
1994	Steven Findlay (USA)
1995	Jason Sutcliffe (Australia)
1996	Francesco Ceresola (Italy)
1997	Mauro Mazzoni (Italy)
1998	Daniel Tofani (Italy)
1999	Adrian Stolzenberg (Germany)
2000	Adrian Stolzenberg (Germany)
2001	Leonardo Pancani (Italy)
2002	Frank Albiez (Germany)
2003	Luca D'Alisera (Italy)
2004	Luca D'Alisera (Italy)
2005	Roberto Riva (Italy)
2006	Roberto Riva (Italy)
2007	Roberto Riva (Italy)
2008	Roberto Riva (Italy)

Women Combined
1992	Rafaela Del Vinaccio (Italy)
1993	Letitia Tinghi (Italy)
1994	April Dayney (USA)
1995	Letitia Tinghi (Italy)
1996	Giusy Loncani (Italy)
1997	Sabrina Tomasini (Italy)
1998	Elke Dederichs (Germany)
1999	Elisa Facciotti (Italy)
2000	Elisa Facciotti (Italy)
2001	Elisa Facciotti (Italy)
2002	Tanja Romano (Italy)
2003	Tanja Romano (Italy)
2004	Tanja Romano (Italy)
2005	Tanja Romano (Italy)
2006	Tanja Romano (Italy)
2007	Tanja Romano (Italy)
2008	Tanja Romano (Italy)

Pairs
1992	Patrick Venerucci/Maura Ferri (Italy)
1993	Patrick Venerucci/Maura Ferri (Italy)
1994	Patrick Venerucci/Beatrice Pallazzi Rossi (Italy)
1995	Patrick Venerucci/Beatrice Pallazzi Rossi (Italy)
1996	Patrick Venerucci/Beatrice Pallazzi Rossi (Italy)
1997	Patrick Venerucci/Beatrice Pallazzi Rossi (Italy)
1998	Patrick Venerucci/Beatrice Pallazzi Rossi (Italy)
1999	Patrick Venerucci/Beatrice Pallazzi Rossi (Italy)
2000	Patrick Venerucci/Beatrice Pallazzi Rossi (Italy)
2001	Patrick Venerucci/Beatrice Pallazzi Rossi (Italy)
2002	Patrick Venerucci/Beatrice Pallazzi Rossi (Italy)
2003	Federico Degli Esposti/Marika Zanforlin (Italy)
2004	Federico Degli Esposti/Marika Zanforlin (Italy)
2005	Federico Degli Esposti/Marika Zanforlin (Italy)
2006	Federico Degli Esposti/Marika Zanforlin (Italy)
2007	Enrico Fabbri/Laura Merzocchini (Italy)
2008	Matteo Guarise/Sara Venerucci (Italy)

Dance
1992	Doug Wait/Deanna Monaham (USA)
1993	Doug Wait/Deanna Monaham (USA)
1994	Tim Patten/Lisa Friday (USA)
1995	Tim Patten/Lisa Friday (USA)
1996	Axel Haber/Swansi Gebauer (Germany)
1997	Axel Haber/Swansi Gebauer (Germany)
1998	Ronald Brenn/Candi Powderly (USA)
1999	Tim Patten/Tara Graney (USA)
2000	Adam White/Melissa Quinn (USA)
2001	Adam White/Melissa Quinn (USA)
2002	Marco Bornati/Emanuela Bornati (Italy)
2003	Fabio Grossi/Michela Pizzi (Italy)
2004	Marco Bornati/Monica Coffele (Italy)
2005	Mirko Pontello/Melissa Comin De Candido (Italy)
2006	Mirko Pontello/Melissa Comin De Candido (Italy)
2007	Marco Bornati/Emanuela Bornati (Italy)
2008	Gabriele Gasparini/Enrica Gasparini (Italy)

Rowing

■ World Championships
First held for men in 1962 and for women in 1974; Olympic champions assume the role of world champion in Olympic years; principal event is the single sculls.

Single Sculls (Men)
1992	Thomas Lange (Germany)
1993	Derek Porter (Canada)
1994	Andre Wilms (Germany)
1995	Iztok Cop (Slovenia)
1996	Xeno Müller (Switzerland)
1997	Jamie Koven (USA)
1998	Rob Waddell (New Zealand)
1999	Rob Waddell (New Zealand)
2000	Rob Waddell (New Zealand)
2001	Olaf Tufte (Norway)
2002	Marcel Hacker (Germany)
2003	Olaf Tufte (Norway)
2004	Olaf Tufte (Norway)
2005	Mahe Drysdale (New Zealand)
2006	Mahe Drysdale (New Zealand)
2007	Mahe Drysdale (New Zealand)
2008	Olaf Tufte (Norway)

Single Sculls (Women)
1992	Elisabeta Lipa (Romania)
1993	Jana Phieme (Germany)
1994	Trine Hansen (Denmark)
1995	Maria Brandin (Sweden)
1996	Ekaterina Khodotovich (Belarus)
1997	Ekaterina Khodotovich (Belarus)
1998	Irina Fedotova (Russia)
1999	Ekaterina Karsten-Khodotovich (Belarus)
2000	Ekaterina Karsten-Khodotovich (Belarus)
2001	Katrin Rutschow-Stomporowski (Germany)
2002	Rumyana Neykova (Bulgaria)
2003	Rumyana Neykova (Bulgaria)
2004	Katrin Rutschow-Stromporowski (Germany)
2005	Ekaterina Karsten-Khodotovich (Belarus)
2006	Ekaterina Karsten-Khodotovich (Belarus)
2007	Ekaterina Karsten-Khodotovich (Belarus)
2008	Rumyana Neykova (Bulgaria)

■ The Boat Race
An annual contest between the crews from the Oxford and Cambridge University rowing clubs; first contested in 1829; the current course is from Putney to Mortlake.

1992	Oxford
1993	Cambridge
1994	Cambridge
1995	Cambridge
1996	Cambridge
1997	Cambridge
1998	Cambridge
1999	Cambridge
2000	Oxford
2001	Cambridge
2002	Oxford
2003	Oxford
2004	Cambridge

Sports and Games

Sports and Games

2005	Oxford
2006	Oxford
2007	Cambridge
2008	Oxford

■ **Diamond Sculls**

Highlight of Henley Royal Regatta held every July; first contested in 1884.

1992	Rorie Henderson (Great Britain)
1993	Thomas Lange (Germany)
1994	Xeno Müller (Switzerland)
1995	Juri Jaanson (Estonia)
1996	Merlin Vervoorn (Netherlands)
1997	Greg Searle (Great Britain)
1998	Jamie Koven (USA)
1999	Marcel Hacker (Germany)
2000	Aquil Abdullah (USA)
2001	Duncan Free (Australia)
2002	Peter Wells (Great Britain)
2003	Alan Campbell (Great Britain)
2004	Marcel Hacker (Germany)
2005	Wyatt Allen (USA)
2006	Mahe Drysdale (New Zealand)
2007	Alan Campbell (Great Britain)
2008	Ian Lawson (Great Britain)

Rugby League

■ **World Cup**

First held in 1954 between Great Britain, France, Australia and New Zealand; played intermittently since and now with the inclusion of other countries. In 1957, 1960 and 1975 (when it was renamed the World Championship) it was played on a league basis. The 1975 tournament stretched over eight months, whereas the winners in 1988 and 1992 lifted the trophy after rounds of games played over three years.

1954	Great Britain
1957	Australia
1960	Great Britain
1968	Australia
1970	Australia
1972	Great Britain
1975	Australia
1977	Australia
1988	Australia
1992	Australia
1995	Australia
2000	Australia
2008	New Zealand

■ **Challenge Cup Final**

First contested in 1897 and won by Batley; first final at Wembley Stadium in 1929.

1992	Wigan
1993	Wigan
1994	Wigan
1995	Wigan
1996	St Helens
1997	St Helens
1998	Sheffield Eagles
1999	Leeds Rhinos
2000	Bradford Bulls
2001	St Helens
2002	Wigan Warriors
2003	Bradford Bulls

2004	St Helens
2005	Hull
2006	St Helens
2007	St Helens
2008	St Helens

■ **Premiership Trophy**

End-of-season knockout competition involving the top eight teams in the first division; first contested at the end of the 1974–5 season; discontinued in 1997.

1992	Wigan
1993	St Helens
1994	Wigan
1995	Wigan
1996	Wigan
1997	Wigan

■ **Engage Super League**

First held in 1996. The top five teams in the league at the end of the season play off for the title; known as the JJB Super League from 1996 to 1999 and Tetley's Super League from 2000 to 2004.

1996	St Helens
1997	Bradford Bulls
1998	Wigan Warriors
1999	St Helens
2000	St Helens
2001	Bradford Bulls
2002	St Helens
2003	Bradford Bulls
2004	Leeds Rhinos
2005	Bradford Bulls
2006	St Helens
2007	Leeds Rhinos
2008	Leeds Rhinos

Rugby Union

■ **World Cup**

The first Rugby Union World Cup was staged in 1987 and won by New Zealand; takes place every four years.

1995	South Africa
1999	Australia
2003	England
2007	South Africa

■ **Six Nations' Championship**

A round robin competition involving England, Ireland, Scotland, Wales, France and, from 2000, Italy; first contested in 1884.

1992	England*
1993	France
1994	Wales
1995	England*
1996	England
1997	France*
1998	France*
1999	Scotland
2000	England
2001	England
2002	France*
2003	England*
2004	France*
2005	Wales*
2006	France
2007	France

Rugby Union pitch

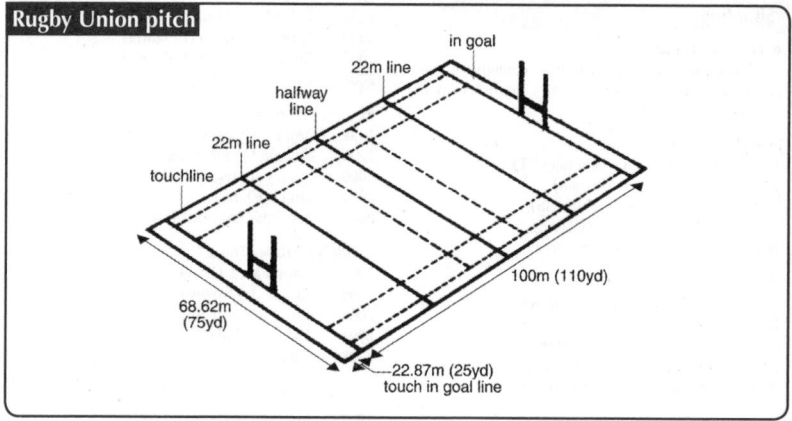

2008   Wales*
* = Grand Slam

■ EDF Energy Cup

An annual knockout competition for English Club sides; first held in the 1971–2 season; known as the John Player Special Cup until 1988, the Pilkington Cup until 1997, the Tetley's Bitter Cup until 2000 and the Powergen Cup until 2006; Welsh clubs introduced in 2006.

1992	Bath
1993	Leicester
1994	Bath
1995	Bath
1996	Bath
1997	Leicester
1998	Saracens
1999	Wasps
2000	Wasps
2001	Newcastle Falcons
2002	London Irish
2003	Gloucester
2004	Newcastle Falcons
2005	Leeds
2006	Wasps
2007	Leicester
2008	Ospreys

■ Welsh Rugby Union Challenge Cup (Konica Minolta Cup)

The knockout tournament for Welsh clubs; first held in 1971–2; formerly known as the Schweppes Welsh Cup, the Swalec Cup and the Principality Cup.

1992	Llanelli
1993	Llanelli
1994	Cardiff
1995	Swansea
1996	Pontypridd
1997	Cardiff
1998	Llanelli
1999	Swansea
2000	Llanelli
2001	Newport
2002	Pontypridd
2003	Llanelli
2004	Neath
2005	Llanelli
2006	Pontypridd
2007	Llandovery
2008	Neath

■ Heineken European Cup

Established in 1996 as a cup competition for major European clubs and provincial teams. English clubs did not take part in 1996 or 1999.

1996	Stade Toulousain
1997	Brive
1998	Bath
1999	Ulster
2000	Northampton
2001	Leicester
2002	Leicester
2003	Stade Toulousain
2004	Wasps
2005	Stade Toulousain
2006	Munster
2007	London Wasps
2008	Munster

Shinty

■ Scottish Hydro Electric Camanachd Cup

The sport's principal trophy, it was first held in 1896 and won by Kingussie. Shinty is the popular name for the original game of Camanachd.

1992	Fort William
1993	Kingussie
1994	Kyles Athletic
1995	Kingussie
1996	Oban
1997	Kingussie
1998	Kingussie
1999	Kingussie
2000	Kingussie
2001	Kingussie
2002	Kingussie
2003	Kingussie
2004	Inverary
2005	Fort William
2006	Kingussie
2007	Fort William
2008	Fort William

Shooting

■ Olympic Games
The Olympic competition is the highlight of the shooting calendar; winners in all categories since 1992 are given below.

Free Pistol (Men)
1992	Konstantine Loukachik (UT)
1996	Boris Kokorev (Russia)
2000	Tanyu Kiryakov (Bulgaria)
2004	Mikhail Nestruev (Russia)
2008	Jin Jong Oh (South Korea)

Rapid-Fire Pistol (Men)
1992	Ralf Schumann (Germany)
1996	Ralf Schumann (Germany)
2000	Sergei Alifirenko (Russia)
2004	Ralf Schumann (Germany)
2008	Oleksandr Petriv (Ukraine)

Small-Bore Rifle (Three Position) (Men)
1992	Grachya Petikiane (UT)
1996	Jean-Pierre Amat (France)
2000	Rajmond Debevec (Slovenia)
2004	Jia Zhanbo (China)
2008	Qiu Jian (China)

Trap (Men)
1992	Petr Hrdlička (Czechoslovakia)
1996	Michael Diamond (Australia)
2000	Michael Diamond (Australia)
2004	Alexei Alipov (Russia)
2008	David Kostelecky (Czech Republic)

Double Trap (Men)
1992	not held
1996	Russell Mark (Australia)
2000	Richard Faulds (Great Britain)
2004	Ahmed Almaktoum (UAE)
2008	Walton Eller (USA)

Skeet (Men)
1992	Zhang Shan (China)
1996	Ennio Falco (Italy)
2000	Mikola Milchev (Ukraine)
2004	Andrea Benelli (Italy)
2008	Vincent Hancock (USA)

Small-Bore Rifle (Prone) (Men)
1992	Lee Eun-chul (South Korea)
1996	Christian Klees (Germany)
2000	Jonas Edman (Sweden)
2004	Matthew Emmons (USA)
2008	Artur Auvazian (Ukraine)

Air Rifle (Men)
1992	Yuri Fedkin (UT)
1996	Artem Khadzhibekov (Russia)
2000	Cai Yalin (China)
2004	Zhu Qinan (China)
2008	Abhinav Bindra (India)

Air Pistol (Men)
1992	Wang Yifu (China)
1996	Roberto di Donna (Italy)
2000	Franck Dumoulin (France)
2004	Wang Yifu (China)
2008	Pang Wei (China)

Sport Pistol (Women)
1992	Marina Logvinenko (UT)

1996	Li Duihong (China)
2000	Maria Grozdeva (Bulgaria)
2004	Maria Grozdeva (Bulgaria)
2008	Chen Ying (China)

Air Rifle (Women)
1992	Yeo Kab Soon (South Korea)
1996	Renata Mauer (Poland)
2000	Nancy Johnson (USA)
2004	Du Li (China)
2008	Katerina Emmous (Czech Republic)

Small-Bore Rifle (Three Position) (Women)
1992	Launa Meili (USA)
1996	Alexandra Ivošev (Yugoslavia)
2000	Renata Mauer-Rozanska (Poland)
2004	Lioubou Galkina (Russia)
2008	Du Li (China)

Air Pistol (Women)
1992	Marina Logvinenko (UT)
1996	Olga Klochneva (Russia)
2000	Tao Luna (China)
2004	Olena Kostevych (Ukraine)
2008	Guo Wenjun (China)

Trap (Women)
1992	not held
1996	not held
2000	Daina Gudzineviciuté (Lithuania)
2004	Suzanne Balogh (Australia)
2008	Satu Makela-Nummela (Finland)

Skeet (Women)
1992	not held
1996	not held
2000	Zemfira Meftakhetdinova (Azerbaijan)
2004	Diana Igaly (Hungary)
2008	Chiara Cainero (Italy)

Skiing

■ World Cup
A season-long competition first organized in 1967; champions are declared in downhill, slalom, giant slalom and super-giant slalom, as well as the overall champion; points are obtained for performances in each category.

Overall winners
Men
1992	Paul Accola (Switzerland)
1993	Marc Girardelli (Luxembourg)
1994	Kjetil-Andre Aamodt (Norway)
1995	Alberto Tomba (Italy)
1996	Lasse Kjus (Norway)
1997	Luc Alphand (France)
1998	Hermann Maier (Austria)
1999	Lasse Kjus (Norway)
2000	Hermann Maier (Austria)
2001	Hermann Maier (Austria)
2002	Stephan Eberharter (Austria)
2003	Stephan Eberharter (Austria)
2004	Hermann Maier (Austria)
2005	Bode Miller (USA)
2006	Benjamin Raich (Austria)
2007	Aksel Lund Svindal (Norway)
2008	Bode Miller (USA)

Women

1992	Petra Kronberger (Austria)
1993	Anita Wachter (Austria)
1994	Vreni Schneider (Switzerland)
1995	Vreni Schneider (Switzerland)
1996	Katja Seizinger (Germany)
1997	Pernilla Wiberg (Sweden)
1998	Katja Seizinger (Germany)
1999	Alexandra Meissnitzer (Austria)
2000	Renate Götschl (Austria)
2001	Janica Kostelic (Croatia)
2002	Michaela Dorfmeister (Austria)
2003	Janica Kostelic (Croatia)
2004	Anja Paerson (Sweden)
2005	Anja Paerson (Sweden)
2006	Janica Kostelic (Croatia)
2007	Nicole Hosp (Austria)
2008	Lindsey Kildow Vonn (USA)

Snooker

■ World Professional Championship

Instituted in the 1926–7 season; a knockout competition open to professional players who are members of the World Professional Billiards and Snooker Association; played at the Crucible Theatre, Sheffield.

1992	Stephen Hendry (Scotland)
1993	Stephen Hendry (Scotland)
1994	Stephen Hendry (Scotland)
1995	Stephen Hendry (Scotland)
1996	Stephen Hendry (Scotland)
1997	Ken Doherty (Ireland)
1998	John Higgins (Scotland)
1999	Stephen Hendry (Scotland)
2000	Mark Williams (Wales)
2001	Ronnie O'Sullivan (England)
2002	Peter Ebdon (England)
2003	Mark Williams (Wales)
2004	Ronnie O'Sullivan (England)
2005	Shaun Murphy (England)
2006	Graeme Dott (Scotland)
2007	John Higgins (Scotland)
2008	Ronnie O'Sullivan (England)

■ World Doubles

First played in 1982; discontinued after 1987.

All winners

1982	Steve Davis (England)/Tony Meo (England)
1983	Steve Davis (England)/Tony Meo (England)
1984	Alex Higgins (Ireland)/Jimmy White (England)
1985	Steve Davis (England)/Tony Meo (England)
1986	Steve Davis (England)/Tony Meo (England)
1987	Mike Hallett (England)/Stephen Hendry (Scotland)

■ The Masters

The Masters is an individual non-ranking tournament but is regarded as one of the game's majors. It has been played at the Wembley Conference Centre since 1979 and was sponsored between 1975 and 2003 by Benson & Hedges.

1992	Stephen Hendry (Scotland)
1993	Stephen Hendry (Scotland)
1994	Alan McManus (Scotland)
1995	Ronnie O'Sullivan (England)

1996	Stephen Hendry (Scotland)
1997	Steve Davis (England)
1998	Mark Williams (Wales)
1999	John Higgins (Scotland)
2000	Matthew Stevens (Wales)
2001	Paul Hunter (England)
2002	Paul Hunter (England)
2003	Mark Williams (Wales)
2004	Paul Hunter (England)
2005	Ronnie O'Sullivan (England)
2006	John Higgins (Scotland)
2007	Ronnie O'Sullivan (England)
2008	Mark Selby (England)

■ World Amateur Championship

First held in 1963; originally took place every two years, but annual since 1984.

1992	Neil Mosley (England)
1993	Chuchat Triratanapradit (Thailand)
1994	Mohamed Yusuf (Pakistan)
1995	Sakchai Sim-Nhan (Thailand)
1996	Stuart Bingham (England)
1997	Marco Fu (China/Hong Kong)
1998	Luke Simmonds (England)
1999	Ian Preece (Wales)
2000	Stephen Maguire (Scotland)
2001	*not held*
2002	Steve Mifsud (Australia)
2003	Pankaj Advani (India)
2004	Mark Allen (Northern Ireland)
2005	*not held*
2006	Kurt Maflin (Norway)
2007	Atthasit Mahitti (Thailand)
2008	Thepchaiya Un Nooh (Thailand)

Softball

■ World Championships

First held for women in 1965 and for men the following year; now usually held every four years.

Men (next 2009)

1992	Canada
1996	New Zealand
2000	New Zealand
2004	New Zealand

Women

1994	USA
1998	USA
2002	USA
2006	USA

Speedway

■ Grand Prix

Individual World Championships inaugurated in 1936; replaced by Grand Prix season in 1995. Team championship (the World Team Cup) instituted in 1960; first official World Pairs Championship in 1970 (threes from 1991); World Team Cup and World Pairs Championship amalgamated in 1994 to become World Team Championship; replaced by Speedway World Cup in 2001.

Individual Grand Prix

1992	Gary Havelock (England)
1993	Sam Ermolenko (USA)
1994	Tony Rickardsson (Sweden)
1995	Hans Nielsen (Denmark)

Sports and Games

Sports and Games

Squash court

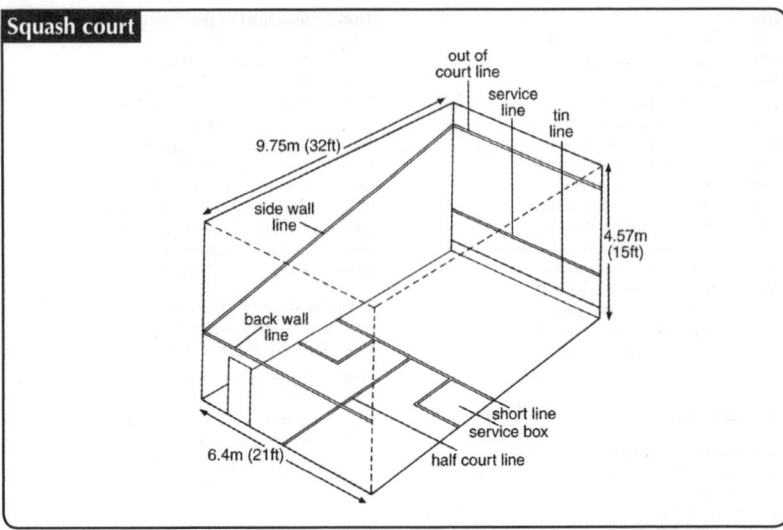

out of court line

service line

tin line

9.75m (32ft)

side wall line

4.57m (15ft)

back wall line

short line
service box

6.4m (21ft)

half court line

1996	Billy Hamill (USA)
1997	Greg Hancock (USA)
1998	Tony Rickardsson (Sweden)
1999	Tony Rickardsson (Sweden)
2000	Mark Loram (England)
2001	Tony Rickardsson (Sweden)
2002	Tony Rickardsson (Sweden)
2003	Nicki Pedersen (Denmark)
2004	Jason Crump (Australia)
2005	Tony Rickardsson (Sweden)
2006	Jason Crump (Australia)
2007	Nicki Pedersen (Denmark)
2008	Nicki Pedersen (Denmark)

Threes

1992   Greg Hancock/Sam Ermolenko/Ronnie Correy (USA)

1993   Greg Hancock/Sam Ermolenko (USA)

- **World Cup**

1994   Per Gustaffson/Tony Rickardsson/Michael Karlsson (Sweden)

1995   Hans Nielsen/Tommy Knudsen/Brian Carger (Denmark)

1996   Tomasz Gollob/ Piotr Protasiewicz/Slawomir Drabik (Poland)

1997   Hans Neilsen/Tommy Knudsen/Jesper Jensen (Denmark)

1998   Greg Hancock/Sam Ermolenko/Billy Hamill (USA)

1999   Jason Crump/Jason Lyons/Leigh Adams/Ryan Sullivan/Todd Wiltshire (Australia)

2000   Tony Rickardsson/Mikael Karlsson/Henrik Gustafsson/Peter Karlsson/Niklas Klingberg (Sweden)

2001   Jason Crump/Leigh Adams/Ryan Sullivan/Todd Wiltshire/Craig Boyce (Australia)

2002   Jason Crump/Leigh Adams/Jason Lyons/Ryan Sullivan/Todd Wiltshire (Australia)

2003   Andreas Jonsson/Mikael Max/Peter Ljung/Peter Karlsson/David Ruud (Sweden)

2004   Andreas Jonsson/Mikael Max/Peter Karlsson/Tony Rickardsson/Antonio Lindback (Sweden)

2005   Grzegorz Walasek/Rune Holta/Piotr Protasiewicz/Jarek Hampel/Tomasz Gollob (Poland)

2006   Niels Kristian Iversen/Nicki Pedersen/Bjarne Pedersen/Hans Andersen/Charlie Gjedde (Denmark)

2007   Krysztof Kasprzak/Jaroslaw Hampel/Tomasz Gollob/Rune Holta/Gregorz Walasek (Poland)

2008   Nicki Pedersen/Bjorne Pedersen/Kenneth Bjerre/Niels Kristian Iversen/Hans Andersen (Denmark)

Squash

- **World Open Championship**

First held in 1976; takes place annually for men and women; every two years for women 1976–89.

Men

1992	Jansher Khan (Pakistan)
1993	Jansher Khan (Pakistan)
1994	Jansher Khan (Pakistan)
1995	Jansher Khan (Pakistan)
1996	Jansher Khan (Pakistan)
1997	Rodney Eyles (Australia)
1998	Jonathon Power (Canada)
1999	Peter Nicol (Scotland)
2000	*not held*
2001	*not held*
2002	David Palmer (Australia)
2003	Amr Shabana (Egypt)

2004	Thierry Lincou (France)
2005	Amr Shabana (Egypt)
2006	David Palmer (Australia)
2007	Amr Shabana (Egypt)
2008	Ramy Ashour (Egypt)

Women

1993	Michelle Martin (Australia)
1994	Michelle Martin (Australia)
1995	Michelle Martin (Australia)
1996	Sarah Fitz-Gerald (Australia)
1997	Sarah Fitz-Gerald (Australia)
1998	Sarah Fitz-Gerald (Australia)
1999	Cassie Campion (Great Britain)
2000	Carol Owens (Australia)
2001	Sarah Fitz-Gerald (Australia)
2002	Sarah Fitz-Gerald (Australia)
2003	Carol Owens (Australia)
2004	Vanessa Atkinson (Netherlands)
2005	Nicol David (Malaysia)
2006	Nicol David (Malaysia)
2007	Rachael Grinham (Australia)
2008	Nicol David (Malaysia)

Surfing

■ **World Professional Championship**
A season-long series of Grand Prix events; first held in 1970.

Men

1992	Kelly Slater (USA)
1993	Derek Ho (USA)
1994	Kelly Slater (USA)
1995	Kelly Slater (USA)
1996	Kelly Slater (USA)
1997	Kelly Slater (USA)
1998	Kelly Slater (USA)
1999	Mark Occhilupo (Australia)
2000	Sunny Garcia (Hawaii)
2001	CJ Hobgood (USA)
2002	Andy Irons (Hawaii)
2003	Andy Irons (Hawaii)
2004	Andy Irons (Hawaii)
2005	Kelly Slater (USA)
2006	Kelly Slater (USA)
2007	Mick Fanning (Australia)
2008	Kelly Slater (USA)

Women

1992	Wendy Botha (Australia)
1993	Pauline Menczer (Australia)
1994	Lisa Andersen (USA)
1995	Lisa Andersen (USA)
1996	Lisa Andersen (USA)
1997	Lisa Andersen (USA)
1998	Layne Beachley (Australia)
1999	Layne Beachley (Australia)
2000	Layne Beachley (Australia)
2001	Layne Beachley (Australia)
2002	Layne Beachley (Australia)
2003	Layne Beachley (Australia)
2004	Sofia Mulanovich (Peru)
2005	Chelsea Georgeson (Australia)
2006	Layne Beachley (Australia)
2007	Stephanie Gilmore (Australia)
2008	Stephanie Gilmore (Australia)

Swimming and diving

■ **Olympic Games**
In 1904 the first 50m freestyle event for men was held (won by Zoltán Halmaj of Hungary), but was then discontinued until 1988. The women's 50m was introduced at the Seoul Games of 1988. The complete list of 2008 Olympic champions is given below.

Men

50m freestyle	César Cielo (Brazil)
100m freestyle	Alain Bernard (France)
200m freestyle	Michael Phelps (USA)
400m freestyle	Park Tae-Hwan (South Korea)
1500m freestyle	Oussama Mellouli (Tunisia)
100m backstroke	Aaron Peirsol (USA)
200m backstroke	Ryan Lochte (USA)
100m breaststroke	Kosuke Kitajima (Japan)
200m breaststroke	Kosuke Kitajima (Japan)
100m butterfly	Michael Phelps (USA)
200m butterfly	Michael Phelps (USA)
200m individual medley	Michael Phelps (USA)
400m individual medley	Michael Phelps (USA)
4 × 100m freestyle relay	USA
4 × 200m freestyle relay	USA
4 × 100m medley relay	USA
10km marathon	Maarten van der Weijden (Netherlands)
3m springboard diving	He Chong (China)
10m platform diving	Matthew Mitcham (Australia)
Synchronized springboard diving	Wang Feng/Qin Kai (China)
Synchronized platform diving	Lin Yue/Huo Liang (China)

Women

50m freestyle	Britta Steffen (Germany)
100m freestyle	Britta Steffen (Germany)
200m freestyle	Federica Pellegrini (Italy)
400m freestyle	Rebecca Adlington (Great Britain)
800m freestyle	Rebecca Adlington (Great Britain)
100m backstroke	Natalie Coughlin (USA)
200m backstroke	Kirsty Coventry (Zimbabwe)
100m breaststroke	Leisel Jones (Australia)
200m breaststroke	Rebecca Soni (USA)
100m butterfly	Lisbeth Trickett (Australia)
200m butterfly	Liu Zige (China)
200m individual medley	Stephanie Rice (Australia)
400m individual medley	Stephanie Rice (Australia)
4 × 100m freestyle relay	Netherlands
4 × 200m freestyle relay	Australia
4 × 100m medley relay	Australia
10km marathon	Larisa Ilchenko (Russia)
3m springboard diving	Guo Jingjing (China)

10m platform diving	Chen Ruolin (China)
Synchronized springboard diving	Guo Jingjing/Wu Minxia (China)
Synchronized platform diving	Wang Xui/Chen Ruolin (China)
Synchronized swimming duet	Anastasia Davydova/Anastasia Ermakova (Russia)
Team	Russia

Table tennis

■ **World Championships**
First held in 1926 and every two years since 1957, with the exception of 1999.

Swaythling Cup (Men's Team)
1993	Sweden
1995	China
1997	China
1999	*not held*
2000	Sweden
2001	China
2004	China
2006	China
2008	China

Corbillon Cup (Women's Team)
1993	China
1995	China
1997	China
1999	*not held*
2000	China
2001	China
2004	China
2006	China
2008	China

Men's Singles
1993	Jean-Philippe Gatien (France)
1995	Kong Linghui (China)
1997	Jan-Ove Waldner (Sweden)
1999	Liu Guoliang (China)
2001	Wang Liqin (China)
2003	Werner Schlager (Austria)
2005	Wang Liqin (China)
2007	Wang Liqin (China)

Women's Singles
1993	Hyun Jung-Hwa (South Korea)
1995	Deng Yaping (China)
1997	Deng Yaping (China)
1999	Wang Nan (China)
2001	Wang Nan (China)
2003	Wang Nan (China)
2005	Zhang Yining (China)
2007	Guo Yue (China)

Men's Doubles
1993	Wang Tao/Lu Lin (China
1995	Wang Tao/Lu Lin (China
1997	Liu Guoliang/Kong Linghui (China)
1999	Liu Guoliang/Kong Linghui (China)
2001	Wang Liqin/Yan Sen (China)
2003	Wang Liqin/Yan Sen (China)
2005	Wang Hao/Kong Linghui (China)
2007	Chen Qi/Ma Lin (China)

Women's Doubles
1993	Liu Wei/Qiao Yunping (China)
1995	Qiao Hong/Deng Yaping (China)
1997	Li Ju/Wang Nan (China)
1999	Wang Nan/Li Ju (China)
2001	Li Ju/Wang Nan (China)
2003	Wang Nan/Zhang Yining (China)
2005	Wang Nan/Zhang Yining (China)
2007	Wang Nan/Zhang Yining (China)

Mixed Doubles
1993	Wang Tao/Liu Wei (China)
1995	Wang Tao/Liu Wei (China)
1997	Kong Linghui/Deng Yaping (China)
1999	Zhang Yingying/Ma Lin (China)
2001	Qin Zhijian/Yang Yin (China)
2003	Wang Nan/Ma Lin (China)
2005	Guo Yue/Wang Liqin (China)
2007	Wang Nan/Ma Lin (China)

Tennis (lawn)

■ **All-England Championships at Wimbledon**
The All-England Championships at Wimbledon are lawn tennis's most prestigious championships; first held in 1877.

Men's Singles
1992	André Agassi (USA)
1993	Pete Sampras (USA)
1994	Pete Sampras (USA)
1995	Pete Sampras (USA)
1996	Richard Krajicek (Netherlands)
1997	Pete Sampras (USA)
1998	Pete Sampras (USA)
1999	Pete Sampras (USA)
2000	Pete Sampras (USA)
2001	Goran Ivanisevic (Croatia)
2002	Lleyton Hewitt (Australia)
2003	Roger Federer (Switzerland)
2004	Roger Federer (Switzerland)
2005	Roger Federer (Switzerland)
2006	Roger Federer (Switzerland)
2007	Roger Federer (Switzerland)
2008	Rafael Nadel (Spain)

Women's Singles
1992	Steffi Graf (Germany)
1993	Steffi Graf (Germany)
1994	Conchita Martínez (Spain)
1995	Steffi Graf (Germany)
1996	Steffi Graf (Germany)
1997	Martina Hingis (Switzerland)
1998	Jana Novotna (Czech Republic)
1999	Lindsay Davenport (USA)
2000	Venus Williams (USA)
2001	Venus Williams (USA)
2002	Serena Williams (USA)
2003	Serena Williams (USA)
2004	Maria Sharapova (Russia)
2005	Venus Williams (USA)
2006	Amélie Mauresmo (France)
2007	Venus Williams (USA)
2008	Venus Williams (USA)

Men's Doubles
1992	John McEnroe (USA)/Michael Stich (Germany)
1993	Todd Woodbridge/Mark Woodforde (Australia)
1994	Todd Woodbridge/Mark Woodforde (Australia)

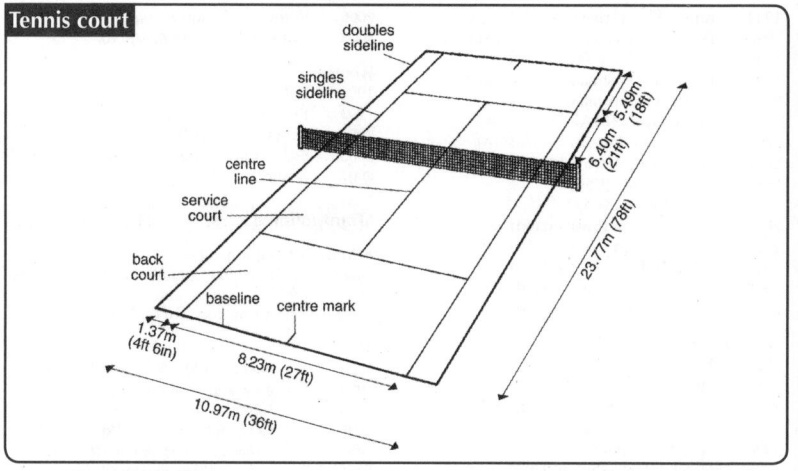

Tennis court

doubles sideline

singles sideline

centre line

service court

back court

baseline   centre mark

6.40m 5.49m (21ft) (18ft)

23.77m (78ft)

1.37m (4ft 6in)

8.23m (27ft)

10.97m (36ft)

Sports and Games

1995	Todd Woodbridge/Mark Woodforde (Australia)
1996	Todd Woodbridge/Mark Woodforde (Australia)
1997	Todd Woodbridge/Mark Woodforde (Australia)
1998	Jacco Eltingh/Paul Haarhuis (Netherlands)
1999	Mahesh Bhupathi/Leander Paes (India)
2000	Todd Woodbridge/Mark Woodforde (Australia)
2001	Donald Johnson/Jared Palmer (USA)
2002	Todd Woodbridge (Australia)/Jonas Bjorkman (Sweden)
2003	Todd Woodbridge (Australia)/Jonas Bjorkman (Sweden)
2004	Todd Woodbridge (Australia)/Jonas Bjorkman (Sweden)
2005	Stephen Huss (Australia)/Wesley Moodie (South Africa)
2006	Bob Bryan/Mike Bryan (USA)
2007	Arnaud Clément/Michaël Llodra (France)
2008	Daniel Nestor (Canada)/Nenad Zimonjic (Serbia)

Women's Doubles

1992	Gigi Fernandez (USA)/Natalya Zvereva (CIS)
1993	Gigi Fernandez (USA)/Natalya Zvereva (CIS)
1994	Gigi Fernandez (USA)/Natalya Zvereva (CIS)
1995	Arantxa Sanchez Vicario (Spain)/Jana Novotna (Czech Republic)
1996	Helena Sukova (Czech Republic)/Martina Hingis (Switzerland)
1997	Gigi Fernandez (USA)/Natalya Zvereva (Belarus)
1998	Jana Novotna (Czech Republic) Martina Hingis (Switzerland)
1999	Lindsay Davenport/Corina Morariu (USA)
2000	Serena Williams/Venus Williams (USA)
2001	Lisa Raymond (USA)/Rennae Stubbs (Australia)
2002	Serena Williams/Venus Williams (USA)
2003	Kim Clijsters (Belgium)/Ai Sugiyama (Japan)

2004	Cara Black (Zimbabwe)/Rennae Stubbs (Australia)
2005	Cara Black (Zimbabwe)/Liezel Huber (South Africa)
2006	Zi Yan/Jie Zheng (China)
2007	Cara Black (Zimbabwe)/Liezel Huber (South Africa)
2008	Serena Williams/Venus Williams (USA)

Mixed Doubles

1992	Larissa Savchenko-Neiland (Latvia)/ Cyril Suk (Czechoslovakia)
1993	Martina Navratilova (USA)/Mark Woodforde (Australia)
1994	Helena Sukova (Czech Republic)/Todd Woodbridge (Australia)
1995	Martina Navratilova/Jonathan Stark (USA)
1996	Helena Sukova/Cyril Suk (Czech Republic)
1997	Helena Sukova/Cyril Suk (Czech Republic)
1998	Serena Williams (USA)/Max Mirnyi (Belarus)
1999	Lisa Raymond (USA)/Leander Paes (India)
2000	Kimberly Po/Donald Johnson (USA)
2001	Daniela Hantuchova (Slovakia)/Leos Friedl (Czech Republic)
2002	Elena Likhovtseva (Russia)/Mahesh Bhupathi (India)
2003	Martina Navratilova (USA)/Leander Paes (India)
2004	Cara Black/Wayne Black (Zimbabwe)
2005	Mary Pierce (France)/Mahesh Bhupathi (India)
2006	Vera Zvonereva (Russia)/Andy Ram (Israel)
2007	Jelena Jankovic (Serbia)/Jamie Murray (Great Britain)
2008	Bob Bryan (USA)/Samantha Stosur (Australia)

■ **United States Open**

First held in 1891 as the United States Championship; became the United States Open in 1968.

Men's Singles

| 1992 | Stefan Edberg (Sweden) |
| 1993 | Pete Sampras (USA) |

Sports and Games

1994	André Agassi (USA)
1995	Pete Sampras (USA)
1996	Pete Sampras (USA)
1997	Pat Rafter (Australia)
1998	Pat Rafter (Australia)
1999	André Agassi (USA)
2000	Marat Safin (Russia)
2001	Lleyton Hewitt (Australia)
2002	Pete Sampras (USA)
2003	Andy Roddick (USA)
2004	Roger Federer (Switzerland)
2005	Roger Federer (Switzerland)
2006	Roger Federer (Switzerland)
2007	Roger Federer (Switzerland)
2008	Roger Federer (Switzerland)

Women's Singles

1992	Monica Seles (Yugoslavia)
1993	Steffi Graf (Germany)
1994	Arantxa Sanchez Vicario (Spain)
1995	Steffi Graf (Germany)
1996	Steffi Graf (Germany)
1997	Martina Hingis (Switzerland)
1998	Lindsay Davenport (USA)
1999	Serena Williams (USA)
2000	Venus Williams (USA)
2001	Venus Williams (USA)
2002	Serena Williams (USA)
2003	Justine Henin-Hardenne (Belgium)
2004	Svetlana Kuznetsova (Russia)
2005	Kim Clijsters (Belgium)
2006	Maria Sharapova (Russia)
2007	Justine Henin (Belgium)
2008	Serena Williams (USA)

■ **Davis Cup**

International team competition organized on a knockout basis; first held in 1900; contested on a challenge basis until 1972.

1992	USA
1993	Germany
1994	Sweden
1995	USA
1996	France
1997	Sweden
1998	Sweden
1999	Australia
2000	Spain
2001	France
2002	Russia
2003	Australia
2004	Spain
2005	Croatia
2006	Russia
2007	USA
2008	Spain

Tenpin bowling

■ **World Championships**

First held in 1923 by the International Bowling Association; since 1954 organized by the Fédération Internationale des Quillieurs (FIQ); now held every two years.

Men

1995	Marc Doi (Canada)
1999	Gery Verbuggen (Belgium)
2003	Mika Luoto (Finland)

2006	Remy Ong (South Korea)
2008	Guy Carninsky (South Africa)

Women

1995	Debby Ship (Canada)
1999	Kelly Kulick (USA)
2003	Zara Glover (England)
2005	Esther Cheah (Malaysia)
2007	Shannon O'Keefe (USA)

Trampolining

■ **World Championships**

First held in 1964 and annually until 1968; since then, every two years until 1998, when the competition was put forward one year.

Men

1992	Aleksandr Moskalenko (Russia)
1994	Aleksandr Moskalenko (Russia)
1996	Dimitri Poliarauch (Belarus)
1998	German Khanytchve (Russia)
1999	Aleksandr Moskalenko (Russia)
2001	Alexsandr Moskalenko (Russia)
2003	Henrik Stehlik (Germany)
2005	Aleksandr Rusakov (Russia)
2007	Ye Shuai (China)

Women

1992	Elena Merkulova (Russia)
1994	Irina Karavaeva (Russia)
1996	Tatyana Kovaleva (Russia)
1998	Irina Karavaeva (Russia)
1999	Irina Karavaeva (Russia)
2001	Anna Dogonadze (Germany)
2003	Karen Cockburn (Canada)
2005	Irina Karavaeva (Russia)
2007	Irina Karavaeva (Russia)

Tug-of-war

■ **World Outdoor Championships**

Instituted in 1975, now usually held every two years; contested at 560kg from 1982.

	720kg	*640kg*	*560kg*
1992	Switzerland	Switzerland	Spain
1994	Netherlands	Switzerland	Spain
1996	Netherlands	Switzerland	Ireland
1998	Netherlands	England	Spain
2000	Switzerland	Switzerland	Switzerland
2002	Netherlands	Switzerland	Switzerland
2004	Netherlands	Switzerland	England
2006	Switzerland	Germany	Switzerland
2008	Switzerland	Switzerland	Sweden

Volleyball

■ **World Championships**

Inaugurated in 1949; first women's championships in 1952; now held every four years, but Olympic champions are also world champions in Olympic years.

Men

1992	Brazil
1994	Italy
1996	Netherlands
1998	Italy
2000	Yugoslavia
2002	Brazil

Volleyball court

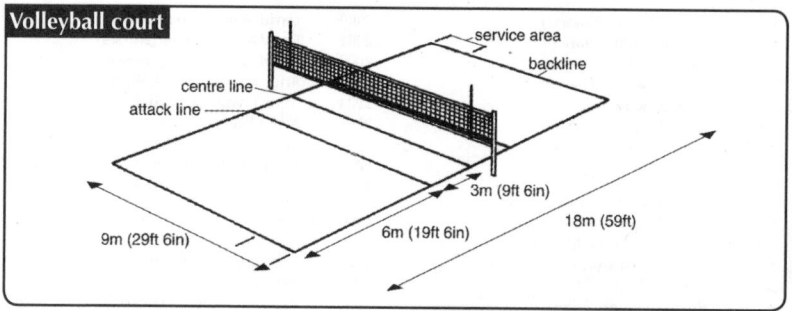

service area
backline
centre line
attack line
3m (9ft 6in)
9m (29ft 6in)
6m (19ft 6in)
18m (59ft)

2004	Brazil
2006	Brazil
2008	USA

Women

1992	Cuba
1994	Cuba
1996	Cuba
1998	Cuba
2000	Cuba
2002	Italy
2004	China
2006	Russia
2008	Brazil

Walking

■ **World Race Walking Cup**
Men
Team competitions for both distances introduced in 1993; contested every two years by national teams.

20km

1993	Mexico
1995	China
1997	Russia
1999	Russia
2002	Russia
2004	China
2006	Spain
2008	Russia

50km

1993	Mexico
1995	Mexico
1997	Russia
1999	Russia
2002	Russia
2004	Russia
2006	Spain
2008	Italy

Women
Team competition introduced in 1979; contested every two years.

20km

1993	Italy
1995	China
1997	Russia
1999	China
2002	Russia
2004	China
2006	Russia
2008	Italy

Water polo

■ **World Championships**
First held in 1973, and sporadically since 1978; formerly included in the World Swimming Championships, now held separately; first women's event in 1986.

Men

1994	Italy
1998	Spain
2001	Spain
2003	Hungary
2005	Serbia and Montenegro
2007	Croatia

Women

1994	Hungary
1998	Italy
2001	Italy
2003	USA
2005	Hungary
2007	USA

■ **World Cup**
Inaugurated in 1979 and held every two years until 2002; now takes place every four years. Women's event unofficial until 1989.

Men

1991	USA
1993	Italy
1995	Hungary
1997	USA
1999	Hungary
2002	Russia
2006	Serbia and Montenegro

Women

1991	Netherlands
1993	Netherlands
1995	Australia
1997	Netherlands
1999	Netherlands
2002	Hungary
2006	Australia

Water skiing

■ **World Championships**
First held in 1949; take place every two years; competitions for Slalom, Tricks, Jumps and the Overall Individual title.

Overall (Men)

1993	Patrice Martin (France)

1995	Patrice Martin (France)
1997	Patrice Martin (France)
1999	Patrice Martin (France)
2001	Jaret Llewellyn (Canada)
2003	Jimmy Siemers (USA)
2005	Jimmy Siemers (USA)
2007	Jaret Llewellyn (Canada)

Overall (Women)

1993	Natalia Rumiantseva (Russia)
1995	Judy Messer (Canada)
1997	Elena Milakova (Russia)
1999	Elena Milakova (Russia)
2001	Elena Milakova (Russia)
2003	Regina Jaquess (USA)
2005	Regina Jaquess (USA)
2007	Clémentine Lucine (France)

Weightlifting

■ **World Championships**
First held in 1898; eleven weight divisions; the most prestigious is the 105kg-plus category (formerly known as Super Heavyweight, then 110kg-plus; in 1993 changed to 108kg-plus; in 1998 reduced to current weight); Olympic champions are automatically world champions in Olympic years.

105kg-plus

1992	Aleksandr Kurlovich (UT)
1993	Ronnie Weller (Germany)
1994	Aleksandr Kurlovich (Belarus)
1995	Andrey Chemerkin (Russia)
1996	Andrey Chemerkin (Russia)
1997	Andrey Chemerkin (Russia)
1998	Andrey Chemerkin (Russia)
1999	Andrey Chemerkin (Russia)
2000	Hossein Rezazadeh (Iran)
2001	Saeed Salem Jaber (Qatar)
2002	Hossein Rezazadeh (Iran)
2003	Hossein Rezazadeh (Iran)
2004	Hossein Rezazadeh (Iran)
2005	Dmitry Klokov (Russia)
2006	Marcin Dolega (Poland)
2007	Viktors Ščerbatihs (Latvia)
2008	Matthias Steiner (Germany)

Wrestling

■ **World Championships**
Graeco-Roman world championships first held in 1921; first freestyle championships in 1951; each style contests ten weight divisions, the heaviest being the 120kg (formerly over 100kg, and until December 2001 130kg) category; Olympic champions become world champions in Olympic years.

Super-heavyweight/120kg
Freestyle

1992	Bruce Baumgartner (USA)
1993	Bruce Baumgartner (USA)
1994	Mahmut Demir (Turkey)
1995	Bruce Baumgartner (USA)
1996	Mahmut Demir (Turkey)
1997	Zekeriya Güglü (Turkey)
1998	Alexis Rodriguez (Cuba)
1999	Stephen Neal (USA)

2000	David Moussoulbes (Russia)
2001	David Moussoulbes (Russia)
2002	David Moussoulbes (Russia)
2003	Artur Taymazov (Uzbekistan)
2004	Artur Taymazov (Uzbekistan)
2005	Aydin Polatci (Turkey)
2006	Artur Taymazov (Uzbekistan)
2007	Beyal Makhov (Russia)
2008	Artur Taymazov (Uzbekistan)

Graeco-Roman

1992	Aleksandr Karelin (UT)
1993	Aleksandr Karelin (Russia)
1994	Aleksandr Karelin (Russia)
1995	Aleksandr Karelin (Russia)
1996	Aleksandr Karelin (Russia)
1997	Aleksandr Karelin (Russia)
1998	Aleksandr Karelin (Russia)
1999	Aleksandr Karelin (Russia)
2000	Rulon Gardner (USA)
2001	Rulon Gardner (USA)
2002	Dremiel Byers (USA)
2003	Khasan Baroev (Russia)
2004	Khasan Baroev (Russia)
2005	Mijain Lopez Nunez (Cuba)
2006	Khasan Baroev (Russia)
2007	Mijain Lopez (Cuba)
2008	Mijain Lopez (Cuba)

Yachting

■ **America's Cup**
One of sport's famous trophies; first won by the schooner *Magic* in 1870; now held approximately every four years, when challengers compete in a series of races to find which of them races against the holder; all 25 winners up to 1983 were from the USA.

Winning yacht (Skipper)

1992	*America* (USA) (Bill Koch)
1995	*Black Magic* (New Zealand) (Russell Coutts)
2000	*Black Magic* (New Zealand) (Russell Coutts)
2003	*Alinghi* (Switzerland) (Russell Coutts)
2007	*Alinghi* (Switzerland) (Brad Butterworth)

■ **Admiral's Cup**
A two-yearly series of races, originally held in the English Channel, around Fastnet rock and at Cowes; originally four national teams of three boats per team, now nine teams of three boats per team (except for the 2003 race, when two-boat teams represented clubs); first held in 1957.

1993	Germany
1995	Italy
1997	USA
1999	Netherlands
2001	*not held*
2003	Australia
2005	*not held*
2007	*not held*

Aaron, Hank (Henry Lewis) (1934–) US baseball player, born Mobile, Alabama. Regarded as one of the greatest batters ever, he set almost every batting record in his 23-season career with the Milwaukee Braves and the Milwaukee Brewers: 2297 runs batted in, 1477 extra-base hits, and 755 home runs (he broke **Babe Ruth**'s long-standing record of 714 in 1974). Named the Most Valuable Player in 1957, he led the Braves to the World Series Championship.

Ali, Muhammad, formerly **Cassius Marcellus Clay** (1942–) US boxer, born Louisville, Kentucky. Won Olympic amateur light-heavyweight title in Rome (1960); turned professional and won world heavyweight title (1964). Stripped of title 1967 for refusing military service on religious grounds, but returned 1970. Made history by regaining the world heavyweight title twice — lost 1971, regained 1974; lost 1978, regained later 1978.

Anquetil, Jacques (1934–87) French racing cyclist, born Normandy. Winner of Tour de France five times (1957, 1961–4); also won Tour of Spain (1963) and of Italy (1964).

Aouita, Said (1959–) Moroccan athlete, born Rabat. Set world records at 1500m and 5000m in 1985 — the first man for 30 years to hold both records. Later broke world records at 2 miles, 2000m, and 3000m. Also Olympic champion (1984), overall Grand Prix winner (1986) and world 5000m champion (1987).

Armstrong, Lance (1971–) US cyclist, born in Plano, Texas. Won the US amateur cycling championship in 1990. Turned professional in 1992 and within a year was ranked fifth in the world. Won stages in the Tour de France in 1993 and 1995 but in 1996 was diagnosed with advanced cancer. Declared clear of cancer in 1997 and went on to win the Tour de France a record seven times in a row (1999–2005).

Beckenbauer, Franz, nicknamed **Kaiser Franz** (1945–) German footballer, coach, manager and administrator, born Munich. European Footballer of the Year in 1972, he captained the West German national side to success in the European Nations Cup (1972) and in the World Cup (1974); he also won three successive European Cup winner's medals with Bayern Munich (1974–6). He coached the West German team (1984–90) and as manager took them to consecutive World Cup finals — as runners up in 1986 and then as winners (for Germany) in 1990. He became President of Bayern Munich in 1994 and led Germany's successful bid to host the 2006 World Cup.

Best, George (1946–2005) Northern Irish footballer, born Belfast. Northern Ireland's greatest individual footballing talent; leading scorer for Manchester United in the Football League First Division (1967–8), and in 1968 winner of a European Cup medal and the title of European Footballer of the Year. Immense career success dwindled early due to pressures of top-class football.

Biondi, Matt(hew) (1965–) US swimmer, born Morego, California. Winner of record seven medals at the 1986 world championships, including three golds; of seven medals at the 1988 Olympics, including five golds; and a silver in the 50m freestyle at the 1992 Olympics. The first to swim a sub-49 seconds 100m freestyle.

Blankers-Koen, Fannie (1918–2004) Dutch athlete, born Baarne. Made Olympic debut in 1946 (high jump) without winning a medal. At the 1948 Olympics she won four gold medals (100m, 200m, 80m hurdles, the rules restricting her to three individual events so she could not contest the high jump or long jump, in both of which she was the world record holder. She set 16 world records at eight different events: 100yd, 100m, 200m, high hurdles, high jump, long jump, pentathlon and 4 × 110yd relay. She also won five European titles between 1946 and 1950.

Border, Allan (1955–) Australian cricketer, born Cremorne, Sydney. Made Test debut for Australia in 1978; team captain 1984–94. Set world records for most Test match and one-day international appearances, and for runs scored in Test matches when his career total reached 10 161 (1993). Played county cricket in England for Gloucestershire and Essex.

Borg, Bjorn Rune (1956–) Swedish tennis player. Swedish Davis Cup team member aged 15, and Wimbledon junior champion aged 16. Winner of five consecutive Wimbledon singles titles (1976–80), two Italian championship titles and six French Open titles (1974–5, 1978–81).

Botham, Ian Terence (1955–) English cricketer, born Heswall, Merseyside. Played for England in 102 Test matches, took 383 wickets, and scored 5200 runs. Held record number of Test wickets (373 wickets at an average of 27.86 runs) until overtaken by **Richard Hadlee**, and four times took ten wickets in a match. Played county cricket in England for Somerset (1974–87), Worcestershire (1987–91) and Durham (1992–3).

Bradman, Don (Sir Donald George) (1908–2001) Australian cricketer, born Cootamundra, New South Wales, regarded as one of the greatest batsmen ever. Played for Australia from 1928 to 1948 (captain 1936–48); made highest aggregate and largest number of centuries in Tests against England, and set record for the highest Australian Test score against England (334 at Leeds in 1930); batting average in Test matches was 99.94 runs per innings.

Bubka, Sergei (1963–) Ukrainian field athlete, born Donetsk. Won gold medal for pole-vaulting at the 1983 world championship, retaining title in 1987, 1991, 1993, 1995 and 1997; also won gold at the 1988 Olympics. Broke 35 world records and in 1994 took the world pole-vault record to 6.14m.

Carson, Willie (William Hunter Fisher) (1942–) Scottish jockey, born Stirling. Rode 17 Classic winners and is fourth in the all-time winners table. First Classic success was on High Top in the 2000 Guineas (1972); recorded a notable royal double for Queen Elizabeth II by winning the Oaks and the St Leger on Dunfermline (1977); won Derby first on Troy (1979), then Henbit (1980), Nashwan (1989) and Erhaab (1994).

Charlton, Bobby (Sir Robert) (1937–) English footballer, born Ashington, Northumberland. He played with Manchester United (1954–73), winning three League championship medals (1956–7, 1964–5, 1966–7) and an FA Cup winner's medal (1963), and captained Manchester United to victory in the 1968 European Cup. Also played 106 games for England between 1957 and 1973, scoring a record 49 goals, and was a member of the victorious World Cup team (1966). In all he played 754 games, scoring 245 goals.

Cobb, Ty(rus Raymond), nicknamed **the Georgia Peach** (1886–1961) US baseball player, born Narrows, Georgia. Regarded as outstanding offensive player of all time; played for the Detroit

Tigers (1905–26) and the Philadelphia Athletics (1926–8), and until Pete Rose in 1985 was the only player with more than 4000 hits in major league baseball. Career batting average was 0.367 (ie he had a hit more than once every three times at bat).

Coe, Sebastian (1956–) English athlete, born Chiswick, London. Winner of 1500m Olympic gold medal and 800m silver medal at both Moscow (1980) and Los Angeles (1984). Broke world record for the 800m, 1000m and the mile in 1981. Between Sep 1976 and June 1983 he did not lose the final of any race over 1500m or a mile.

Comaneci, Nadia (1961–) Romanian gymnast, born Onesti, Moldavia. Winner at the 1976 Olympic Games (aged 14) of gold medals in the parallel bars and beam disciplines and a bronze in the floor, becoming the first to obtain a perfect score of ten for performance on the bars and beam; also won gold medals in the beam at the 1978 world championships and in the beam and the floor exercise at the 1980 Olympics.

Connors, Jimmy (James Scott) (1952–) US tennis player, born East St Louis, Illinois. Winner of the men's singles competition at Wimbledon (1974, 1982), the Australian Open (1974), and the US Open (1974, 1976, 1978, 1982–3). With Ilie Nastase, he won the men's doubles at Wimbledon (1973) and the US Open men's doubles (1975). He was World Championship Tennis champion (1977, 1980), Masters champion (1978), and a US team member in the Davis Cup (1976; 1981 victory).

Court, Margaret Jean Smith, née **Smith** (1942–) Australian tennis player, born Albury, New South Wales. Winner of more Grand Slam events (66) than any other player: 10 Wimbledon titles (including the singles, the first Australian to do so, in 1963, 1965, 1970), 22 US titles (singles in 1962, 1965, 1968–70, 1973), 13 French (singles 1962, 1964, 1969–70, 1973), and 21 Australian (singles 1960–6, 1969–71, 1973). In 1970 she became the second woman (after Maureen Connolly) to win all four major titles in one year.

Davis, Joe (1901–78) English billiards and snooker champion, born Whitwell, near Chesterfield. Made first break of 100 aged 12. World professional snooker champion (1927–46), and billiards champion (1928–33). Attained maximum snooker break of 147 in 1955, later officially recognized as the world record.

Davis, Steve (1957–) English snooker player, born London. World's leading player during the 1980s, and world champion six times (1981, 1983–4, 1987–9).

DiMaggio, Joe (Joseph Paul), nicknamed **Joltin' Joe** and **the Yankee Clipper** (1914–99) US baseball player, born Martinez, California. Played entire career (1936–51) with the New York Yankees. Greatest achievement was hitting safely (recording a hit) at least once in 56 consecutive games in the 1941 season. Was the American League's Most Valuable Player three times and winner of the batting championship twice (1939, 1940). Career total was 361 home runs, with a batting average of 0.325.

Eddery, Pat(rick James John) (1952–) Irish jockey, born Newbridge, Kildare. Champion jockey eleven times between 1974 and 1996. Classics victories include the Derby (1975, 1982, 1990), the Oaks (1979, 1996), the St Leger (1986, 1991, 1994, 1997), 1000 Guineas (1996), 2000 Guineas (1983–4, 1993); also had four Prix de l'Arc de Triomphe wins (1980, 1985–7).

Edwards, Gareth Owen (1947–) Welsh rugby player, born Gwaun-cae-Gurwen, near Swansea. First capped for Wales aged 19 (1967), and became their youngest-ever captain (1968). His 53 consecutive caps set a Welsh record; also played in ten Lions Tests.

Evert, Chris(tine) Marie (1954–) US tennis player, born Fort Lauderdale, Florida. Winner of 157 professional titles, and undefeated on clay from Aug 1973 to May 1979. Her 18 singles Grand Slam titles were: the Australian Open (1982, 1984), the French Open (1974–5, 1979–80, 1983, 1985–6), the All-England Championship at Wimbledon (1974, 1976, 1981) and the US Open (1975–8, 1980, 1982).

Faldo, Nick (Nicholas Alexander) (1957–) English golfer, born Welwyn Garden City, Hertfordshire. Early in career won the Professional Golfers' Association (PGA) championships (1978, 1980–1). Reworked swing and then won the Open championship (1987, 1990, 1992) and the Masters (1989, 1990, 1996). Ryder Cup team member from 1977 to 1997.

Fischer, Bobby (Robert James) (1943–2008) US chess player, born Chicago. Winner of both US junior and senior chess titles aged 14; later world champion (1972–5). He won the title from Boris Spassky in 1972, but was stripped of it in 1975 for failing to agree conditions to defend it against **Anatoly Karpov**. He achieved the highest results rating (Elo 2785) in the history of chess.

Fitzpatrick, Sean (Brian Thomas) (1963–) New Zealand rugby union player, born Auckland. New Zealand's most capped player, and the world's most capped hooker. Set world record of 63 consecutive caps (1986–95). Won 51 caps as captain of New Zealand (1992–7).

Gavaskar, Sunil Manohar, nicknamed **the Little Master** (1949–) Indian cricketer, born Bombay (now Mumbai). Became one of the most prolific run-scorers in Test cricket history. Played for India in 125 Test matches from 1971 to 1997, scoring 10122 runs, including a record 34 Test centuries. Was the first player to score more than 10000 Test runs.

Gebrselassie, Haile (1973–) Ethiopian athlete, born Arssi. Considered by many to be the greatest distance runner ever, he won the gold medal for the 10000m at the 1996 and 2000 Olympics and four World Championships.

Girardelli, Marc (1963–) Luxembourg skier, born LVustenau, Austria. Winner of overall World Cup title more times than any other skier; also eleven world championship medals (four gold, four silver, three bronze) and two Olympic silver medals.

Gooch, Graham (1953–) English cricketer, born London. Made debut for Essex 1973, first capped for England 1975; played in over 100 Test matches, recording his highest score of 333 runs against India in 1990. Captained England 34 times, but resigned July 1993. Scored over 100 centuries, and when he retired from English Test cricket in 1995 had made a career total of 8900 runs.

Grace, W(illiam) G(ilbert) (1848–1915) English cricketer, born Downend, near Bristol. Made first-class debut with Gloucestershire aged 16 (1864) and remained in first-class cricket until 1908, making 126 centuries, scoring 54896 runs and taking 2864 wickets, becoming a national hero. He scored 2739 runs in a season in 1871, 344 runs in an innings in 1876 for MCC, and 100 first-class centuries by 1895.

Graf, Steffi (1969–) German tennis player, born

Sports and Games

Bruehl. In 1988 she won a Golden Grand Slam (the US, French, Australian and Wimbledon singles titles) as well as the gold medal at the Seoul Olympics. Singles wins include the French Open (1987–8, 1993, 1995–6, 1999), the Australian Open (1988–90, 1994), the US Open (1988–9, 1993, 1995–6) and the All-England championship at Wimbledon (1988–9, 1991–3, 1995–6).

Green, Lucinda, née **Prior-Palmer** (1953–) English three-day eventer, born London. She won the Badminton Horse Trials a record six times (1973, 1976–7, 1979, 1983–4) and the Burghley Horse Trials twice (1977, 1981). In the European championships she won an individual gold medal (1975, 1977), a team gold (1977, 1985, 1987), and an individual and team silver (1983). In 1982 she was world champion and won another team gold.

Gretzky, Wayne (1961–) Canadian ice-hockey player, born Brantford, Ontario. Played for the Edmonton Oilers (1978–88), the Los Angeles Kings (1988–96), the St Louis Blues briefly and the New York Rangers (1996–9). He set numerous records including the most goals scored in a season (92 in 1981–2) and most career points (he scored his 2 500th point in 1995 and retired with a total of 2 857). National Hockey League's Most Valuable Player nine times (1980–7, 1989).

Griffith-Joyner, Florence, known as **Flo-Jo** (1959– 98) US track and field sprinter, born Los Angeles, California. Winner of National Collegiate Athletic Association 200m title (1982), an Olympic silver medal in the 200m (1984), and three Olympic gold medals (1988): for the 100m and 200m – setting world records of 10.54 seconds for the former and 21.34 seconds for the latter – and for the 4 × 400m relay.

Hagen, Walter Charles, nicknamed **the Haig** (1892–1969) US golfer, born Rochester, New York State. First US-born winner and four-times winner of the British Open championship (1922, 1924, 1928–9); also won the US Open (1914, 1919), the US Professional Golfers' Association (PGA) a record five times (1921, 1924–7), and captained the first six US Ryder Cup teams (1927–37), which won in 1927, 1931, 1935 and 1937.

Hendry, Stephen (1969–) Scottish snooker player, born Edinburgh. Professional from age 16, became youngest-ever winner of a professional title at the Rothmans Grand Prix (1987). Gained several titles in 1989, including the British Open and, with Mike Hallett, the Fosters World Doubles. Winner of Embassy World Championship (1990, 1992–6, 1999).

Hinault, Bernard, known as **Le Blaireau (the badger)** (1954–) French cyclist, born Yffiniac. Winner of the Tour de France five times (1978–9, 1981–2, 1985). Won Tour of Italy three times and Tour of Spain twice.

Holyfield, Evander (1962–) US boxer, born Alabama. Undisputed heavyweight world champion in 1990–2, 1993–4 and 1996–7. In 2000 he won the WBA belt, becoming the first boxer to become world champion on four separate occasions.

Hutton, Len (Sir Leonard) (1916–90) English cricketer, born Fulneck, Yorkshire. Played for Yorkshire; made debut for England 1937, scoring a century in his first Test against Australia (1938), and in the Oval Test against Australia (also 1938) scored a world record of 364 runs, which stood for 20 years until it was exceeded by one run by **Gary Sobers**. He made 129 first-class centuries,

and captained England in 23 Test matches after World War II.

Johnson, Magic (Earvin) (1959–) US basketball player, born Lansing, Michigan. Played with the Los Angeles Lakers (1979–91 as a guard, 1996 as a forward), when they won five National Basketball Association (NBA) championships (1980, 1982, 1985, 1987–8), and in the 1992 gold medal-winning US Olympic basketball team ('Dream Team'). A member of the NBA All-Star team (1980, 1982–92), he was named NBA Most Valuable Player in 1987, 1989 and 1990.

Johnson, Michael (1967–) US track athlete, born Dallas. He won world championship races in the 200m (1991, 1995) and in the 400m (1993, 1995, 1997, 1999), and at the 1996 Olympics in Atlanta won gold medals in both 200m and 400m events, the first man ever to do so. He won Olympic gold again in the 400m in Sydney 2000 before retiring.

Jones, Bobby (Robert Tyre) (1902–71) US amateur golfer, born Atlanta, Georgia. He won the US Open four times (1923, 1926, 1929, 1930), the British Open three times (1926, 1927, 1930), the US Amateur championship five times and the British Amateur championship once. In 1930 he won the Grand Slam of the US and British Open and Amateur championships. Later he was responsible for the founding of the US Masters in Augusta.

Jordan, Michael Jeffrey (1963–) US basketball player, born Brooklyn, New York City. Played for Chicago Bulls (1984–93, 1995–8), and set many records, including most consecutive seasons leading the league in scoring (1986–7 to 1992–3); also played in US Olympic gold medal-winning basketball teams (1984, 1992). As member of National Basketball Association (NBA) All-Star team (1985–93, 1996–8), was NBA Most Valuable Player in 1988, 1991, 1992, 1996 and 1998.

Kapil Dev, (Nihanj) (1959–) Indian cricketer, born Chandigarh, Punjab. Made first-class debut for Haryana aged 16, and played county cricket in England for Northamptonshire and Worcestershire. Led India to victory in the 1983 World Cup, when he scored 175 not out against Zimbabwe. In 1994 he retired from the game, having set a then world record of 434 Test wickets.

Karpov, Anatoly Yevgenevich (1951–) Soviet chess player, born Zlatoust, in the Urals. Became world champion by default in 1975 after **Bobby Fischer** refused to defend his title; defeated 1985 by **Garry Kasparov**, but won title back in 1993. He held the FIDE (Fédération Internationale des Échecs) world championship from 1994, but lost his title to Alexander Khalifman in 1999.

Kasparov, Garry Kimovich, originally **Gary Weinstein** (1963–) Soviet chess player, born Baku, Azerbaijan. He won the USSR under-18 championship aged twelve and became world junior champion at 16. He was world champion from 1985, when he defeated **Anatoly Karpov**, until 1993, when Karpov won the title back. In 1994 he won the Professional Chess Association world championship, losing the title to Vladimir Kramnik in 2000.

Khan, Jahangir (1963–) Pakistani squash player, born Karachi. Winner of three world amateur titles (1979, 1983, 1985), a record six World Open titles (1981–5, 1988), and ten consecutive British Open titles (1982–91). He was undefeated from Apr 1981 until the World Open final in Nov 1986.

Killy, Jean-Claude (1943–) French ski racer, born St-Cloud. Winner of the downhill and combined gold medals at the world championship in Chile

(1966), and of three gold medals for slalom, giant slalom and downhill at the Winter Olympics (1968).

King, Billie Jean, née **Moffitt** (1943–) US tennis player, born Long Beach, California. She won the ladies doubles title at Wimbledon in 1961 (with Karen Hantze) at her first attempt, and between 1961 and 1979 won a record 20 Wimbledon titles, including the singles in 1966–8, 1972–3 and 1975, and four mixed doubles. She also won 13 US titles (including four singles in 1967, 1971–2, 1974), four French titles (one singles in 1972), and two Australian titles (one singles in 1968).

Klammer, Franz (1953–) Austrian Alpine skier, born Mooswald. Olympic downhill champion (1976), and World Cup downhill champion five times (1975–78, 1983). Between 1974 and 1984 he won a record 25 World Cup downhill races.

Koch, Marita (1957–) German athlete, born Wismar. She won the Olympic 400m title in 1980 and the European title three times, remaining undefeated over 400m between 1977 and 1981. In the 200m race, she won three indoor European championship titles and a World Student Games title. She set 16 world records, including the 400m seven times (which still stands) and the 200m four times.

Korbut, Olga Valentinovna (1956–) Soviet gymnast, born Grodno, Belarus. In the 1972 Olympic Games she won a gold medal as a member of the winning Soviet team, as well as individual golds in the beam and floor exercises and silver for the parallel bars.

Leonard, Sugar Ray (1956–) US boxer, born South Carolina. In 1976 he won an Olympic gold, starting a professional career in which he fought twelve world title fights at various weights and won world titles in each weight. In 35 fights (1977–87) he was beaten once (by Roberto Duran, welterweight title 1980). He became undisputed world welterweight champion again in 1981.

Lewis, Carl (1961–) US track and field athlete, born Birmingham, Alabama. He won four gold medals at the 1984 Olympics (100m, 200m, 4 × 100m relay and long jump), emulating **Jesse Owens**'s achievement of 1936. In 1988 he won an Olympic gold in the long jump and was awarded the 100m gold after Ben Johnson was stripped of the title. In 1992 he won two more Olympic golds in the long jump and the 4 × 100m relay, and in 1996 he earned his ninth and final Olympic gold medal in the long jump.

Louis, Joe, professional name of **Joseph Louis Barrow** (1914–81) US boxer, born Lexington, Alabama. He won the US amateur light-heavyweight title in 1934 and turned professional. He won the world championship in 1937, and held it for a record twelve years, defending his title 25 times. In all he won 68 of his 71 professional fights.

McBride, Willie (William) John (1940–) Irish rugby player, born Toomebridge, County Antrim. He played mostly with the Ballymena team from 1962. A lock forward, he won 45 caps, made a record 17 appearances for the British Lions on five tours, and played for Ireland 63 times.

McEnroe, John Patrick (1959–) US tennis player, born Wiesbaden, Germany. He won the Wimbledon singles title three times (1981, 1983–4), the US Open singles four times (1979–81, 1984), and eight Grand Slam doubles events, seven of them with Peter Fleming, and one at Wimbledon in 1992, with Michael Stich. He was

Grand Prix winner in 1979 and 1984–5, and world championship winner in 1979, 1981 and 1983–4.

Maradona, Diego (1960–) Argentine footballer, born Lanús. One of the best players of his generation, he won over 80 international caps. He played in the 1982 World Cup in Spain, and captained the Argentine side to World Cup victory in 1986 and 1990. He played for Boca Juniors, Barcelona, then Naples (1984–91), leading them to their first-ever Italian championship (1987). After leaving Naples, he played for Seville, Argentina and Boca Juniors again. He became manager of the national team in 2008.

Marciano, Rocky, originally **Rocco Francis Marchegiano** (1923–69) US boxer, born Brockton, Massachusetts. Made his name in 1951 by defeating former world champion **Joe Louis** and won world title from Jersey Joe Walcott in 1952; on retiring in 1956 he was undefeated as world champion with a professional record of 49 bouts and 49 victories.

Matthews, Sir Stanley (1915–2000) English footballer, born Hanley. Joined Stoke City as a winger in 1931, made debut for England aged 20, and over 22 years won 54 international caps. He played for Blackpool (1947–61), winning an FA Cup winner's medal in 1953, then returned to Stoke (1961), playing First Division football until after the age of 50. He was Footballer of the Year twice (1948, 1963), and the inaugural winner of the European Footballer of the Year award (1956).

Merckx, Eddy, known as **the Cannibal** (1945–) Belgian racing cyclist, born Woluwe St Pierre, near Brussels. In the 1969 Tour de France he won the major prize in all three sections – overall, points classification and King of the Mountains. He won the Tour de France five times (1969–72 and 1974); also won the Tour of Italy five times, and all the major classics, including the Milan–San Remo race seven times. World professional road race champion three times, he won more races (445) and more classics than any other rider. Retired 1978.

Montana, Joe (1956–) US American football player, born New Eagle, Pennsylvania. Played as quarterback with San Francisco 49ers (1979–93), then Kansas City Chiefs (1993–5). Member of victorious San Francisco 49ers Super Bowl teams in 1982, 1985, 1989 and 1990; Most Valuable Player in 1982, 1985 and 1990. Retired 1995.

Moore, Bobby (Robert) (1941–93) English footballer, born Barking, Essex. With West Ham (1958–74) and later Fulham (1974–7), he played 1000 matches at senior level, winning an FA Cup winner's medal in 1964 and a European Cup-Winners' Cup medal in 1965. He was capped a record 108 times (107 in succession), 90 of them as captain. He played in the World Cup finals in Chile in 1962 and captained the victorious England side in the 1966 World Cup.

Moser-Pröll, Annemarie, née **Pröll** (1953–) Austrian Alpine skier, born Kleinarl. Winner of a women's record 62 World Cup races (1970–9), she was overall champion (1979), downhill champion (1978, 1979), Olympic downhill champion (1980), world combined champion (1972, 1978), and world downhill champion (1974, 1978, 1980). Retired 1980.

Moses, Ed(win Corley) (1955–) US track athlete, born Dayton, Ohio. The greatest 400m hurdler ever, he was unbeaten from Aug 1977 to June 1987, was Olympic champion twice (1976, 1984) and four times world record holder. Missed 1980 Moscow Olympics due to US boycott.

Navratilova, Martina (1956–) US tennis player, born Prague, Czechoslovakia (Czech Republic).

In 1975 she defected to the USA and turned professional. She won a record nine singles titles at Wimbledon (1978–9, 1982–7, 1990) and the US Open four times (1983–4, 1986–7). Her record of 58 career Grand Slam titles is second only to **Margaret Court**. In 2003 she won the mixed doubles at the Australian Open and Wimbledon with partner Leander Paes.

Nicklaus, Jack, known as **the Golden Bear** (1940–) US golfer, born Columbus, Ohio. His first professional victory was the US Open (1962), which he also won in 1967, 1972 and 1980. Of the other Majors, he won the Masters a record six times (1963, 1965–6, 1972, 1975, 1986); the Open championship three times (1966, 1970, 1978); and the US Professional Golfers' Association (PGA) a record-equalling five times (1963, 1971, 1973, 1975, 1980). He also set a record total of 20 Major victories (including two US Amateurs pre-1962).

Nurmi, Paavo Johannes, known as **the Flying Finn** (1897–1973) Finnish athlete, born Turku. He won nine gold medals at three Olympic Games (1920, 1924, 1928). From 1922 to 1926 he set four world records at 3000m, bringing the time down to 8 minutes 20.4 seconds. He also established world records at six miles (1921, 29:7.1), one mile (1923, 4:10.4) and two miles (1931, 8:59.5).

Oerter, Al(fred) (1936–2007) US athlete and discus-thrower, born Astoria, New York State. An outstanding Olympic competitor, he won four consecutive gold medals for the discus, at Melbourne (1956), Rome (1960), Tokyo (1964) and Mexico (1968), breaking the Olympic record each time.

Owens, Jesse James Cleveland (1913–80) US athlete, born Danville, Alabama; considered the greatest sprinter of his generation. In 1935, while in the Ohio State University team, he set three world records and equalled another, including the long jump (26ft 8⅛in / 8.13m), which lasted 25 years. In 1936 he won four Olympic gold medals (100m, 200m, long jump, and 4 × 100m relay).

Palmer, Arnold (1929–) US golfer, born Youngstown, Pennsylvania. After a brilliant amateur career he turned professional in 1955, but won only eight Majors: the US Amateur (1954), US Masters (1958, 1960, 1962, 1964), US Open (1960) and the Open championship (1961, 1962). He was twice captain of the American Ryder Cup team.

Payton, Walter, nicknamed **Sweetness** (1954–99) US American football player, born Columbia, Mississippi. He played with the Chicago Bears as a running back (1975–87), establishing a National Football League rushing record of 16726 yards (15294m), scoring 125 touchdowns, and winning the Super Bowl in 1986. In one game (1977) he rushed for a record 275 yards (251m).

Pelé, pseudonym of **Edson Arantes do Nascimento** (1940–) Brazilian footballer, born Três Corações, Minas Gerais. He made his international debut for Brazil aged 16, played in four World Cup competitions (1958–70), and led Brazil to victory in 1958, 1962 and 1970. For most of his senior career he played for Santos. Regarded as one of the finest inside-forwards in football history, he attained 1000 goals in first-class football (Nov 1969); his career total was 1281 in 1363 games.

Perry, Fred(erick John) (1909–95) English tennis player, born Stockport, Cheshire. World singles table tennis champion in 1929, he took up lawn tennis aged 19. He won the Wimbledon singles three times (1934–6), the US Open singles three times (1933–4, 1936), and the Australian (1934)

and French (1935) championships, and helped to keep the Davis Cup in Great Britain for four years (1933–6). He was the first man to win all four major titles.

Piggott, Lester Keith (1935–) English jockey, born Wantage. Rode his first winner in 1948, was champion jockey in England on eleven occasions, and in all rode 30 Classic winners, including the Derby nine times. Retired 1995.

Player, Gary (1935–) South African golfer, born Johannesburg. He won the British Open three times (1959, 1968, 1974), the US Masters three times (1961, 1974, 1978), the US Open once (1965), and the US Professional Golfers' Association (PGA) title twice (1962, 1972). He also won the South African Open 13 times, and the Australian Open seven times.

Prost, Alain (1955–) French racing driver, born St Chamond. Won his first Grand Prix in 1981, was world champion four times (1985, 1986, 1989 and 1993), and runner-up four times (1983, 1984, 1988, 1990). Surpassed **Jackie Stewart**'s record of 27 Grand Prix wins in 1987, becoming the most successful driver in the history of the sport. Retired 1994.

Redgrave, Sir Steve (Steven Geoffrey) (1962–) English oarsman and sculler, born Marlow, Buckinghamshire. He won five successive Olympic gold medals (coxed four 1984, coxless pairs 1988, 1992, 1996, coxless four 2000). Nine times world champion, he also won a record three gold medals in the 1986 Commonwealth Games. Together he and Matthew Pinsent (1970–) were world coxless pairs champions (1991, 1993, 1994, 1995), world coxless four champions (1997, 1998, 1999), and Olympic champions (1992, 1996, 2000).

Ruth, Babe, properly **George Herman Ruth** (1895–1948) US baseball player, born Baltimore. Started career as a left-handed pitcher with the Boston Red Sox (1914–19), and became famous for his powerful hitting with the New York Yankees (1920–34); also played for Boston Braves (1935). Considered the greatest all-rounder in baseball history, he scored a record 60 home runs in 1927. In all he played in ten World Series, and hit 714 home runs, a record that stood unsurpassed until **Hank Aaron** broke it in 1974.

Sampras, Pete (1971–) US tennis player, born Washington DC. Five times winner of the US Open singles title (1990, 1993, 1995–6, 2002) and seven times winner of All-England singles title at Wimbledon (1993–5, 1997–2000); with 14 Grand Slam Championships he is the game's most successful male player.

Schumacher, Michael (1969–) German racing driver, born Hürth-Hermülheim. Most successful Formula One driver ever. Seven times world champion (1994–95, 2000–04) who revived the fortunes of manufacturer Ferrari. Finished in the first three 154 times, including winning 91 races, and won pole position 68 times.

Sella, Philippe (1962–) French rugby union player, born Clairac. First capped aged 20, he succeeded Serge Blanco in 1993–4 as the most capped international player of all time with a record 111 caps. During the period 1982–95 he scored 30 international test tries and was France's most capped centre.

Shoemaker, Willie (William Lee) (1931–2003) US jockey, born Fabens, Texas. In the USA his major successes included four Kentucky Derbies, five Belmont Stakes, and two Preakness event wins at

Sports and Games

Baltimore; later, he was successful in Europe too. In 1953 he rode a record 485 winners in a season. The first jockey to saddle more than 8000 winners, he was one of the most successful in racing history and retired in 1990 with 8833 wins.

Smetanina, Raisa Petrovna (1952–) Soviet cross-country skier, born Mokhcha. She won 23 medals between 1974 and 1992, including a record 10 Olympic skiing medals: four gold, five silver and one bronze.

Sobers, Gary, properly **Sir Garfield St Auburn Sobers** (1936–) West Indian cricketer, born Bridgetown, Barbados. In 93 Test matches for the West Indies (captain 1965–74), he scored more than 8000 runs (including 26 centuries), and took 235 wickets and 110 catches. In county cricket he played for Nottinghamshire (captain 1968–74), and in 1968 scored the maximum of 36 runs (six sixes) off one over against Glamorgan at Swansea, a feat equalled by Ravi Shastri in the 1984–5 season.

Spitz, Mark (Andrew) (1950–) US swimmer, born Modesto, California. Winner of seven gold medals at the 1972 Olympics, achieving a world record time in each event, and of two golds in the 1968 Games. He set 26 world records between 1967 and 1972.

Stenmark, Ingemar (1956–) Swedish champion skier, born Tärnaby. In the 1974–5 World Cup he won the slalom and was second overall; he then won the World Cup (1976–8) and became the most successful competitor ever in slalom and grand slalom. He was World Master in 1978 and 1982 and won the Olympic gold medal at Lake Placid in 1980. The first man to win three consecutive slalom titles (1980–2), he won a record 86 World Cup races between 1974 and 1989, when he retired.

Stewart, Sir Jackie (John Young) (1939–) Scottish racing driver, born Dunbartonshire, he won the Dutch, German and US Grands Prix in 1968. World champion in 1969, 1971 and 1973. Knighted 2001.

Tyson, Mike (Michael Gerard) (1966–) US boxer, born New York City. Professional from 1985, he knocked out 15 of his first 25 opponents in the first round. In 1986 he beat Trevor Berbick in the World Boxing Council (WBC) world heavyweight contest, becoming the youngest heavyweight champion (20 years 145 days). In 1987 he defeated James Smith to gain the World Boxing Association title, and then beat Tony Tucker to become world champion. He held the title until defeated by James 'Buster' Douglas in Feb 1990. In 1996 he beat Frank Bruno to reclaim the WBC title, but

later gave it up, and in 1997 was disqualified in his WBA world heavyweight fight against Evander Holyfield for biting his opponent's ear.

Underwood, Rory (1963–) English rugby union player, born Middlesbrough. He was England's most-capped player, and most-capped wing, with 85 caps from 1985 to 1996. Toured Australia (1989) and New Zealand (1993) with the British Lions. At club level he has represented Middlesbrough, Durham, Leicester, Newcastle and Bedford.

Warne, Shane (1969–) Australian cricket player, born Ferntree Gully, Victoria. Selected as one of Wisden's five cricketers of the century, he revived, almost single-handed, the use of leg-spin bowling in attack in Test cricket and holds the record for the most wickets taken. He played in 145 Test matches and took 708 wickets. In one-day internationals he took 293 wickets in 194 matches.

Watson, Tom (Thomas Sturges) (1949–) US golfer, born Kansas City, Missouri. Through the mid-1970s and early 1980s he and **Jack Nicklaus** dominated world golf; Watson won the US Open, two Masters tournaments and five British Opens. He was the US Player of the Year six times and in 1993 captained the US Ryder Cup team to victory.

Woods, Tiger (1976–) US golfer, born Cypress, California. He retained his amateur title for a record three years in a row. Having turned professional in 1996, in 1997 became the youngest, as well as the first black winner of the US Masters. Since then he has won The Open (2000, 2005, 2006), the US Open (2000, 2002, 2008), the US PGA (1999, 2000, 2006, 2007) and The Masters (2001, 2002, 2005). When he won The Masters in 2001, he achieved the unique feat of holding all four Major titles at the same time.

Zatopek, Emil (1922–2000) Czech athlete and middle-distance runner, born Moravia, Czechoslovakia (Czech Republic). He won an Olympic gold medal for the 10000m in the 1948 Olympics and over the next six years broke 13 world records. In the 1952 Olympics he achieved a remarkable golden treble: he retained his gold medal in the 10000m, and also won the 5000m and the marathon.

Zurbriggen, Pirmin (1963–) Swiss skier, born Saas Almagell. Winner of a record number of victories in the downhill during the 1980s, and a total of 40 World Cup victories. In the 1987 World Cup at Crans-Montana he won two gold medals (giant slalom and super G) and two silver medals (downhill and combined) within five days, and in the 1988 Winter Olympics he won a gold in the downhill and a bronze in the giant slalom.

Card, board and other indoor games

baccarat Casino card game; most popular version **baccarat banque**, in which bank plays against players; in another, **chemin de fer**, all players take turns to hold the bank; object is to assemble, either with two or three cards, a points value of nine: picture cards and the 10 = 0; ace = one; other cards face value; if total is a double figure then the first figure is ignored, eg 18 would count as 8. Of 15c derivation, thought to have been introduced into France from Italy during reign of Charles VIII.

backgammon Board game for two players; each has 15 round counters which are moved around the *outer* and *inner tables* on the throw of two dice; aim is to be first to return one's pieces home to inner table and remove them from the board.

Equipment similar to backgammon was found in Tutankhamen's tomb; introduced to Britain by the Crusaders; known as backgammon from c.1750.

bézique Card game played with at least two players; each has a pack but with 2s, 3s, 4s, 5s and 6s taken out; object is to win tricks (rounds of play) and score points on the basis of the cards won. Believed to have originated in Spain and brought to England in 1861; first rules drawn up 1861; a variation is **rubicon bézique**.

blackjack Casino card game with object of accumulating score of 21 (with two cards this is a *blackjack*). Ace = one or eleven; picture cards = ten; others according to face value. Normally four packs of cards are shuffled together and dealt from a wooden 'shoe' by a banker; bets placed before first card is dealt; all cards dealt face up.

bridge Card game developed from whist, using full set of 52 playing cards, played by two pairs of players; thought to have originated in either Greece or India, introduced into Britain in 1880. Most popular forms: **auction bridge** and **contract bridge**. In the former, trumps are decided by preliminary bid or auction. In contract bridge, the most widely played form, trumps are nominated by the highest bidder. Scoring uses chart designed by US inventor, Harold Stirling Vanderbilt, based on tricks (rounds of play) contracted for and won.

canasta Card game similar to **rummy**, where cards are picked up and discarded; uses two packs, including four jokers; object is to collect as many of same denomination as possible. All have points value, but jokers and deuces (2s) are 'wild' (can take any value). Originated in Uruguay in the 1940s, the name deriving from the Spanish word *canasta* ('basket'), probably referring to tray where cards were discarded.

checkers ▶ **draughts**

chemin de fer or **'chemmy'** Casino card game; variant of **baccarat banque**, played by up to nine players; object is to obtain total near as possible to nine with two or three cards; if total is a double figure then the first figure is ignored; 16 would count as 6. Ace = one; picture cards = ten; others face value.

chess Game of strategy for two players using chequered board of 64 squares. Each player has 16 pieces: eight pawns, two castles or rooks, two knights, two bishops, queen and king; object is to capture or *checkmate* opponent's king; all pieces have set moves, queen is most versatile. Played in ancient India as *chaturanga*; earliest reference c.600 AD; current pieces have existed in standard form for over 500 years.

Cluedo® Board game where board is divided into 'rooms' and the players, who are each dealt a few person, place, and implement cards, are characters who must find out the facts concerning a murder (ie murderer, implement used and scene of the crime), which are on cards seen by no-one and hidden in an envelope at the start. Detective work is done by deduction, arranging meetings in the rooms and asking the other character involved to reveal his or her relevant cards.

contract bridge ▶ **bridge**

craps Casino dice game of US origin, adapted from game 'hazard' in 1813. Using two dice, a player loses throwing 2, 3, and 12, but wins with 7 or 11.

cribbage Card game played with two, three or four people with pack of 52 cards and a holed board, the *peg board*, used for scoring. Number of cards dealt to each player is five, six or seven, depending on number of players; cards are discarded into a dummy hand, which each player has in turn; points are scored according to cards dropped (ie for playing a card that makes a pair, a run of three or more, etc); cards are discarded in each round until total of 31 is reached; play continues until the players have discarded all their cards; value of hand then calculated.

dominoes Indoor game, various forms, played by two or more players; dominoes are either wooden or plastic rectangular blocks, with the face of each divided into two halves, each half containing a number of spots, no two identical. In a double-six set of dominoes, every combination between 6–6 and 0–0 is marked on the 28 dominoes. Object of basic game is to lay out sequence or 'line' of dominoes, each player in turn having to put down

a domino of the same value as the one at either end of the line.

draughts or (USA) **checkers** Game played on chess board by two players, each with twelve small, flat, round counters or *pieces*, which are lined up on alternate squares on the first three rows at either side of the board; object is to remove opponent's pieces from board by jumping over them into a vacant diagonal square, having got in a position to do so by moving only forward (until a piece reaches back row of opponent's 'territory', thus becoming a two-piece *king* and permitted to move backwards and forwards) and always on squares of the same colour; believed to have been played in ancient Egypt; first book about draughts published Spain 1547.

gin rummy ▶ **rummy**

go National game of Japan; first played China c.1500 BC; board game for two players played on grid of 19 vertical and 19 horizontal lines (361 intersections); each player has supply of counters and play alternates beginning with black; object is to conquer territory by both encircling vacant intersections and surrounding opponent's counters which are then removed from board; handicapping system exists.

hazard Card game for four players in pairs; similar to **solo**, but to make 25 cards, all cards with face value of two to eight are discarded, and joker is added.

mah-jong Chinese game, originally played with cards, introduced to the West under its present name after World War I; usually played by four people using 144 small tiles divided into six suits. (Sets containing 136 tiles and five suits are also used.) Aim is to collect sequences of tiles. Name means 'sparrow', a bird of mythical great intelligence, which appears on one tile.

Monopoly® Board game for two or more players; aim is acquisition of property; players move a counter each around a board which has some of a capital city's streets, stations and public utility companies on it, which can be bought, built upon, mortgaged etc and for which rent must be paid (using Monopoly money) when landed on as a non-owner. Game ends when all but one player are bankrupt.

pinochle Card game derived from **bézique**; uses two packs of 24 cards, all cards from two to eight having been discarded; object is to win tricks, as in whist, and to score points according to cards won: ace = eleven; ten = ten; king = four; queen = three; jack = two; nine = 0.

poker Gambling card game for two to eight players; object is to get a better hand than opponents (or convince them that you have one). Hands are ranked: best hand is *royal flush* ie 10, Jack, Queen, King, Ace, all of the same suit. Most popular varieties: five-card draw, five-card stud and seven-card stud. Poker started in 19c USA.

pontoon or **vingt-et-un** Card game; a variation of **blackjack**, played by any number of players, but ideally six. Object is to try to obtain a total of 21. A *royal pontoon* consists of a picture card and an ace (ace = eleven or one). Bets are placed and bank held by any player (usually latest royal pontoon winner).

roulette Casino game played with ball and spinning wheel, which is divided into 36 alternately either red or black segments numbered 1 to 36 and a green segment numbered 0 (some wheels in the US also have a segment numbered 00), but not in numerical order. Bets are placed (before the

Sports and Games

wheel is spun) on where ball will come to rest, and can take several forms – on a single number, any two numbers, or any three numbers etc, and on whether winning one will be odd or even.

rummy Domestic card game; possibly derived from **mah-jong**; cards picked up and discarded with object of forming two *hands* of three and four cards, or one of seven; hand obtained must consist of cards of same denomination, or sequence in same suit. A variation is **gin rummy**, where hands are laid face upwards and can be added to by any player during the game. Points are obtained for each card dropped according to its face value, and deducted according to cards remaining in hand when one player wins game by disposing of all his or her cards.

Scrabble ® Word game on special board for two to four players; points scored by placing letter tiles of different values crossword-fashion to form interlocking words; each player has choice of seven tiles until none remain. Scores can be doubled or trebled by making use of premium squares on the board.

shogi Japanese form of **chess**, believed to have originated in India; played on square board with pieces (of which each player has 20) of different powers; object is to *checkmate* king.

solo Card game; a form of **whist**, and similar to **bridge**; players must declare how many tricks they will win before each game; tricks won as in whist.

Trivial Pursuit ® Board game in which players make progress by giving correct answers to general knowledge questions on eg art and literature, entertainment, geography, history, science and nature, and sport and leisure, which are written on special cards. Coloured wedges corresponding to all topics have to be won and the middle space reached to win the game.

whist Non-gambling card game; normally played with four people in pairs; each player receives 13 cards; object is to win more *tricks*, or rounds of play, than the opposing pair; trumps (suit of which cards can win against any card of any other suit) are decided before each game; at *whist drives* trumps are normally played in the following order: hearts, clubs, diamonds, spades; a round of 'no trumps' (where all suits have equal power) is also common.

Hobbies and pastimes

abseiling Descending a steep slope or mountainside; used in mountaineering but now recognized as pursuit in itself. A rope is attached either around the body or through *karabiners* (steel links with spring clips in one side) and is secured from above so that speed of descent can be safely controlled.

aerobics System of exercises which are designed to increase oxygen consumption and speed blood circulation, thereby increasing fitness.

ballooning ▸ hot-air ballooning

batik Ancient folk art of fabric design using a basic wax-resist technique; warm wax is painted onto light-coloured fabric, according to a chosen design, and then dipped into a solution of dye and water – only unwaxed fabric takes dye so when wax is removed design appears against coloured background.

bellringing or **campanology** Ringing church bells; two popular forms; *change ringing* (handpulled method) and *carillon* (uses keyboard connected to the clapper of the bells).

birdwatching or **ornithology** Study and observation of birds in their natural habitat; may involve recording details concerning bird anatomy, behaviour, song and flight patterns.

brass rubbing Duplicating designs on ornamental brass plate, such as is found in churches; brass is covered with paper and then rubbed over with coloured crayons or chalk until copy is produced.

bungee jumping Leaping from river-crossing bridges; person's legs are tied together, covered with protective material, and then clipped with a strong elastic (bungee) rope (adapted to their weight and height), and secured firmly to the bridge; the jumper leaps from a platform on top of the bridge and freefalls, before hanging suspended by the elastic rope, experiencing a series of bouncing movements; jumps also made from cranes, towers, etc.

butterfly-collecting or **lepidoptery** Obtaining butterflies either by catching them in their natural environment or purchasing them already preserved; insects are identified and mounted, usually in a glass display unit.

calligraphy Penmanship, or writing at its most formal; a major art-form in many countries of E Asia and in Arabic-speaking countries; revival of interest in Europe and USA since the 19c; special pen nibs, brushes, ink and paper usually required.

campanology ▸ bellringing

candle-making Producing candles by repeatedly dipping a prepared wick into wax, pouring wax over a wick or pouring wax into moulds; paraffin wax is most often used; candles can be created in any colour, shape, size or fragrance.

climbing Generally refers to scaling anything from a 15m/50ft wall to an assault on the Himalayas, although there should be some level of difficulty in reaching highest point; as well as the physical aspect, climbing also involves psychological thrills of discovery, exploration and avoidance of danger.

coin-collecting ▸ numismatics

cookery Preparing and cooking food; may involve production of exotic and speciality dishes and creation of new recipes.

crochet Making a variety of textile items; uses a special hook to loop yarn in a number of different stitches according to pattern requirements.

dancing The following are just a few of the many forms that dancing takes: **1 ballroom** Social dance form; developed early 20c, revealing strong influence of American ragtime, syncopated rhythms producing the foxtrot and quickstep; also popular were animal dances (eg Turkey Trot, Bunny Hug) and Latin-American dances (cha-cha-cha, tango and samba). **2 country** Historic social dances began to spread across Europe in the 17c, taught by travelling dancing masters, adding 19c forms such as the waltz, quadrille and polka; emphasis on spatial design, with couples in long or circular sets, using simple walking steps. **Traditional dance** In *England*, began 16c; lines, circles, and square sets are common patterns; steps based on simple walking and skipping. In *Ireland*, early forms share the European history of country and court dance; jigs and reels typical, resembling English and Scottish stepping; competitive high stepping form is a 20c creation; arms are held stiffly to the sides; body is erect; there is rapid, complex rhythmic use of the feet; and the knees are sharply lifted. In *Scotland* some country dances are commonly known as **Scottish reels**, but strictly, the reel is an indigenous form of stepping dance performed to bagpipes and showing French aristocratic connections; originally performed in circles as in 'round reels' (threesome, foursome, eightsome etc) and later in lines, 'longwise forms'; feet are in balletic positions with the weight on the balls of the feet; typical steps include slip step, pas de basque, strathspey, and schottische; men's costume is the kilt; women wear dresses with a tartan sash. Other country dances in Scotland also progress in two long lines of male/female couples, and there are square dances (eg quadrille), and circle dances (eg Circassian circle); dances take place to traditional tunes, formerly played on the fiddle, and now also on the accordion; nowadays reels danced to these instruments too. In *Wales*, due to former religious disapproval, there are few traces of traditional dance, but there are some reels and country dances similar to those in England. **3 disco** Popular form of dance mainly for young people, originating 1960s; accompanying music is usually contemporary, often loud, with a rhythmic beat. Definite fashions eg new romantic style, soul, rave, house, punk, break dancing, robotics and gothic style. It takes account of Black music, particularly rapping, and heavy rock. **4 jazz** N American form of vernacular dancing performed to jazz rhythms; a style that swings, owing its origins to African and Caribbean forms of dance, blended with European influences; also used in musical shows on Broadway and in the UK (eg *Cats*). **5 Morris** Ceremonial form of traditional dance found in England. Distinctive features: stamping and hopping; files of performers usually dressed in white and always carrying a stick, handkerchief or garland; some wear bells; accordion or concertina with brass drum accompaniment. Originally exclusively a male domain, women can now take part. **6 step** Social and often competitive form of dance relying on rhythmically complex footwork using parts of the foot, heel, and toe beats, often performed in clogs; maintained through folk festivals both as social and exhibition dance; structure in performance is part fixed and part improvised.

dressmaking Pastime usually undertaken to make low-cost clothes, using a bought tissue-paper pattern and a length of material, but also a creative hobby lending itself to sophisticated fashion design.

electronic games Games programmed and controlled by a small microprocessor; most connected to visual display unit and known as **video games**; many have war themes, others simulate sports; some board games (eg Monopoly®, Scrabble®, Trivial Pursuit®) are available in electronic form; all operated by using a computer keyboard, joystick or joypad attached to a games console or home computer. Larger versions are produced for use in eg amusement arcades.

embroidery Ornamentation of fabric with decorative stitching; dates from very early times, when designs were sewn on to a base fabric by hand; became highly developed eg for rich garments and furnishings, and church vestments in the Middle East, India and Europe; famous example is 11c Bayeux tapestry. Hand embroidery still exists as a craft, but today computer-controlled sewing machines are also used.

fell-walking Trekking on hills or moorland, wearing specialized walking boots and using map and compass to find direction in desolate tracts of land.

gardening Laying out and cultivating plants on a piece of ground for ornamental purposes, rather than for economic gain; type of garden depends not only on gardener's tastes and space available, but also on soil type and fertility, climate, air pollution, and shelter from wind and sun, provided by eg existing trees and rocks. Some special garden types and techniques are: **1 espalier** Technique involving the training of trees on a latticework of wood flat against a wall; tree is carefully tied to the trellis and pruned to control its shape, often creating a decorative effect in limited space. **2 herb garden** Usually includes shrubs as well as herbs, all mostly perennial. The herbs are used primarily for cooking, either fresh or dried (see p 64). **3 Japanese-style garden** Maximum use is made of evergreen plants, the only colour being eg spring-flowering azaleas, and autumn berries; features include stone lanterns, walkways, natural or simulated streams and waterfalls, and occasional stones; **bonsai** technique is associated with Japanese style, though it originated in China; involves dwarfing plants by shallow planting in containers, starvation, root and soil pruning, and the twisting of new shoots with wire to give plants gnarled, aged appearance; pine, fir and maple trees often used. **4 rock garden** or **rockery** Man-made or natural heap of soil and rock fragments in a garden for growing rock plants, usually flowering, hardy perennials, and dwarf trees; rock gardens are often terraced to prevent the topsoil being washed away by rain. **5 water garden** Plants arranged in and around natural or artificial pools and streams, eg water lilies and marsh marigolds. **6 wild-flower garden** Often includes native marsh or bog plants as well as forest-floor wild flowers; usually requires a rich, acid soil.

go-kart racing Driving and racing small, single-seated, motorized vehicles around outdoor tracks; originated USA; has gained a popular following in the UK.

hatha yoga ▶ yoga

horse-riding Involves acquisition of specialized skills learned in order to control the horse from a seated position on its back. Commands are signalled by hand, leg and voice instruction, sometimes reinforced by the use of whip and spurs.

hot-air ballooning Being carried as a passenger through the air by hot-air balloon; may involve navigating the balloon, the mechanics of getting the balloon airborne, and following the balloon in road vehicles.

ikebana Formal Japanese style of flower arrangement; a few blooms or leaves are selected and placed in very careful relationship to one another; popular 1950s and 1960s pastime in W Europe.

kite-flying Flying a light frame covered with paper, cloth or plastic at the end of a length of string, usually requiring windy conditions. Kites can be brightly coloured and of various different shapes; simplest form has only one string, but with two strings, one attached to each side, it can be more easily controlled from the ground and made to do complicated loops and dives in the air.

knitting Ancient craft used for making fabric; loops of yarn are linked together using two or three hand-held needles; machines are now used to produce complex knitted garments and fabrics of many kinds, but they cannot create all the intricate designs commonly produced by skilled hand knitters.

lace-making Most popular method (especially in Europe) of lace production is *bobbin* or *pillow* lace. As many as 1100 bobbins are wound with thread

Sports and Games

and hung on pins which are inserted, according to the design required, into the small holes on a piece of stiff paper attached to a pillow, cushion or polystyrene base; bobbins then looped, plaited and twisted following pattern instructions until the desired item is produced.

lepidoptery ▶ butterfly-collecting

macramé Making a type of coarse lace by knotting and plaiting; widespread revival in mid-19c; used to make decorative fringed borders for costumes as well as furnishings eg window blinds, antimacassars, and cushions.

model-making Mainly the construction of cars, ships, trains and aeroplanes by gluing together preshaped plastic or wooden parts from specialized kits. Some enthusiasts design and produce the parts for their own models.

numismatics Studying and collecting coins, notes and other similar objects, eg medals; dates from Italian Renaissance; 17c collectors were first to catalogue their collections.

origami Making models of animals or other objects by folding sheets of paper into shapes, with minimum use of scissors or other implements; often used as an educational aid for young children; originated 10c Japan.

ornithology ▶ birdwatching

paintball Simulation of military combat; involves firing paint pellets which splatter on contact with clothing to indicate a hit; played by two or more teams; popular in the USA, UK and parts of Europe; believed to be beneficial in the reduction of stress.

panelology Carving thin, wooden panels which may be either framed or lodged between other upright and cross pieces normally stretching across the surface of a wall; pictures are often painted onto these panels; most effective results achieved on panels made from chestnut, oak or white poplar.

paragliding Being towed through the air by a plane whilst wearing an adapted parachute and then being separated in order to glide to the ground.

philately Collecting stamps; one of the world's most popular hobbies; often involves documentation in special books or albums; stamps issued and stamped by the post office on their first day of issue (*first-day covers*) increasingly popular; first philatelist said to have been John Tomlinson, who started collecting the day after the issue of the first postage stamp (the *penny black*) in 1840.

pigeon-fancying Breeding pigeons to exhibit or race, popular in the USA, UK and France.

pigeon racing Pigeons are taken from their loft and released at a starting point that may be hundreds of miles away; their homing instinct takes them back to their loft where a special clock times their arrival, thus establishing the fastest pigeon.

pottery or **potting** Forming clay objects; moist clay is shaped and then dried, usually by *firing* in a *kiln* or oven. Shaping by hand may be aided by using a *potter's wheel*, on which a lump of clay is rotated so it can be *thrown* by the potter's hands; moulding may involve either pressing soft clay into a mould and allowing it to dry, or *slip moulding*, where liquid clay or *slip* is poured into a mould that absorbs the moisture; shaped or moulded objects can be decorated by etching and painted with a colour *glaze*. Pottery tends to be porous and so is protected by a second glaze, which may be transparent or opaque and also gives shiny decorative appearance. Glaze is applied after first firing (when the pottery is called *biscuit*); then object is placed in kiln a second time at a lower temperature.

scuba diving Underwater swimming with the aid of *scuba* (self-contained underwater breathing apparatus) or *aqualung*, first developed in 1942 by Jacques Cousteau and Émil Gagnan; equipment consists of air tank(s), face mask, air regulator, depth gauge, weight belt and buoyancy compensator; divers propel themselves with the legs, wearing large *fins* or *flippers*.

shuffleboard or **shovelboard** Deck game played aboard ship; a larger version of the popular shove-halfpenny; wooden discs, usually c.15cm/6in in diameter, are pushed along deck with long-handled drivers into scoring area.

skateboarding Riding on a single flexible board, longer and wider than the foot, fixed with four small wheels on the underside; speeds of over 100kph/60mph are possible and difficult jumps performed; developed as a way of experiencing surfing thrills on land; became popular in 1960s USA and in UK in 1970s and again in late 1980s.

skin diving Underwater swimming, popularized in the 1930s. Skin-divers use only goggles, face mask, flippers, and short breathing tube or *snorkel*.

skipping Making jumps over a rope, the ends of which are held in each hand so that it can be twirled over the head and under the feet; often thought of as a child's pastime; recognized as good form of exercise.

skittles Game played in several different forms; object is to knock down nine pins with a ball. **Alley skittles** is played in long alleys and **table skittles** is played indoors on a specially constructed table with a swivelled ball attached to a mast by means of a chain; pins are much smaller than those used in tenpin bowling, and are replaced manually, rather than mechanically.

spinning Converting fibres into yarns, originally using distaff and later the spinning wheel, and now often using methods such as friction and rotor spinning; two types of yarn traditionally produced were *woollen* (fibres are randomly arranged), and *worsted* (fibres lie parallel to the length of the yarn).

stamp collecting ▶ philately

tapestry Creation of decorative textiles, originally hand woven, with multi-coloured pictorial designs, made by passing coloured threads among fixed warp threads; Oriental in origin, used for wall hangings, furniture and floor coverings.

taxidermy Preparation and practice of creating lifelike replicas of animals and birds from their treated skins and the careful use of celluloids and other plastics.

trainspotting Identifying locomotives by their numbers or names and ticking them off in special, collectable notebooks.

video games ▶ electronic games

weaving Ancient fabric-producing craft; warp (lengthwise) and weft (crosswise) threads are interlaced on machines called *looms*; hand looms known from very early times; modern industry uses modern weaving looms which have dispensed with *shuttles — bullets, rapiers, water jets* and *air jets* now carry the weft across the warp, with 1500 picks per minute being possible on some machines.

yoga In Indian religious tradition, any of various physical and contemplative techniques designed to free the superior, conscious element in a person from involvement with the inferior material world. **Hatha yoga** most common form in W Hemisphere; importance of physical exercises and positions and breathing-control is stressed in promoting physical and mental wellbeing.

TIME

Perpetual calendar 1801–2040

The calendar for each year is given under the corresponding letter below

Year		Year		Year		Year		Year	
1801	I	1849	C	1897	K	1945	C	1993	K
1802	K	1850	E	1898	M	1946	E	1994	M
1803	M	1851	G	1899	A	1947	G	1995	A
1804	B	1852	J	1900	C	1948	J	1996	D
1805	E	1853	M	1901	E	1949	M	1997	G
1806	G	1854	A	1902	G	1950	A	1998	I
1807	I	1855	C	1903	I	1951	C	1999	K
1808	L	1856	F	1904	L	1952	F	2000	N
1809	A	1857	I	1905	A	1953	I	2001	C
1810	C	1858	K	1906	C	1954	K	2002	E
1811	E	1859	M	1907	E	1955	M	2003	G
1812	H	1860	B	1908	H	1956	B	2004	J
1813	K	1861	E	1909	K	1957	E	2005	M
1814	M	1862	G	1910	M	1958	G	2006	A
1815	A	1863	I	1911	A	1959	I	2007	C
1816	D	1864	L	1912	D	1960	L	2008	F
1817	G	1865	A	1913	G	1961	A	2009	I
1818	I	1866	C	1914	I	1962	C	2010	K
1819	K	1867	E	1915	K	1963	E	2011	M
1820	N	1868	H	1916	N	1964	H	2012	B
1821	C	1869	K	1917	C	1965	K	2013	E
1822	E	1870	M	1918	E	1966	M	2014	G
1823	G	1871	A	1919	G	1967	A	2015	I
1824	J	1872	D	1920	J	1968	D	2016	L
1825	M	1873	G	1921	M	1969	G	2017	A
1826	A	1874	I	1922	A	1970	I	2018	C
1827	C	1875	K	1923	C	1971	K	2019	E
1828	F	1876	N	1924	F	1972	N	2020	H
1829	I	1877	C	1925	I	1973	C	2021	K
1830	K	1878	E	1926	K	1974	E	2022	M
1831	M	1879	G	1927	M	1975	G	2023	A
1832	B	1880	J	1928	B	1976	J	2024	D
1833	E	1881	M	1929	E	1977	M	2025	G
1834	G	1882	A	1930	G	1978	A	2026	I
1835	I	1883	C	1931	I	1979	C	2027	K
1836	L	1884	F	1932	L	1980	F	2028	N
1837	A	1885	I	1933	A	1981	I	2029	C
1838	C	1886	K	1934	C	1982	K	2030	E
1839	E	1887	M	1935	E	1983	M	2031	G
1840	H	1888	B	1936	H	1984	B	2032	J
1841	K	1889	E	1937	K	1985	E	2033	M
1842	M	1890	G	1938	M	1986	G	2034	A
1843	A	1891	I	1939	A	1987	I	2035	C
1844	D	1892	L	1940	D	1988	L	2036	F
1845	G	1893	A	1941	G	1989	A	2037	I
1846	I	1894	C	1942	I	1990	C	2038	K
1847	K	1895	E	1943	K	1991	E	2039	M
1848	N	1896	H	1944	N	1992	H	2040	B

Time

A

JANUARY
```
S  M  T  W  T  F  S
         1  2  3  4  5  6  7
 8  9 10 11 12 13 14
15 16 17 18 19 20 21
22 23 24 25 26 27 28
29 30 31
```

FEBRUARY
```
S  M  T  W  T  F  S
            1  2  3  4
 5  6  7  8  9 10 11
12 13 14 15 16 17 18
19 20 21 22 23 24 25
26 27 28
```

MARCH
```
S  M  T  W  T  F  S
            1  2  3  4
 5  6  7  8  9 10 11
12 13 14 15 16 17 18
19 20 21 22 23 24 25
26 27 28 29 30 31
```

APRIL
```
S  M  T  W  T  F  S
                  1
 2  3  4  5  6  7  8
 9 10 11 12 13 14 15
16 17 18 19 20 21 22
23 24 25 26 27 28 29
30
```

MAY
```
S  M  T  W  T  F  S
    1  2  3  4  5  6
 7  8  9 10 11 12 13
14 15 16 17 18 19 20
21 22 23 24 25 26 27
28 29 30 31
```

JUNE
```
S  M  T  W  T  F  S
               1  2  3
 4  5  6  7  8  9 10
11 12 13 14 15 16 17
18 19 20 21 22 23 24
25 26 27 28 29 30
```

JULY
```
S  M  T  W  T  F  S
                  1
 2  3  4  5  6  7  8
 9 10 11 12 13 14 15
16 17 18 19 20 21 22
23 24 25 26 27 28 29
30 31
```

AUGUST
```
S  M  T  W  T  F  S
         1  2  3  4  5
 6  7  8  9 10 11 12
13 14 15 16 17 18 19
20 21 22 23 24 25 26
27 28 29 30 31
```

SEPTEMBER
```
S  M  T  W  T  F  S
               1  2
 3  4  5  6  7  8  9
10 11 12 13 14 15 16
17 18 19 20 21 22 23
24 25 26 27 28 29 30
```

OCTOBER
```
S  M  T  W  T  F  S
 1  2  3  4  5  6  7
 8  9 10 11 12 13 14
15 16 17 18 19 20 21
22 23 24 25 26 27 28
29 30 31
```

NOVEMBER
```
S  M  T  W  T  F  S
         1  2  3  4
 5  6  7  8  9 10 11
12 13 14 15 16 17 18
19 20 21 22 23 24 25
26 27 28 29 30
```

DECEMBER
```
S  M  T  W  T  F  S
               1  2
 3  4  5  6  7  8  9
10 11 12 13 14 15 16
17 18 19 20 21 22 23
24 25 26 27 28 29 30
31
```

B (leap year)

JANUARY
```
S  M  T  W  T  F  S
 1  2  3  4  5  6  7
 8  9 10 11 12 13 14
15 16 17 18 19 20 21
22 23 24 25 26 27 28
29 30 31
```

FEBRUARY
```
S  M  T  W  T  F  S
            1  2  3
 5  6  7  8  9 10 11
12 13 14 15 16 17 18
19 20 21 22 23 24 25
26 27 28 29
```

MARCH
```
S  M  T  W  T  F  S
               1  2  3
 4  5  6  7  8  9 10
11 12 13 14 15 16 17
18 19 20 21 22 23 24
25 26 27 28 29 30 31
```

APRIL
```
S  M  T  W  T  F  S
 1  2  3  4  5  6  7
 8  9 10 11 12 13 14
15 16 17 18 19 20 21
22 23 24 25 26 27 28
29 30
```

MAY
```
S  M  T  W  T  F  S
         1  2  3  4  5
 6  7  8  9 10 11 12
13 14 15 16 17 18 19
20 21 22 23 24 25 26
27 28 29 30 31
```

JUNE
```
S  M  T  W  T  F  S
                  1  2
 3  4  5  6  7  8  9
10 11 12 13 14 15 16
17 18 19 20 21 22 23
24 25 26 27 28 29 30
```

JULY
```
S  M  T  W  T  F  S
 1  2  3  4  5  6  7
 8  9 10 11 12 13 14
15 16 17 18 19 20 21
22 23 24 25 26 27 28
29 30 31
```

AUGUST
```
S  M  T  W  T  F  S
            1  2  3  4
 5  6  7  8  9 10 11
12 13 14 15 16 17 18
19 20 21 22 23 24 25
26 27 28 29 30 31
```

SEPTEMBER
```
S  M  T  W  T  F  S
                  1
 2  3  4  5  6  7  8
 9 10 11 12 13 14 15
16 17 18 19 20 21 22
23 24 25 26 27 28 29
30
```

OCTOBER
```
S  M  T  W  T  F  S
    1  2  3  4  5  6
 7  8  9 10 11 12 13
14 15 16 17 18 19 20
21 22 23 24 25 26 27
28 29 30 31
```

NOVEMBER
```
S  M  T  W  T  F  S
            1  2  3
 4  5  6  7  8  9 10
11 12 13 14 15 16 17
18 19 20 21 22 23 24
25 26 27 28 29 30
```

DECEMBER
```
S  M  T  W  T  F  S
                  1
 2  3  4  5  6  7  8
 9 10 11 12 13 14 15
16 17 18 19 20 21 22
23 24 25 26 27 28 29
30 31
```

C

JANUARY
```
S  M  T  W  T  F  S
       1  2  3  4  5  6
 7  8  9 10 11 12 13
14 15 16 17 18 19 20
21 22 23 24 25 26 27
28 29 30 31
```

FEBRUARY
```
S  M  T  W  T  F  S
               1  2  3
 4  5  6  7  8  9 10
11 12 13 14 15 16 17
18 19 20 21 22 23 24
25 26 27 28
```

MARCH
```
S  M  T  W  T  F  S
               1  2  3
 4  5  6  7  8  9 10
11 12 13 14 15 16 17
18 19 20 21 22 23 24
25 26 27 28 29 30 31
```

APRIL
```
S  M  T  W  T  F  S
 1  2  3  4  5  6  7
 8  9 10 11 12 13 14
15 16 17 18 19 20 21
22 23 24 25 26 27 28
29 30
```

MAY
```
S  M  T  W  T  F  S
         1  2  3  4  5
 6  7  8  9 10 11 12
13 14 15 16 17 18 19
20 21 22 23 24 25 26
27 28 29 30 31
```

JUNE
```
S  M  T  W  T  F  S
                  1  2
 3  4  5  6  7  8  9
10 11 12 13 14 15 16
17 18 19 20 21 22 23
24 25 26 27 28 29 30
```

JULY
```
S  M  T  W  T  F  S
 1  2  3  4  5  6  7
 8  9 10 11 12 13 14
15 16 17 18 19 20 21
22 23 24 25 26 27 28
29 30 31
```

AUGUST
```
S  M  T  W  T  F  S
            1  2  3  4
 5  6  7  8  9 10 11
12 13 14 15 16 17 18
19 20 21 22 23 24 25
26 27 28 29 30 31
```

SEPTEMBER
```
S  M  T  W  T  F  S
                  1
 2  3  4  5  6  7  8
 9 10 11 12 13 14 15
16 17 18 19 20 21 22
23 24 25 26 27 28 29
30
```

OCTOBER
```
S  M  T  W  T  F  S
    1  2  3  4  5  6
 7  8  9 10 11 12 13
14 15 16 17 18 19 20
21 22 23 24 25 26 27
28 29 30 31
```

NOVEMBER
```
S  M  T  W  T  F  S
            1  2  3
 4  5  6  7  8  9 10
11 12 13 14 15 16 17
18 19 20 21 22 23 24
25 26 27 28 29 30
```

DECEMBER
```
S  M  T  W  T  F  S
                  1
 2  3  4  5  6  7  8
 9 10 11 12 13 14 15
16 17 18 19 20 21 22
23 24 25 26 27 28 29
30 31
```

D (leap year)

JANUARY
```
S  M  T  W  T  F  S
       1  2  3  4  5  6
 7  8  9 10 11 12 13
14 15 16 17 18 19 20
21 22 23 24 25 26 27
28 29 30 31
```

FEBRUARY
```
S  M  T  W  T  F  S
               1  2  3
 4  5  6  7  8  9 10
11 12 13 14 15 16 17
18 19 20 21 22 23 24
25 26 27 28 29
```

MARCH
```
S  M  T  W  T  F  S
                  1  2
 3  4  5  6  7  8  9
10 11 12 13 14 15 16
17 18 19 20 21 22 23
24 25 26 27 28 29 30
31
```

APRIL
```
S  M  T  W  T  F  S
       1  2  3  4  5  6
 7  8  9 10 11 12 13
14 15 16 17 18 19 20
21 22 23 24 25 26 27
28 29 30
```

MAY
```
S  M  T  W  T  F  S
            1  2  3  4
 5  6  7  8  9 10 11
12 13 14 15 16 17 18
19 20 21 22 23 24 25
26 27 28 29 30 31
```

JUNE
```
S  M  T  W  T  F  S
                     1
 2  3  4  5  6  7  8
 9 10 11 12 13 14 15
16 17 18 19 20 21 22
23 24 25 26 27 28 29
```

JULY
```
S  M  T  W  T  F  S
       1  2  3  4  5  6
 7  8  9 10 11 12 13
14 15 16 17 18 19 20
21 22 23 24 25 26 27
28 29 30 31
```

AUGUST
```
S  M  T  W  T  F  S
                  1  2  3
 4  5  6  7  8  9 10
11 12 13 14 15 16 17
18 19 20 21 22 23 24
25 26 27 28 29 30 31
```

SEPTEMBER
```
S  M  T  W  T  F  S
 1  2  3  4  5  6  7
 8  9 10 11 12 13 14
15 16 17 18 19 20 21
22 23 24 25 26 27 28
29 30
```

OCTOBER
```
S  M  T  W  T  F  S
          1  2  3  4  5
 6  7  8  9 10 11 12
13 14 15 16 17 18 19
20 21 22 23 24 25 26
27 28 29 30 31
```

NOVEMBER
```
S  M  T  W  T  F  S
                  1  2
 3  4  5  6  7  8  9
10 11 12 13 14 15 16
17 18 19 20 21 22 23
24 25 26 27 28 29 30
```

DECEMBER
```
S  M  T  W  T  F  S
 1  2  3  4  5  6  7
 8  9 10 11 12 13 14
15 16 17 18 19 20 21
22 23 24 25 26 27 28
29 30 31
```

Time

E

```
JANUARY                  FEBRUARY                 MARCH
S  M  T  W  T  F  S      S  M  T  W  T  F  S      S  M  T  W  T  F  S
         1  2  3  4  5                   1  2                   1  2
 6  7  8  9 10 11 12      3  4  5  6  7  8  9      3  4  5  6  7  8  9
13 14 15 16 17 18 19     10 11 12 13 14 15 16     10 11 12 13 14 15 16
20 21 22 23 24 25 26     17 18 19 20 21 22 23     17 18 19 20 21 22 23
27 28 29 30 31           24 25 26 27 28           24 25 26 27 28 29 30
                                                  31

APRIL                    MAY                      JUNE
S  M  T  W  T  F  S      S  M  T  W  T  F  S      S  M  T  W  T  F  S
       1  2  3  4  5                1  2  3  4                         1
 7  8  9 10 11 12 13      5  6  7  8  9 10 11      2  3  4  5  6  7  8
14 15 16 17 18 19 20     12 13 14 15 16 17 18      9 10 11 12 13 14 15
21 22 23 24 25 26 27     19 20 21 22 23 24 25     16 17 18 19 20 21 22
28 29 30                 26 27 28 29 30 31        23 24 25 26 27 28 29
                                                  30

JULY                     AUGUST                   SEPTEMBER
S  M  T  W  T  F  S      S  M  T  W  T  F  S      S  M  T  W  T  F  S
       1  2  3  4  5                   1  2  3    1  2  3  4  5  6  7
 7  8  9 10 11 12 13      4  5  6  7  8  9 10      8  9 10 11 12 13 14
14 15 16 17 18 19 20     11 12 13 14 15 16 17     15 16 17 18 19 20 21
21 22 23 24 25 26 27     18 19 20 21 22 23 24     22 23 24 25 26 27 28
28 29 30 31              25 26 27 28 29 30 31     29 30

OCTOBER                  NOVEMBER                 DECEMBER
S  M  T  W  T  F  S      S  M  T  W  T  F  S      S  M  T  W  T  F  S
          1  2  3  4                      1  2    1  2  3  4  5  6  7
 6  7  8  9 10 11 12      3  4  5  6  7  8  9      8  9 10 11 12 13 14
13 14 15 16 17 18 19     10 11 12 13 14 15 16     15 16 17 18 19 20 21
20 21 22 23 24 25 26     17 18 19 20 21 22 23     22 23 24 25 26 27 28
27 28 29 30 31           24 25 26 27 28 29 30     29 30 31
```

F (leap year)

```
JANUARY                  FEBRUARY                 MARCH
S  M  T  W  T  F  S      S  M  T  W  T  F  S      S  M  T  W  T  F  S
         1  2  3  4  5                   1  2                      1
 6  7  8  9 10 11 12      3  4  5  6  7  8  9      2  3  4  5  6  7  8
13 14 15 16 17 18 19     10 11 12 13 14 15 16      9 10 11 12 13 14 15
20 21 22 23 24 25 26     17 18 19 20 21 22 23     16 17 18 19 20 21 22
27 28 29 30 31           24 25 26 27 28 29        23 24 25 26 27 28 29
                                                  30 31

APRIL                    MAY                      JUNE
S  M  T  W  T  F  S      S  M  T  W  T  F  S      S  M  T  W  T  F  S
    1  2  3  4  5                   1  2  3       1  2  3  4  5  6  7
 6  7  8  9 10 11 12      4  5  6  7  8  9 10      8  9 10 11 12 13 14
13 14 15 16 17 18 19     11 12 13 14 15 16 17     15 16 17 18 19 20 21
20 21 22 23 24 25 26     18 19 20 21 22 23 24     22 23 24 25 26 27 28
27 28 29 30              25 26 27 28 29 30 31     29 30

JULY                     AUGUST                   SEPTEMBER
S  M  T  W  T  F  S      S  M  T  W  T  F  S      S  M  T  W  T  F  S
    1  2  3  4  5                      1  2       1  2  3  4  5  6
 6  7  8  9 10 11 12      3  4  5  6  7  8  9      7  8  9 10 11 12 13
13 14 15 16 17 18 19     10 11 12 13 14 15 16     14 15 16 17 18 19 20
20 21 22 23 24 25 26     17 18 19 20 21 22 23     21 22 23 24 25 26 27
27 28 29 30 31           24 25 26 27 28 29 30     28 29 30
                         31

OCTOBER                  NOVEMBER                 DECEMBER
S  M  T  W  T  F  S      S  M  T  W  T  F  S      S  M  T  W  T  F  S
       1  2  3  4                         1       1  2  3  4  5  6
 5  6  7  8  9 10 11      2  3  4  5  6  7  8      7  8  9 10 11 12 13
12 13 14 15 16 17 18      9 10 11 12 13 14 15     14 15 16 17 18 19 20
19 20 21 22 23 24 25     16 17 18 19 20 21 22     21 22 23 24 25 26 27
26 27 28 29 30 31        23 24 25 26 27 28 29     28 29 30 31
                         30
```

G

```
JANUARY                  FEBRUARY                 MARCH
S  M  T  W  T  F  S      S  M  T  W  T  F  S      S  M  T  W  T  F  S
             1  2  3  4                      1                      1
 5  6  7  8  9 10 11      2  3  4  5  6  7  8      2  3  4  5  6  7  8
12 13 14 15 16 17 18      9 10 11 12 13 14 15      9 10 11 12 13 14 15
19 20 21 22 23 24 25     16 17 18 19 20 21 22     16 17 18 19 20 21 22
26 27 28 29 30 31        23 24 25 26 27 28        23 24 25 26 27 28 29
                                                  30 31

APRIL                    MAY                      JUNE
S  M  T  W  T  F  S      S  M  T  W  T  F  S      S  M  T  W  T  F  S
         1  2  3  4  5                1  2  3      1  2  3  4  5  6  7
 6  7  8  9 10 11 12      4  5  6  7  8  9 10      8  9 10 11 12 13 14
13 14 15 16 17 18 19     11 12 13 14 15 16 17     15 16 17 18 19 20 21
20 21 22 23 24 25 26     18 19 20 21 22 23 24     22 23 24 25 26 27 28
27 28 29 30              25 26 27 28 29 30 31     29 30

JULY                     AUGUST                   SEPTEMBER
S  M  T  W  T  F  S      S  M  T  W  T  F  S      S  M  T  W  T  F  S
    1  2  3  4  5                      1  2       1  2  3  4  5  6
 6  7  8  9 10 11 12      3  4  5  6  7  8  9      7  8  9 10 11 12 13
13 14 15 16 17 18 19     10 11 12 13 14 15 16     14 15 16 17 18 19 20
20 21 22 23 24 25 26     17 18 19 20 21 22 23     21 22 23 24 25 26 27
27 28 29 30 31           24 25 26 27 28 29 30     28 29 30
                         31

OCTOBER                  NOVEMBER                 DECEMBER
S  M  T  W  T  F  S      S  M  T  W  T  F  S      S  M  T  W  T  F  S
       1  2  3  4                         1       1  2  3  4  5  6
 5  6  7  8  9 10 11      2  3  4  5  6  7  8      7  8  9 10 11 12 13
12 13 14 15 16 17 18      9 10 11 12 13 14 15     14 15 16 17 18 19 20
19 20 21 22 23 24 25     16 17 18 19 20 21 22     21 22 23 24 25 26 27
26 27 28 29 30 31        23 24 25 26 27 28 29     28 29 30 31
                         30
```

H (leap year)

```
JANUARY                  FEBRUARY                 MARCH
S  M  T  W  T  F  S      S  M  T  W  T  F  S      S  M  T  W  T  F  S
             1  2  3  4                      1    1  2  3  4  5  6  7
 5  6  7  8  9 10 11      2  3  4  5  6  7  8      8  9 10 11 12 13 14
12 13 14 15 16 17 18      9 10 11 12 13 14 15     15 16 17 18 19 20 21
19 20 21 22 23 24 25     16 17 18 19 20 21 22     22 23 24 25 26 27 28
26 27 28 29 30 31        23 24 25 26 27 28 29     29 30 31

APRIL                    MAY                      JUNE
S  M  T  W  T  F  S      S  M  T  W  T  F  S      S  M  T  W  T  F  S
       1  2  3  4                      1  2          1  2  3  4  5  6
 5  6  7  8  9 10 11      3  4  5  6  7  8  9      7  8  9 10 11 12 13
12 13 14 15 16 17 18     10 11 12 13 14 15 16     14 15 16 17 18 19 20
19 20 21 22 23 24 25     17 18 19 20 21 22 23     21 22 23 24 25 26 27
26 27 28 29 30           24 25 26 27 28 29 30     28 29 30
                         31

JULY                     AUGUST                   SEPTEMBER
S  M  T  W  T  F  S      S  M  T  W  T  F  S      S  M  T  W  T  F  S
       1  2  3  4                         1          1  2  3  4  5
 5  6  7  8  9 10 11      2  3  4  5  6  7  8      6  7  8  9 10 11 12
12 13 14 15 16 17 18      9 10 11 12 13 14 15     13 14 15 16 17 18 19
19 20 21 22 23 24 25     16 17 18 19 20 21 22     20 21 22 23 24 25 26
26 27 28 29 30 31        23 24 25 26 27 28 29     27 28 29 30
                         30 31

OCTOBER                  NOVEMBER                 DECEMBER
S  M  T  W  T  F  S      S  M  T  W  T  F  S      S  M  T  W  T  F  S
             1  2  3     1  2  3  4  5  6  7                1  2  3  4  5
 4  5  6  7  8  9 10      8  9 10 11 12 13 14      6  7  8  9 10 11 12
11 12 13 14 15 16 17     15 16 17 18 19 20 21     13 14 15 16 17 18 19
18 19 20 21 22 23 24     22 23 24 25 26 27 28     20 21 22 23 24 25 26
25 26 27 28 29 30 31     29 30                    27 28 29 30 31
```

I

JANUARY

S	M	T	W	T	F	S
				1	2	3
4	5	6	7	8	9	10
11	12	13	14	15	16	17
18	19	20	21	22	23	24
25	26	27	28	29	30	31

FEBRUARY

S	M	T	W	T	F	S
1	2	3	4	5	6	7
8	9	10	11	12	13	14
15	16	17	18	19	20	21
22	23	24	25	26	27	28

MARCH

S	M	T	W	T	F	S
1	2	3	4	5	6	7
8	9	10	11	12	13	14
15	16	17	18	19	20	21
22	23	24	25	26	27	28
29	30	31				

APRIL

S	M	T	W	T	F	S
			1	2	3	4
5	6	7	8	9	10	11
12	13	14	15	16	17	18
19	20	21	22	23	24	25
26	27	28	29	30		

MAY

S	M	T	W	T	F	S
					1	2
3	4	5	6	7	8	9
10	11	12	13	14	15	16
17	18	19	20	21	22	23
24	25	26	27	28	29	30
31						

JUNE

S	M	T	W	T	F	S
	1	2	3	4	5	6
7	8	9	10	11	12	13
14	15	16	17	18	19	20
21	22	23	24	25	26	27
28	29	30				

JULY

S	M	T	W	T	F	S
			1	2	3	4
5	6	7	8	9	10	11
12	13	14	15	16	17	18
19	20	21	22	23	24	25
26	27	28	29	30	31	

AUGUST

S	M	T	W	T	F	S
						1
2	3	4	5	6	7	8
9	10	11	12	13	14	15
16	17	18	19	20	21	22
23	24	25	26	27	28	29
30	31					

SEPTEMBER

S	M	T	W	T	F	S
		1	2	3	4	5
6	7	8	9	10	11	12
13	14	15	16	17	18	19
20	21	22	23	24	25	26
27	28	29	30			

OCTOBER

S	M	T	W	T	F	S
				1	2	3
4	5	6	7	8	9	10
11	12	13	14	15	16	17
18	19	20	21	22	23	24
25	26	27	28	29	30	31

NOVEMBER

S	M	T	W	T	F	S
1	2	3	4	5	6	7
8	9	10	11	12	13	14
15	16	17	18	19	20	21
22	23	24	25	26	27	28
29	30					

DECEMBER

S	M	T	W	T	F	S
		1	2	3	4	5
6	7	8	9	10	11	12
13	14	15	16	17	18	19
20	21	22	23	24	25	26
27	28	29	30	31		

J (leap year)

JANUARY

S	M	T	W	T	F	S
				1	2	3
4	5	6	7	8	9	10
11	12	13	14	15	16	17
18	19	20	21	22	23	24
25	26	27	28	29	30	31

FEBRUARY

S	M	T	W	T	F	S
1	2	3	4	5	6	7
8	9	10	11	12	13	14
15	16	17	18	19	20	21
22	23	24	25	26	27	28
29						

MARCH

S	M	T	W	T	F	S
	1	2	3	4	5	6
7	8	9	10	11	12	13
14	15	16	17	18	19	20
21	22	23	24	25	26	27
28	29	30	31			

APRIL

S	M	T	W	T	F	S
				1	2	3
4	5	6	7	8	9	10
11	12	13	14	15	16	17
18	19	20	21	22	23	24
25	26	27	28	29	30	

MAY

S	M	T	W	T	F	S
						1
2	3	4	5	6	7	8
9	10	11	12	13	14	15
16	17	18	19	20	21	22
23	24	25	26	27	28	29
30	31					

JUNE

S	M	T	W	T	F	S
		1	2	3	4	5
6	7	8	9	10	11	12
13	14	15	16	17	18	19
20	21	22	23	24	25	26
27	28	29	30			

JULY

S	M	T	W	T	F	S
				1	2	3
4	5	6	7	8	9	10
11	12	13	14	15	16	17
18	19	20	21	22	23	24
25	26	27	28	29	30	31

AUGUST

S	M	T	W	T	F	S
1	2	3	4	5	6	7
8	9	10	11	12	13	14
15	16	17	18	19	20	21
22	23	24	25	26	27	28
29	30	31				

SEPTEMBER

S	M	T	W	T	F	S
			1	2	3	4
5	6	7	8	9	10	11
12	13	14	15	16	17	18
19	20	21	22	23	24	25
26	27	28	29	30		

OCTOBER

S	M	T	W	T	F	S
					1	2
3	4	5	6	7	8	9
10	11	12	13	14	15	16
17	18	19	20	21	22	23
24	25	26	27	28	29	30
31						

NOVEMBER

S	M	T	W	T	F	S
	1	2	3	4	5	6
7	8	9	10	11	12	13
14	15	16	17	18	19	20
21	22	23	24	25	26	27
28	29	30				

DECEMBER

S	M	T	W	T	F	S
			1	2	3	4
5	6	7	8	9	10	11
12	13	14	15	16	17	18
19	20	21	22	23	24	25
26	27	28	29	30	31	

K

JANUARY

S	M	T	W	T	F	S
					1	2
3	4	5	6	7	8	9
10	11	12	13	14	15	16
17	18	19	20	21	22	23
24	25	26	27	28	29	30
31						

FEBRUARY

S	M	T	W	T	F	S
	1	2	3	4	5	6
7	8	9	10	11	12	13
14	15	16	17	18	19	20
21	22	23	24	25	26	27
28						

MARCH

S	M	T	W	T	F	S
	1	2	3	4	5	6
7	8	9	10	11	12	13
14	15	16	17	18	19	20
21	22	23	24	25	26	27
28	29	30	31			

APRIL

S	M	T	W	T	F	S
				1	2	3
4	5	6	7	8	9	10
11	12	13	14	15	16	17
18	19	20	21	22	23	24
25	26	27	28	29	30	

MAY

S	M	T	W	T	F	S
						1
2	3	4	5	6	7	8
9	10	11	12	13	14	15
16	17	18	19	20	21	22
23	24	25	26	27	28	29
30	31					

JUNE

S	M	T	W	T	F	S
		1	2	3	4	5
6	7	8	9	10	11	12
13	14	15	16	17	18	19
20	21	22	23	24	25	26
27	28	29	30			

JULY

S	M	T	W	T	F	S
				1	2	3
4	5	6	7	8	9	10
11	12	13	14	15	16	17
18	19	20	21	22	23	24
25	26	27	28	29	30	31

AUGUST

S	M	T	W	T	F	S
1	2	3	4	5	6	7
8	9	10	11	12	13	14
15	16	17	18	19	20	21
22	23	24	25	26	27	28
29	30	31				

SEPTEMBER

S	M	T	W	T	F	S
			1	2	3	4
5	6	7	8	9	10	11
12	13	14	15	16	17	18
19	20	21	22	23	24	25
26	27	28	29	30		

OCTOBER

S	M	T	W	T	F	S
					1	2
3	4	5	6	7	8	9
10	11	12	13	14	15	16
17	18	19	20	21	22	23
24	25	26	27	28	29	30
31						

NOVEMBER

S	M	T	W	T	F	S
	1	2	3	4	5	6
7	8	9	10	11	12	13
14	15	16	17	18	19	20
21	22	23	24	25	26	27
28	29	30				

DECEMBER

S	M	T	W	T	F	S
			1	2	3	4
5	6	7	8	9	10	11
12	13	14	15	16	17	18
19	20	21	22	23	24	25
26	27	28	29	30	31	

L (leap year)

JANUARY

S	M	T	W	T	F	S
					1	2
3	4	5	6	7	8	9
10	11	12	13	14	15	16
17	18	19	20	21	22	23
24	25	26	27	28	29	30
31						

FEBRUARY

S	M	T	W	T	F	S
	1	2	3	4	5	6
7	8	9	10	11	12	13
14	15	16	17	18	19	20
21	22	23	24	25	26	27
28	29					

MARCH

S	M	T	W	T	F	S
		1	2	3	4	5
6	7	8	9	10	11	12
13	14	15	16	17	18	19
20	21	22	23	24	25	26
27	28	29	30	31		

APRIL

S	M	T	W	T	F	S
					1	2
3	4	5	6	7	8	9
10	11	12	13	14	15	16
17	18	19	20	21	22	23
24	25	26	27	28	29	30

MAY

S	M	T	W	T	F	S
1	2	3	4	5	6	7
8	9	10	11	12	13	14
15	16	17	18	19	20	21
22	23	24	25	26	27	28
29	30	31				

JUNE

S	M	T	W	T	F	S
			1	2	3	4
5	6	7	8	9	10	11
12	13	14	15	16	17	18
19	20	21	22	23	24	25
26	27	28	29	30		

JULY

S	M	T	W	T	F	S
					1	2
3	4	5	6	7	8	9
10	11	12	13	14	15	16
17	18	19	20	21	22	23
24	25	26	27	28	29	30
31						

AUGUST

S	M	T	W	T	F	S
	1	2	3	4	5	6
7	8	9	10	11	12	13
14	15	16	17	18	19	20
21	22	23	24	25	26	27
28	29	30	31			

SEPTEMBER

S	M	T	W	T	F	S
				1	2	3
4	5	6	7	8	9	10
11	12	13	14	15	16	17
18	19	20	21	22	23	24
25	26	27	28	29	30	

OCTOBER

S	M	T	W	T	F	S
						1
2	3	4	5	6	7	8
9	10	11	12	13	14	15
16	17	18	19	20	21	22
23	24	25	26	27	28	29
30	31					

NOVEMBER

S	M	T	W	T	F	S
		1	2	3	4	5
6	7	8	9	10	11	12
13	14	15	16	17	18	19
20	21	22	23	24	25	26
27	28	29	30			

DECEMBER

S	M	T	W	T	F	S
				1	2	3
4	5	6	7	8	9	10
11	12	13	14	15	16	17
18	19	20	21	22	23	24
25	26	27	28	29	30	31

M

JANUARY	FEBRUARY	MARCH	APRIL	MAY	JUNE
S M T W T F S	S M T W T F S	S M T W T F S	S M T W T F S	S M T W T F S	S M T W T F S
1	1 2 3 4 5	1 2 3 4 5	1 2	1 2 3 4 5 6 7	1 2 3 4
2 3 4 5 6 7 8	6 7 8 9 10 11 12	6 7 8 9 10 11 12	3 4 5 6 7 8 9	8 9 10 11 12 13 14	5 6 7 8 9 10 11
9 10 11 12 13 14 15	13 14 15 16 17 18 19	13 14 15 16 17 18 19	10 11 12 13 14 15 16	15 16 17 18 19 20 21	12 13 14 15 16 17 18
16 17 18 19 20 21 22	20 21 22 23 24 25 26	20 21 22 23 24 25 26	17 18 19 20 21 22 23	22 23 24 25 26 27 28	19 20 21 22 23 24 25
23 24 25 26 27 28 29	27 28	27 28 29 30 31	24 25 26 27 28 29 30	29 30 31	26 27 28 29 30
30 31					

JULY	AUGUST	SEPTEMBER	OCTOBER	NOVEMBER	DECEMBER
S M T W T F S	S M T W T F S	S M T W T F S	S M T W T F S	S M T W T F S	S M T W T F S
1 2	1 2 3 4 5 6	1 2 3	1	1 2 3 4 5	1 2 3
3 4 5 6 7 8 9	7 8 9 10 11 12 13	4 5 6 7 8 9 10	2 3 4 5 6 7 8	6 7 8 9 10 11 12	4 5 6 7 8 9 10
10 11 12 13 14 15 16	14 15 16 17 18 19 20	11 12 13 14 15 16 17	9 10 11 12 13 14 15	13 14 15 16 17 18 19	11 12 13 14 15 16 17
17 18 19 20 21 22 23	21 22 23 24 25 26 27	18 19 20 21 22 23 24	16 17 18 19 20 21 22	20 21 22 23 24 25 26	18 19 20 21 22 23 24
24 25 26 27 28 29 30	28 29 30 31	25 26 27 28 29 30	23 24 25 26 27 28 29	27 28 29 30	25 26 27 28 29 30 31
31			30 31		

N (leap year)

JANUARY	FEBRUARY	MARCH	APRIL	MAY	JUNE
S M T W T F S	S M T W T F S	S M T W T F S	S M T W T F S	S M T W T F S	S M T W T F S
1	1 2 3 4 5	1 2 3 4	1	1 2 3 4 5 6	1 2 3
2 3 4 5 6 7 8	6 7 8 9 10 11 12	5 6 7 8 9 10 11	2 3 4 5 6 7 8	7 8 9 10 11 12 13	4 5 6 7 8 9 10
9 10 11 12 13 14 15	13 14 15 16 17 18 19	12 13 14 15 16 17 18	9 10 11 12 13 14 15	14 15 16 17 18 19 20	11 12 13 14 15 16 17
16 17 18 19 20 21 22	20 21 22 23 24 25 26	19 20 21 22 23 24 25	16 17 18 19 20 21 22	21 22 23 24 25 26 27	18 19 20 21 22 23 24
23 24 25 26 27 28 29	27 28 29	26 27 28 29 30 31	23 24 25 26 27 28 29	28 29 30 31	25 26 27 28 29 30
30 31			30		

JULY	AUGUST	SEPTEMBER	OCTOBER	NOVEMBER	DECEMBER
S M T W T F S	S M T W T F S	S M T W T F S	S M T W T F S	S M T W T F S	S M T W T F S
1	1 2 3 4 5	1 2	1 2 3 4 5 6 7	1 2 3 4	1 2
2 3 4 5 6 7 8	6 7 8 9 10 11 12	3 4 5 6 7 8 9	8 9 10 11 12 13 14	5 6 7 8 9 10 11	3 4 5 6 7 8 9
9 10 11 12 13 14 15	13 14 15 16 17 18 19	10 11 12 13 14 15 16	15 16 17 18 19 20 21	12 13 14 15 16 17 18	10 11 12 13 14 15 16
16 17 18 19 20 21 22	20 21 22 23 24 25 26	17 18 19 20 21 22 23	22 23 24 25 26 27 28	19 20 21 22 23 24 25	17 18 19 20 21 22 23
23 24 25 26 27 28 29	27 28 29 30 31	24 25 26 27 28 29 30	29 30 31	26 27 28 29 30	24 25 26 27 28 29 30
30 31					31

Time

Year equivalents

Jewish[1] (AM)

5756	(25 Sep 1995–13 Sep 1996)
5757	(14 Sep 1996–1 Oct 1997)
5758	(2 Oct 1997–20 Sep 1998)
5759	(21 Sep 1998–10 Sep 1999)
5760	(11 Sep 1999–29 Sep 2000)
5761	(30 Sep 2000–17 Sep 2001)
5762	(18 Sep 2001–6 Sep 2002)
5763	(7 Sep 2002–26 Sep 2003)
5764	(27 Sep 2003–15 Sep 2004)
5765	(16 Sep 2004–3 Oct 2005)
5766	(4 Oct 2005–22 Sep 2006)
5767	(23 Sep 2006–12 Sep 2007)
5768	(13 Sep 2007–29 Sep 2008)
5769	(30 Sep 2008–18 Sep 2009)
5770	(19 Sep 2009–8 Sep 2010)
5771	(9 Sep 2010–28 Sep 2011)
5772	(29 Sep 2011–16 Sep 2012)
5773	(17 Sep 2012–4 Sep 2013)
5774	(5 Sep 2013–24 Sep 2014)
5775	(25 Sep 2014–13 Sep 2015)
5776	(14 Sep 2015–2 Oct 2016)
5777	(3 Oct 2016–20 Sep 2017)
5778	(21 Sep 2017–9 Sep 2018)
5779	(10 Sep 2018–29 Sep 2019)
5780	(30 Sep 2019–18 Sep 2020)

Islamic[2] (H)

1416	(31 May 1995–18 May 1996)
1417	(19 May 1996–8 May 1997)
1418	(9 May 1997–27 Apr 1998)
1419	(28 Apr 1998–16 Apr 1999)
1420	(17 Apr 1999–5 Apr 2000)
1421	(6 Apr 2000–25 Mar 2001)
1422	(26 Mar 2001–14 Mar 2002)
1423	(15 Mar 2002–3 Mar 2003)
1424	(4 Mar 2003–21 Feb 2004)
1425	(22 Feb 2004–9 Feb 2005)
1426	(10 Feb 2005–30 Jan 2006)
1427	(31 Jan 2006–20 Jan 2007)
1428	(21 Jan 2007–9 Jan 2008)
1429	(10 Jan 2008–28 Dec 2008)
1430	(29 Dec 2008–17 Dec 2009)
1431	(18 Dec 2009–6 Dec 2010)
1432	(7 Dec 2010–26 Nov 2011)
1433	(27 Nov 2011–14 Nov 2012)
1434	(15 Nov 2012–4 Nov 2013)
1435	(5 Nov 2013–24 Oct 2014)
1436	(25 Oct 2014–13 Oct 2015)
1437	(14 Oct 2015–1 Oct 2016)
1438	(2 Oct 2016–21 Sep 2017)
1439	(22 Sep 2017–10 Sep 2018)
1440	(11 Sep 2018–31 Aug 2019)
1441	(1 Sep 2019–19 Aug 2020)

Hindu[3] (SE)

1917	(22 Mar 1995–20 Mar 1996)
1918	(21 Mar 1996–21 Mar 1997)
1919	(22 Mar 1997–21 Mar 1998)
1920	(22 Mar 1998–21 Mar 1999)
1921	(22 Mar 1999–20 Mar 2000)
1922	(21 Mar 2000–21 Mar 2001)
1923	(22 Mar 2001–21 Mar 2002)
1924	(22 Mar 2002–21 Mar 2003)
1925	(22 Mar 2003–20 Mar 2004)
1926	(21 Mar 2004–21 Mar 2005)
1927	(22 Mar 2005–21 Mar 2006)
1928	(22 Mar 2006–21 Mar 2007)
1929	(22 Mar 2007–20 Mar 2008)
1930	(21 Mar 2008–21 Mar 2009)
1931	(22 Mar 2009–21 Mar 2010)
1932	(22 Mar 2010–21 Mar 2011)
1933	(22 Mar 2011–20 Mar 2012)
1934	(21 Mar 2012–21 Mar 2013)
1935	(22 Mar 2013–21 Mar 2014)
1936	(22 Mar 2014–21 Mar 2015)
1937	(22 Mar 2015–20 Mar 2016)
1938	(21 Mar 2016–21 Mar 2017)
1939	(22 Mar 2017–21 Mar 2018)
1940	(22 Mar 2018–21 Mar 2019)
1941	(22 Mar 2019–20 Mar 2020)

Hindu[4] (VE)

2052	(14 Mar 1995–13 Mar 1996)
2053	(14 Mar 1996–13 Mar 1997)
2054	(14 Mar 1997–13 Mar 1998)
2055	(14 Mar 1998–13 Mar 1999)
2056	(14 Mar 1999–13 Mar 2000)
2057	(14 Mar 2000–13 Mar 2001)
2058	(14 Mar 2001–13 Mar 2002)
2059	(14 Mar 2002–13 Mar 2003)
2060	(14 Mar 2003–13 Mar 2004)
2061	(14 Mar 2004–13 Mar 2005)
2062	(14 Mar 2005–13 Mar 2006)
2063	(14 Mar 2006–13 Mar 2007)
2064	(14 Mar 2007–13 Mar 2008)
2065	(14 Mar 2008–13 Mar 2009)
2066	(14 Mar 2009–13 Mar 2010)
2067	(14 Mar 2010–13 Mar 2011)
2068	(14 Mar 2011–13 Mar 2012)
2069	(14 Mar 2012–13 Mar 2013)
2070	(14 Mar 2013–13 Mar 2014)
2071	(14 Mar 2014–13 Mar 2015)
2072	(14 Mar 2015–13 Mar 2016)
2073	(14 Mar 2016–13 Mar 2017)
2074	(14 Mar 2017–13 Mar 2018)
2075	(14 Mar 2018–13 Mar 2019)
2076	(14 Mar 2019–13 Mar 2020)

Gregorian equivalents are given in parentheses and are AD (= Anno Domini).

[1] Calculated from 3761 BC, said to be the year of the creation of the world. AM = Anno Mundi.

[2] Calculated from AD 622, the year in which the Prophet went from Mecca to Medina. H = Hegira.

[3] Calculated from AD 78, the beginning of the Saka era (SE), used alongside Gregorian dates in Government of India publications since 22 Mar 1957.

[4] Calculated from 58 BC, the beginning of the Vikrama era (VE). Other important Hindu eras include: Kalacuri era (AD 248), Gupta era (AD 320) and Harsa era (AD 606).

The seasons

N Hemisphere	S Hemisphere	Duration
Spring	Autumn	From vernal/autumnal equinox (c.21 Mar) to summer/winter solstice (c.21 Jun)
Summer	Winter	From summer/winter solstice (c.21 Jun) to autumnal/spring equinox (c.23 Sep)
Autumn	Spring	From autumnal/spring equinox (c.23 Sep) to winter/summer solstice (c.22 Dec)
Winter	Summer	From winter/summer solstice (c.22 Dec) to vernal/autumnal equinox (c.21 Mar)

Chinese animal years and times 1960–2019

Chinese	English	Years					Time of day (hours)
Shu	Rat	1960	1972	1984	1996	2008	2300–0100
Niu	Ox	1961	1973	1985	1997	2009	0100–0300
Hu	Tiger	1962	1974	1986	1998	2010	0300–0500
Tu	Hare	1963	1975	1987	1999	2011	0500–0700
Long	Dragon	1964	1976	1988	2000	2012	0700–0900
She	Serpent	1965	1977	1989	2001	2013	0900–1100
Ma	Horse	1966	1978	1990	2002	2014	1100–1300
Yang	Sheep	1967	1979	1991	2003	2015	1300–1500
Hou	Monkey	1968	1980	1992	2004	2016	1500–1700
Ji	Cock	1969	1981	1993	2005	2017	1700–1900
Gou	Dog	1970	1982	1994	2006	2018	1900–2100
Zhu	Boar	1971	1983	1995	2007	2019	2100–2300

Wedding anniversaries

In many Western countries, different wedding anniversaries have become associated with gifts of different materials. There is some variation between countries, and where modern materials have been added.

1st	Paper, Clocks	14th	Ivory, Gold jewellery
2nd	Cotton, China	15th	Crystal, Watches
3rd	Leather, Crystal/Glass	20th	China, Platinum
4th	Linen, Fruit, Flowers, Appliances	25th	Silver
5th	Wood, Silverware	30th	Pearl, Diamond
6th	Iron, Sugar	35th	Coral, Jade
7th	Copper, Wool, Desk set	40th	Ruby
8th	Bronze, Lace	45th	Sapphire
9th	Pottery, Willow	50th	Gold
10th	Tin, Aluminium, Diamond	55th	Emerald
11th	Steel, Jewellery	60th	Diamond
12th	Silk, Pearls	70th	Platinum
13th	Lace, Textiles		

Months' associations with gems and flowers

In many Western countries, the months are traditionally associated with gemstones and flowers. There is considerable variation between countries. The following combinations are widely recognized in North America and the UK.

Month	Gemstone	Flower
January	Garnet	Carnation, Snowdrop
February	Amethyst	Primrose, Violet
March	Aquamarine, Bloodstone	Jonquil, Violet
April	Diamond	Daisy, Sweet Pea
May	Emerald	Hawthorn, Lily of the Valley
June	Alexandrite, Moonstone, Pearl	Honeysuckle, Rose
July	Ruby	Larkspur, Water Lily
August	Peridot, Sardonyx	Gladiolus, Poppy
September	Sapphire	Aster, Morning Glory
October	Opal, Tourmaline	Calendula, Cosmos
November	Topaz, Zircon	Chrysanthemum
December	Turquoise, Zircon	Holly, Narcissus, Poinsettia

Time

International time differences

The time zones of the world are conventionally measured from longitude 0° at Greenwich Observatory (Greenwich Mean Time, GMT).

Each 15° of longitude east of this point is one hour ahead of GMT (eg when it is 2pm in London it is 3pm or later in time zones to the east). Hours ahead of GMT are shown by a plus sign, eg +3, +4/8.

Each 15° west of this point is one hour behind GMT (eg 2pm in London would be 1pm or earlier in time zones to the west). Hours behind GMT are shown by a minus sign, eg −3, −4/8.

Some countries adopt time zones that vary from standard time. Also, during the summer, several countries adopt Daylight Saving Time (or Summer Time), which is one hour ahead of the times shown below.

Country	GMT	Country	GMT	Country	GMT	Country	GMT
Afghanistan	+4½	Dominican Republic	−4	Libya	+2	Samoa	−11
Albania	+1	East Timor	+8	Liechtenstein	+1	San Marino	+1
Algeria	+1	Ecuador	−5	Lithuania	+2	São Tomé and Príncipe	0
Andorra	+1	Egypt	+2	Luxembourg	+1	Saudi Arabia	+3
Angola	+1	El Salvador	−6	Macedonia	+1	Senegal	0
Antigua and Barbuda	−4	Equatorial Guinea	+1	Madagascar	+3	Serbia	+1
Argentina	−3	Eritrea	+3	Malawi	+2	Seychelles	+4
Armenia	+4	Estonia	+2	Malaysia	+8	Sierra Leone	0
Australia	+8/10	Ethiopia	+3	Maldives	+5	Singapore	+8
Austria	+1	Falkland Is	−4	Mali	0	Slovakia	+1
Azerbaijan	+4	Fiji	+12	Malta	+1	Slovenia	+1
Bahamas	−5	Finland	+2	Marshall Is	+12	Solomon Is	+11
Bahrain	+3	France	+1	Mauritania	0	Somalia	+3
Bangladesh	+6	Gabon	+1	Mauritius	+4	South Africa	+2
Barbados	−4	Gambia	0	Mexico	−6/8	Spain	+1
Belarus	+2	Georgia	+4	Micronesia, Federated States of	+10/11	Sri Lanka	+5½
Belgium	+1	Germany	+1	Moldova	+2	Sudan	+3
Belize	−6	Ghana	0	Monaco	+1	Suriname	−3
Benin	+1	Gibraltar	+1	Mongolia	+7/8	Swaziland	+2
Bermuda	−4	Greece	+2	Montenegro	+1	Sweden	+1
Bhutan	+6	Greenland	−3	Morocco	0	Switzerland	+1
Bolivia	−4	Grenada	−4	Mozambique	+2	Syria	+2
Bosnia and Herzegovina	+1	Guatemala	−6	Myanmar (Burma)	+6½	Taiwan	+8
Botswana	+2	Guinea	0	Namibia	+1	Tajikistan	+5
Brazil	−2/5	Guinea-Bissau	0	Nauru	+12	Tanzania	+3
Brunei	+8	Guyana	−4	Nepal	+5¾	Thailand	+7
Bulgaria	+2	Haiti	−5	Netherlands	+1	Togo	0
Burkina Faso	0	Honduras	−6	New Zealand	+12	Tonga	+13
Burundi	+2	Hong Kong	+8	Nicaragua	−6	Trinidad and Tobago	−4
Cambodia	+7	Hungary	+1	Niger	+1	Tunisia	+1
Cameroon	+1	Iceland	0	Nigeria	+1	Turkey	+2
Canada	−3½/8	India	+5½	Norway	+1	Turkmenistan	+5
Cape Verde	−1	Indonesia	+7/9	Oman	+4	Tuvalu	+12
Central African Republic	+1	Iran	+3½	Pakistan	+5	Uganda	+3
Chad	+1	Iraq	+3	Palau	+9	Ukraine	+2
Chile	−4	Ireland	0	Panama	−5	United Arab Emirates	+4
China	+8	Israel	+2	Papua New Guinea	+10	United Kingdom	0
Colombia	−5	Italy	+1	Paraguay	−4	United States of America	−5/10
Comoros	+3	Jamaica	−5	Peru	−5	Uruguay	−3
Congo	+1	Japan	+9	Philippines	+8	Uzbekistan	+5
Congo, DR	+1/2	Jordan	+2	Poland	+1	Vanuatu	+11
Costa Rica	−6	Kazakhstan	+4/6	Portugal	0	Vatican	+1
Côte d'Ivoire	0	Kenya	+3	Qatar	+3	Venezuela	−4
Croatia	+1	Kiribati	+12/14	Romania	+2	Vietnam	+7
Cuba	−5	Korea, North	+9	Russia	+2/12	Yemen	+3
Cyprus	+2	Korea, South	+9	Rwanda	+2	Zambia	+2
Czech Republic	+1	Kuwait	+3	St Kitts and Nevis	−4	Zimbabwe	+2
Denmark	+1	Kyrgyzstan	+6	St Lucia	−4		
Djibouti	+3	Laos	+7	St Vincent and the Grenadines	−4		
Dominica	−4	Latvia	+2				
		Lebanon	+2				
		Lesotho	+2				
		Liberia	0				

National holidays

National holidays are subject to change. Some holidays are religious feast-days, and even those that occur on fixed dates can vary according to local circumstances or the day of the week on which they fall.

The first part of each country's listing gives the holidays that occur on fixed dates (although these might vary occasionally). Most dates are accompanied by an indication of the purpose of the day, eg Independence = Independence Day; dates which have no gloss are either fixed dates within a religious or civil calendar (for which see below) or bank holidays.

The following fixed dates are shown without gloss:

Jan 1	New Year's Day
Jan 6	Epiphany
Mar 21	Novrus (Persian New Year; various spellings)
May 1	Labour Day (often known by a different name, such as Workers' Day)
Aug 15	Assumption of Our Lady
Nov 1	All Saints' Day
Nov 2	All Souls' Day
Dec 8	Immaculate Conception
Dec 24	Christmas Eve
Dec 25	Christmas Day
Dec 26	Boxing Day/St Stephen's Day
Dec 31	New Year's Eve

The second part of the listing gives holidays whose dates vary, usually depending on religious factors. The following abbreviations are used for variable religious feast-days:

A	Ascension Thursday
Ad	Id-ul-Adha (also found with other spellings — especially Eid-ul-Adha; various names relating to this occasion are used in different countries, such as Tabaski, Id el-Kebir, Hari Raja Haji)
Ar	Arafa
As	Ashora (found with various spellings)
C	Carnival (immediately before Christian Lent, unless otherwise specified)
CC	Corpus Christi
D	Diwali, Deepavali
EM	Easter Monday
ER	End of Ramadan (known generally as Id/Eid-ul-Fitr, but various names relating to this occasion are used in different countries, such as Karite, Hari Raja Puasa)
ES	Easter Sunday
GF	Good Friday
HS	Holy Saturday
HT	Holy Thursday
NY	New Year
PB	Prophet's Birthday (known generally as Maul-id-al-Nabi in various forms and spellings)
R	First day of Ramadan
WM	Whit Monday

A number in brackets such as (Independence) (2) refers to the number of days devoted to the holiday. The listings do not include holidays that affect only certain parts of a country, half-day holidays, or Sundays.

Afghanistan Mar 21, Apr 28 (Victory), May 1, Aug 18 (Independence); Ad (3), As, ER (3), PB, R

Albania Jan 1, 2, Mar 14 (Summer), 21, May 1, Oct 19 (Mother Teresa), Nov 28 (Independence), 29 (Liberation), Dec 25; Ad, EM, EM (Orthodox), ER

Algeria Jan 1, May 1, Jul 5 (Independence), Nov 1 (Revolution); Ad (2), As, ER (2), NY (Muslim), PB

Andorra Jan 1, 6, Mar 14 (Constitution), May 1, Jun 24 (St John), Aug 15, Sep 8 (National), Nov 1, 4 (St Charles), Dec 8, 24, 25, 26, 31; C, EM, GF, HS, WM

Angola Jan 1, 4 (Martyrs of the Colonial Repression), Feb 4 (Beginning of the Armed Struggle), Mar 8 (Women), April 4 (Peace), May 1, 25 (Africa), Jun 1 (Children), Sep 17 (Nation's Founder/National Hero), Nov 2, 11 (Independence), Dec 25

Antigua and Barbuda Jan 1, Nov 1 (Independence), Dec 9 (National Heroes), Dec 25, 26; EM, GF, WM, Labour (1st Mon in May), Carnival (1st Mon and Tues in Aug) (2)

Argentina Jan 1, Mar 24 (Truth and Justice), April 2 (Malvinas), May 1, 25 (First Government), Jun 19 (Flag), Jul 9 (Independence), Aug 17 (San Martín), Oct 12 (Columbus), Dec 8, 25; GF

Armenia Jan 1, 2, 6 (Armenian Orthodox Christmas), 28 (Army), Mar 8 (Women's), Apr 7 (Motherhood and Beauty), 24 (Genocide Memorial), May 1, 9 (Victory and Peace), 28 (Declaration of the First Republic, 1918), Jul 5 (Constitution), Sep 21 (Independence), Dec 7 (Earthquake Memorial), 31

Australia Jan 1, 26 (Australia), Apr 25 (Anzac), Dec 25, 26 (Boxing/Proclamation); Queen's Birthday (Jun, *except Western Australia*, Sept/Oct); EM, GF, HS; *additional days vary between states*

Austria Jan 1, 6, May 1, Aug 15, Oct 26 (National), Nov 1, Dec 8, 25, 26; A, CC, EM, WM

Azerbaijan Jan 1, 2, 20 (Martyrs), Mar 8 (Women), 21 (7), May 9 (Victory), 28 (Republic), June 15 (National Salvation), 26 (Army and Navy), Oct 18 (Independence), Nov 12 (Constitution), 17 (National Revival), Dec

Time

31 (World Azeri Solidarity); Ad, ER

Bahamas, The Jan 1, Jul 10 (Independence), Oct 12 (Discovery), Dec 25, 26; EM, GF, WM; Labour (1st Fri in Jun), Emancipation (1st Mon in Aug)

Bahrain Jan 1, May 1, Dec 16-17 (National); Ad (3), As, ER (3), NY (Muslim), PB

Bangladesh Feb 21 (International Mother Language), Mar 26 (Independence), May 1, Aug 15 (Bangabandhu Memorial), Dec 16 (Victory), 25; Ad (3), As, Buddha Purnima (Apr/May), Durga Puja (Dashami), ER (3), Jamatul Wida, Janmashtami, NY (Bengali), NY (Muslim), PB, Shab-e-Barat, Shab-e-Qadr

Barbados Jan 1, 21 (Errol Barrow), Apr 28 (National Heroes), May 1, Aug 1 (Emancipation), Nov 30 (Independence), Dec 25, 26; EM, GF, WM, Kadooment (Aug)

Belarus Jan 1, 7 (Orthodox Christmas), Mar 8 (Women), May 1, 6 (Memorial/Radounitsa), 9 (Victory), Jul 3 (Independence), Nov 7 (October Revolution), Dec 25; GF, HS, ES, EM, Orthodox Easter

Belgium Jan 1, May 1, Jul 21 (Independence), Aug 15, Nov 1, 11 (Armistice), Dec 25, 26; A, EM, ES, WM; *also community holidays* (Jul 11 Flemish, Sep 27 French, Nov 15 German)

Belize Jan 1, Mar 9 (Baron Bliss), May 1, 24 (Commonwealth), Sep 10 (St George's Caye), 21 (Independence), Oct 12 (Columbus), Nov 19 (Garifuna Settlement), Dec 25, 26; EM, GF, HS

Benin Jan 1, 10 (Traditional religions), May 1, Aug 1 (Independence), 15, Nov 1, 30 (National), Dec 25; A, Ad, EM, ER, PB, WM

Bhutan Aug 8 (Independence), Nov 11 (Birthday of HM Jigme Singye Wangchuk), Dec 17 (National); *all traditional Buddhist holidays*

Bolivia Jan 1, May 1, Aug 7 (National), Nov 2, Dec 25; C (2), CC, GF

Bosnia and Herzegovina Jan 1, 27 (St Sava's Day), Mar 1 (Independence), May 1, Aug 15, Dec 25; EM, GF, Orthodox Christmas (2), Orthodox New Year (2); *much local variation*

Botswana Jan 1, May 1, Jul 1 (Sir Seretse Khama), Sep 30 (Botswana), Dec 25, 26; A, EM, GF, President's Day (Jul) (2)

Brazil Jan 1, Apr 21 (Tiradentes), May 1, Sep 7 (Independence), Oct 12 (Our Lady of Aparecida), Nov 2, 15 (Republic), Dec 25; C (3), CC, GF; *much local variation*

Brunei Jan 1, Feb 23 (National), May 31 (Royal Brunei Malay Regiment), Jul 15 (Sultan's Birthday), Dec 25; Ad, ER (2), Isra' Me'raj, NY (Chinese), NY (Muslim), PB, R, Revelation of the Koran

Bulgaria Jan 1, Mar 3 (National), May 1, 6 (Bulgarian Army), 24 (Culture and Literacy), Sep 6 (Unification), 22 (Independence), Nov 1 (Revival Leaders), Dec 24, 25, 26; Orthodox Easter (Apr/May)

Burkina Faso Jan 1, 3 (1966 Revolution), Mar 8 (Women), May 1, Aug 4 (Revolution), 5 (Independence), 15, Oct 15 (1987 Coup), Nov 1, Dec 11 (National), 25; A, Ad, EM, ER, NY (Muslim), PB

Burma ▶ **Myanmar**

Burundi Jan 1, Feb 5 (Unity), Apr 6 (Ntaryamira Assassination), May 1, Jul 1 (Independence), Aug 15, Oct 13 (Rwagasore Assassination), Oct 21 (Ndadaye Assassination), Nov 1, Dec 25; A, Ad, ER

Cambodia Jan 1, 7 (Victory over Genocide), Mar 8 (Women), Apr 3 (Culture), May 1, 14 (King's Birthday) (3), Jun 1 (Children), 18 (King's Mother's Birthday), Sep 24 (Constitution and Coronation), Oct 30 (Former King Sihanouk's Birthday) (2), Nov 9 (Independence), Dec 10 (Human Rights); Cambodian New Year (Apr) (3), Meak Bochea (Feb), Pchum Ben (Sep) (3), Royal Ploughing Ceremony (May), Visakha Bochea (May), Water/Moon Festival (Nov) (3)

Cameroon Jan 1, Feb 11 (Youth), May 1, 20 (National), Aug 15, Dec 25; A, Ad, ER, GF, ES, EM

Canada Jan 1, Jul 1 (Canada), Nov 11 (Remembrance), Dec 25, 26; EM, GF; Labour (1st Mon in Sep), Thanksgiving (2nd Mon in Oct), Victoria (Mon preceding May 25)

Cape Verde Jan 1, 13 (Democracy), 20 (National Heroes), May 1, Jun 1 (Youth), Jul 5 (Independence), Aug 15, Sep 12 (National), Nov 1, Dec 25; ES, GF

Central African Republic Jan 1, Mar 29 (Death of President Boganda), May 1, Jun 30 (Prayer), Aug 13 (Independence), 15, Nov 1, Dec 1 (National), 25; A, EM, WM

Chad Jan 1, May 1, Aug 11 (Independence), Nov 1, 28 (Republic), Dec 1 (Liberty and Democracy), 25; Ad, EM, ES, ER, PB

Chile Jan 1, May 1, 21 (Navy), Jun 29 (Sts Peter and Paul), Jul 16 (Lady of Carmen), Aug 15, Sep 18 (National), 19 (Army), Oct 12 (Americas), 31 (Reformation), Nov 1, Dec 8, 25; GF, HS

China Jan 1, April 4 (Tomb Sweeping), May 1, Oct 1 (National) (2); Spring Festival (4) (Jan/Feb), NY (Chinese), Dragon Boat Festival (Jun), Mid-Autumn Festival (Sep)

Colombia Jan 1, 6, Mar 19 (St Joseph), May 1, Jun 29 (Sts Peter and Paul), Jul 20 (Independence), Aug 7 (Battle of Boyacá), 15, Oct 12 (Columbus), Nov 1, 11 (Independence of Cartagena), Dec 8, 25; A, CC, GF, HT, Sacred Heart (Jun)

Comoros Jan 1, Mar 18 (Death of President Cheikh), May 1, Jul 6 (Independence), Nov 26 (President Abdallah's Assassination); Ad, As, ER, NY (Muslim), PB, R, Ascension of the Prophet

Congo Jan 1, May 1, Jun 10 (Reconciliation), Aug 15 (Independence), Nov 1, Dec 25; A, EM, ES, WM

Congo, Democratic Republic of the Jan 1, 4 (Martyrs of Independence), 16–17 (National Heroes), May 1, 17 (National Liberation), Jun 30 (Independence) Aug 1 (Parents), Dec 25; ES

Costa Rica Jan 1, Apr 14 (Juan Santamaria), May 1, Jul 25 (Annexation of Guanacaste), Aug 2 (Virgin de Los Angeles), 15 (Mothers), Sep 15 (Independence), Oct 12 (Columbus), Dec 25, 31; ES, GF, HS, HT

Côte d'Ivoire Jan 1, May 1, Aug 7 (Republic), 15, Nov 1, 15 (Peace), Dec 25; A, Ad, EM, ER, GF, PB, WM

Croatia Jan 1, 6, May 1, Jun 22 (Antifascist Resistance), 25 (Statehood), Aug 5 (National Thanksgiving), 15, Oct 8 (Independence), Nov 1, Dec 25, 26; CC, EM

Cuba Jan 1 (Liberation), May 1, Jul 25 (National Rebellion) (2), Oct 10 (Beginning of the Independence Wars), Dec 25

Cyprus Jan 1, 6, Mar 25 (Greek Independence), Apr 1 (Greek Cypriot National), May 1, Aug 15, Oct 1 (Independence), 28 (Greek National Ochi), Dec 24, 25, 26; ES, Green Monday, Kataklysmos, Orthodox Easter (Apr/May) (3)

Czech Republic Jan 1, May 1, 8 (Liberation), Jul 5 (Sts Cyril and Methodius), 6 (Martyrdom of Jan Hus), Sep 28 (Czech Statehood), Oct 28 (Independence), Nov 17 (Freedom and Democracy), Dec 24, 25, 26; EM

Denmark Jan 1, Jun 5 (Constitution), Dec 24, 25, 26; A, EM, GF, HT, WM, General Prayer (Apr/May)

Djibouti Jan 1, May 1, Jun 27 (Independence) (2), Dec 25; Ad (2), ER (2), NY (Muslim), PB, Al-Isra Wal-Mira'age

Dominica Jan 1, May 1, Nov 3 (Independence), 4 (Community Service), Dec 25, 26; C (2), EM, GF, WM, August Monday

Dominican Republic Jan 1, 6, 21 (Our Lady of Altagracia), 26 (Duarte), Feb 27 (Independence), May 1, Aug 16 (Restoration of the Republic), Sep 24 (Our Lady of Mercy), Nov 6 (Constitution), Dec 25; CC, GF

East Timor ▶ Timor-Leste

Ecuador Jan 1, May 1, 24 (Battle of Pichincha), Aug 10 (Independence), Oct 9 (Independence of Guayaquil), Nov 2, 3 (Independence of Cuenca), Dec 25; C (2), GF

Egypt Jan 7 (Coptic Christmas), Apr 25 (Sinai Liberation), May 1, Jul 23 (Revolution), Oct 6 (Armed Forces); Ad (3), ER (2), NY (Muslim), PB, Sham El Nassim (Coptic Easter) (Apr/May)

Eire ▶ Ireland, Republic of

El Salvador Jan 1, May 1, Aug 6 (El Salvador del Mundo), Sep 15 (Independence), Oct 12 (Columbus), Nov 2, 5 (Cry of Independence), Dec 24, 25, 31; ES, GF, HS, HT; *some local variation; public and private sector holidays may differ*

England and Wales Jan 1, Dec 25, 26; EM, GF; Early May (1st Mon), Spring (last Mon in May) and Summer (last Mon in Aug) Bank Holidays

Equatorial Guinea Jan 1, May 1, 25 (Africa), Jun 5 (President's Birthday), Aug 3 (Armed Forces), 15 (Constitution), Oct 12 (Independence), Dec 25; CC, GF

Eritrea Jan 1, Feb 10 (Fenkil), Mar 8 (Women), May 24 (Independence), Jun 20 (Martyrs), Sep 1 (Start of the Armed Struggle), Dec 25; Ad, ER, PB; *Coptic Christmas, Epiphany (Jan), Easter, New Year (Sep) also observed*

Estonia Jan 1, Feb 24 (Independence), May 1 (Spring), Jun 23 (Victory), 24 (St John/Midsummer), Aug 20 (Restoration of Independence), Dec 24, 25, 26; GF, ES, Whit Sunday

Ethiopia Jan 7 (Ethiopian Christmas), 19 (Ethiopian Epiphany), Mar 2 (Victory of Adwa), May 1, 5 (Patriots Victory), 28 (Downfall of the Dergue), Sep 27 (Finding of the True Cross); Ad, ER, NY (Ethiopian) (Sep), PB, Ethiopian Good Friday and Easter Sunday

Fiji Jan 1, Dec 25, 26; D, EM, GF, HS, PB, Queen's Birthday (Jun), National Youth (March), Ratu Sir Lala Sukuna (last Fri in May), Fiji (Oct)

Finland Jan 1, 6, May 1, Nov 1, Dec 6 (Independence), 24, 25, 26; A, EM, ES, GF; Midsummer Day (Jun), Whitsun (May/Jun)

France Jan 1, May 1, 8 (Victory), Jul 14 (Bastille), Aug 15, Nov 1, 11 (Armistice), Dec 25; A, EM, WM

Gabon Jan 1, April 17 (Women), May 1, Aug 15, 16 (Independence) (2), Nov 1, Dec 25; Ad, EM, ER, WM

Gambia, The Jan 1, Feb 18 (Independence), May 1, July 22 (Revolution), Aug 15, Dec 25; Ad, EM, ER, GF, PB

Georgia Jan 1, 7 (Orthodox Christmas), 19 (Orthodox Epiphany), Mar 3 (Mothers), 8 (Women), Apr 9 (National), May 9 (National), 12 (St Andrew), 26 (Independence), Aug 28 (Assumption of the Virgin), Oct 14 (Svetitskhovloba), Nov 23 (St George); EM, ES, GF, HS

Germany Jan 1, May 1, Oct 3 (Unity), Dec 25, 26; A, EM, ES, GF, WM; *much regional variation*

Ghana Jan 1, Mar 6 (Independence), May 1, 25 (Africa), Jul 1 (Republic), Dec 25, 26; Ad, EM, ER, GF, Farmers (1st Fri in Dec)

Greece Jan 1, 6, Mar 25 (Independence), May 1, Aug 15, Oct 28 (Ochi), Dec 25, 26; GF, EM, ES, WM, Orthodox Shrove Monday

Grenada Jan 1, Feb 7 (Independence), May 1, Aug 3 (Emancipation) (2), Oct 25 (Thanksgiving), Dec 25, 26; C, CC, EM, GF, WM

Guatemala Jan 1, May 1, Jun 30 (Army), Sep 15 (Independence), Oct 20 (Revolution), Nov 1, Dec 25, 31; GF, HT, Assumption *(date varies locally)*

Guinea Jan 1, Apr 3 (Second Republic), May 1, 25 (Africa), Aug 15, Oct 2 (Republic), Nov 1, Dec 25; Ad, EM, ER, PB

Guinea-Bissau Jan 1, 20 (Death of Amilcar Cabral), Mar 8 (Women), May 1, Aug 3 (Martyrs of Colonialism), Sep 24 (National), Nov 14 (Readjustment), Dec 25; Ad, ER

Guyana Jan 1, Feb 23 (Republic), May 1, 5 (Arrival Day), 26 (Independence), Aug 1 (Freedom), Dec 25, 26; Ad, D, EM, GF, PB, Phagwah (Mar), Caricom (1st Mon in Jul)

Haiti Jan 1 (Independence), 2 (Ancestors), Apr 14 (Americas), May 1, 18 (Flag/University), Aug 15, Oct 17 (Death of Dessalines), 24 (United Nations), Nov 1, 2, 18 (Battle of Vertières), Dec 25; A, C, CC, GF

Honduras Jan 1, Apr 14 (Americas), May 1, Sep 15 (Independence), Oct 3 (Soldiers), 12 (Americas), 21 (Armed Forces), Dec 25; GF, ES, HS, HT

Hong Kong Jan 1, Apr 4 (Tomb Sweeping), May 1, Jul 1 (Establishment), Oct 1 (National), Dec 25, 26; EM, GF, HS, Lunar New year (3), Buddha's Birthday (May), Dragon Boat Festival (Jun), Day after Chinese Mid-Autumn Festival (Sep), Chung Yeung Festival (Oct)

Hungary Jan 1, Mar 15 (Independence), May 1, Aug 20 (National/St Stephen), Oct 23 (Revolution), Nov 1, Dec 25, 26; EM, WM

Iceland Jan 1, May 1, Jun 17 (National), Dec 25, 26; A, EM, ES, GF, HT, WM, Whit Sunday; First Day of Summer (Apr), Commerce (1st Mon in Aug)

India Jan 1 *(some states)*, 26 (Republic), May 1 *(some states)*, Aug 15 (Independence), Oct 2 (Mahatma Ghandi's Birthday), Dec 25; NY (Parsi, Aug, *some states*); *much regional and religious variation*

Indonesia Jan 1, Aug 17 (Independence), D, Ad, ER (2), GF, NY (Balinese Hindu), NY (Chinese), NY (Muslim), PB, Ascension of the Prophet, Waisak (May)

Iran Feb 11 (Islamic Revolution), Mar 19 (Nationalization of Oil), 21 (3), 31 (Islamic Republic), Apr 1 (Nature), Jun 3 (Death of Imam Khomeini), 4 (1963 Uprising); Ad, As, ER, PB, Eid Ghadir Khom, Tasooah, Arbaeen, Death of the Prophet, Martyrdom of Imam Reza, Martyrdom of Hazrat Fatemah, Birthday of Imam Ali, Prophet's call to mission, Ascension of the Prophet, Birthday of Imam Mahdi, Martyrdom of Imam Ali,

Time

Martyrdom of Imam Sadegh

Iraq Jan 1, 6 (Army), Apr 9 (Baghdad Liberation), 17 (FAO), May 1, Jul 14 (Republic), Aug 8 (Ceasefire), Oct 3 (National); Ad (4), As, ER (3), NY (Muslim), PB

Ireland, Republic of Jan 1, Mar 17 (St Patrick), Dec 25, 26; EM, 1st Mon in May, 1st Mon in Jun, 1st Mon in Aug, last Mon in Oct public holidays

Ireland, Northern ▶ Northern Ireland

Israel NY (Jewish) (Sep/Oct) (2), Purim (Mar), Passover (Apr), Holocaust Memorial (Apr), National Memorial (Apr/May), Independence (Apr/May), Pentecost (May/Jun), Tishah beAv (July/Aug), Yom Kippur (Sep/Oct), Feast of Tabernacles (Sep/Oct), Simchat Tora (Oct), Channukah (Dec)

Italy Jan 1, 6, Apr 25 (Liberation), May 1, Jun 2 (National), Aug 15, Nov 1, Dec 8, 25, 26; EM; *much local variation*

Jamaica Jan 1, May 23 (Labour), Aug 1 (Emancipation), 6 (Independence), Dec 25, 26; Ash Wednesday, EM, GF, National Heroes (3rd Mon in Oct)

Japan Jan 1, Feb 11 (National Foundation), Apr 29 (Showa), May 3 (Constitution Memorial), May 4 (Greenery), 5 (Children), Nov 3 (Culture), 23 (Labour Thanksgiving), Dec 23 (Emperor's Birthday); Autumnal Equinox, Coming-of-Age (2nd Mon in Jan), Marine Day (3rd Mon in Jul), Respect for the Aged (3rd Mon in Sep), Physical Fitness (2nd Mon in Oct), Vernal Equinox

Jordan Jan 1, May 1, 25 (Independence), Jun 10 (Army), Dec 25; Ad (4), R, ER (3), NY (Muslim), PB, Ascension of the Prophet

Kazakhstan Jan 1, 2, 7 (Orthodox Christmas), Mar 8 (Women), 21, May 1 (Unity), 9 (Victory), Aug 30 (Constitution), Oct 25 (Republic), Dec 16 (Independence); Ad

Kenya Jan 1, May 1, Jun 1 (Madaraka), Oct 10 (Moi), 20 (Kenyatta), Dec 12 (Jamhuri), 25, 26; EM, ER, GF

Kiribati Jan 1, Mar 8 (Women), Apr 17 (National Health), Jul 11 (Gospel), 12 (Independence) (3), Aug 6 (Youth), Oct 6 (Teachers), Dec 10 (Human Rights), 25, 26; GF, HS, EM, ES; *length of holidays varies locally*

Korea, Democratic People's Republic of (North Korea) Jan 1, Feb 16 (Kim Jong Il's Birthday) (2), Apr 15 (Kim Il Sung's Birthday), Apr 25 (Army Foundation), May 1, Jul 27 (Fatherland Liberation War Victory), Aug 15 (Liberation), Sep 9 (Foundation of the Republic), Oct 10 (Foundation of the Workers' Party), Dec 27 (Constitution); Lunar NY, Harvest Moon Festival (Sep/Oct)

Korea, Republic of (South Korea) Jan 1, Mar 1 (Independence Movement), May 5 (Children), Jun 6 (Memorial), Aug 15 (Liberation), Oct 3 (National Foundation), Dec 25; Lunar NY, Buddha's Birthday (May), Harvest Moon Festival (Sep/Oct)

Kuwait Jan 1, Feb 25 (National), 26 (Liberation); Ad (4), ER (3), NY (Muslim), PB, Ascension of the Prophet

Kyrgyzstan Jan 1, 7 (Russian Orthodox Christmas), Mar 8 (Women), 21 (Kyrgyz New Year), 24 (Revolution), May 1, 5 (Constitution), 9 (Victory), Aug 31 (Independence), Nov 7 (Social Revolution); Ad, ER

Laos Jan 1, Mar 8 (Women), May 1, Jun 1 (Children), Dec 2 (National); New Year/Water Festival (3) (Apr), Boat Racing Festival (Oct), That Luang Festival (Nov)

Latvia Jan 1, May 1, 4 (Independence), Jun 23 (Ligo), 24 (Janis/Summer Solstice), Nov 18 (Proclamation of the Republic), Dec 25, 26, 31; EM, ES, GF; Mothers (2nd Sun in May)

Lebanon Jan 1, 6 (Armenian Christmas), Feb 9 (St Maron), May 1, 6 (Martyrs), 25 (Resistance and Liberation), Aug 15, Nov 1, 22 (Independence), Dec 25; Ad (3), As, EM, GF, ER (3), NY (Muslim), PB

Lesotho Jan 1, Mar 11 (Moshoeshoe), Apr 4 (Heroes), May 1, Jul 17 (King's Birthday), Oct 4 (Independence), Dec 25, 26; A, EM, GF

Liberia Jan 1, Feb 11 (Armed Forces), Mar 15 (J J Roberts), Apr 12 (Redemption), May 14 (National Unification), 25 (Africa), Jul 26 (Independence), Aug 24 (National Flag), Nov 29 (President Tubman's Birthday), Dec 25; Decoration (Mar), National Fast and Prayer (Apr), Thanksgiving (Nov)

Libya Mar 2 (Declaration of Establishment of Authority of People), 28 (Evacuation of British Troops), Jun 11 (Evacuation of US Troops), Jul 23 (Revolution), Sep 1 (National), Oct 7 (Evacuation of Italian Fascists); Ad (4), As, ER (3), PB

Liechtenstein Jan 1, 2 (Berchtold), 6, Feb 2 (Candlemas), Mar 19 (St Joseph), May 1, Aug 15 (National), Sep 8 (Nativity of Our Lady), Nov 1, Dec 8, 24, 25, 26, 31; A, C, CC, EM, ES, GF, WM, Whit Sunday

Lithuania Jan 1, Feb 16 (Independence), Mar 11 (Restoration of Statehood), May 1, Jun 24 (St John), Jul 6 (Coronation of Mindaugas/Statehood), Aug 15, Nov 1, Dec 25, 26; EM, ES; Mother's Day (1st Sun in May)

Luxembourg Jan 1, May 1, Jun 23 (National), Aug 15, Nov 1, Dec 25, 26; A, C, ES, EM, WM

Macedonia Jan 1 (2), 6 (Orthodox Christmas), May 1, 24 (Sts Cyril and Methodius), Aug 2 (Ilinden), Sep 8 (Independence), Oct 11 (Macedonian Rebellion); Orthodox Easter; *considerable religious variation*

Madagascar Jan 1, Mar 29 (Memorial), May 1, Jun 26 (Independence), Aug 15, Nov 1, Dec 25, 30 (National); A, EM, WM

Malawi Jan 1, 15 (Chilembwe), Mar 3 (Martyrs), May 1, 14 (Kamunzu), Jun 14 (Freedom), Jul 6 (Independence), Oct 15 (Mothers), Dec 25, 26; EM, ER, GF

Malaysia May 1, Aug 31 (National), Dec 25; Ad, D, ER (2), NY (Chinese) (Jan/Feb), NY (Muslim), PB, Wesak; Birthday of Yang Di Pertuan Agong (1st Sat in Jun)

Maldives Jan 1, Jul 26 (Independence), Nov 3 (Victory), 11 (Republic); Ad (4), Ar, ER (3), NY (Muslim), PB, R, Day the Maldives Embraced Islam

Mali Jan 1, 20 (Armed Forces), Mar 26 (Democracy), May 1, 25 (Africa), Sep 22 (Independence), Dec 25; Ad, EM, PB

Malta Jan 1, Feb 10 (St Paul's Shipwreck), Mar 19 (St Joseph), 31 (Freedom), May 1, Jun 7 (Sette Giugno), 29 (Sts Peter and Paul), Aug 15, Sep 8 (Our Lady of the Victories), 21 (Independence), Dec 8, 13 (Republic), 25; GF

Marshall Islands Jan 1, Mar 1 (Nuclear Victims), May 1 (Constitution), Nov 17 (President), Dec 25; Fishermen (1st Fri in Jul), Workers (1st Fri in Sep), Customs (last Fri in Sep), Thanksgiving (3rd Thur in Nov), Gospel (1st Fri in Dec)

Mauritania Jan 1, May 1, 25 (Africa), Nov 28 (National); Ad, ER, NY (Muslim), PB

Mauritius Jan 1, 2, Feb 1 (Abolition of Slavery), Mar 12 (National), May 1, Aug 15, Nov 2 (Arrival of Indentured Labourers), Dec 25; Chinese Spring Festival (Jan/Feb), D, ER, Ganesh Chathurti (Aug/Sep), Maha Shivaratree (Feb/Mar), Ougadi (Mar/Apr), Thaipoosam Cavadee (Jan/Feb)

Mexico Jan 1, Feb 5 (Constitution), 24 (Flag), Mar 21 (Birthday of Benito Juárez), May 1, 5 (Cinco de Mayo), Jun 1 (Navy), Sep 16 (Independence), Nov 20 (Mexican Revolution), Dec 25; HT, GF, EM

Micronesia, Federated States of Jan 1, May 10 (Proclamation of the Federated States of Micronesia), Oct 24 (United Nations), Nov 4 (National Day), Dec 25; *additional days vary between states*

Moldova Jan 1, 7 (Orthodox Christmas) (2), Mar 8 (Women), May 1, 5 (Memorial), 9 (Victory), Aug 27 (Independence), 31 (National Language); EM (Orthodox), ES

Monaco Jan 1, 27 (St Devote), May 1, Aug 15, Nov 1, 19 (National), Dec 8, 25; A, CC, EM, WM

Mongolia Jan 1, Mar 8 (Women), Jun 1 (Mothers and Children), Jul 10 (People's Revolution)' (3), Nov 26 (Independence); NY (lunar)

Montenegro Jan 1 (2), 7 (Orthodox Christmas) (2), May 1 (2), Jul 13 (National) (2); Orthodox Easter

Morocco Jan 1, 11 (Independence Manifesto), May 1, 23 (National), Jul 30 (Throne Day), Aug 14 (Qued-ed-Dahab Allegiance), Aug 20 (King and People), 21 (King's Birthday), Nov 6 (Green March), 18 (Independence); Ad, ER, NY (Muslim), PB

Mozambique Jan 1, Feb 3 (Heroes), Apr 7 (Mozambican Women), May 1, Jun 25 (Independence), Sep 7 (Lusaka Agreement), 26 (Armed Forces), Oct 4 (Peace and Reconciliation), Dec 25 (Christmas/Family)

Myanmar (Burma) Jan 4 (Independence), Feb 12 (Union), Mar 2 (Peasants), 27 (Armed Forces), May 1, Jul 19 (Martyrs), Dec 25; D, 4 Full Moon days, National (Nov/Dec), NY (Burmese), Tazaungdaing Festival (Nov), Thingyan (Apr) (5)

Namibia Jan 1, Mar 21 (Independence), May 1, 4 (Cassinga), 25 (Africa), Aug 26 (Heroes), Dec 10 (Human Rights), Dec 25, 26 (Family/Goodwill); A, GF, EM

Nauru Jan 1, 31 (Independence), May 17 (Constitution), Sep 25 (Youth), Oct 26 (Angam), Dec 25, 26; GF, EM, Easter Tuesday

Nepal Jan 29 (Martyrs), Feb 19 (Democracy), Apr 14 (Ramnawami), May 1, Aug 16 (Janai Purnima), Dec 25; D, NY (Nepalese) (Apr), Shivaratri (Feb/Mar), Restoration of Democracy (Apr), Buddha (May), Krishna Janmasthami (Aug), Ghatasthapana (Sep), Dashain Festival (Oct) (6)

Netherlands Jan 1, Apr 30 (Queen's Birthday), May 5 (Liberation), Dec 25, 26; A, EM, ES, GF, WM

New Zealand Jan 1, 2, Feb 6 (Waitangi), Apr 25 (Anzac), Dec 25, 26; EM, GF, Queen's Birthday (1st Mon in Jun), Labour (4th Mon in Oct)

Nicaragua Jan 1, May 1, Jul 19 (Sandinista Revolution), Sep 14 (Battle of San Jacinto), 15 (Independence), Dec 8, 25; GF, HT

Niger Jan 1, Apr 24 (Concord), May 1, Aug 3 (Independence), Dec 18 (Republic), 25; Ad, EM, ER, PB

Nigeria Jan 1, May 1, 29 (Democracy), Oct 1 (National), Dec 25, 26; Ad, EM, ER, ES, GF, PB

Northern Ireland Jan 1, Mar 17 (St Patrick), Dec 25, 26; GF, EM; Early May and Spring (May) Bank Holidays, Battle of the Boyne/Orangemen (Jul), Summer Bank Holiday (Aug)

Norway Jan 1, May 1, 17 (Constitution), Dec 25, 26; A, EM, GF, HT, Palm Sunday, WM

Oman Jan 1, Nov 18 (National) (2); Ad (5), ER (4), NY (Muslim), PB

Pakistan Mar 23 (Pakistan), Aug 14 (Independence), Nov 9 (Iqbal), Dec 25 (Christmas/Birthday of Quaid-e-Azam); Ad (2), As (2), ER (3), PB; *additional religious optional holidays*

Palau Jan 1, Mar 15 (Youth), May 5 (Senior Citizens), Jun 1 (President), Jul 9 (Constitution), Oct 1 (Independence), 24 (United Nations), Dec 25; Labour Day (1st Mon in Sep), Thanksgiving (last Thurs in Nov)

Panama Jan 1, 9 (Martyrs), May 1, Nov 3 (Independence), 4 (Flag), 10 (First Call for Independence), 28 (Independence from Spain), Dec 8 (Mothers), 25; C, GF; *some local variation*

Papua New Guinea Jan 1, Jul 23 (Remembrance), Sep 16 (Independence), Dec 25, 26; EM, GF; Queen's Birthday (Jun)

Paraguay Jan 1, Mar 1 (Heroes), May 1, 15 (Independence), Jun 12 (Chaco Peace), Aug 15 (Foundation of Asuncion), Sep 29 (Battle of Boqueron), Dec 8, 25; EM, GF, HT

Peru Jan 1, May 1, Jun 29 (Sts Peter and Paul), Jul 28 (Independence), Aug 30 (St Rosa de Lima), Oct 8 (Battle of Angamos), Nov 1, Dec 8, 25; GF, HT

Philippines Jan 1, Apr 9 (Bataan), May 1, Jun 12 (Independence), Nov 1, 30 (Bonifacio), Dec 25, 30 (Rizal), 31; GF, HT, National Heroes (last Sun in Aug)

Poland Jan 1, May 1, 3 (National), Aug 15, Nov 1, 11 (Independence), Dec 25, 26; CC, EM, ES

Portugal Jan 1, Apr 25 (Liberty), May 1, Jun 10 (National), Aug 15, Oct 5 (Republic), Nov 1, Dec 1 (Independence), 8, 25; C, CC, GF

Qatar Sep 3 (Independence), Dec 18 (National); Ad (4), ER (4), NY (Muslim)

Romania Jan 1, 2, May 1, Dec 1 (National), 25, 26; Orthodox Easter (Apr/May) (2); *other major religions each have 2 days for festivals*

Russia Jan 1, 2, 7 (Russian Orthodox Christmas), Feb 24 (Soldiers), Mar 8 (Women), May 1 (Spring and Labour) (2), 9 (Victory), Jun 12 (Independence), Nov 4 (Unity), Dec 25, 26; Russian Orthodox Easter (Apr/May)

Rwanda Jan 1, 28 (Democracy), Feb 1 (National Heroes), Apr 7 (Genocide Memorial), May 1, Jul 1 (Independence), 5 (Freedom), Aug 15, Oct 1 (Patriots), Dec 25, 26; EM, GF

St Christopher and Nevis Jan 1, 2, Sep 16 (National Heroes), 19 (Independence), Dec 25, 26; EM, GF, WM, Labour (May), August Monday, Culturama (day after August Monday)

St Lucia Jan 1, 2, Feb 22 (Independence), May 1, Aug 1 (Emancipation), Oct 6 (Thanksgiving), Dec 13 (National), Dec 25, 26; CC, EM, WM

St Vincent and the Grenadines Jan 1, Mar 14 (National Heroes), Aug 1 (Emancipation), Oct 27 (Independence), Dec 25, 26; C (Jul) (2), EM, GF, WM; Caricom (Jul), Labour (May)

Samoa Jan 1, 2, May 14 (Mothers), Jun 1 (Independence), Aug 11 (Fathers), Dec 25, 26; EM, GF

San Marino Jan 1, 6, Feb 5 (Liberation and St Agatha), Mar 25 (Arengo), Apr 1 (Captains Regents' Ceremony), May 1, Jul 28 (Fall of Fascism), Aug 15, Sep 3 (San Marino and Republic), Oct 1 (Investiture of the New

Time

Captains Regent), Nov 1, 2, Dec 8, 24, 25, 26, 31; CC, EM

São Tomé and Príncipe Jan 1, Feb 3 (Liberty Heroes), May 1, Jul 12 (National Independence), Sep 6 (Armed Forces), 30 (Agricultural Reform), Dec 21 (São Tomé Day), 25

Saudi Arabia Sep 23 (National); Ad (4), ER (3)

Scotland Jan 1, 2, Nov 30 (St Andrew; optional bank holiday), Dec 25, 26; GF; Early May, Spring (May) and Summer (Aug) Bank Holidays

Senegal Jan 1, Apr 4 (National), May 1, Aug 15, Nov 1, Dec 25; A, Ad, As, EM, ER, NY (Muslim), PB, WM

Serbia Jan 1, 2, 7 (Orthodox Christmas), Feb 15 (Statehood), May 1 (2); Orthodox Easter (Apr/May) (4)

Seychelles Jan 1, 2, May 1, Jun 5 (Liberation), 18 (National), 29 (Independence), Aug 15, Nov 1, Dec 8, 25; CC, GF, HS

Sierra Leone Jan 1, Apr 27 (Independence), Dec 25, 26; Ad, EM, ER, GF, PB

Singapore Jan 1, May 1, Aug 9 (National), Dec 25; Ad, D, ER, GF, NY (Chinese, Jan/Feb) (2), Vesak (Apr/May)

Slovakia Jan 1 (New Year/Establishment of Republic), 6, May 1, 8 (Triumph over Fascism), Jul 5 (Sts Cyril and Methodius), Aug 29 (Slovak National Uprising), Sep 1 (Constitution), 15 (Our Lady of the Seven Sorrows), Nov 1, 17 (Freedom and Democracy), Dec 24, 25, 26; GF, EM

Slovenia Jan 1, 2, Feb 8 (Culture), Apr 27 (National Resistance), May 1 (2), Jun 25 (National), Aug 15, Oct 31 (Reformation), Nov 1, Dec 25, 26 (Independence); EM

Solomon Islands Jan 1, Jul 7 (Independence), Dec 25, 26; EM, ES, GF, HS, WM, Queen's Birthday (Jun)

Somalia Jan 1, May 1, Jun 26 (Independence), Jul 1 (Republic), Ad, As, ER, NY (Muslim), PB

South Africa Jan 1, Mar 21 (Human Rights), Apr 27 (Freedom Day), May 1, Jun 16 (Youth), Aug 9 (Women), Sep 24 (Heritage), Dec 16 (Reconciliation), 25, 26 (Goodwill); GF, EM (Family)

Spain Jan 1, 6, May 1, Aug 15, Oct 12 (National), Nov 1, Dec 6 (Constitution), 8, 25; ES, GF, HT (*most areas*); *much regional variation*

Sri Lanka Jan 14 (Tamil Thai Pongal), Feb 4 (National), May 1, Dec 25; Ad, D, ER, GF, NY (Sinhala/Tamil) (Apr) (2), PB, Mahasivarathri (Feb/Mar), Full Moon (*monthly*), day following Vesak Full Moon (May)

Sudan Jan 1 (Independence), 9 (Peace Agreement), Jun 30 (Revolution), Aug 9 (Indigenous People), Dec 25; Ad (4), ER (3), NY (Muslim), PB, Sham al-Naseem (Apr/May), Ascension of the Prophet

Suriname Jan 1, May 1, Jul 1 (Freedom), Aug 9 (Indigenous People), Nov 25 (Independence), Dec 25, 26; EM, ER, GF, Holi Phagwa (Mar)

Swaziland Jan 1, Apr 19 (King's Birthday), 25 (National Flag), May 1, Jul 22 (Birthday of King Sobhuza), Sep 6 (Independence), Dec 25, 26; A, EM, GF; Incwala (Dec/Jan), Umhlanga/Reed Dance (Aug/Sep)

Sweden Jan 1, 6, May 1, Jun 6 (National), Nov 1, Dec 25, 26; A, EM, GF; Midsummer (Jun)

Switzerland Jan 1, 2 (Berchtold), Aug 1 (National), Dec 25, 26; A, EM, GF, WM; *other canton and local holidays*

Syria Jan 1, Mar 8 (Revolution), 21 (Mothers), Apr 17 (Evacuation), May 1, 6 (Martyrs), Oct 6 (Liberation War), Dec 25; Ad (4), ER (3), ES, NY (Muslim), PB; Orthodox Easter (Apr/May)

Taiwan Jan 1 (Foundation of the Republic of China), Feb 28 (Peace Memorial), Apr 5 (Tomb Sweeping), May 1, Oct 10 (National); NY (Chinese) (Jan/Feb) (3), Dragon Boat Festival (Jun), Moon Festival (Sep/Oct)

Tajikistan Jan 1, Mar 8 (Women), 21, May 1, 9 (Victory), Jun 27 (National Unity), Sep 9 (Independence) Nov 6 (Constitution); Ad, ER

Tanzania Jan 1, 12 (Zanzibar Revolution), Apr 26 (Union), May 1, Jul 7 (Industrial), Aug 8 (Farmers), Oct 14 (Nyerere Day), Dec 9 (Independence/Republic), 25, 26; Ad, EM, ER (2), GF, NY (Muslim), PB, R

Thailand Jan 1, Apr 6 (Chakri), 13 (Songkran) (3), May 1, 5 (Coronation), Aug 12 (Queen's Birthday), Oct 23 (Chulalongkorn Memorial), Dec 5 (King's Birthday), 10 (Constitution), 31; Buddhist Lent (Jul), Makha Bucha (Feb), Visakha Bucha (May)

Timor-Leste Jan 1, May 1, 20 (Independence), Aug 30 (Popular Consultation), Nov 1, 2, 12 (Santa Cruz), Dec 8, 25; GF

Togo Jan 1, Apr 27 (Independence), May 1, Jun 21 (Martyrs), Aug 15, Nov 1, Dec 25; A, Ad, EM, ER (2), WM

Tonga Jan 1, Apr 25 (Anzac), Jun 4 (Emancipation), Jul 12 (Crown Prince's Birthday), Aug 1 (King Tupuo V's Birthday and Coronation), Nov 4 (Constitution), Dec 4 (King Tupou I), 25, 26; EM, GF

Trinidad and Tobago Jan 1, Mar 30 (Spiritual Baptist Liberation), May 30 (Indian Arrival), Jun 19 (Labour), Aug 1 (Emancipation), 31 (Independence), Sept 24 (Republic), Dec 25, 26; CC, D, EM, ER, GF

Tunisia Jan 1, Mar 20 (Independence), 21 (Youth), Apr 9 (Martyrs), May 1, Jul 25 (Republic), Aug 13 (Women), Nov 7 (Commemoration); Ad (2), ER (2), NY (Muslim), PB

Turkey Jan 1, Apr 23 (National Sovereignty and Children), May 19 (Atatürk Commemoration/Youth and Sports), Aug 30 (Victory), Oct 29 (Republic); Ad (4), ER (3)

Turkmenistan Jan 1, 12 (Memorial), Feb 19 (Flag Day), Mar 8 (Women), 21, May 9 (Victory), 18 (Revival and Unity), Jun 21 (Election of First President), Oct 6 (Remembrance), 27 (Independence) (2), Dec 12 (Neutrality); Ad, ER

Tuvalu Jan 1, May 12 (Gospel), Aug 5 (Children), Oct 1 (Independence) (2), Nov 11 (Prince of Wales's Birthday), Dec 25, 26; EM, GF; Commonwealth Day (2nd Mon in Mar), Queen's Birthday (Jun)

Uganda Jan 1, 26 (Liberation), Mar 8 (Women), May 1, Jun 3 (Martyrs), 9 (Heroes), Oct 9 (Independence), Dec 25, 26; Ad, EM, ER, GF

UK ▶ England and Wales; Northern Ireland; Scotland

Ukraine Jan 1, 7 (Eastern Orthodox Christmas), Mar 8 (Women), May 1 (2), 9 (Victory), Jun 28 (Constitution), Aug 24 (Independence); Orthodox Easter (Apr/May) (2), Orthodox Pentecost (2)

United Arab Emirates Jan 1, Dec 2 (National); Ad (4), Ascension of the Prophet, ER (3), NY (Muslim), PB

Uruguay Jan 1, 6, Apr 19 (Landing of the 33 Patriots), May 1, 18 (Battle of Las Piedras), Jun 19 (Artigas's Birthday), Jul 18 (Constitution), Aug 25 (Independence), Oct 12 (Americas), Nov 2, Dec 25; C (2), GF, HT

USA Jan 1, Jul 4 (Independence), Nov 11 (Veterans), Dec 25; Martin Luther King's Birthday (3rd Mon in Jan), Washington's Birthday (3rd Mon in Feb), Memorial (last Mon in May), Labor (1st Mon in Sep), Columbus

(2nd Mon in Oct), Thanksgiving (4th Thurs in Nov); *additional days vary between states*

Uzbekistan Jan 1, Mar 8 (Women), 21, May 9 (Memory and Respect), Sep 1 (Independence), Oct 1 (Teachers), Dec 8 (Constitution); Ad, ER

Vanuatu Jan 1, Feb 21 (Father Lini), Mar 5 (Custom Chiefs), May 1, Jul 24 (Children), 30 (Independence), Aug 15, Oct 5 (Constitution), Nov 29 (Unity), Dec 25, 26 (Family); A, EM, ES, GF

Venezuela Jan 1, Apr 19 (Independence), May 1, Jun 24 (Battle of Carabobo), Jul 5 (National), 24 (Bolívar's Birthday), Oct 12 (Indigenous Resistance), Dec 25; C (2), EM, GF, HT

Vietnam Jan 1, Apr 30 (Saigon Liberation), May 1, Sep 2 (National); NY (Vietnamese) (4)

Western Samoa ▶ Samoa

Yemen Jan 1, May 1, 22 (Unity), Sep 26 (Revolution), Oct 14 (National), Nov 30 (Independence); Ad (5), ER (4), NY (Muslim), PB

Yugoslavia ▶ Montenegro; Serbia

Zaire ▶ Congo, Democratic Republic of

Zambia Jan 1, May 1, 25 (African Freedom), Oct 24 (Independence), Dec 25; EM, GF, HS; Youth (2nd Mon in Mar), Heroes (1st Mon in Jul), Unity (1st Tues in Jul), Farmers (1st Mon in Aug)

Zimbabwe Jan 1, Apr 18 (Independence), May 1, 25 (Africa), Aug 11 (Heroes), 12 (Defence Forces), Dec 22 (Unity), 25, 26; EM, GF, HS

COMMUNICATION

Languages: number of speakers

Language families

Estimates of the numbers of speakers in the main language families of the world. The list includes Japanese and Korean, which are not clearly related to any other languages.

Main language families		Main language families	
Indo-European	2 563 000 000	Nilo-Saharan	35 000 000
Sino-Tibetan	1 276 000 000	Uralic	23 000 000
Niger-Congo	358 000 000	Quechuan	10 000 000
Afro-Asiatic	339 000 000	Hmong-Mien	6 000 000
Austronesian	312 000 000	Mayan	6 000 000
Dravidian	222 000 000	Tupi	5 000 000
Altaic	145 000 000	Kartvelian	5 000 000
Japanese	122 000 000	North Caucasian	5 000 000
Austro-Asiatic	101 000 000	Aymaran	2 000 000
Tai-Kadai	78 000 000	Uto-Aztecan	2 000 000
Korean	67 000 000	Oto-Manguean	2 000 000

Specific languages

The first column gives estimates for mother-tongue speakers of the 20 most widely used languages. The second column gives estimates of the total population of all countries where the language has official or semi-official status; these totals are often overestimates, as only a minority of people in countries where a second language is recognized may actually be fluent in it.

Mother-tongue speakers		Official language populations	
Chinese (Mandarin)	873 000 000	English	2 300 000 000
Spanish	322 000 000	Chinese	1 330 000 000
English	309 000 000	Hindi	1 150 000 000
Arabic	206 000 000	Spanish	407 000 000
Hindi	180 000 000	French	367 000 000
Portuguese	177 000 000	Arabic	364 000 000
Bengali	171 000 000	Portuguese	243 000 000
Russian	145 000 000	Bengali	233 000 000
Japanese	122 000 000	Russian	171 000 000
German	95 000 000	Malay	160 000 000
Javanese	76 000 000	Japanese	122 000 000
Telugu	70 000 000	German	100 000 000
Marathi	68 000 000	Urdu	85 000 000
Korean	67 000 000	Italian	60 000 000
Vietnamese	67 000 000	Korean	60 000 000
Tamil	66 000 000	Vietnamese	60 000 000
French	65 000 000	Persian	55 000 000
Bihari	64 000 000	Tagalog	50 000 000
Italian	61 000 000	Thai	50 000 000
Panjabi	60 000 000	Turkish	50 000 000

Speakers of English

The first column gives figures for countries where English is used as a mother tongue or first language; for countries where no figure is given, English is not the first language of a significant number of people. (A question mark indicates that no agreed estimates are available.) An asterisk indicates that the figure includes speakers of an English-based creole. The second column gives total population figures (mainly 1996 estimates) for countries where English has official or semi-official status as a medium of communication. These totals are likely to bear little correlation with the real use of English in the area.

Country	First language speakers of English	Country population	Country	First language speakers of English	Country population
Anguilla*	14 100	14 100	Nepal	?	20 892 000
Antigua and			New Zealand	3 290 000	3 619 000
Barbuda*	84 500	84 500	Nigeria	?	103 912 000
Australia	17 700 000	18 287 000	Pakistan	?	133 500 000
The Bahamas*	307 000	307 000	Papua New Guinea*	2 000 000	5 932 000
Bangladesh	3 200 000	123 100 000	Philippines	30 000	71 750 000
Barbados*	282 000	282 000	Samoa	1 000	214 000
Belize*	111 000	219 000	St Kitts and Nevis*	39 400	39 400
Bermuda	61 000	61 400	St Lucia	1 600	144 000
Bhutan	?	682 000	St Vincent and the		
Botswana	590 000	1 478 000	Grenadines*	100 000+	113 000
Brunei	10 000	290 000	Seychelles	2 000	76 100
Cameroon	2 720 000	13 609 000	Sierra Leone	700 000	4 617 000
Canada	17 100 000	29 784 000	Singapore	1 139 000	3 045 000
Dominica	10 000	73 800	Solomon Islands		396 000
Fiji	15 000	802 000	South Africa	3 800 000	41 734 000
Ghana	?	16 904 000	Sri Lanka	74 000	18 318 000
Gibraltar	24 000	27 100	Suriname		436 000
Grenada*	90 000	97 900	Swaziland		934 000
Guyana*	700 000+	825 000	Tanzania	900 000	29 165 000
India	330 000	952 969 000	Tonga		101 000
Ireland	3 599 000	3 599 000	Trinidad and		
Jamaica*	2 505 000	2 505 000	Tobago*	1 262 000	1 262 000
Kenya		29 137 000	Tuvalu		9 500
Kiribati	500	81 800	Uganda	190 000	20 158 000
Lesotho		2 017 000	UK	57 190 000	58 784 000
Liberia*	570 000	2 110 000	USA	228 700 000	265 455 000
Malawi	540 000	9 453 000	US territories in		
Malaysia	100 000	20 359 000	Pacific	?	196 300
Malta	8 000	373 000	Vanuatu	60 000	172 000
Mauritius	2 000	1 141 000	Zambia	300 000	9 715 000
Montserrat*	8 000	12 000	Zimbabwe	260 000	11 515 000
Namibia	13 000	1 709 000	Other British		
Nauru	700	10 600	territories	?	106 167

Foreign words and phrases

See also Culinary terms of foreign origin p 153.

ab initio (Lat) 'from the beginning'.

à bon marché (Fr) 'good market'; at a good bargain, cheap.

ab ovo (Lat) 'from the egg'; from the beginning.

absit omen (Lat) a superstitious formula; may there be no ill omen (as in a reference just made).

a cappella (Ital) 'in the style of the chapel'; sung without instrumental accompaniment.

Achtung (Ger) 'Look out! Take care!'.

acushla (Ir) term of endearment; darling.

addendum *plural* **addenda** (Lat) 'that which is to be added'; supplementary material for a book.

à deux (Fr) 'for two'; often denotes a dinner or conversation of a romantic nature.

ad hoc (Lat) 'towards this'; for this special purpose.

ad hominem (Lat) 'to the man'; appealing not to logic or reason but to personal preferences or feelings.

ad infinitum (Lat) 'to infinity'; denotes endless repetition.

ad litem (Lat) 'for the lawsuit'; used of a guardian appointed to act in court (eg because of insanity or insufficient years of the litigant).

ad nauseam (Lat) 'to the point of sickness'; disgustingly endless or repetitive.

ad referendum (Lat) 'for reference'; to be further considered.

ad valorem (Lat) 'to value'; 'according to what it is worth'; often used of taxes etc.

advocatus diaboli (Lat) 'devil's advocate'; person opposing an argument in order to expose any flaws in it.

affaire (Fr) liaison, intrigue; an incident arousing speculation and scandal.

afflatus (Lat) 'blowing or breathing'; inspiration (often divine).

aficionado (Span) 'amateur'; an ardent follower; a 'fan'.

a fortiori (Lat) 'from the stronger' (argument);

Communication

Communication

denotes the validity and stronger reason of a proposition.

agent provocateur (Fr) 'provocative agent'; someone who incites others, by pretended sympathy, to commit crimes.

aggiornamento (Ital) 'modernization'; reform (often political).

aide-de-camp (Fr) 'assistant on the field'; an officer who acts as a confidential personal assistant for an officer of higher rank.

aide-mémoire (Fr) 'help-memory'; a reminder; memorandum-book; a written summary of a diplomatic agreement.

à la carte (Fr) 'from the menu'; each dish individually priced.

à la mode (Fr) 'in fashion, fashionable'; also a culinary term.

al fresco (Ital) 'fresh'; painting on fresh or moist plaster; in the fresh, cool or open air.

alma mater (Lat) 'bountiful mother'; one's former school, college, or university; official college or university song (American English).

aloha (Hawaiian) 'love'; a salutation, 'hello' or 'goodbye'.

alumnus *plural* **alumni** (Lat) 'pupil' or 'foster son'; a former pupil or student.

ambiance (Fr) surroundings, atmosphere.

amende honorable (Fr) a public apology satisfying the honour of the injured party.

amour-propre (Fr) 'own love, self-love'; legitimate self-esteem, sometimes exaggerated; vanity, conceit.

ancien régime (Fr) 'old regime'; a superseded and outdated political system or ruling élite.

angst (Ger) 'anxiety'; an unsettling feeling produced by awareness of the uncertainties and paradoxes inherent in the state of being human.

anno Domini (Lat) 'in the year of the Lord'; used in giving dates of the Christian era, counting forward from the year of Christ's birth.

annus mirabilis (Lat) 'year of wonders'; a remarkably successful or auspicious year.

Anschluss (Ger) 'joining together'; union, especially the political union of Germany and Austria in 1938.

antebellum (Lat) 'before the war'; denotes a period before a specific war, especially the American Civil War.

ante meridiem (Lat) 'before midday'; between midnight and noon, abbreviated to am.

à point (Fr) 'into the right condition'; to a nicety, a culinary term.

a posteriori (Lat) 'from the later'; applied to reasoning from experience, from effect to cause; inductive reasoning.

apparatchik (Russ) a Communist spy or agent; (humorous) any bureaucratic hack.

appellation contrôlée (Fr) 'certified name'; used in the labelling of French wines, a guarantee of specified conditions of origin, strength, etc.

après-ski (Fr) 'after-ski'; pertaining to the evening's amusements after skiing.

a priori (Lat) 'from the previous'; denotes argument from the cause to the effect; deductive reasoning.

atelier (Fr) a workshop; an artist's studio.

au contraire (Fr) 'on the contrary'.

au fait (Fr) 'to the point'; highly skilled; knowledgeable or familiar with something.

au fond (Fr) 'at the bottom'; fundamentally.

au naturel (Fr) 'in the natural state'; naked; also a culinary term.

au pair (Fr) 'on an equal basis'; originally an arrangement of mutual service without payment; now used of a girl (usually foreign) who performs domestic duties for board, lodging and pocket money.

auto-da-fé (Port) 'act of the faith'; the public declaration or carrying out of a sentence imposed on heretics in Spain and Portugal by the Inquisition, eg burning at the stake.

avant-garde (Fr) 'front guard'; applied to those in the forefront of an artistic movement.

ave atque vale (Lat) hail and farewell.

babushka (Russ) 'grandmother'; granny; a triangular headscarf worn under the chin.

baksheesh (Persian) a gift or present of money, particularly in the East (India, Turkey, Egypt, etc).

bal costumé (Fr) a fancy-dress ball.

banzai (Jap) a Japanese battle cry, salute to the emperor, or exclamation of joy.

barrio (Span) 'district, suburb'; a community (usually poor) of Spanish-speaking immigrants (esp American English).

batik (Javanese) 'painted'; method of producing patterns on fabric by drawing with wax before dyeing.

beau geste (Fr) 'beautiful gesture'; a magnanimous action.

belle époque (Fr) 'fine period'; the time of gracious living for the well-to-do immediately preceding World War I.

bête noire (Fr) 'black beast'; a bugbear; something one especially dislikes.

Bildungsroman (Ger) 'educational novel'; a novel concerning its hero's early spiritual and emotional development and education.

blasé (Fr) 'cloyed'; dulled to enjoyment.

blitzkrieg (Ger) 'lightning war'; a sudden overwhelming attack by ground and air forces; a burst of intense activity.

bodega (Span) a wine shop that usually sells food as well; a building for wine storage.

bona fides (Lat) 'good faith'; genuineness.

bonne-bouche (Fr) 'good mouth'; a delicious morsel eaten at the end of a meal.

bonsai (Jap) art of growing miniature trees in pots; a dwarf tree grown by this method.

bon vivant (Fr) 'good living (person)'; one who lives well, particularly enjoying good food and wine; a jovial companion.

bon voyage (Fr) have a safe and pleasant journey.

bourgeois (Fr) 'citizen'; a member of the middle class; a merchant; conventional, conservative.

camera obscura (Lat) 'dark room'; a light-free chamber in which an image of outside objects is thrown upon a screen.

canard (Fr) 'duck'; a false rumour; a second wing fitted as a horizontal stabilizer near the nose of an aircraft.

carpe diem (Lat) 'seize the day'; enjoy the pleasures of the present moment while they last.

carte blanche (Fr) 'blank sheet of paper'; freedom of action.

casus belli (Lat) 'occasion of war'; whatever sparks off or justifies a war or quarrel.

cause célèbre (Fr) a very notable or famous trial; a notorious controversy.

caveat emptor (Lat) 'let the buyer beware'; warns the buyer to examine carefully the article about to be purchased.

c'est la vie (Fr) 'that's life'; denotes fatalistic resignation.

chacun à son goût (Fr) 'each to his own taste'; implies surprise at another's choice.

chambré (Fr) 'put into a room'; (of red wine) at room temperature.

chargé-d'affaires (Fr) a diplomatic agent of lesser rank; an ambassador's deputy.

chef d'oeuvre (Fr) a masterpiece; the best piece of

work by a particular artist, writer, etc.

chicano (Span) *mejicano* 'Mexican'; or an American of Mexican descent.

chutzpah (Yiddish) 'effrontery'; nerve to do or say outrageous things.

cinéma vérité (Fr) 'cinema truth'; realism in films usually sought by photographic scenes of real life.

cinquecento (Ital) 'five hundred'; of the Italian art and literature of the 16c Renaissance period.

circa (Lat) 'surrounding'; of dates and numbers: approximately.

cliché (Fr) 'stereotype printing block'; the impression made by a die in any soft metal; a hackneyed phrase or concept.

cognoscente *plural* **cognoscenti** (Ital) 'one who knows'; one who professes critical knowledge of art, music, etc; a connoisseur.

coitus interruptus (Lat) 'interrupted intercourse'; coitus intentionally interrupted by withdrawal before semen is ejaculated; anticlimax when something ends prematurely.

comme il faut (Fr) 'as it is necessary'; correct; genteel.

compos mentis (Lat) 'having control of one's mind'; sane.

contra mundum (Lat) 'against the world'; denotes defiant perseverance despite universal criticism.

cordon bleu (Fr) 'blue ribbon'; denotes food cooked to a very high standard.

coup de foudre (Fr) 'flash of lightning'; a sudden and astonishing happening; love at first sight.

coup de grâce (Fr) 'blow of mercy'; a finishing blow to end pain; a decisive action which ends a troubled enterprise.

coup d'état (Fr) 'blow of state'; a violent overthrow of a government or subversive stroke of state policy.

coupé (Fr) 'cut'; (usually) two-door motor-car with sloping roof.

crème de la crème (Fr) 'cream of the cream'; the very best.

cuisine minceur (Fr) 'slenderness cooking'; a style of cooking characterized by imaginative use of light, simple, low-fat ingredients.

cul-de-sac (Fr) 'bottom of the bag'; a road closed at one end.

cum grano salis (Lat) with a grain (pinch) of salt.

curriculum vitae (Lat) 'course of life'; denotes a summary of someone's educational qualifications and work experience for presenting to a prospective employer.

décolleté (Fr) 'with bared neck and shoulders'; with neck uncovered; (of dress) low-cut.

de facto (Lat) 'from the fact'; in fact; actually; irrespective of what is legally recognized.

de gustibus non est disputandum (Lat) (often in English shortened for convenience to *de gustibus*) 'there is no disputing about tastes'; there is no sense in challenging people's preferences.

déjà vu (Fr) 'already seen'; in any of the arts: unoriginal material; an illusion of having experienced something before; something seen so often it has become tedious.

de jure (Lat) 'according to law'; denotes the legal or theoretical position, which may not correspond with reality.

delirium tremens (Lat) 'trembling delirium'; psychotic condition caused by alcoholism, involving anxiety, shaking, hallucinations, etc.

Deo volente (Lat) 'God willing'; a sort of good-luck talisman.

de rigueur (Fr) 'of strictness'; compulsory; required by strict etiquette.

derrière (Fr) 'behind'; the buttocks.

déshabillé (Fr) 'undressed'; state of being only partially dressed, or of being casually dressed.

de trop (Fr) 'of too much'; superfluous; in the way.

deus ex machina (Lat) 'a god from a machine'; a contrived solution to a difficulty in a plot.

distingué (Fr) 'distinguished'; having an aristocratic or refined demeanour; striking.

dolce far niente (Ital) 'sweet doing nothing'; denotes the pleasure of idleness.

doppelgänger (Ger) 'double goer'; a ghostly duplicate of a living person; a wraith; someone who looks exactly like someone else.

double entendre (Fr) 'double meaning'; ambiguity (normally with indecent connotations).

doyen (Fr) 'dean'; most distinguished member or representative by virtue of seniority, experience, and often also excellence.

droit du seigneur (Fr) 'the lord's right'; originally the alleged right of a feudal superior to take the virginity of a vassal's bride; any excessive claim imposed on a subordinate.

Dummkopf (Ger) 'dumb-head'; blockhead; idiot.

echt (Ger) 'real, genuine'; denotes authenticity, typicality.

Eheu fugaces (Lat); opening of a quotation (Horace *Odes* II, XIV, 1–2) 'Alas! the fleeting years slip away'; bemoans the brevity of human existence.

élan (Fr) 'dash, rush, bound'; flair; flamboyance.

El Dorado (Span) 'the gilded man'; the golden land (or city) imagined by the Spanish conquerors of America; any place which offers the opportunity of acquiring fabulous wealth.

embarras de richesse (Fr) 'embarrassment of wealth'; a perplexing amount of wealth or an abundance of any kind.

embonpoint (Fr) *en bon point* 'in fine form'; well-fed; stout; plump.

emeritus (Lat) 'having served one's time'; eg of a retired professor, honourably discharged from a public duty; holding a position on an honorary basis only.

éminence grise (Fr) 'grey eminence'; someone exerting power through their influence over a superior.

enfant terrible (Fr) 'terrible child'; a precocious child whose sayings embarrass its parents; a person whose behaviour is indiscreet, embarrassing to his associates.

ennui (Fr) 'boredom'; world-weary listlessness.

en passant (Fr) 'in passing'; by the way; incidentally; applied in chess to the taking of a pawn that has just moved two squares as if it had moved only one.

en route (Fr) 'on the way, on the road'; let us go.

entente (Fr) 'understanding'; a friendly agreement between nations.

épater les bourgeois (Fr) 'shock the middle class'; to disconcert the prim and proper; commonly used of artistic productions which defy convention.

erratum *plural* **errata** (Lat) an error in writing or printing.

ersatz (Ger) 'replacement, substitute'; connotes a second-rate substitute; a supplementary reserve from which waste can be made good.

et al (Lat) *et alii* 'and other things'; used to avoid giving a complete and possibly over-lengthy list of all items eg of authors.

Et tu, Brute? (Lat) 'You too, Brutus?' (Caesar's alleged exclamation when he saw Brutus among his assassins); denotes surprise and dismay that a supposed friend has joined in a conspiracy against one.

eureka (Gr) *heureka* 'I have found!'; cry of triumph at a discovery.

Communication

ex cathedra (Lat) 'from the seat'; from the chair of office; authoritatively; judicially.

ex gratia (Lat) 'from favour'; of a payment; one that is made as a favour, without any legal obligation and without admitting legal liability.

ex officio (Lat) 'from office, by virtue of office'; used as a reason for membership of a body.

ex parte (Lat) 'from (one) part, from (one) side'; on behalf of one side only in legal proceedings; partial; prejudiced.

fait accompli (Fr) 'accomplished fact'; already done or settled, and therefore irreversible.

fata Morgana (Ital) a striking kind of mirage, attributed to witchcraft.

fatwa (Arabic) 'the statement of a formal legal opinion'; a formal legal opinion delivered by an Islamic religious leader.

faute de mieux (Fr) 'for lack of anything better'.

faux ami (Fr) 'false friend'; a word in a foreign language that does not mean what it appears to.

faux-naïf (Fr) 'falsely naive'; seeming or pretending to be unsophisticated, innocent, etc.

faux pas (Fr) 'false step'; a social blunder.

femme fatale (Fr) 'fatal woman'; an irresistibly attractive woman who brings difficulties or disasters on men; a siren.

fidus Achates (Lat) 'the faithful Achates' (Aeneas' friend); a loyal follower.

film noir (Fr) 'black film'; a bleak and pessimistic film.

fin de siècle (Fr) 'end of the century'; of the end of the 19c in Western culture or of an era; decadent.

floruit (Lat) 'he or she flourished'; denotes a period during which a person lived.

fons et origo (Lat) 'the source and origin'.

force de frappe (Fr) 'strike force'; equivalent of the 'independent nuclear deterrent'.

force majeure (Fr) 'superior force'; an unforeseeable or uncontrollable course of events, excusing one from fulfilling a contract; a legal term.

Führer (Ger) 'leader, guide'; an insulting term for anyone bossily asserting authority.

Gastarbeiter (Ger) 'guest-worker'; an immigrant worker, especially one who does menial work.

Gauleiter (Ger) 'district leader'; a chief official of a district under the Nazi regime; an overbearing wielder of petty authority.

gemütlich (Ger) amiable; comfortable; cosy.

gestalt (Ger) 'form, shape'; original whole or unit, more than the sum of its parts.

Gesundheit (Ger) 'health', 'your health'; said to someone who has just sneezed.

glasnost (Russ) 'publicity'; the policy of openness and forthrightness followed by the Soviet government, initiated by Mikhail Gorbachev.

Gnothi seauton (Gr) 'Know thyself'.

Götterdämmerung (Ger) 'twilight of the gods'; the downfall of any once powerful system.

goy *plural* **goys** or **goyim** (Hebrew) non-Jewish, a gentile.

grand mal (Fr) 'large illness'; a violently convulsive form of epilepsy.

grand prix (Fr) 'great prize'; any of several international motor races; any competition of similar importance in other sports.

gran turismo (Ital) 'great touring, touring on a grand scale'; a motor car designed for high speed touring in luxury (abbreviation GT).

gratis (Lat) *gratiis* 'kindness, favour'; free of charge.

gravitas (Lat) 'weight'; seriousness; weight of demeanour; avoidance of unseemly frivolity.

gringo (Mexican-Spanish) 'foreigner'.

guru (Hindi) a spiritual leader; a revered instructor or mentor.

habeas corpus (Lat) 'you should have the body'; a writ to a jailer to produce a prisoner in person, and to state the reasons for detention; maintains the right of the subject to protection from unlawful imprisonment.

haiku (Jap) 'amusement poem'; a Japanese poem consisting of only three lines, containing respectively five, seven, and five syllables.

hajj (Arabic) 'pilgrimage'; the Muslim pilgrimage to Mecca.

haka (Maori) a Maori ceremonial war dance; a similar dance performed by New Zealanders eg before a rugby game.

halal (Arabic) 'lawful'; meat from an animal killed in strict accordance with Islamic law.

haute couture (Fr) 'higher tailoring'; fashionable, expensive dress designing and tailoring.

haut monde (Fr) 'high world'; high society; fashionable society; composed of the aristocracy and the wealthy.

hic jacet (Lat) 'here lies'; the first words of an epitaph; memorial inscription.

hoi polloi (Gr) 'the many'; the rabble; the vulgar.

hombre (Span) 'man'.

honoris causa (Lat) 'for the sake of honour'; a token of respect; used to designate honorary university degrees.

hors concours (Fr) 'out of the competition'; not entered for a contest; unequalled.

ibidem (Lat) 'in the same place'; used in footnotes to indicate that the same book (or chapter) has been cited previously.

id (Lat) 'it'; the sum total of the primitive instinctive forces in an individual.

idée fixe (Fr) 'a fixed idea'; an obsession.

idem (Lat) 'the same'.

ikebana (Jap) 'living flowers'; the Japanese art of flower arrangement.

in absentia (Lat) 'in absence'; used for occasions, such as the receiving of a degree award, when the recipient would normally be present.

in camera (Lat) 'in the room'; in a private room; in secret.

incommunicado (Span) 'unable to communicate'; deprived of the right to communicate with others.

in extremis (Lat) 'in the last'; at the point of death; in desperate circumstances.

in flagrante delicto (Lat) 'with the crime blazing'; in the very act of committing the crime.

infra dig (Lat) 'below dignity'; below one's dignity.

in loco parentis (Lat) 'in place of a parent'.

in Shallah (Arabic) 'if God wills'; ▶ **Deo volente**

inter alia (Lat) 'among other things'; used to show that a few examples have been chosen from many possibilities.

in vitro (Lat) 'in glass'; in the test tube.

ipso facto (Lat) 'by the fact itself'; thereby.

je ne sais quoi (Fr) 'I do not know what'; an indefinable something.

jihad (Arabic) 'struggle'; a holy war undertaken by Muslims against unbelievers.

Jugendstil (Ger) 'youth style'; the German term for art nouveau.

kamikaze (Jap) 'divine wind'; Japanese pilots making a suicide attack; any reckless, potentially self-destructive act.

kanaka (Hawaiian) 'man'; used by Europeans (and Australians) to mean South Sea islander.

karaoke (Jap) 'empty orchestra'; in bars, clubs, etc members of the public sing a solo to a recorded backing.

karma (Sanskrit) 'act'; the concept that the actions in a life determine the future condition of an individual.

kibbutz (Hebrew) a Jewish communal agricultural settlement in Israel.

kitsch (Ger) 'rubbish'; work in any of the arts that is pretentious and inferior or in bad taste.

kvetch (Yiddish) 'complain, whine (incessantly)'.

la dolce vita (Ital) 'the sweet life'; the name of a film made by Federico Fellini in 1960 showing a life of wealth, pleasure and self-indulgence.

laissez-faire (Fr) 'let do'; a general principle of non-interference.

Lebensraum (Ger) 'life space'; room to live; used by Hitler to justify his acquisition of land for Germany.

leitmotiv (Ger) 'leading motive'; a recurrent theme.

lèse-majesté (Fr) 'injured majesty'; offence against the sovereign power; treason.

lingua franca (Ital) 'Frankish language'; originally a mixed Italian trading language used in the Levant, subsequently any language chosen as a means of communication among speakers of different languages.

locum tenens (Lat) 'place holder'; a deputy or substitute, especially for a doctor or a clergyman.

macho (Mexican-Spanish) 'male'; originally a positive term denoting masculinity or virility, it has come in English to describe an ostentatious virility.

magnum opus (Lat) 'great work'; a person's greatest achievement, especially a literary work.

maharishi (Sanskrit) a Hindu sage or spiritual leader; a guru.

mañana (Span) 'tomorrow'; an unspecified time in the future.

mea culpa (Lat) 'through my fault'; originally part of the Latin mass; an admission of fault and an expression of repentance.

memento mori (Lat) 'remember that you must die'; an object, such as a skull, or anything to remind one of mortality.

ménage à trois (Fr) 'household of three'; a household comprising a husband and wife and the lover of one of them.

mens sana in corpore sano (Lat) 'a sound mind in a sound body' (Juvenal *Satires* X, 356); the guiding rule of the 19c English educational system.

mirabile dictu (Lat) 'wonderful to tell'; an expression of (sometimes ironic) amazement.

modus operandi (Lat) 'mode of working'; the characteristic methods employed by a particular criminal.

modus vivendi (Lat) 'mode of living'; an arrangement or compromise by means of which those who differ may get on together for a time.

mot juste (Fr) 'exact word'; the word which fits the context exactly.

multum in parvo (Lat) 'much in little'; a large amount in a small space.

mutatis mutandis (Lat) 'with the necessary changes made'.

négociant (Fr) 'merchant, trader'; often used for *négociant en vins* 'wine merchant'.

ne plus ultra (Lat) 'not more beyond'; extreme perfection.

netsuke (Jap) a small Japanese carved ornament used to fasten small objects, eg a purse, tobacco pouch, or medicine box, to the sash of a kimono. They are now collectors' pieces.

noblesse oblige (Fr) 'nobility obliges'; rank imposes obligations.

non sequitur (Lat) 'it does not follow'; a conclusion that does not follow logically from the premise; a remark that has no relation to what has gone before.

nostalgie de la boue (Fr) 'hankering for mud'; a craving for a debased physical life without civilized refinements.

nota bene (Lat) 'observe well, note well'; often abbreviated NB.

nouveau riche (Fr) 'new rich'; one who has only lately acquired wealth (without acquiring good taste).

nouvelle cuisine (Fr) 'new cooking'; a style of simple French cookery that aims to produce dishes that are light and healthy, utilizing fresh fruit and vegetables, and avoiding butter and cream.

nouvelle vague (Fr) 'new wave'; a movement in the French cinema aiming at imaginative quality films.

obiter dictum (Lat) 'something said in passing'; originally a legal term for something said by a trial judge that was incidental to the case in question.

origami (Jap) 'paper-folding'; Japanese art of folding paper to make shapes suggesting birds, boats, etc.

O tempora! O mores! (Lat) 'O the times! O the manners' (Cicero *In Catilinam*); a condemnation of present times, as contrasted with a past which is seen as golden.

outré (Fr) 'gone to excess'; beyond what is customary or proper; eccentric.

pace (Lat) 'peace'; by your leave (indicating polite disagreement).

panem et circenses (Lat) 'bread and circuses', or 'food and the big match' (Juvenal *Satires* X, 80); amusements which divert the populace from unpleasant realities.

passim (Lat) 'everywhere, throughout'; dispersed through a book.

per capita (Lat) 'by heads'; per head of the population in statistical contexts.

perestroika (Russ) 'reconstruction'; restructuring of an organization.

persona non grata (Lat) one who is not welcome or favoured (originally a term in diplomacy).

pied-à-terre (Fr) 'foot to the ground'; a flat, small house etc kept for temporary or occasional accommodation.

plus ça change (Fr) abbreviated form of **plus ça change, plus c'est la même chose** 'the more things change, the more they stay the same'; a comment on the unchanging nature of the world.

post meridiem (Lat) 'after midday, after noon'; abbreviated to pm.

post mortem (Lat) 'after death'; an examination of a body in order to determine the cause of death; an after-the-event discussion.

poule de luxe (Fr) 'luxurious hen'; a sexually attractive promiscuous young woman; a prostitute.

pour encourager les autres (Fr) 'to encourage the others' (Voltaire *Candide*, on the execution of Admiral Byng); exemplary punishment.

premier cru (Fr) 'first growth'; wine of the highest quality in a system of classification.

prêt-à-porter (Fr) 'ready to wear'; refers to 'designer' clothes that are made in standard sizes as opposed to made-to-measure clothes.

prima donna (Ital) 'first lady'; leading female singer in an opera; a person who is temperamental and hard to please.

prima facie (Lat) 'at first sight'; a legal term for evidence that is assumed to be true unless disproved by other evidence.

primus inter pares (Lat) 'first among equals'.

prix fixe (Fr) 'fixed price'; used of a meal in a restaurant offered at a set price for a restricted choice. Compare **table d'hôte**.

pro bono publico (Lat) 'for the public good'; something done for no fee.

quid pro quo (Lat) 'something for something'; something given or taken as equivalent to another, often as retaliation.

Communication

Communication

quod erat demonstrandum (Lat) 'which was to be shown'; often used in its abbreviated form **QED**.

raison d'être (Fr) 'reason for existence'.

rara avis (Lat) 'rare bird' (Juvenal *Satires* VI, 165); something or someone remarkable and unusual.

realpolitik (Ger) 'politics of realism'; practical politics based on the realities and necessities of life, rather than moral or ethical ideas.

recherché (Fr) 'sought out'; carefully chosen; particularly choice; rare or exotic.

reculer pour mieux sauter (Fr) 'move backwards in order to jump better'; a strategic withdrawal to wait for a better opportunity.

reductio ad absurdum (Lat) 'reduction to absurdity'; originally used in logic to mean the proof of a proposition by proving the falsity of its contradictory; the application of a principle so strictly that it is carried to absurd lengths.

répondez, s'il vous plaît (Fr) 'reply, please'; in English mainly in its abbreviated form, **RSVP**, on invitations.

revenons à nos moutons (Fr) 'let us return to our sheep'; let us get back to our subject.

risqué (Fr) 'risky, hazardous'; audaciously bordering on the unseemly.

Rus in urbe (Lat) 'The country in the town' (Martial *Epigrams* XII, 57); the idea of country charm in the centre of a city.

Salus populi suprema est lex (Lat) 'Let the welfare of the people be the chief law' (Cicero *De Legibus* III, 3).

samizdat (Russ) 'self-publisher'; the secret printing and distribution of banned literature in the former USSR and other Eastern European countries previously under Communist rule.

sanctum sanctorum (Lat) 'holy of holies'; the innermost chamber of the temple, where the Ark of the Covenant was kept; any private room reserved for personal use.

sangfroid (Fr) 'cold blood'; self-possession; coolness under stress.

savoir faire (Fr) 'knowing what to do'; knowing what to do and how to do it in any situation.

schadenfreude (Ger) 'hurt joy'; pleasure in others' misfortunes.

schlimazel (Yiddish) 'bad luck'; a persistently unlucky person.

schlock (Yiddish) 'broken or damaged goods'; inferior; shoddy.

schmaltz (Yiddish) 'melted fat, grease'; showy sentimentality, particularly in writing, music, art, etc

schmuck (Yiddish) 'penis'; a (male) stupid person.

shogun (Jap) 'leader of the army'; ruler of feudal Japan.

sic (Lat) 'so, thus'; used in brackets within printed matter to show that the original is faithfully reproduced even if incorrect.

sic transit gloria mundi (Lat) 'so passes away earthly glory'.

sine die (Lat) 'without a day'; the adjournment of a meeting (often in court), indicating that no day has been fixed for its resumption; an indefinite adjournment.

sine qua non (Lat) 'without which not'; an indispensable condition.

sotto voce (Ital) 'below the voice'; in an undertone; aside.

status quo (Lat) 'the state in which'; the existing condition.

sub judice (Lat) 'under a judge'; under consideration by a judge or a court of law.

subpoena (Lat) 'under penalty'; a writ commanding attendance in court.

sub rosa (Lat) 'under the rose'; in secret; privately.

succès de scandale (Fr) 'success of scandal'; the success of a book, film, etc due not to merit but to its connection with, or reference to, a scandal.

summa cum laude (Lat) 'with the highest praise'; with great distinction; the highest class of degree award that can be gained by a US college student.

summum bonum (Lat) 'the chief good'.

table d'hôte (Fr) 'host's table'; a set meal at a fixed price. Compare **prix fixe**.

tabula rasa (Lat) 'scraped table'; a cleaned tablet; a mind not yet influenced by outside impressions and experience.

t'ai chi (Chin) 'great art of boxing'; a system of exercise and self-defence in which good use of balance and co-ordination allows effort to be minimized.

tempus fugit (Lat) 'time flies'; delay cannot be tolerated.

terra incognita (Lat) 'unknown land'; an unknown land (so marked on early maps); an area of study about which very little is known.

touché (Fr) 'touched'; claiming or acknowledging a hit made in fencing; claiming or acknowledging a point scored in an argument.

tour de force (Fr) 'turning movement'; feat of strength or skill.

trompe l'oeil (Fr) 'deceives the eye'; an appearance of reality achieved by the use of perspective and detail in painting, architecture, etc.

tsunami (Jap) 'wave in harbour'; a wave generated by movement of the earth's surface underwater; commonly (and erroneously) called a 'tidal wave'.

Übermensch (Ger) 'over-person'; superman.

ultra vires (Lat) 'beyond strength, beyond powers'; beyond one's power or authority.

urbi et orbi (Lat) 'to the city and the world'; used of the Pope's pronouncements; to everyone.

vade-mecum (Lat) 'go with me'; a handbook; pocket companion.

vin du pays (Fr) 'wine of the country'; a locally produced wine for everyday consumption.

vis-à-vis (Fr) 'face to face'; one who faces or is opposite another; in relation to.

viva voce (Lat) 'with the living voice'; in speech, orally; an oral examination, particularly at a university (commonly 'viva' alone).

volte-face (Fr) 'turn-face'; a sudden and complete change in opinion or in views expressed.

vox populi (Lat) 'voice of the people'; public or popular opinion.

Weltschmerz (Ger) 'world pain'; sympathy with universal misery; thoroughgoing pessimism.

wunderkind (Ger) 'wonder-child'; a 'child prodigy'; one who shows great talent and / or achieves great success at an early (or comparatively early) age.

zeitgeist (Ger) 'time-spirit'; the spirit of the age.

Differences between British and US English

There are many differences of meaning, pronunciation, spelling and syntax between British and US English. Some of the commoner differences in meaning in typical usage are listed below. The increasing influence of US usage on British English is having the effect of blurring distinctions. It should also be remembered that practice differs widely within the USA; and it is becoming increasingly difficult to establish linguistic boundaries between the language used in the USA and the language used in Canada.

There are also a number of general spelling differences between British and US English. Others are less distinct, because both varieties permit variants of form and inflections (for example, the forms **acknowledgement** and **acknowledgment** are found in both US and British English).

British		US		British		US	
-ae-	as in anaesthetic	-e-	as in anesthetic	-ogue	as in catalogue	-og	as in catalog
				-ou-	as in mould	-o-	as in mold
-oe-	as in oestrogen	-e-	as in estrogen	-l-	as in instil, instalment, skilful	-ll-	as in instill, installment, skillful
-ence	as in defence, licence (noun)	-ense	as in defense, license (noun)				
-re	as in centre	-er	as in center	-ll-	as in traveller	-l-	as in traveler
-our	as in flavour	-or	as in flavor				

British	US	British	US
aeroplane	airplane	kerb	curb
aluminium	aluminum	knickers	underpants
anticlockwise	counterclockwise	lavatory	washroom
aubergine	eggplant	lawyer	attorney
autumn	fall	lift	elevator
back garden	yard	lorry	truck
banknote	bill	loudhailer	bullhorn
bath	tub	main road	highway
biscuit (savoury)	cracker	murder	homicide
biscuit (sweet)	cookie	motorway	expressway
bonnet (of a car)	hood (of a car)	number plate (of a vehicle)	license plate (of a vehicle)
braces	suspenders	nappy	diaper
brooch	pin	pavement	sidewalk
bumper (of a car)	fender (of a car)	pedestrian crossing	crosswalk
camp-bed	cot	petrol	gasoline (gas)
caretaker	janitor	pig	hog
chemist's shop	drugstore	plot (of ground)	lot
cheque	check	potato chips	french fries
cinema (building)	movie theater	pram	baby carriage
city centre	downtown	queue	line
coffin	casket	railway	railroad
cornflour	cornstarch	return ticket	round-trip ticket
cotton reel	spool	reverse charge (telephone call)	collect call
courgette	zucchini	rise (in salary)	raise
crisps	potato chips	roundabout (traffic)	rotary
cupboard	closet	rowing-boat	rowboat
current account (bank)	checking account	rubber	eraser
curriculum vitae	résumé	rubbish	trash
curtains	drapes	scone	biscuit
draughts (game)	checkers	season ticket	commutation ticket
drawing pin	thumb tack	shoelace	shoestring
driving licence	driver's license	shop assistant	clerk
dual carriageway	divided highway	silencer (car)	muffler (car)
dustbin	garbage can	spring onions	green onions
engine driver	engineer	sweets	candy
estate agent	realtor	tap	faucet
first floor	second floor	tart	pie
flag day	tag day	terraced house	row house
flat	apartment	tights	pantihose
frying pan	skillet	timber	lumber
grill	broil	traffic jam	gridlock
ground floor	first floor	tram	streetcar
handbag	purse, pocketbook	trolley (at supermarket, etc)	cart
hoarding	billboard	trousers	pants
icing	frosting		
insect	bug		
ironmonger	hardware store		

Communication

Communication

British	US
turn-up (trousers)	cuff (pants)
tyre	tire
underground	subway
undertaker	mortician
verandah	porch

US	British
airplane	aeroplane
aluminum	aluminium
apartment	flat
attorney	lawyer
baby carriage	pram
bill	banknote
billboard	hoarding
billfold	wallet
biscuit	scone
broil	grill
bug	insect
bullhorn	loudhailer
candy	sweets
cart (at supermarket, etc)	trolley
casket	coffin
check	cheque
checkers	draughts
checking account	current account
clerk	shop assistant
closet	cupboard
collect call (telephone)	reverse charge call
commutation ticket	season ticket
cookie	biscuit (sweet)
cornstarch	cornflour
cot	camp-bed
counterclockwise	anticlockwise
cracker	biscuit (savoury)
crosswalk	pedestrian crossing
cuff (pants)	turn-up (trousers)
curb	kerb
diaper	nappy
divided highway	dual carriageway
downtown	city centre
drapes	curtains
drugstore	chemist's shop
eggplant	aubergine
elevator	lift
engineer	engine driver
eraser	rubber
expressway	motorway
fall	autumn
faucet	tap
fender (of a car)	bumper (of a car)
first floor	ground floor
french fries	potato chips
frosting	icing
garbage can	dustbin
gasoline (gas)	petrol
green onions	spring onions
gridlock	traffic jam

British	US
vest	undershirt
waistcoat	vest
wallet	billfold
windscreen	windshield
zip	zipper

US	British
hardware store	ironmonger
highway	main road
hog	pig
homicide	murder
hood (of a car)	bonnet (of a car)
janitor	caretaker
license plate (of a vehicle)	number plate (of a vehicle)
line	queue
lot	plot (of ground)
lumber	timber
mortician	undertaker
movie theater	cinema
muffler (car)	silencer (car)
pantihose	tights
pants	trousers
pie	tart
pin	brooch
pocketbook	handbag, purse
porch	verandah
potato chips	crisps
purse	handbag
railroad	railway
raise (in salary)	rise
realtor	estate agent
résumé	curriculum vitae
rotary (in traffic)	roundabout
round-trip ticket	return ticket
row house	terraced house
second floor	first floor
sidewalk	pavement
skillet	frying pan
spool	cotton reel
streetcar	tram
string	shoelace
subway	underground
suspenders	braces
tag day	flag day
thumb tack	drawing pin
tire	tyre
trash	rubbish
truck	lorry
tub	bath
underpants	knickers
undershirt	vest
vest	waistcoat
washroom	lavatory
windshield	windscreen
yard	back garden
zipper	zip
zucchini	courgette

Proverbs

The date is the first known occurrence in print in English in a recognizable form. In many cases related sentiments are attested earlier, often in Greek and Latin. A number of other proverbs are derived from medieval French sources.

Some of the uses are not in the precise form given here. Proverbs often appear in many forms.

Proverb/Date/Notable uses

absence makes the heart grow fonder 19c

actions speak louder than words 17c

all's well that ends well 14c

an *apple* a day keeps the doctor away 19c

don't throw the *baby* out with the bathwater 19c *Thomas Carlyle*

beauty is in the eye of the beholder 18c *Hume*

beauty is only skin-deep 17c

beggars can't be choosers 16c

the early *bird* catches the worm 17c

a *bird* in the hand is worth two in the bush 15c

birds of a feather flock together 16c *Bible: Ecclesiasticus 27*

once *bitten*, twice shy 19c

when the *blind* lead the blind, both shall fall into the ditch 9c *Bible: Matthew 15*

You can't get *blood* from a stone 17c

blood is thicker than water 19c

brevity is the soul of wit 17c *Shakespeare: Hamlet*

you can't make *bricks* without straw 17c *Bible: Exodus 5*

don't cross your *bridges* until you come to them 19c

a new *broom* sweeps clean 16c

you can't have your *cake* and eat it 16c

if the *cap* fits, wear it 18c

when the *cat's* away, the mice will play 17c

a *change* is as good as a rest 17c *Conan Doyle*

charity begins at home 14c *John Wycliffe*

don't count your *chickens* before they are hatched 16c

clothes make the man 15c

every *cloud* has a silver lining 19c

cut your *coat* according to your cloth 16c

too many *cooks* spoil the broth 16c

curiosity killed the cat 20c

there's none so *deaf* as those that will not hear 16c

needs must when the *devil* drives 15c *Shakespeare: All's Well that Ends Well*

the *devil* finds work for idle hands to do 14c *Chaucer*

the *devil* looks after his own 17c

better the *devil* you know than the devil you don't 16c

discretion is the better part of valour 16c *Shakespeare: Henry IV Pt. 1*

give a *dog* a bad name and hang him 18c

you can't teach an old *dog* new tricks 16c

let sleeping *dogs* lie 14c *Chaucer*

barking *dogs* seldom bite 16c

to *err* is human, to forgive divine 16c

the *exception* proves the rule 17c

familiarity breeds contempt 14c

there are as good *fish* in the sea as ever came out of it 16c

a *fool* and his money are soon parted 16c

there's no *fool* like an old fool 16c

fools rush in where angels fear to tread 18c *Pope*

forewarned is forearmed 15c

a *friend* in need is a friend indeed 11c

those who live in *glass* houses shouldn't throw stones 17c *Chaucer*

all that *glitters* is not gold 13c *Shakespeare: Merchant of Venice, as 'all that glisters...'*

don't teach your *grandmother* to suck eggs 18c

the *grass* is always greener on the other side of the fence 20c

old *habits* die hard 18c *Benjamin Franklin*

many *hands* make light work 14c

first you catch your *hare* 19c *Thackeray*

more *haste* less speed 14c

he who *hesitates* is lost 18c

there is *honour* among thieves 17c

never look a gift *horse* in the mouth 16c

you may take a *horse* to water but you can't make him drink 12c

hunger is the best sauce 16c

where *ignorance* is bliss, 'tis folly to be wise 18c *Thomas Gray*

strike while the *iron* is hot 14c *Chaucer*

a little *knowledge* is a dangerous thing 18c *Pope*

better *late* than never 14c

he who *laughs* last, laughs longest 20c

least said, soonest mended 15c

a *leopard* doesn't change its spots 16c *Bible: Jeremiah 13.23*

many a *little* makes a mickle 13c

half a *loaf* is better than no bread 16c

look before you leap 14c

one man's *meat* is another man's poison 16c

it's no use crying over spilt *milk* 17c

a *miss* is as good as a mile 17c

if the *mountain* won't come to Mahomet, Mahomet must go to the mountain 17c *Bacon*

necessity is the mother of invention 16c

no news is good *news* 17c *James I*

don't cut off your *nose* to spite your face 16c

nothing ventured, nothing gained 17c

great *oaks* from little acorns grow 14c *Chaucer*

you can't make an *omelette* without breaking eggs 19c

out of sight, out of mind 13c

the *pen* is mightier than the sword 16c

take care of the *pence* and the pounds will take care of themselves 18c

in for a *penny*, in for a pound 17c

he that pays the *piper* calls the tune 19c

little *pitchers* have large ears 16c

there's no *place* like home 16c

a watched *pot* never boils 19c *Mrs Gaskell*

practice makes perfect 16c

prevention is better than cure 17c

pride goes before a fall 14c

procrastination is the thief of time 18c *Bible: Proverbs 16*

the *proof* of the pudding is in the eating 14c

you can't make a silk *purse* out of a sow's ear 16c

it never *rains* but it pours 18c

Communication

Proverb/Date/Notable uses	Proverb/Date/Notable uses
the *road* to hell is paved with good intentions 16c	don't put off till *tomorrow* what you can do today 14c *Chaucer*
spare the *rod* and spoil the child 11c *Bible: Proverbs 13*	it's better to *travel* hopefully than to arrive 19c *R L Stevenson*
Rome was not built in a day 16c	the *tree* is known by its fruit 16c *Bible: Matthew 12*
when in *Rome*, do as the Romans do 15c	*trouble* shared is trouble halved 20c *Dorothy L Sayers*
better *safe* than sorry 19c	there's many a good *tune* played on an old fiddle 20c *Samuel Butler*
there is *safety* in numbers 17c *Bible: Proverbs 11*, and *John Bunyan*	one good *turn* deserves another 15c
what's *sauce* for the goose is sauce for the gander 17c	*variety* is the spice of life 18c
as well be hanged for a *sheep* as a lamb 17c	all things come to those who *wait* 16c
there's no *smoke* without fire 14c	*waste* not, want not 18c
speech is silver, but silence is golden 19c *Thomas Carlyle*	still *waters* run deep 15c
it's no use shutting the *stable* door after the horse has bolted 14c	where there's a *will*, there's a way 17c
a *stitch* in time saves nine 18c	it's an ill *wind* that blows nobody any good 16c *Shakespeare: Henry VI, Pt 3*
a rolling *stone* gathers no moss 14c	it's easy to be *wise* after the event 17c *Ben Jonson*
it's the last *straw* that breaks the camel's back 17c	the *wish* is father to the thought 16c *Shakespeare*
little *strokes* fell great oaks 15c	fine *words* butter no parsnips 17c
one *swallow* doesn't make a summer 16c	all *work* and no play makes Jack a dull boy 17c
what you lose on the *swings* you gain on the roundabouts 20c	a bad *workman* blames his tools 17c
you can have too much of a good *thing* 15c	
little *things* please little minds 16c	
time and tide wait for no man 14c *Chaucer, in Latin*	

Some common similes

as bald as a coot
as black as ink *or* pitch
as blind as a bat
as blue as the sky
as bold as brass
as bright as a button
as brown as a berry
as calm as a millpond
as clean as a whistle
as clear as a bell *or* as crystal *or* (*ironically*) as mud
as cold as charity *or* ice
as cool as a cucumber
as cross as two sticks
as daft as a brush
as dead as a dodo *or* a doornail *or* as mutton
as deaf as a post
as different as chalk and cheese
as drunk as a lord *or* a piper
as dry as a bone
as dull as ditchwater
as easy as falling off a log *or* as winking
as fair as a rose
as fit as a fiddle
as flat as a pancake
as free as a bird
as fresh as a daisy *or* as paint
as good as gold
as green as grass
as happy as a lark *or* as a sandboy *or* as Larry
as happy as the day is long
as hard as nails
as high as a kite
as innocent as a lamb
as keen as mustard
as large as life

as light as a feather
as light as down
as like as two peas in a pod *or* (*ironically*) chalk and cheese
as lively as a cricket
as mad as a hatter *or* a March hare
as merry as a grig
as near as a touch
as neat as ninepence
as often as not
as old as Adam *or* Methuselah *or* the hills
as plain as a pikestaff
as pleased as Punch
as poor as a church mouse
as proud as a peacock
as pure as the driven snow
as quick as lightning
as quiet as a mouse
as red as a beetroot
as regular as clockwork
as rich as Croesus
as right as a trivet *or* as rain
as ripe as a cherry
as safe as houses
as sharp as a razor
as sick as a dog *or* a parrot
as silent as the grave
as slippery as an eel
as sober as a judge
as soft as a baby's bottom
as sound as a bell
as sound as a roach
as steady as a rock
as stiff as a poker
as straight as a die

as strong as a horse
as stubborn as a mule
as sure as a gun *or* as eggs is eggs
as thick as a plank
as thick (=conspiratorial) as thieves
as thick (=stupid) as two short planks
as thin as a rake

as tough as leather *or* old boots
as ugly as sin
as warm as toast
as weak as a kitten
as wet as a drowned rat
as white as a sheet *or* as snow
as wise as an owl

-isms

Most of the words included here denote beliefs and practices. Some, however, denote aspects of discrimination; these include **ageism** and **sexism**.

ageism discrimination on the grounds of age

agnosticism belief in the impossibility of knowing God Greek *agnostos* unknown, unknowable

alcoholism addiction to alcohol

altruism unselfish concern for the welfare of others Latin *alteri huic* to this other

atavism reversion to an earlier type Latin *atavus* ancestor

atheism belief that God does not exist Greek *atheos* without god

barbarism state of being coarse or uncivilized Greek *barbaros* foreign, stammering

behaviourism basis of psychology in behaviour of people and animals

cannibalism practice of eating human flesh Spanish *Canibal* Carib

capitalism economic system based on the private ownership of wealth and resources

communism political and economic system based on collective ownership of wealth and resources

conservatism inclination to preserve the status quo

consumerism economic policy of encouraging spending and consuming

Cubism artistic movement using geometrical shapes to represent objects

cynicism belief in the worst in others Greek *kynikos* dog-like

defeatism belief in the inevitability of defeat

dogmatism tendency to present statements of opinion as if unquestionable Greek *dogma* opinion

dynamism state of having limitless energy and enthusiasm

egoism principle that self-interest is the basis of morality Latin *ego* I

elitism belief in the natural superiority of some people Latin *eligere* to elect

empiricism theory that knowledge can only be gained through experiment and observation Greek *empeiria* experience

environmentalism concern to protect the natural environment

escapism tendency to escape from unpleasant reality into fantasy

evangelism practice of trying to persuade someone to adopt a particular belief or cause Greek *evangelion* good news

exhibitionism tendency to behave so as to attract attention to oneself

existentialism philosophy emphasizing freedom of choice and personal responsibility for one's actions

Expressionism artistic movement emphasizing expression of emotions over representation of external reality

extremism adherence to fanatical or extreme opinions

fanaticism excessive enthusiasm for something

Latin *fanaticus* filled with a god, frenzied

favouritism practice of giving unfair preference to a person or group

feminism advocacy of equal rights and opportunities for women

feudalism social system based on tenants' allegiance to a lord

functionalism theory that the intended use of something should determine its design

hedonism belief in the importance of pleasure above all else Greek *hedone* pleasure

heroism quality of showing great courage in one's actions

holism theory that any complex being or system is more than the sum of its parts Greek *holos* whole

humanism philosophy emphasizing human responsibility for moral behaviour

hypnotism practice of inducing a hypnotic state in others Greek *hypnos* sleep

idealism practice of living according to ideals

imperialism principle of extending control over other nations' territory Latin *imperium* sovereignty

Impressionism artistic movement emphasizing artists' impressions of nature

individualism belief in individual freedom and self-reliance

liberalism belief in tolerance of different opinions or attitudes

magnetism state of possessing magnetic attraction

mannerism excessive use of an individual artistic style

Marxism philosophy that political change is brought about by struggle between social classes

masochism derivation of pleasure from one's own pain or suffering named after Sacher-Masoch

materialism excessive interest in material possessions and financial success

monarchism support of the institution of monarchy

monetarism economic theory emphasizing the control of a country's money supply

mysticism practice of gaining direct communication with a deity through prayer and meditation Greek *mystes* initiate

narcissism excessive admiration for oneself or one's appearance

nationalism advocacy of national unity or independence

naturalism realistic and non-idealistic representation of objects

nihilism rejection of moral and religious principles Latin *nihil* nothing

objectivism tendency to emphasize what is objective

opportunism practice of taking advantage of opportunities regardless of principles

Communication

optimism tendency to expect the best possible outcome   Latin *optimus* best

pacifism belief that violence and war are unjustified   Latin *pax* peace, and *facere* to make

paganism belief in a religion which worships many gods   Latin *paganus* peasant, civilian

pantheism doctrine that equates all natural forces and matter with god   Greek *pas* all, *theos* god

parochialism practice of being narrow or provincial in outlook   Latin *parochia* parish

paternalism practice of benevolent but overprotective management or government   Latin *pater* father

patriotism devotion to one's country   Greek *patriotes* compatriot

pessimism tendency to expect the worst possible outcome   Latin *pessimus* worst

plagiarism practice of stealing an idea from another's work and presenting it as one's own   Latin *plagiarius* kidnapper

pluralism co-existence of several ethnic and religious groups in a society   Latin *plus* more

Pointillism artistic movement using small dabs of unmixed colour to suggest shapes   French *pointille* dot

polytheism belief in more than one god   Greek *polys* many, *theos* god

pragmatism a practical, matter-of-fact approach to dealing with problems   Greek *pragma* deed

professionalism practice of showing professional competence and conduct

racism or **racialism** discrimination on the grounds of ethnic origin

realism tendency to present things as they really are

regionalism devotion to or advocacy of one's own region

sadism derivation of pleasure from inflicting pain on others   named after Marquis de Sade

Satanism belief in and worship of the devil

scepticism tendency to question widely-accepted beliefs   Greek *skeptikos* thoughtful

sexism discrimination on the grounds of sex

sizeism discrimination against overweight people

socialism doctrine that a country's wealth belongs to the people as a whole

spiritualism practice of communicating with the spirits of the dead through a medium

stoicism tendency to accept misfortune or suffering without complaint   Greek *Stoa Poikile* Painted Porch (where Zeno taught)

Surrealism artistic movement emphasizing use of images from the unconscious

symbolism use of symbols to express ideas or emotions

terrorism practice of using violence to achieve political ends

Thatcherism political system based on privatization and monetarism advocated by Margaret Thatcher

tokenism practice of doing something once or with minimum effort to appear to comply with a law or principle

tourism practice of travelling to and visiting places for pleasure and relaxation

vandalism practice of inflicting indiscriminate damage on others' property

vegetarianism practice of not eating meat or animal products

ventriloquism practice of making one's voice appear to come from another source   Latin *ventri* belly, *loqui* to speak

voyeurism practice of watching private actions of others for pleasure or sexual gratification

First name meanings in the UK and USA

The meanings of the most popular first names in the UK and USA are given below, along with a few other well-known names.

Name	Original meaning
Aaron	high mountain (*Hebrew*)
Abigail	father rejoices (*Hebrew*)
Adam	redness (*Hebrew*)
Ahmed	more commendable (*Arabic*)
Alan	harmony (*Celtic*)
Albert	nobly bright (*Germanic*)
Alexander	defender of men (*Greek*)
Alexandra	*female form of* Alexander
Alexis	helper (*Greek*)
Alfred	elf counsel (*Germanic*)
Alice	of noble kind (*Germanic*)
Alison	*French diminutive of* Alice
Amanda	fit to be loved (*Latin*)
Amelia	struggling, labour (*Germanic*)
Amy	loved (*French*)
Andrea	*female form of* Andrew
Andrew	manly (*Greek*)
Angela	messenger, angel (*Greek*)
Ann(e)	*English forms of* Hannah
Anthony	*Roman family name*
Antonia	*female form of* Anthony
Arthur	?bear, stone (*Celtic*)
Ashley	*Germanic place name;* ashwood
Austin	*English form of* Augustus; venerated
Barbara	strange, foreign (*Greek*)

Name	Original meaning
Barry	spear, javelin (*Celtic*)
Beatrice	bringer of joy (*Latin*)
Benjamin	son of my right hand (*Hebrew*)
Bernard	bear + brave (*Germanic*)
Beth	*pet form of* Elizabeth
Bethany	*Biblical place name*
Betty	*pet form of* Elizabeth
Bill/Billy	*pet form of* William
Bob	*pet form of* Robert
Brandon	*place name;* broom-covered hill (*Germanic*)
Brian	?hill (?*Celtic*)
Cal(l)um	*Gaelic form of* Columba; dove (*Latin*)
Carl	man, husbandman (*Germanic*)
Carol(e)	*forms of* Caroline
Caroline	*Italian female form of* Charles
Catherine	pure (*Greek*)
Chandra	moon (*Sanskrit*)
Charles	man, husbandman (*Germanic*)
Charlotte	*French female form of* Charles
Chloe	green shoot, verdure (*Greek*)
Christian	follower of Christ
Christine	*French form of* Christina, *ultimately from* Christian
Christopher	carrier of Christ (*Greek*)

Name	Original meaning	Name	Original meaning
Claire	bright, shining (*Latin*)	Jacob	he seized the heel (*Hebrew*)
Colin	*form of* Nicholas	Jacqueline	*French female form of* Jacques
Craig	rock (*Celtic*)		(James)
Daniel	God is my judge (*Hebrew*)	James	*Latin form of* Jacob
Danielle	*female form of* Daniel	Jane	*from Latin* Johanna, *female*
Darren	*Irish surname*		*form of* John
Darryl	*surname; uncertain origin*	Janet	*diminutive form of* Jane
David	beloved, friend (*Hebrew*)	Jasmine	*flower name* (*Persian*)
Dean	*surname*; valley *or* leader	Jason	*form of* Joshua
Deborah	bee (*Hebrew*)	Jeffrey	*alternative spelling of* Geoffrey
Dennis	of Dionysus (*Greek*), *the god*	Jean	*French form of* Johanna, *from*
	of wine		John
Derek	*form of* Theodoric; ruler of the	Jennifer	fair/white + yielding/smooth
	people (*Germanic*)		(*Celtic*)
Diane	*French form of* Diana; divine	Jeremy	*English form of* Jeremiah;
	(*Latin*)		Jehovah exalts (*Hebrew*)
Dipak	little lamp (*Sanskrit*)	Jessica	he beholds (*Hebrew*)
Donald	world mighty (*Gaelic*)	Joan	*contracted form of* Johanna,
Donna	lady (*Latin*)		*from* John
Doreen	*from* Dora, *a short form of*	Joanne	*French form of* Johanna, *from*
	Dorothy		John
Doris	woman from Doris (*Greek*)	John	Jehovah has been gracious
Dorothy	gift of God (*Greek*)		(*Hebrew*)
Edward	property guardian (*Germanic*)	Jonathan	Jehovah's gift (*Hebrew*)
Eileen	*Irish form of* ?Helen	Jordan	flowing down (*Hebrew*)
Elizabeth	oath/perfection of God (*Hebrew*)	Joseph	Jehovah adds (*Hebrew*)
Ella	*dimunitive of* Ellen *or* Eleanor,	Joshua	Jehovah is salvation (*Hebrew*)
	from Helen, *or of* Isabella	Joyce	?joyful (?*Latin*)
Ellie	*dimunitive of* Ellen *or* Eleanor,	Julie	*French female form of Latin*
	from Helen		Julius; descended from Jove
Emily	*Roman family name (Aemilius)*	Karen	Danish *form of* Katarina
Emma	all-embracing (*Germanic*)		(Catherine)
Eric	ruler of all (*Norse*)	Katherine	*alternative spelling of* Catherine
Erica	*female form of* Eric	Kathleen	*English form of Irish* Caitlin
Ethan	strong one, enduring (*Hebrew*)		(*from* Catherine)
Eugene	well-born (*Greek*)	Katie	*pet form of* Catherine
Eugenie	*French female form of* Eugene	Kelly	*Irish surname*; warlike one
Fatima	chaste, motherly (*Arabic*)	Kenneth	*English form of Gaelic*; fair one
Francis/Frances	Frenchman/-woman		or fire-sprung
Frank	*pet form of* Francis	Kerry	*Irish place name*
Frederick	peaceful ruler (*Germanic*)	Kevin	handsome at birth (*Irish*)
Gail	*pet form of* Abigail	Kimberly	*South African place name*
Gareth	gentle (*Welsh*)	Lakisha	La +?Aisha; woman (*Arabic*)
Gary	*US place name*	Latoya	La + *form of* Tonya (Antonia)
Gavin	*Scottish form of* Gawain; hawk	Laura	bay, laurel (*Latin*)
	+ white (*Welsh*)	Lauren	*diminutive of* Laura
Gemma	gem (*Italian*)	Lee	*Germanic place name*; wood,
Geoffrey	?peace (*Germanic*)		clearing
George	husbandman, farmer (*Greek*)	Leslie	*Scottish place name*
Georgia	*female form of* George	Lewis	famous warrior (*Germanic*)
Grace	grace (*French*)	Lilian	lily (*Italian*)
Graham	*Germanic place name*	Lily	*plant name*
Hannah	grace, favour (*Hebrew*)	Linda	serpent (symbol of wisdom)
Harold	army power/ruler (*Germanic*)		(*Germanic*)
Harry	*pet form of* Henry	Lindsay	*Scottish place name*
Has(s)an	good, handsome (*Arabic*)	Lisa	*pet form of* Elizabeth
Hayley	*English place name*; hay-	Lucy	*English form of* Lucia, *from*
	meadow		Lucius; light (*Latin*)
Heather	*plant name*	Luke	of Lucania, in Italy (*Latin*)
Helen	bright/shining one (*Greek*)	Margaret	pearl (*Greek*)
Henry	home ruler (*Germanic*)	Marjorie	*from* Marguerite, *French form*
Holly	*plant name*		*of* Margaret
Hussein	*dimunitive of* Has(s)an	Mark	*English form of* Marcus, *from*
Ian	*modern Scottish form of* John		Mars, *god of war* (*Latin*)
Imran	prosperity (*Arabic*)	Martin	*from* Mars, *god of war* (*Latin*)
Indira	beauty (*Sanskrit*)	Mary	*Greek form of* Miriam (*Hebrew*)
Irene	peace (*Greek*)	Matthew	gift of the Lord (*Hebrew*)
		Megan	*pet form of* Margaret

Communication

Name	Original meaning
Melissa	bee (*Greek*)
Mia	*Scandinavian diminutive of* Maria (Mary)
Michael	like the Lord (*Hebrew*)
Michelle	*English spelling of French* Michèle, *from* Michael
Millicent	hard-working, industrious (*Germanic*)
Millie	*diminutive of* Amelia, Emily *or* Millicent
Miriam	*meaning unknown* (*Hebrew*)
Mohammed	*form of* Muhammad
Molly	*diminutive of* Mary
Morgan	?sea + ?circle (*Welsh*)
Muhammad	commendable (*Arabic*)
Nancy	*pet form of* Ann
Natalie	birthday of the Lord (*Latin*)
Neil	champion (*Irish*)
Nicholas	victory people (*Greek*)
Nicola	*Italian female form of* Nicholas
Nicole	*French female form of* Nicholas
Oliver	olive-tree, *or alteration of* Olaf (*French*)
Olivia	olive (*Latin*)
Omar	flourishing (*Arabic*)
Pamela	?all honey (*Greek*)
Patricia	noble (*Latin*)
Paul	small (*Latin*)
Pauline	*French female form of* Paul
Peter	stone, rock (*Greek*)
Philip	fond of horses (*Greek*)
Rachel	ewe (*Hebrew*)
Rebecca	?noose (*Hebrew*)
Richard	strong ruler (*Germanic*)
Robert	fame bright (*Germanic*)
Ronald	counsel + power (*Germanic*)
Ruby	*name of gemstone*

Name	Original meaning
Ruth	?vision of beauty (*Hebrew*)
Ryan	*Irish surname*
Sally	*pet form of* Sarah
Samantha	*female form of* Samuel
Samuel	heard/name of God (*Hebrew*)
Sandra	*pet form of* Alexandra
Sarah	princess (*Hebrew*)
Scott	*surname*; from Scotland
Sean	*Irish form of* John
Sharon	the plain (*Hebrew*)
Shaun	*English spelling of Irish* Sean
Shirley	bright clearing (*Germanic*)
Simon	*form of* Simeon; listening attentively (*Hebrew*)
Sophie/Sophia	wisdom (*Greek*)
Stephanie	*French female form of* Stephen
Stephen	crown (*Greek*)
Stuart	steward (*Germanic*)
Susan	*short form of* Susannah; lily (*Hebrew*)
T(h)eresa	woman of Theresia (*Greek*)
Thomas	twin (*Hebrew*)
Tiffany	manifestation of God (*Greek*)
Timothy	honouring God (*Greek*)
Trac(e)y	?*pet form of* T(h)eresa
Vera	faith (*Slavic*)
Victoria	victory (*Latin*)
Vincent	conquer (*Latin*)
Virginia	maiden (*Latin*)
Walter	ruling people (*Germanic*)
Wayne	*surname*; wagon-maker
William	will + helmet (*Germanic*)
Zachary	Jehovah has remembered (*Hebrew*)
Zaynab	?*name of fragrant plant* (*Arabic*)
Zoë	life (*Greek*)

Common abbreviations

See also **Computer languages** p 608 and **Abbreviations and acronyms used in e-mail/text messages** p 609

AA	Alcoholics Anonymous
AA	Automobile Association
AAA	Amateur Athletic Association
AAA	American Automobile Association
ABA	Amateur Boxing Association
ABA	American Booksellers Association
ABC	American Broadcasting Corporation
ABC	Australian Broadcasting Corporation
ABM	antiballistic missile
ABTA	Association of British Travel Agents
AC/ac	alternating current
ACAS	Advisory, Conciliation and Arbitration Service
ACE	Arts Council of England
ACLU	American Civil Liberties Union
ACNI	Arts Council of Northern Ireland
ACT	Australian Capital Territory
ACTH	adrenocorticotrophic hormone
ACTU	Australian Council of Trade Unions
ACW	Arts Council of Wales
AD	anno Domini (in the year of Our Lord)
A-D	analog-to-digital (in computing)
ADD	attention deficit disorder

ADH	antidiuretic hormone
ADHD	attention deficit hyperactivity disorder
ADP	adenosine diphosphate
AEA	Atomic Energy Authority (UK)
AEC	Atomic Energy Commission (USA)
AFC	American Football Conference
AFL/CIO	American Federation of Labor/ Congress of Industrial Organizations
AFV	armoured fighting vehicle
AGM	annual general meeting
AGR	advanced gas-cooled reactor
AH	anno Hegirae (in the year of Hegira)
AHF	anti-haemophilic factor
AI	artificial intelligence
AIDS	Acquired Immune Deficiency Syndrome
AIH	artificial insemination by husband
ALCM	air-launched cruise missile
ALP	Australian Labor Party
ALU	arithmetic and logic unit
AM	amplitude modulation
am	ante meridiem (before noon)
AMA	American Medical Association

amu	atomic mass unit
ANC	African National Congress
ANS	autonomic nervous system
ANSI	American National Standards Institute
ANZAC	Australian and New Zealand Army Corps
ANZUS	Australia, New Zealand and the United States
AOB	any other business
AONB	Area of Outstanding Natural Beauty
APEX	Association of Professional, Executive, Clerical, and Computer Staff
APR	annual percentage rate
APRA	Alianza Popular Revolucionaria Americana (American Popular Revolutionary Alliance)
AR	aspect ratio
ARCIC	Anglican-Roman Catholic International Commission
A/S	Advanced/Supplementary
ASA	American Standards Association
ASBO	antisocial behaviour order
ASCII	American Standards Code for Information Interchange
ASDIC	Admiralty Submarine Detection Investigation Committee
ASEAN	Association of South-East Asian Nations
ASL	American Sign Language
ASLEF	Associated Society of Locomotive Engineers and Firemen
ASLIB	Association for Information Management (formerly Association of Special Libraries and Information Bureaux)
ASM	air-to-surface missile
ASPCA	American Society for the Prevention of Cruelty to Animals
ASSR	Autonomous Soviet Socialist Republic
ASTMS	Association of Scientific, Technical, and Managerial Staffs
ATP	adenosine triphosphate
ATS	Auxiliary Territorial Service
ATV	Associated Television
AU	African Union (formerly Organization of African Unity)
AU	astronomical unit
AV	audiovisual
AVC	Additional Voluntary Contribution
AWACS	Airborne Warning and Control System
AWU	Australian Workers' Union
BAFTA	British Academy of Film and Television Arts
BALPA	British Airline Pilots' Association
B&W	black and white
BASIC	(English) British American Scientific International Commercial
BBC	British Broadcasting Corporation
BC	before Christ
BCD	binary coded decimal
BCE	before the Common Era
BCG	bacille (bacillus) Calmette-Guérin
BCS	Bardeen, Cooper & Schrieffer (theory)
BEF	British Expeditionary Force

BEV	Black English Vernacular
BIS	Bank for International Settlements
BLAISE	British Library Automated Information Service
BMA	British Medical Association
BOSS	Bureau of State Security (South Africa)
BP	blood pressure
BSE	bovine spongiform encephalopathy
BSI	British Standards Institution
BST	British Summer Time
btu	British thermal unit
BUF	British Union of Fascists
BUPA	British United Provident Association
CAA	Civil Aviation Authority
CAB	Citizens' Advice Bureau
CACM	Central American Common Market
CAD	computer-aided design
CAI	computer-aided instruction
CAL	computer-aided learning
CAM	computer-aided manufacture
CAP	Common Agricultural Policy
CARICOM	Caribbean Community
CARIFTA	Caribbean Free Trade Area
CATV	cable television
CB	citizens' band (radio)
CBE	Commander of the (Order of the) British Empire
CBI	Confederation of British Industry
CCD	charge-coupled device
CCK	cholecystokinin-pancreozymin
CCR	camera cassette recorder
CCTV	closed circuit television
CD	Civil Defence
CDI	compact disc interactive
CD-R	compact disc recordable
CD-ROM	compact disc read-only memory
CD-RW	compact disc rewritable
CDU	Christian Democratic Union
CE	Common Era
CENTO	Central Treaty Organization
CERN	Organisation Européene pour la Recherche Nucléaire (formerly, Conseil Européen pour la Recherche Nucléaire)
CFC	chlorofluorocarbon
CGS	centimetre-gram-second
CGT	capital gains tax
CGT	Confédération Générale du Travail
CH	Companion of Honour
CHAPS	Clearing House Automated Clearance System
CHIPS	Clearing House Interbank Payments System
CIA	Central Intelligence Agency
CID	Criminal Investigation Department
CIO	Congress of Industrial Organizations
CIS	Commonwealth of Independent States
CJD	Creutzfeldt-Jakob disease
CM	Congregation of the Mission
CMG	Companion of (the Order of) St Michael and St George
CNAA	Council for National Academic Awards
CND	Campaign for Nuclear Disarmament
CNES	Centre National d'Espace
CNN	Cable News Network

Communication

Communication

CNS	central nervous system	ECM	European Common Market
COMECON	Council for Mutual Economic Assistance	ECO	European Coal Organization
		ECOSOC	Economic and Social Council (of the United Nations)
CORE	Congress of Racial Equality		
CP	Congregation of the Passion	ECOWAS	Economic Community of West African States
CPI	Consumer Price Index		
CP/M	control program monitor	ECSC	European Coal and Steel Community
CPR	cardiopulmonary resuscitation	ECT	electroconvulsive therapy
CPU	central processing unit	ECTG	European Channel Tunnel Group
CRO	cathode-ray oscilloscope	ECU	European Currency Unit
CRT	cathode-ray tube	EDC	European Defence Community
CSE	Certificate of Secondary Education	EDF	European Development Fund
CSF	cerebrospinal fluid	EDVAC	Electronic Discrete Variable Automatic Computer
CSIRO	Commonwealth Scientific and Industrial Research Organization		
		EEC	European Economic Community
CSO	colour separation overlay	EEG	electroencephalography
CTT	capital transfer tax	EEOC	Equal Employment Opportunity Commission
CV	cultivar (*cultivated variety*)		
CV	curriculum vitae	EE-ROM	electronically erasable read-only memory
CVO	Commander of the Royal Victorian Order		
		EFA	European Fighter Aircraft
CVS	chorionic villus sampling	EFC	European Forestry Commission
CWA	County Women's Association	EFTA	European Free Trade Association
CWS	Co-operative Wholesale Society	EGF	epidermal growth factor
D-A	digital-to-analog (in computing)	EI	Exposure Index
DAB	digital audio broadcasting	ELDO	European Launcher Development Organization
DALR	dry adiabatic lapse rate		
D&C	dilatation and curettage	ELF	Eritrea Liberation Front
DBE	Dame Commander of the (Order of the) British Empire	emf	electromotive force
		EMS	European Monetary System
DBMS	database management system	EMS	Emergency Medical Service
DBS	direct broadcasting from satellite	emu	electromagnetic units
DC/dc	direct current	EMU	Economic Monetary Union
DCF	discounted cash flow	EMU	European and Monetary Union
DCMG	Dame Commander of (the Order of) St Michael and St George	ENIAC	Electronic Numeral Indicator and Calculator
DCVO	Dame Commander of the Royal Victorian Order	EOKA	Ethniki Organosis Kypriakou Agonos (National Organization of Cypriot Struggle)
DDT	dichloro-diphenyl-trichloroethane		
DES	Department of Education and Science	EP	European Parliament
		EPA	Environmental Protection Agency
DES	diethylstilboestrol	EPR	Einstein-Podolsky-Rosen (paradox)
DFC	Distinguished Flying Cross	EPR	electron paramagnetic resonance
DHA	District Health Authority	EP-ROM	electronically programmable read-only memory
DI	Donor Insemination		
DIA	Defense Intelligence Agency	ERNIE	Electronic Random Number Indicator Equipment
DLP	Democratic Labor Party (Australia)		
DMSO	dimethyl sulphoxide	ERW	enhanced radiation weapon
DNA	deoxyribonucleic acid	ESA	Environmentally Sensitive Area
DOS	Disk Operating System	ESA	European Space Agency
DPP	Director of Public Prosecutions	ESC	electronic stills camera
DSN	Deep Space Network	ESCU	European Space Operations Centre
DSO	Distinguished Service Order	ESO	European Southern Observatory
DST	daylight saving time	ESP	extrasensory perception
DTP	desktop publishing	ESRO	European Space Research Organization
DVD	digital versatile/video disc		
EAC	European Atomic Commission	ESTEC	European Space Research and Technology Centre
EA-ROM	electronically alterable read-only memory		
		ETU	Electricians Trade Union
EBCDIC	Extended Binary-Coded Decimal Interchange Code	EU	European Union
		EUFA	European Union Football Associations
EBU	European Boxing Union		
EBU	European Broadcasting Union	EURATOM	European Atomic Energy Community
EC	European Community	FA	Football Association
ECA	European Commission on Agriculture	FAA	Federal Aviation Administration
		FAO	Food and Agriculture Organization
ECF	extracellular fluid	FBI	Federal Bureau of Investigation
ECG	electrocardiograph	FCA	Farm Credit Administration

FCC	Federal Communications Commission	**HQ**	headquarters
FDIC	Federal Deposit Insurance Corporation	**HR**	House of Representatives
		HRH	His/Her Royal Highness
FIFA	Fédération Internationale de Football Association (International Association Football Federation)	**HRT**	hormone replacement therapy
		IAEA	International Atomic Energy Agency
		IBRD	International Bank for Reconstruction and Development
FIMBRA	Financial Intermediaries, Managers and Brokers Regulatory Association	**IC**	integrated circuit
FLN	Front de Libération Nationale	**ICAO**	International Civil Aviation Organization
FM/fm	frequency modulation	**ICFTU**	International Confederation of Free Trade Unions
FORTRAN	Formula Translation		
FPS	foot-pound-second	**ICI**	Imperial Chemical Industries
FRELIMO	Frente de Libertação de Moçambique	**ICSID**	International Centre for Settlement of Investment Disputes
FSB	Federal'naya Sluzhba Bezopasnosti (Federal Security Service)	**IDA**	International Development Agency
		IFAD	International Fund for Agricultural Development
FSH	follicle-stimulating hormone		
FTC	Federal Trade Commission	**IFC**	International Finance Corporation
GAR	Grand Army of the Republic	**ILO**	International Labour Organization
GATT	General Agreement on Tariffs and Trade	**IMF**	International Monetary Fund
		IMO	International Maritime Organization
GBE	Knight/Dame Grand Cross of the (Order of the) British Empire	**IMRO**	Investment Management Regulatory Organization
GBH	grievous bodily harm	**INLA**	Irish National Liberation Army
GC	George Cross	**INRI**	Iesus Nazarenus Rex Iudeorum (Jesus of Nazareth, King of the Jews)
GCC	Gulf Co-operation Council		
GCE	General Certificate of Education		
GCHQ	Government Communications Headquarters	**IPA**	International Phonetic Alphabet
		IQ	intelligence quotient
GCMG	Knight/Dame Grand Cross of (the Order of) St Michael and St George	**IR**	infrared
		IRA	Irish Republican Army
GCSE	General Certificate of Secondary Education	**IRB**	Irish Republican Brotherhood
		IRBM	intermediate-range ballistic missile
GCVO	Knight/Dame Grand Cross of the Royal Victorian Order	**ISBN**	International Standard Book Number
		ISO	International Organization for Standardization
GDI	gross domestic income		
GDP	gross domestic product	**ISSN**	International Standard Serial Number
GEO	geosynchronous Earth orbit	**ITA**	Initial Teaching Alphabet
GESP	generalized extrasensory perception	**ITAR-Tass**	Informatsionnoe telegrafnoye agentstvo Rossi (Information and Telegraphic Agency of Russia) (previously **TASS**)
GH	growth hormone		
GLC	gas-liquid chromatography		
GLCM	ground-launched cruise missile		
GM	George Medal	**ITC**	Independent Television Commission
GMC	General Medical Council	**ITCZ**	intertropical convergence zone
GMT	Greenwich Mean Time	**ITN**	Independent Television News
GNP	gross national product	**ITO**	International Trade Organization
GnRH	gonadotrophin-releasing hormone	**ITT**	International Telephone and Telegraph Corporation
GP	General Practitioner		
GPSS	General Purpose System Simulator	**ITU**	International Telecommunication Union
GUTS	grand unified theories		
HCG	human chorionic gonadotrophin	**ITV**	Independent Television
HD (TV)	high-definition (television)	**IUCN**	International Union for the Conservation of Nature and Natural Resources
HE	His/Her Excellency		
HEP	hydroelectric power		
HF	high frequency	**IUD**	intrauterine device
HGV	heavy goods vehicle	**IUPAC**	International Union of Pure and Applied Chemistry
HIH	His/Her Imperial Highness		
HIM	His/Her Imperial Majesty	**IUPAP**	International Union of Pure and Applied Physics
HLA	human leucocyte antigen		
HM	His/Her Majesty	**IVF**	in vitro fertilization
HMG	His/Her Majesty's Government	**IVR**	International Vehicle Registration
HMI	His/Her Majesty's Inspectorate	**IWW**	Industrial Workers of the World
HMO	Health Maintenance Organization	**JET**	Joint European Torus
HMS	His/Her Majesty's Ship/Service	**JP**	Justice of the Peace
HMSO	His/Her Majesty's Stationery Office	**JPEG**	Joint Photographic Experts Group
HNC	Higher National Certificate	**KADU**	Kenya African Democratic Union
HND	Higher National Diploma	**KANU**	Kenya African National Union
hp	horsepower	**KB**	Knight Bachelor; Knight of the Bath

Communication

Communication

KBE	Knight Commander of the (Order of the) British Empire
KC	King's Counsel
KCB	Knight Commander of the Bath
KCMG	Knight Commander of (the Order of) St Michael and St George
KCVO	Knight Commander of the Royal Victorian Order
KG	Knight of the (Order of the) Garter
KGB	Komitet Gosudarstvennoye Bezhopaznosti (Committee of State Security) (now **FSB**)
KKK	Ku Klux Klan
KMT	Kuomintang
kpc	kiloparsec
KT	Knight of the Thistle
LAFTA	Latin-American Free Trade Association
LAN	local area network
LAUTRO	Life Assurance and Unit Trust Regulatory Organization
LCD	liquid crystal display
LDC	less developed country
LEA	Local Education Authority
LED	light-emitting diode
LEO	low Earth orbit
LFA	Less Favoured Area
LH	luteinizing hormone
LHRH	luteinizing-hormone-releasing hormone
LIFFE	London International Financial Futures Exchange
LISP	List Processing
LMS	London Missionary Society
LPG	liquefied petroleum gas
LSD	lysergic acid diethylamide
LSI	large-scale integration
LVO	Lieutenant of the Royal Victorian Order
MAC	Multiplexed Analog Component
MAO	monoamine oxidase
MATV	Master Antenna Television
MBE	Member of the (Order of the) British Empire
MC	Master of Ceremonies
MCA	Monetary Compensation Amount
MCC	Marylebone Cricket Club
MDMA	methylenedioxymethamphetamine
ME	myalgic encephalomyelitis
MH	Medal of Honor
MHD	magnetohydrodynamics
MICR	magnetic ink character recognition
MIGA	Multilateral Investment Guarantee Agency
Mired	micro reciprocal degrees
MIRV	multiple independently targeted re- entry vehicle
MKSA	metre-kilogram-second-ampere
MLR	minimum lending rate
mmf	magnetomotive force
MMI	man-machine interaction
MOH	Medal of Honor
mpc	megaparsec
MPEG	Moving Picture Experts Group
MPS	marginal propensity to save
MP3	MPEG-1 Layer 3
MPTP	methylphenyltetrahydropyridine
MRA	Moral Rearmament
MS	multiple sclerosis; manuscript

MSC	Manpower Services Commission
MSG	monosodium glutamate
MSH	melanocyte-stimulating hormone
MVD	Ministerstvo Vnutrennikh Del (Ministry for Internal Affairs)
MVO	Member of the Royal Victorian Order
NAACP	National Association for the Advancement of Colored People
NANC	non-adrenergic, non-cholinergic
NASA	National Aeronautics and Space Administration
NASDA	National Space Development Agency
NATO	North Atlantic Treaty Organization
NDE	near-death experience
NEDO	National Economic Development Office
NEP	New Economic Policy
NF	National Front
NFC	National Football Conference
NGC	New General Catalogue
NGF	nerve growth factor
NHL	National Hockey League
NHS	National Health Service
NIH	National Institutes of Health
NKVD	Narodnyi Komissariat Vnutrennikh Del (People's Commissariat of Internal Affairs)
NLRB	National Labor Relations Board
NMR	nuclear magnetic resonance
NOW	National Organization for Women
NPT	Non-Proliferation Treaty
NRA	National Recovery Administration
NRAO	National Radio Astronomy Observatory
NSF	National Science Foundation
NSPCC	National Society for the Prevention of Cruelty to Children
NTSC	National Television System Commission
NUM	National Union of Mineworkers
NUT	National Union of Teachers
NVC	non-verbal communication
OAPEC	Organization of Arab Petroleum Exporting Countries
OAS	Organisation de l'Armée Secrète (Secret Army Organization)
OAS	Organization of American States
OB	Order of the Bath; outside broadcast
OBE	Officer of the (Order of the) British Empire
OCarm	Order of the Brothers of the Blessed Virgin Mary of Mount Carmel
OCart	Order of Carthusians
OCR	optical character recognition/reader
OCSO	Order of the Reformed Cistercians of the Strict Observance
OD	ordnance datum
ODC	Order of Discalced Carmelites
ODECA	Organización de Estados Centro-americanos (Organization of Central American States)
OECD	Organization for Economic Co-operation and Development
OEEC	Organization for European Economic Co-operation
OEM	Original Equipment Manufacturer
OFM	Order of Friars Minor
OFMCap	Order of Friars Minor Capuchin
OFMConv	Order of Friars Minor Conventual

OGPU	Otdelenie Gosurdarstvenni Politcheskoi Upravi (Special Government Political Administration)
OM	Order of Merit
OMCap	Order of Friars Minor of St Francis Capuccinorum
OOBE	out-of-the-body experience
OP	Order of Preachers
OPEC	Organization of Petroleum Exporting Countries
OSA	Order of the Hermit Friars of St Augustine
OSB	Order of St Benedict
OSFC	Order of Friars Minor of St Francis Capuccinorum
OTC	over-the-counter (stocks and shares, drugs)
OTEC	ocean thermal energy conversion
OU	Open University
OXFAM	Oxford Committee for Famine Relief
PA	personal assistant
PAC	Pan-African Congress
PAC	political action committee
PAL	phase alternation line
PAYE	pay as you earn
pc	parsec
PC	personal computer
PC	Poor Clares
PCP	phenylcyclohexylpiperidine
PDGF	platelet-derived growth factor
PDR	precision depth recorder
PEN	International Association of Poets, Playwrights, Editors, Essayists, and Novelists
PEP	personal equity plan
PEP	Political and Economic Planning
PF	Patriotic Front
PGA	Professional Golfers' Association
PH	Purple Heart
PIN	personal identification number
PK	psychokinesis
PKU	phenylketonuria
PLA	People's Liberation Army
plc	public limited company
PLO	Palestine Liberation Organization
pm	post meridiem (after noon)
PM of F	Presidential Medal of Freedom
PNLM	Palestine National Liberation Movement
POW	prisoner of war
PPI	plan position indicator
PR	proportional representation
PRO	Public Record Office
PRO	public relations officer
PSBR	public sector borrowing requirement
PTA	parent-teacher association
PTO	please turn over
PTFE	polytetrafluoroethylene
PVA	polyvinyl acetate
PVC	polyvinyl chloride
PWA	Public Works Administration
PWR	pressurized-water reactor
PYO	pick-your-own
QC	Queen's Counsel
QCD	quantum chromodynamics
QED	quantum electrodynamics
RA	Royal Academy

R&A	Royal & Ancient Golf Club of St Andrews
RAAF	Royal Australian Air Force
RADA	Royal Academy of Dramatic Art
RAF	Royal Air Force
RAM	random access memory
RAM	Royal Academy of Music
RAN	Royal Australian Navy
RDA	recommended daily allowance
REM	rapid eye movement
RHA	Regional Health Authority
RISC	reduced interaction set computer
RKKA	Rabochekrest'yanshi Krasny (Red Army of Workers and Peasants)
RM	Royal Marines
rms	root-mean-square
RN	Royal Navy
RNA	ribonucleic acid
RNLI	Royal National Lifeboat Institution
ROM	read-only memory
RP	received pronunciation
RPI	retail price index
RPM	resale price maintenance
rpm	revolutions per minute
RRP	recommended retail price
RS	Royal Society
RSI	repetitive strain injury
RSPB	Royal Society for the Protection of Birds
RSPCA	Royal Society for the Prevention of Cruelty to Animals
RSVP	répondez s'il vous plaît (please reply)
RTG	radio-isotope thermoelectric generator
RVO	Royal Victorian Order
SA	Sturm Abteilung (Storm Troopers)
SAC	Scottish Arts Council
sae	stamped addressed envelope
SALR	saturated adiabatic lapse rate
SALT	Strategic Arms Limitation Talks
SAS	Special Air Service
SAT	scholastic aptitude test
SBR	styrene butadiene rubber
SCID	severe combined immuno-deficiency
SCLC	Southern Christian Leadership Conference
SDI	selective dissemination of information
SDI	strategic defense initiative
SDP	Social Democratic Party
SDR	special drawing rights
SDU	Social Democratic Union
SEAQ	Stock Exchange Automated Quotations
SEATO	South East Asia Treaty Organization
SEC	Securities and Exchange Commission
SECAM	Séquence Electronique Couleur avec Mémoire (Electronic Colour Sequence with Memory)
SERPS	State Earnings Related Pension Scheme
SHAEF	Supreme Headquarters Allied Expeditionary Force
SHAPE	Supreme Headquarters Allied Powers, Europe
SHF	super high frequency
SI	Système International (International System)
SIB	Securities and Investments Board
SIOP	Single Integrated Operation Plan

Communication

Communication

SJ	Society of Jesus
SLBN	submarine-launched ballistic missile
SLCM	sea-launched cruise missile
SLE	systemic lupus erythematosus
SLR	single lens reflex
SNCC	Student Non-Violent Co-ordinating Committee
SNP	Scottish National Party
SOCist	Cistercians of Common Observance
SOE	Special Operations Executive
SONAR	sound navigation and ranging
SP	starting price
SQUID	superconducting quantum interference device
SR	Socialist Revolutionaries
SRO	self-regulatory organization
SS	Schutzstaffel (Protective Squad)
SSR	Soviet Socialist Republic
SSSI	Site of Special Scientific Interest
START	Strategic Arms Reduction Talks
STD	subscriber trunk dialling
STD	sexually transmitted disease
STOL	short take-off and landing
SWAPO	South West Africa People's Organization
SWS	slow wave sleep
TAB	Totalisator Agency Board
TARDIS	Time and Relative Dimensions in Space
TASS	Telegrafnoye Agentsvo Sovietskovo Soyuza (Telegraph Agency of the Soviet Union) (now **ITAR-Tass**)
TB	tuberculosis
TCDD	tetrachlorodibenzo-p-dioxin
TEFL	Teaching English as a Foreign Language
TESL	Teaching English as a Second Language
TESOL	Teaching English to Speakers of Other Languages
TGWU	Transport and General Workers Union
TNT	trinitrotoluene
TSB	Trustee Savings Bank
TT	Tourist Trophy
TTL	through the lens
TUC	Trades Union Congress
TV	television
TVA	Tennessee Valley Authority
UAE	United Arab Emirates
UAP	United Australia Party
UCAR	Union of Central African Republics
UCAS	Universities and Colleges Admissions Service
UDA	Ulster Defence Association
UDI	Unilateral Declaration of Independence
UEFA	Union of European Football Associations
UFO	unidentified flying object
UHF	ultra-high frequency
UHT	ultra-high temperature
UK	United Kingdom
UN	United Nations
UNCTAD	United Nations Conference on Trade and Development
UNDP	United Nations Development Programme
UNEP	United Nations Environment Programme

UNESCO	United Nations Educational, Scientific, and Cultural Organization
UNHCR	United Nations High Commission for Refugees
UNHRC	United Nations Human Rights Commission
UNICEF	United Nations Children's Fund (formerly United Nations International Children's Emergency Fund)
UNIDO	United Nations Industrial Development Organization
UNO	United Nations Organization
UNRWA	United Nations Relief and Works Agency for Palestine Refugees in the Near East
UPU	Universal Postal Union
USA	United States of America
USAF	United States Air Force
USCG	United States Coast Guard
USIS	United States Information Service
USSR	Union of Soviet Socialist Republics
UV	ultraviolet
VA	Veterans Administration
VAT	value-added tax
VC	Victoria Cross
VCR	video cassette recorder
VD	venereal disease
VDU	visual display unit
VHF	very high frequency
VHS	Video Home Service
VIP	vasoactive intestinal polypeptide
VIP	very important person
VLF	very low frequency
VLSI	very large scale interpretation
VOA	Voice of America
VSEPR	valence shell electron pair repulsion
VSO	Voluntary Service Overseas
VTOL	vertical take-off and landing
VTR	videotape recorder
WAAC	Women's Auxiliary Army Corps
WAAF	Women's Auxiliary Air Force
WAC	Women's Army Corps
WAP	wireless application protocol
WASP	White Anglo-Saxon Protestant
WBA	World Boxing Association
WBC	World Boxing Council
WCC	World Council of Churches
WEA	Workers' Educational Association
WFTU	World Federation of Trade Unions
WHO	World Health Organization
WI	(National Federation of) Women's Institutes
WIPO	World Intellectual Property Organization
WMO	World Meteorological Organization
WPA	Work Projects Administration
WRAC	Women's Royal Army Corps
WRAF	Women's Royal Air Force
WRNS	Women's Royal Naval Service
WRVS	Women's Royal Voluntary Service
WVS	Women's Voluntary Service
WWF	World Wide Fund for Nature (formerly World Wildlife Fund)
YHA	Youth Hostels Association
YMCA	Young Men's Christian Association
YMHA	Young Men's Hebrew Association
YWCA	Young Women's Christian Association
YWHA	Young Women's Hebrew Association

Alphabets

There is no agreement over the use of a single transliteration system in the case of Hebrew. The equivalents given below are widely used, but several other possibilities can be found.

ARABIC			CYRILLIC			GREEK			HEBREW		
Letter	Name	Transliteration	Letter		Transliteration	Letter	Name	Transliteration	Letter	Name	Transliteration
ﺍ	'alif	'	А	а	a	А α	alpha	a	א	'alef	'
ﺏ	ba	b	Б	б	b	В β	beta	b	ב	bet	b, v
ﺕ	ta	t	В	в	v	Γ γ	gamma	g	ג	gimel	g
ﺙ	tha	th	Г	г	g	Δ δ	delta	d	ד	dalet	d
ﺝ	jim	j	Д	д	d	Е ε	epsilon	e	ה	he	h
ﺡ	ha	h	Е	е	e	Z ζ	zeta	z	ו	vav	v, o, u
ﺥ	kha	kh	Ё	ё	ë	Н η	eta	e, ē	ז	zayin	z
ﺩ	dal	d	Ж	ж	zh	Θ θ	theta	th	ח	chet	ch, h
ﺫ	dhal	dh	З	з	z	Ι ι	iota	i	ט	tet	t
ﺭ	ra	r	И	и	i	К κ	kappa	k	י	yod	y, i
ﺯ	zay	z	Й	й	ï	Λ λ	lambda	l	ךכ	kaf	k, kh
ﺱ	sin	s	К	к	k	М μ	mu	m	ל	lamed	l
ﺵ	shin	sh	Л	л	l	Ν ν	nu	n	םמ	mem	m
ﺹ	sad	s	М	м	m	Ξ ξ	xi	x	ןנ	nun	n
ﺽ	dad	d	Н	н	n	О о	omicron	o	ס	samekh	s
ﻁ	ta	t	О	о	o	Π π	pi	p	ע	ayin	'
ﻅ	za	z	П	п	p	Ρ ρ	rho	r, rh	ףפ	pe	p, f
ﻉ	'ain	'	Р	р	r	Σ σ, ς	sigma	s	ץצ	tzade	s
ﻍ	ghain	gh	С	с	s	Τ τ	tau	t	ק	kof	k
ﻑ	fa	f	Т	т	t	Υ υ	upsilon	u, y	ר	resh	r
ﻕ	qaf	q	У	у	u	Φ φ	phi	ph	שׁ	shin	sh
ﻙ	kaf	k	Ф	ф	f	Χ χ	chi	kh	שׂ	sin	s
ﻝ	lam	l	Х	х	h, kh	Ψ ψ	psi	ps	ת	tav	t
ﻡ	min	m	Ц	ц	ts	Ω ω	omega	ō			
ﻥ	nun	n	Ч	ч	ch						
ﻩ	ha	h	Ш	ш	sh						
ﻭ	waw	w	Щ	щ	shch						
ﻱ	ya	y	Ы	ы	y						
			Ь	ь	'						
			Ъ	ъ	"						
			Э	э	é						
			Ю	ю	yu						
			Я	я	ya						

Runic

The runic alphabet, known as the *futhork*, was made up of 24 basic symbols, although there was considerable regional variation in the overall number of symbols and symbol shapes used. Around 4,000 runic inscriptions and a few manuscripts survive, principally made by the early Scandinavians and Anglo-Saxons.

Letter	Name	Transliteration	Letter	Name	Transliteration	Letter	Name	Transliteration	Letter	Name	Transliteration
ᚠ	feoh	f	ᚷ	gyfu	g	ᛇ	eoh	ï	ᛖ	eoh	e
ᚢ	ur	u	ᚹ	wyn	w	ᛈ	peorð	p	ᛗ	man	m
ᚦ	þorn	þ	ᚻ	hægl	h	ᛉ	eolh	x	ᛚ	lagu	l
ᚩ	os	o	ᚾ	nyd	n	ᛋ	sigel	s	ᛝ	Ing	ng
ᚱ	rad	r	ᛁ	is	i	ᛏ	Tir	t	ᛟ	eþel	œ
ᚳ	cen	k	ᚷ	ger	j	ᛒ	beorc	b	ᛞ	dæg	d

Communication

Semaphore

Semaphore was widely used in visual telegraphy, especially at sea, before the advent of electricity. Old-style railway signals are a simple form of semaphore, with a single arm having two positions to indicate 'stop' and 'go'.

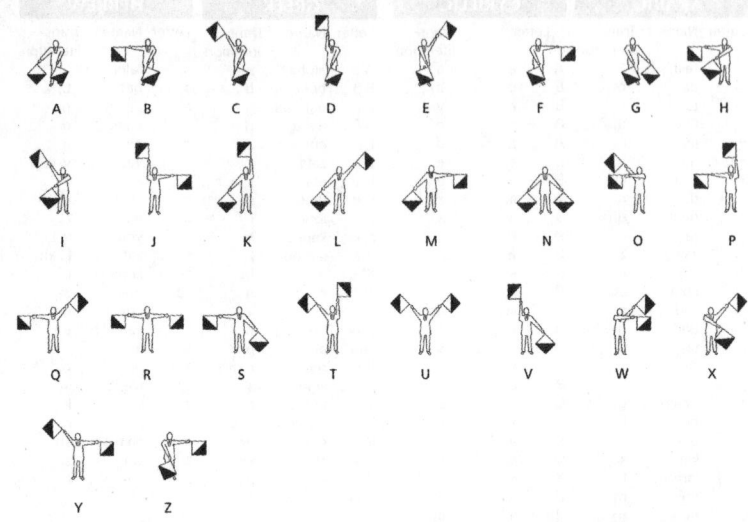

Nato Alphabet

Letter	Code name	Pronunciation
A	Alpha	AL-FAH
B	Bravo	BRAH-VOH
C	Charlie	CHAR-LEE
D	Delta	DELL-TAH
E	Echo	ECK-OH
F	Foxtrot	FOKS-TROT
G	Golf	GOLF
H	Hotel	HOH-TELL
I	India	IN-DEE-AH
J	Juliet	JEW-LEE-ETT
K	Kilo	KEY-LOH
L	Lima	LEE-MAH
M	Mike	MIKE
N	November	NO-VEM-BER
O	Oscar	OSS-CAH
P	Papa	PAH-PAH
Q	Quebec	KEY-BECK
R	Romeo	ROW-ME-OH
S	Sierra	SEE-AIR-RAH
T	Tango	TAN-GO
U	Uniform	YOU-NEE-FORM
V	Victor	VIK-TAH
W	Whiskey	WISS-KEY
X	Xray	ECKS-RAY
Y	Yankee	YANG-KEY
Z	Zulu	ZOO-LOO

Morse and Braille alphabets

Letters	Morse	Braille	Letters	Morse	Braille
A	•—		N	—•	
B	—•••		O	———	
C	—•—•		P	•——•	
D	—••		Q	——•—	
E	•		R	•—•	
F	••—•		S	•••	
G	——•		T	—	
H	••••		U	••—	
I	••		V	•••—	
J	•———		W	•——	
K	—•—		X	—••—	
L	•—••		Y	—•——	
M	——		Z	——••	

British sign language: fingerspelling

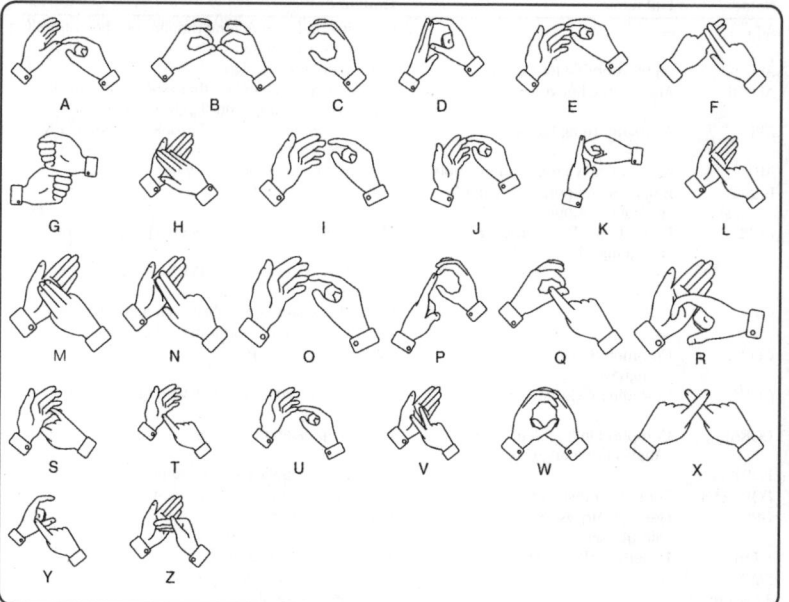

US sign language: fingerspelling

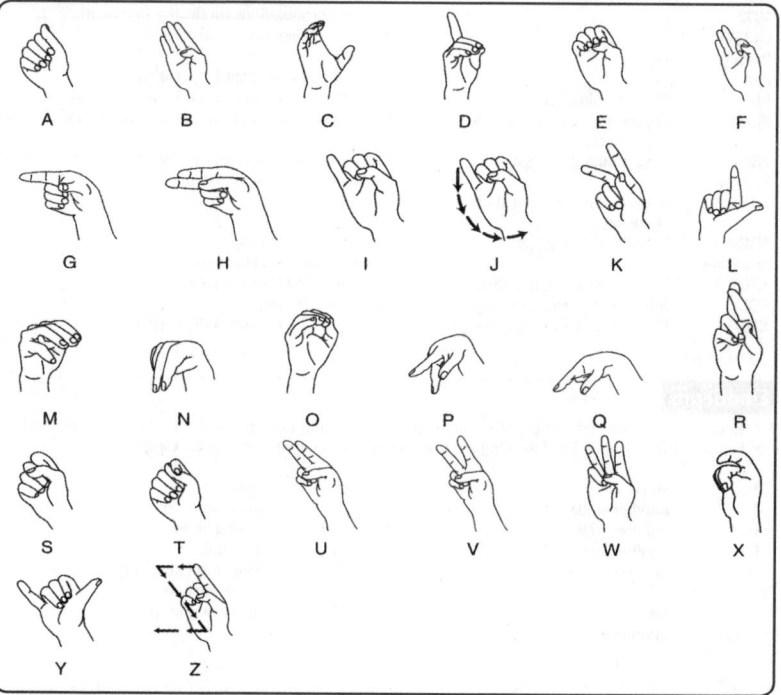

Communication

Communication

Computer languages

Name	Full name	Main use
Ada	—	Complex on-line real-time monitoring and control (eg military applications)
AED	Algol Extended for Design	Computer-aided design
ALGOL	Algorithmic Language	Concise expression of mathematical and logical processes and the control of these processes
APL	A Programming Language	Educational; mathematical problems particularly those concerned with multidimensional arrays
APT	Automatically Programmed Tools	Operate machine tools using numeric codes
BASIC	Beginners All-purpose Symbolic Instruction Code	Education, games
BCPL	B Combined Programming Language	Mathematical, scientific, systems programming
C	—	Operating systems (eg UNIX), business, scientific, games
C++	—	Operating systems, business, scientific, games
C#	—	Object-orientated programming language
COBOL	Common Business Oriented Language	Business data processing
COGO	Co-ordinate Geometry	Solving co-ordinate geometry problems in civil engineering
CORAL	Complex On-line Real-time Application Language	Military applications
FORTH	—	Astronomy, robotics, control applications
FORTRAN	Formula Translation	Mathematical, engineering, scientific
GPSS	General Purpose Systems Simulation	Simulation programs
HTML	Hypertext Mark-up Language	Web page construction
JAVA	—	Internet applications
JavaScript	—	Web development
LISP	List Processing	Linguistics, Artificial Intelligence, manipulation of mathematical and arithmetic logic
LOGO	—	Education, turtle graphics
ML	Meta Language	Functional programming
MO2	—	Parallel computations (derivative of Pascal)
OCCAM	—	Artificial Intelligence applications
Pascal	—	Education
Perl	—	General-purpose scripting language
PL1	Programming Language 1	Educational; commercial and scientific work
PL/M	Programming Language for Microcomputers	Educational; commercial and scientific work
PROLOG	Programming in Logic	Artificial Intelligence, expert systems
Python	—	General-purpose scripting language
SGML	Standard Generalized Mark-up Language	Print applications
SIMULA	Simulation Language	Simulation programs
Smalltalk	—	Object-orientated language
SNOBOL	String Oriented Symbolic Language	Manipulation of textual data
SQL	Structured Query Language	Database querying
XML	Extensible Mark-up Language	Web pages with multimedia content

Emoticons

Emoticons are combinations of keyboard characters that denote personal feelings or expressions, and are used particularly in e-mail. The following are some of the most commonly found examples:

:)	smile	:-		grim
:-)	another smile	: (	unhappy
:o)	another smile	`:)	raising an eyebrow
: D	another smile	: - o	shouting
XD	laughing hard	: - P	tongue sticking out
;)	wink	:'-(	shedding a tear
: *	kiss	>:-(	angry or grumpy
:-) x (- :	another kiss		

Abbreviations and acronyms used in e-mail

AFAIK	As far as I know	IOW	In other words
AFK	Away from keyboard	JTLYK	Just to let you know
ASAP	As soon as possible	KIT	Keep in touch
ATK	At the keyboard	L8R	Later
BAK	Back at keyboard	LOL	Laughing out loud
BBL	Be back later	MYOB	Mind your own business
BBS	Be back soon	NOMDB	Not over my dead body
BFN or B4N	Bye for now	OIC	Oh, I see
BTW	By the way	OOO	Out of order
CYA	See ya	OTOH	On the other hand
F2F	Face to face	POS	Parents over shoulder
FYI	For your information	ROE	Raising one eyebrow
FWIW	For what it's worth	ROTFL	Rolling on the floor laughing
GAL	Get a life	SI	Sarcasm intended
GFN	Gone for now	SWL	Screaming with laughter
GMTA	Great minds think alike	SYS	See you soon
GTGN	Got to go now	TTFN	Ta-ta for now
GTSY	Great to see you	TTYL	Talk to you later
HHOK	Ha, ha, only kidding	TTYT	Talk to you tomorrow
IASA	I am so annoyed	WB	Welcome back
IC	I see	WI	With irony
IMHO	In my humble opinion	WTG	Way to go
IMO	In my opinion	YR	Yeah, right

Abbreviations and acronyms used in text messages

B	Be	POV	Point of view
BCNU	Be seeing you	PPL	People
BFN	Bye for now	PTB	Please text back
B4	Before	R	Are
C	See	RITE	Right
CD	Could	RUOK?	Are you OK?
COZ	Because	SPK	Speak
CU	See you	SUM1	Someone
DA	The	THRU	Through
EVRY1	Everyone	THX	Thanks
EZ	Easy	2DAY	Today
4EVER	Forever	2MORO	Tomorrow
F2F	Face to face	2NITE	Tonight
FWD	Forward	2U2	To you too
GR8	Great	TXT	Text
G2G	Got to go	U	You
H8	Hate	VRI	Very
L8	Late	WAN2	Want to
L8R	Later	WD	Would
LUV	Love	WDYT?	What do you think?
M8	Mate	W8	Wait
MSG	Message	WKND	Weekend
MYOB	Mind your own business	W/O	Without
NE1	Anyone	WOT	What
NETHNG	Anything	WU?	What's up?
NO1	No one	X	Ex
NP	No problem	XLNT	Excellent
OMG	Oh, my God	XTRA	Extra
1CE	Once	YR	Your
PCM	Please call me	YRE	You're
PLS	Please	YYSSW	Yeah yeah sure sure whatever

Communication

Typefaces

The typefaces shown are modern versions of the main groups under which most typefaces may be classified. The dates indicating the introduction of each group are approximate.

Communication

Gothic

𝕬𝕭𝕮𝕯𝕰𝕱𝕲𝕳𝕴𝕵𝕶𝕷𝕸𝕹𝕺𝕻𝕼𝕽𝕾𝕿𝖀𝖁𝖂𝖃𝖄𝖅
abcdefghijklmnopqrstuvwxyz

Fette Fraktur (c.1450)

Sans Serif

ABCDEFGHIJKLMNOPQRSTUVWXYZ
abcdefghijklmnopqrstuvwxyz

Univers (c.1816)

Venetian

ABCDEFGHIJKLMNOPQRSTUVWXYZ
abcdefghijklmnopqrstuvwxyz

Garamond (c.1470)

Egyptian

ABCDEFGHIJKLMNOPQRSTUVWXYZ
abcdefghijklmnopqrstuvwxyz

New Century Schoolbook (c.1830)

Old Face

ABCDEFGHIJKLMNOPQRSTUVWXYZ
abcdefghijklmnopqrstuvwxyz

Caslon Old Face (c.1495)

Old Style

ABCDEFGHIJKLMNOPQRSTUVWXYZ
abcdefghijklmnopqrstuvwxyz

Goudy Old Style (c.1850)

Transitional

ABCDEFGHIJKLMNOPQRSTUVWXYZ
abcdefghijklmnopqrstuvwxyz
Baskerville (c.1761)

Newspaper

ABCDEFGHIJKLMNOPQRSTUVWXYZ
abcdefghijklmnopqrstuvwxyz

Century Bold & Century Roman (c.1890)

Modern

ABCDEFGHIJKLMNOPQRSTUVWXYZ
abcdefghijklmnopqrstuvwxyz

Bodoni (c.1765)

Contemporary

ABCDEFGHIJKLMNOPQRSTUVWXYZ
abcdefghijklmnopqrstuvwxyz

Times New Roman (c.1932)

News agencies

Press name	Full name	Date founded	Location
AAP	Australian Associated Press	1935	Sydney
AE	Agence Europe	1953	Brussels
AFP	Agence France-Presse	1944	Paris
AGI	Agenzia Giornalistica Italia	1950	Rome
AIP	Agence Ivoirienne de Presse	1961	Abidjan
AL	Agencia Lusa	1987	Lisbon
ANA	Athenagence	1896	Athens
ANP	Algemeen Nederlands Persbureau	1934	The Hague
ANSA	Agenzia Nazionale Stampa Associate	1945	Rome
ANTARA	Indonesian National News Agency	1937	Jakarta
AP	Associated Press	1848	New York
APA	African Press Agency	2006	Dakar
APA	Austria Presse-Agentur	1946	Vienna
APP	Associated Press of Pakistan	1948	Islamabad
APS	Agence de Presse Senegalaise	1959	Dakar
APS	Algerie Presse Service	1962	Algiers
ATA	Albanian Telegraphic Agency	1945	Tirana
BELGA	Agence Belga	1920	Brussels
BERNAMA	Malaysian National News Agency	1967	Kuala Lumpur
BOPA	Botswana Press Agency	1981	Gaborone
BSS	Bangladesh Sangbad Sangstha	1972	Dhaka
BTA	Bulgarska Telegrafitscheka Agentzia	1898	Sofia
CANA	Caribbean News Agency	1976	Bridgetown
CNA	Central News Agency	1924	Taipei
CNA	Cyprus News Agency	1976	Nicosia
CNS	China News Service	1952	Beijing
COLPRENSA	Colprensa	1980	Bogota
CP	Canadian Press	1917	Toronto

Press name	Full name	Date founded	Location
CTK	Ceskoslovenska Tiskova Kancelar	1918	Prague
DHA	Dogan News Agency	1999	Istanbul
DPA	Deutsche Presse-Agentur	1949	Hamburg
DyN	Agencia Diarios y Noticias	1982	Buenos Aires
EFE	Agencia EFE	1939	Madrid
FIDES	Agenzia Fides	1926	Vatican City
GNA	Ghana News Agency	1957	Accra
IC	Inforpress Centroamericana	1972	Guatemala
IPS	Inter Press Service	1964	Rome
IRNA	Islamic Republic News Agency	1936	Tehran
ITAR-Tass	Information and Telegraphic Agency of Russia	1992/1904	Moscow
JAMPRESS	Jampress	1984	Kingston
JANA	Jamahiriya News Agency	—	Tripoli
JIJI	Jiji Tsushin-Sha	1945	Tokyo
JTA	Jewish Telegraphic Agency	1919	Jerusalem
KCNA	Korean Central News Agency	1946	Pyongyang
KNA	Kenya News Agency	1963	Nairobi
KPL	Lao News Agency	1968	Vientiane
KUNA	Kuwait News Agency	1976	Kuwait City
KYODO	Kyodo Tsushin	1945	Tokyo
MEDIAFAX	Mediafax News Agency	1991	Bucharest
MENA	Middle East News Agency	1955	Cairo
MNA	Myanmar News Agency	1963	Rangoon
MTI	Magyar Tavariti Iroda	1880	Budapest
NA	Noticias Argentinas	1973	Buenos Aires
NAN	News Agency of Nigeria	1978	Lagos
NINA	National Iraqi News Agency	1959	Baghdad
NOTIMEX	Noticias Mexicanas	1968	Mexico City
NPS	Norsk Presse Service	1960	Oslo
NTB	Norsk Telegrambyra	1867	Oslo
NZPA	New Zealand Press Association	1879	Wellington
ORBE	Agencia Informativa Orbe de Chile	1955	Santiago
PA	Press Association	1868	London
PANAPRESS	Pan-African News Agency	1979	Dakar
PAP	Polska Agencija Prasowa	1944	Warsaw
PETRA	Jordan News Agency	1965	Amman
PNA	Philippines News Agency	1973	Manila
PPI	Pakistan Press International	1959	Karachi
PRELA	Prensa Latina	1959	Havana
PTI	Press Trust of India	1949	Mumbai
RB	Ritzaus Bureau	1866	Copenhagen
REUTERS	Reuters	1851	London
RIA	Russian Information Agency–Novosti	1991	Moscow
SANA	Syrian Arab News Agency	1966	Damascus
SAPA	South African Press Association	1938	Johannesburg
SDA	Schweizerische Depeschenagentur	1894	Berne
SLENA	Sierra Leone News Agency	1987	Freetown
SP	Sofia Press Agency	1967	Sofia
SPA	Saudi Press Agency	1970	Riyadh
STT	Suomen Tietotoimisto	1887	Helsinki
TANJUG	Novinska Agencija Tanjug	1943	Belgrade
TAP	Agence Tunis Afrique Presse	1961	Tunis
TT	Tidningarnas Telegrambyra	1921	Stockholm
UNI	United News of India	1961	New Delhi
UPI	United Press International	1958	New York
UPP	United Press of Pakistan	1949	Karachi
WAFA	Palestine News Agency	1972	Ramallah
XINHUA	Xinhua	1937	Beijing
YONHAP	Yonhap (United) Press Agency	1980	Seoul

Communication

Communication

National newspapers – UK

Name	Location	Circulation[1]	Date founded
Daily Express	London	687000	1900
Daily Mail	London	2077500	1896
Daily Mirror	London	1318200	1903
Daily Record	Glasgow	364800	1895
Daily Star	London	605300	1978
Daily Star Sunday (s)	London	308600	2002
Daily Telegraph	London	799000	1855
Financial Times	London	130700	1880
The Guardian	London	292900	1821
The Herald	Glasgow	61300	1783
The Independent	London	178600	1986
The Independent on Sunday (s)	London	151300	1990
The Mail on Sunday (s)	London	1957000	1982
News of the World (s)	London	2918700	1843
Observer (s)	London	375800	1791
The People (s)	London	577700	1881
Scotland on Sunday (s)	Edinburgh	60000	1988
The Scotsman	Edinburgh	49400	1817
The Sun	London	2896300	1964
The Sunday Express (s)	London	604300	1918
Sunday Mail (s)	Glasgow	444900	1914
The Sunday Mirror (s)	London	1212800	1963
Sunday Sport (s)	Manchester	81600	1986
The Sunday Telegraph (s)	London	580900	1961
The Sunday Times (s)	London	985800	1822
The Times	London	574400	1785

(s) published on Sundays only
[1] June 2008 figures (rounded to nearest 100).

National newspapers – Europe

Name	Location	Circulation[1]	Date founded
ABC	Madrid	242200	1903
AD	Rotterdam	424600	2005
Aftenposten (morning edition)	Oslo	250200	1860
Aujourd'hui en France	Paris	191600	n/a
B.T.	Copenhagen	88200	1916
Berlingske Tidende	Copenhagen	116300	1749
Bild	Hamburg	3499200	1952
Blick	Zürich	231200[2]	1959
Correio do Manhã	Lisbon	118900	1979
Corriere della Sera	Milan	598000[2]	1876
Dagbladet	Oslo	135600	1869
Dagens Nyheter	Stockholm	339700	1864
De Standaard	Brussels	90900	1914
De Telegraaf	Amsterdam	635400	1893
De Volkskrant	Amsterdam	241200	1919
Die Welt	Hamburg	276700	1946
Ekstra Bladet	Copenhagen	99800	1904
El Mundo	Madrid	317800	1989
El País	Madrid	380300	1976
El Periódico	Barcelona	167800[3]	1978
Evening Herald	Dublin	79400[2]	1891
France-Soir	Paris	238000	1944
Frankfurter Allgemeine Sonntagzeitung (s)	Frankfurt	322500	1990
Frankfurter Allgemeine Zeitung	Frankfurt	361500	1949
Gazet Van Antwerpen	Antwerp	107000	1891
Helsingin Sanomat	Helsinki	410400	1889
Het Laatste Nieuws	Brussels	280500	1888
Het Nieuwsblad/De Gentenaar	Brussels	202100	1914
Il Giornale	Milan	197300[2]	1974
Il Sole 24 Ore	Milan	330000[2]	1865
Irish Independent	Dublin	159400[2]	1905
Irish Times	Dublin	119000	1859

Name	Location	Circulation[1]	Date founded
Jornal de Noticias	Porto	93900	1888
Journal du Dimanche (s)	Paris	268800	n/a
Kronen-Zeitung	Vienna	825100	1900
La Dernière Heure	Brussels	82900	1906
La Libre Belgique	Brussels	46000	1884
La Repubblica	Rome	575700[2]	1976
La Stampa	Turin	301400[2]	1867
La Vanguardia	Barcelona	197700	1881
Le Figaro	Paris	344500	1826
Le Monde	Paris	358700	1944
Le Parisien	Paris	534000	1944
Les Echos	Paris	138700	1908
Le Soir	Brussels	92700	1887
L'Humanité	Paris	53500	1904
Libération	Paris	140000	1973
MF Dnes	Prague	290800[2]	1945
Nový Čas	Bratislava	189000[3]	1990
NRC Handelsblad	Rotterdam	229300	1970
Politiken	Copenhagen	110200	1884
Süddeutsche Zeitung	Munich	443900	1945
Sud Presse	Liège	120000	n/a
Sunday Independent (s)	Dublin	283000[2]	1905
Sunday World (s)	Dublin	292100[2]	1973
Tages-Anzeiger	Zurich	216400	1893
VG-Verdens Gang	Oslo	309600	1945
Welt am Sonntag (s)	Hamburg	404300	1948

(s) published on Sundays only
[1] 2007 figures (rounded to nearest 100) for paid circulation of weekday edition.   [2] 2008 figures.   [3] 2006 figures.

Major newspapers – USA

Includes national newspapers and local newspapers having a circulation of 250000 or more. Figures represent the highest circulation of the week, which is often that of the Sunday edition.

Name	Location	Circulation[1]	Date founded
Arizona Republic	Phoenix, AZ	541800	1890
Atlanta Journal-Constitution	Atlanta, GA	523700	1868
Baltimore Sun	Baltimore, MD	377600	1837
Boston Globe	Boston, MA	562300	1872
Chicago Tribune	Chicago, IL	940600	1847
Columbus Dispatch	Columbus, OH	343600	1871
Dallas Morning News	Dallas, TX	702100	1885
Denver Post/Rocky Mountain News	Denver, CO	704200	1859
Detroit News/Free Press	Detroit, MI	640400	1831
Houston Chronicle	Houston, TX	677400	1901
Indianapolis Star	Indianapolis, IN	354300	1903
Kansas City Star	Kansas City, MO	359500	1880
Long Island Newsday	Long Island, NY	464200	1940
Los Angeles Times	Los Angeles, CA	1173100	1881
Miami Herald	Miami, FL	342400	1910
Milwaukee Journal Sentinel	Milwaukee, WI	400300	1995
Minneapolis Star/Tribune	Minneapolis, MN	574400	1867
New York Post	New York, NY	741100	1801
New York Daily News	New York, NY	775500	1919
New York Times[2]	New York, NY	1627700	1851
Newark Star-Ledger	Newark, NJ	570500	1832
Orange County Register	Santa Ana, CA	329500	1905
Philadelphia Inquirer	Washington, DC	688700	1829
Plain Dealer	Cleveland, OH	425500	1842
Portland Oregonian	Portland, OR	375900	1850
St Louis Post-Dispatch	St Louis, MO	407800	1878
St Petersburg Times	St Petersburg, FL	430900	1884
San Antonio Express-News	San Antonio, TX	333900	1865
San Diego Union-Tribune	San Diego, CA	378700	1868
San Francisco Chronicle	San Francisco, CA	438000	1865
Seattle Times	Seattle, WA	423600	1891

Communication

Name	Location	Circulation[1]	Date founded
USA Today[2]	Arlington, VA	2 525 000	1982
Wall Street Journal[2]	New York, NY	2 068 400	1889
Washington Post	Washington, DC	929 900	1877

[1] March 2007 figures (rounded to the nearest 100) for highest circulation of week.
[2] National newspapers.

Symbols in general use

&,	ampersand (*and*)
&c.	et cetera
@	at; per (in costs)
×	by (measuring dimensions, eg 3 × 4)
£	pound
€	euro
$	dollar (also peso, escudo, etc in certain countries)
¢	cent (also centavo, etc in certain countries)
©	copyright
®	registered trademark
¶	new paragraph
§	new section
"	ditto
*	born (in genealogy)
†	died
*	hypothetical or unacceptable form (in linguistics)
☠	poison; danger
♂,□	male
♀,○	female
⌖	bishop's name follows
☏	telephone number follows

☞	this way
✂ ✂···	cut here
♻	recyclable
♻	contains x% of recycled material

In astronomy

●	new moon
☽	moon, first quarter
○	full moon
☾	moon, last quarter

In meteorology

▲▲▲	cold front
●●●	warm front
▼▼▼	stationary front
▲●▲●	occluded front

In cards

♥	hearts
♦	diamonds
♠	spades
♣	clubs

Clothes care symbols

⊠	Do not iron
⌁	Can be ironed with *cool* iron (up to 110°C)
⌁	Can be ironed with *warm* iron (up to 150°C)
⌁	Can be ironed with *hot* iron (up to 200°C)
⊡	Hand wash only
⊞	Can be washed in a washing machine The number shows the most effective washing temperature (in °C)
⊞	Reduced (medium) washing conditions
⊞	Much reduced (minimum) washing conditions (for wool products)
⊠	Do not wash
⊙	Can be tumble dried (one dot within the circle means a low temperature setting; two dots for higher temperatures)

⊠	Do not tumble dry
⊗	Do not dry clean
Ⓐ	Dry cleanable (letter indicates which solvents can be used) A: all solvents
Ⓕ	F: white spirit and solvent 11 can be used
Ⓟ	P: perchloroethylene (tetrachloroethylene), white spirit, solvent 113 and solvent 11 can be used
Ⓟ	Dry cleanable, if special care taken
△	Chlorine bleach may be used with care
△	Do not use chlorine bleach

Car index marks – UK

Between April 1974 and September 2001:

AA	Bournemouth	CR	Portsmouth	FH	Gloucester
AB	Worcester	CS	Glasgow	FJ	Exeter
AC	Coventry	CT	Lincoln	FK	Dudley
AD	Gloucester	CU	Newcastle upon Tyne	FL	Peterborough
AE	Bristol	CV	Truro	FM	Chester
AF	Truro	CW	Preston	FN	Maidstone
AG	Beverley	CX	Leeds	FO	Gloucester
AH	Norwich	CY	Swansea	FP	Leicester
AJ	Middlesbrough	CZ	Belfast	FR	Preston
AK	Sheffield	DA	Birmingham	FS	Edinburgh
AL	Nottingham	DB	Manchester	FT	Newcastle upon Tyne
AM	Swindon	DC	Middlesbrough	FU	Lincoln
AN	Reading	DD	Gloucester	FV	Preston
AO	Carlisle	DE	Swansea	FW	Lincoln
AP	Brighton	DF–DG	Gloucester	FX	Bournemouth
AR	Chelmsford	DH	Dudley	FY	Liverpool
AS	Inverness	DJ	Liverpool	FZ	Belfast
AT	Beverley	DK	Manchester	GA–GB	Glasgow
AU	Nottingham	DL	Portsmouth	GC	Wimbledon
AV	Peterborough	DM	Chester	GD–GE	Glasgow
AW	Shrewsbury	DN	Leeds	GF	Wimbledon
AX	Cardiff	DO	Lincoln	GG	Glasgow
AY	Leicester	DP	Reading	GH	Wimbledon
AZ	Belfast	DR	Exeter	GJ–GK	Wimbledon
BA	Manchester	DS	Glasgow	GL	Truro
BB	Newcastle upon Tyne	DT	Sheffield	GM	Reading
BC	Leicester	DU	Coventry	GN–GP	Wimbledon
BD	Northampton	DV	Exeter	GR	Newcastle upon Tyne
BE	Lincoln	DW	Cardiff	GS	Luton
BF	Stoke-on-Trent	DX	Ipswich	GT	Wimbledon
BG	Liverpool	DY	Brighton	GU	Sidcup
BH	Luton	DZ	Ballymena	GV	Ipswich
BJ	Ipswich	EA	Dudley	GW–GY	Sidcup
BK	Portsmouth	EB	Peterborough	GZ	Belfast
BL	Reading	EC	Preston	HA	Dudley
BM	Luton	ED	Liverpool	HB	Cardiff
BN	Manchester	EE	Lincoln	HC	Brighton
BO	Cardiff	EF	Middlesbrough	HD	Leeds
BP	Portsmouth	EG	Peterborough	HE	Sheffield
BR	Newcastle upon Tyne	EH	Stoke-on-Trent	HF	Liverpool
BS	Inverness	EJ	Swansea	HG	Preston
BT	Leeds	EK	Liverpool	HH	Carlisle
BU	Manchester	EL	Bournemouth	HJ–HK	Chelmsford
BV	Preston	EM	Liverpool	HL	Sheffield
BW	Oxford	EN	Manchester	HM	Wimbledon
BX	Swansea	EO	Preston	HN	Middlesbrough
BY	Stanmore	EP	Swansea	HO	Bournemouth
BZ	Downpatrick	ER	Peterborough	HP	Coventry
CA	Chester	ES	Dundee	HR	Swindon
CB	Manchester	ET	Sheffield	HS	Glasgow
CC	Bangor	EU	Bristol	HT–HU	Bristol
CD	Brighton	EV	Chelmsford	HV	Wimbledon
CE	Peterborough	EW	Peterborough	HW	Bristol
CF	Reading	EX	Norwich	HX	Wimbledon
CG	Bournemouth	EY	Bangor	HY	Bristol
CH	Nottingham	EZ	Belfast	HZ	Omagh
CJ	Gloucester	FA	Stoke-on-Trent	IA	Ballymena
CK	Preston	FB	Bristol	IB	Armagh
CL	Norwich	FC	Oxford	IJ	Downpatrick
CM	Liverpool	FD	Dudley	IL	Enniskillen
CN	Newcastle upon Tyne	FE	Lincoln	IW	Coleraine
CO	Exeter	FF	Bangor	JA	Manchester
CP	Leeds	FG	Brighton	JB	Reading

Communication

JC	Bangor	NM	Luton	SA	Aberdeen
JD	Wimbledon	NN	Nottingham	SB	Glasgow
JE	Peterborough	NO	Chelmsford	SC	Edinburgh
JF	Leicester	NP	Worcester	SCY	Truro (Isles of Scilly)
JG	Maidstone	NR	Leicester	SD	Glasgow
JH	Reading	NS	Glasgow	SE	Aberdeen
JI	Omagh	NT	Shrewsbury	SF–SH	Edinburgh
JJ	Maidstone	NU	Nottingham	SJ	Glasgow
JK	Brighton	NV	Northampton	SK	Inverness
JL	Lincoln	NW	Leeds	SL	Dundee
JM	Reading	NX	Dudley	SM	Carlisle
JN	Chelmsford	NY	Cardiff	SN	Dundee
JO	Oxford	NZ	Coleraine	SO	Aberdeen
JP	Liverpool	OA–OC	Birmingham	SP	Dundee
JR	Newcastle upon Tyne	OD	Exeter	SR	Dundee
JS	Inverness	OE–OH	Birmingham	SS	Aberdeen
JT	Bournemouth	OI	Belfast	ST	Inverness
JU	Leicester	OJ–ON	Birmingham	SU	Glasgow
JV	Lincoln	OO	Chelmsford	SV	*spare*
JW	Birmingham	OP	Birmingham	SW	Carlisle
JX	Leeds	OR	Portsmouth	SX	Edinburgh
JY	Exeter	OS	Glasgow	SY	*spare*
JZ	Downpatrick	OT	Portsmouth	SZ	Downpatrick
KA–KD	Liverpool	OU	Bristol	TA	Exeter
KE	Maidstone	OV	Birmingham	TB	Liverpool
KF	Liverpool	OW	Portsmouth	TC	Bristol
KG	Cardiff	OX	Birmingham	TD–TE	Manchester
KH	Beverley	OY	Stanmore	TF	Reading
KJ–KP	Maidstone	OZ	Belfast	TG	Cardiff
KR	Maidstone	PA–PF	Wimbledon	TH	Swansea
KS	Edinburgh	PG–PH	Guildford	TJ	Liverpool
KT	Maidstone	PJ–PM	Guildford	TK	Exeter
KU	Sheffield	PN	Brighton	TL	Lincoln
KV	Coventry	PO	Portsmouth	TM	Luton
KW	Sheffield	PP	Luton	TN	Newcastle upon Tyne
KX	Luton	PR	Bournemouth	TO	Nottingham
KY	Sheffield	PS	Aberdeen	TP	Portsmouth
KZ	Ballymena	PT	Newcastle upon Tyne	TR	Portsmouth
LA–LF	Stanmore	PU	Chelmsford	TS	Dundee
LG	Chester	PV	Ipswich	TT	Exeter
LH	Stanmore	PW	Norwich	TU	Chester
LJ	Bournemouth	PX	Portsmouth	TV	Nottingham
LK–LP	Stanmore	PY	Middlesbrough	TW	Chelmsford
LR	Stanmore	PZ	Belfast	TX	Cardiff
LS	Edinburgh	QA–QH	Wimbledon	TY	Newcastle upon Tyne
LT–LU	Stanmore	QJ–QN	Wimbledon	TZ	Belfast
LV	Liverpool	QP–QY	Wimbledon	UA–UB	Leeds
LW–LY	Stanmore	RA–RC	Nottingham	UC	Wimbledon
LZ	Armagh	RD	Reading	UD	Oxford
MA–MB	Chester	RE–RF	Stoke-on-Trent	UE	Dudley
MC–MH	Chelmsford	RG	Newcastle upon Tyne	UF	Brighton
MJ	Luton	RH	Beverley	UG	Leeds
MK–MM	Chelmsford	RJ	Manchester	UH	Cardiff
MN	*(not used)*	RK	Stanmore	UI	Londonderry
MO	Reading	RL	Truro	UJ	Shrewsbury
MP	Chelmsford	RM	Carlisle	UK	Birmingham
MR	Swindon	RN	Preston	UL	Wimbledon
MS	Edinburgh	RO	Luton	UM	Leeds
MT–MU	Chelmsford	RP	Northampton	UN–UO	Exeter
MV	Sidcup	RR	Nottingham	UP	Newcastle upon Tyne
MW	Swindon	RS	Aberdeen	UR	Luton
MX–MY	Sidcup	RT	Ipswich	US	Glasgow
NA–NF	Manchester	RU	Bournemouth	UT	Leicester
NG	Norwich	RV	Portsmouth	UU–UW	Wimbledon
NH	Northampton	RW	Coventry	UX	Shrewsbury
NJ	Brighton	RX	Reading	UY	Worcester
NK	Luton	RY	Leicester	UZ	Belfast
NL	Newcastle upon Tyne	RZ	Ballymena	VA	Peterborough

VB	Maidstone	VW–VX	Chelmsford	WT–WU	Leeds
VC	Coventry	VY	Leeds	WV	Brighton
VE	Peterborough	VZ	Omagh	WW–WY	Leeds
VF–VG	Norwich	WA–WB	Sheffield	WZ	Belfast
VH	Leeds	WC	Chelmsford	XI	Belfast
VJ	Gloucester	WD	Dudley	XZ	Belfast
VK	Newcastle upon Tyne	WE–WG	Sheffield	YA–YD	Taunton
VL	Lincoln	WH	Manchester	YE–YF	Wimbledon
VM	Manchester	WJ	Sheffield	YG	Leeds
VN	Middlesbrough	WK	Coventry	YH	Wimbledon
VO	Nottingham	WL	Oxford	YJ	Brighton
VP	Birmingham	WM	Liverpool	YK–YP	Wimbledon
VR	Manchester	WN	Swansea	YR	Wimbledon
VS	Luton	WO	Cardiff	YS	Glasgow
VT	Stoke-on-Trent	WP	Worcester	YT–YY	Wimbledon
VU	Manchester	WR	Leeds	YZ	Coleraine
VV	Northampton	WS	Bristol		

Since September 2001:

AA–AN	Peterborough	HK–HY	Portsmouth	RA–RY	Reading
AO–AU	Norwich	(HW	Isle of Wight)	SA–SJ	Glasgow
AV–AY	Ipswich	KA–KL	Luton	SK–SO	Edinburgh
BA–BY	Birmingham	KM–KY	Northampton	SP–ST	Dundee
CA–CO	Cardiff	LA–LJ	Wimbledon	SU–SW	Aberdeen
CP–CV	Swansea	LK–LT	Stanmore	SX–SY	Inverness
CW–CY	Bangor	LU–LY	Sidcup	VA–VY	Worcester
DA–DK	Chester	MA–MY	Manchester	WA–WJ	Exeter
DL–DY	Shrewsbury	(MN +	Isle of Man)	WK–WL	Truro
EA–EY	Chelmsford	MAN		WM–WY	Bristol
FA–FP	Nottingham	NA–NO	Newcastle	YA–YK	Leeds
FR–FY	Lincoln	NP–NY	Stockton	YL–YU	Sheffield
GA–GO	Maidstone	OA–OY	Oxford	YV–YY	Beverley
GP–GY	Brighton	PA–PT	Preston		
HA–HJ	Bournemouth	PU–PY	Carlisle		

Note that I and Q are not used in the new format.

Car index marks – International

A	Austria	CO	Colombia	GBA	Alderney*
AFG	Afghanistan	CR	Costa Rica	GBG	Guernsey*
AL	Albania	CU	Cuba	GBJ	Jersey*
AM	Armenia	CY	Cyprus*	GBM	Isle of Man*
ANG	Angola	CZ	Czech Republic	GBZ	Gibraltar
AND	Andorra	D	Germany	GCA	Guatemala
AUS	Australia*	DK	Denmark	GE	Georgia
AZ	Azerbaijan	DOM	Dominican Republic	GH	Ghana
B	Belgium	DY	Benin	GR	Greece
BD	Bangladesh*	DZ	Algeria	GUY	Guyana*
BDS	Barbados*	E	Spain	H	Hungary
BF	Burkina Faso	EAK	Kenya*	HK	Hong Kong*
BG	Bulgaria	EAT	Tanzania*	HKJ	Jordan
BIH	Bosnia and Herzegovina	EAU	Uganda*	HR	Croatia
BOL	Bolivia	EAZ	Zanzibar	I	Italy
BR	Brazil	EC	Ecuador	IL	Israel
BRN	Bahrain	ER	Eritrea	IND	India*
BRU	Brunei*	ES	El Salvador	IR	Iran
BS	The Bahamas*	EST	Estonia	IRL	Ireland*
BUR	Myanmar	ET	Egypt	IRQ	Iraq
BVI	British Virgin Islands*	ETH	Ethiopia	IS	Iceland
BY	Belarus	F	France	J	Japan*
BZ	Belize	FIN	Finland	JA	Jamaica*
CAM	Cameroon	FJI	Fiji*	K	Cambodia
CDN	Canada	FL	Liechtenstein	KS	Kyrgyzstan
CH	Switzerland	FØ	Faroe Is	KWT	Kuwait
CI	Côte d'Ivoire	G	Gabon	KZ	Kazakhstan
CL	Sri Lanka*	GB	UK*	L	Luxembourg

Communication

Communication

LAO	Laos	RA	Argentina	SUD	Sudan
LAR	Libya	RB	Botswana*	SY	Seychelles*
LB	Liberia	RC	Taiwan	SYR	Syria
LS	Lesotho*	RCA	Central African	T	Thailand*
LT	Lithuania		Republic	TCH	Chad
LV	Latvia	RCB	Congo	TG	Togo
M	Malta*	RCH	Chile	TJ	Tajikistan
MA	Morocco	RG	Guinea	TM	Turkmenistan
MAL	Malaysia*	RH	Haiti	TN	Tunisia
MC	Monaco	RI	Indonesia*	TR	Turkey
MD	Moldova	RIM	Mauritania	TT	Trinidad and Tobago*
MEX	Mexico	RL	Lebanon	UA	Ukraine
MGL	Mongolia	RM	Madagascar	UAE	United Arab Emirates
MK	Macedonia	RMM	Mali	USA	USA
MOC	Mozambique*	RN	Niger	UZ	Uzbekistan
MS	Mauritius*	RNR	Zambia*	V	Vatican City
MW	Malawi*	RO	Romania	VN	Vietnam
N	Norway	ROK	Korea, Republic of	WAG	The Gambia
NA	Netherlands Antilles	ROU	Uruguay	WAL	Sierra Leone
NAM	Namibia*	RP	Philippines	WAN	Nigeria
NAU	Nauru*	RSM	San Marino	WD	Dominica*
NEP	Nepal*	RU	Burundi	WG	Grenada*
NGR	Nigeria (unofficial)	RUS	Russia	WL	St Lucia*
NIC	Nicaragua	RWA	Rwanda	WS	Samoa
NL	Netherlands	S	Sweden	WV	St Vincent and the
NZ	New Zealand*	SA	Saudi Arabia		Grenadines*
P	Portugal	SD	Swaziland*	YAR	Yemen
PA	Panama	SGP	Singapore*	YV	Venezuela
PE	Peru	SK	Slovakia	Z	Zambia* (unofficial)
PK	Pakistan*	SLO	Slovenia	ZA	South Africa*
PL	Poland	SME	Suriname*	ZRE	Congo, Democratic
PNG	Papua New Guinea*	SN	Senegal		Republic of
PY	Paraguay	SO	Somalia	ZW	Zimbabwe*
Q	Qatar	SRB	Serbia		

*In countries so marked, the rule of the road is to drive on the left; in others, vehicles drive on the right.

Road signs

UK road signs

- *Instruction signs*

Entry to
20 mph zone

End of
20 mph zone

School
crossing patrol

Maximum
speed

National speed
limit applies

Give way to traffic
on major road

No vehicles except
bicycles being pushed

No entry for
vehicular traffic

Give priority to vehicles
from opposite direction

No overtaking

No motor vehicles

No buses
(over 8 passenger seats)

No cycling

No towed caravans

No vehicle or
combination of
vehicles over length
shown

No vehicles over
height shown

No vehicles over
width shown

No vehicles over
maximum gross
weight shown
(in tonnes)

No waiting

No stopping
(Clearway)

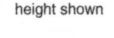

Parking restricted to
permit holders

No stopping during
period indicated
except for buses

No stopping during
times shown except for
as long as necessary
to set down or pick up
passengers

Communication

Communication

■ *Warning signs*

Distance to 'STOP' line ahead

Distance to 'GIVE WAY'

Sharp deviation of route to left (or right if chevrons reversed)

Plate below some signs

Double bend first to left (symbol may be reversed)

Crossroads

Junction on bend ahead

T-junction

Staggered junction

Bend to right (or left if symbol reversed)

The priority through route is indicated by the broader line.

Roundabout

Uneven road

Dual carriageway ends

Road narrows on right (left if symbol reversed)

Road narrows on both sides

Two-way traffic crosses one-way road

Two-way traffic straight ahead

Traffic signals

Traffic signals not in use

Slippery road

Steep hill downwards

Steep hill upwards

US road signs

■ *Instruction signs*

Stop

Do not enter

Yield

Wrong way

No left turn

No U-turn

No parking any time

■ *Warning signs*

Crossroads

Road enters from right

Two-way traffic

Divided highway

Bump

Slippery when wet

Stop ahead

■ *Information signs*

Hospital

Telephone

Information

Camping

Communication

Communication

European road signs

- *Austria*

Diversion

Tram turns at
yellow or red

Federal road
with priority

Federal road
without priority

U-turn
compulsory

Street lights
not on all night

Buses only

- *Belgium*

You may pass
to the right or left

No parking from
1st to 15th of month

No parking from
16th to end of month

Difficult section of road

- *Denmark*

Sight-seeing

Pass either side

Traffic merges

Compulsory
slow lane

Recommended
speed in a bend

- *France*

Keep well over
to the right

Diversion or
relief route

Give way
to traffic

Traffic on the
roundabout has priority

"Priority road"
sign

"End of priority"
sign

Itinéraire Bis (Bison Futé)
Alternative (Holiday) routes

- *Germany*

Diversion

Tram or
bus stop

Autobahn number

Road number

Recommended
speed limit

Emergency diversion
for motorway traffic

- *Italy*

Track for
motorcycles

Snow chains
mandatory

Alternate
one-way
priority

■ *Netherlands*

Cycle track

Danger–trams
crossing

2 hrs maximum
(disc obligatory)

Built-up
area

End of Built-up
area

Parking
prohibited

Stopping
prohibited

■ *Norway*

Tunnel

Parking prohibited
(upper panel)
Allowed (lower)

Parking 2 hrs from
08.00--18.00 hrs
(16.00 hrs Sat.)

Parking 2 hrs from
08.00--17.00 hrs

■ *Spain*

Recommended
maximum speed

Turning permitted

Tourist
accommodation

Compulsory lane
for motorcycles

■ *Sweden*

Tunnel

Slow lane

Meeting point
(narrow roads)

■ *Switzerland*

Postal vehicles
have priority

Parking disc
compulsory

Motorway

Semi-motorway

Tunnel
(lights compulsory)

Flashing red light
(level crossing)

Alternately
flashing lights
(level crossing)

Communication

Communication

UK road distances

Road distances between British centres are given in statute miles, using routes recommended by The Automobile Association based on the quickest travelling time. To convert to kilometres, multiply number given by 1.6093.

	Aberdeen	Birmingham	Bristol	Cambridge	Cardiff	Dover	Edinburgh	Exeter	Glasgow	Holyhead	Hull	Leeds	Liverpool	London	Manchester	Newcastle	Norwich	Nottingham	Penzance	Oxford	Plymouth	Shrewsbury	Southampton	Stranraer
Birmingham	430																							
Bristol	511	85																						
Cambridge	488	101	156																					
Cardiff	532	107	45	191																				
Dover	591	202	202	121	234																			
Edinburgh	130	293	373	337	395	457																		
Exeter	564	157	81	233	119	246	446																	
Glasgow	149	291	372	349	393	490	45	444																
Holyhead	457	151	232	246	209	347	325	305	319															
Hull	361	136	227	157	246	278	229	290	215	163														
Leeds	336	115	238	143	265	285	215	300	220	215	59													
Liverpool	361	98	178	195	200	295	222	250	218	104	127	72												
London	543	118	119	60	155	77	405	170	402	263	215	196	210											
Manchester	354	88	167	153	188	283	218	239	214	123	97	43	34	199										
Newcastle	239	198	291	224	311	346	107	361	150	260	121	91	164	280	141									
Norwich	501	161	217	62	252	165	365	295	379	309	153	173	232	115	183	258								
Nottingham	402	59	151	82	202	202	266	222	281	174	92	73	107	128	71	156	123							
Penzance	696	272	195	346	232	362	561	112	559	419	411	328	355	281	294	407	336	265						
Oxford	497	63	74	82	107	109	362	148	361	232	171	164	153	56	153	253	115	73	253					
Plymouth	624	199	125	275	164	290	488	45	486	347	341	328	294	215	281	346	336	205	78	216				
Shrewsbury	412	48	128	142	110	243	276	201	272	104	164	116	64	162	69	216	205	85	315	113	242			
Southampton	571	128	75	133	123	155	437	114	436	296	253	235	241	76	227	319	192	171	227	67	171	190		
Stranraer	241	307	386	361	408	457	130	457	88	332	259	232	234	419	164	185	440	332	572	406	447	287	447	
York	325	128	221	153	241	274	191	291	208	191	38	24	100	209	71	83	185	86	406	185	340	144	252	228

European road distances

Road distances between some cities, given in kilometres. To convert to statute miles, mulitply by 0.6124.

	Athens	Barcelona	Brussels	Calais	Cherbourg	Cologne	Copenhagen	Geneva	Girbraltar	Hamburg	Hook of Holland	Lisbon	Lyons	Madrid	Marseilles	Milan	Munich	Paris	Rome	Stockholm
Barcelona	3313																			
Brussels	2963	1318																		
Calais	3175	1326	204																	
Cherbourg	3339	1294	583	460																
Cologne	2762	1498	206	409	785															
Copenhagen	3276	2218	966	1136	1545	760														
Geneva	2610	803	677	747	853	1662	1418													
Girbraltar	4485	1172	2256	2224	2047	2436	3196	1975												
Hamburg	2977	2018	597	714	1115	460	460	1118	2897											
Hook of Holland	3030	1490	172	330	731	269	269	895	2428	550										
Lisbon	4532	1304	2084	2052	1827	2290	2971	1936	676	2671	2280									
Lyons	2753	645	690	739	789	714	1458	158	1817	1159	863	1778								
Madrid	3949	636	1558	1550	1347	1764	2498	1439	698	2198	1730	668	1281							
Marseilles	2865	521	1011	1059	1101	1035	1778	425	1693	1479	1183	1762	320	1157						
Milan	2282	1014	925	1077	1209	911	1537	328	2185	1238	1098	2250	328	1724	618					
Munich	2179	1365	747	977	1160	583	1104	591	2565	805	851	2507	724	2010	1109	331				
Paris	3000	1033	285	280	340	465	1176	513	1971	877	457	1799	471	1273	792	856	821			
Rome	817	1460	1511	1662	1794	1497	2050	995	2631	1751	1683	2700	1011	2097	586	946	1476			
Stockholm	3927	2868	1616	1786	2196	1403	650	2068	3886	949	1500	3231	2108	3188	2428	2187	1754	1827	2707	
Vienna	1991	1802	1175	1381	1588	937	1455	1019	2974	1155	1205	2935	1157	2409	1363	898	428	1249	1209	2105

International E-road network ('Euroroutes')

Reference and intermediate roads (class A roads) generally have two-digit numbers (although the extension of the network into Eastern Europe and Asia has necessitated the adoption of three-digit numbers for some class A roads). Branch, link and connecting roads (class B roads, not listed here) have three-digit numbers.

North–South orientated reference roads have two-digit odd numbers ending in the figure 5, and increasing from west to east. East–West orientated roads have two-digit even numbers ending in the figure 0, and increasing from north to south.

Intermediate roads have two-digit odd numbers (for N–S roads) or two-digit even numbers (for E–W roads) falling within the numbers of the reference roads between which they are located.

Only a selection of the towns and cities linked by E-roads are given here.

[...] indicates a sea crossing.

■ West–East orientation

Reference roads

E10	Å — Narvik — Kiruna — Luleå
E20	Shannon — Dublin ... Liverpool — Hull ... Esbjerg — Odense ... Korsør-Køge — Copenhagen ... Malmö — Stockholm ... Tallinn — St Petersburg
E30	Cork — Rosslare ... Fishguard — London — Felixstowe ... Hook of Holland — Utrecht — Hannover — Berlin — Warsaw — Smolensk — Moscow — Samara — Chelyabinsk — Omsk
E40	Calais — Brussels — Aachen — Cologne — Dresden — Krakow — Kiev — Volgograd — Samarkand — Tashkent — Bishkek — Almaty — Ridder
E50	Brest — Paris — Metz — Nuremberg — Prague — Mukačevo — Rostov on Don — Makhachkala
E60	Brest — Tours — Besançon — Basle — Innsbruck — Vienna — Budapest — Bucharest — Agigea ... Poti — Tbilisi — Baku ... Turkmenbashi — Ashgabat — Irkeshtam
E70	La Coruña — Bilbao — Bordeaux — Lyons — Turin — Verona — Trieste — Zagreb — Belgrade — Bucharest — Varna ... Samsun — Poti
E80	Lisbon — Coimbra — Salamanca — Pau — Toulouse — Nice — Genoa — Rome — Pescara ... Dubrovnik — Sofia — Istanbul — Erzincan — Iran
E90	Lisbon — Madrid — Barcelona ... Mazara del Vallo — Messina — Reggio di Calabria — Brindisi ... Igoumenitsa — Thessaloniki — Gelibolu ... Lapseki — Ankara — Iraq

Intermediate roads

E04	Helsingborg — Tornio
E06	Trelleborg — Kirkenes
E08	Tromsø — Turku
E12	Mo i Rana — Umeå ... Vaasa — Helsinki
E14	Trondheim — Sundsvall
E16	Londonderry — Belfast ... Glasgow — Edinburgh ... Bergen — Fagernes — Oslo
E18	Craigavon — Larne ... Stranraer — Newcastle ... Kristiansand — Oslo — Stockholm/Kappelskär ... Mariehamn ... Turku — Helsinki — St Petersburg
E22	Holyhead — Manchester — Immingham ... Amsterdam — Hamburg — Sassnitz ... Trelleborg — Norrköping ... Ventspils — Riga — Moscow — Kazan — Perm — Ishim
E24	Birmingham — Ipswich
E26	Hamburg — Berlin
E28	Berlin — Gdańsk ... Kaliningrad — Minsk — Vilnius
E32	Colchester — Harwich
E34	Zeebrugge — Eindhoven — Bad Oeynhausen
E36	Berlin — Legnica
E38	Glukhov — Shymkent
E42	Dunkirk — Aschaffenburg

E44	Le Havre — Luxembourg — Giessen
E46	Cherbourg — Liège
E48	Schweinfurt — Prague
E52	Strasbourg — Salzburg
E54	Paris — Basle — Munich
E56	Nuremberg — Sattledt
E58	Vienna — Bratislava — Odessa — Rostov on Don
E62	Nantes — Geneva — Milan — Genoa
E64	Turin — Brescia
E66	Fortezza — Graz — Székesfehérvár
E68	Szeged — Braşov
E72	Bordeaux — Toulouse
E74	Nice — Alessandria
E76	Migliarino — Florence
E78	Grosseto — Fano
E82	Porto — Tordesillas
E84	Keşan — Silivri
E86	Krystalopigi — Yefira
E88	Ankara — Refahiye
E92	Igoumenitsa — Volos
E94	Corinth — Athens
E96	Izmir — Sivrihisar
E98	Topbogazi — Syria

Communication

Communication

■ **North–South orientation**

Reference roads

E05	Greenock — Birmingham — Southampton ... Le Havre — Paris — Bordeaux — Madrid — Algeciras
E15	Inverness — Edinburgh — London — Dover ... Calais — Paris — Lyons — Barcelona — Algeciras
E25	Hook of Holland — Luxembourg — Strasbourg — Basle — Geneva — Genoa ... Corsica ... Sardinia ... Palermo
E35	Amsterdam — Cologne — Basle — Milan — Rome
E45	Karesuando — Gothenburg ... Frederikshavn — Hamburg — Munich — Innsbruck — Bologna — Rome — Naples — Villa S Giovanni ... Messina — Gela
E55	Helsingborg ... Heslingør — Copenhagen — Gedser ... Rostock — Berlin — Prague — Salzburg — Rimini — Brindisi ... Igoumenitsa — Kalamata
E65	Malmö — Ystad ... Swinoujście — Prague — Zagreb — Dubrovnik — Skopje — Antirrion ... Rion — Kalamata ... Kissamos — Chania
E75	Vardø — Helsinki ... Gdańsk — Budapest — Belgrade — Athens ... Chania — Sitia
E85	Klaipeda — Černovcy — Bucharest — Alexandropouli
E95	St Petersburg — Kiev — Odessa ... Samsun — Merzifon
E101	Moscow — Kiev
E105	Kirkenes — Murmansk — St Petersburg — Moscow — Yalta
E115	Yaroslavl — Moscow — Rostov on Don — Novorossijsk
E117	Mineraljnie Vodi — Tbilist — Yerevan — Megri
E119	Moscow — Volgograd — Baku — Astara
E121	Samara — Turkmenbashi — Iran
E123	Chelyabinsk — Tashkent — Dushanbe — Nizhny Pyanj
E125	Ishim — Petropavlovsk — Astana — Balkhash — Almaty — Bishkek — Torugart
E127	Omsk — Maikapshagai

Intermediate roads

E01	Larne — Dublin — Rosslare ... La Coruña — Lisbon — Faro — Seville	E51	Berlin — Nuremberg
E03	Cherbourg — La Rochelle	E53	Plzeň — Munich
E07	Pau — Zaragoza	E57	Sattledt — Ljubljana
E09	Orléans — Barcelona	E59	Prague — Zagreb
E11	Vierzon — Montpellier	E61	Villach — Rijeka
E13	Doncaster — London	E63	Sodankylä — Turku
E17	Antwerp — Beaune	E67	Helsinki — Tallinn — Kaunas — Warsaw — Prague
E19	Amsterdam — Brussels — Paris	E69	Nordkapp — Olderfjord
E21	Metz — Geneva	E71	Košice — Budapest — Split
E23	Metz — Lausanne	E73	Budapest — Metković
E27	Belfort — Aosta	E77	Pskov — Budapest
E29	Cologne — Sarreguemines	E79	Miskolc — Calafat — Vidín — Thessaloniki
E31	Rotterdam — Ludwigshafen	E81	Mukacevo — Bucharest — Constanta
E33	Parma — La Spezia	E83	Bjala — Sofia
E37	Bremen — Cologne	E87	Odessa — Eceabat ... Çanakkale — Antalya
E39	Trondheim — Kristiansand — Aalborg	E89	Gerede — Ankara
E41	Dortmund — Altdorf	E91	Toprakkale — Syria
E43	Würzburg — Bellinzona	E97	Kherson — Poti – (missing link) – Trabzon — Aşkale
E47	Helsingborg ... Helsingør — Copenhagen — Rødby ... Lübeck	E99	Şanliurfa — Sadarak
E49	Magdeburg — Vienna		

UK airports

'International' is abbreviated to 'Int'.

Aberdeen (Dyce)	Aberdeen	**Cardiff Int**	Wales
Alderney	Channel Is	**City of Derry (Eglinton)**	N Ireland
Barra	Hebrides	**Coventry**	West Midlands
Belfast City (George Best)	N Ireland	**Doncaster Sheffield (Robin Hood)**	South Yorkshire
Belfast Int	N Ireland		
Benbecula	Hebrides	**Dundee**	Dundee
Birmingham Int	West Midlands	**Durham Tees Valley**	Cleveland
Blackpool Int	Lancashire	**East Midlands Int**	Derbyshire
Bournemouth Int	Dorset	**Edinburgh (Turnhouse)**	Edinburgh
Bristol Int	Avon	**Exeter Int**	Devon
Cambridge	Cambridgeshire	**Glasgow Int**	Glasgow
Campbeltown	Argyll and Bute	**Glasgow Prestwick Int**	Ayrshire

Guernsey	Channel Is	Manchester	Lancashire
Humberside	Lincolnshire	Newcastle Int	Northumbria
Inverness	Highland	Newquay Int	Cornwall
Islay	Hebrides	Norwich Int	Norfolk
Isle of Man (Ronaldsway)		Penzance Heliport	Cornwall
Jersey	Channel Is	Plymouth City	Devon
Kent Int	Thanet	St Mary's	Isle of Scilly
Kirkwall	Orkney	Scatsa	Shetlands
Lands End (St Just)	Cornwall	Shoreham	West Sussex
Leeds-Bradford Int	West Yorkshire	Southampton	Hampshire
Lerwick/Tingwall	Shetlands	Southend	Essex
Liverpool (John Lennon)	Merseyside	Stornoway	Hebrides
London City	London	Sumburgh	Shetlands
London Gatwick	West Sussex	Swansea	Wales
London Heathrow	Middlesex	Tiree	Hebrides
London Luton	Bedfordshire	Tresco	Isles of Scilly
London Stansted	Essex	Wick	Caithness
Lydd	Kent		

Communication

International airports

'International' is abbreviated to 'Int'.

Abadan	Iran	Atlanta (Hartsfield–Jackson Int)	Georgia, USA
Abidjan Int (Felix Houphoet Boigny)	Côte d'Ivoire	Auckland (Int)	New Zealand
Abu Dhabi (Int)	United Arab Emirates	Austin–Bergstrom (Int)	Texas, USA
		Avilés (Asturias)	Spain
Acapulco (General Juan N Alvarez)	Mexico	Baghdad (Int)	Iraq
		Bahrain (Int)	Bahrain
Accra (Kotoka Int)	Ghana	Baltimore (Washington Int)	Maryland, USA
Adana	Turkey	Bamako (Senou Int)	Mali
Addis Ababa (Bole Int)	Ethiopia	Bandar Seri Begawan (Brunei Int)	Brunei
Adelaide	Australia		
Aden (Int)	Yemen	Bangkok (Suvarnabhumi Int)	Thailand
Agadir (Al Massira)	Morocco	Banjul (Int)	Gambia
Akron–Canton	Ohio, USA	Barcelona	Spain
Albany (Int)	New York, USA	Bari (Palese)	Italy
Albuquerque (Int Sunport)	New Mexico, USA	Barranquilla (Ernesto Cortissoz Int)	Colombia
Aleppo (Nejrab)	Syria	Basle-Mulhouse (Euro Airport)	Switzerland
Alexandria (El Nhouza)	Egypt		
Algiers (Houari Boumedienne Int)	Algeria	Beijing (Capital Int)	China
		Beira	Mozambique
Alicante	Spain	Beirut (Rafik Hariri Int)	Lebanon
Almaty (Int)	Kazakhstan	Belfast (Int)	N Ireland (UK)
Almería (Int)	Spain	Belgrade (Nikola Tesla)	Serbia
Amarillo (Rick Husband Int)	Texas, USA	Belize City (Philip Goldson Int)	Belize
Amman (Queen Alia Int)	Jordan		
Amsterdam (Schiphol)	Netherlands	Benghazi (Benina Int)	Libya
Anchorage (Ted Stevens Int)	Alaska, USA	Bergen	Norway
		Berlin (Schönefeld Int)	Germany
Ankara (Esenboga Int)	Turkey	Berlin-Tegel Int (Otto Lilienthal)	Germany
Antananarivo	Madagascar		
Antigua (V C Bird Int)	Antigua	Bermuda (Int)	Bermuda (UK)
Antwerp (Deurne)	Belgium	Berne (Bern–Belp)	Switzerland
Apia (Faleolo)	Samoa	Bilbao	Spain
Archangel (Talagi)	Russia	Billund	Denmark
Arnos Vale (E T Joshua)	St Vincent and the Grenadines	Birmingham (Int)	Alabama, USA
		Bishkek (Manas Int)	Kyrgyzstan
Arrecife (Lanzarote)	Canary Is (Spain)	Bissau (Osvaldo Vieira Int)	Guinea-Bissau
Aruba (Queen Beatrix)	Netherlands Antilles	Bogotá (El Dorado)	Colombia
		Bologna (Guglielmo Marconi)	Italy
Ashgabat	Turkmenistan		
Asmara (Int)	Eritrea	Bordeaux	France
Asunción (Silvio Pettirossi Int)	Paraguay	Boston (Logan Int)	Massachusetts, USA
Athens (Eleftherios Venizelos Int)	Greece	Boulogne	France

Communication

Bourgas	Bulgaria
Brasilia Int (President Juscelino Kubitschek)	Brazil
Bratislava (Letisko M R Štefánika)	Slovakia
Brazzaville (Maya Maya)	Congo
Bremen	Germany
Bridgetown (Grantley Adams Int)	Barbados
Brindisi (Papola Casale)	Italy
Brisbane	Australia
Brussels	Belgium
Brussels South (Charleroi)	Belgium
Bucharest (Baneasa Int)	Romania
Bucharest (Henri Coanda)	Romania
Budapest (Ferihegy Int)	Hungary
Buenos Aires (Ministro Pistarini Int)	Argentina
Buffalo (Niagara Int)	New York, USA
Bujumbura (Int)	Burundi
Bulawayo	Zimbabwe
Cagliari (Elmas)	Sardinia (Italy)
Cairns (Int)	Australia
Cairo (Int)	Egypt
Calabar	Nigeria
Calgary (Int)	Canada
Cali (Alfonso Bonilla Aragón Int)	Colombia
Campinas (Viracopos–Campinas Int)	Brazil
Cancún (Int)	Mexico
Cape Town (Int)	South Africa
Caracas (Simón Bolívar Int)	Venezuela
Casablanca (Mohamed V)	Morocco
Catania (Fontanarossa)	Sicily (Italy)
Cayenne (Rochambeau Int)	French Guiana (France)
Cebu (Mactan–Cebu Int)	Philippines
Charleston (Int)	S Carolina, USA
Charleston (Yeager)	W Virginia, USA
Charlotte (Charlotte–Douglas Int)	N Carolina, USA
Cherbourg (Maupertus)	France
Chicago (Midway Int)	Illinois, USA
Chicago (O'Hare Int)	Illinois, USA
Chittagong (Shah Amanat Int)	Bangladesh
Christchurch (Int)	New Zealand
Cincinnati (Northern Kentucky Int)	Ohio, USA
Cleveland (Hopkins Int)	Ohio, USA
Cologne-Bonn	Germany
Colombo (Bandaranaike)	Sri Lanka
Colorado Springs	Colorado, USA
Columbus (Port Columbus Int)	Ohio, USA
Conakry	Guinea
Congonhas/São Paulo Int	Brazil
Constantine (Ain El Bey)	Algeria
Copenhagen	Denmark
Corfu (Ioannis Kapodistrias Int)	Greece
Cork	Ireland
Cotonou	Benin
Curaçao (Hato Int)	Netherlands Antilles
Dakar (Yoff)	Senegal
Dalaman	Turkey
Dallas–Fort Worth (Int)	Texas, USA
Damascus (Int)	Syria
Dar es Salaam (Int)	Tanzania
Darwin (Int)	Australia
Dayton (James M Cox Int)	Ohio, USA
Denpasar (Ngurah Rai Int)	Indonesia
Denver (Int)	Colorado, USA
Des Moines (Int)	Iowa, USA
Detroit (Metropolitan Wayne County)	Michigan, USA
Dhahran (Int)	Saudi Arabia
Dhaka (Zia Int)	Bangladesh
Djerba (Zarzis)	Tunisia
Djibouti (Ambouli)	Djibouti
Doha (Int)	Qatar
Douala	Cameroon
Dresden	Germany
Dubai (Int)	United Arab Emirates
Dublin	Ireland
Dubrovnik	Croatia
Durban (Int)	South Africa
Düsseldorf (Int)	Germany
Edinburgh (Turnhouse)	Scotland (UK)
Edmonton (Int)	Canada
Eindhoven	Netherlands
El Paso (Int)	Texas, USA
Elat	Israel
Entebbe (Int)	Uganda
Erie (Int)	Pennsylvania, USA
Esbjerg	Denmark
Faro	Portugal
Florence (Peretola)	Italy
Fort de France (Lamentin Int)	Martinique
Fort Lauderdale (Hollywood Int)	Florida, USA
Fort Myers (SW Florida Int)	Florida, USA
Frankfurt	Germany
Freeport (Grand Bahama Int)	Bahamas
Freetown (Lungi Int)	Sierra Leone
Fuerteventura	Canary Is (Spain)
Fukuoka	Japan
Funchal (Madeira)	Madeira (Portugal)
Gaborone (Sir Seretse Khama Int)	Botswana
Gaza (Yaser Arafat Int)	Palestinian Territory
Gdansk (Lech Walesa)	Poland
Geneva (Int)	Switzerland
Genoa (Cristoforo Colombo)	Italy
Georgetown (Cheddi Jagan Int)	Guyana
Gibraltar (North Front)	Gibraltar (UK)
Girona–Costa Brava	Spain
Glasgow (Int)	Scotland (UK)
Glasgow (Prestwick Int)	Scotland (UK)
Gothenburg (Landvetter)	Sweden
Granada	Spain
Grand Cayman (Owen Roberts Int)	Cayman Is (UK)
Grand Rapids (Gerald R Ford Int)	Michigan, USA
Graz	Austria
Guadalajara (Miguel Hidalgo Int)	Mexico
Guam (A B Won Pat Int)	Guam (USA)
Guatemala City (La Aurora Int)	Guatemala
Guayaquil (Simón Bolívar Int)	Ecuador

Halifax Stanfield (Int)	Canada
Hamburg	Germany
Hannover	Germany
Hanoi (Noibai)	Vietnam
Harare (Int)	Zimbabwe
Harrisburg (Int)	Pennsylvania, USA
Hartford (Bradley Int)	Connecticut, USA
Havana (Jose Marti Int)	Cuba
Helsinki–Vantaa	Finland
Heraklion Int (Kazantzakis)	Crete (Greece)
Ho Chi Minh City (Tan Son Nath)	Vietnam
Hong Kong (Int)	Hong Kong (China)
Honiara (Henderson Int)	Solomon Is
Honolulu (Int)	Hawaii, USA
Houston (George Bush Intercontinental)	Texas, USA
Ibiza	Balearic Is (Spain)
Indianapolis (Int)	Indiana, USA
Innsbruck	Austria
Islamabad (Int)	Pakistan
Istanbul (Atatürk Int)	Turkey
Izmir (Adnan Menderes)	Turkey
Jacksonville (Int)	Florida, USA
Jakarta (Halim Perdana Kusama)	Indonesia
Jakarta (Soekarno–Hatta Int)	Indonesia
Jeddah (King Abdulaziz Int)	Saudi Arabia
Jerez de la Frontera	Spain
Johannesburg (O R Tambo Int)	South Africa
Kabul (Khwaja Rawash)	Afghanistan
Kagoshima	Japan
Kalmar	Sweden
Kangerlussuaq (Søndre Strømfjord)	Greenland (Denmark)
Kano (Aminu Kano Int)	Nigeria
Kansas City (Int)	Missouri, USA
Kaohsiung (Int)	Taiwan
Karachi (Jinnah Int)	Pakistan
Karpathos Island	Greece
Kathmandu (Tribhuvan Int)	Nepal
Key West (Int)	Florida, USA
Khartoum	Sudan
Kiev (Boryspil Int)	Ukraine
Kigali	Rwanda
Kingston (Norman Manley Int)	Jamaica
Kinshasa (N'Djili)	Congo (Dem Rep)
Klagenfurt	Austria
Kolkata/Calcutta (Netaji Subhas Chandra Bose Int)	India
Kos Island Int (Hippocrates)	Greece
Košice (Int)	Slovakia
Kota Kinabulu (Int	Sabah, Malaysia
Kraków–Balice (John Paul II Int)	Poland
Kristiansand (Kjevik)	Norway
Kuala Lumpur (Int)	Malaysia
Kuching (Int)	Malaysia
Kuwait (Int)	Kuwait
La Coruña	Spain
La Paz (General Manuel Márquez de Léon Int)	Mexico
Laayoune (Hassan)	Morocco
Lagos (Murtala Muhammed Int)	Nigeria
Lahore (Allama Iqbal Int)	Pakistan

Lamezia Terme (Int)	Italy
Larnaca (Int)	Cyprus
Las Palmas (Gran Canaria)	Canary Is (Spain)
Las Vegas (McCarran Int)	Nevada, USA
Le Havre (Octeville)	France
Leipzig–Halle	Germany
Libreville	Gabon
Liège	Belgium
Liepaja	Latvia
Lille	France
Lilongwe (Int)	Malawi
Lima (Jorge Chávez Int)	Peru
Lincoln	Nebraska, USA
Linköping (Saab)	Sweden
Linz (Blue Danube)	Austria
Lisbon (Portela)	Portugal
Little Rock (National)	Arkansas, USA
Ljubljana	Slovenia
Lomé	Togo
London (City)	England (UK)
London (Gatwick)	England (UK)
London (Heathrow)	England (UK)
London (Stansted)	England (UK)
Long Beach	California, USA
Los Angeles (Int)	California, USA
Louisville (Int)	Kentucky, USA
Lourdes (Tarbes–Lourdes–Pyrenees Int)	France
Luanda	Angola
Lubbock (Preston Smith Int)	Texas, USA
Lubumbashi (Luano Int)	Congo (Dem Rep)
Lugano	Switzerland
Lusaka	Zambia
Luxembourg (Findel)	Luxembourg
Luxor	Egypt
Lviv (Int)	Ukraine
Lyon (Saint Exupéry)	France
Maastricht–Aachen	Netherlands
Madison (Dane County Regional)	Wisconsin, USA
Madrid (Barajas)	Spain
Mahé (Seychelles Int)	Seychelles
Mahón (Menorca Int)	Balearic Is (Spain)
Majunga (Amborovy)	Madagascar
Malabo (St Isabel)	Equatorial Guinea
Málaga	Spain
Malé (Int)	Maldives
Malmö–Sturup	Sweden
Malta (Int)	Malta
Managua (Augusto C Sandino)	Nicaragua
Manaus (Eduardo Gomes)	Brazil
Manchester (Int)	England (UK)
Manchester–Boston (Regional)	New Hampshire, USA
Manila (Ninoy Aquino Int)	Philippines
Manzini (Matsapha Int)	Swaziland
Maputo (Int)	Mozambique
Marrakech (Menara Int)	Morocco
Marseille (Provence)	France
Maseru	Lesotho
Mazatlán (General Rafael Buelna Int)	Mexico
Medan (Polonia Int)	Indonesia
Medina (Mohammad bin Adulaziz)	Saudi Arabia
Melbourne	Australia

Communication

Communication

Memphis (Int)	Tennessee, USA
Mérida (Manuel Crescencio Rejón Int)	Mexico
Mexico City (Benito Juárez Int)	Mexico
Miami (Int)	Florida, USA
Milan (Linate Int)	Italy
Milan (Malpensa)	Italy
Milwaukee (General Mitchell Int)	Wisconsin, USA
Minneapolis–St Paul (Int)	Minneapolis, USA
Minsk (Int)	Belarus
Mogadishu (Int)	Somalia
Mombasa (Moi Int)	Kenya
Monastir	Morocco
Monrovia (Roberts Int)	Liberia
Montego Bay (Sangster Int)	Jamaica
Monterey (Peninsula)	California, USA
Monterrey (General Mariano Escobedo Int)	Mexico
Montevideo (Carrasco Int)	Uruguay
Montpellier (Méditerranée)	France
Montréal-Trudeau	Canada
Montserrat (Gerald's)	Montserrat (UK)
Moroni (Prince Said Ibrahim Int)	Comoros
Moscow (Domodedovo Int)	Russia
Moscow (Sheremetyevo Int)	Russia
Moscow (Vnukovo)	Russia
Mumbai/Bombay (Chhatrapati Shivaji Int)	India
Munich	Germany
Münster/Osnabrück	Germany
Murcia (San Javier)	Spain
Murmansk	Russia
Muscat (Seeb Int)	Oman
Nadi (Int)	Fiji
Nagasaki	Japan
Nagoya (Central Japan Int)	Japan
Nairobi (Jomo Kenyatta Int)	Kenya
Nantes (Atlantique)	France
Naples (Int)	Italy
Narsarsuaq	Greenland
Nashville (Int)	Tennessee, USA
Nassau (Int)	Bahamas
Nauru (Int)	Nauru
N'Djamena	Chad
Newark (Liberty Int)	New Jersey, USA
Newcastle	England (UK)
New Delhi (Indira Gandhi Int)	India
New Orleans (Louis Armstrong Int)	Louisiana, USA
New York (J F Kennedy Int)	New Jersey, USA
New York (La Guardia)	New York, USA
Niamey	Niger
Nice (Côte d'Azure)	France
Niš (Constantin the Great Int)	Serbia
Norfolk (Int)	Virginia, USA
Nørresundby (Aalborg)	Denmark
Norrköping (Kungsangen)	Sweden
Nouadhibou	Mauritania
Nouakchott	Mauritania
Nouméa (Tontouta)	New Caledonia (France)
Nuremberg	Germany
Oakland (Int)	California, USA
Odense	Denmark
Okinawa (Naha)	Japan

Oklahoma City (Will Rogers)	Oklahoma, USA
Olbia (Costa Smeralda)	Sardinia (Italy)
Omaha (Eppley Airfield)	Nebraska, USA
Oran (Es Senia)	Algeria
Örebro	Sweden
Orlando (Int)	Florida, USA
Orlando–Sanford (Int)	Florida, USA
Osaka (Kansai Int)	Japan
Oslo	Norway
Ottawa (Int)	Canada
Ouagadougou	Burkina Faso
Oujda (Les Angades)	Morocco
Pago Pago (Int)	American Samoa (USA)
Palermo (Punta Raisi)	Sicily (Italy)
Palma de Mallorca	Balearic Is (Spain)
Pamplona	Spain
Panama City (Tocumen Int)	Panama
Paphos (Int)	Cyprus
Paris Roïssy (Charles de Gaulle)	France
Paris (Orly)	France
Penang Int (Bayan Lepas)	Malaysia
Perpignan (Llabanère)	France
Perth	Australia
Peshawar	Pakistan
Philadelphia (Int)	Pennsylvania, USA
Phnom Penh (Int)	Cambodia
Phoenix (Sky Harbor Int)	Arizona, USA
Pisa Int (Galileo Galilei)	Italy
Pittsburgh (Int)	Pennsylvania, USA
Point Salines Int	Grenada
Pointe Noire	Congo
Pointe-à-Pitre (Guadeloupe Pôle Caraïbes)	Guadeloupe (France)
Ponta Delgado Int	Azores (Portugal)
Poprad–Tatry	Slovakia
Port-au-Prince (Int)	Haiti
Port Harcourt	Nigeria
Portland (Int)	Oregon, USA
Portland (Int Jetport)	Maine, USA
Port Louis (Sir Seewoosagur Ramgoolam Int)	Mauritius
Port Moresby (Jackson)	Papua New Guinea
Porto	Oporto, Portugal
Pôrto Alegre (Salgado Filho Int)	Brazil
Port Sudan	Sudan
Prague (Ruzyně Int)	Czech Republic
Praia	Cape Verde
Providence (T F Green Int)	Rhode Island, USA
Puerto Vallarta (Gustavo Díaz Ordaz Int)	Mexico
Pula	Croatia
Punta Arenas	Chile
Pyongyang (Sunan)	North Korea
Quebec (Jean-Lesage Int)	Canada
Quito (Mariscal Sucre Int)	Ecuador
Rabat (Sale)	Morocco
Raleigh–Durham (Int)	North Carolina, USA
Ras al Khaimah (Int)	United Arab Emirates
Recife (Guararapes Int)	Brazil
Reggio Calabria (Tito Menniti)	Italy
Regina (Int)	Canada

Reno (Reno–Tahoe Int)	Nevada, USA
Reykjavík (Keflavík Int)	Iceland
Rhodes (Diagoras)	Greece
Richmond (Int)	Virginia, USA
Riga (Int)	Latvia
Rio de Janeiro-Galeão (Antônio Carlos Jobin Int)	Brazil
Rio de Janeiro (Santos Dumont)	Brazil
Riyadh (King Khaled Int)	Saudi Arabia
Rochester (Greater Rochester Int)	New York, USA
Rome (Ciampino)	Italy
Rome (Fiumicino, Leonardo da Vinci)	Italy
Rotterdam	Netherlands
St Denis (Gillot)	Réunion (France)
St Kitts (Robert L Bradshaw Int)	St Kitts and Nevis
St Louis (Lambert–St Louis)	Missouri, USA
St Lucia (Hewanorra Int)	St Lucia
St Petersburg (Pulkovo)	Russia
St Thomas (Cyril E King)	Virgin Islands (USA)
Sal Island (Amilcar Cabral Int)	Cape Verde
Salt Lake City (Int)	Utah, USA
Salvador Int (Deputado Luís Eduardo Magalhães)	Brazil
Salzburg (W A Mozart)	Austria
Sanaa (Int)	Yemen
San Antonio (Int)	Texas, USA
San Diego (Int)	California, USA
San Francisco (Int)	California, USA
San José (Juan Santamaría Int)	Costa Rica
San José Int (Mineta)	California, USA
San Juan (Luis Muñoz Marín Int)	Puerto Rico (USA)
San Pedro Sula (La Mesa Int)	El Salvador
San Salvador (Comalapa Int)	El Salvador
San Sebastian	Spain
Santa Cruz de La Palma	Canary Is (Spain)
Santa Maria	Azores (Portugal)
Santander	Spain
Santiago (Arturo Merino Benitez Int)	Chile
Santiago de Compostela	Spain
Santo Domingo (La Isabela Int)	Dominican Republic
São Paulo-Guarulhos Int	Brazil
São Tomé	São Tomé and Príncipe
Sarajevo (Int)	Bosnia and Herzegovina
Seattle–Tacoma	Washington, USA
Seoul (Incheon Int)	South Korea
Seville	Spain
Sfax	Tunisia
Shanghai (Hongqiao Int)	China
Shanghai (Pudong Int)	China
Shannon	Ireland
Sharjah	United Arab Emirates
Singapore (Changi)	Singapore
Skopje	Macedonia
Sliac	Slovakia
Sofia (Int)	Bulgaria
Split	Croatia
Spokane (Int)	Washington, USA
Stavanger (Sola)	Norway
Stockholm-Arlanda	Sweden
Stockholm-Bromma	Sweden
Strasbourg (Int)	Germany
Stuttgart	Germany
Sydney	Australia
Syracuse (Hancock Int)	New York, USA
Szczecin (Goleniów)	Poland
T'aipei (Chiang Kai Shek)	Taiwan
Tallahassee (Regional)	Florida, USA
Tallinn	Estonia
Tamatve	Madagascar
Tampa (Int)	Florida, USA
Tangier (Boukhalef)	Morocco
Tbilisi (Int)	Georgia
Tegucigalpa (Toncontin Int)	Honduras
Tehran (Mehrabad Int)	Iran
Tel Aviv (Ben Gurion Int)	Israel
Tenerife (Queen Sofia)	Canary Is (Spain)
Thessalonika (Macedonia Int)	Greece
Tijuana (General Abelardo L Rodríguez Int)	Mexico
Timioara (Traian Vuia Int)	Romania
Tirana (Rinas Mother Theresa)	Albania
Tobago (Crown Point)	Trinidad and Tobago
Tokyo Int (Haneda)	Japan
Tokyo (Narita Int)	Japan
Toronto Pearson Int	Canada
Toulouse-Blagnac Int	France
Townsville (Int)	Australia
Trieste (Ronchi dei Legionari)	Italy
Trinidad (Piarco Int)	Trinidad and Tobago
Tripoli (Int)	Libya
Trivandrum Int	India
Tucson (Int)	Arizona, USA
Tunis (Carthage Int)	Tunisia
Turin (Int)	Italy
Turku	Finland
Vaasa	Finland
Vága	Faroe Is (Denmark)
Valencia	Spain
Vancouver (Int)	Canada
Varna (Int)	Bulgaria
Venice (Marco Polo Int)	Italy
Verona (Valerio Catullo)	Italy
Victoria, BC	Canada
Vienna (Int)	Austria
Vientiane (Wattay Int)	Laos
Vigie	St Lucia
Vigo	Spain
Vilnius (Int)	Lithuania
Vitoria (Int)	Spain
Warsaw (Frederic Chopin)	Poland
Washington DC (Dulles Int)	Virginia, USA
Wellington (Int)	New Zealand
Wichita (Mid-Continent)	Kansas, USA
Winnipeg (Int)	Manitoba, Canada
Yangon (Int)	Myanmar/Burma
Zagreb	Croatia
Zakynthos Island	Greece
Zürich (Int)	Switzerland

Airline designators

Communication

Code	Airline	Country
AA	American Airlines	USA
AC	Air Canada	Canada
AF	Air France	France
AH	Air Algérie	Algeria
AI	Air India	India
AM	Aeroméxico	Mexico
AR	Aerolíneas Argentinas	Argentina
AS	Alaska Airlines	USA
AT	Royal Air Maroc	Morocco
AV	Avianca	Colombia
AY	Finnair	Finland
AZ	Alitalia	Italy
BA	British Airways	UK
BD	bmi	UK
BE	Flybe	Channel Is
BG	Biman Bangladesh Airlines	Bangladesh
BH	Hawkair	Canada
BI	Royal Brunei Airlines	Brunei
BL	Pacific Airlines	Vietnam
BP	Air Botswana	Botswana
BT	Air Baltic	Latvia
BU	SAS Braathens	Norway
BY	Thomsonfly	UK
CA	Air China	China
CB	ScotAirways	UK
CI	China Airlines	Taiwan
CK	China Cargo Airlines	China
CM	COPA (Compania Panamena de Aviación)	Panama
CO	Continental Airlines	USA
CS	Continental Micronesia	Mariana Is
CU	Cubana de Aviación	Cuba
CY	Cyprus Airways	Cyprus
CZ	China Southern Airlines	China
DA	Georgian Airways	Georgia
DI	dba	Germany
DL	Delta Air Lines	USA
DP	First Choice Airways	UK
DS	easyJet Switzerland	Switzerland
DT	TAAG Air Angola	Angola
DX	Danish Air Transport	Denmark
EI	Aer Lingus	Ireland
EK	Emirates Airline	United Arab Emirates
EL	Air Nippon	Japan
ET	Ethiopian Airlines	Ethiopia
FG	Ariana Afghan Airlines	Afghanistan
FI	Icelandair	Iceland
FJ	Air Pacific	Fiji
FM	Shanghai Airlines	China
FQ	Thomas Cook Airlines	Belgium
FR	Ryanair	Ireland
FX	FedEx	USA
GA	Garuda Indonesia	Indonesia
GC	Gambia International Airlines	Gambia
GF	Gulf Air	Bahrain
GL	Air Greenland	Greenland
GM	Air Slovakia	Slovakia
GR	Aurigny Air Services	Channel Is (UK)
GY	Guyana Airways 2000	Guyana
HA	Hawaiian Airlines	USA
HM	Air Seychelles	Seychelles
HV	Transavia Airlines	Netherlands

Code	Airline	Country
HY	Uzbekistan Airways	Uzbekistan
IA	Iraqi Airways	Iraq
IB	Iberia Airlines	Spain
IC	Indian Airlines	India
IE	Solomon Airlines	Solomon Is
IF	Islas Airways	Spain
IJ	Great Wall Airlines	China
IL	Lankair	Sri Lanka
IN	MAT Macedonian Airlines	Macedonia
IR	Iran Air	Iran
IY	Yemenia	Yemen
JA	B&H Airlines (Air Bosna)	Bosnia and Herzegovina
JL	Japan Airlines	Japan
JM	Air Jamaica	Jamaica
JP	Adria Airways	Slovenia
JS	Air Koryo	North Korea
JU	JAT Airways	Serbia
KA	Dragonair	Hong Kong
KE	Korean Air	South Korea
KL	KLM Royal Dutch Airlines	Netherlands
KM	Air Malta	Malta
KQ	Kenya Airways	Kenya
KU	Kuwait Airways	Kuwait
KV	Kavminvodyavia	Russia
KX	Cayman Airways	Cayman Is
KZ	Nippon Cargo Airlines	Japan
LA	LAN Airlines	Chile
LG	Luxair	Luxembourg
LH	Lufthansa	Germany
LJ	Sierra National Airlines	Sierra Leone
LN	Libyan Arab Airlines	Libya
LO	LOT Polish Airlines	Poland
LP	LAN Peru	Peru
LR	LACSA	Costa Rica
LT	LTU International	Germany
LV	Albanian Airlines	Albania
LX	Swiss International Airlines	Switzerland
LY	El Al	Israel
MA	Malév Hungarian Airlines	Hungary
MD	Air Madagascar	Madagascar
MH	Malaysian Airlines	Malaysia
MK	Air Mauritius	Mauritius
MN	Comair	South Africa
MS	Egypt Air	Egypt
MT	Thomas Cook Airlines	UK
MX	Mexicana de Aviación	Mexico
NA	North American Airlines	USA
NE	SkyEurope Airlines	Slovakia
NF	Air Vanuatu	Vanuatu
NG	Lauda Air	Austria
NH	All Nippon Airways	Japan
NM	Mount Cook Airline	New Zealand
NU	Japan Transocean Air	Japan
NV	Air Central	Japan
NW	Northwest Airlines	USA
NY	Air Iceland	Iceland
NZ	Air New Zealand	New Zealand
OA	Olympic Airways	Greece
OK	Czech Airlines	Czech Republic
OM	MIAT-Mongolian Airlines	Mongolia
ON	Air Nauru	Australia
OO	SkyWest	USA

Communication

Code	Airline	Country
OS	Austrian Airlines	Austria
OU	Croatia Airlines	Croatia
OV	Estonian Air	Estonia
PC	Air Fiji	Fiji
PE	Air Europe	Italy
PF	Palestinian Airlines	Palestinian Territory
PG	Bangkok Airways	Thailand
PH	Polynesian Airlines	Samoa
PK	Pakistan International Airlines	Pakistan
PQ	Panafrican Airways	Côte d'Ivoire
PR	Philippine Airlines	Philippines
PS	Ukraine International Airlines	Ukraine
PU	Pluna (Lineas Aereas Uruguayas)	Uruguay
PX	Air Niugini	Papua New Guinea
QF	Qantas	Australia
QL	Aero Lanka	Sri Lanka
QM	Air Malawi	Malawi
QR	Qatar Airways	Qatar
QS	Travel Service	Czech Republic
QU	East African Airlines	Uganda
QV	Lao Airlines	Laos
QW	SkyKing Turks and Caicos Airways	Turks and Caicos
QX	Horizon Air	USA
QZ	Indonesia AirAsia	Indonesia
Q3	Zambian Airways	Zambia
RA	Royal Nepal Airlines	Nepal
RB	Syrian Arab Airlines	Syria
RG	Varig	Brazil
RJ	Royal Jordanian	Jordan
RK	Royal Khmer Airlines	Cambodia
RO	Tarom	Romania
RR	Royal Air Force	UK
SA	South African Airways	South Africa
SB	Air Calin	France
SD	Sudan Airways	Sudan
SK	Scandinavian Airlines	Denmark, Norway, Sweden
SN	SN Brussels Airlines	Belgium
SQ	Singapore Airlines	Singapore
SU	Aeroflot	Russia

Code	Airline	Country
SV	Saudia Arabian Airlines	Saudi Arabia
SW	Air Namibia	Namibia
TA	TACA	El Salvador
TC	Air Tanzania	Tanzania
TE	Lithuanian Airlines	Lithuania
TG	Thai Airways International	Thailand
TH	BA Connect	UK
TK	Turkish Airlines	Turkey
TM	LAM (Linhas Aéreas de Moçambique)	Mozambique
TN	Air Tahiti Nui	Tahiti
TO	President Airlines	Cambodia
TP	TAP Portugal	Portugal
TU	Tunis Air	Tunisia
UA	United Airlines	USA
UB	Myanmar Airways International	Myanmar (Burma)
UF	UM Airlines	Ukraine
UL	Sri Lankan Airlines	Sri Lanka
UM	Air Zimbabwe	Zimbabwe
UN	Transaero	Russia
UP	Bahamasair	Bahamas
US	US Airways	USA
VN	Vietnam Airlines	Vietnam
VO	Austrian Arrows/Tyrolean Airways	Austria
VR	TACV (Transportes Aereos de Cabo Verde)	Cape Verde
VS	Virgin Atlantic Airways	UK
VT	Air Tahiti	Tahiti
VV	Aerosvit Airlines	Ukraine
VX	Virgin America	USA
VZ	MyTravel Airways	UK
WA	KLM Cityhopper	Netherlands
WH	China Northwest Airlines	China
WN	Southwest Airlines	USA
WO	World Airways	USA
WW	bmibaby	UK
WX	Cityjet	Ireland
WY	Oman Air	Oman
XL	LAN Ecuador	Ecuador
YK	Air Kibris (Turkish Airlines)	Turkey
YM	Montenegro Airlines	Montenegro
ZB	Monarch Airlines	UK
ZH	Shenzhen Airlines	China
9U	Air Moldova	Moldova

Communication

Air distances

Air distances between some major cities, given in statute miles. To convert to kilometres, multiply number given by 1.6093.

	Amsterdam	Beijing	Buenos Aires	Cairo	Chicago	Delhi	Hong Kong	Honolulu	Istanbul	Johannesburg	Lagos	London	Los Angeles	Mexico City	Montreal	Moscow	Nairobi	Paris	Perth	Rome	Santiago	Sydney	Tokyo
Beijing	6566																						
Buenos Aires	7153	12000																					
Cairo	2042	6685	7468																				
Chicago	4109	7599	5587	6135																			
Delhi	3985	2368	8340	2753	8119																		
Hong Kong	5926	1235	3124	5098	7827	2345																	
Honolulu	8368	6778	8693	9439	4246	7888	5543																
Istanbul	1373	4763	7783	764	5502	2833	5998	9547															
Johannesburg	5606	10108	5725	4012	8705	6765	6728	12892	4776														
Lagos	3161	8030	4832	2443	7065	5196	7541	10367	3207	2854													
London	217	5054	6985	2187	3956	4169	5979	7252	1552	5640	3115												
Los Angeles	5559	6349	6140	7589	1746	8717	7231	2553	6994	10443	7716	5442											
Mexico City	5724	7912	4592	7730	1687	9806	8794	4116	7255	10070	7343	5703	1563										
Montreal	3422	7557	5640	5431	737	7421	8564	4923	4795	8322	5595	3252	2482	2307									
Moscow	1338	3604	8382	1790	5500	2698	4839	8802	1089	6280	4462	1550	6992	6700	4393								
Nairobi	4148	8888	7427	2203	8177	4956	7301	11498	2967	1809	2377	4246	9688	9949	7498	3951							
Paris	261	5108	6892	1995	4140	4089	5987	7463	1394	5422	2922	220	5633	5714	3434	1540	4031						
Perth	9118	4987	9734	7766	11281	5013	3752	7115	7846	5564	9246	9535	11098	12402	8355	7373	12587						
Rome	809	5306	6931	1329	4828	3679	5773	8150	852	4802	2497	898	6340	6601	5431	1478	3349	688	8309				
Santiago	7714	13622	710	8029	5328	12715	3733	8147	10109	5738	6042	8568	5594	4168	5551	10118	7547	461	15129	7548			
Sydney	1039	5689	7760	9196	9324	6495	4586	5078	9883	7601	11700	10565	7498	9061	9980	9425	9410	10150	2037	10149	13092		
Tokyo	6006	1313	13100	6362	6286	3656	1807	3831	5757	8535	9130	6218	5451	7014	6913	4668	8565	6208	4925	6146	11049	4640	
Washington	3854	7930	6097	5859	590	7841	8385	4822	5347	8199	5472	3672	2294	1871	493	4884	7918	3843	11829	4495	5061	9792	6763

Flying times

Approximate flying times between some major cities. Timings quoted (in hours and minutes) are for 'flying time' only. In many cases in order to travel between two points chosen, it is necessary to change aircraft one or more times. Times between flights have not been included.

	Beijing	Buenos Aires	Cairo	Chicago	Delhi	Hong Kong	Honolulu	Istanbul	Johannesburg	Lagos	London	Los Angeles	Mexico City	Montreal	Moscow	Nairobi	Paris	Perth	Rome	Santiago	Sydney	Tokyo
Beijing	16.50																					
Buenos Aires	17.45	28.31																				
Cairo	4.20	13.15	20.40																			
Chicago	8.35	15.15	15.40	18.40																		
Delhi	8.15	6.40	26.20	7.00	20.05																	
Hong Kong	15.15	3.00	29.35	10.55	17.05	6.05																
Honolulu	16.42	10.55	19.00	22.50	9.25	16.50	13.05															
Istanbul	3.15	15.40	18.45	2.00	12.20	7.35	17.35	21.05														
Johannesburg	13.15	20.10	12.30	8.55	21.40	23.45	14.55	30.25	16.30													
Lagos	6.40	22.35	9.55	8.20	14.55	14.55	22.30	23.40	8.05	6.55												
London	1.05	18.05	16.35	5.35	8.30	10.35	16.05	17.15	3.50	13.10	6.25											
Los Angeles	11.15	15.25	13.45	21.00	5.00	19.30	15.50	5.15	14.50	24.25	17.25	11.00										
Mexico City	12.27	18.45	10.25	16.47	5.15	20.42	19.10	8.35	15.42	25.42	19.07	14.35	3.20									
Montreal	7.40	27.30	16.00	12.35	2.20	17.35	23.05	12.50	10.15	20.10	13.25	7.00	6.40	4.45								
Moscow	3.15	8.40	22.05	5.25	12.15	7.35	18.00	21.00	4.40	13.30	10.10	3.45	14.45	18.10	10.45							
Nairobi	8.15	16.00	24.55	4.55	17.00	10.45	12.45	25.45	7.15	3.45	6.20	8.30	19.30	20.42	15.30	12.50						
Paris	1.10	16.35	15.35	5.05	9.00	10.45	16.40	18.05	3.10	15.50	7.45	1.05	12.50	13.25	6.25	4.00	9.20					
Perth	20.35	11.15	25.20	17.10	23.00	9.30	8.15	17.25	15.25	14.20	25.55	19.30	19.30	22.50	26.30	19.40	23.00	21.40				
Rome	2.20	16.10	14.40	3.25	11.35	8.50	15.10	19.13	2.35	12.25	6.55	2.25	14.35	5.35	8.10	4.10	7.20	1.55	20.00			
Santiago	20.50	22.34	2.10	25.10	17.15	29.05	19.15	8.35	21.00	19.55	24.25	16.00	12.00	14.50	24.05	29.05	19.45	26.00	18.50			
Sydney	23.05	16.15	20.45	17.20	21.10	13.50	10.35	11.50	18.40	31.50	28.35	21.55	18.10	18.05	24.50	19.40	31.35	25.05	4.35	23.50		
Tokyo	11.40	3.50	28.30	19.40	12.55	9.45	4.20	7.05	14.05	25.00	18.40	11.50	11.55	16.25	18.55	9.25	19.55	16.45	10.05	17.40	27.55	9.15
Washington	8.55	25.50	11.00	14.20	1.45	20.10	24.15	10.55	11.25	21.20	14.45	8.10	8.10	7.50	2.50	12.30	17.10	9.25	22.45	12.40	17.40	23.35	12.40

Deepwater ports of the world

Aalborg	Denmark	Brindisi	Italy	Duisburg	Germany
Aarhus	Denmark	Brisbane	Australia	Duluth	USA
Abadan	Iran	Bristol	UK	Dundee	UK
Aberdeen	UK	Buena Ventura	Colombia	Dunedin	New Zealand
Abidjan	Côte d'Ivoire	Buenos Aires	Argentina	Dunkirk	France
Abu Dhabi	United Arab Emirates	Buffalo	USA	Durban	South Africa
		Busan	South Korea	Durres	Albania
Acajutla	El Salvador	Cabinda	Angola	East London	South Africa
Acapulco	Mexico	Cadiz	Spain	Elat	Israel
Accra	Ghana	Caen	France	Emden	Germany
Adelaide	Australia	Cagliari	Sardinia	Esbjerg	Denmark
Aden	Yemen	Calabar	Nigeria	Europoort	Netherlands
Agadir	Morocco	Calais	France	Famagusta	Cyprus
Ajaccio	Corsica	Caldera	Costa Rica	Faro	Portugal
Alcudia	Majorca	Calicut	India	Felixstowe	UK
Alexandria	Egypt	Callao	Peru	Flensburg	Germany
Algeciras	Spain	Cannes	France	Flushing	Netherlands
Algiers	Algeria	Cape Town	South Africa	Folkestone	UK
Alicante	Spain	Cap Haitian	Haiti	Fortaleza	Brazil
Almeria	Spain	Cardiff	UK	Fort de France	Martinique
Amsterdam	Netherlands	Cartagena	Colombia	Frankfurt	Germany
Anchorage	USA	Cartagena	Spain	Fray Bentos	Uruguay
Ancona	Italy	Casablanca	Morocco	Fredericia	Denmark
Annaba	Algeria	Catania	Sicily	Frederikshavn	Denmark
Antofagasta	Chile	Cayenne	French Guiana	Fredrikstad	Norway
Antwerp	Belgium			Freeport	Bahamas
Apia	Samoa	Cebu	Philippines	Freeport	USA
Aqaba	Jordan	Charleston	USA	Freetown	Sierra Leone
Archangel	Russia	Chennai		Fremantle	Australia
Arica	Chile	(Madras)	India	Funchal	Madeira
Ashdod	Israel	Cherbourg	France	Galveston	USA
Asunción	Paraguay	Chiba	Japan	Galway	Ireland
Auckland	New Zealand	Chicago	USA	Gateshead	UK
Aveiro	Portugal	Chittagong	Bangladesh	Gavle	Sweden
Aviles	Spain	Cienfuegos	Cuba	Gdańsk	Poland
Bahia Blanca	Argentina	Cleveland	USA	Gdynia	Poland
Baku	Azerbaijan	Coatzacoalcos	Mexico	Geelong	Australia
Balboa	Panama	Cochin	India	Genoa	Italy
Baltimore	USA	Cologne	Germany	Georgetown	Cayman Is
Bandar Abbas	Iran	Colombo	Sri Lanka	Georgetown	Guyana
Bangkok	Thailand	Conakry	Guinea	Ghent	Belgium
Banjul	Gambia	Constanta	Romania	Gibraltar	Gibraltar
Barcelona	Spain	Copenhagen	Denmark	Gijon	Spain
Bari	Italy	Corinth	Greece	Glasgow	UK
Barranquilla	Colombia	Corinto	Nicaragua	Godthaab	Greenland
Basra	Iraq	Cork	Ireland	Goole	UK
Batumi	Georgia	Cotonou	Benin	Gothenburg	Sweden
Beira	Mozambique	Dakar	Senegal	Grangemouth	UK
Beirut	Lebanon	Dalian	China	Gravesend	UK
Belem	Brazil	Dammam	Saudi Arabia	Great	
Belfast	UK	Dampier	Australia	Yarmouth	UK
Belize City	Belize	Dar es Salaam	Tanzania	Greenock	UK
Benghazi	Libya	Darwin	Australia	Grimsby	UK
Bergen	Norway	Davao	Philippines	Guayaquil	Ecuador
Bilbao	Spain	Detroit	USA	Haifa	Israel
Bissau	Guinea-Bissau	Dieppe	France	Hakodate	Japan
		Djibouti	Djibouti	Halifax	Canada
Bizerta	Tunisia	Doha	Qatar	Halmstad	Sweden
Bordeaux	France	Dordrecht	Netherlands	Hamburg	Germany
Boston	USA	Douala	Cameroon	Hamilton	Bermuda
Boulogne	France	Douglas	Isle of Man	Hamilton	Canada
Bourgas	Bulgaria	Dover	UK	Harstad	Norway
Brazzaville	Congo	Dubai	United Arab Emirates	Hartlepool	UK
Bremen	Germany			Harwich	UK
Brest	France	Dublin	Ireland	Havana	Cuba
Bridgetown	Barbados	Dubrovnik	Croatia	Hay Point	Australia

Communication

Helsingborg	Sweden	Lobito	Angola	**New Plymouth**	New Zealand
Helsinki	Finland	Lomé	Togo	Newport	UK
Hiroshima	Japan	London	UK	New York	USA
Hobart	Australia	Long Beach	USA	Nice	France
Ho Chi Minh		Los Angeles	USA	Nouakchott	Mauritania
City	Vietnam	Lowestoft	UK	Noumea	New
Hodeida	Yemen	Luanda	Angola		Caledonia
Holyhead	UK	Lübeck	Germany	Novorossiysk	Russia
Hong Kong	Hong Kong	Lüda	China	Nukualofa	Tonga
Honiari	Solomon Is	Macao	China	Nyborg	Denmark
Honolulu	Hawaii	Malaga	Spain	Oakland	USA
Houston	USA	Malmö	Sweden	Odense	Denmark
Hull	UK	Manama	Bahrain	Odessa	Ukraine
Ibiza	Ibiza	Manaus	Brazil	Oporto	Portugal
Inchon	South Korea	Manchester	UK	Oran	Algeria
Iskenderun	Turkey	Manila	Philippines	Osaka	Japan
Istanbul	Turkey	Mannheim	Germany	Oslo	Norway
Izmir	Turkey	Manzanillo	Mexico	Ostend	Belgium
Jacksonville	USA	Maputo	Mozambique	Oulu	Finland
Jakarta	Indonesia	Mar del Plata	Argentina	Pago Pago	Samoa
Jarrow	UK	Maracaibo	Venezuela	Palermo	Sicily
Jeddah	Saudi Arabia	Mariehamn	Finland	Palma	Majorca
Juneau	USA	Marsala	Sicily	Palm Beach	USA
Kagoshima	Japan	Marseilles	France	Panama Canal	Panama
Kalmar	Sweden	Masan	South Korea	Papeete	Tahiti
Kandla	India	Matanzas	Cuba	Paradip	India
Kaohsiung	Taiwan	Melbourne	Australia	Paramaribo	Suriname
Karachi	Pakistan	Mersin	Turkey	Paranagua	Brazil
Kawasaki	Japan	Messina	Sicily	Paris	France
Khulna	Bangladesh	Miami	USA	Pasajes	Spain
Kiel	Germany	Middlesbrough	UK	Pasir Gudang	Malaysia
Kingston	Jamaica	Milwaukee	USA	Penang	Malaysia
Kirkcaldy	UK	Mina Qaboos	Oman	Philadelphia	USA
Kitakyushu	Japan	Mina Sulman	Bahrain	Phnom Penh	Cambodia
Klaipeda	Lithuania	Mindelo	Cape Verde	Piraeus	Greece
Kobe	Japan	Mizushima	Japan	Plymouth	UK
Kolkata		Mobile	USA	Point-a-Pitre	Guadeloupe
(Calcutta)	India	Mogadishu	Somalia	Pointe-Noire	Congo
Kompong Som	Cambodia	Mombasa	Kenya	Pondicherry	India
Koper	Slovenia	Monrovia	Liberia	Ponta Delgada	Azores
Kota Kinabalu	Malaysia	Montego Bay	Jamaica	Poole	UK
Kowloon	Hong Kong	Montevideo	Uruguay	Port Adelaide	Australia
Kristiansand	Norway	Montreal	Canada	Port-au-Prince	Haiti
Kuching	Malaysia	Mormugao	India	Port Cartier	Canada
Kushiro	Japan	Moulmein	Myanmar	Port Elizabeth	South Africa
Kuwait	Kuwait		(Burma)	Port	
Lagos	Nigeria	Mumbai		Georgetown	Guyana
La Guaira	Venezuela	(Bombay)	India	Port Gentil	Gabon
Langesund	Norway	Murmansk	Russia	Port Harcourt	Nigeria
La Plata	Argentina	Muscat	Oman	Port Hedland	Australia
Larnaca	Cyprus	Nacala	Mozambique	Pork Kelang	Malaysia
Larne	UK	Nagasaki	Japan	Port Kembla	Australia
Las Palmas	Grand Canary	Nagoya	Japan	Portland	USA
La Spezia	Italy	Nampo	North Korea	Port Limon	Costa Rica
Lattakia	Syria	Nantes	France	Port Louis	Mauritius
La Coruña	Spain	Napier	New Zealand	Port Moresby	Papua New
Launceton	Australia	Naples	Italy		Guinea
La Union	El Salvador	Narvik	Norway	Port of Spain	Trinidad
Le Havre	France	Nassau	Bahamas	Port Said	Egypt
Leith	UK	Natal	Brazil	Port Sudan	Sudan
Libreville	Gabon	Nelson	New Zealand	Port Talbot	UK
Liège	Belgium	New		Port Victoria	Seychelles
Limassol	Cyprus	Amsterdam	Guyana	Porto Alegre	Brazil
Limerick	Ireland	Newcastle	Australia	Portsmouth	UK
Lisbon	Portugal	Newcastle	UK	Prince Rupert	Canada
Liverpool	UK	New Haven	USA	Providence	USA
Livingstone	Guatemala	New Mangalore	India	Puerto Cortés	Honduras
Livorno	Italy	New Orleans	USA	Pula	Croatia

Punta Arenas	Chile	Santiago de		Thunder Bay	Canada
Pusan	South Korea	Cuba	Cuba	Timaru	New Zealand
Quebec	Canada	Santo Domingo	Dominican	Tianjin	China
Ramsgate	UK		Republic	Toamasina	Madagascar
Rangoon	Myanmar	Santos	Brazil	Tokyo	Japan
	(Burma)	São Tomé	São Tomé	Toledo	USA
Ravenna	Italy		and Príncipe	Toronto	Canada
Recife	Brazil	Sasebo	Japan	Torshavn	Faroes
Reykjavik	Iceland	Sassandra	Côte d'Ivoire	Toulon	France
Richards Bay	South Africa	Savannah	USA	Townsville	Australia
Richmond	USA	Savona	Italy	Toyama	Japan
Riga	Latvia	Seattle	USA	Trebizond	Turkey
Rijeka	Croatia	Sevastopol	Ukraine	Trieste	Italy
Rimini	Italy	Seville	Spain	Tripoli	Lebanon
Rio de Janeiro	Brazil	Sfax	Tunisia	Tripoli	Libya
Rio Grande	Brazil	Shanghai	China	Trondheim	Norway
Rosaria	Argentina	Shimizu	Japan	Tunis	Tunisia
Rostock	Germany	Singapore	Singapore	Turku	Finland
Rotterdam	Netherlands	Sitra	Bahrain	Tuticorin	India
Rouen	France	Sittwe	Myanmar	Tyre	Lebanon
Sacramento	USA		(Burma)	Ulsan	South Korea
Safi	Morocco	Sousse	Tunisia	Vaasa	Finland
St George's	Grenada	Southampton	UK	Valencia	Spain
St Helier	Jersey	Split	Croatia	Valetta	Malta
St John	Canada	Stavanger	Norway	Valparaíso	Chile
St John's	Antigua	Stockholm	Sweden	Vancouver	Canada
St John's	Canada	Stockton	USA	Varna	Bulgaria
St Malo	France	Stralsund	Germany	Venice	Italy
St Nazaire	France	Suez	Egypt	Velsen	Netherlands
St Petersburg	Russia	Sunderland	UK	Veracruz	Mexico
Sakai	Japan	Sundsvall	Sweden	Vigo	Spain
Salerno	Italy	Surabaya	Indonesia	Visakhapatnam	India
Salina Cruz	Mexico	Suva	Fiji	Vitoria	Brazil
Salonica	Greece	Swansea	UK	Vlaardingen	Netherlands
Salvador	Brazil	Sydney	Australia	Vladivostok	Russia
Samsun	Turkey	Sydney	Canada	Volgograd	Russia
San Diego	USA	Syracuse	Sicily	Walvis Bay	Namibia
San Francisco	USA	Szczecin	Poland	Wellington	New Zealand
San José	Guatemala	Tacoma	USA	Willemstad	Netherlands
San Juan	Puerto Rico	Takamatsu	Japan		Antilles
San Juan del		Takoradi	Ghana	Wilmington	USA
Sur	Nicaragua	Tallinn	Estonia	Xingang	China
San Lorenzo	Argentina	Tampa	USA	Yangon	Myanmar
San Pedro	Côte d'Ivoire	Tampico	Mexico		(Burma)
San Remo	Italy	Tanga	Tanzania	Yokohama	Japan
San Sebastián	Spain	Tangier	Morocco	Zamboanga	Philippines
Santa Cruz de		Taranto	Italy	Zanzibar	Tanzania
Tenerife	Tenerife	Tarragona	Spain	Zeebrugge	Belgium
Santa Fé	Argentina	Tauranga	New Zealand	Zhdanov	Ukraine
Santa Marta	Colombia	Three Rivers			
Santander	Spain	(Trois Rivières)	Canada		

Communication

SOCIAL STRUCTURE

World population estimates

Date (AD)	Millions	Date (AD)	Millions	Date (AD)	Millions
1	300	1900	1650	2010	6907
1000	310	1950	2535	2020	7667
1250	400	1960	3031	2030	8318
1500	500	1970	3699	2040	8824
1750	790	1980	4451	2050	9191
1800	980	1990	5295		
1850	1260	2000	6124		

The above are based on United Nations estimates and predictions (medium variant) published in 2006. The totals are lower than predictions made in the early 1990s (eg 11000 million world population by 2050), mainly due to government-sponsored birth-control schemes in China. By 2050, China is expected to have been overtaken by India as the world's most populous nation (see below).

Population of the six most populous nations

		1950		2050
China	1st	555m	2nd	1409m
India	2nd	372m	1st	1658m
USA	3rd	158m	3rd	402m
USSR/Russian Federation	4th	103m	15th	108m
Japan	5th	84m	16th	103m
Indonesia	6th	80m	5th	297m

Population for 2050 compared against 1950 in medium-variant predictions.

Major cities of the world

Cities are listed alphabetically followed by population figures, with year of estimate (e) or census (c) in brackets. Data is for the city proper, not the metropolitan area, insofar as a distinction can be made.

Abidjan Côte d'Ivoire	3900546 (2008e)
Abu Dhabi United Arab Emirates	1975863 (2008e)
Acapulco Mexico	669366 (2008e)
Accra Ghana	3905009 (2008e)
Adana Turkey	1366027 (2007e)
Addis Ababa Ethiopia	3059000 (2007e)
Adelaide Australia	1039516 (2008e)
Aden Yemen	672514 (2008e)
Agadir Morocco	542130 (2008e)
Agra India	1590073 (2008e)
Ahmadabad India	3867336 (2008e)
Ahvaz Iran	1003162 (2008e)
Ajmer India	542057 (2008e)
Albuquerque USA	504949 (2006e)
Aleppo Syria	2738000 (2007e)
Alexandria Egypt	4110015 (2006c)
Algiers Algeria	3456701 (2008e)
Aligarh India	823085 (2008e)
Allahabad India	1243649 (2008e)
Almaty Kazakhstan	1328362 (2008e)
Amagasaki Japan	455973 (2008e)
Amman Jordan	1135733 (2008e)
Amritsar India	1181790 (2008e)
Amsterdam Netherlands	743393 (2006e)
Ankara Turkey	3763591 (2007e)
Anshan China	1639000 (2007e)
Antananarivo Madagascar	1699114 (2008e)
Antwerp Belgium	472000 (2008e)
Anyang China	887000 (2007e)
Aracaju Brazil	515754 (2008e)
Archangel Russia	341818 (2008e)
Arequipa Peru	887367 (2008e)
Asahikawa Japan	350247 (2008e)
Ashgabat Turkmenistan	891879 (2008e)
Astrakhan Russia	497508 (2008e)
Asunción Paraguay	2014725 (2008e)
Athens Greece	3730000 (2008e)
Atlanta USA	486411 (2006e)
Auckland New Zealand	438000 (2008e)
Austin USA	709893 (2006e)
Baghdad Iraq	6000000 (2008e)
Bakhtaran Iran	784602 (2006c)
Baku Azerbaijan	1892000 (2007e)
Baltimore USA	631366 (2006e)
Bamako Mali	1662786 (2008e)
Bandung Indonesia	6234944 (2008e)
Bangalore India	6660000 (2008e)
Bangkok Thailand	8290000 (2008e)
Bangui Central African Republic	735143 (2006e)
Banjarmasin Indonesia	598518 (2008e)
Banjul The Gambia	33820 (2008e)
Baoding China	1076288 (2008e)
Baoji China	630610 (2008e)
Baotou China	2036000 (2007e)

Barcelona Spain	1 595 110 (2007e)	**Changsha** China	2 211 209 (2008e)	
Bareilly India	812 337 (2008e)	**Changzhou** China	975 848 (2008e)	
Bari Italy	305 843 (2008e)	**Charlotte** USA	630 478 (2006e)	
Barnaul Russia	586 682 (2008e)	**Cheboksary** Russia	450 773 (2008e)	
Barquisimeto Venezuela	1 085 483 (2007e)	**Chelyabinsk** Russia	1 033 637 (2008e)	
Barranquilla Colombia	1 798 000 (2007e)	**Chemnitz** Germany	245 700 (2007e)	
Basra Iraq	2 141 270 (2006e)	**Chengdu** China	3 915 259 (2008e)	
Beijing (Peking) China	12 770 000 (2008e)	**Chennai (Madras)** India	4 562 843 (2008e)	
Beirut Lebanon	1 987 173 (2008e)	**Cherepovets** Russia	311 729 (2008e)	
Belém Brazil	1 522 035 (2008e)	**Chiba** Japan	942 490 (2008e)	
Belfast UK	262 786 (2008e)	**Chicago** USA	2 833 321 (2006e)	
Belgorod Russia	348 536 (2008e)	**Chiclayo** Peru	524 442 (2007c)	
Belgrade Serbia	1 104 240 (2008e)	**Chifeng** China	1 277 000 (2007e)	
Belo Horizonte Brazil	2 480 490 (2008e)	**Chihuahua** Mexico	738 241 (2008e)	
Bengbu China	591 616 (2008e)	**Chimkent** Kazakhstan	454 583 (2008e)	
Benxi China	1 040 148 (2008e)	**Chita** Russia	314 711 (2008e)	
Berlin Germany	3 404 037 (2007e)	**Chittagong** Bangladesh	4 090 809 (2006e)	
Bern Switzerland	956 671 (2006e)	**Chongjin** North Korea	328 493 (2008e)	
Bhavnagar India	589 351 (2008e)	**Chongju** South Korea	643 591 (2006e)	
Bhilai Nagar India	685 863 (2008e)	**Chongqing** China	6 461 000 (2007e)	
Bhopal India	1 712 355 (2008e)	**Chonju** South Korea	729 337 (2006e)	
Bilbao Spain	354 928 (2008e)	**Christchurch** New Zealand	360 765 (2006c)	
Birmingham UK	1 010 200 (2007e)	**Chungho** Taiwan	414 077 (2008e)	
Bissau Guinea-Bissau	408 627 (2008e)	**Cincinnati** USA	332 252 (2006e)	
Bochum Germany	383 743 (2007e)	**Ciudad Guayana** Venezuela	769 243 (2006e)	
Bogota Colombia	7 440 000 (2008e)	**Ciudad Juárez** Mexico	1 537 485 (2008e)	
Bologna Italy	372 380 (2008e)	**Cleveland** USA	444 313 (2006e)	
Bombay ▶ Mumbai		**Cluj-Napoca** Romania	302 644 (2008e)	
Bonn Germany	314 299 (2007e)	**Cochabamba** Bolivia	932 871 (2006e)	
Boston USA	590 763 (2006e)	**Cochin** India	606 223 (2006e)	
Brasilia Brazil	2 406 478 (2008e)	**Coimbatore** India	1 696 000 (2007e)	
Brasov Romania	279 758 (2008e)	**Cologne** Germany	989 766 (2007e)	
Bratislava Slovakia	422 452 (2006e)	**Colombo** Sri Lanka	678 130 (2008e)	
Brazzaville Congo	1 355 000 (2007e)	**Columbus** USA	733 203 (2006e)	
Bremen Germany	547 934 (2007e)	**Conakry** Guinea	1 857 153 (2008e)	
Brisbane Australia	1 823 939 (2008e)	**Constanta** Romania	301 107 (2006e)	
Bristol UK	416 400 (2007e)	**Constantine** Algeria	465 078 (2008e)	
Brno Czech Republic	365 440 (2008e)	**Contagem** Brazil	691 519 (2008e)	
Brussels Belgium	1 018 029 (2006e)	**Copenhagen** Denmark	1 085 000 (2007e)	
Bryansk Russia	418 442 (2008e)	**Córdoba** Argentina	1 669 184 (2006e)	
Bucaramanga Colombia	1 009 000 (2007e)	**Coventry** UK	306 700 (2007e)	
Bucharest Romania	1 921 279 (2008e)	**Cracow** Poland	756 336 (2007e)	
Budapest Hungary	1 666 892 (2008e)	**Cucuta** Colombia	852 000 (2005e)	
Buenos Aires Argentina	12 127 814 (2008e)	**Culiacan** Mexico	809 000 (2007e)	
Buffalo USA	276 059 (2006e)	**Curitiba** Brazil	1 837 036 (2008e)	
Bulawayo Zimbabwe	731 003 (2008e)	**Dakar** Senegal	2 485 851 (2008e)	
Bursa Turkey	1 431 172 (2007e)	**Dalian** China	3 167 000 (2007e)	
Bydgoszcz Poland	362 397 (2007e)	**Dallas** USA	1 232 940 (2006e)	
Cairo Egypt	7 786 640 (2006c)	**Damascus** Syria	2 240 000 (2008e)	
Calcutta ▶ Kolkata		**Da Nang** Vietnam	486 690 (2008e)	
Calgary Canada	988 079 (2006c)	**Dandong** China	870 000 (2007e)	
Cali Colombia	2 139 535 (2007e)	**Daqing** China	1 693 000 (2007e)	
Calicut India	441 123 (2008e)	**Dar es Salaam** Tanzania	2 975 986 (2008e)	
Callao Peru	438 326 (2007c)	**Datong** China	1 873 000 (2007e)	
Caloocan City Philippines	1 378 856 (2007c)	**Davao City** Philippines	1 556 270 (2008e)	
Campinas Brazil	1 095 220 (2008e)	**Delhi** India	18 000 000 (2008e)	
Campo Grande Brazil	791 209 (2008e)	**Denver** USA	566 974 (2006e)	
Campos Brazil	403 804 (2008e)	**Detroit** USA	871 121 (2006e)	
Canberra Australia	329 200 (2008e)	**Dhaka** Bangladesh	7 310 000 (2008e)	
Cape Town South Africa	3 481 156 (2008e)	**Diyarbakir** Turkey	592 557 (2007e)	
Caracas Venezuela	2 985 000 (2007e)	**Dnepropetrovsk** Ukraine	1 046 922 (2008e)	
Cardiff UK	321 000 (2007e)	**Doha** Qatar	398 017 (2008e)	
Cartagena Colombia	871 342 (2007e)	**Donetsk** Ukraine	990 132 (2008e)	
Casablanca Morocco	3 239 585 (2008e)	**Dortmund** Germany	587 624 (2007e)	
Catania Italy	293 093 (2008e)	**Douala** Cameroon	1 978 650 (2008e)	
Cebu City Philippines	811 365 (2008e)	**Dresden** Germany	504 795 (2007e)	
Chandigarh India	1 003 301 (2008e)	**Dubai** United Arab Emirates	1 674 527 (2008e)	
Changchun China	2 688 669 (2008e)	**Dublin** Ireland	1 044 726 (2006c)	

Social Structure

Duisburg Germany	499111 (2007e)	**Harare** Zimbabwe	1661675 (2008e)
Dukou China	462953 (2006e)	**Harbin** China	3621000 (2007e)
Duque de Caxias Brazil	862267 (2008e)	**Havana** Cuba	2144040 (2008e)
Durban South Africa	3306631 (2008e)	**Hefei** China	2035000 (2007e)
Durgapur India	538306 (2008e)	**Hegang** China	761228 (2008e)
Dushanbe Tajikistan	689123 (2008e)	**Helsinki** Finland	568146 (2007e)
Düsseldorf Germany	577505 (2007e)	**Hengyang** China	1016000 (2007e)
Dzhambul Kazakhstan	398233 (2008e)	**Hermosillo** Mexico	627378 (2008e)
Edinburgh UK	468100 (2007e)	**Higashiosaka** Japan	512133 (2008e)
Edmonton Canada	1034945 (2006c)	**Himeji** Japan	483205 (2008e)
El Giza Egypt	2681863 (2006c)	**Hirakata** Japan	407092 (2006e)
El Mahalla el-Koubra Egypt	442884 (2006c)	**Hiroshima** Japan	1165870 (2008e)
El Mansoura Egypt	450267 (2006c)	**Ho Chi Minh City** Vietnam	6710000 (2008e)
El Paso USA	609415 (2006e)	**Hohhot** China	1726000 (2007e)
Eskisehir Turkey	570825 (2007e)	**Homs** Syria	1005000 (2007e)
Essen Germany	583198 (2007e)	**Hong Kong** China	7175596 (2008e)
Faisalabad Pakistan	2708944 (2008e)	**Honolulu** USA	377357 (2006e)
Faridabad India	1407265 (2008e)	**Houston** USA	2144491 (2006e)
Feira de Santana Brazil	535300 (2006e)	**Howrah** India	1033158 (2008e)
Fez Morocco	1008782 (2008e)	**Huaibei** China	976220 (2008e)
Florence Italy	376714 (2008e)	**Huainan** China	1451000 (2007e)
Fortaleza Brazil	2468165 (2008e)	**Huangshi** China	703152 (2008e)
Fort Worth USA	653320 (2006e)	**Hubli-Dharwar** India	879506 (2008e)
Frankfurt am Main Germany	652610 (2007e)	**Hull ▶ Kingston upon Hull**	
Freetown Sierra Leone	819634 (2008e)	**Hunjiang** China	789000 (2005e)
Fujisawa Japan	403788 (2008e)	**Hyderabad** India	3980938 (2008e)
Fukuoka Japan	1433418 (2008e)	**Hyderabad** Pakistan	1496163 (2008e)
Fukuyama Japan	384217 (2006e)	**Iasi** Romania	315214 (2007e)
Funabashi Japan	578116 (2008e)	**Ibadan** Nigeria	2550600 (2006c)
Fushun China	1470000 (2007e)	**Icel** Turkey	629635 (2008e)
Fuxin China	694525 (2008e)	**Ichikawa** Japan	474166 (2008e)
Fuzhou China	2606000 (2007e)	**Inchon** South Korea	2550000 (2007e)
Ganzhou China	258786 (2008e)	**Indianapolis** USA	785597 (2006e)
Gaziantep Turkey	1175042 (2007e)	**Indore** India	2026000 (2007e)
Gdańsk Poland	456103 (2007e)	**Irkutsk** Russia	584442 (2006e)
Genoa Italy	588450 (2008e)	**Isfahan** Iran	1583609 (2006c)
Georgetown Guyana	247588 (2008e)	**Istanbul** Turkey	10757327 (2007e)
Gifu Japan	396889 (2008e)	**Ivanovo** Russia	412884 (2008e)
Glasgow UK	581900 (2007e)	**Iwaki** Japan	356829 (2006e)
Goiânia Brazil	1247525 (2008e)	**Izhevsk** Russia	615114 (2008e)
Gomel Belarus	477161 (2008e)	**Izmir** Turkey	2606294 (2007e)
Gorakhpur India	707516 (2008e)	**Jabalpur** India	1285000 (2007e)
Gorlovka Ukraine	270526 (2008e)	**Jaboatão** Brazil	790815 (2008e)
Gothenburg Sweden	827000 (2005e)	**Jacksonville** USA	794555 (2006e)
Grozny Russia	185600 (2008e)	**Jaipur** India	2997114 (2008e)
Guadalajara Mexico	1616581 (2008e)	**Jakarta** Indonesia	8576788 (2008e)
Guangzhou (Canton) China	8829000 (2007e)	**Jalandhar** India	857717 (2008e)
Guarulhos Brazil	1286855 (2008e)	**Jamshedpur** India	655290 (2008e)
Guatemala City Guatemala	1074410 (2008e)	**Jedda** Saudi Arabia	3088558 (2008e)
Guayaquil Ecuador	2530000 (2008e)	**Jerusalem** Israel	750892 (2008e)
Guilin China	987000 (2007e)	**Jiamusi** China	1020000 (2007e)
Guiyang China	3662000 (2007e)	**Jiaozuo** China	857000 (2007e)
Gujranwala Pakistan	1484172 (2008e)	**Jilin** China	2396000 (2007e)
Guntur India	540011 (2008e)	**Jinan** China	2798000 (2007e)
Gwalior India	978000 (2007e)	**Jingdezhen** China	312350 (2006e)
Gwangju South Korea	1440000 (2007e)	**Jinzhou** China	956000 (2007e)
Hachioji Japan	588315 (2006e)	**Jixi** China	965000 (2007e)
The Hague Netherlands	475197 (2006e)	**João Pessoa** Brazil	693094 (2008e)
Haiphong Vietnam	1969000 (2007e)	**Jodhpur** India	987124 (2008e)
Hakodate Japan	293265 (2008e)	**Johannesburg** South Africa	3888180 (2007e)
Hamamatsu Japan	609786 (2006e)	**Juiz de Fora** Brazil	509100 (2006e)
Hamburg Germany	1754182 (2007e)	**Kabul** Afghanistan	3000000 (2008e)
Hamhung North Korea	575463 (2008e)	**Kaesong** North Korea	348176 (2008e)
Hamilton Canada	504559 (2006c)	**Kagoshima** Japan	607701 (2008e)
Handan China	1631000 (2007e)	**Kaifeng** China	872000 (2007e)
Hangzhou China	3410000 (2008e)	**Kaliningrad** Russia	436762 (2006e)
Hanoi Vietnam	4378000 (2007e)	**Kaluga** Russia	340475 (2006e)
Hanover Germany	516343 (2007e)	**Kampala** Uganda	1507042 (2008e)

Kanazawa Japan	459 488 (2006e)	**Liaoyang** China	794 000 (2007e)
Kano Nigeria	2 950 000 (2008e)	**Liaoyuan** China	468 146 (2006e)
Kanpur India	3 067 663 (2008e)	**Libreville** Gabon	713 167 (2008e)
Kansas City USA	447 306 (2006e)	**Lima** Peru	7 804 611 (2008e)
Kaohsiung Taiwan	1 522 399 (2008e)	**Lipetsk** Russia	519 026 (2006e)
Karachi Pakistan	12 130 000 (2007e)	**Lisbon** Portugal	491 888 (2008e)
Karaganda Kazakhstan	429 202 (2008e)	**Liupanshui** China	1 221 000 (2007e)
Karaj Iran	1 468 773 (2008e)	**Liuzhou** China	1 497 000 (2007e)
Kathmandu Nepal	911 084 (2008e)	**Liverpool** UK	435 500 (2007e)
Katowice Poland	341 322 (2006e)	**Ljubljana** Slovenia	254 188 (2006e)
Kaunas Lithuania	358 111 (2007e)	**Lodz** Poland	756 666 (2007e)
Kawaguchi Japan	489 236 (2008e)	**Lomé** Togo	1 501 777 (2008e)
Kawasaki Japan	1 362 976 (2008e)	**London** Canada	457 720 (2006c)
Kayseri Turkey	696 833 (2007e)	**London (Greater)** UK	7 556 900 (2007e)
Kazan Russia	1 113 000 (2006e)	**Londrina** Brazil	505 932 (2008e)
Keelung Taiwan	401 453 (2006e)	**Long Beach** USA	472 494 (2006e)
Kemerovo Russia	478 788 (2008e)	**Los Angeles** USA	3 849 378 (2006e)
Kenitra Morocco	388 375 (2008e)	**Luanda** Angola	4 800 000 (2007e)
Khabarovsk Russia	593 578 (2008e)	**Lublin** Poland	352 786 (2007e)
Kharkov Ukraine	1 460 446 (2008e)	**Lucknow** India	2 621 063 (2008e)
Khartoum Sudan	4 600 000 (2008e)	**Ludhiana** India	1 662 325 (2008e)
Kherson Ukraine	313 587 (2008e)	**Luhansk** Ukraine	446 959 (2008e)
Khulna Bangladesh	1 355 354 (2007e)	**Luoyang** China	1 715 000 (2007e)
Kiev Ukraine	2 700 000 (2007e)	**Lusaka** Zambia	1 377 130 (2008e)
Kigali Rwanda	904 779 (2008e)	**Luxembourg** Luxembourg	75 552 (2008e)
Kingston Jamaica	585 300 (2006e)	**Lyons** France	482 717 (2008e)
Kingston upon Hull UK	257 000 (2007e)	**Maceió** Brazil	1 073 565 (2008e)
Kinshasa Democratic	7 843 000 (2007e)	**Machida** Japan	420 414 (2008e)
Republic of Congo		**Madras ▶ Chennai**	
Kirkuk Iraq	835 927 (2008e)	**Madrid** Spain	3 128 600 (2006e)
Kirov Russia	458 004 (2008e)	**Madurai** India	1 294 000 (2007e)
Kishinyov Moldova	598 355 (2008e)	**Magnitogorsk** Russia	402 375 (2008e)
Kitakyushu Japan	982 094 (2008e)	**Makassar** Indonesia	1 410 551 (2008e)
Kitchener Canada	451 235 (2006c)	**Makeyevka** Ukraine	367 403 (2008e)
Kitwe Zambia	488 426 (2008e)	**Makhachkala** Russia	510 775 (2006e)
Kobe Japan	1 538 324 (2008e)	**Malaga** Spain	566 319 (2008e)
Kochi Japan	336 592 (2006e)	**Malang** Indonesia	964 000 (2005e)
Kolhapur India	553 815 (2008e)	**Managua** Nicaragua	1 165 000 (2005e)
Kolkata (Calcutta) India	5 021 458 (2008e)	**Manaus** Brazil	1 766 820 (2008e)
Komsomolosk Russia	278 649 (2008e)	**Manchester** UK	458 100 (2007e)
Konya Turkey	967 055 (2007e)	**Mandalay** Myanmar (Burma)	1 329 943 (2008e)
Koriyama Japan	339 741 (2008e)	**Manila** Philippines	1 660 714 (2007c)
Kota India	810 509 (2008e)	**Maputo** Mozambique	1 099 102 (2007c)
Krasnodar Russia	710 000 (2006e)	**Maracaibo** Venezuela	2 447 096 (2008e)
Krasnoyarsk Russia	902 142 (2008e)	**Maracay** Venezuela	1 007 000 (2007e)
Krivoy Rog Ukraine	714 453 (2008e)	**Mar del Plata** Argentina	584 702 (2008e)
Kuala Lumpur Malaysia	1 458 790 (2008e)	**Mariupol** Ukraine	476 860 (2008e)
Kumamoto Japan	684 505 (2006e)	**Marrakesh** Morocco	887 192 (2008e)
Kumasi Ghana	1 765 712 (2008e)	**Marseilles** France	1 400 000 (2007e)
Kunming China	2 931 000 (2007e)	**Masan** South Korea	316 344 (2008e)
Kurashiki Japan	475 693 (2008e)	**Matsudo** Japan	480 785 (2008e)
Kurgan Russia	336 749 (2008e)	**Matsuyama** Japan	487 890 (2006e)
Kursk Russia	400 172 (2008e)	**Mecca** Saudi Arabia	1 421 715 (2008e)
Kuwait City Kuwait	32 403 (2005c)	**Medan** Indonesia	2 300 000 (2008e)
Kyoto Japan	1 474 764 (2005c)	**Medellin** Colombia	3 080 000 (2008e)
Lagos Nigeria	9 494 045 (2008e)	**Meerut** India	1 398 000 (2007e)
Lahore Pakistan	6 747 238 (2008e)	**Meknes** Morocco	576 152 (2008e)
Lanzhou China	2 561 000 (2007e)	**Melbourne** Australia	3 810 000 (2007e)
La Paz Bolivia	1 590 000 (2007e)	**Memphis** USA	674 126 (2008e)
La Plata Argentina	731 458 (2008e)	**Mendoza** Argentina	919 824 (2008e)
Las Palmas Grand Canary	377 056 (2006e)	**Meshed** Iran	2 410 800 (2006c)
Las Vegas USA	552 536 (2006e)	**Mexicali** Mexico	885 000 (2007e)
Leeds UK	761 100 (2007e)	**Mexico City** Mexico	8 836 000 (2008e)
Leicester UK	292 600 (2007e)	**Miami** USA	404 048 (2006e)
Leipzig Germany	506 578 (2007e)	**Milan** Italy	1 299 633 (2008e)
Leon Mexico	1 488 000 (2007e)	**Milwaukee** USA	573 358 (2006e)
Leshan China	1 157 000 (2007e)	**Minneapolis** USA	372 833 (2006e)
Lianyungang China	806 000 (2007e)	**Minsk** Belarus	1 810 000 (2007e)

Mogadishu Somalia	1609050 (2008e)	Omiya Japan	404000 (2006e)
Mogilyov Belarus	366763 (2006e)	Omsk Russia	1139000 (2006e)
Mombasa Kenya	867028 (2008e)	Oporto Portugal	240773 (2008e)
Monrovia Liberia	1144018 (2008e)	Oran Algeria	680947 (2008e)
Monterrey Mexico	1123799 (2006e)	Ordzhonikidze Russia	315608 (2002c)
Montevideo Uruguay	1311358 (2008e)	Orenburg Russia	550552 (2006e)
Montreal Canada	3635571 (2006c)	Oryol Russia	323036 (2008e)
Moradabad India	785105 (2008e)	Osaka Japan	2636874 (2008e)
Moscow Russia	13260700 (2008e)	Osasco Brazil	715000 (2006e)
Mosul Iraq	2721096 (2008e)	Osijek Croatia	86412 (2008e)
Mudanjiang China	1244000 (2007e)	Oslo Norway	839423 (2007e)
Multan Pakistan	1528075 (2008e)	Ostrava Czech Republic	311963 (2008e)
Mumbai (Bombay) India	13662885 (2008e)	Ottawa-Gatineau Canada	1130761 (2006c)
Munich Germany	1294608 (2007e)	Oujda Morocco	419154 (2008e)
Murcia Spain	432133 (2008e)	Padang Indonesia	929429 (2008e)
Murmansk Russia	321000 (2006e)	Palembang Indonesia	1749000 (2007e)
Mysore India	973856 (2008e)	Palermo Italy	663173 (2008e)
Naberezhnye Chelny Russia	507000 (2006e)	Palma Majorca	381285 (2006e)
Nagano Japan	378811 (2008e)	Panama City Panama	1281000 (2007e)
Nagasaki Japan	433772 (2008e)	Panchiao Taiwan	490082 (2006e)
Nagoya Japan	3230000 (2007e)	Panshan China	657731 (2008e)
Nagpur India	2359331 (2008e)	Paris France	2177528 (2008e)
Naha Japan	316302 (2008e)	Patna India	2030000 (2008e)
Nairobi Kenya	3038553 (2008e)	Pavlodar Kazakhstan	354809 (2008e)
Namangan Uzbekistan	439359 (2006e)	Penza Russia	510851 (2006e)
Nanchang China	2310000 (2008e)	Perm Russia	975920 (2008e)
Nanjing China	4150000 (2008e)	Perth Australia	1555000 (2007e)
Nanning China	2167000 (2007e)	Peshawar Pakistan	1344967 (2008e)
Nantong China	947000 (2007e)	Philadelphia USA	1448394 (2006e)
Naples Italy	965421 (2008e)	Phoenix USA	1512986 (2006e)
Nara Japan	368238 (2008e)	Pingdingshan China	849000 (2007e)
Nashville-Davidson USA	552120 (2006e)	Pingxiang China	961000 (2007e)
Nassau The Bahamas	235102 (2008e)	Pittsburgh USA	312819 (2006e)
Natal Brazil	808713 (2008e)	Plovdiv Bulgaria	346727 (2007e)
N'Djamena Chad	989000 (2007e)	Phnom Pénh Cambodia	1398449 (2006e)
Ndola Zambia	467397 (2008e)	Poltava Ukraine	317931 (2006e)
Newark USA	281378 (2006e)	Pontianak Indonesia	466090 (2008e)
Newcastle Australia	500085 (2006e)	Port-au-Prince Haiti	1998000 (2007e)
New Delhi India	321883 (2006e)	Port Elizabeth (Nelson Mandela Metropole) South Africa	1112768 (2008e)
New Orleans USA	454207 (2006e)		
New York USA	8214426 (2006e)		
Nezahualcóyotl Mexico	1220062 (2008e)	Portland USA	537081 (2006e)
Niamey Niger	907178 (2008e)	Port Louis Mauritius	154477 (2008e)
Nice France	347900 (2006e)	Port Moresby Papua New Guinea	301817 (2008e)
Nicosia Cyprus	213027 (2008e)		
Niigata Japan	785067 (2005c)	Porto Alegre Brazil	1441000 (2006e)
Nikolayev Ukraine	507213 (2008e)	Port of Spain Trinidad	49959 (2008e)
Ningbo China	1923000 (2007e)	Port Said Egypt	546776 (2006e)
Niš Serbia	173835 (2006e)	Poznań Poland	564035 (2007e)
Nishinomiya Japan	479429 (2008e)	Prague Czech Republic	1181032 (2008e)
Niteroi Brazil	476700 (2006e)	Pretoria (Tshwane) South Africa	1633569 (2008e)
Nizhny Novgorod (Gorky) Russia	1241032 (2008e)		
		Puebla Mexico	2195000 (2007e)
Nizhny Tagil Russia	374844 (2008e)	Pune (Poona) India	3230322 (2008e)
Nova Iguaçu Brazil	844600 (2006e)	Pusan South Korea	3402335 (2008e)
Nouakchott Mauritania	775758 (2008e)	Pyongyang North Korea	3300000 (2007e)
Novokuznetsk Russia	562000 (2006e)	Qinhuangdao China	1003000 (2007e)
Novosibirsk Russia	1417389 (2008e)	Qiqihar China	1641000 (2007e)
Nuremberg Germany	500855 (2007e)	Qom Iran	957496 (2006c)
Oakland USA	393632 (2006e)	Quebec Canada	715515 (2006e)
Odessa Ukraine	994739 (2008e)	Quezon City Philippines	2679450 (2007c)
Ogbomosho Nigeria	951000 (2007e)	Quito Ecuador	1594883 (2008e)
Oita Japan	468215 (2008e)	Rabat Morocco	1754425 (2008e)
Okayama Japan	686749 (2008e)	Raipur India	875000 (2007e)
Oklahoma City USA	537734 (2006e)	Rajkot India	1335397 (2008e)
Olinda Brazil	387500 (2006e)	Ranchi India	1021628 (2008e)
Omaha USA	417809 (2006e)	Rangoon Myanmar (Burma)	4886305 (2008e)
Omdurman Sudan	3128000 (2007e)	Rawalpindi Pakistan	1877580 (2008e)

Recife Brazil	1 530 404 (2008e)	**Shijiazhuang** China	2 270 000 (2008e)
Reykjavik Iceland	201 008 (2008e)	**Shiraz** Iran	1 233 146 (2008e)
Ribeirao Preto Brazil	586 216 (2008e)	**Shizuoka** Japan	697 113 (2008e)
Riga Latvia	738 386 (2006e)	**Sholapur** India	1 094 553 (2008e)
Rio de Janeiro Brazil	6 193 265 (2008e)	**Shoubra el-Kheima** Egypt	1 016 722 (2006c)
Riyadh Saudi Arabia	4 606 888 (2008e)	**Shuangyashan** China	554 760 (2008e)
Rome Italy	2 740 000 (2008e)	**Sialkot** Pakistan	494 591 (2008e)
Rosario Argentina	1 228 978 (2008e)	**Sian (Xian)** China	4 305 536 (2008e)
Rostov-na-Donu Russia	1 055 000 (2006e)	**Simferopol** Ukraine	340 877 (2008e)
Rotterdam Netherlands	592 995 (2008e)	**Singapore** Singapore	4 974 232 (2008e)
Sacramento USA	453 781 (2006e)	**Sinuiju** North Korea	350 000 (2006e)
Safi Morocco	298 361 (2008e)	**Skopje** Macedonia	589 307 (2008e)
Sagamihara Japan	657 699 (2006e)	**Smolensk** Russia	314 061 (2008e)
St Catharines-Niagara Canada	390 317 (2006c)	**Sochi** Russia	327 224 (2006e)
		Sofia Bulgaria	1 126 389 (2007e)
St Louis USA	347 181 (2006e)	**Songnam** South Korea	1 016 969 (2008e)
St Petersburg Russia	4 570 000 (2008e)	**Sorocaba** Brazil	613 650 (2008e)
Sakai Japan	780 367 (2006e)	**Srinagar** India	1 140 000 (2007e)
Salem India	849 444 (2008e)	**Stavropol** Russia	365 936 (2006e)
Salonika Greece	351 367 (2008e)	**Stockholm** Sweden	1 737 995 (2008e)
Salvador Brazil	2 899 965 (2008e)	**Stuttgart** Germany	593 923 (2007e)
Samara Russia	1 143 000 (2006e)	**Suita** Japan	356 368 (2008e)
Samarkand Uzbekistan	315 939 (2006e)	**Surabaya** Indonesia	2 845 000 (2007e)
San'a Yemen	1 876 669 (2008e)	**Surakarta** Indonesia	762 000 (2005e)
San Antonio USA	1 296 682 (2006e)	**Surat** India	3 842 000 (2007e)
San Cristobal Venezuela	247 876 (2006e)	**Suva** Fiji	85 691 (2007c)
San Diego USA	1 256 951 (2006e)	**Suwon** South Korea	1 333 428 (2008e)
San Francisco USA	744 041 (2006e)	**Suzhou** China	1 650 000 (2007e)
San José USA	929 936 (2006e)	**Sverdlovsk** Russia	1 293 058 (2008e)
San Juan Puerto Rico	409 262 (2008e)	**Sydney** Australia	4 327 000 (2007e)
San Luis Potosí Mexico	1 067 668 (2008e)	**Szczecin** Poland	408 583 (2007e)
San Miguel de Tucumán Argentina	818 672 (2008e)	**Tabriz** Iran	1 409 077 (2008e)
		Taegu South Korea	2 460 000 (2007e)
San Pedro Sula Honduras	592 187 (2008e)	**Taejon** South Korea	1 468 000 (2007e)
San Salvador El Salvador	1 433 000 (2007e)	**Taichung** Taiwan	1 078 000 (2007e)
Santa Cruz de la Sierra Bolivia	1 545 161 (2008e)	**Tainan** Taiwan	767 596 (2008e)
		Taipei Taiwan	2 603 000 (2007e)
Santiago Chile	5 630 000 (2008e)	**Taiyuan** China	2 913 000 (2007e)
Santiago de Cuba Cuba	563 001 (2006e)	**Takamatsu** Japan	337 900 (2008e)
Santo André Brazil	679 464 (2008e)	**Takatsuki** Japan	353 872 (2006e)
Santo Domingo Dominican Republic	2 429 851 (2008e)	**Tallinn** Estonia	394 898 (2008e)
		Tambov Russia	290 055 (2006e)
Santos Brazil	418 400 (2006e)	**Tangier** Morocco	730 849 (2008e)
São Bernardo do Campo Brazil	803 906 (2006e)	**Tangshan** China	1 879 000 (2007e)
		Tanta Egypt	421 076 (2006e)
São Gonçalo Brazil	985 283 (2008e)	**Tashkent** Uzbekistan	2 450 000 (2008e)
São João de Meriti Brazil	467 000 (2006e)	**Tbilisi** Georgia	1 103 300 (2006e)
São José dos Campos Brazil	672 262 (2008e)	**Tegucigalpa** Honduras	1 021 661 (2008e)
São Luis Brazil	998 400 (2006e)	**Tehran** Iran	7 711 230 (2006c)
São Paulo Brazil	11 105 000 (2008e)	**Tel Aviv** Israel	389 344 (2008e)
Sapporo Japan	1 904 216 (2008e)	**Teresina** Brazil	907 000 (2007e)
Saragossa Spain	658 186 (2006e)	**Tetouan** Morocco	341 689 (2008e)
Sarajevo Bosnia and Herzegovina	737 350 (2006e)	**Thane** India	1 673 465 (2008e)
		Tianjin (Tientsin) China	7 200 000 (2008e)
Saransk Russia	299 689 (2008e)	**Tijuana** Mexico	1 553 000 (2007e)
Saratov Russia	839 788 (2008e)	**Timisoara** Romania	307 347 (2007e)
Seattle USA	582 454 (2006e)	**Tirana** Albania	400 000 (2008e)
Semarang Indonesia	1 396 000 (2007e)	**Tiruchchirapalli** India	951 000 (2007e)
Semipalatinsk Kazakhstan	312 136 (2008e)	**Tokyo** Japan	8 648 655 (2008e)
Sendai Japan	1 362 000 (2005e)	**Toledo** USA	305 292 (2006e)
Seoul South Korea	9 796 000 (2007e)	**Tolyatti** Russia	729 626 (2008e)
Shanchung Taiwan	357 920 (2006e)	**Tomsk** Russia	484 765 (2006e)
Shanghai China	15 584 627 (2008e)	**Tonghua** China	562 466 (2008e)
Shantou China	1 601 000 (2007e)	**Toronto** Canada	5 790 000 (2008e)
Shaoguan China	702 904 (2008e)	**Toulouse** France	448 000 (2008e)
Sheffield UK	530 300 (2007e)	**Toyama** Japan	421 156 (2005c)
Shenyang China	4 787 000 (2007e)	**Toyohasi** Japan	381 108 (2006e)
Shihezi China	590 662 (2008e)	**Toyonaka** Japan	382 956 (2006e)

Social Structure

Social Structure

Toyota Japan	364620 (2006e)		Warangal India	582350 (2008e)
Tripoli Libya	2189000 (2007e)		Warsaw Poland	1704717 (2007e)
Trivandrum India	813460 (2008e)		Washington USA	581530 (2006e)
Trujillo Peru	804505 (2008e)		Weifang China	1553000 (2007e)
Tucson USA	518956 (2006c)		Wellington New Zealand	179466 (2006c)
Tula Russia	634490 (2006e)		Wenzhou China	2350000 (2007e)
Tulsa USA	379833 (2006e)		Windhoek Namibia	296366 (2008e)
Tunis Tunisia	941020 (2006e)		Winnipeg Canada	633451 (2006c)
Turin Italy	908263 (2008e)		Wroclaw Poland	633950 (2007e)
Tver Russia	391316 (2008e)		Wuhan China	7243000 (2007e)
Tyumen Russia	528370 (2008e)		Wuhu China	810000 (2007e)
Ufa Russia	1030000 (2006e)		Wuppertal Germany	358330 (2007e)
Ulan Bator Mongolia	903273 (2008e)		Wuxi China	1749000 (2007e)
Ulan-Ude Russia	348000 (2006e)		Xiamen China	2519000 (2007e)
Ulsan South Korea	1061000 (2007e)		Xiangfan China	1069000 (2007e)
Ulyanovsk Russia	642257 (2006e)		Xiangtan China	676218 (2006e)
Urawa Japan	516700 (2006e)		Xiangyang China	1126000 (2007e)
Urumqi China	2151000 (2007e)		Xining China	1048000 (2007e)
Ust-Kamenogorsk	344421 (2008e)		Xinxiang China	903000 (2007e)
Kazakhstan			Xuzhou China	2091000 (2007e)
Utsunomiya Japan	462752 (2008e)		Yakeshi China	113458 (2006e)
Vadodara India	1756000 (2007e)		Yangquan China	692797 (2006e)
Valencia Spain	805304 (2006e)		Yantai China	2116000 (2007e)
Valencia Venezuela	1770000 (2007e)		Yaoundé Cameroon	1676588 (2008e)
Valladolid Spain	379454 (2006e)		Yaroslavl Russia	600525 (2008e)
Vancouver Canada	2254397 (2008e)		Yerevan Armenia	1195519 (2008e)
Varanasi India	1487556 (2008e)		Yichang (Ichang) China	875000 (2007e)
Vargas Venezuela	329742 (2008e)		Yichun (Ichun) China	982000 (2007e)
Varna Bulgaria	323296 (2007e)		Yinchuan China	991000 (2007e)
Venice Italy	266667 (2008e)		Yingkou China	795000 (2007e)
Veracruz Mexico	586355 (2008e)		Yogyakarta Indonesia	686716 (2008e)
Victoria Seychelles	22198 (2008e)		Yokohama Japan	3648851 (2008e)
Vienna Austria	1664146 (2007e)		Yokosuka Japan	426162 (2005c)
Vientiane Laos	747321 (2008e)		Zagreb Croatia	703185 (2008e)
Vijayawada India	1132644 (2008e)		Zamboanga City Philippines	774407 (2007c)
Vilnius Lithuania	542782 (2007e)		Zaporozhye Ukraine	789548 (2008e)
Viña del Mar Chile	297041 (2006e)		Zarqa Jordan	483270 (2006e)
Vinnitsa Ukraine	350075 (2006e)		Zhangjiakou China	1046000 (2007e)
Virginia Beach USA	435619 (2006e)		Zhengzhou China	2636000 (2007e)
Visakhapatnam India	1489211 (2008e)		Zhenjiang China	854000 (2007e)
Vitebsk Belarus	341462 (2008e)		Zhuzhou China	1080000 (2007e)
Vladimir Russia	301876 (2008e)		Zibo China	3061000 (2007e)
Vladivostok Russia	584496 (2006e)		Zigong China	1105000 (2007e)
Volgograd Russia	992000 (2006e)		Zürich Switzerland	353067 (2008e)
Voronezh Russia	822300 (2008e)			
Wakayama Japan	367827 (2008e)			

Largest cities by population

■ World

Delhi India	18000000	Buenos Aires Argentina	12218000
Shanghai China	15585000	Karachi Pakistan	12130000
Mumbai (Bombay) India	13663000	São Paulo Brazil	11105000
Moscow Russia	13260000	Istanbul Turkey	10757000
Beijing (Peking) China	12770000	Seoul South Korea	9796000

■ Europe

Moscow Russia	13260000	Berlin Germany	3404000
Istanbul Turkey	10757000	Madrid Spain	3129000
London UK	7557000	Rome Italy	2740000
St Petersburg Russia	4570000	Kiev Ukraine	2700000
Athens Greece	3730000	Paris France	2178000

■ USA

New York New York	8214000	**Philadelphia** Pennsylvania	1448000
Los Angeles California	3849000	**San Antonio** Texas	1297000
Chicago Illinois	2833000	**San Diego** California	1257000
Houston Texas	2145000	**Dallas** Texas	1233000
Phoenix Arizona	1513000	**San José** California	929936

Largest metropolitan areas by population

Metropolitan areas can be difficult to define; usually they are considered to be a city plus the suburban areas immediately surrounding it. In some densely populated areas, several major cities may be close enough to be considered one metropolitan area. However, the appropriateness of boundaries and the consistency of the criteria used to define them can vary widely from country to country. The following data, mostly taken from the United Nations report *World Urbanization Prospects: 2007 Revision*, are very approximate.

Greater Tokyo (metropolitan area) Japan	35676000	**Greater São Paulo (metropolitan area)** Brazil	18845000
Seoul (National Capital Area) South Korea	22800000	**Delhi (National Capital Territory)** India	15926000
New York (metropolitan area) USA	19040000	**Shanghai (municipality)** China	14987000
Greater Mexico City (metropolitan area) Mexico	19028000	**Kolkata (Calcutta) (metropolitan area)** India	14787000
Greater Mumbai (Bombay) (metropolitan area) India	18978000	**Moscow (municipality)** Russia	10452000

United Nations (UN)

The United Nations was formed to maintain world peace and foster international co-operation. It was formally established in 1945 with 51 member states. It has six 'principal organs': the General Assembly, the Security Council, the Secretariat, the International Court of Justice, the Economic and Social Council, and the Trusteeship Council.

■ Membership

Member countries are grouped by year of entry. There are currently 191 member states.

1945	Argentina, Australia, Belgium, Byelorussian SSR (Belarus, 1991), Bolivia, Brazil, Canada, Chile, China (Taiwan to 1971), Colombia, Costa Rica, Cuba, Czechoslavakia (to 1993), Denmark, Dominican Republic, Ecuador, Egypt, El Salvador, Ethiopia, France, Greece, Guatemala, Haiti, Honduras, India, Iran, Iraq, Lebanon, Liberia, Luxembourg, Mexico, Netherlands, New Zealand, Nicaragua, Norway, Panama, Paraguay, Peru, Philippines, Poland, Saudi Arabia, South Africa, Syria, Turkey, Ukrainian SSR (Ukraine, 1991), USSR (Russia, 1991), UK, USA, Uruguay, Venezuela, Yugoslavia (to 1992)
1946	Afghanistan, Iceland, Sweden, Thailand
1947	Pakistan, Yemen (N, to 1990)
1948	Burma (Myanmar, 1989)
1949	Israel
1950	Indonesia
1955	Albania, Austria, Bulgaria, Kampuchea (Cambodia, 1989), Ceylon (Sri Lanka, 1970), Finland, Hungary, Ireland, Italy, Jordan, Laos, Libya, Nepal, Portugal, Romania, Spain
1956	Japan, Morocco, The Sudan, Tunisia
1957	Ghana, Malaya (Malaysia, 1963)
1958	Guinea
1960	Cameroon, Central African Republic, Chad, Congo, Côte d'Ivoire (Ivory Coast), Cyprus, Dahomey (Benin, 1975), Gabon, Madagascar, Mali, Niger, Nigeria, Senegal, Somalia, Togo, Upper Volta (Burkina Faso, 1984), Zaïre (Democratic Republic of the Congo, 1997)
1961	Mauritania, Mongolia, Sierra Leone, Tanganyika (within Tanzania, 1964)
1962	Algeria, Burundi, Jamaica, Rwanda, Trinidad and Tobago, Uganda
1963	Kenya, Kuwait, Zanzibar (within Tanzania, 1964)
1964	Malawi, Malta, Zambia, Tanzania
1965	The Gambia, Maldives, Singapore
1966	Barbados, Botswana, Guyana, Lesotho
1967	Yemen (S, to 1990)
1968	Equatorial Guinea, Mauritius, Swaziland
1970	Fiji
1971	Bahrain, Bhutan, China (People's Republic), Oman, Qatar, United Arab Emirates
1973	The Bahamas, German Democratic Republic (within GFR 1990), German Federal Republic
1974	Bangladesh, Grenada, Guinea-Bissau
1975	Cape Verde, Comoros, Mozambique, Papua New Guinea, São Tomé and Príncipe, Suriname

Social Structure

Social Structure

1976	Angola, Seychelles, Western Samoa (Samoa, 1997)
1977	Djibouti, Vietnam
1978	Dominica, Solomon Islands
1979	St Lucia
1980	St Vincent and the Grenadines, Zimbabwe
1981	Antigua and Barbuda, Belize, Vanuatu
1983	St Kitts and Nevis
1984	Brunei
1990	Liechtenstein, Namibia, Yemen (formerly N Yemen and S Yemen)
1991	Estonia, Federated States of Micronesia, Latvia, Lithuania, Marshall Islands, N Korea, S Korea
1992	Armenia, Azerbaijan, Bosnia-Herzegovina, Croatia, Georgia, Kazakhstan, Kyrgyzstan, Moldova, San Marino, Slovenia, Tajikistan, Turkmenistan, Uzbekistan
1993	Andorra, Czech Republic, Eritrea, Former Yugoslav Republic of Macedonia, Monaco, Slovakia
1994	Palau
1999	Kiribati, Nauru, Tonga
2000	Tuvalu, Yugoslavia (Serbia, 2006)
2002	Switzerland, East Timor
2006	Montenegro

■ **UN specialized agencies**

Abbreviated form	Full title	Area of concern
FAO	Food and Agriculture Organization	Improvement of the production and distribution of agricultural products
IAEA	International Atomic Energy Agency	Promotes safe, secure and peaceful nuclear technologies
IBRD[1]	International Bank for Reconstruction and Development	Aid of development through investment
ICAO	International Civil Aviation Organization	Encouragement of safety measures in international flight
ICSID[1]	International Centre for Settlement of Investment Disputes	Settlement of investment disputes between governments and foreign investors
IDA[1]	International Development Association	Credit on special terms to provide assistance for less developed countries
IFAD	International Fund for Agricultural Development	Increase of food production in developing countries by the generation of grants or loans
IFC[1]	International Finance Corporation	Promotion of the international flow of private capital
ILO	International Labour Organization	Social justice
IMF	International Monetary Fund	Promotion of international monetary co-operation
IMO	International Maritime Organization	Co-ordination of safety at sea
ITU	International Telecommunication Union	Allocation of frequencies and regulation of procedures
MIGA[1]	Multilateral Investment Guarantee Agency	Promotion of foreign investment in economies of developing countries
UNESCO	United Nations Educational, Scientific and Cultural Organization	Stimulation of popular education and the spread of culture
UNIDO	United Nations Industrial Development Organization	Assists developing countries in improving their economies and growth
UPU	Universal Postal Union	Uniting members within a single postal territory
WHO	World Health Organization	Promotion of the highest standards of health for all people
WMO	World Meteorological Organization	Standardization and utilization of meteorological observations
WIPO	World Intellectual Property Organization	Protection of copyright, designs, inventions, etc

[1] This institution is part of the World Bank Group.

■ UN Secretaries-General

Term of office	Name and *nation of origin*	Term of office	Name and *nation of origin*
1946–53	Trygve Lie *Norway*	1982–91	Javier Pérez de Cuéllar *Peru*
1953–61	Dag Hammarskjöld *Sweden*	1992–6	Boutros Boutros-Ghali *Egypt*
1962–71	U Thant *Burma*	1997–2006	Kofi Annan *Ghana*
1972–81	Kurt Waldheim *Austria*	2006–	Ban Ki-moon *South Korea*

The Commonwealth

The Commonwealth is an informal association of autonomous states most of which have been under British rule at some point in their history. It was formally established in 1931 and meets frequently to discuss matters of common interest and concern. Its head is Queen Elizabeth II.

■ Membership

Member countries are grouped by year of entry. There are currently 53 member states.

1931	Australia, Canada, New Zealand, United Kingdom, South Africa (left 1961, rejoined 1994)
1947	India, Pakistan (left 1972, rejoined 1989; suspended 1999, readmitted 2004; suspended 2007, readmitted 2008)
1948	Sri Lanka
1957	Ghana, Malaysia
1960	Nigeria (suspended 1995, readmitted 1999)
1961	Cyprus, Sierra Leone, Tanzania
1962	Jamaica, Trinidad and Tobago, Uganda
1963	Kenya
1964	Malawi, Malta, Zambia
1965	The Gambia, Singapore
1966	Barbados, Botswana, Guyana, Lesotho
1968	Mauritius, Nauru*, Swaziland
1970	Tonga, Samoa (formerly Western Samoa), Fiji (left 1987, rejoined 1997; suspended 2000, readmitted 2001, suspended 2006)
1972	Bangladesh
1973	The Bahamas
1974	Grenada
1975	Papua New Guinea
1976	Seychelles
1978	Dominica, Solomon Islands, Tuvalu*
1979	Kiribati, St Lucia, St Vincent and the Grenadines
1980	Vanuatu, Zimbabwe (suspended 2002, left 2003)
1981	Antigua and Barbuda, Belize
1982	Maldives
1983	St Kitts and Nevis
1984	Brunei
1990	Namibia
1995	Cameroon, Mozambique

* Nauru is a member in arrears; Tuvalu joined as a special member and became a full member in 2000.
The Republic of Ireland resigned from the Commonwealth in 1949.

■ Commonwealth Secretaries-General

Term of office	Name and *nation of origin*	Term of office	Name and *nation of origin*
1965–75	Arnold Smith *Canada*	2000–2008	Donald C McKinnon *New Zealand*
1975–90	Shridath Ramphal *Guyana*	2008	Karmalesh Sharma *India*
1990–2000	Emeka Anyaoku *Nigeria*		

Commonwealth of Independent States (CIS)

The organization is a grouping of twelve independent states formed in 1991 from the 15 republics that formerly made up the Soviet Union. It acts as a co-ordinating body for foreign, defence and economic policies and as a forum for addressing problems arising from the break-up of the Soviet Union.

1991	Armenia, Azerbaijan, Belarus, Kazakhstan, Kyrgyzstan, Moldova, Russia, Tajikistan, Turkmenistan*, Ukraine**, Uzbekistan
1993	Georgia (in August 2008 Georgia announced its withdrawal from the CIS)

* Turkmenistan withdrew in 2005 and became an associate member.
** Ukraine has never ratified the CIS treaty

Social Structure

Social Structure

European Union (EU)

This was established as the European Economic Community (EEC) by the Treaty of Rome in 1957. In 1967 the EEC merged with the European Coal and Steel Community and the European Atomic Energy Community to form the European Community (EC). It became the European Union (EU) in 1993 under the terms of the Treaty of Maastricht (1991).

■ Membership

Member countries are grouped by year of entry. There are currently 27 member states.

1958	Belgium, France, Germany, Italy, Luxembourg, The Netherlands
1973	Denmark, Republic of Ireland, United Kingdom
1981	Greece
1986	Portugal, Spain
1995	Austria, Finland, Sweden
2004	Cyprus, Czech Republic, Estonia, Hungary, Latvia, Lithuania, Malta, Poland, Slovakia, Slovenia
2007	Bulgaria, Romania

Candidate countries: Croatia, Macedonia, Turkey.

■ EU institutions

Title	Task
Council of the European Union	represents the member states
Court of Auditors	checks the financing of the EU
European Court of Justice	upholds European law
European Central Bank	responsible for EU monetary policy
European Commission	upholds the interests of the EU
European Investment Bank	finances EU investment projects
European Parliament	represents the EU citizens

■ Presidents of the European Commission

The European Commission is an executive body of 25 Commissioners from EU member states, headed by a president.

Term of office	Name and *country of origin*
1958–67	Walter Hallstein *West Germany*
1967–70	Jean Rey *Belgium*
1970–2	Franco Malfatti *Italy*
1972–3	Sicco Mansholt *Netherlands*
1973–7	François-Xavier Ortoli *France*
1977–81	Roy Jenkins *UK*
1981–5	Gaston Thorn *Luxembourg*
1985–95	Jacques Delors *France*
1995–9	Jacques Santer *Luxembourg*
1999–2004	Romano Prodi *Italy*
2004–	José Manuel Barroso *Portugal*

■ European Parliament political groupings

Seats held as at 27 January 2009.

Country	PES	EPP-ED	UEN	ALDE	EUL/NGL	Greens/EFA	IND/DEM	NM	Total
Austria	7	6		1		2		2	18
Belgium	7	6		6		2		3	24
Bulgaria	5	5		5				3	18
Cyprus		3		1	2				6
Czech Rep	2	14			6		1	1	24
Denmark	5	1	1	4	1	1	1		14
Estonia	3	1		2					6
Finland	3	4		5	1	1			14
France	31	18		10	3	6	3	7	78
Germany	23	49		7	7	13			99
Greece	8	11			4		1		24
Hungary	9	13		2					24

Country	PES	EPP-ED	UEN	ALDE	EUL/NGL	Greens/ EFA	IND/DEM	NM	Total
Ireland	1	5	4	1	1		1		13
Italy	17	24	13	12	7	2		3	78
Latvia		3	4	1		1			9
Lithuania	2	2	2	7					13
Luxembourg	1	3		1		1			6
Malta	3	2							5
Netherlands	7	7		5	2	4	2		27
Poland	9	15	20	6			3	1	54
Portugal	12	9			3				24
Romania	10	18		6		1			35
Slovakia	3	8						3	14
Slovenia	1	4		2					7
Spain	24	24		2	1	3			54
Sweden	5	6		3	2	1	2		19
UK	19	27		11	1	5	8	7	78
Total	217	288	44	100	41	43	22	30	785

PES = Party of European Socialists (including the British Labour Party, the French Socialist Party and the German Social Democratic Party)
EPP-ED = European People's Party (Christian Democrats) and European Democrats (including the British Conservative Party, the Uster Unionist Party and the Swedish Moderate Party)
UEN = Union for Europe of the Nations (including the Irish Fianna Fáil and the Italian Alleanza Nazionale)
ALDE = Alliance of Liberals and Democrats for Europe (including the British Liberal Democrats, the Union for French Democracy and the German Free Democratic Party)
EUL/NGL = Confederal Group of the European United Left/Nordic Green Left (including the French Communist Party and the Dutch Socialist Party)
Greens/EFA = European Federation of Green Parties/European Free Alliance (including the Green parties, Scottish Nationalist Party and Plaid Cymru)
IND/DEM = Independence/Democracy Group (including the UK Independence Party)
NM = Non-attached Members

Europe – administrative divisions

■ Austria

State	Area sq km	sq mi	Population (2008 est)	Capital
Burgenland	3966	1531	280880	Eisenstadt
Carinthia (Kärnten)	9533	3681	558872	Klagenfurt
Lower Austria (Niederösterreich)	19172	7402	1598839	Sankt Pölten
Salzburg	7154	2762	531330	Salzburg
Styria (Steiermark)	16387	6327	1204434	Graz
Tyrol (Tirol)	12647	4883	704514	Innsbruck
Upper Austria (Oberösterreich)	11980	4626	1408751	Linz
Vienna (Wien)	415	160	1682971	—
Vorarlberg	2601	1004	367015	Bregenz

■ Belgium

Province	Area sq km	sq mi	Population (1 Jan 2008)	Capital
Antwerp	2867	1107	1715707	Antwerp
E Flanders	2982	1151	1408484	Ghent
Flemish Brabant	2106	813	1060232	Leuven
Hainaut	3787	1462	1300097	Mons
Liège	3862	1491	1053722	Liège
Limbourg	2422	935	826690	Hasselt
Luxembourg	4441	1715	264084	Arlon
Namur	3665	1415	465380	Namur
Walloon Brabant	1091	421	373492	Wavre
W Flanders	3314	1210	1150487	Bruges

Social Structure

Social Structure

■ Bulgaria

Province	Area sq km	sq mi	Population (1 Jan 2007 est)	Capital
Burgas	7748	2992	423547	Burgas
Khaskovo	5533	2136	277478	Khaskovo
Lovech	4129	1594	169951	Lovech
Montana	3636	1404	182258	Montana (formerly Mikhailovgrad)
Plovdiv	5973	2692	715816	Plovdiv
Ruse	2803	1082	266157	Ruse
Sofiya	8411	3248	1444082	Sofia (Sofiya)
Varna	3819	1475	462013	Varna

■ Cyprus

District	Area sq km	sq mi	Population (2006 est)	Capital
Famagusta	1979	764	43000	Famagusta
Larnaca	1126	435	130100	Larnaca
Limassol	1393	538	223600	Limassol
Nicosia	2717	1049	307100	Nicosia
Paphos	1395	539	74900	Paphos

■ Czech Republic

Region	Area sq km	sq mi	Population (31 March 2008)
C Bohemia (St ední echy)	11016	4253	1208145
C Moravia (St ední Morava)	9123	3523	1232637
Moravia-Silesia (Moravskoslezsko)	5535	2137	1249844
North East (Severovýchod)	12440	4803	1499981
North West (Severozápad)	8649	3340	1141193
Prague (city)	496	192	1218644
South East (Jihovýchod)	13990	5402	1656159
South West (Jihozápad)	17618	6802	1196533

■ Denmark

Region	Area sq km	sq mi	Population (1 Jan 2008)	Capital
Capital (Hovedstaden)	2561	989	1645825	Copenhagen (København)
Mid Jutland (Midtjylland)	13053	5040	1237041	Viborg
North Jutland (Nordjylland)	8020	3097	578839	Aalborg (Aelborg)
Zealand (Sjælland)	7273	2808	819427	Sorø
South Denmark (Syddanmark)	12191	4707	1194659	Vejle

■ Estonia

County	Area sq km	sq mi	Population (1 Jan 2008)	Capital
Harju	4332	1673	523277	Tallinn
Hiiu	1023	395	10118	Kardla
Ida-Viru	3364	1299	170719	Jõhvi
Jõgeva	2604	1005	36922	Jõgeva
Järva	2623	1013	36208	Paide
Lääne	2383	920	27552	Haapsalu
Lääne-Viru	3465	1338	67375	Rakvere
Põlva	2165	836	31175	Põlva
Pärnu	4806	1856	88563	Pärnu
Rapla	2980	1151	36684	Rapla
Saare	2922	1128	34845	Kuressaare
Tartu	3089	1193	149283	Tartu
Valga	2047	790	34265	Valga
Viljandi	3589	1386	55877	Viljandi
Võru	2305	890	38072	Võru

■ Finland

Province	Area sq km	sq mi	Population (31 Dec 2007)	Capital
Åland	1527	590	27153	Mariehamn
Eastern Finland	14000	5405	573478	Mikkeli
Lapland	93057	35929	184390	Rovaniemi
Oulu	56868	21957	467190	Oulu
Southern Finland	30229	11671	2173509	Hämeenlinna
Western Finland	74186	28643	1874764	Turku

■ France

Region	Area sq km	sq mi	Population (1 Jan 2007 est)	Capital
Alsace	8280	3197	1829000	Strasbourg
Aquitaine	41309	15950	3123000	Bordeaux
Auvergne	26013	10044	1337000	Clermont-Ferrand
Brittany (Bretagne)	27209	10505	3103000	Rennes
Burgundy (Bourgogne)	31582	12194	1630000	Dijon
Centre	39151	15116	2515000	Orléans
Champagne-Ardenne	25606	9887	1337000	Reims
Corsica (Corse)	8680	3351	281000	Ajaccio
Franche-Comté	16202	6256	1151000	Besançon
Ile de France	12011	4637	11577000	Paris
Languedoc-Roussillon	27376	10570	2548000	Montpellier
Limousin	16942	6541	727000	Limoges
Lorraine	23547	9092	2343000	Nancy
Midi-Pyrénées	45349	17509	2782000	Toulouse
Nord-Pas-de-Calais	12413	479	4048000	Lille
Normandy, Lower (Basse-Normandie)	17589	6791	1453000	Caen
Normandy, Upper (Haute-Normandie)	12318	4756	1815000	Rouen
Pays de la Loire	32082	1237	3455000	Nantes
Picardy (Picardie)	19399	7490	1890000	Amiens
Poitou-Charentes	25809	9965	1722000	Poitiers
Provence-Alpes-Côte d'Azur	31400	12124	4818000	Marseilles
Rhône-Alpes	43698	16872	6058000	Lyons

■ Germany

District	Area sq km	sq mi	Population (31 Dec 2006)	Capital
Baden-Württemberg	35751	13804	10738753	Stuttgart
Bavaria	70546	27239	12492658	Munich
Berlin	889	340	3404037	Berlin
Brandenburg	29481	11379	2547772	Potsdam
Bremen	404	156	663979	Bremen
Hamburg	755	292	1754182	Hamburg
Hesse	21114	8152	6075359	Wiesbaden
Mecklenburg-Vorpommern	23170	8944	1693754	Schwerin
Lower Saxony (Niedersachsen)	47609	18271	7982685	Hannover
North Rhine-Westphalia (Nordrhein-Westfalen)	34070	13155	18028745	Düsseldorf
Rheinland-Pfalz	19849	7664	4052860	Mainz
Saarland	2570	992	1043167	Saarbrücken
Saxony (Sachsen)	18412	7080	4249774	Dresden
Saxony-Anhalt (Sachsen-Anhalt)	20445	7894	2441787	Magdeburg
Schleswig-Holstein	15739	6077	2834254	Kiel
Thüringia (Thüringen)	16171	6242	2311140	Erfurt

■ Greece

Region	Area sq km	sq mi	Population (1 Jan 2007 est)	Capital
Attica (Attikí)	3808	1470	4032456	Athens
C Greece (Stereá Ellás)	15549	6004	556441	Lamia

Social Structure

Social Structure

Region	Area sq km	sq mi	Population (1 Jan 2007 est)	Capital
C Macedonia (Kedrikí Makedhonía)	19147	7393	1927823	Thessaloniki
Crete (Kríti)	8336	3218	604469	Heraklion
E Macedonia and Thrace (Anatolikí Makedhonía kaí Thráki)	14157	5466	607205	Comotini
Epirus (Ípiros)	9203	3553	348520	Ioannina
Ionian Is (Iónioi Nísoi)	2307	891	225879	Corfu
N Aegean (Vóreion Aiyaíon)	3836	1481	201083	Mytilene
Peloponnese (Pelopónnisos)	15490	5981	595092	Tripolis
S Aegean (Nótion Aiyaíon)	5286	2041	304975	Hermoupolis
Thessaly (Thessalía)	14037	5420	737034	Larissa
W Greece (Dhytikí Ellás)	11350	4382	736899	Patras
W Macedonia (Dhytikí Makedhonía)	9451	3649	293864	Kozani

■ Hungary

County	Area sq km	sq mi	Population (1 Jan 2008)	Capital
Baranya	4487	1732	396633	Pécs
Bács-Kiskun	8362	3229	533710	Kecskemét
Békés	5632	2175	376657	Bekéscsaba
Borsod-Abaúj-Zemplén	7247	2798	709634	Miskolc
Budapest[1]	525	203	1702297	—
Csongrád	4263	1646	424139	Szeged
Fejér	4373	1688	428572	Székesfehérvár
Györ-Moson-Sopron	4062	1568	444384	Györ
Hajdú-Bihar	6211	2398	543802	Debrecen
Heves	3637	1404	316874	Eger
Jász-Nagykún-Szolnok	5607	2165	399200	Szolnok
Komárom-Esztergom	2251	869	314649	Tatabánya
Nógrád	2544	982	210182	Salgótarján
Pest	6394	2469	1195020	Budapest
Somogy	6036	2331	325024	Kapsovár
Szabolcs-Szatmár-Bereg	5938	2293	571018	Nyíregyháza
Tolna	3704	1430	238431	Szekszárd
Vas	3337	1288	261877	Szombathely
Vezprém	4639	1791	361620	Veszprém
Zala	3784	1461	291678	Zalaegerszeg

[1] Budapest has county status.

■ Iceland

Region	Area sq km	sq mi	Population (2008)	Capital
Austurland	21991	8491	13919	Egilsstadir
Höfudborgarsvaedi	19821	7651	196564	Reykjavik
Nordurland eystra	22368	8636	28618	Akureyri
Nordurland vestra	13093	5055	7810	Saudárkrókur
Sudurland	25214	9735	23505	Selfoss
Sudurnes	—[1]	—[1]	20446	Keflavik
Vestfirdir	9470	3657	7299	Ísafjördur
Vesturland	8701	3360	15462	Borgarnes

[1] Höfudborgarsvaedi includes Sudurnes.

■ Ireland

County	Area sq km	sq mi	Population (2006)	Administrative centre
Carlow	896	346	50349	Carlow
Cavan	1891	730	64003	Cavan
Clare	3188	1231	110950	Ennis
Cork	7459	2880	481295	Cork
Donegal	4830	1865	147264	Lifford
Dublin	922	356	1187176	Dublin

County	Area sq km	sq mi	Population (2006)	Administrative centre
Galway	5939	2293	231670	Galway
Kerry	4701	1815	139835	Tralee
Kildare	1694	654	186335	Naas
Kilkenny	2062	796	87558	Kilkenny
Laoighis (Leix)	1720	664	67059	Portlaoise
Leitrim	1526	589	28950	Carrick
Limerick	2686	1037	184055	Limerick
Longford	1044	403	34391	Longford
Louth	821	317	111267	Dundalk
Mayo	5398	2084	123839	Castlebar
Meath	2339	903	162831	Trim
Monaghan	1290	498	55997	Monaghan
Offaly	1997	771	70868	Tullamore
Roscommon	2463	951	58768	Roscommon
Sligo	1795	693	60894	Sligo
Tipperary	4254	1642	149244	Clonmel
Waterford	1839	710	107961	Waterford
Westmeath	1764	681	79346	Mullingar
Wexford	2352	908	131749	Wexford
Wicklow	2025	782	126194	Wicklow

■ Italy

Region	Area sq km	sq mi	Population (31 Dec 2007)	Capital
Abruzzi	10794	4168	1309797	L'Aquila
Basilicata	9992	3858	591338	Potenza
Calabria	15080	5823	1998052	Catanzaro
Campania	13595	5249	5790187	Naples (Napoli)
Emilia-Romagna	22124	8542	4223264	Bologna
Friuli-Venezia Giulia	7844	3029	1212602	Trieste
Lazio	17227	6649	5493308	Rome (Roma)
Liguria	5418	2092	1607878	Genoa (Genova)
Lombardy (Lombardia)	23859	9214	9545441	Milan (Milano)
Marche	9693	3743	1536098	Ancona
Molise	4438	1713	320074	Campobasso
Piedmont (Piemonte)	25399	9807	4352828	Turin (Torino)
Puglia	19357	7473	4069869	Bari
Sardinia (Sardegna)	24090	9301	1659443	Cagliari
Sicily (Sicilia)	25707	9926	5016861	Palermo
Tuscany (Toscana)	22992	8877	3638211	Florence (Firenze)
Trentino-Alto Adige	13607	5252	994703	Bozen (Bolzano)[1], Trent, Trient (Trento)[1]
Umbria	8456	3265	872967	Perugia
Valle d'Aosta	3262	1259	124812	Aosta
Veneto	18365	7090	4773554	Venice (Venezia)

[1] Joint regional capitals.

■ Latvia

Region	Area sq km	sq mi	Population (1 Jan 2008)
Aizkraukle Rajons (district)	2565	990	39971
Alūksnes Rajons (district)	2243	866	24159
Balvu Rajons (district)	2386	921	26823
Bauskas Rajons (district)	1882	727	50811
Cēsu Rajons (district)	3067	1184	56265
Daugavpils (municipality)	72	28	105958
Daugavpils Rajons (district)	2525	975	38574
Dobeles Rajons (district)	1633	631	37713
Gulbenes Rajons (district)	1877	725	25864
Jēkabpils Rajons (district)	2998	1158	52076
Jelgava (municipality)	60	23	65635
Jelgavas Rajons (district)	1604	619	37278
Jūrmala (municipality)	100	39	55580
Kraslavas Rajons (district)	2285	882	32699

Social Structure

Social Structure

Region	Area sq km	sq mi	Population (1 Jan 2008)
Kuldīgas Rajons (district)	2502	966	35541
Liepāja (municipality)	60	23	85050
Liepājas Rajons (district)	3594	1388	43306
Limbaži Rajons (district)	2602	1005	37429
Ludzas Rajons (district)	2412	931	30807
Madonas Rajons (district)	3346	1292	42263
Ogres Rajons (district)	1840	710	64811
Preiļu Rajons (district)	2041	788	37743
Rēzekne (municipality)	17	7	35883
Rēzeknes Rajons (district)	2812	1086	39784
Rīga (municipality)	307	119	717371
Rīgas Rajons (district)	3059	1181	167774
Saldus Rajons (district)	2182	842	36324
Talsu Rajons (district)	2751	1062	46280
Tukuma Rajons (district)	2447	945	54753
Valkaa Rajons (district)	2437	941	31314
Valmieras Rajons (district)	2365	913	57938
Ventspils (municipality)	46	18	43299
Ventspils Rajons (district)	2472	954	13818

■ Lithuania

County	Area sq km	sq mi	Population (1 Jan 2008)	Capital
Alytus	5425	2095	177040	Alytus
Kaunas	8090	3124	673706	Kaunas
Klaipėda	5207	2010	378843	Klaipėda
Marijampolė	4467	1725	181219	Marijampolė
Panevežys	7881	3043	284235	Panevežys
Šiauliai	8589	3316	349876	Šiauliai
Taurage	4411	1703	127378	Taurage
Telšiai	4303	1661	173383	Telšiai
Utena	7206	2782	172580	Utena
Vilnius	9730	3757	848097	Vilnius

■ Luxembourg

District/canton	Area sq km	sq mi	Population (1 Jan 2008)
Diekirch (district)	1157	447	74863
Clervaux	332	128	14032
Diekirch	239	92	28138
Redange	267	103	15344
Vianden	54	21	4264
Wiltz	265	102	13085
Grevenmacher (district)	525	203	58109
Echternach	186	72	15606
Grevenmacher	211	82	24081
Remich	128	49	18422
Luxembourg (district)	904	349	350827
Capellen	199	77	39605
Esch-sur-Alzette	243	94	146484
Luxembourg (city)	238	92	139390
Mersch	224	86	25348

■ Malta

District	Area sq km	sq mi	Population (31 Dec 2006 est)
Gozo and Comino	70	27	31280
Northern	78	30	58086
Northern Harbour	32	12	120291
South Eastern	53	20	59795
Southern Harbour	15	6	81057
Western	69	27	57301

■ The Netherlands

Province	Area sq km	sq mi	Population (1 Jan 2007)	Capital
Drenthe	2680	1025	486197	Assen
Flevoland	2412	549	374424	Lelijstad
Friesland	5741	1295	642209	Leeuwarden
Gelderland	5143	1935	1979059	Arnhem
Groningen	2967	906	573614	Groningen
Limburg	2196	838	1127805	Maastricht
N Brabant (Noord-Brabant)	5016	1910	2419042	's-Hertogenbosch
N Holland (Noord-Holland)	4059	1029	2613070	Haarlem
Overijssel	3420	1289	1116374	Zwolle
S Holland (Zuid-Holland)	3446	1123	3455097	The Hague
Utrecht	1434	514	1190604	Utrecht
Zeeland	2932	692	380497	Middelburg

■ Poland

Voivodships (Provinces)	Area sq km	sq mi	Population (30 June 2007)
Dolnoslaskie	19948	7700	2879758
Kujawsko-Pomorskie	17970	6936	2065540
Łódzkie	18219	7033	2560903
Lubelskie	25115	9694	2168993
Lubuskie	13984	5398	1008461
Malopolskie	15144	5846	3274627
Mazowieckie	35597	13740	5178480
Opolskie	9412	3633	1039427
Podkarpackie	17926	6919	2097281
Podlaskie	20180	7792	1194529
Pomorskie	18293	7061	2206600
Slaskie	12294	4745	4662302
Swietokrzyskie	11672	4505	1277494
Warminsko-Mazurskie	24203	9342	1426609
Wielkopolskie	29826	11513	3382189
Zachodniopomorskie	22902	8840	1692774

■ Portugal

Region	Area sq km	sq mi	Population (31 Dec 2007 est)	Capital
Aveiro	2808	1084	734195	Aveiro
Beja	10225	3948	153091	Beja
Braga	2695	1041	862191	Braga
Bragança	6597	2546	142049	Bragança
Castelo Branco	6616	2553	199094	Castelo Branco
Coimbra	3971	1532	434311	Coimbra
Évora	7393	2854	169788	Évora
Faro	4986	1924	426386	Faro
Guarda	5540	2138	172304	Guarda
Leiria	3508	1354	479499	Leiria
Lisboa	2758	1064	2232700	Lisboa (Lisbon)
Portalegre	6065	2342	118141	Portalegre
Porto	2341	904	1820752	Porto
Santarém	6707	2588	466011	Santarém
Setúbal	5064	1955	853445	Setúbal
Viana do Castelo	2210	853	251676	Viano do Costelo
Vila Real	4305	1661	217338	Vila Real
Viseu	5007	1933	393909	Viseu
Autonomous regions				
The Azores	2247	868	244006	Ponta Delgada
Madeira	794	306	246689	Funchal

Social Structure

■ Romania

County	Area sq km	sq mi	Population (1 July 2005)	Capital
Alba	6242	2409	379189	Alba Iulia
Arad	7754	2993	459286	Arad
Argeş	6826	2634	646320	Piteşti
Bacău	6621	2555	723518	Bacău
Bihor	7544	2911	595685	Oradea
Bistriţa-Năsăud	5355	2067	317254	Bistriţa
Botoşani	4986	1924	459900	Botoşani
Brăila	4766	1840	370428	Brăila
Braşov	5363	2070	595211	Braşov
Buzău	6103	2355	494052	Buzău
Caraş-Severin	8520	3288	331876	Reşiţa
Călăraşi	5088	1964	317652	Călăraşi
Cluj	6674	2576	694511	Cluj-Napoka
Constanţa	7071	2729	715148	Constanţa
Covasna	3705	1431	223886	Sfîntu Gheorghe
Dîmboviţa	4054	1565	537090	Tîrgovişte
Dolj	7413	2862	718874	Craiova
Galaţi	4466	1721	620500	Galaţi
Giurgiu	3526	1361	286208	Giurgiu
Gorj	5602	2163	384852	Tîrgu Jiu
Harghita	6639	2562	326558	Miercurea-Ciuc
Hunedoara	7063	2726	480459	Deva
Ialomiţa	4453	1720	292666	Slobozia
Iaşi	5476	2113	813943	Iaşi
Ilfov	1583	611	293409	—
Maramureş	6304	2433	515610	Baia Mare
Mehedinţi	4933	1904	303869	Drobeta-Turnu-Severin
Mureş	6714	2592	583383	Tîrgu Mureş
Neamţ	5896	2276	570682	Piatra Neamţ
Olt	5498	2129	483674	Slatina
Prahova	4716	1819	827512	Ploieşti
Sălaj	3864	1492	245638	Zalău
Satu Mare	4418	1705	368702	Satu Mare
Sibiu	5432	2097	422259	Sibiu
Suceava	8555	3303	705752	Suceava
Teleorman	5790	2235	422314	Alexandria
Timiş	8697	3358	658837	Timişoara
Tulcea	8499	3280	252485	Tulcea
Vaslui	5318	2053	460751	Vaslui
Vâlcea	5765	2225	415181	Râmnicu Vâlcea
Vrancea	4857	1874	393766	Focşani
Municipality				
Bucharest	1821	703	1924959	Bucharest

■ Slovakia

Region	Area sq km	sq mi	Population (31 Dec 2006)	Capital
Banska Bystrica (Banskobystrický kraj)	9455	3651	655762	Banska Bystrica
Bratislava (Bratislavský kraj)	2053	793	606753	Bratislava
Kosice (Košický kraj)	6753	2607	773086	Kosice
Nitra (Nitriansky kraj)	6343	2449	707305	Nitra
Presov (Prešovský kraj)	8993	3472	800483	Presov
Trencin (Trenčiansky kraj)	4501	1738	599847	Trencin
Trnava (Trnavský kraj)	4148	1602	555075	Trnava
Zilina (Žilinský kraj)	6788	2621	695326	Zilina

Social Structure

■ Slovenia

Region	Area sq km	sq mi	Population (31 Dec 2007)	Capital
Gorenjska	2137	825	201254	Kranj
Goriška	2325	898	120329	Nova Gorica
Jugovzhodna Slovenija	1690	653	141547	Novo Mesto
Koroška	1041	402	73714	Slovenj Gradec
Notranjsko-kraška	1456	562	52083	Postojna
Obalno-kraška	1044	403	107905	Koper
Osrednjeslovenska	3540	1367	508607	Ljubljana
Podravska	2170	838	321781	Maribor
Pomurska	1337	516	121824	Murska Sobota
Savinjska	2384	920	261243	Celje
Spodnjeposavska	885	342	70353	Krško
Zasavska	264	102	45226	Trbovlje

■ Spain

Province	Area sq km	sq mi	Population (1 Jan 2007)	Capital
Álava	3047	1176	305459	Vitoria Gasteiz
Albacete	14862	5737	392110	Albacete
Alicante	5863	2263	1825264	Alicante
Almería	8774	3387	646633	Almería
Asturias	10565	4078	1074862	Oviedo
Ávila	8048	3106	168638	Ávila
Badajoz	21657	8360	678459	Badajoz
Baleares (Balearic Is)	5014	1935	1030650	Palma
Barcelona	7733	2985	5332513	Barcelona
Burgos	14309	5523	365972	Burgos
Cáceres	19945	7699	411531	Cáceres
Cádiz	7385	2850	1207343	Cádiz
Cantabria	5289	2041	572824	Santander
Castellón	6679	2579	573282	Castellón
Ciudad Real	19749	7519	510122	Ciudad Real
Córdoba	13718	5295	792182	Córdoba
La Coruña	7876	3040	1132792	La Coruña
Cuenca	17061	6585	211375	Cuenca
Girona (Gerona)	5886	2272	706185	Girona
Granada	12531	4387	884099	Granada
Guadalajara	12190	4705	224076	Guadalajara
Guipúzcoa	1997	771	694944	San Sebastián
Huelva	10885	4202	497671	Huelva
Huesca	15613	6027	220107	Huesca
Jaén	13498	5210	664742	Jáen
León	15468	5971	497387	León
Lléida (Lérida)	12028	4642	414015	Lléida
Lugo	9803	3784	355176	Lugo
Madrid	7995	3086	6081689	Madrid
Málaga	7276	2808	1517523	Málaga
Murcia	11317	4368	1392117	Murcia
Navarra	10421	4022	605876	Pamplona
Ourense	7278	2809	336926	Orense
Palencia	8035	3101	173281	Palencia
Las Palmas	4072	1572	1042131	Las Palmas
Pontevedra	4477	1728	947639	Vigo
La Rioja	5034	1943	308968	Logrono
Salamanca	12336	4761	351326	Salamanca
Santa Cruz de Tenerife	3170	1224	983820	Santa Cruz de Tenerife
Segovia	6949	2682	159322	Segovia
Sevilla	14001	5404	1849268	Sevilla
Soria	10287	3971	93593	Soria
Tarragona	6283	2425	757795	Tarragona
Teruel	14785	5707	144046	Teruel
Toledo	15368	5932	639621	Toledo
Valencia	10763	4154	2486483	Valencia
Valladolid	8202	3166	521661	Valladolid

Social Structure

Social Structure

Province	Area sq km	sq mi	Population (1 Jan 2007)	Capital
Vizcaya	2217	856	1141457	Bilbao
Zamora	10559	4076	197237	Zamora
Zaragoza	17252	6659	932502	Zaragoza

■ Sweden

County	Area sq km	sq mi	Population (31 Dec 2007)	Capital
Blekinge	2941	1136	151900	Karlskrona
Dalarna	28194	10886	275618	Falun
Gävleborg	18191	7024	275556	Gävle
Gotland	3140	1212	57122	Visby
Halland	5454	2106	291393	Halmstad
Jämtland	49443	19090	126937	Östersund
Jönköping	9944	3839	333610	Jönköping
Kalmar	11170	4313	233834	Kalmar
Kronoberg	8458	3266	180787	Växjö
Norrbotten	98913	39191	250602	Lulece
Örebro	8519	3289	276067	Örebro
Östergötland	10562	4078	420809	Linköping
Skåne	10025	3870	1199357	Malmö
Södermanland	6060	2340	265190	Nyköping
Stockholm	6488	2505	1949516	Stockholm
Uppsala	6989	2698	323270	Uppsala
Värmland	17584	6789	273826	Karlstad
Västerbotten	55401	21390	257593	Umeå
Västernorrland	21678	8370	243449	Härnösand
Västmanland	6302	2433	249193	Västeraces
Västra Götalands	23942	9244	1547298	Gothenburg

■ Switzerland

Canton	Area sq km	sq mi	Population (31 Dec 2007 est)	Capital
Aargau	1395	540	581600	Aarau
Appenzell Ausser-Rhoden[1]	243	94	52700	Herisau
Appenzell Inner-Rhoden[1]	172	66	15500	Appenzell
Basle (Basel-Landschaft)[1]	428	165	269100	Liestal
Basle (Basel-Stadt)[1]	37	14	185200	Basel
Berne	5932	2290	963000	Berne
Fribourg	1591	614	263200	Fribourg
Geneva (Genève)	245	94	438200	Geneva
Glarus	684	264	38200	Glarus
Graubünden (Fr: Grisons)	7106	2744	188800	Chur (Coire)
Jura	837	323	69600	Delémont
Lucerne (Luzern)	1429	552	363500	Lucerne
Neuenberg (Neuchâtel)	716	276	169800	Neuchâtel
Nidwalden[1]	241	93	40300	Stans
Obwalden[1]	480	186	34000	Sarnen
St Gall (Sankt Gallen)	1950	752	465900	St Gall
Schaffhausen	298	115	74500	Schaffhausen
Schwyz	851	328	141000	Schwyz
Solothurn	791	305	250200	Solothurn
Thurgau	863	333	238300	Frauenfeld
Ticino	2738	1056	328600	Bellinzona
Uri	1057	408	35000	Altdorf
Valais	5213	2015	298600	Sion
Vaud	2822	1090	672000	Lausanne
Zug	207	80	109100	Zug
Zürich	1661	641	1307600	Zürich

[1] Demicanton — functions as a full canton.

■ United Kingdom

▶ **County and unitary councils of England**, **Council areas of Wales**, **Council areas of Scotland** and **Districts of Northern Ireland**, which follow

County and unitary councils of England

	Abbreviation[1]	Area sq km	sq mi	Population[2]	Persons per sq km
Non-metropolitan counties					
Bedfordshire	Beds	1 192	460	407 000	341
Buckinghamshire	Bucks	1 568	605	490 600	313
Cambridgeshire	Cambs	3 056	1 180	597 400	195
Cheshire	Ches	2 081	803	688 700	331
Cornwall and Isles of Scilly	none	3 559	1 374	531 700	149
Cumbria	[Cumb]	6 824	2 635	496 900	73
Derbyshire	Derby	2 551	985	758 200	297
Devon	[Dev]	6 562	2 534	750 100	114
Dorset	[Dors]	2 542	981	406 800	160
Durham	Dur	2 232	862	504 900	226
East Sussex	[E Suss]	1 713	661	508 300	297
Essex	[Ess]	3 469	1 339	1 376 400	397
Gloucestershire	Glos	2 653	1 024	582 600	220
Hampshire	Hants	3 689	1 424	1 276 800	346
Hertfordshire	Herts	1 639	633	1 066 100	650
Kent	none	3 543	1 368	1 394 700	394
Lancashire	Lancs	2 897	1 119	1 168 100	403
Leicestershire	Leics	2 084	805	641 000	308
Lincolnshire	Lincs	5 921	2 286	692 800	117
London[3]	none	1 579	610	7 556 900	4 786
Norfolk	[Norf]	5 372	2 074	840 700	156
Northamptonshire	Northants	2 367	914	678 300	287
Northumberland	Northumb	5 026	1 941	310 600	62
North Yorkshire	N Yorks	8 038	3 103	595 500	74
Nottinghamshire	Notts	2 085	805	771 900	370
Oxfordshire	Oxon	2 606	1 006	635 500	244
Shropshire	[Shrops]	3 197	1 234	290 900	91
Somerset	Som	3 452	1 333	522 800	151
Staffordshire	Staffs	2 623	1 013	825 800	315
Suffolk	[Suff]	3 798	1 466	709 400	187
Surrey	[Sur]	1 677	647	1 098 200	655
Warwickshire	War	1 979	764	526 700	266
West Sussex	[W Suss]	1 988	768	776 300	390
Wiltshire	Wilts	3 246	1 253	452 600	139
Worcestershire	Worcs	1 761	680	555 400	315
Metropolitan boroughs					
Barnsley	none	329	127	224 600	683
Birmingham	none	268	103	1 010 200	3 769
Bolton	none	140	54	262 300	1 874
Bradford	none	366	141	497 400	1 359
Bury	none	99	38	183 300	1 852
Calderdale	none	364	141	200 100	550
Coventry	none	99	38	306 700	3 098
Doncaster	none	568	219	291 100	513
Dudley	none	98	38	305 400	3 116
Gateshead	none	142	55	190 500	1 340
Kirklees	none	409	158	401 000	980
Knowsley	none	86	33	150 900	1 755
Leeds	none	552	213	761 100	1 378
Liverpool	none	112	43	435 500	3 888
Manchester	none	116	45	458 100	3 949
Newcastle upon Tyne	none	113	44	271 600	2 404
North Tyneside	none	82	32	196 000	2 390
Oldham	none	142	55	219 500	1 546
Rochdale	none	158	61	206 100	1 304
Rotherham	none	286	110	253 400	886
St Helens	none	136	53	177 400	1 304
Salford	none	97	37	219 200	2 260
Sandwell	none	86	33	287 500	3 343
Sefton	none	153	59	276 200	1 805
Sheffield	none	368	142	530 300	1 441
Solihull	none	178	69	203 600	1 144

Social Structure

Social Structure

	Abbreviation[1]	Area		Population[2]	Persons per sq km
		sq km	sq mi		
South Tyneside	none	64	25	151 000	2 359
Stockport	none	126	47	280 900	2 229
Sunderland	none	137	53	280 300	2 046
Tameside	none	103	40	214 400	2 082
Trafford	none	106	41	212 800	2 008
Wakefield	none	339	131	321 600	949
Walsall	none	104	40	254 500	2 447
Wigan	none	188	73	305 600	1 626
Wirral	none	157	61	310 200	1 976
Wolverhampton	none	69	27	236 000	3 420
Unitary authorities					
Bath and North East Somerset	none	351	136	178 300	508
Blackburn with Darwen	none	137	53	140 900	1 028
Blackpool	none	35	14	142 500	4 071
Bournemouth	none	46	18	163 200	3 548
Bracknell Forest	none	109	42	113 500	1 041
Brighton and Hove	none	82	32	253 500	3 091
Bristol, City of	none	110	42	416 400	3 785
Darlington	none	197	76	100 000	508
Derby	none	78	30	237 900	3 050
East Riding of Yorkshire	none	2 415	932	333 300	138
Halton	none	74	29	119 500	1 615
Hartlepool	none	94	36	91 400	972
Herefordshire, County of	[Herefs]	2 162	835	178 400	83
Isle of Wight	IOW	380	147	139 500	367
Kingston upon Hull, City of	none	71	27	257 000	3 620
Leicester	none	73	28	292 600	4 008
Luton	none	43	17	188 800	4 391
Medway	none	192	74	252 200	1 314
Middlesbrough	none	54	21	138 700	2 569
Milton Keynes	none	309	119	228 400	739
North East Lincolnshire	none	192	74	158 400	825
North Lincolnshire	none	833	322	159 400	191
North Somerset	N Som	373	144	204 700	549
Nottingham	none	75	29	288 700	3 849
Peterborough	none	344	133	163 300	475
Plymouth	none	80	31	250 700	3 134
Poole	none	65	25	138 100	2 125
Portsmouth	none	40	15	197 700	4 943
Reading	none	40	15	143 700	3 593
Redcar and Cleveland	none	245	95	139 400	569
Rutland	none	394	152	38 400	97
Slough	none	27	10	120 100	4 448
Southampton	none	50	19	231 200	4 624
South Gloucestershire	S Glos	497	192	256 500	516
Southend-on-Sea	none	42	16	162 000	3 857
Stockton-on-Tees	none	204	79	190 200	932
Stoke-on-Trent	none	93	36	239 000	2 570
Swindon	none	230	89	189 500	824
Telford and Wrekin	none	290	112	161 700	558
Thurrock	none	164	63	150 000	915
Torbay	none	63	24	134 200	2 130
Warrington	none	176	68	195 200	1 109
West Berkshire	W Berks	704	272	150 700	214
Windsor and Maidenhead	none	198	76	141 000	712
Wokingham	none	179	69	156 600	875
York	none	271	105	193 300	713
TOTAL		130 423	50 354	51 092 000	392

[1] Square brackets denote that the abbreviation is not generally regarded as established. Those without are generally accepted abbreviations.

[2] Mid-2007 population estimates.

[3] Greater London comprises 32 boroughs (divided into Inner London and Outer London boroughs) and the City of London.

Note: Figures do not add exactly because of rounding. Total area includes inland, but not tidal, water.

Population data source: ONS, © Crown copyright 2008.

Council areas of Wales

Unitary authority	Administrative centre	Area sq km	Population[1]	Persons per sq km
Blaenau Gwent	Ebbw Vale	109	69 170	636
Bridgend	Bridgend	251	133 917	534
Caerphilly	Hengoed	277	171 824	619
Cardiff	Cardiff	140	321 000	2 288
Carmarthenshire	Carmarthen	2 372	179 539	76
Ceredigion	Aberaeron	1 790	77 777	43
Conwy	Conwy	1 130	111 709	99
Denbighshire	Ruthin	838	97 009	116
Flintshire	Mold	438	150 537	344
Gwynedd	Caernarfon	2 548	118 374	46
Merthyr Tydfil	Merthyr Tydfil	111	55 619	501
Monmouthshire	Cwmbran	851	88 200	104
Neath Port Talbot	Port Talbot	442	137 376	311
Newport	Newport	190	140 203	736
Pembrokeshire	Haverfordwest	1 619	117 921	73
Powys	Llandrindod Wells	5 196	131 963	25
Rhondda, Cynon, Taff	Clydach Vale	424	233 734	551
Swansea	Swansea	378	228 086	603
Torfaen	Pontypool	126	91 086	722
Vale of Glamorgan	Barry	331	124 017	374
Wrexham	Wrexham	504	131 963	262
Ynys Mon (Isle of Anglesey)	Llangefni	714	69 003	97
TOTAL		20 780	2 979 975	143

[1] 2007 mid-year population estimates published 2008. Figures may not add exactly because of rounding.
Population data source: Statistical Directorate, Welsh Assembly Government © Crown copyright 2008.

Council areas of Scotland

Unitary authority[1]	Administrative centre	Area sq km	Population[2]	Persons per sq km
Aberdeen City	Aberdeen	186	209 260	1 127
Aberdeenshire	Aberdeen	6 313	239 160	38
Angus	Forfar	2 182	109 870	50
Argyll and Bute	Lochgilphead	6 909	91 350	13
Clackmannanshire	Alloa	159	49 900	315
Dumfries and Galloway	Dumfries	6 426	148 300	23
Dundee City	Dundee	60	142 150	2 376
East Ayrshire	Kilmarnock	1 262	119 570	95
East Dunbartonshire	Kirkintilloch	175	104 850	600
East Lothian	Haddington	679	94 440	139
East Renfrewshire	Giffnock	174	89 260	514
Edinburgh, City of	Edinburgh	264	468 070	1 775
Eilean Siar[4]	Stornoway	3 071	26 300	9
Falkirk	Falkirk	297	150 720	507
Fife	Glenrothes	1 325	360 500	272
Glasgow City	Glasgow	175	581 940	3 316
Highland	Inverness	25 659	217 440	8
Inverclyde	Greenock	160	81 080	505
Midlothian	Dalkeith	354	79 510	225
Moray	Elgin	2 238	86 870	39
North Ayrshire	Irvine	885	135 760	153
North Lanarkshire	Motherwell	470	324 680	691
Orkney Islands	Kirkwall	990	19 860	20
Perth and Kinross	Perth	5 286	142 140	27
Renfrewshire	Paisley	261	169 600	650
Scottish Borders	Newton St Boswells	4 732	111 430	24
Shetland Islands	Lerwick	1 466	21 950	15
South Ayrshire	Ayr	1 222	111 690	91
South Lanarkshire	Hamilton	1 772	309 500	175
Stirling	Stirling	2 187	88 190	40

Social Structure

Unitary authority[1]	Administrative centre	Area sq km	Population[2]	Persons per sq km
West Dunbartonshire	Dumbarton	159	91 090	573
West Lothian	Livingston	427	167 770	393
TOTAL[3]		77 925	5 144 200	66

[1] The counties of Scotland were replaced by 9 regional and 53 district councils in 1975; these in turn became 29 Unitary Authorities or Council Areas on 1 April 1996, the 3 island councils remaining as before.
[2] 2007 mid-year population estimates published 24 Jul 2008.
[3] Figures may not add exactly because of rounding. Area revised according to digital boundaries used in 2001 census.
[4] Formerly known as Western Isles.
Data obtained from the General Register Office for Scotland, © Crown copyright 2008.

Districts of Northern Ireland

Name	Administrative centre	Area sq km	Population[1]	Persons per sq km
Antrim	Antrim	421	52 621	125
Ards	Newtownards	380	77 117	203
Armagh	Armagh	671	57 685	86
Ballymena	Ballymena	630	62 118	99
Ballymoney	Ballymoney	416	29 741	72
Banbridge	Banbridge	451	46 449	103
Belfast	—	110	267 535	2 440
Carrickfergus	Carrickfergus	81	40 026	495
Castlereagh	Belfast	85	65 562	771
Coleraine	Coleraine	486	56 815	117
Cookstown	Cookstown	514	35 429	69
Craigavon	Craigavon	282	88 820	316
Derry	—	381	108 535	285
Down	Downpatrick	649	69 188	107
Dungannon	Dungannon	772	54 306	70
Fermanagh	Enniskillen	1 699	61 291	36
Larne	Larne	336	31 344	93
Limavady	Limavady	586	34 428	59
Lisburn	Lisburn	447	113 520	254
Magherafelt	Magherafelt	564	43 099	77
Moyle	Ballycastle	494	16 740	34
Newry and Mourne	Newry	898	95 494	106
Newtownabbey	Newtownabbey	151	81 690	542
North Down	Bangor	81	78 657	973
Omagh	Omagh	1 130	51 508	46
Strabane	Strabane	862	39 430	46
TOTAL		13 576	1 759 148	130

[1] 2007 mid-year population estimates. Figures may not add exactly due to rounding.
Population data source: Northern Ireland Statistics and Research Agency, © Crown Copyright 2008.

British islands

Name	Adminstrative centre	Area[1] sq km	sq mi	Population[2]	Persons per sq km
Isle of Man	Douglas	572	221	75 831	133
Jersey	St Helier	116	45	91 321	787
Guernsey	St Peter Port	63	24	65 573	1 041
Alderney (dependency of Guernsey)	St Anne's	8	3	2 400[3]	300
Sark	—	4	2	600	150

[1] Data obtained from: States of Guernsey, Advisory and Finance Committee, © States of Guernsey 2002; Economic Affairs Division, Isle of Man Government Treasury, © Isle of Man Government 2002; Statistics Unit, States of Jersey Policy and Resources Department.
[2] 2007 estimated figures.
[3] Official estimate.

Political definitions

Politics is the science of government: it studies and regulates the creation of legislation, as well as defining the role of the individual within society. Below are 50 concise definitions of the most widely used political terms.

Act of Parliament Bill passed through both houses of the UK Parliament.

Anarchism Rejection of the state and other forms of authority.

Authoritarianism Government not dependent on the consent of society.

Bill, parliamentary Draft of proposed new law for consideration by legislature.

Cabinet Group of senior ministers usually heading government departments.

Civil disobedience Strategy to achieve political goals by refusing to co-operate with a government or its agents.

Civil rights Rights guaranteed by a state to its citizens.

Coalition Arrangement between countries or political parties to pursue a common goal.

Communism Political ideology featuring common ownership of property, associated with the theories of Karl Marx (1818–83), published in his *Communist Manifesto* (1848).

Conservatism Political beliefs stressing adherence to established authority.

Constitution Principles that determine the way a country may be governed, usually in the form of a written document.

Democracy Rule by the people, usually with decision-making in the hands of popularly elected representatives.

Devolution Delegation of authority from central government to a subordinate elected institution.

Dictatorship Rule by a single person, or several people (eg military dictatorship), unelected and authoritarian in character.

Dissidents People who oppose a regime and may suffer discrimination.

Fascism Nationalistic and authoritarian movement associated with the 1930s.

Federalism Territorial political organization aiming to maintain national unity while permitting regional diversity.

Green Movement opposing ecological and environmental effects caused by technological and economic policies.

House of Commons Lower (and effectively ruling) chamber of UK Parliament.

House of Lords Non-elected house of UK Parliament, containing hereditary and life peers.

House of Representatives One of the two chambers of the US legislature.

Human rights Fundamental rights beyond those prescribed by law.

Ideology Set of beliefs and attitudes that support particular interests.

Imperialism Extension of state power through acquisition of other territories.

Left wing Political position occupied by those with radical and reforming tendencies towards social and political order.

Legislature Institution with power to pass laws.

Liberalism Doctrine that urges freedom of the individual, religion, trade and economics (*laissez faire*).

Nationalism Doctrine that views the nation as the principal unit of political organization.

Nationalization Taking an industry into state ownership.

Ombudsman Official who investigates complaints regarding government actions.

Pluralism Existence within a society of a variety of groups, limiting the power of any one group.

Pressure group Organization formed to support a particular political interest.

Privatization Transfer to private ownership of organizations owned by the state.

Privy Council Body advising the British monarch, appointed by the Crown.

Proletariat In socialist philosophy, term denoting working class.

Proportional representation Voting system ensuring that the representation of voters is in proportion to their numbers.

Racism Ideology alleging inferiority of racial or ethnic groups in terms of their biological or physical characteristics.

Radicalism Ideology arguing for substantial political and social change.

Referendum Device whereby the electorate can vote on a measure put before it by a government.

Right wing Political position of support for established institutions and opposition to socialist developments.

Sanction Penalty imposed by one state against another, such as denial of trade.

Sectarianism Excessive loyalty or attachment to a particular sect or party.

Senate One of the two chambers of a national or state legislature.

Separatism Demand for separation from territorial and political sovereignty of the state to which the separatists belong.

Socialism Doctrine favouring state intervention to create an egalitarian society.

Terrorism Violent behaviour to promote a particular political cause, often aimed at overthrow of the established order.

Totalitarianism System in which political opposition is suppressed and decision-making is highly centralized.

Trade union Association of people, usually in the same trade, joining together to improve pay and working conditions.

Tribunal Official body appointed to inquire into and give judgement on some matter of dispute.

Welfare state System whereby state is responsible for protecting and promoting citizens' welfare in areas such as health, employment, pensions and education.

Legislative systems of government

A bicameral political system is one in which there are two chambers in the legislature, whereas a unicameral system has only one chamber.

Social Structure

■ **Bicameral**

Africa
Algeria, Burundi, Congo, Democratic Republic of the Congo, Ethiopia, Gabon, Lesotho, Liberia, Madagascar, Mauritania, Morocco, Namibia, Nigeria, Rwanda, South Africa, Sudan, Swaziland, Tunisia, Zimbabwe

The Americas
Antigua and Barbuda, Argentina, The Bahamas, Barbados, Belize, Bolivia, Brazil, Canada, Chile, Colombia, Dominican Republic, Grenada, Haiti, Jamaica, Mexico, Paraguay, St Lucia, Trinidad and Tobago, Uruguay, USA

Asia
Afghanistan, Bahrain, Bhutan, Cambodia, India, Indonesia, Japan, Jordan, Kazakhstan, Malaysia, Pakistan, Philippines, Tajikistan, Thailand, Uzbekistan

Australasia
Australia, Fiji, Palau

Europe
Austria, Belarus, Belgium, Bosnia and Herzegovina, Czech Republic, France, Germany, Ireland, Italy, Netherlands, Poland, Romania, Russian Federation, Spain, Switzerland, UK

■ **Unicameral**

Africa
Angola, Benin, Botswana, Burkino Faso, Cameroon, Cape Verde, Central African Republic, Chad, Comoros, Côte d'Ivoire, Djibouti, Egypt, Equatorial Guinea, Eritrea, The Gambia, Ghana, Guinea, Guinea-Bissau, Kenya, Libya, Malawi, Mali, Mauritius, Mozambique, Niger, São Tomé and Príncipe, Senegal, Seychelles, Sierra Leone, Somalia, Tanzania, Togo, Uganda, Zambia

The Americas
Costa Rica, Cuba, Dominica, Ecuador, El Salvador, Guatemala, Guyana, Honduras, Nicaragua, Panama, Peru, St Christopher and Nevis, St Vincent and the Grenadines, Suriname, Venezuela

Asia
Armenia, Azerbaijan, Bangladesh, Brunei, China, East Timor, Iran, Iraq, Israel, Kuwait, Kyrgyzstan, Laos, Lebanon, Maldives, Mongolia, Myanmar (Burma), Nepal, North Korea, Qatar, Singapore, South Korea, Sri Lanka, Syria, Taiwan, Turkey, Turkmenistan, United Arab Emirates, Vietnam, Yemen

Australasia
Federated States of Micronesia, Kiribati, Marshall Islands, Nauru, New Zealand, Papua New Guinea, Samoa, Solomon Islands, Tonga, Tuvalu, Vanuatu

Europe
Albania, Andorra, Bulgaria, Croatia, Cyprus, Denmark, Estonia, Finland, Georgia, Greece, Hungary, Iceland, Latvia, Liechtenstein, Lithuania, Luxembourg, Macedonia, Malta, Moldova, Monaco, Montenegro, Norway, Portugal, San Marino, Serbia, Slovakia, Slovenia, Sweden, Ukraine

Passage of a public bill to law in the UK

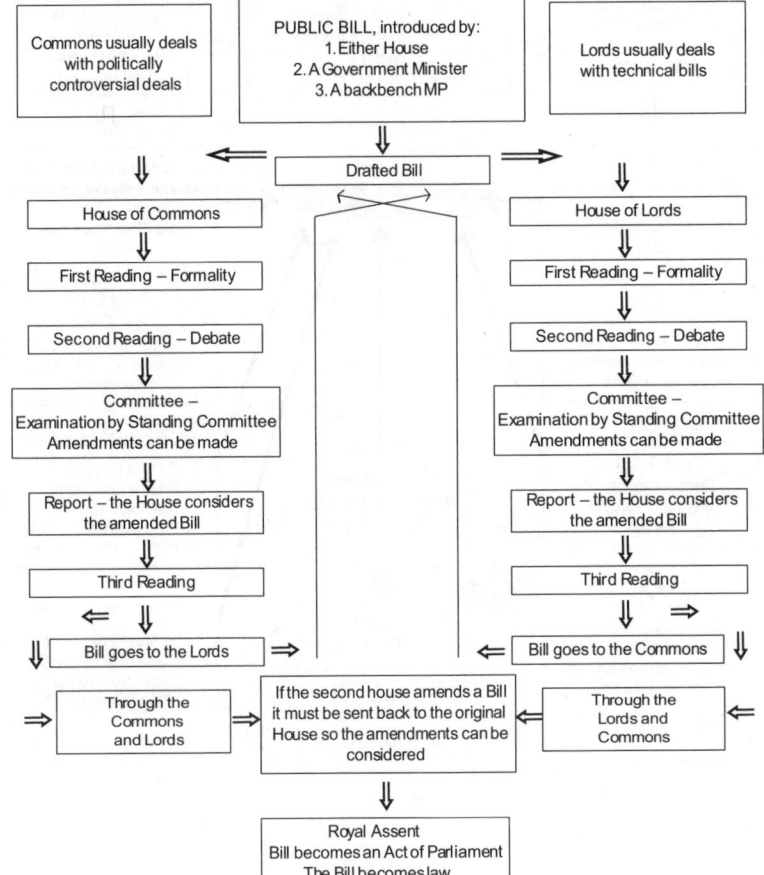

Passage of a public bill to law in the USA

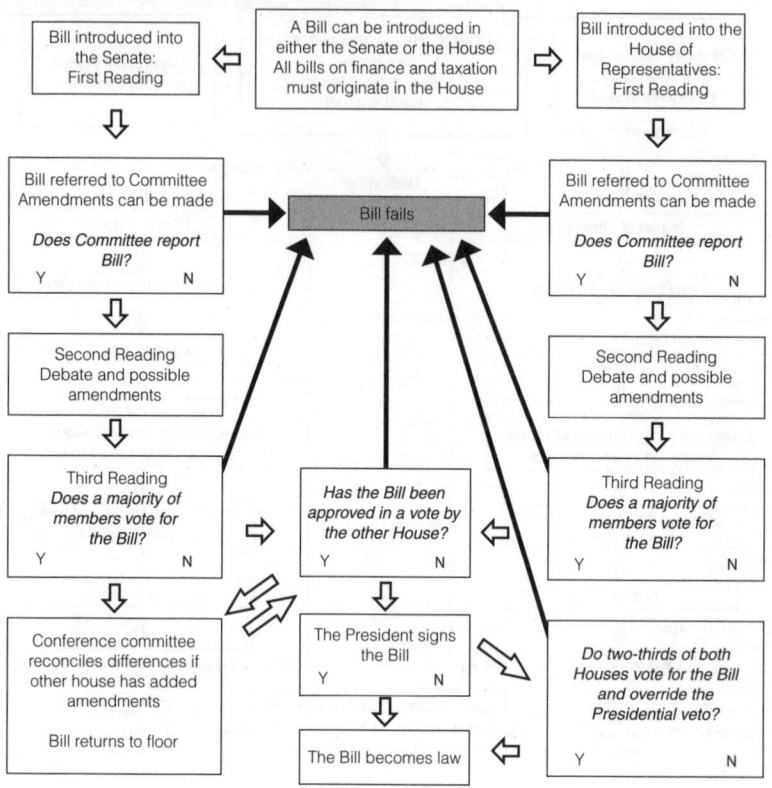

Military ranks

Navy	Army	Air Force
UK		
Admiral of the Fleet	Field Marshal	Marshal of the Royal Air Force
Admiral	General	Air Chief Marshal
Vice-Admiral	Lieutenant-General	Air Marshal
Rear-Admiral	Major-General	Air Vice-Marshal
Commodore Admiral	Brigadier	Air Commodore
Captain RN	Colonel	Group Captain
Commander	Lieutenant-Colonel	Wing Commander
Lieutenant Commander	Major	Squadron Leader
Lieutenant	Captain	Flight Lieutenant
Sub-Lieutenant	Lieutenant	Flying Officer
Midshipman	Second Lieutenant	Pilot Officer
France		
Amiral	Général d'Armée	Général d'Armée Aérienne
Vice-Amiral d'Escadre	Général de Corps d'Armée	Général de Corps Aérien
Vice-Amiral	Général de Division	Général de Division Aérienne
Contre-Amiral	Général de Brigade	Général de Brigade Aérienne
Capitaine de Vaisseau	Colonel	Colonel
Capitaine de Frégate	Lieutenant-Colonel	Lieutenant-Colonel
Capitaine de Corvette	Commandant	Commandant
Lieutenant de Vaisseau	Capitaine	Capitaine
Enseigne de Vaisseau de 1ère classe	Lieutenant	Lieutenant
Enseigne de 2ème classe	Sous-Lieutenant	Sous-Lieutenant
Germany		
Admiral	General	General
Vizeadmiral	Generalleutnant	Generalleutnant
Konteradmiral	Generalmajor	Generalmajor
Flotillenadmiral	Brigadegeneral	Brigadegeneral
Kapitan zur See	Oberst	Oberst
Fregattenkapitän	Oberstleutnant	Oberstleutnant
Korvettenkapitän	Major	Major
Kapitänleutnant	Hauptmann	Hauptmann
Oberleutnant zur See	Oberleutnant	Leutnant
Leutnant zur See	Leutnant	Oberfahnrich
Russia		
Admiral of the Fleet of the Russian Federation	Marshal of the Army of the Russian Federation	Marshal of the Air Force of the Russian Federation
Admiral of the Fleet	Army General	General of the Air Force
Admiral	Colonel-General	Colonel-General
Vice-Admiral	Lieutenant-General	Lieutenant-General
Rear-Admiral	Major-General	Major-General
Captain 1st class	Colonel	Colonel
Captain 2nd class	Lieutenant-Colonel	Lieutenant-Colonel
Captain 3rd class	Major	Major
Captain-Lieutenant	Captain	Captain
Senior Lieutenant	Senior Lieutenant	Senior Lieutenant
Lieutenant	Lieutenant	Lieutenant
Junior Lieutenant	Junior Lieutenant	Junior Lieutenant
USA		
Fleet Admiral	General of the Army	General of the Air Force
Admiral	General	General
Vice-Admiral	Lieutenant-General	Lieutenant-General
Rear-Admiral	Major-General	Major-General
Commodore Admiral	Brigadier-General	Brigadier-General
Captain	Colonel	Colonel
Commander	Lieutenant-Colonel	Lieutenant-Colonel
Lieutenant-Commander	Major	Major
Lieutenant	Captain	Captain
Lieutenant Junior Grade	First Lieutenant	First-Lieutenant
Ensign	Second Lieutenant	Second-Lieutenant

Social Structure

Royal and aristocratic ranks

England	France	Holy Roman Empire (Germany)	Italy	Spain
king	roi	Kaiser	re	rey
prince	prince	Herzog	duca	duque
duke	duc	Pfalzgraf	principe	principe
marquess	marquis	Markgraf	marchese	marques
earl	comte	Landgraf	conde	conde
viscount	vicomte		visconte	vizconde
baron				

Honours: UK

CBE ▶ The Most Excellent Order of the British Empire

The Distinguished Service Order (DSO) Established in 1886; bestowed as a reward for the distinguished service in action of commissioned officers in the Navy, Army and Royal Air Force; extended in 1942 to cover officers of the Merchant Navy.

The George Cross (GC) Instituted in 1940 as a reward for gallantry, and conferred upon those responsible for 'acts of the greatest heroism or of the most conspicuous courage in circumstances of extreme danger'.

The Imperial Service Order (ISO) Instituted in 1902 to reward members of the Civil Service; one class of membership; numbers limited to 1700 in total, 1100 belonging to the Home Civil Service, and 600 coming from the Overseas Civil Service.

MBE ▶ The Most Excellent Order of the British Empire

The Most Ancient and Most Noble Order of the Thistle (KT) An ancient order revived by King James II in 1687, and re-established by Queen Anne in 1703; limited to 16 knights.

The Most Distinguished Order of St Michael and St George Founded in 1818 by King George III; conferred upon British subjects for services abroad or in the British Commonwealth, with the motto 'Auspicium melioris aevi' (Token of a better age), and divided into three classes: Knight Grand Cross (GCMG), Knight Commander (KCMG) and Companion (CMG).

The Most Excellent Order of the British Empire An order of knighthood, the first to be granted to both sexes equally; instituted 1917; divided into military and civil divisions in 1918, with five divisions: Knight or Dame Grand Cross (GBE), Knight or Dame Commander (KBE/DBE), Commander (CBE), Officer (OBE) and Member (MBE).

The Most Honourable Order of the Bath Founded in 1399, revived by King George in 1725; originally a military order, the civil branch was established in 1847; women became eligible in 1971; the order has three divisions: Knight or Dame Grand Cross (GCB), Knight or Dame Commander (KCB/DCB), and Companion (CB).

The Most Noble Order of the Garter (KG) Instituted in 1348 by Edward III; limited to 24 knights companion only, and with the motto 'Honi soit qui mal y pense' (Shame on him who thinks evil of it).

OBE ▶ The Most Excellent Order of the British Empire

The Order of Merit (OM) Instituted in 1902, with civil and military divisions, and limited to 24 in number.

The Order of the Companions of Honour Instituted in 1917 at the same time as the Most Excellent Order of the British Empire; it carries no title or precedence and consists of one class ranking immediately after the first class of the Order of the British Empire; membership is limited to 65 in number, excluding honorary members.

The Royal Red Cross Instituted by Queen Victoria in 1883; the first military order designed solely for women, and conferred upon members of the nursing services for their efforts in the field, and for others undertaking voluntary work on behalf of the sick or wounded or on behalf of the Red Cross.

The Royal Victorian Chain Founded in 1902 by King Edward VII, it confers no precedence on the holder, and is largely, although not exclusively, awarded to foreign monarchs.

The Royal Victorian Order Established by Queen Victoria in 1896, with no limit to the number of members; conferred for services to the sovereign or Royal Family; bestowed upon foreigners as well as British subjects; women became eligible in 1936.

The Victoria Cross (VC) Instituted by Queen Victoria in 1856 to reward conspicuous bravery, and the most highly coveted of British military decorations.

Honours: Europe

▪ Denmark

Order of Dannebrog Believed to have been founded in 1219 and one of the oldest orders in existence, revived in 1671, with six main classes: Grand Commanders, Knights Grand Cross, Commanders of the First Degree, Commanders, Knights of the First Degree and Knights, and an auxiliary class known as the Badge of Honour.

Order of the Elephant Founded in 1462 and revived by King Christian V in 1693; the premier order of Denmark.

▪ France

Croix de Guerre Military award established in 1915 to commemorate individuals mentioned in despatches.

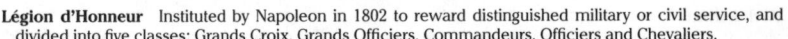

Légion d'Honneur   Instituted by Napoleon in 1802 to reward distinguished military or civil service, and divided into five classes: Grands Croix, Grands Officiers, Commandeurs, Officiers and Chevaliers.

■ Germany

The Iron Cross   Established by Frederick William in 1813 as an award for gallantry in action; various grades of award.

Order of Merit   Instituted by the Federal German Republic in 1951, and divided into eight classes: Grand Cross (three grades), Large Merit Cross (three grades) and Merit Cross (two grades).

■ Italy

Ordine al Merito della Repubblica Italiana   Established in 1952, with five classes of award: Grand Cross, Grand Officer, Commander, Officer and Member.

■ Netherlands

Huisorde van Oranje   Established in 1905, awarded for outstanding services to the Royal House; corresponds to the Royal Victorian Order in the United Kingdom.

Militaire Willemsorde   Founded by King William I in 1815; the highest military decoration open to members of the forces of all ranks and to civilians for acts of bravery and devotion to duty.

Nederlandsche Leeuw   Founded by King William I in 1815, awarded to those of proven patriotism, outstanding zeal and devotion to civil duty, and to those with extraordinary ability in the arts and sciences; open to civilians, members of the military and foreigners; divided into three classes: Grand Cross, Commander and Knight, with an attached brotherhood whose members are nominated for acts of distinction, self-sacrifice and philanthropy.

Orde van Oranje Nassau   Established in 1892; awarded to Netherlanders and foreigners for distinguished performance to the state or society; open to civilians or members of the forces; divided into five classes: Grand Cross, Grand Officer, Knight Commander, Officer and Knight.

Honours: USA

The Bronze Star   Established in 1944; awarded to members of the forces for acts of heroism or merit and for services beyond the call of duty, but not sufficiently outstanding to merit the Silver Star or Legion of Merit.

The Congressional Medal of Honor   Instituted in 1861/1862, and first awarded during the American Civil War; conferred upon members of the forces showing exceptional gallantry and bravery in action.

The Distinguished Service Cross   Instituted in 1918; confined to the army, and awarded to those showing extraordinary heroism in circumstances which do not justify the Congressional Medal of Honor.

The Legion of Merit   Instituted in 1942; awarded to members of both the United States and foreign forces for distinguished service and meritorious conduct over a period of time.

The Purple Heart   First instituted by George Washington in 1782 and reinstituted by Congress in 1932; awarded to those wounded in military action, and bears the inscription 'For Military Merit'.

The Medal for Merit   Established by President Roosevelt in 1942 to award civilians of the USA or her allies for distinguished and meritorious service.

The Silver Star   First authorized during World War I, it takes precedence over the Legion of Merit.

Forms of address

In the fomulae given below, *F* stands for forename and *S* for surname.

■ Very formal ceremonial styles for closing letters are now seldom used: 'Yours faithfully' is assumed below, unless otherwise indicated.

■ Forms of spoken address are given only where a special style is followed.

■ Holders of courtesy titles are addressed according to their rank, but without 'The', 'The Right Hon.', or 'The Most Hon.'.

■ Ranks in the armed forces, and ecclesiastical and ambassadorial ranks, precede titles in the peerage, eg 'Colonel the Earl of —' or 'The Rev the Marquess of —'.

■ Although the correct forms of address are given below for members of the Royal Family, it is more normal practice for letters to be addressed to their private secretary, equerry, or lady-in-waiting.

■ More detailed information about forms of address is to be found in Debrett's *Correct Form* and Black's *Titles and Forms of Address*.

Ambassadors (foreign)
Address on envelope: 'His/Her Excellency the Ambassador of —' or 'His/Her Excellency the — Ambassador'. (The wife of an ambassador is not entitled to the style 'Her Excellency'.) *Begin*: 'Your Excellency'. (Within the letter, refer to 'Your Excellency' once, thereafter as 'you'.) *Close*: 'I have the honour to be, Sir/Madam (or according to rank), Your Excellency's obedient servant'. *Spoken address*: 'Your Excellency' at least once, and then 'Sir' or 'Madam' by name.

Archbishop (Anglican communion)
Address on envelope: 'The Most Reverend the Lord Archbishop of —'. (The Archbishops of Canterbury and York are Privy Counsellors, and should be addressed as 'The Most Reverend and Right Hon. the Lord Archbishop of —'.) *Begin*: 'Dear Archbishop' or 'My Lord Archbishop'. *Spoken address*: 'Your Grace'. *Begin an official speech*: 'My Lord Archbishop'.

Archbishop (Roman Catholic)
Address on envelope: 'His Grace the Archbishop of —'. *Begin*: 'My Lord Archbishop'. *Close*: 'I remain, Your Grace, Yours faithfully' or 'Yours faithfully'. *Spoken address*: 'Your Grace'.

Social Structure

Social Structure

Archdeacon
Address on envelope: 'The Venerable the Archdeacon of —'. *Begin*: 'Dear Archdeacon' or 'Venerable Sir'. *Spoken address*: 'Archdeacon'. *Begin an official speech*: 'Venerable Sir'.

Baron
Address on envelope: 'The Right Hon. the Lord —'. *Begin*: 'My Lord'. *Spoken address*: 'My Lord'.

Baron's wife (Baroness)
Address on envelope: 'The Right Hon. the Lady [S—]'. *Begin*: 'Dear Lady'. *Spoken address*: 'Madam'.

Baroness (in her own right)
Address on envelope: either as for Baron's wife, or 'The Right Hon. the Baroness [S—]'. Otherwise, as for Baron's wife.

Baronet
Address on envelope: 'Sir [F—S—], Bt'. *Begin*: 'Dear Sir'. *Spoken address*: 'Sir [F—]'.

Baronet's wife
Address on envelope: 'Lady [S—]'. If she has the title 'Lady' by courtesy, 'Lady [F—S—]'. If she has the courtesy style 'The Hon.', this precedes 'Lady'. *Begin*: 'Dear Madam'. *Spoken address*: 'Madam'.

Bishop (Anglican communion)
Address on envelope: 'The Right Reverend the Lord Bishop of —'. (The Bishop of London is a Privy Counsellor, so is addressed as 'The Right Rev and Right Hon. the Lord Bishop of London'. The Bishop of Meath is styled 'The Most Reverend'.) *Begin*: 'Dear Bishop' or 'My Lord'. *Spoken address*: 'Bishop'. *Begin an official speech*: 'My Lord'.

Bishop (Episcopal Church in Scotland)
Address on envelope: 'The Right Reverend [F—S—], Bishop of —'. Otherwise as for a bishop of the Anglican communion. The bishop who holds the position of Primus is addressed as 'The Most Reverend the Primus'. *Begin*: 'Dear Primus'. *Spoken address*: 'Primus'.

Bishop (Roman Catholic)
Address on envelope: 'His Lordship the Bishop of —' or 'The Right Reverend [F—S—], Bishop of —'. In Ireland, 'The Most Reverend' is used instead of 'The Right Reverend'. If an auxiliary bishop, address as 'The Right Reverend [F—S—], Auxiliary Bishop of —'. *Begin*: 'My Lord' or (more rarely) 'My Lord Bishop'. *Close*: 'I remain, My Lord' or (more rarely), 'My Lord Bishop, Yours faithfully', or simply 'Yours faithfully'. *Spoken address*: 'My Lord' or (more rarely) 'My Lord Bishop'.

Cabinet Minister ▶ Secretary of State

Canon (Anglican communion)
Address on envelope: 'The Reverend Canon [F—S—]'. *Begin*: 'Dear Canon' or 'Dear Canon [S—]'. *Spoken address*: 'Canon' or 'Canon [S—]'.

Canon (Roman Catholic)
Address on envelope: 'The Very Reverend Canon [F—S—]'. *Begin*: 'Very Reverend Sir'. *Spoken address*: 'Canon [S—]'.

Cardinal
Address on envelope: 'His Eminence Cardinal [S—]'. If an archbishop, 'His Eminence the Cardinal Archbishop of —'. *Begin*: 'Your Eminence' or (more rarely) 'My Lord Cardinal'. *Close*: 'I remain, Your Eminence (or 'My Lord Cardinal'), Yours faithfully'. *Spoken*: 'Your Eminence'.

Clergy (Anglican communion)
Address on envelope: 'The Reverend [F—S—]'. *Begin*: 'Dear Sir/Madam' or 'Dear Mr/Mrs [S—]'.

Clergy (Roman Catholic)
Address on envelope: 'The Reverend [F—S—]'. If a member of a religious order, the initials of the order should be added after the name. *Begin*: 'Dear Reverend Father'.

Clergy (Other churches)
Address on envelope: 'The Reverend [F—S—]'. *Begin*: 'Dear Sir/Madam' or 'Dear Mr/Mrs [S—]'.

Countess
Address on envelope: 'The Right Hon. the Countess of —'. *Begin*: 'Dear Madam'. *Spoken address*: 'Madam'.

Dean (Anglican)
Address on envelope: 'The Very Reverend the Dean of —'. *Begin* 'Dear Dean' or 'Very Reverend Sir/Madam'. *Spoken address*: 'Dean'. *Begin an official speech*: 'Very Reverend Sir/Madam'.

Doctor
Physicians, anaesthetists, pathologists and radiologists are addressed as 'Doctor'. Surgeons, whether they hold the degree of Doctor of Medicine or not, are known as 'Mr/Mrs'. In England and Wales, obstetricians and gynaecologists are addressed as 'Mr/Mrs', but in Scotland, Ireland and elsewhere as 'Doctor'. In addressing a letter to the holder of a doctorate, the initials DD, MD, etc are placed after the ordinary form of address, eg 'The Rev John Smith DD', the 'Rev Dr Smith' and 'Dr John Brown' are also used.

Dowager
Address on envelope: On the marriage of a peer or baronet, the widow of the previous holder of the title becomes 'Dowager' and is addressed 'The Right Hon. the Dowager Countess of —', 'The Right Hon. the Dowager Lady —', etc. If there is already a Dowager still living, she retains this title, the later widow being addressed 'The Most Hon. [F—], Marchioness of —', 'The Right Hon. [F—], Lady —', etc. However, many Dowagers prefer the style which includes their Christian names to that including the title Dowager. *Begin*, etc as for a peer's wife.

Duchess
Address on envelope: 'Her Grace the Duchess of —'. *Begin*: 'Dear Madam'. *Spoken address*: 'Your Grace'. (For Royal Duchess ▶ **Princess**.)

Duke
Address on envelope: 'His Grace the Duke of —'. *Begin*: 'My Lord Duke'. *Spoken address*: 'Your Grace'. (For Royal Duke ▶ **Prince**.)

Earl
Address on envelope: 'The Right Hon. the Earl of —'. *Begin*: 'My Lord'. *Spoken address*: 'My Lord'. (For Earl's wife ▶ **Countess**.)

Governor of a colony or Governor-General
Address on envelope: 'His Excellency [ordinary designation], Governor(-General) of —'. (The Governor-General of Canada has the rank of 'Right Honourable', which he retains for life.) The wife of a Governor-General is styled 'Her Excellency' within the country her husband administers. *Begin*: according to rank. *Close*: 'I have the honour to be, Sir (or 'My Lord', if a peer), Your Excellency's obedient servant'. *Spoken address*: 'Your Excellency'.

Judge, High Court
Address on envelope: if a man, 'The Hon. Mr Justice [S—]'; if a woman, 'The Hon. Mrs Justice [S—]'. *Begin*: 'Dear Sir/Madam'; if on judicial matters, 'My Lord/Lady'. *Spoken address*: 'Sir/Madam'; only on the bench or when dealing with judicial matters should a High Court Judge be addressed as 'My Lord/Lady' or referred to as 'Your Lordship/Ladyship'.

Judge, Circuit
Address on envelope: 'His/Her Honour Judge [S—]'. If a Knight, 'His Honour Judge Sir [F—S—]'. *Begin*: 'Dear Sir/Madam'. *Spoken address*: 'Sir/Madam'; address as 'Your Honour' only when on the bench or dealing with judicial matters.

Justice of the Peace (England and Wales)
When on the bench, refer to and address as 'Your Worship'; otherwise according to rank. The letters 'JP' may be added after the person's name in addressing a letter, if desired.

Knight Bachelor
As Baronet, except that 'Bt' is omitted. Knight of the Bath, of St Michael and St George, etc. *Address on envelope*: 'Sir [F—S—]', with the initials 'GCB', 'KCB', etc added. *Begin*: 'Dear Sir'.

Knight's wife
As Baronet's wife, or according to rank.

Lady Mayoress
Address on envelope: 'The Lady Mayoress of —'. *Begin*: 'My Lady Mayoress'. *Spoken address*: '(My) Lady Mayoress'.

Lord Mayor
Address on envelope: The Lord Mayors of London, York, Belfast, Cardiff, Dublin and also Melbourne, Sydney, Adelaide, Perth, Brisbane and Hobart are styled 'The Right Hon. the Lord Mayor of —'. Other Lord Mayors are styled 'The Right Worshipful the Lord Mayor of —'. *Begin*: 'My Lord Mayor', even if the holder of the office is a woman. *Spoken address*: '(My) Lord Mayor'.

Marchioness
Address on envelope: 'The Most Hon. the Marchioness of —'. *Begin*: 'Dear Madam'. *Spoken address*: 'Madam'.

Marquess
Address on envelope: 'The Most Hon. the Marquess of —'. *Begin*: 'My Lord'. *Spoken address*: 'My Lord'.

Mayor
Address on envelope: 'The Worshipful the Mayor of —'; in the case of cities and certain towns, 'The Right Worshipful'. *Begin*: 'Mr Mayor'. *Spoken address*: 'Mr Mayor'.

Mayoress
Address on envelope: 'The Mayoress of —'. *Begin*: 'Madam Mayoress' is traditional, but some now prefer 'Madam Mayor'. *Spoken address*: 'Mayoress' (or 'Madam Mayor').

Member of Parliament
Address on envelope: Add 'MP' to the usual form of address. *Begin*: according to rank.

Monsignor
Address on envelope: 'The Reverend Monsignor [F—S—]'. If a canon, 'The Very Reverend Monsignor (Canon) [F—S—]'. *Begin*: 'Reverend Sir'. *Spoken address*: 'Monsignor [S—]'.

Officers in the Armed Forces
Address on envelope: The professional rank is prefixed to any other rank, eg 'Admiral the Right Hon. the Earl of —', 'Lieut.-Col. Sir [F—S—], KCB'. Officers below the rank of Rear-Admiral, and Marshal of the Royal Air Force, are entitled to 'RN' (or 'Royal Navy') and 'RAF' respecively after their name. Army officers of the rank of Colonel or below may follow their name with the name of their regiment or corps (which may be abbreviated). Officers in the women's services add 'WRNS', 'WRAF', 'WRAC'. *Begin*: according to social rank.

Officers (retired and former)
Address on envelope: Officers above the rank of Lieutenant (in the Royal Navy), Captain (in the Army) and Flight Lieutenant (in the Royal Air Force) may continue to use and be addressed by their armed forces rank after being placed on the retired list. The word 'retired' (or in an abbreviated form) should not normally be placed after the person's name. Former officers in the women's services do not normally continue to use their ranks.

Pope
Address on envelope: 'His Holiness, the Pope'. *Begin*: 'Your Holiness' or 'Most Holy Father'. *Close*: if a Roman Catholic, 'I have the honour to be your Holiness's most devoted and obedient child' (or 'most humble child'); if not Roman Catholic, 'I have the honour to be (or 'remain') Your Holiness's obedient servant'. *Spoken address*: 'Your Holiness'.

Prime Minister
Address on envelope: according to rank. The Prime Minister is a Privy Counsellor (see separate entry) and the letter should be addressed accordingly. *Begin*, etc according to rank.

Prince
Address on envelope: If a Duke, 'His Royal Highness the Duke of —'; if not a Duke, 'His Royal Highness the

Prince [F—]', if a child of the sovereign; otherwise 'His Royal Highness Prince [F—] of [Kent or Gloucester]'. *Begin*: 'Sir'. Refer to as 'Your Royal Highness'. *Close*: 'I have the honour to remain (or 'be'), Sir, Your Royal Highness's most humble and obedient servant'. *Spoken address*: 'Your Royal Highness' once, thereafter 'Sir'.

Princess
Address on envelope: If a Duchess, 'Her Royal Highness the Duchess of —'; if not a Duchess, the daughter of a sovereign is addressed as 'Her Royal Highness the Princess [F—]', followed by any title she holds by marriage. 'The' is omitted in addressing a princess who is not the daughter of a sovereign. A Princess by marriage is addressed 'HRH Princess [husband's F—] of —'. *Begin*: 'Madam'. Refer to as 'Your Royal Highness'. *Close*: as for Prince, substituting 'Madam' for 'Sir'. *Spoken address*: 'Your Royal Highness' once, thereafter 'Ma'am'.

Privy Counsellor
Address on envelope: If a peer, 'The Right Hon. the Earl of —, PC'; if not a peer, 'The Right Hon. [F—S—]', without the 'PC'. *Begin*, etc according to rank.

Professor
Address on envelope: 'Professor [F—S—]'; the styles 'Professor Lord [S—]' and 'Professor Sir [F—S—]' are often used, but are deprecated by some people. If the professor is in holy orders, 'The Reverend Professor'. *Begin*: 'Dear Sir/Madam', or according to rank. *Spoken address*: according to rank.

Queen
Address on envelope: 'Her Majesty The Queen'. *Begin*: 'Madam, with my humble duty'. Refer to as 'Your Majesty'. *Close*: 'I have the honour to remain (or 'be'), Madam, Your Majesty's most humble and obedient servant'. *Spoken address*: 'Your Majesty' once, thereafter 'Ma'am'. *Begin an official speech*: 'May it please Your Majesty'.

Rabbi
Address on envelope: 'Rabbi [initial and S—]' or, if a doctor, 'Rabbi Doctor [initial and S—]'. *Begin*: 'Dear Sir'. *Spoken address*: 'Rabbi [S—]' or '[Doctor S—]'.

Secretary of State
Address on envelope: 'The Right Hon. [F—S—], MP, Secretary of State for —', or 'The Secretary of State for —'. Otherwise according to rank.

Viscount
Address on envelope: 'The Right Hon. the Viscount —'. *Begin*: 'My Lord'. *Spoken address*: 'My Lord'.

Viscountess
Address on envelope: 'The Right Hon. the Viscountess —'. *Begin*: 'Dear Madam'. *Spoken address*: 'Madam'.

NATIONS OF THE WORLD

A–Z of nations

In the following table, there is variation in the spelling of names and currencies for countries that do not use the Roman alphabet (such as the Arabic countries), depending on the system of transliteration used.

Population figures are estimates for 2008 unless otherwise stated.

English name	Area (sq km)	Population	Capital (English name in parentheses)	Currency
Afghanistan	647497	32738000	Kābul	1 Afghani (Af) = 100 puls
Albania	28748	3620000	Tiranë (Tirana)	1 Lek (Lk) = 100 qindarka
Algeria	2460500	33770000	El Djazâir (Algiers)	1 Algerian Dinar (AD, DA) = 100 centimes
Andorra	468	82627	Andorra la Vella	1 Euro (€) = 100 cents
Angola	1245790	12531000	Luanda	1 Kwanza (Kzrl) = 100 lwei
Antigua and Barbuda	442	84500	St John's	1 East Caribbean Dollar (EC$) = 100 cents
Argentina	2766890	40482000	Buenos Aires	1 Peso ($) = 100 australes
Armenia	29800	2968000	Yerevan	1 Dram (Drm) =100 lumas
Australia	7682300	21007000	Canberra	1 Australian Dollar ($A) = 100 cents
Austria	83854	8206000	Vienna	1 Euro (€) = 100 cents
Azerbaijan	86600	8178000	Baku	1 New Manat =100 gopik
The Bahamas	13934	307000	Nassau	1 Bahamian Dollar (BA$, B$) = 100 cents
Bahrain	678	718000	Al-Manāmah (Manama)	1 Bahrain Dinar (BD) = 1000 fils
Bangladesh	143998	153547000	Dhaka	1 Taka (Tk) = 100 poisha
Barbados	431	282000	Bridgetown	1 Barbadian Dollar (BD$) = 100 cents
Belarus	207600	9686000	Minsk	1 Belarusian Rouble (BR) =100 kopeks
Belgium	32545	10404000	Bruxelles/ Brussel (Brussels)	1 Euro (€) = 100 cents
Belize	22963	301000	Belmopan	1 Belizean Dollar (BZ$) = 100 cents
Benin	112622	8536000	Porto Novo	1 CFA Franc (CFAFr)= 100 centimes
Bhutan	46600	682000	Thimphu	1 Ngultrum (Nu) = 100 chetrum
Bolivia	1098580	9248046	La Paz/Sucre	1 Boliviano ($b) = 100 centavos
Bosnia and Herzegovina	51129	4590000	Sarajevo	1 Konvertible Marka (KM) = 100 pfennige
Botswana	582096	1842000	Gaborone	1 Pula (P, Pu) = 100 thebe
Brazil	8511965	196343000	Brasília	1 Real (R$) = 100 centavos
Brunei	5765	381000	Bandar Seri Begawan	1 Brunei Dollar (B$) = 100 sen
Bulgaria	110912	7263000	Sofija (Sofia)	1 Lev (Lv) = 100 stotinki
Burkina Faso	274540	15265000	Ouagadougou	1 CFA Franc (CFAFr) = 100 centimes
Burma ▶ Myanmar				
Burundi	27834	8691000	Bujumbura	1 Burundi Franc (BuFr, FBu) = 100 centimes
Cambodia	181035	14242000	Phnum Pénh (Phnom Penh)	1 Riel (CRI) = 100 sen
Cameroon	475439	18468000	Yaoundé	1 CFA Franc (CFAFr) = 100 centimes

Nations of the World

English name	Area (sq km)	Population	Capital (English name in parentheses)	Currency
Canada	9970610	33213000	Ottawa	1 Canadian Dollar (C$, Can$) = 100 cents
Cape Verde	4033	427000	Praia	1 Escudo Caboverdiano (CVEsc) = 100 centavos
Central African Republic	622984	4444000	Bangui	1 CFA Franc (CFAFr) = 100 centimes
Chad	1284640	10111000	N'Djamena	1 CFA Franc (CFAFr) = 100 centimes
Chile	756626	16454000	Santiago	1 Chilean Peso (Ch$) = 100 centavos
China	9597000	1330044000	Beijing	1 Renminbi or Yuan (RMBY, $, Y) = 10 jiao = 100 fen
Colombia	1140105	45014000	Bogotá	1 Colombian Peso (Col$) = 100 centavos
Comoros	1862	732000	Moroni	1 Comoran Franc (KMF) = 100 centimes
Congo	341945	3903000	Brazzaville	1 CFA Franc (CFAFr) = 100 centimes
Congo, Democratic Republic of the	2343950	66514000	Kinshasa	1 Congolese Franc (CF) = 100 centimes
Costa Rica	51022	4196000	San José	1 Costa Rican Colón (CRℂ) = 100 céntimos
Côte d'Ivoire (Ivory Coast)	320633	20180000	Yamoussoukro	1 CFA Franc (CFAFr) = 100 centimes
Croatia	56538	4492000	Zagreb	1 Kuna (Kn) = 100 lipa
Cuba	110860	11424000	La Habana (Havana)	1 Cuban Peso (Cub$) = 100 centavos
Cyprus	9251	793000	Lefkosía/ Lefkoşa (Nicosia)	1 Euro (€) = 100 cents
Czech Republic	78864	10221000	Praha (Prague)	1 Koruna (CZK) = 100 haléřů
Denmark	43076[1]	5485000	København (Copenhagen)	1 Danish Krone (Dkr) = 100 øre
Djibouti	23310	506000	Djibouti	1 Djibouti Franc (DF, DjFr) = 100 centimes
Dominica	751	72000	Roseau	1 East Caribbean Dollar (EC$) = 100 cents
Dominican Republic	48442	9507000	Santo Domingo	1 Dominican Republic Peso (RD$, DR$) = 100 centavos
East Timor	14874	1109000	Dili	1 US Dollar ($) = 100 cents
Ecuador	270699	13928000	Quito	1 US Dollar ($) = 100 cents
Egypt	1001449	81713000	El-Qāhirah (Cairo)	1 Egyptian Pound (£E, LE) = 100 piastres
El Salvador	21476	7066000	San Salvador	1 US Dollar ($) = 100 cents
Equatorial Guinea	26016	616000	Malabo	1 CFA Franc (CFAFr) = 100 centimes
Eritrea	121320	5502000	Asmara	1 Nakfa (Nfa) = 100 cents
Estonia	45100	1308000	Tallinn	1 Kroon (KR) = 100 sents
Ethiopia	1128497	82545000	Ādīs Ābeba (Addis Ababa)	1 Ethiopian Birr (EB) = 100 cents
Federated States of Micronesia ▶ Micronesia				
Fiji	18333	932000	Suva	1 Fiji Dollar (F$) = 100 cents
Finland	338145	5245000	Helsinki	1 Euro (€) = 100 cents
France	551000	62151000	Paris	1 Euro (€) = 100 cents
Gabon	267667	1486000	Libreville	1 CFA Franc (CFAFr) = 100 centimes
The Gambia	11295	1735000	Banjul	1 Dalasi (GMD) = 100 butut
Georgia	69700	4631000	Tbilisi	1 Lari (GEL) = 100 tetri
Germany	357868	82369000	Berlin	1 Euro (€) = 100 cents
Ghana	238686	23383000	Accra	1 Cedi (₵) = 100 pesewas

English name	Area (sq km)	Population	Capital (English name in parentheses)	Currency
Greece	131957	10723000	Athínai (Athens)	1 Euro (€) = 100 cents
Grenada	344	90300	St George's	1 East Caribbean Dollar (EC$) = 100 cents
Guatemala	108889	13002000	Guatemala City	1 Quetzal (Q) = 100 centavos
Guinea	246048	9806000	Conakry	1 Guinea Franc (GFr) = 100 centimes
Guinea-Bissau	36260	1503000	Bissau	1 CFA Franc (CFAFr) = 100 centimes
Guyana	214969	771000	Georgetown	1 Guyana Dollar (G$) = 100 cents
Haiti	27750	8924000	Port-au-Prince	1 Gourde (G, Gde) = 100 centimes
Holland ▶ Netherlands, The				
Honduras	112088	7639000	Tegucigalpa	1 Lempira (L, La) = 100 centavos
Hungary	93030	9931000	Budapest	1 Forint (Ft) = 100 fillér
Iceland	103000	304400	Reykjavík	1 Króna (IKr, ISK) = 100 aurar
India	3287590	1147996000	Nī Dillī (New Delhi)	1 Indian Rupee (Re, Rs) = 100 paise
Indonesia	1906240	237512000	Jakarta	1 Rupiah (Rp) = 100 sen
Iran	1648000	65875000	Tehrān (Tehran)	1 Iranian Rial (Rls,RI) = 100 dinars
Iraq	434925	28221000	Baghdād (Baghdad)	1 New Iraqi Dinar (ID) = 1000 fils
Ireland	70282	4156000	Baile Átha Cliath (Dublin)	1 Euro (€) = 100 cents
Israel	20770	7112000	Tel Aviv	1 New Israeli Shekel (NIS) = 100 agora
Italy	301225	58145000	Roma (Rome)	1 Euro (€) = 100 cents
Ivory Coast ▶ Côte d'Ivoire				
Jamaica	10957	2804000	Kingston	1 Jamaican Dollar (J$) = 100 cents
Japan	381945	127288000	Tōkyō (Tokyo)	1 Yen (Y, ¥) = 100 sen
Jordan	89213	6199000	'Ammān (Amman)	1 Jordanian Dinar (JD) = 1000 fils
Kazakhstan	2717300	15340000	Astana	1 Tenge = 100 tiyn
Kenya	580370	37954000	Nairobi	1 Kenyan Shilling (Ksh) = 100 cents
Kiribati	811	110400	Tawara	1 Australian Dollar ($A) = 100 cents
Korea, North	122098	23479000	P'yŏngyang (Pyongyang)	1 Won (NKW) = 100 chon
Korea, South	98913	48379000	Sŏul (Seoul)	1 Won (W) = 100 jeon
Kuwait	17818	2597000	Al-Kuwayt (Kuwait City)	1 Kuwaiti Dinar (KD) = 1000 fils
Kyrgyzstan	198500	5357000	Biškek (Bishkek)	1 Som (Kgs) = 100 tyjyn
Laos	236800	6677000	Viangchan (Vientiane)	1 New Kip (Kp) = 100 at
Latvia	64100	2245000	Riga	1 Lat (Ls) = 100 santims
Lebanon	10452	3972000	Bayrūt (Beirut)	1 Lebanese Pound (LL, L£) = 100 piastres
Lesotho	30460	2128000	Maseru	1 Loti (*plural* Maloti) (M, LSM) = 100 lisente
Liberia	111370	3335000	Monrovia	1 Liberian Dollar (L$) = 100 cents
Libya	1758610	6174000	Tarābulus (Tripoli)	1 Libyan Dinar (LD) = 1000 dirhams
Liechtenstein	160	34500	Vaduz	1 Swiss Franc (SFr, SwF) = 100 centimes = 100 rappen
Lithuania	65200	3565000	Vilnius	1 Litas (Lt) = 100 centas
Luxembourg	2586	486000	Luxembourg	1 Euro (€) = 100 cents

Nations of the World

English name	Area (sq km)	Population	Capital (English name in parentheses)	Currency
Macedonia	25713	2061000	Skopje	1 Denar (D, den) = 100 deni
Madagascar	587040	20043000	Antananarivo	1 Ariary (A) = 5 Iraimbilanja
Malawi	118484	13932000	Lilongwe	1 Kwacha (MK) = 100 tambala
Malaysia	329749	25274000	Kuala Lumpur	1 Malaysian Ringgit (dollar) (M$) = 100 cents
Maldives	300	385900	Malé	1 Rufiyaa (MRf, Rf) = 100 laarees
Mali	1240192	12324000	Bamako	1 CFA Franc (CFAFr)= 100 centimes
Malta	316	403500	Valletta	1 Euro (€) = 100 cents
Marshall Islands	180	63000	Majuro	1 US Dollar ($, US$) = 100 cents
Mauritania	1029920	3365000	Nouakchott	1 Ouguiya (U, UM) = 5 khoums
Mauritius	1865	1274000	Port Louis	1 Mauritian Rupee (MR, MauRe) = 100 cents
Mexico	1978800	10995500	Ciudad de México (Mexico City)	1 Mexican Peso (Mex $) = 100 centavos
Micronesia	702	108000	Palikir	1 US Dollar (US$) = 100 cents
Moldova	33843	4324000	Chişinău (Chisinau)	1 Leu (Mld) = 100 bani
Monaco	2	32800	Monaco	1 Euro (€) = 100 cents
Mongolia	1564619	2996000	Ulaanbaatar (Ulan Bator)	1 Tugrik (T) = 100 möngö
Montenegro	13812	678000	Podgorica/ Cetinje	1 Euro (€) = 100 cents
Morocco	446550	34343000	Ar Ribāṭ (Rabat)	1 Dirham (DH) = 100 centimes
Mozambique	799390	21285000	Maputo	1 Metical (Mt, MZM) = 100 centavos
Myanmar (Burma)	678576	47758000	Naypyitaw	1 Kyat (K) = 100 pyas
Namibia	823144	2089000	Windhoek	1 Namibian Dollar (N$) = 100 cents
Nauru	21	13700	Yaren District	1 Australian Dollar ($A) = 100 cents
Nepal	145391	29519000	Kathmandu	1 Nepalese Rupee (NRp, NRs) = 100 paise/pice
The Netherlands	41526	16645000	Amsterdam	1 Euro (€) = 100 cents
New Zealand	268812	4173000	Wellington	1 New Zealand Dollar (NZ$) = 100 cents
Nicaragua	130668	5786000	Managua	1 Gold Córdoba (C$) = 100 centavos = 10 reales
Niger	1267000	13273000	Niamey	1 CFA Franc (CFAFr) = 100 centimes
Nigeria	923768	146255000	Abuja	1 Naira (N, ₦) = 100 kobo
Norway	323895	4644000	Oslo	1 Norwegian Krone (NKr) = 100 øre
Oman	300000	3312000	Masqat (Muscat)	1 Omani Rial (RO) = 1000 baisas
Pakistan	803943	172800000	Islāmābād (Islamabad)	1 Pakistan Rupee (PRs, Rp) = 100 paisa
Palau	494	21000	Melekeok	1 US Dollar ($, US$) = 100 cents
Panama	77381	3310000	Cuidad de Panamá (Panama City)	1 Balboa (B, Ba) = 100 centésimos; US$ also in use
Papua New Guinea	462840	5932000	Port Moresby	1 Kina (K) = 100 toea
Paraguay	406750	6831000	Asunción	1 Guaraní (Gs) = 100 céntimos
Peru	1284640	29181000	Lima	1 Nuevo Sol (Pes) = 100 cénts
Philippines	299679	91062000	Manila	1 Philippine Peso (PHP) = 100 centavos

English name	Area (sq km)	Population	Capital (English name in parentheses)	Currency
Poland	312612	38501000	Warszawa (Warsaw)	1 Złoty (Zl) = 100 groszy
Portugal	91982	10677000	Lisboa (Lisbon)	1 Euro = 100 cents
Qatar	11437	824000	Ad-Dawhah (Doha)	1 Qatari Riyal (QR) = 100 dirhams
Romania	237500	22247000	Bucureşti (Bucharest)	1 New Leu (L, *plural* Lei) = 100 bani
Russia	17075400	140702000	Moskva (Moscow)	1 Rouble (R) = 100 kopeks
Rwanda	26338	10186000	Kigali	1 Rwanda Franc (RF, RWFr) = 100 centimes
St Christopher and Nevis	269	38100	Basseterre	1 East Caribbean Dollar (EC$) = 100 cents
St Lucia	616	160000	Castries	1 East Caribbean Dollar (EC$) = 100 cents
St Vincent and the Grenadines	390	118400	Kingstown	1 East Caribbean Dollar (EC$) = 100 cents
Samoa	2842	217000	Apia	1 Tala (ST$) = 100 sene
San Marino	61	29900	San Marino	1 Euro (€) = 100 cents
São Tomé and Príncipe	1001	206000	São Tomé	1 Dobra (Db) = 100 centavos
Saudi Arabia	2331000	28147000	Ar-Riyād (Riyadh)	1 Saudi Arabian Riyal (SR, SRls) = 20 qursh = 100 halala
Senegal	196840	12853000	Dakar	1 CFA Franc (CFAFr) = 100 centimes
Serbia	77474	10159000	Beograd (Belgrade)	1 Dinar (D, Din) = 100 paras
Seychelles	453	82200	Victoria	1 Seychelles Rupee (SR) = 100 cents
Sierra Leone	72325	6295000	Freetown	1 Leone (Le) = 100 cents
Singapore	647	4608000	Singapura (Singapore City)	1 Singapore Dollar (S$) = 1 Ringgit = 100 cents
Slovakia	49035	5455000	Bratislava	1 Euro (€) = 100 cents
Slovenia	20251	2008000	Ljubljana	1 Euro (€) =100 cents
Solomon Islands	27556	581300	Honiara	1 Solomon Islands Dollar (SI$) = 100 cents
Somalia	637657	9559000	Muqdisho (Mogadishu)	1 Somali Shilling (SoSh) = 100 cents
South Africa	1228376	48783000	Pretoria/ Cape Town	1 Rand (R) = 100 cents
Spain	504782	40491000	Madrid	1 Euro (€) = 100 cents
Sri Lanka	65610	21129000	Colombo	1 Sri Lankan Rupee (SLR, SLRs) = 100 cents
Sudan	2504530	40218000	Al-Khartūm (Khartoum)	1 Sudanese Dinar (SD) = 10 pounds
Suriname	163265	476000	Paramaribo	1 Suriname Dollar (SRD, $) = 100 cents
Swaziland	17363	1129000	Mbabane	1 Lilangeni (*plural* Emalangeni) (Li, E) = 100 cents
Sweden	411479	9045000	Stockholm	1 Swedish Krona (SKr) = 100 øre
Switzerland	41228	7581000	Bern (Berne)	1 Swiss Franc (SFr, SwF) = 100 centimes = 100 rappen
Syria	185180	19748000	Dimashq (Damascus)	1 Syrian pound (LS, S$) = 100 piastres
Taiwan	36000	22921000	T'aipei (Taipei)	1 New Taiwan Dollar (NT$) = 100 cents
Tajikistan	143100	7212000	Dušanbe (Dushanbe)	1 Somoni (S) = 100 dirams

Nations of the World

English name	Area (sq km)	Population	Capital (English name in parentheses)	Currency
Tanzania	945087	40213000	Dodoma	1 Tanzanian Shilling (TSh) = 100 cents
Thailand	513115	65493000	Bangkok	1 Baht (B) = 100 satang
Togo	56600	5859000	Lomé	1 CFA Franc (CFAFr) = 100 centimes
Tonga	748	119000	Nuku'alofa	1 Pa'anga/Tongan Dollar (T$) = 100 seniti
Trinidad and Tobago	5128	1047000	Port of Spain	1 Trinidad and Tobago Dollar (TT$) = 100 cents
Tunisia	164150	10384000	Toûnis (Tunis)	1 Tunisian Dinar (TD, D) = 1000 millimes
Turkey	779452	71893000	Angora (Ankara)	1 New Turkish Lira (TRY) = 100 kurus
Turkmenistan	488100	5179000	Ašgabat (Ashgabat)	1 Manat (TMM) = 100 tenesi
Tuvalu	26	12200	Funafuti	1 Australian Dollar (A$) = 100 cents
Uganda	238461	31368000	Kampala	1 Uganda Shilling (USh) = 100 cents
Ukraine	603700	45994000	Kyïv (Kiev)	1 Hryvnia = 100 kopiykas
United Arab Emirates	83600	4621000	Abū Zhaby (Abu Dhabi)	1 Dirham (DH) = 100 fils
United Kingdom	242495	60944000	London	1 Pound Sterling (£) = 100 pence
United States of America	9160454	303825000	Washington, DC	1 US Dollar ($, US$) = 100 cents
Uruguay	176215	3478000	Montevideo	1 Uruguayan Peso (Ur$, Urug$) = 100 centésimos
Uzbekistan	447400	27345000	Toškent (Tashkent)	1 Sum = 100 tiyin
Vanuatu	12336	215000	Port Vila	1 Vatu (V, VT) = 100 centimes
Vatican City State	0.4	824	Vatican City	1 Euro (€) = 100 cents
Venezuela	912050	26415000	Caracas	1 Bolívar (Bs) = 100 céntimos
Vietnam	329566	86116000	Hà Nôi (Hanoi)	1 Dông (D) = 10 hào = 100 xu
Western Samoa ▶ Samoa				
Yemen	531570	23013000	Sana'a	1 Yemeni Riyal (YR, YRI) = 100 fils
Zaire ▶ Congo, Democratic Republic of				
Zambia	752613	11669000	Lusaka	1 Kwacha (K) = 100 ngwee
Zimbabwe	391090	11350000	Harare	1 Zimbabwe Dollar (Z$) = 100 cents

[1] Excluding Faroe Islands (1399 sq km) and Greenland (2175600 sq km).

AFGHANISTAN

Official name Islamic Republic of Afghanistan
Local name Afghânestân (Dari), Afğänistän (Pashto)
Location A landlocked, mountainous republic in south-central Asia, bounded to the north by Turkmenistan, Uzbekistan and Tajikistan; to the east and south by Pakistan; to the west by Iran; and in the extreme north-east by China and India
Area 647 497 sq km/249 934 sq mi
Capital Kabul

Chief towns Herat, Jalalabad, Kandahar, Mazar-e Sharif
Population 32 738 000 (2008e), although 1.9 million are still refugees in Pakistan or Iran
Time zone GMT +4.5
Currency 1 Afghani (Af) = 100 puls
Languages Dari, Pashto
Religions Islam 99% (Sunni 80%, Shia 19%), others 1%
Ethnic groups Pushtun 42%, Tajik 27%, Hazara 9%, Uzbek 9%, others 13%

Physical description

A mountainous country centred on the Hindu Kush system which reaches over 7000m/23 000ft in the centre and north-east; highest point is Nowshak (7485m/24 557ft); many secondary ranges; north-west of the Hindu Kush, heights decrease towards the Turkmenistan border; also north-west is the fertile valley of Herat; arid uplands lie to the south of the Hindu Kush descending into desert in the south-west.

Climate

Continental climate with winter severity increased by altitude; summers are warm everywhere except on the highest peaks; protected from summer monsoons by the southern mountains; rain mostly occurs during spring and autumn; annual rainfall averages 338mm; lower levels have a desert or semi-arid climate.

Government

Since 2004, governed by an executive President, a Council of Ministers, and a bicameral legislature (*Jirga*), comprising the House of the People and the House of Elders. There are no formal political parties.

Economy

Economy devastated by decades of civil war; based on agriculture, especially grain, rice, fruit, nuts, vegetables and livestock; small-scale industries, including textiles, carpets, handicrafts and food processing; natural gas production in the north, largely for export; major source of illegally produced opium.

History

The nation first formed in 1747 under Ahmad Shah Durrani. In the 19c and early 20c Britain saw Afghanistan as a bridge between India and the Middle East, but failed to gain control during the Afghan Wars. The feudal monarchy survived until after World War II, when the constitution became more liberal under several Soviet-influenced five-year economic plans. In 1973 the king was deposed and a republic was formed. A new constitution was adopted in 1977, but a coup in 1978 installed a new government under the communist leader, Nur Muhammad Taraki; a further coup in 1979 led to invasion by Soviet forces, which was fiercely resisted by the Mujahedin. In 1989 the Soviet troops finally withdrew, and in 1992 Mujahedin groups forced the resignation of the communist government of Muhammad Najibullah and proclaimed the Islamic State of Afghanistan. Fighting between factions continued, until the rise in 1994 of the Taliban, who sought to replace factionalism with Islamic law; this included repression of women, public floggings and executions. Within two years the Taliban had taken Kabul, executed Najibullah, and the civil war had resulted in up to 45 000 Afghan deaths. By 1998 the country was mainly under Taliban control, but fierce resistance from the opposition Northern Alliance meant the civil war continued. In 2001 a US-led coalition began military action against the Taliban, believing them to harbour senior members of Al Qaeda responsible for terror attacks on the USA. The Taliban regime was overthrown and a UN-brokered deal saw a power-sharing administration installed, led by Hamid Karzai. Presidential elections were held in 2004, and parliamentary elections in 2005. The government's control of the country outside Kabul is tenuous and dependent on the presence of international forces. In the southern provinces in particular, Taliban-inspired violence since 2001 and especially since 2005, is hindering reconstruction.

ALBANIA

Official name Republic of Albania
Local name Shqipëria
Location A mountainous republic in the western part of the Balkan Peninsula, bounded to the west by the Adriatic Sea; to the north-west by Montenegro; to the north-east by the Serbian province of Kosovo; to the east by Macedonia; and to the south-east by Greece
Area 28 748 sq km/11 097 sq mi
Capital Tirana

Chief towns Shkodër, Durrës, Vlorë, Korçë, Elbasan
Population 3 620 000 (2008e)
Time zone GMT +1
Currency 1 Lek (Lk) = 100 qindarka
Language Albanian
Religions Islam 70% (Sunni), Christianity 30% (Orthodox 20%, RC 10%)
Ethnic groups Albanian 95%, Greek 3%, others 2%

Physical description

Mountainous and relatively inaccessible; the northern Albanian Alps rise to 2692m/8832ft; highest point is Maja e Korabit (Golem Korab; 2753m/9032ft); rivers include the Drin, Shkumbin, Seman, Vijosë; half the population is concentrated in the western low-lying area, which occupies only one quarter of the country.

Climate

Mediterranean-type climate: hot and dry on the plains in summer (average July temperature 24°–25°C), with frequent thunderstorms; winters are mild, damp and cyclonic (average January temperature 8°–9°C); winters in the mountains are often severe, with snow cover lasting for several months; annual mountain precipitation exceeds 1000mm.

Government

Governed by a President, a Prime Minister and Council of Ministers, with a unicameral People's Assembly.

Economy

Completing transition from planned to market economy; dependent on remittances from expatriate workers and foreign aid; agriculture still the main employer, producing wheat, maize, sugar beet, potatoes and fruit; main industries are agricultural product processing, textiles, oil products, cement, production of crude oil, minerals and natural gas; hydroelectric power plants on several rivers.

History

The history of the Albanians dates back to the 2c AD, when Ptolemy referred to a tribe, the Albanoi, in the region of modern Albania. The Albanian Ghegs and Tosks speak two forms of an Indo-European language now considered a dialect of Illyrian, the Albanians being recognized as descendants of the ancient Illyrians but with Slav, Greek, Vlach and Turkish blood. In the Middle Ages they were included within the empires of Byzantium, Samuel (of Macedonia) and Stephen I Nemanja of Serbia, but from the 12c an independent Albanian enclave developed around Krujë. Their decentralized tribal way of life was little changed under Ottoman rule (1503–1913) and was only destroyed with the establishment of the communist regime (1945). After local uprisings, the Albanian national movement formally began with the League of Prizren (1878–81). The first general uprising resulted in independence in 1912, and in 1913 the first independent Albanian state was established. Its boundaries excluded many Albanians, many of whom still live in Kosovo. Albania's independence was short-lived at first, as Italian forces occupied the country from 1914 until 1920; however, it became a republic in 1925, and a monarchy, under King Zog I, in 1928. During World War II Albania was occupied by Germany and Italy and it became a republic again in 1946. After being involved in a dispute with the USSR in 1961, it withdrew from the Warsaw Pact in 1968 but maintained close links with communist China until 1978. The Socialist People's Republic was instituted in 1976. The country gradually began to move towards democratic reform and westernization, and the first free elections were held in 1991, the communists losing power in the 1992 election. In the early 1990s the economy declined and severe food shortages led to violent rioting. Further rioting broke out in early 1997 after many Albanians lost money in the collapse of investment schemes. An influx of refugees from Kosovo in 1999 was an additional economic burden. In 2003 Albania began talks with the EU about membership.

ALGERIA

Official name People's Democratic Republic of Algeria
Local name Al-Jazã 'ir (Arabic), Algérie (French)
Location A North African republic, bounded to the west by Morocco; to the south-west by Western Sahara, Mauritania and Mali; to the south-east by Niger; to the east by Libya; to the north-east by Tunisia; and to the north by the Mediterranean Sea
Area 2 460 500 sq km/949 753 sq mi
Capital Algiers

Chief towns Constantine, Oran, Skikda, Annaba, Mostaganem, Blida, Tlemcen
Population 33 770 000 (2008e)
Time zone GMT +1
Currency 1 Algerian Dinar (AD, DA) = 100 centimes
Language Arabic; Berber dialects are widely spoken and French is also used
Religions Islam 99% (Sunni), others 1%
Ethnic groups Arab-Berber 99%, European 1%

Physical description

From the Mediterranean coast, the mountains rise in a series of ridges and plateaux to the Atlas Saharien; 91% of the population is located on the narrow coastal plain; part of the Sahara Desert lies to the south of the Atlas Saharien; in the north-east of this region is a major depression, the Chott Melrhir, which extends east into Tunisia; the Hoggar Mountains in the far south rise to 2918m/9573ft at Mount Tahat.

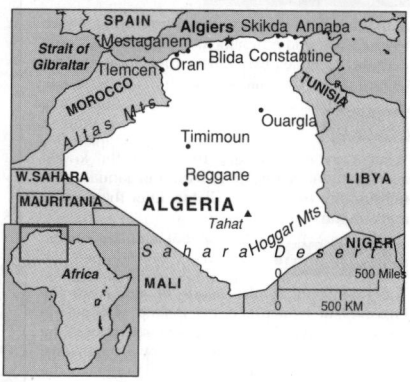

Climate

Typical Mediterranean climate on the north coast; annual average rainfall of 400–800mm (mostly November–March); snow on the higher ground; Algiers, representative of the coastal region, has an annual rainfall of 760mm with average maximum daily temperatures of 15°–29°C; the rest of the country has an essentially rainless Saharan climate.

Government

Governed by a President, a Prime Minister and Council of Ministers, and a bicameral Parliament, comprising a National People's Assembly and a National Council.

Economy

Large-scale 1960s nationalization reversed in 1990s, promoting economic growth; oil and natural gas production and products account for c.30% of GDP; other industries are mining, electrical goods, light industries and food processing; agriculture is mainly on the north coast (wheat, barley, oats, grapes, citrus fruits, vegetables).

History

The indigenous peoples of Algeria (Berbers) have been driven back from the coast by many invaders, including the Phoenicians, Romans (Algeria became a province of the Roman Empire), Vandals, Arabs, Turks and French. Islam and Arabic were introduced by the Arabs in the 8–11c, and Islam (Sunni Muslim) is now the chief religion. The Turkish invasion took place in the 16c, and the French colonial campaign in the 19c resulted in control by 1902. The National Liberation Front (FLN) engaged in guerrilla war with French forces in 1954–62, and Algeria gained independence in 1962. The first president of the republic, Ahmed Ben Bella, was replaced after a coup in 1965 led by Houari Boumédienne, who governed by decree until 1976, when elections were held and a new constitution declared him president. He was succeeded in 1979 by Chadli Benjedid. In 1992 a state of emergency was declared as a result of clashes between government forces and the Islamic Salvation Front, and for the rest of the 1990s Algeria was wracked by a bloody civil war between its secular government and Islamic fundamentalist insurgents in which an estimated 100 000 people died. The level of violence fell after 1999, when the newly elected President Bouteflika instituted a policy of reconciliation with the Islamists. Recent years have also seen increased agitation for recognition of the Berber community, and the Berber language Tamazight, both of which have been granted by the government.

■ **American Samoa▶ United States of America**

ANDORRA

Official name Principality of Andorra; also sometimes known as the Valleys of Andorra
Local name Andorra
Location A small, mountainous, semi-independent, neutral state on the southern slopes of the central Pyrenees between France and Spain
Area 468 sq km/181 sq mi
Capital Andorra la Vella

Population 82 627 (2008e)
Time zone GMT +1
Currency 1 Euro (€) = 100 cents
Language Catalan; French, Castilian and Portuguese are also spoken
Religions Christianity 95% (RC)
Ethnic groups Spanish 43%, Andorran 33%, Portuguese 11%, French 7%, others 6%

Physical description

A mountainous country, the whole lying above 840m/2750ft and reaching 2947m/9669ft at Coma Pedrosa; occupies two valleys (del Norte and del Orient) of the River Valira.

Climate

Winters are cold but dry and sunny; the lowest average monthly rainfall is 34mm in January; the midsummer months are slightly drier than spring and autumn.

Government

The Co-Princes (titular heads of state) are the President of France and the Bishop of Urgel (in Spain), represented by permanent delegates in the principality; Andorra is governed by an Executive Council and the unicameral General Council of the Valleys.

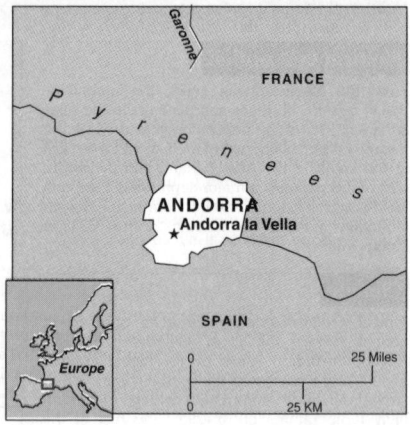

Economy

Based on banking and financial services (no direct or value-added taxes; no currency exchange restrictions) and tourism (especially skiing), which account for over 80% of economic activity; other industries are construction, forestry and agriculture (tobacco and livestock breeding); hydroelectric power produced on the river.

History

One of the oldest states in Europe, Andorra has been under the joint protection of France and Spain since 1278, and became an independent parliamentary democracy in 1993.

ANGOLA

Official name Republic of Angola
Local name Angola
Location A republic in south-west Africa, bounded to the south by Namibia; to the east by Zambia; and to the north by the Democratic Republic of the Congo; with the separate province of Cabinda enclosed by the Congo
Area 1 245 790 sq km/480 875 sq mi
Capital Luanda
Chief towns Huambo, Benguela, Lobito, Namibe

(Moçâmedes), Cabinda, Malanje, Lubango
Population 12 531 000 (2008e)
Time zone GMT +1
Currency 1 Kwanza (Kzrl) = 100 lwei
Language Portuguese; Bantu and other African languages are also spoken
Religions Christianity 53% (RC 38%, Prot 15%), traditional beliefs 47%
Ethnic groups Ovimbundu 37%, Kimbundu 25%, Bakongo 13%, others 25%

Physical description

A narrow coastal plain, widening in the north towards the Congo Delta; high plateau inland with an average elevation of 1200m/3937ft; the highest point is Serro Môco (2619m/8592ft); numerous rivers rise in the plateau but few are navigable for any length. The south is desert and semi-desert.

Climate

Mostly a tropical plateau climate, with a single wet season in October–March and a long dry season; more temperate above 1500m; Huambo is representative of the upland region with an average annual rainfall of 1450mm and average daily temperatures of 24°–29°C; temperature and rainfall are much reduced on the coast, which is semi-desert as far north as Luanda (eg Namibe in the south has an average annual rainfall of 55mm; in the far north it is 600mm).

Government

Governed by an executive President, a Prime Minister and Council of Ministers and a unicameral National Assembly; the first elections since 1992 took place in 2008.

Economy

More stable and growing economy since end of civil war; rich in natural resources (oil, diamonds, gold, uranium, other minerals); oil extraction and refining provides 85% of GDP; other industries are mining, forestry, fishing, cement, tobacco products and ship repair; agriculture mostly at subsistence level; export crops are coffee, sisal and cotton.

History

The area became a Portuguese colony after exploration in 1483; an estimated 3 million slaves were sent to Brazil during the next 300 years. Boundaries were formally defined during the Congress of Berlin in 1884–5. Angola became an Overseas Province of Portugal in 1951 and gained independence in 1975. Shortly afterwards, civil war broke out between three factions: the Marxist MPLA (Popular Movement for the Liberation of Angola) government, UNITA (National Union for the Total Independence of Angola) and the FNLA (National Front for the Liberation of Angola). The FNLA and UNITA received arms from the USA in 1975–6, and in 1976 Cuban combat troops arrived to back up the MPLA. South African forces occupied an area along the Angola–Namibia frontier in 1975–6, and were active again in support of UNITA in 1981–4. Meanwhile, Angola backed the Namibian independence movement SWAPO (South West Africa People's Organization), which launched attacks on Namibia from Angolan territory in the 1970s. Eventually an international agreement signed in 1988 linked arrangements for the independence of Namibia with the withdrawal of Cuban troops and the cessation of South African support for UNITA. In 1991 a peace agreement between UNITA and the government was followed by multi party elections, but UNITA did not accept the results and fighting resumed. The conflict continued, despite another peace agreement (1994), the deployment of UN peacekeeping forces (1995–8), and UNITA's proposed inclusion in a government of national unity (1997), until 2002, when a ceasefire was agreed after the death of UNITA leader Jonas Savimbi. UNITA gradually demobilized its forces and transformed itself into a political party. Repatriation of refugees began in 2003, and in 2004 preparations began for elections in 2006, but these were delayed until 2008 as damaged infrastructure and landmines left parts of the country inaccessible.

■ Anguilla▶United Kingdom

ANTIGUA AND BARBUDA

Official name Antigua and Barbuda
Local name Antigua and Barbuda
Location An independent group of three tropical islands in the Leeward group of the Lesser Antilles in the eastern Caribbean Sea: Antigua, Barbuda and the uninhabited Redonda
Area 442 sq km/171 sq mi
Capital St John's
Chief town Codrington (on Barbuda)
Population 84 500 (2008e)

Time zone GMT –4
Currency 1 East Caribbean Dollar (EC$) = 100 cents
Language English
Religions Christianity 92% (Prot 82%, RC 10%), others 2%, none/unaffiliated 1%
Ethnic groups black 91%, mixed 4%, white 2%, others 3%

Physical description

Antigua is flatter than the other Leeward Islands, rising to 402m/1319ft at Boggy Peak; Barbuda is a flat, coral island reaching only 44m/144ft at its highest point, with a large lagoon on its western side.

Climate

Tropical, with temperatures ranging from 24°C in January, to 27°C in August–September, and an average annual rainfall of 1000mm; subject to tropical storms and hurricanes between August and October.

Government

Governed by a Governor-General (representing the British monarch, who is head of state), a Prime Minister and Cabinet, and a bicameral Parliament, consisting of a Senate and a House of Representatives.

Economy

Tourism (provides over 50% of GDP), offshore financial services, construction and light manufacturing; agricultural production mostly for local consumption.

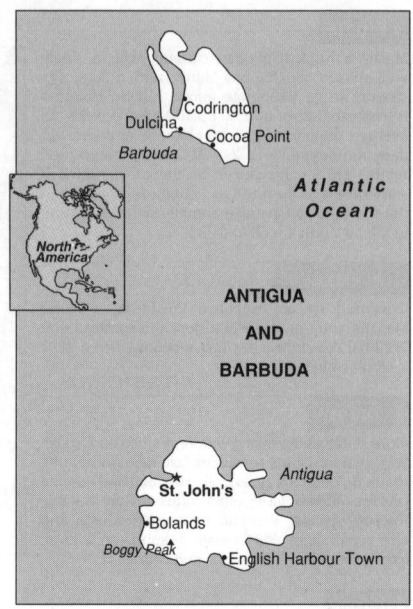

History

Columbus visited Antigua in 1493. It was colonized by the English in 1632 and ceded to England in 1667. Barbuda was colonized from Antigua in 1661. Administered as part of the Leeward Islands Federation from 1871 until 1956, it became an associated state of the UK in 1967. Full independence of Antigua and Barbuda was achieved in 1981. The Prime Minister at independence was Vere Cornwall Bird of the Antigua Labour Party, whose family continued to dominate the country's politics until 2004.

ARGENTINA

Official name Argentine Republic
Local name Argentina
Location A republic in south-eastern South America, bounded to the east by the southern Atlantic Ocean; to the west by Chile; to the north by Bolivia and Paraguay; and to the north-east by Brazil and Uruguay
Area 2766890 sq km/1068296 sq mi
Capital Buenos Aires
Chief towns Córdoba, Rosario, Mendoza, La Plata, Mar del Plata, San Miguel de Tucumán
Population 40482000 (2008e)
Time zone GMT –3
Currency 1 Peso ($) = 100 australes
Language Spanish
Religions Christianity 94% (RC 92% (less than 20% practising), Prot 2%), Judaism 2%, others 4%
Ethnic groups European (mostly Spanish and Italian) 97%, mestizo, Amerindian and others 3%

Physical description

The Andes stretch the entire length of Argentina (north to south), forming the boundary with Chile; the mountains extend far to the east in north Argentina, but their breadth decreases towards the south; high ranges, plateaux and rocky spurs are found in the north-west; the highest peak is Aconcagua (6960m/22835ft); a grassy, treeless plain (the *pampa*) is to the east; uneven, arid steppes lie to the south; the island of Tierra del Fuego is situated off the southern tip; north Argentina is drained by the Paraguay, Paraná and Uruguay rivers, which join in the River Plate estuary; several rivers flow to the Atlantic Ocean in the south; there are many lakes in the *pampa* and Patagonia regions, the largest being Lago Argentino (1415 sq km/546 sq mi).

Climate

Most of Argentina lies in the rain shadow of the Andes; dry steppe or elevated desert in the north-west corner; moderately humid sub-tropical climate in the north-east; the central *pampa* region and a strip along the foot of the mountains are semi-arid with temperatures ranging from tropical to moderately cool, with average annual temperature 16°C and rainfall 500–1000mm at Buenos Aires; between these two semi-arid areas lies the rain shadow; desert plateau extends to the coast; some rainfall prevents absolute barrenness; the southern part is directly influenced by strong prevailing westerlies.

South America

BOLIVIA

PARAGUAY

BRAZIL

CHILE

San Miguel de Tucumán

Resistencia

Paraná

Salado

Uruguay

ARGENTINA

L. Mar Chiquita

Córdoba

Rosario

Paraná

URUGUAY

Aconcagua

Mendoza

Buenos Aires ★

Rio de la Plata

La Plata

San Rafael

P
a
m
p
a
s

Pacific

Ocean

Mar del Plata

Bahía Blanca

Colorado

Negro

Neuquén

Gulf of San Matias

San Carlos
de Bariloche

A
N
D
E
S

Atlantic

Ocean

Rawson

P
a
t
a
g
o
n
i
a

Comodoro Rivadavia

**Gulf of
San Jorge**

Falkland Islands
(UK)

Puerto Santa Cruz

Strait of Magellan

Tierra del Fuego

Ushuaia

0   250 Miles

0   250 KM

Nations of the World

Government

Governed by an executive President, a Cabinet and a bicameral National Congress, comprising a Chamber of Deputies and a Senate.

Economy

Strong economic growth since collapse of 2001–2; rich in natural resources; oil and gas are extracted, chiefly off coast of Patagonia; fertile *pampa* supports export-orientated agriculture (grain, oil-bearing seeds, fruit, tea, tobacco, livestock), wine production and meat, flour and sugar processing industries; other industries include vehicles, consumer goods, textiles, chemicals, petrochemicals, printing, metallurgy and steel.

History

The majority of the population is of European origin and the remainder is of mestizo or South American Indian origin. Argentina was settled in the 16c by the Spanish. It declared its independence in 1816, and the United Provinces of the Río de la Plata were established. Following a war with Paraguay in 1865–70, Argentina acquired the Gran Chaco plain. In the 19c and 20c, power swung between powerful political factions and between civilian and military regimes. An attempt to gain control of the Falkland Islands in 1982 resulted in defeat in the Falklands War with the UK, and precipitated the downfall of the military junta in power since 1976. Civilian rule was re-established in 1983 and has endured, despite political instability in the early 21c following an economic collapse in 2001–2. Economic recovery began in 2003, although a third of Argentines remain in poverty.

ARMENIA

Official name Republic of Armenia
Local name Hayastan
Location A mountainous republic in southern Transcaucasia, bounded to the north by Georgia; to the east and south-west by Azerbaijan; to the south-east by Iran; and to the west by Turkey
Area 29 800 sq km/11 500 sq mi
Capital Yerevan
Chief towns Vanadzor, Gyumri

Population 2 968 000 (2008e)
Time zone GMT +4
Currency 1 Dram (Drm) = 100 lumas
Language Armenian; Russian is also used
Religions Christianity 99% (Orthodox 95%, other 4%), others 1%
Ethnic groups Armenian 98%, Kurd 1%, Russian and others 1%

Physical description

Mountainous, rising to 4090m/13 418ft at Mount Aragats in the west; the largest lake is the Sevan in the east; the chief river is the Araks; the country is in an earthquake zone.

Climate

Dry and hot in summer, cold in winter.

Government

Governed by a President, a Prime Minister and Cabinet, and a unicameral National Assembly.

Economy

Emerging market economy, achieving sustained growth but dependent on foreign aid; subject to trade embargos over conflict with Azerbaijan; main industries are mining (diamonds, other minerals), machinery, textiles, chemicals, vehicles, microelectronics, jewellery, foodstuffs; main cash crops are grain, fruit, vegetables and livestock.

History

The Armenians are a Christian nation of Indo-European origin, speaking a language of that family with some Caucasian features. Their history goes back to the Roman period and includes years of relative independence; their highly developed ancient culture, particularly in fine art, architecture and sculpture, reached its zenith in the 14c. Their resentment of foreign domination during the 19c provoked their Russian and Turkish rulers, and those who were not retained under Turkish control were taken over by the Russians in 1828. During World War I, the Turks deported two-thirds of Armenians (1.75 million) to Syria and Palestine; 600 000 were either killed or died of starvation during the journey; later, many settled in Europe, the USA and the USSR. Galvanized by earlier Turkish massacres and encouraged by Lenin, Armenia declared its independence in 1918; however, it lost it again on Lenin's orders in 1920 for allegedly consorting with Soviet enemies. Armenia was proclaimed a Soviet Socialist

Republic in 1920, and became a constituent republic of the USSR in 1936. At this time Soviet Armenia laid claim to Turkish Armenia. In 1988 a severe earthquake harmed the country's economy, and further damage was done from 1991 by the dispute with neighbouring Azerbaijan over Nagorno-Karabakh, a mountainous autonomous region ruled by Azerbaijan since 1923 despite having a mainly Armenian population. With the disintegration of the USSR, Armenia declared its independence in 1991 as the Republic of Armenia and became a member of the CIS (Commonwealth of Independent States). The following year a state of emergency was declared as a result of the worsening economic situation, and the dispute with Azerbaijan over Nagorno-Karabakh escalated into war. A ceasefire agreement was reached in 1994 and talks to find a peaceful resolution continue. In 1999 Armenia's parliament was stormed by gunmen who killed the prime minister, parliamentary speaker and six others.

■ Aruba▶Netherlands, The

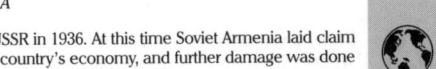

AUSTRALIA

Official name Commonwealth of Australia
Local name Australia
Location An independent country and the smallest continent in the world, entirely in the southern hemisphere
Area 7 682 300 sq km / 2 966 136 sq mi
Capital Canberra
Chief towns Melbourne, Brisbane, Perth, Adelaide, Sydney

Population 21 007 000 (2008e)
Time zone GMT +8/+10
Currency 1 Australian Dollar ($A) = 100 cents
Language English; Aboriginal languages are also spoken
Religions Christianity 67% (RC 26%, Prot 41%), others 4%, unspecified 13%, none 15%
Ethnic groups European 92%, Asian 7%, aboriginal and others 1%

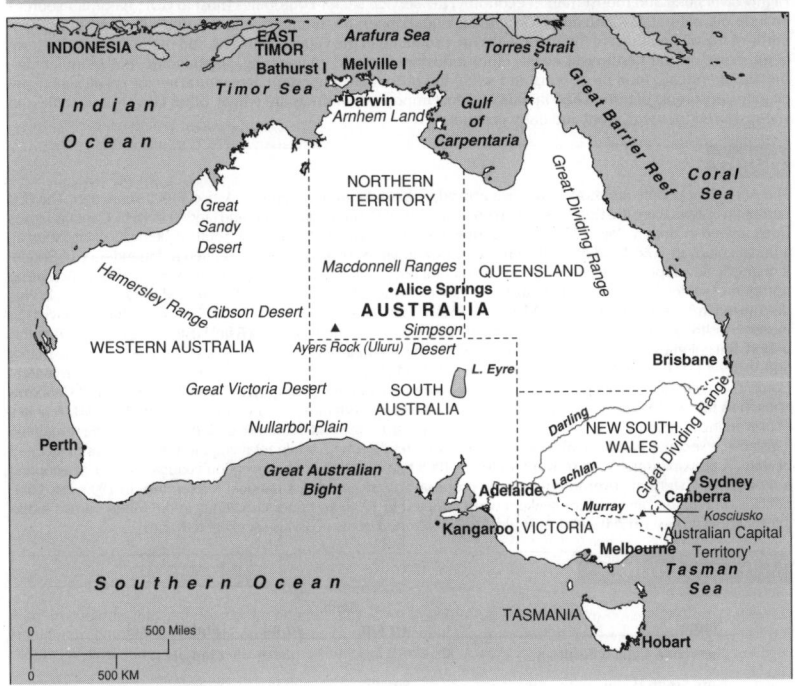

Physical description

Almost 40% of its land mass is north of the Tropic of Capricorn; the Australian continent consists largely of plains and plateaux, most of which average 600m/1968ft above sea level; the West Australian Plateau occupies nearly half the whole area; in the centre are the MacDonnell Ranges, in the north-west the Kimberley Plateau, and in the west the Hamersley Ranges; most of the plateau is dry and barren desert, notably the Gibson Desert in the west, the Great Sandy Desert in the north-west, the Great Victoria Desert in the south and the Simpson Desert in the central area; in the south is the Nullarbor Plain; the Eastern Highlands or Great Dividing Range lie parallel to the eastern seaboard, rising to 2228m/7310ft at Mount Kosciusko (Australia's highest point), in the Australian Alps; between the Western Plateau and the Eastern Highlands lies a broad lowland belt extending south into the Murray–Darling plains; off the north-east coast, stretching for over 1900km/1200mi, is the Great

Barrier Reef; the island of Tasmania, a southern extension of the Eastern Highlands, rises to 1617m/5305ft at Mount Ossa, and is separated from the mainland by the Bass Strait; Australia's longest river is the Murray, its chief tributaries being the Darling, Murrumbidgee and Lachlan. Fertile land with a temperate climate and reliable rainfall is limited to the lowlands and valleys near the coast in the east and south-east, and to a small part of the south-west corner. The population is concentrated in these two regions.

Climate

There are four main climatic zones: a tropical zone in the north and north-east, with rainfall concentrated in the summer months; a warm-temperate zone in the south-east, with rainfall distributed throughout the year; a Mediterranean-type zone in the south and south-west, with moderate amounts of rain which fall mainly in winter; and a continental zone in interior and semi-desert areas, with wide daily variations in temperature and scanty and unreliable rainfall. Warm or hot throughout the year. More than one third of the country receives under 260mm average annual rainfall; less than one third receives over 500mm; half the country has a rainfall variability of more than 30%, with many areas experiencing prolonged drought. Tasmania has a temperate climate, without the extremes of heat of the mainland and with more regular rainfall, although conditions vary greatly between mountain and coast.

Government

Governed by a Governor-General (representing the British monarch, who is head of state), a Prime Minister and Cabinet, and a bicameral federal Parliament, comprising a Senate and a House of Representatives. Each of the six states and two territories has its own governor, executive council and legislative assembly.

Economy

Highly diversified and robust market economy; the service sector contributes most to GDP; natural resources include oil, natural gas, bauxite, nickel, lead, zinc, copper, tin, uranium, iron ore and other minerals; two-thirds of the oil and most of the natural gas are produced in the Gippsland basin, and major discoveries have been made off the north-west coast; other industries include engineering, shipbuilding, car manufacture, metals, chemicals, food processing and wine; the historically important agricultural sector is still significant despite constraints of terrain and rainfall; its most important products are wheat, other cereals and cattle and sheep, raised for meat, wool and dairy products.

History

The Aboriginal people are thought to have arrived in Australia from South-East Asia c.40000 years ago. The first European visitors were the Dutch, who explored the Gulf of Carpentaria in 1606 and landed in 1642. Captain James Cook arrived in Botany Bay in 1770, and claimed the east coast for Britain. New South Wales was established as a penal colony in 1788. In 1829 all the territory now known as Australia was constituted a dependency of Britain. It originally developed as several widely-spread colonies, relating to Britain more than to one another. Increasing numbers of settlers were attracted to Australia, especially after the introduction of Spanish Merino sheep. Gold was discovered in New South Wales and Victoria (1851), and in Western Australia (1892). Transportation of convicts to eastern Australia ended in 1840, but continued until 1853 in Tasmania and 1868 in Western Australia. During this period, the colonies drafted their own constitutions and set up governments: New South Wales (1855), Tasmania and Victoria (1856), South Australia (1857), Queensland (1860) and Western Australia (1890). In 1901 a federal Commonwealth of Australia was established by agreement between the colonies, with the new city of Canberra chosen as the site for its capital, and Australia became independent within the Commonwealth in 1931. A policy of preventing immigration by non-whites stayed in force from the end of the 19c until 1974. In 1986, the remaining legislative, executive and judicial links with the UK were abolished, while retaining the British monarch as head of state. A growing republican movement led in 1998 to a constitutional convention voting in favour of adopting a republican system of government, but the proposal was rejected in a national referendum in 1999. Hard-line policies on refugees and asylum seekers were adopted in 1992, and poor conditions in detention camps led to international protests in 2001 after Australia forcibly diverted boats of asylum seekers to Nauru.

States and territories

Name	Area sq km	sq mi	State capital
Australian Capital Territory	2432	939	Canberra
New South Wales	801427	309431	Sydney
Northern Territory	1346200	519768	Darwin
Queensland	1732700	668995	Brisbane
South Australia	984376	380070	Adelaide
Tasmania	68331	26383	Hobart
Victoria	227600	87876	Melbourne
Western Australia	2525500	975096	Perth

AUSTRIA

Official name Republic of Austria
Local name Österreich
Location A mountainous republic in central
Europe, bounded to the north by Germany, the
Czech Republic and Slovakia; to the south by
Italy and Slovenia; to the west by Switzerland
and Liechtenstein; and to the east by Hungary
Area 83 854 sq km/32 368 sq mi
Capital Vienna
Chief towns Graz, Linz, Salzburg, Innsbruck,
Klagenfurt

Population 8 206 000 (2008e)
Time zone GMT +1
Currency 1 Euro (€) = 100 cents
Language German; Slovene, Croatian and
Hungarian are also official languages in certain
provinces
Religions Christianity 79% (RC 74%, Prot 5%), Islam
4%, none/unaffiliated 14%, others 3%
Ethnic groups Austrian 91%, former Yugoslavs 4%,
others 5%

Physical description

Situated at the eastern end of the Alps, the country
is almost entirely mountainous; the ranges of the
Ötztal, Zillertal, Hohe Tauern and Niedere Tauern
stretch eastwards from the main Alpine massif; the
highest point is Grossglockner, at 3797m/12 457ft;
chief passes into Italy are the Brenner and Plöcken;
most of the country is in the drainage basin of the
River Danube; the Neusiedler See on the Hungarian
border is the largest lake in Austria.

Climate

There are three climatic regions: the Alps (often
sunny in winter but cloudy in summer); the Danube
valley and the Vienna basin (the driest region); and the south-east, a region of heavy thunderstorms, with
often severe winters but warmer summers than north of the Alps. In general, most rain falls in the summer
months; winters are cold; there is a warm, dry wind (the Föhn) in some north-to-south valleys, especially in
autumn and spring, which can be responsible for fires and snow-melt leading to avalanches.

Government

Governed by a federal President, a federal Chancellor and government, and a bicameral Federal Assembly,
comprising a National Council and a Federal Council. Each of the nine *Länder* is administered by its own
government, headed by a governor elected by the provincial legislature.

Economy

Highly diversified market economy with a large services sector; major industries include tourism, foodstuffs,
luxury commodities, mechanical engineering, steel construction, machinery, forestry, mining and metal
products; the principal agricultural areas along the River Danube and north of the Alps produce crops, cattle,
fruit and grapes for wine-making; natural resources include oil, natural gas, minerals and hydroelectric
power.

History

Austria was part of the Roman Empire until the 5c, then was occupied by Germanic tribes and in the late
8c became a frontier area of Charlemagne's empire. It became a duchy and passed to the Habsburg family
(1282), who made it the foundation of their empire; the head of the Habsburg house was almost continually
the Holy Roman Emperor, making Austria the leading German state. Habsburg defeats in the 19c (notably
the Austro–Prussian War) and Hungarian nationalism led to the Dual Monarchy of Austria-Hungary. The
assassination of Archduke Franz Ferdinand by Serbian nationalists triggered World War I. Following the
collapse of Austria-Hungary at the end of the war, those German-speaking lands of the Habsburg Empire
not annexed by other successor states constituted themselves on 12 Nov 1918 as 'German Austria', renamed
Austria on the insistence of the victor powers. Between the wars the republic led an uneasy existence, with
most of public opinion and most politicians seeking union with Germany. Union with Hitler's Germany, which
occurred when Austria was annexed by the German Reich in Mar 1938 (*Anschluss*), under the name *Ostmark*,
was more controversial. After World War II, Austria was reconstituted as a distinct territory by the Allies and
administered as four occupied zones until 1955, when the occupying powers withdrew and it became an
independent, neutral, democratic state. Austria joined the EC in 1995 and replaced the schilling with the euro
in 2002. In 2000, the inclusion of the extreme right-wing Freedom Party in a coalition government led the EU
to impose diplomatic sanctions for seven months.

AZERBAIJAN

Official name Republic of Azerbaijan
Local name Azarbaycan
Location A republic in eastern Transcaucasia, bounded to the east by the Caspian Sea and to the south by Iran; Armenia splits the country in the south-west and forms the western boundary of the main part; Georgia and Russia lie to the north
Area 86 600 sq km/33 428 sq mi
Capital Baku

Chief towns Gäncä, Sumqayit
Population 8 178 000 (2008e)
Time zone GMT +4
Currency 1 New Manat = 100 gopik
Language Azerbaijani (Azeri)
Religions Islam 93% (Shia), Christianity 5% (Orthodox), others 2%
Ethnic groups Azeri 91%, Dagestani 2%, Russian 2%, Armenian 1%, others 4%

Physical description

Crossed by the Greater Caucasus mountains in the north and the Lesser Caucasus in the south-west; the ranges are separated by the plain of the River Kura, much of it below sea level; the highest peak is Mount Bazar-Dyuzi (4480m/14 698ft) in the north-east; forests cover 10.5% of the total area.

Climate

Continental; hot in summer, with winters that are mild in the lowlands but cold and snowy in the mountains.

Government

Governed by an executive President, a Prime Minister and Cabinet of Ministers, and a unicameral National Assembly (*Milli Majlis*).

Economy

In transition from command to market economy; dominated by oil and natural gas extraction (90% of exports) and related industries; agriculture is main employer; main crops are cotton, cereals, fruit, vegetables, tea, silk and livestock.

History

The Azeris have a long history, mainly of subjection to the neighbouring empires. A Turkish people converted to Islam, they came under Tsarist Russian rule in 1813. The development of the oil industry in and around Baku produced leaders who, encouraged by Lenin, declared independence in 1918. However, in 1920 they were reconquered on his instructions for allegedly siding with Soviet enemies, and Azerbaijan was proclaimed a Soviet Socialist Republic; it became a constituent republic of the USSR in 1936. Between Dec 1988 and Jan 1990 riots promoted by the nationalist Azerbaijan Popular Front culminated in an anti-Armenian pogrom in the capital, and Soviet troops mounted a violent assault on the city to restore order. Before emerging as an independent republic in 1991 following the disintegration of the USSR, Azerbaijan became locked in a struggle with Armenia over the autonomous region that Stalin had set up for the latter's co-nationals in Nagorno-Karabakh. This degenerated into war in 1992. A ceasefire was announced in 1994 and talks to effect a peaceful resolution continue. Azerbaijan joined the CIS (Commonwealth of Independent States) in 1993. Despite the introduction of multiparty democracy in 1995, Azerbaijan was effectively under the rule of President Heydar Aliyev from 1992 until his death in 2003, when his equally authoritarian son, Ilham Aliyev, was elected to succeed him.

■ Azores ▶ Portugal

THE BAHAMAS

Official name Commonwealth of the Bahamas
Local name The Bahamas
Location An independent archipelago of c.700 low-lying islands and over 2000 cays, forming a chain extending c.800km/500mi south-east from the coast of Florida
Area 13 934 sq km/5379 sq mi
Capital Nassau
Chief town Freeport

Population 307 000 (2008e)
Time zone GMT −5
Currency 1 Bahamian Dollar (BA$, B$) = 100 cents
Language English
Religions Christianity 96% (Prot and others 83%, RC 14%), none/unaffiliated 3%, others 1%
Ethnic groups black 85%, white 12%, Asian and Hispanic 3%

Physical description

The low-lying coralline limestone islands of the Bahamas comprise the two oceanic banks of Little Bahama and Great Bahama; the highest point, Mt Alvernia on Cat Island, is only 63m/207ft above sea level.

Climate

Subtropical, with average temperatures of 21°C in winter and 27°C in summer; the average annual rainfall is 750–1500mm; hurricanes are frequent in June–November.

Government

Governed by a Governor-General (representing the British monarch, who is head of state), a Prime Minister and Cabinet, and a bicameral Parliament, consisting of a House of Assembly and a Senate.

Economy

Developing country; main economic activities are tourism (60% of GDP) and offshore financial services (tax-haven status); other industries include oil trans-shipment and refining, fishing, rum and liqueur distilling, salt, chemicals, fruit, vegetables.

History

Columbus reached the Bahamas in 1492, but the first permanent European settlement was established in 1647 by English and Bermudan religious refugees. The Bahamas became a British Crown Colony in 1717, and were a notorious rendezvous for buccaneers and pirates. They gained independence in 1973. The Prime Minister at independence was Sir Lynden Pindling, who was regarded as the founding father of The Bahamas.

BAHRAIN

Official name Kingdom of Bahrain
Local name Al-Bahrayn
Location A monarchy comprising a group of 33 islands in the Persian Gulf, midway between the Qatar Peninsula and mainland Saudi Arabia; a causeway (25km/16mi in length) connects Bahrain to Saudi Arabia
Area 678 sq km/262 sq mi
Capital Manama
Chief town Al Muharraq

Population 718 000 (2008e)
Time zone GMT +3
Currency 1 Bahrain Dinar (BD) = 1000 fils
Language Arabic; English, Farsi and Urdu are also spoken
Religions Islam 81% (of whom Shia 70%, Sunni 30%), Christian 9%, others 10%
Ethnic groups Bahraini 62%, non-Bahraini (mostly Asian and Arab) 38%

Physical description

Bahrain comprises 33 islands; the largest, Bahrain Island, is c.48km/30mi long and 13–16km/8–10mi wide; the highest point is Jabal Dukhan (135m/443ft); largely bare and infertile; causeways link the four main islands, and connect Bahrain Island to Saudi Arabia.

Nations of the World

Nations of the World

Climate

Hot, humid climate, with average temperatures of 30°C–40°C in May–October and 20°C–30°C in winter; cool north/north-east winds, with a little rain in December–March; rest of the year dominated by either a moist north-east wind (the *Shamal*) or the hot, sand-bearing *Qaws* from the south.

Government

A hereditary constitutional monarchy; governed by the King, a Prime Minister and Council of Ministers, and a bicameral National Assembly, comprising a Council of Representatives and a Consultative Council.

Economy

Prosperous economy based on oil (on- and offshore) but now diversified; regional banking, financial services and commercial centre; natural gas, lime, gypsum; oil refining, aluminium smelting, ship repairing.

History

Bahrain was a flourishing trade centre in 2000–1800 BC. It was ruled by Iran from 1602 until the Iranian rulers were ousted in 1783 by the al-Khalifa family, who rule to this day. Political control of Bahrain was held by Britain from 1820 to 1971, and oil was discovered during this time, in 1932. In 1971 Bahrain gained independence and Isa ibn Sulman became ruler. He dissolved the National Assembly in 1975 as a result of disputes between Sunni and Shia Muslim communities. On his death in 1999 he was succeeded by his son, Hamad bin Isa. Following a referendum on political reform in 2001, the country became a constitutional monarchy with a partially elected parliament, and the Emir adopted the title of King. Elections to a new legislative assembly were held in 2002.

■ **Balearic Islands ► Spain**

BANGLADESH

Official name People's Republic of Bangladesh
Local name Banladesh
Location An Asian republic lying between the foothills of the Himalayas and the Indian Ocean, bounded to the west, north-west and east by India; to the south-east by Myanmar; and to the south by the Bay of Bengal
Area 143 998 sq km/55 583 sq mi
Capital Dhaka

Chief towns Chittagong, Khulna, Narayanganj
Population 153 547 000 (2008e)
Time zone GMT +6
Currency 1 Taka (Tk) = 100 poisha
Language Bangla (Bengali); English is the second language
Religions Islam 83% (mostly Sunni), Hinduism 16%, others 1%
Ethnic groups Bengali 98%, others 2%

Physical description

Mainly a vast, low-lying alluvial plain, cut by a network of rivers and marshes; main rivers are the Ganges (Padma), Brahmaputra (Jamuna) and Meghna, joining in the south to form the largest delta in the world; subject to frequent flooding; in the east, fertile valleys and peaks of Chittagong Hill Tracts rise to c.1000m/3280ft; highest point is Keokradong (1230m/4035ft); vast areas of the southern delta are covered in mangroves and hardwood forest.

Climate

Tropical monsoon climate; a hot season in March–June with heavy thunderstorms; very humid, with higher temperatures inland; the main rainy season is June–September; cyclones in the Bay of Bengal cause sea surges and frequent widespread flooding of coastal areas.

Government

Governed by a President, a Prime Minister and Cabinet, and a unicameral Parliament, with a number of seats reserved for women.

Economy

Poor country dependent on foreign aid and remittances of expatriate workers; recent growth in energy sector (natural gas), garments and knitwear (over 50% of export earnings), jute goods, leather, processing agricultural products; 60% of workforce employed in agriculture, especially cotton, jute (supplies 80% of world's jute), tea, sugar, fish and seafood.

History

Bangladesh formed part of the state of Bengal in British India until Muslim East Bengal was created in 1905, separate from Hindu West Bengal. Reunited in 1911, East and West Bengal were again partitioned in 1947, with West Bengal remaining in India and East Bengal forming East Pakistan. Disparity in investment and development between East and West Pakistan (separated by over 1000mi/1600km), coupled with language differences, caused East Pakistan to seek autonomy. The suspension of democracy following a sweeping electoral victory by the Awami League in East Pakistan in 1970, the devastation of this province of Pakistan by a cyclone in the same year (it is one of the world's most densely populated areas), and the Dhaka government's ineffectual response to the disaster — which claimed 220 000

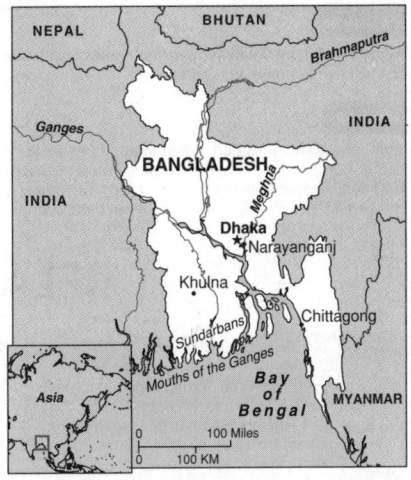

lives and countless homes and crops — triggered fighting, which developed into a full-scale civil war in 1971. Following a popular uprising and military intervention by India, which had accepted huge numbers of Bengali refugees, Pakistan surrendered the territory, which became the independent republic of Bangladesh. Political instability in the 1970s and 1980s led to a number of coups, the assassination of two presidents, and periods under martial law (1975–8, 1982–6) or a state of emergency (1987–8). Following the restoration of the constitution (1986) and parliamentary rule (1991), power alternated between the Bangladesh National Party, led by Khaleda Zia, and the Awami League, led by Sheikh Hasina Wajed. The BNP government stepped down in 2006 when its term of office expired but violent protests over electoral preparations caused the president to declare a state of emergency in 2007, and to remain in office after the expiry of his term. Elections were held in December 2008, and were won by the Awami League.

BARBADOS

Official name Barbados	Population 282 000 (2008e)
Local name Barbados	Time zone GMT –4
Location An independent state and the most easterly of the Caribbean Islands, situated in the Atlantic Ocean	Currency 1 Barbadian Dollar (BD$) = 100 cents
	Language English
Area 431 sq km/166 sq mi	Religions Christianity 75% (Prot and others 71%, RC 4%), none/unaffiliated 21%, others 5%
Capital Bridgetown	Ethnic groups black 90%, white 4%, Asian and others 6%
Chief town Speightstown	

Physical description

A small, triangular island, 32km/20mi long (north-west to south-east); it rises to 340m/1115ft at Mount Hillaby and is ringed by a coral reef.

Climate

Tropical, with an average annual temperature of 27°C and an average annual rainfall of 1420mm; the hurricane season is July–November.

Government

Governed by a Governor-General (representing the British monarch, who is head of state), a Prime Minister and Cabinet, and a bicameral Parliament, comprising a Senate and a House of Assembly.

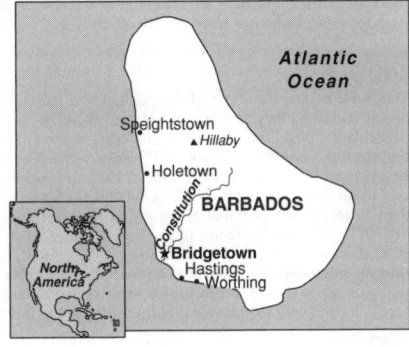

Nations of the World

Economy

Tourism, offshore financial services, sugar, light manufacturing, component assembly (electronic and electrical equipment), garments.

History

Early inhabitants included Amerindians from South America, who arrived c.350 AD, Arawak Indians and Caribs, but the island was uninhabited when colonized by the English in 1627. It was a Crown colony from 1652 and attained self-government in 1961, becoming independent in 1966. Since independence, power has alternated between the Barbados Labour Party and the Democratic Labour Party.

BELARUS

Official name Republic of Belarus
Local name Belarus
Location A republic in eastern Europe, bounded to the west by Poland; to the north-west by Lithuania; to the north by Latvia; to the east by Russia; and to the south by the Ukraine
Area 207 600 sq km/80 134 sq mi
Capital Minsk
Chief towns Gomel, Vitebsk, Mogilev, Bobruysk, Grodno, Brest

Population 9 686 000 (2008e)
Time zone GMT +2
Currency 1 Belarusian Rouble (BR) = 100 kopeks
Languages Belarusian, Russian
Religions Orthodox Christianity 40%, RC 7%, other Christian 1%, others 2% (including Islam and Judaism), unaffliated 50%
Ethnic groups Belarusian 81%, Russian 11%, Polish 4%, Ukrainian 3%, others 1%

Physical description

Mostly a large plain, with many lakes (c.11 000) and marshes, and low hills in the north-west rising to 345m/1132ft; rivers include the Dnieper, Zapadnaya Dvina and Neman; one-third of the country is covered by forests.

Climate

Continental, with cold winters and warm, humid summers.

Government

Governed by a President, a Prime Minister and
Council of Minister, and a bicameral National Assembly consisting of a Council of the Republic and a House of Representatives.

Economy

Much of economy is still under state control; dependent on Russia for energy needs and oil for industry and re-export; main industries are machine building, metalworking, chemicals, petrochemicals, textiles, food, woodworking, radio-electronics, agriculture (grain, potatoes, vegetables, sugar beet, flax, beef, milk).

History

The Belorussians were one of the original Slav tribes, like the Russians themselves. They remained slightly distinct because they lived in the exposed western border area and were subject to long periods of foreign, particularly Polish, rule. Under Tsarist control from 1795, they eventually developed a national movement that declared independence in 1917. However, a feeble Belorussia had a troubled existence; it declared a Belorussian Soviet Socialist Republic in 1919 and was incorporated into the USSR in 1921. In 1945 its territory was expanded at the expense of Poland and, for Soviet political reasons, it was given separate membership of the UN. Yet its sense of national identity remained comparatively undeveloped until it achieved independence in 1991 on the disintegration of the Soviet Union; also that year it became a founding member of the CIS (Commonwealth of Independent States). Alyaksandr Lukashenka, President since 1994, has resisted economic reform, precipitating economic collapse in the late 1990s, and has become increasingly authoritarian. He has pursued closer relations with Russia, committing Belarus to greater political and economic integration with Russia in 1997 and 1999 treaties, although there has been little real progress towards this.

BELGIUM

Official name Kingdom of Belgium
Local name Belgique (French), België (Flemish),
 Belgien (German)
Location A kingdom in north-western Europe,
 bounded to the north by the Netherlands; to the
 south by France; to the east by Germany and
 Luxembourg; and to the west by the North Sea
Area 32 545 sq km/12 562 sq mi
Capital Brussels
Chief towns Antwerp, Ghent, Charleroi, Liège,
Bruges, Namur, Mons
Population 10 404 000 (2008e)
Time zone GMT +1
Currency 1 Euro (€) = 100 cents
Languages Flemish (Dutch), French, German
 (mainly on the eastern border); Brussels is
 officially a bilingual city (French and Flemish)
Religions Christianity 85% (RC 75%, Prot 10%),
 Islam 2%, none/unaffiliated 10%, others 3%

Physical description

Low-lying and fertile in the west, with some hills
in the south-east region (Ardennes); highest point
is Signal de Botrange (694m/2277ft); the main
river systems, the Sambre–Meuse and the Scheldt,
drain across the Dutch border and are linked by a
complex network of canals.

Climate

Temperate with strong maritime influences; mild
winters, warm summers and frequent rainfall.

Government

A hereditary constitutional monarchy with a King
as head of state; governed by a Prime Minister
and Council of Ministers, and a bicameral Federal Chambers, comprising a Chamber of Representatives
and a Senate. There are three communities (Flemish, Francophone, Germanophone), each with its own
community government and assembly. There are three regions (Flanders, Wallonia, Brussels), each with its
own regional government and assembly.

Economy

A long-standing centre of European trade and one of the earliest countries in Europe to industrialize; now
a highly developed and diversified market economy with a large service sector owing to the location in
Brussels of several major international organizations; with few natural resources apart from coal (no longer
produced), industries developed based on processing imported raw materials for export, eg the iron and
steel industry imports raw materials from Luxembourg and Germany; other industries include metallurgical
and engineering products, motor vehicle assembly, processed food and beverages, chemicals, textiles, glass
and petroleum; major trade in gemstones (especially diamonds); agriculture is mainly livestock, sugar beet,
vegetables, fruit, grain and tobacco.

History

A line drawn east to west just to the south of Brussels divides the population by race and language into
two approximately equal parts; north of the line the inhabitants are Flemings of Teutonic stock who speak
Flemish, while south of the line they are French-speaking Latins known as
Walloons. Belgium was part of the Roman Empire until the 2c AD, and after
being invaded by Germanic tribes it became part of the Frankish Empire. In
the early Middle Ages, some semi-independent provinces and cities grew up
and from 1385 were absorbed by the House of Burgundy. They were known as
the Spanish Netherlands, and were ruled by the Habsburgs from 1477 until the
Peace of Utrecht (1713); the Spanish provinces were then transferred to Austria
as the Austrian Netherlands. The country was conquered by the French in 1794
and formed part of the First French Republic and Empire until in 1815 it united
with the northern (Dutch) provinces under King William I of the Netherlands.
The southern (Belgian) provinces were unhappy with the union because of
William's religious, linguistic and economic policies. The Belgian Revolution
began with riots in Brussels on 25 Aug 1830. A provisional government, called
a National Convention, declared the independence of Belgium and drafted a
new constitution (7 Feb 1831), which made Belgium a constitutional monarchy
with Leopold of Saxe-Coburg as its first king (Leopold I). The Great Powers
recognized Belgian independence at the Conference of London (20 Jan 1831).
However, William I refused to co-operate; as a result an armed standoff dragged
on for most of the 1830s. Finally in 1839 the Dutch government capitulated and

Ethnic groups

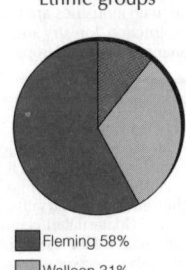

■ Fleming 58%
□ Walloon 31%
■ others 11%

signed a treaty which completed the independence of Belgium. During the 20c, Belgium was occupied by Germany in both world wars, and in the post-war period political tension between Walloons and Flemings caused the collapse of several governments until federalization began in the 1980s with the creation of regional 'subgovernments' for Wallonia and Flanders. In 1989 a new federal constitution divided Belgium into three autonomous regions: the Walloon Region (Wallonia), the Flemish Region (Flanders) and the bilingual Brussels-Capital Region; constitutional amendments in 1993 completed federalization. Belgium joined with Luxembourg and the Netherlands to form the Benelux economic union in 1948. It was a founder member of the EEC in 1958, and replaced the Belgian franc with the euro in 2002.

BELIZE

Official name Belize
Local name Belize
Location An independent state in Central America, bounded to the north by Mexico; to the west and south by Guatemala; and to the east by the Caribbean Sea
Area 22963 sq km/8864 sq mi
Capital Belmopan
Chief towns Belize City, Dangriga, Punta Gorda, San Ignacio

Population 301 000 (2008e)
Time zone GMT –6
Currency 1 Belizean Dollar (BZ$) = 100 cents
Language English; Spanish and Creole predominate; Mayan dialects and Carib are also spoken
Religions Christianity 77% (RC 50%, Prot 27%), others 14%, none/unaffiliated 9%
Ethnic groups mestizo 49%, Creole 25%, Maya 11%, Garifuna 6%, others 9%

Physical description

The country has an extensive coastal plain, swampy in the north, more fertile in the south; the Maya Mountains extend almost to the east coast, rising to 1120m/3674ft at Victoria Peak; they are flanked by pine ridges, tropical forests, savannahs and farm land; the Belize River flows west to east; inner coastal waters are protected by the world's fifth longest barrier reef.

Climate

Generally subtropical but tempered by trade winds; coastal temperatures vary between 10°C and 36°C, with a greater range in the mountains; there is variable rainfall with an average of 1295mm in the north and 4445mm in the south; drier season in February–April; hurricanes have caused severe damage.

Government

Governed by a Governor-General (representing the British monarch, who is head of state), a Prime Minister and Cabinet, and a bicameral National Assembly, comprising a Senate and a House of Representatives.

Economy

The main industries are tourism, garment manufacturing, food processing (sugar refining, citrus processing), construction, forestry and marine products; significant agricultural sector produces main export items (sugar, bananas, citrus and tropical fruit, shrimp, fish); crude oil production began in 2006.

History

There is evidence of early Maya settlement in Belize, and its coast was colonized in the 17c by shipwrecked British sailors and disbanded soldiers from Jamaica, who defended the territory against the Spanish. Created a British colony in 1862, it was administered from Jamaica, but the tie with Jamaica was severed in 1884. A ministerial system of government was introduced in 1961, and in 1964 full internal self-government was achieved. The country changed its name from British Honduras to Belize in 1973 and gained full independence in 1981. Guatemalan claims over Belize territory led to a British military presence until, in the early 1990s, Guatemala established diplomatic relations with Belize. Almost all of the British presence was withdrawn in 1993. Talks sponsored by the Organization of American States (OAS) continue in search of a final resolution to the dispute with Guatemala.

BENIN

Official name Republic of Benin
Local name Bénin
Location A republic in West Africa, bounded to
the north by Niger; to the east by Nigeria; to the
south by the Bight of Benin; to the west by Togo;
and to the north-west by Burkina Faso
Area 112 622 sq km/43 472 sq mi
Capital Porto Novo (constitutional), Cotonou (seat
of government)
Chief towns Ouidah, Abomey, Kandi, Parakou,
Natitingou
Population 8 536 000 (2008e)
Time zone GMT +1
Currency 1 CFA Franc (CFAFr) = 100 centimes
Language French; Fon, Yoruba and several other
local languages are also spoken
Religions Christianity 43% (27% RC), Islam 24%,
traditional beliefs 17%, others 16%
Ethnic groups Fon 39%, Adja 15%, Yoruba 12%,
others 34%

Physical description

Rises from a 100km/62mile sandy coast with
lagoons, to low-lying plains, then to a savannah
plateau at c.400m/1300ft; the Atakora Mountains
rise to over 500m/1640ft in the north-west; highest
point is Mt Sokbaro (658m/2159ft); several rivers
flow south to the Gulf of Guinea.

Climate

Tropical climate, divided into three zones; in the
south, there is rain throughout the year, especially
during the 'Guinea Monsoon' (May–October); in
the central area there are two rainy seasons (peaks
in May–June and October); in the north, there is
one (July–September); the northern dry season
(October–April) is hot, has low humidity, and is
subject to the dry *harmattan* wind from the north-
east.

Government

Governed by an executive President, a Council of
Ministers and a unicameral National Assembly.

Economy

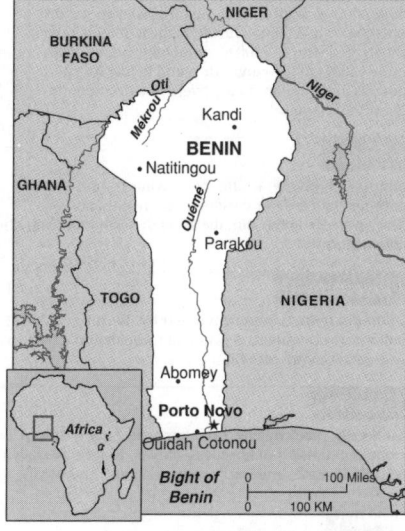

Underdeveloped and dependent on foreign aid, with a high trade deficit and massive foreign debt; main
activities are cotton growing, palm products, food processing, textiles, crude oil production.

History

As the Kingdom of Dahomey, it was based on its capital at Abomey, and in the late 17c and early 18c extended
its authority from the coast to the interior, to the west of the Yoruba states. In the 1720s the cavalry of the Oyo
Kingdom of the Yoruba devastated Dahomey, but when the Oyo Empire collapsed in the early 19c, Dahomey
regained its power. The state was annexed by the French in 1883 and constituted a territory of French West
Africa in 1904, but regained its independence in 1960. In 1972 it was declared a Marxist–Leninist state under
the leadership of President Mathieu Kérékou, who renamed it Benin in 1975. The country gradually achieved
stability and moved towards democratic government, abandoning Marxism–Leninism in 1989. A multiparty
democratic constitution was adopted in 1991. In 2004, a 40-year border dispute with neighbouring Nigeria
was resolved and the border redrawn.

■ **Bermuda ▶ United Kingdom**

Nations of the World

BHUTAN

Official name Kingdom of Bhutan
Local name Druk Yul
Location A small state in the eastern Himalayas, bounded to the north by China and to the south by India
Area 46 600 sq km/18 000 sq mi
Capital Thimphu
Chief town Phuntsholing

Population 682 000 (2008e)
Time zone GMT +6
Currency 1 Ngultrum (Nu) = 100 chetrum
Language Dzongkha
Religions Buddhism 75%, Hinduism 25%
Ethnic groups Bhote 50%, Nepalese 35%, others 15%

Physical description

Mountainous north, with east Himalayan peaks reaching over 7000m/22 966ft; highest point is Kula Kangri (7553m/24 780ft); mountain ridges with fertile valleys in the centre descend to low forested foothills in the south; many rivers flow to meet the River Brahmaputra.

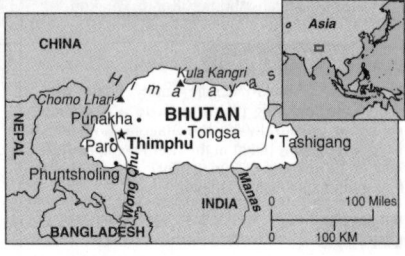

Climate

Subtropical in the south; cool winters and hot summers in the central valleys; severe winters and cool summers in the Himalayas, with permanent snowfields and glaciers; rainfall is heavy owing to frequent violent storms.

Government

A hereditary monarchy; governed by the King, a Prime Minister and Council of Ministers, and a bicameral Parliament comprising a National Council and a National Assembly. The King's position must be confirmed by legislative vote every three years.

Economy

Cautiously modernizing economy still largely based on agriculture; main crops are rice, wheat, maize, mountain barley, potatoes, vegetables, fruit (especially oranges) and cardamom (main export); small-scale industry includes mining, forestry, cement, chemicals, hydroelectric power and tourism.

History

Remoteness limited outside contact until modern times. A treaty of cooperation between Bhutan and the East India Company was signed in 1774; the southern part of the country was annexed by Britain in 1865. In 1910 Britain agreed not to interfere in internal affairs, transferring the supervision of Bhutan's external affairs to British India, and in 1949 Bhutan signed a similar treaty with India. In 1990 large numbers of ethnic Nepalese moved to Nepal and India following the introduction of strict cultural laws. Bhutan has been governed since 1907 by maharajahs, now addressed as King of Bhutan. The absolute monarchy was replaced in 1969 by a form of democratic monarchy, with the King as the head of the government. He relinquished this role in 1998, when further reforms were introduced. A constitution promulgated in 2005 introduced further democratization, including parliamentary elections in 2008.

BOLIVIA

Official name Republic of Bolivia
Local name Bolivia
Location A landlocked republic in western central South America, bounded to the north and east by Brazil; to the west by Peru; to the south-west by Chile; to the south by Argentina; and to the south-east by Paraguay
Area 1 098 580 sq km/424 052 sq mi

Capital La Paz (seat of government), Sucre (legal)
Chief towns Cochabamba, El Alto, Oruro, Potosí, Santa Cruz
Population 9 248 000 (2008e)
Time zone GMT –4
Currency 1 Boliviano ($b) = 100 centavos
Languages Spanish, Quechua, Ayamará
Religions Christianity 100% (RC 95%, Prot 5%)

Physical description

Bounded to the west by the Cordillera Occidental of the Andes, rising to 6542m/21 463ft at Nevado Sajarna, and to the east by the Cordillera Real; between the mountains lies the 400km/250mi central Altiplano Plateau, at 3600m/11 811ft above sea level; major lakes in this region are Titicaca and Poopó; several rivers flow from the Andes towards the Brazilian frontier.

Climate

Varies, according to altitude; humid and semi-tropical in the lowlands, cold and semi-arid in the mountains.

Government

Governed by an executive President, a Cabinet and a bicameral National Congress, comprising a Chamber of Senators and a Chamber of Deputies.

Ethnic groups

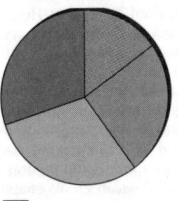

Economy

Poor country dependent on foreign aid; abundant mineral resources, including 20% of world's tin; main industries are mining (zinc, tin, gold) and smelting, natural gas and oil production, agriculture (soya beans, coffee, coca, cotton, cereals, sugar) and forestry; world's third largest producer of illegal cocaine.

History

Bolivia formed part of the Inca Empire in the 15c, and there is evidence of earlier civilization. It was conquered by the Spanish in the 16c, and achieved independence after the war of liberation in 1825. Much territory was lost after wars with neighbouring countries, with the Chaco War (1932–5) in particular having a devastating effect. In 1952 the *Movimiento Nacionalista Revolucionario* (National Revolutionary Movement), an alliance of mineworkers and peasants, overthrew the military dictatorship and came to power. It brought about some far-reaching social reforms during the 1950s, including universal suffrage, nationalization of the tin mines, and the improvement in status of the South American Indians. However, Bolivia's instability continued, with several more changes of government and military coups during the 20c. Economic collapse in the 1980s caused many of the poor to turn to cultivation of coca, the basis of cocaine, and crop-eradication programmes, essential to obtain overseas aid, have provoked protests and strikes in recent years. Fierce opposition to greater political power for Amerindians caused political turmoil in 2007–8.

- Quechua 30%
- mestizo 30%
- Aymará 25%
- white 15%

BOSNIA AND HERZEGOVINA

Official name Bosnia and Herzegovina
Local name Bosna i Hercegovina
Location A republic in the western part of the Balkan Peninsula, bounded to the west and north by Croatia; to the east by Serbia and to the south by Montenegro
Area 51 129 sq km/19 736 sq mi
Capital Sarajevo

Chief towns Banja Luka, Zenica, Tuzla, Mostar
Population 4 590 000 (2008e)
Time zone GMT +1
Currency 1 Konvertible Marka (KM) = 100 pfennige
Languages Bosnian, Croatian, Serbian
Religions Christianity 46% (Orthodox 31%, RC 15%), Islam 40%, others 14%

Physical description

The mountainous centre includes part of the Dinaric Alps; highest point is Maglic (2386m/7828ft); it is split by its limestone gorges; in the north the land falls to the River Sava valley; there is 20km of coastline on the Adriatic Sea.

Climate

Continental, with hot summers and cold winters.

Government

Governed by a collective presidency (which rotates among the three members), a Prime Minister and Council of Ministers, and a bicameral Parliamentary Assembly, consisting of a House of Peoples and a House of Representatives. Each of the two self-governing entities within the republic, the Federation of Bosnia and Herzegovina (Bosniac/Croat) and the Republika Srpska (Serb), has its own president, executive council and legislature.

Economy

Recovery from devastation of civil war hampered by inefficiency and uneasy relations between different national and local political entities; largely dependent on foreign aid; most agricultural output consumed domestically; mining (minerals, metals, coal), steel, textiles, assembly of domestic appliances, vehicles and military equipment; hydro-electric power exported.

History

In Mar 1992, Bosnia–Herzegovina followed the republics of Slovenia and Croatia in declaring its independence from Yugoslavia. Civil war broke out between communist and nationalist elements from the Yugoslav National Army and extreme nationalist paramilitary groups, gradually and brutally engulfing the civilian population until all civil order dissolved. A three-sided civil war raged between the Muslims loyal to the government, and the Serbs and Croats who proclaimed themselves independent and began fighting for territory. By the end of 1992 the Serbs had besieged Sarajevo and were carrying out a brutal policy of ethnic cleansing, which UN peacekeeping forces attempted to stop. An alliance made in 1994 between Bosnian Muslims and Bosnian Croats enabled the recapture of territory during 1995, and NATO air-strikes helped to end the Sarajevo siege. The signing of the Dayton Peace Accord in Dec 1995 brought relative, if rather tense, peace. It created a federal multi-ethnic Bosnian government with a rotating presidency and two separate administrations divided along ethnic and geographic lines into the Republic Srpska (Bosnian Serb) and the Bosniac/Croat Federation. Civilian aspects of the Accord are overseen by the Office of the UN High Representative. Military aspects of the Accord have been overseen by peacekeeping and stabilizing forces of the UN (1995), NATO (1995–2005) and the EU (since 2005). The Hague war crimes tribunal has convicted a number of people for the atrocities committed between 1992 and 1995.

Ethnic groups

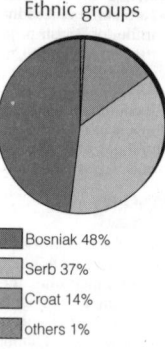

- Bosniak 48%
- Serb 37%
- Croat 14%
- others 1%

BOTSWANA

Official name Republic of Botswana
Local name Botswana
Location A landlocked republic in southern Africa, bounded to the south by South Africa; to the west and north by Namibia; and to the east by Zimbabwe
Area 582 096 sq km/224 689 sq mi
Capital Gaborone
Chief towns Francistown, Lobatse, Selebi-Phikwe, Orapa, Jwaneng

Population 1 842 000 (2008e)
Time zone GMT +2
Currency 1 Pula (P, Pu) = 100 thebe
Languages English; Setswana, Kalanga, Sekgalagadi
Religions Christianity 72%, traditional beliefs 6%, other 1%, none/unaffiliated 21%
Ethnic groups Tswana (Setswana) 79%, Kalanga 11%, Basarwa 3%, others 7%

Physical description

Undulating sandy plateau with an average elevation of c.1100m/3609ft; the most fertile and most densely populated area, in the east, falls to the River Limpopo; the terrain in the south and west progresses through savannah and dry scrubland to the aridity of the Kalahari Desert; to the north and north-west are the swamps of the Okavango Delta and deciduous forests.

Climate

Sub-tropical in the north, increasingly arid in the south and west, and more temperate in the east; rainfall in the north and east falls almost totally in summer (October–April) with an annual average of 450mm; average maximum daily temperatures range between 23°C and 32°C; annual rainfall is erratic in the Kalahari Desert, decreasing south and west to below 200mm.

Government

Governed by an executive President, a Cabinet and a unicameral National Assembly; a House of Chiefs acts as an advisory council on tribal matters and constitutional changes.

Economy

Relatively prosperous owing to mineral resources, chiefly diamonds (over 30% of GDP), copper, nickel (second largest African producer), salt, soda ash, potash and coal; agriculture mainly subsistence level, except cattle-rearing (80% of sector output; beef is a major export); diversifying into safari tourism and financial services.

History

The area was visited by missionaries in the 19c and came under British protection in 1885. The southern part became a British Crown Colony, then part of Cape Colony in 1895, while the northern part became the Bechuanaland Protectorate. In 1964 it achieved self-government, and in 1966 it gained independence and changed its name to Botswana. Although stable and relatively prosperous since independence, it faces serious demographic and social problems owing to the high level of HIV/AIDS infection, which the government has developed programmes to counter.

BRAZIL

Official name Federative Republic of Brazil
Local name Brasil
Location A republic in eastern and central South America, bounded to the north by French Guiana, Suriname, Guyana and Venezuela; to the north-west by Colombia; to the west by Peru, Bolivia and Paraguay; to the south-west by Argentina; to the south by Uruguay; and to the east by the Atlantic Ocean
Area 8 511 965 sq km/3 285 618 sq mi
Capital Brasília

Chief towns São Paulo, Rio de Janeiro, Belo Horizonte, Recife, Salvador
Population 196 343 000 (2008e)
Time zone GMT −2/−5
Currency 1 Real (R$) = 100 centavos
Language Portuguese; Spanish and English are widely spoken
Religions Christianity 89% (RC 74% (nominal), Prot 15%), Spiritualism 1%, others 2%, none/unaffiliated 8%

Physical description

Nearly 60% of the country is taken up by the low-lying Amazon basin in the north, drained by rivers that carry 20% of the Earth's running water; north of the Amazon are the Guiana Highlands, including the country's highest peak, Pico da Neblina (3014m/9888ft); south of the Amazon and occupying Brazil's centre is the Brazilian Plateau, with vegetation varying from thorny scrub forest to wooded savannah (campo cerrado); between the plateau and the east coast lie the Brazilian Highlands, rising to 2890m/9482ft at Pico da Bandeira; on the Atlantic coast a thin strip of land, c.100km/62mi wide, contains 30% of the population; there are eight river systems, notably the Amazon in the north, the São Francisco in the centre, and the Paraguay, Paraná and Uruguay in the south; Brazil contains the world's biggest rainforest; where forest canopy has been cleared, soils are susceptible to erosion.

Climate

Almost entirely tropical; the Equator passes through the northern region, and the Tropic of Capricorn through the south-eastern; in the Amazon basin the annual rainfall is 1500–2000mm, with no dry season; the average midday temperatures are 27°–32°C; there are more distinct wet and dry seasons on the Brazilian Plateau; the dry region in the north-east is susceptible to long droughts, with daily temperatures 21°–36°C, and monthly rainfall as little as 3mm in August, rising to 185mm in March; on the narrow coastal strip, the climate is hot and tropical, with rainfall varying greatly north to south; the southern states lie outside the tropics, with a seasonal, temperate climate.

Government

A federal republic governed by an executive President, a Cabinet and a bicameral National Congress, consisting of the Federal Senate and the Chamber of Deputies. Each of the 26 states has a governor and legislative assembly.

Economy

A diversified middle-income economy stabilized by recent reforms; one of the world's largest farming countries, especially in coffee (the world's largest exporter), cocoa and soya beans (the second largest exporter), maize, rice, wheat, sugar, citrus fruit and beef; its rich natural resources include iron ore (reserves possibly the world's largest), manganese, bauxite, beryllium, chrome, nickel, gold, gemstones; oil and natural gas; steel, chemicals, petrochemicals, food processing, wood products, footwear, textiles, motor and aerospace vehicles, financial services, electronics, tourism; large investments in hydro-electric power, alcohol fuel, coal and nuclear power; timber reserves are the third largest in the world but expansion of agriculture and forestry hastens continuing destruction of the Amazon rainforest, to worldwide concern; a road network is being extended through the rainforest.

Ethnic groups

- white 54%
- mulatto 38%
- black 6%
- others 2%

History

The territory was claimed for the Portuguese after a fortuitous landfall by Pedro Cabral in 1500, and the first settlement was at Salvador da Bahia. There were 13 feudal grants, which were replaced in 1572 by a viceroyalty. The country was divided into north and south, with capitals at Salvador and Rio de Janeiro. During the Napoleonic Wars, the Portuguese court transferred to Brazil. Brazilian independence was declared in 1822, and a monarchy was established. In 1889 there was a coup, which was followed in 1891 by the declaration of a republic. Large numbers of European immigrants arrived in the early 20c. A revolution, headed by Getúlio Vargas, established a dictatorship in 1930–45, but a liberal republic was restored in 1946. Another coup in 1964 led to a military-backed presidential regime, and a military junta was established in 1969. Under President Figueiredo (1979–85) the military government began a process of liberalization, allowing the return of political exiles to stand for state and federal offices, and in 1985 elections restored civilian government. Subsequent governments and leaders have faced a particularly difficult economic situation, but plans to develop the Amazon basin have attracted controversy because of the threat posed to environmentally important rainforest.

- ■ **British Antarctic Territory▶ United Kingdom**

- ■ **British Indian Ocean Territory▶ United Kingdom**

- ■ **British Virgin Islands▶ United Kingdom**

BRUNEI

Official name Brunei Darussalam
Local name Brunei
Location A state on the north-west coast of Borneo, south-eastern Asia, bounded by the South China Sea in the north-west, and on all other sides by Malaysia's Sarawak state
Area 5765 sq km/2225 sq mi
Capital Bandar Seri Begawan
Chief towns Kuala Belait, Seria, Bangar

Population 381 000 (2008e)
Time zone GMT +8
Currency 1 Brunei Dollar (B$) = 100 sen
Language Malay; English and Chinese are widely spoken
Religions Islam 67%, Buddhism 13%, Christianity 10%, traditional beliefs and others 10%
Ethnic groups Malay 66%, Chinese 11%, indigenous 4%, others 19%

Physical description

The country is divided in two by the Limbang River valley in Sarawak (Malaysia); swampy coastal plains rise through foothills to a mountainous region on the Malaysian border; highest point is Bukit Pagon (1850m/6098ft); equatorial rainforest covers 75% of the land area.

Climate

Tropical climate, with high temperatures and humidity, and no marked seasons; average daily temperature ranges between 24°C and 30°C; annual average rainfall is 2540mm on the coast, doubling in the interior.

Government

A hereditary monarchy; governed by the Sultan, advised by a Privy Council, a Council of Cabinet Ministers and a Religious Council. The unicameral Legislative Council was reconvened in 2004 (for the first time in 20 years) and passed constitutional changes enlarging it and making it partially elected in future.

Economy

Largely dependent on oil and gas (nearly 50% of GDP) and income from overseas investments; now diversifying into financial services and tourism; main crops are rice, vegetables, fruit, poultry.

History

Formerly a powerful Muslim sultanate, it came under British protection in 1888, achieved internal self-government in 1971, and gained independence in 1984. In 2004 the Sultan reconvened the Legislative Council, which had been disbanded 20 years earlier.

BULGARIA

Official name Republic of Bulgaria
Local name Bãlgarija
Location A republic in the east of the Balkan Peninsula in south-eastern Europe, bounded to the north by Romania; to the west by Serbia and Macedonia; to the south by Greece; to the south-east by Turkey; and to the east by the Black Sea
Area 110912 sq km/42812 sq mi
Capital Sofia
Chief towns Plovdiv, Varna, Ruse, Burgas, Stara Zagora, Pleven
Population 7263000 (2008e)
Time zone GMT +2
Currency 1 Lev (Lv) = 100 stotinki
Language Bulgarian; Turkish and Roma are also spoken
Religions Christianity 84% (Orthodox 83%, other 1%), Islam 12%, others 4%
Ethnic groups Bulgarian 84%, Turk 9%, Roma 5%, others 2%

Physical description

The centre is traversed west to east by the Balkan Mountains, rising to over 2000m/6562ft; the Rhodope Mountains in the south-west rise to nearly 3000m/9842ft; highest point is Musala (2925m/9596ft); the lowland plains are in the basins of the main rivers, the Danube in the north and the Maritsa in the south-east; other rivers are the Iskur, Yantra and Struma.

Climate

Largely continental, with hot summers and cold winters, and average temperatures lower at altitude; winters are slightly warmer on the Black Sea coast and summers there can resemble the Mediterranean.

Government

Governed by a President, a Prime Minister and Cabinet, and a unicameral National Assembly.

Economy

Completing transition to industrialized market economy; industries include power generation (including nuclear power), machine building, metal working, oil refining and petrochemicals, food processing, chemicals, construction materials, metals, textiles and garments; fertile agricultural land produces fruit, vegetables, tobacco, grapes for wine-making, wheat, barley, sunflower seeds and livestock; tourism is expanding.

History

In the 7c Bulgars crossed the Danube and gradually merged in with the Slavonic population and established the Kingdom of Bulgaria, which was continually at war with the Byzantine Empire until it was destroyed by the Turks in the 14c. It was under Turkish rule until 1878, when a principality was created, but full independence was only achieved in 1908, when it became a kingdom. It was aligned with Germany in both world wars and in 1944 was occupied by the USSR. The monarchy was abolished in 1946 and it was proclaimed a Socialist

People's Republic. In the early 1990s a multiparty government introduced political and economic reforms, which initially caused some difficulties. Political stability was achieved in the late 1990s, and Bulgaria made sufficient progress to join the EU in 2007.

BURKINA FASO

Official name Burkina Faso
Local name Burkina Faso
Location A landlocked republic in West Africa, bounded to the north and west by Mali; to the east by Niger; to the south-east by Benin; to the south by Togo and Ghana; and to the south-west by Côte d'Ivoire
Area 274 540 sq km/105 972 sq mi
Capital Ouagadougou
Chief towns Bobo-Dioulasso, Koudougou,
Ouahigouya, Tenkodogo
Population 15 265 000 (2008e)
Time zone GMT
Currency 1 CFA Franc (CFAFr) = 100 centimes
Language French; many local languages are also spoken
Religions Islam 50%, traditional beliefs 40%, Christianity (mainly RC) 10%
Ethnic groups Mossi 50%, others (c.60 ethnic groups, including Mande, Fulani and Bobo) 50%

Physical description

Low-lying plateau, falling away to the south; highest point is Tena Kourou (749m/2457ft); many rivers are seasonal; wooded savannahs in the south; semi-desert in the north.

Climate

Tropical climate, with an average temperature of 27°C in the dry season (December–May); rainy season (June–October), with violent storms (August); the *harmattan* wind blows from the north-east (December–March); rainfall higher in the south and decreases further north.

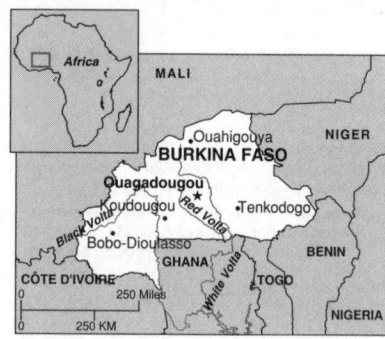

Government

Governed by a President, a Prime Minister and Council of Ministers, and a unicameral National Assembly.

Economy

Very poor country, dependent on foreign aid; agriculture mostly at subsistence level and subject to drought; main cash crops are cotton (world's third largest producer) and livestock; industries include gold mining (third largest export), processing cotton and agricultural products, soap, cigarettes, textiles.

History

The area was part of the Mossi Empire in the 18–19c before becoming a French protectorate in 1898. At first it was part of French Sudan (now Mali), then in 1919 it was made into Upper Volta. This was abolished in 1932, with most land joined to the Côte d'Ivoire. In 1947 its original borders were reconstituted, and in 1958 it gained autonomy within the French Community, followed by independence as Upper Volta in 1960. It was renamed Burkina Faso in 1984. In the first three decades of independence there were several military coups, the last by Blaise Compaoré in 1987; military rule ended in 1991 with multiparty elections which were won by Compaoré and the Popular Front.

■ Burma▶Myanmar

BURUNDI

Official name Republic of Burundi
Local name Burundi
Location A small landlocked republic in central Africa, bounded to the north by Rwanda; to the east and south by Tanzania; to the south-west by Lake Tanganyika; and to the west by the Democratic Republic of the Congo
Area 27 834 sq km/10 744 sq mi
Capital Bujumbura
Chief towns Bubanza, Ngozi, Muyinga, Muramvya,
Gitega, Bururi, Rutana
Population 8 691 000 (2008e)
Time zone GMT +2
Currency 1 Burundi Franc (BuFr, FBu) = 100 centimes
Languages French, Kirundi
Religions Christianity 67% (RC 62%, Prot 5%), traditional beliefs 23%, Islam 10%
Ethnic groups Hutu 85%, Tutsi 14%, others 1%

Physical description

Mostly a plateau with an average height of c.1500m/4921ft, lying across the Nile–Congo watershed and sloping east towards Tanzania; bounded to the west by Lake Tanganyika and to the north-west by the narrow River Ruizi plain; the River Akanyaru forms the northern border; the highest point is at Mount Heha (2670m/8760ft).

Climate

Equatorial climate, varying with altitude and season; moderately wet, except during the dry season (June–Sept); the average annual rainfall at Bujumbura is 850mm.

Government

Governed by an executive President, a Council of Ministers and a bicameral Parliament, consisting of a National Assembly and a Senate. The 2005 constitution specifies the proportions of Hutu and Tutsi and of women members in each chamber and in the Council of Ministers.

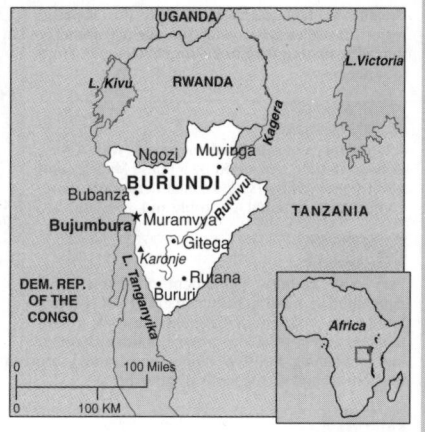

Economy

A very poor country, dependent on foreign aid; agriculture is mostly at subsistence level but with coffee, tea, sugar, cotton and hides the main cash crops; small-scale industry includes light manufacturing, food processing, assembly of imported components and public sector construction; reserves of oil, nickel, copper and other resources not exploited.

History

From the 16c the country was ruled by Tutsi kings who dominated a Hutu population. Germany annexed the area in 1890, and included it in German East Africa. After World War I it became a League of Nations mandated territory, being administered by the Belgians from 1919. In 1946 it joined with Rwanda to become the UN Trust Territory of Ruanda–Urundi, but broke this union on gaining independence in 1962; it became a republic in 1966. Civil war broke out in 1972 and there were military coups in 1976 and 1987. A multiparty constitution was adopted in 1992 and the following year saw the end of Tutsi dominance with the election of a Hutu head of state and a Hutu majority in the National Assembly. Soon after the election, however, the Tutsi-dominated army staged a coup in which the president was killed, and his successor was killed with the Rwandan president when their plane was shot down in 1994. These deaths sparked off fierce ethnic conflict and led to the loss of hundreds of thousands of lives during the ensuing decade. In 1996 the incumbent Hutu President was ousted by another coup and a multi-ethnic government was formed. Talks from 1999 resulted in 2001 in the inauguration of a transitional power-sharing government, and presidential and legislative elections were held in 2005. Most rebel groups have ceased activities, but one clashed with the army in 2008.

CAMBODIA

Official name Kingdom of Cambodia
Local name Kâmpuchéa
Location A republic in South-East Asia, bounded to the north-west by Thailand; to the north by Laos; to the east and south by Vietnam; and to the south and south-west by the Gulf of Thailand
Area 181035 sq km/69880 sq mi
Capital Phnom Penh
Chief towns Battambang, Kâmpŏng Som, Kâmpŏng Chhnăng
Population 14242000 (2008e)
Time zone GMT +7
Currency 1 Riel (CRI) = 100 sen
Language Khmer; French and English are also spoken
Religions Buddhism 95%, others 5%
Ethnic groups Khmer 90%, Vietnamese 5%, Chinese 1%, others 4%

Physical description

Occupies a plain surrounding the Tonlé Sap (lake), a freshwater depression on the Cambodian Plain, which is crossed by the flood plain of the Mekong River; the highest land lies in the south-west, where the Cardamom Mountains run for 160km/100mi across the Thailand border, rising to 1813m/5948ft at Phnom Aôral.

Climate

Tropical monsoon climate, with a wet season in May–November; heavy rainfall in the south-western mountains; high temperatures in the lowland region throughout the year; the average monthly rainfall at Phnom Penh is 257mm in October, 7mm in January.

Government

A hereditary constitutional monarchy with a King as head of state; governed by a Prime Minister and government ministers, and a bicameral Parliament, comprising a National Assembly and a Senate.

Economy

Very poor country, dependent on foreign aid; agriculture is main activity, largely at subsistence level; main crops are rice, rubber, livestock, maize, tobacco and vegetables; growing industrial sector includes fishing, forestry, mining (gemstones), construction, manufacturing of garments, footwear, tourism; offshore oil and gas deposits discovered.

History

Originally part of the Kingdom of Funan, it was taken over by the Khmers in the 6c. From the 15c it was in dispute with the Vietnamese and the Thais. In 1863 it was established as a French protectorate, and it became part of Indochina in 1887. It gained independence from France in 1953, with Prince Sihanouk as Prime Minister. From the late 1960s there was growing insurgency led by the Khmer Rouge, a communist guerrilla force, and in 1970 the monarchy was overthrown in a right-wing coup and the country was renamed the Khmer Republic. Fighting throughout the country between communist and nationalist factions also involved troops from North and South Vietnam and the USA. In 1975 Phnom Penh surrendered to the Khmer Rouge, and the following year the Republic of Democratic Kampuchea was proclaimed. An attempt to reform the economy on cooperative lines and the introduction of an extreme and brutal regime by Pol Pot in 1975–8 caused the deaths of an estimated 2.5 million people. There was further fighting in 1977–8, and Phnom Penh was captured by the Vietnamese in 1979, causing the Khmer Rouge to flee. The Vietnamese immediately established a government in Cambodia led by Heng Samrin, but fighting with the Khmer Rouge guerrillas and Sihanouk's nationalist forces did not stop until the Vietnamese withdrawal in 1987–9. In 1983 an anti-Vietnamese government-in-exile (the Coalition Government of Democratic Kampuchea) was recognized by the UN. In 1989 the name of Cambodia was restored. Under a UN peace plan agreed in 1991 and after a period of transitional government under the UN, in 1993 a new constitution was adopted and multiparty elections took place. In the new democratic monarchy, Prince Sihanouk became king, his son Prince Norodom Ranariddh was appointed Prime Minister, and Hun Sen, a former leader of the Vietnamese-backed government, became second Prime Minister. The Khmer Rouge continued guerrilla warfare until 1996, when internal divisions caused it to weaken; Pol Pot died in 1998 and the remaining Khmer Rouge surrendered in 1999. Meanwhile the ruling coalition suffered divisions; in 1997 Hun Sen and his armed supporters ousted Prince Ranariddh, but in the 1998 election Hun Sen's party failed to win a large enough majority to form a government and the coalition with the royalist party has continued since. King Sihanouk abdicated in 2004 in favour of his son Norodom Sihamoni.

CAMEROON

Official name Republic of Cameroon
Local name Cameroun
Location A republic in West Africa, bounded to the south-west by Equatorial Guinea; to the south by Gabon; to the south-east by Congo; to the east by the Central African Republic; to the north-east by Chad; and to the north-west by Nigeria
Area 475 439 sq km/183 519 sq mi
Capital Yaoundé
Chief town Douala
Population 18 468 000 (2008e)

Time zone GMT +1
Currency 1 CFA Franc (CFAFr) = 100 centimes
Languages French, English; many local languages are also spoken
Religions Christianity 40%, traditional beliefs 40%, Islam 20%
Ethnic groups Cameroon Highlanders 31%, Equatorial Bantu 19%, Kirdi 11%, Fulani 10%, North-western Bantu 8%, Eastern Nigritic 7%, other African 13%, non-African 1%

Physical description

Equatorial rainforest on the low coastal plain rising to a central plateau of over 1300m/4265ft; the western region is forested and mountainous, rising to 4070m/13352ft at Mount Cameroon, an active volcano and the highest peak in West Africa; the north-central land rises towards the Massif d'Adamaoua; low savannah and semi-desert plains in the north towards Lake Chad; rivers flowing from the central plateau to the Gulf of Guinea include the River Sanaga.

Climate

The north has a wet season in April–September, with the remainder of the year being dry; annual rainfall in the north is 1000–1750mm; the equatorial south experiences rain throughout the year, with two wet seasons and two dry seasons; Yaoundé, in the south, has an average annual rainfall of 4030mm and maximum daily temperatures ranging between 27°C and 30°C; a small part of Mount Cameroon receives over 10000mm of rain annually.

Government

Governed by a President, a Prime Minister and government ministers, and a unicameral National Assembly; a 1996 constitutional amendment providing for a second legislative chamber has not been implemented.

Economy

Poor country, dependent on foreign aid; main industries based on natural resources, including oil and petroleum products, timber, aluminium and agricultural products; agriculture employs c.70% of the workforce; cash crops are cocoa (world's fifth largest producer), coffee, cotton and rubber; tourism is growing, especially to national parks and reserves.

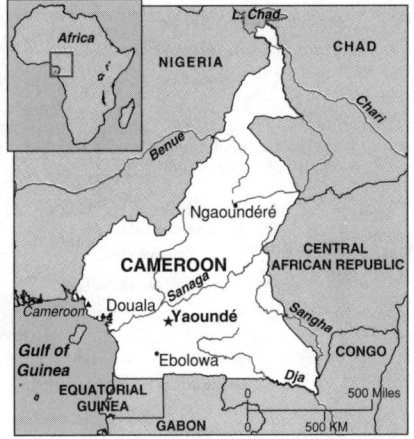

History

The country was first explored by the Portuguese navigator Fernando Po, and later by traders from Spain, the Netherlands and Britain. It became a German protectorate, Kamerun, in 1884, and after World War I was divided into French and British Cameroon in 1919, which was confirmed by the League of Nations mandate in 1922. The UN turned mandates into trusteeships in 1946. French Cameroon became independent as the Republic of Cameroon in 1960, while the northern sector of British Cameroon voted to become part of Nigeria, and the southern sector part of Cameroon; the Federal Republic of Cameroon was established, with separate parliaments, in 1961. The federal system was abolished in 1972, and the country's name was changed to the United Republic of Cameroon; the word 'United' was dropped from the name in 1984. From 1972 to 1992 it was ruled by one party, the Cameroon People's Democratic Movement, with Paul Biya as President from 1982. Political pluralism was restored in 1992, and in multiparty elections Biya was re-elected president and the ruling party was returned to power. Both have continued to hold power since in elections whose fairness has been disputed by the opposition. Cameroon joined the Commonwealth of Nations in 1995, the first country to do so that has never been fully under British rule at any point in its history.

CANADA

Official name Canada
Local name Canada
Location An independent country in North America, bounded to the south by the USA; to the west by the Pacific Ocean; to the north-west by Alaska; to the north by the Arctic Ocean and Baffin Bay; to the north-east by the Davis Strait; and to the east by the Labrador Sea and the Atlantic Ocean
Area 9970610 sq km/3848655 sq mi

Capital Ottawa
Chief towns Calgary, Edmonton, Montréal, Québec, Toronto, Vancouver, Victoria, Winnipeg
Population 33213000 (2008e)
Time zone –3.5/–8
Currency 1 Canadian Dollar (C$, Can$) = 100 cents
Languages English, French
Religions Christianity 70% (RC 43%, Prot 23%, other Christian 4%), Islam 2%, others/unaffiliated 12%, none 16%

Physical description

Main topographical divisions are: the mountainous Appalachian-Acadian region (Nova Scotia, New Brunswick); the Canadian Shield, which comprises over half the country, in the north and east; the St Lawrence–Great Lakes lowlands (south Quebec, Ontario); the interior plains (prairies) south and west of the Shield; the western mountains, including the Rocky, Cassiar, Mackenzie and Coast ranges; and the Arctic archipelago (Nunavut); the Coast Mountains flank a rugged, heavily-indented Pacific coastline, rising to 5950m/19520ft at Mount Logan, the highest peak in Canada; the Arctic coast is permanently ice-bound or obstructed by ice floes, except for Hudson Bay (frozen for c.9 months each year); major rivers include the Yukon and Mackenzie in the west, North Saskatchewan, South Saskatchewan, Saskatchewan and Athabasca in the centre, and Ottawa and St Lawrence in the east; the Great Lakes occupy the south-east of Ontario; 44% of land area is forested.

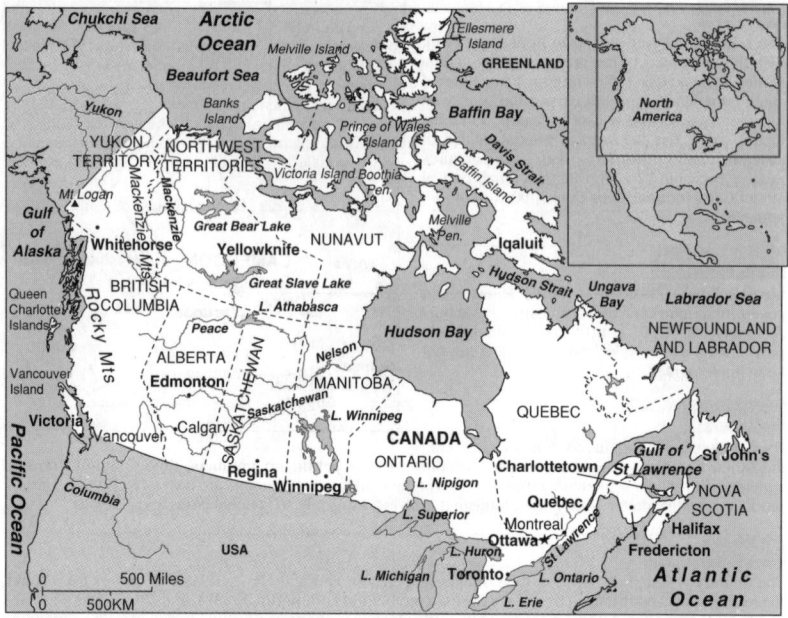

Climate

Varies, from arctic and sub-arctic in the north to temperate in the south; cold air from the Arctic sweeps south and east in winter and spring; mild winters and warm summers on the west coast and some inland valleys of British Columbia; winter temperatures on the Atlantic shores are warmer than those of the interior, but summer temperatures are lower; much of the southern interior has warm summers and long, cold winters; tornadoes occur in the southern interior in May–September.

Government

Governed by a Governor-General (representing the British monarch, who is head of state), a Prime Minister and Federal Cabinet, and a bicameral Federal Parliament, comprising a Senate and a House of Commons. Each of the ten provinces and three territories has its own Lieutenant-Governor (Commissioner in the territories), executive council and legislative assembly.

Economy

Highly developed industrialized and diversified market economy, with services (finance, real estate, tourism) the largest sector; abundant natural resources are basis of major industries, including timber, pulp and newsprint (world's largest exporter), minerals, especially uranium (world's largest producer), diamonds (world's third largest producer), asbestos, zinc, silver, nickel, potash, gypsum, molybdenum, sulphur, oil (especially Alberta), natural gas and fisheries; manufacturing industries produce motor vehicles and parts, iron and steel, industrial machinery, aircraft and telecommunications equipment, chemicals and plastics; leading agricultural producer, particularly of wheat (world's second largest exporter), barley, oilseed, fruit, vegetables and dairy products.

Ethnic groups

- British origin 28%
- mixed 26%
- French origin 23%
- other European 15%
- Amerindian 2%
- others 6%

History

There is evidence of Viking settlement in c.1000. The country was visited by Cabot in 1497, and in 1528 St John's, Newfoundland, was established as the shore base for the English fisheries. The St Lawrence was explored for France by Cartier in 1534, and Newfoundland was claimed for England in 1583, making it England's first overseas colony. Champlain founded the city of Quebec in 1608. The Hudson's Bay Company was founded in 1670, and in the late 17c there was conflict between the British and the colonists of New France. Britain gained large areas from the 1713 Treaty of Utrecht. After the Seven Years' War, during which Wolfe captured Quebec (1759), the Treaty of Paris gave Britain almost all of France's possessions in North America. The province of Quebec was created in 1774, and migration of loyalists from the USA after the American Revolution led to the division of Quebec into Upper and Lower Canada, reunited as Canada in 1841. The Dominion of Canada was created in 1867 by a confederation of Quebec, Ontario, Nova Scotia and New Brunswick. Rupert's Land and Northwest Territories were bought from the Hudson's Bay Company in 1869–70, and were later joined by Manitoba (1870), British Columbia (1871, after promise of a transcontinental railroad), Prince Edward Island (1873), Yukon (1898, following the Klondike Gold Rush), Alberta and Saskatchewan (1905) and Newfoundland (1949). In 1982 the Canada Act gave Canada full responsibility for its constitution. There was recurring political tension in the latter part of the 20c arising from the French-Canadian separatist movement in Quebec, and from the desire for autonomy of the Native American and Inuit populations; a 1992 referendum approved the creation of the vast autonomous territory of Nunavut for the Inuit people, and this was implemented in 1999. Although independence for Quebec was rejected in a 1995 referendum in the province, in 2006 the parliament agreed that the Quebecois should be considered a 'nation' within Canada.

Provinces

Province († Territory)	Area sq km	sq mi	Provincial capital
Alberta	661 848	255 472	Edmonton
British Columbia	944 735	364 667	Victoria
Manitoba	647 797	250 050	Winnipeg
New Brunswick	72 908	28 142	Fredericton
Newfoundland and Labrador	405 212	156 412	St John's
Northwest Territories†	1 346 106	519 597	Yellowknife
Nova Scotia	55 284	21 340	Halifax
Nunavut†	2 093 190	807 971	Iqaluit
Ontario	1 076 395	415 488	Toronto
Prince Edward Island	5 660	2 185	Charlottetown
Quebec	1 542 056	595 234	Quebec City
Saskatchewan	651 036	251 300	Regina
Yukon Territory†	482 443	186 223	Whitehorse

■ Canary Islands ▶ Spain

CAPE VERDE

Official name Republic of Cape Verde
Local name Cabo Verde
Location An island group in the Atlantic Ocean, lying off the west coast of Africa
Area 4033 sq km/1557 sq mi
Capital Praia
Chief town Mindelo
Population 427 000 (2008e)

Time zone GMT –1
Currency 1 Escudo Caboverdiano (CVEsc) = 100 centavos
Language Portuguese; Crioulo is widely spoken
Religions Christianity 98% (RC), others 1%, none/unaffiliated 1%
Ethnic groups Creole (mixed) 71%, African 28%, European 1%

Physical description

The islands are of volcanic origin, mostly mountainous; the highest peak is Pico do Cano at 2829m/9281ft, an active volcano on Fogo Island; coastal plains are semi-desert; savannah or thin forest lies on the mountains; fine, sandy beaches on most islands.

Climate

Located at the northern limit of the tropical rain belt; low and unreliable rainfall, mainly in August–October; cooler and damper in the uplands; severe drought can occur; the tropical heat is subject to only a small temperature range throughout the year.

Government

Governed by a President, a Prime Minister and Council of Ministers, and a unicameral National Assembly.

Economy

Poor country, dependent on foreign aid and remittances from expatriate workers; recent growth based on service sector (tourism, shipping, transport); industry includes food processing, beverages, garments, footwear, fishing and fish processing, salt mining; agriculture constrained by aridity and drought, causing periodic food shortages; irrigated land produces bananas, sweet potatoes, sugar cane, coffee, peanuts.

History

The islands were colonized by the Portuguese in the 15c and used as a penal colony. Administered with Portuguese Guinea until 1879, the group became an overseas province of Portugal in 1951. It gained independence in 1975 after a campaign by the African Party for the Independence of Cape Verde and Guinea-Bissau (PAICV), which remained the only legal party (dropping Guinea-Bissau from its name in 1980) until multiparty elections took place in 1991. That year the new Movement for Democracy came to power. The PAICV returned to power in the 2001 elections.

■ **Cayman Islands ▶ United Kingdom**

CENTRAL AFRICAN REPUBLIC

Official name Central African Republic
Local name République Centrafricaine (French), Ködörösêse tî Bêafrîka (Sango)
Location A republic in central Africa, bounded to the north by Chad; to the north-east by Sudan; to the south by the Democratic Republic of the Congo and Congo; and to the west by Cameroon
Area 622 984 sq km / 240 534 sq mi
Capital Bangui

Chief towns Berbérati, Bouar, Bossangoa
Population 4 444 000 (2008e)
Time zone GMT +1
Currency 1 CFA Franc (CFAFr) = 100 centimes
Language French, Sangho
Religions Christianity 50% (Prot 25%, RC 25%), traditional beliefs 35%, Islam 15%
Ethnic groups Baya 33%, Banda 27%, Mandjia 13%, Sara 10%, Mboum 7%, others 10%

Physical description

Occupies a plateau forming the watershed between the Chad and Congo river basins; most northern rivers drain towards Lake Chad, and southbound rivers flow towards the River Ubangi; the highest ground is in the north-east (Massif des Bongos) and north-west; highest point is Mont Ngaoui (1420m / 4659ft).

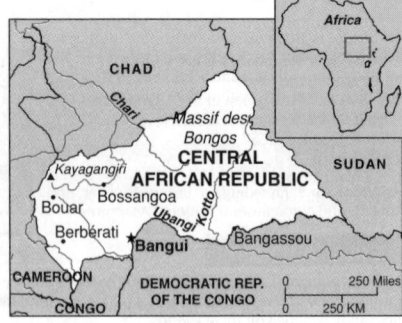

Climate

Tropical, with a rainy season in the north between May and September; average annual rainfall between 875mm and 1000mm; more equatorial climate in the south.

Government

Governed by a President, a Prime Minister and government ministers, and a unicameral National Assembly.

Economy

Very poor country, dependent on foreign aid; rich natural resources, much unexploited, although diamond-mining and forestry are major industries; economic mainstay is agriculture, accounting for over 50% of GDP; c.85% of the workforce is engaged in subsistence agriculture; cash crops are cotton, coffee and tobacco.

History

For a time part of French Equatorial Africa (known as Ubangi Shari), it became an autonomous republic within the French community in 1958 and gained independence in 1960 with David Dacko as president. He was overthrown in 1966 in a coup led by Col. Bokassa, who established a monarchy known as the Central African Empire in 1976 with himself as emperor. Bokassa was deposed and fled in 1979 (he returned in 1986 for trial and was found guilty of murder and other crimes in 1987). The country reverted to a republic and David Dacko became President until he was ousted by a military coup in 1981. Civilian rule returned in 1986, and in 1992 the constitution was amended to allow for opposition parties and to reduce the powers of the president. Elections the following year brought in a coalition government. The political situation remained unstable, with several coup attempts in recent years, culminating in a successful coup in 2003 which installed General François Bozize as President. A new constitution was approved in 2004 and in 2005 Bozize was elected president.

CHAD

Official name Republic of Chad
Local name Tchad
Location A landlocked republic in north central Africa, bounded to the north by Libya; to the east by Sudan; to the south by the Central African Republic; and to the west by Cameroon, Nigeria and Niger
Area 1 284 640 sq km/495 871 sq mi
Capital N'Djamena (also Ndjamena)
Chief towns Moundou, Sarh, Abéché

Population 10 111 000 (2008e)
Time zone GMT +1
Currency 1 CFA Franc (CFAFr) = 100 centimes
Languages French, Arabic; many local languages are also spoken, of which the most widely used is Sara
Religions Islam 53%, Christianity 34%, traditional beliefs 7%, others 6%
Ethnic groups Over 200 ethnic groups, of which the largest are Sara (28%) and Arab (13%)

Physical description

A mostly arid, semi-desert plateau at the edge of the Sahara Desert with an average altitude of 200–500m/656–1640ft; isolated massifs along the eastern border with Sudan rise to 1500m/4921ft; the Tibesti Mountains in the north rise to 3415m/11 204ft at Emi Koussi; vegetation is generally desert scrub or steppe; the Logone and Chari rivers drain from the southern hills into Lake Chad; most people live in the fertile south.

Climate

The south is tropical, with moderate rainfall in May–October, but dry for the rest of the year; the hot and arid north is almost rainless; the central plain is hot and dry, with a brief rainy season in June–September.

Government

Governed by a President, a Prime Minister and Cabinet, and a unicameral National Assembly.

Economy

Poor country, formerly dependent on international aid and agriculture but starting to experience an oil boom since fields in the Doba basin began production in 2003; subsistence agriculture, herding and fishing employ 80% of the workforce; main cash crops are cotton and livestock; salt is mined around Lake Chad.

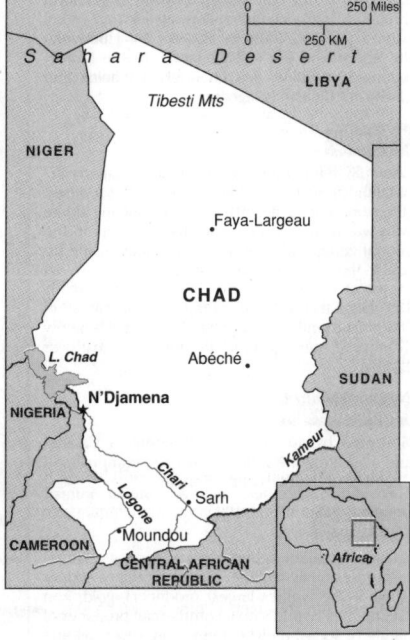

History

Chad was part of French Equatorial Africa in the 19c, became a French colony in 1920, and gained independence in 1960. Since independence it has been politically unstable, owing to tension between the Muslim Arab north and the Christian and animist African south, different factions attracting support from Libya and France. After a number of coups in the 1960s and 1970s, factional fighting led to civil war until 1987, when Libya was forced to withdraw. In 1990 another Libyan-backed coup brought to power Idriss Déby. Under Déby, there was gradual democratization and a new constitution was introduced in 1996. A rebellion by the

Nations of the World

Movement for Democracy and Justice in Chad led to civil war in 1998, and despite several peace agreements, violence continues and Déby's regime was nearly overthrown in 2006 and 2008. Chad has also experienced an influx of thousands of Sudanese refugees from Darfur since early 2004, and its forces have clashed with Sudanese militia on the border.

■ **Channel Islands ► United Kingdom**

CHILE

Official name Republic of Chile
Local name Chile
Location A republic in south-western South America, bounded to the west by the Pacific Ocean; to the east by Argentina; to the north-east by Bolivia; and to the north-west by Peru
Area 756 626 sq km / 292 058 sq mi
Capital Santiago
Chief towns Valparaíso, Concepción, Talcahuano, Antofagasta, Viña del Mar
Population 16 454 000 (2008e)
Time zone GMT −4
Currency 1 Chilean Peso (Ch$) = 100 centavos
Language Spanish
Religions Christianity 87% (RC 70%, Prot 15%), others 5%, none 8%
Ethnic groups white and white–Amerindian 95%, Mapuche 4%, other Amerindian 1%

Physical description

A long narrow country lying between the Andes and the South Pacific Ocean; the highest point is Ojos del Salado (6910m/22 660ft); the Andes rise in the north to 6732m/22 057ft at Llullaillaco, declining in height in the centre and south; Chile extends from the arid Atacama Desert in the north through a fertile central valley, 40–60km/25–40mi wide at 1200m/3937ft in altitude, lying between the Andes and the coastal range, to the heavily indented coastline, sea channels, ice-fields and glaciers of Chilean Patagonia.

Climate

Generally temperate but highly varied (spans 37° of latitude); extreme aridity in the northern desert (the world's driest desert); a Mediterranean climate with warm, wet winters and dry summers in the central zone; and cool, wet and windy in the far south; the average temperature at Valparaíso on the coast varies from below 12°C (July) to nearly 18°C (January), with an average annual rainfall of 505mm; at Santiago (high altitude), rainfall is below 375mm; at Antofagasta in the north, it is just over 12mm.

Government

Governed by an executive President, a Cabinet and a bicameral National Congress, comprising a Chamber of Deputies and a Senate.

Economy

Emerging market economy; based on its natural resources and agriculture; mining produces copper (Chile is the world's largest producer), gold, iron ore, nitrates (world's only commercial producer of nitrate of soda), molybdenum, iron, silver; oil and gas production declining; other major industries are forestry and wood products, fishing and fish products, agriculture (fruit, vegetables, cereals, meat, wool) and wine-making.

History

Originally occupied by South American Indians, the arrival of the Spanish in the 16c made Chile part

of the Viceroyalty of Peru. In 1810 it declared its independence from Spain, which resulted in war until the Spanish were defeated in 1818. Border disputes with Bolivia, Peru and Argentina brought a Chilean victory in the War of the Pacific (1879–84). In the late 1920s economic unrest led to a military dictatorship until 1931. The Marxist coalition government of President Allende was ousted in 1973 and replaced by a military junta led by General Pinochet, who banned all political activity, resulting in considerable political opposition, both at home and abroad. A constitution providing for an eventual return to democracy came into effect in 1981, and after 1988 there were limited political reforms. Free elections were held in late 1989, and in 1990 the National Congress was restored and Pinochet's rule ended. Various attempts were made to bring Pinochet to trial for human rights atrocities committed during his time in office, but none had been successful by the time of his death in 2006. Since the return to democracy, the military's influence on government has been reduced and the country has been relatively stable.

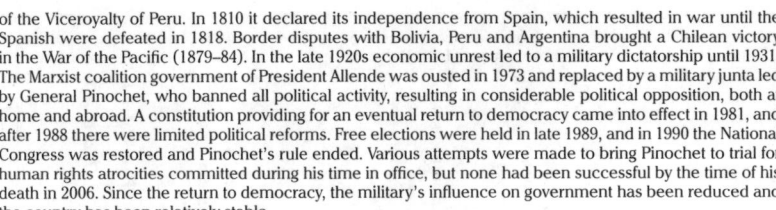

CHINA

Official name People's Republic of China
Local name Zhong Guo
Location A socialist state in central and eastern Asia, bounded to the north-west by Kyrgyzstan and Kazakhstan; to the north by Mongolia; to the north-east by Russia; to the east by North Korea, the Yellow Sea and the East China Sea; to the south by the South China Sea, Vietnam, Laos, Myanmar (Burma), India, Bhutan and Nepal; and to the west by India, Pakistan, Afghanistan and Tajikistan
Area 9 597 000 sq km / 3 704 000 sq mi
Capital Beijing
Chief towns Shanghai, Tianjin, Shenyang, Wuhan, Guangzhou
Population 1 330 044 000 (2008e)
Time zone GMT +8
Currency 1 Renminbi or Yuan (RMBY, $, Y) = 10 jiao = 100 fen
Languages standard Chinese (Putonghua) or Mandarin, also Yue (Cantonese), Wu, Minbei, Minnan, Xiang, Gan, Hakka; minority languages
Religions Officially atheist; five state-registered religions include Daoism, Buddhism, Christianity (RC and Prot) 4%, Islam 2%
Ethnic groups Han 92%, others (includes Zhuang, Uygur, Hui, Tujia, Yi, Tibetan, Miao, Manchu, Mongol, Dong, Yao, Buyi, Korean) 8%

Physical description

Over two-thirds of the country is upland hill, mountain and plateau; the highest mountains are in the west, where the Tibetan Plateau rises to an average altitude of 4000m/13 123ft ('the roof of the world'); the highest point is Mount Everest (8850m/29 035ft); the land descends to the desert or semi-desert of Sinkiang and Inner Mongolia north and east of the Tibetan Plateau; the broad and fertile plains of Manchuria lie in the north-east, separated from North Korea by the densely forested Changpai Shan uplands; further east and south, the prosperous Sichuan Basin is drained by the Yangtze River; the southern plains and east coast, with rich, fertile soils, are heavily populated.

Climate

Varied, with seven zones: (1) north-east China has cold winters, with strong north winds and warm, humid summers, but unreliable rainfall; in Manchuria, the rivers are frozen for four to six months each year, and snow lies for 100–150 days; (2) central China has warm and humid summers, sometimes with typhoons or tropical cyclones on the coast; (3) south China, partly within the tropics, is the wettest area in summer; frequent typhoons (especially in July–October); (4) south-west China has summer temperatures moderated by altitude, winters are mild with little rain; summers are wet in the mountains; (5) Tibet autonomous region, a high plateau surrounded by mountains, has severe winters with frequent light snow and hard frost, summers are warm, but nights are cold; (6) Xinjiang and the western interior has an arid desert climate, cold winters, and well distributed rainfall throughout the year; (7) Inner Mongolia has an extreme continental-type climate, with cold winters and warm summers, and strong winds in winter and spring.

Government

Governed by an elected National People's Congress of c.3000 deputies, who appoint a State Council (led by a Prime Minister) and elect a President. The Chinese Communist Party is the ruling party and its leadership is formally elected by the party congress, held every five years.

Economy

Centrally planned economy liberalized since 1980s to quasi-market economy with large private sector and strong international trade; industrial sector now highly diversified and includes heavy industry (iron, steel, minerals, machinery, armaments, textiles), manufacturing (garments, household goods, consumables) and construction; coal, oil and hydro-electric power production (from Three Gorges Dam) increasing; agriculture still employs about 40% of workforce, producing rice, cereals, vegetables, peanuts, tea, fruit, cotton, silk, oilseed, livestock; financial sector and tourism of growing economic importance.

History

Chinese civilization is believed to date from the Xia Dynasty of c.2200–1767 BC; the Shang Dynasty (c.1766–

Nations of the World

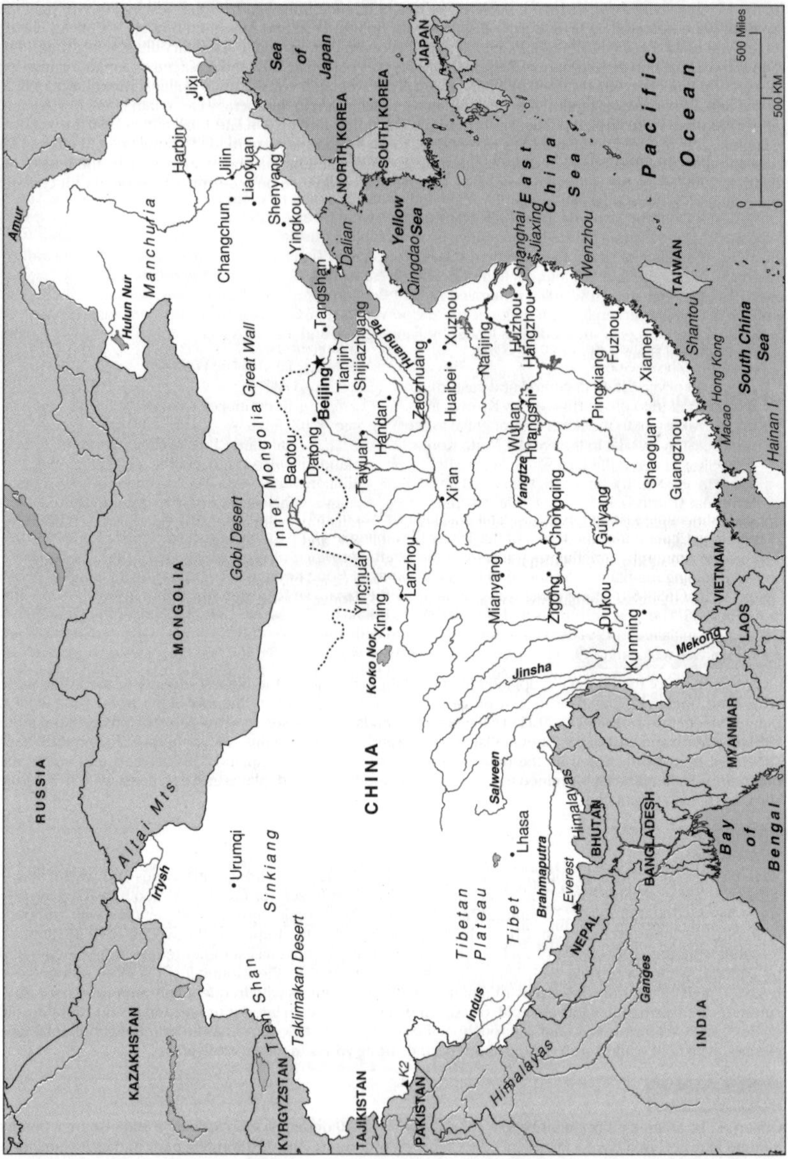

Map of China with surrounding countries including RUSSIA, KAZAKHSTAN, KYRGYZSTAN, TAJIKISTAN, PAKISTAN, INDIA, NEPAL, BHUTAN, BANGLADESH, MYANMAR, LAOS, VIETNAM, MONGOLIA, NORTH KOREA, SOUTH KOREA, JAPAN, TAIWAN.

1122 BC) saw the introduction of bronze, and was presided over by a chariot-riding warrior aristocracy; the Western Zhou Dynasty ruled over a prosperous feudal agricultural society (c.1066–771 BC); the Eastern Zhou Dynasty (770–256 BC) was the era of Confucius and Lao Zi (Lao-tzu); the Qin Dynasty (221–206 BC) unified the warring states and provided a system of centralized control; there was expansion west during the Western and Eastern Han dynasties (206 BC–AD 220). From the 4c, a series of northern dynasties was set up by invaders, with several dynasties in the south; these were gradually reunited during the Sui (581–618) and Tang (618–907) dynasties. After a period of partition into Five Dynasties (907–60) there emerged the Song Dynasty (960–1279), remembered for literature, philosophy and inventions (eg movable type, gunpowder); Genghis Khan established the Mongol Yuan Dynasty (1279–1368). There followed visits by Europeans, such as Marco Polo, in the 13–14c, and the Ming Dynasty (1368–1644) increased contacts with the West. It was overthrown by Manchus, who ruled until 1911, and enlarged the empire to include Manchuria, Mongolia, Tibet, Taiwan and parts of Turkestan. Opposition to foreign penetration led to the Opium Wars (1839–42, 1858–60), in which defeat compelled China

to open ports to foreign trade. The Sino–Japanese War (1895) gave control of Taiwan and Korea to Japan. The Boxer Rising (1898–1900) was a massive protest against foreign influence. The Republic of China was founded by Sun Yat-sen (1912) after the fall of the Qing Dynasty, but was followed by chaos and an era of regional warlords. Unification came under Jiang Jieshi (Chiang Kai-shek), who made Nanjing the capital in 1928. Conflict between nationalists and communists led to the Long March (1934–5), with the communists moving to north-west China under Mao Zedong (Mao Tse-tung). The deeply corrupt nationalist regime was defeated in 1950 and withdrew to Taiwan. The People's Republic of China was proclaimed in 1949, with its capital at Beijing (Peking). The first Five-Year Plan (1953–7) was a period of nationalization and collectivization; the Great Leap Forward (1958–9) emphasized local authority and the establishment of rural communes, but this attempt to accelerate industrial and agricultural progress resulted in a famine in which 30–40 million died; the Cultural Revolution was initiated by Mao Zedong in 1966 and plunged the country into ten years of political and social turmoil ended only by Mao's death in 1976. Many policies were reversed after Mao's death, and with the return to power of Deng Xiaoping there began a drive towards rapid industrialization and greater trade relations with the West. The killing of student-led pro-democracy protesters in Tiananmen Square, Beijing, in 1989 provoked international outrage and the introduction of economic sanctions, but these had no effect and were relaxed after 1990. Gradual steps towards a controlled market economy continued throughout the 1990s and by the early 21c China was emerging as a major economic power. In 1997 China entered a new era with the death of Deng Xiaoping, who was succeeded as leader by Jiang Zemin, and the handover in July of the former British Crown Colony of Hong Kong.

❖Hong Kong

Area 16 sq km/6 sq mi	Population 7 019 000 (2008e)

History

Britain first occupied Hong Kong during the first Opium War in 1841, and it was officially ceded 'in perpetuity' to Britain by China under the terms of the Treaty of Nanjing in 1842. Under British rule, Hong Kong became a free-trade entrepôt, attracting migrants from the nearby province of Guangdong. The Kowloon Peninsula on the adjoining mainland was added to Britain's colony of Hong Kong in 1860, following the second of the Opium Wars (1856–60). Hong Kong was occupied by the Japanese in World War II, but re-occupied by the British in 1945. The New Territories had been leased to Britain for 99 years in 1898, and, under the Sino–British Declaration initialled in 1984 by which Britain agreed to cede the whole of Hong Kong at the end of the lease, the region was restored to China in 1997. Tung Chee-Hwa was appointed the first chief executive of the new Hong Kong Special Administrative Region and pledged to abide by the 'one country, two systems' plan, also outlined in the 1984 declaration, to preserve the existing way of life.

❖Macao

Area 1067 sq km/412 sq mi	Population 545 700 (2008e)

History

Macao was used as a base for Catholic missionaries in the 17c and 18c as well as being a port of call for British traders on their way to Canton in the early 19c. Until the 19c, Macao was a flourishing trade centre, but the silting of its harbour and increasing competition from Hong Kong led to its decline. With the overthrow of the Salazar dictatorship in Portugal in 1975 and the new government's commitment to decolonization, China exercised greater influence in the colony. In 1987 it was agreed that Macao would be formally returned to Chinese control in 1999 under the same arrangements applying to the British return of Hong Kong to China in 1997 (ie that the capitalist system should remain in place).

COLOMBIA

Official name Republic of Colombia
Local name Colombia
Location A republic in the north-west of South America. It is bounded to the north by Panama and the Caribbean Sea; to the west by the Pacific Ocean; to the east by Venezuela; to the south-east by Brazil; and to the south by Ecuador and Peru
Area 1 140 105 sq km/440 080 sq mi
Capital Bogotá

Chief towns Medellín, Cali, Barranquilla
Population 45 014 000 (2008e)
Time zone GMT −5
Currency 1 Colombian Peso (Col$) = 100 centavos
Language Spanish
Religions Christianity 90% (mainly RC), others 10%
Ethnic groups mestizo 58%, white 20%, mulatto 14%, black 4%, mixed black–Amerindian 3%, Amerindian 1%

Physical description

Caribbean and Pacific coastlines, with several island possessions; on the mainland, the Andes run north to south, branching into three ranges dividing narrow coastal plains in the north and west from the extensive forested lowlands of the Amazon basin; the highest peaks are Pico Cristóbal Colón and Pico Simón Bolívar, both 5775m/18947ft; the Cordillera Oriental in the east surrounds large areas of plateau; rivers flow to the Pacific Ocean, Caribbean Sea and Amazon.

Climate

Mostly tropical, modified by altitude; hot and humid in the north-west and west, with annual rainfall of over 2500mm; the Caribbean coast has less rainfall and a dry period (December–April); the annual rainfall of the Andes is 1000–2500mm, falling evenly throughout the year; hot and humid tropical lowlands in the east, with annual rainfall of 2000–2500mm.

Government

Governed by an executive President, a Cabinet and a bicameral Congress, comprising a Senate and a Chamber of Representatives).

Economy

Growing and diversifying economy; development of the interior hampered by lack of transport infrastructure; exploits coal, oil, natural gas and hydro-electric resources, gold, platinum, silver, emeralds, iron ore and other minerals; major cash crops are coffee, sugar, rice, bananas, cut flowers, cotton, livestock products; manufactures textiles, paper products and leather goods. Widespread illegal drug trafficking (especially cocaine).

History

From the early 16c the country was conquered by the Spanish, who dominated the Amerindian peoples. Governed by Spain within the Viceroyalty of Peru, it later became part of the Viceroyalty of New Granada. After the campaigns of Simón Bolívar, it gained independence in 1819, and formed a union with Ecuador, Venezuela and Panama as Gran Colombia; the union ended with the secession of Venezuela in 1829, and Ecuador in 1830, leaving New Granada to adopt the name Colombia. Colombia suffered civil war (known as La Violencia) in the 1950s, and there has been considerable political unrest since the 1980s because of left-wing insurgency and the activities of drugs cartels. There is widespread illegal cocaine trafficking, which successive governments have been attempting to eradicate with help from the USA since 1989. A new constitution was adopted in 1991, but a state of emergency was declared in 1992 because of violence by the drugs traffickers, insurgents and paramilitaries. These have presented less of a threat to civil order in recent years, but the government has been unable to suppress or reach a negotiated settlement with the insurgents, although paramilitary groups are being disarmed.

COMOROS

Official name Union of the Comoros	Capital Moroni
Local name Comores	Population 732 000 (2008e)
Location A group of three volcanic islands (Ngazidja (formerly Grand Comore), Anjouan and Mohéli) at the northern end of the Mozambique Channel, between Mozambique and Madagascar	Time zone GMT +3
	Currency 1 Comoran Franc (KMF) = 100 centimes
	Languages French, Arabic, Shikomoro or Comoran (a local Arabic–Swahili dialect)
	Religions Islam 98% (Sunni), Christianity 2% (RC)
Area 1862 sq km/719 sq mi	Ethnic groups Comorian 97%, others 3%

Physical description

The island interiors vary from steep mountains to low hills; the highest point is Le Karthala (2360m/7743ft), an active volcano on Ngazidja.

Climate

Tropical; May–October is the dry season and November–April is the hot, humid season; average temperatures are 20°C in July and 28°C in November.

Government

Governed by an executive President of the Union (the post rotates among the elected presidents of the three main islands), a Cabinet and a unicameral Assembly of the Union. Each of the three main islands has its own President, government and legislative assembly.

Economy

Very poor country, dependent on foreign aid and remittances from expatriate workers; main activities are agriculture (vanilla, copra, cloves, coconuts, bananas, cassava), tourism and perfume distillation.

History

Under French control from 1843 to 1912, it became a French Overseas Territory in 1947. Internal political autonomy was achieved in 1961, and unilateral independence was declared in 1975 by the Comorian President Ahmed Abdallah, who was deposed later that year. The island of Mayotte, however, decided to remain under French administration. Political instability has dogged the republic since independence, with a number of coups between 1976 and 1999, some supported by European mercenaries, and demands for greater autonomy by the three main islands. In 1997, Anjouan and Mohéli demanded to secede from the Comoros and return to French rule. Following a coup in 1999, the military took control and reunited the country. A new constitution in 2002 created a federal Union of the Comoros, with greater autonomy and individual presidents for the three islands.

CONGO

Official name Republic of the Congo; also sometimes known as Congo (Brazzaville)
Local name Congo
Location A west central African republic, bounded to the west by Gabon; to the north-west by Cameroon; to the north by the Central African Republic; to the east and south by the Democratic Republic of the Congo; and to the south-west by the Atlantic Ocean
Area 341 945 sq km/131 990 sq mi

Capital Brazzaville
Chief towns Pointe-Noire, Loubomo, Nkayi
Population 3 903 000 (2008e)
Time zone GMT +1
Currency 1 CFA Franc (CFAFr) = 100 centimes
Languages French, Kikongo, Lingala, Monokutuba
Religions Christianity 50% (mainly RC), traditional beliefs 48%, Islam 2%
Ethnic groups Kongo 48%, Sangha 20%, Teke 17%, Mbochi 12%, others 3%

Physical description

A short Atlantic coastline fringes a broad mangrove plain that rises inland to mountains reaching 900m/2953ft; the inland mountain ridge is deeply cut by the River Congo flowing south-west to the coast; beyond this ridge, the Niari Valley rises up through terraced hills to reach 1040m/3412ft at Mont de la Lékéti on the Gabon frontier; mainly covered by dense grassland, mangrove and rainforest; several rivers flow east and south to meet the Oubangui and Congo rivers, which form the eastern and southern borders.

Climate

Hot, humid, equatorial climate; annual rainfall is 1250–1750mm, decreasing near the Atlantic coast and in the south; temperatures vary little, with average daily maximum temperatures at Brazzaville 28°–33°C; the dry season is June–September.

Government

Governed by an executive President, a Cabinet and a bicameral Parliament consisting of a National Assembly and a Senate.

717

Economy

Poor country, with high external debt; dependent on oil; also produces phosphates, natural gas, lead, zinc, gold, diamonds; main industries are oil refining, forestry and wood processing, agriculture; main cash crops are sugar cane, cocoa and coffee.

History

The first European visitors to the area were the Portuguese, in the 15c. The French established a colonial presence there in the late 19c, and from 1908 to 1958 it was part of French Equatorial Africa, known as the 'Middle Congo'. It gained independence as the Republic of Congo in 1960, and in 1968 a military coup created the first Marxist state in Africa, renaming the country the People's Republic of the Congo. Marxism was renounced in 1990 and opposition parties were permitted. Elections took place in 1993 but the results were disputed and fighting between opposing ethnic and political groups ensued. A military coup in 1997 initiated a civil war that lasted until 2003. The subsequent peace is fragile, and some rebels remain active in the south, where many have turned to banditry.

DEMOCRATIC REPUBLIC OF THE CONGO

Official name Democratic Republic of the Congo
Local name Congo
Location A central African republic, bounded to the west by the Congo and the Atlantic Ocean; to the south-west by Angola; to the south-east by Zambia; to the east by Tanzania, Burundi, Rwanda and Uganda; to the north-east by Sudan; and to the north and north-west by the Central African Republic
Area 2 343 950 sq km/904 765 sq mi
Capital Kinshasa

Chief towns Lubumbashi, Kisangani, Mbuji-Mayi, Kananga
Population 66 514 000 (2008e)
Time zone GMT +1/+2
Currency 1 Congolese Franc (CF) = 100 centimes
Languages French, Kikongo, Kingwana, Lingala, Tshiluba
Religions Christianity 70% (RC 50%, Prot 20%), Islam 10%, others and traditional beliefs 20%
Ethnic groups Bantu and Hamitic 44%, others 56%

Physical description

The country lies mostly in the low-lying basin of the River Congo and its principal tributaries, the Lualaba and the Kasai; it rises in the east to a densely-forested plateau, which is bounded to the east by a chain of lakes (Albert, Edward, Kivu and Tanganyika) and volcanic mountains; the Ruwenzori Mountains in the north-east rise to 5110m/16765ft at Pic Marguerite on Mt Ngaliema (Mt Stanley); the Mitumbar Mountains lie further south; a narrow strip of land follows the River Congo to the Atlantic Ocean and a short 43km/27mi coastline.

Climate

Equatorial, with high temperatures, humidity and rainfall; the Equator crosses the north of the country, creating different climatic cycles either side of it, with the dry season falling in December–February in the north and May–September in the south; the average annual rainfall at Kisangani is 1700mm; the average maximum daily temperatures range between 28°C and 31°C.

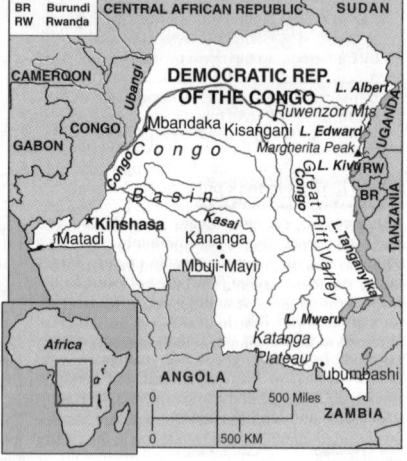

Government

Governed by a President, a Prime Minister and Cabinet, and a bicameral Parliament, comprising a National Assembly and a Senate.

Economy

Devastated by decades of mismanagement and civil war; renewed economic activity since 2002; rich natural resources (copper, cobalt, diamonds, tin, manganese, zinc, gold, silver, iron ore, rare-earth metals, offshore oil, hydro-electric power, timber); main industries are mining (diamonds, cobalt, copper, zinc), mineral processing, oil production, textiles, footwear, food processing, beverages, cigarettes, cement, forestry, ship repair; most of the population is involved in subsistence farming; cash crops include coffee, sugar, palm oil, rubber, tea, quinine.

History

The Bantu had settled most of the country by AD 1000, and the first Europeans to visit were the Portuguese, in 1482. There were expeditions by Henry Morton Stanley in 1874–7, and the country was claimed by King Leopold II of Belgium and recognized in 1885 at the Congress of Berlin as the Congo Free State. In 1908 it became a Belgian colony and was renamed the Belgian Congo. On gaining independence in 1960 it was renamed the Democratic Republic of the Congo, and the mineral-rich Katanga (later, Shaba) province claimed independence; this resulted in civil war which destroyed the new government of Patrice Lumumba. A UN peacekeeping force entered the country and remained until 1964. The following year President Mobutu Sese Seko seized power in a coup. He renamed the country Zaire in 1971 and at first was credited with introducing a hitherto unknown degree of stability; however, his regime became increasingly corrupt and unpopular. Further conflict erupted in 1977–8, and there were power struggles in the early 1990s, with violent ethnic unrest in Shaba, Kivu and Kasai provinces in 1993. In addition, over 1 million refugees from the civil war in Rwanda entered Zaire in 1994. In 1996 Zaire was invaded by a rebel army led by Laurent Kabila, an ethnic Tutsi, who the following year overthrew the government, forcing Mobutu into exile. Kabila was installed as head of state and the country was renamed the Democratic Republic of the Congo, but civil war with extensive foreign intervention continued. Kabila was assassinated in 2001 and succeeded by his son Joseph. Following disengagement in 2001 and peace talks in 2002, an interim government was formed in 2003, and elections took place in 2006. The presidential election was won by Joseph Kabila. A fragile peace has held in much of the country, except the eastern provinces, which have been subject to continued violence against civilians by a renegade militia, and a new insurgency in 2008.

COSTA RICA

Official name Republic of Costa Rica
Local name Costa Rica
Location The second smallest republic in Central America, bounded to the west by the Pacific Ocean; to the north by Nicaragua; to the east by the Caribbean; and to the south-east by Panama
Area 51 022 sq km/19 694 sq mi
Capital San José
Chief towns Cartago, Heredia, Liberia, Puntarenas, Limón

Population 4 196 000 (2008e)
Time zone GMT –6
Currency 1 Costa Rican Colón (CR₡) = 100 céntimos
Language Spanish
Religions Christianity 92% (RC 76%, Prot 16%), others 5%, none 3%
Ethnic groups white and mestizo 94%, black and mulatto 3%, Amerindian 1%, Chinese 1%, others 1%

Physical description

A chain of volcanic mountain ranges runs the length of Costa Rica (some volcanoes are active); the highest peak is Chirripó Grande (3819m/12529ft) in the Cordillera de Talamanca; the central plateau, the Meseta Central, covers an area of 5200 sq km/2000 sq mi at an altitude of 800–1400m/2600–4600ft; it is drained in the west by the Rio Grande into the Pacific and in the north-east by the River Reventazón into the Caribbean; between the mountains and the coast the land is low and swampy, with tropical forest as the land rises and lowland savannah in the north-west.

Climate

Tropical climate, with a small temperature range and abundant rainfall; more temperate in the central uplands; dry season is December–May; average annual rainfall is 3300mm, with much local variation; the average annual temperature is 26°–28°C.

Government

Governed by an executive President, a Cabinet and a unicameral Legislative Assembly.

Economy

Overcame 1990s economic problems, largely through diversification, and now prospering; main industry is tourism, especially 'eco-tourism' (one-third of area is national parkland or nature reserve); main industries produce computer components, medical supplies, textiles, foodstuffs, garments, construction materials, plastic goods; agriculture produces coffee, bananas, sugar, pineapples, beef and timber.

Nations of the World

Nations of the World

History

Visited by Columbus in 1502, it was named Costa Rica ('rich coast') in the belief that vast gold treasures existed. It was under Spanish rule from 1530 until it gained its independence in 1821, and was a member of the Central American Federation in 1824–39. During the 20c there was political unrest, with civil war in 1948, following which the army was disbanded. Since the civil war, power has alternated between the two main political parties. The 2006 presidential election was won by Arias Sánchez, president in 1986–90 and winner of the 1987 Nobel Peace Prize for devising a peace plan that ended the civil wars in neighbouring Nicaragua and in El Salvador.

CÔTE D'IVOIRE

Official name Republic of Côte d'Ivoire
Local name Côte d'Ivoire
Location A republic in West Africa, bounded to the south-west by Liberia; to the north-west by Guinea; to the north by Mali and Burkina Faso; to the east by Ghana; and to the south by the Gulf of Guinea
Area 320633 sq km/123764 sq mi
Capital Yamoussoukro
Chief towns Abidjan (former capital; still the administrative centre), Bouaké, Daloa, Man, Korhogo, Gagnoa
Population 20180000 (2008e)
Time zone GMT
Currency 1 CFA Franc (CFAFr) = 100 centimes
Language French; many local languages are also spoken
Religions Islam 39%, Christianity 33%, traditional beliefs 12%, none 16%
Ethnic groups Akan 42%, Voltaic 18%, Northern Mande 16%, Krou 11%, Southern Mande 10%, others 3%

Physical description

Sandy beaches and lagoons, backed by a broad rainforest-covered coastal plain in the south; the land rises towards savannah at 300–350m/980–1150ft in the centre; the Mount Nimba massif in the north-west is 1752m/5748ft at the highest point; rivers generally flow north to south.

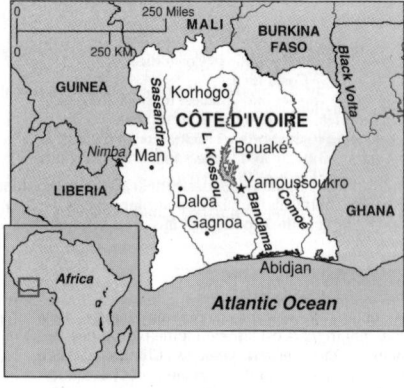

Climate

Tropical, varying with distance from the coast; rainfall decreases towards the north; the average annual rainfall at Abidjan is 2100mm; average temperatures are 25°–27°C.

Government

Governed by an executive President, a Prime Minister and Cabinet, and a unicameral National Assembly.

Economy

In decline owing to civil war; largely based on agriculture, which employs c.68% of the population; main cash crops are cocoa (world's largest producer), coffee (fifth largest robusta coffee producer), bananas, palm oil, rice, sugar, cotton, pineapples, rubber; industries include food processing, textiles, forestry, fishing, production of oil and hydro-electric power; oil refining, vehicle assembly.

History

Explored by the Portuguese in the 15c and the centre of the ivory trade from the 16c, the area came under French influence from 1842. Declared a French protectorate in 1889 and a French colony in 1893, it became a territory within French West Africa in 1904. It gained independence in 1960 as a one-party republic, with Felix Houphouët-Boigny as President. He introduced a multiparty system in 1990, when the elections were won by his Democratic Party of the Côte d'Ivoire (PDCI). He was succeeded on his death in 1993 by Henri Konan-Bédié, who ruled until overthrown in a 1999 coup by Robert Guëi. Guëi fled in 2000 after popular protests against rigged elections and Laurent Gbagbo, believed to be the winning candidate, became President. Political turmoil continued, leading to civil war from 2002 until 2003, when a ceasefire left the country divided between the government-controlled south and the rebel-held north, with international peacekeeping troops deployed in a buffer zone. Clashes have continued, however, and the peace agreement has not been fully implemented. A transitional coalition government was formed in 2005, and a new peace accord was signed in 2007. The 2005 elections have been delayed repeatedly but are now expected in early 2009.

CROATIA

Official name Republic of Croatia
Local name Hrvatska
Location A mountainous republic in eastern
Europe, bounded to the south-west and west by
the Adriatic Sea; to the north by Slovenia; to the
north-east by Hungary; to the east by Serbia; and
to the south-east by Bosnia and Herzegovina,
and Montenegro
Area 56 538 sq km/21 824 sq mi

Capital Zagreb
Chief towns Rijeka, Cakovec, Split, Zadar
Population 4 492 000 (2008e)
Time zone GMT +1
Currency 1 Kuna (Kn) = 100 lipa
Language Croatian
Religions Christianity 93% (RC 88%, Orthodox 5%),
Islam 1%, others 1%, none 5%
Ethnic groups Croat 90%, Serb 4%, others 6%

Physical description

The Adriatic coastline is 1778km/1105mi in length
with over 1180 islands and islets, backed by long
mountain ranges dividing the coast from the fertile
north-eastern plains; the highest point is Dinara
(1830m/6004ft); the main river is the Sava, flowing
across the northern plain.

Climate

Continental; hot summers and cold winters; milder
on coast.

Government

Governed by a President, a Prime Minister and Cabinet, and a unicameral assembly, the House of
Representatives.

Economy

Industrialized market economy; main activities are shipbuilding, textiles, food processing, wood processing,
cement, chemicals, fertilizers, pharmaceuticals, tourism, fishing, mining, production of oil and hydro-electric
power; agriculture produces grains, fruit, vegetables, livestock and tobacco.

History

Croatia includes the region lying between Bosnia and Hungary, called Slavonia, which was recorded as a
kingdom in its own right in 1240 and was administered by the Hungarian King Béla IV as a *banovina* with its
own *ban* (viceroy) within the Kingdom of Croatia in 1260. In the 13–14c Slavonia was ruled by members of
the ruling dynasty in Hungary, but was returned to the Croatian ban in 1476. The Slavonian *sabor* (parliament)
was joined to that of Croatia in the mid-16c but Slavonia was then occupied by the Ottomans until the Treaty
of Karlowitz (1699), when it passed to the Habsburg Emperor and was absorbed into the Military Frontier.
The Croatian people were originally Slav settlers who migrated (6–7c) from White Croatia in the Ukraine to
the old Roman provinces of Pannonia and Dalmatia. Their independent kingdom, ruled by Croatian kings,
existed from 910 until 1102, when the Croatian crown passed to the Hungarian Árpád Dynasty. From 1526 to
1918 the Croatian and Hungarian crowns were joined under the Habsburg Dynasty, but during the 15–16c
the Croats became divided between three empires: the Croats in Croatia and Slavonia were subject to the
Habsburgs; those in Dalmatia were subject to Venice; and those in Bosnia and Herzegovina to the Ottomans.
In 1868 Croatia and Slavonia were made a joint crown land under Hungarian rule. Not until 1918 and the
creation of the Kingdom of Serbs, Croats and Slovenes (later Yugoslavia) were the Croats all subject to one
government. During occupation by the Axis powers in 1941–5, after the disintegration of Yugoslavia, part of
Croatia and Bosnia-Herzegovina formed the Independent State of Croatia, a satellite state of the Axis powers.
Benito Mussolini chose Prince Aimone of Saxony, the Duke of Spoleto, to be King, but the Prince never took
over his kingdom. The state was, instead, subject to the brutal regime of Ante Pavelić, the leader of the Ustaša,
a fascist movement. In 1945 Croatia became one of the constituent republics of the Socialist Federal Republic
of Yugoslavia. In 1991 the Croatian President Franjo Tudjman declared Croatia's independence from the
Yugoslav Federation, which was followed by confrontation with the National Army and civil war; an official
ceasefire was declared in 1992 but fighting restarted in 1993. From 1992 Croatian forces were involved in
the war in Bosnia-Herzegovina, where there is a large Croat population. Since the death of the authoritarian
Tudjman in 1999, Croatia has been more outward looking. It has joined the World Trade Organization, and is
expected to accede to the EU in 2010.

CUBA

Official name Republic of Cuba
Local name Cuba
Location An island republic in the Caribbean Sea
Area 110 860 sq km / 42 792 sq mi
Capital Havana
Chief towns Santiago de Cuba, Camagüey, Holguín, Santa Clara, Guantánamo
Population 11 424 000 (2008e)

Time zone GMT –5
Currency 1 Cuban Peso (Cub$) = 100 centavos
Language Spanish
Religions Christianity (RC mainly) and Santeria (a mixture of Christianity and African religions)
Ethnic groups white 65%, mulatto 25%, black 10%

Physical description

An archipelago, comprising the island of Cuba, Isla de la Juventud, and c.1600 islets and cays; the main island is 1250km / 777mi long, varying in width from 191km / 119mi in the east to 31km / 19mi in the west; heavily indented coastline; the south coast is generally low and marshy and the north coast is steep and rocky, with some fine harbours; the main ranges are the Sierra del Escambray in the centre, the Sierra de los Organos in the west, and the Sierra Maestra in the east; the highest peak is Pico Turquino (2005m / 6578ft); the island is mostly flat, with wide, fertile valleys and plains.

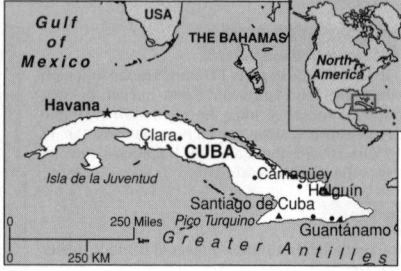

Climate

Subtropical, warm and humid; the average annual temperature is 25°C; the dry season is November–April; the average annual rainfall is 1375mm; hurricanes usually occur in June–November.

Government

Governed by an executive President, a Council of Ministers and a unicameral National Assembly of the People's Power; a Council of State, elected by the National Assembly, represents it between sessions. The Cuban Communist Party is the only legal political party.

Economy

Nationalized and centrally planned economy since 1959; extremely run-down owing to international trade embargos and loss of Soviet subsidies; crisis caused by collapse of communism in Europe led to limited privatization and market reforms in 1990s; now attracting foreign investment; main cash crops are sugar (world's second largest producer) and tobacco; chief industries are tourism, sugar refining, oil production, tobacco processing, nickel mining (world's fifth largest producer), biotechnology.

History

The island was visited by Columbus in 1492, and was a Spanish colony until 1898. Spain relinquished its rights over Cuba following a US-supported revolution led by José Martí. Cuba gained independence in 1902, with the USA retaining naval bases and reserving the right of intervention in domestic affairs. The struggle against the dictatorship of General Batista led by Fidel Castro, unsuccessful in 1953, was finally successful in 1959, and a communist state was established. In 1961 an invasion by US-supported Cuban exiles was defeated at the Bay of Pigs, and in 1962 the discovery of the installation of Soviet missile bases in Cuba prompted a US naval blockade. The collapse of the Soviet Union in 1991 meant that Cuba lost the commercial, military and economic support that it had enjoyed since 1960, and Castro was forced to reduce public services and introduce food rationing. After emigration was permitted (1980), many Cubans settled in Florida, leading to the need for an agreement between Cuba and the USA (1994) to regulate the flow of asylum seekers. For over 30 years the USA maintained a continually tightening economic and military blockade of Castro's Cuba, cemented by the Helms–Burton Act of 1996. However, this has failed to destroy the economy, which has benefited in recent years from the relaxation of state controls and increased overseas investment and tourism. Fidel Castro stood down as president in 2008, and his brother Raul was elected to succeed him, having been acting president since 2006.

CYPRUS

Official name Republic of Cyprus
Local name Kipros (Greek), Kibris (Turkish)
Location An island republic in the north-east Mediterranean Sea
Area 9251 sq km/3571 sq mi
Capital Nicosia
Chief towns Larnaca, Limassol, Kyrenia; Famagusta (the chief port prior to the 1974 Turkish invasion) is under Turkish Cypriot control, and has been declared closed by the Cyprus government
Population 793 000 (2008e)
Time zone GMT +2
Currency 1 Euro (€) = 100 cents
Languages Greek, Turkish, with English widely spoken
Religions Christianity 78% (Orthodox), Islam 18%, others 4%
Ethnic groups Greek 77%, Turkish 18%, others 5%

Physical description

The Kyrenia Mountains extend 150km/90mi along the north coast, rising to 1024m/3360ft at Mount Kyparissovouno; the forest-covered Troödos Mountains are in the centre and south-west, rising to 1951m/6401ft at Mount Olympus; the fertile Mesaoria plain extends across the island's centre; the coastline is indented, with several long, sandy beaches.

[Map: TURKEY, Mediterranean Sea, under Turkish administration, CYPRUS, Nicosia, Kyrenia, Famagusta, Olympus, Larnaca, Limassol, Asia; 0 100 Miles, 0 100 KM]

Climate

Mediterranean climate, with hot, dry summers and warm, wet winters; average annual rainfall is 500mm, with great local variation; average daily temperatures (July–August) range from 22°C on the Troödos Mountains to 29°C on the central plain; winters are mild, with an average temperature of 4°C in higher parts of the mountains, and 10°C on the plain; there is snow on higher land in winter.

Government

Governed by an executive President, a Council of Ministers and a unicameral House of Representatives; Turkish members ceased to attend in 1983, when the Turkish community declared itself independent (as the 'Turkish Republic of Northern Cyprus', recognized only by Turkey).

Economy

The Greek Cypriot area has a diverse market economy dominated by the services sector; main industries are tourism, financial services, shipping services, food and wine, textiles and garments, chemicals, pharmaceuticals, metal products, wood products; main agricultural products are citrus fruits, potatoes, grapes, vegetables. The Turkish Cypriot economy is internationally isolated and heavily dependent on Turkish financial support; largely agricultural, exporting citrus fruits, potatoes and textiles; small tourist industry.

History

Cyprus has a recorded history of 4000 years, with its rulers having included the Greeks, Ptolemaic Egyptians, Persians, Romans, Byzantines, Arabs, Franks, Venetians, Turks and British. Byzantine control of the island ended at the time of the Third Crusade when Richard I, the Lionheart, conquered Cyprus on his way to Palestine and established Guy of Lusignan as King of Cyprus. This marked the beginning of a long period in which aspiring Crusaders could look on Cyprus as a relatively safe haven. In the 15c, because piracy out of the island had remained a constant threat to Muslim seaborne trade in the eastern Mediterranean, the Circassian Mamluk, Sultan al-Ashraf Barsbay, mounted an attack and established Mamluk influence. Later, when Cyprus became effectively a protectorate of the Venetian empire, it still paid tribute to the Mamluk Sultan. The last vestige of Frankish influence in the eastern Mediterranean, the island fell to the Ottoman Sultan, Selim II, in 1571 and remained under Ottoman control until ceded to the British in 1878. It became a British Crown Colony in 1925. Greek Cypriot demands for union with Greece (*enosis*) led in the 1950s to guerrilla warfare waged against the British administration by EOKA, and a four-year state of emergency (1955–9). Cyprus achieved independence in 1960, with Britain retaining sovereignty over the military bases at Akrotiri and Dhekelia. Despite a constitution providing for power-sharing between the Greek and Turkish Cypriots, there were intercommunal clashes throughout the 1960s and in 1971; a UN peacekeeping force was deployed in 1964. The 1974 Turkish invasion led to occupation of the northern third of the island, causing the displacement of over 160 000 Greek Cypriots; the island was partitioned into two parts, from the north-west coast above Pomos to Famagusta in the east, cutting through Nicosia where it is called the Green Line. Famagusta (the chief port prior to the 1974 Turkish invasion) remains under Turkish Cypriot control, and has been declared closed by the Cyprus government. Turkish government members ceased to attend government in 1983, when the Turkish Cypriot community declared itself independent (as the 'Turkish Republic of Northern Cyprus'). Reunification talks in the 1980s and 1990s were inconclusive, but the impetus provided by Cyprus's approaching admission to the EU led to UN-sponsored talks from 1999 onwards that resulted in 2004 in the Annan plan for a united republic with a two-state federal structure. This was accepted in a referendum by the Turkish Cypriots but rejected by the Greek Cypriots, and only the southern part of the island joined the EU in 2004.

CZECH REPUBLIC

Official name Czech Republic
Local name Cesko
Location A landlocked republic in eastern Europe, bounded to the west by Germany; to the north and east by Poland; to the south-east by Slovakia; and to the south by Austria
Area 78864 sq km/30441 sq mi
Capital Prague
Chief towns Brno, Plzen, Ostrava, Olomouc

Population 10221000 (2008e)
Time zone GMT +1
Currency 1 Koruna (CZK) = 100 haléřů
Language Czech
Religions Christianity 29% (RC 27%, Prot 2%), others 3%, unspecified 9%, none/unaffiliated 59%
Ethnic groups Czech 90%, Moravian 4%, Slovak 2%, others 4%

Physical description

Bohemia (west and centre) comprises rolling fertile plains and plateaux surrounded by low mountains; Moravia (east) is mostly hilly, rising to the western range of the Carpathian mountains in the east, and is divided by the River Morava valley; the highest point is Sněžka (1602m/5256ft) in the north; drained by the Morava, Vitava, Elbe and Oder rivers; there are many lakes; forests and woods cover one-third of the land.

Climate

Continental, with warm, humid summers and cold, dry winters.

Government

Governed by a President, a Prime Minister and Council of Ministers, and a bicameral Parliament consisting of a Chamber of Deputies and a Senate.

Economy

Has become a prosperous market economy since 1990; industrialized in 19c; major industries produce iron, steel, machinery, motor vehicles, chemicals, glass, armaments, hydro-electric power, timber and wood products; main crops are wheat, potatoes, sugar beets, hops, fruit, pigs and poultry.

History

The republic comprises the former provinces of Bohemia, Silesia and Moravia, and from 1918 to 1993 it formed part of Czechoslovakia. It became an independent republic on 1 Jan 1993 following the dissolution of Czechoslovakia, and Václav Havel, formerly President of Czechoslovakia, became President. In 1999 the Czech Republic was admitted to NATO and in 2004 it joined the EU.

DENMARK

Official name Kingdom of Denmark
Local name Danmark
Location A kingdom in northern Europe, it is the smallest of the Scandinavian countries and consists of most of the Jutland Peninsula, several islands in the Baltic Sea (the largest include Zealand, Fyn, Lolland, Falster and Bornholm), and some of the northern Frisian Islands in the North Sea
Area (excluding dependencies) 43076 sq km/16627 sq mi

Capital Copenhagen
Chief towns Århus, Odense, Ålborg, Esbjerg, Randers, Kolding
Population 5485000 (2008e)
Time zone GMT +1
Currency 1 Danish Krone (Dkr) = 100 øre
Language Danish; English is widely spoken
Religions Christianity 83% (Lutheran 82%), Islam 4%, other 13%
Ethnic groups Danish 96%, Faroese and Inuit 1%, others 3%

Physical description

Uniformly low-lying; the highest point (Ejer Bavnehøj in east Jylland) is only 173m/567ft; there are no large rivers and few lakes; the shoreline is indented by many lagoons and fjords (the largest of which is Lim Fjord, which cut off the northern extremity of Denmark in 1825).

Climate

Cool maritime climate, giving cold and cloudy winters and warm, sunny summers; annual rainfall is usually below 675mm.

Government

A hereditary constitutional monarchy with a Queen as head of state; governed by a Prime Minister and Cabinet and a unicameral Parliament (*Folketing*), at which the Faroe Islands and Greenland each have two representatives.

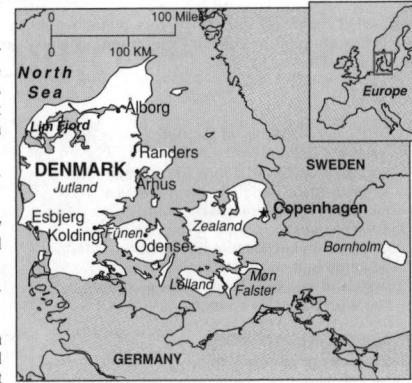

Economy

Highly industrialized and diversified market economy based on intensive agriculture, forestry, energy and processing industries; agricultural exports include grains, meat, dairy products, fish; industry produces electronic appliances, foodstuffs, beer, chemicals, furniture, ships, windmills; oil, natural gas and electricity are exported.

History

Denmark formed part of Viking kingdoms in the 8–10c and was the centre of the Danish Empire under Canute in the 11c. In 1397 the Union of Kalmar brought Sweden and Norway under Danish rule; Sweden separated from the union in the 16c, and Norway was ceded to Sweden in 1814. Schleswig-Holstein was lost to Germany in 1864, but northern Schleswig was returned after a plebiscite in 1920. Denmark was occupied by Germany during World War II. Iceland became independent of Danish rule in 1944; the Faroe Islands and Greenland remain dependencies but were granted internal self-government in 1948 and 1979 respectively. Denmark joined the EC in 1973. A referendum in 2000 rejected a proposal to replace the krone with the euro.

❖Faroe Islands

Location A group of islands lying in the North Atlantic Ocean, between the Shetland Islands and Iceland, and subject to the Danish crown
Area 1399 sq km/540 sq mi
Capital Torshavn
Population 48 700 (2008e)

❖Greenland

Location The second-largest island in the world (after Australia), lying north-east of North America in the North Atlantic and Arctic oceans, and subject to the Danish crown
Area 2 175 600 sq km/839 780 sq mi
Capital Nuuk (Godthåb)
Population 57 600 (2008e)

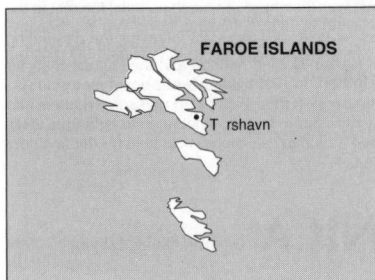

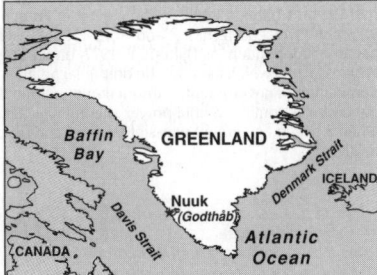

Nations of the World

DJIBOUTI

Official name Republic of Djibouti
Local name Djibouti
Location A republic in north-east Africa, bounded to the north by Eritrea; to the north-west, west and south by Ethiopia; to the south-east by Somalia; and to the east by the Gulf of Aden
Area 23310 sq km/8998 sq mi
Capital Djibouti
Chief towns Tadjoura, Dikhil, Obock, Ali-Sabieh

Population 506000 (2008e)
Time zone GMT +3
Currency 1 Djibouti Franc (DF, DjFr) = 100 centimes
Languages Arabic, French
Religions Islam 94% (Sunni), Christianity 6% (RC 4%, Prot 2%)
Ethnic groups Issa 60%, Afar 35%, Arab and others 5%

Physical description

A series of plateaux dropping down from mountains to flat low-lying rocky desert; 350km/220mi of fertile coastal strip around the Gulf of Tadjoura, which juts deep into the country; the highest point, Moussa Ali, rises to 2020m/6627ft in the north; the lowest point is 155m/508ft below sea level (Lake Abbé).

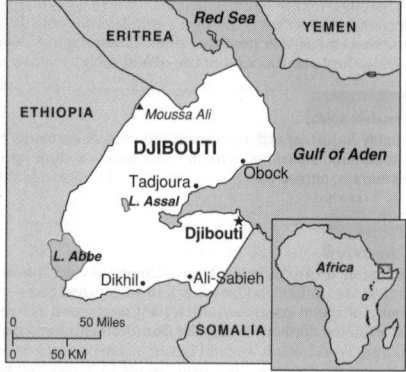

Climate

Semi-arid, with a hot season in May–September; very high temperatures on coastal plains all year round, maximum average daily temperature dropping below 30°C for only three months (December–February); slightly lower humidity and temperatures in the interior highlands (over 600m); rainfall average 130mm annually at Djibouti.

Government

Governed by a President, a Prime Minister and Council of Ministers, and a unicameral National Assembly.

Economy

Poor, and dependent on foreign aid; large service sector (80% of GDP) based on strategic location as military base for European forces and the port of Djibouti's role as a transit port for landlocked neighbouring countries and commercial hub of free trade zone in north-east Africa; aridity restricts agriculture to irrigated areas (date palms, fruit, vegetables) and livestock-rearing by nomads; some fishing and tourism.

History

Settled by the Afars and Issas about 2000 years ago, the area was the object of French colonial interest in the mid-19c and Djibouti became the capital of French Somaliland in 1892. Following World War II it became a French Overseas Territory, and from 1967 was called the French Territory of the Afars and the Issas. It became independent as Djibouti in 1977, under President Hassan Gouled Aptidon and the Popular Rally for Progress Party, which became the only legal political party in 1981. In 1991 fighting broke out in protest at Issa domination of government; introduction of a limited multiparty system in 1992 failed to resolve matters and the civil war continued until power-sharing was agreed in 1994. Some factions continued to fight until 2000, when a peace agreement was signed. Free and unrestricted multiparty elections were held for the first time in 2003.

DOMINICA

Official name Commonwealth of Dominica
Local name Dominica
Location An independent republic located in the Windward Islands, in the east Caribbean Sea
Area 751 sq km/290 sq mi
Capital Roseau
Chief towns Portsmouth, Grand Bay
Population 72000 (2008e)

Time zone GMT –4
Currency 1 East Caribbean Dollar (EC$) = 100 cents
Language English; French Creole is also spoken
Religions Christianity 91% (RC 61%), Rastafarian 1%, others 2%, none 6%
Ethnic groups black 87%, mixed 9%, Amerindian 3%, others 1%

Physical description

Roughly rectangular in shape, with a deeply-indented coastline; the island is c.50km/30mi long and 26km/16mi wide, rising to 1447m/4747ft at Morne Diablotin; volcanic origin, with many fumaroles and sulphur springs; it has a central ridge, with lateral spurs and deep valleys, with several rivers; forests covers 67% of the land area.

Climate

Tropical; warm and humid; average monthly temperatures are 26°–32°C; average annual rainfall is 1750mm on the coast and 6250mm in the mountains; subject to hurricanes in July–November.

Government

Governed by a President, a Prime Minister and Cabinet, and a unicameral House of Assembly.

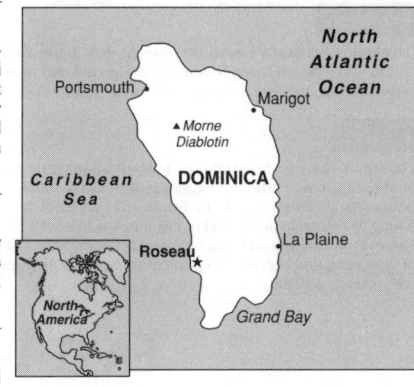

Economy

Largely based on agriculture and produce processing; tourism is growing; diversifying into fishing, forestry and light industry; main products are bananas, fruit juices, soap, coconut oil, lime oil, bay oil, copra, rum, vegetables, citrus fruits.

History

Columbus reached the island in 1493, and there were attempts at colonization by the French and British in the 18c. It became a British Crown Colony in 1805. It was part of the Federation of the West Indies from 1958 to 1962, and gained independence in 1978. Edison James became Prime Minister in 1995, ending the 15-year tenure of Dame Eugenia Charles, the Caribbean's first woman prime minister, but James's United Workers' Party lost the 2000 election to the Dominica Labour Party.

DOMINICAN REPUBLIC

Official name Dominican Republic
Local name La Dominicana
Location A republic of the West Indies, comprising the eastern two-thirds of the island of Hispaniola, and bordering Haiti to the west
Area 48 442 sq km/18 699 sq mi
Capital Santo Domingo
Chief towns Santiago, La Vega, San Juan, San Francisco de Macorís, La Romana

Population 9 507 000 (2008e)
Time zone GMT –4
Currency 1 Dominican Republic Peso (RD$, DR$) = 100 centavos
Language Spanish
Religions Christianity 87% (69% RC, 18% Prot), none 11%, other 2%
Ethnic groups mixed 73%, white 16%, black 11%

Physical description

Crossed by the Cordillera Central, a heavily-wooded range with many peaks over 3000m/9840ft; the Pico Duarte (3175m/10 417ft) is the highest peak in the Caribbean; in the south-west, Lake Enriquillo lies in a broad valley cutting east to west; there is a wide coastal plain to the east.

Climate

Tropical maritime, with a rainy season from May to November; the average temperature at Santo Domingo ranges between 24°C (January) and 27°C (July); average annual rainfall is 1400mm; hurricanes may occur in June–November.

Government

Governed by an executive President, a Cabinet and a bicameral National Congress consisting of a Senate and a Chamber of Deputies.

Nations of the World

Economy

Developing economy based on tourism, free trade zones and agriculture (sugar, coffee, cocoa, bananas, cotton and tobacco); dependent on foreign aid and remittances from expatriate workers; industries include sugar refining, cement, mining (ferronickel, gold, silver), light manufacturing, textiles.

History

Columbus reached the island in 1492 and it became a Spanish colony in the 16–17c; the eastern province of Santo Domingo remained Spanish after the partition of Hispaniola in 1697. Taken over by Haiti on several occasions, it gained independence in 1844 under its modern name, but was reoccupied by Spain in 1861–5. A long dictatorship at the end of the 19c was followed by revolution and bankruptcy. The dictatorship of Gen. Rafael Trujillo (1930–61) was followed by a period of instability and then from the mid-1960s by a succession of right-wing and centre-right governments. Political crises and allegations of fraud and corruption dominated the 1980s and 1990s.

EAST TIMOR

Official name Democratic Republic of East Timor
Local name Timor-Leste (Portuguese), Timor Lorosa'e (Tetum)
Location A republic in South-East Asia occupying the eastern half of the island of Timor and the enclave of Oecusse in the west of the island
Area 14 874 sq km/5743 sq mi
Capital Dili
Chief towns Baucau, Pante Macassar

Population 1 109 000 (2008e)
Time zone GMT +9
Currency 1 US Dollar ($) = 100 cents
Language Portuguese, Tetum; English, Indonesian and local languages are also spoken
Religions Christianity 99% (RC 98%, Prot 1%), Islam 1%
Ethnic groups Malayo-Polynesian, Papuan

Physical description

Mountainous and forested, with numerous rivers; the highest peak is Tata Mailau (2950m/9678ft); the state includes the smaller islands of Pulau Atauro and Jaco.

Climate

Hot and humid equatorial climate; dry season (June–September), rainy season (December–March); the average temperature is 27°C on the coast, falling inland and with altitude.

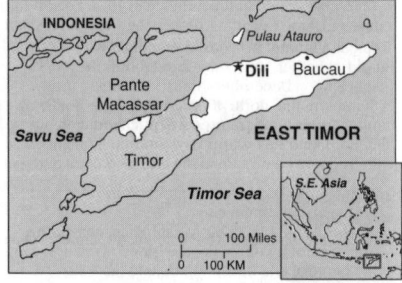

Government

Governed by a President, a Prime Minister and Council of Ministers, and a unicameral National Parliament.

Economy

Very poor country, dependent on foreign aid; largely agrarian; main products are coffee, sandalwood, marble, vanilla; offshore oil and natural gas exploitation generates revenue but few jobs.

History

Colonized by the Portuguese in the 16c, it remained an overseas territory of Portugal after World War II when the western part of Timor became part of Indonesia. Colonial administration withdrew following the 1974 coup in Portugal and in 1975 it declared itself independent as the Democratic Republic of East Timor. After a civil war between supporters of independence and those advocating integration into Indonesia, East Timor was annexed by Indonesia in 1976. The annexation was not recognized by the UN. Resistance to Indonesian rule was met with severe repression. In a 1999 plebiscite, 78 per cent of the population voted for independence; the vote was ratified by Indonesia but provoked violence by pro-Indonesian factions. After a period under a UN transitional administration, East Timor became independent in 2002. UN peacekeeping troops returned in 2006 after clashes with sacked army personnel developed into widespread factional violence. Instability has continued, with violent protests in 2007 and attacks on the president and prime minister in 2008.

ECUADOR

Official name Republic of Ecuador
Local name Ecuador
Location A republic straddling the Equator in the north-west of South America. It is bounded to the north by Colombia; to the south and east by Peru; and to the west by the Pacific Ocean, and its territory includes the Galápagos Islands in the Pacific Ocean
Area 270 699 sq km / 104 490 sq mi
Capital Quito

Chief towns Guayaquil, Cuenca, Riobamba, Esmeraldas
Population 13 928 000 (2008e)
Time zone GMT −5
Currency 1 US Dollar ($) = 100 cents
Language Spanish; Quechua is also spoken
Religions Christianity 95% (mainly RC), others 5%
Ethnic groups mestizo 65%, Amerindian 25%, Spanish and others 7%

Physical description

The Andes run north to south down the centre of the country; three main ranges rise to peaks which include Cotopaxi (5896m/19344ft) and enclose high plateaux *Sierra*; highest point is Mount Chimborazo (6267m/20560ft); the Andes divide the broad coastal plain (*Costa*) of the west from the eastern alluvial plains (*Oriente*), covered with rainforest and dissected by rivers flowing from the Andes towards the Amazon; frequent serious earthquakes; the Galápagos Islands comprise six main volcanic islands.

Climate

Tropical climate in coastal regions, with hot, humid weather and rain throughout the year (especially December–April); varies from 2000mm in the north to 200mm in the south; central Andes temperatures are much reduced by altitude; Quito has warm days and chilly nights, with frequent heavy rain in the afternoon; hot and wet equatorial climate in the east.

Government

Governed by an executive President, a Cabinet and a unicameral National Assembly.

Economy

Based on oil (50% of export earnings) and agriculture; main cash crops are bananas (world's leading exporter), cut flowers, coffee, cocoa, fish (tuna), shrimps, vegetables; industries process food and timber products; oil piped from the *Oriente* to refineries at Esmeraldas.

History

Formerly part of the Inca Empire, it was conquered by the Spanish in 1527 and included in the Viceroyalty of New Granada. On gaining independence in 1822, it joined with Panama, Colombia and Venezuela to form Gran Colombia, but left the union to become an independent republic in 1830. The country was politically unstable throughout the 20c (there were 22 presidents between 1925 and 1948, none completing a term in office), and the volatility has continued owing to economic difficulties since the 1980s and popular protests at economic reforms. Ecuador adopted the US dollar in 2000 in an attempt to stabilize the economy. A new constitution was approved by popular vote in September 2008.

EGYPT

Official name Arab Republic of Egypt
Local name Misr
Location A republic in north-east Africa, bounded to the west by Libya; to the south by Sudan; to the east by the Red Sea; to the north-east by Israel; and to the north by the Mediterranean Sea
Area 1 001 449 sq km/386 559 sq mi
Capital Cairo

Chief towns Alexandria, Port Said, Aswan, Suez, El Gîza
Population 81 713 000 (2008e)
Time zone GMT +2
Currency 1 Egyptian Pound (£E, LE) = 100 piastres
Language Arabic
Religions Islam 90% (mostly Sunni), Christianity 10% (mostly Coptic)
Ethnic groups Egyptian 99%, others 1%

Physical description

The River Nile flows north from the Sudan, dammed south of Aswan to create Lake Nasser, to its huge delta, 250km/160mi across and 160km/100mi north to south, on the Mediterranean coast; it divides the mainly flat and arid country into the narrow, sparsely inhabited Eastern Desert between the Nile valley and the Red Sea and the broad Western Desert, which covers over two-thirds of the country and contains seven major depressions; the largest and lowest of these is the Qattara Depression (133m/436ft below sea level); the Sinai Peninsula to the east of the Red Sea is a desert region with mountains rising to 2637m/8651ft at Gebel Katherîna, Egypt's highest point; 90% of the population lives on the Nile flood plain (c.3% of the country's area).

Climate

Mainly desert, except for an 80km/50mile-wide Mediterranean coastal fringe, where annual rainfall is 100–200mm; very hot on the coast when the dust-laden *khamsin* wind blows north from the Sahara (March–June); Alexandria, on the coast, has an annual average rainfall of 180mm; elsewhere, rainfall is less than 50mm.

Government

Governed by an executive President, a Prime Minister and Council of Ministers, and a unicameral People's Assembly; a Consultative Council has an advisory role. Political parties based on religious adherence are banned.

Economy

Based on services (tourism, Suez Canal revenues, remittances), oil and agriculture; land under cultivation increased by irrigation; main crops are cotton, rice, maize, wheat, vegetables, fruit and livestock; chief industries produce crude oil and petroleum products, natural gas, textiles, processed food, chemicals, pharmaceuticals, metals (iron ore, phosphates, manganese, gypsum) and metal products.

History

The history of Egypt can be traced as far back as c.6000 BC, to Neolithic cultures on the River Nile. A unified kingdom embracing lower and upper Egypt was first created in c.3100 BC, ruled by Pharaonic dynasties; the pyramids at El Gîza were constructed during the Fourth Dynasty. Egyptian power was greatest during the New Empire period (1567–1085 BC). It became a Persian province in the 6c BC and was conquered by Alexander the Great in the 4c BC. Ptolemaic Pharaohs ruled Egypt until 30 BC, when it was conquered and ruled by the Roman Empire (30 BC to AD 324) and the Byzantine Empire. It was conquered by Arabs in AD 672. From 1798 until 1801, it was occupied by France under Napoleon. The Suez Canal was constructed in 1869. A revolt in 1879 against the ruling Khedive was put down by British intervention in 1882. Egypt became a formal British protectorate in 1914, but declared its independence in 1922. It was used as a base for Allied forces during World War II. King Farouk was deposed by the army in 1952, and Egypt was declared a republic in 1953. Nationalization of the Suez Canal in 1956 provoked a joint Anglo–French and Israeli invasion, the forces being obliged to withdraw by international pressure. War with Israeli in 1967 resulted in the loss of the Sinai Peninsula and control of part of the Suez Canal (regained following negotiations in the 1970s). In 1981 President Sadat was assassinated, and relations with Arab nations were strained by Egypt's recognition of Israel, but they improved again during the 1980s. Sadat's successor, President Hosni Mubarak, has followed a policy of moderation and reconciliation, playing an active role in the Middle East peace process to resolve the Arab–Israeli conflict in the 1990s, but has been unable to stem terrorism at home. During the 1990s there were violent clashes between Muslims and Coptic Christians. The Islamic fundamentalists (mainly the Islamic Group and al-Jihad organizations) grew increasingly violent in their campaign against the government, and by the end of the decade foreign tourists as well as Egyptians were among their targets. Although Mubarak's presidency has been approved by national referendum every six years since 1981 and there are direct legislative elections, lack of general political freedom has aroused increasing frustration and resentment, expressed in public demonstrations in recent years.

EL SALVADOR

Nations of the World

Official name Republic of El Salvador	Chief towns Santa Ana, San Miguel, Mejicanos
Local name El Salvador	Population 7 066 000 (2008e)
Location The smallest of the Central American republics, bounded to the north and east by Honduras; to the west by Guatemala; and to the south by the Pacific Ocean	Time zone GMT –6
	Currency 1 US Dollar ($) = 100 cents
	Language Spanish
	Religions Christianity 81% (RC 57%, Prot 24%), others 2%, none 17%
Area 21 476 sq km/8290 sq mi	
Capital San Salvador	Ethnic groups mestizo 90%, white 9%, Amerindian 1%

Physical description

Two volcanic ranges running east to west divide El Salvador into three geographical regions, ranging from a narrow coastal belt in the south through upland valleys and plateaux to mountains in the north (highest point, Cerro El Pital, is 2730m/8957ft); the River Lempa, dammed for hydroelectricity, flows south to the Pacific; many volcanic lakes; earthquakes are common.

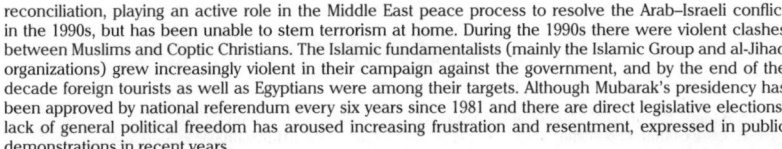

Climate

Varies greatly with altitude; hot and tropical on the coastal lowlands; single rainy season (May–October); temperate uplands; average annual temperature at San Salvador is 23°C; average annual rainfall is 1775mm.

Government

Governed by an executive President, a Council of State and a unicameral Legislative Assembly.

Economy

Largely based on the service sector (commerce, financial services), manufacturing and agriculture (coffee, sugar, shrimps); main industries are food processing, beverages, petroleum products, chemicals; fertilizers; textiles, furniture, metals.

History

Originally part of the Aztec kingdom, it was conquered by the Spanish in 1526, and achieved independence from Spain in 1821. A member of the Central American Federation until its dissolution in 1839, it became an independent republic in 1841. In the mid-20c it was ruled by dictatorships, suffered political unrest, and waged war with Honduras in 1965 and 1969. There was also considerable political unrest in the 1970s, with guerrilla activity against the US-supported government intensifying from 1977 into a civil war in which 75 000 died and many became refugees. A peace agreement was signed in 1992 in which the left-wing guerrilla group *Frente Farabundo Marti de Liberación Nacional* (FMLN) was recognized as a political party; it won a few seats in the 1994 elections in which the right-wing *Alianza Republicana Nacionalista* (ARENA) came to power. Since then, FMLN has increased its share of the vote, often being the largest party in parliament, but it has never held office, as ARENA has always formed coalition governments with smaller right-wing parties. Severe earthquakes in early 2001 and a volcanic eruption and a tropical storm in late 2005 caused widespread devastation.

■ **England▶United Kingdom**

EQUATORIAL GUINEA

Official name Republic of Equatorial Guinea
Local name Guinea Ecuatorial
Location A republic in western central Africa, comprising a mainland area (Río Muni) and several islands (notably Bioko and Annabón) in the Gulf of Guinea
Area 26016 sq km/10042 sq mi
Capital Malabo, on Bioko
Chief towns Bata and Evinayong on the mainland,
Luba and Riaba on Bioko
Population 616000 (2008e)
Time zone GMT +1
Currency 1 CFA Franc (CFAFr) = 100 centimes
Languages Spanish, French; pidgin English, Fang and other local languages are also spoken
Religions Christianity 93% (mainly RC), traditional beliefs 5%, Islam 1%, none/unspecified 1%
Ethnic groups Fang 86%, Bubi 6%, others 8%

Physical description

The mainland rises sharply from a narrow coastal plain of mangrove swamps towards a heavily forested mountainous plateau; deeply cut by several rivers; the islands are volcanic; Bioko Island, about 160km/100mi north-west of the mainland, rises to 3007m/9865ft at Pico de Basilé.

Climate

Hot and humid equatorial; average annual rainfall is c.2000mm; average maximum daily temperature is 29°–32°C.

Government

Governed by a President, a Prime Minister and Council of Ministers, and a unicameral House of Representatives of the People.

Economy

Transformed by discovery of oil and natural gas off Bioko in 1990s; other activities are agriculture (mostly subsistence level except for cocoa production), fishing, forestry and wood processing.

History

Equatorial Guinea was first visited by Europeans in the 15c. The island of Fernando Po (Bioko) was claimed by Portugal in 1494 and held until 1788. Occupied by Britain from 1781 until 1843, the rights to the area were acquired by Spain in 1844. It gained independence in 1968 and was ruled by President Macias Nguema until a military coup in 1979 led by his nephew, Obiang Nguema, ended his repressive regime. A new constitution was approved in 1991 and multiparty democracy was legalized in 1992. Even so, Nguema's Equatorial Guinea Democratic Party (PDGE) has maintained its grip on power, most of the elections since 1992 being boycotted because of irregularities by the opposition parties, some of which have been banned. Opposition leaders were imprisoned in 2002 for allegedly taking part in an attempted coup, and in 2003 some set up a government-in-exile in Spain.

ERITREA

Official name State of Eritrea
Local name Eretra
Location A country in north-east Africa, bounded to the north and north-west by Sudan; to the west and south-west by Ethiopia; to the south by Djibouti; and to the east by the Red Sea
Area 121320 sq km/46841 sq mi
Capital Asmara
Chief towns Assab, Massawa, Keren, Tessenai
Population 5502000 (2008e)
Time zone GMT +3
Currency 1 Nakfa (Nfa) = 100 cents
Languages Arabic, Tigrinya; several local languages are also spoken
Religions Islam 60% (Sunni), Christianity 37% (Coptic etc 32%, RC 5%), others 3%
Ethnic groups Tigrinya 50%, Tigrean 35%, Afar 4%, Saho 3%, Kunama 3%, others 5%

Physical description

Low-lying coastal plain stretching 1000km/620mi along the Red Sea, rising to an inland plateau; highest point is Soira (3018m/9901ft).

Climate

Hot and dry desert along the Red Sea coast; cooler and wetter in the central highlands; semi-arid in the western hills and lowlands.

Government

Governed by an executive President, a State Council and a unicameral National Assembly; transitional arrangements put in place at independence remain in operation, and elections under the constitution approved in 1997 have been postponed indefinitely.

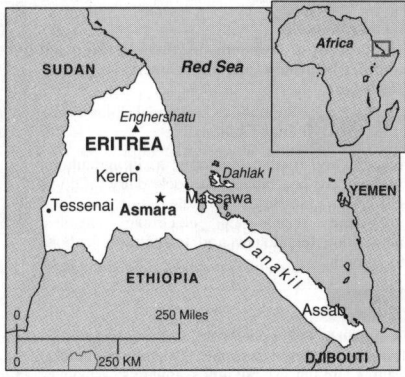

Economy

Reconstructing after the war for independence; command economy dependent on foreign aid and expatriates' remittances; subsistence agriculture supports 80% of the population, but subject to drought and famine; industries include food processing, beverages, textiles, garments, salt, cement.

History

The area was under the control of the Ottoman Empire from the mid 16c. Occupied by Italy in 1884, it became an Italian colony in 1890. It was used as a base for the Italian invasion of Abyssinia in 1935, and became part of Italian East Africa in 1936. It was then taken by the British in 1941, federated with Ethiopia at the request of the UN in 1952, and made a province of Ethiopia in 1962. This galvanized the Eritrean Liberation Front (ELF), which had been founded as the Eritrean Liberation Movement in 1958, and it waged guerrilla warfare against the government throughout the 1960s and 1970s. In 1970 a communist faction broke away to form the Eritrean People's Liberation Front (EPLF), which emerged during the 1980s as the dominant rebel group. Despite this division and much fighting between rebel groups, it managed, through support from the Eastern bloc and some Arab countries, to prevent its destruction both while Haile Selassie was Emperor and when Mengistu was President. When Soviet support waned, the EPLF joined with other Ethiopian rebel groups, including the Tigray People's Liberation Front, and overthrew the Mengistu regime in 1991. The EPLF immediately formed a separate provisional Eritrean government. A referendum on independence in 1993 recorded a massive vote in favour, and Eritrea's independence was declared the following month. The EPLF became the ruling political party, renaming itself the People's Front for Democracy and Justice. The post-independence regime has become increasingly authoritarian; elections scheduled for 2001 did not take place and have not been rescheduled and the transitional government remains in power. Since 1998, Eritrea and Ethiopia have clashed frequently over border territory, especially in Tigray, and international arbitration has been unable to resolve the dispute so far.

ESTONIA

Official name Republic of Estonia
Local name Eesti (Estonian), Estonskaya (Russian)
Location A republic in eastern Europe, bounded to the west by the Baltic Sea; to the north by the Gulf of Finland; to the east by Russia; and to the south by Latvia
Area 45 100 sq km/17 409 sq mi
Capital Tallinn
Chief towns Tartu, Narva, Kohtla-Järve, Pärnu
Population 1 308 000 (2008e)

Time zone GMT +2
Currency 1 Kroon (KR) = 100 sents
Language Estonian; Russian is widely known
Religions Christianity 28% (Lutheran 14%, Orthodox 13%, other Christian 1%), others 6%, none 66%
Ethnic groups Estonian 68%, Russian 26%, Ukrainian 2%, Belarusian 1%, Finnish 1%, others 2%

Physical description

Mostly a plain of marshes, over 1500 lakes and forests (36% of land area); highest point is Suur Munamagi (318m/1043ft); there are many islands on the coast, notably Saaremaa, Hiiumaa and Muhu.

Climate

Cool summers, wet winters.

Government

Governed by a President, a Prime Minister and Council of Ministers, and a unicameral Parliament (*Riigikogu*).

Economy

Industrialized market economy; main agricultural products are vegetables, livestock, dairy products and fish; industries include forestry, food processing, engineering, electronics, textiles, information technology and telecommunications equipment.

History

Occupied by Vikings in the 9c, during its history it has been ruled by Denmark, Sweden, Poland, Russia and the Teutonic Knights of Germany. For a time it was divided into two areas: northern Estonia and Livonia (southern Estonia and Latvia), but was ceded to Russia in its entirety by Sweden in 1721. It achieved independence in 1918, was annexed by the Soviet Union and declared a Soviet Socialist Republic in 1940, and was occupied by Germany during World War II. Soviet forces re-annexed the country in 1944 and it remained part of the Soviet Union until 1991 when, following a resurgence of the nationalist movement in the 1980s, it declared its independence. A new constitution was agreed in 1992, and the last Russian troops were withdrawn in 1994. Since independence, Estonia has pursued pro-western policies, joining the EU and NATO in 2004.

ETHIOPIA

Official name Federal Democratic Republic of Ethiopia
Local name Ityopya
Location A landlocked republic in north-east Africa, bounded to the west and south-west by Sudan; to the south by Kenya; to the east and north-east by Somalia; and to the north by Djibouti and Eritrea
Area 1 128 497 sq km/435 600 sq mi
Capital Addis Ababa

Chief towns Dire Dawa, Harer
Population 82 545 000 (2008e)
Time zone GMT +3
Currency 1 Ethiopian Birr (EB) = 100 cents
Language Amharic, Tigrinya, Oromigna; 70 local languages are also spoken
Religions Christianity 55% (Coptic 45%, Prot 10%), Islam 40%, animist 4%, other 1%
Ethnic groups Oromo 32%, Amhara 30%, Southern peoples 10%, Tigre 6%, Somali 6 %, others 16%

Physical description

Dominated by a mountainous central plateau; split diagonally by the Great Rift Valley; the highest point is Ras Dashen (4620m/15 157ft); the plateau is crossed east to west by the Blue Nile, which has its source in Lake Tana; the north and east are relatively low-lying; in the north-east the Danakil Depression dips to 116m/381ft below sea level; became landlocked when its former province of Eritrea became independent.

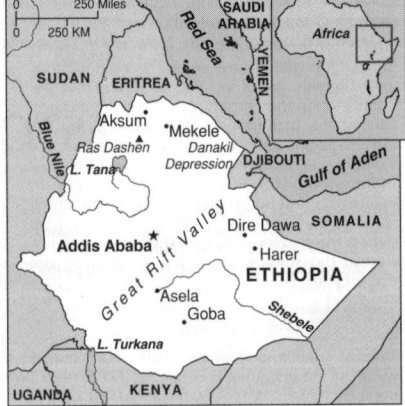

Climate

Tropical, moderated by higher altitudes; distinct wet season (April–September); temperatures warm, but rarely hot all year round; annual rainfall generally over 1000mm; hot, semi-arid north-east and south-east lowlands receive less than 500mm annually; subject to severe droughts since the 1980s.

Government

Governed by a President, a Prime Minister and Council of Ministers, and a bicameral Parliament, consisting of a House of the Federation and a House of People's Representatives.

Economy

One of the world's poorest countries, dependent on foreign aid; progress often reversed by severe drought and resulting famine, deaths and resettlement; agriculture employs over 80% of the population, especially in subsistence farming and herding; small food processing industry; some natural resources but little exploited; exports mainly coffee, qat, gold, leather goods, livestock, oilseeds.

History

Ethiopia, formerly Abyssinia, is the oldest independent country in sub-Saharan Africa, and the first African country to be Christianized. Abyssinian independence was recognized by the League of Nations in 1923, but after the invasion of Italy in 1935 the country was annexed as Italian East Africa from 1936 to its liberation in 1941, when Emperor Haile Selassie returned from exile. A military coup in 1974 led to the establishment of the Marxist Provisional Military Administrative Council (PMAC) or Dergue, and opposition was met by mass arrests and executions in 1977–8. In addition to war with Somalia over the Ogaden district during the 1970s and 1980s, there was internal conflict with separatist Eritrean and Tigrean forces, who secured victories over government troops in the early 1980s, while the country suffered severe famine. The PMAC dissolved in 1987, with the transfer of power to the People's Democratic Republic, but an attempted coup in 1989 was followed by the complete collapse of the regime in 1991 and renewed famine in 1992. Eritrea secured its independence in 1993. A transitional government ruled until a new federal system was established in 1995. Relative stability and economic growth slowly returned, although since 1998 there have been frequent clashes with Eritrea over border territory, especially in Tigray, and international arbitration has been unable to resolve the dispute so far. In late 2006, Ethiopia intervened militarily in Somalia in support of its transitional government and its troops withdrew at the start of 2009.

■ **Falkland Islands ▶ United Kingdom**

■ **Faroe Islands ▶ Denmark**

FIJI

Official name Republic of the Fiji Islands
Local name Viti
Location A Melanesian island group of around 332 islands (c.100 permanently inhabited) and over 500 islets in the south-west Pacific Ocean, forming an independent republic
Area 18 333 sq km / 7076 sq mi
Capital Suva

Chief towns Lautoka, Ba, Labasa, Nadi, Nausori
Population 932 000 (2008e)
Time zone GMT +12
Currency 1 Fiji Dollar (F$) = 100 cents
Languages Fijian, English, Hindi
Religions Christianity 53% (Prot 46%, mainly Methodist, RC 7%), Hinduism 34%, Islam 7%, others 6%

Physical description

The larger islands are generally mountainous and rugged; areas of flat land suitable for cultivation in the coastal plains, river deltas and valleys; the highest peak, Tomaniivi, is on Viti Levu (1324m/4348ft); there are hot springs in isolated places; most smaller islands consist of limestone, with little vegetation; there is an extensive coral reef (Great Sea Reef) stretching for 500km/300mi along the western fringe; dense, tropical forest lies on the wet, windward side in the south-east; mainly treeless on the dry, leeward side.

Climate

Tropical maritime climate, with hot, humid weather; temperatures average 20°–29°C; winds are variable in the wet season (November–April), when tropical cyclones can occur; the annual rainfall varies from 1900mm to 3050mm, the higher rainfall falling in the east and south-east.

Government

Governed by a President (appointed by the Great Council of Chiefs), a Prime Minister and Cabinet, and a bicameral Parliament consisting of a Senate and a House of Representatives.

Economy

Developed and diversified economy but dependent on foreign aid and expatriates' remittances after political instability and stagnation since 1980s; agriculture employs 70% of the workforce; main industries are tourism (which is growing), sugar production and milling, garment manufacturing and gold mining (all in decline), fishing, forestry.

History

Fiji was visited by Tasman in 1643, and by Cook in 1774. It became a British colony in 1874. It gained independence in 1970 as a constitutional monarchy, and became a republic after the 1987 coup. Initially stable, the country became politically volatile in the 1980s owing to tensions between the native Melanesians and the growing ethnic Indian population. The 1987 election brought to power an Indian-dominated coalition, which led to military coups in May and Sep; a civilian government was restored in Dec. A new constitution upholding ethnic Melanesian political power was effected in 1990, but was attacked by opposition parties as racist and the racist elements were removed in 1997. The 1999 election brought to power a multiracial coalition government headed by an Indian prime minister and he and most of the Cabinet were held hostage for several weeks in 2000 by ethnic Fijians; the military intervened and imposed military government. Elections restored civilian government in 2001, but in 2006 attempts by the government to reduce the military's influence in politics resulted in another military coup.

Ethnic groups

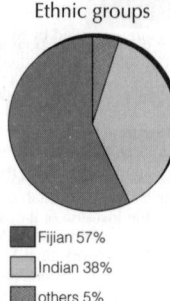

■ Fijian 57%
☐ Indian 38%
▨ others 5%

FINLAND

Official name Republic of Finland
Local name Suomi (Finnish), Finland (Swedish)
Location A republic in northern Europe, bounded to the east by Russia; to the south by the Gulf of Finland; to the west by the Gulf of Bothnia and Sweden; and to the north by Norway
Area 338 145 sq km/130 524 sq mi
Capital Helsinki
Chief towns Tampere, Turku, Espoo, Vantaa

Population 5 245 000 (2008e)
Time zone GMT +2
Currency 1 Euro (€) = 100 cents
Languages Finnish, Swedish; Sami and Russian are spoken by minorities
Religions Christianity 85% (Lutheran 83%, Orthodox 1%, other Christian 1%), none 15%
Ethnic groups Finnish 93%, Swedish 6%, others 1%

Physical description

A low-lying glaciated plain, with an average height of 150m/492ft; highest peak is a spur of Halti Fell (1328m/4356ft) on the north-west border; there are over 60 000 shallow lakes in the south-east, providing a system of inland navigation; with land still rising from the sea, the area is increasing by 7 sq km/2.7 sq mi each year; over one quarter of the country lies north of the Arctic Circle; chief rivers are the Tornio, Kemi and Oulu; the archipelago of Saaristomeri is in the south-west, with over 17 000 islands and skerries; the Ahvenanmaa islands are in the west; forest land covers 65% of the country, and water 10%.

Climate

The country's northern location is ameliorated by the Baltic Sea; western winds bring warm air currents in summer; Eurasian winds bring cold spells in winter and heatwaves in summer; annual precipitation in the south is 600–700mm, and 500–600mm in the north, with half of it falling as snow; during summer the sun stays above the horizon for over 70 days.

Government

Governed by a President, a Prime Minister and Council of State, and a unicameral Parliament (*Eduskunta*).

Economy

Highly industrialized market economy; traditional timber and metals industries now supplemented by cutting-edge telecommunications and electronics manufacturing; main exports are electronic and electrical goods, chemicals, metals, timber, paper, wood pulp; terrain and climate restrict agriculture, and foodstuffs (especially grain) and energy are major imports.

History

Finland was ruled by Sweden from 1157 until it was ceded to Russia in 1809 and became an autonomous grand duchy of the Russian Empire. A nationalist movement developed in the 19c and after the Bolshevik Revolution in 1917, it declared its independence. It resisted invasion by the USSR in 1939 but was defeated in 1940 and forced to cede territory; in the hope of recovering this territory it joined Germany's attack on the Soviet Union in 1941, and lost territory to the USSR under the treaty concluded after the 1944 armistice. Under a 1948 treaty with the USSR, Finland was obliged to demilitarize its Soviet border and to adopt a neutral stance in international affairs; these terms lasted until the Soviet Union collapsed in 1991. Finland joined the EU in 1995, and replaced the markka with the euro in 2002.

FRANCE

Official name French Republic
Local name France
Location A republic in western Europe, bounded to the north and north-east by the English Channel, Belgium and Luxembourg; to the east by Germany, Switzerland, Italy and Monaco; to the south by the Mediterranean Sea, Spain and Andorra; and to the west by the Bay of Biscay
Area 551 000 sq km/213 000 sq mi
Capital Paris

Chief towns Marseilles, Lyons, Toulouse, Nice, Strasbourg
Population 62 151 000 (2008e)
Time zone GMT +1
Currency 1 Euro (€) = 100 cents
Language French
Religions Christianity 54% (RC 51%, Prot 3%), Islam 9% Judaism 1%, Buddhism 1%, others/none 35%
Ethnic groups European, with North African, German, Indochinese and Basque minorities

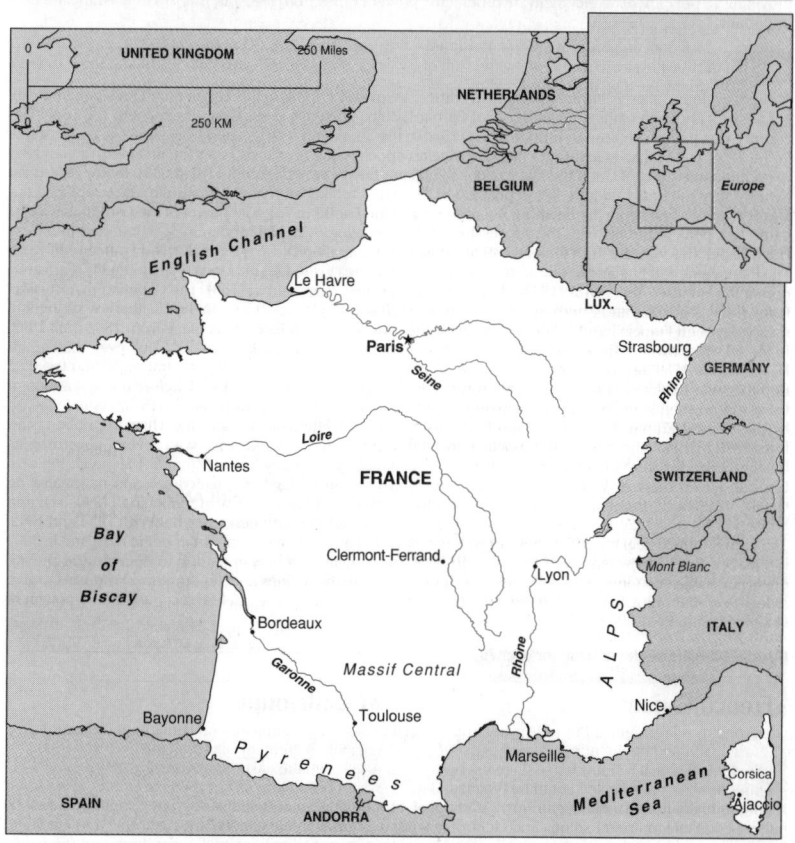

Physical description

A country of low and medium-sized hills and plateaux deeply cut by rivers; bounded to the south and east by large mountain ranges, notably (in the interior) the Armorican Massif, the Massif Central, the Cévennes, the Vosges and the Ardennes; in the east the Jura and the Alps (rising to 4807m/15771ft at Mont Blanc, the highest point); in the south the Pyrenees; chief rivers include the Loire, Rhône, Seine and Garonne; also includes the island of Corsica in the Mediterranean Sea.

Climate

The south has a Mediterranean climate, with warm, wet winters and hot, dry summers; in the north-west the climate is maritime, with an average annual rainfall of 573mm; the east has a continental climate with an average annual rainfall of 786mm.

Government

Governed by a President, a Prime Minister and Council of Ministers, and a bicameral Parliament consisting of a National Assembly and a Senate.

Economy

Highly industrialized and diversified economy with strong services sector; currently in transition from extensive state ownership to greater market orientation; western Europe's foremost producer of agricultural products, chiefly cereals, beef, sugar beet, potatoes, wine, grapes and dairy products; metal and chemical industries are based on reserves of iron ore, bauxite, potash, salt and sulphur; heavy industry (steel, machinery, textiles, clothing, chemicals, vehicles) is based around northern coalfields; other industry includes aircraft, motor vehicles, electronic goods, textiles, plastics, pharmaceuticals, food processing; several nuclear power sites, providing 75 per cent of all electricity; hydroelectric power comes from the Alps; tourism and fishing are also important.

History

There is evidence of prehistoric settlement in France, as revealed in Paleolithic carvings and rock paintings (eg at Lascaux) and in Neolithic megaliths (eg at Carnac). Celtic-speaking Gauls were dominant by the 5c BC. The country was part of the Roman Empire from 125BC to the 5c AD, and was invaded by several Germanic tribes in the 3–5c. The Franks inaugurated the Merovingian epoch in the 5c. Clovis I was the first Merovingian king to control large parts of Gaul; the last to hold significant power was Dagobert I (died 638), though the royal dynasty survived until Childeric III's deposition in 751. The Carolingian ruling dynasty ultimately replaced the Merovingians when Pepin III, the Short, became King of the Franks in 751. The power of the Carolingian kings came to a peak in the 8c, with the succession of Charlemagne. A feudal monarchy was founded in 987 by Hugh Capet; this was the third Frankish royal dynasty (the Capetian Dynasty), which ruled France until 1328. The Plantagenets of England acquired several French territories in the 12c, but lands were gradually recovered during the Hundred Years' War (1337–1453), apart from Calais (regained in 1558). The Capetian dynasty was followed by the Valois and Bourbon dynasties, from 1328 and 1589 respectively. In the 16c there was ongoing rivalry between Francis I and Emperor Charles V, then the Wars of Religion took place from 1562 until 1598. In the 17c the power of the monarchy was restored, reaching its peak under Louis XIV. However, the French Revolution of 1789 dismantled the *ancien régime* in the name of liberty, equality and fraternity, and the First Republic was declared in 1792. The First Empire (1804–14) was ruled by Napoleon I, before the restoration of the Bourbon monarchy for a period between 1814 and 1848. The Second Republic (1848–52) was followed by the Second Empire (1852–70), ruled by Louis Napoleon (Napoleon III), and the Third Republic lasted from 1870 to 1940. There was great political instability between the world wars, with several governments holding office for short periods. The country was occupied by Germany from 1940 until 1944, with the pro-German government at Vichy and the Free French in London under the conservative and nationalist de Gaulle. The Fourth Republic began in 1946; shortly afterwards there was war in Indochina (1946–54), and conflict in Algeria (1954–62). Most of France's colonies were granted independence between 1954 and 1962. The Fifth Republic began in 1958; that same year, France became a founding member of the EEC, and in 2002 it replaced the French franc with the euro. In 2003, the constitution was amended to decentralize power, devolving some economic, education and transport powers to the regions and departments. Proposals to give a degree of autonomy to Corsica were defeated in 2003, however, and separatists resumed the campaign of violence begun in the 1970s.

Overseas departments / regions

❖French Guiana

Location Situated on the north-eastern coast of South America, it is bounded to the west by Suriname; to the east and south by Brazil; and to the north by the Atlantic Ocean
Area 90909 sq km/35091 sq mi
Capital Cayenne
Population 199500 (2006e)

❖Guadeloupe

Location A group of islands in the central Lesser Antilles, in the east Caribbean Sea
Area 1704 sq km/658 sq mi
Capital Basse-Terre
Population 405000 (2006e)

❖Martinique

Location An island in the Windward group of the
Lesser Antilles, east Caribbean Sea, between
Dominica and St Lucia
Area 1079 sq km/416 sq mi
Capital Fort-de-France
Population 436 100 (2006e)

❖Réunion

Location An island in the Indian Ocean, to the east
of Madagascar
Area 2510 sq km/969 sq mi
Capital St-Denis
Population 787 500 (2006e)

Territorial collectivities

❖French Polynesia

Location A grouping of five scattered
archipelagoes in the south-east Pacific Ocean,
between the Cook Islands in the west and the
Pitcairn Islands in the east
Area 3941 sq km/1521 sq mi
Capital Papeete (on Tahiti)
Population 283 000 (2008e)

❖Mayotte

Location A small island group of volcanic origin,
east of Comoros, in the west Indian Ocean
Area 374 sq km/144 sq mi
Capital Mamoudzou
Population 216 300 (2008e)

❖St Barthélemy

Location An island in the central Lesser Antilles,
in the east Caribbean Sea, north-west of
Guadeloupe
Area 21 sq km/8 sq mi
Capital Gustavia
Population 7 490 (2008e)

❖St Martin

Location The northern part of the island of St
Martin, in the east Caribbean Sea, north-west of
Guadeloupe
Area 54 sq km/21 sq mi
Capital Marigot
Population 29 370 (2008e)

❖St Pierre and Miquelon

Location Two small groups of islands in the
North Atlantic Ocean, south of Newfoundland
(Canada)
Area 240 sq km/93 sq mi
Capital St-Pierre
Population 7000 (2008e)

❖Wallis and Futuna Islands

Location Two groups of islands in the south-
central Pacific Ocean, lying north-east of Fiji
Area 274 sq km/106 sq mi
Capital Matu-Utu (on Uvéa)
Population 15 200 (2008e)

Sui generis collectivity

❖New Caledonia

Location A large island with a group of small
islands as dependencies in the south-west
Pacific Ocean, 1100km/680mi east of Australia
Area 18 575 sq km/7170 sq mi
Capital Nouméa
Population 224 800 (2008e)

Overseas territory

❖French Southern and Antarctic Territories

Location A group of islands in the southern Indian
Ocean, and Adélie Land in Antarctica
Area 507 781 sq km/196 003 sq mi
Population Scientific staff only

GABON

Official name Gabonese Republic
Local name Gabon
Location A republic in west equatorial Africa,
bounded to the south, east and north-east by
Congo; to the north by Cameroon; to the north-
west by Equatorial Guinea; and to the west by
the Atlantic Ocean
Area 267 667 sq km/103 319 sq mi
Capital Libreville
Chief towns Lambaréné, Franceville, Port Gentil

Population 1 486 000 (2008e)
Time zone GMT +1
Currency 1 CFA Franc (CFAFr) = 100 centimes
Language French; local languages are widely
spoken
Religions Christianity over 55%, traditional beliefs
and Islam 1%
Ethnic groups Bantu tribes (Fang, Bapounou, Nzebi
and Obamba are the main groupings) 89%,
other Africans and Europeans 11%

Physical description

On the Equator for 880km/550mi west to east; land rises from narrow coastal plain with lagoons and estuaries towards the African central plateau, cut by several rivers, notably the Ogooué; highest point is Mont Ibounji (1575m/5167ft); c.85% of land is rainforest, with savannah in the east and south.

Climate

Equatorial climate; annual average rainfall is 1250–2000mm, rising to 2500mm near the coast and at altitude; dry season in June–August; average maximum daily temperatures at Libreville are 33°–37°C.

Government

Governed by a President, a Prime Minister and Council of Ministers, and a bicameral Parliament consisting of a Senate and a National Assembly.

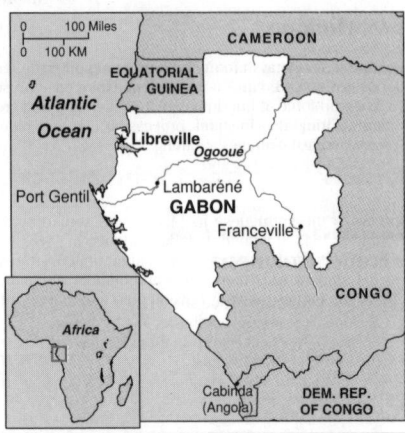

Economy

Prosperous economy based on oil (50% of GDP), natural gas, minerals (manganese, iron ore, uranium) and forestry; industries mostly process the energy, mineral, timber and agricultural products; agriculture, largely at subsistence level, employs 60% of the workforce; main products are cocoa, coffee, sugar, palm oil, rubber, cattle, fish.

History

Gabon was visited by the Portuguese in the 15c and was under French control from the mid-19c. Libreville was founded in 1849 by slaves liberated from a slave ship captured by the French. The country was occupied by France in 1885, and became one of four territories of French West Africa in 1910. It gained independence in 1960. President Bongo assumed power in 1967 and in 1968 a one-party state was established. Unrest in the late 1980s led to the introduction in 1991 of a new constitution allowing a multiparty system. The president's party has remained the ruling party under the multiparty system (amid allegations of electoral fraud), although it has formed coalition governments that include opposition party members since 1994.

THE GAMBIA

Official name Republic of the Gambia
Local name Gambia
Location A republic situated in west Africa, bounded on all sides by Senegal except for the Atlantic Ocean coastline in the west
Area 11 295 sq km/4015 sq mi
Capital Banjul
Chief towns Serrekunda, Brikama, Bakau, Georgetown
Population 1 753 000 (2006e)

Time zone GMT
Currency 1 Dalasi (GMD) = 100 butut
Language English; Mandinka, Fula, Wolof and other local languages are also spoken
Religions Islam 90%, Christianity 8%, traditional beliefs 2%
Ethnic groups Mandinka 42%, Fula 18%, Wolof 16%, Dyola 10%, Serahuli 9%, other African 4%, non-African 1%

Physical description

The Gambia is a strip of land stretching 322km/200mi east to west along the River Gambia; mostly a flood plain flanked by savannah and low hills, not rising above 90m/295ft.

Climate

Tropical, with a hot rainy season in June–September; there is high humidity in the wet season with high night temperatures; the average annual rainfall at Banjul is 1295mm, average temperatures range from 23°C in January, to 27°C in July; average temperatures rise to over 40°C inland and rainfall decreases.

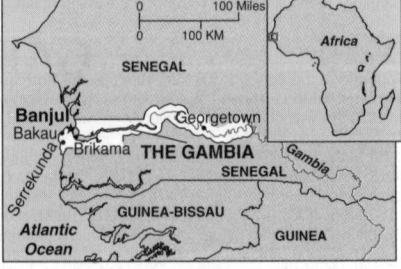

Government

Governed by an executive President, a Cabinet and a unicameral National Assembly.

Economy

Economic mainstays are agriculture, re-export trade with neighbouring countries and tourism; offshore oil deposits discovered in 2004, though unexploited at present; agriculture, largely at subsistence level, employs 75% of workforce; groundnuts are the chief crop and groundnut processing is the main industry; small-scale manufacturing also includes processing fish and hides, agricultural machinery assembly, metalworking, woodworking, beverages, clothing.

History

Visited by the Portuguese in 1455, it was settled by the English in the 17c and became a British Crown Colony in 1843. It gained its independence in 1965, and became a republic in 1970 under the presidency of Sir Dawda Jawara, who was president until overthrown in a 1994 military coup. The country has enjoyed relative stability, but the regime is authoritarian and although multiparty elections have been held since 2001, opposition parties regularly boycott polls and there is intimidation of the opposition and the media.

GEORGIA

Official name Georgia
Local name Sak'art'velo
Location A republic in central and western Transcaucasia. It is bounded to the south-east by Azerbaijan; to the south by Armenia; to the south-west by Turkey; to the west by the Black Sea; and to the north by Russia
Area 69 700 sq km/26 900 sq mi
Capital Tbilisi
Chief towns Kutaisi, Rustavi, Batumi, Sukhumi, Poti

Population 4 631 000 (2008e)
Time zone GMT +4
Currency 1 Lari (GEL) = 100 tetri
Languages Georgian, Abkhaz; Russian, Armenian and Azeri are also spoken
Religions Christianity 83% (Georgian Orthodox 65%, Russian Orthodox 10%, Armenian Orthodox 8%), Islam 11%, unknown 6%
Ethnic groups Georgian 84%, Azeri 6%, Armenian 6%, Russian 1%, others 3%

Physical description

Mostly mountainous, with the Greater Caucasus in the north and the Lesser Caucasus in the south; the highest point is Mount Shkhara (5201m/17 063ft); chief rivers are the Kura and Rioni; forest covers c.39% of the republic.

Climate

Subtropical, warm and humid in the west; continental in the east with hot summers and cold winters.

Government

Governed by a President, a Prime Minister and Council of Ministers, and a unicameral Parliament.

Economy

Recovering from near collapse of 1990s; agriculture is largest sector, employing 55% of workforce and producing wines, tea, tobacco and citrus fruits; main industries are steel, aircraft, machine tools, vehicles, textiles, footwear, chemicals, wood products, financial services, re-export of oil and gas (transit state for pipelines to Black Sea from landlocked eastern neighbours).

History

Founded in the 4c BC, it was later ruled by the Romans and then the Arabs. An independent empire in the 11c later fell to Persia and Turkey. Part of the Russian empire from the early 19c, it declared independence in 1918 but was occupied by Soviet troops in 1921 and proclaimed a Soviet Socialist Republic. It formed the Transcaucasian Republic with Armenia and Azerbaijan before becoming a separate republic of the USSR in 1936. In the 1980s growing demands for autonomy or independence were brutally suppressed, but nevertheless led to independence being declared in 1991. Clashes between supporters of President Zviad Gamsakhurdia and the National Guard developed into a civil war that resulted in the deposition of the President and the suspension of parliament. Gamsakhurdia was replaced in 1992 by Eduard Shevardnadze, who set about restoring stability to the nation. In addition to the civil conflict, which continued throughout 1993, there was fighting by secessionists in the regions of Abkhazia, to whom Shevardnadze agreed in 1994 to give a measure of autonomy, and South Ossetia. Shevardnadze was forced to resign in Nov 2003 after demonstrations over alleged electoral fraud, and the presidential election in 2004 was won by Mikhail Saakashvili. In 2008, clashes between the army and South Ossetian separatists led Georgia to attack the region. Russia retaliated in support of the secessionists and invaded Georgia. The short-lived conflict was ended by a ceasefire.

GERMANY

Official name Federal Republic of Germany
Local name Deutschland
Location It is bounded to the east by Poland and
the Czech Republic; to the south-east and south
by Austria; to the south-west by Switzerland; to
the west by France, Luxembourg, Belgium and
the Netherlands; and to the north by the North
Sea, Denmark and the Baltic Sea
Area 357 868 sq km/138 137 sq mi
Capital Berlin

Chief towns Bonn, Hamburg, Munich, Cologne,
Essen, Leipzig, Frankfurt (am Main)
Population 82 369 000 (2008e)
Time zone GMT +1
Currency 1 Euro (€) = 100 cents
Language German; Sorbian (a Slavic language) is
spoken by a few
Religions Christianity 68% (Prot 34%, RC 34%),
Islam 4%, others and unaffiliated 28%
Ethnic groups German 92%, Turkish 2%, others 6%

Map of Germany showing cities including Hamburg, Berlin, Essen, Düsseldorf, Cologne, Bonn, Frankfurt, Karlsruhe, Stuttgart, Munich, Nuremberg, Leipzig, Dresden; neighbouring countries Denmark, Netherlands, Belgium, Lux., France, Switzerland, Liech., Austria, Italy, Czech Republic, Poland; features North Sea, Baltic Sea, Frisian Islands, Rügen, Rhine, Weser, Elbe, Main, Danube, Black Forest, Bodensee, Zugspitze; inset map of Europe.

Physical description

The Baltic coastline is backed by a fertile low-lying plain, low hills and many glacial lakes; the central uplands include the Rhenish Slate Mountains, the Black Forest and the Odenwald and Spessart; the land rises in the south in several ranges, notably the Bavarian Alps (highest peak is the Zugspitze, 2962m/9717ft), and the Harz Mountains of the Thüringian Forest; major rivers include the Rhine (south to north), Elbe, Ems, Weser, Ruhr, Danube, Oder and Neisse; a complex canal system links the chief rivers.

Climate

Temperate in the north-west, with mild but stormy winters; elsewhere, the climate is continental (more temperate in the east); the east and south have lower winter temperatures, with considerable snowfall and some freezing of canals; average winter temperature in the north is 2°C, and in the south it is –3°C; average summer temperature in the north is 16°C, and slightly higher in the south; the average annual rainfall on the plains is 600–700mm, increasing in parts of the Alps to 2000mm.

Government

Governed by a federal President, a federal Chancellor and government, and a bicameral legislature, comprising the Federal Assembly (*Bundestag*) and the Federal Council (*Bundesrat*). Each of the 16 states (*Länder*) has its own government and legislature.

Economy

A diverse, highly industrialized and technologically advanced economy, although reunification in the 1990s caused recession and stagnation; in the north and the centre there is substantial heavy industry, especially iron and steel (in the Ruhr Valley), coal mining, cement, metal products, chemicals, textiles, machinery, electrical goods, food processing, precision and optical equipment, motor vehicles, shipbuilding and textiles; coal, iron ore, zinc, lead and potash are mined; agriculture includes arable and livestock farming, fruit, wheat, barley, potatoes, sugar beet and forestry; the Rhine and Mosel valleys are major wine-producing areas; tourism is increasing, especially in the south.

History

A central European state formed by the political unification of West Germany and East Germany in 1990. It was the location of ancient Germanic tribes united within the Frankish Empire of Charlemagne in the 8c and of an elective monarchy after 918 under Otto I, with the Holy Roman Empire divided into several hundred states. Many reforms and territorial changes took place during the Napoleonic era, and after the Congress of Vienna (1814–15) a German Confederation of 39 states under Austria was formed. Under Bismarck, Prussia succeeded Austria as the leading German power and excluded her from the North German Confederation. The union of Germany and foundation of the Second Reich (1871), with the King of Prussia as hereditary German Emperor, gave rise, from around 1900, to an aggressive foreign policy which eventually led to World War I. After the German defeat, the Second Reich was replaced by the democratic Weimar Republic and, in 1933, political power passed to the Nazi Party. Hitler's acts of aggression as Chancellor and Leader (*Führer*) of the totalitarian Third Reich eventually led to World War II and a second defeat for Germany, with the collapse of the German political regime. The area of Germany was subsequently reduced, and occupied by the UK, USA, France, USSR and Poland, whose zone is now recognized as sovereign Polish territory. This Western occupation softened with the creation of the Federal Republic of Germany (1949) out of the three western zones, and a socialist German Democratic Republic (East Germany) out of the Soviet-occupied zone. Western forces continued to occupy West Berlin, which became a province of West Germany, while East Germany was governed on the communist Soviet model, with the Socialist Unity Party (SED) guaranteed a pre-eminent role. Anti-Soviet demonstrations in East Germany were put down in 1953, and both republics were recognized as sovereign states the following year. In 1958 West Germany was a founder-member of the EEC, and in 2002 it replaced the Deutsche Mark with the euro. The flow of refugees from East to West Germany continued until 1961, but was largely stopped by the building of the Berlin Wall. East Germany was accorded diplomatic recognition and membership of the UN after signing a treaty with West Germany in 1973. In East Germany the movement for democratic reform, as well as mounting economic crisis, culminated (Nov 1989) in the opening of the Berlin Wall and other border crossings to the West, and a more open government policy. Free elections (Mar 1990) led first to economic union with West Germany (July) and then full political unification (Oct), in which West Germany's federal system of government, built around 10 states (*Länder*) with considerable powers, absorbed East Germany as five additional states. Germany is a leading industrial and trading nation, and a dominant force in the European Union (EU), but since reunification has experienced economic problems and outbreaks of racial violence by the far right. Chancellor Helmut Kohl and the CDU (Christian Democratic Union) held power for 16 years from 1982, and were defeated in 1998 by the SPD (Social Democratic Party) led by Gerhard Schröder. Schröder lost a vote of confidence in 2005 and called an early election which resulted in a narrow victory for the opposition; the three main political parties formed a 'grand coalition' under the opposition leader Angela Merkel, who became Germany's first female Chancellor.

GHANA

Official name Republic of Ghana
Local name Ghana
Location A republic in West Africa, bounded to the west by the Côte d'Ivoire; to the north by Burkina Faso; to the east by Togo; and to the south by the Gulf of Guinea
Area 238 686 sq km/92 133 sq mi
Capital Accra
Chief towns Sekondi-Takoradi, Kumasi, Tamale
Population 23 383 000 (2008e)

Time zone GMT
Currency 1 Cedi (₵) = 100 pesewas
Language English; several African languages are also spoken
Religions Christianity 69% (Prot 43%, RC 15%, other 11%), Islam 16%, traditional beliefs 8%, other 1%, none 6%
Ethnic groups African 92% (of whom Akan 45%, Mole-Dagbon 15%, Ewe 12%, Ga-Dangme 7%, Guan 4%, Gurma 3%, Grusi 3%), others 8%

Physical description

Coastline of sand bars and lagoons; low-lying grassy plains inland, leading to the Ashanti plateau in the west and the River Volta basin in the east, dammed to form Lake Volta; mountains rise in the east to 885m/2904ft at Afadjato.

Climate

Tropical climate, including a warm, dry coastal belt in the south-east, a hot, humid south-west corner, and hot, dry savannah in the north; Kumasi has an average annual rainfall of 1400mm.

Government

Governed by an executive President, a Council of Ministers and a unicameral Parliament.

Economy

Poor country, dependent on international aid; economy based on gold, cocoa (world's second largest producer), forestry and tuna fishing; diamonds, manganese and bauxite also mined; agriculture largely at subsistence level; industries include light manufacturing, aluminium smelting and food processing.

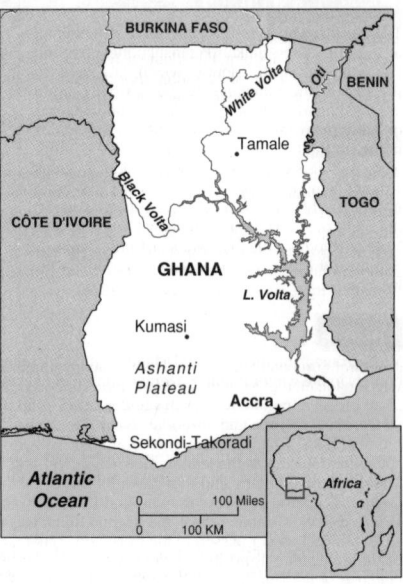

History

Ghana was discovered by Europeans in the 15c, and became the centre of the slave trade in the 18c. The modern state was created by the union of two former British territories, British Gold Coast (Crown Colony in 1874) and British Togoland in 1957, and the name was taken from the ancient Kingdom of Ghana. It became independent in 1957 and a republic in 1960, the first British colony in Africa to achieve independence. The country was mostly under military rule, interspersed with short-lived civilian governments, from 1966 until 1992, when a multiparty constitution was approved. In 2002–4, a reconciliation commission investigated human rights abuses during military rule. Since the mid 1990s there have been clashes between different ethnic groups in the north, mostly over land ownership.

■ Gibraltar▶United Kingdom

GREECE

Official name Hellenic Republic
Local name Ellas, Ellada
Location A republic in south-eastern Europe, occupying the southern part of the Balkan Peninsula and numerous islands in the Aegean and Ionian seas
Area 131 957 sq km/50 935 sq mi
Capital Athens
Chief towns Thessaloniki, Patras, Heraklion (on

Crete), Volos, Larisa, Piraieus
Population 10 723 000 (2008e)
Time zone GMT +2
Currency 1 Euro (€) = 100 cents
Language Greek
Religions Christianity 98% (Orthodox), Islam 1%, others 1%
Ethnic groups Greek 93%, others 7%

Physical description

The country consists of a large area of mainland at the end of the Balkan Peninsula, including the Peloponnese in the south, which is linked to the rest of the mainland by the narrow Corinth Isthmus; nearly 80% of the country is mountainous or hilly; main ranges are the Pindhos Mountains in the north, the Rhodope Mountains in the north-east, and the east coast range, which includes Mount Olympus (2917m/9570ft), the highest point in Greece; there are several rivers and small lakes; there are over 1400 islands, notably Crete, Euboea, Lesbos, Rhodes, Chios, Cephalonia, Corfu, Lemnos, Samos and Naxos, also with hilly or mountainous interiors.

Climate

Mediterranean on the coast and islands, with mild, rainy winters and hot, dry summers; rainfall occurs almost entirely in the winter months; average annual rainfall in Athens is 414mm.

Government

Governed by a President, a Prime Minister and Cabinet, and a unicameral Parliament; Mount Athos, in Macedonia region, is a self-governing community of 20 monasteries.

Economy

Market economy with a large public sector; the service sector accounts for 72% of GDP and employs 68% of the workforce, mainly in tourism and shipping; agriculture is based on cereals, vegetables, fruit, tobacco, beef and dairy products; industries include food and tobacco processing, textiles, metal products, chemicals, mining (iron, magnesite, bauxite, lignite), oil refining and petroleum products.

History

Greece has been inhabited since Palaeolithic times, and its prehistoric civilization culminated in the remarkable Minoan culture of Crete (3400–1100 BC). The Dorians (a sub-group of Hellenic peoples) invaded from the north in the 12c BC, and Greek colonies were established along the north and south Mediterranean coasts and on the shores of the Black Sea. In the 8–6c BC the Greeks settled throughout the eastern Mediterranean, establishing colonies along the shores of Asia Minor and the adjoining islands. There were many city states on the mainland, notably Sparta and Athens. In the southern part of the Balkan Peninsula, a distinctive Greek culture has persisted unbroken since antiquity; the Slav and Avar invaders who arrived in waves in the 6c and later settled in the southern part of the Balkan Peninsula were Hellenized and assimilated into the original population. In the 5c BC Persian invasions were repelled at Marathon, Salamis, Plataea and Mycale, and Greek literature and art flourished. Conflict between Sparta and Athens (the Peloponnesian War, 431–404 BC) weakened the country, which was overwhelmed by the Macedonians (4c BC) under Philip II of Macedon, who unified the Greek city states under their hegemony. Military expeditions under Philip's son, Alexander III, the Great, penetrated Asia and Africa. Macedonian power was broken by the Romans in 197 BC. After the fall of the western Roman Empire, Greece and Crete formed part of the Greek-speaking Byzantine Empire which stretched deep into Asia Minor and the Middle East. The Byzantine Age (330–1204) was a period of political and cultural hegemony for the Greeks in the Balkans and eastern Mediterranean. After the sack of Constantinople (1204), the Balkan Greeks fell prey to the ambitions of the Franks and Venetians, and finally to the Turks who occupied Greece from 1460 to 1830. Crete was purchased by the Venetian Republic in 1210 and enjoyed an artistic renaissance, but after it too fell to the Ottomans (1669), it went into a long decline. The Greek national revival began in the late 18c, and led to the Greek War of Independence (1821–8) against the Turks. By the end of the war Greece, though ravaged, was a free state, and it gained formal recognition of its independence from the Ottoman Empire in 1832. During the war, the Cretans joined the insurgents but were quickly crushed and made subject to the Egyptian Viceroy, Ali Pasha. Once again under Ottoman control from 1840, Cretan demands for *enosis* (union with Greece) grew apace, with several revolts (1858, 1866–9 and 1895), but these were handled cautiously by the Greek government lest it antagonize the Ottoman Empire. After a brief military campaign, Crete was declared independent under a High Commissioner appointed by the Great Powers (1898). The Cretan assembly declared its *enosis* in 1908, but not until the Treaties of London (1913) was it joined to the Kingdom of Greece. After gaining independence, Greek society was riddled with divisions, with the 19c seeing continuous arguments over the constitution and form of government. In the early 20c the Greeks were at war from 1912 to 1922: first the Balkan Wars, then World War I, both of which brought substantial territorial gains, and then the disastrous war against the Turks in Anatolia (1919–22) during which c.30 000 Christians were killed in Izmir (Smyrna) in Sep 1922, and over a million Greeks were forced to leave Asia Minor. The Greek Republic was established in 1924 and the monarchy restored in 1935. Meanwhile, Crete became a stronghold of support for its native son, Eleuthérios Venizélos, and rebelled against Metaxas (1938). During World War II, Greece and Crete were occupied by the Germans, and Greece was afterwards ravaged by a bloody civil war (1944–9) between monarchists and communists. Following a tentative period of democracy, a military coup in 1967 led to the right-wing dictatorship of the Greek Colonels (1967–74). The monarchy was formally abolished and democracy restored in 1974, since when there has been relative peace and stability. Greece joined the EC in 1981 and replaced the drachma with the euro in 2002.

■ Greenland ▶ Denmark

GRENADA

Official name Grenada
Local name Grenada
Location An independent constitutional monarchy of the West Indies and the most southerly of the Windward Islands, in the eastern Caribbean Sea
Area 344 sq km/133 sq mi
Capital St George's
Chief towns Gouyave, Victoria, Grenville

Population 90 300 (2008e)
Time zone GMT –4
Currency 1 East Caribbean Dollar (EC$) = 100 cents
Language English
Religions Christianity 100% (RC 53%, Prot 47%)
Ethnic groups African descent 82%, mixed 13%, European and East Indian 5%

Physical description

Comprises the main island of Grenada (34km/21mi long and 19km/12mi wide) and the South Grenadines (including Carriacou), an arc of small islands extending from Grenada north to St Vincent; Grenada is of volcanic origin, with a ridge of mountains along its entire length; the highest point is Mount St Catherine, which rises to 843m/2766ft.

Climate

Subtropical; the average annual temperature is 23°C; the annual rainfall varies from 1270mm on the coast to 5000mm in the interior; the rainy season is June–December.

Government

Governed by a Governor-General (representing the British monarch, who is head of state), a Prime Minister and Cabinet, and a bicameral Parliament comprising a Senate and a House of Representatives.

Economy

Poor country, dependent on international aid; main activities are tourism, financial services, agriculture (chiefly nutmeg, bananas, cocoa, fruit, vegetables, mace, fish), processing agricultural products, textiles and light assembly industries.

History

Columbus discovered the island in 1498. Settled by the French in the mid-17c, it was ceded to Britain in 1763 by the Treaty of Paris, but retaken by France in 1779, and ceded again to Britain in 1783. It became a British Crown Colony in 1877 and gained its independence in 1974 under Prime Minister Eric Gairy. The government was overthrown in 1979 by Maurice Bishop, who became Prime Minister but was deposed and killed in a further uprising in 1983.

These events prompted an invasion by US troops to restore stable government, which has been maintained since elections in 1984, with power alternating between the two main political parties.

■ Guadeloupe▶France

■ Guam▶United States of America

GUATEMALA

Official name Republic of Guatemala
Local name Guatemala
Location The northernmost of the central American republics, bounded to the north and west by Mexico; to the south-west by the Pacific Ocean; to the east by Belize and the Caribbean Sea; and to the south-east by Honduras and El Salvador
Area 108 889 sq km/42 031 sq mi
Capital Guatemala City
Chief towns Quezaltenango, Escuintla, Antigua, Mazatenango
Population 13 002 000 (2008e)
Time zone GMT –6
Currency 1 Quetzal (Q) = 100 centavos
Language Spanish; 23 indigenous languages are also officially recognized
Religions Christianity 88% (RC 57%, Prot 31%), traditional beliefs (Mayan) 5%, others 7%
Ethnic groups mestizo (Ladino) and European 59%, Amerindian 40%, others 1%

Physical description

Over two-thirds is mountainous with extensive forests; from the narrow Pacific coastal plain, the highlands rise steeply to heights of 2500–3000m/8200–9840ft; there are many volcanoes on the southern edge of the highlands; rivers flow to both the Pacific Ocean and the Caribbean Sea; the highest point is Tajumulco (4220m/13 845ft).

Climate

Tropical in the lowlands and on the Caribbean coast, cooler at altitude; rainy season in May–October; Guatemala City average temperatures are 17°C in January and 21°C in July; average annual rainfall is 1316mm; much higher rainfall on exposed slopes; subject to severe hurricanes and earthquakes.

Government

Governed by an executive President, a Cabinet, and a unicameral Congress of the Republic.

Economy

Developing country, still dependent on international aid and remittances; agriculture is most important sector, accounting for c.40% of exports, chiefly coffee, sugar, bananas, cardamon, fruit, vegetables; industries include textiles, garments, ceramics; tourism is growing.

History

Mayan and Aztec civilizations flourished before the Spanish conquest of 1523–4. Guatemala gained independence from Spain as part of the Central American Federation in 1821. The Federation was officially dissolved in 1840, following which the country had a series of dictatorships broken by short periods of representative government. In 1985 civilian rule was restored and has survived attempted coups in 1989 and 1993. In 1996, after 35 years of fighting between left-wing Guatemalan National Revolutionary Unity guerrillas and the government, a peace agreement was finally reached, ending Latin America's longest civil war. Guatemala's long-standing dispute regarding its claim to Belize edged closer to resolution in 1991, when Guatemala recognized Belize's independence. Talks in 2002 led to agreement on a draft settlement to the border dispute.

■ Guiana, French▶France

GUINEA

Official name Republic of Guinea
Local name Guinée
Location A republic in West Africa, bounded to the north-west by Guinea-Bissau; to the north by Senegal and Mali; to the east by Côte d'Ivoire; . to the south by Liberia and Sierra Leone; and to the south-west by the Atlantic Ocean
Area 246 048 sq km/94 974 sq mi
Capital Conakry
Chief towns Kankan, Kindia, Labé

Population 9 860 000 (2008e)
Time zone GMT
Currency 1 Guinea Franc (GFr) = 100 centimes
Language French; eight local languages are also spoken widely
Religions Islam 85%, Christianity 8%, traditional beliefs 7%
Ethnic groups Peulh 40%, Malinke 30%, Soussou 20%, others 10%

Physical description

The coast is characterized by mangrove forests, rising to a forested and widely cultivated narrow coastal plain; the Fouta Djallon massif in the north-west lies c.900m/2952ft above the coastal plain; the highest point is Mount Nimba (1752m/5748ft); savannah plains in the east are cut by rivers flowing towards the upper basin of the River Niger; the Guinea Highlands in the south-east are forested and generally rise above 1000m/3280ft.

Climate

Tropical climate (wet season May–October); the average temperature in the dry season on the coast is 32°C, dropping to 23°C in the wet season; cooler inland and drier in the east; the average annual rainfall at Conakry is 4923mm.

Government

Governed by an executive President, a Prime Minister and Council of Ministers and a unicameral National Assembly.

Economy

Undeveloped and dependent on international aid; agriculture, mostly at subsistence level, employs 76% of workforce; chief cash crops are coffee, tropical fruits and fish; main industries are mining (bauxite, iron ore, gold, diamonds), alumina refining, processing agricultural produce and light manufacturing.

History

Part of the Mali Empire in the 16c, it became a French protectorate in 1849 and was governed with Senegal as Rivières du Sud. It became a separate colony in 1893, and a constituent territory within French West Africa in 1904. It reverted to separate colonial status as an Overseas Territory in 1946, and became independent in 1958. The first president, Ahmed Sékou Touré, established a one-party state pursuing Marxist policies and remained in power until his death in 1984. Shortly after his death a coup established a Military Committee for National Recovery under Lansana Conté, who introduced economic liberalization and in 1993 reintroduced a multiparty system. Conté was elected president and has retained office in subsequent elections. Since 2000, an influx of refugees from conflicts in neighbouring countries has created an additional economic burden, and increasing ethnic tension.

GUINEA-BISSAU

Official name Republic of Guinea-Bissau
Local name Guiné-Bissau
Location A republic in West Africa, bounded to the south-east and east by Guinea; to the north by Senegal; and to the south-west by the Atlantic Ocean
Area 36 260 sq km/14 000 sq mi
Capital Bissau
Chief towns Bafatá, Bolama, Mansôa
Population 1 503 000 (2008e)

Time zone GMT
Currency 1 CFA Franc (CFAFr) = 100 centimes
Languages Portuguese, Guinean Creole (Crioulo); many African languages are also spoken
Religions Islam 50%, traditional beliefs 40%, Christianity 10%
Ethnic groups Balante 30%, Fula 20%, Malinke 14%, Mandyako 13%, Pepel 7%, other African 15%, others 1%

Physical description

An indented coast typified by islands and mangrove-lined estuaries, backed by forested coastal plains; a low-lying country with savannah-covered plateaus in the south and east, rising to 310m/1017ft on the Guinea border; chief rivers are the Cacheu, Geba and Corubal; includes the heavily-forested Bijagos Archipelago.

Climate

Tropical climate with a wet season in June–October; average annual rainfall at Bissau is 1950mm and the temperature range is 24°–27°C.

Government

Governed by an executive President, a Prime Minister and Council of Ministers, and a unicameral National People's Assembly.

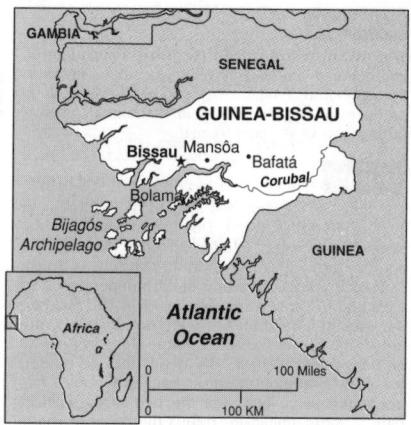

Economy

Very poor, and dependent on international aid; based on agriculture, mostly at subsistence level, and fishing; chief cash crops are groundnuts, palm kernels, cashew nuts, rice, fish, timber; small-scale industry processes agricultural produce and produces beer and soft drinks; unexploited mineral reserves.

History

Discovered by the Portuguese in 1446, Guinea Bissau was administered as part of the Cape Verde islands until 1879, when it became a separate Portuguese colony. After becoming an Overseas Territory of Portugal in 1952, it gained independence in 1973, with Luís Cabral as President from 1974. He was deposed by a military coup led by João Vieira in 1980, and the constitution was changed in 1984 to make Vieira President. A multiparty system was introduced in 1990, and the first multiparty elections were held in 1994; they were won by the ruling party and Vieira was re-elected. An army mutiny in 1998 developed into a civil war until Vieira was ousted in 1999 but the president elected in 2000, Kumba Yalla, was deposed in a military coup in 2003. Constitutional government was reintroduced with a legislative election in 2004 and a presidential election in 2005 that was won by Vieira.

GUYANA

Official name Co-operative Republic of Guyana	Time zone GMT –4
Local name Guyana	Currency 1 Guyana Dollar (G$) = 100 cents
Location A republic on the northern coast of South America, bounded to the east by Suriname; to the west by Venezuela; to the south by Brazil; and to the north by the Atlantic Ocean	Language English; Creole, Hindi, Urdu and Amerindian dialects are also spoken
Area 214 969 sq km/82 978 sq mi	Religions Christianity 57% (Prot 49%, RC 8%), Hinduism 28%, Islam 7%, others 4%, none 4%
Capital Georgetown	Ethnic groups East Indian 43%, black 30%, mixed 17%, Amerindian 9%, other 1%
Population 771 000 (2008e)	

Physical description

Narrow coastal plains rise to highlands in the west and savannah in the south; the highest peak is Mount Roraima (2810m/9219ft) in the Pakaraima Mountains; much of the interior (c.85%) is covered with rainforest; the coastal plain, below sea level at high tide, is protected by sea defences, dams and canals; main rivers are the Essequibo, Demerara and Berbice, with many rapids and waterfalls in the upper courses.

Climate

Equatorial climate, moderated by north-east trade winds; the lowlands are hot and wet, with high humidity; Georgetown, in the coastal lowland area, has average temperatures of 22°C–31°C and two seasons of high rainfall (May–July, November–January); lower temperatures and less rainfall on the high plateau inland.

Government

Governed by an executive President, a Prime Minister and Cabinet, and a unicameral National Assembly.

Economy

Slow recovery from 1990s problems; dependent on international aid and remittances; main activities are agriculture (sugar, rice), processing agricultural products, mining (bauxite, gold, diamonds), forestry, fishing (shrimps); some tourism.

History

The coast of Guyana was sighted by Columbus in 1498 and settled by the Dutch from the late 16c. Several areas were ceded to Britain in 1815, and the country formally came under British rule as British Guiana in 1831. Guyana gained independence in 1966 and became a republic in 1970. The first two decades of independence were dominated by the autocratic Forbes Burnham, Prime Minister 1966–80 and President 1980–5. His death in 1985 ended his party's monopoly of power, and power has alternated since between the two main political parties. Party affiliations reflect the racial divisions between those of African descent and those of Indian descent, and the persistent tension between the two has a destabilizing effect on politics.

HAITI

Official name Republic of Haiti	Population 8 924 000 (2008e)
Local name Haïti	Time zone GMT –5
Location A republic in the West Indies occupying the western third of the island of Hispaniola in the Caribbean Sea	Currency 1 Gourde (G, Gde) = 100 centimes
	Languages French, Creole
	Religions Christianity 96% (RC 80%, Prot 16%), others 3%, none/unaffiliated 1%
Area 27 750 sq km/10 712 sq mi	
Capital Port-au-Prince	Note: Around half the population practises voodoo
Chief towns Port-de-Paix, Cap-Haïtien, Gonaïves, Les Cayes, Jacmel, Jérémie	Ethnic groups black 95%, mulatto and white 5%

Physical description

Consists of two mountainous peninsulas (the Massif du Nord in the north and the Massif de la Hotte in the south), separated by a deep structural depression, the Plaine du Cul-de-Sac; to the east is the Massif de la Selle, with Haiti's highest peak, La Selle (2680m/8792ft); Haiti includes the islands of Gonâve off the west coast and Tortue off the north coast.

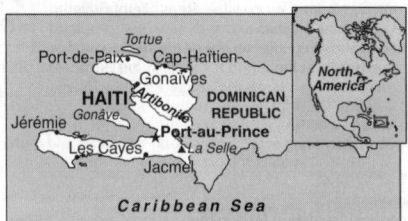

Climate

Tropical maritime; average monthly temperatures range from 24°C to 29°C; annual average rainfall for the north coast and mountains is 1475–1950mm, but only 500mm in the west; the wet season is May–September; hurricanes are common.

Government

Governed by a President, a Prime Minister and Council of Ministers, and a bicameral National Assembly comprising a Chamber of Deputies and a Senate.

Economy

Poorest country in the western hemisphere; heavily dependent on international aid and expatriates' remittances; nearly 70% of population depends on subsistence agriculture; chief activities are agriculture (coffee, cocoa, mangoes, sugar), fishing, garments, leather goods, electronic components, food processing, beverages, tobacco products.

History

Columbus reached Hispaniola in 1492, and Haiti was created when the western third of the island was ceded to France in 1697. In 1791–1804 the Haitian Revolution, the only successful slave revolution in the New World, took place. It culminated in the independence of Haiti (1804). From 1822 to 1844 Haiti was united with Santo Domingo (Dominican Republic). In the late 19c it experienced great instability, with 22 changes of government between 1843 and 1915, when it came under US occupation for 19 years, until 1934. From 1957 to 1986 the Duvalier family had absolute power, their rule being enforced by a civilian militia known as the Tonton Macoute. After Jean-Claude Duvalier fled the country in 1986, it came under military rule until Jean-Bertrand Aristide was elected president in 1990. Aristide was deposed in 1991 in a military coup that instigated a period of repressive rule. Following UN-led negotiations with the military leaders, and amid fears of a US-led invasion, Aristide was restored to power in 1994. He was voted out of office in the elections the following year and René Préval became President in 1996. Aristide was re-elected in 2000, but in 2004 he went into exile after mounting protests at government corruption developed into an armed rebellion. René Préval was elected president again in 2006.

HONDURAS

Official name Republic of Honduras
Local name Honduras
Location A republic in Central America, bounded to the south-west by El Salvador; to the west by Guatemala; to the east and south-east by Nicaragua; to the north by the Caribbean Sea; and to the south by the Pacific Ocean
Area 112 088 sq km/43 266 sq mi
Capital Tegucigalpa
Chief towns San Pedro Sula, Choluteca, La Ceiba,
El Progreso
Population 7 639 000 (2008e)
Time zone GMT –6
Currency 1 Lempira (L, La) = 100 centavos
Language Spanish; Amerindian dialects are also spoken
Religions Christianity 100% (RC 97%, Prot 3%)
Ethnic groups mestizo 90%, Amerindian 7%, black 2%, white 1%

Physical description

The interior is mountainous (c.75% of the land area), with lower-lying land only along the Caribbean and Pacific coasts; the southern plateau rises to 2870m/9416ft at Cerro Las Minas; the Laguna Caratasca lies in the extreme north-east; the Bay Islands in the Caribbean Sea and a group of nearly 300 islands in the Gulf of Fonseca also belong to Honduras.

Climate

Tropical climate in coastal areas, temperate in the centre and west; two wet seasons in upland areas (May–July, September–October); variable temperatures in the interior, 15°–24°C; on the coastal plains the average is c.30°C.

Government

Governed by an executive President, a Cabinet and a unicameral National Congress.

Economy

Poor country, dependent on international aid; agriculture, fishing and forestry are the main activities and basis of most industry; chief products are coffee, shrimps, bananas, gold, palm oil, fruit, lobster, timber, textiles, garments; offshore assembly for re-export and tourism are growing.

History

The centre of Maya culture in the 4–9c, it was settled by the Spanish in the early 16c, and became a province of Guatemala. Honduras gained independence from Spain in 1821 and joined the Central American Federation. It became an independent sovereign state in 1838. The country experienced periods of instability interspersed with military rule until 1981, when a civilian government was elected. During the 1980s it became embroiled in the civil wars in El Salvador and Nicaragua, providing training bases for the counter-insurgents supported by the USA. This provoked internal unrest, which continued after the external wars ended, lasting throughout the 1990s and raising concerns about human rights abuses. In 1998–9 the police and armed forces were brought under civilian control, but the problem of gang warfare continues.

■ Hong Kong ▶ China

Nations of the World

HUNGARY

Official name Republic of Hungary

Local name Magyarorszag

Location A landlocked republic in the Danube basin, central Europe, bounded to the north by Slovakia; to the north-east by the Ukraine; to the east by Romania; to the south by Serbia; to the south-west by Croatia; and to the west by Slovenia and Austria

Area 93 030 sq km/35 910 sq mi

Capital Budapest

Chief towns Debrecen, Miskolc, Szeged, Pécs, Györ

Population 9 931 000 (2008e)

Time zone GMT +1

Currency 1 Forint (Ft) = 100 fillér

Language Magyar (Hungarian)

Religions Christianity 75% (RC 52%, Prot 19%, other Christian 4%), others 11%, none/unaffiliated 14%

Ethnic groups Magyar 92%, Roma 2%, others 6%

Physical description

Mostly low-lying, with low mountains in the north, north-east and north-west; the highest peak is Kékes (1014m/3327ft); the north-west highlands are a spur of the Alps and separate the Little Hungarian Plain from Lake Balaton and the central plains; drained by the River Danube and its tributaries (flowing north to south); frequent flooding, especially in the Great Plains, east of the Danube.

Climate

Extreme continental climate with a marked difference between summer and winter; wettest in spring and early summer; winters are cold with snow lying for 30–40 days and the River Danube is sometimes frozen over for long periods; fog is frequent during settled winter weather.

Government

Governed by a President, a Prime Minister and Cabinet, and a unicameral National Assembly.

Economy

Transformed since 1989 into a market economy with strong growth; nearly half of land is cultivated; agricultural products include cereals, sunflower seeds, vegetables, livestock and grapes for wine-making; large industrial sector includes mining, metallurgy, construction materials, food processing, textiles, chemicals, pharmaceuticals and motor vehicles, logistics and business services.

History

The Magyars probably settled the Hungarian plain in the 9c and a kingdom was formed under St Stephen I in the 11c. This was conquered by the Turks in 1526, then became part of the Habsburg Empire in the 17c. Austria and Hungary were reconstituted as the Dual Monarchy of Austria-Hungary in 1867. The year 1869 was declared the Hungarian Millennium to celebrate the 1000th anniversary of the Magyars' original settlement; it was used by the Hungarian government within Austria-Hungary not only to celebrate the political and economic achievements of the previous half century, but also as an anti-Habsburg demonstration, and it marked an intensification of the attempt to Magyarize Hungary's subject nationalities. Protests were made by the Magyar poor, as well as by Slavs and Romanians. After World War I Hungary became a republic, but a communist revolt introduced a new regime in 1919. A nominally monarchical constitution under a regent, Admiral Miklós Horthy, was restored in 1920, but after the failure of its policy of alliance with Germany in World War II, a new republic under communist government was formed in 1949. In 1956 there was a national insurrection known as the Hungarian Uprising, which followed the denunciation of Stalin at the 20th Congress of the Soviet Communist Party for his oppressive rule. Rioting students and workers demanded radical reform. When the new Prime Minister Imre Nagy announced plans for Hungary's withdrawal from the Warsaw Pact, among other things, Soviet troops and tanks crushed the uprising. Many were killed, thousands fled abroad, and Nagy was executed. Reform was set back for more than a decade, but in the 1960s János Kádár introduced limited liberalization which encouraged the development of the most prosperous and liberal regime in the Soviet bloc. In 1989 pressure for political change was led from within the Communist Party; the same year Hungary was declared a democratic state and in 1990 multiparty elections were held. Since the elections of 1994, when the Hungarian Democratic Forum (MDF) were ousted by a Hungarian Socialist Party-led coalition under Prime Minister Gyula Horn, Hungary has experienced gradual economic growth. Hungary joined NATO in 1999 and the EU in 2004.

ICELAND

Official name Republic of Iceland
Local name Ísland
Location An island state lying between the northern Atlantic Ocean and the Arctic Ocean, south-east of Greenland and 900km/550mi west of Norway
Area 103 000 sq km/40 000 sq mi
Capital Reykjavík
Chief towns Akureyri, Húsavík, Akranes, Keflavík, Ísafjördur

Population 304 400 (2008e)
Time zone GMT
Currency 1 Króna (IKr, ISK) = 100 aurar
Language Icelandic
Religions Christianity 91% (Prot 86%, RC 2%, other Christian 3%), unaffiliated 3%, others 6%
Ethnic groups Icelandic 94%, Danish 1%, others 5%

Physical description

A volcanic island of relatively recent geological origin, at the northern end of the mid-Atlantic Ridge, with several active volcanoes (eg Hekla); the coastline is heavily indented, with many long fjords; an inland plateau of glaciers, lakes and lava fields covers 80% of the interior, rising to mountainous ridges in the north, centre and south; the highest point is Hvannadalshnúkur (2119m/6952ft) in the south-east; famous for its hot springs and geysers, notably *Geysir* from which the term is derived; subterranean hot water provides geothermal power.

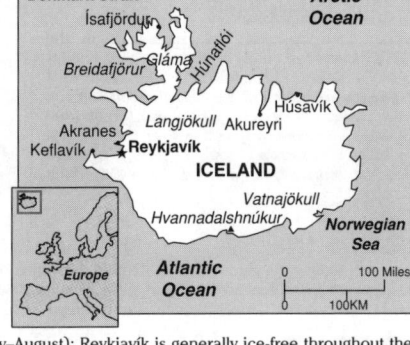

Climate

Temperate, owing to influence of Gulf Stream, but changeable, with relatively mild winters; average daily temperatures are –2°C (January) to 14°C (July–August); Reykjavík is generally ice-free throughout the year; summers are cool and cloudy; average monthly rainfall reaches 94mm (October).

Government

Governed by a President, a Prime Minister and Cabinet, and a unicameral legislature (*Althing*).

Economy

Market economy based largely on inshore and deep-water fishing (70% of export earnings); stock farming, dairy farming, horse-breeding and tourism are important; diversifying into aluminium and diatomite production, information technology and bio-genetics. Badly affected by the 2008 banking collapse.

History

The island was settled by the Norse in the 9c, and in the 10c was the seat of the world's oldest parliament, the *Althing*. It united with Norway in 1262, and with Norway came under Danish rule in 1397. When Norway was ceded to Sweden in 1814, Iceland remained Danish. In 1918 Iceland became an independent kingdom with the same sovereign as Denmark, and since 1944 it has been an independent republic. The extension of the fishing limit around Iceland in 1958, 1972 and 1975 precipitated the 'Cod War' disputes with the UK. Subsequent attempts to restrict fishing in Icelandic waters have allowed stocks to recover from the overfishing of the 1980s, and economic dependence on fisheries is being reduced by diversification. But the economy was affected badly by the failure of a number of banks in 2008.

INDIA

Official name Republic of India
Local name Bhārat (Hindi)
Location A federal republic in southern Asia,
bounded to the north-west by Pakistan; to the
north by China, Nepal and Bhutan; to the east
by Myanmar (Burma) and Bangladesh; to the
south-east by the Bay of Bengal; and to the
south-west by the Arabian Sea
Area 3 287 590 sq km/1 269 338 sq mi
Capital New Delhi
Chief towns Ahmadabad, Bangalore, Chennai,
Hyderabad, Jaipur, Kanpur, Kolkata, Lucknow,
Mumbai, Nagpur, Poona.

*India has renamed several of its cities and states
in recent years, reverting to pre-colonial names;
Bombay is now known as Mumbai, Calcutta as
Kolkata, and Madras as Chennai.*
Population 1 147 996 000 (2008e)
Time zone GMT +5.5
Currency 1 Indian Rupee (Re, Rs) = 100 paise
Languages Hindi, English and 14 other official
languages; Hindustani is spoken widely in
northern India
Ethnic groups Indo-Aryan 72%, Dravidian 25%,
others 3%

Physical description

The second largest state in Asia, bordered to the north by the mountain ridges and valleys of the Himalayas;
the highest peaks are over 7000m/22 966ft in the Karakoram Range and the Ladakh Plateau; Kanchenjunga
(8598m/28 298ft) is the highest point; east of Bangladesh lie the plains and mountainous uplands of Assam;
the central river plains formed by the basins of the Indus, Ganges and Brahmaputra rivers rise to low hills;
south of these is the Deccan Peninsula, with coastal plains rising to a central plateau bounded by the Western
and Eastern Ghats hills; the Thar Desert north-west of Rajasthan is bordered by semi-desert areas.

Climate

Dominated by the Asiatic monsoon; rains come from the south-west (June–October); rainfall decreases (December–February) as winds blow in from the north, followed by drought until March or May; temperatures in the northern mountains vary greatly with altitude; rainfall decreases east to west on the northern plains, with desert conditions in the extreme west; temperatures vary with altitude on the Deccan Plateau, although towards the south of the plateau region the climate is tropical, even in the cool season; the west coast is subject to rain throughout the year, particularly in the south, where humidity is high; cyclones and storms on the south-east coast (especially October–December), with high temperatures and humidity during the monsoon season; Assam has a similar climate to the northern plains and Himalayas but such heavy rainfall in June–October that Cherrapunji is one of the three wettest places in the world, with annual rainfall averaging 10800mm/425in.

Religions

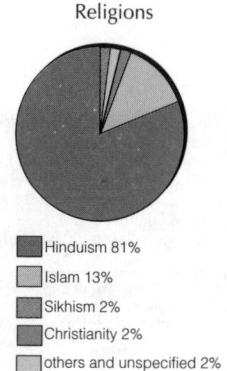

- Hinduism 81%
- Islam 13%
- Sikhism 2%
- Christianity 2%
- others and unspecified 2%

Government

A federal democratic republic; governed by the President of the Union, a Prime Minister and Cabinet, and a bicameral Houses of Parliament (*Sansad*), consisting of a Council of States (*Rajya Sabha*) and a House of the People (*Lok Sabha*). There are 28 states, six union territories and the national capital territory. Each state has a Governor, Council of Ministers and legislative assembly. Each territory is administered by an Administrator or Lieutenant-Governor.

Economy

Formerly a closed economy which opened up in the 1990s, initiating sustained growth and transformation from a largely agricultural economy to one based on services (information technology, telecommunications, tourism) and manufacturing (textiles, garments, chemicals, pharmaceuticals, food processing, steel, transport equipment, cement, machinery, software, jewellery, leather goods); other industries include mining (coal, iron ore, diamonds, other gems), oil and natural gas production; agriculture, fishing and forestry support 60% of the population; main crops are rice, cereals and pulses for subsistence and sugar, jute, cotton and tea as cash crops.

History

The Indus civilization, which emerged in c.2500 BC, was destroyed in 1500 BC by the Aryans, who developed the Brahminic caste system. The Mauryan Emperor Asoka unified most of India, and established Buddhism as the state religion in the 3c BC. Hinduism spread in the 2c BC, and there were Muslim influences during the 7–8c, with a sultanate established at Delhi. Delhi was captured by Timur in 1398 and the Mughal Empire was established by Babur in 1526, and extended by Akbar and Aurangzeb. The Portuguese, French, Dutch and British had footholds in India in the 18c, which led to conflict between France and Britain in 1746–63. The development of British interests was represented by the British East India Company, and British power was established after the Indian Uprising (1857) was crushed. A movement for independence arose in the late 19c, and the Government of India Act in 1919 allowed the election of Indian ministers to share power with appointed British governors; a further Act in 1935 allowed the election of independent provincial governments. Passive resistance campaigns led by Mahatma Gandhi began in the 1920s, and independence was granted in 1948, on the basis of a partition which established a Muslim state (Pakistan). Indian states were later reorganized on a linguistic basis. There was a Pakistan–India war over the disputed territory of Kashmir and Jammu in 1948; this still unresolved issue underlay further India–Pakistan conflict in 1965 and 1971 (the Indo–Pakistan Wars), as well as periods of tension in 1999 and 2000–2 that were heightened by the fact that both countries now possessed nuclear weapons. There has been sporadic Hindu–Muslim hostility internally too, notably in 1978, but also in 1992 and 2002, when the mosque at Ayodhya was the focus of violent rioting that claimed many lives. Separatist movements continue, especially that of the Sikhs' demand for an independent Sikh state in the Punjab. The suppression of the militant Sikh movement in 1984 led to the assassination of Indira Gandhi. Also in 1984, a major gas leak in the city of Bhopal caused c.2500 deaths. Rajiv Gandhi, leader of the Congress (I) Party, was assassinated in 1991 during the general election. Increasing tension generally resulted in inter-communal violence and the declaration in 1993 of a national state of emergency. The Congress (I) Party was heavily defeated in 1996, and a period of political instability followed in which there were several general elections and allegations of widespread corruption in public life. Economic reforms, begun in the early 1990s, continued and India is emerging as a major world economy with a growing middle class. The Congress (I) Party was eclipsed by the Hindu nationalist Bharatiya Janata Party (BJP) in the 1990s, won a surprise victory in the 2004 general election under Sonia Gandhi; she refused the premiership and Manmohan Singh became Prime Minister, the first Sikh to hold the office. In recent years, the main security threats have been from Kashmiri separatists and Islamic extremists; terrorist attacks in Mumbai in 2008 left nearly 200 dead.

INDONESIA

Official name Republic of Indonesia
Local name Indonesia
Location A republic in South-East Asia comprising the world's largest island group
Area 1906240 sq km/735809 sq mi
Capital Jakarta
Chief towns Jayapura, Bandung, Semarang, Surabaya, Medan, Palembang
Population 237512000 (2008e)
Time zones GMT +7/+9
Currency 1 Rupiah (Rp) = 100 sen
Language Bahasa Indonesia; English, Dutch, Javanese and other local dialects are widely spoken; 300 regional languages

Physical description

Five main islands and 30 smaller archipelagos totalling 13677 islands and islets, of which c.6000 are inhabited; most have narrow coastal plains with hilly or mountainous interiors; over 100 volcanic peaks on Java, of which 15 are active; the highest point is Puncak Jaya (5030m/16503ft); over 50% of country is covered with rainforest.

Climate

Equatorial climate (hot and humid), affected alternatively by the north monsoon (November–March) and south monsoon (May–September) and often particularly wet in April and October; annual rainfall of 1500–4000mm/60–160in; the average temperature is 27°C on island coasts, falling inland and with altitude.

Government

Governed by an executive President, a Cabinet and a bicameral People's Consultative Assembly, comprising a House of Representatives and a House of Representatives of the Regions.

Economy

Recovering from financial and political crises of 1990s, Bali bombings and Indian Ocean tsunami; growth based on mineral assets and agricultural production; main activities are oil and natural gas production, mining (coal, minerals, metals), forestry, fishing, production of rubber, coffee and rice, textiles, chemicals, electrical appliances and tourism.

History

Indonesia includes the island group of the Moluccas, also called the Spice Islands; Kalimantan, four provinces in the Indonesian part of Borneo; Sumatra, which is the fifth-largest island in the world and was the centre of the Buddhist kingdom of Sri Vijaya in the 7–13c; and was discovered by Marco Polo in the 13c; and the western half of the mountainous island of Timor. The Indonesian islands were settled in early times by Hindus and Buddhists, whose power lasted until the 14c. Islam was introduced in the 14–15c. Portuguese settlers arrived in the early 16c, and the Dutch East India Company was established in 1602. Occupied by the Japanese in World War II, Indonesia declared its independence in 1945, under Dr Sukarno. The 1945 constitution established a federal system that was replaced by

Religions

- Islam 86%
- Christianity 9%
- Hinduism 2%
- Buddhism 1%
- others 1%

unified control in 1950. The expulsion of Dutch citizens led to a breakdown of the economy, causing hardship and unrest. Sukarno's rule became increasingly authoritarian; in the disarray following an unsuccessful military coup in 1965, General Suharto deposed Sukarno in 1967 and made himself President. Suharto's period in office was dogged by Islamic fundamentalist uprisings, ethnic violence, and the long-running separatist war in East Timor. Following an economic collapse and calls for political reform, Suharto was replaced in 1998 by his deputy, B J Habibie. Habibie's caution and the debacle in East Timor further damaged government prestige, and in 1999, in the first democratically held elections for 44 years, Habibie was succeeded by Abdurrahman Wahid. Allegations of corruption persisted and Wahid was impeached in 2001 and replaced by the Vice-President, Megawati Sukarnoputri. She was defeated in the 2004 presidential election by Susilo Bambang Yudhoyono. Since independence in 1945, several islands have developed separatist movements: the Moluccas fought an unsuccessful separatist war in the 1950s; East Timor, a Portuguese colony until 1975, was illegally annexed by Indonesia from 1976 until 1999, when it regained its independence after a long and violent separatist campaign; Irian Jaya (now Papua) was granted a degree of autonomy in 2002 but separatist agitation continues; and Aceh province in Sumatra was granted a degree of autonomy in 2005. Since the mid 1990s, ethnic and religious tensions have emerged, resulting in intercommunal violence in Kalimantan, Sulawesi and the Moluccas; and Islamic extremists linked to al-Qaeda have been held responsible for bombings in Bali in 2002, 2003 and 2005. Sumatra, and in particular Aceh, was devastated in 2004 by the Indian Ocean tsunami, which killed over 200 000 people in Indonesia.

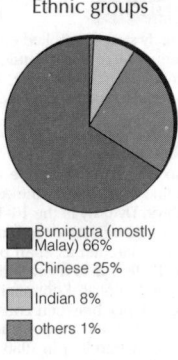

Ethnic groups

- Bumiputra (mostly Malay) 66%
- Chinese 25%
- Indian 8%
- others 1%

IRAN

Official name Islamic Republic of Iran
Local name Îrân
Location A republic in south-west Asia, bounded to the north by Armenia, Azerbaijan, Turkmenistan and the Caspian Sea; to the east by Afghanistan and Pakistan; to the south by the Gulf of Oman and the Persian Gulf; to the west by Iraq; and to the north-west by Turkey
Area 1 648 000 sq km/636 128 sq mi
Capital Tehran
Chief towns Mashhad, Isfahan, Tabriz, Shiraz,

Abadan
Population 65 875 000 (2008e)
Time zone GMT +3.5
Currency 1 Iranian Rial (Rls, RI) = 100 dinars
Language Farsi (Persian); Turkic and several minority languages are also spoken
Religions Islam 98% (Shia 89%, Sunni 9%), others 2%
Ethnic groups Persian 51%, Azeri 24%, Gilaki and Mazandarani 8%, Kurdish 7%, others 10%

Physical description

Largely composed of a vast arid central plateau, average elevation of 1200m/3936ft, with many salt and sand basins; rimmed by mountain ranges that drop down to narrow coastal lowlands; bound to the north by the Elburz Mountains, rising to 5670m/18 602ft at Mount Damavend; the Zagros Mountains in the west and south rise to 3000–4600m/9843–15 092ft; prone to earthquakes.

Climate

Mainly a desert climate, with annual rainfall below 300mm; average temperatures at Tehran are 2°C (January), 29°C (July), average annual rainfall is 246mm; the Caspian coastal strip is much wetter (800–2000mm) than the interior and rain is more widely distributed throughout the year; hot and humid on the shores of the Persian Gulf.

Government

Governed by an executive President, a Council of Ministers and a unicameral Consultative Council (*Majlis al-Shoura*); legislation passed by the Majlis must be approved by the Council of Guardians of the Constitution; the Assembly of Experts elects the Spiritual Leader of the Revolution (*Wali-e Faqih*), who exercises overall authority.

Economy

Largely state-controlled economy, based on exploitation of oil (80% of export earnings) and natural gas, and production of petrochemicals; other activities include mining (iron ore, copper, manganese, chromium, coal), agriculture (cereals, rice, sugar, fruit, nuts, silk), manufacturing (chemicals, textiles, carpets, construction materials, food processing, metal fabrication, armaments) and forestry.

History

Iran was an early centre of civilization and its dynasties include the aggressive Sassanids (from 3c) and its first royal house, the Achaemenids (from 7c). It was ruled by the Arabs, Turks and Mongols until the Safavid Dynasty in the 16–18c and the Qajar Dynasty in the 19–20c. The Qajar monarchy was overthrown in 1921 in a military coup led by Reza Shah Pahlavi, who was elected Shah in 1925. He was deposed in 1941 and succeeded as Shah by his son Muhammad Reza Shah Pahlavi. Protests against the Shah's regime in the 1970s led to a revolution in 1978. The Shah went into exile and an Islamic Republic was proclaimed under Ayatollah Khomeini in 1979. Since Khomeini's death in 1989, there has been a struggle for political ascendency between conservatives and more liberal reformers; although liberalization has generally been blocked by the religious authorities and the judiciary, there is a vocal popular pro-democracy movement. The Iran–Iraq War in 1980–8 claimed possibly one million Iranian lives. During the Gulf War (1991) and the Iraq War (2003) Iran remained neutral, although it is suspected of supporting Shia insurgents in Iraq since 2003. Since 1979 relations between Iran and the West, particularly the USA, have been strained over Iran's alleged abuses of human rights, its hostility to the Middle East peace process and its rumoured involvement in both international terrorism and the development of nuclear weapons. Relations have deteriorated further since 2002 because of concerns over Iran's development of nuclear power. The resumption of its uranium enrichment programme in 2005 was condemned by the IAEA and led to the UN Security Council imposing limited trade sanctions in 2006 and 2007.

IRAQ

Official name Republic of Iraq
Local name Al-Iraq
Location A republic in south-west Asia, bounded to the east by Iran; to the north by Turkey; to the north-west by Syria; to the west by Jordan; to the south-west and south by Saudi Arabia; and to the south-east by Kuwait and the Persian Gulf

Area 434 925 sq km/167 881 sq mi
Capital Baghdad
Chief towns Basra, Kirkuk, Mosul
Population 28 221 000 (2008e)
Time zone GMT +3
Currency 1 New Iraqi Dinar (ID) = 1000 fils
Language Arabic; Kurdish is also spoken

Physical description

Largely comprises the vast alluvial tract of the Tigris–Euphrates lowland (which is equal to ancient Mesopotamia); the two rivers are separated in their upper courses by the plateau of Al Jazirah, which rises to 1547m/5075ft, but join about 190km/118mi from the Persian Gulf; the lowland here has swamp vegetation; mountains in the north-east rise to over 3000m/9843ft; the highest point is an unnamed peak of 3611m/11 846ft; desert in other areas.

Climate

Mainly arid; summers are very hot and dry; winters are often cold; average temperatures at Baghdad are 10°C in January and 35°C in July, with an average annual rainfall of 140mm; rainfall is highest in the north-east, where the average is 400–600mm.

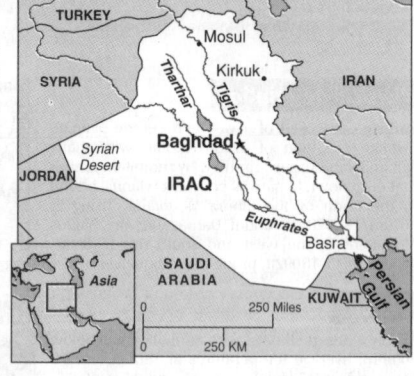

Government

Governed by a President, a Prime Minister and Council of Ministers, and a unicameral Council of Representatives in which 69 seats are set aside for women.

Economy

Impoverished by three decades of war, trade sanctions and under-investment; reconstruction after 2003 undermined by insurgency but economic activity has benefited from drop in violence since 2007; economy based on oil and natural gas production, now back to pre-war levels; other industries include textiles, chemicals, construction materials, food processing, metals; main agricultural products are grains, rice, vegetables, dates, cotton and livestock.

History

Iraq was part of the Ottoman Empire from the 16c until World War I. It was captured by British forces in 1916 and became a British-administered mandated territory in 1921. It gained independence under the Hashemite Dynasty in 1932, but the monarchy was overthrown and replaced by military rule in 1958. Since the 1960s, Kurdish nationalists in the north-east have been fighting to establish a separate state; the north became autonomous after 2003. Saddam Hussein came to power as President in 1979. His invasion of Iran in 1980 led to the Iran–Iraq War, which lasted until 1988. The invasion of Kuwait in 1990 led to UN sanctions, the Gulf War in 1991, and Iraqi withdrawal. Tension in the area remained, and Iraqi attacks on Kurdish settlements and Shiite refugees continued. UN sanctions remained in place owing to Iraq's refusal to cooperate with proposed UN inspections and verification of the destruction of its weapons of mass destruction (WMD), and in 2003 a US-led military force invaded and occupied the country, toppling Saddam Hussein, who was captured in Dec 2003, tried for crimes against humanity and executed in Dec 2006. From May 2003 onwards, an insurgency developed with the apparent aim of destabilizing the country. Despite deteriorating internal security, sovereignty was handed over to an interim government in 2004. This was replaced in Apr 2006 by a multi-ethnic and multi-racial coalition, following elections in Dec 2005 to a permanent legislature. The brutal sectarian violence of 2005 onwards began to decline in 2007.

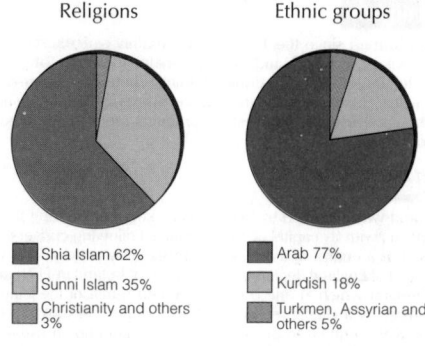

Religions
- ■ Shia Islam 62%
- ■ Sunni Islam 35%
- ■ Christianity and others 3%

Ethnic groups
- ■ Arab 77%
- ■ Kurdish 18%
- ■ Turkmen, Assyrian and others 5%

IRELAND

Official name Ireland
Local name Éire
Location A republic occupying southern, central and north-western Ireland, separated from Great Britain by the Irish Sea and St George's Channel, and bounded to the north-east by Northern Ireland, part of the UK
Area 70 282 sq km/27 129 sq mi
Capital Dublin
Chief towns Cork, Limerick, Waterford, Galway, Drogheda, Dundalk, Sligo

Population 4 156 000 (2008e)
Time zone GMT
Currency 1 Euro (€) = 100 cents
Languages Irish (Gaelic), English; the Gaelic-speaking areas, mostly in the west, are known as the *Gaeltacht*
Religions Christianity 92% (RC 87%, Prot 3%, other Christian 2%), others and unspecified 4%, none 4%
Ethnic groups Celtic and English

Physical description

Much of the interior comprises a central plain surrounded by hills and low mountains and containing expanses of bog and many lakes; it is drained by slow-moving rivers such as the Shannon, Liffey and Slaney; there are long east-to-west valleys in the south; the mountains on the west coast are part of the Caledonian system of Scandinavia and Scotland, with quartzite peaks weathered into conical mountains such as Croagh Patrick (765m/2510ft); a younger mountain system in the south creates a landscape of ridges and valleys; the highest point is Carrauntoohil (1041m/3415ft).

Climate

Mild and changeable, with few extremes of temperature; rainfall is heaviest in the west, often over 3000mm; it is drier in the east and south, the Dublin annual average being 785mm.

Government

Governed by a President, a Prime Minister (*Taoiseach*) and Cabinet, and a bicameral National Parliament (*Oireachtas*) comprising a House of Representatives (*Dáil Éireann*) and a Senate (*Seanad Éireann*).

Economy

Transformed since the 1980s from a mainly agricultural economy to one based on services (information technology, tourism) and industry; major industries are metals and minerals extraction and processing, production of food and drink, clothing, chemicals, pharmaceuticals, machinery, transport equipment and vehicles, computer software and hardware; agriculture, fishing and forestry less significant than previously, although livestock and livestock products are a major export; some natural gas and hydro-electric power production.

History

Ireland was occupied by Goidelic-speaking Celts during the Iron Age, and a high kingship was established c.200 AD, with its capital at Tara (Meath). Following conversion to Christianity by St Patrick in the 5c, Ireland became a centre of learning and missionary activity. The south-east was attacked by Vikings from c.800. Henry I of England declared himself Lord of Ireland in 1171, and Anglo-Norman expansion created a Lordship of Ireland which at one point dominated much of the island before being pushed back into Munster and Leinster by a Gaelic revival in 14–15c. Henry VIII took the title 'King of Ireland' in 1542, but direct Crown rule was confined to the area around Dublin known as the Pale, though the Anglo-Norman vassals of the Crown ruled over much more. Elizabethan conquest unified the island under English control, which was shaken by a Catholic rebellion during the War of the Three Kingdoms in the 1640s. Parliamentary forces under Oliver Cromwell reconquered Catholic Ireland in 1649–50. The Protestant communities in Ulster continued to survive this turmoil, as they did later on when supporters of the deposed Catholic King James VII and II were defeated by William III at the Battle of the Boyne (1690). Following a century of suppression, the struggle for Irish freedom developed in the 18–19c, including such revolutionary movements as Wolfe Tone's United Irishmen (1796–8), and later Young Ireland (1848) and the Fenians (1866–7). The Act of Union, uniting Ireland and Britain, came into effect in 1801; the Catholic Relief Act (1829) enacted Catholic emancipation and enabled Catholics to sit in Parliament; and Land Acts (1870–1903) attacked Irish poverty (prior to these acts, the Irish Famine in 1845–7 had drastically reduced the population). Two Home Rule Bills were introduced by Gladstone (1886, 1893), and a third Home Rule Bill was passed in 1914, but never came into effect because of World War I. In 1916 there was an armed rebellion against British rule (the Easter Rising), and in 1919 a republic was proclaimed by Sinn Féin. A partition proposed by Britain in 1920 was largely ignored by the Irish Republic. In 1921 a treaty gave Ireland dominion status as the Irish Free State, subject to the right of Northern Ireland to opt out; this right was exercised, and a frontier was agreed in 1925. The Irish constitution of 1937 renamed the country Éire and declared the country a sovereign, independent and democratic state with a directly elected President. All constitutional links between the Irish Republic and the UK were severed with the declaration of the republic in 1948, although under the Republic of Ireland Act 1949 (Ireland) and the Ireland Act 1949 (UK), the republic retained special citizenship arrangements and trade preference with Britain. Since 1973 Ireland has been a member of the EC, and replaced the Irish pound or punt with the euro in 2002. Since the 1990s Irish Prime Ministers Albert Reynolds (1992–4), John Bruton (1994–7) and Bertie Ahern (1997–2008) have been involved in the Northern Ireland peace process.

■ Isle of Man▶ United Kingdom

ISRAEL

Official name State of Israel	*Note: Israel claims Jerusalem as its capital, but*
Local name Yisra'el	*this is not recognized internationally*
Location A democratic republic in the Middle	Chief towns Jerusalem, Haifa, Beersheba, Acre,
East, bounded to the north by Lebanon; to the	Holon
north-east by Syria; to the east by Jordan; to	Population 7 112 000 (2008e)
the south-west by Egypt; and to the west by the	Time zone GMT +2
Mediterranean Sea	Currency 1 New Israeli Shekel (NIS) = 100 agora
Area 20 770 sq km/8017 sq mi	Languages Hebrew, Arabic
Capital Tel Aviv	

Physical description

Extends 420km/260mi north to south; width varies from 20km/12mi to 116km/72mi; the narrow coastal plain is crossed by several rivers; mountainous interior, rising to 1208m/3963ft at Mount Meron; mountains in Galilee and Samaria, dissected by faults, dropping east to below sea level in the Jordan–Red Sea Rift Valley; the River Jordan forms part of the eastern border; the Negev Desert in the south occupies c.60% of the country's area.

Climate

Typically Mediterranean in the north and centre, with hot, dry summers and mild, wet winters; average temperatures at Tel Aviv-Jaffa are 14°C in January and 27°C in July; average annual rainfall is 550mm; rainfall is heavier inland, with occasional snow; low rainfall in Negev, decreasing in the south.

Government

Governed by a President, a Prime Minister and Cabinet, and a unicameral legislature (*Knesset*).

Economy

Highly developed and diversified economy, based on technically advanced industry and agriculture developed intensively since 1970s; major industries are technology (aviation, electronics, biotechnology, computer software, telecommunications, alternative energy sources), manufacturing (wood and paper products, food, drink, tobacco products, metal goods, chemicals, plastics, cement, textiles, footwear), oil refining, potash, phosphates, construction, diamond-cutting, agriculture (citrus and other fruits, vegetables, cotton, tobacco, meat, dairy products) and tourism, primarily to religious centres; irrigation schemes have greatly extended the area under cultivation.

History

Zionists settled in Palestine in the 1880s when it was under Ottoman rule, and the British declared support for a Jewish 'national home' there in 1917. However, Zionist ambitions were never satisfied under the League of Nations mandate given to Britain (1918–47), although Jewish immigration in the 1930s and 1940s increased greatly due to Nazi persecution. The British evacuated Palestine after World War II, unable to control a new flood of Jewish immigration strongly supported by the USA. Tension between Arabs and Jews led the UN in 1947 to support the formation of two states in Palestine, one Jewish and the other Arab. When the Arab side rejected this, David Ben-Gurion announced the creation of the independent State of Israel on 14 May 1948. Military conflict with surrounding countries ensued in which Israeli forces were victorious. Further wars took place in 1956 (Suez Crisis) and 1967 (Six-Day War), when Israel gained control of the Gaza Strip, the Sinai Peninsula as far as the

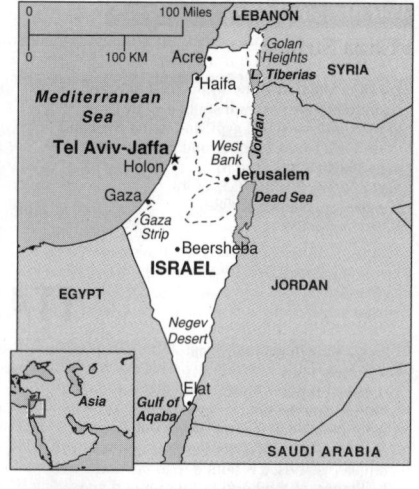

Religions

Ethnic groups

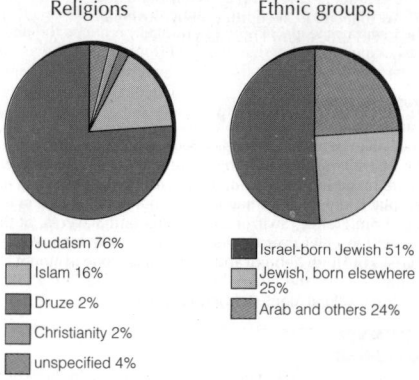

■ Judaism 76%
□ Islam 16%
■ Druze 2%
□ Christianity 2%
□ unspecified 4%

■ Israel-born Jewish 51%
□ Jewish, born elsewhere 25%
■ Arab and others 24%

Suez Canal, the West Bank of the River Jordan (including the eastern sector of Jerusalem), and the Golan Heights in Syria; these areas have since been referred to as the 'occupied territories'. Wars also broke out in 1973 (Yom Kippur War) and in 1982 (Lebanon War), which forced the PLO to leave Beirut in 1982–5. In contrast, a peace agreement was reached with Egypt in 1979 (under which Sinai was returned) and with Jordan in 1994. During the 1990s there were several attempts to resolve the Israeli–Palestinian conflict. The Oslo Accords (1993) led to the establishment of the Palestinian Autonomous Areas in Jericho and the Gaza Strip (1994–5), Hebron (1997) and six West Bank towns (1998). However, violence continued, with suicide bombings in Israeli cities, an armed struggle in south Lebanon (until Israeli troops withdrew in 1999), and clashes between Palestinians and Israeli forces. Efforts to negotiate a final settlement have been hindered since 2001 by the election of Israeli governments critical of the peace process, the outbreak of a second intifada in 2000, the Israeli refusal to negotiate with Yasser Arafat because of the Palestinian authorities' failure to rein in the violence of extremists, and Israel's construction of a wall between Israeli and Palestinian areas despite international protests. Negotiations with the Palestinians resumed in 2005 after Arafat's death (2004) and the election of his moderate successor, Mahmoud Abbas, and were boosted by the evacuation of Israeli settlements and withdrawal of Israeli forces from the Gaza Strip in 2005. But they stalled again in early 2006 with the victory of the extremist Hamas movement in the Palestinian legislative elections. The situation deteriorated dramatically in summer 2006 when the kidnapping of Israeli soldiers in the Gaza Strip and on the Lebanon border prompted Israeli military invasions of Gaza and southern Lebanon. The Palestinians' internal power struggle in 2006–7 prevented the resumption of negotiations until late 2007, but the intransigence of Hamas has led Israel to tighten its blockade of Gaza and respond militarily to Hamas' rocket attacks, culminating in a massive bombardment and invasion of Gaza by Israel at the close of 2008, which ended in a fragile ceasefire in January 2009.

Nations of the World

Palestinian Autonomous Areas

❖Gaza Strip

Location Situated to the south-west of Israel; bounded to the east and south-east by Israel, to the south-west by Egypt, and to the west and north-west by the Mediterranean Sea
Area 360 sq km/139 sq mi
Seat of administration Gaza City
Population 1 500 000 (2008e)

❖West Bank

Location Situated to the east of Israel; bounded to the north, west and south by Israel, and to the east by Jordan and the Dead Sea
Area 5860sq km/2262 sq mi
Population 2 408 000 (2008e)

ITALY

Official name Italian Republic
Local name Italia
Location A republic in southern Europe, comprising the boot-shaped peninsula extending south into the Mediterranean Sea and the islands of Sicily, Sardinia and about 70 smaller islands. It is bounded to the north-west by France; to the north by Switzerland and Austria; and to the north-east by Slovenia
Area 301 225 sq km/116 273 sq mi
Capital Rome

Chief towns Milan, Turin, Genoa, Naples, Bologna, Palermo, Florence, Venice
Population 58 145 000 (2008e)
Time zone GMT +1
Currency 1 Euro (€) = 100 cents
Language Italian; German, French and Slovene are also spoken in some parts
Religions Christianity 83% (mostly RC), Islam 1%, others 16%
Ethnic groups Italian 94%, others 6%

Physical description

The Italian peninsula extends c.800km/500mi south-east from the Lombardy plains; it is mostly mountainous, the Apennine range forming a spine along its length that rises to peaks above 2000m/6562ft; to the north of the range lies the broad, fertile Lombardo–Venetian plain in the basin of the River Po and to its east are the plains of Emilia-Romagna in the north and Apulia in the south; the Alps and Dolomite mountains divide Italy from France, Switzerland, Austria and Slovenia; at the foot of the Alps lie lakes Maggiore, Como and Garda; the chief rivers include the Po, Tiber, Arno, Volturno, Liri and Adige; Sicily includes the limestone massifs of Monti Nebrodi and the volcanic cone of Mount Etna (3323m/10 902ft), one of three active volcanos in the country, the others being Vesuvius (1277m/4190ft) and Stromboli (926m/3038ft); Sardinia rises to 1835m/6020ft at Monti del Gennargentu.

Climate

The climate is predominantly Mediterranean (mild, wet winters and hot, dry summers), but with Alpine conditions in the north and colder, wetter and often snowy winters in the higher areas of peninsular Italy; the west coast is warmer than the Adriatic coast and receives more rainfall.

Government

Governed by a President, a Prime Minister and Council of Ministers, and a bicameral Parliament consisting of a Chamber of Deputies and a Senate.

Economy

A diversified market economy, with industry largely concentrated in the north and agriculture in the south; main industry is tourism; other industries are based on processing imported raw materials and manufacturing goods (precision machinery, motor vehicles, chemicals, pharmaceuticals, electrical goods, textiles, fashion, clothing and footwear); agricultural products, wine, minerals and non-ferrous metals are also exported.

History

In pre-Roman times, Italy, which was not a concept covering the racially-mixed Po Valley, was inhabited by Etruscans in the north, Latins in the centre of the country and Greeks in the south. Most regions were part of the Roman Empire by the 3c BC; barbarian tribes invaded in the 4c AD, and the last Roman emperor was deposed in AD476. Italy was later ruled by the Lombards and by the Franks under Charlemagne, who was crowned Emperor of the Romans in 800. It became part of the Holy Roman Empire under Otto I, the Great, in 962, and popes and emperors were in conflict throughout the Middle Ages. There were disputes between Guelfs and Ghibellines in the 12c. Italy was divided amongst five main powers during the 14–15c (Kingdom of Naples, Duchy of Milan, republics of Florence and Venice, and the papacy). The country made a major contribution to European culture through the Renaissance. Four satellite republics were set up after a successful French invasion during the wars of the French Revolution, and Napoleon I was crowned King of Italy in 1805. The 19c saw the upsurge of liberalism and nationalism (the Risorgimento); unification was achieved by 1870 under

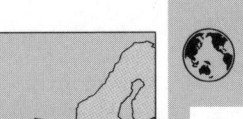

GERMANY

AUSTRIA

SWITZERLAND

LIECH.

A l p s

Adige

Dolomites

SLOVENIA

L. Maggiore

L. Como

L. Garda

Mont Blanc

Milan •

ITALY

Po

Venice

Turin

CROATIA

Genoa

• Bologna

San Marino

BOSNIA-HERZEGOVINA

A

Arno

Florence

FRANCE

Ligurian Sea

Adriatic Sea

Elba

p

Corsica (France)

n

Tiber

n

★ **Rome**

i

Voltumo

n

e

Naples ▲▲ *Vesuvius*

Sardinia

s

Cagliari

Tyrrhenian Sea

Stromboli

Mediterranean Sea

Palermo

Etna ▲

Sicily

Ionian Sea

0   100 Miles

0   100 KM

ALGERIA

TUNISIA

Pantelleria

Europe

Victor Emmanuel II of Sardinia, aided by Cavour and Garibaldi; colonies were established in Eritrea (1870–89) and Somaliland (1889), but the attempt to secure a protectorate over Abyssinia was defeated at the Battle of Adowa (1896). During World War I, Italy fought alongside the Allies. The Fascist movement brought Mussolini to power in 1922, and he led the conquest of Abyssinia (1935–6) and occupation of Albania (1939). The alliance with Hitler in World War II led to the end of the Italian Empire. Italy became a democratic republic in 1946, but political instability resulted in 45 governments in 47 years until partial reform of the voting system in 1993 produced longer-lasting governments. Italy was a founding member of the EEC in 1958, and in 2002 replaced the lira with the euro. Following corruption scandals, in the early 1990s there was a drive to reform the political establishment, although Silvio Berlusconi (Prime Minister 1994, 2001–6, 2008–   ) was dogged by accusations of corruption, of which he was acquitted in 2004 following a four-year trial.

JAMAICA

Official name Jamaica
Local name Jamaica
Location An island nation of the West Indies in the Caribbean Sea
Area 10957 sq km/4229 sq mi
Capital Kingston
Chief towns Montego Bay, Spanish Town
Population 2804000 (2008e)

Time zone GMT −5
Currency 1 Jamaican Dollar (J$) = 100 cents
Language English; Jamaican Creole is also spoken
Religions Christianity 65% (Prot 62% (about half Church of God), RC 3%), other/unspecified 14%, none 21%
Ethnic groups black 91%, mixed 6%, others 3%

Physical description

The third largest island in the Caribbean Sea, with a maximum length of 234km/145mi and width varying from 35km/22mi to 82km/51mi; mountainous and rugged, particularly in the east where the Blue Mountains rise to 2256m/7401ft at Blue Mountain Peak; more than 100 small rivers.

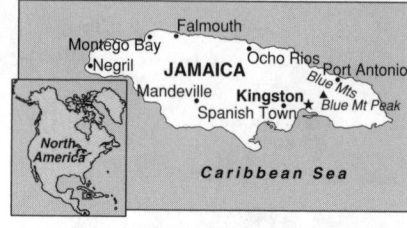

Climate

Tropical climate at sea level, more temperate at higher altitudes; coastal temperatures range from 21°C to 34°C, with an average annual rainfall of 1980mm; virtually no rainfall on the south and south-west plains; the island lies within the hurricane belt.

Government

Governed by a Governor-General (representing the British monarch, who is head of state), a Prime Minister and Cabinet, and a bicameral Parliament consisting of a House of Representatives and a Senate.

Economy

Weak economy, dependent on international aid and expatriates' remittances; main activities are tourism, bauxite and alumina production, agriculture (sugar, bananas, coffee, yams), clothing, food processing, rum, metal, paper, chemicals.

History

The island was visited by Columbus in 1494 and settled by the Spanish in 1509. From 1640, West African slave labour was imported for work on the sugar plantations. Jamaica was occupied by the British in 1655. Self-government was introduced in 1944, and independence was achieved in 1962. Post-independence politics has been dominated by the Jamaican Labour Party and the People's National Party. Fraught relations between the two deteriorated into violence in the 1970s. Despite greater political stability in recent years, there are high levels of crime and violence, largely connected with drugs.

JAPAN

Official name Japan
Local name Nihon/Nippon
Location An island state off the east coast of Asia. It comprises the four large islands of Hokkaido, Honshu, Kyushu and Shikoku, and many small islands
Area 381945 sq km/147431 sq mi
Capital Tokyo
Chief towns Yokohama, Osaka, Nagoya, Sapporo,

Kyoto, Kobe
Population 127288000 (2008e)
Time zone GMT +9
Currency 1 Yen (Y, ¥) = 100 sen
Language Japanese
Religions Shintoism 84%/Buddhism 70%, Christianity 1%, others 15%
Ethnic groups Japanese 99%, others 1%

Physical description

The islands have narrow coastal plains rising to wooded, mountainous interiors, so less than 20% of the land can be cultivated; on Hokkaido the central range rises to over 2000m/6562ft; Honshu includes Japan's highest point, Mount Fuji (3776m/12388ft); there are many volcanoes, mainly extinct or dormant; the more southerly islands of Shikoku and Kyushu have low cones and rolling hills; further south are the Ryukyu chain of volcanic islands, of which Okinawa is the largest; Japan lies on the boundaries of three tectonic plates and 20% of the world's earthquakes occur here.

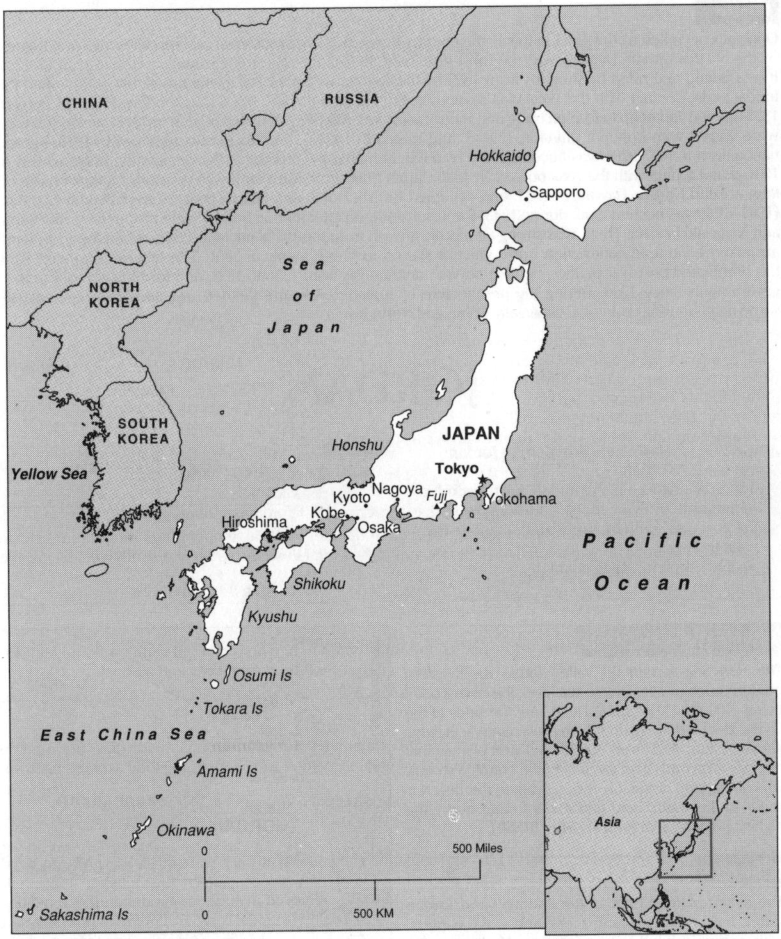

Climate

An oceanic climate, influenced by the Asian monsoon, with temperatures reduced by altitude; in the north there are short, warm summers and severe winters with heavy snow, and heavy rainfall on western coasts; in the south there are mild, almost subtropical winters with light rainfall, and very warm summers whose heat is often oppressive, especially in the cities; typhoons occur in summer and early autumn; Akita in north Honshu has an average daily temperature of −5°–2°C in January, 19°–28°C in August, and rainfall in this area is a minimum of 104mm in February–March and a maximum of 211mm in September. ;

Government

A hereditary constitutional monarchy with an Emperor as head of state; governed by a Prime Minister and Cabinet, and a bicameral Diet (*Kokkai*), comprising a House of Representatives (*Shugiin*) and a House of Councillors (*Sangiin*).

Economy

Highly industrialized market economy, now recovering from 14 years of stagnation; main activities are financial services and banking, and industries producing high-technology electronic products, motor vehicles, office machinery, chemicals, machine tools, steel and other metals, ships, textiles and processed food; intensive agriculture, rice being the principal crop; fishing; forestry.

History

Originally occupied by the Ainu, in the 4c the country developed from individual communities into small states; by the 5c, the Yamato Dynasty was the most dominant. Its culture was strongly influenced by China (8–12c). It was united and ruled by shoguns from 1603 by the Tokugawa Dynasty of military dictators, who tamed the feudal lords. Contact with the West was severely restricted until the visit of US Commodore Matthew Perry in 1853 opened Japan up to foreign trade and industrialization. After the Meiji Restoration in 1868, successful wars were waged with imperial China in 1894–5, and Russia in 1904–5, and Korea was annexed in 1910. Intense nationalism in the 1920s was accompanied by a rise in militarism, leading to the occupation of Manchuria in 1931–2 and a pact with the Axis powers in 1940. Japan entered World War II with a surprise attack on the US fleet at Pearl Harbor, Hawaii, in 1941, and occupied British, Dutch and French possessions in South-East Asia (1941–2). It was pushed back during 1943–5 and surrendered after atomic bombs were dropped on Hiroshima and Nagasaki in 1945. There was strong economic growth from the 1960s until the 1990s, when Japan suffered a marked economic contraction from which it started to emerge only in 2001. The Liberal Democrat Party has dominated post-war politics, holding power continuously from 1955 to 1993, and forming part of coalition governments since 1995. During the premiership of Junichiro Koizumi (2001–6) relations deteriorated with some neighbouring countries, especially China and North Korea.

JORDAN

Official name Hashemite Kingdom of Jordan
Local name Al'Urdunn
Location A kingdom in the Middle East, bounded to the north by Syria; to the north-east by Iraq; to the east and south by Saudi Arabia; and to the west by Israel
Area 89 213 sq km/34 445 sq mi
Capital Amman

Chief towns Irbid, Zarqa, Salt, Karak, Aqaba
Population 6 199 000 (2008e)
Time zone GMT +2
Currency 1 Jordanian Dinar (JD) = 1000 fils
Language Arabic
Religions Islam 92% (Sunni), Christianity 6%, others 2%
Ethnic groups Arab 98%, others 2%

Physical description

The Red Sea–Jordan rift valley forms the western border; much of it lies below sea level, the lowest point being –400m/–1312ft at the Dead Sea; the sides of the rift rise steeply through undulating hill country to heights above 1000m; land levels out into a desert plateau that extends eastwards over the rest of the country, so only 25% of the land is suitable for cultivation; the desert is sandy in the south, hard and rocky further north; the highest point is Jabal Rum (1754m/5755ft).

Climate

The desert plateau (90% of the country) and Jordan valley have very hot summers and cold winters, with annual rainfall below 200mm; Mediterranean climate elsewhere, with hot, dry summers and cool, wet winters; temperatures at Amman are 7°C (January), 25°C (July); average annual rainfall is 290mm.

Government

A hereditary monarchy; governed by the King, a Prime Minister and Council of Ministers, and a bicameral National Assembly consisting of a Senate and a House of Deputies.

Economy

Growing economy, although still dependent on international aid; few natural resources; main activities are tourism, mining (potash, phosphate), oil refining, textiles, garments, pharmaceuticals, machinery, agriculture (vegetables, fruit, nuts); developing irrigation schemes in the Jordan valley.

History

Jordan was part of the Roman Empire, and came under Arab control in the 7c. It was the centre of Crusader activity in the 11–12c, and part of the Turkish Ottoman Empire from the 16c until World War I. With the collapse of the empire in 1918, the area was divided into Palestine (west of the River Jordan) and Transjordan (east of the River Jordan), both administered by Britain. Transjordan gained independence in 1946, changing its name to Jordan. After the British mandate over Palestine ended in 1948, the newly created State of Israel fought to control the West Bank area. An armistice in 1949 left Jordan in control of the West Bank, and the West and East Banks united within Jordan in 1951. However, Israel took control of the West Bank after the Six-Day War in 1967. Following attempts by the Jordanian army to expel Palestinian guerrillas from the West

Bank in 1970–1, civil war erupted; an amnesty was declared in 1973, and claims to the West Bank were ceded to the PLO (Palestine Liberation Organization) in 1974. Legal and administrative links with the West Bank were cut in 1988, and Jordan formally renounced sovereignty over the West Bank and East Jerusalem in 1999. Following internal unrest in 1989, political, social and economic reforms were initiated and the first elections since 1967 took place. A ban on political parties ended in 1991 and the first multiparty elections since 1956 took place in 1993. King Hussein, who ruled from 1952 to 1998, was succeeded on his death by his son, Abdullah II, who has instituted economic reforms in association with the International Monetary Fund. Since 2003, Jordan has experienced a number of terrorist attacks that appear to be the work of Islamic extremists, possibly linked to al-Qaeda.

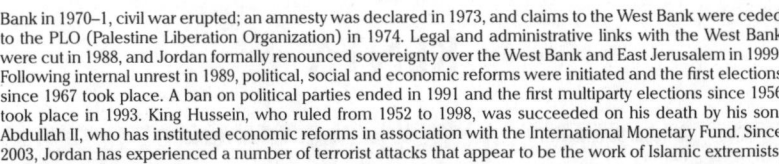

KAZAKHSTAN

Official name Republic of Kazakhstan
Local name Qazaqstan
Location A republic in western Asia, bounded to the north by Russia; to the south by Turkmenistan, Uzbekistan and Kyrgyzstan; to the east by China; and to the west by the Caspian Sea
Area 2 717 300 sq km / 1 048 878 sq mi
Capital Astana
Chief towns Karaganda, Semipalatinsk, Chimkent, Petropavlovsk
Population 15 340 000 (2008e)
Time zone GMT +5/+6
Currency 1 Tenge = 100 tiyn
Language Kazakh, Russian
Religions Islam 47%, Christianity 46% (Orthodox 44%, Prot 2%), others 7%
Ethnic groups Kazakh 53%, Russian 30%, Ukrainian 4%, Uzbek 3%, German 2%, others 8%

Physical description

Steppeland in the north gives way to desert in the south; the lowest elevation is near the eastern shore of the Caspian Sea (–132m/–433ft); mountain ranges in the east and south-east; the highest point is Khan Tengri (6995m/22 949ft); the chief rivers are the Irtysh, Syrdarya, Ural, Emba and Ili; the largest lake is Lake Balkhash; the Aral Sea lies on the south border with Uzbekistan.

Climate

Continental; hot summers and cold winters.

Government

Governed by a President, a Prime Minister and Cabinet, and a bicameral Parliament consisting of a Senate and an Assembly (*Majilis*).

Economy

Fast-growing economy owing to oil boom, with export pipelines opened to Black Sea ports (2001) and China (2006); other industries include mining (coal, phosphates, chrome, lead, zinc, silver, ferrous metals) and mineral processing, agriculture (grain, wool, cotton, livestock); machine-building (construction equipment, tractors, agricultural machinery, electric motors), chemicals.

History

Formerly the home of nomadic Kazakhs and ruled by Mongol khans, it was taken over by Tsarist Russia during the 19c. In the early 20c a nationalist movement was violently suppressed and it became an autonomous republic of the Soviet Union in 1920 and a full republic in 1936. In 1991 it became an independent republic, and was a founding member of the CIS (Commonwealth of Independent States). Economic reform began in 1993, but the country has serious economic and environmental problems. Nursultan Nazarbayev, head of state since 1990, presides over an authoritarian regime with poor human rights and civil liberties records.

KENYA

<div class="sidebar">

</div>

Official name Republic of Kenya
Local name Kenya
Location A republic in East Africa, bounded to the south by Tanzania; to the west by Uganda; to the north-west by Sudan; to the north by Ethiopia; to the north-east by Somalia; and to the east by the Indian Ocean
Area 580 370 sq km/224 080 sq mi
Capital Nairobi
Chief towns Mombasa, Kisumu, Nakuru, Malindi

Population 37 954 000 (2008e)
Time zone GMT +3
Currency 1 Kenyan Shilling (Ksh) = 100 cents
Languages English and Kiswahili, with many tribal languages spoken
Religions Christianity 78% (Prot 45%, RC 33%), traditional beliefs 10%, Islam 10%, others 2%
Ethnic groups Kikuyu 22%, Luhya 14%, Luo 13%, Kalenjin 12%, Kamba 11%, other African 27%, others 1%

Physical description

Crossed by the Equator; the Great Rift Valley in the west runs north to south; the south-west plateau includes the highest point, Mount Kenya (5200m/17060ft), and the Aberdare range; arid semi-desert in the north, generally under 600m/1969ft; numerous lakes, including part of Lake Victoria in the south-west and Lake Turkana, the largest body of water, in the north; the Chalbi Desert lies south-east of Lake Turkana; the coastal strip south of the River Tana is typified by coral reefs, mangrove swamps and small island groups.

Climate

Tropical climate on the coast, with high temperatures and humidity; more temperate at altitude; in Mombasa the average annual rainfall is 1200mm, the average daily temperatures are 27°–31°C; annual rainfall decreases from 500mm in the south to 250mm in the far north; frost and snow lie in the high mountains.

Government

Governed by an executive President, a Prime Minister and Cabinet, and a unicameral National Assembly.

Economy

Very poor country, dependent on international aid; agriculture and horticulture employ 75% of the workforce; chief cash crops are tea (world's fourth largest producer), coffee, vegetables; other activities include food processing, small-scale manufacturing (consumer goods, textiles), tourism, oil refining, fishing.

History

Anthropologists have found very early fossil hominids in the region. The coast was settled by Arabs in the 7c, and the country came under Portuguese control in the 16–17c, and under British control as an East African Protectorate in 1895. After it became a British colony in 1920, an independence movement grew, culminating in the Mau Mau rebellion in 1952–60. Led by KANU (the Kenya African National Union), it gained independence in 1963 under Prime Minister Jomo Kenyatta, who became President when Kenya became a republic in 1964. He was succeeded on his death in 1978 by Daniel T arap Moi. In 1991 a multiparty system was legalized. Moi won the elections of 1992 and 1998 amid allegations of electoral fraud, and during the 1990s there were sporadic outbreaks of violent unrest fuelled by demands for constitutional change. Moi's long rule came to an end in 2001, when KANU lost elections to opposition parties and the National Rainbow Coalition's Mwai Kibaki was elected President. The declaration of Kibaki's re-election in Dec 2007 triggered serious violence, amid claims of election rigging. After international mediation, Kibaki and opposition leader Raila Odinga agreed to form a coalition government with Kibaki as President and Odinga as Prime Minister.

KIRIBATI

Official name Republic of Kiribati
Local name Kiribati (pronounced 'keer-ree-bahss')
Location A group of 33 low-lying coral islands scattered over c.3 million sq km/1.2 million sq mi of the central Pacific Ocean
Area 811 sq km/313 sq mi
Capital Tawara

Population 110400 (2008e)
Time zone GMT +12/+14
Currency 1 Australian Dollar ($A) = 100 cents
Languages English, I-Kiribati
Religions Christianity 92% (RC 52%, Prot 40%), others 8%
Ethnic groups Micronesian 99%, others 1%

Physical description

The islands seldom rise to more than 4m/13ft and usually consist of a reef enclosing a lagoon; Banaba, a solid coral outcrop with a fringing reef, rises to 87m/285ft.

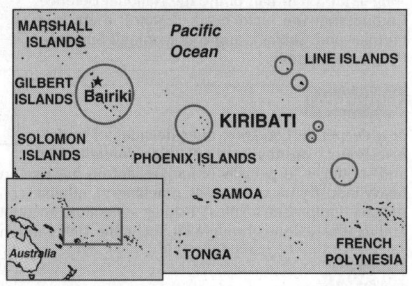

Climate

Maritime equatorial climate in the central islands; the islands further north and south are tropical; the average annual temperature is 27°C; the average annual rainfall varies from 500mm south of the Equator to 3000mm in the north; the rainy season is June–November north of the Equator and November–April south of it; some islands suffer from periodic drought.

Government

Governed by an executive President, a Cabinet and a unicameral House of Assembly.

Economy

Weak economy since phosphate deposits ran out in 1979; dependent on international aid, expatriates' remittances, copra, coconuts, seaweed, fish and tourism.

History

The Gilbert and Ellice Islands were visited by British seafarers in the 18c, proclaimed a British protectorate in 1892, and annexed in 1916. The two island groups separated in 1975, and the Gilbert Islands achieved independence in 1979 under the name of Kiribati. In 1999, Kiribati joined the UN. Kiribati is threatened by rising sea levels; two atolls were reported submerged in 1999. In 2002 Kiribati, with Tuvalu and the Maldives, announced its intention to take legal action against the USA over its refusal to sign the Kyoto Protocol.

NORTH KOREA

Official name Democratic People's Republic of Korea
Local name Chosun
Location A socialist state in eastern Asia, in the northern half of the Korean Peninsula, bounded to the north by China; to the north-east by Russia; to the west by Korea Bay and the Yellow Sea; to the east by the Sea of Japan; and to the south by South Korea
Area 122098 sq km/47130 sq mi

Capital Pyongyang
Chief towns Chongjin, Sinuiju, Wonsan, Kaesong
Population 23479000 (2008e)
Time zone GMT +9
Currency 1 Won (NKW) = 100 chon
Language Korean
Religions traditional beliefs 16%, Chondogyo 14%, Buddhism 2%, Christianity 1%, none/unaffiliated 67% (all figures are estimates)
Ethnic groups Korean 100%

Physical description

Lies on a high plateau occupying the north part of a mountainous peninsula; many areas rise to over 2000m/6562ft; the highest point is Mount Paektu (2744m/9003ft); lower mountains and foothills in the south descend to narrow coastal plains in the east and wider coastal plains in the west.

Climate

Temperate, with warm summers and severely cold winters; rivers freeze for 3–4 months, and ice blocks harbours; daily temperatures at Pyongyang in the west range from –3°C to –13°C in January, and from 20°C to 29°C in July–August; average rainfall in Pyongyang ranges between a minimum of 11mm in February and a maximum of 237mm in July.

Government

A totalitarian republic, nominally Communist (Korean Workers' Party) but with political control maintained through the personality cult created by the late Kim Il-sung (died 1994; declared 'Eternal President' in 1998) and continued by his son, Kim Jong-il, the Chairman of the the National Defence Commission (de facto head of state); there is a Premier and Cabinet, and a unicameral Supreme People's Assembly.

Economy

In a desperate condition after decades of under-investment, mismanagement, high foreign debt and shortages, especially of fuel; reliant on massive amounts of international food aid; main activities are heavy industry (steel, cement, machinery), mining (coal, minerals, metals), manufacturing (machine tools, military equipment, textiles), fishing; agriculture accounts for over 25% of economic activity but inefficiencies and natural disasters brought famine in the 1990s and malnutrition is still widespread.

History

The peninsula was united in the 7c by the Silla Dynasty, which was succeeded by the Koryo Dynasty in 935 and then by the Yi Dynasty, which ruled (1392–1910) as a vassel of China. In 1910 it was formally annexed by Japan, and after Japan's defeat in World War II it was partitioned along the 38th parallel (latitude 38°N), the north being occupied by Soviet troops and the south by US troops. The Korean War (1950–3) was fought after North Korea (supported by China) invaded South Korea to prevent its independence, and it was rebuffed by a multinational UN force. Reunification talks have taken place intermittently since 1980. Power in North Korea lies in the hands of the Korean Workers' (Communist) Party, whose leader was the President. Kim Il Sung was President from 1972 until his death in 1994, and in 1998 was declared 'Eternal President'; since 1998, as the Chairman of the National Defence Committee, his son Kim Jong Il has held power. A combination of natural disasters and economic mismanagement led to acute food shortages in the 1990s and the country is still dependent on international food and fuel aid. International concerns in the 1990s over North Korea's attempts to develop a nuclear capacity were heightened by its decision to reactivate its nuclear programme in 2002 and its withdrawal from the Nuclear Non-Proliferation Treaty in 2003. Diplomatic efforts to resolve the nuclear issue began in 2003, and in 2007 two denuclearization agreements were concluded.

SOUTH KOREA

Official name Republic of Korea
Local name Han'guk
Location A republic in eastern Asia occupying the southern half of the Korean Peninsula, bounded to the west by the Yellow Sea; to the east by the Sea of Japan; to the south by the Korean Strait; and to the north by North Korea, from which it is separated by a demilitarized zone
Area 98 913 sq km/38 180 sq mi

Capital Seoul
Chief towns Inchon, Pusan, Taegu
Population 48 379 000 (2008e)
Time zone GMT +9
Currency 1 Won (W) = 100 jeon
Language Korean
Religions Christianity 26% (Prot 20%, RC 6%), Buddhism 23%, others 1%, none 49%
Ethnic groups Korean 100%

Physical description

The Taebaek Sanmaek Range runs north to south along the east coast, reaching heights of over 900m/2953ft; it descends through a series of ridges to broad, undulating coastal lowlands; c.3000 islands off the west and south coasts; the largest is Cheju-do, on which is situated the highest peak, Halla-san (1950m/6398ft).

Climate

Extreme continental climate, with cold winters and hot summers; typhoons possible in the wettest months (June–September); average daily temperatures at Seoul are −9° to –0°C (January), 22°–31°C (August); rainfall minimum 20mm (February), maximum 376mm (July).

Government

Governed by a President, a Prime Minister and State Council, and a unicameral National Assembly.

Economy

Transformed since 1960s from a largely agrarian into a highly industrialized economy; initially based on heavy industry (steel, motor vehicles, shipbuilding, petrochemicals) and electrical goods but widened from the 1980s to include electronics, telecommunications equipment, computers, textiles, clothing, leather goods, chemicals; tourism is growing.

History

The peninsula was united in the 7c by the Silla Dynasty, which was succeeded by the Koryo Dynasty in 935 and then by the Yi Dynasty, which ruled (1392–1910) as a vassel of China. In 1910 it was formally annexed by Japan, and after Japan's defeat in World War II it was partitioned along the 38th parallel (latitude 38°N), the north being occupied by Soviet troops and the south by US troops. In a bid to prevent South Korea becoming an independent state, North Korean forces invaded in 1950, sparking off the Korean War (1950–3) between communist and non-communist forces. After 1948, South Korea experienced mostly authoritarian, often military, rule. There was a military coup in 1961, led by Park Chung-hee, whose repressive regime introduced military law in 1972, and he was assassinated in 1979. Pro-democracy agitation led to the first multiparty elections in 1988 but politics continued to be dogged by allegations of corruption and electoral fraud and by military influence. Reunification talks with North Korea have taken place intermittently since 1980, but tensions remain because of the North's nuclear programme and concern over its weak economy, and the prospect of US troop withdrawals from the demilitarized zone.

■ Kosovo ▶ Serbia

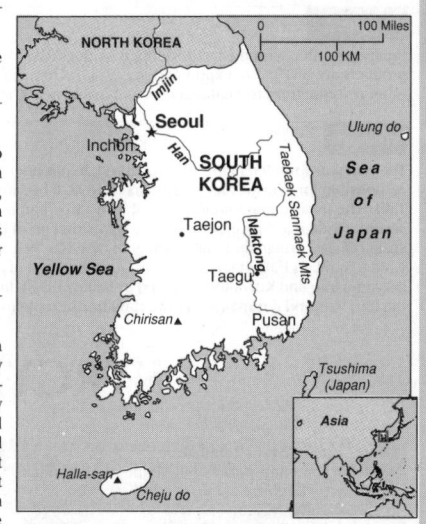

Nations of the World

KUWAIT

Official name State of Kuwait
Local name Al-Kuwayt
Location An independent state at the head of the Persian Gulf, bounded to the north and west by Iraq; to the south by Saudi Arabia; and to the east by the Persian Gulf
Area 17818 sq km/6878 sq mi
Capital Kuwait City
Chief towns Shuwaikh, Mina al Ahmadi

Population 2 579 000 (2008e)
Time zone GMT +3
Currency 1 Kuwaiti Dinar (KD) = 1000 fils
Language Arabic; English is also widely spoken
Religions Islam 85% (Sunni 60%, Shia 25%), others 15%
Ethnic groups Kuwaiti 45%, other Arab 35%, South Asian 9%, Iranian 4%, others 7%

Physical description

Consists of the mainland and nine islands; the terrain is flat or gently undulating, rising in the south-west to 271m/889ft; the Wadi al Batin runs along the western border with Iraq; terrain is generally stony with sparse vegetation.

Climate

Hot, dry climate, with an average annual rainfall of 111mm; summer temperatures are very high, often above 45°C (July–August); winter daytime temperatures often exceed 20°C; humidity is generally high; sandstorms are common throughout the year.

Government

A hereditary monarchy; governed by the Emir, a Prime Minister and Council of Ministers, and a unicameral National Assembly.

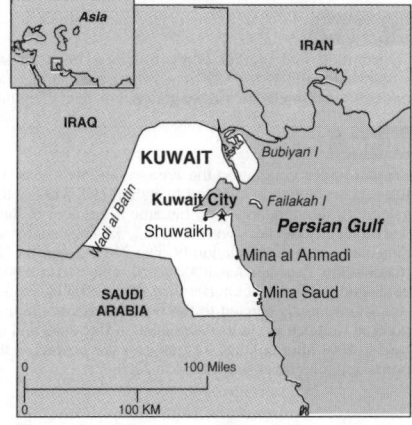

Economy

Prospered after oil industry developed in the 1940s; now recovered from effects of 1991 Gulf War; main products are oil (95% of export earnings), petrochemicals, processed food, fertilizers, construction materials; other revenue from foreign reserves and investments, shipbuilding and repair.

History

The port was founded in the 18c, and the state has been ruled since 1756 by the Sabah family. Britain became responsible for Kuwait's foreign affairs in 1899. It became a British protectorate in 1914, and independent in 1961. The invasion and annexation of Kuwait by Iraq in Aug 1990 led to the Gulf War in Jan–Feb 1991, with severe damage to Kuwait City and the infrastructure of the country. Major post-war problems included large-scale refugee emigration, the burning of oil wells by Iraq (all capped by Nov 1991) and the pollution of Gulf waters by oil. In 1992 the port of Umm Quasr and part of an oilfield were passed to Kuwait when the boundary between Iraq and Kuwait was moved by 600m/1970ft. In 2003 Kuwait was a base for the build-up of forces for the Iraq War and it remains an important transit route for military and civilian traffic into and out of Iraq.

KYRGYZSTAN

Official name Kyrgyz Republic
Kyrgyz is sometimes also spelt Kirghiz; sometimes known as Kirghizia
Local name Kyrgyzstan
Location A landlocked republic in north-east Central Asia, bounded to the north by Kazakhstan; to the west by Uzbekistan; to the south and south-west by Tajikistan; and to the south-east and east by China.
Area 198 500 sq km/76 621 sq mi
Capital Bishkek

Chief towns Osh, Przhevalsk, Kyzyl-Kiya
Population 5 357 000 (2008e)
Time zone GMT +6
Currency 1 Som (Kgs) = 100 tyjyn (*sometimes transliterated as tyin or tyiyn*)
Languages Kyrgyz, Russian
Religions Islam 75%, Christianity 20% (Orthodox), others 5%
Ethnic groups Kyrgyz 67%, Uzbek 14%, Russian 11%, Ukrainian 1%, others 7%

Physical description

Lies in the Tien Shan Mountains with the Pamirs to the south; c.75% of land is mountainous; the highest point is Jengish Chokusu/Pik Pobedy (7439m/24 406ft); the chief river is the Naryn and Lake Issyk-Kul is the largest lake.

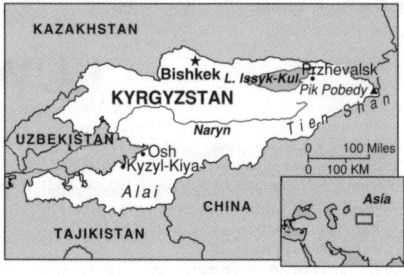

Climate

Varies according to location; sub-tropical in the south-west, dry in the north and west, continental to polar in the mountainous east.

Government

Governed by a President, a Prime Minister and Cabinet, and a unicameral Supreme Council.

Economy

Transformed into market economy since 1991 but struggling; main activities are agriculture (55% of employment and 34% of GDP; cash crops are cotton, wool, meat, tobacco), mining (coal, gold, mercury, tin, uranium), hydro-electric power generation, light manufacturing (machinery, footwear).

History

Russian forces conquered the area in the late 19c and it was incorporated into the Russian Empire. The Russian Revolution in 1917 led to a short civil war but the area became part of the USSR in 1921. In 1991 it gained its independence and became a member of the CIS (Commonwealth of Independent States). The first multiparty elections were held in 1995. The country has implemented economic reforms, but not without difficulties, including inflation of over 700 per cent in 1993, high levels of unemployment and widespread malnutrition. President Askar Akayev, first elected in 1990, was deposed in 2005 in a popular uprising in protest at alleged government interference in the 2005 election. Kurmanbek Bakiyev became acting president and was subsequently elected to the post. His government's failure to address corruption or the rising level of political violence led to its resignation in Dec 2006 and the calling of early elections. These were eventually held in 2007 after political turmoil over the powers of the presidency led to three new constitutions being promulgated in rapid succession in 2006–7.

LAOS

Official name Lao People's Democratic Republic
Local name Lao
Location A landlocked republic in South-East Asia,
  bounded to the east by Vietnam; to the south
  by Cambodia; to the west by Thailand and
  Myanmar (Burma); and to the north by China
Area 236 800 sq km/91 405 sq mi
Capital Vientiane
Chief towns Luang Prabang, Pakse, Savannakhét

Population 6 677 000 (2008e)
Time zone GMT +7
Currency 1 New Kip (Kp) = 100 at
Language Lao
Religions Buddhism 67%, Christianity 1%,
  other/unspecified 32%
Ethnic groups Lao 55%, Khmu 11%, Hmong 8%,
  others (other 100 ethnic groups) 26%

Physical description

The land rises from the fertile valley of the Mekong River, which follows much of the border with Thailand in the west, to rugged hills and mountains covered with dense jungle in the east; the highest point is Phou Bia (2820m/9252ft).

Climate

Monsoonal with heavy rain in May–September; hot and dry February–April; average annual temperatures in Vientiane are 14°–34°C, but it is cooler in the mountains.

Government

Governed by a President, a Prime Minister and Council of Ministers, and a unicameral National Assembly; the Lao People's Revolutionary Party (LPRP) is the only legal political party.

Economy

Very poor, and dependent on international aid; agriculture, mostly at subsistence level, employs over 75% of the workforce; main cash crop is coffee; other activities include infrastructure construction projects, food processing, garment manufacture, low-tech assembly, forestry, mining (tin, copper, gypsum), hydro-electric power.

History

Small principalities were united in the 14c into the kingdom of Lan Xang, which dominated until 1713, when it split into three kingdoms that became tributaries of Siam (Thailand) in the late 18c, and then a French protectorate in 1893. Occupied by the Japanese in World War II, it gained independence from France as a constitutional monarchy in 1953, but much of the next 20 years was spent in civil war between the pro-Western and royalist parties, and the communist-supported Pathet Lao (now the LPRP). The country was partitioned between the two sides in 1973 but in 1975 the Pathet Lao seized power and established a communist republic. Although still officially a communist state, Laos initiated economic liberalization in 1986 and joined the Association of South East Asian Nations (ASEAN) in 1997. Civil disturbances, including bombings and armed attacks on buses, in 2000 and 2003 were attributed to insurgents from the Hmong people or anti-government groups.

LATVIA

Official name Republic of Latvia
Local name Latvija
Location A republic in north-eastern Europe,
  bounded to the west by the Baltic Sea; to the
  north-west by the Gulf of Riga; to the north by
  Estonia; to the east by Russia; to the south-east
  by Belarus, and to the south by Lithuania
Area 64 100 sq km/24 749 sq mi
Capital Riga

Chief towns Daugavpils, Liepaja
Population 2 245 000 (2008e)
Time zone GMT +2
Currency 1 Lat (Ls) = 100 santims
Language Latvian; Russian is also spoken
Religions Christianity 57% (Lutheran 20%,
  Orthodox 15%), other, unaffiliated and none 43%
Ethnic groups Latvian 57%, Russian 30%,
  Belarusian 4%, Ukrainian 3%, others 6%

Physical description

Flat and low-lying; the highest point is Gaizinkalns at 312m/1024ft; over 40% of the land is forested; the north-west coast is indented by the Gulf of Riga; the chief river is the Daugava

Climate

Moderate winters; cool, rainy summers.

Government

Governed by a President, a Prime Minister and Cabinet of Ministers, and a unicameral legislature (*Saeima*).

Economy

Transformed into market economy since 1991, although some enterprises still state-owned; services (transit, banking) now largest sector; other activities include forestry, manufacturing (vehicles, textiles, machinery, fertilizers, domestic appliances, electronics, pharmaceuticals, food processing).

History

Incorporated into Russia in 1721, it became an independent state in 1918, but was annexed by the Soviet Union in 1940. It was occupied by Germany during World War II and re-annexed by the USSR on liberation. Nationalism grew in the 1980s, and in 1990 independence talks began with the USSR. Independence was declared in 1991 and the last Russian troops left Latvia in 1994, but tensions remain between the Russian and Latvian communities. Since the restoration of democracy in 1993, Latvia has had a succession of centre-right coalition governments. It joined NATO and the EU in 2004.

LEBANON

Official name Republic of Lebanon
Local name Al-Lubnän (Arabic), Liban (French)
Location A republic on the eastern coast of the Mediterranean Sea in south-west Asia, bounded to the north and east by Syria, and to the south by Israel
Area 10452 sq km/4034 sq mi
Capital Beirut

Chief towns Tripoli, Saida, Zahle
Population 3972000 (2008e)
Time zone GMT +2
Currency 1 Lebanese Pound (LL, L£) = 100 piastres
Language Arabic, French; English and Armenian are also spoken
Ethnic groups Arab 95%, Armenian 4%, others 1%

Physical description

The narrow coastal plain rises gradually east to the Lebanon Mountains, which extend along most of the country; peaks include the Qornet es-Sauda (3087m/10137ft); the arid eastern slopes fall abruptly to the fertile El Beqaa plateau (c.1000m/3280ft); the Anti-Lebanon range lies in the east; the River Litani flows south between the ranges.

Climate

Mediterranean, varying with altitude, with hot, dry summers and warm, moist winters, except in the mountains, where heavy snow is usual; average rainfall at Beirut is 920mm and average temperatures are 13°–27°C. It is much cooler and drier in the Beqaa valley and irrigation is essential.

Government

Governed by a President (who must be a Maronite Christian), a Prime Minister (who must be a Sunni Muslim) and Council of Ministers, and a unicameral National Assembly (divided equally between Christians and Muslims).

Economy

Reconstruction after civil war was restoring position as regional entrepôt and financial services centre; recovery devastated by Israeli attacks on Hezbollah in 2006, and internal political tensions; services (banking, tourism) are largest sector; main industries are food processing, wine-making, jewellery, cement, textiles, mineral and chemical products, timber, furniture, oil refining, metals; agriculture produces fruit, vegetables, tobacco, livestock.

History

The area was part of the Phoenician Empire from 5c BC until 1c AD, when it came under Roman rule. It was contested between Christians and Muslims during the Crusades before becoming part of the Ottoman Empire from the 16c until the empire's collapse after World War I. In 1920 the state of Greater Lebanon was created, based upon the autonomous Maronite Christian area around Jabal Lubnan and incorporating the Muslim coastal regions to the north and south, and the Beqaa valley.

Religions

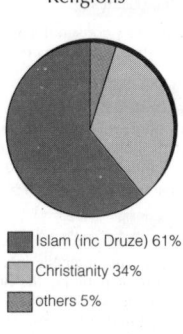

■ Islam (inc Druze) 61%
□ Christianity 34%
■ others 5%

This was administered by France under a League of Nations mandate until 1941, when it declared its independence. The 1943 constitution enshrined power-sharing by all the country's religions but tensions between Christians and Muslims erupted in 1975 into a civil war pitching a coalition of Christian groups against Druze and Muslim militias. Conflict continued for 15 years, drawing in the Palestinian Liberation Organization (based in Beirut until forced to withdraw from Lebanon by Israel in 1982), Syrian troops (in support of Muslim factions) and Israeli forces, which invaded in 1978 and 1982 in reprisal for Palestinian guerrilla raids on Israel. A ceasefire came into effect in 1989, and a peace plan – the Ta'if Accord – reduced the domination of Maronite Christians in government. Resistance to the Ta'if Accord was crushed by Syria and a fragile peace was achieved in 1991, followed by elections in 1992. Syria exerted a strong influence on Lebanese politics after the civil war, with pro-Syrian governments in office and Syrian troops remaining in the country, until 2005, when the assassination of a leading politician provoked huge rallies that brought down the pro-Syrian government and obliged Syria to withdraw its remaining troops and agents. Despite this, the government's control of the country remained weak. Clashes in southern Lebanon between Israeli troops (or the Israel-backed South Lebanon Army between 1985 and 2000) and Hizbullah guerrillas had continued since the end of the civil war, and in summer 2006 Hizbullah activities provoked massive Israeli air, sea and land strikes that devastated the country's infrastructure. The subsequent deployment of UN peacekeepers and then the Lebanese army extended government control in the south, and it gained greater control in the north in 2007.

LESOTHO

Official name Kingdom of Lesotho
Local name Lesotho
Location An African kingdom completely bounded by South Africa
Area 30 460 sq km / 11 758 sq mi
Capital Maseru
Chief towns Mafeteng, Quthing
Population 2 128 000 (2008e)

Time zone GMT +2
Currency 1 Loti (plural Maloti) (M, LSM) = 100 lisente
Languages Sesotho, English; Zulu and Xhosa are also spoken
Religions Christianity 90% (RC 45%, Prot 45%), others 10%
Ethnic groups Sotho 99%, others 1%

Physical description

Small country, 230km/140mi east to west, 200km/120mi north to south; the Drakensberg Mountains lie in the north-east and east and include Lesotho's highest peak, Thabana-Ntlenyana (3482m/11 424ft); the Mulati Mountains run south to west from the north-east border forming a steep escarpment; only 13% of the land, mostly in the west, is cultivable; the population mainly lives west of the highlands at an altitude of 1500–1800m/4920–5900ft; serious soil erosion, especially in the west; the main rivers are the Orange and the Caledon.

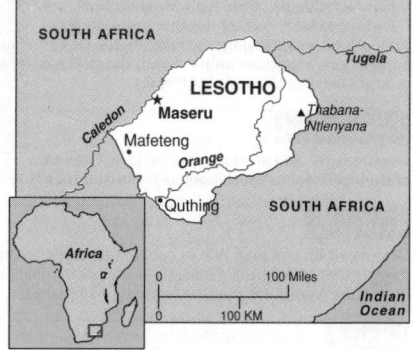

Climate

Mild, dry winters at lower altitudes but snow is frequent in the mountains; the warm summer season is October–April; the lowland summer maximum temperature is 32°C, the winter minimum is 7°C; annual average rainfall is 725mm.

Nations of the World

Government

A hereditary constitutional monarchy with a King as head of state; governed by a Prime Minister and Council of Ministers, and a bicameral Parliament consisting of a National Assembly and a Senate.

Economy

Very poor; revenues derive from customs dues, expatriates' remittances and exporting water and hydro-electric power to South Africa; small manufacturing base (processing agricultural products) and tourism developing; agriculture, mostly at subsistence level, employs 86% of the workforce, but productivity declining owing to drought, soil erosion and loss of workforce to HIV/AIDS; recent slump in garment manufacturing.

History

Lesotho was originally inhabited by hunting and gathering San (Bushmen). Bantu peoples arrived in the 16c, and the nation of the Basotho was organized in 1824 by Moshoeshoe I. After fighting both the Afrikaners and the British, Moshoeshoe put his country under British protection as Basutoland in 1868, and it was administered until 1880 from the Cape Colony. In 1884 it came under direct control of the British government as a British High Commission Territory. The kingdom gained independence as a hereditary monarchy in 1966. Chief Jonathan, prime minister since 1966 and effectively a dictator since 1970, was overthrown in a military coup in 1986. Military rule ended after another coup in 1991 led to the restoration of democracy in 1993. Protests after the 1998 election led to the revision of the constitution before the 2002 election. Lesotho faces serious problems owing to the high level of HIV/AIDS infection (among the highest in the world) and food shortages caused by successive years of drought.

LIBERIA

Official name Republic of Liberia
Local name Liberia
Location A tropical republic in West Africa, bounded to the north-west by Sierra Leone; to the north by Guinea; to the east by Côte d'Ivoire; and to the south by the Atlantic Ocean
Area 111370 sq km/42999 sq mi
Capital Monrovia
Chief towns Harper, Greenville, Buchanan, Robertsport

Population 3335000 (2008e)
Time zone GMT
Currency 1 Liberian Dollar (L$) = 100 cents
Language English; many local languages are also spoken
Religions traditional beliefs 40%, Christianity 40%, Islam 20%
Ethnic groups African 95% (includes Kpelle, Bassa, Grebo, Gio, Kru, Mano), Americo-Liberian 2.5%, Congo People 2.5%

Physical description

Low coastal belt with lagoons, beaches, and mangrove marshes; a rolling plateau (500–800m/1640–2624ft) with grasslands and rainforest; land rises inland to mountains; the highest point is Mount Wuteve (1380m/4528ft); rivers cut south-west through the plateau.

Climate

Equatorial climate, with high temperatures and abundant rainfall; rainfall declines from south to north; high humidity during the rainy season (April–September), especially on the coast; the average annual rainfall at Monrovia is 4150mm.

Government

Governed by an executive President, a Cabinet, and a bicameral National Assembly consisting of a House of Representatives and a Senate.

Economy

Devastated by civil war; rich in natural resources; main activities are agriculture (cocoa, coffee, palm oil), forestry (timber, rubber), mining (iron, diamonds, gold), processing rubber and palm oil; the largest merchant fleet in the world, including the registration of many foreign ships.

History

Mapped by the Portuguese in the 15c, it originated as a result of the activities of the philanthropic American Colonization Society wishing to establish a homeland for former slaves. The country was first settled in

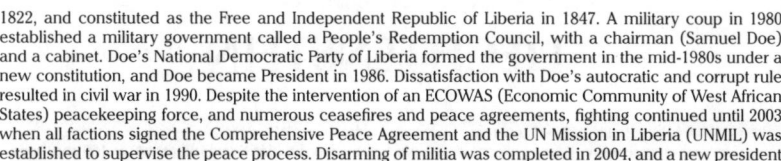

1822, and constituted as the Free and Independent Republic of Liberia in 1847. A military coup in 1980 established a military government called a People's Redemption Council, with a chairman (Samuel Doe) and a cabinet. Doe's National Democratic Party of Liberia formed the government in the mid-1980s under a new constitution, and Doe became President in 1986. Dissatisfaction with Doe's autocratic and corrupt rule resulted in civil war in 1990. Despite the intervention of an ECOWAS (Economic Community of West African States) peacekeeping force, and numerous ceasefires and peace agreements, fighting continued until 2003 when all factions signed the Comprehensive Peace Agreement and the UN Mission in Liberia (UNMIL) was established to supervise the peace process. Disarming of militia was completed in 2004, and a new president and legislature were elected in 2005. In 2006 a commission was set up to investigate human rights abuses between 1979 and 2003.

LIBYA

Official name Great Socialist People's Libyan Arab Jamahiriya
Local name Lībyā
Location A north African state, bounded to the north-west by Tunisia; to the west by Algeria; to the south-west by Niger; to the south by Chad; to the south-east by Sudan; to the east by Egypt; and to the north by the Mediterranean Sea
Area 1 758 610 sq km/678 823 sq mi

Capital Tripoli
Chief towns Misratah, Benghazi, Tobruk
Population 6 174 000 (2008e)
Time zone GMT +2
Currency 1 Libyan Dinar (LD) = 1000 dirhams
Language Arabic
Religions Islam 97% (Sunni), others 3%
Ethnic groups Arab and Berber 97%, others 3%

Physical description

Mainly low-lying Saharan desert or semi-desert; the land rises in the south to over 2000m/6561ft in the Tibesti Massif; the highest point is Pic Bette (2286m/7500ft); surface water is limited to infrequent oases.

Climate

Mediterranean climate on the coast; the coastal city of Tripoli has an average annual rainfall of 385mm with average maximum daily temperatures of 16°–30°C; annual rainfall in the desert seldom exceeds 100mm; temperatures in the south are over 40°C for three months of the year.

Government

In principle, the state is governed by the masses, through the appointed, unicameral General People's Congress, which appoints the General People's Committee; in practice, power rests in the hands of the 'Leader of the Revolution', Colonel Gaddafi.

Economy

Largely state-controlled economy; dominated by oil (95% of total exports) and natural gas; diversifying into production of petrochemicals, iron, steel and aluminium as well as processing agricultural products; agricultural sector is small and 75% of food is imported.

History

Controlled at various times by Phoenicians, Carthaginians, Greeks, Vandals and Byzantines, Libya came under Arab domination during the 7c. It was under Turkish rule from the 16c until the Italians gained control in 1911, and it was named Libya by them in 1934. It suffered heavy fighting during World War II, then came under British and French control. It became the independent Kingdom of Libya in 1951. A military coup established a republic under Muammar Gaddafi in 1969, and it was governed by a Revolutionary Command Council. Government policy since the revolution has been based on the promotion of Arab unity and the furtherance of Islam. Relations with other countries were strained from the 1970s until 2003 by controversial activities, including the alleged organization of international terrorism: diplomatic relations were severed by the UK after the murder of a policewoman in London in 1984; Tripoli and Benghazi were bombed by the US Air Force in response to alleged terrorist activity in 1986; two Libyan fighter planes were shot down by US aircraft off the north African coast in 1989; and sanctions were imposed by the UN Security Council in 1992 following Libya's refusal to extradite for trial two men suspected of the bombing of a PanAm aircraft over Lockerbie in 1988. Sanctions were suspended in 1999 after the suspects were handed over for trial, and lifted in 2003 after Libya admitted responsibility for the bombing. Since 2003, Gaddafi has sought to end Libya's international isolation, abandoning its WMD programmes and promising in 2004 to allow UN nuclear weapons inspections.

Nations of the World

LIECHTENSTEIN

Official name Principality of Liechtenstein
Local name Liechtenstein
Location A small landlocked independent
  principality in central Europe, lying between the
  Austrian state of Voralberg to the east and the
  Swiss cantons of St Gallen and Graubünden to
  the west
Area 160 sq km/62 sq mi
Capital Vaduz
Population 34 500 (2008e)

Time zone GMT +1
Currency 1 Swiss Franc (SFr, SwF) = 100 centimes
  = 100 rappen
Language German, Alemannic dialect
Religions Christianity 87% (RC 78%, Prot 9%), Islam
  5%, unaffiliated 7%, others 1%
Ethnic groups Liechtensteiner 66%, Italian, Turkish
  and others 34%

Physical description

Situated in the Alps; bounded to the west by the River
Rhine, its valley occupying c.40% of the country;
much of the rest consists of forested mountains,
rising to 2599m/8527ft in the Grauspitz.

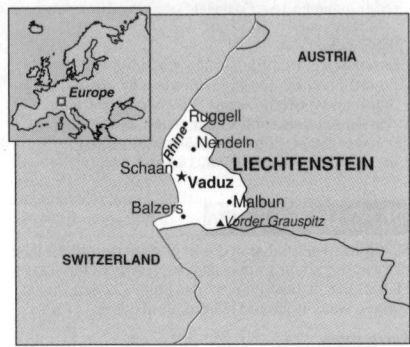

Climate

Alpine, moderated by a warm south wind (the
Föhn); average high temperature of 20°–28°C in
summer; average annual rainfall is 1050–1200mm.

Government

A hereditary constitutional monarchy; governed
by the Prince, a Head of Government and Cabinet,
and a unicameral legislature (*Landtag*).

Economy

Highly industrialized and diversified economy; largest sectors are services (banking, financial services,
tourism, postage stamps) and specialized and high-technology industries such as dental products, electronics,
metal manufacturing, textiles, ceramics, pharmaceuticals, food products, precision and optical instruments.

History

Originally the medieval counties of Vaduz and Schellenberg, this small territory came into the hands of
the princes of Liechtenstein between 1699 and 1712. A principality of the Holy Roman Empire from 1719,
Liechtenstein became a member of the Confederation of the Rhine in 1806 and of the German Confederation
from 1815 until 1866, when it became fully independent. Its neutrality, declared in 1868, was respected in both
world wars. Close economic and political ties have existed at different times with Austria and Switzerland.

LITHUANIA

Official name Republic of Lithuania
Local name Lietuva
Location A republic in north-eastern Europe,
  bounded to the north by Latvia; to the east and
  south by Belarus; to the south-west by Poland
  and the Kaliningrad region of Russia, and to the
  west by the Baltic Sea
Area 65 200 sq km/25 167 sq mi
Capital Vilnius
Chief towns Kaunas, Klaipėda, Šiauliai

Population 3 565 000 (2008e)
Time zone GMT +2
Currency 1 Litas (Lt) = 100 centas
Language Lithuanian; Russian and Polish are also
  spoken
Religions Christianity 85% (RC 79%, Russian
  Orthodox 4%, Prot 2%), others and unspecified
  5%, none 10%
Ethnic groups Lithuanian 83%, Polish 7%, Russian
  6%, others 4%

Physical description

Rolling plains with low hills in the west and south-east and over 2800 lakes; the highest point is Juozapine Hill
(294m/965ft); the chief river is the Neman.

Climate

Varies between maritime and continental; wet, with moderate winters and summers.

Government

Governed by a President, a Prime Minister and Cabinet, and a unicameral legislature (*Seimas*).

Economy

Transformed since 1991 into a diverse, largely private-sector market economy; main industries are textiles and clothing, oil processing, forestry, food processing, manufacturing (machinery, machine tools, electric and electronic equipment and components, chemicals, furniture), shipbuilding, amber extraction and jewellery-making.

History

The last part of Europe to become fully Christian (15c), by the 14c Lithuania formed a large grand duchy in central and eastern Europe. It was confederated with Poland from the 16c until 1795, when it came under imperial Russian control following the partition of Poland. Intensive Russification led to revolts in the 19c and early 20c. Occupied by Germany in World War I, it became an independent republic in 1918 but was annexed by the USSR in 1940 before a second German occupation in 1941. Soviet control was re-established in 1944. Nationalism in the 1980s led to a unilateral declaration of independence in 1990; independence was recognized internationally in 1991 and the last Russian troops left the country in 1993. Since independence there has been a succession of short-lived, mostly centre-right coalition governments. Lithuania joined NATO and the EU in 2004.

LUXEMBOURG

Official name Grand Duchy of Luxembourg
Local name Lëtzeberg (Letz), Luxembourg (Fr), Luxemburg (Ger)
Location An independent duchy in north-western Europe, bounded to the east by Germany; to the west by Belgium; and to the south by France
Area 2586 sq km/998 sq mi
Capital Luxembourg
Chief towns Esch-sur-Alzette, Dudelange, Differdange

Population 486 000 (2008e)
Time zone GMT +1
Currency 1 Euro (€) = 100 cents
Languages Lëtzebuergesch, German, French
Religions Christianity 90% (RC), Islam 2%, others and none 8%
Ethnic groups Luxembourger 63%, Portuguese 13%, French 5%, Italian 4%, German 2%, other EU 7%, others 6%

Physical description

Divides into the wooded hilly region of Ösling in the north and the flatter, more fertile Gutland; the highest point is Buurgplaatz (559m/1833ft); water resources have been developed by canalization of the River Mosel, by hydroelectric dams on the River Our, and by reservoirs on the River Sûre.

Climate

It is drier and sunnier in the south, but winters can be severe; in the sheltered Mosel Valley, summers and autumns are warm enough for cultivation of vines.

Government

A hereditary constitutional monarchy with a Grand Duke as head of state; governed by a Prime Minister and Council of Ministers, and a unicameral Chamber of Deputies; a State Council has an advisory role.

Economy

Very prosperous economy based on service sector (banking, financial services, tourism); industry still dominated by iron and steel but diversifying into information technology, telecommunications, freight transport, food processing, chemicals, metal products, engineering, rubber, glass.

History

After being occupied by the Romans and then the Franks (in the 5c), Luxembourg came under the control of the House of Luxembourg in the 11c. The first Count of Luxembourg was created in 1060; the family, which owned lands in the area between the Maas and the Mosel from the 13c, took its name from the Castle of Lützelburg, and came to prominence when Henry VII was elected Holy Roman Emperor in 1308. Although they lost the imperial crown after Henry's death, his son John gained control of Bohemia and the Luxemburgers' power grew comparable with that of the Habsburgs. Their most important representative was Emperor Charles IV, who elevated Luxembourg to a duchy in 1354. From 1346 until 1437 (when the dynasty died out in the male line with the death of Sigismund), all but one of the German kings came from the House of Luxembourg. The country of Luxembourg was then controlled by various European powers (Burgundy 1443–77, Habsburgs 1477–1555, Spain 1555–1684, France 1684–97) before returning to Habsburg control after the War of the Spanish Succession. It was made a Grand Duchy and passed to the Netherlands following the Congress of Vienna in 1815. In 1830 much of Luxembourg joined the Belgians in the revolt against William I; this resulted in the division of the country, with the western, French-speaking region joining Belgium. The remaining Grand Duchy was granted political autonomy in 1838, and recognized as a neutral independent state in 1867. Occupied by Germany in both world wars, it entered into economic union with Belgium in 1921, joined the Benelux economic union in 1948, and abandoned neutrality on joining NATO in 1949. Luxembourg was a founding member of the EEC in 1958, and the Luxembourg franc was replaced by the euro in 2002.

■ Macao ► China

MACEDONIA

Official name Republic of Macedonia; known internationally as the former Yugoslav Republic of Macedonia (FYROM or FYR Macedonia)
Local name Makedonija
Location A landlocked republic in the Balkan Peninsula in southern Europe, bounded to the west by Albania; to the south by Greece; to the east by Bulgaria; and to the north by Serbia and Kosovo
Area 25 713 sq km/9925 sq mi

Capital Skopje
Chief towns Bitola, Gostivar, Tetovo, Kumanovo
Population 2 061 000 (2008e)
Time zone GMT +1
Currency 1 Denar (D, den) = 100 deni
Language Macedonian, Albanian
Religions Christianity 65% (Orthodox), Islam 33%, others 2%
Ethnic groups Macedonian 64%, Albanian 25%, Turkish 4%, others 7%

Physical description

Mountainous, with deep basins and valleys and two large lakes, Ohrid and Prespa, on the south-west border with Albania; bisected by the River Vardar; the highest point is Golem Korab (Maja e Korabit; 2753m/9032ft).

Climate

Mediterranean, with cold winters and warm summers.

Government

Governed by a President, a Prime Minister and government ministers (who are elected by, but not members of, the legislature), and a unicameral Assembly (*Sobranje*). Ethnic Albanians have considerable local autonomy in areas where they predominate.

Economy

Made a slow transition to a market economy after 1991 and remains poor; main activities are agriculture (tobacco, vegetables, dairy products), wine-making, food processing, textiles, chemicals, mining (iron), steel-making, cement, pharmaceuticals.

History

The area of ancient Macedonia (consisting of the present region of Macedonia in northern Greece and the former Yugoslav Republic of Macedonia) was inhabited by Macedonians who spoke a Slav language closer to Bulgarian than Serbo-Croat. Through the centuries, many tribes and nations settled in Macedonia and its ethnic composition is accordingly complex; the French *macédoine* is a synonym for 'medley' or 'mixture'. Slav tribes arrived in the 7c and mixed with the Greek and romanized Illyrians and Thracians, while the Byzantine rulers established settlements of Scythians and christianized Turks. In the 9c the Bulgars conquered Macedonia but the region returned to Byzantine rule until the Ottoman conquest (1355). Under the Turks, Sasi, Tartars, Cerkezi, Gypsies and Jews all settled and mixed with the local population. At the end of the 19c, a nationalist movement emerged, its members insisting that the Macedonians were neither Bulgars nor Serbs, but a distinct Slav nation with its own language; this was a claim which the neighbouring Serbs, Bulgars and Greeks, nations all bent on territorial expansion, were determined to discount. After the Balkan Wars in 1913, Macedonia was divided between Greece and Serbia. It is the Serbian part that was given to Yugoslavia by the Treaty of Neuilly in 1919, an act confirmed by the treaties signed at the Paris Peace Conference in 1947, when the region was named the Republic of Macedonia within the Federal Republic of Yugoslavia. Despite claims to parts of it by Albania and Bulgaria, and deteriorating relations with Greece (which claims that its region called Macedonia is the only one entitled to the name), Macedonia formally seceded from Yugoslavia in 1991 and was admitted to the UN in 1993. There was ongoing tension and sporadic violence between ethnic Albanians and Macedonians throughout the 1990s. Violence intensified in 2001, with a short-lived uprising by ethnic Albanian rebel groups demanding more rights. A peace deal in Aug led to constitutional changes that improved the status and rights of ethnic Albanians and in 2004 ethnic Albanian areas were given greater autonomy. NATO forces oversaw disarmament of the rebels in 2001; it handed over peacekeeping duties to the EU in 2003. Macedonia is formally a candidate for membership of NATO and the EU.

MADAGASCAR

Official name Republic of Madagascar
Local name Madagasikara (Malagasy), Madagascar (French)
Location An island republic in the Indian Ocean, separated from East Africa by the Mozambique Channel
Area 587 040 sq km/226 656 sq mi
Capital Antananarivo
Chief towns Toamasina, Mahajanga, Fianarantsoa, Antsiranana, Toliara

Population 20 043 000 (2008e)
Time zone GMT +3
Currency 1 Ariary (A) = 5 Iraimbilanja
Language Malagasy, French, English
Religions Traditional beliefs 52%, Christainity 41%, Islam 7%
Ethnic groups Merina 26%, Betsimisaraka 16%, Betsileo 12%, Tsimihety 7%, Sakalava 7%, others 32%

Physical description

Bisected north to south by a ridge of mountains rising to 2876m/9436ft at Maromokotra; cliffs to the east drop down to a coastal plain through tropical forest; a terraced descent to the west through savannah to the coast, which is heavily indented in the north; great bio-diversity, with high proportion of species unique to island.

Climate

Temperate climate in the highlands; the average annual rainfall is 1000–1500mm; tropical coastal region with an annual rainfall at Toamasina in the east of 3500mm; cyclones occur regularly.

Government

Governed by a President, a Prime Minister and Council of Ministers, and a bicameral Parliament comprising a National Assembly and a Senate.

Economy

Poor country, dependent on agriculture and fishing; chief cash crops are coffee, vanilla, fish, sugar, cocoa, cloves, pepper, cotton; other activities are mining (chromite, graphite, sapphires), manufacturing (garments, soap, beverages, glassware), food processing, chemicals, oil refining, cement, metalworking, car assembly.

Nations of the World

History

Madagascar was settled by Indonesians in the 1c AD and by African traders in the 8c. The French established trading posts in the late 18c and claimed the island as a protectorate in 1885. After becoming an autonomous overseas French territory (the Malagasy Republic) in 1958, it gained independence in 1960 and was named Madagascar again in 1975. Following anti-government riots, in 1992 a new constitution was approved which reduced the powers of the President, Didier Ratsiraka, who had held office since 1975. He was defeated in 1993 but returned to office in 1997 after winning the 1996 elections. Disputed elections in 2001 led to several months of political confusion and unrest that brought the country close to civil war; Marc Ravalomanana emerged as the winner, and Ratsiraka then fled into exile. Ravalomanana was re-elected in the 2006 presidential election.

■ Madeira▶Portugal

MALAWI

Official name Republic of Malawi
Local name Malaŵi
Location A landlocked republic in south-eastern Africa, bounded to the south-west and south-east by Mozambique; to the east by Lake Nyasa (Lake Malawi); to the north by Tanzania; and to the west by Zambia
Area 118 484 sq km/45 735 sq mi
Capital Lilongwe

Chief towns Blantyre, Zomba, Limbe, Salima
Population 13 932 000 (2008e)
Time zone GMT +2
Currency 1 Kwacha (MK) = 100 tambala
Languages English, Chichewa
Religions Christianity 70%, Islam 20% (Sunni), others 10%
Ethnic groups African (mainly Chewa and Nguni); small Asian and European minorites

Physical description

Crossed north to south by the Great Rift Valley in which lies Africa's third-largest lake, Lake Nyasa (Lake Malawi); high plateaux on either side; Shire highlands in the south rise to 3002m/9849ft at Sapitwa Peak on Mount Mulanje.

Climate

Tropical climate in the south, with high year-round temperatures (28°–37°C); average annual rainfall, 740mm; more moderate temperatures in centre; higher rainfall in the mountains overlooking Lake Nyasa (1500–2000mm).

Government

Governed by an executive President, a Cabinet and a unicameral National Assembly.

Economy

Very poor country, dependent on international aid; agriculture, mostly at subsistence level, employs 85% of the workforce but is vulnerable to drought, flooding and soil degradation; chief cash crops are tobacco (53% of export earnings), tea, sugar, coffee, cotton and groundnuts; manufacturing (agricultural processing, textiles, garments, consumer products), forestry and sawmill products.

History

The area was explored by the Portuguese in the 17c, and European contact was established by David Livingstone in 1859. Scottish church missions were established in the area, and it was claimed as the British Nyasaland Districts Protectorate in 1891, and then called the British Central Africa Protectorate in 1893. It was established as the British colony of Nyasaland in 1907, and in the 1950s it joined with Northern and Southern Rhodesia (now Zambia and Zimbabwe) to form the Federation of Rhodesia and Nyasaland. After gaining independence in 1964 with Hastings Banda as Prime Minister, it became a republic in 1966 and a one-party state with Banda as President. As a result of international pressure and growing unrest within the country, a referendum was held in 1993 in which the population voted for a multiparty system. Bakili Muluzi was elected president in 1994 and served until 2004, when Bingu wa Mutharika took office and launched an anti-corruption campaign. Malawi faces serious problems because of the high level of HIV/AIDS infection among the population and recent crop failures owing to drought.

MALAYSIA

Official name Federation of Malaysia
Local name Malaysia
Location An independent federation of states in South-East Asia, comprising most of the lower part of the Malay Peninsula, bounded by Thailand to the north, and part of the island of Borneo, bounded by Indonesia to the south and Brunei in the north-east
Area 329 749 sq km/127 283 sq mi
Capital Kuala Lumpur; Putrajaya is the administrative capital
Chief towns George Town, Ipoh, Malacca, Johor Baharu, Kuching, Kota Kinabalu

Population 25 274 000 (2008e)
Time zone GMT +8
Currency 1 Malaysian Ringgit (dollar) (M$) = 100 cents
Language Bahasa Malaysia (Malay); Chinese, English, Tamil and local languages are also spoken
Religions Islam 60%, Buddhism 19%, Christianity 9%, Hinduism 6%, traditional Chinese religions 3%, others 3%
Ethnic groups Malay 50%, Chinese 24%, indigenous people 11%, Indian 7%, others 8%

Physical description

Peninsular Malaysia consists of a mountain chain running north to south, rising to Mount Tahan (2189m/7182ft); there are narrow east and broader west coastal plains; mostly tropical rainforest and mangrove swamp; a coastline of long, narrow beaches; the chief river is the Pahang (456km/283mi long). Sarawak, on the north-west coast of Borneo, has a narrow, swampy coastal belt backed by foothills rising sharply towards

mountain ranges on the Indonesian frontier; Sabah, in the north-east corner of Borneo, has a deeply indented coastline and a narrow western coastal plain, rising sharply into the Crocker Range, reaching 4094m/13 432ft at Mount Kinabalu, Malaysia's highest peak.

Climate

Tropical, with little variation in temperature and high humidity; strongly influenced by the monsoon winds (April–September or November–February); the wet seasons are March–May and September–November; it is cooler and wetter in the mountains.

Government

Governed by a supreme head of state, a Prime Minister and Cabinet, and a bicameral Parliament, consisting of a Senate and a House of Representatives; the supreme head of state is elected by the rulers of the nine states of peninsular Malaysia from among their number. Each of the eleven states is a hereditary constitutional monarchy governed by its sultan or raja, an executive council and a legislative assembly.

Economy

Diversified emerging economy driven by exports; agriculture, forestry and mining produce raw materials (rubber, palm oil, metals, timber) for processing and manufacturing industries; also produces electronic equipment, textiles and chemicals; oil and natural gas production and processing, especially in Sarawak and Sabah; tourism is a major industry.

History

Malaysia formed part of the Srivijaya Empire in the 9–14c and experienced Hindu and Muslim influences in the 14–15c. From the 16c, Portugal, the Netherlands and Britain vied for control. Singapore, Malacca and Penang were formally incorporated into the British Colony of the Straits Settlements in 1826. British protection was extended over Perak, Selangor, Negeri Sembilan and Pahang, constituted into the Federated Malay States, in 1895, and protection treaties with several other states (Unfederated Malay States) were agreed in 1885–1930. The region was occupied by the Japanese in World War II, after which Sarawak became a British colony, Singapore became a separate colony, the colony of North Borneo was formed, and the Malay Union was established, uniting the Malay states and the Straits Settlements of Malacca and Penang. In 1948 the nine peninsular states were federated as the Federation of Malaya. Growing resentment by the Chinese-dominated Malayan Communist Party (MCP) of Malay dominance within the Federation led to an insurrection led by the MCP against British rule. The insurrection and the campaign to crush it, the Malayan Emergency, lasted from 1948 until 1960, although the insurrection was effectively broken by the mid-1950s. Malaya gained independence in 1957, and in 1963 it combined with Singapore, Sarawak and Sabah to form the Federation of Malaysia; Singapore withdrew from the Federation in 1965. Post-independence politics has been dominated by the United Malay National Organization, initially as the governing party and since 1971 as the dominant partner in coalition governments. Mahathir bin Muhammad served as Prime Minister for 22 years (1981–2003), a period which saw increasingly authoritarian rule and considerable tension between ethnic groups because of policies favouring Malays. Parts of the country were devastated by the 2004 Indian Ocean tsunami.

MALDIVES

Official name Republic of Maldives
Local name Dhivehi Raajje
Location A republic consisting of an island archipelago in the Indian Ocean
Area 300 sq km/120 sq mi
Capital Malé
Population 385 900 (2008e)

Time zone GMT +5
Currency 1 Rufiyaa (MRf, Rf) = 100 laarees
Language Dhivehi; English is spoken widely
Religions Islam 100% (Sunni)
Ethnic groups Maldivian (mixture of South Indian, Sinhalese and Arab) with African minorities

Physical description

Small, flat, low-lying islands; highest point is only 2.4m above sea level.

Climate

Generally warm and humid; affected by south-west monsoons (April–October); the average annual rainfall is 2100mm and the average daily temperature is 22°C.

Government

Governed by an executive President, a Cabinet and a unicameral People's Assembly.

Economy

Undeveloped, but experiencing steady growth until devastated by 2004 tsunami; main activities are tourism (28% of GDP), shipping, fishing, manufacturing (garments, accessories), boat-building, coconut processing, handicrafts; agriculture constrained by lack of cultivable land, so most food is imported.

History

A former dependency of Ceylon (now Sri Lanka), it was a British protectorate from 1887 until 1965, when it gained independence. Its sultanate was abolished in 1968 when it became a republic under President Ibrahim Masir. He was succeeded in 1978 by Maumoon Abdul Gayoom, who remained in office until 2008. His tenure allowed economic development, although his regime was accused of repression and human rights abuses. Pro-democracy demonstrations in 2003–4 led to the legalization of political parties in 2005. In recent years, the Maldivian authorities have expressed concern over the impact of global warming and rising sea levels, as 80% of the land is one metre or less above sea level. Most of the islands were devastated by the Indian Ocean tsunami in 2004.

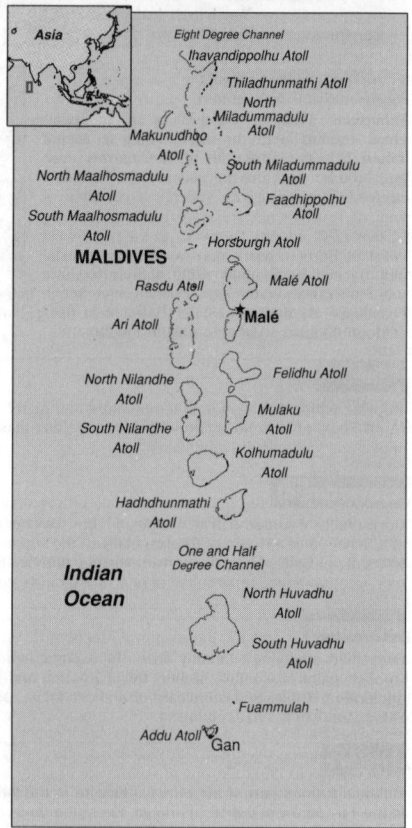

Asia

Eight Degree Channel
Ihavandippolhu Atoll
Thiladhunmathi Atoll
North Miladummadulu Atoll
Makunudhoo Atoll
North Maalhosmadulu Atoll
South Miladummadulu Atoll
South Maalhosmadulu Atoll
Faadhippolhu Atoll
Horsburgh Atoll
MALDIVES
Rasdu Atoll
Malé Atoll
Ari Atoll
Malé
North Nilandhe Atoll
Felidhu Atoll
South Nilandhe Atoll
Mulaku Atoll
Kolhumadulu Atoll
Hadhdhunmathi Atoll
One and Half Degree Channel
Indian Ocean
North Huvadhu Atoll
South Huvadhu Atoll
Fuammulah
Addu Atoll Gan

MALI

Official name Republic of Mali
Local name Mali
Location A landlocked republic in West Africa, bounded to the north-east by Algeria; to the north-west by Mauritania; to the west by Senegal; to the south-west by Guinea; to the south by Côte d'Ivoire; to the south-east by Burkina Faso; and to the east by Niger
Area 1 240 192 sq km/478 714 sq mi
Capital Bamako
Chief towns Ségou, Mopti, Sikasso, Kayes, Gao, Timbuktu
Population 12 324 000 (2008e)
Time zone GMT
Currency 1 CFA Franc (CFAFr) = 100 centimes
Language French; Bambara and other local languages are spoken widely
Religions Islam 90% (mostly Sunni), traditional beliefs or none 5%, Christianity 5%
Ethnic groups Mande 50% (includes Bambara, Malinke, Soninke), Peul 17%, Voltaic 12%, Songhai 6%, Tuareg and Moor 10%, others 5%

Physical description

On the fringe of the Sahara; the lower part of the Hoggar massif is located in the north; arid plains lie between 300m/984ft and 500m/1640ft; there is arid desert in the north with sand dunes; mainly savannah in the south; the main rivers are the Niger and Sénégal; the highest point is Hombori Tondo (1155m/3789ft).

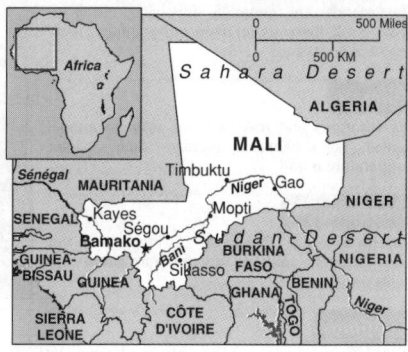

Climate

Subtropical in south; arid in north; in the south the rainy season lasts for five months (June–October); the annual average rainfall is c.1000mm in the south, decreasing to almost zero in the Saharan north.

Government

Governed by a President, a Prime Minister and Council of Ministers, and a unicameral National Assembly.

Economy

Very poor; dependent on international aid and expatriates' remittances; agriculture and herding, mainly at subsistence level, employ 80% of the workforce; usual self-sufficiency in food recently undermined by drought and locust attacks; cash crops are cotton (35% of export earnings) and livestock; other activities include mining (gold (50% of export earnings) and phosphates), food and cotton processing and construction.

History

Between the 13c and 15c the medieval Kingdom of Mali flourished in the Western Sudan, dominating the trade routes of the Sahara with North Africa. The kingdom reached its peak in the 14c and declined in the 15c. Although it had a quasi-Islamic ruling group, it was dominated by Muslim merchants, and it became an important factor in the Islamicization of West Africa. Mali was governed by France from 1881 to 1895 and was a territory of French Sudan (part of French West Africa) until 1959, when it entered a partnership with Senegal as the Federation of Mali. It achieved independence as a separate nation in 1960. Its first President, Modibo Keita, was overthrown in 1968 in a military coup led by Moussa Traoré, who held power until ousted by the military in 1991 following pro-democracy rioting. In 1992 a new multiparty constitution was introduced and the elections were won by the Alliance for Democracy in Mali Party and President Alpha Oumar Konaré, who soon faced a rebellion by Tuareg tribesmen (the Tuareg Unified Movements and Fronts of Azawad) in the north of the country; a peace agreement was signed in 1994, and greater autonomy was granted in 2006. Konaré was succeeded as President by Amadou Toumani Touré in 2002.

MALTA

Official name Republic of Malta
Local name Malta
Location An archipelago republic in the central Mediterranean Sea
Area 316 sq km/122 sq mi
Capital Valletta
Chief towns Sliema, Birkirkara, Qormi, Rabat, Victoria
Population 403 500 (2008e)

Time zone GMT +1
Currency 1 Euro (€) = 100 cents
Languages Maltese, English; there are many Arabic words in the local vocabulary
Religions Christianity 98% (RC), Islam 1%, others/none 1%
Ethnic groups Maltese 98%, British 2%

Physical description

The islands are generally low-lying, rising to 253m/830ft; there are no rivers or mountains; well-indented coastline.

Climate

Dry summers and mild winters; average annual rainfall is c.400mm; average daily winter temperature is 13°C.

Government

Governed by a President, a Prime Minister and Cabinet, and a unicameral House of Representatives.

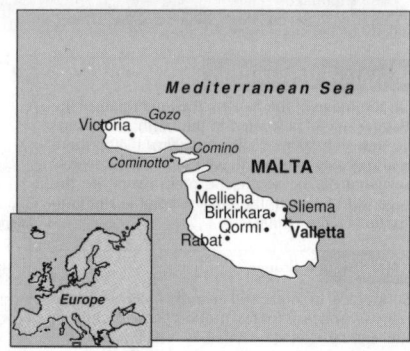

Economy

Market economy now dominated by service sector (tourism, financial services, freight trans-shipment, retailing); main industries are manufacturing (electronics, textiles, beverages), ship repair (the former naval dockyards having been converted to commercial use) and food processing; agricultural sector produces only 20% of food requirements.

History

Malta has at various times been controlled by Phoenicians, Greeks, Carthaginians and Romans. It was conquered by Arabs in the 9c, and later by Spain, and under Emperor Charles V it was given to the Knights Hospitallers in 1530. Captured by the British during the Napoleonic Wars, and a Crown Colony from 1815, it was an important strategic base in both world wars, and particularly in World War II when it was blockaded and subject to aerial bombardment for five months; its resistance led to the people of Malta being awarded the George Cross in 1942. It achieved independence in 1964 and became a republic in 1974, developing links with communist and Arab countries from the early 1970s. It became more pro-European from the late 1980s, and joined the EU in 2004.

■ Man, Isle of▶ United Kingdom

■ Mariana Islands, Northern▶ United States of America

MARSHALL ISLANDS

Official name Republic of the Marshall Islands
Local name Marshall Islands
Location An independent archipelago republic in the central Pacific Ocean
Area c.180 sq km/70 sq mi
Capital Majuro
Population 63 000 (2008e)

Time zone GMT +12
Currency 1 US Dollar ($, US$) = 100 cents
Languages Marshallese, English
Religions Christianity 93% (Prot 85%, RC 8%), Baha'i 1%, unaffiliated 2%, others 4%
Ethnic groups Marshallese 92%, mixed 6%, other 2%

Physical description

Low-lying coral, limestone and sand islands, atolls and reefs, with few natural resources.

Climate

Hot and humid; the wet season is from May to November; occasional typhoons.

Government

Governed by an executive President, a Cabinet and a unicameral Parliament. A Council of Chiefs has a consultative role on land and customs.

Economy

Subsistence economy based on copra and other coconut products, and dependent on US aid; government is largest employer (64%); activities include farming, fishing, tourism, services to US military bases, shipping registration.

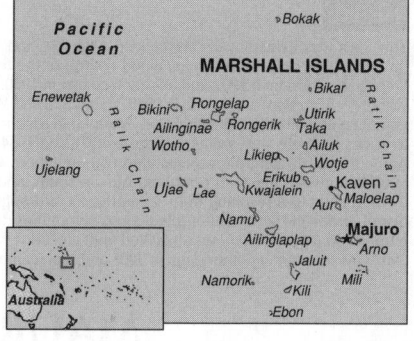

History

Originally settled by Micronesians, the islands were explored by the Spanish in 1529 and became a German protectorate in 1886. After World War I they came under Japanese control, and after World War II the group became a UN Trust Territory (1947–78), administered by the USA; the UN trusteeship ended in 1990. Between 1946 and 1962 US nuclear weapon tests were held on the Bikini and Enewetak atolls. After the Marshall Islands became a self-governing republic in 1979, a compact of free association with the USA was signed in 1982, and came into force in 1986, giving the republic its independence; under this compact the USA retained control of external security and defence and gave financial help. A renegotiated compact came into force in 2004.

■ Martinique▶France

MAURITANIA

Official name Islamic Republic of Mauritania
Local name Mauritanie (French), Mūrītāniyā (Arabic)
Location A republic in north-west Africa, bounded to the south-west by Senegal; to the south and east by Mali; to the north-east by Algeria; to the north by Western Sahara; and to the west by the Atlantic Ocean
Area 1 029 920 sq km / 397 549 sq mi
Capital Nouakchott

Chief towns Nouadhibou, Atar
Population 3 365 000 (2008e)
Time zone GMT
Currency 1 Ouguiya (U, UM) = 5 khoums
Language Arabic, Pulaar, Soninke, Wolof; French and other local languages are also widely spoken
Religions Islam 100%
Ethnic groups mixed Arab and black 40%, Arab 30%, black 30%

Physical description

The Saharan zone in the north covers two-thirds of the country with sand dunes, mountainous plateaux and occasional oases; the coastal area has minimal rainfall and little vegetation; savannah grasslands lie in the Sahelian zone; the Sénégal River valley is the chief agricultural region; the highest point is Kediet Ijill (915m / 3002ft) in the north-west.

Climate

Dry and tropical with sparse rainfall; temperatures can rise to over 49°C in the Sahara.

Government

Governed by a President, a Prime Minister and Council of Ministers, and a bicameral Parliament comprising a Senate and a National Assembly.

Economy

Very poor country; agriculture and animal husbandry, mostly at subsistence level, employ 50% of the workforce; susceptible to drought and affected recently by locusts; main industries are mining (iron ore (nearly 40% of export earnings), gold), fishing and fish processing; offshore oil and gas to be exploited.

History

The coast was sighted by the Portuguese in the 15c, and European trading settlements were established from the 16c. In the mid 19c, France gained control of the territory and it became a French protectorate within French West Africa in 1903 and a French colony in 1920. It gained independence in 1960. When the Spanish withdrew from Western Sahara in 1976, Mauritania and Morocco divided the territory between them, but after conflict with Polisario Front guerrillas, Mauritania renounced all rights to the region in 1979, leaving Morocco to annex it. There were military coups in 1978 and 1984, the latter bringing to power Col. Maaouya ould Sid Ahmed Taya. Civilian rule was restored with multiparty elections in 1992. During the 1990s there was ethnic tension between the Arab north and African south, and internal unrest by opposition groups, exacerbated by food shortages resulting from several years of drought and a locust infestation in 2004. There were civil disturbances and several attempted coups before President Taya was deposed in a military coup in 2005, and a transitional government was installed until elections were held in 2006 and 2007. The president elected in 2007 was ousted in another coup in 2008 and replaced by an army general.

MAURITIUS

Official name Republic of Mauritius
Local name Mauritius
Location A small island nation in the Indian Ocean
Area 1865 sq km/720 sq mi
Capital Port Louis
Population 1 274 000 (2008e)
Time zone GMT +4

Currency 1 Mauritian Rupee (MR, MauRe) = 100 cents
Language English; Creole is spoken by the majority
Religions Hinduism 48%, Christianity 32% (RC 24%), Islam 17%, others 3%
Ethnic groups Indo-Mauritian 68%, Creole 27%, others 5%

Physical description

A volcanic island, with a central plateau; it falls steeply to narrow coastlands in the south and south-west; the highest peak is Piton de la Petite Rivière Noire (828m/2717ft); dry, lowland coast, with wooded savannah, mangrove swamp and bamboo in the east; surrounded by coral reefs enclosing lagoons and sandy beaches.

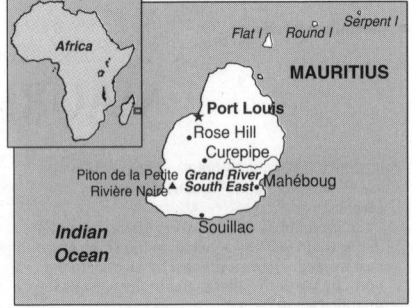

Climate

Tropical-maritime, with temperatures averaging between 22°C and 26°C; there is a wide variation in rainfall, with most rain falling in the central plateau; lies in the cyclone belt (November–April).

Government

Governed by a President, a Prime Minister and Council of Ministers, and a unicameral National Assembly.

Economy

Traditional industries of sugar (15% of export earnings) and textiles and garment manufacture supplemented by tourism, chemicals, metal products, transport equipment; diversifying into financial services, information technology and telecommunications as sugar and textile exports decline.

History

The island was visited by Arabs in the 10c and discovered by the Portuguese in the 16c. The Dutch took possession in 1598–1710, followed by the French in 1710–1810, and the British in 1810. It was formally ceded to Britain by the Treaty of Paris in 1814, and governed jointly with the Seychelles as a single colony until 1903. It became an independent state in 1968 and a republic in 1992. The Mauritian Socialist Party held power from 1982 to 1995, returning to power in 2000 in coalition with the Mouvement Militant Mauricien. The coalition lost the 2005 election to the Socialist Alliance.

■ Mayotte ▶ France

MEXICO

Nations of the World

Official name United Mexican States

Local name México

Location A federal republic in the south of North America, bounded to the north by the USA; to the west by the Gulf of California; to the west and south-west by the Pacific Ocean; to the south by Guatemala and Belize; and to the east by the Gulf of Mexico

Area 1 978 800 sq km/763 817 sq mi

Capital Mexico City

Chief towns Guadalajara, Léon, Monterrey, Ciudad Juárez

Population 109 955 000 (2008e)

Time zone GMT −6/−8

Currency 1 Mexican Peso (Mex$) = 100 centavos

Language Spanish; Mayan and other indigenous languages are also spoken

Religions Christianity 82% (RC 76%, Prot 6%), others/unspecified 14%, none 3%

Physical description

Bisected by the Tropic of Cancer; situated at the south end of the North American Western Cordillera; narrow coastal plains border the Pacific Ocean and the Gulf of Mexico; land rises steeply to a central plateau, reaching a height of c.2400m/7874ft around Mexico City; the plateau is bounded by the Sierra Madre Occidental in the west and Sierra Madre Oriental in the east; volcanic peaks lie to the south, notably Citlaltépetl (5699m/18697ft); limestone lowlands of the Yucatán peninsula stretch into the Gulf of Mexico in the south-east; the country is subject to earthquakes.

Climate

Great climatic variation between the coasts and mountains; desert or semi-desert conditions in the north-west; typically tropical climate on the east coast; generally wetter on the west coast; extreme temperature variations in the north, very cold in winter, very warm in summer.

Government

Governed by an executive President, a Cabinet and a bicameral Congress of the Union comprising a Senate and a Chamber of Deputies. Each of the 31 states has its own constitution, a Governor and a Chamber of Deputies.

Nations of the World

Economy

Diverse market economy closely linked to USA; main activities are oil and natural gas extraction, petrochemicals, iron and steel production, manufacturing (food, beverages, textiles, garments, tobacco, chemicals, motor vehicles, consumer durables), offshore assembly for US market, mining (especially silver), tourism and financial services; agriculture produces maize, wheat, soya beans, rice, beans, cotton, coffee, fruit, tomatoes, beef, poultry and dairy products.

History

Mexico was at the centre of Mesoamerican civilizations for over 2500 years: the Gulf Coast Olmecs were based at La Venta; Zapotecs at Monte Albán near Oaxaca; Mixtecs at Mitla; Toltecs at Tula; Mayas in the Yucatán; and Aztecs at Tenochtitlán. These peoples were subjugated from the 13c by the Aztecs, who were destroyed by the Spanish under Hernan Cortés in 1519–21. As the Viceroyalty of New Spain, Mexico came under Spanish rule until the 19c. The struggle for independence began in 1810 and Mexico became a federal republic in 1824. It lost nearly a third of its territory in all to the USA in 1836 and after the Mexican War (1846–8). There was civil war in 1858–61, and another Mexican War in 1862–7 during which French forces occupied Mexico City in 1863, declaring Archduke Maximilian of Austria to be Emperor of Mexico. The French withdrew and Maximilian was executed in 1867. The presidency of Porfirio Díaz (1876–80, 1884–1911) saw material progress but his dictatorial regime provoked the Mexican Revolution, which began in 1910 and did not end until 1920, and the establishment of a constitutional republic. Lázaro Cárdenas, President from 1934 to 1940, nationalized foreign-owned oil and railway companies, and carried out massive land reforms. After his presidency, however, the radicalism of the Institutional Revolutionary Party (PRI), which came to dominate political life, increasingly became more rhetoric than reality; it formed a succession of authoritarian governments until it lost its parliamentary majority in 1997 (for the first time since 1929) and PAN candidates have won the presidential elections since 2000. The second half of the 20c was rendered difficult due to economic problems, only partially relieved by mass emigration to the USA. Mexico became part of NAFTA in 1994. Marginalization of indigenous peoples provoked an armed uprising in the south in 1994–5, led by the Zapatista National Liberation Army (EZLN). A renewed, civil campaign in 2001 supported a bill of indigenous rights but after the legislation was passed, the Zapatistas claimed the provisions had been watered down.

Ethnic groups

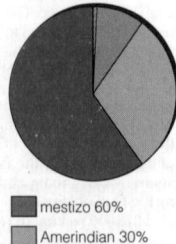

■ mestizo 60%
□ Amerindian 30%
■ white 9%
■ others 1%

FEDERATED STATES OF MICRONESIA

Official name Federated States of Micronesia
Local name Micronesia
Location A federal republic consisting of 607 islands divided into four states – Yap, Chuuk (formerly Truk), Pohnpei (formerly Ponape) and Kosrae (formerly Kosaie) – in the western Pacific Ocean
Area 702 sq km/271 sq mi
Capital Palikir, on Pohnpei

Population 108 000 (2008e)
Time zone GMT +10/+11
Currency 1 US Dollar (US$) = 100 cents
Language English; eight major indigenous languages are also spoken
Religions Christianity 97% (RC 50%, Prot 47%), others 3%
Ethnic groups Chuukese 49%, Pohnpeian 24%, Kosraean 6%, Yapese 5%, others 16%

Physical description

Islands vary geologically, from low coral atolls to mountainous volcanic islands; Pohnpei, Kosrae and Chuuk have volcanic outcroppings; highest point is Totolom (791m/2595ft).

Climate

Tropical; heavy rainfall all year round, especially in the eastern islands; subject to typhoons.

Government

Governed by an executive President, a Cabinet and a unicameral Congress. Each of the four states has its own government and traditional leadership council. There are no political parties.

Economy

Subsistence economy based on farming and fishing; dependent on US aid; tourism is growing but constrained by remoteness; other activities are construction, fish processing, specialized aquaculture, handicrafts.

History

The islands were probably first settled by eastern Melanesians in 1500 BC. The Spanish colonized them in the 17c and sold them to Germany in 1898. Japan occupied the islands for the Allies in World War I and administered them as a mandated territory from 1920 until ousted in 1944 by US forces. In 1947 the islands became part of the UN Trust Territory of the Pacific Islands, administered by the USA. From 1965 there was a growing campaign for independence, and Micronesia became a self-governing federation in 1979. A compact of free association with the USA came into force in 1986, when Micronesia became independent, with the USA responsible for its security and defence; a renegotiated compact came into force in 2004. Micronesia was admitted to the UN in 1991.

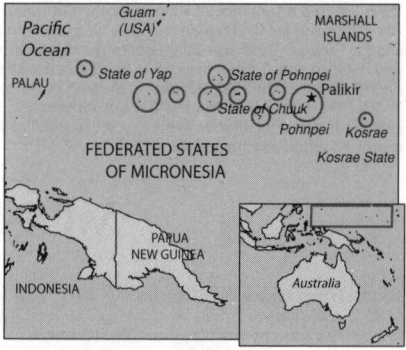

MOLDOVA

Official name Republic of Moldova
Local name Moldova
Location A landlocked republic in eastern Europe, bounded to the west by Romania, and to the north, east and south by the Ukraine
Area 33 843 sq km/13 066 sq mi
Capital Chisinau
Chief towns Tiraspol, Bendery, Beltsy

Population 4 324 000 (2008e)
Time zone GMT +2
Currency 1 Leu (Mld) = 100 bani
Language Moldovan
Religions Christianity 98% (Orthodox), Judaism 2%
Ethnic groups Moldovan/Romanian 78%, Ukrainian 8%, Russian 6%, Gagauz 4%, Bulgarian 2%, others 2%

Physical description

The terrain consists of a hilly plain, reaching a height of 429m/1407ft at Mount Balanesti in the centre; chief rivers are the Dniester and Prut.

Climate

Continental, with cold to moderate winters and warm summers.

Government

Governed by a President, a Prime Minister and Cabinet, and a unicameral Parliament.

Economy

Poorest country in Europe, dependent on remittances from expatriates working abroad (c.30% of workforce); most industry lies in breakaway Transdniestria region; agriculture contributes 18% of GDP, producing grains, tobacco, sugar beet, vegetables, fruit, beef and dairy products; other activities are wine-making, food processing, agricultural machinery, foundry equipment, domestic appliances, hosiery, footwear, garments.

History

An independent principality in the 14–15c, the territory was disputed by several powers, principally Russia and the Ottoman Empire, from the 16c to the early 19c. In 1812 Russia was granted control of Bessarabia (most of present-day Moldova) and the remainder came under Ottoman rule, subsequently becoming part of Romania. Following a nationalist movement, Bessarabia declared its independence from Russia in 1918 and united with Romania, but in 1940 Romania was forced to cede Bessarabia to the USSR, and it was incorporated with another small strip of land as the Moldavian Soviet Socialist Republic. Moldavia achieved independence from the USSR as the Republic of Moldova in 1991 and became a member of the CIS (Commonwealth of Independent States). The ineffectualness of the moderate reformist governments of the

1990s led to a resurgence of support for the Communist Party, which has won all the elections since 1998. Ethnic tensions led the Russian and Ukrainian ethnic minorities in the Dnestr region (east of the River Dnestr) and the Gagauz (Turkic-speaking) minority in the south-west to declare independence in 1990, although this was not recognized. There was fierce fighting in Dnestr in 1991–2, where Russian troops have been stationed since to maintain the 1992 ceasefire while talks continue. Both regions were granted special autonomy status in the 1994 constitution, but this has not satisfied the Dnestr region, which has reasserted its demand for independence; the failure to achieve a settlement has left the region in a state of limbo, prey to corruption, organized crime and smuggling.

MONACO

Official name Principality of Monaco
Local name Monaco
Location A small principality on the Mediterranean Riviera, close to the Italian frontier with France
Area 1.9 sq km/0.75 sq mi
Capital Monaco
Chief town Monte Carlo
Population 32 800 (2008e)

Time zone GMT +1
Currency 1 Euro (€) = 100 cents
Language French; English, Italian and Monégasque are also spoken
Religions Christianity 95% (RC 90%, Prot 5%), others 5%
Ethnic groups French 47%, Monégasque 16%, Italian 16%, others 21%

Physical description

Hilly, rugged and rocky, rising to 63m/206ft; expanded into the sea by infilling; almost entirely urban.

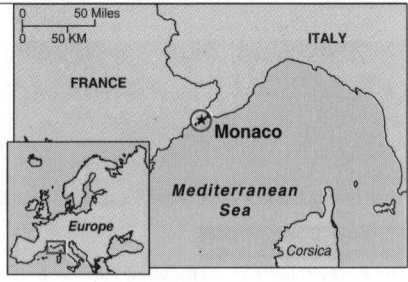

Climate

Warm, dry summers and mild winters.

Government

A hereditary constitutional monarchy; governed by the Prince, a Council of Government and a unicameral National Council; close political ties with France.

Economy

Prosperous economy based on services (tourism, gambling, financial services, real estate) and light industries manufacturing consumer products.

History

In 1297 the Grimaldi family won Monaco from the Genoese, who had held it since 1191, but they did not secure full possession until 1419. Though the Grimaldis were allies of France (except when they were under Spanish protection in 1524–1641), Monaco was formally annexed by France in 1793 during the French Revolutionary regime. It has been under French protection ever since, apart from a period under Sardinia in 1815–61. In 2002 the French franc was replaced by the euro as the official currency.

MONGOLIA

Official name Mongolia
Local name Mongol Uls
Location A landlocked republic in eastern central Asia, bounded to the north by Russia and on other sides by China
Area 1 564 619 sq km/604 099 sq mi
Capital Ulan Bator
Chief towns Darhan, Erdenet

Population 2 996 000 (2008e)
Time zone GMT +8
Currency 1 Tugrik (T) = 100 möngö
Language Khalkha Mongol
Religions Buddhist Lamaism 50%, Shamanism and Christianity 6%, Islam 4%, none 40%
Ethnic groups Mongol 94%, Turkic 5%, Chinese, Russian and others 1%

Physical description

One of the highest countries in the world, with an average height of 1580m/5184ft; the highest point is the Khuiten peak of Altai Tavan Bogd at 4373m/14350ft; terrain ranges from desert in the south (the Gobi Desert covers the southern third of the country) through grassy steppes to the Mongolian Altai and Hangai mountains in the west, and taiga; the largest lakes are found in the north-west; major rivers flow north and north-east.

Climate

Climatic conditions are extreme, with long, severe winters and short, warm summers; the average temperature at Ulan Bator is −27° in January and 11°–22°C in July; rainfall is generally low; arid desert conditions prevail in the south.

Government

Governed by a President, a Prime Minister and Cabinet, and a unicameral State Great Hural.

Economy

Difficult transition from planned to market economy; main activities are mining (copper, gold, tin, coal, uranium, tungsten), cashmere production, agriculture (livestock, wool, hides), processing animal products, manufacturing (construction materials, food, beverages, textiles) and construction.

History

Originally the homeland of nomadic tribes, which united under Genghis Khan in the 13c to become part of the great Mongol Empire, Mongolia was assimilated into China, and divided into Inner and Outer Mongolia. Inner Mongolia remains an autonomous region of China, but Outer Mongolia declared itself an independent monarchy in 1911 when China's imperial regime collapsed. Although Chinese rule was reasserted in 1915, Mongolian revolutionaries, with Soviet support, overthrew the Chinese in 1921 and formed a government. When the king died in 1924, the Mongolian People's Republic was formed and aligned itself with the USSR, following similar policies. With Soviet support it resisted Japanese attacks in the late 1930s, but in a 1946 plebiscite voted for independence from Soviet control. A pro-democracy campaign led to multiparty elections in 1990 and economic liberalization followed. The former communist party has continued to dominate politics since 1990, although it lost power to an alliance of nationalists and social democrats in 1996–2001.

MONTENEGRO

Official name Montenegro
Local name Crna Gora
Location A republic in the Balkan Peninsula, bounded to the north-west by Bosnia and Herzegovina; to the north-east by Serbia; to the east by Kosovo; to the south by Albania; to the west by Croatia; and to the south-west by the Adriatic Sea
Area 13 812 sq km/5333 sq mi
Capital Podgorica (administrative centre); Cetinje (historic and cultural capital)

Chief towns Nikšic, Bar
Population 678 000 (2008e)
Time zone GMT +1
Currency 1 Euro (€) = 100 cents
Language Montenegrin (Ijekavian dialect of Serbian), Serbian and Albanian
Religions Christianity 78% (Orthodox 74%, RC 4%), Islam 17%, others 5%
Ethnic groups Montenegrin 43%, Serb 32%, Bosniak 8%, Albanian 5%, others 12%

Physical description

Densely forested mountains in the interior are cut by river valleys and canyons; the highest point is Bobotov Kuk (2522m/8274ft); fertile lowlands lie alongside lakes and in river valleys; the low-lying, 293km-long Adriatic coastline is highly indented; the main river is the Tara.

Climate

Mediterranean, with hot, dry summers and autumns; there is a colder upland climate inland, with heavy winter snow.

Government

Governed by a President, a Prime Minister and Cabinet, and a unicameral Assembly of Montenegro.

Economy

Economic and fiscal autonomy since 1990s; reform has stimulated some recovery from effects of wars with Croatia and Bosnia and Herzegovina; main activities are tourism, aluminium production, steel-making, processing agricultural products and manufacturing (consumer goods); agriculture produces cereals, tobacco, potatoes, fruit, livestock products; wine-making.

History

The area was part of the Roman province of Illyria, settled by Slavs in the 7c and established as the independent province of Zeta. In the late 12c it was incorporated into the Serbian empire. Montenegrin independence was recognized at the Congress of Berlin in 1878, and it retained its independent monarchy until 1918, when King Nicholas was deposed and Montenegro was absorbed into Serbia. With Serbia and territories of the former Austro-Hungarian empire, it formed the Kingdom of Serbs, Croats and Slovenes (renamed Yugoslavia in 1929), which was united under the Serbian monarch, Peter I. Yugoslavia was occupied by Axis forces in 1941 and re-established in 1945 as the communist Federal People's Republic (comprising Croatia, Slovenia, Bosnia-Herzegovina, Macedonia, Montenegro and Serbia) under President Josip Tito. After Tito's death in 1980, nationalisms resurfaced and the federation eventually disintegrated when Croatia and Slovenia seceded in 1991 and Bosnia-Herzegovina and Macedonia in 1992. Serbia and Montenegro remained as the Federal Republic of Yugoslavia, which was declared on 27 Apr 1992. Montenegrin desire for independence led to a restructuring in 2003 into a looser federation of the two republics, called Serbia and Montenegro. Following a referendum, Montenegro declared its independence in Jun 2006.

MOROCCO

Official name Kingdom of Morocco
Local name Al Maghrib
Location A kingdom in North Africa, bounded to the south-west by Western Sahara, over which Morocco claims sovereignty; to the south-east and east by Algeria; to the north-east by the Mediterranean Sea; and to the west by the Atlantic Ocean
Area 446 550 sq km/172 412 sq mi
Capital Rabat

Chief towns Casablanca, Fez, Marrakesh, Tangier, Meknès, Kenitra, Tétouan, Oujda, Agadir
Population 34 343 000 (2008e)
Time zone GMT
Currency 1 Dirham (DH) = 100 centimes
Language Arabic; Berber and French are also spoken
Religions Islam 99% (mostly Sunni), Christianity and Judaism 1%
Ethnic groups Arab–Berber 99%, others 1%

Physical description

Dominated by a series of mountain ranges, rising in the High Atlas in the south to 4165m/13665ft at Mount Toubkal; the Atlas Mountains descend south-east to the north-west edge of the Sahara Desert; the broad coastal plain is bounded to the west by the Atlantic Ocean.

Climate

Mediterranean climate on the north coast; it is settled and hot in May–September; the average annual rainfall is 400–800mm, decreasing towards the Sahara, which is virtually rainless; Rabat, on the Atlantic coast, has average maximum daily temperatures of 17°–28°C; heavy winter snowfall in the High Atlas; the desert region experiences extreme heat in summer, with chilly winter nights.

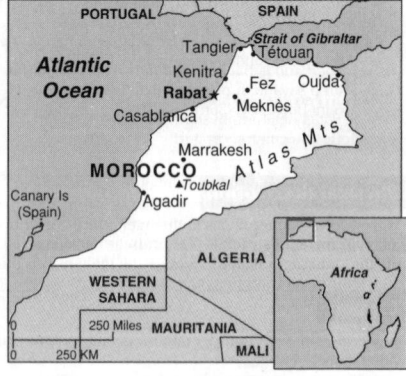

Government

A hereditary constitutional monarchy; governed by the King, a Prime Minister and a Cabinet, and a bicameral Parliament consisting of a House of Representatives and a House of Councillors.

Economy

Poor country; many dependent on remittances from expatriate workers; large public sector; main sector is agriculture, which employs 40% of the workforce and produces cereals, citrus fruits, vegetables, wine, olives, livestock; other activities are mining (especially phosphate) and mineral processing, food processing, fishing, manufacturing (leather goods, garments, transistors, telecommunications equipment), oil refining, chemicals, construction and tourism.

History

From the 12c BC the northern coast was occupied by Phoenicians, Carthaginians and Romans. Arabs invaded in the 7c AD, and Europeans began to establish an interest in the region in the 19c. The Treaty of Fez in 1912 established Spanish Morocco (capital, Tétouan) and French Morocco (capital, Rabat), and the international zone of Tangier was created in 1923; the protectorates gained independence in 1956 as a monarchy under the Alawite Dynasty, still the ruling house, although the coastal towns of Ceuta and Melilla remain Spanish. Since the accession of Muhammad VI in 1999, Morocco has started to move away from absolute monarchy. In 1975 the former Spanish Sahara (Western Sahara) was annexed and partitioned by Morocco and Mauritania; Mauritania withdrew in 1979 and Morocco annexed the rest of the territory. Fighting continued until 1991, when a ceasefire came into effect, but an impasse over a proposed referendum on the territory's future status has prevented progress towards a resolution.

MOZAMBIQUE

Official name Republic of Mozambique
Local name Moçambique
Location A republic in south-eastern Africa, bounded to the south by Swaziland; to the south and south-west by South Africa; to the west by Zimbabwe; to the north-west by Zambia and Malawi; to the north by Tanzania; and to the east by the Mozambique Channel and the Indian Ocean
Area 799 390 sq km / 306 644 sq mi
Capital Maputo

Chief towns Nampula, Beira, Pemba
Population 21 285 000 (2008e)
Time zone GMT +2
Currency 1 Metical (Mt, MZM) = 100 centavos
Language Portuguese; over 16 local languages
Religions Christianity 41% (RC 24%, others 17%), Islam 18%, others 18%, none 23%; some aspects of traditional beliefs are widespread
Ethnic groups African Makua 99%, (includes Tsonga, Lomwe, Sena), others 1%

Physical description

The main rivers are the Zambezi and Limpopo, providing irrigation and hydroelectricity; south of the Zambezi, the coast is low-lying, with sandy beaches and mangroves; low hills of volcanic origin are found inland; the Zimbabwe Plateau lies further north; the coast north of the Zambezi is more rugged and is backed by a narrower coastal plain, with a savannah plateau inland; the highest peak, Mount Binga, is 2436m/7992ft.

Climate

Tropical, with relatively low rainfall in the coastal lowlands; average annual rainfall at Beira, in the central coast zone, is 1520mm, with maximum daily temperatures of 25°–32°C; in the drier areas of the interior lowlands, rainfall decreases to 500–750mm; Mozambique has one rainy season in December–March.

Government

Governed by an executive President, a Prime Minister and Council of Ministers, and a unicameral Assembly of the Republic.

Economy

Very poor, and dependent on international aid; recovery from civil war (1977–92) hindered by natural disasters (2000–3, 2006–8) and high level of HIV/AIDS infection; agriculture and fishing employs 81% of the workforce; chief cash crops are prawns, fish, cotton, cashew nuts, sugar, citrus fruits; growing

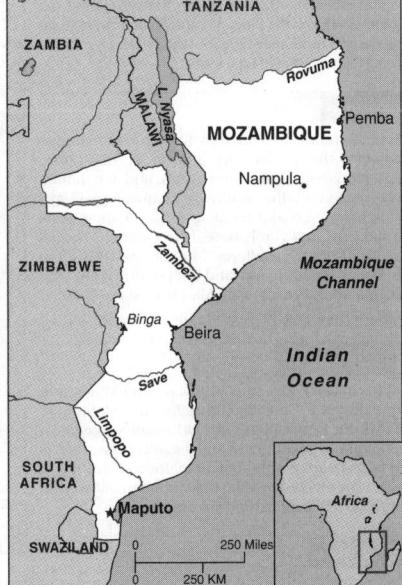

Nations of the World

industrial base, especially minerals (aluminium processing), natural gas, hydro-electric power, forestry, garment manufacturing, food processing.

History

The country was originally inhabited by Bantu peoples from the north in the 1–4c. By the late 15c the coast had been settled by Arab traders and discovered by Portuguese explorers. Administered as part of Portuguese India from 1751, Mozambique acquired separate colonial status as Portuguese East Africa in the late 19c, and became an overseas province of Portugal in 1951. An independence movement, the *Frente de Libertação de Moçambique* (Frelimo), formed in 1962 and began a guerrilla war against the Portuguese in 1964. Independence was gained in 1975 and Mozambique became a socialist one-party state. A brutal civil war erupted between the ruling party Frelimo and the opposition group Renamo until in 1992 a peace agreement was signed and Renamo became a political party. A new constitution under a multiparty system was implemented in 1990, and in 1994 the first multiparty elections were won by Frelimo. Reconstruction was slowed by natural catastrophes in 2000–3; the legacy of landmines and resulting amputees, and a high level of HIV/AIDS infection are also serious problems.

MYANMAR (BURMA)

Official name Union of Myanmar; still often referred to internationally as Burma

Local name Myanmar

Location A republic in South-East Asia, bounded to the north and north-east by China; to the east by Laos and Thailand; to the north-west by India; to the west by Bangladesh; and to the south and west by the Bay of Bengal and the Andaman Sea

Area 678 576 sq km/261 930 sq mi

Capital Nay Pyi Taw (administrative capital)

Chief towns Rangoon, Mandalay, Henzada, Pegu, Myingyan

Population 47 758 000 (2008e)

Time zone GMT +6.5

Currency 1 Kyat (K) = 100 pyas

Language Burmese; several minority languages are also spoken

Religions Buddhism 89%, Christianity 4%, Islam 4%, animist 1%, others 2%

Ethnic groups Burman 68%, Shan 9%, Karen 7%, Rakhine 4%, Chinese 3%, Indian 2%, Mon 2%, others 5%

Physical description

Rimmed in the north, east and west by mountain ranges rising in the north to Hkakabo Razi (5881m/19294ft) and descending in a series of ridges and valleys to central lowlands drained by the Irrawaddy and the Chindwin rivers; the Salween and Sittang rivers drain the eastern mountains; the Irrawaddy's delta extends over 240km/150mi of tidal forest.

Climate

Tropical monsoon climate, with a marked change between the cooler, dry season of the north-east monsoon (November–April) and the hotter, wet season of the south-west monsoon (May–September); coastal areas and higher mountains in the east and north have heavy annual rainfall (2500–5000mm); sheltered interior lowlands often as low as 1000mm; lowland temperatures are high all year round (especially March to May); there is high humidity on the coast.

Government

Under military rule since 1962; a State Peace and Development Council (formerly the State Law and Order Restoration Council) of senior generals appoints the government and the SPDC chairman is de facto head of state. The unicameral Constituent Assembly elected in 1990 has not been allowed to convene. Political parties are banned.

Economy

Very poor; international aid withdrawn owing to military regime's human rights abuses; agriculture employs 70% of the workforce and contributes 42% of GDP; chief cash crops are rice, beans, pulses and fish; other activities include forestry, mining (minerals, gemstones), oil and gas production; manufacturing and services are struggling; tourism is growing; major producer of illegal drugs.

History

The country was first unified in the 11c by King Anawrahta. Kublai Khan invaded in 1287. A second dynasty was established in 1486, but it was plagued by internal disunity and wars with Siam from the 16c. A new dynasty under King Alaunghpaya was founded in 1752. Burma was annexed to British India in 1886 following the Anglo–Burmese Wars of 1824–85. It was separated from India in 1937, becoming a Crown colony, and was occupied by the Japanese in World War II. It gained independence as the Union of Burma in 1948. The government was overthrown in 1962 in a military coup which introduced a single-party socialist state, and the country has remained under military rule since. Following pro-democracy demonstrations in 1987–8, martial law was imposed, the country's name was changed to Myanmar and Aung San Suu Kyi, the leader of the opposition National League for Democracy (NLD) party, was placed under house arrest; she has been under house arrest almost constantly since 1989. The 1990 election, the country's first multiparty election for 30 years, was won by the NLD but the result was ignored by the military rulers and persecution of pro-democracy demonstrators has continued despite international protests. The NLD and other opposition groups boycotted a constitutional convention held in 2004–7; the government claimed 92% of the 99% turnout supported the new constitution put to a referendum only weeks after Cyclone Nargis devastated the Irrawaddy basin in May 2008. There has been fighting since independence with armed insurgent groups, mostly derived from ethnic groups. Since 1992, 15 ethnic groups have signed ceasefire agreements following offensives against them by the government, and the largest, the Kayin (Karen), began talks in 2004 about a ceasefire.

NAMIBIA

Official name Republic of Namibia
Local name Namibia
Location A republic in south-western Africa, bounded to the north by Angola; to the north-east by Zambia; to the east by Botswana; to the south by South Africa; and to the west by the Atlantic Ocean; the narrow Caprivi Strip in the north-east connects Namibia with Zambia and Zimbabwe
Area 823 144 sq km/317 734 sq mi
Capital Windhoek

Chief towns Lüderitz, Keetmanshoop, Grootfontein
Population 2 894 000 (2008e)
Time zone GMT +1
Currency 1 Namibian Dollar (N$) = 100 cents
Language English; Afrikaans, German and local languages are also widely spoken
Religions Christianity 85%, traditional beliefs 15%
Ethnic groups Ovambo 50%, Kavango 9%, Damara 7%, Herero 7%, white 6%, mixed 6%, Nama 5%, others 10%

Physical description

The Namib Desert runs along the Atlantic coast; the inland plateau has a mean elevation of 1500m/4921ft; the highest point is Konigstein peak on Brandberg (2574m/8445ft); the Kalahari Desert lies to the east and south; the Orange River forms the southern frontier with South Africa.

Climate

Arid with low rainfall and cooler temperatures on the coast; higher temperatures and rainfall in the interior; the average annual rainfall at Windhoek, in the interior, is 360mm and the average maximum daily temperature range is 20°–30°C.

Government

Governed by an executive President, a Prime Minister and Cabinet, and a bicameral Parliament consisting of a National Assembly and a National Council.

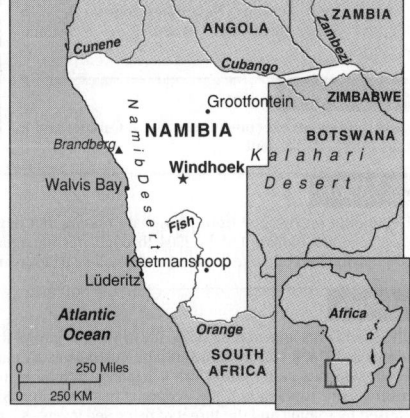

Economy

Main industrial activity is exploitation of rich mineral deposits (over 50% of export earnings), including diamonds, copper, zinc, lead, uranium, tin, silver, tungsten; agricultural sector employs about half the workforce, mostly at subsistence level, but cattle-ranching and fishing produce exports; diversifying into tourism and manufacturing.

History

Pre-colonial Namibia was inhabited by Bantu tribes and San (Bushmen). It became the German protectorate of South West Africa in 1884, and from 1904 the Germans waged near-genocidal wars to crush the Herero and Nama peoples. Occupied by South African troops in 1914, it was mandated to South Africa by the League of

Nations in 1920. After World War II, South Africa continued to administer the area as South West Africa, and refused the UN's demand in 1961 that it terminate the mandate. The South West Africa People's Organization (SWAPO) began a guerrilla war against South Africa in 1966, and the UN challenged South African rule, changing the country's name to Namibia in 1968, and recognizing SWAPO as representative of the Namibian people in 1972. In 1988 South Africa agreed to Namibian independence in exchange for the withdrawal of Cuban troops from Angola, and Namibia gained its independence in 1990. In 1994 the Walvis Bay area, a major port and South African enclave, was returned to Namibia. The country has enjoyed stability since 1990, apart from a brief secessionist campaign in the Caprivi Strip in 1998–9.

NAURU

Official name Republic of Nauru
Local name Naoero (Nauruan), Nauru (English)
Location An independent republic formed by a small, isolated island in the west-central Pacific Ocean, 42km/26mi to the south of the Equator and 4000km/2500mi north-east of Sydney, Australia
Area 21 sq km/8 sq mi
Capital There is no official capital, but government offices are situated in Yaren District

Population 13 700 (2008e)
Time zone GMT +12
Currency 1 Australian Dollar ($A) = 100 cents
Language Nauruan; English is also widely used
Religions Christianity 79% (Prot 46%, RC 33%), Buddhism and others 14%, unspecified 2%, none 5%
Ethnic groups Nauruan 58%, other Pacific Islanders 26%, Chinese and Vietnamese 8%, European 8%

Physical description

The ground rises from sandy beaches to form a fertile coastal belt, c.100–300m/330–980ft wide, the only cultivable soil; a central plateau inland, which reaches 65m/213ft at its highest point, is composed largely of phosphate-bearing rocks.

Climate

Tropical, with average daily temperatures of 24°–34°C, and average humidity between 70 and 80 per cent; annual rainfall averages 1524mm and falls mainly in the monsoon season (November–February), with marked yearly deviations; experiences occasional cyclones.

Government

Governed by an executive President, a Cabinet and a unicameral Parliament.

Economy

Dependent on revenue from phosphate mining, but deposits close to exhaustion; trust funds created with past revenue bankrupted in 2004 through mismanagement; limited subsistence agriculture and fishing; diversifying into offshore banking and small-scale tourism.

History

The island was annexed by Germany in 1888 as part of the Marshall Islands Protectorate. Occupied by Allied troops in 1914, it was administered by Australia as a League of Nations mandate after World War I, and as a UN trust territory after World War II. It gained independence in 1968. Nauru's future is uncertain as phosphate reserves are running out, the economy has been in crisis since 2004, and it faces environmental problems caused by mining and the threat of rising sea levels as a result of global warming.

NEPAL

Official name Federal Democratic Republic of
  Nepal
Local name Nepāl
Location A landlocked independent state lying
  along the southern slopes of the Himalayas in
  central Asia, bounded to the north by the Tibet
  region of China, and to the east, south and west
  by India
Area 145391 sq km/56121 sq mi
Capital Kathmandu

Chief towns Patan, Bhadgaon
Population 29519000 (2008e)
Time zone GMT +5.75
Currency 1 Nepalese Rupee (NRp, NRs) = 100
  paise/pice
Language Nepali; around 70 dialects and
  languages are also spoken
Religions Hinduism 81%, Buddhism 11%, Islam
  4%, others 4%
Ethnic groups Nepali 65%, others and unspecified 35%

Physical description

Rises steeply from the plains of the Ganges
basin; high fertile valleys in the hill country at
c.1300m/4265ft, such as the Vale of Kathmandu,
are enclosed by mountain ranges; the country
is dominated by the glaciated peaks of the
Himalayas, the highest of which is Mount Everest
at 8848m/29035ft.

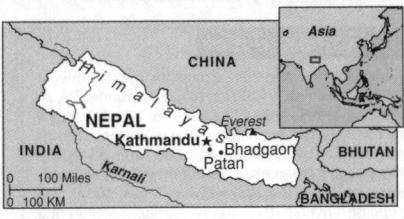

Climate

Varies from subtropical lowland, with hot, humid summers and mild winters, to an alpine climate over
3300m, where peaks are permanently snow-covered; temperatures at Kathmandu vary from 40°C in May to
2°C in December; the monsoon season occurs during summer (June–September); average annual rainfall
decreases from 1778mm in the east to 889mm in the west.

Government

A republic since the abolition of the hereditary monarchy in May 2008; governed by a President, a Prime
Minister and Council of Ministers, and a unicameral Constituent Assembly.

Economy

One of the least developed countries in Asia; dependent on international aid, trade with India and expatriates'
remittances; agriculture employs 76% of the people and generates 38% of GDP; main industry is tourism;
other activities include manufacturing (especially carpets, garments, leather goods), processing agricultural
products (rice, jute, sugar, oilseed).

History

Nepal was ruled from about the 4c to the 10c by the Licchavi Dynasty, then from the 10c to 18c by the
Malla Dynasty, under which Hinduism became the dominant religion. Modern Nepal was formed from a
group of independent hill states which were united in the 18c. In 1769 the Shah Dynasty came to power
following an invasion by Gurkhas, who moved the capital to Kathmandu. War with the British in 1815–16
curtailed Nepal's expansion; its independence was formally recognized by Britain in 1923. The Rana family
held power as hereditary chief ministers from 1846 until 1950–1, when the monarchy was restored to power.
Apart from 1959–60, when a parliamentary system of government was in place, the kings ruled as absolute
monarchs until 1990, when a new constitution introduced a multiparty parliamentary system and a reduction
in the king's powers, following pro-democracy riots. But the factionalized nature of the country's politics
led to frequent changes of government, and the instability was exacerbated by a Maoist insurrection which
began in 1996, spreading from the remote west to the rest of the country. The government attempted to
suppress the insurgents by often brutal methods but with little success. King Gyanendra (who succeeded to
the throne in 2001 after the murder of his brother, King Birendra, by Crown Prince Dipendra, who committed
suicide) assumed direct power in 2005–6 in an attempt to defeat the insurgents but found himself isolated
as the political class allied itself with the insurgents to demand the restoration of democracy. The legislature,
reinstated in Apr 2006, voted to reduce the king's political powers and in Nov the government signed a peace
agreement with the insurgents that ended the insurgency, included insurgents in a transitional government
and allowed the UN to supervise disarmament. The Constituent Assembly elected in Apr 2008 declared the
country a republic at its inaugural meeting.

Nations of the World

THE NETHERLANDS

Official name Kingdom of the Netherlands
Local name Nederlanden
Location A maritime kingdom in north-western Europe, bounded to the west and north by the North Sea; to the east by Germany; and to the south by Belgium
Area 41 526 sq km/16 033 sq mi
Capital Amsterdam; The Hague (Den Haag) is the seat of government,
Chief towns The Hague, Rotterdam, Utrecht, Haarlem, Eindhoven, Arnhem, Groningen

Population 16 645 000 (2008e)
Time zone GMT +1
Currency 1 Euro (€) = 100 cents
Language Dutch, Frisian in Friesland; English is widely spoken
Religions Christianity 50% (RC 30%, Prot 20%), Islam 6%, others 2%, none/unaffiliated 42%
Ethnic groups Dutch 81%, EU 5%, Indonesian 2%, Turks 2%, Surinamese 2%, Moroccans 2%, Antilleans 1%, others 5%

Physical description

Generally low and flat, except in the south-east where hills rise to 321m/1053ft; around 27% of the land area is below sea level, an area inhabited by c.60% of the population, and is protected from submersion by coastal dunes and artificial dykes; the country is largely a delta comprising silt from the mouths of the Rhine, Waal, Maas, IJssel and Schelde rivers; the many canals connecting the rivers total 6340km/3940mi in length; land reclamation from the sea by polder dykes has been carried out for centuries; reclamation of the Zuiderzee (the remnant of which now forms the IJsselmeer) began in 1920.

Climate

Temperate maritime climate; average temperatures are 1.7°C (January) and 17°C (July); annual rainfall, distributed fairly evenly throughout the year, exceeds 700mm.

Government

A hereditary constitutional monarchy with a Queen as head of state; governed by a Prime Minister and Council of Ministers, and a bicameral States-General (*Staten-Generaal*), which consists of a First Chamber and a Second Chamber.

Economy

Highly developed and diversified market economy based on foreign trade through its role as a European trans-shipment hub (Rotterdam and the Europort); main industries are food processing, oil refining and production of electrical machinery and equipment, metal and engineering products, chemicals and microelectronics, and fishing; highly intensive agricultural sector includes animal husbandry, horticulture, potatoes, sugar beet and cereals; the Netherlands is the world's third largest exporter of agricultural produce; Amsterdam is a world diamond centre.

History

The Netherlands was part of the Roman Empire until the 4c AD, and part of the Frankish Empire by the 8c before being incorporated into the Holy Roman Empire. The Netherlands passed to the Dukes of Burgundy in the 15c and then to Philip II, who succeeded to Spain and the Netherlands in 1555. Attempts to stamp out Protestantism led to rebellion in 1572, and the seven northern provinces united against Spain in 1579. These United Provinces of the Netherlands achieved independence, which was finally recognized by Spain in 1648 at the end of the Eighty Years' War, and so founded the modern Dutch state. Between 1795 and 1813 it was overrun by the French, who established the Batavian Republic. Thereafter, it was united with Belgium as the Kingdom of the United Netherlands, until Belgium broke away to form a separate kingdom in 1830. The country was neutral in World War I, but there was strong Dutch resistance to German occupation during World War II. In the late 1940s there were conflicts over the independence of Dutch colonies in South-East Asia, particularly Indonesia. The Netherlands joined with Belgium and Luxembourg to form the Benelux economic union in 1948. It was a founding member of the EEC in 1958, and in 2002 replaced the guilder with the euro.

Overseas territories

❖Aruba

Location An island in the Caribbean Sea, about 30km/19mi north of Venezuela, and 70km/44mi west of Curaçao (The Netherlands)
Area 193 sq km/75 sq mi
Capital Oranjestad

Population 101 500 (2008e)

❖St Maarten

Location The southern third of the island of St Martin in the Leeward group of the Lesser Antilles
Area 34 sq km/13 sq mi
Capital Philipsburg
Population 38 900 (2007e)

❖Curaçao

Location An island in the Caribbean Sea, north of the Venezuelan Coast, and east of Aruba
Area 444 sq km/171 sq mi
Capital Willemstad
Population 137 000 (2007e)

❖Netherlands Antilles

A group of islands in the Caribbean Sea, the federation was dissolved in 2008; Curaçao and St Maarten became autonomous, and Bonaire, St Eustatius and Saba were given city status within the Netherlands

■ New Caledonia ▶ France

NEW ZEALAND

Official name New Zealand
Local name New Zealand (English), Aotearoa (Maori)
Location An independent state comprising a group of islands in the Pacific Ocean to the south-east of Australia
Area 268 812 sq km/103 761 sq mi
Capital Wellington
Chief towns Auckland, Christchurch, Dunedin,
Hamilton
Population 4 173 000 (2008e)
Time zone GMT +12
Currency 1 New Zealand Dollar (NZ$) = 100 cents
Languages English, Maori
Religions Christianity 53% (Prot 32%, RC 12%, other Christian 9%), others 3%, none/unaffiliated 44%
Ethnic groups European 70%, Maori 8%, mixed 8%, Asian 6%, Pacific Islanders 4%, others 4%

Physical description

The two principal islands, North and South, are separated by the Cook Strait; there is also Stewart Island, and several minor islands; North Island is mountainous in the centre, with many hot springs; peaks rise to 2797m/9176ft at Mount Ruapehu and there are several volcanoes; South Island is mountainous for its whole length, rising in the Southern Alps to 3753m/12312ft at Mount Cook (Aoraki); there are many glaciers and mountain lakes; the largest area of level lowland is the Canterbury Plain on the eastern side of South Island.

Climate

Temperate, and highly changeable, with all months moderately wet; it is almost subtropical in the north and on the east coast, with mild winters and warm, humid summers; Auckland daily temperatures are 8°–13°C (July), 16°–23°C (January), average monthly rainfall 145mm (July), 79mm (December–January); the temperatures in South Island are generally lower.

Government

Governed by a Governor-General (representing the British monarch, who is head of state), a Prime Minister and Cabinet, and a unicameral House of Representatives.

Economy

Mixed, trade-orientated economy; highly efficient agricultural sector provides most exports, chiefly dairy products, meat, fish, wool (world's third largest exporter), fruit, wine; other industries are food processing, wood and paper products, textiles, iron and steel, machinery, transport equipment, banking and insurance, tourism and mining; natural gas and hydro-electric power generation.

History

The islands are thought to have been settled by Polynesian explorers about 1000 years ago. The first European sighting was in 1642 by Abel Tasman, who named it Staten Landt; it later became known as Nieuw Zeeland, after the Dutch province. Captain Cook sighted it in 1769, and British settlement began in 1792. The country remained a dependency of New South Wales until 1841. Outbreaks of war in the 1840s and 1860s between immigrants and Maori, known as the Maori Wars, were disastrous for the Maori, much of whose land was taken. The country became the self-governing Dominion of New Zealand in 1907, and its independence was formally acknowledged in 1947. During the 1990s Maori activists demanded compensation for land lost to European settlers, and the government agreed either to pay compensation to certain tribes or to give them areas of land.

NICARAGUA

Official name Republic of Nicaragua
Local name Nicaragua
Location The largest of the Central American republics, bounded to the north by Honduras; to the east by the Caribbean Sea; to the south by Costa Rica; and to the west by the Pacific Ocean
Area 130668 sq km/50451 sq mi
Capital Managua
Chief towns León, Granada, Masaya, Chinandega, Matagalpa, Corinto

Population 5786000 (2008e)
Time zone GMT –6
Currency 1 Gold Córdoba (C$) = 100 centavos = 10 reales
Language Spanish; English and local languages are also spoken
Religions Christianity 82% (RC 58%, Prot 22%, other Christian 2%), others 2%, none 16%
Ethnic groups mestizo 69%, white 17%, black 9%, Amerindian 5%

Physical description

Mountainous western half with volcanic ranges rising to over 2000m/6562ft in the north-west; highest point is the Mogotón peak (2103m/6899ft); two large lakes, Lake Nicaragua and Lake Managua, lie between the central mountains and the coastal mountain range; rolling uplands and forested plains lie to the east; many short rivers flow into the Pacific Ocean and the lakes.

Climate

Tropical, with average annual temperatures ranging from 15°–35°C according to altitude; there is a rainy season from May–November when humidity is high; the average annual rainfall at Managua is 1140mm; subject to devastating hurricanes.

Government

Governed by an executive President, a Cabinet and a unicameral National Assembly.

Economy

Poorest Latin American country; agriculture and fisheries account for largest share of export earnings; main cash crops are coffee, beef, shellfish, tobacco, sugar, peanuts; other activities include food processing, forestry, gold-mining, oil refining, manufacturing (chemicals, machinery, metal products, textiles, garments, beverages, footwear).

History

The Pacific coast was colonized by the Spanish in the early 16c. Nicaragua gained independence from Spain in 1821 and left the Central American Federation in 1838. The plains of eastern Nicaragua, the Mosquito Coast, remained largely undeveloped and were under British protection until 1860. In the late 19c and early 20c the country was ruled by the dictatorial José Santos Zelaya, who was overthrown in 1909 by a coup supported by the USA. The USA continued to exert its influence until the 1930s, when another dictator, Anastasio Somoza (García) came to power in 1938; he ruled until his assassination in 1956. He was succeeded by first one son, Luis Somoza Debayle, and then another, Anastasio Somoza Debayle, the latter ruling from 1967 until the Sandinista National Liberation Front (FSLN) seized power in 1979 and established a socialist junta of national reconstruction. The former supporters of the Somoza government (the Contras), based in Honduras and supported by the USA until 1989, carried on a guerrilla war against the junta from 1979. Ceasefires and disarmament were agreed in 1990 and 1994. The ceasefires were the result of the Sandinistas' unexpected defeat in the 1990 elections by the National Opposition Union. From the late 1990s, governments were liberal or liberal-dominated coalitions, keeping the FSLN from power even though it was often the largest party in the National Assembly. In 2006 the FSLN candidate Daniel Ortega (president 1985–1990) was elected president and the FSLN became the largest parliamentary party.

NIGER

Official name Republic of Niger
Local name Niger
Location A landlocked republic in West Africa, bounded to the north-east by Libya; to the north-west by Algeria; to the west by Mali; to the south-west by Burkina Faso; to the south by Benin and Nigeria; and to the east by Chad
Area 1 267 000 sq km/489 189 sq mi
Capital Niamey
Chief towns Agadès, Diffa, Dosso, Maradi, Tahoua, Zinder
Population 13 273 000 (2008e)
Time zone GMT +1
Currency 1 CFA Franc (CFAFr) = 100 centimes
Language French; Hausa and Djerma are spoken widely
Religions Islam 80%, Christianity, traditional beliefs and others 20%
Ethnic groups Hausa 55%, Djerma Sonrai 21%, Tuareg 9%, Peuhl 9%, Kanouri Manga 5%, other 1%

Physical description

Niger lies on the southern fringe of the Sahara Desert, on a high plateau; the Hamada Manguene Plateau lies in the far north; the Aïr Massif is in the centre; the Ténéré du Tafassasset Desert is in the east; the Western Talk Desert occupies the centre and north; water in quantity is found only in the south-west around the River Niger and in the south-east around Lake Chad; the highest point is Mt Idoukal-n-Taghès (2 022m/6 634ft).

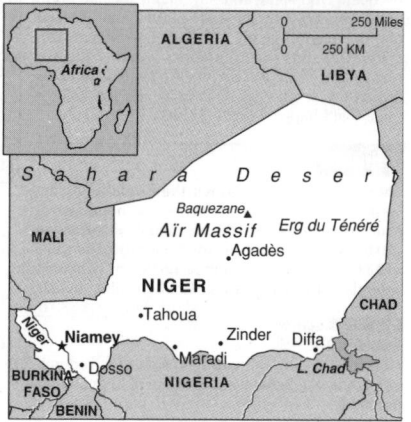

Climate

One of the hottest countries in the world; marked rainy season in the south from June to October; rainfall decreases in the north to almost negligible levels in desert areas; the annual rainfall at Niamey is 554mm; drought can occur.

Government

Governed by a President, a Prime Minister and Council of Ministers, and a unicameral National Assembly.

Economy

Poorest country in the world, dependent on international economic and food aid; agriculture and herding, mostly at subsistence level, engage 90% of the workforce; production affected by recurrent droughts, locusts and desertification; main commercial crops are cotton, livestock and vegetables; the other main activity is mining of uranium ore (30% of export earnings).

History

Inhabited, according to archaeological evidence, during the Palaeolithic period, it was ruled by the Tuaregs from the 11c, the Zerma from the 17c, and the Hausa from the 14c, who ousted the Tuaregs in the 18c, but were themselves ousted by the Fulani. The first European occupiers were the French from 1883. Niger became a territory within French West Africa in 1904, and gained independence in 1960. A military coup in 1974 heralded a military dictatorship until 1989, when civilian government was restored but under a one-party system. Civil unrest in 1990 led to the approval of a multiparty constitution in 1992. The government elected in 1993 was ousted in 1996 by a military coup led by Ibrahim Baré Maïnassara; he was assassinated in 1999, and Daouda Wanke became President. Constitution changes later in 1999 restored democracy and Mamadou Tandja was elected President; he was re-elected in 2004 and his party remained the largest parliamentary party. Locust infestations in 2004 and drought since 2005 caused severe food shortages from 2005 and the UN appealed for food aid several times in 2005–6.

NIGERIA

Official name Federal Republic of Nigeria
Local name Nigeria
Location A republic in West Africa, bounded to the west by Benin; to the north by Niger; to the north-east by Chad; to the east by Cameroon; and to the south by the Gulf of Guinea and the Bight of Benin
Area 923 768 sq km/356 574 sq mi
Capital Abuja

Chief towns Lagos, Ibadan, Ogbomosho, Kano, Oshogbo, Ilorin, Abeokuta, Port Harcourt
Population 146 255 000 (2008e)
Time zone GMT +1
Currency 1 Naira (N, ₦) = 100 kobo
Language English; Hausa, Yoruba, Igbo and Fulani are also spoken
Religions Islam 50% (Sunni), Christianity 40%, traditional beliefs 10%

Physical description

The coastal strip has a long, sandy shoreline with mangrove swamps, dominated by the River Niger delta; an undulating area of tropical rainforest and oil palm bush lie north of the coastal strip; the relatively dry central plateau is characterized by open woodland and savannah; the far north of the country is on the edge of the Sahara Desert and is largely a gently undulating savannah with tall grasses; there are numerous rivers in Nigeria, notably the Niger and Benue; the Gotel Mountains are on the south-eastern frontier and the highest point is at Chappal Waddi (2419m/7936ft).

Climate

There are two rainy seasons in the coastal areas; the wettest part is the Niger delta and the mountainous south-eastern border, with an annual rainfall above 2500mm, decreasing towards the west; Ibadan, in the south-east, has an average daily maximum temperature of 31°C and an average annual rainfall of 1120mm; there is only one rainy season in the north; the dry season extends from October to April, when little rain falls.

Government

Governed by an executive President, a Federal Executive Council and a bicameral National Assembly consisting of a Senate and a House of Representatives. Each of the 36 states has a Governor and a legislative assembly.

Economy

Low-income country; heavily dependent on oil (95% of foreign exchange earnings) and liquified natural gas; reforms introduced to stimulate non-oil sector; agriculture, mostly at subsistence level, engages 70% of the workforce but Nigeria is a net food importer; cash crops include cocoa and rubber; other major activities are mining, processing agricultural products, manufacturing, printing, shipbuilding and repair.

History

There are over 250 tribal groups, notably the Hausa and Fulani in the north, Yoruba in the south, and Igbo in the east. Nigeria was at the centre of the Nok culture in 500 BC–AD 200. Several African kingdoms developed throughout the area in the Middle Ages (eg the Hausa and Yoruba), and Muslim immigrants arrived in the 15–16c. European settlers arrived and participated in the gold and slave trades. A British colony was established at Lagos in 1861, and protectorates of North and South Nigeria were created in 1900. These were amalgamated as the Colony and Protectorate of Nigeria in 1914, which became a federation in 1954 and gained independence in 1960. Nigeria was declared a federal republic in 1963 under President Azikiwe. A military coup took place in 1966, and the Igbo people in the east formed the Republic of Biafra in 1967, resulting in the Biafran War and eventually the surrender of Biafra in 1970. There were further military coups in 1983 and 1985, after which governments were military or military-dominated until 1999. In 1999, civilian rule was reintroduced and the first civilian-run elections in 20 years were held in 2003. Ethnic and religious tensions and violence have

Ethnic groups

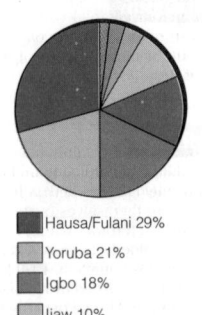

■ Hausa/Fulani 29%
□ Yoruba 21%
■ Igbo 18%
□ Ijaw 10%
■ Kanuri 4%
■ Ibibio 3%
■ Tiv 2%
■ others 13%

increased since 1999; the main division is between the mainly Muslim north and the predominantly Christian south, but there are also groups calling for secession or greater autonomy.

- **Northern Ireland► United Kingdom**

- **Northern Mariana Islands► United States of America**

- **North Korea► Korea, North**

NORWAY

Official name Kingdom of Norway
Local name Norge
Location A kingdom in north-west Europe, bounded to the north by the Arctic Ocean; to the east by Sweden, Finland and Russia; to the west by the North Sea and Norwegian Sea; and to the south by the Skagerrak; includes the dependencies of Svalbard and Jan Mayen Island (Arctic) and Bouvet Island, Peter I Island and Queen Maud Land (Antarctica)
Area 323 895 sq km / 125 023 sq mi
Capital Oslo
Chief towns Bergen, Trondheim, Stavanger, Kristiansand
Population 4 644 000 (2008e)
Time zone GMT +1
Currency 1 Norwegian Krone (NKr) = 100 øre
Language Norwegian, in Bokmål and Nynorsk varieties; Sami and Finnish are spoken by minorities
Religions Christianity 90% (Prot 87% (mainly Lutheran), RC 1%, other Christian 2%), Islam 2%, others and none/unaffiliated 8%
Ethnic groups Norwegian 94%, Sami (Lapp) 1%, others 5%

Physical description

The interior is covered by mountains and elevated barren tablelands (especially in the south-west and centre) separated by deep, narrow valleys; much of the interior rises above 1500m/4921ft; the highest point is Galdhøpiggen (2469m/8100ft); there are numerous lakes, the largest of which is Lake Mjøsa, and some of the highest waterfalls in the world; major rivers include the Glåma, Dramselv and Lågen; the coastline is irregular, with many long, deep fjords, and fringed by small islands; the two largest island groups, off the north-west coast, are the Lofoten and Vesterålen groups; half the country lies inside the Arctic Circle; c.25% is forested.

Climate

An Arctic winter climate in the interior highlands, with snow, strong winds and severe frosts; comparatively mild winter conditions exist on the coast; rainfall is heavy on the west coast; average annual rainfall at Bergen is 1958mm; there are colder winters and warmer, drier summers in the southern lowlands.

Government

A hereditary constitutional monarchy with a King as head of state; governed by a Prime Minister and Council of State, and a unicameral Parliament (*Storting*) which divides into an Upper House (*Lagting*) and a Lower House (*Odelsting*) to debate legislative matters.

Economy

Prosperous market economy based primarily on oil and gas extraction and processing and on fisheries; the other main activities are engineering (shipping, telecommunications and hydro-electric power equipment), shipping freight services, food processing, forestry, pulp and paper products, metals, chemicals, mining, textiles and tourism; less than 3% of the land is under cultivation.

History

A noble family from Sweden settled in southern Norway in the 7c, and the establishment of Norway as a united kingdom was achieved c.900 by Harald the Fair-Haired. Canute brought Norway under Danish rule in 1029 but after his death the throne reverted to Magnus I. When the royal house died out in the 14c, the Danish monarch was the nearest heir and in 1397 Norway, Sweden and Denmark were united under a single monarch. Sweden seceded in 1523 but Norway remained Danish until 1814, when it was ceded to Sweden; it continued to have its own legislature although the government was appointed by the Swedish monarch. Growing nationalism resulted in the dissolution of the union and independence in 1905. Norway declared neutrality in both world wars, but was occupied by Germany in 1940–4. The Labour Party has dominated post-war political life, governing on its own or in coalitions for most of the period since 1945. Norway joined NATO in 1949 but has rejected membership of the EC/EU in referendums in 1972 and 1994.

OMAN

Official name Sultanate of Oman
Local name 'Umān
Location An independent state in the extreme south-eastern corner of the Arabian Peninsula. It is bounded to the north-west by the United Arab Emirates; to the west by Saudi Arabia; to the south-west by Yemen; to the north-east by the Gulf of Oman; and to the south-east and east by the Arabian Sea
Area 300 000 sq km/115 800 sq mi

Capital Muscat
Chief towns Matrah, Nazwa, Salalah
Population 3 312 000 (2008e)
Time zone GMT +4
Currency 1 Omani Rial (RO) = 1000 baisas
Language Arabic
Religions Islam 86% (Ibadhi 75%), Hinduism 13%, others 1%
Ethnic groups Arab 74%, Pakistani 22%, others 4%

Physical description

The tip of the Musandam peninsula in the Strait of Hormuz is separated from the rest of the country by an 80km/50mi strip belonging to the United Arab Emirates; over 80% of the country is desert, with mountains in the north and south-west; the highest point is Jebel Shams (3075m/10 088ft); the alluvial plain of the Batinah lies east and north of the Hajar mountains, along the Gulf coast.

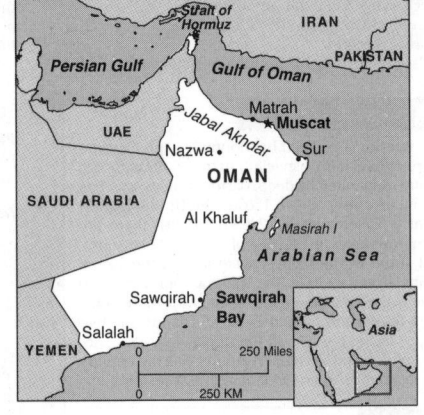

Climate

A desert climate with much regional variation; hot and humid coast from April to October with a maximum temperature of 47°C; hot and dry interior during this summer period; relatively temperate in mountains; light monsoon rains in the south from June to September.

Government

A hereditary absolute monarchy; ruled by the Sultan, who legislates by decree, implemented by a Council of Ministers. An elected Consultative Council and appointed Council of State have advisory roles. There are no political parties. Women have participated in politics since 1997.

Economy

Prosperity based on oil and gas; other activities include oil refining, construction, agriculture (dates, limes, bananas, alfalfa, vegetables), fishing, cement, copper, steel, chemicals and optic fibre; developing liquified natural gas production and trans-shipment ports, metal manufacturing, petrochemicals, information and communication technology, fisheries, manufacturing and tourism.

History

Oman was a dominant maritime power of the western Indian Ocean in the 16c. A sultanate ruled by the present dynasty was established in 1749, and came under British influence in the 19c. It suffered internal dissension in 1913–20 between supporters of the Sultanate and members of the Ibadhi sect who wanted to be ruled exclusively by their religious leader. This flared up again in the 1950s but by 1959 the sultan had established control over the whole country. An insurrection in the south from the mid 1960s was defeated with external military assistance in 1975. In 1970 Sultan Qaboos bin Said overthrew his father in a bloodless coup and initiated a modernization programme.

PAKISTAN

Official name Islamic Republic of Pakistan
Local name Pākistān
Location An Asian state, bounded to the east by India; to the west by Afghanistan and Iran; and to the north by China; the disputed area of Jammu and Kashmir lies to the north-east.
Area 803 943 sq km / 310 322 sq mi
Capital Islamabad

Chief towns Karachi, Lahore, Faisalabad, Rawalpindi
Population 172 800 000 (2008e)
Time zone GMT +5
Currency 1 Pakistan Rupee (PRs, Rp) = 100 paisa
Language Urdu, English; Punjabi and several local languages are also spoken

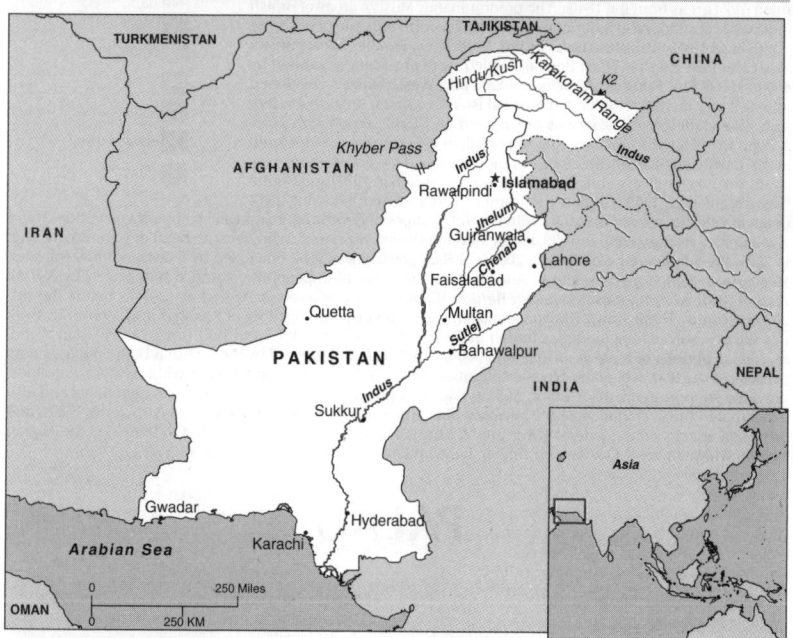

Physical description

Mostly lying on the alluvial flood plain of the River Indus; bounded to the north and west by mountains rising to 8611m/28 254ft at K2; largely flat plateau, low-lying plains, and arid desert to the south of the Karakoram range.

Climate

Dominated by the Asiatic monsoon; in the mountains and foothills of the north and west, the climate is cool with summer rain and winter snow; in the upland plateaux, summers are hot and winters are cool, with the possibility of some winter rain; in summer the Indus Valley is extremely hot and is fanned by dry winds, often carrying sand; throughout the country, the hottest season lasts from March to June, with the highest temperatures occurring in the south; the rainy season lasts from late June to early October and coincides with the south-western monsoon.

Government

Governed by a President, a Prime Minister and Cabinet, and a bicameral Parliament consisting of a National Assembly and a Senate. Four of the six provinces have a Governor, executive and legislative assembly; the Federal Capital Territory and the Tribal Areas are administered by the federal government.

Religions

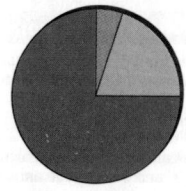

■ Sunni Islam 75%
■ Shia Islam 20%
■ Christianity, Hinduism and others 5%

Economy

Poor country, developing with international assistance; agriculture employs 42% of the workforce, producing cotton, wheat, rice, sugar and livestock products; cotton supports the major industries of cotton processing (spinning, weaving) and textile manufacturing (cotton yarn and fabrics, garments, bedlinen); other activities are food processing, pharmaceuticals, construction materials, paper products, fertilizer, leather goods, rugs.

History

Pakistan's walled cities at Mohenjo-Daro, Harappa and Kalibangan are evidence of civilization in the Indus Valley over 4000 years ago. Muslims ruled the region under the Mughal Empire from 1526 to 1761, and the British ruled most areas from the 1840s. The predominantly Muslim areas of British India were partitioned at independence in 1947 to form the state of Pakistan, consisting of West Pakistan (Baluchistan, North-West Frontier, West Punjab, Sind) and East Pakistan (East Bengal), which were physically separated by 1000mi/1600km. Differences between East and West Pakistan developed into civil war in 1971, resulting in East Pakistan becoming an independent state (Bangladesh). Pakistan was proclaimed an Islamic republic in 1956. A coup in 1958 led to military rule until civilian government was restored in 1971 with Zulfikar Ali Bhutto as Prime Minister. This government was overthrown in a military coup led by General Zia ul-Haq in 1977, and Bhutto was executed in 1979. Civilian government was restored following Zia's death in 1988 but proved unstable, with several changes of government amid allegations of corruption. There was another military coup in 1999, led by General Pervez Musharraf, who became head of government and, in 2001, President; after elections in 2002 a civilian government took office, led by a civilian prime minister. Musharraf resigned as President in Aug 2008, under threat of impeachment, and was replaced by Asif Ali Zardari, widower of opposition leader Benazir Bhutto, who was assassinated a few months before the Feb 2008 elections. There was a Pakistan–India war over the disputed territory of Kashmir and Jammu in 1948; this still unresolved issue underlay further India–Pakistan conflict in 1965 and 1971 (the Indo–Pakistan Wars), as well as periods of tension in 1999 and 2000–2 that were heightened by the fact that both countries now possessed nuclear weapons. Since September 2001, Pakistan has aligned itself with Western countries, provided support to the allies in the Afghan War. This policy angered the government's opponents and also exacerbated the sectarian violence between Shia and Sunni extremists, which had begun in the 1980s, and provoked attacks on the federal government, Christians and Westerners. It also led to unrest on the Afghan border, where many al-Qaeda- and Taliban-linked militants have established bases.

Ethnic Groups

- Punjabi 45%
- Pashtun 15%
- Sindhi 14%
- Sariaki 8%
- Muhajir 7%
- Balochi 4%
- Other 7%

PALAU

Official name Republic of Palau	Languages Palauan; in certain islands, Sonsoralese, Tobi, Angaur, English and Japanese are also official languages
Local name Belau	
Location A group of c.350 small islands and islets in the west Pacific Ocean, 960km/600mi east of the Philippines	Religions Christianity 65% (RC 42%, Prot 23%), traditional beliefs (Modekngei) 9%, others 10%, none/unaffiliated 16%
Area 494 sq km/191 sq mi	
Capital Melekeok; government institutions began moving from Koror to the new capital in 2006	Ethnic groups Palauan (Micronesian with Malaysian and Melanesian admixtures) 70%, Filipino 15%, Chinese 5%, other Asian 2%, white 2%, others 6%
Population 21 000 (2008e)	
Time zone GMT +9	
Currency 1 US Dollar ($, US$) = 100 cents	

Physical description

Varies from the high, mountainous main island of Babelthuap to low-lying coral islands, often surrounded by coral reefs; highest point is Mount Ngerchelchuus (242m/794ft).

Climate

Tropical; hot all year, with high humidity; the wet season is in May–November; the average annual temperature is 27°C and the average annual rainfall is 3810mm; typhoons are common.

Government

Governed by an executive President, a Cabinet and a bicameral National Congress consisting of a House of Delegates and a Senate.

Economy

Dependent on US aid; main activities are tourism, subsistence agriculture (coconuts, copra, cassava, sweet potatoes), fishing.

History

The islands were nominally Spanish until 1899, when control passed to Germany. Japan occupied the islands on behalf of the Allies in 1914 and administered them as a League of Nations mandate from 1920 until ousted by US forces in 1944. In 1947 the islands became part of a UN trust territory administered by the USA. They became a self-governing republic in 1981, and achieved independence in 1994 under a compact of free association with the USA, by which the USA retained responsibility for Palau's defence.

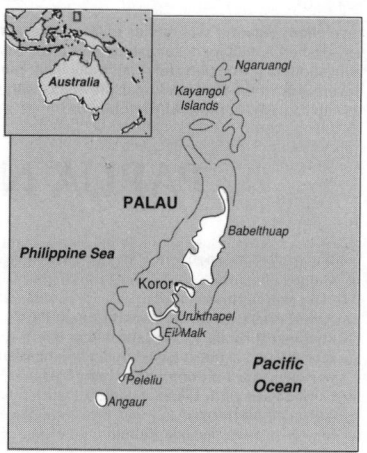

PANAMA

Official name Republic of Panama
Local name Panamá
Location A republic occupying the south-eastern end of the isthmus of Central America, bounded to the north by the Caribbean Sea; to the south by the Pacific Ocean; to the west by Costa Rica; and to the east by Colombia
Area 77 381 sq km/29 762 sq mi
Capital Panama City
Chief towns David, Colón, Santiago

Population 3 310 000 (2008e)
Time zone GMT –5
Currency 1 Balboa (B, Ba) = 100 centésimos; the US dollar is also in use
Language Spanish
Religions Christianity 100% (RC 85%, Prot 15%)
Ethnic groups mestizo (Amerindian and white) 70%, Amerindian and mixed (West Indian) 14%, white 10%, Amerindian 6%

Physical description

Mostly mountainous, with coastal plains either side of the central range; the Serranía de Tabasará in the west rises to over 2000m/6562ft; the highest point is Barú volcano in Chiriqui (3475m/11 400ft); the Azuero peninsula lies to the south; lake-studded lowland cuts across the isthmus; dense tropical forests lie on the Caribbean coast.

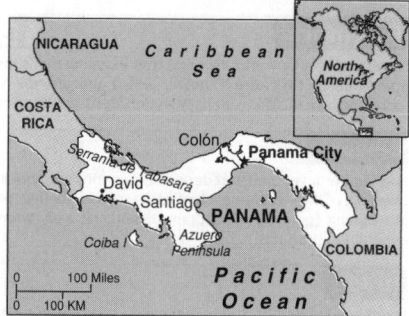

Climate

Tropical, with a mean annual temperature of 32°C; the rainy season is May–December; average annual rainfall at Colón, on the Caribbean coast, is 3280mm, while in Panama City it is 1780mm.

Government

Governed by an executive President, a Cabinet and a unicameral Legislative Assembly.

Economy

Based on a large services sector (77% of GDP) centred around operation of the Panama Canal, the Colón free trade zone, financial services and ship registration; expansion of canal approved in 2006; other activities are construction, brewing, manufacturing (construction materials, textiles), sugar refining, agriculture (bananas, rice, coffee, sugar cane), which employs 15% of the workforce, and fishing.

History

The area was visited by Columbus in 1502 and quickly gained strategic importance as a centre of Spanish trade movement, a vital link between the Caribbean and Pacific. It remained under Spanish colonial rule until 1821, when it gained its independence and joined the union known as Gran Colombia. After this split up in 1830, Panama became part of Colombia until 1903, when it achieved its independence after a US-inspired revolution. Panama was under military rule almost constantly from 1968, when General Omar Torrijos established a military dictatorship, until 1989, when General Manuel Noriega was ousted by US forces after allegations of corruption and drugs trafficking; Panama abolished its standing army in 1991. Panama assumed sovereignty of the Panama Canal, previously administered by the USA, in 1999, and in 2006 a plan to double its capacity was approved by referendum.

PAPUA NEW GUINEA

Official name Independent State of Papua New Guinea
Local name Papuaniugini
Location An independent island group in the south-west Pacific Ocean; the part of the territory occupying the eastern half of the island of New Guinea is bordered by Indonesia
Area 462 840 sq km/178 656 sq mi
Capital Port Moresby
Chief towns Lae, Madang, Rabaul

Population 5 932 000 (2008e)
Time zone GMT +10
Currency 1 Kina (K) = 100 toea
Language Pidgin English; English, Motu and over 800 other languages are spoken
Religions Christianity 96% (Prot and others 69%, RC 27%), traditional beliefs and other 4%
Ethnic groups Papuan 85%, Melanesian 1%, others 14%

Physical description

On the island of New Guinea, mountains densely covered with tropical rainforest run across the centre, with snow-covered peaks rising above 4000m/13 123ft; the highest point is Mount Wilhelm (4509m/14 793ft); large rivers flow to the south, north and east; vast mangrove swamps lie along the coast; the archipelago islands are mountainous, mostly volcanic, and fringed with coral reefs.

Climate

Tropical monsoon climate, with temperatures and humidity constantly high; the average temperature range is 22°–33°C; high rainfall, which averages 2000–3000mm but can be 5000mm in the mountains.

Government

Governed by a Governor-General (representing the British monarch, who is head of state), a Prime Minister and National Executive Council, and a unicameral National Parliament. Bougainville has had internal autonomy since 2005, with its own president, government and legislative assembly.

Economy

Poor, underdeveloped and dependent on international aid; agriculture, mainly at subsistence level, employs over 80% of the workforce; chief cash crops are coffee, palm oil, copra, cocoa and vanilla; the main industries are mining (gold, silver, copper, nickel), oil and natural gas production, forestry, fishing and processing agricultural products.

History

Possibly inhabited by South-East Asians who came to Papua New Guinea via Indonesia many thousands of years ago, it was visited by the Portuguese and the Spanish in the 16c before being colonized by the British and Dutch in the late 18c. In 1884 Britain proclaimed a protectorate in the south-east, while Germany proclaimed the north-east quadrant to be a German protectorate. German New Guinea was established in the north-east in 1899. The German colony was occupied by Australia in World War I, and Australia administered the British and German areas as mandated territories from 1920 until independence, except during the Japanese occupation of 1942–5. The territories were combined in 1949 as the UN Trust Territory of Papua and New Guinea. In 1963 the UN transferred the western part of New Guinea to Indonesia. The remaining territory was renamed Papua New Guinea in 1971 and gained its independence in 1975. The island of Bougainville attempted to secede at independence, and the separatist campaign became an armed conflict in 1989, with fighting continuing until a ceasefire in 1998. A peace agreement signed in 2001 provided autonomy for the island and guaranteed a referendum on the island's status in 10 to 15 years; the first autonomous government was elected in 2005. Papua New Guinea suffers from rampant crime, and in 2004 an Australian study judged it to be on the brink of social and economic collapse.

PARAGUAY

Official name Republic of Paraguay
Local name Paraguay
Location A landlocked country in central South America, bounded to the north-west by Bolivia; to the north and east by Brazil; and to the south-west by Argentina
Area 406 750 sq km / 157 000 sq mi
Capital Asunción
Chief towns Villarrica, Concepción

Population 6 831 000 (2008e)
Time zone GMT –4
Currency 1 Guaraní (Gs) = 100 céntimos
Language Spanish, Guaraní
Religions Christianity 97% (RC 90%, Prot 6% (mostly Mennonite), other Christian 1%), others 2%, none 1%
Ethnic groups mestizo 95%, others 5%

Physical description

Divided into two regions by the River Paraguay, lying mostly at altitudes below 450m/1476ft; bordered to the south and east by the River Paraná; the Gran Chaco in the west is mostly grassy plains or scrub forest; more fertile land lies in the east; the Paraná Plateau is mainly wet, treeless savannah; the highest point is Cerro Pero (842m/2762ft).

Climate

Tropical in the north-west, with hot summers, warm winters, and rainfall up to 1250mm; lower temperatures in the south-east, with rainfall up to 1750mm; the temperature at Asunción ranges from 12°C in winter to 35°C in summer.

Government

Governed by an executive President, a Council of Ministers and a bicameral Congress consisting of a Chamber of Deputies and a Senate.

Economy

Poor country; agriculture, mostly at subsistence level, employs 31% of the workforce; chief cash crops are soya beans, cassava, cotton, sugar, cereals, vegetables, fruit and meat; other activities include hydro-electric power generation, forestry, processing agricultural and forestry products and manufacturing (basic consumer goods, textiles, chemicals).

History

Originally inhabited by Guaranís, the area was settled by the Spanish after 1537, and by Jesuit missionaries who arrived in 1609. It gained independence from Spain in 1811. During the disastrous War of the Triple Alliance (1864–70) against Brazil, Argentina and Uruguay, Paraguay lost over half of its population. In 1935 it regained territory disputed with Bolivia after the three-year Chaco War. Civil war broke out in 1947, and in 1954 General Alfredo Stroessner seized power and became President. His autocratic and increasingly repressive regime was ousted in a coup in 1989. The first multiparty elections were held in 1993, but political instability has persisted since the 1990s, with assassinations, a coup attempt, widespread corruption and organized crime.

PERU

Official name Republic of Peru
Local name Perú
Location A republic on the west coast of South America, bounded to the north by Ecuador; to the north-east by Colombia; to the east by Brazil and Bolivia; to the south by Chile; and to the west by the Pacific Ocean
Area 1 284 640 sq km / 495 871 sq mi
Capital Lima
Chief towns Arequipa, Chiclayo, Cuzco, Trujillo

Population 29 181 000 (2008e)
Time zone GMT –5
Currency 1 Nuevo Sol (Pes) = 100 cénts
Languages Spanish, Quechua; Aymara is also widely spoken
Religions Christianity 83% (RC 81%, other Christian 2%), others 1%, none/unaffiliated 16%
Ethnic groups Amerindian 45% (principally Quechua), mestizo 37%, white 15%, black, Japanese, Chinese and others 3%

Physical description

Arid plains and foothills on the coast, with areas of desert and fertile river valleys; the central sierra, with an average altitude of 3000m/9842ft, contains 50% of the population; the highest point is Huascarán (6768m/22204ft); rivers cut through the plateau, forming deep canyons; the forested Andes and the Amazon basin lie to the east; the major rivers flow to the Amazon.

Climate

Mild temperatures all year on the coast; dry, arid desert in the south; in the north, the coastal region has bursts of torrential rain every 10 years or so with rising sea temperatures and the cold current retreats south; this phenomenon is known as El Niño. Andean temperatures never rise above 23°C, with a large daily temperature range and night frost in the dry season; in the Peruvian portion of the Amazon basin to the east, the climate is typically wet and tropical.

Government

Governed by an executive President, a Council of Ministers and a unicameral Congress of the Republic.

Economy

Poor but developing market economy; the main industries are mining (copper, gold, zinc, silver), oil and natural gas extraction and oil refining; other activities include steel and metal fabrication, fishing and fish processing, manufacturing (textiles, garments), food processing, tourism; agricultural products include coffee, cotton, sugar, rice).

History

Peru had a highly developed Inca civilization by the 15c, but this empire fell to the Spanish in 1531–3, and the Viceroyalty of Peru was established. Its gold and silver mines made Peru the principal source of wealth in Spain's American empire. After declaring its independence in 1821, Peru entered into several border disputes during the 19c (eg the War of the Pacific in 1879–83); disputes with Ecuador and Chile were only resolved in 1998 and 1999. Following independence, military dictatorships alternated with periods of democratic rule until 1980, since when democratic civilian rule has prevailed. Terrorist activities, principally by the Maoist *Sendero Luminoso* (Shining Path) guerrilla movement, and drug-related violence destabilized the government and the economy in the 1980s and 1990s; the violence and the retaliation by the authorities led to over 60000 deaths and widespread human rights abuses. The legacy of criminal violence and lawlessness, much of it related to drug-trafficking, remains. In 2007 President Garcia was granted emergency powers to rule by decree on issues related to organized crime and drug-trafficking.

PHILIPPINES

Official name Republic of the Philippines
Local name Pilipinas
Location A republic consisting of an archipelago of more than 7100 islands and islets, situated to the north-east of Borneo (Indonesia) and to the south of Taiwan
Area 299679 sq km/115676 sq mi
Capital Manila
Chief towns Quezon City, Basilan, Cebu, Bacolod, Davao, Iloilo
Population 91062000 (2008e)
Time zone GMT +8
Currency 1 Philippine Peso (PHP) = 100 centavos
Language Filipino (based on Tagalog), English; eight major dialects and many local dialects are also spoken
Religions Christianity 93% (RC 81%, Prot 12%), Islam 5%, others 2%

Physical description

Largely mountainous, with north to south ridges rising to over 2500m/8200ft; the highest point is Mount Apo (2954m/9691ft); there are narrow coastal plains and broad interior plateaux; forests cover half the land area; some islands are ringed by coral reefs.

Climate

Tropical; warm and humid throughout the year, with an average temperature of 27°C; average rainfall at Manila is 2080mm; lying astride the typhoon belt, the Philippines are affected by c.15 cyclonic storms annually.

Government

Governed by an executive President, a Cabinet and a bicameral Congress, comprising a Senate and a House of Representatives. The Mindanao region has autonomy, with its own governor and legislative assembly.

Economy

Poor but developing; remittances of c.9 million expatriate workers vital to economy; main industries are electronics assembly, garments, footwear, pharmaceuticals, chemicals, wood products, oil refining, mining (copper), fishing; growing services sector (tourism, information technology and other call centre operations, finance); agriculture and fisheries employ 35% of the workforce.

History

The Philippines was claimed for Spain by Magellan in 1521 but ceded to the USA after the Spanish–American War of 1898. It became self-governing in 1935, was occupied by the Japanese during World War II, and achieved independence in 1946. During the period 1945–53 the communist-dominated Huk rebellion was suppressed. Ferdinand Marcos seized power in 1965 and imposed martial law in 1972–81. His regime became increasingly repressive and corrupt, and was believed responsible for the assassination of the exiled political leader Benigno Aquino on his return to Manila in 1983. Marcos was ousted by mass protests after he falsified results to deny Corazon Aquino's victory in the 1986 presidential election. President Aquino survived political unrest and several attempted coups to introduce a new constitution and entrench democracy. Her successor, Fidel Ramos, instigated peace talks with the communist and Muslim rebels responsible for long-running insurgencies. The Moro National Liberation Front, Muslim separatists in the southern islands, ended its activities after a 1996 agreement created an autonomous Muslim region in Mindanao and three other islands. This agreement was not accepted by the Moro Islamic Liberation Front, which has been in talks with the government since 2003, although the ceasefire was breached in 2005. Clashes with communist insurgents have continued despite peace talks in 2004. After September 2001, Abu Sayyaf, an Islamic group suspected of links with al-Qaeda, emerged on the island of Jolo.

■ **Pitcairn Islands ▶ United Kingdom**

Ethnic groups

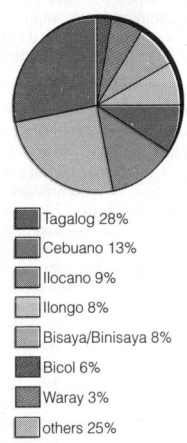

- Tagalog 28%
- Cebuano 13%
- Ilocano 9%
- Ilongo 8%
- Bisaya/Binisaya 8%
- Bicol 6%
- Waray 3%
- others 25%

POLAND

Official name Republic of Poland
Local name Polska
Location A republic in central Europe, bounded to the north by the Kaliningrad region of Russia and the Baltic Sea; to the west by Germany; to the south-west by the Czech Republic; to the south by Slovakia; to the south-east by the Ukraine; and to the north-east by Belarus and Lithuania
Area 312 612 sq km / 120 668 sq mi
Capital Warsaw

Chief towns Łódz, Kraków, Wrocław, Poznań, Gdańsk, Katowice, Lublin
Population 38 501 000 (2008e)
Time zone GMT +1
Currency 1 Złoty (Zl) = 100 groszy
Language Polish
Religions Christianity 92% (RC 90%, Orthodox and Prot 2%), none/unaffiliated 8%
Ethnic groups Polish 97%, German, Belarusian, Ukrainian and others 3%

Nations of the World

Physical description

Mostly part of the great European plain, lying at less than 200m above sea level; the Carpathian and Sudetes Mountains in the south rise in the High Tatra to 2499m/8199ft at Mount Rysy; the Polish plateau to the north of the Tatra is cut by the Bug, San and Vistula rivers; Europe's richest coal basin lies in the west (Silesia); north of the plateau there are lowlands with many lakes; the Baltic coastal area is flat, with sandy heathland and numerous lagoons (coastline length is 491km/305mi); the main rivers are the Vistula and Oder; rivers are often frozen in winter and liable to flood; forests cover one-fifth of the land.

Climate

Continental climate, with severe winters and hot summers; rain falls chiefly in summer and seldom exceeds 650mm annually.

Government

Governed by a President, a Prime Minister and Council of Ministers, and a bicameral National Assembly, comprising a Diet (*Sejm*) and a Senate.

Economy

Transformed from planned to market economy in 1990s; the main industries are machine building, iron and steel, mining (coal, sulphur, copper, silver, lead), chemicals, shipbuilding, food processing, glass, beverages and textiles; modernized but inefficient agricultural sector employs 16% of workforce, producing vegetables, fruit, cereals, meat and dairy products.

History

Poland was inhabited from 2000 BC or earlier and became an independent kingdom in the 9c. Under the Piast Dynasty the Poles emerged as the most powerful of a number of Slavic groups in 1025. Towards the end of Jagiełłon rule Poland formed a union with Lithuania (1569), at which point it stretched from the Baltic to the Black Sea. This Commonwealth was weakened by attacks from Russia, Brandenburg, Turkey and Sweden, and eventually in 1772, 1793 and 1795 Poland was partitioned between Prussia, Russia and Austria, and was deprived of its independent statehood; Russia gained the lion's share of its territories. Following the 1815 Congress of Vienna, Poland became a semi-independent state called the Congress Kingdom of Poland, and was incorporated into the Russian Empire under Alexander I. The Poles constantly struggled for national liberation, and there were uprisings in 1830, 1846–9 and 1863, which led to the kingdom being fully absorbed and subjected to a repressive campaign of Russification. However, the struggle was eventually won at the end of World War I in 1918 when an independent Polish state emerged. Germany invaded Poland in 1939, precipitating World War II, and Poland was partitioned between Germany and the USSR in the same year. The country was liberated by Soviet forces in 1944, when a People's Democracy was established under Soviet influence, and by 1947 communists controlled the government. In 1980 a mass movement for civil and national rights coalesced around the independent trade union Solidarity. Its leaders were detained in 1981–3, and a state of martial law was imposed. The economic situation worsened, and there was continuing unrest in the 1980s, resulting in talks between the government, Solidarity and the Roman Catholic Church in 1989. In multiparty elections later that year, the communist government lost power and Solidarity helped to form a coalition government, its leader, Lech Wałesa, becoming President in 1990. The transition to a market economy in the 1990s was accompanied by popular discontent, political difficulties and recession, but nevertheless a private sector developed within the economy and democratic government is entrenched. Poland joined NATO in 1999 and the EU in 2004.

■ **Polynesia, French▶France**

PORTUGAL

Official name Portuguese Republic
Local name Portugal
Location A country in south-western Europe on the western side of the Iberian Peninsula, bounded to the north and east by Spain; and to the south and west by the Atlantic Ocean
Area 91 982 sq km/35 142 sq mi
Capital Lisbon

Chief towns Oporto, Setúbal, Coimbra
Population 10 677 000 (2008e)
Time zone GMT
Currency 1 Euro (€) = 100 cents
Language Portuguese
Religions Christianity 87% (RC 85%, other Christian 2%), others/unaffiliated 9%, none 4%
Ethnic groups Portuguese 95%, others 5%

Physical description

There are several mountain ranges formed by the west spurs of the Spanish mountain system; the chief range is the Serra da Estrêla in the north, rising to 1991m/6532ft; the highest point in Portuguese territory is Mount Pico on Ilha do Pico (Pico Island) in the Azores (2351m/7713ft); the coast and the areas south of the Tagus are lower-lying; the four main rivers (the Douro, Minho, Tagus and Guadiana) are the lower courses of rivers beginning in Spain; large forests of pine, oak, cork-oak, eucalyptus and chestnut cover about 20% of the country.

Climate

Temperate maritime, with increased variation between summer and winter temperatures inland; the west coast is relatively cool in summer; there is most rainfall in winter.

Government

Governed by a President, a Prime Minister and Council of Ministers, and a unicameral Assembly of the Republic.

Economy

Diversified and increasingly service-based economy; main activities are tourism, manufacturing (vehicle components, textiles, footwear, pulp and paper, cork, ceramics, chemicals, food processing), metals and metalworking, oil refining, wine-making, shipbuilding, forestry, fishing and agriculture; hydro-electric power and other sustainable energy sources increasingly exploited.

History

Portugal became a kingdom under Alphonso I in 1139. The Portuguese Empire began in the 15c, a time of world exploration by the Portuguese. Portugal came under Spanish domination from 1580 to 1640, and was invaded by the French in 1807. The monarchy was overthrown and the First Republic established in 1910. A military coup took place in 1926, and in the early 1930s the country came under the Estado Novo regime of Dr Antonio Salazar, whose dictatorship lasted over 35 years (1932–68). His successor was overthrown in 1974 in a military coup that caused great turmoil until with elections in 1976 the situation began to stabilize. Civilian government was formally restored in 1982. Portugal joined the EC in 1986, and replaced the escudo with the euro in 2002.

❖Azores

Location An archipelago of nine islands of volcanic origin in the North Atlantic Ocean, lying 1400–1800km/870–1100mi to the west of the Cabo da Roca on mainland Portugal
Area 2300 sq km/900 sq mi
Chief town Ponta Delgada, on São Miguel
Population 240 000 (2003e)

❖Madeira

Location An archipelago of six islands off the coast of North Africa, 990km/615mi south-west of Lisbon
Area 796 sq km/307 sq mi
Capital Funchal, on Madeira
Population 243 000 (2003e)

■ **Puerto Rico ► United States of America**

QATAR

Official name State of Qatar
Local name Qatar
Location A low-lying state on the east coast of the Arabian Peninsula, comprising the Qatar Peninsula and numerous small offshore islands. It is bounded to the south by Saudi Arabia, and elsewhere by the Persian Gulf
Area 11 437 sq km/4415 sq mi
Capital Doha

Chief towns Dukhan, Al Khawr, Umm Sai'd, Al Wakrah
Population 824 800 (2008e)
Time zone GMT +3
Currency 1 Qatari Riyal (QR) = 100 dirhams
Language Arabic; English is also spoken
Religions Islam 78%, Christianity 8%, others 14%
Ethnic groups Arab 40%, Pakistani 18%, Indian 18%, Iranian 10%, others 14%

Physical description

The peninsula, 160km/100mi long and 55–80km/34–50mi wide, slopes gently from the Dukhan Heights (98m/322ft) to the east shore; the highest point is Qurayn Abu al Bawl (103m/338ft); barren terrain, mainly sand and gravel; coral reefs offshore.

Climate

Desert climate with average temperatures of 23°C in the winter and 35°C in the summer; high humidity; sparse annual rainfall not exceeding 75mm per annum.

Government

A hereditary absolute monarchy; ruled by the Emir, assisted by a Council of Ministers and advised by an appointed Advisory Council. A constitution promulgated in 2004 will introduce a partially elected legislative council.

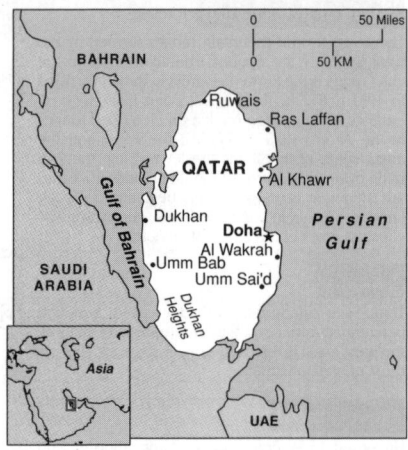

Economy

Prosperity based on oil and liquified natural gas (85% of export earnings); diversified into oil refining, petrochemicals and fertilizers; other activities are steel-making, cement, ship repair, fishing; agriculture is constrained by terrain and climate and contributes less than 1% of GDP.

History

Under the suzerainty of Bahrain for most of the 19c, Qatar was then ruled by the Ottoman Empire before becoming a British protectorate after the Turkish withdrawal in 1916. It declared its independence in 1971. Sheikh Khalifa bin Hamad al-Thani ruled from 1972 until 1995, when he was deposed by his son, Sheikh Hamad bin Khalifa al-Thani. The latter has introduced liberal reforms, including extending the franchise to women (1999) and promulgating a new constitution (2004) that provides for a partially elected legislative council.

■ **Réunion► France**

■ **Republic of China► Taiwan**

ROMANIA

Official name Romania
Local name România
Location A republic in south-eastern Europe, bounded to the south by Bulgaria; to the west by Serbia and Hungary; to the east by Moldova and the Black Sea; and to the north and east by the Ukraine.
Area 237 500 sq km/91 675 sq mi
Capital Bucharest
Chief towns Braşov, Constanţa, Iaşi, Timişoara,

Cluj-Napoca
Population 22 247 000 (2008e)
Time zone GMT +2
Currency 1 New Leu (L, plural Lei) = 100 bani
Language Romanian
Religions Christianity 99% (Orthodox 87%, Prot 7%, RC 5%), Islam and others 1%
Ethnic groups Romanian 89%, Magyar 7%, Roma 2%, others 2%

Physical description

The Carpathian Mountains separate Old Romania from Transylvania, and form the heart of the country; the Eastern Carpathians, between the northern frontier and the Prahova Valley, constitute an area of extensive forest cut by many passes; the higher Southern Carpathians are situated between the Prahova Valley and the Timis-Cerna gorges; the Western Carpathians lie between the River Danube and the River Somes; the highest peak is Mount Moldoveanu (2544m/8349ft); the Romanian Plain in the south includes the Baragan Plain (to the east), the richest arable area, and the Oltenian Plain (to the west), crossed by many rivers; there are c.3500 glacial ponds, lakes and coastal lagoons; over one-quarter of the land is forested.

Climate

Continental, with cold, snowy winters and hot, dry summers; the mildest area in winter is along the Black Sea coast; the plains of the north and east can suffer from drought; average annual rainfall is 1000mm (in the mountains) and 400mm (in the Danube delta).

Government

Governed by a President, a Prime Minister and Cabinet, and a bicameral Parliament comprising a Senate and a Chamber of Deputies.

Economy

Transition from planned to market economy has quickened since 2004; main industries are electrical equipment, textiles and footwear, light machinery, vehicle assembly, mining (especially coal, iron ore), forestry, metals and metal products, chemicals, food processing, oil and gas extraction, oil refining, wine-making; agriculture contributes 8% of GDP but is largely at subsistence level and inefficient; chief crops are cereals, sugar beet, vegetables, sunflower seeds, fruit and livestock.

History

The Romanian people are descended from the Dacians, Romans, Vlachs, Slavs and the other settlers in Moldavia and Wallachia (modern Romania) who speak Romanian. While the culture of the Slav settlers came to dominate elsewhere in the north Balkans, the Romanians' ancestors assimilated to the Latin culture of the earlier Romanized inhabitants. Under the Ottoman Empire (15–19c), the Romanians began their movement for national independence in the 1820s, aspiring to the unification of Moldavia, Wallachia and Transylvania. In 1862 Moldavia and Wallachia merged to form the Principality of Romania, and a monarchy was created in 1866. Romania joined the Allies in World War I, and acquired Transylvania, Bessarabia and Bukovina in the post-war settlement. Romania supported Germany in World War II and Soviet forces occupied the country in 1944. After the war it lost territories to Russia, Hungary and Bulgaria. The monarchy was abolished and a communist People's Republic established in 1947. Under the autocratic President Nicolae Ceauşescu, leader of the Romanian Communist Party from 1965, Romania became increasingly independent of the USSR, forming relationships with China and several Western countries. In 1989 violent repression of protests, resulting in the deaths of thousands of demonstrators, sparked a popular uprising and the overthrow of the Ceauşescu regime and execution of the President and his wife. Although Romania became a multiparty democracy in 1991, governments were dominated by former communists until 1996, when Ion Iliescu was defeated in the presidential election by Emil Constantinescu. Iliescu was re-elected president in 2000 but lost the 2004 election to Traian Basescu. Romania joined NATO in 2004 and the EU in 2007.

RUSSIA

Official name Russian Federation
Local name Rossiya
Location A republic occupying much of eastern Europe and northern Asia, bounded to the north by the Arctic Ocean; to the west by Norway, Finland, Estonia, Latvia, Belarus, Ukraine and the Black Sea; to the south-west by Georgia, Azerbaijan and the Caspian Sea; to the south by Kazakhstan, China and Mongolia; to the south-east by North Korea and the Sea of Japan; and to the east by the Sea of Okhotsk and the Bering Sea. The Kaliningrad enclave borders Lithuania and Poland
Area 17 075 400 sq km/6 591 104 sq mi
Capital Moscow
Chief towns St Petersburg, Nizhniy Novgorod, Rostov-on-Don, Volgograd, Yekaterinburg, Novosibirsk, Chelyabinsk, Kazan, Samara, Omsk
Population 140 702 000 (2008e)
Time zone GMT +2/+12
Currency 1 Rouble (R) = 100 kopeks
Language Russian; many minority languages are also spoken

B	BELARUS
E	ESTONIA
G	GERMANY
L	LITHUANIA
LAT	LATVIA
P	POLAND
R	RUSSIA

Physical description

Vast plains dominate the western half of the country; the Ural Mountains separate the East European Plain in the west from the West Siberian Lowlands in the east; the Central Siberian Plateau lies east of the River Yenisey; further east lies the North Siberian Plain; the Caucasus, Tien Shan and Pamir ranges lie along the southern frontier; the Lena, Ob, Severnaya Dvina, Pechora, Yenisey, Indigirka and Kolyma rivers flow to the Arctic Ocean; the Amur, Amgun and rivers of the Kamchatka Peninsula flow to the Pacific Ocean; the Caspian Sea basin includes the Volga and Ural rivers; there are over 20 000 lakes, the largest being the Caspian Sea, Lake Taymyr and Lake Baikal, the highest point is Mount Elbrus (5642m/18 510ft).

Climate

There are several different climate regions; variable weather in the north and the centre; throughout the country, winters are cold, with temperatures increasingly severe in the east and north, and summers are hot in the south and warm elsewhere; average temperature in Moscow is 9°C in January and 18°C in July; average annual rainfall is 630mm; Siberia has a continental climate, with very cold and prolonged winters, and short, often warm summers.

Government

Governed by a President, a Prime Minister and Council of Ministers, and a bicameral Federal Assembly, consisting of the Council of the Federation and the State *Duma*. The regime has become increasingly authoritarian and centralized since 2000.

Economy

Post-Communist transition from a planned to a market economy partially reversed by renationalization of key industries after 2000; main industries are oil, natural gas, forestry, mining (coal, iron ore, non-ferrous metals, gemstones) and metallurgy; machine-building (including aircraft, space vehicles and defence, transport, communications, agricultural and construction equipment), shipbuilding, power generation and transmission equipment, medical and scientific instruments, consumer durables, textiles, food processing; agricultural production reflects the highly varied terrain and climate, and includes cereals, cotton, vines, tobacco and stock-breeding.

History

Russia was settled by many ethnic groups, initially Slavs, Turks and Bulgars (3–7c AD) and in the 13c came under the overlordship of the Mongols. Moscow was established as a centre of political power in the north during the 14c and the grand duchy of Moscovy threw off Mongol overlordship, beginning a process of unification and expansion. Internal disorder and constant warfare with neighbouring countries (eg

Religions

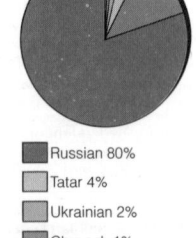

Islam 15%
Christianity 22%
none or non-practising 63%

Ethnic groups

Russian 80%
Tatar 4%
Ukrainian 2%
Chuvash 1%
Bashkir 1%
others 12%

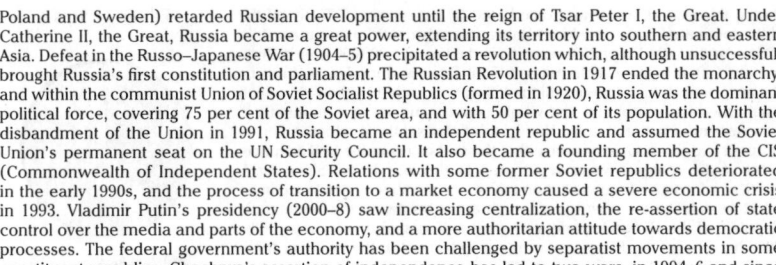

Poland and Sweden) retarded Russian development until the reign of Tsar Peter I, the Great. Under Catherine II, the Great, Russia became a great power, extending its territory into southern and eastern Asia. Defeat in the Russo–Japanese War (1904–5) precipitated a revolution which, although unsuccessful, brought Russia's first constitution and parliament. The Russian Revolution in 1917 ended the monarchy, and within the communist Union of Soviet Socialist Republics (formed in 1920), Russia was the dominant political force, covering 75 per cent of the Soviet area, and with 50 per cent of its population. With the disbandment of the Union in 1991, Russia became an independent republic and assumed the Soviet Union's permanent seat on the UN Security Council. It also became a founding member of the CIS (Commonwealth of Independent States). Relations with some former Soviet republics deteriorated in the early 1990s, and the process of transition to a market economy caused a severe economic crisis in 1993. Vladimir Putin's presidency (2000–8) saw increasing centralization, the re-assertion of state control over the media and parts of the economy, and a more authoritarian attitude towards democratic processes. The federal government's authority has been challenged by separatist movements in some constituent republics. Chechnya's assertion of independence has led to two wars, in 1994–6 and since 1999; direct rule from Moscow was imposed in 2000.

RWANDA

Official name Republic of Rwanda
Local name Rwanda
Location A landlocked republic in central Africa, bounded to the north by Uganda; to the east by Tanzania; to the south by Burundi; and to the west by the Democratic Republic of the Congo and Lake Kivu
Area 26338 sq km/10166 sq mi
Capital Kigali

Chief towns Butare, Ruhengeri
Population 10186000 (2008e)
Time zone GMT +2
Currency 1 Rwanda Franc (RF, RWFr) = 100 centimes
Languages Kinyarwanda, English, French; Swahili is widely used in commerce
Religions Christianity 93% (RC 56%, Prot 37%), Islam 5%, traditional beliefs and none 2%

Physical description

The country is situated at a relatively high altitude, the highest point being Karisimbi volcano (4507m/14787ft) in the Virunga range; the western third of the country drains into Lake Kivu and then the River Congo, the remainder drains towards the River Nile; there are many lakes.

Climate

Tropical highland climate; two wet seasons (October–December and March–May), with the highest rainfall in the west, decreasing in the central uplands and to the north and east; the average annual rainfall at Kigali is 1000mm.

Government

Governed by a President, a Prime Minister and Council of Ministers, and a bicameral Parliament consisting of a Chamber of Deputies and a Senate.

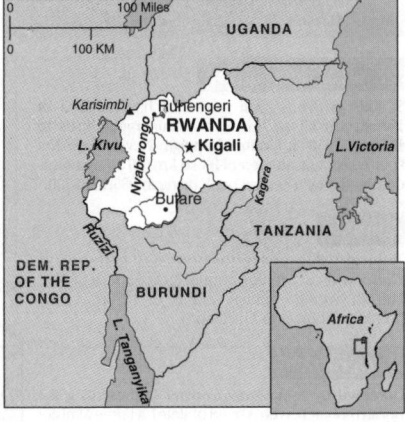

Economy

Poor country, dependent on international aid; agriculture, mostly at subsistence level, engages c.90% of the population; chief cash crops are coffee, tea and livestock products; small-scale industries include mining (coltan, cassiterite, tin), processing of agricultural products, light manufacturing and small-scale tourism.

History

The Hutu peoples who settled the country came under the dominance of Tutsi peoples, who migrated into the area and established a monarchy in the 15c. The country became a German protectorate in 1899, and was mandated with Burundi to Belgium as the Territory of Ruanda–Urundi after World War I. It became a UN Trust Territory administered by Belgium after World War II. Unrest in 1959 led to a Hutu revolt and the overthrow of Tutsi rule, and in 1962 the union with Burundi was broken when both nations gained independence. A military coup took place in 1973, and there was a gradual return to stability under the new Hutu President Habyarimana, whose party, the National Revolutionary Movement for Development (MRND), was the only legal party until 1991. Successive incursions by Tutsi rebels from the 1960s onwards were defeated by the army until 1990, when the advance of the *Front Patriotique Rwandaise* (FPR) forced the government to negotiate a power-sharing accord, signed in 1993; ethnic unrest continued unabated

Nations of the World

during this period, and was exacerbated by massacres of Tutsis by the Hutu-dominated army. President Habyarimana's death in an air crash in 1994 reignited ethnic conflict, resulting in the loss of c.800 000 lives in three months (often in large-scale massacres of Tutsis and moderate Hutus by the army and Hutu militias) until the killing was ended by the FPR, which established its control over the whole country and set up a multi-ethnic government of national unity. Hundreds of thousands of refugees fled to Burundi and Tanzania to escape either the massacres or the FPR advance; most of the refugees were repatriated in the late 1990s. Since 1994, political reforms and reconciliation measures have been introduced in an effort to stabilize the country, although areas bordering the Democratic Republic of the Congo experienced great suffering and tension in 1998–2002 because of the Rwandan army's involvement in the civil war there and remain volatile.

Ethnic groups

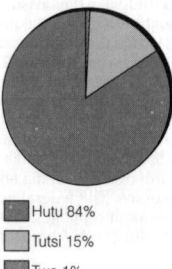

■ Hutu 84%
□ Tutsi 15%
■ Twa 1%

ST CHRISTOPHER AND NEVIS

Official name Federation of St Christopher and Nevis; also known as St Kitts and Nevis
Local name St Kitts and Nevis
Location An independent state in the North Leeward Islands in the eastern Caribbean Sea. It comprises the islands of St Christopher (St Kitts), Nevis and Sombrero
Area 269 sq km / 104 sq mi
Capital Basseterre

Population 39 800 (2008e)
Time zone GMT –4
Currency 1 East Caribbean Dollar (EC$) = 100 cents
Language English
Religions Christianity 75% (Prot 50%, RC 25%), others 25%
Ethnic groups black 93%, mulatto 4%, white 1%, others 2%

Physical description

St Kitts is 37km / 23mi long and has an area of 168 sq km / 65 sq mi; a mountain range rises to 1156m / 3793ft at Mount Liamuiga; Nevis, 3km / 2mi south-east, has an area of 93 sq km / 36 sq mi and is dominated by a central peak rising to 985m / 3232ft.

Climate

Tropical, influenced by the north-east trade winds; warm, with an average annual temperature of 26°C and an average annual rainfall of 1375mm; low humidity; subject to hurricanes.

Government

Governed by a Governor-General (representing the British monarch, who is head of state), a Prime Minister and Cabinet, and a unicameral National Assembly.

Atlantic Ocean

▲ *Misery*

Basseterre ★ *St Kitts*

ST KITTS AND NEVIS *The Narrows*

Newcastle

Nevis Peak ▲ *Nevis*

Caribbean

North America

Sea

Economy

Sugar industry, historically the economic mainstay, closed in 2005 as unviable; main activities are tourism, offshore financial services and light manufacturing (distilling, food processing, garments, electronics); Nevis is developing a sea-cotton industry.

History

Originally inhabited by Caribs, the islands were visited by Christopher Columbus in 1493, who named the larger one Saint Christopher. The name was shortened to St Kitts by English settlers when the island became the first British colony in the West Indies, in 1623. Control was disputed between France and Britain in the 17–18c, and the island was ceded to Britain in 1783. St Kitts and Nevis were united in 1882, along with Anguilla (which became a separate British dependency in 1980). They became internally self-governing in 1967 and gained independence in 1983. In 1997 the government of Nevis voted to secede from St Kitts but in 1998 a referendum on the issue failed to secure the necessary two-thirds majority.

■ St Helena ▶ United Kingdom

ST LUCIA

Official name St Lucia
Local name St Lucia
Location An independent constitutional monarchy and the second-largest of the Windward Islands, situated in the eastern Caribbean Sea
Area 616 sq km/238 sq mi
Capital Castries
Chief towns Vieux Fort, Soufrière
Population 160 000 (2008e)

Time zone GMT –4
Currency 1 East Caribbean Dollar (EC$) = 100 cents
Language English; French patois is also spoken
Religions Christianity 91% (RC 67%, Prot 10%, other Christian 14%), Rastafarian 2%, other 1%, none/unaffiliated 6%
Ethnic groups black 83%, mixed 12%, East Indian 2%, other/unspecified 3%

Physical description

The island is 43km/27mi long and 23km/14mi wide; mountainous centre, rising to 950m/3117ft at Mount Gimie; the twin volcanic peaks of Gros Piton and Petit Piton rise steeply from the sea on the south-west coast of the island.

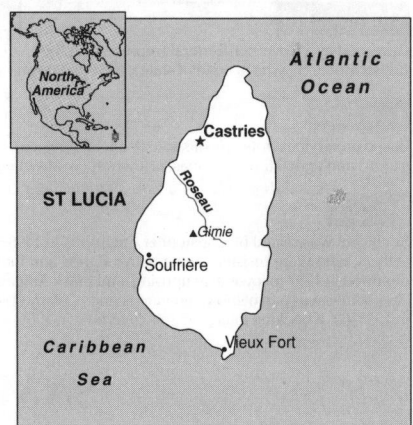

Climate

Tropical; annual temperatures range from 18°C to 34°C; the wet season is June–December; average annual rainfall is 1500mm on the north coast and 4000mm in the interior.

Government

Governed by a Governor-General (representing the British monarch, who is head of state), a Prime Minister and Cabinet, and a bicameral Parliament consisting of a House of Assembly and a Senate.

Economy

Services (tourism, offshore financial services) are the largest sector of the economy; other activities include agriculture (bananas, cocoa, vegetables, fruit, coconuts), light manufacturing (garments, beverages, corrugated cardboard boxes, food processing) and assembling electronic components.

History

Originally inhabited by Arawak Indians who were displaced by Caribs, the island was reputedly sighted by Christopher Columbus in 1502. It was settled by the French in the 17c, but ownership was disputed between Britain and France from 1659 until it was ceded to Britain in 1814. It became internally self-governing in 1967 and gained independence in 1979.

■ **St Pierre and Miquelon▶France**

ST VINCENT AND THE GRENADINES

Official name St Vincent and the Grenadines
Local name St Vincent and the Grenadines
Location An independent state in the Windward Islands, situated in the eastern Caribbean Sea
Area 390 sq km/150 sq mi
Capital Kingstown
Population 118 400 (2008e)
Time zone GMT –4

Currency 1 East Caribbean Dollar (EC$) = 100 cents
Language English; French patois is also spoken
Religions Christianity 88% (Prot 75%, RC 13%), others 12%
Ethnic groups black 66%, mixed 19%, East Indian 6%, Carib Amerindian 2%, others 7%

Nations of the World

Physical description

Comprises the island of St Vincent (length 29km/18mi; width 16km/10mi) and the northern Grenadine Islands; St Vincent is volcanic in origin and hilly; the highest peak is Soufrière, an active volcano rising to a height of 1234m/4049ft; the most recent eruption was in 1997; the Grenadines are low-lying coral reefs.

Climate

Tropical, with an average annual temperature of 25°C, and an average annual rainfall of 1500mm on the coast, 3800mm in the interior.

Government

Governed by a Governor-General (representing the British monarch, who is head of state), a Prime Minister and Cabinet, and a unicameral House of Assembly.

Economy

Based on services (tourism, offshore financial services), manufacturing (food processing, furniture, garments, starch) and agriculture (bananas, arrowroot (world's largest producer), coconuts).

History

St Vincent was visited by Christopher Columbus in 1498. The first European settlement was in 1762 by British settlers, who were resisted by the native Caribs and the French but defeated both. Most of the Caribs were deported in 1797 following an uprising, and black Africans were imported as slave labour. St Vincent and the Grenadines was part of the Windward Islands Colony (1880–1958) and then joined the West Indies Federation in 1958–62. It became internally self-governing in 1969, and gained its independence in 1979.

SAMOA

Official name Independent State of Samoa
Local name Samoa
Location An island nation in the south-west Pacific Ocean, 2600km/1600mi north-east of Auckland, New Zealand
Area 2842 sq km/1097 sq mi
Capital Apia
Population 217 000 (2008e)

Time zone GMT –11
Currency 1 Tala (ST$) = 100 sene
Languages Samoan, English
Religions Christianity 98% (Prot 57%, RC 20%, other Christian 21%), others/unspecified 2%
Ethnic groups Samoan 93%, mixed 6%, European 1%

Physical description

The islands are formed from ranges of extinct volcanoes, rising to 1829m/6000ft on Savai'i; many dormant volcanoes; highest point is Mount Silisili (1857m/6092ft) thick tropical vegetation; several coral reefs.

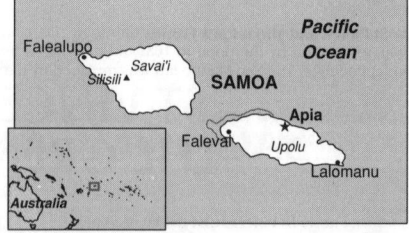

Climate

Tropical; the rainy season is November–April; average annual temperatures are 22°–30°C; average annual rainfall is 2775mm; cyclones occur.

Government

Governed by an elected monarch as head of state, a Prime Minister and Cabinet, and a unicameral Legislative Assembly.

Economy

Poor country dependent on international aid, expatriates' remittances, fishing and largely subsistence agriculture; chief cash crops are fish, coconuts, copra, taro; diversifying into tourism, offshore financial services and light manufacturing (vehicle parts, garments and beer).

History

Inhabited since around 1000 BC, Samoa was visited by the Dutch in 1772, and in 1889 was divided between Germany (which acquired Western Samoa) and the USA (which acquired Tutuila and adjacent small islands, now known as American Samoa). After 1914 Western Samoa was administered by New Zealand, from 1919 to 1946 under a League of Nations mandate, and then as a UN Trust Territory, until it gained independence in 1962. Malietoa Tanumafili II became head of state for life in 1963. The legislative assembly voted to change the country's name to Samoa in 1997.

■ **Samoa, American ▶ United States of America**

SAN MARINO

Official name Republic of San Marino
Local name San Marino
Location A very small landlocked republic completely surrounded by central Italy, lying 20km/12mi from the Adriatic Sea
Area 61 sq km/24 sq mi
Capital San Marino
Chief towns Serravalle

Population 29 900 (2008e)
Time zone GMT +1
Currency 1 Euro (€) = 100 cents
Language Italian
Religions Christianity 95% (RC), unaffiliated, others and none 5%
Ethnic groups Sammarinese 88%, Italian 11%, others 1%

Physical description

Ruggedly mountainous, centred on the limestone ridges of Mount Titano (755m/2477ft) and the valley of the River Ausa.

Climate

Mediterranean climate modified by altitude, with cold, often snowy, winters and warm summers (20°–30°C); rainfall is moderate, with an annual average of 880mm.

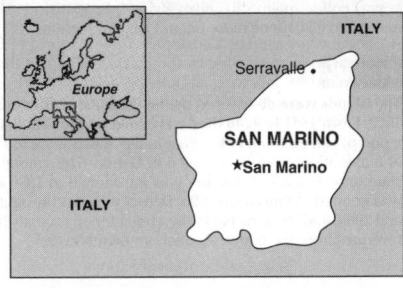

Government

Governed by two captains-regent (*capitani reggenti*) elected for six-month terms as joint heads of state, a Congress of State (cabinet) and the unicameral Great and General Council.

Economy

Based on tourism (over 50% of GDP), sale of postage stamps and coins, agriculture (wine, cheeses), banking and manufacturing (garments, electronics, ceramics).

History

Reputedly founded in the 4c by a Christian stonecutter as a refuge from religious persecution, its independence was recognized by the pope in 1631, and in 1862 a treaty of friendship with Italy preserved San Marino's independence. The San Marino lira was replaced by the euro in 2002 as the official currency.

SÃO TOMÉ AND PRÍNCIPE

Official name Democratic Republic of São Tomé and Príncipe
Local name São Tomé e Príncipe
Location An equatorial island republic in the Gulf of Guinea, off the coast of west Africa
Area 1001 sq km/386 sq mi
Capital São Tomé
Chief town Santo António

Population 206 000 (2008e)
Time zone GMT
Currency 1 Dobra (Db) = 100 centavos
Language Portuguese
Religions Christianity 77% (RC 70%, Prot 7%), others 3%, none 20%
Ethnic groups black 90%, Portuguese and Creole 10%

Nations of the World

Physical description

Volcanic, densely forested islands; São Tomé lies c.440km/275mi off the north coast of Gabon, has an area of 860 sq km/332 sq mi and reaches a height of 2024m/6640ft at Pico de São Tomé; Príncipe, the smaller of the two islands, lies c.200km/125mi off the north coast of Gabon, covers 140sq km/54sq mi and has similar terrain.

Climate

Tropical; the average annual temperature is 27°C on the coast, 20°C in the mountains; there is a rainy season from October to May; the annual average rainfall varies from 500mm to 1000mm.

Government

Governed by a President, a Prime Minister and Cabinet, and a unicameral National Assembly.

Economy

Poor country, dependent on international aid; based on agriculture (cocoa (80% of export earnings), copra, coffee, palm oil); diversifying into tourism and (from c.2010) offshore oil and gas production.

Africa

Santo António
Príncipe · Ilha Caroço
Tinhosa Pequena
Tinhosa Grande

Atlantic Ocean

SÃO TOMÉ AND PRÍNCIPE

São Tomé
São Tomé
Santana
▲ Pico de São Tomé
Porto Alegre · Santa Cruz
Ilha das Rôlas

History

The islands were discovered by the Portuguese between 1469 and 1472, and became a Portuguese colony in 1522. From 1641 to 1740 they were held by the Dutch, then were recovered by Portugal. They later became a port of call en route to the East Indies. Resistance to Portuguese rule led to riots in 1953, and the formation of a liberation movement based in Gabon. The colony gained independence in 1975, and was a one-party state until a new constitution was introduced in 1990 and multiparty elections were held in 1991. Príncipe was granted autonomy in 1995. Democracy has brought a degree of instability, with short-lived coups in 1995 and 2003, and tensions have been heightened recently by political disagreement over control of the expected revenues from the country's offshore oil reserves.

SAUDI ARABIA

Official name Kingdom of Saudi Arabia
Local name Al-'Arabīyah as-Sa'ūdīyah
Location An Arabic kingdom comprising about four-fifths of the Arabian Peninsula, bounded to the west by the Red Sea; to the north-west by Jordan; to the north by Iraq; to the north-east by Kuwait; to the east by the Persian Gulf, Qatar and the United Arab Emirates; to the south-east and south by Oman; and to the south and south-west by Yemen
Area 2331000 sq km/899766 sq mi
Capital Riyadh

Chief towns Jeddah, Mecca, Medina, Ta'if, Ad Dammam, Abha
Population 28147000 (2008e)
Time zone GMT +3
Currency 1 Saudi Arabian Riyal (SR, SRls) = 20 qursh = 100 halala
Language Arabic
Religions Islam 100% (Sunni 90%, Shia 10%); public practice of any religion other than Islam is forbidden
Ethnic groups Arab 90%, Afro-Asian 10%

Physical description

The Red Sea coastal plain is bounded by mountains; the highlands in the south-west include Jabal Sawda' (3133m/10278ft), Saudi Arabia's highest peak; the Arabian Peninsula slopes gently north and east towards the oil-rich Al Hasa plain on the Persian Gulf; the interior comprises two extensive areas of sand desert, the Nafud in the north and the Great Sandy Desert in the south; the central Najd has some large oases; salt flats are numerous in the eastern lowlands; a large network of wadis drains north to east.

Climate

Hot and dry, with average temperatures varying from 21°C in the north, to 26°C in the south; day temperatures may rise to 50°C in the interior sand deserts; night frosts are common in the north and highlands; the Red Sea coast is hot and humid; average rainfall is low.

Government

A hereditary absolute monarchy based on Islamic teachings and Arab Bedouin tradition; ruled by the King, assisted by a Council of Ministers and advised by an appointed Consultative Council. There are no political parties.

Economy

Prosperity based on oil (world's leading oil exporter and largest proven reserves) and gas; diversified since 1970s so non-oil sector now contributes 60% of GDP, through petrochemicals, financial services, construction, building materials, mining (gold, iron ore, copper) and metal fabrication, ship and aircraft repair, and services for the pilgrimage trade; agricultural productivity increased by irrigation, desalination and aquifers; main products are cereals, fruit, meat and dairy products.

History

Famed as the birthplace of Islam with the holy cities of Mecca, Medina and Jeddah, the modern state was founded by Saudi Arabia's first king, Ibn Saud, leader of the fundamentalist Wahhabi sect, who by 1932 had united the four tribal provinces of Hejaz, Asir, Najd and Al Hasa. The ruling family has preserved stability by suppressing dissent, and has resisted the growing calls for greater democracy for many years, making limited concessions in 2005. Internal tension also grew in the 1990s because of the continuing presence of foreign troops in the country after the 1991 Gulf War, and these troops and other foreign nationals became terrorist targets. Despite redeployment of foreign troops to Qatar, attacks increased after the start of the war with Iraq in 2003 and included Saudi as well as foreign victims. Some dissident groups are believed to have links to al-Qaeda.

■ Scotland▶United Kingdom

SENEGAL

Official name Republic of Senegal
Local name Sénégal
Location A country in West Africa, bounded to the north by Mauritania; to the east by Mali; to the south by Guinea and Guinea-Bissau; and to the west by the Atlantic Ocean. It surrounds The Gambia on three sides
Area 196 840 sq km/75 980 sq mi
Capital Dakar
Chief towns Thiès, Kaolack, St Louis, Ziguinchor

Population 12 853 000 (2008e)
Time zone GMT
Currency 1 CFA Franc (CFAFr) = 100 centimes
Languages French; Malinke, Wolof, Serere, Soninke and Peul are 'national languages'
Religions Islam 94% (Sunni), Christianity 5% (mostly RC), traditional beliefs 1%
Ethnic groups Wolof 43%, Pular 24%, Serer 15%, Jola 4%, others 14%

Physical description

The most westerly country in mainland Africa; the coast is characterized by dunes, mangrove forests and mudbanks; an extensive low-lying basin of savannah and semi-desert vegetation lies to the north; seasonal streams drain to the River Sénégal; the south rises to c.500m/1640ft.

Climate

Tropical, with a rainy season between June and September; high humidity levels and high night-time temperatures, especially on the coast; rainfall decreases from the south (1000–1500mm) to the north (300–350mm); the average annual rainfall at Dakar is 541mm and the average temperature ranges from 22°C to 28°C.

Government

Governed by an executive President, a Prime Minister and Council of Ministers, and a unicameral National Assembly.

Economy

Poor country, dependent on international aid; agriculture and fishing employ c.75% of the workforce; main cash crops are fish, peanuts and cotton; main industries are food and fish processing, mining (phosphate, iron ore, zircon, gold), oil refining, production of fertilizer and construction materials, tourism.

History

Senegal was part of the Mali Empire in the 14–15c. The French established a fort at Saint-Louis in 1659, and it was incorporated as a territory within French West Africa in 1902. It became an autonomous state in 1958, and joined with French Sudan as the independent Federation of Mali in Jun 1960, but withdrew in Aug to become a separate independent republic. It became a one-party state in 1966 and the Socialist Party dominated political life for 40 years until Abdoulaye Wade was elected president in 2000 and his Senegalese Democratic Party won the 2001 legislative election. A separatist uprising led by the Movement of Democratic Forces of Casamance began in southern Senegal in the 1980s and continued sporadically throughout the 1990s; a peace deal with the rebels was signed in 2004, although a rebel faction continues to fight.

SERBIA

Official name Republic of Serbia
Local name Srbija
Location A republic in the Balkan Peninsula of south-eastern Europe, bounded to the south-west by Montenegro; to the west by Croatia, and Bosnia and Herzegovina; to the north by Hungary; to the north-east by Romania; to the east by Bulgaria; and to the south by Macedonia and Albania; includes the province of Kosovo, which declared independence in 2008, and Vojvodina
Area 77 474 sq km / 29 905 sq mi

Capital Belgrade
Chief towns Kragujevac, Nis, Novi Sad, Priština (in Kosovo), Subotica
Population 10 159 000 (2008e)
Time zone GMT +1
Currency 1 Dinar (D, Din) = 100 paras
Language Serbian; Romanian, Hungarian, Slovak, Ukrainian and Croatian are all official in Vojvodina
Religions Christianity 92% (Orthodox 85%, RC 6%, Prot 1%), Islam 3%, other, unknown or none 5%

Physical description

Dominated in the north by the Danube, Tisza and Sava rivers, with fertile plains in the north-east; drained in the centre by the River Morava; mountain ranges in the south are cut by deep river valleys; there are several great lakes in the south.

Climate

A continental climate in the north and north-east; rain falls throughout the year; there is a colder upland climate, with winter snow.

Government

Governed by a President, a Prime Minister and Council of Ministers, and the unicameral National Assembly.

Economy

Fragile recovery from 1990s war with Bosnia, insurgencies and economic sanctions; still requires international aid; economic mainstay is agriculture, which employs 30% of the workforce and produces cereals, sugar beet, sunflowers, meat and dairy products; industries include processing agricultural and forestry products (sugar, pulp and paper), machine building, mining (lead), metallurgy, manufacturing (consumer goods, electronics, pharmaceuticals), petroleum products, chemicals.

History

The medieval kingdom of Serbia, originally a vassal state of the Byzantine Empire, grew to form a large and prosperous state in the Balkans until it fell to the Turks in 1389. It gained autonomy within the Ottoman Empire in 1815 and achieved independence in 1878, becoming a kingdom in 1881. After World War I Serbia joined with Montenegro and territories of the former Austro-Hungarian Empire to form the Kingdom of Serbs, Croats and Slovenes (renamed Yugoslavia in 1929), which was united under the Serbian monarch, Peter I. Yugoslavia was occupied by Axis forces in 1941 and re-established in 1945 as the communist Federal

People's Republic (comprising Croatia, Slovenia, Bosnia-Herzegovina, Macedonia, Montenegro and Serbia) under President Josip Tito. After Tito's death in 1980, nationalisms resurfaced and the federation eventually disintegrated when Croatia and Slovenia seceded in 1991 and Bosnia-Herzegovina and Macedonia in 1992. Serbia and Montenegro remained as the Federal Republic of Yugoslavia, which was declared on 27 Apr 1992. Slobodan Milosevic, President of Serbia from 1989, became President of Yugoslavia in 1997. In 1999 Serbian violence in suppressing secessionism in Kosovo and the ethnic cleansing of the province's Albanian population led to the bombing of Serbia by NATO in Mar–Jun. During the conflict, Milosevic was indicted by the UN war crimes tribunal for his part in the atrocities carried out in the province; his trial at the Hague tribunal began in 2002 and was ended by his death in 2006. Kosovo was a UN-administered autonomous province within Serbia with its own parliament and the euro as its currency from 1999 to 2008. Milosevic was defeated in the 2000 presidential election by Vojislav Kostunica. The federation was restructured in 2003 into a looser union of the two republics, called Serbia and Montenegro. In Jun 2006, the union was dissolved following Montenegro's vote in favour of independence, and Serbia suceeded to the union's membership of international bodies.

Ethnic groups

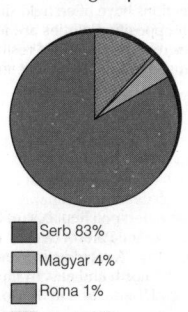

■ Serb 83%
▨ Magyar 4%
▣ Roma 1%
▨ others 12%

❖Kosovo

Location Province of Serbia adjoining Montenegro, Albania and Macedonia; declared independence unilaterally in 2008; independence recognized by over 40 countries but not by UN
Area 10 887 sq km/4 202 sq mi
Seat of administration Pristina
Population 2 127 000 (2007e)

SEYCHELLES

Official name Republic of Seychelles
Local name Seychelles
Location A state of 115 islands in the south-west Indian Ocean, north of Madagascar
Area 453 sq km/175 sq mi
Capital Victoria
Population 82 200 (2008e)

Time zone GMT +4
Currency 1 Seychelles Rupee (SR) = 100 cents
Language Creole, English
Religions Christianity 93% (RC 82%, Prot and others 11%), Hinduism 2%, Islam 1%, others 4%
Ethnic groups mulatto 94%, Malagasy 3%, Chinese 2%, English 1%

Physical description

The islands fall into two main groups; the first, a compact group of 41 steep granitic islands, are mountainous, rising to 906m/2969ft at Morne Seychellois on Mahé; the steep forest-clad slopes drop down to coastal lowlands with a vegetation of grass and dense scrub; the second is a group of low-lying coralline islands and atolls which are situated to the south-west.

Africa

Praslin
SEYCHELLES
La Digue
Silhouette
Victoria
Mahé
Indian
Ocean

Climate

Tropical, with a rainfall that varies with altitude and is higher on the southern sides of the islands; the wettest months are November to March; rarely affected by tropical storms.

Government

Governed by an executive President, a Council of Ministers and a unicameral National Assembly.

Economy

Developing economy, based on tourism and fishing; diversified into agriculture (coconuts, cinnamon) and manufacturing (processing fish and agricultural products, consumer goods).

History

The islands were visited by Vasco da Gama in 1502, and colonized by the French in 1768. The population is largely descended from 18c French colonists and their freed African slaves. Captured by Britain in 1794, it was incorporated as a dependency of Mauritius in 1814 and became a separate British Crown Colony in 1903. It became an independent republic in 1976. Following a coup in 1977, it became a one-party state under

Nations of the World

President France-Albert René. Opposition parties have been permitted since 1991, however, and multiparty elections have been held since 1993. The Seychelles People's Progressive Front has remained the ruling party but opposition parties are increasing their share of the vote in elections. President René retired in 2004 and was replaced by Vice-President James Michel, who was elected president in 2006. Widespread damage was caused by the Indian Ocean tsunami in 2004.

SIERRA LEONE

Official name Republic of Sierra Leone
Local name Sierra Leone
Location A republic in West Africa, bounded to the north and east by Guinea; to the south-east by Liberia; and to the south and west by the Atlantic Ocean
Area 72325 sq km/27917 sq mi
Capital Freetown
Chief towns Bo, Sefadu, Makeni, Kenema, Lunsar

Population 6295000 (2008e)
Time zone GMT
Currency 1 Leone (Le) = 100 cents
Languages English, Mende, Temne; Krio (a Creole language) is also widely spoken
Religions Islam 60% (Sunni), traditional beliefs 30%, Christianity 10%
Ethnic groups African 90% (20 ethnic groups, including Mende 30%, Temne 30%), others 10%

Physical description

Narrow coastal plain with mangrove swamps and beaches; behind this is low-lying wooded land, rising in the west to an average height of 500m/1640ft in the Loma Mountains; the highest point is Loma Mansa (also called Bintimani; 1948m/6391ft); the Tingi Mountains in the south-east rise to 1853m/6079ft.

Climate

Tropical, with a rainy season from May to November; the highest rainfall is on the coast; temperatures are uniformly high throughout the year, c.27°C; the average annual rainfall at Freetown is 3436mm.

Government

Governed by an executive President, a Cabinet and a unicameral Parliament.

Economy

Very poor country, dependent on international aid; slow recovery from civil war; main activities are mining (diamonds, rutile), agriculture, which is mostly at subsistence level but through cash crops (coffee, cocoa) provides c.50% of GDP, fishing, oil refining, ship repair, processing agricultural products, light manufacturing.

History

The area was visited by Portuguese navigators in the 15c and British slave traders in the 16c and 17c. In the 1780s coastal land was bought from local chiefs by English philanthropists who established settlements, including Freetown, for freed slaves. Sierra Leone became a British Crown Colony in 1808, and the hinterland was declared a British protectorate in 1896. The country gained independence in 1961 and became a republic in 1971 under the one-party regime of President Siaka Stevens, who retired in 1985 and was succeeded as president by Joseph Momoh. Transition to multiparty democracy under a new constitution adopted in 1991 was aborted by a military coup in 1992 led by Captain Valentine Strasser. The country returned to civilian rule in 1996 but the government was ousted by another coup in 1997, although it was restored to power the following year with the help of a Nigerian-led coalition of West African forces. The return to multiparty and civilian rule was complicated by a civil war which had begun in 1991. A 1999 peace accord could not be implemented at first, as the ceasefire collapsed in 2000 despite the presence of UN peacekeeping forces, who were drawn into the fighting. A 2001 ceasefire was more effective and disarmament of rebel forces was completed by 2004. President Kabbah, first elected in 1996, was re-elected in 2002, and progress began towards restoring stability to the country. A war crimes tribunal was set up in 2004.

SINGAPORE

Official name Republic of Singapore
Local name Singapore
Location A republic at the southern tip of the Malay Peninsula, in South-East Asia. It consists of the island of Singapore (linked to Malaysia by a causeway) and about 50 adjacent islets
Area 647 sq km/250 sq mi
Capital Singapore
Population 4 608 000 (2008e)
Time zone GMT +8

Currency 1 Singapore Dollar (S$) = 1 Ringgit = 100 cents
Languages Chinese (mainly Mandarin), English, Malay, Tamil, various Chinese dialects
Religions Buddhism 42%, Islam 15%, Christianity 15% (RC 5%, other Christian 10%), Taoism 9%, Hinduism 4%, none/unaffiliated 15%
Ethnic groups Chinese 77%, Malay 14%, Indian 8%, others 1%

Physical description

The highest point of low-lying Singapore Island is at Bukit Timah (177m/581ft); the island measures c.42km/26mi by 22km/14mi at its widest; an important deep-water harbour lies to the south-east.

Climate

Equatorial, with high humidity, an average annual rainfall of 2438mm, and a daily temperature range from 21°C to 34°C.

Government

Governed by a President, a Prime Minister and Cabinet, and a unicameral Parliament.

Economy

Highly industrialized and diverse economy based on the service sector (entrepôt trade, banking, financial and business services, tourism, retail and consumer services); major trans-shipment centre; main industries are manufacturing (electronics, engineering, biomedical sciences, chemicals) oil refining, rubber processing, food processing, ship repair.

History

Originally part of the Sumatran Sri Vijaya kingdom, in 1819 it was leased by the British East India Company from the Sultan of Johore. Singapore, Malacca and Penang were incorporated as the Straits Settlements in 1826; they became a British Crown Colony in 1867, and were occupied by the Japanese during World War II. Self-governing from 1959, Singapore was part of the Federation of Malaya from 1963 until it withdrew and became an independent republic in 1965. Although Singapore is a multiparty state, the People's Action Party (PAP) has dominated political life since 1959; opposition candidates were elected for the first time in 1984. The PAP leader Lee Kuan Yew was Prime Minister from 1959 until he retired in 1990. His son Lee Hsien Loong became Prime Minister in 2004.

SLOVAKIA

Official name Slovak Republic
Local name Slovensko
Location A landlocked republic in eastern Europe, bounded to the north by Poland; to the east by the Ukraine; to the south by Hungary; to the south-west by Austria; and to the west by the Czech Republic
Area 49 035 sq km/18 927 sq mi
Capital Bratislava

Chief towns Košice, Banská Bystrica, Prešov
Population 5 455 000 (2008e)
Time zone GMT +1
Currency 1 Euro (€) = 100 cents
Language Slovak
Religions Christianity 84% (RC 69%, Prot 11%, Orthodox 4%), other/unaffiliated 3%, none 13%
Ethnic groups Slovak 86%, Magyar 10%, Roma 2%, others 2%

Physical description

Lowlands in the south; Tatra Mountains in the north rise to 2655m/8710ft at Gerlachovsky Stit.

Climate

Continental; hot in summer, cold in winter.

Government

Governed by a President, a Prime Minister and Cabinet, and a unicameral National Council.

Economy

Industrialized and diverse economy; completing transition to market economy; main activities are mining (coal, iron ore, metals, minerals) and metal products, agriculture (cereals, sugar beet, hops, fruit, livestock), beverages (wine, beer), fuels and energy (natural gas, coke, oil, nuclear), chemicals, synthetic fibres, machinery, paper, printing, ceramics, transport vehicles; textiles, electrical and optical equipment, rubber products.

History

The area formed part of Great Moravia in the 9c, belonged to the Magyar Empire from the 10c, and came under Habsburg rule from the 16c. A Slovak national movement gradually grew during the 19c and broke away from Hungarian rule when the Austro-Hungarian Empire collapsed after World War I. It became a province of Czechoslovakia in 1918, but many Slovaks objected to the centralized nature of the state established in 1918 and the greater prosperity of the Czech lands. In 1939, on Hitler's instructions, a supposedly independent republic under German protection was carved out of Czechoslovakia. After liberation by Soviet forces in 1945, Slovakia was returned to Czechoslovakia, where a communist regime assumed power in 1948. Little was done by the communists to meet Slovak aspirations, but with the collapse of communism in 1989, nationalist demands intensified again and the federation was dissolved into two separate states, with Slovakia becoming an independent republic in Jan 1993. The Movement for a Democratic Slovakia dominated the coalition governments of the early 1990s, but the centre-right coalition that came to power in 1998 and was re-elected in 2002 introduced the constitutional and economic reforms required for NATO and EU membership; Slovakia joined both in 2004 and in 2009 replaced the Koruna with the euro.

SLOVENIA

Official name Republic of Slovenia
Local name Slovenija
Location A republic in central Europe, bounded to the north by Austria; to the west by Italy; to the south by Croatia; to the east by Hungary, and with a short coastline on the Adriatic Sea
Area 20 251 sq km/7817 sq mi
Capital Ljubljana
Chief towns Maribor, Kranj, Celje, Koper

Population 2 008 000 (2008e)
Time zone GMT +1
Currency 1 Euro (€) = 100 cents
Language Slovene
Religions Christianity 61% (RC 58%, Orthodox 2%, other Christian 1%), Islam 2%, others 23%, none/unaffiliated 14%
Ethnic groups Slovene 83%, Serb 2%, Croat 2%, Bosniak 1%, others 12%

Physical description

The land is mountainous, with Mount Triglav (2864m/9396ft) as its highest point; it drops towards the Adriatic coast and the valleys of the chief rivers, the Sava and Drava; over 50% is forested.

Climate

Continental, with hot summers and cold winters, in the plateaux and valleys in the east; Mediterranean climate on the Adriatic coast.

Government

Governed by a President, a Prime Minister and Cabinet, and a unicameral National Assembly. A National Council has an advisory role.

Economy

Smooth transition to market economy in 1990s, though much still in state ownership; main industries are mining (coal, iron ore, lead, zinc), metal processing, electronic and optical equipment, vehicles, electric power equipment, forestry and timber processing, textiles, chemicals, rubber, plastics, machinery production, tourism; agriculture produces potatoes, hops, cereals, sugar beet and grapes.

History

Settled by Slovenians in the 6c, it was later controlled by Slavs and Franks, and was part of the Austro-Hungarian Empire until 1918 when it joined with Croatia, Montenegro, Serbia and Bosnia-Herzegovina to form the Kingdom of Serbs, Croats and Slovenes. This was renamed Yugoslavia in 1929 and became a communist republic after World War II. In July 1991, President Milan Kucan declared Slovenia's independence from the Yugoslav Federation. The Yugoslav National Army intervened, leading to the so-called 'Ten-Day War' with Slovenian forces, but the federal forces withdrew under an EU-brokered ceasefire. Elections in 1992 saw Milan Kucan re-elected as president, an office he held until 2002. All the governments since 1991 have been coalitions; the Liberal Democracy of Slovenia party was the major party in every coalition from 1991 until 2004. Slovenia joined the EU and NATO in 2004, and in 2007 replaced the tolar with the euro.

SOLOMON ISLANDS

Official name Solomon Islands
Local name Solomon Islands
Location An independent country consisting of an archipelago of six main islands and 400 smaller islands in the south-west Pacific Ocean
Area 27 556 sq km/10 637 sq mi
Capital Honiara
Chief towns Gizo, Auki, Kirakira
Population 581 300 (2008e)

Time zone GMT +11
Currency 1 Solomon Islands Dollar (SI$) = 100 cents
Language English; Melanesian pidgin and over 100 local languages are also spoken
Religions Christianity 97% (Prot 62%, RC 19%, others 16%), others 3%
Ethnic groups Melanesian 94%, Polynesian 3%, Micronesian 1%, others 2%

Physical description

The six larger islands (Choiseul, Guadalcanal, Makira, Malaita, New Georgia, Santa Isabel) have densely forested mountain ranges of mainly volcanic origin, deep, narrow valleys, and coastal belts lined with coconut palms; they are ringed by reefs; the highest point is Mount Makarakomburu (2477m/8127ft) on Guadalcanal.

Climate

Equatorial; the average temperature is 27°C; high humidity; rainfall averages c.3500mm per year.

Government

Governed by a Governor-General (representing the British monarch, who is head of state), a Prime Minister and Cabinet, and a unicameral National Parliament.

Economy

Poor country, dependent on international aid; still recovering from ethnic unrest and lawlessness (1998–2003); agriculture, mainly at subsistence level, provides over 40% of GDP; main activities are forestry, fishing, mining (gold production currently suspended), production of copra and palm oil.

History

Inhabited since at least 1500 BC, the islands were discovered by the Spanish in 1568. The southern Solomon Islands were placed under British protection in 1893, and the outer islands were added to the protectorate in 1899. The islands were captured by the Japanese in 1942 and recaptured by US forces in 1943 after fierce fighting, especially on the island of Guadalcanal. The islands gained their independence in 1978. Tension between different ethnic groups on Guadalcanal in the late 1990s led to conflict between two rival militias from 1998 and an attempted coup in 2000. A fragile peace was brokered in 2000 but worsening economic and social problems in 2002 led to growing lawlessness. In mid 2003 the government requested assistance from neighbouring countries and order was restored and the militias disarmed.

SOMALIA

Official name Somali Republic
Local name Soomaaliya
Location A north-east African state, bounded
to the north-west by Djibouti; to the west by
Ethiopia; to the south-west by Kenya; to the east
by the Indian Ocean; and to the north by the
Gulf of Aden
Area 637 657 sq km/246 199 sq mi
Capital Mogadishu

Chief towns Hargeysa, Berbera, Kismayu, Baidoa
Population 9 559 000 (2008e)
Time zone GMT +3
Currency 1 Somali Shilling (SoSh) = 100 cents
Languages Somali; Arabic, English and Italian are
also spoken widely
Religions Islam 98% (Sunni), Christianity 2%
Ethnic groups Somali 85%, Bantu, Arab and others
15%

Physical description

Occupies the eastern Horn of Africa where an arid coastal plain broadens to the south and rises inland to a plateau at nearly 1000m/3280ft; forested mountains on the Gulf of Aden coast rise to 2416m/7926ft at Mount Shimbiris.

Climate

Considerable variation in climate between the north coast (hot, humid, low rainfall), the east coast (cooler with less variation in temperature, humid, higher rainfall) and inland (very hot, low humidity, very little rain); serious and persistent threat of drought.

Government

A transitional federal government was created in 2004, comprising a President, a Prime Minister and Cabinet, and a unicameral National Assembly; it controls little of the country.

Economy

Very poor country, with many dependent on remittances from emigrant workers; political situation prevents economic development or delivery of international aid; thriving entrepreneurial informal economy in some sectors (telecommunications, trade); main activity is agriculture, primarily livestock-raising by nomads and semi-nomads which provides 40% of GDP and 65% of export earnings; also cultivation of bananas and fishing.

History

The country was settled by Arabs in the 7–10c, and was the object of Italian, French and British interest after the opening of the Suez Canal in 1869. Modern Somalia was formed by the amalgamation of the Italian and British protectorates upon independence in 1960. In 1969 a military coup led by Muhammad Siad Barre established a socialist Islamic regime which became a one-party state in 1979. In 1988, civil war began with fighting between government forces and rebel groups, particularly the Somali National Movement (SNM), forcing Barre to flee in 1991. Attempts to establish a new central government were unsuccessful as political and clan rivalries split the former rebels. The SNM declared the north-west region independent as the Somaliland Republic in 1991, and in 1998 the north-east declared its autonomy as the region of Puntland; neither has received international recognition but each has a functioning government and relative stability. Elsewhere, the state effectively disintegrated amid clan-based factional conflict between rival 'warlords'. Agriculture was disrupted by severe drought as well as the fighting in the south in the early 1990s; UN relief convoys and the multinational forces sent to protect them came under attack and were withdrawn in 1995. The fighting, famines and disease caused an estimated one million deaths. Talks in 2002–4 resulted in an agreement to establish a federal government and transitional institutions to govern until elections in 2007. Members of the transitional government and legislature only began to return to Somalia in 2005, and were based in Baidoa, 250km from the capital, because of the security situation. Muslim militias loyal to the Union of Islamic Courts (UIC) took control of Mogadishu and other parts of the south in Jul 2006 after defeating local warlords. The UIC advanced on Baidoa in Dec but was driven back and then out of all the territory it held by government troops supported by Ethiopian forces. A resurgence by the UIC in 2008 enabled it to recapture much of the south.

SOUTH AFRICA

Official name Republic of South Africa
Local name South Africa
Location A republic in the south of the African continent. It is bounded to the north-west by Namibia; to the north by Botswana; to the north-east by Zimbabwe, Mozambique and Swaziland; to the east and south-east by the Indian Ocean; and to the south-west and west by the southern Atlantic Ocean; Lesotho is landlocked within its borders
Area 1 228 376 sq km/474 275 sq mi
Capital Pretoria (administrative), Cape Town

(legislative), Bloemfontein (judicial)
Chief towns Durban, Johannesburg, Port Elizabeth
Population 48 783 000 (2008e)
Time zone GMT +2
Currency 1 Rand (R) = 100 cents
Languages IsiZulu, IsiXosa, Afrikaans, Sepedi, English, Setswana, Sesotho, Xitsonga are the main languages; other local languages are also spoken
Religions Christianity 80% (Prot 37%, RC 7%, other Christian 36%), Islam 1%, others 2%, none/unaffiliated 17%

Physical description

Occupies the southern extremity of the African plateau, fringed by mountains and a lowland coastal margin to the west, east and south; the northern interior comprises the Kalahari Basin, scrub grassland and arid desert, at an altitude 650–1250m/2133–4101ft; the peripheral highlands rise to over 1200m/3937ft; the Great Escarpment rises east to 3482m/11 424ft at Thabana Ntlenyana, Lesotho; the highest point is Mafadi (3451m/11 322ft); the Orange River flows west to meet the Atlantic; its chief tributaries are the Vaal and Caledon rivers.

Climate

Subtropical in the east, with lush vegetation; the average monthly rainfall at Durban is 28mm in July, 130mm in March, the annual average is 1101mm; dry moistureless climate on the west coast; Mediterranean climate in southern tip; the annual average rainfall at Cape Town is 510mm, with minimum daily temperatures of 7°C in July, to an average maximum of 26°C in January–February; desert region further north, with an annual average rainfall of less than 30mm.

Ethnic groups

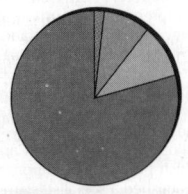

■ black African 79%
■ white 10%
□ coloured 9%
■ Indian/Asian 2%

Government

Governed by an executive President, a Cabinet and a bicameral Parliament consisting of a National Assembly and a National Council of Provinces. Each of the nine provinces has its own constitution, executive and legislature.

Economy

Developed, diversified industrial economy but wide wealth disparity so subsistence agriculture supports the very poor; main activities are mining (platinum, gold, chromium, diamonds, other metals, non-metallic minerals), vehicle assembly, metalworking, iron and steel, manufacturing (machinery, textiles, chemicals, fertilizers), fuels and energy (coal, natural gas, nuclear), financial services, tourism, agriculture (cereals, sugar, fruits, vegetables, livestock), wine-making, fishing, forestry; inadequate water resources supplemented by imports.

History

South Africa was originally inhabited by Khoisan tribes, and many Bantu tribes arrived from the north after c.1000. The Portuguese reached the Cape of Good Hope in the late 15c, and it was settled by the Dutch in 1652. The British arrived in 1795 and annexed the Cape in 1814. In 1836 the Boers (descendants of Dutch colonists) undertook the Great Trek north-east across the Orange River to Natal, where the first Boer republic was founded in 1839. Natal was annexed by the British in 1846, but the Boer republics of Transvaal (founded 1852) and Orange Free State (1854) received recognition. The discovery of diamonds in 1866 and gold in 1886 led to rivalry between the British and the Boers, which resulted in the Boer Wars of 1880–1 and 1899–1902. In 1910 Transvaal, Natal, Orange Free State and Cape Province were united to form the Union of South Africa, a dominion of the British Empire. It became a sovereign state within the Commonwealth of Nations in 1931, but left the Commonwealth and became a republic in 1961. Post-war, South African politics became dominated by the treatment of the non-white majority. Between 1948 and 1991 the apartheid policy resulted in the development of separate political institutions for different racial groups, eg Africans were considered permanent citizens of the 'homelands' to which each tribal group was assigned and were given no representation in the South African parliament. Continuing racial violence and strikes led to the declaration of a state of emergency in 1986. Several countries imposed economic and cultural sanctions in protest at the apartheid system. The progressive dismantling of apartheid by the government of F W de Klerk took place from 1990, but negotiations towards a non-racial democracy were marked by continuing violent clashes. In 1993 a new constitution gave the vote to all South African adults, and in 1994 free democratic elections resulted in the formation of an ANC-led multiracial government, and Nelson Mandela became President. In the same year, South Africa rejoined the Commonwealth and took its UN seat again. The ANC has remained in power since 1994. President Mandela was succeeded in 1999 by Thabo Mbeki, who was re-elected in 2004 but resigned in 2008 over allegations of interference in legal cases. A Truth and Reconciliation Commission began hearings in 1996 on human rights abuses committed by the former government and liberation movements during the apartheid era.

- South Georgia ▶ United Kingdom

- South Korea ▶ Korea, South

- South Sandwich Islands ▶ United Kingdom

SPAIN

Official name Kingdom of Spain	Chief towns Barcelona, Valencia, Seville, Zaragoza,
Local name España	Málaga
Location A country in south-western Europe,	Population 40 491 000 (2008e)
occupying most of the Iberian Peninsula;	Time zone GMT +1
bordered to the north-east by France and	Currency 1 Euro (€) = 100 cents
Andorra; to the west by Portugal; to the north-	Language Spanish (Castilian); Catalan, Galician
west and north by the Atlantic Ocean; and to the	(Gallego) and Basque (Euskera) are also official
east by the Mediterranean Sea	languages in certain regions
Area 504 782 sq km/190 078 sq mi	Religions Christianity 94% (RC), others 6%
Capital Madrid	

Physical description

The country consists mainly of a central plateau (the Meseta, average height 700m/2297ft) crossed and surrounded by mountains; the Andalusian or Baetic Mountains in the south-east rise to 3478m/11 410ft at Mulhacén; the Pyrenees in the north rise to 3404m/11 168ft at Pico de Aneto; the main rivers are the Duero, Tajo (Tagus), Guadiana, Guadalquivir, Ebro and Miño; the highest point is Pico de Teide (3718m/12 198ft) on the island of Tenerife in the Canary Islands.

Climate

The Meseta has a continental climate, with hot summers, cold winters and low rainfall; there is high rainfall in the mountains, with deep winter snow; the south Mediterranean coast has the warmest winter temperatures on the European mainland.

Government

A hereditary constitutional monarchy with a King as head of state; governed by a Prime Minister and Council of Ministers, and a bicameral National Assembly (*Cortes Generales*) comprising a Congress of Deputies and

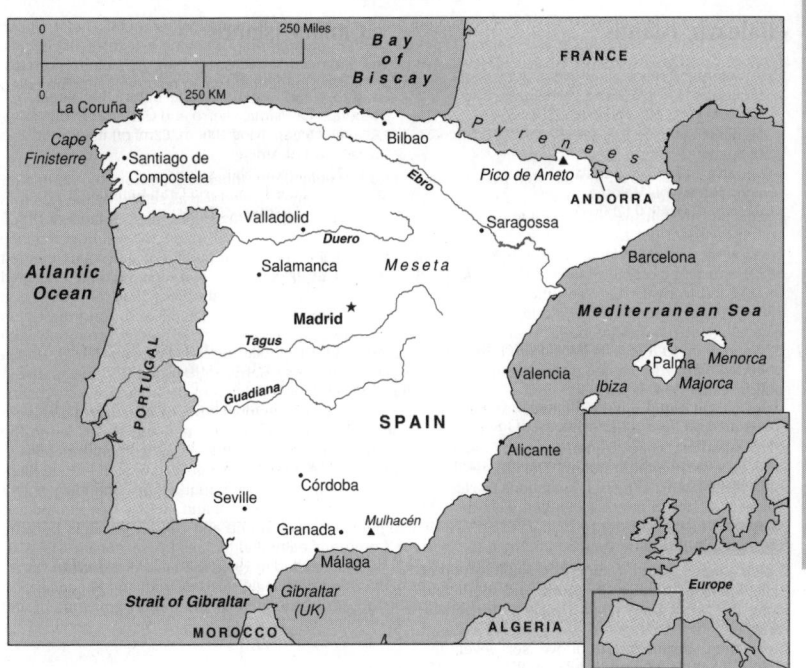

a Senate. Each of the 19 autonomous regions has its own executive and legislature.

Economy

Industrialized and diversified market economy; main activities are tourism, mining (coal, iron ore, copper, zinc, lead, uranium, tungsten), steel-making, fishing (one of Europe's largest fleets), manufacturing (metal products, textiles, garments and footwear, chemicals, vehicles, machine tools, ceramics, pharmaceuticals, medical equipment, food processing), shipbuilding, agriculture, wine-making.

History

Early inhabitants included Iberians, Celts, Phoenicians, Greeks and Romans. From the 8c there was Muslim domination, and then Christian reconquest, which was completed by 1492. Spain assumed its modern form with the dynastic union of the crowns of Aragon and Castile, a union that was effective by 1479. In the 16c Spanish exploration of the New World led to the growth of the Spanish Empire. There was a period of decline after the Revolt of the Netherlands in 1581. Significant set-backs included the defeat of the Spanish Armada in 1588, defeat by France, acknowledged in the Treaty of the Pyrenees (1659), the War of the Spanish Succession in 1702–13, Spain's involvement in the Peninsular War against Napoleon I in 1808–14, and the Spanish–American War in 1898 that led to the loss of Cuba, Puerto Rico and the remaining Pacific possessions. The dictatorship of Miguel Primo de Rivera (1923–30) was followed by the exile of the King and the establishment of the Second Republic in 1931. A military revolt headed by General Franco in 1936 led to the Spanish Civil War and a Fascist dictatorship until Franco's death in 1975. At this point Spain became a constitutional monarchy, with Prince Juan Carlos of Bourbon, nominated as Franco's successor in 1969, acceding to the throne. The transition to democracy began with free elections in 1977 and the introduction of a democratic constitution in 1978, and survived attempted military coups in 1978 and 1981. Spain joined the EC in 1986, and replaced the peseta with the euro in 2002. From the 1960s onwards, the Basque separatist movement, ETA, has carried out a terrorist campaign of bombings, assassinations and kidnappings in an attempt to win independence for the Basque country; numerous ceasefires, the most recent in 2006, have been broken, and attempts to negotiate a settlement have failed. Increasing degrees of autonomy have been granted to 19 regions, including the Basque country, since 1978.

Languages

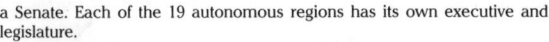

■ Castilian Spanish 74%
■ Catalan 17%
■ Galician 7%
■ Basque 2%

❖Balearic Islands

Location An archipelago of five major islands (Majorca, Minorca, Ibiza, Formentera and Cabrera) and eleven islets in the west Mediterranean Sea, situated near the east coast of Spain
Area 5014 sq km/1935 sq mi
Capital Palma, on Majorca
Population 1 001 000 (2006e)

❖Canary Islands

Location An island archipelago of seven major islands (Gran Canaria, Fuerteventura, Lanzarote, Tenerife, La Palma, Hierro and Gomera) in the Atlantic Ocean, lying 100km/62mi off the north-west coast of Africa
Area 7273 sq km/2807 sq mi
Chief town Las Palmas, on Gran Canaria
Population 1 996 000 (2006e)

SRI LANKA

Official name Democratic Socialist Republic of Sri Lanka
Local name Sri Lanka
Location An island state in the Indian Ocean situated off the south-east coast of India
Area 65 610 sq km/25 325 sq mi
Capital Colombo, Sri Jayawardenapura Kotte (legislative)

Chief towns Jaffna, Kandy, Galle, Trincomalee
Population 21 129 000 (2008e)
Time zone GMT +5.5
Currency 1 Sri Lankan Rupee (SLR, SLRs) = 100 cents
Languages Sinhala, Tamil; English and other local languages are spoken

Physical description

A pear-shaped island, lying off the southern tip of India; low-lying areas in the north and south, and along the coasts; the coastal plain is fringed by sandy beaches and lagoons; the centre is a massif more than 1500m/4921ft above sea level; the highest peak is Pidurutalagala at 2524m/8281ft; the northern region is generally arid in the dry season; nearly half the country is forest, jungle or scrubland.

Climate

High temperatures and humidity in the northern plains; temperatures in the interior are reduced by altitude; affected by the south-west monsoon (May–September) and the north-east monsoon (November–March); the average daily temperatures at Trincomalee are 24°–33°C; rainfall is heavy, particularly on the south-west coast and in the mountains.

Government

Governed by an executive President, a Prime Minister and Cabinet, and a unicameral Parliament.

Economy

Poor country; economy damaged by civil war and 2004 tsunami; largest sector is services (tourism, telecommunications, banking, insurance); agriculture employs c.34% of workforce; cash crops are tea, spices, coconut, rubber, tobacco; main industries are forestry, fishing, mining (coal, diamonds, emeralds, rubies), oil refining, manufacturing (textiles, garments), processing agricultural products.

History

The Sinhalese (from northern India) colonized part of the island in the 5c BC and dominated the northern plain until around AD 1200, when they gradually moved south-westwards due to the many Tamil invasions from southern India. Buddhism spread amongst the Sinhalese from about 200 BC. Some coastal areas of the country were conquered by the Portuguese in the 15c, then it was taken over by the Dutch in 1658. British occupation began in 1796, and the island became a British colony in 1802. The whole island was united for the first time in 1815, when

Religions

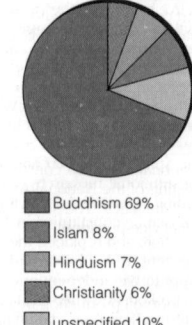

- Buddhism 69%
- Islam 8%
- Hinduism 7%
- Christianity 6%
- unspecified 10%

it was named Ceylon. Tamil labourers were brought in from southern India during colonial rule, to work on coffee and tea plantations. Ceylon gained independence as a dominion within the Commonwealth in 1948, and became a republic in 1972, when it adopted the name Sri Lanka. Acute tension exists between the Buddhist Sinhalese majority and the Hindu Tamil minority, who live predominantly in the north and east of the island. Separatist movements began to campaign for an independent Tamil state in the Tamil majority areas in the 1970s, and in the early 1980s the Liberation Tigers of Tamil Eelam (LTTE) began a guerrilla war against government forces for control of these areas. The fighting has remained mainly in the Jaffna Peninsula, though sporadic terrorist attacks have taken place elsewhere. Attempts to negotiate a settlement in the 1980s and 1990s were unsuccessful. A number of normalization measures resulted from talks in 2002–3 but these stalled owing to disagreement within the government over concessions made to the Tamils, who withdrew because of the slow progress; an attempt to reopen the talks in 2006 failed. The 2002 ceasefire held until early 2006, since when conflict has escalated. The 2004 Indian Ocean tsunami killed over 30 000 people and caused widespread devastation in Sri Lanka.

Ethnic groups

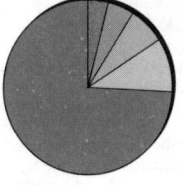

- ■ Sinhalese 74%
- □ Sri Lankan Moor 7%
- ■ Indian Tamil 5%
- ■ Sri Lankan Tamil 4%
- □ others 10%

Nations of the World

SUDAN

Official name Republic of the Sudan
Local name As-Sūdān
Location A north-east African republic, bounded to the north by Egypt; to the north-west by Libya; to the west by Chad; to the south-west by the Central African Republic; to the south by the Democratic Republic of the Congo, Uganda and Kenya; to the east by Ethiopia; and to the north-east by the Red Sea

Area 2 504 530 sq km/966 749 sq mi
Capital Khartoum
Chief towns Port Sudan, Wad Medani, Omdurman
Population 40 218 000 (2008e)
Time zone GMT +3
Currency 1 Sudanese Dinar (SD) = 10 pounds
Language Arabic, English; a number of local languages and dialects are also spoken

Physical description

The largest country in Africa; largely desert, except where crossed by the middle reaches of the River Nile; the eastern edge is formed by the Nubian Highlands and an escarpment rising to over 2000m/6562ft on the Red Sea; the Imatong Mountains in the south rise to 3187m/10 456ft at Kinyeti, the country's highest point; the Darfur Massif is located in the west; the White Nile flows north to meet the Blue Nile at Khartoum.

Climate

Desert conditions in the north, with minimal annual rainfall of 160mm at Port Sudan, increasing in the tropical south to 1000mm; in the hottest months (July–August), the temperature rarely falls below 24°C in the north.

Government

Transitional; the 2005 constitution established an executive President, a Cabinet and a National Legislature consisting of the National Assembly and the Council of States; elections were to be held by 2008 but have yet to take place. The south has a largely autonomous government with a president who also serves as the national vice-president.

Economy

Very poor; oil production began in 1999 and oil and petroleum products are now major exports; agriculture, mostly at subsistence level, employs c.80% of the workforce and provides 32% of GDP; cultivatable area extended by irrigation schemes; chief cash crops are cotton, sesame, livestock, groundnuts, gum arabic, sugar cane; industries are oil refining, processing of cotton, edible oils and sugar, manufacturing (textiles, cement, soap, footwear, pharmaceuticals, armaments), vehicle assembly.

History

Sudan was Christianized in the 6c. Islam was introduced in the 7c, but only became widespread from the 13c. Egypt established control of northern Sudan in the early 19c but the Mahdi Revolt in the 1880s led to a combined British–Egyptian campaign to subdue the country, resulting in a jointly administered condominium under a British governor from 1899 until 1955. Sudan gained its independence in 1956. The post-independence period has been dominated by conflict arising from tensions between the Arab Muslim north and the African Christian and animist south. The first civil war (1955–72) resulted in greater autonomy for the south. The second civil war (1983–2004) ended with an agreement creating a largely autonomous administration (installed in 2005) and a power-sharing national government; under the agreement, a referendum on independence for the south will be held after six years. The civil wars caused political instability in the whole country, resulting in several coups, and Sudan was under military rule for most of the period from 1955 to 1996. An estimated 1.5 million died in the conflicts and famines caused by war and drought. There has been a separate conflict in the western region of Darfur since 2003, arising from intercommunal violence between Arab nomads and African farmers. The severe reprisals against African rebels by government-backed Arab militias, and government obstruction of aid agencies' relief work have left thousands dead and over two million people displaced. The government has failed to disarm the militias, and resisted until late 2006 international pressure to extend the limited mandate of African Union peacekeeping troops and allow their replacement by UN peacekeepers.

Religions

Ethnic groups

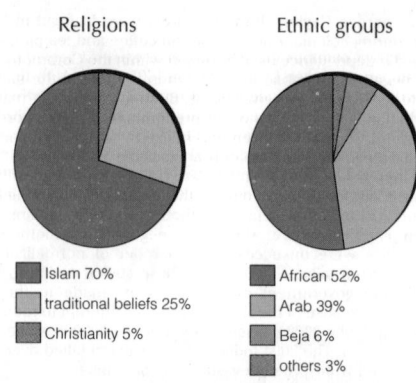

Religions:
- Islam 70%
- traditional beliefs 25%
- Christianity 5%

Ethnic groups:
- African 52%
- Arab 39%
- Beja 6%
- others 3%

SURINAME

Official name Republic of Suriname
Local name Suriname
Location A republic in north-eastern South America, bounded to the west by Guyana; to the south by Brazil; to the east by French Guiana; and to the north by the Atlantic Ocean
Area 163 265 sq km/63 020 sq mi
Capital Paramaribo
Chief towns Brokopondo, Nieuw Amsterdam
Population 476 000 (2008e)

Time zone GMT –3
Currency 1 Surinamese Dollar (SRD, $) =100 cents
Language Dutch; English, Sranang Tongo (Surinamese), Hindustani and Javanese are also spoken
Religions Christianity 48% (Prot 25%, RC 23%), Hinduism 27%, Islam 20%, traditional beliefs 5%
Ethnic groups Hindustani 37%, Creole 31%, Javanese 15%, black 10%, Amerindian 2%, Chinese 2%, others 3%

Physical description

Diverse natural regions, ranging from coastal lowland through savannah to mountainous upland; the coastal strip is mostly covered by swamp; the highland interior in the south is covered with dense tropical rainforest; the highest point is Julianatop (1230m/4035ft).

Climate

Tropical, moderated by trade winds; hot and humid, with two rainy seasons (March–July and December–January); Paramaribo temperatures range from 22°–33°C; the average monthly rainfall is 310mm in the north and 67mm in the south.

Government

Governed by an executive President, a Council of Ministers and a unicameral National Assembly.

Economy

Developing country, still in receipt of international aid; economy dominated by mining (bauxite, gold) and alumina production; other activities are oil extraction, forestry, fishing, agriculture (rice, bananas) and food processing.

History

Sighted by Columbus in 1498, Suriname was first settled by the Dutch in 1602 and the British in 1651. The British part was taken by the Dutch in 1667, captured by the British in 1799, and restored to the Netherlands in 1818. It became an independent republic in 1975, after which around 40% of the population emigrated to the Netherlands. There were military coups in 1980 and 1982. A guerrilla campaign for a return to democracy began in 1986 and civilian government was restored in 1988, but another coup was staged in 1990. Democracy was restored with elections in 1991 which brought to power the New Front for Democracy and Development coalition, led by Ronald Venetiaan, who served as president until 1996 and again from 2000. In 2004, the Surinamese dollar replaced the guilder as the official currency.

SWAZILAND

Official name Kingdom of Swaziland
Local name Swatini
Location A landlocked monarchy in south-east Africa, bounded to the north, west, south and south-east by South Africa, and to the north-east and east by Mozambique
Area 17 363 sq km/6702 sq mi
Capital Mbabane, Lobamba (royal and legislative capital)

Population 1 129 000 (2008e)
Time zone GMT +2
Currency 1 Lilangeni (plural Emalangeni) (Li, E) = 100 cents
Languages English, SiSwati
Religions Zionism 40%, RC 20%, Islam 10%, others (including Prot) 30%
Ethnic groups African 97%, European 3%

Physical description

A small country, with mountainous Highveld in the west; the highest point is Emblembe at 1862m/6109ft; the more populated Middleveld in the centre descends to 600–700m/1970–2300ft; the rolling, bush-covered Lowveld in the east is irrigated by river systems; the Lubombo runs along the east of the Lowveld.

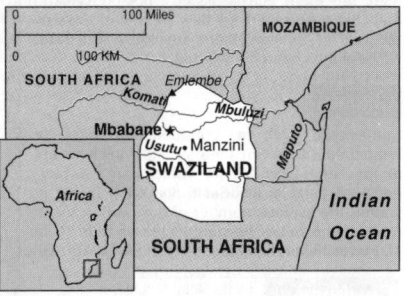

Climate

The Highveld is humid and near temperate, with an average annual rainfall of 1000–2280mm; the Middleveld and Lubombo are subtropical and drier; the Lowveld is tropical, with relatively little rain (500–890mm, susceptible to drought); the average annual temperature is 16°C in the west and 22°C in the east.

Government

A hereditary monarchy; governed by the King, a Prime Minister and Cabinet, and a bicameral Parliament comprising a Senate and a House of Assembly.

Economy

Poor, and dependent on customs union revenues and expatriates' remittances; agriculture, mostly at subsistence level, employs 70% of the workforce; chief cash crops are sugar cane, cotton, citrus fruits and pineapples; main activities are mining (coal, stone), wood pulp, processing agricultural products (sugar, soft drink concentrate), manufacturing (textiles, garments, consumer durables).

History

The Swazi people probably arrived in the area in the 16c. Boundaries with the Transvaal were decided in the 19c, and independence was guaranteed in 1881 and again in 1884, when the country became a South African protectorate. The British agreed to the Transvaal administration of Swaziland in 1894 but, after the Second Boer War, Swaziland, though retaining its monarchy, came under British rule as a British High Commission territory in 1903. It gained independence in 1968 under King Sobhuza II, who assumed absolute power in 1973. Mswati III acceded to the throne in 1986 and has faced increasingly strong demands for democratization, reinforced by demonstrations and strikes; a new constitution introduced in 2005 maintains the ban on political parties.

SWEDEN

Official name Kingdom of Sweden
Local name Sverige
Location A constitutional monarchy in northern Europe, occupying the eastern side of the Scandinavian Peninsula, bounded to the east by Finland, the Gulf of Bothnia and the Baltic Sea; to the south-west by the Skagerrak and Kattegat; and to the west and north-west by Norway
Area 411 479 sq km/158 830 sq mi
Capital Stockholm
Chief towns Gothenburg, Malmö, Uppsala, Norrköping, Västerås, Örebro, Linköping
Population 9 045 000 (2008e)
Time zone GMT +1
Currency 1 Swedish Krona (Skr) = 100 øre
Language Swedish; Sami and Finnish are spoken by minorities
Religions Lutheran Christianity 87%, other Christian and other faiths 13%
Ethnic groups Swedish 90%, Finnish and Lapp 3%, others 7%

Physical description

The terrain is mostly flat or undulating lowlands in the south and east, with mountains in the west; the Kjölen Mountains form much of the boundary with Norway; the highest peak is Kebnekaise (2111m/6926ft); there are many lakes (9% of land area), the chief being Vänern, Vättern and Mälaren; there are many coastal islands, notably Gotland and Öland; several rivers flow south-east towards the Gulf of Bothnia; there are many waterfalls; c.57% of the country is forested.

Climate

Continental, with a considerable range of temperature between summer and winter, except in the south-west, where winters are warmer; enclosed parts of the Baltic Sea often freeze in winter; the average number of days with a mean temperature below freezing increases from 71 in Malmö to 184 at Haparanda near the Arctic Circle.

Government

A hereditary constitutional monarchy with a King as head of state; governed by a Prime Minister and Cabinet, and a unicameral legislature (*Riksdag*).

Economy

Highly industrialized and diversified economy; industries such as forestry (wood products, pulp and paper), mining (iron ore, copper, uranium), steel-making and hydro-electric power generation supplemented in late 20c by engineering and high-technology manufacturing (specialized machinery and systems, motor vehicles, aircraft, electrical and electronic equipment, pharmaceuticals, plastics, chemicals) and telecommunications.

History

Formed from the union of the kingdoms of the Goths and Svears in the 7c, it did not include the southern parts of the peninsula (Skåne, Halland and Blekinge), which were part of Denmark, until these were conquered in 1658. Sweden established sovereignty over Finland in the 13c. With Norway, Sweden was brought under Danish rule in 1397, but it regained its independence after a rebellion in 1521 and the election to the throne of Gustav I Vasa. Sweden's power reached its height in the 17c but later waned; Finland was lost to Russia in 1809. Norway was ceded to Sweden in 1814, but the union was dissolved in 1905 when Norway became independent. Sweden has been a neutral country since 1814. It became a member of the EU in 1995, but in 2003 decided against replacing the krona with the euro.

SWITZERLAND

Official name Swiss Confederation
Local name Schweiz (German), Suisse (French),
Svizzera (Italian), Svizra (Romansch)
Location A landlocked republic, bounded to the
east by Liechtenstein and Austria; to the south
by Italy; to the west by France; and to the north
by Germany
Area 41 228 sq km/15 914 sq mi
Capital Berne
Chief towns Zurich, Lucerne, St Gallen, Lausanne,
Basle, Geneva

Population 7 581 000 (2008e)
Time zone GMT +1
Currency 1 Swiss Franc (SFr, SwF) = 100 centimes
= 100 rappen
Languages German, French, Italian and Romansch;
many of the Swiss speak more than one of these
languages
Religions Christianity 79% (RC 42%, Prot 35%,
other Christian 2%), Islam 4%, others 1%,
none/unaffiliated 16%

Physical description

The most mountainous country in Europe, with the Alps occupying about two-thirds of the country, in the south and east; the highest peak is Dufourspitze (4634m/15 203ft); the average height of the Pre-Alps in the north-west is 2000m/6562ft; the Jura Mountains run along the western border with France; the central plateau, at an average altitude of 580m/1903ft, is fringed by large lakes; major lakes include Constance, Zurich, Lucerne, Neuchâtel and Geneva; chief rivers are the Rhine, Rhône, Adige, Inn, and the tributaries of the Po; there are c.3000 sq km/1160 sq mi of glaciers, notably the Aletsch; densely forested.

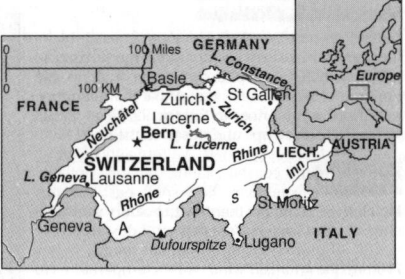

Climate

Temperate, varying greatly with relief and altitude; there are warm summers, with considerable rainfall; winter temperatures average 0°C; average annual rainfall in the central plateau is c.1000mm; average annual temperature is 7–9°C; the Föhn, a warm wind, is noticeable in the Alps during late winter and spring.

Government

Governed by a President (elected annually), who chairs the Federal Council, and a bicameral Federal Assembly comprising a Council of States and a National Council. Each of the 20 cantons and six half-cantons has its own government and considerable autonomy.

Economy

Highly industrialized and diversified economy with large service sector (banking, insurance, financial and corporate services, tourism); main industries are precision engineering, pharmaceuticals, chemicals, telecommunications, food processing and packaging, graphic machinery, electrical and mechanical engineering, metalworking.

Ethnic groups

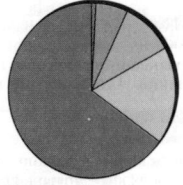

German 65%
French 18%
Italian 10%
Romansch 1%
others 6%

History

Part of the Holy Roman Empire in the 10c, the Swiss Confederation was created in 1291, when the cantons of Uri, Schwyz and Unterwalden formed a defensive league. The Confederation expanded during the 14c and was the centre of the Reformation in the 16c. Swiss independence and neutrality was recognized under the Treaty of Westphalia in 1648. The country was conquered by Napoleon I, who in 1798 instituted the Helvetian Republic. In 1815 it was organized as a confederation of 22 cantons, and in 1848 a federal constitution was adopted. Switzerland has been neutral for two centuries, including during both world wars, but joined the UN in 2002. Many policy decisions are made by national referenda.

SYRIA

Official name Syrian Arab Republic
Local name As-Sūriyya
Location A republic in the Middle East, bounded to the west by the Mediterranean Sea and Lebanon; to the south-west by Israel; to the south by Jordan; to the east by Iraq; and to the north by Turkey
Area 185 180 sq km/71 479 sq mi
Capital Damascus
Chief towns Halab (Aleppo), Homs, Hama, Latakia

Population 19 748 000 (2008e)
Time zone GMT +2
Currency 1 Syrian pound (LS, S$) = 100 piastres
Language Arabic; Kurdish, Armenian, Aramaic and Circassian are also spoken
Religions Islam 90% (Sunni 74%, others 16%), Christianity 10%
Ethnic groups Arab 90%, Kurds, Armenians and others 10%

Physical description

Behind a narrow Mediterranean coastal plain, the Jabal al Nusayriyah mountain range rises to c.1500m/4921ft; steep drop in the east to the Euphrates River valley; the Anti-Lebanon range in the south-west rises to 2814m/9232ft at Mount Hermon; open steppe and desert to the east.

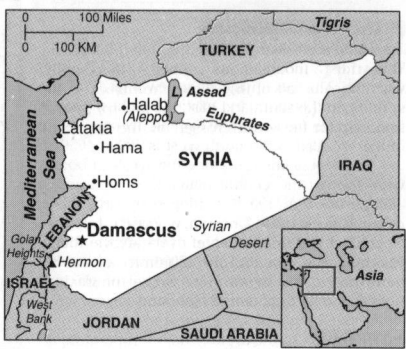

Climate

Mediterranean on the coast, with hot, dry summers and mild, wet winters; desert or semi-desert climate in 60% of country, with an annual rainfall below 200mm; the *khamsin* wind causes temperatures to rise to 43°–49°C; in Damascus the average annual rainfall is 225mm, and average temperatures range from 7°C in January to 27°C in July.

Government

Governed by an executive President, a Prime Minister and Council of Ministers, and a unicameral People's Assembly. The Ba'ath Party has dominated politics since 1963.

Economy

Moving slowly away from state control and state ownership of the economy; main industries are oil (55–60% of export earnings), gas, mining (phosphate), petroleum products, textiles, garments, food processing, beverages, tobacco; agricultural sector produces cotton, fruit, vegetables, wheat, meat, livestock.

History

The country was part of the Phoenician, Persian, Roman and Byzantine empires. It was conquered by Muslim Arabs in the 7c, when Damascus became the capital of the Umayyad Dynasty, and was subsequently ruled by foreign dynasties including the Egyptian Fatimids and Mamluks, before being conquered by Turks in the 11c. The scene of many battles during the Crusades in the Middle Ages, it was part of the Ottoman Empire in 1517 and enjoyed a brief period of independence in 1920, before being made a French mandate. Syria gained its independence in 1946. It merged with Egypt and Yemen to form the United Arab Republic in 1958, but re-established itself as an independent state under its present name in 1961. Syria was involved in the Arab–Israeli wars in 1948, 1967 and 1973, losing the Golan Heights region to Israel in 1967. Syrian intervention in Lebanon began in 1976, when Syrian troops were sent to restore order during the civil war; its military presence influenced politics there after the civil war ended until the troops were withdrawn in 2005. Many Western states accuse Syria of continuing to support militants in Lebanon and Iraq. President Hafez al-Asad seized power in a coup in 1970, formally taking office in 1971. On his death in 2000, he was succeeded by his son, Bashar. Bashar al-Asad introduced some openness into political life but the results alarmed the establishment and restrictions have been reimposed.

TAIWAN

Official name Republic of China
Local name T'aiwan
Location An island republic consisting of Taiwan Island and several smaller islands, lying c.130km/80mi off the south-east coast of China
Area 36 000 sq km/13 896 sq mi
Capital Taipei
Chief towns Chilung, Kaohsiung, Taichung
Population 22 921 000 (2008e)

Time zone GMT +8
Currency 1 New Taiwan Dollar (NT$) = 100 cents
Language Chinese (Mandarin); Taiwanese and Hakka are also spoken
Religions Buddhism 35%/Taoism 33%, Christianity 4%, Islam and others 3% (many also believe in traditional Chinese religions)
Ethnic groups Taiwanese Chinese (including Hakka) 84%, mainland Chinese 14%, Ainu 2%

Physical description

The island is c.395km/245mi long, 100–145km/60–90mi wide; a mountain range runs north to south, covering over half of the island; the highest peak is Yu Shan (3997m/13 113ft); the low-lying land is mainly on the west; crossed by the Tropic of Cancer.

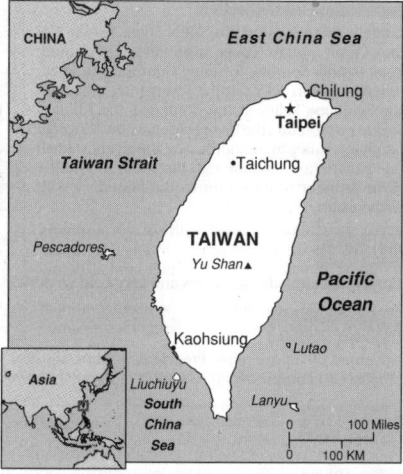

Climate

Subtropical, except in far south, where it is tropical; affected by the monsoon (May–November); high rainfall, averaging over 2000mm a year in the lowlands and much more in the mountains; especially heavy rain in the typhoon season (July–September); summers are hot and humid; mild and short winters; the average daily temperature at Taipei is 12°–19°C in January, and 24°–33°C in July–August; the monthly rainfall is 71mm in December and 290mm in June.

Government

Governed by a President, a Premier and Executive Yuan, and a unicameral Legislative Yuan. The National Assembly, a largely ad hoc ceremonial body, was disbanded in 2005.

Economy

Highly industrialized and diverse market economy; main industries are high-technology manufacturing (electronics, computer products), oil refining, chemicals, textiles, iron and steel, machinery, cement and food processing.

History

Taiwan was discovered by the Portuguese in 1590 and conquered by the Chinese in the 17c. Ceded to Japan in 1895, it was returned to China in 1945. The Nationalist government (the Guomindang) withdrew to Taiwan after being defeated by the communists in mainland China in 1949. Emergency measures adopted in 1949 froze political life on the island until the late 1980s, when demands grew for democratization of the authoritarian one-party state; martial law was lifted in 1987; Taiwan ended its state of war with China in 1991, officially recognizing the communist People's Republic of China for the first time; and the first multiparty elections were held in 1992. Since then, power has shifted from the mainlanders to the native Taiwanese, and 50 years of Guomindang rule ended when the Democratic Progressive Party won the presidency in 2000 and the 2001 legislative election, although the Guomindang regained both the presidency and a legislative majority in 2008. China regards Taiwan as a province of the People's Republic and has sanctioned the use of force to prevent Taiwan declaring itself independent.

TAJIKISTAN

Official name Republic of Tajikistan
Local name Toçikiston
Location A landlocked republic in south-eastern Central Asia, bounded to the west and north by Uzbekistan; to the north by Kyrgyzstan; to the east by China; and to the south by Afghanistan
Area 143 100 sq km/55 200 sq mi
Capital Dushanbe

Chief towns Khudzand, Kulyab, Kurgan-Tyube
Population 7 212 000 (2008e)
Time zone GMT +5
Currency 1 Somoni (S) = 100 dirams
Languages Tajik; Russian is widely used
Religions Islam 90% (Sunni 85%, Shia 5%), others 10%
Ethnic groups Tajik 80%, Uzbek 15%, Russian 1%, Kyrgyz 1%, others 3%

Physical description

Largely mountainous; the Tien Shan, Gissar-Alai and Pamir ranges cover over 90% of the area; Peak Ismoili Somoni, formerly Communism Peak, reaches 7495m/24 590ft; the lower-lying areas are the Ferghana Valley in the north and the Khatlon region in the south; the River Syrdarya flows through Ferghana Valley in the north, and the rivers Vakhsh and Kolamihon flow through the south to join the River Amudarya, which forms the boundary with Afghanistan.

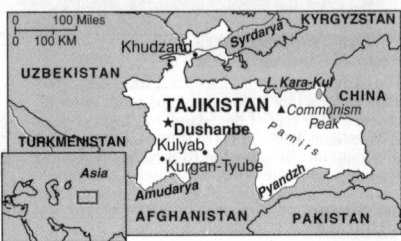

Climate

Continental; hot, dry summers and very cold winters.

Government

Governed by an executive President, a Prime Minister and Council of Ministers, and a bicameral legislature (*Majlisi Oli*) comprising an Assembly of Representatives and a National Assembly.

Economy

Poor, with a fragile economy; dependent on expatriates' remittances and international aid; large agricultural sector employs 67% of workforce, producing cotton, fruit and livestock as cash crops; main industries are aluminium production, hydro-electric power generation, mining (zinc, lead), food processing (vegetable oil), textiles, fertilizers, cement, machine tools, domestic appliances.

History

Inhabited by Tajiks, who originated in Iran, it was conquered by Arabs in the 7c and 8c, then by the Mongol Empire in the 13c, remaining under the control of various khanates until the 19c. In 1868 the north was subsumed into the Russian Empire, which the south was annexed by the Emirate of Bukhara. At the time of the Russian Revolution in 1917, the central Asian emirates attempted to assert their independence but Bolshevik control was established in northern Tajikistan in 1918 and in the Bukhara emirate in 1920. Tajikistan was given full republic status within the USSR in 1929. It became independent in 1991, and joined the CIS (Commonwealth of Independent States). In 1992 anti-government demonstrations escalated into civil war between pro-government forces and Muslim and pro-democracy groups. A peace treaty signed in 1997 was implemented by 2000, although assassinations and bombings targeting government ministers and buildings have continued. Former communists have dominated the presidency and governments since 1991. The regime is authoritarian, stifling dissent, and recent elections have been deemed neither free nor fair.

TANZANIA

Official name United Republic of Tanzania
Local name Tanzania
Location An East African republic, consisting of the mainland region of Tanganyika, and Zanzibar, just off the coast in the Indian Ocean, which includes Zanzibar Island, Pemba Island and some small islets
Area 945 087 sq km/364 898 sq mi
Capital Dodoma
Chief towns Dar es Salaam, Zanzibar, Mwanza, Tanga, Arusha
Population 40 213 000 (2008e)

Time zone GMT +3
Currency 1 Tanzanian Shilling (TSh) = 100 cents
Languages Kiswahili, English; Arabic is also spoken in Zanzibar, and there are many local languages
Religions Tanganyika: Islam 35%, traditional beliefs 35%, Christianity 30%; Zanzibar: Islam 99%, others 1%
Ethnic groups Tanganyika: Bantu 95% (includes over 120 tribes, none more than 10% of population), other African 4%, Asian, European, Arab and others 1%; Zanzibar: Arab, African, mixed

Physical description

The largest East African country, just south of the Equator; the coast is fringed by long sandy beaches protected by coral reefs; the coastal plain rises towards a central plateau with an average elevation of 1000m/3280ft; high grasslands and mountain ranges lie to the centre and south; the Rift Valley branches around Lake Victoria in the north, where there are several high volcanic peaks, notably Mount Kilimanjaro (5895m/19 340ft); the extensive Serengeti plain lies to the west; the eastern branch of the Rift Valley runs through central Tanzania from north to east of Lake Victoria, containing several lakes; the western branch runs south down the west side of Lake Victoria, and includes Lake Tanganyika and Lake Rukwa.

Climate

Tropical, modified by altitude; hot and humid on the coast and offshore islands; the average temperatures are c.23°C in June–September and 27°C in December–March; average annual rainfall is over 1100mm; hot and dry on the central plateau, with an average annual rainfall of 250mm; semi-temperate at altitudes above 1500m; permanent snow on high peaks.

Government

Governed by an executive President, a Prime Minister and Cabinet and a unicameral National Assembly. Zanzibar is semi-autonomous, with its own president and legislature.

Economy

Very poor, and dependent on international aid; agriculture contributes 42% of GDP and employs c.80% of the workforce; main cash crops are coffee, cashew nuts, cotton, tea, sugar cane, beer, tobacco and, on Zanzibar, cloves and coconuts; main industries are tourism, mining (gold, diamonds, iron) and manufacturing (processing agricultural products, cement, petroleum products, footwear, garments, wood products, fertilizer).

History

Inhabited by Caucasoid peoples and then in the 5c by Bantus from western Africa, the area had early links with Arab, Indian and Persian traders. The Swahili culture developed in the 10–15c, and Portuguese explorers arrived in the 15c. The island of Zanzibar was the capital of the Omani empire in the 1840s. Penetration of the interior by German missionaries and British explorers took place in the mid-19c, and Zanzibar became a British protectorate in 1890. German East Africa was established on the mainland in 1891 and by 1907 Germany controlled the whole country. After World War I, Tanganyika (mainland Tanzania) became a mandated territory under British administration (1919) and in 1961 it gained independence; it became a republic in 1962. Zanzibar was granted independence as a constitutional monarchy, with the Sultan as head of state; the Sultan was overthrown in 1964, and Zanzibar united with Tanganyika to form the United Republic of Tanzania. The country was a one-party state under the Revolutionary Party of Tanzania (CCM) from 1977 to 1992, when a multiparty system was approved. The first multiparty elections were held in 1995 and were won by the CCM, which continues to dominate politics.

THAILAND

Nations of the World

Official name Kingdom of Thailand
Local name Prathet Thai
Location A kingdom in South-East Asia, bounded
to the west by the Andaman Sea; to the west
and north-west by Myanmar (Burma); to the
north-east and east by Laos; to the south-east
by Cambodia; and to the south by the Gulf of
Thailand and Malaysia
Area 513 115 sq km/198 062 sq mi

Capital Bangkok
Chief towns Chiang Mai, Nakhon Ratchasima
Population 65 493 000 (2008e)
Time zone GMT +7
Currency 1 Baht (B) = 100 satang
Language Thai
Religions Buddhism 95%, Islam 4%, others 1%
Ethnic groups Thai 75%, Chinese 14%, others 11%

Physical description

The centre is dominated by the fertile flood plain
of the Chao Phraya River; a north-eastern plateau
rises above 300m/984ft and covers one-third of
the country; mountainous northern region rises
to 2595m/8514ft at Doi Inthanon; the narrow,
low-lying southern Kra Isthmus with a spine of
mountains separates the Andaman Sea from
the Gulf of Thailand and is covered in tropical
rainforest; mangrove-forested islands off the coast.

Climate

Equatorial climate in the south; tropical monsoon
climate in the north and centre; rainfall mostly
during south-west monsoon (May–October) except
in Kra Isthmus, which is wetter during the north-
east monsoon (November–April), when the rest of
the country has less rainfall.

Government

A hereditary constitutional monarchy with a
King as head of state; governed by a Prime
Minister and Cabinet, and a bicameral National
Assembly consisting of a Senate and a House of
Representatives.

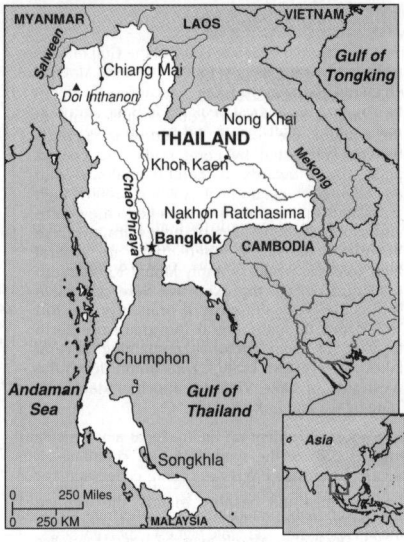

Economy

Developing economy; main industry is tourism; agriculture employs nearly half the workforce and produces
rice, cassava, rubber, maize, sugar cane, coconuts, soya beans, livestock; other activities include fishing,
mining (tin, tungsten), processing agricultural products, manufacturing (textiles, garments, computers and
parts, furniture, plastics, vehicles and parts, electronics, jewellery, electrical appliances).

History

There is evidence that Thailand had Bronze Age communities in c.4000 BC. By the 7c Buddhism had spread
to the country from India; Thailand's successful nationalist and reform movements have often had Buddhist
leaders, and the work of the monastic order or *sangha* remains highly regarded in social terms. The Thai
nation was founded in the 13c, and is the only country in south and south-east Asia to have escaped
colonization by a European power. It was occupied by the Japanese during World War II, and had military or
military-controlled governments for most of the time from 1945 until mass demonstrations in 1992 resulted in
a return to civilian government and a reduction in the power of the military. After months of political turmoil,
the military staged a coup in 2006 and established an interim government to rule until elections in 2007.
The government formed after the elections saw many changes in its first year in office as various ministers
(including the first two prime ministers) were obliged to stand down or were banned from political life by the
constitutional court, which also ordered the dissolution of a number of political parties; most had been found
guilty of electoral fraud or other irregularities. Thailand was struck by the 2004 Indian Ocean tsunami, which
killed thousands of people and caused widespread devastation.

TOGO

Official name Togolese Republic
Local name Togo
Location A republic in West Africa, bounded to the west by Ghana; to the north by Burkina Faso; to the east by Benin; and to the south by the Gulf of Guinea
Area 56 600 sq km/21 848 sq mi
Capital Lomé
Chief towns Sokodé, Kpalimé, Atakpamé

Population 5 859 000 (2008e)
Time zone GMT
Currency 1 CFA Franc (CFAFr) = 100 centimes
Language French; Ewe, Mina, Kabye and Dagomba are the main local languages
Religions traditional beliefs 51%, Christianity 29%, Islam 20%
Ethnic groups African 99% (mainly Ewe, Mina and Kabye), others 1%

Physical description

Togo rises from the lagoon coast of the Gulf of Guinea, through low-lying plains to the Atakora Mountains, which run north-east to south-west across the centre of the country; the highest peak is Pic Baumann (Mount Agou; 986m/3235ft); semi-arid savannah lies north of the mountains.

Climate

Tropical; one rainy season in the north (May–September) and two on the coast (April–June, October); the average annual rainfall at Lomé on the coast is 875mm.

Government

Governed by a President, a Prime Minister and Council of Ministers, and a unicameral National Assembly.

Economy

Very poor, dependent on international aid; agriculture, employs 65% of the workforce and contributes 40% of GDP; chief cash crops are cotton, coffee and cocoa; industries are phosphate mining, processing agricultural products and light manufacturing; regional trans-shipment and re-exports now generate highest export earnings.

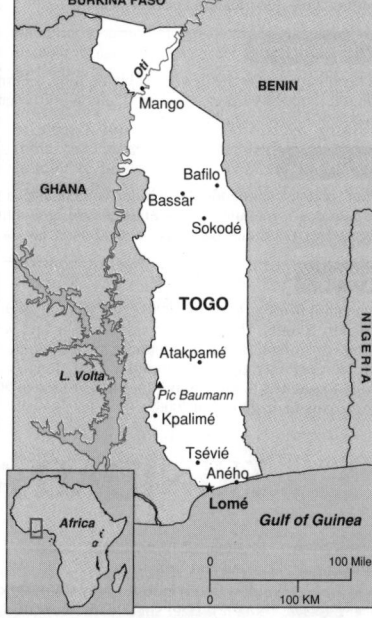

History

Formerly part of the Kingdom of Togoland, it was a German protectorate from 1884 to 1914. After World War I, it was divided between France (French Togo) and Britain (part of British Gold Coast) by mandate of the League of Nations (1922). In 1946 the British and French governments placed their territories under UN trusteeships. British Togoland integrated with Ghana when it became independent in 1957. French Togo gained its independence as Togo in 1960. There were military coups in Togo in 1963 and 1967, the latter bringing General Gnassingbé Eyadéma to power. In 1979 a new constitution was adopted making the country a one-party state. Eyadéma was forced by violent demonstrations to legalize other political parties in 1992, but he and his party won the first multiparty elections in 1993 and all subsequent elections, maintaining their brutal suppression of opposition, particularly at the time of the 1998 elections. When Eyadéma died in 2005, his son Faure Gnassingbé was elected president. Reconciliation talks in 2006 agreed to the participation of opposition parties in a government of national unity pending credible elections. The elections were won by the ruling party.

TONGA

Official name Kingdom of Tonga
Local name Tonga; also sometimes known as the Friendly Islands
Location An independent monarchy of 176 islands in the south-west Pacific Ocean
Area 748 sq km/289 sq mi
Capital Nuku'alofa, on Tongatapu

Population 119 000 (2008e)
Time zone GMT +13
Currency 1 Pa'anga/Tongan Dollar (T$) = 100 seniti
Languages Tongan, English
Religions Christianity 79% (Prot 63%, RC 16%), others 21%
Ethnic groups Tongan 98%, others 2%

Nations of the World

Physical description

Tonga consists of c.169 islands, 36 of which are inhabited, divided into three main groups (coral formations of Ha'apai and Tongatapu-Eua, and mountainous Vava'u); the largest island is Tongatapu, with two-thirds of the population and an area of 260 sq km/100 sq mi; the western islands are mainly volcanic and some are still active; they rise to a height of 500–1000m/1640–3280ft; the highest point is the extinct volcano on Kao Island (1046m/3432ft).

Climate

Semi-tropical; the average annual temperature at Tongatapu is 23°C and the average annual rainfall is 1750mm; occasional cyclones (November–April), earthquakes and offshore volcanic activity.

Government

A hereditary monarchy; governed by the King, a Prime Minister and Privy Council (cabinet), and a unicameral Legislative Assembly (*Fale Alea*).

Economy

Poor country, dependent on international aid and expatriates' remittances; main activities are agriculture (squashes, coconuts, bananas, vanilla beans, cocoa, coffee, ginger, black pepper), fishing and tourism.

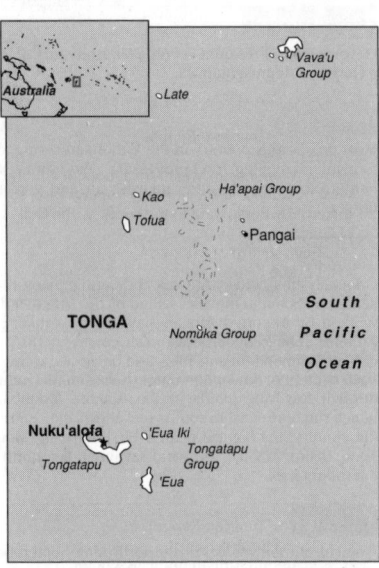

History

Inhabited from as early as 1000 BC, the islands were visited by Captain James Cook in 1773 and named the Friendly Islands. They received missionaries and were established as a nation under King George Tupou I. Tonga became a British protectorate in 1899, under its own monarchy, and gained independence in 1970. A pro-democracy movement started in 1992, Tonga's first political party was formed in 1994, and elected MPs were appointed to the cabinet for the first time in 2005. Further reform was promised after demonstrations, some violent, in 2005 and 2006.

TRINIDAD AND TOBAGO

Official name Republic of Trinidad and Tobago
Local name Trinidad and Tobago
Location A republic comprising the southernmost islands of the Lesser Antilles chain in the south-east Caribbean Sea, just north of the South American mainland
Area 5128 sq km/1979 sq mi
Capital Port of Spain
Chief towns San Fernando, Arima, Scarborough
Population 1 047 000 (2008e)

Time zone GMT –4
Currency 1 Trinidad and Tobago Dollar (TT$) = 100 cents
Language English
Religions Christianity 58% (RC 26%, Prot 22%, other Christian 10%), Hinduism 22%, Islam 6%, others 11%, none/unaffiliated 3%
Ethnic groups East Indian 40%, black 37%, mixed 20%, others 3%

Physical description

The island of Trinidad is roughly rectangular in shape; separated from Venezuela to the south by the 11km/7mi Gulf of Paria; crossed by three mountain ranges; the highest point is El Cerro del Aripo (940m/3084ft); the remainder of the land is low-lying, with large coastal mangrove swamps; Pitch Lake in the south-west is the world's largest reservoir of natural asphalt; Tobago lies 30km/19mi north-east; the Main Ridge extends along most of the island, rising to 576m/1890ft.

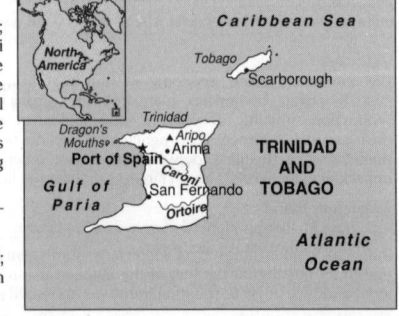

Climate

Tropical, with an annual average temperature of 29°C; the average rainfall is 1270mm in the west, 3048mm in the north-east.

Government

Governed by a President, a Prime Minister and Cabinet, and a bicameral Parliament, comprising a Senate and a House of Representatives.

Economy

Most prosperous country in the Caribbean owing to oil and natural gas production; other activities include tourism, oil refining, food processing, petroleum products, chemicals (ammonia, methanol), steel products, cement, beverages, cotton textiles, car and appliance assembly, agriculture (cocoa, coffee, citrus fruits, flowers).

History

Originally inhabited by Arawak and Carib Indians, the islands were visited by Columbus in 1498. Trinidad was settled by Spain in the 16c, raided by the Dutch and French in the 17c, when tobacco and sugar plantations worked by imported African slaves were established, and ceded to Britain in 1802 under the Treaty of Amiens. Tobago became a British colony in 1814. The two islands became a joint British colony in 1899, gained independence in 1962, and became a republic in 1976. The republic has been politically stable since independence, power alternating between the two main political parties.

TUNISIA

Official name Tunisian Republic
Local name Tūnisiya
Location A north African republic, bounded to the west by Algeria; to the south-east by Libya; and to the north-east and north by the Mediterranean Sea
Area 164 150 sq km/63 362 sq mi
Capital Tunis
Chief towns Bizerta, Sousse, Sfax, Gabes

Population 10 384 000 (2008e)
Time zone GMT +1
Currency 1 Tunisian Dinar (TD, D) = 1000 millimes
Language Arabic; French is also spoken
Religions Islam 98%, Christianity 1%, Judaism and others 1%
Ethnic groups Arab and Berber 98%, European 1%, Jewish and others 1%

Physical description

The Atlas Mountains in the north-west rise to 1544m/5066ft at Jebel Chambi; the central depression runs west to east, containing several salty lakes; dry, sandy upland lies to the south.

Climate

Mediterranean climate on the coast, with hot, dry summers and wet winters; the daily maximum temperature is 14°–33°C; the average annual rainfall is 420mm at Tunis and over twice this level in the Atlas Mountains; further south, rainfall decreases and temperatures can be extreme.

Government

Governed by an executive President, a Prime Minister and Council of Ministers, and a bicameral Parliament comprising a Chamber of Deputies and a Chamber of Councillors.

Economy

Diverse industrialized economy in transition from state to private ownership; main industries are oil production, mining (especially phosphate, iron ore), tourism, processing agricultural products, manufacturing (textiles, footwear, beverages, mechanical goods, chemicals); agriculture is of declining importance; the world's fourth largest producer of olive oil.

History

Ruled at various times by Phoenicians, Carthaginians, Romans, Byzantines, Arabs, Spanish and Turks due to its situation at the hub of the Mediterranean, it became a French protectorate in 1883 and gained independence in 1956. The monarchy was abolished in 1957 and the country became a republic under one-party rule with Habib Bourguiba as president. The government's refusal to meet demands for the legalization of other political parties led to serious unrest in the 1970s, and a multiparty system was introduced in 1981, although the ruling party has retained its grip on power, tolerating little dissent. Bourguiba was deposed in 1987 by Zine el-Abidine Ben Ali, who remains president.

TURKEY

Official name Republic of Turkey
Local name Türkiye
Location A republic lying partly in Europe and partly in Asia. The European area (Thrace) is bounded to the west by the Aegean Sea and Greece, and to the north by Bulgaria and the Black Sea; the Asian area (Anatolia) is bounded to the east by Georgia, Armenia, Azerbaijan and Iran, and to the south by Iraq, Syria and the Mediterranean Sea

Area 779 452 sq km/300 868 sq mi
Capital Ankara
Chief towns Istanbul, Izmir, Adana, Bursa, Gaziantep
Population 71 893 000 (2008e)
Time zone GMT +2
Currency 1 New Turkish Lira (TRY) = 100 kurus
Language Turkish
Religions Islam 99% (mostly Sunni), others 1%
Ethnic groups Turkish 80%, Kurdish 16%, others 4%

Physical description

A mountainous country with ranges extending along the north and south coasts of Anatolia; average altitude of the high central plateau is 1000–2000m/3281–6562ft; the Taurus Mountains cover the entire southern part of Anatolia; east Anatolia is the highest region, and the highest peak is Mount Ararat (5165m/16945ft); the alluvial coastal plains are 2030km/1219mi wide; chief rivers include the Kizil Irmak, Sakarya and Seyhan; the Tigris and the Euphrates rivers have their origins in Turkey; the Turkish Straits (the Dardanelles, Sea of Marmara and Bosporus), which connect the Black Sea and the Mediterranean Sea, separate the European and Asian parts of Turkey.

Climate

Mediterranean climate on the Aegean and Mediterranean coasts, with hot, dry summers and warm, wet winters; on the Black Sea coast, rainfall becomes heavy in summer and autumn; rainfall is low on the interior plateau, with cold winters, hot summers and occasional thunderstorms; susceptible to severe earthquakes, especially in northern Anatolia.

Government

Governed by a President, a Prime Minister and Cabinet, and a unicameral Grand National Assembly.

Economy

Developing, industrialized economy, although many emigrant workers; main industries are textiles and clothing manufacture, vehicle assembly, iron and steel, electrical machinery, food processing, mining (coal, iron ore, chromium, copper, boron), steel-making, metal manufactures, forestry, paper, tourism; trans-shipment point for oil and gas from Central Asian countries; agriculture employs 36% of the workforce; the chief crops are tobacco, cotton, cereals, olives, sugar beets, citrus and other fruits, mohair, wool, hides.

History

Modern Turkey developed out of the Ottoman Empire and includes the area known as Asia Minor. It was formerly part of the empire of Alexander I, and of the Byzantine Empire. In the 13c the Seljuk Sultanate was replaced by the Ottoman Sultanate in north-west Asia Minor. The Turkish invasion of Europe began with the Balkans in 1375, and in 1453 Constantinople fell to the Turks. The empire was at its peak in the 16c, but in the 17c began a slow decline, losing most of its European territory in the 19c and early 20c. During World War I, Turkey allied with Germany and after the defeat its remaining territory was partitioned. Following a revolution, the sultanate was abolished and the Republic of Turkey was proclaimed in 1923, led by Kemal Atatürk, who introduced policies of westernization, economic development and secularism. Turkey was neutral throughout most of World War II, before siding with the Allies in 1945. It joined NATO in 1952. There were military coups in 1960, 1971, 1980 and 1997, and the military's political influence remains considerable, although measures to reduce this have been introduced to satisfy EU requirements since Turkey became a candidate for membership in 1999. Relations with Greece have been strained since 1974, when Turkey invaded northern Cyprus in support of Turkish Cypriots and subsequently recognized the regime established there. Since the 1980s the south-east of Anatolia has suffered fierce fighting between government forces and

Kurdish separatists, especially the PKK (Kurdish Workers' Party), who want to establish an independent state for Turkey's 12 million Kurds. The policy of secularism, enshrined in the constitution, has been a source of political tension in recent years as support for Islamist parties has grown.

Nations of the World

TURKMENISTAN

Official name Turkmenistan
Local name Turkmenostan
Location A republic in south-west Central Asia, bounded to the north by Kazakhstan and Uzbekistan; to the south by Iran and Afghanistan; and to the west by the Caspian Sea
Area 488 100 sq km/188 400 sq mi
Capital Ashgabat
Chief towns Chardzhou, Mary, Türkmenbashi,

Nebit-Dag
Population 5 179 000 (2008e)
Time zone GMT +5
Currency 1 Manat (TMM) = 100 tenesi
Languages Turkmen, Russian, Uzbek
Religions Islam 89% (mostly Sunni), Christianity 9% (Orthodox), others 2%
Ethnic groups Turkmen 85%, Uzbek 5%, Russian 4%, others 6%

Physical description

Principally composed of the Kara Kum desert (c.80%), with hills and mountains in the south; the highest point is Ayrybaba (3139m/10 298ft); some areas below sea level by the Caspian Sea; the chief river is the Amudarya.

Climate

Continental; hot and arid in the desert areas.

Government

Governed by an executive President, a Council of Ministers and a unicameral Parliament.

Economy

State-controlled and inefficient; hydrocarbon exports restricted by lack of pipelines, now under construction; agriculture employs 48% of workforce; chief crops are cotton, cereals and livestock; main industries are oil and gas production, oil refining, petrochemicals, processing agricultural products and textiles.

History

The area was invaded and occupied by many empires, including the Persian, Greek (under Alexander the Great), Parthian and Mongol. In the 19c it was incorporated into the Russian Empire. A brief period of autonomy ended in 1921, when it became part of the USSR. In 1991 it gained its independence and became a member of the CIS (Commonwealth of Independent States). Saparmurad Niyazov became leader of the Turkmen Communist Party in 1985 and was elected president in 1990. He remained in power until his death in 2006, his autocratic regime preventing the development of political pluralism or press freedom and promoting a personality cult. Kurbanguly Berdymukhamedov was elected president in 2007, and has introduced some economic and social welfare reforms.

■ **Turks and Caicos Islands▶United Kingdom**

TUVALU

Official name Tuvalu
Local name Tuvalu
Location An independent island group in the south-west Pacific, 1050km/650mi north of Fiji
Area 26 sq km/10 sq mi
Capital Funafuti (in Vaiaku village on Fongafale islet)

Population 12 200 (2008e)
Time zone GMT +12
Currency 1 Australian Dollar (A$) = 100 cents
Languages Tuvaluan, English
Religions Christianity 97%, Baha'i 1%, others 2%
Ethnic groups Polynesian 96%, others 4%

Physical description

Comprises nine low-lying coral atolls, running north-west to south-east in a chain 580km/360mi long.

Nations of the World

Climate

Tropical; the average annual temperature is 30°C and the average annual rainfall is 3535mm.

Government

Governed by a Governor-General (representing the British monarch, who is head of state), a Prime Minister and Cabinet, and a unicameral Parliament.

Economy

Undeveloped, with few resources; revenues from government investments, expatriates' remittances, sale of fishing licences, postage stamps and coins, leasing its international telephone code and internet suffix, fishing and subsistence agriculture; only cash crop is coconuts (copra); small-scale tourism.

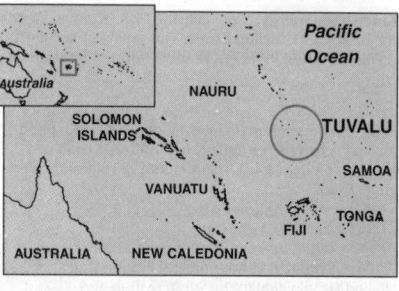

History

Settled by Polynesians in the 16c, the islands became a British protectorate as the Ellice Islands in 1877, were part of the British Protectorate of the Gilbert and Ellice Islands from 1892, and were annexed as the Gilbert and Ellice Islands Colony in 1916. Following a 1974 referendum the colonies were separated, and the Ellice Islands gained independence as Tuvalu in 1978. Tuvalu is threatened by rising sea levels, which have already damaged its agriculture. In 2002, with Kiribati and the Maldives, it began legal action against the USA over its refusal to sign the Kyoto Protocol.

UGANDA

Official name Republic of Uganda
Local name Uganda
Location A landlocked East African republic, bounded to the south by Rwanda, Tanzania and Lake Victoria; to the east by Kenya; to the north by Sudan; and to the west by the Democratic Republic of the Congo
Area 238461 sq km/92069 sq mi
Capital Kampala
Chief towns Jinja, Mbale, Tororo, Soroti, Entebbe
Population 31368000 (2008e)

Time zone GMT +3
Currency 1 Uganda Shilling (USh) = 100 cents
Language English; Ganda/Luganda, Swahili and other local languages are also spoken
Religions Christianity 84% (Prot 42%, RC 42%), Islam 12%, others 3%, none 1%
Ethnic groups Baganda 17%, Banyankole 9%, Basoga 8%, Bakiga 7%, Iteso 6%, Langi 6%, Bagisu 5%, Acholi 5%, Lugbara 4%, Bunyoro 3%, others 29%

Physical description

Mainly on a plateau with an elevation of 900–1000m/2953–3281ft; dry savannah or semi-desert north of Lake Kyoga; the population is concentrated in the fertile Lake Victoria basin; the Western Rift Valley runs along Uganda's frontier with the Democratic Republic of Congo; straddling the frontier is the Mount Stanley massif, including Margherita Peak (5110m/16765ft), the highest point in Uganda; c.20% of the country is lakes, rivers and wetlands; contains half of lakes Victoria, Edward and Albert as well as lakes Kwania, Kyoga, George and Bisina (formerly Lake Salisbury); the two main rivers are the upper reaches of the River Nile (the Victoria Nile and the Albert Nile).

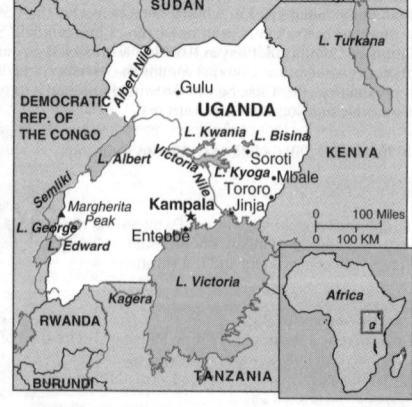

Climate

Tropical; the highest rainfall is in the mountains to the west and south-west and along the shores of Lake Victoria, exceeding 1500mm a year; daily temperatures at Entebbe on the north shore of the lake are 24°–28°C; central and north-eastern areas treceive less than 1000mm of rain annually.

Government

Governed by a President, a Prime Minister and Cabinet, and a unicameral Parliament.

Economy

Poor, and dependent on international aid; agriculture and fishing support c.80% of the population and provide the main exports of coffee, fish and fish products, tea, cotton, tobacco and fresh flowers; other activities include mining (gold), manufacturing (cotton textiles, cement), steel production and hydro-electric power generation.

History

Bantu-speaking peoples migrated into south-west Uganda c.500 BC, and by the 14c were organized into several kingdoms. Uganda was discovered by Arab traders and British explorers in the 19c and granted to the Imperial British East Africa Company in 1888. The Kingdom of Buganda became a British protectorate in 1893, and other territory was included by 1903. Uganda gained its independence in 1962 as a federation of the kingdoms of Ankole, Buganda, Bunyoro, Busoga and Toro. It became a federal republic in 1963 but the federal status was dropped in 1966 after a coup by the Prime Minister, Dr Milton Obote, who became President. He was deposed in a 1971 military coup led by General Idi Amin Dada, whose repressive regime was overthrown in 1979. Obote returned to power but failed to restore stability and another military coup took place in 1985 in the midst of a civil war with rebels led by Yoweri Museveni. The rebels took control of the country in 1986 and Museveni became President, beginning a process of reconstruction that has resulted in relative peace and stability for the past 20 years. Museveni and his National Resistance Movement have retained power in subsequent elections. The ban on political parties was lifted in 1995 and they were allowed to contest elections for the first time in 2006. The Lord's Resistance Army (LRA) has conducted an insurgency in the north from the late 1980s, massacring or mutilating thousands, abducting over 20 000 children to serve in its forces and displacing over 1.6 million people; peace talks began in 2006, and a permanent ceasefire was signed in 2008.

UKRAINE

Official name Ukraine
Local name Ukraïna
Location A republic in eastern Europe, bounded to the south-west by Moldova and Romania; to the west by Hungary, Slovakia and Poland; to the north by Belarus; to the east by Russia; and to the south by the Black Sea
Area 603 700 sq km/233 028 sq mi
Capital Kiev
Chief towns Kharkov, Donetsk, Odessa, Dnepropetrovsk, Lvov, Zaporozhye, Krivoy Rog
Population 45 994 000 (2008e)
Time zone GMT +2
Currency 1 Hryvnia = 100 kopiykas
Languages Ukrainian, Russian
Religions Christianity 96% (Orthodox 92%, Prot/RC 4%), others 4%
Ethnic groups Ukrainian 78%, Russian 17%, others (including Tatar) 5%

Physical description

Most of the country lies in a plain, rising to plateaux in the west, south and south-east; the Ukrainian Carpathian Mountains in the west rise to 2061m/6762ft at Hora Hoverla; the Crimean Peninsula separates the Black Sea from the Sea of Azov; the Crimean Mountains lie along the south coast of the peninsula; chief rivers are the Dnieper, Dniester, Severskiy Donets and Prut; there are many reservoirs and lakes.

Climate

Temperate continental, with cold winters and warm summers; Mediterranean on the south Crimean coast, with cool winters and hot summers.

Government

Governed by a President, a Prime Minister and Council of Ministers, and a unicameral Supreme Council.

Economy

Industrialized economy; growth inhibited by slow pace of economic reform; agriculture employs c.25% of the workforce; chief crops are wheat, sugar beet, sunflowers, vegetables, livestock; main industry is mining (coal, iron ore, non-ferrous minerals) and metallurgy, steel being the top export; other industries are electricity generation, petrochemicals, chemicals, machinery and transport equipment, shipbuilding, engineering, food processing (especially sugar).

History

Inhabited by Scythians in ancient times, the country was then invaded by Goths, Huns and Khazars. Kiev became the centre of power of a Slavic state in the 9c, but it was overrun by the Golden Horde in the 14c. Ruled by Lithuania in the 14–15c, Ukraine came under Polish rule in the 16c, when many people fled and formed resistance movements (Cossacks). It gradually became part of Russia in the 17–18c. Ukraine declared its independence in 1918, but Kiev was occupied by Soviet troops and the country became a Soviet Socialist Republic in 1922. After World War II, Ukraine gained territory in the west, and in 1954 the largely Russian-populated Crimea was transferred from Russia to Ukraine. In 1986 the Chernobyl nuclear disaster occurred, leaving c.8% of the country contaminated. Ukraine became independent in 1991 and a founding member of the CIS (Commonwealth of Independent States). There is a marked divide between the Russian-influenced east and the European-influenced west, which is reflected in political divisions. These came to a head after the presidential election in 2004, when mass demonstrations and civil disobedience greeted the announcement of the Russian-backed Viktor Yanukovych's victory; the result was eventually overturned because of voting irregularities and the rerun election was won by pro-European Viktor Yushchenko. Ukraine accepted the Crimea's declaration of autonomy in 1991, but rejected its 1992 vote for independence, imposing direct rule in 1994–5; considerable autonomy was granted in 1999.

UNITED ARAB EMIRATES

Official name United Arab Emirates
Local name Al-Imārāt al-'Arabīyah al-Muttahida
Location A federation of seven autonomous emirates in the eastern central Arabian Peninsula. It is bounded to the north by the Persian Gulf; to the east by Oman; and to the south and west by Saudi Arabia
Area 83 600 sq km/32 300 sq mi
Capital Abu Dhabi
Chief towns Dubai, Sharjah, Ras al-Khaimah

Population 4 621 000 (2008e)
Time zone GMT +4
Currency 1 Dirham (DH) = 100 fils
Languages Arabic; English, Persian, Hindi and Urdu are also spoken
Religions Islam 96% (Sunni 80%, Shia 16%), others 4%
Ethnic groups Arab 55% (UAE citizens c.20%), South Asian 28%, Iranian 8%, others 9%

Physical description

Comprises the emirates of Abu Dhabi, Ajman, Dubai, Fujairah, Ras al-Khaimah, Sharjah and Umm al-Qaiwan; located along the southern shore (Trucial Coast) of the Persian Gulf; Fujairah has a coastline along the Gulf of Oman; salt marshes predominate on the coast; barren desert and gravel plain inland; the Hajar Mountains in Fujairah rise to over 1000m/3281; the highest point is Jabal Yibir (1527m/5010ft).

Climate

Dry subtropical, hot with limited rainfall; winter temperatures average 21°C, with high humidity (in excess of 70%); less humid in summer, with maximum temperatures rising to 45°C; sandstorms are common; the average annual rainfall in Abu Dhabi is 32mm.

Government

Governed by a Supreme Council comprising the hereditary rulers of the seven emirates. The Council elects a President and Vice-President from among its number, and the President appoints the Prime Minister and Council of Ministers; an appointed Federal National Council, which has a consultative role, became partially elected in 2006. Each emirate has its own government.

Economy

Prosperity based on oil and gas production; diversified into petrochemicals, construction, manufacturing (aluminium, cement, chemicals, fertilizer, pharmaceuticals, construction materials, handicrafts, textiles); fishing, ship repair, boat-building, financial services, tourism, agriculture (dates, vegetables, fruit); Abu Dhabi is the main oil and gas producer; Dubai is a regional entrepôt, tourist centre and free trade zone; other emirates dependent on Abu Dhabi and federal government, although Sharjah is a manufacturing base.

History

As early as the third millennium BC the area was crossed by many Sumerian trade routes. It came under

Muslim influence from the 7c and was visited by the Portuguese in the 16c. The British East India Company arrived in the 17c. Various peace treaties with Britain were signed from 1820 by the ruling sheikhs of what became known as the Trucial States, which accepted British protection in 1892. Abu Dhabi's huge oilfields were discovered in 1958. A federal state was formed by six emirates on independence in 1971; the emirate of Ras al Khaimah joined the following year. Sheik Zayed of Abu Dhabi was president from independence until his death in 2004. He was succeeded as Sultan of Abu Dhabi by his son, Sheikh Khalifa, who was also elected president of the UAE. A limited degree of democracy was introduced with indirect elections to the consultative Federal National Council in 2006.

Nations of the World

UNITED KINGDOM

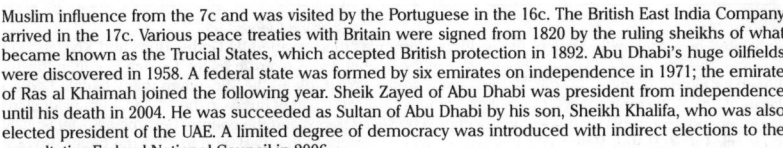

Official name United Kingdom of Great Britain and Northern Ireland	**Chief towns** Belfast, Birmingham, Bradford, Cardiff, Edinburgh, Glasgow, Leeds, Liverpool, Manchester, Newcastle upon Tyne
Local name United Kingdom	**Population** 60944000 (2008e)
Location A kingdom in Western Europe, comprising England, Scotland, Wales and Northern Ireland	**Time zone** GMT
Area 242495 sq km/93627 sq mi	**Currency** 1 Pound Sterling (£) = 100 pence
Capital London	**Language** English; Welsh and Gaelic are spoken by minorities

Climate

Temperate maritime climate, moderated by prevailing south-west winds; generally wetter and warmer in the west.

Government

A hereditary constitutional monarchy with a Queen as head of state; governed by a Prime Minister and Cabinet, and a bicameral Parliament comprising a House of Commons and a House of Lords.

Economy

Highly developed and technologically advanced economy, now based on services and trade; first industrialized economy, in 19c; heavy industry and manufacturing declined in late 20c; services (especially banking, insurance and business services; electronics; telecommunications; tourism) are now the largest economic sector, contributing 75% of GDP and employing 80% of the workforce; industry is declining in importance, contributing 23% of GDP and employing 18% of the workforce; industrial output is predominantly of manufactured goods (machine tools; electronics, communications, automation, transport and electric power equipment; motor vehicles and parts; chemicals; paper and paper products; textiles; garments; other consumer goods), the rest being fuels (coal, North Sea oil and natural gas), processed food and agricultural raw materials, ores and metals; intensive, highly mechanized agricultural sector produces 60% of food needs with less than 2% of the workforce, contributing 1% of GDP.

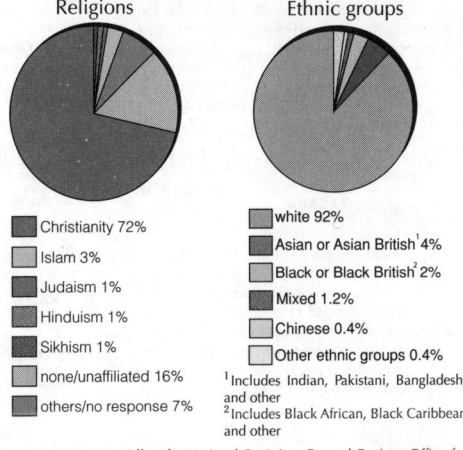

Religions

Ethnic groups

Christianity 72%
Islam 3%
Judaism 1%
Hinduism 1%
Sikhism 1%
none/unaffiliated 16%
others/no response 7%

white 92%
Asian or Asian British[1] 4%
Black or Black British[2] 2%
Mixed 1.2%
Chinese 0.4%
Other ethnic groups 0.4%

[1] Includes Indian, Pakistani, Bangladeshi and other
[2] Includes Black African, Black Caribbean and other

Sources: Census 2001, Office for National Statistics, General Register Office for Scotland, Northern Ireland Statistics and Research Agency © Crown copyright 2006

History

Wales was effectively joined to England in 1301, then Scotland was joined under one crown in 1603 (and by legislative union in 1707) and Ireland in 1801 (the United Kingdom of Great Britain and Ireland). The present name dates from 1922, following the establishment of the Irish Free State. There was major colonial expansion in the 18c and 19c; most colonies were granted independence in the 20c. The UK joined the EC in 1973.

Shetland Islands

Atlantic Ocean

Orkney Islands

North Sea

Outer Hebrides

L. Ness
Inverness
Spey
Ben Nevis
Tay
Grampian Mts
L. Lomond
Aberdeen
Dundee
SCOTLAND
Inner Hebrides
Glasgow
Clyde
Edinburgh

Cheviot Hills
Newcastle upon Tyne
Londonderry
L. Neagh
N. IRELAND
Belfast
Scafell Pike
UNITED KINGDOM
Isle of Man

Irish Sea

IRELAND
Liverpool
Bradford
Manchester
Leeds
Sheffield
Trent
The Wash

Snowdon
Cambrian Mts
Birmingham
Leicester
Norwich
Severn
WALES
ENGLAND
Great Ouse

Cardiff
Swansea
Bristol
London
Thames
Southampton
Dover

Europe

Plymouth
Isle of Wight
English Channel

0   100 Miles
0   100 KM

Channel Islands

FRANCE

❖England

Area 130 279 sq km / 50 301 sq mi	Liverpool, Manchester, Newcastle upon Tyne
Capital London	Population 50 763 000 (2006e)
Chief towns Birmingham, Bradford, Leeds,	

Physical description

Largely undulating lowland, rising in the south to the Mendips, Cotswolds, Chilterns and North Downs, in the north to the north–south ridge of the Pennines and in the north-west to the Cumbrian mountains; the highest point is Scafell Pike at 978m/3209ft; drained in the east by the Tyne, Tees, Humber, Ouse and Thames rivers, and in the west by the Eden, Ribble, Mersey and Severn rivers; the Lake District in the north-west includes Derwent Water, Ullswater, Windermere and Bassenthwaite.

History

England was conquered by the Roman Empire in the 1c AD. From the 4c Germanic tribes raided and then occupied the country, forcing many of the Romano-British westwards into Cornwall and Wales. Various kingdoms were established, some coming under attack and eventual occupation by the Vikings in the 9c. England was retaken in the 10c and unified under the kings of Wessex, although it was conquered and ruled by Danish kings in the early 11c. English rule was restored in 1042, but the country was conquered by William I, the Conqueror, in 1066. The Magna Carta, which began the nation's constitutional development, was signed during the reign of King John in 1215. Under Edward I, England succeeded in conquering Wales by 1283. The Wars of the Roses from 1455 until 1485 resulted in the House of Tudor becoming the ruling family until 1603. There was major colonial expansion in the 16c. In the 17c there was a seven-year war between Royalists and Parliamentarians (the English Civil Wars), at the end of which Charles I was executed (1649). In the 18c the first Act of Union was signed in 1707, joining England in legislative union with Scotland; the second, which was signed in 1800, joined England and Scotland with Ireland, creating the United Kingdom (UK).

❖Northern Ireland

Area 13 576 sq km/5242 sq mi
Capital Belfast

Chief towns Armagh, Londonderry
Population 1 741 600 (2006e)

Physical description

Northern Ireland occupies the north-eastern part of Ireland, and is centred on Lough Neagh; to the north and east are the Antrim Mountains; the Mourne Mountains are in the south-east the highest point is Slieve Donard at 852m/2795ft.

History

A separate parliament to the rest of Ireland (Stormont) was established in 1920, with a House of Commons and a Senate. There is a Protestant majority in the population, generally supporting political union with Great Britain; many of the Roman Catholic minority look for union with the Republic of Ireland. Violent conflict between the communities broke out in 1968 (the Ulster 'Troubles'), leading to the establishment of a British Army peacekeeping force. Sectarian murders and bombings continued both within and outside the province, and as a result of the disturbances the Northern Irish parliament was abolished in 1972. Legislative and executive powers were vested in the UK Secretary of State for Northern Ireland from 1972 to 1999 and from 2002 to 2007. Negotiations between the political parties took place in Belfast in 1991 and 1992, leading to the Downing Street Declaration by UK and Irish governments in 1993. An IRA ceasefire was announced in 1994–6, but there was renewed violence in 1996–7 until the ceasefire recommenced in 1997. Further cross-party talks resulted in the Good Friday Agreement in 1998, under which the Northern Ireland Assembly with devolved powers was established in 1999. Devolved government was suspended in late 2002 after the Unionists refused to work with Sinn Fein following the discovery of its apparent involvement in intelligence gathering for terrorist purposes. Devolution was restored in May 2007 after a new power-sharing agreement was reached.

❖Scotland

Area 77 907 sq km/30 080 sq mi
Capital Edinburgh

Chief towns Aberdeen, Dundee, Glasgow
Population 5 116 900 (2006e)

Physical description

Divided into the Southern Uplands (rising to 843m/2766ft at Merrick), the Central Lowlands (formed by the valleys of the Clyde, Forth and Tay rivers, and the most densely populated area) and the Northern Highlands (divided by the fault line following the Great Glen, and rising to 1344m/4406ft at Ben Nevis); there are 787 islands, most of which lie off the heavily-indented west coast and only c.60 exceed 8 sq km/3 sq mi; there are several wide estuaries on the east coast, primarily the Firths of Forth, Tay and Moray; the interior has many freshwater lochs, the largest being Loch Lomond (70 sq km/27 sq mi) and the deepest Loch Morar (310m/1017ft); the major rivers are the Clyde, Tay (the longest, at 192km/119mi), Dee, Spey and Tweed.

History

Roman attempts to limit incursions of northern tribes were marked by the building of the Antonine Wall (AD 142), which extended from the Forth estuary to the Clyde, and Hadrian's Wall (AD 122–8), which extended from the Solway Firth to the River Tyne and was the principal northern frontier of the Roman province of Britain. The unification of the area now comprising Scotland began in the 9c and was completed in the 12c, with the Norse-controlled islands added in the 13c–16c. From the 11c there were frequent wars with England over territory and the extent of English influence, which amounted to overlordship in the late 13c. Scottish independence was restored by Robert Bruce, and recognized by England in 1328. The Stuarts succeeded to the throne in the 14c and united the crowns of Scotland and England in 1603; the parliaments were united under the Act of Union in 1707 although Scotland has always retained a separate legal and educational system. There were unsuccessful Jacobite rebellions in 1715 and 1745. A proposal for devolution failed in a referendum in 1979, but another in 1997 gave it overwhelming approval and a Scottish parliament with tax-raising powers was elected, officially opening in 1999.

❖Wales

Area 20733 sq km/8005 sq mi	Chief towns Swansea, Wrexham
Capital Cardiff	Population 2965900 (2006e)

Physical description

Mostly high plateaux with short mountain ranges divided by deep river valleys; rises in the north-west to 1085m/3560ft at Snowdon in the Snowdonia range (the highest point); the Cambrian Mountains rise in the centre, and the Brecon Beacons in the south; drained by the Severn, Clwyd, Conwy, Dee, Dovey, Taff, Tawe, Teifi, Towy, Usk and Wye rivers.

History

The Celtic peoples of Wales resisted the Roman invasion but were subjugated c.78AD. With the retreat of the Romans, Wales became a refuge for the Romano-British driven westwards by Germanic invaders of southern Britain from the 4c. In the 8c Welsh territory was lost to Offa, King of Mercia, who built a frontier dyke from the Dee to the Wye. Although in the 9c Rhodri Mawr united Wales against the Saxons, Norse and Danes, union was never maintained permanently, weakening resistance to English incursions. Edward I of England established authority over Wales, building several castles in the 12–13c, and his son was created the first Prince of Wales (1301). Nationalist feeling remained strong, with a revolt against Henry IV led by Owen Glendower in the early 15c, but was tempered by the accession of the Tudors to the English throne in 1485. Wales was politically united with England at the Act of Union in 1535, which extended English laws to Wales and gave it parliamentary representation for the first time. Wales became a centre of Nonconformist religion in the 18c. A political nationalist movement developed, embodied in Plaid Cymru, which returned its first MP in 1966. A referendum in 1979 opposed devolution, but another in 1997 narrowly approved it, and the opening session of the Welsh Assembly was held in June 1999.

British Islands

❖Channel Islands

Location An island group of the British Isles in the English Channel, west of the Cotentin Peninsula of Normandy. A dependent territory of the British Crown, it is divided into the Bailiwicks of Jersey and of Guernsey and dependencies. English, French and a Norman-French *patois* are spoken Area 194 sq km/75 sq mi	Capital St Helier (Jersey); St Peter Port (Guernsey) Population 159510 (2006e) Time zone GMT Main islands Jersey, Guernsey, and the dependencies of Guernsey: Alderney, Brecqhou, Great Sark, Little Sark, Herm, Jethou, Lihou, the Caskets, the Minquiers and the Chauseys

Government

There are legislative assemblies in Jersey, Guernsey, Alderney (the States) and Sark (the Chief Pleas) and each Bailiwick has its own legal system and Royal Court. A Crown-appointed Bailiff presides over the States and the Royal Court of each Bailiwick.

Economy

Financial services (used as a tax haven); agriculture and horticulture (fruit, vegetables; flowers; dairy produce, Jersey and Guernsey cattle); tourism.

History

The islands were granted to the Dukes of Normandy in the 10c, and were the only part of Normandy remaining with the English Crown after 1204. They were occupied by Germany in World War II (1940–5).

❖Isle of Man

Location A British Crown dependency in the Irish Sea, west of England and east of Northern Ireland Area 572 sq km/221 sq mi	Capital Douglas Population 75441 (2006c) Time zone GMT

Government

The island has its own parliamentary, legal and administrative systems. The legislature, the Court of Tynwald, consists of the elected House of Keys and the Legislative Council (composed of the the President of Tynwald, the Bishop of Sodor and Man, the Attorney-General and eight members elected by the House of Keys). Acts of the British Parliament do not generally apply to the Isle of Man.

Economy

Financial services (used as a tax haven); tourism; light manufacturing; agriculture.

History

Ruled by the Welsh from the 6c until the 9c, then by the Scandinavians, Scots and English, the island was purchased by the British government partly in 1765 and wholly in 1828. Manx survived as an everyday language until the 19c.

UK dependent territories

⬦Anguilla

Location The most northerly of the Leeward Islands, in the east Caribbean Sea	Population 14 100 (2008e)
Area 90 sq km/35 sq mi	Time zone GMT –4
Capital The Valley	Currency 1 Eastern Caribbean Dollar (EC$) = 100 cents

Government

Internally self-governing; the British monarch is represented by a Governor; assisted by an Executive Council and a unicameral House of Assembly.

Economy

Tourism, fishing; boat-building; offshore financial services, agriculture (peas, corn, sweet potatoes, cattle, tobacco).

History

Colonized by English settlers in 1650, Anguilla was linked administratively with St Christopher and Nevis for most of its history until 1980.

⬦Bermuda

Location A group of c.138 low-lying, coral islands and islets situated in the west Atlantic Ocean c.900km/560mi east of Cape Hatteras, North Carolina (USA)	Capital Hamilton
	Population 66 500 (2008e)
	Time zone GMT –4
Area 53 sq km/20 sq mi	Currency 1 Bermudan Dollar = 100 cents

Government

Internally self-governing; the British monarch is represented by a Governor-General; assisted by a Cabinet and a bicameral Parliament (Senate and House of Assembly).

Economy

Financial and business services (especially insurance and as corporate business centre); tourism; manufacturing (petroleum products, pharmaceuticals, perfumes), boat-building, ship repair; vegetables; citrus and banana plantations; flowers; fish processing.

History

Discovered by Spanish mariner, Juan Bermudez, in the early 16c, the island was colonized by English settlers in 1612, becoming an important naval station and (until 1862) penal settlement. Internal self-government was granted in 1968. A movement for independence caused tension in the 1970s, including the assassination of the Governor-General in 1973, but a referendum rejected independence in 1995.

⬦British Antarctic Territory

Location A British territory which includes the South Orkney Islands, the South Shetland Islands, the Graham Land Peninsula in	Antarctica, and the part of the Antarctic land mass extending to the South Pole
	Area 1 709 400 sq km/659 999 sq mi

Government

Administered by a Commissioner based at the Foreign and Commonwealth Office in London.

Nations of the World

Economy

Economy

The territory (which lies 20°–80° W and south of 60°S) is populated solely by scientists of the British Antarctic Survey; some tourism; postage stamps.

History

First sighted by explorers in the early 19c, it was part of the Falkland Islands Dependencies when the British Antarctic Survey arrived in 1943–4, and became the British Antarctic Territory in 1962.

❖British Indian Ocean Territory

Location A British territory consisting of the Chagos Archipelago in the Indian Ocean, covering 54 400 sq km/21 003 sq mi of ocean	and lying 1900km/1180mi north-east of Mauritius Area 60 sq km/23 sq mi

Government

Administered by a Commissioner based at the Foreign and Commonwealth Office in London.

Economy

Construction projects and services in support of the military base on Diego Garcia.

History

Acquired by France in the 18c, the islands were annexed by Britain in 1814 and administered as dependencies of Mauritius and the Seychelles until 1965. The Territory was established to meet UK and US defence requirements in the Indian Ocean; Diego Garcia was evacuated in 1967–73 to allow the construction of a UK–US naval support facility.

❖British Virgin Islands

Location A group of over 40 islands, islets and cays at the north-western end of the Lesser Antilles chain in the east Caribbean Sea Area 153 sq km/59 sq mi	Capital Road Town Population 24 040 (2008e) Time zone GMT –4 Currency 1 US Dollar ($, US$)= 100 cents

Government

Internally self-governing; the British monarch is represented by a Governor; assisted by a Premier and Cabinet, and a unicameral House of Assembly.

Economy

Tourism; financial services; rum; gravel and stone extraction; manufacturing (concrete, paint); livestock; coconuts; sugar cane; fruit; vegetables; fish.

History

Tortola was colonized by British planters in 1666, and a constitutional government was granted in 1774. The islands became part of the Leeward Islands in 1872, a separate Crown Colony in 1956, and gained internal self-government in 1977.

❖Cayman Islands

Location An island group in the west Caribbean Sea, comprising the islands of Grand Cayman, Cayman Brac and Little Cayman, c.240km/150mi south of Cuba Area 260 sq km/100 sq mi	Capital George Town Population 47 800 (2008e) Time zone GMT –5 Currency 1 Caymanian Dollar = 100 cents

Government

Mainly internally self-governing; the British monarch is represented by a Governor; assisted by a Cabinet and a unicameral Legislative Assembly.

Economy

Financial services; tourism (including cruise ship traffic); property development; oil trans-shipment; crafts, jewellery; cattle, poultry; vegetables; tropical fish; turtle products.

History

The islands were discovered by Columbus in 1503. They were ceded to Britain in 1670 and colonized by British settlers from Jamaica in the 18c. They became part of a federal territory in 1959 and a separate colony in 1962.

❖Falkland Islands

Location An archipelao of around 700 islands situated in the South Atlantic Ocean, c.650km/400mi north-east of the Magellan Strait
Area 12 173 sq km/4700 sq mi

Capital Stanley
Population 3 140 (2008e)
Time zone GMT –4
Currency 1 Falkland Island Pound = 100 pence

Government

Internally self-governing; the British monarch is represented by a Governor; assisted by an Executive Council and a unicameral Legislative Council.

Economy

Fishing; tourism; agriculture; fish and wool processing; services to British military presence.

History

The islands were seen by several early navigators, including Capt John Strong in 1689–90, who named them. There is a long history of occupation by European countries, including France, Spain and Britain, which established its first settlement in 1765. Argentina occupied the islands in 1820 but the settlement was destroyed in 1831. Britain asserted possession in 1833 and the islands were permanently colonized. Argentina's claims to sovereignty over the whole area resulted in invasion by its military forces in 1982; a British naval and military task force recaptured the islands two months later.

❖Gibraltar

Location A narrow peninsula rising steeply from the low-lying coast of south-west Spain at the eastern end of the Strait of Gibraltar, which is an important strategic point of control for the western Mediterranean Sea

Area 6.5 sq km/2.5 sq mi
Population 28 000 (2008e)
Time zone GMT +1
Currency 1 Gibraltar Pound = 100 pence

Government

Internally self-governing; the British monarch is represented by a Governor; assisted by a Council of Ministers and a unicameral Parliament.

Economy

Financial services; trans-shipment trade; shipping services; tourism; retail; manufacturing; telecommunications (internet businesses).

History

Settled by the Moors in 711, Gibraltar was taken by Spain in 1462, and ceded to Britain in 1713, becoming a British Crown Colony in 1830. As a Crown Colony, it played a key role in Allied naval operations during both world wars. A proposal to end British rule was defeated by a referendum in 1967 and a joint sovereignty arrangement with Spain was rejected in 2002. Since then, Spain has moderated its claims to sovereignty and the bilateral Anglo-Spanish talks about the territory became tripartite with the inclusion of the Gibraltarian government from 2003.

❖Montserrat

Location A volcanic island in the Leeward Islands in the east Caribbean Sea
Area 102 sq km/39 sq mi
Capital Brades. *Note: The original capital, Plymouth, lies within the Exclusion Zone, an area into which entry is prohibited since a devastating volcanic eruption from the Soufrière*

Hills volcano in 1997 made it uninhabitable.
Population 5 000 (2008e). *Note: The population has dropped from 10 639 in 1991 as a result of an exodus after the 1997 eruption.*
Time zone GMT –4
Currency 1 Eastern Caribbean Dollar (EC$) = 100 cents

Government

Internally self-governing; the British monarch is represented by a Governor; assisted by an Executive Council and a unicameral Legislative Council.

Economy

Before the 1997 volcanic eruption the main activity was tourism, with small-scale manufacturing and agriculture. The burial of over half the island in 1997 and continuing volcanic activity has left the economy largely moribund.

History

Visited by Columbus in 1493, the island was colonized by English and Irish settlers in 1632. Possession was disputed between the French and British in the 17c and 18c but the island was assigned to Britain in 1783 and became a Crown Colony in 1871. It was part of the Federation of the West Indies in 1958–62. Activity by the Chances Peak and Soufrière Hills volcanoes, especially in 1997, led to the evacuation of many residents and has made over half of the island uninhabitable.

❖Pitcairn Islands

Location An island group in the south-east Pacific Ocean, east of French Polynesia, comprising Pitcairn Island and the uninhabited islands of Ducie, Henderson and Oeno
Area 4.5 sq km/2 sq mi

Capital Adamstown
Population 48 (2008e)
Time zone GMT –8.5
Currency 1 New Zealand Dollar (NZ$) = 100 cents

Government

Internal affairs managed through a unicameral Island Council; the British High Commissioner to New Zealand is non-resident Governor.

Economy

Sales of postage stamps, internet domain names and handicrafts; subsistence fishing and horticulture.

History

The island was visited by the British in 1767 and settled by mutineers from HMS *Bounty* in 1790. Overpopulation led to emigration to Norfolk Island in 1856 but some islanders returned in 1859 and 1864. The settlement was administered from Fiji from 1952 to 1970, when responsibility was transferred to the British High Commissioner to New Zealand.

❖St Helena and Dependencies

Location The territory comprises the islands of St Helena, Ascension and Tristan da Cunha, all volcanic, lying in the South Atlantic Ocean. St Helena is 1920km/1200mi from the south-west coast of Africa; Ascension lies 1200km/745mi north-west of St Helena, and Tristan da Cunha 2333km/1449mi south-west of St Helena.
Area St Helena 122 sq km/47 sq mi; Ascension 90 sq km/35 sq mi; Tristan da Cunha 98 sq km/38

sq mi
Capital St Helena: Jamestown; Ascension: Georgetown; Tristan da Cunha: Edinburgh of the Seven Seas
Population St Helena 4 000 (2006e); Ascension 1000; Tristan da Cunha 275
Time zone GMT
Currency 1 St Helena Pound ($) = 100 pence, or 1 UK Pound Sterling ($) = 100 pence

Government

St Helena has an Executive Council and a unicameral Legislative Council. Ascension and Tristan da Cunha both have an Island Council, chaired by the island's Administrator; the Administrators are the local representatives of the Governor of St Helena, who is the representative of the British monarch.

Economy

Fishing and fish processing; sales of postage stamps; Ascension provides services for RAF aircraft in transit to the Falkland Islands.

History

St Helena was discovered by the Portuguese in 1502. It was annexed by the Dutch in 1633 but not occupied by them, and the British East India Company seized it in 1659. It was lent to the British government as a place of exile for Napoleon Bonaparte from 1815 until 1821, and became a Crown Colony in 1834. Ascension Island (discovered c.1501 but uninhabited until 1815) and Tristan da Cunha (discovered in 1506; annexed by Britain in 1816; evacuated in 1963 because of volcanic activity) were made dependencies of St Helena in 1922 and 1938 respectively.

❖South Georgia and the South Sandwich Islands

Location South Georgia is a mountainous ice-covered island in the South Atlantic Ocean, about 1390km/300mi south-east of the Falkland Islands. The South Sandwich Islands are a group of 11 uninhabited volcanic islands in the South Atlantic Ocean, c.720km/450mi south-east of South Georgia.

Area South Georgia: c.3750 sq km/1450 sq mi; South Sandwich Islands: 1152 sq km/445 sq mi
Administrative centre King Edward Point
Population Inhabited solely by scientists at the research stations on South Georgia and neighbouring Bird Island, government officers and the museum curators

Government

Administered by a Commissioner, who is the Governor of the Falkland Islands.

Economy

Sale of fishing licences, postage stamps and commemorative coins; customs and harbour dues.

History

Captain Cook landed on the islands in 1775. They were annexed by Britain in 1908 and 1917, and were a sealing and whaling centre until 1965. In 1982 they were invaded by Argentina and recaptured by Britain. The explorer Ernest Shackleton is buried on South Georgia.

❖Turks and Caicos Islands

Location A pair of island groups which lie c.80km/50mi south-east of the Bahamas, of which archipelago they form the south-eastern part; they lie 920km/570mi south-east of Miami (USA)

Area 430 sq km/166 sq mi
Capital Grand Turk (Cockburn Town)
Population 22 300 (2008e)
Time zone GMT −5
Currency 1 US Dollar ($, US$) = 100 cents

Government

Internally self-governing; the British monarch is represented by a Governor; assisted by an Executive Council and a unicameral House of Parliament.

Economy

Tourism; property development; financial services; fishing and fish-processing.

History

Sighted by the Spanish in 1512, the islands were linked formally to the Bahamas in 1799 and then annexed by Jamaica in 1872. They became a British Crown colony in 1962, were administered from the Bahamas in 1965–73, and achieved internal self-government in 1976.

UNITED STATES OF AMERICA

Official name United States of America
Local name United States
Location A federal republic in North America and the fourth-largest country in the world. It includes the detached states of Alaska and Hawaii. The mainland is bounded to the north by Canada; to the east by the Atlantic Ocean; to the south by the Gulf of Mexico; and to the west by the Pacific Ocean

Area 9 160 454 sq km/3 535 935 sq mi
Capital Washington, DC (District of Columbia)
Chief towns New York City, Chicago, Los Angeles, Philadelphia, Detroit, Houston
Population 303 825 000 (2008e)
Time zone GMT −5/ −10
Currency 1 US Dollar ($, US$) = 100 cents
Language English; there is a sizeable Spanish-speaking minority

Physical description

The East Atlantic coastal plain is backed by the Appalachian Mountains from the Great Lakes in the north to Alabama in the south; this series of parallel ranges includes the Allegheny, Blue Ridge and Catskill mountains;

Nations of the World

to the south the plain broadens out towards the Gulf of Mexico and into the Florida Peninsula; to the west, the Gulf Plains stretch north to meet the higher Great Plains from which they are separated by the Ozark Mountains; further west, the Rocky Mountains rise to over 4500m/14760ft; the highest point is Mount McKinley, Alaska, at 6194m/20322ft; the lowest point is in Death Valley (−86m/−282ft); drainage in the north is into the St Lawrence River or the Great Lakes; in the east, the Hudson, Delaware, Potomac and other rivers flow east into the Atlantic Ocean; the central plains of the United States are drained by the great Red River–Missouri–Mississippi river system and by other rivers flowing into the Gulf of Mexico; in the west the main rivers are the Columbia and Colorado.

Religions

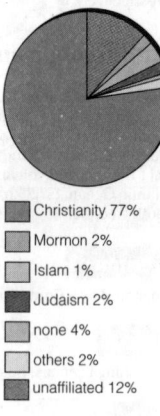

Climate

Temperate in most parts, but tropical in Florida and Hawaii, arctic in Alaska, semi-arid in the Great Plains and arid in the deserts of the south-west; most regions are affected by westerly depressions that can bring changeable weather; rainfall is heaviest in the Pacific north-west, lightest in the south-west; in the Great Plains, wide temperature variation is the result of cold air from the Arctic as well as warm tropical air from the Gulf of Mexico; on the west coast the influence of the Pacific Ocean results in a smaller range of temperatures between summer and winter; on the east coast there is a gradual increase in winter temperatures southwards; the states bordering the Gulf of Mexico and the Atlantic Ocean are subject to hurricanes moving north-east from the Caribbean Sea; tornadoes occur in the mid-west and south-east; states bordering the Pacific and Hawaii are affected by earthquakes and volcanic activity.

- Christianity 77%
- Mormon 2%
- Islam 1%
- Judaism 2%
- none 4%
- others 2%
- unaffiliated 12%

Government

Governed by a President, who is elected every four years by a college of state representatives and appoints a Cabinet, subject to confirmation by the Senate. The bicameral Congress comprises a House of Representatives, elected for two-year terms, and a Senate, elected for six-year terms. Each of the 50 states has a governor, executive and legislature; the District of Columbia has a Mayor.

Ethnic groups

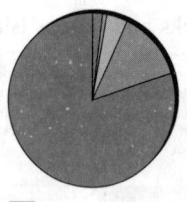

Economy

Highly diversified and technologically advanced economy, becoming in the 20c the leading industrial nation in the world; despite prosperity, has large budget and trade deficits, with increasingly uneven distribution of wealth; vast mineral and agricultural resources; service sector (banking, financial and corporate services; real estate; tourism etc) accounts for 79% of GDP and 77% of employment; main industries are oil and natural gas production, oil refining, steel, motor vehicles, aircraft and aerospace equipment, telecommunications equipment, chemicals, pharmaceuticals, electronic equipment, consumer goods, food processing, forestry, mining; agriculture and fisheries produce wheat, maize, other cereals, fruit, vegetables, cotton, soya beans, fish, meat and dairy products, contributing 1% to GDP.

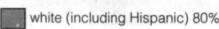

- white (including Hispanic) 80%
- black 13%
- Asian 4%
- Amerindian, Alaskan native, native Hawaiian or Pacific islander 1%
- two or more races 2%

History

The country was first settled by migrant groups from Asia over 25000 years ago. These Native Americans remained undisturbed until the country was explored by the Norse (9c) and the Spanish (16c), who settled in Florida and Mexico. In the 17c, there were settlements by the British, French, Dutch, Germans and Swedish. Many black Africans were introduced as slaves to work on the plantations. In the following century, British control grew throughout the area. A revolt of the English-speaking colonies in the American Revolution (1775–83) led to the creation of the United States of America, which then lay between the Great Lakes, the Mississippi and Florida; the Declaration of Independence was made on 4 July 1776. Louisiana was sold to the USA by France in 1803 (the Louisiana Purchase) and the westward movement of settlers began. Florida was ceded by Spain in 1819, and other Spanish states joined the Union between 1821 and 1853. In 1860–1, 11 Southern states left the Union over the slavery issue, and formed the Confederacy; the Civil War (1861–5) ended in victory for the North, and the Southern states later rejoined the Union. As a result of the North's victory, slavery was abolished in 1865. In 1867 Alaska was purchased from Russia, and the Hawaiian Islands were annexed in 1898 (both admitted as states in 1959). The USA entered World War I on the side of the Allies in 1917. Native Americans were given the right to become US citizens in 1924. In 1929 the stockmarket on Wall Street crashed, resulting in the Great Depression. After the Japanese attack on Pearl Harbor in 1941, the USA entered World War II. The campaign for black civil rights developed in the 1960s, accompanied by much civil disturbance. From 1964 to 1975 the USA intervened in the Vietnam War, supporting non-communist South Vietnam. The USA led the space exploration programme of the 1960s and 1970s (in 1969 US astronaut Neil Armstrong was the first person on the moon). The Cold War between the USA and the USSR came to an end in 1990; since then US military forces have been deployed in UN peacekeeping missions in countries

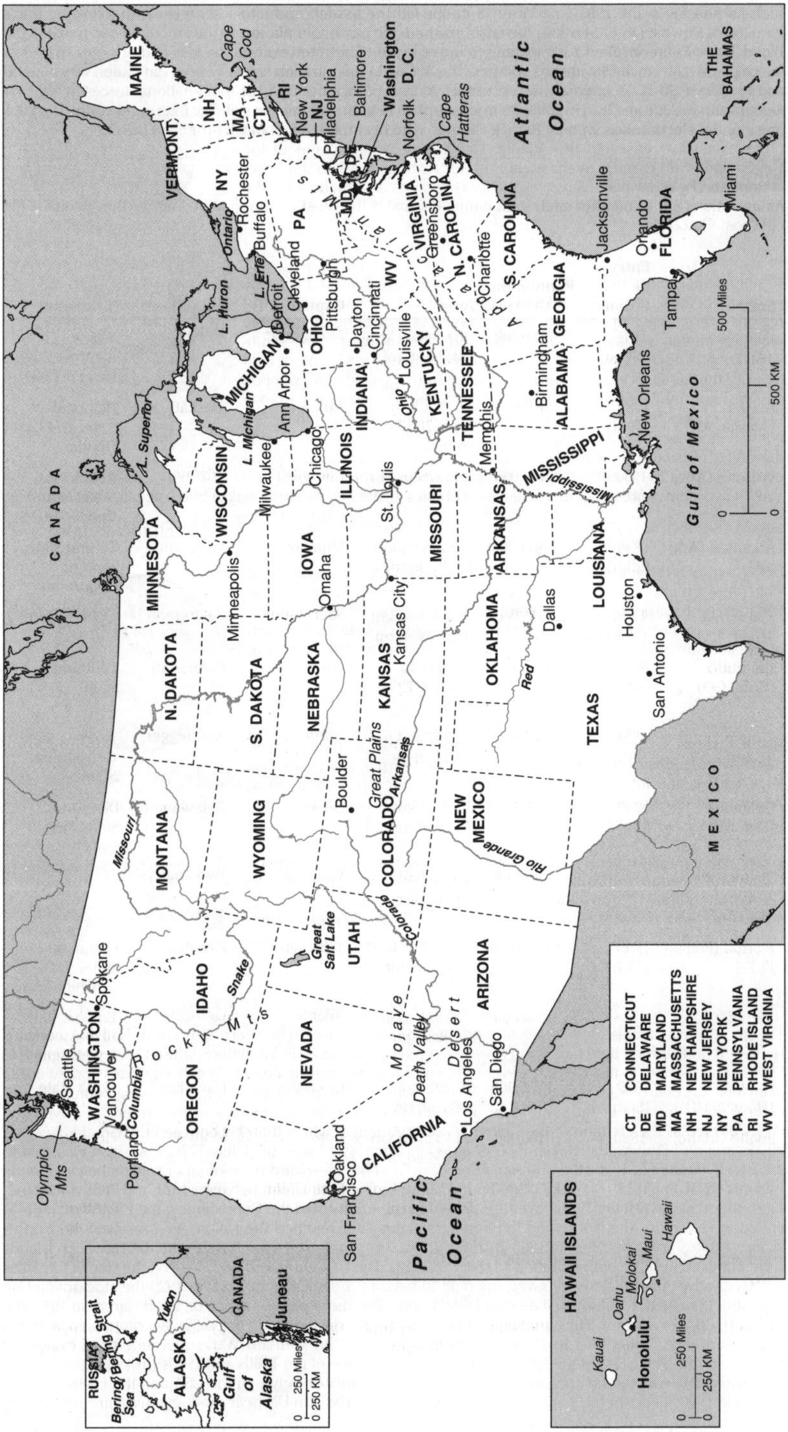

Nations of the World

such as Bosnia. In the 1991 Gulf War, US troops led the assault against Saddam Hussein following Iraq's invasion of Kuwait. On 11 Sep 2001 terrorists crashed one passenger plane into the Pentagon and two into the World Trade Center in New York, leading to the collapse of both towers and the loss of thousands of lives; a fourth plane also crashed without survivors. The Al Qaeda organization led by Osama bin Laden was blamed and President Bush declared a 'war on terror'. As part of this, the USA led multi-national forces in wars on Afghanistan in 2001 and Iraq in 2003; US troops remain in both countries to stabilize internal security. The 2008 presidential election was won by Barack Obama, who became the first black American president.

States of the USA

Abbreviations are given after each state name: the first is the most common abbreviation, the second is the ZIP (postal) code.

State	Entry to Union	Population (2006e)	Area	Capital	Inhabitant	Nickname
Alabama (Ala; AL)	1819 (22nd)	4599000	131443 sq km/ 50750 sq mi	Montgomery	Alabamian	Yellow-hammer State, Heart of Dixie
Alaska (Alaska; AK)	1959 (49th)	670000	1477268 sq km/570373 sq mi	Juneau	Alaskan	Mainland State, The Last Frontier
Arizona (Ariz; AZ)	1912 (48th)	6166000	295276 sq km/ 114006 sq mi	Phoenix	Arizonan	Apache State, Grand Canyon State
Arkansas (Ark; AR)	1836 (25th)	2811000	137754 sq km/ 53187 sq mi	Little Rock	Arkansan	Natural State, Land of Opportunity
California (Calif; CA)	1850 (31st)	36458000	403971 sq km/ 155973 sq mi	Sacramento	Californian	Golden State
Colorado (Colo; CO)	1876 (38th)	4753000	268658 sq km/103729 sq mi	Denver	Coloradan	Centennial State
Connecticut (Conn; CT)	1788 (5th)	3505000	12547 sq km/ 4844 sq mi	Hartford	Nutmegger	Nutmeg State, Constitution State
Delaware (Del; DE)	1787 (1st)	853000	5133 sq km/ 1985 sq mi	Dover	Delawarean	Diamond State, First State
District of Columbia (DC; DC)		581000	159 sq km/ 61 sq mi	Washington	Washington-ian	
Florida (Fla; FL)	1845 (27th)	18090000	139697 sq km/ 53937 sq mi	Tallahassee	Floridian	Everglade State, Sunshine State
Georgia (Ga; GA)	1788 (4th)	9364000	152571 sq km/ 58908 sq mi	Atlanta	Georgian	Empire State of the South, Peach State
Hawaii (Hawaii; HI)	1959 (50th)	1285000	16636 sq km/ 6423 sq mi	Honolulu	Hawaiian	Aloha State
Idaho (Idaho; ID)	1890 (43rd)	1466000	214325 sq km/ 82751 sq mi	Boise	Idahoan	Gem State
Illinois (Ill; IL)	1818 (21st)	12832000	144123 sq km/ 55646 sq mi	Springfield	Illinoisan	Prairie State, Land of Lincoln
Indiana (Ind; IN)	1816 (19th)	6313000	92903 sq km/35870 sq mi	Indianapolis	Hoosier	Hoosier State
Iowa (Iowa; IA)	1846 (29th)	2982000	144716 sq km/ 55875 sq mi	Des Moines	Iowan	Hawkeye State, Corn State

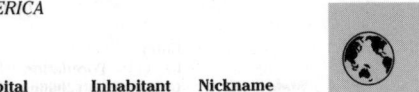

State	Entry to Union	Population (2006e)	Area	Capital	Inhabitant	Nickname
Kansas (Kans; KS)	1861 (34th)	2 764 000	211 922 sq km/ 81 823 sq mi	Topeka	Kansan	Sunflower State, Jayhawker State
Kentucky (Ky; KY)	1792 (15th)	4 206 000	102 907 sq km/ 39 732 sq mi	Frankfort	Kentuckian	Bluegrass State
Louisiana (La; LA)	1812 (18th)	4 288 000	112 836 sq km/ 43 566 sq mi	Baton Rouge	Louisianian	Pelican State, Sugar State, Creole State
Maine (Maine, ME)	1820 (23rd)	1 321 000	79 931 sq km/ 30 861 sq mi	Augusta	Downeaster	Pine Tree State
Maryland (Md; MD)	1788 (7th)	5 616 000	25 316 sq km/ 9 775 sq mi	Annapolis	Marylander	Old Line State, Free State
Massachusetts (Mass; MA)	1788 (6th)	6 437 000	20 300 sq km/ 7 838 sq mi	Boston	Bay Stater	Bay State, Old Colony
Michigan (Mich; MI)	1837 (26th)	10 096 000	150 544 sq km/ 58 125 sq mi	Lansing	Michigander	Wolverine State, Great Lake State
Minnesota (Minn; MN)	1858 (32nd)	5 167 000	206 207 sq km/ 79 617 sq mi	St Paul	Minnesotan	Gopher State, North Star State
Mississippi (Miss; MS)	1817 (20th)	2 910 000	123 510 sq km/ 47 687 sq mi	Jackson	Mississipp-ian	Magnolia State
Missouri (Mo; MO)	1821 (24th)	5 843 000	178 446 sq km/ 68 898 sq mi	Jefferson City	Missourian	Bullion State, Show Me State
Montana (Mont; MT)	1889 (41st)	945 000	376 991 sq km/ 145 556 sq mi	Helena	Montanan	Treasure State, Big Sky Country
Nebraska (Nebr; NE)	1867 (37th)	1 768 000	199 113 sq km/ 76 878 sq mi	Lincoln	Nebraskan	Cornhusker State, Beef State
Nevada (Nev; NV)	1864 (36th)	2 495 000	273 349 sq km/ 105 540 sq mi	Carson City	Nevadan	Silver State, Sagebrush State
New Hampshire (NH; NH)	1788 (9th)	1 315 000	23 292 sq km/ 8 993 sq mi	Concord	New Hampshirite	Granite State
New Jersey (NJ; NJ)	1787 (3rd)	8 724 000	19 210 sq km/ 7 417 sq mi	Trenton	New Jerseyite	Garden State
New Mexico (N Mex; NM)	1912 (47th)	1 955 000	314 334 sq km/ 121 364 sq mi	Santa Fe	New Mexican	Sunshine State, Land of Enchantment
New York (NY; NY)	1788 (11th)	19 306 000	122 310 sq km/ 47 224 sq mi	Albany	New Yorker	Empire State
North Carolina (NC; NC)	1789 (12th)	8 856 000	126 180 sq km/ 48 718 sq mi	Raleigh	North Carolinian	Old North State, Tar Heel State
North Dakota (N Dak; ND)	1889 (39th)	636 000	178 695 sq km/ 68 994 sq mi	Bismarck	North Dakotan	Flickertail State, Sioux State, Peace Garden State
Ohio (Ohio; OH)	1803 (17th)	11 478 000	106 067 sq km/ 40 952 sq mi	Columbus	Ohioan	Buckeye State
Oklahoma (Okla; OK)	1907 (46th)	3 579 000	177 877 sq km/ 68 678 sq mi	Oklahoma City	Oklahoman	Sooner State

Nations of the World

State	Entry to Union	Population (2006e)	Area	Capital	Inhabitant	Nickname
Oregon (Oreg; OR)	1859 (33rd)	3 701 000	251 385 sq km/ 97 060 sq mi	Salem	Oregonian	Sunset State, Beaver State
Pennsylvania (Pa; PA)	1787 (2nd)	12 441 000	116 083 sq km/ 44 820 sq mi	Harrisburg	Pennsyl-vanian	Keystone State
Rhode Island (RI; RI)	1790 (13th)	1 068 000	2 707 sq km/ 1 045 sq mi	Providence	Rhode Islander	Ocean State, Plantation State
South Carolina (SC; SC)	1788 (8th)	4 321 000	77 988 sq km/ 30 111 sq mi	Columbia	South Carolinian	Palmetto State
South Dakota (S Dak; SD)	1889 (40th)	781 000	196 576 sq km/ 75 898 sq mi	Pierre	South Dakotan	Mount Rushmore State, Coyote State
Tennessee (Tenn; TN)	1796 (16th)	6 039 000	106 759 sq km/ 41 220 sq mi	Nashville	Tennessean	Volunteer State
Texas (Tex; TX)	1845 (28th)	23 508 000	678 358 sq km/ 261 914 sq mi	Austin	Texan	Lone Star State
Utah (Utah; UT)	1896 (45th)	2 550 000	212 816 sq km/ 82 168 sq mi	Salt Lake City	Utahn	Mormon State, Beehive State
Vermont (Vt; VT)	1791 (14th)	624 000	23 955 sq km/ 9 249 sq mi	Montpelier	Vermonter	Green Mountain State
Virginia (Va; VA)	1788 (10th)	7 643 000	102 558 sq km/ 39 598 sq mi	Richmond	Virginian	Old Dominion State, Mother of Presidents
Washington (Wash; WA)	1889 (42nd)	6 396 000	172 447 sq km/ 66 582 sq mi	Olympia	Washington-ian	Evergreen State, Chinook State
West Virginia (W Va; WV)	1863 (35th)	1 818 000	62 758 sq km/ 24 231 sq mi	Charleston	West Virginian	Panhandle State, Mountain State
Wisconsin (Wis; WI)	1848 (30th)	5 556 000	145 431 sq km/ 56 151 sq mi	Madison	Wisconsinite	Badger State, America's Dairyland
Wyoming (Wyo; WY)	1890 (44th)	515 000	251 501 sq km/ 97 105 sq mi	Cheyenne	Wyomingite	Equality State, Cowboy State

Non-self-governing territories and commonwealths

❖American Samoa (AS)

Location A group of islands in the South Pacific Ocean, some 3500km/2175mi north-east of New Zealand
Area 199 sq km/77 sq mi

Capital Pago Pago
Population 65 000 (2008e)
Time zone GMT –11

Government

Has a measure of self-government, with a bicameral legislature (the *Fono*) which comprises a Senate and a House of Representatives; the directly elected Governor is the head of the executive; a representative is elected every two years to represent the territory in the US House of Representatives.

Economy

Principal activities are tuna fishing; fish processing and canning; small-scale agriculture; handicrafts.

History

The USA acquired rights to American Samoa in 1899, and the islands were ceded by their chiefs in 1900–25.

❖Guam

Location The largest and southernmost of the Mariana Islands, in the north-west Pacific Ocean
Area 541 sq km/209 sq mi

Capital Hagatna (Agaña)
Population 176000 (2008e)
Time zone GMT +10

Government

Has a measure of internal self-government, with a unicameral legislature directly elected every two years; the directly elected Governor is head of the executive; a delegate is elected every two years to represent the territory in the US House of Representatives.

Economy

Highly dependent on US defence expenditure (military installations cover 35% of the island) and tourism; diversifying into trans-shipment services, construction, printing, food processing and textiles.

History

A Spanish colony for centuries, it was ceded to the USA in 1898; it was occupied by Japan from 1941 to 1944.

❖Northern Mariana Islands

Location A territory comprising 14 islands in the north-west Pacific Ocean, c.2400km/1500mi to the east of the Philippines
Area 477 sq km/184 sq mi

Capital Saipan
Population 86600 (2008e)
Time zone GMT +10

Government

Internally self-governing, with a directly elected bicameral legislature (Senate and House of Representatives); a directly elected Governor presides over the executive; the commonwealth has a resident representative in Washington but no delegate in the US Congress.

Economy

Tourism; garment manufacture; agriculture (cattle, coconuts, fruit, vegetables), handicrafts.

History

From 1947 to 1986, the islands were administered by the USA under UN mandate as part of the US Trust Territory of the Pacific Islands. They became a self-governing commonwealth of the USA in 1978.

❖Puerto Rico

Location The easternmost island of the Greater Antilles, situated between the Dominican Republic in the west and the US Virgin Islands in the east, c.1600km/1000miles south-east of Miami (USA)

Area 8870 sq km/3424 sq mi
Capital San Juan
Chief towns Ponce, Bayamón, Mayaguez
Population 3958000 (2008e)
Time zone GMT –4

Government

Internally self-governing, with a directly elected bicameral Legislative Assembly consisting of a Senate and a House of Representatives; a directly elected Governor is head of the executive; a Resident Commissioner is elected every four years to represent the territory in the US House of Representatives.

Economy

Tourism; manufacturing (textiles, clothing, electrical and electronic equipment, food processing, chemicals); agriculture (dairy farming, livestock, sugar cane, coffee, tropical fruits); fishing and canning; rum and other beverages.

History

Originally occupied by Carib and Arawaks, the island was visited by Columbus in 1493. It remained a Spanish colony until ceded to the USA in 1898, and became a semi-autonomous commonwealth in association with the USA in 1952.

❖ US Virgin Islands

Location A group of more than 50 islands in the south and west of the Virgin Islands group of the Lesser Antilles in the Caribbean Sea, 64km/40mi east of Puerto Rico (USA). There are three main islands: St Thomas, St Croix and St John

Area 342 sq km/132 sq mi
Capital Charlotte Amalie, on St Thomas
Population 109 800 (2008e)
Time zone GMT −4

Government

Internally self-governing, with a unicameral Senate; a directly elected Governor heads the executive; a representative is elected every two years to represent the territory in the US House of Representatives.

Economy

Tourism; oil-refining; manufacturing (watch assembly, rum, construction, pharmaceuticals, textiles, electronics); small-scale agriculture; growing business and financial services sector.

History

Denmark colonized St Thomas and St John in 1671, and bought St Croix from France in 1733. The islands were purchased by the USA in 1917.

URUGUAY

Official name Oriental [Eastern] Republic of Uruguay
Local name Uruguay
Location A republic in eastern South America, bounded to the south and south-east by the Atlantic Ocean; to the north and north-east by Brazil; and to the west by Argentina
Area 176 215 sq km/68 018 sq mi
Capital Montevideo
Chief towns Salto, Paysandú, Mercedes, Las

Piedras
Population 3 478 000 (2008e)
Time zone GMT −3
Currency 1 Uruguayan Peso (Ur$, Urug$) = 100 centésimos
Language Spanish
Religions Christianity 56% (RC 45%), unaffliated 28%, others/none 15%
Ethnic groups white 88%, mestizo 8%, black 4%

Physical description

Grass-covered plains in the south rise northwards to a high sandy plateau; the River Negro flows south to west to meet the River Uruguay on the Argentine frontier; the highest point is Cerro Catedral (514m/1686ft).

Climate

Temperate, with warm summers and mild winters; the average annual rainfall at Montevideo is 978mm with an average temperature of 16°C.

Government

Governed by an executive President, a Council of Ministers and a bicameral General Assembly consisting of a Chamber of Representatives and a Chamber of Senators.

```
0        100 Miles
0     100 KM
                          South
                BRAZIL    America
  Salto
        Río Negro
        Reservoir
  Paysandú
                        L. Mirim
        Negro
  Mercedes  Durazno
            URUGUAY
  Río de la Plata  Las Piedras
ARGENTINA        Montevideo    Atlantic
                               Ocean
```

Economy

Developing economy, based on agriculture, especially ranching and livestock products; main exports are meat, wool, hides, skins and rice; other activities include tourism, offshore financial services, food processing, brewing and wine-making, fishing, forestry, manufacturing (electrical machinery, transport equipment, petroleum products, textiles, chemicals), mining.

History

Originally occupied by various Indian tribes known collectively as the Charrúas people, the area was discovered by the Spanish in 1515 and became part of the Spanish Viceroyalty of Río de la Plata in 1726. Between 1814 and 1825 it was a province of Brazil, and it gained independence in 1828. During the 19c there was a struggle for political control between the liberals (the 'redshirts', or *Colorados*), and the conservatives (the 'whites', or *Blancos*), which was resolved when the former took office for 86 years (1872–1958). Unrest caused by the Marxist Tupamaros guerrillas lasted from 1962 to 1973, and military rule prevailed from 1973 until civilian rule was restored in 1985 after violent demonstrations. The Colorado and National (*Blanco*) parties' dominance of politics has been eroded in recent years by left-wing parties and coalitions such as the Progressive Encounter–Broad Front (EP-FA), which won the 2004 election and whose candidate won the presidency in 2004.

UZBEKISTAN

Official name Republic of Uzbekistan

Local name Özbekiston

Location A landlocked republic in central and northern Central Asia, bounded to the south by Afghanistan; to the south-west by Turkmenistan; to the west, north and east by Kazakhstan; to the north by the Aral Sea; and to the east by Kyrgyzstan and Tajikistan

Area 447 400 sq km/172 696 sq mi

Capital Tashkent

Chief towns Samarkand, Andizhan, Namangan

Population 27 345 000 (2006e)

Time zone GMT +5

Currency 1 Sum = 100 tiyin

Language Uzbek; Russian and Tajik are also spoken

Religions Islam 88% (mostly Sunni), Christianity 9% (Orthodox), others/unaffiliated 3%

Ethnic groups Uzbek 71%, Russian 8%, Tajik 5%, Kazakh 4%, Tatars 3%, others 9%

Physical description

The Tien Shan and Pamir mountains in the east and south-east drop through foothills to the fertile Fergana Valley and the Kyzyl-Kum desert, east of the Aral Sea; west of the desert is the Ustyurt Plateau and the delta of the Amudarya river; the highest point is Beshtor Peak (4299m/14 104ft).

Climate

Long, hot summers, mild winters; temperatures are lower in the mountains; low rainfall.

Government

Governed by an executive President, a Prime Minister and Cabinet, and a bicameral Supreme Assembly consisting of a Legislative Chamber and a Senate.

Economy

Centrally planned and state-controlled economy; intensive agriculture produces cotton, vegetables, fruit, cereals and livestock; main industries are mining (especially for gold and coal), oil and natural gas production (exports restricted by lack of pipelines at present), hydro-electric power generation, textiles and food processing.

History

The area formed part of the 'silk road' trade route linking China with Asia Minor and Europe in the 1c BC. Islam was introduced by Arab invaders in the 7c–8c. In the 12c–13c it was the centre of Genghis Khan's empire, and its cities of Samarkand and Tashkent grew rich from the silk caravan trade. It later divided into the khanates of Bukhara, Khiva and Kokand, which were subjected to attacks by Russia from the early 18c until they were annexed in 1876. The Uzbeks rebelled against Russian rule in 1918 but were suppressed and the country was proclaimed a Soviet Socialist Republic in 1924. It declared its independence from the USSR in 1991, and became a member of the CIS (Commonwealth of Independent States). Post-independence politics is still dominated by the former communist People's Democratic Party and its allies; opposition parties are barred from participation in elections, the two main opposition parties are banned, and other forms of dissent are suppressed. The former communist leader Islam Karimov was elected president in 1991 and has retained the office since. The government has used a Muslim insurgency, which began in 1996 and is largely confined to the Fergana valley, as an excuse to curtail human rights and suppress political opposition and protests.

VANUATU

Official name Republic of Vanuatu
Local name Vanuatu
Location An independent republic comprising an irregular Y-shaped island chain scattered over 860 000 sq km/332 046 sq mi of the south-west Pacific Ocean, 400km/250mi north-east of the French islands of New Caledonia
Area 12 336 sq km/4763 sq mi
Capital Port Vila, on Éfaté

Population 215 000 (2008e)
Time zone GMT +11
Currency 1 Vatu (V, VT) = 100 centimes
Languages Over 100 local languages, Bislama (pidgin), English, French
Religions Christianity 83% (RC 13%), traditional beliefs 6%, others/none 11%
Ethnic groups Melanesian 95%, others 5%

Physical description

Mainly volcanic and rugged, with raised coral beaches fringed by reefs; the highest peak (Tabwemasana on Espiritu Santo) rises to 1888m/6194ft; there are several active volcanoes; densely forested, with narrow strips of cultivated land on the coast.

Climate

Tropical, with a hot and rainy season in November–April when cyclones may occur; annual temperatures at Port Vila are 16°–33°C, and the average annual rainfall is 2310mm.

Government

Governed by a President, a Prime Minister and Council of Ministers, and a unicameral Parliament.

Economy

Poor country, dependent on international aid; agriculture, largely at subsistence level, engages 65% of the population; chief cash crops are coconuts (yielding copra and oil), beef, cocoa, kava and coffee; other activities include forestry, food processing, tourism and offshore financial services.

History

Visited by the Portuguese in 1606, the islands were named the New Hebrides in 1775 by Capt Cook. They were settled in 19c by the British and French, who established plantations, and from 1906 were jointly administered as the Condominium of the New Hebrides. This gained independence as the Republic of Vanuatu in 1980.

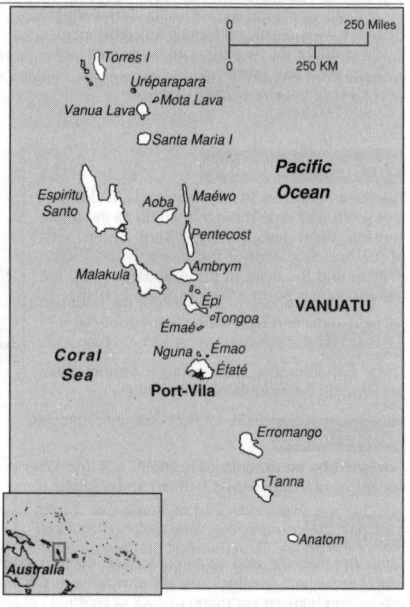

VATICAN CITY STATE

Official name Vatican City State; The Holy See is the term used to indicate the Pope and others concerned in the government of the Roman Catholic Church at its headquarters
Local name Città del Vaticano; Santa Sede
Location A papal sovereign state, and the smallest independent state in the world. Surrounded on all sides by Rome, Italy, it is a World Heritage Site and includes St Peter's Basilica, the Vatican Palace and Museum, several buildings in Rome,

and the Pope's summer villa at Castel Gandolfo
Area 0.4 sq km/0.2 sq mi
Capital Vatican City
Population 824 (2008e)
Time zone GMT +1
Currency 1 Euro (€) = 100 cents
Language Latin; Italian is widely spoken
Religions Christianity 100% (RC)
Ethnic groups predominantly European, especially Italian

Climate

Mediterranean; hot summers and mild winters.

Government

The head of state is the Supreme Pontiff of the Roman Catholic Church, the Pope, who is elected for life by a conclave of members of the Sacred College of Cardinals. Administration is carried out by the Secretariat of State and the Pontifical Commission, appointed by the Pope. There is no legislature.

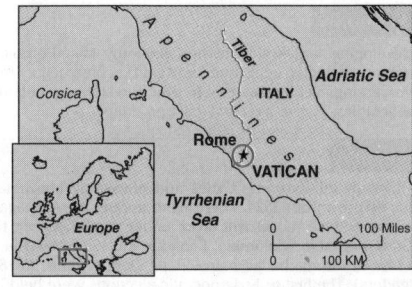

Economy

Unique, predominantly non-commercial economy; supported by financial contributions (known as *Peter's Pence*) from Roman Catholics around the world; some sales of postage stamps, tourist items, publications and museum fees.

History

The Vatican City State was created in 1929 by the Lateran Pacts signed by Pope Pius XI and Mussolini. In these pacts or treaties Italy recognized the Pope's sovereignty over the city of the Vatican and declared the state to be neutral and inviolable territory. The treaties resolved the dispute arising from the newly unified Italy's annexation of the Papal States in 1860 and capture of Rome in 1870; the papacy had always refused to recognize the loss of the Papal States and their incorporation into Italy. The Vatican is now protected by the 1954 La Haye Convention. In 2002 the Italian lira was replaced by the euro as the official currency.

VENEZUELA

Official name Bolivarian Republic of Venezuela
Local name Venezuela
Location The most northerly country in South America, bounded to the north by the Caribbean Sea; to the east by Guyana; to the south by Brazil; and to the south-west and west by Colombia
Area 912050 sq km/352051 sq mi
Capital Caracas
Chief towns Maracaibo, Ciudad Guayana, Valencia, Barquisimeto
Population 26415000 (2008e)
Time zone GMT –4.5
Currency 1 Bolívar (Bs) = 100 céntimos
Language Spanish; local dialects are also spoken
Religions Christianity 98% (RC 96%, Prot 2%), others /unaffiliated 2%
Ethnic groups mestizo 67%, white 21%, black 10%, Amerindian 2%

Physical description

The Guiana Highlands in the south-east cover over half the country; the Venezuelan Highlands, part of the Andes, lie in the west and separate the coast from the interior, reaching heights of over 5000m/16400ft; the highest point is Pico Bolívar (5007m/16427ft); there are lowlands around Lake Maracaibo and in the valley of the Orinoco River, which runs through the centre of the country between the two mountain ranges.

Climate

Tropical, though temperatures and humidity are lower at altitude; generally hot and humid in the lowlands; one rainy season (April–October); annual temperatures at Caracas are 13°–27°C, monthly rainfall between 10mm and 109mm; annual rainfall on the coast increases from very low amounts around Lake Maracaibo to 1000mm in the east; in the Guiana Highlands to the south-east, annual rainfall is c.1500mm.

Government

Governed by an executive President, a Council of Ministers and a unicameral National Assembly.

Economy

Developing, largely state-owned economy, based on oil and gas (90% of exports); other industries include mining (bauxite, coal, iron ore, gold), construction materials, textiles, metals (steel, aluminium), food processing, vehicle assembly and forestry; agriculture produces cereals, sugar cane, rice, bananas, vegetables, coffee, beef and dairy products.

History

Originally inhabited by Caribs and Arawaks, Venezuela was seen by Columbus in 1498, and settled by the Spanish from 1520. There were frequent revolts against Spanish colonial rule, and in the early 19c an independence movement arose under Simón Bolívar; this led to the formal establishment of the state of Gran Colombia (Colombia, Ecuador and Venezuela) in 1821. Following the collapse of Gran Colombia in 1829, Venezuela became an independent republic in 1830 under the first of a series of *caudillos* (military leaders). The first truly democratic elections were held in 1947 but the government was overthrown by the military within months. An enduring civilian democracy was established in 1958 and from the 1960s there was relative political stability, with power alternating between the two major parties, the Democratic Action and the Christian Democrats. In 1998 Hugo Chávez, imprisoned for his part in an attempted coup in 1992, became president. He introduced radical economic reforms that polarized Venezuelan society but he survived an attempted coup in 2002 and a national referendum on his tenure of office in 2004 to win a third term in 2006. He has nationalized major industries, and has pledged to implement '21st-century socialism'.

VIETNAM

Official name Socialist Republic of Vietnam
Local name Viêt Nam
Location An independent socialist state in South-East Asia, bounded to the east by the South China Sea (including the Gulf of Tongking in the north); to the west by Laos and Cambodia; and to the north by China
Area 329 566 sq km / 127 213 sq mi
Capital Hanoi
Chief towns Ho Chi Minh City (formerly Saigon),

Haiphong, Da Nang, Nha Trang
Population 86 116 000 (2006e)
Time zone GMT +7
Currency 1 Dồng (D) = 10 hào = 100 xu
Language Vietnamese
Religions Buddhism 12%, Christianity 8%, Cao Dai 3%, Hao Hao 1%, others, unaffiliated or none 76%
Ethnic groups Kinh Vietnamese 86%, others (53 ethnic groups) 14%

Physical description

Occupies a narrow mountainous strip along the coast of the Gulf of Tongking and the South China Sea, 1600km/994mi long but only 40km/25mi at its widest; broader and lower-lying at the Mekong River delta in the south and along the Red River Valley in the north; mountains in the north-west; the highest peak is Fan si Pan at 3143m/10312ft; a limestone plateau in the south stretches west into Cambodia.

Climate

Tropical monsoon, dominated by south to south-east winds during May–September and north to north-east winds during October–April; the rainy season (May–September) causes high humidity; the average annual rainfall is 1000mm in the lowlands, 2500mm in the uplands; temperatures are high in the south, cooler in the north during October–April.

Government

Governed by a President, a Prime Minister and Council of Ministers, and a unicameral National Assembly (*Quoc-Hoi*). The Communist Party of Vietnam, through its Politburo and the Secretariat of the Central Committee, elected by the Party Congress every five years, exercises the real power.

Economy

Poor but developing; in receipt of international aid; agriculture and fishing, largely at subsidence level, employ 56% of the workforce; chief cash crops are fish, seafood, rice, coffee, rubber, cotton, tea; industries are food processing, machine building, coal-mining, forestry, manufacturing (garments, footwear, steel, cement, fertilizer, glass, tyres, paper) and offshore oil and gas production.

History

Under the influence of China for many centuries, the area was visited by the Portuguese in 1535. Dutch, French and English traders arrived in the 17c, with missionaries. In 1802 the regions of Tongking in the north, Annam in the centre, and Cochin-China in the south united as the Vietnamese Empire, which was conquered by the French from the 1860s. French protectorates were established in Cochin-China in 1867, and in Annam and Tongking in 1884, and the French Indo-Chinese Union with Cambodia and Laos was formed in 1887. Vietnam was occupied during World War II by the Japanese, who were resisted by the communist Viet Minh League under Ho Chi Minh. The Viet Minh declared independence in 1945, but this was not recognized by France, which attempted to reassert its control. The Indo-China War (1946–54) resulted in the withdrawal of the French and an armistice that divided the country between the communist 'Democratic Republic' in the north and the 'State' of Vietnam in the south. In 1957 a communist insurgency in South Vietnam escalated into a civil war between communist North Vietnam and US-backed South Vietnam, which broadened to involve the USA directly from 1964 until US troops were withdrawn in 1973 following a peace agreement with North Vietnam. North Vietnam violated the peace agreement to capture Saigon (now Ho Chi Minh City) and took control of the south in 1975. The country was reunified as the Socialist Republic of Vietnam in 1976. After the collapse of the USSR in 1991, Vietnam improved its relations with China and the USA. A new constitution was adopted in 1992 which approved many economic and political reforms. Although power remains with the ruling Communist Party, in 2006 the party leadership requested comments on its political platform, prompting an open debate on the party's role, criticism of the government and some calls for political pluralism. A younger leadership was subsequently appointed.

- **Virgin Islands, British▶United Kingdom**

- **Virgin Islands, United States▶United States of America**

- **Wales▶United Kingdom**

- **Wallis and Futuna▶France**

YEMEN

Official name Republic of Yemen
Local name Al-Yamaniyya
Location A republic in the south of the Arabian Peninsula, bounded to the north by Saudi Arabia; to the west by the Red Sea; to the south by the Gulf of Aden; and to the east by Oman
Area 531 570 sq km/205 186 sq mi
Capital Sana'a

Chief towns Aden, Hodeida, Mukalla, Ta'iz
Population 23 013 000 (2008e)
Time zone GMT +3
Currency 1 Yemeni Riyal (YR, YRI) = 100 fils
Language Arabic
Religions Islam 100% (Sunni 70%, Shia 30%)
Ethnic groups Arab 96%, others 4%

Physical description

A narrow desert plain bordering the Red Sea rises abruptly to mountains at 3000–3700m/9840–12 140ft; the highest point is Jabal an Nabi Shu'ayb (3760m/12 336ft); a flat, narrow coastal plain in the south is backed by mountains rising to almost 2500m; to the north, a plateau merges with the gravel plains and sand wastes of the Rub al Khali Basin.

Climate

Hot and humid on the coastal strip in the west, with an annual temperature of 29°C; milder in the highlands, where winters can be cold; annual rainfall is higher in the north and west than in the east and south; hot all year round in the south, with maximum temperatures over 40°C in July and August; very high humidity in this area; average temperatures at Aden are 24°C in January, 32°C in July.

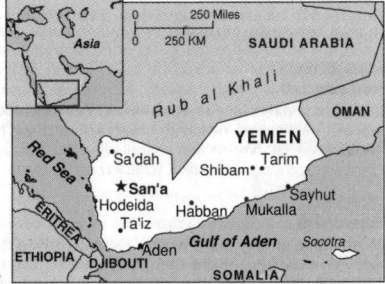

Government

Governed by a President, a Prime Minister and Council of Ministers, and a unicameral House of Representatives.

Economy

Poorest country in the Middle East, despite oil resources; agriculture and fishing, largely at subsistence level, engage c.75% of the population; chief cash crops are coffee and fish; main industries are oil production and refining, manufacturing (textiles, leather goods, aluminium products), food processing and ship repair.

History

From c.750 BC there were advanced civilizations in southern Arabia. The area came under the control of the Muslim caliphate in the 7c AD, and was ruled by Egyptian caliphs from c.1000. North Yemen was part of the Ottoman Empire from the 16c until 1918, it was then ruled by the Hamid al-Din Dynasty until a revolution in 1962, when the Yemen Arab Republic (North Yemen) was proclaimed by the army. Fighting between royalists and republicans continued until 1967, when the republican regime was recognized. Aden was under British occupation from 1839, and a protectorate over the neighbouring emirates of the southern hinterland was gradually established in the late 19c. A rebellion against British rule began in 1963 and after British troops withdrew in 1967, power was seized by the National Liberation Front, which established the People's Republic of Yemen (South Yemen); it was renamed the People's Democratic Republic of Yemen in 1970. Following negotiations, which began in 1979, in 1990 the two countries united as the Republic of Yemen. The first free, multiparty elections took place in 1993. There was a brief civil war between the north and south in 1994 after the south attempted to secede, and tensions remain. There was a religious uprising in the north-west in 2004–5, and rioting in 2005 over the economic situation. Ali Abdullah Saleh, president of North Yemen from 1978, became president of the united country in 1990 and has retained the office at each election.

ZAMBIA

Official name Republic of Zambia
Local name Zambia
Location A landlocked republic in southern Africa, bounded to the west by Angola; to the south by Namibia, Zimbabwe and Mozambique; to the east by Malawi; to the north-east by Tanzania; and to the north by the Democratic Republic of the Congo
Area 752 613 sq km/290 509 sq mi
Capital Lusaka

Chief towns Ndola, Kitwe, Kabwe, Livingstone
Population 11 669 000 (2008e)
Time zone GMT +2
Currency 1 Kwacha (K) = 100 ngwee
Language English; local languages are also spoken
Religions Christianity 87%, Islam and Hinduism 1%, others 7%, unspecified 5%
Ethnic groups African 99% (over 70 ethnic groups, including Bemba, Maravi, Tonga and Lozi), European and others 1%

Physical description

Occupies a high plateau at an altitude of 1000–1400m/3281–4590ft; the highest point is 2067m/6781ft, south-east of Mbala; the Zambezi River rises in the north extremity of North-West Province; includes parts of lakes Tanganyika, Mweru and Kariba.

Climate

Temperate on upland plateau; tropical in low-lying areas; rainy season is October–March; at Lusaka the average rainfall is 840mm and the maximum average daily temperatures range between 23°C and 35°C.

Government

Governed by an executive President, a Cabinet and a unicameral National Assembly.

Economy

Very poor, and receiving international aid; dependent on copper and cobalt mining and processing (64% of export earnings); agriculture, mostly at subsistence level, and horticulture engage 85% of the workforce; chief cash crops are tobacco, cut flowers and cotton; other activities are electricity generation, food processing, manufacturing (beverages, chemicals, textiles, fertilizer) and tourism.

History

Most ethnic groups at present in Zambia arrived there between the 16c and the 18c. Arab slave-traders arrived in the 19c, as did European settlers. The country was administered by the British South Africa Company under Cecil Rhodes. Known as Barotseland, it was declared a British sphere of influence in 1888 and named Northern Rhodesia in 1911. It became a British protectorate in 1924. Massive copper deposits were discovered in late 1920s. Between 1953 and 1963 Northern Rhodesia was joined with Southern Rhodesia (now Zimbabwe) and Nyasaland (now Malawi) as the Federation of Rhodesia and Nyasaland. Northern Rhodesia gained its independence in 1964 as the Republic of Zambia. Kenneth Kaunda became president at independence and remained in power until 1991. Zambia was a one-party state from 1972 until 1991, when multiparty elections were held. These resulted in victory for a pro-democracy party and its candidate, Frederick Chiluba, became President. He was re-elected in 1996, surviving coup attempts in 1993 and 1997. Levy Mwanawasa became President in 2002 and initiated an anti-corruption campaign; he was re-elected in 2006 but died in office in 2008 and was succeeded by his vice-president.

ZIMBABWE

Official name Republic of Zimbabwe
Local name Zimbabwe
Location A landlocked republic in southern Africa, bounded to the south by South Africa; to the south-west by Botswana; to the north-west by Zambia; and to the north-east, east and south-east by Mozambique
Area 391 090 sq km/150 961 sq mi
Capital Harare
Chief towns Bulawayo, Gweru, Mutare
Population 11 350 000 (2008e)

Time zone GMT +2
Currency 1 Zimbabwe Dollar (Z$) = 100 cents
Language English; Shona, Sindebele and other local languages are also spoken
Religions mixture of Christian and traditional beliefs 50%, Christianity 25%, traditional beliefs 24%, Islam and others 1%
Ethnic groups African 98% (Shona 82%, Ndebele 14%, other 2%), mixed and Asian 1%, white less than 1%

Physical description

High plateau country with the Middleveld at 900–1200m/2950–3940ft and the Highveld running south-west to north-east, with an altitude of 1200–1500m/3940–4920ft; the land dips towards the Zambezi River in the north and the Limpopo River in the south; the mountains on the eastern frontier rise to 2592m/8504ft at Mount Inyangani.

Climate

Generally subtropical, strongly influenced by altitude; warm and dry in the lowlands, with an annual rainfall of between 400mm and 600mm; the mountains in the east receive 1500–2000mm of rain annually; the average maximum daily temperatures at Harare, in the Highveld, range between 21°C and 29°C.

Government

Governed by an executive President, a Cabinet and a bicameral Parliament consisting of a House of Assembly and a Senate. The post of Prime Minister was revived for the opposition leader Morgan Tsvangirai in the power-sharing agreement signed in 2008.

Economy

Once-flourishing economy close to collapse; most people dependent on food aid; agriculture severely disrupted by seizure of white-owned farms (2000–1); main cash crops are cotton, tobacco and maize; other activities include mining (gold, coal, platinum, copper, nickel, tin, iron ore), metal processing and manufacturing (garments, footwear, food processing).

History

From the 12c to 16c the country was a Bantu kingdom, with its capital at Great Zimbabwe. In the 19c it was taken over by the Ndebele people and named the Kingdom of Matabeleland; this was often in dispute with the Shona people of Mashonaland to the north. It came under British influence in the 1880s, when the British South Africa Company under Cecil Rhodes began its exploitation of the rich mineral resources of the area. The Company invaded Mashonaland in 1890 and by 1900 controlled much of Central Africa. Its area was divided into Northern and Southern Rhodesia in 1911. Southern Rhodesia became a self-governing British colony in 1923, and formed part of the Central African Federation with Northern Rhodesia (Zambia) and Nyasaland (Malawi) from 1953 to 1963. Opposition to the independence of Southern Rhodesia under African rule resulted in a unilateral declaration of independence by the white-dominated government in 1965. Economic sanctions and internal guerrilla activity forced the government to negotiate with the main African groups of the Patriotic Front. Power transferred to the African majority and the country gained its independence as Zimbabwe in 1980. Robert Mugabe became Prime Minister on independence, and President in 1987. His regime has become increasingly autocratic, suppressing internal dissent, especially by the opposition Movement for Democratic Change (MDC) and the media, and rejecting international criticism of human rights and other abuses. Zimbabwe withdrew from the Commonwealth in 2003 because its membership had been suspended indefinitely over the political situation. The agricultural collapse following the appropriation of white-owned farms since 2000 has resulted in widespread food shortages since 2001; international food aid is not distributed equitably, malnutrition is widespread, and a cholera outbreak began in late 2008. The 2008 legislative election was won by the MDC, whose candidate is believed to have won the simultaneous presidential election, but President Mugabe was declared re-elected. After weeks of violent clashes between rival supporters, the government and the MDC agreed to share power, but the agreement was only implemented in early 2009 because of disagreement over the composition of the cabinet.

INDEX

The main page reference relating to a subject is indicated in **bold type**.
Illustrations are indicated in *italic type*.

A

Aachen Cathedral 53
Aalto, Alvar 454
aardvark 80
Aaron, Hank 559
abalone 110
Abba 417
abbreviations 598
  e-mail 609
  text messages 609
abdominal pain 131, 133, 135
Abelard, Peter 246, 503
abelia 72
Abelson, Philip Hauge 201
Aberdeen 661
  museums and galleries 461
Aberdeenshire 661
aberration 164
Abhidhamma Pitaka 492
Abidjan 638
abnormal growths 177
ABO blood group system 126
Aboukir Bay, Battle of 277
Abraham 500, 503
Abraham, F Murray 398
Abrahams, Peter 341
Abrikosov, Alexei A 187
Abse, Dannie 356
abseiling 566
absolute alcohol 164
absolute zero **164**, 169
absorption 164
Abstract Art 437
Abstract Expressionism 437
Abts, Tomma 444
Abu Bakr 499
Abu Dhabi 638
  political leaders 335
Abu Simbel 53
abutilon 72
Abyssinia 274
  Italian invasion of 278
ac 164
AC/DC (rock group) 417
acacia 72
Academy Awards 397
Academy of Ancient
  Music 407
Academy of St Martin-in-the-
  Fields 407
acanthus 70
Acapulco 638
Accademia galleries 460, 461
acceleration 208
accentor 91
accipiters 516
Accra 638
Accused, The 398
ACE inhibitor drugs 141
acerola 64
acetals 203
acetylcholine 182
Achebe, Chinua 341
Achernar 7
Achilles **471**, 472, 473, 474,
  477, 480, 481, 483, 484, 487
acid **164**, 169
acidanthera 69

acidifiers 152
acidity 170
  E numbers 152
  wine 160
acid rain *45*, 47
  definition 164
Ackroyd, Peter 341
Aconcagua 28, 34, 35
aconite 64
acoustic imaging 164
acoustics 174
acquired character 164
acquired immune deficiency
  syndrome 131
  discovery 135
acre 209
Acre, capture of 246, 276
Acrisius 474
acronyms 598
  e-mail 609
  text messages 609
Acropolis 54
Acropolis Museum 459
Actaeon 471
actinium 199
actinobiology 174
Action Painting 271, 437
Actium, Battle of 275
activity, energy
  expended 148
Act of Parliament 663
Act of Union:
  (1535) 858
  (1707) 258, 857
  (1801) 760
actors 363,
acupoints 139
acupressure 139
acupuncture **139**, 140, 231
Ada computer language 608
Adad 471
Adam, Adolphe 433
Adam, Robert 454
Adam, William 454
Adams, Ansel 445
Adams, Bryan 417
Adams, Douglas 341
Adams, John 399
Adams, Marcus 445
Adams, Richard 341
Adamson, Robert 445
Adana 638
Adapa 471
adaptation 164
Adcock, Fleur 356
Addams, Jane 458
Adderley, 'Cannonball' 409
addictions 139, 140
adding machine 188, 257
Addis Ababa 638
address, forms of 669
Adelaide 638
Aden 638
adenoviruses 131, 133
Ader, Clement 188
adhesive, epoxy resin 188
adhesive, rubber-based
  glue 188
adiabatic process 164

Adichie, Chimamanda
  Ngozi 355
Adiga, Aravind 355
adipose 149
Aditi 471
Adjani, Isabelle 363
Admetus 471
Admiral's Cup 519
  fixture results 558
admittance 209
Adonis 469, **471**
Adrastus 485
adrenal gland 135
adrenaline 135
adsorption 164
adult females' daily energy
  requirements 147
adult males' daily energy
  requirements 148
adult shoe sizes,
  international 222
Advent 493, 494
Adventists 502
AED computer language 608
Aeetes 480
Aegean Captain 48
Aegean Sea 48
Aegir 470, 471
Aegisthus **471**, 474, 482, 487
Aeneas **471**, 472, 475, 483,
  486
Aeneid 480
Aeolian Islands 29
Aeolic branch of Greek
  race 477
Aeolus 469, **471**, 477
aeons, geological 22
aeration 152
aerial feeders 97
aerobics 566
aerodynamics 174
aerology 174
aeronautics 174
aeroplane 188
  steam powered 188
  swing-wing 188
Aerosmith 417
aerosol 188
  defined 164
aerospace 164
aerothermodynamics 174
Aeschylus 360
Aesculapius 471
Aesir 470
aetiology 174
Afghanistan 673, **679**
  allied invasion 279
  civil war 279
  national holidays 577
  political leaders 289
  Soviet invasion 279
  UN membership 645
  World Heritage sites 51
Africa 28
  causes of death 135
  exploration 274
African elephant 89, 120
African lily 69
African Queen, The 397

AZ

Index

African trypanosomiasis 134
African tulip tree 76
African violet 70
Afrika Corps 268, 278
Afro-Asiatic languages 584
Afsluitdijk Sea dam 227
Agadir 638
Agamemnon 471, 473, 475, 478, 482
agapanthus 69
agate 27
ageing process 175
Agenor 473, 476
age of the Earth 19
Agincourt, Battle of 252, 276
Aglaia 476
Agnelli, Giovanni 192
Agni 471
Agnon, Shmuel Yosef 458
Agra 638
World Heritage site 54
Agre, Peter 187
Agricola 253, 274, 275
agrimony 64
Agutter, Jenny 363
Ahimsa 499
Ahmadabad 638
Ahmad Shah, Emperor 283
Ahmad Shah Durrani 679
Ahriman 503
Ahtisaari, Martti 459
Ahura Mazda 471, 503, 509
Ahvaz 638
Aïda 405
AIDS 131
discovery 135
Aiello, Danny 363
Aiken, Conrad 356
aikido 514
Aimée, Anouk 363
aïoli 153
Aiolos 477
air distances 634
air force ranks 667
airline designation codes 632
airports:
international 627
UK 626
airship, non-rigid 188
airship, rigid 188
Airy, Sir George 177
Astronomer Royal 18
Ajax 471
Ajmer 638
Akashi–Kaikyo bridge 224
Akbar I (the Great) 283
Akbar II 283
Akerlof, George A 459
Akhmatova, Anna 356
Akhnaten 405
Aki tunnel 226
Akiyama, Shotaro 445
Aksum 235
World Heritage site 53
Alabama 866
Alabama Song 356
à la carte 153
Alamgir II 283

Alamo, Battle of the 277
à la mode 153
Åland Islands 29
Alashan Desert 33
Alaska 866
albacore 105
Albania 673, **680**
national holidays 577
political leaders 289
UN membership 645
World Heritage sites 51
albatross 95
golf 516
Albee, Edward 360
Albemarle, Duke of 515
Albéniz, Isaac 399
Albert, Eddie 363
Alberta 709
Albert Herring 405
Alberti, Leon Battista 253, 454
Alberto Lleras dam 227
Albigensian Crusade 276
Albuquerque 638
Alcazar of Toledo, Museum of the 461
Alceste 405
Alcestis 471
Alcinous 481
Alcis 470
Alcmaeon 471
Alcmene 471
alcohol intake 149
alcoholism 139
Alcott, Louisa May 341
Alcyone 471
Alda, Alan 363
Aldebaran 7
al dente 153
alder, common 74
Alder, Kurt 186
Alderney 29, **662, 858**
Aldiss, Brian 341
Aldrich, Robert 392
Aldridge, James 341
Aldrin, Buzz 275
alecost 64
Alecto 475
Aleppo 638
World Heritage site 58
Aleutian Islands 29
Alexander, F M 140
Alexander Islands 29
Alexander technique 140
Alexander the Great 231, 232, 280, 745, 851
conquests of 275
exploration 274
Alexandre, Vicente 459
Alexandria 638
alexandrite 27
month association 575
Alex Fraser bridge 224
Alferov, Zhores I 187
Alfvén, Hannes Olof 186
algae 164, 166
geological record
study of 174, 176
algebra 175, 253

Algeria 673, **681**
national holidays 577
political leaders 290
UN membership 645
World Heritage sites 51
Algiers 638
World Heritage site 51
ALGOL computer language 608
algology 174
Alhambra 249
World Heritage site 57
Ali 499, **503**
Ali, Muhammad 559
Alice Doesn't Live Here Anymore 398
Aligarh 638
alimentary canal 125
alkali 164, 165, 169
alkalinity 170
E numbers 152
al-Khalifa family 692
alkyl nitrites 143
Alkyone 484
All About Eve 397
Allahabad 638
Allais, Maurice 459
Allen, Edgar 137
Allen, Sir Thomas 406
Allen, Woody 363, 392
Academy Awards 398
Allende, Salvador 270, 713
allergic reactions 141, 168
E numbers 152
allergies 135
allergy treatments 140
Alley, Kirstie 363
alligator 102
allium 69
allotropy 164
alloy 164
alloys 175
All Quiet on the Western Front 397
All Saints' Day 493
national holidays 577
All Souls' Day 493
national holidays 583
All Souls' Festival (Chinese) 498
allspice 66
All's Well That Ends Well 362
All the King's Men 397
Allyson, June 363
Almaty 638
Almas Tower 228
Almodóvar, Pedro 392
almond:
nutritional value 150
tree 74
almond, dwarf 72
Aloadi 476
aloe 64
Alpert, Herb 429
alphabets 605, 606
Alpha Centauri A 8
Alpha Centauri B 8
alpha particle 164
Alpha-Scorpiids meteor

shower 9
Alphito 469
Alpine skiing 519
Al Qaeda 279, 679, 866
Alsace 159
Alston, Richard 432
  Dance Company 437
Altaic languages 584
Altair (star) 7
Altair (computer) 271
Altamira Cave 57
Altdorfer, Albrecht 439
Alte Pinakothek 460
alternating current 164
Althaea 480
Altman, Robert 392
Altman, Sidney 187
altocumulus clouds 44
Altona Museum 460
Altos de Campana 49
altostratus clouds 44
aluminium 199
  properties 202
  wedding anniversary 575
alum root 70
Alvarez, Alfred 341
Alvarez, Luis W 186
Alvin Ailey American Dance
  Theater 436
alyssum 70
Alzheimer, Alois 177
Alzheimer's disease 177
Amadeus 398
Amagasaki 638
amaryllis 69
Amaterasu 471, 479
Amazing Adventures of
  Kavalier & Clay, The 356
Amazonia national park/
  nature reserve 49
Amazon rainforest 702
Amazon River 33
  exploration 274
Amazons 471, 478, 487
ambassadors, form of
  address 669
Ambassador bridge 224
amber 27
Ambler, Eric 341
ambulance 188
Ameche, Don 363
Amen 471
American Ballet Theater 436
American Beauty 399
American Civil War 278, 864
American cockroach 114
American Declaration of
  Independence 260
American Express Travel
  Agency 192
American football 516
  fixture results 535
American Friends Service
  Committee, The 458
American in Paris, An 397
American Museum of Natural
  History 462
American Museum of the
  Moving Image 462

American Pastoral 356
American presidents 340
American Samoa 868
America's Cup 519
  fixture results 558
American Telegraph and
  Telephone Co 192
American vice-
  presidents 340
American War of
  Independence 277
americium 199
amethyst 27
  month association 575
Amette, Jacques-Pierre 356
AM frequency 164
Amiens, Battle 278
Amiens Cathedral 53
Amies, Sir Hardy 450
Amin Dada, Idi 279, 853
amino acid 164, 171
Amis, Martin 341
Amis, Sir Kingsley 341
Amitabha 471
Amma 471
Amman 638
Ammon 471
ammonites 24
  geological record 23
Amnesty International 459
Amoco Cadiz 48
amoebiasis 131
Amon 471
amorphous 164
ampelopsis 72
Ampère, André 177
  inventions 189
Ampex Co 192
amphetamines 143
Amphiaros 471
Amphiarus 485
Amphibia 79
amphibians 100
  endangered species 119
  geological record 23
amphibolite 25
amphibolite banks 26
Amphitrite 471, 485, 487
Amphitryon 471
amplitude modulation 169
Amritsar 254, 638
Amsterdam (city) 638
  museums and galleries 459
Amsterdam (novel) 355
Amte, Baba 509
amu 164
Amundsen, Roald 275
Amun-Re 470, 471
Amur River 33
anabolic steroids 141
anaconda 102
anaemia 130
anaerobic 164
anaesthetic 135, 136, 137
Anahita 471
analgesic drugs 141
analysis (mathematics) 175
Anand, Mulk Raj 341
anaphylaxis 136

anarchism 663
Anastasia (ballet) 433
Anastasia (film) 398
Anat 473
Anaxagoras 464
Anaximander 464
Ancestor-worship 500
Anchises 472
anchovy 105
anchusa 70
Ancient Egyptian
  dynasties 280
Ancient Orient, Museum of
  the 460
Andaman Islands 29
Andaman Sea 32
Andean condor 90
Anderson, Dame Judith 363
Anderson, Marian 406
Anderson, Michael 398
Anderson, Philip W 187
andesite 26
Ando, Tadao 454
Andorra 673, 682
  national holidays 577
  political leaders 290
  UN membership 646
  World Heritage sites 51
Andre, Carl 444
Andrea Chénier 405
Andress, Ursula 363
Andrew, St (disciple) 492
Andrews, Anthony 363
Andrews, Dame Julie 363
  Academy Awards 398
Andric, Ivo 458
Androcles 472
Andromache 472, 477, 481
Andromeda 472, 483
Andromeda constellation 6,
  7
androsterone 136
anemone 69, 70
Anfinsen, Christian B 186
angel, angels 472, 476
Angel Falls 33, 49
Angelico, Fra 439
Angell, Sir Norman 458
Angelou, Maya 341, 356
angel's trumpet 76
angina 141, 142
angiology 174
Angkor 247, 252
  World Heritage site 52
anglerfish 105
Anglesey, Isle of 661
angling 514
  fixture results 521
Anglo-Australian Telescope 9
Angola 673, 682
  civil war 279
  national holidays 577
  political leaders 290
  UN membership 646
Angostura bridge 224
Angra Mainyu 472
ångström 209
anguid 102
Anguilla 859

A-Z

Index

English speakers 585
Angus 661
animal behaviour 175
animal distribution 177
Animalia 61, **79**
  invertebrates 110
animal kingdom 61, **79**
animals 61, 79
  classification 61, 79
  collective names 118
  species under threat 119
  study of 177
Animals, The 417
animism 500
anion 164
aniseed 64
anisotropic 164
Ankara 638
  museums and galleries 459
Annacis bridge 224
Annan, Kofi 647
  Nobel prize 459
Anna Perenna 472
Annapurna I 34
Annapurna II 34
annatto 66
Anne Frank's House 459
Annie Hall 398
annihilation 164, 165
anniversaries, wedding 575
Ann-Margret 363
annual 164
annual meteor showers 9
annular solar eclipses 4
annulus 164
anode 164
anorexia 139
anorthosite 26
Anouilh, Jean 360
Anquetil, Jacques 559
Anschütz, Ottomar 445
Anselm, St 503
Anshan 638
ant, ants 116
  army 116
  collective names 118
  honeypot 116
  weaver 116
antacid drugs 141
Antananarivo 638
Antarctica 28
  exploration 275
Antares 7
antbird 98
anteater 80
antelope, dwarf 80
anthelminthic drugs 141
Anthemias of Tralles 454
anthrax 131
  bacillus discovery 136
  serum discovery 136
anthroposophy 502
anthyllis 72
antianxiety drugs 141
antibacterial drugs 141
antibacterial
  preservatives 152
antibiotics 141
  discovery 138

antibodies 125, 126
  defined **164**, 168
anti-caking agents 152
anticancer drugs 141
anticoagulant drugs 141
anticyclone 164
antidepressant drugs 141
antidiarrhoeal drugs 141
antiemetic drugs 141
anti-foaming agents 152
antifungal drugs 141
antigen, antigens **164**, 168
  blood groups 126
Antigone **472**, 474, 479, 484, 487
Antigua and Barbuda 673, **683**
  Commonwealth
    membership 647
  English speakers 585
  exploration 274
  national holidays 577
  political leaders 290
  UN membership 646
antihistamine 136
antihistamine drugs 141
antihypertensive drugs 142
Antilles, Greater 29
Antilles, Lesser 29
antimanic drugs 142
antimicrobial agent 138
antimicrobial
  preservatives 152
antimony 201
  properties 202
antimuscarinic drugs 142
Antioch, capture of 276
antioxidants 152
antiparticle 164
antipasto 153
antipopes 287
antiproliferation drugs 142
antipsychotic drugs 142
antipyretic agent 136
antiquities museums:
  Europe 459
  UK 461
  USA 462
antirheumatic drugs 142
antisepsis 136
antispasmodic drugs 142
antiviral drugs 142
Antlia constellation 6, 7
antlion 115
Antonine Wall 234, 857
Antonioni, Michelangelo 392
Antony and Cleopatra 275
Antony and Cleopatra
  (play) 362
Antrim 662
Antwerp 638
  museums and galleries 459
Antwerp, Battle 278
Anu 471, **472**
Anubis 470, **472**
Anuradhapura 57
anus, inflammation of 133
anxiety 140, 141, 143
Anyang 638

Anzio, Battle of 279
Aon Center 228
A-1 Asterix satellite 11
Aouita, Said 559
apartheid 834
Apartment, The 398
apatite 27
  Mohs' hardness scale 28
aperitif 153
aperture **165**, 167
apes 118
aphid 115
Aphrodite 469, 471, **472**, 475, 483
Apis 470, 472, 485
Apkallu 471
APL computer language 608
Apollinaire, Guillaume 356
Apollo 469, 471, **472**, 473, 474, 478, 480, 481, 484
Apollodorus of
  Damascus 454
Apollon Musagète 433
Apollo-Soyuz Test Project 14, 15
Apollo spacecraft
  missions 13, 14
Apopis 485
Appalachian Spring 433
appellation contrôlée 160
appendicitis **131**, 133, 183
Appert, Leon 189
Appert, Nicolas 188, 263
appetite loss 132, 144
apple 63
  nutritional value 150
apple, crab 74
Appleton, Sir Edward 177
  Nobel prize 186
apple tree 74
appliances, wedding
  anniversary 575
applied mathematics 175
Après-midi d'un faune,
  L' 433
apricot 63
  nutritional value 150
APT computer language 608
Apuleius, Lucius 341
Apus constellation 6, 7
aqualung 568
aquamarine 27
  month association 575
Aquarius constellation 6, 7
aqua vitae 153
Aquila constellation 6, 7
Aquinas, St Thomas 248, 503
Aquino, Benigno 813
Ara constellation 6, 7
Arabia 274
Arabian Desert 33
Arabian Gulf 32
Arabian Nights 483
Arabian Sea 32
Arabic alphabet 605
Arabic language 584
Arabic numbers 207
Arab-Israeli wars 279, 280
Arabs 275

Aracaju 638
Arachne 472
Arachnida 113
Arafa 577
Arafat, Yasser 761
Nobel prize 459
Arafura Sea 32
Aragon 48
aragonite 27
Aral Sea 32
Ararat 35
Arber, Werner 187
arboreal birds 96
Arbus, Diane 445
Arc-et-Senans 53
Archaea 61
archaeological museums:
Europe 459
UK 461
USA 462
Archangel (city) 638
archangels 472
archbishop, form of
address 669
archdeacon, form of
address 670
Archer, Anne 363
Archer, Jeffrey 341
archery 514
fixture results 522
Archimedes 177
inventions 188, 191
Archimedes' principle 165
architects 454
architectural styles 453
Arctic exploration 275
arctic hare 84
Arctic Monkeys 417
Arctic National Wildlife
Refuge 49
Arctic Ocean 32
arctic tern 100
Arcturus 7
Ards 662
area:
areas of common
shapes 205
common measures 212
conversion factors 209, 214
conversion tables 216
SI units 208
area of the Earth 19
Arecibo Telescope 9
Arend-Roland comet 8
Arequipa 638
World Heritage site 56
Ares 469, 471, **472**, 473, 475,
485, 487
Arethusa 469, 472
Arfvedson, Johan 200
Argentina 673, **684**
national holidays 577
political leaders 290
UN membership 645
World Heritage sites 51
Argo 479
argol 160
argon 199
Argonauts **472**, 474

Argus **472**, 478
Argyll and Bute 661
Ariadne **472**, 481
Ariadne auf Naxos 405
Ariane space missions 12
Arias Sánchez, Oscar 459
Ariel 3
Aries constellation 6, 7
Ariosto, Ludovico 356
Aristaeus 472
aristocracy, ranks of 668
Aristophanes 233, 360
Aristotle:
philosophy 464
science 177
Arius 503
Arizona 866
Arjuna 472
ark 500
Arkansas 866
Arkwright, Richard 191
Arlen, Harold 403
Arles 53
Arliss, George 397
armadillo 80
armadillo, giant 80
Armagh 662
Armani, Giorgio 450
Armati, Salvino degli 191,
249
Armatrading, Joan 417
Armenia 673, **686**
CIS membership 647
national holidays 577
political leaders 290
UN membership 646
World Heritage sites 51
Armide et Renaud 405
Armitage, Kenneth 444
Armory Museum 460
Armstrong, Lance 532, 559
Armstrong, Louis 409
Armstrong, Neil 13, 14, 275
army ranks 667
army museums 459
Arnhem, Battle of 279
Arnold, Eve 445
Arnold, Sir Malcolm 399
Arnoldson, Klas 457
aromatherapy 140
aromatic compounds 165
Around the World in 80
Days 398
Arp, Hans 444
Arquette, Rosanna 363
ar-Razi 243
Arrow, Kenneth 458
arsenic 199
Arsonval, Arsene D' 189
Arsuf, Battle of 276
Artemis 469, 471, **472**, 473,
479, 480, 482, 484
Artemis, temple of 280
art galleries:
Europe 459
UK 461
USA 462
arthritis 139, 140, 142
Arthropoda 112, 113, 114

Arthur **472**, 479, 488
Arthur Ravenel Jr bridge 224
artichoke, Chinese 67
artichoke, globe 67
artichoke, Jerusalem 67
Art Institute of Chicago 462
artists 439
Art Nouveau 453
art therapy 139
Aruba 801
Aryans 755
asafoetida 66
Asahikawa 638
Asara be-Tevet 500
Ascension Island 862
Ascension Thursday 577
Asclepius 469, **472**, 478
ascorbic acid 130
asepsis 136
As Good as it Gets 399
ash, common 74
Ashante traditional
buildings 54
Ashcroft, Dame Peggy 363
Asher, Jane 363
Ashgabat 638
Ashley, Laura 450
Ashley, Merrill 435
Ashmolean Museum of Art
and Archaeology 462
Ashora 577
Ashton, Sir Frederick 432
ballets 433, 434, 435
Ash Wednesday 493, 494
Asia 28
causes of death 135
Asimov, Isaac 341
asparagus 67
nutritional value 150
Aspdin, Joseph 188
aspen 74
asphodel 70
asphyxiation 131
aspirin 142
introduction of 188
Asplund, Erik Gunnar 454
Asquith, Anthony 392
ass 80, 341
Asser, Tobias 457
Association football 516
fixture results 535
Assumption of Our Lady 577
Astaire, Fred 363
Astarte 473
astatine 199
aster 70
month association 575
asteroid, asteroids **165**,
169, 172
space missions 12
Asterope 484
asthenosphere 20
asthma 142
astigmatism 129, 165
astilbe 70
Asti Spumante 159
Astor, John, 1st Baron 192
Astor, Mary 364
Astor, William, 1st

Viscount 192
Astoria bridge 224
Astrakhan 638
astronautics 174
Astronomers Royal 18
astronomical unit 165
  SI conversion factors 209
astronomy 174
  space missions 11
astrophysics 174
Asturias, Miguel Angel 458
Asunción 638
Aswan High Dam 227
asymmetrical bars 517
As You Like It 362
Atacama Desert 33
Atalanta 473
Atatürk, Kemal 850
Atatürk dam 227
Aten 470, **473**
Atget, Eugène 445
Athanasius, St 503
Athavale, Pandurang
  Shastri 509
Athene 469, 472, **473**, 483
Athens 638, 644
  ancient city state 275
  museums and galleries 459
  World Heritage site 54
athlete's foot 141
athletics 514
  fixture results 522
Athol, House of 285
Atkinson, Rowan 364
Atlanta 638
  museums and galleries 462
Atlantic Empress 48
Atlantic Ocean 32
  exploration 274
Atlantis space shuttle 14, 15
Atlas 469, **473**, 478, 484
Atlas Mountains 681, 794
Atli 477
atmosphere 164, 165
  Earth 19, 20
  pressure 20
  study of 174, 175
  temperature 19, 20
atmospheric pressure 164
atom, atoms 164, **165**, 166,
  167, 168, 169, 170, 171, 173
atomic bomb 188
  development 182, 183, 185
atomic constants 196
atomic mass unit 165
  SI conversion factors 209
atomic number **165**, 170
  metals 202
  table of elements 199
atomic structure 178
atomic transformation 184
atomic weight 199
Atreus **473**, 487
atria 126
atropine 136
Atropos 473
Attenborough, Richard,
  Baron 364, 392
  Academy Awards 398

Attila (Norse myth) 477
Attila the Hun 275
Attis 469, 473
Atwood, Margaret 341
  literary prizes 355
Atys 473
Auber, Daniel 434
aubergine 67
  nutritional value 150
aubrietia 70
Auchincloss, Louis 341
Auckland 638
auction bridge (game) 565
Auden, W H 356
Auer, Karl 200, 201
Auerbach, Frank 439
au gratin 153
Auguste Rodin Museum 460
Augustine of Hippo, St 236,
  504
Augustiner Museum 460
auk 94
Aumann, Robert J 459
au naturel 153
Aung San Suu Kyi 797
  Nobel prize 459
aura therapy 140
Aurangzeb (Alamgir) 283
auricles 126
Auriga constellation 6, 7
Aurora (goddess) 473
aurora 165
aurora australis 165
aurora borealis 165
Auschwitz concentration
  camp 56
Auslese 159
Austen, Jane 341
Austerlitz, Battle of 277
Austin (city) 638
Austin, Alfred 359
Austin, John L 464
Austin (of Longbridge),
  Herbert, 1st Baron 192
Austral, Florence 406
Australasia 135
Australia 28, 673, **687**
  Commonwealth
  membership 647
  English speakers 585
  exploration 274
  national holidays 577
  political leaders 291
  states and territories 688
  UN membership 645
  World Heritage sites 51
Australian Ballet, The 436
Australian Capital
  Territory 688
Australian Chamber
  Orchestra 407
Australian Dance
  Theatre 436
Australian Rules football 516
  fixture results 536
Australia Telescope 9
Austria 673, **689**
  administrative divisions 649
  EU membership 648

  monarchs 283
  national holidays 577
  political leaders 291
  road signs 622
  UN membership 645
  World Heritage sites 51
Austrian Succession, War of
  the 260, 277
Austro-Asiatic languages 584
Austronesian languages 584
autecology 174
authoritarianism 663
autogenics 140
autograph tree 76
Autolycus 473
autonomic nervous
  system 123
autonomics 174
autosuggestion 140
Autumn 575
autumnal equinox 575
Avalon, Frankie 364
Avedon, Richard 445
average daily energy
  requirements 147
Averroës, Ibn Rushd 464
Aves 79, **89**
Avignon 53
Ávila 57
Avildsen, John G 398
Avis, House of 285
avocado:
  fruit 64
  nutritional value 150
  tree 76
  vegetable 67
avocet 94
Avogadro, Amedeo 177
avoirdupois ounce 210
Awami League 693
Awu (volcano) 35
Axel, Richard 187
Axelrod, Julius 177
  Nobel prize 186
axial rotation period
  (planets) 2
Ayatollah Khomeini 279
ayatollahs 499
Ayckbourn, Sir Alan 360
Ayer, Sir Alfred 464
Ayers Rock *see* Uluru
Aykroyd, Dan 364
Ayler, Albert 409
Aymaran languages 584
azalea 72
Azerbaijan 673, **690**
  CIS membership 647
  national holidays 577
  political leaders 291
  UN membership 645
  World Heritage sites 51
azo dyes 152
Azores 29, **815**
Aztecs 247, 250, 790

B

Baal 473
Babbage, Charles 177

inventions 188
Babi Yar Massacre 278
baboon 80
collective names 118
Babur 254, 283, **755**
Babylonia 191, 231
Bacall, Lauren 364
baccarat 564
Bacchus 469, 470, 473
Bach, Edward 140
Bach, Johann Sebastian 261, **399**
ballets 433, 434
Bacharach, Burt 403
Bach flower healing 140
Bach remedies 140
bacillus 136
backgammon 564
background radiation 165
back problems 139, 140, 141
backstroke 520
baclava 153
bacon 150
Bacon, Francis 439
Bacon, Francis, Viscount St Albans:
science 177
philosophy 464
Bacon, Kevin 364
Bacon, Roger 249, 464
bacteria 165
classification 61
geological record 22, 23
study of 174, 175
bacterial infections 131
bacteriology **174**, 184
bacteriophage 165
bacterium 170
badger 80
collective names 118
Badham, John 392
Badlands 49
badminton 514
energy expenditure 148
fixture results 524
Baeyer, Adolf von 188
Baez, Joan 417
Baffin Bay 274
Baffin Island 28, 29
Baffin, William 274
bagatelle 514
baggataway 518
Baghdad 638
Bahadur Shah I 283
Bahadur Shah II 283
Baha'i 492
distribution of adherents 489
sacred texts 501
Bahamas, The 673, **691**
Commonwealth membership 647
English speakers 585
island group 29
national holidays 578
political leaders 291
UN membership 645
Baha'u'llah 492, **504**
Bahrain 673, **691**
national holidays 578

political leaders 291
UN membership 645
World Heritage sites 51
Baikal, Lake 32, 57
Bailey, David 445
Bailey, Norman 406
Bailey shipping forecast area 59
Bainbridge, Dame Beryl 341
bain-marie 153
Baird, John Logie 177
inventions 192
Baishazhou bridge 224
Bajer, Fredrik 457
Baker, Chet 409
Baker, Dame Janet 406
Baker, Josephine 435
Baker, Sir Herbert 454
Baker, Tom 364
baked foods 152
Bakhtaran 638
baklava 153
Baku (city) 638
Baku (monster) 479
Bakun dam 227
Balaclava, Battle of 278
Baläifossen 33
Balanchine, George 432
ballets 433, 434, 435
Balard, Antoine 199
Balboa, Vasco Núñez de 274
Balch, Emily 458
Balder 470, 473
Baldwin, Alec 364
Baldwin, James 341
Balearic Islands 29, **836**
Balenciaga, Cristóbal 450
Balfour Declaration 268
Balkhash, Lake 32
Ball, Lucille 364
Ballantyne, R M 341
Ballard, J G 341
ballet:
ballets 433
choreographers 432
companies 436
dancers 435
Ballet du XXe siècle 436
Ballet Gulbenkian 436
Ballet Joos 436
Ballet Rambert 436
Ballet Russe de Monte Carlo 436
Ballets de Paris 436
Ballets des Champs Élysées 436
Ballets Russes de Sergei Diaghilev 436
Ballets Trockadero de Monte Carlos 436
Ballet-Théâtre Contemporain 436
Ballet West 436
Balliol, House of 285
ballistics 174
Ballo in Maschera, Un 405
balloon, first manned flight 188, 261
ballooning 567

ballroom dancing 566
Balluet, Paul 457
Ballymena 662
Ballymoney 662
Balmain, Pierre 450
balneology 174
balthazar (bottle) 163
balti 153
Baltic Sea 32
Baltimore 638
museums and galleries 462
Baltimore, David 187
Balzac, Honoré de 341
Bamako 638
bamboo 76
Ban, King 479
banana:
fruit 64
nutritional value 150
tree 76
Banbridge 662
Bancroft, Anne 364
Academy Awards 398
Banda, Hastings 782
bandicoot 79
Bandung 638
Banff 49
Bangalore 638
Bangkok 638
Bangladesh 673, **692**
Commonwealth membership 647
English speakers 585
national holidays 578
political leaders 291
UN membership 645
World Heritage sites 51
Bangor (Wales) 461
Bangui 638
Banjarmasin 638
Banjul 638
Bankhead, Tallulah 364
bank holidays 577
Bank of America Tower 228
Bank of China Tower 228
Banks, Iain 341
Banks, Lynne Reid 342
Banksy 439
Bannockburn, Battle of 250, 276
Banting, Frederick Grant 137
Banville, John 342
literary prizes 355
banyan tree 76
baobab tree 76
Baoding 638
Baoji 638
Baotou 638
baptism 493
Baptist Church 493
bar (conversion factor) 209
Barbados 673, **693**
Commonwealth membership 647
English speakers 585
national holidays 578
political leaders 292
UN membership 645
Barbarelli, Giorgio 441

Barbary apes 85
barbed wire, first patent 188
barbed wire,
manufacture 188
Barber Institute of Fine Arts,
The 461
Barber of Seville, The 263,
405
barbet 96
Barbieri, Gato 409
barbiturates 143
preparation of barbituric
acid 188
Barbour, Ian Graeme 509
Barcelona 639
museums and galleries 460
World Heritage site 57
Barclay, Robert 192
Bardeen, John 192
Nobel prizes 186, 187
Bardini Museum 460
Bardot, Brigitte 364
Bardo Thodol 492
Bareilly 639
Barents Sea 32
Bargello Museum 460
Bari 639
barium 199
discovery 179
properties 202
Barker, Pat 342
literary prizes 355
Barkin, Ellen 364
Barlach, Ernst 444
barley 62
barn (conversion factor) 209
barnacle, acorn 112
Barnard, Christiaan 177, 271
Barnard's Star 8
Barnaul 639
Barnes, Julian 342
Barnsley 659
barometer 188
baron 668
form of address 670
baroness, form of
address 670
baronet, form of
address 670
baronet's wife, form of
address 670
baron's wife, form of
address 670
Baroque architecture 453
Baroque art 437
Barotseland 876
Barquisimeto 639
Barra 30
barracuda 105
Barranquilla 639
barrel (conversion
factors) 209
Barré-Sinoussi,
Françoise 188
Barrier Reef, Great 51
Barrow, John 275
Barrow, John D 509
Barrow Straits 275
Barry, Sir Charles 454

Barrymore, Drew 364
Barrymore, Ethel 364
Barrymore, John 364
Barrymore, Lionel 364
Academy Awards 397
Barstow, Dame
Josephine 406
Barstow, Stan 342
Bartered Bride, The 405
Barth, John 342
Barth, Karl 268, 504
Bartholomew, St
(disciple) 492
Bartók, Béla 399
ballet music 434
operas 405
Bartoli, Cecilia 406
Barton, Sir Derek 186
Baryshnikov, Mikhail 435
barytes 27
basalt 26
base 165
baseball 514
fixture results 525
baseball field *525*
base pairs (DNA) 121
bases (E numbers) 152
base toadstool 77
BASIC computer
language 608
Basie, 'Count' 409
basil 64
Basilisk 473
Basinger, Kim 364
basketball 514
fixture results 526
Basle 460
Basov, Nicolay 186
Basque separatism 835
Basra 639
Basra, Battle of 275
Bassey, Dame Shirley 417
Basutoland 776
bat 80
Bates, Alan 364
Bates, H E 342
Bates, Kathy 365
Academy Awards 398
Bath:
museums and galleries 461
World Heritage site 58
Bath, Order of the 668
Bath and North East
Somerset 660
bathing 174
batik 566
battery, electric 188
Battistini, Mattia 406
Battle, Kathleen 406
battles, major 275
Baudelaire, Charles 356
Bauhaus 53
Bauhaus Archives and
Museum of Design,
The 460
Bausch, Pina 435
Bavarian National
Museum 460
Bawden, Nina 342

Baxter, Warner 397
bay (spice) 66
Bayadère, La 433
Bayan 492
Bayeux Tapestry 245
Bay Islands 29
Bay of Bengal 32
Bay of Pigs invasion 279
Bayonne bridge 224
bays, lunar 3
BBC National Orchestra of
Wales 407
BBC Philharmonic
Orchestra 407
BBC Scottish Symphony
Orchestra 407
BBC Symphony
Orchestra 407
BCG vaccine 269
BCPL computer
language 608
Beach Boys, The 417
beach heliotrope 76
Beadle, George 186
beam (gymnastics) 517
beans 67
nutritional value 150
bean sprouts 67
bean tree, Red Indian 74
bear:
American black 120
black 80
brown 81
collective names 118
grizzly 81
bear, polar 86
endangered species 120
Beard, James 156
Beardsley, Aubrey 439
béarnaise 153
Béart, Emmanuelle 365
Beatles, The 271, **417**
Grammy awards 429
Beaton, Sir Cecil 445
Beaton, Robert 398
Béatrice et Bénédict 405
Beatty, Ned 365
Beatty, Warren 365, 392
Beaufort, Sir Francis 177
Beaufort scale 41
Beaujolais 159
Beaujolais Nouveau 159
Beaumont, Sir Francis 360
Beaumont, Harry 397
Beaune 159
beautiful clavaria 77
Beautiful Mind, A 399
beaver 81
beaver, mountain 81
Beaverbrook, Max Aitken, 1st
Baron 193
béchamel 153
Bechet, Sidney 409
Bechuanaland 701
Beckenbauer, Franz 559
Becker, Gary 459
Becket, St Thomas (à) 504
Beckett, Samuel 271, 360
Nobel prize 458

Becquerel, Antoine
  Henri 177
bedbug 115
Bede, St 504
Bedelia, Bonnie 365
Bedford, Sybille 342
Bedfordshire 659
Bednorz, J Georg 187
bee, bumble 116
bee, honey 117
beech 74
bee-eater 96
beef 150
beefsteak fungus 77
Bee Gees, The 417
  Grammy awards 429
bee hummingbird 100
Beer, Patricia 356
Beerbohm, Sir Max 342
Beernaert, August 457
Beery, Wallace 397
bees 116
  collective names 118
Beethoven, Ludwig van 399
  operas 405
beetles 117
Beeton, Mrs Isabella
  Mary 156
beetroot 67
  nutritional value 150
Beggar's Opera, The 405
Begin, Menachem 459
begonia 70
Behan, Brendan 360
Behn, Aphra 259, 342
Behrens, Peter 454
Behring, Emil Adolf von:
  inventions 191
  medical discoveries 136,
  138
Beiderbecke, Bix 409
Beijing (Peking) 639, 644
  World Heritage site 52
Beinn Eighe 49
Beirut 639
Béjart, Maurice 432
  ballets 433, 434, 435
Béjart Ballet Lausanne 436
Békésy, Georg von 136
  Nobel prize 186
Belarus 673, 694
  CIS membership 647
  national holidays 578
  political leaders 292
  UN membership 645
  World Heritage sites 51
Bel Canto 355
Belém 639
  World Heritage site 57
belemnites 24
Belém Tower 57
Belfast 639
  district 662
  museums and galleries 461
Belgium 673, 695
  administrative divisions 649
  EU membership 648
  monarchs 283
  national holidays 578

political leaders 292
road signs 622
UN membership 645
World Heritage sites 51
Belgorod 639
Belgrade 639
beliefs, distribution of
  adherents 489
Belize 673, 696
  Commonwealth
  membership 647
  English speakers 585
  national holidays 578
  political leaders 292
  UN membership 646
  World Heritage sites 51
Bell, Alexander Graham 178
  inventions 190, 192
Bell, Vanessa 439
belladonna lily 69
bellbird 98
Bellerophon 473, 483
bellflower 70
Bellini, Gentile 439
Bellini, Vincenzo 405
Belloc, Hillaire 356
Bellona 469
Bellow, Saul 342
  Nobel prize 459
bellringing 566
Belmondo, Jean-Paul 365
Belo, Carlos Filipe
  Ximenes 459
Belo Horizonte 639
Beloved 356
Belushi, James 365
Belushi, John 365
Belvedere Gallery 461
Bely, Andrei 342
Benacerraf, Baruj 187
Benavente y Martinez,
  Jacinto 458
Benbecula 30
Bendigeid Vran 473
Bendorf bridge 224
Benedict XVI 287
Benedictus, David 342
Benelux 800
Benesch, Alfred 192
Bengali language 584
Bengbu 639
Ben-Gurion, David 761
Ben-Hur 398
Benigni, Roberto 399
Benin 673, 697
  national holidays 578
  political leaders 292
  UN membership 645
  World Heritage sites 51
Benjamin Franklin
  bridge 224
Bennett, Alan 360
Bennett, Arnold 342
Bennett, Rodney 433
Bennett, Tony 409
  Grammy awards 429
Bennett comet 8
Benson, George 429
Bentham, Jeremy 262, 464

benthos 165
Benxi 639
Benz, Karl 193
  inventions 188
benzene 165
benzodiazepines 142, 143
  discovery 136
berberis 72
Berbers 681
Berenger, Tom 365
Beresford, Bruce 398
Berg, Alban 399
  operas 405, 406
Berg, Paul 187
bergamot 70
Berganza, Teresa 406
Bergen, Candice 365
Berger, Hans 136
Berger, John 342
Berger, Thomas 342
Bergman, Ingmar 392
Bergman, Ingrid 365
  Academy Awards 397, 398
Bergonzi, Carlo 406
Bergson, Henri 458
Bergström, Sune K 187
beri-beri 130
Bering Sea 32
Bering Strait 274
Berio, Luciano 399
Berkeley, Bishop
  George 258, 464
berkelium 199
Berkoff, Stephen 365
Berlage, Hendrick Petrus 454
Berlin 639, 644
  museums and galleries 460
  World Heritage sites 53
Berlin, Irving 403
Berlin, Sir Isaiah 464
Berliner, Emil 191
Berliner Philharmoniker
  Orchestra 407
Berlin Wall 270, 743
Berlioz, Hector 265, 399
  ballet music 434
  operas 405, 406
Bermuda 859
  English speakers 585
  World Heritage site 58
Bernadotte, House of 286
Bernard, Claude 136
Berne 639
  World Heritage site 58
Berne, Suzanne 355
Berners, Gerald 435
Bernhardt, Sarah 365
Bernina Hotel 189
Bernini, Gian Lorenzo:
  architecture 454
  sculpture 444
Bernstein, Leonard 399
  ballet music 433
  songwriting 403
Berry, Chuck 417
Berry, Halle 365
  Academy Awards 399
Berryman, John 356
Berserker 473

A-Z Index

Bertolucci, Bernardo 392
  Academy Awards 398
beryl 27
beryllium 199
  properties 202
Berzelius, Jöns Jacob 199,
  201, 202, 263
Bes 473
Besant, Annie 504
Bessarabia 791
Bessemer, Henry 191, 265
Bessmertnova, Natalia 435
Besson, Luc 392
Best, Charles 137
Best, George 559
Best Years of Our Lives,
  The 397
Beta-blocker drugs, beta-
  blockers 142
Beta Crucis 7
beta particle 165
beta-ray radioactivity 180
Betelgeuse 7
Bethe, Hans Albrecht 186
Betjeman, Sir John 356
  Poets laureate 359
Bet-Pak-Dala desert 33
Beuys, Joseph 444
bézique 564
Bezymianny volcano 35
Bhagavad Gita 498
bhaji 153
Bhaktivedanta Swami
  Prabhupada, A C 270, 502
Bhavnagar 639
Bhilai Nagar 639
Bhopal 639
  disaster 46
Bhutan 673, **698**
  English speakers 585
  national holidays 578
  political leaders 293
  UN membership 645
Bhutto, Benazir 808
Bhutto, Zulfikar Ali 808
Biafra 804
Białowieza national park/
  nature reserve 49
biathlon 514, 519
  fixture results 526
Bible 492, 500, 501, 502
bicameral legislatures 664
Biches, Les (ballet) 433
bicycle 188
biennial 165
bifocal lens 188
Big Bang 165, 169, 181
  study of 174
Bihari language 584
Bikini atoll 787
Bilbao 639
  museums and galleries 460
bilberry 63
bilharzia 131
bilharziasis 131
Bill, parliamentary 663
  passage into law (UK) 665
  passage into law (USA) 666
billiards 514

fixture results 527
Billy Budd 405
Billy the Kid (ballet) 433
binary notation 165
binary numbers 207
Binchy, Maeve 342
Binnig, Gerd 190
  Nobel prize 187
binomial system of
  nomenclature 182
bioassay 165
biochemic tissue salts 140
bioclimatology 174
biogenesis 165
biology 174
bioluminescence 165
biomechanics 139
biometeorology 174
Biondi, Matt 559
biophysics 174
biosphere 165
biosystematics 174
biotechnology 174
biotin 130
biotite 26
Birch, L Charles 509
birch, silver 74
Birch, Thomas 138
bird-eating spider 113
birdie 516
bird of paradise 91
birds 79, **89**
  aerial feeders 97
  arboreal birds 96
  collective names 118
  endangered species 119
  flightless birds 89
  game-birds and cranes 99
  infection by 133
  records 100
  seabirds 95
  shorebirds 94
  songbirds 91
  study of 176
  waterfowl 93
Birdseye, Clarence 193
birds of prey 90
  sport 516
birdwatching 566
birdwing butterfly 115
biriani 153
Birmingham 639
  council 659
  museums and galleries 461
Birmingham Royal Ballet 436
Biro, Laszlo 190
Birtwistle, Sir Harrison 399
  operas 405
biryani 153
Biscay shipping forecast
  area 59
Bischof, Werner 445
biscuits 149, 150
bishop, form of address 670
Bishop, Elizabeth 356
Bishop, Katherine Scott 139
Bishop, J Michael 178
  Nobel prize 187
Bishops' Wars 277

Bismarck Archipelago 29
bismuth 199
  properties 202
bison, American 81
bison, European 81
  endangered species 120
bisque 153
Bissagos Islands 29
Bissau 639
Bissell, Melville 188
Bisset, Jacqueline 365
bistort 70
bit (computing) 165
bivalves 110, 111
  fossils 24
Bizet, Georges 267, 400
  ballet music 433, 434
  operas 405
Björk 417
Björling, Jussi 406
Black, Sir James 187
Blackadder, Elizabeth 439
blackberry 63
  nutritional value 150
Blackburn with Darwen 660
blackcurrant 63
  nutritional value 150
Black Death 250, 251
Blackett, Baron (Patrick) 186
Black-headed Taoists 501
black hole **165**, 171
blackjack 564
Blackmore, R D 342
Blackpool 660
Black Sabbath 417
Black Sea 32
black widow 113
bladder, irritable 142
Bladud 473, 480
Blaenau Gwent 661
Blahnik, Manolo 450
Blake, Peter 439
Blake, William:
  art 439
  poetry 356
Blakey, Art 409
Blanc, Anjou 159
Blanc, Raymond 156
blanch 153
Blanchett, Cate 365
blancmange 153
Blankers-Koen, Fannie 559
blanquette 153
Blavatsky, Helena 504
bleaching agents 152
Bleasdale, Alan 342
bleeding heart 70
Blenheim, Battle of 277
Blenheim Palace 58
blenny 105
Blessed, Brian 365
Bley, Carla 409
Blind Assassin, The 355
Bliss, Sir Arthur 433
Bliss, Nathaniel 18
blisters 131, 134
Blobel, Günter 187
Bloch, Felix 186
Bloembergen, Nicolaas 187

Blois, House of 283
Blondie 417
blood 174
  artificial 188
blood cells, red 138
blood circulation 127
  discovery 136
blood clots 141, 142
blood groups 126
  discovery 136
blood pressure 136
  treatment 141
bloodstone 27
  month association 575
Blood, Sweat and Tears 429
Bloom, Claire 365
Blount, Herman 415
bluebell 69
blueberry 63
Blue Nile 274
blues 409
Blue Sky 399
blue whale 88, 89
Blum, V 138
Blumberg, Baruch S 178
  Nobel prize 187
Blumenfeld, Erwin 445
Blumenthal, Heston 156
Blunden, Edmund 356
Blur 417
blusher 77
Blyton, Enid 342
BMI 147
boa 102
boar 81
  Chinese calendar 575
Boateng, Ozwald 450
Boat Race, The 547
bobsledding 515
bobsleighing 515
  fixture results 527
Bocage, André 138
Boccaccio, Giovanni 251
Bochum 639
Böcklin, Arnold 439
Bocuse, Paul 156
Bodhidharma 504
bodhisattva 492
body mass index 147
body posture 140, 141
body weight 147, 149
Boeing, William 193
Boer Wars 278, 834
Boer-Zulu War 277
Boethius, Anicius Manlius
  Severinus 238, 464
Boff, Leonardo 504
Bogarde, Sir Dirk 365
Bogart, Humphrey 365
  Academy Awards 397
Bogdanovich, Peter 392
bogey 516
Bogota 639
Bohème, La 405
Bohemia 724
Bohemian Protestants 277
Bohr, Aage N 187
Bohr, Niels 178, 199
  inventions 188

bohrium 199
Boisbaudran, Paul Émile
  Lecoq de 199, 200, 201
Boito, Arrigo 403
Boj-Bulok cave 34
Bokassa, Emperor 711
Bolan, Marc (and T Rex) 418
bolas spider 113
Bolero (ballet) 433
Bolívar, Simón 716
Bolivia 673, 698
  national holidays 578
  political leaders 293
  UN membership 645
  World Heritage sites 51
Böll, Heinrich 342
  Nobel prize 458
Bolm, Adolph 433
Bologna 639
Bologna, Giovanni da 444
bolognese 153
Bolshoi Ballet 436
Bol'shoi Teleskop
  Azimutal'nyi 9
Bolson de Mapimi desert 33
Bolton 659
Boltzmann, Ludwig
  Eduard 178
bombax tree 76
bombe 153
Bomberg, David 439
Bonaparte, Napoleon 259,
  262, 284, 862
  battles 277
Bonci, Alessandro 406
Bond, Edward 360
bones 122
  study of 176
Bonham-Carter, Helena 365
Bonhoeffer, Dietrich 504
bonito 105
Bonn 639
Bonnard, Pierre 439
bonne femme 153
Bonnie Prince Charlie 277
bonsai gardening 567
Booker Prize see Man
  Booker Prize
Booker T and the MGs 418
Book of Kells 241
Boorman, John 392
boosters, immunization 144
Boötes 7
Boot Hill Museum 462
Booth, Hubert 192
Booth, Shirley 397
Booth, William 504
Bor 470
borage 64
Bordas, Georges 189
Bordeaux 159
  World Heritage site 53
Border, Allan 559
boreal zone 39
Boreas 469
borecole 67
Borel, Jean-Francois 136
Borg, Björn 559
Borgatti, Giuseppe 406

Borges, Jorge Luis 342
Borghese Gallery 461
Borgioli, Dino 406
Borgnine, Ernest 365
  Academy Awards 398
Boris Godunov 405
Borlaug, Norman 458
Born, Max 186
Borneo 28, 30
Born Yesterday 397
Borodin, Mikhail 434
boron 199, 850
Borovansky Ballet 436
Borromini, Francesco 454
Bosch, Hieronymus 439
Bosnia and Herzegovina 673,
  699
  Federation of 700
  national holidays 578
  political leaders 293
  UN membership 646
  World Heritage sites 52
Bosphorus bridges 224
Boston 639
  museums and galleries 462
Boston Ballet 436
Boston bean 67
Boston Symphony
  Orchestra 407
Bosworth Field, Battle
  of 252, 276
botany 174
Botany Bay 274
Botham, Ian 559
Bothe, Walther 186
bo tree 76
Botswana 673, 700
  Commonwealth
    membership 647
  English speakers 585
  national holidays 578
  political leaders 294
  UN membership 645
  World Heritage sites 52
Botticelli, Sandro 439
bottlebrush shrub 72
bottlebrush tree 76
bottle sizes, wine 163
Bottom the Weaver 487
Boucher, François 439
Boudicca 234
Bougainville, Louis de 274
bougainvillea 72
bouillabaisse 153
bouillon 153
Boulez, Pierre 400
Boullée, Étienne-Louis 454
Boumédienne, Houari 681
bouquet 160
bouquet garni 153
Bourbon, House of:
  France 284, 738
  Spain 286
Bourdeaux, Michael 509
Bourgeois, Léon 457
Bourgeois, Louise 444
Bourges Cathedral 53
bourguignon 153
Bourke-White, Margaret 446

Bourne, Matthew 432
Bournemouth 660
Bournemouth Symphony
  Orchestra 407
Bournonville, August 432
  ballets 434, 435
Boutique Fantasque, La 433
Bovet, Daniel 186
  discoveries 136
Bow, Clara 365
Bowen, Elizabeth 342
bowerbird 91
Bowie, David 366, 418
Bowles, Paul 342
bowling 515
bowls 515
  fixture results 527
Bowman, James 406
box (tree) 74
Boxer Uprising 278, 715
boxing 515
  fixture results 528
Boxing Day 577
Box tunnel 226
Boyd, William 342
Boyd Orr of Brechin,
  Baron 458
Boyer, Paul D 187
Boyle, The Hon Robert 178
  inventions 190
Boyle's law 178
Boyne, Battle of the 258,
  277, 760
Boys Don't Cry 399
Boys' Town 397
brachiopods 24
Bracknell Forest 660
Bradbury, Sir Malcolm 342
Bradbury, Ray 342
Bradford 659
Bradford, Barbara
  Taylor 342
Bradley, James 18
Bradman, Don 559
Brady, Matthew B 446
Braer 48
Braganza, House of 285
Bragg, Melvyn 342
Bragi 470
Brahe, Tycho 178, 255
Brahma 473, 485
Brahman 498
Brahmanism 501
Brahms, Johannes 400
Braille alphabet 606
brain 123, 124
  discoveries 136
Braine, John 342
brain mushroom 77
braise 153
Bramante, Donato 454
bramble 63
Bran 473
Branagh, Kenneth 366
Brancusi, Constantin 444
Brand, Hennig 201, 259
Brandauer, Klaus Maria 366
Brandes, Rudolph 136
Brando, Marlon 366

Academy Awards 398
Brandt, Bill 446
Brandt, Georg 199
Brandt, Willy 458
Brannigan, Owen 406
Branson, Sir Richard 193
Branting, Karl 458
Braque, Georges 437, 439
Brasilia 639
  World Heritage sites 52
Brasov 639
Brassaï 446
brass rubbing 566
Bratislava 639
Brattain, Walter 192
  Nobel prize 186
Braveheart 399
Brazil 673, 701
  exploration 274
  national holidays 578
  political leaders 294
  UN membership 645
  World Heritage sites 52
Brazil nut 150
Brazil nut tree 74
Brazzaville 639
bread 150
breadfruit 64
breadfruit tree 76
break-bone fever 131
bream 105
Brearley, Henry 191
breastfeeding women, daily
  energy requirements 147
breast stroke 520
breathing 127Breathing
  Lessons 356
Brebbel, Cornelis 191
breccia 25
Brecht, Bertolt 360
Breguet, Louis and
  Jacques 189
Bremen 639
  World Heritage site 53
Brenner, Sydney 178
  Nobel prize 187
Brera Picture Gallery 460
Bresson, Robert 392
Breuer, Marcel Lajos 454
brewing 213
Briand, Aristide 458
bridge 565
  contract 565
  fixture results 529
Bridgend 661
Bridge of Sighs 224
Bridge on the River Kwai,
  The 398
bridges 224
Bridges, Jeff 366
Bridges, Lloyd 366
Bridges, Robert 359
Bridgman, Percy
  Williams 186
Brie 163
  nutritional value 150
Brief Wondrous Life of Oscar
  Wao, The 356
Brierley, Sir Ron 193

Brieux, Eugène 360
Brighid 473
Bright, William Rohl 509
brightest stars 7
Brighton and Hove 660
Brigit 473
brill 105
Brink, André 343
Brink, Norman 138
brioche 153
Brisbane 639
bristlemouth 109
Bristol 639
  council 660
  museums and galleries 461
Britain 274
Britain, Battle of 278
Britannia tubular rail
  bridge 224
British Antarctic
  Territory 859
British Challenger
  expedition 275
British Columbia 709
British East India
  Company 755
British Empire Games 514
British Empire, Order of
  the 668
British English, differences
  from US English 591
British Indian Ocean
  Territory 860
British Museum, The 461
British prime ministers 339
British sign language 607
British thermal unit 209
British Virgin Islands 860
Brittain, Vera 343
Britten (of Aldeburgh),
  Benjamin, Baron 400
  ballet music 433, 434
  operas 405, 406
Brno 639
  World Heritage site 53
broad jump 518
Broad Peak Central 34
Broad Peak I 34
broadbill 98
Broadway Melody, The 397
broccoli 67
  nutritional value 150
brochette 153
Brockhouse, Bertram N 187
Broderick, Matthew 366
Brodsky, Joseph 356
  Nobel prize 459
Brody, Adrien 399
Bromfield, Louis 343
bromine 199
bronchiolitis 131
bronchitis 47, 142
bronchodilator drugs 142
bronco riding 519
Bronson, Charles 366
Brontë, Anne 343
Brontë, Charlotte 343
Brontë, Emily 343
bronze 188

wedding anniversary 575
Bronze Star 669
Brook, Peter 392
Brooke, Rupert 356
Brooke-Rose, Christine 343
Brooklyn bridge 224
Brookner, Anita 343
Brooks, Geraldine 356
Brooks, Gwendolyn 356
Brooks, James L 398
Brooks, Louise 366
Brooks, Mel 366, 392
broom 72
Broonzy, Big Bill 409
Brophy, Brigid 343
Brosse, Salomon de 454
brotulid 109
Brown, Bryan 366
Brown, George Douglas 343
Brown, George Mackay 343
Brown, Harold P 189
Brown, Herbert C 187
Brown, James 418
Brown, John 278
Brown, Michael S 187
Brown, Nacio Herb 403
Brown, Sandy 409
brown bear 81
brownea tree 76
Browne Falls 33
Browning, Elizabeth
  Barrett 356
Browning, Robert 356
brown rat 89
Browns Ferry 46
Brubeck, Dave 409
Bruce, Christopher 432
Bruce, David 138
Bruce, House of 285
Bruce, James 274
Bruce, Robert 250, 857
brucellosis 131
Bruckner, Anton 400
Brueghel, Pieter (the
  Elder) 439
Bruges 460
  World Heritage site 51
brûlé 153
Brunei 673, **702**
  Commonwealth
    membership 647
  English speakers 585
  national holidays 578
  political leaders 294
  UN membership 646
Brunel, Isambard
  Kingdom 178
  inventions 191
Brunelleschi, Filippo 454
Brunhild, Brunhilde 473
Brunner, Emil 504
Brunswick 460
Brussels 639
  museums and galleries 460
  World Heritage sites 51
Brussels sprout 67
  nutritional value 150
Brutalism 453
Bryansk 639

Bryce, David 454
Brynhild 473
Brynner, Yul 366
  Academy Awards 398
Buber, Martin 504
Bubka, Sergei 559
bubonic plague 131
Bucaramanga 639
Buchan, John 343
Buchanan, James 459
Bucharest 639
Buck, Linda B 187
Buck, Pearl 343
  Nobel prize 458
Buckinghamshire 659
buckler agaric 77
buckminsterfullerene 165
Buck's fizz 161
buckthorn 72
buckyballs 165
Budapest 639
  museums and galleries 460
  World Heritage site 54
Buddha 492, **504**
Buddhism 492
  distribution of adherents
    489
  festivals 492
  sacred texts 501
Buddhist art 437
Budding, Edwin Beard 190
buddleia 72
Buenos Aires 639, 644
  exploration 274
Buffalo 639
  museums and galleries 462
buffalo 118
buffalo, wild water 81
buffers 152
bugbane 70
bugs 115
buildings, tallest
  inhabited 228
Buisson, Ferdinand 458
Bujones, Fernando 435
Bulawayo 639
bulbs 69
bulbul 91
Bulgakov, Mikhail 343
Bulgaria 673, **703**
  EU membership 648
  administrative divisions 650
  national holidays 578
  political leaders 294
  UN membership 645
  World Heritage sites 52
Bulgars 703
Bulge, Battle of the 279
bulimia nervosa 142
bulking agents 152
Bull, Deborah 435
bull-fighting 515
Bullock, Sandra 366
Bullock, Wynn 446
bulrush millet 62
Bultman, Rudolf Karl 504
Bunche, Ralph 458
bungee jumping 566
Bunin, Ivan 458

Bunker Hill, Battle of 277
Bunsen, Robert 188, 199,
  201, 265
bunsen burner 188, 265
bunting 91
Buñuel, Luis 392
Bunyan, John 259, 343
Bunyip 473
Buoninsegna, Duccio di 249,
  440
Buran space shuttle 12
Bureau International
  Permanent de la Paix 457
Burgess, Anthony 343
Burgin, Victor 446
burglar alarm 188
Burgos Cathedral 57
Burgundy 159
Burhoe, Ralph Wendell 509
Burke, Edmund 464
Burke, Robert 275
Burkina Faso 673, **704**
  national holidays 578
  political leaders 295
  UN membership 645
Burma campaigns 278
Burmah Agate 48
Burne-Jones, Sir Edward 439
Burnet, Sir MacFarlane 186
burnet moth 116
Burnett, Frances
  Hodgson 343
Burney, Fanny 261, 343
Burnham, David Hudson 454
Burns, Robert 263, 356
Burra, Edward 439
Burrell, Sir William 193
Burrell Collection, The 461
Burren 49
Burroughs, Edgar Rice 343
Burroughs, William 188
Burroughs, William
  Seward 343
Burrow, The 433
Burrows, Jonathan 434
Bursa 639
Burstyn, Ellen 398
Burt, William 192
Burton, Decimus 454
Burton, Gary 409
Burton, Richard (actor) 366
Burton, Richard
  (explorer) 275
Burton, Tim 392
Burton, W Leigh 189
Burundi 673, **704**
  national holidays 578
  political leaders 295
  UN membership 645
Bury 659
Bush, George W 866
Bush, Kate 418
bushbaby 81
bushbuck 81
bushels 219
Bushnell, David 191
Bussell, Darcey 435
Bussy, Antoine 200
bustard 99

busy lizzie 70
butcherbird 91
Butenandt, Adolf 136, 137
  Nobel prize 186
Butler, Nicholas 458
Butler, Robert Olen 356
Butlin, Sir William (Billy) 193
Butt, Dame Clara 406
butter 150
buttercup 70
Butterfield, William 454
Butterfield 8 398
butterflies 115
butterfly-collecting 566
butterfly fish 105
butterfly stroke 520
buzzard 90
**Byatt, A S (Dame
  Antonia)** 343
  literary prizes 355
Bydgoszcz 639
Byrd, Charlie 409
Byrds, The 418
**Byron, George, 6th
  Baron** 356
byte 165
Byzantine architecture 453
Byzantine Empire 276, 745
Byzantine Museum 459
Byzantium 276

C

computer language 608
C++ computer language 608
C# computer language 608
Caan, James 366
Caballé, Montserrat 406
Cabaret 398
cabbage 67
  nutritional value 150
cabbage white butterfly 115
caber tossing 515
Cabernet Sauvignon 159
Cabinet 663
  cabinet minister, form of
    address 670
cable-car 188
Cabot, John 253, 274
Cabot, Sebastian 274
Cabral, Pedro Alvares 274
cacciatora 153
cacciatore 153
cactus 72
Cadbury, George 193
Cadbury, John 193
Cadiz, sack of 277
cadmium 199
  properties 202
Cadmus 473
Caelum constellation 6, 7
Caelus 488
Caerphilly 661
Caesar, conquests of 275
Caesar's mushroom 77
caesium 182, **199**
  properties 202
Cage, John 271, 400
Cage, Nicolas 366

Academy Awards 399
Cagney, James 366
  Academy Awards 397
Cahn, Sammy 403
Cailler, François-Louis 188
Cain and Abel 433
Caine, Sir Michael 366
Cairo 639
  World Heritage site 53
calabash 76
calamari 153
Calatrava, Santiago 454
Calchas 473
calciferols 130
calcite 27
  Mohs' hardness scale 28
calcium 179, **199**
  E numbers 152
  in diet 130
  properties 202
calcium carbonate 25
**calcium carbonate
  deposits** 172
**calcium channel blocker
  drugs** 142
calculating machines 177,
  183
calculus **165**, 182
Calder, Alexander 444
Calderdale 659
calendar, modern 188
calendars 569
  Chinese 498
  Christian 493
  Gregorian 574
  Hindu 498, 574
  Indian 574
  Islamic 499, 574
  Japanese 500
  Jewish 500, 574
calendula 575
Calgary 639
Cali 639
calico bush 72
Calicut 639
California 866
**California Submillimetre
  Observatory** 9
californium 199
caliphs 499
Callao 639
Callas, Maria 406
Callicrates 455
calligraphy 566
Calliope **473**, 481
Callisto (nymph) 473
Callisto (satellite) 2
Callow, Simon 366
Calloway, Cab 409
Caloocan City 639
calorie 209
calorific values of food 150,
  151
**Calouste Gulbenkian
  Museum** 460
Calvin, John 254, 504
Calvin, Melvin 186
Calvino, Italo 343
calzone 153

Camargo, Maria Anna de 435
Camargue 49
camassia 69
Cambodia 673, **705**
  national holidays 578
  political leaders 295
  UN membership 645
  World Heritage sites 52
Cambodian War 279
Cambrian period 23
  fossils 24
Cambridge 461
Cambridge (USA) 462
Cambridgeshire 659
camel 81
  length of pregnancy 89
Camelford 46
camellia (flower) 72
camellia (tree) 74
**Camelopardalis
  constellation** 6, 7
Camembert 163
camera, polaroid 188
camera lens 165
Cameron, James 399
Cameron, Julia Margaret 446
Cameroon 674, **706**
  Commonwealth
    membership 647
  English speakers 585
  national holidays 578
  political leaders 296
  UN membership 645
  World Heritage sites 52
camomile 64
campanology 566
Campbell, Glen 429
Campbells 277
Campen, Jacob van 454
Campinas 639
Campo Grande 639
Campos 639
Camus, Albert 343
  Nobel prize 458
Canada 674, **707**
  Commonwealth
    membership 647
  English speakers 585
  national holidays 578
  political leaders 296
  provinces 709
  territories 709
  UN membership 645
  World Heritage sites 52
**Canada-France-Hawaii
  Telescope** 9
**Canadian Arctic
  Archipelago** 29
Canadian canoe 515
**Canaima national park/nature
  reserve** 49
Canaletto 261, 439
canapé 153
Canary Islands 29, **836**
canasta 565
Canberra 266, 639
cancer 165
  causes of death 135
  drugs 141

preventative measures 149
study of 176
Cancer constellation 6, 7
Candela, Felix 454
candidiasis 134
candle-making 566
candlenut tree 76
Canes Venatici
constellation 6, 7
Canetti, Elias 343
Nobel prize 459
Canis Major constellation 6, 7
Canis Minor constellation 6, 7
cannabis 65
illegal use 143
cannelloni 153
canning 188
cannon 188
cannonball tree 76
canoeing 515
fixture results 529
canon, form of address 670
Canopus 7
Canova, Antonio 444
Canterbury Cathedral 246
World Heritage site 58
Cantrell, J F 190
canvasback goose 100
**Canyonlands national park/
nature reserve** 49
Capa, Robert 446
capacitance 209
capacity:
conversion factors 214
conversion tables 218
wine bottle sizes 163
Capaneus 485
Cape Bojadar 274
Capecchi, Mario R 188
Cape gooseberry 63
Capella 7
Cape of Good Hope 274
Cape of Storms 274
Cape Province 834
caper 66
Capet, House of 284, 738
Cape Town 639
Cape Verde 674, **709**
national holidays 578
political leaders 296
UN membership 645
Cape Verde Islands 29
exploration 274
Capote (film) 399
Capote, Truman 343
cappuccino 153
Capra, Frank 392
Academy Awards 397
Capriccio 405
Capricornus constellation 6, 7
Captain and Tennille 429
Captains Courageous 397
capybara 81
car:
air-conditioning 188
disc brakes 188

internal combustion 188
petrol-driven 188
speedometer 188
three-wheeled steam
tractor 188
Caracas 639
World Heritage site 59
carambola 64
carat 165
Caravaggio 255, **439**
caraway 66
carbohydrate 165
amount in food 150, 151
dietary
recommendations 149
carbon 165
in Sun 1
table of elements 199
carbon cycle **61**
carbon dating 165
carbon dioxide 167, 168
carbon fibres 188
Carboniferous period 23
fossils 24
carburettor 188
carcinogen 165
cardamom 66
Carden, Joan 406
**Cárdenas, García López
de** 274
Cárdenas, Lázaro 790
cardiac muscle 123, 126
cardiac muscular activity 174
Cardiff 639
council 661
museums and galleries 461
Cardin, Pierre 450
cardinal (bird) 91
**cardinal, form of
address** 670
Cardinale, Claudia 366
cardiology 174
**cardio-pulmonary
resuscitation** 128
cardoon 67
Carducci, Giosuè 457
Carey, Peter 343
literary prizes 355
Caribbean Sea 32
Carignan 159
Carina constellation 6, 7
car index marks:
international 617
UK 615
Carlier, François 189
**Carlsbad Caverns National
Park** 58
Carlson, Carolyn 435
Carlson, Chester 192
Carlsson, Arvid 187
Carluccio, Antonio 156
Carlyle, Robert 367
Carmarthenshire 661
Carmen (ballet) 433
Carmen (opera) 405
Carmichael, Hoagy 403
Carnap, Rudolf 464
**Carnarvon national park/
nature reserve** 49

carnation 70
month association 575
Carnavalet Museum 461
Carné, Marcel 392
Carnegie, Andrew 193
Carnegie Museum of Art 463
**Carnegie Museum of Natural
History** 463
Carnes, Kim 429
Carney, Art 398
Carnival 577
carnivore 165
Caro, Sir Anthony 444
Caroline Islands 29
Caron, Leslie 367
Carothers, Wallace H 190
carp 105
Carpathian Mountains 817
World Heritage site 58
Carpenter, John 393
Carpenters, The 418
Carpentier, Pierre 189
carpet sweeper 188
Carradine, John 367
Carré, Ferdinand 191
Carreras, José 406
Carrey, Jim 367
Carrickfergus 662
Carroll, Lewis 343, 446
carrot 67
nutritional value 150
Carson, Willie 559
Carswell, E A 138
Cartagena 639
World Heritage site 52
Carter 433
Carter, Angela 343
Carter, Betty 409
Carter, Elliott, Jr 400
Carter, Jimmy 459
Cartesian geometry 179
Carthage 275
World Heritage site 58
Cartier, Jacques 274
Cartier-Bresson, Henri 446
cartilage 122
Cartland, Barbara 343
Cartwright, Edmund 190, 263
Caruso, Enrico 406
Carver, Raymond 343
caryopteris 72
Casablanca (city) 639
Casablanca (film) 397
Cascade tunnel 226
Cash, Johnny 418
cash register 188
Caspian Sea 32
Cassandra **473**, 477
Cassatt, Mary 440
Cassavetes, John 367
Cassin, René 458
**Cassini–Huygens space
mission** 12
exploration 275
Cassiopeia constellation 6, 7
cassowary 89
Castillo de Bellver 48
Castle of the Sforzas 460
Castlereagh 662

A-Z

Index

Castor **474**, 480
castor-oil tree, prickly 74
Castro, Fidel 270, 272, 722
casuarina 77
cat 81
  collective names 118
  length of pregnancy 89
Catalan Museum of Art 460
catalysis **165**, 166, 167
catalyst 165
Catania 639
catarrh 131
Cat Ballou 398
caterpillars 118
catfish 105
Catharine Convent State
  Museum 461
Cathars 276
Cather, Willa 343
cathode 164, 165
cation 166
catmint 70
Caton, Richard 136
cattle 81
  collective names 118
Catullus, Gaius Valerius 357
Caucasian languages 584
cauliflower 67
  nutritional value 150
Causley, Charles 357
caustic 166
Cauwelaert, Didier van 356
Cavalcade 397
Cavalleria Rusticana 405
Cavendish, Henry 200, 261
caves:
  deepest 34
  exploration 518
  study of flora and fauna 177
caviar 120
Caxton, William 253
cayenne 66
Cayley, George 189
Cayman Islands 860
CBE 668
C Donald Shane Telescope 9
ceanothus 72
Ceaușescu, Nicolae 817
Cebu City 639
Cech, Thomas R 187
Cecrops 474
cedar, smooth Tasmanian 74
cedar, white 74
cedar of Lebanon 74
Cehi 2 cave 34
Cela, Camilo José 343
  Nobel prize 459
celandine 64
celandine, giant 70
Celebes 28
celeriac 67
celery 64, 67
  nutritional value 150
cell 165, **166**, 167, 169, 170,
  171
cell cycle regulation 181, 183
Cellini, Benvenuto 444
cell structure and
  function 174

cellular division 136
celluloid 188
cellulose 166
  properties 203
Celsius, Anders 178
  exploration 274
Celsius temperature
  scale 166
  SI conversion factors 209
  conversion table 211
Celtic tribes (Gaul) 275
cement 188
Cenerentola, La 405
Cenozoic era 23
  fossils 24
  ice ages 24
Centaur, Centaurs 472, **474**,
  479, 481, 484
Centaurus constellation 6, 7
centigrade temperature
  scale 166, 178
  conversion table 211
  SI conversion factors 209
Centimetre-Gram-Second
  unit 166
Central African Republic 674,
  710
  national holidays 578
  political leaders 296
  UN membership 645
  World Heritage sites 52
Central Ballet of China 436
central nervous system **123**,
  124
  study of 175
Central Plaza building 228
centrifuge 166
Cephalopoda 110, **111**
Cepheus 472
Cepheus constellation 6, 7
ceratostigma 72
Cerberus 474
cereals 62
cerebellum 124
cerebral cortex 124
cerebral hemispheres 124
Ceredigion 661
Ceres (dwarf planet) **3**, 199
Ceres (goddess) 469, 470,
  475
cerium 199
  properties 202
Cernunnos 474
Certas Co 188
Cervantes, Saavedra, Miguel
  de 343
cesium 199
Cetus constellation 6, 7
ceviche 153
Ceylon 837
Cézanne, Paul 440
CFCs 166
CGRO 12
CGS unit 166
Chablis 159
Chabon, Michael 356
Chabrier, Emmanuel 400
Chabrol, Claude 393
Chac 474

Chaco War 699, 811
Chad 674, **711**
  national holidays 578
  political leaders 296
  UN membership 645
Chad, Lake 32
  exploration 275
Chadwick, Sir James 178
  Nobel prize 186
chaffinch 92
Chagall, Marc 440
Chagos Archipelago 29
Chain, Sir Ernest Boris 186
chakras 140
chalcedony 27
Chalfie, Martin 188
chalk 25
Chamaeleon constellation 6,
  7
Chamberlain, Sir Austen 458
Chamberlain, Owen 186
Chamberlain, Richard 367
Chamberlen, Peter 189
Chambers, Sir William 454
chameleon 102
chameleon, tiger 120
chamois 81
Chamoiseau, Patrick 356
Champ, The 397
champions:
  100 greatest 559
  winners 1992–2008 521
Chandigarh 639
Chandler, Raymond 343
Chandos, Oliver Lyttelton, 1st
  Viscount 193
Chandrasekhar,
  Subrahmanyan 178
  Nobel prize 187
Chanel, Gabrielle (Coco) 450
Chang Jiang, River 33
Changchun 639
Changsha 639
Changzhou 639
Channel Islands 29, **858**
Channel tunnel 226
Chant du rossignol, Le 433
chanterelle 77
Chaos 482
chaos theory 166
chapati, chapatti 153
Chaplin, Charlie 367
Chaplin, Geraldine 367
Chapman, George 360
Chapman, W H 191
Chapman and Hall
  publishers 190
Chardonnay 159
Chariots of Fire 398
charismatic movement 502
Charisse, Cyd 367
Charlemagne 286
  conquests 275
Charles I 256, 277
Charles IV 263, 780
Charles IX 276
Charles, Jacques-Alexandre-
  César 178
Charles, Ray 409, 418

Grammy awards 429
Charles's law 178
Charles the Great 275
Charleston 462
Charlotte (city) 639
Charlton, Bobby 559
Charly 398
Charon 474
Charpak, Georges 187
Chartres Cathedral 246, 453
World Heritage site 53
Chase, Chevy 367
chasseur 153
château 159, 161
Chateaubriand 153
Château de Versailles 461
Chateauneuf-du-Pape 159
chaturanga 565
Chatwin, Bruce 343
Chaucer, Geoffrey 251, 357
Chausson, Ernest 400
Chauvin, Yves 187
Chauviré, Yvette 435
Chávez Frías, Hugo 874
chayote 67
Cheboksary 639
Chechen wars 819
Chechnya 819
checkers 565
Checkmate (ballet) 433
Cheddar 163
nutritional value 150
cheese 163
nutritional value 150
cheetah 81
records 89
chefs 156
Cheiron 471, 472, **474**, 484
Chekhov, Anton 267, 360
chelating agents 152
Chelonia 102
Chelwood, Viscount Cecil
of 458
Chelyabinsk 639
chemical composition of
Sun's photosphere 1
chemical sediments 25
chemin de fer 565
chemistry 174
Chemnitz 639
Chengdu 639
Chenin Blanc 159
Chennai (Madras) 639
Chen Ning-Yang 186
Chen Yuan-ping 517
Cher 367, 418
Academy Awards 398
Cherenkov, Pavel 186
Cherepovets 639
cherimoya 64
Chermayeff, Serge 454
Chernobyl 46
cherry (fruit):
nutritional value 150
sour 63
sweet 63
cherry (sour) tree 74
cherry, cornelian (shrub) 72
Cherry, Don 409

cherry, morello (tree) 74
cherry, wild (tree) 74
chert 25
cherubim 472
chervil 64
Chesapeake Bay Bridge-
Tunnel 226
Chesbrough tunnel 226
Cheshire 659
Cheshire cheese 163
chess 565
fixture results 529
Chesterton, G K 344
chestnut, horse 74
chestnut, Spanish 74
chestnut, sweet 74
chest pain 133, 134
Chevalier, Maurice 367
Cheyenne 278
Chi 139
Chianti 159
Chiba 639
Chicago 639, 645
museums and galleries 462
Chicago (film) 399
Chicago, Judy 440
Chicago Symphony
Orchestra 407
chicken 150
collective names 118
chicken pox 131
chickpea 67
nutritional value 150
Chiclayo 639
Chicoasén dam 227
chicory 64, 67
Chifeng 639
chiffon 153
Chihuahua 639
Chihuahuan Desert 33
Child, Julia 157
childbirth, study of 176
childbirth infections 133
children, daily energy
requirements 147
Children of a Lesser God 398
children's shoe sizes,
international 222
Childs, Lucinda 432
Chile 674, **712**
national holidays 578
political leaders 297
UN membership 645
World Heritage sites 52
chilli pepper 66
Chim, David Seymour 446
Chimaera, Chimera 474
Chimkent 639
chimpanzee 81
length of pregnancy 89
China 674, **713**
civil war 279
dynasties 281
inventions 188, 190, 191
most populous nations 638
national holidays 578
political leaders 297
revolution 278
UN membership 645

World Heritage sites 52
chinaberry tree 76
china wedding
anniversary 575
chinchilla 82
Chin dynasties 281
Ch'in dynasties 281
Chinese calendar 575
Chinese festivals 498
Chinese language 584
Chinese lantern 72
chinese leaf 67
Chinese New Year 498
chionodoxa 69
chip (computing) 166
chipmunk 87
Chirico, Giorgio de 440
Chiron Corporation research
team 137
chiropody 139
chiropractic 139
Chita 639
Chittagong 639
Chitwan national park/nature
reserve 49
chives 64, 67
Chivor dam 227
chlorine 199
chlorofluorocarbons 166
chloroform 136
chlorophylls 164, **166**
chocho 67
chocolate 188
nutritional value 150
Choi Hong Hi, General 520
cholecalciferol 130
cholera 131
immunization 144
cholera vibrion 136
cholesterol 166
cholesterol-lowering
drugs 142
Cholmondeleys, The 436
Chongjin 639
Chongju 639
Chongqing 639
Chonju 639
Chonos Archipelago 29
Choo, Jimmy 450
Cho Oyu 34
Chopin, Frédéric 400
ballet music 434
choreographers 432
works 433
Chou dynasties 281
choux pastry 153
Christadelphians 502
Christchurch 639
Christ Church Picture
Gallery 462
Christian, Charlie 409
Christian calendar 493, 577
Christian denominations 493
Christian feasts:
immovable 493
movable 493
Christianity 492
denominations 493
distribution of adherents 489

sacred texts 501
Christian names,
meanings 596
Christie, Dame Agatha 344
Christie, James 193
Christie, Julie 367
Academy Awards 398
Christie, Sir William 18
Christmas-berry 76
Christmas Day 493, 577
Christmas Eve 577
Christmas rose 70
Christo 440
chromatics 174
chromium 199
in diet 130
properties 202
chromosomal abnormalities,
study of 174
chromosome,
chromosomes 121, **166**,
167, 168, 172
discovery 136
chromosome X 136
chromosphere 1
chronometer 188
chrysanthemum 70
month association 575
chrysoprase 27
Chthonia 475
Chu, Steven 187
Chuang-tzu 501
chub 106
chukka 518
Chulaki 433
Chungho 639
Churchill, Sir Winston 458
Church of England 493
Church of Jesus Christ of
Latter-Day Saints 502
Churriguera, Don José 454
Chu'un Ch'iu 498
ciabatta 153
Cibber, Colley 359
cicada 115
Ciechanover, Aaron 187
Cimabue 440
Cimarron 397
Cimino, Michael 398
Cincinnati 639
museums and galleries 462
Cinderella 433
cinema 188
wide screen 188
cinnamon 66
cinquefoil 70
Cinsault 159
Cipasang dam 227
circadian rhythm 136
Circe **474**, 479, 485
Circinus constellation 6, 7
circle 205
conic sections 206
circulation of the blood **127**
discovery 180
circumnavigation of the
globe 274
cirrocumulus clouds 45
cirrostratus clouds 45

cirrus clouds 45
cistus 72
CITES 120
CITIC Plaza building 228
citrates 152
citrine 27
Citroën, André 193
city, cities 638
largest by population 644
City Ballet of London 436
City of Birmingham Symphony
Orchestra 407
Ciudad Guayana 639
Ciudad Juárez 639
civet 82
civet, African 120
civil disobedience 663
civil rights 663
civil wars 277, 278, 279
Angola 683
Bosnia and Herzegovina 700
El Salvador 731
Guatemala 747
Laos 773
Pakistan 693
Somalia 832
Sudan 838
Clackmannanshire 661
cladistics 174
Claiborne, Craig 157
Claiborne, Liz 450
Clair, René 393
Clampitt, Amy 357
clams 118
Clapton, Eric 418
Grammy awards 429
Clare, John 357
claret 161
Clark, Michael 435
Clark, Petula 367
Clark, Steven 137
Clark, William 275
Clark and Gollan 188
Clarke, Sir Arthur C 344
Clarke, Kenny 410
Clash, The 418
classification:
organisms 61
sedimentary rocks 25
clastic rocks 25
Claude, Albert 187
Claude, Georges 190
Claude Lorraine 440
Claus, Carl Ernst 201
Clausius, Rudolf 182
Clavell, James 344
clay 25
Clay, Cassius 559
clay-pigeon shooting 515
clean mycena 77
Cleary, Jon 344
Cleese, John 367
clematis 72
Clemens, Samuel
Langhorne 354
clementine 63
Clementine space mission 12
Clement of Alexandria 504
Clemenza di Tito, La 405

Clergue, Lucien 446
clergy, forms of address 670
clerodendron 72
Cleve, Per Teodor 200, 202
Cleveland 639
museums and galleries 462
Cleveland Symphony
Orchestra 407
click beetle 117
Clift, Montgomery 367
Clifton suspension
bridge 224
construction 178
climate, study of 174
climate change 119
climatic conditions, study
of 176
climatic zones 39
climatology 174
climbing 566
Clio **474**, 481
clock:
mechanical 188
pendulum 188
quartz 188
wedding anniversary 575
clone 166
Clooney, George 367
Close, Glenn 367
cloth, measures of 213
clothes care symbols 614
clothes moth 116
clothes sizes,
international 222
Clotho 474
clouded agaric 77
clouds 44, 45
cloves 66
Cluedo® 565
Cluj-Napoca 639
Cluster II 12
clustered woodlover 79
Clytemnestra 471, **474**, 475,
477, 478, 480, 482
coagulation 136
coal 25
coalition 663
Coal Miner's Daughter 398
coal tar dyes 152
Coase, Ronald 459
Coates, Wells Wintemute 454
cobalt 199
properties 202
Cobb, Lee J 367
Cobb, Ty 559
COBOL computer
language 608
Coburn, Alvin 446
Coburn, James 367
cocaine 143
cocaine, crack 144
Cochabamba 639
Cochin 639
cochlea 136
Cochran, Eddie 418
cock 575
Cockatrice 474
Cockcroft, Sir John 186
Cocker, Joe 418

Cockerell, Charles 454
Cockerell, Christopher 189
cockle, common 111
Cockran, Mrs W A 189
cockroaches 114
  collective names 118
cocoa 66
coconut (spice) 66
coconut palm (tree) 76
Cocteau, Jean 393
cod 106
  nutritional value 150
Cod War 753
codeine 141
Coe, Sebastian 560
Coen, Ethan 393
  Academy Awards 399
Coen, Joel 393
  Academy Awards 399
Coetzee, J M 344
  literary prizes 355
  Nobel prize 459
coffee, instant 188
coffee tree 76
COGO computer
  language 608
Cohan, George M 403
Cohen, Leonard 418
Cohen, Stanley 187
Cohen-Tannoudji,
  Claude 187
Cohn, Edwin Joseph 137
Coimbatore 639
coin-collecting 566
Colbert, Claudette 397
cold, common 131
cold-blooded reptiles 102
Coldplay 418
  Grammy awards 429
Cole, Natalie 429
Cole, Nat 'King' 410
  Grammy awards 429
Coleman, Ornette 410
Coleoptera 110, 117
Coleraine 662
Coleridge, Samuel Taylor 357
Colette, Sidonie
  Gabrielle 344
Coll 30
Collatinus 480
collective names for
  mammals, fish and
  birds 118
Collier, Marie 406
Colline Gate 488
Collins, Albert 410
Collins, Joan 367
Collins, Phil 429
Collins, Wilkie 344
colloid 164, 166, 167
Colman, Ronald 397
Cologne 639
  museums and galleries 460
Cologne Cathedral 53
Colombard 159
Colombia 674, 715
  national holidays 578
  political leaders 298
  UN membership 645

World Heritage sites 52
Colombo 639
Colorado 866
Colorado beetle 117
Color of Money, The 398
Colossus of Rhodes 233, 280
colours, E numbers 152
colours, study of 174
colour therapy 140
colquhounia 72
Colson, Charles W 509
Colt, Samuel 191
Coltrane, John 410
Coltrane, Robbie 368
colugo 82
Columba constellation 6, 7
Columbia River 275
Columbia space shuttle 14,
  15
  record 18
columbine 70
Columbus (city) 639
Columbus, Christopher 274
Colvin, Shawn 429
coma (comets) 8
coma (medical) 133, 134, 135
Coma Berenices
  constellation 6, 7
Comaneci, Nadia 560
Combescot, Pierre 356
combined oral
  contraceptives 142
Come Back, Little Sheba 397
Comedy of Errors, The 362
comet 166, 172
comets 8
  space missions 12
Coming Home 398
Comité International de la
  Croix-Rouge 457, 458
Commander Islands 29
Commandments, Ten 493
commensalism 166
Commodore Barry
  bridge 224
common abbreviations 598
common cold 131
common earthball 77
common grisette 78
common illegal drugs 143
commonly prescribed
  drugs 141
common maple 75
common measures 212
common morel 78
common oak 75
common puffball 78
common similes 594
common spadefoot 100
common stinkhorn 78
Commonwealth 647
  membership 647
  Secretaries-General 647
Commonwealth Games 514
Commonwealth of
  Independent States 647
  membership 647
communication, study of 177
communication

problems 139
communications 197
communications satellites 11
Communism 663
Communism Peak 34
Communist rebellion in
  China 278
Comoro Islands 29
Comoros 674, 716
  national holidays 578
  political leaders 298
  UN membership 645
compact disc 188
Compaoré, Blaise 704
comparative anatomy 178
compass:
  discovery of magnetite 188
  first record of 188
complementary
  medicine 139
composers 399
composition of selected
  foods 150
Compton-Burnett, Dame
  Ivy 344
computer 189
  electronic digital 189
computer languages 608
Comte, Auguste 464
Conakry 639
conception, prevention 142
Concertgebouw
  Orchestra 407
Concerto Barocco 433
conch 110
Conchobhar 474
Concorde aircraft 271
concrete 189
condensation 44
Condon, Richard 344
condor 90
conductance 209
conductor 164, 165, 166,
  167, 172
cone 205
  conic sections 206
cone shell 110
Confederacy 864
Confederate states 278
Confidence pour
  confidence 356
Confucianism 498
  sacred texts 501
Confucius (K'ung Fu-
  tse) 498, 504
confusion 131, 132, 143
congenital 166
conger eel 106
conglomerate 25
Congo 674, 717
  national holidays 578
  political leaders 298
  UN membership 645
Congo, Democratic Republic
  of the 674, 718
  civil wars 279
  national holidays 578
  political leaders 299
  UN membership 645

World Heritage sites 52
Congo River 33
  exploration 275
Congressional Medal of
  Honor 669
Congreve, William 360
conic sections 206
conjunctivitis 131, 134
Connecticut 866
Connell, Evan S 344
Connery, Sir Sean 368
Connors, Jimmy 560
Conrad, Joseph 344
Conran, Jasper 451
Conran, Sir Terence 193
Consentes Dii 474
Conservatism 663
consommé 153
Constable, John 440
Constant, Paule 356
Constanta 639
Constantine 639
Constantinople, fall of 252,
  276
constellations 6
constitution 663
constricting snakes 102
Constructivism 437
Consul, The 405
consumption 210
Consus 469
contact lenses 189
Contagem 639
Conté, Nicholas 190
contemporary art museums:
  Europe 459
  UK 461
  USA 462
Conti, Tom 368
continental drift 22, 166
continents 28
  formation 22
contraceptive drugs 142
contraceptive pill 189
contract bridge 565
  fixture results 529
Contras 279, 802
convection 166
convenience foods 149
conversion factors 214
  SI factors 209
conversion tables:
  area 216
  capacity 218
  length 215
  tyre pressures 220
  volume 217
  weight 220
  temperature 211
convulsions 133
Conwy 661
Cook, James 274
Cook, Thomas 192
Cooke, Sam 418
cookery 566
cookery writers 156
Cook Islands 29
Cook pine (tree) 76
Cookson, Dame

Catherine 344
Cookstown 662
Cooper, Alice 418
Cooper, Daniel M 192
Cooper, Gary 368
  Academy Awards 397
Cooper, Geoffrey 137
Cooper, Jilly 344
Cooper, Leon 186
Cooper, William 344
coot 99
Copenhagen 639
  museums and galleries 460
Copernican theory 178, 180
Copernicus, Nicolaus 178,
  255
Copland, Aaron 400
  ballet music 433, 434
Coppélia 433
copper 199
  in diet 130
  properties 202
  wedding anniversary 575
copper beech (tree) 74
Coppola, Francis Ford 393
  Academy Awards 398
Coquette 397
coral, corals 28
  fossils 23, 24
  geological record 23
  wedding anniversary 575
CORAL computer
  language 608
Coralli 433
coral reefs 120
Coral Sea 32
coral shower tree 76
coral tree 76
Corbett national park/nature
  reserve 49
Corbières 159
Cordelia 480
Córdoba (Argentina) 639
  World Heritage site 51
Córdoba (Spain) 243
  World Heritage site 57
cordon bleu 153
Corea, Chick 410
Corelli, Arcangelo 400
Corey, Elias James 187
Cori, Carl 186
Cori, Gerty 186
coriander 65, 66
Corinth 275
Coriolanus 362
Coriolis effect 166
Cormack, Allan M 187
Corman, Roger 393
cormorant 95
corms 69
corn (cereal) 62
corn on the cob 150
cornea, scarring of 134
Corneille, Pierre 360
cornelian cherry 72
Cornell, Eric A 187
Corner, George
  Washington 137
Cornforth, Sir John

Warcup 187
Corning, James Leonard 135
Cornwall 659
corona (Sun) 1
Corona Australis
  constellation 6, 7
Corona Borealis
  constellation 6, 7
coronaviruses 133
coronilla 72
Corot, Jean Baptiste
  Camille 440
Corpus Christi 493, 494
  national holidays 577
Correggio 440
Correr Museum 461
corrida de toros 515
Corrigan, Mairead 459
corrugated iron 189
Corsica 53
Corson, Dale 199
Corte Real, Gaspar 274
corticosteroid drugs 142
cortisone 136
Cortona, Pietro Berrettini
  da 454
corundum 27
  Mohs' hardness scale 28
Corunna, Battle of 277
Corvus constellation 6, 7
corylopsis 72
coryza 131
Così Fan Tutte 405
Cosindas, Marie 446
cosmic rays 166
cosmology 174
cosmos (flower) 575
Cosmos 186/188 11
Costa Rica 674, 718
  national holidays 578
  political leaders 299
  UN membership 645
  World Heritage sites 52
Costello, Elvis 418
Coster, Dirk 200
costmary 64
Costner, Kevin 368
  Academy Awards 398
Côte d'Ivoire (Ivory
  Coast) 674, 720
  national holidays 578
  political leaders 299
  UN membership 645
  World Heritage sites 52
Côtes du Rhône 159
Cotillard, Marion 399
cotton, wild (tree) 76
cougar 86
coughing 132, 135
Coulomb, Charles Augustin
  de 178
Council of the European
  Union 648
councils:
  England 659
  Northern Ireland 662
  Scotland 661
  Wales 661
countess, form of

address 670
countries 679
 areas 673
 currencies 673
 populations 673
country dancing 566
Country Girl, The 398
county councils, England 659
coupe 154
Couperin, François 400
Courbet, Gustave 440
courgette 67
 nutritional value 150
Cournand, André 186
Courrèges, André 451
Courrier, Robert 137
courser 94
Court, Margaret 560
Courtaulds Ltd 188
Courtenay, Tom 368
Court of Auditors (EU) 648
Courtois, Bernard 200
'court' tennis 519
couscous 154
Cousin, Victor 464
Cousteau, Jacques 269, 568
Coventry 639
 council 659
 museums and galleries 461
cow 89
Coward, Sir Noël:
 plays 360
 songwriting 403
cowbird 91
Cowdray Park 546
Cowper, William 357
cowrie 110
coxswain 519
coyote 82
coypu 82
CPR 128
crab 150
 edible 112
 fiddler 112
 hermit 112
 robber 112
crab apple tree 74
Crabbe, George 357
crab spider 113
crack cocaine 144
cracking 166
Cracow 639
 World Heritage site 56
Cragg, Tony 444
Craig, Charles 406
Craigavon 662
Cram, Donald J 187
Cranach, Lucas, (the
 Elder) 255, 440
cranberry 63
crane 99
 collective names 118
crane, Siberian 120
Crane, Stephen 344
cranefly 116
cranial osteopathy 140
craniosacral therapy 140
Cranko, John 432
 ballets 434

crape myrtle 76
craps 565
Crash 399
Crater constellation 6, 7
Crawford, Broderick 397
Crawford, Joan 368
 Academy Awards 397
Crawford, Osbert 446
Cray, Robert 410
crayfish, noble 112
cream 150
Cream (pop group) 419
Crécy, Battle of 276
credit card 189
Creed, Martin 444
Creedence Clearwater
 Revival 419
crème 154
crème fraîche 154
Creon 472, 474, 484
crêpe 154
Cressida 474, 482, 487
Cretaceous period 23
 fossils 24
cretinism 130
cribbage 565
Crick, Francis 136, 178
 Nobel prize 186
cricket 515
 fixture results 530
cricket, bush 114
cricket, house 114
cricket field positions 530
crickets 114, 421
Crimean War 264, 278
Crime in the Neighborhood,
 A 355
crinum 69
crisps 150
Cristofori, Bartolomeo 190
criteriums 515
Croatia 674, 721
 EU membership 648
 national holidays 578
 political leaders 299
 UN membership 645
 World Heritage sites 52
Croats 721
Croce, Benedetto 464
crochet 566
crocodile 89, 102
 collective names 118
Crocodylia 102
crocosmia 69
crocus 69
Crohn's disease 142
croissant 154
Cro-Magnon man 229
Cromarty shipping forecast
 area 59
Crompton, Samuel 191
Cromwell, Oliver 256, 286
 military campaigns 277
Cromwell, Richard 286
Cronenberg, David 393
Cronin, James W 187
Cronstedt, Baron Axel
 Fredrik 200
Cronus 469, 474, 485, 488

Crookes, William 202
croquante 154
croquet 515
 fixture results 531
croquette 154
Crosby, Bing 368
 Academy Awards 397
Crosby, Stills, Nash and
 Young 419
Cross, Christopher 429
cross-country running
 fixture results 531
cross-country skiing 519
crosses 510
crossword puzzle 189
croûte 154
croûton 154
crow 91
 collective names 118
Crow, Sheryl 419
 Grammy awards 429
Crowe, Russell 368
 Academy Awards 399
crown green bowls 515
crown imperial 69
cru 161
crude oil 213
Cruise, Tom 368
Cruls comet 8
Crusades, The 276
crust 20, 21
Crustacea 112
crustaceans 112
Crutzen, Paul J 187
Crux constellation 6, 7
Cruz, Penélope 368
cryogenics 174
crystal 189
 wedding anniversary 575
Crystal, Billy 368
crystal healing 140
crystallography 174
CST 140
Ctesibius 189, 192
Cuba 674, 722
 island group 28, 29
 national holidays 578
 political leaders 299
 UN membership 645
 World Heritage sites 52
cube roots 204
cubes of numbers 204
Cubism 437
Cu Chulainn 474
cuckoo 96
cuckoo-roller 96
cuckoo-spit 115
cucumber 67
 nutritional value 150
Cucuta 639
Cudworth, Ralph 464
Cugnot, Nicolas 188
Cukor, George 398
Culiacan 639
culinary terms of foreign
 origin 153
Culloden, Battle of 277
Cullum, Jamie 410
Culp, Robert 368

A-Z Index

Cultural Revolution 270, 715
Culture Club 419
Cumberland Mountain tunnel 226
Cumbria 659
cumin 66
cummings, e e 357
cumulonimbus clouds 44
cumulus clouds 44
Cunard, Sir Samuel 193
cuneiform writing 231
Cunning Little Vixen, The 405
Cunningham, Imogen 446
Cunningham, Merce 432
  ballets 434
Cunningham, Michael 356
Cupid 469, **474**
Cupid's dart (flower) 70
Cupitt, Don 505
Curaçao 801
curassow 99
Cure, The 419
Curiatii 478
curie 209
Curie, Marie **178**, 199, 201, 267
Curie, Pierre **178**, 199, 201, 267
Curitiba 639
curium 178, **199**
Curl, Robert, Jr 182
  Nobel prize 187
curlew, stone 94
curling 515
  fixture results 532
currant, flowering 72
currencies, world 673
current, currents (electrical) 164, **166**, 169
curry leaf 66
Curtis, Edward 446
Curtis, Jamie Lee 368
Curtis, Tony 368
Curtiz, Michael 393
  Academy Awards 397
curtonus 69
Cusack, Cyril 368
Cushing, Peter 368
Custer, General 278
Custer's Last Stand 278
cuttle-bone 111
cuttlefish, common 111
Cuvier, Georges 178
Cuvilliés, François de 454
Cuzco 254
  World Heritage sites 56
cyanocobalamin 130
Cybele 469, 473, **474**
cybernetics 174
Cyclades 29
cyclamen 69
cycling 515
  energy expenditure 148
  fixture results 532
cyclocross 515
  fixture results 532
cyclone 166
  windstorms 42

Cyclopes **474**, 477, 482, 484
Cyclops **474**, 476, 484
cyclosporin-A 136
cyclotron 178, 182
Cygnus constellation 6, 7
cylinder, area 205
Cymbeline 362
cypress, Lawson 74
Cyprus 674, **723**
  administrative divisions 650
  Commonwealth membership 647
  Crusader conquest 276
  EU membership 648
  national holidays 578
  political leaders 300
  Turkish invasion 279
  UN membership 645
  World Heritage sites 53
Cyrano de Bergerac (film) 397
Cyrillic alphabet 239, 605
cystitis 135
cytogenetics 174
cytology 174
cytotoxic drugs 141
Czech Republic 674, **724**
  administrative divisions 650
  EU membership 648
  national holidays 578
  political leaders 300
  UN membership 646
  World Heritage sites 53
Czechoslovakia:
  political leaders 300
  Soviet invasion 279
  UN membership 645

D

dab 106
dace 106
Dada art 437
Daedalus **474**, 478, 481
daffodil 69
Dafoe, Willem 368
Daguerre, Louis 446
Dahl, Roald 344
dahlia 70
Dahomey 697
Daily Express 612
Daily Mail 612
Daily Mirror 612
Daily Record 612
Daily Star 612
Daily Star Sunday 612
Daily Telegraph 612
Daimler, Gottlieb 188, 190
Dai-shimizu tunnel 226
daisy 70
  month association 575
Dakar 639
Dalí, Salvador 269, 440
Dalí Museum 460
dal, dahl 154
Dalai Lama 272, 505
  Nobel prize 459
Dale, Henry Hallet 137
Dalian 639

Dallas 639, 645
  museums and galleries 462
Dalton, John 178
Dalton, Timothy 369
Dalton's law 178
Dam, Henrik 139, 186
Damascus 639
  World Heritage site 58
Dambulla (Golden Rock Temple) 57
Damnation of Faust, The 405
Damon, Matt 369
dams 227
damselfish 106
damson 63
Danaans 474
Danae 474
Da Nang 639
Danaoi 474
dance:
  choreographers 432
  companies 436
  dancers 435
Dance, Charles 369
Dance, George (the Elder) 454
Dance, George (the Younger) 454
dance movement therapy 140
Dances with Wolves 398
Dance Theater of Harlem 436
dancing 566
dandelion 65
Dandong 639
Dangerous (film) 397
Daniel Johnson dam 227
Daniels, Jeff 369
Danilova, Alexandra 435
Dankworth, Sir John 410
Danson, Ted 369
Dante, Joe 393
Dante Alighieri 251, 357
Danu 474
Danube delta 57
Dão 159
Daphne 474
Daphnis 474
Da Ponte, Lorenzo 403
Daqing 639
Dar es Salaam 639
d'Arblay, Mme (Fanny) 343
Darby, Abraham 191, 259
Darby, John Nelson 503
Dardanelles campaign 278
Darfur 838
  conflict 280
Darin, Bobby 429
Darling 398
Darlington 660
Darrell, Peter 432
  ballets 434
darter 95
Dartmoor 49
darts 516
  fixture results 533
Darwin, Charles 179, 265
Darwinian theory **166**, 169

date (fruit) 63
  nutritional value 150
date palm (tree) 76
date-plum 63
dates, national holidays 577
Datong 639
Dauberval 433
Daumier, Honoré 440
Dausset, Jean 137
  Nobel prize 187
Davaine, Casimir Joseph 136
Davao City 639
Davenant, Sir William 359
Davenport, Nigel 369
Davey, Grenville 444
David, Elizabeth 157
David, J 138
David, Jacques Louis 440
Davidson, Bruce 446
Davidson, Donald 465
Davidson, Lionel 344
Davies, Paul 509
Davies, Robertson 344
Davies, Ryland 406
Davies, Siobhan 432
Davis Strait 274
Davis, Bette 369
  Academy Awards 397
Davis, Geena 369
Davis, Joe 560
Davis, John 274
Davis, Judy 369
Davis, Marguerite 138
Davis, Miles 410
Davis, Raymond, Jr 187
Davis, Robert H 189
Davis, Sammy, Jr 419
Davis, Steve 560
Davis, Stuart 440
Davisson, Clinton 186
Davy, Sir Humphry **179**, 199,
  200, 201
  medical discoveries 137
Dawes, Charles 458
Dawkins, Richard 179
Day, Doris 369
Day-Lewis, Cecil 357
  Poets laureate 359
Day-Lewis, Daniel 369
  Academy Awards 398, 399
Daylight comet 8
daylight saving time 576
Day of Atonement 500
D-Day invasion 279
Deacon, Richard 444
  Turner prize 444
Dead Kennedys, The 419
deadly nightshade 65
Dead Man Walking 399
dead rat's tree 76
dean, form of address 670
Dean, James 369
death, causes of 135
death cap 78
Death in Venice (opera) 405
death's-head hawk moth 116
Death Valley national park/
  nature reserve 49
deathwatch beetle 117

de Beauvoir, Simone 344, 465
Debierne, André-Louis 199
Debreu, Gerard 459
Debussy, Claude 400
  ballet music 433
  operas 405
DeCarava, Roy 446
decathlon 516
deceiver, common
  laccaria 78
De Chéseaux comet 8
decibel scale 197
decimal numbers 207
Declaration of Independence,
  American 864
decompression chamber 189
decorative arts museums:
  Europe 459
  UK 461
  USA 462
de Duve, Christian 187
Deepavali 577
deepest caves 34
deepest diver (bird) 100
deepest dweller (fish) 109
Deep Purple 419
Deep Space 1 12
deepwater ports 635
deer 82
  collective names 118
deer, red 82
Deer Hunter, The 398
deficiency symptoms,
  minerals 130
deficiency symptoms,
  vitamins 130
definitions, political 663
Defoe, Daniel 259, 344
deforestation 46
Degas, Edgar 440
de Gaulle, Charles 738
de Gennes, Pierre-Gilles 187
degradation of habitats 119
degree (temperature) 209
De Havilland, Olivia 369
  Academy Awards 397
de Hevesy, George 186
Dehmelt, Hans G 187
Deighton, Len 344
Deimos 2
Deirdre 474
Deisenhofer, Johann 187
De Keersmaeker, Anne
  Teresa 435
Dekker, Thomas 360
de Klerk, F W 834
  Nobel prize 459
de Kooning, Willem 440
de la Mare, Walter 357
De la Renta, Oscar 451
Delacroix, Eugène 440
Delafield, E M 344
Delaware 866
Delaware Aqueduct
  tunnel 226
Delbrück, Max 179
  Nobel prize 186
Delhi 639, 644, 645
  World Heritage sites 54

d'Elhujar, Don Fausto 202
Delibes, Léo 433
DeLillo, Don 344
delirium 134
Delius, Frederick 400
  ballet music 434, 435
Deller, Alfred 406
Deller, Jeremy 444
Del Monaco, Mario 406
Delmonico, Lorenzo 157
Delorme, Philibert 454
Delos 480
  World Heritage site 54
Delphi:
  museums and galleries 460
  World Heritage site 54
delphinium 70
Delphinus constellation 6, 7
Delta Aquariids meteor
  shower 9
de Luca, Giuseppe 406
De Lucia, Fernando 406
Demarcay, Eugène 199
Demeter 469, **475**
demijohn 161
Demikhov, Vladimir P 189
Demme, Jonathan 393
  Academy Awards 399
de Mille, Agnes 432
  ballets 433, 434
de Mille, Cecil B 393
  Academy Awards 397
democracy 663
Democritus 465
demon, demons 472, **475**,
  476, 478, 480, 481, 485
De Mornay, Rebecca 369
Denbighshire 661
Dench, Dame Judi 369
dendrochronology 174
Deneb 7
Deneuve, Catherine 369
dengue fever 131
De Niro, Robert 369
  Academy Awards 398
denitrification 60
Denmark 674, **724**
  administrative divisions 650
  EU membership 648
  honours 668
  islands 29
  monarchs 283
  national holidays 579
  political leaders 300
  road signs 622
  territories 725
  UN membership 645
  World Heritage sites 53
density, SI units 208
density of polymers 203
density of the Sun 1
dental plate 189
Denver 639
  museums and galleries 462
Denver, John 419
deodar tree 74
deoxyribonucleic acid 121,
  167
  discovery 136

A-Z

Index

de Palma, Brian   393
Depardieu, Gérard   369
Departed, The   399
Depeche Mode   419
dependence on drugs   143,
   144
Depp, Johnny   369
depressants (drugs)   143
depression (medical)   131,
   141, 142, 143
depression
   (meteorological)   166
de Quincey, Thomas   344
Derain, André Louis   440
Derby   660
Derby, The   539
Derbyshire   659
de Reszke, Jean   406
Dergue   579, 735
dermatitis   130
dermatology   174
dermis   123
Dern, Bruce   369
Dern, Laura   370
Derrida, Jacques   270, 465
Derry   662
Desai, Anita   344
Desai, Kiran   355
Descartes, René:
   philosophy   465
   science   179
desertification   166
deserts, formation   166
deserts, largest   33
desfontainia   72
designers, fashion   450
desk set, wedding
   anniversary   575
Des Moines   462
Destiny's Child   419
destroying angel   78
destruction of habitats   119
detergents   189
detoxification
   treatments   141
Detroit   639
   museums and galleries   462
Detroit River tunnel   226
Detroit Symphony
   Orchestra   407
Deucalion   475, 477, 478
Deutsches Museum   460
deutzia   72
de Valois, Dame Ninette   432
   ballets   433, 434
devil's coach-horse   117
devil's hole pupfish   109
DeVito, Danny   370
devolution   663
Devon   659
   World Heritage sites   58
Devonian period   23
   fossils   24
De Vries, Peter   344
Dewey, John   465
Dhaka   639
dhal   154
dharma   498
Dhaulagiri (mountain)   34

diabetes   135, 142
Diaghilev, Sergei   432
diameters:
   planets   2
   Sun   1
diamond   27
   Mohs' hardness scale   28
   month association   575
   wedding anniversary   575
Diamond, Neil   419
Diamond Grace   48
Diamond Sculls   548
Diana   469, 470, 475
diarrhoea   46, 131, 132, 134
Dias, Bartolomeu   253, 274
Dias, Dinis   274
Dias, Diogo   274
Diat, Louis Felix   157
Diaz, Cameron   370
Diaz, Junot   356
DiCaprio, Leonardo   370
Dickens, Charles   344
   invention   190
Dickens, Monica   344
Dickinson, Emily   357
Dickson Wright, Clarissa   157
dictatorship   663
Diddley, Bo   419
Didion, Joan   344
Dido (myth)   475
Dido and Aeneas   405
Diels, Otto Paul
   Hermann   186
Diesel, Rudolf   189, 267
diesel engine   189, 267
diet   149
   macrobiotic   140
Dieterle, William   397
dietetics   139
dieting tips   149
Dietrich, Marlene   370
diffraction   166
diffusion   166
Digambara   499
digestive problems   141
digestive system   *125*
   discoveries   136
dill   65
Dillon, Matt   370
DiMaggio, Joe   560
Dimbleby, Josceline
   Rose   157
dimorphism   166
Dinesen, Isak   344
dingo   82
dingy agaric   78
dinosaurs   23
Diocesan Museum   460
Diogenes   465
Diomedes   475, 483
Dion, Celine   429
Dione   2
Dionysius Exiguus   188
Dionysus   469, 472, 475, 480,
   483, 485, 486
Dior, Christian   451
diorite   26
Dipavali   498
diphtheria   131

bacillus discovered   136
   immunization   144
   serum against   136
diplera   72
dipper   91
Diptera   110, 116
Dirac, Paul Adrien
   Maurice   179
direct current   166
directors   392
Dire Straits   419
Dis   470
disciples   492
disco dancing   567
discolouration   152
Discovery space shuttle   14,
   15
discus   516
disease, diseases   131
   complementary medical
      treatments   139
   immunization   144
   study of   174, 175, 176, 177
Disgrace   355
dishwasher, automatic   189
disinfection   136
dispersion   166
Disraeli (film)   397
Disraeli, Benjamin   344
dissidents   663
distances, air   634
distances, road   624
Di Stefano, Giuseppe   406
Distinguished Service
   Cross   669
Distinguished Service
   Order   668
District of Columbia   866
diuretic drugs   142
diurnal   166
diver   94
diving   516
   fixture results   553
Divorcee, The   397
Diwali   498
   national holidays   579
Dix, Otto   440
Dixie Chicks   429
Diyarbakir   639
Djibouti   674, 726
   national holidays   579
   political leaders   301
   UN membership   646
DNA   121, 165, 167, 170, 173
   discovery   136, 178, 185, 271
DNA fingerprinting   181, 273
Dnepropetrovsk   639
DOC   161
DOCG   161
docking in space   11
doctor, form of address   670
Dodecanese Islands   29
Dodge City   462
Dodgson, Charles   343, 446
Doesburg, Theo van   454
dog   82
   Chinese calendar   575
   collective names   118
   in space   11

length of pregnancy 89
dogfish 106
Dogger shipping forecast area 59
dogtooth violet 69
dogwood (shrub) 72
dogwood, common (tree) 74
Doha 639
Doherty, Peter C 179
Nobel prize 187
Doisneau, Robert 446
Doisy, Edward 137
Nobel prize 186
Dolayatra 498
Dolcelatte 163
dolerite 26
Dolin, Sir Anton 435
choreography 434
dolomite 25, 27
dolorite 25
dolphin 82
collective names 118
length of pregnancy 89
dolphin, river 82
dolphinfish 106
Dolphy, Eric 410
Domagk, Gerhard 138
Nobel prize 186
Dome of the Rock, Jerusalem 241
Domesday Book 244
domestic chicken 100
dominant 167
Domingo, Placido 406
Dominica 674, 726
Commonwealth membership 647
English speakers 585
national holidays 579
political leaders 301
UN membership 646
World Heritage sites 53
Dominican Republic 674, 727
national holidays 579
political leaders 301
UN membership 645
World Heritage sites 53
dominions 472
Domino, Fats 410
dominoes 565
Donald, Ian 192
Doñana national park/nature reserve 49
Donar 470
Donat, Robert 370
Academy Awards 397
Donatello 253, 444
Donati comet 8
Don Carlos 405
Doncaster 659
doner kebab 154
Donetsk 639
Don Giovanni 405
Donizetti, Gaetano 405
Donleavy, J P 344
Donne, John 257, 357
Donner, Richard 393
Donohoe, Amanda 370
Donovan, Terence Daniel 446

Don Pasquale 405
Don Quixote (ballet) 433
Doobie Brothers, The 429
Doolittle, Hilda 357
Doors, The 419
Doppler, Christian Johann 179
Doppler effect 167, 179
Dorado constellation 6, 7
dorado 106
Doré, Gustave 440
Dorians 477, 745
dormouse 82
Dorn, Friedrich 201
Doros 477
Dors, Diana 370
Dorset 659
World Heritage sites 58
Dorsey, Tommy 410
Dortmund 639
dory 106
Dorylaeum, battles of 276
Doshi, Balkrishna 454
Dos Passos, John Roderigo 344
Dostoevsky, Fyodor 344
Douala 639
Doubleday, Abner 514
Double Life, A 397
Double Ninth Festival 498
Double Palmtree, The 461
Douglas, Kirk 370
Douglas, Michael 370
Academy Awards 398
dove 118
Dover shipping forecast area 59
dowager, form of address 670
Dowell, Sir Anthony 435
Down (N Ireland) 662
Downing Street Declaration 857
Down's Syndrome 136
Doyle, Sir Arthur Conan 345
Doyle, Roddy 345
literary prizes 355
Dr Jekyll and Mr Hyde (film) 397
Drabble, Margaret 345
Draco constellation 6, 7
dragon, dragons 475
Chinese calendar 575
Dragon Boat Festival 498
dragonfly 114
dragon tree 76
Drake, Francis 255, 274, 277
dramatherapy 139
Draper, Henry 446
draughts 565
fixture results 533
Dravidian languages 584
Dresden 639
museums and galleries 460
World Heritage site 53
dressage 533
Dressler, Marie 397
dressmaking 567
Drew, Richard 191

Dreyfuss, Richard 370
Academy Awards 398
Drigo 433
drill, electric hand 189
drill, pneumatic 189
Driving Miss Daisy 398
dromedary 82
drongo 91
drug abuse symptoms 143, 144
drug dependence 143, 144
drugs:
commonly prescribed 141
illegal 143
study of effects 176
Druze 775
distribution of adherents 490
dryad, dryads 475, 482
dryad's saddle 78
Dryden, John 259, 357, 360
Poets laureate 359
dry ice 167
Dubai 639
Dubin, Al 404
Dublin 640
museums and galleries 460
Dubna, Russia 199, 201
dubnium 199
Dubrovnik 52
Duchamp, Marcel 440
Duchenne, Guillaume 179
duchess, form of address 670
duck 93
collective names 118
Duclos du Hauron, Louis 446
Dudley 659
Dudok, Willem 454
Duffy, Carol Ann 357
Duffy, Maureen 345
Du Fu 238, 241
Dufy, Raoul 440
du Gard, Roger Martin 458
duiker 82
Duisburg 640
Dukas, Paul 400
duke 668
form of address 670
Duke Bluebeard's Castle 405
Dukou 640
Dulbecco, Renato 179
Nobel prize 187
Dumas, Alexandre (fils) 345
Dumas, Alexandre (père) 345
du Maurier, Dame Daphne 345
Dumfries and Galloway 661
Dummer, Geoffrey 189
Dunaway, Faye 370
Academy Awards 398
Dunbar, William 357
Duncan, Isadora 435
Dundee 661
Dungannon 662
Dunham, Katherine 435
dunite 26
Dunkirk evacuation 278
Dunlop, John Boyd 193

inventions 192
Dunmore, Helen 345
Dunn, Douglas (dancer) 435
Dunn, Douglas (poet) 357
Dunn, Nell 345
Duns Scotus, John 248, 465
Duo Concertant 433
Dupond, Patrick 435
Du Pont, Pierre 193
Du Pont Nemours,
 Eleuthère 193
Duque de Caxias 640
Duran Duran 419
Durban 640
Durbin, Deanna 370
Dürer, Albrecht 440
Durga 475
Durga-puja 498
Durgapur 640
Durham 659
 World Heritage site 58
durian 76
Durrell, Gerald 345
Durrell, Lawrence 345
Dushanbe 640
Düsseldorf 640
Dutch art 437
Dutch elm 74
Dutch National Ballet 436
Dutch Wars of
 Independence 276
Dutilleux, Henri 400
Dutton, Geoffrey 357
Duvall, Robert 370
 Academy Awards 398
Duvall, Shelley 370
du Vigneaud, Vincent 186
DV8 Physical Theatre 436
Dvořák, Antonin 400
dwarf planet **167**, 171, 172
 planets 3
dwarf star 167
Dylan, Bob 403, 420
 Grammy awards 429
dynamics 174
dynamite 189
Dynamite, Ms 420
dynasties, ancient
 Egyptian 280
dynasties, Chinese 281
dyne 209
dysentery 131
Dyson, Freeman J 509
Dyson, Sir Frank 18
dysprosium 199
Dzhambul 640
Dzungaria 33

E

Ea 471, **475**
eagle:
 bald 90
 collective names 118
 golden 90
 harpy 90
 in golf 516
 sea 90
eagle ray 106

Eagles, The 420
 Grammy awards 429
Eakins, Thomas 447
Eanes, Gil 274
ear *128*
 study of 176
Eardley, Joan 440
earl 668
 form of address 671
Early Bird satellite 11
Earth 2, **19**, 165
 age 19
 area 19
 atmosphere 19, 20
 circumference 19
 mass 19
 pressure 20
 satellite 2, 3, 4
 space missions 11
 structure 20
 study of 175, 176
 temperature 19, 20
earthquake,
 earthquakes 167
 major 36
 plate tectonics 21
 severity measurement 37
 study of 176
 tsunamis 38
earthquake severity
 measurement 37
Earth, Wind and Fire 420
earwig 114
East Ayrshire 661
East China Sea 32
East Dunbartonshire 661
Easter 493, 494
Easter Island 31
 World Heritage sites 52
Easter Monday 577
Easter Rising 268, 278, 760
Easter Sunday 577
East Frisian Islands 30
East Germany 743
East Lothian 661
Eastman, George 447
 inventions 190
East Renfrewshire 661
East Riding of Yorkshire 660
East Sea 32
East Sussex 659
East Timor 674, 728
 Indonesia 757
 national holidays 579
 political leaders 301
 UN membership 646
Eastwood, Clint 370, 393
 Academy Awards 399
Ebadi, Shirin 459
Eberth, Karl Joseph 138
ebony 76
Ebony Concerto 433
Ebro River, Battle of 278
Eccles, Sir John 186
Echenoz, Jean 356
Echidna (myth) **475**, 478
echidna, long-beaked 79
echidna, short-beaked 79
echinacea 70

echinoderms 24
Echo 475
echolocation 80, 86
ECHO 1 satellite 11
Eckert, J Presper 189
Eckhart, Johannes 250, 505
eclogite 25
Eco, Umberto 273, 345
E. coli bacteria 131, 133
ecology 174
econometrics 174
economics 175
ecophysiology 174
ecosystem 167
 endangered 119, 120
Ecstasy (drug) 144
ectothermic 102
Ecuador 674, **729**
 national holidays 579
 political leaders 301
 UN membership 645
 World Heritage sites 53
ecumenism 502
eczema 142
Edam cheese 163
 nutritional value 150
Eddery, Pat 560
Edelman, Gerald M 186
edelweiss 70
Eden, Barbara 370
Edgerton, Harold 447
Edgeworth, Maria 345
edible fruits 63, 64
edible fungi 77
Edinburgh 640
 council 661
 museums and galleries 461
 World Heritage site 58
Edinburgh Missionary
 Conference 502
Edison, Thomas 179
 inventions 189, 190, 192
Edmonton 640
Edvard Munch Museum 460
Edwards, Gareth 560
EEG 136
eel 106
Effelsberg Radio Telescope 9
egg, nutritional value 150
egg-laying mammals 79
eggplant 67
 nutritional value 150
Eglevsky, André 435
Egreria 469
Egypt 674, **730**
 ancient dynasties 280
 inventions 188, 189, 191, 192
 national holidays 579
 political leaders 302
 UN membership 645
 World Heritage sites 53
Egyptian art 438
Egyptian gods 470
Egyptian Helen, The 405
Ehrlich, Paul 179
eider duck 100
Eid-ul-Adha 577
Eid-ul-Fitr 577
Eiffel Tower 267

Eigen, Manfred   186
Eigg   30
Eightfold Path   492
Eijkman, Christiaan   138
Eilean Siar council   661
Eileithyia   469
Einstein, Albert   **179**, 199
einsteinium   179, **199**
Einstein on the Beach   405
Einthoven, Willem   189
Eisenstaedt, Alfred   447
Eisenstein, Sergei   393
Ekberg, Anita   371
Ekeberg, Anders Gustaf   201
Ekland, Britt   371
Ekofisk   48
El Alamein, Battle of   278
eland   82
elasticity   176
ElBaradei, Mohamed   459
El Chichón volcano   35
El Cid   244
   battles   275
elderberry   65
Eldfell   35
Eldridge, Roy   410
electrical currents, study
   of   174
electric chair   189
electric charge, electric
   charges   **166**, 178
   study of   174
electric current   167, 172
   SI units   208
electric eel   106
electric field   167
electric flat iron   189
electric generator   189
electric guitar   189
electric heater   189
electricity   183
electric light bulb   189
Electric Light Orchestra   420
electric motor (AC)   189
electric motor (DC)   189
electric oven   189
electric ray   106
electrocardiography   174
   inventions   189
electrode   167
electrodynamics   177
electro-encephalogram   136
electrokinetics   174
electrolysis   167
electromagnet   189
electromagnetic
   constants   196
electromagnetic
   induction   179
   discoveries   181, 183
electromagnetics   174
electromagnetic waves   **167**,
   168, 169, 170, 171, 172
electromagnetism   174
   discoveries   181, 182, 183
electromyography   174
electron, electrons   164, 165,
   166, **167**, 168, 169, 170, 171
   physical constants   196

study of   174, 177
electronic games   567
electronics   174
electronvolt   209
electrophysiology   174
electrostatics   174
electrotherapeutics   179
Elegy for Young Lovers   405
Elektra (myth)   **475**, 484
Elektra (opera)   405
element, elements   164, 166,
   167, 170, 171
   atomic numbers   199
   Periodic table   198
   symbols   199
   table   199
elephant, African   83
   endangered species   120
   length of pregnancy   89
   records   89
elephant, Asian   120
elephant, collective
   names   118
elephant's-ear (tree)   76
Elgar, Sir Edward   400
   ballet music   433
El Giza   640
El Greco Museum   461
Elhujar, Don Fausto d'   202
Elias, Brian   433
Elion, Gertrude B   187
Eliot, George   345
Eliot, T S   357, 360
   Nobel prize   458
Elis, Don   410
Elite Syncopations   433
Elizabeth II   286
elk   82
   collective names   118
Elkin, Stanley   345
Ellesmere Island   28
Ellice Islands   29
Ellington, 'Duke'   403, 410
Elliott, Denholm   371
Elliott, Missy   420
ellipse   206
   conic sections   206
Ellis, Alice Thomas   345
Ellis, George F R   509
elm   74
El Mahalla el-Koubra   640
El Mansoura   640
Elmer Gantry   398
El Niño   **167**, 812
El Paso   640
El Salvador   674, **731**
   national holidays   579
   political leaders   302
   UN membership   645
   World Heritage sites   53
Elvehjem, Conrad   138
embryology   174
embryos   174
emerald   27
   month association   575
   wedding anniversary   575
Emerson, Ralph Waldo   357
emetic russula   78
Emin, Tracey   440

Eminem   420
Emirates Office Tower   228
Emmenthal cheese   163
emoticons   608
Empedocles   465
emperor penguin   100
emperors:
   Holy Roman Empire   286
   Japanese   281
   Mughal   283
   Roman   282
emphysema   140
Empire Falls   356
Empire State Building   228
Empson, Sir William   357
emu   89
emulsifiers   152
emulsifying salts   152
emulsion   167
Enceladus   2
enchilada   154
Encke comet   8
en croûte   154
encyclopedia   189
endangered species   119
Endeavour space shuttle   14,
   15
Enders, John   186
endive   67
endocrine system   124
   study of   174
endocrinology   174
endorphins   136
endoscope   189
endoskeleton   122
endothermic   167
endothermic animals   79
Endymion   475
energetics   174
energy   165
   daily energy
   requirements   147
   energy expenditure   148
   SI conversion factors   209
   SI units   208
energy consumed   148, 149
Engel, Johann   454
Engineering:
   bridges   224
   dams   227
   tallest buildings   228
   tunnels   226
England   856
   county councils   659
   monarchs   283
   national holidays   579
   unitary authorities   660
Engle, Robert F III   459
English Chamber
   Orchestra   407
English Civil War   246, 277
English elm   74
English language:
   differences between British
   and US English   591
   speakers   584, 585
English National Ballet   436
English Patient, The:
   film   399

novel 355
English speakers 584, 585
enhancers (flavour) 152
Enigma Variations 433
Enki 475, 478
Enlil 475
Eno, Brian 420
Enrico Fermi reactor 46
Enright, Anne 355
entomology 174
entrée 154
entrecôte 154
entrepreneurs 192
entropy 167
E numbers 152
  allergic reactions to 152
environmental disasters:
  land 46
  sea 48
enzyme, enzymes 167
  discoveries 136, 137
enzyme-catalyzed
  reactions 183
Eos 469, **475**, 478, 480, 482
epazote 65
épée 516
épée fencing 518
epicentre 167
Epicurus 465
epidemiology 174
epidermis 123
Epigoni 471, **475**, 485
epilepsy treatment 137
Epiphany 493
  national holidays 577
epistemics 175
epochs 23
Epona 469, **475**
Epsilon Eridani 8
Epsilon Indi 8
Epstein, Sir Jacob 444
equator 19
Equatorial Guinea 674, **732**
  national holidays 579
  political leaders 303
  UN membership 645
equestrian events 533
equinox 167
  seasons 575
Equuleus constellation 6, 7
eras 22, 23
Erasmus, Desiderius 255,
  505
Erato **475**, 481
erbium 199
Erebus 35
Erechtheum 474, 475
Erechtheus 475
erg 209
ergonomics 175
Erickson, Arthur 454
Ericsson, Leif 274
Eridanus constellation 6, 7
Erie, Lake 32
Eriksen, Gunn 157
Erik the Red 244, 274
Erin Brockovich 399
Erinyes 471, **475**
Eris (dwarf planet) 3

Eris (myth) 475
Eritrea 674, **732**
  national holidays 579
  political leaders 303
  UN membership 646
Erlanger, Joseph 186
ermine 87
Ernst, Max 440
Ernst, Richard R 179
  Nobel prize 187
E-road network 625
Eros 469, **475**, 484
Ertan dam 227
Ertl, Gerhard 188
eruptions, volcanic 35
erythronium 69
Eryx, Mount 474
Esaki, Leo 187
escalator 189
escallonia 72
escalope 154
Escher, M C 440
Escoffier, Auguste 157
Eskisehir 640
Esmeralda dam 227
ESO New Technology
  Telescope 9
ESO 3.6m telescope 9
ESP 176
espresso 154
Esquivel, Adolfo Pérez 459
Essen 640
  museums and galleries 460
  World Heritage site 54
Essex 659
Esson, Louis 360
Estevez, Emilio 371
Estonia 674, **733**
  administrative divisions 650
  EU membership 648
  national holidays 579
  political leaders 303
  UN membership 646
  World Heritage sites 53
ETA 835
Eta Aquariids meteor
  shower 9
Eteocles **475**, 479, 485
ethanol 164, **167**
ether 137
Ethiopia 674, **734**
  national holidays 579
  political leaders 303
  UN membership 645
  World Heritage sites 53
ethnic cleansing 279
ethnology museums:
  Europe 459
  UK 461
  USA 462
ethology 175, 180, 182, 185
ethyl alcohol 167
etiology 174
Etna 35
Eton College 516
Etosha national park/nature
  reserve 49
Eubacteria 61
Eucharist 493

euchryphia 72
Eucken, Rudolf 457
Euclid 179
Eugene Onegin (opera) 405
eugenics 175
Eugenides, Jeffrey 356
Euler, Leonhard 179
Eumenes II of
  Pergamum 190
Eumenides 476
Eupalinus tunnel 226
euphoria 143, 144
Euphrosyne 476
Euripides 360
Europa (myth) 473, **476**, 485
Europa (satellite) 2
Europe 28
  administrative divisions 649
  causes of death 135
  largest cities 644
  myth 476
  newspapers 612
European Central Bank 648
European Commission 648
  presidents 648
European Community 648
European Court of
  Justice 648
European Economic
  Community 648
European flea 116
European Investment
  Bank 648
European Parliament 648
  political groupings 648
European road signs 622
European Union 648
  institutions 648
  membership 648
  members' administrative
  divisions 649
europium 199
Euroroutes 625
Euryale 476
Eurydice 472, 476
euryops 72
Eurystheus 477
Eurythmics 420
Eusden, Laurence 359
Eusebius of Caesarea 237,
  505
Euterpe **476**, 481
evangelicalism 502
Evans, Bill 410
Evans, Dame Edith 371
Evans, Sir Geraint 406
Evans, Gil 410
Evans, Herbert McLean 137
Evans, Sir Martin J 188
Evans, Ray 404
Evans, Walker 447
evaporation 44
evening primrose 70
Everest 34
  conquest 275
Everett, Rupert 371
Everglades National Park 49
  World Heritage site 58
Evergreen Point bridge 224

Everitt, Percival 192
everlasting flower
  (immortelle) 70
everlasting flower, pearly 70
Everly Brothers, The 420
Evert, Chris 560
evolution, theory of 167,
  178, 179, 181
Evren Gunay Dudeni cave 34
Ewing, Maria 406
Excalibur 472
excitability 133
exercise 148
exhaustion 131
exobiology 175
exothermic 167
exploitation of species 119
exploration 274
Explorer space missions 11
explosives (invention) 189
expression marks,
  musical 431
Expressionism 438
extinction of species 119
extinguisher 189
Exxon Valdez 48
Eyck, Jan van 253, 440
eye, eyes 128, *129*, 165
  Purkinje's figure 184
  study of 176
eyesight 197
Eyre, Lake 32
Eysenck, Hans Jurgen 179

F

fabiana 72
Façade 433
facsimile machine (fax) 189
FA Cup 516
Fafnir 470
Fahrenheit, Gabriel 179
  inventions 192
Fahrenheit temperature
  scale 167
  conversion table 211
  SI conversion factors 209
Fairbairns, Zoë 345
Fairbanks, Douglas, Jr 371
Fairbanks, Douglas, Sr 371
fairies' bonnets 78
Fair Isle shipping forecast
  area 59
Fair Maid of Perth, The 405
fairy-ring champignon 78
Faisalabad 640
Faith, Percy 429
faiths, distribution of
  adherents 489
falcon, falcons 90
  trade in 120
falconry 516
Faldo, Nick 560
Falk, Peter 371
Falkirk 248, 661
Falkland Islands 29, **861**
Falklands War 272, 279, 686
Falla, Manuel de 400
  ballet music 435

Fall of Khartoum 278
Fallopian tubes, infection
  of 133
Fall River Legend 433
false blusher 78
false sunbird 98
Falstaff 405
Family (biology) 168
  classification 61
Famished Road, The 355
Fancy Free 433
Fang Feng 192
Fanthorpe, U A 357
FAO 646
Faraday, Michael 179
  inventions 189, 192
farce 154
farci 154
Fargo 399
Farhi, Nicole 451
Faridabad 640
Farmer, Fannie Merritt 157
Farmer, Philip José 345
Farmer's Daughter, The 397
Faroe Islands, Faroes 29, **725**
  shipping forecast area 59
Farrar, Geraldine 406
Farrell, Eileen 406
Farrell, Suzanne 435
Farrow, Mia 371
Farruk-siyar 283
Fascism 663
fashion designers 450
Fassbinder, Rainer
  Werner 393
Fast, Howard 345
fastest animal on two
  legs 100
fastest fish 109
fastest flyer (bird) 100
fastest mammals (on
  land) 89
Fastnet shipping forecast
  area 59
fat in diet 149
  nutritional value of
  foods 150, 151
fat soluble vitamins 130
Fates 476
fathom 210
FATIMA tunnel 226
Faulkner, William 345
  Nobel prize 458
fault (geology) 167
fault systems 21
Fauna 469
Faunus 469, **476**, 480
Fauré, Gabriel 400
  ballet music 433, 434
Faust (opera) 405
Fauvism 438
Fearnley-Whittingstall,
  Hugh 157
feathers, most (bird) 100
federalism 663
feedback 167
Fein, Wilhelm 189
Feininger, Andreas 447
Feinstein, Elaine 345

Feira de Santana 640
Feld Ballet NY 436
Feldenkrais method 140
Feldman 434
feldspar 25, 26
Fell, Norman 371
Fellini, Federico 393
fell walking 520, 567
female reproductive
  system 129
Feminist Art 438
fencing 516
  fixture results 534
Fenguoshan tunnel 226
Fenians 760
Fenn, John B 187
fennel 66
fennel, Florentine 65, 67
Fenton, Roger 447
fenugreek 66
Fermanagh 662
Fermat, Pierre de 179, 185
Fermat's 'last theorem' 179,
  185, 273
fermentation 167
fermi 210
Fermi, Enrico 179, 200
  Nobel prize 186
fermium 180, 200
Feronia 469
Ferrara 55
Ferrer, Jose 397
ferret 87
  collective names 118
  length of pregnancy 89
Ferret (myth) 476
Ferrier, Kathleen 406
Ferry, Bryan 420
Fert, Albert 188
fertilization 168
  discoveries 137
Festival of Pure
  Brightness 498
festivals:
  Buddhist 492
  Chinese 498
  Christian 493
  Hindu 498
  Islamic 499
  Japanese 500
  Jewish 500
feta cheese 163
fettuccine 154
Feuerbach, Ludwig 465
fever 131, 132, 133, 134, 135
feverfew 65
Feynman, Richard 180
  Nobel prize 186
Fez 640
  World Heritage site 56
Fibonacci, Leonardo 249
fibre in diet 149
  nutritional value of
  foods 150, 151
fibre optics 167
fibrin formation 136
Fichte, Johann Gottlieb 465
Fick, Adolph E 189
Fidelio 405

A-Z

Index

Fides 469
Field, Sally 371
  Academy Awards 398
field events (athletics) 514
field hockey 517
Fielding, Henry 345
field mushroom 78
Fields, Dorothy 403
Fields, W C 371
fields of scientific study 174
field theory 167
Fiennes, Ralph 371
Fife 661
5th Dimension 429
fig (fruit) 63
  nutritional value 150
fig (tree) 74
Figes, Eva 345
figure skating 517
figures of myth and
  legend 471
Fiji 674, **735**
  Commonwealth
    membership 647
  English speakers 585
  islands 30
  national holidays 579
  political leaders 303
  UN membership 645
filariae transmission 137
file fish 106
Fille du Régiment, La 405
Fille mal gardée, La 433
film (invention) 189
film and TV actors 363
film directors 392
Financial Times 612
finch 91
Finch, Peter 371
  Academy Awards 398
fine art museums:
  Europe 459
  UK 461
  USA 462
fines herbes 154
finfoot 99
fingerspelling, British 607
fingerspelling, US 607
Finisterre shipping forecast
  area 59
Finland 674, **736**
  administrative divisions 651
  EU membership 648
  monarchs 284
  national holidays 579
  political leaders 303
  UN membership 645
  World Heritage sites 53
Finlay, Carlos Juan 139
Finn mac Cumhal 476
Finney, Albert 371
Finnish Architecture, Museum
  of 460
Fiordland national park/
  nature reserve 49
fir, Douglas 75
fir, red 75
Fire, Andrew Z 187
  discoveries 138

Firearms Museum of 460
Firebird, The 433
Firestone, Harvey 193
firethorn 72
firming agents 152
first landing on Mars 275
first landing on the
  moon 275
first man in space 11, 275
first manned space flight 15,
  17
first names, meanings 596
first spacewalk 13, 15
first use of stone 280
first woman in space 11, 15
Firth, Colin 371
Firth, Peter 371
firwood agaric 78
Fischer, Bobby 560
Fischer, Edmond H 182
  Nobel prize 187
Fischer, Ernst Otto 187
Fischer-Dieskau,
  Dietrich 406
Fischer von Erlach,
  Johann 454
fish 79, **105**
  collective names 118
  endangered species 119
  records 109
Fisher, Carrie 371
Fisher, F(rances)
  K(ennedy) 157
Fisher King 483
fisher marten 85
Fisher shipping forecast
  area 59
fishing 516
fission 167, 170
Fitch, Val L 187
Fitou 159
Fitzgerald, Edward 357
Fitzgerald, Ella 411
Fitzgerald, F Scott 269, 345
Fitzgerald, Penelope 345
Fitzpatrick, Sean 560
FitzRoy shipping forecast
  area 59
Five Dynasties and Ten
  Kingdoms period 242, 281
Five pillars of faith 499
fives 516
Fjorgynn 470
Flack, Roberta 420
  Grammy awards 429
flagon 163
Flagstad, Kirsten 406
flambé 154
flame tree 77
flamingo 93
  collective names 118
Flamsteed, John 18
Flanders, Battle of 278
Flathead tunnel 226
flat racing 517
Flaubert, Gustave 265, 345
Flauergues comet 8
flavour modifiers 152
fleabane 70

fleas 116
  infection by 131, 134
Fledermaus, Die 405
Fleet debtors' prison 519
Fleetwood Mac 420
  Grammy awards 429
Fleming, Sir Alexander 180
  discoveries 137
  Nobel prize 186
Fleming, Ian 345
Fleming, Renée 406
Fleming, Victor 393
  Academy Awards 397
Flemings 695
Flemish 695
Fletcher, John 360
Fletcher, Louise 371
  Academy Awards 398
flies 116
  collective names 118
  infection by 133
flight 89
flightless birds 89
flint 25
Flintshire 661
Flixborough disaster 46
FLN (National Liberation
  Front) 681
Flodden, Battle of 276
floor exercise
  (gymnastics) 517
Flora 469, **476**
Florence 640
  museums and galleries 460
  World Heritage site 55
florentine 154
Florey, Baron (Howard) 186
Florida 866
  exploration 274
Flory, Paul J 187
flotation therapy 140
flounder 106
flour, nutritional value 150
flour treatment agents 152
flowering plants 69
flowerpecker 91
flowers:
  bulbs, corms, rhizomes and
    tubers 69
  herbaceous 70
  month associations 575
  shrubs 72
  wedding anniversary 575
Floyd, Keith 157
flu 132
fluid 166, **167**
fluid retention 142
fluidics 175
fluids, study of 175
fluoride in diet 130
fluorine 199
fluorite 27
  Mohs' hardness scale 28
fly agaric 78
flycatcher:
  New World 98
  Old World 91
  silky 91
  tyrant 98

fly fishing 521
Flying Dutchman, The 405
flying fish 106
flying times 634
Flynn, Errol 371
FNLA 683
f-number 167
Fo, Dario 360
Nobel prize 459
focaccia 154
Fogel, Robert 459
foil (fencing) 516
Fokine, Michel 432
ballets 433, 434
folic acid 130
folk museums:
Europe 459
UK 461
USA 462
Folkers, Karl 139
Folkwang Museum 460
Fomalhaut 7
Fomoiri 480
Fonda, Henry 371
Academy Awards 398
Fonda, Jane 371
Academy Awards 398
Fonda, Peter 372
fondue 154
Fontaine, Joan 372
Academy Awards 397
Fontainebleau 53
Fonteyn, Dame Margot 435
food, composition of 150
Food and Agriculture
Organization 646
food decay, inhibition 152
food poisoning,
inhibition 152
food storage time,
improvement 152
foot (unit of
measurement) 209, 210
football 516
energy expenditure 148
fixture results 535
football pitch 536
Football Association 516
foot massage 141
foot problems 139
Foraminifera 24
Forbes, Bryan 393
force 174
SI conversion factors 209
SI units 208
forceps (obstetric) 189
Ford, Ford Madox 345
Ford, Harrison 372
Ford, Henry 193
Ford, Henry, II 193
Ford, John 393
Academy Awards 397
Ford, John (playwright) 360
Ford, Richard 345
literary prizes 356
foreign phrases 585
foreign words 585
forenames, meanings 596
forensic science 197

Forest, Lee De 189, 190
Forester, C S 345
forests 46
rate of deforestation 46
forget-me-not 70
Forman, Miloš 394
Academy Awards 398
forms of address 669
Formula One racing 518
fixture results 544
Fornax constellation 6, 7
Forrest Gump 399
Forrester, Maureen 406
Forssmann, Werner 186
Forster, E M 267, 345
Forsyth, Frederick 345
forsythia 72
Fortaleza 640
World Heritage site 58
Forth Bridge (rail) 224
FORTH computer
language 608
Forth Road Bridge 224
Forth shipping forecast
area 59
Forties shipping forecast
area 59
Fort Lauderdale 462
Fort Myers 462
FORTRAN computer
language 608
Fortuna 469, **476**
Fort Worth 640
fossil, fossils 167
geological record 22, 23, **24**
study of 175
Foster, Jodie 372
Academy Awards 398
Foster, Norman, Baron 455
Fottinger, Hermann 189
Foucault, Jean 180
Foucault, Michel 465
Four Noble Truths 492
Four Seasons, The
(ballet) 433
Four Temperaments, The 433
Fowler, William A 187
Fowles, John 345
fox 83
collective names 118
length of pregnancy 89
Fox, George 256, 503, **505**
Fox, James 372
Fox, Michael J 372
foxglove 65, 70
foxhunting 516
foxtail millet 62
Foxx, Jamie 399
Fracci, Carla 435
fractal 167
fractions 207
fractography 175
Fragonard, Jean Honoré 440
Frame, Janet 345
France 674, **737**
administrative divisions 651
EU membership 648
honours 668
military ranks 667

monarchs 284
national holidays 579
overseas collectivities 739
overseas departments 738
overseas territories 739
political leaders 304
road signs 622
UN membership 645
World Heritage sites 53
France, Anatole 458
Francesca, Piero della 442
Francis, Dick 346
Francis of Assisi, St 248, 505
francium 200
Franck, César 400
ballet music 434
Franco, General 835
Franey, Pierre 157
frangipani 72
Frank, Il'ja 186
Frank, Robert 447
Frankfurt (am Main) 640
museums and galleries 460
frankfurter 154
Frankie Goes to
Hollywood 420
Franklin, Aretha 411, 420
Franklin, Benjamin 188, 190
Franklin, John 275
Franklin, Rosalind 180
medical discoveries 136
Franks 238, 239, 240, 738
Franz Ferdinand 420
Franz Josef Land 30
Frascati 159
Fraser, Lady Antonia 346
fraternal twins 167
fraxinella 70
Frayn, Michael 346
Frears, Stephen 394
Fredhällstunneln 226
freefalling 519
Free French forces 738
Freeling, Nicholas 346
Freeman, Morgan 372
Freemasonry 502
Freer Gallery of Art 463
Free Soul, A 397
freestyle (swimming) 520
Freetown 640
freeze-drying 189
Frege, Gottlob 465
Freiburg im Breisgau 460
Fréjus tunnel 226
Frelimo 796
Fremstad, Olive 406
French, Marilyn 346
French Connection, The 398
French Guiana 738
French language 584
French marigold 71
French Polynesia 31, **739**
French Revolution 262, 277,
738
French Revolutionary
Wars 277
French Southern and
Antarctic Territories 739
French Wars of Religion 254,

A–Z Index

276
Freni, Mirella   406
frequency   167
  SI units   209
frequency modulation
  (FM)   169
Freud, Lucian   440
Freud, Sigmund   180
Frey   470, **476**
Freya   202
Freyja   470, **476**, 482
Freyr   **476**, 482
fricassee   154
Frick, Henry   193
Frick Collection   462
Fried, Alfred   457
Friedkin, William   394
  Academy Awards   398
Friedman, Jerome I   187
Friedman, Milton   459
Friedrich, Caspar David   440
Friends, Society of   256, 503
Friends Service Council,
  The   458
frigatebird   95
Frigg   470, 473, **476**
Frigga   476
Frink, Dame Elizabeth   444
Frisch, Karl von   180
  Nobel prize   187
Frisch, Otto   188
Frisch, Ragnar   458
Frisian Islands   30
Frith, Francis   447
fritillaria   69
fritillary butterfly   115
frog:
  collective names   118
  common   100
  edible   100
  goliath   100
  leopard   100
  marsh   100
  painted   101
  parsley   101
  poison-arrow   101
froghopper   115
frogmouth   97
fromage frais   154
From Here to Eternity   398
front crawl   520
Frost, Robert   357
fruit   63, 64
  dietary
  recommendations   149
  wedding anniversary   575
Fry, Stephen   372
fuchsia   72
Fucino tunnel   226
Fuerteventura   29
Fuji, Mt   35
Fuji-Hakone-Izu national
  park/nature reserve   49
Fujisawa   640
Fukui, Kenichi   187
Fukuoka   640
Fukuyama   640
Fulani   803, 804
Fuller, Roy   346

fulmar   95
Funabashi   640
fundamentalism   502
fungal infection   131
fungi   77
  classification   61
  edible   77
  poisonous   77
  study of   175
Funk, Casimir   138
funnel-web spider   113
Funny Girl   398
Furchgott, Robert F   187
Furies, The   476
furniture beetle   117
furthest migrator (bird)   100
furze   72
Fuseli, Henri   440
Fushun   640
fusilli   154
fusion   167, 170
Fuxin   640
Fuzhou   640

G

gabbro   26
Gabin, Jean   372
Gable, Clark   372
  Academy Awards   397
Gabo, Naum   444
Gabon   674, **739**
  national holidays   579
  political leaders   305
  UN membership   645
  World Heritage sites   53
Gabor, Dennis   189
  Nobel prize   186
Gabor, Zsa Zsa   372
Gabriel, Ange-Jacques   455
Gaddafi, Muammar   777
Gaddis, William   346
Gadolin, Johan   **180**, 200, 202
gadolinium   180, **200**
Gaea   476
Gaelic Athletic
  Association   517
Gaelic football   516
  fixture results   536
Gagarin, Yuri   15, 17, 271, 275
Gahn, Johan Gottlieb   200
Gaia   469, **476**, 478, 482, 487
Gainsborough, Thomas   261,
  440
Gainsville   462
Gajdusek, Daniel   180
  Nobel prize   187
Galahad, Sir   **476**, 479
galantine   154
Galápagos Islands   30
  national park/nature
  reserve   49
Galatea   476
galaxy   165, **167**, 171
Galen   **180**, 237
Galilei, Galileo   180, 255
Galliano, John   451
Galli-Curci, Amelita   406
Gallic Wars   275

Galli-Marie, Celestine   406
Gallipoli campaign   278
gallium   200
  properties   202
gallon   210
Galsworthy, John   346, 360
  Nobel prize   458
galtonia   69
Galunggung volcano   35
Galvani, Luigi   180
galvanized iron   168
galvanometer   189
Gama, Vasco da   274
Gambia, The   674, **740**
  Commonwealth
  membership   647
  national holidays   579
  political leaders   305
  UN membership   645
  World Heritage sites   53
Gambon, Sir Michael   372
gamebirds   99
gamma radiation   167, 168
gamma-ray, gamma rays   176
  radiation   197
gamma-ray astronomy   12
Gandhi (film)   398
Gandhi, Mahatma   270, **505**,
  755
Ganesha   476
gangrene   137
ganja   65
gannet   95
Ganymede (myth)   469, **476**
Ganymede (satellite)   2
Ganzhou   640
Gao Xingjian   459
garam masala   154
Garavani, Valentino   452
Garbarek, Jan   411
Garbo, Greta   372
García Márquez, Gabriel   346
  Nobel prize   459
gardenia   72
gardening   567
  energy expenditure   148
garden spider   113
Gardner, Ava   372
Garland, Judy   372
  Grammy awards   429
garland flower   72
garlic   65
garlic marosmius   78
Garner, Erroll   411
Garner, Helen   346
Garner, James   372
Garnerin, André-Jacques   190
garnet   26, 27
  month association   575
garnet, red   25
garni   154
Garnier, Tony   455
Garr, Teri   372
Garrett, Lesley   406
garrya   72
Garson, Greer   397
Garter, Order of the
  (KG)   668
Garvey, Marcus   505

gas lighting 189
Gasherbrum I 34
Gasherbrum II 34
Gasherbrum III 34
Gaskell, Mrs Elizabeth 346
Gaslight 397
Gasser, Herbert 186
Gassman, Vittorio 372
gastroenteritis 131
Gastropoda 110
gateau 154
Gates, Bill 193
Gateshead 659
Gathering, The 355
Gaudé, Laurent 356
Gaudí, Antoni 455
Gaudier-Brzeska, Henri 444
Gaugamela, Battle of 275
Gauguin, Paul 440
Gaultier, Jean-Paul 451
gauss 210
Gauss, Carl Friedrich 180
Gautier, Marthe 136
Gavaskar, Sunil 560
Gawain, Gawayne 476
Gaye, Marvin 420
Gay-Lussac, Joseph
  Louis 180
Gay-Lussac's law 180
Gaynor, Janet 397
Gaza Strip 761, 762
gazelle 83
Gaziantep 640
Gdańsk 640
Ge 476
gean (tree) 74
gearbox, automatic 189
Geb 470
Gebrselassie, Haile 560
gecko 102
gecko, giant bronze 120
Ged, William 191
Gedda, Nicolai 406
Geddes, Sir Patrick 455
geese, collective names 118
Gefion 470
Gehry, Frank 455
Geiger, Hans Wilhelm 180
Geitel, Hans F 190
Gell-Mann, Murray 180
  Nobel prize 186
Gemara 500
Gemini constellation 6, 7
Geminids meteor shower 9
Gemini spacecraft
  mission 11, 13
Gemini Telescopes 9
gemstones 27
  month association 575
gene, genes 166, 167, 168,
  170, 171
  discoveries 137
  DNA 121
genecology 175
Genée, Dame Adeline 435
General Theory of
  Relativity 172
Genesis 420
Genet, Jean 360

genetic code 168, 271
genetic engineering 168
  study of 175
genetic material 167
genetics 178, 179, 183
  study of 175
Geneva 460
Genghis Khan 248, 249
  conquests 276
Genii 476
Genius 469
Genoa 640
  museums and galleries 460
  World Heritage site 55
genome 168, 172, 273
genotype 166, 168
Genthe, Arnold 447
gentian 65, 70
Gentleman Golfers of
  Edinburgh 516
Gentleman's Agreement 397
genus 168
  classification 61
  flowering plants 69
geochronology 175
Geoffrey of Monmouth's
  History 247, 476
geological time scale 22
geology 175, 181
geometry 179, 183
geomorphology 168
geophysics 175
George Cross (GC) 668
  Malta 786
George Ellery Hale
  Telescope 9
Georgetown 640
George Washington
  bridge 224
Georgia 674, 741
  CIS membership 647
  national holidays 579
  political leaders 305
  UN membership 646
  World Heritage sites 53
Georgia (US state) 866
geostationary 168
geothermal power 168
geranium 70
gerbil 83
Gere, Richard 372
gerenuk 83
Gerhardie, William 346
Géricault, Théodore 440
German Bight shipping
  forecast area 59
germanium 200
German language 584
German measles 131
  immunization 144
German Resistance, Memorial
  Museum of the 460
Germany 674, 742
  administrative divisions 651
  EU membership 648
  honours 668
  military ranks 667
  monarchs 284
  national holidays 579

political leaders 305
road signs 622
UN membership 645
World Heritage sites 53
gerontology 175
Gershwin, George 400, 403
  operas 405
Gershwin, Ira 403
gestation 168
gestation periods
  (mammals) 89
Getty, Jean Paul 194
Getty Center 462
Gettysburg, Battle of 278
Getz, Stan 411
  Grammy awards 429
geum 70
Gewürztraminer 159
Ghana 675, 744
  Commonwealth
  membership 647
  English speakers 585
  national holidays 579
  political leaders 306
  UN membership 645
  World Heritage sites 54
Ghazali, Abu Hamid
  Mohammed al- 505
ghee 154
Ghegs 680
Ghiberti, Lorenzo 444
Ghiorso, Albert 199, 200
Ghirlandaio, Domenico 441
Ghost Road, The 355
Giacconi, Riccardo 187
Giacometti, Alberto 444
Giaever, Ivar 187
Giambologna 444
giant anteater 80
giant armadillo 80
giants 476
Giant's Causeway 58
giant star 168
Giauque, William Francis 186
Gibb, James 192
gibbon 83
Gibbon, Lewis Grassic 346
Gibbons, Stella 346
Gibbs, James 455
Giberto, Astrud 429
Gibraltar 861
  English speakers 585
Gibson, Mel 373
  Academy Awards 399
Gide, André 346
  Nobel prize 458
Gielgud, Sir John 373
Giffard, Henri 188
Gifu 640
Gigantes 476
Gigantomachy 476
Gigi 398
Gigli, Beniamino 406
Gilbert, Cass 455
Gilbert, Sir William 403
  operettas 405
Gilbert, Walter 187
Gilbert Islands 30
Gilead 356

Gilgamesh 231, 471, **476**
Gill, Sir David 447
Gillespie, 'Dizzy' 411
Gillette, King Camp 191
Gilliam, Terry 394
Gilliat, Penelope 346
Gilly, Friedrich 455
Gilman, Alfred G 187
Gilpin, John 435
ginger 66
ginkgo 75
gin rummy 566
Ginsberg, Allen 357
ginseng 65
Ginzburg, Vitaly 187
Gioconda, La 405
Giordano, Umberto 405
Giorgio, Francesco di 455
Giorgione (da
   Castelfranco) 441
Giotto (di Bondone) 249, 441
Giotto space mission 12
giraffe 83
   collective names 118
   length of pregnancy 89
   records 89
Girardelli, Marc 560
Giraudoux, Jean 360
Gir national park/nature
   reserve 49
Giselle 433
Gish, Lillian 373
Gissing, George 346
Giulio Romano 455
Givenchy, Hubert 451
Gjellerup, Karl 457
glacé 154
glacial periods 24
glaciation 24
Glacier national park/nature
   reserve 49
Gladesville bridge 224
Gladiator 399
gladiator spider 113
gladiolus 69
   month association 575
glands *124*, 168
glandular fever 131
Glaser, Donald A 186
Glasgow 640
   council 661
   museums and galleries 461
Glasgow, Ellen 346
Glashow, Sheldon L 187
Glass, Philip 271, 400
   operas 405
glass 26
   inventions 189
   wedding anniversary 575
glass fibre 189
glassware 189
Glauber, Roy J 187
glazing agents 152
Glazunov, Alexander 434
Glencoe Massacre 258, 277
Glendower, Owen 276
Glidden, Joseph 188
glider 189
gliding 537

Glima 521
Glorious Revolution 258, 277
glory of the snow 69
Gloucestershire 659
Glover, Danny 373
glow-worm 117
Gluck, Christoph 261, 400
   operas 405
glucose level reduction 142
glühwein 161
glycogen enzymes 182
GMT 576
gnat, collective names 118
gnateater 98
Gnawl 485
gneiss 25
gnocchi 154
gnu 83
go (game) 565
Goa 254
   World Heritage site 54
goat:
   collective names 118
   length of pregnancy 89
   mountain 83
   wild 83
goatfish 108
goat's-beard 70
goat willow 76
Gobbi, Tito 406
Gobi Desert 33
   exploration 274
Gobind Singh 258, 505
goby 106
Godard, Jean-Luc 394
Godden, Rumer 346
Gödel, Kurt 465
Godfather, The, Parts I and
   II 398
God of Small Things,
   The 355
gods:
   Egyptian 470
   Greek 469
   Norse 470
   Roman 469
Gods Go A-Begging, The 433
Godwin, Fay 447
Godwin, William 346
Goeppert-Mayer, Maria 186
Goes, Hugo van der 441
Goethe, Johann Wolfgang
   von 346, 360
Goethe Museum 460
Gogol, Nikolai 346, 360
Goiânia 640
Going My Way 397
goitre 130
go-kart racing 567
gold 165, 199
   properties 202
   wedding anniversary 575
Gold, Herbert 346
Goldberg, Whoopi 373
Goldblum, Jeff 373
Golden Age 474, 485
Golden Apples 478, 481
Golden Cockerel, The 405
Golden Eagle 487

Golden Fleece 472, 474, 475,
   479, 480
Golden Gate bridge 224
golden rain (tree) 77
golden rod 70
golden shower (tree) 77
goldfinch, collective
   names 118
goldfish 106
Golding, Sir William 346
   Nobel prize 459
Goldman, William 346
Goldmark, Peter 191, 192
Goldsmith, Oliver 346, 360
Goldstein, Joseph L 187
Goldsworthy, Andy 445
gold tree 77
golf 516
   energy expenditure 148
   fixture results 537
goliath beetle 117
Gomel 640
Gondoliers, The 405
Goneril 480
Gone with the Wind
   (film) 397
goniatites 24
gonococcus 137
gonorrhoea 132, 133
González, Julio 445
Gooch, Graham 560
Goodall, Howard 400
Goodbye Girl, The 398
Goodbye Mr Chips 397
Good Earth, The 397
Good Friday 494
   national holidays 577
Good Friday Agreement 272,
   857
Goodman, Benny 411
Goodman, John 373
Goodpasture, Ernest
   William 138
Good Scent From A Strange
   Mountain, A 356
Goodyear, Charles 189, 191
goose 93
gooseberry 63
gopher 83
Gorakhpur 640
Gorbachev, Mikhail 272, 459
Gorboduc 476
Gordimer, Nadine 346
   Nobel prize 459
Gordon, David 434
Gordon, Dexter 411
Gordon, Douglas 444
Gordon, General 278
Gore, Al 459
Gore, Walter 435
Gorgias 465
Gorgon, Gorgons 472, **476**,
   480, 483
Gorgonzola cheese 163
gorilla 83
   collective names 118
   endangered species 120
Gorky, Arshile 441
Gorky, Maxim 346

Gorlovka 640
Gormley, Antony 445
  Turner prize 444
gorse 72
Gorsky, Alexander 435
Gosainthan 34
Gosse, Sir Edmund 346
Gothenburg 640
Gothic architecture 453
Gothic art 438
Gotland 30
Gouda cheese 163
Gouffre Mirolda cave 34
gougère 154
goujons 154
Goulandris Natural History
  Museum 459
Gould, Charles Henry 191
Gould, Morton 433
Gould, Stephen Jay 180
Goulding, Edmund 397
Gounod, Charles 400
  operas 405
government 663
  legislative systems 664
governor, form of
  address 671
governor-general, form of
  address 671
Goya (y Lucientes), Francisco
  de 441
GPSS computer
  language 608
Grace, W G 560
Graces 476
grade 210
Graeco-Roman wrestling 521
Graf, Steffi 560
Graham, Martha 432
  ballets 433, 434
Graham, William ('Billy') 505
  Templeton prize 509
Graham, Winston 346
Grahame, Kenneth 346
Graham-Smith, Sir Francis 18
Graiae 476
Grail 479
grain conversion factors 210
grain weevil 117
Grainger, Percy 400
Gramme, Zenobe 189
Grammy awards 429
gramophone 179, 189
Granada 276
  World Heritage site 57
Gran Canaria 29
Grand Canyon 274
Grand Canyon National
  Park 50
  World Heritage site 58
Grand Coulee dam 227
Grand Dixence dam 227
Grand Hotel 397
Grand Macabre, Le 405
Grand National 520
  fixture results 540
Grands Ballets Canadiens de
  Montreal 436
Grand Trunk rail-road

bridge 224
Granger, Clive W J 459
Granger, Stewart 373
Granicus, Battle of 275
Granit, Ragnar 186
granite 25, 26
granny's bonnet 70
Gran Paradiso national park/
  nature reserve 49
Grant, Cary 373
Grant, Hugh 373
Grant, Lee 373
Grant, Linda 355
Gran Telescopio Canarias 9
Granth, Adi 256, 501
grape, grapes 63
  nutritional value 150
  wine-making 159
grapefruit 63
  nutritional value 150
grapefruit tree 75
Grapelli, Stephane 411
graphite 27
graptolites 24
Grass, Günter 346
  Nobel prize 459
grasshoppers 114
Grateful Dead, The 421
gratin 154
gratiné 154
gratinate 154
Graves (wine area) 159
Graves, Robert 346, 357
gravitational waves 168
gravity 11
Gray, Alasdair 346
Gray, Rose 157
Gray, Thomas 357
Great Apennine tunnel 226
great auk 94
Greatbach, Wilson 190
Great Barrier Reef 51
Great Basin Desert 33
Great Bear constellation 6, 7
Great Bear Lake 32
Great Belt (Storebælt) East
  bridge 224
Great Britain 28
Great Comet 8
great crested newt 101
Greater New Orleans
  bridge 224
greatest migration (fish) 109
Greatest Show on Earth,
  The 397
greatest wingspan 100
Great Lakes of Canada 274
great northern diver 93
  records 100
Great Sandy Desert 33
Great Slave Lake 32
Great Smoky Mountains
  National Park 50
  World Heritage site 58
Great Trek 264, 834
Great Victoria Desert 33
Great Wall of China 233
  World Heritage site 52
Great Ziegfeld, The 397

grebe 93
Greco, El 441
Greece 675, 745
  administrative divisions 651
  EU membership 648
  monarchs 284
  national holidays 579
  political leaders 306
  UN membership 645
  World Heritage sites 54
Greek art 438
Greek alphabet 605
Greek city states 275
Greek fire 241
Greek gods 469
Greek numbers 207
Greek War of
  Independence 277, 745
Greek architecture 453
Green (politics) 663
Green, Howard 191
  discoveries 138
Green, Lucinda 561
Greenaway, Peter 394
Green Day 429
Greene, Graham 347
Greene, Robert 360
greengage 63
Greengard, Paul 187
greenhouse effect 168
Greenland 28, 30, 725
  exploration 274
Greenland Sea 32
greensand 25
Greenway, Francis 455
Greenwich Mean Time 177
  International time
  differences 576
Greenwich Observatory 576
Greenwood, Joan 373
Grégoir, Marc 190
Gregor, William 202
Gregorian calendar 261, 493
  year equivalents 574
Gregory, Cynthia 435
gremolata 154
Grenache 159
Grenada 675, 746
  Commonwealth
  membership 647
  English speakers 585
  invasion of 279
  national holidays 579
  political leaders 307
  UN membership 645
grenadier 107
Grenville, Kate 347
  literary prizes 355
Gretzky, Wayne 561
Grey, Dame Beryl 435
grey mullet 106
greyhound racing 516
  fixture results 537
greywacke 25
Grieg, Edvard 400
Griffin 476
Griffith, D W 269, 394
Griffith, Melanie 373
Griffith-Joyner, Florence 561

AZ

Index

AZ

Index

Griffiths, Richard 373
Grigorovich, Yuri 433, 434
Grigson, Heather 157
Grigson, Sophie 157
Grimaldi family 792
Grimm's Fairy Tales 263
Grimoin-Sanson, Raoul 188
Grímsvötn 35
griping toadstool 79
Gris, Juan 441
Grisi, Carlotta 435
gritstone 25
grizzly bear 81
Groeninge Museum 460
Gropius, Walter 455
Gross, David J 187
Grossman, Loyd 157
Grossmith, George 347
Grosz, George 441
ground-based telescopes 9
grouper 106
grouse 99
    collective names 118
    endangered species 120
growth hormone
    secretion 137
Grozny 640
Grubbs, Robert H 187
Grünberg, Peter 188
Grünewald, Matthias 441
Grus constellation 6, 7
Gruyère cheese 163
Gryphon 476
Guadalajara 640
    World Heritage site 55
Guadalcanal 831
Guadeloupe 738
guaiacum 65
Guam 869
Guan Di 477
Guangzhou (Canton) 640
Guangzhou West Tower 228
Guardian, The 612
Guarini, Guarino 455
Guarulhos 640
Guatemala 675, **747**
    national holidays 579
    political leaders 308
    UN membership 645
    World Heritage sites 54
Guatemala City 640
guava 64
    tree 77
Guavio dam 227
Guayaquil 640
Gudrun 477
Guérard, Michel Etienne 157
Guernsey 29, **662**, 858
Guess Who's Coming to
    Dinner 398
Guggenheim Museum 460
Guggenheim Museum,
    Solomon 462
Guiana 274
Guiana, French 738
Guibal, Théophile 192
Guilin 640
Guillemin, Roger 136, 137
    Nobel prize 187

guillemot 95
Guillet's goby 109
Guinea 675, **748**
    national holidays 579
    political leaders 308
    UN membership 645
    World Heritage sites 54
guinea fowl, guineafowl 99
guinea pig 84
    length of pregnancy 89
Guinea-Bissau 675, **748**
    national holidays 579
    political leaders 308
    UN membership 645
Guinevere **477**, 479
Guinness, Sir Alec 373
    Academy Awards 398
Guinness, Sir Benjamin 194
Guinness Museum 460
Guise, Duc de 276
Guiyang 640
Gujranwala 640
Gulbenkian, Calouste 194
Gulf oil spill 48
Gulf of Alaska 32
Gulf of Guinea 32
Gulf of Mexico 32
Gulf of St Lawrence 274
Gulf War 272, 279, 772
gull 94
gum, blue 75
gum, cider 75
gum, snow 75
gun (invention) 189
Gunn, Thom 357
Gunpowder Plot 256, 277
Guns n' Roses 421
Guntur 640
Gupta era 574
Gurkha War 277
Gurkhas 277, 799
gurnard 106
Guru Dev 503
Guru Nanak 252, 501, **505**
Guru Nanak Jananti 498
gurus 501
Gutenberg, Johannes 253
    inventions 191
Guterson, David 347
Gutiérrez, Gustavo 270, 505
gutta-percha tree 75
Guttenberg, Steve 373
Guy, Buddy 411
Guyana 675, **749**
    Commonwealth
        membership 647
    English speakers 585
    national holidays 579
    political leaders 308
    UN membership 645
Gwalior 640
Gwangju 640
Gwynedd 661
    World Heritage site 58
Gwynne, Fred 373
György, Paul 138
Györgyi, Albert von 139
Gyanendra, King 799
Gyatso, Tenzin 459

gymnastics 517
    energy expenditure 148
    fixture results 538
gynaecology, gynecology 175
gypsophila 70
gypsum 27
    Mohs' hardness scale 28
gypsy mushroom 78
gyro-compass 189
gyroscope **168**, 180

H

Haas, Ernst 447
Haavelmo, Trygve 459
Haberlandt, Ludwig 137
Habermas, Jürgen 465
habitat destruction 119
Habsburg dynasty:
    Austria 283
    Portugal 285
    Spain 285
Habsburg–Valois Wars 276
Hachioji 640
Hackman, Gene 373
    Academy Awards 398
Hadad 471, **477**
Hadar 7
haddock, nutritional
    value 150
Haddon, Mark 347
Hades 469, 475, 476, **477**,
    483, 486
Hadid, Zaha 455
Hadith 499
Hadrian's Wall 234
    World Heritage site 58
haemoglobin 184
Haemophilus influenzae type
    b vaccine 144
hafnium 200
Hagen, Walter 561
Haggard, Sir Rider 347
Haggis, Paul 399
Hagia Sophia Museum 460
Hagman, Larry 374
Hague, The 640
    museums and galleries 461
Hahn, Otto 201
    Nobel prize 186
Haile Selassie 278, 735
Hailey, Arthur 347
Haiphong 640
Haiti 675, **750**
    civil war 279
    national holidays 579
    political leaders 308
    UN membership 645
    World Heritage sites 54
Hajj 499
hake 106
Hakodate 640
Halász, Gyula 446
Halcyone 477
halcyons 477
Hale-Bopp comet 8
Hales, Stephen 136
Haley, Bill 421
half marathon 518

Half of a Yellow Sun 355
halibut 107
Hall, John L 187
Hall, Sir Peter 394
Hallé Orchestra 407
Halley, Edmond 180, 259
  Astronomer Royal 18
Halley's comet 8
  space missions 12
hallucinations 143
hallucinogens 143
Hals, Frans 441
Halsman, Philippe 447
Halton 660
ham, nutritional value 150
hamadryads 477
Hamamatsu 640
Hamburg 640
  museums and galleries 460
hamerkop 93
Hamhung 640
Hamill, Mark 374
Hamilton (Canada) 640
Hamilton, Gordon 435
Hamilton, Richard 441
Hamilton, Thomas 455
Hamilton, Sir William 465
Hamlet (ballet) 433
Hamlet (film) 397
Hamlet, Prince of Denmark
  (play) 362
Hamlin, Harry 374
Hammarskjöld, Dag 647
  Nobel prize 458
Hammarsten, Olaf 136
Hammer, Armand 194
hammer throw 517
Hammerstein, Oscar, II 404
Hammett, Dashiell 347
Hammond Innes, Ralph 347
Hamnett, Katharine 451
Hampshire 659
Hampton, Lionel 411
hamster 84
  length of pregnancy 89
Hamsun, Knut 457
Han, Kyung-Chik 509
Hancock, Herbie 411
  Grammy awards 429
Handan 640
handball 517
  fixture results 538
Handel, George Frideric 400
  ballet music 433
  operas 405
Handy, W C 411
Han dynasties 281
hanepoot 161
hang gliding 517
  fixture results 538
Hanging Gardens of
  Babylon 280
Hangzhou 640
Hanks, Tom 374
  Academy Awards 399
Hannah, Daryl 374
Hannibal 232
Hanno 274
Hanoi 640

Hanover 640
Hanover, House of 286
Hänsch, Theodor W 187
Hansel and Gretel
  (opera) 405
Hansen, Gerhard 137
Hanukkah 500
Hanuman 477
Harare 640
Harbin 640
Hardangervidda national
  park/nature reserve 50
Hardie, Keir 266
Hardy, Sir Alister 509
Hardy, Bert 447
Hardy, Oliver 374
Hardy, Thomas 347
hare 84
  Chinese calendar 575
  collective names 118
  Patagonian 84
Hare, David 360
harebell 69
Hare Krishna 270, 502
Hargreaves, James 191, 261
Hari Raja Haji 577
Hari Raja Puasa 577
Harlan J Smith Telescope 9
Harlaw, Battle of 276
Harlequinade 433
Harlow, Jean 374
harmattan wind 697
Harmsworth, Harold see
  Rothermere
harness racing 517
Harold II 244, 275
Harper, Heather 406
Harpers Ferry raid 278
Harpies 477
Harpocrates 477
Harrelson, Woody 374
harrier 90
Harris, Emmylou 421
Harris, Julie 374
Harris, Richard 374
Harrison, George 421
Harrison, James 191
Harrison, John 188
Harrison, Sir Rex 374
  Academy Awards 398
Harrow school 520
Harry and Tonto 398
Harsa era 574
Harsanyi, John 459
Hart, Lorenz 404
hartebeest 84
Hartford 462
Hartlepool 660
Hartley, L P 347
Hartline, Haldan Keffer 186
Hartnell, Sir Norman 451
Hartwell, Leland H 187
Haruka 12
Harvey, Frederick 157
Harvey, William 180, 257
  medical discoveries 136
Hass, Earl 192
Hassel, Odd 186
hassium 200

Hastings, Battle of 244, 245,
  275
Hatchett, Charles 200
hatha yoga 568
Hathor 470, 477
Hattie's pincushion 71
Hauer, Rutger 374
Hauptman, Herbert A 187
Hauptmann, Gerhart 360
  Nobel prize 457
Hausa 803, 804
Hausen, Harald zur 188
Haussmann, Georges 455
haute cuisine 154
Havana 640
  World Heritage site 53
Havel, Václav 724
Hawaii 866
Hawaii Volcanoes National
  Park 58
Hawaiian islands 30, 274
Hawaiian Patriot 48
hawk 118
hawking 517
Hawking, Stephen
  William 181
Hawkins, Coleman 411
Hawks, Howard 394
Hawksmoor, Nicholas 455
Hawn, Goldie 374
Haworth, Sir Norman 186
hawthorn:
  month association 575
  shrubs 72
  tree 75
Hawthorne, Nathaniel 347
Hawthorne, Sir Nigel 374
Hay, Will 374
Haydée, Marcia 435
Haydn, Joseph 400
Hayes, Helen 397
hay fever, hayfever 168
  treatment 141
Hayward, Susan 374
  Academy Awards 398
Hayworth, Rita 374
hazard 565
hazel, common 75
Hazzard, Shirley 347
headache 130, 132, 133, 134,
  135, 139
Heaney, Seamus 273, 357
  Nobel prize 459
hearing 128
heart *126*
  artificial 189
  dietary
    recommendations 149
  study of 174
heart attack 141, 142
heartburn 141
heart disease 135
heart failure 141
heart's-ease 65
heart transplant, first 177, 271
heat 177
  SI units 208
heat capacity 203
heath, winter-flowering 73

A–Z

Index

Heathcote, Paul 157
heather 73
heat pump 189
heaviest flying bird 100
heavyweight champions 528
Hebbel, Friedrich 360
Hebe (myth) 469, **477**
hebe (shrub) 73
Hebei Spirit 48
Hebrew alphabet 605
Hebrides 30
Hebrides shipping forecast
area 59
Hecabe 477
Hecate 469, **477**
Heckman, James 459
hectare 210
Hector 471, 472, 477, 483, 484
Hecuba **477**, 484, 487
hedgehog 84
length of pregnancy 89
hedgehog mushroom 78
Heeger, Alan J 187
Hefei 640
Hegang 640
Hegel, Georg 262, 465
Hegira 238, 574
Heidegger, Martin 268, 465
height 147
Heimdall 470
Heimdallr 477
Heinlein, Robert A 347
Heinz, Henry 194
Heiress, The 397
Heisei era 281
Heisenberg, Werner Karl 181
Hekla 35
Hel 470, **477**
Hela 477
Helen 472, 474, **477**, 480, 483
Helheim 477
helichrysum 73
helicopter 189
heliopsis 71
Helios 469, 475, **477**, 478, 483
helium 164
in Sun 1
table of elements 200
hellbender 101
hellebore 71
Hellen 477
Hellenes 477
Heller, Joseph 347
Heller, Michael 509
Helmholtz, Hermann 181, 265
Helpmann, Sir Robert 435
ballets 433
Helsinki 640
museums and galleries 460
Hemingway, Ernest 269, 347
Nobel prize 458
hemlock 65
hemlock, Western 75
hemp 65
hen, collective names 118
henbane 65
Hench, Philip 186
Henderson, Arthur 458

Henderson, Fletcher 411
Henderson, Joe 411
Hendricks, Barbara 406
Hendrix, Jimi 421
Hendry, Stephen 561
Hengyang 640
Henle, Friedrich Gustav
Jakob 181
Henley Royal Regatta 548
henna 65
Hennebique, François 189
Henri, Adrian 357
Henry IV Part One 362
Henry IV Part Two 362
Henry V 276
play 362
Henry VI Part One 362
Henry VI Part Three 362
Henry VI Part Two 362
Henry VII 276
Henry VIII 493
play 362
Henry Ford Museum 462
Henryson, Robert 357
Henry the Navigator 274
Henze, Hans Werner 405
ballet music 434
heparin 137
hepatitis 132, 143
immunization 144
hepatitis B vaccine 178
hepatitis-C virus 137
Hepburn, Audrey 375
Academy Awards 398
Hepburn, Katharine 374
Academy Awards 397, 398
Hephaestus 469, **477**
heptathlon 517
Hepworth, Dame
Barbara 445
Hera 469, 472, 473, 475, 476,
477, 478, 484, 488
Heracles 471, 472, 473, 474,
477, 478, 481, 483
Heraclitus 465
Herald, The 612
herbaceous 168
flowering plants 70
herbalism 140
herbal medicine 140
herb Christopher 71
Herbert (of Cherbury),
Edward, 1st Baron 465
Herbert, George 357
herbivore 168
herbs 64
complementary
medicine 139
Hercules 477
Hercules constellation 6, 7
Herd Boy and Weaving Maid
Festival 498
heredity 137
Herefordshire 660
Herman, Jerry 403
Herman, Woody 411
Hermanas, Las 433
hermaphrodite 168
Hermaphroditus **477**

Hermes 469, 472, 473, **477**,
478, 483, 487
Hermitage Museum,
State 461
Hermod 470
Hermosillo 640
Hero 478
heroin 143
heron 93
collective names 118
Heron Island national park/
nature reserve 50
Herrick, Robert 357
herring 107
Herschbach, Dudley R 187
Herschel, Sir John 181
Herschel, Sir William 181
radiation 197
Hershey, Alfred D 186
Hershey, Barbara 374
Hershko, Avram 187
Hertfordshire 659
Hertwig, Oskar 137
Hertz, Heinrich 181
inventions 191
medical discoveries 139
radiation 197
Herzberg, Gerhard 186
Hesperides 473, **478**, 482
Hess, Alfred 139
Hess, Walter 186
Hesse, Hermann 347
Nobel prize 458
Hestia 469, **478**
Heston, Charlton 375
Academy Awards 398
Hevesey, Georg 200
Hewett, Dorothy 360
Hewish, Antony 187
Hewson, William 136
Heyer, Georgette 347
Heymans, Corneille 186
Heyrovsky, Jaroslav 186
Heywood, Thomas 360
Hiawatha 478
Hib (vaccine) 144
Hibberd, Jack 360
hibiscus 73
Hick, John 505
Hicks, Sir John 458
Hidden Words 492
hieroglyphics 230
Higashiosaka 640
high bar (gymnastics) 517
High Coast bridge 224
highest flyer (bird) 100
highest mountains 34
highest waterfalls 33
high jump **517**, 518
Highland council 661
Highland Games 515
High Noon 397
High Renaissance art 438
Highsmith, Patricia 347
High Tech architecture 453
Hijuelos, Oscar 356
Hildebrandt, Johann
von 455
Hill, David 447

Hill, Geoffrey 357
Hill, George Roy 394
  Academy Awards 398
Hill, Lauryn 429
Hill, Susan 347
Hillary, Edmund 275
Hiller, Dame Wendy 375
Hilliard, Nicholas 441
Hilton, Conrad 194
Hilton, James 347
Himeji 640
Hinault, Bernard 561
Hindemith, Paul 433
Hindi language 584
Hindu calendars 574
Hindu festivals 498
Hinduism 498
  distribution of adherents 490
  sacred texts 501
Hindu Kush 679
Hine, Lewis W 447
Hines, Barry 347
Hines, Earl 412
Hinshelwood, Sir Cyril 186
Hipparchos 235
hippeastrum 69
Hippocrates 181, 233
  discoveries 136
Hippodameia 483
Hippolyta 471, 478, 487
Hippolytus 473, **478**, 483
Hippomedon 485
Hippomenes 473
hippopotamus 84
  collective names 118
  endangered species 120
Hirakata 640
Hiro (Yasuhiro
  Wakabayashi) 447
Hiroshima 270, 640
Hiroshima Peace
  Memorial 55
Hirst, Damien 273, 441
  Turner prize 444
Hispaniola 28, 29
histamine 168
histology 175, 259
Hitchcock, Sir Alfred 394
  Academy Awards 397
Hitchings, George H 187
Hittites 190, 230, 231
HIV virus 131, 143
  medical discoveries 137
Hizbullah 775
Hjelm, Peter 200
HLA 137
Hmong-Mien languages 584
HMS Pinafore 405
hoarseness 132
hoatzin 99
Hoban, Russell 347
Hobbes, Thomas 258, 466
Hobby-Eberly Telescope 10
Ho Chi Minh 875
Ho Chi Minh City 640
hock (wine) 161
hockey 517
  energy expenditure 148
  fixture results 538

hockey pitch *539*
Hockney, David 441
Hoder 470
Hodges, Johnny 412
Hodgkin, Sir Alan 186
Hodgkin, Dorothy 186
Hodgkin, Sir Howard 441
Hodgson, Ralph 357
Hoe, Richard 191
Hoenir 470
Hoff, Marcian E 190
Hoffman, Dustin 375
  Academy Awards 398
Hoffman, Philip
  Seymour 399
Hoffman, Roald 187
Hoffmann, Felix 188
  discoveries 136
Hoffmann, Josef 455
Hofstadter, Robert 186
hog, collective names 118
Hogan, Paul 375
Hogarth, William 261, 441
Hoge Veluwe national park/
  nature reserve 50
Hogg, James 347
Hohhot 640
Hokkaido 28
Hokuriku tunnel 226
Hokusai, Katsushika 441
Holbein, Hans, 'the
  Younger' 441
Holbrook, Hal 375
Holden, William 375
  Academy Awards 398
hole in one 516
Holi 498
Holiday, Billie 412
Holland, Henry 455
Holland tunnel 226
Holley, Robert W 186
Holliday, Judy 397
Hollies, The 421
Hollinghurst, Alan 355
holly 75
  month association 575
Holly, Buddy 421
hollyhock 71
Holm, Wilhelm Christian 435
Holm, Sir Ian 375
Holmes, Edwin T 188
holmium 200
hologram 168
holography 189
Holst, Gustav 269, 401
Holt, Victoria 347
Holtby, Winifred 347
Holyfield, Evander 561
Holy Grail 476, 483
Holy Places (crusades) 276
Holy Roman Emperors 286
Holy Saturday 494
  national holidays 577
Holy Spirit 492, 502, 503
Holy Thursday 577
Hom, Ken 157
homeopathy 140
Homer 233, 357
Homo sapiens 229

Homs 640
Honda, Soichiro 194
Honduras 675, **751**
  exploration 274
  national holidays 579
  political leaders 309
  UN membership 645
  World Heritage sites 54
Honduras, British 696
Honegger, Arthur 401
honey, nutritional value 150
honey bee 117
honeycreeper, Hawaiian 91
honeyeater 92
honey fungus 78
honeyguide 96
honeysuckle 73
  month association 575
Hong Kong 640, **715**
  national holidays 579
Hong Kong Ballet 436
Honolulu 640
  museums and galleries 462
honours and decorations:
  Europe 668
  UK 668
  USA 669
Honshu (Hondo) 28
Hooke, Robert 181
Hooker, John Lee 412
Hooke's Law 181
hoopoe 96, 484
Hoosac tunnel 226
Hoover, William 194
Hoover dam 227
hop, step and jump 520
Hope, Bob 375
Hopkins, Kenyon 434
Hopkins, Sir Anthony 375
  Academy Awards 399
Hopkins, Sir Frederick 139
Hopkins, Gerard Manley 357
Hopkins, Lightnin' 412
Hopper, Dennis 375
Horace, Quintus Horatius
  Flaccus 357
Horae **478**, 479, 487
Horatii 478
Hordern, Sir Michael 375
Horgan, Paul 347
hormone 124, 168
  discoveries 137
hornbeam 75
hornbill 96
hornblende 25, 26
Horne, Marilyn 406
hornet, European 117
hornfels 25
horn of plenty 78
Horologium constellation 6,
  7
horology 175
hors d'oeuvre 154
horse 84
  Chinese calendar 575
  collective names 118
  length of pregnancy 89
  measurement 213
horse chestnut 74

horse mushroom 78
horsepower 210
horse racing 517
  fixture results 539
horseradish 65, 66
horse-riding 567
horse vault 517
Horus 470, **478**, 479
Horvitz, H Robert 187
Hoshi matsuri 500
hosiery 222
Hoskins, Bob 375
hosta 71
hot-air ballooning 567
Hotter, Hans 406
hoummos, houmus 154
hound, collective names 118
Hounsfield, Godfrey N 191
  Nobel prize 187
Houphouët-Boigny, Felix 720
Hours, The (novel) 356
Hours, The (film) 399
housefly 116
House for Art 461
house mouse 89
House of Commons 663
House of Lancaster 276
House of Lords 663
House of
  Representatives 663
House of York 276
house spider 113
housework, energy
  expenditure 148
Housman, A E 357
Houssay, Bernardo 186
Houston 640, 645
  museums and galleries 462
Houston, Whitney 421
  Grammy awards 429
Houston Ballet 436
hovercraft 189
hoverfly 116
Howard, Sir Ebenezer 455
Howard, Elizabeth Jane 347
Howard, Leslie 375
Howard, Ron 399
Howard, Sidney 360
Howard, Trevor 375
How Green Was My
  Valley 397
How late it was, how late 355
Howards End (film) 399
Howlin' Wolf 412
Howrah 640
Howrah bridge 224
Hsia Dynasty 488
Hsi Ling Shi 191
Hsuehshan tunnel 226
Hsun Tzu 498
HTML computer
  language 608
Huaibei 640
Huainan 640
Huang He (Yellow) River 33
Huangshi 640
Huang-ti 478
Hubbard, L Ron 270, 503
Hubble, Edwin 181

inventions 192
Hubble Space Telescope 12,
  14, 273
Hubel, David H 187
Huber, Robert 187
Hubli-Dharwar 640
Hud 398
Huddleston, Trevor 505
Hudson, Henry 274
Hudson, Hugh 398
Hudson, Rock 375
Hudson Bay 32, 707
  exploration 274
Hudson River 274
Hudson volcano 35
Huggins, Charles 186
Hughes, Howard 194
Hughes, John 136
Hughes, Ted 273, 358
  Poets laureate 359
Hughes, Thomas 347
Hugh the Drover 405
Hugo, Victor 347
Huguenots 276
Huitzilopochtli 478
Hulanicki, Barbara 451
Hulce, Tom 375
Hull, Cordell 458
Hulme, Keri 347
Hulse, Russell A 187
human immunodeficiency
  virus 131
Human League 421
human leucocyte antigen 137
human rights 663
humans 79
  geological record 23
  length of pregnancy 89
  records 89
Humason comet 8
Humayun 283
  World Heritage site 54
Humber Estuary bridge 224
Humber shipping forecast
  area 59
Hume, David 260, 466
Hume, John 459
humectants 152
Humen bridge 224
hummingbird 97
hummingbird hawk
  moth 116
hummus 154
Humperdinck, Engelbert 405
Hundertwasser,
  Friedensreich 441
Hun raids 275
hundredweight 221
Hundred Years' War 250,
  252, 276
Hungarian National
  Museum 460
Hungarian Revolution 278
Hungarian Uprising 752
Hungary 675, **752**
  administrative divisions 652
  EU membership 648
  national holidays 579
  political leaders 309

UN membership 645
  World Heritage sites 54
Hunjiang 640
Hunt, Helen 399
Hunt, Holman 441
Hunt, R Timothy 187
Hunt, Sir Tim 181
Hunt, Walter 191
Hunter, Evan 347
Hunter, Holly 375
  Academy Awards 399
Hunter, Kim 376
Hunterian Art Gallery and
  Museum 461
hunting 119
Huppert, Isabelle 376
hurdles (athletics) 516,
  517, 518
hurdles (horse racing) 517
hurdling 517
hurley 517
Hurley Machine Co 192
hurling 517
  fixture results 540
Huron, Lake 32
hurricane 42
Hurston, Zora Neale 347
Hurt, John 376
Hurt, William 376
  Academy Awards 398
Hurwicz, Leonid 459
Hussein, Saddam 759
Husserl, Edmund 466
Hussey, Olivia 376
Huston, Anjelica 376
Huston, John 394
Hutter, Jakob 505
Hutton, James 181
Hutton, Len 561
Hutu 705, 819
Huxley, Aldous 269, 347
Huxley, Sir Andrew 186
Huxley, Thomas Henry 181
Huygens, Christiaan 181, 257
  inventions 188
hyacinth 69
  grape 69
  wild 69
Hyakutake comet 8
Hyatt, John W 188, 190
hybrid 168
Hyderabad 640
Hyde-White, Wilfrid 376
Hydra 475, **478**
Hydra constellation 6, 7
hydrangea 73
hydraulics 175
hydrodynamics 175
hydrogen 165
  in Sun 1
  table of elements 200
hydrogen ion
  concentration 185
hydrogeology 175
hydrography 175
hydrological cycle *44*
hydrology 175
hydroponics 175
hydrostatics 175

hydrotherapy 140
Hydrus constellation 6, 7
hyena 84
 collective names 118
 length of pregnancy 89
Hygeia 478
Hymen 478
Hymenoptera 110, **116**
Hypatia 239
hyperactivity 143, 152
hyperbola 206
Hyperboreans 478
Hyperion (myth) 478
Hyperion (satellite) 2
Hyperion tunnel 226
Hypnos 469
hypnosis 140
hypnotherapy 140
hypoglycaemic drugs 142
hyssop 65, 73

I

Iacocca, Lee 194
IAEA 646
Iapetus 478
Iapetus satellite 2
Iasi 640
Ibadan 640
ibex 84
ibis 93
Ibiza 29
IBM 192
Ibn Saud 825
Ibrahim (emperor) 283
Ibrahim, Abdullah 412
IBRD 646
Ibsen, Henrik 267, 360
ICAO 646
Icarian Sea 478
Icarus 474, **478**
ice ages 24
Ice Break, The 405
ice hockey 517
 fixture results 540
ice hockey rink *541*
Icel 640
Iceland 28, 675, **753**
 administrative divisions 652
 national holidays 579
 political leaders 310
 UN membership 645
 World Heritage sites 54
ice skating 517
 fixture results 541
ice speedway 520
Ichikawa 640
I Ching 498, 501
ichneumon 117
ICSID 646
IDA 646
Idaho 866
Id al-Adha 499, 577
Id al-Fitr 499, 577
Idea of Perfection, The 355
Id el-Kebir 577
identical twins 173
ideology 663
Iders, Ijsbrand 274

Idomeneo 405
Idomeneus 478
Id-ul-Adha 499, 577
Id-ul-Fitr 499, 577
Idunn 470
IFAD 646
IFC 646
Igbo 804
Ignarro, Louis J 187
Ignatius Loyola, St 254, 505
igneous rocks 26, 168
iguana 102
iguana, common 120
Iguazú/Iguaçu national park/
 nature reserve 50
I-Hsing 188, 241
ikebana 567
Ikeya-Seki comet 8
Iliad 233, 484, 485
illegal drugs 143
Illinois 866
illuminance 210
Illumination (ballet) 433
illumination (SI units) 209
Illyuzia-Mezhonnogo-
 Snezhnaya cave 34
ILO 646
imams 499
Imeni Ismail Samani Peak 34
IMF 646
Immaculate Conception 493
 national holidays 577
Immortals 501
immortelle (everlasting
 flower) 70
immovable feasts 493
immune system 142, 179
immunity 168
immunization:
 for travel 144
 of children 144
immunology 175
immunosuppressant
 drugs 142
IMO 646
impala 84 ·
impedance 209
imperialism 663
Imperial Service Order 668
Imperial War Museum 461,
 462
important discoveries in
 medicine 135
Impressionism 438
imprinting 168
improving agents 152
Inanna 478
Incas 252, 253, 254, 255
inch 209, 210
Inchon 640
Incoronazione di Poppea,
 L' 405
incubation 131
Independence Day
 (novel) 356
Independent, The 612
Independent on Sunday 612
index marks (cars):
 international 617

UK 615
India 638, 675, **754**
 civil war 279
 Commonwealth
 membership 647
 English speakers 585
 exploration 274
 national holidays 579
 political leaders 310
 UN membership 645
 World Heritage sites 54
Indiana 866
Indianapolis 640
 museums and galleries 462
Indian corn 62
Indian Mutiny 263, 264
Indian Ocean 32
 exploration 274
Indian states 275
Indian Uprising 755
indicator 169
indigenous 168
indigofera 73
indium 200
Indochina 270, 706
 French war of 279
Indo-China War 875
Indo-European
 languages 584
Indonesia 30, 638, 675, **756**
 East Timor 272, 728
 national holidays 579
 political leaders 310
 UN membership 645
 World Heritage sites 54
Indo-Pakistan Wars 755
Indore 640
Indra 478
inductance 209
Indus constellation 6, 7
industrialists 192
Industrial Revolution 261
inert gases 170
inertia 168
 SI units 208
infections 131
infectious diseases 131
 causes of death 135
infectious
 mononucleosis 131
infinity 168
influenza 132
Informer, The 397
infrared radiation 167, **168**,
 169
Infrared Space
 Observatory 12
infrasound 168
Inge, William 361
Ingres, Jean 441
Inguri dam 227
Inheritance of Loss, The 355
inhibin 137
injuries 135
Inner Hebrides 30
Innes, Michael *see* Stewart,
 J I M
In Old Arizona 397
inorganic 168

insect, leaf 114
insect, stick 114
insects 113
  endangered species 119
  study of 174
Institute of Contemporary
  Arts 461
insulin 137
integer **168**, 169, 171
integrated circuit 166, **168**
  concept 189
Intel 190
interference 185
interferometer 189
interferometry 189
interferon 137
interglacial periods 24
Intergovernmental Panel on
  Climate Change 459
interleukin 137
international airports 627
International Atomic Energy
  Agency 646
  Nobel prize 459
International Bank for
  Reconstruction and
  Development 646
International Campaign to
  Ban Landmines 459
International Centre for
  Settlement of Investment
  Disputes 646
International Civil Aviation
  Organization 646
international clothing
  sizes 222
International Development
  Association 646
International Finance
  Corporation 646
International Fund
  for Agricultural
  Development 646
International Gothic art 438
International Labour
  Organization 646
  Nobel prize 458
International Maritime
  Organization 646
International Modern
  architecture 453
International Monetary
  Fund 646
international paper sizes 223
international pattern
  sizes 222
International Physicians for
  the Prevention of Nuclear
  War 459
International Society
  for Krishna
  Consciousness 270, 502
International Space
  Station 14, 15
International Style
  (architecture) 453
International system of
  units 208
International

Telecommunication
  Union 646
international time
  differences 576
Interpreter of Maladies 356
In the Heat of the Night 398
intifada 761
invasion of Grenada 279
invasion of Sicily 278
invasive species 119
inventions 188
Inverclyde 661
invertebrates 110
  crustaceans 112
  insects 113
  molluscs 110
  spiders 113
Invitation, The 433
in vitro fertilization 168
INXS 421
Io (myth) 472, **478**
Io (satellite) 2
iodine 200
  in diet 130
ion, ions 164, **168**
  complementary
  medicine 139
Iona 30, 238
Ionesco, Eugène 361
Ionian branch of Greeks 477
Ionian Islands 30
ionization 165, 167, **168**
Iowa 866
Iphigeneia 473, **478**
Iphigénie en Tauride 405
ipomoea 73
Ipsus, Battle of 275
IRAM Array telescope 10
Iran 675, **757**
  national holidays 579
  political leaders 311
  UN membership 645
  World Heritage sites 54
Iranian Revolution 279
Iran–Iraq War 272, 279, 758,
  759
Iraq 675, **758**
  national holidays 580
  political leaders 311
  UN membership 645
  World Heritage sites 54
Iraq War 280, 759
IRAS-Araki-Alcock comet 8
Ireland 28
Ireland, John 401
Ireland, Republic of 675, **759**
  administrative divisions 652
  English speakers 585
  national holidays 580
  political leaders 311
  UN membership 645
  World Heritage sites 54
Irenaeus, St 506
Irene 479
Irénée du Pont Telescope 10
iridium 200
  properties 202
Iridium space missions 12
iridology 140

iris (flower) 69
Iris (myth) 469, **479**
iris diaphragm 165
irises, patterns on 140
Irish Famine 264, 760
Irish Rebellion, Great 277
Irish Sea shipping forecast
  area 59
Irkutsk 640
iron 200
  in diet 130
  in Sun 1
  properties 202
  working of 189
Ironbridge 224
Iron Maiden 421
Irons, Jeremy 376
  Academy Awards 398
ironstone 25
ironwood 77
irrational number 168
irritable bowel
  syndrome 142
Irving, John 347
Isaac Newton Telescope 10
Isaacs, Alick 137
Isadora (ballet) 433
ISEE-C space mission 12
Isfahan 640
Isherwood, Christopher 348
Ishiguro, Kazuo 348
  literary prizes 355
Ishtar 233, 479
Isis 470, **479**, 482
Islam 499
  distribution of adherents 490
  sacred texts 501
Islamic art 438
Islamic calendar 238, 574
Islamic festivals 499
Islamic Salvation Front 681
islands 28
  British 662
  major groups 29
Islay 30
Isle of Man 662, **858**
Isle of Wight 660
Isley Brothers, The 421
Ismailis 499
-isms 595
isobar 169
Isolde 479, 487
isomer 169
isotope, isotopes 164, 165,
  169, 172
Israel 675, **760**
  national holidays 580
  political leaders 311
  UN membership 645
  World Heritage sites 54
Israelites 230, 500
Israel Philharmonic
  Orchestra 407
Issus, Battle of 275
Istanbul 640, 644
  museums and galleries 460
  World Heritage site 58
Itaipú dam 227
Italian invasion of

Abyssinia 278
Italian language 584
Italian millet 62
Italian War of Unification 278
Italy 675, **762**
  administrative divisions 653
  EU membership 648
  monarchs 284
  national holidays 580
  political leaders 312
  road signs 622
  UN membership 645
  World Heritage sites 54
It Happened One Night 397
Ithuriel's spear 69
Itkinos 455
ITU 646
Itylos 484
Itys 484
Itzamma 479
IUCN 119
Iuppiter 479
Ivanov, Lev 432
  ballets 434
Ivanovo 640
  World Heritage site 52
Ivan the Terrible 254, 433
Ives, Charles 401
IVF 168
ivory:
  trade in 120
  wedding anniversary 575
Ivory, James 394
Iwaki 640
I Want to Live! 398
Iwo Jima, Battle of 279
Ixion 479
Ixtoc 48
Izanagi no Mikoto 479
Izanami no Mikoto 479
Izhevsk 640
Izmir 640
Iztaccíhuatl-Popocatépetl
  national park/nature
  reserve 50

J

Jabalpur 640
Jaboatão 640
jacamar 96
jacana 94
jacaranda 77
jack (tree) 77
jackal 84
jackfruit 77
jackrabbit 84
Jackson (city) 462
Jackson, Charles 135
Jackson, Glenda 376
  Academy Awards 398
Jackson, Gordon 376
Jackson, Michael 421
  Grammy awards 429
Jackson, Milt 412
Jackson, Peter 394
  Academy Awards 399
Jacksonville 640
Jacob, François 186

Jacobi, Sir Derek 376
Jacobite Rebellion 258,
  260, 277
Jacobs, Marc 451
Jacobsen, Arne 455
jade 27
Jaffrey, Madhur 157
jaguar 84
Jahandar Shah 283
Jahangir 283
Jainism 232, 499
  sacred texts 501
Jaipur 640
Jakarta 640
Jaki, Stanley L 509
Jakobovits, Lord 509
Jalandhar 640
jam, nutritional value 150
Jam, The 421
Jamaica 29, 675, **764**
  Commonwealth
  membership 647
  English speakers 585
  exploration 274
  national holidays 580
  political leaders 312
  UN membership 645
James Clerk Maxwell
  Telescope 10
James, Elmore 412
James, Henry 348
James, P D 348
James, Ralph 199
James, St (disciple) 492
James, William 466
James I and VI 277
James II 256, 258, 277
James of Alphaeus, St
  (disciple) 492
Jamin, J-C 189
Jammu 755, 807, 808
Jamshedpur 640
Janáček, Leoš 401
  operas 405
Janamashtami 498
Jannings, Emil 397
Jansen, Cornelius 506
Jansky, Karl Guthe 181
Janssen, Jules 189
Janssen, Zacharias 190, 255
Janus 469, **479**
Japan 638, 675, **764**
  emperors 281
  islands 30
  invasion of Korea 277
  national holidays 580
  political leaders 312
  UN membership 645
  World Heritage sites 55
Japanese encephalitis 144
Japanese festivals 500
Japanese folk religions 500
Japanese language 584
Japhet 478
japji 501
japonica 73
jardinière 154
Jarman, Derek 394
Jarre, Jean-Michel 421

Jarrett, Keith 412
Jarvik, Robert 189
Jasinski, Roman 435
jasmine 73
Jason 472, 474, **479**, 480
jasper 27
Jaspers, Karl 466
jaundice 132, 135
Java 28, 30
JAVA computer language 608
Javanese language 584
JavaScript computer
  language 608
Java Trench 32, 38
javelin 516, **517**
jazz 409
jazz dance 567
Je m'en vais 356
Jean Bernard cave 34
Jean-Claude (de
  Guillebon) 440
Jeanneret, Charles
  Édouard 455
jeans 190
Jeans, Sir James
  Hopwood 181
Jedda 640
Jefferson, Blind Lemon 412
Jefferson, Thomas 455
Jeffreys, Sir Alec 181
Jehovah's Witnesses 266, 502
Jelinek, Elfriede 348
  Nobel prize 459
jellyfish, collective
  names 118
Jenkins, David 506
Jenkins' Ear, War of 277
Jenner, Edward 181, 263
  discoveries 138
Jenney, William Le
  Baron 191
Jennings, Elizabeth 358
Jensen, Hans 186
Jensen, Johannes
  Vilhelm 458
Jenufa 405
jerboa 84
Jericho 229
Jerne, Niels K 187
jeroboam (wine) 163
Jersey 29, 662, **858**
Jerusalem 640
  capture of 276
  siege of 275
  World Heritage site 54
Jerusalem sage 73
Jesus Christ 492, 502, **506**
jet 25
  properties 27
jet stream 169
Jeu de cartes (ballet) 433
jeu de paume 516, 518, 519
Jeune homme et la mort,
  Le 433
jewellery wedding
  anniversary 575
Jewels (ballet) 433
Jewish calendar 574
Jewish festivals 500

Az

Index

Jewison, Norman 398
Jew's ear fungus 78
Jezebel 397
Jhabvala, Ruth Prawer 348
Jhulanayatra 498
Jiamusi 640
Jiangyin Yangtze bridge 224
jiao 501
Jiaozuo 640
Jilin 640
Jiménez, Juan Ramón 458
Jimmu Tenno 479
Jinan 640
jinas 499
Jin dynasty 236, 246, 281
jinga Shinto 500
Jingdezhen 640
Jin Mao Building 228
Jinzhou 640
Jixi 640
Joan Miró Foundation 460
Joan of Arc 252, 276
João Pessoa 640
Jobs, Steven 194
Jocasta 474, **479**
jockey, jockeys 517
  fixture results 539
Jodhpur 640
Joel, Billy 421
  Grammy awards 429
Joffrey Ballet of Chicago 436
jogging, energy
  expenditure 148
Johannesburg 640
Johansson, Scarlett 376
John, Augustus 441
John, Sir Elton 421
John, Gwen 441
John, St (disciple) 492
Johnny Belinda 397
John of the Cross, St 506
Johns, Jasper 441
Johnson, Don 376
Johnson, Eyvind 458
Johnson, J J 412
Johnson, James P 412
Johnson, Lonnie 412
Johnson, Magic (Earvin) 561
Johnson, Michael 561
Johnson, Philip 455
Johnson, Robert 412
Johnson, Samuel 261, 358
Johnstone, (Christian)
  Isobel 157
joints 122
  study of 176
Jolie, Angelina 376
Jones, Bobby 561
Jones, Edward P 356
Jones, Elvin 413
Jones, Sir Harold 18
Jones, Inigo 455
Jones, James Earl 376
Jones, Jennifer 376
  Academy Awards 397
Jones, Norah 422
  Grammy Awards 429
Jones, Quincy 413
  Grammy awards 429

Jones, Tom 422
Jong, Erica 348
jonquil 575
Jonson, Ben 257, 361
  Poets laureate 359
Jooss, Kurt 432
Joplin, Janis 422
Joplin, Scott 413
  ballet music 433
Jordan 675, **766**
  civil war 279
  national holidays 580
  political leaders 313
  UN membership 645
  World Heritage sites 55
Jordan, Michael 561
Jordan, Neil 394
Jorullo volcano 35
José Limón Dance
  Company 436
Josephson, Brian D 187
Joshua-tree 75
Jouhaux, Léon 458
Joule, James Prescott 181
Joyce, James 348
Juan Carlos, King 835
Juan Fernández Islands 30
Judaism 500
  distribution of adherents 491
  sacred texts 501
Judas Iscariot 492
Judas-tree 75
Judas Tree, The 433
judge, form of address 671
Judgement at
  Nuremberg 398
judo 517
  fixture results 542
judogi 517
Judson, Whitcomb L 192
Juguertia, King of
  Numidia 275
Juiz de Fora 640
jujitsu 517
Julia, Raul 376
Julian Calendar 493
Julich Succession, War of
  the 277
Julius Caesar 234, 275
  inventions 190
  play 362
Julunggul 479
jumping spider 113
Jung, Carl 181
juniper (herb) 65
juniper, common (tree) 75
Juno 469, 470, 479
Jupiter (myth) 469, 470, 479
Jupiter (planet) 2
  satellites 2
  space missions 12, 13
Jura 30
Jurassic period 23
  fossils 24
Jurchen dynasty 246, 281
Jurinac, Sena 406
jus 154
justice of the peace, form of
  address 671

Jutland, Battle of 278

K

Kabul 640
Kaesong 640
Kaffir corn 62
kaffir lily 71
Kafka, Franz 269, 348
Kafue national park/nature
  reserve 50
Kagoshima 640
kagu 99
Kahn, Louis 455
Kahneman, Daniel 459
Kaifeng 640
Kain, Karen 435
Kaiser, Georg 361
Kaiser Chiefs 422
Kakadu national park/nature
  reserve 50
kala-azar 132
Kalacuri era 574
Kalahari Desert 33
kale 67
Kalevala 480
Kaliningrad 640
Kaliya 479
Kaluga 640
Kama 479
Kambarantinsk dam 227
Kamet 34
kami 479, 500
Kampala 640
Kampuchea 706
  UN membership 645
Kanazawa 641
Kandel, Eric 187
Kandinsky, Wassily 269, 441
Kandy 57
Kane 479
Kane, Sarah 361
kangaroo 79
  collective names 118
  length of pregnancy 89
kangaroo, rat 80
Kangchenjunga 34
Kangchenjunga South
  Peak 34
Kangchenjunga West
  Peak 34
Kanmon tunnel 226
Kano 641
Kano, Dr Jigoro 517
Kanpur 641
Kansas 867
Kansas City 641
  museums and galleries 462
Kant, Immanuel:
  philosophy 466
  science 181
Kantorovich, Leonid 458
Kaohsiung 641
Kapany, Navinder S 190
Kapil Dev, Nihanj 561
Kapitsa, Pyotr 187
Kaplan, Johanna 348
kapok tree 77
Kapoor, Anish 445

Turner prize 444
Kap Shui Mun bridge 224
Karachi 641, 644
Karaganda 641
Karaj 641
Kara Kum 33
Karan, Donna 451
Kara Sea 32
karat 165
karate 517
  fixture results 543
Karite 577
Karle, Jerome 187
Karlfeldt, Erik Axel 458
Karloff, Boris 376
karma:
  Buddhism 492
  Hinduism 498
  Jainism 499
Karpov, Anatoly 561
Karrer, Paul 186
Karsavina, Tamara 435
Karsh, Yousuf 447
Kartvelian languages 584
Karzai, Hamid 679
Kasdan, Lawrence 394
Kashmir 755, 807, 808
Kasparov, Gary 561
Kastler, Alfred 186
Kathmandu 641
  World Heritage site 56
Kathmandu Valley 56
Katmai volcano 35
Katowice 641
Katse dam 227
Katya Kabanova 405
katydids 114
Katz, Sir Bernard 182
  Nobel prize 186
Kaufman, Philip 394
Kaunas 641
Kaunda, Kenneth 876
Kavanagh, Patrick 358
Kavir desert 33
Kawaguchi 641
Kawasaki 641
kayak 515
Kaye, Danny 376
Kaye, Nora 435
Kayseri 641
Kazakhstan 675, 767
  CIS membership 647
  national holidays 580
  political leaders 313
  UN membership 645
  World Heritage sites 55
Kazan 641
  World Heritage site 57
Kazan, Elia 394
  Academy Awards 397, 398
Kazantazakis, Nikos 348
Kaziranga national park/
  nature reserve 50
Keane, Molly 348
Keaton, Buster 376
Keaton, Diane 377
  Academy Awards 398
Keaton, Michael 377
Keats, John 265, 358

Keck Telescope 10
Keelung 641
Keijo tunnel 226
Keitel, Harvey 377
Kekrops 479
Kelaino 484
Kellogg, Frank B 458
Kelly, Gene 377
Kelly, Grace 377
  Academy Awards 398
Kelly, William 191
Kelman, James 348
  literary prizes 355
Kelvin, William Thomson, 1st
  Baron 182
  inventions 189, 192
Kelvingrove Art Gallery and
  Museum 461
Kelvin temperature scale 169
  conversion table 211
Kemerovo 641
Kempis, Thomas à 252, 506
Kendall, Edward 136, 138
  Nobel prize 186
Kendall, Henry W 187
kendo 517
kendokas 517
Kendrew, Sir John
  Cowdery 186
Keneally, Thomas 348
Keneun 487
Kenitra 641
Kenneally, E A 189
Kennedy, Joseph W 201
Kennedy, George 377
Kennedy, John F 270
Kennedy, Margaret 348
Kent 659
Kent, Allegra 435
Kenton, Stan 413
Kentucky 867
Kenya 675, 768
  Commonwealth
    membership 647
  English speakers 585
  national holidays 580
  political leaders 314
  UN membership 645
  World Heritage sites 55
Kenzo Takada 451
Keo 48
Kepler, Johannes 182
Kérékou, Mathieu 697
Kerguelen Islands 30
Kern, Jerome 403
Kerouac, Jack 271, 348
Kerr, Deborah 377
Kerr, Graham 157
kerria 73
Kerr-McGee 47
Kertész, André 447
Kertész, Imre 459
Kesey, Ken 348
Keshan disease 130
ketamine 143
Kettering, Charles F 191
Ketterle, Wolfgang 187
Kettle's Yard 461
Keyes, Sidney 358

K-feldspars 26
Kgalagadi national park/
  nature reserve 50
Khabarovsk 641
Khachaturian 434
Khalsa 258, 501
Khan, Inamullah 509
Khan, Jahangir 561
Khao Yai national park/nature
  reserve 50
Khark 5 48
Kharkov 641
Khartoum 641
  fall of 278
Kherson 641
Khmer Rouge 279, 706
Khmers 247, 706
Khnum 470
Khonsou 470
Khorana, Har Gobind 186
Khulna 641
Kidd, Carol 413
Kidman, Nicole 377
  Academy Awards 399
kidney, artificial 190
kidney failure 135
kidney infection 133
Kiefer, Anselm 441
Kierkegaard, Søren
  Aabye 466
Kieslowski, Krzystof 394
Kiev 641, 644
  World Heritage site 58
Kiev dam 227
Kigali 641
Kikuyu revolt 279
Kilauea volcano 35
Kilby, Jack 190
  Nobel prize 187
Kilimanjaro 35
Kilimanjaro national park/
  nature reserve 50
Kill von Kull bridge 224
Killiecrankie, Battle of 277
killifish 110
Killy, Jean-Claude 561
kilocalories:
  daily energy
    requirements 147
  energy expenditure 148
kilogram-force 210
kilojoules:
  daily energy
    requirements 147
  energy expenditure 148
Kilsby Ridge tunnel 226
kimberlite 26
Kim Dae Jung 459
Kim Il-sung 770
Kim Jong-il 770
Kinabalu national park/nature
  reserve 50
Kincardine bridge 224
kinematics 175
kinesiology 140
kinetics 174
kinetic theory of gases 178
king 668
King, B B 413, 422

King, Ben E 422
King, Billie Jean 562
King, Charles Glen 139
King, Carole 422
  Grammy awards 429
King, Francis 348
King, Harold 138
King (of Wartnaby), John,
  Baron 194
King, Martin Luther 270, 506
  Nobel prize 458
King, Stephen 250, 348
King and I, The 398
kingdoms 61
  ancient Egyptian 280
  animal 61, 79
  Animalia 61, **79**
  Archaea 61
  bacteria 61
  Eubacteria 61
  Fungi 61
  plant 61, 62
  Plantae 61, **62**
  Protista, protoctista 61
kingfisher, kingfishers 96
  in myth
King John (play) 362
King Lear, The Tragedy
  of 362
King Priam 405
Kings, Battle of the 275
kings, Roman 282
Kingsley, Sir Ben 377
  Academy Awards 398
Kingsley, Charles 348
Kingston 641
Kingston upon Hull 641
  council 660
Kinks, The 422
Kinshasa 641
Kinski, Klaus 377
Kinski, Nastassja 377
Kipling, Rudyard 348
  Nobel prize 457
Kirch comet 8
Kirchhoff, Gustav Robert 182
Kirchner, Ernst 441
kirengeshoma 71
Kiribati 675, **769**
  Commonwealth
    membership 647
  English speakers 585
  national holidays 580
  political leaders 314
  UN membership 646
Kirk, Roland 413
Kirki 48
Kirkland, Gelsey 435
Kirklees 659
Kirkuk 641
Kirov 641
Kirov Ballet 261, 436
Kishau dam 227
Kishinyov 641
Kiss 422
Kissinger, Henry 458
Kiss of the Spider
  Woman 398
Kitaj, R B 441

Kitakyushu 641
Kitchener 641
kite 90
kite-flying 567
kittens, collective names 118
Kitty Foyle 397
Kitwe 641
kiwi 89
kiwi fruit 63
Klammer, Franz 562
Klaproth, Martin
  Heinrich 202
Klebs, Edwin 136
Klee, Paul 441
Klein, Anne 451
Klein, Calvin 451
Klein, Lawrence 459
Klimt, Gustav 441
Kline, Franz 441
Kline, Kevin 377
Klug, Sir Aaron 187
Klute 398
Klyuchevskoy volcano 35
Knight, Gladys 422
Knight, J P 192
knight bachelor, form of
  address 671
Knight Errant 433
Knightley, Keira 377
Knights Hospitallers 786
Knights Templar 246
knight's wife, form of
  address 671
knitting 567
Knoll, Max 190
Knossos 231
knot 210
Knowles, William S 187
Known World, The 356
Knowsley 659
Knox, John 493, **506**
Knussen, Oliver 406
koa (tree) 77
koala 80
Kobayashi, Makoto 188
Kobe 641
Koch, Marita 562
Koch, Robert 136, 138
Kochi 641
kofta 154
Kohl, Helmut 743
Köhler, Georges J F 187
kohlrabi 67
Kohn, Walter 187
Kohoutek comet 8
Kojiki 500, 501
Kokoschka, Oskar 441
Kolff, Willem 190
Kolhapur 641
Kolkata (Calcutta) 641, 645
kolkwitzia 73
Kollo, René 406
Komodo dragon 103
Komsomolosk 641
Koniuszy, Frank 138
Konya 641
Koolhaas, Rem 455
Koopmans, Tjalling 458
Koran 499

Korbut, Olga 562
Kore 483
Korea, Democratic People's
  Republic of (North
  Korea) 675, **769**
  national holidays 580
  political leaders 314
  UN membership 646
  World Heritage sites 55
Korea, Republic of (South
  Korea) 675, **770**
  national holidays 580
  political leaders 314
  UN membership 646
  World Heritage sites 55
Korean language 584
Korean War 270, 279, 770, 771
kori bustard 100
Koriyama 641
Korn, Arthur 189
Kornberg, Arthur 186
Kornberg, Roger D 187
Korsakov's syndrome 130
Kos 29
Kosciusko national park/
  nature reserve 50
Koshiba, Masatoshi 187
Kosovo 272, 826, 827
  political leaders 314
  World Heritage site 57
Kostunica, Vojislav 827
Kota 641
Kraftwerk 422
Krakatoa 35
Kramer vs Kramer 398
Krasnodar 641
Krasnoyarsk 641
Kraus, Alfredo 406
Krebs, Sir Edwin 182
  Nobel prize 187
Krebs, Sir Hans 182
  Nobel prize 186
Krebs cycle 182
Kreon 479
Kriemhild 477
krill 112
Krishna 270, 479, 498, 502
Kristall spacecraft
  mission 16
Krivoy Rog 641
Kroemer, Herbert 187
Kronos 479
Kroto, Sir Harold 182
  Nobel prize 187
Krubera-Voronja cave 34
Kruger national park/nature
  reserve 50
Krupa, Gene 413
Krupp, Alfred 194
krypton 200
kshatriya warriors 483
K2 34
Kuala Lumpur 641
Kuan Ti 479
Kublai Khan 248, 249
Kubrick, Stanley 394
Kucan, Milan 831
Kuhn, Richard 138
  Nobel prize 186

Kumamoto 641
Kumarbi 479
Kumasi 641
kumquat 63
Kundera, Milan 271, 348
Küng, Hans 506
kung fu 518
K'ung Fu-tse 498
Kunming 641
Kupka, Frantisek 441
Kurashiki 641
Kurgan 641
Kuril Islands 30
Kurosawa, Akira 394
Kursk 641
Kurushima-Kaikyo II
  bridge 224
Kusch, Polykarp 186
Kushner, Tony 361
Kushti 521
Kuwait 675, 771
  environmental disaster 47
  national holidays 580
  political leaders 314
  UN membership 645
Kuwait City 641
Kuznets, Simon 458
Kvant spacecraft missions 16
Kvasir 470
Kyd, Thomas 361
Kydland, Finn E 459
kyoko Shinto 500
Kyoto 641
  World Heritage site 55
Kyrgyzstan 675, 772
  CIS membership 647
  national holidays 580
  political leaders 315
  UN membership 646
Kyu 517
Kyzyl Kum desert 33

L

Labarraque, Antoine 136
La Bataille 356
Laborit, Henri 192
Labour Day 577
Labrador 709
  exploration 274
Labrouste, Henri 455
laburnum (shrub) 73
laburnum, common (tree) 75
Laccadive Islands 30
lace (wedding
  anniversary) 575
lace-making 567
Lacerta constellation 6, 7
lacewings 115
Lachesis 479
Laclos, Pierre Choderlos
  de 348
Lacroix, Christian 451
lacrosse 518
  fixture results 543
Lacus Mortis 3
Lacus Somniorum 3
Lacy, Steve 413
Ladd, Alan 377

Ladenis, Nico 157
Ladoga, Lake 32
Ladon 474, 478
Lady and the Fool, The 434
ladybird 117
'Lady Day' 412
Lady Macbeth of
  Mtsensk 405
lady mayoress, form of
  address 671
Lady of Shallot 434
Lady of the Lake 481
Ladysmith, Battle of 278
Laennec, René 191
Laerdal tunnel 226
Laertes 483
La Fayette, Marie, Comtesse
  de 348
La Fontaine, Henri 457
La Fontaine, Jean de 358
Lagerfeld, Karl 451
Lagerkvist, Pär 458
Lagerlöf, Selma 457
Lagos 641
Lahiri, Jhumpa 356
Lahore 641
  World Heritage site 56
Laika space missions 11
Lainzer Tiergarten national
  park/nature reserve 50
Laius 479
lake, lakes:
  largest 32
  lunar 3
  study of 175
Lake Chad 275
Lake District National
  Park 50
Lake Ngami 275
Lake Pontchartrain
  Causeway 224
Lake Tanganyika 275
Lakshmi 479
Lakshmi-puja 498
Lalande 21185 8
Lalo, Édouard 401
Lamaism 492
La maîtresse de Brecht 356
Lamarck, Jean, Chevalier
  de 182
Lamarr, Hedy 377
Lamas, Carlos Saavedra 458
Lamb, Willis 186
lamb chop, nutritional
  value 150
Lambert, Christopher 377
Lambert, Constant 434
Lambinet Museum 461
Lambrusco 159
Lament of the Waves 434
Lamington volcano 35
Lamming, George 348
Lamour, Dorothy 377
Lampedusa, Giuseppe di 348
Lamprechtsofen Vogelschacht
  cave 34
lamprey 107
Lamprophyre 26
Lancashire 659

Lancashire cheese 163
Lancaster, Burt 377
  Academy Awards 398
Lancaster, House of 283
Lancelot, Sir 476, 477, 479
Lanchbery 434
Lanchester, Frederick W 188
Land, Edwin 188
Landau, Lev Davidovich 186
land forms 168
Landis, John 394
Landseer, Sir Edwin 441
landslides 38
Landsteiner, Karl 136, 138,
  267
Lang, Fritz 395
Lang, Helmut 451
lang, k d 422
langar 501
Lange, Christian 458
Lange, Dorothea 447
Lange, Hope 378
Lange, Jessica 378
  Academy Awards 399
Langer, Suzanne K 466
Langland, William 251, 358
langlaufing 519
Langmuir, Irving 182
language, languages:
  computer 608
  e-mail 609
  text messages 609
  families 584
  speakers 584
Languedoc (Canal du Midi)
  tunnel 226
La Niña 169
Lansbury, Angela 378
Lantern Festival 498
lanternfish 107
lanthanum 200
  properties 202
Lanza, Mario 406
Lanzarote 29
Lanzhou 641
Laocoon 479
Laodicea, Battle of 276
Laomedon 484
Laos 675, 773
  national holidays 580
  political leaders 315
  UN membership 645
  World Heritage sites 55
Lao-tzu 232, 501, 506
La Paz 641
lapeirousia 69
lapis lazuli 27
Lapiths 479
Laplace, Pierre Simon,
  Marquis de 182
Lapland 274
La Plata 641
larch, European 75
larch, golden 75
larch boletus 78
Lares 469, 479, 483
Large Binocular
  Telescope 10
largest cities of the

world 644
largest deserts 33
largest fish 109
largest ground-based
    telescopes 9
largest islands 28
largest lakes 32
largest mammals 89
largest metropolitan
    areas 645
largest seas 32
lark 92
    collective names 118
Larkin, Philip 358
larkspur 575
Lar Lubovitch Dance
    Company 436
Larne 662
Laroche, Guy 451
Larrey, Jean Dominique 188
Larry's Party 355
Lartigue, Jacques-Henri 448
Larvikite 26
laryngitis 132
laryngology 175
larynx 175
lasagne 154
La Scala Museum of Theatre
    History 460
Lasdun, Sir Denys 455
laser 168, **169**, 271
    inventions 190
Las Palmas 641
lassa fever 132
Lassen Peak volcano 35
Last Command, The 397
Last Emperor, The 398
Last King of Scotland,
    The 399
Last Orders 355
Las Vegas 641
Latinus 479
Latmos, Mount 475
Latona 480
La Tour, Georges de 257, 441
Latvia 675, **773**
    EU membership 648
    administrative divisions 653
    national holidays 580
    political leaders 315
    UN membership 645
    World Heritage sites 55
laughing gas 137, 179
Laughlin, Robert B 187
Laughton, Charles 378
    Academy Awards 397
Launcelot du Lac 480
launchers, space 11
launderette 190
Laurel, Stan 378
Lauren, Ralph 451
Laurie, Piper 378
Lauterbur, Paul C 187
lava 26, 169
lavender 65, 73
laver 67
Laveran, Charles-Louis-
    Alphonse 137
La Vie en Rose 399

Lavinia 480
Lavoisier, Antoine 182
    medical discoveries 138
Lavrovsky 434
law:
    passage, UK 665
    passage, USA 666
Law, Jude 378
Lawler, Ray 361
lawn bowls 515
lawnmower 190
Lawrence, D H 348
Lawrence, Ernest 182, 200
    Nobel prize 186
Lawrence of Arabia
    (film) 398
lawrencium 200
Lawson, Nigella 158
lawyer's wig 78
Laxness, Halldór 458
Laylat al-Miraj 499
Laylat al-Qadr 499
lead 201
    properties 202
Leadbelly, Lead Belly 413
leafbird 92
leaf insect 114
League of Augsburg, War of
    the 277
Lean, Sir David 395
    Academy Awards 398
Leander 478
Leaning Tower of Pisa 247
Lear 480
Lear, Edward 358
leather 575
leatherjacket 116
leatherwood 75
Leaving Las Vegas 399
Lebanon 675, **774**
    civil war 279
    Israeli invasions 279, 280
    national holidays 580
    political leaders 315
    UN membership 645
    World Heritage sites 55
Le Carré, John 348
Le Chasseur Zéro 356
Leckey, Mark 444
Le Clézio, Jean-Marie
    Gustave 459
Le Corbusier 455
LED 169
Leda 474, 477, **480**
Lederberg, Joshua 186
Lederman, Leon M 187
Ledoux, Claude Nicolas 455
Le Duc Tho 458
Led Zeppelin 422
Lee, Ang 395
Lee, Bruce 378
Lee, Christopher 378
Lee, David M 187
Lee, Harper 348
Lee, Laurie 348
Lee, Peggy 422
Lee, Sonny 415
Lee, Spike 378, 395
Lee, Yuan Tseh 187

Leeds 641
    council 659
    museums and galleries 461
leek 65, 68
    nutritional value 150
Lee Kuan Yew 829
lees 161
Leeuwenhoek, Anton
    van 136, 137, 138
Le Fanu, Sheridan 348
left wing 663
legend 471
Legend of Joseph 434
Legend of Judith 434
Léger, Fernand 441
Leggett, Anthony J 187
legionnaire's disease 132
Legion of Merit 669
legislation:
    passage, UK 665
    passage, USA 666
legislative systems of
    government 664
legislature 663
Le Guin, Ursula K 348
Lehár, Franz 405
Lehmann, Lilli 406
Lehmann, Lotte 406
Lehmann, Rosamond 348
Lehn, Jean-Marie 187
Leibniz, Gottfried:
    philosophy 466
    science 182
Leibovitz, Annie 448
Leicester 641
    council 660
    legend 480
    museums and galleries 461
Leicester cheese 163
Leicestershire 659
Leigh, Janet 378
Leigh, Mike 395
Leigh, Vivien 378
    Academy Awards 397
Leipzig 641
    museums and galleries 460
Leishman, Sir William 182
leishmaniasis 132
Leith, Prue 158
Lejeune, Jérôme 136
Leloir, Luis Federico 186
Lely, Sir Peter 441
lemming 84
Lemminkäinen 480
lemon:
    fruit 63
    herb 65
    tree 75
Lemmon, Jack 378
    Academy Awards 398
lemon balm 65
lemon sole 107
lemur 84
Lemures 480
Lena River 33
length 212
    conversion factors 214
    conversion tables 215
    SI conversion factors 209

SI units 208
**length of pregnancy in some
mammals** 89
Lenin Museum, Central 460
Lennon, John 404, 422
Grammy awards 429
lens, lenses 167
discoveries 180
Lent 494
national holidays 577
lentil 68
nutritional value 150
Leo constellation 6, 7
Leo Minor constellation 6, 7
Leon 641
Leonard, Robert Z 397
Leonard, Sugar Ray 562
Leonardo da Vinci:
architecture 455
art 441
sculpture 445
**Leonardo da Vinci
Museum of Science and
Technology** 460
Leonard Trophy 528
Leoncavallo, Ruggero 405
Leone, Sergio 395
Leonids meteor shower 9
Leontief, Wassily 458
leopard 85
collective names 118
Lepanto, Battle of 254, 276
Lepidoptera 110, **115**
lepidoptery 566
Le Prince, Louis 189
leprosy 132
bacillus discovered 137
leptospermum 73
Lepus constellation 6, 7
Lerner, Alan Jay 404
Le Rocher de Tanios 356
Leroy, Gilles 356
Lesage, Georges Louis 192
Les Bienveillantes 356
Les Champs d'Honneur 356
Lescot, Pierre 455
Les Filles du Calvaire 356
Leshan 641
World Heritage site 52
Le soleil des Scorta 356
Lesotho 675, **775**
Commonwealth
membership 647
English speakers 585
national holidays 580
political leaders 316
UN membership 645
Les ombres errantes 356
lespedeza 73
Lessing, Doris 349
Nobel prize 459
Le Testament français 356
Lethaby, William 455
lethargy 131
Lethe 474
Leto **480**, 482
lettuce 68
nutritional value 150
Levan, Albert 136

Le Vau, Louis 455
Levi, Primo 349
Leviathan (book) 258
Leviathan (monster) 480
Levi-Montalcini, Rita 187
Levine, Philip 136, 138
Levinson, Barry 395
Academy Awards 398
Levi-Strauss 190
Levitt, Helen 448
Levy, Andrea 355
Lewis 30
Lewis, Sir Arthur 459
Lewis, Carl 562
Lewis, C S 349
Lewis, Edward B 187
Lewis, Jerry 378
Lewis, Jerry Lee 422
Lewis, John 413
Lewis, Meriwether 275
Lewis, Sinclair 349
Nobel prize 458
Lexell comet 8
L'Exposition coloniale 356
leycesteria 73
Lhasa 52
Lhotse 34
Lhotse E Peak 34
Lianyungang 641
Liaoyang 641
Liaoyuan 641
liatris 71
Libby, Willard Frank 186
Liber Pater 469
liberalism 663
Liberia 675, **776**
English speakers 585
national holidays 580
political leaders 316
UN membership 645
liberty cap 78
Libeskind, Daniel 455
Libitina 469
Li Bo 238, 241
Libra constellation 6, 7
librettists 403
Libreville 641
Libya 675, **777**
national holidays 580
political leaders 316
UN membership 645
World Heritage sites 55
**Lichfield, Patrick, 5th
Earl** 448
Lichine, David 435
Li Ching 498
Lichtenstein, Roy 441
Liebfraumilch 159
Liechtenstein 675, **778**
national holidays 580
political leaders 316
UN membership 646
Liège 460
Liège, Battle of 278
Lierasen tunnel 226
Lif 480
Life is Beautiful 399
Life of Émile Zola 397
Life of Pi 355

lift (mechanical) 190
Lifthrasir 480
ligaments 122
Ligeti, György 401
operas 405
light 176
SI units 209
light bulb 179
light-emitting diode 169
lightning conductor 190
light-year 169
brightest stars 7
SI conversion factors 210
lignite 25
**Ligue des Sociétés de la
Croix-Rouge** 458
lilac 73
Lilies of the Field 398
Lilith 480
lily 69
belladonna 69
lily-of-the-Nile 69
lily-of-the-valley 69
month association 575
lily trotter 94
Limón, José 432
ballets 434
Lima 641
World Heritage site 56
Limavady 662
lime:
fruit 63
herbs 65
small-leafed 75
tree 75
limestone 25
limnology 175
limpet, common 110
limpet, slipper 110
limpkin 99
Lincolnshire 659
Lind, James 138
Lind, Jenny 406
Lindemann, J 137
Line Islands 30
**linen wedding
anniversary** 575
Line of Beauty, The 355
Linnaeus, Carolus 182, 261
linoleum 190
lion 85
collective names 118
length of pregnancy 89
Lion in Winter, The 398
Lion's Gate bridge 224
lion's tail 73
Lipetsk 641
lipids, lipoids 169
Lipmann, Fritz 186
Lippershey, Hans 192, 257
Lippi, Fra Filippo 442
Lipscomb, William N 187
lipstick tree 77
liquid flow 175
liquid volume 212, 213
liquorice 65
Lisbon 641
museums and galleries 460
World Heritage site 57

Lisburn 662
LISP computer language 608
Lister, Joseph 182
  discoveries 136, 137
Liszt, Franz 401
  ballet music 434
literary prizes 355
Lithgow, John 378
lithium 200
  properties 202
  antimanic drugs 142
lithography 190
lithology 175
lithosphere 20
Lithuania 676, **778**
  EU membership 648
  administrative divisions 654
  national holidays 580
  political leaders 316
  UN membership 645
  World Heritage sites 55
litmus 169
litre 210
Littel, Jonathan 356
Little, Alastair 158
Little Bear constellation 6, 7
Little Bighorn, Battle of 278
Little Jazz 410
Little Richard 422
Liupanshui 641
Liuzhou 641
Lively, Penelope 349
liver, nutritional value 150
liver enlargement 132
Liverpool 641
  council 659
  museums and galleries 461
  World Heritage site 58
Livingston, Jay 404
Livingstone, David 275, 782
lizard, Aran rock 120
lizard, beaded 102
lizard, blind 102
lizard, Bornean earless 103
lizard, chisel-tooth 103
lizard, girdle-tailed 103
lizard, monitor 103
lizard, night 103
lizard, snake 103
lizard, wall and sand 103
lizard, worm 103
Ljubljana 641
llama 85
Lloyd, Christopher 378
Lloyd, Frank 397
Lloyd, Harold 378
Lloyd-Webber, Andrew,
  Baron 401
Llyr 473
loach 107
lobelia 71
lobster:
  common 112
  Norway 112
  nutritional value 151
  spiny 112
local anaesthetics 141
Lochhead, Liz 361
Lochner, Stefan 442

lock 190
Locke, John 258, 466
Lockerbie bombing 777
lockjaw 134
Lockwood, Margaret 378
locomotive 190
locust:
  collective names 118
  desert 114
  migratory 114
locust tree 75
Lodge, David 349
Lodz 641
loess 25
Loesser, Frank 404
Loewe, Frederick 404
Loewi, Otto 137
Löffler, Friedrich 136
Lofoten Islands 30
loganberry 63
logarithms 183, 257
Logi 470
LOGO computer
  language 608
Lohengrin (myth) 480
Lohengrin (opera) 405
Loki 470, 473, 477, **480**
Lollobrigida, Gina 378
Lom, Herbert 378
Lomé 641
London 641, 644
  Bridge 224
  council 659
  legend 480
  museums and galleries 461
  World Heritage sites 58
London (Canada) 641
London, Jack 349
London and Southwark
  Subway 226
London Festival Ballet 436
London Philharmonic
  Orchestra 407
London Symphony
  Orchestra 407
London Transport
  Museum 461
Londrina 641
Long, Crawford 135
Long, Richard 444
Long Beach 641
longest rivers 33
longest-lived fish 109
Longfellow, Henry
  (Wadsworth) 358
longitude 576
long jump 516, 517, **518**
Long March 715
Long March satellite 11
Longtan dam 227
loom, power 190, 263
looms 568
loon 94
  record 100
Loos, Adolf 455
Loos, Battle of 278
loosestrife 71
loquat 63
Lorca, Federico García 269,

361
lord mayor, form of
  address 671
Lord of the Rings, The (The
  Return of the King) 399
Lord's Resistance Army 853
Lord's Supper 493
Loren, Sophia 379
  Academy Awards 398
Lorentz, Hendrik 182
Lorenz, Konrad **182**, 185
  Nobel prize 187
Lorimer, Sir Robert 455
Loring, Eugene 432
  ballets 433
Lorre, Peter 379
Lorsch 53
Los Angeles 641, 645
  museums and galleries 462
Los Angeles, Victoria de 407
Los Angeles Philharmonic
  Orchestra 408
Los Glaciares national park/
  nature reserve 50
Lost Weekend, The 397
Lot, King 476
Lotophagi 480
Lötschberg tunnel 226
lotus 71
Lotus-eaters 480
loudspeaker 190
Louis, Joe 562
Louis XI 515
Louis XIV 277
Louisiana 867
Louisiana Purchase 262
louse 134
Louvre, The 231, 460
lovage 65
Love for Three Oranges,
  The 405
Lovell Telescope 10
Løvenskjold 434
Love's Labours Lost 362
Lowe, Rob 379
Lowell, Amy 358
Lowell, Robert 358
Lower Austria Museum
  of 461
Lowry, L S 442
Lowry, Malcolm 349
LSD 143
Luanda 641
Lübeck 53
Lubich, Chiara 509
Lublin 641
Lucas, George 271, 395
Lucas, Robert, Jr 459
Lucia di Lammermoor 405
Lucknow 641
Lucrece, Lucretia 480
Lucrezia Borgia 405
Lud 480
Luddites 262
Ludgate 480
Ludhiana 641
Ludwig, Christa 407
Lug 480
lugeing, luge

tobogganing 515, 518
fixture results 527
Lugosi, Bela 379
Luhansk 641
Lukacs, George 466
Lukas, Paul 397
Lully, Jean-Baptiste 405
Lulu (opera) 405
Lumbye 435
Lumet, Sidney 395
Lumière, Auguste and
Louis 188
luminescence **169**, 170
luminous flux 209
luminous intensity 208
Lumley, Joanna 379
Lumumba, Patrice 719
Luna 469
Luna, La 434
lunar bays 3
lunar eclipses *5*, 253
lunar lakes 3
lunar landings 11, 12
lunar marshes 3
lunar module 13, 14
Lunar Orbiter 1 11
Lunar Prospector 12
lunar seas *3*
Luna space missions 11
Lunceford, Jimmie 413
Lundy shipping forecast
area 59
lungs *127*
Luoyang 234, 641
lupin 71
Lupu bridge 224
Lupus constellation 6, 7
Luria, Salvador E 186
lurid boletus 78
Lurie, Alison 349
Lusaka 641
lutetium 200
Luther, Martin 493, **506**
Lutheran Church 493
Luton 660
Lutuli, Albert 458
Lutyens, Sir Edwin 455
Luxembourg 676, **779**
administrative divisions 654
city 641 EU
membership 648
monarchs 284
national holidays 580
political leaders 317
UN membership 645
World Heritage sites 55
Luxon, Benjamin 407
Luyten 8
Luzon 28
Lwoff, André 186
lychee 63
lychee tree 77
Lycurgus 480
Lyell, Sir Charles 182
lymphatic system *125*
lymph gland
enlargement 131, 132
lymph node
enlargement 131, 134

lymph nodes 125, 131
lymph vascular system, study
of 174
Lynch, David 395
Lynen, Feodor 186
lynx 85
Lynx constellation 6, 7
Lynyrd Skynyrd 422
lyonnaise 154
Lyons 641
World Heritage site 53
Lyons, Sir Joseph 194
Lyra 7
lyrebird 98
Lyrids meteor shower 9
lysergic acid
diethulamide 143
Lyttelton, Humphrey 413

M

Maalouf, Amin 356
Maat 470, **480**
Maathai, Wangari 459
macadamia nut 77
Macao 254, 256, **715**
World Heritage site 52
macaque monkeys 85
macaroni 155
Macaulay, Dame Rose 349
Macaulay, Thomas 358
McBean, Angus 448
Macbeth 244
Macbeth (opera) 405
Macbeth (play) 362
McBride, Jim 395
MacBride, Seán 458
McBride, Willie John 562
MacCaig, Norman 358
McCall's Ferry bridge 224
McCallum, David 379
McCarey, Leo 397
McCarthy, Andrew 379
McCarthy, Cormac 356
McCartney, Sir Paul 404, 422
McCartney, Stella 451
McClintock, Barbara 187
MacColl, Ewan 404
McCollum, Elmer Verner 138
McCord, James I 509
McCormack, John 407
McCowen, Alec 379
McCullin, Don 448
MacDiarmid, Alan G 187
MacDiarmid, Hugh 358
MacDonald, George 349
McDonald clan 277
McDormand, Frances 399
MacDowell, Andie 379
mace 66
Macedonia 676, **780**
EU membership 648
national holidays 580
political leaders 317
UN membership 645
World Heritage sites 55
Macedonians 745
Maceió 641
McEnroe, John 562

maceration 161
McEwan, Ian 349
literary prizes 355
McFadden, Daniel 459
McFerrin, Bobby 429
McGaffrey, Ives W 192
McGoohan, Patrick 379
McGough, Roger 358
McGregor, Ewan 379
Macgregor, John 515
Mach, Ernst:
philosophy 466
science 182
Machida 641
machine gun 190, 267
Mach number 169
McHugh, Jimmy 404
Machu Picchu 56
McIlvanney, William 349
MacInnes, Colin 349
MacIntyre, Alasdair
Chalmers 466
Macke, August 442
McKellen, Sir Ian 379
Mackenzie, Kenneth 199
MacKenzie, Sir Compton 349
MacKenzie, Henry 349
Mackenzie River 33
mackerel 107
nutritional value 151
McKern, Leo 379
Mackerras 434
Mackinac Straits bridge 224
MacKinnon, Roderick 187
Mackintosh, Charles
Rennie 456
Mackmurdo, Arthur 456
McLaglen, Victor 397
MacLaine, Shirley 379
Academy Awards 398
McLaughlin, John 413
MacLean, Alistair 349
McLean, Don 422
McLean, Jay 137
MacLean, Sorley 358
McLeod, John James 137
MacLeod of Fiunary,
Lord 509
McMillan, Edwin 201
Nobel prize 186
MacMillan, James 401
Macmillan, Sir Kenneth 432
ballets 433, 434
MacMillan, Kirkpatrick 188
Macnee, Patrick 379
MacNeice, Louis 358
Mâcon 160
McQueen, Alexander 452
McQueen, Steve (actor) 379
McQueen, Steve
(sculptor) 444
macramé 568
macrobiotics 140
Madagascar 28, 676, **781**
exploration 274
national holidays 580
political leaders 317
UN membership 645
World Heritage sites 55

Madama Butterfly 405
Madden, John 399
Madden, R J 138
Madeira 30, 815
  exploration 274
  wines 160
Maderna, Carlo 456
Madesani, Grazia
  Deledda 458
Madness 422
Madonna 379, 423
Madrid 641, 644
  museums and galleries 460
Madurai 641
Maenads **480**, 483
Maeterlinck, Maurice 361
  Nobel prize 457
Mafeking, Battle of 278
Magee, Carlton C 190
Magellan, Ferdinand 254, 274
Magerøy tunnel 226
Magherafelt 662
Magic Flute, The 405
magic mushroom 78
magma 168, **169**
Magna Carta 248, 857
Magnani, Anna 398
magnesium 179, **200**
  in diet 130
  in Sun 1
  properties 202
magnesium carbonate 25
magnesium salts 152
magnetic field, magnetic
  fields 167, **169**
  study of 175
magnetic field strength:
  SI conversion factors 210
  SI units 209
magnetic flux density 209,
  210
magnetism 175, 179
magnetohydrodynamics 175
magnetometer 180
magnetostatics 175
Magnitogorsk 641
magnitude 169
  stars 7
magnolia (shrub) 73
magnolia (tree) 75
magnum 163
magpie 118
magpie lark 92
Magritte, René 442
Magyars 242, 752
Mahabharata 498
Maharishi Mahesh Yogi 268,
  503, **506**
Maha-sivaratri 498
Mahavira, Vardhamana 232,
  506
Mahayana Buddhism 492
Mahayana Sutras 492
Mahdi 266, 278, 838
Mahfouz, Naguib 349
  Nobel prize 459
mah-jong 565
Mahler, Gustav 401
  ballet music 434

mahogany 77
  American 120
  bigleaf 120
mahonia 73
Maia 469, 484
Mailer, Norman 349
Mail on Sunday 612
Maiman, Theodore 190, 271
Maimonides, Moses 246, 466
Mainbocher 452
Maine 867
main trace minerals 130
main types of vitamin 130
maize 62
Major, Dame Malvina 407
major battles and wars 275
major beliefs, distribution of
  adherents 489
Majorca 29
major causes of death 135
major earthquakes 36
major island groups 29
major oil spills at sea 48
major painting styles 437
major tsunamis 38
major volcanoes 35
Makalu I 34
Makarova, Natalia 435
Makassar 641
Makeyevka 641
Makhachkala 641
Makine, Andréï 356
malachite 27
malacology 175
Malade imaginaire, Le
  (ballet) 434
Malaga (city) 641
Malaga (wines) 160
Malagasy Republic 782
Malamud, Bernard 349
Malang 641
malaria 132
  carriers 116
  discoveries 137
Malawi 676, **782**
  Commonwealth
    membership 647
  English speakers 585
  national holidays 580
  political leaders 317
  UN membership 645
  World Heritage sites 55
Malawi/Nyasa, Lake 32
Malayan Emergency 783
Malay Archipelago 30
Malay language 584
Malaysia 676, **783**
  Commonwealth
    membership 647
  English speakers 585
  national holidays 580
  political leaders 317
  UN membership 645
  World Heritage sites 55
Malaysian giant turtle 104
Maldives 676, **784**
  Commonwealth
    membership 647
  islands 30

national holidays 580
  political leaders 317
  UN membership 645
Male 30
male reproductive
  system 129
malformations,
  biological 177
Mali 676, **785**
  national holidays 580
  political leaders 318
  UN membership 645
  World Heritage sites 55
malic acid 161
Malin shipping forecast
  area 59
Malkovich, John 380
Mallarmé, Stéphane 358
malmsey 161
Malory, Thomas 253, 477
Malouf, David 349
Malpighi, Marcello 183, 259
Malta 676, **786**
  administrative divisions 654
  Commonwealth
    membership 647
  English speakers 585
  EU membership 648
  national holidays 580
  political leaders 318
  UN membership 645
  World Heritage sites 55
Maltese Islands 30
malus 73
Maly Ballet 436
Mamas and the Papas,
  The 423
Mambo Kings Play Songs of
  Love, The 356
Mamelles de Tirésias,
  Les 405
Mamet, David 361
mammals 79
  animal kingdom 79
  collective names 118
  endangered species 119
  geological record 23
  length of pregnancy 89
  records 89
mammary glands 79
Man Booker Prize 355
Man, Isle of 858
Managua 641
manakin 98
Manaslu 34
Manaus 641
Manchego cheese 163
Manchester 641
  council 659
  museums and galleries 462
Manchu dynasty 278, 281
Mancini, Henry 404
  Grammy awards 429
Mandalay 641
mandarin 63
Mandarin 584
Mandela, Nelson 834
  Nobel prize 459
mandrake 65

mandrake leaves   135
mandrill   80
Manes   480
Manes (prophet)   506
Manet, Édouard   265, 442
Man for All Seasons, A
   (film)   398
Manfred Mann   423
Manfredi, Bartholomew   192
manganese   200
   in diet   130
   properties   202
mango   64
mango tree   77
mangrove forests   120
Manic Street Preachers   423
Manila   641
Manilow, Barry   423
Manitoba   709
Mankiewicz, Joseph   395
   Academy Awards   397
Mankowitz, Wolf   349
Mann, Delbert   398
Mann, Thomas   269, 349
   Nobel prize   458
Mannerism   438
Manning, Olivia   349
Manon (ballet)   434
Manon (opera)   405
Manon Lescaut (opera)   405
Mansard, François   456
Mansard, Jules   456
Mansfield, Jayne   380
Mansfield, Katherine   269,
   349
Mansfield, Sir Peter   187
Manson, Patrick   137
manta ray   107
Mantegna, Andrea   442
mantids   114
mantle (Earth)   20, 21
mantra   140
Mantuan Succession, War of
   the   277
Manu national park/nature
   reserve   50
Manuel M Torres dam   227
MAOIs   142
Maori   801
Maori Wars   278, 802
maple, common   75
maple, field   75
maple, sugar   75
Mapplethorpe, Robert   448
maps   190
Maputo   641
Mar, Earl of   277
Maracaibo   641
Maracaibo, Lake   32
Maracay   641
Maradona, Diego   562
Marathi language   584
marathon   518
Marathon, Battle of   275
marble   25
Marburg (or green monkey)
   disease   132
marc   161
March (novel)   356

March, Fredric   397
marchioness, form of
   address   671
Marchoux, Émile   136
Marciano, Rocky   562
Marconi, Guglielmo   183
   inventions   191
Marcos, Ferdinand   813
Marcus, Rudolph A   187
Marcuse, Herbert   466
Mar del Plata   641
Marduk   480, 481, 487
Mare Australe   3
Mare Crisium   3
Mare Fecunditatis   3
Mare Frigoris   3
Mare Humboldtianum   3
Mare Humorum   3
Mare Imbrium   3
Mare Ingenii   3
Mare Marginis   3
Mare Moscoviense   3
Mare Nectaris   3
Mare Nubium   3
Mare Orientale   3
Mare Serenitatis   3
Mare Smythii   3
Mare Spumans   3
Mare Tranquillitatis   3
Mare Undarum   3
Mare Vaporum   3
Marey, Étienne   448
margarine   190
   nutritional value   151
Mariana Islands   30
Mariana Islands,
   Northern   869
Mariana Trench   32
Marignac, Jean Charles
   Galissard de   200, 202
marigold, African   71
marigold, pot   71
marijuana   65, 143
Mariner space missions   11,
   12
maritime museums:
   Europe   459
   UK   461
   USA   462
Mariupol   641
marjoram   65
Markandaya, Kamala   349
Mark Morris Dance
   Group   436
Markova, Dame Alicia   435
Markowitz, Harry   459
Marks (of Broughton), Simon,
   1st Baron   194
marl   25
Marley, Bob   423
marlin   109
Marlowe, Christopher   255,
   361
marmoset   85
marmot   87
Marne, Battle of the   278
Marquesas Islands   30
marquess   668
   form of address   671

Marrakesh   244, 641
   World Heritage site   56
Marriage of Figaro, The   263,
   405
Marrison, Warren Alvin   188
marrow   68
Mars (myth)   469, 470, 472,
   480
Mars (planet)   2
   satellites   2
   space missions   11, 12, 13
Marsala   160, 636
Marsalis, Wynton   413
Marseilles   641
Mars Express mission   13
Mars Global Survey   12
Marsh, Ngaio   349
Marshall, Barry J   183
   Nobel prize   187
Marshall, George C   458
Marshall, Rob   399
Marshall Islands   676, 786
   islands   30
   national holidays   580
   political leaders   318
   UN membership   646
marshes   3
marsh mallow   65
Mars-Jones, Adam   349
Mars landing, first   275
Mars Pathfinder
   expedition   12, 275
Mars Rover mission   13
Marston, John   361
Marston Moor, Battle of   277
marsupials   79
Marsyas   480
Martel, Yann   349
   literary prizes   355
marten   85
Martha and the
   Vandellas   425
Martha Graham Dance
   Company   436
martial art(s)   518
Martin   433
Martin, A J P   186
Martin, Paul   448
Martin, Steve   380
Martin, Valerie   355
Martin Dressler: The Tale of
   an American Dreamer   356
Martinelli, Giovanni   407
Martini, Simone   442
Martinique   739
Martins, Peter   435
Martinson, Harry   458
Martinu, Bohuslav   433
Marty   398
Marvell, Andrew   259, 358
Marvin, Lee   380
   Academy Awards   398
Marx, Karl   466
Marx Brothers, The   380
Mary II   258, 277
Mary Poppins   398
Maryland   867
Marylebone Cricket Club   515
Masaccio   442

A–Z

Index

Masan 641
Mascagni, Pietro 405
Mascarene Islands 30
mascarpone 155
Masefield, John 358
  Poets laureate 359
Maskarade 405
Maskawa, Toshihide 188
Maskelyne, Nevil 18
Maskin, Eric S 459
Mask of Orpheus, The 405
Mason, James 380
masonry damage (earthquake
  severity measurement) 37
Masques, The 434
mass:
  Earth 19
  SI conversion factors 209
  SI units 208
  Sun 1
Mass 493
Massachusetts 867
Massacre of Wounded
  Knee 278
massage 139, **140**, 141
Massenet, Jules:
  ballet music 434
  operas 405, 406
Massey, Raymond 380
Massie, Allan 349
Massine, Léonide 432
  ballets 433, 434, 435
Masson, Gérard 434
Masson, André 442
Masters of Methods 501
Mastroianni, Marcello 380
matadors 515
matamata 104
match 190
match, safety 190
maté 65
mathematical signs and
  symbols 204
mathematics 175
Mather, John C 187
Mathilde 434
Matisse, Henri 442
Matlin, Marlee 398
matrix 169
Matsudo 641
Matsuo Basho 259
Matsuyama 641
Matthau, Walter 380
Matthew, St (disciple) 492
Matthews, Sir Stanley 562
Mature, Victor 380
Mauchly, John W 189
Maugham, Somerset 349
Maul-id-al-Nabi 577
Mau-Mau uprisings 279
Mauna Loa 35
Maupassant, Guy de 349
Maura, Carmen 380
Mauri, Rosita 435
Mauriac, François 349
  Nobel prize 458
Mauritania 252, 676, **787**
  national holidays 580
  political leaders 318

UN membership 645
World Heritage sites 55
Mauritius 676, **788**
  Commonwealth
    membership 647
  English speakers 585
  islands 30
  national holidays 581
  political leaders 318
  UN membership 645
  World Heritage sites 55
Mausoleum at
  Halicarnassus 280
Mauvoisin dam 227
Mawlid al-Nabi 499
Maximilian 790
maxwell 210
Maxwell, James Clerk 181,
  183
  inventions 190
Maxwell, Robert 194
Maxwell Davies, Sir
  Peter 273, 401
Maya culture 751
Mayall, John 423
Mayan languages 584
Maya ruins of Copan 54
Mayas 790
Mayerbeer 434
Mayerling (ballet) 434
mayfly 114
Mayon 35
mayonnaise 155
mayor, form of address 671
mayoress, form of
  address 671
Mayotte 739
MBE 668
Mbeki, Thabo 834
Mbiti, John Samuel 506
MCO 12
Meade, James 459
Meader, Vaughn 429
meadow rue 71
meadow vole 89
measles 132
  immunization 144
Measure for Measure 362
measurement:
  earthquake severity 37
  sea disturbance 41
  windspeed 41
measures 212, 213
measuring, study of 175
Mecca 499, 641, 825
mechanical vibrations, study
  of 177
mechanical waves, study
  of 174
mechanics 175
Mechnikov, Ilya 137
Medal for Merit 669
Medan 641
Medawar, Sir Peter 183
  Nobel prize 186
Medea 233, 480
Medellin 641
medical discoveries 135
Médecins sans

Frontières 459
medicine:
  complementary 139
  important discoveries 135
  supplementary
    treatment 139
Medieval art 438
Medina 825
meditation 140
meditation buddhas 471
**Mediterranean climatic
  zone** 39
Mediterranean Sea 32
medlar 63
medlar tree 75
Médoc 160
Medusa 476, 480, 483
Medway 660
Meerut 641
Mega Bridge (Dipangkorn
  Rasmijoti) 224
Megara 475
Meiko Chuo bridge 224
Meistersinger von Nürnberg,
  Die 405
Meitner, Lise 200, 201
meitnerium 200
Meknes 641
  World Heritage site 56
Mekong River 33
melancholy gentleman 71
Melanchthon, Philip 506
Melanesia 30
Melba, Dame Nellie 407
Melbourne 641
Melbourne Symphony
  Orchestra 408
Melchior, Lauritz 407
Meleager 480
Melias 480, 482
Mellanby, Edward 139
Mello, Craig C 187
  discoveries 138
melon 63
  nutritional value 151
Melpomene 480
melting point of metals 202
Melville, Herman 265, 349
Member of Parliament, form
  of address 671
Memling, Hans 442
Memling Museum 460
Memnon 475, **480**
Memphis (Egypt) 53
Memphis (USA) 641
  museums and galleries 462
men on moon 14
Menai Strait bridge 224
Menchú Tum, Rigoberta 459
Mencius (Meng-tzu) 506
Mendel, Gregor 183
  discoveries 137
Mendel, Lafayette 138
mendelevium 200
Mendeleyev, Dmitri 183, 200
Mendel's laws 183
Mendelsohn, Eric 456
Mendelssohn, Felix 401
  ballet music 434

Mendes, Sam 399
Mendoza 641
Mendoza, Pedro de 274
Menelaus 473, **480**, 484, 486
Menes 472
meningitis **132**, 133
  immunization of
    children 144
  immunization for travel 145
Menorca 29
Menotti, Gian-Carlo 405
Mensa constellation 6, 7
men's shirt sizes,
  international 222
men's sock sizes,
  international 222
men's suit and overcoat sizes,
  international 222
mental activity, study of 176
mental illnesses 139, 140
mental impairment 143
menziesa 73
Mercalli intensity scale 37
Mercantour national park/
  nature reserve 50
Merce Cunningham Dance
  Company 436
Mercer, Johnny 404
Merchant of Venice, The 362
Merckx, Eddy 562
Mercouri, Melina 380
mercury (element) 200
  properties 202
Mercury (myth) 469, 470,
  477, 481
Mercury (planet) 2
  space missions 12, 13
Meredith, George 349
merganser, red-breasted 100
Mergé-Mouriès,
  Hippolyte 190
meridian (Earth) 19
meridians 139, 141
meringue 155
Merleau-Ponty, Maurice 466
Merlin 472, **481**
MERLIN telescope 10
Merlot 160
mermaid 481
mermen 481, 487
Merope 484
Merrifield, Robert B 187
Merry Widow, The 405
Merry Wives of Windsor, The
  (opera) 405
Merry Wives of Windsor, The
  (play) 362
Merryman, Jerry D 190
Mersey tunnel 226
Merthyr Tydfil 661
Merton, Robert 459
mesclun 155
Meshed 641
mesite 99
Mesoamericans 790
Mesopotamia 758
  inventions 190, 192
Mesozoic era 23
mesquite 77

Messiaen, Olivier 401
metallography 175
metals 202
  study of 175
metamorphic rocks 25, 169
meteor, meteors **169**, 172
  annual showers 9
meteorological extremes 39
meteorology 175
Metheny, Pat 413
Methodist Church 493
methuselah 163
methylamphetamine 144
metric carat 210
metrology 175
metropolitan areas,
  largest 645
metropolitan borough
  councils, England 659
Metropolitan Museum of
  Art 462
Mexicali 641
Mexican Revolution 790
Mexican War 278
Mexico 676, **789**
  national holidays 581
  political leaders 318
  UN membership 645
  World Heritage sites 55
Mexico City 641, 645
  World Heritage sites 56
Mezzrow, Mezz 413
Miami 641
Miami City Ballet 436
mica 25, 26
Mica dam 227
Michael, George 423
  Grammy awards 429
Michaelis, Leonor 183
Michel, Hartmut 187
Michelangelo:
  art 442
  sculpture 445
Michelozzo di
  Bartolommeo 253, 456
Michelson, Albert
  Abraham 183
Michener, James A 350
Michigan 867
Michigan, Lake 32
microbes 137
microchip 190
microfossils 175
micro-light 517
micron 210
Micronesia 30
Micronesia, Federated States
  of 676, **790**
  national holidays 581
  political leaders 319
  UN membership 646
micropalaeontology 175
microphone 190
microprocessor 190
microscope 181, 190
Microscopium
  constellation 6, 7
microwave, microwaves 167,
  169, 171

  radiation 197
microwave background 169
microwave oven 190
Midas 481
Mid-Autumn Festival 498
Middlesbrough 660
Middlesex 356
Midler, Bette 380
  Grammy awards 429
Midlothian 661
Midnight Cowboy 398
Midsummer Marriage,
  The 405
Midsummer Night's Dream, A:
  ballet 434
  myth 484, 487
  play 362
Midway Island, Battle of 278
Miescher, Johann
  Friedrich 137
Mies van der Rohe,
  Ludwig 456
MIGA 646
Migenes-Johnson, Julia 407
migmatite 25
migraine 140, 141
migratory species, convention
  on 120
Mikado, The 405
Milan 641
  museums and galleries 460
  World Heritage sites 55
Milanion 473
Milan La Scala Orchestra 408
Milanov, Zinka 407
Mildred Pierce 397
mile 210
Milestone, Lewis 397
milfoil 66
Milhaud, Darius 401
Milindapanha 492
military ranks 667
  forms of address 671
milk, nutritional value 151
Milky Way 168,
  myths 488
Mill, J S 466
Millais, Sir John 442
Milland, Ray 397
Millau bridge 224
Millay, Edna St Vincent 358
Miller, Arthur 361
Miller, George 395
Miller, Glenn 414
Miller, Henry 269, 350
Miller, Jonathan 395
Miller, Lee 448
Miller, Merton 459
Miller, Steve 423
Miller, William 503
millet 62
Millet, Jean-François 442
Millhauser, Steven 356
Millikan, Robert
  Andrews 183
Million Dollar Baby 399
Mills, Hayley 380
Mills, Sir John 380
Milne, A A 350

Milosevic, Slobodan 827
Miłosz, Czesław 459
Milstein, César 183
Nobel prize 187
Milton, John 259, 358
Milton Keynes 660
Milwaukee 641
Mimas 2
Mimir 470
mimosa 72
mimosa tree 75
mimulus 73
Min and Bill 397
Minami Bisan-Seto
bridge 224
Mindanao 28
mineralogy 175
minerals 27
E numbers 152
in diet 130
study of 175
Minerva 469, 470, 472, 473,
474, 481
Minervois 160
minestrone 155
Ming dynasty 281
Minghella, Anthony 399
Mingus, Charles (Jr) 414
mink 87
length of pregnancy 89
Minkus 433
Minneapolis 641
museums and galleries 462
Minnehaha 478
Minnelli, Liza 380
Academy Awards 398
Minnelli, Vincente 395
Academy Awards 397, 398
minneola 63
Minnesota 867
Minnesota Orchestra 408
minnow 107
Minoan culture 230, 745
Minogue, Kylie 423
minor planet 169
Minos 472, 474, 476, 478,
481, 483
Minotaur 231, 481, 483, 487
Minot, George 138
Minsk 641
minute 210
Miracle Worker, The 398
Miralles, Enric 456
Miranda 3
MIR docking 14
mirin 161
Miró, Joan 442
Mirren, Dame Helen 380
Academy Awards 399
Mirrlees, James 459
MIR space station 14, 16
Mirza ali Mohammed 492
Mirza Husayn Ali 264, 492,
504
Misery 398
Mishima, Yukio 350
Mishna 500
missile, air-to-air 190
missile guidance

systems 197
Mississippi 867
Mississippi River 33
exploration 274
Missoni, Tai 452
Missouri 867
Missouri River 275
Mistral, Gabriela 458
Mitchell, Joni 423
Mitchell, Julian 350
Mitchell, Margaret 350
Mitchell, Peter D 187
Mitchell, William 515
Mitchison, Naomi 350
Mitchum, Robert 380
mite 134
Mitford, Nancy 350
Mithra 481
Mithras 469
MIT Museum 462
Mixtecs 790
Miyake, Issey 452
MKSA 169
ML computer language 608
Mnemosyne 481
Mo, Timothy 350
Mobutu Sese Seko 719
mockernut 75
mockingbird 92
mock orange 73
model-making 568
modern art galleries:
Europe 459
UK 461
USA 462
modern dance:
dancers 435
choreographers 432
companies 436
modern pentathlon 518
fixture results 543
modifiers, flavour 152
Modigliani, Amedeo 442
Modigliani, Franco 459
Modimo 481
Modine, Matthew 381
Modugno, Domenico 429
modulation 169
Moerae 481, 482, 487
Moffat tunnel 226
Mogadishu 642
Mogilyov 642
Moholy-Nagy, László 448
Mohs, Friedrich 28
Mohs' hardness scale 28
Moldova 676, 791
CIS membership 647
national holidays 581
political leaders 319
UN membership 646
World Heritage sites 56
mole 85
collective names 118
marsupial 80
mole (SI unit) 169
molecule, molecules 164,
165, 166, 168, 169, 173
Molière 361
Molina, Mario J 187

Molloy Deep 32
Mollusca 110
molluscs 110
endangered species 119
study of 175
Moloch 481
moltkia 73
Moltmann, Jürgen 506
molybdenum 200
in diet 130
properties 202
Molyneux, Edward 452
Mombasa 642
momentum 208
Monaco 676, 792
national holidays 581
political leaders 319
UN membership 646
monarch butterfly 115
World Heritage site 56
monarchs, European 283
Mondrian, Piet 442
Moneo, José Rafael 456
Monet, Claude 267, 442
Moneta, Ernesto 457
money 673
first use 233, 245
money spider 113
Mongol dynasty 281
Mongol empire 248, 276
Mongolia 676, 792
national holidays 581
political leaders 319
UN membership 645
World Heritage sites 56
Mongolian gerbil 83
Mongols 191, 248, 249, 250
mongoose 85
Moniz, Antonio Egas 186
Monk, Thelonious 414
Monkees, The 423
monkey 85
Chinese calendar 575
collective names 118
capuchin 85
rhesus 89
monkeypod 77
monkey puzzle tree 75
monkfish 107
monkshood 64
Monmouthshire 661
Monoamine oxidase
inhibitors 142
Monoceros constellation 6, 7
monoclonal antibodies 142,
183
Monod, Jacques 137
Nobel prize 186
Monongahela River
disaster 47
Monopoly® 565
monotremes 79
Monroe, Marilyn 271, 381
Monroe Doctrine 264
Monrovia 642
Monsarrat, Nicholas 350
Mons Graupius, Battle of 275
monsignor, form of
address 671

monsoon 755
Monster (film) 399
monsters 481
Monster's Ball 399
Montagu, Lady Mary
 Wortley 138
Montagnier, Luc 137
 Nobel prize 188
Montale, Eugenio 458
Montana 867
Montana, Claude 452
Montana, Joe 562
Montand, Yves 381
Mont Blanc 274
Mont Blanc tunnel 226
Monte Cassino, Battle of 279
Montenegro 676, **793**
 national holidays 581
 political leaders 319
 UN membership 645
 World Heritage sites 56
Monterrey 642
Montesquieu, Charles-Louis,
 Baron de la Brède et
 de 466
Monteverdi, Claudio 401
 operas 405
Montevideo 642
 siege of 277
Montgolfier, Jacques and
 Joseph 188
Montgomery, Wes 414
Month in the Country, A 434
months' association with
 flowers and gems 575
Montreal 642
Mont St Michel 53
Montserrat 861
 English speakers 585
Montserrat volcano 35
Monumentum pro
 Gesualdo 434
mood, mood swings 142, 143
Moody Blues, The 423
mooli 68
Moon 4
 phases *4*
 satellite 2
 space missions 11
 landings 14, 275
moonstone 27
 month association 575
Moonstruck 398
Moorcock, Michael 350
Moore, Bobby (Robert) 562
Moore, Brian 350
Moore, Charles 456
Moore, Demi 381
Moore, Dudley 381
Moore, George 467
Moore, Henry 269, 445
Moore, James 515
Moore, Sir John 277
Moore, Marianne 358
Moore, Roger 381
Moore, Stanford 186
Moorehead, Agnes 381
moorish idol 107
Moors 246, 276

Moor's Pavane, The 434
moose 82
Moradabad 642
Moranis, Rick 381
Morath, Inge 448
Moravia 724
Moray council 661
moray eel 107
Mordecai 434
More, Henry 467
Moreau, Gustave 442
Moreau, Jeanne 381
Morehouse comet 8
morel 78
Morgan, Frank 381
Morgan, Harry 381
Morgan, Thomas Hunt 136
Morgan le Fay 481
Morisot, Berthe 442
Morissette, Alanis 429
Morita, Akio 194
Mormon Utah War 278
Mormons 264, 278, **502**
morning glory 73
 month association 575
Morning Glory (film) 397
Morocco 676, **794**
 national holidays 581
 political leaders 319
 UN membership 645
 World Heritage sites 56
Morpheus 469, **481**
morphine 141
 discovery 137
morphology 175
Morpurgo, Michael 350
Morris, Mark 432
Morris, William 442
Morris dancing 567
Morrison, Toni 350
 literary prizes 356
 Nobel prize 459
Morrison, Van 423
Morse, Samuel F B 192
Morse alphabet 606
Mortensen, Erik 452
Mortimer, Penelope 350
Mortimer, Sir John 350
Morton, Jelly Roll 414
Morton, William Thomas 137
Mosander, Carl Gustaf 199,
 200, 201
Moscatello 160
Moscow 642, 644, 645
 museums and galleries 460
 World Heritage site 57
Moscow, Battle of 278
Mosel, Moselle 160
Moser-Pröll, Annemarie 562
Moses 230, 246, 248, 260,
 500, 506
Moses, Ed 562
Moses und Aron 405
Mosimann, Anton 158
Mosley, Nicholas 350
mosquito 116
 infection 132, 135
 medical discoveries 137,
 139

Mössbauer, Rudolf 186
Mossi Empire 704
most abundant bird 100
Most Holy Book 492
most prolific breeder
 (mammal) 89
most restricted distribution
 (fish) 109
most widespread
 mammal 89
most widespread fish 109
Mosul 642
mother-of-pearl shrub 73
mother tongues 584
Motherwell, Robert 442
moths 116
Motion, Andrew 273, 358
 Poets laureate 359
motion, study of 174
motion picture Academy
 Awards 397
motmot 96
motocross 518
motorcycle (invention) 190
motorcycle racing 518, 520
 fixture results 544
Motörhead 423
motor neurones 123, 124
motor racing 518, 520
 fixture results 544
Motorola 192
Mott, John R 458
Mott, Sir Neville 187
motte and bailey castle 243
Mottelson, Ben R 187
MO2 computer language 608
mountain ash (shrub) 73
mountain ash (tree) 75
mountain biking 518
mountaineering 518
mountain formation 20,
 21, 23
mountain laurel 72
mountains, highest 34
Mount Apo national park/
 nature reserve 50
Mount Cook national park/
 nature reserve 50
Mountford, Charles 448
Mount MacDonald
 tunnel 226
Mount Olympus national
 park/nature reserve 50
mouse 85
 length of pregnancy 89
 records 89
mousebird 97
moussaka 155
mousse 155
movable feasts 493
movements, religious 502
moxa 140
moxibustion 140
Moyle 662
Mozambique 676, **795**
 Commonwealth
 membership 647
 exploration 274
 national holidays 581

political leaders 319
UN membership 645
World Heritage sites 56
Mozambique War of
Independence 279
Mozart, Wolfgang
Amadeus 263, 401
operas 405
Mozart's Birthplace 461
mozzarella 155
MPLA 683
MPL space missions 12
Mrkos comet 8
MRSA 132
Mrs Miniver 397
Mubarak, Hosni 730
Much Ado About Nothing 362
Mudanjiang 642
Muddus national park/nature
reserve 50
mudpuppy 101
mudstone 25
muesli 155
Mugabe, Robert 877
Mughal emperors 283
Mughal Empire 755
mugwort 65
Muhammad 492, 499, **507**
Muhammad, Elijah 507
Muhammad Shah 283
Muir, Edwin 358
Muir, Jean 452
Mujahedin 679
mulberry 63
common 75
white 75
mule, collective names 118
Mull 30
mullahs 499
mullein 71
Müller, Franz Joseph 201
Muller, Hermann Joseph 186
Müller, K Alexander 187
Müller, Paul Hermann 186
Müller-Thurgau 160
Mulligan, Gerry 414
mulligatawny 155
Mulliken, Robert S 186
Mullis, Kary Banks 183, 187
Nobel prize 187
Multan 642
Multilateral Investment
Guarantee Agency 646
multiple mirror telescope 10
multiplication table 208
Mumbai (Bombay) 642,
644, 645
mumps 132
immunization 144
Munch, Edvard 442
Mundell, Robert 459
Muni, Paul 397
Munich 642
museums and galleries 460
Munro, Hector Hugh 352
Münster cheese 163
muon 196
Murad, Ferid 187
Murcia 642

Murdoch, Dame Iris 350, 467
Murdoch, Rupert 194
Murdock, William 189
Murmansk 642
Murphy, E A 191
Murphy, Eddie 381
Murphy, William 138
Murray, Bill 381
Murray, Joseph E 187
Murray Louis and Nikolais
Dance Company 436
Musée d'Orsay 461
Musca constellation 6, 7
Muscadelle 160
Muscadet 160
Muscat 160
muscatel 161
muscle, muscles *122*
study of 175
muscle aches 131, 132
muscle cramps 131
muscle problems 139, 140, 141
muscle repair 141
musculo-skeletal
complaints 139, 140, 141
Muse, Muses 473, 474, 475,
480, 484, 486, 488
Muses-A space mission 12
Museum Boijmans Van
Beuningen 461
Museum of Childhood 461
Museum of Welsh
Antiquities 461
museums:
Europe 459
UK 461
USA 462
Museveni, Yoweri 853
Musharraf, Pervez 808
mushroom 68
nutritional value 151
musical symbols, terms and
abbreviations 430
musicians:
jazz and blues 409
pop and rock 417
music therapy 139
mussel, common 111
nutritional value 151
Mussolini 278
Mussorgsky, Modest 401
operas 405
mustard, black 66
mustard, white 66
mutation 169
Mutiny on the Bounty 397
Muybridge, Eadweard 448
Muz Tag Ata 34
Myanmar (Burma) 676, **796**
national holidays 581
political leaders 319
UN membership 645
mycology 175
Myerson, Roger B 459
My Fair Lady (film) 398
My Left Foot 398
myofibrils 122
myology 175
Myrdal, Alva 459

Myrdal, Gunnar 458
Myrmidons 481
myrrh 65
Myrrha 471
myrtle (herb) 65
myrtle (shrub) 73
myrtle, orange bark 75
Mysore 642
Mystic River 399
mythological figures 471
mythology:
Egyptian 470
Greek 469
Norse 470
Roman 469

N

Naberezhnye Chelny 642
Nabokov, Vladimir 271, 350
Nabucco 405
Nadar 448
nadir 169
Nagano 642
Nagarjuna 507
Nagasaki 642
Nagorno-Karabakh 687, 690
Nagoya 642
Nagpur 642
Nagy, Imre 752
Naha 642
Naiad, Naiads 481
Naipaul, (Sir) V S 350
Nobel prize 459
Nairn, Nick 158
Nairobi 642
Naismith, James 514
Najibullah, Muhammad 679
naked ladies 69
naked mushroom 78
Namangan 642
Nambu, Yoichiro 188
names, meanings 596
Namib Desert 33
Namibia 676, **797**
Commonwealth
membership 647
English speakers 585
national holidays 581
political leaders 320
UN membership 646
World Heritage sites 56
Namib-Naukluft national park/
nature reserve 50
nan 155
Nanchang 642
Nanda Devi 34
Nanga Parbat 34
Nanjing 642
Nanjing bridges 225
Nanjing Greenland Financial
Center 228
Nanna 470
Nanning 642
Nansen, Fridtjof 275
Nobel prize 458
Nantong 642
Naoise 474
Napier, John 183, 257

Naples 642
  museums and galleries 460
  World Heritage site 55
Napoleon 259, 262, 264, 266, 284, 738
Napoleonic Wars 277
Nara 642
  World Heritage sites 55
narcissus 69
  month association 575
Narcissus (myth) 475, **481**
narcotic analgesics 143
narwhal 85
NASA:
  inventions 191
  space launches 13
NASA Infrared Telescope Facility 10
Nash, Heddle 407
Nash, John (architect) 456
Nash, John (economist) 459
Nash, Ogden 358
Nash, Paul 442
Nashville-Davidson 642
Nassau 642
nasturtium 65, 71
Natal (city) 642
Natal (province) 834
Nathans, Daniel 187
National Air and Space Museum 463
National Archives (USA) 463
national art galleries:
  Europe 459
  UK 461
  USA 462
National Ballet 436
National Ballet of Canada 436
National Ballet of Cuba 436
National Ballet of Mexico 436
National Gallery 461
National Gallery of Art 463
National Gallery of Scotland 461
national holidays 577
National Hunt racing 517
nationalism 663
nationalization 663
National Maritime Museum 461
National Museum of American Art 463
National Museum of American History 463
National Museum of Scotland 461
national museums:
  Europe 459
  UK 461
  USA 462
national parks 49
National Portrait Gallery, The 461
National Railway Museum 462
National Symphony Orchestra 408
nations of the world 673

Native Americans' uprising 277
NATO alphabet 606
Natta, Guilio 186
natterjack 101
Natural History Museum 461
natural history museums:
  Europe 459
  UK 461
  USA 462
natural selection 169
nature reserves 49
naturopathy 140
Naufraga balearica 120
Nauru 676, **798**
  Commonwealth membership 647
  English speakers 585
  national holidays 581
  political leaders 320
  UN membership 646
nausea 131, 132, 135, 141
Nausicaa 481
nautical measures 213
naval ranks 667
Navaratri 498
navarin 155
navigation satellite 11
Navigator Islands 274
Navratilova, Martina 562
Nazi Party 743
NBC Symphony Orchestra 408
N'Djamena 642
Ndola 642
Neal, Patricia 381
  Academy Awards 398
Neanderthal man 229
neap tides 169
nearest stars 8
NEAR space mission 12
Neary, Patricia 435
NEAT (Lötschberg Base) tunnel 226
NEAT (St Gotthard) tunnel 226
Neath Port Talbot 661
Nebraska 867
nebuchadnezzar 163
nebula 168, **169**
neck problems 139
Neckam, Alexander 188, 247
nectarine 63
  nutritional value 151
needle sharing 143
Néel, Louis Eugène 186
Neeson, Liam 381
negative ion therapy 140
Nehallenia 470
Neher, Erwin 187
Neill, Sam 381
Neisser, Albert Ludwig Siegmund 137
Neku-siyar 283
Nelson, Admiral 277
Nelson, Ricky 423
Nemchinova, Vera 435
Nemesis 469, **481**
Neoclassicism (architecture) 453

Neoclassicism (art) 438
neodymium 200
Neo-Expressionism 438
neon 200
  in Sun 1
neon lamp 190
Neo-Plasticism 438
Neoptolemus 472, **481**, 484
Nepal 676, **799**
  English speakers 585
  national holidays 581
  political leaders 320
  UN membership 645
  World Heritage sites 56
Nephthys 470, **481**
Neptune (myth) 469, 470, 481, 484
Neptune (planet) **2**, 201
  satellites 3
  space missions 12
neptunium 201
Nereid 3
Nereids **481**, 482
Nereus 469, 481
Nergal 481
nerine 69
Nerthus 470
Neruda, Pablo 458
nerve cells 123, 124
nerve impulses **123**, 184
nerve reflexes 123
Nervi, Pier Luigi 456
nervous conduction 174
nervousness 141
nervous reaction 137
nervous system 123
  study of 175
Nesbit, Edith 350
Nessebar 52
Nessus 481
Nestlé 188
Nestor 482, 486
netball 518
  fixture results 545
Netherland Dance Theatre 436
Netherlands, The 676, **800**
  administrative divisions 655
  EU membership 648
  honours 669
  monarchs 284
  national holidays 581
  political leaders 320
  road signs 623
  territories 801
  UN membership 645
  World Heritage sites 56
Netherlands Antilles 801
Netherlands Costume Museum 461
Netherlands Railway Museum 461
Network 398
Neumann, Balthasar 456
neuralgia 140
neuroendocrinology 175
neurological disorders 130
neurology 175
neuron, neurone 170

neuropathology 176
Neuroptera 110, **115**
neurotransmitters 142
neutrino 170
neutron, neutrons 165, 167, 169, **170**, 171
physical constants 196
neutron star 170
Nevada 867
Neveu 191
New Age beliefs 502
Newark 642
New Brunswick 709
Newby, P H 350
New Caledonia 739
Newcastle 642
council 659
museums and galleries 462
New China dam 227
Newcomen, Thomas 191, 259
New Delhi 642
Newfoundland 28, 30, 709
exploration 274
New Guinea 28
New Hampshire 867
Newhart, Bob 429
New Haven 462
New Hebrides 30
New Jersey 867
Newman, Arnold 448
Newman, Barnett 442
Newman, John Henry 266, 507
Newman, Paul 381
Academy Awards 398
Newman, Randy 423
New Mexico 867
New Orleans 642
museums and galleries 462
New Orleans Philharmonic Symphony Orchestra 408
Newport 661
New River Gorge bridge 225
Newry and Mourne 662
news agencies 610
New Siberian Islands 30
News of the World 612
New South Wales 688
newspapers 190
Europe 612
UK 612
USA 613
newt, newts:
alpine 101
Bosca's 101
marbled 101
palmate 101
smooth 101
warty 101
Newton, Helmut 448
Newton, Sir Isaac 183, 259
Newton comet 8
Newton-John, Olivia 429
Newtownabbey 662
New World 274
New Year:
Chinese 498
Islamic 499
Japanese 500

Jewish 500
national holidays 577
New Year's Eve 577
New York (city) 642, 645
museums and galleries 462
New York (state) 867
New York Bay 274
New York City Ballet 436
New York Philharmonic Orchestra 408
New York Symphony Orchestra 408
New Zealand 676, **801**
Commonwealth membership 647
English speakers 585
exploration 274
islands 31
national holidays 581
political leaders 321
UN membership 645
World Heritage sites 56
Nezahualcóyotl 642
Ngami, Lake 275
Ngorongoro national park/ nature reserve 50
Ngugi wa Thiong'o 350
Ngugi, James T 350
niacin 130
discovery 138
Niamey 642
Nibelungen 473, 482
Nicaragua 676, **802**
civil war 279
national holidays 581
political leaders 321
UN membership 645
World Heritage sites 56
Nice 642
Nichiren 248, 492
Nicholas U Mayall Telescope 10
Nichols, Mike 395
Nicholson, Ben 442
Nicholson, Jack 381
Academy Awards 398
nickel 200
properties 202
Nicklaus, Jack 563, 564
Nicobar Islands 31
Nicolai, Otto 405
Nicosia 642
Nidud 488
Niebuhr, Carsten 274
Niebuhr, Reinhold 507
Nielsen, Carl 401
operas 405
Nielsen, Leslie 382
Niemeyer, Oscar 456
Niepce, Joseph
Nicéphore 448
inventions 190
Niersteiner 160
Nietzsche, Friedrich 467
Niger 676, **803**
national holidays 581
political leaders 321
UN membership 645
World Heritage sites 56

Niger River 33
exploration 274
Niger-Congo languages 584
Nigeria 676, **804**
Commonwealth membership 647
English speakers 585
national holidays 581
political leaders 321
UN membership 645
World Heritage sites 56
Nigerian–Biafran War 279
night blindness 130
nightingale 484
collective names 118
Nightingale, Florence 265
nightjar 97
nightjar, owlet- 98
Night Journey 434
Night Shadow 434
Nihon Shoki 500
Niigata 642
Nijinska, Bronislova 432
ballets 433, 434, 435
Nijinsky, Vaslav 435
ballets 433, 434
Nike 469, **482**
Nikolais, Alwin 432
Nikolayev 642
Nile, Battle of the 277
Nile, Blue 274
Nile, White 274
Nile–Red Sea canal 280
Nile River 33
Nilo-Saharan languages 584
Nilson, Lars Fredrik 201
Nilsson, Birgit 407
Nilsson, Lennart 448
nimbostratus clouds 44
Nimoy, Leonard 382
Ningbo 642
Ninurta 482
Niobe 200, **482**
niobium 200
Nirenberg, Marshall 186
Nirvana 492
Nirvana (rock band) 423
Niš 642
Nishinomiya 642
Niteroi 642
nitrates 60
nitrification 60
nitrites 60
nitrogen 182, **200**
in Sun 1
nitrogen cycle *60*
nitrous oxide 137
Niven, David 382
Academy Awards 398
Niwano, Nikkyo 509
Nix 482
Nixie 482
Nixon in China 405
Nizhny Novgorod (Gorky) 642
Nizhny Tagil 642
Njord 470, **482**
Nobel, Alfred **194**, 200
inventions 189

nobelium 200
Nobel prizes 186, 457
Nobeyama Millimetre Array
 (telescope) 10
Nobeyama Radio
 Telescope 10
noble beech 74
noble gases 170
noble rot 161
Noces, Les 434
No Country for Old Men 399
Nocturne 434
Noddack, Walter 201
node 170
Noel-Baker, Philip 458
Nokomis 478
Nolde, Emil 442
Nolte, Nick 382
non-steroidal anti-
 inflammatory drugs 142
non-stick pan 190
noradrenaline 142
Nordsund bridge 225
Nordic Museum 461
Nordic skiing 519
Norfolk 659
Norfolk Island pine 77
Norgay, Tenzing 275
Noriega, Manuel 810
Norma (opera) 405
Norma constellation 6, 7
Norman, Jessye 407
Norman Conquest 244, 275
Normandie bridge 225
Normandy landings 268, 279
Normandy, House of 283
Norma Rae 398
Norns 470, 482
Norrish, Ronald 186
Norse gods 470
North, Douglass 459
North America 28
North American meadow
 vole 89
Northamptonshire 659
North Ayrshire 661
North Cape tunnel 226
North Carolina 867
North Dakota 867
North Down 662
North East Greenland national
 park 50
North East Lincolnshire 660
Northern Ballet Theatre 436
Northern Ireland 662, 857
 districts 661
 museums and galleries 461
 national holidays 581
Northern Ireland
 Assembly 857
Northern Mariana
 Islands 869
Northern Sinfonia 408
Northern States Power
 Company disaster 48
Northern Territory 688
North Frisian Islands 30
North Island 28
North Lanarkshire 661

North Lincolnshire 660
North Pole 275
Northrop, John Howard 186
North Sea 32
North Somerset 660
North Tyneside 659
Northumberland 659
North Utsire shipping forecast
 area 59
North-west America 274
North West Passage 274, 275
Northwest Territories 709
North Yorkshire 659
Norway 676, 805
 national holidays 581
 political leaders 322
 road signs 623
 UN membership 645
 World Heritage sites 56
Norway lemming 84
Norwegian Folk Museum 460
Norwegian Sea 32
nose 176
nose (wine-tasting) 161
nosology 176
Nottingham 660
Nottinghamshire 659
Nouakchott 642
nougat 155
Nouvel, Jean 456
nouvelle cuisine 155
nova 170, 173
Nova Iguaçu 642
Novak, Michael 509
Nova Scotia 709
 exploration 274
Novaya Zemlya 28, 31
novelists 341
Novelli, Jean-Christophe 158
Novello, Ivor 404
novel serialization 190
Novgorod 242, 251
 World Heritage site 57
Novokuznetsk 642
Novosibirsk 642
Novrus 577
Nowruz 48
Nox 482
Noye's Fludde 405
Noyori, Ryoji 187
NSAIDs 141, 142
Nubian Desert 33
nuclear energy 168, 170
nuclear explosion 167
nuclear fission 170
nuclear fusion 170, 172
nuclear reaction 168, 170,
 171
nuclear reactor 180
nuclear studies 176
nucleic acid 137
nucleon 170
nucleonics 176
nucleus 164, 166, 170, 171
Nuffield, William Morris, 1st
 Viscount 194
numerical data, study of 177
numerical equivalents 207
Numidian War 275

numismatics 568
Nunavut 709
Nurek dam 227
Nuremberg 642
Nureyev, Rudolf 435
Nurmi, Paavo 563
Nurse, Sir Paul M 183
 Nobel prize 187
Nüsslein-Volhard,
 Christiane 187
Nut 470
Nutcracker, The 434
nuthatch 92
nutmeg 66
 California 75
Nux 482
Nyamuragira volcano 35
Nyasa/Malawi, Lake 32
Nyasaland 782
Nye, Robert 350
nylon 203, 269
 invention 190
Nymph, Nymphs 471, 472,
 473, 474, 475, 476, 477, 481,
 482, 485, 486
Nyx 482

O

oak:
 California live 75
 common 75
 cork 75
 English 75 red 75
Oakland 642
Oaks, The 539
Oasis 423
Oates, Joyce Carol 350
oatmeal 151
oats 62
 porridge 151
Ob (river) 33
OBE 668
Obermeier, Otto 138
Oberon (myth) 482
Oberon (satellite) 3
Oberon, Merle 382
obesity:
 body mass index 147
 dietary
 recommendations 149
Obon 500
Obote, Milton 853
O'Brien, Edna 350
O'Brien, Flann 350
Observer, The 612
obsidian 26
obstetrics 176
O'Casey, Sean 361
OCCAM computer
 language 608
occupational therapy 139
occupations, patron saints
 of 497
ocean cooling 169
Oceania 28
oceanic trenches 21
Oceanid, Oceanids 474, 482
ocean floor 275

Ocean of Storms 3
  NASA moon landings 14
oceanography 175, **176**
oceans 32
  study of 176
Oceanus 469, **482**
Oceanus Procellarum 3
ocean warming 167
Ochoa, Severo 186
Ockham, William of 250, 467
Octans constellation 6, 7
Octavian 282
  battles 275
octopus 111
  blue-ringed 111
  common 111
octopush 518
octopus tree 77
Odessa 642
Odin 470, 473, 476, 477, 482, 487
odontology 176
Odysseus 233, 471, 472, 473, 474, 475, 480, 481, **482**, 483, 485, 486
Odyssey 482, 485, 486
Oë, Kenzaburo 350
  Nobel prize 459
oedema 142
Oedipus 474, 475, 479, **482**, 484, 487
Oedipus Rex (opera) 405
Oedipus Tyrranus (play) 405
oenology 161
Oenone 483
oenophile 161
oersted 210
Oerter, Al 563
oestrogen 137, 142
oestrone 137
Offa's Dyke 241
Offenbach, Jacques 265, 401
  ballet music 434
  operas 405
Office International Nansen pour les Réfugiés 458
Office of the UN High Commissioner for Refugees 458, 459
officers in armed forces, forms of address 671
Ofili, Chris 444
O'Flaherty, Liam 350
Ogbomosho 642
Ogmios 482
O'Hara, John 350
ohi' a lehua 77
Ohinamatsuri 500
Ohio 867
Ohlin, Bertil 459
Ohm, Georg Simon 183
Ohm's law 183
oil spills 48
oil, vegetable 151
oilbird 98
Oileus 471
Oita 642
Ojos del Salado 34
okapi 85

World Heritage site 52
Okayama 642
Oklahoma 867
Oklahoma City 642
  museums and galleries 463
okra 68
Okri, Ben 351
  literary prizes 355
Olah, George 187
Oldenburg, Claes 445
Oldenburg-Holstein-Gottorp, House of 286
Oldfield, Bruce 452
Oldfield, Mike 424
Oldham 659
Oldman, Gary 382
old man of the woods 78
oleander 73
olearia 73
oleaster 73
Olinda 642
  World Heritage sites 52
Oliphant, Margaret 351
olive (tree) 75
Oliver! 398
Oliver, George 135, 528
Oliver, Isaac 444
Oliver, Jamie 158
Oliver, King 414
Olivetti, Adriano 195
Olivier, Laurence, Baron 395
  Academy Awards 397
olivine 26
Olmecs 231, 790
Olo'upena Falls 33
Olympia:
  museum 460
  World Heritage site 54
Olympians 469, 473, **482**
Olympic Games 512, 513
  legend 475, 483
Olympic National Park 50
Olympus, Mount 482
Omagh 662
Omaha 642
Oman 676, **806**
  national holidays 581
  political leaders 322
  UN membership 645
  World Heritage sites 56
Omar Khayyám 245
ombudsman 663
Omdurman 642
omelette 155
Omiya 642
omnivore 170
Omsk 642
Onassis, Aristotle 195
On Beauty 355
onchocerciasis 133
oncogene, oncogenes 170
  discoveries 137, 178, 185
oncology 176
Ondaatje, Michael 351
  literary prizes 355
Ondine 434
O'Neal, Ryan 382
O'Neal, Tatum 382
One Flew Over the Cuckoo's

Nest 398
Onega, Lake 32
Onegin 434
O'Neill, Eugene 361
  Nobel prize 458
On Golden Pond 398
onion 65, 68
  nutritional value 151
Ono, Yoko 429
Onsager, Lars 186
Ontario 709
Ontario, Lake 32
On the Waterfront 398
onyx 27
oölogy 176
opal 27
  month association 575
operas 405
opera singers 406
operettas 405
Ophiuchus constellation 6, 7
opium poppy 65
Opium Wars 264, 277, 278, 714
Oporto 642
  World Heritage site 57
opossum 80
  length of pregnancy 89
Oppenheimer, Robert 183
  inventions 188
Ops 469, 470, 482
ophthalmology 176
optical fibre, optical fibres 170
  invention 190
optical sound recording 190
optics, study of 176
optimum weight 147
oral contraceptive drugs 142
Oran 642
orange 63
  nutritional value 151
Orange, House of 284
orange, sweet (tree) 75
Orange-Fish River tunnel 226
Orange Free State 834
orange juice 151
orange-peel fungus 78
Orange Prize for Fiction 355
orang-utan 85
  length of pregnancy 89
  trade in 120
Orbison, Roy 424
orbital flight (space) 13
orb-web spider 113
orchestra layout 408
orchestras 407
Orchestre Symphonique de Montréal 408
orchid 71
  endangered species 120
orchitis 132
Orcus 469
order 61
order of magnitude 170
Order of Merit 668
Order of the Companions of Honour 668
orders of chivalry 668

Ordinary People 398
Ordos Desert 33
Ordovician period 23
  fossils 24
Ordzhonikidze 642
Oreads 482
oregano 65
Oregon 868
Orenburg 642
Orestes 471, 474, 475, 479, **482**
Øresund bridge 225
Øresund tunnel 226
Orfeo ed Euridice 405
Orff, Carl 401
organ failure 144
organic 170
organic compound 171
organic material 165
organic molecule 164
organic sediments 25
organic substances 167, 173
organisms, classification of 61
organography 176
orienteering 518
  fixture results 545
origami 568
Origen 507
Origin of Species by Means of Natural Selection, The 179
Orinoco River 274
oriole (Old World) 92
Orion 482
Orion constellation 6, 7
Orionids meteor shower 9
Orkney council 661
Orkney Islands 31
Orleans, siege of 276
ornithogalum 69
ornithology 176
  hobby 566
orogenesis 170
Oroville dam 227
Orpheus 472, 473, 476, **482**
Orpheus (ballet) 434
Orpheus in the Underworld 265, 405
Orsenna, Erik 356
Ortega y Gasset, José 467
orthoclase 28
Orthodox Church 493
orthogenesis 170
orthopaedics, orthopedics 176
Orthoptera 110, **114**
Orton, Joe 361
Orwell, George 271, 351
Ory, Kid 414
Oryol 642
Osaka 642
Osasco 642
Osborne, John 271, 361
Osborne, Thomas Burr 138
Osbourne, Ozzy 424
Oscar and Lucinda 355
Oscars 397
Osheroff, Douglas D 187
Oshogatsu 500

Oshumi satellite 11
Osijek 642
Osiris 230, 470, **482**, 485
Oslo 642
  museums and galleries 460
Oslo Philharmonic Orchestra 408
osmanthus 73
osmium 201
  properties 202
osmosis 170
osprey 90
Ossa, Mount 476
Ossian 261
osteology 176
osteomalacia 130
osteomyelitis 133
osteopathy 139
osteoporosis 130
ostracods 24
Ostrava 642
ostrich 89
  record 100
O'Sullivan, Maureen 382
Otello 405
Othello 362
Othello oil spill 48
Otis, Elisha G 190
otology 176
Oto-Manguean languages 584
O'Toole, Peter 382
otorhinolaryngology 176
Otr 470
Ottawa-Gatineau 642
otter 85
  collective names 118
Otterburn, Battle of 276
Otto, Rudolf 507
Otway, Thomas 361
Oud, Jacobus 456
Oudney, Walter 275
Oughtred, William 191, 257
Ouida 351
Oujda 642
ounce 210
Ouranus 482, 488
Outer Hebrides 30
OutKast 429
Out of Africa 398
ova, study of 176
ovenbird 98
overdose 143
over-exploitation 119
over-fishing 119
over-harvesting 119
overweight 147
Ovid 235, 358
ovulation 137
Owen, Wilfred 269, 358
Owens, Jesse 563
Owens Illinois Glass Co 189
Owingsburg Landing tunnel 226
owl 90
  barn 90
  collective names 118
ox:
  Chinese calendar 575

collective names 118
ox-eye 71
Oxford 462
Oxfordshire 659
oxidation **170**, 171
  E numbers 152
  wine 162
oxygen 182, **201**
  in Sun 1
oyster 111
  collective names 118
oystercatcher 94
oyster mushroom 78
Ozbeck, Rifat 452
Ozick, Cynthia 351
ozone layer 166, **170**

P

pacemaker 190
Pacific Ocean 32
  exploration 274
Pacino, Al 382
  Academy Awards 399
Packer, Kerry 195
Pactolus, River 481
Padang 642
paddle tennis 518
Paddy Clarke, Ha Ha Ha 355
Padua 55
paella 155
Page, Geraldine 382
  Academy Awards 398
Page, Ruth 435
Pagliacci 405
pagoda-tree 75
Päijänne tunnel 226
pain 133, 134, 135
pain-relieving drugs 141, 142
paint 190
paintball 568
painting 437
Pakistan 676, **807**
  civil war 279
  Commonwealth membership 647
  English speakers 585
  national holidays 581
  political leaders 322
  UN membership 645
  World Heritage sites 56
pakora 155
Palace of El Pardo 460
Palade, George E 187
palaeoclimatology 176
palaeoecology 176
palaeogeography 176
palaeontology 176, 178
palaeopathology 176
Palaeozoic era 23
  ice ages 24
palaeozoology 176
Palance, Jack 382
palate 162
Palau 676, **808**
  national holidays 581
  political leaders 322
  UN membership 646
Palazzo Bianco 460

AZ

Index

Palazzo Capodimonte 460
Palazzo Rosso 460
Palembang 642
Palermo 642
Pales 469
Palestine 761, **762**, 766, 767
Palestinian Autonomous
  Areas 761, **762**
  political leaders 323
Palestrina, Giovanni 401
Paley, William 507
Pali Canon 492
Palin, Michael 382
Palladio, Andrea 456
palladium 201
  properties 202
Pallas 201
Palma 642
palmchat 92
Palmer, Arnold 563
Palmer, Robert 424
Palmer, Samuel 442
palm Pritchardia 120
Palm (Passion) Sunday 494
Paltrow, Gwyneth 382
  Academy Awards 399
Palus Epidemiarum 3
Palus Nebularum 3
Palus Putredinis 3
Palus Somnii 3
palynology 176
Pamuk, Orhan 351
  Nobel prize 459
Pan 469, 474, **482**, 486
Panama 676, **809**
  exploration 274
  national holidays 581
  political leaders 323
  UN membership 645
  World Heritage sites 56
Panama Canal 269, 810
Panama City 642
Panchiao 642
panda, giant 85
  World Heritage site 52
pandanus 77
Pandarus 482
Pandion 483
Pandora 482, 484
panelology 568
Pan Gu 483
Panjabi language 584
Pannenberg, Wolfhart 507
Panov, Valery 435
Panova, Galina 435
Panshan 642
pansy 71
Pantheon 235
panther cap 78
pantothenic acid 130
Panufnik, Sir Andrej 433
Paolozzi, Sir Eduardo 445
papaya 64
paper 190
  international sizes 223
  measures 213
  wedding anniversary 575
paperbark tree 77
paper clip 190

paper sizes 223
Papillons, Les 434
papillote 155
Papin, Denis 191
Papposileni 486
paprika 66
Papua New Guinea 676, **810**
  Commonwealth
    membership 647
  English speakers 585
  national holidays 581
  political leaders 323
  UN membership 645
  World Heritage sites 56
parabola 206
paracetamol 141
parachute 190
parachuting 518
Parade (ballet) 434
paragliding 568
Paraguay 677, **811**
  national holidays 581
  political leaders 323
  UN membership 645
  World Heritage sites 56
Paraguay River 274
parallel bars
  (gymnastics) 517
parallelogram 205
Paralympic Games 513
paralysis 133
Parana River 274
paranoia 143, 144
paranormal, study of 176
parapsychology 176
parasite, parasites 170
  study of 176
parasitic diseases 135
parasitic worms 141
parasitology 176
parasol mushroom 78
Parasurama 483
Parcae 481, 483
parchment 190
Paricutín volcano 35
Paris (city) 642, 644
  museums and galleries 460
  World Heritage site 53
Paris (myth) 471, 472, 477,
  483
Paris Opéra Ballet 436
Park, Mungo 274
Parke, L F J 138
Parker, Alan 395
Parker, Charlie 414
Parkes Radio Telescope 10
parking meter 190
Parkinson, James 183
Parkinson, Norman 448
Parkinson's disease 142, 183
Parks, Gordon 449
Parmenides 467
Parmesan cheese 155
Parmigianino 442
Parnassus 475
parotid gland 132
parotitis 133
parrot, parrots 97
  collective names 118

  infection by 133
parrotfish 107
Parry, Sir Hubert 401
parsec 170
  SI conversion factors 210
Parsifal (myth) 483
Parsifal (opera) 249, 405
parsley 65
parsnip 68
  nutritional value 151
Parsons, Charles 191
parthenogenesis 170
Parthenopaeus 485
Parton, Dolly 424
partridge 118
Parzival 249, 483
Pasadena 463
Pascal, Blaise 183, 257
  inventions 191
Pascal computer
  language 608
Pasiphae 481, **483**
Pasmore, Victor 442
Pasolini, Pier Paolo 395
Pass, Joe 414
passage of bills:
  UK 665
  USA 666
passata 155
Passchendaele, Battle of 278
Passeriformes 100
Passerines 98
passion fruit 64
Passover 500
pasta 155
  nutritional value 151
Pasternak, Boris 351
  Nobel prize 458
Pasteur, Louis 184, 265
  discoveries 136, 137, 138
  inventions 190
pasteurization 170, 190
pastimes 566
Patagonian Desert 33
Patchett, Ann 355
pâté 155
Paterson, Jennifer 158
pathogen 170, 173
pathology 176
Pati dam 227
Patineurs, Les 434
patisserie 155
Patna 642
Paton, Allan 351
Patos, Lake 32
Patou, Jean 452
Patrick, John 361
Patroclus 483, 485
patron saints of
  occupations 497
Patten, Brian 358
Patten, Marguerite 158
pattern sizes,
  international 222
Patti, Adelina 407
Patton (film) 398
Paul, St 507
Paul, Wolfgang 187
Paulescu, Nicolae 137

Pauli, Wolfgang 184
Nobel prize 186
Pauling, Linus 184
Nobel prizes 186, 458
Pavarotti, Luciano 407
Pavelić, Ante 721
Pavlodar 642
Pavlov, Ivan Petrovich 184
Pavo constellation 6, 7
Paxton, Sir Joseph 456
Payen, Anselme 137
payload 14, 18
Payton, Walter 563
Paz, Octavio 358
Nobel prize 459
pea 68
nutritional value 151
peach 63
nutritional value 151
peacock (bird) 118
peacock (flower) 69
Peacock, Thomas Love 351
Peacocke, Arthur 509
Peake, Mervyn 351
peanuts, nutritional
value 151
pear 63
nutritional value 151
tree 75
pearl 28
month association 575
wedding anniversary 575
pearl bush 73
Pearl Fishers, The 405
Pearl Harbor 268, 278
Pears, Sir Peter 407
Pearson, Charles 191
Pearson, Lester B 458
Peary, Robert 275
peat 25
Peck, Gregory 382
Academy Awards 398
Peckinpah, Sam 395
pecks 220
Pedersen, Charles J 187
Pedersen, Niels-Henning
Ørsted 414
pedology 176
Pegasus 7, 473, **483**
Pegasus constellation 6, 7
pegmatite 26
Pegsat space mission 12
Pei, I M 456
Peierls, Rudolf 188
Peirce, Charles 467
Peking Man site 52
Pelagian Islands 31
Pelé 563
Pelée, Mont 35
Peleus 471, 475, **483**
Pelias 479
pelican 95
Pelion, Mount 476
Pelléas et Mélisande 405
Peloponnesian Wars 275
Pelops 483, 486, 487
pelota 518
Pelote Basque 518
Pembrokeshire 661

pen 190
Penates 469, **483**
penates publici 483
pencil 190
Penderecki, Krzysztof 401
pendulum 180,
Peneios 474
Penelope 483, 486
penguin 96
collective names 118
penicillin 137, 180, 269
Peninsular War 277
Penn, Irving 449
Penn, Sean 383
Academy Awards 399
Penn, William 503
Pennsylvania 868
Pennsylvania Ballet 437
penny-bun fungus 78
Pentateuch 500
pentathlon 517, **518**
Pentecost 492, 493, 494
Pentecostalism 266, 493, **503**
Pentheus 483
pentium processor 190
penumbra 1
Penza 642
Penzias, Arno A 187
peony:
flower 71
herb 65
shrub 73
People, The 612
People's Palace Museum 461
Pepi II 280
pepper (spice) 66
pepper (vegetable) 68
nutritional value 151
peppermint 65
pepsin 184
peptic ulcers 141
Pepusch, Johann
Christoph 405
percentages 207
Perceval, Sir 480, **483**
perch 107
Percy, Sir Henry 276
peregrine falcon 90
records 100
sport 516
perennial 170
Peres, Shimon 459
Perey, Marguerite 200
Pergamon Museum 460
Peri 483
pericarditis 133
pericardium 133
Pericles 362
peridot 28
month association 575
peridotite 26
Perier, Jacques C 191
périgord truffle 78
periodic law 183
periodic table 170, **198**
periods, geological 22, 23
peripheral nervous
system 123
peristalsis 125

Perithous 479
peritonitis 133
periwinkle, common 110
Perkins, Anthony 383
Perl computer language 608
Perl, Martin L 187
Perm 642
permeability 209
Permian period 23
fossils 24
permittivity 209
perpetual calendar 569
Perret, Auguste 456
Perrier, Carlo 201
Perrot, Jules 433
ballets 433
Perry, Fred 563
Perry, Grayson 444
Perse, Saint-John 458
Perseids meteor shower 9
Persephone 469, 471, 475,
483, 486
Persepolis 54
Perseus 472, 474, 476, **483**
Perseus constellation 6, 7
Persia 275
Persian Gulf 274
Persian language 584
Persian Wars 239, 275
persimmon 63
Persoz, Jean-François 137
Perth 642
Perth and Kinross 661
pertussis 144
Peru 677, **811**
national holidays 581
political leaders 323
UN membership 645
World Heritage sites 56
Perugino 442
Perun 483, 485
Perutz, Max 184
Nobel prize 186
Peruvian lily 71
Pesach 500
Pesci, Joe 383
Peshawar 642
pesto 155
Peter, Daniel 188
Peter, St (disciple) 492
Peterborough 660
Peter Grimes 405
Peter, Paul and Mary 424
Petersburg, battles of
(USA) 278
Peterson, Oscar 414
Petipa, Lucien 435
Petipa, Marie 435
Petipa, Marius 433
ballets 433, 434
Petit, Roland 433
ballets 433
petit four 155
Petra 55
Petrarch 251, 358
petrel, diving 96
petrel, storm 96
Petrified Forest national park/
nature reserve 50

AZ

Index

petrology 176
Petronas Twin Towers 228
Petronio, Stephen 435
Petroushka 434
petunia 71
Pfälzerwald national park/ nature reserve 50
Pfeiffer, Michelle 383
Phaedra 478, **483**
Phaethon 483
phage 170
phagocytes 137
phalarope 95
Phanerozoic aeon 22
pharmacodynamics 176
pharmacokinetics 176
pharmacology 176
Pharos of Alexandria 280
Pharsalus, Battle of 275
pharyngitis 133
pheasant 99
collective names 118
Pheidias 445
Pheidippides 518
Phelps, Edmund S 459
Phenix 483
phenol 137
phenology 176
phenomenology 176
Phenytoin 137
Philadelphia (city) 642, 645
museums and galleries 463
Philadelphia (film) 399
Philadelphia Orchestra 408
Philadelphia Story, The 397
philately 568
Philemon 483
Philharmonia, The 408
Philip, St (disciple) 492
Philip II of Macedon 745
Philip II of Spain 254, 276
Philipe, Gérard 383
Philippine Sea 32
Philippines, The 676, **812**
English speakers 585
exploration 274
islands 31
national holidays 581
political leaders 325
UN membership 645
World Heritage sites 56
Philips 188
Phillips, William D 187
Philo Judeaus 467
Philoctetes 481, 483
Philomel 483
Philomela 483
philosophers 464
philosophy 179
phlox 71
Phnom Penh 642
phobias 145
treatments 140
Phobos 2
Phoebe 484
Phoenix (city) 642, 645
Phoenix (myth) 484
Phoenix, River 383

Phoenix constellation 6, 7
Phoenix Islands 31
phonetics 176
phonograph 190
phosphates 152
phosphorescence 170
phosphorus 201, 259
minerals in diet 130
phot 210
photobiology 176
photochemical reaction 170
photoelectric cell 190
photoelectric effect 170
photograph 168
photographers 445
photographic film 190
photographic lens 190
photography 190
photography, colour 190
photon 170
photosensitive 170
photosynthesis 166, **170**
carbon cycle 61
phototypesetting 190
Phu Rua national park/nature reserve 50
pH value 164, 169, **170**, 185
phycology 176
phyllite 25
phylum 61
physalis 63
physical constants 196
physico-chemical constants 197
physics 176
physiography 176
physiology 174
dietary recommendations 149
physiotherapy 139
phytology 176
phytomenadione 130
phytopathology 176
phytosociology 176
Pianist, The 399
Piano, The 399
pianoforte 190
Picabia, Francis 442
picadors 515
Picasso, Pablo 267, 442
Picasso Museum 460
Pickett, Wilson 424
Pickford, Mary 383
Academy Awards 397
Pictor constellation 6, 7
Picus 469
piddock 111
Piedmont truffle 78
pieris 73, 115
Pierre, D B C 355
pig:
collective names 118
length of pregnancy 89
pigeon 97
pink 120
pigeon-fancying 568
pigeon racing 568
Piggott, Lester 563
pike 107

record 109
pilaf, pilaff 155
Pilates 140
Pilates, Joseph 141
pilau 155
pilchard 107
piles 133
Pilkington, Sir Alastair 195
Pilobolus Dance Theater 437
pimple 131
Pinatubo, Mount 35
Pincus, Gregory 189
pine (tree):
Austrian 75
Corsican 75
Monterey 75
Scots 75
Pine, Courtney 414
pineapple 64
nutritional value 151
Pineapple Poll 434
pine processionary moth 116
Pingdingshan 642
ping pong 520
Pingxiang 642
Pink Floyd 424
Pinochet, General 713
pinochle 565
Pinot 160
Pinotage 160
pint 210
Pinter, Harold 361
Nobel prize 459
Pinza, Ezio 407
Pioneer space missions 12
pipe 162
pipefish 107
Piper, John 442
pipesnake 103
Pirandello, Luigi 361
Nobel prize 458
Piranesi, Giambattista 456
Pire, Georges 458
Pirquet, Clemens Peter von 135
Pisa 247, 249
World Heritage sites 55
Pisano, Andrea 445
Pisano, Giovanni 445
Pisano, Nicola 249, 445, 456
Pisces constellation 6, 7
Piscis Austrinus constellation 6, 7
Pissarro, Camille 442
pistol shooting 518, 519
Pitcairn Islands 31, **862**
Pitney, Gene 424
Pitt, Brad 383
pitta 98
Pitti Palace 460
Pittsburgh 642
museums and galleries 463
Pittsburgh Ballet Theater 437
Pittsburgh Symphony Orchestra 408
pituitary 137
pizza 155
placental mammals 79, **80**

Places in the Heart 398
plagioclase 26
plaice 107
Plaidy, Jean 351
plains wanderer 99
Planck, Max Karl Ernst 184
plane angle 209
planet, planets 2, 170
  satellites 2
  study of 176
planetary motion 182
planetology 176
plane tree:
  London 75
  Oriental 75
plankton 171
plant, plants 61, **62,** 175, 176
  classification 61, **62**
  endangered species 119
  geological record 23
Plantae 61, **62**
Plantagenet, House of 252, 283
plantcutter 98
plant diseases 176
plant gums 152
plant kingdom 61, **62**
plant oils 140
Plantson, Anthony A 189
plant species
  distribution 176
plasma 171
plasma membrane 171
plasticity 176
plasticizers 152
plastics 190
Plata River 33
plate tectonics 21, 171
platform diving 516
Plath, Sylvia 358
platinum 201
  properties 202
  wedding anniversary 575
Plato:
  philosophy 467
  science 184
Platoon 398
platypus 79
Plautus, Titus Maccius 361
Player, Gary 563
Playfair, William 456
plays of Shakespeare 362
playwrights 360
Pleasence, Donald 383
Pleiades 477, 482, **484**
Plenciz, M A 137
Pliny the Elder 135
Plisetskaya, Maya 435
PL/M computer language 608
PL1 computer language 608
Plotinus 236, 467
Plovdiv 642
plover 95
  collective names 118
  crab 95
Plowright, Joan 383
plum 63
  tree 75
Plummer, Christopher 383

pluralism 663
Pluto (dwarf planet) **3,** 201
  space missions 12, 13
Pluto (myth) 469, 470, 477, 484
plutonium 201
  properties 202
Plymouth 660
  shipping forecast area 59
Plymouth (USA) 463
Plymouth Brethren 503
pneumococcal infection 144
pneumonia 133, 134
P.91 (STEP 2) space mission 12
Pobedy Peak 34
pocket calculator 190
podiatry 139
Poe, Edgar Allan 351
Poelzig, Hans 456
poets 356
poets laureate 359
Pogues, The 424
poinsettia 73
  month association 575
point-to-point 518
Poiret, Paul 452
poise 210
poisonous fungi 77
poisons, study of 177
Poitier, Sidney 383
  Academy Awards 398
Poitiers, Battle of 276
poker 565
Pol Pot 706
Poland 677, **813**
  administrative divisions 655
  EU membership 648
  national holidays 581
  political leaders 325
  UN membership 645
  World Heritage sites 56
Polanski, Roman 395
Polanyi, John C 187
polar bear 86
  endangered species 120
polar caps 39
polarization 171
Polaroid 171
polecat 87
polenta 155
  discoveries 135
pole vault 516, **518**
Police, The 424
polio, poliomyelitis 133
  immunization 144, 145
Polisario Front 788
political definitions 663
political leaders 289
Politzer, H David 187
Polkinghorne, John C 509
Pollack, Sydney 395
  Academy Awards 398
Pollock, Jackson 271, 442
pollution 164
  endangered species 119
  environmental disasters 46, 48
Pollux (myth) **474,** 477,

480, 484
Pollux (star) 7
polo 518
  fixture results 546
Polo, Marco 249, 714, 756
polo field *546*
polonium 178, **201,** 267
Poltava 642
polyacrylonitrile 203
Polybus 482
polycarbonates 203
polyethylene 203
polygons 205
Polyhymnia 481, **484**
polyisoprene 203
polymer, polymers 171
  properties 203
polymerase chain reaction 183
polymorphism 171
Polyneices 484
Polynesia 31
Polynesia, French 739
Polynices 474, 475, 479, **484**
Polyphemus 474, 476, **484**
polypropylene 203
polystyrene 203
polythene 203
polyurethane 203
polyvinylchloride 203
pomegranate 63
pomelo 63
Pomerol 160
pommel horse 517
Pomona 470, 484
Pompeii 234
  World Heritage site 55
Pompey 234, 275
Pompidou Centre, Museum of Modern Art at the 461
Ponchielli, Amilcare 405
Pond, John 18
pondskater 115
Ponselle, Rosa 407
Pons-Winnecke comet 8
Pont d'Avignon (bridge) 225
Pont du Gard 53
Ponte Infante Dom Henrique (bridge) 225
Pontiac's War 277
Pontianak 642
Pont l'Évêque cheese 163
pontoon 565
Pontoppidan, Henrik 457
Pontormo, Jacopo da 442
Pontypridd bridge 225
pony, collective names 118
pool 518
Poole 660
Pop, Iggy 424
Pop Art 438
Pope, Alexander 259, 358
Pope Benedict XVI 272, 288
popes 287
  form of address 671
poplar:
  balsam 75
  black 75
  Lombardy 75

white 75
Pople, John A 187
pop musicians and
  singers 417
Popocatèpetl volcano 35
Popp, Lucia 407
poppadom, poppadum 155
Popper, Sir Karl 467
poppy 71
  month association 575
  opium 65
population:
  adherents of major
    faiths 489
  largest cities 644
  most populous nations 638
  nations 673
  world 638
population growth 119
porcelain 190, 251
porcupine 86
  collective names 118
  New World 86
  Old World 86
Porgy and Bess 405
pork chop, nutritional
  value 151
porpoise 86
  collective names 118
Porrex 476
port (wine) 162
Portal, Michel 414
Port-au-Prince 642
Port Elizabeth 642
Porter, Cole 404
Porter, Eliot 449
Porter, Harold 351
Porter, Katherine 351
Porter, Peter 358
Porter, Rodney R 186
Porter of Luddenham, Baron
  (George) 186
Portier, Paul 136
Portland 642
  museums and galleries 463
Portland shipping forecast
  area 59
Port Louis 642
Port Moresby 642
Porto Alegre 642
Port of Spain 642
ports, deepwater 635
Port Said 642
Port Salut cheese 163
Portsmouth 660
Portugal 677, 815
  administrative divisions 655
  EU membership 648
  monarchs 284
  national holidays 581
  overseas territory 815
  political leaders 325
  UN membership 645
  World Heritage sites 56
Portuguese language 584
Portunus 470
Porzott, Eugene 190
Poseidon 469, 471, 472, 473,
  475, 476, 477, 483, 484, 487

Posilipo tunnel 226
positron, positrons 164,
  166, 171
Possession]355
possum, brushtail 80
Post-Impressionism 438
Post-Modernism
  (architecture) 453
Post-Modernism (art) 438
potassium 179, 200
  in diet 130
  properties 202
potato 68
  nutritional value 151
potentilla 73
potholing 518
potoo 98
Potter, Dennis 361
pottery 229, 231
  hobby 568
pottery wedding
  anniversary 575
potting 568
Poulenc, Francis 401
  ballet music 433, 434, 435
  operas 405
pound (weight) 210
Pound, Ezra 358
poundal 210
Poussin, Nicolas 442
powderpuff (tree) 77
Powell, Anthony 351
Powell, Bud 414
Powell, Cecil Frank 186
Powell, Michael 395
Powell, Robert 383
powerboat racing 519
  fixture results 546
powerlifting 521
Powers, Stefanie 383
Powys 661
Powys, John Cowper 351
Poznań 642
prädikat 162
Prada, Miucca 452
Prado Museum, The 460
Prague 642
  museums and galleries 461
  World Heritage sites 53
Prajapati 484
praline 155
praseodymium 201
Pratchett, Terry 351
Pravaz, Charles Gabriel 192
prawn, common 112
  nutritional value 151
Praxiteles 233, 445
praying mantis 114
Precambrian aeon 22
  ice ages 24
precession of the
  equinoxes 171
precipitation 44
pregnancy 168
  length in some mammals 89
  management of 176
pregnant women, daily energy
  requirements 147
Prelog, Vladimir 187

Pre-Raphaelite art 438
Presbyterian Church 493
Prescot, Edward C 459
Present Histories 434
preservatives 152
Presidents of the European
  Commission 648
presidents of the USA 340
Presley, Elvis 271, 383, 424
Pressburger, Emeric 395
pressure 20
  SI conversion factors 209
  SI units 208
pressure cooker 191, 259
pressure group 663
Prestige oil spill 48
Prestonpans, Battle of 277
Pretenders, The 424
Pretoria 642
pretzel 155
Prey, Hermann 407
Priam 471, 473, 477, 481, 483,
  484, 487
Priapus 484
Price, Leontyne 407
Price, Vincent 383
Priestley, J B 351
Priestley, Joseph 137, 201,
  261
Prigogine, Ilya 187
primary colours 171
prime ministers, British 339
  form of address 671
Prime of Miss Jean Brodie,
  The 398
Primitivism 439
Primo de Rivera 835
primrose 71
  month association 575
primula 71
prince 668
  form of address 671
Prince (musician) 424
Prince Edward Island 30,
  709
Prince Igor 434
Prince of the Pagodas,
  The 434
princess, form of
  address 672
Princess Elsa 480
principal Greek gods 469
principal igneous rocks 26
principal metamorphic
  rocks 25
principalities 472
printing measures 213
printing press 191, 253
prion 137
Pritchett, (Sir) V S 351
Private Life of Henry VIII,
  The 397
privatization 663
Privy Council 663
privy counsellor, form of
  address 672
Prix de l'Arc de
  Triomphe 540
Prix Goncourt 356

prizes:
Academy Awards 397
Grammy Awards 429
literary 355
Nobel prizes 186, 457
Templeton prize 509
Turner prize 444
probability theory 182, 183, 257
processed foods 149
Procne 483
Procrustes 484
proctitis 133
Procyon A 7, 8
Procyon B 8
Prodigal Son, The 434
professor, form of address 672
profiterole 155
progesterone 137
progestogens 142
Progne 483
Progress M1 space mission 12
Prokhorov, Aleksandr 186
Prokofiev, Sergei 269, 401
ballet music 433, 434
operas 405
proletariat 663
PROLOG computer language 608
Prometheus 201, 475, 478, **484**, 487
promethium 201
pronghorn 89
propeller (ship) 191
properties:
gemstones 27
metals 202
minerals 27
polymers 203
Property 355
Prophet's Birthday 577
proportional representation 663
prosciutto 155
Proserpina 470, 483, 484
Prospero satellite 12
Prost, Alain 544, 563
prosthetics 176
protactinium 201
Protagoras 467
protein 164, 171
nutritional value of foods 150, 151
Protestantism 254, 489
Proteus (myth) 472, **484**
Proteus (satellite) 3
Protista, protoctista 61
proton, protons 165, 166, 169, 170, **171**
physical constants 196
protozoa 61, 137
Proulx, E Annie 351
literary prizes 356
Proust, Marcel 269, 351
provençale 155
proverbs 593
proxemics 176

Proxima Centauri 8
Prudhomme, Paul 158
prunes 151
Prusiner, Stanley 137
Nobel prize 187
Prussia 258, 260, 262, 266, 743
Pryor, Richard 383
psittacosis 133
Psyche 484
psychedelic drugs 143
psychiatry 176
psychoanalysis 180
psychodynamics 176
psychokinesis 176
psychological disorders 176
psychometrics 176
psychopathology 176
psychopharmacology 176
psychophysics 176
psychosis 144
psychotherapeutic drugs 141, 142
psychotic disorders 142
Ptah 470, **484**, 485
pterodactyl 102
Ptolemaic system 184
Ptolemy (astronomer) 184, 237, 243, 245
Ptolemy I 232
Public Enemy 424
Pucci, Emilio, Marchese di Barsento 452
Puccini, Giacomo 267, 401
operas 405, 406
Puckle, James 190
Puebla 642
World Heritage site 56
puerperal fever 133
Puerto Rico 29, **869**
exploration 274
Puerto Rico Trench 32
puffbird 97
puffer (fish) 107
puffin 96
Pugin, Augustus 456
Pugwash Conferences on Science and World Affairs 459
puja 498, 499
Pulitzer, Joseph 195
Pulitzer Prize 356
Pullman, Philip 351
Pulp 424
pulse rate 126
puma 86
pumice 26
pumpernickel 155
pumpkin 68
Punch and Judy 405
Pune (Poona) 642
Punic Wars 232, 275
Punjab 755
Puppis constellation 6, 7
Purcell, Edward Mills 186
Purcell, Henry 259, 401
ballet music 434
operas 405
purée 155

puri 155
Purim 500
Puritani, I 405
Purkinje, Jan 184
Purkinje's figure 184
purple blewit 78
Purple Heart 669
purslane 65
Purusha 484
pus 131
Pusan 642
Pushkin, Aleksandr 358
Pushkin Museum of Fine Arts 460
Putin, Vladimir 819
Pu'uka'oku Falls 33
Puzo, Mario 351
PVC 203
Pwyll 484, 485
Pye, Henry 359
pyelitis 133
Pygmalion 484
pygmy hippopotamus 120
pygmy shrew, Savi's 89
Pylades 475
Pynchon, Thomas 271, 351
Pyongyang 642
pyramids 230, 280
building of 280
Pyramus 484
Pyrenees 53, 57
pyridoxine 130
pyrite 27
pyroxene 25, 26
Pyrrha 475
Pythagoras
philosophy 467
science 184
Pythagoras' theorem 184, 206
Pythian games 484
Python computer language 608
Python (myth) 484
python (snake) 103
Pyxis constellation 6, 7

Q

Qaboos bin Said 806
Qat 484
Qatar 677, **816**
national holidays 581
political leaders 326
UN membership 645
Qi 139, 140, 141
Qin dynasty 281, 714
Qing dynasty 256, 258, 264, 268, 281, 715
Qingzhou Min River bridge 225
Qinhuangdao 642
Qiqihar 642
Qom 642
Quadrantids meteor shower 9
Quaid, Dennis 383
Quaid, Randy 384
quail 100

button 100
collective names 118
Quakers 256, 503
Nobel prize 458
Quant, Mary 452
quantum
electrodynamics 180
quantum mechanics 176
quantum theory 171, 184
quark 171
quart 213, 220
quartz 25, 26
Mohs' hardness scale 28
properties 27
quartzite 25
quasar 171
Quasimodo, Salvatore 458
Quaternary period 23
Quayle, Sir Anthony 384
Quebec (city) 642
World Heritage site 52
Quebec (province) 709
Quebec, Battle of 277
Quebec bridge 225
Quechuan languages 584
Queen (rock band) 425
Queen, Ellery 351
queen, form of address 672
Queen, The 399
Queen Anne's War 277
Queen Charlotte Islands 31
Queensland 688
World Heritage sites 51
quenelle 155
Querinus 484
quesadilla 155
Quetzalcoatl 484
Quezon City 642
Qufu 52
quiche 155
Quidde, Ludwig 458
Quignard, Pascal 356
Qui-Lim-Choo 137
quince 63
quince tree 75
Quine, Willard Van
Orman 467
Quinn, Anthony 384
quinoline 138
Quito 642
World Heritage sites 53
quoits 519

R

Ra 485
Rabat 642
rabbis 500
form of address 672
rabbit 86
collective names 118
length of pregnancy 89
Rabbit at Rest 356
Rabi, Isidore Isaac 186
rabies 133
rabies carriers 87
rabies vaccination 138, 145
Rabin, Yitzhak 459
raccoon 86

Rachmaninov, Sergei 267,
402
ballet music 434
Racine, Jean 259, 361
racism 663
rackets, racquets 519
rad 210
radar 171
invention 191
Radcliffe, Ann 351
Radhakrishnan, Sir
Sarvepalli 509
radiation 165, 167, 168, 169,
170, 171, 173
study of 176
wavelengths 197
radicalism 663
radio 191
radioactivity 171, 177, 178
radio astronomy 181
radiobiology 176
radio broadcasting 267,
269, 197
radiocarbon dating 165
radio galaxy 171
Radiohead 425
radiology 176
radio telegraphy 191
radio wave, radio waves 167,
169, 171
radiation 197
radish 68
radium 178, 201, 267
radon 201
Raeburn, Sir Henry 442
Rafid-ud-Darajat 283
Rafi-ud-Daulat 283
raft spider 113
Raging Bull 398
Ragnarok 473
ragout 155
Rahimi, Atiq 356
Rahner, Karl 507
rails, iron 191
railway, electric 191
railway, underground 191,
265
railway museums:
Europe 459
UK 461
USA 462
rain, study of 175
Rainbow bridge 225
Rainbow Snake 473, 485
Raine, Kathleen 358
Rainer, Luise 397
Rainey, Gertrude ('Ma
Rainey') 414
rainfall 44
acid rain 45
meteorological extremes 39
rainforests 46
deforestation 46
Rainier, Mount 35
Rain Man 398
rain tree 77
Rainwater, L James 187
Raipur 642
raisins, nutritional value 151

Raitt, Bonnie 429
Rajkot 642
Rajneesh, Bhagwan
Shree 507
Rakaposhi 34
Rake's Progress, The
(ballet) 434
Rake's Progress, The
(opera) 405
Rakshabandhana 498
Raleigh, Walter 255, 274
rallying 519
Rama 485, 486
Rama IX bridge 225
Ramadan 499
national holidays 581
Ramakrishna
Paramahasa 507
Ramanavami 498
Ramayana 498
Rambaud, Patrick 356
Rambert, Dame Marie 435
Rameau, Jean Philippe 261,
402
ramekin 155
Ramnefjellsfossen 33
Ramón y Cajal, Santiago 184
Ramos-Horta, José 459
Rampling, Charlotte 384
Ramsay, Allan 443
Ramsay, Gordon 158
Ramsay, Sir William 199,
200, 202
Nobel prize 184
Ramsey, Ian Thomas 507
Ramsey, Norman F 187
Ran 470
Ranchi 642
Ranger VII space mission 11
Rangoon 642
Rankin (photographer) 449
Rankin, Ian 351
Rankine temperature scale:
conversion table 211
SI conversion factors 209
ranks of the aristocracy 668
Ransome, Arthur 351
Rao, Raja 351
raoul (tree) 75
Rape of Lucretia, The 405
Raphael 443
Raphael, Frederic 351
rare gases 170
rash 132, 133, 134
raspberry 63
nutritional value 151
Rastafarianism 491
rat 86
Chinese calendar 575
collective names 118
length of pregnancy 89
record 89
ratafia 155
ratatouille 155
Rathayatra 498
Rathbone, Basil 384
Rathke, Martin Heinrich 184
rational number 171
Ratites 89

rat-tail (fish) 107
rattan ball 519
Rattigan, Sir Terence 361
Ravel, Maurice 402
  ballet music 433, 435
raven, collective names 118
Ravenna 55
Ravenswood (William S
  Ritchie) bridge 225
ravioli 155
Rawalpindi 642
Rawls, John 467
ray 108
Ray (film) 399
Ray, Johnnie 425
Ray, Man 449
Ray, Satyajit 395
Rayleigh, John 184, 199
Raymonda 434
rayon 191
razor 191
razor-shell, pod 111
Re 485
reactance 209
Read, Piers Paul 351
Reading 660
  museums and galleries 462
Reagan, Ronald 340, 384
Realism 439
real tennis 519
  fixture results 546
Réaumur, René de 184
  inventions 189
Réaumur temperature
  scale 211
Rebecca 397
Reblochon cheese 163
recessive 171
Recife 643
recombination 171
record (music) 191
record holders:
  birds 100
  fish 109
  mammals 89
rectal bleeding 131
rectangle 205
rectum, inflammation 133
red-billed quelea 100
red blood cells 126, 138
red-breasted merganser 100
Redcar and Cleveland 660
Red Cross, International
  Committee of the 457, 458
Red Cross, League of
  Societies of the 458
redcurrant 63
red deer 82
Redding, Otis 425
Redford, Robert 384, 395
  Academy Awards 398
red garnet 25
red giant 171
Redgrave, Sir Michael 384
Redgrave, Sir Steve 563
Redgrave, Vanessa 384
Red-headed Taoists 501
red-hot poker 71
Red List of Threatened

Species 119
red mullet 108
Redon, Odilon 443
Red Sea 32
redshift 171, 181
reduction 170, 171
Redwood National Park 50
  World Heritage site 58
Reed, Lou 425
Reed, Oliver 384
Reed, Sir Carol 396
  Academy Awards 398
reedbuck 86
Rees, Sir Martin 18
Reeve, Christopher 384
Reeves, Keanu 384
Reeves, Martha (and The
  Vandellas) 425
Reeves Ltd 190
referendum 663
reflexology 141
Reformation 252, 254, 493
refraction 171
refrigerator 191, 266
Regan 480
registration marks (cars):
  international 617
  UK 615
Regulus 7
rehoboam 163
Reich, Ferdinand 200
Reichenbach, Hans 467
Reichenstein, Baron von 201
Reichstein, Tadeus 186
reiki 141
Reina Sofía 460
reindeer 82
  length of pregnancy 89
Reiner, Carl 396
Reiner, Rob 396
Reines, Frederick 187
Reinhardt, Django 415
relapsing fever 138
relative atomic mass 172
relativity 172
relativity, theory of 172, 179,
  183, 267
relaxation therapies 140, 141
release agents 152
Religion and Atheism,
  Museum of the History
  of 461
religions 492, 502
  distribution of adherents 489
  sacred texts 501
religious leaders 503
religious movements 502
religious sects 502
religious symbols 510
rem 210
REM (pop group) 425
Remains of the Day, The 355
Remarque, Erich Maria 351
Rembrandt 257, 443
remora 108
remote sensing 172
Remus 485
Renaissance
  architecture 453

Renaissance art 439
Renamo 796
Renard, Le 434
Renault, Louis 457
Renault, Mary 351
Rendell, Ruth, Baroness 351
Rendezvous, Les 434
Renfrewshire 661
Rennsteig tunnel 227
Reno 463
Reno, Jesse W 189
Renoir, Auguste 443
Renoir, Jean 396
Renwick, James 456
reproductive organs 129
reptiles 79, 102
  animal kingdom 79
  endangered species 119
  geological record 23
Reptilia 79, 102
Republika Srpska 700
Requiem 434
Residence Gallery 461
Residence Museum 460
resins 203
resistivity 203
resonance 172
Respighi, Ottorino 433
respiration 172
  carbon cycle 61
  discoveries 138
respiratory ailments 135
restaurateurs 156
Reticulum constellation 6, 7
retinol 130
retsina 162
Réunion 30, 739
Reversal of Fortune 398
revolver 191
Reykjavik 643
Reymont, Wladslaw 458
Reynolds, Burt 384
Reynolds, Sir Joshua 443
Rhadamanthus 476, 485
Rhadamanthys 485
Rhapsody 434
rhea (bird) 89
Rhea (myth) 469, 482, 485
Rhea (satellite) 2
Rheia 485
Rheims 53
Rhenish wine 162
rhenium 201
rheology 176
Rhesus factor 126
  discovery 138
Rhesus monkey 85
  length of pregnancy 89
rheumatoid arthritis 142
Rhiannon 485
Rhine, Battle of the 279
Rhine wine 162
rhinoceros 86
  collective names 118
  southern white 120
rhinoviruses 131
rhizomes 69
Rhode Island 868
Rhodes 29

World Heritage site 54
Rhodes, Gary 158
Rhodes, Zandra 452
Rhodesia, Northern 876
Rhodesia, Southern 877
rhodium 201
rhododendron 73
rhombus 205
Rhondda, Cynon, Taff 661
rhubarb 63
rhus 73
Rhynchocephalia 102
rhyolite 26
Rhys, Jean 351
Riabouchinska, Tatiana 435
Rialto 225, 255
ribbon woods 73
Ribeirao Preto 643
riboflavin 130
  discovery 138
ribonucleic acid 172
Ricci, Nina 452
rice 62
  nutritional value 151
Rice, Sir Tim 404
Rich, Adrienne 358
Richard II (play) 362
Richard III 252, 276
  play 362
Richard, Sir Cliff 425
Richard Alston Dance
  Company 437
Richards, Dickinson W 186
Richardson, Dorothy M 352
Richardson, Harry
  Handel 352
Richardson, Miranda 384
Richardson, Sir Ralph 384
Richardson, Robert C 187
Richardson, Samuel 261, 352
Richardson, Tony 398
Richet, Charles Robert 136
Richie, Lionel 425
  Grammy awards 429
Richler, Mordecai 352
Richter, Burton 187
Richter, Charles 184, 269
  inventions 191
Richter, Hieronymous 200
Richter seismographic
  scale 172, 191
Rickenbacker, Adolph 189
Rickes, Edward 138
rickets 130, 139
Rickman, Alan 384
Ricoeur, Paul 467
Riding, Laura 358
Riesling 160
Rieti 434
Rietveld, Gerrit 456
rifle shooting 514, **519**
Riga 643
  World Heritage site 55
Rigel 7
Rigg, Dame Diana 385
Righteous Brothers, The 425
right wing 663
Rigoletto 405
rigor 133, 134, 135

Rijksmuseum 459
rijsttafel 155
Riley, Bridget 443
Rilke, Rainer Maria 358
Rimbaud, Arthur 358
Rimmon 471
Rimsky-Korsakov,
  Nikolai 402
  ballet music 434
  operas 405
Ring, The 405
Rings (gymnastics) 517
ringworm 141
Rio de Janeiro 643
Rio de la Plata 274
Rioja 160
Rio-Niteroi bridge 225
Risorgimento 762
risotto 155
Rite of Spring, The 434
Ritter, Johann 197
Ritter, W 188
Ritts, Herb 449
Rituals 434
Rivera, Diego 443
river blindness 133
rivers, longest 33
Riyadh 643
RNA, ribonucleic acid 165,
  172, 173
  mapping 185
  interference 138
roach 108
Roach, Max 415
road distances:
  European 624
  UK 624
Road, The 355
Road Home, The 355
road network,
  international 625
road races 515
  fixture results 532
road signs:
  Europe 622
  UK 619
  USA 621
Robards, Jason 385
Robbia, Luca della 445
Robbins, Frederick 186
Robbins, Harold 352
Robbins, Jerome 433
  Academy Award 398
  ballets 433
Robbins, Tim 385, 396
Roberts, Julia 385
  Academy Awards 399
Roberts, Richard J 185
  Nobel prize 187
Robertson, Cliff 398
robin 92
robinia 73
Robinson, Edward G 385
Robinson, Henry Peach 449
Robinson, John A T 507
Robinson, Marilynne 356
Robinson, Sir Robert 186
Robinson, Smokey 425
Robles, Alfonso García 459

robotics 176
robots 176
Robuchon, Joël 158
Roc 485
Rochdale 659
Rochester 463
Rochester, John Wilmot, Earl
  of 359
Rochester Gas and Electric
  Company 47
Rockall shipping forecast
  area 59
rock climbing 518
Rockefeller, John 195
rocket (missile) 191
rock musicians and
  singers 417
rock rose 73
rocks, study of 175, 176, 177
Rocky 398
Rocky Mountain Parks 52
Rococo architecture 453
Rococo art 439
Rod 485
Rodbell, Martin 187
Rodchenko, Alexander 449
Roddick, Anita 195
Roden, Claudia 158
rodeo 519
Rodeo (ballet) 434
Rodgers, Richard 269, 404
Rodin, Auguste 267, 445
Roeg, Nicolas 396
Roerich 434
Roethke, Theodore
  Huebner 359
Roger, Brother 507
  Templeton Prize 509
Rogers, Ginger 385
  Academy Awards 397
Rogers, Richard, Baron 456
Rogers, Ruth 158
Rogers, Will 385
Rogers Pass tunnels 227
Rogun dam 227
Rohe, Ludwig Mies van
  der 456
Rohini satellite 12
Rohrer, Heinrich 190
  Nobel prize 187
Rokko tunnel 227
Roland, F Sherwood 187
Rolex 192
Rolf, Dr Ida 141
Rolfe, Frederick 352
rolfing 141
Rolland, Romain 457
roller (bird) 97
roller skating 519
  fixture results 546
Rolling Stones, The 425
Rollins, Sonny 415
Rolls, Charles 195
Rolston III, Holmes 509
Roman architecture 453
Roman Catholic Church 493
  distribution of adherents 489
Roman emperors 282
Roman Empire 234

AZ

Index

Romanesque 453
Roman gods 469
Roman Holiday 398
Romania 677, **816**
  administrative divisions 656
  EU membership 648
  national holidays 581
  political leaders 326
  UN membership 645
  World Heritage sites 57
Roman kings 282
Roman numbers 207
Romano cheese 163
Romanov, House of 285
Romanticism (art) 439
Rombauer, Irma 158
Romberg, Sigmund 404
Rome 643, 644
  battles and wars 275
  monarchs 282
  museums and galleries 461
  World Heritage site 55
Romeo and Juliet
  (ballet) 434
Romeo and Juliet (play) 362
Romeril, John 361
Rommel, General 278
Romulus 238, 282, 472, **485**
röntgen 210
Röntgen, Wilhelm von 184
  medical discoveries 139,
  267
  radiation 197
röntgenology 176
rook, collective names 118
Room at the Top 398
Rooms 434
Rooney, Mickey 385
Roosevelt, F D R 340
Roosevelt, Theodore 340
  Nobel prize 457
Root, Elihu 457
roots of numbers 204
Roquefort cheese 163
Rorty, Richard 467
Rosa, Salvator 443
Rosario 643
rose 73
  month association 575
rosé 162
Rose, Irwin 187
rosemary 65, 73
Rosenberg, Isaac 359
Rosenberg, Steven 137
Rosenblum, Walter 449
Rosenkavalier, Der 405
Rosensweig, Ronald 189
Roses, Wars of the 252,
  276, 857
Rose Tattoo, The 398
Rosetta Stone 185, 263
rosewood, Brazilian 120
Rosh Hashana 500
Rosmerta 485
Ross (star) 8
Ross, Diana 425
Ross, John 275
Ross, Ronald 137, 139
Rossellini, Isabella 385

Rossellini, Roberto 396
Rossen, Robert 397
Rossetti, Dante Gabriel 443
Rossignol, Le 405
Rossini, Gioacchino 263, 402
  ballet music 433
  operas 405, 406
Rostov-na-Donu 643
Rota, Nino 434
rotation (Sun) 1
Rotblat, Joseph 459
Roth, Henry 352
Roth, Philip 352
  literary prizes 356
Roth, Tim 385
Rotheim, Erik 188
Rotherham 659
Rothermere, Harold
  Harmsworth, 1st
  Viscount 195
Rothko, Mark 443
Rothstein, Arthur 449
roti 155
Rotterdam 643
  museums and galleries 461
Rouaud, Jean 356
rouge, giant 69
Rouge Brésil 356
roulade 156
roulette 565
rounders 519
roundworms 141
Rourke, Mickey 385
Rous, Peyton 186
Rousseau, Henri 443
Rousseau, Jean Jacques 260,
  467
roux 156
Roux, Albert Henri 158
Roux, Pierre Émile 136
Roux, Pierre-Paul-Émile 138
rowan 73
  tree 75
Rowe, Nicholas 359
rowing 519
  fixture results 547
Rowling, J K 273, 352
Rowntree, Joseph 195
Roxy Music 426
Roy, Arundhati 355
Royal Ballet 437
Royal Danish Ballet 437
royal flush 565
royal houses, European 283
Royalists 277
Royal Liverpool Philharmonic
  Orchestra 408
Royal national park/nature
  reserve 50
Royal New Zealand
  Ballet 437
royal palm 77
Royal Philharmonic
  Orchestra 408
Royal Red Cross 668
Royal Scottish National
  Orchestra 408
Royal Swedish Ballet 437
'royal' tennis 519

Royal Victorian Chain 668
Royal Victorian Order 668
Royal Winnipeg Ballet 437
Royce, Sir Henry 195
Roze, Pascale 356
Ruapehu volcano 35
rubber 203
  inventions 191
Rubbia, Carlo 187
rubella 131
  immunization 144
Rubens, Sir Peter Paul 443
Rubens's House 459
rubidium 182, **201**
  properties 202
Rubik, Erno 191
Rubik cube 191
Rubinstein, Ida Lvovna 435
ruby 28
  month association 575
  wedding anniversary 575
Rudolf, Lake 32
Rudra 485
rue 65
Ruether, Rosemary
  Radford 508
Rufin, Jean-Christophe 356
rugby, energy
  expenditure 148
Rugby fives 516
Rugby League 519
  fixture results 548
Rugby Union 519
  fixture results 548
Rugby Union field
  549
rugelach, ruggelach 156
Ruggles, Wesley 397
Rumina 470
rummy 566
Runge, Friedlieb
  Ferdinand 138
Runic alphabet 605
runny nose 131
Runyang bridge 225
Ruppell's griffon 100
Rush, Geoffrey 399
Rushdie, Salman 273, 352
Ruska, Ernst 190
  Nobel prize 187
Russell, Bertrand 269, 467
  Nobel prize 458
Russell, Charles Taze 266,
  502, 508
Russell, Jane 385
Russell, Ken 396
Russell, Kurt 385
Russell, Willy 361
Russia 677, **817**
  CIS membership 647
  military ranks 667
  monarchs 285
  national holidays 581
  political leaders 326
  UN membership 645
  World Heritage sites 57
Russian language 584
Russian Museum 461
Russian Revolution 268,

278, 819
Russian Soldier   434
Russian/USSR space
   launches   15
Russo, Richard   356
Russo-Finnish War   737
Russo-Japanese War   266,
   819
Ruth, Babe   563
ruthenium   201
Rutherford, Daniel   200
Rutherford, Ernest   **184**, 201
   radiation   197
Rutherford, Joseph
   Franklin   502
Rutherford, Dame
   Margaret   385
rutherfordium   201
Rutland   29, 660
Ružička, Leopold   138
   Nobel prize   186
Rwanda   677, **819**
   civil war   279
   national holidays   581
   political leaders   326
   UN membership   645
Rwenzori national park/
   nature reserve   51
Ryan, Meg   385
Ryan, Robert   385
Ryder, Winona   385
Ryder Cup   537
rye   62
Ryle, Gilbert   468
Ryle, Sir Martin: 18
   Astronomer Royal   18
   Nobel prize   187

S

Saarinen, Eero   456
Saarinen, Eliel   456
Sabines   486
sabre   516
Sabu   386
Sachs, Nelly   458
sack (wine)   162
Sackville, Thomas   361
Sackville-West, Vita   352
Sacramento   643
Sacre du printemps, Le   434
Sacred Hunger   355
sacred religious texts   501
Sadat, Anwar   730
   Nobel prize   459
Sade, Donatien, Comte
   de   352
Sadler's Wells Ballet   436, 437
safety-pin   191
saffron   65
saffron milk cap   78
Safi   643
Sagamihara   643
Sagarmatha national park/
   nature reserve   50
sage   65
sage, common   73
Sagitta constellation   6, 7
Sagittarius constellation   6, 7

Sahara Desert   33
sailfish   108
   record   109
sailing   519
Sainsbury (of Drury Lane),
   Alan Sainsbury, Baron   195
St Albans, Battle of   276
St Barthélemy   739
St Bartholomew's Day
   Massacre   276
St Benedict   238
St Catharines-Niagara   643
St Christopher and
   Nevis   677, **820**
   Commonwealth
      membership   647
   English speakers   585
   national holidays   581
   political leaders   327
   UN membership   646
   World Heritage sites   57
St-Émilion   160
Saint-Exupéry, Antoine
   de   352
St George's mushroom   78
St Gotthard tunnels   227
St Helena   862
St Helens   659
St Helens, Mount   35
St Ives   462
Saint-John Perse   359
St John's wort   73
Saint Joseph, John   449
St Kilda   58
Saint Laurent, Yves   452
St Lawrence, Gulf of   32
St Lawrence River   274
St Leger   540
St-Léon, Arthur   433
   ballets   433
St Louis   643
St Lucia   677, **821**
   Commonwealth
      membership   647
   English speakers   585
   national holidays   581
   political leaders   327
   UN membership   646
   World Heritage sites   57
St Maarten   801
St Martin   739
St Michael and St George,
   Order of   668
St Patrick   760
St Paulin cheese   163
St Peter   492
St Petersburg   643, 644
   museums and galleries   461
   World Heritage sites   57
St Petersburg Philharmonic
   Orchestra   408
St Pierre and Miquelon   739
saints, patron   497
Saint-Saëns, Camille   402
   operas   405
saints' days   494
St Stephen's Day   577
St Vincent and the
   Grenadines   677, **821**

Commonwealth
   membership   647
English speakers   585
national holidays   581
political leaders   327
UN membership   646
Saisons, Les   434
Saka era   574
Sakai   643
Sakhalin   28
Sakharov, Andrei   458
Sakhmet   485
Saki   352
Sakmann, Bert   187
Saladin   246, 248, 276
Salam, Abdus   187
Salamanca   57
salamander:
   alpine   101
   Chinese giant   101
   fire   101
   goldstriped   101
   spectacled   101
salami   156
salat   499
Salazar, Dr Antonio   815
Salazar bridge   225
Salem   258, 643
Salerno, Battle of   278
Salford   659
Salgado, Sebastião   449
Salinger, J D   271, 352
Salle, Robert Cavelier de
   la   257, 274
sallow willow   76
Salmacis   477
salmanazar   163
salmon   108
   nutritional value   151
Salome   405
Salomon, Erich   449
Salonika   643
salpingitis   133
salsa   156
salsa verde   156
salsify   68
salt   149
salt imbalance   140
salt lagoons   32
Salt Lake City   502
   museums and galleries   463
salt lakes   32
Salvador   643
   World Heritage site   52
salvarsan   179, 180
salvia   71
Salyut spacecraft
   missions   15, 16
Salzburg:
   museums and galleries   461
   World Heritage site   51
Samara   643
samarium   201
Samarkand   643
   fall of   276
   World Heritage site   59
sambo   521
Samoa   677, **822**
   Commonwealth

membership 647
English speakers 585
islands 31
national holidays 581
political leaders 327
UN membership 646
samosa 156
Sampras, Pete 563
samsara 498
Samson et Dalila 405
Samuelson, Paul 458
Samuelsson, Bengt I 187
samurai 517
San'a 643
World Heritage site 59
San Andreas fault 21
San Antonio 643, 645
Sancerre 160
San Cristobal 643
sanction 663
Sand, George 352
sandalwood (spice) 66
sandalwood (tree) 77
sand-box tree 77
sandeel 108
Sander, August 449
Sanders, George 386
sandfly 132
sandgrouse 97
San Diego 643, 645
Sandinistas 279, 802, 803
Sandoz disaster 46
sandpiper 95
Sands, Julian 386
sandstone 25
Sandwell 659
San Francisco 643
museums and galleries 463
San Francisco Ballet 437
San Francisco Orchestra 408
Sanger, Frederick 186, 187
sangria 162
San José 643, 645
San Juan 643
World Heritage site 58
Sankara 508
San Luis Potosí 643
San Marino 677, 823
national holidays 581
political leaders 327
UN membership 646
World Heritage site 57
San Marino (USA) 463
Sanmichele, Michele 456
San Miguel de Tucumán 643
San Pedro Sula 643
San Roque dam 227
San Salvador 643
Sansovino, Jacopo 456
Santa Cecilia Academy
Orchestra 408
Santa Cruz de la Sierra 643
Santa Fe 463
Santana, Carlos 426
Grammy awards 429
Santayana, George 468
Sante Maria delle Grazie 55
Santiago 643
Santiago de Cuba 643

World Heritage site 53
Santo André 643
Santo Domingo 643
Santoriní/Thíra 35
Santos 643
São Bernardo do Campo 643
São Gonçalo 643
São João de Meriti 643
São José dos Campos 643
São Luis 643
World Heritage site 52
São Paulo 643, 644, 645
São Tomé and Príncipe 677,
823
islands 31
national holidays 582
political leaders 327
UN membership 645
sapodilla plum 64
sapphire 28
month association 575
wedding anniversary 575
Sapporo 643
saprobe 172
saprophyte 172
saprotroph 172
Sapsago cheese 163
Saragossa 643
Sarajevo 643
Saramago, José 459
Sarandon, Susan 386
Academy Awards 399
Saransk 643
Sarapis 485
Sarasota 463
Sarasvati 473, 485
Sarasvati-puja 498
Saratoga, Battle of 277
Saratov 643
Sardar Sarovar dam 228
Sardi, Melchior Pio Vi 158
sardine 107, 108
sardonyx 575
Sarek national park/nature
reserve 50
Sargent, John Singer 443
Sark 29, 662, 858
Sarma cave 34
Saroyan, William 352
Sarpedon 485
SARS 133
Sarto, Andrea del 439
Sartre, Jean-Paul:
literature 352, 361
Nobel prize 458
philosophy 268, 468
Saskatchewan 709
sassafras 67
sassafras, American 75
Sassoon, Siegfried 359
Satan 475, 499
Satan's boletus 78
satellite, artificial 168
first in orbit 11
invention 191
Satie, Erik 402
ballet music 434
Sato, Eisaku 458
satsuma 64

saturated compounds 172
saturated fats 149
Saturn (myth) 470, 479,
482, 485
Saturn (planet) 2, 181
satellites 2
space missions 12
satyr, satyrs 476, 480, 485
Saudi Arabia 677, 824
national holidays 582
political leaders 327
UN membership 645
World Heritage sites 57
sauerkraut 156
saum 499
Saumur 160
Saunders, Dame Cecily 509
sausage tree 77
Saussure, Horace 274
sauté 156
Sauternes 160
Sauvignon Blanc 160
Savalas, Telly 386
Save the Tiger 398
Savery, Thomas 191, 259
Savi's pygmy shrew 89
Savoy, Guy 158
saw 191
sawfly 117
Saxe-Coburg-Gotha, House
of 286
Saxons 237, 275
Sayansk dam 228
Sayers, Dorothy L 352
scalar 172
scallop, great 111
scandium 201
scanner 191
scarab beetle 117
Scarborough 643
Scarlatti, Domenico 402
scarlet fever 133
scarlet-stemmed boletus 78
Scènes de ballet 434
Scent of a Woman 399
Schaffner, Franklin J 398
Schally, Andrew V 187
Schawlow, Arthur L 187
Scheele, Carl Wilhelm 199
Schéhérazade 434
Scheider, Ralph 189
Scheider, Roy 386
Schell, Maximilian 398
Schelling, Friedrich von 468
Schelling, Thomas C 459
Schiaparelli, Elsa 452
Schick, Jacob 191
Schickard, Wilhelm 188
Schielandshuis 461
Schiele, Egon 443
Schiller, Johann von 361
Schindler's List 399
Schinkel, Karl 456
schist 25
schistosoma 131
schizophrenia 142
Schleiermacher,
Friedrich 508
Schlesinger, John 396

A-Z Index

Academy Awards 398
Schlick, Moritz 468
Schmalkaldic League, War of the 276
Schnabel, Julian 443
schnapps 156
schnitzel 156
Schnütgen Museum 460
Scholes, Myron 459
Scholl, Andreas 407
Schönberg, Arnold 402
operas 405
Schönbrunn 51
Schønheyder, Fritz 139
Schopenhauer, Arthur 262, 468
Schreiner, Olive 352
Schrieffer, J Robert 186
Schrock, Richard R 187
Schrödinger, Erwin 184
Schrotter, Anton von 190
Schubert, Franz 402
ballet music 434
Schueller, Eugène 191
Schuhl, Jean-Jacques 356
Schultz, Theodore 459
Schumacher, Michael 563
Schumann, Elisabeth 407
Schumann, Robert 402
ballet music 434
Schwann, Theodor 184
Schwartz, Melvin 187
Schwarz, Delmore 359
Schwarzenegger, Arnold 386
Schwarzkopf, Dame Elisabeth 407
Schwassmann-Wachmann 1 comet 8
Schweitzer, Albert 508
Nobel prize 458
Schwingen 521
Schwinger, Julian 186
Schwitters, Kurt 445
science, fields of study 174
science museums
Europe 459
UK 461
USA 462
scientific terms 164
scientists 177
Scientology 270, 503
Scilly Isles 31
scimitar bill 97
Sclavo, Achille 136
Scofield, Paul 386
Academy Awards 398
scorpionfish 108
scorpion fly 115
Scorpius constellation 6, 7
Scorsese, Martin 396
Academy Awards 399
Scotch Symphony 434
scotch tape 191
Scotland 857
councils 661
monarchs 285
museums and galleries 461
national holidays 582
Scotland on Sunday 612

Scotsman, The 612
Scott, George C 386
Academy Awards 398
Scott, Robert 275
Scott, Sir George Gilbert 456
Scott, Sir Ridley 396
Academy Awards 399
Scott, Sir Walter 263, 352
Scottish Ballet 437
Scottish Borders council 661
Scottish Chamber Orchestra 408
Scottish National Gallery of Modern Art 461
Scottish National Portrait Gallery 461
Scottish Parliament 272, 857
Scotto, Renata 407
Scrabble® 566
scrambled egg tree 77
scrambling 518
screamer (bird) 94
screw 191
screw pine 77
Scriabin, Alexander 402
scrub-bird 99
Scruton, Roger 468
scuba diving 568
sculling 519
Sculptor constellation 6, 7
sculptors 444
scurvy 130
discoveries 138
Scutum constellation 6, 7
Scylla 485
sea, seas 32
disturbance measurement 41
lunar 3
study of 175
Sea, The 355
sea bass 108
seabirds 95
Seaborg, Glenn Theodore 199, 200, 201
Nobel prize 186
seaborgium 201
sea-bream 108
sea buckthorn 73
sea butterfly 110
sea disturbance measurement 41
Sea Empress 49
sea holly 71
seahorse 108
seal 86
collective names 118
northern fur 89
southern fur 120
Seal (musician) 429
Sea of Japan 32
Sea of Okhotsk 32
Sea of Tranquillity 3
moon landings 14
sea robin 106
Sears Tower 228
seasons 575
Sea Star 49
Seattle 643

museums and galleries 463
Seattle Symphony Orchestra 408
second 210
Secretaries-General:
Commonwealth 647
United Nations 646
secretary bird 91
secretary of state, form of address 672
sectarianism 663
sects 502
Sedaka, Neil 426
sedatives 142
sedimentary rocks 172
classification 25
seedsnipe 95
Seeley, Henry W 189
Seferis, George 458
Sefström, Nils Gabriel 202
Sefton 659
Segalas, Pierre 189
Segovia 57
Segrè, Emilio 199, 201
Nobel prize 186
Seiber, Matyas 433
Seifert, Jaroslav 359
Nobel prize 459
Seikan tunnel 227
seismic activity 20
seismic sea waves 38
seismic waves, study of 176
seismology 175, **176**
Sekhmet 470, **485**
Seki-Lines comet 8
Selby, Hubert, Jr 352
selective serotonin re-uptake inhibitors 142
Selendang oil spill 49
Selene 469, 475, 478, **485**
selenium 201
in diet 130
self-defence 514
self-hypnotherapy 140
Selfridge, Harry Gordon 195
Sella, Philippe 563
Selleck, Tom 386
Sellers, Peter 386
Selten, Reinhard 459
semaphore 606
Semarang 643
Semele (myth) 485
Semele (opera) 405
Semenov, Nikolay 186
semiconductor 168, 169, **172**
Sémillon 160
semiology 177
semiotics 177
Semipalatinsk 643
Semiramis 485
Semper Gallery 460
Sen, Amartya 459
Senate 663
Sendai 643
Sendero Luminoso 812
Seneca, Lucius Annaeus 361
senecio 73
Senefelder, Aloys 190
Senegal 677, **825**

national holidays 582
political leaders 327
UN membership 645
World Heritage sites 57
Senegal River 274
sense organs 124
ear 124, 128
eye 124, 128
sensory neurones 123
Seoul 643, 644, 645
Separate Tables 398
separatism 663
sepek takraw 519
September 11 attacks 866
sequestrants 152
Sequoia and Kings Canyon
national park/nature
reserve 50
Sequoyah 1 disaster 47
seraphim 472
Serapis 485
Serbia 677, **826**
national holidays 582
NATO attacks 272, 279
political leaders 328
UN membership 645
World Heritage sites 57
Serbia and Montenegro 328
Serenade 434
Serengeti National Park 50
World Heritage site 58
Sergeant York 397
seriema 100
series, geological 22, 23
Serlio, Sebastiano 456
serology 177
serotherapy 191
serotonin 142
Serpens constellation 6, 7
serpent (Chinese
calendar) 575
serpentine 25, 28
serpentinite 25
Serturner, Friedrich 137
serums 177
service tree, true 75
Servius Tullius 476
sesame 67
Sesostris 485
Seth 470, 478, 481, 482, **485**
Seth, Vikram 352
Seurat, Georges 443
Seven against Thebes 475,
484, **485**
Seven Deadly Sins, The 403,
432, 434
Seven Sleepers of
Ephesus 485
Seventh Day Adventists 503
7th Heaven 397
Seven Valleys 492
Seven Weeks' War 278
Seven Wonders of the
World 280
Seven Years' War 260, 277
Severe Acute Respiratory
Syndrome 133
Severn bridges 225
Severnaya Zemlya 31

Seville 57
Sewaren 49
sewing machine 191
sex determination 172
Sex Pistols, The 426
Sextans constellation 6, 7
sexton beetle 117
Sextus 480
Seychelles 677, **827**
Commonwealth
membership 647
English speakers 585
islands 31
national holidays 582
political leaders 328
UN membership 646
World Heritage sites 57
Seymour, Alan 361
Seymour, Jane 386
Seymour, Lynn 436
SGML computer
language 608
Shackleton, Ernest 275
Shadows, The 426
Shadwell, Thomas 359
Shaffer, Peter 361
Shaftesbury, Anthony Ashley
Cooper, 3rd Earl of 468
shag 95
shaggy ink cap 78
Shah Alam I 283
Shah Alam II 283
Shah Jahan 257, 283
Shajin Telescope 10
Shakespeare in Love 399
Shakespeare, William 361
plays 362
Shakta Vjacheslav Pantjukhina
cave 34
Shakti 498
shale 25
shamans 500
Shamash 486
Shanchung 643
Shang dynasty 281
Shanghai 643, 644, 645
Shango 486
Shangri-las, The 426
Shannon, Del 426
Shannon shipping forecast
area 59
Shantou 643
Shaoguan 643
Shaolin Temple 518
shapes 205
Shari'a 499
Sharif, Omar 386
shark, sharks:
basking 108
collective names 118
great white 108
gulper 120
hammerhead 108
record 109
tiger 108
whale 108
Sharp, Phillip A 185
Nobel prize 187
Sharpe, Tom 352

Sharpe, William 459
Sharpey-Schafer,
Edward 135
Sharpless, K Barry 187
Shatner, William 386
Shavuot 500
Shaw, Artie 415
Shaw, George Bernard 361
Nobel prize 458
Shaw, Norman 456
Shaw, Sandie 426
Shearer, Moira 436
Shearer, Norma 397
Shearer, Sybil 436
shearwater 96
sheathbill 95
Sheeler, Charles 449
Sheen, Charlie 386
Sheen, Martin 386
sheep:
American bighorn 86
barbary 86
blue 86
Chinese calendar 575
collective names 118
length of pregnancy 89
Sheffield 643
council 659
museums and galleries 462
Shelley, Mary 263, 352
Shelley, Percy Bysshe 359
Shemini Atzeret 500
Shenyang 643
World Heritage site 52
Shenzhou space
missions 12, 13
Shepard, Sam 362, 386
Shepherd, Cybill 386
Shepp, Archie 415
Sher, Sir Anthony 387
Sheridan, Richard
Brinsley 362
Sherrifmuir, Battle of 277
sherry 162
Sherwood, Robert 362
Shetland council 661
Shetland Islands 31
Shevardnadze, Eduard 741
shiatsu 141
Shibanpo bridge 225
Shibasaburo Kitasato 136,
138
Shields, Carol 352
literary prizes 355
Shih Ching 498
Shihezi 643
Shiites 499
Shijiazhuang 643
Shiloh, Battle of 278
Shimomura, Osamu 188
shinai 517
Shine 399
shingles 134
Shining Path 812
Shin-shimizu tunnel 227
Shintoism 500
distribution of adherents 491
sacred texts 501
shinty 519

fixture results 549
ship 191
shipping forecast areas 59
Shipping News, The 356
Shirakawa, Hideki 187
Shiraz (city) 643
Shiraz (wine) 160
Shirley-Quick, John 407
shirt sizes, international 222
Shiva 475, 486, 498
Shiva Asar be-Tammuz 500
Shizuoka 643
Shockley, William 192
  Nobel prize 186
shoebill 94
Shoemaker-Levy 9 comet 8
Shoemaker, Willie 563
shoe sizes, international 222
shogi 566
shogun, shoguns 246, 256, 766
Sholapur 643
Sholokhov, Mikhail 352
  Nobel prize 458
shooting 519
  fixture results 550
shooting star 169
shorebirds 94
Short, Horace 190
Shorter, Wayne 415
shortest-lived fish 109
Shostakovich, Dmitri 402
  operas 405
shot put 516, 517, 518, **519**
Shoubra el-Kheima 643
shovelboard 568
Showa era 281
show jumping 533
shrew 87
  elephant 120
  endangered species 87
  pygmy Savi's 89
Shrewsbury, Battle of 276
shrike 92
  cuckoo 92
  vanga 92
shrimp, common 112
Shriver, Lionel 355
Shropshire 659
shrubs 72
Shuangyashan 643
shuffleboard 568
Shull, Clifford G 187
Shun Hing Square building 228
Shute, Nevil 352
shuttle flights 14
SI 166, 169, **172**
  conversion factors 209
  prefixes 211
  units 208
Sialkot 643
Sian (Xian) 643
Sibelius, Jean 402
  ballet music 434
Sibley, Dame Antoinette 436
Sibyl 486
Sibylla 486
Sibylline Books 486

Sicilian Vespers, War of the 276
Sicily, invasion of 278
sickener (fungus) 78
Sickert, Walter 443
sidalcea 71
Siddharta Gautama, Prince 492, **504**
sidereal period 2
sidereal time 172
Sidney, Sir Philip 359
Sieff (of Brimpton), Israel, Baron 195
Siegbahn, Kai M 187
Siegel, Don 396
sieges:
  Granada 276
  Jerusalem 275
  Montevideo 277
  Orleans 276
  Perilous 476
Siegfried 486
Sielmann, Heinz 449
Siemens, Ernst Werner von 191
Siena:
  museums and galleries 461
  World Heritage site 55
Siepi, Cesare 407
Sierra Leone 677, **828**
  civil war 279
  Commonwealth membership 647
  English speakers 585
  national holidays 582
  political leaders 328
  UN membership 645
Sif 470
Siffre, Michel 136
sight 128
Sigmund the Volsung 486
sign language:
  British 607
  US 607
Signoret, Simone 398
signs:
  mathematical 204
  road 619
  zodiac 511
Sigurd 473, 477, **486**
Sigyn 470
Sihanouk 706
Sikhism 501
  distribution of adherents 491
  sacred texts 501
Sikkens Museum of Signs 461
Silence of the Lambs, The 399
Sileni 486
Silenus 486
Silesia 724
silicon 201
  in Sun 1
silicon chip 172
  invention 191
silk 191
  wedding anniversary 575
silk moth 116

Sillanpää, Frans Emil 458
Sillitoe, Alan 352
siltstone 25
Silurian period 23
  fossils 24
Silvanus 470, 486
silver 199
  properties 202
  wedding anniversary 575
Silver, Horace 415
silver birch 74
silver fir, common 75
silverfish 114
Silver Star 669
silverware 575
Sim, Alastair 387
Sima de la Cornisa cave 34
Simchat Torah 500
Simenon, Georges 352
Simferopol 643
similes 594
Simmons, Jean 387
Simon, Carly 426
Simon, Claude 352
  Nobel prize 459
Simon, Herbert 459
Simon, Paul 404, 426
  Grammy awards 429
Simon and Garfunkel 429
Simon Boccanegra 405
Simone, Nina 415
Simon the Canaanite (disciple) 492
Simon 'the Zealot' (disciple) 492
Simplon tunnels 227
Simply Red 426
Simpson Desert 33
Simpson, James 136
SIMULA computer language 608
Sin 486
Sinai Peninsula 730
Sinatra, Frank 387, 426
  Grammy awards 429
Sinclair, Sir Clive 195
Sinden, Sir Donald 387
sine wave 172
Singapore 677, **829**
  city 643
  Commonwealth membership 647
  English speakers 585
  national holidays 582
  political leaders 328
  UN membership 645
Singapore, Battle of 278
Singer, Isaac Bashevis 352
  Nobel prize 459
Singer, Marc 387
singers:
  jazz and blues 409
  opera 406
  pop and rock 417
Singh 501
Sinhalese 836
Sinn Féin 760
Sin of Madelon Claudet, The 397

Sino-Japanese War 715
Sino-Tibetan languages 584
Sinuiju 643
sinus 134
Sinus Aestuum 3
Sinus Iridum 3
sinusitis 134
Sinus Medii 3
Sinus Roris 3
Sioux 278
Sirens 481, 482, **486**
Sirius A 7, 8
Sirius B 8
Siskind, Aaron 449
Sisley, Alfred 443
Sistema Cheve cave 34
Sistema del Trave cave 34
Sistema Huautla cave 34
Sisyphus 486
Sita 486
Sitwell, Dame Edith 359
Six-Day War 270, 279
61 Cygni A 8
61 Cygni B 8
Siza, Álvaro 456
Skanda 486
Skarnsundet bridge 225
skate 108
skateboarding 568
skating, ice 517
skeleton *122*
Ski Museum 460
ski-flying 519
skiing 519
  cross-country 514
  fixture results 550
skijoring 519
skimmer 95
skimmia 73
skin *123*
  artificial 191
  study of 174
skin culture 138
skin disorders 130
skin diving 568
skin grafting 183
skink 103
skipper butterfly 116
skipping 568
skittles 568
Skopje 643
Skou, Jens C 187
skua 95
Skuld 482
skull 122, 124
skunk 87
  length of pregnancy 89
Sky Train Bridge 225
Skyamsen 486, 487
skydiving 519
Skye 30
Skylab space missions 14
skyscraper 191
slate 25
Slater, Christian 387
slaters 113
slaves' revolt 275
Sleep, Wayne 436
Sleeping Beauty, The 434

sleeping sickness 134
  carriers 116
discovery 138
slide rule 191, 257
slimming products 152
slippery jack 79
sloth:
  Hoffmann's two-toed 120
  pygmy 120
  three-toed 87
  two-toed 87
Slough 660
Slovakia 677, **829**
  administrative divisions 656
  EU membership 648
  national holidays 582
  political leaders 328
  UN membership 646
  World Heritage sites 57
Slovenia 677, **830**
  administrative divisions 657
  national holidays 582
  political leaders 328
  UN membership 646
  World Heritage sites 57
slug (unit) 210
slug, slugs 110
  great grey 111
Sluys, Battle of 276
Sly and the Family Stone 426
Small Island 355
smallest bird 100
smallest fish 109
smallest mammal 89
Smalley, Richard E 182
  Nobel prize 187
smallpox 134
  discoveries 138
Smalltalk computer
  language 608
Smart, Christopher 359
smelt 108
Smetana, Bedřich 405
Smetanina, Raisa 564
Smiley, Jane 356
Smirke, Sir Robert 456
Smith, Alexander McCall 352
Smith, Bessie 414, 415
Smith, Sir C Aubrey 387
Smith, Delia 158
Smith, E L 138
Smith, Hamilton 137, 187
  Nobel prize 187
Smith, Iain Crichton 352
Smith, Joseph 508
Smith, Lucien B 188
Smith, Dame Maggie 387
  Academy Awards 398
Smith, Michael 183
  Nobel prize 187
Smith, Patti 426
Smith, Stevie 359
Smith, Tommy 415
Smith, Vernon L 459
Smith, W E 449
Smith, Will 387
Smith, Zadie 353
  literary prizes 355
Smithies, Oliver 188

Smiths, The 426
Smithsonian Institute 463
Smolensk 643
Smollett, Tobias 353
Smoot, George F 187
smooth muscle 123, 168
Smyth, John 493
Smythe, Francis 449
Smythson, Robert 456
snail, snails 110
  giant African 111
  great ramshorn 111
  roman 111
snake, snakes 101
  dawn blind 103
  front fanged 103
  harmless 103
  shieldtail 103
  thread 104
  typical blind 104
snake-bird 95
snake's-head 69
snapdragon 71
sneezing 131
Snell, George D 187
snipe, painted 95
SNOBOL computer
  language 608
snooker 519
  fixture results 551
Snow, C P 353
snow, study of 175
snow and ice climbing 518
snowberry 73
snowboarding 519
Snowdon, Antony Armstrong-
  Jones, 1st Earl of 449
Snowdonia National Park 51
snowdrop 69
  month association 575
snowflake 26, 69
Soane, Sir John 456
soap 191
soapstone 28
Soave 160
Sobers, Gary 561, **564**
Sobrero, Ascanio 189
soccer 516
Sochi 643
social interaction, study
  of 176
Socialism 663
Society Islands 31
  exploration 274
Society of Friends 503
Socrates 232, 468
soda 191
sodalite 27
Soderbergh, Steven 396
Söderblom, Nathan 458
Söderström, Elisabeth 407
sodium 179, **200**
  in diet 130
  properties 202
Sofia 643
softball 520
  fixture results 551
soil, study of 176
Soka Gakkai 492

Sokolow, Anna 434
Solal, Martial 415
Solar I oil spill 49
solar eclipses *4*
solar imaging 13
solar mass 210
solar system 165, **172**
  planets 2
  satellites 2
  space missions 11
sole 108
Sole shipping forecast
  area 59
solfaterre 70
Solferino, Battle of 278
Solidarity 814
Solihull 659
Sol Invictus 477
solo 566
Solomon Islands 677, **831**
  Commonwealth
    membership 647
  English speakers 585
  islands 31
  national holidays 582
  political leaders 329
  UN membership 646
  World Heritage sites 57
Solomon's seal 70
Solow, Robert 459
solstice 172
  seasons 575
solvent abuse 143
solvents 143
Solway Moss, Battle of 276
Solzhenitsyn, Aleksandr 353
  Nobel prize 458
  Templeton Prize 509
Soma 486
Somalia 677, **832**
  national holidays 582
  political leaders 329
  UN membership 645
Somaliland 275
somatic nervous system 123
Somerset 659
Somes, Michael 436
Somme, Battle of the 269,
  278
Sommelier, Germain 189
Somoza, Anastasio 802
sonar 164, **172**
Sondheim, Stephen 404
songbirds 91
Song dynasty 242, 248, 249,
  281
Songnam 643
Song of Bernadette, The 397
Song of Hiawatha, The 478
Song of the Earth 434
songwriters 403
sonic boom 172
sonics 177
Sonnambula, La 405
Sonoran Desert 33
Sony® 188
Sophie's Choice 398
Sophocles 233, 362
sorbet 156

Sörensen, Sören Peter
  Lauritz 185
sore throat 131, 132, 133, 134
sorghum 62
Sorocaba 643
sorrel 65, 68
Soto, Hernando de 274
Sottsass, Ettore, Jr 457
soufflé 156
Soufflot, Jacques 457
Soufrière volcano 35
Soufrière Hills volcano 35
Sound of Music, The 398
sour cherry (tree) 74
soursop 64
South Africa 677, **833**
  Commonwealth
    membership 647
  English speakers 585
  national holidays 582
  political leaders 329
  UN membership 645
  World Heritage sites 57
South African Large
  Telescope 10
South America 28
  exploration 274
Southampton 660
  museums and galleries 462
South Australia 688
South Ayrshire 661
South Carolina 868
South China (Nan) Sea 32
South Dakota 868
South-East Iceland shipping
  forecast area 59
Southend-on-Sea 660
Southern Ocean 32
Southey, Robert 359
South Georgia 863
  exploration 274
South Gloucestershire 660
South Island 28
South Lanarkshire 661
South Orkney Islands 31
South Pole 275
South Sandwich Islands 863
  exploration 274
South Sandwich Trench 32
South Sea Bubble 260
South Shetland Islands 31
South Tyneside 660
South Utsire shipping forecast
  area 59
sowbugs 113
soya 67
soya bean 67
Soyer, Alexis 158
Soyinka, Wole 362
  Nobel prize 459
Soyuz spacecraft
  missions 11, 12, 14, 15,
  16, 17
space, first man in 11, 275
space flight 174
  first 15
Spacek, Sissy 387
  Academy Awards 398
Spacelab 14

space launchers 11
space missions 11
  NASA 13
  USSR/Russian 15
space records 17
space shuttle 12
  invention 191
space station 15, 16
space telescope 12, 273
spacewalk, first 13, 15
Spacey, Kevin 387
  Academy Awards 399
Spader, James 387
spaghetti 156
Spain 677, **834**
  administrative divisions 657
  EU membership 648
  monarchs 285
  national holidays 582
  political leaders 329
  road signs 623
  UN membership 645
  World Heritage sites 57
Spanish Armada 254, 255,
  277
Spanish chestnut 74
Spanish Civil War 268, 269,
  278
Spanish language 584
Spanish Succession, War of
  the 258, 277
Spark, Dame Muriel 353
Sparks, William 191
sparrow 91, **92**
  collective names 118
sparrowhawk 91
Sparta 231, 232, 275, 745
Spartacus 275
  ballet 434
Spätlese 160
speakers of English 585
spearmint 65
Spears, Britney 426
species 168, **172**
  classification 61
  endangered 119
species under threat 119
specific gravity 27
Speckled Cape tortoise 104
spectacles 191, 249
Spectre de la Rose, Le 434
spectroscopy 179
speech, study of 176
speech and language
  therapy 139
speed of light 196
speed skating 517
speedway 520
  fixture results 551
speedwell 71
Speke, John 275
spelaeology, speleology 177
spelunking 518
Spence, Sir Basil 457
Spence, Michael 459
Spencer, Herbert 264, 468
Spencer, Percy Le Baron 190
Spencer, Sir Stanley 443
Spender, Sir Stephen 359

Spenser, Edmund 255, 359
spermatozoa 138
Sperry, Elmer A 189
Sperry, Roger W 187
Spessivtseva, Olga 436
sphere 205
Spica 7
Spice Girls, The 426
Spice Islands 756
spices 66
spiders 113
spiderwort 71
Spielberg, Steven 396
  Academy Awards 399
Spina, Alessandro della 191, 249
spinach 68
  nutritional value 151
spinal cord 123, 124
spinel 27
spinning 568
spinning frame 191
spinning jenny 191, 261
spinning-mule 191
Spinoza, Baruch 468
spiraea 73
Spirit Cloud Taoists 501
spiritual gifts 503
Spitteler, Carl 457
spitting spider 113
Spitz, Mark 564
spleen enlargement 132
Split 52
sponges 23
spoonbill 93
spore 172
'sport of kings' 517
sports 514
  100 champions 559
sports-car racing 518
sports injuries 139
Sports Museum of Finland 460
sprat 108
Spring 575
Spring, Howard 353
springboard diving 516
springbok 87
spring equinox 575
Springfield, Dusty 426
springhare 87
Springsteen, Bruce 426
spring tides 172
spritzer 162
spruce, Norway 75
spruce, sitka 75
Spry, Constance 158
spur-thighed tortoise 104
spur-winged goose 100
Sputnik space missions 11
SQL computer language 608
Squalius keadicus 120
Squamata 102
square (areas) 205
square roots 204
squares of numbers 204
squash (sport) 520
  energy expenditure 148
  fixture results 552

squash (vegetable) 68
squash court 552
squash rackets 520
squid, squids 111
  common 111
  giant 112
squill 70
squirrel 87
  collective names 118
  grey 87
  length of pregnancy 89
squirrelfish 108
Sri Lanka 677, 836
  civil war 279
  Commonwealth membership 647
  English speakers 585
  islands 31
  national holidays 582
  political leaders 330
  UN membership 645
  World Heritage sites 57
Srinagar 643
Srivijaya Empire 783
SSRIs 142
Staatskapelle Orchestra 408
stabilizers 152
stachyurus 74
Staffa 30
Staffordshire 659
stag beetle 117
stage races 515
stalactite 172
stalagmite 172
Stalag 17 398
Stalingrad, Battle of 278
Stallone, Sylvester 387
Stamp, Terence 387
stamp collecting 568
standard atmosphere 210
Stanford, Sir Charles 402
Stanislavsky Ballet 437
Stanley, Henry Morton 275, 719
Stanley, Wendell Meredith 186
Stanton, Harry Dean 387
Stanwyck, Barbara 387
staphylea 74
Staphylococcus 138
stapler 191
star, stars 165, 169, 170, 171, 172, 173
  brightest 7
  nearest 8
  study of 174
starches 165
Stardust space mission 12
starling 92
  collective names 118
Starling, Simon 444
starter motor 191
Star Wars (film) 271
State Hermitage Museum 461
State Jewish Museum 461
states of the USA 866
statics, study of 177
statistics, study of 177
Statue of Liberty 58, 267

Statue of Zeus 233, 280
Status Quo 426
Staub, Hans 136
Staudinger, Hermann 186
Staunton, Imelda 387
Stavropol 643
Stead, C K 353
steam engine 181, 185
  inventions 191
steamship 178, 191, 262
Stedelijk Museum of Modern Art 459
steel 191
  wedding anniversary 575
Steely Dan 426
  Grammy Awards 429
Steen, Jan 443
Steenbock, Harry 139
steeplechase 520
steer wrestling 519
Steichen, Edward 449
Steiger, Rod 388
  Academy Awards 398
Stein, Gertrude 353
Stein, Rick 159
Stein, William H 186
Steinbeck, John 353
  Nobel prize 458
Steinberger, Jack 187
Steiner, Rudolf 268, 502, 508
stellar evolution 172
Stendhal 353
Stenmark, Ingemar 564
step dancing 567
stere 210
stereotype 191
Stern, Otto 186
Sternbach, Leo 136
Sternberg, Sir Sigmund 509
sternbergia 70
Sterne, Lawrence 353
stethoscope 191, 263
Stevens, Cat 426
Stevens, Wallace 359
Stevenson, Juliet 388
Stevenson, Robert Louis 353
Stewart, House of 285
Stewart, J I M 353
Stewart, Jackie 563, 564
Stewart, James 388
  Academy Awards 397
Stewart, Mary 353
Stewart, Rod 427
Stheno 476
stick insect 114
stickleback 108
Stieglitz, Alfred 449
Stigler, George 459
Stiglitz, Joseph E 459
stilb 210
Stillwater, Battle of 277
stilt 94
Stilton cheese 163
stimulants 143
Sting, The 398
stingray 108
stinkhorn, common 78
stinking russula 78
Stirling 661

A-Z

Index

Stirling, Sir James 457
stock-car racing 518, **520**
Stockhausen, Karlheinz 402
Stockholm 643
   museums and galleries 461
Stockport 660
Stockton-on-Tees 660
Stockwell, Dean 388
Stoics Quartet 434
Stoke-on-Trent 660
Stoker, Bram 353
stokes 210
stokesia 71
Stoltz, Eric 388
Stolze 434
stomach acids 141
stomach ulcers 183
Stone Diaries, The 356
stone, first use of 280
Stone, Oliver 396
   Academy Awards 398
Stone, Robert 353
Stone, Sharon 388
Stone, Sir Richard 459
Stonehenge 230
   World Heritage site 58
Stoppard, Sir Tom 362
Storey, David 353
stork 94
   collective names 118
Störmer, Horst L 187
Story of Louis Pasteur,
   The 397
stout agaric 78
Stowe, Harriet Beecher 265,
   353
Strabane 662
Straits of Magellan 274
Strand, Paul 450
Stranglers, The 427
Strasbourg 53
Stratas, Teresa 407
stratigraphy 175, **177**
stratocumulus clouds 44
stratus clouds 44
Strauss, David Friedrich 508
Strauss, Johann, (the
   Younger) 402
   operas 405
Strauss, Richard 402
   ballet music 433, 434
   operas 405
Stravinsky, Igor 402
   ballet music 433, 434, 435
   operas 405
strawberry 64
   nutritional value 151
strawberry tree 76
Streep, Meryl 388
   Academy Awards 398
Street, George 457
Street Angel 397
Streetcar Named Desire, A
   (film) 397
street hockey 520
Streets, The 427
Streisand, Barbra 388, 427
   Academy Awards 398
   Grammy awards 429

streptococcus bacteria 132,
   133, 134
streptomycin 138
Stresemann, Gustav 458
stress 140, 141
Strindberg, August 362
striped squill 70
Strite, Charles 192
Stroessner, Alfredo 811
stroganoff 156
stroke 141
Stromboli 35
Stromeyer, Friedrich 199
Strong, Frank 138
strong scented garlic 78
Strontian, Scotland 201
strontium 179, **201**
Strowger, Alman B 192
structure of the Earth 20
strudel 156
Strupenfossen 33
Struve Geodectic Arc 59
STS (space shuttle
   flights) 12, 14
Stuart, Charles Edward 277
Stuart, House of 258, 286
Stuart, James 457
Stubbs, George 443
Studer, Cheryl 407
sturgeon 108
   endangered species 120
   record 109
   trade in 120
Sturgeon, William 189
Sturt Desert 33
Stuttgart 643
Stuttgart Ballet 437
Styne, Jule 404
Styron, William 353
Styx, River 471, 474
Subaru Telescope 10
subatomic particle 170,
   171, **172**
submarine 191
suborbital flight 13
subsonic 169, **172**
subtropical climatic zone 39
succession, wars of 277
Sucellus 486
Sucre 52
Sudan 677, **837**
   national holidays 582
   political leaders 330
   UN membership 645
   World Heritage sites 57
Suenens, Cardinal Leon 509
Suez Canal 266, 730
Suez Crisis 270
Suez Invasion 279
Suffolk 659
Sufis 499
sugar, sugars 165
   dietary
   recommendations 149
   nutritional value 151
   wedding anniversary 575
Sugar, Alan 195
sugar substitutes 152
Sui dynasty 238, 281

Suita 643
suit sizes, international 222
Sukkot 500
Sukla 498
sulfur 201
sulfurous acid 162
sulky 517
Sullivan, Sir Arthur 403, 405
   ballet music 434
Sullivan, Louis 457
sulphonamides 138
sulphur 201
   in Sun 1
sulphur tuft 79
sulphurous acid 162
Sulston, John E 187
Sumatra 28, 30
Summer 575
Summer, Donna 427
summer solstice 172
   seasons 575
Summerspace 434
summer squash 68
Summer Time 576
summer truffle 79
Sumner, James
   Batcheller 186
sumo wrestling 520
Sun 1
   comets 8
Sun, The 612
sunbird 92
sunbird, false 98
sun bittern 100
Sunday Express 612
Sunday Mail 612
Sunday Mirror 612
Sunday Sport 612
Sunday Telegraph 612
Sunday Times 612
Sunderland 660
sunfish 108
sunflower 71
Sung dynasty 281
Sunni 499
Sun Ra 415
Sunrise 397
sun rose 73
sunshine 39
sunspot umbra 1
sunstone 28
sun-tan cream 191
superaerodynamics 177
Super Bowl 535
superconductivity 172
supergiant star 173
Superior, Lake 32
supernova 173
supersonic 169, 172, **173**
supplementary medical
   treatments 139
supplementary medicine 139
Surabaya 643
Surakarta 643
Surat 643
surface tension 208
surfing 520
   fixture results 553
surgeonfish 109

Surinam cherry (tree) 77
Suriname 677, **838**
  English speakers 585
  national holidays 582
  political leaders 330
  UN membership 645
  World Heritage sites 58
Surman, John 415
Surrealism 437
Surrey 659
Surtsey 35
  World Heritage sites 54
Surveyor 1 space mission 11
Susa-no-o 471
susceptance 209
suspension bridge 191
Suspicion 397
Sutcliffe, Frank Meadow 450
Sutherland, Donald 388
Sutherland, Earl W Jr 186
Sutherland, Graham 443
Sutherland, Dame Joan 407
Sutherland, Kiefer 388
Sutong bridge 225
Suva 643
Suwon 643
Suzhou 643
  World Heritage sites 52
Svarog 486
Sventovit 486
Sverdlovsk 643
Svetambara 499
swallow 93
  myth 484
swallowtail butterfly 116
Swami Vivekananda 508
swan 94
  collective names 118
  record 100
Swan, Joseph 191
Swan Lake 434
Swank, Hilary 388
  Academy Awards 399
Swansea 661
  museums and galleries 462
Swanson, Gloria 388
SWAPO 798
Swayze, Patrick 388
Swaziland 677, **839**
  Commonwealth
    membership 647
  English speakers 585
  national holidays 582
  political leaders 331
  UN membership 645
swede 68
  nutritional value 151
Sweden 677, **840**
  administrative divisions 658
  EU membership 648
  monarchs 286
  national holidays 582
  political leaders 331
  road signs 623
  UN membership 645
  World Heritage sites 58
Swedenborg, Emanuel 260, 508
Swedish Nightingale,

The 406
Swedish/European
  Submillimetre
  Telescope 10
sweet chestnut tree 74
sweetcorn 62
sweeteners 152
sweet pea 71
  month association 575
sweet potato 68
sweet william 71
swift 98
  crested 98
Swift, Graham 353
  literary prizes 355
Swift, Jonathan 261, 353
Swift-Tuttle comet 8
swimming 520
  energy expenditure 148
  fixture results 553
Swinburne, Algernon
  Charles 359
Swindon 660
swine, collective names 118
Swinton, Ernest 192
swiss chard 68
Swiss National Museum 461
Swiss national park/nature
  reserve 50
Switzer, Joe and Bob 190
Switzerland 677, **841**
  administrative divisions 658
  national holidays 582
  political leaders 331
  road signs 623
  UN membership 645
  World Heritage sites 58
swordfish 109
sycamore 76
Sydney 643
Sydney Dance Company 437
Sydney Harbour bridge 225
Sydney Opera House 271
  World Heritage sites 51
Sydney Symphony
  Orchestra 408
syenite 26
Sylphide, La 434
Sylphides, Les 434
Sylvaner 160
Sylvanus 486
symbiosis 173
symbols:
  astronomy 614
  clothes care 614
  general 614
  mathematical 204
  meteorology 614
  musical 430
  religious 510
Symons, Julian 353
Symphonic Variations 434
Symphonie fantastique 265, 434
Symphony in C 434
Symphony in Three
  Movements 434
symptomatology 177
symptoms 131

  study of 177
synagogue 500
synecology 177
Synge, J M 362
Synge, Richard 186
Syngué Sabour: Pierre de
  Patience 356
syphilis 134
Syracuse 472
  World Heritage sites 55
Syrah 160
Syratalviadukt bridge 225
Syria 678, **842**
  inventions 192
  national holidays 582
  political leaders 332
  UN membership 645
  World Heritage sites 58
Syrian Desert 33
syringa 73
syringe, hypodermic 192
syringe, scientific 191
Syrinx 486
Système International
  d'Unités 172
systematics 177
Szczecin 643
Szent-Györgyi, Albert von
  Nagyrapolt 185
  Nobel prize 186
Szymborska, Wislawa 359
  Nobel prize 459

T

Taal volcano 35
Taanit Esther 500
Tabaski 577
table d'hôte 156
table of elements 199
table tennis 520
  fixture results 554
  invention 192
Tabriz 643
Tacke Noddack, Ida 201
Tacoma Narrows (New)
  bridge 225
Taegu 643
Taejon 643
taekwondo 520
Tagalog language 584
tagliatelle 156
Taglioni, Marie 436
Tagore, Rabindranath 457
Tago-Sato-Kosaka comet 8
Tagus II bridge 225
Tahiti 31, 236
t'ai chi ch'uan 141
Tai-Kadai languages 584
Taichung 643
Tainan 643
Taipei 643
Taipei 101 building 228
Taiping Rebellion 264
Taiwan 678, **843**
  islands 31
  national holidays 582
  political leaders 332
  UN membership 645

Az

Index

Taiyuan 643
Tajikistan 678, **844**
  CIS membership 647
  national holidays 582
  political leaders 333
  UN membership 646
Taj Mahal 54, 257
Takamatsu 643
Takamine, Jokichi 135
Takatsuki 643
Takla Makan desert 33
Talbot, William Fox 450
  inventions 190
talc 27
  Mohs' hardness scale 28
Tale of the Genji 243
Tales of Hoffman, The
  (ballet) 434
Tales of Hoffmann, The
  (opera) 405
Taliban 272, 679
Talking Heads 427
Tallchief, Maria 436
tallest inhabited
  buildings 228
tallest mammals 89
Tallinn 643
  World Heritage sites 53
Talmud 238, 500
tamarack 76
tamarind 64
  spice 67
tamarins 85
tamarisk 74
Tambora volcano 35
Tambov 643
Tamerlane 276
Tameside 660
Tamil language 584
Tamil separatism 837
Taming of the Shrew, The
  (ballet) 434
Taming of the Shrew, The
  (play) 362
Tamm, Igor 186
Tammuz 486
tampon 192
Tanabata 500
Tanaka, Koichi 187
tandoori 156
Tandy, Jessica 388
  Academy Awards 398
Tane 486
tang 109
Tanganyika 845
Tanganyika, Lake 32
  exploration 275
Tang dynasty 238, 239, 242,
  281
Tange, Kenzo 457
tangelo 64
tangerine 64
Tangier 643
Tango no Sekku 500
Tangshan 643
Tanguy, Yves 443
tank 192, 269
Tannenberg, Battle of 278
Tanner, John 191

Tannhäuser 405
tannin 162
tansy 65
Tanta 643
tantalum 201
Tantalus 201, **486**
Tanzania 678, **845**
  Commonwealth
   membership 647
  English speakers 585
  national holidays 582
  political leaders 333
  UN membership 645
  World Heritage sites 58
Taoism 232, 478, **501**
  distribution of adherents 491
  sacred texts 501
Tao masters 501
Tao-te-ching 501
tapaculo 99
tapas 156
tapestry 568
tapeworms 141
tapir 87
Taranis 486
Tarantino, Quentin 396
tarantula 113
Tarawera volcano 35
Tarpeia 486
Tarquinius Superbus 480
Tarquinus Priscus 486
tarragon, French 65
Tarragona 160
tarsier 87
Tarski, Alfred 468
tartar 162
tartrates 152
Tashkent 643
Tasman, Abel Janszoon 257,
  274
Tasmania 31, 257, 688
  exploration 274
Tasman Spirit 49
Tassell, James Van 190
Tatara bridge, Great 225
Tate, Nahum 359
Tate, Sir Henry 195
Tate Britain 462
Tate galleries 462
Tate Modern 273, 462
Tati, Jacques 396
Tatlin, Vladimir
  Yevgrafovich 443
Tatra national park/nature
  reserve 50
Tatum, Art 415
Tatum, Edward 186
Taube, Henry 187
Tauber, Richard 407
Taupin, Bernie 404
Taurids meteor shower 9
Taurus constellation 6, 7
Tavener, Sir John 402
Tavernier, Bertrand 396
taxa 174
taxidermy 568
taxonomy 61, 174
Tay bridge 225
Taygete 484

Taylor, A Hoyt 191
Taylor, Cecil 415
Taylor, Charles 509
Taylor, Dame Elizabeth 388
  Academy Awards 398
Taylor, James 427
Taylor, Joseph H, Jr 187
Taylor, Richard E 187
Taylor, Robert 388
Taylor, Rod 389
Tbilisi 643
TCDD gas 47
Tchaikovsky, Piotr 402
  ballet music 433, 434
  operas 405
Teagarden, Jack 415
teak tree 77
teal, Campbell Islands 120
teal, collective names 118
team roping 519
Tear, Robert 407
Tearle, Sir Godfrey 389
tears 162
Tebaldi, Renata 407
Tebbutt comet 8
technetium 201
technology museums:
  Europe 459
  UK 461
  USA 462
tectonics 177
tectonics, plate 21
teeth, study of 176
Tegucigalpa 643
Tehran 643
Tehri dam 228
Teilhard de Chardin,
  Pierre 508
Te Kanawa, Dame Kiri 407
Tel Aviv 643
Telamon 471
telegraph 192, 265, 267
telegraph code 192
telegraphy 183, 191
Telemachus 486
Telemann, George
  Philipp 402
telephone 178, 192, 262, 267
telescope, telescopes 180,
  181
  inventions 192
  large ground-based
   telescopes 9
Telescopium constellation 6,
  7
television 192
television image, first 177,
  269
Telford and Wrekin 660
tellurium 201
Tellus 476
Telugu language 584
Temin, Howard 187
temperate climatic zone 39
temperature:
  atmosphere 20
  conversion tables 211
  Earth 19
  meteorological extremes 39

SI conversion factors 209
SI units 209
Sun 1
wine 162
world temperature 40
world temperature
change 41
temperature scales 178, 179,
182, 184
conversion tables 211
Tempest, The 362
Temple, Shirley 389
Temple of Artemis 280
Templeton Prize 509
tempo marks 431
Temptations, The 427
Ten Commandments 493
Tendai 492
Tender Mercies 398
tendons 122
Tenerife 29
Tengri 486
Tennant, Emma 353
Tennant, Smithson 200, 201
Tennessee 868
tennis, lawn 520
energy expenditure 148
invention 192
fixture results 554
tennis court *555*
Tennyson, Alfred, Lord 359
Poets laureate 359
tenpin bowling 515
fixture results 556
tensile strength
(polymers) 203
teratology 177
terbium 201
Teresa of Ávila, St 508
**Teresa of Calcutta,
Mother** 508
Nobel prize 459
Templeton Prize 509
Tereshkova, Valentina 15
Teresina 643
Tereus 483
Terfel, Bryn 407
Terminus 486
termites 115
terms:
musical 430, 431
wine-making and wine-
tasting 160
Terms of Endearment 398
Terpsichore 481, 486
terrapin 104
Terrier, Louis-Félix 136
Terrillon, Octave 136
terrorism 663
Terry-Thomas 389
Tertiary period 23
Tertullian 508
Teshub 479, **487**
Tesla, Nikola 185
inventions 189, 191
Testino, Mario 450
test matches 515
testosterone 138
tetanus 134

discoveries 138
immunization 144, 145
Tethys (myth) 482
Tethys (satellite) 2
Tetley, Glen 433
ballets 435
Tet offensive 279
Tetouan 643
Tetrazzini, Luisa 407
Teutates 487
Teutonic Knights 734
Texaco 356
**Texan War of
Independence** 277
Texas 868
Texas Instruments 191
textiles wedding
anniversary 575
text messages 609
Teyte, Dame Maggie 407
Tezcatlipoca 487
Thíra volcano 35
**Thackeray, William
Makepeace** 353
Thaddeus (disciple) 492
Thailand 678, **846**
national holidays 582
political leaders 333
UN membership 645
World Heritage sites 58
Thai language 584
thalassotherapy 141
Thaleia 487
Thales 233, 468
Thalia 481, **487**
thallium 202
Thames barrier 228
**Thames shipping forecast
area** 59
Thames tunnel 178
first 227
Thammuz 487
Thanatos 469
Thane 643
Thar Desert 33
Tharp, Twyla 433
**Thatcher Ferry (Bridge of the
Americas) bridge** 225
theatre museums:
Europe 459
UK 461
USA 462
Thebes (city) 53
Thebes (myth) 473
Theiler, Max 186
Themis 487
theologians 503
**Theorell, Axel Hugo
Theodor** 186
theory of evolution 178,
179, 181
theory of relativity **172**, 179,
183, 267
**Theotocopoulos, Domenico
(El Greco)** 441
Theravada Buddhism 492
There Will Be Blood 399
therm 210
thermal energy 168

thermidor 156
thermionics 177
thermodynamics 177, 182,
184
thermometer 179, 192
thermonuclear energy 173
Theron, Charlize 389
Academy Awards 399
Theroux, Paul 353
Theseus 231, 472, 478, 481,
483, 484, **487**
Thessalonika 54
Thessaloniki 461
Thetis 471, 475, 483, **487**
thiamin 130
discovery 138
thickeners 152
thick knee 94
Thielemans, 'Toots' 415
Thimonnier, Barthelemy 191
Thin Lizzy 427
Thirty Years' War 256, 257,
277
Thisbe 484
thistle:
globe 71
Scotch 71
**Thistle, Order of the
(KT)** 668
Thivolet, Jacques 191
Thomas, D M 353
Thomas, Dylan 359
Thomas, E Donnall 187
Thomas, Edward 359
Thomas, John 502
Thomas, R S 359
Thomas, Robert 191
Thomas, St (disciple) 492
Thomas Cup 524
Thompson, Emma 389
Academy Awards 399
Thomson, Sir George 186
Thomson, James 359
Thomson, Sir Joseph 185
Thomson, Robert 192
Thomson, Sir William *see*
Kelvin, William Thomson,
1st Baron
't Hooft, Gerardus 187
Thor 201, 470, **487**
thorium 201
Thorpe and Salter 188
Thoth 470, **487**
Thousand Acres, A 356
threadworms 141
threatened species 119
**Three-Cornered Hat,
The** 435
Three Day Event 533
Three Faces of Eve, The 398
Three Gorges dam 227
**Three Henries, War of
the** 276
Three Kingdoms period 236,
281
Three Mile Island 47
Threepenny Opera, The 405
thrips 115
throat, study of 176

Index

thrombolytic drugs 142
thrush (bird) 93
thrush (infection) 133, **134**
 treatment 141
thulium 202
Thunderbird 487
thunder-bugs 115
Thurman, Uma 389
Thurrock 660
Thyestes 471, 473, **487**
thyme 65, 74
thyroxine 138
Tiamat 487
Tiananmen Square 272, 715
Tianjin (Tientsin) 643
Tibbett, Lawrence 407
tick 134
tidal waves 38
tides, study of 175
tierce 162
Tierney, Gene 389
Tierra del Fuego 28, 31
Tiffany, Charles 195
tiger 87
 Bengal 120
 Chinese calendar 575
 collective names 118
 length of pregnancy 89
tiger flower 69
tiger lily 70
tiger moth 116
tiger's claw 77
Tijuana 643
Tikal national park/nature
 reserve 50
tikka 156
Tillich, Paul 508
Tilly, Meg 389
Tilsit cheese 163
timbale 156
timber measures 213
Timbuktu 55
time:
 geological 22
 international differences 576
 SI units 208
timeclock 192
time measurement 175
Times, The 612
time trials 515
time zones 576
Timisoara 643
Timon of Athens 362
Timor-Leste 579, 582
tin 201
 properties 202
 wedding anniversary 575
tinamou 90
Tinbergen, Jan 458
Tinbergen, Nikolaas 185
 Nobel prize 187
Ting, Samuel Chao
 Chung 187
Tinguely, Jean 445
Tintoretto 443
Tippett, Sir Michael 402
 operas 405
Tirana 643
Tiree 30

Tiresias 487
Tirich Mir 34
TIROS satellite 11
Tiruchchirapalli 643
Tiselius, Arne Wilhelm
 Kaurin 186
Tishah beAv 500
Tisiphone 475
tissue 169, 173
 study of 175
tit 93
Titan, Titans (myth) 469, 473,
 474, 478, 480, 481, 482, 484,
 485, **487**
Titan (satellite) 2
 space missions 12
Titania (myth) 487
Titania (satellite) 3
Titanic (film) 399
titanium 202
 properties 202
Titian 255, 443
Titicaca, Lake 32
Titus Andronicus 362
Tjio, Joe Hin 136
Tlaloc 487
Tlazolteotl 487
T-lymphocytes 138
TNF 138
toad, toads:
 collective names 118
 common 101
 green 101
 marine 101
 midwife 101
 Mount Nimba 120
 Surinam 101
 yellow-bellied 101
toaster 192
Tobin, James 459
tobogganing 515
 fixture results 527
Tobruk, Battle of 278
Todd, Lord Alexander 186
tody 97
To Each His Own 397
Togo 678, **847**
 national holidays 582
 political leaders 333
 UN membership 645
 World Heritage sites 58
Tokelau 31
To Kill a Mockingbird 398
Tokyo 643, 645
Toledo 643
 museums and galleries 461
 World Heritage sites 58
Toledo (USA) 463
Tolkien, J R R 271, 353
Tolstoy, Count Leo 353
Toltecs 242, 790
Tolyatti 643
tomato 68
 nutritional value 151
Tomiki-ryo 514
Tom Jones (film) 398
Tom Jones (novel) 261
Tomlin, Lily 389
tomography 138

Tomonaga, Sin-itiro 186
Tomsk 643
ton, tons 210
 conversion tables 221
Tone, Wolfe 760
Tonegawa, Susumu 187
Tonga 678, **847**
 Commonwealth
 membership 647
 English speakers 585
 national holidays 582
 political leaders 333
 UN membership 646
Tonghua 643
tonne, tonnes:
 conversion tables 221
 SI conversion factors 210
tonsillitis 134
tonsils 131, 134
Tonton Macoute 751
tooth decay 130
topaz 28
 Mohs' hardness scale 28
 month association 575
Topkapi Palace Museum 460
topology 175, **177**
Torah 500
Torbay 660
Torca del Cerro del Cuevon
 cave 34
Torfaen 661
Tormé, Mel 415
tornado 173
 windstorms 42
Toronto 643
Toronto Symphony Orchestra
 408
torpedo ray 106
torque 208
torr 210
Torrance, Thomas F 509
Torrey Canyon 49
Torricelli, Evangelista 188,
 257
tortilla 156
tortoise, tortoises 104
Tosca 267, 406
Tosks 680
totalitarianism 663
total solar eclipses 4
Toto 429
Toubkal national park/nature
 reserve 50
toucan 97
Touch of Class, A 398
Toulouse 643
Toulouse-Lautrec, Henri 443
Tour de France 532
tourmaline 27, 28
 month association 575
Tournachon, Gaspard-
 Felix 448
tournedos 156
Tower Bridge 225
Tower of London 58
Tower Subway 227
Townes, Charles H:
 Nobel prize 186
 Templeton Prize 509

toxicology 177
Toyama 643
Toyohasi 643
Toyonaka 643
Toyota 644
trace minerals 130
Tracey, Stan 416
trachoma 134
trachyte 26
track events (athletics) 514
track racing 515
Tracy, Spencer 389
  Academy Awards 397
trade in endangered
  species 120
trade union 663
traditional beliefs 491
traditional dance 566
Trafalgar, Battle of 262, 277
Trafalgar shipping forecast
  area 59
traffic lights 192
Trafford 660
Tragedy of King Lear,
  The 362
Training Day 399
trainspotting 568
trampolining 520
  fixture results 556
tranquillizers 136, 192
Transbay (San Francisco-
  Oakland Bay) bridge 225
transcendental
  meditation 268, 503
Transfiguration 493
transformer 192
transistor 192, 271
transition element 173
transition metal 173
Transit 1B satellite 11
transmission of disease 131
transmutation 182
transpiration 44
transplant rejection 137, 183
transport museums:
  Europe 459
  UK 461
  USA 462
Trans-Tokyo Bay Highway
  bridge 225
transuranic elements 173
Transvaal 834
Transylvania 817
Tranter, Nigel 353
trapdoor spider 114
trapezium 205
trap shooting 515
travel agency 192
traveller's cheques 192
Travers, Morris William 200,
  202
Traviata, La 265, 406
Travolta, John 389
Treasury of St Mark's 461
Treasury of the Holy Roman
  Empire 461
Treaty of Maastricht 648
Treaty of Rome 270
tree, trees:

temperate and
  Mediterranean 74
  tropical 76
treecreeper 93
  Australian 93
treefrog, common 101
tree-nighthawk 98
tree of heaven 76
Trefilova, Vera
  Alexandrovna 436
Tremain, Rose 353
  literary prizes 355
Tres Hermanas falls 33
Tres Marías 31
Trevithick, Richard 190
Trevor, William 353
triangle 205
Triangulum constellation 6, 7
Triangulum Australe
  constellation 6, 7
Triassic period 23
  fossils 24
tribunal 663
tricyclic drugs 142
Trier 54
triggerfish 109
Triglav 487
trilobites 24
  geological record 23
Trimble, David 459
Trinidad 274
Trinidad and Tobago 678, 848
  Commonwealth
    membership 647
  English speakers 585
  national holidays 582
  political leaders 334
  UN membership 645
Trinity Sunday 493, 494
trinquete 518
Tripitaka 492
  World Heritage site 55
triple jump 520
Tripoli 644
Trip to Bountiful, The 398
Tristan 487
Tristan da Cunha 31, 862
Tristano, Lennie 416
Tristan und Isolde 406
Trivandrum 644
Trivial Pursuit® 566
trogon 97
Troilus 474, 482, 487
Troilus and Cressida 362
Trois jours chez ma
  mère 356
Trois-Rivières (Laviolette)
  bridge 225
Trojan War(s) 275, 480
Trojans, The (opera) 406
Trollope, Anthony 353
Trollope, Joanna 353
Tronquoy tunnel 227
tropical climatic zone 39
tropical rainforests 45, 46
tropicbird 96
Tros 476

'Troubles, the' 857
trout 109
  collective names 118
Trovatore, Il 265, 406
troy ounce 210
Trucial States 855
true flies 116
True Grit 398
True History of the Kelly
  Gang 355
Truffaut, François 396
Trujillo 644
Truman Doctrine 270
Trump, Donald 195
Trump International Hotel 228
trumpeter (bird) 100
trumpet of the dead 78
trumps 566
Ts'ai Lun 190
Tsavo national park/nature
  reserve 50
tsetse fly 116
  discoveries 138
  infection by 134
Tsien, Roger Y 188
Tsing Ma bridge 225
Tsui, Daniel C 187
tsunami, tsunamis 173
  major 38
Tsung-Dao Lee 186
Tuamotu Archipelago 31
Tuareg 785, 803
tuatara 102, 104
Tuatha de Danann 487
tuberculin 135
tuberculosis 134
  medical discoveries 138
  immunization 145
tubers 69
tubocurarine 138
Tucana constellation 6, 7
Tuckett 434
Tucson 644
Tudjman, Franjo 721
Tudor, Antony 433
  ballets 433
Tudor, House of 283, 857
tufa 25
tuff 26
Tugela Falls 33
tug-of-war 520
  fixture results 556
Tula 644
tulip 70
tulip tree 76
Tullus Hostilius 478
Tulsa 644
  museums and galleries 463
tumblebugs 117
tumbling 520
Tumor Necrosis Factor 138
tumours 176
tuna:
  bluefin 110
  nutritional value 151
  skipjack 109
  yellowfin 109
tungsten 202
  properties 202

tungsten lamp 182
Tunis 248, 644
  World Heritage site 58
Tunisia 678, **849**
  national holidays 582
  political leaders 334
  UN membership 645
  World Heritage sites 58
tunnels 226
tunny 109
Tuntex Sky Tower 228
Tuohy, Frank 353
Tupamaros guerrillas 871
Tupi languages 584
turaco 97
Turandot 401, 406
turbojet 192
turbot 109
turbulence 173
Turgenev, Ivan 354
Turin 644
  World Heritage site 55
turkey 100
  collective names 118
  nutritional value 151
Turkey 678, **850**
  EU membership 648
  national holidays 582
  political leaders 334
  UN membership 645
  World Heritage sites 58
Turkish language 584
Turkmenistan 678, **851**
  CIS membership 647
  national holidays 582
  political leaders 334
  UN membership 646
  World Heritage sites 58
Turks and Caicos Islands 863
turmeric 67
Turner, Dame Eva 407
Turner, J M W 443
Turner, Kathleen 389
Turner, Lana 389
Turner, Ted 195
Turner, Tina 427
  Grammy awards 429
Turner Prize 444
turnip 68
  nutritional value 151
Turn of the Screw, The
  (opera) 406
Turpin, Raymond 136
turquoise 28
  month association 575
turtle, turtles:
  Afro-American side-
    necked 104
  American mud and
    musk 104
  Austro-American side-
    necked 104
  big-headed 104
  box 104
  Central American river 104
  collective names 118
  endangered species 120
  Hawksbill 120
  Mexican musk 104

pig-nosed softshell 104
  pond and river 104
  sea 104
  snapping 104
  softshell 105
Turturro, John 389
Tushingham, Rita 389
Tutankhamun 231
Tutsi 279, 705, 819
Tutu, Desmond 508
  Nobel prize 459
Tutuola, Amos 354
Tuvalu 678, **851**
  Commonwealth
    membership 647
  English speakers 585
  national holidays 582
  political leaders 334
  UN membership 646
TV actors 363
TV broadcasting 197
Tver 644
Twain, Mark 267, 354
Twain, Shania 427
Twelfth Night 362
twenty brightest stars 7
twenty nearest stars 8
twins 173
Two Fat Ladies 159
Two Gentlemen of Verona,
  The 362
Two International Finance
  Centre 228
Two Women (film) 398
Tyche 487
Tycho comet 8
Tycho's star 178
Tydeus 485
Tyler, Anne 354
  literary prizes 356
Tyndareus 474
Tyne shipping forecast
  area 59
Tyner, McCoy 416
typefaces 610
typewriter 192
Typhoeus 487
typhoid 134
  immunization 145
  vaccination 182
typhoon 173
  windstorms 42
Typhon (myth) 478, **487**
typhus 134
  discoveries 138
Tyr 470, **487**
tyre 192
tyre pressure conversion
  tables 220
Tyrone's Rebellion 277
Tyson, Keith 444
Tyson, Mike 564
Tyumen 644
Tzom Gedaliahu 500

U

Uber Cup 525
UB40 427

Uccello, Paolo 443
Ufa 644
Uffizi Gallery 460
Uganda 678, **852**
  civil war 279
  Commonwealth
    membership 647
  English speakers 585
  national holidays 582
  political leaders 334
  UN membership 645
  World Heritage sites 58
ugli 64
ugly toadstool 77
Uist, North 30
Uist, South 30
Ujung-Kulon national park/
  nature reserve 50
UK *see* United Kingdom
Ukraine 678, **853**
  CIS membership 647
  national holidays 582
  political leaders 335
  UN membership 645
  World Heritage sites 58
Ulan Bator 644
Ulanova, Galina 436
Ulan-Ude 644
Ull 470
ullage 162
Ullmann, Liv 389
Ulloa, Antonio de 201
Ulsan 644
Ulster Museum 461
Ulster Orchestra 408
ultrasonic 173
ultrasonography 192
ultrasound 173
ultraviolet radiation 167,
  170, **173**
  wavelengths 197
Ulugh Muztagh 34
Uluru-Kata Tjuta National
  Park 51
  World Heritage site 51
Ulyanovsk 644
Ulysses 482, 488
Ulysses (novel) 269
Umbriel 3
Un Aller simple 356
uncertainty principle 173,
  181
underweight 147
Underwood, Rory 564
Undset, Sigrid 458
UNESCO 646
  World Heritage sites 51
Unforgiven 399
Ungaro, Emanuel 452
Un Grand Pas vers le Bon
  Dieu 356
UN High Commissioner
  for Refugees, Office of
  the 458, 459
unicameral legislatures 664
unicorn 488
UNIDO 646
unified field theory 173
Union Carbide disaster 46

Union of Soviet Socialist Republics 819
  political leaders 335
  population growth 638
  UN membership 645
Union of the Crowns 285
Union states (USA) 278
UNITA 683
unitary authorities:
  England 660
  Scotland 661
  Wales 661
United Arab Emirates 678, **854**
  national holidays 582
  political leaders 335
  UN membership 645
United Church of Christ 493
United Irishmen 262
United Kingdom 678, **855**
  administrative divisions 659
  airports 626
  Commonwealth membership 647
  dependent territories 859
  English speakers 585
  EU membership 648
  islands 662
  military ranks 667
  monarchs 286
  national holidays 582
  newspapers 612
  political leaders 339
  road signs 619
  UN membership 645
  World Heritage sites 58
United Kingdom Infrared Telescope 10
United Nations 645
  membership 645
  Nobel prize 459
  Secretaries-General 647
United Nations Children's Fund 458
United Nations Educational Scientific and Cultural Organization 646
United Nations Industrial Development Organization 646
United Nations peacekeeping forces 459
United States of America 678, **863**
  English speakers 585
  largest cities 645
  military ranks 667
  national holidays 582
  newspapers 613
  political leaders 340
  population growth 638
  road signs 621
  sign language 607
  states 866
  territories 868
  UN membership 645
  Virgin Islands 870
  War of Independence 264, 277

World Heritage sites 58
universal constants 196
universal joint 192
Universal Postal Union 646
universe, study of 174
unmanned Moon rover 11
unsaturated compounds 173
Unsworth, Barry 355
Unzen volcano 35
Upanishads 232, 498
Updike, John 354
  literary prizes 356
Uposatha Days 492
upper respiratory tract, study of 175
Upper Volta 704
UPU 646
Upward, Edward 354
Uralic languages 584
Urania 481, 488
uranium 202
  properties 202
Uranus (myth) 474, 476, 478, 482, 488
Uranus (planet) 2, 181, 182, 202
  satellites 3
  space missions 12
Urawa 644
Urbain, Georges 200
Urdr 482
Urdu language 584
urea cycle 182
urethra, discharge from 132
urethritis 135
urinary tract, study of 177
urination, discomfort 132
urine flow, study of 177
Uris, Leon 354
urodynamics 177
urology 177
Urquiola oil spill 49
Ursa Major constellation 6, 7, 473
Ursa Minor constellation 6, 7
Ursids meteor shower 9
urticaria 141
Uruguay 678, **870**
  national holidays 583
  political leaders 336
  UN membership 645
  World Heritage sites 59
Urumqi 644
US, USA see United States of America
USA for Africa 429
US English, differences from British English 591
USSR see Union of Soviet Socialist Republics
Ustinov, Sir Peter 389
Ust-Kamenogorsk 644
Ust'-Urt desert 33
US Virgin Islands 870
Utah 868
Utamaro, Kitagawa 443
Uther Pendragon 488
Utigardsfossen 33
Uto-Aztecan languages 584

Utrecht 258, 461
Utsire shipping forecast areas 59
Utsunomiya 644
U2 427
  Grammy awards 429
Utzon, Jørn 457
UV726-8B 8
Uzbekistan 678, **871**
  CIS membership 647
  national holidays 583
  political leaders 336
  UN membership 646
  World Heritage sites 59

V

Vaaler, Johann 190
vaccination,
  vaccinations 181, 182, 184
  discoveries 138
  immunization of children 144
vacherin 156
Vacherin cheese 163
vacuum 209, 257
vacuum cleaner 192
Vadodara 644
vaginal discharge 132, 133, 134
Vaglia tunnel 227
Vahagn 488
Väinämöinen 488
Vainqueurs, Les 435
Vaiont dam 228
valence number 202
Valencia 244, 644
  World Heritage site 57
valency 173
Valens, Ritchie 427
Valentine, Basil 199
Valentino (fashion designer) 452
Valentino, Rudolph 389
Vale of Glamorgan 661
valerian 65
Valetta 55
valkyrie, valkyries 470, 473, **488**
Valladolid 644
Valmy, Battle of 277
Valois, House of 284
Valpolicella 160
Valse, La 435
Vanadis 202
vanadium 202
  properties 202
Van Allen radiation belts 173
  space missions 11
Vanbrugh, Sir John 457
Van Cleef, Lee 389
Vancouver 644
Vancouver, George 274
Van Dam, José 407
Van Damme, Jean-Claude 390
Van de Graaff, Robert Jemison 185
Vanderbilt, Harold

A–Z

Index

Stirling 565
Van der Elsken, Ed 450
van der Meer, Simon 187
Van der Post, Sir
  Laurens 354
Van der Weyden, Rogier 443
Van Diemen's Land 274
Vandross, Luther 427
Van Dyck, Sir Anthony 257,
  443
Van Dyke, Dick 390
Vane, Sir John R 187
Van Gogh, Vincent 443
Van Gogh Museum 459
Vanguard space mission 11
Van Halen 427
vanilla 67
Vanir 470
Vansittart, Peter 354
Vanuatu 678, **872**
  Commonwealth
    membership 647
  English speakers 585
  national holidays 583
  political leaders 336
  UN membership 646
  World Heritage sites 59
van Vleck, John H 187
Varanasi 644
Vardhamana Mahavira 499
Varèse, Edgard 402
Vargas 644
Vargas Llosa, Mario 354
variation 172, 173
Variations (ballet) 435
varicella 131
varieties of wines and
  grapes 159
Varmus, Harold E 185
  Nobel prize 187
Varna 644
Varro, Marcus Terentius 189,
  235
Varuna 488
Vasa, House of 286
Vasco da Gama bridge 225
Vasistha 488
Vassy, massacre of 276
Vatican City 678, **872**
  World Heritage sites 59
Vatican Museums 461
Vaughan, Sarah 416
Vaughn, Robert 390
Vaughan Williams, Ralph 402
  operas 405
vault 162
Vauquelin, Nicolas-Louis 199
Vautrin, Jean 356
Vayu 477
VDQS 162
vector 173
Veda, Vedas 485, 498
Vedic religion 498
Vega (star) 7
Vega, Suzanne 428
Vega 1 space mission 12
vegetables 67
  dietary
    recommendations 149

Vela constellation 6, 7
Velázquez, Diego 443
Velde, Henri van de 457
velocity:
  SI conversion factors 210
  SI units 208
  of light 180
velouté 156
Veltman, Martinus J G 187
velvet shank 79
Velvet Underground, The 428
vending machine 192
Venera space missions 11, 12
venereal infection 135
Venezuela 678, **873**
  national holidays 583
  political leaders 337
  UN membership 645
  World Heritage sites 59
Venice 644
  inventions 189
  museums and galleries 461
  World Heritage site 55
Ventana, La 435
ventilator 192
ventricles 126
Venturi, Robert 457
Venus (myth) 470, 472
Venus (planet) 2
  space missions 11, 12, 13
Venus de Milo 235
Veracruz 644
Verdandi 482
Verdi, Giuseppe 265, 402
  ballet music 433, 434
  operas 405, 406
Verdun, Battle of 278
Verlaine, Paul 359
Vermeer, Jan 259, 443
vermicelli 156
Vermont 868
vermouth 162
vernal equinox 575
Verne, Jules 354
Vernon God Little 355
Veronese 443
veronica 74
Verrazano, Giovanni da 274
Verrazano Narrows
  bridge 225
Verrocchio, Andrea del 443
Versace, Gianni 453
Versailles:
  museums and galleries 461
  World Heritage site 53
vertebrates 79, 182
Vertumnus 470
vervain 66
Verve, The 428
very high frequencies 173
Very Large Array
  (telescope) 10
Vespri Siciliani, I 406
Vespucci, Amerigo 274
Vesta 470, 478, 488
Vesterålen Islands 31
Vesuvius 35, 234
Veterans Memorial
  bridge 225

VHF 173
viburnum 74
vice-presidents of the
  USA 340
Vichy government 738
Vickers, Jon 407
Vickrey, William 459
Victor Blanco Telescope 10
Victoria (city) 644
Victoria (myth) 470, 482
Victoria (state) 688
Victoria, Lake 32
Victoria and Albert
  Museum 462
Victoria Cross 668
Victoria Falls 275
  national park/nature
    reserve 50
  World Heritage site 59
Victoria Island 28
Victoria Jubilee bridge 225
Vidal, Gore 354
Vidar 470
video games 567
videophone 192
video recorder 192
Vienna 644
  museums and galleries 461
Vienna Philharmonic
  Orchestra 408
Vienna Symphony
  Orchestra 408
Vientiane 644
Viet Cong 279
Vietnam 678, **874**
  national holidays 583
  political leaders 337
  UN membership 646
  World Heritage sites 59
Vietnamese language 584
Vietnam War 270, 279, 864,
  875
Vignola, Giacomo Barozzi
  da 457
Vijayawada 644
Viking 1 space mission 12
Viking raids 240, 275
Viking shipping forecast
  area 59
Vikrama era 574
Villella, Edward 436
Vilnius 644
  World Heritage sites 55
Viña del Mar 644
vinaigrette 156
Vinaya Pitaka 492
Vincent, Gene 428
Vincent, Jan-Michael 390
vine 162
Vine, Barbara 354
vineyard 162
vingt-et-un 565
vinho verde 162
viniculture 162
Vinland 274
Vinnitsa 644
Vinnufossen 33
vinosity 162
vintage 163

vintner 163
violet 72
  month association 575
Viollet-le-Duc, Eugène 457
viper 105
  collective names 118
Viracocha 488
viral infections 131
Virchow, Rudolph 136
vireo 93
Virgil 235, 359
Virginia 868
Virginia Beach 644
Virginia creeper 74
Virgin Islands 31
  British 860
  US 870
Virgo constellation 6, 7
virology 177
Virtanen, Artturi Ilmari 186
virtual reality 173
virtues 472
Virunga national park/nature
  reserve 51
virus, viruses 165, 170, 172,
  173
  discoveries 138
  infections 131
  study of 175, 177
Visakhapatnam 644
Visconti, Luchino 396
viscosity:
  SI conversion factors 210
  SI units 208
  study of 176
viscount 668
  form of address 672
viscountess, form of
  address 672
Vishnu 485, 488, 498, 502
visible light 166
Visvamitra 488
vitamin, vitamins 173
  dietary
  recommendations 149
  discoveries 138
vitamin A 130
vitamin B$_1$ 130
vitamin B$_2$ 130
vitamin B$_3$ 130
vitamin B$_5$ 130
vitamin B$_6$ 130
vitamin B$_7$ 130
vitamin B$_9$ 130
vitamin B$_{12}$ 130
vitamin C 130, 185
vitamin D 130
vitamin E 130
vitamin K 130
Vitebsk 644
viticulture 163
Vitruvius 457
Vivaldi, Antonio 261, 402
Vladimir 644
Vladivostok 644
Vlaminck, Maurice de 443
Voight, Jon 398
Volans constellation 6, 7
vol-au-vent 156

volcanic activity 26
  eruptions 38
  geological record 20, 23
  plate tectonics 21
volcanoes 35
Volcanus 477, 488
vole 87, 89
Volgograd 644
volleyball 520
  fixture results 556
volleyball court 557
Volta, Alessandro, Count 185
  inventions 188
Voltaire, François-Marie
  de 354
Voltaire Museum 460
voltamperes 209
volume:
  conversion factors 214
  conversion tables 217
  measures 212, 213
  SI conversion factors 209
  SI units 208
  Sun 1
Volundr 470
Voluntaries 435
vomiting 131, 132, 133, 141
von Euler, Ulf 186
von Hayek, Friedrich 458
von Heidenstam, Verner 457
von Heyse, Paul 457
von Klitzing, Klaus 187
Vonnegut, Kurt, Jr 354
von Neumann, John 185
  inventions 189
von Ossietzky, Carl 458
von Otter, Anne Sofie 407
von Stroheim, Erich 390
von Sydow, Max 390
von Weizsäcker, Carl
  Friedrich 509
Voronezh 644
Voshkod space missions 15
Vostok space missions 11, 15
Vouvray 160
Voyager space missions 12
Voysey, Charles 457
Vrtra 478
Vulcan 470, 477, 488
Vulcano 35
vulnerable species 119
Vulpecula constellation 6, 7
Vulpian 135
vulture
  Asian 120
  New World 91
  Old World 91
  Ruppell's griffon 100

W

Waals, Johannes van der 185
Wagner, Herbert 190
Wagner, Otto 457
Wagner, Richard 403, 482
  ballet music 434, 435
  operas 405, 406
Wagner, Robert 390
Wagner-Jauregg,

Theodor 138
wagtail 93
Wahhabis 499, 825
Wahl 201
Wain, John 354
waipiti 82
Waits, Tom 428
Wak 488
Wakayama 644
Wakefield 660
Waksman, Selman 138
  Nobel prize 186
Walcott, Derek 359
  Nobel prize 459
Wald, George 186
Wales 858
  councils 661
  museums and galleries 461,
  462
  national holidays 583
Wałesa, Lech 814
  Nobel prize 459
Walken, Christopher 390
Walker, Alice 273, 354
Walker, John E 187
Walker, T-Bone 416
Walker Art Gallery 461
walking 520
  energy expenditure 148
  fixture results 557
Walk the Line 399
Walk to the Paradise Garden,
  The 435
wallaby 80
Wallace Collection, The 462
Wallace, William 248, 250,
  276
Waller, Fats 416
Wallinger, Mark 444
Wallis and Futuna
  Islands 739
Wallis, Barnes 188
Walloon Life, Museum of 460
Walloons 695, 696
Wall Street (film) 398
walnut, walnuts:
  black 76
  common 76
  nutritional values 151
Walpole, Horace 354
walrus 87
Walsall 660
Walters, Julie 390
Walton, Ernest 186
Walton, Frederick 190
Walton, Sir William 402
  ballet music 433
Wanamaker, Sam 390
wandering albatross 100
wand flower 70
Wang, An 195
Wanxian bridge 225
Warangal 644
warbler, American 93
Warburg, Otto Heinrich 185
Warhol, Andy 271, 443
warm-blooded animals 79
Warne, Shane 564
Warner, David 390

Warner, Marina 354
War of Jenkins' Ear 277
War of the Austrian
 Succession 260, 277
War of the Julich
 Succession 277
War of the League of
 Augsburg 277
War of the Mantuan
 Succession 277
War of the Pacific 278, 713,
 812
War of the Schmalkaldic
 League 276
War of the Sicilian
 Vespers 276
War of the Spanish
 Succession 258, 277
War of the Three
 Henries 276
War of the Triple
 Alliance 811
Warren, Harry 404
Warren, J Robin 183
 Nobel prize 187
Warren, Robert Penn 354
Warring states period 281
Warrington 660
wars, major 275
wars of succession 277
Wars of the Roses 252, 276,
 857
Warsaw 644
 museums and galleries 461
 World Heritage site 56
warthog 81
Warton, Thomas 359
Warwick, Dionne 428
Warwickshire 659
washing machine 192
Washington (city) 644
 museums and galleries 463
Washington (state) 868
Washington, Denzel 390
 Academy Awards 399
Washington, Dinah 416
wasps 116
watch, watches 192
 wedding anniversary 575
Watch on the Rhine 397
water, study of 175
waterbuck 87
water chestnut 72
watercress 66, 68
waterfalls, highest 33
water flea 112
waterfowl 93
Waterhouse, Alfred 457
Waterhouse, Keith 354
water lily 72
 month association 575
Waterloo, Battle of 277
Waterloo Handicap 528
Waterman, Lewis 190
watermelon 64
water polo 520
 fixture results 557
Waters, Ethel 416
Waters, Muddy 416

water skiing 521
 fixture results 557
water soluble vitamins 130
water spider 114
water therapies 140, 141
Waterton Lakes national park/
 nature reserve 51
water vapour 168
Watson, James D 185
 discoveries 136
 Nobel prize 186
Watson, Tom 564
Watt, James 185
 inventions 191
Watteau, Antoine 444
wattle 72
wattle-bird 93
Waugh, Evelyn 354
wave frequency 179
wavelength, wavelengths 166
 radiation 197
wave mechanics 184
wave theory of light 184, 185
waxbill 93
waxwing 93
Wayland 470, 488
Wayne, John 390
 Academy Awards 398
Way of All Flesh 397
Waza national park/nature
 reserve 51
We Need to Talk About
 Kevin 355
Wearing, Gillian 444
weasel 87
weather:
 acid rain 45
 clouds 44
 extremes 39
 sea disturbance 41
 space missions 11
 study of 175
 wind force 41
 windstorms 42
weather forecasting 197
Weaver, Sigourney 390
weaving 568
Webb, Sir Aston 457
Webb, Francis 359
Webb, Philip 457
Webb Ellis, William 519
Weber, Bruce 450
Weber, Carl Maria von 403
 ballet music 434
Weber, Eberhard 416
Webern, Anton von 403
Webster, Ben 416
Webster, John 257, 362
wedding anniversaries 575
Wedding Bouquet, A 435
Weegee 450
Weifang 644
weigela 74
weight:
 Body Mass Index 147
 conversion factors 214, 215
 conversion tables 220
 measures 212, 213
 optimum body weight 147

weightlifting 521
 fixture results 558
weight loss 131, 134, 149
Weil, Simone 468
Weiland 470
Weill, Kurt 403, 404
 ballet music 434
 operas 405
Weinberg, Robert 137
Weinberg, Steven 185
 Nobel prize 187
Weinstock, Mildred 139
Weir, Peter 396
Weland 470
Welch, Raquel 390
Weldon, Fay 354
welfare state 663
Wellcome Museum of the
 History of Medicine,
 The 462
Weller, Thomas 186
Welles, Orson 269, 390, 396
Wellington 644
Wellington, Duke of 277
Wellman, William A 397
Wells, H G 354
Wells, Horace 135
Welsbach, Baron von 200,
 201
Welsh, Irvine 354
Welsh Assembly 272, 858
Welty, Eudora 354
Wenders, Wim 396
Wenzhou 644
Werther 406
Wesker, Arnold 362
Wesley, John 260, 493, **508**
Wesley, Mary 354
West, Mae 390
West, Morris 354
West, Dame Rebecca 354
West Bank 761, **762**, 766
West Berkshire 660
West comet 8
West Dunbartonshire 662
West-Eastern Divan
 Orchestra 408
Western Australia 688
Western Isles 662
Western Theatre Ballet 437
West Frisian Islands 30
West Germany 270, 272, 743
Westlife 428
West Lothian 662
Westminster palace and
 abbey 58
Weston, Edward 450
West Saxon kings 283
West Side Story 398
West Sussex 659
West Virginia 868
Westwood, Vivienne 453
Weyergans, François 356
whale, whales:
 beaked 87
 beluga 88
 blue 88
 collective names 118
 endangered species 120

grey 88
humpback 88
killer 88
length of pregnancy 89
long-finned pilot 88
record 89
sperm 88
western grey 120
white 88
whale-headed stork 94
whale shark 109
Wham! 428
Wharton, Edith 354
What You Will 362
wheat 62
wheel 192
Wheeling bridge 225
whelk 111
**When I Lived in Modern
Times** 355
**Where the Wild Things
Are** 406
whin 72
whiptail and racerunner 105
whirlwind 173
whist 566
Whistler, James McNeill 444
Whitaker, Forest 399
White, Antonia 354
White, Barry 428
White, Ellen Gould 264, 503
White, Marco Pierre 159
White, Margaret 446
White, Minor 450
White, Patrick 355
Nobel prize 458
White, T H 355
whitebeam 76
white currant 64
white dwarf 173
white-eye 93
Whitehead, A N 468
Whitehead, Gillian 403
Whitehead, William 359
white laurel 75
**White Mountain, Battle of
the** 277
White Nile 274
Whiteread, Rachel 273, 445
Turner prize 444
White Stripes, The 428
White Tiger, The 355
white truffle 79
Whitman, Walt 359
Whit Monday 577
Whit Sunday 493, 494
Whittle, Frank 192, 269
Whitworth Art Gallery 462
WHO 646
Who, The 428
whooping cough 135
immunization 144
**Who's Afraid of Virginia
Woolf?** 398
Widmark, Richard 391
Wieman, Carl E 187
Wien, Wilhelm 185
Wiener, Otto 407
Wieschaus, Eric F 187

Wiesel, Elie 459
Wiesel, Torsten N 187
Wigan 660
**Wight shipping forecast
area** 59
Wigler, Michael 137
Wilczek, Frank 187
wild cat 88
Wilde, Oscar 267, 355, 362
Wilder, Billy 396
Academy Awards 397, 398
Wilder, Gene 391
Wilder, Thornton 355, 362
wild flower preparations 140
Wilding, Michael 355
wild pansy 65
wild pig 81
Wiles, Sir Andrew 185
Wilkins, Maurice 185
discoveries 136
Nobel prize 186
Wilkinson, Sir Geoffrey 187
Wilkinson, J 188
William III 258, 277
**William Herschel
Telescope** 10
Williams, Sir Bernard 468
Williams, Betty 459
Williams, Jody 459
Williams, Kenneth 391
Williams, Robbie 428
Williams, Robin 391
**Williams, Roger
(Baptist)** 493
**Williams, Roger
(scientist)** 138
Williams, Tennessee 362
Williams, Tony 416
Williams, Treat 391
Williamsburg 463
Williamson, David 362
Williamson, Nicol 391
William Tell 406
William the Conqueror 244,
275
Williamstown 463
Willis, Bruce 391
Willis Tower 228
willow:
pussy 76
weeping 76
wedding anniversary 575
white 76
Wills, Lucy 138
Wills, William 275
Nobel prize 457
Wilson, A N 355
Wilson, Jacqueline 355
Wilson, Kenneth G 187
Wilson, Robert W 187
Wilson, T Woodrow 340
Wiltshire 659
Winchester fives 516
wind:
extremes 39
speed measurement 41
storms 42
wind force scale 41
Windhoek 644

Winding, Kai 416
windmill 192
Windscale disaster 46
Windsor, House of 286
**Windsor and
Maidenhead** 660
windstorms 42
wine 159
bottle sizes 163
terminology 160
wine bottle sizes 163
Winehouse, Amy 428
Grammy awards 429
**wine-making
terminology** 160
wine-tasting terminology 160
wing chun 518
Winger, Debra 391
Winger, Eugene P 186
Wingfield, Walter G 192, 520
Wings (film) 397
**Winkler, Clemens
Alexander** 200
Winnipeg 644
Winnipeg, Lake 32
Winogrand, Garry 450
Winslet, Kate 391
Academy Awards 399
winter 575
winter aconite 64, 70
winter fungus 79
Winter Olympic Games 513
Winters, Shelley 391
winter solstice 172
seasons 575
Winter Solstice Festival 498
Winterson, Jeanette 355
winter squash 68
Winter's Tale, The 362
winter sweet 74
Winwood, Steve 429
WIPO 646
wireless transmissions 184
wireworm 117
Wirral 660
Wisconsin 868
Wisdom, Sir Norman 391
Wise, Robert 396
Academy Awards 398
Wishart, Martin 159
wisteria 74
witch-hazel 66, 74
Witherspoon, Reese 391
Academy Awards 399
Wittgenstein, Ludwig 268, 468
Wittig, Georg 187
WMO 646
Wodehouse, (Sir) P G 355
Woden 470, 482, 488
Wöhler, Friedrich 199
Wokingham 660
wolf, wolves:
collective names 118
grey 88
Wolf comet 8
Wolfe, Thomas 355
Wolfe, Tom 355
Wolfendale, Sir Arnold 18
Wolff, Tobias 355

AZ

Index

wolfram 202
wolfsbane 72
wolf spider 113
Wollaston, William H 201
   inventions 190
Wolong national park/nature
   reserve 51
Wolverhampton 660
wolverine 88
woman in space, first 11, 15
wombat 80
Women in Love (film) 398
women's clothes sizes,
   international 222
women's hosiery sizes,
   international 222
Wonder, Stevie 428
   Grammy awards 429
wonders of the world,
   seven 280
wood, formation of 62
Wood, Grant 444
Wood, John (the Elder) 457
Wood, John (the
   Younger) 457
Wood, Natalie 391
Wood, Thomas 139
wood agaric 79
Wood Buffalo national park/
   nature reserve 51
woodcock, collective
   names 118
woodcreeper 99
Wooden Horse 479
woodhoopoe 97
woodlouse 113
wood mushroom 79
woodpecker 97
   collective names 118
Woods, James 391
Woods, Tiger 564
wood swallow 93
Woodward, Joanne 391
   Academy Awards 398
Woodward, Robert
   Burns 186
wood wedding
   anniversary 575
woodworm 117
wool wedding
   anniversary 575
Woolf, Virginia 355
Woolley, Dilworth Wayne 138
Woolley, Sir Richard 18
woolly milk-cap 79
Woolworth, Frank
   Winfield 195
Worcestershire 659
word processor 192
Wordsworth, William 263,
   359
   Poets laureate 359
Workers' Day 577
World Council of
   Churches 502
World Cup (football) 516
   fixture results 535
World Equestrian Games 533
World Financial Centre

building 228
World Glory oil spill 49
World Health
   Organization 646
World Heritage sites 51
World Intellectual Property
   Organization 646
world languages 584
World Meteorological
   Organization 646
world population:
   estimates 638
   largest cities 644
world ports 635
world religions 492
   distribution of adherents 489
   sacred texts 501
world temperatures 40
   temperature change 41
World-Tree 488
World War I 278
World War II 278
World Wide Web 273
wormwood 66
Worrall Thompson,
   Antony 159
Worth, Charles 453
Wotan 470, 482, 488
Wouk, Herman 355
Wounded Knee, massacre
   of 278
Wozzeck 406
wrasse 109
wren 93
   New Zealand 99
Wren, Sir Christopher 457
WRESAT satellite 11
wrestling 521
   fixture results 558
Wrexham 661
Wright, Frank Lloyd 457
Wright (of Derby),
   Joseph 444
Wright, Judith 359
Wright, Orville and
   Wilbur 188
Wright, Richard
   Nathaniel 355
writing (pictography) 192
Wroclaw 644
   World Heritage sites 56
Wuhan 644
Wuhu 644
Wuppertal 644
wurst 156
Wushan bridge 225
Wüthrich, Kurt 187
Wuxi 644
Wyatt, James 457
Wyatt, Sir Thomas 359
wych elm 74
Wycherly, William 362
Wycliffe, John 250, **508**
Wyeth, Andrew 444
Wyler, William 397
   Academy Awards 397, 398
Wyman, Jane 397
Wyndham, John 355
Wynne, Arthur 189

Wyoming 868

X

X-chromosome 173
Xenakis, Iannis 403
xenon 202
xenosaur 105
xerography 192, 269
Xia dynasty 281
Xiamen 644
Xiangfan 644
Xiangtan 644
Xiangyang 644
Xiaolangdi dam 228
Xihoumen bridge 225
Xiling Yangtze bridge 225
Xining 644
Xinxiang 644
Xipe Totec 488
Xiuhtecuhtli 488
XML computer language 608
X-ray crystallography 180,
   185
X-rays 167, **173**, 184, 267
   discoveries 139
   radiation 197
   study of 176
Xuthos 477
Xuzhou 644

Y

yachting 519
   fixture results 558
Yagli 521
Yakeshi 644
yakitori 156
Yale Art Gallery, The 462
Yalow, Rosalyn 187
yam 68
Yama 488
Yamamoto, Yohji 453
yang 140
Yangquan 644
Yankee Doodle Dandy 397
Yannas, Ioannis 191
Yantai 644
Yaoundé 644
yard 209, 210
Yardbirds 428
Yaroslavl 644
   World Heritage sites 57
yarrow 66, 72
Yasunari, Kawabata 458
Y-chromosome 173
years:
   Chinese calendar 575
   Gregorian equivalents 574
Yeats, W B 359
   Nobel prize 458
yellow-brown boletus 79
yellow fever 135
   discoveries 139
   immunization 145
yellow oleander 77
yellow stainer 79
Yellowstone National
   Park 49, 51

World Heritage site   58
Yeltsin, Boris   819
Yemen   678, **875**
   national holidays   583
   political leaders   337
   UN membership   645, 646
   World Heritage sites   59
Yenisey River   33
Yerby, Frank   355
Yerevan   644
Yes   428
yew, Asian   120
yew, common   76
Ygerna   488
Yggdrasil   488
Yichang (Ichang)   644
Yichun (Ichun)   644
yin   140
Yinchuan   644
Yin dynasty   281
Yingkou   644
Yin-Yang   501
Ynys Mon   661
yoga   568
   treatment   141
yogurt, nutritional value   151
Yogyakarta   644
Yokohama   644
Yokohama Bay bridge   225
Yokosuka   644
Yomi   479
Yom Kippur   500
Yom Kippur War   270
York   660
   museums and galleries   462
York, House of   252, 283
York, Michael   391
Yorktown, Battle of   277
Yoruba   247, 804
Yosemite National Park   51
   World Heritage site   59
You Can't Take It with
   You   397
Young, Brigham   509
Young, Leo C   191
Young, Lester   416
Young, Loretta   397
Young, Neil   428
Young, Thomas   185
   inventions   189
Yourcenar, Marguerite   355
Ypres, Battle of   278
ytterbium   202
Ytterby, Sweden   199, 201, 202
yttria   180
yttrium   202
Yuan dynasty   281, 714
Yu Chang Yang   137

Yugoslavia:
   civil war   272, 279
   Montenegro   794
   political leaders   338
   Serbia   826
   UN membership   645, 646
Yukawa, Hideki   186
Yukon Territory   709
Yunus, Muhammad   459
Yu the Great   488

Z

zabaglione   156
Zagreb   644
Zaire   718
zakat   499
Zambesi River   275
Zambia   678, **876**
   Commonwealth
      membership   647
   English speakers   585
   national holidays   583
   political leaders   338
   UN membership   645
   World Heritage sites   59
Zamboanga City   644
Zamyatin, Evgeny   355
Zanhary   488
Zanzibar   31, 845
Zapatistas   790
Zaporozhye   644
Zapotecs   790
Zappa, Frank   428
Zarco, João Gonçalves   274
Zardari, Asif Ali   808
Zarqa   644
Zarya space mission   12
Zatopek, Emil   564
zebra   88
   collective names   118
zebra spider   114
Zeffirelli, Franco   397
Zeiss, Carl   189
Zellweger, Renée   391
Zemeckis, Robert   397
   Academy Awards   399
Zemlya Frantsa-Iosifa   31
Zen   246, 248, 492
zenith   173
Zeno of Elea   468
Zephaniah, Benjamin   359
Zeppelin, Graf Ferdinand
   von   188
Zernike, Frederik   186
Zeta-Jones, Catherine   391
Zeus   469, 471, 472, 473, 474,
   475, 476, 477, 478, 479, 480,

481, 482, 483, 485, 486, **488**
   Seven Wonders of the
      World   233, 280
Zewail, Ahmed H   187
Zhangjiakou   644
Zheng He, Admiral   252, 274
Zhengzhou   644
Zhenjiang   644
Zhon-gyual   501
Zhoukoudian   52
Zhuzhou   644
Zia ul-Haq   808
Zibo   644
Ziegler, Karl   186
Zigong   644
Zimbabwe   678, **877**
   Commonwealth
      membership   647
   English speakers   585
   national holidays   583
   political leaders   339
   UN membership   646
   World Heritage sites   59
zinc   202
   in diet   130
   properties   202
Zinfandel   160
Zinkernagel, Rolf M   179
   Nobel prize   187
Zinnemann, Fred   397
   Academy Awards   398
Zionists   268, 761
zip-fastener   192
zircon   27, 28
   month association   575
zirconium   202
zodiac   173
   signs   511
Zog I   680
Zola, Émile   355
Zond 5 space mission   11
Zoo bridge   225
zoogeography   177
zoology   177
zootaxy   177
Zoroaster   232, 503, **509**
Zoroastrianism   503
zucchini   67
Zulu War   278
Zurbriggen, Pirmin   564
Zürich   644
   museums and galleries   461
Zvezda space mission   12
Zweibrucken, House of   286
Zwingli, Huldreich   254, 509
ZZ Top   428